LITERATURE AND ITS WRITERS

An Introduction to Fiction, Poetry, and Drama

LITERATURE AND ITS WRITERS

An Introduction to Fiction, Poetry, and Drama

Ann Charters
UNIVERSITY OF CONNECTICUT

Samuel Charters

BEDFORD BOOKS 〽 Boston

For Bedford Books
President and Publisher: Charles H. Christensen
General Manager and Associate Publisher: Joan E. Feinberg
Managing Editor: Elizabeth M. Schaaf
Developmental Editor: Stephen A. Scipione
Editorial Assistant: Rebecca Jerman
Production Editor: Lori Chong Roncka
Production Assistant: Ellen Thibault
Copyeditor: Barbara Sutton
Text Design: Anna George
Cover Design: Hannus Design Associates
Cover Painting: Vanessa Bell, *Leonard Sydney Woolf,* oil on canvas, 1940. By courtesy of the
   National Portrait Gallery, London.

Library of Congress Catalog Card Number: 96–86766

Manufactured in the United States of America.

1   0   9   8   7
f   e   d   c

For information, write: Bedford Books, 75 Arlington Street, Boston, MA 02116 (617-426-7440)

ISBN: 0–312–13770–2

Acknowledgments

FICTION

Jack Agueros. "Dominoes" from *Dominoes and Other Stories from the Puerto Rican.* Copyright © 1993 by Jack Agueros.
   Reprinted with the permission of Curbstone Press. Distributed by Consortium.
Woody Allen. "The Kugelmass Episode" from *Side Effects.* Copyright © 1977 by Woody Allen. Reprinted with the permis-
   sion of Random House, Inc.
Dorothy Allison. "Lupus" from *Trash.* Copyright © 1988 by Dorothy Allison. Reprinted with the permission of Firebrand
   Books, Ithaca, New York.
Margaret Atwood. "Happy Endings" from *Murder in the Dark*, published in the United States as *Good Bones and Simple Mur-
   ders.* Copyright © 1983 by Margaret Atwood. Reprinted with the permission of Doubleday, a division of Bantam Dou-
   bleday Dell Publishing Group, Inc. and Coach House Press.
Isaac Babel. "My First Goose," translated by Walter Morison, from *The Collected Stories of Isaac Babel.* Copyright © 1955 by
   S. G. Philips, Inc. Reprinted with the permission of the publishers.

*Acknowledgments and copyrights are continued at the back of the book on pages 2120–2130, which constitute an extension of the copy-
right page. It is a violation of the law to reproduce these selections by any means whatsoever without the written permission of the copyright holder.*

PREFACE FOR INSTRUCTORS

Literature and Its Writers invites students to explore a variety of ways to read, think, and write about short fiction, poetry, and drama. It differs from other anthologies in its pervasive emphasis on what writers, not textbook editors, have to say about literary works.

Those who write literature generally offer the most useful insights into it. Although recent critical debate has helped us gain new perspectives on the literary canon and has encouraged us to reconsider many of our attitudes and opinions, most students find sophisticated critical theory less illuminating than an approach that allows them to trace the connections between the works and their authors. Such as approach helps students think usefully about two questions fundamental to the study of literature: How is it made, and how is it related to us?

Literary theorists will continue to debate the efficacy of an author-centered study of literature, but this approach works in most classrooms. Not all students have the knowledge to appreciate critical theory, but all of them are capable of appreciating literature as the creation of talented human beings like themselves. And if some students have the courage to try to become professional writers, they can take heart from the examples of established authors, whose lives not only inspire young writers but also suggest the many directions their careers can take.

A DISTINCTIVE EMPHASIS ON WRITERS

We have structured *Literature and Its Writers* to keep students' attention focused on what storytellers, poets, and playwrights have to say about the art and craft of literature. In addition to more than seventy stories, three hundred poems, and almost twenty plays, the book features 160 commentaries that discuss specific literary works, literary form and influence, and the creative process. Students encounter not only "A Rose for Emily," but also what William Faulkner had to say about his famous story; not just the poetry of Emily Dickinson, but also Dickinson's remarks about her poetry in letters to Thomas Wentworth Higginson; not just Lorraine Hansberry's *A Raisin in the Sun*, but also Hansberry's admiring tribute to Shakespeare. The commentaries provide numerous discussion and writing opportunities, as well as models of how writers think, read, and write about literature.

The focus on writers does not stop with the commentaries. We also include full biographical headnotes for individual authors, with the words of the writers themselves often interwoven. We have prepared unique chapters on how storytellers, poets, and playwrights respond to each other and to their historical contexts. We have provided discussion of the traditional elements of literature, but no more than students need to know in order to understand what the writers themselves have to say about literature. Finally, we have shifted all questions and writing suggestions from the book itself to the Instructor's Manual, where the apparatus will not influence students' interpretations but can be drawn on by instructors who so choose.

HOW THE BOOK IS ORGANIZED

Literature and Its Writers is divided into the three literary genres of short fiction, poetry, and drama. Within each section, introductory chapters discuss the genre, its elements, how writers respond to each other and to their times, and reading, critical thinking, and writing. Then comes the literature — the fiction and drama sections prepared by Ann Charters and the poetry section by Samuel Charters. Seventy-seven stories, arranged alphabetically by author, represent the most extensive and diverse selection of the type of literature students most enjoy..It includes a stimulating range of authors, from Washington Irving to Sandra Cisneros, eleven of whom are represented by at least two stories. Three hundred seventeen poems, appearing within the discussion chapters and in an alphabetically arranged anthology of forty-nine poets, include familiar classics, such as the sonnets of Shakespeare and the odes of Keats, alongside many examples of fresh and noncanonical poetry, such as the selection from a West African griot epic by Alhaji Fabala Kanuteh. As in the fiction section, many of the individual poets are represented by enough works to facilitate in-depth study. Nineteen plays, from enduring works by Sophocles and Arthur Miller to contemporary plays by Marsha Norman, August Wilson, and David Henry Hwang, are arranged chronologically so the headnotes can trace the development of dramatic tradition. Among the many one-act works in this section is a fifteenth-century Nō play that represents an important dramatic tradition not usually included in introductory textbooks.

Following the literature in each section are the commentaries: fifty-five on stories and storytellers, sixty-one on poetry and poets, and forty-four on plays and playwrights. Although they mainly present the remarks of short story writers, poets, and dramatists, the commentaries also include a sampling of contemporary criticism for instructors who wish to give their students a taste of how a feminist or deconstructive critic, for example, might read one of the literary works in the book. Each section closes with casebooks of commentaries that provide an in-depth look — in the authors' own words and the words of other writers, scholars, and critics — at three storytellers (Raymond Carver, Sandra Cisneros, and Flannery O'Connor), four poets (Emily Dickinson, Robert Frost, Langston Hughes, and Sylvia Plath) and two playwrights (William Shakespeare and Lorraine Hansberry).

HELP FOR STUDENT WRITERS

In addition to the chapters on reading, critical thinking, and writing mentioned above, *Literature and Its Writers* concludes with an appendix that offers a lengthy discussion of the writing process in general and an analysis of specific ways of writing about literature. The appendix contains seven student papers along with examples of journal keeping, free writing, lists, and other aids to help students get started on their essays. Throughout the anthology, the commentaries, casebooks, and authors treated in-depth offer a wealth of stimulating topics for student writers.

INSTRUCTOR'S MANUAL

An accompanying Instructor's Manual for *Literature and Its Writers* presents a wide range of teaching resources, including essays that offer interpretations of individual works to explore in the classroom, questions to prompt student discussion, topics for writing, and a section on audiovisual resources.

ACKNOWLEDGMENTS

We acknowledge the help of many people, beginning with the publisher of Bedford Books, Charles Christensen, who had the idea for this textbook; editor Steve Scipione, who offered invaluable support and encouragement throughout the project; and production editor Lori Roncka, who resourcefully and attentively saw it through the production process. We would also like to express our appreciation to others at Bedford: to Joan Feinberg, Karen Henry, Kathy Retan, and Elizabeth Schaaf for their insightful comments; and to Rebecca Jerman for her tireless research and assistance. Fred Courtright cleared permissions on a dauntingly tight schedule. We are also grateful for the comments of the hundreds of teachers who helped refine the selections in Ann Charters's *The Story and Its Writers* in its various editions and whose insights contributed to our conception and choice of selections in *Literature and Its Writers*. We would like to thank our reviewers: Linda Bensel-Meyers, University of Tennessee at Knoxville; Irene Fairley, Northeastern University; Iris Ray

Hart, Santa Fe Community College; William Sheidley, University of Southern Colorado; and Robert Wallace, Case Western Reserve University.

For material included in the chapter "What Is a Short Story?" we are indebted to the University of Connecticut Library and the New York Public Library, whose archives traced a copy of Thomas Roscoe's English translation of J. C. C. Nachtigal's transcription of the German folktale "Peter Klaus the Goatherd," published in *The German Novelists: Tales Selected from Ancient and Modern Authors in That Language* (London, 1820).

At the University of Connecticut in Storrs, Susan Abbotson gave excellent suggestions to clarify the introductory chapters and headnotes in the drama section. She also wrote the drama section of the instructor's manual. Students Haruko Do, Teryn Johnson, and Steven Silvester wrote new papers included in the discussions of writing about literature. Miranda Marvin of Wellesley College and Jim and Janet Robertson of Storrs supplied information about the audiences of classic Greek plays. Finally, at the English Institute in Uppsala University, Professor Rolf Lunden strengthened our resolve to include a play by Eugene O'Neill in the textbook and read an early draft of the first chapter on the short story.

Ann Charters
University of Connecticut, Storrs
Samuel Charters

BRIEF CONTENTS

Part Three • DRAMA   1379

CONTENTS

Part Two • POETRY 871

Part Three • DRAMA   *1379*

Introduction

LITERATURE AND ITS WRITERS

Camerado, I give you my hand!
I give you my love more precious than money,
I give you myself before preaching or law;
Will you give me yourself? will you come travel with me?
Shall we stick by each other as long as we live?
                    –WALT WHITMAN, "Song of the Open Road"

The great American poet Walt Whitman extends an invitation to the reader in "Song of the Open Road," proposing a journey together that is as much an open-ended way of traveling as the promise of an open road. You can accept Whitman's invitation and read fiction, poetry, and drama for many reasons, including the pleasure of companionship and the promise of enlightenment. The more knowledgeable you are about what and how you read, the farther you can travel in the world of literature and the larger realms of the imagination.

Studying literature also helps you to become a better thinker and writer. The American poet Robert Frost aptly described the journey on which you are about to embark when he said, "To learn to write is to learn to have ideas." Reading closely and thinking critically about the stories, poems, and plays in this anthology will suggest ideas that you can develop in class discussions and in your essays. For many students, this will be the primary use of *Literature and Its Writers*.

At first you may suppose that you have little in common with the distinguished authors gathered here, but bear in mind that each of them was once a beginner. The short story writer Raymond Carver described taking his first college course in "Creative Writing 101." After reading his commentary, one student recognized a connection with Carver's experience in this short essay.

Raymond Carver's "Creative Writing 101"
We all have several turning points in our life. These turning points may include getting married, losing loved ones, having chil-

dren, and changing jobs. However, we can have other turning points which exert more subtle effects on us and are no less significant.

The American writer Raymond Carver married young and had two children. He eked out a living to support his family, but he wanted to go to college because of his desire to be a writer. He felt in his bones that he had to get an education in order to learn more about being a writer. When he finally could enroll in a college writing course, he was fortunate to have John Gardner, a published novelist, as his teacher.

Studying with Gardner was a significant turing point in Carver's life. Gardner became aware of Carver's difficulty in finding a place to work, so he offered his student the key to his office, where Carver could begin what he remembered as his "first serious attempts at writing." Just as important, Gardner read Carver's first stories seriously. Sometimes Carver had to revise a sentence several times to satisfy his teacher. Gardner insisted that a writer must be honest. He couldn't "fake it" by writing about something he didn't believe in.

Carver learned what he called "a writer's values and craft" from his first writing teacher. These were what Gardner taught him in Creative Writing 101, Carver's most important turning point as a writer.

Recognizing Carver's experience in Creative Writing 101 as an important turning point was the connection the student made between her own knowledge of life and Carver's essay. Going on to analyze the "values and craft" exemplified by works of literature can help you to develop your own skills as a reader and writer. You can read about the American playwright Lorraine Hansberry's "Shakespearean Experience" and compare it in an essay with your own thoughts about *Hamlet*. You can analyze the dazzling sparks of ideas about the themes of love and death in the lyrics of Emily Dickinson or Sylvia Plath, or interpret the genius of Langston Hughes as he translates the pain of racism into poetry accessible to everyone. You can make connections between short plays by the modern writers Samuel Beckett and David Henry Hwang and the ancient text of a Japanese Nō play. In your study of literature you can begin to understand how writers respond to their times and analyze how writers respond to other writers, as you do when you think about the texts in this book and exchange comments with your instructor and classmates.

READING LITERATURE

Regardless of where you start to study and write about literature — whether you begin with short stories, poems, or plays — the important thing to remember is that you must try to read your assignments slowly and carefully. When you become a student of literature, you do not read in the same casual way you pick up a newspaper or a magazine, or even in the way you may skim the pages of required reading for your other courses, trying to find and underline passages in which the author has stated the meaning or main ideas about the subject in words that you then memorize for a quiz or exam.

Try to read your assignments twice, the first time enjoying the experience of *arriving* at the end of the text, seeing how the author resolves the plot of a story or play or develops the subject of a poem. The second time you read a text, you can focus on *getting there,* seeing how authors create their work by using the elements of their craft. This is called *close reading,* and it is essential for understanding what an author has created in the text. This process will assist you in interpreting accurately what you have read, which is the first step in thinking critically about it.

THINKING AND WRITING ABOUT LITERATURE

With literature, *you* help to create the meaning. The truth of a story, poem, or play, or its vision or reflection of the world, is in part a result of the reader's response to it. Literature becomes meaningful when you read actively, taking the time to think about what you have read so that you can relate the author's personal vision to your own experience of life and the questions you ask of it.

To help you develop your critical thinking and express your ideas, this anthology includes individual chapters on thinking and writing about fiction, poetry, and drama, as well as an appendix on writing about literature that describes the writing process step by step.

Just as the student understood that there was a parallel between Raymond Carver's essay "Creative Writing 101" and her experience of life's "turning points," you create the meaning in a literary work as you refine your thoughts about it. Expressing your ideas in words will help you to clarify your response for yourself and others. You write to discover what you know, hoping "to find truth at the end of a pencil," as Ernest Hemingway described it. You will find more detailed suggestions to help you think and write about what you read in the introductory chapters to each of the three literary genres as you embark on your journey in *Literature and Its Writers.*

LITERATURE AND ITS WRITERS

An Introduction to Fiction, Poetry, and Drama

PART ONE

FICTION

WHAT IS A SHORT STORY?

Fiction is like the spider's web, attached ever so slightly perhaps, but still
attached to life at all four corners.
                                    —VIRGINIA WOOLF, *A Room of One's Own*

People have told stories to each other since before the dawn of history,
but the literary genre that we call the short story is a relatively recent phenomenon, much younger than the genres of poetry and drama. Most of us
have spent our lives listening to, telling, watching, and reading stories, and
we think we can recognize them. They seem as familiar to us as our reflection
in a mirror. Stories could even be said to resemble people, appearing in all
shapes and sizes. Consider, for example, the following narrative or act of
storytelling:

Peter Klaus the Goatherd

In the village of Littendorf at the foot of a mountain lived Peter Klaus, a
goatherd, who was in the habit of pasturing his flock upon the Kyffhausen
hills. Towards evening he generally let them browse upon a green plot not far
off, surrounded with an old ruined wall from which he could take a muster of
his whole flock.

For some days past he had observed that one of his prettiest goats, soon
after its arrival at this spot, usually disappeared, nor joined the fold again until late in the evening. He watched her again and again, and at last found that
she slipped through a gap in the old wall, whither he followed her. It led into
a passage which widened as he went into a cavern; and here he saw the goat
employed in picking up the oats that fell through some crevices in the place

above. He looked up, shook his ears at this odd shower of oats, but could discover nothing. Where the deuce could it come from? At length he heard over his head the neighing and stamping of horses; he listened, and concluded that the oats must have fallen through the manger when they were fed. The poor goatherd was sadly puzzled what to think of these horses in this uninhabited part of the mountain, but so it was, for a groom making his appearance, without saying a word beckoned him to follow him. Peter obeyed, and followed him up some steps which brought him into an open court-yard surrounded by old walls. At the side of this was a still more spacious cavern, surrounded by rocky heights which only admitted a kind of twilight, through the overhanging trees and shrubs. He went on, and came to a smooth shaven green, where he saw twelve ancient knights none of whom spoke a word, engaged in playing at nine pins. His guide now beckoned to Peter in silence, to pick up the nine pins and went his way. Trembling in every joint Peter did not venture to disobey, and at times he cast a stolen glance at the players, whose long beards and slashed doublets were not at all in the present fashion. By degrees his looks grew bolder; he took particular notice of every thing around him; among other things observing a tankard near him filled with wine, whose odour was excellent, he took a good draught. It seemed to inspire him with life; and whenever he began to feel tired of running, he applied with fresh ardour to the tankard, which always renewed his strength. But finally it quite overpowered him, and he fell asleep.

When he next opened his eyes, he found himself on the grass-plot again, in the old spot where he was in the habit of feeding his goats. He rubbed his eyes, he looked round, but could see neither dog nor flock; he was surprised at the long rank grass that grew around him, and at trees and bushes which he had never before seen. He shook his head and walked a little farther, looking for the old sheep path and the hillocks and roads where he used daily to drive his flock; but he could find no traces of them left. Yet he saw the village just before him; it was the same Littendorf, and scratching his head he hastened at a quick pace down the hill to enquire after his flock.

All the people whom he met going into the place were strangers to him, were differently dressed, and even spoke in a different style to his old neighbors. When he asked about his goats, they only stared at him, and fixed their eyes upon his chin. He put his hand unconsciously to his mouth, and to his great surprise found that he had got a beard, at least a foot long. He now began to think that both he and all the world about him were in a dream; and yet he knew the mountain for that of the Kyffhausen (for he had just come down it) well enough. And there were the cottages, with their gardens and grass-plots, much as he had left them. Besides the lads who had all collected round him, answered to the enquiry of a passenger, what place it was: "Littendorf, sir."

Still shaking his head, he went farther into the village to look for his own house. He found it, but greatly altered for the worse; a strange goatherd in an old tattered frock lay before the door, and near him his old dog, which growled and showed its teeth at Peter when he called him. He went through the entrance which had once a door, but all within was empty and deserted;

Peter staggered like a drunken man out of the house, and called for his wife and children by their names. But no one heard him, and no one gave him any answer.

Soon, however, a crowd of women and children got round the inquisitive stranger, with the long hoary beard; and asked him what it was he wanted. Now Peter thought it was such a strange kind of thing to stand before his own house, enquiring for his own wife and children, as well as about himself, that evading these inquiries he pronounced the first name that came into his head: "Kurt Steffen, the blacksmith?" Most of the spectators were silent, and only looked at him wistfully, till an old woman at last said, "Why, for these twelve years he has been at Sachsenburg, whence I suppose you are not come today." "Where is Valentine Meier, the tailor?" "The Lord rest his soul," cried another woman leaning on her crutch, "he has been lying more than fifteen years in a house he will never leave."

Peter recognized in the speakers, two of his young neighbours who seemed to have grown old very suddenly, but he had no inclination to enquire any farther. At this moment there appeared making her way through the crowd of spectators, a sprightly young woman with a year old baby in her arms, and a girl about four taking hold of her hand, all three as like his wife he was seeking for as possible. "What are your names?" he enquired in a tone of great surprise. "Mine is Maria." "And your father's?" continued Peter. "God rest his soul! Peter Klaus for sure. It's now twenty years ago since we were all looking for him day and night upon the Kyffhausen; for his flock came home without him, and I was then," continued the woman, "only seven years old."

The goatherd could no longer bear this. "I am Peter Klaus," he said. "Peter and no other," and he took his daughter's child and kissed it. The spectators appeared struck dumb with astonishment, until first one and then another began to say, "Yes, indeed, this is Peter Klaus! Welcome, good neighbour, after twenty years' absence, welcome home."

Most readers would say that this narrative about Peter Klaus's twenty-year sleep in the mountains of Germany is a story. It is, using the definition of the English novelist E. M. Forster, a narrative of events arranged in a time sequence. Yet comparing it in your mind with other stories you have read, you may suspect that it doesn't quite fit into the literary genre of a *short story*. Considering the narrative's brevity and old-fashioned language, an informed reader would call it a *tale*, a narrative sequence less developed than a short story.

What you have just read is Thomas Roscoe's 1820 translation of "Peter Klaus the Goatherd," a traditional narrative collected in Germany at the end of the eighteenth century by the folklorist J. C. C. Nachtigal. The German folktale was originally published in Bremen in 1800 in a collection titled *Folkssagen, Nacherzhaht von Otmar (Folktales, Transcribed by Otmar —* Nachtigal's pseudonym). Nachtigal's transcription of the German folktale became the source of what most literary historians acknowledge as the first American short story, "Rip Van Winkle," by Washington Irving (p. 296).

The connection between "Rip Van Winkle" and "Peter Klaus the

Goatherd" is so clear that Irving was charged by hostile critics with plagiarism when he published his version of the story in *The Sketch Book* in 1819–20. The story of a person who disappears from the world in order to experience what Joseph Campbell described in *Hero with a Thousand Faces* as a "life-enhancing return" is common to the mythology of many cultures. Irving never denied that he had used a German source for his story. He even suggested as much at the end of "Rip Van Winkle," even if he tried to obscure his debt to Nachtigal.

Like the more famous Brothers Grimm who published their collections of German folktales a dozen years after him, Nachtigal believed in the importance of the oral tradition of storytelling. In the preface to his book, he explained that "the popular stories here offered my countrymen . . . are real tales of the people, collected among them with much care, as they were fast dropping into oblivion, and are here narrated in the most simple and faithful language."

When you read "Peter Klaus the Goatherd," you probably sensed that it was a story, but how did you know this? In 1842 the American author Edgar Allan Poe was one of the first writers to attempt an analysis of the aesthetic properties of what he called "the prose tale." He stressed its *length* and its *unity of effect* as its most characteristic features. Aware that the quality of the reader's attention to works of literature was important, Poe insisted that a prose narrative had to be brief enough to be read in one sitting. He argued that any interruption would destroy the unity of the work's emotional effect on the reader.

Most readers feel that literary works don't always need to be read in one sitting to achieve their effect, but Poe's "unity of effect" is an important standard. It can be found in all successful works of art, including poetry and drama as well as short fiction. In particular, you can see that "Peter Klaus the Goatherd" is unified in its plot, characters, setting, point of view, style, and theme, the six elements of fiction that give stories their unity.

In the early years of the nineteenth century when authors like J. C. C. Nachtigal and Washington Irving began to publish their prose tales, they found a receptive audience of readers willing to suspend disbelief and enter the imaginative world of their fiction. In the previous century the novel had emerged as a new literary genre, and it also helped to create an audience of readers for entertaining short narratives. You will find that writers using the elements of fiction have powerful resources to shape both the form and the meaning of their stories.

RELATED STORY: *Washington Irving, "Rip Van Winkle," page 296.*

RELATED COMMENTARIES: *John Cheever, "Why I Write Short Stories," page 736; Grace Paley, "A Conversation with Ann Charters," page 782; Edgar Allan Poe, "The Importance of the Single Effect in a Prose Tale," page 787; Leslie Marmon Silko, "Language and Literature from a Pueblo Indian Perspective," page 793.*

2

THE ELEMENTS OF FICTION: A STORYTELLER'S MEANS

A true work of fiction is a wonderfully simple thing — so simple that most so-called serious writers avoid trying it, feeling they ought to do something more important and ingenious, never guessing how incredibly difficult it is. A true work of fiction does all of the following things, and does them elegantly, efficiently: it creates a vivid and continuous dream in the reader's mind; it is implicitly philosophical; it fulfills or at least deals with all of the expectations it sets up; and it strikes us, in the end, not simply as a thing done but as a shining performance.

–JOHN GARDNER, "What Writers Do"

PLOT

Since the short story is defined as a prose narrative usually involving one unified episode or a sequence of related events, plot is basic to this literary form. Plot is the sequence of events in a story and their relation to one another. Writers usually present the events of the plot in a coherent time frame that the reader can follow easily. As we read, we sense that the events are related by causation, and their meaning lies in this relation. To the casual reader, causation (or why something in the plot happened next) seems to result only from the writer's organization of the events into a chronological sequence. A more thoughtful reader understands that causation in the plot of a memorable short story reveals a good deal about the author's use of the other elements of fiction as well, especially characterization.

As E. M. Forster realized, plot not only answers *what* happened next, but it also suggests *why*. The psychologist James Hillman has explained in *Healing Fiction* that plot reveals "human intentions. Plot shows how it all hangs together and makes sense. Only when a narrative receives inner coherence in terms of the depths of human nature do we have fiction, and for this fiction we have to have plot. . . . To plot is to move from asking the question *and then what happened?* to the question *why did it happen?*"

A short story can dramatize the events of a brief episode or compress a longer period of time. Analyzing why a short story is short, the critic Norman Friedman suggests that it "may be short not because its action is inherently small, but rather because the author has chosen — in working with an episode or plot — to omit certain of its parts. In other words, an action may be large in size and still be short in the telling because not all of it is there." A short story can describe something that happens in a few minutes or encompass action that takes years to conclude. The narrative possibilities are endless, as the writer may omit or condense complex episodes to intensify their dramatic effect or expand a single incident to make a relatively long story.

Regardless of length, the plot of a short story usually has what critics term an **end orientation** — the outcome of the action or the conclusion of the plot — inherent in its opening paragraphs. As Mark Twain humorously observed, "Fiction is obliged to stick to possibilities. Truth isn't." The novelist may conclude a single episode long before the end of a novel and then pick up the thread of another narrative, or interpret an event from another angle in a different character's point of view, linking episode to episode and character to character so that each illuminates the others. But a story stops earlier. As Poe recognized in 1842, its narrative dramatizes a single effect complete unto itself.

The events in the plot of a short story usually involve a conflict or struggle between opposing forces. When you analyze a plot, you can often (but not always) see it develop in a pattern during the course of the narration. Typically you find that the first paragraphs of the story or **exposition** give the background or setting of the conflict. The **rising action** dramatizes the specific events that set the conflict in motion. Often there is a **turning point** in the story midway before further **complications** prolong the suspense of the conflict's resolution. The **climax** is the emotional high point of the narration. In the **falling action**, the events begin to wind down and point the reader toward the **conclusion** or **denouement** at the end of the story, which resolves the conflict to a greater or lesser degree. Sometimes the conclusion introduces an unexpected turn of events or a surprise ending. In successful stories the writer shapes these stages into a complex structure that may impress you with its balance and proportion.

The plot of "Peter Klaus the Goatherd" relates a sequence of events about a man who falls asleep for twenty years after a supernatural encounter in the mountains and then awakens to return to his family and friends, whose lives have gone on without him. The first part, or *exposition*, of the folktale introduces character, setting, and time. This all occurs in the first short paragraph of Nachtigal's version. The next, much longer paragraph introduces the *rising action*, the events that lead to Peter Klaus's mysterious encounter with the "twelve ancient knights." The *turning point* occurs when he wakes up. *Complications* make up the second half of the story, when Peter Klaus returns to his village and finds himself a stranger there. This leads to the *climax*, the emotional high point when the old goatherd hears the story of his disappearance from his daughter and "could no longer bear this. 'I am Peter Klaus,' he said, 'Peter and no other.' " This moment of recognition may cause the sympathetic reader to wince with pity for the old man. The *falling action* and *conclusion* immediately follow the goatherd's pathetic recognition of what has happened to him. In this short tale, the conclusion is the final sentence of the narrative.

When Washington Irving transformed "Peter Klaus the Goatherd" into the American story "Rip Van Winkle," it became four times as long. You might say that the difference between the treatment of the plot in the two versions is that Nachtigal's folktale tends to summarize the action, while Irving's short story develops it. Irving invented many new details to create elaborate twists and turns in the basic plot as well as to transform its characters and setting.

In modern stories, plot most often evolves as the interaction of characters with circumstances. Authors develop it through dialogue and commentary as well as description of action. They can also add **foreshadowing** and **verbal irony** to the narration, anticipating a turn of events that may or may not go along with our expectations. The opening paragraph of "Rip Van Winkle" is a good example of Irving's leisurely approach to his plot, containing examples of both foreshadowing and verbal irony:

> The following Tale was found among the papers of the late Diedrich Knickerbocker, an old gentleman of New York, who was very curious in the Dutch history of the province, and the manners of the descendants from its primitive settlers. His historical researches, however, did not lie so much among books as among men; for the former are lamentably scanty on his favorite topics; whereas he found the old burghers, and still more their wives, rich in that legendary lore so invaluable to true history. Whenever, therefore, he happened upon a genuine Dutch family, snugly shut up in its low-roofed farmhouse, under a spreading sycamore, he looked upon it as a little clasped volume of black-letter, and studied it with the zeal of a book-worm.

As the reader will learn in a few more paragraphs, Rip Van Winkle himself is one such "old burgher" (foreshadowing), a character whose life experience is rich in "legendary lore." But in Irving's tale, Rip's wife is not allowed to tell her story, so we are given a different reality than the literal meaning of the author's words in his introduction (verbal irony).

Regardless of the author's method of developing the plot, the goal is the same: The writer of short stories must *show* the reader something about human nature through the dramatic action of the plot and the other elements of the story, and not just *tell* the reader what to think. A good plot engages our curiosity, surprises us, and keeps us in suspense. As the contemporary American writer Eudora Welty understood, "A narrative line is in its deeper sense, of course, the tracing out of a meaning, and the real continuity of a story lies in this probing forward." A storyteller must sustain the illusion of reality until the end of the story, unfolding events with the continuing revelation of an apparently endless silk handkerchief drawn from a skillful magician's coat sleeve.

CHARACTER

If you are like most people, plot is what keeps you going when you first read a story, and character is what stays with you after you have finished reading it. The title of the German folktale "Peter Klaus the Goatherd" is named after its memorable **protagonist** or central character. Characters are usually the people who are involved in what happens in a story. Writers can use animals as characters, or even such inanimate objects as trees, chairs, and shoes, but with the term *character* we usually mean a human being with emotions whose mind works something like our own.

When we ask Why? of the plot of a story, we usually find the answer in the characters, who are convincing if we can understand their actions. Peter Klaus does not always understand why he acts as he does. Yet the reasons are there, and we may know them before the fictional characters do. We instinctively strive to connect the events of a story by more than their simple chronological sequence, because assuming connection between the events and the inner life of the characters makes the story seem coherent.

How are the characters in a short story to be understood? Any discussion of character tends to drift into a value judgment, as our principles of definition and evaluation for fictional characters are based on the ones we use for real people, tentative and confused as they may be. We must remember that we are reading about *fictional* characters in a short story, not real ones. The only evidence we have about characters is what the author puts into the story.

We are on firmer ground in literary discussions when we analyze the writer's method of characterization as well as the character's personality. Nachtigal's method is one of economy. We know from the title that Peter Klaus is the central person in the action. A little more than a dozen words into the story, we are told all we need to know about him — he is a goatherd. Only one sparse adjective, *a*, modifies the noun. We are in the fictional world of the oral folk tradition, where characters are known primarily by what they do. They are defined by their actions, not by their sensitive introspection, their subtle responses to other people, or their being described as good or bad.

Characters are sometimes called **round** or **flat**. For characters to emerge as round, the reader must feel the play and pull of their actions and responses to situations. Peter Klaus is a flat character. He does not have complex responses to his situation; he is acted upon by his circumstances.

 Even as a flat character, Peter Klaus is not **static**. He is a **dynamic** character who changes during the narrative because something significant happens to him. However, his daughter Maria, a minor character in his story, is both flat and static. She makes such a brief appearance that she doesn't appear as an individual. She doesn't come alive on the page because there is no accumulation of detail about her actions and responses.

Writers of short fiction suggest their philosophical view of the world in the way they present their characters. In such early tales as "Peter Klaus the Goatherd" authors create worlds of fantasy where the characters tend to be flat; they have little control over their environment. Later writers of realistic stories create more rounded protagonists because they put more emphasis on the choices that their fictional characters make, granting them more control over their fates.

Different fictional worlds make different demands on the reader's imagination, but what is most important is the emotional truth of the fictional character, flat or round, dynamic or static. To avoid **sentimentality** (emotional overindulgence) and **stereotyping** (generalized, oversimplified judgment) in creating characters, the writer must be able to suggest enough complexity to engage the reader's emotions, or the story will not succeed.

SETTING

Setting is the place and time of the story. To set the scene and suggest a mood or atmosphere for the events to follow, the writer attempts to create in the reader's visual imagination the illusion of a solid world in which the story takes place. Setting is so important that the opening words of "Peter Klaus the Goatherd" are "In the Village of Littendorf at the foot of a mountain lived Peter Klaus." Since this tale is based on legendary material about a human being's encounter with the spirit world, it could easily have started with the phrase "Once upon a time." Instead, the storyteller brings it out of the realm of fantasy and suggests it happens in the real world by mentioning the name of the village where the events allegedly took place to make the tale seem more credible to the reader.

In "Peter Klaus the Goatherd" the setting is secondary to the action; in "Rip Van Winkle" it is central. Irving's description of the countryside is so virtuosic that you could award him the first Harry Houdini magician's prize for excellence among sleight-of-hand scene painters. Irving spends an entire paragraph describing the Catskills' "magical hues and shapes" before introducing Rip Van Winkle. Then when Rip climbs the mountains hunting squirrel, the beauties of nature are described again through his eyes:

> In a long ramble of the kind on a fine autumnal day, Rip had unconsciously scrambled to one of the highest parts of the Kaatskill mountains. He was after his favorite sport of squirrel-shooting, and the still solitudes had echoed and re-echoed with the reports of his gun. Panting and fatigued, he threw himself, late in the afternoon, on a green knoll, covered with mountain herbage, that crowned the brow of a precipice. From an opening between the trees he could overlook all the lower country for many a mile of rich woodland. He saw at a distance the lordly Hudson, far, far below him, moving on its silent but majestic course, with the reflection of a purple cloud, or the sail of a lagging bark, here and there sleeping on its glassy bosom, and at last losing itself in the blue highlands.
>
> On the other side he looked down into a deep mountain glen, wild, lonely, and shagged, the bottom filled with fragments from the impending cliffs, and scarcely lighted by the reflected rays of the setting sun. For some time Rip lay musing on this scene; evening was gradually advancing; the mountains began to throw their long blue shadows over the valleys; he saw that it would be dark long before he could reach the village.

Like other early-nineteenth-century American authors such as Nathaniel Hawthorne, Irving contrasts the countryside in the New World tamed by its human occupants (the peaceful "rich woodland" and "lordly Hudson") with the untamed territory (the "wild, lonely" mountainside) outside the settled villages. When Rip sees the mountains, those specters of the wild landscape, throwing their "long blue shadows" over the peaceful valleys, Irving uses the setting to suggest a symbolic meaning in the plot. The description of nature tamed and untamed, different in daytime and at night, foreshadows Rip's mysterious meeting with the spirit world.

When the writer locates the narrative in a physical setting, the reader is moved step by step toward acceptance of the fiction. The *external* reality of the setting is always an illusion, our mental images that correspond to the words that the writer has put on paper. Yet this invented setting is essential if we are to share the *internal* emotional life of the characters involved in the plot. The setting of a story furnishes the location for its world of feeling. A sense of place engages us in the fictional characters' situations.

Place helps make the characters seem real, but, to be most effective, the setting must also have a dramatic use. It must be perceived to affect character or plot. When Klaus the goatherd returns after his twenty-year sleep and sees his house "greatly altered for the worse" and "empty and deserted," he staggers "like a drunken man." In "Rip Van Winkle," Irving begins his story in the decade before the American Revolution, not in a vague "once upon a time." After Rip's twenty years' absence, the momentous change in his Hudson River village is evident in the new sign he notices hanging above the tavern he had frequented with his cronies — the "ruby face of King George" has been replaced by a portrait of General Washington. By giving precise details about the setting, writers share their vision of their fictional world with their readers, creating the illusion that the story unfolds in the real world.

POINT OF VIEW

Point of view refers to the author's choice of a narrator for the story. At the start, the writer must decide whether to employ **first-person narration,** using the pronoun *I,* or **third-person narration,** using the pronouns *he, she,* and *they.* (Second-person narration, *you,* is less common, although the dramatic intimacy of second-person narrative address is often used in poetry and song lyrics.) The writer's choice of a point of view to narrate stories usually falls into two major categories:

FIRST-PERSON NARRATION (NARRATOR APPARENTLY
A PARTICIPANT IN THE STORY)

1. A major character
2. A minor character

THIRD-PERSON NARRATION (NARRATOR A NONPARTICIPANT IN THE STORY)

1. Omniscient — seeing into the minds of all characters
2. Limited omniscient — seeing into one or, sometimes, two characters' minds
3. Objective — seeing into none of the characters' minds

First-Person Narration

The tale of "Peter Klaus the Goatherd" uses third-person narration, but you can imagine how it might have sounded in the first-person *I* if the author had let us imagine that Peter Klaus had told it himself:

I don't want to sound crazy or anything, but it did happen to me. It was a long time ago, but I can still remember everything just as clear as a bell. I was watching my goats late one afternoon in the mountains, and I saw one stray through the wall. I went after her into a cave, and then suddenly I heard a lot of horses. A strange-looking man appeared and I followed him to a group of knights who were playing a game of ninepins. They made me help them, but I found something to drink, and I don't know how it happened, but I fell sound asleep. When I woke up and went home, I found everything had changed. My wife had died and my little girl had grown up. I had been asleep for twenty years!

Since Peter Klaus is presented as such a simple character, there is no magic to his first-person account. The storyteller in a first-person narration can be either a major or a minor character. If Peter is too tongue-tied to tell you his own tale, the author could let you hear it from a minor participant on the sidelines of the action, his daughter Maria. Her view of what happened to her father might sound something like this:

Yes, you can ask me about him, but I was very young when he disappeared, only seven or so. I don't remember that much about him. All of us went out to look for him, and my mother cried bitterly when the search party from our village came back and told her that they'd failed to find him. His flock of goats came home all right, but somebody else took charge of it, and we became very poor. My mother slaved to keep us fed and warm. When she died, poor thing, I was raised by my aunt. It must have been twenty years before I saw my dear father again standing in front of our house. I must admit that I didn't even recognize him until he spoke to me!

To be effective as a story, the biased report of the first-person narrator must have a dramatic significance. This usually occurs in a subtle discrepancy between the way he or she sees characters or events and the reader's sense of what really happened. Peter Klaus's laconic first-person narrative has the authority of an eye-witness account, of course, but Maria was only a little girl when her father disappeared, and she can't tell us much about his fantastic adventure away from home.

From the way Peter and his daughter describe what happened to them in these different versions of the tale, it appears that they both lack artistry as storytellers. You will discover that writers in this anthology such as Edgar Allan Poe, Charlotte Perkins Gilman, William Faulkner, Grace Paley, and Sandra Cisneros use first-person narration to magnificent effect in their stories, adding to the emotional impact of the events they describe.

Third-Person Narration

Third-person narration means that the author tells the story using the pronouns *he* or *she* instead of the presumably more subjective *I*. Narrated in the third person, the folktale begins, "In the village of Littendorf at the foot of a mountain lived Peter Klaus, a goatherd, who was in the habit of pasturing his flock upon the Kyffhausen hills."

There can be significant differences, however, in the way authors handle third-person narration. "Peter Klaus the Goatherd" is an example of *limited omniscient* narration, because Nachtigal confines himself to revealing the thoughts of only one character, his protagonist. The folklorist tells his story with such scrupulous regard for his source in the oral tradition that he doesn't present an interior, subjective view of Peter Klaus's experience. When the goatherd sees the "odd shower of oats" in the cavern ("Where the deuce could it come from?"), we are told that he was "sadly puzzled what to think" about the idea of a stable of horses in that part of the mountains, but we are told mostly what he did, rather than what he thought or felt. At the climax of his story, when he meets his daughter, the emotional content of Peter's response is summarized in a single sentence: "The goatherd could no longer bear this."

Irving took a different approach to third-person narration. As you have read in the opening paragraph of "Rip Van Winkle," Irving chose to take the third-person *omniscient* point of view toward his materials. This approach signals to the reader that the storyteller is omniscient, ready to tell you everything there is to know about all the characters in his tale, what they think and feel as well as what they do. Fairy tales beginning "Once upon a time" are the most familiar examples of omniscient narration.

There are several other varieties of third-person narration, since authors are highly conscious of the different effects on the reader resulting from their choice of a particular point of view. Discussing her approach to writing fiction, the South African writer Nadine Gordimer once said, "I have the writer's healthy selfish instinct to keep open the multiple vision that the fly's eye of the writer had brought me." A writer can tell a story using *objective narration*, attempting to create a totally detached perspective on the characters and the plot of the story. Setting, action, and dialogue appear on the page without the narrator's comments or the characters' reflection.

When Joseph Conrad suggested that the nineteenth-century French author Guy de Maupassant was interested in using only *facts* to tell his story, Conrad was implying that Maupassant was attempting objective narration. Yet Maupassant himself insisted on his "personal view" as a writer and on his selectivity in presenting what he called "the illusion of reality" in fiction. For example, in his famous story "The Necklace," Maupassant's "personal view" included a snobbish disdain for a social-climbing wife from a modest background.

The American writer Ernest Hemingway attempted an even more rigorous use of objective narration. In "Hills Like White Elephants," he presents only enough background information to introduce the physical setting and his two characters; then he narrates his story through their dialogue. You must read between the lines to understand what the characters are discussing.

Narration can be classified into further subcategories (for example, first- and third-person stream-of-consciousness narration), but a writer's handling of different points of view is always more flexible than the rigid categories imply. Franz Kafka, who tells the story of "The Metamorphosis" through the thoughts of his central character, Gregor Samsa, continues in the last pages of the narrative to describe events after Gregor's death so the reader can get a harrowing sense of how his uncaring family went on without him.

STYLE

Style is the characteristic way an author uses language to create literature. Style is the result of the writer's habitual use of certain rhetorical patterns, including <u>sentence length and complexity</u>, <u>word choice</u> and <u>placement</u>, <u>and punctuation</u>. Nachtigal uses simple sentence construction and choice of words in "Peter Klaus the Goatherd" to suggest that his tale had originated among uneducated people. Irving, on the other hand, wrote to show off his virtuosity as a prose stylist to his educated readers. He used much more <u>complicated sentence structure</u> and a much more sophisticated vocabulary.

You might think of the author's prose style as a projection of his or her <u>voice as a writer</u>, as if you were hearing the story instead of reading it. Voice, as the Canadian writer Margaret Atwood described it, is "a speaking voice, like the singing voice in music, that moves not across a space, across the page, but through time. Surely every written story is, in the final analysis, a score for voice. These little black marks on the page mean nothing without their retranslation into sound."

Of course, the voice brought to life by the words resonating in the mind of the reader is not necessarily the literal voice of the author. When Nachtigal told his story, his voice was flat and matter-of-fact, devoid of emotional resonance, the voice of a folklorist and scholar who respected his material. The German peasant who originally narrated the sad tale of Peter Klaus to him might have been a virtuoso performer in the oral tradition of her village, using a dramatic voice, physical gestures, and perhaps even music or props for an impressive effect. But transcribed and printed on the page, the bare words of the tale are all that remain to us.

<u>Tone is the way the author</u> conveys his or her unstated attitudes <u>toward the story</u>. We assume that Nachtigal's serious tone was present in the original German version of his tale, but since we read it in an English translation, we must be cautious in describing his authorial voice and tone. Since Irving wrote in English, we stand on firmer ground, understanding that he chose to put on a performance in "Rip Van Winkle." As you saw in the opening paragraph of his story, he adopted a humorous tone to amuse his readers.

<u>Irony</u> is another means by which writers tell stories. Irony makes the <u>reader aware of a reality that differs from the reality</u> the characters perceive (*dramatic irony*) or from the literal meaning of the author's words (*verbal irony*). Irving's prose style is rich in irony. You have already noticed an example of verbal irony in his opening paragraph to "Rip Van Winkle" when he refers to the wives "rich in that legendary lore so invaluable to true history." A good example of dramatic irony occurs at the end of the story, when Rip returns to his village after his long sleep. On the street he meets "a precise counterpart of himself, as he went up the mountain; apparently as lazy, and certainly as ragged." Here is a situation full of dramatic irony because Rip doesn't know

he is looking at his son. He sees the shiftless young man only as a mirror of himself twenty years before.

The use of **symbolism** can also be an aspect of a writer's style. A literary symbol can be anything in a story's setting, plot, or characterization that suggests an abstract meaning to the reader in addition to its literal significance. We have already seen how Irving's description of the late-afternoon shadows of the mountains symbolized the mysterious fantasy world that Rip entered shortly afterwards. Symbols are more eloquent as specific images — visual ideas — than any paraphrase, suggesting infinitely more than they state. They are not always interpreted the same way by all readers. For example, the mountain shadows may suggest to another reader a symbol that foreshadows Rip's long sleep and his awakening into old age.

An entire story can also suggest a symbolic as well as a literal meaning. A story becomes an **allegory** when all the characters, places, things, and events represent symbolic qualities and their interactions are meant to reveal a moral truth. Whereas symbolism results from the multiple meanings inherent in a good story, an allegorical interpretation tends to simplify the meaning. We can easily interpret the folktale "Peter Klaus the Goatherd" as an allegory. Its traditional source suggests that centuries ago in Europe it could have served as a medieval Christian moral fable reminding listeners about the brevity of human life, or warning them about the dangers of pagan worship or alcohol.

THEME

Theme is a generalization about the meaning of a story. Whereas the plot of a story can be summarized by stating what happened in the action, the theme is the general idea behind the events of the plot that expresses the meaning of the story. Nachtigal and Irving's stories about the mysterious nature of time and human mortality, are relatively easy to boil down to a phrase that summarizes their meaning, because both authors were writing at a time when readers expected to be taught a moral lesson when they read prose narratives. When Irving was criticized for basing his stories on a German source, he pointed out that Shakespeare had also borrowed the plots of his plays and that great writers succeeded not because they invented new stories but "because they have rooted themselves in the unchanging principles of human nature."

The stories we encounter daily do much more than entertain us; they also play a central role in our lives. Students of the media tell us that the narratives told to us by parents, friends, teachers, books, audio recordings, radio, television, and film are the real authors of what we take to be our "common" sense, helping us arrive at an understanding of ourselves and our place in the world. As James Hillman has explained, our stories provide "dynamic coherence and meaning to the dispersed narratives of our lives." At the same time, fiction also has the power to challenge our everyday sense of reality by reminding us of our mortality and suggesting that anything might happen, since the universe is ultimately beyond our control and comprehension.

Theme comes last in a discussion of the elements of fiction because all the other elements must be accounted for in determining it. The structure and theme of a story are fused like the body and soul of a reader; their interaction creates a living pattern. While the various actions of the plot must strike us as realistic and inevitable, the complete truth that it reveals is in essence indefinable and untranslatable outside the story. The storyteller says, "Let me tell you how it is," and we pay attention because we want to know what the story can show us about the complexities of human experience. Theme is an abstract formulation of the author's vision of the meaning of life.

One of the pleasures of a good story is figuring out what has pulled us into it. The ways authors use the elements of fiction to create their stories will reflect their philosophical view of the meaning of our common experience, what the Russian writer Isaac Babel called "the secret curve" behind the author's "straight line." The summary of a writer's theme is no substitute for the story in its entirety, but our attempt to state it can help us understand the story better. As the Southern writer Flannery O'Connor said, "A story is a way to say something that can't be said any other way, and it takes every word in the story to say what the meaning is. . . . When anybody asks what a story is about, the only proper thing is to tell him to read the story."

RELATED COMMENTARIES: *Sherwood Anderson, "Form, Not Plot, in the Short Story," page 730; Anton Chekhov, "Technique in Writing the Short Story," page 738; James Hillman, "A Note on Story," page 756; D. H. Lawrence, "Draft Passage from 'Odour of Chrysanthemums,' " page 765; Flannery O'Connor, "The Element of Suspense in 'A Good Man Is Hard to Find,' " page 854; Frank O'Connor, "Style and Form in Joyce's 'The Dead,' " page 780; Peter Rudy, "Tolstoy's Revisions in 'The Death of Ivan Ilych,' " page 790; Eudora Welty, "Plot and Character in Chekhov's 'The Darling,' " page 811.*

3

STORYTELLERS AND HISTORY

Fiction is history, human history, or it is nothing. But it is also more than that; it stands on firmer ground, being based on the reality of forms and the observation of social phenomena, whereas history is based on documents, and the reading of print and handwriting — on second-hand impression. Thus fiction is nearer truth.

–JOSEPH CONRAD, *Notes on Life and Letters*

Your understanding of the elements of fiction can help you to interpret the meaning of a story, but you can also appreciate that what you are reading is always much more than a self-contained, self-referential text printed on the page before you. When writers create an imaginary world in a story, they are also referring to the world outside the text, what students often call "the real world." Literature's link to the events of human history is as real as the paper it is printed on.

In the first half of the twentieth century, readers practicing what they had begun to call **formalism,** or the New Criticism, concentrated on the meaning and form that exists within each poem, play, or story. For a variety of reasons they divorced literature from its larger biographical, historical, or psychological contexts. With considerable skill they explicated images and symbols, traced patterns of ambiguity, and tabulated the stylistic characteristics of the authors they studied. The critic Ross Murfin has summarized the reaction against their practices:

> About 1970 the New Criticism came under attack by reader-response critics (who believe that the meaning of a work is not inherent in its internal form but rather is cooperatively produced by the reader and the text) and poststructuralists (who, following the philosophy of Jacques Derrida, argue that texts are inevitably self-contradictory and that we can find form in them only by ignoring or suppressing conflicting details or elements). In retrospect it is clear that, in their outspoken opposition to the New Criticism notwith-

standing, the reader-response critics and poststructuralists of the 1970s were very much *like* their formalist predecessors in two important respects: for the most part, they ignored the world beyond the text and its reader, and, for the most part, they ignored the historical contexts within which literary works are written and read.

Appreciating the historical context of a story does not mean that you should abandon a close reading of the text or ignore your increasing awareness that as a reader you undoubtedly approach it with your own prejudices and blind spots. As you read, you should remain on the alert for the multiple, sometimes self-contradictory meanings that you find in a literary work — meanings that resist a final interpretation.

The New Historicism — an approach to literature that builds on formalism, reader-response theory, and poststructuralism — is essentially a practical criticism. It recognizes, as the critic Terry Eagleton has said, that "human meanings are in a deep sense historical: they are not a question of intuiting the universal essence of what it is to be an onion, but a matter of changing, practical transactions between social individuals. . . . Understanding is radically historical: it is always caught up with the concrete situation I am in, and that I am trying to surpass."

Recent feminist, cultural, and social critics have pointed out that history is not necessarily linear and progressive, and that there is rarely a consistent zeitgeist ("spirit of the times") to use as a convenient label for a particular historical period. It is notoriously difficult to reconstruct the past, as we are all biased by our own vantage point and our own individual agendas, whether we realize it or not. Our situation as subjective individuals trying to interpret meaning in our daily life and in the literature we read suggests the dilemma of scientists whose physical means of studying phenomena in laboratory experiments inevitably introduce an element of error and distortion into their research data.

Nevertheless, even if as historians we agree that events seldom have any single or central cause, we can learn from the approach taken by New Historicist critics that individual works can be approached as part of a larger literary, biographical, historical, and cultural context. For example, stories by Nachtigal, Irving, Hawthorne, and Poe illustrate ways that the new genre of short fiction developed in its earliest years. In addition to studying the history of a literary genre, we can study an individual story in the context of its author's entire career, appreciating, for example, how D. H. Lawrence developed from his early realistic style in "Odour of Chrysanthemums" to his later symbolic style in "The Rocking-Horse Winner."

The interaction of writers, as with John Steinbeck's recasting of Lawrence's early story in "The Chrysanthemums," is another aspect of the historical study of short fiction, as authors continue to create a living tradition of storytelling. Finally, authors themselves sometimes interact with their readers by elucidating their thematic intentions in individual stories, as William Faulkner does in commenting on "A Rose for Emily" and Flannery O'Connor does in her remarks about "A Good Man Is Hard to Find." These explicit statements of authorial intent are part of the historical background of these stories.

Reading short fiction closely, most of us are conscious that stories have a literal as well as a literary context. From the headnotes to the individual authors and the essays by writers and critics in the Commentaries section (p. 726), you will learn that occasionally storytellers create work based on their personal experience of a specific historic event, as Stephen Crane did in "The Open Boat," when he fictionalized what happened to him as a passenger after the shipwreck of the steamship *Commodore* off the Florida coast in January 1897.

For other writers, the inspiration for their fiction may be a personal story that they tell in order to communicate their suffering to others in an attempt to expose social injustice, as Charlotte Perkins Gilman did when she wrote "The Yellow Wallpaper." This story emerged from Gilman's own experience of a nervous breakdown, the result of a "rest cure" prescribed by an eminent physician in Philadelphia who, like others of the time, refused to recognize a woman's need for intellectual stimulation.

Literary critics point out that history penetrates literature in a variety of ways, and the closer a fictional work is to our own time, the more we take for granted its historical context. For example, the setting of Joyce Carol Oates's "Where Are You Going, Where Have You Been?" includes many details about teen culture in the early 1960s. When fifteen-year-old Connie hangs out with her friends at the drive-in restaurant across the street from the shopping mall, they would listen to "the music that made everything so good: the music was always in the background like music at a church service, it was something to depend upon."

If you research the historical context of this short story, you will learn that Connie is listening to such jukebox hits as "Kisses Sweeter than Wine," "Chantilly Lace," "Do You Wanna Dance," and "Ten Commandments of Love." The escapist lyrics of romantic songs like these echo in her mind when a menacing visitor, Arnold Friend, turns up unexpectedly in her driveway and psychologically bullies her into submission. Oates dedicated the story to Bob Dylan, who redefined popular music in the mid-1960s when he wrote songs containing a tougher representation of American society — songs like "It Ain't Me, Babe," "The Times They Are A-Changin'," and "Blowin' in the Wind."

Most of the stories in this anthology are ideal for studying how storytellers respond to the social and political issues of their time, from the description of war in the fiction of Isaac Babel, Frank O'Connor, and Tim O'Brien to the depiction of the effect desegregation has on a Georgia city bus in a Flannery O'Connor story, the misery of AIDS in a story by Susan Sontag, and a sudden Puerto Rican ghetto killing in a story by Jack Agueros. Ralph Ellison dramatizes the courage of a black youth enduring racial prejudice in the Midwest, Amy Tan charts the tension between a Chinese mother and her California-born daughter, Tillie Olsen projects the thoughts of a single parent anxious about her child's future after high school. These and other works of fiction contain our human history, as Joseph Conrad realized. That storytellers reflect the truth of our lives at actual historical moments is evident to every attentive reader.

4

STORYTELLER
TO STORYTELLER

For spite of all the Indian-summer sunlight on the hither side of Hawthorne's soul, the other side — like the dark half of the physical sphere — is shrouded in blackness, ten times black. . . . Now, it is that blackness in Hawthorne, of which I have spoken, that so fixes and fascinates me.
–HERMAN MELVILLE in the Berkshires, reviewing
Nathaniel Hawthorne's *Mosses from an Old Manse*

If what makes a writer distinctive is an individual voice, then why do we study the ways writers interact with one another? We can trace a direct line of influence between "Peter Klaus the Goatherd" and "Rip Van Winkle" because we know that Irving translated Nachtigal's transcription of the folktale. In fact, Irving's copy of *Folks-sagen, Nacherzhaht von Otmar,* the German book he used for his translation, is in his library at Sunnyside, Irving's home (now a museum) in Tarrytown, New York. When Irving recast the folktale, he enlarged the thematic content by creating an archetypal figure who has appealed to generations of readers. Peter Klaus was a tragic victim, a man whose life was devastated by the twenty years he lost in an enchanted sleep; Rip Van Winkle was a comic hero, a free soul who triumphed over his long sleep in the mountains by becoming the village storyteller and transforming his life into story. Irving's originality was in creating an unforgettable comic character.

The example of Irving and Nachtigal teaches us something about the importance of history and tradition in short story literature. We prize originality and diversity in our culture, but we live in a complex web of relationships with other people, and our literature reflects the interdependence of all human beings, including writers. The French anthropologist Claude Lévi-Strauss wrote in *The Way of the Masks* that "When he claims to be solitary, the artist lulls himself in a perhaps fruitful illusion, but the privilege he grants himself is not real. When he thinks he is expressing himself spontaneously, creating an original work, he is answering other past or present, actual or potential creators. Whether one knows it or not, one never walks alone along the path of creativity."

We appreciate writers for their individuality, but we also hear their voices as storytellers in company with a chorus of their peers. In the essay "Tradition and the Individual Talent," the American poet T. S. Eliot discussed the nature of the responses of writers to other writers. Eliot understood that in our literary tradition, instances of memorable writing rarely originate in the direct influence between two writers, as we have seen with Irving and Nachtigal. Eliot believed that tradition is "a matter of much wider significance." Usually writers read other writers to gain a historical sense, a perception "not only of the pastness of the past, but of its presence."

Eliot's insight into the ways writers interact with the past is also helpful as an explanation of why tradition is a living presence for readers of literature as well as for the authors who create it. For Eliot,

> what happens when a new work of art is created is something that happens simultaneously to all the works of art which preceded it. The existing monuments form an ideal order among themselves, which is modified by the introduction of the new (the really new) work of art among them. The existing order is complete before the new work arrives; for order to persist after the supervention of novelty, the *whole* existing order must be, if ever so slightly, altered. . . . The past should be altered by the present as much as the present is directed by the past.

Irving's fanciful story changes the way we regard Nachtigal's faithful transcription of the German folktale. "Rip Van Winkle" comes at the beginning of a new phase of literary history, the metamorphosis of anonymous works from the oral tradition of storytelling into the published form of short stories credited to individual authors.

Nearly two hundred years after Nachtigal and Irving, the tradition of one writer influencing another continues. In the literary magazine *Antaeus* in the spring of 1989, the editor Daniel Halpern described how he polled "a hundred or so" contemporary authors and asked them to list a few of the classic writers who had in "some crucial way" influenced their own work. Halpern found that the top ten most influential short story writers were as follows:

1. *Anton Chekhov* (influenced fifteen of the polled contemporary authors, including Raymond Carver, Nadine Gordimer, Tim O'Brien, Susan Sontag, and Eudora Welty)
2. *William Faulkner* (influenced twelve authors, including Joyce Carol Oates)
3. *Ernest Hemingway* (influenced ten authors, including Carver)
4. *James Joyce* (influenced ten authors, including Oates and O'Brien)
5. *Franz Kafka* (influenced ten authors, including Oates and Sontag)
6. *Henry James* (influenced seven authors)
7. *Isaac Babel* (influenced five authors)
8. *Jorge Luis Borges* (influenced five authors, including Sandra Cisneros)
9. *Edgar Allan Poe* (influenced five authors)
10. *Sherwood Anderson* (influenced four authors)

Using the headnotes and commentary in this anthology, you can trace several different lines of influence among storytellers. Most of them are less direct than the link between Irving and Nachtigal. From Eudora Welty's perspective, as she observes in her commentary on how plot and character function in Chekhov's work, "The fact that stories have plots in common is of no more account than that many people have blue eyes." Welty was concerned with analyzing what she considered the "deeper" depths of fiction, the way "characters in the plot connect us with the vastness of our secret life, which is endlessly explorable."

How the influence of one author on another can help to shape the latter's creation of what Welty would term an "awe-inspiring" character can be seen by recognizing the effect of Nathaniel Hawthorne's short stories on Herman Melville. In 1850 Melville confessed his admiration for the dark side of Hawthorne when he reviewed a book of Hawthorne's tales, *Mosses from an Old Manse*. Then, a few years later, when Melville began writing magazine fiction, he created one of the darkest characters in American literature — the despairing Wall Street clerk in "Bartleby, the Scrivener."

In late-nineteenth-century short fiction, a thematic influence is discernible between the Russian writers Anton Chekhov and Leo Tolstoy. In Chekhov's creation of the title character of "The Darling," he seems to have deliberately challenged Tolstoy's patriarchal view of the role of women, at least as we understand it from Tolstoy's commentary on the story. Sometimes writers agree; sometimes they disagree. If they express their response to each other's ideas in a short story or a commentary, then the line of influence between the two writers may deepen your understanding of a specific work. What is most important is *the work* as an expression of the writer. Remember the warning of the American philosopher George Santayana, "To understand how the artist felt, however, is not criticism; criticism is an investigation of what the work is good for."

Early in the twentieth century, when the short story was flourishing as a literary form, the work of older writers often inspired younger ones. For example, the American writer Willa Cather expressed her admiration for Sarah Orne Jewett in an introduction to Jewett's collected stories, where in an eloquent paragraph Cather explained what had drawn her to her predecessor's short fiction in the first place:

> When we find ourselves on shipboard, among hundreds of strangers, we very soon recognize those who are sympathetic to us. We find our own books in the same way. We like a writer much as we like individuals; for what he is, simply, underneath his accomplishments. More often than we realize, it is for some moral quality, some ideal which he himself cherishes, though it may be little discernible in his behavior in the world. It is the light behind his books and is the living quality in his sentences.

The American modernist writer Sherwood Anderson explained in *A Story Teller's Story* that he was emboldened to experiment with the form of his short stories after reading a book by Gertrude Stein. As the literary tradition developed, specific works of short fiction also served as the source of new stories. You can see this happening when the Irish writer Frank O'Connor credits the Russian writer Isaac Babel's "My First Goose," about the Soviet revolution, as the inspiration for O'Connor's antiwar story "Guests of the Nation," about the Irish struggle to break free from English rule. More recently, the American writer Joyce Carol Oates recast Katherine Anne Porter's "He" in her story "Heat," taking a different point of view toward the characters. Studying a story's source can help us to understand it as one writer's response to another writer's prose, not imitating the earlier writer's style or plot but using it as a way to express a personal voice and a different interpretation of human experience.

Short story writers can also create stories using sources and materials other than fiction. The contemporary American author Raymond Carver wrote "Errand" as a tribute to Anton Chekhov, after reading a biography of the Russian author by Henri Troyat. The details about Chekhov's life that Carver took from the biography and the ones he invented to give shape and form to his story of Chekhov's death all help us appreciate Carver's genius as a storyteller. The American writer Susan Glaspell used her play *Trifles* (1916) as the basis of her story "A Jury of Her Peers." The playwright Tennessee Williams dramatized the idea for his play *The Glass Menagerie* (1945) from his early story "Portrait of a Girl in Glass."

Finally, in this anthology, we can see the operation of influence in the way the Native American writer Leslie Marmon Silko wrote "Yellow Woman" as her version of one of the legends of her Laguna tribe. She retold the traditional story as a deliberate extension of the creative spirit of her own heritage, unlike Irving's appropriation nearly two hundred years earlier of what he called "the rich mine of German literature" to advance his own career as a writer. As the critic Guy Davenport recognized in his book *Every Force Evolves a Form,* "We live in, or seem to live in, a century whose art summarizes, or explores to the limits of art, forms developed in other times."

The French critic Julia Kristeva and the Russian critic Mikhail Bakhtin coined the term *intertextuality* to refer to the presence or aspects of one or more earlier texts within a new work. Examples of **intertextuality** could be actual quotations from an older work, as in Carver's use of Troyat's biography of Chekhov in "Errand." It could also be **allusion**, as when the Latina writer Sandra Cisneros refers to Rip Van Winkle in "The Monkey Garden" or when the southern writer Dorothy Allison creates a character who summarizes the plot of a Flannery O'Connor story in "Lupus." **Parody** is another instance of intertextuality, as when Jane Smiley imagines a humorous new ending for Kafka's "The Metamorphosis." Some critics use the concept of intertextuality more broadly to include influences on a writer inside a specific literary tradition. Reading Flannery O'Connor could remind us of other southern writers in the grotesque tradition, such as William Faulkner.

Throughout the history of the short story, authors have been interacting with one another and their culture in a variety of ways. You can enjoy the stories in this anthology without tracing their influences or becoming aware of intertextuality. But as you study short fiction, you may find that, rather than narrowing your sense of the literary tradition by constraining it to a hierarchy of influences, knowledge of these interactions gives you a broader perspective in which to enjoy this literary genre, as storytellers continue to create and revitalize the tradition in a complex web of tales.

RELATED COMMENTARIES: *Raymond Carver, "On 'Errand,' " page 823; Kate Chopin, "How I Stumbled upon Maupassant," page 740; Herman Melville, "Blackness in Hawthorne's 'Young Goodman Brown,' " page 768; Jay Parini, "Lawrence's and Steinbeck's 'Chrysanthemums,' " page 786; Jane Smiley, "Gregor: My Life as a Bug," page 798; Leo Tolstoy, "Chekhov's Intent in 'The Darling,' " page 801.*

5

READING, THINKING, AND WRITING ABOUT SHORT FICTION

General rules in art are useful chiefly as a lamp in a mine, or a handrail down a black stairway; they are necessary for the sake of the guidance they give, but it is a mistake, once they are formulated, to be too much in awe of them.
—EDITH WHARTON, *The Writing of Fiction*

Read literature for the pleasure of it, Ernest Hemingway once told an interviewer, adding that "whatever else you find will be the measure of what you brought to the reading." We all have different personalities and come from different backgrounds, but we all look forward to being entertained when we turn to a story. Anything else you find there comes from you. A story becomes more meaningful when you read actively, relating the author's personal vision embodied in the form and content of the narrative to your own experience of life and the questions you ask of it.

Reading short fiction attentively and imaginatively promises the further enjoyment of discovering how the storyteller uses language to create a work of art. This way of reading brings you closer to understanding the achievement of the stories in this anthology and their writers. Literature is invention, and storytellers are inventors, whether they appear in the guise of entertainers, teachers, or enchanters. The authors whose stories are collected here are experts at invention. They delight us most completely when we apprehend the genius of their art by studying how they select the details and shape the patterns of their fiction.

What is the best way to read a story? The writer Vladimir Nabokov once suggested that the ideal reader should develop "a combination of the artistic and the scientific [temperament]. The enthusiastic artist alone is apt to be too subjective in his attitude toward a book, and so a scientific coolness of judgment will temper the intuitive heat." Read a story the first time for pleasure; bring out your "scientific coolness" when you study it the second time.

The first time you read a story, you may find yourself concerned primarily with *arriving* at the end of the narrative, seeing how the author resolves the plot. On your second reading you can focus on *getting there*, seeing how the author invents and shapes the narrative by using the elements of fiction. Ideally, you should remain a little aloof, a little detached when reading the second time. Cherish the details of the story's pattern. Enjoy the pleasure of beginning to understand its magic by taking notes on your responses to the author's use of the different elements of fiction.

When you read a story for the first time, you may find it relatively easy to see the elements of plot, character, and setting interact on the page. They stand out because they seem to make the story happen, and — at least for the casual reader — they appear to be what the story is about. Point of view, style, and theme, on the other hand, are less visible elements. Many readers regard them with dread as part of what they call the "hidden meaning" of a story. While it is true that you may have to look for these particular elements deliberately, you will find that this hunt is worth the treasure. The more you read attentively, the easier it will be to appreciate how all the elements operate in short fiction. You will begin to understand more fully that *how* a story is written is an essential part of *what* it is saying.

If you make the effort, you will find that reading literature is an activity that challenges your intellect and emotions to the highest degree. After finishing a story for the first time, you may feel contradictory responses to it, uncertain how to interpret what you have read. A second or third reading may help clarify your impressions, or you may find you have to close your book and think about the story if it doesn't fit easily into your preconceptions about human experience. The effort is worthwhile. As the critic Ray Carey has explained, the different forms of storytelling can "point a way out of some of the traps of received forms of thinking and feeling. Every artist makes a fresh effort of awareness. He [or she] offers new forms of caring. He [or she] can point out the processed emotions and canned understandings that deceive us. He [or she] can reveal the emotional lies that ensnare us. He [or she] can help us to new and potentially revolutionary understandings of our lives." Because reading a good story is potentially an enlightening experience, you will find that analyzing the means available to the storyteller is one of the best ways to make the story accessible to you.

The great eighteenth-century English critic Samuel Johnson said that the great majority of people needed to be reminded more often than instructed. Remember to read each story at least once in its entirety. The best way to give short stories a chance to entertain and enchant you is to sit down and grant them your full attention. Read them carefully straight through from beginning to end.

Stories are shorter than novels, but they're not necessarily easier to read. The editor Charles McGrath cautions that

> stories aren't just *brief*, they're *different*; and they require of the reader something like the degree of concentration they require of the writer. . . . You can't skim or coast or leap ahead, and if you have to put a story down, it's not always easy to pick up — emotionally, that

is — where you left off. You have to backtrack a little, or even start over. It's not enough to read a story the way you read a book or a newspaper. Stories ask of us that we surrender ourselves to them.

GUIDELINES FOR STUDYING SHORT FICTION

1. Make an entry in your notebook for each story assigned in class, writing down the author's name and the story's title and date. As you begin to read, remember T. S. Eliot's advice in his essay "Tradition and the Individual Talent" that "criticism is as inevitable as breathing, and that we should be none the worse for articulating what passes in our minds when we read a book and feel an emotion about it, for criticizing our own minds in their work of criticism."

2. Use a dictionary to look up words in both the headnote and the story that you do not understand.

3. After you have read the story, make notes about the way the author has used the elements of fiction; this will help you remember and review the story later. Note, for example, the names of the characters, the geographical setting, the author's choice of a point of view, and the literary style in which it is written. Try summing up the story's theme in a phrase or sentence.

4. If you have difficulty understanding the story's meaning or how any of the elements of fiction work within it, write down your questions so you can ask them in class.

5. In class, take notes on the important material about the story that you learn from lectures and discussions and ask the questions you recorded after you read the assignment. You may be able to develop these notes in later writing assignments.

6. Review technical words about short fiction that were used in class; this will help you to understand them better.

7. If you have particularly enjoyed a story, go to the library to check out other works by that writer. Reading on your own will enrich the class assignments.

CRITICAL THINKING ABOUT SHORT FICTION

You will find that reading a story and discussing it in class are only part of the process of understanding it. Usually your thinking about a story begins with interpreting it, clarifying what the author is saying in the action of the plot, and making sure you understand the characters and have a clear idea of the theme of the story. Critical thinking goes a step further beyond interpretation when you discuss how the form of the story is related to its content or when you analyze how the story relates to your own experience.

Thinking about a story for an essay assignment will help you to focus your thoughts. Ideas for writing can come from any number of sources. Sometimes your instructor will give you a specific assignment; other times you will be asked to generate the idea for the paper yourself. Whatever the case, your reading notes and the class discussions will help you prepare for writing about the story.

Before you can start thinking about writing a response to literature, you should feel that you thoroughly understand the story as a whole. Read it again to remind yourself of the passages that strike you with particular force. Underline the words and sentences you consider significant — or, even better, make a list in your notebook of what seems important while you are rereading the story. These can be outstanding descriptions of the characters or settings, passages of meaningful dialogue, details showing the way the author builds toward the story's climax, or hints that foreshadow the conclusion. To stimulate ideas about topics, you may want to jot down answers to the following questions about the elements of the story as you reread it.

Plot. Does the plot depend on chance, or coincidence? Or does it grow out of the personalities of the characters? Are any later incidents foreshadowed early in the story? Are the episodes presented in chronological order? If not, why is this so? Does the climax indicate a change in a situation or a change in a character? How dramatic is this change? Or is there no change at all?

Character. Are the characters believable? Are they stereotypes? Do they suggest real people, or abstract qualities? Is there one protagonist or are there several? Does the story have an antagonist? How does the author tell you about the main character — through description of physical appearance, actions, thoughts, and emotions, or through contrast with a minor character? Does the main character change in the course of the story? If so, how? Why?

Setting. How does the setting influence the plot and the characters? Does it help to suggest or develop the meaning of the story?

Point of View. How does the point of view shape the theme? Would the story change if told from a different viewpoint? In first-person narration, can you trust the narrator?

Style. Is the author's prose style primarily literal or figurative? Can you find examples of irony in dialogue or narrative passages? If dialect or colloquial speech is used, what is its effect? Does the author call attention to the way he or she uses words, or is the literary style inconspicuous?

Theme. Does the story's title help explain its meaning? Can you find a suggestion of the theme in specific passages of dialogue or description? Are certain symbols or repetitions of images important in revealing the author's intent in the story, what Edgar Allan Poe would call "the single effect"?

Now put the text aside and look over the notes in your journal. Can you see any pattern in them? You may find that you have been most impressed by the way the author developed characterizations, for example. Then you will have a possible topic for your paper. Certainly if you have a choice, you should pick whatever appeals to you the most in the story and concentrate on it.

WRITING ABOUT SHORT FICTION

In the appendix, "Writing about Literature" (p. 2081) you will find a discussion of the most frequently assigned methods of writing essays about short fiction: explication, analysis, and comparison and contrast. Brainstorming ideas for your paper, organizing your thoughts into a coherent outline, and creating rough and finished drafts are some of the topics discussed in this section, which is intended to help you work your way through the various stages of the writing process.

Different assignments for writing about short fiction may involve specific critical approaches to literature. For example, you may be asked to analyze your own response to the author's voice or the symbolism in a story as a "reader response" critic, or you may decide to express your ideas about a story from a feminist or historical perspective. These different approaches are an excellent way to develop your critical thinking about literature. The titles of several commentaries in Chapter 7 (p. 726) indicate that they were written using specific critical strategies.

Finally, the headnotes and commentary on the various authors and stories in this anthology suggest a range of topics exploring the intertextual and cultural background of works of short fiction for a research paper. Whatever your assignments, you will find that writing about literature will intensify your involvement with it, clarifying your responses and sharpening your critical thinking.

RELATED COMMENTARIES: *Wayne C. Booth, "A Rhetorical Reading of O'Connor's 'Everything That Rises Must Converge,' " page 867; Ralph Ellison, "The Influence of Folklore on 'Battle Royal,' " page 744; Sandra M. Gilbert and Susan Gubar, "A Feminist Reading of Gilman's 'The Yellow Wallpaper,' " page 749; J. Hillis Miller, "A Deconstructive Reading of Melville's 'Bartleby the Scrivener,' " page 770; Flannery O'Connor, "Writing Short Stories," page 849; Eudora Welty, "Is Phoenix Jackson's Grandson Really Dead?" page 809.*

6

STORIES AND STORYTELLERS

JACK AGUEROS *(b. 1934) was born and raised in East Harlem, New York City. He grew up in a multicultural neighborhood and attended local schools, where a Jewish friend taught him about the prevalence of prejudice in the world by talking about Hitler's efforts to exterminate the Jews during World War II. "I had thought that prejudice meant discrimination against Puerto Ricans . . . ," he remembers. "[My friend] made me think it wasn't so bad to be Puerto Rican, even though I definitely did not look American."*

In the 1960s Agueros was a political activist ("rabble-rouser" is his term) for Puerto Rican rights, serving as New York City deputy commissioner of the Community Development Agency, appointed by then-mayor John Lindsay. In 1967 he resigned his position and began a hunger strike, vowing to fast until the city government changed its practice of excluding Puerto Ricans from advisory and decision-making boards. From 1976 to 1986 Agueros was the director of El Museo del Barrio in New York, the oldest Puerto Rican cultural institution in the United States. During these years he thought of himself as "working the other side of the cultural angle" in his efforts to promote working-class art and to make visual arts more accessible to the Puerto Rican community.

Agueros has written television dramas for children about Puerto Rican life that were produced on "Sesame Street," but in recent years he has concentrated on writing autobiographical essays, short fiction, and poetry, including a translation of the early-twentieth-century Puerto Rican poet Julia de Burgos. Dominoes and Other Stories from the Puerto Rican, Agueros's first collection of stories, was published in 1993.

31

Commenting on "Dominoes," he has compared the rules of the game to the social rules that bind the men playing it:

> *I've seen it happen many times — over a game of stickball or asking a girl to dance. These men are not depraved or crazy. They're trapped in the culture. It's very systematic. You mention my mother and we have to go to blows. Just the way the double-six domino has to lead to the Dead Man's Box.*

Agueros portrays his working-class characters sympathetically, but he is skeptical of the writer's role in stimulating significant social change: "I don't know how the role of a writer relates to the advancement of his community. A lot of people think that when they're doing better, it means that the community is doing better. I don't believe that at all."

JACK AGUEROS

Dominoes

1993

DOUBLE SIX: THE BOX OF TEETH

Ebarito liked to hold six dominoes in his left hand. And he wished his hands were larger so that he might span all seven at once. But even Paco with his large hands could not hold seven dominoes.

He tapped the single domino he held in his right hand once on the board. It was a signal that meant he passed. It was irritating to pass at his first turn in the first game.

Paco, sitting to Ebarito's right, laughed a simple "ha," and said nothing.

Tito, the next player, played his domino at a right angle to the double six that Paco had led with. And he also kept another domino spinning at his right hand by periodically snapping his index finger and his thumb.

Wilson, the fourth player, liked to lay his dominoes on their sides in one semicircle. He took one and placed it on the board, then tightened the semicircle.

Paco laughed two loud "ha's" and slapped his domino down on the board. When he took his hand away Ebarito could see he would have to pass again since the game was at sixes at both ends.

"*No voy,*" he said in Spanish, without tapping his domino.

Paco laughed one "ha."

Tito, playing one and spinning one, said, "Remember, many of one, few of another."

Ebarito took a long drink from his can of beer.

Wilson looked at his little round wall and played a domino. Then he said, "Only three of those."

Paco played and said, "You know how to count, but the game was invented by a mute."

Another round had gone by and Ebarito saw that he was controlling the threes. But it was too late in this game. He had passed twice and might have to pass once more. There was no doubt about it — Paco had the luck and the skill. It was very hard to beat him in a game of dominoes. And especially when he teamed up with Tito — or even worse when he teamed up with Wilson. Luckily today Wilson was Ebarito's partner and so Ebarito had expectations of making a decent showing — perhaps even coming in under the one hundred point handicap that Paco had offered. If Paco had teamed with Wilson, Ebarito could have gotten a handicap of 200 points — but so what — nobody could beat Paco and Wilson, not even with a 250 point handicap. And with a handicap that large there was no purpose to the game. A handicap only meant something if it was the element that wobbled the wheel of fortune.

Ebarito finished his beer. Decided he would not drink another one. None of them drank, why should he? Or maybe they just wouldn't drink with him.

DOUBLE FIVE

Alma leaned on the ledge of her second floor window. With a cushion under her elbows she could sit like this for hours, enjoying the street life. The boys were not yet playing stoop ball. But by the *bodega*, near the empty yard, she could see her uncle Paco playing dominoes with of all people, Ebarito. Most of the men disliked Ebarito. And even though he had a reputation as a good barber the men avoided him. And as he also had a reputation as a lousy domino player it was strange to see him sitting there teamed up with Wilson. Her uncle Paco had told her once, "Ebarito is nothing but a barber and a pretty boy. He can't play dominoes and he's always trying. In the merchant marine we were all barbers."

She had learned the game out of curiosity — she couldn't see what was in it that kept the men sitting there day and night playing and playing. In the summer in the street and in the winter in her kitchen.

She had begged uncle Paco to teach her the game and one Saturday evening, when her old boyfriend Sammy had stood her up, he took the dominoes out and said, "Sit down." He was a man like that — couldn't express too many things and yet he was smart. For twenty years he sailed around the world visiting many interesting places, reading when he was not playing. But he just didn't talk very much.

Dominoes seemed to Alma a ridiculous game. Whoever got the double six played first if you were just starting. Once you played the first game whoever won started the second game. Then it was just a matter of following the numbers. Your opponent put down a six, you played a six. Your opponent put down a two, you put down a two. If you didn't have something you passed. But her uncle said it wasn't like that at all. He said there was strategy. If you had a two-five and a four-five and you could play a five, which one would you play? Well, that was strategy. You looked over the board, you counted all the fours, you counted all the twos, you looked at your own hand, and you decided which one to play. That wasn't luck, that was skill. That was how you controlled the game.

But Alma didn't like the game — if she wanted to kill time she preferred looking out the window, and in the winter she liked cards now and then — especially a game called "Casino." For the moment she was more interested in her new boyfriend PeeWee. She was hoping he would come over from 112th Street, where he lived near Third Avenue. And perhaps he would invite her for a walk in Central Park or better still, to a movie. She hadn't been to a movie in a few weeks, and the Star Theater on 107th and Lexington was playing two good films. But PeeWee did not come around the corner.

DOUBLE FOUR

Paco shifted his weight on the milk crate he was sitting on.

Ebarito played one of his threes.

Tito knocked on the board, close to where his domino was spinning.

"Oh, oh, somebody's got no threes or sixes," said Wilson.

Ebarito said, "I believe Paco said this was a game invented by a mute."

Paco slapped down his domino with great force, and when he removed his ham-sized hand he said, *"Lo tranque.* I locked it at sixes — let's go, count up."

Tito took everyone's dominoes and counted forty-two points, then turned them all face down.

Paco mixed the dominoes driving his left hand clockwise, and his right hand counterclockwise, slightly out of synchronization.

Tito said, "I like a hand where I have four of something and they don't come out until the second or third play."

"Take your dominoes," said Paco leaving his hands at the side of the board. This meant he would take last — take whatever remained. It was like a boxer dropping his gloves to his sides and daring his opponent to hit him.

Ebarito took his seven, skipping around hoping to get a better selection. But he was feeling worse and worse. He had no business in this foursome. This was strictly a losing proposition for him. His game was women; the barber shop. His hand was terrible, three doubles. *"La caja de muerto,"* the dead man's box, meaning the double blank, and *"La caja de dientes,"* meaning the box of teeth, or the double six, and the double three. This was going to be another painful and embarrassing loss. He could see that he would lose by 250 points — the 100 point handicap would be just another humiliation.

"No voy," said Tito furiously spinning his domino.

"Already?" said Wilson.

By the next play Ebarito had to pass and he struck his domino down with a hard sharp blow — like an angry gaveling. And he wished it were a nail that he could drive through the board and into the ground. He knew he was going to lose, knew he had but one recourse now — to lose gracefully — be a good sport — offer to buy everyone a beer, a cigar or a drink — say the obvious out loud — "You are too good for me" — but Goddammit he couldn't do it — it stuck in his craw like a thing he could not swallow, could not spit.

DOUBLE THREE

Of all the sounds on the street the sharp blow of a domino on a wooden board caught Alma's attention. It was a sound she had heard many times before, and which she disliked. When she looked over at the game Ebarito looked angry, but she still couldn't see Paco's face. She could see Wilson, whom she didn't like although she had known him all her life. He was her uncle's best friend. A master domino player and a very hard man. He believed in fate. "Men who are real men can live their lives anyway they like — because their destiny is clear. To be a *macho* is the destiny. The trouble for you Alma is that you fool around with men who are not *machos*," he had told her once in her kitchen. "And for a woman, Wilson, what is the fate for a woman?" "I don't know," he had answered, "I don't know anything about women. For women I recommend an *espiritista* and the church. One will tell you the future and the other will console you about it. But I'm not sure which does what."

After that pronouncement both Wilson and Paco had broken into very heavy prolonged laughter. Tito was not like that. He was kinder and he talked more, but he was not as strong as they were. They could make him do the opposite of what he believed. But they genuinely liked him — not because they influenced him, but because they seemed to enjoy his company — he was what they were not — social and friendly, fun loving and relaxed. But he had not left Puerto Rico to join the merchant marine when he was sixteen — like Wilson or Paco. They were just *jíbaro* kids — country boys suddenly with mean men and dangerous work and thirty years at sea always looking to see who was standing behind you. Tito had steady legs, like a man used to walking on the earth. Wilson and Paco had a strange gait, always waiting for the sea to pitch!

DOUBLE TWO

Tito played and was talking. "You know my father used to say when we were watching the baseball games — 'The ball is round, son, the game is not over until the last out.' But in dominoes, especially in double-six, the game is over as soon as you get your hand. Isn't it?"

Paco grimaced. He believed in skill.

"I know, I know, the game was invented by a mute. But I can't be like you Paco — I can't sit through a whole game and not say a word — to me part of this game is talking — about this about that."

"Oh yeah — some people even say that that is your strategy as a team. You yak yak to distract them while Paco . . ." Ebarito let his voice trail off.

"While Paco what?" asked Tito and Wilson at the same time.

"Yeah, while Paco what, little barber?" asked Paco.

"Something the matter with being a barber?" asked Ebarito while playing his double six.

Paco stared at the board.

"Apparently barbers can't count," said Paco.

"Right," said Tito, the domino perfectly still under his right index finger, "you passed on six before — it's called reneging."

"You calling me a cheater?" asked Ebarito standing up.

"No," said Paco, "but then you better admit you can't count."

"Perhaps your mother can't count," said Ebarito. And in the moment that his words were being formed in his mouth he bent over, picked up the metal milk crate he had been sitting on and swung it at Paco's head.

Paco was already rising, his straightening legs upending the board, the dominoes scattering, and with his left arm he grabbed the milk crate and pushed it back into Ebarito's chest. And Ebarito went backward, losing his balance, down. And Paco was on top of him, both massive hands tightly around Ebarito's throat.

Tito went to break it up, but Wilson pulled him by the arm, and hissed, "Fuck the pretty boy barber," and Tito just stopped, as if Wilson's venom had paralyzed him.

Then Paco started to lift Ebarito's head and strike it against the sidewalk at the same time that he tightened his hands ever more around his neck. Ebarito reached into his jacket and pulled out the long thin trimming scissor with the loop that cradles the pinky and adds balance and control to the tool. He began to drive the scissor into Paco's rib cage with a circular motion from the elbow, for the rest of his arm was immobilized by Paco's knee.

"They are killing each other," gasped Tito to Wilson who was still holding them.

DOUBLE ONE

Alma broke out of a reverie to see PeeWee across the street calling her and yelling and pointing over to the vacant lot. When Alma looked she let go a scream and yelled, "Paco, Paco, stop it, stop it, Wilson stop them. Tito for God's sake do something. PeeWee call the police." And she screamed again. But no one moved.

She screamed again, her hands covering her ears as if she could not tolerate her own penetrating wail. And then she turned into the apartment. When she was no longer visible in the window PeeWee came to life again, for he had been more startled by the screaming than by the fight. The screaming turned the fight into something more serious than he had at first thought.

He looked in two directions trying to remember where the nearest phone was. And then he headed for the corner drugstore, before he could see Alma come screaming out of her hallway like a train out of a tunnel onto the street.

Wilson still held Tito's arm in a vise-like grip. "They are *machos*," said Wilson, seeming to speak through clenched teeth, "they know what they want."

But at the sight of Alma pulling at Paco, Tito broke loose and kicked the scissor from Ebarito's hand and pulled at Paco too.

Paco stood up thinking Ebarito was dead. He took a few staggering steps and then found his balance, and began walking off in no particular direction. But his left rib cage looked like a colander with blood pouring out of twelve scissor holes, some spurting, some just trickling down over the already forming clots. And when he reached the fire hydrant Paco crumbled down into a pile like a pneumatic tire that had a blow out.

He was dead.

He was dead before he fell.

He was dead even before he stood up and walked.

The body had its habits and in a man who spoke very little, his body had spoken last — it had refused to die where fate had ordained — he didn't want to be near Ebarito. Death wanted him there, but he would go here.

Alma in tears, in terror and hysteria was on her knees crying and screaming next to the body of the wrong man, for it was inconceivable to her that Ebarito could be alive and her uncle dead. She screamed over the bloody head, face and body of Ebarito, "You killed him, you let him be killed, you killers." She screamed at everyone. She screamed at no one.

DOUBLE BLANK
THE DEAD MAN'S BOX

Ebarito awoke. Pain played over his body head to throat to arm. And he realized he had his eyes closed.

He tried to open his eyes and found it difficult to do. He could not turn his head and his neck seemed very stiff. As he tried to feel his body beyond the pain he discovered that he could not lift his head, and while he did not seem to be tied down, he couldn't shift his weight at all. He could curl his fingers and wiggle his toes. His tongue felt huge in his mouth: as if he had a wash-cloth stuffed there rather than a tongue. His left arm was more mobile but he could only raise it somewhat. He tried to open his eyes again.

And when he opened them everything seemed to be clouded and out of focus. And there was nothing but white to see, but there was the unmistakable smell of hospital — like there was the unmistakable smell of barbershop, of dentist, of laundry.

Then he heard a squeaky wheel, footsteps, and heard someone speaking. The doctor was asking, "Do you understand English? — Do you speak English? English?"

Painfully he tried to shake his head yes, as he could not find his voice. He could not move the wash rag in his mouth, nor spit it out. And he could not shake his head either.

The doctor was saying, "Lucky boy you are to be alive — your skull was cracked — do you remember?"

"No," said the doctor, "you can't speak — he wrecked your trachea, larynx? — you know — voice box? Adam's apple? With a little oxygen deprivation — maybe asphyxia. Drove your cricoid up against the 7th in the neck — you understand? You have cracks in your trachea. Severe damage to the vocal cords from bone and cartilage pushing up against them, tearing through them. You may never be able to speak — maybe growl. I did some marvelous work in there — you understand — *vida* — life? Serious concussion, on your *cabeza* — you know — head, *cabeza*? One eye is fine — a matter of a few days, maybe two weeks and we will know the whole story on the eyes. There is a little infection there now — *infección*, you know?"

Ebarito tried to point to his mouth, but his left arm was manacled to the bed.

∞

WOODY ALLEN *was born Allen Stewart Konigsberg in 1935 and grew up in what he calls "a typical, noisy ethnic family" in Brooklyn, New York. "Probably if my parents had pushed me along more cultural lines, I might have started out being a serious writer, because that's what has always interested me. But I had no cultural background whatsoever. . . . I didn't go to a play until I was about eighteen years old, almost never went to a museum, listened only to popular music, and never read at all." After graduating from high school, Allen attended and dropped out of both New York University and the City College of New York. While still a student he sold jokes to newspaper columnists, and at the age of seventeen, in 1952, he joined NBC as a staff writer.*

In 1964 Allen wrote his first screenplay, What's New Pussycat? *Since then he has written, directed, and often starred in more than thirty films. He is one of the few major American filmmakers to insist on total control over his productions, which he equates with artistic freedom. "I'm only making films because I'm as free there as if I were writing novels," he says. "You can't create unless you're completely free." Writing was important to Allen even as a child: "From the first grade, I was always the class writer. I remember very distinctly, I'd buy those little black and white notebooks and say, 'Today I'll write a mystery story.' I'd go home and write, and invariably they'd come out funny. I certainly couldn't care less if I ever performed again, and don't care much if I ever direct another film, but I would not like to be in a position not to write."*

In addition to screenplays, Allen has published three books of comic stories and sketches: Getting Even *(1971),* Without Feathers *(1975), and* Side Effects *(1980).* The Complete Prose of Woody Allen *appeared in 1991. Like his films, his short fiction reveals a humorously skeptical yet romantic mind. He is also an astute analyzer of his own work: "If it's successful, the laughs don't come from jokes, they come from characters in emotionally desperate circumstances." "The Kugelmass Episode," which first appeared in* The New Yorker, *won the 1978 O. Henry Award.*

RELATED PLAY: *Woody Allen, "Two Monologues from* Annie Hall *and* Manhattan," *page 1897.*

WOODY ALLEN

The Kugelmass Episode   1977

Kugelmass, a professor of humanities at City College, was unhappily married for the second time. Daphne Kugelmass was an oaf. He also had two dull sons by his first wife, Flo, and was up to his neck in alimony and child support.

"Did I know it would turn out so badly?" Kugelmass whined to his analyst one day. "Daphne had promised. Who suspected she'd let herself go and swell up like a beach ball? Plus she had a few bucks, which is not in itself a healthy reason to marry a person, but it doesn't hurt, with the kind of operating nut I have. You see my point?"

Kugelmass was bald and as hairy as a bear, but he had soul.

"I need to meet a new woman," he went on. "I need to have an affair. I need not look the part, but I'm a man who needs romance. I need softness, I need flirtation. I'm not getting younger, so before it's too late I want to make love in Venice, trade quips at '21,'° and exchange coy glances over red wine and candlelight. You see what I'm saying?"

Dr. Mandel shifted in his chair and said, "An affair will solve nothing. You're so unrealistic. Your problems run much deeper."

"And also this affair must be discreet," Kugelmass continued. "I can't afford a second divorce. Daphne would really sock it to me."

"Mr. Kugelmass — "

"But it can't be anyone at City College, because Daphne also works there. Not that anyone on the faculty at C.C.N.Y. is any great shakes, but some of those coeds . . ."

"Mr. Kugelmass — "

"Help me. I had a dream last night. I was skipping through a meadow holding a picnic basket and the basket was marked 'Options.' And then I saw there was a hole in the basket."

"Mr. Kugelmass, the worst thing you could do is act out. You must simply express your feelings here, and together we'll analyze them. You have been in treatment long enough to know there is no overnight cure. After all, I'm an analyst, not a magician."

"Then perhaps what I need is a magician," Kugelmass said, rising from his chair. And with that he terminated his therapy.

A couple of weeks later, while Kugelmass and Daphne were moping around in their apartment one night like two pieces of old furniture, the phone rang.

"I'll get it," Kugelmass said. "Hello."

"Kugelmass?" a voice said. "Kugelmass, this is Persky."

"Who?"

"Persky. Or should I say The Great Persky?"

"Pardon me?"

"I hear you're looking all over town for a magician to bring a little exotica into your life? Yes or no?"

"Sh-h-h," Kugelmass whispered. "Don't hang up. Where are you calling from, Persky?"

Early the following afternoon, Kugelmass climbed three flights of stairs in a broken-down apartment house in the Bushwick section of Brooklyn. Peering through the darkness of the hall, he found the door he was looking for and pressed the bell. I'm going to regret this, he thought to himself.

Seconds later, he was greeted by a short, thin, waxy-looking man.

"*You're* Persky the Great?" Kugelmass said.

"The Great Persky. You want a tea?"

"No, I want romance. I want music. I want love and beauty."

"But not tea, eh? Amazing. O.K., sit down."

Persky went to the back room, and Kugelmass heard the sounds of boxes and furniture being moved around. Persky reappeared, pushing before him a large object on squeaky roller-skate wheels. He removed some old silk

---

21: A famous restaurant in New York City.

handkerchiefs that were lying on its top and blew away a bit of dust. It was a cheap-looking Chinese cabinet, badly lacquered.

"Persky," Kugelmass said, "what's your scam?"

"Pay attention," Persky said. "This is some beautiful effect. I developed it for a Knights of Pythias date last year, but the booking fell through. Get into the cabinet."

"Why, so you can stick it full of swords or something?"

"You see any swords?"

Kugelmass made a face and, grunting, climbed into the cabinet. He couldn't help noticing a couple of ugly rhinestones glued onto the raw plywood just in front of his face. "If this is a joke," he said.

"Some joke. Now, here's the point. If I throw any novel into this cabinet with you, shut the doors, and tap it three times, you will find yourself projected into that book."

Kugelmass made a grimace of disbelief.

"It's the emess,"° Persky said. "My hand to God. Not just a novel, either. A short story, a play, a poem. You can meet any of the women created by the world's best writers. Whoever you dreamed of. You could carry on all you like with a real winner. Then when you've had enough you give a yell, and I'll see you're back here in a split second."

"Persky, are you some kind of outpatient?"

"I'm telling you it's on the level," Persky said.

Kugelmass remained skeptical. "What are you telling me — that this cheesy homemade box can take me on a ride like you're describing?"

"For a double sawbuck."°

Kugelmass reached for his wallet. "I'll believe this when I see it," he said.

Persky tucked the bills in his pants pocket and turned toward his bookcase. "So who do you want to meet? Sister Carrie? Hester Prynne? Ophelia? Maybe someone by Saul Bellow? Hey, what about Temple Drake?° Although for a man your age she'd be a workout."

"French, I want to have an affair with a French lover."

"Nana?"°

"I don't want to have to *pay* for it."

"What about Natasha in *War and Peace*?"

"I said French. I know! What about Emma Bovary?° That sounds to me perfect."

"You got it, Kugelmass. Give me a holler when you've had enough." Persky tossed in a paperback copy of Flaubert's novel.

---

emess: The truth.
double sawbuck: $20.
Sister Carrie . . . Temple Drake: Carrie Meeber is the heroine of Theodore Dreiser's novel *Sister Carrie* (1900); Hester Prynne is in Nathaniel Hawthorne's novel *The Scarlet Letter* (1850); Ophelia is in Shakespeare's *Hamlet* (c. 1600); and Temple Drake is a character in William Faulkner's novel *Sanctuary* (1931).
Nana: The title character in Émile Zola's novel *Nana* (1880).
Emma Bovary: The heroine of Gustave Flaubert's novel *Madame Bovary* (1865).

"You sure this is safe?" Kugelmass asked as Persky began shutting the cabinet doors.

"Safe. Is anything safe in this crazy world?" Persky rapped three times on the cabinet and then flung open the doors.

Kugelmass was gone. At the same moment, he appeared in the bedroom of Charles and Emma Bovary's house at Yonville. Before him was a beautiful woman standing alone with her back turned to him as she folded some linen. I can't believe this, thought Kugelmass, staring at the doctor's ravishing wife. This is uncanny. I'm here. It's her.

Emma turned in surprise. "Goodness, you startled me," she said. "Who are you?" She spoke in the same fine English translation as the paperback.

It's simply devastating, he thought. Then, realizing that it was he whom she had addressed, he said, "Excuse me, I'm Sidney Kugelmass. I'm from City College. A professor of humanities. C.C.N.Y.? Uptown. I — oh, boy!"

Emma Bovary smiled flirtatiously and said, "Would you like a drink? A glass of wine, perhaps?"

She is beautiful, Kugelmass thought. What a contrast with the troglodyte who shared his bed! He felt a sudden impulse to take this vision into his arms and tell her she was the kind of woman he had dreamed of all his life.

"Yes, some wine," he said hoarsely. "White. No, red. No, white. Make it white."

"Charles is out for the day," Emma said, her voice full of playful implication.

After the wine, they went for a stroll in the lovely French countryside. "I've always dreamed that some mysterious stranger would appear and rescue me from the monotony of this crass rural existence," Emma said, clasping his hand. They passed a small church. "I love what you have on," she murmured. "I've never seen anything like it around here. It's so . . . so modern."

"It's called a leisure suit," he said romantically. "It was marked down." Suddenly he kissed her. For the next hour they reclined under a tree and whispered together and told each other deeply meaningful things with their eyes. Then Kugelmass sat up. He had just remembered he had to meet Daphne at Bloomingdale's. "I must go," he told her. "But don't worry. I'll be back."

"I hope so," Emma said.

He embraced her passionately, and the two walked back to the house. He held Emma's face cupped in his palms, kissed her again, and yelled, "O.K., Persky! I got to be at Bloomingdale's by three-thirty."

There was an audible pop, and Kugelmass was back in Brooklyn.

"So? Did I lie?" Persky asked triumphantly.

"Look, Persky, I'm right now late to meet the ball and chain at Lexington Avenue, but when can I go again? Tomorrow?"

"My pleasure. Just bring a twenty. And don't mention this to anybody."

"Yeah. I'm going to call Rupert Murdoch."°

Kugelmass hailed a cab and sped off to the city. His heart danced on point. I am in love, he thought, I am the possessor of a wonderful secret. What

---

Rupert Murdoch: The Australian newspaper tycoon (b. 1931).

he didn't realize was that at this very moment students in various classrooms across the country were saying to their teachers, "Who is this character on page 100? A bald Jew is kissing Madame Bovary?" A teacher in Sioux Falls, South Dakota, sighed and thought, Jesus, these kids, with their pot and acid. What goes through their minds!

Daphne Kugelmass was in the bathroom-accessories department at Bloomingdale's when Kugelmass arrived breathlessly. "Where've you been?" she snapped. "It's four-thirty."

"I got held up in traffic," Kugelmass said.

Kugelmass visited Persky the next day, and in a few minutes was again passed magically to Yonville. Emma couldn't hide her excitement at seeing him. The two spent hours together, laughing and talking about their different backgrounds. Before Kugelmass left, they made love. "My God, I'm doing it with Madame Bovary!" Kugelmass whispered to himself. "Me, who failed freshman English."

As the months passed, Kugelmass saw Persky many times and developed a close and passionate relationship with Emma Bovary. "Make sure and always get me into the book before page 120," Kugelmass said to the magician one day. "I always have to meet her before she hooks up with this Rodolphe character."

"Why?" Persky asked. "You can't beat his time?"

"Beat his time. He's landed gentry. Those guys have nothing better to do than flirt and ride horses. To me, he's one of those faces you see in the pages of *Women's Wear Daily*. With the Helmut Berger hairdo. But to her he's hot stuff."

"And her husband suspects nothing?"

"He's out of his depth. He's a lack-lustre little paramedic who's thrown in his lot with a jitterbug. He's ready to go to sleep by ten, and she's putting on her dancing shoes. Oh, well. . . . See you later."

And once again Kugelmass entered the cabinet and passed instantly to the Bovary estate at Yonville. "How you doing, cupcake?" he said to Emma.

"Oh, Kugelmass," Emma sighed. "What I have to put up with. Last night at dinner, Mr. Personality dropped off to sleep in the middle of the dessert course. I'm pouring my heart out about Maxim's and the ballet, and out of the blue I hear snoring."

"It's O.K., darling, I'm here now," Kugelmass said, embracing her. I've earned this, he thought, smelling Emma's French perfume and burying his nose in her hair. I've suffered enough. I've paid enough analysts. I've searched till I'm weary. She's young and nubile, and I'm here a few pages after Léon and just before Rodolphe. By showing up during the correct chapters, I've got the situation knocked.

Emma, to be sure, was just as happy as Kugelmass. She had been starved for excitement, and his tales of Broadway night life, of fast cars and Hollywood and TV stars, enthralled the young French beauty.

"Tell me again about O. J. Simpson," she implored that evening, as she and Kugelmass strolled past Abbé Bournisien's church.

"What can I say? The man is great. He sets all kinds of rushing records. Such moves. They can't touch him."

"And the Academy Awards?" Emma said wistfully. "I'd give anything to win one."

"First you've got to be nominated."

"I know. You explained it. But I'm convinced I can act. Of course, I'd want to take a class or two. With Strasberg maybe. Then, if I had the right agent — "

"We'll see, we'll see. I'll speak to Persky."

That night, safely returned to Persky's flat, Kugelmass brought up the idea of having Emma visit him in the big city.

"Let me think about it," Persky said. "Maybe I could work it. Stranger things have happened." Of course, neither of them could think of one.

"Where the hell do you go all the time?" Daphne Kugelmass barked at her husband as he returned home late that evening. "You got a chippie stashed somewhere?"

"Yeah, sure, I'm just the type," Kugelmass said wearily. "I was with Leonard Popkin. We were discussing Socialist agriculture in Poland. You know Popkin. He's a freak on the subject."

"Well, you've been very odd lately," Daphne said. "Distant. Just don't forget about my father's birthday. On Saturday?"

"Oh, sure, sure," Kugelmass said, heading for the bathroom.

"My whole family will be there. We can see the twins. And Cousin Hamish. You should be more polite to Cousin Hamish — he likes you."

"Right, the twins," Kugelmass said, closing the bathroom door and shutting out the sound of his wife's voice. He leaned against it and took a deep breath. In a few hours, he told himself, he would be back in Yonville again, back with his beloved. And this time, if all went well, he would bring Emma back with him.

At three-fifteen the following afternoon, Persky worked his wizardry again. Kugelmass appeared before Emma, smiling and eager. The two spent a few hours at Yonville with Binet and then remounted the Bovary carriage. Following Persky's instructions, they held each other tightly, closed their eyes, and counted to ten. When they opened them, the carriage was just drawing up at the side door of the Plaza Hotel, where Kugelmass had optimistically reserved a suite earlier in the day.

"I love it! It's everything I dreamed it would be," Emma said as she whirled joyously around the bedroom, surveying the city from their window. "There's F.A.O. Schwarz. And there's Central Park, and the Sherry is which one? Oh, there — I see. It's too divine."

On the bed there were boxes from Halston and Saint Laurent. Emma unwrapped a package and held up a pair of black velvet pants against her perfect body.

"The slacks suit is by Ralph Lauren," Kugelmass said. "You'll look like a million bucks in it. Come on, sugar, give us a kiss."

"I've never been so happy!" Emma squealed as she stood before the mirror. "Let's go out on the town. I want to see *Chorus Line* and the Guggenheim and this Jack Nicholson character you always talk about. Are any of his flicks showing?"

"I cannot get my mind around this," a Stanford professor said. "First a strange character named Kugelmass, and now she's gone from the book. Well, I guess the mark of a classic is that you can reread it a thousand times and always find something new."

The lovers passed a blissful weekend. Kugelmass had told Daphne he would be away at a symposium in Boston, and would return Monday. Savoring each moment, he and Emma went to the movies, had dinner in Chinatown, passed two hours at a discothèque, and went to bed with a TV movie. They slept till noon on Sunday, visited SoHo, and ogled celebrities at Elaine's. They had caviar and champagne in their suite on Sunday night and talked until dawn. That morning, in the cab taking them to Persky's apartment, Kugelmass thought, It was hectic, but worth it. I can't bring her here too often, but now and then it will be a charming contrast with Yonville.

At Persky's, Emma climbed into the cabinet, arranged her new boxes of clothes neatly around her, and kissed Kugelmass fondly. "My place next time," she said with a wink. Persky rapped three times on the cabinet. Nothing happened.

"Hmm," Persky said, scratching his head. He rapped again, but still no magic. "Something must be wrong," he mumbled.

"Persky, you're joking!" Kugelmass cried. "How can it not work?"

"Relax, relax. Are you still in the box, Emma?"

"Yes."

Persky rapped again — harder this time.

"I'm still here, Persky."

"I know, darling. Sit tight."

"Persky, we *have* to get her back," Kugelmass whispered. "I'm a married man, and I have a class in three hours. I'm not prepared for anything more than a cautious affair at this point."

"I can't understand it," Persky muttered. "It's such a reliable little trick."

But he could do nothing. "It's going to take a little while," he said to Kugelmass. "I'm going to have to strip it down. I'll call you later."

Kugelmass bundled Emma into a cab and took her back to the Plaza. He barely made it to his class on time. He was on the phone all day, to Persky and to his mistress. The magician told him it might be several days before he got to the bottom of the trouble.

"How was the symposium?" Daphne asked him that night.

"Fine, fine," he said, lighting the filter end of a cigarette.

"What's wrong? You're as tense as a cat."

"Me? Ha, that's a laugh. I'm as calm as a summer night. I'm just going to take a walk." He eased out the door, hailed a cab, and flew to the Plaza.

"This is no good," Emma said. "Charles will miss me."

"Bear with me, sugar," Kugelmass said. He was pale and sweaty. He kissed her again, raced to the elevators, yelled at Persky over a pay phone in the Plaza lobby, and just made it home before midnight.

"According to Popkin, barley prices in Kraków have not been this stable since 1971," he said to Daphne, and smiled wanly as he climbed into bed.

• • •

The whole week went by like that. On Friday night, Kugelmass told Daphne there was another symposium he had to catch, this one in Syracuse. He hurried back to the Plaza, but the second weekend there was nothing like the first. "Get me back into the novel or marry me," Emma told Kugelmass. "Meanwhile, I want to get a job or go to class, because watching TV all day is the pits."

"Fine. We can use the money," Kugelmass said. "You consume twice your weight in room service."

"I met an Off Broadway producer in Central Park yesterday, and he said I might be right for a project he's doing," Emma said.

"Who is this clown?" Kugelmass asked.

"He's not a clown. He's sensitive and kind and cute. His name's Jeff Something-or-Other, and he's up for a Tony."

Later that afternoon, Kugelmass showed up at Persky's drunk.

"Relax," Persky told him. "You'll get a coronary."

"Relax. The man says relax. I've got a fictional character stashed in a hotel room, and I think my wife is having me tailed by a private shamus."°

"O.K., O.K. We know there's a problem." Persky crawled under the cabinet and started banging on something with a large wrench.

"I'm like a wild animal," Kugelmass went on. "I'm sneaking around town, and Emma and I have had it up to here with each other. Not to mention a hotel tab that reads like the defense budget."

"So what should I do? This is the world of magic," Persky said. "It's all nuance."

"Nuance, my foot. I'm pouring Dom Pérignon and black eggs into this little mouse, plus her wardrobe, plus she's enrolled at the Neighborhood Playhouse and suddenly needs professional photos. Also, Persky, Professor Fivish Kopkind, who teaches Comp Lit and who has always been jealous of me, has identified me as the sporadically appearing character in the Flaubert book. He's threatened to go to Daphne. I see ruin and alimony; jail. For adultery with Madame Bovary, my wife will reduce me to beggary."

"What do you want me to say? I'm working on it night and day. As far as your personal anxiety goes, that I can't help you with. I'm a magician, not an analyst."

By Sunday afternoon, Emma had locked herself in the bathroom and refused to respond to Kugelmass's entreaties. Kugelmass stared out the window at the Wollman Rink and contemplated suicide. Too bad this is a low floor, he thought, or I'd do it right now. Maybe if I ran away to Europe and started life over. . . . Maybe I could sell the *International Herald Tribune*, like those young girls used to.

The phone rang. Kugelmass lifted it to his ear mechanically.

"Bring her over," Persky said. "I think I got the bugs out of it."

Kugelmass's heart leaped. "You're serious?" he said. "You got it licked?"

---

private shamus: Detective.

"It was something in the transmission. Go figure."

"Persky, you're a genius. We'll be there in a minute. Less than a minute."

Again the lovers hurried to the magician's apartment, and again Emma Bovary climbed into the cabinet with her boxes. This time there was no kiss. Persky shut the doors, took a deep breath, and tapped the box three times. There was the reassuring popping noise, and when Persky peered inside, the box was empty. Madame Bovary was back in her novel. Kugelmass heaved a great sigh of relief and pumped the magician's hand.

"It's over," he said. "I learned my lesson. I'll never cheat again, I swear it." He pumped Persky's hand again and made a mental note to send him a necktie.

Three weeks later, at the end of a beautiful spring afternoon, Persky answered his doorbell. It was Kugelmass, with a sheepish expression on his face.

"O.K., Kugelmass," the magician said. "Where to this time?"

"It's just this once," Kugelmass said. "The weather is so lovely, and I'm not getting any younger. Listen, you've read *Portnoy's Complaint?* Remember The Monkey?"°

"The price is now twenty-five dollars, because the cost of living is up, but I'll start you off with one freebie, due to all the trouble I caused you."

"You're good people," Kugelmass said, combing his few remaining hairs as he climbed into the cabinet again. "This'll work all right?"

"I hope. But I haven't tried it much since all that unpleasantness."

"Sex and romance," Kugelmass said from inside the box. "What we go through for a pretty face."

Persky tossed in a copy of *Portnoy's Complaint* and rapped three times on the box. This time, instead of a popping noise there was a dull explosion, followed by a series of crackling noises and a shower of sparks. Persky leaped back, was seized by a heart attack, and dropped dead. The cabinet burst into flames, and eventually the entire house burned down.

Kugelmass, unaware of this catastrophe, had his own problems. He had not been thrust into *Portnoy's Complaint,* or into any other novel, for that matter. He had been projected into an old textbook, *Remedial Spanish,* and was running for his life over a barren, rocky terrain as the word *tener* "to have") — a large and hairy irregular verb — raced after him on its spindly legs.

ର

DOROTHY ALLISON (b. 1949) *was born in Greenville, South Carolina, the first child of a fifteen-year-old unwed mother who dropped out of the seventh grade to work as a waitress. Allison was raised in extreme poverty by her mother's family; she remembers "hiding out under the porch" so she could listen to her grandmother and aunts tell randy stories. Her childhood was scarred from the time she was five to eleven years old, when she was often beaten and raped by her abusive stepfather. Allison writes of her lasting sense of shame and guilt:*

The Monkey: The sexually liberated heroine of Philip Roth's novel *Portnoy's Complaint* (1969).

*Most of my life I have despised myself, the child who didn't tell her mother she
was being raped. The only defense I ever found was sending my little sisters
in to him, because I knew he wasn't as bad with them as he was with me. So I
grew up convinced that I was an evil creature. Because I put people in harm's
way to escape harm just a little bit.*

*After attending Florida Presbyterian College on a National Merit scholarship,
Allison joined a feminist collective when the radical women's movement surfaced in
the early 1970s. "Feminism saved my life. It was a substitute religion that made
sense." She did not try to see her family until 1981, when she chose to return to her
roots. She understands that her first book of poetry,* The Women Who Hate Me,
*(1983) "wouldn't have happened if I hadn't started talking to my mother and my sis-
ters again." The story "Lupus" is from her second book,* Trash *(1988), a collection of
short stories originally published by small lesbian presses and alternative magazines
which won two Lambda Literary Awards. Four years later Allison received mainstream recognition with her autobiographical novel* Bastard Out of Carolina, *a fi-
nalist for the 1992 National Book Award. Allison's fourth book,* Two or Three
Things I Know for Sure, *was published in 1994, and she is currently working on a
novel, another collection of short stories, and a fictionalized portrait of Janis Joplin.*

In the preface to Trash, *Allison describes her childhood as "that long terrible
struggle to simply survive, to escape my stepfather, uncles, speeding Pontiacs, broken
glass and rotten floorboards." She watched as the members of her family succumbed to
what she considered the diseases of the poor — "diseases that come from working in
mills, bad food, stress, exposure to chemicals. My great-grandmother lived to 110. In
the next generation, nobody reached sixty." She says that she had to come to terms
with her feelings of "survivor guilt" for her family members who could not escape the
destructive cycle of backwater poverty as she had done by going to college: "Everything I survived became one more reason to want to die." Writing about her life became Allison's way to come to terms with her past, honoring the attempt to make
literature out of "the condensed and reinvented experience of a cross-eyed, working-
class lesbian, addicted to violence, language, and hope."*

RELATED STORY: *Flannery O'Connor, "A Good Man Is Hard to Find," page 558.*

DOROTHY ALLISON

Lupus°

1988

"You don't get home often enough."

It is August and high summer has fattened all the trees on Old Henderson
Road, dried the road to powder and grey loose loam, coating the myrtle
and dogwood trees with a flat white alkali stain. Temple sits on her
porch while her oldest girl rinses her hairpins in a tub of bleach and

---

Lupus: Any of various skin diseases; especially a chronic tuberculous disease of the skin or
mucous membranes; a particularly dangerous disease of metabolical origin — incurable but
sometimes controlled by steroid drugs — which exhausts the energies of its victims and ne-
cessitates an extremely careful and restricted life. [Allison's note]
Lupus: A wolf, from "eating into the substance of"; cancer. [Allison's note]

spring water. Off in the yard, the dogs raise a dust cloud. I wipe sweat off my mouth and drink tea like I never left home.

Temple slides her palms on the worn porch steps, flat and smooth under her hands, back and forth. We watch a long green trailer turn the corner, shear the leaves on the myrtle, just miss the leaning porch, the poplar, the young dogwood.

"That would have done it," Temple laughs softly, open-mouthed and happy. "I could have put in the new plumbing this year 'stead of next. Anything that big's got to be insured."

I nod, scratch chigger bites on my ankles, unable to relax to pissing in the weeds, hoping that trailer comes back and pays for more than the plumbing. She married late, Cousin Temple did, married late and well — steady boy, one of those Roberts from Ashville, a lean, freckled, still boy, as steady as she was and as quiet, a good son who loved his mother and never ran around like the other boys all the other cousins married early.

Temple rolls a little hair between two fingers and turns her red-tan face up into the sun slanting past the porch beams. This house, yard, dirt road, myrtle trees, kudzu holding the screens on the windows — none of it would stand up to a Northern winter, a Yankee tax assessor, or an estate sale. But it puts Temple outside them, a property owner, something none of the rest of the family can imagine becoming. Temple has been an outsider all her life, though living on her own since her mama left her with her own mother when Temple was barely seven — a quiet red-faced seven as she is now a quiet red-faced woman whose hair shows grey where it lays close to her skull.

"You were a bean when you were a girl," Temple tells me, "a string bean, and your sister was a butter bean. Your mama was a stretch of stringy pork, and together you didn't make a decent Sunday dinner."

When Temple laughs, her head goes back. Her long red hair shakes out, and all the grey she has so skillfully tried to hide flows loose and flashes at me, silver and white. "Temple," I tell her, "you're finally getting old."

"Bullshit," she flares. "And apple butter. I'm just more woman than the men in this town can handle. And I've more left to me than most people get to start out." Then she smiles, oh she smiles! The skin around her mouth that's aged so dry and tight flushes and fills like the grin on a mewling baby. But her teeth slip loose, and her hand flies up to hide the wolf grin.

"Goddamn," she sighs. Her daughter doesn't look up. Temple's hand caresses her porch, strokes the soft, worn wood like the lover she barely remembers. "It ain't Robert, you know, but it is, I'd swear. All I have of him anyway. Nights, I seem to hear him breathing, but it's the walls. They sweat so, they smell just the way he did. And I got to where I don't care if I'm crazy. I talk to this house like it was him."

Somehow it is. There was an army insurance policy, a thousand-dollar burial, and a four-thousand-dollar mortgage, plus two more for the plumbing which never worked anyway. In the North, it would have brought nothing; in Ashville only a little more; but out here off Old Henderson Road in 1959 it was an estate for three orphans and a red-headed woman suddenly going grey.

"Lupus," she says, "it was Lupus." An old story I have heard many times these twenty-five years. Temple scratches herself, and spits, angry now as she was angry then. "Damn doctors, damn hospitals, never said what else. Lupus, you know, kills slow, takes a long time—years. But Robert, Lord, Robert sank into that bed. He died so fast. Weeks seemed like no time. He just melted away."

Maryat stirs her hairpins. Claire brings a pitcher of tea to the door. I wipe my mouth again, saying nothing, watching the sweat shine on Temple's cheeks. When I was a child and slept in her bed, I would lie awake and watch the line — eyelids to cheekbones to mouth. Never touched it, never once reached out to touch her cheekbone, though I dreamed of pulling her into my neck, sucking her throat, and licking her eyes. Now I curl my fingers around my hipbones, hug myself, and don't quite reach out to her trembling hands.

"You never saw the store, did you?" Little flecks of broken woodgrain pull up under Temple's fingernails. "Your mama wouldn't bring you girls around. Hell, your mama thought you girls were meant to be special, wasn't gonna carry you around to no honky-tonk roadhouse." She reaches for me, touching my sun-warmed thigh.

"But it wasn't like that, not really. The store was across from the high school and clean as a dried peach pit. Scrubbed hollow, hell, I scrubbed me raw. We had pinball machines, and a candy counter, Coke coolers, chip racks, and billiards. No liquor 'cept for Robert's beer in the back cooler."

"But we lost it, of course. We lost everything."

Temple pauses, pulls at her tea and frowns. "Hard to remember all that, hard times and craziness. I was crazy, you know, oh yes. We lost the store, the car, even the baby's bed — all those weeks with Robert lying still, breathing like a train going up a hill. All that slow, crazy time, and me crazy. Me just out of my head. I was howling at Granny, screaming at the girls, tearing at myself. Hated myself, like I'd done it, like I'd brought it on him. Nobody in his family had it, but Granny said we'd had a cousin with it, so maybe it had come through me."

"It was important then, how it had come on us. Later I didn't care, but then it was like that was the only thing that mattered."

Dust drifts down in the sunlight. Another truck turns the corner and shakes the porch. It's a shortcut, this road and Temple's lot. Truckers come through and wave. Temple ignores them, slaps her porch, watches the dirty paint flake down. The dogs in the yard, tied off to a tree, howl and kick and lie down again, panting in the heat.

"I got mustard grass, you know, and yellow nettles. Grow 'em 'cause it makes people mad, 'cause ain't nobody can tell me anything. It keeps people away, makes sure no one touches what's mine."

They still have fireflies in Greenville, and green tree frogs, katydids, and rock-sucking worms. The muscadines still hang in sheets off the trees behind Old Henderson Road. Once every few years, Temple takes up with some traveling man, someone she can't see staying around. She wants nobody permanent now, not after Robert and the girls, that first baby, everybody she ever loved.

"Temple's nothing but trouble," the cousins claim. They complain of her life, her girls. "Hard-assed, cold-hearted woman." Everybody agrees. "Thinks more of that ratty-walled house than her family, thinks more of herself than a woman should."

Off Old Henderson Road, the porches tilt. The paint chips off. Temple's bathroom is still out back of the pines. She has the cousins come over to prop the windows, wire back the roof where the slats are sliding down. Where the paint has gone, the wood stays bare and rain-marked. She won't paint again, says it will just flake off in the heat.

Kids come over from West Greenville, drive their pickups right up on the grass, hide behind the dead vines that shield the shed out back; stare in where Temple stores broken chairs, empty boxes, an extra bed. They giggle a lot, smoke dope, and occasionally fall through the rotten boards.

You gonna pay for that you white-eyed sonofabitch!

Temple threatens to pen that shed for chickens, set traps, loose the dogs. All she really does is talk to the uncles real loud on the phone.

Come up here and shoot me a few of these bastards!

Sometimes she doesn't bother to dial. Sometimes she doesn't bother to roll over or get up, lies in bed for a day, her face set and angry so the girls know to stay away. Gets up thinner but quiet. Goes back to work as the crossing guard at Greenville South-East, the only work she's had since Robert died.

"You ever read that Flannery O'Connor? I got the book from Macon a few years back. Heard she'd had the Lupus, thought it might be in there, but God knows it ain't. You read that crazy woman? Made me think people're worse than I thought, and I thought bad enough. But the worst was some of it made me laugh and then made me 'shamed. Thinking, what kind of woman laughs at such troubles? Babies drowning themselves for Jesus, preachers and old ladies getting their whole families shot dead 'cause they forgot the right highway."

Flat, flat, her hand, her face, the sunlight on the porch. Temple's memory of a
boy dead now twenty-five years. "I'd hate to think it was the Lupus."

"Get her to think of something else," Mama asked me. "People say she's going crazy out on that old porch."

Nobody really knows Temple. The women smile about her, say, *Lord God, but
she loved that man.* Everybody says it's a pity, how she sits, how she
doesn't get on with her life, take another husband, have another child,
plant zinnias or baby's breath and go on. Go on.

I sit on Temple's porch and drink coffee, drink tea when the morning heats up,
talk to her of New York and California, of cities she's never seen. I watch
how she laughs, her red hair swinging from side to side, bringing the
grey and white to the surface, bringing out the shadows and wrinkles
under her eyes.

"How can you live in a city? All those pictures like to make my heart hurt. I
could smell it — hot concrete, tar, and piss. No green for miles. No color
a'tall. Lord, where's the life in it?"

I tell her about the color of night, the lights on the bridges, the hot shine in the
women's eyes, the cold glare of metal moving fast. I tell her about the
cold winter light shining on flat stacks of slate, hanging over the New
Jersey highways, the cars growling rock music out their vents — how
tight the people wear their clothes, how tall the buildings, how sweet the
dawn after you do not sleep for days.

The silence answers me, I wipe my fingertips on the porch, smell myrtle and
crushed onion through the dust of passing trucks, watch Claire cross the
yard, how she swings her arms and throws back her head, her white face
with the black eyebrows etched as high and fierce as crows across the
highway. I have not been this still in years, have not heard my own heart
when I was not shadowed by full dark and bourbon, not looked into a
face that mirrored mine as Temple's does — bone to bone, ancient grief
to daily rage.

"How do you do it?" I ask her. "How do you live this far from the rest of the
world?"

"What do I need the world for?" Temple laughs at me. "Besides I got sugar,
just like Granny. Came on two years ago, and 'pressure, they say, though
I an't checking. What good is it to know you gonna die sooner than
later? It makes me think the world's too damn close on me anyway."

"Claire, honey, pour me another glass of tea."

Claire, the wire child, thin as the poplar on the corner, pale as the birch peeling in the backyard, brings the jug in two hands and smiles at me. The
little reddish-brown nodules on her shoulders could be freckles but are
not. The flush under Temple's skin deepens, and her hands start to

shake on the glass. She is seeing what I am watching — Claire's smile and those deadly little warts.

"You know, a lot of famous people died of the Lupus. But then people have it for years and never die, or at least, don't die of just that." She sighs, rolls the ragged ends of her hair between fingers suddenly flushed pink.

"You know what I did?" She looks away, away from me, away from her daughter, away from the dogs who paw restlessly at the bare patches near the trees. "I let them take his body. Told them to go ahead, do anything they had to. When it came down to it, I said, just tell me what it was. The girls, of course, I was thinking of the girls. And they took him, did their stuff to him, things I can't even imagine. I don't think, in the end, we buried more than the frame of him."

Temple's hands shake, her tea spills over the splintered boards of the porch. Leaning forward makes her face go a deeper red. "Doctors, like lawyers you know, they don't hurry."

"I thought it would be a while, weeks maybe, even months. But Lord, years! I never thought they'd take years, and then tell me nothing. Just the Lupus, 'cause of the spots and the strangling. Lupus like with Claire or that cousin I don't know that I really believe ever existed. But hell, they didn't really know what killed him. Lupus kills slow, and Robert died fast."

"Sometimes, sometimes, I dream sometimes, oh God!" Temple rocks her head back and forth, casts a glance at her daughters and looks quickly away, speaking in a whisper that does not carry to where they sit. "I dream sometimes I lead the children out in front of a big old semi, a row of hearses following easy as you please, all their daddies nodding at me as they're mowed down!"

She shakes her head, shakes her shoulders, her whole torso following, the pink in her cheeks going brighter than sunburn.

"But, sometimes, too, I dream I am alone, walking through Greenville as it burns, the sparks coming down on my neck but nothing burning me. No one sees me. They come out and throw water and yell. I just walk through and grin. Imagine the kind of woman I am to take pleasure in that kind of thing!"

Imagine the kind of woman she is, Temple on her porch with the paint flaking down. Temple with her hands still on her knees, ridged and knobby, the veins blue-purple and high. Her face a permanent red-tan flush. Her daughters going in and out, slowly, carefully, the deadly warts on the pale skin of their necks and calves burning her eyes.

Imagine what kind of woman sits still, safe in her own mind, slow as myrtle leaves turning. Sugar thickening the blood in her veins, pressure pinking her skin. Wanting nothing more than new plumbing and her daughters' slow movement forward, alive. Some man to come along now and then, never quite as real as the man who lives behind her eyes.

Temple writes me once a year, a letter that lists who's died, who's been born, a letter that ends with a reminder of who she is. She is my favorite cousin, after me the most remarkable, the one who lived with us the year I was seven, the year mama almost died, the year she first had cancer and I fell in love with the very idea of red-headed women.

"Do you hear from Temple?" Mama always asks me. "She say anything about the girls? Heard from Dot that Maryat was planning on getting married and Claire wasn't doing very well at all."

Every year I do not go home, it hurts me. I think of Temple, the year I was seven and she was eighteen; the year I was eleven and she lost her lover; the year she lost her teeth and her baby girl; the years I realized she would never be mine.

"Do you hear from Temple?" My mama, my cousins, my aunts always ask. I am the one she writes to, and if I have not heard from her then no one has. Sometimes I do not answer, I fall into Temple's white-eyed memories, the silence of her flushed cheeks, her thin face and hot eyes. The wolf in my neck bares his teeth, stretches, lays one paw on the other, dreaming of fire and sparks raining down, myrtle leaves blackening in the heat. I fight him with my love for Temple, hug to myself the warmth and stillness of her porch, the certainty that she does not fear the wolf in her, the wolf who hides his teeth but watches, watches out of her eyes.

ಬಜ

SHERWOOD ANDERSON *(1876–1941) was born to a jack-of-all-trades father in Camden, Ohio. He did not publish his first book until he was over forty, after working for many years as a newsboy, farm laborer, stable boy, factory hand, and advertising copywriter. Dissatisfied with the commercial spirit of the advertising business, Anderson made friends with writers in Chicago and began to publish his own poetry and fiction. The poet Carl Sandburg encouraged him, but Anderson's literary style was most influenced by* Three Lives *(1909), an experimental book by the expatriate American writer Gertrude Stein, which he felt revolutionized the language of narrative.*

In 1916 Anderson published his first novel, Windy McPherson's Son. *He followed it with another novel and a volume of poetry, but he did not receive wide recognition until 1919, with the book* Winesburg, Ohio. *This collection of related stories, including "Hands," about life in a small town explores the devastating consequences of the repressive conventions of a provincial society. It was followed by other important collections of stories:* The Triumph of the Egg *(1921),* Horses and Men *(1923), and* Death in the Woods and Other Stories *(1933). In his time Anderson was a strong influence on Ernest Hemingway, William Faulkner, Richard Wright, and John Steinbeck. The editor Martha Foley wrote in 1941 that*

> *Sherwood Anderson set out on new paths at a time when the American short story seemed doomed to a formula-ridden, conventionalized, mechanized, and commercialized concept. When* Winesburg, Ohio *appeared in 1919 it was intensely influential on writers who either had lost heart or had not yet found*

their way. His vision was his own; his characters were people into whose hearts and minds he seemed intuitively to peer; his prose was simple, deceptively simple, sensuous, rich, and evocative.

As literary critics have observed, the characteristic tone of Anderson's short fiction is melancholy reminiscence. In an understated fashion, he wove carefully selected realistic details into such narratives as "Hands," which moves by apparently formless associations of thought and feeling but is actually a controlled progression of fully dramatized situations. Anderson's importance in our literature is suggested by Richard Wright's acknowledgment that Anderson's stories made him see that through the powers of fiction, "America could be shaped nearer to the hearts of those who lived in it."

RELATED COMMENTARY: *Sherwood Anderson, "Form, Not Plot, in the Short Story," page 730.*

SHERWOOD ANDERSON

Hands   1919

Upon the half decayed veranda of a small frame house that stood near the edge of a ravine near the town of Winesburg, Ohio, a fat little old man walked nervously up and down. Across a long field that had been seeded for clover but that had produced only a dense crop of yellow mustard weeds, he could see the public highway along which went a wagon filled with berry pickers returning from the fields. The berry pickers, youths and maidens, laughed and shouted boisterously. A boy clad in a blue shirt leaped from the wagon and attempted to drag after him one of the maidens who screamed and protested shrilly. The feet of the boy in the road kicked up a cloud of dust that floated across the face of the departing sun. Over the long field came a thin girlish voice. "Oh, you Wing Biddlebaum, comb your hair, it's falling into your eyes," commanded the voice to the man, who was bald and whose nervous little hands fiddled about the bare white forehead as though arranging a mass of tangled locks.

Wing Biddlebaum, forever frightened and beset by a ghostly band of doubts, did not think of himself as in any way a part of the life of the town where he had lived for twenty years. Among all the people of Winesburg but one had come close to him. With George Willard, son of Tom Willard, the proprietor of the new Willard House, he had formed something like a friendship. George Willard was the reporter on the *Winesburg Eagle* and sometimes in the evenings he walked out along the highway to Wing Biddlebaum's house. Now as the old man walked up and down on the veranda, his hands moving nervously about, he was hoping that George Willard would come and spend the evening with him. After the wagon containing the berry pickers had passed, he went across the field through the tall mustard weeds and climbing a rail fence peered anxiously along the road to the town. For a moment he stood thus, rubbing his hands together and looking up and down the road, and then, fear overcoming him, ran back to walk again upon the porch of his own house.

In the presence of George Willard, Wing Biddlebaum, who for twenty years had been the town mystery, lost something of his timidity, and his shadowy personality, submerged in a sea of doubts, came forth to look at the world. With the young reporter at his side, he ventured in the light of day into Main Street or strode up and down on the rickety front porch of his own house, talking excitedly. The voice that had been low and trembling became shrill and loud. The bent figure straightened. With a kind of wriggle, like a fish returned to the brook by the fisherman, Biddlebaum the silent began to talk, striving to put into words the ideas that had been accumulated by his mind during long years of silence.

Wing Biddlebaum talked much with his hands. The slender expressive fingers, forever active, forever striving to conceal themselves in his pockets or behind his back, came forth and became the piston rods of his machinery of expression.

The story of Wing Biddlebaum is a story of hands. Their restless activity, like unto the beating of the wings of an imprisoned bird, had given him his name. Some obscure poet of the town had thought of it. The hands alarmed their owner. He wanted to keep them hidden away and looked with amazement at the quiet inexpressive hands of other men who worked beside him in the fields, or passed, driving sleepy teams on country roads.

When he talked to George Willard, Wing Biddlebaum closed his fists and beat with them upon a table or on the walls of his house. The action made him more comfortable. If the desire to talk came to him when the two were walking in the fields, he sought out a stump or the top board of a fence and with his hands pounding busily talked with renewed ease.

The story of Wing Biddlebaum's hands is worth a book itself. Sympathetically set forth it would tap many strange, beautiful qualities in obscure men. It is a job for a poet. In Winesburg the hands had attracted attention merely because of their activity. With them Wing Biddlebaum had picked as high as a hundred and forty quarts of strawberries in a day. They became his distinguishing feature, the source of his fame. Also they made more grotesque an already grotesque and elusive individuality. Winesburg was proud of the hands of Wing Biddlebaum in the same spirit in which it was proud of Banker White's new stone house and Wesley Moyer's bay stallion, Tony Tip, that had won the two-fifteen trot at the fall races in Cleveland.

As for George Willard, he had many times wanted to ask about the hands. At times an almost overwhelming curiosity had taken hold of him. He felt that there must be a reason for their strange activity and their inclination to keep hidden away and only a growing respect for Wing Biddlebaum kept him from blurting out the questions that were often in his mind.

Once he had been on the point of asking. The two were walking in the fields on a summer afternoon and had stopped to sit upon a grassy bank. All afternoon Wing Biddlebaum had talked as one inspired. By a fence he had stopped and beating like a giant woodpecker upon the top board had shouted at George Willard, condemning his tendency to be too much influenced by the people about him. "You are destroying yourself," he cried.

"You have the inclination to be alone and to dream and you are afraid of dreams. You want to be like others in town here. You hear them talk and you try to imitate them."

On the grassy bank Wing Biddlebaum had tried again to drive his point home. His voice became soft and reminiscent, and with a sigh of contentment he launched into a long rambling talk, speaking as one lost in a dream.

Out of the dream Wing Biddlebaum made a picture for George Willard. In the picture men lived again in a kind of pastoral golden age. Across a green open country came clean-limbed young men, some afoot, some mounted upon horses. In crowds the young men came to gather about the feet of an old man who sat beneath a tree in a tiny garden and who talked to them.

Wing Biddlebaum became wholly inspired. For once he forgot the hands. Slowly they stole forth and lay upon George Willard's shoulders. Something new and bold came into the voice that talked. "You must try to forget all you have learned," said the old man. "You must begin to dream. From this time on you must shut your ears to the roaring of the voices."

Pausing in his speech, Wing Biddlebaum looked long and earnestly at George Willard. His eyes glowed. Again he raised the hands to caress the boy and then a look of horror swept over his face.

With a convulsive movement of his body, Wing Biddlebaum sprang to his feet and thrust his hands deep into his trousers pockets. Tears came to his eyes. "I must be getting along home. I can talk no more with you," he said nervously.

Without looking back, the old man had hurried down the hillside and across a meadow, leaving George Willard perplexed and frightened upon the grassy slope. With a shiver of dread the boy arose and went along the road toward town. "I'll not ask him about his hands," he thought, touched by the memory of the terror he had seen in the man's eyes. "There's something wrong, but I don't want to know what it is. His hands have something to do with his fear of me and of everyone."

And George Willard was right. Let us look briefly into the story of the hands. Perhaps our talking of them will arouse the poet who will tell the hidden wonder story of the influence for which the hands were but fluttering pennants of promise.

In his youth Wing Biddlebaum had been a school teacher in a town in Pennsylvania. He was not then known as Wing Biddlebaum, but went by the less euphonic name of Adolph Myers. As Adolph Myers he was much loved by the boys of his school.

Adolph Myers was meant by nature to be a rare teacher of youth. He was one of those rare, little-understood men who rule by a power so gentle that it passes as a lovable weakness. In their feeling for the boys under their charge such men are not unlike the finer sort of women in their love of men.

And yet that is but crudely stated. It needs the poet there. With the boys of his school, Adolph Myers had walked in the evening or had sat talking until dusk upon the schoolhouse steps lost in a kind of dream. Here and there went his hands, caressing the shoulders of the boys, playing about the tousled heads. As he talked his voice became soft and musical. There was a caress in that also. In a way the voice and the hands, the stroking of the shoulders and the touching of the hair was a part of the schoolmaster's effort to carry a dream into the young minds. By the caress that was in his fingers he expressed himself. He was one of those men in whom the force that creates life is diffused, not centralized. Under the caress of his hands doubt and disbelief went out of the minds of the boys and they began also to dream.

And then the tragedy. A half-witted boy of the school became enamored of the young master. In his bed at night he imagined unspeakable things and in the morning went forth to tell his dreams as facts. Strange, hideous accusations fell from his loose-hung lips. Through the Pennsylvania town went a shiver. Hidden, shadowy doubts that had been in men's minds concerning Adolph Myers were galvanized into beliefs.

The tragedy did not linger. Trembling lads were jerked out of bed and questioned. "He put his arms about me," said one. "His fingers were always playing in my hair," said another.

One afternoon a man of the town, Henry Bradford, who kept a saloon, came to the schoolhouse door. Calling Adolph Myers into the school yard he began to beat him with his fists. As his hard knuckles beat down into the frightened face of the schoolmaster, his wrath became more and more terrible. Screaming with dismay, the children ran here and there like disturbed insects. "I'll teach you to put your hands on my boy, you beast," roared the saloon keeper, who, tired of beating the master, had begun to kick him about the yard.

Adolph Myers was driven from the Pennsylvania town in the night. With lanterns in their hands a dozen men came to the door of the house where he lived alone and commanded that he dress and come forth. It was raining and one of the men had a rope in his hands. They had intended to hang the schoolmaster, but something in his figure, so small, white, and pitiful, touched their hearts and they let him escape. As he ran away into the darkness they repented of their weakness and ran after him, swearing and throwing sticks and great balls of soft mud at the figure that screamed and ran faster and faster into the darkness.

For twenty years Adolph Myers had lived alone in Winesburg. He was but forty but looked sixty-five. The name Biddlebaum he got from a box of goods seen at a freight station as he hurried through an eastern Ohio town. He had an aunt in Winesburg, a black-toothed old woman who raised chickens, and with her he lived until she died. He had been ill for a year after the experience in Pennsylvania, and after his recovery worked as a day laborer in the fields, going timidly about and striving to conceal his hands. Although he did not understand what had happened he felt that the hands must be to blame. Again and again the fathers of the boys had talked of the hands. "Keep your hands to yourself," the saloon keeper had roared, dancing with fury in the schoolhouse yard.

Upon the veranda of his house by the ravine, Wing Biddlebaum continued to walk up and down until the sun had disappeared and the road beyond the field was lost in the grey shadows. Going into his house he cut slices of bread and spread honey upon them. When the rumble of the evening train that took away the express cars loaded with the day's harvest of berries had passed and restored the silence of the summer night, he went again to walk upon the veranda. In the darkness he could not see the hands and they became quiet. Although he still hungered for the presence of the boy, who was the medium through which he expressed his love of man, the hunger became again a part of his loneliness and his waiting. Lighting a lamp, Wing Biddlebaum washed the few dishes soiled by his simple meal and, setting up a folding cot by the screen door that led to the porch, prepared to undress for the night. A few stray white bread crumbs lay on the cleanly washed floor by the table; putting the lamp upon a low stool he began to pick up the crumbs, carrying them to his mouth one by one with unbelievable rapidity. In the dense blotch of light beneath the table, the kneeling figure looked like a priest engaged in some service of his church. The nervous expressive fingers, flashing in and out of the light, might well have been mistaken for the fingers of the devotee going swiftly through decade after decade of his rosary.

༙༙

MARGARET ATWOOD (b. 1939) is a Canadian writer of poetry and fiction. Born in Ottawa, Ontario, she spent the first eleven years of her life in the sparsely settled "bush" country of northern Ontario and Quebec, where her father, an entomologist, did research. She remembers that

> I did not spend a full year in school until I was in Grade Eight. I began to write at the age of five — poems, "novels," comic books, and plays — but I had no thought of being a professional writer until I was sixteen. I entered Victoria College, University of Toronto, when I was seventeen and graduated in 1961. I won a Woodrow Wilson Fellowship to Harvard, where I studied Victorian Literature, and spent the next ten years in one place after another: Boston, Montreal, Edmonton, Toronto, Vancouver, England, and Italy, alternately teaching and writing.

Atwood's first poem was published when she was nineteen. To date she has published two collections of short stories, several novels — including the best-sellers Surfacing (1972), The Handmaid's Tale (1986), Cat's Eye (1989), and The Robber Bride (1993) — and more than a dozen books of poetry. She was encouraged to write as a young woman because Canadians of her generation felt a strong need to develop a national literature.

Atwood has compared writing stories to telling riddles and jokes, all three requiring "the same mystifying buildup, the same surprising twist, the same impeccable sense of timing." She took pleasure in writing "Happy Endings," but she was puzzled by the form the story took:

> When I wrote "Happy Endings" — the year was, I think, 1982, and I was writing a number of short fictions then — I did not know what sort of creature it was. It was not a poem, a short story, or a prose poem. It was not quite a condensation, a commentary, a questionnaire, and it missed being a parable, a proverb, a paradox. It was a mutation. Writing it gave me a sense of furtive glee, like scribbling anonymously on a wall with no one looking.
>   This summer I saw a white frog. It would not have been startling if I didn't know that this species of frog is normally green. This is the way such a

mutant literary form unsettles us. We know what is expected, in a given arrangement of words; we know what is supposed to come next. And then it doesn't.

It was a little disappointing to learn that other people had a name for such aberrations [metafiction], and had already made up rules.

MARGARET ATWOOD

Happy Endings
1983

John and Mary meet.
What happens next?
If you want a happy ending, try A.

A

John and Mary fall in love and get married. They both have worthwhile and remunerative jobs which they find stimulating and challenging. They buy a charming house. Real estate values go up. Eventually, when they can afford live-in help, they have two children, to whom they are devoted. The children turn out well. John and Mary have a stimulating and challenging sex life and worthwhile friends. They go on fun vacations together. They retire. They both have hobbies which they find stimulating and challenging. Eventually they die. This is the end of the story.

B

Mary falls in love with John but John doesn't fall in love with Mary. He merely uses her body for selfish pleasure and ego gratification of a tepid kind. He comes to her apartment twice a week and she cooks him dinner, you'll notice that he doesn't even consider her worth the price of a dinner out, and after he's eaten the dinner he fucks her and after that he falls asleep, while she does the dishes so he won't think she's untidy, having all those dirty dishes lying around, and puts on fresh lipstick so she'll look good when he wakes up, but when he wakes up he doesn't even notice, he puts on his socks and his shorts and his pants and his shirt and his tie and his shoes, the reverse order from the one in which he took them off. He doesn't take off Mary's clothes, she takes them off herself, she acts as if she's dying for it every time, not because she likes sex exactly, she doesn't, but she wants John to think she does because if they do it often enough surely he'll get used to her, he'll come to depend on her and they will get married, but John goes out the door with hardly so much as a good-night and three days later he turns up at six o'clock and they do the whole thing over again.

Mary gets run-down. Crying is bad for your face, everyone knows that and so does Mary but she can't stop. People at work notice. Her friends tell her John is a rat, a pig, a dog, he isn't good enough for her, but she can't believe it. Inside John, she thinks, is another John, who is much nicer. This other John will emerge like a butterfly from a cocoon, a Jack from a box, a pit from a prune, if the first John is only squeezed enough.

One evening John complains about the food. He has never complained about the food before. Mary is hurt.

Her friends tell her they've seen him in a restaurant with another woman, whose name is Madge. It's not even Madge that finally gets to Mary: it's the restaurant. John has never taken Mary to a restaurant. Mary collects all the sleeping pills and aspirins she can find, and takes them and a half a bottle of sherry. You can see what kind of a woman she is by the fact that it's not even whiskey. She leaves a note for John. She hopes he'll discover her and get her to the hospital in time and repent and then they can get married, but this fails to happen and she dies.

John marries Madge and everything continues as in A.

C

John, who is an older man, falls in love with Mary, and Mary, who is only twenty-two, feels sorry for him because he's worried about his hair falling out. She sleeps with him even though she's not in love with him. She met him at work. She's in love with someone called James, who is twenty-two also and not yet ready to settle down.

John on the contrary settled down long ago: this is what is bothering him. John has a steady, respectable job and is getting ahead in his field, but Mary isn't impressed by him, she's impressed by James, who has a motorcycle and a fabulous record collection. But James is often away on his motorcycle, being free. Freedom isn't the same for girls, so in the meantime Mary spends Thursday evenings with John. Thursdays are the only days John can get away.

John is married to a woman called Madge and they have two children, a charming house which they bought just before the real estate values went up, and hobbies which they find stimulating and challenging, when they have the time. John tells Mary how important she is to him, but of course he can't leave his wife because a commitment is a commitment. He goes on about this more than is necessary and Mary finds it boring, but older men can keep it up longer so on the whole she has a fairly good time.

One day James breezes in on his motorcycle with some top-grade California hybrid and James and Mary get higher than you'd believe possible and they climb into bed. Everything becomes very underwater, but along comes John, who has a key to Mary's apartment. He finds them stoned and entwined. He's hardly in any position to be jealous, considering Madge, but nevertheless he's overcome with despair. Finally he's middle-aged, in two years he'll be bald as an egg and he can't stand it. He purchases a handgun, saying he needs it for target practice — this is the thin part of the plot, but it can be dealt with later — and shoots the two of them and himself.

Madge, after a suitable period of mourning, marries an understanding man called Fred and everything continues as in A, but under different names.

D

Fred and Madge have no problems. They get along exceptionally well and are good at working out any little difficulties that may arise. But their charming house is by the seashore and one day a giant tidal wave approaches. Real estate values go down. The rest of the story is about what caused the tidal wave and how they escape from it. They do, though thousands drown, but Fred and Madge are virtuous and lucky. Finally on high ground they clasp each other, wet and dripping and grateful, and continue as in A.

E

Yes, but Fred has a bad heart. The rest of the story is about how kind and understanding they both are until Fred dies. Then Madge devotes herself to charity work until the end of A. If you like, it can be "Madge," "cancer," "guilty and confused," and "bird watching."

F

If you think this is all too bourgeois, make John a revolutionary and Mary a counterespionage agent and see how far that gets you. Remember, this is Canada. You'll still end up with A, though in between you may get a lustful brawling saga of passionate involvement, a chronicle of our times, sort of.

You'll have to face it, the endings are the same however you slice it. Don't be deluded by any other endings, they're all fake, either deliberately fake, with malicious intent to deceive, or just motivated by excessive optimism if not by downright sentimentality.

The only authentic ending is the one provided here:

John and Mary die. John and Mary die. John and Mary die.

So much for endings. Beginnings are always more fun. True connoisseurs, however, are known to favor the stretch in between, since it's the hardest to do anything with.

That's about all that can be said for plots, which anyway are just one thing after another, a what and a what and a what.

Now try How and Why.

ରେଷ

ISAAC BABEL *(1894–1939?) was born in the Moldavanka district of Odessa, in Russia. His father, a Jewish businessman, made him study Yiddish, the Bible, and the Talmud, but his favorite subject was French literature. By the time Babel was fifteen he began to write stories in French, "à la Maupassant," and his later story "Guy de Maupassant" (1932) is a tribute to the influence of this writer. In 1915 Babel moved to St. Petersburg and tried unsuccessfully to publish his stories. His only encouragement came from the Russian writer Maxim Gorky, who advised him to get more life experience: "Go to the people." For six years Babel took Gorky at his word. He became a soldier on the Romanian front in World War I, worked as a press correspondent attached to the Soviet Cavalry, and found other jobs as a reporter and a printer during the chaotic period of civil war that followed the Russian Revolution of 1917. In 1924 he began to publish his stories in* Left, *a Soviet avant-garde literary magazine devoted to revolution in politics and the arts. A year later he published a col-*

lection of his tales, The Story of My Dove-Cote, *and in 1925 his best work appeared* — Red Cavalry, *thirty-four sketches depicting scenes of bravery and suffering during the Polish campaign of 1920, when Babel was with the Soviet Cavalry.*

Babel's literary style has been called "as terse as algebra," but its lyricism is also unmistakable. He juxtaposed poetic and natural details in his descriptions, often stressing the grotesque and sensual, as in "My First Goose." Critics have noted that these tactics are Babel's way of catching us off guard and breaking down our defenses so that we will be more receptive to his main theme as a writer — the complex relationship between our illusions about life and the truth of life.

Babel often revised his stories several times before he was satisfied. When his books first appeared, he was hailed in the Soviet Union as a master prose stylist, but during Stalin's purges in the 1930s he was attacked for his ideological shortcomings. When he was asked by his Soviet critics in 1937 why he wrote so little, he replied that he could manage only short things: "Let me put it this way; the point is that Tolstoy was able to describe what happened to him minute by minute, he remembered it all, whereas I, evidently, only have it in me to describe the most interesting five minutes I've experienced in twenty-four hours." The tone of Babel's reply is joking, but underneath is a sense of his bitterness and frustration. He also wrote, "No steel can pierce the human heart so chillingly as a period at the right moment," a pun on Stalin's name as "the man of steel." Babel's brave affirmation of individuality was unacceptable to the Soviet authorities, and in May 1939 he was arrested and disappeared into a concentration camp.

ISAAC BABEL

My First Goose   1925

TRANSLATED BY WALTER MORISON

Savitsky, Commander of the VI Division, rose when he saw me, and I wondered at the beauty of his giant's body. He rose, the purple of his riding-breeches and the crimson of his little tilted cap and the decorations stuck on his chest cleaving the hut as a standard cleaves the sky. A smell of scent and sickly sweet freshness of soap emanated from him. His long legs were like girls sheathed to the neck in shining riding-boots.

He smiled at me, struck his riding-whip on the table, and drew toward him an order that the Chief of Staff had just finished dictating. It was an order for Ivan Chesnokov to advance on Chugunov-Dobryvodka with the regiment entrusted to him, to make contact with the enemy and destroy the same.

"For which destruction," the Commander began to write, smearing the whole sheet, "I make this same Chesnokov entirely responsible, up to and including the supreme penalty, and will if necessary strike him down on the spot; which you, Chesnokov, who have been working with me at the front for some months now, cannot doubt."

The Commander signed the order with a flourish, tossed it to his orderlies, and turned upon me grey eyes that danced with merriment.

I handed him a paper with my appointment to the Staff of the Division.

"Put it down in the Order of the Day," said the Commander. "Put him down for every satisfaction save the front one. Can you read and write?"

"Yes, I can read and write," I replied, envying the flower and iron of that youthfulness. "I graduated in law from St. Petersburg University."

"Oh, are you one of those grinds?" he laughed. "Specs on your nose, too! What a nasty little object! They've sent you along without making any inquiries; and this is a hot place for specs. Think you'll get on with us?"

"I'll get on all right," I answered, and went off to the village with the quartermaster to find a billet for the night.

The quartermaster carried my trunk on his shoulder. Before us stretched the village street. The dying sun, round and yellow as a pumpkin, was giving up its roseate ghost to the skies.

We went up to a hut painted over with garlands. The quartermaster stopped, and said suddenly, with a guilty smile:

"Nuisance with specs. Can't do anything to stop it, either. Not a life for the brainy type here. But you go and mess up a lady, and a good lady too, and you'll have the boys patting you on the back."

He hesitated, my little trunk on his shoulder; then he came quite close to me, only to dart away again despairingly and run to the nearest yard. Cossacks were sitting there, shaving one another.

"Here, you soldiers," said the quartermaster, setting my little trunk down on the ground. "Comrade Savitsky's orders are that you're to take this chap in your billets, so no nonsense about it, because the chap's been through a lot in the learning line."

The quartermaster, purple in the face, left us without looking back. I raised my hand to my cap and saluted the Cossacks. A lad with long straight flaxen hair and the handsome face of the Ryazan Cossacks went over to my little trunk and tossed it out at the gate. Then he turned his back on me and with remarkable skill emitted a series of shameful noises.

"To your guns — number double-zero!" an older Cossack shouted at him, and burst out laughing. "Running fire!"

His guileless art exhausted, the lad made off. Then, crawling over the ground, I began to gather together the manuscripts and tattered garments that had fallen out of the trunk. I gathered them up and carried them to the other end of the yard. Near the hut, on a brick stove, stood a cauldron in which pork was cooking. The steam that rose from it was like the far-off smoke of home in the village, and it mingled hunger with desperate loneliness in my head. Then I covered my little broken trunk with hay, turning it into a pillow, and lay down on the ground to read in *Pravda* Lenin's speech at the Second Congress of the Comintern. The sun fell upon me from behind the toothed hillocks, the Cossacks trod on my feet, the lad made fun of me untiringly, the beloved lines came toward me along a thorny path and could not reach me. Then I put aside the paper and went out to the landlady, who was spinning on the porch.

"Landlady," I said, "I've got to eat."

The old woman raised to me the diffused whites of her purblind eyes and lowered them again.

"Comrade," she said, after a pause, "what with all this going on, I want to go and hang myself."

"Christ!" I muttered, and pushed the old woman in the chest with my fist. "You don't suppose I'm going to go into explanations with you, do you?"

And turning around I saw somebody's sword lying within reach. A severe-looking goose was waddling about the yard, inoffensively preening its feathers. I overtook it and pressed it to the ground. Its head cracked beneath my boot, cracked and emptied itself. The white neck lay stretched out in the dung, the wings twitched.

"Christ!" I said, digging into the goose with my sword. "Go and cook it for me, landlady."

Her blind eyes and glasses glistening, the old woman picked up the slaughtered bird, wrapped it in her apron, and started to bear it off toward the kitchen.

"Comrade," she said to me, after a while. "I want to go and hang myself." And she closed the door behind her.

The Cossacks in the yard were already sitting around their cauldron. They sat motionless, stiff as heathen priests at a sacrifice, and had not looked at the goose.

"The lad's all right," one of them said, winking and scooping up the cabbage soup with his spoon.

The Cossacks commenced their supper with all the elegance and restraint of peasants who respect one another. And I wiped the sword with sand, went out at the gate, and came in again, depressed. Already the moon hung above the yard like a cheap earring.

"Hey, you," suddenly said Surovkov, an older Cossack. "Sit down and feed with us till your goose is done."

He produced a spare spoon from his boot and handed it to me. We supped up the cabbage soup they had made, and ate the pork.

"What's in the newspaper?" asked the flaxen-haired lad, making room for me.

"Lenin writes in the paper," I said, pulling out *Pravda*. "Lenin writes that there's a shortage of everything."

And loudly, like a triumphant man hard of hearing, I read Lenin's speech out to the Cossacks.

Evening wrapped about me the quickening moisture of its twilight sheets; evening laid a mother's hand upon my burning forehead. I read on and rejoiced, spying out exultingly the secret curve of Lenin's straight line.

"Truth tickles everyone's nostrils," said Surovkov, when I had come to the end. "The question is, how's it to be pulled from the heap. But he goes and strikes at it straight off like a hen pecking at a grain!"

This remark about Lenin was made by Surovkov, platoon commander of the Staff Squadron; after which we lay down to sleep in the hayloft. We slept, all six of us, beneath a wooden roof that let in the stars, warming one another, our legs intermingled. I dreamed: and in my dreams saw women. But my heart, stained with bloodshed, grated and brimmed over.

ೞ

JAMES BALDWIN *(1924–1987) was born the son of a clergyman in Harlem, where he attended Public School 24, Frederick Douglass Junior High School, and De-Witt Clinton High School. While still a high school student he preached at the Fireside Pentecostal Assembly, but when he was seventeen he renounced the ministry. Two years later, living in Greenwich Village, he met Richard Wright, who encouraged him to be a writer and helped him win a Eugene Saxton Fellowship. Soon afterward Baldwin moved to France, as Wright had, to escape the stifling racial oppression he found in the United States. Although France was his more or less permanent residence until his death from cancer nearly forty years later, Baldwin regarded himself as a "commuter" rather than an expatriate. He said,*

> *Only white Americans can consider themselves to be expatriates. Once I found myself on the other side of the ocean, I could see where I came from very clearly, and I could see that I carried myself, which is my home, with me. You can never escape that. I am the grandson of a slave, and I am a writer. I must deal with both.*

Baldwin began his career by publishing novels and short stories. Go Tell It on the Mountain, *his first novel, was highly acclaimed when it appeared in 1953. It was based on his childhood in Harlem and his fear of his tyrannical father. Baldwin's frank depiction of homosexuality in the novels* Giovanni's Room *(1956) and* Another Country *(1962) drew criticism, but during the civil rights movement a few years later, he established himself as a brilliant essayist. In his lifetime Baldwin published several collections of essays, three more novels, and a book of five short stories,* Going to Meet the Man *(1965).*

"Sonny's Blues," from that collection, is one of Baldwin's strongest psychological dramatizations of the frustrations of African American life in our times. Like Wright's autobiographical books, Baldwin's work is an inspiration to young writers struggling to express their experience of racism. The African writer Chinua Achebe has said that "as long as injustice exists . . . the words of James Baldwin will be there to bear witness and to inspire and elevate the struggle for human freedom."

RELATED COMMENTARY: *James Baldwin, "Autobiographical Notes," page 732.*

JAMES BALDWIN

Sonny's Blues

1957

I read about it in the paper, in the subway, on my way to work. I read it, and I couldn't believe it, and I read it again. Then perhaps I just stared at it, at the newsprint spelling out his name, spelling out the story. I stared at it in the swinging lights of the subway car, and in the faces and bodies of the people, and in my own face, trapped in the darkness which roared outside.

It was not to be believed and I kept telling myself that, as I walked from the subway station to the high school. And at the same time I couldn't doubt it. I was scared, scared for Sonny. He became real to me again. A great block of ice got settled in my belly and kept melting there slowly all day long, while I taught my classes algebra. It was a special kind of ice. It kept melting, sending trickles of ice water all up and down my veins, but it never got less. Sometimes it hardened and seemed to expand until I felt my guts were going to come spilling out or that I was going to choke or scream. This would always be at a moment when I was remembering some specific thing Sonny had once said or done.

When he was about as old as the boys in my classes his face had been bright and open, there was a lot of copper in it; and he'd had wonderfully direct brown eyes, and great gentleness and privacy. I wondered what he looked like now. He had been picked up, the evening before, in a raid on an apartment downtown, for peddling and using heroin.

I couldn't believe it: but what I mean by that is that I couldn't find any room for it anywhere inside me. I had kept it outside me for a long time. I hadn't wanted to know. I had had suspicions, but I didn't name them, I kept putting them away. I told myself that Sonny was wild, but he wasn't crazy. And he'd always been a good boy, he hadn't ever turned hard or evil or disrespectful, the way kids can, so quick, so quick, especially in Harlem. I didn't want to believe that I'd ever see my brother going down, coming to nothing, all that light in his face gone out, in the condition I'd already seen so many others. Yet it had happened and here I was, talking about algebra to a lot of boys who might, every one of them for all I knew, be popping off needles every time they went to the head. Maybe it did more for them than algebra could.

I was sure that the first time Sonny had ever had horse, he couldn't have been much older than these boys were now. These boys, now, were living as we'd been living then, they were growing up with a rush and their heads bumped abruptly against the low ceiling of their actual possibilities. They were filled with rage. All they really knew were two darknesses, the darkness of their lives, which was now closing in on them, and the darkness of the movies, which had blinded them to that other darkness, and in which they now, vindictively, dreamed, at once more together than they were at any other time, and more alone.

When the last bell rang, the last class ended, I let out my breath. It seemed I'd been holding it for all that time. My clothes were wet — I may have looked as though I'd been sitting in a steam bath, all dressed up, all afternoon. I sat alone in the classroom a long time. I listened to the boys outside, downstairs, shouting and cursing and laughing. Their laughter struck me for perhaps the first time. It was not the joyous laughter which — God knows why — one associates with children. It was mocking and insular, its intent to denigrate. It was disenchanted, and in this, also, lay the authority of their curses. Perhaps I was listening to them because I was thinking about my brother and in them I heard my brother. And myself.

One boy was whistling a tune, at once very complicated and very simple, it seemed to be pouring out of him as though he were a bird, and it sounded very cool and moving through all that harsh, bright air, only just holding its own through all those other sounds.

I stood up and walked over to the window and looked down into the courtyard. It was the beginning of the spring and the sap was rising in the boys. A teacher passed through them every now and again, quickly, as though he or she couldn't wait to get out of that courtyard, to get those boys out of their sight and off their minds. I started collecting my stuff. I thought I'd better get home and talk to Isabel.

The courtyard was almost deserted by the time I got downstairs. I saw this boy standing in the shadow of a doorway, looking just like Sonny. I almost called his name. Then I saw that it wasn't Sonny, but somebody we used to know, a boy from around our block. He'd been Sonny's friend. He'd never been mine, having been too young for me, and, anyway, I'd never liked him. And now, even though he was a grown-up man, he still hung around that block, still spent hours on the street corners, was always high and raggy. I used to run into him from time to time and he'd often work around to asking me for a quarter or fifty cents. He always had some real good excuse, too, and I always gave it to him, I don't know why.

But now, abruptly, I hated him. I couldn't stand the way he looked at me, partly like a dog, partly like a cunning child. I wanted to ask him what the hell he was doing in the school courtyard.

He sort of shuffled over to me, and he said, "I see you got the papers. So you already know about it."

"You mean about Sonny? Yes, I already know about it. How come they didn't get you?"

He grinned. It made him repulsive and it also brought to mind what he'd looked like as a kid. "I wasn't there. I stay away from them people."

"Good for you." I offered him a cigarette and I watched him through the smoke. "You come all the way down here just to tell me about Sonny?"

"That's right." He was sort of shaking his head and his eyes looked strange, as though they were about to cross. The bright sun deadened his damp dark brown skin and it made his eyes look yellow and showed up the dirt in his kinked hair. He smelled funky. I moved a little away from him and I said, "Well, thanks. But I already know about it and I got to get home."

"I'll walk you a little ways," he said. We started walking. There were a couple of kids still loitering in the courtyard and one of them said goodnight to me and looked strangely at the boy beside me.

"What're you going to do?" he asked me. "I mean, about Sonny?"

"Look. I haven't seen Sonny for over a year. I'm not sure I'm going to do anything. Anyway, what the hell *can* I do?"

"That's right," he said quickly, "ain't nothing you can do. Can't much help old Sonny no more, I guess."

It was what I was thinking and so it seemed to me he had no right to say it.

"I'm surprised at Sonny, though," he went on — he had a funny way of talking, he looked straight ahead as though he were talking to himself — "I thought Sonny was a smart boy, I thought he was too smart to get hung."

"I guess he thought so too," I said sharply, "and that's how he got hung. And how about you? You're pretty goddamn smart, I bet."

Then he looked directly at me, just for a minute. "I ain't smart," he said. "If I was smart, I'd have reached for a pistol a long time ago."

"Look. Don't tell *me* your sad story, if it was up to me, I'd give you one." Then I felt guilty — guilty, probably, for never having supposed that the poor bastard *had* a story of his own, much less a sad one, and I asked, quickly, "What's going to happen to him now?"

He didn't answer this. He was off by himself some place. "Funny thing," he said, and from his tone we might have been discussing the quickest way to get to Brooklyn, "when I saw the papers this morning, the first thing I asked myself was if I had anything to do with it. I felt sort of responsible."

I began to listen more carefully. The subway station was on the corner, just before us, and I stopped. He stopped, too. We were in front of a bar and he ducked slightly, peering in, but whoever he was looking for didn't seem to be there. The juke box was blasting away with something black and bouncy and I half watched the barmaid as she danced her way from the juke box to her place behind the bar. And I watched her face as she laughingly responded to something someone said to her, still keeping time to the music. When she smiled one saw the little girl, one sensed the doomed, still-struggling woman beneath the battered face of the semi-whore.

"I never *give* Sonny nothing," the boy said finally, "but a long time ago I come to school high and Sonny asked me how it felt." He paused, I couldn't bear to watch him, I watched the barmaid, and I listened to the music which seemed to be causing the pavement to shake. "I told him it felt great." The music stopped, the barmaid paused and watched the juke box until the music began again. "It did."

All this was carrying me some place I didn't want to go. I certainly didn't want to know how it felt. It filled everything, the people, the houses, the music, the dark, quicksilver barmaid, with menace; and this menace was their reality.

"What's going to happen to him now?" I asked again.

"They'll send him away some place and they'll try to cure him." He shook his head. "Maybe he'll even think he's kicked the habit. Then they'll let him loose" — he gestured, throwing his cigarette into the gutter. "That's all."

"What do you mean, that's *all*?"

But I knew what he meant.

"I *mean*, that's *all*." He turned his head and looked at me, pulling down the corners of his mouth. "Don't you know what I mean?" he asked, softly.

"How the hell *would* I know what you mean?" I almost whispered it, I don't know why.

"That's right," he said to the air, "how would *he* know what I mean?" He turned toward me again, patient and calm, and yet I somehow felt him shaking, shaking as though he were going to fall apart. I felt that ice in my guts again, the dread I'd felt all afternoon; and again I watched the barmaid, moving about the bar, washing glasses, and singing. "Listen. They'll let him out and then it'll just start all over again. That's what I mean."

"You mean — they'll let him out. And then he'll just start working his way back in again. You mean he'll never kick the habit. Is that what you mean?"

"That's right," he said, cheerfully. "*You* see what I mean."

"Tell me," I said at last, "why does he want to die? He must want to die, he's killing himself, why does he want to die?"

He looked at me in surprise. He licked his lips. "He don't want to die. He wants to live. Don't nobody want to die, ever."

Then I wanted to ask him — too many things. He could not have answered, or if he had, I could not have borne the answers. I started walking. "Well, I guess it's none of my business."

"It's going to be rough on old Sonny," he said. We reached the subway station. "This is your station?" he asked. I nodded. I took one step down. "Damn!" he said, suddenly. I looked up at him. He grinned again. "Damn it if I didn't leave all my money home. You ain't got a dollar on you, have you? Just for a couple of days, is all."

All at once something inside gave and threatened to come pouring out of me. I didn't hate him any more. I felt that in another moment I'd start crying like a child.

"Sure," I said. "Don't sweat." I looked in my wallet and didn't have a dollar, I only had a five. "Here," I said. "That hold you?"

He didn't look at it — he didn't want to look at it. A terrible closed look came over his face, as though he were keeping the number on the bill a secret from him and me. "Thanks," he said, and now he was dying to see me go. "Don't worry about Sonny. Maybe I'll write him or something."

"Sure," I said. "You do that. So long."

"Be seeing you," he said. I went on down the steps.

And I didn't write Sonny or send him anything for a long time. When I finally did, it was just after my little girl died, he wrote me back a letter which made me feel like a bastard.

Here's what he said:

> Dear brother,
> You don't know how much I needed to hear from you. I wanted to write you many a time but I dug how much I must have hurt you and so I didn't write. But now I feel like a man who's been trying to climb up out of some deep, real deep and funky hole and just saw the sun up there, outside. I got to get outside.
> I can't tell you much about how I got here. I mean I don't know how to tell you. I guess I was afraid of something or I was trying to escape from something and you know I have never been very strong in the head (smile). I'm glad Mama and Daddy are dead and can't see what's happened to their son and I swear if I'd known what I was doing I would never have hurt you so, you and a lot of other fine people who were nice to me and who believed in me.
> I don't want you to think it had anything to do with me being a musician. It's more than that. Or maybe less than that. I can't get anything straight in my head down here and I try not to think about what's going to happen to me when I get outside again. Sometime I think I'm going to flip and *never* get outside and sometime I think I'll

come straight back. I tell you one thing, though, I'd rather blow my brains out than go through this again. But that's what they all say, so they tell me. If I tell you when I'm coming to New York and if you could meet me, I sure would appreciate it. Give my love to Isabel and the kids and I was sure sorry to hear about little Gracie. I wish I could be like Mama and say the Lord's will be done, but I don't know it seems to me that trouble is the one thing that never does get stopped and I don't know what good it does to blame it on the Lord. But maybe it does some good if you believe it.

Your brother,
Sonny

Then I kept in constant touch with him and I sent him whatever I could and I went to meet him when he came back to New York. When I saw him many things I thought I had forgotten came flooding back to me. This was because I had begun, finally, to wonder about Sonny, about the life that Sonny lived inside. This life, whatever it was, had made him older and thinner and it had deepened the distant stillness in which he had always moved. He looked very unlike my baby brother. Yet, when he smiled, when we shook hands, the baby brother I'd never known looked out from the depths of his private life, like an animal waiting to be coaxed into the light.

"How you been keeping?" he asked me.

"All right. And you?"

"Just fine." He was smiling all over his face. "It's good to see you again."

"It's good to see you."

The seven years' difference in our ages lay between us like a chasm: I wondered if these years would ever operate between us as a bridge. I was remembering, and it made it hard to catch my breath, that I had been there when he was born; and I had heard the first words he had ever spoken. When he started to walk, he walked from our mother straight to me. I caught him just before he fell when he took the first steps he ever took in this world.

"How's Isabel?"

"Just fine. She's dying to see you."

"And the boys?"

"They're fine, too. They're anxious to see their uncle."

"Oh, come on. You know they don't remember me."

"Are you kidding? Of course they remember you."

He grinned again. We got into a taxi. We had a lot to say to each other, far too much to know how to begin.

As the taxi began to move, I asked, "You still want to go to India?"

He laughed. "You still remember that. Hell, no. This place is Indian enough for me."

"It used to belong to them," I said.

And he laughed again. "They damn sure knew what they were doing when they got rid of it."

Years ago, when he was around fourteen, he'd been all hipped on the idea of going to India. He read books about people sitting on rocks, naked, in all kinds of weather, but mostly bad, naturally, and walking barefoot through hot coals and arriving at wisdom. I used to say that it sounded to me as though they were getting away from wisdom as fast as they could. I think he sort of looked down on me for that.

"Do you mind," he asked, "if we have the driver drive alongside the park? On the west side — I haven't seen the city in so long."

"Of course not," I said. I was afraid that I might sound as though I were humoring him, but I hoped he wouldn't take it that way.

So we drove along, between the green of the park and the stony, lifeless elegance of hotels and apartment buildings, toward the vivid, killing streets of our childhood. These streets hadn't changed, though housing projects jutted up out of them now like rocks in the middle of a boiling sea. Most of the houses in which we had grown up had vanished, as had the stores from which we had stolen, the basements in which we had first tried sex, the rooftops from which we had hurled tin cans and bricks. But houses exactly like the houses of our past yet dominated the landscape, boys exactly like the boys we once had been found themselves smothering in these houses, came down into the streets for light and air and found themselves encircled by disaster. Some escaped the trap, most didn't. Those who got out always left something of themselves behind, as some animals amputate a leg and leave it in the trap. It might be said, perhaps, that I had escaped, after all, I was a school teacher; or that Sonny had, he hadn't lived in Harlem for years. Yet, as the cab moved uptown through streets which seemed, with a rush, to darken with dark people, and as I covertly studied Sonny's face, it came to me that what we both were seeking through our separate cab windows was that part of ourselves which had been left behind. It's always at the hour of trouble and confrontation that the missing member aches.

We hit 110th Street and started rolling up Lenox Avenue. And I'd known this avenue all my life, but it seemed to me again, as it had seemed on the day I'd first heard about Sonny's trouble, filled with a hidden menace which was its very breath of life.

"We almost there," said Sonny.

"Almost." We were both too nervous to say anything more.

We live in a housing project. It hasn't been up long. A few days after it was up it seemed uninhabitably new, now, of course, it's already rundown. It looks like a parody of the good, clean, faceless life — God knows the people who live in it do their best to make it a parody. The beat-looking grass lying around isn't enough to make their lives green, the hedges will never hold out the streets, and they know it. The big windows fool no one, they aren't big enough to make space out of no space. They don't bother with the windows, they watch the TV screen instead. The playground is most popular with the children who don't play at jacks, or skip rope, or roller skate, or swing, and they can be found in it after dark. We moved in partly because it's not too far from where I teach, and partly for the kids; but it's really just like the houses in which Sonny and I grew up. The same things happen, they'll have the same things to remember. The moment Sonny and I started into the house I had the feeling that I was simply bringing him back into the danger he had almost died trying to escape.

Sonny has never been talkative. So I don't know why I was sure he'd be dying to talk to me when supper was over the first night. Everything went fine, the oldest boy remembered him, and the youngest boy liked him, and Sonny had remembered to bring something for each of them; and Isabel, who is really much nicer than I am, more open and giving, had gone to a lot of trouble about dinner and was genuinely glad to see him. And she's always been able to tease Sonny in a way that I haven't. It was nice to see her face so vivid again and to hear her laugh and watch her make Sonny laugh. She wasn't, or, anyway, she didn't seem to be, at all uneasy or embarrassed. She chatted as though there were no subject which had to be avoided and she got Sonny past his first, faint stiffness. And thank God she was there, for I was filled with that icy dread again. Everything I did seemed awkward to me, and everything I said sounded freighted with hidden meaning. I was trying to remember everything I'd heard about dope addiction and I couldn't help watching Sonny for signs. I wasn't doing it out of malice. I was trying to find out something about my brother. I was dying to hear him tell me he was safe.

"Safe!" my father grunted, whenever Mama suggested trying to move to a neighborhood which might be safer for children. "Safe, hell! Ain't no place safe for kids, nor nobody."

He always went on like this, but he wasn't, ever, really as bad as he sounded, not even on weekends, when he got drunk. As a matter of fact, he was always on the lookout for "something a little better," but he died before he found it. He died suddenly, during a drunken weekend in the middle of the war, when Sonny was fifteen. He and Sonny hadn't ever got on too well. And this was partly because Sonny was the apple of his father's eye. It was because he loved Sonny so much and was frightened for him, that he was always fighting with him. It doesn't do any good to fight with Sonny. Sonny just moves back, inside himself, where he can't be reached. But the principal reason that they never hit it off is that they were so much alike. Daddy was big and rough and loud-talking, just the opposite of Sonny, but they both had — that same privacy.

Mama tried to tell me something about this, just after Daddy died. I was home on leave from the army.

This was the last time I ever saw my mother alive. Just the same, this picture gets all mixed up in my mind with pictures I had of her when she was younger. The way I always see her is the way she used to be on a Sunday afternoon, say, when the old folks were talking after the big Sunday dinner. I always see her wearing pale blue. She'd be sitting on the sofa. And my father would be sitting in the easy chair, not far from her. And the living room would be full of church folks and relatives. There they sit, in chairs all around the living room, and the night is creeping up outside, but nobody knows it yet. You can see the darkness growing against the windowpanes and you hear the street noises every now and again, or maybe the jangling beat of a tambourine from one of the churches close by, but it's real quiet in the room. For a moment nobody's talking, but every face looks darkening, like the sky outside. And my mother rocks a little from the waist, and my father's eyes are closed. Everyone is looking at something a child can't see. For a minute they've forgotten the children. Maybe a kid is lying on the rug, half asleep. Maybe somebody's got a kid in his lap and is absent-mindedly stroking the kid's head. Maybe there's a kid, quiet and big-eyed, curled up in a big chair in the corner. The silence, the darkness coming, and the darkness in the faces frightens the child obscurely. He hopes that the hand which strokes his forehead will never stop — will never die. He hopes that there will never come a time when the old folks won't be sitting around the living room, talking about where they've come from, and what they've seen, and what's happened to them and their kinfolk.

But something deep and watchful in the child knows that this is bound to end, is already ending. In a moment someone will get up and turn on the light. Then the old folks will remember the children and they won't talk any more that day. And when light fills the room, the child is filled with darkness. He knows that every time this happens he's moved just a little closer to that darkness outside. The darkness outside is what the old folks have been talking about. It's what they've come from. It's what they endure. The child knows that they won't talk any more because if he knows too much about what's happened to *them*, he'll know too much too soon, about what's going to happen to *him*.

The last time I talked to my mother, I remember I was restless. I wanted to get out and see Isabel. We weren't married then and we had a lot to straighten out between us.

There Mama sat, in black, by the window. She was humming an old church song, *Lord, you brought me from a long ways off.* Sonny was out somewhere. Mama kept watching the streets.

"I don't know," she said, "if I'll ever see you again, after you go off from here. But I hope you'll remember the things I tried to teach you."

"Don't talk like that," I said, and smiled. "You'll be here a long time yet."

She smiled, too, but she said nothing. She was quiet for a long time. And I said, "Mama, don't you worry about nothing. I'll be writing all the time, and you be getting the checks. . . ."

"I want to talk to you about your brother," she said, suddenly. "If anything happens to me he ain't going to have nobody to look out for him."

"Mama," I said, "ain't nothing going to happen to you *or* Sonny. Sonny's all right. He's a good boy and he's got good sense."

"It ain't a question of his being a good boy," Mama said, "nor of his having good sense. It ain't only the bad ones, nor yet the dumb ones that gets sucked under." She stopped, looking at me. "Your Daddy once had a brother," she said, and she smiled in a way that made me feel she was in pain. "You didn't never know that, did you?"

"No," I said, "I never knew that," and I watched her face.

"Oh, yes," she said, "your Daddy had a brother." She looked out of the window again. "I know you never saw your Daddy cry. But *I* did — many a time, through all these years."

I asked her, "What happened to his brother? How come nobody's ever talked about him?"

This was the first time I ever saw my mother look old.

"His brother got killed," she said, "when he was just a little younger than you are now. I knew him. He was a fine boy. He was maybe a little full of the devil, but he didn't mean nobody no harm."

Then she stopped and the room was silent, exactly as it had sometimes been on those Sunday afternoons. Mama kept looking out into the streets.

"He used to have a job in the mill," she said, "and, like all young folks, he just liked to perform on Saturday nights. Saturday nights, him and your father would drift around to different places, go to dances and things like that, or just sit around with people they knew, and your father's brother would sing, he had a fine voice, and play along with himself on his guitar. Well, this particular Saturday night, him and your father was coming home from some place, and they were both a little drunk and there was a moon that night, it was bright like day. Your father's brother was feeling kind of good, and he was whistling to himself, and he had his guitar slung over his shoulder. They was coming down a hill and beneath them was a road that turned off from the highway. Well, your father's brother, being always kind of frisky, decided to run down this hill, and he did, with that guitar banging and clanging behind him, and he ran across the road, and he was making water behind a tree. And your father was sort of amused at him and he was still coming down the hill, kind of slow. Then he heard a car motor and that same minute his brother stepped from behind the tree, into the road, in the moonlight. And he started to cross the road. And your father started to run down the hill, he says he don't know why. This car was full of white men. They was all drunk, and when they seen your father's brother they let out a great whoop and holler and they aimed the car straight at him. They was having fun, they just wanted to scare him, the way they do sometimes, you know. But they was drunk. And I guess the boy, being drunk, too, and scared, kind of lost his head. By the time he jumped it was too late. Your father says he heard his brother scream when the car rolled over him, and he heard the wood of that guitar when it give, and he heard them strings go flying, and he heard them white men shouting, and the car kept on a-going and it ain't stopped till this day. And, time your father got down the hill, his brother weren't nothing but blood and pulp."

Tears were gleaming on my mother's face. There wasn't anything I could say.

"He never mentioned it," she said, "because I never let him mention it before you children. Your Daddy was like a crazy man that night and for many a night thereafter. He says he never in his life seen anything as dark as that road after the lights of that car had gone away. Weren't nothing, weren't nobody on that road, just your Daddy and his brother and that busted guitar. Oh, yes. Your Daddy never did really get right again. Till the day he died he weren't sure but that every white man he saw was the man that killed his brother."

She stopped and took out her handkerchief and dried her eyes and looked at me.

"I ain't telling you all this," she said, "to make you scared or bitter or to make you hate nobody. I'm telling you this because you got a brother. And the world ain't changed."

I guess I didn't want to believe this. I guess she saw this in my face. She turned away from me, toward the window again, searching those streets.

"But I praise my Redeemer," she said at last, "that He called your Daddy home before me. I ain't saying it to throw no flowers at myself, but, I declare, it keeps me from feeling too cast down to know I helped your father get safely through this world. Your father always acted like he was the roughest, strongest man on earth. And everybody took him to be like that. But if he hadn't had *me* there — to see his tears!"

She was crying again. Still, I couldn't move. I said, "Lord, Lord, Mama, I didn't know it was like that."

"Oh, honey," she said, "there's a lot that you don't know. But you are going to find it out." She stood up from the window and came over to me. "You got to hold on to your brother," she said, "and don't let him fall, no matter what it looks like is happening to him and no matter how evil you gets with him. You going to be evil with him many a time. But don't you forget what I told you, you hear?"

"I won't forget," I said. "Don't you worry, I won't forget. I won't let nothing happen to Sonny."

My mother smiled as though she were amused at something she saw in my face. Then, "You may not be able to stop nothing from happening. But you got to let him know you's *there*."

Two days later I was married, and then I was gone. And I had a lot of things on my mind and I pretty well forgot my promise to Mama until I got shipped home on a special furlough for her funeral.

And, after the funeral, with just Sonny and me alone in the empty kitchen, I tried to find out something about him.

"What do you want to do?" I asked him.

"I'm going to be a musician," he said.

For he had graduated, in the time I had been away, from dancing to the juke box to finding out who was playing what, and what they were doing with it, and he had bought himself a set of drums.

"You mean, you want to be a drummer?" I somehow had the feeling that being a drummer might be all right for other people but not for my brother Sonny.

"I don't think," he said, looking at me very gravely, "that I'll ever be a good drummer. But I think I can play a piano."

I frowned. I'd never played the role of the older brother quite so seriously before, had scarcely ever, in fact, *asked* Sonny a damn thing. I sensed myself in the presence of something I didn't really know how to handle, didn't understand. So I made my frown a little deeper as I asked: "What kind of musician do you want to be?"

He grinned. "How many kinds do you think there are?"

"Be *serious*," I said.

He laughed, throwing his head back, and then looked at me. "I *am* serious."

"Well, then, for Christ's sake, stop kidding around and answer a serious question. I mean, do you want to be a concert pianist, you want to play classical music and all that, or — or what?" Long before I finished he was laughing again. "For Christ's *sake*, Sonny!"

He sobered, but with difficulty. "I'm sorry. But you sound so — *scared!*" and he was off again.

"Well, you may think it's funny now, baby, but it's not going to be so funny when you have to make your living at it, let me tell you *that*." I was furious because I knew he was laughing at me and I didn't know why.

"No," he said, very sober now, and afraid, perhaps, that he'd hurt me, "I don't want to be a classical pianist. That isn't what interests me. I mean" — he paused, looking hard at me, as though his eyes would help me to understand, and then gestured helplessly, as though perhaps his hand would help — "I mean, I'll have a lot of studying to do, and I'll have to study *everything*, but, I mean, I want to play *with* — jazz musicians." He stopped. "I want to play jazz," he said.

Well, the word had never before sounded as heavy, as real, as it sounded that afternoon in Sonny's mouth. I just looked at him and I was probably frowning a real frown by this time. I simply couldn't see why on earth he'd want to spend his time hanging around nightclubs, clowning around on bandstands, while people pushed each other around a dance floor. It seemed — beneath him, somehow. I had never thought about it before, had never been forced to, but I suppose I had always put jazz musicians in a class with what Daddy called "good-time people."

"Are you *serious*?"

"Hell, *yes*, I'm serious."

He looked more helpless than ever, and annoyed, and deeply hurt.

I suggested, helpfully: "You mean — like Louis Armstrong?"

His face closed as though I'd struck him. "No. I'm not talking about none of that old-time, down home crap."

"Well, look, Sonny, I'm sorry, don't get mad. I just don't altogether get it, that's all. Name somebody — you know, a jazz musician you admire."

"Bird."

"Who?"

"Bird! Charlie Parker! Don't they teach you nothing in the goddamn army?"

I lit a cigarette. I was surprised and then a little amused to discover that I was trembling. "I've been out of touch," I said. "You'll have to be patient with me. Now. Who's this Parker character?"

"He's just one of the greatest jazz musicians alive," said Sonny, sullenly, his hands in his pockets, his back to me. "Maybe *the* greatest," he added, bitterly, "that's probably why *you* never heard of him."

"All right," I said, "I'm ignorant. I'm sorry. I'll go out and buy all the cat's records right away, all right?"

"It don't," said Sonny, with dignity, "make any difference to me. I don't care what you listen to. Don't do me no favors."

I was beginning to realize that I'd never seen him so upset before. With another part of my mind I was thinking that this would probably turn out to be one of those things kids go through and that I shouldn't make it seem important by pushing it too hard. Still, I didn't think it would do any harm to ask: "Doesn't all this take a lot of time? Can you make a living at it?"

He turned back to me and half leaned, half sat, on the kitchen table. "Everything takes time," he said, "and — well, yes, sure, I can make a living at it. But what I don't seem to be able to make you understand is that it's the only thing I want to do."

"Well, Sonny," I said, gently, "you know people can't always do exactly what they *want* to do — "

"*No*, I don't know that," said Sonny, surprising me. "I think people *ought* to do what they want to do, what else are they alive for?"

"You getting to be a big boy," I said desperately, "it's time you started thinking about your future."

"I'm thinking about my future," said Sonny, grimly. "I think about it all the time."

I gave up. I decided, if he didn't change his mind, that we could always talk about it later. "In the meantime," I said, "you got to finish school." We had already decided that he'd have to move in with Isabel and her folks. I knew this wasn't the ideal arrangement because Isabel's folks are inclined to be dicty and they hadn't especially wanted Isabel to marry me. But I didn't know what else to do. "And we have to get you fixed up at Isabel's."

There was a long silence. He moved from the kitchen table to the window. "That's a terrible idea. You know it yourself."

"Do you have a *better* idea?"

He just walked up and down the kitchen for a minute. He was as tall as I was. He had started to shave. I suddenly had the feeling that I didn't know him at all.

He stopped at the kitchen table and picked up my cigarettes. Looking at me with a kind of mocking, amused defiance, he put one between his lips. "You mind?"

"You smoking already?"

He lit the cigarette and nodded, watching me through the smoke. "I just wanted to see if I'd have the courage to smoke in front of you." He grinned and blew a great cloud of smoke to the ceiling. "It was easy." He looked at my face. "Come on, now. I bet you was smoking at my age, tell the truth."

I didn't say anything but the truth was on my face, and he laughed. But now there was something very strained in his laugh. "Sure. And I bet that ain't all you was doing."

He was frightening me a little. "Cut the crap," I said. "We already decided that you was going to go and live at Isabel's. Now what's got into you all of a sudden?"

"*You* decided it," he pointed out. "*I* didn't decide nothing." He stopped in front of me, leaning against the stove, arms loosely folded. "Look, brother. I don't want to stay in Harlem no more, I really don't." He was very earnest. He looked at me, then over toward the kitchen window. There was something in his eyes I'd never seen before, some thoughtfulness, some worry all his own. He rubbed the muscle of one arm. "It's time I was getting out of here."

"Where do you want to *go*, Sonny?"

"I want to join the army. Or the navy, I don't care. If I say I'm old enough, they'll believe me."

Then I got mad. It was because I was so scared. "You must be crazy. You goddamn fool, what the hell do you want to go and join the *army* for?"

"I just told you. To get out of Harlem."

"Sonny, you haven't even finished *school*. And if you really want to be a musician, how do you expect to study if you're in the *army*?"

He looked at me, trapped, and in anguish. "There's ways. I might be able to work out some kind of deal. Anyway, I'll have the G.I. Bill when I come out."

"*If* you come out." We stared at each other. "Sonny, please. Be reasonable. I know the setup is far from perfect. But we got to do the best we can."

"I ain't learning nothing in school," he said. "Even when I go." He turned away from me and opened the window and threw his cigarette out into the narrow alley. I watched his back. "At least, I ain't learning nothing you'd want me to learn." He slammed the window so hard I thought the glass would fly out, and turned back to me. "And I'm sick of the stink of these garbage cans!"

"Sonny," I said, "I know how you feel. But if you don't finish school now, you're going to be sorry later that you didn't." I grabbed him by the shoulders. "And you only got another year. It ain't so bad. And I'll come back and I swear I'll help you do *whatever* you want to do. Just try to put up with it till I come back. Will you please do that? For me?"

He didn't answer and he wouldn't look at me.

"Sonny. You hear me?"

He pulled away. "I hear you. But you never hear anything *I* say."

I didn't know what to say to that. He looked out of the window and then back at me. "OK," he said, and sighed. "I'll try."

Then I said, trying to cheer him up a little, "They got a piano at Isabel's. You can practice on it."

And as a matter of fact, it did cheer him up for a minute. "That's right," he said to himself. "I forgot that." His face relaxed a little. But the worry, the thoughtfulness, played on it still, the way shadows play on a face which is staring into the fire.

But I thought I'd never hear the end of that piano. At first, Isabel would write me, saying how nice it was that Sonny was so serious about his music and how, as soon as he came in from school, or wherever he had been when he was supposed to be at school, he went straight to that piano and stayed there until suppertime. And, after supper, he went back to that piano and stayed there until everybody went to bed. He was at the piano all day Saturday and all day Sunday. Then he bought a record player and started playing records. He'd play one record over and over again, all day long sometimes, and he'd improvise along with it on the piano. Or he'd play one section of the record, one chord, one change, one progression, then he'd do it on the piano. Then back to the record. Then back to the piano.

Well, I really don't know how they stood it. Isabel finally confessed that it wasn't like living with a person at all, it was like living with sound. And the sound didn't make any sense to her, didn't make any sense to any of them — naturally. They began, in a way, to be afflicted by this presence that was living in their home. It was as though Sonny were some sort of god, or monster. He moved in an atmosphere which wasn't like theirs at all. They fed him and he ate, he washed himself, he walked in and out of their door; he certainly wasn't nasty or unpleasant or rude, Sonny isn't any of those things; but it was as though he were all wrapped up in some cloud, some fire, some vision all his own; and there wasn't any way to reach him.

At the same time, he wasn't really a man yet, he was still a child, and they had to watch out for him in all kinds of ways. They certainly couldn't throw him out. Neither did they dare to make a great scene about that piano because even they dimly sensed, as I sensed, from so many thousands of miles away, that Sonny was at that piano playing for his life.

But he hadn't been going to school. One day a letter came from the school board and Isabel's mother got it — there had, apparently, been other letters but Sonny had torn them up. This day, when Sonny came in, Isabel's mother showed him the letter and asked where he'd been spending his time. And she finally got it out of him that he'd been down in Greenwich Village, with musicians and other characters, in a white girl's apartment. And this scared her and she started to scream at him and what came up, once she began — though she denies it to this day — was what sacrifices they were making to give Sonny a decent home and how little he appreciated it.

Sonny didn't play the piano that day. By evening, Isabel's mother had calmed down but then there was the old man to deal with, and Isabel herself. Isabel says she did her best to be calm but she broke down and started crying. She says she just watched Sonny's face. She could tell, by watching him, what was happening with him. And what was happening was that they penetrated his cloud, they had reached him. Even if their fingers had been a thousand times more gentle than human fingers ever are, he could hardly help feeling that they had stripped him naked and were spitting on that nakedness. For he also had to see that his presence, that music, which was life or death to him, had been torture for them and that they had endured it, not at all for his sake, but only for mine. And Sonny couldn't take that. He can take it a little better today than he could then but he's still not very good at it and, frankly, I don't know anybody who is.

The silence of the next few days must have been louder than the sound of all the music ever played since time began. One morning, before she went to work, Isabel was in his room for something and she suddenly realized that all of his records were gone. And she knew for certain that he was gone. And he was. He went as far as the navy would carry him. He finally sent me a post-card from some place in Greece and that was the first I knew that Sonny was still alive. I didn't see him any more until we were both back in New York and the war had long been over.

He was a man by then, of course, but I wasn't willing to see it. He came by the house from time to time, but we fought almost every time we met. I didn't like the way he carried himself, loose and dreamlike all the time, and I didn't like his friends, and his music seemed to be merely an excuse for the life he led. It sounded just that weird and disordered.

Then we had a fight, a pretty awful fight, and I didn't see him for months. By and by I looked him up, where he was living, in a furnished room in the Village, and I tried to make it up. But there were lots of people in the room and Sonny just lay on his bed, and he wouldn't come downstairs with me, and he treated these other people as though they were his family and I weren't. So I got mad and then he got mad, and then I told him that he might just as well be dead as live the way he was living. Then he stood up and he told me not to worry about him any more in life, that he *was* dead as far as I was concerned. Then he pushed me to the door and the other people looked on as though nothing were happening, and he slammed the door behind me. I stood in the hallway, staring at the door. I heard somebody laugh in the room and then the tears came to my eyes. I started down the steps, whistling to keep from crying, I kept whistling to myself, *You going to need me, baby, one of these cold, rainy days.*

I read about Sonny's trouble in the spring. Little Grace died in the fall. She was a beautiful little girl. But she only lived a little over two years. She died of polio and she suffered. She had a slight fever for a couple of days, but it didn't seem like anything and we just kept her in bed. And we would certainly have called the doctor, but the fever dropped, she seemed to be all right. So we thought it had just been a cold. Then, one day, she was up, playing, Isabel was in the kitchen fixing lunch for the two boys when they'd come in from school, and she heard Grace fall down in the living room. When you have a lot of children you don't always start running when one of them falls, unless they start screaming or something. And, this time, Grace was quiet. Yet, Isabel says that when she heard that *thump* and then that silence, something happened in her to make her afraid. And she ran to the living room and there was little Grace on the floor, all twisted up, and the reason she hadn't screamed was that she couldn't get her breath. And when she did scream, it was the worst sound, Isabel says, that she'd ever heard in all her life, and she still hears it sometimes in her dreams. Isabel will sometimes wake me up with a low, moaning, strangled sound and I have to be quick to awaken her and hold her to me and where Isabel is weeping against me seems a mortal wound.

I think I may have written Sonny the very day that little Grace was buried. I was sitting in the living room in the dark, by myself, and I suddenly thought of Sonny. My trouble made his real.

One Saturday afternoon, when Sonny had been living with us, or, anyway, been in our house, for nearly two weeks, I found myself wandering aimlessly about the living room, drinking from a can of beer, and trying to work up the courage to search Sonny's room. He was out, he was usually out whenever I was home, and Isabel had taken the children to see their grandparents. Suddenly I was standing still in front of the living room window, watching Seventh Avenue. The idea of searching Sonny's room made me still. I scarcely dared to admit to myself what I'd be searching for. I didn't know what I'd do if I found it. Or if I didn't.

On the sidewalk across from me, near the entrance to a barbecue joint, some people were holding an old-fashioned revival meeting. The barbecue cook, wearing a dirty white apron, his conked hair reddish and metallic in the pale sun, and a cigarette between his lips, stood in the doorway, watching them. Kids and older people paused in their errands and stood there, along with some older men and a couple of very tough-looking women who watched everything that happened on the avenue, as though they owned it, or were maybe owned by it. Well, they were watching this, too. The revival was being carried on by three sisters in black, and a brother. All they had were their voices and their Bibles and a tambourine. The brother was testifying and while he testified two of the sisters stood together, seeming to say, amen, and the third sister walked around with the tambourine outstretched and a couple of people dropped coins into it. Then the brother's testimony ended and the sister who had been taking up the collection dumped the coins into her palm and transferred them to the pocket of her long black robe. Then she raised both hands, striking the tambourine against the air, and then against one hand, and she started to sing. And the two other sisters and the brother joined in.

It was strange, suddenly, to watch, though I had been seeing these street meetings all my life. So, of course, had everybody else down there. Yet, they paused and watched and listened and I stood still at the window. *"Tis the old ship of Zion,"* they sang, and the sister with the tambourine kept a steady, jangling beat, *"it has rescued many a thousand!"* Not a soul under the sound of their voices was hearing this song for the first time, not one of them had been rescued. Nor had they seen much in the way of rescue work being done around them. Neither did they especially believe in the holiness of the three sisters and the brother, they knew too much about them, knew where they lived, and how. The woman with the tambourine, whose voice dominated the air, whose face was bright with joy, was divided by very little from the woman who stood watching her, a cigarette between her heavy, chapped lips, her hair a cuckoo's nest, her face scarred and swollen from many beatings, and her black eyes glittering like coal. Perhaps they both knew this, which was why, when, as rarely, they addressed each other, they addressed each other as Sister. As the singing filled the air the watching, listening faces underwent a change, the eyes focusing on something within; the music seemed to soothe a poison out of them; and time seemed, nearly, to fall away from the sullen, belligerent, battered faces, as though they were fleeing back to their first condition, while dreaming of their last. The barbecue cook half shook his head and smiled, and dropped his cigarette and disappeared into his joint. A man fumbled in his pockets for change and stood holding it in his hand impatiently, as though he had just remembered a pressing appointment further up the avenue. He looked furious. Then I saw Sonny, standing on the edge of the crowd. He was carrying a wide, flat notebook with a green cover, and it made him look, from where I was standing, almost like a schoolboy. The coppery sun brought out the copper in his skin, he was very faintly smiling, standing very still. Then the singing stopped, the tambourine turned into a collection plate again. The furious man dropped in his coins and vanished, so did a couple of the women, and Sonny dropped some change in the plate, looking directly at the woman with a little smile. He started across the avenue, toward the house. He has a slow, loping walk, something like the way Harlem hipsters walk, only he's imposed on this his own half-beat. I had never really noticed it before.

I stayed at the window, both relieved and apprehensive. As Sonny disappeared from my sight, they began singing again. And they were still singing when his key turned in the lock.

"Hey," he said.

"Hey, yourself. You want some beer?"

"No. Well, maybe." But he came up to the window and stood beside me, looking out. "What a warm voice," he said.

They were singing *If I could only hear my mother pray again!*

"Yes," I said, "and she can sure beat that tambourine."

"But what a terrible song," he said, and laughed. He dropped his notebook on the sofa and disappeared into the kitchen. "Where's Isabel and the kids?"

"I think they went to see their grandparents. You hungry?"

"No." He came back into the living room with his can of beer. "You want to come some place with me tonight?"

I sensed, I don't know how, that I couldn't possibly say no. "Sure. Where?"

He sat down on the sofa and picked up his notebook and started leafing through it. "I'm going to sit in with some fellows in a joint in the Village."

"You mean, you're going to play, tonight?"

"That's right." He took a swallow of his beer and moved back to the window. He gave me a sidelong look. "If you can stand it."

"I'll try," I said.

He smiled to himself and we both watched as the meeting across the way broke up. The three sisters and the brother, heads bowed, were singing *God be with you till we meet again.* The faces around them were very quiet. Then the song ended. The small crowd dispersed. We watched the three women and the lone man walk slowly up the avenue.

"When she was singing before," said Sonny, abruptly, "her voice reminded me for a minute of what heroin feels like sometimes — when it's in your veins. It makes you feel sort of warm and cool at the same time. And distant. And — and sure." He sipped his beer, very deliberately not looking at me. I watched his face. "It makes you feel — in control. Sometimes you've got to have that feeling."

"Do you?" I sat down slowly in the easy chair.

"Sometimes." He went to the sofa and picked up his notebook again. "Some people do."

"In order," I asked, "to play?" And my voice was very ugly, full of contempt and anger.

"Well" — he looked at me with great, troubled eyes, as though, in fact, he hoped his eyes would tell me things he could never otherwise say — "they *think* so. And *if* they think so — !"

"And what do *you* think?" I asked.

He sat on the sofa and put his can of beer on the floor. "I don't know," he said, and I couldn't be sure if he were answering my question or pursuing his thoughts. His face didn't tell me. "It's not so much to *play*. It's to *stand* it, to be able to make it at all. On any level." He frowned and smiled: "In order to keep from shaking to pieces."

"But these friends of yours," I said, "they seem to shake themselves to pieces pretty goddamn fast."

"Maybe." He played with the notebook. And something told me that I should curb my tongue, that Sonny was doing his best to talk, that I should listen. "But of course you only know the ones that've gone to pieces. Some don't — or at least they haven't *yet* and that's just about all *any* of us can say." He paused. "And then there are some who just live, really, in hell, and they know it and they see what's happening and they go right on. I don't know." He sighed, dropped the notebook, folded his arms. "Some guys, you can tell from the way they play, they on something *all* the time. And you can see that, well, it makes something real for them. But of course," he picked up his beer from the floor and sipped it and put the can down again, "they *want* to, too, you've got to see that. Even some of them that say they don't — *some*, not all."

"And what about you?" I asked — I couldn't help it. "What about you? Do *you* want to?"

He stood up and walked to the window and remained silent for a long time. Then he sighed. "Me," he said. Then: "While I was downstairs before, on my way here, listening to that woman sing, it struck me all of a sudden how much suffering she must have had to go through — to sing like that. It's *repulsive* to think you have to suffer that much."

I said: "But there's no way not to suffer — is there, Sonny?"

"I believe not," he said and smiled, "but that's never stopped anyone from trying." He looked at me. "Has it?" I realized, with this mocking look, that there stood between us, forever, beyond the power of time or forgiveness, the fact that I had held silence — so long! — when he had needed human speech to help him. He turned back to the window. "No, there's no way not to suffer. But you try all kinds of ways to keep from drowning in it, to keep on top of it, and to make it seem — well, like *you*. Like you did something, all right, and now you're suffering for it. You know?" I said nothing. "Well you know," he said, impatiently, "why *do* people suffer? Maybe it's better to do something to give it a reason, *any* reason."

"But we just agreed," I said, "that there's no way not to suffer. Isn't it better, then, just to — take it?"

"But nobody just takes it," Sonny cried, "that's what I'm telling you! *Everybody* tries not to. You're just hung up on the *way* some people try — it's not *your* way!"

The hair on my face began to itch, my face felt wet. "That's not true," I said, "that's not true. I don't give a damn what other people do, I don't even care how they suffer. I just care how *you* suffer." And he looked at me. "Please believe me," I said, "I don't want to see you — die — trying not to suffer."

"I won't," he said, flatly, "die trying not to suffer. At least, not any faster than anybody else."

"But there's no need," I said, trying to laugh, "is there? in killing yourself."

I wanted to say more, but I couldn't. I wanted to talk about will power and how life could be — well, beautiful. I wanted to say that it was all within; but was it? or, rather, wasn't that exactly the trouble? And I wanted to promise that I would never fail him again. But it would all have sounded — empty words and lies.

So I made the promise to myself and prayed that I would keep it.

"It's terrible sometimes, inside," he said, "that's what's the trouble. You walk these streets, black and funky and cold, and there's not really a living ass to talk to, and there's nothing shaking, and there's no way of getting it out — that storm inside. You can't talk it and you can't make love with it, and when you finally try to get with it and play it, you realize *nobody's* listening. So *you've* got to listen. You got to find a way to listen."

And then he walked away from the window and sat on the sofa again, as though all the wind had suddenly been knocked out of him. "Sometimes you'll do *anything* to play, even cut your mother's throat." He laughed and looked at me. "Or your brother's." Then he sobered. "Or your own." Then: "Don't worry. I'm all right now and I think I'll *be* all right. But I can't forget — where I've been. I don't mean just the physical place I've been, I mean where I've *been*. And *what* I've been."

"What have you been, Sonny?" I asked.

He smiled — but sat sideways on the sofa, his elbow resting on the back, his fingers playing with his mouth and chin, not looking at me. "I've been something I didn't recognize, didn't know I could be. Didn't know anybody could be." He stopped, looking inward, looking helplessly young, looking old. "I'm not talking about it now because I feel *guilty* or anything like that — maybe it would be better if I did, I don't know. Anyway, I can't really talk about it. Not to you, not to anybody," and now he turned and faced me. "Sometimes, you know, and it was actually when I was most *out* of the world, I felt that I was in it, that I was *with* it, really, and I could play or I didn't really have to *play*, it just came out of me, it was there. And I don't know how I played, thinking about it now, but I know I did awful things, those times, sometimes, to people. Or it wasn't that I *did* anything to them — it was that they weren't real." He picked up the beer can; it was empty; he rolled it between his palms: "And other times — well, I needed a fix, I needed to find a place to lean, I needed to clear a space to *listen* — and I couldn't find it, and I — went crazy, I did terrible things to *me*, I was terrible *for* me." He began pressing the beer can between his hands, I watched the metal begin to give. It glittered, as he played with it, like a knife, and I was afraid he would cut himself, but I said nothing. "Oh well. I can never tell you. I was all by myself at the bottom of something, stinking and sweating and crying and shaking, and I smelled it, you know? *my* stink, and I thought I'd die if I couldn't get away from it and yet, all the same, I knew that everything I was doing was just locking me in with it. And I didn't know," he paused, still flattening the beer can, "I didn't know, I still *don't* know, something kept telling me that maybe it was good to smell your own stink, but I didn't think that *that* was what I'd been trying to do — and — who can stand it?" and he abruptly dropped the ruined beer can, looking at me with a small, still smile, and then rose, walking to the window as though it were the lodestone rock. I watched his face, he watched the avenue. "I couldn't tell you when Mama died — but the reason I wanted to leave Harlem so bad was to get away from drugs. And then, when I ran away, that's what I was running from — really. When I came back, nothing had changed, *I* hadn't changed, I was just — older." And he stopped, drumming with his fingers on the windowpane. The sun had vanished, soon darkness would fall. I watched his face. "It can come again," he said, almost as though speaking to himself. Then he turned to me. "It can come again," he repeated. "I just want you to know that."

"All right," I said, at last. "So it can come again, All right."

He smiled, but the smile was sorrowful. "I had to try to tell you," he said.

"Yes," I said. "I understand that."

"You're my brother," he said, looking straight at me, and not smiling at all.

"Yes," I repeated, "yes. I understand that."

He turned back to the window, looking out. "All that hatred down there," he said, "all that hatred and misery and love. It's a wonder it doesn't blow the avenue apart."

We went to the only nightclub on a short, dark street, downtown. We squeezed through the narrow, chattering, jam-packed bar to the entrance of the big room, where the bandstand was. And we stood there for a moment, for the lights were very dim in this room and we couldn't see. Then, "Hello, boy," said a voice and an enormous black man, much older than Sonny or myself, erupted out of all that atmospheric lighting and put an arm around Sonny's shoulder. "I been sitting right here," he said, "waiting for you."

He had a big voice, too, and heads in the darkness turned toward us.

Sonny grinned and pulled a little away, and said, "Creole, this is my brother. I told you about him."

Creole shook my hand. "I'm glad to meet you, son," he said, and it was clear that he was glad to meet me *there*, for Sonny's sake. And he smiled, "You got a real musician in *your* family," and he took his arm from Sonny's shoulder and slapped him, lightly, affectionately, with the back of his hand.

"Well. Now I've heard it all," said a voice behind us. This was another musician, and a friend of Sonny's, a coal-black, cheerful-looking man, built close to the ground. He immediately began confiding to me, at the top of his lungs, the most terrible things about Sonny, his teeth gleaming like a light-house and his laugh coming up out of him like the beginning of an earth-quake. And it turned out that everyone at the bar knew Sonny, or almost everyone; some were musicians, working there, or nearby, or not working, some were simply hangers-on, and some were there to hear Sonny play. I was introduced to all of them and they were all very polite to me. Yet, it was clear that, for them, I was only Sonny's brother. Here, I was in Sonny's world. Or, rather: his kingdom. Here, it was not even a question that his veins bore royal blood.

They were going to play soon and Creole installed me, by myself, at a table in a dark corner. Then I watched them, Creole, and the little black man, and Sonny, and the others, while they horsed around, standing just below the bandstand. The light from the bandstand spilled just a little short of them and, watching them laughing and gesturing and moving about, I had the feeling that they, nevertheless, were being most careful not to step into that circle of light too suddenly: that if they moved into the light too suddenly, without thinking, they would perish in flame. Then, while I watched, one of them, the small, black man, moved into the light and crossed the bandstand and started fooling around with his drums. Then — being funny and being, also, ex-tremely ceremonious — Creole took Sonny by the arm and led him to the pi-ano. A woman's voice called Sonny's name and a few hands started clapping. And Sonny, also being funny and being ceremonious, and so touched, I think, that he could have cried, but neither hiding it nor showing it, riding it like a man, grinned, and put both hands to his heart and bowed from the waist.

Creole then went to the bass fiddle and a lean, very bright-skinned brown man jumped up on the bandstand and picked up his horn. So there they were, and the atmosphere on the bandstand and in the room began to change and tighten. Someone stepped up to the microphone and announced them. Then there were all kinds of murmurs. Some people at the bar shushed others. The waitress ran around, frantically getting in the last orders, guys and chicks got closer to each other, and the lights on the bandstand, on the quartet, turned to a kind of indigo. Then they all looked different there. Creole looked about him for the last time, as though he were making certain that all his chickens were in the coop, and then he — jumped and struck the fiddle. And there they were.

All I know about music is that not many people ever really hear it. And even then, on the rare occasions when something opens within, and the music enters, what we mainly hear, or hear corroborated, are personal, private, van-ishing evocations. But the man who creates the music is hearing something else, is dealing with the roar rising from the void and imposing order on it as it hits the air. What is evoked in him, then, is of another order, more terrible be-cause it has no words, and triumphant, too, for that same reason. And his tri-umph, when he triumphs, is ours. I just watched Sonny's face. His face was troubled, he was working hard, but he wasn't with it. And I had the feeling that, in a way, everyone on the bandstand was waiting for him, both waiting for him and pushing him along. But as I began to watch Creole, I realized that it was Creole who held them all back. He had them on a short rein. Up there, keeping the beat with his whole body, wailing on the fiddle, with his eyes half closed, he was listening to everything, but he was listening to Sonny. He was having a dialogue with Sonny. He wanted Sonny to leave the shoreline and strike out for the deep water. He was Sonny's witness that deep water and drowning were not the same thing — he had been there, and he knew. And he wanted Sonny to know. He was waiting for Sonny to do the things on the keys which would let Creole know that Sonny was in the water.

And, while Creole listened, Sonny moved, deep within, exactly like someone in torment. I had never before thought of how awful the relationship must be between the musician and his instrument. He has to fill it, this instrument, with the breath of life, his own. He has to make it do what he wants it to do. And a piano is just a piano. It's made out of so much wood and wires and little hammers and big ones, and ivory. While there's only so much you can do with it, the only way to find this out is to try; to try and make it do everything.

And Sonny hadn't been near a piano for over a year. And he wasn't on much better terms with his life, not the life that stretched before him now. He and the piano stammered, started one way, got scared, stopped; started another way, panicked, marked time, started again; then seemed to have found a direction, panicked again, got stuck. And the face I saw on Sonny I'd never seen before. Everything had been burned out of it, and, at the same time, things usually hidden were being burned in, by the fire and fury of the battle which was occurring in him up there.

Yet, watching Creole's face as they neared the end of the first set, I had the feeling that something had happened, something I hadn't heard. Then they finished, there was scattered applause, and then, without an instant's warning, Creole started into something else, it was almost sardonic, it was *Am I Blue.* And, as though he commanded, Sonny began to play. Something began to happen. And Creole let out the reins. The dry, low, black man said something awful on the drums, Creole answered, and the drums talked back. Then the horn insisted, sweet and high, slightly detached perhaps, and Creole listened, commenting now and then, dry, and driving, beautiful and calm and old. Then they all came together again, and Sonny was part of the family again. I could tell this from his face. He seemed to have found, right there beneath his fingers, a damn brand-new piano. It seemed that he couldn't get over it. Then, for awhile, just being happy with Sonny, they seemed to be agreeing with him that brand-new pianos certainly were a gas.

Then Creole stepped forward to remind them that what they were playing was the blues. He hit something in all of them, he hit something in me, myself, and the music tightened and deepened, apprehension began to beat the air. Creole began to tell us what the blues were all about. They were not about anything very new. He and his boys up there were keeping it new, at the risk of ruin, destruction, madness, and death, in order to find new ways to make us listen. For, while the tale of how we suffer, and how we are delighted, and how we may triumph is never new, it always must be heard. There isn't any other tale to tell, it's the only light we've got in all this darkness.

And this tale, according to that face, that body, those strong hands on those strings, has another aspect in every country, and a new depth in every generation. Listen, Creole seemed to be saying, listen. Now these are Sonny's blues. He made the little black man on the drums know it, and the bright, brown man on the horn. Creole wasn't trying any longer to get Sonny in the water. He was wishing him Godspeed. Then he stepped back, very slowly, filling the air with the immense suggestion that Sonny speak for himself.

Then they all gathered around Sonny and Sonny played. Every now and again one of them seemed to say, amen. Sonny's fingers filled the air with life, his life. But that life contained so many others. And Sonny went all the way back, he really began with the spare, flat statement of the opening phrase of the song. Then he began to make it his. It was very beautiful because it wasn't hurried and it was no longer a lament. I seemed to hear with what burning he had made it his, with what burning we had yet to make it ours, how we could cease lamenting. Freedom lurked around us and I understood, at last, that he could help us to be free if we would listen, that he would never be free until we did. Yet, there was no battle in his face now. I heard what he had gone through, and would continue to go through until he came to rest in earth. He had made it his: that long line, of which we knew only Mama and Daddy. And he was giving it back, as everything must be given back, so that, passing through death, it can live forever. I saw my mother's face again, and felt, for the first time, how the stones of the road she had walked on must have bruised her feet. I saw the moonlit road where my father's brother died. And it brought something else back to me, and carried me past it. I saw my little girl again and felt Isabel's tears again, and I felt my own tears begin to rise. And I was yet aware that this was only a moment, that the world waited outside, as hungry as a tiger, and that trouble stretched above us, longer than the sky.

Then it was over. Creole and Sonny let out their breath, both soaking wet, and grinning. There was a lot of applause and some of it was real. In the dark, the girl came by and I asked her to take drinks to the bandstand. There was a long pause, while they talked up there in the indigo light and after awhile I saw the girl put a Scotch and milk on top of the piano for Sonny. He didn't seem to notice it, but just before they started playing again, he sipped from it and looked toward me, and nodded. Then he put it back on top of the piano. For me, then, as they began to play again, it glowed and shook above my brother's head like the very cup of trembling.

፠

TONI CADE BAMBARA *(1939–1996) was born in New York City and grew up in Harlem and Bedford-Stuyvesant. As a child she began scribbling stories on the margins of her father's copies of the* New York Daily News *and the squares of thin white cardboard her mother's stockings came wrapped around. She has said of herself,*

> I was raised by my family and community to be a combatant. Forays to the Apollo [Theater in Harlem] with my daddy and hanging tough on Speakers Corner with my mama taught me the power of the word, the importance of the resistance tradition, and the high standards our [black] community had regarding verbal performance. While my heart is a laughing gland and my fa-

vorite thing to be doing is laughing so hard I have to lower myself on the wall to keep from falling down, near that chamber is a blast furnace where a rifle pokes from the ribs.

In high school and at Queens College, Bambara remembered that she "hogged the lit journal." She took writing courses and wrote novels, stories, plays, film scripts, operas, "you-name-its." After graduating from Queens, she worked various jobs and studied for her M.A. at the City College of New York while she wrote fiction in "the predawn in-betweens." She began to publish her stories, and in 1972 she collected them in her first book, Gorilla, My Love. It wasn't until Bambara returned from a trip to Cuba in 1973 that she thought of herself as a writer: "There I learned what Langston Hughes and others, most especially my colleagues in the Neo-Black Arts Movement, had been teaching for years — that writing is a legitimate way, an important way, to participate in the empowerment of the community that names me." Her books of stories include The Black Woman (1970), Tales and Stories for Black Folks (1971), and The Sea Birds Are Still Alive: Collected Stories (1977). She has also published two novels, The Salt Eaters (1980) and If Blessing Comes (1987).

Like Zora Neale Hurston, whom Bambara credited with giving her new ways to consider literary material (folkways as the basis of art) and new categories of perception (women's images), Bambara often used humor in her fiction. She said that "what I enjoy most in my work is the laughter and the outrage and the attention to language." Her stories, like "The Lesson," were often about children, but Bambara tried to avoid sentimentality. She attempted to keep her torrents of language and feeling under control by remembering the premises from which she proceeded as a black writer: "One, we are at war. Two, the natural response to oppression, ignorance, evil, and mystification is wide-awake resistance. Three, the natural response to stress and crisis is not breakdown and capitulation, but transformation and renewal."

TONI CADE BAMBARA

The Lesson   1972

Back in the days when everyone was old and stupid or young and foolish and me and Sugar were the only ones just right, this lady moved on our block with nappy hair and proper speech and no makeup. And quite naturally we laughed at her, laughed the way we did at the junk man who went about his business like he was some big-time president and his sorry-ass horse his secretary. And we kinda hated her too, hated the way we did the winos who cluttered up our parks and pissed on our handball walls and stank up our hallways and stairs so you couldn't halfway play hide-and-seek without a goddamn gas mask. Miss Moore was her name. The only woman on the block with no first name. And she was black as hell, cept for her feet, which were fish-white and spooky. And she was always planning these boring-ass things for us to do, us being my cousin, mostly, who lived on the block cause we all moved North the same time and to the same apartment then spread out gradual to breathe. And our parents would yank our heads into some kinda shape and crisp up our clothes so we'd be presentable for travel with Miss Moore, who always looked like she was going to church, though she never did. Which is just one of the things the grownups talked about when they talked behind her back like a dog. But when she came calling with some sachet she'd sewed up or some gingerbread she'd made or some book, why then they'd all be too embarrassed to turn her down and we'd get handed over all spruced up. She'd been to college and said it was only right that she should take responsibility for the young ones' education, and she not even related by marriage or blood. So they'd go for it. Specially Aunt Gretchen. She was the main gofer in the family. You got some ole dumb shit foolishness you want somebody to go for, you send for Aunt Gretchen. She been screwed into the go-along for so long, it's a blood-deep natural thing with her. Which is how she got saddled with me and Sugar and Junior in the first place while our mothers were in a la-de-da apartment up the block having a good ole time.

So this one day, Miss Moore rounds us all up at the mailbox and it's puredee hot and she's knockin herself out about arithmetic. And school suppose to let up in summer I heard, but she don't never let up. And the starch in my pinafore scratching the shit outta me and I'm really hating this nappy-head bitch and her goddamn college degree. I'd much rather go to the pool or to the show where it's cool. So me and Sugar leaning on the mailbox being surly, which is a Miss Moore word. And Flyboy checking out what everybody brought for lunch. And Fat Butt already wasting his peanut-butter-and-jelly sandwich like the pig he is. And Junebug punchin on Q.T.'s arm for potato chips. And Rosie Giraffe shifting from one hip to the other waiting for somebody to step on her foot or ask her if she from Georgia so she can kick ass, preferably Mercedes'. And Miss Moore asking us do we know what money is, like we a bunch of retards. I mean real money, she say, like it's only poker chips or monopoly papers we lay on the grocer. So right away I'm tired of this and say so. And would much rather snatch Sugar and go to the Sunset and terrorize the West Indian kids and take their hair ribbons and their money too. And Miss Moore files that remark away for next week's lesson on brotherhood, I can tell. And finally I say we oughta get to the subway cause it's cooler and besides we might meet some cute boys. Sugar done swiped her mama's lipstick, so we ready.

So we heading down the street and she's boring us silly about what things cost and what our parents make and how much goes for rent and how money ain't divided up right in this country. And then she gets to the part about we all poor and live in the slums, which I don't feature. And I'm ready to speak on that, but she steps out in the street and hails two cabs just like that. Then she hustles half the crew in with her and hands me a five-dollar bill and tells me to calculate 10 percent tip for the driver. And we're off. Me and Sugar and Junebug and Flyboy hangin out the window and hollering to everybody, putting lipstick on each other cause Flyboy a faggot anyway, and making farts with our sweaty armpits. But I'm mostly trying to figure how to spend this money. But they all fascinated with the meter ticking and Junebug starts laying bets as to how much it'll read when Flyboy can't hold his breath no more. Then Sugar lays bets as to how much it'll be when we get there. So I'm stuck.

Don't nobody want to go for my plan, which is to jump out at the next light and run off to the first bar-b-que we can find. Then the driver tells us to get the hell out cause we there already. And the meter reads eighty-five cents. And I'm stalling to figure out the tip and Sugar say give him a dime. And I decide he don't need it bad as I do, so later for him. But then he tries to take off with Junebug foot still in the door so we talk about his mama something ferocious. Then we check out that we on Fifth Avenue and everybody dressed up in stockings. One lady in a fur coat, hot as it is. White folks crazy.

"This is the place," Miss Moore say, presenting it to us in the voice she uses at the museum. "Let's look in the windows before we go in."

"Can we steal?" Sugar asks very serious like she's getting the ground rules squared away before she plays. "I beg your pardon," say Miss Moore, and we fall out. So she leads us around the windows of the toy store and me and Sugar screamin, "This is mine, that's mine, I gotta have that, that was made for me, I was born for that," till Big Butt drowns us out.

"Hey, I'm going to buy that there."

"That there? You don't even know what it is, stupid."

"I do so," he say punchin on Rosie Giraffe. "It's a microscope."

"Whatcha gonna do with a microscope, fool?"

"Look at things."

"Like what, Ronald?" ask Miss Moore. And Big Butt ain't got the first notion. So here go Miss Moore gabbing about the thousands of bacteria in a drop of water and the somethinorother in a speck of blood and the million and one living things in the air around us is invisible to the naked eye. And what she say that for? Junebug go to town on that "naked" and we rolling. Then Miss Moore ask what it cost. So we all jam into the window smudgin it up and the price tag say $300. So then she ask how long'd take for Big Butt and Junebug to save up their allowances. "Too long," I say. "Yeh," adds Sugar, "outgrown it by that time." And Miss Moore say no, you never outgrow learning instruments. "Why, even medical students and interns and," blah, blah, blah. And we ready to choke Big Butt for bringing it up in the first damn place.

"This here costs four hundred eighty dollars," say Rosie Giraffe. So we pile up all over her to see what she pointin out. My eyes tell me it's a chunk of glass cracked with something heavy, and different-color inks dripped into the splits, then the whole thing put into a oven or something. But for $480 it don't make sense.

"That's a paperweight made of semi-precious stones fused together under tremendous pressure," she explains slowly, with her hands doing the mining and all the factory work.

"So what's a paperweight?" ask Rosie Giraffe.

"To weigh paper with, dumbbell," say Flyboy, the wise man from the East.

"Not exactly," say Miss Moore, which is what she say when you warm or way off too. "It's to weigh paper down so it won't scatter and make your desk untidy." So right away me and Sugar curtsy to each other and then to Mercedes who is more the tidy type.

"We don't keep paper on top of the desk in my class," say Junebug, figuring Miss Moore crazy or lyin one.

"At home, then," she say. "Don't you have a calendar and a pencil case and a blotter and a letter-opener on your desk at home where you do your homework?" And she know damn well what our homes look like cause she nosys around in them every chance she gets.

"I don't even have a desk," say Junebug. "Do we?"

"No. And I don't get no homework neither," says Big Butt.

"And I don't even have a home," says Flyboy like he do at school to keep the white folks off his back and sorry for him. Send this poor kid to camp posters, is his specialty.

"I do," says Mercedes. "I have a box of stationery on my desk and a picture of my cat. My godmother bought the stationery and the desk. There's a big rose on each sheet and the envelopes smell like roses."

"Who wants to know about your smelly-ass stationery," say Rosie Giraffe fore I can get my two cents in.

"It's important to have a work area all your own so that . . ."

"Will you look at this sailboat, please," say Flyboy, cutting her off and pointin to the thing like it was his. So once again we tumble all over each other to gaze at this magnificent thing in the toy store which is just big enough to maybe sail two kittens across the pond if you strap them to the posts tight. We all start reciting the price tag like we in assembly. "Handcrafted sailboat of fiberglass at one thousand one hundred ninety-five dollars."

"Unbelievable," I hear myself say and am really stunned. I read it again for myself just in case the group recitation put me in a trance. Same thing. For some reason this pisses me off. We look at Miss Moore and she lookin at us, waiting for I dunno what.

"Who'd pay all that when you can buy a sailboat set for a quarter at Pop's, a tube of glue for a dime, and a ball of string for eight cents? It must have a motor and a whole lot else besides," I say. "My sailboat cost me about fifty cents."

"But will it take water?" say Mercedes with her smart ass.

"Took mine to Alley Pond Park once," say Flyboy. "String broke. Lost it. Pity."

"Sailed mine in Central Park and it keeled over and sank. Had to ask my father for another dollar."

"And you got the strap," laugh Big Butt. "The jerk didn't even have a string on it. My old man wailed on his behind."

Little Q.T. was staring hard at the sailboat and you could see he wanted it bad. But he too little and somebody'd just take it from him. So what the hell. "This boat for kids, Miss Moore?"

"Parents silly to buy something like that just to get all broke up," say Rosie Giraffe.

"That much money it should last forever," I figure.

"My father'd buy it for me if I wanted it."

"Your father, my ass," say Rosie Giraffe getting a chance to finally push Mercedes.

"Must be rich people shop here," say Q.T.

"You are a very bright boy," say Flyboy. "What was your first clue?" And he rap him on the head with the back of his knuckles, since Q.T. the only one he could get away with. Though Q.T. liable to come up behind you years later and get his licks in when you half expect it.

"What I want to know is," I says to Miss Moore though I never talk to her, I wouldn't give the bitch that satisfaction, "is how much a real boat costs? I figure a thousand'd get you a yacht any day."

"Why don't you check that out," she says, "and report back to the group?" Which really pains my ass. If you gonna mess up a perfectly good swim day least you could do is have some answers. "Let's go in," she say like she got something up her sleeve. Only she don't lead the way. So me and Sugar turn the corner to where the entrance is, but when we get there I kinda hang back. Not that I'm scared, what's there to be afraid of, just a toy store. But I feel funny, shame. But what I got to be shamed about? Got as much right to go in as anybody. But somehow I can't seem to get hold of the door, so I step away from Sugar to lead. But she hangs back too. And I look at her and she looks at me and this is ridiculous. I mean, damn, I have never been shy about doing nothing or going nowhere. But then Mercedes steps up and then Rosie Giraffe and Big Butt crowd in behind and shove, and next thing we all stuffed into the doorway with only Mercedes squeezing past us, smoothing out her jumper and walking right down the aisle. Then the rest of us tumble in like a glued-together jigsaw done all wrong. And people lookin at us. And it's like the time me and Sugar crashed into the Catholic church on a dare. But once we got in there and everything so hushed and holy and the candles and the bowin and the handkerchiefs on all the drooping heads, I just couldn't go through with the plan. Which was for me to run up to the altar and do a tap dance while Sugar played the nose flute and messed around in the holy water. And Sugar kept given me the elbow. Then later teased me so bad I tied her up in the shower and turned it on and locked her in. And she'd be there till this day if Aunt Gretchen hadn't finally figured I was lying about the boarder takin a shower.

Same thing in the store. We all walkin on tiptoe and hardly touchin the games and puzzles and things. And I watched Miss Moore who is steady watchin us like she waitin for a sign. Like Mama Drewery watches the sky and sniffs the air and takes note of just how much slant is in the bird formation. Then me and Sugar bump smack into each other, so busy gazing at the toys, 'specially the sailboat. But we don't laugh and go into our fat-lady bump-stomach routine. We just stare at that price tag. Then Sugar run a finger over the whole boat. And I'm jealous and want to hit her. Maybe not her, but I sure want to punch somebody in the mouth.

"Watcha bring us here for, Miss Moore?"

"You sound angry, Sylvia. Are you mad about something?" Givin me one of them grins like she tellin a grown-up joke that never turns out to be funny. And she's lookin very closely at me like maybe she plannin to do my portrait from memory. I'm mad, but I won't give her that satisfaction. So I slouch around the store being very bored and say, "Let's go."

Me and Sugar at the back of the train watchin the tracks whizzin by large then small then getting gobbled up in the dark. I'm thinkin about this tricky toy I saw in the store. A clown that somersaults on a bar then does chin-ups just cause you yank lightly at his leg. Cost $35. I could see me askin my mother for a $35 birthday clown. "You wanna who that costs what?" she'd say, cocking her head to the side to get a better view of the hole in my head. Thirty-five dollars could buy new bunk beds for Junior and Gretchen's boy. Thirty-five dollars and the whole household could go visit Grand-daddy Nelson in the country. Thirty-five dollars would pay for the rent and the piano bill too. Who are these people that spend that much for performing clowns and $1000 for toy sailboats? What kinda work they do and how they live and how come we ain't in on it? Where we are is who we are, Miss Moore always pointin out. But it don't necessarily have to be that way, she always adds then waits for somebody to say that poor people have to wake up and demand their share of the pie and don't none of us know what kind of pie she talking about in the first damn place. But she ain't so smart cause I still got her four dollars from the taxi and she sure ain't gettin it. Messin up my day with this shit. Sugar nudges me in my pocket and winks.

Miss Moore lines us up in front of the mailbox where we started from, seem like years ago, and I got a headache for thinkin so hard. And we lean all over each other so we can hold up under the draggy-ass lecture she always finishes us off with at the end before we thank her for borin us to tears. But she just looks at us like she readin tea leaves. Finally she say, "Well, what did you think of F.A.O. Schwarz?"

Rosie Giraffe mumbles, "White folks crazy."

"I'd like to go there again when I get my birthday money," says Mercedes, and we shove her out the pack so she has to lean on the mailbox by herself.

"I'd like a shower. Tiring day," say Flyboy.

Then Sugar surprises me by sayin, "You know, Miss Moore, I don't think all of us here put together eat in a year what that sailboat costs." And Miss Moore lights up like somebody goosed her "And?" she say, urging Sugar on. Only I'm standin on her foot so she don't continue.

"Imagine for a minute what kind of society it is in which some people can spend on a toy what it would cost to feed a family of six or seven. What do you think?"

"I think," say Sugar pushing me off her feet like she never done before, cause I whip her ass in a minute, "that this is not much of a democracy if you ask me. Equal chance to pursue happiness means an equal crack at the dough, don't it?" Miss Moore is besides herself and I am disgusted with Sugar's treachery. So I stand on her foot one more time to see if she'll shove me. She shuts up, and Miss Moore looks at me, sorrowfully I'm thinkin. And somethin weird is goin on, I can feel it in my chest.

"Anybody else learn anything today?" lookin dead at me. I walk away and Sugar has to run to catch up and don't even seem to notice when I shrug her arm off my shoulder.

"Well, we got four dollars anyway," she says.

"Uh, hunh."

"We could go to Hascombs and get half a chocolate layer and then go to the Sunset and still have plenty money for potato chips and ice cream sodas."

"Uh, hunh."

"Race you to Hascombs," she say.

We start down the block and she gets ahead which is O.K. by me cause I'm going to the West End and then over to the Drive to think this day through. She can run if she want to and even run faster. But ain't nobody gonna beat me at nuthin.

ᔕᔕ

JORGE LUIS BORGES *(1899–1986), the eminent Argentinean writer of fiction, poetry, and criticism, was born in Buenos Aires. His father, a professor of psychology, amused him in childhood with various philosophical puzzles that continued to intrigue Borges when he grew up. Educated in Europe, he began to write as a member of a Spanish avant-garde literary movement called* ultráisme, *a development of expressionism in which image and metaphor are exaggerated to become more important than plot, character, or theme. Borges rejected this extreme view when he matured as an artist. At the age of twenty-two he returned to Buenos Aires, where he published three books of poetry and worked as a municipal librarian. A champion of freedom unaffiliated with any political party, Borges was hounded out of his job by the dictator Juan Perón, who made him a poultry inspector. After the fall of Perón, Borges was named director of the National Library of Argentina in Buenos Aires, where he worked until his progressive blindness circumscribed his activities.*

Borges's international reputation as a prose writer was established in 1944 with Fictions, *a brilliant collection of stories and sketches. In dreamlike works of short fiction, he created fantastic worlds dramatizing his view that in our unexplainable universe, all identity is an illusion.* Labyrinths *(1962),* Dreamtigers *(1964),* The Aleph and Other Stories *(1970),* Doctor Brodie's Report *(1974), and several other volumes followed.* Borges on Writing *(1973) contains the author's views on fiction, poetry, and translation. As the critic Victor Langue wrote in his preface to* Dreamtigers, *"Borges's narratives . . . are thought-games about an infinite and always delusive universe, fictions in which arguments, subtle changes in pace, color, and perspective disintegrate the objective world."*

"Everything and Nothing," Borges's sketch based on the life of William Shakespeare, is one of the short prose and poetry selections collected in Dreamtigers. *In the epilogue to that volume, Borges wrote that "of all the books I have delivered to the presses, none, I think, is as personal as the straggling collection mustered for this hodge-podge, precisely because it abounds in reflections and interpolations. Few things have happened to me, and I have read a great many. Or rather, few things have happened to me more worth remembering than . . . the music of England's words."*

RELATED PLAY: *William Shakespeare,* Hamlet, Prince of Denmark, *page 1474.*

RELATED COMMENTARY: *John Keats, "From a Letter to George and Thomas Keats, 21 December 1817," page 2048.*

JORGE LUIS BORGES

Everything and Nothing   1964

TRANSLATED BY MILDRED BOYER

There was no one in him; behind his face (which even in the poor paintings of the period is unlike any other) and his words, which were copious, imaginative, and emotional, there was nothing but a little chill, a dream not dreamed by anyone. At first he thought everyone was like him, but the puzzled look on a friend's face when he remarked on that emptiness told him he was mistaken and convinced him forever that an individual must not differ from his species. Occasionally he thought he would find in books the cure for his ill, and so he learned the small Latin and less Greek of which a contemporary was to speak. Later he thought that in the exercise of an elemental human rite he might well find what he sought, and he let himself be initiated by Anne Hathaway° one long June afternoon. At twenty-odd he went to London. Instinctively, he had already trained himself in the habit of pretending that he was someone, so it would not be discovered that he was no one. In London he hit upon the profession to which he was predestined, that of the actor, who plays on stage at being someone else. His playacting taught him a singular happiness, perhaps the first he had known; but when the last line was applauded and the last corpse removed from the stage, the hated sense of unreality came over him again. He ceased to be Ferrex or Tamburlaine° and again became a nobody. Trapped, he fell to imagining other heroes and other tragic tales. Thus, while in London's bawdyhouses and taverns his body fulfilled its destiny as body, the soul that dwelled in it was Caesar, failing to heed the augurer's admonition, and Juliet, detesting the lark, and Macbeth, conversing on the heath with the witches, who are also the fates. Nobody was ever as many men as that man, who like the Egyptian Proteus managed to exhaust all the possible shapes of being. At times he slipped into some corner of his work a confession, certain that it would not be deciphered; Richard affirms that in his single person he plays many parts, and Iago° says with strange words, "I am not what I am." His passages on the fundamental identity of existing, dreaming, and acting are famous.

Twenty years he persisted in that controlled hallucination, but one morning he was overcome by the surfeit and the horror of being so many kings who die by the sword and so many unhappy lovers who converge, diverge, and melodiously agonize. That same day he disposed of his theater. Before a week was out he had returned to the village of his birth, where he recovered the trees and the river of his childhood; and he did not bind them to

---

Anne Hathaway: Shakespeare's wife.
Ferrex or Tamburlaine: Ferrex is a character in Thomas Norton and Thomas Sackville's play *Gorboduc* (561). Tamburlaine is the eponymous hero of Christopher Marlowe's *Tamburlaine the Great* (1587).
Caesar ... Juliet ... Macbeth ... Richard ... Iago: Characters in Shakespeare's plays *Julius Caesar, Romeo and Juliet, Macbeth, Richard III,* and *Othello.*

those others his muse had celebrated, those made illustrious by mythological allusions and Latin phrases. He had to be someone; he became a retired impresario who has made his fortune and who interests himself in loans, lawsuits, and petty usury. In this character he dictated the arid final will and testament that we know, deliberately excluding from it every trace of emotion and of literature. Friends from London used to visit his retreat, and for them he would take on again the role of poet.

The story goes that, before or after he died, he found himself before God and he said: "I, who have been so many men in vain, want to be one man: myself." The voice of God replied from a whirlwind: "Neither am I one self; I dreamed the world as you dreamed your work, my Shakespeare, and among the shapes of my dream are you, who, like me, are many persons — and none."

ॐ

RAYMOND CARVER *(1938–1988) grew up in a logging town in Oregon, where his father worked in a sawmill and his mother held odd jobs. After graduating from high school, Carver married at the age of nineteen and had two children. Working hard to support his wife and family, he managed to enroll briefly in 1958 as a student at Chico State College in California, where he took a creative writing course from a then nearly unknown young novelist named John Gardner. Carver remembered that he decided to try to become a writer because he liked to read pulp novels and magazines about hunting and fishing. He credited Gardner for giving him a strong sense of direction as a writer: "A writer's values and craft. This is what the man taught and what he stood for, and this is what I've kept by me in the years since that brief but all-important time."*

In 1963 Carver received his B.A. from Humboldt State College in northern California. The following year he studied writing at the University of Iowa. But the 1960s, he said, were difficult for him and his wife:

> I learned a long time ago when my kids were little and we had no money, and we were working our hearts out and weren't getting anywhere, even though we were giving it our best, my wife and I, that there were more important things than writing a poem or a story. That was a very hard realization for me to come to. But it came to me, and I had to accept it or die. Getting milk and food on the table, getting the rent paid, if a choice had to be made, then I had to forgo writing.

Carver's desire to be a writer was so strong that he kept on writing long after the "cold facts" of his life told him he ought to quit. His first collection of stories, Will You Please Be Quiet, Please?, *was nominated for the National Book Award in 1976. Four more collections of stories followed, along with five books of poetry, before his death from lung cancer.*

Critics have noted that the rapid evolution of Carver's style causes his fiction to fall into three distinct periods. The tentative writing in his first book of stories — many of which he subsequently revised and republished — was followed by a paring down of his prose. This resulted in the hard-edged and detached minimalist style of his middle period, exemplified by the stories in his collection What We Talk About

When We Talk About Love *(1981). In his final period, Carver developed a more ex-pansive style, as in the collection* Cathedral *(1983) and the new stories in his last col-lection,* Where I'm Calling From: New and Selected Stories *(1988), from which* "Errand" *is taken.*

Influenced by the cadence of Ernest Hemingway's sentences, Carver also be-lieved in simplicity. He wrote,

> It's possible, in a poem or a short story, to write about commonplace things
> and objects using commonplace but precise language, and to endow those
> things — a chair, a window curtain, a fork, a stone, a woman's earring —
> with immense, even startling power.... If the words are heavy with the
> writer's own unbridled emotions, or if they are imprecise and inaccurate for
> some other reason — if the words are in any way blurred — the reader's eyes
> will slide right over them and nothing will be achieved. The reader's own
> artistic sense will simply not be engaged.

RELATED COMMENTARIES: *See Casebook on Raymond Carver, pages 814–832, including Raymond Carver, "On Writing," page 815; "Creative Writing 101," page 818; "The Ashtray," page 821; "On 'Errand,' " page 823; Olga Knipper, "Remem-bering about Chekhov," page 824; Edward Sanders, "From Chekhov," page 825; Henri Troyat, "Chekhov's Last Days," page 826; Tom Jenks, "The Origin of 'Cathe-dral,' " page 829; Arthur M. Saltzman, "A Reading of 'What We Talk About When We Talk About Love,' " page 830.*

RAYMOND CARVER

Cathedral

1981

This blind man, an old friend of my wife's, he was on his way to spend the night. His wife had died. So he was visiting the dead wife's relatives in Connecticut. He called my wife from his in-laws'. Arrangements were made. He would come by train, a five-hour trip, and my wife would meet him at the station. She hadn't seen him since she worked for him one summer in Seattle ten years ago. But she and the blind man had kept in touch. They made tapes and mailed them back and forth. I wasn't enthusiastic about his visit. He was no one I knew. And his being blind bothered me. My idea of blindness came from the movies. In the movies, the blind moved slowly and never laughed. Sometimes they were led by seeing-eye dogs. A blind man in my house was not something I looked forward to.

That summer in Seattle she had needed a job. She didn't have any money. The man she was going to marry at the end of the summer was in of-ficers' training school. He didn't have any money, either. But she was in love with the guy, and he was in love with her, etc. She'd seen something in the pa-per: HELP WANTED — *Reading to Blind Man,* and a telephone number. She phoned and went over, was hired on the spot. She'd worked with this blind man all summer. She read stuff to him, case studies, reports, that sort of thing. She helped him organize his little office in the county social-service depart-ment. They'd become good friends, my wife and the blind man. How do I know these things? She told me. And she told me something else. On her last day in the office, the blind man asked if he could touch her face. She agreed to this. She told me he touched his fingers to every part of her face, her nose — even her neck! She never forgot it. She even tried to write a poem about it. She was always trying to write a poem. She wrote a poem or two every year, usually after something really important had happened to her.

When we first started going out together, she showed me the poem. In the poem, she recalled his fingers and the way they had moved around over her face. In the poem, she talked about what she had felt at the time, about what went through her mind when the blind man touched her nose and lips. I can remember I didn't think much of the poem. Of course, I didn't tell her that. Maybe I just don't understand poetry. I admit it's not the first thing I reach for when I pick up something to read.

Anyway, this man who'd first enjoyed her favors, the officer-to-be, he'd been her childhood sweetheart. So okay. I'm saying that at the end of the summer she let the blind man run his hands over her face, said goodbye to him, married her childhood etc., who was now a commissioned officer, and she moved away from Seattle. But they'd kept in touch, she and the blind man. She made the first contact after a year or so. She called him up one night from an Air Force base in Alabama. She wanted to talk. They talked. He asked her to send him a tape and tell him about her life. She did this. She sent the tape. On the tape, she told the blind man about her husband and about their life together in the military. She told the blind man she loved her husband but she didn't like it where they lived and she didn't like it that he was a part of the military-industrial thing. She told the blind man she'd written a poem and he was in it. She told him that she was writing a poem about what it was like to be an Air Force officer's wife. The poem wasn't finished yet. She was still writing it. The blind man made a tape. He sent her the tape. She made a tape. This went on for years. My wife's officer was posted to one base and then another. She sent tapes from Moody AFB, McGuire, McConnell, and finally Travis, near Sacramento, where one night she got to feeling lonely and cut off from people she kept losing in that moving-around life. She got to feeling she couldn't go it another step. She went in and swallowed all the pills and capsules in the medicine chest and washed them down with a bottle of gin. Then she got into a hot bath and passed out.

But instead of dying, she got sick. She threw up. Her officer — why should he have a name? he was the childhood sweetheart, and what more does he want? — came home from somewhere, found her, and called the ambulance. In time, she put it all on a tape and sent the tape to the blind man. Over the years, she put all kinds of stuff on tapes and sent the tapes off lickety-split. Next to writing a poem every year, I think it was her chief means of recreation. On one tape, she told the blind man she'd decided to live away from her officer for a time. On another tape, she told him about her divorce. She and I began going out, and of course she told her blind man about it. She told him everything, or so it seemed to me. Once she asked me if I'd like to hear the latest tape from the blind man. This was a year ago. I was on the tape, she said. So I said okay, I'd listen to it. I got us drinks and we settled down in the living room. We made ready to listen. First she inserted the tape into the player and adjusted a couple of dials. Then she pushed a lever. The tape squeaked and someone began to talk in this loud voice. She lowered the volume. After a few minutes of harmless chitchat, I heard my own name in the mouth of this stranger, this blind man I didn't even know! And then this: "From all you've said about him, I can only conclude — " But we were interrupted, a knock at the door, something, and we didn't ever get back to the tape. Maybe it was just as well. I'd heard all I wanted to.

Now this same blind man was coming to sleep in my house.

"Maybe I could take him bowling," I said to my wife. She was at the draining board doing scalloped potatoes. She put down the knife she was using and turned around.

"If you love me," she said, "you can do this for me. If you don't love me, okay. But if you had a friend, any friend, and the friend came to visit, I'd make him feel comfortable." She wiped her hands with the dish towel.

"I don't have any blind friends," I said.

"You don't have *any* friends," she said. "Period. Besides," she said, "goddamn it, his wife's just died! Don't you understand that? The man's lost his wife!"

I didn't answer. She'd told me a little about the blind man's wife. Her name was Beulah. Beulah! That's a name for a colored woman.

"Was his wife Negro?" I asked.

"Are you crazy?" my wife said. "Have you just flipped or something?" She picked up a potato. I saw it hit the floor, then roll under the stove. "What's wrong with you?" she said. "Are you drunk?"

"I'm just asking," I said.

Right then my wife filled me in with more detail than I cared to know. I made a drink and sat at the kitchen table to listen. Pieces of the story began to fall into place.

Beulah had gone to work for the blind man the summer after my wife had stopped working for him. Pretty soon Beulah and the blind man had themselves a church wedding. It was a little wedding — who'd want to go to such a wedding in the first place? — just the two of them, plus the minister and the minister's wife. But it was a church wedding just the same. It was what Beulah had wanted, he'd said. But even then Beulah must have been carrying the cancer in her glands. After they had been inseparable for eight years — my wife's word, *inseparable* — Beulah's health went into a rapid decline. She died in a Seattle hospital room, the blind man sitting beside the bed and holding on to her hand. They'd married, lived and worked together, slept together — had sex, sure — and then the blind man had to bury her. All this without his having ever seen what the goddamned woman looked like. It was beyond my understanding. Hearing this, I felt sorry for the blind man for a little bit. And then I found myself thinking what a pitiful life this woman must have led. Imagine a woman who could never see herself as she was seen in the eyes of her loved one. A woman who could go on day after day and never receive the smallest compliment from her beloved. A woman whose husband could never read the expression on her face, be it misery or something better.

Someone who could wear makeup or not — what difference to him? She could, if she wanted, wear green eye-shadow around one eye, a straight pin in her nostril, yellow slacks and purple shoes, no matter. And then to slip off into death, the blind man's hand on her hand, his blind eyes streaming tears — I'm imagining now — her last thought maybe this: that he never even knew what she looked like, and she on an express to the grave. Robert was left with a small insurance policy and half of a twenty-peso Mexican coin. The other half of the coin went into the box with her. Pathetic.

So when the time rolled around, my wife went to the depot to pick him up. With nothing to do but wait — sure, I blamed him for that — I was having a drink and watching the TV when I heard the car pull into the drive. I got up from the sofa with my drink and went to the window to have a look.

I saw my wife laughing as she parked the car. I saw her get out of the car and shut the door. She was still wearing a smile. Just amazing. She went around to the other side of the car to where the blind man was already starting to get out. This blind man, feature this, he was wearing a full beard! A beard on a blind man! Too much, I say. The blind man reached into the back seat and dragged out a suitcase. My wife took his arm, shut the car door, and, talking all the way, moved him down the drive and then up the steps to the front porch. I turned off the TV. I finished my drink, rinsed the glass, dried my hands. Then I went to the door.

My wife said, "I want you to meet Robert. Robert, this is my husband. I've told you all about him." She was beaming. She had this blind man by his coat sleeve.

The blind man let go of his suitcase and up came his hand.

I took it. He squeezed hard, held my hand, and then he let it go.

"I feel like we've already met," he boomed.

"Likewise," I said. I didn't know what else to say. Then I said, "Welcome. I've heard a lot about you." We began to move then, a little group, from the porch into the living room, my wife guiding him by the arm. The blind man was carrying his suitcase in his other hand. My wife said things like, "To your left here, Robert. That's right. Now watch it, there's a chair. That's it. Sit down right here. This is the sofa. We just bought this sofa two weeks ago."

I started to say something about the old sofa. I'd liked that old sofa. But I didn't say anything. Then I wanted to say something else, small-talk, about the scenic ride along the Hudson. How going *to* New York, you should sit on the right-hand side of the train, and coming *from* New York, the left-hand side.

"Did you have a good train ride?" I said. "Which side of the train did you sit on, by the way?"

"What a question, which side!" my wife said. "What's it matter which side?" she said.

"I just asked," I said.

"Right side," the blind man said. "I hadn't been on a train in nearly forty years. Not since I was a kid. With my folks. That's been a long time. I'd nearly forgotten the sensation. I have winter in my beard now," he said. "So I've been told, anyway. Do I look distinguished, my dear?" the blind man said to my wife.

"You look distinguished, Robert," she said. "Robert," she said. "Robert, it's just so good to see you."

My wife finally took her eyes off the blind man and looked at me. I had the feeling she didn't like what she saw. I shrugged.

I've never met, or personally known, anyone who was blind. This blind man was late forties, a heavy-set, balding man with stooped shoulders, as if he carried a great weight there. He wore brown slacks, brown shoes, a light-brown shirt, a tie, a sports coat. Spiffy. He also had this full beard. But he didn't use a cane and he didn't wear dark glasses. I'd always thought dark glasses were a must for the blind. Fact was, I wished he had a pair. At first glance, his eyes looked like anyone else's eyes. But if you look close, there was something different about them. Too much white in the iris, for one thing, and the pupils seemed to move around in the sockets without his knowing it or being able to stop it. Creepy. As I stared at his face, I saw the left pupil turn in toward his nose while the other made an effort to keep in one place. But it was only an effort, for that eye was on the roam without his knowing it or wanting it to be.

I said, "Let me get you a drink. What's your pleasure? We have a little of everything. It's one of our pastimes."

"Bub, I'm a Scotch man myself," he said fast enough in this big voice. "Right," I said. Bub! "Sure you are, I knew it."

He let his fingers touch his suitcase, which was sitting alongside the sofa. He was taking his bearings. I didn't blame him for that.

"I'll move that up to your room," my wife said.

"No, that's fine," the blind man said loudly. "It can go up when I go up."

"A little water with the Scotch?" I said.

"Very little," he said.

"I knew it," I said.

He said, "Just a tad. The Irish actor, Barry Fitzgerald? I'm like that fellow. When I drink water, Fitzgerald said, I drink water. When I drink whiskey, I drink whiskey." My wife laughed. The blind man brought his hand up under his beard. He lifted his beard slowly and let it drop.

I did the drinks, three big glasses of Scotch with a splash of water in each. Then we made ourselves comfortable and talked about Robert's travels. First the long flight from the West Coast to Connecticut, we covered that. Then from Connecticut up here by train. We had another drink concerning that leg of the trip.

I remembered having read somewhere that the blind didn't smoke because, as speculation had it, they couldn't see the smoke they exhaled. I thought I knew that much and that much only about blind people. But this blind man smoked his cigarette down to the nubbin and then lit another one. This blind man filled his ashtray and my wife emptied it.

When we sat down at the table for dinner, we had another drink. My wife heaped Robert's plate with cube steak, scalloped potatoes, green beans. I buttered him up two slices of bread. I said, "Here's bread and butter for you." I swallowed some of my drink. "Now let us pray," I said, and the blind man lowered his head. My wife looked at me, her mouth agape. "Pray the phone won't ring and the food doesn't get cold," I said.

We dug in. We ate everything there was to eat on the table. We ate like there was no tomorrow. We didn't talk. We ate. We scarfed. We grazed that table. We were into serious eating. The blind man had right away located his foods, he knew just where everything was on his plate. I watched with admiration as he used his knife and fork on the meat. He'd cut two pieces of meat, fork the meat into his mouth, and then go all out for the scalloped potatoes, the beans next, and then he'd tear off a hunk of buttered bread and eat that. He'd follow this up with a big drink of milk. It didn't seem to bother him to use his fingers once in a while, either.

We finished everything, including half a strawberry pie. For a few moments, we sat as if stunned. Sweat beaded on our faces. Finally, we got up from the table and left the dirty plates. We didn't look back. We took ourselves into the living room and sank into our places again. Robert and my wife sat on the sofa. I took the big chair. We had us two or three more drinks while they talked about the major things that had come to pass for them in the past ten years. For the most part, I just listened. Now and then I joined in. I didn't want him to think I'd left the room, and I didn't want her to think I was feeling left out. They talked of things that had happened to them — to them! — these past ten years. I waited in vain to hear my name on my wife's sweet lips: "And then my dear husband came into my life" — something like that. But I heard nothing of the sort. More talk of Robert. Robert had done a little of everything, it seemed, a regular blind jack-of-all-trades. But most recently he and his wife had had an Amway distributorship, from which, I gathered, they'd earned their living, such as it was. The blind man was also a ham radio operator. He talked in his loud voice about conversations he'd had with fellow operators in Guam, in the Philippines, in Alaska, and even in Tahiti. He said he'd have a lot of friends there if he ever wanted to go visit those places. From time to time, he'd turn his blind face toward me, put his hand under his beard, ask me something. How long had I been in my present position? (Three years.) Did I like my work? (I didn't.) Was I going to stay with it? (What were the options?) Finally, when I thought he was beginning to run down, I got up and turned on the TV.

My wife looked at me with irritation. She was heading toward a boil. Then she looked at the blind man and said, "Robert, do you have a TV?"

The blind man said, "My dear, I have two TVs. I have a color set and a black-and-white thing, an old relic. It's funny, but if I turn the TV on, and I'm always turning it on, I turn on the color set. It's funny, don't you think?"

I didn't know what to say to that. I had absolutely nothing to say to that. No opinions. So I watched the news program and tried to listen to what the announcer was saying.

"This is a color TV," the blind man said. "Don't ask me how, but I can tell."

"We traded up a while ago," I said.

The blind man had another taste of his drink. He lifted his beard, sniffed it, and let it fall. He leaned forward on the sofa. He positioned his ashtray on the coffee table, then put the lighter to his cigarette. He leaned back on the sofa and crossed his legs at the ankles.

My wife covered her mouth, and then she yawned. She stretched. She said, "I think I'll go upstairs and put on my robe. I think I'll change into something else. Robert, you make yourself comfortable," she said.

"I'm comfortable," the blind man said.

"I want you to feel comfortable in this house," she said.

"I am comfortable," the blind man said.

After she'd left the room, he and I listened to the weather report and then to the sports roundup. By that time, she'd been gone so long I didn't know if she was going to come back. I thought she might have gone to bed. I wished she'd come back downstairs. I didn't want to be left alone with a blind man. I asked him if he wanted another drink, and he said sure. Then I asked if he wanted to smoke some dope with me. I said I'd just rolled a number. I hadn't, but I planned to do so in about two shakes.

"I'll try some with you," he said.

"Damn right," I said. "That's the stuff."

I got our drinks and sat down on the sofa with him. Then I rolled us two fat numbers. I lit one and passed it. I brought it to his fingers. He took it and inhaled.

"Hold it as long as you can," I said. I could tell he didn't know the first thing.

My wife came back downstairs wearing her pink robe and her pink slippers.

"What do I smell?" she said.

"We thought we'd have us some cannabis," I said.

My wife gave me a savage look. Then she looked at the blind man and said, "Robert, I didn't know you smoked."

He said, "I do now, my dear. There's a first time for everything. But I don't feel anything yet."

"This stuff is pretty mellow," I said. "This stuff is mild. It's dope you can reason with," I said. "It doesn't mess you up."

"Not much it doesn't, bub," he said, and laughed.

My wife sat on the sofa between the blind man and me. I passed her the number. She took it and toked and then passed it back to me. "Which way is this going?" she said. Then she said, "I shouldn't be smoking this. I can hardly keep my eyes open as it is. That dinner did me in. I shouldn't have eaten so much."

"It was the strawberry pie," the blind man said. "That's what did it," he said, and he laughed his big laugh. Then he shook his head.

"There's more strawberry pie," I said.

"Do you want some more, Robert?" my wife said.

"Maybe in a little while," he said.

We gave our attention to the TV. My wife yawned again. She said, "Your bed is made up when you feel like going to bed, Robert. I know you must have had a long day. When you're ready to go to bed, say so." She pulled his arm. "Robert?"

He came to and said, "I've had a real nice time. This beats tapes, doesn't it?"

I said, "Coming at you," and I put the number between his fingers. He inhaled, held the smoke, and then let it go. It was like he'd been doing it since he was nine years old.

"Thanks, bub," he said. "But I think this is all for me. I think I'm beginning to feel it," he said. He held the burning roach out for my wife.

"Same here," she said. "Ditto. Me, too." She took the roach and passed it to me. "I may just sit here for a while between you two guys with my eyes closed. But don't let me bother you, okay? Either one of you. If it bothers you, say so. Otherwise, I may just sit here with my eyes closed until you're ready to go to bed," she said. "Your bed's made up, Robert, when you're ready. It's right next to our room at the top of the stairs. We'll show you up when you're ready. You wake me up now, you guys, if I fall asleep." She said that and then she closed her eyes and went to sleep.

The news program ended. I got up and changed the channel. I sat back down on the sofa. I wished my wife hadn't pooped out. Her head lay across the back of the sofa, her mouth open. She'd turned so that her robe had slipped away from her legs, exposing a juicy thigh. I reached to draw her robe back over her, and it was then that I glanced at the blind man. What the hell! I flipped the robe open again.

"You say when you want some strawberry pie," I said.

"I will," he said.

I said, "Are you tired? Do you want me to take you up to your bed? Are you ready to hit the hay?"

"Not yet," he said. "No, I'll stay up with you, bub. If that's all right. I'll stay up until you're ready to turn in. We haven't had a chance to talk. Know what I mean? I feel like me and her monopolized the evening." He lifted his beard and he let it fall. He picked up his cigarettes and his lighter.

"That's all right," I said. Then I said, "I'm glad for the company."

And I guess I was. Every night I smoked dope and stayed up as long as I could before I fell asleep. My wife and I hardly ever went to bed at the same time. When I did go to sleep, I had these dreams. Sometimes I'd wake up from one of them, my heart going crazy.

Something about the church and the Middle Ages was on the TV. Not your run-of-the-mill TV fare. I wanted to watch something else. I turned to the other channels. But there was nothing on them, either. So I turned back to the first channel and apologized.

"Bub, it's all right," the blind man said. "It's fine with me. Whatever you want to watch is okay. I'm always learning something. Learning never ends. It won't hurt me to learn something tonight. I got ears," he said.

We didn't say anything for a time. He was leaning forward with his head turned at me, his right ear aimed in the direction of the set. Very disconcerting. Now and then his eyelids drooped and then they snapped open again. Now and then he put his fingers into his beard and tugged, like he was thinking about something he was hearing on the television.

On the screen, a group of men wearing cowls was being set upon and tormented by men dressed in skeleton costumes and men dressed as devils.

The men dressed as devils wore devil masks, horns, and long tails. This pageant was part of a procession. The Englishman who was narrating the thing said it took place in Spain once a year. I tried to explain to the blind man what was happening.

"Skeletons," he said. "I know about skeletons," he said, and he nodded.

The TV showed this one cathedral. Then there was a long, slow look at another one. Finally, the picture switched to the famous one in Paris, with its flying buttresses and its spires reaching up to the clouds. The camera pulled away to show the whole of the cathedral rising above the skyline.

There were times when the Englishman who was telling the thing would shut up, would simply let the camera move around over the cathedrals. Or else the camera would tour the countryside, men in fields walking behind oxen. I waited as long as I could. Then I felt I had to say something. I said, "They're showing the outside of this cathedral now. Gargoyles. Little statues carved to look like monsters. Now I guess they're in Italy. Yeah, they're in Italy. There's paintings on the walls of this one church."

"Are those fresco paintings, bub?" he asked, and he sipped from his drink.

I reached for my glass. But it was empty. I tried to remember what I could remember. "You're asking me are those frescoes?" I said. "That's a good question. I don't know."

The camera moved to a cathedral outside Lisbon. The differences in the Portuguese cathedral compared with the French and Italian were not that great. But they were there. Mostly the interior stuff. Then something occurred to me, and I said, "Something has occurred to me. Do you have any idea what a cathedral is? What they look like, that is? Do you follow me? If somebody says cathedral to you, do you have any notion what they're talking about? Do you know the difference between that and a Baptist church, say?"

He let the smoke dribble from his mouth. "I know they took hundreds of workers fifty or a hundred years to build," he said. "I just heard the man say that, of course. I know generations of the same families worked on a cathedral. I heard him say that too. The men who began their life's work on them, they never lived to see the completion of their work. In that wise, bub, they're no different from the rest of us, right?" He laughed. Then his eyelids drooped again. His head nodded. He seemed to be snoozing. Maybe he was imagining himself in Portugal. The TV was showing another cathedral now. This one was in Germany. The Englishman's voice droned on. "Cathedrals," the blind man said. He sat up and rolled his head back and forth. "If you want the truth, bub, that's about all I know. What I just said. What I heard him say. But maybe you could describe one to me? I wish you'd do it. I'd like that. If you want to know, I really don't have a good idea."

I stared hard at the shot of the cathedral on the TV. How could I even begin to describe it? But say my life depended on it. Say my life was being threatened by an insane guy who said I had to do it or else.

I stared some more at the cathedral before the picture flipped off into the countryside. There was no use. I turned to the blind man and said, "To begin with, they're very tall." I was looking around the room for clues. "They reach

way up. Up and up. Toward the sky. They're so big, some of them, they have
to have these supports. To help hold them up, so to speak. These supports are
called buttresses. They remind me of viaducts, for some reason. But maybe
you don't know viaducts, either? Sometimes the cathedrals have devils and
such carved into the front. Sometimes lords and ladies. Don't ask me why this
is," I said.

He was nodding. The whole upper part of his body seemed to be moving back and forth.

"I'm not doing so good, am I?" I said.

He stopped nodding and leaned forward on the edge of the sofa. As he
listened to me, he was running his fingers through his beard. I wasn't getting
through to him, I could see that. But he waited for me to go on just the same.
He nodded, like he was trying to encourage me. I tried to think what else to
say. "They're really big," I said. "They're massive. They're built of stone. Marble, too, sometimes. In those olden days, when they built cathedrals, men
wanted to be close to God. In those olden days, God was an important part of
everyone's life. You could tell this from their cathedral-building. I'm sorry," I
said, "but it looks like that's the best I can do for you. I'm just no good at it."

"That's all right, bub," the blind man said. "Hey, listen. I hope you don't
mind my asking you. Can I ask you something? Let me ask you a simple question, yes or no. I'm just curious and there's no offense. You're my host. But let
me ask if you are in any way religious? You don't mind my asking?"

I shook my head. He couldn't see that, though. A wink is the same as a
nod to a blind man. "I guess I don't believe in it. In anything. Sometimes it's
hard. You know what I'm saying?"

"Sure I do," he said.

"Right," I said.

The Englishman was still holding forth. My wife sighed in her sleep. She
drew a long breath and went on with her sleeping.

"You'll have to forgive me," I said. "But I can't tell you what a cathedral
looks like. It just isn't in me to do it. I can't do any more than I've done."

The blind man sat very still, his head down, as he listened to me.

I said, "The truth is, cathedrals don't mean anything special to me.
Nothing. Cathedrals. They're something to look at on late-night TV. That's all
they are."

It was then that the blind man cleared his throat. He brought something
up. He took a handkerchief from his back pocket. Then he said, "I get it, bub.
It's okay. It happens. Don't worry about it," he said. "Hey, listen to me. Will
you do me a favor? I got an idea. Why don't you find us some heavy paper?
And a pen. We'll do something. We'll draw one together. Get us a pen and
some heavy paper. Go on, bub, get the stuff," he said.

So I went upstairs. My legs felt like they didn't have any strength in
them. They felt like they did after I'd done some running. In my wife's room,
I looked around. I found some ballpoints in a little basket on her table. And
then I tried to think where to look for the kind of paper he was talking about.

Downstairs, in the kitchen, I found a shopping bag with onion skins in
the bottom of the bag. I emptied the bag and shook it. I brought it into the liv-

ing room and sat down with it near his legs. I moved some things, smoothed the wrinkles from the bag, spread it out on the coffee table.

The blind man got down from the sofa and sat next to me on the carpet.

He ran his fingers over the paper. He went up and down the sides of the paper. The edges, even the edges. He fingered the corners.

"All right," he said. "All right, let's do her."

He found my hand, the hand with the pen. He closed his hand over my hand. "Go ahead, bub, draw," he said. "Draw. You'll see. I'll follow along with you. It'll be okay. Just begin now like I'm telling you. You'll see. Draw," the blind man said.

So I began. First I drew a box that looked like a house. It could have been the house I lived in. Then I put a roof on it. At either end of the roof, I drew spires. Crazy.

"Swell," he said. "Terrific. You're doing fine," he said.

"Never thought anything like this could happen in your lifetime, did you, bub? Well, it's a strange life, we all know that. Go on now. Keep it up."

I put in windows with arches. I drew flying buttresses. I hung great doors. I couldn't stop. The TV station went off the air. I put down the pen and closed and opened my fingers. The blind man felt round over the paper. He moved the tips of his fingers over the paper, all over what I had drawn, and he nodded.

"Doing fine," the blind man said.

I took up the pen again, and he found my hand. I kept at it. I'm no artist. But I kept drawing just the same.

My wife opened up her eyes and gazed at us. She sat up on the sofa, her robe hanging open. She said, "What are you doing? Tell me, I want to know."

I didn't answer her.

The blind man said, "We're drawing a cathedral. Me and him are working on it. Press hard," he said to me. "That's right. That's good," he said. "Sure. You got it, bub. I can tell. You didn't think you could. But you can, can't you? You're cooking with gas now. You know what I'm saying? We're going to really have us something here in a minute. How's the old arm?" he said. "Put some people in there now. What's a cathedral without people?"

My wife said, "What's going on? Robert, what are you doing? What's going on?"

"It's all right," he said to her. "Close your eyes now," the blind man said to me.

I did it. I closed them just like he said.

"Are they closed? he said. "Don't fudge."

"They're closed," I said.

"Keep them that way," he said. He said, "Don't stop now. Draw."

So we kept on with it. His fingers rode my fingers as my hand went over the paper. It was like nothing else in my life up to now.

Then he said, "I think that's it. I think you got it," he said. "Take a look. What do you think?"

But I had my eyes closed. I thought I'd keep them that way for a little longer. I thought it was something I ought to do.

"Well?" he said. "Are you looking?"

My eyes were still closed. I was in my house. I knew that. But I didn't feel like I was inside anything.

"It's really something," I said.

RAYMOND CARVER

Errand

1987

Chekhov. On the evening of March 22, 1897, he went to dinner in Moscow with his friend and confidant Alexei Suvorin. This Suvorin was a very rich newspaper and book publisher, a reactionary, a self-made man whose father was a private at the battle of Borodino. Like Chekhov, he was the grandson of a serf. They had that in common: each had peasant's blood in his veins. Otherwise, politically and temperamentally, they were miles apart. Nevertheless, Suvorin was one of Chekhov's few intimates, and Chekhov enjoyed his company.

Naturally, they went to the best restaurant in the city, a former town house called the Hermitage — a place where it could take hours, half the night even, to get through a ten-course meal that would, of course, include several wines, liqueurs, and coffee. Chekhov was impeccably dressed, as always — a dark suit and waistcoat, his usual pince-nez. He looked that night very much as he looks in the photographs taken of him during this period. He was relaxed, jovial. He shook hands with the maître d', and with a glance took in the large dining room. It was brilliantly illuminated by ornate chandeliers, the tables occupied by elegantly dressed men and women. Waiters came and went ceaselessly. He had just been seated across the table from Suvorin when suddenly, without warning, blood began gushing from his mouth. Suvorin and two waiters helped him to the gentlemen's room and tried to stanch the flow of blood with ice packs. Suvorin saw him back to his own hotel and had a bed prepared for Chekhov in one of the rooms of the suite. Later, after another hemorrhage, Chekhov allowed himself to be moved to a clinic that specialized in the treatment of tuberculosis and related respiratory infections. When Suvorin visited him there, Chekhov apologized for the "scandal" at the restaurant three nights earlier but continued to insist there was nothing seriously wrong. "He laughed and jested as usual," Suvorin noted in his diary, "while spitting blood into a large vessel."

Maria Chekhov, his younger sister, visited Chekhov in the clinic during the last days of March. The weather was miserable; a sleet storm was in progress, and frozen heaps of snow lay everywhere. It was hard for her to wave down a carriage to take her to the hospital. By the time she arrived she was filled with dread and anxiety.

"Anton Pavlovich lay on his back," Maria wrote in her *Memoirs*. "He was not allowed to speak. After greeting him, I went over to the table to hide my emotions." There, among bottles of champagne, jars of caviar, bouquets of flowers from well-wishers, she saw something that terrified her: a freehand drawing, obviously done by a specialist in these matters, of Chekhov's lungs. It was the kind of sketch a doctor often makes in order to show his patient what he thinks is taking place. The lungs were outlined in blue, but the upper parts were filled in with red. "I realized they were diseased," Maria wrote.

Leo Tolstoy was another visitor. The hospital staff were awed to find themselves in the presence of the country's greatest writer. The most famous man in Russia? Of course they had to let him in to see Chekhov, even though "nonessential" visitors were forbidden. With much obsequiousness on the part of the nurses and resident doctors, the bearded, fierce-looking old man was shown into Chekhov's room. Despite his low opinion of Chekhov's abilities as a playwright (Tolstoy felt the plays were static and lacking in any moral vision. "Where do your characters take you?" he once demanded of Chekhov. "From the sofa to the junk room and back"), Tolstoy liked Chekhov's short stories. Furthermore, and quite simply, he loved the man. He told Gorky, "What a beautiful, magnificent man: modest and quiet, like a girl. He even walks like a girl. He's simply wonderful." And Tolstoy wrote in his journal (everyone kept a journal or a diary in those days), "I am glad I love . . . Chekhov."

Tolstoy removed his woollen scarf and bearskin coat, then lowered himself into a chair next to Chekhov's bed. Never mind that Chekhov was taking medication and not permitted to talk, much less carry on a conversation. He had to listen, amazedly, as the Count began to discourse on his theories of the immortality of the soul. Concerning that visit, Chekhov later wrote, "Tolstoy assumes that all of us (humans and animals alike) will live on in a principle (such as reason or love) the essence and goals of which are a mystery to us. . . . I have no use for that kind of immortality. I don't understand it, and Lev Niko-layevich [Tolstoy] was astonished I didn't."

Nevertheless, Chekhov was impressed with the solicitude shown by Tolstoy's visit. But, unlike Tolstoy, Chekhov didn't believe in an afterlife and never had. He didn't believe in anything that couldn't be apprehended by one or more of his five senses. And as far as his outlook on life and writing went, he once told someone that he lacked "a political, religious, and philosophical world view. I change it every month, so I'll have to limit myself to the description of how my heroes love, marry, give birth, die, and how they speak."

Earlier, before his t.b. was diagnosed, Chekhov had remarked, "When a peasant has consumption, he says, 'There's nothing I can do. I'll go off in the spring with the melting of the snows.' " (Chekhov himself died in the summer, during a heat wave.) But once Chekhov's own tuberculosis was discovered he continually tried to minimize the seriousness of his condition. To all appearances, it was as if he felt, right up to the end, that he might be able to throw off the disease as he would a lingering catarrh. Well into his final days, he spoke with seeming conviction of the possibility of an improvement. In fact, in a letter written shortly before his end, he went so far as to tell his sister that he was "getting fat" and felt much better now that he was in Badenweiler.

Badenweiler is a spa and resort city in the western area of the Black Forest, not far from Basel. The Vosges are visible from nearly anywhere in the city, and in those days the air was pure and invigorating. Russians had been going there for years to soak in the hot mineral baths and promenade on the boulevards. In June, 1904, Chekhov went there to die.

Earlier that month, he'd made a difficult journey by train from Moscow to Berlin. He traveled with his wife, the actress Olga Knipper, a woman he'd met in 1898 during rehearsals for *The Seagull*. Her contemporaries describe her as an excellent actress. She was talented, pretty, and almost ten years younger than the playwright. Chekhov had been immediately attracted to her, but was slow to act on his feelings. As always, he preferred a flirtation to marriage. Finally, after a three-year courtship involving many separations, letters, and the inevitable misunderstandings, they were at last married, in a private ceremony in Moscow, on May 25, 1901. Chekhov was enormously happy. He called Olga his "pony," and sometimes "dog" or "puppy." He was also fond of addressing her as "little turkey" or simply as "my joy."

In Berlin, Chekhov consulted with a renowned specialist in pulmonary disorders, a Dr. Karl Ewald. But, according to an eyewitness, after the doctor examined Chekhov he threw up his hands and left the room without a word. Chekhov was too far gone for help: this Dr. Ewald was furious with himself for not being able to work miracles, and with Chekhov for being so ill.

A Russian journalist happened to visit the Chekhovs at their hotel and sent back this dispatch to his editor: "Chekhov's days are numbered. He seems mortally ill, is terribly thin, coughs all the time, gasps for breath at the slightest movement, and is running a high temperature." This same journalist saw the Chekhovs off at Potsdam Station when they boarded their train for Badenweiler. According to his account, "Chekhov had trouble making his way up the small staircase at the station. He had to sit down for several minutes to catch his breath." In fact, it was painful for Chekhov to move: his legs ached continually and his insides hurt. The disease had attacked his intestines and spinal cord. At this point he had less than a month to live. When Chekhov spoke of his condition now, it was, according to Olga, "with an almost reckless indifference."

Dr. Schwöhrer was one of the many Badenweiler physicians who earned a good living by treating the well-to-do who came to the spa seeking relief from various maladies. Some of his patients were ill and infirm, others simply old and hypochondriacal. But Chekhov's was a special case: he was clearly beyond help and in his last days. He was also very famous. Even Dr. Schwöhrer knew his name: he'd read some of Chekhov's stories in a German magazine. When he examined the writer early in June, he voiced his appreciation of Chekhov's art but kept his medical opinions to himself. Instead, he prescribed a diet of cocoa, oatmeal drenched in butter, and strawberry tea. This last was supposed to help Chekhov sleep at night.

On June 13, less than three weeks before he died, Chekhov wrote a letter to his mother in which he told her his health was on the mend. In it he said, "It's likely that I'll be completely cured in a week." Who knows why he said this? What could he have been thinking? He was a doctor himself, and he knew better. He was dying, it was as simple and as unavoidable as that. Nevertheless, he sat out on the balcony of his hotel room and read railway timetables. He asked for information on sailings of boats bound for Odessa from Marseilles. But he *knew*. At this stage he had to have known. Yet in one of the last letters he ever wrote he told his sister he was growing stronger by the day.

He no longer had any appetite for literary work, and hadn't for a long time. In fact, he had very nearly failed to complete *The Cherry Orchard* the year before. Writing that play was the hardest thing he'd ever done in his life. Toward the end, he was able to manage only six or seven lines a day. "I've started losing heart," he wrote Olga. "I feel I'm finished as a writer, and every sentence strikes me as worthless and of no use whatever." But he didn't stop. He finished his play in October, 1903. It was the last thing he ever wrote, except for letters and a few entries in his notebook.

A little after midnight on July 2, 1904, Olga sent someone to fetch Dr. Schwöhrer. It was an emergency: Chekhov was delirious. Two young Russians on holiday happened to have the adjacent room, and Olga hurried next door to explain what was happening. One of the youths was in his bed asleep, but the other was still awake, smoking and reading. He left the hotel at a run to find Dr. Schwöhrer. "I can still hear the sound of the gravel under his shoes in the silence of that stifling July night," Olga wrote later on in her memoirs. Chekhov was hallucinating, talking about sailors, and there were snatches of something about the Japanese. "You don't put ice on an empty stomach," he said when she tried to place an ice pack on his chest.

Dr. Schwöhrer arrived and unpacked his bag, all the while keeping his gaze fastened on Chekhov, who lay gasping in the bed. The sick man's pupils were dilated and his temples glistened with sweat. Dr. Schwöhrer's face didn't register anything. He was not an emotional man, but he knew Chekhov's end was near. Still, he was a doctor, sworn to do his utmost, and Chekhov held on to life, however tenuously. Dr. Schwöhrer prepared a hypodermic and administered an injection of camphor, something that was supposed to speed up the heart. But the injection didn't help — nothing, of course, could have helped. Nevertheless, the doctor made known to Olga his intention of sending for oxygen. Suddenly, Chekhov roused himself, became lucid, and said quietly, "What's the use? Before it arrives I'll be a corpse."

Dr. Schwöhrer pulled on his big moustache and stared at Chekhov. The writer's cheeks were sunken and gray, his complexion waxen; his breath was raspy. Dr. Schwöhrer knew the time could be reckoned in minutes. Without a word, without conferring with Olga, he went over to an alcove where there was a telephone on the wall. He read the instructions for using the device. If he activated it by holding his finger on a button and turning a handle on the side of the phone, he could reach the lower regions of the hotel — the kitchen. He picked up the receiver, held it to his ear, and did as the instructions told him. When someone finally answered, Dr. Schwöhrer ordered a bottle of the hotel's best champagne. "How many glasses?" he was asked. "Three glasses!" the doctor shouted into the mouthpiece. "And hurry, do you hear?" It was one of those rare moments of inspiration that can easily enough be overlooked later on, because the action is so entirely appropriate it seems inevitable.

The champagne was brought to the door by a tired-looking young man whose blond hair was standing up. The trousers of his uniform were wrinkled, the creases gone, and in his haste he'd missed a loop while buttoning his jacket. His appearance was that of someone who'd been resting (slumped in a chair, say, dozing a little), when off in the distance the phone had clamored in the early-morning hours — great God in Heaven! — and the next thing he knew he was being shaken awake by a superior and told to deliver a bottle of Moët to Room 211. "And hurry, do you hear?"

The young man entered the room carrying a silver ice bucket with the champagne in it and a silver tray with three cut-crystal glasses. He found a place on the table for the bucket and glasses, all the while craning his neck, trying to see into the other room, where someone panted ferociously for breath. It was a dreadful, harrowing sound, and the young man lowered his chin into his collar and turned away as the ratchety breathing worsened. Forgetting himself, he stared out the open window toward the darkened city. Then this big imposing man with a thick moustache pressed some coins into his hand — a large tip, by the feel of it — and suddenly the young man saw the door open. He took some steps and found himself on the landing, where he opened his hand and looked at the coins in amazement.

Methodically, the way he did everything, the doctor went about the business of working the cork out of the bottle. He did it in such a way as to minimize, as much as possible, the festive explosion. He poured three glasses and, out of habit, pushed the cork back into the neck of the bottle. He then took the glasses of champagne over to the bed. Olga momentarily released her grip on Chekhov's hand — a hand, she said later, that burned her fingers. She arranged another pillow behind his head. Then she put the cool glass of champagne against Chekhov's palm and made sure his fingers closed around the stem. They exchanged looks — Chekhov, Olga, Dr. Schwöhrer. They didn't touch glasses. There was no toast. What on earth was there to drink to? To death? Chekhov summoned his remaining strength and said, "It's been so long since I've had champagne." He brought the glass to his lips and drank. In a minute or two Olga took the empty glass from his hand and set it on the nightstand. Then Chekhov turned onto his side. He closed his eyes and sighed. A minute later, his breathing stopped.

Dr. Schwöhrer picked up Chekhov's hand from the bedsheet. He held his fingers to Chekhov's wrist and drew a gold watch from his vest pocket, opening the lid of the watch as he did so. The second hand on the watch moved slowly, very slowly. He let it move around the face of the watch three times while he waited for signs of a pulse. It was three o'clock in the morning and still sultry in the room. Badenweiler was in the grip of its worst heat wave in years. All the windows in both rooms stood open, but there was no sign of a breeze. A large, black-winged moth flew through a window and banged wildly against the electric lamp. Dr. Schwöhrer let go of Chekhov's wrist. "It's over," he said. He closed the lid of his watch and returned it to his vest pocket.

At once Olga dried her eyes and set about composing herself. She thanked the doctor for coming. He asked if she wanted some medication — laudanum, perhaps, or a few drops of valerian. She shook her head. She did have one request, though: before the authorities were notified and the newspapers found out, before the time came when Chekhov was no longer in her keeping, she wanted to be alone with him for a while. Could the doctor help with this? Could he withhold, for a while anyway, news of what had just occurred?

Dr. Schwöhrer stroked his moustache with the back of a finger. Why not? After all, what difference would it make to anyone whether this matter became known now or a few hours from now? The only detail that remained was to fill out a death certificate, and this could be done at his office later on in the morning, after he'd slept a few hours. Dr. Schwöhrer nodded his agreement and prepared to leave. He murmured a few words of condolence. Olga inclined her head. "An honor," Dr. Schwöhrer said. He picked up his bag and left the room and, for that matter, history.

It was at this moment that the cork popped out of the champagne bottle; foam spilled down onto the table. Olga went back to Chekhov's bedside. She sat on a footstool, holding his hand, from time to time stroking his face. "There were no human voices, no everyday sounds," she wrote. "There was only beauty, peace, and the grandeur of death."

She stayed with Chekhov until daybreak, when thrushes began to call from the garden below. Then came the sound of tables and chairs being moved about down there. Before long, voices carried up to her. It was then a knock sounded at the door. Of course she thought it must be an official of some sort — the medical examiner, say, or someone from the police who had questions to ask and forms for her to fill out, or maybe, just maybe, it could be Dr. Schwöhrer returning with a mortician to render assistance in embalming and transporting Chekhov's remains back to Russia.

But, instead, it was the same blond young man who'd brought the champagne a few hours earlier. This time, however, his uniform trousers were neatly pressed, with stiff creases in front, and every button on his snug green jacket was fastened. He seemed quite another person. Not only was he wide awake but his plump cheeks were smooth-shaven, his hair was in place, and he appeared anxious to please. He was holding a porcelain vase with three long-stemmed yellow roses. He presented these to Olga with a smart click of his heels. She stepped back and let him into the room. He was there, he said, to collect the glasses, ice bucket, and tray, yes. But he also wanted to say that, because of the extreme heat, breakfast would be served in the garden this morning. He hoped this weather wasn't too bothersome; he apologized for it.

The woman seemed distracted. While he talked, she turned her eyes away and looked down at something in the carpet. She crossed her arms and held her elbows. Meanwhile, still holding his vase, waiting for a sign, the young man took in the details of the room. Bright sunlight flooded through the open windows. The room was tidy and seemed undisturbed, almost untouched. No garments were flung over chairs, no shoes, stockings, braces, or stays were in evidence, no open suitcases. In short, there was no clutter, nothing but the usual heavy pieces of hotel-room furniture. Then, because the woman was still looking down, he looked down, too, and at once spied a cork near the toe of his shoe. The woman did not see it — she was looking somewhere else. The young man wanted to bend over and pick up the cork, but he was still holding the roses and was afraid of seeming to intrude even more by drawing any further attention to himself. Reluctantly, he left the cork where it was and raised his eyes. Everything was in order except for the uncorked, half-empty bottle of champagne that stood alongside two crystal glasses over on the little table. He cast his gaze about once more. Through an open door he saw that the third glass was in the bedroom, on the nightstand. But someone still occupied the bed! He couldn't see a face, but the figure under the covers lay perfectly motionless and quiet. He noted the figure and looked elsewhere. Then, for a reason he couldn't understand, a feeling of uneasiness took hold of him. He cleared his throat and moved his weight to the other leg. The woman still didn't look up or break her silence. The young man felt his cheeks grow warm. It occurred to him, quite without his having thought it through, that he should perhaps suggest an alternative to breakfast in the garden. He coughed, hoping to focus the woman's attention, but she didn't look at him. The distinguished foreign guests could, he said, take breakfast in their rooms this morning if they wished. The young man (his name hasn't survived, and it's likely he perished in the Great War) said he would be happy to bring up a tray. Two trays, he added, glancing uncertainly once again in the direction of the bedroom.

He fell silent and ran a finger around the inside of his collar. He didn't understand. He wasn't even sure the woman had been listening. He didn't know what else to do now; he was still holding the vase. The sweet odor of the roses filled his nostrils and inexplicably caused a pang of regret. The entire time he'd been waiting, the woman had apparently been lost in thought. It was as if all the while he'd been standing there, talking, shifting his weight, holding his flowers, she had been someplace else, somewhere far from Badenweiler. But now she came back to herself, and her face assumed another expression. She raised her eyes, looked at him, and then shook her head. She seemed to be struggling to understand what on earth this young man could be doing there in the room holding a vase with three yellow roses. Flowers? She hadn't ordered flowers.

The moment passed. She went over to her handbag and scooped up some coins. She drew out a number of banknotes as well. The young man touched his lips with his tongue; another large tip was forthcoming, but for what? What did she want him to do? He'd never before waited on such guests. He cleared his throat once more.

No breakfast, the woman said. Not yet, at any rate. Breakfast wasn't the important thing this morning. She required something else. She needed him to go out and bring back a mortician. Did he understand her? Herr Chekhov was dead, you see. *Comprenez-vous?* Young man? Anton Chekhov was dead. Now listen carefully to me, she said. She wanted him to go downstairs and ask someone at the front desk where he could go to find the most respected mortician in the city. Someone reliable, who took great pains in his work and whose manner was appropriately reserved. A mortician, in short, worthy of a great artist. Here, she said, and pressed the money on him. Tell them downstairs that I have specifically requested you to perform this duty for me. Are you listening? Do you understand what I'm saying to you?

The young man grappled to take in what she was saying. He chose not to look again in the direction of the other room. He had sensed that something was not right. He became aware of his heart beating rapidly under his jacket, and he felt perspiration break out on his forehead. He didn't know where he should turn his eyes. He wanted to put the vase down.

Please do this for me, the woman said. I'll remember you with gratitude. Tell them downstairs that I insist. Say that. But don't call any unnecessary attention to yourself or to the situation. Just say that this is necessary, that I request it — and that's all. Do you hear me? Nod if you understand. Above all, don't raise an alarm. Everything else, all the rest, the commotion — that'll come soon enough. The worst is over. Do we understand each other?

The young man's face had grown pale. He stood rigid, clasping the vase. He managed to nod his head.

After securing permission to leave the hotel he was to proceed quietly and resolutely, though without any unbecoming haste, to the mortician's. He was to behave exactly as if he were engaged on a very important errand, nothing more. He *was* engaged on an important errand, she said. And if it would help keep his movements purposeful he should imagine himself as someone moving down the busy sidewalk carrying in his arms a porcelain vase of roses that he had to deliver to an important man. (She spoke quietly, almost confidentially, as if to a relative or a friend.) He could even tell himself that the man he was going to see was expecting him, was perhaps impatient for him to arrive with his flowers. Nevertheless, the young man was not to become excited and run, or otherwise break his stride. Remember the vase he was carrying! He was to walk briskly, comporting himself at all times in as dignified a manner as possible. He should keep walking until he came to the mortician's house and stood before the door. He would then raise the brass knocker and let it fall, once, twice, three times. In a minute the mortician himself would answer.

This mortician would be in his forties, no doubt, or maybe early fifties — bald, solidly built, wearing steel-frame spectacles set very low on his nose. He would be modest, unassuming, a man who would ask only the most direct and necessary questions. An apron. Probably he would be wearing an apron. He might even be wiping his hands on a dark towel while he listened to what was being said. There'd be a faint whiff of formaldehyde on his clothes. But it was all right, and the young man shouldn't worry. He was nearly a grownup now and shouldn't be frightened or repelled by any of this. The mortician would hear him out. He was a man of restraint and bearing, this mortician, someone who could help allay people's fears in this situation, not increase them. Long ago he'd acquainted himself with death in all its various guises and forms; death held no surprises for him any longer, no hidden secrets. It was this man whose services were required this morning.

The mortician takes the vase of roses. Only once while the young man is speaking does the mortician betray the least flicker of interest, or indicate that he's heard anything out of the ordinary. But the one time the young man mentions the name of the deceased, the mortician's eyebrows rise just a little. Chekhov, you say? Just a minute, and I'll be with you.

Do you understand what I'm saying, Olga said to the young man. Leave the glasses. Don't worry about them. Forget about crystal wineglasses and such. Leave the room as it is. Everything is ready now. We're ready. Will you go?

But at that moment the young man was thinking of the cork still resting near the toe of his shoe. To retrieve it he would have to bend over, still gripping the vase. He would do this. He leaned over. Without looking down, he reached out and closed it into his hand.

RAYMOND CARVER

What We Talk About When We Talk About Love
1981

My friend Mel McGinnis was talking. Mel McGinnis is a cardiologist, and sometimes that gives him the right.

The four of us were sitting around his kitchen table drinking gin. Sunlight filled the kitchen from the big window behind the sink. There were Mel and me and his second wife, Teresa — Terri, we called her — and my wife, Laura. We lived in Albuquerque then. But we were all from somewhere else.

There was an ice bucket on the table. The gin and the tonic water kept going around, and we somehow got on the subject of love. Mel thought real love was nothing less than spiritual love. He said he'd spent five years in a seminary before quitting to go to medical school. He said he still looked back on those years in the seminary as the most important years in his life.

Terri said the man she lived with before she lived with Mel loved her so much he tried to kill her. Then Terri said, "He beat me up one night. He dragged me around the living room by my ankles. He kept saying, 'I love you, I love you, you bitch.' He went on dragging me around the living room. My head kept knocking on things." Terri looked around the table. "What do you do with love like that?"

She was a bone-thin woman with a pretty face, dark eyes, and brown hair that hung down her back. She liked necklaces made of turquoise, and long pendant earrings.

"My God, don't be silly. That's not love, and you know it," Mel said. "I don't know what you'd call it, but I sure know you wouldn't call it love."

"Say what you want to, but I know it was," Terri said. "It may sound crazy to you, but it's true just the same. People are different, Mel. Sure, sometimes he may have acted crazy. Okay. But he loved me. In his own way maybe, but he loved me. There was love there, Mel. Don't say there wasn't."

Mel let out his breath. He held his glass and turned to Laura and me. "The man threatened to kill me," Mel said. He finished his drink and reached for the gin bottle. "Terri's a romantic. Terri's of the kick-me-so-I'll-know-you-love-me school. Terri, hon, don't look that way." Mel reached across the table and touched Terri's cheek with his fingers. He grinned at her.

"Now he wants to make up," Terri said.

"Make up what?" Mel said. "What is there to make up? I know what I know. That's all."

"How'd we get started on this subject, anyway?" Terri said. She raised her glass and drank from it. "Mel always has love on his mind," she said. "Don't you, honey?" She smiled, and I thought that was the last of it.

"I just wouldn't call Ed's behavior love. That's all I'm saying, honey," Mel said. "What about you guys?" Mel said to Laura and me. "Does that sound like love to you?"

"I'm the wrong person to ask," I said. "I didn't even know the man. I've only heard his name mentioned in passing. I wouldn't know. You'd have to know the particulars. But I think what you're saying is that love is an absolute."

Mel said, "The kind of love I'm talking about is. The kind of love I'm talking about, you don't try to kill people."

Laura said, "I don't know anything about Ed, or anything about the situation. But who can judge anyone else's situation?"

I touched the back of Laura's hand. She gave me a quick smile. I picked up Laura's hand. It was warm, the nails polished, perfectly manicured. I encircled the broad wrist with my fingers, and I held her.

"When I left, he drank rat poison," Terri said. She clasped her arms with her hands. "They took him to the hospital in Sante Fe. That's where we lived then, about ten miles out. They saved his life. But his gums went crazy from it. I mean they pulled away from his teeth. After that, his teeth stood out like fangs. My God," Terri said. She waited a minute, then let go of her arms and picked up her glass.

"What people won't do!" Laura said.

"He's out of the action now," Mel said. "He's dead."

Mel handed me the saucer of limes. I took a section, squeezed it over my drink, and stirred the ice cubes with my finger.

"It gets worse," Terri said. "He shot himself in the mouth. But he bungled that too. Poor Ed," she said. Terri shook her head.

"Poor Ed nothing," Mel said. "He was dangerous."

Mel was forty-five years old. He was tall and rangy with curly soft hair. His face and arms were brown from the tennis he played. When he was sober, his gestures, all his movements, were precise, very careful.

"He did love me though, Mel. Grant me that," Terri said. "That's all I'm asking. He didn't love me the way you love me. I'm not saying that. But he loved me. You can grant me that, can't you?"

"What do you mean, he bungled it?" I said.

Laura leaned forward with her glass. She put her elbows on the table and held her glass in both hands. She glanced from Mel to Terri and waited with a look of bewilderment on her open face, as if amazed that such things happened to people you were friendly with.

"How'd he bungle it when he killed himself?" I said.

"I'll tell you what happened," Mel said. "He took this twenty-two pistol he'd bought to threaten Terri and me with. Oh, I'm serious, the man was always threatening. You should have seen the way we lived in those days. Like fugitives. I even bought a gun myself. Can you believe it? A guy like me? But I did. I bought one for self-defense and carried it in the glove compartment. Sometimes I'd have to leave the apartment in the middle of the night. To go to the hospital, you know? Terri and I weren't married then, and my first wife had the house and kids, the dog, everything, and Terri and I were living in this apartment here. Sometimes, as I say, I'd get a call in the middle of the night and have to go in to the hospital at two or three in the morning. It'd be dark out there in the parking lot, and I'd break into a sweat before I could even get to my car. I never knew if he was going to come up out of the shrubbery or from behind a car and start shooting. I mean, the man was crazy. He was capable of wiring a bomb, anything. He used to call my service at all hours and say he needed to talk to the doctor, and when I'd return the call, he'd say, 'Son of a bitch, your days are numbered.' Little things like that. It was scary, I'm telling you."

"I still feel sorry for him," Terri said.

"It sounds like a nightmare," Laura said. "But what exactly happened after he shot himself?"

Laura is a legal secretary. We'd met in a professional capacity. Before we knew it, it was a courtship. She's thirty-five, three years younger than I am. In addition to being in love, we like each other and enjoy one another's company. She's easy to be with.

"What happened?" Laura said.

Mel said, "He shot himself in the mouth in his room. Someone heard the shot and told the manager. They came in with a passkey, saw what had happened, and called an ambulance. I happened to be there when they brought him in, alive but past recall. The man lived for three days. His head swelled up to twice the size of a normal head. I'd never seen anything like it, and I hope I never do again. Terri wanted to go in and sit with him when she found out about it. We had a fight over it. I didn't think she should see him like that. I didn't think she should see him, and I still don't."

"Who won the fight?" Laura said.

"I was in the room with him when he died," Terri said. "He never came up out of it. But I sat with him. He didn't have anyone else."

"He was dangerous," Mel said. "If you call that love, you can have it."

"It was love," Terri said. "Sure, it's abnormal in most people's eyes. But he was willing to die for it. He did die for it."

"I sure as hell wouldn't call it love," Mel said. "I mean, no one knows what he did it for. I've seen a lot of suicides, and I couldn't say anyone ever knew what they did it for."

Mel put his hands behind his neck and tilted his chair back. "I'm not interested in that kind of love," he said. "If that's love, you can have it."

Terri said, "We were afraid. Mel even made a will out and wrote to his brother in California who used to be a Green Beret. Mel told him who to look for if something happened to him."

Terri drank from her glass. She said, "But Mel's right — we lived like fugitives. We were afraid. Mel was, weren't you, honey? I even called the police at one point, but they were no help. They said they couldn't do anything until Ed actually did something. Isn't that a laugh?" Terry said.

She poured the last of the gin into her glass and waggled the bottle. Mel got up from the table and went to the cupboard. He took down another bottle.

"Well, Nick and I know what love is," Laura said. "For us, I mean," Laura said. She bumped my knee with her knee. "You're supposed to say something now," Laura said, and turned her smile on me.

For an answer, I took Laura's hand and raised it to my lips. I made a big production out of kissing her hand. Everyone was amused.

"We're lucky," I said.

"You guys," Terri said. "Stop that now. You're making me sick. You're still on the honeymoon, for God's sake. You're still gaga, for crying out loud. Just wait. How long have you been together now? How long has it been? A year? Longer than a year?"

"Going on a year and a half," Laura said, flushed and smiling.

"Oh, now," Terri said. "Wait awhile."

She held her drink and gazed at Laura.

"I'm only kidding," Terri said.

Mel opened the gin and went around the table with the bottle.

"Here, you guys," he said. "Let's have a toast. I want to propose a toast. A toast to love. To true love," Mel said.

We touched glasses.

"To love," we said.

Outside in the backyard, one of the dogs began to bark. The leaves of the aspen that leaned past the window ticked against the glass. The afternoon sun was like a presence in this room, the spacious light of ease and generosity. We could have been anywhere, somewhere enchanted. We raised our glasses again and grinned at each other like children who had agreed on something forbidden.

"I'll tell you what real love is," Mel said. "I mean, I'll give you a good example. And then you can draw your own conclusions." He poured more gin into his glass. He added an ice cube and a sliver of lime. We waited and sipped our drinks. Laura and I touched knees again. I put a hand on her warm thigh and left it there.

"What do any of us really know about love?" Mel said. "It seems to me we're just beginners at love. We say we love each other and we do, I don't doubt it. I love Terri and Terri loves me, and you guys love each other too. You know the kind of love I'm talking about now. Physical love, that impulse that drives you to someone special, as well as love of the other person's being, his or her essence, as it were. Carnal love and, well, call it sentimental love, the day-to-day caring about the other person. But sometimes I have a hard time accounting for the fact that I must have loved my first wife too. But I did, I know I did. So I suppose I am like Terri in that regard. Terri and Ed." He thought about it and then he went on. "There was a time when I thought I loved my first wife more than life itself. But now I hate her guts. I do. How do you explain that? What happened to that love? What happened to it, is what I'd like to know. I wish someone could tell me. Then there's Ed. Okay, we're back to Ed. He loves Terri so much he tries to kill her and he winds up killing himself." Mel stopped talking and swallowed from his glass. "You guys have been together eighteen months and you love each other. It shows all over you. You glow with it. But you both loved other people before you met each other. You've both been married before, just like us. And you probably loved other people before that too, even. Terri and I have been together five years, been married for four. And the terrible thing, the terrible thing is, but the good thing too, the saving grace, you might say, is that if something happened to one of us — excuse me for saying this — but if something happened to one of us tomorrow I think the other one, the other person, would grieve for a while, you know, but then the surviving party would go out and love again, have someone else soon enough. All this, all of this love we're talking about, it would just be a memory. Maybe not even a memory. Am I wrong? Am I way off base? Because I want you to set me straight if you think I'm wrong. I want to know. I mean, I don't know anything, and I'm the first one to admit it."

"Mel, for God's sake," Terri said. She reached out and took hold of his wrist. "Are you getting drunk? Honey? Are you drunk?"

"Honey, I'm just talking," Mel said. "All right? I don't have to be drunk to say what I think. I mean, we're all just talking, right?" Mel said. He fixed his eyes on her.

"Sweetie, I'm not criticizing," Terri said.

She picked up her glass.

"I'm not on call today," Mel said. "Let me remind you of that. I am not on call," he said.

"Mel, we love you," Laura said.

Mel looked at Laura. He looked at her as if he could not place her, as if she was not the woman she was.

"Love you too, Laura," Mel said. "And you, Nick, love you too. You know something?" Mel said. "You guys are our pals," Mel said.

He picked up his glass.

Mel said, "I was going to tell you about something. I mean, I was going to prove a point. You see, this happened a few months ago, but it's still going on right now, and it ought to make us feel ashamed when we talk like we know what we're talking about when we talk above love."

"Come on now," Terri said. "Don't talk like you're drunk if you're not drunk."

"Just shut up for once in your life," Mel said very quietly. "Will you do me a favor and do that for a minute? So as I was saying, there's this old couple who had this car wreck out on the interstate. A kid hit them and they were all torn to shit and nobody was giving them much chance to pull through."

Terri looked at us and then back at Mel. She seemed anxious, or maybe that's too strong a word.

Mel was handing the bottle around the table.

"I was on call that night," Mel said. "It was May or maybe it was June. Terri and I had just sat down to dinner when the hospital called. There'd been this thing out on the interstate. Drunk kid, teenager, plowed his dad's pickup into this camper with this old couple in it. They were up in their mid-seventies, that couple. The kid — eighteen, nineteen, something — he was DOA. Taken the steering wheel through his sternum. The old couple, they were alive, you understand. I mean, just barely. But they had everything. Multiple fractures, internal injuries, hemorrhaging, contusions, lacerations, the works, and they each of them had themselves concussions. They were in a bad way, believe me. And, of course, their age was two strikes against them. I'd say she was worse off than he was. Ruptured spleen along with everything else. Both kneecaps broken. But they'd been wearing their seatbelts and, God knows, that's what saved them for the time being."

"Folks, this is an advertisement for the National Safety Council," Terri said. "This is your spokesman, Dr. Melvin R. McGinnis, talking." Terri laughed. "Mel," she said, "sometimes you're just too much. But I love you, hon," she said.

"Honey, I love you," Mel said.

He leaned across the table. Terri met him halfway. They kissed.

"Terri's right," Mel said as he settled himself again. "Get those seatbelts on. But seriously, they were in some shape, those oldsters. By the time I got down there, the kid was dead, as I said. He was off in a corner, laid out on a gurney. I took one look at the old couple and told the ER nurse to get me a neurologist and an orthopedic man and a couple of surgeons down there right away."

He drank from his glass. "I'll try to keep this short," he said. "So we took the two of them up to the OR and worked like fuck on them most of the night. They had these incredible reserves, those two. You see that once in a while. So we did everything that could be done, and toward morning we're giving them a fifty-fifty chance, maybe less than that for her. So here they are, still alive the next morning. So, okay, we move them into the ICU, which is where they both kept plugging away at it for two weeks, hitting it better and better on all the scopes. So we transfer them out to their own room."

Mel stopped talking. "Here," he said, "let's drink this cheapo gin the hell up. Then we're going to dinner, right? Terri and I know a new place. That's where we'll go, to this new place we know about. But we're not going until we finish up this cut-rate, lousy gin."

Terri said, "We haven't actually eaten there yet. But it looks good. From the outside, you know."

"I like food," Mel said. "If I had it to do all over again, I'd be a chef, you know? Right, Terri?" Mel said.

He laughed. He fingered the ice in his glass.

"Terri knows," he said. "Terri can tell you. But let me say this. If I could come back again in a different life, a different time and all, you know what? I'd like to come back as a knight. You were pretty safe wearing all that armor. It was all right being a knight until gunpowder and muskets and pistols came along."

"Mel would like to ride a horse and carry a lance," Terri said.

"Carry a woman's scarf with you everywhere," Laura said.

"Or just a woman," Mel said.

"Shame on you," Laura said.

Terri said, "Suppose you came back as a serf. The serfs didn't have it so good in those days," Terri said.

"The serfs never had it good," Mel said. "But I guess even the knights were vessels to someone. Isn't that the way it worked? But then everyone is always a vessel to someone. Isn't that right? Terri? But what I liked about knights, besides their ladies, was that they had that suit of armor, you know, and they couldn't get hurt very easy. No cars in those days, you know? No drunk teenagers to tear into your ass."

"Vassals," Terri said.

"What?" Mel said.

"Vassals," Terri said. "They were called vassals, not vessels."

"Vassals, vessels," Mel said, "what the fuck's the difference? You knew what I meant anyway. All right," Mel said. "So I'm not educated. I learned my stuff. I'm a heart surgeon, sure, but I'm just a mechanic. I go in and I fuck around and I fix things. Shit," Mel said.

"Modesty doesn't become you," Terri said.

"He's just a humble sawbones," I said. "But sometimes they suffocated in all that armor, Mel. They'd even have heart attacks if it got too hot and they were too tired and worn out. I read somewhere that they'd fall off their horses and not be able to get up because they were too tired to stand with all that armor on them. They got trampled by their own horses sometimes."

"That's terrible," Mel said. "That's a terrible thing, Nicky. I guess they'd just lay there and wait until somebody came along and made a shish kebab out of them."

"Some other vessel," Terri said.

"That's right," Mel said. "Some vassal would come along and spear the bastard in the name of love. Or whatever the fuck it was they fought over in those days."

"Same things we fight over these days," Terri said.

Laura said, "Nothing's changed."

The color was still high in Laura's cheeks. Her eyes were bright. She brought her glass to her lips.

Mel poured himself another drink. He looked at the label closely as if studying a long row of numbers. Then he slowly put the bottle down on the table and slowly reached for the tonic water.

• • •

"What about the old couple?" Laura said. "You didn't finish that story you started."

Laura was having a hard time lighting her cigarette. Her matches kept going out.

The sunshine inside the room was different now, changing, getting thinner. But the leaves outside the window were still shimmering, and I stared at the pattern they made on the panes and on the Formica counter. They weren't the same patterns, of course.

"What about the old couple?" I said.

"Older but wiser," Terri said.

Mel stared at her.

Terri said, "Go on with your story, hon. I was only kidding. Then what happened?"

"Terri, sometimes," Mel said.

"Please, Mel," Terri said. "Don't always be so serious, sweetie. Can't you take a joke?"

"Where's the joke?" Mel said.

He held his glass and gazed steadily at his wife.

"What happened?" Laura said.

Mel fastened his eyes on Laura. He said, "Laura, if I didn't have Terri and if I didn't love her so much, and if Nick wasn't my best friend, I'd fall in love with you, I'd carry you off, honey," he said.

"Tell your story," Terri said. "Then we'll go to that new place, okay?"

"Okay," Mel said. "Where was I?" he said. He stared at the table and then he began again.

"I dropped in to see each of them every day, sometimes twice a day if I was up doing other calls anyway. Casts and bandages, head to foot, the both of them. You know, you've seen it in the movies. That's just the way they looked, just like in the movies. Little eye-holes and nose-holes and mouth-holes. And she had to have her legs slung up on top of it. Well, the husband was very depressed for the longest while. Even after he found out that his wife was going to pull through, he was still very depressed. Not about the accident, though. I mean, the accident was one thing, but it wasn't everything. I'd get up to his mouth-hole, you know, and he'd say no, it wasn't the accident exactly but it was because he couldn't see her through his eye-holes. He said that was what was making him feel so bad. Can you imagine? I'm telling you, the man's heart was breaking because he couldn't turn his goddamn head and *see* his goddamn wife."

Mel looked around the table and shook his head at what he was going to say.

"I mean, it was killing the old fart just because he couldn't *look* at the fucking woman."

We all looked at Mel.

"Do you see what I'm saying?" he said.

Maybe we were a little drunk by then. I know it was hard keeping things in focus. The light was draining out of the room, going back through the window where it had come from. Yet nobody made a move to get up from the table to turn on the overhead light.

"Listen," Mel said. "Let's finish this fucking gin. There's about enough left here for one shooter all around. Then let's go eat. Let's go to the new place."

"He's depressed," Terri said. "Mel, why don't you take a pill?"

Mel shook his head. "I've taken everything there is."

"We all need a pill now and then," I said.

"Some people are born needing them," Terri said.

She was using her finger to rub at something on the table. Then she stopped rubbing.

"I think I want to call my kids," Mel said. "Is that all right with everybody? I'll call my kids," he said.

Terri said, "What if Marjorie answers the phone? You guys, you've heard us on the subject of Marjorie? Honey, you know you don't want to talk to Marjorie. It'll make you feel even worse."

"I don't want to talk to Marjorie," Mel said. "But I want to talk to my kids."

"There isn't a day goes by that Mel doesn't say he wishes she'd get married again. Or else die," Terri said. "For one thing," Terri said, "she's bankrupting us. Mel says it's just to spite him that she won't get married again. She has a boyfriend who lives with her and the kids, so Mel is supporting the boyfriend too."

"She's allergic to bees," Mel said. "If I'm not praying she'll get married again, I'm praying she'll get herself stung to death by a swarm of fucking bees."

"Shame on you," Laura said.

"Bzzzzzzz," Mel said, turning his fingers into bees and buzzing them at Terri's throat. Then he let his hands drop all the way to his sides.

"She's vicious," Mel said. "Sometimes I think I'll go up there dressed like a beekeeper. You know, that hat that's like a helmet with the plate that comes down over your face, the big gloves, and the padded coat? I'll knock on the door and let loose a hive of bees in the house. But first I'd make sure the kids were out, of course."

He crossed one leg over the other. It seemed to take him a lot of time to do it. Then he put both feet on the floor and leaned forward, elbows on the table, his chin cupped in his hands.

"Maybe I won't call the kids, after all. Maybe it isn't such a hot idea. Maybe we'll just go eat. How does that sound?"

"Sounds fine to me," I said. "Eat or not eat. Or keep drinking. I could head right on out into the sunset."

"What does that mean, honey?" Laura said.

"It just means what I said," I said. "It means I could just keep going. That's all it means."

"I could eat something myself," Laura said. "I don't think I've ever been so hungry in my life. Is there something to nibble on?"

"I'll put out some cheese and crackers," Terri said.

But Terri just sat there. She did not get up to get anything.
Mel turned his glass over. He spilled it out on the table.
"Gin's gone," Mel said.
Terri said, "Now what?"
I could hear my heart beating. I could hear everyone's heart. I could hear the human noise we sat there making, not one of us moving, not even when the room went dark.

⚬⚬⚬

JOHN CHEEVER *(1912–1982), the leading exponent of the kind of carefully fashioned story of modern suburban manners that* The New Yorker *popularized, has been called "the Chekhov of the suburbs" by the reviewer John Leonard. Cheever spent most of his life in New York City and in suburban towns similar to the ones he described in much of his fiction. Born in Quincy, Massachusetts, he was raised by parents who owned a prosperous business that failed after the 1929 stock market crash. His parents enjoyed reading literature to him, so at an early age he was acquainted with the fiction of Charles Dickens, Jack London, and Robert Louis Stevenson. He started his career at an unusually young age. Expelled from Thayer Academy for being, by his own account, a "quarrelsome, intractable . . . and lousy student," he moved to New York City, lived in a cell of a room on a bread-and-buttermilk diet, and wrote stories. When his first one, "Expelled," was accepted for publication by Malcolm Cowley, then editor of the* New Republic, *Cheever was launched as a teenager into a career as a writer of fiction. Earlier Cowley had told him that his stories were too long to get published by magazines that paid, so, to encourage discipline, he made Cheever write a story of not more than a thousand words every day for four days.*

Cheever's first collection of stories, The Way Some People Live, *appeared in 1942, while he was serving in the army. In 1953 he strengthened his literary reputation with* The Enormous Radio and Other Stories, *a collection of fourteen of his* New Yorker *pieces. Six years later appeared another story collection,* The Housebreaker of Shady Hill. *In the 1960s and 1970s he published three more books of short stories and two widely acclaimed novels,* Bullet Park *(1969) and* Falconer *(1977).* The Stories of John Cheever, *published in 1978, won both the Pulitzer Prize and the National Book Critics Circle Award and became one of the few collections of short stories ever to make the* New York Times *best-seller list. In more than fifty years, Cheever published more than 200 magazine stories; he figured that he earned "enough money to feed the family and buy a new suit every other year."*

Usually a rapid writer, Cheever said he liked best the stories that he wrote in less than a week, although he spent months working on "The Swimmer" (1964). He originally wrote a draft of the plot as "a perfectly good" novel, but then he burned it. "I could very easily have sold the book," he said, "but the trick was to get the winter constellations in the midsummer sky without anyone knowing about it, and it didn't take 250 pages to do that."

RELATED COMMENTARY: *John Cheever, "Why I Write Short Stories," page 736.*

JOHN CHEEVER

The Swimmer   1964

It was one of those midsummer Sundays when everyone sits around saying, "I *drank* too much last night." You might have heard it whispered by the parishioners leaving church, heard it from the lips of the priest himself, struggling with his cassock in the *vestiarium*, heard it from the golf links and the tennis courts, heard it from the wild-life preserve where the leader of the Audubon group was suffering from a terrible hangover. "I *drank* too much," said Donald Westerhazy. "We all *drank* too much," said Lucinda Merrill. "It must have been the wine," said Helen Westerhazy. "I *drank* too much of that claret."

This was the edge of the Westerhazys' pool. The pool, fed by an artesian well with a high iron content, was a pale shade of green. It was a fine day. In the west there was a massive stand of cumulus cloud so like a city seen from a distance — from the bow of an approaching ship — that it might have had a name. Lisbon. Hackensack. The sun was hot. Neddy Merrill sat by the green water, one hand in it, one around a glass of gin. He was a slender man — he seemed to have the especial slenderness of youth — and while he was far from young he had slid down his banister that morning and given the bronze backside of Aphrodite on the hall table a smack, as he jogged toward the smell of coffee in his dining room. He might have been compared to a summer's day, particularly the last hours of one, and while he lacked a tennis racket or a sail bag the impression was definitely one of youth, sport, and clement weather. He had been swimming and now he was breathing deeply, sterorously as if he could gulp into his lungs the components of that moment, the heat of the sun, the intenseness of his pleasure. It all seemed to flow into his chest. His own house stood in Bullet Park, eight miles to the south, where his four beautiful daughters would have had their lunch and might be playing tennis. Then it occurred to him that by taking a dogleg to the southwest he could reach his home by water.

His life was not confining and the delight he took in this observation could not be explained by its suggestion of escape. He seemed to see, with a cartographer's eye, that string of swimming pools, that quasi-subterranean stream that curved across the county. He had made a discovery, a contribution to modern geography; he would name the stream Lucinda after his wife. He was not a practical joker nor was he a fool but he was determinedly original and had a vague and modest idea of himself as a legendary figure. The day was beautiful and it seemed to him that a long swim might enlarge and celebrate its beauty.

He took off a sweater that was hung over his shoulders and dove in. He had an inexplicable contempt for men who did not hurl themselves into pools. He swam a choppy crawl, breathing either with every stroke or every fourth stroke and counting somewhere well in the back of his mind the one-two one-two of a flutter kick. It was not a serviceable stroke for long distances but the domestication of swimming had saddled the sport with some customs and in his part of the world a crawl was customary. To be embraced and sustained by the light green water was less a pleasure, it seemed, than the resumption of a natural condition, and he would have liked to swim without trunks, but this was not possible, considering his project. He hoisted himself up on the far curb — he never used the ladder — and started across the lawn. When Lucinda asked where he was going he said he was going to swim home.

The only maps and charts he had to go by were remembered or imaginary but these were clear enough. First there were the Grahams, the Hammers, the Lears, the Howlands, and the Crosscups. He would cross Ditmar Street to the Bunkers and come, after a short portage, to the Levys, the Welchers, and the public pool in Lancaster. Then there were the Hallorans, the Sachses, the Biswangers, Shirley Adams, the Gilmartins, and the Clydes. The day was lovely, and that he lived in a world so generously supplied with water seemed like a clemency, a beneficence. His heart was high and he ran across the grass. Making his way home by an uncommon route gave him the feeling that he was a pilgrim, an explorer, a man with a destiny, and he knew that he would find friends all along the way; friends would line the banks of the Lucinda River.

He went through a hedge that separated the Westerhazys' land from the Grahams', walked under some flowering apple trees, passed the shed that housed their pump and filter, and came out at the Grahams' pool. "Why, Neddy," Mrs. Graham said, "what a marvelous surprise. I've been trying to get you on the phone all morning. Here, let me get you a drink." He saw then, like any explorer, that the hospitable customs and traditions of the natives would have to be handled with diplomacy if he was ever going to reach his destination. He did not want to mystify or seem rude to the Grahams nor did he have the time to linger there. He swam the length of their pool and joined them in the sun and was rescued, a few minutes later, by the arrival of two carloads of friends from Connecticut. During the uproarious reunions he was able to slip away. He went down by the front of the Grahams' house, stepped over a thorny hedge, and crossed a vacant lot to the Hammers'. Mrs. Hammer, looking up from her roses, saw him swim by although she wasn't quite sure who it was. The Lears heard him splashing past the open windows of their living room. The Howlands and the Crosscups were away. After leaving the Howlands' he crossed Ditmar Street and started for the Bunkers', where he could hear, even at that distance, the noise of a party.

The water refracted the sound of voices and laughter and seemed to suspend it in midair. The Bunkers' pool was on a rise and he climbed some stairs to a terrace where twenty-five or thirty men and women were drinking. The only person in the water was Rusty Towers, who floated there on a rubber raft. Oh, how bonny and lush were the banks of the Lucinda River! Prosperous men and women gathered by the sapphire-colored waters while caterer's men in white coats passed them cold gin. Overhead a red de Haviland trainer was circling around and around and around in the sky with something like the glee of a child in a swing. Ned felt a passing affection for the scene, a tenderness for the gathering, as if it was something he might touch. In the distance he heard thunder. As soon as Enid Bunker saw him she began to scream: "Oh, look who's here! What a marvelous surprise! When Lucinda said you couldn't come I thought I'd *die*." She made her way to him through the crowd, and when they had finished kissing she led him to the bar, a progress that was slowed by the fact that he stopped to kiss eight or ten other women and shake the hands of as many men. A smiling bartender he had seen at a hundred parties gave him a gin and tonic and he stood by the bar for a moment, anxious not to get stuck in any conversation that would delay his voyage. When he seemed about to be surrounded he dove in and swam close to the side to avoid colliding with Rusty's raft. At the far end of the pool he bypassed the Tomlinsons with a broad smile and jogged up the garden path. The gravel cut his feet but this was only unpleasantness. The party was confined to the pool, and as he went toward the house he heard the brilliant, watery sound of voices fade, heard the noise of a radio from the Bunkers' kitchen, where someone was listening to a ball game. Sunday afternoon. He made his way through the parked cars and down the grassy border of their driveway to Alewives Lane. He did not want to be seen on the road in his bathing trunks but there was no traffic and he made the short distance to the Levys' driveway, marked with a PRIVATE PROPERTY sign and a green tube for the *New York Times.* All the doors and windows of the big house were open but there were no signs of life; not even a dog barked. He went around the side of the house to the pool and saw that the Levys had only recently left. Glasses and bottles and dishes of nuts were on a table at the deep end, where there was a bathhouse or gazebo, hung with Japanese lanterns. After swimming the pool he got himself a glass and poured a drink. It was his fourth or fifth drink and he had swum nearly half the length of the Lucinda River. He felt tired, clean, and pleased at that moment to be alone; pleased with everything.

It would storm. The stand of cumulus cloud — that city — had risen and darkened, and while he sat there he heard the percussiveness of thunder again. The de Haviland trainer was still circling overhead and it seemed to Ned that he could almost hear the pilot laugh with pleasure in the afternoon; but when there was another peal of thunder he took off for home. A train whistle blew and he wondered what time it had gotten to be. Four? Five? He thought of the provincial station at that hour, where a waiter, his tuxedo concealed by a raincoat, a dwarf with some flowers wrapped in newspaper, and a woman who had been crying would be waiting for the local. It was suddenly growing dark; it was that moment when the pin-headed birds seemed to organize their song into some acute and knowledgeable recognition of the storm's approach. Then there was a fine noise of rushing water from the crown of an oak at his back, as if a spigot there had been turned. Then the noise of fountains came from the crowns of all the tall trees. Why did he love storms, what was the meaning of his excitement when the door sprang open and the rain wind fled rudely up the stairs, why had the simple task of shutting the windows of an old house seemed fitting and urgent, why did the first watery notes of a storm wind have for him the unmistakable sound of good news, cheer, glad tidings? Then there was an explosion, a smell of cordite, and rain lashed the Japanese lanterns that Mrs. Levy had bought in Kyoto the year before last, or was it the year before that?

He stayed in the Levys' gazebo until the storm had passed. The rain had cooled the air and he shivered. The force of the wind had stripped a maple of its red and yellow leaves and scattered them over the grass and the water. Since it was midsummer the tree must be blighted, and yet he felt a peculiar sadness at this sign of autumn. He braced his shoulders, emptied his glass, and started for the Welchers' pool. This meant crossing the Lindleys' riding ring and he was surprised to find it overgrown with grass and all the jumps dismantled. He wondered if the Lindleys had sold their horses or gone away for the summer and put them out to board. He seemed to remember having heard something about the Lindleys and their horses but the memory was unclear. On he went, barefoot through the wet grass, to the Welchers', where he found their pool was dry.

This breach in his chain of water disappointed him absurdly, and he felt like some explorer who seeks a torrential headwater and finds a dead stream. He was disappointed and mystified. It was common enough to go away for the summer but no one ever drained his pool. The Welchers had definitely gone away. The pool furniture was folded, stacked, and covered with a tarpaulin. The bathhouse was locked. All the windows of the house were shut, and when he went around to the driveway in front he saw a FOR SALE sign nailed to a tree. When had he last heard from the Welchers — when, that is, had he and Lucinda last regretted an invitation to dine with them? It seemed only a week or so ago. Was his memory failing or had he so disciplined it in the repression of unpleasant facts that he had damaged his sense of the truth? Then in the distance he heard the sound of a tennis game. This cheered him, cleared away all his apprehensions and let him regard the overcast sky and the cold air with indifference. This was the day that Neddy Merrill swam across the county. That was the day! He started off then for his most difficult portage.

Had you gone for a Sunday afternoon ride that day you might have seen him, close to naked, standing on the shoulders of Route 424, waiting for a chance to cross. You might have wondered if he was the victim of foul play, had his car broken down, or was he merely a fool. Standing barefoot in the deposits of the highway — beer cans, rags, and blowout patches — exposed to all kinds of ridicule, he seemed pitiful. He had known when he started that this was a part of his journey — it had been on his maps — but confronted with the lines of traffic, worming through the summery light, he found himself unprepared. He was laughed at, jeered at, a beer can was thrown at him, and he had no dignity or humor to bring to the situation. He could have gone back, back to the Westerhazys', where Lucinda would still be sitting in the sun. He had signed nothing, vowed nothing, pledged nothing, not even to himself. Why, believing as he did, that all human obduracy was susceptible to common sense, was he unable to turn back? Why was he determined to complete his journey even if it meant putting his life in danger? At what point had this prank, this joke, this piece of horseplay become serious? He could not go back, he could not even recall with any clearness the green water at the Westerhazys', the sense of inhaling the day's components, the friendly and relaxed voices saying that they had *drunk* too much. In the space of an hour, more or less, he had covered a distance that made his return impossible.

An old man, tooling down the highway at fifteen miles an hour, let him get to the middle of the road, where there was a grass divider. Here he was exposed to the ridicule of the northbound traffic, but after ten or fifteen minutes he was able to cross. From here he had only a short walk to the Recreation Center at the edge of the village of Lancaster, where there were some handball courts and a public pool.

The effect of the water on voices, the illusion of brilliance and suspense, was the same here as it had been at the Bunkers' but the sounds here were louder, harsher, and more shrill, and as soon as he entered the crowded enclosure he was confronted with regimentation. "ALL SWIMMERS MUST TAKE A SHOWER BEFORE USING THE POOL. ALL SWIMMERS MUST USE THE FOOTBATH. ALL SWIMMERS MUST WEAR THEIR IDENTIFICATION DISKS." He took a shower, washed his feet in a cloudy and bitter solution, and made his way to the edge of the water. It stank of chlorine and looked to him like a sink. A pair of lifeguards in a pair of towers blew police whistles at what seemed to be regular intervals and abused the swimmers through a public address system. Neddy remembered the sapphire water at the Bunkers' with longing and thought that he might contaminate himself — damage his own prosperousness and charm — by swimming in this murk, but he reminded himself that he was an explorer, a pilgrim, and that this was merely a stagnant bend in the Lucinda River. He dove, scowling with distaste, into the chlorine and had to swim with his head above water to avoid collisions, but even so he was bumped into, splashed, and jostled. When he got to the shallow end both lifeguards were shouting at him: "Hey, you, you without the identification disk, get outa the water." He did, but they had no way of pursuing him and he went through the reek of suntan oil and chlorine out through the hurricane fence and passed the handball courts. By crossing the road he entered the wooded part of the Halloran estate. The woods were not cleared and the footing was treacherous and difficult until he reached the lawn and the clipped beech hedge that encircled their pool.

The Hallorans were friends, an elderly couple of enormous wealth who seemed to bask in the suspicion that they might be Communists. They were zealous reformers but they were not Communists, and yet when they were accused, as they sometimes were, of subversion, it seemed to gratify and excite them. Their beech hedge was yellow and he guessed this had been blighted like the Levys' maple. He called hullo, hullo, to warn the Hallorans of his approach, to palliate his invasion of their privacy. The Hallorans, for reasons that had never been explained to him, did not wear bathing suits. No explanations were in order, really. Their nakedness was a detail in their uncompromising zeal for reform and he stepped politely out of his trunks before he went through the opening in the hedge.

Mrs. Halloran, a stout woman with white hair and a serene face, was reading the *Times*. Mr. Halloran was taking beech leaves out of the water with a scoop. They seemed not surprised or displeased to see him. Their pool was perhaps the oldest in the county, a fieldstone rectangle, fed by a brook. It had no filter or pump and its waters were the opaque gold of the stream.

"I'm swimming across the county," Ned said.

"Why, I didn't know one could," exclaimed Mrs. Halloran.

"Well, I've made it from the Westerhazys'," Ned said. "That must be about four miles."

He left his trunks at the deep end, walked to the shallow end, and swam this stretch. As he was pulling himself out of the water he heard Mrs. Halloran say, "We've been *terribly* sorry to hear about all your misfortunes, Neddy."

"My misfortunes?" Ned asked. "I don't know what you mean."

"Why we heard that you'd sold the house and that your poor children. . . ."

"I don't recall having sold the house," Ned said, "and the girls are at home."

"Yes," Mrs. Halloran sighed. "Yes. . . ." Her voice filled the air with an unseasonable melancholy and Ned spoke briskly. "Thank you for the swim."

"Well, have a nice trip," said Mrs. Halloran.

Beyond the hedge he pulled on his trunks and fastened them. They were loose and he wondered if, during the space of an afternoon, he could have lost some weight. He was cold and he was tired and the naked Hallorans and their dark water had depressed him. The swim was too much for his strength but how could he have guessed this, sliding down the banister that morning and sitting in the Westerhazys' sun? His arms were lame. His legs felt rubbery and ached at the joints. The worst of it was the cold in his bones and the feeling that he might never be warm again. Leaves were falling down around him and he smelled wood smoke on the wind. Who would be burning wood at this time of the year?

He needed a drink. Whiskey would warm him, pick him up, carry him through the last of his journey, refresh his feeling that it was original and valorous to swim across the county. Channel swimmers took brandy. He needed a stimulant. He crossed the lawn in front of the Hallorans' house and went down a little path to where they had built a house for their only daughter, Helen, and her husband, Eric Sachs. The Sachses' pool was small and he found Helen and her husband there.

"Oh, *Neddy*," Helen said. "Did you lunch at Mother's?"

"Not *really*," Ned said. "I *did* stop to see your parents." This seemed to be explanation enough. "I'm terribly sorry to break in on you like this but I've taken a chill and I wonder if you'd give me a drink."

"Why, I'd *love* to," Helen said, "but there hasn't been anything in this house to drink since Eric's operation. That was three years ago."

Was he losing his memory, had his gift for concealing painful facts let him forget that he had sold his house, that his children were in trouble, and that his friend had been ill? His eyes slipped from Eric's face to his abdomen, where he saw three pale, sutured scars, two of them at least a foot long. Gone was his navel, and what, Neddy thought, would the roving hand, bed-checking one's gifts at 3 A.M., make of a belly with no navel, no link to birth, this breach in the succession?

"I'm sure you can get a drink at the Biswangers'," Helen said. "They're having an enormous do. You can hear it from here. Listen!"

She raised her head and from across the road, the lawns, the gardens, the woods, the fields, he heard again the brilliant noise of voices over water. "Well, I'll get wet," he said, still feeling that he had no freedom of choice about his means of travel. He dove into the Sachses' cold water, and gasping, close to drowning, made his way from one end of the pool to the other. "Lucinda and I want *terribly* to see you," he said over his shoulder, his face set toward the Biswangers'. "We're sorry it's been so long and we'll call you *very* soon."

He crossed some fields to the Biswangers' and the sounds of revelry there. They would be honored to give him a drink, they would be happy to give him a drink. The Biswangers invited him and Lucinda for dinner four times a year, six weeks in advance. They were always rebuffed and yet they continued to send out their invitations, unwilling to comprehend the rigid and undemocratic realities of their society. They were the sort of people who discussed the price of things at cocktails, exchanged market tips during dinner, and after dinner told dirty stories to mixed company. They did not belong to Neddy's set — they were not even on Lucinda's Christmas card list. He went toward their pool with feelings of indifference, charity, and some unease, since it seemed to be getting dark and these were the longest days of the year. The party when he joined it was noisy and large. Grace Biswanger was the kind of hostess who asked the optometrist, the veterinarian, the real-estate dealer, and the dentist. No one was swimming and the twilight, reflected on the water of the pool, had a wintry gleam. There was a bar and he started for this. When Grace Biswanger saw him she came toward him, not affectionately as he had every right to expect, but bellicosely.

"Why, this party has everything," she said loudly, "including a gate crasher."

She could not deal him a social blow — there was no question about this and he did not flinch. "As a gate crasher," he asked politely, "do I rate a drink?"

"Suit yourself," she said. "You don't seem to pay much attention to invitations."

She turned her back on him and joined some guests, and he went to the bar and ordered a whiskey. The bartender served him but he served him rudely. His was a world in which the caterer's men kept the social score, and to be rebuffed by a part-time barkeep meant that he had suffered some loss of social esteem. Or perhaps the man was new and uninformed. Then he heard Grace at his back say: "They went for broke overnight — nothing but income — and he showed up drunk one Sunday and asked us to loan him five thousand dollars. . . ." She was always talking about money. It was worse than eating your peas off a knife. He dove into the pool, swam its length, and went away.

The next pool on his list, the last but two, belonged to his old mistress,

Shirley Adams. If he had suffered any injuries at the Biswangers' they would be cured here. Love — sexual roughhouse in fact — was the supreme elixir, the pain killer, the brightly colored pill that would put the spring back into his step, the joy of life in his heart. They had had an affair last week, last month, last year. He couldn't remember. It was he who had broken it off, his was the upper hand, and he stepped through the gate of the wall that surrounded her pool with nothing so considered as self-confidence. It seemed in a way to be his pool, as the lover, particularly the illicit lover, enjoys the possessions of his mistress with an authority unknown to holy matrimony. She was there, her hair the color of brass, but her figure, at the edge of the lighted, cerulean water, excited in him no profound memories. It had been, he thought, a light-hearted affair, although she had wept when he broke it off. She seemed confused to see him and he wondered if she was still wounded. Would she, God forbid, weep again?

"What do you want?" she asked.

"I'm swimming across the county."

"Good Christ. Will you ever grow up?"

"What's the matter?"

"If you've come here for money," she said, "I won't give you another cent."

"You could give me a drink."

"I could but I won't. I'm not alone."

"Well, I'm on my way."

He dove in and swam the pool, but when he tried to haul himself up onto the curb he found that the strength in his arms and shoulders had gone, and he paddled to the ladder and climbed out. Looking over his shoulder he saw, in the lighted bathhouse, a young man. Going out onto the dark lawn he smelled chrysanthemums or marigolds — some stubborn autumnal fragrance — on the night air, strong as gas. Looking overhead he saw that the stars had come out, but why should he seem to see Andromeda, Cepheus, and Cassiopeia? What had become of the constellations of midsummer? He began to cry.

It was probably the first time in his adult life that he had ever cried, certainly the first time in his life that he had ever felt so miserable, cold, tired, and bewildered. He could not understand the rudeness of the caterer's barkeep or the rudeness of a mistress who had come to him on her knees and showered his trousers with tears. He had swum too long, he had been immersed too long, and his nose and his throat were sore from the water. What he needed then was a drink, some company, and some clean, dry clothes, and while he could have cut directly across the road to his home he went on to the Gilmartins' pool. Here, for the first time in his life, he did not dive but went down the steps into the icy water and swam a hobbled sidestroke that he might have learned as a youth. He staggered with fatigue on his way to the Clydes' and paddled the length of their pool, stopping again and again with his hand on the curb to rest. He climbed up the ladder and wondered if he had the strength to get home. He had done what he wanted, he had swum the county, but he was so stupefied with exhaustion that his triumph seemed vague. Stooped, holding on to the gateposts for support, he turned up the driveway of his own house.

The place was dark. Was it so late that they had all gone to bed? Had Lucinda stayed at the Westerhazys' for supper? Had the girls joined her there or gone someplace else? Hadn't they agreed, as they usually did on Sunday, to regret all their invitations and stay at home? He tried the garage doors to see what cars were in but the doors were locked and rust came off the handles onto his hands. Going toward the house, he saw the force of the thunderstorm had knocked one of the rain gutters loose. It hung down over the front door like an umbrella rib, but it could be fixed in the morning. The house was locked, and he thought that the stupid cook or the stupid maid must have locked the place up until he remembered that it had been some time since they had employed a maid or a cook. He shouted, pounded on the door, tried to force it with his shoulder, and then, looking in at the windows, saw that the place was empty.

∞

ANTON CHEKHOV *(1860–1904), the Russian short story writer and playwright, wrote his first stories while he was a medical student at Moscow University, to help his family pay off debts. His grandfather had been a serf who had bought his freedom. His father was an unsuccessful grocer in Taganrog, in the southwestern part of the country. After completing medical school, Chekhov became an assistant to the district doctor in a provincial town. His early stories were mostly humorous sketches that he first published in newspapers under various pseudonyms, keeping his own name for his medical articles. But the popularity of these sketches made him decide to become a writer.*

Chekhov's first two collections of short stories, published in 1886 and 1887, were acclaimed by readers, and from that time on he was able to devote all his time to writing. He bought a small estate near Moscow, where he lived with his family and treated sick peasants at no charge. Chekhov's kindness and good works were not a matter of any political program or religious impulse but, as Vladimir Nabokov put it, "the natural coloration of his talent." He was extremely modest about his extraordinary ability to empathize with his characters. Once he said to a visitor, "Do you know how I write my stories? Here's how!" And he glanced at his table, took up the first object that he saw — it was an ashtray — and said, "If you want it, you'll have a story tomorrow. It will be called 'The Ashtray.' " And it seemed to the visitor that Chekhov was conjuring up a story in front of his eyes: "Certain indefinite situations, adventures which had not yet found concrete form, were already beginning to crystallize about the ashtray."

Chekhov's story-writing technique appears disarmingly simple. Yet, as Virginia Woolf recognized, "as we read these little stories about nothing at all, the horizon widens; the soul gains an astonishing sense of freedom." Chekhov's remarkable absence of egotism can be seen in masterpieces such as "The Darling" and "The Lady with the Pet Dog," both of which he wrote toward the end of his life. He once sent a sketch describing himself to the editor who first encouraged him in which he gave a sense of the depth of his self-knowledge:

Write a story, do, about a young man, the son of a serf, a former grocery boy, a choir singer, a high school pupil and university student, brought up to respect rank, to kiss the hands of priests, to truckle to the ideas of others — a young man who expressed thanks for every piece of bread, who was whipped many times, who went without galoshes to do his tutoring, who used his fists, tortured animals, was fond of dining with rich relatives, was a hypocrite in his dealings with God and men, needlessly, solely out of a realization of his own insignificance — write how this young man squeezes the slave out of himself, drop by drop, and how, on awaking one fine morning, he feels that the blood coursing through his veins is no longer that of a slave but that of a real human being.

Chekhov's more than 800 stories have immensely influenced writers of short fiction. Unconcerned with giving a social or ethical message in his work, he championed what he called "the holy of holies" — "love and absolute freedom — freedom from violence and lies, whatever their form."

RELATED PLAY: Anton Chekhov, The Bear, *page 1661.*

RELATED COMMENTARIES: *Raymond Carver, "The Ashtray," page 821; Anton Chekhov, "Technique in Writing the Short Story," page 738; Vladimir Nabokov, "A Reading of Chekhov's 'The Lady with the Little Dog,'" page 775; Leo Tolstoy, "Chekhov's Intent in 'The Darling,'" page 801; Henri Troyat, "Chekhov's Last Days," page 826; Eudora Welty, "Plot and Character in Chekhov's 'The Darling,'" page 811.*

ANTON CHEKHOV

The Darling

1899

TRANSLATED BY CONSTANCE GARNETT

Olenka, the daughter of the retired collegiate assessor, Plemyanniakov, was sitting in her back porch, lost in thought. It was hot, the flies were persistent and teasing, and it was pleasant to reflect that it would soon be evening. Dark rainclouds were gathering from the east, and bringing from time to time a breath of moisture in the air.

Kukin, who was the manager of an open-air theatre called the Tivoli, and who lived in the lodge, was standing in the middle of the garden looking at the sky.

"Again!" he observed despairingly. "It's going to rain again! Rain every day, as though to spite me. I might as well hang myself! It's ruin! Fearful losses every day."

He flung up his hands, and went on, addressing Olenka:

"There! that's the life we lead, Olga Semyonovna. It's enough to make one cry. One works and does one's utmost; one wears oneself out, getting no sleep at night, and racks one's brain what to do for the best. And then what happens? To begin with, one's public is ignorant, boorish. I give them the very best operetta, a dainty masque, first rate music-hall artists. But do you suppose that's what they want! They don't understand anything of that sort. They want a clown; what they ask for is vulgarity. And then look at the weather! Almost every evening it rains. It started on the tenth of May, and it's kept it up all May and June. It's simply awful! The public doesn't come, but I've to pay the rent just the same, and pay the artists."

The next evening the clouds would gather again, and Kukin would say with an hysterical laugh:

"Well, rain away, then! Flood the garden, drown me! Damn my luck in this world and the next! Let the artists have me up! Send me to prison! — to Siberia! — the scaffold! Ha, ha, ha!"

And next day the same thing.

Olenka listened to Kukin with silent gravity, and sometimes tears came into her eyes. In the end his misfortunes touched her; she grew to love him. He was a small thin man, with a yellow face, and curls combed forward on his forehead. He spoke in a thin tenor; as he talked his mouth worked on one side, and there was always an expression of despair on his face; yet he aroused a deep and genuine affection in her. She was always fond of some one, and could not exist without loving. In earlier days she had loved her papa, who now sat in a darkened room, breathing with difficulty; she had loved her aunt who used to come every other year from Bryansk; and before that, when she was at school, she had loved her French master. She was a gentle, soft-hearted, compassionate girl, with mild, tender eyes and very good health. At the sight of her full rosy cheeks, her soft white neck with a little dark mole on it, and the kind, naïve smile, which came into her face when she listened to anything pleasant, men thought, "Yes, not half bad," and smiled too, while lady visitors could not refrain from seizing her hand in the middle of a conversation, exclaiming in a gush of delight, "You darling!"

The house in which she had lived from her birth upwards, and which was left her in her father's will, was at the extreme end of the town, not far from the Tivoli. In the evenings and at night she could hear the band playing, and the crackling and banging of fireworks, and it seemed to her that it was Kukin struggling with his destiny, storming the entrenchments of his chief foe, the indifferent public; there was a sweet thrill at her heart, she had no desire to sleep, and when he returned home at daybreak, she tapped softly at her bedroom window, and showing him only her face and one shoulder through the curtain, she gave him a friendly smile. . . .

He proposed to her, and they were married. And when he had a closer view of her neck and her plump, fine shoulders, he threw up his hands, and said:

"You darling!"

He was happy, but as it rained on the day and night of his wedding, his face still retained an expression of despair.

They got on very well together. She used to sit in his office, to look after things in the Tivoli, to put down the accounts and pay the wages. And her rosy cheeks, her sweet, naïve, radiant smile, were to be seen now at the office window, now in the refreshment bar or behind the scenes of the theatre. And already she used to say to her acquaintances that the theatre was the chief and most important thing in life, and that it was only through the drama that one could derive true enjoyment and become cultivated and humane.

"But do you suppose the public understands that?" she used to say.

"What they want is a clown. Yesterday we gave 'Faust Inside Out,' and almost all the boxes were empty; but if Vanitchka and I had been producing some vulgar thing, I assure you the theatre would have been packed. Tomorrow Vanitchka and I are doing 'Orpheus in Hell.' Do come."

And what Kukin said about the theatre and the actors she repeated. Like him she despised the public for their ignorance and their indifference to art; she took part in the rehearsals, she corrected the actors, she kept an eye on the behavior of the musicians, and when there was an unfavorable notice in the local paper, she shed tears, and then went to the editor's office to set things right.

The actors were fond of her and used to call her "Vanitchka and I," and "the darling"; she was sorry for them and used to lend them small sums of money, and if they deceived her, she used to shed a few tears in private, but did not complain to her husband.

They got on well in the winter too. They took the theatre in the town for the whole winter, and let it for short terms to a Little Russian company, or to a conjurer, or to a local dramatic society. Olenka grew stouter, and was always beaming with satisfaction, while Kukin grew thinner and yellower, and continually complained of their terrible losses, although he had not done badly all the winter. He used to cough at night, and she used to give him hot raspberry tea or lime-flower water, to rub him with eau-de-Cologne and to wrap him in her warm shawls.

"You're such a sweet pet!" she used to say with perfect sincerity, stroking his hair. "You're such a pretty dear!"

Towards Lent he went to Moscow to collect a new troupe, and without him she could not sleep, but sat all night at her window, looking at the stars, and she compared herself with the hens, who are awake all night and uneasy when the cock is not in the hen-house. Kukin was detained in Moscow, and wrote that he would be back at Easter, adding some instructions about the Tivoli. But on the Sunday before Easter, late in the evening, came a sudden ominous knock at the gate; some one was hammering on the gate as though on a barrel — boom, boom, boom! The drowsy cook went flopping with her bare feet through the puddles, as she ran to open the gate.

"Please open," said some one outside in a thick bass. "There is a telegram for you."

Olenka had received telegrams from her husband before, but this time for some reason she felt numb with terror. With shaking hands she opened the telegram and read as follows:

> "Ivan Petrovitch died suddenly to-day. Awaiting immate instructions fufuneral Tuesday."

That was how it was written in the telegram — "fufuneral," and the utterly incomprehensible word "immate." It was signed by the stage manager of the operatic company.

"My darling!" sobbed Olenka. "Vanitchka, my precious, my darling! Why did I ever meet you! Why did I know you and love you! Your poor heartbroken Olenka is all alone without you!"

Kukin's funeral took place on Tuesday in Moscow, Olenka returned home on Wednesday, and as soon as she got indoors she threw herself on her bed and sobbed so loudly that it could be heard next door, and in the street.

"Poor darling!" the neighbors said, as they crossed themselves. "Olga Semyonovna, poor darling! How she does take on!"

Three months later Olenka was coming home from mass, melancholy and in deep mourning. It happened that one of her neighbors, Vassily Andreitch Pustovalov, returning home from church, walked back beside her. He was the manager at Babakayev's, the timber merchant's. He wore a straw hat, a white waistcoat, and a gold watch-chain, and looked more like a country gentleman than a man in trade.

"Everything happens as it is ordained, Olga Semyonovna," he said gravely, with a sympathetic note in his voice; "and if any of our dear ones die, it must be because it is the will of God, so we ought to have fortitude and bear it submissively."

After seeing Olenka to her gate, he said good-bye and went on. All day afterwards she heard his sedately dignified voice, and whenever she shut her eyes she saw his dark beard. She liked him very much. And apparently she had made an impression on him too, for not long afterwards an elderly lady, with whom she was only slightly acquainted, came to drink coffee with her, and as soon as she was seated at table began to talk about Pustovalov, saying that he was an excellent man whom one could thoroughly depend upon, and that any girl would be glad to marry him. Three days later Pustovalov came himself. He did not stay long, only about ten minutes, and he did not say much, but when he left, Olenka loved him — loved him so much that she lay awake all night in a perfect fever, and in the morning she sent for the elderly lady. The match was quickly arranged, and then came the wedding.

Pustovalov and Olenka got on very well together when they were married.

Usually he sat in the office till dinner-time, then he went out on business, while Olenka took his place, and sat in the office till evening, making up accounts and booking orders.

"Timber gets dearer every year; the price rises twenty per cent," she would say to her customers and friends. "Only fancy we used to sell local timber, and now Vassitchka always has to go for wood to the Mogilev district. And the freight!" she would add, covering her cheeks with her hands in horror. "The freight!"

It seemed to her that she had been in the timber trade for ages and ages, and that the most important and necessary thing in life was timber; and there was something intimate and touching to her in the very sound of words such as "baulk," "post," "beam," "pole," "scantling," "batten," "lath," "plank," etc.

At night when she was asleep she dreamed of perfect mountains of planks and boards, and long strings of wagons, carting timber somewhere far away. She dreamed that a whole regiment of six-inch beams forty feet high, standing on end, was marching upon the timber-yard; that logs, beams, and boards knocked together with the resounding crash of dry wood, kept falling and getting up again, piling themselves on each other. Olenka cried out in her sleep, and Pustovalov said to her tenderly: "Olenka, what's the matter, darling? Cross yourself!"

Her husband's ideas were hers. If he thought the room was too hot, or that business was slack, she thought the same. Her husband did not care for entertainments, and on holidays he stayed at home. She did likewise.

"You are always at home or in the office," her friends said to her. "You should go to the theatre, darling, or to the circus."

"Vassitchka and I have no time to go to theatres," she would answer sedately. "We have no time for nonsense. What's the use of these theatres?"

On Saturdays Pustovalov and she used to go to the evening service; on holidays to early mass, and they walked side by side with softened faces as they came home from church. There was a pleasant fragrance about them both, and her silk dress rustled agreeably. At home they drank tea, with fancy bread and jams of various kinds, and afterwards they ate pie. Every day at twelve o'clock there was a savory smell of beet-root soup and of mutton or duck in their yard, and on fast-days of fish, and no one could pass the gate without feeling hungry. In the office the samovar was always boiling, and customers were regaled with tea and cracknels. Once a week the couple went to the baths and returned side by side, both red in the face.

"Yes, we have nothing to complain of, thank God," Olenka used to say to her acquaintances. "I wish every one were as well off as Vassitchka and I."

When Pustovalov went away to buy wood in the Mogilev district, she missed him dreadfully, lay awake and cried. A young veterinary surgeon in the army, called Smirnin, to whom they had let their lodge, used sometimes to come in in the evening. He used to talk to her and play cards with her, and this entertained her in her husband's absence. She was particularly interested in what he told her of his home life. He was married and had a little boy, but was separated from his wife because she had been unfaithful to him, and now he hated her and used to send her forty rubles a month for the maintenance of their son. And hearing of all this, Olenka sighed and shook her head. She was sorry for him.

"Well, God keep you," she used to say to him at parting, as she lighted him down the stairs with a candle. "Thank you for coming to cheer me up, and may the Mother of God give you health."

And she always expressed herself with the same sedateness and dignity, the same reasonableness, in imitation of her husband. As the veterinary surgeon was disappearing behind the door below, she would say:

"You know, Vladimir Platonitch, you'd better make it up with your wife. You should forgive her for the sake of your son. You may be sure the little fellow understands."

And when Pustovalov came back, she told him in a low voice about the veterinary surgeon and his unhappy home life, and both sighed and shook their heads and talked about the boy, who, no doubt, missed his father, and by some strange connection of ideas, they went up to the holy icons, bowed to the ground before them, and prayed that God would give them children.

And so the Pustovalovs lived for six years quietly and peaceably in love and complete harmony.

But behold! one winter day after drinking hot tea in the office, Vassily Andreitch went out into the yard without his cap on to see about sending off some timber, caught cold, and was taken ill. He had the best doctors, but he grew worse and died after four months' illness. And Olenka was a widow once more.

"I've nobody, now you've left me, my darling," she sobbed, after her husband's funeral. "How can I live without you, in wretchedness and misery! Pity me, good people, all alone in the world!"

She went about dressed in black with long "weepers," and gave up wearing hat and gloves for good. She hardly ever went out, except to church, or to her husband's grave, and led the life of a nun. It was not till six months later that she took off the weepers and opened the shutters of the windows. She was sometimes seen in the mornings, going with her cook to market for provisions, but what went on in her house and how she lived now could only be surmised. People guessed, from seeing her drinking tea in her garden with the veterinary surgeon, who read the newspaper aloud to her, and from the fact that, meeting a lady she knew at the post-office, she said to her:

"There is no proper veterinary inspection in our town, and that's the cause of all sorts of epidemics. One is always hearing of people's getting infection from the milk supply, or catching diseases from horses and cows. The health of domestic animals ought to be as well cared for as the health of human beings."

She repeated the veterinary surgeon's words, and was of the same opinion as he about everything. It was evident that she could not live a year without some attachment, and had found new happiness in the lodge. In any one else this would have been censured, but no one could think ill of Olenka; everything she did was so natural. Neither she nor the veterinary surgeon said anything to other people of the change in their relations, and tried, indeed, to conceal it, but without success, for Olenka could not keep a secret. When he had visitors, men serving in his regiment, and she poured out tea or served the supper, she would begin talking of the cattle plague, of the foot and mouth disease, and of the municipal slaughter-houses. He was dreadfully embarrassed, and when the guests had gone, he would seize her by the hand and hiss angrily:

"I've asked you before not to talk about what you don't understand. When we veterinary surgeons are talking among ourselves, please don't put your word in. It's really annoying."

And she would look at him with astonishment and dismay, and ask him in alarm: "But, Voloditchka, what *am* I to talk about?"

And with tears in her eyes she would embrace him, begging him not to be angry, and they were both happy.

But this happiness did not last long. The veterinary surgeon departed, departed for ever with his regiment, when it was transferred to a distant place — to Siberia, it may be. And Olenka was left alone.

Now she was absolutely alone. Her father had long been dead, and his armchair lay in the attic, covered with dust and lame of one leg. She got thinner and plainer, and when people met her in the street they did not look at her as they used to, and did not smile to her; evidently her best years were over and left behind, and now a new sort of life had begun for her, which did not bear thinking about. In the evening Olenka sat in the porch, and heard the band playing and the fireworks popping in the Tivoli, but now the sound stirred no response. She looked into her yard without interest, thought of nothing, wished for nothing, and afterwards, when night came on she went to bed and dreamed of her empty yard. She ate and drank as it were unwillingly.

And what was worst of all, she had no opinions of any sort. She saw the objects about her and understood what she saw, but could not form any opinion about them, and did not know what to talk about. And how awful it is not to have any opinions! One sees a bottle, for instance, or the rain, or a peasant driving in his cart, but what the bottle is for, or the rain, or the peasant, and what is the meaning of it, one can't say, and could not even for a thousand rubles. When she had Kukin, or Pustovalov, or the veterinary surgeon, Olenka could explain everything, and give her opinion about anything you like, but now there was the same emptiness in her brain and in her heart as there was in her yard outside. And it was as harsh and as bitter as wormwood in the mouth.

Little by little the town grew in all directions. The road became a street, and where the Tivoli and the timber-yard had been, there were new turnings and houses. How rapidly time passes! Olenka's house grew dingy, the roof got rusty, the shed sank on one side, and the whole yard was overgrown with docks and stinging-nettles. Olenka herself had grown plain and elderly; in summer she sat in the porch, and her soul, as before, was empty and dreary and full of bitterness. In winter she sat at her window and looked at the snow. When she caught the scent of spring, or heard the chime of the church bells, a sudden rush of memories from the past came over her, there was a tender ache in her heart, and her eyes brimmed over with tears; but this was only for a minute, and then came emptiness again and the sense of the futility of life. The black kitten, Briska, rubbed against her and purred softly, but Olenka was not touched by these feline caresses. That was not what she needed. She wanted a love that would absorb her whole being, her whole soul and reason — that would give her ideas and an object in life, and would warm her old blood. And she would shake the kitten off her skirt and say with vexation:

"Get along; I don't want you!"

And so it was, day after day and year after year, and no joy, and no opinions. Whatever Mavra, the cook, said she accepted.

One hot July day, towards evening, just as the cattle were being driven away, and the whole yard was full of dust, some one suddenly knocked at the gate. Olenka went to open it herself and was dumbfounded when she looked out; she saw Smirnin, the veterinary surgeon, grey-headed, and dressed as a civilian. She suddenly remembered everything. She could not help crying and letting her head fall on his breast without uttering a word, and in the violence of her feeling she did not notice how they both walked into the house and sat down to tea.

"My dear Vladimir Platonitch! What fate has brought you?" she muttered, trembling with joy.

"I want to settle here for good, Olga Semyonovna," he told her. "I have resigned my post, and have come to settle down and try my luck on my own account. Besides, it's time for my boy to go to school. He's a big boy. I am reconciled with my wife, you know."

"Where is she?" asked Olenka.

"She's at the hotel with the boy, and I'm looking for lodgings."

"Good gracious, my dear soul! Lodgings? Why not have my house? Why shouldn't that suit you? Why, my goodness, I wouldn't take any rent!" cried Olenka in a flutter, beginning to cry again. "You live here, and the lodge will do nicely for me. Oh dear! how glad I am!"

Next day the roof was painted and the walls were whitewashed, and Olenka, with her arms akimbo, walked about the yard giving directions. Her face was beaming with her old smile, and she was brisk and alert as though she had waked from a long sleep. The veterinary's wife arrived — a thin, plain lady, with short hair and a peevish expression. With her was her little Sasha, a boy of ten, small for his age, blue-eyed, chubby, with dimples in his cheeks. And scarcely had the boy walked into the yard when he ran after the cat, and at once there was the sound of his gay, joyous laugh.

"Is that your puss, auntie?" he asked Olenka. "When she has little ones, do give us a kitten. Mamma is awfully afraid of mice."

Olenka talked to him, and gave him tea. Her heart warmed and there was a sweet ache in her bosom, as though the boy had been her own child. And when he sat at the table in the evening, going over his lessons, she looked at him with deep tenderness and pity as she murmured to herself:

"You pretty pet! . . . my precious! . . . Such a fair little thing, and so clever."

" 'An island is a piece of land which is entirely surrounded by water,' " he read aloud.

"An island is a piece of land," she repeated, and this was the first opinion to which she gave utterance with positive conviction after so many years of silence and dearth of ideas.

Now she had opinions of her own, and at supper she talked to Sasha's parents, saying how difficult the lessons were at the high schools, but that yet the high school was better than a commercial one, since with a high-school education all careers were open to one, such as being a doctor or an engineer.

Sasha began going to the high school. His mother departed to Harkov to her sister's and did not return; his father used to go off every day to inspect cattle, and would often be away from home for three days together, and it seemed to Olenka as though Sasha was entirely abandoned, that he was not wanted at home, that he was being starved, and she carried him off to her lodge and gave him a little room there.

And for six months Sasha had lived in the lodge with her. Every morning Olenka came into his bedroom and found him fast asleep, sleeping noiselessly with his hand under his cheek. She was sorry to wake him.

"Sashenka," she would say mournfully, "get up, darling. It's time for school."

He would get up, dress and say his prayers, and then sit down to breakfast, drink three glasses of tea, and eat two large cracknels and half a buttered roll. All this time he was hardly awake and a little ill-humored in consequence.

"You don't quite know your fable, Sashenka," Olenka would say, looking at him as though he were about to set off on a long journey. "What a lot of trouble I have with you! You must work and do your best, darling, and obey your teachers."

"Oh, do leave me alone!" Sasha would say.

Then he would go down the street to school, a little figure, wearing a big cap and carrying a satchel on his shoulder. Olenka would follow him noiselessly.

"Sashenka!" she would call after him, and she would pop into his hand a date or a caramel. When he reached the street where the school was, he would feel ashamed of being followed by a tall, stout woman; he would turn round and say:

"You'd better go home, auntie. I can go the rest of the way alone."

She would stand still and look after him fixedly till he had disappeared at the school-gate.

Ah, how she loved him! Of her former attachments not one had been so deep; never had her soul surrendered to any feeling so spontaneously, so disinterestedly, and so joyously as now that her maternal instincts were aroused. For this little boy with the dimple in his cheek and the big school cap, she would have given her whole life, she would have given it with joy and tears of tenderness. Why? Who can tell why?

When she had seen the last of Sasha, she returned home, contented and serene, brimming over with love; her face, which had grown younger during the last six months, smiled and beamed; people meeting her looked at her with pleasure.

"Good-morning, Olga Semyonovna, darling. How are you, darling?"

"The lessons at the high school are very difficult now," she would relate at the market. "It's too much; in the first class yesterday they gave him a fable to learn by heart, and a Latin translation and a problem. You know it's too much for a little chap."

And she would begin talking about the teachers, the lessons, and the school books, saying just what Sasha said.

At three o'clock they had dinner together: in the evening they learned their lessons together and cried. When she put him to bed, she would stay a long time making the Cross over him and murmuring a prayer; then she would go to bed and dream of that far-away misty future when Sasha would finish his studies and become a doctor or an engineer, would have a big house of his own with horses and a carriage, would get married and have children. . . . She would fall asleep still thinking of the same thing, and tears would run down her cheeks from her closed eyes, while the black cat lay purring beside her: "Mrr, mrr, mrr."

Suddenly there would come a loud knock at the gate.

Olenka would wake up breathless with alarm, her heart throbbing. Half a minute later would come another knock.

"It must be a telegram from Harkov," she would think, beginning to tremble from head to foot. "Sasha's mother is sending for him from Harkov. . . . Oh, mercy on us!"

She was in despair. Her head, her hands, and her feet would turn chill, and she would feel that she was the most unhappy woman in the world. But another minute would pass, voices would be heard: it would turn out to be the veterinary surgeon coming home from the club.

"Well, thank God!" she would think.

And gradually the load in her heart would pass off, and she would feel at ease. She would go back to bed thinking of Sasha, who lay sound asleep in the next room, sometimes crying out in his sleep:

"I'll give it you! Get away! Shut up!"

ANTON CHEKHOV

The Lady with the Pet Dog   *1899*

TRANSLATED BY AVRAHM YARMOLINSKY

I

A new person, it was said, had appeared on the esplanade: a lady with a pet dog. Dmitry Dmitrich Gurov, who had spent a fortnight at Yalta and had got used to the place, had also begun to take an interest in new arrivals. As he sat in Vernet's confectionery shop, he saw, walking on the esplanade, a fair-haired young woman of medium height, wearing a beret; a white Pomeranian was trotting behind her.

And afterwards he met her in the public garden and in the square several times a day. She walked alone, always wearing the same beret and always with the white dog; no one knew who she was and everyone called her simply "the lady with the pet dog."

"If she is here alone without husband or friends," Gurov reflected, "it wouldn't be a bad thing to make her acquaintance."

He was under forty, but he already had a daughter twelve years old, and two sons at school. They had found a wife for him when he was very young, a student in his second year, and by now she seemed half as old again as he. She was a tall, erect woman with dark eyebrows, stately and dignified and, as she said of herself, intellectual. She read a great deal, used simplified spelling in her letters, called her husband, not Dmitry, but Dimitry, while he privately considered her of limited intelligence, narrow-minded, dowdy, was afraid of her, and did not like to be at home. He had begun being unfaithful to her long ago — had been unfaithful to her often and, probably for that reason, almost always spoke ill of women, and when they were talked of in his presence used to call them "the inferior race."

It seemed to him that he had been sufficiently tutored by bitter experience to call them what he pleased, and yet he could not have lived without "the inferior race" for two days together. In the company of men he was bored and ill at ease, he was chilly and uncommunicative with them; but when he was among women he felt free, and knew what to speak to them about and how to comport himself; and even to be silent with them was no strain on him. In his appearance, in his character, in his whole make-up there was something attractive and elusive that disposed women in his favor and allured them. He knew that, and some force seemed to draw him to them, too.

Oft-repeated and really bitter experience had taught him long ago that with decent people — particularly Moscow people — who are irresolute and slow to move, every affair which at first seems a light and charming adventure inevitably grows into a whole problem of extreme complexity, and in the end a painful situation is created. But at every new meeting with an interesting woman this lesson of experience seemed to slip from his memory, and he was eager for life, and everything seemed so simple and diverting.

One evening while he was dining in the public garden the lady in the beret walked up without haste to take the next table. Her expression, her gait, her dress, and the way she did her hair told him that she belonged to the upper class, that she was married, that she was in Yalta for the first time and alone, and that she was bored there. The stories told of the immorality in Yalta are to a great extent untrue; he despised them, and knew that such stories were made up for the most part by persons who would have been glad to sin themselves if they had had the chance; but when the lady sat down at the next table three paces from him, he recalled these stories of easy conquests, of trips to the mountains, and the tempting thought of a swift, fleeting liaison, a romance with an unknown woman of whose very name he was ignorant, suddenly took hold of him.

He beckoned invitingly to the Pomeranian, and when the dog approached him, shook his finger at it. The Pomeranian growled; Gurov threatened it again.

The lady glanced at him and at once dropped her eyes.

"He doesn't bite," she said and blushed.

"May I give him a bone?" he asked; and when she nodded he inquired affably, "Have you been in Yalta long?"

"About five days."

"And I am dragging out the second week here."

There was a short silence.

"Time passes quickly, and yet it is so dull here!" she said, not looking at him.

"It's only the fashion to say it's dull here. A provincial will live in Belyov or Zhizdra and not be bored, but when he comes here it's 'Oh, the dullness! Oh, the dust!' One would think he came from Granada."

She laughed. Then both continued eating in silence, like strangers, but after dinner they walked together and there sprang up between them the light banter of people who are free and contented, to whom it does not matter where they go or what they talk about. They walked and talked of the strange light on the sea: the water was a soft, warm, lilac color, and there was a golden band of moonlight upon it. They talked of how sultry it was after a hot day. Gurov told her that he was a native of Moscow, that he had studied languages and literature at the university, but had a post in a bank; that at one time he had trained to become an opera singer but had given it up, that he owned two

houses in Moscow. And he learned from her that she had grown up in Petersburg, but had lived in S —— since her marriage two years previously, that she
was going to stay in Yalta for about another month, and that her husband,
who needed a rest, too, might perhaps come to fetch her. She was not certain
whether her husband was a member of a Government Board or served on a
Zemstvo Council,° and this amused her. And Gurov learned too that her name
was Anna Sergeyevna.

Afterwards in his room at the hotel he thought about her — and was certain that he would meet her the next day. It was bound to happen. Getting into
bed he recalled that she had been a schoolgirl only recently, doing lessons like
his own daughter; he thought how much timidity and angularity there was
still in her laugh and her manner of talking with a stranger. It must have been
the first time in her life that she was alone in a setting in which she was followed, looked at, and spoken to for one secret purpose alone, which she could
hardly fail to guess. He thought of her slim, delicate throat, her lovely gray
eyes.

"There's something pathetic about her, though," he thought, and
dropped off.

II

A week had passed since they had struck up an acquaintance. It was a
holiday. It was close indoors, while in the street the wind whirled the dust
about and blew people's hats off. One was thirsty all day, and Gurov often
went into the restaurant and offered Anna Sergeyevna a soft drink or ice
cream. One did not know what to do with oneself.

In the evening when the wind had abated they went out on the pier
to watch the steamer come in. There were a great many people walking
about the dock; they had come to welcome someone and they were carrying bunches of flowers. And two peculiarities of a festive Yalta crowd stood
out: the elderly ladies were dressed like young ones and there were many
generals.

Owing to the choppy sea, the steamer arrived late, after sunset, and it
was a long time tacking about before it put in at the pier. Anna Sergeyevna
peered at the steamer and the passengers through her lorgnette as though
looking for acquaintances, and whenever she turned to Gurov her eyes were
shining. She talked a great deal and asked questions jerkily, forgetting the next
moment what she had asked; then she lost her lorgnette in the crush.

The festive crowd began to disperse; it was now too dark to see people's
faces; there was no wind anymore, but Gurov and Anna Sergeyevna still stood
as though waiting to see someone else come off the steamer. Anna Sergeyevna
was silent now, and sniffed her flowers without looking at Gurov.

"The weather has improved this evening," he said. "Where shall we go
now? Shall we drive somewhere?"

She did not reply.

Then he looked at her intently, and suddenly embraced her and kissed

---

Zemstvo Council: County council.

her on the lips, and the moist fragrance of her flowers enveloped him; and at once he looked round him anxiously, wondering if anyone had seen them.

"Let us go to your place," he said softly. And they walked off together rapidly.

The air in her room was close and there was the smell of the perfume she had bought at the Japanese shop. Looking at her, Gurov thought: "What encounters life offers!" From the past he preserved the memory of carefree, good-natured women whom love made gay and who were grateful to him for the happiness he gave them, however brief it might be; and of women like his wife who loved without sincerity, with too many words, affectedly, hysterically, with an expression that it was not love or passion that engaged them but something more significant; and of two or three others, very beautiful, frigid women, across whose faces would suddenly flit a rapacious expression — an obstinate desire to take from life more than it could give, and these were women no longer young, capricious, unreflecting, domineering, unintelligent, and when Gurov grew cold to them their beauty aroused his hatred, and the lace on their lingerie seemed to him to resemble scales.

But here there was the timidity, the angularity of inexperienced youth, a feeling of awkwardness; and there was a sense of embarrassment, as though someone had suddenly knocked at the door. Anna Sergeyevna, "the lady with the pet dog," treated what had happened in a peculiar way, very seriously, as though it were her fall — so it seemed, and this was odd and inappropriate. Her features drooped and faded, and her long hair hung down sadly on either side of her face; she grew pensive and her dejected pose was that of a Magdalene in a picture by an old master.

"It's not right," she said. "You don't respect me now, you first of all."

There was a watermelon on the table. Gurov cut himself a slice and began eating it without haste. They were silent for at least half an hour.

There was something touching about Anna Sergeyevna; she had the purity of a well-bred, naive woman who has seen little of life. The single candle burning on the table barely illumined her face, yet it was clear that she was unhappy.

"Why should I stop respecting you, darling?" asked Gurov. "You don't know what you're saying."

"God forgive me," she said, and her eyes filled with tears. "It's terrible."

"It's as though you were trying to exonerate yourself."

"How can I exonerate myself? No. I am a bad, low woman; I despise myself and I have no thought of exonerating myself. It's not my husband but myself I have deceived. And not only just now; I have been deceiving myself for a long time. My husband may be a good, honest man, but he is a flunkey! I don't know what he does, what his work is, but I know he is a flunkey! I was twenty when I married him. I was tormented by curiosity; I wanted something better. 'There must be a different sort of life,' I said to myself. I wanted to live! To live, to live! Curiosity kept eating at me — you don't understand it, but I swear to God I could no longer control myself; something was going on in me; I could not be held back. I told my husband I was ill, and came here.

And here I have been walking about as though in a daze, as though I were mad; and now I have become a vulgar, vile woman whom anyone may despise."

Gurov was already bored with her; he was irritated by her naive tone, by her repentance, so unexpected and so out of place, but for the tears in her eyes he might have thought she was joking or play-acting.

"I don't understand, my dear," he said softly. "What do you want?"

She hid her face on his breast and pressed close to him.

"Believe me, believe me, I beg you," she said, "I love honesty and purity, and sin is loathsome to me; I don't know what I'm doing. Simple people say, 'The Evil One has led me astray.' And I may say of myself now that the Evil One has led me astray."

"Quiet, quiet," he murmured.

He looked into her fixed, frightened eyes, kissed her, spoke to her softly and affectionately, and by degrees she calmed down, and her gaiety returned; both began laughing.

Afterwards when they went out there was not a soul on the esplanade. The town with its cypresses looked quite dead, but the sea was still sounding as it broke upon the beach; a single launch was rocking on the waves and on it a lantern was blinking sleepily.

They found a cab and drove to Oreanda.

"I found out your surname in the hall just now: it was written on the board — von Dideritz," said Gurov. "Is your husband German?"

"No; I believe his grandfather was German, but he is Greek Orthodox himself."

At Oreanda they sat on a bench not far from the church, looked down at the sea, and were silent. Yalta was barely visible through the morning mist; white clouds rested motionlessly on the mountaintops. The leaves did not stir on the trees, cicadas twanged, and the monotonous muffled sound of the sea that rose from below spoke of the peace, the eternal sleep awaiting us. So it rumbled below when there was no Yalta, no Oreanda here; so it rumbles now, and it will rumble as indifferently and as hollowly when we are no more. And in this constancy, in this complete indifference to the life and death of each of us, there lies, perhaps, a pledge of our eternal salvation, of the unceasing advance of life upon earth, of unceasing movement towards perfection. Sitting beside a young woman who in the dawn seemed so lovely, Gurov, soothed and spellbound by these magical surroundings — the sea, the mountains, the clouds, the wide sky — thought how everything is really beautiful in this world when one reflects: everything except what we think or do ourselves when we forget the higher aims of life and our own human dignity.

A man strolled up to them — probably a guard — looked at them, and walked away. And this detail, too, seemed so mysterious and beautiful. They saw a steamer arrive from Feodosia, its lights extinguished in the glow of dawn.

"There is dew on the grass," said Anna Sergeyevna, after a silence.

"Yes, it's time to go home."

They returned to the city.

Then they met every day at twelve o'clock on the esplanade, lunched and dined together, took walks, admired the sea. She complained that she slept badly, that she had palpitations, asked the same questions, troubled now by jealousy and now by the fear that he did not respect her sufficiently. And often in the square or the public garden, when there was no one near them, he suddenly drew her to him and kissed her passionately. Complete idleness, these kisses in broad daylight exchanged furtively in dread of someone's seeing them, the heat, the smell of the sea, and the continual flitting before his eyes of idle, well-dressed, well-fed people, worked a complete change in him; he kept telling Anna Sergeyevna how beautiful she was, how seductive, was urgently passionate; he would not move a step away from her, while she was often pensive and continually pressed him to confess that he did not respect her, did not love her in the least, and saw in her nothing but a common woman. Almost every evening rather late they drove somewhere out of town, to Oreanda or to the waterfall; and the excursion was always a success, the scenery invariably impressed them as beautiful and magnificent.

They were expecting her husband, but a letter came from him saying that he had eye-trouble, and begging his wife to return home as soon as possible. Anna Sergeyevna made haste to go.

"It's a good thing I am leaving," she said to Gurov. "It's the hand of Fate!"

She took a carriage to the railway station, and he went with her. They were driving the whole day. When she had taken her place in the express, and when the second bell had rung, she said, "Let me look at you once more — let me look at you again. Like this."

She was not crying but was so sad that she seemed ill and her face was quivering.

"I shall be thinking of you — remembering you," she said. "God bless you; be happy. Don't remember evil against me. We are parting forever — it has to be, for we ought never to have met. Well, God bless you."

The train moved off rapidly, its lights soon vanished, and a minute later there was no sound of it, as though everything had conspired to end as quickly as possible that sweet trance, that madness. Left alone on the platform, and gazing into the dark distance, Gurov listened to the twang of the grasshoppers and the hum of the telegraph wires, feeling as though he had just waked up. And he reflected, musing, that there had now been another episode or adventure in his life, and it, too, was at an end, and nothing was left of it but a memory. He was moved, sad, and slightly remorseful: this young woman whom he would never meet again had not been happy with him; he had been warm and affectionate with her, but yet in his manner, his tone, and his caresses there had been a shade of light irony, the slightly coarse arrogance of a happy male who was, besides, almost twice her age. She had constantly called him kind, exceptional, high-minded; obviously he had seemed to her different from what he really was, so he had involuntarily deceived her.

Here at the station there was already a scent of autumn in the air; it was a chilly evening.

"It is time for me to go north, too," thought Gurov as he left the platform. "High time!"

III

At home in Moscow the winter routine was already established; the stoves were heated, and in the morning it was still dark when the children were having breakfast and getting ready for school, and the nurse would light the lamp for a short time. There were frosts already. When the first snow falls, on the first day the sleighs are out, it is pleasant to see the white earth, the white roofs; one draws easy, delicious breaths, and the season brings back the days of one's youth. The old limes and birches, white with hoar-frost, have a good-natured look; they are closer to one's heart than cypresses and palms, and near them one no longer wants to think of mountains and the sea.

Gurov, a native of Moscow, arrived there on a fine frosty day, and when he put on his fur coat and warm gloves and took a walk along Petrovka, and when on Saturday night he heard the bells ringing, his recent trip and the places he had visited lost all charm for him. Little by little he became immersed in Moscow life, greedily read three newspapers a day, and declared that he did not read the Moscow papers on principle. He already felt a longing for restaurants, clubs, formal dinners, anniversary celebrations, and it flattered him to entertain distinguished lawyers and actors, and to play cards with a professor at the physicians' club. He could eat a whole portion of meat stewed with pickled cabbage and served in a pan, Moscow style.

A month or so would pass and the image of Anna Sergeyevna, it seemed to him, would become misty in his memory, and only from time to time he would dream of her with her touching smile as he dreamed of others. But more than a month went by, winter came into its own, and everything was still clear in his memory as though he had parted from Anna Sergeyevna only yesterday. And his memories glowed more and more vividly. When in the evening stillness the voices of his children preparing their lessons reached his study, or when he listened to a song or to an organ playing in a restaurant, or when the storm howled in the chimney, suddenly everything would rise up in his memory; what had happened on the pier and the early morning with the mist on the mountains, and the steamer coming from Feodosia, and the kisses. He would pace about his room a long time, remembering and smiling; then his memories passed into reveries, and in his imagination the past would mingle with what was to come. He did not dream of Anna Sergeyevna, but she followed him about everywhere and watched him. When he shut his eyes he saw her before him as though she were there in the flesh, and she seemed to him lovelier, younger, tenderer than she had been, and he imagined himself a finer man than he had been in Yalta. Of evenings she peered out at him from the bookcase, from the fireplace, from the corner — he heard her breathing, the caressing rustle of her clothes. In the street he followed the women with his eyes, looking for someone who resembled her.

Already he was tormented by a strong desire to share his memories with someone. But in his home it was impossible to talk of his love, and he had no one to talk to outside; certainly he could not confide in his tenants or in anyone at the bank. And what was there to talk about? He hadn't loved her then, had he? Had there been anything beautiful, poetical, edifying, or simply interesting in his relations with Anna Sergeyevna? And he was forced to talk vaguely of love, of women, and no one guessed what he meant; only his wife would twitch her black eyebrows and say, "The part of a philanderer does not suit you at all, Dimitry."

One evening, coming out of the physicians' club with an official with whom he had been playing cards, he could not resist saying:

"If you only knew what a fascinating woman I became acquainted with at Yalta!"

The official got into his sledge and was driving away, but turned suddenly and shouted:

"Dmitry Dmitrich!"

"What is it?"

"You were right this evening: the sturgeon was a bit high."

These words, so commonplace, for some reason moved Gurov to indignation, and struck him as degrading and unclean. What savage manners, what mugs! What stupid nights, what dull, humdrum days! Frenzied gambling, gluttony, drunkenness, continual talk always about the same thing! Futile pursuits and conversations always about the same topics take up the better part of one's time, the better part of one's strength, and in the end there is left a life clipped and wingless, an absurd mess, and there is no escaping or getting away from it — just as though one were in a madhouse or a prison.

Gurov, boiling with indignation, did not sleep all night. And he had a headache all the next day. And the following nights too he slept badly; he sat up in bed, thinking, or paced up and down his room. He was fed up with his children, fed up with the bank; he had no desire to go anywhere or to talk of anything.

In December during the holidays he prepared to take a trip and told his wife he was going to Petersburg to do what he could for a young friend — and he set off for S——. What for? He did not know, himself. He wanted to see Anna Sergeyevna and talk with her, to arrange a rendezvous if possible.

He arrived at S—— in the morning, and at the hotel took the best room, in which the floor was covered with gray army cloth, and on the table there was an inkstand, gray with dust and topped by a figure on horseback, its hat in its raised hand and its head broken off. The porter gave him the necessary information: von Dideritz lived in a house of his own on Staro-Goncharnaya Street, not far from the hotel: he was rich and lived well and kept his own horses; everyone in the town knew him. The porter pronounced the name: "Dridiritz."

Without haste Gurov made his way to Staro-Goncharnaya Street and found the house. Directly opposite the house stretched a long gray fence studded with nails.

"A fence like that would make one run away," thought Gurov, looking now at the fence, now at the windows of the house.

He reflected: this was a holiday, and the husband was apt to be at home. And in any case, it would be tactless to go into the house and disturb her. If he were to send her a note, it might fall into her husband's hands, and that might spoil everything. The best thing was to rely on chance. And he kept walking up and down the street and along the fence, waiting for the chance. He saw a beggar go in at the gate and heard the dogs attack him; then an hour later he heard a piano, and the sound came to him faintly and indistinctly. Probably it was Anna Sergeyevna playing. The front door opened suddenly, and an old woman came out, followed by the familiar white Pomeranian. Gurov was on the point of calling to the dog, but his heart began beating violently, and in his excitement he could not remember the Pomeranian's name.

He kept walking up and down, and hated the gray fence more and more, and by now he thought irritably that Anna Sergeyevna had forgotten him, and was perhaps already diverting herself with another man, and that that was very natural in a young woman who from morning till night had to look at that damn fence. He went back to his hotel room and sat on the couch for a long while, not knowing what to do, then he had dinner and a long nap.

"How stupid and annoying all this is!" he thought when he woke and looked at the dark windows: it was already evening. "Here I've had a good sleep for some reason. What am I going to do at night?"

He sat on the bed, which was covered with a cheap gray blanket of the kind seen in hospitals, and he twitted himself in his vexation:

"So there's your lady with the pet dog. There's your adventure. A nice place to cool your heels in."

That morning at the station a playbill in large letters had caught his eye. *The Geisha* was to be given for the first time. He thought of this and drove to the theater.

"It's quite possible that she goes to first nights," he thought.

The theater was full. As in all provincial theaters, there was a haze above the chandelier, the gallery was noisy and restless; in the front row, before the beginning of the performance the local dandies were standing with their hands clasped behind their backs; in the Governor's box the Governor's daughter, wearing a boa, occupied the front seat, while the Governor himself hid modestly behind the portiere and only his hands were visible; the curtain swayed; the orchestra was a long time tuning up. While the audience was coming in and taking their seats, Gurov scanned the faces eagerly.

Anna Sergeyevna, too, came in. She sat down in the third row, and when Gurov looked at her his heart contracted, and he understood clearly that in the whole world there was no human being so near, so precious, and so important to him; she, this little, undistinguished woman, lost in a provincial crowd, with a vulgar lorgnette in her hand, filled his whole life now, was his sorrow and his joy, the only happiness that he now desired for himself, and to the sounds of the bad orchestra, of the miserable local violins, he thought how lovely she was. He thought and dreamed.

A young man with small side-whiskers, very tall and stooped, came in with Anna Sergeyevna and sat down beside her; he nodded his head at every step and seemed to be bowing continually. Probably this was the husband whom at Yalta, in an access of bitter feeling, she had called a flunkey. And there really was in his lanky figure, his side-whiskers, his small bald patch, something of a flunkey's retiring manner; his smile was mawkish, and in his buttonhole there was an academic badge like a waiter's number.

During the first intermission the husband went out to have a smoke; she remained in her seat. Gurov, who was also sitting in the orchestra, went up to her and said in a shaky voice, with a forced smile:

"Good evening!"

She glanced at him and turned pale, then looked at him again in horror, unable to believe her eyes, and gripped the fan and the lorgnette tightly together in her hands, evidently trying to keep herself from fainting. Both were silent. She was sitting, he was standing, frightened by her distress and not daring to take a seat beside her. The violins and the flute that were being tuned up sang out. He suddenly felt frightened: it seemed as if all the people in the boxes were looking at them. She got up and went hurriedly to the exit; he followed her, and both of them walked blindly along the corridors and up and down stairs, and figures in the uniforms prescribed for magistrates, teachers, and officials of the Department of Crown Lands, all wearing badges, flitted before their eyes, as did also ladies, and fur coats on hangers; they were conscious of drafts and the smell of stale tobacco. And Gurov, whose heart was beating violently, thought:

"Oh, Lord! Why are these people here and this orchestra!"

And at that instant he suddenly recalled how when he had seen Anna Sergeyevna off at the station he had said to himself that all was over between them and that they would never meet again. But how distant the end still was!

On the narrow, gloomy staircase over which it said "To the Amphitheatre," she stopped.

"How you frightened me!" she said, breathing hard, still pale and stunned. "Oh, how you frightened me! I am barely alive. Why did you come? Why?"

"But do understand, Anna, do understand — " he said hurriedly, under his breath. "I implore you, do understand — "

She looked at him with fear, with entreaty, with love; she looked at him intently, to keep his features more distinctly in her memory.

"I suffer so," she went on, not listening to him. "All this time I have been thinking of nothing but you; I live only by the thought of you. And I wanted to forget, to forget; but why, oh, why have you come?"

On the landing above them two high school boys were looking down and smoking, but it was all the same to Gurov; he drew Anna Sergeyevna to him and began kissing her face and hands.

"What are you doing, what are you doing!" she was saying in horror, pushing him away. "We have lost our senses. Go away today; go away at once — I conjure you by all that is sacred, I implore you — People are coming this way!"

Someone was walking up the stairs.

"You must leave," Anna Sergeyevna went on in a whisper. "Do you hear, Dmitry Dmitrich? I will come and see you in Moscow. I have never been happy; I am unhappy now, and I never, never shall be happy, never! So don't make me suffer still more! I swear I'll come to Moscow. But now let us part. My dear, good, precious one, let us part!"

She pressed his hand and walked rapidly downstairs, turning to look round at him, and from her eyes he could see that she really was unhappy. Gurov stood for a while, listening, then when all grew quiet, he found his coat and left the theater.

IV

And Anna Sergeyevna began coming to see him in Moscow. Once every two or three months she left S —— telling her husband that she was going to consult a doctor about a woman's ailment from which she was suffering — and her husband did and did not believe her. When she arrived in Moscow she would stop at the Slavyansky Bazar Hotel, and at once send a man in a red cap to Gurov. Gurov came to see her, and no one in Moscow knew of it.

Once he was going to see her in this way on a winter morning (the messenger had come the evening before and not found him in). With him walked his daughter, whom he wanted to take to school; it was on the way. Snow was coming down in big wet flakes.

"It's three degrees above zero,° and yet it's snowing," Gurov was saying to his daughter. "But this temperature prevails only on the surface of the earth; in the upper layers of the atmosphere there is quite a different temperature."

"And why doesn't it thunder in winter, papa?"

He explained that, too. He talked, thinking all the while that he was on his way to a rendezvous, and no living soul knew of it, and probably no one would ever know. He had two lives, an open one, seen and known by all who needed to know it, full of conventional truth and conventional falsehood, exactly like the lives of his friends and acquaintances; and another life that went on in secret. And through some strange, perhaps accidental, combination of circumstances, everything that was of interest and importance to him, everything that was essential to him, everything about which he felt sincerely and did not deceive himself, everything that constituted the core of his life, was going on concealed from others; while all that was false, the shell in which he hid to cover the truth — his work at the bank, for instance, his discussions at the club, his references to the "inferior race," his appearances at anniversary celebrations with his wife — all that went on in the open. Judging others by himself, he did not believe what he saw, and always fancied that every man led his real, most interesting life under cover of secrecy as under cover of night. The personal life of every individual is based on secrecy, and perhaps it is partly for that reason that civilized man is so nervously anxious that personal privacy should be respected.

Having taken his daughter to school, Gurov went on to the Slavyansky Bazar Hotel. He took off his fur coat in the lobby, went upstairs, and knocked

---

three degrees above zero: On the Celsius scale — about thirty-seven degrees Fahrenheit.

gently at the door. Anna Sergeyevna, wearing his favorite gray dress, exhausted by the journey and by waiting, had been expecting him since the previous evening. She was pale, and looked at him without a smile, and he had hardly entered when she flung herself on his breast. That kiss was a long, lingering one, as though they had not seen one another for two years.

"Well, darling, how are you getting on there?" he asked. "What news?"

"Wait; I'll tell you in a moment — I can't speak."

She could not speak; she was crying. She turned away from him, and pressed her handkerchief to her eyes.

"Let her have her cry; meanwhile I'll sit down," he thought, and he seated himself in an armchair.

Then he rang and ordered tea, and while he was having his tea she remained standing at the window with her back to him. She was crying out of sheer agitation, in the sorrowful consciousness that their life was so sad; that they could only see each other in secret and had to hide from people like thieves! Was it not a broken life?

"Come, stop now, dear!" he said.

It was plain to him that this love of theirs would not be over soon, that the end of it was not in sight. Anna Sergeyevna was growing more and more attached to him. She adored him, and it was unthinkable to tell her that their love was bound to come to an end some day; besides, she would not have believed it!

He went up to her and took her by the shoulders, to fondle her and say something diverting, and at that moment he caught sight of himself in the mirror.

His hair was already beginning to turn gray. And it seemed odd to him that he had grown so much older in the last few years, and lost his looks. The shoulders on which his hands rested were warm and heaving. He felt compassion for this life, still so warm and lovely, but probably already about to begin to fade and wither like his own. Why did she love him so much? He always seemed to women different from what he was, and they loved in him not himself, but the man whom their imagination created and whom they had been eagerly seeking all their lives; and afterwards, when they saw their mistake, they loved him nevertheless. And not one of them had been happy with him. In the past he had met women, come together with them, parted from them, but he had never once loved; it was anything you please, but not love. And only now when his head was gray he had fallen in love, really, truly — for the first time in his life.

Anna Sergeyevna and he loved each other as people do who are very close and intimate, like man and wife, like tender friends; it seemed to them that Fate itself had meant them for one another, and they could not understand why he had a wife and she a husband; and it was as though they were a pair of migratory birds, male and female, caught and forced to live in different cages. They forgave each other what they were ashamed of in their past, they forgave everything in the present, and felt that this love of theirs had altered them both.

Formerly in moments of sadness he had soothed himself with whatever logical arguments came into his head, but now he no longer cared for logic; he felt profound compassion, he wanted to be sincere and tender.

"Give it up now, my darling," he said. "You've had your cry; that's enough. Let us have a talk now, we'll think up something."

Then they spent a long time taking counsel together, they talked of how to avoid the necessity for secrecy, for deception, for living in different cities, and not seeing one another for long stretches of time. How could they free themselves from these intolerable fetters?

"How? How?" he asked, clutching his head. "How?"

And it seemed as though in a little while the solution would be found, and then a new and glorious life would begin; and it was clear to both of them that the end was still far off, and that what was to be most complicated and difficult for them was only just beginning.

ᔕᔕ

KATE CHOPIN *(1851–1904) was born in St. Louis. Her father died when she was four, and she was raised by her Creole mother's family. In 1870 she married Oscar Chopin, a cotton broker. They lived in Louisiana, first in New Orleans and then on a large plantation among the French-speaking Acadians. When her husband died in 1882, Chopin moved with her six children back to St. Louis. Friends encouraged her to write, and when she was nearly forty she published her first novel,* At Fault *(1890). Her stories began to appear in* Century *and* Harper's Magazine, *and two collections followed:* Bayou Folk *(1894) and* A Night in Acadie *(1897). Her last major work, the novel* The Awakening *(1899), is her masterpiece, but its sympathetic treatment of adultery shocked reviewers and readers throughout America. In St. Louis the novel was taken out of the libraries, and Chopin was denied membership in the St. Louis Fine Arts Club. When her third collection of stories was rejected by her publisher at the end of 1899, Chopin felt herself a literary outcast; she wrote very little in the last years of her life.*

What affronted the genteel readers of the 1890s was Chopin's attempt to write frankly about women's emotions in their relations with men, children, and their own sexuality. After her mother's death in 1885, she stopped being a practicing Catholic and accepted the Darwinian view of human evolution. Seeking God in nature rather than through the church, Chopin wrote freely on the subjects of sex and love, but she said she learned to her sorrow that, for American authors, "the limitations imposed upon their art by their environment hamper a full and spontaneous expression." Magazine editors turned down her work if it challenged conventional social behavior, as does "The Story of an Hour," which feminist critics championed more than half a century after Chopin's death.

Chopin adopted Guy de Maupassant as a model after translating his stories from the French. "Here was life, not fiction," she wrote, "for where were the plots, the old fashioned mechanism and stage trappings that in a vague, unthinking way I had fancied were essential to the art of story making?"

RELATED COMMENTARY: *Kate Chopin, "How I Stumbled upon Maupassant,"* page 740.

KATE CHOPIN

The Story of an Hour   1894

Knowing that Mrs. Mallard was afflicted with a heart trouble, great care was taken to break to her as gently as possible the news of her husband's death.

It was her sister Josephine who told her, in broken sentences; veiled hints that revealed in half concealing. Her husband's friend Richards was there, too, near her. It was he who had been in the newspaper office when intelligence of the railroad disaster was received, with Brently Mallard's name leading the list of "killed." He had only taken the time to assure himself of its truth by a second telegram, and had hastened to forestall any less careful, less tender friend in bearing the sad message.

She did not hear the story as many women have heard the same, with a paralyzed inability to accept its significance. She wept at once, with sudden, wild abandonment, in her sister's arms. When the storm of grief had spent itself she went away to her room alone. She would have no one follow her.

There stood, facing the open window, a comfortable, roomy armchair. Into this she sank, pressed down by a physical exhaustion that haunted her body and seemed to reach into her soul.

She could see in the open square before her house the tops of trees that were all aquiver with the new spring life. The delicious breath of rain was in the air. In the street below a peddler was crying his wares. The notes of a distant song which some one was singing reached her faintly, and countless sparrows were twittering in the eaves.

There were patches of blue sky showing here and there through the clouds that had met and piled one above the other in the west facing her window.

She sat with her head thrown back upon the cushion of the chair, quite motionless, except when a sob came up into her throat and shook her, as a child who had cried itself to sleep continues to sob in its dreams.

She was young, with a fair, calm face, whose lines bespoke repression and even a certain strength. But now there was a dull stare in her eyes, whose gaze was fixed away off yonder on one of those patches of blue sky. It was not a glance of reflection, but rather indicated a suspension of intelligent thought.

There was something coming to her and she was waiting for it, fearfully. What was it? She did not know; it was too subtle and elusive to name. But she felt it, creeping out of the sky, reaching toward her through the sounds, the scents, the color that filled the air.

Now her bosom rose and fell tumultuously. She was beginning to recognize this thing that was approaching to possess her, and she was striving to beat it back with her will — as powerless as her two white slender hands would have been.

When she abandoned herself a little whispered word escaped her slightly parted lips. She said it over and over under her breath: "free, free,

free!" The vacant stare and the look of terror that had followed it went from her eyes. They stayed keen and bright. Her pulses beat fast, and the coursing blood warmed and relaxed every inch of her body.

She did not stop to ask if it were or were not a monstrous joy that held her. A clear and exalted perception enabled her to dismiss the suggestion as trivial.

She knew that she would weep again when she saw the kind, tender hands folded in death; the face that had never looked save with love upon her, fixed and gray and dead. But she saw beyond that bitter moment a long procession of years to come that would belong to her absolutely. And she opened and spread her arms out to them in welcome.

There would be no one to live for her during those coming years: she would live for herself. There would be no powerful will bending hers in that blind persistence with which men and women believe they have a right to impose a private will upon a fellow-creature. A kind intention or a cruel intention made the act seem no less a crime as she looked upon it in that brief moment of illumination.

And yet she had loved him — sometimes. Often she had not. What did it matter! What could love, the unsolved mystery, count for in face of this possession of self-assertion which she suddenly recognized as the strongest impulse of her being!

"Free! Body and soul free!" she kept whispering.

Josephine was kneeling before the closed door with her lips to the keyhole, imploring for admission. "Louise, open the door! I beg; open the door — you will make yourself ill. What are you doing, Louise? For heaven's sake open the door."

"Go away. I am not making myself ill." No; she was drinking in a very elixir of life through that open window.

Her fancy was running riot along those days ahead of her. Spring days, and summer days, and all sorts of days that would be her own. She breathed a quick prayer that life might be long. It was only yesterday she had thought with a shudder that life might be long.

She arose at length and opened the door to her sister's importunities. There was a feverish triumph in her eyes, and she carried herself unwittingly like a goddess of Victory. She clasped her sister's waist, and together they descended the stairs. Richards stood waiting for them at the bottom.

Some one was opening the front door with a latchkey. It was Brently Mallard who entered, a little travel-stained, composedly carrying his gripsack and umbrella. He had been far from the scene of accident, and did not even know there had been one. He stood amazed at Josephine's piercing cry; at Richards' quick motion to screen him from the view of his wife.

But Richards was too late.

When the doctors came they said she had died of heart disease — of joy that kills.

☙

SANDRA CISNEROS *(b. 1954), the daughter of a Mexican father and a Chicana mother, grew up in ghetto neighborhoods in Chicago and began writing poetry when she was ten. Her six brothers so dominated the household that she remembers that she felt she had "seven fathers." Cisneros spoke Spanish at home with her father and on her frequent trips to Mexico to visit her grandmother, but she did not think of herself as a Chicana writer until she began a series of autobiographical sketches in reaction to what she was being taught in the M.F.A. program at the University of Iowa's Writers Workshop in 1977. Then she discovered her literary voice, realizing the uniqueness of her experience growing up as a poor Latina in Chicago:*

> *Everyone seemed to have some communal knowledge which I did not have. . . . This caused me to question myself, to become defensive. What did I, Sandra Cisneros, know? What could I know? My classmates were from the best schools in the country. They had been bred as fine hothouse flowers. I was a yellow weed among the city's cracks.*

Cisneros says that she became a writer because she was "determined to fill a literary void . . . trying to write the stories that haven't been written." These early sketches developed into the book published as The House on Mango Street *(1983), more than forty short narratives that were highly praised by critics and won the 1985 Before Columbus Foundation's American Book Award. Cisneros had found a way to write stories*

> *that were a cross between poetry and fiction. . . . [I] wanted to write a collection which could be read at any random point without having any knowledge of what came before or after. Or, that could be read in a series to tell one big story. I wanted stories like poems, compact and lyrical and ending with reverberation.*

As Joyce Carol Oates has observed, Cisneros's "emotionally rich subject is the Latino community, specifically the experience of growing up female in a male-dominated society; her work . . . might be as readily classified as prose poetry as prose fiction." To date Cisneros has published three books of poetry and Woman Hollering Creek and Other Stories *(1991), a collection of more than twenty lyrical narratives about Mexican Americans in San Antonio who have different experiences living on both sides of the border with Mexico. The five short, interrelated stories presented here are part of the "one big story" of Cisneros's* The House on Mango Street, *a collection that she says was modeled on Jorge Luis Borges's* Dreamtigers *(1964).*

RELATED STORY: *Jorge Luis Borges, "Everything and Nothing," page 96.*

RELATED COMMENTARIES: *See Casebook on Sandra Cisneros, pages 832–847, including Sandra Cisneros, "Straw into Gold," page 832; Ellen McCracken, "On Cisneros's* The House on Mango Street," *page 835; Julián Olivares, "The House on Mango Street and the Poetics of Space," page 839; Alvina E. Quintana, "The House as Symbol," page 842; and Mark Zimmerman, "U.S. Latino Literature: History and Development," page 844.*

SANDRA CISNEROS

The House on Mango Street

We didn't always live on Mango Street. Before that we
on the third floor, and before that we lived on Keeler. Before Keeler it was
Paulina, and before that I can't remember. But what I remember most is moving a lot. Each time it seemed there'd be one more of us. By the time we got
to Mango Street we were six — Mama, Papa, Carlos, Kiki, my sister Nenny,
and me.

The house on Mango Street is ours, and we don't have to pay rent to
anybody, or share the yard with the people downstairs, or be careful not to
make too much noise, and there isn't a landlord banging on the ceiling with a
broom. But even so, it's not the house we'd thought we'd get.

We had to leave the flat on Loomis quick. The water pipes broke and the
landlord wouldn't fix them because the house was too old. We had to leave
fast. We were using the washroom next door and carrying water over in
empty milk gallons. That's why Mama and Papa looked for a house, and
that's why we moved into the house on Mango Street, far away, on the other
side of town.

They always told us that one day we would move into a house, a real
house that would be ours for always so we wouldn't have to move each year.
And our house would have running water and pipes that worked. And inside
it would have real stairs, not hallway stairs, but stairs inside like the houses on
T.V. And we'd have a basement and at least three washrooms so when we took
a bath we wouldn't have to tell everybody. Our house would be white with
trees around it, a great big yard and grass growing without a fence. This was
the house Papa talked about when he held a lottery ticket and this was the
house Mama dreamed up in the stories she told us before we went to bed.

But the house on Mango Street is not the way they told it at all. It's small
and red with tight steps in front and windows so small you'd think they were
holding their breath. Bricks are crumbling in places, and the front door is so
swollen you have to push hard to get in. There is no front yard, only four little
elms the city planted by the curb. Out back is a small garage for the car we
don't own yet and a small yard that looks smaller between the two buildings
on either side. There are stairs in our house, but they're ordinary hallway
stairs, and the house has only one washroom. Everybody has to share a bedroom — Mama and Papa, Carlos and Kiki, me and Nenny.

Once when we were living on Loomis, a nun from my school passed by
and saw me playing out front. The laundromat downstairs had been boarded
up because it had been robbed two days before and the owner had painted on
the wood YES WE'RE OPEN so as not to lose business.

Where do you live? she asked.

There, I said pointing up to the third floor.

You live *there?*

There. I had to look to where she pointed — the third floor, the paint
peeling, wooden bars Papa had nailed on the windows so we wouldn't fall

. You live *there?* The way she said it made me feel like nothing. *There.* I lived *there.* I nodded.

I knew then I had to have a house. A real house. One I could point to. But this isn't it. The house on Mango Street isn't it. For the time being, Mama says. Temporary, says Papa. But I know how those things go.

SANDRA CISNEROS

Hairs

1983

Everybody in our family has different hair. My Papa's hair is like a broom, all up in the air. And me, my hair is lazy. It never obeys barrettes or bands. Carlos' hair is thick and straight. He doesn't need to comb it. Nenny's hair is slippery — slides out of your hand. And Kiki, who is the youngest, has hair like fur.

But my mother's hair, my mother's hair, like little rosettes, like little candy circles all curly and pretty because she pinned it in pincurls all day, sweet to put your nose into when she is holding you, holding you and you feel safe, is the warm smell of bread before you bake it, is the smell when she makes room for you on her side of the bed still warm with her skin, and you sleep near her, the rain outside falling and Papa snoring. The snoring, the rain, and Mama's hair that smells like bread.

SANDRA CISNEROS

My Name

1983

In English my name means hope. In Spanish it means too many letters. It means sadness, it means waiting. It is like the number nine. A muddy color. It is the Mexican records my father plays on Sunday mornings when he is shaving, songs like sobbing.

It was my great-grandmother's name and now it is mine. She was a horse woman too, born like me in the Chinese year of the horse — which is supposed to be bad luck if you're born female — but I think this is a Chinese lie because the Chinese, like the Mexicans, don't like their women strong.

My great-grandmother. I would've liked to have known her, a wild horse of a woman, so wild she wouldn't marry. Until my great-grandfather threw a sack over her head and carried her off. Just like that, as if she were a fancy chandelier. That's the way he did it.

And the story goes she never forgave him. She looked out the window her whole life, the way so many women sit their sadness on an elbow. I wonder if she made the best with what she got or was she sorry because she couldn't be all the things she wanted to be. Esperanza. I have inherited her name, but I don't want to inherit her place by the window.

At school they say my name funny as if the syllables were made out of tin and hurt the roof of your mouth. But in Spanish my name is made out of a softer something, like silver, not quite as thick as sister's name — Magdalena — which is uglier than mine. Magdalena who at least can come home and become Nenny. But I am always Esperanza.

I would like to baptize myself under a new name, a name more like the real me, the one nobody sees. Esperanza as Lisandra or Maritza or Zeze the X. Yes. Something like Zeze the X will do.

SANDRA CISNEROS

The Monkey Garden   1983

The monkey doesn't live there anymore. The monkey moved — to Kentucky — and took his people with him. And I was glad because I couldn't listen anymore to his wild screaming at night, the twangy yakkety-yak of the people who owned him. The green metal cage, the porcelain table top, the family that spoke like guitars. Monkey, family, table. All gone.

And it was then we took over the garden we had been afraid to go into when the monkey screamed and showed its yellow teeth.

There were sunflowers big as flowers on Mars and thick cockscombs bleeding the deep red fringe of theater curtains. There were dizzy bees and bow-tied fruit flies turning somersaults and humming in the air. Sweet sweet peach trees. Thorn roses and thistle and pears. Weeds like so many squinty-eyed stars and brush that made your ankles itch and itch until you washed with soap and water. There were big green apples hard as knees. And everywhere the sleepy smell of rotting wood, damp earth and dusty hollyhocks thick and perfumy like the blue-blond hair of the dead.

Yellow spiders ran when we turned rocks over and pale worms blind and afraid of light rolled over in their sleep. Poke a stick in the sandy soil and a few blue-skinned beetles would appear, an avenue of ants, so many crusty lady bugs. This was a garden, a wonderful thing to look at in the spring. But bit by bit, after the monkey left, the garden began to take over itself. Flowers stopped obeying the little bricks that kept them from growing beyond their paths. Weeds mixed in. Dead cars appeared overnight like mushrooms. First one and then another and then a pale blue pickup with the front windshield missing. Before you knew it, the monkey garden became filled with sleepy cars.

Things had a way of disappearing in the garden, as if the garden itself ate them, or, as if with its old-man memory, it put them away and forgot them. Nenny found a dollar and a dead mouse between two rocks in the stone wall where the morning glories climbed, and once when we were playing hide and seek, Eddie Vargas laid his head beneath a hibiscus tree and fell asleep there like a Rip Van Winkle until somebody remembered he was in the game and went back to look for him.

This, I suppose, was the reason why we went there. Far away from where our mothers could find us. We and a few old dogs who lived inside the empty cars. We made a club-house once on the back of that old blue pickup.

And besides, we liked to jump from the roof of one car to another and pretend they were giant mushrooms.

Somebody started the lie that the monkey garden had been there before anything. We liked to think the garden could hide things for a thousand years. There beneath the roots of soggy flowers were the bones of murdered pirates and dinosaurs, the eye of a unicorn turned to coal.

This is where I wanted to die and where I tried one day but not even the monkey garden would have me. It was the last day I would go there.

Who was it that said I was getting too old to play the games? Who was it I didn't listen to? I only remember that when the others ran, I wanted to run too, up and down and through the monkey garden, fast as the boys, not like Sally who screamed if she got her stockings muddy.

I said, Sally, come on, but she wouldn't. She stayed by the curb talking to Tito and his friends. Play with the kids if you want, she said, I'm staying here. She could be stuck-up like that if she wanted to, so I just left.

It was her own fault too. When I got back Sally was pretending to be mad . . . something about the boys having stolen her keys. Please give them back to me, she said punching the nearest one with a soft fist. They were laughing. She was too. It was a joke I didn't get.

I wanted to go back with the other kids who were still jumping on cars, still chasing each other through the garden, but Sally had her own game.

One of the boys invented the rules. One of Tito's friends said you can't get the keys back unless you kiss us and Sally pretended to be mad at first but she said yes. It was that simple.

I don't know why, but something inside me wanted to throw a stick. Something wanted to say no when I watched Sally going into the garden with Tito's buddies all grinning. It was just a kiss, that's all. A kiss for each one. So what, she said.

Only how come I felt angry inside. Like something wasn't right. Sally went behind that old blue pickup to kiss the boys and get her keys back, and I ran up three flights of stairs to where Tito lived. His mother was ironing shirts. She was sprinkling water on them from an empty pop bottle and smoking a cigarette.

Your son and his friends stole Sally's keys and now they won't give them back unless she kisses them and right now they're making her kiss them, I said all out of breath from the three flights of stairs.

Those kids, she said, not looking up from her ironing.

That's all?

What do you want me to do, she said, call the cops? And kept on ironing.

I looked at her a long time, but couldn't think of anything to say, and ran back down the three flights to the garden where Sally needed to be saved. I took three big sticks and a brick and figured this was enough.

But when I got there Sally said go home. Those boys said, leave us alone. I felt stupid with my brick. They all looked at me as if *I* was the one that was crazy and made me feel ashamed.

And then I don't know why but I had to run away. I had to hide myself at the other end of the garden, in the jungle part, under a tree that wouldn't mind if I lay down and cried a long time. I closed my eyes like tight stars so that I wouldn't, but I did. My face felt hot. Everything inside hiccupped.

I read somewhere in India there are priests who can will their heart to stop beating. I wanted to will my blood to stop, my heart to quit its pumping. I wanted to be dead, to turn into the rain, my eyes melt into the ground like two black snails. I wished and wished. I closed my eyes and willed it, but when I got up my dress was green and I had a headache.

I looked at my feet in their white socks and ugly round shoes. They seemed far away. They didn't seem to be my feet anymore. And the garden that had been such a good place to play didn't seem mine either.

SANDRA CISNEROS

Mango Says Goodbye Sometimes   *1983*

I like to tell stories. I tell them inside my head. I tell them after the mailman says, Here's your mail. Here's your mail he said.

I make a story for my life, for each step my brown shoe takes. I say, "And so she trudged up the wooden stairs, her sad brown shoes taking her to the house she never liked."

I like to tell stories. I am going to tell you a story about a girl who didn't want to belong.

We didn't always live on Mango Street. Before that we lived on Loomis on the third floor, and before that we lived on Keeler. Before Keeler it was Paulina, but what I remember most is Mango Street, sad red house, the house I belong but do not belong to.

I put it down on paper and then the ghost does not ache so much. I write it down and Mango says goodbye sometimes. She does not hold me with both arms. She sets me free.

One day I will pack my bags of books and paper. One day I will say goodbye to Mango. I am too strong for her to keep me here forever. One day I will go away.

Friends and neighbors will say, What happened to that Esperanza? Where did she go with all those books and paper? Why did she march so far away?

They will not know I have gone away to come back. For the ones I left behind. For the ones who cannot out.

တ္တ

STEPHEN CRANE (1871–1900) *wrote some of the most memorable fiction and poetry ever created by an American, publishing fourteen books in his short lifetime. The poet John Berryman, who wrote a biography of Crane, observed the essential truth about him: "Crane was a writer and nothing else: a man alone in a room with the English language, trying to get human feelings right." Crane's style in his short* *stories is as intensely personal as Edgar Allan Poe's or Nathaniel Hawthorne's, but he did not use the techniques of fantasy and allegory. "His eyes remained wide open on his world," according to Berryman. "He was almost illusionless, whether about his subjects or himself. Perhaps his sole illusion was the heroic one; and not even this, especially if he was concerned in it himself as a man, escaped his irony."*

Crane was born in Newark, New Jersey, the youngest of fourteen children. His father, a Methodist minister, died when Crane was a boy, and his mother supported the family by writing articles for Methodist newspapers and reporting for the New York Tribune and the Philadelphia Press. Crane briefly attended Lafayette College and Syracuse University before going to work in New York City as a freelance journalist. He became interested in life in the Bowery, one of the worst slums in New York, and he used this setting for his novel Maggie: A Girl of the Streets, a work so grimly naturalistic in its portrayal of slum life and so frank in its treatment of sex that Crane had to publish it at his own expense in 1893. Two years later he sold a long story about the Civil War to a syndicate for less than a hundred dollars. That work, The Red Badge of Courage, was such a vivid account of wartime experience — even though Crane had never been in a battle himself — that it established his literary reputation.

In the last five years of his life, before he died of tuberculosis in Germany, Crane traveled extensively as a reporter, first to the American West, then to Florida. He could not keep away from scenes of war or revolution, believing — as did Ernest Hemingway after him — that "the nearer a writer gets to life, the greater he becomes as an artist." Crane was en route to Florida on the steamship Commodore when the ship was wrecked on New Year's Day, 1897. He based one of his finest short stories, "The Open Boat," on what happened to him in a lifeboat with the other survivors. He had first reported the disaster in an article for his newspaper shortly after the shipwreck. Joseph Conrad admired Crane's writing and said of "The Open Boat" that "by the deep and simple humanity of its presentation, [the story] seems somehow to illustrate the essentials of life itself, like a symbolic tale."

RELATED COMMENTARY: *Stephen Crane, "The Sinking of the* Commodore," *page 741.*

STEPHEN CRANE

The Open Boat

1897

**A Tale Intended to Be after the Fact,
Being the Experience of Four Men from
the Sunk Steamer** *Commodore*

I

None of them knew the color of the sky. Their eyes glanced level, and were fastened upon the waves that swept toward them. These waves were of the hue of slate, save for the tops, which were of foaming white, and all of the men knew the colors of the sea. The horizon narrowed and widened, and dipped and rose, and at all times its edge was jagged with waves that seemed thrust up in points like rocks.

Many a man ought to have a bath-tub larger than the boat which here rode upon the sea. These waves were most wrongfully and barbarously abrupt and tall, and each froth-top was a problem in small boat navigation.

The cook squatted in the bottom and looked with both eyes at the six inches of gunwale which separated him from the ocean. His sleeves were rolled over his fat forearms, and the two flaps of his unbuttoned vest dangled as he bent to bail out the boat. Often he said: "Gawd! That was a narrow clip." As he remarked it he invariably gazed eastward over the broken sea.

The oiler, steering with one of the two oars in the boat, sometimes raised himself suddenly to keep clear of water that swirled in over the stern. It was a thin little oar and it seemed often ready to snap.

The correspondent, pulling at the other oar, watched the waves and wondered why he was there.

The injured captain, lying in the bow, was at this time buried in that profound dejection and indifference which comes, temporarily at least, to even the bravest and most enduring when, willy nilly, the firm fails, the army loses, the ship goes down. The mind of the master of a vessel is rooted deep in the timbers of her, though he command for a day or a decade, and this captain had on him the stern impression of a scene in the grays of dawn of seven turned faces, and later a stump of a top-mast with a white ball on it that slashed to and fro at the waves, went low and lower, and down. Thereafter there was something strange in his voice. Although steady, it was deep with mourning, and of a quality beyond oration or tears.

"Keep 'er a little more south, Billie," said he.

" 'A little more south,' sir," said the oiler in the stern.

A seat in this boat was not unlike a seat upon a bucking broncho, and, by the same token, a broncho is not much smaller. The craft pranced and reared, and plunged like an animal. As each wave came, and she rose for it, she seemed like a horse making at a fence outrageously high. The manner of her scramble over these walls of water is a mystic thing, and, moreover, at the top of them were ordinarily these problems in white water, the foam racing down from the summit of each wave, requiring a new leap, and a leap from the air. Then, after scornfully bumping a crest, she would slide, and race, and splash down a long incline and arrive bobbing and nodding in front of the next menace.

A singular disadvantage of the sea lies in the fact that after successfully surmounting one wave you discover that there is another behind it just as important and just as nervously anxious to do something effective in the way of swamping boats. In a ten-foot dingey one can get an idea of the resources of the sea in the line of waves that is not probable to the average experience, which is never at sea in a dingey. As each slaty wall of water approached, it shut all else from the view of the men in the boat, and it was not difficult to imagine that this particular wave was the final outburst of the ocean, the last effort of the grim water. There was a terrible grace in the move of the waves, and they came in silence, save for the snarling of the crests.

In the wan light, the faces of the men must have been gray. Their eyes must have glinted in strange ways as they gazed steadily astern. Viewed from a balcony, the whole thing would doubtlessly have been weirdly picturesque. But the men in the boat had no time to see it, and if they had had leisure there were other things to occupy their minds. The sun swung steadily up the sky, and they knew it was broad day because the color of the sea changed from slate to emerald-green, streaked with amber lights, and the foam was like tumbling snow. The process of the breaking day was unknown to them. They were aware only of this effect upon the color of the waves that rolled toward them.

In disjointed sentences the cook and the correspondent argued as to the difference between a life-saving station and a house of refuge. The cook had said: "There's a house of refuge just north of the Mosquito Inlet Light, and as soon as they see us, they'll come off in their boat and pick us up."

"As soon as who see us?" said the correspondent.

"The crew," said the cook.

"Houses of refuge don't have crews," said the correspondent. "As I understand them, they are only places where clothes and grub are stored for the benefit of shipwrecked people. They don't carry crews."

"Oh, yes, they do," said the cook.

"No, they don't," said the correspondent.

"Well, we're not there yet, anyhow," said the oiler, in the stern.

"Well," said the cook, "perhaps it's not a house of refuge that I'm thinking of as being near Mosquito Inlet Light. Perhaps it's a life-saving station."

"We're not there yet," said the oiler, in the stern.

II

As the boat bounced from the top of each wave, the wind tore through the hair of the hatless men, and as the craft plopped her stern down again the spray slashed past them. The crest of each of these waves was a hill, from the top of which the men surveyed, for a moment, a broad tumultuous expanse, shining and wind-riven. It was probably splendid. It was probably glorious, this play of the free sea, wild with lights of emerald and white and amber.

"Bully good thing it's an on-shore wind," said the cook. "If not where would we be? Wouldn't have a show."

"That's right," said the correspondent.

The busy oiler nodded his assent.

Then the captain, in the bow, chuckled in a way that expressed humor, contempt, tragedy, all in one. "Do you think we've got a show, now, boys?" said he.

Whereupon the three went silent, save for a trifle of hemming and hawing. To express any particular optimism at this time they felt to be childish and stupid, but they all doubtless possessed this sense of the situation in their mind. A young man thinks doggedly at such times. On the other hand, the ethics of their condition was decidedly against any open suggestion of hopelessness. So they were silent.

"Oh, well," said the captain, soothing his children, "we'll get ashore all right."

But there was that in his tone which made them think, so the oiler quoth: "Yes! If this wind holds!"

The cook was bailing. "Yes! If we don't catch hell in the surf."

Canton flannel gulls flew near and far. Sometimes they sat down on the sea, near patches of brown sea-weed that rolled over the waves with a movement like carpets on a line in a gale. The birds sat comfortably in groups, and they were envied by some in the dingey, for the wrath of the sea was no more to them than it was to a covey of prairie chickens a thousand miles inland. Often they came very close and stared at the men with black bead-like eyes. At these times they were uncanny and sinister in their unblinking scrutiny, and the men hooted angrily at them, telling them to be gone. One came, and evidently decided to alight on the top of the captain's head. The bird flew parallel to the boat and did not circle, but made short sidelong jumps in the air in chicken-fashion. His black eyes were wistfully fixed upon the captain's head. "Ugly brute," said the oiler to the bird. "You look as if you were made with a jack-knife." The cook and the correspondent swore darkly at the creature. The captain naturally wished to knock it away with the end of the heavy painter, but he did not dare do it, because anything resembling an emphatic gesture would have capsized this freighted boat, and so with his open hand, the captain gently and carefully waved the gull away. After it had been discouraged from the pursuit the captain breathed easier on account of his hair, and others breathed easier because the bird struck their minds at this time as being somehow gruesome and ominous.

In the meantime the oiler and the correspondent rowed. And also they rowed.

They sat together in the same seat, and each rowed an oar. Then the oiler took both oars; then the correspondent took both oars; then the oiler; then the correspondent. They rowed and they rowed. The very ticklish part of the business was when the time came for the reclining one in the stern to take his turn at the oars. By the very last star of truth, it is easier to steal eggs from under a hen than it was to change seats in the dingey. First the man in the stern slid his hand along the thwart and moved with care, as if he were of Sèvres.° Then the man in the rowing seat slid his hand along the other thwart. It was all done with the most extraordinary care. As the two sidled past each other, the whole party kept watchful eyes on the coming wave, and the captain cried: "Look out now! Steady there!"

The brown mats of sea-weed that appeared from time to time were like islands, bits of earth. They were travelling, apparently, neither one way nor the other. They were, to all intents, stationary. They informed the men in the boat that it was making progress slowly toward the land.

The captain, rearing cautiously in the bow, after the dingey soared on a great swell, said that he had seen the light-house at Mosquito Inlet. Presently the cook remarked that he had seen it. The correspondent was at the oars, then, and for some reason he too wished to look at the light-house, but his back was toward the far shore and the waves were important, and for some time he could not seize an opportunity to turn his head. But at last there came

---

Sèvres: A delicate French porcelain.

a wave more gentle than the others, and when at the crest of it he swiftly scoured the western horizon.

"See it?" said the captain.

"No," said the correspondent, slowly, "I didn't see anything."

"Look again," said the captain. He pointed. "It's exactly in that direction."

At the top of another wave, the correspondent did as he was bid, and this time his eyes chanced on a small still thing on the edge of the swaying horizon. It was precisely like the point of a pin. It took an anxious eye to find a light-house so tiny.

"Think we'll make it, Captain?"

"If this wind holds and the boat don't swamp, we can't do much else," said the captain.

The little boat, lifted by each towering sea, and splashed viciously by the crests, made progress that in the absence of sea-weed was not apparent to those in her. She seemed just a wee thing wallowing, miraculously, top-up, at the mercy of five oceans. Occasionally, a great spread of water, like white flames, swarmed into her.

"Bail her, cook," said the captain, serenely.

"All right, Captain," said the cheerful cook.

III

It would be difficult to describe the subtle brotherhood of men that was here established on the seas. No one said that it was so. No one mentioned it. But it dwelt in the boat, and each man felt it warm him. They were a captain, an oiler, a cook, and a correspondent, and they were friends, friends in a more curiously iron-bound degree than may be common. The hurt captain, lying against the water-jar in the bow, spoke always in a low voice and calmly, but he could never command a more ready and swiftly obedient crew than the motley three of the dingey. It was more than a mere recognition of what was best for the common safety. There was surely in it a quality that was personal and heartfelt. And after this devotion to the commander of the boat there was this comradeship that the correspondent, for instance, who had been taught to be cynical of men, knew even at the time was the best experience of his life. But no one said that it was so. No one mentioned it.

"I wish we had a sail," remarked the captain. "We might try my overcoat on the end of an oar and give you two boys a chance to rest." So the cook and the correspondent held the mast and spread wide the overcoat. The oiler steered, and the little boat made good way with her new rig. Sometimes the oiler had to scull sharply to keep a sea from breaking into the boat, but otherwise sailing was a success.

Meanwhile the light-house had been growing slowly larger. It had now almost assumed color, and appeared like a little gray shadow on the sky. The man at the oars could not be prevented from turning his head rather often to try for a glimpse of this little gray shadow.

At last, from the top of each wave the men in the tossing boat could see land. Even as the light-house was an upright shadow on the sky, this land seemed but a long black shadow on the sea. It certainly was thinner than paper. "We must be about opposite New Smyrna," said the cook, who had coasted this shore often in schooners. "Captain, by the way, I believe they abandoned that life-saving station there about a year ago."

"Did they?" said the captain.

The wind slowly died away. The cook and the correspondent were not now obliged to slave in order to hold high the oar. But the waves continued their old impetuous swooping at the dingey, and the little craft, no longer under way, struggled woundily over them. The oiler or the correspondent took the oars again.

Shipwrecks are *apropos* of nothing. If men could only train for them and have them occur when the men had reached pink condition, there would be less drowning at sea. Of the four in the dingey none had slept any time worth mentioning for two days and two nights previous to embarking in the dingey, and in the excitement of clambering about the deck of a foundering ship they had also forgotten to eat heartily.

For these reasons, and for others, neither the oiler nor the correspondent was fond of rowing at this time. The correspondent wondered ingenuously how in the name of all that was sane could there be people who thought it amusing to row a boat. It was not an amusement; it was a diabolical punishment, and even a genius of mental aberrations could never conclude that it was anything but a horror to the muscles and a crime against the back. He mentioned to the boat in general how the amusement of rowing struck him, and the weary-faced oiler smiled in full sympathy. Previously to the foundering, by the way, the oiler had worked double-watch in the engine-room of the ship.

"Take her easy, now, boys," said the captain. "Don't spend yourselves. If we have to run a surf you'll need all your strength, because we'll sure have to swim for it. Take your time."

Slowly the land arose from the sea. From a black line it became a line of black and a line of white — trees and sand. Finally, the captain said that he could make out a house on the shore. "That's the house of refuge, sure," said the cook. "They'll see us before long, and come out after us."

The distant light-house reared high. "The keeper ought to be able to make us out now, if he's looking through a glass," said the captain. "He'll notify the life-saving people."

"None of those other boats could have got ashore to give word of the wreck," said the oiler, in a low voice. "Else the life-boat would be out hunting us."

Slowly and beautifully the land loomed out of the sea. The wind came again. It had veered from the northeast to the southeast. Finally, a new sound struck the ears of the men in the boat. It was the low thunder of the surf on the shore. "We'll never be able to make the light-house now," said the captain. "Swing her head a little more north, Billie."

" 'A little more north,' sir," said the oiler.

Whereupon the little boat turned her nose once more down the wind, and all but the oarsman watched the shore grow. Under the influence of this expansion doubt and direful apprehension were leaving the minds of the men. The management of the boat was still most absorbing, but it could not prevent a quiet cheerfulness. In an hour, perhaps, they would be ashore.

Their back-bones had become thoroughly used to balancing in the boat and they now rode this wild colt of a dingey like circus men. The correspondent thought that he had been drenched to the skin, but happening to feel in the top pocket of his coat, he found therein eight cigars. Four of them were soaked with sea-water; four were perfectly scatheless. After a search, somebody produced three dry matches, and thereupon the four waifs rode impudently in their little boat, and with an assurance of an impending rescue shining in their eyes, puffed at the big cigars and judged well and ill of all men. Everybody took a drink of water.

IV

"Cook," remarked the captain, "there don't seem to be any signs of life about your house of refuge."

"No," replied the cook. "Funny they don't see us!"

A broad stretch of lowly coast lay before the eyes of the men. It was of dunes topped with dark vegetation. The roar of the surf was plain, and sometimes they could see the white lip of a wave as it spun up the beach. A tiny house was blocked out black upon the sky. Southward, the slim light-house lifted its little gray length.

Tide, wind, and waves were swinging the dingey northward. "Funny they don't see us," said the men.

The surf's roar was here dulled, but its tone was, nevertheless, thunderous and mighty. As the boat swam over the great rollers, the men sat listening to this roar. "We'll swamp sure," said everybody.

It is fair to say here that there was not a life-saving station within twenty miles in either direction, but the men did not know this fact and in consequence they made dark and opprobrious remarks concerning the eyesight of the nation's life-savers. Four scowling men sat in the dingey and surpassed records in the invention of epithets.

"Funny they don't see us."

The light-heartedness of a former time had completely faded. To their sharpened minds it was easy to conjure pictures of all kinds of incompetency and blindness and, indeed, cowardice. There was the shore of the populous land, and it was bitter and bitter to them that from it came no sign.

"Well," said the captain, ultimately, "I suppose we'll have to make a try for ourselves. If we stay out here too long, we'll none of us have strength left to swim after the boat swamps."

And so the oiler, who was at the oars, turned the boat straight for the shore. There was a sudden tightening of muscles. There was some thinking.

"If we don't all get ashore — " said the captain. "If we don't all get ashore, I suppose you fellows know where to send news of my finish?"

They then briefly exchanged some addresses and admonitions. As for the reflections of the men, there was a great deal of rage in them. Perchance they might be formulated thus: "If I am going to be drowned — if I am going to be drowned — if I am going to be drowned, why, in the name of the seven mad gods who rule the sea, was I allowed to come thus far and contemplate sand and trees? Was I brought here merely to have my nose dragged away as I was about to nibble the sacred cheese of life? It is preposterous. If this old ninny-woman, Fate, cannot do better than this, she should be deprived of the management of men's fortunes. She is an old hen who knows not her intention. If she has decided to drown me, why did she not do it in the beginning and save me all this trouble. The whole affair is absurd. . . . But, no, she cannot mean to drown me. She dare not drown me. She cannot drown me. Not after all this work." Afterward the man might have had an impulse to shake his fist at the clouds. "Just you drown me, now, and then hear what I call you!"

The billows that came at this time were more formidable. They seemed always just about to break and roll over the little boat in a turmoil of foam. There was a preparatory and long growl in the speech of them. No mind unused to the sea would have concluded that the dingey could ascend these sheer heights in time. The shore was still afar. The oiler was a wily surfman. "Boys," he said, swiftly, "she won't live three minutes more and we're too far out to swim. Shall I take her to sea again, Captain?"

"Yes! Go ahead!" said the captain.

This oiler, by a series of quick miracles, and fast and steady oarsmanship, turned the boat in the middle of the surf and took her safely to sea again.

There was a considerable silence as the boat bumped over the furrowed sea to deeper water. Then somebody in gloom spoke. "Well, anyhow, they must have seen us from the shore by now."

The gulls went in slanting flight up the wind toward the gray desolate east. A squall, marked by dingy clouds, and clouds brick-red, like smoke from a burning building, appeared from the southeast.

"What do you think of those life-saving people? Ain't they peaches?"

"Funny they haven't seen us."

"Maybe they think we're out here for sport! Maybe they think we're fishin'. Maybe they think we're damned fools."

It was a long afternoon. A changed tide tried to force them southward, but wind and wave said northward. Far ahead, where coast-line, sea, and sky formed their mighty angle, there were little dots which seemed to indicate a city on the shore.

"St. Augustine?"

The captain shook his head. "Too near Mosquito Inlet."

And the oiler rowed, and then the correspondent rowed. Then the oiler rowed. It was a weary business. The human back can become the seat of more aches and pains than are registered in books for the composite anatomy of a regiment. It is a limited area, but it can become the theatre of innumerable muscular conflicts, tangles, wrenches, knots, and other comforts.

"Did you ever like to row, Billie?" asked the correspondent.

"No," said the oiler, "Hang it."

When one exchanged the rowing-seat for a place in the bottom of the

boat, he suffered a bodily depression that caused him to be careless of everything save an obligation to wiggle one finger. There was cold sea-water swash-
ing to and fro in the boat, and he lay in it. His head, pillowed on a thwart, was
within an inch of the swirl of a wave crest, and sometimes a particularly obstreperous sea came in-board and drenched him once more. But these matters
did not annoy him. It is almost certain that if the boat had capsized he would
have tumbled comfortably out upon the ocean as if he felt sure that it was a
great soft mattress.

"Look! There's a man on the shore!"

"Where?"

"There! See 'im? See 'im?"

"Yes, sure! He's walking along."

"Now he's stopped. Look! He's facing us!"

"He's waving at us!"

"So he is! By thunder!"

"Ah, now, we're all right! There'll be a boat out here for us in half an
hour."

"He's going on. He's running. He's going up to that house there."

The remote beach seemed lower than the sea, and it required a searching
glance to discern the little black figure. The captain saw a floating stick and
they rowed to it. A bath-towel was by some weird chance in the boat, and, tying this on the stick, the captain waved it. The oarsman did not dare turn his
head, so he was obliged to ask questions.

"What's he doing now?"

"He's standing still again. He's looking, I think. . . . There he goes again.
Toward the house. . . . Now he's stopped again."

"Is he waving at us?"

"No, not now! He was, though."

"Look! There comes another man!"

"He's running."

"Look at him go, would you."

"Why, he's on a bicycle. Now he's met the other man. They're both waving at us. Look!"

"There comes something up the beach."

"What the devil is that thing?"

"Why, it looks like a boat."

"Why, certainly it's a boat."

"No, it's on wheels."

"Yes, so it is. Well, that must be the life-boat. They drag them along shore
on a wagon."

"That's the life-boat, sure."

"No, by, it's — it's an omnibus."

"I tell you it's a life-boat."

"It is not! It's an omnibus. I can see it plain. See? One of those big hotel
omnibuses."

"By thunder, you're right. It's an omnibus, sure as fate. What do you

suppose they are doing with an omnibus? Maybe they are going around collecting the life-crew, hey?"

"That's it, likely. Look! There's a fellow waving a little black flag. He's
standing on the steps of the omnibus. There come those other two fellows.
Now they're all talking together. Look at the fellow with the flag. Maybe he
ain't waving it!"

"That ain't a flag, is it? That's his coat. Why, certainly, that's his coat."

"So it is. It's his coat. He's taken it off and is waving it around his head.
But would you look at him swing it!"

"Oh, say, there isn't any life-saving station there. That's just a winter resort hotel omnibus that has brought over some of the boarders to see us
drown."

"What's that idiot with the coat mean? What's he signaling, anyhow?"

"It looks as if he were trying to tell us to go north. There must be a life-
saving station up there."

"No! He thinks we're fishing. Just giving us a merry hand. See? Ah,
there, Willie."

"Well, I wish I could make something out of those signals. What do you
suppose he means?"

"He don't mean anything. He's just playing."

"Well, if he'd just signal us to try the surf again, or to go to sea and wait,
or go north, or go south, or go to hell — there would be some reason in it. But
look at him. He just stands there and keeps his coat revolving like a wheel. The
ass!"

"There come more people."

"Now there's quite a mob. Look! Isn't that a boat?"

"Where? Oh, I see where you mean. No, that's no boat."

"That fellow is still waving his coat."

"He must think we like to see him do that. Why don't he quit it. It don't
mean anything."

"I don't know. I think he is trying to make us go north. It must be that
there's a life-saving station there somewhere."

"Say, he ain't tired yet. Look at 'im wave."

"Wonder how long he can keep that up. He's been revolving his coat
ever since he caught sight of us. He's an idiot. Why aren't they getting men to
bring a boat out. A fishing boat — one of those big yawls — could come out
here all right. Why don't he do something?"

"Oh, it's all right, now."

"They'll have a boat out here for us in less than no time, now that
they've seen us."

A faint yellow tone came into the sky over the low land. The shadows on
the sea slowly deepened. The wind bore coldness with it, and the men began
to shiver.

"Holy smoke!" said one, allowing his voice to express his impious
mood, "if we keep on monkeying out here! If we've got to flounder out here
all night!"

"Oh, we'll never have to stay here all night! Don't you worry. They've seen us now, and it won't be long before they'll come chasing out after us."

The shore grew dusky. The man waving a coat blended gradually into this gloom, and it swallowed in the same manner the omnibus and the group of people. The spray, when it dashed uproariously over the side, made the voyagers shrink and swear like men who were being branded.

"I'd like to catch the chump who waved the coat. I feel like soaking him one, just for luck."

"Why? What did he do?"

"Oh, nothing, but then he seemed so damned cheerful."

In the meantime the oiler rowed, and then the correspondent rowed, and then the oiler rowed. Gray-faced and bowed forward, they mechanically, turn by turn, plied the leaden oars. The form of the light-house had vanished from the southern horizon, but finally a pale star appeared, just lifting from the sea. The streaked saffron in the west passed before the all-merging darkness, and the sea to the east was black. The land had vanished, and was expressed only by the low and drear thunder of the surf.

"If I am going to be drowned — if I am going to be drowned — if I am going to be drowned, why, in the name of the seven mad gods who rule the sea, was I allowed to come thus far and contemplate sand and trees? Was I brought here merely to have my nose dragged away as I was about to nibble the sacred cheese of life?"

The patient captain, drooped over the water-jar, was sometimes obliged to speak to the oarsman.

"Keep her head up! Keep her head up!"

" 'Keep her head up,' sir." The voices were weary and low.

This was surely a quiet evening. All save the oarsman lay heavily and listlessly in the boat's bottom. As for him, his eyes were just capable of noting the tall black waves that swept forward in a most sinister silence, save for an occasional subdued growl of a crest.

The cook's head was on a thwart, and he looked without interest at the water under his nose. He was deep in other scenes. Finally he spoke. "Billie," he murmured, dreamfully, "what kind of pie do you like best?"

V

"Pie," said the oiler and the correspondent, agitatedly. "Don't talk about those things, blast you!"

"Well," said the cook, "I was just thinking about ham sandwiches, and — "

A night on the sea in an open boat is a long night. As darkness settled finally, the shine of the light, lifting from the sea in the south, changed to full gold. On the northern horizon a new light appeared, a small bluish gleam on the edge of the waters. These two lights were the furniture of the world. Otherwise there was nothing but waves.

Two men huddled in the stern, and distances were so magnificent in the dingey that the rower was enabled to keep his feet partly warmed by thrusting them under his companions. Their legs indeed extended far under the rowing-seat until they touched the feet of the captain forward. Sometimes, despite the efforts of the tired oarsman, a wave came piling into the boat, an icy wave of the night, and the chilling water soaked them anew. They would twist their bodies for a moment and groan, and sleep the dead sleep once more, while the water in the boat gurgled about them as the craft rocked.

The plan of the oiler and the correspondent was for one to row until he lost the ability, and then arouse the other from his sea-water couch in the bottom of the boat.

The oiler plied the oars until his head drooped forward, and the overpowering sleep blinded him. And he rowed yet afterward. Then he touched a man in the bottom of the boat, and called his name. "Will you spell me for a little while?" he said, meekly.

"Sure, Billie," said the correspondent, awakening and dragging himself to a sitting position. They exchanged places carefully, and the oiler, cuddling down in the sea-water at the cook's side, seemed to go to sleep instantly.

The particular violence of the sea had ceased. The waves came without snarling. The obligation of the man at the oars was to keep the boat headed so that the tilt of the rollers would not capsize her, and to preserve her from filling when the crests rushed past. The black waves were silent and hard to be seen in the darkness. Often one was almost upon the boat before the oarsman was aware.

In a low voice the correspondent addressed the captain. He was not sure that the captain was awake, although this iron man seemed to be always awake. "Captain, shall I keep her making for that light north, sir?"

The same steady voice answered him. "Yes. Keep it about two points off the port bow."

The cook had tied a life-belt around himself in order to get even the warmth which this clumsy cork contrivance could donate, and he seemed almost stove-like when a rower, whose teeth invariably chattered wildly as soon as he ceased his labor, dropped down to sleep.

The correspondent, as he rowed, looked down at the two men sleeping under foot. The cook's arm was around the oiler's shoulders, and, with their fragmentary clothing and haggard faces, they were the babes of the sea, a grotesque rendering of the old babes in the wood.

Later he must have grown stupid at his work, for suddenly there was a growling of water, and a crest came with a roar and a swash into the boat, and it was a wonder that it did not set the cook afloat in his life-belt. The cook continued to sleep, but the oiler sat up, blinking his eyes and shaking with the new cold.

"Oh, I'm awful sorry, Billie," said the correspondent, contritely.

"That's all right, old boy," said the oiler, and lay down again and was asleep.

Presently it seemed that even the captain dozed, and the correspondent thought that he was the one man afloat on all the oceans. The wind had a voice as it came over the waves, and it was sadder than the end.

There was a long, loud swishing astern of the boat, and a gleaming trail of phosphorescence, like blue flame, was furrowed on the black waters. It might have been made by a monstrous knife.

Then there came a stillness, while the correspondent breathed with the open mouth and looked at the sea.

Suddenly there was another swish and another long flash of bluish light, and this time it was alongside the boat, and might almost have been reached with an oar. The correspondent saw an enormous fin speed like a shadow through the water, hurling the crystalline spray and leaving the long glowing trail.

The correspondent looked over his shoulder at the captain. His face was hidden, and he seemed to be asleep. He looked at the babes of the sea. They certainly were asleep. So, being bereft of sympathy, he leaned a little way to one side and swore softly into the sea.

But the thing did not then leave the vicinity of the boat. Ahead or astern, on one side or the other, at intervals long or short, fled the long sparkling streak, and there was to be heard the whirroo of the dark fin. The speed and power of the thing were greatly to be admired. It cut the water like a gigantic and keen projectile.

The presence of this biding thing did not affect the man with the same horror that it would if he had been a picnicker. He simply looked at the sea dully and swore in an undertone.

Nevertheless, it is true that he did not wish to be alone with the thing. He wished one of his companions to awaken by chance and keep him company with it. But the captain hung motionless over the water-jar and the oiler and the cook in the bottom of the boat were plunged in slumber.

VI

"If I am going to be drowned — if I am going to be drowned — if I am going to be drowned, why, in the name of the seven mad gods who rule the sea, was I allowed to come thus far and contemplate sand and trees?"

During this dismal night, it may be remarked that a man would conclude that it was really the intention of the seven mad gods to drown him, despite the abominable injustice of it. For it was certainly an abominable injustice to drown a man who had worked so hard, so hard. The man felt it would be a crime most unnatural. Other people had drowned at sea since galleys swarmed with painted sails, but still —

When it occurs to a man that nature does not regard him as important, and that she feels she would not maim the universe by disposing of him, he at first wishes to throw bricks at the temple, and he hates deeply the fact that there are no bricks and no temples. Any visible expression of nature would surely be pelleted with his jeers.

Then, if there be no tangible thing to hoot he feels, perhaps, the desire to confront a personification and indulge in pleas, bowed to one knee, and with hands supplicant, saying: "Yes, but I love myself."

A high cold star on a winter's night is the word he feels that she says to him. Thereafter he knows the pathos of his situation.

The men in the dingey had not discussed these matters, but each had, no doubt, reflected upon them in silence and according to his mind. There was seldom any expression upon their faces save the general one of complete weariness. Speech was devoted to the business of the boat.

To chime the notes of his emotion, a verse mysteriously entered the correspondent's head. He had even forgotten that he had forgotten this verse, but it suddenly was in his mind.

> A soldier of the Legion lay dying in Algiers,
> There was lack of woman's nursing, there was dearth of woman's tears;
> But a comrade stood beside him, and he took that comrade's hand,
> And he said: "I never more shall see my own, my native land."

In his childhood, the correspondent had been made acquainted with the fact that a soldier of the Legion lay dying in Algiers, but he had never regarded it as important. Myriads of his school-fellows had informed him of the soldier's plight, but the dinning had naturally ended by making him perfectly indifferent. He had never considered it his affair that a soldier of the Legion lay dying in Algiers, nor had it appeared to him as a matter for sorrow. It was less to him than the breaking of a pencil's point.

Now, however, it quaintly came to him as a human, living thing. It was no longer merely a picture of a few throes in the breast of a poet, meanwhile drinking tea and warming his feet at the grate; it was an actuality — stern, mournful, and fine.

The correspondent plainly saw the soldier. He lay on the sand with his feet out straight and still. While his pale left hand was upon his chest in an attempt to thwart the going of his life, the blood came between his fingers. In the far Algerian distance, a city of low square forms was set against a sky that was faint with the last sunset hues. The correspondent, plying the oars and dreaming of the slow and slower movements of the lips of the soldier, was moved by a profound and perfectly impersonal comprehension. He was sorry for the soldier of the Legion who lay dying in Algiers.

The thing which had followed the boat and waited had evidently grown bored at the delay. There was no longer to be heard the slash of the cut-water, and there was no longer the flame of the long trail. The light in the north still glimmered, but it was apparently no nearer to the boat. Sometimes the boom of the surf rang in the correspondent's ears, and he turned the craft seaward then and rowed harder. Southward, some one had evidently built a watch-fire on the beach. It was too low and too far to be seen, but it made a shimmering, roseate reflection upon the bluff back of it, and this could be discerned from the boat. The wind came stronger, and sometimes a wave suddenly raged out like a mountain-cat and there was to be seen the sheen and sparkle of a broken crest.

The captain, in the bow, moved on his water-jar and sat erect. "Pretty long night," he observed to the correspondent. He looked at the shore. "Those life-saving people take their time."

"Did you see that shark playing around?"

"Yes, I saw him. He was a big fellow, all right."

"Wish I had known you were awake."

Later the correspondent spoke into the bottom of the boat.

"Billie!" There was a slow and gradual disentanglement. "Billie, will you spell me?"

"Sure," said the oiler.

As soon as the correspondent touched the cold comfortable sea-water in the bottom of the boat, and had huddled close to the cook's life-belt he was deep in sleep, despite the fact that his teeth played all the popular airs. This sleep was so good to him that it was but a moment before he heard a voice call his name in a tone that demonstrated the last stages of exhaustion. "Will you spell me?"

"Sure, Billie."

The light in the north had mysteriously vanished, but the correspondent took his course from the wide-awake captain.

Later in the night they took the boat farther out to sea, and the captain directed the cook to take one oar at the stern and keep the boat facing the seas. He was to call out if he should hear the thunder of the surf. This plan enabled the oiler and the correspondent to get respite together. "We'll give those boys a chance to get into shape again," said the captain. They curled down and, after a few preliminary chatterings and trembles, slept once more the dead sleep. Neither knew they had bequeathed to the cook the company of another shark, or perhaps the same shark.

As the boat caroused on the waves, spray occasionally bumped over the side and gave them a fresh soaking, but this had no power to break their repose. The ominous slash of the wind and the water affected them as it would have affected mummies.

"Boys," said the cook, with the notes of every reluctance in his voice, "she's drifted in pretty close. I guess one of you had better take her to sea again." The correspondent, aroused, heard the crash of the toppled crests.

As he was rowing, the captain gave him some whiskey and water, and this steadied the chills out of him. "If I ever get ashore and anybody shows me even a photograph of an oar — "

At last there was a short conversation.

"Billie. . . . Billie, will you spell me?"

"Sure," said the oiler.

VII

When the correspondent again opened his eyes, the sea and the sky were each of the gray hue of the dawning. Later, carmine and gold was painted upon the waters. The morning appeared finally, in its splendor, with a sky of pure blue, and the sunlight flamed on the tips of the waves.

On the distant dunes were set many little black cottages, and a tall white wind-mill reared above them. No man, nor dog, nor bicycle appeared on the beach. The cottages might have formed a deserted village.

The voyagers scanned the shore. A conference was held in the boat.

"Well," said the captain, "if no help is coming, we might better try a run through the surf right away. If we stay out here much longer we will be too weak to do anything for ourselves at all." The others silently acquiesced in this reasoning. The boat was headed for the beach. The correspondent wondered if none ever ascended the tall wind-tower, and if then they never looked seaward. This tower was a giant, standing with its back to the plight of the ants. It represented in a degree, to the correspondent, the serenity of nature amid the struggles of the individual — nature in the wind, and nature in the vision of men. She did not seem cruel to him then, nor beneficent, nor treacherous, nor wise. But she was indifferent, flatly indifferent. It is, perhaps, plausible that a man in this situation, impressed with the unconcern of the universe, should see the innumerable flaws of his life and have them taste wickedly in his mind and wish for another chance. A distinction between right and wrong seems absurdly clear to him, then, in this new ignorance of the grave-edge, and he understands that if he were given another opportunity he would mend his conduct and his words, and be better and brighter during an introduction, or at a tea.

"Now, boys," said the captain, "she is going to swamp sure. All we can do is to work her in as far as possible, and then when she swamps, pile out and scramble for the beach. Keep cool now, and don't jump until she swamps sure."

The oiler took the oars. Over his shoulders he scanned the surf. "Captain," he said, "I think I'd better bring her about, and keep her head-on to the seas and back her in."

"All right, Billie," said the captain. "Back her in." The oiler swung the boat then and, seated in the stern, the cook and the correspondent were obliged to look over their shoulders to contemplate the lonely and indifferent shore.

The monstrous inshore rollers heaved the boat high until the men were again enabled to see the white sheets of water scudding up the slanted beach. "We won't get in very close," said the captain. Each time a man could wrest his attention from the rollers, he turned his glance toward the shore, and in the expression of the eyes during this contemplation there was a singular quality. The correspondent, observing the others, knew that they were not afraid, but the full meaning of their glances was shrouded.

As for himself, he was too tired to grapple fundamentally with the fact. He tried to coerce his mind into thinking of it, but the mind was dominated at this time by the muscles, and the muscles said they did not care. It merely occurred to him that if he should drown it would be a shame.

There were no hurried words, no pallor, no plain agitation. The men simply looked at the shore. "Now, remember to get well clear of the boat when you jump," said the captain.

Seaward the crest of a roller suddenly fell with a thunderous crash, and the long white comber came roaring down upon the boat.

"Steady now," said the captain. The men were silent. They turned their eyes from the shore to the comber and waited. The boat slid up the incline, leaped at the furious top, bounced over it, and swung down the long back of the wave. Some water had been shipped and the cook bailed it out.

But the next crest crashed also. The tumbling boiling flood of white water caught the boat and whirled it almost perpendicular. Water swarmed in from all sides. The correspondent had his hands on the gunwale at this time, and when the water entered at that place he swiftly withdrew his fingers, as if he objected to wetting them.

The little boat, drunken with this weight of water, reeled and snuggled deeper into the sea.

"Bail her out, cook! Bail her out," said the captain.

"All right, Captain," said the cook.

"Now boys, the next one will do for us, sure," said the oiler. "Mind to jump clear of the boat."

The third wave moved forward, huge, furious, implacable. It fairly swallowed the dingey, and almost simultaneously the men tumbled into the sea. A piece of life-belt had lain in the bottom of the boat, and as the correspondent went overboard he held this to his chest with his left hand.

The January water was icy, and he reflected immediately that it was colder than he had expected to find it off the coast of Florida. This appeared to his dazed mind as a fact important enough to be noted at the time. The coldness of the water was sad; it was tragic. This fact was somehow so mixed and confused with his opinion of his own situation that it seemed almost a proper reason for tears. The water was cold.

When he came to the surface he was conscious of little but the noisy water. Afterward he saw his companions in the sea. The oiler was ahead in the race. He was swimming strongly and rapidly. Off to the correspondent's left, the cook's great white and corked back bulged out of the water, and in the rear the captain was hanging with his one good hand to the keel of the overturned dingey.

There is a certain immovable quality to a shore, and the correspondent wondered at it amid the confusion of the sea.

It seemed also very attractive, but the correspondent knew that it was a long journey, and he paddled leisurely. The piece of life-preserver lay under him, and sometimes he whirled down the incline of a wave as if he were on a hand-sled.

But finally he arrived at a place in the sea where travel was beset with difficulty. He did not pause swimming to inquire what manner of current had caught him, but there his progress ceased. The shore was set before him like a bit of scenery on a stage, and he looked at it and understood with his eyes each detail of it.

As the cook passed, much farther to the left, the captain was calling to him, "Turn over on your back, cook! Turn over on your back and use the oar."

"All right, sir." The cook turned on his back, and, paddling with an oar, went ahead as if he were a canoe.

Presently the boat also passed to the left of the correspondent with the captain clinging with one hand to the keel. He would have appeared like a man raising himself to look over a board fence, if it were not for the extraordinary gymnastics of the boat. The correspondent marvelled that the captain could still hold to it.

They passed on, nearer to shore — the oiler, the cook, the captain — and following them went the water-jar, bouncing gayly over the seas.

The correspondent remained in the grip of this strange new enemy — a current. The shore, with its white slope of sand and its green bluff, topped with little silent cottages, was spread like a picture before him. It was very near to him then, but he was impressed as one who in a gallery looks at a scene from Brittany or Holland.

He thought: "I am going to drown? Can it be possible? Can it be possible? Can it be possible?" Perhaps an individual must consider his own death to be the final phenomenon of nature.

But later a wave perhaps whirled him out of his small deadly current, for he found suddenly that he could again make progress toward the shore. Later still, he was aware that the captain, clinging with one hand to the keel of the dingey, had his face turned away from the shore and toward him, and was calling his name. "Come to the boat! Come to the boat!"

In his struggle to reach the captain and the boat, he reflected that when one gets properly wearied, drowning must really be a comfortable arrangement, a cessation of hostilities accompanied by a large degree of relief, and he was glad of it, for the main thing in his mind for some moments had been the horror of the temporary agony. He did not wish to be hurt.

Presently he saw a man running along the shore. He was undressing with most remarkable speed. Coat, trousers, shirt, everything flew magically off him.

"Come to the boat," called the captain.

"All right, Captain." As the correspondent paddled, he saw the captain let himself down to bottom and leave the boat. Then the correspondent performed his one little marvel of the voyage. A large wave caught him and flung him with ease and supreme speed completely over the boat and far beyond it. It struck him even then as an event in gymnastics, and a true miracle of the sea. An overturned boat in the surf is not a plaything to a swimming man.

The correspondent arrived in water that reached only to his waist, but his condition did not enable him to stand for more than a moment. Each wave knocked him into a heap, and the under-tow pulled at him.

Then he saw the man who had been running and undressing, and undressing and running, come bounding into the water. He dragged ashore the cook, and then waded toward the captain, but the captain waved him away, and sent him to the correspondent. He was naked, naked as a tree in winter, but a halo was about his head, and he shone like a saint. He gave a strong pull, and a long drag, and a bully heave at the correspondent's hand. The correspondent, schooled in the minor formulae, said: "Thanks, old man." But suddenly the man cried: "What's that?" He pointed a swift finger. The correspondent said: "Go."

In the shallows, face downward, lay the oiler. His forehead touched sand that was periodically, between each wave, clear of the sea.

The correspondent did not know all that transpired afterward. When he achieved safe ground he fell, striking the sand with each particular part of his body. It was as if he had dropped from a roof, but the thud was grateful to him.

It seems that instantly the beach was populated with men with blankets, clothes, and flasks, and women with coffee-pots and all the remedies sacred to their minds. The welcome of the land to the men from the sea was warm and generous, but a still and dripping shape was carried slowly up the beach, and the land's welcome for it could only be the different and sinister hospitality of the grave.

When it came night, the white waves paced to and fro in the moonlight, and the wind brought the sound of the great sea's voice to the men on shore, and they felt that they could then be interpreters.

ജ

RALPH ELLISON *(1914–1994) was born in Oklahoma City, Oklahoma. His father, a small-time vendor of ice and coal, died when Ellison was three, and thereafter his mother worked as a domestic servant to support herself and her son. Ellison later credited his mother, who recruited black votes for the Socialist Party, for turning him into an activist. She also brought home discarded books and phonograph records from the white households where she worked, and as a boy Ellison developed an interest in literature and music. He played trumpet in his high school band, and it was at this time that he began to relate the works of fiction he was reading to real life. "I began to look at my own life through the lives of fictional characters," he observed. "When I read Stendhal, I would search until I began to find patterns of a Stendhalian novel within the Negro communities in which I grew up. I began, in other words, quite early to connect the worlds projected in literature . . . with the life in which I found myself."*

In 1933 Ellison entered Tuskegee Institute in Alabama, where he studied music for three years. Then he went to New York City and met the black writers Langston Hughes and Richard Wright, whose encouragement helped him to become a writer. Wright turned Ellison's attention to writing short stories and reading "those works in which writing was discussed as a craft . . . to Henry James's prefaces, to Conrad," and to other authors. In 1939 Ellison's short stories, essays, and reviews began to appear in periodicals. After World War II, he settled down to work on the novel Invisible Man. *Published in 1952, it received the National Book Award for fiction and was listed in a 1965* Book Week *poll as the most distinguished American novel of the preceding twenty years. As the critic Richard D. Lyons recognized, the novel was "a chronicle of a young black man's awakening to racial discrimination and his battle against the refusal of Americans to see him apart from his ethnic background, which in turn leads to humiliation and disillusionment." "Battle Royal," an excerpt from* Invisible Man, *is often anthologized. It appears after the prologue describing the underground chamber in which the nameless protagonist has retreated from the chaos of life aboveground.*

Insisting that "art by its nature is social," Ellison began Invisible Man *with the words "I am an invisible man. No, I am not a spook like those who haunted Edgar*

Allan Poe; nor am I one of your Hollywood-movie ectoplasms. I am a man of sub-stance, of flesh and bone, fiber and liquids — and I might even be said to possess a mind. I am invisible, understand, simply because people refuse to see me." At the time of his death from cancer, Ellison left an unfinished novel started in the late 1950s. His initial work on the manuscript was destroyed in a fire, and it was difficult for him to complete the book. In addition to Invisible Man, *Ellison published a few short stories and two collections of essays,* Shadow and Act *(1964) and* Going to the Territory *(1986). He was also Albert Schweitzer Professor of Contemporary Literature and Cul-ture at New York University.*

RELATED COMMENTARY: *Ralph Ellison, "The Influence of Folklore on 'Battle Royal,' " page 744.*

RALPH ELLISON

Battle Royal   1952

It goes a long way back, some twenty years. All my life I had been look-ing for something, and everywhere I turned someone tried to tell me what it was. I accepted their answers too, though they were often in contradiction and even self-contradictory. I was naïve. I was looking for myself and asking everyone except myself questions which I, and only I, could answer. It took me a long time and much painful boomeranging of my expectations to achieve a realization everyone else appears to have been born with: That I am nobody but myself. But first I had to discover that I am an invisible man!

And yet I am no freak of nature, nor of history. I was in the cards, other things having been equal (or unequal) eighty-five years ago. I am not ashamed of my grandparents for having been slaves. I am only ashamed of myself for having at one time been ashamed. About eighty-five years ago they were told that they were free, united with others of our country in everything pertaining to the common good, and, in everything social, separate like the fingers of the hand. And they believed it. They exulted in it. They stayed in their place, worked hard, and brought up my father to do the same. But my grandfather is the one. He was an odd old guy, my grandfather, and I am told I take after him. It was he who caused the trouble. On his deathbed he called my father to him and said, "Son, after I'm gone I want you to keep up the good fight. I never told you, but our life is a war and I have been a traitor all my born days, a spy in the enemy's country ever since I give up my gun back in the Reconstruction. Live with your head in the lion's mouth. I want you to overcome 'em with yeses, undermine 'em with grins, agree 'em to death and destruction, let 'em swoller you till they vomit or bust wide open." They thought the old man had gone out of his mind. He had been the meekest of men. The younger children were rushed from the room, the shades drawn, and the flame of the lamp turned so low that it sputtered on the wick like the old man's breathing. "Learn it to the younguns," he whispered fiercely; then he died.

But my folks were more alarmed over his last words than over his dying. It was as though he had not died at all, his words caused so much anxiety. I was warned emphatically to forget what he had said and, indeed, this is the first time it has been mentioned outside the family circle. It had a tremendous effect upon me, however. I could never be sure of what he meant. Grandfather had been a quiet old man who never made any trouble, yet on his deathbed he had called himself a traitor and a spy, and he had spoken of his meekness as a dangerous activity. It became a constant puzzle which lay unanswered in the back of my mind. And whenever things went well for me I remembered my grandfather and felt guilty and uncomfortable. It was as though I was carrying out his advice in spite of myself. And to make it worse, everyone loved me for it. I was praised by the most lily-white men of the town. I was considered an example of desirable conduct — just as my grandfather had been. And what puzzled me was that the old man had defined it as *treachery*. When I was praised for my conduct I felt a guilt that in some way I was doing something that was really against the wishes of the white folks, that if they had understood they would have desired me to act just the opposite, that I should have been sulky and mean, and that that really would have been what they wanted, even though they were fooled and thought they wanted me to act as I did. It made me afraid that some day they would look upon me as a traitor and I would be lost. Still I was more afraid to act any other way because they didn't like that at all. The old man's words were like a curse. On my graduation day I delivered an oration in which I showed that humility was the secret, indeed, the very essence of progress. (Not that I believed this — how could I, remembering my grandfather? — I only believed that it worked.) It was a great success. Everyone praised me and I was invited to give the speech at a gathering of the town's leading white citizens. It was a triumph for our whole community.

It was in the main ballroom of the leading hotel. When I got there I discovered that it was on the occasion of a smoker, and I was told that since I was to be there anyway I might as well take part in the battle royal to be fought by some of my schoolmates as part of the entertainment. The battle royal came first.

All of the town's big shots were there in their tuxedoes, wolfing down the buffet foods, drinking beer and whiskey and smoking black cigars. It was a large room with a high ceiling. Chairs were arranged in neat rows around three sides of a portable boxing ring. The fourth side was clear, revealing a gleaming space of polished floor. I had some misgivings over the battle royal, by the way. Not from a distaste for fighting, but because I didn't care too much for the other fellows who were to take part. They were tough guys who seemed to have no grandfather's curse worrying their minds. No one could mistake their toughness. And besides, I suspected that fighting a battle royal might detract from the dignity of my speech. In those pre-invisible days I visualized myself as a potential Booker T. Washington. But the other fellows didn't care too much for me either, and there were nine of them. I felt superior to them in my way, and I didn't like the manner in which we were all crowded together into the servants' elevator. Nor did they like my being there. In fact, as the warmly lighted floors flashed past the elevator we had words over the fact that I, by taking part in the fight, had knocked one of their friends out of a night's work.

We were led out of the elevator through a rococo hall into an anteroom and told to get into our fighting togs. Each of us was issued a pair of boxing gloves and ushered out into the big mirrored hall, which we entered looking cautiously about us and whispering, lest we might accidentally be heard above the noise of the room. It was foggy with cigar smoke. And already the whiskey was taking effect. I was shocked to see some of the most important men of the town quite tipsy. They were all there — bankers, lawyers, judges, doctors, fire chiefs, teachers, merchants. Even one of the more fashionable pastors. Something we could not see was going on up front. A clarinet was vibrating sensuously and the men were standing up and moving eagerly forward. We were a small tight group, clustered together, our bare upper bodies touching and shining with anticipatory sweat; while up front the big shots were becoming increasingly excited over something we still could not see. Suddenly I heard the school superintendent, who had told me to come, yell, "Bring up the shines, gentlemen! Bring up the little shines!"

We were rushed up to the front of the ballroom, where it smelled even more strongly of tobacco and whiskey. Then we were pushed into place. I almost wet my pants. A sea of faces, some hostile, some amused, ringed around us, and in the center, facing us, stood a magnificent blonde — stark naked. There was dead silence. I felt a blast of cold air chill me. I tried to back away, but they were behind me and around me. Some of the boys stood with lowered heads, trembling. I felt a wave of irrational guilt and fear. My teeth chattered, my skin turned to goose flesh, my knees knocked. Yet I was strongly attracted and looked in spite of myself. Had the price of looking been blindness, I would have looked. The hair was yellow like that of a circus kewpie doll, the face heavily powdered and rouged, as though to form an abstract mask, the eyes hollow and smeared a cool blue, the color of a baboon's butt. I felt a desire to spit upon her as my eyes brushed slowly over her body. Her breasts were firm and round as the domes of East Indian temples, and I stood so close as to see the fine skin texture and beads of pearly perspiration glistening like dew around the pink and erected buds of her nipples. I wanted at one and the same time to run from the room, to sink through the floor, or go to her and cover her from my eyes and the eyes of the others with my body; to feel the soft thighs, to caress her and destroy her, to love her and murder her, to hide from her, and yet to stroke where below the small American flag tattooed upon her belly her thighs formed a capital V. I had a notion that of all in the room she saw only me with her impersonal eyes.

And then she began to dance, a slow sensuous movement; the smoke of a hundred cigars clinging to her like the thinnest of veils. She seemed like a fair bird-girl girdled in veils calling to me from the angry surface of some gray and threatening sea. I was transported. Then I became aware of the clarinet playing and the big shots yelling at us. Some threatened us if we looked and others if we did not. On my right I saw one boy faint. And now a man grabbed a silver pitcher from a table and stepped close as he dashed ice water upon him and stood him up and forced two of us to support him as his head hung and moans issued from his thick bluish lips. Another boy began to plead to go home. He was the largest of the group, wearing dark red fighting trunks much too small to conceal the erection which projected from him as though in answer to the insinuating low-registered moaning of the clarinet. He tried to hide himself with his boxing gloves.

And all the while the blonde continued dancing, smiling faintly at the big shots who watched her with fascination, and faintly smiling at our fear. I noticed a certain merchant who followed her hungrily, his lips loose and drooling. He was a large man who wore diamond studs in a shirtfront which swelled with the ample paunch underneath, and each time the blonde swayed her undulating hips he ran his hand through the thin hair of his bald head and, with his arms upheld, his posture clumsy like that of an intoxicated panda, wound his belly in a slow and obscene grind. This creature was completely hypnotized. The music had quickened. As the dancer flung herself about with a detached expression on her face, the men began reaching out to touch her. I could see their beefy fingers sink into her soft flesh. Some of the others tried to stop them and she began to move around the floor in graceful circles, as they gave chase, slipping and sliding over the polished floor. It was mad. Chairs went crashing, drinks were spilt, as they ran laughing and howling after her. They caught her just as she reached a door, raised her from the floor, and tossed her as college boys are tossed at a hazing, and above her red fixed-smiling lips I saw the terror and disgust in her eyes, almost like my own terror and that which I saw in some of the other boys. As I watched, they tossed her twice and her soft breasts seemed to flatten against the air and her legs flung wildly as she spun. Some of the more sober ones helped her to escape. And I started off the floor, heading for the anteroom with the rest of the boys.

Some were still crying and in hysteria. But as we tried to leave we were stopped and ordered to get into the ring. There was nothing to do but what we were told. All ten of us climbed under the ropes and allowed ourselves to be blindfolded with broad bands of white cloth. One of the men seemed to feel a bit sympathetic and tried to cheer us up as we stood with our backs against the ropes. Some of us tried to grin. "See that boy over there?" one of the men said. "I want you to run across at the bell and give it to him right in the belly. If you don't get him, I'm going to get you. I don't like his looks." Each of us was told the same. The blindfolds were put on. Yet even then I had been going over my speech. In my mind each word was as bright as flame. I felt the cloth pressed into place, and frowned so that it would be loosened when I relaxed.

But now I felt a sudden fit of blind terror. I was unused to darkness. It was as though I had suddenly found myself in a dark room filled with poisonous cottonmouths. I could hear the bleary voices yelling insistently for the battle royal to begin.

"Get going in there!"

"Let me at that big nigger!"

I strained to pick up the school superintendent's voice, as though to squeeze some security out of that slightly more familiar sound.

"Let me at those black sonsabitches!" someone yelled.

"No, Jackson, no!" another voice yelled. "Here, somebody, help me hold Jack."

"I want to get at that ginger-colored nigger. Tear him limb from limb," the first voice yelled.

I stood against the ropes trembling. For in those days I was what they called ginger-colored, and he sounded as though he might crunch me between his teeth like a crisp ginger cookie.

Quite a struggle was going on. Chairs were being kicked about and I could hear voices grunting as with a terrific effort. I wanted to see, to see more desperately than ever before. But the blindfold was as tight as a thick skin-puckering scab and when I raised my gloved hands to push the layers of white aside a voice yelled, "Oh, no you don't, black bastard! Leave that alone!"

"Ring the bell before Jackson kills him a coon!" someone boomed in the sudden silence. And I heard the bell clang and the sound of the feet scuffling forward.

A glove smacked against my head. I pivoted, striking out stiffly as someone went past, and felt the jar ripple along the length of my arm to my shoulder. Then it seemed as though all nine of the boys had turned upon me at once. Blows pounded me from all sides while I struck out as best I could. So many blows landed upon me that I wondered if I were not the only blindfolded fighter in the ring, or if the man called Jackson hadn't succeeded in getting me after all.

Blindfolded, I could no longer control my motions. I had no dignity. I stumbled about like a baby or a drunken man. The smoke had become thicker and with each new blow it seemed to sear and further restrict my lungs. My saliva became like hot bitter glue. A glove connected with my head, filling my mouth with warm blood. It was everywhere. I could not tell if the moisture I felt upon my body was sweat or blood. A blow landed hard against the nape of my neck. I felt myself going over, my head hitting the floor. Streaks of blue light filled the black world behind the blindfold. I lay prone, pretending that I was knocked out, but felt myself seized by hands and yanked to my feet. "Get going, black boy! Mix it up!" My arms were like lead, my head smarting from blows. I managed to feel my way to the ropes and held on, trying to catch my breath. A glove landed in my mid-section and I went over again, feeling as though the smoke had become a knife jabbed into my guts. Pushed this way and that by the legs milling around me, I finally pulled erect and discovered that I could see the black, sweat-washed forms weaving in the smoky-blue atmosphere like drunken dancers weaving to the rapid drum-like thuds of blows.

Everyone fought hysterically. It was complete anarchy. Everybody fought everybody else. No group fought together for long. Two, three, four, fought one, then turned to fight each other, were themselves attacked. Blows landed below the belt and in the kidney, with the gloves open as well as closed, and with my eye partly opened now there was not so much terror. I moved carefully, avoiding blows, although not too many to attract attention, fighting from group to group. The boys groped about like blind, cautious crabs crouching to protect their mid-sections, their heads pulled in short against their shoulders, their arms stretched nervously before them, with their fists testing the smoke-filled air like the knobbed feelers of hypersensitive snails. In one corner I glimpsed a boy violently punching the air and heard him scream in pain as he smashed his hand against a ring post. For a second I saw him bent over holding his hand, then going down as a blow caught his unprotected head. I played one group against the other, slipping in and throwing a punch then stepping out of range while pushing the others into the melee to take the blows blindly aimed at me. The smoke was agonizing and there were no rounds, no bells at three minute intervals to relieve our exhaustion. The room spun round me, a swirl of lights, smoke, sweating bodies surrounded by tense white faces. I bled from both nose and mouth, the blood spattering upon my chest.

The men kept yelling, "Slug him, black boy! Knock his guts out!"

"Uppercut him! Kill him! Kill that big boy!"

Taking a fake fall, I saw a boy going down heavily beside me as though we were felled by a single blow, saw a sneaker-clad foot shoot into his groin as the two who had knocked him down stumbled upon him. I rolled out of range, feeling a twinge of nausea.

The harder we fought the more threatening the men became. And yet, I had begun to worry about my speech again. How would it go? Would they recognize my ability? What would they give me?

I was fighting automatically and suddenly I noticed that one after another of the boys was leaving the ring. I was surprised, filled with panic, as though I had been left alone with an unknown danger. Then I understood. The boys had arranged it among themselves. It was the custom for the two men left in the ring to slug it out for the winner's prize. I discovered this too late. When the bell sounded two men in tuxedoes leaped into the ring and removed the blindfold. I found myself facing Tatlock, the biggest of the gang. I felt sick at my stomach. Hardly had the bell stopped ringing in my ears than it clanged again and I saw him moving swiftly toward me. Thinking of nothing else to do I hit him smash on the nose. He kept coming, bringing the rank sharp violence of stale sweat. His face was a black blank of a face, only his eyes alive — with hate of me and aglow with a feverish terror from what had happened to us all. I became anxious. I wanted to deliver my speech and he came at me as though he meant to beat it out of me. I smashed him again and again, taking his blows as they came. Then on a sudden impulse I struck him lightly and as we clinched, I whispered, "Fake like I knocked you out, you can have the prize."

"I'll break your behind," he whispered hoarsely.

"For *them*?"

"For *me*, sonofabitch!"

They were yelling for us to break it up and Tatlock spun me half around with a blow, and as a joggled camera sweeps in a reeling scene, I saw the howling red faces crouching tense beneath the cloud of blue-gray smoke. For a moment the world wavered, unraveled, flowed, then my head cleared and Tatlock bounced before me. That fluttering shadow before my eyes was his jabbing left hand. Then falling forward, my head against his damp shoulder, I whispered,

"I'll make it five dollars more."

"Go to hell!"

But his muscles relaxed a trifle beneath my pressure and I breathed, "Seven!"

"Give it to your ma," he said, ripping me beneath the heart.

And while I still held him I butted him and moved away. I felt myself bombarded with punches. I fought back with hopeless desperation. I wanted to deliver my speech more than anything else in the world, because I felt that only these men could judge truly my ability, and now this stupid clown was ruining my chances. I began fighting carefully now, moving in to punch him and out again with my greater speed. A lucky blow to his chin and I had him going too — until I heard a loud voice yell, "I got my money on the big boy."

Hearing this, I almost dropped my guard. I was confused: Should I try to win against the voice out there? Would not this go against my speech, and was not this a moment for humility, for nonresistance? A blow to my head as I danced about sent my right eye popping like a jack-in-the-box and settled my dilemma. The room went red as I fell. It was a dream fall, my body languid and fastidious as to where to land, until the floor became impatient and smashed up to meet me. A moment later I came to. An hypnotic voice said FIVE emphatically. And I lay there, hazily watching a dark red spot of my own blood shaping itself into a butterfly, glistening and soaking into the soiled gray world of the canvas.

When the voice drawled TEN I was lifted up and dragged to a chair. I sat dazed. My eye pained and swelled with each throb of my pounding heart and I wondered if now I would be allowed to speak. I was wringing wet, my mouth still bleeding. We were grouped along the wall now. The other boys ignored me as they congratulated Tatlock and speculated as to how much they would be paid. One boy whimpered over his smashed hand. Looking up front, I saw attendants in white jackets rolling the portable ring away and placing a small square rug in the vacant space surrounded by chairs. Perhaps, I thought, I will stand on the rug to deliver my speech.

Then the M.C. called to us, "Come on up here boys and get your money."

We ran forward to where the men laughed and talked in their chairs, waiting. Everyone seemed friendly now.

"There it is on the rug," the man said. I saw the rug covered with coins of all dimensions and a few crumpled bills. But what excited me, scattered here and there, were the gold pieces.

"Boys, it's all yours," the man said. "You get all you grab."

"That's right, Sambo," a blond man said, winking at me confidentially.

I trembled with excitement, forgetting my pain. I would get the gold and the bills, I thought. I would use both hands. I would throw my body against the boys nearest me to block them from the gold.

"Get down around the rug now," the man commanded, "and don't anyone touch it until I give the signal."

"This ought to be good," I heard.

As told, we got around the square rug on our knees. Slowly the man raised his freckled hand as we followed it upward with our eyes.

I heard, "These niggers look like they're about to pray!"

Then, "Ready," the man said. "Go!"

I lunged for a yellow coin lying on the blue design of the carpet, touching it and sending a surprised shriek to join those rising around me. I tried frantically to remove my hand but could not let go. A hot, violent force tore through my body, shaking me like a wet rat. The rug was electrified. The hair bristled up on my head as I shook myself free. My muscles jumped, my nerves jangled, writhed. But I saw that this was not stopping the other boys. Laughing in fear and embarrassment, some were holding back and scooping up the coins knocked off by the painful contortions of the others. The men roared above us as we struggled.

"Pick it up, goddamnit, pick it up!" someone called like a bass-voiced parrot. "Go on, get it!"

I crawled rapidly around the floor, picking up the coins, trying to avoid the coppers and to get greenbacks and the gold. Ignoring the shock by laughing, as I brushed the coins off quickly, I discovered that I could contain the electricity — a contradiction, but it works. Then the men began to push us onto the rug. Laughing embarrassedly, we struggled out of their hands and kept after the coins. We were all wet and slippery and hard to hold. Suddenly I saw a boy lifted into the air, glistening with sweat like a circus seal, and dropped, his wet back landing flush upon the charged rug, heard him yell and saw him literally dance upon his back, his elbows beating a frenzied tatoo upon the floor, his muscles twitching like the flesh of a horse stung by many flies. When he finally rolled off, his face was gray and no one stopped him when he ran from the floor amid booming laughter.

"Get the money," the M.C. called. "That's good hard American cash!"

And we snatched and grabbed, snatched and grabbed. I was careful not to come too close to the rug now, and when I felt the hot whiskey breath descend upon me like a cloud of foul air I reached out and grabbed the leg of a chair. It was occupied and I held on desperately.

"Leggo, nigger! Leggo!"

The huge face wavered down to mine as he tried to push me free. But my body was slippery and he was too drunk. It was Mr. Colcord, who owned a chain of movie houses and "entertainment palaces." Each time he grabbed me I slipped out of his hands. It became a real struggle. I feared the rug more than I did the drunk, so I held on, surprising myself for a moment by trying to topple *him* upon the rug. It was such an enormous idea that I found myself actually carrying it out. I tried not to be obvious, yet when I grabbed his leg, trying to tumble him out of the chair, he raised up roaring with laughter, and, looking at me with soberness dead in the eye, kicked me viciously in the chest. The chair leg flew out of my hand. I felt myself going and rolled. It was as though I had rolled through a bed of hot coals. It seemed a whole century would pass before I would roll free, a century in which I was seared through the deepest levels of my body to the fearful breath within me and the breath seared and heated to the point of explosion. It'll all be over in a flash, I thought as I rolled clear. It'll all be over in a flash.

But not yet, the men on the other side were waiting, red faces swollen as though from apoplexy as they bent forward in their chairs. Seeing their fingers coming toward me I rolled away as a fumbled football rolls off the receiver's fingertips, back into the coals. That time I luckily sent the rug sliding out of place and heard the coins ringing against the floor and the boys scuffling to pick them up and the M.C. calling, "All right, boys, that's all. Go get dressed and get your money."

I was limp as a dish rag. My back felt as though it had been beaten with wires.

When we had dressed the M.C. came in and gave us each five dollars, except Tatlock, who got ten for being last in the ring. Then he told us to leave. I was not to get a chance to deliver my speech, I thought. I was going out into the dim alley in despair when I was stopped and told to go back. I returned to the ballroom, where the men were pushing back their chairs and gathering in groups to talk.

The M.C. knocked on a table for quiet. "Gentlemen," he said, "we almost forgot an important part of the program. A most serious part, gentlemen. This boy was brought here to deliver a speech which he made at his graduation yesterday. . . ."

"Bravo!"

"I'm told that he is the smartest boy we've got out there in Greenwood. I'm told that he knows more big words than a pocket-sized dictionary."

Much applause and laughter.

"So now, gentlemen, I want you to give him your attention."

There was still laughter as I faced them, my mouth dry, my eye throbbing. I began slowly, but evidently my throat was tense, because they began shouting, "Louder! Louder!"

"We of the younger generation extol the wisdom of that great leader and educator," I shouted, "who first spoke these flaming words of wisdom: 'A ship lost at sea for many days suddenly sighted a friendly vessel. From the mast of the unfortunate vessel was seen a signal: "Water, water; we die of thirst!" The answer from the friendly vessel came back: "Cast down your bucket where you are." The captain of the distressed vessel, at last heeding the injunction, cast down his bucket, and it came up full of fresh sparkling water from the mouth of the Amazon River.' And like him I say, and in his words, 'To those of my race who depend upon bettering their condition in a foreign land, or who underestimate the importance of cultivating friendly relations with the Southern white man, who is his next-door neighbor, I would say: "Cast down your bucket where you are" — cast it down in making friends in every manly way of the people of all races by whom we are surrounded. . . .' "

I spoke automatically and with such fervor that I did not realize that the men were still talking and laughing until my dry mouth, filling up with blood from the cut, almost strangled me. I coughed, wanting to stop and go to one of the tall brass, sand-filled spittoons to relieve myself, but a few of the men, especially the superintendent, were listening and I was afraid. So I gulped it down, blood, saliva, and all, and continued. (What powers of endurance I had during those days! What enthusiasm! What a belief in the rightness of things!) I spoke even louder in spite of the pain. But still they talked and still they laughed, as though deaf with cotton in dirty ears. So I spoke with greater emotional emphasis. I closed my ears and swallowed blood until I was nauseated. The speech seemed a hundred times as long as before, but I could not leave out a single word. All had to be said, each memorized nuance considered, rendered. Nor was that all. Whenever I uttered a word of three or more syllables a group of voices would yell for me to repeat it. I used the phrase "social responsibility" and they yelled:

"What's the word you say, boy?"

"Social responsibility," I said.

"What?"

"Social . . ."

"Louder."

". . . responsibility."

"More!"

"Respon — "

"Repeat!"

" — sibility."

The room filled with the uproar of laughter until, no doubt, distracted by having to gulp down my blood, I made a mistake and yelled a phrase I had often seen denounced in newspaper editorials, heard debated in private.

"Social . . ."

"What?" they yelled.

". . . equality — "

The laughter hung smokelike in the sudden stillness. I opened my eyes, puzzled. Sounds of displeasure filled the room. The M.C. rushed forward. They shouted hostile phrases at me. But I did not understand.

A small dry mustached man in the front row blared out, "Say that slowly, son!"

"What sir?"

"What you just said!"

"Social responsibility, sir," I said.

"You weren't being smart, were you, boy?" he said, not unkindly.

"No, sir!"

"You sure that about 'equality' was a mistake?"

"Oh, yes, sir," I said. "I was swallowing blood."

"Well, you had better speak more slowly so we can understand. We mean to do right by you, but you've got to know your place at all times. All right, now, go on with your speech."

I was afraid. I wanted to leave but I wanted also to speak and I was afraid they'd snatch me down.

"Thank you, sir," I said, beginning where I had left off, and having them ignore me as before.

Yet when I finished there was a thunderous applause. I was surprised to see the superintendent come forth with a package wrapped in white tissue paper, and, gesturing for quiet, address the men.

"Gentlemen, you see that I did not overpraise this boy. He makes a good speech and some day he'll lead his people in the proper paths. And I don't have to tell you that that is important in these days and times. This is a good, smart boy, and so to encourage him in the right direction, in the name of the Board of Education I wish to present him a prize in the form of this . . ."

He paused, removing the tissue paper and revealing a gleaming calfskin brief case.

". . . in the form of this first-class article from Shad Whitmore's shop."

"Boy," he said, addressing me, "take this prize and keep it well. Consider it a badge of office. Prize it. Keep developing as you are and some day it will be filled with important papers that will help shape the destiny of your people."

I was so moved that I could hardly express my thanks. A rope of bloody saliva forming a shape like an undiscovered continent drooled upon the leather and I wiped it quickly away. I felt an importance that I had never dreamed.

"Open it and see what's inside," I was told.

My fingers a-tremble, I complied, smelling the fresh leather and finding an official-looking document inside. It was a scholarship to the state college for Negroes. My eyes filled with tears and I ran awkwardly off the floor.

I was overjoyed; I did not even mind when I discovered that the gold pieces I had scrambled for were brass pocket tokens advertising a certain make of automobile.

When I reached home everyone was excited. Next day the neighbors came to congratulate me. I even felt safe from grandfather, whose deathbed curse usually spoiled my triumphs. I stood beneath his photograph with my brief case in hand and smiled triumphantly into his stolid black peasant's face. It was a face that fascinated me. The eyes seemed to follow everywhere I went.

That night I dreamed I was at a circus with him and that he refused to laugh at the clowns no matter what they did. Then later he told me to open my brief case and read what was inside and I did, finding an official envelope stamped with the state seal; and inside the envelope I found another and another, endlessly, and I thought I would fall of weariness. "Them's years," he said. "Now open that one." And I did and in it I found an engraved document containing a short message in letters of gold. "Read it," my grandfather said. "Out loud."

"To Whom It May Concern," I intoned. "Keep This Nigger-Boy Running."

I awoke with the old man's laughter ringing in my ears.

(It was a dream I was to remember and dream again for many years after. But at the time I had no insight into its meaning. First I had to attend college.)

∾

LOUISE ERDRICH *(b. 1954) is of German and Native American descent. She grew up in Wahpeton, North Dakota, as a member of the Turtle Mountain Band of Chippewa. For many years her grandfather was tribal chair of the reservation. At Dartmouth College, Erdrich won several prizes for her fiction and poetry, including the American Academy of Poets Prize. After graduating in 1976, she returned to North Dakota, where she taught in the Poetry in the Schools Program. In 1979 she received her M.A. in creative writing from Johns Hopkins University. Erdrich is married to Michael Dorris, a professor of Native American studies at Dartmouth College who is also a writer. They collaborated on the novel* The Crown of Columbus *(1992).*

Erdrich has been an editor of the Boston Indian Council newspaper, The Circle. *Her stories have appeared in* Redbook, *the* New England Review, *and the* Mississippi Valley Review *and have been included in* Earth Power Coming, *an anthology of Native American literature, as well as* That's What She Said: Contemporary Poetry and Fiction by Native American Women. *In 1984 a collection of her poetry,* Jacklight, *was published and her first work of fiction,* Love Medicine, *won the National Book Critics Circle Award. Her novels* Beet Queen *(1986) and* Tracks *(1988) continue the* Love Medicine *series of stories, and her fourth novel,* The Bingo Palace, *appeared in 1994.* The Blue Jay's Dance: A Birth Year *(1995) is her celebration of motherhood, and* Tales of Burning Love *(1996) is her most recent novel.*

"The Red Convertible" is a chapter from Love Medicine. *Each chapter is a self-enclosed narrative that also functions as a separate short story about the lives of two families, the Kashpaws and the Lamartines, on a North Dakota reservation between 1934 and 1984. "The Red Convertible" takes place in 1974 and is narrated by Lyman Lamartine.*

Erdrich's work has won praise for its psychological depth and its literary excellence; it is a landmark achievement in its depiction of the lives of contemporary Native Americans. As the novelist Peter Matthiessen has observed, Love Medicine *is "quick with agile prose, taut speech, poetry, and power, conveying unflinchingly the funkiness, humor, and great unspoken sadness of the Indian reservations, and a people exiled to a no-man's-land between two worlds."*

LOUISE ERDRICH

The Red Convertible   1984

I was the first one to drive a convertible on my reservation. And of course it was red, a red Olds. I owned that car along with my brother Henry Junior. We owned it together until his boots filled with water on a windy night and he bought out my share. Now Henry owns the whole car, and his younger brother Lyman (that's myself), Lyman walks everywhere he goes.

How did I earn enough money to buy my share in the first place? My own talent was I could always make money. I had a touch for it, unusual in a Chippewa. From the first I was different that way, and everyone recognized it. I was the only kid they let in the American Legion Hall to shine shoes, for example, and one Christmas I sold spiritual bouquets for the mission door to door. The nuns let me keep a percentage. Once I started, it seemed the more money I made the easier the money came. Everyone encouraged it. When I was fifteen I got a job washing dishes at the Joliet Café, and that was where my first big break happened.

It wasn't long before I was promoted to busing tables, and then the short-order cook quit and I was hired to take her place. No sooner than you know it I was managing the Joliet. The rest is history. I went on managing. I soon became part owner, and of course there was no stopping me then. It wasn't long before the whole thing was mine.

After I'd owned the Joliet for one year, it blew over in the worst tornado ever seen around here. The whole operation was smashed to bits. A total loss. The fryalator was up in a tree, the grill torn in half like it was paper. I was only sixteen. I had it all in my mother's name, and I lost it quick, but before I lost it I had every one of my relatives, and their relatives, to dinner, and I also bought that red Olds I mentioned, along with Henry.

The first time we saw it! I'll tell you when we first saw it. We had gotten a ride up to Winnipeg, and both of us had money. Don't ask me why, because we never mentioned a car or anything, we just had all our money. Mine was cash, a big bankroll from the Joliet's insurance. Henry had two checks — a week's extra pay for being laid off, and his regular check from the Jewel Bearing Plant.

We were walking down Portage anyway, seeing the sights, when we saw it. There it was, parked, large as life. Really as *if* it was alive. I thought of the word *repose,* because the car wasn't simply stopped, parked, or whatever. That car reposed, calm and gleaming, a FOR SALE sign in its left front window. Then, before we had thought it over at all, the car belonged to us and our pockets were empty. We had just enough money for gas back home.

We went places in that car, me and Henry. We took off driving all one whole summer. We started off toward the Little Knife River and Mandaree in Fort Berthold and then we found ourselves down in Wakpala somehow, and then suddenly we were over in Montana on the Rocky Boy, and yet the summer was not even half over. Some people hang on to details when they travel, but we didn't let them bother us and just lived our everyday lives here to there.

I do remember this one place with willows. I remember I laid under those trees and it was comfortable. So comfortable. The branches bent down all around me like a tent or a stable. And quiet, it was quiet, even though there was a powwow close enough so I could see it going on. The air was not too still, not too windy either. When the dust rises up and hangs in the air around the dancers like that, I feel good. Henry was asleep with his arms thrown wide. Later on, he woke up and we started driving again. We were somewhere in Montana, or maybe on the Blood Reserve — it could have been anywhere. Anyway it was where we met the girl.

All her hair was in buns around her ears, that's the first thing I noticed about her. She was posed alongside the road with her arm out, so we stopped. That girl was short, so short her lumber shirt looked comical on her, like a nightgown. She had jeans on and fancy moccasins and she carried a little suitcase.

"Hop on in," says Henry. So she climbs in between us.

"We'll take you home," I says. "Where do you live?"

"Chicken," she says.

"Where the hell's that?" I ask her.

"Alaska."

"Okay," says Henry, and we drive.

We got up there and never wanted to leave. The sun doesn't truly set there in summer, and the night is more a soft dusk. You might doze off, sometimes, but before you know it you're up again, like an animal in nature. You never feel like you have to sleep hard or put away the world. And things would grow up there. One day just dirt or moss, the next day flowers and long grass. The girl's name was Susy. Her family really took to us. They fed us and put us up. We had our own tent to live in by their house, and the kids would be in and out of there all day and night. They couldn't get over me and Henry being brothers, we looked so different. We told them we knew we had the same mother, anyway.

One night Susy came in to visit us. We sat around in the tent talking of this and that. The season was changing. It was getting darker by that time, and the cold was even getting just a little mean. I told her it was time for us to go. She stood up on a chair.

"You never seen my hair," Susy said.

That was true. She was standing on a chair, but still, when she unclipped her buns the hair reached all the way to the ground. Our eyes opened. You couldn't tell how much hair she had when it was rolled up so neatly. Then my brother Henry did something funny. He went up to the chair and said, "Jump on my shoulders." So she did that, and her hair reached down past his waist, and he started twirling, this way and that, so her hair was flung out from side to side.

"I always wondered what it was like to have long pretty hair," Henry says. Well we laughed. It was a funny sight, the way he did it. The next morning we got up and took leave of those people.

On to greener pastures, as they say. It was down through Spokane and across Idaho then Montana and very soon we were racing the weather right along under the Canadian border through Columbus, Des Lacs, and then we were in Bottineau County and soon home. We'd made most of the trip, that summer, without putting up the car hood at all. We got home just in time, it turned out, for the army to remember Henry had signed up to join it.

I don't wonder that the army was so glad to get my brother that they turned him into a Marine. He was built like a brick outhouse anyway. We liked to tease him that they really wanted him for his Indian nose. He had a nose big and sharp as a hatchet, like the nose on Red Tomahawk, the Indian who killed Sitting Bull, whose profile is on signs all along the North Dakota highways. Henry went off to training camp, came home once during Christmas, then the next thing you know we got an overseas letter from him. It was 1970, and he said he was stationed up in the northern hill country. Whereabouts I did not know. He wasn't such a hot letter writer, and only got off two before the enemy caught him. I could never keep it straight, which direction those good Vietnam soldiers were from.

I wrote him back several times, even though I didn't know if those letters would get through. I kept him informed all about the car. Most of the time I had it up on blocks in the yard or half taken apart, because that long trip did a hard job on it under the hood.

I always had good luck with numbers, and never worried about the draft myself. I never even had to think about what my number was. But Henry was never lucky in the same way as me. It was at least three years before Henry came home. By then I guess the whole war was solved in the government's mind, but for him it would keep on going. In those years I'd put his car into almost perfect shape. I always thought of it as his car while he was gone, even though when he left he said, "Now it's yours," and threw me his key.

"Thanks for the extra key," I'd said. "I'll put it up in your drawer just in case I need it." He laughed.

When he came home, though, Henry was very different, and I'll say this: the change was no good. You could hardly expect him to change for the better, I know. But he was quiet, so quiet, and never comfortable sitting still anywhere but always up and moving around. I thought back to times we'd sat still for whole afternoons, never moving a muscle, just shifting our weight along the ground, talking to whoever sat with us, watching things. He'd always had a joke, then, too, and now you couldn't get him to laugh, or when he did it was more the sound of a man choking, a sound that stopped up the throats of other people around him. They got to leaving him alone most of the time, and I didn't blame them. It was a fact: Henry was jumpy and mean.

I'd bought a color TV set for my mom and the rest of us while Henry was away. Money still came very easy. I was sorry I'd ever bought it though, because of Henry. I was also sorry I'd bought color, because with black-and-white the pictures seem older and farther away. But what are you going to do? He sat in front of it, watching it, and that was the only time he was completely still. But it was the kind of stillness that you see in a rabbit when it freezes and before it will bolt. He was not easy. He sat in his chair gripping the armrests with all his might, as if the chair itself was moving at a high speed and if he let go at all he would rocket forward and maybe crash right through the set.

Once I was in the room watching TV with Henry and I heard his teeth click at something. I looked over, and he'd bitten through his lip. Blood was going down his chin. I tell you right then I wanted to smash that tube to pieces. I went over to it but Henry must have known what I was up to. He rushed from his chair and shoved me out of the way, against the wall. I told myself he didn't know what he was doing.

My mom came in, turned the set off real quiet, and told us she had made something for supper. So we went and sat down. There was still blood going down Henry's chin, but he didn't notice it and no one said anything, even though every time he took a bit of his bread his blood fell onto it until he was eating his own blood mixed in with the food.

While Henry was not around we talked about what was going to happen to him. There were no Indian doctors on the reservation, and my mom was afraid of trusting the old man, Moses Pillager, because he courted her long ago and was jealous of her husbands. He might take revenge through her son. We were afraid that if we brought Henry to a regular hospital they would keep him.

"They don't fix them in those places," Mom said; "they just give them drugs."

"We wouldn't get him there in the first place," I agreed, "so let's just forget about it."

Then I thought about the car.

Henry had not even looked at the car since he'd gotten home, though like I said, it was in tip-top condition and ready to drive. I thought the car might bring the old Henry back somehow. So I bided my time and waited for my chance to interest him in the vehicle.

One night Henry was off somewhere. I took myself a hammer. I went out to that car and I did a number on its underside. Whacked it up. Bent the tail pipe double. Ripped the muffler loose. By the time I was done with the car it looked worse than any typical Indian car that has been driven all its life on reservation roads, which they always say are like government promises — full of holes. It just about hurt me, I'll tell you that! I threw dirt in the carburetor and I ripped all the electric tape off the seats. I made it look just as beat up as I could. Then I sat back and waited for Henry to find it.

Still, it took him over a month. That was all right, because it was just getting warm enough, not melting, but warm enough to work outside.

"Lyman," he says, walking in one day, "that red car looks like shit."

"Well it's old," I says. "You got to expect that."

"No way!" says Henry. "That car's a classic! But you went and ran the piss right out of it, Lyman, and you know it don't deserve that. I kept that car in A-one shape. You don't remember. You're too young. But when I left, that car was running like a watch. Now I don't even know if I can get it to start again, let alone get it anywhere near its old condition."

"Well you try," I said, like I was getting mad, "but I say it's a piece of junk."

Then I walked out before he could realize I knew he'd strung together more than six words at once.

After that I thought he'd freeze himself to death working on that car. He was out there all day, and at night he rigged up a little lamp, ran a cord out the window, and had himself some light to see by while he worked. He was better than he had been before, but that's still not saying much. It was easier for him to do the things the rest of us did. He ate more slowly and didn't jump up and down during the meal to get this or that or look out the window. I put my hand in the back of the TV set, I admit, and fiddled around with it good, so that it was almost impossible now to get a clear picture. He didn't look at it very often anyway. He was always out with that car or going off to get parts for it. By the time it was really melting outside, he had it fixed.

I had been feeling down in the dumps about Henry around this time. We had always been together before. Henry and Lyman. But he was such a loner now that I didn't know how to take it. So I jumped at the chance one day when Henry seemed friendly. It's not that he smiled or anything. He just said, "Let's take that old shitbox for a spin." Just the way he said it made me think he could be coming around.

We went out to the car. It was spring. The sun was shining very bright. My only sister, Bonita, who was just eleven years old, came out and made us stand together for a picture. Henry leaned his elbow on the red car's windshield, and he took his other arm and put it over my shoulder, very carefully, as though it was heavy for him to lift and he didn't want to bring the weight down all at once.

"Smile," Bonita said, and he did.

That picture, I never look at it anymore. A few months ago, I don't know why, I got his picture out and tacked it on the wall. I felt good about Henry at the time, close to him. I felt good having his picture on the wall, until one night when I was looking at television. I was a little drunk and stoned. I looked up at the wall and Henry was staring at me. I don't know what it was, but his smile had changed, or maybe it was gone. All I know is I couldn't stay in the same room with that picture. I was shaking. I got up, closed the door, and went into the kitchen. A little later my friend Ray came over and we both went back into that room. We put the picture in a brown bag, folded the bag over and over tightly, then put it way back in a closet.

I still see that picture now, as if it tugs at me, whenever I pass that closet door. The picture is very clear in my mind. It was so sunny that day Henry had to squint against the glare. Or maybe the camera Bonita held flashed like a mirror, blinding him, before she snapped the picture. My face is right out in the sun, big and round. But he might have drawn back, because the shadows on his face are deep as holes. There are two shadows curved like little hooks around the ends of his smile, as if to frame it and try to keep it there — that one, first smile that looked like it might have hurt his face. He has his field jacket on and the worn-in clothes he'd come back in and kept wearing ever since. After Bonita took the picture, she went into the house and we got into the car. There was a full cooler in the trunk. We started off, east, toward Pembina and the Red River because Henry said he wanted to see the high water.

The trip over there was beautiful. When everything starts changing, drying up, clearing off, you feel like your whole life is starting. Henry felt it, too. The top was down and the car hummed like a top. He'd really put it back in shape, even the tape on the seats was very carefully put down and glued back in layers. It's not that he smiled again or even joked, but his face looked to me as if it was clear, more peaceful. It looked as though he wasn't thinking of anything in particular except the bare fields and windbreaks and houses we were passing.

The river was high and full of winter trash when we got there. The sun was still out, but it was colder by the river. There were still little clumps of dirty snow here and there on the banks. The water hadn't gone over the banks yet, but it would, you could tell. It was just at its limit, hard swollen glossy like an old gray scar. We made ourselves a fire, and we sat down and watched the current go. As I watched it I felt something squeezing inside me and tightening and trying to let go all at the same time. I knew I was not just feeling it myself; I knew I was feeling what Henry was going through at that moment. Except that I couldn't stand it, the closing and opening. I jumped to my feet. I took Henry by the shoulders and I started shaking him. "Wake up," I says, "wake up, wake up, wake up!" I didn't know what had come over me. I sat down beside him again.

His face was totally white and hard. Then it broke, like stones break all of a sudden when water boils up inside them.

"I know it," he says. "I know it. I can't help it. It's no use."

We start talking. He said he knew what I'd done with the car. It was obvious it had been whacked out of shape and not just neglected. He said he wanted to give the car to me for good now, it was no use. He said he'd fixed it just to give it back and I should take it.

"No way," I says, "I don't want it."

"That's okay," he says, "you take it."

"I don't want it, though," I says back to him, and then to emphasize, just to emphasize, you understand, I touch his shoulder. He slaps my hand off.

"Take that car," he says.

"No," I say. "Make me," I say, and then he grabs my jacket and rips the arm loose. That jacket is a class act, suede with tags and zippers. I push Henry backwards, off the log. He jumps up and bowls me over. We go down in a clinch and come up swinging hard, for all we're worth, with our fists. He socks my jaw so hard I feel like it swings loose. Then I'm at his rib cage and land a good one under his chin so his head snaps back. He's dazzled. He looks at me and I look at him and then his eyes are full of tears and blood and at first I think he's crying. But no, he's laughing. "Ha! Ha!" he says. "Ha! Ha! Take good care of it."

"Okay," I says, "okay, no problem. Ha! Ha!"

I can't help it, and I start laughing, too. My face feels fat and strange, and after a while I get a beer from the cooler in the trunk, and when I hand it to Henry he takes his shirt and wipes my germs off. "Hoof-and-mouth disease," he says. For some reason this cracks me up, and so we're really laughing for a while, and then we drink all the rest of the beers one by one and throw them in the river and see how far, how fast, the current takes them before they fill up and sink.

"You want to go on back?" I ask after a while. "Maybe we could snag a couple nice Kashpaw girls."

He says nothing. But I can tell his mood is turning again.

"They're all crazy, the girls up here, every damn one of them."

"You're crazy too," I say, to jolly him up. "Crazy Lamartine boys!"

He looks as though he will take this wrong at first. His face twists, then clears, and he jumps up on his feet. "That's right!" he says. "Crazier 'n hell. Crazy Indians!"

I think it's the old Henry again. He throws off his jacket and starts swinging his legs out from the knees like a fancy dancer. He's down doing something between a grass dance and a bunny hop, no kind of dance I ever saw before, but neither has anyone else on all this green growing earth. He's wild. He wants to pitch whoopee! He's up and at me and all over. All this time I'm laughing so hard, so hard my belly is getting tied up in a knot.

"Got to cool me off!" he shouts all of a sudden. Then he runs over to the river and jumps in.

There's boards and other things in the current. It's so high. No sound comes from the river after the splash he makes, so I run right over. I look around. It's getting dark. I see he's halfway across the water already, and I know he didn't swim there but the current took him. It's far. I hear his voice, though, very clearly across it.

"My boots are filling," he says.

He says this in a normal voice, like he just noticed and he doesn't know what to think of it. Then he's gone. A branch comes by. Another branch. And I go in.

By the time I get out of the river, off the snag I pulled myself onto, the sun is down. I walk back to the car, turn on the high beams, and drive it up the bank. I put it in first gear and then I take my foot off the clutch. I get out, close the door, and watch it plow softly into the water. The headlights reach in as they go down, searching, still lighted even after the water swirls over the back end. I wait. The wires short out. It is all finally dark. And then there is only the water, the sound of it going and running and going and running and running.

ಙಙ

WILLIAM FAULKNER *(1897–1962) was born in New Albany, Mississippi, into an old southern family. When he was a child, his parents moved to the isolated town of Oxford, Mississippi, and except for his service in World War I and some time in New Orleans and Hollywood, he spent the rest of his life there. "I discovered my own little postage stamp of native soil was worth writing about, and that I would never live long enough to exhaust it." His literary career began in New Orleans, where he lived for six months and wrote newspaper sketches and stories for the* Times-Picayune. *He met Sherwood Anderson in New Orleans, and Anderson helped him publish his first novel,* Soldier's Pay, *in 1926. Faulkner's major work was written in the late 1920s and the 1930s, when he created an imaginary county adjacent to Oxford, calling it Yoknapatawpha County and chronicling its history in a series of experimental novels. In* The Sound and the Fury *(1929),* As I Lay Dying *(1930),* Sanctuary *(1931),* Light in August *(1932),* Absalom, Absalom! *(1936), and The*

Hamlet *(1940), he showed himself to be a writer of genius, although "a willfully and perversely chaotic one," as Jorge Luis Borges noted, whose "labyrinthine world" required a no less labyrinthine prose technique to describe in epic manner the disintegration of the South through many generations. Faulkner was awarded the Nobel Prize for literature in 1952.*

Faulkner experimented with using a child's point of view in "That Evening Sun," but he rarely included poetic imagery or stream-of-consciousness narration in his stories, which he wrote, he often said, to help him pay his rent. His biographer Frederick Karl has noted that he used short fiction "as a means of working through, or toward, larger ideas." He wrote nearly a hundred stories, often revising them later to fit as sections into a novel. Four books of his stories were published in his lifetime. When Faulkner revised "That Evening Sun" after its initial appearance in the American Mercury *in March 1931 for inclusion in* These 13, *his first story collection published that same year, he omitted a paragraph after the father and the three children have left Nancy in her cabin. The story originally read:*

> *Then we had crossed the ditch, walking out of Nancy's life. Then her life was sitting there with the door open and the lamp lit, waiting, and the ditch between us and us going on, the white people going on, dividing the impinged lives of us and Nancy.*
> *"Who will do our washing now, father?" I said.*

Although some readers found symbolism in "A Rose for Emily" that suggested he was implying a battle between the North (the character Homer Barron) and the South (Miss Emily herself), Faulkner denied a schematic interpretation. He said he had intended to write a ghost story, and "I think that the writer is too busy trying to create flesh-and-blood people that will stand up and cast a shadow to have time to be conscious of all the symbolism that he may put into what he does or what people may read into it."

RELATED COMMENTARY: *William Faulkner, "The Meaning of 'A Rose for Emily,' " page 748.*

WILLIAM FAULKNER

A Rose for Emily   *1931*

I

When Miss Emily Grierson died, our whole town went to her funeral: the men through a sort of respectful affection for a fallen monument, the women mostly out of curiosity to see the inside of her house, which no one save an old manservant — a combined gardener and cook — had seen in at least ten years.

It was a big, squarish frame house that had once been white, decorated with cupolas and spires and scrolled balconies in the heavily lightsome style of the seventies, set on what had once been our most select street. But garages and cotton gins had encroached and obliterated even the august names of that neighborhood; only Miss Emily's house was left, lifting its stubborn and coquettish decay above the cotton wagons and the gasoline pumps — an eyesore among eyesores. And now Miss Emily had gone to join the representatives of those august names where they lay in the cedar-bemused cemetery among the ranked and anonymous graves of Union and Confederate soldiers who fell at the battle of Jefferson.

Alive, Miss Emily had been a tradition, a duty, and a care; a sort of hereditary obligation upon the town, dating from that day in 1894 when Colonel Sartoris, the mayor — he who fathered the edict that no Negro woman should appear on the streets without an apron — remitted her taxes, the dispensation dating from the death of her father on into perpetuity. Not that Miss Emily would have accepted charity. Colonel Sartoris invented an involved tale to the effect that Miss Emily's father had loaned money to the town, which the town, as a matter of business, preferred this way of repaying. Only a man of Colonel Sartoris' generation and thought could have invented it, and only a woman could have believed it.

When the next generation, with its more modern ideas, became mayors and aldermen, this arrangement created some little dissatisfaction. On the first of the year they mailed her a tax notice. February came, and there was no reply. They wrote her a formal letter, asking her to call at the sheriff's office at her convenience. A week later the mayor wrote her himself, offering to call or to send his car for her, and received in reply a note on paper of an archaic shape, in a thin, flowing calligraphy in faded ink, to the effect that she no longer went out at all. The tax notice was also enclosed, without comment.

They called a special meeting of the Board of Aldermen. A deputation waited upon her, knocked at the door through which no visitor had passed since she ceased giving china-painting lessons eight or ten years earlier. They were admitted by the old Negro into a dim hall from which a stairway mounted into still more shadow. It smelled of dust and disuse — a close, dank smell. The Negro led them into the parlor. It was furnished in heavy, leather-covered furniture. When the Negro opened the blinds of one window, they could see that the leather was cracked; and when they sat down, a faint dust rose sluggishly about their thighs, spinning with slow motes in the single sunray. On a tarnished gilt easel before the fireplace stood a crayon portrait of Miss Emily's father.

They rose when she entered — a small, fat woman in black, with a thin gold chain descending to her waist and vanishing into her belt, leaning on an ebony cane with a tarnished gold head. Her skeleton was small and spare; perhaps that was why what would have been merely plumpness in another was obesity in her. She looked bloated, like a body long submerged in motionless water, and of that pallid hue. Her eyes, lost in the fatty ridges of her face, looked like two small pieces of coal pressed into a lump of dough as they moved from one face to another while the visitors stated their errand.

She did not ask them to sit. She just stood in the door and listened quietly until the spokesman came to a stumbling halt. Then they could hear the invisible watch ticking at the end of the gold chain.

Her voice was dry and cold. "I have no taxes in Jefferson. Colonel Sartoris explained it to me. Perhaps one of you can gain access to the city records and satisfy yourselves."

"But we have. We are the city authorities, Miss Emily. Didn't you get a notice from the sheriff, signed by him?"

"I received a paper, yes," Miss Emily said. "Perhaps he considers himself the sheriff. . . . I have no taxes in Jefferson."

"But there is nothing on the books to show that, you see. We must go by the — "

"See Colonel Sartoris. I have no taxes in Jefferson."

"But, Miss Emily — "

"See Colonel Sartoris." (Colonel Sartoris had been dead almost ten years.) "I have no taxes in Jefferson. Tobe!" The Negro appeared. "Show these gentlemen out."

II

So she vanquished them, horse and foot, just as she had vanquished their fathers thirty years before about the smell. That was two years after her father's death and a short time after her sweetheart — the one we believed would marry her — had deserted her. After her father's death she went out very little; after her sweetheart went away, people hardly saw her at all. A few of the ladies had the temerity to call, but were not received, and the only sign of life about the place was the Negro man — a young man then — going in and out with a market basket.

"Just as if a man — any man — could keep a kitchen properly," the ladies said; so they were not surprised when the smell developed. It was another link between the gross, teeming world and the high and mighty Griersons.

A neighbor, a woman, complained to the mayor, Judge Stevens, eighty years old.

"But what will you have me do about it, madam?" he said.

"Why, send her word to stop it," the woman said. "Isn't there a law?"

"I'm sure that won't be necessary," Judge Stevens said. "It's probably just a snake or a rat that nigger of hers killed in the yard. I'll speak to him about it."

The next day he received two more complaints, one from a man who came in diffident deprecation. "We really must do something about it, Judge. I'd be the last one in the world to bother Miss Emily, but we've got to do something." That night the Board of Aldermen met — three graybeards and one younger man, a member of the rising generation.

"It's simple enough," he said. "Send her word to have her place cleaned up. Give her a certain time to do it in, and if she don't. . . ."

"Dammit, sir," Judge Stevens said, "will you accuse a lady to her face of smelling bad?"

So the next night, after midnight, four men crossed Miss Emily's lawn and slunk about the house like burglars, sniffing along the base of the brickwork and at the cellar openings while one of them performed a regular sowing motion with his hand out of a sack slung from his shoulder. They broke open the cellar door and sprinkled lime there, and in all the outbuildings. As they recrossed the lawn, a window that had been dark was lighted and Miss

Emily sat in it, the light behind her, and her upright torso motionless as that of an idol. They crept quietly across the lawn and into the shadow of the locusts that lined the street. After a week or two the smell went away.

That was when people had begun to feel really sorry for her. People in our town, remembering how old lady Wyatt, her great-aunt, had gone completely crazy at last, believed that the Griersons held themselves a little too high for what they really were. None of the young men were quite good enough for Miss Emily and such. We had long thought of them as a tableau, Miss Emily a slender figure in white in the background, her father a spraddled silhouette in the foreground, his back to her and clutching a horsewhip, the two of them framed by the backflung front door. So when she got to be thirty and was still single, we were not pleased exactly, but vindicated; even with insanity in the family she wouldn't have turned down all of her chances if they had really materialized.

When her father died, it got about that the house was all that was left to her; and in a way, people were glad. At last they could pity Miss Emily. Being left alone, and a pauper, she had become humanized. Now she too would know the old thrill and the old despair of a penny more or less.

The day after his death all the ladies prepared to call at the house and offer condolence and aid, as is our custom. Miss Emily met them at the door, dressed as usual and with no trace of grief on her face. She told them that her father was not dead. She did that for three days, with the ministers calling on her, and the doctors, trying to persuade her to let them dispose of the body. Just as they were about to resort to law and force, she broke down, and they buried her father quickly.

We did not say she was crazy then. We believed she had to do that. We remembered all the young men her father had driven away, and we knew that with nothing left, she would have to cling to that which had robbed her, as people will.

III

She was sick for a long time. When we saw her again, her hair was cut short, making her look like a girl, with a vague resemblance to those angels in colored church windows — sort of tragic and serene.

The town had just let the contracts for paving the sidewalks, and in the summer after her father's death they began the work. The construction company came with niggers and mules and machinery, and a foreman named Homer Barron, a Yankee — a big, dark, ready man, with a big voice and eyes lighter than his face. The little boys would follow in groups to hear him cuss the niggers, and the niggers singing in time to the rise and fall of picks. Pretty soon he knew everybody in town. Whenever you heard a lot of laughing anywhere about the square, Homer Barron would be in the center of the group. Presently, we began to see him and Miss Emily on Sunday afternoons driving in the yellow-wheeled buggy and the matched team of bays from the livery stable.

At first we were glad that Miss Emily would have an interest, because the ladies all said, "Of course a Grierson would not think seriously of a Northerner, a day laborer." But there were still others, older people, who said that even grief could not cause a real lady to forget *noblesse oblige* — without calling it *noblesse oblige*. They just said, "Poor Emily. Her kinsfolk should come to her." She had some kin in Alabama; but years ago her father had fallen out with them over the estate of old lady Wyatt, the crazy woman, and there was no communication between the two families. They had not even been represented at the funeral.

And as soon as the old people said, "Poor Emily," the whispering began. "Do you suppose it's really so?" they said to one another. "Of course it is. What else could. . . ." This behind their hands; rustling of craned silk and satin behind jalousies closed upon the sun of Sunday afternoon as the thin, swift clop-clop-clop of the matched team passed: "Poor Emily."

She carried her head high enough — even when we believed that she was fallen. It was as if she demanded more than ever the recognition of her dignity as the last Grierson; as if it had wanted that touch of earthiness to reaffirm her imperviousness. Like when she bought the rat poison, the arsenic. That was over a year after they had begun to say "Poor Emily," and while the two female cousins were visiting her.

"I want some poison," she said to the druggist. She was over thirty then, still a slight woman, though thinner than usual, with cold, haughty black eyes in a face the flesh of which was strained across the temples and about the eyesockets as you imagine a lighthouse-keeper's face ought to look. "I want some poison," she said.

"Yes, Miss Emily. What kind? For rats and such? I'd recom —— "

"I want the best you have. I don't care what kind."

The druggist named several. "They'll kill anything up to an elephant. But what you want is —— "

"Arsenic," Miss Emily said. "Is that a good one?"

"Is . . . arsenic? Yes, ma'am. But what you want —— "

"I want arsenic."

The druggist looked down at her. She looked back at him, erect, her face like a strained flag. "Why, of course," the druggist said. "If that's what you want. But the law requires you to tell what you are going to use it for."

Miss Emily just stared at him, her head tilted back in order to look him eye for eye, until he looked away and went and got the arsenic and wrapped it up. The Negro delivery boy brought her the package; the druggist didn't come back. When she opened the package at home there was written on the box, under the skull and bones: "For rats."

IV

So the next day we all said, "She will kill herself"; and we said it would be the best thing. When she had first begun to be seen with Homer Barron, we had said, "She will marry him." Then we said, "She will persuade him yet," because Homer himself had remarked — he liked men, and it was known that he drank with the younger men in the Elks' Club — that he was not a marrying man. Later we said, "Poor Emily" behind the jalousies as they passed on Sunday afternoon in the glittering buggy, Miss Emily with her head high and

Homer Barron with his hat cocked and a cigar in his teeth, reins and whip in a yellow glove.

Then some of the ladies began to say that it was a disgrace to the town and a bad example to the young people. The men did not want to interfere, but at last the ladies forced the Baptist minister — Miss Emily's people were Episcopal — to call upon her. He would never divulge what happened during that interview, but he refused to go back again. The next Sunday they again drove about the streets, and the following day the minister's wife wrote to Miss Emily's relations in Alabama.

So she had blood-kin under her roof again and we sat back to watch developments. At first nothing happened. Then we were sure that they were to be married. We learned that Miss Emily had been to the jeweler's and ordered a man's toilet set in silver, with the letters H.B. on each piece. Two days later we learned that she had bought a complete outfit of men's clothing, including a nightshirt, and we said, "They are married." We were really glad. We were glad because the two female cousins were even more Grierson than Miss Emily had ever been.

So we were not surprised when Homer Barron — the streets had been finished some time since — was gone. We were a little disappointed that there was not a public blowing-off, but we believed that he had gone on to prepare for Miss Emily's coming, or to give her a chance to get rid of the cousins. (By that time it was a cabal, and we were all Miss Emily's allies to help circumvent the cousins.) Sure enough, after another week they departed. And, as we had expected all along, within three days Homer Barron was back in town. A neighbor saw the Negro man admit him at the kitchen door at dusk one evening.

And that was the last we saw of Homer Barron. And of Miss Emily for some time. The Negro man went in and out with the market basket, but the front door remained closed. Now and then we would see her at the window for a moment, as the men did that night when they sprinkled the lime, but for almost six months she did not appear on the streets. Then we knew that this was to be expected too; as if that quality of her father which had thwarted her woman's life so many times had been too virulent and too furious to die.

When we next saw Miss Emily, she had grown fat and her hair was turning gray. During the next few years it grew grayer and grayer until it attained an even pepper-and-salt iron-gray, when it ceased turning. Up to the day of her death at seventy-four it was still that vigorous iron-gray, like the hair of an active man.

From that time on her front door remained closed, save during a period of six or seven years, when she was about forty, during which she gave lessons in china-painting. She fitted up a studio in one of the downstairs rooms, where the daughters and granddaughters of Colonel Sartoris' contemporaries were sent to her with the same regularity and in the same spirit that they were sent to church on Sundays with a twenty-five-cent piece for the collection plate. Meanwhile her taxes had been remitted.

Then the newer generation became the backbone and the spirit of the town, and the painting pupils grew up and fell away and did not send their children to her with boxes of color and tedious brushes and pictures cut from the ladies' magazines. The front door closed upon the last one and remained closed for good. When the town got free postal delivery, Miss Emily alone refused to let them fasten the metal numbers above her door and attach a mailbox to it. She would not listen to them.

Daily, monthly, yearly we watched the Negro grow grayer and more stooped, going in and out with the market basket. Each December we sent her a tax notice, which would be returned by the post office a week later, unclaimed. Now and then we would see her in one of the downstairs windows — she had evidently shut up the top floor of the house — like the carven torso of an idol in a niche, looking or not looking at us, we could never tell which. Thus she passed from generation to generation — dear, inescapable, impervious, tranquil, and perverse.

And so she died. Fell ill in the house filled with dust and shadows, with only a doddering Negro man to wait on her. We did not even know she was sick; we had long since given up trying to get any information from the Negro. He talked to no one, probably not even to her, for his voice had grown harsh and rusty, as if from disuse.

She died in one of the downstairs rooms, in a heavy walnut bed with a curtain, her gray head propped on a pillow yellow and moldy with age and lack of sunlight.

V

The Negro met the first of the ladies at the front door and let them in, with their hushed, sibilant voices and their quick, curious glances, and then he disappeared. He walked right through the house and out the back and was not seen again.

The two female cousins came at once. They held the funeral on the second day, with the town coming to look at Miss Emily beneath a mass of bought flowers, with the crayon face of her father musing profoundly above the bier and the ladies sibilant and macabre; and the very old men — some in their brushed Confederate uniforms — on the porch and the lawn, talking of Miss Emily as if she had been a contemporary of theirs, believing that they had danced with her and courted her perhaps, confusing time with its mathematical progression, as the old do, to whom all the past is not a diminishing road but, instead, a huge meadow which no winter ever quite touches, divided from them now by the narrow bottleneck of the most recent decade of years.

Already we knew that there was one room in that region above stairs which no one had seen in forty years, and which would have to be forced. They waited until Miss Emily was decently in the ground before they opened it.

The violence of breaking down the door seemed to fill this room with pervading dust. A thin, acrid pall as of the tomb seemed to lie everywhere upon this room decked and furnished as for a bridal: upon the valance curtains of faded rose color, upon the rose-shaded lights, upon the dressing table, upon the delicate array of crystal and the man's toilet things backed with tarnished silver, silver so tarnished that the monogram was obscured. Among them lay a collar and tie, as if they had just been removed, which, lifted, left upon the surface a pale crescent in the dust. Upon a chair hung the suit, carefully folded; beneath it the two mute shoes and the discarded socks.

The man himself lay in the bed.

For a long while we just stood there, looking down at the profound and fleshless grin. The body had apparently once lain in the attitude of an embrace, but now the long sleep that outlasts love, that conquers even the grimace of love, had cuckolded him. What was left of him, rotted beneath what was left of the nightshirt, had become inextricable from the bed in which he lay; and upon him and upon the pillow beside him lay that even coating of the patient and biding dust.

Then we noticed that in the second pillow was the indentation of a head. One of us lifted something from it, and leaning forward, that faint and invisible dust dry and acrid in the nostrils, we saw a long strand of iron-gray hair.

WILLIAM FAULKNER

That Evening Sun   1931

I

Monday is no different from any other weekday in Jefferson now. The streets are paved now, and the telephone and electric companies are cutting down more and more of the shade trees — the water oaks, the maples and locusts and elms — to make room for iron poles bearing clusters of bloated and ghostly and bloodless grapes, and we have a city laundry which makes the rounds on Monday morning, gathering the bundles of clothes into bright-colored, specially-made motor cars: the soiled wearing of a whole week now flees apparitionlike behind alert and irritable electric horns, with a long diminishing noise of rubber and asphalt like tearing silk, and even the Negro women who still take in white people's washing after the old custom, fetch and deliver it in automobiles.

But fifteen years ago, on Monday morning the quiet, dusty, shady streets would be full of Negro women with, balanced on their steady, turbaned heads, bundles of clothes tied up in sheets, almost as large as cotton bales, carried so without touch of hand between the kitchen door of the white house and the blackened washpot beside a cabin door in Negro Hollow.

Nancy would set her bundle on the top of her head, then upon the bundle in turn she would set the black straw sailor hat which she wore winter and summer. She was tall, with a high, sad face sunken a little where her teeth were missing. Sometimes we would go a part of the way down the lane and across the pasture with her, to watch the balanced bundle and the hat that never bobbed nor wavered, even when she walked down into the ditch and up the other side and stooped through the fence. She would go down on her hands and knees and crawl through the gap, her head rigid, uptilted, the bundle steady as a rock or a balloon, and rise to her feet again and go on.

Sometimes the husbands of the washing women would fetch and deliver the clothes, but Jesus never did that for Nancy, even before father told him to stay away from our house, even when Dilsey was sick and Nancy would come to cook for us.

And then about half the time we'd have to go down the lane to Nancy's cabin and tell her to come on and cook breakfast. We would stop at the ditch, because father told us to not have anything to do with Jesus — he was a short black man, with a razor scar down his face — and we would throw rocks at Nancy's house until she came to the door, leaning her head around it without any clothes on.

"What yawl mean, chunking my house?" Nancy said. "What you little devils mean?"

"Father says for you to come on and get breakfast," Caddy said. "Father says it's over a half an hour now, and you've got to come this minute."

"I aint studying no breakfast," Nancy said. "I going to get my sleep out."

"I bet you're drunk," Jason said. "Father says you're drunk. Are you drunk, Nancy?"

"Who says I is?" Nancy said. "I got to get my sleep out. I ain't studying no breakfast."

So after a while we quit chunking the cabin and went back home. When she finally came, it was too late for me to go to school. So we thought it was whisky until that day they arrested her again and they were taking her to jail and they passed Mr Stovall. He was the cashier in the bank and a deacon in the Baptist church, and Nancy began to say:

"When you going to pay me, white man? When you going to pay me, white man? It's been three times now since you paid me a cent — " Mr Stovall knocked her down, but she kept on saying, "When you going to pay me, white man? It's been three times now since — " until Mr Stovall kicked her in the mouth with his heel and the marshal caught Mr Stovall back, and Nancy lying in the street, laughing. She turned her head and spat out some blood and teeth and said, "It's been three times now since he paid me a cent."

That was how she lost her teeth, and all that day they told about Nancy and Mr Stovall, and all that night the ones that passed the jail could hear Nancy singing and yelling. They could see her hands holding to the window bars, and a lot of them stopped along the fence, listening to her and to the jailer trying to make her stop. She didn't shut up until almost daylight, when the jailer began to hear a bumping and scraping upstairs and he went up there and found Nancy hanging from the window bar. He said that it was cocaine and not whisky, because no nigger would try to commit suicide unless he was full of cocaine, because a nigger full of cocaine wasn't a nigger any longer.

The jailer cut her down and revived her; then he beat her, whipped her. She had hung herself with her dress. She had fixed it all right, but when they arrested her she didn't have on anything except a dress and so she didn't have anything to tie her hands with and she couldn't make her hands let go of the window ledge. So the jailer heard the noise and ran up there and found Nancy hanging from the window, stark naked, her belly already swelling out a little, like a little balloon.

When Dilsey was sick in her cabin and Nancy was cooking for us, we could see her apron swelling out; that was before father told Jesus to stay away from the house. Jesus was in the kitchen, sitting behind the stove, with his razor scar on his black face like a piece of dirty string. He said it was a watermelon that Nancy had under her dress.

"It never come off of your vine, though," Nancy said.

"Off of what vine?" Caddy said.

"I can cut down the vine it did come off of," Jesus said.

"What makes you want to talk like that before these chillen?" Nancy said. "Whyn't you go on to work? You done et. You want Mr Jason to catch you hanging around his kitchen, talking that way before these chillen?"

"Talking what way?" Caddy said. "What vine?"

"I cant hang around white man's kitchen," Jesus said. "But white man can hang around mine. White man can come in my house, but I cant stop him. When white man want to come in my house, I aint got no house. I cant stop him, but he cant kick me outen it. He cant do that."

Dilsey was still sick in her cabin. Father told Jesus to stay off our place. Dilsey was still sick. It was a long time. We were in the library after supper.

"Isn't Nancy through in the kitchen yet?" mother said. "It seems to me that she has had plenty of time to have finished the dishes."

"Let Quentin go and see," father said. "Go and see if Nancy is through, Quentin. Tell her she can go on home."

I went to the kitchen. Nancy was through. The dishes were put away and the fire was out. Nancy was sitting in a chair, close to the cold stove. She looked at me.

"Mother wants to know if you are through," I said.

"Yes," Nancy said. She looked at me. "I done finished." She looked at me.

"What is it?" I said. "What is it?"

"I aint nothing but a nigger," Nancy said. "It aint none of my fault."

She looked at me, sitting in the chair before the cold stove, the sailor hat on her head. I went back to the library. It was the cold stove and all, when you think of a kitchen being warm and busy and cheerful. And with a cold stove and the dishes all put away, and nobody wanting to eat at that hour.

"Is she through?" mother said.

"Yessum," I said.

"What is she doing?" mother said.

"She's not doing anything. She's through."

"I'll go and see," father said.

"Maybe she's waiting for Jesus to come and take her home," Caddy said.

"Jesus is gone," I said. Nancy told us how one morning she woke up and Jesus was gone.

"He quit me," Nancy said. "Done gone to Memphis, I reckon. Dodging them city *po*-lice for a while, I reckon."

"And a good riddance," father said. "I hope he stays there."

"Nancy's scaired of the dark," Jason said.

"So are you," Caddy said.

"I'm not," Jason said.

"Scairy cat," Caddy said.

"I'm not," Jason said.

"You, Candace!" mother said. Father came back.

"I am going to walk down the lane with Nancy," he said. "She says that Jesus is back."

"Has she seen him?" mother said.

"No. Some Negro sent her word that he was back in town. I wont be long."

"You'll leave me alone, to take Nancy home?" mother said. "Is her safety more precious to you than mine?"

"I wont be long," father said.

"You'll leave these children unprotected, with that Negro about?"

"I'm going too," Caddy said. "Let me go, Father."

"What would he do with them, if he were unfortunate enough to have them?" father said.

"I want to go, too," Jason said.

"Jason!" mother said. She was speaking to father. You could tell that by the way she said the name. Like she believed that all day father had been trying to think of doing the thing she wouldn't like the most, and that she knew all the time that after a while he would think of it. I stayed quiet, because father and I both knew that mother would want him to make me stay with her if she just thought of it in time. So father didn't look at me. I was the oldest. I was nine and Caddy was seven and Jason was five.

"Nonsense," father said. "We wont be long."

Nancy had her hat on. We came to the lane. "Jesus always been good to me," Nancy said. "Whenever he had two dollars, one of them was mine." We walked in the lane. "If I can just get through the lane," Nancy said, "I be all right then."

The lane was always dark. "This is where Jason got scared on Hallowe'en," Caddy said.

"I didn't," Jason said.

"Cant Aunt Rachel do anything with him?" father said. Aunt Rachel was old. She lived in a cabin beyond Nancy's, by herself. She had white hair and she smoked a pipe in the door, all day long; she didn't work any more. They said she was Jesus' mother. Sometimes she said she was and sometimes she said she wasn't any kin to Jesus.

"Yes, you did," Caddy said. "You were scairder than Frony. You were scairder than T.P. even. Scairder than niggers."

"Cant nobody do nothing with him," Nancy said. "He say I done woke up the devil in him and aint but one thing going to lay it down again."

"Well, he's gone now," father said. "There's nothing for you to be afraid of now. And if you'd just let white men alone."

"Let what white men alone?" Caddy said. "How let them alone?"

"He aint gone nowhere," Nancy said. "I can feel him. I can feel him now, in this lane. He hearing us talk, every word, hid somewhere, waiting. I aint seen him, and I aint going to see him again but once more, with that razor in his mouth. That razor on that string down his back, inside his shirt. And then I aint going to be even surprised."

"I wasn't scaired," Jason said.

"If you'd behave yourself, you'd have kept out of this," father said. "But it's all right now. He's probably in St. Louis now. Probably got another wife by now and forgot all about you."

"If he has, I better not find out about it," Nancy said. "I'd stand there right over them, and every time he wropped her, I'd cut that arm off. I'd cut his head off and I'd slit her belly and I'd shove — "

"Hush," father said.

"Slit whose belly, Nancy?" Caddy said.

"I wasn't scaired," Jason said. "I'd walk right down this lane by myself."

"Yah," Caddy said. "You wouldn't dare to put your foot down in it if we were not here too."

II

Dilsey was still sick, so we took Nancy home every night until mother said, "How much longer is this going on? I to be left alone in this big house while you take home a frightened Negro?"

We fixed a pallet in the kitchen for Nancy. One night we waked up, hearing the sound. It was not singing and it was not crying, coming up the dark stairs. There was a light in mother's room and we heard father going down the hall, down the back stairs, and Caddy and I went into the hall. The floor was cold. Our toes curled away from it while we listened to the sound. It was like singing and it wasn't like singing, like the sounds that Negroes make.

Then it stopped and we heard father going down the back stairs, and we went to the head of the stairs. Then the sound began again, in the stairway, not loud, and we could see Nancy's eyes halfway up the stairs, against the wall. They looked like cat's eyes do, like a big cat against the wall, watching us. When we came down the steps to where she was, she quit making the sound again, and we stood there until father came back up from the kitchen, with his pistol in his hand. He went back down with Nancy and they came back with Nancy's pallet.

We spread the pallet in our room. After the light in mother's room went off, we could see Nancy's eyes again. "Nancy," Caddy whispered, "are you asleep, Nancy?"

Nancy whispered something. It was oh or no, I dont know which. Like nobody had made it, like it came from nowhere and went nowhere, until it was like Nancy was not there at all; that I had looked so hard at her eyes on the stairs that they had got printed on my eyeballs, like the sun does when you have closed your eyes and there is no sun. "Jesus," Nancy whispered. "Jesus."

"Was it Jesus?" Caddy said. "Did he try to come into the kitchen?"

"Jesus," Nancy said. Like this: Jeeeeeeeeeeeeeeeesus, until the sound went out, like a match or a candle does.

"It's the other Jesus she means," I said.

"Can you see us, Nancy?" Caddy whispered. "Can you see our eyes too?"

"I aint nothing but a nigger," Nancy said. "God knows. God knows."

"What did you see down there in the kitchen?" Caddy whispered. "What tried to get in?"

"God knows," Nancy said. We could see her eyes. "God knows."

Dilsey got well. She cooked dinner. "You'd better stay in bed a day or two longer," father said.

"What for?" Dilsey said. "If I had been a day later, this place would be to rack and ruin. Get on out of here now, and let me get my kitchen straight again."

Dilsey cooked supper too. And that night, just before dark, Nancy came into the kitchen.

"How do you know he's back?" Dilsey said. "You aint seen him."

"Jesus is a nigger," Jason said.

"I can feel him," Nancy said. "I can feel him laying yonder in the ditch."

"Tonight?" Dilsey said. "Is he there tonight?"

"Dilsey's a nigger too," Jason said.

"You try to eat something," Dilsey said.

"I dont want nothing," Nancy said.

"I aint a nigger," Jason said.

"Drink some coffee," Dilsey said. She poured a cup of coffee for Nancy. "Do you know he's out there tonight? How come you know it's tonight?"

"I know," Nancy said. "He's there, waiting. I know. I done lived with him too long. I know what he is fixing to do fore he know it himself."

"Drink some coffee," Dilsey said. Nancy held the cup to her mouth and blew into the cup. Her mouth pursed out like a spreading adder's, like a rubber mouth, like she had blown all the color out of her lips with blowing the coffee.

"I aint a nigger," Jason said. "Are you a nigger, Nancy?"

"I hellborn, child," Nancy said. "I wont be nothing soon. I going back where I come from soon."

III

She began to drink the coffee. While she was drinking, holding the cup in both hands, she began to make the sound again. She made the sound into the cup and the coffee sploshed out onto her hands and her dress. Her eyes looked at us and she sat there, her elbows on her knees, holding the cup in both hands, looking at us across the wet cup, making the sound. "Look at Nancy," Jason said. "Nancy cant cook for us now. Dilsey's got well now."

"You hush up," Dilsey said. Nancy held the cup in both hands, looking at us, making the sound, like there were two of them: one looking at us and the other making the sound. "Whyn't you let Mr Jason telefoam the marshal?" Dilsey said. Nancy stopped then, holding the cup in her long brown hands. She tried to drink some coffee again, but it sploshed out of the cup, onto her hands and her dress, and she put the cup down. Jason watched her.

"I cant swallow it," Nancy said. "I swallows but it wont go down me."

"You go down to the cabin," Dilsey said. "Frony will fix you a pallet and I'll be there soon."

"Wont no nigger stop him," Nancy said.

"I aint a nigger," Jason said. "Am I, Dilsey?"

"I reckon not," Dilsey said. She looked at Nancy. "I dont reckon so. What you going to do, then?"

Nancy looked at us. Her eyes went fast, like she was afraid there wasn't time to look, without hardly moving at all. She looked at us, at all three of us at one time. "You member that night I stayed in yawls' room?" she said. She told about how we waked up early the next morning, and played. We had to play quiet, on her pallet, until father woke up and it was time to get breakfast. "Go and ask your maw to let me stay here tonight," Nancy said. "I wont need no pallet. We can play some more."

Caddy asked mother. Jason went too. "I cant have Negroes sleeping in the bedrooms," mother said. Jason cried. He cried until mother said he couldn't have any dessert for three days if he didn't stop. Then Jason said he would stop if Dilsey would make a chocolate cake. Father was there.

"Why dont you do something about it?" mother said. "What do we have officers for?"

"Why is Nancy afraid of Jesus?" Caddy said. "Are you afraid of father, mother?"

"What could the officers do?" father said. "If Nancy hasn't seen him, how could the officers find him?"

"Then why is she afraid?" mother said.

"She says he is there. She says she knows he is there tonight."

"Yet we pay taxes," mother said. "I must wait here alone in this big house while you take a Negro woman home."

"You know that I am not lying outside with a razor," father said.

"I'll stop if Dilsey will make a chocolate cake," Jason said. Mother told us to go out and father said he didn't know if Jason would get a chocolate cake or not, but he knew what Jason was going to get in about a minute. We went back to the kitchen and told Nancy.

"Father said for you to go home and lock the door, and you'll be all right," Caddy said. "All right from what, Nancy? Is Jesus mad at you?" Nancy was holding the coffee cup in her hands again, her elbows on her knees and her hands holding the cup between her knees. She was looking into the cup. "What have you done that made Jesus mad?" Caddy said. Nancy let the cup go. It didn't break on the floor, but the coffee spilled out, and Nancy sat there with her hands still making the shape of the cup. She began to make the sound again, not loud. Not singing and not unsinging. We watched her.

"Here," Dilsey said. "You quit that, now. You get aholt of yourself. You wait here. I going to get Versh to walk home with you." Dilsey went out.

We looked at Nancy. Her shoulders kept shaking, but she quit making the sound. We watched her. "What's Jesus going to do to you?" Caddy said. "He went away."

Nancy looked at us. "We had fun that night I stayed in yawls' room, didn't we?"

"I didn't," Jason said. "I didn't have any fun."

"You were asleep in mother's room," Caddy said. "You were not there."

"Let's go down to my house and have some more fun," Nancy said.

"Mother wont let us," I said. "It's too late now."

"Dont bother her," Nancy said. "We can tell her in the morning. She wont mind."

"She wouldn't let us," I said.

"Dont ask her now," Nancy said. "Dont bother her now."

"She didn't say we couldn't go," Caddy said.

"We didn't ask," I said.

"If you go, I'll tell," Jason said.

"We'll have fun," Nancy said. "They won't mind, just to my house. I been working for yawl a long time. They won't mind."

"I'm not afraid to go," Caddy said. "Jason is the one that's afraid. He'll tell."

"I'm not," Jason said.

"Yes, you are," Caddy said. "You'll tell."

"I won't tell," Jason said. "I'm not afraid."

"Jason ain't afraid to go with me," Nancy said. "Is you, Jason?"

"Jason is going to tell," Caddy said. The lane was dark. We passed the pasture gate. "I bet if something was to jump out from behind that gate, Jason would holler."

"I wouldn't," Jason said. We walked down the lane. Nancy was talking loud.

"What are you talking so loud for, Nancy?" Caddy said.

"Who; me?" Nancy said. "Listen at Quentin and Caddy and Jason saying I'm talking loud."

"You talk like there was five of us here," Caddy said. "You talk like father was here too."

"Who; me talking loud, Mr Jason?" Nancy said.

"Nancy called Jason 'Mister,' " Caddy said.

"Listen how Caddy and Quentin and Jason talk," Nancy said.

"We're not talking loud," Caddy said. "You're the one that's talking like father — "

"Hush," Nancy said; "hush, Mr Jason."

"Nancy called Jason 'Mister' aguh — "

"Hush," Nancy said. She was talking loud when we crossed the ditch and stooped through the fence where she used to stoop through with the clothes on her head. Then we came to her house. We were going fast then. She opened the door. The smell of the house was like the lamp and the smell of Nancy was like the wick, like they were waiting for one another to begin to smell. She lit the lamp and closed the door and put the bar up. Then she quit talking loud, looking at us.

"What're we going to do?" Caddy said.

"What do yawl want to do?" Nancy said.

"You said we would have some fun," Caddy said.

There was something about Nancy's house; something you could smell besides Nancy and the house. Jason smelled it, even. "I don't want to stay here," he said. "I want to go home."

"Go home, then," Caddy said.

"I don't want to go by myself," Jason said.

"We're going to have some fun," Nancy said.

"How?" Caddy said.

Nancy stood by the door. She was looking at us, only it was like she had emptied her eyes, like she had quit using them. "What do you want to do?" she said.

"Tell us a story," Caddy said. "Can you tell a story?"

"Yes," Nancy said.

"Tell it," Caddy said. We looked at Nancy. "You don't know any stories."

"Yes," Nancy said. "Yes, I do."

She came and sat in a chair before the hearth. There was a little fire there. Nancy built it up, when it was already hot inside. She built a good blaze. She told a story. She talked like her eyes looked, like her eyes watching us and her voice talking to us did not belong to her. Like she was living somewhere else, waiting somewhere else. She was outside the cabin. Her voice was inside and the shape of her, the Nancy that could stoop under a barbed wire fence with a bundle of clothes balanced on her head as though without weight, like a balloon, was there. But that was all. "And so this here queen come walking up to the ditch, where that bad man was hiding. She was walking up to the ditch, and she say, 'If I can just get past this here ditch,' was what she say . . ."

"What ditch?" Caddy said. "A ditch like that one out there? Why did a queen want to go into a ditch?"

"To get to her house," Nancy said. She looked at us. "She had to cross the ditch to get into her house quick and bar the door."

"Why did she want to go home and bar the door?" Caddy said.

IV

Nancy looked at us. She quit talking. She looked at us. Jason's legs stuck straight out of his pants where he sat on Nancy's lap. "I don't think that's a good story," he said. "I want to go home."

"Maybe we had better," Caddy said. She got up from the floor. "I bet they are looking for us right now." She went toward the door.

"No," Nancy said. "Don't open it." She got up quick and passed Caddy. She didn't touch the door, the wooden bar.

"Why not?" Caddy said.

"Come back to the lamp," Nancy said. "We'll have fun. You don't have to go."

"We ought to go," Caddy said. "Unless we have a lot of fun." She and Nancy came back to the fire, the lamp.

"I want to go home," Jason said. "I'm going to tell."

"I know another story," Nancy said. She stood close to the lamp. She looked at Caddy, like when your eyes look up at a stick balanced on your nose.

She had to look down to see Caddy, but her eyes looked like that, like when you are balancing a stick.

"I won't listen to it," Jason said. "I'll bang on the floor."

"It's a good one," Nancy said. "It's better than the other one."

"What's it about?" Caddy said. Nancy was standing by the lamp. Her hand was on the lamp, against the light, long and brown.

"Your hand is on that hot globe," Caddy said. "Don't it feel hot to your hand?"

Nancy looked at her hand on the lamp chimney. She took her hand away, slow. She stood there, looking at Caddy, wringing her long hand as though it were tied to her wrist with a string.

"Let's do something else," Caddy said.

"I want to go home," Jason said.

"I got some popcorn," Nancy said. She looked at Caddy and then at Jason and then at me and then at Caddy again. "I got some popcorn."

"I don't like popcorn," Jason said. "I'd rather have candy."

Nancy looked at Jason. "You can hold the popper." She was still wringing her hand; it was long and limp and brown.

"All right," Jason said. "I'll stay a while if I can do that. Caddy can't hold it. I'll want to go home again if Caddy holds the popper."

Nancy built up the fire. "Look at Nancy putting her hands in the fire," Caddy said. "What's the matter with you, Nancy?"

"I got popcorn," Nancy said. "I got some." She took the popper from under the bed. It was broken. Jason began to cry.

"Now we can't have any popcorn," he said.

"We ought to go home, anyway," Caddy said. "Come on, Quentin."

"Wait," Nancy said; "wait. I can fix it. Don't you want to help me fix it?"

"I don't think I want any," Caddy said. "It's too late now."

"You help me, Jason," Nancy said. "Don't you want to help me?"

"No," Jason said. "I want to go home."

"Hush," Nancy said; "hush. Watch. Watch me. I can fix it so Jason can hold it and pop the corn." She got a piece of wire and fixed the popper.

"It won't hold good," Caddy said.

"Yes, it will," Nancy said. "Yawl watch. Yawl help me shell some corn."

The popcorn was under the bed too. We shelled it into the popper and Nancy helped Jason hold the popper over the fire.

"It's not popping," Jason said. "I want to go home."

"You wait," Nancy said. "It'll begin to pop. We'll have fun then." She was sitting close to the fire. The lamp was turned up so high it was beginning to smoke.

"Why don't you turn it down some?" I said.

"It's all right," Nancy said. "I'll clean it. Yawl wait. The popcorn will start in a minute."

"I don't believe it's going to start," Caddy said. "We ought to start home, anyway. They'll be worried."

"No," Nancy said. "It's going to pop. Dilsey will tell um yawl with me.

I been working for yawl long time. They won't mind if yawl at my house. You wait, now. It'll start popping any minute now."

Then Jason got some smoke in his eyes and he began to cry. He dropped the popper into the fire. Nancy got a wet rag and wiped Jason's face, but he didn't stop crying.

"Hush," she said. "Hush." But he didn't hush. Caddy took the popper out of the fire.

"It's burned up," she said. "You'll have to get some more popcorn, Nancy."

"Did you put all of it in?" Nancy said.

"Yes," Caddy said. Nancy looked at Caddy. Then she took the popper and opened it and poured the cinders into her apron and began to sort the grains, her hands long and brown, and we watching her.

"Haven't you got any more?" Caddy said.

"Yes," Nancy said; "yes. Look. This here ain't burnt. All we need to do is — "

"I want to go home," Jason said. "I'm going to tell."

"Hush," Caddy said. We all listened. Nancy's head was already turned toward the barred door, her eyes filled with red lamplight. "Somebody is coming," Caddy said.

Then Nancy began to make that sound again, not loud, sitting there above the fire, her long hands dangling between her knees; all of a sudden water began to come out on her face in big drops, running down her face, carrying in each one a little turning ball of firelight like a spark until it dropped off her chin. "She's not crying," I said.

"I ain't crying," Nancy said. Her eyes were closed. "I ain't crying. Who is it?"

"I don't know," Caddy said. She went to the door and looked out. "We've got to go now," she said. "Here comes father."

"I'm going to tell," Jason said. "Yawl made me come."

The water still ran down Nancy's face. She turned in her chair. "Listen. Tell him. Tell him we going to have fun. Tell him I take good care of yawl until in the morning. Tell him to let me come home with yawl and sleep on the floor. Tell him I won't need no pallet. We'll have fun. You member last time how we had so much fun?"

"I didn't have fun," Jason said. "You hurt me. You put smoke in my eyes. I'm going to tell."

V

Father came in. He looked at us. Nancy did not get up.

"Tell him," she said.

"Caddy made us come down here," Jason said. "I didn't want to."

Father came to the fire. Nancy looked up at him. "Can't you go to Aunt Rachel's and stay?" he said. Nancy looked up at father, her hands between her knees. "He's not here," father said. "I would have seen him. There's not a soul in sight."

"He in the ditch," Nancy said. "He waiting in the ditch yonder."

"Nonsense," father said. He looked at Nancy. "Do you know he's there?"

"I got the sign," Nancy said.

"What sign?"

"I got it. It was on the table when I come in. It was a hogbone, with blood meat still on it, laying by the lamp. He's out there. When yawl walk out that door, I gone."

"Gone where, Nancy?" Caddy said.

"I'm not a tattletale," Jason said.

"Nonsense," father said.

"He out there," Nancy said. "He looking through that window this minute, waiting for yawl to go. Then I gone."

"Nonsense," father said. "Lock up your house and we'll take you on to Aunt Rachel's."

" 'Twont do no good," Nancy said. She didn't look at father now, but he looked down at her, at her long, limp, moving hands. "Putting it off wont do no good."

"Then what do you want to do?" father said.

"I don't know," Nancy said. "I can't do nothing. Just put it off. And that don't do no good. I reckon it belong to me. I reckon what I going to get ain't no more than mine."

"Get what?" Caddy said. "What's yours?"

"Nothing," father said. "You all must get to bed."

"Caddy made me come," Jason said.

"Go on to Aunt Rachel's," father said.

"It won't do no good," Nancy said. She sat before the fire, her elbows on her knees, her long hands between her knees. "When even your own kitchen wouldn't do no good. When even if I was sleeping on the floor in the room with your chillen, and the next morning there I am, and blood — "

"Hush," father said. "Lock the door and put out the lamp and go to bed."

"I scared of the dark," Nancy said. "I scared for it to happen in the dark."

"You mean you're going to sit right here with the lamp lighted?" father said. Then Nancy began to make the sound again, sitting before the fire, her long hands between her knees. "Ah, damnation," father said. "Come along, chillen. It's past bedtime."

"When yawl go home, I gone," Nancy said. She talked quieter now, and her face looked quiet, like her hands. "Anyway, I got my coffin money saved up with Mr. Lovelady." Mr. Lovelady was a short, dirty man who collected the Negro insurance, coming around to the cabins or the kitchens every Saturday morning, to collect fifteen cents. He and his wife lived at the hotel. One morning his wife committed suicide. They had a child, a little girl. He and the child went away. After a week or two he came back alone. We would see him going along the lanes and the back streets on Saturday mornings.

"Nonsense," father said. "You'll be the first thing I'll see in the kitchen tomorrow morning."

"You'll see what you'll see, I reckon," Nancy said. "But it will take the Lord to say what that will be."

VI

"Come and put the bar up," father said. But she didn't move. She didn't look at us again, sitting quietly there between the lamp and the fire. From some distance down the lane we could look back and see her through the open door.

"What, Father?" Caddy said. "What's going to happen?"

"Nothing," father said. Jason was on father's back, so Jason was the tallest of all of us. We went down into the ditch. I looked at it, quiet. I couldn't see much where the moonlight and the shadows tangled.

"If Jesus is hid here, he can see us, cant he?" Caddy said.

"He's not there," father said. "He went away a long time ago."

"You made me come," Jason said, high; against the sky it looked like father had two heads, a little one and a big one. "I didn't want to."

We went up out of the ditch. We could still see Nancy's house and the open door, but we couldn't see Nancy now, sitting before the fire with the door open, because she was tired. "I just done got tired," she said. "I just a nigger. It ain't no fault of mine."

But we could hear her, because she began just after we came up out of the ditch, the sound that was not singing and not unsinging. "Who will do our washing now, Father?" I said.

"I'm not a nigger," Jason said, high and close above father's head.

"You're worse," Caddy said, "you are a tattletale. If something was to jump out, you'd be scairder than a nigger."

"I wouldn't," Jason said.

"You'd cry," Caddy said.

"Caddy," father said.

"I wouldn't!" Jason said.

"Scairy cat," Caddy said.

"Candace!" father said.

ನಿ

GABRIEL GARCÍA MÁRQUEZ *(b. 1928) was born in the remote town of Aracataca in Magdalena province, near the Caribbean coast of Colombia. The oldest of twelve children of a poverty-stricken telegraph operator and his wife, he was raised by his maternal grandparents. When he was eight, he was sent to school near Bogotá, and after his graduation in 1946 he studied law. A writer from childhood, García Márquez published his first book,* Leaf Storm and Other Stories, *which includes "A Very Old Man with Enormous Wings," in 1955. He spent the next few years in Paris, where he wrote two short novels. After the Cuban Revolution, he returned to Central America and worked as a journalist and screenwriter. His comic masterpiece, the novel* One

Hundred Years of Solitude *(1967), was written while he lived in Mexico City. His other novels include* The Autumn of the Patriarch *(1975), a novel about the life of a Latin American dictator, and the best-seller* Love in the Time of Cholera *(1988). In 1982 he received the Nobel Prize for literature.*

García Márquez mingles realistic and fantastic details in all his fiction, including "A Very Old Man with Enormous Wings." He has said that the origin of his stories is always an image, "not an idea or a concept. The image grows in my head until the whole story takes shape as it might in real life." Leaf Storm *was written after García Márquez returned from visiting the place where he grew up. As he later explained to an interviewer from the* Paris Review,

> *The atmosphere, the decadence, the heat in the village were roughly the same as what I had felt in Faulkner. It was a banana plantation region inhabited by a lot of Americans from the fruit companies which gave it the same sort of atmosphere I had found in the writers of the Deep South. Critics have spoken of the literary influence of Faulkner but I see it as a coincidence: I had simply found material that had to be dealt with in the same way that Faulkner had treated similar material. . . .*
>
> *What really happened to me in that trip to Aracataca was that I realized that everything that had occurred in my childhood had a literary value that I was only now appreciating. From the moment I wrote* Leaf Storm *I realized I wanted to be a writer and that nobody could stop me and that the only thing left for me to do was to be the best writer in the world.*

Other collections of short fiction by García Márquez are No One Writes to the Colonel and Other Stories *(1968),* Innocent Eréndira and Other Stories *(1978),* Collected Stories *(1984), and* Strange Pilgrims *(1993).*

In 1988 García Márquez coauthored (with Fernando Birri) a screenplay of "A Very Old Man with Enormous Wings" for Television Española. In a scene added to the film version of the story, the old man is revealed as a trickster or confidence man who takes off his wings when he is alone. The film also begins with a quotation from Hebrews 13:2: "Be not forgetful to entertain strangers: for thereby some have entertained angels unaware."

GABRIEL GARCÍA MÁRQUEZ

A Very Old Man with Enormous Wings 1955

TRANSLATED BY GREGORY RABASSA

On the third day of rain they had killed so many crabs inside the house that Pelayo had to cross his drenched courtyard and throw them into the sea, because the newborn child had a temperature all night and they thought it was due to the stench. The world had been sad since Tuesday. Sea and sky were a single ash-gray thing and the sands of the beach, which on March nights glimmered like powdered light, had become a stew of mud and rotten shellfish. The light was so weak at noon that when Pelayo was coming back to the house after throwing away the crabs, it was hard for him to see what it was that was moving and groaning in the rear of the courtyard. He had to go very close to see that it was an old man, a very old man, lying face down in the mud, who, in spite of his tremendous efforts, couldn't get up, impeded by his enormous wings.

Frightened by that nightmare, Pelayo ran to get Elisenda, his wife, who was putting compresses on the sick child, and he took her to the rear of the courtyard. They both looked at the fallen body with mute stupor. He was dressed like a ragpicker. There were only a few faded hairs left on his bald skull and very few teeth in his mouth, and his pitiful condition of a drenched great-grandfather had taken away any sense of grandeur he might have had. His huge buzzard wings, dirty and half-plucked, were forever entangled in the mud. They looked at him so long and so closely that Pelayo and Elisenda very soon overcame their surprise and in the end found him familiar. Then they dared speak to him, and he answered in an incomprehensible dialect with a strong sailor's voice. That was how they skipped over the inconvenience of the wings and quite intelligently concluded that he was a lonely castaway from some foreign ship wrecked by the storm. And yet, they called in a neighbor woman who knew everything about life and death to see him, and all she needed was one look to show them their mistake.

"He's an angel," she told them. "He must have been coming for the child, but the poor fellow is so old that the rain knocked him down."

On the following day everyone knew that a flesh-and-blood angel was held captive in Pelayo's house. Against the judgment of the wise neighbor woman, for whom angels in those times were the fugitive survivors of a celestial conspiracy, they did not have the heart to club him to death. Pelayo watched over him all afternoon from the kitchen, armed with his bailiff's club, and before going to bed he dragged him out of the mud and locked him up with the hens in the wire chicken coop. In the middle of the night, when the rain stopped, Pelayo and Elisenda were still killing crabs. A short time afterward the child woke up without a fever and with a desire to eat. Then they felt magnanimous and decided to put the angel on a raft with fresh water and provisions for three days and leave him to his fate on the high seas. But when they went out into the courtyard with the first light of dawn, they found the whole neighborhood in front of the chicken coop having fun with the angel, without the slightest reverence, tossing him things to eat through the openings in the wire as if he weren't a supernatural creature but a circus animal.

Father Gonzaga arrived before seven o'clock, alarmed at the strange news. By that time onlookers less frivolous than those at dawn had already arrived and they were making all kinds of conjectures concerning the captive's future. The simplest among them thought that he should be named mayor of the world. Others of sterner mind felt that he should be promoted to the rank of five-star general in order to win all wars. Some visionaries hoped that he could be put to stud in order to implant on earth a race of winged wise men who could take charge of the universe. But Father Gonzaga, before becoming a priest, had been a robust woodcutter. Standing by the wire, he reviewed his catechism in an instant and asked them to open the door so that he could take a close look at that pitiful man who looked more like a huge decrepit hen among the fascinated chickens. He was lying in a corner drying his open wings in the sunlight among the fruit peels and breakfast leftovers that the early risers had thrown him. Alien to the impertinences of the world, he only lifted his antiquarian eyes and murmured something in his dialect when Father Gonzaga went into the chicken coop and said good morning to him in Latin. The parish priest had his first suspicion of an impostor when he saw that he did not understand the language of God or know how to greet His ministers. Then he noticed that seen close up he was much too human: he had an unbearable smell of the outdoors, the back side of his wings was strewn with parasites and his main feathers had been mistreated by terrestrial winds, and nothing about him measured up to the proud dignity of angels. Then he came out of the chicken coop and in a brief sermon warned the curious against the risks of being ingenuous. He reminded them that the devil had the bad habit of making use of carnival tricks in order to confuse the unwary. He argued that if wings were not the essential element in determining the difference between a hawk and an airplane, they were even less so in the recognition of angels. Nevertheless, he promised to write a letter to his bishop so that the latter would write to his primate so that the latter would write to the Supreme Pontiff in order to get the final verdict from the highest courts.

His prudence fell on sterile hearts. The news of the captive angel spread with such rapidity that after a few hours the courtyard had the bustle of a marketplace and they had to call in troops with fixed bayonets to disperse the mob that was about to knock the house down. Elisenda, her spine all twisted from sweeping up so much marketplace trash, then got the idea of fencing in the yard and charging five cents admission to see the angel.

The curious came from far away. A traveling carnival arrived with a flying acrobat who buzzed over the crowd several times, but no one paid any attention to him because his wings were not those of an angel but, rather, those of a sidereal° bat. The most unfortunate invalids on earth came in search of health: a poor woman who since childhood had been counting her heartbeats and had run out of numbers; a Portuguese man who couldn't sleep because the noise of the stars disturbed him; a sleep-walker who got up at night to undo the things he had done while awake; and many others with less serious ailments. In the midst of that shipwreck disorder that made the earth tremble, Pelayo and Elisenda were happy with fatigue, for in less than a week they had crammed their rooms with money and the line of pilgrims waiting their turn to enter still reached beyond the horizon.

The angel was the only one who took no part in his own act. He spent his time trying to get comfortable in his borrowed nest, befuddled by the hellish heat of the oil lamps and sacramental candles that had been placed along the wire. At first they tried to make him eat some mothballs, which, according to the wisdom of the wise neighbor woman, were the food prescribed for angels. But he turned them down, just as he turned down the papal lunches that the penitents brought him, and they never found out whether it was because he

---

sidereal: Coming from the stars.

was an angel or because he was an old man that in the end he ate nothing but eggplant mush. His only supernatural virtue seemed to be patience. Especially during the first days, when the hens pecked at him, searching for the stellar parasites that proliferated in his wings, and the cripples pulled out feathers to touch their defective parts with, and even the most merciful threw stones at him, trying to get him to rise so they could see him standing. The only time they succeeded in arousing him was when they burned his side with an iron for branding steers, for he had been motionless for so many hours that they thought he was dead. He awoke with a start, ranting in his hermetic language and with tears in his eyes, and he flapped his wings a couple of times, which brought on a whirlwind of chicken dung and lunar dust and a gale of panic that did not seem to be of this world. Although many thought that his reaction had been one not of rage but of pain, from then on they were careful not to annoy him, because the majority understood that his passivity was not that of a hero taking his ease but that of a cataclysm in repose.

Father Gonzaga held back the crowd's frivolity with formulas of maidservant inspiration while awaiting the arrival of a final judgment on the nature of the captive. But the mail from Rome showed no sense of urgency. They spent their time finding out if the prisoner had a navel, if his dialect had any connection with Aramaic, how many times he could fit on the head of a pin, or whether he wasn't just a Norwegian with wings. Those meager letters might have come and gone until the end of time if a providential event had not put an end to the priest's tribulations.

It so happened that during those days, among so many other carnival attractions, there arrived in town the traveling show of the woman who had been changed into a spider for having disobeyed her parents. The admission to see her was not only less than the admission to see the angel, but people were permitted to ask her all manner of questions about her absurd state and to examine her up and down so that no one would ever doubt the truth of her horror. She was a frightful tarantula the size of a ram and with the head of a sad maiden. What was most heart-rending, however, was not her outlandish shape but the sincere affliction with which she recounted the details of her misfortune. While still practically a child she had sneaked out of her parents' house to go to a dance, and while she was coming back through the woods after having danced all night without permission, a fearful thunderclap rent the sky in two and through the crack came the lightning bolt of brimstone that changed her into a spider. Her only nourishment came from the meatballs that charitable souls chose to toss into her mouth. A spectacle like that, full of so much human truth and with such a fearful lesson, was bound to defeat without even trying that of a haughty angel who scarcely deigned to look at mortals. Besides, the few miracles attributed to the angel showed a certain mental disorder, like the blind man who didn't recover his sight but grew three new teeth, or the paralytic who didn't get to walk but almost won the lottery, and the leper whose sores sprouted sunflowers. Those consolation miracles, which were more like mocking fun, had already ruined the angel's reputation when the woman who had been changed into a spider finally crushed him completely. That was how Father Gonzaga was cured forever of his insomnia and Pelayo's courtyard went back to being as empty as during the time it had rained for three days and crabs walked through the bedrooms.

The owners of the house had no reason to lament. With the money they saved they built a two-story mansion with balconies and gardens and high netting so that crabs wouldn't get in during the winter, and with iron bars on the windows so that angels wouldn't get in. Pelayo also set up a rabbit warren close to town and gave up his job as bailiff for good, and Elisenda bought some satin pumps with high heels and many dresses of iridescent silk, the kind worn on Sunday by the most desirable women in those times. The chicken coop was the only thing that didn't receive any attention. If they washed it down with creolin and burned tears of myrrh inside it every so often, it was not in homage to the angel but to drive away the dungheap stench that still hung everywhere like a ghost and was turning the new house into an old one. At first, when the child learned to walk, they were careful that he not get too close to the chicken coop. But then they began to lose their fears and got used to the smell, and before the child got his second teeth he'd gone inside the chicken coop to play, where the wires were falling apart. The angel was no less standoffish with him than with other mortals, but he tolerated the most ingenious infamies with the patience of a dog who had no illusions. They both came down with chicken pox at the same time. The doctor who took care of the child couldn't resist the temptation to listen to the angel's heart, and he found so much whistling in the heart and so many sounds in his kidneys that it seemed impossible for him to be alive. What surprised him most, however, was the logic of his wings. They seemed so natural on that completely human organism that he couldn't understand why other men didn't have them too.

When the child began school it had been some time since the sun and rain had caused the collapse of the chicken coop. The angel went dragging himself about here and there like a stray dying man. They would drive him out of the bedroom with a broom and a moment later find him in the kitchen. He seemed to be in so many places at the same time that they grew to think that he'd been duplicated, that he was reproducing himself all through the house, and the exasperated and unhinged Elisenda shouted that it was awful living in that hell full of angels. He could scarcely eat and his antiquarian eyes had also become so foggy that he went about bumping into posts. All he had left were the bare cannulae° of his last feathers. Pelayo threw a blanket over him and extended him the charity of letting him sleep in the shed, and only then did they notice that he had a temperature at night, and was delirious with the tongue twisters of an old Norwegian. That was one of the few times they became alarmed, for they thought he was going to die and not even the wise neighbor woman had been able to tell them what to do with dead angels.

And yet he not only survived his worst winter, but seemed improved with the first sunny days. He remained motionless for several days in the far-

---

cannulae: The tubular pieces by which feathers are attached to a body.

thest corner of the courtyard, where no one would see him, and at the beginning of December some large, stiff feathers began to grow on his wings, the feathers of a scarecrow, which looked more like another misfortune of decrepitude. But he must have known the reason for those changes, for he was quite careful that no one should notice them, that no one should hear the sea chanteys that he sometimes sang under the stars. One morning Elisenda was cutting some bunches of onions for lunch when a wind that seemed to come from the high seas blew into the kitchen. Then she went to the window and caught the angel in his first attempts at flight. They were so clumsy that his fingernails opened a furrow in the vegetable patch and he was on the point of knocking the shed down with the ungainly flapping that slipped on the light and couldn't get a grip on the air. But he did manage to gain altitude. Elisenda let out a sigh of relief, for herself and for him, when she saw him pass over the last houses, holding himself up in some way with the risky flapping of a senile vulture. She kept watching him even when she was through cutting the onions and she kept on watching until it was no longer possible for her to see him, because then he was no longer an annoyance in her life but an imaginary dot on the horizon of the sea.

സ്

CHARLOTTE PERKINS GILMAN *(1860–1935) was born in Hartford, Connecticut. Her father deserted the family shortly after she was born and provided her mother with only meager support. As a teenager Gilman attended the Rhode Island School of Design for a brief period and worked as a commercial artist and teacher. Like her great-aunt Harriet Beecher Stowe, she was concerned at an early age with social injustice and wrote poetry about the hardship of women's lives.*

In 1884 she married the artist Charles Walter Stetson. Suffering extreme depression after the birth of a daughter, she left her husband and moved to California in 1888. They were divorced, and she later married George Houghton Gilman, with whom she lived for thirty-four years. In the 1890s Gilman established her reputation as a lecturer and writer of feminist tracts. Her book Women and Economics *(1898) is considered one of the most important works of the early years of the women's movement in the United States. Gilman's later books —* Concerning Children *(1900),* The Home *(1904), and* Human Work *(1904) — argue that women should be educated to become financially independent, which would enable them to contribute more to the amelioration of systems of justice and the improvement of society. From 1909 to 1917 Gilman published her own journal,* The Forerunner, *for which she wrote voluminously. At the end of her life, suffering from cancer, she committed suicide with chloroform.*

Today Gilman's best-known work is her early story "The Yellow Wallpaper," written around 1890, shortly after her own nervous breakdown. It is part fantasy and part autobiography, a vivid account of her illness and treatment by the physician S. Weir Mitchell, who forbade her any activity, especially writing, the thing she most wanted to do. In setting the story Gilman used elements of the conventional gothic romances that were a staple in women's popular fiction — an isolated mansion, a distant but dominating male figure, and a mysterious household — all of which force the heroine into the role of passive victim of circumstances. But Gilman gave her own twist to the form. Using the brief paragraphs and simple sentences of popular fiction, she narrated her story with a clinical precision that avoided the trite language of conventional Gothic romances.

RELATED COMMENTARIES: *Sandra M. Gilbert and Susan Gubar, "A Feminist Reading of Gilman's 'The Yellow Wallpaper,' " page 749; Charlotte Perkins Gilman, "Undergoing the Cure for Nervous Prostration," page 752.*

CHARLOTTE PERKINS GILMAN

The Yellow Wallpaper   1892

It is very seldom that mere ordinary people like John and myself secure ancestral halls for the summer.

A colonial mansion, a hereditary estate, I would say a haunted house and reach the height of romantic felicity — but that would be asking too much of fate!

Still I will proudly declare that there is something queer about it.

Else, why should it be let so cheaply? And why have stood so long untenanted?

John laughs at me, of course, but one expects that.

John is practical in the extreme. He has no patience with faith, an intense horror of superstition, and he scoffs openly at any talk of things not to be felt and seen and put down in figures.

John is a physician, and *perhaps* — (I would not say it to a living soul, of course, but this is dead paper and a great relief to my mind) — *perhaps* that is one reason I do not get well faster.

You see, he does not believe I am sick! And what can one do?

If a physician of high standing, and one's own husband, assures friends and relatives that there is really nothing the matter with one but temporary nervous depression — a slight hysterical tendency — what is one to do?

My brother is also a physician, and also of high standing, and he says the same thing.

So I take phosphates or phosphites — whichever it is — and tonics, and air and exercise, and journeys, and am absolutely forbidden to "work" until I am well again.

Personally, I disagree with their ideas.

Personally, I believe that congenial work, with excitement and change, would do me good.

But what is one to do?

I did write for a while in spite of them; but it *does* exhaust me a good deal — having to be so sly about it, or else meet with heavy opposition.

I sometimes fancy that in my condition, if I had less opposition and more society and stimulus — but John says the very worst thing I can do is to think about my condition, and I confess it always makes me feel bad.

So I will let it alone and talk about the house.

The most beautiful place! It is quite alone, standing well back from the road, quite three miles from the village. It makes me think of English places that you read about, for there are hedges and walls and gates that lock, and lots of separate little houses for the gardeners and people.

There is a *delicious* garden! I never saw such a garden — large and shady, full of box-bordered paths, and lined with long grape-covered arbors with seats under them.

There were greenhouses, but they are all broken now.

There was some legal trouble, I believe, something about the heirs and co-heirs; anyhow, the place has been empty for years.

That spoils my ghostliness, I am afraid, but I don't care — there is something strange about the house — I can feel it.

I even said so to John one moonlight evening, but he said what I felt was a draught, and shut the window.

I get unreasonably angry with John sometimes. I'm sure I never used to be so sensitive. I think it is due to this nervous condition.

But John says if I feel so I shall neglect proper self-control; so I take pains to control myself — before him, at least, and that makes me very tired.

I don't like our room a bit. I wanted one downstairs that opened onto the piazza and had roses all over the window, and such pretty old-fashioned chintz hangings! But John would not hear of it.

He said there was only one window and not room for two beds, and no near room for him if he took another.

He is very careful and loving, and hardly lets me stir without special direction.

I have a schedule prescription for each hour in the day; he takes all care from me, and so I feel basely ungrateful not to value it more.

He said he came here solely on my account, that I was to have perfect rest and all the air I could get. "Your exercise depends on your strength, my dear," said he, "and your food somewhat on your appetite; but air you can absorb all the time." So we took the nursery at the top of the house.

It is a big, airy room, the whole floor nearly, with windows that look all ways, and air and sunshine galore. It was nursery first, and then playroom and gymnasium, I should judge, for the windows are barred for little children, and there are rings and things in the walls.

The paint and paper look as if a boys' school had used it. It is stripped off — the paper — in great patches all around the head of my bed, about as far as I can reach, and in a great place on the other side of the room low down. I never saw a worse paper in my life. One of those sprawling, flamboyant patterns committing every artistic sin.

It is dull enough to confuse the eye in following, pronounced enough constantly to irritate and provoke study, and when you follow the lame uncertain curves for a little distance they suddenly commit suicide — plunge off at outrageous angles, destroy themselves in unheard-of contradictions.

The color is repellent, almost revolting: a smouldering unclean yellow, strangely faded by the slow-turning sunlight. It is a dull yet lurid orange in some places, a sickly sulphur tint in others.

No wonder the children hated it! I should hate it myself if I had to live in this room long.

There comes John, and I must put this away — he hates to have me write a word.

We have been here two weeks, and I haven't felt like writing before, since that first day.

I am sitting by the window now, up in this atrocious nursery, and there is nothing to hinder my writing as much as I please, save lack of strength.

John is away all day, and even some nights when his cases are serious.

I am glad my case is not serious!

But these nervous troubles are dreadfully depressing.

John does not know how much I really suffer. He knows there is no reason to suffer, and that satisfies him.

Of course it is only nervousness. It does weigh on me so not to do my duty in any way!

I meant to be such a help to John, such a real rest and comfort, and here I am a comparative burden already!

Nobody would believe what an effort it is to do what little I am able — to dress and entertain, and order things.

It is fortunate Mary is so good with the baby. Such a dear baby!

And yet I *cannot* be with him, it makes me so nervous.

I suppose John never was nervous in his life. He laughs at me so about this wallpaper!

At first he meant to repaper the room, but afterward he said that I was letting it get the better of me, and that nothing was worse for a nervous patient than to give way to such fancies.

He said that after the wallpaper was changed it would be the heavy bedstead, and then the barred windows, and then that gate at the head of the stairs, and so on.

"You know the place is doing you good," he said, "and really, dear, I don't care to renovate the house just for a three months' rental."

"Then do let us go downstairs," I said. "There are such pretty rooms there."

Then he took me in his arms and called me a blessed little goose, and said he would go down cellar, if I wished, and have it whitewashed into the bargain.

But he is right enough about the beds and windows and things.

It is as airy and comfortable a room as anyone need wish, and, of course, I would not be so silly as to make him uncomfortable just for a whim.

I'm really getting quite fond of the big room, all but that horrid paper.

Out of one window I can see the garden — those mysterious deep-shaded arbors, the riotous old-fashioned flowers, and bushes and gnarly trees.

Out of another I get a lovely view of the bay and a little private wharf belonging to the estate. There is a beautiful shaded lane that runs down there from the house. I always fancy I see people walking in these numerous paths and arbors, but John has cautioned me not to give way to fancy in the least. He says that with my imaginative power and habit of story-making, a nervous weakness like mine is sure to lead to all manner of excited fancies, and that I ought to use my will and good sense to check the tendency. So I try.

I think sometimes that if I were only well enough to write a little it would relieve the press of ideas and rest me.

But I find I get pretty tired when I try.

It is so discouraging not to have any advice and companionship about my work. When I get really well, John says we will ask Cousin Henry and Julia down for a long visit; but he says he would as soon put fireworks in my pillow-case as to let me have those stimulating people about now.

I wish I could get well faster.

But I must not think about that. This paper looks to me as if it *knew* what a vicious influence it had!

There is a recurrent spot where the pattern lolls like a broken neck and two bulbous eyes stare at you upside down.

I get positively angry with the impertinence of it and the everlastingness. Up and down and sideways they crawl, and those absurd unblinking eyes are everywhere. There is one place where two breadths didn't match, and the eyes go all up and down the line, one a little higher than the other.

I never saw so much expression in an inanimate thing before, and we all know how much expression they have! I used to lie awake as a child and get more entertainment and terror out of blank walls and plain furniture than most children could find in a toy-store.

I remember what a kindly wink the knobs of our big old bureau used to have, and there was one chair that always seemed like a strong friend.

I used to feel that if any of the other things looked too fierce I could always hop into that chair and be safe.

The furniture in this room is no worse than inharmonious, however, for we had to bring it all from downstairs. I suppose when this was used as a playroom they had to take the nursery things out, and no wonder! I never saw such ravages as the children have made here.

The wallpaper, as I said before, is torn off in spots, and it sticketh closer than a brother — they must have had perseverance as well as hatred.

Then the floor is scratched and gouged and splintered, the plaster itself is dug out here and there, and this great heavy bed, which is all we found in the room, looks as if it had been through the wars.

But I don't mind it a bit — only the paper.

There comes John's sister. Such a dear girl as she is, and so careful of me! I must not let her find me writing.

She is a perfect and enthusiastic housekeeper, and hopes for no better profession. I verily believe she thinks it is the writing which made me sick!

But I can write when she is out, and see her a long way off from these windows.

There is one that commands the road, a lovely shaded winding road, and one that just looks off over the country. A lovely country, too, full of great elms and velvet meadows.

This wallpaper has a kind of subpattern in a different shade, a particularly irritating one, for you can only see it in certain lights, and not clearly then.

But in the places where it isn't faded and where the sun is just so — I can see a strange, provoking, formless sort of figure that seems to skulk about behind that silly and conspicuous front design.

There's sister on the stairs!

Well, the Fourth of July is over! The people are all gone, and I am tired out. John thought it might do me good to see a little company, so we just had Mother and Nellie and the children down for a week.

Of course I didn't do a thing. Jennie sees to everything now.

But it tired me all the same.

John says if I don't pick up faster he shall send me to Weir Mitchell° in the fall.

But I don't want to go there at all. I had a friend who was in his hands once, and she says he is just like John and my brother, only more so!

Besides, it is such an undertaking to go so far.

I don't feel as if it was worthwhile to turn my hand over for anything, and I'm getting dreadfully fretful and querulous.

I cry at nothing, and cry most of the time.

Of course I don't when John is here, or anybody else, but when I am alone.

And I am alone a good deal just now. John is kept in town very often by serious cases, and Jennie is good and lets me alone when I want her to.

So I walk a little in the garden or down that lovely lane, sit on the porch under the roses, and lie down up here a good deal.

I'm getting really fond of the room in spite of the wallpaper. Perhaps *because* of the wallpaper.

It dwells in my mind so!

I lie here on this great immovable bed — it is nailed down, I believe — and follow that pattern about by the hour. It is as good as gymnastics, I assure you. I start, we'll say, at the bottom, down in the corner over there where it has not been touched, and I determine for the thousandth time that I *will* follow that pointless pattern to some sort of a conclusion.

I know a little of the principle of design, and I know this thing was not arranged on any laws of radiation, or alternation, or repetition, or symmetry, or anything else that I ever heard of.

It is repeated, of course, by the breadths, but not otherwise.

Weir Mitchell: Dr. S. Weir Mitchell (1829–1914) was an eminent Philadelphia neurologist who advocated "rest cures" for nervous disorders. He was the author of *Diseases of the Nervous System, Especially of Women* (1881).

Looked at in one way, each breadth stands alone; the bloated curves and flourishes — a kind of "debased Romanesque" with delirium tremens go waddling up and down in isolated columns of fatuity.

But, on the other hand, they connect diagonally, and the sprawling outlines run off in great slanting waves of optic horror, like a lot of wallowing seaweeds in full chase.

The whole thing goes horizontally, too, at least it seems so, and I exhaust myself trying to distinguish the order of its going in that direction.

They have used a horizontal breadth for a frieze, and that adds wonderfully to the confusion.

There is one end of the room where it is almost intact, and there, when the crosslights fade and the low sun shines directly upon it, I can almost fancy radiation after all — the interminable grotesque seems to form around a common center and rush off in headlong plunges of equal distraction.

It makes me tired to follow it. I will take a nap, I guess.

I don't know why I should write this.

I don't want to.

I don't feel able.

And I know John would think it absurd. But I *must* say what I feel and think in some way — it is such a relief!

But the effort is getting to be greater than the relief.

Half the time now I am awfully lazy, and lie down ever so much. John says I mustn't lose my strength, and has me take cod liver oil and lots of tonics and things, to say nothing of ale and wines and rare meat.

Dear John! He loves me very dearly, and hates to have me sick. I tried to have a real earnest reasonable talk with him the other day, and tell him how I wish he would let me go and make a visit to Cousin Henry and Julia.

But he said I wasn't able to go, nor able to stand it after I got there; and I did not make out a very good case for myself, for I was crying before I had finished.

It is getting to be a great effort for me to think straight. Just this nervous weakness, I suppose.

And dear John gathered me up in his arms, and just carried me upstairs and laid me on the bed, and sat by me and read to me till it tired my head.

He said I was his darling and his comfort and all he had, and that I must take care of myself for his sake, and keep well.

He says no one but myself can help me out of it, that I must use my will and self-control and not let any silly fancies run away with me.

There's one comfort — the baby is well and happy, and does not have to occupy this nursery with the horrid wallpaper.

If we had not used it, that blessed child would have! What a fortunate escape! Why, I wouldn't have a child of mine, an impressionable little thing, live in such a room for worlds.

I never thought of it before, but it is lucky that John kept me here after all; I can stand it so much easier than a baby, you see.

Of course I never mention it to them any more — I am too wise — but I keep watch for it all the same.

There are things in the wallpaper that nobody knows about but me, or ever will.

Behind that outside pattern the dim shapes get clearer every day.

It is always the same shape, only very numerous.

And it is like a woman stooping down and creeping about behind that pattern. I don't like it a bit. I wonder — I begin to think — I wish John would take me away from here!

It is so hard to talk with John about my case, because he is so wise, and because he loves me so.

But I tried it last night.

It was moonlight. The moon shines in all around just as the sun does.

I hate to see it sometimes, it creeps so slowly, and always comes in by one window or another.

John was asleep and I hated to waken him, so I kept still and watched the moonlight on that undulating wallpaper till I felt creepy.

The faint figure behind seemed to shake the pattern, just as if she wanted to get out.

I got up softly and went to feel and see if the paper *did* move, and when I came back John was awake.

"What is it, little girl?" he said. "Don't go walking about like that — you'll get cold."

I thought it was a good time to talk, so I told him that I really was not gaining here, and that I wished he would take me away.

"Why, darling!" said he. "Our lease will be up in three weeks, and I can't see how to leave before.

"The repairs are not done at home, and I cannot possibly leave town just now. Of course, if you were in any danger, I could and would, but you really are better, dear, whether you can see it or not. I am a doctor, dear, and I know. You are gaining flesh and color, your appetite is better, I feel really much easier about you."

"I don't weigh a bit more," said I, "nor as much; and my appetite may be better in the evening when you are here but it is worse in the morning when you are away!"

"Bless her little heart!" said he with a big hug. "She shall be as sick as she pleases! But now let's improve the shining hours by going to sleep, and talk about it in the morning!"

"And you won't go away?" I asked gloomily.

"Why, how can I, dear? It is only three weeks more and then we will take a nice little trip for a few days while Jennie is getting the house ready. Really, dear, you are better!"

"Better in body perhaps — " I began, and stopped short, for he sat up straight and looked at me with such a stern, reproachful look that I could not say another word.

"My darling," said he, "I beg you, for my sake and for our child's sake, as well as for your own, that you will never for one instant let that idea enter your mind! There is nothing so dangerous, so fascinating, to a temperament like yours. It is a false and foolish fancy. Can you trust me as a physician when I tell you so?"

So of course I said no more on that score, and we went to sleep before long. He thought I was asleep first, but I wasn't, and lay there for hours trying to decide whether that front pattern and the back pattern really did move together or separately.

On a pattern like this, by daylight, there is a lack of sequence, a defiance of law, that is a constant irritant to a normal mind.

The color is hideous enough, and unreliable enough, and infuriating enough, but the pattern is torturing.

You think you have mastered it, but just as you get well under way in following, it turns a back-somersault and there you are. It slaps you in the face, knocks you down, and tramples upon you. It is like a bad dream.

The outside pattern is a florid arabesque, reminding one of a fungus. If you can imagine a toadstool in joints, an interminable string of toadstools, budding and sprouting in endless convolutions — why, that is something like it.

That is, sometimes!

There is one marked peculiarity about this paper, a thing nobody seems to notice but myself, and that is that it changes as the light changes.

When the sun shoots in through the east window — I always watch for that first long, straight ray — it changes so quickly that I never can quite believe it.

That is why I watch it always.

By moonlight — the moon shines in all night when there is a moon — I wouldn't know it was the same paper.

At night in any kind of light, in twilight, candlelight, lamplight, and worst of all by moonlight, it becomes bars! The outside pattern, I mean, and the woman behind it is as plain as can be.

I didn't realize for a long time what the thing was that showed behind, that dim subpattern, but now I am quite sure it is a woman.

By daylight she is subdued, quiet. I fancy it is the pattern that keeps her so still. It is so puzzling. It keeps me quiet by the hour.

I lie down ever so much now. John says it is good for me, and to sleep all I can.

Indeed he started the habit by making me lie down for an hour after each meal.

It is a very bad habit, I am convinced, for you see, I don't sleep.

And that cultivates deceit, for I don't tell them I'm awake — oh, no!

The fact is I am getting a little afraid of John.

He seems very queer sometimes, and even Jennie has an inexplicable look.

It strikes me occasionally, just as a scientific hypothesis, that perhaps it is the paper!

I have watched John when he did not know I was looking, and come into the room suddenly on the most innocent excuses, and I've caught him several times *looking at the paper!* And Jennie too. I caught Jennie with her hand on it once.

She didn't know I was in the room, and when I asked her in a quiet, a very quiet voice, with the most restrained manner possible, what she was doing with the paper, she turned around as if she had been caught stealing, and looked quite angry — asked me why I should frighten her so!

Then she said that the paper stained everything it touched, that she had found yellow smooches on all my clothes and John's and she wished we would be more careful!

Did not that sound innocent? But I know she was studying that pattern, and I am determined that nobody shall find it out but myself!

Life is very much more exciting now than it used to be. You see, I have something more to expect, to look forward to, to watch. I really do eat better, and am more quiet than I was.

John is so pleased to see me improve! He laughed a little the other day, and said I seemed to be flourishing in spite of my wallpaper.

I turned it off with a laugh. I had no intention of telling him it was *because* of the wallpaper — he would make fun of me. He might even want to take me away.

I don't want to leave now until I have found it out. There is a week more, and I think that will be enough.

I'm feeling so much better!

I don't sleep much at night, for it is so interesting to watch developments; but I sleep a good deal during the daytime.

In the daytime it is tiresome and perplexing.

There are always new shoots on the fungus, and new shades of yellow all over it. I cannot keep count of them, though I have tried conscientiously.

It is the strangest yellow, that wallpaper! It makes me think of all the yellow things I ever saw — not beautiful ones like buttercups, but old, foul, bad yellow things.

But there is something else about that paper — the smell! I noticed it the moment we came into the room, but with so much air and sun it was not bad. Now we have had a week of fog and rain, and whether the windows are open or not, the smell is here.

It creeps all over the house.

I find it hovering in the dining-room, skulking in the parlor, hiding in the hall, lying in wait for me on the stairs.

It gets into my hair.

Even when I go to ride, if I turn my head suddenly and surprise it — there is that smell!

Such a peculiar odor, too! I have spent hours in trying to analyze it, to find what it smelled like.

It is not bad — at first — and very gentle, but quite the subtlest, most enduring odor I ever met.

In this damp weather it is awful. I wake up in the night and find it hanging over me.

It used to disturb me at first. I thought seriously of burning the house — to reach the smell.

But now I am used to it. The only thing I can think of that it is like is the *color* of the paper! A yellow smell.

There is a very funny mark on this wall, low down, near the mopboard. A streak that runs round the room. It goes behind every piece of furniture, except the bed, a long, straight, even *smooch*, as if it had been rubbed over and over.

I wonder how it was done and who did it, and what they did it for. Round and round and round — round and round and round — it makes me dizzy!

I really have discovered something at last.

Through watching so much at night, when it changes so, I have finally found out.

The front pattern *does* move — and no wonder! The woman behind shakes it!

Sometimes I think there are a great many women behind, and sometimes only one, and she crawls around fast, and her crawling shakes it all over.

Then in the very bright spots she keeps still, and in the very shady spots she just takes hold of the bars and shakes them hard.

And she is all the time trying to climb through. But nobody could climb through that pattern — it strangles so; I think that is why it has so many heads.

They get through and then the pattern strangles them off and turns them upside down, and makes their eyes white!

If those heads were covered or taken off it would not be half so bad.

I think that woman gets out in the daytime!

And I'll tell you why — privately — I've seen her!

I can see her out of every one of my windows!

It is the same woman, I know, for she is always creeping, and most women do not creep by daylight.

I see her in that long shaded lane, creeping up and down. I see her in those dark grape arbors, creeping all round the garden.

I see her on that long road under the trees, creeping along, and when a carriage comes she hides under the blackberry vines.

I don't blame her a bit. It must be very humiliating to be caught creeping by daylight!

I always lock the door when I creep by daylight. I can't do it at night, for I know John would suspect something at once.

And John is so queer now that I don't want to irritate him. I wish he would take another room! Besides, I don't want anybody to get that woman out at night but myself.

I often wonder if I could see her out of all the windows at once.

But, turn as fast as I can, I can only see out of one at one time.

And though I always see her, she *may* be able to creep faster than I can turn! I have watched her sometimes away off in the open country, creeping as fast as a cloud shadow in a wind.

If only that top pattern could be gotten off from the under one! I mean to try it, little by little.

I have found out another funny thing, but I shan't tell it this time! It does not do to trust people too much.

There are only two more days to get this paper off, and I believe John is beginning to notice. I don't like the look in his eyes.

And I heard him ask Jennie a lot of professional questions about me. She had a very good report to give.

She said I slept a good deal in the daytime.

John knows I don't sleep very well at night, for all I'm so quiet!

He asked me all sorts of questions too, and pretended to be very loving and kind.

As if I couldn't see through him!

Still, I don't wonder he acts so, sleeping under this paper for three months.

It only interests me, but I feel sure John and Jennie are affected by it.

Hurrah! This is the last day, but it is enough. John is to stay in town over night, and won't be out until this evening.

Jennie wanted to sleep with me — the sly thing; but I told her I should undoubtedly rest better for a night all alone.

That was clever, for really I wasn't alone a bit! As soon as it was moonlight and that poor thing began to crawl and shake the pattern, I got up and ran to help her.

I pulled and she shook. I shook and she pulled, and before morning we had peeled off yards of that paper.

A strip about as high as my head and half around the room.

And then when the sun came and that awful pattern began to laugh at me, I declared I would finish it today!

We go away tomorrow, and they are moving all my furniture down again to leave things as they were before.

Jennie looked at the wall in amazement, but I told her merrily that I did it out of pure spite at the vicious thing.

She laughed and said she wouldn't mind doing it herself, but I must not get tired.

How she betrayed herself that time!

But I am here, and no person touches this paper but Me — not *alive!*

She tried to get me out of the room — it was too patent! But I said it was so quiet and empty and clean now that I believed I would lie down again and sleep all I could, and not to wake me even for dinner — I would call when I woke.

So now she is gone, and the servants are gone, and the things are gone, and there is nothing left but that great bedstead nailed down, with the canvas mattress we found on it.

We shall sleep downstairs tonight, and take the boat home tomorrow.

I quite enjoy the room, now it is bare again.

How those children did tear about here!

This bedstead is fairly gnawed!

But I must get to work.

I have locked the door and thrown the key down into the front path.

I don't want to go out, and I don't want to have anybody come in, till John comes.

I want to astonish him.

I've got a rope up here that even Jennie did not find. If that woman does get out, and tries to get away, I can tie her!

But I forgot I could not reach far without anything to stand on!

This bed will *not* move!

I tried to lift and push it until I was lame, and then I got so angry I bit off a little piece at one corner — but it hurt my teeth.

Then I peeled off all the paper I could reach standing on the floor. It sticks horribly and the pattern just enjoys it! All those strangled heads and bulbous eyes and waddling fungus growths just shriek with derision!

I am getting angry enough to do something desperate. To jump out of the window would be admirable exercise, but the bars are too strong even to try.

Besides I wouldn't do it. Of course not. I know well enough that a step like that is improper and might be misconstrued.

I don't like to *look* out of the windows even — there are so many of those creeping women, and they creep so fast.

I wonder if they all come out of that wallpaper as I did!

But I am securely fastened now by my well-hidden rope — you don't get *me* out in the road there!

I suppose I shall have to get back behind the pattern when it comes night, and that is hard!

It is so pleasant to be out in this great room and creep around as I please!

I don't want to go outside. I won't, even if Jennie asks me to.

For outside you have to creep on the ground, and everything is green instead of yellow.

But here I can creep smoothly on the floor, and my shoulder just fits in that long smooch around the wall, so I cannot lose my way.

Why, there's John at the door!

It is no use, young man, you can't open it!

How he does call and pound!

Now he's crying to Jennie for an axe.

It would be a shame to break down that beautiful door!

"John, dear!" said I in the gentlest voice. "The key is down by the front steps, under a plantain leaf!"

That silenced him for a few moments.

Then he said, very quietly indeed, "Open the door, my darling!"

"I can't," said I. "The key is down by the front door under a plantain leaf!" And then I said it again, several times, very gently and slowly, and said it so often that he had to go and see, and he got it of course, and came in. He stopped short by the door.

"What is the matter?" he cried. "For God's sake, what are you doing!"

I kept on creeping just the same, but I looked at him over my shoulder.

"I've got out at last," said I, "in spite of you and Jane. And I've pulled off most of the paper, so you can't put me back!"

Now why should that man have fainted? But he did, and right across my path by the wall, so that I had to creep over him every time!

ର୍ଷ

SUSAN **GLASPELL** *(1876–1948) was born in Davenport, Iowa, into a family that had been among the state's first settlers a generation before. After her graduation from high school, she worked as a reporter and society editor for various newspapers before enrolling at Drake University in Des Moines. There she studied literature, philosophy, and history; edited the college newspaper; and began to write short stories. In 1899 she took a job as statehouse reporter for the Des Moines* Daily News. *Years later she claimed that the discipline of newspaper work helped her to become a creative writer.*

At the age of twenty-five, Glaspell returned to Davenport to live with her family, determined, as she said, to "boldly" quit journalism and "give all my time to my own writing. I say 'boldly,' because I had to earn my living." Slowly she began to publish her fiction, mostly sentimental magazine pieces and an undistinguished first novel — work that, as her biographer C. W. E. Bigsby noted, "suggested little of the originality and power which were to mark her work in the theater." In 1909 Glaspell met George Cram Cook, a novelist and utopian socialist from a wealthy family who divorced his second wife and left his two children to marry her. They moved to Greenwich Village and collaborated on a play for the Washington Square Players in 1915, Suppressed Desires. *The following year, after the Players had moved to Provincetown on Cape Cod, Cook urged Glaspell to write a new play for the theater company, renamed the Provincetown Players. Her memory of a murder trial in Iowa that she had covered as a newspaper reporter served as the inspiration for the short play* Trifles *(1916). Glaspell recalled that she "had meant to do it as a short story, but the stage took it for its own."*

Trifles *was so successful as an experimental play that Glaspell turned it into a short story a year later, retitling it "A Jury of Her Peers." Her choice of a limited-omniscient, third-person point of view (via the character Martha Hale's perspective) and her description of the harsh realities of the rural setting in "A Jury of Her Peers" suggest the local-color tradition of such earlier writers as Sarah Orne Jewett, although Glaspell's suffragist sympathies were more radical than the views of nineteenth-century women writers. In 1912 Glaspell published her first book of stories,* Lifted Masks, *and she continued to write fiction as well as plays for most of her life. In her forty-seven-year career, she published fifty short stories, nine novels, and thirteen plays, including the Pulitzer Prize–winning play* Alison's House *(1931), based on Genevieve Taggart's biography of Emily Dickinson.*

RELATED PLAY: *Susan Glaspell,* Trifles, *page 1673.*
RELATED COMMENTARY: *Leonard Mustazza, "Generic Translation and Thematic Shift in Susan Glaspell's* Trifles *and 'A Jury of Her Peers,' " page 2002.*

SUSAN GLASPELL

A Jury of Her Peers   1917

When Martha Hale opened the storm-door and got a cut of the north wind, she ran back for her big woolen scarf. As she hurriedly wound that round her head her eye made a scandalized sweep of her kitchen. It was no ordinary thing that called her away — it was probably further from ordinary than anything that had ever happened in Dickson County. But what her eye took in was that her kitchen was in no shape for leaving: her bread all ready for mixing, half the flour sifted and half unsifted.

She hated to see things half done; but she had been at that when the team from town stopped to get Mr. Hale, and then the sheriff came running in to say his wife wished Mrs. Hale would come too — adding, with a grin, that he guessed she was getting scary and wanted another woman along. So she had dropped everything right where it was.

"Martha!" now came her husband's impatient voice. "Don't keep folks waiting out here in the cold."

She again opened the storm-door, and this time joined the three men and the one woman waiting for her in the big two-seated buggy.

After she had the robes tucked around her she took another look at the woman who sat beside her on the back seat. She had met Mrs. Peters the year before at the county fair, and the thing she remembered about her was that she didn't seem like a sheriff's wife. She was small and thin and didn't have a strong voice. Mrs. Gorman, sheriff's wife before Gorman went out and Peters came in, had a voice that somehow seemed to be backing up the law with every word. But if Mrs. Peters didn't look like a sheriff's wife, Peters made it up in looking like a sheriff. He was to a dot the kind of man who could get himself elected sheriff — a heavy man with a big voice, who was particularly genial with the law-abiding, as if to make it plain that he knew the difference between criminals and non-criminals. And right there it came into Mrs. Hale's mind, with a stab, that this man who was so pleasant and lively with all of them was going to the Wrights' now as a sheriff.

"The country's not very pleasant this time of year," Mrs. Peters at last ventured, as if she felt they ought to be talking as well as the men.

Mrs. Hale scarcely finished her reply, for they had gone up a little hill and could see the Wright place now, and seeing it did not make her feel like talking. It looked very lonesome this cold March morning. It had always been a lonesome-looking place. It was down in a hollow, and the poplar trees around it were lonesome-looking trees. The men were looking at it and talking about what had happened. The county attorney was bending to one side of the buggy, and kept looking steadily at the place as they drew up to it.

"I'm glad you came with me," Mrs. Peters said nervously, as the two women were about to follow the men in through the kitchen door.

Even after she had her foot on the door-step, her hand on the knob, Martha Hale had a moment of feeling she could not cross that threshold. And the reason it seemed she couldn't cross it now was simply because she hadn't crossed it before. Time and time again it had been in her mind, "I ought to go over and see Minnie Foster" — she still thought of her as Minnie Foster, though for twenty years she had been Mrs. Wright. And then there was always something to do and Minnie Foster would go from her mind. But *now* she could come.

The men went over to the stove. The women stood close together by the door. Young Henderson, the county attorney, turned around and said, "Come up to the fire, ladies."

Mrs. Peters took a step forward, then stopped. "I'm not — cold," she said.

And so the two women stood by the door, at first not even so much as looking around the kitchen.

The men talked for a minute about what a good thing it was the sheriff had sent his deputy out that morning to make a fire for them, and then Sheriff Peters stepped back from the stove, unbuttoned his outer coat, and leaned his hands on the kitchen table in a way that seemed to mark the beginning of official business. "Now, Mr. Hale," he said in a sort of semi-official voice, "before we move things about, you tell Mr. Henderson just what it was you saw when you came here yesterday morning."

The county attorney was looking around the kitchen.

"By the way," he said, "has anything been moved?" He turned to the sheriff. "Are things just as you left them yesterday?"

Peters looked from cupboard to sink; from that to a small worn rocker a little to one side of the kitchen table.

"It's just the same."

"Somebody should have been left here yesterday," said the county attorney.

"Oh — yesterday," returned the sheriff, with a little gesture as of yesterday having been more than he could bear to think of. "When I had to send Frank to Morris Center for that man who went crazy — let me tell you. I had my hands full *yesterday*. I knew you could get back from Omaha by today, George, and as long as I went over everything here myself — "

"Well, Mr. Hale," said the county attorney, in a way of letting what was past and gone go, "tell just what happened when you came here yesterday morning."

Mrs. Hale, still leaning against the door, had that sinking feeling of the mother whose child is about to speak a piece. Lewis often wandered along and got things mixed up in a story. She hoped he would tell this straight and plain, and not say unnecessary things that would just make things harder for Minnie Foster. He didn't begin at once, and she noticed that he looked queer — as if standing in that kitchen and having to tell what he had seen there yesterday morning made him almost sick.

"Yes, Mr. Hale?" the county attorney reminded.

"Harry and I had started to town with a load of potatoes," Mrs. Hale's husband began.

Harry was Mrs. Hale's oldest boy. He wasn't with them now, for the very good reason that those potatoes never got to town yesterday and he was taking them this morning, so he hadn't been home when the sheriff stopped to say he wanted Mr. Hale to come over to the Wright place and tell the county attorney his story there, where he could point it all out. With all Mrs. Hale's other emotions came the fear now that maybe Harry wasn't dressed warm enough — they hadn't any of them realized how that north wind did bite.

"We come along this road," Hale was going on, with a motion of his hand to the road over which they had just come, "and as we got in sight of the house I says to Harry, 'I'm goin' to see if I can't get John Wright to take a telephone.' You see," he explained to Henderson, "unless I can get somebody to go in with me they won't come out this branch road except for a price I can't pay. I'd spoke to Wright about it once before; but he put me off, saying folks talked too much anyway, and all he asked was peace and quiet — guess you know about how much he talked himself. But I thought maybe if I went to the house and talked about it before his wife, and said all the women-folks liked the telephones, and that in this lonesome stretch of road it would be a good thing — well, I said to Harry that that was what I was going to say — though I said at the same time that I didn't know as what his wife wanted made much difference to John — "

Now there he was! — saying things he didn't need to say. Mrs. Hale tried to catch her husband's eye, but fortunately the county attorney interrupted with:

"Let's talk about that a little later, Mr. Hale. I do want to talk about that, but I'm anxious now to get along to just what happened when you got here."

When he began this time, it was very deliberately and carefully:

"I didn't see or hear anything. I knocked at the door. And still it was all quiet inside. I knew they must be up — it was past eight o'clock. So I knocked again, louder, and I thought I heard somebody say, 'Come in.' I wasn't sure — I'm not sure yet. But I opened the door — this door," jerking a hand toward the door by which the two women stood, "and there, in that rocker" — pointing to it — "sat Mrs. Wright."

Everyone in the kitchen looked at the rocker. It came into Mrs. Hale's mind that that rocker didn't look in the least like Minnie Foster — the Minnie Foster of twenty years before. It was a dingy red, with wooden rungs up the back, and the middle rung was gone, and the chair sagged to one side.

"How did she — look?" the county attorney was inquiring.

"Well," said Hale, "she looked — queer."

"How do you mean — queer?"

As he asked it he took out a note-book and pencil. Mrs. Hale did not like the sight of that pencil. She kept her eye fixed on her husband, as if to keep him from saying unnecessary things that would go into that note-book and make trouble.

Hale did speak guardedly, as if the pencil had affected him too.

"Well, as if she didn't know what she was going to do next. And kind of — done up."

"How did she seem to feel about your coming?"

"Why, I don't think she minded — one way or other. She didn't pay much attention. I said, 'Ho' do, Mrs. Wright? It's cold, ain't it?' And she said, 'Is it?' — and went on pleatin' at her apron.

"Well, I was surprised. She didn't ask me to come up to the stove, or to sit down, but just set there, not even lookin' at me. And so I said: 'I want to see John.'

"And then she — laughed. I guess you would call it a laugh.

"I thought of Harry and the team outside, so I said, a little sharp, 'Can I see John?' 'No,' says she — kind of dull like. 'Ain't he home?' says I. Then she looked at me. 'Yes,' says she, 'he's home.' 'Then why can't I see him?' I asked her, out of patience with her now. 'Cause he's dead' says she, just as quiet and dull — and fell to pleatin' her apron. 'Dead?' says I, like you do when you can't take in what you've heard.

"She just nodded her head, not getting a bit excited, but rockin' back and forth.

" 'Why — where is he?' says I, not knowing *what* to say.

"She just pointed upstairs — like this" — pointing to the room above.

"I got up, with the idea of going up there myself. By this time I — didn't know what to do. I walked from there to here; then I says: 'Why, what did he die of?'

" 'He died of a rope around his neck,' says she; and just went on pleatin' at her apron."

Hale stopped speaking, and stood staring at the rocker, as if he were still seeing the woman who had sat there the morning before. Nobody spoke; it was as if every one were seeing the woman who had sat there the morning before.

"And what did you do then?" the county attorney at last broke the silence.

"I went out and called Harry. I thought I might — need help. I got Harry in, and we went upstairs." His voice fell almost to a whisper. "There he was — lying over the — "

"I think I'd rather have you go into that upstairs," the county attorney interrupted, "where you can point it all out. Just go on now with the rest of the story."

"Well, my first thought was to get that rope off. It looked — "

He stopped, his face twitching.

"But Harry, he went up to him, and he said, 'No, he's dead all right, and we'd better not touch anything.' So we went downstairs.

"She was still sitting that same way. 'Has anybody been notified?' I asked. 'No,' says she, unconcerned.

" 'Who did this, Mrs. Wright?' said Harry. He said it businesslike, and she stopped pleatin' at her apron. 'I don't know,' she says. 'You don't *know*?' says Harry. 'Weren't you sleepin' in the bed with him?' 'Yes,' says she, 'but I was on the inside.' 'Somebody slipped a rope round his neck and strangled him, and you didn't wake up?' says Harry. 'I didn't wake up,' she said after him.

"We may have looked as if we didn't see how that could be, for after a minute she said, 'I sleep sound.'

"Harry was going to ask her more questions, but I said maybe that weren't our business; maybe we ought to let her tell her story first to the coroner or the sheriff. So Harry went fast as he could over to High Road — the Rivers' place, where there's a telephone."

"And what did she do when she knew you had gone for the coroner?" The attorney got his pencil in his hand all ready for writing.

"She moved from that chair to this one over here" — Hale pointed to a small chair in the corner — "and just sat there with her hands held together and looking down. I got a feeling that I ought to make some conversation, so I said I had come in to see if John wanted to put in a telephone; and at that she started to laugh, and then she stopped and looked at me — scared."

At the sound of a moving pencil the man who was telling the story looked up.

"I dunno — maybe it wasn't scared," he hastened: "I wouldn't like to say it was. Soon Harry got back, and then Dr. Lloyd came, and you, Mr. Peters, and so I guess that's all I know that you don't."

He said that last with relief, and moved a little, as if relaxing. Everyone moved a little. The county attorney walked toward the stair door.

"I guess we'll go upstairs first — then out to the barn and around there." He paused and looked around the kitchen.

"You're convinced there was nothing important here?" he asked the sheriff. "Nothing that would — point to any motive?"

The sheriff too looked all around, as if to re-convince himself.

"Nothing here but kitchen things," he said, with a little laugh for the insignificance of kitchen things.

The county attorney was looking at the cupboard — a peculiar, ungainly structure, half closet and half cupboard, the upper part of it being built in the wall, and the lower part just the old-fashioned kitchen cupboard. As if its queerness attracted him, he got a chair and opened the upper part and looked in. After a moment he drew his hand away sticky.

"Here's a nice mess," he said resentfully.

The two women had drawn nearer, and now the sheriff's wife spoke.

"Oh — her fruit," she said, looking to Mrs. Hale for sympathetic understanding. She turned back to the county attorney and explained: "She worried about that when it turned so cold last night. She said the fire would go out and her jars might burst."

Mrs. Peters' husband broke into a laugh.

"Well, can you beat the women! Held for murder, and worrying about her preserves!"

The young attorney set his lips.

"I guess before we're through with her she may have something more serious than preserves to worry about."

"Oh, well," said Mrs. Hale's husband, with good-natured superiority, "women are used to worrying over trifles."

The two women moved a little closer together. Neither of them spoke. The county attorney seemed suddenly to remember his manners — and think of his future.

"And yet," said he, with the gallantry of a young politician, "for all their worries, what would we do without the ladies?"

The women did not speak, did not unbend. He went to the sink and began washing his hands. He turned to wipe them on the roller towel — whirled it for a cleaner place.

"Dirty towels! Not much of a housekeeper, would you say, ladies?"

He kicked his foot against some dirty pans under the sink.

"There's a great deal of work to be done on a farm," said Mrs. Hale stiffly.

"To be sure. And yet" — with a little bow to her — "I know there are some Dickson County farm-houses that do not have such roller towels." He gave it a pull to expose its full length again.

"Those towels get dirty awful quick. Men's hands aren't always as clean as they might be."

"Ah, loyal to your sex, I see," he laughed. He stopped and gave her a keen look. "But you and Mrs. Wright were neighbors. I suppose you were friends, too."

Martha Hale shook her head.

"I've seen little enough of her of late years. I've not been in this house — it's more than a year."

"And why was that? You didn't like her?"

"I liked her well enough," she replied with spirit. "Farmers' wives have their hands full, Mr. Henderson. And then — " She looked around the kitchen.

"Yes?" he encouraged.

"It never seemed a very cheerful place," said she, more to herself than to him.

"No," he agreed; "I don't think anyone would call it cheerful. I shouldn't say she had the home-making instinct."

"Well, I don't know as Wright had, either," she muttered.

"You mean they didn't get on very well?" he was quick to ask.

"No; I don't mean anything," she answered, with decision. As she turned a little away from him, she added: "But I don't think a place would be any the cheerfuller for John Wright's bein' in it."

"I'd like to talk to you about that a little later, Mrs. Hale," he said. "I'm anxious to get the lay of things upstairs now."

He moved toward the stair door, followed by the two men.

"I suppose anything Mrs. Peters does'll be all right?" the sheriff inquired. "She was to take in some clothes for her, you know — and a few little things. We left in such a hurry yesterday."

The county attorney looked at the two women whom they were leaving alone there among the kitchen things.

"Yes — Mrs. Peters," he said, his glance resting on the woman who was not Mrs. Peters, the big farmer woman who stood behind the sheriff's wife. "Of course Mrs. Peters is one of us," he said, in a manner of entrusting responsibility. "And keep your eye out, Mrs. Peters, for anything that might be of use. No telling; you women might come upon a clue to the motive — and that's the thing we need."

Mr. Hale rubbed his face after the fashion of a showman getting ready for a pleasantry.

"But would the women know a clue if they did come upon it?" he said; and, having delivered himself of this, he followed the others through the stair door.

The women stood motionless and silent, listening to the footsteps, first upon the stairs, then in the room above them.

Then, as if releasing herself from something strange. Mrs. Hale began to arrange the dirty pans under the sink, which the county attorney's disdainful push of the foot had deranged.

"I'd hate to have men comin' into my kitchen," she said testily — "snoopin' round and criticizin'."

"Of course it's no more than their duty," said the sheriff's wife, in her manner of timid acquiescence.

"Duty's all right," replied Mrs. Hale bluffly; "but I guess that deputy sheriff that come out to make the fire might have got a little of this on." She gave the roller towel a pull. "Wish I'd thought of that sooner! Seems mean to talk about her for not having things slicked up, when she had to come away in such a hurry."

She looked around the kitchen. Certainly it was not "slicked up." Her eye was held by a bucket of sugar on a low shelf. The cover was off the wooden bucket, and beside it was a paper bag — half full.

Mrs. Hale moved toward it.

"She was putting this in there," she said to herself — slowly.

She thought of the flour in her kitchen at home — half sifted, half not sifted. She had been interrupted, and had left things half done. What had interrupted Minnie Foster? Why had that work been left half done? She made a move as if to finish it, — unfinished things always bothered her, — and then she glanced around and saw that Mrs. Peters was watching her — and she didn't want Mrs. Peters to get that feeling she had got of work begun and then — for some reason — not finished.

"It's a shame about her fruit," she said, and walked toward the cupboard that the county attorney had opened, and got on the chair, murmuring: "I wonder if it's all gone."

It was a sorry enough looking sight, but "Here's one that's all right," she said at last. She held it toward the light. "This is cherries, too." She looked again. "I declare I believe that's the only one."

With a sigh, she got down from the chair, went to the sink, and wiped off the bottle.

"She'll feel awful bad, after all her hard work in the hot weather. I remember the afternoon I put up my cherries last summer."

She set the bottle on the table, and, with another sigh, started to sit down in the rocker. But she did not sit down. Something kept her from sitting down in that chair. She straightened — stepped back, and, half turned away, stood looking at it, seeing the woman who had sat there "pleatin' at her apron."

The thin voice of the sheriff's wife broke in upon her: "I must be getting those things from the front-room closet." She opened the door into the other room, started in, stepped back. "You coming with me, Mrs. Hale?" she asked nervously. "You — you could help me get them."

They were soon back — the stark coldness of that shut-up room was not a thing to linger in.

"My!" said Mrs. Peters, dropping the things on the table and hurrying to the stove.

Mrs. Hale stood examining the clothes the woman who was being detained in town had said she wanted.

"Wright was close!"° she exclaimed, holding up a shabby black skirt that bore the marks of much making over. "I think maybe that's why she kept so much to herself. I s'pose she felt she couldn't do her part; and then, you don't enjoy things when you feel shabby. She used to wear pretty clothes and be lively — when she was Minnie Foster, one of the town girls, singing in the choir. But that — oh, that was twenty years ago."

With a carefulness in which there was something tender, she folded the shabby clothes and piled them at one corner of the table. She looked up at Mrs. Peters, and there was something in the other woman's look that irritated her.

"She don't care," she said to herself. "Much difference it makes to her whether Minnie Foster had pretty clothes when she was a girl."

Then she looked again, and she wasn't so sure; in fact, she hadn't at any time been perfectly sure about Mrs. Peters. She had that shrinking manner, and yet her eyes looked as if they could see a long way into things.

"This all you was to take in?" asked Mrs. Hale.

"No," said the sheriff's wife; "she said she wanted an apron. Funny thing to want," she ventured in her nervous little way, "for there's not much to get you dirty in jail, goodness knows. But I suppose just to make her feel more natural. If you're used to wearing an apron — . She said they were in the bottom drawer of this cupboard. Yes — here they are. And then her little shawl that always hung on the stair door."

She took the small gray shawl from behind the door leading upstairs, and stood a minute looking at it.

Suddenly Mrs. Hale took a quick step toward the other woman.

---

close: Frugal, tightfisted.

"Mrs. Peters!"

"Yes, Mrs. Hale?"

"Do you think she — did it?"

A frightened look blurred the other thing in Mrs. Peters' eyes.

"Oh, I don't know," she said, in a voice that seemed to shrink away from the subject.

"Well, I don't think she did," affirmed Mrs. Hale stoutly. "Asking for an apron, and her little shawl. Worryin' about her fruit."

"Mr. Peters says — ." " Footsteps were heard in the room above; she stopped, looked up, then went on in a lowered voice: "Mr. Peters says — it looks bad for her. Mr. Henderson is awful sarcastic in a speech, and he's going to make fun of her saying she didn't — wake up."

For a moment Mrs. Hale had no answer. Then, "Well, I guess John Wright didn't wake up — when they was slippin' that rope under his neck," she muttered.

"No, it's *strange*," breathed Mrs. Peters. "They think it was such a — funny way to kill a man."

She began to laugh; at the sound of the laugh, abruptly stopped.

"That's just what Mr. Hale said," said Mrs. Hale, in a resolutely natural voice. "There was a gun in the house. He says that's what he can't understand."

"Mr. Henderson said, coming out, that what was needed for the case was a motive. Something to show anger — or sudden feeling."

"Well, I don't see any signs of anger around here," said Mrs. Hale, "I don't — " She stopped. It was as if her mind tripped on something. Her eye was caught by a dishtowel in the middle of the kitchen table. Slowly she moved toward the table. One half of it was wiped clean, the other half messy. Her eyes made a slow, almost unwilling turn to the bucket of sugar and the half empty bag beside it. Things begun — and not finished.

After a moment she stepped back, and said, in that manner of releasing herself:

"Wonder how they're finding things upstairs? I hope she had it a little more red up° up there. You know," — she paused, and feeling gathered, — "it seems kind of *sneaking:* locking her up in town and coming out here to get her own house to turn against her!"

"But, Mrs. Hale," said the sheriff's wife, "the law is the law."

"I s'pose 'tis," answered Mrs. Hale shortly.

She turned to the stove, saying something about that fire not being much to brag of. She worked with it a minute, and when she straightened up she said aggressively:

"The law is the law — and a bad stove is a bad stove. How'd you like to cook on this?" — pointing with the poker to the broken lining. She opened the oven door and started to express her opinion of the oven; but she was swept

---

red up: Neat.

into her own thoughts, thinking of what it would mean, year after year, to have that stove to wrestle with. The thought of Minnie Foster trying to bake in that oven — and the thought of her never going over to see Minnie Foster — .

She was startled by hearing Mrs. Peters say: "A person gets discouraged — and loses heart."

The sheriff's wife had looked from the stove to the sink — to the pail of water which had been carried in from outside. The two women stood there silent, above them the footsteps of the men who were looking for evidence against the woman who had worked in that kitchen. That look of seeing into things, of seeing through a thing to something else, was in the eyes of the sheriff's wife now. When Mrs. Hale next spoke to her, it was gently:

"Better loosen up your things, Mrs. Peters. We'll not feel them when we go out."

Mrs. Peters went to the back of the room to hang up the fur tippet she was wearing. A moment later she exclaimed, "Why, she was piecing a quilt," and held up a large sewing basket piled high with quilt pieces.

Mrs. Hale spread some of the blocks on the table.

"It's log-cabin pattern," she said, putting several of them together. "Pretty, isn't it?"

They were so engaged with the quilt that they did not hear the footsteps on the stairs. Just as the stair door opened Mrs. Hale was saying:

"Do you suppose she was going to quilt it or just knot it?"

The sheriff threw up his hands.

"They wonder whether she was going to quilt it or just knot it!"

There was a laugh for the ways of women, a warming of hands over the stove, and then the county attorney said briskly:

"Well, let's go right out to the barn and get that cleared up."

"I don't see as there's anything so strange," Mrs. Hale said resentfully, after the outside door had closed on the three men — "our taking up our time with little things while we're waiting for them to get the evidence. I don't see as it's anything to laugh about."

"Of course they've got awful important things on their minds," said the sheriff's wife apologetically.

They returned to an inspection of the block for the quilt. Mrs. Hale was looking at the fine, even sewing, and preoccupied with thoughts of the woman who had done that sewing, when she heard the sheriff's wife say, in a queer tone:

"Why, look at this one."

She turned to take the block held out to her.

"The sewing," said Mrs. Peters, in a troubled way. "All the rest of them have been so nice and even — but — this one. Why, it looks as if she didn't know what she was about!"

Their eyes met — something flashed to life, passed between them; then, as if with an effort, they seemed to pull away from each other. A moment Mrs. Hale sat there, her hands folded over that sewing which was so unlike all the rest of the sewing. Then she had pulled a knot and drawn the threads.

"Oh, what are you doing, Mrs. Hale?" asked the sheriff's wife, startled.

"Just pulling out a stitch or two that's not sewed very good," said Mrs. Hale mildly.

"I don't think we ought to touch things," Mrs. Peters said, a little help-lessly.

"I'll just finish up this end," answered Mrs. Hale, still in that mild, matter-of-fact fashion.

She threaded a needle and started to replace bad sewing with good. For a little while she sewed in silence. Then, in that thin, timid voice, she heard:

"Mrs. Hale!"

"Yes, Mrs. Peters?"

"What do you suppose she was so — nervous about?"

"Oh, *I* don't know," said Mrs. Hale, as if dismissing a thing not impor-tant enough to spend much time on. "I don't know as she was — nervous. I sew awful queer sometimes when I'm just tired."

She cut a thread, and out of the corner of her eye looked up at Mrs. Peters. The small, lean face of the sheriff's wife seemed to have tightened up. Her eyes had that look of peering into something. But next moment she moved, and said in her thin, indecisive way:

"Well, I must get those clothes wrapped. They may be through sooner than we think. I wonder where I could find a piece of paper — and string."

"In that cupboard, maybe," suggested Mrs. Hale, after a glance around.

One piece of the crazy sewing remained unripped. Mrs. Peter's back turned, Martha Hale now scrutinized that piece, compared it with the dainty, accurate sewing of the other blocks. The difference was startling. Holding this block made her feel queer, as if the distracted thoughts of the woman who had perhaps turned to it to try and quiet herself were communicating themselves to her.

Mrs. Peters' voice roused her.

"Here's a bird-cage," she said. "Did she have a bird, Mrs. Hale?"

"Why, I don't know whether she did or not." She turned to look at the cage Mrs. Peters was holding up. "I've not been here in so long." She sighed. "There was a man round last year selling canaries cheap — but I don't know as she took one. Maybe she did. She used to sing real pretty herself."

Mrs. Peters looked around the kitchen.

"Seems kind of funny to think of a bird here." She half laughed — an at-tempt to put up a barrier. "But she must have had one — or why would she have a cage? I wonder what happened to it."

"I suppose maybe the cat got it," suggested Mrs. Hale, resuming her sewing.

"No; she didn't have a cat. She's got that feeling some people have about cats — being afraid of them. When they brought her to our house yes-terday, my cat got in the room, and she was real upset and asked me to take it out."

"My sister Bessie was like that," laughed Mrs. Hale.

The sheriff's wife did not reply. The silence made Mrs. Hale turn round. Mrs. Peters was examining the bird-cage.

"Look at this door," she said slowly. "It's broke. One hinge has been pulled apart."

Mrs. Hale came nearer.

"Looks as if someone must have been — rough with it."

Again their eyes met — startled, questioning, apprehensive. For a moment neither spoke nor stirred. Then Mrs. Hale, turning away, said brusquely:

"If they're going to find any evidence, I wish they'd be about it. I don't like this place."

"But I'm awful glad you came with me, Mrs. Hale." Mrs. Peters put the bird-cage on the table and sat down. "It would be lonesome for me — sitting here alone."

"Yes, it would, wouldn't it?" agreed Mrs. Hale, a certain determined naturalness in her voice. She had picked up the sewing, but now it dropped in her lap, and she murmured in a different voice: "But I tell you what I *do* wish, Mrs. Peters. I wish I had come over sometimes when she was here. I wish — I had."

"But of course you were awful busy, Mrs. Hale. Your house — and your children."

"I could've come," retorted Mrs. Hale shortly. "I stayed away because it weren't cheerful — and that's why I ought to have come. I" — she looked around — "I've never liked this place. Maybe because it's down in a hollow and you don't see the road. I don't know what it is, but it's a lonesome place, and always was. I wish I had come over to see Minnie Foster sometimes. I can see now — " She did not put it into words.

"Well, you mustn't reproach yourself," counseled Mrs. Peters. "Somehow, we just don't see how it is with other folks till — something comes up."

"Not having children makes less work," mused Mrs. Hale, after a silence, "but it makes a quiet house — and Wright out to work all day — and no company when he did come in. Did you know John Wright, Mrs. Peters?"

"Not to know him. I've seen him in town. They say he was a good man."

"Yes — good," conceded John Wright's neighbor grimly. "He didn't drink, and kept his word as well as most, I guess, and paid his debts. But he was a hard man, Mrs. Peters. Just to pass the time of day with him — ." She stopped, shivered a little. "Like a raw wind that gets to the bone." Her eye fell upon the cage on the table before her, and she added, almost bitterly: "I should think she would've wanted a bird!"

Suddenly she leaned forward, looking intently at the cage. "But what do you s'pose went wrong with it?"

"I don't know," returned Mrs. Peters; "unless it got sick and died."

But after she said it she reached over and swung the broken door. Both women watched it as if somehow held by it.

"You didn't know — her?" Mrs. Hale asked, a gentler note in her voice.

"Not till they brought her yesterday," said the sheriff's wife.

"She — come to think of it, she was kind of like a bird herself. Real sweet and pretty, but kind of timid and — fluttery. How — she — did — change."

That held her for a long time. Finally, as if struck with a happy thought and relieved to get back to everyday things, she exclaimed:

"Tell you what, Mrs. Peters, why don't you take the quilt in with you? It might take up her mind."

"Why, I think that's a real nice idea, Mrs. Hale," agreed the sheriff's wife, as if she too were glad to come into the atmosphere of a simple kindness. "There couldn't possibly be any objection to that, could there? Now, just what will I take? I wonder if her patches are in here — and her things?"

They turned to the sewing basket.

"Here's some red," said Mrs. Hale, bringing out a roll of cloth. Underneath that was a box. "Here, maybe her scissors are in here — and her things." She held it up. "What a pretty box! I'll warrant that was something she had a long time ago — when she was a girl."

She held it in her hand a moment; then, with a little sigh, opened it.

Instantly her hand went to her nose.

"Why — !"

Mrs. Peters drew nearer — then turned away.

"There's something wrapped up in this piece of silk," faltered Mrs. Hale.

"This isn't her scissors," said Mrs. Peters, in a shrinking voice.

Her hand not steady, Mrs. Hale raised the piece of silk. "Oh, Mrs. Peters!" she cried. "It's — "

Mrs. Peters bent closer.

"It's the bird," she whispered.

"But, Mrs. Peters!" cried Mrs. Hale. "*Look* at it! Its *neck* — look at its neck! It's all — other side *to*."

She held the box away from her.

The sheriff's wife again bent closer.

"Somebody wrung its neck," said she, in a voice that was slow and deep.

And then again the eyes of the two women met — this time clung together in a look of dawning comprehension, of growing horror. Mrs. Peters looked from the dead bird to the broken door of the cage. Again their eyes met. And just then there was a sound at the outside door.

Mrs. Hale slipped the box under the quilt pieces in the basket, and sank into the chair before it. Mrs. Peters stood holding to the table. The county attorney and the sheriff came in from outside.

"Well, ladies," said the county attorney, as one turning from serious things to little pleasantries, "have you decided whether she was going to quilt it or knot it?"

"We think," began the sheriff's wife in a flurried voice, "that she was going to — knot it."

He was too preoccupied to notice the change that came in her voice on that last.

"Well, that's very interesting, I'm sure," he said tolerantly. He caught sight of the bird-cage. "Has the bird flown?"

"We think the cat got it," said Mrs. Hale in a voice curiously even.

He was walking up and down, as if thinking something out.

"Is there a cat?" he asked absently.

Mrs. Hale shot a look up at the sheriff's wife.

"Well, not *now*," said Mrs. Peters. "They're superstitious, you know; they leave."

She sank into her chair.

The county attorney did not heed her. "No sign at all of anyone having come in from the outside," he said to Peters, in the manner of continuing an interrupted conversation. "Their own rope. Now let's go upstairs again and go over it, piece by piece. It would have to have been someone who knew just the — "

The stair door closed behind them and their voices were lost.

The two women sat motionless, not looking at each other, but as if peering into something and at the same time holding back. When they spoke now it was as if they were afraid of what they were saying, but as if they could not help saying it.

"She liked the bird," said Martha Hale, low and slowly. "She was going to bury it."

"When I was a girl," said Mrs. Peters, under her breath, "my kitten — there was a boy took a hatchet, and before my eyes — before I could get there — " She covered her face an instant. "If they hadn't held me back I would have" — she caught herself, looked upstairs where footsteps were heard, and finished weakly — "hurt him."

Then they sat without speaking or moving.

"I wonder how it would seem," Mrs. Hale at last began, as if feeling her way over strange ground — "never to have had any children around?" Her eyes made a slow sweep of the kitchen, as if seeing what that kitchen had meant through all the years. "No, Wright wouldn't like the bird," she said after that — "a thing that sang. She used to sing. He killed that too." Her voice tightened.

Mrs. Peters moved uneasily.

"Of course we don't know who killed the bird."

"I knew John Wright," was Mrs. Hale's answer.

"It was an awful thing was done in this house that night, Mrs. Hale," said the sheriff's wife. "Killing a man while he slept — slipping a thing round his neck that choked the life out of him."

Mrs. Hale's hand went out to the bird-cage.

"His neck. Choked the life out of him."

"We don't *know* who killed him," whispered Mrs. Peters wildly. "We don't *know*."

Mrs. Hale had not moved. "If there had been years and years of — nothing, then a bird to sing to you, it would be awful — still — after the bird was still."

It was as if something within her not herself had spoken, and it found in Mrs. Peters something she did not know as herself.

"I know what stillness is," she said, in a queer, monotonous voice. "When we homesteaded in Dakota, and my first baby died — after he was two years old — and me with no other then — "

Mrs. Hale stirred.

"How soon do you suppose they'll be through looking for the evidence?"

"I know what stillness is," repeated Mrs. Peters, in just the same way. Then she too pulled back. "The law has got to punish crime, Mrs. Hale," she said in her tight little way.

"I wish you'd seen Minnie Foster," was the answer, "when she wore a white dress with blue ribbons, and stood up there in the choir and sang."

The picture of that girl, the fact that she had lived neighbor to that girl for twenty years, and had let her die for lack of life, was suddenly more than she could bear.

"Oh, I *wish* I'd come over here once in a while!" she cried. "That was a crime! Who's going to punish that?"

"We mustn't take on," said Mrs. Peters, with a frightened look toward the stairs.

"I might 'a' *known* she needed help! I tell you, it's *queer,* Mrs. Peters. We live close together, and we live far apart. We all go through the same things — it's all just a different kind of the same thing! If it weren't — why do you and I *understand?* Why do we *know* — what we know this minute?"

She dashed her hand across her eyes. Then, seeing the jar of fruit on the table, she reached for it and choked out:

"If I was you I wouldn't *tell* her her fruit was gone! Tell her it *ain't.* Tell her it's all right — all of it. Here — take this in to prove it to her! She — she may never know whether it was broke or not."

She turned away.

Mrs. Peters reached out for the bottle of fruit as if she were glad to take it — as if touching a familiar thing, having something to do, could keep her from something else. She got up, looked about for something to wrap the fruit in, took a petticoat from the pile of clothes she had brought from the front room, and nervously started winding that round the bottle.

"My!" she began, in a high, false voice, "it's a good thing the men couldn't hear us! Getting all stirred up over a little thing like a — dead canary." She hurried over that. "As if that could have anything to do with — with — My, wouldn't they *laugh?*"

Footsteps were heard on the stairs.

"Maybe they would," muttered Mrs. Hale — "maybe they wouldn't."

"No, Peters," said the county attorney incisively; "it's all perfectly clear, except the reason for doing it. But you know juries when it comes to women. If there was some definite thing — something to show. Something to make a story about. A thing that would connect up with this clumsy way of doing it."

In a covert way Mrs. Hale looked at Mrs. Peters. Mrs. Peters was looking at her. Quickly they looked away from each other. The outer door opened and Mr. Hale came in.

"I've got the team round now," he said. "Pretty cold out there."

"I'm going to stay here awhile by myself," the county attorney suddenly announced. "You can send Frank out for me, can't you?" he asked the sheriff. "I want to go over everything. I'm not satisfied we can't do better."

Again, for one brief moment, the two women's eyes found one another. The sheriff came up to the table.

"Did you want to see what Mrs. Peters was going to take in?"

The county attorney picked up the apron. He laughed.

"Oh, I guess they're not very dangerous things the ladies have picked out."

Mrs. Hale's hand was on the sewing basket in which the box was concealed. She felt that she ought to take her hand off the basket. She did not seem able to. He picked up one of the quilt blocks which she had piled on to cover the box. Her eyes felt like fire. She had a feeling that if he took up the basket she would snatch it from him.

But he did not take it up. With another little laugh, he turned away, saying:

"No; Mrs. Peters doesn't need supervising. For that matter, a sheriff's wife is married to the law. Ever think of it that way, Mrs. Peters?"

Mrs. Peters was standing beside the table. Mrs. Hale shot a look up at her; but she could not see her face. Mrs. Peters had turned away. When she spoke, her voice was muffled.

"Not — just that way," she said.

"Married to the law!" chuckled Mrs. Peters' husband. He moved toward the door into the front room, and said to the county attorney:

"I just want you to come in here a minute, George. We ought to take a look at these windows."

"Oh — windows," said the county attorney scoffingly.

"We'll be right out, Mr. Hale," said the sheriff to the farmer, who was still waiting by the door.

Hale went to look after the horses. The sheriff followed the county attorney into the other room. Again — for one final moment — the two women were alone in that kitchen.

Martha Hale sprang up, her hands tight together, looking at that other woman, with whom it rested. At first she could not see her eyes, for the sheriff's wife had not turned back since she turned away at that suggestion of being married to the law. But now Mrs. Hale made her turn back. Her eyes made her turn back. Slowly, unwillingly, Mrs. Peters turned her head until her eyes met the eyes of the other woman. There was a moment when they held each other in a steady, burning look in which there was no evasion nor flinching. Then Martha Hale's eyes pointed the way to the basket in which was hidden the thing that would make certain the conviction of the other woman — that woman who was not there and yet who had been there with them all through that hour.

For a moment Mrs. Peters did not move. And then she did it. With a rush forward, she threw back the quilt pieces, got the box, tried to put it in her handbag. It was too big. Desperately she opened it, started to take the bird out. But there she broke — she could not touch the bird. She stood there help-less, foolish.

There was the sound of a knob turning in the inner door. Martha Hale snatched the box from the sheriff's wife, and got it in the pocket of her big coat just as the sheriff and the county attorney came back into the kitchen.

"Well, Henry," said the county attorney facetiously, "at least we found out that she was not going to quilt it. She was going to — what is it you call it, ladies?"

Mrs. Hale's hand was against the pocket of her coat.

"We call it — knot it, Mr. Henderson."

ॐ

NADINE GORDIMER (b. 1923), *the recipient of the 1991 Nobel Prize for Literature, was born in the small town of Springs, near Johannesburg, South Africa. Her mother was English, and her father, a Jewish watchmaker, emigrated to Africa from the Baltic states. Gordimer attended a convent school and studied at the University of the Witwatersrand, getting what she has called "a scrappy and uninspiring minimal education." Growing up in South Africa, she never recognized herself in any of the English books she read until she encountered the stories of the New Zealand writer Katherine Mansfield. Then, Gordimer says, "I realized here was somebody who was writing about this other world, whose seasons at least I shared. Then I understood it was possible to be a writer even if you didn't live in England."*

Gordimer began to write stories before she attempted a novel. She acknowledges three writers as her guides: D. H. Lawrence, who influenced her way of looking at the natural world; Henry James, who gave her a consciousness of form; and Ernest Hemingway, who taught her to hear what is essential in dialogue. Her early stories, such as "The Kindest Thing To Do," appeared in The New Yorker, Harper's, *and other American magazines and were first collected in* Face to Face *(1949) and* The Soft Voice of the Serpent *(1952). Since her first novel,* The Lying Days, *was published in 1953, she has continued to write novels and short fiction collections. In her stories, Gordimer rarely experiments beyond the realistic rendering of her subject, but her decision to write in the form of the short story or the novel depends on the shape the material takes as a narrative:*

> *Whether it sprawls or neatly bites its own tail, a short story is a concept that the writer can "hold" fully realized in his imagination at one time. A novel is, by comparison, staked out, and must be taken possession of stage by stage; it is impossible to contain, all at once, the proliferation of concepts it ultimately may use. For this reason I cannot understand how people can suppose one makes a conscious choice, after knowing what one wants to write about, between writing a novel or a short story. A short story occurs, in the imaginative sense. To write one is to express from a situation in the exterior or interior world the life-giving drop — sweat, tear, semen, saliva — that will spread an intensity on the page; burn a hole in it.*

NADINE GORDIMER

The Kindest Thing to Do   *1950*

In the warm stupor of early Sunday afternoon, when the smell of Sunday roast still hangs about the house, and the servants have banged the kitchen door closed behind them and gone off, gleaming and sweaty in tight Sunday clothes, to visit at the Location, the family comes out dreamily, slackly, to lie upon the lawn. The hour has drained them of will; they come out at the pull of some instinct, like that which sends animals creeping away to die. They lie, suspended in the hour, with the cushions and books about them. The big wheels have turned slower and slower; now they cease to turn, and hang motionless. Only the tiny wheels still turn; silent and busy and scarcely noticeable, the beetles climbing in the grass blades, the flowers fingered gently by small currents, as they lift, breathing up to the sun. The little world is still running, where the birds peck, stepping daintily on their twigs of claws in the flower beds.

"Have you got Micky there?" The voice came clearly from the bedroom window and it almost made her wince, it almost penetrated, but there was no resistance to it: in the fluid, heavy, resurgent air the steel blade of sound slid through and was lost. Her head, drooping near the drooping, bee-heavy, crumpled paper chalices of the poppies, lifted half-protestingly, her lazy hand brushed the grey specks of insects which flecked the pages of Petrarch's "Laura in Death." In her mind's eye, she saw Micky, head to tail, asleep, somewhere near ... On the grass, at her back, at her side; somewhere ... She grunted and waved in assent, already back in the book, in the mazy spell of steady warmth and flowers fixed in the hypnosis of the sun, and grass blades, seen from their own level, consumed in dark, blazing light along the edges. The pulses slackened and the blood ran sweet and heavy in the veins; the print danced and the mind almost swooned. It swerved away, off into thoughts half-formed, that trailed and merged.

In one of the neighbouring houses that enclosed the garden on three sides, some poor child began to practise the piano. The unsure notes came hesitantly across the air, a tiny voice that disturbed the afternoon no more than would a fly, buzzing about the ear of a sleeping giant. The Sunday paper lay about. The father lay rolled on to his back, suddenly asleep in the defenceless fashion of the middle aged, with his mouth half open and the stretched folds of his neck relaxed like the neck of an old turkey. The little boy had grass in his hair, that was itself like winter grass, pale and rough. The others read, dozed, dreamed, and lay on their backs, the sky and the trees and the house and the bright dots of poppies reflected in their eyes as in an old-fashioned convex mirror — the kind of mirror that in Victorian days reflected the room it looked down upon as another world into which one might climb, like *Alice Through the Looking-glass*. There it was, the shining white house, the shining green fir, the shining blue sky, in the little round mirror of each eye.

She read on, lost, drowsing, flicking minute creatures from the pages, scratching mechanically at her leg, where the grass pricked her.

And the next moment it was gone; the beautiful lassitude turned sick and sour within her, the exquisite torpor hung heavy around her neck, she struggled free of the coils of the dead afternoon. "But I was sure . . ." she said, stunned; feeling beaten down before the figure of her mother. Her mother stood, almost too much to bear, purposeful and hard as reality, demanding and urgent. Her glance was too insistent, it came like a pain, piercing the spell. "Well, there you are . . ." the mother spoke with scornful resignation, angrily, "I might have known you wouldn't bother to look."

"But I thought . . ."

"Yes, of course 'you thought' — surely it wasn't asking too much of you to see whether the dog was with you? Well, it's done now, and the poor little bird's bleeding and half torn to bits and still alive, too."

The girl sat up. She was dizzy. The afternoon suddenly sang and was orange-coloured. The great wheels started turning, the world creaked and groaned and rushed into confusion and activity, the clamour started up again.

Yesterday they had found a bird — an injured dove, its wing damaged by some small boy's catapult. Once before they had found a hurt bird, and had kept it in a cage and fed it until it was able to fly again, and so this time they brought out the old cage and put the sullen soft grey dove inside with food and water, confident that with care it would soon be healed. Now this afternoon, the mother — always mindful of the small responsibilities that everyone else so easily forgot after the first ardour of sympathy — had gone out to the shed to see how the bird was progressing, and seeing it sulking, puffed up resentfully in a corner of its cage, had decided to let it out to peck about the back garden for a while, intending to return it to the cage if it were still unable to fly. But of course Micky, who eyed the doves upon the wall longingly, and chased them ineffectually when they alighted upon the path or the grass, must be kept out of the way. The mother had made sure that Micky was safely on the front lawn with the family. She had called out of the bedroom window . . .

"I was sure he was here," the girl repeated. "I felt sure he was here. I thought . . ."

"I had a feeling he'd gone round there after the bird, and when I went out, sure enough, there he was worrying it as if it were a bone."

"Little beast . . ." the girl shuddered.

"It's alive, poor creature, too — I'm sure I don't know what's to be done for it now." The mother kept her accusing gaze on the girl, washing her hands of the whole affair.

"You didn't kill it . . . ?" the girl asked, almost pleadingly.

"*I* can't kill the thing," she said. She had always done everything unpleasant for her children; she had always stood between them and the ugliness of life: death, sickness, despair.

The girl looked for something in her mother's face and this time did not find it.

Suddenly she wished, wished she could have the last half-hour back, she wanted it over again, desperately, childishly, uselessly, so that she might look up from her book and say: No, Micky isn't here.

In a kind of sulky horror she got up and started to walk round the side of the house. "Where?" she said drearily, pausing and turning. Her hair was rumpled and grass clung to her clothes, her right cheek was flushed with sun. "Just near the hedge," said the mother.

She tried to prepare herself to imagine what the bird would look like, but her mind turned away from the thought. It was upset, too lately, roughly woken to serve her. The narcotic sun stared hatefully upon her and she sickened from it, as a man turns from the smell of liquor he has drunk too freely the night before. She did not *care* about the bird; she did not want to be bothered with it. She wanted to go away into the house, or out, somewhere, and pretend it hadn't happened. If you ignored something, put it utterly from you, and went on to the next thing, it was as if it had never happened. If she walked away now, life would grow over the incident, covering it, hiding it smoothly.

I am weak, she said, self-pitying.

I'll have to kill it.

Something lifted and turned over inside her as she realized the thought. Fear prickled right over her body, from her head to her toes.

Then she came out round the screen of the hedge and into the shade of the hedge and she looked upon the ground, that was damp and mossy in patches, and she could not see the bird. She looked here and there, and poked at a drift of dead leaves with her foot, but she did not find it.

And then she turned and there it was, lying in a stony hollow just behind her. There it was, and it was not a bird, it was a flattened mess of dusty feathers, torn and wet with the dog's saliva, oozing dark blood from wounds that lay hidden, making sodden the close soft down of — ah, what was it, was it the breast, the tail; what part was recognizable in the crushed wad of that small body . . .

Only the head. And as she saw the head a thrill of such vivid, terrifying, utter anguish contracted in her that she felt that some emotion she had never used before had been called up from her soul. It was unbearable. It was the emotion that bursts the human heart. The emotion from which men hide their heads in despair. For the head of the bird lay sunken in the last humility, down upon its broken breast; the beak rested piteously in the feathers, and the eyes were closed strangely, resignedly, in the final martyrdom of suffering. A passionate desperation of agony had passed over that small grey head, had blazed up in the little being of the bird, making it great, bigger than itself, and breaking it, bringing its head down upon its broken breast.

She felt that nothing could expiate this, ever; nothing, nothing; no tears, no sorrowing, no compensation of other joys could wipe out this thing that existed in life.

She saw that the bird still lived; that it was; that it experienced the awfulness of its own annihilation. And cowardly and trembling, knowing that each moment she delayed out of cowardice it suffered to the full, she slowly drew off her sandal. Very slowly, almost whimpering, she lifted the sandal and brought it down upon the bird's head. She had not known it would be so terrible — that beneath the blow of the sandal she would feel the shape of the small grey head, the particular horror of the resistance of the delicate-boned skull and the softness of the outer covering of feathers, all at once, at the moment of contact. And in an agonized instant life asserted itself vainly and for the last time in the tiny creature, and it half-raised itself, opening the thin mute beak in a wild flutter. Wildly she brought the sandal down again; once, twice, three times. The bird was dead.

And now it was nothing; it was a dead bird.

She put her sandal on again, feeling the dust on her bare foot uncomfortable against the inner sole.

She looked at the bird. How strange a thing that was — she had killed, had battered the life out of something. She thought: killing is a strange thing; it is terrible, until you do it, right up to the moment of doing it.

She had read so many times of murder, and it had meant nothing to her; it was as emotionally incomprehensible to her as a passionate love affair would be to a child of seven. But now with a slow cold trickle of fear that ran — and could not be checked, could not be fought — through her soul, leaving its cold awful imprint, a dark knowledge came to her. She felt it open, a Lethean flower of knowledge, that she feared and did not want, chilling her soul with a strange cold sap. It came coldly because it was a dreadful cold thing, the understanding of the fulfillment of the will to kill. I could kill anything now, she thought, and the words seemed light and easy. They were the words of no-feeling, and she was afraid of them. She was deadened under the weight of this cold knowledge, that would never leave her now, once it was discovered. Ah, the hopelessness, the awfulness of knowing . . . The passion of pity she had felt for the bird was nothing compared with this; gladly, gladly would she feel that again. But she could not; only the calm reasonableness of the clear thought: I could kill anything now.

She came round to the front garden, breathing warmly, with her face drawn in a wry frown. They watched her from the lawn. "Well, what happened?" they asked, watching her face. "I killed it. It's dead," she said.

"Ugh . . . How awful . . . How could you?"

"It was the kindest thing to do," said someone else sensibly. "She had to put the poor thing out of its misery — what else could she do?" The mother got up and went round to the back to dispose of the body.

She went inside because she could not bear the lazy, sprawling sun, that blazed as horribly now as an electric light left burning right on into daylight. She washed, and combed her hair, and let the water run over her hands. And later, in the evening, she went out, and laughing and talking in a group of those social acquaintances who are vaguely referred to as "friends," she said with a grimace — "I had to do something ghastly this afternoon — I had to kill a bird." "How brave of you!" said the young man, laughing, with mock heroic emphasis. "For a girl — yes," said another, spearing an olive on a coloured toothpick. "Women are terrified of squashing a beetle. God knows, they can be cruel and ruthless in their own devious subtle fashions — but when it comes to killing any sort of little creature, they're the most craven cowards." "Well, I did," she said stoutly, carelessly; and laughing like a woman of spirit, she took the olive from him and popped it into her mouth.

NATHANIEL HAWTHORNE *(1804–1864), writer of short stories and novels, was born in Salem, Massachusetts, into an eminent family who traced their lineage back to the Puritans. After his graduation from Bowdoin College in 1825, Hawthorne lived at home while he wrote short fiction he called "tales" or "articles" that he tried to sell to periodicals. American magazines of the time were mostly interested in publishing ghost stories, Indian legends, and "village tales" based on historical anecdotes. Hawthorne (like his contemporary Edgar Allan Poe) created stories that transcended the limitations of these conventions; his imagination was stirred by what he called "an inveterate love of allegory."*

Hawthorne published his first collection of stories, Twice-Told Tales, *in 1837; a second book of stories,* Mosses from an Old Manse, *appeared in 1846. That year he stopped writing to earn a better living for his family as surveyor of customs for the port of Salem. This was a political appointment, and after the Whigs won the presidency three years later, Hawthorne — a Democrat — was out of a job. He returned to writing fiction, sketching his "official life" at the Custom House in the introduction to his novel* The Scarlet Letter *in 1850. During the last decade of his career as a writer he published three other novels, several books for children, and another collection of tales. In "The Custom House," Hawthorne humorously suggested that his profession would not have impressed his Puritan ancestors:*

> *"What is he?" murmurs one grey shadow of my forefathers to the other. "A writer of story-books! What kind of business in life, what manner of glorifying God, or being serviceable to mankind in his day and generation, may that be? Why, the degenerate fellow might as well have been a fiddler!" Such are the compliments bandied between my great-grandsires and myself across the gulf of time! And yet, let them scorn me as they will, strong traits of their nature have intertwined themselves with mine.*

Despite Hawthorne's portrait of himself as an unappreciated artist, he was recognized by contemporaries such as Herman Melville and Edgar Allan Poe as a "genius of a very lofty order." Hawthorne wrote about 120 short tales and sketches in addition to his novels. His notebooks are filled with ideas for stories, more often jottings of abstract ideas than detailed observations of "real" individuals. "The Hollow of the Three Hills" and "Young Goodman Brown" are two of his moral tales set in the distant past.

RELATED COMMENTARIES: *Herman Melville, "Blackness in Hawthorne's 'Young Goodman Brown,' " page 768; Edgar Allan Poe, "The Importance of the Single Effect in a Prose Tale," page 787.*

NATHANIEL HAWTHORNE

The Hollow of the Three Hills   1830

In those strange old times, when fantastic dreams and madmen's reveries were realized among the actual circumstances of life, two persons met together at an appointed hour and place. One was a lady, graceful in form and fair of feature, though pale and troubled, and smitten with an untimely blight in what should have been the fullest bloom of her years; the other was an ancient and meanly dressed woman, of ill-favored aspect, and so withered, shrunken and decrepit, that even the space since she began to decay must have exceeded the ordinary term of human existence. In the spot where they encountered, no mortal could observe them. Three little hills stood near each other, and down in the midst of them sunk a hollow basin, almost mathematically circular, two or three hundred feet in breadth, and of such depth that a stately cedar might but just be visible above the sides. Dwarf pines were numerous upon the hills, and partly fringed the outer verge of the intermediate hollow; within which there was nothing but the brown grass of October, and here and there a tree-trunk, that had fallen long ago, and lay mouldering with no green successor from its roots. One of these masses of decaying wood, formerly a majestic oak, rested close beside a pool of green and sluggish water at the bottom of the basin. Such scenes as this (so gray tradition tells) were once the resort of a Power of Evil and his plighted subjects; and here, at midnight or on the dim verge of evening, they were said to stand round the mantling pool, disturbing its putrid waters in the performance of an impious baptismal rite. The chill beauty of an autumnal sunset was now gilding the three hill-tops, whence a paler tint stole down their sides into the hollow.

"Here is our pleasant meeting come to pass," said the aged crone, "according as thou hast desired. Say quickly what thou wouldst have of me, for there is but a short hour that we may tarry here."

As the old withered woman spoke, a smile glimmered on her countenance, like lamplight on the wall of a sepulchre. The lady trembled, and cast her eyes upward to the verge of the basin, as if meditating to return with her purpose unaccomplished. But it was not so ordained.

"I am stranger in this land, as you know," said she at length. "Whence I come it matters not; — but I have left those behind me with whom my fate was intimately bound, and from whom I am cut off forever. There is a weight in my bosom that I cannot away with, and I have come hither to inquire of their welfare."

"And who is there by this green pool, that can bring thee news from the ends of the Earth?" cried the old woman, peering into the lady's face. "Not from my lips mayst thou hear these tidings; yet, be thou bold, and the daylight shall not pass away from yonder hill-top, before thy wish be granted."

"I will do your bidding though I die," replied the lady desperately.

The old woman seated herself on the trunk of the fallen tree, threw aside the hood that shrouded her gray locks, and beckoned her companion to draw near.

"Kneel down," she said, "and lay your forehead on my knees."

She hesitated a moment, but the anxiety, that had long been kindling, burned fiercely up within her. As she knelt down, the border of her garment was dipped into the pool; she laid her forehead on the old woman's knees, and the latter drew a cloak about the lady's face, so that she was in darkness. Then she heard the muttered words of a prayer, in the midst of which she started, and would have arisen.

"Let me flee, — let me flee and hide myself, that they may not look upon me!" she cried. But, with returning recollection, she hushed herself, and was still as death.

For it seemed as if other voices — familiar in infancy, and unforgotten through many wanderings, and in all the vicissitudes of her heart and fortune — were mingling with the accents of the prayer. At first the words were faint and indistinct, not rendered so by distance, but rather resembling the dim pages of a book, which we strive to read by an imperfect and gradually brightening light. In such a manner, as the prayer proceeded, did those voices strengthen upon the ear; till at length the petition ended, and the conversation of an aged man, and of a woman broken and decayed like himself, became distinctly audible to the lady as she knelt. But those strangers appeared not to stand in the hollow depth between the three hills. Their voices were encompassed and re-echoed by the walls of a chamber, the windows of which were rattling in the breeze; the regular vibration of a clock, the crackling of a fire, and the tinkling of the embers as they fell among the ashes, rendered the scene almost as vivid as if painted to the eye. By a melancholy hearth sat these two old people, the man calmly despondent, the woman querulous and tearful, and their words were all of sorrow. They spoke of a daughter, a wanderer they knew not where, bearing dishonor along with her, and leaving shame and affliction to bring their gray heads to the grave. They alluded also to other and more recent woe, but in the midst of their talk, their voices seemed to melt into the sound of the wind sweeping mournfully among the autumn leaves; and when the lady lifted her eyes, there was she kneeling in the hollow between three hills.

"A weary and lonesome time yonder old couple have of it," remarked the old woman, smiling in the lady's face.

"And did you also hear them!" exclaimed she, a sense of intolerable humiliation triumphing over her agony and fear.

"Yea; and we have yet more to hear," replied the old woman. "Wherefore, cover thy face quickly."

Again the withered hag poured forth the monotonous words of a prayer that was not meant to be acceptable in Heaven; and soon, in the pauses of her breath, strange murmurings began to thicken, gradually increasing so as to drown and overpower the charm by which they grew. Shrieks pierced through the obscurity of sound, and were succeeded by the singing of sweet female voices, which in their turn gave way to a wild roar of laughter, broken suddenly by groanings and sobs, forming altogether a ghastly confusion of terror and mourning and mirth. Chains were rattling, fierce and stern voices uttered threats, and the scourge resounded at their command. All these noises deepened and became substantial to the listener's ear, till she could distinguish every soft and dreamy accent of the love songs, that died causelessly into funeral hymns. She shuddered at the unprovoked wrath which blazed up like the spontaneous kindling of flame, and she grew faint at the fearful merriment, raging miserably around her. In the midst of this wild scene, where unbound passions jostled each other in a drunken career, there was one solemn voice of a man, and a manly and melodious voice it might once have been. He went to-and-fro continually, and his feet sounded upon the floor. In each member of that frenzied company, whose own burning thoughts had become their exclusive world, he sought an auditor for the story of his individual wrong, and interpreted their laughter and tears as his reward of scorn or pity. He spoke of woman's perfidy, of a wife who had broken her holiest vows, of a home and heart made desolate. Even as he went on, the shout, the laugh, the shriek, the sob, rose up in unison, till they changed into the hollow, fitful, and uneven sound of the wind, as it fought among the pine-trees on those three lonely hills. The lady looked up, and there was the withered woman smiling in her face.

"Couldst thou have thought there were such merry times in a Mad House?" inquired the latter.

"True, true," said the lady to herself; "there is mirth within its walls, but misery, misery without."

"Wouldst thou hear more?" demanded the old woman.

"There is one other voice I would fain listen to again," replied the lady faintly.

"Then lay down thy head speedily upon my knees, that thou may'st get thee hence before the hour be past."

The golden skirts of day were yet lingering upon the hills, but deep shades obscured the hollow and the pool, as if sombre night were rising thence to overspread the world. Again that evil woman began to weave her spell. Long did it proceed unanswered, till the knolling of a bell stole in among the intervals of her words, like a clang that had travelled far over valley and rising ground, and was just ready to die in the air. The lady shook upon her companion's knees, as she heard that boding sound. Stronger it grew and sadder, and deepened into the tone of a death-bell, knolling dolefully from some ivy-mantled tower, and bearing tidings of mortality and woe to the cottage, to the hall, and to the solitary wayfarer, that all might weep for the doom appointed in turn to them. Then came a measured tread, passing slowly, slowly on, as of mourners with a coffin, their garments trailing on the ground, so that the ear could measure the length of their melancholy array. Before them went the priest, reading the burial-service, while the leaves of his book were rustling in the breeze. And though no voice but his was heard to speak aloud, still there were revilings and anathemas, whispered but distinct, from women and from men, breathed against the daughter who had wrung the aged hearts of her parents, — the wife who had betrayed the trusting fondness of her husband, — the mother who had sinned against natural affection, and left her child to die. The sweeping sound of the funeral train faded away like a thin vapour, and the wind, that just before had seemed to shake the coffin-pall, moaned sadly round the verge of the Hollow between three Hills. But when the old woman stirred the kneeling lady, she lifted not her head.

"Here has been a sweet hour's sport!" said the withered crone, chuckling to herself.

NATHANIEL HAWTHORNE

Young Goodman Brown   *1835*

Young Goodman Brown came forth at sunset into the street at Salem village; but put his head back, after crossing the threshold, to exchange a parting kiss with his young wife. And Faith, as the wife was aptly named, thrust her own pretty head into the street, letting the wind play with the pink ribbons of her cap while she called to Goodman Brown.

"Dearest heart," whispered she, softly and rather sadly, when her lips were close to his ear, "prithee put off your journey until sunrise and sleep in your own bed to-night. A lone woman is troubled with such dreams and such thoughts that she's afeared of herself sometimes. Pray tarry with me this night, dear husband, of all nights in the year."

"My love and my Faith," replied young Goodman Brown, "of all nights in the year, this one night must I tarry away from thee. My journey, as thou callest it, forth and back again, must needs be done 'twixt now and sunrise. What, my sweet, pretty wife, dost thou doubt me already, and we but three months married?"

"Then God bless you!" said Faith, with the pink ribbons; "and may you find all well when you come back."

"Amen!" cried Goodman Brown. "Say thy prayers, dear Faith, and go to bed at dusk, and no harm will come to thee."

So they parted; and the young man pursued his way until, being about to turn the corner by the meeting-house, he looked back and saw the head of Faith still peeping after him with a melancholy air, in spite of her pink ribbons.

"Poor little Faith!" thought he, for his heart smote him. "What a wretch am I to leave her on such an errand! She talks of dreams, too. Methought as she spoke there was trouble in her face, as if a dream had warned her what work is to be done to-night. But no, no; 't would kill her to think it. Well, she's a blessed angel on earth, and after this one night I'll cling to her skirts and follow her to heaven."

With this excellent resolve for the future, Goodman Brown felt himself justified in making more haste on his present evil purpose. He had taken a dreary road, darkened by all the gloomiest trees of the forest, which barely stood aside to let the narrow path creep through, and closed immediately behind. It was all as lonely as could be; and there is this peculiarity in such a solitude, that the traveller knows not who may be concealed by the innumerable trunks and the thick boughs overhead; so that with lonely footsteps he may yet be passing through an unseen multitude.

"There may be a devilish Indian behind every tree," said Goodman Brown to himself; and he glanced fearfully behind him as he added, "What if the devil himself should be at my very elbow!"

His head being turned back, he passed a crook of the road, and, looking forward again, beheld the figure of a man, in grave and decent attire, seated at the foot of an old tree. He arose at Goodman Brown's approach and walked onward side by side with him.

"You are late, Goodman Brown," said he. "The clock of the Old South was striking as I came through Boston, and that is full fifteen minutes agone."

"Faith kept me back a while," replied the young man, with a tremor in his voice, caused by the sudden appearance of his companion, though not wholly unexpected.

It was now deep dusk in the forest, and deepest in that part of it where these two were journeying. As nearly as could be discerned, the second traveller was about fifty years old, apparently in the same rank of life as Goodman Brown, and bearing a considerable resemblance to him, though perhaps more in expression than features. Still they might have been taken for father and son. And yet, though the elder person was as simply clad as the younger, and as simple in manner too, he had an indescribable air of one who knew the world, and who would not have felt abashed at the governor's dinner table or in King William's court, were it possible that his affairs should call him thither. But the only thing about him that could be fixed upon as remarkable was his staff, which bore the likeness of a great black snake, so curiously wrought that it might almost be seen to twist and wriggle itself like a living serpent. This, of course, must have been an ocular deception, assisted by the uncertain light.

"Come, Goodman Brown," cried his fellow-traveller, "this is a dull pace for the beginning of a journey. Take my staff, if you are so soon weary."

"Friend," said the other, exchanging his slow pace for a full stop, "having kept covenant by meeting thee here, it is my purpose now to return whence I came. I have scruples touching the matter thou wot'st of."

"Sayest thou so?" replied he of the serpent, smiling apart. "Let us walk on, nevertheless, reasoning as we go; and if I convince thee not thou shalt turn back. We are but a little way in the forest yet."

"Too far! too far!" exclaimed the goodman, unconsciously resuming his walk. "My father never went into the woods on such an errand, nor his father before him. We have been a race of honest men and good Christians since the days of the martyrs; and shall I be the first of the name of Brown that ever took this path and kept" —

"Such company, thou wouldst say," observed the elder person, interpreting his pause. "Well said, Goodman Brown! I have been as well acquainted with your family as with ever a one among the Puritans; and that's no trifle to say. I helped your grandfather, the constable, when he lashed the Quaker woman so smartly through the streets of Salem; and it was I that brought your father a pitch-pine knot, kindled at my own hearth, to set fire to an Indian village, in King Philip's war.° They were my good friends, both; and many a pleasant walk have we had along this path, and returned merrily after midnight. I would fain be friends with you for their sake."

"If it be as thou sayest," replied Goodman Brown, "I marvel they never spoke of these matters; or, verily, I marvel not, seeing that the least rumor of the sort would have driven them from New England. We are a people of prayer, and good works to boot, and abide no such wickedness."

King Philip's war: King Philip, a Wampanoag chief, spearheaded the most destructive Indian war ever waged against the New England colonists (1675–76).

"Wickedness or not," said the traveller with the twisted staff, "I have a very general acquaintance here in New England. The deacons of many a church have drunk the communion wine with me; the selectmen of divers towns make me their chairman; and a majority of the Great and General Court are firm supporters of my interest. The governor and I, too — But these are state secrets."

"Can this be so?" cried Goodman Brown, with a stare of amazement at his undisturbed companion. "Howbeit, I have nothing to do with the governor and council; they have their own ways, and are no rule for a simple husbandman like me. But, were I to go on with thee, how should I meet the eye of that good old man, our minister, at Salem village? Oh, his voice would make me tremble both Sabbath day and lecture day."

Thus far the elder traveller had listened with due gravity; but now burst into a fit of irrepressible mirth, shaking himself so violently that his snake-like staff actually seemed to wriggle in sympathy.

"Ha! ha! ha!" shouted he again and again; then composing himself, "Well, go on, Goodman Brown, go on; but, prithee, don't kill me with laughing."

"Well, then, to end the matter at once," said Goodman Brown, considerably nettled, "there is my wife, Faith. It would break her dear little heart; and I'd rather break my own."

"Nay, if that be the case," answered the other, "e'en go thy ways, Goodman Brown. I would not for twenty old women like the one hobbling before us that Faith should come to any harm."

As he spoke he pointed his staff at a female figure on the path, in whom Goodman Brown recognized a very pious and exemplary dame, who had taught him his catechism in youth, and was still his moral and spiritual adviser, jointly with the minister and Deacon Gookin.

"A marvel, truly that Goody Cloyse should be so far in the wilderness at nightfall," said he. "But with your leave, friend, I shall take a cut through the woods until we have left this Christian woman behind. Being a stranger to you, she might ask whom I was consorting with and whither I was going."

"Be it so," said his fellow-traveller. "Betake you to the woods, and let me keep the path."

Accordingly the young man turned aside, but took care to watch his companion, who advanced softly along the road until he had come within a staff's length of the old dame. She, meanwhile, was making the best of her way, with singular speed for so aged a woman, and mumbling some indistinct words — a prayer, doubtless — as she went. The traveller put forth his staff and touched her withered neck with what seemed the serpent's tail.

"The devil!" screamed the pious old lady.

"Then Goody Cloyse knows her old friend?" observed the traveller, confronting her and leaning on his writhing stick.

"Ah, forsooth, and is it your worship indeed?" cried the good dame. "Yea, truly is it, and in the very image of my old gossip, Goodman Brown, the grandfather of the silly fellow that now is. But — would your worship believe it? — my broomstick hath strangely disappeared, stolen, as I suspect, by that unhanged witch, Goody Cory, and that, too, when I was all anointed with the juice of smallage, and cinquefoil, and wolf's bane" —

"Mingled with fine wheat and the fat of a new-born babe," said the shape of old Goodman Brown.

"Ah, your worship knows the recipe," cried the old lady, cackling aloud. "So, as I was saying, being all ready for the meeting, and no horse to ride on, I made up my mind to foot it; for they tell me there is a nice young man to be taken into communion to-night. But now your good worship will lend me your arm, and we shall be there in a twinkling."

"That can hardly be," answered her friend. "I may not spare you my arm, Goody Cloyse; but here is my staff, if you will."

So saying, he threw it down at her feet, where, perhaps, it assumed life, being one of the rods which its owner had formerly lent to the Egyptian magi. Of this fact, however, Goodman Brown could not take cognizance. He had cast up his eyes in astonishment, and, looking down again, beheld neither Goody Cloyse nor the serpentine staff, but his fellow-traveller alone, who waited for him as calmly as if nothing had happened.

"That old woman taught me my catechism," said the young man; and there was a world of meaning in this simple comment.

They continued to walk onward, while the elder traveller exhorted his companion to make good speed and persevere in the path, discoursing so aptly that his arguments seemed rather to spring up in the bosom of his auditor than to be suggested by himself. As they went, he plucked a branch of maple to serve for a walking stick, and began to strip it of the twigs and little boughs, which were wet with evening dew. The moment his fingers touched them they became strangely withered and dried up as with a week's sunshine. Thus the pair proceeded, at a good free pace, until suddenly, in a gloomy hollow of the road, Goodman Brown sat himself down on the stump of a tree and refused to go any farther.

"Friend," he said, stubbornly, "my mind is made up. Not another step will I budge on this errand. What if a wretched old woman do choose to go to the devil when I thought she was going to heaven: is that any reason why I should quit my dear Faith and go after her?"

"You will think better of this by and by," said his acquaintance, composedly. "Sit here and rest yourself a while; and when you feel like moving again, there is my staff to help you along."

Without more words, he threw his companion the maple stick, and was as speedily out of sight as if he had vanished into the deepening gloom. The young man sat a few moments by the roadside, applauding himself greatly, and thinking with how clear a conscience he should meet the minister in his morning walk, nor shrink from the eye of good old Deacon Gookin. And what calm sleep would be his that very night, which was to have been spent so wickedly, but so purely and sweetly now, in the arms of Faith! Amidst these pleasant and praiseworthy meditations, Goodman Brown heard the tramp of horses along the road, and deemed it advisable to conceal himself within the verge of the forest, conscious of the guilty purpose that had brought him thither, though now so happily turned from it.

On came the hoof tramps and the voices of the riders, two grave old voices, conversing soberly as they drew near. These mingled sounds appeared to pass along the road, within a few yards of the young man's hiding-place; but, owing doubtless to the depth of the gloom at that particular spot, neither the travellers nor their steeds were visible. Though their figures brushed the small boughs by the wayside, it could not be seen that they intercepted, even for a moment, the faint gleam from the strip of bright sky athwart which they must have passed. Goodman Brown alternately crouched and stood on tiptoe, pulling aside the branches and thrusting forth his head as far as he durst without discerning so much as a shadow. It vexed him the more, because he could have sworn, were such a thing possible, that he recognized the voices of the minister and Deacon Gookin, jogging along quietly, as they were wont to do, when bound to some ordination or ecclesiastical council. While yet within hearing, one of the riders stopped to pluck a switch.

"Of the two, reverend sir," said the voice like the deacon's, "I had rather miss an ordination dinner than to-night's meeting. They tell me that some of our community are to be here from Falmouth and beyond, and others from Connecticut and Rhode Island, besides several of the Indian powwows, who, after their fashion, know almost as much deviltry as the best of us. Moreover, there is a goodly young woman to be taken into communion."

"Mighty well, Deacon Gookin!" replied the solemn old tones of the minister. "Spur up, or we shall be late. Nothing can be done, you know, until I get on the ground."

The hoofs clattered again; and the voices, talking so strangely in the empty air, passed on through the forest, where no church had ever been gathered or solitary Christian prayed. Whither, then, could these holy men be journeying so deep into the heathen wilderness? Young Goodman Brown caught hold of a tree for support, being ready to sink down on the ground, faint and overburdened with the heavy sickness of his heart. He looked up to the sky, doubting whether there really was a heaven above him. Yet there was the blue arch, and the stars brightening in it.

"With heaven above and Faith below, I will yet stand firm against the devil!" cried Goodman Brown.

While he still gazed upward into the deep arch of the firmament and had lifted his hands to pray, a cloud, though no wind was stirring, hurried across the zenith and hid the brightening stars. The blue sky was still visible, except directly overhead, where this black mass of cloud was sweeping swiftly northward. Aloft in the air, as if from the depths of the cloud, came a confused and doubtful sound of voices. Once the listener fancied that he could distinguish the accents of towns-people of his own, men and women, both pious and ungodly, many of whom he had met at the communion table, and had seen others rioting at the tavern. The next moment, so indistinct were the sounds, he doubted whether he had heard aught but the murmur of the old forest, whispering without a wind. Then came a stronger swell of those familiar tones, heard daily in the sunshine at Salem village, but never until now from a cloud of night. There was one voice, of a young woman, uttering lamentations, yet with an uncertain sorrow, and entreating for some favor, which, perhaps, it would grieve her to obtain; and all the unseen multitude, both saints and sinners, seemed to encourage her onward.

"Faith!" shouted Goodman Brown, in a voice of agony and desperation; and the echoes of the forest mocked him, crying, "Faith! Faith!" as if bewildered wretches were seeking her all through the wilderness.

The cry of grief, rage, and terror was yet piercing the night, when the unhappy husband held his breath for a response. There was a scream, drowned immediately in a louder murmur of voices, fading into far-off laughter, as the dark cloud swept away, leaving the clear and silent sky above Goodman Brown. But something fluttered lightly down through the air and caught on the branch of a tree. The young man seized it, and beheld a pink ribbon.

"My Faith is gone!" cried he after one stupefied moment. "There is no good on earth; and sin is but a name. Come, devil; for to thee is this world given."

And, maddened with despair, so that he laughed loud and long, did Goodman Brown grasp his staff and set forth again, at such a rate that he seemed to fly along the forest path rather than to walk or run. The road grew wilder and drearier and more faintly traced, and vanished at length, leaving him in the heart of the dark wilderness, still rushing onward with the instinct that guides mortal man to evil. The whole forest was peopled with frightful sounds — the creaking of the trees, the howling of wild beasts, and the yell of Indians; while sometimes the wind tolled like a distant church bell, and sometimes gave a broad roar around the traveller, as if all Nature were laughing him to scorn. But he was himself the chief horror of the scene, and shrank not from its other horrors.

"Ha! ha! ha!" roared Goodman Brown when the wind laughed at him. "Let us hear which will laugh loudest. Think not to frighten me with your deviltry. Come witch, come wizard, come Indian powwow, come devil himself, and here comes Goodman Brown. You may as well fear him as he fear you."

In truth, all through the haunted forest there could be nothing more frightful than the figure of Goodman Brown. On he flew among the black pines, brandishing his staff with frenzied gestures, now giving vent to an inspiration of horrid blasphemy, and now shouting forth such laughter as set all the echoes of the forest laughing like demons around him. The fiend in his own shape is less hideous than when he rages in the breast of man. Thus sped the demoniac on his course, until, quivering among the trees, he saw a red light before him, as when the felled trunks and branches of a clearing have been set on fire, and throw up their lurid blaze against the sky, at the hour of midnight. He paused, in a lull of the tempest that had driven him onward, and heard the swell of what seemed a hymn, rolling solemnly from a distance with the weight of many voices. He knew the tune; it was a familiar one in the choir of the village meeting-house. The verse died heavily away, and was lengthened by a chorus, not of human voices, but of all the sounds of the benighted wilderness pealing in awful harmony together. Goodman Brown cried out, and his cry was lost to his own ear by its unison with the cry of the desert.

In the interval of silence he stole forward until the light glared full upon his eyes. At one extremity of an open space, hemmed in by the dark wall of the forest, arose a rock, bearing some rude, natural resemblance either to an altar or a pulpit, and surrounded by four blazing pines, their tops aflame, their stems untouched, like candles at an evening meeting. The mass of foliage that had overgrown the summit of the rock was all on fire, blazing high into the night and fitfully illuminating the whole field. Each pendent twig and leafy festoon was in a blaze. As the red light arose and fell, a numerous congregation alternately shone forth, then disappeared in shadow, and again grew, as it were, out of the darkness, peopling the heart of the solitary woods at once.

"A grave and dark-clad company," quoth Goodman Brown.

In truth they were such. Among them, quivering to and fro between gloom and splendor, appeared faces that would be seen next day at the council board of the province, and others which, Sabbath after Sabbath, looked devoutly heavenward, and benignantly over the crowded pews, from the holiest pulpits in the land. Some affirm that the lady of the governor was there. At least there were high dames well known to her, and wives of honored husbands, and widows, a great multitude, and ancient maidens, all of excellent repute, and fair young girls, who trembled lest their mothers should espy them. Either the sudden gleams of light flashing over the obscure field bedazzled Goodman Brown, or he recognized a score of the church members of Salem village famous for their especial sanctity. Good old Deacon Gookin had arrived, and waited at the skirts of that venerable saint, his revered pastor. But, irreverently consorting with these grave, reputable, and pious people, these elders of the church, these chaste dames and dewy virgins, there were men of dissolute lives and women of spotted fame, wretches given over to all mean and filthy vice, and suspected even of horrid crimes. It was strange to see that the good shrank not from the wicked, nor were the sinners abashed by the saints. Scattered also among their pale-faced enemies were the Indian priests, or powwows, who had often scared their native forest with more hideous incantations than any known to English witchcraft.

"But where is Faith?" thought Goodman Brown; and, as hope came into his heart, he trembled.

Another verse of the hymn arose, a slow and mournful strain, such as the pious love, but joined to words which expressed all that our nature can conceive of sin, and darkly hinted at far more. Unfathomable to mere mortals is the lore of fiends. Verse after verse was sung; and still the chorus of the desert swelled between like the deepest tone of a mighty organ; and with the final peal of that dreadful anthem there came a sound, as if the roaring wind, the rushing streams, the howling beasts, and every other voice of the unconcerted wilderness were mingling and according with the voice of guilty man in homage to the prince of all. The four blazing pines threw up a loftier flame, and obscurely discovered shapes and visages of horror on the smoke wreaths above the impious assembly. At the same moment the fire on the rock shot redly forth and formed a flowing arch above its base, where now appeared a figure. With reverence be it spoken, the figure bore no slight similitude, both in garb and manner, to some grave divine of the New England churches.

"Bring forth the converts!" cried a voice that echoed through the field and rolled into the forest.

At the word, Goodman Brown stepped forth from the shadow of the trees and approached the congregation, with whom he felt a loathful brotherhood by the sympathy of all that was wicked in his heart. He could have well-nigh sworn that the shape of his own dead father beckoned him to advance, looking downward from a smoke wreath, while a woman, with dim features of despair, threw out her hand to warn him back. Was it his mother? But he had no power to retreat one step, nor to resist, even in thought, when the minister and good old Deacon Gookin seized his arms and led him to the blazing rock. Thither came also the slender form of a veiled female, led between Goody Cloyse, that pious teacher of the catechism, and Martha Carrier, who had received the devil's promise to be queen of hell. A rampant hag was she. And there stood the proselytes beneath the canopy of fire.

"Welcome, my children," said the dark figure, "to the communion of your race. Ye have found thus young your nature and your destiny. My children, look behind you!"

They turned; and flashing forth, as it were, in a sheet of flame, the fiend worshippers were seen; the smile of welcome gleamed darkly on every visage.

"There," resumed the sable form, "are all whom ye have reverenced from youth. Ye deemed them holier than yourselves and shrank from your own sin, contrasting it with their lives of righteousness and prayerful aspirations heavenward. Yet here are they all in my worshipping assembly. This night it shall be granted you to know their secret deeds: how hoary-bearded elders of the church have whispered wanton words to the young maids of their households; how many a woman, eager for widows' weeds, has given her husband a drink at bedtime and let him sleep his last sleep in her bosom; how beardless youths have made haste to inherit their fathers' wealth; and how fair damsels — blush not, sweet ones — have dug little graves in the garden, and bidden me, the sole guest, to an infant's funeral. By the sympathy of your human hearts for sin ye shall scent out all the places — whether in church, bedchamber, street, field, or forest — where crime has been committed, and shall exult to behold the whole earth one stain of guilt, one mighty blood spot. Far more than this. It shall be yours to penetrate, in every bosom, the deep mystery of sin, the fountain of all wicked arts, and which inexhaustibly supplies more evil impulses than human power — than my power at its utmost — can make manifest in deeds. And now, my children, look upon each other."

They did so; and, by the blaze of the hell-kindled torches, the wretched man beheld his Faith, and the wife her husband, trembling before that unhallowed altar.

"Lo, there ye stand, my children," said the figure, in a deep and solemn tone, almost sad with its despairing awfulness, as if his once angelic nature could yet mourn for our miserable race. "Depending upon one another's hearts, ye had still hoped that virtue were not all a dream. Now are ye undeceived. Evil is the nature of mankind. Evil must be your only happiness. Welcome again, my children, to the communion of your race."

"Welcome," repeated the fiend worshippers, in one cry of despair and triumph.

And there they stood, the only pair, as it seemed, who were yet hesitating on the verge of wickedness in this dark world. A basin was hallowed, naturally, in the rock. Did it contain water, reddened by the lurid light? or was it blood? or, perchance, a liquid flame? Herein did the shape of evil dip his hand and prepare to lay the mark of baptism upon their foreheads, that they might be partakers of the mystery of sin, more conscious of the secret guilt of others, both in deed and thought, than they could now be of their own. The husband cast one look at his pale wife, and Faith at him. What polluted wretches would the next glance show them to each other, shuddering alike at what they disclosed and what they saw!

"Faith! Faith!" cried the husband, "look up to heaven, and resist the wicked one."

Whether Faith obeyed he knew not. Hardly had he spoken when he found himself amid calm night and solitude, listening to a roar of the wind which died heavily away through the forest. He staggered against the rock, and felt it chill and damp; while a hanging twig, that had been all on fire, besprinkled his cheek with the coldest dew.

The next morning young Goodman Brown came slowly into the street of Salem village, staring around him like a bewildered man. The good old minister was taking a walk along the graveyard to get an appetite for breakfast and meditate his sermon, and bestowed a blessing, as he passed, on Goodman Brown. He shrank from the venerable saint as if to avoid an anathema. Old Deacon Gookin was at domestic worship, and the holy words of his prayer were heard through the open window. "What God doth the wizard pray to?" quoth Goodman Brown. Goody Cloyse, that excellent old Christian, stood in the early sunshine at her own lattice, catechizing a little girl who had brought her a pint of morning's milk. Goodman Brown snatched away the child as from the grasp of the fiend himself. Turning the corner by the meeting-house, he spied the head of Faith, with the pink ribbons, gazing anxiously forth, and bursting into such joy at sight of him that she skipped along the street and almost kissed her husband before the whole village. But Goodman Brown looked sternly and sadly into her face, and passed on without a greeting.

Had Goodman Brown fallen asleep in the forest and only dreamed a wild dream of a witch-meeting?

Be it so if you will; but, alas! it was a dream of evil omen for young Goodman Brown. A stern, a sad, a darkly meditative, a distrustful, if not a desperate man did he become from the night of that fearful dream. On the Sabbath day, when the congregation were singing a holy psalm, he could not listen because an anthem of sin rushed loudly upon his ear and drowned all the blessed strain. When the minister spoke from the pulpit with power and fervid eloquence, and, with his hand on the open Bible, of the sacred truths of our religion, and of saint-like lives and triumphant deaths, and of future bliss or misery unutterable, then did Goodman Brown turn pale, dreading lest the roof should thunder down upon the gray blasphemer and his hearers. Often, awaking suddenly at midnight, he shrank from the bosom of Faith; and at morning or eventide, when the family knelt down at prayer, he scowled and muttered to himself, and gazed sternly at his wife, and turned away. And when he had lived long, and was borne to his grave a hoary corpse, followed by Faith, an aged woman, and children and grandchildren, a goodly procession, besides neighbors not a few, they carved no hopeful verse upon his tombstone, for his dying hour was gloom.

ɷ

BESSIE HEAD *(1937–1986) was born in Pietermaritzburg, South Africa, the daughter of a white mother and a black father. Raised by foster parents, she was placed in a mission orphanage at the age of thirteen. A lonely child, she was comforted by reading, which invited her into what she called "a world of magic beyond your own." In her early twenties she taught in an elementary school and wrote stories for a local newspaper. After her marriage in 1961, she left South Africa, seeking political refuge from apartheid on an agricultural commune in Serowe in Botswana.*

The journalist Betty Fradkin has described Head's life as a refugee: "There is no electricity yet. At night Bessie types by the light of six candles. Fruit trees and vegetables surround the house. Bessie makes guava jam to sell, and will sell vegetables when the garden is enlarged." Despite the devastating experiences of racial oppression and the dislocation and economic hardship of exile, Head found the peace of mind necessary to create fiction: "In South Africa, all my life I lived in shattered little bits. All those shattered bits began to grow together here. . . . I have a peace against which all the turmoil is worked out." In 1969 she published her first novel, When Rain Clouds Gather. *Two other novels followed, along with a collection of related stories titled* The Collector of Treasures and Other Botswana Village Tales *(1977) and a history of her village,* Serowe: Village of the Rain Wind *(1981). Her last novel,* A Bewitched Crossroad *(1984), is a chronicle combining history and folklore. Two years later, Head died of hepatitis while working on her autobiography.*

Highly sensitive to the enduring power of ritual and tradition in contemporary African life, Head was also concerned with the often precarious role of women in the patriarchal systems of African tribal society. "Looking for a Rain God" dramatizes the conflict between traditional and contemporary codes of behavior in the villages and cities she had known.

BESSIE HEAD

Looking for a Rain God   1977

It is lonely at the lands where the people go to plough. These lands are vast clearings in the bush, and the wild bush is lonely too. Nearly all the lands are within walking distance from the village. In some parts of the bush where the underground water is very near the surface, people made little rest camps for themselves and dug shallow wells to quench their thirst while on their journey to their own lands. They experienced all kinds of things once they left the village. They could rest at shady watering places full of lush, tangled trees with delicate pale-gold and purple wild flowers springing up between soft green moss and the children could hunt around for wild figs and any berries that might be in season. But from 1958, a seven-year drought fell upon the land and even the watering places began to look as dismal as the dry open thorn-bush country; the leaves of the trees curled up and withered; the moss became dry and hard and, under the shade of the tangled trees, the ground turned a powdery black and white, because there was no rain. People said rather humorously that if you tried to catch the rain in a cup it would only fill a teaspoon. Towards the beginning of the seventh year of drought, the summer had become an anguish to live through. The air was so dry and moisture-free that it burned the skin. No one knew what to do to escape the heat and tragedy was in the air. At the beginning of that summer, a number of men just went out of their homes and hung themselves to death from trees. The major-ity of the people had lived off crops, but for two years past they had all re-turned from the lands with only their rolled-up skin blankets and cooking utensils. Only the charlatans, incanters, and witch-doctors made a pile of money during this time because people were always turning to them in des-peration for little talismans and herbs to rub on the plough for the crops to grow and the rain to fall.

The rains were late that year. They came in early November, with a promise of good rain. It wasn't the full, steady downpour of the years of good rain, but thin, scanty, misty rain. It softened the earth and a rich growth of green things sprang up everywhere for the animals to eat. People were called to the village kgotla to hear the proclamation of the beginning of the plough-ing season; they stirred themselves and whole families began to move off to the lands to plough.

The family of the old man, Mokgobja, were among those who left early for the lands. They had a donkey cart and piled everything onto it, Mokgobja — who was over seventy years old; two little girls, Neo and Boseyong; their mother Tiro and an unmarried sister, Nesta; and the father and supporter of the family, Ramadi, who drove the donkey cart. In the rush of the first hope of rain, the man, Ramadi, and the two women, cleared the land of thorn-bush and then hedged their vast ploughing area with this same thorn-bush to pro-tect the future crop from the goats they had brought along for milk. They cleared out and deepened the old well with its pool of muddy water and still in this light, misty rain, Ramadi inspanned two oxen and turned the earth over with a hand plough.

The land was ready and ploughed, waiting for the crops. At night, the earth was alive with insects singing and rustling about in search of food. But suddenly, by mid-November, the rain fled away; the rain-clouds fled away and left the sky bare. The sun danced dizzily in the sky, with a strange cruelty. Each day the land was covered in a haze of mist as the sun sucked up the last drop of moisture out of the earth. The family sat down in despair, waiting and waiting. Their hopes had run so high; the goats had started producing milk, which they had eagerly poured on their porridge, now they ate plain porridge with no milk. It was impossible to plant the corn, maize, pumpkin and water-melon seeds in the dry earth. They sat the whole day in the shadow of the huts and even stopped thinking, for the rain had fled away. Only the children, Neo and Boseyong, were quite happy in their little girl world. They carried on with their game of making house like their mother and chattered to each other in light, soft tones. They made children from sticks around which they tied rags, and scolded them severely in an exact imitation of their own mother. Their voices could be heard scolding the day long: "You stupid thing, when I send you to draw water, why do you spill half of it out of the bucket!" "You stupid thing! Can't you mind the porridge-pot without letting the porridge burn!" And then they would beat the rag-dolls on their bottoms with severe expressions.

The adults paid no attention to this; they did not even hear the funny chatter; they sat waiting for rain; their nerves were stretched to breaking-point willing the rain to fall out of the sky. Nothing was important, beyond that. All their animals had been sold during the bad years to purchase food, and of all their herd only two goats were left. It was the women of the family who finally broke down under the strain of waiting for rain. It was really the two women who caused the death of the little girls. Each night they started a weird, high-pitched wailing that began on a low, mournful note and whipped up to a frenzy. Then they would stamp their feet and shout as though they had lost their heads. The men sat quiet and self-controlled; it was important for men to maintain their self-control at all times but their nerve was breaking too. They knew the women were haunted by the starvation of the coming year.

Finally, an ancient memory stirred in the old man, Mokgobja. When he was very young and the customs of the ancestors still ruled the land, he had been witness to a rain-making ceremony. And he came alive a little, struggling to recall the details which had been buried by years and years of prayer in a Christian church. As soon as the mists cleared a little, he began consulting in whispers with his youngest son, Ramadi. There was, he said, a certain rain god who accepted only the sacrifice of the bodies of children. Then the rain would fall; then the crops would grow, he said. He explained the ritual and as he talked, his memory became a conviction and he began to talk with unshak-able authority. Ramadi's nerves were smashed by the nightly wailing of the women and soon the two men began whispering with the two women. The children continued their game: "You stupid thing! How could you have lost the money on the way to the shop! You must have been playing again!"

After it was all over and the bodies of the two little girls had been spread across the land, the rain did not fall. Instead, there was a deathly silence at night and the devouring heat of the sun by day. A terror, extreme and deep, overwhelmed the whole family. They packed, rolling up their skin blankets and pots, and fled back to the village.

People in the village soon noted the absence of the two little girls. They had died at the lands and were buried there, the family said. But people noted their ashen, terror-stricken faces and a murmur arose. What had killed the children, they wanted to know? And the family replied that they had just died. And people said amongst themselves that it was strange that the two deaths had occurred at the same time. And there was a feeling of great unease at the unnatural looks of the family. Soon the police came around. The family told them the same story of death and burial at the lands. They did not know what the children had died of. So the police asked to see the graves. At this, the mother of the children broke down and told everything.

Throughout that terrible summer the story of the children hung like a dark cloud of sorrow over the village, and the sorrow was not assuaged when the old man and Ramadi were sentenced to death for ritual murder. All they had on the statute books was that ritual murder was against the law and must be stamped out with the death penalty. The subtle story of strain and starvation and breakdown was inadmissible evidence at court; but all the people who lived off crops knew in their hearts that only a hair's breadth had saved them from sharing a fate similar to that of the Mokgobja family. They could have killed something to make the rain fall.

∞

ERNEST HEMINGWAY *(1898–1961) was born in Oak Park, Illinois, but he spent most of his boyhood in Michigan, where his father, a doctor, encouraged his enthusiasm for camping and hunting. Active as a reporter for his high school newspaper, Hemingway decided not to go on to college. Instead he worked as a reporter on the* Kansas City Star *for a few months before volunteering to serve in an American ambulance unit in France during World War I. Then he went to Italy, served at the front, and was severely wounded in action just before his nineteenth birthday. After the war he was too restless to settle down in the United States, so he lived in Paris and supported himself and his wife as a newspaper correspondent. He worked hard at learning how to write fiction; as he later said, "I found the greatest difficulty, aside from knowing what you really felt, rather than what you were supposed to feel, or had been taught to feel, was to put down what really happened in action: what the actual things were which produced the emotion that you experienced."*

In America Hemingway had admired the work of Sherwood Anderson, especially the colloquial, "unliterary" tone of his stories, and in Paris he came under the influence of Gertrude Stein, telling Anderson in a letter of 1922 that "Gertrude Stein and me are just like brothers." As the critic A. Walton Litz and many others have recognized, Hemingway was receptive to several diverse influences as a young writer forging his literary style, including the work of the experimental poet Ezra Pound, whose advice in essays written in 1913 on the composition of imagist poetry is suggested in the style developed in Hemingway's early fiction:

1. *Direct treatment of the "thing," without evasion or cliché.*
2. *The use of absolutely no word that does not contribute to the general design.*
3. *Fidelity to the rhythms of natural speech.*
4. *The natural object is always the adequate symbol.*

Hemingway's first book, In Our Time *(1925), is a collection of stories and sketches. His early novels,* The Sun Also Rises *(1926) and* A Farewell to Arms *(1929), established him as a master stylist, probably the most influential writer of American prose in the first half of the twentieth century. In 1938 he collected what he considered his best short fiction in* The Fifth Column and the First Forty-Nine Stories. *After publication of* The Old Man and the Sea, *he was awarded the Nobel Prize for Literature in 1954. Seven years later, in poor health and haunted by the memory of the suicide of his father, who had shot himself with a Civil War pistol in 1929, Hemingway killed himself with a shotgun in his Idaho hunting lodge.*

Hemingway's concise way of developing a plot through dialogue, as in "Hills Like White Elephants," attracted many imitators. He once explained how he achieved an intense compression by comparing his method to the principle of the iceberg: "There is seven-eighths of it under water for every part that shows. Anything you know you can eliminate and it only strengthens your iceberg. It is the part that doesn't show. If a writer omits something because he does not know it then there is a hole in the story." The most authoritative collection of Hemingway's stories, The Complete Short Stories of Ernest Hemingway: The Finca-Vigia Edition, *was published in 1991.*

RELATED COMMENTARY: *Ezra Pound, "On the Principles of Imagism," page 1297.*

ERNEST HEMINGWAY

Hills Like White Elephants
1927

The hills across the valley of the Ebro were long and white. On this side there was no shade and no trees and the station was between two lines of rails in the sun. Close against the side of the station there was the warm shadow of the building and a curtain, made of strings of bamboo beads, hung across the open door into the bar, to keep out flies. The American and the girl with him sat at a table in the shade, outside the building. It was very hot and the express from Barcelona would come in forty minutes. It stopped at this junction for two minutes and went on to Madrid.

"What should we drink?" the girl asked. She had taken off her hat and put it on the table.

"It's pretty hot," the man said.

"Let's drink beer."

"*Dos cervezas,*" the man said into the curtain.

"Big ones?" a woman asked from the doorway.

"Yes. Two big ones."

The woman brought two glasses of beer and two felt pads. She put the felt pads and the beer glasses on the table and looked at the man and the girl. The girl was looking off at the line of hills. They were white in the sun and the country was brown and dry.

"They look like white elephants," she said.

"I've never seen one," the man drank his beer.

"No, you wouldn't have."

"I might have," the man said. "Just because you say I wouldn't have doesn't prove anything."

The girl looked at the bead curtain. "They've painted something on it," she said. "What does it say?"

"Anis del Toro. It's a drink."

"Could we try it?"

The man called "Listen" through the curtain. The woman came out from the bar.

"Four reales."

"We want two Anis del Toro."

"With water?"

"Do you want it with water?"

"I don't know," the girl said. "Is it good with water?"

"It's all right."

"You want them with water?" asked the woman.

"Yes, with water."

"It tastes like licorice," the girl said and put the glass down.

"That's the way with everything."

"Yes," said the girl. "Everything tastes of licorice. Especially all the things you've waited so long for, like absinthe."

"Oh, cut it out."

"You started it," the girl said. "I was being amused. I was having a fine time."

"Well, let's try and have a fine time."

"All right. I was trying. I said the mountains looked like white elephants. Wasn't that bright?"

"That was bright."

"I wanted to try this new drink: That's all we do, isn't it — look at things and try new drinks?"

"I guess so."

The girl looked across at the hills.

"They're lovely hills," she said. "They don't really look like white elephants. I just meant the coloring of their skin through the trees."

"Should we have another drink?"

"All right."

The warm wind blew the bead curtain against the table.

"The beer's nice and cool," the man said.

"It's lovely," the girl said.

"It's really an awfully simple operation, Jig," the man said. "It's not really an operation at all."

The girl looked at the ground the table legs rested on.

"I know you wouldn't mind it, Jig. It's really not anything. It's just to let the air in."

The girl did not say anything.

"I'll go with you and I'll stay with you all the time. They just let the air in and then it's all perfectly natural."

"Then what will we do afterward?"

"We'll be fine afterward. Just like we were before."

"What makes you think so?"

"That's the only thing that bothers us. It's the only thing that's made us unhappy."

The girl looked at the bead curtain, put her hand out, and took hold of two of the strings of beads.

"And you think then we'll be all right and be happy."

"I know we will. You don't have to be afraid. I've known lots of people that have done it."

"So have I," said the girl. "And afterward they were all so happy."

"Well," the man said, "if you don't want to you don't have to. I wouldn't have you do it if you didn't want to. But I know it's perfectly simple."

"And you really want to?"

"I think it's the best thing to do. But I don't want you to do it if you don't really want to."

"And if I do it you'll be happy and things will be like they were and you'll love me?"

"I love you now. You know I love you."

"I know. But if I do it, then it will be nice again if I say things are like white elephants, and you'll like it?"

"I'll love it. I love it now but I just can't think about it. You know how I get when I worry."

"If I do it you won't ever worry?"

"I won't worry about that because it's perfectly simple."

"Then I'll do it. Because I don't care about me."

"What do you mean?"

"I don't care about me."

"Well, I care about you."

"Oh, yes. But I don't care about me. And I'll do it and then everything will be fine."

"I don't want you to do it if you feel that way."

The girl stood up and walked to the end of the station. Across, on the other side, were fields of grain and trees along the banks of the Ebro. Far away, beyond the river, were mountains. The shadow of a cloud moved across the field of grain and she saw the river through the trees.

"And we could have all this," she said. "And we could have everything and every day we make it more impossible."

"What did you say?"

"I said we could have everything."

"We can have everything."

"No, we can't."

"We can have the whole world."

"No, we can't."

"We can go everywhere."

"No, we can't. It isn't ours any more."

"It's ours."

"No, it isn't. And once they take it away, you never get it back."

"But they haven't taken it away."

"We'll wait and see."

"Come on back in the shade," he said. "You mustn't feel that way."

"I don't feel any way," the girl said. "I just know things."

"I don't want you to do anything that you don't want to do —— "

"Nor that isn't good for me," she said. "I know. Could we have another beer?"

"All right. But you've got to realize —— "

"I realize," the girl said. "Can't we maybe stop talking?"

They sat down at the table and the girl looked across at the hills on the dry side of the valley and the man looked at her and at the table.

"You've got to realize," he said, "that I don't want you to do it if you don't want to. I'm perfectly willing to go through with it if it means anything to you."

"Doesn't it mean anything to you? We could get along."

"Of course it does. But I don't want anybody but you. I don't want any one else. And I know it's perfectly simple."

"Yes, you know it's perfectly simple."

"It's all right for you to say that, but I do know it."

"Would you do something for me now?"

"I'd do anything for you."

"Would you please please please please please please please stop talking?"

He did not say anything but looked at the bags against the wall of the station. There were labels on them from all the hotels where they had spent nights.

"But I don't want you to," he said, "I don't care anything about it."

"I'll scream," the girl said.

The woman came out through the curtains with two glasses of beer and put them down on the damp felt pads. "The train comes in five minutes," she said.

"What did she say?" asked the girl.

"That the train is coming in five minutes."

The girl smiled brightly at the woman, to thank her.

"I'd better take the bags over to the other side of the station," the man said. She smiled at him.

"All right. Then come back and we'll finish the beer."

He picked up the two heavy bags and carried them around the station to the other tracks. He looked up the tracks but could not see the train. Coming back, he walked through the barroom, where people waiting for the train were drinking. He drank an Anis at the bar and looked at the people. They were all waiting reasonably for the train. He went out through the bead curtain. She was sitting at the table and smiled at him.

"Do you feel better?" he asked.

"I feel fine," she said. "There's nothing wrong with me. I feel fine."

∞

ZORA NEALE HURSTON *(1901?–1960) was born in 1901 or 1902 (the records are lost, and she gave different birth dates in her writing) in Eatonville, Florida, a town founded by African Americans. When her mother died in 1912, her fa-*

ther, *a Baptist minister, could not raise their eight children, so Hurston was forced to move from one relative's home to another. She never finished grade school, but when she was old enough to support herself, she attended Howard University in Washington, D.C. In 1921 she published her first story, "John Redding Goes to Sea," in the student literary magazine.*

In 1925 Hurston went to New York City and became active in the cultural renaissance in Harlem, collaborating with Langston Hughes on a folk comedy, Mule Bone. *Like Hughes and several other writers of that time, she was deeply interested in the abiding folk spirit inherent in southern life. After Hurston studied with the famous anthropologist Franz Boas at Barnard College, she returned to Florida to record the oral traditions of her native community. As critics have noted, from this time to the end of her life she tried to achieve a balance in her literary work between the folk culture of her background and her expression as an individual artist. Realizing that many white people used stereotypes to keep African Americans, Asian Americans, Hispanic Americans, and Native Americans in their "place," Hurston insisted it was*

> *urgent to realize that minorities do think, and think about something other than the race problem. That they are very human and internally, according to natural endowment, are just like everybody else. So long as this is not conceived, there must remain that feeling of unsurmountable difference, and difference to the average man means something bad. If people were made right, they would be just like him.*

During the 1930s Hurston turned all her energies to writing. She published Mules and Men *(1935), based on material from her field trips to Florida, and* Their Eyes Were Watching God *(1937), a novel about a woman's search for love and personal identity, in addition to several other books, including an autobiography. Although she published more than any other African American woman writer of her time, in the last two decades of her life she earned very little from her writing, and she died penniless in Florida. Fifteen years after Hurston's death, her work was rediscovered by the women's movement, and she is now regarded as an important American writer. "Sweat" is from* The Eatonville Anthology *(1927), the collection that brought Hurston to national attention.*

RELATED COMMENTARIES: *Zora Neale Hurston, "What White Publishers Won't Print," page 758; Alice Walker, "Zora Neale Hurston: A Cautionary Tale and a Partisan View," page 807.*

ZORA NEALE HURSTON

Sweat

1926

I

It was eleven o'clock of a Spring night in Florida. It was Sunday. Any other night, Delia Jones would have been in bed for two hours by this time. But she was a washwoman, and Monday morning meant a great deal to her. So she collected the soiled clothes on Saturday when she returned the clean things. Sunday night after church, she sorted and put the white things to soak. It saved her almost a half-day's start. A great hamper in the bedroom held the clothes that she brought home. It was so much neater than a number of bundles lying around.

She squatted on the kitchen floor beside the great pile of clothes, sorting them into small heaps according to color, and humming a song in a mournful key, but wondering through it all where Sykes, her husband, had gone with her horse and buckboard.

Just then something long, round, limp, and black fell upon her shoulders and slithered to the floor beside her. A great terror took hold of her. It softened her knees and dried her mouth so that it was a full minute before she could cry out or move. Then she saw that it was the big bull whip her husband liked to carry when he drove.

She lifted her eyes to the door and saw him standing there bent over with laughter at her fright. She screamed at him.

"Sykes, what you throw dat whip on me like dat? You know it would skeer me — looks just like a snake, an' you knows how skeered Ah is of snakes."

"Course Ah knowed it! That's how come Ah done it." He slapped his leg with his hand and almost rolled on the ground in his mirth. "If you such a big fool dat you got to have a fit over a earth worm or a string, Ah don't keer how bad Ah skeer you."

"You ain't got no business doing it. Gawd knows it's a sin. Some day Ah'm gointuh drop dead from some of yo' foolishness. 'Nother thing, where you been wid mah rig? Ah feeds dat pony. He ain't fuh you to be drivin' wid no bull whip."

"You sho' is one aggravatin' nigger woman!" he declared and stepped into the room. She resumed her work and did not answer him at once. "Ah done tole you time and again to keep them white folks' clothes outa dis house."

He picked up the whip and glared at her. Delia went on with her work. She went out into the yard and returned with a galvanized tub and set it on the washbench. She saw that Sykes had kicked all of the clothes together again, and now stood in her way truculently, his whole manner hoping, *praying*, for an argument. But she walked calmly around him and commenced to re-sort the things.

"Next time, Ah'm gointer kick 'em outdoors," he threatened as he struck a match along the leg of his corduroy breeches.

Delia never looked up from her work, and her thin, stooped shoulders sagged further.

"Ah ain't for no fuss t'night, Sykes. Ah just come from taking sacrament at the church house."

He snorted scornfully. "Yeah, you just come from de church house on a Sunday night, but heah you is gone to work on them clothes. You ain't nothing but a hypocrite. One of them amen-corner Christians — sing, whoop, and shout, then come home and wash white folks' clothes on the Sabbath."

He stepped roughly upon the whitest pile of things, kicking them helter-skelter as he crossed the room. His wife gave a little scream of dismay, and quickly gathered them together again.

"Sykes, you quit grindin' dirt into these clothes! How can Ah git through by Sat'day if Ah don't start on Sunday?"

"Ah don't keer if you never git through. Anyhow, Ah done promised Gawd and a couple of other men, Ah ain't gointer have it in mah house. Don't gimme no lip neither, else Ah'll throw 'em out and put mah fist up side yo' head to boot."

Delia's habitual meekness seemed to slip from her shoulders like a blown scarf. She was on her feet; her poor little body, her bare knuckly hands bravely defying the strapping hulk before her.

"Looka heah, Sykes, you done gone too fur. Ah been married to you fur fifteen years, and Ah been takin' in washin' fur fifteen years. Sweat, sweat, sweat! Work and sweat, cry and sweat, pray and sweat!"

"What's that got to do with me?" he asked brutally.

"What's it got to do with you, Sykes? Mah tub of suds is filled yo' belly with vittles more times than yo' hands is filled it. Mah sweat is done paid for this house and Ah reckon Ah kin keep on sweatin' in it."

She seized the iron skillet from the stove and struck a defensive pose, which act surprised him greatly, coming from her. It cowed him and he did not strike her as he usually did.

"Naw you won't," she panted, "that ole snaggle-toothed black woman you runnin' with ain't comin' heah to pile up on *mah* sweat and blood. You ain't paid for nothin' on this place, and Ah'm gointer stay right heah till Ah'm toted out foot foremost."

"Well, you better quit gittin' me riled up, else they'll be totin' you out sooner than you expect. Ah'm so tired of you Ah don't know whut to do. Gawd! How Ah hates skinny wimmen!"

A little awed by this new Delia, he sidled out of the door and slammed the back gate after him. He did not say where he had gone, but she knew too well. She knew very well that he would not return until nearly daybreak also. Her work over, she went on to bed but not to sleep at once. Things had come to a pretty pass!

She lay awake, gazing upon the debris that cluttered their matrimonial trail. Not an image left standing along the way. Anything like flowers had long ago been drowned in the salty stream that had been pressed from her heart. Her tears, her sweat, her blood. She had brought love to the union and he had brought a longing after the flesh. Two months after the wedding, he had given her the first brutal beating. She had the memory of his numerous trips to Orlando with all of his wages when he had returned to her penniless, even before the first year had passed. She was young and soft then, but now she thought of her knotty, muscled limbs, her harsh knuckly hands, and drew herself up into an unhappy little ball in the middle of the big feather bed. Too late now to hope for love, even if it were not Bertha it would be someone else. This case differed from the others only in that she was bolder than the others. Too late for everything except her little home. She had built it for her old days, and planted one by one the trees and flowers there. It was lovely to her, lovely.

Somehow, before sleep came, she found herself saying aloud: "Oh well, whatever goes over the Devil's back, is got to come under his belly. Sometime or ruther, Sykes, like everybody else, is gointer reap his sowing." After that she was able to build a spiritual earthworks against her husband. His shells could no longer reach her. AMEN. She went to sleep and slept until he announced his presence in bed by kicking her feet and rudely snatching the covers away.

"Gimme some kivah heah, an' git yo' damn foots over on yo' own side! Ah oughter mash you in yo' mouf fuh drawing dat skillet on me."

Delia went clear to the rail without answering him. A triumphant indifference to all that he was or did.

II

The week was full of work for Delia as all other weeks, and Saturday found her behind her little pony, collecting and delivering clothes.

It was a hot, hot day near the end of July. The village men on Joe Clarke's porch even chewed cane listlessly. They did not hurl the cane-knots as usual. They let them dribble over the edge of the porch. Even conversation had collapsed under the heat.

"Heah come Delia Jones," Jim Merchant said, as the shaggy pony came 'round the bend of the road toward them. The rusty buckboard was heaped with baskets of crisp, clean laundry.

"Yep," Joe Lindsay agreed. "Hot or col', rain or shine, jes'ez reg'lar ez de weeks roll roun' Delia carries 'em an' fetches 'em on Sat'day."

"She better if she wanter eat," said Moss. "Jones ain't wuth de shot an' powder hit would tek tuh kill 'em. Not to *huh* he ain't."

"He sho' ain't," Walter Thomas chimed in. "It's too bad, too, cause she wuz a right pretty li'l trick when he got huh. Ah'd uh mah'ied huh mahself if he hadnter beat me to it."

Delia nodded briefly at the men as she drove past.

"Too much knockin' will ruin *any* 'oman. He done beat huh 'nough tuh kill three women, let 'lone change they looks," said Elijah Moseley. "How Syke kin stommuck dat big black greasy Mogul he's layin' roun' wid, gits me. Ah swear dat eight-rock couldn't kiss a sardine can Ah done thowed out de back do' 'way las' yeah."

"Aw, she's fat, thass how come. He's allus been crazy 'bout fat women," put in Merchant. "He'd a' been tied up wid one long time ago if he could a' found one tuh have him. Did Ah tell yuh 'bout him come sidlin' roun' *mah* wife — bringin' her a basket uh peecans outa his yard fuh a present? Yessir, mah wife! She tol' him tuh take 'em right straight back home, 'cause Delia works so hard ovah dat washtub she reckon everything on de place taste lak sweat an' soapsuds. Ah jus' wisht Ah'd a' caught 'im 'roun' dere! Ah'd a' made his hips ketch on fiah down dat shell road."

"Ah know he done it, too. Ah sees 'im grinnin' at every 'oman dat passes," Walter Thomas said. "But even so, he useter eat some mighty big hunks uh humble pie tuh git dat li'l 'oman he got. She wuz ez pritty ez a speckled pup! Dat wuz fifteen years ago. He useter be so skeered uh losin' huh, she could make him do some parts of a husband's duty. Dey never wuz de same in de mind."

"There oughter be a law about him," said Lindsay. "He ain't fit tuh carry guts tuh a bear."

Clarke spoke for the first time. "Tain't no law on earth dat kin make a man be decent if it ain't in 'im. There's plenty men dat takes a wife lak dey do a joint uh sugar-cane. It's round, juicy, an' sweet when dey gits it. But dey squeeze an' grind, squeeze an' grind an' wring tell dey wring every drop uh pleasure dat's in 'em out. When dey's satisfied dat dey is wrung dry, dey treats 'em jes' lak dey do a cane-chew. Dey thows 'em away. Dey knows whut dey is doin' while dey is at it, an' hates theirselves fuh it but they keeps on hangin' after huh tell she's empty. Den dey hates huh fuh bein' a cane-chew an' in de way."

"We oughter take Syke an' dat stray 'oman uh his'n down in Lake Howell swamp an' lay on de rawhide till they cain't say Lawd' a' mussy. He allus wuz uh ovahbearin niggah, but since dat white 'oman from up north done teached 'im how to run a automobile, he done got too beggety to live — an' we oughter kill 'im," Old Man Anderson advised.

A grunt of approval went around the porch. But the heat was melting their civic virtue and Elijah Moseley began to bait Joe Clarke.

"Come on, Joe, git a melon outa dere an' slice it up for yo' customers. We'se all sufferin' wid de heat. De bear's done got *me*!"

"Thass right, Joe, a watermelon is jes' whut Ah needs tuh cure de eppizudicks," Walter Thomas joined forces with Moseley. "Come on dere, Joe. We all is steady customers an' you ain't set us up in a long time. Ah chooses dat long, bowlegged Floridy favorite."

"A god, an' be dough. You all gimme twenty cents and slice away," Clarke retorted. "Ah needs a col' slice m'self. Heah, everybody chip in. Ah'll lend y'all mah meat knife."

The money was all quickly subscribed and the huge melon brought forth. At that moment, Sykes and Bertha arrived. A determined silence fell on the porch and the melon was put away again.

Merchant snapped down the blade of his jacknife and moved toward the store door.

"Come on in, Joe, an' gimme a slab uh sow belly an' uh pound uh coffee — almost fuhgot 'twas Sat'day. Got to git on home." Most of the men left also.

Just then Delia drove past on her way home, as Sykes was ordering magnificently for Bertha. It pleased him for Delia to see.

"Git whutsoever yo' heart desires, Honey. Wait a minute, Joe. Give huh two bottles uh strawberry soda-water, uh quart parched ground-peas, an' a block uh chewin' gum."

With all this they left the store, with Sykes reminding Bertha that this was his town and she could have it if she wanted it.

The men returned soon after they left, and held their watermelon feast.

"Where did Syke Jones git da 'oman from nohow?" Lindsay asked.

"Ovah Apopka. Guess dey musta been cleanin' out de town when she lef'. She don't look lak a thing but a hunk uh liver wid hair on it."

"Well, she sho' kin squall," Dave Carter contributed. "When she gits ready tuh laff, she jes' opens huh mouf an' latches it back tuh de las' notch. No ole granpa alligator down in Lake Bell ain't got nothin' on huh."

III

Bertha had been in town three months now. Sykes was still paying her room-rent at Della Lewis' — the only house in town that would have taken her in. Sykes took her frequently to Winter Park to "stomps." He still assured her that he was the swellest man in the state.

"Sho' you kin have dat li'l ole house soon's Ah git dat 'oman outa dere. Everything b'longs tuh me an' you sho' kin have it. Ah sho' 'bominates uh skinny 'oman. Lawdy, you sho' is got one portly shape on you! You kin git *anything* you wants. Dis is *mah* town an' you sho' kin have it."

Delia's work-worn knees crawled over the earth in Gethsemane° and up the rocks of Calvary many, many times during these months. She avoided the villagers and meeting places in her efforts to be blind and deaf. But Bertha nullified this to a degree, by coming to Delia's house to call Sykes out to her at the gate.

Delia and Sykes fought all the time now with no peaceful interludes. They slept and ate in silence. Two or three times Delia had attempted a timid friendliness, but she was repulsed each time. It was plain that the breaches must remain agape.

The sun had burned July to August. The heat streamed down like a million hot arrows, smiting all things living upon the earth. Grass withered, leaves browned, snakes went blind in shedding, and men and dogs went mad. Dog days!

Delia came home one day and found Sykes there before her. She wondered, but started to go on into the house without speaking, even though he was standing in the kitchen door and she must either stoop under his arm or ask him to move. He made no room for her. She noticed a soap box beside the steps, but paid no particular attention to it, knowing that he must have brought it there. As she was stooping to pass under his outstretched arm, he suddenly pushed her backward, laughingly.

"Look in de box dere Delia, Ah done brung yuh somethin'!"

She nearly fell upon the box in her stumbling, and when she saw what it held, she all but fainted outright.

"Syke! Syke, mah Gawd! You take dat rattlesnake 'way from heah! You *gottuh*. Oh, Jesus, have mussy!"

"Ah ain't got tuh do nuthin' uh de kin' — fact is Ah ain't got tuh do nothin' but die. Tain't no use uh you puttin' on airs makin' out lak you skeered uh dat snake — he's gointer stay right heah tell he die. He wouldn't bite me cause Ah knows how tuh handle 'im. Nohow he wouldn't risk breakin' out his fangs 'gin *yo* skinny laigs."

"Naw, now Syke, don't keep dat thing 'round tryin' tuh skeer me tuh

---

Gethsemane: A reference to the garden where Jesus was betrayed (in the Gospels) before being tried and crucified on Calvary or Golgotha, the "hill of skulls."

death. You knows Ah'm even feared uh earth worms. Thass de biggest snake Ah evah did se. Kill 'im Syke, please."

"Doan ast me tuh do nothin' fuh yuh. Goin' 'round tryin' tuh be so damn asterperious. Naw, Ah ain't gonna kill it. Ah think uh damn sight mo' uh him dan you! Dat's a nice snake an' anybody doan lak 'im kin jes' hit de grit."

The village soon heard that Sykes had the snake, and came to see and ask questions.

"How de hen-fire did you ketch dat six-foot rattler, Syke?" Thomas asked.

"He's full uh frogs so he cain't hardly move, thass how Ah eased up on 'm. But Ah'm a snake charmer an' knows how tuh handle 'em. Shux, dat ain't nothin'. Ah could ketch one eve'y day if Ah so wanted tuh."

"Whut he needs is a heavy hick'ry club leaned real heavy on his head. Dat's de bes' way tuh charm a rattlesnake."

"Naw, Walt, y'all jes' don't understand dese diamon' backs lak Ah do," said Sykes in a superior tone of voice.

The village agreed with Walter, but the snake stayed on. His box remained by the kitchen door with its screen wire covering. Two or three days later it had digested its meal of frogs and literally came to life. It rattled at every movement in the kitchen or the yard. One day as Delia came down the kitchen steps she saw his chalky-white fangs curved like scimitars hung in the wire meshes. This time she did not run away with averted eyes as usual. She stood for a long time in the doorway in a red fury that grew bloodier for every second that she regarded the creature that was her torment.

That night she broached the subject as soon as Sykes sat down to the table.

"Syke, Ah wants you tuh take dat snake 'way fum heah. You done starved me an' Ah put up widcher, you done beat me an Ah took dat, but you don kilt all mah insides bringin' dat varmint heah."

Sykes poured out a saucer full of coffee and drank it deliberately before he answered her.

"A whole lot Ah keer 'bout how you feels inside uh out. Dat snake ain't goin' no damn wheah till Ah gits ready fuh 'im tuh go. So fur as beatin' is concerned, yuh ain't took near all dat you gointer take ef yuh stay 'round me."

Delia pushed back her plate and got up from the table. "Ah hates you, Sykes," she said calmly. "Ah hates you tuh de same degree dat Ah useter love yuh. Ah done took an' took till mah belly is full up tuh mah neck. Dat's de reason Ah got mah letter fum de church an' moved mah membership tuh Woodbridge — so Ah don't haftuh take no sacrament wid yuh. Ah don't wantuh see yuh 'round me atall. Lay 'round wid dat 'oman all yuh wants tuh, but gwan 'way from me an' mah house. Ah hates yuh lak uh suck-egg dog."

Sykes almost let the huge wad of corn bread and collard greens he was chewing fall out of his mouth in amazement. He had a hard time whipping himself up to the proper fury to try to answer Delia.

"Well, Ah'm glad you does hate me. Ah'm sho' tiahed uh you hangin' ontuh me. Ah don't want yuh. Look at yuh stringey ole neck! Yo' rawbony laigs an' arms is enough tuh cut uh man tuh death. You looks jes' lak de devvul's doll-baby tuh *me*. You cain't hate me no worse dan Ah hates you. Ah been hatin' *you* fuh years."

"Yo' ole black hide don't look lak nothin' tuh me, but uh passle uh wrinkled up rubber, wid yo' big ole yeahs flappin' on each side lak uh paih uh buzzard wings. Don't think Ah'm gointuh be run 'way fum mah house neither. Ah'm goin' tuh de white folks 'bout *you*, mah young man, de very nex' time you lay yo' han's on me. Mah cup is done run ovah." Delia said this with no signs of fear and Sykes departed from the house, threatening her, but made not the slightest move to carry out any of them.

That night he did not return at all, and the next day being Sunday, Delia was glad she did not have to quarrel before she hitched up her pony and drove the four miles to Woodbridge.

She stayed to the night service — "love feast" — which was very warm and full of spirit. In the emotional winds her domestic trials were borne far and wide so that she sang as she drove homeward,

> *Jurden water, black an' col*
> *Chills de body, not de soul*
> *An'Ah wantah cross Jurden in uh calm time.*

She came from the barn to the kitchen door and stopped.

"Whut's de mattah, ol' Satan, you ain't kicken' up yo' racket?" She addressed the snake's box. Complete silence. She went on into the house with a new hope in its birth struggles. Perhaps her threat to go to the white folks had frightened Sykes! Perhaps he was sorry! Fifteen years of misery and suppression had brought Delia to the place where she would hope *anything* that looked towards a way over or through her wall of inhibitions.

She felt in the match-safe behind the stove at once for a match. There was only one there.

"Dat niggah wouldn't fetch nothin' heah tuh save his rotten neck, but he kin run thew whut Ah brings quick enough. Now he done toted off nigh on tuh haff uh box uh matches. He done had dat 'oman heah in mah house, too."

Nobody but a woman could tell how she knew this even before she struck the match. But she did and it put her into a new fury.

Presently she brought in the tubs to put the white things to soak. This time she decided she need not bring the hamper out of the bedroom; she would go in there and do the sorting. She picked up the pot-bellied lamp and went in. The room was small and the hamper stood hard by the foot of the white iron bed. She could sit and reach through the bedposts — resting as she worked.

"Ah wantah cross Jurden in uh calm time." She was singing again. The mood of the "love feast," had returned. She threw back the lid of the basket almost gaily. Then, moved by both horror and terror, she sprang back toward the door. *There lay the snake in the basket!* He moved sluggishly at first, but even as she turned round and round, jumped up and down in an insanity of fear, he began to stir vigorously. She saw him pouring his awful beauty from the basket upon the bed, then she seized the lamp and ran as fast as she could to the kitchen. The wind from the open door blew out the light and the darkness added to her terror. She sped to the darkness of the yard, slamming the door after her before she thought to set down the lamp. She did not feel safe even on the ground, so she climbed up in the hay barn.

There for an hour or more she lay sprawled upon the hay a gibbering wreck.

Finally she grew quiet, and after that came coherent thought. With this stalked through her a cold, bloody rage. Hours of this. A period of introspection, a space of retrospection, then a mixture of both. Out of this an awful calm.

"Well, Ah done de bes' Ah could. If things ain't right, Gawd knows tain't mah fault."

She went to sleep — a twitch sleep — and woke up to a faint gray sky. There was a loud hollow sound below. She peered out. Sykes was at the wood-pile, demolishing a wire-covered box.

He hurried to the kitchen door, but hung outside there some minutes before he entered, and stood some minutes more inside before he closed it after him.

The gray in the sky was spreading. Delia descended without fear now, and crouched beneath the low bedroom window. The drawn shade shut out the dawn, shut in the night. But the thin walls held back no sound.

"Dat ol' scratch is woke up now!" She mused at the tremendous whirr inside, which every woodsman knows, is one of the sound illusions. The rattler is a ventriloquist. His whirr sounds to the right, to the left, straight ahead, behind, close under foot — everywhere but where it is. Woe to him who guesses wrong unless he is prepared to hold up his end of the argument! Sometimes he strikes without rattling at all.

Inside, Sykes heard nothing until he knocked a pot lid off the stove while trying to reach the match-safe in the dark. He had emptied his pockets at Bertha's.

The snake seemed to wake up under the stove and Sykes made a quick leap into the bedroom. In spite of the gin he had had, his head was clearing now.

"Mah Gawd!" he chattered, "ef Ah could on'y strack uh light!"

The rattling ceased for a moment as he stood paralyzed. He waited. It seemed that the snake waited also.

"Oh, fuh de light! Ah thought he'd be too sick" — Sykes was muttering to himself when the whirr began again, closer, right underfoot this time. Long before this, Sykes' ability to think had been flattened down to primitive instinct and he leaped — onto the bed.

Outside Delia heard a cry that might have come from a maddened chimpanzee, a stricken gorilla. All the terror, all the horror, all the rage that man possibly could express, without a recognizable human sound.

A tremendous stir inside there, another series of animal screams, the intermittent whirr of the reptile. The shade torn violently down from the window, letting in the red dawn, a huge brown hand seizing the window stick, great dull blows upon the wooden floor punctuating the gibberish of sound long after the rattle of the snake had abruptly subsided. All this Delia could see and hear from her place beneath the window, and it made her ill. She crept over to the four o'clocks and stretched herself on the cool earth to recover.

She lay there. "Delia, Delia!" She could hear Sykes calling in a most despairing tone as one who expected no answer. The sun crept on up, and he called. Delia could not move — her legs had gone flabby. She never moved, he called, and the sun kept rising.

"Mah Gawd!" She heard him moan, "Mah Gawd fum Heben!" She heard him stumbling about and got up from her flower-bed. The sun was growing warm. As she approached the door she heard him call out hopefully, "Delia, is dat you Ah heah?"

She saw him on his hands and knees as soon as she reached the door. He crept an inch or two toward her — all that he was able, and she saw his horribly swollen neck and his one open eye shining with hope. A surge of pity too strong to support bore her away from that eye that must, could not, fail to see the tubs. He would see the lamp. Orlando with its doctors was too far. She could scarcely reach the chinaberry tree, where she waited in the growing heat while inside she knew the cold river was creeping up and up to extinguish that eye which must know by now that she knew.

ഇൻ

WASHINGTON IRVING *(1783–1859), named after George Washington, u as the youngest of eleven children born in New York City to a mother of English descent and a Scottish father who was a prosperous merchant. After studying law with a judge, Josiah Hoffman, Irving went on a Grand Tour of Europe for two years, visiting France, Italy, Switzerland, Belgium, Holland, and England. Returning to New York City, he took the eighteenth-century English prose writers as his models when he published the* Salmagundi Papers *(1807–08) and a comic* History of New York *(1809), in which he invented the figure of a talkative elderly narrator named Diedrich Knickerbocker who told raucous anecdotes about the early political history of the Dutch colony. Irving's* History *was so successful that his comical gentleman "Knickerbocker" came to personify New York City. The name survives today in the professional basketball team the New York Knicks.*

Anguished by the death of his fiancée, Judge Hoffman's daughter Matilda, Irving left New York in 1815 to join his brother Peter in the European branch of the family's hardware business in Liverpool. When the venture failed, Irving — describing himself as "harassed and hag-ridden by the cares and anxieties of business" — decided to stay in England and try to make his living as a writer. He moved to London and began to meet British authors, including Sir Walter Scott, one of the most successful novelists of his time, whom Irving visited in his country house in 1818. They shared an enthusiasm for German literature, which Irving had read in translation. Scott had based the subplot of a play he was writing on a German folktale, and when Irving returned to London he immersed himself in an intensive study of German. He wrote his friend Henry Breevort,

> I have been for some time past engaged in the study of the German language,
> and have got so far as to be able to read and sputter a little. It is a severe task,
> and has required hard study; but the rich mine of German literature holds
> forth abundant reward.

As he put it, Irving started "scribbling" short prose tales based on his own translations. In one especially inspired day he produced "Rip Van Winkle," which was published in London in 1819–20 as part of his two-volume collection The Sketch Book.

Irving's source for "Rip Van Winkle" was the German folktale of "Peter Klaus the Goatherd," but he went to ingenious lengths to disguise his borrowing. First he invented the tongue-in-cheek character "Geoffrey Crayon" as the author of The Sketch Book, attempting to hide that he was an American writer trying to interest English readers in his work. In his preface, Irving said that Geoffrey Crayon was a traveler "unsettled in his abode," making impressionistic, quick "crayon" sketches while journeying in Europe and the United States. Then Irving created a frame for "Rip Van Winkle," with Crayon telling the reader that he found the tale "among the papers of the late Diedrich Knickerbocker, an old gentleman of New York." Irving's use of pseudonyms and mock-documentation in the opening and closing paragraphs of "Rip Van Winkle" underscores the humorous tone of his tale, which gave the story an enduring new life as an American legend. He followed "Rip Van Winkle" in The Sketch Book with another short story masterpiece based on German folklore, "The Legend of Sleepy Hollow," and completed the collection with travel sketches and informal essays.

Irving didn't write many tales after The Sketch Book, but it was so popular that Scott followed his lead and published the first short story in British literature, "The Two Drovers," in 1827. When Irving was charged with plagiarism by hostile critics, he defended himself by explaining that he considered folktales "fair foundations for authors of fiction to build upon." He insisted that

> much of what I value myself upon in writing, escapes the observation of the
> great mass of my readers, who are intent more upon the story than the way in
> which it is told. For my part I consider a story merely as a frame on which to
> stretch my materials. It is the play of thought, and sentiment and language;
> the weaving in of characters, lightly yet expressively delineated; the familiar
> and faithful exhibition of scenes of common life, and the half concealed vein of
> humor that is often playing through the whole — these are among what I aim
> at, and which I felicitate myself in proportion as I think I succeed.

Irving was the first American short story author to attain a European audience. When the English writer Mary Mitford Russell edited her Stories of American Life (1830) in London, she excluded Irving from her list of American authors because she felt that "his writings are essentially European and must be content to take their station amongst the Spectators and Tatlers of the mother country." After seventeen years abroad Irving returned to New York in 1832 and settled in Tarrytown on the Hudson. He involved himself in politics and continued to publish books, most notably the travel sketches A Tour on the Prairies in 1835 and the multivolume Life of Washington, completed shortly before his death in 1859.

RELATED STORY: J. C. C. Nachtigal, "Peter Klaus the Goatherd," page 3.

WASHINGTON IRVING

Rip Van Winkle

1819–20

A Posthumous Writing of Diedrich Knickerbocker

By Woden, God of Saxons,
From whence comes Wensday, that is Wodensday,
Truth is a thing that ever I will keep
Unto thylke day in which I creep into
My sepulchre —
— CARTWRIGHT°

[The following Tale was found among the papers of the late Diedrich Knickerbocker, an old gentleman of New York, who was very curious in the Dutch history of the province, and the manners of the descendants from its primitive settlers. His historical researches, however, did not lie so much among books as among men; for the former are lamentably scanty on his favorite topics; whereas he found the old burghers, and still more their wives, rich in that legendary lore so invaluable to true history. Whenever, therefore, he happened upon a genuine Dutch family, snugly shut up in its low-roofed farmhouse, under a spreading sycamore, he looked upon it as a little clasped volume of black-letter, and studied it with the zeal of a book-worm.

The result of all these researches was a history of the province during the reign of the Dutch governors, which he published some years since. There have been various opinions as to the literary character of his work, and, to tell the truth, it is not a whit better than it should be. Its chief merit is its scrupulous accuracy, which indeed was a little questioned on its first appearance, but has since been completely established; and it is now admitted into all historical collections as a book of unquestionable authority.

The old gentleman died shortly after the publication of his work; and now that he is dead and gone, it cannot do much harm to his memory to say that his time might have been much better employed in weightier labors. He, however, was apt to ride his hobby his own way; and though it did now and then kick up the dust a little in the eyes of his neighbors, and grieve the spirit of some friends, for whom he felt the truest deference and affection, yet his errors and follies are remembered "more in sorrow than in anger," and it begins to be suspected that he never intended to offend. But however his memory may be appreciated by critics, it is still held dear by many folk whose good opinion is well worth having; particularly by certain biscuit-makers, who have gone so far as to imprint his likeness on their New-Year cakes; and have thus given him a chance for immortality, almost equal to being stamped on a Waterloo Medal, or a Queen Anne's Farthing.]

Whoever has made a voyage up the Hudson must remember the Kaatskill mountains. They are a dismembered branch of the great Ap-

---

° This author has never been identified.

palachian family, and are seen away to the west of the river, swelling up to a noble height, and lording it over the surrounding country. Every change of season, every change of weather, indeed, every hour of the day, produces some change in the magical hues and shapes of these mountains, and they are regarded by all the good wives, far and near, as perfect barometers. When the weather is fair and settled, they are clothed in blue and purple, and print their bold outlines on the clear evening sky; but sometimes, when the rest of the landscape is cloudless, they will gather a hood of gray vapors about their summits, which, in the last rays of the setting sun, will glow and light up like a crown of glory.

At the foot of these fairy mountains, the voyager may have descried the light smoke curling up from a village, whose shingle-roofs gleam among the trees, just where the blue tints of the upland melt away into the fresh green of the nearer landscape. It is a little village, of great antiquity, having been founded by some of the Dutch colonists in the early times of the province, just about the beginning of the government of the good Peter Stuyvesant, (may he rest in peace!) and there were some of the houses of the original settlers standing within a few years, built of small yellow bricks brought from Holland, having latticed windows and gable fronts, surmounted with weathercocks.

In that same village, and in one of these very houses (which, to tell the precise truth, was sadly time-worn and weather-beaten), there lived, many years since, while the country was yet a province of Great Britain, a simple, good-natured fellow, of the name of Rip Van Winkle. He was a descendant of the Van Winkles who figured so gallantly in the chivalrous days of Peter Stuyvesant, and accompanied him to the siege of Fort Christina. He inherited, however, but little of the martial character of his ancestors. I have observed that he was a simple, good-natured man; he was, moreover, a kind neighbor, and an obedient, hen-pecked husband. Indeed, to the latter circumstance might be owing that meekness of spirit which gained him such universal popularity; for those men are most apt to be obsequious and conciliating abroad, who are under the discipline of shrews at home. Their tempers, doubtless, are rendered pliant and malleable in the fiery furnace of domestic tribulation; and a curtain-lecture is worth all the sermons in the world for teaching the virtues of patience and long-suffering. A termagant wife may, therefore, in some respects, be considered a tolerable blessing; and if so, Rip Van Winkle was thrice blessed.

Certain it is, that he was a great favorite among all the good wives of the village, who, as usual with the amiable sex, took his part in all family squabbles; and never failed, whenever they talked those matters over in their evening gossipings, to lay all the blame on Dame Van Winkle. The children of the village, too, would shout with joy whenever he approached. He assisted at their sports, made their playthings, taught them to fly kites and shoot marbles, and told them long stories of ghosts, witches, and Indians. Whenever he went dodging about the village, he was surrounded by a troop of them, hanging on his skirts, clambering on his back, and playing a thousand tricks on him with impunity; and not a dog would bark at him throughout the neighborhood.

The great error in Rip's composition was an insuperable aversion to all kinds of profitable labor. It could not be from the want of assiduity or perseverance; for he would sit on a wet rock, with a rod as long and heavy as a Tar-

tar's lance, and fish all day without a murmur, even though he should not be encouraged by a single nibble. He would carry a fowling-piece on his shoulder for hours together, trudging through woods and swamps, and up hill and down dale, to shoot a few squirrels or wild pigeons. He would never refuse to assist a neighbor even in the roughest toil, and was a foremost man at all country frolics for husking Indian corn, or building stone fences; the women of the village, too, used to employ him to run their errands, and to do such little odd jobs as their less obliging husbands would not do for them. In a word, Rip was ready to attend to anybody's business but his own; but as to doing family duty, and keeping his farm in order, he found it impossible.

In fact, he declared it was of no use to work on his farm; it was the most pestilent little piece of ground in the whole country; everything about it went wrong, and would go wrong, in spite of him. His fences were continually falling to pieces; his cow would either go astray, or get among the cabbages; weeds were sure to grow quicker in his fields than anywhere else; the rain always made a point of setting in just as he had some out-door work to do; so that though his patrimonial estate had dwindled away under his management, acre by acre, until there was little more left than a mere patch of Indian corn and potatoes, yet it was the worst conditioned farm in the neighborhood.

His children, too, were as ragged and wild as if they belonged to nobody. His son Rip, an urchin begotten in his own likeness, promised to inherit the habits, with the old clothes, of his father. He was generally seen trooping like a colt at his mother's heels, equipped in a pair of his father's cast-off galligaskins, which he had much ado to hold up with one hand, as a fine lady does her train in bad weather.

Rip Van Winkle, however, was one of those happy mortals, of foolish, well-oiled dispositions, who take the world easy, eat white bread or brown, whichever can be got with least thought or trouble, and would rather starve on a penny than work for a pound. If left to himself, he would have whistled life away in perfect contentment; but his wife kept continually dinning in his ears about his idleness, his carelessness, and the ruin he was bringing on his family. Morning, noon and night, her tongue was incessantly going, and everything he said or did was sure to produce a torrent of household eloquence. Rip had but one way of replying to all lectures of the kind, and that, by frequent use, had grown into a habit. He shrugged his shoulders, shook his head, cast up his eyes, but said nothing. This, however, always provoked a fresh volley from his wife; so that he was fain to draw off his forces, and take to the outside of the house — the only side which, in truth, belongs to a henpecked husband.

Rip's sole domestic adherent was his dog Wolf, who was as much henpecked as his master; for Dame Van Winkle regarded them as companions in idleness, and even looked upon Wolf with an evil eye, as the cause of his master's going so often astray. True it is, in all points of spirit befitting an honorable dog, he was as courageous an animal as ever scoured the woods; but what courage can withstand the ever-enduring and all-besetting terrors of a woman's tongue? The moment Wolf entered the house his crest fell, his tail drooped to the ground, or curled between his legs, he sneaked about with a gallows air, casting many a sidelong glance at Dame Van Winkle, and at the least flourish of a broomstick or ladle he would fly to the door with yelping precipitation.

Times grew worse and worse with Rip Van Winkle as years of matrimony rolled on; a tart temper never mellows with age, and a sharp tongue is the only edged tool that grows keener with constant use. For a long while he used to console himself, when driven from home, by frequenting a kind of perpetual club of the sages, philosophers, and other idle personages of the village, which held its sessions on a bench before a small inn, designated by a rubicund portrait of His Majesty George the Third. Here they used to sit in the shade through a long, lazy summer's day, talking listlessly over village gossip, or telling endless sleepy stories about nothing. But it would have been worth any statesman's money to have heard the profound discussions that sometimes took place, when by chance an old newspaper fell into their hands from some passing traveller. How solemnly they would listen to the contents, as drawled out by Derrick Van Bummel, the schoolmaster, a dapper learned little man, who was not to be daunted by the most gigantic word in the dictionary; and how sagely they would deliberate upon public events some months after they had taken place.

The opinions of this junto° were completely controlled by Nicholas Vedder, patriarch of the village, and landlord of the inn, at the door of which he took his seat from morning till night, just moving sufficiently to avoid the sun and keep in the shade of a large tree; so that the neighbors could tell the hour by his movements as accurately as by a sun-dial. It is true he was rarely heard to speak, but smoked his pipe incessantly. His adherents, however (for every great man has his adherents), perfectly understood him, and knew how to gather his opinions. When anything that was read or related displeased him, he was observed to smoke his pipe vehemently, and to send forth short, frequent, and angry puffs; but when pleased, he would inhale the smoke slowly and tranquilly, and emit it in light and placid clouds; and sometimes, taking the pipe from his mouth, and letting the fragrant vapor curl about his nose, would gravely nod his head in token of perfect approbation.

From even this stronghold the unlucky Rip was at length routed by his termagant wife, who would suddenly break in upon the tranquillity of the assemblage and call the members all to naught; nor was that august personage, Nicholas Vedder himself, sacred from the daring tongue of this terrible virago, who charged him outright with encouraging her husband in habits of idleness.

Poor Rip was at last reduced almost to despair; and his only alternative, to escape from the labor of the farm and clamor of his wife, was to take gun in hand and stroll away into the woods. Here he would sometimes seat himself at the foot of a tree, and share the contents of his wallet with Wolf, with whom he sympathized as a fellow-sufferer in persecution. "Poor Wolf," he would say, "thy mistress leads thee a dog's life of it, but never mind, my lad, whilst I

---

junto: A group brought together by a common purpose.

live thou shalt never want a friend to stand by thee!" Wolf would wag his tail, look wistfully in his master's face, and if dogs can feel pity, I verily believe he reciprocated the sentiment with all his heart.

In a long ramble of the kind on a fine autumnal day, Rip had unconsciously scrambled to one of the highest parts of the Kaatskill mountains. He was after his favorite sport of squirrel-shooting, and the still solitudes had echoed and re-echoed with the reports of his gun. Panting and fatigued, he threw himself, late in the afternoon, on a green knoll, covered with mountain herbage, that crowned the brow of a precipice. From an opening between the trees he could overlook all the lower country for many a mile of rich woodland. He saw at a distance the lordly Hudson, far, far below him, moving on its silent but majestic course, with the reflection of a purple cloud, or the sail of a lagging bark, here and there sleeping on its glassy bosom, and at last losing itself in the blue highlands.

On the other side he looked down into a deep mountain glen, wild, lonely, and shagged, the bottom filled with fragments from the impending cliffs, and scarcely lighted by the reflected rays of the setting sun. For some time Rip lay musing on this scene; evening was gradually advancing; the mountains began to throw their long blue shadows over the valleys; he saw that it would be dark long before he could reach the village, and he heaved a heavy sigh when he thought of encountering the terrors of Dame Van Winkle.

As he was about to descend, he heard a voice from a distance, hallooing, "Rip Van Winkle, Rip Van Winkle!" He looked around, but could see nothing but a crow winging its solitary flight across the mountain. He thought his fancy must have deceived him, and turned again to descend, when he heard the same cry ring through the still evening air: "Rip Van Winkle! Rip Van Winkle!" — at the same time Wolf bristled up his back, and giving a low growl, skulked to his master's side, looking fearfully down into the glen. Rip now felt a vague apprehension stealing over him; he looked anxiously in the same direction, and perceived a strange figure slowly toiling up the rocks, and bending under the weight of something he carried on his back. He was surprised to see any human being in this lonely and unfrequented place; but supposing it to be some one of the neighborhood in need of his assistance, he hastened down to yield it.

On nearer approach he was still more surprised at the singularity of the stranger's appearance. He was a short, square-built old fellow, with thick bushy hair, and a grizzled beard. His dress was of the antique Dutch fashion, — a cloth jerkin strapped around the waist — several pair of breeches, the outer one of ample volume, decorated with rows of buttons down the sides, and bunches at the knees. He bore on his shoulders a stout keg, that seemed full of liquor, and made signs for Rip to approach and assist him with the load. Though rather shy and distrustful of this new acquaintance, Rip complied with his usual alacrity; and mutually relieving one another, they clambered up a narrow gully, apparently the dry bed of a mountain torrent. As they ascended, Rip every now and then heard long, rolling peals, like distant thunder, that seemed to issue out of a deep ravine, or rather cleft, between lofty rocks, toward which their rugged path conducted. He paused for an instant, but supposing it to be the muttering of one of those transient thunder-showers which often take place in mountain heights, he proceeded. Passing through the ravine, they came to a hollow, like a small amphitheatre, sur-rounded by perpendicular precipices, over the brinks of which impending trees shot their branches, so that you only caught glimpses of the azure sky and the bright evening cloud. During the whole time Rip and his companion had labored on in silence; for though the former marvelled greatly what could be the object of carrying a keg of liquor up this wild mountain, yet there was something strange and incomprehensible about the unknown, that inspired awe and checked familiarity.

On entering the amphitheatre, new objects of wonder presented them-selves. On a level spot in the centre was a company of odd-looking personages playing at ninepins. They were dressed in a quaint, outlandish fashion; some wore short doublets, others jerkins, with long knives in their belts, and most of them had enormous breeches, of similar style with that of the guide's. Their visages, too, were peculiar: one had a large beard, broad face, and small pig-gish eyes; the face of another seemed to consist entirely of nose, and was sur-mounted by a white sugar-loaf hat, set off with a little red cock's tail. They all had beards, of various shapes and colors. There was one who seemed to be the commander. He was a stout old gentleman, with a weather-beaten counte-nance; he wore a laced doublet, broad belt and hanger, high crowned hat and feather, red stockings, and high-heeled shoes, with roses in them. The whole group reminded Rip of the figures in an old Flemish painting, in the parlor of Dominie Van Shaick, the village parson, and which had been brought over from Holland at the time of the settlement.

What seemed particularly odd to Rip was, that, though these folks were evidently amusing themselves, yet they maintained the gravest faces, the most mysterious silence, and were, withal, the most melancholy party of plea-sure he had ever witnessed. Nothing interrupted the stillness of the scene but the noise of the balls, which, whenever they rolled, echoed along the moun-tains like rumbling peals of thunder.

As Rip and his companion approached them, they suddenly desisted from their play, and stared at him with such fixed, statue-like gaze, and such strange, uncouth, lack-lustre countenances, that his heart turned within him, and his knees smote together. His companion now emptied the contents of the keg into large flagons, and made signs to him to wait upon the company. He obeyed with fear and trembling; they quaffed the liquor in profound silence, and then returned to their game.

By degrees Rip's awe and apprehension subsided. He even ventured, when no eye was fixed upon him, to taste the beverage, which he found had much of the flavor of excellent Hollands. He was naturally a thirsty soul, and was soon tempted to repeat the draught. One taste provoked another; and he reiterated his visits to the flagon so often that at length his senses were over-powered, his eyes swam in his head, his head gradually declined, and he fell into a deep sleep.

On waking, he found himself on the green knoll whence he had first seen the old man of the glen. He rubbed his eyes — it was a bright sunny morning. The birds were hopping and twittering among the bushes, and the eagle was wheeling aloft, and breasting the pure mountain breeze. "Surely," thought Rip, "I have not slept here all night." He recalled the occurrences before he fell asleep. The strange man with a keg of liquor — the mountain ravine — the wild retreat among the rocks — the woe-begone party at ninepins — the flagon — "Oh! that flagon! that wicked flagon!" thought Rip, "what excuse shall I make to Dame Van Winkle?"

He looked round for his gun, but in place of the clean, well-oiled fowling-piece, he found an old firelock lying by him, the barrel encrusted with rust, the lock falling off, and the stock worm-eaten. He now suspected that the grave roisters of the mountains had put a trick upon him, and, having dosed him with liquor, had robbed him of his gun. Wolf, too, had disappeared, but he might have strayed away after a squirrel or partridge. He whistled after him, and shouted his name, but all in vain; the echoes repeated his whistle and shout, but no dog was to be seen.

He determined to revisit the scene of the last evening's gambol, and if he met with any of the party, to demand his dog and gun. As he rose to walk, he found himself stiff in the joints, and wanting in his usual activity. "These mountain beds do not agree with me," thought Rip, "and if this frolic should lay me up with a fit of the rheumatism, I shall have a blessed time with Dame Van Winkle." With some difficulty he got down into the glen: he found the gully up which he and his companion had ascended the preceding evening; but to his astonishment a mountain stream was now foaming down it, leaping from rock to rock, and filling the glen with babbling murmurs. He, however, made shift to scramble up its sides, working his toilsome way through thickets of birch, sassafras, and witch-hazel, and sometimes tripped up or entangled by the wild grape-vines that twisted their coils or tendrils from tree to tree, and spread a kind of network in his path.

At length he reached to where the ravine had opened through the cliffs to the amphitheatre; but no traces of such opening remained. The rocks presented a high, impenetrable wall, over which the torrent came tumbling in a sheet of feathery foam, and fell into a broad deep basin, black from the shadows of the surrounding forest. Here, then, poor Rip was brought to a stand. He again called and whistled after his dog; he was only answered by the cawing of a flock of idle crows, sporting high in air about a dry tree that overhung a sunny precipice; and who, secure in their elevation, seemed to look down and scoff at the poor man's perplexities. What was to be done? the morning was passing away, and Rip felt famished for want of his breakfast. He grieved to give up his dog and gun; he dreaded to meet his wife; but it would not do to starve among the mountains. He shook his head, shouldered the rusty firelock, and, with a heart full of trouble and anxiety, turned his footsteps homeward.

As he approached the village he met a number of people, but none whom he knew, which somewhat surprised him, for he had thought himself acquainted with every one in the country round. Their dress, too, was of a different fashion from that to which he was accustomed. They all stared at him with equal marks of surprise, and whenever they cast their eyes upon him, invariably stroked their chins. The constant recurrence of this gesture induced Rip, involuntarily, to do the same, when, to his astonishment, he found his beard had grown a foot long!

He had now entered the skirts of the village. A troop of strange children ran at his heels, hooting after him, and pointing at his gray beard. The dogs, too, not one of which he recognized for an old acquaintance, barked at him as he passed. The very village was altered; it was larger and more populous. There were rows of houses which he had never seen before, and those which had been his familiar haunts had disappeared. Strange names were over the doors — strange faces at the windows — everything was strange. His mind now misgave him; he began to doubt whether both he and the world around him were not bewitched. Surely this was his native village, which he had left but the day before. There stood the Kaatskill mountains — there ran the silver Hudson at a distance — there was every hill and dale precisely as it had always been. Rip was sorely perplexed. "That flagon last night," thought he, "has addled my poor head sadly!"

It was with some difficulty that he found the way to his own house, which he approached with silent awe, expecting every moment to hear the shrill voice of Dame Van Winkle. He found the house gone to decay — the roof fallen in, the windows shattered, and the doors off the hinges. A half-starved dog that looked like Wolf was skulking about it. Rip called him by name, but the cur snarled, showed his teeth, and passed on. This was an unkind cut indeed. "My very dog," sighed poor Rip, "has forgotten me!"

He entered the house, which to tell the truth, Dame Van Winkle had always kept in neat order. It was empty, forlorn, and apparently abandoned. This desolateness overcame all his connubial fears — he called loudly for his wife and children — the lonely chambers rang for a moment with his voice, and then all again was silence.

He now hurried forth, and hastened to his old resort, the village inn, but it too was gone. A large rickety wooden building stood in its place, with great gaping windows, some of them broken and mended with old hats and petticoats, and over the door was painted, "The Union Hotel, by Jonathan Doolittle." Instead of the great tree that used to shelter the quiet little Dutch inn of yore, there now was reared a tall naked pole, with something on top that looked like a red night-cap, and from it was fluttering a flag, on which was a singular assemblage of stars and stripes — all this was strange and incomprehensible. He recognized on the sign, however, the ruby face of King George, under which he had smoked so many a peaceful pipe; but even this was singularly metamorphosed. The red coat was changed for one of blue and buff, a sword was held in the hand instead of a sceptre, the head was decorated with a cocked hat, and underneath was painted in large characters, GENERAL WASHINGTON.

There was, as usual, a crowd of folk about the door, but none that Rip recollected. The very character of the people seemed changed. There was a busy, bustling, disputatious tone about it, instead of the accustomed phlegm and drowsy tranquillity. He looked in vain for the sage Nicholas Vedder, with his broad face, double chin, and fair long pipe, uttering clouds of tobacco-smoke instead of idle speeches; or Van Bummel, the schoolmaster, doling forth the contents of an ancient newspaper. In place of these, a lean, bilious-looking fellow, with his pockets full of handbills, was haranguing vehemently about rights of citizens — elections — members of congress — liberty — Bunker's Hill — heroes of seventy-six — and other words, which were a perfect Babylonish jargon to the bewildered Van Winkle.

The appearance of Rip, with his long, grizzled beard, his rusty fowling-piece, his uncouth dress, and an army of women and children at his heels, soon attracted the attention of the tavern-politicians. They crowded round him, eyeing him from head to foot with great curiosity. The orator bustled up to him, and, drawing him partly aside, inquired "On which side he voted?" Rip stared in vacant stupidity. Another short but busy little fellow pulled him by the arm, and, rising on tiptoe, inquired in his ear, "Whether he was Federal or Democrat?" Rip was equally at a loss to comprehend the question; when a knowing, self-important old gentleman, in a sharp cocked hat, made his way through the crowd, putting them to the right and left with his elbows as he passed, and planting himself before Van Winkle, with one arm akimbo, the other resting on his cane, his keen eyes and sharp hat penetrating, as it were, into his very soul, demanded in an austere tone, "What brought him to the election with a gun on his shoulder, and a mob at his heels; and whether he meant to breed a riot in the village?" — "Alas! gentlemen," cried Rip, somewhat dismayed, "I am a poor quiet man, a native of the place, and a loyal subject of the King, God bless him!"

Here a general shout burst from the by-standers — "A tory! a tory! a spy! a refugee! hustle him! away with him!" It was with great difficulty that the self-important man in the cocked hat restored order; and, having assumed a tenfold austerity of brow, demanded again of the unknown culprit, what he came there for, and whom he was seeking? The poor man humbly assured him that he meant no harm, but merely came there in search of some of his neighbors, who used to keep about the tavern.

"Well — who are they? — name them."

Rip bethought himself a moment, and inquired, "Where's Nicholas Vedder?"

There was a silence for a little while, when an old man replied, in a thin piping voice, "Nicholas Vedder! why, he is dead and gone these eighteen years! There was a wooden tombstone in that churchyard that used to tell all about him, but that's rotten and gone too."

"Where's Brom Dutcher?"

"Oh, he went off to the army in the beginning of the war; some say he was killed at the storming of Stony Point — others say he was drowned in a squall at the foot of Antony's Nose. I don't know — he never came back again."

"Where's Van Bummel, the schoolmaster?"

"He went off to the wars too, was a great militia general, and is now in congress."

Rip's heart died away at hearing of these sad changes in his home and friends, and finding himself thus alone in the world. Every answer puzzled him too, by treating of such enormous lapses of time, and of matters which he could not understand: war — congress — Stony Point — he had no courage to ask after any more friends, but cried out in despair, "Does nobody here know Rip Van Winkle?"

"Oh, Rip Van Winkle!" exclaimed two or three. "Oh, to be sure! that's Rip Van Winkle yonder, leaning against the tree."

Rip looked, and he beheld a precise counterpart of himself, as he went up the mountain; apparently as lazy, and certainly as ragged. The poor fellow was now completely confounded. He doubted his own identity, and whether he was himself or another man. In the midst of his bewilderment, the man in the cocked hat demanded who he was, and what was his name.

"God knows," exclaimed he, at his wit's end; "I'm not myself — I'm somebody else — that's me yonder — no — that's somebody else got into my shoes — I was myself last night, but I fell asleep on the mountain, and they've changed my gun, and everything's changed, and I'm changed, and I can't tell what's my name, or who I am!"

The by-standers began now to look at each other, nod, wink significantly, and tap their fingers against their foreheads. There was a whisper, also, about securing the gun, and keeping the old fellow from doing mischief, at the very suggestion of which the self-important man in the cocked hat retired with some precipitation. At this critical moment a fresh, comely woman pressed through the throng to get a peep at the gray-bearded man. She had a chubby child in her arms, which, frightened at his looks, began to cry. "Hush, Rip," cried she, "hush, you little fool; the old man won't hurt you." The name of the child, the air of the mother, the tone of her voice, all awakened a train of recollections in his mind. "What is your name, my good woman?" asked he.

"Judith Gardenier."

"And your father's name?"

"Ah, poor man, Rip Van Winkle was his name, but it's twenty years since he went away from home with his gun, and never has been heard of since — his dog came home without him; but whether he shot himself, or was carried away by the Indians, nobody can tell. I was then but a little girl."

Rip had but one question more to ask; but he put it with a faltering voice:

"Where's your mother?"

"Oh, she too died but a short time since; she broke a blood vessel in a fit of passion at a New England peddler."

There was a drop of comfort, at least, in this intelligence. The honest man could contain himself no longer. He caught his daughter and her child in his arms. "I am your father!" cried he — "Young Rip Van Winkle once — old Rip Van Winkle now! — Does nobody know poor Rip Van Winkle?"

All stood amazed, until an old woman, tottering out from among the crowd, put her hand to her brow, and peering under it in his face for a moment, exclaimed, "Sure enough! it is Rip Van Winkle — it is himself! Welcome home again, old neighbor. Why, where have you been these twenty long years?"

Rip's story was soon told, for the whole twenty years had been to him but as one night. The neighbors stared when they heard it; some were seen to wink at each other, and put their tongues in their cheeks: and the self-important man in the cocked hat, who, when the alarm was over, had returned to the field, screwed down the corners of his mouth, and shook his head — upon which there was a general shaking of the head throughout the assemblage.

It was determined, however, to take the opinion of old Peter Vanderdonk, who was seen slowly advancing up the road. He was a descendant of the historian of that name, who wrote one of the earliest accounts of the province. Peter was the most ancient inhabitant of the village, and well versed in all the wonderful events and traditions of the neighborhood. He recollected Rip at once, and corroborated his story in the most satisfactory manner. He assured the company that it was a fact, handed down from his ancestor the historian, that the Kaatskill mountains had always been haunted by strange beings. That it was affirmed that the great Hendrick Hudson, the first discoverer of the river and country, kept a kind of vigil there every twenty years, with his crew of the *Half-moon;* being permitted in this way to revisit the scenes of his enterprise, and keep a guardian eye upon the river and the great city called by his name. That his father had once seen them in their old Dutch dresses playing at ninepins in a hollow of the mountain; and that he himself had heard, one summer afternoon, the sound of their balls, like distant peals of thunder.

To make a long story short, the company broke up and returned to the more important concerns of the election. Rip's daughter took him home to live with her; she had a snug, well-furnished house, and a stout, cheery farmer for a husband, whom Rip recollected for one of the urchins that used to climb upon his back. As to Rip's son and heir, who was the ditto of himself, seen leaning against the tree, he was employed to work on the farm; but evinced an hereditary disposition to attend to anything else but his business.

Rip now resumed his old walks and habits; he soon found many of his former cronies, though all rather the worse for the wear and tear of time; and preferred making friends among the rising generation, with whom he soon grew into great favor.

Having nothing to do at home, and being arrived at that happy age when a man can be idle with impunity, he took his place once more on the bench at the inn-door, and was reverenced as one of the patriarchs of the village, and a chronicle of the old times "before the war." It was some time before he could get into the regular track of gossip, or could be made to comprehend the strange events that had taken place during his torpor. How that there had been a revolutionary war — that the country had thrown off the yoke of old England — and that, instead of being a subject of his Majesty George the Third, he was now a free citizen of the United States. Rip, in fact, was no politician; the changes of states and empires made but little impression to him; but there was one species of despotism under which he long groaned, and that was — petticoat government. Happily that was at an end; he had got his neck out of the yoke of matrimony, and could go in and out whenever he pleased, without dreading the tyranny of Dame Van Winkle. Whenever her name was mentioned, however, he shook his head, shrugged his shoulders, and cast up his eyes; which might pass either for an expression of resignation to his fate, or joy at his deliverance.

He used to tell his story to every stranger that arrived at Mr. Doolittle's hotel. He was observed, at first, to vary on some points every time he told it, which was, doubtless, owing to his having so recently awaked. It at last settled down precisely to the tale I have related, and not a man, woman, or child in the neighborhood but knew it by heart. Some always pretended to doubt the reality of it, and insisted that Rip had been out of his head, and that this was one point on which he always remained flighty. The old Dutch inhabitants, however, almost universally gave it full credit. Even to this day they never hear a thunderstorm of a summer afternoon about the Kaatskill, but they say Hendrick Hudson and his crew are at their game of ninepins; and it is a common wish of all hen-pecked husbands in the neighborhood, when life hangs heavy on their hands, that they might have a quieting draught out of Rip Van Winkle's flagon.

NOTE

The foregoing Tale, one would suspect, had been suggested to Mr. Knickerbocker by a little German superstition about the Emperor Frederick *der Rothbart,* and the Kypphäuser mountain: the subjoined note, however, which he had appended to the tale, shows that it is an absolute fact, narrated with his usual fidelity.

"The story of Rip Van Winkle may seem incredible to many, but nevertheless I give it my full belief, for I know the vicinity of our old Dutch settlements to have been very subject to marvellous events and appearances. Indeed, I have heard many stranger stories than this, in the villages along the Hudson; all of which were too well authenticated to admit of a doubt. I have even talked with Rip Van Winkle myself, who, when last I saw him, was a very venerable old man, and so perfectly rational and consistent on every other point, that I think no conscientious person could refuse to take this into the bargain; nay, I have seen a certificate on the subject taken before a country justice and signed with a cross, in the justice's own handwriting. The story, therefore, is beyond the possibility of doubt."

"D. K."

∞

SHIRLEY JACKSON *(1919–1965) was born in San Francisco, California, her mother a housewife and her father an employee of a lithographing company. Most of her early life was spent in Burlingame, California, which she later used as the setting for her first novel,* The Road Through the Wall *(1948). As a child she was interested in writing; she won a poetry prize at age twelve, and in high school she began keeping a diary to record her writing progress. After high school she briefly attended the University of Rochester but left because of an attack of the mental depression that was to recur periodically in her later years. She recovered her health by living quietly at home and writing, conscientiously turning out 1,000 words of prose a day. In 1937 she entered Syracuse University, where she published stories in the student literary magazine. There she met Stanley Edgar Hyman, who was to become a noted literary critic.*

They were married in 1940, the year she received her degree. They had four children while both continued active literary careers, settling to raise their family in a large Victorian house in Vermont, where Hyman taught literature at Bennington College.

Jackson's first national publication was a humorous story written after a job at a department store during the Christmas rush: "My Life with R. H. Macy" appeared in The New Republic *in 1941. Her first child was born the next year, but she wrote every day on a disciplined schedule, selling her stories to magazines and publishing three novels. She refused to take herself too seriously as a writer: "I can't persuade myself that writing is honest work. It is a very personal reaction, but 50 percent of my life is spent washing and dressing the children, cooking, washing dishes and clothes, and mending. After I get it all to bed, I turn around to my typewriter and try to — well, to create concrete things again. It's great fun, and I love it. But it doesn't tie any shoes."*

Jackson's best-known work, "The Lottery," is often anthologized, dramatized, and televised. She regarded it as a tale in the sense that Nathaniel Hawthorne used the term — a moral allegory revealing the hidden evil of the human soul. She wrote later that "explaining just what I had hoped the story to say is very difficult. I supposed, I hoped, by setting a particularly brutal ancient rite in the present and in my own village, to shock the story's readers with a graphic dramatization of the pointless violence and general inhumanity in their own lives."

RELATED COMMENTARY: *Shirley Jackson, "The Morning of June 28, 1948, and 'The Lottery,' " page 762.*

Shirley Jackson

The Lottery

1948

The morning of June 27th was clear and sunny, with the fresh warmth of a full-summer day; the flowers were blossoming profusely and the grass was richly green. The people of the village began to gather in the square, between the post office and the bank, around ten o'clock; in some towns there were so many people that the lottery took two days and had to be started on June 26th, but in this village, where there were only about three hundred people, the whole lottery took less than two hours, so it could begin at ten o'clock in the morning and still be through in time to allow the villagers to get home for noon dinner.

The children assembled first, of course. School was recently over for the summer, and the feeling of liberty sat uneasily on most of them; they tended to gather together quietly for a while before they broke into boisterous play, and their talk was still of the classroom and teacher, of books and reprimands. Bobby Martin had already stuffed his pockets full of stones, and the other boys soon followed his example, selecting the smoothest and roundest stones; Bobby and Harry Jones and Dickie Delacroix — the villagers pronounced this name "Dellacroy" — eventually made a great pile of stones in one corner of the square and guarded it against the raids of the other boys. The girls stood aside, talking among themselves, looking over their shoulders at the boys, and the very small children rolled in the dust or clung to the hands of their older brothers or sisters.

Soon the men began to gather, surveying their own children, speaking of planting and rain, tractors and taxes. They stood together, away from the pile of stones in the corner, and their jokes were quiet and they smiled rather than laughed. The women, wearing faded house dresses and sweaters, came shortly after their menfolk. They greeted one another and exchanged bits of gossip as they went to join their husbands. Soon the women, standing by their husbands, began to call to their children, and the children came reluctantly, having to be called four or five times. Bobby Martin ducked under his mother's grasping hand and ran, laughing, back to the pile of stones. His father spoke up sharply, and Bobby came quickly and took his place between his father and his oldest brother.

The lottery was conducted — as were the square dances, the teen-age club, the Halloween program — by Mr. Summers, who had time and energy to devote to civic activities. He was a round-faced, jovial man and he ran the coal business, and people were sorry for him, because he had no children and his wife was a scold. When he arrived in the square, carrying the black wooden box, there was a murmur of conversation among the villagers, and he waved and called, "Little late today, folks." The postmaster, Mr. Graves, followed him, carrying a three-legged stool, and the stool was put in the center of the square and Mr. Summers set the black box down on it. The villagers kept their distance, leaving a space between themselves and the stool, and when Mr. Summers said, "Some of you fellows want to give me a hand?" there was a hesitation before two men, Mr. Martin and his oldest son, Baxter, came forward to hold the box steady on the stool while Mr. Summers stirred up the papers inside it.

The original paraphernalia for the lottery had been lost long ago, and the black box now resting on the stool had been put into use even before Old Man Warner, the oldest man in town, was born. Mr. Summers spoke frequently to the villagers about making a new box, but no one liked to upset even as much tradition as was represented by the black box. There was a story that the present box had been made with some pieces of the box that had preceded it, the one that had been constructed when the first people settled down to make a village here. Every year, after the lottery, Mr. Summers began talking again about a new box, but every year the subject was allowed to fade off without anything's being done. The black box grew shabbier each year; by now it was no longer completely black but splintered badly along one side to show the original wood color, and in some places faded or stained.

Mr. Martin and his oldest son, Baxter, held the black box securely on the stool until Mr. Summers had stirred the papers thoroughly with his hand. Because so much of the ritual had been forgotten or discarded, Mr. Summers had been successful in having slips of paper substituted for the chips of wood that had been used for generations. Chips of wood, Mr. Summers had argued, had been all very well when the village was tiny, but now that the population was more than three hundred and likely to keep on growing, it was necessary to use something that would fit more easily into the black box. The night before the lottery, Mr. Summers and Mr. Graves made up the slips of paper and put them in the box, and it was then taken to the safe of Mr. Summers's coal company and locked up until Mr. Summers was ready to take it to the square next morning. The rest of the year, the box was put away, sometimes one place, sometimes another; it had spent one year in Mr. Graves's barn and another year underfoot in the post office, and sometimes it was set on a shelf in the Martin grocery and left there.

There was a great deal of fussing to be done before Mr. Summers declared the lottery open. There were the lists to make up — of heads of families, heads of households in each family, members of each household in each family. There was the proper swearing-in of Mr. Summers by the postmaster, as the official of the lottery; at one time, some people remembered, there had been a recital of some sort, performed by the official of the lottery, a perfunctory, tuneless chant that had been rattled off duly each year; some people believed that the official of the lottery used to stand just so when he said or sang it, others believed that he was supposed to walk among the people, but years and years ago this part of the ritual had been allowed to lapse. There had been, also, a ritual salute, which the official of the lottery had had to use in addressing each person who came up to draw from the box, but this also had changed with time, until now it was felt necessary only for the official to speak to each person approaching. Mr. Summers was very good at all this; in his clean white shirt and blue jeans, with one hand resting carelessly on the black box, he seemed very proper and important as he talked interminably to Mr. Graves and the Martins.

Just as Mr. Summers finally left off talking and turned to the assembled villagers, Mrs. Hutchinson came hurriedly along the path to the square, her sweater thrown over her shoulders, and slid into place in the back of the crowd. "Clean forgot what day it was," she said to Mrs. Delacroix, who stood next to her, and they both laughed softly. "Thought my old man was out back stacking wood," Mrs. Hutchinson went on, "and then I looked out the window and the kids was gone, and then I remembered it was the twenty-seventh and came a-running." She dried her hands on her apron, and Mrs. Delacroix said, "You're in time, though. They're still talking away up there."

Mrs. Hutchinson craned her neck to see through the crowd and found her husband and children standing near the front. She tapped Mrs. Delacroix on the arm as a farewell and began to make her way through the crowd. The people separated good-humoredly to let her through; two or three people said, in voices just loud enough to be heard across the crowd, "Here comes your Missus, Hutchinson," and "Bill, she made it after all." Mrs. Hutchinson reached her husband, and Mr. Summers, who had been waiting, said cheerfully, "Thought we were going to have to get on without you, Tessie." Mrs. Hutchinson said, grinning, "Wouldn't have me leave m'dishes in the sink, now, would you, Joe?" and soft laughter ran through the crowd as the people stirred back into position after Mrs. Hutchinson's arrival.

"Well, now," Mr. Summers said soberly, "guess we better get started, get this over with, so's we can go back to work. Anybody ain't here?"

"Dunbar," several people said. "Dunbar, Dunbar."

Mr. Summers consulted his list. "Clyde Dunbar," he said. "That's right. He's broke his leg, hasn't he? Who's drawing for him?"

"Me, I guess," a woman said, and Mr. Summers turned to look at her. "Wife draws for her husband," Mr. Summers said. "Don't you have a grown boy to do it for you, Janey?" Although Mr. Summers and everyone else in the village knew the answer perfectly well, it was the business of the official of the lottery to ask such questions formally. Mr. Summers waited with an expression of polite interest while Mrs. Dunbar answered.

"Horace's not but sixteen yet," Mrs. Dunbar said regretfully. "Guess I gotta fill in for the old man this year."

"Right," Mr. Summers said. He made a note on the list he was holding. Then he asked, "Watson boy drawing this year?"

A tall boy in the crowd raised his hand. "Here," he said. "I'm drawing for m'mother and me." He blinked his eyes nervously and ducked his head as several voices in the crowd said things like "Good fellow, Jack," and "Glad to see your mother's got a man to do it."

"Well," Mr. Summers said, "guess that's everyone. Old Man Warner make it?"

"Here," a voice said, and Mr. Summers nodded.

A sudden hush fell on the crowd as Mr. Summers cleared his throat and looked at the list. "All ready?" he called. "Now, I'll read the names — heads of families first — and the men come up and take a paper out of the box. Keep the paper folded in your hand without looking at it until everyone has had a turn. Everything clear?"

The people had done it so many times that they only half listened to the directions; most of them were quiet, wetting their lips, not looking around. Then Mr. Summers raised one hand high and said, "Adams." A man disengaged himself from the crowd and came forward. "Hi, Steve," Mr. Summers said, and Mr. Adams said, "Hi, Joe." They grinned at one another humorlessly and nervously. Then Mr. Adams reached into the black box and took out a folded paper. He held it firmly by one corner as he turned and went hastily back to his place in the crowd, where he stood a little apart from his family, not looking down at his hand.

"Allen," Mr. Summers said, "Anderson. . . . Bentham."

"Seems like there's no time at all between lotteries any more," Mrs. Delacroix said to Mrs. Graves in the back row. "Seems like we got through with the last one only last week."

"Time sure goes fast," Mrs. Graves said.

"Clark. . . . Delacroix."

"There goes my old man," Mrs. Delacroix said. She held her breath while her husband went forward.

"Dunbar," Mr. Summers said, and Mrs. Dunbar went steadily to the box while one of the women said, "Go on, Janey," and another said, "There she goes."

"We're next," Mrs. Graves said. She watched while Mr. Graves came around from the side of the box, greeted Mr. Summers gravely, and selected a slip of paper from the box. By now, all through the crowd there were men holding the small folded papers in their large hands, turning them over and over nervously. Mrs. Dunbar and her two sons stood together, Mrs. Dunbar holding the slip of paper.

"Harburt. . . . Hutchinson."

"Get up there, Bill," Mrs. Hutchinson said, and the people near her laughed.

"Jones."

"They do say," Mr. Adams said to Old Man Warner, who stood next to him, "that over in the north village they're talking of giving up the lottery."

Old Man Warner snorted. "Pack of crazy fools," he said. "Listening to the young folks, nothing's good enough for *them*. Next thing you know, they'll be wanting to go back to living in caves, nobody work any more, live *that* way for a while. Used to be a saying about 'Lottery in June, corn be heavy soon.' First thing you know, we'd all be eating stewed chickweed and acorns. There's *always* been a lottery," he added petulantly. "Bad enough to see young Joe Summers up there joking with everybody."

"Some places have already quit lotteries," Mrs. Adams said.

"Nothing but trouble in *that*," Old Man Warner said stoutly. "Pack of young fools."

"Martin." And Bobby Martin watched his father go forward. "Overdyke. . . . Percy."

"I wish they'd hurry," Mrs. Dunbar said to her older son. "I wish they'd hurry."

"They're almost through," her son said.

"You get ready to run tell Dad," Mrs. Dunbar said.

Mr. Summers called his own name and then stepped forward precisely and selected a slip from the box. Then he called, "Warner."

"Seventy-seventh year I been in the lottery," Old Man Warner said as he went through the crowd. "Seventy-seventh time."

"Watson." The tall boy came awkwardly through the crowd. Someone said. "Don't be nervous, Jack," and Mr. Summers said, "Take your time, son."

"Zanini."

After that, there was a long pause, a breathless pause, until Mr. Summers, holding his slip of paper in the air, said, "All right, fellows." For a minute, no one moved, and then all the slips of paper were opened. Suddenly, all the women began to speak at once, saying, "Who is it?" "Who's got it?" "Is it the Dunbars?" "Is it the Watsons?" Then the voices began to say, "It's Hutchinson. It's Bill," "Bill Hutchinson's got it."

"Go tell your father," Mrs. Dunbar said to her older son.

People began to look around to see the Hutchinsons. Bill Hutchinson was standing quiet, staring down at the paper in his hand. Suddenly, Tessie Hutchinson shouted to Mr. Summers, "You didn't give him time enough to take any paper he wanted. I saw you. It wasn't fair!"

"Be a good sport, Tessie," Mrs. Delacroix called, and Mrs. Graves said, "All of us took the same chance."

"Shut up, Tessie," Bill Hutchinson said.

"Well, everyone," Mr. Summers said, "that was done pretty fast, and now we've got to be hurrying a little more to get done in time." He consulted his next list. "Bill," he said, "you draw for the Hutchinson family. You got any other households in the Hutchinsons?"

"There's Don and Eva," Mrs. Hutchinson yelled. "Make *them* take their chance!"

"Daughters drew with their husbands' families, Tessie," Mr. Summers said gently. "You know that as well as anyone else."

"It wasn't *fair*," Tessie said.

"I guess not, Joe," Bill Hutchinson said regretfully. "My daughter draws with her husband's family, that's only fair. And I've got no other family except the kids."

"Then, as far as drawing for families is concerned, it's you," Mr. Summers said in explanation, "and as far as drawing for households is concerned, that's you, too. Right?"

"Right," Bill Hutchinson said.

"How many kids, Bill?" Mr. Summers asked formally.

"Three," Bill Hutchinson said. "There's Bill, Jr., and Nancy, and little Dave. And Tessie and me."

"All right, then," Mr. Summers said. "Harry, you got their tickets back?"

Mr. Graves nodded and held up the slips of paper. "Put them in the box, then," Mr. Summers directed. "Take Bill's and put it in."

"I think we ought to start over," Mrs. Hutchinson said, as quietly as she could. "I tell you it wasn't *fair*. You didn't give him time enough to choose. *Every*body saw that."

Mr. Graves had selected the five slips and put them in the box, and he dropped all the papers but those onto the ground, where the breeze caught them and lifted them off.

"Listen, everybody," Mrs. Hutchinson was saying to the people around her.

"Ready, Bill?" Mr. Summers asked, and Bill Hutchinson, with one quick glance around at his wife and children, nodded.

"Remember," Mr. Summers said, "take the slips and keep them folded until each person has taken one. Harry, you help little Dave." Mr. Graves took the hand of the little boy, who came willingly with him up to the box. "Take a paper out of the box, Davy," Mr. Summers said. Davy put his hand into the box and laughed. "Take just *one* paper," Mr. Summers said. "Harry, you hold it for him." Mr. Graves took the child's hand and removed the folded paper from the tight fist and held it while little Dave stood next to him and looked up at him wonderingly.

"Nancy next," Mr. Summers said. Nancy was twelve, and her school friends breathed heavily as she went forward, switching her skirt, and took a slip daintily from the box. "Bill, Jr.," Mr. Summers said, and Billy, his face red and his feet overlarge, nearly knocked the box over as he got a paper out.

"Tessie," Mr. Summers said. She hesitated for a minute, looking around defiantly, and then set her lips and went up to the box. She snatched a paper out and held it behind her.

"Bill," Mr. Summers said, and Bill Hutchinson reached into the box and felt around, bringing his hand out at last with the slip of paper in it.

The crowd was quiet. A girl whispered, "I hope it's not Nancy," and the sound of the whisper reached the edges of the crowd.

"It's not the way it used to be," Old Man Warner said clearly. "People ain't the way they used to be."

"All right," Mr. Summers said. "Open the papers. Harry, you open little Dave's."

Mr. Graves opened the slip of paper and there was a general sigh through the crowd as he held it up and everyone could see that it was blank. Nancy and Bill, Jr., opened theirs at the same time, and both beamed and laughed, turning around to the crowd and holding their slips of paper above their heads.

"Tessie," Mr. Summers said. There was a pause, and then Mr. Summers looked at Bill Hutchinson, and Bill unfolded this paper and showed it. It was blank.

"It's Tessie," Mr. Summers said, and his voice was hushed. "Show us her paper, Bill."

Bill Hutchinson went over to his wife and forced the slip of paper out of her hand. It had a black spot on it, the black spot Mr. Summers had made the night before with the heavy pencil in the coal-company office. Bill Hutchinson held it up and there was a stir in the crowd.

"All right, folks," Mr. Summers said. "Let's finish quickly."

Although the villagers had forgotten the ritual and lost the original black box, they still remembered to use stones. The pile of stones the boys had made earlier was ready; there were stones on the ground with the blowing scraps of paper that had come out of the box. Mrs. Delacroix selected a stone so large she had to pick it up with both hands and turned to Mrs. Dunbar. "Come on," she said. "Hurry up."

Mrs. Dunbar had small stones in both hands, and she said, gasping for breath, "I can't run at all. You'll have to go ahead and I'll catch up with you."

The children had stones already, and someone gave little Davy Hutchinson a few pebbles.

Tessie Hutchinson was in the center of a cleared space by now, and she held her hands out desperately as the villagers moved in on her. "It isn't fair," she said. A stone hit her on the side of the head.

Old Man Warner was saying, "Come on, come on, everyone." Steve Adams was in the front of the crowd of villagers, with Mrs. Graves beside him.

"It isn't fair, it isn't right," Mrs. Hutchinson screamed and then they were upon her.

SARAH ORNE JEWETT (1849–1909) was born in South Berwick, Maine. Her father was a country doctor, and she often accompanied him on his horse-and-buggy rounds among sick people on the local farms. She later said that she got her real education from these trips, rather than from her classes at Miss Rayne's School and the Berwick Academy. She had a fine ear for local speech and the native idiom, which she used to good effect in her stories. Impressed as a girl by the sympathetic depiction of local color (the people and life of a particular geographical setting) in the fiction of Harriet Beecher Stowe, Jewett began to write stories herself, publishing her earliest one, "Jenny Garrow's Lovers," in a Boston weekly when she was eighteen years old. Shortly after her twentieth birthday, her work was accepted by the prestigious Atlantic Monthly, and her career was launched. Jewett published her first collection of stories, Deephaven, in 1877. She read the work of Gustave Flaubert, Émile Zola, Leo Tolstoy, and Henry James, and her style gradually matured, as is evident in the stories that make up the 1886 volume A White Heron and Other Stories. Jewett took her favorite motto from Flaubert, "One should write of ordinary life as if one were writing history." Her masterpiece, The Country of the Pointed Firs (1896), is a book of scrupulously observed short sketches linked by the narrator's account of her stay in a Maine seacoast village and her growing involvement in the quiet lives of its people.

Many stories were written about New England in Jewett's time, but hers have a unique quality stemming from her deep sympathy for the native characters and her ear for local speech. Once she laughingly told the younger writer Willa Cather that her head was full of dear old houses and dear old women, and when an old house and an old woman came together in her brain with a click, she knew a story was under way.

Although it is true that Jewett's realism heightens the attractive aspects of the rural New England character at the same time that it diminishes the harsher qualities, her literary technique is so candid that the darker undercurrents of deprivation, both physical and psychological, are evident beneath the surface of her descriptions. Henry James recognized that Jewett was "surpassed only by Hawthorne as producer of the most finished and penetrating of the numerous 'short stories' that have the domestic life of New England for their general and their doubtless somewhat lean subject." In her time she was lauded for possessing an exquisitely simple, natural, and graceful style; now she is regarded as the most distinguished American regionalist writer of the Nineteenth Century, as evidenced by her finest tale, "A White Heron."

SARAH ORNE JEWETT

A White Heron

1886

I

The woods were already filled with shadows one June evening, just before eight o'clock, though a bright sunset still glimmered faintly among the trunks of the trees. A little girl was driving home her cow, a plodding, dilatory, provoking creature in her behavior, but a valued companion for all that. They were going away from the western light, and striking deep into the dark woods, but their feet were familiar with the path, and it was no matter whether their eyes could see it or not.

There was hardly a night the summer through when the old cow could be found waiting at the pasture bars; on the contrary, it was her greatest pleasure to hide herself away among the high huckleberry bushes, and though she wore a loud bell she had made the discovery that if one stood perfectly still it would not ring. So Sylvia had to hunt for her until she found her and call Co'! Co'! with never an answering Moo, until her childish patience was quite spent. If the creature had not given good milk and plenty of it, the case would have seemed very different to her owners. Besides, Sylvia had all the time there was, and very little use to make of it. Sometimes in pleasant weather it was a consolation to look upon the cow's pranks as an intelligent attempt to play hide and seek, and as the child had no playmates she lent herself to this amusement with a good deal of zest. Though this chase had been so long that the wary animal herself had given an unusual signal of her whereabouts, Sylvia had only laughed when she came upon Mistress Moolly at the swampside, and urged her affectionately homeward with a twig of birch leaves. The old cow was not inclined to wander farther, she even turned in the right direction for once as they left the pasture, and stepped along the road at a good pace. She was quite ready to be milked now, and seldom stopped to browse. Sylvia wondered what her grandmother would say because they were so late. It was a great while since she had left home at half past five o'clock, but everybody knew the difficulty of making this errand a short one. Mrs. Tilley had chased the horned torment too many summer evenings herself to blame any one else for lingering, and was only thankful as she waited that she had Sylvia, nowadays, to give such valuable assistance. The good woman suspected that Sylvia loitered occasionally on her own account; there never was such a child for straying about out-of-doors since the world was made! Everybody said that it was a good change for a little maid who had tried to grow for eight years in a crowded manufacturing town, but, as for Sylvia herself, it seemed as if she never had been alive at all before she came to live at the farm. She thought often with wistful compassion of a wretched dry geranium that belonged to a town neighbor.

" 'Afraid of folks,' " old Mrs. Tilley said to herself, with a smile, after she had made the unlikely choice of Sylvia from her daughter's houseful of children, and was returning to the farm. " 'Afraid of folks,' they said! I guess she won't be troubled no great with 'em up to the old place!" When they reached the door of the lonely house and stopped to unlock it, and the cat came to purr loudly, and rub against them, a deserted pussy, indeed, but fat with young robins, Sylvia whispered that this was a beautiful place to live in, and she never should wish to go home.

The companions followed the shady wood-road, the cow taking slow steps, and the child very fast ones. The cow stopped long at the brook to drink, as if the pasture were not half a swamp, and Sylvia stood still and waited, letting her bare feet cool themselves in the shoal water, while the great twilight moths struck softly against her. She waded on through the brook as the cow moved away, and listened to the thrushes with a heart that beat fast with pleasure. There was a stirring in the great boughs overhead. They were full of little birds and beasts that seemed to be wide-awake, and going about their world, or else saying good-night to each other in sleepy twitters. Sylvia herself felt sleepy as she walked along. However, it was not much farther to the house, and the air was soft and sweet. She was not often in the woods so late as this, and it made her feel as if she were a part of the gray shadows and the moving leaves. She was just thinking how long it seemed since she first came to the farm a year ago, and wondering if everything went on in the noisy town just the same as when she was there; the thought of the great red-faced boy who used to chase and frighten her made her hurry along the path to escape from the shadow of the trees.

Suddenly this little woods-girl is horror-stricken to hear a clear whistle not very far away. Not a bird's whistle, which would have a sort of friendliness, but a boy's whistle, determined, and somewhat aggressive. Sylvia left the cow to whatever sad fate might await her, and stepped discreetly aside into the bushes, but she was just too late. The enemy had discovered her, and called out in a very cheerful and persuasive tone, "Halloa, little girl, how far is it to the road?" and trembling Sylvia answered almost inaudibly, "A good ways."

She did not dare to look boldly at the tall young man, who carried a gun over his shoulder, but she came out of her bush and again followed the cow, while he walked alongside.

"I have been hunting for some birds," the stranger said kindly, "and I have lost my way, and need a friend very much. Don't be afraid," he added gallantly. "Speak up and tell me what your name is, and whether you think I can spend the night at your house, and go out gunning early in the morning."

Sylvia was more alarmed than before. Would not her grandmother consider her much to blame? But who could have foreseen such an accident as this? It did not appear to be her fault, and she hung her head as if the stem of it were broken, but managed to answer, "Sylvy," with much effort when her companion again asked her name.

Mrs. Tilley was standing in the doorway when the trio came into view. The cow gave a loud moo by way of explanation.

"Yes, you'd better speak up for yourself, you old trial! Where'd she tucked herself away this time, Sylvy?" Sylvia kept an awed silence; she knew by instinct that her grandmother did not comprehend the gravity of the situation. She must be mistaking the stranger for one of the farmer-lads of the region.

The young man stood his gun beside the door, and dropped a heavy game-bag beside it; then he bade Mrs. Tilley good-evening, and repeated his wayfarer's story, and asked if he could have a night's lodging.

"Put me anywhere you like," he said. "I must be off early in the morning, before day; but I am very hungry, indeed. You can give me some milk at any rate, that's plain."

"Dear sakes, yes," responded the hostess, whose long slumbering hospitality seemed to be easily awakened. "You might fare better if you went out on the main road a mile or so, but you're welcome to what we've got. I'll milk right off, and you make yourself at home. You can sleep on husks or feathers," she proffered graciously. "I raised them all myself. There's good pasturing for geese just below here towards the ma'sh. Now step round and set a plate for the gentleman, Sylvy!" And Sylvia promptly stepped. She was glad to have something to do, and she was hungry herself.

It was a surprise to find so clean and comfortable a little dwelling in this New England wilderness. The young man had known the horrors of its most primitive housekeeping, and the dreary squalor of that level of society which does not rebel at the companionship of hens. This was the best thrift of an old-fashioned farmstead, though on such a small scale that it seemed like a hermitage. He listened eagerly to the old woman's quaint talk, he watched Sylvia's pale face and shining gray eyes with ever growing enthusiasm, and insisted that this was the best supper he had eaten for a month; then, afterward, the new-made friends sat down in the doorway together while the moon came up.

Soon it would be berry-time, and Sylvia was a great help at picking. The cow was a good milker, though a plaguy thing to keep track of, the hostess gossiped frankly, adding presently that she had buried four children, so that Sylvia's mother, and a son (who might be dead) in California were all the children she had left. "Dan, my boy, was a great hand to go gunning," she explained sadly. "I never wanted for pa'tridges or gray squer'ls while he was to home. He's been a great wand'rer, I expect, and he's no hand to write letters. There, I don't blame him, I'd ha' seen the world myself if it had been so I could.

"Sylvia takes after him," the grandmother continued affectionately, after a minute's pause. "There ain't a foot o' ground she don't know her way over, and the wild creatur's counts her one o' themselves. Squer'ls she'll tame to come an' feed right out o' her hands, and all sorts o' birds. Last winter she got the jay-birds to bangeing here, and I believe she'd 'a' scanted herself of her own meals to have plenty to throw out amongst 'em, if I hadn't kep' watch. Anything but crows, I tell her, I'm willin' to help support, — though Dan he went an' tamed one o' them that did seem to have reason same as folks. It was round here a good spell after he went away. Dan an' his father they didn't hitch, — but he never held up his head ag'in after Dan had dared him an' gone off."

The guest did not notice this hint of family sorrows in his eager interest in something else.

"So Sylvy knows all about birds, does she?" he exclaimed, as he looked round at the little girl who sat, very demure but increasingly sleepy, in the moonlight. "I am making a collection of birds myself. I have been at it ever since I was a boy." (Mrs. Tilley smiled.) "There are two or three very rare ones I have been hunting for these five years. I mean to get them on my own ground if they can be found."

"Do you cage 'em up?" asked Mrs. Tilley doubtfully, in response to this enthusiastic announcement.

"Oh, no, they're stuffed and preserved, dozens and dozens of them," said the ornithologist, "and I have shot or snared every one myself. I caught a glimpse of a white heron three miles from here on Saturday, and I have followed it in this direction. They have never been found in this district at all. The little white heron, it is," and he turned again to look at Sylvia with the hope of discovering that the rare bird was one of her acquaintances.

But Sylvia was watching a hop-toad in the narrow footpath.

"You would know the heron if you saw it," the stranger continued eagerly. "A queer tall white bird with soft feathers and long thin legs. And it would have a nest perhaps in the top of a high tree, made of sticks, something like a hawk's nest."

Sylvia's heart gave a wild beat; she knew that strange white bird, and had once stolen softly near where it stood in some bright green swamp grass, away over at the other side of the woods. There was an open place where the sunshine always seemed strangely yellow and hot, where tall, nodding rushes grew, and her grandmother had warned her that she might sink in the soft black mud underneath and never be heard of more. Not far beyond were the salt marshes and beyond those was the sea, the sea which Sylvia wondered and dreamed about, but never had looked upon, though its great voice could often be heard above the noise of the woods on stormy nights.

"I can't think of anything I should like so much as to find that heron's nest," the handsome stranger was saying. "I would give ten dollars to anybody who could show it to me," he added desperately, "and I mean to spend my whole vacation hunting for it if need be. Perhaps it was only migrating, or had been chased out of its own region by some bird of prey."

Mrs. Tilley gave amazed attention to all this, but Sylvia still watched the toad, not divining, as she might have done at some calmer time, that the creature wished to get to its hole under the doorstep, and was much hindered by the unusual spectators at that hour of the evening. No amount of thought, that night, could decide how many wished-for treasures the ten dollars, so lightly spoken of, would buy.

The next day the young sportsman hovered about the woods, and Sylvia kept him company, having lost her first fear of the friendly lad, who proved to be most kind and sympathetic. He told her many things about the birds and what they knew and where they lived and what they did with themselves. And he gave her a jack-knife, which she thought as great a treasure as if she were a desert-islander. All day long he did not once make her troubled or afraid except when he brought down some unsuspecting singing creature from its bough. Sylvia would have liked him vastly better without his gun; she could not understand why he killed the very birds he seemed to like so much. But as the day waned, Sylvia still watched the young man with loving admiration. She had never seen anybody so charming and delightful; the woman's heart, asleep in the child, was vaguely thrilled by a dream of love. Some premonition of that great power stirred and swayed these young foresters who traversed the solemn woodlands with soft-footed silent care. They stopped to listen to a bird's song; they pressed forward again eagerly, parting the branches — speaking to each other rarely and in whispers; the young man going first and Sylvia following, fascinated, a few steps behind, with her gray eyes dark with excitement.

She grieved because the longed-for white heron was elusive, but she did not lead the guest, she only followed, and there was no such thing as speaking first. The sound of her own unquestioned voice would have terrified her — it was hard enough to answer yes or no when there was need of that. At last evening began to fall, and they drove the cow home together, and Sylvia smiled with pleasure when they came to the place where she heard the whistle and was afraid only the night before.

II

Half a mile from home, at the farther edge of the woods, where the land was highest, a great pine-tree stood, the last of its generation. Whether it was left for a boundary mark, or for what reason, no one could say; the woodchoppers who had felled its mates were dead and gone long ago, and a whole forest of sturdy trees, pines and oaks and maples, had grown again. But the stately head of this old pine towered above them all and made a landmark for sea and shore miles and miles away. Sylvia knew it well. She had always believed that whoever climbed to the top of it could see the ocean; and the little girl had often laid her hand on the great rough trunk and looked up wistfully at those dark boughs that the wind always stirred, no matter how hot and still the air might be below. Now she thought of the tree with a new excitement, for why, if one climbed it at break of day, could not one see all the world, and easily discover whence the white heron flew, and mark the place, and find the hidden nest?

What a spirit of adventure, what wild ambition! What fancied triumph and delight and glory for the later morning when she could make known the secret! It was almost too real and too great for the childish heart to bear.

All night the door of the little house stood open, and the whippoorwills came and sang upon the very step. The young sportsman and his old hostess were sound asleep, but Sylvia's great design kept her broad awake and watching. She forgot to think of sleep. The short summer night seemed as long as the winter darkness, and at last when the whippoorwills ceased, and she was afraid the morning would after all come too soon, she stole out of the house and followed the pasture path through the woods, hastening toward the open ground beyond, listening with a sense of comfort and companionship to the drowsy twitter of a half-awakened bird, whose perch she had jarred in passing. Alas, if the great wave of human interest which flooded for the first time this dull little life should sweep away the satisfactions of an existence heart to heart with nature and the dumb life of the forest!

There was the huge tree asleep yet in the paling moonlight, and small and hopeful Sylvia began with utmost bravery to mount to the top of it, with tingling, eager blood coursing the channels of her whole frame, with her bare feet and fingers, that pinched and held like bird's claws to the monstrous ladder reaching up, up, almost to the sky itself. First she must mount the white oak tree that grew alongside, where she was almost lost among the dark branches and the green leaves heavy and wet with dew; a bird fluttered off its nest, and a red squirrel ran to and fro and scolded pettishly at the harmless housebreaker. Sylvia felt her way easily. She had often climbed there, and knew that higher still one of the oak's upper branches chafed against the pine trunk, just where its lower boughs were set close together. There, when she made the dangerous pass from one tree to the other, the great enterprise would really begin.

She crept out along the swaying oak limb at last, and took the daring step across into the old pine-tree. The way was harder than she thought; she must reach far and hold fast, the sharp dry twigs caught and held her and scratched her like angry talons, the pitch made her thin little fingers clumsy and stiff as she went round and round the tree's great stem, higher and higher upward. The sparrows and robins in the woods below were beginning to wake and twitter to the dawn, yet it seemed much lighter there aloft in the pine-tree, and the child knew that she must hurry if her project were to be of any use.

The tree seemed to lengthen itself out as she went up, and to reach farther and farther upward. It was like a great main-mast to the voyaging earth; it must truly have been amazed that morning through all its ponderous frame as it felt this determined spark of human spirit creeping and climbing from higher branch to branch. Who knows how steadily the least twigs held themselves to advantage this light, weak creature on her way! The old pine must have loved his new dependent. More than all the hawks, and bats, and moths, and even the sweet-voiced thrushes, was the brave, beating heart of the solitary gray-eyed child. And the tree stood still and held away the winds that June morning while the dawn grew bright in the east.

Sylvia's face was like a pale star, if one had seen it from the ground, when the last thorny bough was past, and she stood trembling and tired but wholly triumphant, high in the tree-top. Yes, there was the sea with the dawning sun making a golden dazzle over it, and toward that glorious east flew two hawks with slow-moving pinions. How low they looked in the air from that height when before one had only seen them far up, and dark against the blue sky. Their gray feathers were as soft as moths; they seemed only a little way from the tree, and Sylvia felt as if she too could go flying away among the clouds. Westward, the woodlands and farms reached miles and miles into the distance; here and there were church steeples, and white villages; truly it was a vast and awesome world.

The birds sang louder and louder. At last the sun came up bewilderingly bright. Sylvia could see the white sails of ships out at sea, and the clouds that were purple and rose-colored and yellow at first began to fade away. Where was the white heron's nest in the sea of green branches, and was this wonderful sight and pageant of the world the only reward for having climbed to such a giddy height? Now look down again, Sylvia, where the green marsh is set among the shining birches and dark hemlocks; there where you saw the white heron once you will see him again; look, look! a white spot of him like a single floating feather comes up from the dead hemlock and grows larger, and rises, and comes close at last, and goes by the landmark pine with steady sweep of wing and outstretched slender neck and crested head. And wait! wait! do not move a foot or a finger, little girl, do not send an arrow of light and conscious- ness from your two eager eyes, for the heron has perched on a pine bough not far beyond yours, and cries back to his mate on the nest, and plumes his feath- ers for the new day!

The child gives a long sigh a minute later when a company of shouting cat-birds comes also to the tree, and vexed by their fluttering and lawlessness the solemn heron goes away. She knows his secret now, the wild, light, slender bird that floats and wavers, and goes back like an arrow presently to his home in the green world beneath. Then Sylvia, well satisfied, makes her perilous way down again, not daring to look far below the branch she stands on, ready to cry sometimes because her fingers ache and her lamed feet slip. Wondering over and over again what the stranger would say to her, and what he would think when she told him how to find his way straight to the heron's nest.

"Sylvy, Sylvy!" called the busy old grandmother again and again, but nobody answered, and the small husk bed was empty, and Sylvia had disap- peared.

The guest waked from a dream, and remembering his day's pleasure hurried to dress himself that it might sooner begin. He was sure from the way the shy little girl looked once or twice yesterday that she had at least seen the white heron, and now she must really be persuaded to tell. Here she comes now, paler than ever, and her worn old frock is torn and tattered, and smeared with pine pitch. The grandmother and the sportsman stand in the door to- gether and question her, and the splendid moment had come to speak of the dead hemlock-tree by the green marsh.

But Sylvia does not speak after all, though the old grandmother fretfully rebukes her, and the young man's kind appealing eyes are looking straight in her own. He can make them rich with money; he has promised it, and they are poor now. He is so well worth making happy, and he waits to hear the story she can tell.

No, she must keep silence! What is it that suddenly forbids her and makes her dumb? Has she been nine years growing, and now, when the great world for the first time puts out a hand to her, must she thrust it aside for a bird's sake? The murmur of the pine's green branches is in her ears, she re- members how the white heron came flying through the golden air and how they watched the sea and the morning together, and Sylvia cannot speak; she cannot tell the heron's secret and give its life away.

Dear loyalty, that suffered a sharp pang as the guest went away disap- pointed later in the day, that could have served and followed him and loved him as a dog loves! Many a night Sylvia heard the echo of his whistle haunt- ing the pasture path as she came home with the loitering cow. She forgot even her sorrow at the sharp report of his gun and the piteous sight of thrushes and sparrows dropping silent to the ground, their songs hushed and their pretty feathers stained and wet with blood. Were the birds better friends than their hunter might have been, — who can tell? Whatever treasures were lost to her, woodlands and summer-time, remember! Bring your gifts and graces and tell your secrets to this lonely country child!

ॐ

CHARLES R. JOHNSON *(b. 1948) was born in Evanston, Illinois, the son of a construction worker. His mother encouraged his early interest in drawing, and at the age of seventeen he published his first book of cartoons. Six years later he created, coproduced, and hosted the PBS series "Charlie's Pad." He also found the time to complete a B.A. in journalism at Southern Illinois University in Carbondale, where he was inspired by the visit to campus of the black activist poet Amiri Baraka (LeRoi Jones). Johnson, who was still drawing cartoons, took Baraka's words to heart: "Baraka said a black artist should bring his talent back home to black people. I cut classes for a week and just drew, all day, all night." Johnson went on to earn an M.A. in philosophy at Southern Illinois University while studying creative writing with the novelist John Gardner, who had been Raymond Carver's teacher fifteen years before.*

According to the critic Mayemma Graham, it was Gardner who helped Johnson "to draw the connection between the Afro-American historical experience and various philosophical ideas — African, Eastern and Western — by appropriating different fictional modes." During this time Johnson devoted himself to developing what he calls "a genuinely philosophical black American fiction, which I don't think existed before the work of Jean Toomer, Richard Wright, and Ralph Ellison." Johnson's first novel, Faith and the Good Thing *(1974), reflects this stage of his development. His second novel,* Oxherding Tale *(1982), is a modern slave narrative, influenced in part by Frederick Douglass's autobiography and Herman Melville's story "Benito Cereno." In 1988 he published a book of essays,* Being and Race: Black Writing Since 1970, *and two years later he won the National Book Award for his novel* Middle Passage.

In the late 1970s Johnson began to publish short fiction in various periodicals. "Menagerie, A Child's Fable" appeared in the Indiana Review *in 1984. It was later collected in his volume of short stories,* The Sorcerer's Apprentice *(1986). Currently Johnson teaches creative writing at the University of Washington and martial arts at a Seattle kung fu club, and he makes frequent public appearances around the country as a lecturer, encouraging what he calls "ambitious, carefully wrought, innovative, intelligent fiction by writers who exhibit what Northrop Frye once called 'an educated imagination.' " Despite his demanding schedule, he says: "I should work twice as hard as I do. You create your essence through what you do. I really believe that work is prayer."*

CHARLES JOHNSON

Menagerie, A Child's Fable 1984

Among watchdogs in Seattle, Berkeley was known generally as one of the best. Not the smartest, but steady. A pious German shepherd (Black Forest origins, probably) with big shoulders, black gums, and weighing more than some men, he sat guard inside the glass door of Tilford's Pet Shoppe, watching the pedestrians scurry along First Avenue, wondering at the derelicts who slept ever so often inside the foyer at night, and sometimes he nodded when things were quiet in the cages behind him, lulled by the bubbling of the fish-tanks, dreaming of an especially fine meal he'd once had, or the little female poodle, a real flirt, owned by the aerobic dance teacher (who was no saint her-self) a few doors down the street; but Berkeley was, for all his woolgathering, never asleep at the switch. He took his work seriously. Moreover, he knew ex-actly where he was at every moment, what he was doing, and why he was do-ing it, which was more than can be said for most people, like Mr. Tilford, a real gumboil, whose ways were mysterious to Berkeley. Sometimes he treated the animals cruelly, or taunted them; he saw them not as pets but profit. Never-theless, no vandals, or thieves, had ever brought trouble through the doors or windows of Tilford's Pet Shoppe, and Berkeley, confident of his power but never flaunting it, faithful to his master though he didn't deserve it, was cer-tain that none ever would.

At closing time, Mr. Tilford, who lived alone, as most cruel men do, al-ways checked the cages, left a beggarly pinch of food for all the animals, and a single biscuit for Berkeley. The watchdog always hoped for a pat on his head, or for Tilford to play with him, some sign of approval to let him know he was appreciated, but such as this never came. Mr. Tilford had thick glasses and a thin voice, was stubborn, hot-tempered, a drunkard and a loner who, sliding toward senility, sometimes put his shoes in the refrigerator, and once — Berkeley winced at the memory — put a Persian he couldn't sell in the Mix Master during one of his binges. Mainly, the owner drank and watched televi-sion, which was something else Berkeley couldn't understand. More than once he'd mistaken gunfire on screen for the real thing (a natural error, since no one told him violence was entertainment for some), howled loud enough to bring down the house, and Tilford booted him outside. Soon enough, Berkeley stopped looking for approval; he didn't bother to get up from biting fleas behind the counter when he heard the door slam.

But it seemed one night too early for closing time. His instincts on this had never been wrong before. He trotted back to the darkened storeroom; then his mouth snapped shut. His feeding bowl was as empty as he'd last left it.

"Say, Berkeley," said Monkey, whose cage was near the storeroom. "What's goin' on? Tilford didn't put out the food."

Berkeley didn't care a whole lot for Monkey, and usually he ignored him. He was downright wicked, a comedian always grabbing his groin to get a laugh, throwing feces, or fooling with the other animals, a clown who'd do anything to crack up the iguana, Frog, Parrot, and the Siamese, even if it meant aping Mr. Tilford, which he did well, though Berkeley found this par-ody frightening, like playing with fire, or literally biting the hand that fed you. But he, too, was puzzled by Tilford's abrupt departure.

"I don't know," said Berkeley. "He'll be back, I guess."

Monkey, his head through his cage, held onto the bars like a movie in-mate. "Wanna bet?"

"What're you talking about?"

"Wake *up*," said Monkey. "Tilford's sick. I seen better faces on dead guppies in the fishtank. You ever see a pulmonary embolus?" Monkey ballooned his cheeks, then started breathing hard enough to hyperventilate, rolled up both red-webbed eyes, then crashed back into his cage, howling.

Not thinking this funny at all, Berkeley padded over to the front door, gave Monkey a grim look, then curled up against the bottom rail, waiting for Tilford's car to appear. Cars of many kinds, and cars of different sizes, came and went, but that Saturday night the owner did not show. Nor the next morning, or the following night, and on the second day it was not only Monkey but every beast, bird, and fowl in the Shoppe that shook its cage or tank and howled at Berkeley for an explanation — an ear-shattering babble of tongues, squawks, trills, howls, mewling, bellows, hoots, blorting, and belly growls because Tilford had collected everything from baby alligators to zebra-striped fish, an entire federation of cultures, with each animal having its own distinct, inviolable nature (so they said), the rows and rows of counters screaming with a plurality of so many backgrounds, needs, and viewpoints that Berkeley, his head splitting, could hardly hear his own voice above the din.

"Be patient!" he said. "Believe me, he's comin' back!"

"Come *off* it," said one of three snakes. "Monkey says Tilford's *dead*. Question is, what're we gonna *do* about it?"

Berkeley looked, witheringly, toward the front door. His empty stomach gurgled like a sewer. It took a tremendous effort to untangle his thoughts. "If we can just hold on a — "

"We're *hungry*!" shouted Frog. "We'll starve before old Tilford comes back!"

Throughout this turmoil, the shouting, beating of wings, which blew feathers everywhere like confetti, and an angry slapping of fins that splashed water to the floor, Monkey simply sat quietly, taking it all in, stroking his chin as a scholar might. He waited for a space in the shouting, then pushed his head through the cage again. His voice was calm, studied, like an old-time barrister before the bar. "Berkeley? Don't get mad now, but I think it's obvious that there's only one solution."

"What?"

"Let us out," said Monkey. "Open the cages."

"No!"

"We've got a crisis situation here." Monkey sighed like one of the elderly, tired lizards, as if his solution bothered even him. "It calls for courage, radical decisons. You're in charge until Tilford gets back. That means you gotta feed us, but you can't do that, can you? Only one here with hands is *me*. See, we all have different talents, unique gifts. If you let us out, we can pool our resources. I can *open* the feed bags!"

"You can?" The watchdog swallowed.

"Uh-huh." He wiggled his fingers dexterously, then the digits on his feet. "But somebody's gotta throw the switch on this cage. I can't reach it. Dog, I'm asking you to be democratic! Keeping us locked up is fascist!"

The animals clamored for release; they took up Monkey's cry, "Self-determination!" But everything within Berkeley resisted this idea, the possibility of chaos it promised, so many different, quarrelsome creatures uncaged, set loose in a low-ceilinged Shoppe where even he had trouble finding room to turn around between the counters, pens, displays of paraphernalia, and heavy, bubbling fishtanks. The chances for mischief were incalculable, no question of that, but slow starvation was certain if he didn't let them in the storeroom. Furthermore, he didn't want to be called a fascist. It didn't seem fair, Monkey saying that, making him look bad in front of the others. It was the one charge you couldn't defend yourself against. Against his better judgment, the watchdog rose on his hindlegs and, praying this was the right thing, forced open the cage with his teeth. For a moment Monkey did not move. He drew breath loudly and stared at the open door. Cautiously, he stepped out, stood up to his full height, rubbed his bony hands together, then did a little dance and began throwing open the other cages one by one.

Berkeley cringed. "The tarantula, too?"

Monkey gave him a cold glance over one shoulder. "You should get to know him, Berkeley. Don't be a bigot."

Berkeley shrank back as Tarantula, an item ordered by a Hell's Angel who never claimed him, shambled out — not so much an insect, it seemed to Berkeley, as Pestilence on legs. ("Be fair!" he scolded himself. "He's okay, I'm okay, we're all okay.") He watched helplessly as Monkey smashed the ant farm, freed the birds, and then the entire troupe, united by the spirit of a bright, common future, slithered, hopped, crawled, bounded, flew, and clawed its way into the storeroom to feed. All except crankled, old Tortoise, whom Monkey hadn't freed, who, in fact, didn't want to be released and snapped at Monkey's fingers when he tried to open his cage. No one questioned it. Tortoise had escaped the year before, remaining at large for a week, and then he returned mysteriously on his own, his eyes strangely unfocused, as if he'd seen the end of the world, or a vision of the world to come. He hadn't spoken in a year. Hunched inside his shell, hardly eating at all, Tortoise lived in the Shoppe, but you could hardly say he was part of it, and even the watchdog was a little leery of him. Berkeley, for his part, had lost his hunger. He dragged himself, wearily, to the front door, barked frantically when a woman walked by, hoping she would stop, but after seeing the window sign, which read–CLOSED–from his side, she stepped briskly on. His tail between his legs, he went slowly back to the storeroom, hoping for the best, but what he found there was no sight for a peace-loving watchdog.

True to his word, Monkey had broken open the feed bags and boxes of food, but the animals, who had always been kept apart by Tilford, discovered as they crowded into the tiny storeroom and fell to eating that sitting down to table with creatures so different in their gastronomic inclinations took the edge off their appetites. The birds found the eating habits of the reptiles, who thought eggs were a delicacy, disgusting and drew away in horror; the reptiles, who were proud of being cold-blooded, and had an elaborate theory of beauty based on the aesthetics of scales, thought the body heat of the mammals cloying and nauseating, and refused to feed beside them, and this was fine for the mammals, who, led by Monkey, distrusted anyone odd enough to be born in an egg, and dismissed them as lowlifes on the evolutionary scale;

they were shoveling down everything — bird food, dog biscuits, and even the thin wafers reserved for the fish.

"Don't touch that!" said Berkeley. "The fish have to eat, too! They can't leave the tanks!"

Monkey, startled by the watchdog, looked at the wafers in his fist thoughtfully for a second, then crammed them into his mouth. "That's their problem."

Deep inside, Berkeley began a rumbling bark, let it build slowly, and by the time it hit the air it was a full-throated growl so frightening that Monkey jumped four, maybe five feet into the air. He threw the wafers at Berkeley. "Okay — okay, give it to 'em! But remember one thing, dog: You're a mammal, too. It's unnatural to take sides against your own kind."

Scornfully, the watchdog turned away, trembling with fury. He snuffled up the wafers in his mouth, carried them to the huge, man-sized tanks, and dropped them in amongst the sea horses, guppies, and jellyfish throbbing like hearts. Goldfish floated toward him, his voice and fins fluttering. He kept a slightly startled expression. "What the hell is going on? Where's Mr. Tilford?"

Berkeley strained to keep his voice steady. "Gone."

"For good?" asked Goldfish. "Berkeley, we heard what the others said. They'll let us starve — "

"No," he said. "I'll protect you."

Goldfish bubbled relief, then looked panicky again. "What if Tilford doesn't come back ever?"

The watchdog let his head hang. The thought seemed too terrible to consider. He said, more to console himself than Goldfish, "It's his Shoppe. He has to come back."

"But suppose he *is* dead, like Monkey says." Goldfish's unblinking, lidless eyes grabbed at Berkeley and refused to release his gaze. "Then it's our Shoppe, right?"

"Eat your dinner."

Goldfish called, "Berkeley, wait — "

But the watchdog was deeply worried now. He returned miserably to the front door. He let fly a long, plaintive howl, his head tilted back like a mountaintop wolf silhouetted by the moon in a Warner Brothers cartoon — he did look like that — his insides hurting with the thought that if Tilford was dead, or indifferent to their problems, that if no one came to rescue them, then they were dead, too. True, there was a great deal of Tilford inside Berkeley, what he remembered from his training as a pup, but this faint sense of procedure and fair play hardly seemed enough to keep order in the Shoppe, maintain the peace, and more important provide for them as the old man had. He'd never looked upon himself as a leader, preferring to attribute his distaste for decision to a rare ability to see all sides. He was no hero like Old Yeller, or the legendary Gellert, and testing his ribs with his teeth, he wondered how much weight he'd lost from worry. Ten pounds? Twenty pounds? He covered both eyes with his black paws, whimpered a little, feeling a failure of nerve, a soft white core of fear like a slug in his stomach. Then he drew breath and, with it, new determination. The owner couldn't be dead. Monkey would never convince him of that. He simply had business elsewhere. And when he returned, he would expect to find the Shoppe as he left it. Maybe even running more smoothly, like an old Swiss watch that he had wound and left ticking. When the watchdog tightened his jaws, they creaked at the hinges, but he tightened them all the same. His eyes narrowed. No evil had visited the Shoppe from outside. He'd seen to that. None, he vowed, would destroy it from within.

But he could not be everywhere at once. The corrosion grew day by day. Cracks, then fissures began to appear, it seemed to Berkeley, everywhere, and in places where he least expected them. Puddles and pyramidal plops were scattered underfoot like traps. Bacterial flies were everywhere. Then came maggots. Hamsters gnawed at electrical cords in the storeroom. Frog fell sick with a genital infection. The fish, though the gentlest of creatures, caused undertow by demanding day-and-night protection, claiming they were handicapped in the competition for food, confined to their tanks, and besides, they were from the most ancient tree; all life came from the sea, they argued, the others owed *them*.

Old blood feuds between beasts erupted, too, grudges so tired you'd have thought them long buried, but not so. The Siamese began to give Berkeley funny looks, and left the room whenever he entered. Berkeley let him be, thinking he'd come to his senses. Instead, he jumped Rabbit when Berkeley wasn't looking, the product of this assault promising a new creature — a cabbit — with jack-rabbit legs and long feline whiskers never seen in the Pet Shoppe before. Rabbit took this badly. In the beginning she sniffed a great deal, and with good reason — rape was a vicious thing — but her grief and pain got out of hand, and soon she was lost in it with no way out, like a child in a dark forest, and began organizing the females of every species to stop cohabiting with the males. Berkeley stood back, afraid to butt in because Rabbit said that it was none of his damned business and he was as bad as all the rest. He pleaded reason, his eyes burnt-out from sleeplessness, with puffy bags beneath them, and when that did no good, he pleaded restraint.

"The storeroom's half-empty," he told Monkey on the fifth day. "If we don't start rationing the food, we'll starve."

"There's always food."

Berkeley didn't like the sound of that. "Where?"

Smiling, Monkey swung his eyes to the fishtanks.

"Don't you go near those goldfish!"

Monkey stood at bay, his eyes tacked hatefully on Berkeley, who ground his teeth, possessed by the sudden, wild desire to bite him, but knowing, finally, that he had the upper hand in the Pet Shoppe, the power. In other words, bigger teeth. As much as he hated to admit it, his only advantage, if he hoped to hold the line, his only trump, if he truly wanted to keep them afloat, was the fact that he outweighed them all. They were afraid of him. Oddly enough, the real validity of his values and viewpoint rested, he realized, on his having the biggest paw. The thought fretted him. For all his idealism, truth was decided in the end by those who could be bloodiest in fang and claw. Yet and still, Monkey had an arrogance that made Berkeley weak in the knees.

"Dog," he said, scratching under one arm, "you got to sleep *some*time."

And so Berkeley did. After hours of standing guard in the storeroom, or trying to console Rabbit, who was now talking of aborting the cabbit, begging her to reconsider, or reassuring the birds, who crowded together in one corner against, they said, threatening moves by the reptiles, or splashing various medicines on Frog, whose sickness had now spread to the iguana — after all this, Berkeley did drop fitfully to sleep by the front door. He slept greedily, dreaming of better days. He twitched and woofed in his sleep, seeing himself schtupping the little French poodle down the street, and it was good, like making love to lightning, she moved so well with him; and then of his puppyhood, when his worst problems were remembering where he'd buried food from Tilford's table, or figuring out how to sneak away from his mother, who told him all dogs had cold noses because they were late coming to the Ark and had to ride next to the rail. His dream cycled on, as all dreams do, with greater and greater clarity from one chamber of vision to the next until he saw, just before waking, the final drawer of dream-work spill open on the owner's return. Splendidly dressed, wearing a bowler hat and carrying a walking stick, sober, with a gentle smile for Berkeley (Berkeley was sure), Tilford threw open the Pet Shoppe door in a blast of wind and burst of preternatural brilliance that rayed the whole room, evaporated every shadow, and brought the squabbling, the conflict of interpretations, mutations, and internecine battles to a halt. No one dared move. They stood frozen like a fish in ice, or a bird caught in the crosswinds, the colorless light behind the owner so blinding it obliterated their outlines, blurred their precious differences, as if each were a rill of the same ancient light somehow imprisoned in form, with being-formed itself the most preposterous of conditions, outrageous, when you thought it through, because it occasioned suffering, meant separation from other forms, and the illusion of identity, but even this ended like a dream within the watchdog's dream, and only he and the owner remained. Reaching down, he stroked Berkeley's head. And at last he said, like God whispering to Samuel: *Well done.* It was all Berkeley had ever wanted. He woofed again, snoring like a sow, and scratched in his sleep; he heard the owner whisper *begun,* which was a pretty strange thing for him to say, even for Tilford, even in a dream. His ears strained forward; *begun,* Tilford said again. And for an instant Berkeley thought he had the tense wrong, intending to say, "Now we can begin," or something prophetically appropriate like that, but suddenly he was awake, and Parrot was flapping his wings and shouting into Berkeley's ear.

"The gun," said Parrot. "Monkey has it."

Berkeley's eyes, still phlegmed by sleep, blearily panned the counter. The room was swimming, full of smoke from a fire in the storeroom. He was short of wind. And, worse, he'd forgotten about the gun, a Smith and Wesson, that Tilford had bought after pet shop owners in Seattle were struck by thieves who specialized in stealing exotic birds. Monkey had it now. Berkeley's water ran down his legs. He'd propped the pistol between the cash register and a display of plastic dog collars, and his wide, yellow grin was frighteningly like that of a general Congress has just given the go-ahead to on a scorched-earth policy.

"Get it!" said Parrot. "You promised to protect us, Berkeley!"

For a few fibrous seconds he stood trembling paw-deep in dung, the odor of decay burning his lungs, but he couldn't come full awake, and still he felt himself to be on the fringe of a dream, his hair moist because dreaming of the French poodle had made him sweat. But the pistol . . . There was no power balance now. He'd been outplayed. No hope unless he took it away. Circling the counter, head low and growling, or trying to work up a decent growl, Berkeley crept to the cash register, his chest pounding, bunched his legs to leap, then sprang, pretending the black explosion of flame and smoke was like television gunfire, though it ripped skin right off his ribs, sent teeth flying down his throat, and blew him back like an empty pelt against Tortoise's cage. He lay still. Now he felt nothing in his legs. Purple blood like that deepest in the body cascaded to the floor from his side, rushing out with each heartbeat, and he lay twitching a little, only seeing now that he'd slept too long. Flames licked along the floor. Fish floated belly up in a dark, unplugged fishtank. The females had torn Siamese to pieces. Speckled lizards were busy sucking baby canaries from their eggs. And in the holy ruin of the Pet Shoppe the tarantula roamed free over the corpses of Frog and Iguana. Beneath him, Berkeley heard the ancient Tortoise stir, clearing a rusty throat clogged from disuse. Only he would survive the spreading fire, given his armor. His eyes burning from the smoke, the watchdog tried to explain his dream before the blaze reached them. "We could have endured, we had enough in common — for Christ's sake, we're *all* animals."

"Indeed," said Tortoise grimly, his eyes like headlights in a shell that echoed cavernously. "Indeed."

ର୍ଦ୍ଦ

JAMES JOYCE *(1882–1941) was born James Augustine Aloysius Joyce in Rathgar, a suburb of Dublin, during a turbulent era of political change in Ireland. His parents sent him at the age of six to the best Jesuit school, Clongowes Wood College, where he spent three years; but in 1891 his father was no longer able to afford the tuition, and he was withdrawn. During the period of his parents' financial decline, Joyce — a brilliant student — was educated at home and then given free tuition at Belvedere College, where he won prizes for his essays. Shortly after taking his bachelor's degree in 1902 from University College, Dublin, he left Ireland for Paris, where he attended one class at the Collège de Médecine but dropped out because he could not afford the fees. Nearly starving, he remained in Paris and wrote what he called "Epiphanies." These were notebook jottings of overheard conversations or passing observations that he later incorporated into his fiction, thinking that they illuminated in a flash the meaning of a group of apparently unrelated phenomena. In April 1903 Joyce returned to Dublin because his mother was dying. He remained in Ireland for a short time as a teacher, but the following year he went to live abroad again, disillusioned by his home country's political corruption and religious hypocrisy.*

Dubliners (1916), a group of fifteen short stories begun in 1904, was Joyce's attempt to "write a chapter of the moral history" of Ireland. He chose Dublin for the setting because that city seemed to him "the center of paralysis," but he also thought of following the book with another entitled "Provincials." As if to prove his perception

of the extent of stifling moral repression in his country, he had great difficulties getting the book published — a struggle lasting nine years. This so angered and frustrated Joyce that he never again lived in Ireland; he settled in Trieste, Zurich, and
Paris and wrote the novels that established him as one of the greatest authors of modern times: A Portrait of the Artist as a Young Man (1916), Ulysses (1922), and
Finnegan's Wake (1939).

Joyce's stories about the lives of young people, servants, politicians, and the
complacent middle class were intended to represent a broad spectrum of Dublin life —
not "a collection of tourist impressions" but a penetrating account of the spiritual
waste of his times. Today's reader finds it difficult to believe that some stories in
Dubliners could have appeared so scandalous to Joyce's publishers that at one point
the plates were destroyed at the printers. "Araby" and "The Dead" suggest the periods of adolescence and maturity which Joyce depicted in his book. As a stylist, he
blended a detached sympathy for his subject with a "scrupulous meanness" of observed detail. Instead of dramatic plots, he structured his stories around "epiphanies"
— evanescent moments that reveal "a sudden spiritual manifestation, whether in the
vulgarity of speech or of gesture or in a memorable expression of the mind itself."

RELATED COMMENTARIES: Richard Ellmann, "A Biographical Perspective on
Joyce's 'The Dead,' " page 746; Frank O'Connor, "Style and Form in Joyce's 'The
Dead,' " page 780.

JAMES JOYCE

Araby   1916

North Richmond Street, being blind, was a quiet street except at the
hour when the Christian Brothers' School set the boys free. An uninhabited
house of two storeys stood at the blind end, detached from its neighbours in a
square ground. The other houses of the street, conscious of decent lives within
them, gazed at one another with brown imperturbable faces.

The former tenant of our house, a priest, had died in the back drawing-
room. Air, musty from having been long enclosed, hung in all the rooms, and
the waste room behind the kitchen was littered with old useless papers.
Among these I found a few paper-covered books, the pages of which were
curled and damp: The Abbot, by Walter Scott, The Devout Communicant, and The
Memoirs of Vidocq. I liked the last best because its leaves were yellow. The wild
garden behind the house contained a central apple-tree and a few straggling
bushes under one of which I found the late tenant's rusty bicycle-pump. He
had been a very charitable priest; in his will he had left all his money to institutions and the furniture of his house to his sister.

When the short days of winter came dusk fell before we had well eaten
our dinners. When we met in the street the houses had grown sombre. The
space of sky above us was the colour of ever-changing violet and towards it
the lamps of the street lifted their feeble lanterns. The cold air stung us and we
played till our bodies glowed. Our shouts echoed in the silent street. The career of our play brought us through the dark muddy lanes behind the houses

where we ran the gauntlet of the rough tribes from the cottages, to the back doors of the dark dripping gardens where odours arose from the ashpits, to the dark odorous stables where a coachman smoothed and combed the horse or shook music from the buckled harness. When we returned to the street light from the kitchen windows had filled the areas. If my uncle was seen turning the corner we hid in the shadow until we had seen him safely housed. Or if Mangan's sister came out on the doorstep to call her brother in to his tea we watched her from our shadow peer up and down the street. We waited to see whether she would remain or go in and, if she remained, we left our shadow and walked up to Mangan's steps resignedly. She was waiting for us, her figure defined by the light from the half-opened door. Her brother always teased her before he obeyed and I stood by the railings looking at her. Her dress swung as she moved her body and the soft rope of her hair tossed from side to side.

Every morning I lay on the floor in the front parlour watching her door. The blind was pulled down to within an inch of the sash so that I could not be seen. When she came out on the doorstep my heart leaped. I ran to the hall, seized my books, and followed her. I kept her brown figure always in my eye and, when we came near the point at which our ways diverged, I quickened my pace and passed her. This happened morning after morning. I had never spoken to her, except for a few casual words, and yet her name was like a summons to all my foolish blood.

Her image accompanied me even in places the most hostile to romance. On Saturday evenings when my aunt went marketing I had to go to carry some of the parcels. We walked through the flaring streets, jostled by drunken men and bargaining women, amid the curses of labourers, the shrill litanies of shop-boys who stood on guard by the barrel of pigs' cheeks, the nasal chanting of street-singers, who sang a *come-all-you* about O'Donovan Rossa,° or a ballad about the troubles in our native land. These noises converged in a single sensation of life for me: I imagined that I bore my chalice safely through a throng of foes. Her name sprang to my lips at moments in strange prayers and praises which I myself did not understand. My eyes were often full of tears (I could not tell why) and at times a flood from my heart seemed to pour itself out into my bosom. I thought little of the future. I did not know whether I would ever speak to her or not or, if I spoke to her, how I could tell her of my confused adoration. But my body was like a harp and her words and gestures were like fingers running upon the wires.

One evening I went into the back drawing-room in which the priest had died. It was a dark rainy evening and there was no sound in the house. Through one of the broken panes I heard the rain impinge upon the earth, the fine incessant needles of water playing in the sodden beds. Some distant lamp or lighted window gleamed below me. I was thankful that I could see so little.

O'Donovan Rossa: Jeremiah O'Donovan (1831–1915), born in Ross Carberry of County Cork, was nicknamed "Dynamite Rossa" for championing violent means to achieve Irish independence.

All my senses seemed to desire to veil themselves and, feeling that I was about to slip from them, I pressed the palms of my hands together until they trembled, murmuring: *"O love! O love!"* many times.

At last she spoke to me. When she addressed the first words to me I was so confused that I did not know what to answer. She asked me was I going to *Araby.* I forgot whether I answered yes or no. It would be a splendid bazaar, she said she would love to go.

"And why can't you?" I asked.

While she spoke she turned a silver bracelet round and round her wrist. She could not go, she said, because there would be a retreat that week in her convent. Her brother and two other boys were fighting for their caps and I was alone at the railings. She held one of the spikes, bowing her head towards me. The light from the lamp opposite our door caught the white curve of her neck, lit up her hair that rested there and, falling, lit up the hand upon the railing. It fell over one side of her dress and caught the white border of a petticoat, just visible as she stood at ease.

"It's well for you," she said.

"If I go," I said, "I will bring you something."

What innumerable follies laid waste my waking and sleeping thoughts after that evening! I wished to annihilate the tedious intervening days. I chafed against the work of school. At night in my bedroom and by day in the classroom her image came between me and the page I strove to read. The syllables of the word *Araby* were called to me through the silence in which my soul luxuriated and cast an Eastern enchantment over me. I asked for leave to go to the bazaar on Saturday night. My aunt was surprised and hoped it was not some Freemason affair. I answered few questions in class. I watched my master's face pass from amiability to sternness; he hoped I was not beginning to idle. I could not call my wandering thoughts together. I had hardly any patience with the serious work of life which, now that it stood between me and my desire, seemed to me child's play, ugly monotonous child's play.

On Saturday morning I reminded my uncle that I wished to go to the bazaar in the evening. He was fussing at the hallstand, looking for the hatbrush, and answered me curtly:

"Yes, boy, I know."

As he was in the hall I could not go into the front parlour and lie at the window. I left the house in bad humour and walked slowly towards the school. The air was pitilessly raw and already my heart misgave me.

When I came home to dinner my uncle had not yet been home. Still it was early. I sat staring at the clock for some time and, when its ticking began to irritate me, I left the room. I mounted the staircase and gained the upper part of the house. The high cold empty gloomy rooms liberated me and I went from room to room singing. From the front window I saw my companions playing below in the street. Their cries reached me weakened and indistinct and, leaning my forehead against the cool glass, I looked over at the dark house where she lived. I may have stood there for an hour, seeing nothing but the brown-clad figure cast by my imagination, touched discreetly by the lamplight at the curved neck, at the hand upon the railings and at the border below the dress.

When I came downstairs again I found Mrs. Mercer sitting at the fire. She was an old garrulous woman, a pawnbroker's widow, who collected used stamps for some pious purpose. I had to endure the gossip of the tea-table. The meal was prolonged beyond an hour and still my uncle did not come. Mrs. Mercer stood up to go: she was sorry she couldn't wait any longer, but it was after eight o'clock and she did not like to be out late, as the night air was bad for her. When she had gone I began to walk up and down the room, clenching my fists. My aunt said:

"I'm afraid you may put off your bazaar for this night of Our Lord."

At nine o'clock I heard my uncle's latchkey in the halldoor. I heard him talking to himself and heard the hallstand rocking when it had received the weight of his overcoat. I could interpret these signs. When he was midway through his dinner I asked him to give me the money to go to the bazaar. He had forgotten.

"The people are in bed and after their first sleep now," he said.

I did not smile. My aunt said to him energetically:

"Can't you give him the money and let him go? You've kept him late enough as it is."

My uncle said he was very sorry he had forgotten. He said he believed in the old saying: "All work and no play makes Jack a dull boy." He asked me where I was going and, when I had told him a second time he asked me did I know *The Arab's Farewell to his Steed.* When I left the kitchen he was about to recite the opening lines of the piece to my aunt.

I held a florin° tightly in my hand as I strode down Buckingham Street towards the station. The sight of the streets thronged with buyers and glaring with gas recalled to me the purpose of my journey. I took my seat in a third-class carriage of a deserted train. After an intolerable delay the train moved out of the station slowly. It crept onward among ruinous houses and over the twinkling river. At Westland Row Station a crowd of people pressed to the carriage doors; but the porters moved them back, saying that it was a special train for the bazaar. I remained alone in the bare carriage. In a few minutes the train drew up beside an improvised wooden platform. I passed out on to the road and saw by the lighted dial of a clock that it was ten minutes to ten. In front of me was a large building which displayed the magical name.

I could not find any sixpenny entrance and, fearing that the bazaar would be closed, I passed in quickly through a turnstile, handing a shilling to a weary-looking man. I found myself in a big hall girdled at half its height by a gallery. Nearly all the stalls were closed and the greater part of the hall was in darkness. I recognised a silence like that which pervades a church after a service. I walked into the centre of the bazaar timidly. A few people were gathered about the stalls which were still open. Before a curtain, over which the words *Café Chantant* were written in coloured lamps, two men were counting money on a salver. I listened to the fall of the coins.

---

florin: A silver coin worth two shillings.

Remembering with difficulty why I had come I went over to one of the stalls and examined porcelain vases and flowered tea-sets. At the door of the stall a young lady was talking and laughing with two young gentlemen. I remarked their English accents and listened vaguely to their conversation.

"O, I never said such a thing!"

"O, but you did!"

"O, but I didn't!"

"Didn't she say that?"

"Yes. I heard her."

"O, there's a . . . fib!"

Observing me the young lady came over and asked me did I wish to buy anything. The tone of her voice was not encouraging; she seemed to have spoken to me out of a sense of duty. I looked humbly at the great jars that stood like eastern guards at either side of the dark entrance to the stall and murmured:

"No, thank you."

The young lady changed the position of one of the vases and went back to the two young men. They began to talk of the same subject. Once or twice the young lady glanced at me over her shoulder.

I lingered before her stall, though I knew my stay was useless, to make my interest in her wares seem the more real. Then I turned away slowly and walked down the middle of the bazaar. I allowed the two pennies to fall against the sixpence in my pocket. I heard a voice call from one end of the gallery that the light was out. The upper part of the hall was now completely dark.

Gazing up into the darkness I saw myself as a creature driven and derided by vanity; and my eyes burned with anguish and anger.

JAMES JOYCE

The Dead   1916

Lily, the caretaker's daughter, was literally run off her feet. Hardly had she brought one gentleman into the little pantry behind the office on the ground floor and helped him off with his overcoat than the wheezy hall-door bell clanged again and she had to scamper along the bare hallway to let in another guest. It was well for her she had not to attend to the ladies also. But Miss Kate and Miss Julia had thought of that and had converted the bathroom upstairs into a ladies' dressing-room. Miss Kate and Miss Julia were there, gossiping and laughing and fussing, walking after each other to the head of the stairs, peering down over the banisters and calling down to Lily to ask her who had come.

It was always a great affair, the Misses Morkan's annual dance. Everybody who knew them came to it, members of the family, old friends of the family, the members of Julia's choir, any of Kate's pupils that were grown up enough and even some of Mary Jane's pupils too. Never once had it fallen flat.

For years and years it had gone off in splendid style as long as anyone could remember; ever since Kate and Julia, after the death of their brother Pat, had left the house in Stoney Batter and taken Mary Jane, their only niece, to live with them in the dark gaunt house on Usher's Island, the upper part of which they had rented from Mr Fulham, the corn-factor on the ground floor. That was a good thirty years ago if it was a day. Mary Jane, who was then a little girl in short clothes, was now the main prop of the household for she had the organ in Haddington Road. She had been through the Academy and gave a pupils' concert every year in the upper room of the Antient Concert Rooms. Many of her pupils belonged to better-class families on the Kingstown and Dalkey line. Old as they were, her aunts also did their share. Julia, though she was quite grey, was still the leading soprano in Adam and Eve's, and Kate, being too feeble to go about much, gave music lessons to beginners on the old square piano in the back room. Lily, the caretaker's daughter, did housemaid's work for them. Though their life was modest they believed in eating well; the best of everything: diamond-bone sirloins, three-shilling tea and the best bottled stout. But Lily seldom made a mistake in the orders so that she got on well with her three mistresses. They were fussy, that was all. But the only thing they would not stand was back answers.

Of course they had good reason to be fussy on such a night. And then it was long after ten o'clock and yet there was no sign of Gabriel and his wife. Besides they were dreadfully afraid that Freddy Malins might turn up screwed. They would not wish for worlds that any of Mary Jane's pupils should see him under the influence; and when he was like that it was sometimes very hard to manage him. Freddy Malins always came late but they wondered what could be keeping Gabriel: and that was what brought them every two minutes to the banisters to ask Lily had Gabriel or Freddy come.

— O, Mr Conroy, said Lily to Gabriel when she opened the door for him, Miss Kate and Miss Julia thought you were never coming. Good-night, Mrs Conroy.

— I'll engage they did, said Gabriel, but they forget that my wife here takes three mortal hours to dress herself.

He stood on the mat, scraping the snow from his goloshes, while Lily led his wife to the foot of the stairs and called out:

— Miss Kate, here's Mrs Conroy.

Kate and Julia came toddling down the dark stairs at once. Both of them kissed Gabriel's wife, said she must be perished alive and asked was Gabriel with her.

— Here I am as right as the mail, Aunt Kate! Go on up. I'll follow, called out Gabriel from the dark.

He continued scraping his feet vigorously while the three women went upstairs, laughing, to the ladies' dressing-room. A light fringe of snow lay like a cape on the shoulders of his overcoat and like toecaps on the toes of his goloshes; and, as the buttons of his overcoat slipped with a squeaking noise through the snow-stiffened frieze, a cold fragrant air from out-of-doors escaped from crevices and folds.

— Is it snowing again, Mr Conroy? asked Lily.

She had preceded him into the pantry to help him off with his overcoat. Gabriel smiled at the three syllables she had given his surname and glanced at her. She was a slim, growing girl, pale in complexion and with hay-coloured hair. The gas in the pantry made her look still paler. Gabriel had known her when she was a child and used to sit on the lowest step nursing a rag doll.

— Yes, Lily, he answered, and I think we're in for a night of it.

He looked up at the pantry ceiling, which was shaking with the stamping and shuffling of feet on the floor above, listened for a moment to the piano and then glanced at the girl, who was folding his overcoat carefully at the end of a shelf.

— Tell me, Lily, he said in a friendly tone, do you still go to school?

— O no, sir, she answered. I'm done schooling this year and more.

— O, then, said Gabriel gaily, I suppose we'll be going to your wedding one of these fine days with your young man, eh?

The girl glanced back at him over her shoulder and said with great bitterness:

— The men that is now is only all palaver and what they can get out of you.

Gabriel coloured as if he felt he had made a mistake and, without looking at her, kicked off his goloshes and flicked actively with his muffler at his patent-leather shoes.

He was a stout tallish young man. The high colour of his cheeks pushed upwards even to his forehead where it scattered itself in a few formless patches of pale red; and on his hairless face there scintillated restlessly the polished lenses and the bright gilt rims of the glasses which screened his delicate and restless eyes. His glossy black hair was parted in the middle and brushed in a long curve behind his ears where it curled slightly beneath the groove left by his hat.

When he had flicked lustre into his shoes he stood up and pulled his waistcoat down more tightly on his plump body. Then he took a coin rapidly from his pocket.

— O Lily, he said, thrusting it into her hands, it's Christmas-time, isn't it? Just . . . here's a little. . . .

He walked rapidly towards the door.

— O no, sir! cried the girl, following him. Really, sir, I wouldn't take it.

— Christmas-time! Christmas-time! said Gabriel, almost trotting to the stairs and waving his hand to her in deprecation.

The girl, seeing that he had gained the stairs, called out after him:

— Well, thank you, sir.

He waited outside the drawing-room door until the waltz should finish, listening to the skirts that swept against it and to the shuffling of feet. He was still discomposed by the girl's bitter and sudden retort. It had cast a gloom over him which he tried to dispel by arranging his cuffs and the bows of his tie. Then he took from his waistcoat pocket a little paper and glanced at the headings he had made for his speech. He was undecided about the lines from Robert Browning for he feared they would be above the heads of his hearers. Some quotation that they could recognise from Shakespeare or from the

Melodies° would be better. The indelicate clacking of the men's heels and the shuffling of their soles reminded him that their grade of culture differed from his. He would only make himself ridiculous by quoting poetry to them which they could not understand. They would think that he was airing his superior education. He would fail with them just as he had failed with the girl in the pantry. He had taken up a wrong tone. His whole speech was a mistake from first to last, an utter failure.

Just then his aunts and his wife came out of the ladies' dressing-room. His aunts were two small plainly dressed old women. Aunt Julia was an inch or so the taller. Her hair, drawn low over the tops of her ears, was grey; and grey also, with darker shadows, was her large flaccid face. Though she was stout in build and stood erect her slow eyes and parted lips gave her the appearance of a woman who did not know where she was or where she was going. Aunt Kate was more vivacious. Her face, healthier than her sister's, was all puckers and creases, like a shrivelled red apple, and her hair, braided in the same old-fashioned way, had not lost its ripe nut colour.

They both kissed Gabriel frankly. He was their favourite nephew, the son of their dead elder sister, Ellen, who had married T. J. Conroy of the Port and Docks.

— Gretta tells me you're not going to take a cab back to Monkstown to-night, Gabriel, said Aunt Kate.

— No, said Gabriel, turning to his wife, we had quite enough of that last year, hadn't we? Don't you remember, Aunt Kate, what a cold Gretta got out of it? Cab windows rattling all the way, and the east wind blowing in after we passed Merrion. Very jolly it was. Gretta caught a dreadful cold.

Aunt Kate frowned severely and nodded her head at every word.

— Quite right, Gabriel, quite right, she said. You can't be too careful.

— But as for Gretta there, said Gabriel, she'd walk home in the snow if she were let.

Mrs Conroy laughed.

— Don't mind him, Aunt Kate, she said. He's really an awful bother, what with green shades for Tom's eyes at night and making him do the dumb-bells, and forcing Eva to eat the stirabout. The poor child! And she simply hates the sight of it! . . . O, but you'll never guess what he makes me wear now!

She broke out into a peal of laughter and glanced at her husband, whose admiring and happy eyes had been wandering from her dress to her face and hair. The two aunts laughed heartily too, for Gabriel's solicitude was a standing joke with them.

— Goloshes! said Mrs Conroy. That's the latest. Whenever it's wet underfoot I must put on my goloshes. To-night even he wanted me to put them on, but I wouldn't. The next thing he'll buy me will be a diving suit.

Gabriel laughed nervously and patted his tie reassuringly while Aunt Kate nearly doubled herself, so heartily did she enjoy the joke. The smile soon

---

the Melodies: *Irish Melodies* is a collection of poems by Thomas Moore (1779–1852) that generated goodwill and support for Irish nationalists.

faded from Aunt Julia's face and her mirthless eyes were directed towards her nephew's face. After a pause she asked:

— And what are goloshes, Gabriel?

— Goloshes, Julia! exclaimed her sister. Goodness me, don't you know what goloshes are? You wear them over your ... over your boots, Gretta, isn't it?

— Yes, said Mrs Conroy. Guttapercha things. We both have a pair now. Gabriel says everyone wears them on the continent.

— O, on the continent, murmured Aunt Julia, nodding her head slowly.

Gabriel knitted his brows and said, as if he were slightly angered:

— It's nothing very wonderful but Gretta thinks it very funny because she says the word reminds her of Christy Minstrels.

— But tell me, Gabriel, said Aunt Kate, with brisk tact. Of course, you've seen about the room. Gretta was saying ...

— O, the room is all right, replied Gabriel. I've taken one in the Gresham.

— To be sure, said Aunt Kate, by far the best thing to do. And the children, Gretta, you're not anxious about them?

— O, for one night, said Mrs Conroy. Besides, Bessie will look after them.

— To be sure, said Aunt Kate again. What a comfort it is to have a girl like that, one you can depend on! There's that Lily, I'm sure I don't know what has come over her lately. She's not the girl she was at all.

Gabriel was about to ask his aunt some questions on this point but she broke off suddenly to gaze after her sister who had wandered down the stairs and was craning her neck over the banisters.

— Now, I ask you, she said, almost testily, where is Julia going? Julia! Julia! Where are you going?

Julia, who had gone halfway down one flight, came back and announced blandly:

— Here's Freddy.

At the same moment a clapping of hands and a final flourish of the pianist told that the waltz had ended. The drawing-room door was opened from within and some couples came out. Aunt Kate drew Gabriel aside hurriedly and whispered into his ear:

— Slip down, Gabriel, like a good fellow and see if he's all right, and don't let him up if he's screwed. I'm sure he's screwed. I'm sure he is.

Gabriel went to the stairs and listened over the banisters. He could hear two persons talking in the pantry. Then he recognised Freddy Malins' laugh. He went down the stairs noisily.

— It's such a relief, said Aunt Kate to Mrs Conroy, that Gabriel is here. I always feel easier in my mind when he's here. . . . Julia, there's Miss Daly and Miss Power will take some refreshment. Thanks for your beautiful waltz, Miss Daly. It made lovely time.

A tall wizen-faced man, with a stiff grizzled moustache and swarthy skin, who was passing out with his partner said:

— And may we have some refreshment, too, Miss Morkan?

— Julia, said Aunt Kate summarily, and here's Mr Browne and Miss Furlong. Take them in, Julia, with Miss Daly and Miss Power.

— I'm the man for the ladies, said Mr Browne, pursing his lips until his moustache bristled and smiling in all his wrinkles. You know, Miss Morkan, the reason they are so fond of me is —

He did not finish his sentence, but, seeing that Aunt Kate was out of earshot, at once led the three young ladies into the back room. The middle of the room was occupied by two square tables placed end to end, and on these Aunt Julia and the caretaker were straightening and smoothing a large cloth. On the sideboard were arrayed dishes and plates, and glasses and bundles of knives and forks and spoons. The top of the closed square piano served also as a sideboard for viands and sweets. At a smaller sideboard in one corner two young men were standing, drinking hop-bitters.

Mr Browne led his charges thither and invited them all, in jest, to some ladies' punch, hot, strong and sweet. As they said they never took anything strong he opened three bottles of lemonade for them. Then he asked one of the young men to move aside, and, taking hold of the decanter, filled out for himself a goodly measure of whisky. The young men eyed him respectfully while he took a trial sip.

— God help me, he said, smiling, it's the doctor's orders.

His wizened face broke into a broader smile, and the three young ladies laughed in musical echo to his pleasantry, swaying their bodies to and fro, with nervous jerks of their shoulders. The boldest said:

— O, now, Mr Browne, I'm sure the doctor never ordered anything of the kind.

Mr Browne took another sip of his whisky and said, with sidling mimicry:

— Well, you see, I'm like the famous Mrs Cassidy, who is reported to have said: *Now, Mary Grimes, if I don't take it, make me take it, for I feel I want it.*

His hot face had leaned forward a little too confidentially and he had assumed a very low Dublin accent so that the young ladies, with one instinct, received his speech in silence. Miss Furlong, who was one of Mary Jane's pupils, asked Miss Daly what was the name of the pretty waltz she had played; and Mr Browne, seeing that he was ignored, turned promptly to the two young men who were more appreciative.

A red-faced young woman, dressed in pansy, came into the room, excitedly clapping her hands and crying:

— Quadrilles! Quadrilles!

Close on her heels came Aunt Kate, crying:

— Two gentlemen and three ladies, Mary Jane!

— O, here's Mr Bergin and Mr Kerrigan, said Mary Jane. Mr Kerrigan, will you take Miss Power? Miss Furlong, may I get you a partner, Mr Bergin. O, that'll just do now.

— Three ladies, Mary Jane, said Aunt Kate.

The two young gentlemen asked the ladies if they might have the pleasure, and Mary Jane turned to Miss Daly.

— O, Miss Daly, you're really awfully good, after playing for the last two dances, but really we're so short of ladies to-night.

— I don't mind in the least, Miss Morkan.

— But I've a nice partner for you, Mr Bartell D'Arcy, the tenor. I'll get him to sing later on. All Dublin is raving about him.

— Lovely voice, lovely voice! said Aunt Kate.

As the piano had twice begun the prelude to the first figure Mary Jane led her recruits quickly from the room. They had hardly gone when Aunt Julia wandered slowly into the room, looking behind her at something.

— What is the matter, Julia? asked Aunt Kate anxiously. Who is it?

Julia, who was carrying in a column of table-napkins, turned to her sister and said, simply, as if the question had surprised her:

— It's only Freddy, Kate, and Gabriel with him.

In fact right behind her Gabriel could be seen piloting Freddy Malins across the landing. The latter, a young man of about forty, was of Gabriel's size and build, with very round shoulders. His face was fleshy and pallid, touched with colour only at the thick hanging lobes of his ears and at the wide wings of his nose. He had coarse features, a blunt nose, a convex and receding brow, tumid and protruded lips. His heavy-lidded eyes and the disorder of his scanty hair made him look sleepy. He was laughing heartily in a high key at a story which he had been telling Gabriel on the stairs and at the same time rubbing the knuckles of his left fist backwards and forwards into his left eye.

— Good-evening, Freddy, said Aunt Julia.

Freddy Malins bade the Misses Morkan good-evening in what seemed an offhand fashion by reason of the habitual catch in his voice and then, seeing that Mr Browne was grinning at him from the sideboard, crossed the room on rather shaky legs and began to repeat in an undertone the story he had just told to Gabriel.

— He's not so bad, is he? said Aunt Kate to Gabriel.

Gabriel's brows were dark but he raised them quickly and answered:

— O no, hardly noticeable.

— Now, isn't he a terrible fellow! she said. And his poor mother made him take the pledge on New Year's Eve. But come on, Gabriel, into the drawing-room.

Before leaving the room with Gabriel she signalled to Mr Browne by frowning and shaking her forefinger in warning to and fro. Mr Browne nodded in answer and, when she had gone, said to Freddy Malins:

— Now, then, Teddy, I'm going to fill you out a good glass of lemonade just to buck you up.

Freddy Malins, who was nearing the climax of his story, waved the offer aside impatiently but Mr Browne, having first called Freddy Malins' attention to a disarray in his dress, filled out and handed him a full glass of lemonade. Freddy Malins' left hand accepted the glass mechanically, his right hand being engaged in the mechanical readjustment of his dress. Mr Browne, whose face was once more wrinkling with mirth, poured out for himself a glass of whisky while Freddy Malins exploded, before he had well reached the climax of his story, in a kink of high-pitched bronchitic laughter and, setting down his un-tasted and overflowing glass, began to rub the knuckles of his left fist back-wards and forwards into his left eye, repeating words of his last phrase as well as his fit of laughter would allow him.

Gabriel could not listen while Mary Jane was playing her Academy piece, full of runs and difficult passages, to the hushed drawing-room. He liked music but the piece she was playing had no melody for him and he doubted whether it had any melody for the other listeners, though they had begged Mary Jane to play something. Four young men, who had come from the refreshment-room to stand in the doorway at the sound of the piano, had gone away quietly in couples after a few minutes. The only persons who seemed to follow the music were Mary Jane herself, her hands racing along the key-board or lifted from it at the pauses like those of a priestess in mo-mentary imprecation, and Aunt Kate standing at her elbow to turn the page.

Gabriel's eyes, irritated by the floor, which glittered with beeswax under the heavy chandelier, wandered to the wall above the piano. A picture of the balcony scene in *Romeo and Juliet* hung there and beside it was a picture of the two murdered princes in the Tower which Aunt Julia had worked in red, blue and brown wools when she was a girl. Probably in the school they had gone to as girls that kind of work had been taught, for one year his mother had worked for him as a birthday present a waistcoat of purple tabinet, with little foxes' heads upon it, lined with brown satin and having round mulberry but-tons. It was strange that his mother had had no musical talent though Aunt Kate used to call her the brains carrier of the Morkan family. Both she and Ju-lia had always seemed a little proud of their serious and matronly sister. Her photograph stood before the pierglass. She held an open book on her knees and was pointing out something in it to Constantine who, dressed in a man-o'-war suit, lay at her feet. It was she who had chosen the names for her sons for she was very sensible of the dignity of family life. Thanks to her, Constan-tine was now senior curate in Balbriggan and, thanks to her, Gabriel himself had taken his degree in the Royal University. A shadow passed over his face as he remembered her sullen opposition to his marriage. Some slighting phrases she had used still rankled in his memory; she had once spoken of Gretta as being country cute and that was not true of Gretta at all. It was Gretta who had nursed her during all her last long illness in their house at Monkstown.

He knew that Mary Jane must be near the end of her piece for she was playing again the opening melody with runs of scales after every bar and while he waited for the end the resentment died down in his heart. The piece ended with a trill of octaves in the treble and a final deep octave in the bass. Great applause greeted Mary Jane as, blushing and rolling up her music ner-vously, she escaped from the room. The most vigorous clapping came from the four young men in the doorway who had gone away to the refreshment-room at the beginning of the piece but had come back when the piano had stopped.

Lancers were arranged. Gabriel found himself partnered with Miss Ivors. She was a frank-mannered talkative young lady, with a freckled face and prominent brown eyes. She did not wear a low-cut bodice and the large brooch which was fixed in the front of her collar bore on it an Irish device.

When they had taken their places she said abruptly:

— I have a crow to pluck with you.

— With me? said Gabriel.

She nodded her head gravely.

— What is it? asked Gabriel, smiling at her solemn manner.

— Who is G.C.? answered Miss Ivors, turning her eyes upon him.

Gabriel coloured and was about to knit his brows, as if he did not understand, when she said bluntly:

— O, innocent Amy! I have found out that you write for *The Daily Express.* Now, aren't you ashamed of yourself?

— Why should I be ashamed of myself? asked Gabriel, blinking his eyes and trying to smile.

— Well, I'm ashamed of you, said Miss Ivors frankly. To say you'd write for a rag like that. I didn't think you were a West Briton.

A look of perplexity appeared on Gabriel's face. It was true that he wrote a literary column every Wednesday in *The Daily Express,* for which he was paid fifteen shillings. But that did not make him a West Briton surely. The books he received for review were almost more welcome than the paltry cheque. He loved to feel the covers and turn over the pages of newly printed books. Nearly every day when his teaching in the college was ended he used to wander down the quays to the second-hand booksellers, to Hickey's on Bachelor's Walk, to Webb's or Massey's on Aston's Quay, or to O'Clohissey's in the by-street. He did not know how to meet her charge. He wanted to say that literature was above politics. But they were friends of many years' standing and their careers had been parallel, first at the University and then as teachers: he could not risk a grandiose phrase with her. He continued blinking his eyes and trying to smile and murmured lamely that he saw nothing political in writing reviews of books.

When their turn to cross had come he was still perplexed and inattentive. Miss Ivors promptly took his hand in a warm grasp and said in a soft friendly tone:

— Of course, I was only joking. Come, we cross now.

When they were together again she spoke of the University question and Gabriel felt more at ease. A friend of hers had shown her his review of Browning's poems. That was how she had found out the secret: but she liked the review immensely. Then she said suddenly:

— O, Mr Conroy, will you come for an excursion to the Aran Isles this summer? We're going to stay there a whole month. It will be splendid out in the Atlantic. You ought to come. Mr Clancy is coming, and Mr Kilkelly and Kathleen Kearney. It would be splendid for Gretta too if she'd come. She's from Connacht, isn't she?

— Her people are, said Gabriel shortly.

— But you will come, won't you? said Miss Ivors, laying her warm hand eagerly on his arm.

— The fact is, said Gabriel, I have already arranged to go —

— Go where? asked Miss Ivors.

— Well, you know, every year I go for a cycling tour with some fellows and so —

— But where? asked Miss Ivors.

— Well, we usually go to France or Belgium or perhaps Germany, said Gabriel awkwardly.

— And why do you go to France and Belgium, said Miss Ivors, instead of visiting your own land?

— Well, said Gabriel, it's partly to keep in touch with the languages and partly for a change.

— And haven't you your own language to keep in touch with — Irish? asked Miss Ivors.

— Well, said Gabriel, if it comes to that, you know, Irish is not my language.

Their neighbours had turned to listen to the cross-examination. Gabriel glanced right and left nervously and tried to keep his good humour under the ordeal which was making a blush invade his forehead.

— And haven't you your own land to visit, continued Miss Ivors, that you know nothing of, your own people, and your own country?

— O, to tell you the truth, retorted Gabriel suddenly, I'm sick of my own country, sick of it!

— Why? asked Miss Ivors.

Gabriel did not answer for his retort had heated him.

— Why? repeated Miss Ivors.

They had to go visiting together and, as he had not answered her, Miss Ivors said warmly:

— Of course, you've no answer.

Gabriel tried to cover his agitation by taking part in the dance with great energy. He avoided her eyes for he had seen a sour expression on her face. But when they met in the long chain he was surprised to feel his hand firmly pressed. She looked at him from under her brows for a moment quizzically until he smiled. Then, just as the chain was about to start again, she stood on tiptoe and whispered into his ear:

— West Briton!

When the lancers were over Gabriel went away to a remote corner of the room where Freddy Malins' mother was sitting. She was a stout feeble old woman with white hair. Her voice had a catch in it like her son's and she stuttered slightly. She had been told that Freddy had come and that he was nearly all right. Gabriel asked her whether she had had a good crossing. She lived with her married daughter in Glasgow and came to Dublin on a visit once a year. She answered placidly that she had had a beautiful crossing and that the captain had been most attentive to her. She spoke also of the beautiful house her daughter kept in Glasgow, and of all the nice friends they had there. While her tongue rambled on Gabriel tried to banish from his mind all memory of the unpleasant incident with Miss Ivors. Of course the girl or woman, or whatever she was, was an enthusiast but there was a time for all things. Perhaps he ought not to have answered her like that. But she had no right to call him a West Briton before people, even in joke. She had tried to make him ridiculous before people, heckling him and staring at him with her rabbit's eyes.

He saw his wife making her way towards him through the waltzing couples. When she reached him she said into his ear:

— Gabriel, Aunt Kate wants to know won't you carve the goose as usual. Miss Daly will carve the ham and I'll do the pudding.

— All right, said Gabriel.

— She's sending in the younger ones first as soon as this waltz is over so that we'll have the tables to ourselves.

— Were you dancing? asked Gabriel.

— Of course I was. Didn't you see me? What words had you with Molly Ivors?

— No words. Why? Did she say so?

— Something like that. I'm trying to get that Mr D'Arcy to sing. He's full of conceit, I think.

— There were no words, said Gabriel moodily, only she wanted me to go for a trip to the west of Ireland and I said I wouldn't.

His wife clasped her hands excitedly and gave a little jump.

— O, do go, Gabriel, she cried. I'd love to see Galway again.

— You can go if you like, said Gabriel coldly.

She looked at him for a moment, then turned to Mrs Malins and said:

— There's a nice husband for you, Mrs Malins.

While she was threading her way back across the room Mrs Malins, without adverting to the interruption, went on to tell Gabriel what beautiful places there were in Scotland and beautiful scenery. Her son-in-law brought them every year to the lakes and they used to go fishing. Her son-in-law was a splendid fisher. One day he caught a fish, a beautiful big big fish, and the man in the hotel boiled it for their dinner.

Gabriel hardly heard what she said. Now that supper was coming near he began to think again about his speech and about the quotation. When he saw Freddy Malins coming across the room to visit his mother Gabriel left the chair free for him and retired into the embrasure of the window. The room had already cleared and from the back room came the clatter of plates and knives. Those who still remained in the drawing-room seemed tired of dancing and were conversing quietly in little groups. Gabriel's warm trembling fingers tapped the cold pane of the window. How cool it must be outside! How pleasant it would be to walk out alone, first along by the river and then through the park! The snow would be lying on the branches of the trees and forming a bright cap on the top of the Wellington Monument. How much more pleasant it would be there than at the supper-table!

He ran over the headings of his speech: Irish hospitality, sad memories, the Three Graces, Paris, the quotation from Browning. He repeated to himself a phrase he had written in his review: *One feels that one is listening to a thought-tormented music.* Miss Ivors had praised the review. Was she sincere? Had she really any life of her own behind all her propagandism? There had never been any ill-feeling between them until that night. It unnerved him to think that she would be at the supper-table, looking up at him while he spoke with her critical quizzing eyes. Perhaps she would not be sorry to see him fail in his speech. An idea came into his mind and gave him courage. He would say, alluding to Aunt Kate and Aunt Julia: *Ladies and Gentlemen, the generation which is now on the wane among us may have had its faults but for my part I think it had certain qualities of hospitality, of humour, of humanity, which the new and very serious and hypereducated generation that is growing up around us seems to me to lack.* Very good: that was one for Miss Ivors. What did he care that his aunts were only two ignorant old women?

A murmur in the room attracted his attention. Mr Browne was advancing from the door, gallantly escorting Aunt Julia, who leaned upon his arm, smiling and hanging her head. An irregular musketry of applause escorted her also as far as the piano and then, as Mary Jane seated herself on the stool, and Aunt Julia, no longer smiling, half turned so as to pitch her voice fairly into the room, gradually ceased. Gabriel recognised the prelude. It was that of an old song of Aunt Julia's — *Arrayed for the Bridal.* Her voice, strong and clear in tone, attacked with great spirit the runs which embellish the air and though she sang very rapidly she did not miss even the smallest of the grace notes. To follow the voice, without looking at the singer's face, was to feel and share the excitement of swift and secure flight. Gabriel applauded loudly with all the others at the close of the song and loud applause was borne in from the invisible supper-table. It sounded so genuine that a little colour struggled into Aunt Julia's face as she bent to replace in the music-stand the old leather-bound song-book that had her initials on the cover. Freddy Malins, who had listened with his head perched sideways to hear her better, was still applauding when everyone else had ceased and talking animatedly to his mother who nodded her head gravely and slowly in acquiescence. At last, when he could clap no more, he stood up suddenly and hurried across the room to Aunt Julia whose hand he seized and held in both his hands, shaking it when words failed him or the catch in his voice proved too much for him.

— I was just telling my mother, he said, I never heard you sing so well, never. No, I never heard your voice so good as it is to-night. Now! Would you believe that now? That's the truth. Upon my word and honour that's the truth. I never heard your voice sound so fresh and so . . . so clear and fresh, never.

Aunt Julia smiled broadly and murmured something about compliments as she released her hand from his grasp. Mr Browne extended his open hand towards her and said to those who were near him in the manner of a showman introducing a prodigy to an audience:

— Miss Julia Morkan, my latest discovery!

He was laughing very heartily at this himself when Freddy Malins turned to him and said:

— Well, Browne, if you're serious you might make a worse discovery.

All I can say is I never heard her sing half so well as long as I am coming here. And that's the honest truth.

— Neither did I, said Mr Browne. I think her voice has greatly improved.

Aunt Julia shrugged her shoulders and said with meek pride:

— Thirty years ago I hadn't a bad voice as voices go.

— I often told Julia, said Aunt Kate emphatically, that she was simply thrown away in that choir. But she never would be said by me.

She turned as if to appeal to the good sense of the others against a refractory child while Aunt Julia gazed in front of her, a vague smile of reminiscence playing on her face.

— No, continued Aunt Kate, she wouldn't be said or led by anyone, slaving there in that choir night and day, night and day. Six o'clock on Christmas morning! And all for what?

— Well, isn't it for the honour of God, Aunt Kate? asked Mary Jane, twisting round on the piano-stool and smiling.

Aunt Kate turned fiercely on her niece and said:

— I know all about the honour of God, Mary Jane, but I think it's not at all honourable for the pope to turn out the women out of the choirs that have slaved there all their lives and put little whipper-snappers of boys over their heads. I suppose it is for the good of the Church if the pope does it. But it's not just, Mary Jane, and it's not right.

She had worked herself into a passion and would have continued in defence of her sister for it was a sore subject with her but Mary Jane, seeing that all the dancers had come back, intervened pacifically:

— Now, Aunt Kate, you're giving scandal to Mr Browne who is of the other persuasion.

Aunt Kate turned to Mr Browne, who was grinning at this allusion to his religion, and said hastily:

— O, I don't question the pope's being right. I'm only a stupid old woman and I wouldn't presume to do such a thing. But there' such a thing as common everday politeness and gratitude. And if I were in Julia's place I'd tell that Father Healy straight up to his face. . . .

— And besides, Aunt Kate, said Mary Jane, we really are all hungry and when we are hungry we are all very quarrelsome.

— And when we are thirsty we are also quarrelsome, added Mr Browne.

— So that we had better go to supper, said Mary Jane, and finish the discussion afterwards.

On the landing outside the drawing-room Gabriel found his wife and Mary Jane trying to persuade Miss Ivors to stay for supper. But Miss Ivors, who had put on her hat and was buttoning her cloak, would not stay. She did not feel in the least hungry and she had already overstayed her time.

— But only for ten minutes, Molly, said Mrs Conroy. That won't delay you.

— To take a pick itself, said Mary Jane, after all your dancing.

— I really couldn't, said Miss Ivors.

— I am afraid you didn't enjoy yourself at all, said Mary Jane hopelessly.

— Ever so much, I assure you, said Miss Ivors, but you really must let me run off now.

— But how can you get home? asked Mrs Conroy.

— O, it's only two steps up the quay.

Gabriel hesitated a moment and said:

— If you will allow me, Miss Ivors, I'll see you home if you really are obliged to go.

But Miss Ivors broke away from them.

— I won't hear of it, she cried. For goodness sake go in to your suppers and don't mind me. I'm quite well able to take care of myself.

— Well, you're the comical girl, Molly, said Mrs Conroy frankly.

— *Beannacht libh,*° cried Miss Ivors, with a laugh, as she ran down the staircase.

Mary Jane gazed after her, a moody puzzled expression on her face, while Mrs Conroy leaned over the banisters to listen for the hall-door. Gabriel asked himself was he the cause of her abrupt departure. But she did not seem to be in ill humour: she had gone away laughing. He stared blankly down the staircase.

At that moment Aunt Kate came toddling out of the supper-room, almost wringing her hands in despair.

— Where is Gabriel? she cried. Where on earth is Gabriel? There's everyone waiting in there, stage to let, and nobody to carve the goose!

— Here I am, Aunt Kate! cried Gabriel, with sudden animation, ready to carve a flock of geese, if necessary.

A fat brown goose lay at one end of the table and at the other end, on a bed of creased paper strewn with sprigs of parsley, lay a great ham, stripped of its outer skin and peppered over with crust crumbs, a neat paper frill round its shin and beside this was a round of spiced beef. Between these rival ends ran parallel lines of side-dishes: two little minsters of jelly, red and yellow; a shallow dish full of blocks of blancmange and red jam, a large green leaf-shaped dish with a stalk-shaped handle, on which lay bunches of purple raisins and peeled almonds, a companion dish on which lay a solid rectangle of Smyrna figs, a dish of custard topped with grated nutmeg, a small bowl full of chocolates and sweets wrapped in gold and silver papers and a glass vase in which stood some tall celery stalks. In the centre of the table there stood, as sentries to a fruit-stand which upheld a pyramid of oranges and American apples, two squat old-fashioned decanters of cut glass, one containing port and the other dark sherry. On the closed square piano a pudding in a huge yellow dish lay in waiting and behind it were three squads of bottles of stout and ale and minerals, drawn up according to the colours of their uniforms, the first

---

Beannacht libh: "A blessing on you" (Irish — traditional way of saying "farewell").

two black, with brown and red labels, the third and smallest squad white, with transverse green sashes.

Gabriel took his seat boldly at the head of the table and, having looked to the edge of the carver, plunged his fork firmly into the goose. He felt quite at ease now for he was an expert carver and liked nothing better than to find himself at the head of a well-laden table.

— Miss Furlong, what shall I send you? he asked. A wing or a slice of the breast?

— Just a small slice of the breast.

— Miss Higgins, what for you?

— O, anything at all, Mr Conroy.

While Gabriel and Miss Daly exchanged plates of goose and plates of ham and spiced beef Lily went from guest to guest with a dish of hot floury potatoes wrapped in a white napkin. This was Mary Jane's idea and she had also suggested apple sauce for the goose but Aunt Kate had said that plain roast goose without apple sauce had always been good enough for her and she hoped she might never eat worse. Mary Jane waited on her pupils and saw that they got the best slices and Aunt Kate and Aunt Julia opened and carried across from the piano bottles of stout and ale for the gentlemen and bottles of minerals for the ladies. There was a great deal of confusion and laughter and noise, the noise of orders and counter-orders, of knives and forks, of corks and glass-stoppers. Gabriel began to carve second helpings as soon as he had finished the first round without serving himself. Everyone protested loudly so that he compromised by taking a long draught of stout for he had found the carving hot work. Mary Jane settled down quietly to her supper but Aunt Kate and Aunt Julia were still toddling round the table, walking on each other's heels, getting in each other's way and giving each other unheeded orders. Mr Browne begged of them to sit down and eat their suppers and so did Gabriel but they said there was time enough so that, at last, Freddy Malins stood up and, capturing Aunt Kate, plumped her down on her chair amid general laughter.

When everyone had been well served Gabriel said, smiling:

— Now, if anyone wants a little more of what vulgar people call stuffing let him or her speak.

A chorus of voices invited him to begin his own supper and Lily came forward with three potatoes which she had reserved for him.

— Very well, said Gabriel amiably, as he took another preparatory draught, kindly forget my existence, ladies and gentlemen, for a few minutes.

He set to his supper and took no part in the conversation with which the table covered Lily's removal of the plates. The subject of talk was the opera company which was then at the Theatre Royal. Mr Bartell D'Arcy, the tenor, a dark-complexioned young man with a smart moustache, praised very highly the leading contralto of the company but Miss Furlong thought she had a rather vulgar style of production. Freddy Malins said there was a negro chieftain singing in the second part of the Gaiety pantomime who had one of the finest tenor voices he had ever heard.

— Have you heard him? he asked Mr Bartell D'Arcy across the table.

— No, answered Mr Bartell D'Arcy carelessly.

— Because, Freddy Malins explained, now I'd be curious to hear your opinion of him. I think he has a grand voice.

— It takes Teddy to find out the really good things, said Mr Browne familiarly to the table.

— And why couldn't he have a voice too? asked Freddy Malins sharply. Is it because he's only a black?

Nobody answered this question and Mary Jane led the table back to the legitimate opera. One of her pupils had given her a pass for *Mignon*. Of course it was very fine, she said, but it made her think of poor Georgina Burns. Mr Browne could go back farther still, to the old Italian companies that used to come to Dublin — Tietjens, Ilma de Murzka, Campanini, the great Trebelli, Giuglini, Ravelli, Aramburo. Those were the days, he said, when there was something like singing to be heard in Dublin. He told too of how the top gallery of the old Royal used to be packed night after night, of how one night an Italian tenor had sung five encores to *Let Me Like a Soldier Fall*, introducing a high C every time, and of how the gallery boys would sometimes in their enthusiasm unyoke the horses from the carriage of some great *prima donna* and pull her themselves through the streets to her hotel. Why did they never play the grand old operas now, he asked, *Dinorah, Lucrezia Borgia?* Because they could not get the voices to sing them: that was why.

— O, well, said Mr Bartell D'Arcy, I presume there are as good singers to-day as there were then.

— Where are they? asked Mr Browne defiantly.

— In London, Paris, Milan, said Mr Bartell D'Arcy warmly. I suppose Caruso, for example, is quite as good, if not better than any of the men you have mentioned.

— Maybe so, said Mr Browne. But I may tell you I doubt it strongly.

— O, I'd give anything to hear Caruso sing, said Mary Jane.

— For me, said Aunt Kate, who had been picking a bone, there was only one tenor. To please me, I mean. But I suppose none of you ever heard of him.

— Who was he, Miss Morkan? asked Mr Bartell D'Arcy politely.

— His name, said Aunt Kate, was Parkinson. I heard him when he was in his prime and I think he had then the purest tenor voice that was ever put into a man's throat.

— Strange, said Mr Bartell D'Arcy. I never even heard of him.

— Yes, yes, Miss Morkan is right, said Mr Browne. I remember hearing of old Parkinson but he's too far back for me.

— A beautiful pure sweet mellow English tenor, said Aunt Kate with enthusiasm.

Gabriel having finished, the huge pudding was transferred to the table. The clatter of forks and spoons began again. Gabriel's wife served out spoonfuls of the pudding and passed the plates down the table. Midway down they were held up by Mary Jane, who replenished them with raspberry or orange jelly or with blancmange and jam. The pudding was of Aunt Julia's making and she received praises for it from all quarters. She herself said that it was not quite brown enough.

— Well, I hope, Miss Morkan, said Mr Browne, that I'm brown enough for you because, you know, I'm all brown.

All the gentlemen, except Gabriel, ate some of the pudding out of compliment to Aunt Julia. As Gabriel never ate sweets the celery had been left for him. Freddy Malins also took a stalk of celery and ate it with his pudding. He had been told that celery was a capital thing for the blood and he was just then under the doctor's care. Mrs Malins, who had been silent all through the supper, said that her son was going down to Mount Melleray in a week or so. The table then spoke of Mount Melleray, how bracing the air was down there, how hospitable the monks were and how they never asked for a penny-piece from their guests.

— And do you mean to say, asked Mr Browne incredulously, that a chap can go down there and put up there as if it were a hotel and live on the fat of the land and then come away without paying a farthing?

— O, most people give some donation to the monastery when they leave, said Mary Jane.

— I wish we had an institution like that in our Church, said Mr Browne candidly.

He was astonished to hear that the monks never spoke, got up at two in the morning and slept in their coffins. He asked what they did it for.

— That's the rule of the order, said Aunt Kate firmly.

— Yes, but why? asked Mr Browne.

Aunt Kate repeated that it was the rule, that was all. Mr Browne still seemed not to understand. Freddy Malins explained to him, as best he could, that the monks were trying to make up for the sins committed by all the sinners in the outside world. The explanation was not very clear for Mr Browne grinned and said:

— I like that idea very much but wouldn't a comfortable spring bed do them as well as a coffin?

— The coffin, said Mary Jane, is to remind them of their last end.

As the subject had grown lugubrious it was buried in a silence of the table during which Mrs Malins could be heard saying to her neighbour in an indistinct undertone:

— They are very good men, the monks, very pious men.

The raisins and almonds and figs and apples and oranges and chocolates and sweets were now passed about the table and Aunt Julia invited all the guests to have either port or sherry. At first Mr Bartell D'Arcy refused to take either but one of his neighbours nudged him and whispered something to him upon which he allowed his glass to be filled. Gradually as the last glasses were being filled the conversation ceased. A pause followed, broken only by the noise of the wine and by unsettlings of chairs. The Misses Morkan, all three, looked down at the tablecloth. Someone coughed once or twice and then a few gentlemen patted the table gently as a signal for silence. The silence came and Gabriel pushed back his chair and stood up.

The patting at once grew louder in encouragement and then ceased altogether. Gabriel leaned his ten trembling fingers on the tablecloth and smiled nervously at the company. Meeting a row of upturned faces he raised his eyes to the chandelier. The piano was playing a waltz tune and he could hear the skirts sweeping against the drawing-room door. People, perhaps, were standing in the snow on the quay outside, gazing up at the lighted windows and listening to the waltz music. The air was pure there. In the distance lay the park where the trees were weighted with snow. The Wellington Monument wore a gleaming cap of snow that flashed westward over the white field of Fifteen Acres.

He began:

— Ladies and Gentlemen.

— It has fallen to my lot this evening, as in years past, to perform a very pleasing task but a task for which I am afraid my poor powers as a speaker are all too inadequate.

— No, no! said Mr Browne.

— But, however that may be, I can only ask you to-night to take the will for the deed and to lend me your attention for a few moments while I endeavour to express to you in words what my feelings are on this occasion.

— Ladies and Gentlemen. It is not the first time that we have gathered together under this hospitable roof, around this hospitable board. It is not the first time that we have been the recipients — or perhaps, I had better say, the victims — of the hospitality of certain good ladies.

He made a circle in the air with his arm and paused. Everyone laughed or smiled at Aunt Kate and Aunt Julia and Mary Jane who all turned crimson with pleasure. Gabriel went on more boldly:

— I feel more strongly with every recurring year that our country has no tradition which does it so much honour and which it should guard so jealously as that of its hospitality. It is a tradition that is unique as far as my experience goes (and I have visited not a few places abroad) among the modern nations. Some would say, perhaps, that with us it is rather a failing than anything to be boasted of. But granted even that, it is, to my mind, a princely failing, and one that I trust will long be cultivated among us. Of one thing, at least, I am sure. As long as this one roof shelters the good ladies aforesaid — and I wish from my heart it may do so for many and many a long year to come — the tradition of genuine warm-hearted courteous Irish hospitality, which our forefathers have handed down to us and which we in turn must hand down to our descendants, is still alive among us.

A hearty murmur of assent ran round the table. It shot through Gabriel's mind that Miss Ivors was not there and that she had gone away discourteously: and he said with confidence in himself:

— Ladies and Gentlemen.

— A new generation is growing up in our midst, a generation actuated by new ideas and new principles. It is serious and enthusiastic for these new ideas and its enthusiasm, even when it is misdirected, is, I believe, in the main sincere. But we are living in a sceptical and, if I may use the phrase, a thought-tormented age: and sometimes I fear that this new generation, educated or hypereducated as it is, will lack those qualities of humanity, of hospitality, of kindly humour which belonged to an older day. Listening tonight to the names of all those great singers of the past it seemed to me, I must confess, that we were living in a less spacious age. Those days might, without exaggeration, be called spacious days: and if they are gone beyond recall let us hope, at least, that in gatherings such as this we shall still speak of them with pride and affection, still cherish in our hearts the memory of those dead and gone great ones whose fame the world will not willingly let die.

— Hear, hear! said Mr Browne loudly.

— But yet, continued Gabriel, his voice falling into a softer inflection, there are always in gatherings such as this sadder thoughts that will recur to our minds: thoughts of the past, of youth, of changes, of absent faces that we miss here to-night. Our path through life is strewn with many such sad memories: and were we to brood upon them always we could not find the heart to go on bravely with our work among the living. We have all of us living duties and living affections which claim, and rightly claim, our strenuous endeavours.

— Therefore, I will not linger on the past. I will not let any gloomy moralising intrude upon us here to-night. Here we are gathered together for a brief moment from the bustle and rush of our everyday routine. We are met here as friends, in the spirit of good-fellowship, as colleagues, also to a certain extent, in the true spirit of *camaraderie*, and as the guests of — what shall I call them? — the Three Graces of the Dublin musical world.

The table burst into applause and laughter at this sally. Aunt Julia vainly asked each of her neighbours in turn to tell her what Gabriel had said.

— He says we are the Three Graces, Aunt Julia, said Mary Jane.

Aunt Julia did not understand but she looked up, smiling, at Gabriel, who continued in the same vein:

— Ladies and Gentlemen.

— I will not attempt to play to-night the part that Paris played on another occasion. I will not attempt to choose between them. The task would be an invidious one and one beyond my poor powers. For when I view them in turn, whether it be our chief hostess herself, whose good heart, whose too good heart, has become a byword with all who knew her, or her sister, who seems to be gifted with perennial youth and whose singing must have been a surprise and a revelation to us all to-night, or, last but not least, when I consider our youngest hostess, talented, cheerful, hard-working and the best of nieces, I confess, Ladies and Gentlemen, that I do not know to which of them I should award the prize.

Gabriel glanced down at his aunts and, seeing the large smile on Aunt Julia's face and the tears which had risen to Aunt Kate's eyes, hastened to close. He raised his glass of port gallantly, while every member of the company fingered a glass expectantly, and said loudly:

— Let us toast them all three together. Let us drink to their health, wealth, long life, happiness and prosperity and may they long continue to hold the proud and self-won position which they hold in their profession and the position of honour and affection which they hold in our hearts.

All the guests stood up, glass in hand, and, turning towards the three seated ladies, sang in unison, with Mr Browne as leader:

For they are jolly gay fellows,
For they are jolly gay fellows,
For they are jolly gay fellows,
Which nobody can deny.

Aunt Kate was making frank use of her handkerchief and even Aunt Julia seemed moved. Freddy Malins beat time with his pudding-fork and the singers turned towards one another, as if in melodious conference, while they sang, with emphasis:

Unless he tells a lie,
Unless he tells a lie.

Then, turning once more towards their hostesses, they sang:

For they are jolly gay fellows,
For they are jolly gay fellows,
For they are jolly gay fellows,
Which nobody can deny.

The acclamation which followed was taken up beyond the door of the supper-room by many of the other guests and renewed time after time, Freddy Malins acting as officer with his fork on high.

The piercing morning air came into the hall where they were standing so that Aunt Kate said:
— Close the door, somebody. Mrs Malins will get her death of cold.
— Browne is out there, Aunt Kate, said Mary Jane.
— Browne is everywhere, said Aunt Kate, lowering her voice.
Mary Jane laughed at her tone.
— Really, she said archly, he is very attentive.
— He has been laid on here like the gas, said Aunt Kate in the same tone, all during the Christmas.
She laughed herself this time good-humouredly and then added quickly:
— But tell him to come in, Mary Jane, and close the door. I hope to goodness he didn't hear me.
At that moment the hall-door was opened and Mr Browne came in from the doorstep, laughing as if his heart would break. He was dressed in a long green overcoat with mock astrakhan cuffs and collar and wore on his head an oval fur cap. He pointed down the snow-covered quay from where the sound of shrill prolonged whistling was borne in.
— Teddy will have all the cabs in Dublin out, he said.
Gabriel advanced from the little pantry behind the office, struggling into his overcoat and, looking round the hall, said:
— Gretta not down yet?

— She's getting on her things, Gabriel, said Aunt Kate.

— Who's playing up there? asked Gabriel.

— Nobody. They're all gone.

— O no, Aunt Kate, said Mary Jane. Bartell D'Arcy and Miss O'Callaghan aren't gone yet.

— Someone is strumming at the piano, anyhow, said Gabriel.

Mary Jane glanced at Gabriel and Mr Browne and said with a shiver:

— It makes me feel cold to look at you two gentlemen muffled up like that. I wouldn't like to face your journey home at this hour.

— I'd like nothing better this minute, said Mr Browne stoutly, than a rattling fine walk in the country or a fast drive with a good spanking goer between the shafts.

— We used to have a very good horse and trap at home, said Aunt Julia sadly.

— The never-to-be-forgotten Johnny, said Mary Jane, laughing.

Aunt Kate and Gabriel laughed too.

— Why, what was wonderful about Johnny? asked Mr Browne.

— The late lamented Patrick Morkan, our grandfather, that is, explained Gabriel, commonly known in his later years as the old gentleman, was a glue-boiler.

— O, now, Gabriel, said Aunt Kate, laughing, he had a starch mill.

— Well, glue or starch, said Gabriel, the old gentleman had a horse by the name of Johnny. And Johnny used to work in the old gentleman's mill, walking round and round in order to drive the mill. That was all very well; but now comes the tragic part about Johnny. One fine day the old gentleman thought he'd like to drive out with the quality to a military review in the park.

— The Lord have mercy on his soul, said Aunt Kate compassionately.

— Amen, said Gabriel. So the old gentleman, as I said, harnessed Johnny and put on his very best tall hat and his very best stock collar and drove out in grand style from his ancestral mansion somewhere near Back Lane, I think.

Everyone laughed, even Mrs Malins, at Gabriel's manner and Aunt Kate said:

— O now, Gabriel, he didn't live in Back Lane, really. Only the mill was there.

— Out from the mansion of his forefathers, continued Gabriel, he drove with Johnny. And everything went on beautifully until Johnny came in sight of King Billy's statue: and whether he fell in love with the horse King Billy sits on or whether he thought he was back again in the mill, anyhow he began to walk round the statue.

Gabriel paced in a circle round the hall in his goloshes amid the laughter of the others.

— Round and round he went, said Gabriel, and the old gentleman, who was a very pompous old gentleman, was highly indignant. *Go on, sir! What do you mean, sir? Johnny! Johnny! Most extraordinary conduct! Can't understand the horse!*

The peals of laughter which followed Gabriel's imitation of the incident were interrupted by a resounding knock at the hall-door. Mary Jane ran to open it and let in Freddy Malins. Freddy Malins, with his hat well back on his head and his shoulders humped with cold, was puffing and steaming after his exertions.

— I could only get one cab, he said.

— O, we'll find another along the quay, said Gabriel.

— Yes, said Aunt Kate. Better not keep Mrs Malins standing in the draught.

Mrs Malins was helped down the front steps by her son and Mr Browne and, after many manœuvres, hoisted into the cab. Freddy Malins clambered in after her and spent a long time settling her on the seat, Mr Browne helping him with advice. At last she was settled comfortably and Freddy Malins invited Mr Browne into the cab. There was a good deal of confused talk, and then Mr Browne got into the cab. The cabman settled his rug over his knees, and bent down for the address. The confusion grew greater and the cabman was directed differently by Freddy Malins and Mr Browne, each of whom had his head out through a window of the cab. The difficulty was to know where to drop Mr Browne along the route and Aunt Kate, Aunt Julia and Mary Jane helped the discussion from the doorstep with cross-directions and contradictions and abundance of laughter. As for Freddy Malins he was speechless with laughter. He popped his head in and out of the window every moment, to the great danger of his hat, and told his mother how the discussion was progressing till at last Mr Browne shouted to the bewildered cabman above the din of everybody's laughter:

— Do you know Trinity College?

— Yes, sir, said the cabman.

— Well, drive bang up against Trinity College gates, said Mr Browne, and then we'll tell you where to go. You understand now?

— Yes, sir, said the cabman.

— Make like a bird for Trinity College.

— Right, sir, cried the cabman.

The horse was whipped up and the cab rattled off along the quay amid a chorus of laughter and adieus.

Gabriel had not gone to the door with the others. He was in a dark part of the hall gazing up the staircase. A woman was standing near the top of the first flight, in the shadow also. He could not see her face but he could see the terracotta and salmonpink panels of her skirt which the shadow made appear black and white. It was his wife. She was leaning on the banisters, listening to something. Gabriel was surprised at her stillness and strained his ear to listen also. But he could hear little save the noise of laughter and dispute on the front steps, a few chords struck on the piano and a few notes of a man's voice singing.

He stood still in the gloom of the hall, trying to catch the air that the voice was singing and gazing up at his wife. There was grace and mystery in her attitude as if she were a symbol of something. He asked himself what is a woman standing on the stairs in the shadow, listening to distant music, a symbol of. If he were a painter he would paint her in that attitude. Her blue felt hat would show off the bronze of her hair against the darkness and the dark panels of her skirt would show off the light ones. *Distant Music* he would call the picture if he were a painter.

The hall-door closed; and Aunt Kate, Aunt Julia and Mary Jane came down the hall, still laughing.

— Well, isn't Freddy terrible? said Mary Jane. He's really terrible.

Gabriel said nothing but pointed up the stairs towards where his wife was standing. Now that the hall-door was closed the voice and the piano could be heard more clearly. Gabriel held up his hand for them to be silent. The song seemed to be in the old Irish tonality and the singer seemed uncertain both of his words and of his voice. The voice, made plaintive by distance and by the singer's hoarseness, faintly illuminated the cadence of the air with words expressing grief:

> *O, the rain falls on my heavy locks*
> *And the dew wets my skin,*
> *My babe lies cold . . .*

— O, exclaimed Mary Jane. It's Bartell D'Arcy singing and he wouldn't sing all the night. O, I'll get him to sing a song before he goes.

— O do, Mary Jane, said Aunt Kate.

Mary Jane brushed past the others and ran to the staircase but before she reached it the singing stopped and the piano was closed abruptly.

— O, what a pity! she cried. Is he coming down, Gretta?

Gabriel heard his wife answer yes and saw her come down towards them. A few steps behind her were Mr Bartell D'Arcy and Miss O'Callaghan.

— O, Mr D'Arcy, cried Mary Jane, it's downright mean of you to break off like that when we were all in raptures listening to you.

— I have been at him all the evening, said Miss O'Callaghan, and Mrs Conroy too and he told us he had a dreadful cold and couldn't sing.

— O, Mr D'Arcy, said Aunt Kate, now that was a great fib to tell.

— Can't you see that I'm as hoarse as a crow? said Mr D'Arcy roughly.

He went into the pantry hastily and put on his overcoat. The others, taken aback by his rude speech, could find nothing to say. Aunt Kate wrinkled her brows and made signs to the others to drop the subject. Mr D'Arcy stood swathing his neck carefully and frowning.

— It's the weather, said Aunt Julia, after a pause.

— Yes, everybody has colds, said Aunt Kate readily, everybody.

— They say, said Mary Jane, we haven't had snow like it for thirty years; and I read this morning in the newspapers that the snow is general all over Ireland.

— I love the look of snow, said Aunt Julia sadly.

— So do I, said Miss O'Callaghan. I think Christmas is never really Christmas unless we have the snow on the ground.

— But poor Mr D'Arcy doesn't like the snow, said Aunt Kate, smiling.

Mr D'Arcy came from the pantry, fully swathed and buttoned, and in a repentant tone told them the history of the cold. Everyone gave him advice and said it was a great pity and urged him to be very careful of his throat in the night air. Gabriel watched his wife who did not join in the conversation. She was standing right under the dusty fanlight and the flame of the gas lit up the rich bronze of her hair which he had seen her drying at the fire a few days before. She was in the same attitude and seemed unaware of the talk about her. At last she turned towards them and Gabriel saw that there was colour on her cheeks and that her eyes were shining. A sudden tide of joy went leaping out of his heart.

— Mr D'Arcy, she said, what is the name of that song you were singing?

— It's called *The Lass of Aughrim*, said Mr D'Arcy, but I couldn't remember it properly. Why? Do you know it?

— *The Lass of Aughrim*, she repeated. I couldn't think of the name.

— It's a very nice air, said Mary Jane. I'm sorry you were not in voice tonight.

— Now, Mary Jane, said Aunt Kate, don't annoy Mr D'Arcy. I won't have him annoyed.

Seeing that all were ready to start she shepherded them to the door where good-night was said:

— Well, good-night, Aunt Kate, and thanks for the pleasant evening.

— Good-night, Gabriel. Good-night, Gretta!

— Good-night, Aunt Kate, and thanks ever so much. Good-night, Aunt Julia.

— O, good-night, Gretta, I didn't see you.

— Good-night, Mr D'Arcy. Good-night, Miss O'Callaghan.

— Good-night, Miss Morkan.

— Good-night, again.

— Good-night, all. Safe home.

— Good-night. Good-night.

The morning was still dark. A dull yellow light brooded over the houses and the river; and the sky seemed to be descending. It was slushy underfoot; and only streaks and patches of snow lay on the roofs, on the parapets of the quay and on the area railings. The lamps were still burning redly in the murky air and, across the river, the palace of the Four Courts stood out menacingly against the heavy sky.

She was walking on before him with Mr Bartell D'Arcy, her shoes in a brown parcel tucked under one arm and her hands holding her skirt up from the slush. She had no longer any grace of attitude but Gabriel's eyes were still bright with happiness. The blood went bounding along his veins; and the thoughts were rioting through his brain, proud, joyful, tender, valorous.

She was walking on before him so lightly and so erect that he longed to run after her noiselessly, catch her by the shoulders and say something foolish and affectionate into her ear. She seemed to him so frail that he longed to defend her against something and then to be alone with her. Moments of their secret life together burst like stars upon his memory. A heliotrope envelope was lying beside his breakfast-cup and he was caressing it with his hand. Birds were twittering in the ivy and the sunny web of the curtain was shimmering along the floor: he could not eat for happiness. They were standing on the crowded platform and he was placing a ticket inside the warm palm of her glove. He was standing with her in the cold, looking in through a grated window at a man making bottles in a roaring furnace. It was very cold. Her face, fragrant in the cold air, was quite close to his; and suddenly she called out to the man at the furnace.

— Is the fire hot, sir?

But the man could not hear her with the noise of the furnace. It was just as well. He might have answered rudely.

A wave of yet more tender joy escaped from his heart and went coursing in warm flood along his arteries. Like the tender fires of stars moments of their life together, that no one knew of or would ever know of, broke upon and illumined his memory. He longed to recall to her those moments, to make her forget the years of their dull existence together and remember only their moments of ecstasy. For the years, he felt, had not quenched his soul or hers. Their children, his writing, her household cares had not quenched all their souls' tender fire. In one letter that he had written to her then he had said: *Why is it that words like these seem to me so dull and cold? Is it because there is no word tender enough to be your name?*

Like distant music these words that he had written years before were borne towards him from the past. He longed to be alone with her. When the others had gone away, when he and she were in their room in the hotel, then they would be alone together. He would call her softly:

— Gretta!

Perhaps she would not hear at once: she would be undressing. Then something in his voice would strike her. She would turn and look at him. . . .

At the corner of Winetavern Street they met a cab. He was glad of its rattling noise as it saved him from conversation. She was looking out of the window and seemed tired. The others spoke only a few words, pointing out some building or street. The horse galloped along wearily under the murky morning sky, dragging his old rattling box after his heels, and Gabriel was again in a cab with her, galloping to catch the boat, galloping to their honeymoon.

As the cab drove across O'Connell Bridge° Miss O'Callaghan said:

— They say you never cross O'Connell Bridge without seeing a white horse.

— I see a white man this time, said Gabriel.

— Where? asked Mr Bartell D'Arcy.

Gabriel pointed to the statue, on which lay patches of snow. Then he nodded familiarly to it and waved his hand.

— Good-night, Dan, he said gaily.

When the cab drew up before the hotel Gabriel jumped out and, in spite of Mr Bartell D'Arcy's protest, paid the driver. He gave the man a shilling over his fare. The man saluted and said:

— A prosperous New Year to you, sir.

O'Connell Bridge: The central bridge in Dublin, named after the patriot Daniel O'Connell (1775–1847) whose statue stands nearby.

— The same to you, said Gabriel cordially.

She leaned for a moment on his arm in getting out of the cab and while standing at the curbstone, bidding the others good-night. She leaned lightly on his arm, as lightly as when she had danced with him a few hours before. He had felt proud and happy then, happy that she was his, proud of her grace and wifely carriage. But now, after the kindling again of so many memories, the first touch of her body, musical and strange and perfumed, sent through him a keen pang of lust. Under cover of her silence he pressed her arm closely to his side; and, as they stood at the hotel door, he felt that they had escaped from their lives and duties, escaped from home and friends and run away together with wild and radiant hearts to a new adventure.

An old man was dozing in a great hooded chair in the hall. He lit a candle in the office and went before them to the stairs. They followed him in silence, their feet falling in soft thuds on the thickly carpeted stairs. She mounted the stairs behind the porter, her head bowed in the ascent, her frail shoulders curved as with a burden, her skirt girt tightly about her. He could have flung his arms about her hips and held her still for his arms were trembling with desire to seize her and only the stress of his nails against the palms of his hands held the wild impulse of his body in check. The porter halted on the stairs to settle his guttering candle. They halted too on the steps below him. In the silence Gabriel could hear the falling of the molten wax into the tray and the thumping of his own heart against his ribs.

The porter led them along a corridor and opened a door. Then he set his unstable candle down on a toilet-table and asked at what hour they were to be called in the morning.

— Eight, said Gabriel.

The porter pointed to the tap of the electric-light and began a muttered apology but Gabriel cut him short.

— We don't want any light. We have enough light from the street. And I say, he added, pointing to the candle, you might remove that handsome article, like a good man.

The porter took up his candle again, but slowly for he was surprised by such a novel idea. Then he mumbled good-night and went out. Gabriel shot the lock to.

A ghostly light from the street lamp lay in a long shaft from one window to the door. Gabriel threw his overcoat and hat on a couch and crossed the room towards the window. He looked down into the street in order that his emotion might calm a little. Then he turned and leaned against a chest of drawers with his back to the light. She had taken off her hat and cloak and was standing before a large swinging mirror, unhooking her waist. Gabriel paused for a few moments, watching her, and then said:

— Gretta!

She turned away from the mirror slowly and walked along the shaft of light towards him. Her face looked so serious and weary that the words would not pass Gabriel's lips. No, it was not the moment yet.

— You look tired, he said.

— I am a little, she answered.

— You don't feel ill or weak?

— No, tired: that's all.

She went on to the window and stood there, looking out. Gabriel waited again and then, fearing that diffidence was about to conquer him, he said abruptly:

— By the way, Gretta!

— What is it?

— You know that poor fellow Malins? he said quickly.

— Yes. What about him?

— Well, poor fellow, he's a decent sort of chap after all, continued Gabriel in a false voice. He gave me back that sovereign I lent him and I didn't expect it really. It's a pity he wouldn't keep away from that Browne, because he's not a bad fellow at heart.

He was trembling now with annoyance. Why did she seem so abstracted? He did not know how he could begin. Was she annoyed, too, about something? If she would only turn to him or come to him of her own accord! To take her as she was would be brutal. No, he must see some ardour in her eyes first. He longed to be master of her strange mood.

— When did you lend him the pound? she asked, after a pause.

Gabriel strove to restrain himself from breaking out into brutal language about the sottish Malins and his pound. He longed to cry to her from his soul, to crush her body against his, to overmaster her. But he said:

— O, at Christmas, when he opened that little Christmas-card shop in Henry Street.

He was in such a fever of rage and desire that he did not hear her come from the window. She stood before him for an instant, looking at him strangely. Then, suddenly raising herself on tiptoe and resting her hands lightly on his shoulders, she kissed him.

— You are a very generous person, Gabriel, she said.

Gabriel, trembling with delight at her sudden kiss and at the quaintness of her phrase, put his hands on her hair and began smoothing it back, scarcely touching it with his fingers. The washing had made it fine and brilliant. His heart was brimming over with happiness. Just when he was wishing for it she had come to him of her own accord. Perhaps her thoughts had been running with his. Perhaps she had felt the impetuous desire that was in him and then the yielding mood had come upon her. Now that she had fallen to him so easily he wondered why he had been so diffident.

He stood, holding her head between his hands. Then, slipping one arm swiftly about her body and drawing her towards him, he said softly:

— Gretta dear, what are you thinking about?

She did not answer nor yield wholly to his arm. He said again, softly:

— Tell me what it is, Gretta. I think I know what is the matter. Do I know?

She did not answer at once. Then she said in an outburst of tears:

— O, I am thinking about that song, *The Lass of Aughrim*.

She broke loose from him and ran to the bed and, throwing her arms across the bed-rail, hid her face. Gabriel stood stock-still for a moment in astonishment and then followed her. As he passed in the way of the cheval-glass he caught sight of himself in full length, his broad, well-filled shirtfront, the face whose expression always puzzled him when he saw it in a mirror and his glimmering gilt-rimmed eyeglasses. He halted a few paces from her and said:

— What about the song? Why does that make you cry?

She raised her head from her arms and dried her eyes with the back of her hand like a child. A kinder note than he had intended went into his voice.

— Why, Gretta? he asked.

— I am thinking about a person long ago who used to sing that song.

— And who was the person long ago? asked Gabriel, smiling.

— It was a person I used to know in Galway when I was living with my grandmother, she said.

The smile passed away from Gabriel's face. A dull anger began to gather again at the back of his mind and the dull fires of his lust began to glow angrily in his veins.

— Someone you were in love with? he asked ironically.

— It was a young boy I used to know, she answered, named Michael Furey. He used to sing that song, *The Lass of Aughrim*. He was very delicate.

Gabriel was silent. He did not wish her to think that he was interested in this delicate boy.

— I can see him so plainly, she said after a moment. Such eyes as he had: big dark eyes! And such an expression in them — an expression!

— O, then, you were in love with him? said Gabriel.

— I used to go out walking with him, she said, when I was in Galway.

A thought flew across Gabriel's mind.

— Perhaps that was why you wanted to go to Galway with that Ivors girl? he said coldly.

She looked at him and asked in surprise:

— What for?

Her eyes made Gabriel feel awkward. He shrugged his shoulders and said:

— How do I know? To see him perhaps.

She looked away from him along the shaft of light towards the window in silence.

— He is dead, she said at length. He died when he was only seventeen. Isn't that a terrible thing to die so young as that?

— What was he? asked Gabriel, still ironically.

— He was in the gasworks, she said.

Gabriel felt humiliated by the failure of his irony and by the evocation of this figure from the dead, a boy in the gasworks. While he had been full of memories of their secret life together, full of tenderness and joy and desire, she had been comparing him in her mind with another. A shameful consciousness of his own person assailed him. He saw himself as a ludicrous figure, acting as a pennyboy for his aunts, a nervous well-meaning sentimentalist, orating to vulgarians and idealising his own clownish lusts, the pitiable fatuous fellow he had caught a glimpse of in the mirror. Instinctively he turned his back more to the light lest she might see the shame that burned upon his forehead.

He tried to keep up his tone of cold interrogation but his voice when he spoke was humble and indifferent.

— I suppose you were in love with this Michael Furey, Gretta, he said.

— I was great with him at that time, she said.

Her voice was veiled and sad. Gabriel, feeling now how vain it would be to try to lead her whither he had purposed, caressed one of her hands and said, also sadly:

— And what did he die of so young, Gretta? Consumption, was it?

— I think he died for me, she answered.

A vague terror seized Gabriel at this answer as if, at that hour when he had hoped to triumph, some impalpable and vindictive being was coming against him, gathering forces against him in its vague world. But he shook himself free of it with an effort of reason and continued to caress her hand. He did not question her again for he felt that she would tell him of herself. Her hand was warm and moist: it did not respond to his touch but he continued to caress it just as he had caressed her first letter to him that spring morning.

— It was in the winter, she said, about the beginning of the winter when I was going to leave my grandmother's and come up here to the convent. And he was ill at the time in his lodgings in Galway and wouldn't be let out and his people in Oughterard were written to. He was in decline, they said, or something like that. I never knew rightly.

She paused for a moment and sighed.

— Poor fellow, she said. He was very fond of me and he was such a gentle boy. We used to go out together, walking, you know, Gabriel, like the way they do in the country. He was going to study singing only for his health. He had a very good voice, poor Michael Furey.

— Well; and then? asked Gabriel.

— And then when it came to the time for me to leave Galway and come up to the convent he was much worse and I wouldn't be let see him so I wrote a letter saying I was going up to Dublin and would be back in the summer and hoping he would be better then.

She paused for a moment to get her voice under control and then went on:

— Then the night before I left I was in my grandmother's house in Nuns' Island, packing up, and I heard gravel thrown up against the window. The window was so wet I couldn't see so I ran downstairs as I was and slipped out the back into the garden and there was the poor fellow at the end of the garden, shivering.

— And did you not tell him to go back? asked Gabriel.

— I implored of him to go home at once and told him he would get his death in the rain. But he said he did not want to live. I can see his eyes as well as well! He was standing at the end of the wall where there was a tree.

— And did he go home? asked Gabriel.

— Yes, he went home. And when I was only a week in the convent he died and he was buried in Oughterard where his people came from. O, the day I heard that, that he was dead!

She stopped, choking with sobs, and, overcome by emotion, flung herself face downward on the bed, sobbing in the quilt. Gabriel held her hand for a moment longer, irresolutely, and then, shy of intruding on her grief, let it fall gently and walked quietly to the window.

She was fast asleep.

Gabriel, leaning on his elbow, looked for a few moments unresentfully on her tangled hair and half-open mouth, listening to her deep-drawn breath. So she had had that romance in her life: a man had died for her sake. It hardly pained him now to think how poor a part he, her husband, had played in her life. He watched her while she slept as though he and she had never lived together as man and wife. His curious eyes rested long upon her face and on her hair: and, as he thought of what she must have been then, in that time of her first girlish beauty, a strange friendly pity for her entered his soul. He did not like to say even to himself that her face was no longer beautiful but he knew that it was no longer the face for which Michael Furey had braved death.

Perhaps she had not told him all the story. His eyes moved to the chair over which she had thrown some of her clothes. A petticoat string dangled to the floor. One boot stood upright, its limp upper fallen down: the fellow of it lay upon its side. He wondered at his riot of emotions of an hour before. From what had it proceeded? From his aunt's supper, from his own foolish speech, from the wine and dancing, the merry-making when saying good-night in the hall, the pleasure of the walk along the river in the snow. Poor Aunt Julia! She, too, would soon be a shade with the shade of Patrick Morkan and his horse. He had caught that haggard look upon her face for a moment when she was singing *Arrayed for the Bridal*. Soon, perhaps, he would be sitting in that same drawing-room, dressed in black, his silk hat on his knees. The blinds would be drawn down and Aunt Kate would be sitting beside him, crying and blowing her nose and telling him how Julia had died. He would cast about his mind for some words that might console her, and would find only lame and useless ones. Yes, yes: that would happen very soon.

The air of the room chilled his shoulders. He stretched himself cautiously along under the sheets and lay down beside his wife. One by one they were all becoming shades. Better pass boldly into that other world, in the full glory of some passion, than fade and wither dismally with age. He thought of how she who lay beside him had locked in her heart for so many years that image of her lover's eyes when he had told her that he did not wish to live.

Generous tears filled Gabriel's eyes. He had never felt like that himself towards any woman but he knew that such a feeling must be love. The tears gathered more thickly in his eyes and in the partial darkness he imagined he saw the form of a young man standing under a dripping tree. Other forms were near. His soul had approached that region where dwell the vast hosts of the dead. He was conscious of, but could not apprehend, their wayward and flickering existence. His own identity was fading out into a grey impalpable world: the solid world itself which these dead had one time reared and lived in was dissolving and dwindling.

A few light taps upon the pane made him turn to the window. It had begun to snow again. He watched sleepily the flakes, silver and dark, falling obliquely against the lamplight. The time had come for him to set out on his journey westward. Yes, the newspapers were right: snow was general all over Ireland. It was falling on every part of the dark central plain, on the treeless hills, falling softly upon the Bog of Allen and, farther westward, softly falling into the dark mutinous Shannon waves. It was falling, too, upon every part of the lonely churchyard on the hill where Michael Furey lay buried. It lay thickly drifted on the crooked crosses and headstones, on the spears of the little gate, on the barren thorns. His soul swooned slowly as he heard the snow falling faintly through the universe and faintly falling, like the descent of their last end, upon all the living and the dead.

ʊɔɿ

FRANZ KAFKA *(1883–1924) led a life whose events are simple and sad. He was born into a Jewish family in Prague, and from youth onward he feared his authoritarian father so much that he stuttered in his presence, although he spoke easily with others. In 1906 he received a doctorate in jurisprudence, and for many years he worked a tedious job as a civil service lawyer investigating claims at the state Worker's Accident Insurance Institute. He never married and lived for the most part with his parents, writing fiction at night (he was an insomniac) and publishing only a few slim volumes of stories during his lifetime.* Meditation, *a collection of sketches, appeared in 1912;* The Stoker: A Fragment *in 1913;* The Metamorphosis *in 1915;* The Judgment *in 1916;* In the Penal Colony *in 1919; and* A Country Doctor *in 1920. Only a few of his friends knew that Kafka was also at work on the great novels that were published after his death from tuberculosis:* The Trial *(1925),* The Castle *(1926), and* Amerika *(1927). (He asked his literary executor, Max Brod, to burn these works in manuscript, but Brod refused.)*

Kafka's despair with his writing, his job, his father, and his life was complete. Like Gustave Flaubert — whom he admired — he used his fiction as a "rock" to which he clung in order not to be drowned in the waves of the world around him. With typical irony, however, he saw the effort as futile: "By scribbling I run ahead of myself in order to catch myself up at the finishing post. I cannot run away from myself." In his diaries Kafka recorded his obsession with literature: "What will be my fate as a writer is very simple. My talent for portraying my dreamlike inner life has thrust all other matters into the background." Kafka created striking "parables of alienation," as his biographer Ernst Pawel has noted, but the "dreamlike" quality of his imagination is apparent in all his work.

Kafka is perhaps best known as the author of the waking nightmare "The Metamorphosis," whose remarkable first sentence is one of the most famous in short story literature. The hero of the story, Gregor Samsa (pronounced Zamza), is the son of philistine, middle-class parents in Prague, as was Kafka, and literary critics have tended to interpret the story as an autobiographical fiction, using the "monstrous insect" as a Freudian symbol that characterizes Kafka's sense of inadequacy before his demanding father. Kafka himself considered psychoanalysis "a helpless error," regarding Freud's theories as very rough pictures that do not do justice to either the details or the essence of life. Perhaps the greatest literary influence on Kafka was Flaubert; both writers used language with ironic precision and without explicit intrusion of their private sentiments. The visionary, nightmarish quality of Kafka's fiction is in striking contrast to its precise and formal style, the clarity of which intensifies the dark richness of the fantasy.

RELATED COMMENTARIES: *Jane Smiley, "Gregor: My Life as a Bug," page 798; John Updike, "Kafka and 'The Metamorphosis,' " page 804.*

FRANZ KAFKA

The Metamorphosis

1915

TRANSLATED BY WILLA MUIR AND EDWIN MUIR

I

As Gregor Samsa awoke one morning from uneasy dreams he found himself transformed in his bed into a gigantic insect. He was lying on his hard, as it were armor-plated, back and when he lifted his head a little he could see his dome-like brown belly divided into stiff arched segments on top of which the bed quilt could hardly keep in position and was about to slide off completely. His numerous legs, which were pitifully thin compared to the rest of his bulk, waved helplessly before his eyes.

What has happened to me? he thought. It was no dream. His room, a regular human bedroom, only rather too small, lay quiet between the four familiar walls. Above the table on which a collection of cloth samples was unpacked and spread out — Samsa was a commercial traveler — hung the picture which he had recently cut out of an illustrated magazine and put into a pretty gilt frame. It showed a lady, with a fur cap on and a fur stole, sitting upright and holding out to the spectator a huge fur muff into which the whole of her forearm had vanished!

Gregor's eyes turned next to the window, and the overcast sky — one could hear rain drops beating on the window gutter — made him quite melancholy. What about sleeping a little longer and forgetting all this nonsense, he thought, but it could not be done, for he was accustomed to sleep on his right side and in his present condition he could not turn himself over. However violently he forced himself towards his right side he always rolled on to his back again. He tried it at least a hundred times, shutting his eyes to keep from seeing his struggling legs, and only desisted when he began to feel in his side a faint dull ache he had never experienced before.

Oh God, he thought, what an exhausting job I've picked on! Traveling about day in, day out. It's much more irritating work than doing the actual business in the office, and on top of that there's the trouble of constant traveling, of worrying about train connections, the bed and irregular meals, casual acquaintances that are always new and never become intimate friends. The devil take it all! He felt a slight itching up on his belly; slowly pushed himself on his back nearer to the top of the bed so that he could lift his head more easily; identified the itching place which was surrounded by many small white spots the nature of which he could not understand and made to touch it with a leg, but drew the leg back immediately, for the contact made a cold shiver run through him.

He slid down again into his former position. This getting up early, he thought, makes one quite stupid. A man needs his sleep. Other commercials live like harem women. For instance, when I come back to the hotel of a morning to write up the orders I've got, these others are only sitting down to breakfast. Let me just try that with my chief; I'd be sacked on the spot. Anyhow, that might be quite a good thing for me, who can tell? If I didn't have to hold my hand because of my parents I'd have given notice long ago, I'd have gone to the chief and told him exactly what I think of him. That would knock him endways from his desk! It's a queer way of doing, too, this sitting on high at a desk and talking down to employees, especially when they have to come quite near because the chief is hard of hearing. Well, there's still hope; once I've saved enough money to pay back my parents' debts to him — that should take another five or six years — I'll do it without fail. I'll cut myself completely loose then. For the moment, though, I'd better get up, since my train goes at five.

He looked at the alarm clock ticking on the chest. Heavenly Father! he thought. It was half-past six o'clock and the hands were quietly moving on, it was even past the half-hour, it was getting on toward a quarter to seven. Had the alarm clock not gone off? From the bed one could see that it had been properly set for four o'clock; of course it must have gone off. Yes, but was it possible to sleep quietly through that ear-splitting noise? Well, he had not slept quietly, yet apparently all the more soundly for that. But what was he to do now? The next train went at seven o'clock; to catch that he would need to hurry like mad and his samples weren't even packed up, and he himself wasn't feeling particularly fresh and active. And even if he did catch the train he wouldn't avoid a row with the chief, since the firm's porter would have been waiting for the five o'clock train and would have long since reported his failure to turn up. The porter was a creature of the chief's, spineless and stupid. Well, supposing he were to say he was sick? But that would be most unpleasant and would look suspicious, since during his five years' employment he had not been ill once. The chief himself would be sure to come with the sick-insurance doctor, would reproach his parents with their son's laziness and would cut all excuses short by referring to the insurance doctor, who of course regarded all mankind as perfectly healthy malingerers. And would he be so far wrong on this occasion? Gregor really felt quite well, apart from a drowsiness that was utterly superfluous after such a long sleep, and he was even unusually hungry.

As all this was running through his mind at top speed without his being able to decide to leave his bed — the alarm clock had just struck a quarter to seven — there came a cautious tap at the door behind the head of his bed. "Gregor," said a voice — it was his mother's — "it's a quarter to seven. Hadn't you a train to catch?" That gentle voice! Gregor had a shock as he heard his own voice answering hers, unmistakably his own voice, it was true, but with a persistent horrible twittering squeak behind it like an undertone, that left the words in their clear shape only for the first moment and then rose up reverberating round them to destroy their sense, so that one could not be sure one

had heard them rightly. Gregor wanted to answer at length and explain everything, but in the circumstances he confined himself to saying: "Yes, yes, thank
you, Mother, I'm getting up now." The wooden door between them must have
kept the change in his voice from being noticeable outside, for his mother contented herself with this statement and shuffled away. Yet this brief exchange of
words had made the other members of the family aware that Gregor was still
in the house, as they had not expected, and at one of the side doors his father
was already knocking, gently, yet with his fist. "Gregor, Gregor," he called,
"what's the matter with you?" And after a little while he called again in a
deeper voice: "Gregor! Gregor!" At the other side door his sister was saying in
a low, plaintive tone: "Gregor? Aren't you well? Are you needing anything?"
He answered them both at once: "I'm just ready," and did his best to make his
voice sound as normal as possible by enunciating the words very clearly and
leaving long pauses between them. So his father went back to his breakfast, but
his sister whispered: "Gregor, open the door, do." However, he was not thinking of opening the door, and felt thankful for the prudent habit he had acquired
in traveling of locking all doors during the night, even at home.

His immediate intention was to get up quietly without being disturbed,
to put on his clothes and above all eat his breakfast, and only then to consider
what else was to be done, since in bed, he was well aware, his meditations
would come to no sensible conclusion. He remembered that often enough in
bed he had felt small aches and pains, probably caused by awkward postures,
which had proved purely imaginary once he got up, and he looked forward
eagerly to seeing this morning's delusions gradually fall away. That the
change in his voice was nothing but the precursor of a severe chill, a standing
ailment of commercial travelers, he had not the least possible doubt.

To get rid of the quilt was quite easy; he had only to inflate himself a little and it fell off by itself. But the next move was difficult, especially because
he was so uncommonly broad. He would have needed arms and hands to
hoist himself up; instead he had only the numerous little legs which never
stopped waving in all directions and which he could not control in the least.
When he tried to bend one of them it was the first to stretch itself straight; and
did he succeed at last in making it do what he wanted, all the other legs meanwhile waved the more wildly in a high degree of unpleasant agitation. "But
what's the use of lying idle in bed," said Gregor to himself.

He thought that he might get out of bed with the lower part of his body
first, but this lower part, which he had not yet seen and of which he could
form no clear conception, proved too difficult to move; it shifted so slowly;
and when finally, almost wild with annoyance, he gathered his forces together
and thrust out recklessly, he had miscalculated the direction and bumped
heavily against the lower end of the bed, and the stinging pain he felt informed him that precisely this lower part of his body was at the moment probably the most sensitive.

So he tried to get the top part of himself out first, and cautiously moved
his head towards the edge of the bed. That proved easy enough, and despite
its breadth and mass the bulk of his body at last slowly followed the movement of his head. Still, when he finally got his head free over the edge of the

bed he felt too scared to go on advancing, for after all if he let himself fall in this way it would take a miracle to keep his head from being injured. And at all costs he must not lose consciousness now, precisely now; he would rather stay in bed.

But when after a repetition of the same efforts he lay in his former position again, sighing, and watched his little legs struggling against each other more wildly than ever, if that were possible, and saw no way of bringing any order into this arbitrary confusion, he told himself again that it was impossible to stay in bed and that the most sensible course was to risk everything for the smallest hope of getting away from it. At the same time he did not forget meanwhile to remind himself that cool reflection, the coolest possible, was much better than desperate resolves. In such moments he focused his eyes as sharply as possible on the window, but, unfortunately, the prospect of the morning fog, which muffled even the other side of the narrow street, brought him little encouragement and comfort. "Seven o'clock already," he said to himself when the alarm clock chimed again, "seven o'clock already and still such a thick fog." And for a little while he lay quiet, breathing lightly, as if perhaps expecting such complete repose to restore all things to their real and normal condition.

But then he said to himself: "Before it strikes a quarter past seven I must be quite out of this bed, without fail. Anyhow, by that time someone will have come from the office to ask for me, since it opens before seven." And he set himself to rocking his whole body at once in a regular rhythm, with the idea of swinging it out of the bed. If he tipped himself out in that way he could keep his head from injury by lifting it at an acute angle when he fell. His back seemed to be hard and was not likely to suffer from a fall on the carpet. His biggest worry was the loud crash he would not be able to help making, which would probably cause anxiety, if not terror, behind all the doors. Still, he must take the risk.

When he was already half out of the bed — the new method was more a game than an effort, for he needed only to hitch himself across by rocking to and fro — it struck him how simple it would be if he could get help. Two strong people — he thought of his father and the servant girl — would be amply sufficient; they would only have to thrust their arms under his convex back, lever him out of the bed, bend down with their burden and then be patient enough to let him turn himself right over on to the floor, where it was to be hoped his legs would then find their proper function. Well, ignoring the fact that the doors were all locked, ought he really to call for help? In spite of his misery he could not suppress a smile at the very idea of it.

He had got so far that he could barely keep his equilibrium when he rocked himself strongly, and he would have to nerve himself very soon for the final decision since in five minutes' time it would be a quarter past seven — when the front doorbell rang. "That's someone from the office," he said to himself, and grew almost rigid, while his little legs only jigged about all the faster. For a moment everything stayed quiet. "They're not going to open the door," said Gregor to himself, catching at some kind of irrational hope. But then of course the servant girl went as usual to the door with her heavy tread and opened it. Gregor needed only to hear the first good morning of the visitor to know immediately who it was — the chief clerk himself. What a fate, to be condemned to work for a firm where the smallest omission at once gave rise to the gravest suspicion! Were all employees in a body nothing but scoundrels, was there not among them one single loyal devoted man who, had he wasted only an hour or so of the firm's time in a morning, was so tormented by conscience as to be driven out of his mind and actually incapable of leaving his bed? Wouldn't it really have been sufficient to send an apprentice to inquire — if any inquiry were necessary at all — did the chief clerk himself have to come and thus indicate to the entire family, an innocent family, that this suspicious circumstance could be investigated by no one less versed in affairs than himself? And more through the agitation caused by these reflections than through any act of will Gregor swung himself out of bed with all his strength. There was a loud thump, but it was not really a crash. His fall was broken to some extent by the carpet, his back, too, was less stiff than he thought, and so there was merely a dull thud, not so very startling. Only he had not lifted his head carefully enough and had hit it; he turned it and rubbed it on the carpet in pain and irritation.

"That was something falling down in there," said the chief clerk in the next room to the left. Gregor tried to suppose to himself that something like what had happened to him today might some day happen to the chief clerk; one really could not deny that it was possible. But as if in brusque reply to this supposition the chief clerk took a couple of firm steps in the next-door room and his patent leather boots creaked. From the right-hand room his sister was whispering to inform him of the situation: "Gregor, the chief clerk's here." "I know," muttered Gregor to himself; but he didn't dare to make his voice loud enough for his sister to hear it.

"Gregor," said his father now from the left-hand room, "the chief clerk has come and wants to know why you didn't catch the early train. We don't know what to say to him. Besides, he wants to talk to you in person. So open the door, please. He will be good enough to excuse the untidiness of your room." "Good morning, Mr. Samsa," the chief clerk was calling amiably meanwhile. "He's not well," said his mother to the visitor, while his father was still speaking through the door, "he's not well, sir, believe me. What else would make him miss a train! The boy thinks about nothing but his work. It makes me almost cross the way he never goes out in the evenings; he's been here the last eight days and has stayed at home every single evening. He just sits there quietly at the table reading a newspaper or looking through railway timetables. The only amusement he gets is doing fretwork. For instance, he spent two or three evenings cutting out a little picture frame; you would be surprised to see how pretty it is; it's hanging in his room; you'll see it in a minute when Gregor opens the door. I must say I'm glad you've come, sir; we should never have got him to unlock the door by ourselves; he's so obstinate; and I'm sure he's unwell, though he wouldn't have it to be so this morning." "I'm just coming," said Gregor slowly and carefully, not moving an inch for fear of losing one word of the conversation. "I can't think of any other explanation, madam," said the chief clerk, "I hope it's nothing serious. Although on the other hand I must say that we men of business — fortunately or unfortunately — very often simply have to ignore any slight indisposition, since business must be attended to." "Well, can the chief clerk come in now?" asked Gregor's father impatiently, again knocking on the door. "No," said Gregor. In the left-hand room a painful silence followed this refusal, in the right-hand room his sister began to sob.

Why didn't his sister join the others? She was probably newly out of bed and hadn't even begun to put on her clothes yet. Well, why was she crying? Because he wouldn't get up and let the chief clerk in, because he was in danger of losing his job, and because the chief would begin dunning his parents again for the old debts? Surely these were things one didn't need to worry about for the present. Gregor was still at home and not in the least thinking of deserting the family. At the moment, true, he was lying on the carpet and no one who knew the condition he was in could seriously expect him to admit the chief clerk. But for such a small discourtesy, which could plausibly be explained away somehow later on, Gregor could hardly be dismissed on the spot. And it seemed to Gregor that it would be much more sensible to leave him in peace for the present than to trouble him with tears and entreaties. Still, of course, their uncertainty bewildered them all and excused their behavior.

"Mr. Samsa," the chief clerk called now in a louder voice, "what's the matter with you? Here you are, barricading yourself in your room, giving only 'yes' and 'no' for answers, causing your parents a lot of unnecessary trouble and neglecting — I mention this only in passing — neglecting your business duties in an incredible fashion. I am speaking here in the name of your parents and of your chief, and I beg you quite seriously to give me an immediate and precise explanation. You amaze me, you amaze me. I thought you were a quiet, dependable person, and now all at once you seem bent on making a disgraceful exhibition of yourself. The chief did hint to me early this morning a possible explanation for your disappearance — with reference to the cash payments that were entrusted to you recently — but I almost pledged my solemn word of honor that this could not be so. But now that I see how incredibly obstinate you are, I no longer have the slightest desire to take your part at all. And your position in the firm is not so unassailable. I came with the intention of telling you all this in private, but since you are wasting my time so needlessly I don't see why your parents shouldn't hear it too. For some time past your work has been most unsatisfactory; this is not the season of the year for a business boom, of course, we admit that, but a season of the year for doing no business at all, that does not exist, Mr. Samsa, must not exist."

"But, sir," cried Gregor, beside himself and in his agitation forgetting everything else, "I'm just going to open the door this very minute. A slight illness, an attack of giddiness, has kept me from getting up. I'm still lying in bed. But I feel all right again. I'm getting out of bed now. Just give me a moment or two longer! I'm not quite so well as I thought. But I'm all right, really. How a thing like that can suddenly strike one down! Only last night I was quite well, my parents can tell you, or rather I did have a slight presentiment. I must have showed some sign of it. Why didn't I report it at the office! But one always thinks that an indisposition can be got over without staying in the house. Oh sir, do spare my parents! All that you're reproaching me with now has no foundation; no one has ever said a word to me about it. Perhaps you haven't looked at the last orders I sent in. Anyhow, I can still catch the eight o'clock train, I'm much the better for my few hours' rest. Don't let me detain you here, sir; I'll be attending to business very soon, and do be good enough to tell the chief so and to make my excuses to him!"

And while all this was tumbling out pell-mell and Gregor hardly knew what he was saying, he had reached the chest quite easily, perhaps because of the practice he had had in bed, and was now trying to lever himself upright by means of it. He meant actually to open the door, actually to show himself and speak to the chief clerk; he was eager to find out what the others, after all their insistence, would say at the sight of him. If they were horrified then the responsibility was no longer his and he could stay quiet. But if they took it calmly, then he had no reason either to be upset, and could really get to the station for the eight o'clock train if he hurried. At first he slipped down a few times from the polished surface of the chest, but at length with a last heave he stood upright; he paid no more attention to the pains in the lower part of his body, however they smarted. Then he let himself fall against the back of a near-by chair, and clung with his little legs to the edges of it. That brought him into control of himself again and he stopped speaking, for now he could listen to what the chief clerk was saying.

"Did you understand a word of it?" the chief clerk was asking; "surely he can't be trying to make fools of us?" "Oh dear," cried his mother, in tears, "perhaps he's terribly ill and we're tormenting him. Grete! Grete!" she called out then. "Yes, Mother?" called his sister from the other side. They were calling to each other across Gregor's room. "You must go this minute for the doctor. Gregor is ill. Go for the doctor, quick. Did you hear how he was speaking?" "That was no human voice," said the chief clerk in a voice noticeably low beside the shrillness of the mother's. "Anna! Anna!" his father was calling through the hall to the kitchen, clapping his hands, "get a locksmith at once!" And the two girls were already running through the hall with a swish of skirts — how could his sister have got dressed so quickly? — and were tearing the front door open. There was no sound of its closing again; they had evidently left it open, as one does in houses where some great misfortune has happened.

But Gregor was now much calmer. The words he uttered were no longer understandable, apparently, although they seemed clear enough to him, even clearer than before, perhaps because his ear had grown accustomed to the sound of them. Yet at any rate people now believed that something was wrong with him, and were ready to help him. The positive certainty with which these first measures had been taken comforted him. He felt himself drawn once more into the human circle and hoped for great and remarkable results from both the doctor and the locksmith, without really distinguishing precisely between them. To make his voice as clear as possible for the decisive conversation that was now imminent he coughed a little, as quietly as he could, of course, since this noise too might not sound like a human cough for all he was able to judge. In the next room meanwhile there was complete silence. Per-

haps his parents were sitting at the table with the chief clerk, whispering, perhaps they were all leaning against the door and listening.

Slowly Gregor pushed the chair towards the door, then let go of it,
caught hold of the door for support — the soles at the end of his little legs
were somewhat sticky — and rested against it for a moment after his efforts.
Then he set himself to turning the key in the lock with his mouth. It seemed,
unhappily, that he hadn't really any teeth — what could he grip the key with?
— but on the other hand his jaws were certainly very strong; with their help
he did manage to set the key in motion, heedless of the fact that he was undoubtedly damaging them somewhere, since a brown fluid issued from his
mouth, flowed over the key and dripped on the floor. "Just listen to that," said
the chief clerk next door; "he's turning the key." That was a great encouragement to Gregor; but they should all have shouted encouragement to him, his
father and mother too: "Go on, Gregor," they should have called out, "keep
going, hold on to that key!" And in the belief that they were all following his
efforts intently, he clenched his jaws recklessly on the key with all the force at
his command. As the turning of the key progressed he circled round the lock,
holding on now only with his mouth, pushing on the key, as required, or
pulling it down again with all the weight of his body. The louder click of the
finally yielding lock literally quickened Gregor. With a deep breath of relief he
said to himself: "So I didn't need the locksmith," and laid his head on the handle to open the door wide.

Since he had to pull the door towards him, he was still invisible when it
was really wide open. He had to edge himself slowly round the near half of
the double door, and to do it very carefully if he was not to fall plump upon
his back just on the threshold. He was still carrying out this difficult manoeuvre, with no time to observe anything else, when he heard the chief clerk utter
a loud "Oh!" — it sounded like a gust of wind — and now he could see the
man, standing as he was nearest to the door, clapping one hand before his
open mouth and slowly backing away as if driven by some invisible steady
pressure. His mother — in spite of the chief clerk's being there her hair was
still undone and sticking up in all directions — first clasped her hands and
looked at his father, then took two steps towards Gregor and fell on the floor
among her outspread skirts, her face hidden on her breast. His father knotted
his fist with a fierce expression on his face as if he meant to knock Gregor back
into his room, then looked uncertainly round the living room, covered his eyes
with his hands and wept till his great chest heaved.

Gregor did not go now into the living room, but leaned against the inside of the firmly shut wing of the door, so that only half his body was visible
and his head above it bending sideways to look at the others. The light had
meanwhile strengthened; on the other side of the street one could see clearly a
section of the endlessly long, dark gray building opposite — it was a hospital
— abruptly punctuated by its row of regular windows; the rain was still
falling, but only in large singly discernible and literally singly splashing
drops. The breakfast dishes were set out on the table lavishly, for breakfast
was the most important meal of the day to Gregor's father, who lingered it out
for hours over various newspapers. Right opposite Gregor on the wall hung a

photograph of himself on military service, as a lieutenant, hand on sword, a carefree smile on his face, inviting one to respect his uniform and military bearing. The door leading to the hall was open, and one could see that the front door stood open too, showing the landing beyond and the beginning of the stairs going down.

"Well," said Gregor, knowing perfectly that he was the only one who had retained any composure, "I'll put my clothes on at once, pack up my samples and start off. Will you only let me go? You see, sir, I'm not obstinate, and I'm willing to work; traveling is a hard life, but I couldn't live without it. Where are you going, sir? To the office? Yes? Will you give a true account of all this? One can be temporarily incapacitated, but that's just the moment for remembering former services and bearing in mind that later on, when the incapacity has been got over, one will certainly work with all the more industry and concentration. I'm loyally bound to serve the chief, you know that very well. Besides, I have to provide for my parents and my sister. I'm in great difficulties, but I'll get out of them again. Don't make things any worse for me than they are. Stand up for me in the firm. Travelers are not popular there, I know. People think they earn sacks of money and just have a good time. A prejudice there's no particular reason for revising. But you, sir, have a more comprehensive view of affairs than the rest of the staff, yes, let me tell you in confidence, a more comprehensive view than the chief himself, who, being the owner, lets his judgment easily be swayed against one of his employees. And you know very well that the traveler, who is never seen in the office almost the whole year round, can so easily fall a victim to gossip and ill luck and unfounded complaints, which he mostly knows nothing about, except when he comes back exhausted from his rounds, and only then suffers in person from their evil consequences, which he can no longer trace back to the original causes. Sir, sir, don't go away without a word to me to show that you think me in the right at least to some extent!"

But at Gregor's very first words the chief clerk had already backed away and only stared at him with parted lips over one twitching shoulder. And while Gregor was speaking he did not stand still one moment but stole away towards the door, without taking his eyes off Gregor, yet only an inch at a time, as if obeying some secret injunction to leave the room. He was already at the hall, and the suddenness with which he took his last step out of the living room would have made one believe he had burned the sole of his foot. Once in the hall he stretched his right arm before him towards the staircase, as if some supernatural power were waiting there to deliver him.

Gregor perceived that the chief clerk must on no account be allowed to go away in this frame of mind if his position in the firm were not to be endangered to the utmost. His parents did not understand this so well; they had convinced themselves in the course of years that Gregor was settled for life in this firm, and besides they were so occupied with their immediate troubles that all foresight had forsaken them. Yet Gregor had this foresight. The chief clerk must be detained, soothed, persuaded and finally won over; the whole future of Gregor and his family depended on it! If only his sister had been there! She was intelligent; she had begun to cry while Gregor was still lying quietly on his back. And no doubt the chief clerk, so partial to ladies, would have been guided by her; she would have shut the door of the flat and in the hall talked him out of his horror. But she was not there, and Gregor would have to handle the situation himself. And without remembering that he was still unaware what powers of movement he possessed, without even remembering that his words in all possibility, indeed in all likelihood, would again be unintelligible, he let go the wing of the door, pushed himself through the opening, started to walk towards the chief clerk, who was already ridiculously clinging with both hands to the railing on the landing; but immediately, as he was feeling for a support, he fell down with a little cry upon all his numerous legs. Hardly was he down when he experienced for the first time this morning a sense of physical comfort; his legs had firm ground under them; they were completely obedient, as he noted with joy; they even strove to carry him forward in whatever direction he chose; and he was inclined to believe that a final relief from all his sufferings was at hand. But in the same moment as he found himself on the floor, rocking with suppressed eagerness to move, not far from his mother, indeed just in front of her, she, who had seemed so completely crushed, sprang all at once to her feet, her arms and fingers outspread, cried: "Help, for God's sake, help!" bent her head down as if to see Gregor better, yet on the contrary kept backing senselessly away; had quite forgotten that the laden table stood behind her; sat upon it hastily, as if in absence of mind, when she bumped into it; and seemed altogether unaware that the big coffee pot beside her was upset and pouring coffee in a flood over the carpet.

"Mother, Mother," said Gregor in a low voice, and looked up at her. The chief clerk, for the moment, had quite slipped from his mind; instead, he could not resist snapping his jaws together at the sight of the streaming coffee. That made his mother scream again, she fled from the table and fell into the arms of his father, who hastened to catch her. But Gregor had now no time to spare for his parents; the chief clerk was already on the stairs; with his chin on the banisters he was taking one last backward look. Gregor made a spring, to be as sure as possible of overtaking him; the chief clerk must have divined his intention, for he leaped down several steps and vanished; he was still yelling "Ugh!" and it echoed through the whole staircase.

Unfortunately, the flight of the chief clerk seemed completely to upset Gregor's father, who had remained relatively calm until now, for instead of running after the man himself, or at least not hindering Gregor in his pursuit, he seized in his right hand the walking stick which the chief clerk had left behind on a chair, together with a hat and greatcoat, snatched in his left hand a large newspaper from the table and began stamping his feet and flourishing the stick and the newspaper to drive Gregor back into his room. No entreaty of Gregor's availed, indeed no entreaty was even understood, however humbly he bent his head his father only stamped on the floor the more loudly. Behind his father his mother had torn open a window, despite the cold weather, and was leaning far out of it with her face in her hands. A strong draught set in from the street to the staircase, the window curtains blew in, the newspapers on the table fluttered, stray pages whisked over the floor. Pitilessly Gregor's father drove him back, hissing and crying "Shoo!" like a savage. But Gregor was quite unpracticed in walking backwards, it really was a slow business. If he only had a chance to turn round he could get back to his room at once, but he was afraid of exasperating his father by the slowness of such a rotation and at any moment the stick in his father's hand might hit him a fatal blow on the back or on the head. In the end, however, nothing else was left for him to do since to his horror he observed that in moving backwards he could not even control the direction he took; and so, keeping an anxious eye on his father all the time over his shoulder, he began to turn round as quickly as he could, which was in reality very slowly. Perhaps his father noted his good intentions, for he did not interfere except every now and then to help him in the manoeuvre from a distance with the point of the stick. If only he would have stopped making that unbearable hissing noise! It made Gregor quite lose his head. He had turned almost completely round when the hissing noise so distracted him that he even turned a little the wrong way again. But when at last his head was fortunately right in front of the doorway, it appeared that his body was too broad simply to get through the opening. His father, of course, in his present mood was far from thinking of such a thing as opening the other half of the door, to let Gregor have enough space. He had merely the fixed idea of driving Gregor back into his room as quickly as possible. He would never have suffered Gregor to make the circumstantial preparations for standing up on end and perhaps slipping his way through the door. Maybe he was now making more noise than ever to urge Gregor forward, as if no obstacle impeded him; to Gregor, anyhow, the noise in his rear sounded no longer like the voice of one single father; this was really no joke, and Gregor thrust himself — come what might — into the doorway. One side of his body rose up, he was tilted at an angle in the doorway, his flank was quite bruised, horrid blotches stained the white door, soon he was stuck fast and, left to himself, could not have moved at all, his legs on one side fluttered trembling to the air, those on the other were crushed painfully to the floor — when from behind his father gave him a strong push which was literally a deliverance and he flew far into the room, bleeding freely. The door was slammed behind him with the stick, and then at last there was silence.

II

Not until it was twilight did Gregor awake out of a deep sleep, more like a swoon than a sleep. He would certainly have waked up of his own accord not much later, for he felt himself sufficiently rested and well-slept, but it seemed to him as if a fleeting step and a cautious shutting of the door leading into the hall had aroused him. The electric lights in the street cast a pale sheen here and there on the ceiling and the upper surfaces of the furniture, but down below, where he lay, it was dark. Slowly, awkwardly trying out his feelers, which he now first learned to appreciate, he pushed his way to the door to see what had been happening there. His left side felt like one single long, unpleasant tense scar, and he had actually to limp on his two rows of legs. One little leg, moreover, had been severely damaged in the course of that morning's events — it was almost a miracle that only one had been damaged — and trailed uselessly behind him.

He had reached the door before he discovered what had really drawn him to it: the smell of food. For there stood a basin filled with fresh milk in which floated little sops of white bread. He could almost have laughed with joy, since he was now still hungrier than in the morning, and he dipped his head almost over the eyes straight into the milk. But soon in disappointment he withdrew it again; not only did he find it difficult to feed because of his tender left side — and he could only feed with the palpitating collaboration of his whole body — he did not like the milk either, although milk had been his favorite drink and that was certainly why his sister had set it there for him, indeed it was almost with repulsion that he turned away from the basin and crawled back to the middle of the room.

He could see through the crack of the door that the gas was turned on in the living room, but while usually at this time his father made a habit of reading the afternoon newspaper in a loud voice to his mother and occasionally to his sister as well, not a sound was now to be heard. Well, perhaps his father had recently given up this habit of reading aloud, which his sister had mentioned so often in conversation and in her letters. But there was the same silence all around, although the flat was certainly not empty of occupants. "What a quiet life our family has been leading," said Gregor to himself, and as he sat there motionless staring into the darkness he felt great pride in the fact that he had been able to provide such a life for his parents and sister in such a fine flat. But what if all the quiet, the comfort, the contentment were now to end in horror? To keep himself from being lost in such thoughts Gregor took refuge in movement and crawled up and down the room.

Once during the long evening one of the side doors was opened a little and quickly shut again, later the other side door too; someone had apparently wanted to come in and then thought better of it. Gregor now stationed himself immediately before the living room door, determined to persuade any hesitating visitor to come in or at least to discover who it might be; but the door was not opened again and he waited in vain. In the early morning, when the doors were locked, they had all wanted to come in, now that he had opened one door and the other had apparently been opened during the day, no one came in and even the keys were on the other side of the doors.

It was late at night before the gas went out in the living room, and Gregor could easily tell that his parents and his sister had all stayed awake until then, for he could clearly hear the three of them stealing away on tiptoe. No one was likely to visit him, not until the morning, that was certain; so he had plenty of time to meditate at his leisure on how he was to arrange his life afresh. But the lofty, empty room in which he had to lie flat on the floor filled him with an apprehension he could not account for, since it had been his very own room for the past five years — and with a half-unconscious action, not without a slight feeling of shame, he scuttled under the sofa, where he felt comfortable at once, although his back was a little cramped and he could not lift his head up, and his only regret was that his body was too broad to get the whole of it under the sofa.

He stayed there all night, spending the time partly in a light slumber, from which his hunger kept waking him up with a start, and partly in worrying and sketching vague hopes, which all led to the same conclusion, that he must lie low for the present and, by exercising patience, and the utmost consideration, help the family to bear the inconvenience he was bound to cause them in his present condition.

Very early in the morning, it was still almost night, Gregor had the chance to test the strength of his new resolutions, for his sister, nearly fully dressed, opened the door from the hall and peered in. She did not see him at once, yet when she caught sight of him under the sofa — well, he had to be somewhere, he couldn't have flown away, could he? — she was so startled that without being able to help it she slammed the door shut again. But as if regretting her behavior she opened the door again immediately and came in on tiptoe, as if she were visiting an invalid or even a stranger. Gregor had pushed his head forward to the very edge of the sofa and watched her. Would she notice that he had left the milk standing, and not for lack of hunger, and would she bring in some other kind of food more to his taste? If she did not do it of her own accord, he would rather starve than draw her attention to the fact, although he felt a wild impulse to dart out from under the sofa, throw himself at her feet and beg her for something to eat. But his sister at once noticed, with surprise, that the basin was still full, except for a little milk that had been spilt all around it, she lifted it immediately, not with her bare hands, true, but with a cloth and carried it away. Gregor was wildly curious to know what she would bring instead, and made various speculations about it. Yet what she actually did next, in the goodness of her heart, he could never have guessed at. To find out what he liked she brought him a whole selection of food, all set out on an old newspaper. There were old, half-decayed vegetables, bones from last night's supper covered with a white sauce that had thickened; some raisins and almonds; a piece of cheese that Gregor would have called uneatable two days ago; a dry roll of bread, a buttered roll, and a roll both buttered and salted. Besides all that, she set down again the same basin, into which she had poured some water, and which was apparently to be reserved for his exclusive use. And with fine tact, knowing that Gregor would not eat in her presence, she withdrew quickly and even turned the key, to let him understand that he could take his ease as much as he liked. Gregor's legs all whizzed towards the food. His wounds must have healed completely, moreover, for he felt no disability, which amazed him and made him reflect how more than a month ago he had cut one finger a little with a knife and had still suffered pain from the wound only the day before yesterday. Am I less sensitive now? he thought, and sucked greedily at the cheese, which above all the other edibles attracted him at once and strongly. One after another and with tears of satisfaction in his eyes he quickly devoured the cheese, the vegetables and the sauce; the fresh food, on the other hand, had no charms for him, he could not even stand the smell of it and actually dragged away to some little distance the things he could eat. He had long finished his meal and was only lying lazily on the same spot when his sister turned the key slowly as a sign for him to retreat. That roused him at once, although he was nearly asleep, and he hurried under the sofa again. But it took considerable self-control for him to stay under the sofa, even for the short time his sister was in the room, since the large meal had swollen his body somewhat and he was so cramped he could hardly breathe. Slight attacks of breathlessness afflicted him and his eyes were starting a little out of his head as he watched his unsuspecting sister sweeping together with a broom not only the remains of what he had eaten but even the things he had not touched, as if these were now of no use to anyone, and hastily shoveling it all into a bucket, which she covered with a wooden lid and carried away. Hardly had she turned her back when Gregor came from under the sofa and stretched and puffed himself out.

In this manner Gregor was fed, once in the early morning while his parents and the servant girl were still asleep, and a second time after they had all had their midday dinner, for then his parents took a short nap and the servant girl could be sent out on some errand or other by his sister. Not that they would have wanted him to starve, of course, but perhaps they could not have borne to know more about his feeding than from hearsay, perhaps too his sister wanted to spare them such little anxieties wherever possible, since they had quite enough to bear as it was.

Under what pretext the doctor and the locksmith had been got rid of on that first morning Gregor could not discover, for since what he had said was not understood by the others it never struck any of them, not even his sister, that he could understand what they said, and so whenever his sister came into his room he had to content himself with hearing her utter only a sigh now and then and an occasional appeal to the saints. Later on, when she had got a little used to the situation — of course she could never get completely used to it — she sometimes threw out a remark which was kindly meant or could be so interpreted. "Well, he liked his dinner today," she would say when Gregor had made a good clearance of his food; and when he had not eaten, which gradually happened more and more often, she would say almost sadly: "Everything's been left standing again."

But although Gregor could get no news directly, he overheard a lot from the neighboring rooms, and as soon as voices were audible, he would run to the door of the room concerned and press his whole body against it. In the first few days especially there was no conversation that did not refer to him somehow, even if only indirectly. For two whole days there were family consultations at every mealtime about what should be done; but also between meals the same subject was discussed, for there were always at least two members of the family at home, since no one wanted to be alone in the flat and to leave it quite empty was unthinkable. And on the very first of these days the household cook — it was not quite clear what and how much she knew of the situation — went down on her knees to his mother and begged leave to go, and when she departed, a quarter of an hour later, gave thanks for her dismissal with tears in her eyes as if for the greatest benefit that could have been conferred on her, and without any prompting swore a solemn oath that she would never say a single word to anyone about what had happened.

Now Gregor's sister had to cook too, helping her mother; true, the cooking did not amount to much, for they ate scarcely anything. Gregor was always hearing one of the family vainly urging another to eat and getting no answer but: "Thanks, I've had all I want," or something similar. Perhaps they drank nothing either. Time and again his sister kept asking his father if he wouldn't like some beer and offered kindly to go and fetch it herself, and when he made no answer suggested that she could ask the concierge to fetch it, so that he need feel no sense of obligation, but then a round "No" came from his father and no more was said about it.

In the course of that very first day Gregor's father explained the family's financial position and prospects to both his mother and his sister. Now and then he rose from the table to get some voucher or memorandum out of the small safe he had rescued from the collapse of his business five years earlier. One could hear him opening the complicated lock and rustling papers out and shutting it again. This statement made by his father was the first cheerful information Gregor had heard since his imprisonment. He had been of the opinion that nothing at all was left over from his father's business, at least his father had never said anything to the contrary, and of course he had not asked him directly. At the time Gregor's sole desire was to do his utmost to help the family to forget as soon as possible the catastrophe which had overwhelmed the business and thrown them all into a state of complete despair. And so he had set to work with unusual ardor and almost overnight had become a commercial traveler instead of a little clerk, with of course much greater chances of earning money, and his success was immediately translated into good round coin which he could lay on the table for his amazed and happy family. These had been fine times, and they had never recurred, at least not with the same sense of glory, although later on Gregor had earned so much money that he was able to meet the expenses of the whole household and did so. They had simply got used to it, both the family and Gregor; the money was gratefully accepted and gladly given, but there was no special uprush of warm feeling. With his sister alone had he remained intimate, and it was a secret plan of his that she, who loved music, unlike himself, and could play movingly on the violin, should be sent next year to study at the Conservatorium, despite the great expense that would entail, which must be made up in some other way. During his brief visits home the Conservatorium was often mentioned in the talks he had with his sister, but always merely as a beautiful dream which could never come true, and his parents discouraged even these innocent references to it; yet Gregor had made up his mind firmly about it and meant to announce the fact with due solemnity on Christmas Day.

Such were the thoughts, completely futile in his present condition, that went through his head as he stood clinging upright to the door and listening. Sometimes out of sheer weariness he had to give up listening and let his head fall negligently against the door, but he always had to pull himself together again at once, for even the slight sound his head made was audible next door and brought all conversation to a stop. "What can he be doing now?" his father would say after a while, obviously turning towards the door, and only then would the interrupted conversation gradually be set going again.

Gregor was now informed as amply as he could wish — for his father tended to repeat himself in his explanations, partly because it was a long time since he had handled such matters and partly because his mother could not always grasp things at once — that a certain amount of investments, a very small amount it was true, had survived the wreck of their fortunes and had even increased a little because the dividends had not been touched meanwhile. And besides that, the money Gregor brought home every month — he had kept only a few dollars for himself — had never been quite used up and now amounted to a small capital sum. Behind the door Gregor nodded his head eagerly, rejoiced at this evidence of unexpected thrift and foresight. True, he could really have paid off some more of his father's debts to the chief with his extra money, and so brought much nearer the day on which he could quit his job, but doubtless it was better the way his father had arranged it.

Yet this capital was by no means sufficient to let the family live on the interest of it; for one year, perhaps, or at the most two, they could live on the principal, that was all. It was simply a sum that ought not to be touched and should be kept for a rainy day; money for living expenses would have to be earned. Now his father was still hale enough but an old man, and he had done no work for the past five years and could not be expected to do much; during these five years, the first years of leisure in his laborious though unsuccessful life, he had grown rather fat and become sluggish. And Gregor's old mother, how was she to earn a living with her asthma, which troubled her even when she walked through the flat and kept her lying on a sofa every other day panting for breath beside an open window? And was his sister to earn her bread, she who was still a child of seventeen and whose life hitherto had been so pleasant, consisting as it did in dressing herself nicely, sleeping long, helping in the housekeeping, going out to a few modest entertainments and above all playing the violin? At first whenever the need for earning money was mentioned Gregor let go his hold on the door and threw himself down on the cool leather sofa beside it, he felt so hot with shame and grief.

Often he just lay there the long nights through without sleeping at all, scrabbling for hours on the leather. Or he nerved himself to the great effort of pushing an armchair to the window, then crawled up over the window sill and, braced against the chair, leaned against the windowpanes, obviously in some recollection of the sense of freedom that looking out of a window always used to give him. For in reality day by day things that were even a little way off were growing dimmer to his sight; the hospital across the street, which he used to execrate for being all too often before his eyes, was now quite beyond his range of vision, and if he had not known that he lived in Charlotte Street, a quiet street but still a city street, he might have believed that his window gave on a desert waste where gray sky and gray land blended indistinguishably into each other. His quick-witted sister only needed to observe twice that the armchair stood by the window; after that whenever she had tidied the room she always pushed the chair back to the same place at the window and even left the inner casements open.

If he could have spoken to her and thanked her for all she had to do for him, he could have borne her ministrations better; as it was, they oppressed him. She certainly tried to make as light as possible of whatever was disagreeable in her task, and as time went on she succeeded, of course, more and more, but time brought more enlightenment to Gregor too. The very way she came in distressed him. Hardly was she in the room when she rushed to the window, without even taking time to shut the door, careful as she was usually to shield the sight of Gregor's room from the others, and as if she were almost suffocating tore the casements open with hasty fingers, standing then in the open draught for a while even in the bitterest cold and drawing deep breaths. This noisy scurry of hers upset Gregor twice a day; he would crouch trembling under the sofa all the time, knowing quite well that she would certainly have spared him such a disturbance had she found it at all possible to stay in his presence without opening a window.

On one occasion, about a month after Gregor's metamorphosis, when there was surely no reason for her to be still startled at his appearance, she came a little earlier than usual and found him gazing out of the window, quite motionless, and thus well placed to look like a bogey. Gregor would not have been surprised had she not come in at all, for she could not immediately open the window while he was there, but not only did she retreat, she jumped back as if in alarm and banged the door shut; a stranger might well have thought that he had been lying in wait for her there meaning to bite her. Of course he hid himself under the sofa at once, but he had to wait until midday before she came again, and she seemed more ill at ease than usual. This made him realize how repulsive the sight of him still was to her, and that it was bound to go on being repulsive, and what an effort it must cost her not to run away even from the sight of the small portion of his body that stuck out from under the sofa. In order to spare her that, therefore, one day he carried a sheet on his back to the sofa — it cost him four hours' labor — and arranged it there in such a way as to hide him completely, so that even if she were to bend down she could not see him. Had she considered the sheet unnecessary, she would certainly have stripped it off the sofa again, for it was clear enough that this curtaining and confining of himself was not likely to conduce Gregor's comfort, but she left it where it was, and Gregor even fancied that he caught a thankful glance from her eye when he lifted the sheet carefully a very little with his head to see how she was taking the new arrangement.

For the first fortnight his parents could not bring themselves to the point of entering his room, and he often heard them expressing their appreciation of his sister's activities, whereas formerly they had frequently scolded her for being as they thought a somewhat useless daughter. But now, both of them often waited outside the door, his father and his mother, while his sister tidied his room, and as soon as she came out she had to tell them exactly how things were in the room, what Gregor had eaten, how he had conducted himself this time and whether there was not perhaps some slight improvement in his condition. His mother, moreover, began relatively soon to want to visit him, but his father and sister dissuaded her at first with arguments which Gregor listened to very attentively and altogether approved. Later, however, she had to be held back by main force, and when she cried out: "Do let me in to Gregor, he is my unfortunate son! Can't you understand that I must go to him?" Gregor thought that it might be well to have her come in, not every day, of course, but perhaps once a week; she understood things, after all, much better than his sister, who was only a child despite the efforts she was making and had perhaps taken on so difficult a task merely out of childish thoughtlessness.

Gregor's desire to see his mother was soon fulfilled. During the daytime he did not want to show himself at the window, out of consideration for his parents, but he could not crawl very far around the few square yards of floor space he had, nor could he bear lying quietly at rest all during the night, while he was fast losing any interest he had ever taken in food, so that for mere recreation he had formed the habit of crawling crisscross over the walls and ceiling. He especially enjoyed hanging suspended from the ceiling; it was much better than lying on the floor; one could breathe more freely; one's body swung and rocked lightly; and in the almost blissful absorption induced by this suspension it could happen to his own surprise that he let go and fell plump on the floor. Yet he now had his body much better under control than formerly, and even such a big fall did him no harm. His sister at once remarked the new distraction Gregor had found for himself — he left traces behind him of the sticky stuff on his soles wherever he crawled — and she got the idea in her head of giving him as wide a field as possible to crawl in and of removing the pieces of furniture that hindered him, above all the chest of drawers and the writing desk. But that was more than she could manage all by herself; she did not dare ask her father to help her; and as for the servant girl, a young creature of sixteen who had had the courage to stay on after the cook's departure, she could not be asked to help, for she had begged as an especial favor that she might keep the kitchen door locked and open it only on a definite summons; so there was nothing left but to apply to her mother at an hour when her father was out. And the old lady did come, with exclamations of joyful eagerness, which, however, died away at the door of Gregor's room. Gregor's sister, of course, went in first, to see that everything was in order before letting his mother enter. In great haste Gregor pulled the sheet lower and rucked it more in folds so that it really looked as if it had been thrown accidentally over the sofa. And this time he did not peer out from under it; he renounced the pleasure of seeing his mother on this occasion and was only glad that she had come at all. "Come in, he's out of sight," said his sister, obviously leading her mother in by the hand. Gregor could now hear the two women struggling to shift the heavy old chest from its place, and his sister claiming the greater part of the labor for herself, without listening to the admonitions of her mother who feared she might overstrain herself. It took a long time. After at least a quarter of an hour's tugging his mother objected that the chest had better be left where it was, for in the first place it was too heavy and could never be got out before his father came home, and standing in the middle of the room like that it would only hamper Gregor's movements, while in the second place it was not at all certain that removing the furniture would be doing a service to Gregor. She was inclined to think to the contrary; the sight of the naked walls made her own heart heavy, and why shouldn't Gregor have the same feeling, considering that he had been used to his furniture for so long and might feel forlorn without it. "And doesn't it look," she concluded in a low voice — in fact she had been almost whispering all the time as if to avoid letting Gregor, whose exact whereabouts she did not know, hear even the tones of her voice, for she was convinced that he could not understand her words — "doesn't it look as if we were showing him, by taking away his furniture, that we have given up hope of his ever getting better and are just leaving him coldly to himself? I think it would be best to keep his room exactly as it has always been, so that when he comes back to us he will find everything unchanged and be able all the more easily to forget what has happened in between."

On hearing these words from his mother Gregor realized that the lack of all direct human speech for the past two months together with the monotony of family life must have confused his mind, otherwise he could not account for the fact that he had quite earnestly looked forward to having his room emptied of furnishing. Did he really want his warm room, so comfortably fitted with old family furniture, to be turned into a naked den in which he would certainly be able to crawl unhampered in all directions but at the price of shedding simultaneously all recollection of his human background? He had indeed been so near the brink of forgetfulness that only the voice of his mother, which he had not heard for so long, had drawn him back from it. Nothing should be taken out of his room; everything must stay as it was; he could not dispense with the good influence of the furniture on his state of mind; and even if the furniture did hamper him in his senseless crawling round and round, that was no drawback but a great advantage.

Unfortunately his sister was of the contrary opinion; she had grown accustomed, and not without reason, to consider herself an expert in Gregor's affairs as against her parents, and so her mother's advice was now enough to make her determined on the removal not only of the chest and the writing desk, which had been her first intention, but of all the furniture except the indispensable sofa. This determination was not, of course, merely the outcome of childish recalcitrance and of the self-confidence she had recently developed so unexpectedly and at such cost; she had in fact perceived that Gregor needed a lot of space to crawl about in, while on the other hand he never used the furniture at all, so far as could be seen. Another factor might have been also the enthusiastic temperament of an adolescent girl, which seeks to indulge itself on every opportunity and which now tempted Grete to exaggerate the horror of her brother's circumstances in order that she might do all the more for him. In a room where Gregor lorded it all alone over empty walls no one save herself was likely ever to set foot.

And so she was not to be moved from her resolve by her mother who seemed moreover to be ill at ease in Gregor's room and therefore unsure of herself, was soon reduced to silence and helped her daughter as best she could to push the chest outside. Now, Gregor could do without the chest, if need be, but the writing desk he must retain. As soon as the two women had got the chest out of his room, groaning as they pushed it, Gregor stuck his head out from under the sofa to see how he might intervene as kindly and cautiously as possible. But as bad luck would have it, his mother was the first to return, leaving Grete clasping the chest in the room next door where she was trying to shift it all by herself, without of course moving it from the spot. His mother however was not accustomed to the sight of him, it might sicken her and so in alarm Gregor backed quickly to the other end of the sofa, yet could not prevent the sheet from swaying a little in front. That was enough to put her on the alert. She paused, stood still for a moment and then went back to Grete.

Although Gregor kept reassuring himself that nothing out of the way was happening, but only a few bits of furniture were being changed round, he soon had to admit that all this trotting to and fro of the two women, their little ejaculations and the scraping of furniture along the floor affected him like a vast disturbance coming from all sides at once, and however much he tucked in his head and legs and cowered to the very floor he was bound to confess that he would not be able to stand it for long. They were clearing his room out; taking away everything he loved; the chest in which he kept his fret saw and other tools was already dragged off; they were now loosening the writing desk which had almost sunk into the floor, the desk at which he had done all his homework when he was at the commercial academy, at the grammar school before that, and, yes, even at the primary school — he had no more time to waste in weighing the good intentions of the two women, whose existence he had by now almost forgotten, for they were so exhausted that they were laboring in silence and nothing could be heard but the heavy scuffling of their feet.

And so he rushed out — the women were just leaning against the writing desk in the next room to give themselves a breather — and four times changed his direction, since he really did not know what to rescue first, then on the wall opposite, which was already otherwise cleared, he was struck by the picture of the lady muffled in so much fur and quickly crawled up to it and pressed himself to the glass, which was a good surface to hold on to and comforted his hot belly. This picture at least, which was entirely hidden beneath him, was going to be removed by nobody. He turned his head towards the door of the living room so as to observe the women when they came back.

They had not allowed themselves much of a rest and were already coming; Grete had twined her arm round her mother and was almost supporting her. "Well, what shall we take now?" said Grete, looking round. Her eyes met Gregor's from the wall. She kept her composure, presumably because of her mother, bent her head down to her mother, to keep her from looking up, and said, although in a fluttering, unpremeditated voice: "Come, hadn't we better go back to the living room for a moment?" Her intentions were clear enough to Gregor, she wanted to bestow her mother in safety and then chase him down from the wall. Well, just let her try it! He clung to his picture and would not give it up. He would rather fly in Grete's face.

But Grete's words had succeeded in disquieting her mother, who took a step to one side, caught sight of the huge brown mass on the flowered wallpaper, and before she was really conscious that what she saw was Gregor screamed in a loud, hoarse voice: "Oh God, oh God!" fell with outspread arms over the sofa as if giving up and did not move. "Gregor!" cried his sister, shaking her fist and glaring at him. This was the first time she had directly addressed him since his metamorphosis. She ran into the next room for some aromatic essence with which to rouse her mother from her fainting fit. Gregor wanted to help too — there was still time to rescue the picture — but he was stuck fast to the glass and had to tear himself loose; he then ran after his sister into the next room as if he could advise her, as he used to do; but then had to stand helplessly behind her; she meanwhile searched among various small bottles and when she turned round started in alarm at the sight of him; one bottle fell on the floor and broke; a splinter of glass cut Gregor's face and some kind of corrosive medicine splashed him; without pausing a moment longer Grete gathered up all the bottles she could carry and ran to her mother with them; she banged the door shut with her foot. Gregor was now cut off from his mother, who was perhaps nearly dying because of him; he dared not open the door for fear of frightening away his sister, who had to stay with her mother; there was nothing he could do but wait; and harassed by self-reproach and worry he began now to crawl to and fro, over everything, walls, furniture and ceiling, and finally in his despair, when the whole room seemed to be reeling round him, fell down onto the middle of the big table.

A little while elapsed, Gregor was still lying there feebly and all around was quiet, perhaps that was a good omen. Then the doorbell rang. The servant girl was of course locked in her kitchen, and Grete would have to open the door. It was his father. "What's been happening?" were his first words; Grete's face must have told him everything. Grete answered in a muffled voice, apparently hiding her head on his breast: "Mother has been fainting, but she's better now. Gregor's broken loose." "Just what I expected," said his father, "just what I've been telling you, but you women would never listen." It was clear to Gregor that his father had taken the worst interpretation of Grete's all too brief statement and was assuming that Gregor had been guilty of some violent act. Therefore Gregor must now try to propitiate his father, since he had neither time nor means for an explanation. And so he fled to the door of his own room and crouched against it, to let his father see as soon as he came in from the hall that his son had the good intention of getting back into his room immediately and that it was not necessary to drive him there, but that if only the door were opened he would disappear at once.

Yet his father was not in the mood to perceive such fine distinctions. "Ah!" he cried as soon as he appeared, in a tone which sounded at once angry and exultant. Gregor drew his head back from the door and lifted it to look at his father. Truly, this was not the father he had imagined to himself; admittedly he had been too absorbed of late in his new recreation of crawling over the ceiling to take the same interest as before in what was happening elsewhere in the flat, and he ought really to be prepared for some changes. And yet, and yet, could that be his father? The man who used to lie wearily sunk in bed whenever Gregor set out on a business journey; who welcomed him back of an evening lying in a long chair in a dressing gown; who could not really rise to his feet but only lifted his arms in greeting, and on the rare occasions when he did go out with his family, on one or two Sundays a year and on high holidays, walked between Gregor and his mother, who were slow walkers anyhow, even more slowly than they did, muffled in his old greatcoat, shuffling laboriously forward with the help of his crook-handled stick which he set down most cautiously at every step and, whenever he wanted to say anything, nearly always came to a full stop and gathered his escort around him? Now he was standing there in fine shape; dressed in a smart blue uniform with gold buttons, such as bank messengers wear; his strong double chin bulged over the stiff high collar of his jacket; from under his bushy eyebrows his black eyes darted fresh and penetrating glances; his onetime tangled white hair had been combed flat on either side of a shining and carefully exact parting. He pitched his cap, which bore a gold monogram, probably the badge of some bank, in a wide sweep across the whole room on to a sofa and with the tail-ends of his jacket thrown back, his hands in his trouser pockets, advanced with a grim visage towards Gregor. Likely enough he did not himself know what he meant to do; at any rate he lifted his feet uncommonly high, and Gregor was dumbfounded at the enormous size of his shoe soles. But Gregor could not risk standing up to him, aware as he had been from the very first day of his new life that his father believed only the severest measures suitable for dealing with him. And so he ran before his father, stopping when he stopped and scuttling forward again when his father made any kind of move. In this way they circled the room several times without anything decisive happening; indeed the whole operation did not even look like a pursuit because it was carried out so slowly. And so Gregor did not leave the floor, for he feared that his father might take as a piece of peculiar wickedness any excursion of his over the walls or the ceiling. All the same, he could not stay this course much longer, for while his father took one step he had to carry out a whole series of movements. He was already beginning to feel breathless, just as in his former life his lungs had not been very dependable. As he was staggering along, trying to concentrate his energy on running, hardly keeping his eyes open; in his dazed state never even thinking of any other escape than simply going forward; and having almost forgotten that the walls were free to him, which in this room were well provided with finely carved pieces of furniture full of knobs and crevices — suddenly something lightly flung landed close behind him and rolled before him. It was an apple; a second apple followed immediately; Gregor came to a stop in alarm; there was no point in running on, for his father was determined to bombard him. He had filled his pockets with fruit from the dish on the sideboard and was now shying apple after apple, without taking particularly good aim for the moment. The small red apples rolled about the floor as if magnetized and cannoned into each other. An apple thrown without much force grazed Gregor's back and glanced off harmlessly. But another following immediately landed right on his back and sank in; Gregor wanted to drag himself forward, as if this startling, incredible pain could be left behind him: but he felt as if nailed to the spot and flattened himself out in a complete derangement of all his senses. With his last conscious look he saw the door of his room being torn open and his mother rushing out ahead of his screaming sister, in her underbodice, for her daughter had loosened her clothing to let her breathe more freely and recover from her swoon, he saw his mother rushing towards his father, leaving one after another behind her on the floor her loosened petticoats, stumbling over her petticoats straight to his father and embracing him, in complete union with him

— but here Gregor's sight began to fail — with her hands clasped round his father's neck as she begged for her son's life.

III

The serious injury done to Gregor, which disabled him for more than a month — the apple went on sticking in his body as a visible reminder, since no one ventured to remove it — seemed to have made even his father recollect that Gregor was a member of the family, despite his present unfortunate and repulsive shape, and ought not to be treated as an enemy, that, on the contrary, family duty required the suppression of disgust and the exercise of patience, nothing but patience.

And although his injury had impaired, probably forever, his power of movement, and for the time being it took him long, long minutes to creep across his room like an old invalid — there was no question now of crawling up the wall — yet in his own opinion he was sufficiently compensated for this worsening of his condition by the fact that towards evening the living-room door, which he used to watch intently for an hour or two beforehand, was always thrown open, so that lying in the darkness of his room, invisible to the family, he could see them all at the lamp-lit table and listen to their talk, by general consent as it were, very different from his earlier eavesdropping.

True, their intercourse lacked the lively character of former times, which he had always called to mind with a certain wistfulness in the small hotel bedrooms where he had been wont to throw himself down, tired out, on damp bedding. They were now mostly very silent. Soon after supper his father would fall asleep in his armchair; his mother and sister would admonish each other to be silent; his mother, bending low over the lamp, stitched at fine sewing for an underwear firm; his sister, who had taken a job as a salesgirl, was learning shorthand and French in the evenings on the chance of bettering herself. Sometimes his father woke up, and as if quite unaware that he had been sleeping said to his mother: "What a lot of sewing you're doing today!" and at once fell asleep again, while the two women exchanged a tired smile.

With a kind of mulishness his father persisted in keeping his uniform on even in the house; his dressing gown hung uselessly on its peg and he slept fully dressed where he sat, as if he were ready for service at any moment and even here only at the beck and call of his superior. As a result, his uniform, which was not brand-new to start with, began to look dirty, despite all the loving care of the mother and sister to keep it clean, and Gregor often spent whole evenings gazing at the many greasy spots on the garment, gleaming with gold buttons always in a high state of polish, in which the old man sat sleeping in extreme discomfort and yet quite peacefully.

As soon as the clock struck ten his mother tried to rouse his father with gentle words and to persuade him after that to get into bed, for sitting there he could not have a proper sleep and that was what he needed most, since he had to go to duty at six. But with the mulishness that had obsessed him since he became a bank messenger he always insisted on staying longer at the table, although he regularly fell asleep again and in the end only with the greatest trouble could be got out of his armchair and into his bed. However insistently

Gregor's mother and sister kept urging him with gentle reminders, he would go on slowly shaking his head for a quarter of an hour, keeping his eyes shut, and refuse to get to his feet. The mother plucked at his sleeve, whispering endearments in his ear, the sister left her lessons to come to her mother's help, but Gregor's father was not to be caught. He would only sink down deeper in his chair. Not until the two women hoisted him up by the armpits did he open his eyes and look at them both, one after the other, usually with the remark: "This is a life. This is the peace and quiet of my old age." And leaning on the two of them he would heave himself up, with difficulty, as if he were a great burden to himself, suffer them to lead him as far as the door and then wave them off and go on alone, while the mother abandoned her needlework and the sister her pen in order to run after him and help him farther.

Who could find time, in this overworked and tired-out family, to bother about Gregor more than was absolutely needful? The household was reduced more and more; the servant girl was turned off; a gigantic bony charwoman with white hair flying round her head came in morning and evening to do the rough work; everything else was done by Gregor's mother, as well as great piles of sewing. Even various family ornaments, which his mother and sister used to wear with pride at parties and celebrations, had to be sold, as Gregor discovered of an evening from hearing them all discuss the prices obtained. But what they lamented most was the fact that they could not leave the flat which was much too big for their present circumstances, because they could not think of any way to shift Gregor. Yet Gregor saw well enough that consideration for him was not the main difficulty preventing the removal, for they could have easily shifted him in some suitable box with a few air holes in it; what really kept them from moving into another flat was rather their own complete hopelessness and the belief that they had been singled out for a misfortune such as had never happened to any of their relations or acquaintances. They fulfilled to the uttermost all that the world demands of poor people, the father fetched breakfast for the small clerks in the bank, the mother devoted her energy to making underwear for strangers, the sister trotted to and fro behind the counter at the behest of customers, but more than this they had not the strength to do. And the wound in Gregor's back began to nag at him afresh when his mother and sister, after getting his father into bed, came back again, left their work lying, drew close to each other and sat cheek by cheek; when his mother, pointing towards his room, said: "Shut that door now, Grete," and he was left again in darkness, while next door the women mingled their tears or perhaps sat dry-eyed staring at the table.

Gregor hardly slept at all by night or by day. He was often haunted by the idea that next time the door opened he would take the family's affairs in hand again just as he used to do; once more, after this long interval, there appeared in his thoughts the figures of the chief and the chief clerk, the commercial travelers and the apprentices, the porter who was so dull-witted, two or three friends in other firms, a chambermaid in one of the rural hotels, a sweet and fleeting memory, a cashier in a milliner's shop, whom he had wooed earnestly but too slowly — they all appeared, together with strangers or people he had quite forgotten, but instead of helping him and his family they were one and all unapproachable and he was glad when they vanished. At other times he would not be in the mood to bother about his family, he was only filled with rage at the way they were neglecting him, and although he had no clear idea of what he might care to eat he would make plans for getting into the larder to take the food that was after all his due, even if he were not hungry. His sister no longer took thought to bring him what might especially please him, but in the morning and at noon before she went to business hurriedly pushed into his room with her foot any food that was available, and in the evening cleared it out again with one sweep of the broom, heedless of whether it had been merely tasted, or — as most frequently happened — left untouched. The cleaning of his room, which she now did always in the evenings, could not have been more hastily done. Streaks of dirt stretched along the walls, here and there lay balls of dust and filth. At first Gregor used to station himself in some particularly filthy corner when his sister arrived, in order to reproach her with it, so to speak. But he could have sat there for weeks without getting her to make any improvements; she could see the dirt as well as he did, but she had simply made up her mind to leave it alone. And yet, with a touchiness that was new to her, which seemed anyhow to have infected the whole family, she jealously guarded her claim to be the sole caretaker of Gregor's room. His mother once subjected his room to a thorough cleaning, which was achieved only by means of several buckets of water — all this dampness of course upset Gregor too and he lay widespread, sulky and motionless on the sofa — but she was well punished for it. Hardly had his sister noticed the changed aspect of his room than she rushed in high dudgeon into the living room and, despite the imploringly raised hands of her mother, burst into a storm of weeping, while her parents — her father had of course been startled out of his chair — looked on at first in helpless amazement; then they too began to go into action; the father reproached the mother on his right for not having left the cleaning of Gregor's room to his sister; shrieked at the sister on his left that never again was she to be allowed to clean Gregor's room; while the mother tried to pull the father into his bedroom, since he was beyond himself with agitation; the sister, shaken with sobs, then beat upon the table with her small fists; and Gregor hissed loudly with rage because not one of them thought of shutting the door to spare him such a spectacle and so much noise.

Still, even if the sister, exhausted by her daily work, had grown tired of looking after Gregor as she did formerly, there was no need for his mother's intervention or for Gregor's being neglected at all. The charwoman was there. This old widow, whose strong bony frame had enabled her to survive the worst a long life could offer, by no means recoiled from Gregor. Without being in the least curious she had once by chance opened the door of his room and at the sight of Gregor, who, taken by surprise, began to rush to and fro although no one was chasing him, merely stood there with her arms folded. From that time she never failed to open his door a little for a moment, morning and evening, to have a look at him. At first she even used to call him to her, with words which apparently she took to be friendly, such as: "Come along, then, you old dung beetle!" or "Look at the old dung beetle, then!" To such allocutions Gregor made no answer, but stayed motionless where he was, as if the door had never been opened. Instead of being allowed to disturb him so senselessly whenever the whim took her, she should rather have been ordered to clean out his room daily, that charwoman! Once, early in the morning — heavy rain was lashing on the windowpanes, perhaps a sign that spring was on the way — Gregor was so exasperated when she began addressing him again that he ran at her, as if to attack her, although slowly and feebly enough. But the charwoman instead of showing fright merely lifted high a chair that happened to be beside the door, and as she stood there with her mouth wide open it was clear that she meant to shut it only when she brought the chair down on Gregor's back. "So you're not coming any nearer?" she asked, as Gregor turned away again, and quietly put the chair back into the corner.

Gregor was now eating hardly anything. Only when he happened to pass the food laid out for him did he take a bit of something in his mouth as a pastime, kept it there for an hour at a time and usually spat it out again. At first he thought it was chagrin over the state of his room that prevented him from eating, yet he soon got used to the various changes in his room. It had become a habit in the family to push into his room things there was no room for elsewhere, and there were plenty of these now, since one of the rooms had been let to three lodgers. These serious gentlemen — all three of them with full beards, as Gregor once observed through a crack in the door — had a passion for order, not only in their own room but, since they were now members of the household, in all its arrangements, especially in the kitchen. Superfluous, not to say dirty, objects they could not bear. Besides, they had brought with them most of the furnishings they needed. For this reason many things could be dispensed with that it was no use trying to sell but that should not be thrown away either. All of them found their way into Gregor's room. The ash can likewise and the kitchen garbage can. Anything that was not needed for the moment was simply flung into Gregor's room by the charwoman, who did everything in a hurry; fortunately Gregor usually saw only the object, whatever it was, and the hand that held it. Perhaps she intended to take the things away again as time and opportunity offered, or to collect them until she could throw them all out in a heap, but in fact they just lay wherever she happened to throw them, except when Gregor pushed his way through the junk heap and shifted it somewhat, at first out of necessity, because he had not room enough to crawl, but later with increasing enjoyment, although after such excursions, being sad and weary to death, he would lie motionless for hours. And since the lodgers often ate their supper at home in the common living room, the living room door stayed shut many an evening, yet Gregor reconciled himself quite easily to the shutting of the door, for often enough on evenings when it was opened he had disregarded it entirely and lain in the darkest corner of his room, quite unnoticed by the family. But on one occasion the charwoman left the door open a little and it stayed ajar even when the lodgers came in for supper and the lamp was lit. They set themselves at the top end of the table where formerly Gregor and his father and mother had eaten their meals, unfolded their napkins and took knife and fork in hand. At once his mother appeared in the other doorway with a dish of meat and close behind her his sister with a dish of potatoes piled high. The food steamed with a thick vapor. The lodgers bent over the food set before them as if to scrutinize it before eating, in fact the man in the middle, who seemed to pass for an authority with the other two, cut a piece of meat as it lay on the dish, obviously to discover if it were tender or should be sent back to the kitchen. He showed satisfaction, and Gregor's mother and sister, who had been watching anxiously, breathed freely and began to smile.

The family itself took its meals in the kitchen. Nonetheless, Gregor's father came into the living room before going in to the kitchen and with one prolonged bow, cap in hand, made a round of the table. The lodgers all stood up and murmured something in their beards. When they were alone again they ate their food in almost complete silence. It seemed remarkable to Gregor that among the various noises coming from the table he could always distinguish the sound of their masticating teeth, as if this were a sign to Gregor that one needed teeth in order to eat, and that with toothless jaws even of the finest make one could do nothing. "I'm hungry enough," said Gregor sadly to himself, "but not for that kind of food. How these lodgers are stuffing themselves, and here am I dying of starvation!"

On that very evening — during the whole of his time there Gregor could not remember ever having heard the violin — the sound of violin-playing came from the kitchen. The lodgers had already finished their supper, the one in the middle had brought out a newspaper and given the other two a page apiece, and now they were leaning back at ease reading and smoking. When the violin began to play they pricked up their ears, got to their feet, and went on tiptoe to the hall door where they stood huddled together. Their movements must have been heard in the kitchen, for Gregor's father called out: "Is the violin-playing disturbing you, gentlemen? It can be stopped at once." "On the contrary," said the middle lodger, "could not Fräulein Samsa come and play in this room, beside us, where it is much more convenient and comfortable?" "Oh certainly," cried Gregor's father, as if he were the violin-player. The lodgers came back into the living room and waited. Presently Gregor's father arrived with the music stand, his mother carrying the music and his sister with the violin. His sister quietly made everything ready to start playing; his parents, who had never let rooms before and so had an exaggerated idea of the courtesy due to lodgers, did not venture to sit down on their own chairs; his father leaned against the door, the right hand thrust between two buttons of his livery coat, which was formally buttoned up; but his mother was offered a chair by one of the lodgers and, since she left the chair just where he had happened to put it, sat down in a corner to one side.

Gregor's sister began to play; the father and mother, from either side, intently watched the movements of her hands. Gregor, attracted by the playing, ventured to move forward a little until his head was actually inside the living room. He felt hardly any surprise at his growing lack of consideration for the others; there had been a time when he prided himself on being considerate. And yet just on this occasion he had more reason than ever to hide himself, since owing to the amount of dust which lay thick in his room and rose into the air at the slightest movement, he too was covered with dust; fluff and hair and remnants of food trailed with him, caught on his back and along his sides; his indifference to everything was much too great for him to turn on his back and scrape himself clean on the carpet, as once he had done several times a day. And in spite of his condition, no shame deterred him from advancing a little over the spotless floor of the living room.

To be sure, no one was aware of him. The family was entirely absorbed in the violin-playing; the lodgers, however, who first of all had stationed themselves, hands in pockets, much too close behind the music stand so that they could all have read the music, which must have bothered his sister, had soon retreated to the window, half-whispering with downbent heads, and stayed there while his father turned an anxious eye on them. Indeed, they were making it more than obvious that they had been disappointed in their expectation of hearing good or enjoyable violin-playing, that they had had more than enough of the performance and only out of courtesy suffered a continued disturbance of their peace. From the way they all kept blowing the smoke of their cigars high in the air through nose and mouth one could divine their irritation. And yet Gregor's sister was playing so beautifully. Her face leaned sideways, intently and sadly her eyes followed the notes of music. Gregor crawled a little farther forward and lowered his head to the ground so that it might be possible for his eyes to meet hers. Was he an animal, that music had such an effect upon him? He felt as if the way were opening before him to the unknown nourishment he craved. He was determined to push forward till he reached his sister, to pull at her skirt and so let her know that she was to come into his room with her violin, for no one here appreciated her playing as he would appreciate it. He would never let her out of his room, at least, not so long as he lived; his frightful appearance would become, for the first time, useful to him; he would watch all the doors of his room at once and spit at intruders; but his sister should need no constraint, she should stay with him of her own free will; she should sit beside him on the sofa, bend down her ear to him and hear him confide that he had had the firm intention of sending her to the Conservatorium, and that, but for his mishap, last Christmas — surely Christmas was long past? — he would have announced it to everybody without allowing a single objection. After this confession his sister would be so touched that she would burst into tears, and Gregor would then raise himself to her shoulder and kiss her on the neck, which, now that she went to business, she kept free of any ribbon or collar.

"Mr. Samsa!" cried the middle lodger, to Gregor's father, and pointed, without wasting any more words, at Gregor, now working himself slowly forwards. The violin fell silent, the middle lodger first smiled to his friends with a shake of the head and then looked at Gregor again. Instead of driving Gregor out, his father seemed to think it more needful to begin by soothing down the lodgers, although they were not at all agitated and apparently found Gregor more entertaining than the violin-playing. He hurried toward them and, spreading out his arms, tried to urge them back into their own room and at the same time to block their view of Gregor. They now began to be really a little angry, one could not tell whether because of the old man's behavior or because it had just dawned on them that all unwittingly they had such a neighbor as Gregor next door. They demanded explanations of his father, they waved their arms like him, tugged uneasily at their beards, and only with reluctance backed towards their room. Meanwhile Gregor's sister, who stood there as if lost when her playing was so abruptly broken off, came to life again, pulled herself together all at once after standing for a while holding violin and bow in nervelessly hanging hands and staring at her music, pushed her violin into the lap of her mother, who was still sitting in her chair fighting asthmatically for breath, and ran into the lodgers' room to which they were now being shepherded by her father rather more quickly than before. One could see the pillows and blankets on the beds flying under her accustomed fingers and being laid in order. Before the lodgers had actually reached their room she had finished making the beds and slipped out.

The old man seemed once more to be so possessed by his mulish self-assertiveness that he was forgetting all the respect he should show to his lodgers. He kept driving them on and driving them on until in the very door of the bedroom the middle lodger stamped his foot loudly on the floor and so brought him to a halt. "I beg to announce," said the lodger, lifting one hand and looking also at Gregor's mother and sister, "that because of the disgusting conditions prevailing in this household and family" — here he spat on the floor with emphatic brevity — "I give you notice on the spot. Naturally I won't pay you a penny for the days I have lived here, on the contrary I shall consider bringing an action for damages against you, based on claims — believe me — that will be easily susceptible of proof." He ceased and stared straight in front of him, as if he expected something. In fact his two friends at once rushed into the breach with these words: "And we too give notice on the spot." On that he seized the door-handle and shut the door with a slam.

Gregor's father, groping with his hands, staggered forward and fell into his chair; it looked as if he were stretching himself there for his ordinary evening nap, but the marked jerkings of his head, which was as if uncontrollable, showed that he was far from asleep. Gregor had simply stayed quietly all the time on the spot where the lodgers had espied him. Disappointment at the failure of his plan, perhaps also the weakness arising from extreme hunger, made it impossible for him to move. He feared, with a fair degree of certainty, that at any moment the general tension would discharge itself in a combined attack upon him, and he lay waiting. He did not react even to the noise made by the violin as it fell off his mother's lap from under her trembling fingers and gave out a resonant note.

"My dear parents," said his sister, slapping her hand on the table by way of introduction, "things can't go on like this. Perhaps you don't realize that, but I do. I won't utter my brother's name in the presence of this creature, and so all I say is: we must try to get rid of it. We've tried to look after it and to put up with it as far as is humanly possible, and I don't think anyone could reproach us in the slightest."

"She is more than right," said Gregor's father to himself. His mother, who was still choking for lack of breath, began to cough hollowly into her hand with a wild look in her eyes.

His sister rushed over to her and held her forehead. His father's thoughts seemed to have lost their vagueness at Grete's words, he sat more upright, fingering his service cap that lay among the plates still lying on the table from the lodgers' supper, and from time to time looked at the still form of Gregor.

"We must try to get rid of it," his sister now said explicitly to her father, since her mother was coughing too much to hear a word, "it will be the death of both of you, I can see that coming. When one has to work as hard as we do, all of us, one can't stand this continual torment at home on top of it. At least I can't stand it any longer." And she burst into such a passion of sobbing that her tears dropped on her mother's face, where she wiped them off mechanically.

"My dear," said the old man sympathetically, and with evident understanding, "but what can we do?"

Gregor's sister merely shrugged her shoulders to indicate the feeling of helplessness that had now overmastered her during her weeping fit, in contrast to her former confidence.

"If he could understand us," said her father, half questioningly; Grete, still sobbing, vehemently waved a hand to show how unthinkable that was.

"If he could understand us," repeated the old man, shutting his eyes to consider his daughter's conviction that understanding was impossible, "then perhaps we might come to some agreement with him. But as it is — "

"He must go," cried Gregor's sister. "That's the only solution, Father. You must just try to get rid of the idea that this is Gregor. The fact that we've believed it for so long is the root of all our trouble. But how can it be Gregor? If this were Gregor, he would have realized long ago that human beings can't live with such a creature, and he'd have gone away on his own accord. Then we wouldn't have any brother, but we'd be able to go on living and keep his memory in honor. As it is, this creature persecutes us, drives away our lodgers, obviously wants the whole apartment to himself and would have us all sleep in the gutter. Just look, Father," she shrieked all at once, "he's at it again!" And in an access of panic that was quite incomprehensible to Gregor she even quitted her mother, literally thrusting the chair from her as if she would rather sacrifice her mother than stay so near to Gregor, and rushed behind her father, who also rose up, being simply upset by her agitation, and half-spread his arms out as if to protect her.

Yet Gregor had not the slightest intention of frightening anyone, far less his sister. He had only begun to turn round in order to crawl back to his room, but it was certainly a startling operation to watch, since because of his disabled condition he could not execute the difficult turning movements except by lifting his head and then bracing it against the floor over and over again. He paused and looked round. His good intentions seemed to have been recognized; the alarm had only been momentary. Now they were all watching him in melancholy silence. His mother lay in her chair, her legs stiffly outstretched and pressed together, her eyes almost closing for sheer weariness; his father and his sister were sitting beside each other, his sister's arm around the old man's neck.

Perhaps I can go on turning round now, thought Gregor, and began his labors again. He could not stop himself from panting with the effort, and had to pause now and then to take breath. Nor did anyone harass him, he was left entirely to himself. When he had completed the turn-round he began at once to crawl straight back. He was amazed at the distance separating him from his room and could not understand how in his weak state he had managed to accomplish the same journey so recently, almost without remarking it. Intent on crawling as fast as possible, he barely noticed that not a single word, not an ejaculation from his family, interfered with his progress. Only when he was already in the doorway did he turn his head round, not completely, for his neck muscles were getting stiff, but enough to see that nothing had changed behind him except that his sister had risen to her feet. His last glance fell on his mother, who was not quite overcome by sleep.

Hardly was he well inside his room when the door was hastily pushed shut, bolted, and locked. The sudden noise in his rear startled him so much that his little legs gave beneath him. It was his sister who had shown such haste. She had been standing ready waiting and had made a light spring forward, Gregor had not even heard her coming, and she cried "At last!" to her parents as she turned the key in the lock.

"And what now?" said Gregor to himself, looking round in the darkness. Soon he made the discovery that he was now unable to stir a limb. This did not surprise him, rather it seemed unnatural that he should ever actually have been able to move on these feeble little legs. Otherwise he felt relatively comfortable. True, his whole body was aching, but it seemed that the pain was gradually growing less and would finally pass away. The rotting apple in his back and the inflamed area around it, all covered with soft dust, already hardly troubled him. He thought of his family with tenderness and love. The decision that he must disappear was one that he held to even more strongly than his sister, if that were possible. In this state of vacant and peaceful meditation he remained until the tower clock struck three in the morning. The first broadening of light in the world outside the window entered his consciousness once more. Then his head sank to the floor of its own accord and from his nostrils came the last faint flicker of his breath.

When the charwoman arrived early in the morning — what between her strength and her impatience she slammed all the doors so loudly, never mind how often she had been begged not to do so, that no one in the whole apartment could enjoy any quiet sleep after her arrival — she noticed nothing unusual as she took her customary peep into Gregor's room. She thought he was lying motionless on purpose, pretending to be in the sulks; she credited him with every kind of intelligence. Since she happened to have the long-handled broom in her hand she tried to tickle him up with it from the doorway. When that too produced no reaction she felt provoked and poked at him a little harder, and only when she had pushed him along the floor without meeting any resistance was her attention aroused. It did not take her long to establish the truth of the matter, and her eyes widened, she let out a whistle, yet did not waste much time over it but tore open the door of the Samsas' bedroom and yelled into the darkness at the top of her voice: "Just look at this, it's dead; it's lying here dead and done for!"

Mr. and Mrs. Samsa started up in their double bed and before they realized the nature of the charwoman's announcement had some difficulty in overcoming the shock of it. But then they got out of bed quickly, one on either side, Mr. Samsa throwing a blanket over his shoulders, Mrs. Samsa in nothing but her nightgown; in this array they entered Gregor's room. Meanwhile the door of the living room opened, too, where Grete had been sleeping since the advent of the lodgers; she was completely dressed as if she had not been to bed, which seemed to be confirmed also by the paleness of her face. "Dead?" said Mrs. Samsa, looking questioningly at the charwoman, although she could have investigated for herself, and the fact was obvious enough without investigation. "I should say so," said the charwoman, proving her words by pushing Gregor's corpse a long way to one side with her broomstick. Mrs. Samsa made a movement as if to stop her, but checked it. "Well," said Mr. Samsa, "now thanks be to God." He crossed himself, and the three women followed his example. Grete, whose eyes never left the corpse, said: "Just see how thin he was. It's such a long time since he's eaten anything. The food came out again just as it went in." Indeed, Gregor's body was completely flat and dry, as could only now be seen when it was no longer supported by the legs and nothing prevented one from looking closely at it.

"Come in beside us, Grete, for a little while," said Mrs. Samsa with a tremulous smile, and Grete, not without looking back at the corpse, followed her parents into their bedroom. The charwoman shut the door and opened the window wide. Although it was so early in the morning a certain softness was perceptible in the fresh air. After all, it was already the end of March.

The three lodgers emerged from their room and were surprised to see no breakfast; they had been forgotten. "Where's our breakfast?" said the middle lodger peevishly to the charwoman. But she put her finger to her lips and hastily, without a word, indicated by gestures that they should go into Gregor's room. They did so and stood, their hands in the pockets of their somewhat shabby coats, around Gregor's corpse in the room where it was now fully light.

At that the door of the Samsas' bedroom opened and Mr. Samsa appeared in his uniform, his wife on one arm, his daughter on the other. They all looked a little as if they had been crying; from time to time Grete hid her face on her father's arm.

"Leave my house at once!" said Mr. Samsa, and pointed to the door without disengaging himself from the women. "What do you mean by that?" said the middle lodger, taken somewhat aback, with a feeble smile. The two others put their hands behind them and kept rubbing them together, as if in gleeful expectation of a fine set-to in which they were bound to come off the winners. "I mean just what I say," answered Mr. Samsa, and advanced in a straight line with his two companions towards the lodger. He stood his ground at first quietly, looking at the floor as if his thoughts were taking a new pattern in his head. "Then let us go, by all means," he said, and looked up at Mr. Samsa as if in a sudden access of humility he were expecting some renewed sanction for this decision. Mr. Samsa merely nodded briefly once or twice with meaning eyes. Upon that the lodger really did go with long strides

into the hall, his two friends had been listening and had quite stopped rubbing their hands for some moments and now went scuttling after him as if
afraid that Mr. Samsa might get into the hall before them and cut them off
from their leader. In the hall they all three took their hats from the rack, their
sticks from the umbrella stand, bowed in silence and quitted the apartment.
With a suspiciousness which proved quite unfounded Mr. Samsa and the two
women followed them out to the landing; leaning over the banister they
watched the three figures slowly but surely going down the long stairs, vanishing from sight at a certain turn of the staircase on every floor and coming
into view again after a moment or so; the more they dwindled, the more the
Samsa family's interest in them dwindled, and when a butcher's boy met
them and passed them on the stairs coming up proudly with a tray on his
head, Mr. Samsa and the two women soon left the landing and as if a burden
had been lifted from them went back into their apartment.

They decided to spend this day in resting and going for a stroll; they had
not only deserved such a respite from work but absolutely needed it. And so
they sat down at the table and wrote three notes of excuse, Mr. Samsa to his
board of management, Mrs. Samsa to her employer and Grete to the head of
her firm. While they were writing, the charwoman came in to say that she was
going now, since her morning's work was finished. At first they only nodded
without looking up, but as she kept hovering there they eyed her irritably.
"Well?" said Mr. Samsa. The charwoman stood grinning in the doorway as if
she had good news to impart to the family but meant not to say a word unless
properly questioned. The small ostrich feather standing upright on her hat,
which had annoyed Mr. Samsa ever since she was engaged, was waving gaily
in all directions. "Well, what is it then?" asked Mrs. Samsa, who obtained
more respect from the charwoman than the others. "Oh," said the charwoman, giggling so amiably that she could not at once continue, "just this,
you don't need to bother about how to get rid of the thing next door. It's been
seen to already." Mrs. Samsa and Grete bent over their letters again, as if preoccupied; Mr. Samsa, who perceived that she was eager to begin describing it
all in detail, stopped her with a decisive hand. But since she was not allowed
to tell her story, she remembered the great hurry she was in, being obviously
deeply huffed: "Bye, everybody," she said, whirling off violently, and departed with a frightful slamming of doors.

"She'll be given notice tonight," said Mr. Samsa, but neither from his
wife nor his daughter did he get any answer, for the charwoman seemed to
have shattered again the composure they had barely achieved. They rose,
went to the window and stayed there, clasping each other tight. Mr. Samsa
turned in his chair to look at them and quietly observed them for a little. Then
he called out: "Come along, now, do. Let bygones be bygones. And you might
have some consideration for me." The two of them complied at once, hastened
to him, caressed him and quickly finished their letters.

Then they all three left the apartment together, which was more than
they had done for months, and went by tram into the open country outside the
town. The tram, in which they were the only passengers, was filled with warm
sunshine. Leaning comfortably back in their seats they canvassed their

prospects for the future, and it appeared on closer inspection that these were not at all bad, for the jobs they had got, which so far they had never really discussed with each other, were all three admirable and likely to lead to better things later on. The greatest immediate improvement in their condition would of course arise from moving to another house; they wanted to take a smaller and cheaper but also better situated and more easily run apartment than the one they had, which Gregor had selected. While they were thus conversing, it struck both Mr. and Mrs. Samsa, almost at the same moment, as they became aware of their daughter's increasing vivacity, that in spite of all the sorrow of recent times, which had made her cheeks pale, she had bloomed into a pretty girl with a good figure. They grew quieter and half unconsciously exchanged glances of complete agreement, having come to the conclusion that it would soon be time to find a good husband for her. And it was like a confirmation of their new dreams and excellent intentions that at the end of their journey their daughter sprang to her feet first and stretched her young body.

℞℞

JAMAICA KINCAID (b. 1949) *was born and educated in St. Johns, Antigua, in the West Indies. Her father was a carpenter, and her family doted upon her, the only child. Kincaid remembers:*

> My mother did keep everything I ever wore, and basically until I was quite grown up my past was sort of a museum to me. Clearly, the way I became a writer was that my mother wrote my life for me and told it to me. I can't help but think that it made me interested in the idea of myself as an object. I can't account for the reason I became a writer any other way, because I certainly didn't know writers. And not only that. I thought writing was something that people just didn't do anymore, that went out of fashion, like the bustle. I really didn't read a book that was written in the twentieth century until I was about seventeen and away from home.

Kincaid left Antigua to study in the United States, but she found college "a dismal failure," so she educated herself. She began writing and published her stories in Rolling Stone, *the* Paris Review, *and* The New Yorker, *where she became a staff writer in 1978. Six years later she published her first book,* At the Bottom of the River, *a collection of stories, which won the Morton Dauwen Zabel Award of the American Academy and Institute of Arts and Letters. In 1985* Annie John, *her book of interrelated stories about a girl's coming of age in the West Indies, was also much praised. In her autobiographical writing, Kincaid often explores the idea that her deep affection for her family and her native country developed into a conflicting need for separation and independence as she grew up.*

Typically Kincaid writes in a deliberately precise rhythmic style about intense emotions, as in her story "Girl" (1984). Her fiction is free from conventional plots, characters, and dialogue. The critic Suzanne Freeman has recognized that "what Kincaid has to tell me, she tells, with her singsong style, in a series of images that are as sweet and mysterious as the secrets that children whisper in your ear." Although Kincaid is married to an American and lives in New York City, she feels that the British West Indies will continue to be the source for her fiction. "What I really feel about

America is that it's given me a place to be myself — but myself as I was formed some-where else." A Small Place *(1989), another book about the West Indies, was described by the novelist Salman Rushdie as "a jeremiad of great clarity and a force that one might have called torrential were the language not so finely controlled." Her latest books are* Lucy *(1990) and* The Autobiography of My Mother *(1996).*

JAMAICA KINCAID

Girl

1984

Wash the white clothes on Monday and put them on the stone heap; wash the color clothes on Tuesday and put them on the clothesline to dry; don't walk barehead in the hot sun; cook pumpkin fritters in very hot sweet oil; soak your little cloths right after you take them off; when buying cotton to make yourself a nice blouse, be sure that it doesn't have gum on it, because that way it won't hold up well after a wash; soak salt fish overnight before you cook it; is it true that you sing benna° in Sunday school?; always eat your food in such a way that it won't turn someone else's stomach; on Sundays try to walk like a lady and not like the slut you are so bent on becoming; don't sing benna in Sunday school; you mustn't speak to wharf-rat boys, not even to give directions; don't eat fruits on the street — flies will follow you; *but I don't sing benna on Sundays at all and never in Sunday school;* this is how to sew on a but-ton; this is how to make a button-hole for the button you have just sewed on; this is how to hem a dress when you see the hem coming down and so to prevent yourself from looking like the slut I know you are so bent on becom-ing; this is how you iron your father's khaki shirt so that it doesn't have a crease; this is how you iron your father's khaki pants so that they don't have a crease; this is how you grow okra — far from the house, because okra tree harbors red ants; when you are growing dasheen, make sure it gets plenty of water or else it makes your throat itch when you are eating it; this is how you sweep a corner; this is how you sweep a whole house; this is how you sweep a yard; this is how you smile to someone you don't like too much; this is how you smile to someone you don't like at all; this is how you smile to someone you like completely; this is how you set a table for tea; this is how you set a table for dinner; this is how you set a table for dinner with an important guest; this is how you set a table for lunch; this is how you set a table for breakfast; this is how to behave in the presence of men who don't know you very well, and this way they won't recognize immediately the slut I have warned you against becoming; be sure to wash every day, even if it is with your own spit; don't squat down to play marbles — you are not a boy, you know; don't pick people's flowers — you might catch something; don't throw stones at black-birds, because it might not be a blackbird at all; this is how to make a bread pudding; this is how to make doukona;° this is how to make pepper pot; this

---

benna: Calypso music.
doukona: A spicy plantain pudding.

is how to make a good medicine for a cold; this is how to make a good medicine to throw away a child before it even becomes a child; this is how to catch a fish; this is how to throw back a fish you don't like, and that way something bad won't fall on you; this is how to bully a man; this is how a man bullies you; this is how to love a man, and if this doesn't work there are other ways, and if they don't work don't feel too bad about giving up; this is how to spit up in the air if you feel like it, and this is how to move quick so that it doesn't fall on you; this is how to make ends meet; always squeeze bread to make sure it's fresh; *but what if the baker won't let me feel the bread?*; you mean to say that after all you are really going to be the kind of woman who the baker won't let near the bread?

జ్ఞ

D[AVID] H[ERBERT] LAWRENCE *(1885–1930) was born the son of a coal miner in the industrial town of Eastwood, in Nottinghamshire, England. His mother had been a schoolteacher, and she was frustrated by the hard existence of a coal miner's wife. Through her financial sacrifices, Lawrence was able to complete high school; then he studied to become a teacher. He finished his university studies and was licensed as a teacher at the age of twenty-three. Moving to South London, he allied himself with the young literary rebels there, and his first novel,* The White Peacock, *was published in 1910. In 1912 Lawrence fell in love with an older married woman, Frieda von Richthofen, who abandoned her husband and children to run off with him to her native Germany. English society never forgave either of them, although the pair eventually married in 1914 and maintained their exceedingly stormy union, punctuated with frequent affairs, until Lawrence's death. In 1913, Lawrence was established as a major literary figure with the publication of* Sons and Lovers.

Much of his fiction, like this novel and the story "Odour of Chrysanthemums," is about characters caught between their unsatisfactory relationships with others and their struggle to break free. Lawrence sought an ideal balance or, as he wrote in the novel Women in Love *(1920), a "star equilibrium," in which two beings are attracted to each other but never lose their individuality. He felt that "no emotion is supreme, or exclusively worth living for. All emotions go to the achieving of a living relationship between a human being and the other human being or creature or thing he becomes purely related to."*

A prolific writer, Lawrence suffered from tuberculosis and spent years wandering in Italy, Australia, Mexico, New Mexico, and southern France, seeking a warm, sunny climate. He also fled to primitive societies to escape the industrialization and commercialism of Western life. A virulent social critic, he was frequently harassed by censorship because his short stories, novels, and poetry were often explicitly sexual and he always challenged conventional moral attitudes. Literature, for Lawrence, had two great functions: providing an emotional experience, and then, if the reader had the courage of his or her own feelings and could live imaginatively, becoming "a mine of practical truth."

Lawrence wrote stories all his life, publishing a first collection, The Prussian Officer, *in 1914; it was followed by four other collections. In 1961 his stories were compiled in a three-volume paperback edition that has gone through numerous reprintings. The style of the early stories is harshly realistic, but Lawrence's depiction of his characters' emotional situations changed in his later work, where he created fantasies like his famous and chilling story "The Rocking-Horse Winner."*

RELATED STORY: *John Steinbeck, "The Chrysanthemums," page 632.*

RELATED COMMENTARIES: *D. H. Lawrence, Draft Passage from "Odour of Chrysanthemums," page 765; Janice H. Harris, "Levels of Meaning in Lawrence's 'The Rocking-Horse Winner,'" page 754; Jay Parini, "Lawrence's and Steinbeck's 'Chrysanthemums,'" page 786.*

D. H. LAWRENCE

The Rocking-Horse Winner

1926

There was a woman who was beautiful, who started with all the advantages, yet she had no luck. She married for love, and the love turned to dust. She had bonny children, yet she felt they had been thrust upon her, and she could not love them. They looked at her coldly, as if they were finding fault with her. And hurriedly she felt she must cover up some fault in herself. Yet what it was that she must cover up she never knew. Nevertheless, when her children were present, she always felt the center of her heart go hard. This troubled her, and in her manner she was all the more gentle and anxious for her children, as if she loved them very much. Only she herself knew that at the center of her heart was a hard little place that could not feel love, no, not for anybody. Everybody else said of her: "She is such a good mother. She adores her children." Only she herself, and her children themselves, knew it was not so. They read it in each other's eyes.

There were a boy and two little girls. They lived in a pleasant house, with a garden, and they had discreet servants, and felt themselves superior to anyone in the neighborhood.

Although they lived in style, they felt always an anxiety in the house. There was never enough money. The mother had a small income, and the father had a small income, but not nearly enough for the social position which they had to keep up. The father went into town to some office. But though he had good prospects, these prospects never materialized. There was always the grinding sense of the shortage of money, though the style was always kept up.

At last the mother said: "I will see if *I* can't make something." But she did not know where to begin. She racked her brains, and tried this thing and the other, but could not find anything successful. The failure made deep lines come into her face. Her children were growing up, they would have to go to school. There must be more money, there must be more money. The father, who was always very handsome and expensive in his tastes, seemed as if he never *would* be able to do anything worth doing. And the mother, who had a great belief in herself, did not succeed any better, and her tastes were just as expensive.

And so the house came to be haunted by the unspoken phrase: *There must be more money! There must be more money!* The children could hear it all the time though nobody said it aloud. They heard it at Christmas, when the expensive and splendid toys filled the nursery. Behind the shining modern rocking horse, behind the smart doll's house, a voice would start whispering: "There *must* be more money! There *must* be more money!" And the children would stop playing, to listen for a moment. They would look into each other's eyes, to see if they had all heard. And each one saw in the eyes of the other two that they too had heard. "There *must* be more money! There *must* be more money!"

It came whispering from the springs of the still-swaying rocking horse, and even the horse, bending his wooden, champing head, heard it. The big doll, sitting so pink and smirking in her new pram, could hear it quite plainly, and seemed to be smirking all the more self-consciously because of it. The foolish puppy, too, that took the place of the teddy bear, he was looking so extraordinarily foolish for no other reason but that he heard the secret whisper all over the house: "There *must* be more money!"

Yet nobody ever said it aloud. The whisper was everywhere, and therefore no one spoke it. Just as no one ever says: "We are breathing!" in spite of the fact that breath is coming and going all the time.

"Mother," said the boy Paul one day, "why don't we keep a car of our own? Why do we always use Uncle's, or else a taxi?"

"Because we're the poor members of the family," said the mother.

"But why *are* we, Mother?"

"Well — I suppose," she said slowly and bitterly, "it's because your father has no luck."

The boy was silent for some time.

"Is luck money, Mother?" he asked rather timidly.

"No, Paul. Not quite. It's what causes you to have money."

"Oh!" said Paul vaguely. "I thought when Uncle Oscar said *filthy lucker*, it meant money."

"*Filthy lucre* does mean money," said the mother. "But it's lucre, not luck."

"Oh!" said the boy. "Then what *is* luck, Mother?"

"It's what causes you to have money. If you're lucky you have money. That's why it's better to be born lucky than rich. If you're rich, you may lose your money. But if you're lucky, you will always get more money."

"Oh! Will you? And is Father not lucky?"

"Very unlucky, I should say," she said bitterly.

The boy watched her with unsure eyes.

"Why?" he asked.

"I don't know. Nobody ever knows why one person is lucky and another unlucky."

"Don't they? Nobody at all? Does *nobody* know?"

"Perhaps God. But He never tells."

"He ought to, then. And aren't you lucky either, Mother?"

"I can't be, if I married an unlucky husband."

"But by yourself, aren't you?"

"I used to think I was, before I married. Now I think I am very unlucky indeed."

"Why?"

"Well — never mind! Perhaps I'm not really," she said.

The child looked at her, to see if she meant it. But he saw, by the lines of her mouth, that she was only trying to hide something from him.

"Well, anyhow," he said stoutly, "I'm a lucky person."

"Why?" said his mother, with a sudden laugh.

He stared at her. He didn't even know why he had said it.

"God told me," he asserted, brazening it out.

"I hope He did, dear!" she said, again with a laugh, but rather bitter.

"He did, Mother!"

"Excellent!" said the mother.

The boy saw she did not believe him; or, rather, that she paid no attention to his assertion. This angered him somewhat, and made him want to compel her attention.

He went off by himself, vaguely, in a childish way, seeking for the clue to "luck." Absorbed, taking no heed of other people, he went about with a sort of stealth, seeking inwardly for luck. He wanted luck, he wanted it, he wanted it. When the two girls were playing dolls in the nursery, he would sit on his big rocking horse, charging madly into space, with a frenzy that made the little girls peer at him uneasily. Wildly the horse careered, the waving dark hair of the boy tossed, his eyes had a strange glare in them. The little girls dared not speak to him.

When he had ridden to the end of his mad little journey, he climbed down and stood in front of his rocking horse, staring fixedly into its lowered face. Its red mouth was slightly open, its big eye was wide and glassy-bright.

Now! he could silently command the snorting steed. Now, take me to where there is luck! Now take me!

And he would slash the horse on the neck with the little whip he had asked Uncle Oscar for. He *knew* the horse could take him to where there was luck, if only he forced it. So he would mount again, and start on his furious ride, hoping at last to get there. He knew he could get there.

"You'll break your horse, Paul!" said the nurse.

"He's always riding like that! I wish he'd leave off!" said his elder sister Joan.

But he only glared down on them in silence. Nurse gave him up. She could make nothing of him. Anyhow he was growing beyond her.

One day his mother and his uncle Oscar came in when he was on one of his furious rides. He did not speak to them.

"Hallo, you young jockey! Riding a winner?" said his uncle.

"Aren't you growing too big for a rocking horse? You're not a very little boy any longer, you know," said his mother.

But Paul only gave a blue glare from his big, rather close-set eyes. He would speak to nobody when he was in full tilt. His mother watched him with an anxious expression on her face.

At last he suddenly stopped forcing his horse into the mechanical gallop, and slid down.

"Well, I got there!" he announced fiercely, his blue eyes still flaring, and his sturdy long legs straddling apart.

"Where did you get to?" asked his mother.

"Where I wanted to go," he flared back at her.

"That's right, son!" said Uncle Oscar. "Don't you stop till you get there. What's the horse's name?"

"He doesn't have a name," said the boy.

"Gets on without all right?" asked the uncle.

"Well, he has different names. He was called Sansovino last week."

"Sansovino, eh? Won the Ascot. How did you know his name?"

"He always talks about horse races with Bassett," said Joan.

The uncle was delighted to find that his small nephew was posted with all the racing news. Bassett, the young gardener, who had been wounded in the left foot in the war and had got his present job through Oscar Cresswell, whose batman he had been, was a perfect blade of the "turf." He lived in the racing events, and the small boy lived with him.

Oscar Cresswell got it all from Bassett.

"Master Paul comes and asks me, so I can't do more than tell him, sir," said Bassett, his face terribly serious, as if he were speaking of religious matters.

"And does he ever put anything on a horse he fancies?"

"Well — I don't want to give him away — he's a young sport, a fine sport, sir. Would you mind asking him himself? He sort of takes a pleasure in it, and perhaps he'd feel I was giving him away, sir, if you don't mind."

Bassett was serious as a church.

The uncle went back to his nephew and took him off for a ride in the car.

"Say, Paul, old man, do you ever put anything on a horse?" the uncle asked.

The boy watched the handsome man closely.

"Why, do you think I oughtn't to?" he parried.

"Not a bit of it! I thought perhaps you might give me a tip for the Lincoln."

The car sped on into the country, going down to Uncle Oscar's place in Hampshire.

"Honor bright?" said the nephew.

"Honor bright, son!" said the uncle.

"Well, then, Daffodil."

"Daffodil! I doubt it, sonny. What about Mirza?"

"I only know the winner," said the boy. "That's Daffodil."

"Daffodil, eh?"

There was a pause. Daffodil was an obscure horse comparatively.

"Uncle!"

"Yes, son?"

"You won't let it go any further, will you? I promised Bassett."

"Bassett be damned, old man! What's he got to do with it?"

"We're partners. We've been partners from the first. Uncle, he lent me my first five shillings, which I lost. I promised him, honor bright, it was only between me and him; only you gave me that ten-shilling note I started winning with, so I thought you were lucky. You won't let it go any further, will you?"

The boy gazed at his uncle from those big, hot, blue eyes, set rather close together. The uncle stirred and laughed uneasily.

"Right you are, son! I'll keep your tip private. Daffodil, eh? How much are you putting on him?"

"All except twenty pounds," said the boy. "I keep that in reserve."

The uncle thought it a good joke.

"You keep twenty pounds in reserve, do you, you young romancer? What are you betting, then?"

"I'm betting three hundred," said the boy gravely. "But it's between you and me, Uncle Oscar! Honor bright?"

The uncle burst into a roar of laughter.

"It's between you and me all right, you young Nat Gould,"° he said, laughing. "But where's your three hundred?"

"Bassett keeps it for me. We're partners."

"You are, are you! And what is Bassett putting on Daffodil?"

"He won't go quite as high as I do, I expect. Perhaps he'll go a hundred and fifty."

"What, pennies?" laughed the uncle.

"Pounds," said the child, with a surprised look at his uncle. "Bassett keeps a bigger reserve than I do."

Between wonder and amusement Uncle Oscar was silent. He pursued the matter no further, but he determined to take his nephew with him to the Lincoln races.

"Now, son," he said, "I'm putting twenty on Mirza, and I'll put five for you on any horse you fancy. What's your pick?"

"Daffodil, Uncle."

"No, not the fiver on Daffodil!"

"I should if it was my own fiver," said the child.

"Good! Good! Right you are! A fiver for me and a fiver for you on Daffodil."

The child had never been to a race meeting before, and his eyes were blue fire. He pursed his mouth tight, and watched. A Frenchman just in front had put his money on Lancelot. Wild with excitement, he flailed his arms up and down, yelling *Lancelot! Lancelot!* in his French accent.

Daffodil came in first, Lancelot second, Mirza third. The child, flushed and with eyes blazing, was curiously serene. His uncle brought him four five-pound notes, four to one.

"What am I to do with these?" he cried, waving them before the boy's eyes.

"I suppose we'll talk to Bassett," said the boy. "I expect I have fifteen hundred now; and twenty in reserve; and this twenty."

His uncle studied him for some moments.

"Look here, son!" he said. "You're not serious about Bassett and that fifteen hundred, are you?"

Nat Gould: Nathaniel Gould (1857–1919) was a British novelist and sports columnist known best for a series of novels about horse racing.

"Yes, I am. But it's between you and me, Uncle. Honor bright!"

"Honor bright all right, son! But I must talk to Bassett."

"If you'd like to be a partner, Uncle, with Bassett and me, we could all be partners. Only, you'd have to promise, honor bright, Uncle, not to let it go beyond us three. Bassett and I are lucky, and you must be lucky, because it was your ten shillings I started winning with. . . ."

Uncle Oscar took both Bassett and Paul into Richmond Park for an afternoon, and there they talked.

"It's like this, you see, sir," Bassett said. "Master Paul would get me talking about racing events, spinning yarns, you know, sir. And he was always keen on knowing if I'd made or if I'd lost. It's about a year since, now, that I put five shillings on Blush of Dawn for him — and we lost. Then the luck turned, with that ten shillings he had from you, that we put on Singhalese. And since then, it's been pretty steady, all things considering. What do you say, Master Paul?"

"We're all right when we're sure," said Paul. "It's when we're not quite sure that we go down."

"Oh, but we're careful then," said Bassett.

"But when are you *sure*?" Uncle Oscar smiled.

"It's Master Paul, sir," said Bassett, in a secret, religious voice. "It's as if he had it from heaven. Like Daffodil, now, for the Lincoln. That was as sure as eggs."

"Did you put anything on Daffodil?" asked Oscar Cresswell.

"Yes, sir. I made my bit."

"And my nephew?"

Bassett was obstinately silent, looking at Paul.

"I made twelve hundred, didn't I, Bassett? I told Uncle I was putting three hundred on Daffodil."

"That's right," said Bassett, nodding.

"But where's the money?" asked the uncle.

"I keep it safe locked up, sir. Master Paul he can have it any minute he likes to ask for it."

"What, fifteen hundred pounds?"

"And twenty! And *forty*, that is, with the twenty he made on the course."

"It's amazing!" said the uncle.

"If Master Paul offers you to be partners, sir, I would, if I were you; if you'll excuse me," said Bassett.

Oscar Cresswell thought about it.

"I'll see the money," he said.

They drove home again, and sure enough, Bassett came round to the garden house with fifteen hundred pounds in notes. The twenty pounds reserve was left with Joe Glee, in the Turf Commission deposit.

"You see, it's all right, Uncle, when I'm *sure*! Then we go strong, for all we're worth. Don't we, Bassett?"

"We do that, Master Paul."

"And when are you sure?" said the uncle, laughing.

"Oh, well, sometimes I'm *absolutely* sure, like about Daffodil," said the boy; "and sometimes I have an idea; and sometimes I haven't even an idea, have I, Bassett? Then we're careful, because we mostly go down."

"You do, do you! And when you're sure, like about Daffodil, what makes you sure, sonny?"

"Oh, well, I don't know," said the boy uneasily. "I'm sure, you know, Uncle; that's all."

"It's as if he had it from heaven, sir," Bassett reiterated.

"I should say so!" said the uncle.

But he became a partner. And when the Leger was coming on, Paul was "sure" about Lively Spark, which was a quite inconsiderable horse. The boy insisted on putting a thousand on the horse, Bassett went for five hundred, and Oscar Cresswell two hundred. Lively Spark came in first, and the betting had been ten to one against him. Paul had made ten thousand.

"You see," he said, "I was absolutely sure of him."

Even Oscar Cresswell had cleared two thousand.

"Look here, son," he said, "this sort of thing makes me nervous."

"It needn't, Uncle! Perhaps I shan't be sure again for a long time."

"But what are you going to do with your money?" asked the uncle.

"Of course," said the boy. "I started it for Mother. She said she had no luck, because Father is unlucky, so I thought if *I* was lucky, it might stop whispering."

"What might stop whispering?"

"Our house. I *hate* our house for whispering."

"What does it whisper?"

"Why — why" — the boy fidgeted — "why, I don't know. But it's always short of money, you know, Uncle."

"I know it, son, I know it."

"You know people send Mother writs, don't you, Uncle?"

"I'm afraid I do," said the uncle.

"And then the house whispers, like people laughing at you behind your back. It's awful, that is! I thought if I was lucky. . . ."

"You might stop it," added the uncle.

The boy watched him with big blue eyes, that had an uncanny cold fire in them, and he said never a word.

"Well, then!" said the uncle. "What are we doing?"

"I shouldn't like Mother to know I was lucky," said the boy.

"Why not, son?"

"She'd stop me."

"I don't think she would."

"Oh!" — and the boy writhed in an odd way — "I *don't* want her to know, Uncle."

"All right, son! We'll manage it without her knowing."

They managed it very easily. Paul, at the other's suggestion, handed over five thousand pounds to his uncle, who deposited it with the family lawyer, who was then to inform Paul's mother that a relative had put five thousand pounds into his hands, which sum was to be paid out a thousand pounds at a time, on the mother's birthday, for the next five years.

"So she'll have a birthday present of a thousand pounds for five successive years," said Uncle Oscar. "I hope it won't make it all the harder for her later."

Paul's mother had her birthday in November. The house had been "whispering" worse than ever lately, and, even in spite of his luck, Paul could not bear up against it. He was very anxious to see the effect of the birthday letter, telling his mother about the thousand pounds.

When there were no visitors, Paul now took his meals with his parents, as he was beyond the nursery control. His mother went into town nearly every day. She had discovered that she had an odd knack of sketching furs and dress materials, so she worked secretly in the studio of a friend who was the chief artist for the leading drapers. She drew the figures of ladies in furs and ladies in silk and sequins for the newspaper advertisements. This young woman artist earned several thousand pounds a year, but Paul's mother only made several hundreds, and she was again dissatisfied. She so wanted to be first in something, and she did not succeed, even in making sketches for drapery advertisements.

She was down to breakfast on the morning of her birthday. Paul watched her face as she read her letters. He knew the lawyer's letter. As his mother read it, her face hardened and became more expressionless. Then a cold, determined look came on her mouth. She hid the letter under the pile of others, and said not a word about it.

"Didn't you have anything nice in the post for your birthday, Mother?" said Paul.

"Quite moderately nice," she said, her voice cold and absent.

She went away to town without saying more.

But in the afternoon Uncle Oscar appeared. He said Paul's mother had had a long interview with the lawyer, asking if the whole five thousand could not be advanced at once, as she was in debt.

"What do you think, Uncle?" said the boy.

"I leave it to you, son."

"Oh, let her have it, then! We can get some more with the other," said the boy.

"A bird in the hand is worth two in the bush, laddie!" said Uncle Oscar.

"But I'm sure to *know* for the Grand National; or the Lincolnshire; or else the Derby. I'm sure to know for *one* of them," said Paul.

So Uncle Oscar signed the agreement, and Paul's mother touched the whole five thousand. Then something very curious happened. The voices in the house suddenly went mad, like a chorus of frogs on a spring evening. There were certain new furnishings, and Paul had a tutor. He was *really* going to Eton, his father's school, in the following autumn. There were flowers in the winter, and a blossoming of the luxury Paul's mother had been used to. And yet the voices in the house, behind the sprays of mimosa and almond blossom, and from under the piles of iridescent cushions, simply trilled and screamed in a sort of ecstasy: "There *must* be more money! Oh-h-h; there *must* be more money. Oh, now, now-w! Now-w-w — there *must* be more money! — more than ever! More than ever!"

It frightened Paul terribly. He studied away at his Latin and Greek. But his intense hours were spent with Bassett. The Grand National had gone by; he had not "known," and had lost a hundred pounds. Summer was at hand. He was in agony for the Lincoln. But even for the Lincoln he didn't "know," and he lost fifty pounds. He became wild-eyed and strange, as if something were going to explode in him.

"Let it alone, son! Don't you bother about it!" urged Uncle Oscar. But it was as if the boy couldn't really hear what his uncle was saying.

"I've got to know for the Derby! I've got to know for the Derby!" the child reiterated, his big blue eyes blazing with a sort of madness.

His mother noticed how overwrought he was.

"You'd better go to the seaside. Wouldn't you like to go now to the seaside, instead of waiting? I think you'd better," she said, looking down at him anxiously, her heart curiously heavy because of him.

But the child lifted his uncanny blue eyes. "I couldn't possibly go before the Derby, Mother!" he said. "I couldn't possibly!"

"Why not?" she said, her voice becoming heavy when she was opposed. "Why not? You can still go from the seaside to see the Derby with your uncle Oscar, if that's what you wish. No need for you to wait here. Besides, I think you care too much about these races. It's a bad sign. My family has been a gambling family, and you won't know till you grow up how much damage it has done. But it has done damage. I shall have to send Bassett away, and ask Uncle Oscar not to talk racing to you, unless you promise to be reasonable about it; go away to the seaside and forget it. You're all nerves!"

"I'll do what you like, Mother, so long as you don't send me away till after the Derby," the boy said.

"Send you away from where? Just from this house?"

"Yes," he said, gazing at her.

"Why, you curious child, what makes you care about this house so much, suddenly? I never knew you loved it."

He gazed at her without speaking. He had a secret within a secret, something he had not divulged, even to Bassett or to his uncle Oscar.

But his mother, after standing undecided and a little bit sullen for some moments, said:

"Very well, then! Don't go to the seaside till after the Derby, if you don't wish it. But promise me you won't let your nerves go to pieces. Promise you won't think so much about horse racing and *events*, as you call them!"

"Oh, no," said the boy casually. "I won't think much about them, Mother. You needn't worry. I wouldn't worry, Mother, if I were you."

"If you were me and I were you," said his mother, "I wonder what we *should* do!"

"But you know you needn't worry, Mother, don't you?" the boy repeated.

"I should be awfully glad to know it," she said wearily.

"Oh, well you *can*, you know. I mean, you *ought* to know you needn't worry," he insisted.

"Ought I? Then I'll see about it," she said.

Paul's secret of secrets was his wooden horse, that which had no name.

Since he was emancipated from a nurse and a nursery governess, he had had his rocking horse removed to his own bedroom at the top of the house.

"Surely, you're too big for a rocking horse!" his mother had remonstrated.

"Well, you see, Mother, till I can have a *real* horse, I like to have *some* sort of animal about," had been his quaint answer.

"Do you feel he keeps you company?" She laughed.

"Oh, yes! He's very good, he always keeps me company, when I'm there," said Paul.

So the horse, rather shabby, stood in an arrested prance in the boy's bedroom.

The Derby was drawing near, and the boy grew more and more tense. He hardly heard what was spoken to him, he was very frail, and his eyes were really uncanny. His mother had sudden strange seizures of uneasiness about him. Sometimes, for half an hour, she would feel a sudden anxiety about him that was almost anguish. She wanted to rush to him at once, and know he was safe.

Two nights before the Derby, she was at a big party in town, when one of her rushes of anxiety about her boy, her firstborn, gripped her heart till she could hardly speak. She fought with the feeling, might and main, for she believed in common sense. But it was too strong. She had to leave the dance and go downstairs to telephone to the country. The children's nursery governess was terribly surprised and startled at being rung up in the night.

"Are the children all right, Miss Wilmot?"

"Oh, yes, they are quite all right."

"Master Paul? Is he all right?"

"He went to bed as right as a trivet. Shall I run up and look at him?"

"No," said Paul's mother reluctantly. "No! Don't trouble. It's all right. Don't sit up. We shall be home fairly soon." She did not want her son's privacy intruded upon.

"Very good," said the governess.

It was about one o'clock when Paul's mother and father drove up to their house. All was still. Paul's mother went to her room and slipped off her white fur cloak. She had told her maid not to wait up for her. She heard her husband downstairs, mixing a whisky and soda.

And then, because of the strange anxiety at her heart, she stole upstairs to her son's room. Noiselessly she went along the upper corridor. Was there a faint noise? What was it?

She stood, with arrested muscles, outside his door, listening. There was a strange, heavy, and yet not loud noise. Her heart stood still. It was a soundless noise, yet rushing and powerful. Something huge, in violent, hushed motion. What was it? What in God's name was it? She ought to know. She felt that she knew the noise. She knew what it was.

Yet she could not place it. She couldn't say what it was. And on and on it went, like a madness.

Softly, frozen with anxiety and fear, she turned the door handle.

The room was dark. Yet in the space near the window, she heard and saw something plunging to and fro. She gazed in fear and amazement.

Then suddenly she switched on the light, and saw her son, in his green pajamas, madly surging on the rocking horse. The blaze of light suddenly lit him up, as he urged the wooden horse, and lit her up, as she stood, blonde, in her dress of pale green and crystal, in the doorway.

"Paul!" she cried. "Whatever are you doing?"

"It's Malabar!" he screamed, in a powerful, strange voice. "It's Malabar!"

His eyes blazed at her for one strange and senseless second, as he ceased urging his wooden horse. Then he fell with a crash to the ground, and she, all her tormented motherhood flooding upon her, rushed to gather him up.

But he was unconscious, and unconscious he remained, with some brain fever. He talked and tossed, and his mother sat stonily by his side.

"Malabar! It's Malabar! Bassett, Bassett, I *know*! It's Malabar!"

So the child cried, trying to get up and urge the rocking horse that gave him his inspiration.

"What does he mean by Malabar?" asked the heart-frozen mother.

"I don't know," said the father stonily.

"What does he mean by Malabar?" she asked her brother Oscar.

"It's one of the horses running for the Derby," was the answer.

And, in spite of himself, Oscar Cresswell spoke to Bassett, and himself put a thousand on Malabar: at fourteen to one.

The third day of the illness was critical: they were waiting for a change. The boy, with his rather long, curly hair, was tossing ceaselessly on the pillow. He never slept nor regained consciousness, and his eyes were like blue stones. His mother sat, feeling her heart had gone, turned actually into a stone.

In the evening, Oscar Cresswell did not come, but Bassett sent a message, saying could he come up for one moment, just one moment? Paul's mother was very angry at the intrusion, but on second thought she agreed. The boy was the same. Perhaps Bassett might bring him to consciousness.

The gardener, a shortish fellow with a little brown mustache, and sharp little brown eyes, tiptoed into the room, touched his imaginary cap to Paul's mother, and stole to the bedside, staring with glittering, smallish eyes at the tossing, dying child.

"Master Paul!" he whispered. "Master Paul! Malabar came in first all right, a clean win. I did as you told me. You've made over seventy thousand pounds, you have; you've got over eighty thousand. Malabar came in all right, Master Paul."

"Malabar! Malabar! Did I say Malabar, Mother? Did I say Malabar? Do you think I'm lucky, Mother? I knew Malabar, didn't I? Over eighty thousand pounds! I call that lucky, don't you, Mother? Over eighty thousand pounds! I knew, didn't I know I knew? Malabar came in all right. If I ride my horse till I'm sure, then I tell you, Bassett, you can go as high as you like. Did you go for all you were worth, Bassett?"

"I went a thousand on it, Master Paul."

"I never told you, Mother, that if I can ride my horse, and *get there*, then I'm absolutely sure — oh, absolutely! Mother, did I ever tell you? I *am* lucky!"

"No, you never did," said the mother.

But the boy died in the night.

And even as he lay dead, his mother heard her brother's voice saying to her: "My God, Hester, you're eighty-odd thousand to the good, and a poor devil of a son to the bad. But, poor devil, poor devil, he's best gone out of a life where he rides his rocking horse to find a winner."

D. H. Lawrence

Odour of Chrysanthemums   1909

I

The small locomotive engine, Number 4, came clanking, stumbling down from Selston with seven full wagons. It appeared round the corner with loud threats of speed, but the colt that it startled from among the gorse, which still flickered indistinctly in the raw afternoon, out-distanced it at a canter. A woman, walking up the railway line to Underwood, drew back into the hedge, held her basket aside, and watched the footplate° of the engine advancing. The trucks thumped heavily past, one by one, with slow inevitable movement, as she stood insignificantly trapped between the jolting black wagons and the hedge; then they curved away towards the coppice where the whithered oak leaves dropped noiselessly, while the birds, pulling at the scarlet hips beside the track, made off into the dusk that had already crept into the spinney. In the open, the smoke from the engine sank and cleaved to the rough grass. The fields were dreary and forsaken, and in the marshy strip that led to the whimsey, a reedy pit-pond, the fowls had already abandoned their run among the alders, to roost in the tarred fowl-house. The pit-bank loomed up beyond the pond, flames like red sores licking its ashy sides, in the afternoon's stagnant light. Just beyond rose the tapering chimneys and the clumsy black headstocks of Brinsley Colliery. The two wheels were spinning fast up against the sky, and the winding engine rapped out its little spasms. The miners were being turned up.

The engine whistled as it came into the wide bay of railway lines beside the colliery, where rows of trucks stood in harbour.

Miners, single, trailing and in groups, passed like shadows diverging home. At the edge of the ribbed level of sidings squat a low cottage, three steps down from the cinder track. A large bony vine clutched at the house, as if to claw down the tiled roof. Round the bricked yard grew a few wintry primroses. Beyond, the long garden sloped down to a bush-covered brook course. There were some twiggy apple trees, winter-crack trees, and ragged cabbages. Beside the path hung dishevelled pink chrysanthemums, like pink cloths hung on bushes. A woman came stooping out of the felt-covered fowl-house, half-way down the garden. She closed and padlocked the door, then drew herself erect, having brushed some bits from her white apron.

She was a tall woman of imperious mien, handsome, with definite black eyebrows. Her smooth black hair was parted exactly. For a few moments she stood steadily watching the miners as they passed along the railway: then she

---

footplate: Platform on early locomotives for the engineer to stand on.

turned towards the brook course. Her face was calm and set, her mouth was closed with disillusionment. After a moment she called:

"John!" There was no answer. She waited, and then said distinctly:

"Where are you?"

"Here!" replied a child's sulky voice from among the bushes. The woman looked piercingly through the dusk.

"Are you at that brook?" she asked sternly.

For answer the child showed himself before the raspberry-canes that rose like whips. He was a small, sturdy boy of five. He stood quite still, defiantly.

"Oh!" said the mother, conciliated. "I thought you were down at that wet brook — and you remember what I told you — "

The boy did not move or answer.

"Come, come on in," she said more gently, "it's getting dark. There's your grandfather's engine coming down the line!"

The lad advanced slowly, with resentful, taciturn movement. He was dressed in trousers and waistcoat of cloth that was too thick and hard for the size of the garments. They were evidently cut down from a man's clothes.

As they went slowly towards the house he tore at the ragged wisps of chrysanthemums and dropped the petals in handfuls among the path.

"Don't do that — it does look nasty," said his mother. He refrained, and she, suddenly pitiful, broke off a twig with three or four wan flowers and held them against her face. When mother and son reached the yard her hand hesitated, and instead of laying the flower aside, she pushed it in her apron-band. The mother and son stood at the foot of the three steps looking across the bay of lines at the passing home of the miners. The trundle of the small train was imminent. Suddenly the engine loomed past the house and came to a stop opposite the gate.

The engine-driver, a short man with round grey beard, leaned out of the cab high above the woman.

"Have you got a cup of tea?" he said in a cheery, hearty fashion.

It was her father. She went in, saying she would mash. Directly, she returned.

"I didn't come to see you on Sunday," began the little grey-bearded man.

"I didn't expect you," said his daughter.

The engine-driver winced; then, reassuming his cheery, airy manner, he said:

"Oh, have you heard then? Well, and what do you think — ?"

"I think it is soon enough," she replied.

At her brief censure the little man made an impatient gesture, and said coaxingly, yet with dangerous coldness:

"Well, what's a man to do? It's no sort of life for a man of my years, to sit at my own hearth like a stranger. And if I'm going to marry again it may as well be soon as late — what does it matter to anybody?"

The woman did not reply, but turned and went into the house. The man in the engine-cab stood assertive, till she returned with a cup of tea and a piece of bread and butter on a plate. She went up the steps and stood near the foot-plate of the hissing engine.

"You needn't 'a' brought me bread an' butter," said her father. "But a cup of tea" — he sipped appreciatively — "it's very nice." He sipped for a moment or two, then: "I hear as Walter's got another bout on," he said.

"When hasn't he?" said the woman bitterly.

"I heerd tell of him in the 'Lord Nelson' braggin' as he was going to spend that b —— afore he went: half a sovereign that was."

"When?" asked the woman.

"A' Sat'day night — I know that's true."

"Very likely," she laughed bitterly. "He gives me twenty-three shillings."

"Aye, it's a nice thing, when a man can do nothing with his money but make a beast of himself!" said the grey-whiskered man. The woman turned her head away. Her father swallowed the last of his tea and handed her the cup.

"Aye," he sighed, wiping his mouth. "It's a settler, it is —— "

He put his hand on the lever. The little engine strained and groaned, and the train rumbled towards the crossing. The woman again looked across the metals. Darkness was settling over the spaces of the railway and trucks: the miners, in grey sombre groups, were still passing home. The winding engine pulsed hurriedly, with brief pauses. Elizabeth Bates looked at the dreary flow of men, then she went indoors. Her husband did not come.

The kitchen was small and full of firelight; red coals piled glowing up the chimney mouth. All the life of the room seemed in the white, warm hearth and the steel fender reflecting the red fire. The cloth was laid for tea; cups glinted in the shadows. At the back, where the lowest stairs protruded into the room, the boy sat struggling with a knife and a piece of white wood. He was almost hidden in the shadow. It was half-past four. They had but to await the father's coming to begin tea. As the mother watched her son's sullen little struggle with the woods, she saw herself in his silence and pertinacity; she saw the father in her child's indifference to all but himself. She seemed to be occupied by her husband. He had probably gone past his home, slunk past his own door, to drink before he came in, while his dinner spoiled and wasted in waiting. She glanced at the clock, then took the potatoes to strain them in the yard. The garden and fields beyond the brook were closed in uncertain darkness. When she rose with the saucepan, leaving the drain steaming into the night behind her, she saw the yellow lamps were lit along the high road that went up the hill away beyond the space of the railway lines and the field.

Then again she watched the men trooping home, fewer now and fewer.

Indoors the fire was sinking and the room was dark red. The woman put her saucepan on the hob, and set a batter-pudding near the mouth of the oven. Then she stood unmoving. Directly, gratefully, came quick young steps to the door. Someone hung on the latch a moment, then a little girl entered and began pulling off her outdoor things, dragging a mass of curls, just ripening from gold to brown, over her eyes with her hat.

Her mother chid her for coming late from school, and said she would have to keep her at home the dark winter days.

"Why, mother, it's hardly a bit dark yet. The lamp's not lighted, and my father's not home."

"No, he isn't. But it's a quarter to five! Did you see anything of him?"

The child became serious. She looked at her mother with large, wistful blue eyes.

"No, mother, I've never seen him. Why? Has he come up an' gone past, to Old Brinsley? He hasn't, mother, 'cos I never saw him."

"He'd watch that," said the mother bitterly, "he'd take care as you didn't see him. But you may depend upon it, he's seated in the 'Prince o' Wales.' He wouldn't be this late."

The girl looked at her mother piteously.

"Let's have our teas, mother, should we?" said she.

The mother called John to table. She opened the door once more and looked out across the darkness of the lines. All was deserted: she could not hear the winding-engines.

"Perhaps," she said to herself, "he's stopped to get some ripping done."

They sat down to tea. John, at the end of the table near the door, was almost lost in the darkness. Their faces were hidden from each other. The girl crouched against the fender slowly moving a thick piece of bread before the fire. The lad, his face a dusky mark on the shadow, sat watching her who was transfigured in the red glow.

"I do think it's beautiful to look in the fire," said the child.

"Do you?" said her mother. "Why?"

"It's so red, and full of little caves —— and it feels so nice, and you can fair smell it."

"It'll want mending directly," replied her mother, "and then if your father comes he'll carry on and say there never is a fire when a man comes home sweating from the pit. A public house is always warm enough."

There was silence till the boy said complainingly: "Make haste, our Annie."

"Well, I am doing! I can't make the fire do it no faster, can I?"

"She keeps wafflin' it about so's to make 'er slow," grumbled the boy.

"Don't have such an evil imagination, child," replied the mother.

Soon the room was busy in the darkness with the crisp sound of crunching. The mother ate very little. She drank her tea determinedly, and sat thinking. When she rose her anger was evident in the stern unbending of her head. She looked at the pudding in the fender and broke out:

"It is a scandalous thing as a man can't even come home to his dinner! If it's crozzled up to a cinder I don't see why I should care. Past his very door he goes to get to a public-house, and here I sit with his dinner waiting for him — "

She went out. As she dropped piece after piece of coal on the red fire, the shadows fell on the walls, till the room was almost in total darkness.

"I canna see," grumbled the invisible John. In spite of herself, the mother laughed.

"You know the way to your mouth," she said. She set the dust-pan outside the door. When she came again like a shadow on the hearth, the lad repeated, complaining sulkily:

"I canna see."

"Good gracious!" cried the mother irritably, "you're as bad as your father if it's a bit dusk!"

Nevertheless, she took a paper spill from a sheaf on the mantelpiece and proceeded to light the lamp that hung from the ceiling in the middle of the room. As she reached up, her figure displayed itself just rounding with maternity.

"Oh, mother —— !" exclaimed the girl.

"What?" said the woman, suspended in the act of putting the lamp-glass over the flame. The copper reflector shone handsomely on her, as she stood with uplifted arm, turning to face her daughter.

"You've got a flower in your apron!" said the child, in a little rapture at this unusual event.

"Goodness me!" exclaimed the woman, relieved. "One would think the house was afire." She replaced the glass and waited a moment before turning up the wick. A pale shadow was seen floating vaguely on the floor.

"Let me smell!" said the child, still rapturously, coming forward and putting her face to her mother's waist.

"Go along, silly!" said the mother, turning up the lamp. The light revealed their suspense so that the woman felt it almost unbearable. Annie was still bending at her waist. Irritably, the mother took the flowers out from her apron-band.

"Oh, mother — don't take them out!" Annie cried, catching her hand and trying to replace the sprig.

"Such nonsense!" said the mother, turning away. The child put the pale chrysanthemums to her lips, murmuring:

"Don't they smell beautiful!"

Her mother gave a short laugh.

"No," she said, "not to me. It was chrysanthemums when I married him, and chrysanthemums when you were born, and the first time they ever brought him home drunk, he'd got brown chrysanthemums in his buttonhole."

She looked at the children. Their eyes and their parted lips were wondering. The mother sat rocking in silence for some time. Then she looked at the clock.

"Twenty minutes to six!" In a tone of fine bitter carelessness she continued: "Eh, he'll not come now till they bring him. There he'll stick! But he needn't come rolling in here in his pit-dirt, for *I* won't wash him. He can lie on the floor —— Eh, what a fool I've been, what a fool! And this is what I came here for, to this dirty hole, rats and all, for him to slink past his very door. Twice last week — he's begun now —— "

She silenced herself, and rose to clear the table.

While for an hour or more the children played, subduedly intent, fertile of imagination, united in fear of the mother's wrath, and in dread of their father's home-coming, Mrs. Bates sat in her rocking-chair making a "singlet" of thick cream-coloured flannel, which gave a dull wounded sound as she tore off the grey edge. She worked at her sewing with energy, listening to the children, and her anger wearied itself, lay down to rest, opening its eyes from time to time and steadily watching, its ears raised to listen. Sometimes even her anger quailed and shrank, and the mother suspended her sewing, tracing the footsteps that thudded along the sleepers outside: she would lift her head sharply to bid the children "hush," but she recovered herself in time, and the footsteps went past the gate, and the children were not flung out of their play-world.

But at last Annie sighed, and gave in. She glanced at her wagon of slippers, and loathed the game. She turned plaintively to her mother.

"Mother!" — but she was inarticulate.

John crept out like a frog from under the sofa. His mother glanced up. "Yes," she said, "just look at those shirt-sleeves!"

The boy held them out to survey them, saying nothing. Then somebody called in a hoarse voice away down the line, and suspense bristled in the room, till two people had gone by outside, talking.

"It is time for bed," said the mother.

"My father hasn't come," wailed Annie plaintively. But her mother was primed with courage.

"Never mind. They'll bring him when he does come — like a log." She meant there would be no scene. "And he may sleep on the floor till he wakes himself. I know he'll not go to work to-morrow after this!"

The children had their hands and faces wiped with a flannel. They were very quiet. When they had put on their night-dresses, they said their prayers, the boy mumbling. The mother looked down at them, at the brown silken bush of intertwining curls in the nape of the girl's neck, at the little black head of the lad, and her heart burst with anger at their father, who caused all three such distress. The children hid their faces in her skirts for comfort.

When Mrs. Bates came down, the room was strangely empty, with a tension of expectancy. She took up her sewing and stitched for some time without raising her head. Meantime her anger was tinged with fear.

II

The clock struck eight and she rose suddenly, dropping her sewing on her chair. She went to the stair-foot door, opened it, listening. Then she went out, locking the door behind her.

Something scuffled in the yard, and she started, though she knew it was only the rats with which the place was over-run. The night was very dark. In the great bay of railway lines, bulked with trucks, there was no trace of light, only away back she could see a few yellow lamps at the pit-top, and the red smear of the burning pit-bank on the night. She hurried along the edge of the track, then, crossing the converging lines, came to the stile by the white gates, whence she emerged on the road. Then the fear which had led her shrank. People were walking up to New Brinsley; she saw the lights in the houses; twenty yards farther on were the broad windows of the "Prince of Wales," very warm and bright, and the loud voices of men could be heard distinctly. What a fool she had been to imagine that anything had happened to him! He was merely drinking over there at the "Prince of Wales." She faltered. She had never yet been to fetch him, and she never would go. So she continued her walk towards the long straggling line of houses, standing back on the highway. She entered a passage between the dwellings.

"Mr. Rigley? — Yes! Did you want him? No, he's not in at this minute."

The raw-boned woman leaned forward from her dark scullery and peered at the other, upon whom fell a dim light through the blind of the kitchen window.

"Is it Mrs. Bates?" she asked in a tone tinged with respect.

"Yes. I wondered if your Master was at home. Mine hasn't come yet."

" 'Asn't 'e! Oh, Jack's been 'ome an' 'ad 'is dinner an' gone out. 'E's just gone for 'alf an hour afore bed-time. Did you call at the 'Prince of Wales'? "

"No —— "

"No, you didn't like —— ! It's not very nice." The other woman was indulgent. There was an awkward pause. "Jack never said nothink about — about your Master," she said.

"No! — I expect he's stuck in there!"

Elizabeth Bates said this bitterly, and with recklessness. She knew that the woman across the yard was standing at her door listening, but she did not care. As she turned:

"Stop a minute! I'll just go an' ask Jack if 'e knows anythink," said Mrs. Rigley.

"Oh no — I wouldn't like to put —— !"

"Yes, I will, if you'll just step inside an' see as th' childer doesn't come downstairs and set theirselves afire."

Elizabeth Bates, murmuring a remonstrance, stepped inside. The other woman apologised for the state of the room.

The kitchen needed apology. There were little frocks and trousers and childish undergarments on the squab and on the floor, and a litter of playthings everywhere. On the black American cloth of the table were pieces of bread and cake, crusts, slops, and a teapot with cold tea.

"Eh, ours is just as bad," said Elizabeth Bates, looking at the woman, not at the house. Mrs. Rigley put a shawl over her head and hurried out, saying:

"I shanna be a minute."

The other sat, noting with faint disapproval the general untidiness of the room. Then she fell to counting the shoes of various sizes scattered over the floor. There were twelve. She sighed and said to herself: "No wonder!" — glancing at the litter. There came the scratching of two pairs of feet on the yard, and the Rigleys entered. Elizabeth Bates rose. Rigley was a big man, with very large bones. His head looked particularly bony. Across his temple was a blue scar, caused by a wound got in the pit, a wound in which the coaldust remained blue like tattooing.

" 'Asna 'e come whoam yit?" asked the man, without any form of greeting, but with deference and sympathy. "I couldna say wheer he is — 'e's non ower theer!" — he jerked his head to signify the "Prince of Wales."

" 'E's 'appen gone up to th' 'Yew,' " said Mrs. Rigley.

There was another pause. Rigley had evidently something to get off his mind:

"Ah left 'im finishin' a stint," he began. "Loose-all 'ad bin gone about ten minutes when we com'n away, an' I shouted: 'Are ter comin', Walt?' an' 'e said: 'Go on, Ah shanna be but a' ef a minnit,' so we com'n ter th' bottom, me an' Bowers, thinkin' as 'e wor just behint, an' 'ud come up i' th' next bantle —— "

He stood perplexed, as if answering a charge of deserting his mate. Elizabeth Bates, now again certain of disaster, hastened to reassure him:

"I expect 'e's gone up to th' 'Yew Tree,' as you say. It's not the first time.

I've fretted myself into a fever before now. He'll come home when they carry him."

"Ay, isn't it too bad!" deplored the other woman.

"I'll just step up to Dick's an' see if 'e *is* theer," offered the man, afraid of appearing alarmed, afraid of taking liberties.

"Oh, I wouldn't think of bothering you that far," said Elizabeth Bates, with emphasis, but he knew she was glad of his offer.

As they stumbled up the entry, Elizabeth Bates heard Rigley's wife run across the yard and open her neighbour's door. At this, suddenly all the blood in her body seemed to switch away from her heart.

"Mind!" warned Rigley. "Ah've said many a time as Ah'd fill up them ruts in this entry, sumb'dy 'll be breakin' their legs yit."

She recovered herself and walked quickly along with the miner.

"I don't like leaving the children in bed, and nobody in the house," she said.

"No, you dunna!" he replied courteously. They were soon at the gate of the cottage.

"Well, I shanna be many minnits. Dunna you be frettin' now, 'e'll be all right," said the butty.°

"Thank you very much, Mr. Rigley," she replied.

"You're welcome!" he stammered, moving away. "I shanna be many minnits."

The house was quiet. Elizabeth Bates took off her hat and shawl, and rolled back the rug. When she had finished, she sat down. It was a few minutes past nine. She was startled by the rapid chuff of the winding-engine at the pit, and the sharp whirr of the brakes on the rope as it descended. Again she felt the painful sweep of her blood, and she put her hand to her side, saying aloud: "Good gracious! — it's only the nine o'clock deputy going down," rebuking herself.

She sat still listening. Half an hour of this, and she was wearied out.

"What am I working myself up like this for?" she said pitiably to herself, "I s'll only be doing myself some damage."

She took out her sewing again.

At a quarter to ten there were footsteps. One person! She watched for the door to open. It was an elderly woman, in a black bonnet and a black woollen shawl — his mother. She was about sixty years old, pale, with blue eyes, and her face all wrinkled and lamentable. She shut the door and turned to her daughter-in-law peevishly.

"Eh, Lizzie, whatever shall we do, whatever shall we do!" she cried.

Elizabeth drew back a little, sharply.

"What is it, mother?" she said.

The elder woman seated herself on the sofa.

"I don't know, child, I can't tell you!" — she shook her head slowly. Elizabeth sat watching her, anxious and vexed.

"I don't know," replied the grandmother, sighing very deeply. "There's

---

butty: A fellow workman in a colliery.

no end to my troubles, there isn't. The things I've gone through, I'm sure it's enough —— !" She wept without wiping her eyes, the tears running.

"But, mother," interrupted Elizabeth, "what do you mean? What is it?"

The grandmother slowly wiped her eyes. The fountains of her tears were stopped by Elizabeth's directness. She wiped her eyes slowly.

"Poor child! Eh, you poor thing!" she moaned. "I don't know what we're going to do, I don't — and you as you are — it's a thing, it is indeed!"

Elizabeth waited.

"Is he dead?" she asked, and at the words her heart swung violently, though she felt a slight flush of shame at the ultimate extravagance of the question. Her words sufficiently frightened the old lady, almost brought her to herself.

"Don't say so, Elizabeth! We'll hope it's not as bad as that; no, may the Lord spare us that, Elizabeth. Jack Rigley came just as I was sittin' down to a glass afore going to bed, an' 'e said: "Appen you'll go down th' line, Mrs. Bates. Walt's had an accident. 'Appen you'll go an' sit wi' 'er till we can get him home.' I hadn't time to ask him a word afore he was gone. An' I put my bonnet on an' come straight down, Lizzie. I thought to myself: 'Eh, that poor blessed child, if anybody should come an' tell her of a sudden, there's no knowin' what'll 'appen to 'er.' You mustn't let it upset you, Lizzie — or you know what to expect. How long is it, six months — or is it five, Lizzie? Ay!" — the old woman shook her head — "time slips on, it slips on! Ay!"

Elizabeth's thoughts were busy elsewhere. If he was killed — would she be able to manage on the little pension and what she could earn? — she counted up rapidly. If he was hurt — they wouldn't take him to the hospital — how tiresome he would be to nurse! — but perhaps she'd be able to get him away from the drink and his hateful ways. She would — while he was ill. The tears offered to come to her eyes at the picture. But what sentimental luxury was this she was beginning? She turned to consider the children. At any rate she was absolutely necessary for them. They were her business.

"Ay!" repeated the old woman, "it seems but a week or two since he brought me his first wages. Ay — he was a good lad, Elizabeth, he was, in his way. I don't know why he got to be such a trouble, I don't. He was a happy lad at home, only full of spirits. But there's no mistake he's been a handful of trouble, he has! I hope the Lord'll spare him to mend his ways. I hope so, I hope so. You've had a sight o' trouble with him, Elizabeth, you have indeed. But he was a jolly enough lad wi' me, he was, I can assure you. I don't know how it is. . . ."

The old woman continued to muse aloud, a monotonous irritating sound, while Elizabeth thought concentratedly, startled once, when she heard the winding-engine chuff quickly, and the brakes skirr with a shriek. Then she heard the engine more slowly, and the brakes made no sound. The old woman did not notice. Elizabeth waited in suspense. The mother-in-law talked, with lapses into silence.

"But he wasn't your son, Lizzie, an' it makes a difference. Whatever he was, I remember him when he was little, an' I learned to understand him and to make allowances. You've got to make allowances for them —— "

It was half-past ten, and the old woman was saying: "But it's trouble

from beginning to end; you're never too old for trouble, never too old for that
—— " when the gate banged back, and there were heavy feet on the steps.

"I'll go, Lizzie, let me go," cried the old woman, rising. But Elizabeth
was at the door. It was a man in pit-clothes.

"They're bringin' 'im, Misses," he said. Elizabeth's heart halted a moment. Then it surged on again, almost suffocating her.

"Is he — is it bad?" she asked.

The man turned away, looking at the darkness:

"The doctor says 'e'd been dead hours. 'E saw 'im i' th' lamp-cabin."

The old woman, who stood just behind Elizabeth, dropped into a chair,
and folded her hands, crying: "Oh, my boy, my boy!"

"Hush!" said Elizabeth, with a sharp twitch of a frown. "Be still, mother,
don't waken th' children: I wouldn't have them down for anything!"

The old woman moaned softly, rocking herself. The man was drawing
away. Elizabeth took a step forward.

"How was it?" she asked.

"Well, I couldn't say for sure," the man replied, very ill at ease. " 'E wor
finishin' a stint an' th' butties 'ad gone, an' a lot o' stuff come down atop 'n 'im."

"And crushed him?" cried the widow, with a shudder.

"No," said the man, "it fell at th' back of 'im. 'E wor under th' face, an' it
niver touched 'im. It shut 'im in. It seems 'e wor smothered."

Elizabeth shrank back. She heard the old woman behind her cry:

"What? — what did 'e say it was?"

The man replied, more loudly: " 'E wor smothered!"

Then the old woman wailed aloud, and this relieved Elizabeth.

"Oh, mother," she said, putting her hand on the old woman, "don't
waken th' children, don't waken th' children."

She wept a little, unknowing, while the old mother rocked herself and
moaned. Elizabeth remembered that they were bringing him home, and she
must be ready. "They'll lay him in the parlour," she said to herself, standing a
moment pale and perplexed.

Then she lighted a candle and went into the tiny room. The air was cold
and damp, but she could not make a fire, there was no fireplace. She set down
the candle and looked round. The candlelight glittered on the lustre-glasses,
on the two vases that held some of the pink chrysanthemums, and on the dark
mahogany. There was a cold, deathly smell of chrysanthemums in the room.
Elizabeth stood looking at the flowers. She turned away, and calculated
whether there would be room to lay him on the floor, between the couch and
the chiffonier. She pushed the chairs aside. There would be room to lay him
down and to step round him. Then she fetched the old red tablecloth, and another old cloth, spreading them down to save her bit of carpet. She shivered
on leaving the parlour; so, from the dresser drawer she took a clean shirt and
put it at the fire to air. All the time her mother-in-law was rocking herself in the
chair and moaning.

"You'll have to move from there, mother," said Elizabeth. "They'll be
bringing him in. Come in the rocker."

The old mother rose mechanically, and seated herself by the fire, continuing to lament. Elizabeth went into the pantry for another candle, and there, in the little pent-house under the naked tiles, she heard them coming. She stood still in the pantry doorway, listening. She heard them pass the end of the house, and come awkwardly down the three steps, a jumble of shuffling footsteps and muttering voices. The old woman was silent. The men were in the yard.

Then Elizabeth heard Matthews, the manager of the pit, say: "You go in first, Jim. Mind!"

The door came open, and the two women saw a collier backing into the room, holding one end of a stretcher, on which they could see the nailed pit-boots of the dead man. The two carriers halted, the man at the head stooping to the lintel of the door.

"Wheer will you have him?" asked the manager, a short, white-bearded man.

Elizabeth roused herself and came from the pantry carrying the un-lighted candle.

"In the parlour," she said.

"In there, Jim!" pointed the manager, and the carriers backed round into the tiny room. The coat with which they had covered the body fell off as they awkwardly turned through the two doorways, and the women saw their man, naked to the waist, lying stripped for work. The old woman began to moan in a low voice of horror.

"Lay th' stretcher at th' side," snapped the manager, "an' put 'im on th' cloths. Mind now, mind! Look you now ——!"

One of the men had knocked off a vase of chrysanthemums. He stared awkwardly, then they set down the stretcher. Elizabeth did not look at her husband. As soon as she could get in the room, she went and picked up the broken vase and the flowers.

"Wait a minute!" she said.

The three men waited in silence while she mopped up the water with a duster.

"Eh, what a job, what a job, to be sure!" the manager was saying, rub-bing his brow with trouble and perplexity. "Never knew such a thing in my life, never! He'd no business to ha' been left. I never knew such a thing in my life! Fell over him clean as a whistle, an' shut him in. Not four foot of space, there wasn't — yet it scarce bruised him."

He looked down at the dead man, lying prone, half naked, all grimed with coal-dust.

" ' 'Sphyxiated,' the doctor said. It *is* the most terrible job I've ever known. Seems as if it was done o' purpose. Clean over him, an' shut 'im in, like a mouse-trap" — he made a sharp, descending gesture with his hand.

The colliers standing by jerked aside their heads in hopeless comment. The horror of the thing bristled upon them all.

Then they heard the girl's voice upstairs calling shrilly: "Mother, mother — who is it? Mother, who is it?"

Elizabeth hurried to the foot of the stairs and opened the door:

"Go to sleep!" she commended sharply. "What are you shouting about? Go to sleep at once — there's nothing ——"

Then she began to mount the stairs. They could hear her on the boards, and on the plaster floor of the little bedroom. They could hear her distinctly:

"What's the matter now? — what's the matter with you, silly thing?" — her voice was much agitated, with an unreal gentleness.

"I thought it was some men come," said the plaintive voice of the child. "Has he come?"

"Yes, they've brought him. There's nothing to make a fuss about. Go to sleep now, like a good child."

They could hear her voice in the bedroom, they waited whilst she covered the children under the bedclothes.

"Is he drunk?" asked the girl, timidly, faintly.

"No! No — he's not! He — he's asleep."

"Is he asleep downstairs?"

"Yes — and don't make a noise."

There was silence for a moment, then the men heard the frightened child again:

"What's that noise?"

"It's nothing, I tell you, what are you bothering for?"

The noise was the grandmother moaning. She was oblivious of everything, sitting on her chair rocking and moaning. The manager put his hand on her arm and bade her "Sh — sh!!"

The old woman opened her eyes and looked at him. She was shocked by this interruption, and seemed to wonder.

"What time is it?" the plaintive thin voice of the child, sinking back unhappily into sleep, asked this last question.

"Ten o'clock," answered the mother more softly. Then she must have bent down and kissed the children.

Matthews beckoned to the men to come away. They put on their caps and took up the stretcher. Stepping over the body, they tiptoed out of the house. None of them spoke till they were far from the wakeful children.

When Elizabeth came down she found her mother alone on the parlour floor, leaning over the dead man, the tears dropping on him.

"We must lay him out," the wife said. She put on the kettle, then returning knelt at the feet, and began to unfasten the knotted leather laces. The room was clammy and dim with only one candle, so that she had to bend her face almost to the floor. At last she got off the heavy boots and put them away.

"You must help me now," she whispered to the old woman. Together they stripped the man.

When they arose, saw him lying in the naïve dignity of death, the women stood arrested in fear and respect. For a few moments they remained still, looking down, the old mother whimpering. Elizabeth felt countermanded. She saw him, how utterly inviolable he lay in himself. She had nothing to do with him. She could not accept it. Stooping, she laid her hand on him, in claim. He was still warm, for the mine was hot where he had died. His mother had his face between her hands, and was murmuring incoherently. The old tears fell in succession as drops from wet leaves; the mother was not weeping, merely her tears flowed. Elizabeth embraced the body of her husband, with cheek and lips. She seemed to be listening, inquiring, trying to get some connection. But she could not. She was driven away. He was impregnable.

She rose, went into the kitchen, where she poured warm water into a bowl, brought soap and flannel and a soft towel.

"I must wash him," she said.

Then the old mother rose stiffly, and watched Elizabeth as she carefully washed his face, carefully brushing the big blond moustache from his mouth with the flannel. She was afraid with a bottomless fear, so she ministered to him. The old woman, jealous, said:

"Let me wipe him!" — and she kneeled on the other side drying slowly as Elizabeth washed, her big black bonnet sometimes brushing the dark head of her daughter-in-law. They worked thus in silence for a long time. They never forgot it was death, and the touch of the man's dead body gave them strange emotions, different in each of the women; a great dread possessed them both, the mother felt the lie was given to her womb, she was denied; the wife felt the utter isolation of the human soul, the child within her was a weight apart from her.

At last it was finished. He was a man of handsome body, and his face showed no traces of drink. He was blond, full-fleshed, with fine limbs. But he was dead.

"Bless him," whispered his mother, looking always at his face, and speaking out of sheer terror. "Dear lad — bless him!" She spoke in a faint, sibilant ectasy of fear and mother love.

Elizabeth sank down again to the floor, and put her face against his neck, and trembled and shuddered. But she had to draw away again. He was dead, and her living flesh had no place against his. A great dread and weariness held her: she was so unavailing. Her life was gone like this.

"White as milk he is, clear as a twelve-month baby, bless him, the darling!" the old mother murmured to herself. "Not a mark on him, clear and clean and white, beautiful as ever a child was made," she murmured with pride. Elizabeth kept her face hidden.

"He went peaceful, Lizzie — peaceful as sleep. Isn't he beautiful, the lamb? Ay — he must ha' made his peace, Lizzie. 'Appen he made it all right, Lizzie, shut in there. He'd have time. He wouldn't look like this if he hadn't made his peace. The lamb, the dear lamb. 'Eh, but he had a hearty laugh. I loved to hear it. He had the heartiest laugh, Lizzie, as a lad ―― "

Elizabeth looked up. The man's mouth was fallen back, slightly open under the cover of the moustache. The eyes, half shut, did not show glazed in the obscurity. Life with its smoky burning gone from him, had left him apart and utterly alien to her. And she knew what a stranger he was to her. In her womb was ice of fear, because of this separate stranger with whom she had been living as one flesh. Was this what it all meant — utter, intact separateness, obscured by heat of living? In dread she turned her face away. The fact was too deadly. There had been nothing between them, and yet they had come together, exchanging their nakedness repeatedly. Each time he had taken her, they had been two isolated beings, far apart as now. He was no more responsible than she. The child was like ice in her womb. For as she looked at the dead man, her mind, cold and detached, said clearly: "Who am I? What have I been doing? I have been fighting a husband who did not exist. *He* existed all the time. What wrong have I done? What was that I have been living with? There lies the reality, this man." And her soul died in her for fear: she knew she had never seen him, he had never seen her, they had met in the dark and had fought in the dark, not knowing whom they met nor whom they fought. And now she saw, and turned silent in seeing. For she had been wrong. She had said he was something he was not; she had felt familiar with him. Whereas he was apart all the while, living as she never lived, feeling as she never felt:

In fear and shame she looked at his naked body, that she had known falsely. And he was the father of her children. Her soul was torn from her body and stood apart. She looked at his naked body and was ashamed, as if she had denied it. After all, it was itself. It seemed awful to her. She looked at his face, and she turned her own face to the wall. For his look was other than hers, his way was not her way. She had denied him what he was — she saw it now. She had refused him as himself. And this had been her life, and his life. She was grateful to death, which restored the truth. And she knew she was not dead.

And all the while her heart was bursting with grief and pity for him. What had he suffered? What stretch of horror for this helpless man! She was rigid with agony. She had not been able to help him. He had been cruelly injured, this naked man, this other being, and she could make no reparation. There were the children — but the children belonged to life. This dead man had nothing to do with them. He and she were only channels through which life had flowed to issue in the children. She was a mother — but how awful she knew it now to have been a wife. And he, dead now, how awful he must have felt it to be a husband. She felt that in the next world he would be a stranger to her. If they met there, in the beyond, they would only be ashamed of what had been before. The children had come, for some mysterious reason, out of both of them. But the children did not unite them. Now he was dead, she knew how eternally he was apart from her, how eternally he had nothing more to do with her. She saw this episode of her life closed. They had denied each other in life. Now he had withdrawn. An anguish came over her. It was finished then: it had become hopeless between them long before he died. Yet he had been her husband. But how little!

"Have you got his shirt, 'Lizabeth?"

Elizabeth turned without answering, though she strove to weep and behave as her mother-in-law expected. But she could not, she was silenced. She went into the kitchen and returned with the garment.

"It is aired," she said, grasping the cotton shirt here and there to try. She was almost ashamed to handle him; what right had she or anyone to lay hands on him; but her touch was humble on his body. It was hard work to clothe him. He was so heavy and inert. A terrible dread gripped her all the while: that he could be so heavy and utterly inert, unresponsive, apart. The horror of the distance between them was almost too much for her — it was so infinite a gap she must look across.

At last it was finished. They covered him with a sheet and left him lying, with his face bound. And she fastened the door of the little parlour, lest the children should see what was lying there. Then, with peace sunk heavy on her heart, she went about making tidy the kitchen. She knew she submitted to life, which was her immediate master. But from death, her ultimate master, she winced with fear and shame.

ΩΩ

CLARICE LISPECTOR *(1925–1977) was born of Russian parents in the Ukraine, but two months after her birth, her family moved to Brazil. As a teenager growing up in Rio de Janeiro, she began to write stories and plays while embarking on an ambitious study of contemporary Brazilian and European literature, particularly the fiction of Katherine Mansfield and Virginia Woolf, with whom she felt a special affinity, and the existentialist philosophy of Albert Camus and Jean-Paul Sartre. In 1944 she graduated from the National Faculty of Law and worked as one of Brazil's first woman journalists. Shortly afterward Lispector married a diplomat and published her first novel,* Close to the Savage Heart *(1944).*

Living in Europe and the United States with her husband from 1945 to 1960, Lispector wrote many stories and novels in which she explored her preoccupation with existential themes. Literary critics singled out the stories in Family Ties *(1960), from which "The Smallest Woman in the World" is taken, for particular praise. In this story Lispector created a world both miraculous and familiar, dramatizing the instinct for survival that directs the thoughts and actions of every living creature. As the critic Giovanni Pontiero has observed, Lispector's stories suggest a surreal quality in their portrayal of the everyday lives of her characters. "Free from psychological conflicts, they show a greater participation in what is real — the greater space that includes all spaces."*

Lispector believed that the essence of all art and literature is experimental, and she was fascinated by the creative process. Her prize-winning novels and collections of stories established her as a leading Brazilian author. An Apprenticeship, or the Book of Pleasures *(1969) was one of the books that introduced her work in translation to an American audience. Her last novel,* The Hour of the Star, *was published the same year as her death from cancer. Lispector's most recently translated collection of short fiction is* The Foreign Legion: Stories and Chronicles *(1986).*

RELATED COMMENTARY: *Julia Alvarez, "On Lispector's 'The Smallest Woman in the World,' " page 727.*

CLARICE LISPECTOR

The Smallest Woman in the World   *1960*

TRANSLATED BY ELIZABETH BISHOP

In the depths of Equatorial Africa the French explorer, Marcel Pretre, hunter and man of the world, came across a tribe of surprisingly small pygmies. Therefore he was even more surprised when he was informed that a still smaller people existed, beyond forests and distances. So he plunged farther on.

In the Eastern Congo, near Lake Kivu, he really did discover the smallest pygmies in the world. And — like a box within a box within a box — obedient, perhaps, to the necessity nature sometimes feels of outdoing herself — among the smallest pygmies in the world there was the smallest of the smallest pygmies in the world.

Among mosquitoes and lukewarm trees, among leaves of the most rich and lazy green, Marcel Pretre found himself facing a woman seventeen and three-quarter inches high, full-grown, black, silent — "Black as a monkey," he informed the press — who lived in a treetop with her little spouse. In the tepid miasma of the jungle, that swells the fruits so early and gives them an almost intolerable sweetness, she was pregnant.

So there she stood, the smallest woman in the world. For an instant, in the buzzing heat, it seemed as if the Frenchman had unexpectedly reached his final destination. Probably only because he was not insane, his soul neither wavered nor broke its bounds. Feeling an immediate necessity for order and for giving names to what exists, he called her Little Flower. And in order to be able to classify her among the recognizable realities, he immediately began to collect facts about her.

Her race will soon be exterminated. Few examples are left of this species, which, if it were not for the sly dangers of Africa, might have multiplied. Besides disease, the deadly effluvium of the water, insufficient food, and ranging beasts, the great threat to the Likoualas are the savage Bahundes, a threat that surrounds them in the silent air, like the dawn of battle. The Bahundes hunt them with nets, like monkeys. And eat them. Like that: they catch them in nets and *eat* them. The tiny race, retreating, always retreating, has finished hiding away in the heart of Africa, where the lucky explorer discovered it. For strategic defense, they live in the highest trees. The women descend to grind and cook corn and to gather greens; the men, to hunt. When a child is born, it is left free almost immediately. It is true that, what with the beasts, the child frequently cannot enjoy this freedom for very long. But then it is true that it cannot be lamented that for such a short life there had been any long, hard work. And even the language that the child learns is short and simple, merely the essentials. The Likoualas use few names; they name things by gestures and animal noises. As for things of the spirit, they have a drum. While they dance to the sound of the drum, a little male stands guard against the Bahundes, who come from no one knows where.

That was the way, then, that the explorer discovered, standing at his very feet, the smallest existing human thing. His heart beat, because no emerald in the world is so rare. The teachings of the wise men of India are not so rare. The richest man in the world has never set eyes on such strange grace. Right there was a woman that the greed of the most exquisite dream could never have imagined. It was then that the explorer said timidly, and with a delicacy of feeling of which his wife would never have thought him capable: "You are Little Flower."

At that moment, Little Flower scratched herself where no one scratches. The explorer — as if he were receiving the highest prize for chastity to which an idealistic man dares aspire — the explorer, experienced as he was, looked the other way.

A photograph of Little Flower was published in the colored supplement of the Sunday Papers, life-size. She was wrapped in a cloth, her belly already very big. The flat nose, the black face, the splay feet. She looked like a dog.

On that Sunday, in an apartment, a woman seeing the picture of Little Flower in the paper didn't want to look a second time because "It gives me the creeps."

In another apartment, a lady felt such perverse tenderness for the smallest of the African women that — an ounce of prevention being worth a pound of cure — Little Flower could never be left alone to the tenderness of that lady. Who knows to what murkiness of love tenderness can lead? The woman was upset all day, almost as if she were missing something. Besides, it was spring and there was a dangerous leniency in the air.

In another house, a little girl of five, seeing the picture and hearing the comments, was extremely surprised. In a houseful of adults, this little girl had been the smallest human being up until now. And, if this was the source of all caresses, it was also the source of the first fear of the tyranny of love. The existence of Little Flower made the little girl feel — with a deep uneasiness that only years and years later, and for very different reasons, would turn into thought — made her feel, in her first wisdom, that "sorrow is endless."

In another house, in the consecration of spring, a girl about to be married felt an ecstasy of pity: "Mama, look at her little picture, poor little thing! Just look how sad she is!"

"But," said the mother, hard and defeated and proud, "it's the sadness of an animal. It isn't human sadness."

"Oh, Mama!" said the girl, discouraged.

In another house, a clever little boy had a clever idea: "Mummy, if I could put this little woman from Africa in little Paul's bed when he's asleep? When he woke up wouldn't he be frightened? Wouldn't he howl? When he saw her sitting on his bed? And then we'd play with her! She would be our toy!"

His mother was setting her hair in front of the bathroom mirror at the moment, and she remembered what a cook had told her about life in an orphanage. The orphans had no dolls, and, with terrible maternity already throbbing in their hearts, the little girls had hidden the death of one of the children from the nun. They kept the body in a cupboard and when the nun went out they played with the dead child, giving her baths and things to eat, punishing her only to be able to kiss and console her. In the bathroom, the mother remembered this, and let fall her thoughtful hands, full of curlers. She considered the cruel necessity of loving. And she considered the malignity of our desire for happiness. She considered how ferociously we need to play. How many times we will kill for love. Then she looked at her clever child as if she were looking at a dangerous stranger. And she had a horror of her own soul that, more than her body, had engendered that being, adept at life and happiness. She looked at him attentively and with uncomfortable pride, that child who had already lost two front teeth, evolution evolving itself, teeth falling out to give place to those that could bite better. "I'm going to buy him a new suit," she decided, looking at him, absorbed. Obstinately, she adorned her gap-toothed son with fine clothes; obstinately, she wanted him very clean, as if his cleanliness could emphasize a soothing superficiality, obstinately perfecting the polite side of beauty. Obstinately drawing away from, and drawing him away from, something that ought to be "black as a monkey." Then, looking in the bathroom mirror, the mother gave a deliberately refined and social smile, placing a distance of insuperable millenniums between the abstract lines of her features and the crude face of Little Flower. But, with years of practice, she knew that this was going to be a Sunday on which she would have to hide from herself anxiety, dreams, and lost millenniums.

In another house, they gave themselves up to the enthralling task of measuring the seventeen and three-quarter inches of Little Flower against the wall. And, really, it was a delightful surprise: she was even smaller than the sharpest imagination could have pictured. In the heart of each member of the family was born, nostalgic, the desire to have that tiny and indomitable thing for itself, that thing spared having been eaten, that permanent source of charity. The avid family soul wanted to devote itself. To tell the truth, who hasn't wanted to own a human being just for himself? Which, it is true, wouldn't always be convenient; there are times when one doesn't want to have feelings.

"I bet if she lived here it would end in a fight," said the father, sitting in the armchair and definitely turning the page of the newspaper. "In this house everything ends in a fight."

"Oh, you, José — always a pessimist," said the mother.

"But, Mama, have you thought of the size her baby's going to be?" said the oldest little girl, aged thirteen, eagerly.

The father stirred uneasily behind his paper.

"It should be the smallest black baby in the world," the mother answered, melting with pleasure. "Imagine her serving our table, with her big little belly!"

"That's enough!" growled father.

"But you have to admit," said the mother, unexpectedly offended, "that it is something very rare. You're the insensitive one."

And the rare thing itself?

In the meanwhile, in Africa, the rare thing herself, in her heart — and who knows if the heart wasn't black, too, since once nature has erred she can no longer be trusted — the rare thing herself had something even rarer in her heart, like the secret of her own secret: a minimal child. Methodically, the explorer studied that little belly of the smallest mature human being. It was at this moment that the explorer, for the first time since he had known her, instead of feeling curiosity, or exhalation, or victory, or the scientific spirit, felt sick.

The smallest woman in the world was laughing.

She was laughing, warm, warm — Little Flower was enjoying life. The rare thing herself was experiencing the ineffable sensation of not having been eaten yet. Not having been eaten yet was something that at any other time would have given her the agile impulse to jump from branch to branch. But, in this moment of tranquility, amid the thick leaves of the Eastern Congo, she was not putting this impulse into action — it was entirely concentrated in the smallness of the rare thing itself. So she was laughing. It was a laugh such as only one who does not speak laughs. It was a laugh that the explorer, constrained, couldn't classify. And she kept on enjoying her own soft laugh, she who wasn't being devoured. Not to be devoured is the most perfect feeling. Not to be devoured is the secret goal of a whole life. While she was not being eaten, her bestial laughter was as delicate as joy is delicate. The explorer was baffled.

In the second place, if the rare thing herself was laughing, it was because, within her smallness, a great darkness had begun to move.

The rare thing herself felt in her breast a warmth that might be called love. She loved that sallow explorer. If she could have talked and had told him that she loved him, he would have been puffed up with vanity. Vanity that would have collapsed when she added that she also loved the explorer's ring very much, and the explorer's boots. And when that collapse had taken place, Little Flower would not have understood why. Because her love for the explorer — one might even say "profound love," since, having no other resources, she was reduced to profundity — her profound love for the explorer would not have been at all diminished by the fact that she also loved his boots. There is an old misunderstanding about the word love, and, if many children are born from this misunderstanding, many others have lost the unique chance of being born, only because of the susceptibility that demands that it be me! me! that is loved, and not my money. But in the humidity of the forest these cruel refinements do not exist, and love is not to be eaten, love is to find a boot pretty, love is to like the strange color of a man who isn't black, is to laugh for love of a shiny ring. Little Flower blinked with love, and laughed warmly, small, gravid, warm.

The explorer tried to smile back, without knowing exactly to what abyss his smile responded, and then he was embarrassed as only a very big man can be embarrassed. He pretended to adjust his explorer's hat better; he colored, prudishly. He turned a lovely color, a greenish-pink, like a lime at sunrise. He was undoubtedly sour.

Perhaps adjusting the symbolic helmet helped the explorer to get control of himself, severely recapture the discipline of his work, and go on with his note-taking. He had learned how to understand some of the tribe's few articulate words, and to interpret their signs. By now, he could ask questions.

Little Flower answered "Yes." That it was very nice to have a tree of her own to live in. Because — she didn't say this but her eyes became so dark that they said it — because it is good to own, good to own, good to own. The explorer winked several times.

Marcel Pretre had some difficult moments with himself. But at least he kept busy taking notes. Those who didn't take notes had to manage as best they could:

"Well," suddenly declared one old lady, folding up the newspaper decisively, "well, as I always say: God knows what He's doing."

෨෨

KATHERINE MANSFIELD (1888–1923) *was born Kathleen Mansfield Beauchamp in Wellington, New Zealand. In 1903 she persuaded her father, a banker and industrialist, to send her to London to study the cello. After a brief return to New Zealand, she went back to London with a small allowance from her family, deciding to become a writer instead of a musician after meeting D. H. Lawrence and Virginia Woolf. Mansfield's first book of short stories,* In a German Pension, *was published in*

1911. In the same year she met the literary critic John Middleton Murry, who became her husband in 1918. Bliss and Other Stories (1920) established her reputation and was followed by The Garden-Party (1922).

Mansfield took Anton Chekhov as her model, but after she was stricken with tuberculosis in 1918 she found it difficult to work. In her posthumously published Journal (1927), she often upbraided herself when she felt too ill to write: "Look at the stories that wait and wait just at the threshold. Why don't I let them in? And their place would be taken by others who are lurking beyond just there — waiting for the chance." Finally she sought a cure for her illness at the Gurdjieff Institute in France, run by the noted Armenian mystic Georges Ivanovitch Gurdjieff, whose methods combined spiritual and physical healing. She died at the institute a few months after her thirty-fourth birthday.

Eighty-eight of Mansfield's stories have been published (including fifteen left unfinished), and they have had a great influence on the development of the literary form. As did Chekhov and James Joyce, Mansfield simplified plot to intensify its emotional impact, dramatizing small moments to reveal the larger significance in people's lives, or, as Willa Cather observed, approaching "the major forces of life through comparatively trivial incidents." Mansfield developed her own technique of narration in which she transformed a chance incident into a terse psychological drama. As would a symbolist poet, she used concrete images — such as the fur piece in "Miss Brill" — to convey her characters' feelings, or what she called "the state of the soul." Her stories have affected later writers as powerfully as Chekhov's affected her.

KATHERINE MANSFIELD

Miss Brill   1922

Although it was so brilliantly fine — the blue sky powdered with gold and great spots of light like white wine splashed over the Jardins Publiques — Miss Brill was glad that she had decided on her fur. The air was motionless, but when you opened your mouth there was just a faint chill, like a chill from a glass of iced water before you sip, and now and again a leaf came drifting — from nowhere, from the sky. Miss Brill put up her hand and touched her fur. Dear little thing! It was nice to feel it again. She had taken it out of its box that afternoon, shaken out the moth-powder, given it a good brush, and rubbed the life back into the dim little eyes. "What has been happening to me?" said the sad little eyes. Oh, how sweet it was to see them snap at her again from the red eiderdown! . . . But the nose, which was of some black composition, wasn't at all firm. It must have had a knock, somehow. Never mind — a little dab of black sealing-wax when the time came — when it was absolutely necessary. . . . Little rogue! Yes, she really felt like that about it. Little rogue biting its tail just by her left ear. She could have taken it off and laid it on her lap and stroked it. She felt a tingling in her hands and arms, but that came from walking, she supposed. And when she breathed, something light and sad — no, not sad, exactly — something gentle seemed to move in her bosom.

There were a number of people out this afternoon, far more than last Sunday. And the band sounded louder and gayer. That was because the Season had begun. For although the band played all the year round on Sundays, out of season it was never the same. It was like some one playing with only the family to listen; it didn't care how it played if there weren't any strangers present. Wasn't the conductor wearing a new coat, too? She was sure it was new. He scraped with his foot and flapped his arms like a rooster about to crow, and the bandsmen sitting in the green rotunda blew out their cheeks and glared at the music. Now there came a little "flutey" bit — very pretty! — a little chain of bright drops. She was sure it would be repeated. It was; she lifted her head and smiled.

Only two people shared her "special" seat: a fine old man in a velvet coat, his hands clasped over a huge carved walking-stick, and a big old woman, sitting upright, with a roll of knitting on her embroidered apron. They did not speak. This was disappointing, for Miss Brill always looked forward to the conversation. She had become really quite expert, she thought, at listening as though she didn't listen, at sitting in other people's lives just for a minute while they talked round her.

She glanced, sideways, at the old couple. Perhaps they would go soon. Last Sunday, too, hadn't been as interesting as usual. An Englishman and his wife, he wearing a dreadful Panama hat and she button boots. And she'd gone on the whole time about how she ought to wear spectacles; she knew she needed them; but that it was no good getting any; they'd be sure to break and they'd never keep on. And he'd been so patient. He'd suggested everything — gold rims, the kind that curved round your ears, little pads inside the bridge. No, nothing would please her. "They'll always be sliding down my nose!" Miss Brill had wanted to shake her.

The old people sat on the bench, still as statues. Never mind, there was always the crowd to watch. To and fro, in front of the flower beds and the band rotunda, the couples and groups paraded, stopped to talk, to greet, to buy a handful of flowers from the old beggar who had his tray fixed to the railings. Little children ran among them, swooping and laughing; little boys with big white silk bows under their chins, little girls, little French dolls, dressed up in velvet and lace. And sometimes a tiny staggerer came suddenly rocking into the open from under the trees, stopped, stared, as suddenly sat down "flop," until its small high-stepping mother, like a young hen, rushed scolding to its rescue. Other people sat on the benches and green chairs, but they were nearly always the same, Sunday after Sunday, and — Miss Brill had often noticed — there was something funny about nearly all of them. They were odd, silent, nearly all old, and from the way they stared they looked as though they'd just come from dark little rooms or even — even cupboards!

Behind the rotunda the slender trees with yellow leaves down drooping, and through them just a line of sea, and beyond the blue sky with gold-veined clouds.

Tum-tum-tum tiddle-um! tiddle-um! tum tiddley-um tum ta! blew the band.

Two young girls in red came by and two young soldiers in blue met them, and they laughed and paired and went off arm-in-arm. Two peasant women with funny straw hats passed, gravely, leading beautiful smoke-coloured donkeys. A cold, pale nun hurried by. A beautiful woman came along and dropped her bunch of violets, and a little boy ran after to hand them to her, and she took them and threw them away as if they'd been poisoned. Dear me! Miss Brill didn't know whether to admire that or not! And now an ermine toque and a gentleman in grey met just in front of her. He was tall, stiff, dignified, and she was wearing the ermine toque she'd bought when her hair was yellow. Now everything, her hair, her face, even her eyes, was the same colour as the shabby ermine, and her hand, in its cleaned glove, lifted to dab her lips, was a tiny yellowish paw. Oh, she was so pleased to see him — delighted! She rather thought they were going to meet that afternoon. She described where she'd been — everywhere, here, there, along by the sea. The day was so charming — didn't he agree? And wouldn't he, perhaps? . . . But he shook his head, lighted a cigarette, slowly breathed a great deep puff into her face, and, even while she was still talking and laughing, flicked the match away and walked on. The ermine toque was alone; she smiled more brightly than ever. But even the band seemed to know what she was feeling and played more softly, played tenderly, and the drum beat, "The Brute! The Brute!" over and over. What would she do? What was going to happen now? But as Miss Brill wondered, the ermine toque turned, raised her hand as though she'd seen some one else, much nicer, just over there, and pattered away. And the band changed again and played more quickly, more gaily than ever, and the old couple on Miss Brill's seat got up and marched away, and such a funny old man with long whiskers hobbled along in time to the music and was nearly knocked over by four girls walking abreast.

Oh, how fascinating it was! How she enjoyed it! How she loved sitting here, watching it all! It was like a play. It was exactly like a play. Who could believe the sky at the back wasn't painted? But it wasn't till a little brown dog trotted on solemn and then slowly trotted off, like a little "theatre" dog, a little dog that had been drugged, that Miss Brill discovered what it was that made it so exciting. They were all on the stage. They weren't only the audience, not only looking on; they were acting. Even she had a part and came every Sunday. No doubt somebody would have noticed if she hadn't been there; she was part of the performance after all. How strange she'd never thought of it like that before! And yet it explained why she made such a point of starting from home at just the same time each week — so as not to be late for the performance — and it also explained why she had quite a queer, shy feeling at telling her English pupils how she spent her Sunday afternoons. No wonder! Miss Brill nearly laughed out loud. She was on the stage. She thought of the old invalid gentleman to whom she read the newspaper four afternoons a week while he slept in the garden. She had got quite used to the frail head on the cotton pillow, the hollowed eyes, the open mouth and the high pinched nose. If he'd been dead she mightn't have noticed for weeks; she wouldn't have minded. But suddenly he knew he was having the paper read to him by an actress! "An actress!" The old head lifted; two points of light quivered in the old eyes. "An actress — are ye?" And Miss Brill smoothed the newspaper as though it were the manuscript of her part and said gently: "Yes, I have been an actress for a long time."

The band had been having a rest. Now they started again. And what they played was warm, sunny, yet there was just a faint chill — a something, what was it? — not sadness — no, not sadness — a something that made you want to sing. The tune lifted, lifted, the light shone; and it seemed to Miss Brill that in another moment all of them, all the whole company, would begin singing. The young ones, the laughing ones who were moving together, they would begin, and the men's voices, very resolute and brave, would join them. And then she too, she too, and the others on the benches — they would come in with a kind of accompaniment — something low, that scarcely rose or fell, something so beautiful — moving. . . . And Miss Brill's eyes filled with tears and she looked smiling at all the other members of the company. Yes, we understand, we understand, she thought — though what they understood she didn't know.

Just at that moment a boy and a girl came and sat down where the old couple had been. They were beautifully dressed; they were in love. The hero and heroine, of course, just arrived from his father's yacht. And still soundlessly singing, still with that trembling smile, Miss Brill prepared to listen.

"No, not now," said the girl. "Not here, I can't."

"But why? Because of that stupid old thing at the end there?" asked the boy. "Why does she come here at all — who wants her? Why doesn't she keep her silly old mug at home?"

"It's her fu-fur which is so funny," giggled the girl. "It's exactly like a fried whiting."

"Ah, be off with you!" said the boy in an angry whisper. Then: "Tell me, ma petite chérie — "

"No, not here," said the girl. "Not yet."

On her way home she usually bought a slice of honey-cake at the baker's. It was her Sunday treat. Sometimes there was an almond in her slice, sometimes not. It made a great difference. If there was an almond it was like carrying home a tiny present — a surprise — something that might very well not have been there. She hurried on the almond Sundays and struck the match for the kettle in quite a dashing way.

But to-day she passed the baker's by, climbed the stairs, went into the little dark room — her room like a cupboard — and sat down on the red eiderdown. She sat there for a long time. The box that the fur came out of was on the bed. She unclasped the necklet quickly; quickly, without looking, laid it inside. But when she put the lid on she thought she heard something crying.

ର

GUY DE MAUPASSANT (1850–1893) *was born in Normandy, the son of a wealthy stockbroker. Unable to accept discipline in school, he joined the army during the Franco-Prussian War of 1870–1871. Then for seven years he apprenticed himself to Gustave Flaubert, a distant relative, who attempted to teach him to write. Maupassant remembered, "I wrote verses, short stories, longer stories, even a wretched play. Nothing survived. The master read everything. Then, the following Sunday at lunch,* he developed his criticisms." Flaubert taught Maupassant that talent "is nothing other than a long patience. Work."

The essence of Flaubert's now famous teaching is that the writer must look at everything to find some aspect of it that no one has yet seen or expressed. "Everything contains some element of the unexplored because we are accustomed to use our eyes only with the memory of what other people before us have thought about the object we are looking at. The least thing has a bit of the unknown about it. Let us find this."

In 1880 Maupassant caused a sensation with the publication of his story "Boule de Suif" ("Ball of Fat"), a dramatic account of prostitution and bourgeois hypocrisy. During the next decade, before his gradual incapacitation and death from syphilis, he published nearly 300 stories. Characterized by compact and dramatic narrative lines, they read as modern short stories, eliminating the moral judgments and the long digressions used by many earlier writers. Along with his younger contemporary Anton Chekhov, Maupassant is responsible for technical advances that moved the short story toward an austerity that has marked it ever since. These two writers influenced nearly everyone who has written short fiction after them. As Joseph Conrad recognized, "Facts, and again facts, are his [Maupassant's] unique concern. That is why he is not always properly understood." Maupassant's lack of sentimentality toward his characters, as in his depiction of the wife in "The Necklace," laid him open to charges of cynicism and hardness. Even if Maupassant's stories display a greater distance from his characters and a less sympathetic irony than Chekhov's, both writers were the most accomplished of narrators, equal in their powers of exact observation and independent judgment and in their supple, practiced knowledge of their craft.

RELATED COMMENTARY: *Kate Chopin, "How I Stumbled upon Maupassant," page 740.*

GUY DE MAUPASSANT

The Necklace

1884

TRANSLATED BY MARJORIE LAURIE

She was one of those pretty and charming girls who are sometimes, as if by a mistake of destiny, born in a family of clerks. She had no dowry, no expectations, no means of being known, understood, loved, wedded by any rich and distinguished man; and she let herself be married to a little clerk at the Ministry of Public Instructions.

She dressed plainly because she could not dress well, but she was as unhappy as though she had really fallen from her proper station, since with women there is neither caste nor rank: and beauty, grace, and charm act instead of family and birth. Natural fineness, instinct for what is elegant, suppleness of wit, are the sole hierarchy, and make from women of the people the equals of the very greatest ladies.

She suffered ceaselessly, feeling herself born for all the delicacies and all the luxuries. She suffered from the poverty of her dwelling, from the wretched look of the walls, from the worn-out chairs, from the ugliness of the curtains. All those things, of which another woman of her rank would never even have been conscious, tortured her and made her angry. The sight of the little Breton peasant, who did her humble housework aroused in her regrets which were despairing, and distracted dreams. She thought of the silent antechambers hung with Oriental tapestry, lit by tall bronze candelabra, and of the two great footmen in knee breeches who sleep in the big armchairs, made drowsy by the heavy warmth of the hot-air stove. She thought of the long *salons* fitted up with ancient silk, of the delicate furniture carrying priceless curiosities, and of the coquettish perfumed boudoirs made for talks at five o'clock with intimate friends, with men famous and sought after, whom all women envy and whose attention they all desire.

When she sat down to dinner, before the round table covered with a tablecloth three days old, opposite her husband, who uncovered the soup tureen and declared with an enchanted air, "Ah, the good *pot-au-feu*! I don't know anything better than that," she thought of dainty dinners, of shining silverware, of tapestry which peopled the walls with ancient personages and with strange birds flying in the midst of a fairy forest; and she thought of delicious dishes served on marvelous plates, and of the whispered gallantries which you listen to with a sphinxlike smile, while you are eating the pink flesh of a trout or the wings of a quail.

She had no dresses, no jewels, nothing. And she loved nothing but that; she felt made for that. She would so have liked to please, to be envied, to be charming, to be sought after.

She had a friend, a former schoolmate at the convent, who was rich, and whom she did not like to go and see any more, because she suffered so much when she came back.

But one evening, her husband returned home with a triumphant air, and holding a large envelope in his hand.

"There," said he. "Here is something for you."

She tore the paper sharply, and drew out a printed card which bore these words:

"The Minister of Public Instruction and Mme. Georges Ramponneau request the honor of M. and Mme. Loisel's company at the palace of the Ministry on Monday evening, January eighteenth."

Instead of being delighted, as her husband hoped, she threw the invitation on the table with disdain, murmuring:

"What do you want me to do with that?"

"But, my dear, I thought you would be glad. You never go out, and this is such a fine opportunity. I had awful trouble to get it. Everyone wants to go; it is very select, and they are not giving many invitations to clerks. The whole official world will be there."

She looked at him with an irritated glance, and said, impatiently:

"And what do you want me to put on my back?"

He had not thought of that; he stammered:

"Why, the dress you go to the theater in. It looks very well, to me."

He stopped, distracted, seeing his wife was crying. Two great tears descended slowly from the corners of her eyes toward the corners of her mouth. He stuttered:

"What's the matter? What's the matter?"

But, by violent effort, she had conquered her grief, and she replied, with a calm voice, while she wiped her wet cheeks:

"Nothing. Only I have no dress and therefore I can't go to this ball. Give your card to some colleague whose wife is better equipped than I."

He was in despair. He resumed:

"Come, let us see, Mathilde. How much would it cost, a suitable dress, which you could use on other occasions. Something very simple?"

She reflected several seconds, making her calculations and wondering also what sum she could ask without drawing on herself an immediate refusal and a frightened exclamation from the economical clerk.

Finally, she replied, hesitatingly:

"I don't know exactly, but I think I could manage it with four hundred francs."

He had grown a little pale, because he was laying aside just that amount to buy a gun and treat himself to a little shooting next summer on the plain of Nanterre, with several friends who went to shoot larks down there, of a Sunday.

But he said:

"All right. I will give you four hundred francs. And try to have a pretty dress."

The day of the ball drew near, and Mme. Loisel seemed sad, uneasy, anxious. Her dress was ready, however. Her husband said to her one evening:

"What is the matter? Come, you've been so queer these last three days."

And she answered:

"It annoys me not to have a single jewel, not a single stone, nothing to put on. I shall look like distress. I should almost rather not go at all."

He resumed:

"You might wear natural flowers. It's very stylish at this time of the year. For ten francs you can get two or three magnificent roses."

She was not convinced.

"No; there's nothing more humiliating than to look poor among other women who are rich."

But her husband cried:

"How stupid you are! Go look up your friend Mme. Forestier, and ask her to lend you some jewels. You're quite thick enough with her to do that."

She uttered a cry of joy:

"It's true. I never thought of it."

The next day she went to her friend and told of her distress.

Mme. Forestier went to a wardrobe with a glass door, took out a large jewelbox, brought it back, opened it, and said to Mme. Loisel:

"Choose, choose, my dear."

She saw first of all some bracelets, then a pearl necklace, then a Venetian cross, gold and precious stones of admirable workmanship. She tried on the ornaments before the glass, hesitated, could not make up her mind to part with them, to give them back. She kept asking:

"Haven't you any more?"

"Why, yes. Look. I don't know what you like."

All of a sudden she discovered, in a black satin box, a superb necklace of diamonds, and her heart began to beat with an immoderate desire. Her hands trembled as she took it. She fastened it around her throat, outside her high necked dress, and remained lost in ecstasy at the sight of herself.

Then she asked, hesitating, filled with anguish:

"Can you lend me that, only that?"

"Why, yes, certainly."

She sprang upon the neck of her friend, kissed her passionately, then fled with her treasure.

The day of the ball arrived. Mme. Loisel made a great success. She was prettier than them all, elegant, gracious, smiling, and crazy with joy. All the men looked at her, asked her name, endeavored to be introduced. All the attachés of the Cabinet wanted to waltz with her. She was remarked by the minister himself.

She danced with intoxication, with passion, made drunk by pleasure, forgetting all, in the triumph of her beauty, in the glory of her success, in a sort of cloud of happiness composed of all this homage, of all this admiration, of all these awakened desires, and of that sense of complete victory which is so sweet to a woman's heart.

She went away about four o'clock in the morning. Her husband had been sleeping since midnight, in a little deserted anteroom, with three other gentlemen whose wives were having a good time. He threw over her shoulders the wraps which he had brought, modest wraps of common life, whose poverty contrasted with the elegance of the ball dress. She felt this, and wanted to escape so as not to be remarked by the other women, who were enveloping themselves in costly furs.

Loisel held her back.

"Wait a bit. You will catch cold outside. I will go and call a cab."

But she did not listen to him, and rapidly descended the stairs. When they were in the street they did not find a carriage; and they began to look for one, shouting after the cabmen whom they saw passing by at a distance.

They went down toward the Seine, in despair, shivering with cold. At last they found on the quay one of those ancient noctambulant coupés° which, exactly as if they were ashamed to show their misery during the day, are never seen round Paris until after nightfall.

It took them to their door in the Rue des Martyrs, and once more, sadly, they climbed up homeward. All was ended, for her. And as to him, he reflected that he must be at the Ministry at ten o'clock.

She removed the wraps which covered her shoulders before the glass, so as once more to see herself in all her glory. But suddenly she uttered a cry. She no longer had the necklace around her neck!

Her husband, already half undressed, demanded:

"What is the matter with you?"

---

coupés: Enclosed four-wheeled carriages.

She turned madly toward him:

"I have — I have — I've lost Mme. Forestier's necklace."

He stood up, distracted.

"What! — how? — impossible!"

And they looked in the folds of her dress, in the folds of her cloak, in her pockets, everywhere. They did not find it.

He asked:

"You're sure you had it on when you left the ball?"

"Yes, I felt it in the vestibule of the palace."

"But if you had lost it in the street we should have heard it fall. It must be in the cab."

"Yes. Probably. Did you take his number?"

"No. And you, didn't you notice it?"

"No."

They looked, thunderstruck, at one another. At last Loisel put on his clothes.

"I shall go back on foot," said he, "over the whole route which we have taken to see if I can find it."

And he went out. She sat waiting on a chair in her ball dress, without strength to go to bed, overwhelmed, without fire, without a thought.

Her husband came back about seven o'clock. He had found nothing.

He went to Police Headquarters, to the newspaper offices, to offer a reward; he went to the cab companies — everywhere, in fact, whither he was urged by the least suspicion of hope.

She waited all day, in the same condition of mad fear before this terrible calamity.

Loisel returned at night with a hollow, pale face; he had discovered nothing.

"You must write to your friend," said he, "that you have broken the clasp of her necklace and that you are having it mended. That will give us time to turn round."

She wrote at his dictation.

At the end of a week they had lost all hope.

And Loisel, who had aged five years, declared:

"We must consider how to replace that ornament."

The next day they took the box which had contained it, and they went to the jeweler whose name was found within. He consulted his books.

"It was not I, madame, who sold that necklace; I must simply have furnished the case."

Then they went from jeweler to jeweler, searching for a necklace like the other, consulting their memories, sick both of them with chagrin and anguish.

They found, in a shop at the Palais Royal, a string of diamonds which seemed to them exactly like the one they looked for. It was worth forty thousand francs. They could have it for thirty-six.

So they begged the jeweler not to sell it for three days yet. And they made a bargain that he should buy it back for thirty-four thousand francs, in case they found the other one before the end of February.

Loisel possessed eighteen thousand francs which his father had left him. He would borrow the rest.

He did borrow, asking a thousand francs of one, five hundred of another, five louis here, three louis there. He gave notes, took up ruinous obligations, dealt with usurers and all the race of lenders. He compromised all the rest of his life, risked his signature without even knowing if he could meet it; and, frightened by the pains yet to come, by the black misery which was about to fall upon him, by the prospect of all the physical privation and of all the moral tortures which he was to suffer, he went to get the new necklace, putting down upon the merchant's counter thirty-six thousand francs.

When Mme. Loisel took back the necklace, Mme. Forestier said to her, with a chilly manner:

"You should have returned it sooner; I might have needed it."

She did not open the case, as her friend had so much feared. If she had detected the substitution, what would she have thought, what would she have said? Would she not have taken Mme. Loisel for a thief?

Mme. Loisel now knew the horrible existence of the needy. She took her part, moreover, all of a sudden, with heroism. That dreadful debt must be paid. She would pay it. They dismissed their servant; they changed their lodgings; they rented a garret under the roof.

She came to know what heavy housework meant and the odious cares of the kitchen. She washed the dishes, using her rosy nails on the greasy pots and pans. She washed the dirty linen, the shirts, and the dishcloths, which she dried upon a line; she carried the slops down to the street every morning, and carried up the water, stopping for breath at every landing. And, dressed like a woman of the people, she went to the fruiterer, the grocer, the butcher, her basket on her arm, bargaining, insulted, defending her miserable money sou by sou.

Each month they had to meet some notes, renew others, obtain more time.

Her husband worked in the evening making a fair copy of some tradesman's accounts, and late at night he often copied manuscript for five sous a page.

And this life lasted for ten years.

At the end of ten years, they had paid everything, everything, with the rates of usury, and the accumulations of the compound interest.

Mme. Loisel looked old now. She had become the woman of impoverished households — strong and hard and rough. With frowsy hair, skirts askew, and red hands, she talked loud while washing the floor with great swishes of water. But sometimes, when her husband was at the office, she sat down near the window, and she thought of that gay evening of long ago, of that ball where she had been so beautiful and so fêted.

What would have happened if she had not lost that necklace? Who knows? Who knows? How life is strange and changeful! How little a thing is needed for us to be lost or to be saved!

But, one Sunday, having gone to take a walk in the Champs Elysées to refresh herself from the labor of the week, she suddenly perceived a woman who was leading a child. It was Mme. Forestier, still young, still beautiful, still charming.

Mme. Loisel felt moved. Was she going to speak to her? Yes, certainly. And now that she had paid, she was going to tell her all about it. Why not?

She went up.

"Good-day, Jeanne."

The other, astonished to be familiarly addressed by this plain goodwife, did not recognize her at all, and stammered.

"But — madam! — I do not know — you must be mistaken."

"No. I am Mathilde Loisel."

Her friend uttered a cry.

"Oh, my poor Mathilde! How you are changed!"

"Yes, I have had days hard enough, since I have seen you, days wretched enough — and that because of you!"

"Of me! How so?"

"Do you remember that diamond necklace which you lent me to wear at the ministerial ball?"

"Yes. Well?"

"Well, I lost it."

"What do you mean? You brought it back."

"I brought you back another just like it. And for this we have been ten years paying. You can understand that it was not easy for us, who had nothing. At last it is ended, and I am very glad."

Mme. Forestier had stopped.

"You say that you bought a necklace of diamonds to replace mine?"

"Yes. You never noticed it, then! They were very like."

And she smiled with a joy which was proud and naïve at once.

Mme. Forestier, strongly moved, took her two hands.

"Oh, my poor Mathilde! Why, my necklace was paste. It was worth at most five hundred francs!"

෪

HERMAN MELVILLE *(1819–1891) published his first short story in 1853 as "Bartleby, the Scrivener: A Story of Wall Street." Behind him were seven years of writing novels beginning with the burst of creative energy that produced his early books of sea adventure:* Typee *(1846),* Omoo *(1847),* Mardi *(1849),* Redburn *(1849), and* White-Jacket *(1850). All of these were based on his experiences on board ship. Melville had been left in poverty at the age of fifteen when his father went bankrupt, and in 1839 he went to sea as a cabin boy. Two years later he sailed on a whaler bound for the Pacific, but he deserted in the Marquesas Islands and lived for a time with cannibals. Having little formal education, Melville later boasted that "a whale ship was my Yale College and my Harvard." His most ambitious book was* Moby-Dick *(1851), a work of great allegorical complexity heavily indebted to the influence of Nathaniel Hawthorne, Melville's neighbor in the Berkshires at the time he wrote it.* Moby-Dick *was not a commercial success, however, and the novel that followed it,* Pierre *(1852), was dismissed by critics as incomprehensible trash.*

It was at this point that Melville turned to the short story. Between 1853 and 1856 he published fifteen sketches and stories and a serialized historical novel, promising the popular magazines that his stories would "contain nothing of any sort to shock the fastidious." But when this work and another novel (The Confidence Man, 1857) failed to restore his reputation, he ceased trying to support his family by his pen. He moved from his farm in the Berkshires to a house in New York City bought for him by his father-in-law, and worked for more than twenty years as an inspector of customs. He published a few books of poems and wrote a short novel, Billy Budd, which critics acclaimed as one of his greatest works when it was published — thirty years after his death.

Melville stood at the crossroads in the early history of American short fiction. When he began to publish in magazines, Hawthorne and Edgar Allan Poe had already done their best work in the romantic vein of tales and sketches, and the realistic local-color school of short stories had not yet been established. Melville created something new in "Bartleby, the Scrivener," a fully developed, if discursive, short story set in a contemporary social context. It baffled readers of Putnam's Monthly Magazine in 1853, when it was published in two installments. One reviewer called it "a Poeish tale with an infusion of more natural sentiment." For the rest of his stories, Melville used the conventional form of old-fashioned tales mostly set in remote times or places.

RELATED COMMENTARIES: *Herman Melville, "Blackness in Hawthorne's 'Young Goodman Brown,' " page 768; J. Hillis Miller, "A Deconstructive Reading of Melville's 'Bartleby, the Scrivener,' " page 770.*

HERMAN MELVILLE

Bartleby, the Scrivener

1853

A Story of Wall Street

I am a rather elderly man. The nature of my avocations, for the last thirty years, has brought me into more than ordinary contact with what would seem an interesting and somewhat singular set of men, of whom, as yet, nothing, that I know of, has ever been written — I mean, the law-copyists, or scriveners. I have known very many of them, professionally and privately, and, if I pleased, could relate divers histories, at which good-natured gentlemen might smile, and sentimental souls might weep. But I waive the biographies of all other scriveners, for a few passages in the life of Bartleby, who was a scrivener, the strangest I ever saw, or heard of. While, of other law-copyists, I might write the complete life, of Bartleby nothing of that sort can be done. I believe that no materials exist, for a full and satisfactory biography of this man. It is an irreparable loss to literature. Bartleby was one of those beings of whom nothing is ascertainable, except from the original sources, and, in his case, those are very small. What my own astonished eyes saw of Bartleby, *that* is all I know of him, except, indeed, one vague report, which will appear in the sequel.

Ere introducing the scrivener, as he first appeared to me, it is fit I make some mention of myself, my *employés*, my business, my chambers, and general surroundings, because some such description is indispensable to an adequate understanding of the chief character about to be presented. Imprimis:° I am a man who, from his youth upwards, has been filled with a profound conviction that the easiest way of life is the best. Hence, though I belong to a profession proverbially energetic and nervous, even to turbulence, at times, yet nothing of that sort have I ever suffered to invade my peace. I am one of those unambitious lawyers who never address a jury, or in any way draw down public applause; but, in the cool tranquillity of a snug retreat, do a snug business among rich men's bonds, and mortgages, and title-deeds. All who know me, consider me an eminently *safe* man. The late John Jacob Astor, a personage little given to poetic enthusiasm, had no hesitation in pronouncing my first grand point to be prudence; my next, method. I do not speak it in vanity, but simply record the fact, that I was not unemployed in my profession by the late John Jacob Astor; a name which, I admit, I love to repeat; for it hath a rounded and orbicular sound to it, and rings like unto bullion. I will freely add, that I was not insensible to the late John Jacob Astor's good opinion.

Some time prior to the period at which this little history begins, my avocations had been largely increased. The good old office, now extinct in the State of New York, of a Master in Chancery, had been conferred upon me. It was not a very arduous office, but very pleasantly remunerative. I seldom lose my temper; much more seldom indulge in dangerous indignation at wrongs and outrages; but I must be permitted to be rash here and declare, that I consider the sudden and violent abrogation of the office of Master in Chancery, by the new Constitution, as a —— premature act; inasmuch as I had counted upon a life-lease of the profits, whereas I only received those of a few short years. But this is by the way.

My chambers were up stairs, at No. — Wall Street. At one end, they looked upon the white wall of the interior of a spacious skylight shaft, penetrating the building from top to bottom.

This view might have been considered rather tame than otherwise, deficient in what landscape painters call "life." But, if so, the view from the other end of my chambers offered, at least, a contrast, if nothing more. In that direction, my windows commanded an unobstructed view of a lofty brick wall, black by age and everlasting shade; which wall required no spy-glass to bring out its lurking beauties, but, for the benefit of all near-sighted spectators, was pushed up to within ten feet of my window-panes. Owing to the great height of the surrounding buildings, and my chambers being on the second floor, the interval between this wall and mine not a little resembled a huge square cistern.

At the period just preceding the advent of Bartleby, I had two persons as copyists in my employment, and a promising lad as an office-boy. First, Turkey; second, Nippers; third, Ginger Nut. These may seem names, the like of which are not usually found in the Directory. In truth, they were nicknames, mutually conferred upon each other by my three clerks, and were deemed ex-

---

Imprimis: In the first place (Latin).

pressive of their respective persons or characters. Turkey was a short, pursy Englishman, of about my own age — that is, somewhere not far from sixty. In the morning, one might say, his face was of a fine florid hue, but after twelve o'clock, meridian — his dinner hour — it blazed like a grate full of Christmas coals; and continued blazing — but, as it were, with a gradual wane — till six o'clock, P.M., or thereabouts; after which, I saw no more of the proprietor of the face, which, gaining its meridian with the sun, seemed to set with it, to rise, culminate, and decline the following day, with the like regularity and undiminished glory. There are many singular coincidences I have known in the course of my life, not the least among which was the fact, that, exactly when Turkey displayed his fullest beams from his red and radiant countenance, just then, too, at that critical moment, began the daily period when I considered his business capacities as seriously disturbed for the remainder of the twenty-four hours. Not that he was absolutely idle, or averse to business then; far from it. The difficulty was, he was apt to be altogether too energetic. There was a strange, inflamed, flurried, flighty recklessness of activity about him. He would be incautious in dipping his pen into his inkstand. All his blots upon my documents were dropped there after twelve o'clock, meridian. Indeed, not only would he be reckless, and sadly given to making blots in the afternoon, but, some days, he went further, and was rather noisy. At such times, too, his face flamed with augmented blazonry, as if cannel coal had been heaped on anthracite. He made an unpleasant racket with his chair; spilled his sand-box; in mending his pens, impatiently split them all to pieces, and threw them on the floor in a sudden passion; stood up, and leaned over his table, boxing his papers about in a most indecorous manner, very sad to behold in an elderly man like him. Nevertheless, as he was in many ways a most valuable person to me, and all the time before twelve o'clock, meridian, was the quickest, steadiest creature, too, accomplishing a great deal of work in a style not easily to be matched — for these reasons, I was willing to overlook his eccentricities, though, indeed, occasionally, I remonstrated with him. I did this very gently, however, because, though the civilest, nay, the blandest and most reverential of men in the morning, yet, in the afternoon, he was disposed, upon provocation, to be slightly rash with his tongue — in fact, insolent. Now, valuing his morning services as I did, and resolved not to lose them — yet, at the same time, made uncomfortable by his inflamed ways after twelve o'clock — and being a man of peace, unwilling by my admonitions to call forth unseemly retorts from him, I took upon me, one Saturday noon (he was always worse on Saturdays) to hint to him, very kindly, that, perhaps, now that he was growing old, it might be well to abridge his labors; in short, he need not come to my chambers after twelve o'clock, but, dinner over, had best go home to his lodgings, and rest himself till tea-time. But no; he insisted upon his afternoon devotions. His countenance became intolerably fervid, as he oratorically assured me — gesticulating with a long ruler at the other end of the room — that if his services in the morning were useful, how indispensable, then, in the afternoon?

"With submission, sir," said Turkey, on this occasion, "I consider myself your right-hand man. In the morning I but marshal and deploy my columns; but in the afternoon I put myself at their head, and gallantly charge the foe, thus" — and he made a violent thrust with the ruler.

"But the blots, Turkey," intimated I.

"True; but, with submission, sir, behold these hairs! I am getting old. Surely, sir, a blot or two of a warm afternoon is not to be severely urged against gray hairs. Old age — even if it blot the page — is honorable. With submission, sir, we *both* are getting old."

This appeal to my fellow-feeling was hardly to be resisted. At all events, I saw that go he would not. So, I made up my mind to let him stay, resolving, nevertheless, to see to it that, during the afternoon, he had to do with my less important papers.

Nippers, the second on my list, was a whiskered, sallow, and, upon the whole, rather piratical-looking young man, of about five-and-twenty. I always deemed him the victim of two evil powers — ambition and indigestion. The ambition was evinced by a certain impatience of the duties of a mere copyist, an unwarrantable usurpation of strictly professional affairs such as the original drawing up of legal documents. The indigestion seemed betokened in an occasional nervous testiness and grinning irritability, causing the teeth to audibly grind together over mistakes committed in copying; unnecessary maledictions, hissed, rather than spoken, in the heat of business; and especially by a continual discontent with the height of the table where he worked. Though of a very ingenious mechanical turn, Nippers could never get this table to suit him. He put chips under it, blocks of various sorts, bits of pasteboard, and at last went so far as to attempt an exquisite adjustment, by final pieces of folded blotting paper. But no invention would answer. If, for the sake of easing his back, he brought the table-lid at a sharp angle well up towards his chin, and wrote there like a man using the steep roof of a Dutch house for his desk, then he declared that it stopped the circulation in his arms. If now he lowered the table to his waistbands, and stooped over it in writing, then there was a sore aching in his back. In short, the truth of the matter was, Nippers knew not what he wanted. Or, if he wanted anything, it was to be rid of a scrivener's table altogether. Among the manifestations of his diseased ambition was a fondness he had for receiving visits from certain ambiguous-looking fellows in seedy coats, whom he called his clients. Indeed, I was aware that not only was he, at times, considerable of a ward-politician, but he occasionally did a little business at the justices' courts, and was not unknown on the steps of the Tombs.° I have good reason to believe, however, that one individual who called upon him at my chambers, and who, with a grand air, he insisted was his client, was no other than a dun, and the alleged title-deed, a bill. But, with all his failings, and the annoyances he caused me, Nippers, like his compatriot Turkey, was a very useful man to me; wrote a neat, swift hand; and, when he chose, was not deficient in a gentlemanly sort of deportment. Added to this, he always dressed in a gentlemanly sort of way; and so, incidentally, reflected

---

the Tombs: A prison in New York City.

credit upon my chambers. Whereas, with respect to Turkey, I had much ado to keep him from being a reproach to me. His clothes were apt to look oily, and smell of eating-houses. He wore his pantaloons very loose and baggy in summer. His coats were execrable, his hat not to be handled. But while the hat was a thing of indifference to me, inasmuch as his natural civility and deference, as a dependent Englishman, always led him to doff it the moment he entered the room, yet his coat was another matter. Concerning his coats, I reasoned with him; but with no effect. The truth was, I suppose, that a man with so small an income could not afford to sport such a lustrous face and a lustrous coat at one and the same time. As Nippers once observed, Turkey's money went chiefly for red ink. One winter day, I presented Turkey with a highly respectable-looking coat of my own — a padded gray coat, of a most comfortable warmth, and which buttoned straight up from the knee to the neck. I thought Turkey would appreciate the favor, and abate his rashness and obstreperousness of afternoons. But no; I verily believe that buttoning himself up in so downy and blanket-like a coat had a pernicious effect upon him upon the same principle that too much oats are bad for horses. In fact, precisely as a rash, restive horse is said to feel his oats, so Turkey felt his coat. It made him insolent. He was a man whom prosperity harmed.

Though, concerning the self-indulgent habits of Turkey, I had my own private surmises, yet, touching Nippers, I was well persuaded that, whatever might be his faults in other respects, he was, at least, a temperate young man. But, indeed, nature herself seemed to have been his vintner, and, at his birth, charged him so thoroughly with an irritable, brandy-like disposition, that all subsequent potations were needless. When I consider how, amid the stillness of my chambers, Nippers would sometimes impatiently rise from his seat, and stooping over his table, spread his arms wide apart, seize the whole desk, and move it, and jerk it, with a grim, grinding motion on the floor, as if the table were a perverse voluntary agent, intent on thwarting and vexing him, I plainly perceive that, for Nippers, brandy-and-water were altogether superfluous.

It was fortunate for me that, owing to its peculiar cause — indigestion — the irritability and consequent nervousness of Nippers were mainly observable in the morning, while in the afternoon he was comparatively mild. So that, Turkey's paroxysms only coming on about twelve o'clock, I never had to do with their eccentricities at one time. Their fits relieved each other, like guards. When Nippers' was on, Turkey's was off; and *vice versa*. This was a good natural arrangement, under the circumstances.

Ginger Nut, the third on my list, was a lad, some twelve years old. His father was a carman, ambitious of seeing his son on the bench instead of a cart, before he died. So he sent him to my office, as student at law, errand-boy, cleaner, and sweeper, at the rate of one dollar a week. He had a little desk to himself, but he did not use it much. Upon inspection, the drawer exhibited a great array of the shells of various sorts of nuts. Indeed, to this quick-witted youth, the whole noble science of the law was contained in a nutshell. Not the least among the employments of Ginger Nut, as well as one which he discharged with the most alacrity, was his duty as cake and apple purveyor for

Turkey and Nippers. Copying lawpapers being proverbially a dry, husky sort of business, my two scriveners were fain to moisten their mouths very often with Spitzenbergs, to be had at the numerous stalls nigh the Custom House and Post Office. Also, they sent Ginger Nut very frequently for that peculiar cake — small, flat, round, and very spicy — after which he had been named by them. Of a cold morning, when business was but dull, Turkey would gobble up scores of these cakes, as if they were mere wafers — indeed, they sell them at the rate of six or eight for a penny — the scrape of his pen blending with the crunching of the crisp particles in his mouth. Of all the fiery afternoon blunders and flurried rashness of Turkey, was his once moistening a ginger-cake between his lips, and clapping it on to a mortgage, for a seal. I came within an ace of dismissing him then. But he mollified me by making an oriental bow, and saying —

"With submission, sir, it was generous of me to find you in stationery on my own account."

Now my original business — that of a conveyancer and title hunter, and drawer-up of recondite documents of all sorts — was considerably increased by receiving the Master's office. There was now great work for scriveners. Not only must I push the clerks already with me, but I must have additional help.

In answer to my advertisement, a motionless young man one morning stood upon my office threshold, the door being open, for it was summer. I can see that figure now — pallidly neat, pitiably respectable, incurably forlorn! It was Bartleby.

After a few words touching his qualifications, I engaged him, glad to have among my corps of copyists a man of so singularly sedate an aspect, which I thought might operate beneficially upon the flighty temper of Turkey, and the fiery one of Nippers.

I should have stated before that ground-glass folding-doors divided my premises into two parts, one of which was occupied by my scriveners, the other by myself. According to my humor, I threw open these doors, or closed them. I resolved to assign Bartleby a corner by the folding-doors, but on my side of them, so as to have this quiet man within easy call, in case any trifling thing was to be done. I placed his desk close up to a small side-window in that part of the room, a window which originally had afforded a lateral view of certain grimy brickyards and bricks, but which, owing to subsequent erections, commanded at present no view at all, though it gave some light. Within three feet of the panes was a wall, and the light came down from far above, between two lofty buildings, as from a very small opening in a dome. Still further to a satisfactory arrangement, I procured a high green folding screen, which might entirely isolate Bartleby from my sight, though not remove him from my voice. And thus, in a manner, privacy and society were conjoined.

At first, Bartleby did an extraordinary quantity of writing. As if long famishing for something to copy, he seemed to gorge himself on my documents. There was no pause for digestion. He ran a day and night line, copying by sunlight and by candle-light. I should have been quite delighted with his application, had he been cheerfully industrious. But he wrote on silently, palely, mechanically.

It is, of course, an indispensable part of a scrivener's business to verify the accuracy of his copy, word by word. Where there are two or more scriveners in an office, they assist each other in this examination, one reading from the copy, the other holding the original. It is a very dull, wearisome, and lethargic affair. I can readily imagine that, to some sanguine temperaments, it would be altogether intolerable. For example, I cannot credit that the mettlesome poet, Byron, would have contentedly sat down with Bartleby to examine a law document of, say five hundred pages, closely written in a crimpy hand.

Now and then, in the haste of business, it had been my habit to assist in comparing some brief document myself, calling Turkey or Nippers for this purpose. One object I had, in placing Bartleby so handy to me behind the screen, was, to avail myself of his services on such trivial occasions. It was on the third day, I think, of his being with me, and before any necessity had arisen for having his own writing examined, that, being much hurried to complete a small affair I had in hand, I abruptly called to Bartleby. In my haste and natural expectancy of instant compliance, I sat with my head bent over the original on my desk, and my right hand sideways, and somewhat nervously extended with the copy, so that, immediately upon emerging from his retreat, Bartleby might snatch it and proceed to business without the least delay.

In this very attitude did I sit when I called to him, rapidly stating what it was I wanted him to do — namely, to examine a small paper with me. Imagine my surprise, nay, my consternation, when, without moving from his privacy, Bartleby, in a singularly mild, firm voice, replied, "I would prefer not to."

I sat awhile in perfect silence, rallying my stunned faculties. Immediately it occurred to me that my ears had deceived me, or Bartleby had entirely misunderstood my meaning. I repeated my request in the clearest tone I could assume; but in quite as clear a one came the previous reply, "I would prefer not to."

"Prefer not to," echoed I, rising in high excitement, and crossing the room with a stride. "What do you mean? Are you moonstruck? I want you to help me compare this sheet here — take it," and I thrust it towards him.

"I would prefer not to," said he.

I looked at him steadfastly. His face was leanly composed; his gray eye dimly calm. Not a wrinkle of agitation rippled him. Had there been the least uneasiness, anger, impatience, or impertinence in his manner; in other words, had there been anything ordinarily human about him, doubtless I should have violently dismissed him from the premises. But as it was, I should have as soon thought of turning my pale plaster-of-paris bust of Cicero out of doors. I stood gazing at him awhile, as he went on with his own writing, and then reseated myself at my desk. This is very strange, thought I. What had one best do? But my business hurried me. I concluded to forget the matter for the present, reserving it for my future leisure. So, calling Nippers from the other room, the paper was speedily examined.

A few days after this, Bartleby concluded four lengthy documents, being quadruplicates of a week's testimony taken before me in my High Court of Chancery. It became necessary to examine them. It was an important suit, and great accuracy was imperative. Having all things arranged, I called Turkey, Nippers, and Ginger Nut, from the next room, meaning to place the four copies in the hands of my four clerks, while I should read from the original. Accordingly, Turkey, Nippers, and Ginger Nut had taken their seats in a row, each with his document in his hand, when I called to Bartleby to join this interesting group.

"Bartleby! quick, I am waiting."

I heard a slow scrape of his chair legs on the uncarpeted floor, and soon he appeared standing at the entrance of his hermitage.

"What is wanted?" said he, mildly.

"The copies, the copies," said I, hurriedly. "We are going to examine them. There" — and I held towards him the fourth quadruplicate.

"I would prefer not to," he said, and gently disappeared behind the screen.

For a few moments I was turned into a pillar of salt, standing at the head of my seated column of clerks. Recovering myself, I advanced towards the screen, and demanded the reason for such extraordinary conduct.

"*Why* do you refuse?"

"I would prefer not to."

With any other man I should have flown outright into a dreadful passion, scorned all further words, and thrust him ignominiously from my presence. But there was something about Bartleby that not only strangely disarmed me, but, in a wonderful manner, touched and disconcerted me. I began to reason with him.

"These are your own copies we are about to examine. It is labor saving to you, because one examination will answer for your four papers. It is common usage. Every copyist is bound to help examine his copy. Is it not so? Will you not speak? Answer!"

"I prefer not to," he replied in a flute-like tone. It seemed to me that, while I had been addressing him, he carefully revolved every statement that I made; fully comprehended the meaning; could not gainsay the irresistible conclusion; but, at the same time, some paramount consideration prevailed with him to reply as he did.

"You are decided, then, not to comply with my request — a request made according to common usage and common sense?"

He briefly gave me to understand, that on that point my judgment was sound. Yes: his decision was irreversible.

It is not seldom the case that, when a man is browbeaten in some unprecedented and violently unreasonable way, he begins to stagger in his own plainest faith. He begins, as it were, vaguely to surmise that, wonderful as it may be, all the justice and all the reason is on the other side. Accordingly, if any disinterested persons are present, he turns to them for some reinforcement for his own faltering mind.

"Turkey," said I, "what do you think of this? Am I not right?"

"With submission, sir," said Turkey, in his blandest tone, "I think that you are."

"Nippers," said I, "what do *you* think of it?"

"I think I should kick him out of the office."

(The reader of nice perceptions will have perceived that, it being morning, Turkey's answer is couched in polite and tranquil terms, but Nippers replies in ill-tempered ones. Or, to repeat a previous sentence, Nippers' ugly mood was on duty, and Turkey's off.)

"Ginger Nut," said I, willing to enlist the smallest suffrage in my behalf, "what do *you* think of it?"

"I think, sir, he's a little *luny*," replied Ginger Nut, with a grin.

"You hear what they say," said I, turning towards the screen, "come forth and do your duty."

But he vouchsafed no reply. I pondered a moment in sore perplexity. But once more business hurried me. I determined again to postpone the consideration of this dilemma to my future leisure. With a little trouble we made out to examine the papers without Bartleby, though at every page or two Turkey deferentially dropped his opinion, that this proceeding was quite out of the common; while Nippers, twitching in his chair with a dyspeptic nervousness, ground out, between his set teeth, occasional hissing maledictions against the stubborn oaf behind the screen. And for his (Nippers') part, this was the first and the last time he would do another man's business without pay.

Meanwhile Bartleby sat in his hermitage, oblivious to everything but his own peculiar business there.

Some days passed, the scrivener being employed upon another lengthy work. His late remarkable conduct led me to regard his ways narrowly. I observed that he never went to dinner; indeed, that he never went anywhere. As yet I had never, of my personal knowledge, known him to be outside of my office. He was a perpetual sentry in the corner. At about eleven o'clock though, in the morning, I noticed that Ginger Nut would advance towards the opening in Bartleby's screen, as if silently beckoned thither by a gesture invisible to me where I sat. The boy would then leave the office, jingling a few pence, and reappear with a handful of ginger-nuts, which he delivered in the hermitage, receiving two of the cakes for his trouble.

He lives, then, on ginger-nuts, thought I; never eats a dinner, properly speaking; he must be a vegetarian, then; but no; he never eats even vegetables, he eats nothing but ginger-nuts. My mind then ran on in reveries concerning the probable effects upon the human constitution of living entirely on ginger-nuts. Ginger-nuts are so called, because they contain ginger as one of their peculiar constituents, and the final flavoring one. Now, what was ginger? A hot, spicy thing. Was Bartleby hot and spicy? Not at all. Ginger, then, had no effect upon Bartleby. Probably he preferred it should have none.

Nothing so aggravates an earnest person as a passive resistance. If the individual so resisted be of a not inhumane temper, and the resisting one perfectly harmless in his passivity, then, in the better moods of the former, he will endeavor charitably to construe to his imagination what proves impossible to be solved by his judgment. Even so, for the most part, I regarded Bartleby and his ways. Poor fellow! thought I, he means no mischief; it is plain he intends no insolence; his aspect sufficiently evinces that his eccentricities are involuntary. He is useful to me. I can get along with him. If I turn him away, the chances are he will fall in with some less indulgent employer, and then he will be rudely treated, and perhaps driven forth miserably to starve. Yes. Here I can cheaply purchase a delicious self-approval. To befriend Bartleby; to humor him in his strange wilfulness, will cost me little or nothing, while I lay up in my soul what will eventually prove a sweet morsel for my conscience. But this mood was not invariable with me. The passiveness of Bartleby sometimes irritated me. I felt strangely goaded on to encounter him in new opposition — to elicit some angry spark from him answerable to my own. But, indeed, I might as well have essayed to strike fire with my knuckles against a bit of Windsor soap. But one afternoon the evil impulse in me mastered me, and the following little scene ensued:

"Bartleby," said I, "when those papers are all copied, I will compare them with you."

"I would prefer not to."

"How? Surely you do not mean to persist in that mulish vagary?"

No answer.

I threw open the folding-doors nearby, and turning upon Turkey and Nippers, exclaimed:

"Bartleby a second time says, he won't examine his papers. What do you think of it, Turkey?"

It was afternoon, be it remembered. Turkey sat glowing like a brass boiler; his bald head steaming; his hands reeling among his blotted papers.

"Think of it?" roared Turkey. "I think I'll just step behind his screen, and black his eyes for him!"

So saying, Turkey rose to his feet and threw his arms into a pugilistic position. He was hurrying away to make good his promise, when I detained him, alarmed at the effect of incautiously rousing Turkey's combativeness after dinner.

"Sit down, Turkey," said I, "and hear what Nippers has to say. What do you think of it, Nippers? Would I not be justified in immediately dismissing Bartleby?"

"Excuse me, that is for you to decide, sir. I think his conduct quite unusual, and, indeed, unjust, as regards Turkey and myself. But it may only be a passing whim."

"Ah," exclaimed I, "you have strangely changed your mind, then — you speak very gently of him now."

"All beer," cried Turkey; "gentleness is effects of beer — Nippers and I dined together to-day. You see how gentle *I* am, sir. Shall I go and black his eyes?"

"You refer to Bartleby, I suppose. No, not to-day, Turkey," I replied; "pray, put up your fists."

I closed the doors, and again advanced towards Bartleby. I felt additional incentives tempting me to my fate. I burned to be rebelled against again. I remembered that Bartleby never left the office.

"Bartleby," said I, "Ginger Nut is away; just step around to the Post Office, won't you?" (it was but a three minutes' walk) "and see if there is anything for me."

"I would prefer not to."

"You *will* not?"

"I *prefer* not."

I staggered to my desk, and sat there in a deep study. My blind inveteracy returned. Was there any other thing in which I could procure myself to be ignominiously repulsed by this lean, penniless wight? my hired clerk? What added thing is there, perfectly reasonable, that he will be sure to refuse to do?

"Bartleby!"

No answer.

"Bartleby," in a louder tone.

No answer.

"Bartleby," I roared.

Like a very ghost, agreeably to the laws of magical invocation, at the third summons, he appeared at the entrance of his hermitage.

"Go to the next room, and tell Nippers to come to me."

"I would prefer not to," he respectfully and slowly said, and mildly disappeared.

"Very good, Bartleby," said I, in a quiet sort of serenely-severe self-possessed tone, intimating the unalterable purpose of some terrible retribution very close at hand. At the moment I half intended something of the kind. But upon the whole, as it was drawing towards my dinner-hour, I thought it best to put on my hat and walk home for the day, suffering much from perplexity and distress of mind.

Shall I acknowledge it? The conclusion of this whole business was, that it soon became a fixed fact of my chambers, that a pale young scrivener, by the name of Bartleby, had a desk there; that he copied for me at the usual rate of four cents a folio (one hundred words); but he was permanently exempt from examining the work done by him, that duty being transferred to Turkey and Nippers, out of compliment, doubtless, to their superior acuteness; moreover, said Bartleby was never, on any account, to be dispatched on the most trivial errand of any sort; and that even if entreated to take upon him such a matter, it was generally understood that he would "prefer not to" — in other words, that he would refuse point blank.

As days passed on, I became considerably reconciled to Bartleby. His steadiness, his freedom from all dissipation, his incessant industry (except when he chose to throw himself into a standing revery behind his screen), his great stillness, his unalterableness of demeanor under all circumstances, made him a valuable acquisition. One prime thing was this — *he was always there* — first in the morning, continually through the day, and the last at night. I had a singular confidence in his honesty. I felt my most precious papers perfectly safe in his hands. Sometimes, to be sure, I could not, for the very soul of me, avoid falling into sudden spasmodic passions with him. For it was exceeding difficult to bear in mind all the time those strange peculiarities, privileges, and unheard-of exemptions, forming the tacit stipulations on Bartleby's part under which he remained in my office. Now and then, in the eagerness of dispatching pressing business, I would inadvertently summon Bartleby, in a short, rapid tone, to put his finger, say, on the incipient tie of a bit of red tape with which I was about compressing some papers. Of course, from behind the screen the usual answer, "I prefer not to," was sure to come; and then, how could a human creature, with the common infirmities of our nature, refrain from bitterly exclaiming upon such perverseness — such unreasonableness? However, every added repulse of this sort which I received only tended to lessen the probability of my repeating the inadvertence.

Here it must be said, that, according to the custom of most legal gentlemen occupying chambers in densely populated law buildings, there were several keys to my door. One was kept by a woman residing in the attic, which person weekly scrubbed and daily swept and dusted my apartments. Another was kept by Turkey for convenience sake. The third I sometimes carried in my own pocket. The fourth I knew not who had.

Now, one Sunday morning I happened to go to Trinity Church, to hear a celebrated preacher, and finding myself rather early on the ground I thought I would walk round to my chambers for a while. Luckily I had my key with me; but upon applying it to the lock, I found it resisted by something inserted from the inside. Quite surprised, I called out; when to my consternation a key was turned from within; and thrusting his lean visage at me, and holding the door ajar, the apparition of Bartleby appeared, in his shirt-sleeves, and otherwise in a strangely tattered *deshabille*, saying quietly that he was sorry, but he was deeply engaged just then, and preferred not admitting me at present. In a brief word or two, he moreover added, that perhaps I had better walk round the block two or three times, and by that time he would probably have concluded his affairs.

Now, the utterly unsurmised appearance of Bartleby, tenanting my law-chambers of a Sunday morning, with his cadaverously gentlemanly *nonchalance*, yet withal firm and self-possessed, had such a strange effect upon me, that incontinently I slunk away from my own door, and did as desired. But not without sundry twinges of impotent rebellion against the mild effrontery of this unaccountable scrivener. Indeed, it was his wonderful mildness chiefly, which not only disarmed me, but unmanned me, as it were. For I consider that one, for the time, is sort of unmanned when he tranquilly permits his hired clerk to dictate to him, and order him away from his own premises. Furthermore, I was full of uneasiness as to what Bartleby could possibly be doing in my office in his shirt-sleeves, and in an otherwise dismantled condition on a Sunday morning. Was anything amiss going on? Nay, that was out of the question. It was not to be thought of for a moment that Bartleby was an immoral person. But what could he be doing there? — copying? Nay again, whatever might be his eccentricities, Bartleby was an eminently decorous person. He would be the last man to sit down to his desk in any state approaching to nudity. Besides, it was Sunday; and there was something about Bartleby that forbade the supposition that he would by any secular occupation violate the proprieties of the day.

Nevertheless, my mind was not pacified; and full of a restless curiosity, at last I returned to the door. Without hindrance I inserted my key, opened it, and entered. Bartleby was not to be seen. I looked round anxiously, peeped behind his screen; but it was very plain that he was gone. Upon more closely examining the place, I surmised that for an indefinite period Bartleby must have ate, dressed, and slept in my office, and that too without plate, mirror, or bed. The cushioned seat of a rickety old sofa in one corner bore the faint impress of a lean, reclining form. Rolled away under his desk, I found a blanket; under the empty grate, a blacking box and brush; on a chair, a tin basin, with soap and a ragged towel; in a newspaper a few crumbs of ginger-nuts and a morsel of cheese. Yes, thought I, it is evident enough that Bartleby has been making his home here, keeping bachelor's hall all by himself. Immediately then the thought came sweeping across me, what miserable friendlessness and loneliness are here revealed! His poverty is great; but his solitude, how horrible! Think of it. Of a Sunday, Wall Street is deserted as Petra;° and every night of every day it is an emptiness. This building, too, which of week-days hums with industry and life, at nightfall echoes with sheer vacancy, and all through Sunday is forlorn. And here Bartleby makes his home; sole spectator of a solitude which he has seen all populous — a sort of innocent and transformed Marius° brooding among the ruins of Carthage!

For the first time in my life a feeling of overpowering stinging melancholy seized me. Before, I had never experienced aught but a not unpleasing sadness. The bond of a common humanity now drew me irresistibly to gloom. A fraternal melancholy! For both I and Bartleby were sons of Adam. I remembered the bright silks and sparkling faces I had seen that day, in gala trim, swan-like sailing down the Mississippi of Broadway; and I contrasted them with the pallid copyist, and thought to myself, Ah, happiness courts the light, so we deem the world is gay; but misery hides aloof, so we deem that misery there is none. These sad fancyings — chimeras, doubtless, of a sick and silly brain — led on to other and more special thoughts, concerning the eccentricities of Bartleby. Presentiments of strange discoveries hovered round me. The scrivener's pale form appeared to me laid out, among uncaring strangers, in its shivering winding-sheet.

Suddenly I was attracted by Bartleby's closed desk, the key in open sight left in the lock.

I mean no mischief, seek the gratification of no heartless curiosity, thought I; besides, the desk is mine, and its contents, too, so I will make bold to look within. Everything was methodically arranged, the papers smoothly placed. The pigeon-holes were deep, and removing the files of documents, I groped into their recesses. Presently I felt something there, and dragged it out. It was an old bandanna handkerchief, heavy and knotted. I opened it, and saw it was a saving's bank.

I now recalled all the quiet mysteries which I had noted in the man. I remembered that he never spoke but to answer; that, though at intervals he had considerable time to himself, yet I had never seen him reading — no, not even

---

Petra: A city in what is now Jordan, once the center of an Arab kingdom. It was deserted for more than ten centuries, until its rediscovery by explorers in 1812.
Marius: Gaius Marius (157?–86 B.C.) was a Roman general, several times elected consul. Marius's greatest military successes came in the Jugurthine War, in Africa. Later, when his opponents gained power and he was banished, he fled to Africa. Carthage was a city in North Africa.

a newspaper; that for long periods he would stand looking out, at his pale window behind the screen, upon the dead brick wall; I was quite sure he never visited any refectory or eating-house; while his pale face clearly indicated that he never drank beer like Turkey; or tea and coffee even, like other men; that he never went anywhere in particular that I could learn; never went out for a walk, unless, indeed, that was the case at present; that he had declined telling who he was, or whence he came, or whether he had any relatives in the world; that though so thin and pale, he never complained of ill-health. And more than all, I remembered a certain unconscious air of pallid — how shall I call it? — of pallid haughtiness, say, or rather an austere reserve about him, which has positively awed me into my tame compliance with his eccentricities, when I had feared to ask him to do the slightest incidental thing for me, even though I might know, from his long-continued motionlessness, that behind his screen he must be standing in one of those dead-wall reveries of his.

Revolving all these things, and coupling them with the recently discovered fact, that he made my office his constant abiding place and home, and not forgetful of his morbid moodiness; revolving all these things, a prudential feeling began to steal over me. My first emotions had been those of pure melancholy and sincerest pity; but just in proportion as the forlornness of Bartleby grew and grew to my imagination, did that same melancholy merge into fear, that pity into repulsion. So true it is, and so terrible, too, that up to a certain point the thought or sight of misery enlists our best affections; but, in certain special cases, beyond that point it does not. They err who would assert that invariably this is owing to the inherent selfishness of the human heart. It rather proceeds from a certain hopelessness of remedying excessive and organic ill. To a sensitive being, pity is not seldom pain. And when at last it is perceived that such pity cannot lead to effectual succor, common sense bids the soul be rid of it. What I saw that morning persuaded me that the scrivener was the victim of innate and incurable disorder. I might give alms to his body; but his body did not pain him; it was his soul that suffered, and his soul I could not reach.

I did not accomplish the purpose of going to Trinity Church that morning. Somehow, the things I had seen disqualified me for the time from church-going. I walked homeward, thinking what I would do with Bartleby. Finally, I resolved upon this — I would put certain calm questions to him the next morning, touching his history, etc., and if he declined to answer them openly and unreservedly (and I supposed he would prefer not), then to give him a twenty dollar bill over and above whatever I might owe him, and tell him his services were no longer required; but that if in any other way I could assist him, I would be happy to do so, especially if he desired to return to his native place, wherever that might be, I would willingly help to defray the expenses. Moreover, if, after reaching home, he found himself at any time in want of aid, a letter from him would be sure of a reply.

The next morning came.

"Bartleby," said I, gently calling to him behind his screen.

No reply.

"Bartleby," said I, in a still gentler tone, "come here; I am not going to ask you to do anything you would prefer not to do — I simply wish to speak to you."

Upon this he noiselessly slid into view.

"Will you tell me, Bartleby, where you were born?"

"I would prefer not to."

"Will you tell me *anything* about yourself?"

"I would prefer not to."

"But what reasonable objection can you have to speak to me? I feel friendly towards you."

He did not look at me while I spoke, but kept his glance fixed upon my bust of Cicero, which, as I then sat, was directly behind me, some six inches above my head.

"What is your answer, Bartleby?" said I, after waiting a considerable time for a reply, during which his countenance remained immovable, only there was the faintest conceivable tremor of the white attenuated mouth.

"At present I prefer to give no answer," he said, and retired into his hermitage.

It was rather weak in me I confess, but his manner, on this occasion, nettled me. Not only did there seem to lurk in it a certain calm disdain, but his perverseness seemed ungrateful, considering the undeniable good usage and indulgence he had received from me.

Again I sat ruminating what I should do. Mortified as I was at his behavior, and resolved as I had been to dismiss him when I entered my office, nevertheless I strangely felt something superstitious knocking at my heart, and forbidding me to carry out my purpose, and denouncing me for a villain if I dared to breathe one bitter word against this forlornest of mankind. At last, familiarly drawing my chair behind his screen, I sat down and said: "Bartleby, never mind, then, about revealing your history; but let me entreat you, as a friend, to comply as far as may be with the usages of this office. Say now, you will help to examine papers tomorrow or next day: in short, say now, that in a day or two you will begin to be a little reasonable: — say so, Bartleby."

"At present I would prefer not to be a little reasonable," was his mildly cadaverous reply.

Just then the folding-doors opened, and Nippers approached. He seemed suffering from an unusually bad night's rest, induced by severer indigestion than common. He overheard those final words of Bartleby.

"*Prefer not*, eh?" gritted Nippers — "I'd *prefer* him, if I were you, sir," addressing me — "I'd *prefer* him; I'd give him preferences, the stubborn mule! What is it, sir, pray, that he *prefers* not to do now?"

Bartleby moved not a limb.

"Mr. Nippers," said I, "I'd prefer that you would withdraw for the present."

Somehow, of late, I had got into the way of involuntarily using this word "prefer" upon all sorts of not exactly suitable occasions. And I trembled to think that my contact with the scrivener had already and seriously affected me in a mental way. And what further and deeper aberration might it not yet produce? This apprehension had not been without efficacy in determining me to summary measures.

As Nippers, looking very sour and sulky, was departing, Turkey blandly and deferentially approached.

"With submission, sir," said he, "yesterday I was thinking about Bartleby here, and I think that if he would but prefer to take a quart of good ale every day, it would do much towards mending him, and enabling him to assist in examining his papers."

"So you have got the word, too," said I, slightly excited.

"With submission, what word, sir?" asked Turkey, respectfully crowding himself into the contracted space behind the screen, and by so doing, making me jostle the scrivener. "What word, sir?"

"I would prefer to be left alone here," said Bartleby, as if offended at being mobbed in his privacy.

"*That's* the word, Turkey," said I — "*that's* it."

"Oh, *prefer*? oh yes — queer word. I never use it myself. But, sir, as I was saying, if he would but prefer — "

"Turkey," interrupted I, "you will please withdraw."

"Oh certainly, sir, if you prefer that I should."

As he opened the folding-door to retire, Nippers at his desk caught a glimpse of me, and asked whether I would prefer to have a certain paper copied on blue paper or white. He did not in the least roguishly accent the word "prefer." It was plain that it involuntarily rolled from his tongue. I thought to myself, surely I must get rid of a demented man, who already has in some degree turned the tongues, if not the heads of myself and clerks. But I thought it prudent not to break the dismission at once.

The next day I noticed that Bartleby did nothing but stand at his window in his dead-wall revery. Upon asking him why he did not write, he said that he had decided upon doing no more writing.

"Why, how now? what next?" exclaimed I, "do no more writing?"

"No more."

"And what is the reason?"

"Do you not see the reason for yourself?" he indifferently replied.

I looked steadfastly at him, and perceived that his eyes looked dull and glazed. Instantly it occurred to me, that his unexampled diligence in copying by his dim window for the first few weeks of his stay with me might have temporarily impaired his vision.

I was touched. I said something in condolence with him. I hinted that of course he did wisely in abstaining from writing for a while; and urged him to embrace that opportunity of taking wholesome exercise in the open air. This, however, he did not do. A few days after this, my other clerks being absent, and being in a great hurry to dispatch certain letters by the mail, I thought that, having nothing else earthly to do, Bartleby would surely be less inflexible than usual, and carry these letters to the Post Office. But he blankly declined. So, much to my inconvenience, I went myself.

Still added days went by. Whether Bartleby's eyes improved or not, I could not say. To all appearance, I thought they did. But when I asked him if they did he vouchsafed no answer. At all events, he would do no copying. At last, in replying to my urgings, he informed me that he had permanently given up copying.

"What!" exclaimed I; "suppose your eyes should get entirely well — better than ever before — would you not copy then?"

"I have given up copying," he answered, and slid aside.

He remained as ever, a fixture in my chamber. Nay — if that were possible — he became still more of a fixture than before. What was to be done? He would do nothing in the office; why should he stay there? In plain fact, he had now become a millstone to me, not only useless as a necklace, but afflictive to bear. Yet I was sorry for him. I speak less than truth when I say that, on his own account, he occasioned me uneasiness. If he would but have named a single relative or friend, I would instantly have written, and urged their taking the poor fellow away to some convenient retreat. But he seemed alone, absolutely alone in the universe. A bit of wreck in the mid-Atlantic. At length, necessities connected with my business tyrannized over all other considerations. Decently as I could, I told Bartleby that in six days' time he must unconditionally leave the office. I warned him to take measures, in the interval, for procuring some other abode. I offered to assist him in this endeavor, if he himself would but take the first step towards a removal. "And when you finally quit me, Bartleby," added I, "I shall see that you go not away entirely unprovided. Six days from this hour, remember."

At the expiration of that period, I peeped behind the screen, and lo! Bartleby was there.

I buttoned up my coat, balanced myself; advanced slowly towards him, touched his shoulder, and said, "The time has come; you must quit this place; I am sorry for you; here is money; but you must go."

"I would prefer not," he replied, with his back still towards me.

"You *must*."

He remained silent.

Now I had an unbounded confidence in this man's common honesty. He had frequently restored to me sixpences and shillings carelessly dropped upon the floor, for I am apt to be very reckless in such shirt-button affairs. The proceeding, then, which followed will not be deemed extraordinary.

"Bartleby," said I, "I owe you twelve dollars on account; here are thirty-two; the odd twenty are yours — Will you take it?" and I handed the bills towards him.

But he made no motion.

"I will leave them here, then," putting them under a weight on the table. Then taking my hat and cane and going to the door, I tranquilly turned and added — " After you have removed your things from these offices, Bartleby, you will of course lock the door — since every one is now gone for the day but you — and if you please, slip your key underneath the mat, so that I may have it in the morning. I shall not see you again; so good-bye to you. If, hereafter, in your new place of abode, I can be of any service to you, do not fail to advise me by letter. Good-bye, Bartleby, and fare you well."

But he answered not a word; like the last column of some ruined temple, he remained standing mute and solitary in the middle of the otherwise deserted room.

As I walked home in a pensive mood, my vanity got the better of my pity. I could not but highly plume myself on my masterly management in getting rid of Bartleby. Masterly I call it, and such it must appear to any dispassionate thinker. The beauty of my procedure seemed to consist in its perfect quietness. There was no vulgar bullying, no bravado of any sort, no choleric hectoring, and striding to and fro across the apartment, jerking out vehement commands for Bartleby to bundle himself off with his beggarly traps. Nothing of the kind. Without loudly bidding Bartleby depart — as an inferior genius might have done — I *assumed* the ground that depart he must; and upon that assumption built all I had to say. The more I thought over my procedure, the more I was charmed with it. Nevertheless, next morning, upon awakening, I had my doubts — I had somehow slept off the fumes of vanity. One of the coolest and wisest hours a man has, is just after he awakes in the morning. My procedure seemed as sagacious as ever — but only in theory. How it would prove in practice — there was the rub. It was truly a beautiful thought to have assumed Bartleby's departure; but, after all, that assumption was simply my own, and none of Bartleby's. The great point was, not whether I had assumed that he would quit me, but whether he would prefer to do so. He was more a man of preferences than assumptions.

After breakfast, I walked down town, arguing the probabilities *pro* and *con*. One moment I thought it would prove a miserable failure, and Bartleby would be found all alive at my office as usual; the next moment it seemed certain that I should find his chair empty. And so I kept veering about. At the corner of Broadway and Canal Street, I saw quite an excited group of people standing in earnest conversation.

"I'll take odds he doesn't," said a voice as I passed.

"Doesn't go? — done!" said I, "put up your money."

I was instinctively putting my hand in my pocket to produce my own, when I remembered that this was an election day. The words I had overheard bore no reference to Bartleby, but to the success or non-success of some candidate for the mayoralty. In my intent frame of mind, I had, as it were, imagined that all Broadway shared in my excitement, and were debating the same question with me. I passed on, very thankful that the uproar of the street screened my momentary absent-mindedness.

As I had intended, I was earlier than usual at my office door. I stood listening for a moment. All was still. He must be gone. I tried the knob. The door was locked. Yes, my procedure had worked to a charm; he indeed must be vanished. Yet a certain melancholy mixed with this: I was almost sorry for my brilliant success. I was fumbling under the door mat for the key, which Bartleby was to have left there for me, when accidentally my knee knocked against a panel, producing a summoning sound, and in response a voice came to me from within — "Not yet; I am occupied."

It was Bartleby.

I was thunderstruck. For an instant I stood like the man who, pipe in mouth, was killed one cloudless afternoon long ago in Virginia, by summer lightning; at his own warm open window he was killed, and remained leaning out there upon the dreamy afternoon, till someone touched him, when he fell.

"Not gone!" I murmured at last. But again obeying that wondrous ascendancy which the inscrutable scrivener had over me, and from which ascendancy, for all my chafing, I could not completely escape, I slowly went down stairs and out into the street, and while walking round the block, considered what I should next do in this unheard-of perplexity. Turn the man out by an actual thrusting I could not; to drive him away by calling him hard names would not do; calling in the police was an unpleasant idea; and yet, permit him to enjoy his cadaverous triumph over me — this, too, I could not think of. What was to be done? or, if nothing could be done, was there anything further that I could *assume* in the matter? Yes, as before I had prospectively assumed that Bartleby would depart, so now I might retrospectively assume that departed he was. In the legitimate carrying out of this assumption, I might enter my office in a great hurry, and pretending not to see Bartleby at all, walk straight against him as if he were air. Such a proceeding would in a singular degree have the appearance of a home-thrust. It was hardly possible that Bartleby could withstand such an application of the doctrine of assumption. But upon second thoughts the success of the plan seemed rather dubious. I resolved to argue the matter over with him again.

"Bartleby," said I, entering the office, with a quietly severe expression, "I am seriously displeased. I am pained, Bartleby. I had thought better of you. I had imagined you of such a gentlemanly organization, that in any delicate dilemma a slight hint would suffice — in short, an assumption. But it appears I am deceived. Why," I added, unaffectedly starting, "You have not even touched that money yet," pointing to it, just where I had left it the evening previous.

He answered nothing.

"Will you, or will you not, quit me?" I now demanded in a sudden passion, advancing close to him.

"I would prefer *not* to quit you," he replied, gently emphasizing the *not*.

"What earthly right have you to stay here? Do you pay any rent? Do you pay my taxes? Or is this property yours?"

He answered nothing.

"Are you ready to go on and write now? Are your eyes recovered? Could you copy a small paper for me this morning? or help examine a few lines? or step round to the Post Office? In a word, will you do anything at all, to give a coloring to your refusal to depart the premises?"

He silently retired into his hermitage.

I was now in such a state of nervous resentment that I thought it but prudent to check myself at present from further demonstrations. Bartleby and I were alone. I remembered the tragedy of the unfortunate Adams and the still more unfortunate Colt in the solitary office of the latter; and how poor Colt, being dreadfully incensed by Adams, and imprudently permitting himself to get wildly excited, was at unawares hurried into his fatal act — an act which certainly no man could possibly deplore more than the actor himself.° Often it had occurred to me in my ponderings upon the subject that had that altercation taken place in the public street, or at a private residence, it would not have terminated as it did. It was the circumstance of being alone in a solitary office, up stairs, of a building entirely unhallowed by humanizing domestic associations — an uncarpeted office, doubtless, of a dusty, haggard sort of appearance — this it must have been, which greatly helped to enhance the irritable desperation of the hapless Colt.

But when this old Adam of resentment rose in me and tempted me concerning Bartleby, I grappled him and threw him. How? Why, simply by recalling the divine injunction: "A new commandment give I unto you, that ye love one another." Yes, this it was that saved me. Aside from higher considerations, charity often operates as a vastly wise and prudent principle — a great safeguard to its possessor. Men have committed murder for jealousy's sake, and anger's sake, and hatred's sake, and selfishness' sake, and spiritual pride's sake; but no man, that ever I heard of, ever committed a diabolical murder for sweet charity's sake. Mere self-interest, then, if no better motive can be enlisted, should, especially with high-tempered men, prompt all beings to charity and philanthropy. At any rate, upon the occasion in question, I strove to drown my exasperated feelings towards the scrivener by benevolently construing his conduct. Poor fellow, poor fellow! thought I, he don't mean anything; and besides, he has seen hard times, and ought to be indulged.

I endeavored, also, immediately to occupy myself, and at the same time to comfort my despondency. I tried to fancy, that in the course of the morning, at such time as might prove agreeable to him, Bartleby, of his own free accord, would emerge from his hermitage and take up some decided line of march in the direction of the door. But no. Half-past twelve o'clock came; Turkey began to glow in the face, overturn his inkstand, and become generally obstreperous; Nippers abated down into quietude and courtesy; Ginger Nut munched his noon apple; and Bartleby remained standing at his window in one of his profoundest dead-wall reveries. Will it be credited? Ought I to acknowledge it? That afternoon I left the office without saying one further word to him.

Some days now passed, during which, at leisure intervals I looked a little into "Edwards on the Will,"° and "Priestley° on Necessity." Under the cir-

---

the actor himself: John C. Colt murdered Samuel Adams in January 1842. Later that year, after his conviction, Colt committed suicide a half-hour before he was to be hanged. The case received wide and sensationalistic press coverage at the time.

Edwards on the Will: Jonathan Edwards was an important American theologian, a rigidly orthodox Calvinist who believed in the doctrine of predestination and a leader of the Great Awakening, the religious revival that swept the North American colonies in the 1740s. The work being alluded to here is *Freedom of the Will* (1754).

Priestley on Necessity: Joseph Priestley (1733–1803) was an English scientist and clergyman who began as a Unitarian but developed his own radical ideas on "natural determinism." As a scientist, he did early experiments with electricity and was one of the first to discover the existence of oxygen. As a political philosopher, he championed the French Revolution — a cause so unpopular in England that he had to flee that country and spend the last decade of his life in the United States.

cumstances, those books induced a salutary feeling. Gradually I slid into the persuasion that these troubles of mine, touching the scrivener, had been all predestined from eternity, and Bartleby was billeted upon me for some mysterious purpose of an all-wise Providence, which it was not for a mere mortal like me to fathom. Yes, Bartleby, stay there behind your screen, thought I; I shall persecute you no more; you are harmless and noiseless as any of these old chairs; in short, I never feel so private as when I know you are here. At last I see it, I feel it; I penetrate to the predestined purpose of my life. I am content. Others may have loftier parts to enact; but my mission in this world, Bartleby, is to furnish you with office-room for such period as you may see fit to remain.

I believe that this wise and blessed frame of mind would have continued with me, had it not been for the unsolicited and uncharitable remarks obtruded upon me by my professional friends who visited the rooms. But thus it often is, that the constant friction of illiberal minds wears out at last the best resolves of the more generous. Though to be sure, when I reflected upon it, it was not strange that people entering my office should be struck by the peculiar aspect of the unaccountable Bartleby, and so be tempted to throw out some sinister observations concerning him. Sometimes an attorney, having business with me, and calling at my office, and finding no one but the scrivener there, would undertake to obtain some sort of precise information from him touching my whereabouts; but without heeding his idle talk, Bartleby would remain standing immovable in the middle of the room. So after contemplating him in that position for a time, the attorney would depart, no wiser than he came.

Also, when a reference was going on, and the room full of lawyers and witnesses, and business driving fast, some deeply-occupied legal gentleman present, seeing Bartleby wholly unemployed, would request him to run round to his (the legal gentleman's) office and fetch some papers for him. Thereupon, Bartleby would tranquilly decline, and yet remain idle as before. Then the lawyer would give a great stare, and turn to me. And what could I say? At last I was made aware that all through the circle of my professional acquaintance, a whisper of wonder was running round, having reference to the strange creature I kept at my office. This worried me very much. And as the idea came upon me of his possibly turning out a long-lived man, and keeping occupying my chambers, and denying my authority; and perplexing my visitors; and scandalizing my professional reputation; and casting a general gloom over the premises; keeping soul and body together to the last upon his savings (for doubtless he spent but half a dime a day), and in the end perhaps outlive me, and claim possession of my office by right of his perpetual occupancy: as all these dark anticipations crowded upon me more and more, and my friends continually intruded their relentless remarks upon the apparition in my room; a great change was wrought in me. I resolved to gather all my faculties together, and forever rid me of this intolerable incubus.

Ere revolving any complicated project, however, adapted to this end, I first simply suggested to Bartleby the propriety of his permanent departure. In a calm and serious tone, I commended the idea to his careful and mature consideration. But, having taken three days to meditate upon it, he apprised me, that his original determination remained the same; in short, that he still preferred to abide with me.

What shall I do? I now said to myself, buttoning up my coat to the last button. What shall I do? what ought I to do? what does conscience say I *should* do with this man, or, rather, ghost. Rid myself of him, I must; go, he shall. But how? You will not thrust him, the poor, pale, passive mortal you will not thrust such a helpless creature out of your door? you will not dishonor yourself by such cruelty? No, I will not, I cannot do that. Rather would I let him live and die here, and then mason up his remains in the wall. What, then, will you do? For all your coaxing, he will not budge. Bribes he leaves under your own paper-weight on your table; in short, it is quite plain that he prefers to cling to you.

Then something severe, something unusual must be done. What! surely you will not have him collared by a constable, and commit his innocent pallor to the common jail? And upon what ground could you procure such a thing to be done? — a vagrant, is he? What! he a vagrant, a wanderer, who refuses to budge? It is because he will not be a vagrant, then, that you seek to count him *as* a vagrant. That is too absurd. No visible means of support: there I have him. Wrong again: for indubitably he *does* support himself, and that is the only unanswerable proof that any man can show of his possessing the means so to do. No more, then. Since he will not quit me, I must quit him. I will change my offices; I will move elsewhere, and give him fair notice, that if I find him on my new premises I will then proceed against him as a common trespasser.

Acting accordingly, next day I thus addressed him: "I find these chambers too far from the City Hall; the air is unwholesome. In a word, I propose to remove my offices next week, and shall no longer require your services. I tell you this now, in order that you may seek another place."

He made no reply, and nothing more was said.

On the appointed day I engaged carts and men, proceeded to my chambers, and, having but little furniture, everything was removed in a few hours. Throughout, the scrivener remained standing behind the screen, which I directed to be removed the last thing. It was withdrawn; and, being folded up like a huge folio, left him the motionless occupant of a naked room. I stood in the entry watching him a moment, while something from within me upbraided me.

I re-entered, with my hand in my pocket — and — and my heart in my mouth.

"Good-bye, Bartleby; I am going — good-bye, and God some way bless you; and take that," slipping something in his hand. But it dropped upon the floor, and then — strange to say — I tore myself from him whom I had so longed to be rid of.

Established in my new quarters, for a day or two I kept the door locked, started at every footfall in the passages. When I returned to my rooms, after any little absence, I would pause at the threshold for an instant, and attentively listen, ere applying my key. But these fears were needless. Bartleby never came nigh me.

I thought all was going well, when a perturbed-looking stranger visited me, inquiring whether I was the person who had recently occupied rooms at No. — Wall Street.

Full of forebodings, I replied that I was.

"Then, sir," said the stranger, who proved a lawyer, "you are responsible for the man you left there. He refuses to do any copying; he refuses to do anything; he says he prefers not to; and he refuses to quit the premises."

"I am very sorry, sir," said I, with assumed tranquillity, but an inward tremor, "but, really, the man you allude to is nothing to me — he is no relation or apprentice of mine, that you should hold me responsible for him."

"In mercy's name, who is he?"

"I certainly cannot inform you. I know nothing about him. Formerly I employed him as a copyist; but he has done nothing for me now for some time past."

"I shall settle him, then — good morning, sir."

Several days passed, and I heard nothing more; and, though I often felt a charitable prompting to call at the place and see poor Bartleby, yet a certain squeamishness, of I know not what, withheld me.

All is over with him, by this time, thought I, at last, when, through another week, no further intelligence reached me. But, coming to my room the day after, I found several persons waiting at my door in a high state of nervous excitement.

"That's the man here — he comes," cried the foremost one, whom I recognized as the lawyer who had previously called upon me alone.

"You must take him away, sir, at once," cried a portly person among them, advancing upon me, and whom I knew to be the landlord of No. — Wall Street. "These gentlemen, my tenants, cannot stand it any longer; Mr. B —— " pointing to the lawyer, "has turned him out of his room, and he now persists in haunting the building generally, sitting upon the banisters of the stairs by day, and sleeping in the entry by night. Everybody is concerned; clients are leaving the offices; some fears are entertained of a mob; something you must do, and that without delay."

Aghast at this torrent, I fell back before it, and would fain have locked myself in my new quarters. In vain I persisted that Bartleby was nothing to me — no more than to any one else. In vain — I was the last person known to have anything to do with him, and they held me to the terrible account. Fearful, then, of being exposed in the papers (as one person present obscurely threatened), I considered the matter, and, at length, said, that if the lawyer would give me a confidential interview with the scrivener, in his (the lawyer's) own room, I would, that afternoon, strive my best to rid them of the nuisance they complained of.

Going up stairs to my old haunt, there was Bartleby silently sitting upon the banister at the landing.

"What are you doing here, Bartleby?" said I.

"Sitting upon the banister," he mildly replied.

I motioned him into the lawyer's room, who then left us.

"Bartleby," said I, "are you aware that you are the cause of great tribulation to me, by persisting in occupying the entry after being dismissed from the office?"

No answer.

"Now one of two things must take place. Either you must do something, or something must be done to you. Now what sort of business would you like to engage in? Would you like to re-engage in copying for some one?"

"No; I would prefer not to make any change."

"Would you like a clerkship in a dry-goods store?"

"There is too much confinement about that. No, I would not like a clerkship; but I am not particular."

"Too much confinement," I cried, "why, you keep yourself confined all the time!"

"I would prefer not to take a clerkship," he rejoined, as if to settle that little item at once.

"How would a bar-tender's business suit you? There is no trying of the eye-sight in that."

"I would not like it at all; though, as I said before, I am not particular."

His unwonted wordiness inspirited me. I returned to the charge.

"Well, then, would you like to travel through the country collecting bills for the merchants? That would improve your health."

"No, I would prefer to be doing something else."

"How, then, would going as a companion to Europe, to entertain some young gentleman with your conversation — how would that suit you?"

"Not at all. It does not strike me that there is anything definite about that. I like to be stationary. But I am not particular."

"Stationary you shall be, then," I cried, now losing all patience, and, for the first time in all my exasperating connections with him, fairly flying into a passion. "If you do not go away from these premises before night, I shall feel bound — indeed, I *am* bound — to — to — to quit the premises myself!" I rather absurdly concluded, knowing not with what possible threat to try to frighten his immobility into compliance. Despairing of all further efforts, I was precipitately leaving him, when a final thought occurred to me — one which had not been wholly unindulged before.

"Bartleby," said I, in the kindest tone I could assume under such exciting circumstances, "will you go home with me now not to my office, but my dwelling — and remain there till we can conclude upon some convenient arrangement for you at our leisure? Come, let us start now, right away."

"No: at present I would prefer not to make any change at all."

I answered nothing; but, effectually dodging every one by the suddenness and rapidity of my flight, rushed from the building, ran up Wall Street towards Broadway, and, jumping into the first omnibus, was soon removed from pursuit. As soon as tranquillity returned, I distinctly perceived that I had now done all that I possibly could, both in respect to the demands of the landlord and his tenants, and with regard to my own desire and sense of duty, to benefit Bartleby, and shield him from rude persecution. I now strove to be entirely care-free and quiescent; and my conscience justified me in the attempt; though, indeed, it was not so successful as I could have wished. So fearful was I of being again hunted out by the incensed landlord and his exasperated tenants, that, surrendering my business to Nippers, for a few days, I drove about the upper part of the town and through the suburbs, in my rockaway; crossed over to Jersey City and Hoboken, and paid fugitive visits to Manhattanville and Astoria. In fact, I almost lived in my rockaway for the time.

When again I entered my office, lo, a note from the landlord lay upon the desk. I opened it with trembling hands. It informed me that the writer had sent to the police, and had Bartleby removed to the Tombs as a vagrant. Moreover, since I knew more about him than any one else, he wished me to appear at that place, and make a suitable statement of the facts. These tidings had a conflicting effect upon me. At first I was indignant; but, at last, almost approved. The landlord's energetic, summary disposition, had led him to adopt a procedure which I do not think I would have decided upon myself; and yet, as a last resort, under such peculiar circumstances, it seemed the only plan.

As I afterwards learned, the poor scrivener, when told that he must be conducted to the Tombs, offered not the slightest obstacle, but, in his pale, unmoving way, silently acquiesced.

Some of the compassionate and curious by-standers joined the party; and headed by one of the constables arm-in-arm with Bartleby, the silent procession filed its way through all the noise, and heat, and joy of the roaring thoroughfares at noon.

The same day I received the note, I went to the Tombs, or, to speak more properly, the Halls of Justice. Seeking the right officer, I stated the purpose of my call, and was informed that the individual I described was, indeed, within. I then assured the functionary that Bartleby was a perfectly honest man, and greatly to be compassionated, however unaccountably eccentric. I narrated all I knew, and closed by suggesting the idea of letting him remain in as indulgent confinement as possible, till something less harsh might be done — though, indeed, I hardly knew what. At all events, if nothing else could be decided upon, the alms-house must receive him. I then begged to have an interview.

Being under no disgraceful charge, and quite serene and harmless in all his ways, they had permitted him freely to wander about the prison, and, especially, in the inclosed grass-platted yards thereof. And so I found him there, standing all alone in the quietest of the yards, his face towards a high wall, while all around, from the narrow slits of the jail windows, I thought I saw peering out upon him the eyes of murderers and thieves.

"Bartleby!"

"I know you," he said, without looking round — "and I want nothing to say to you."

"It was not I that brought you here, Bartleby," said I, keenly pained at his implied suspicion. "And to you, this should not be so vile a place. Nothing reproachful attaches to you by being here. And see, it is not so sad a place as one might think. Look, there is the sky, and here is the grass."

"I know where I am," he replied, but would say nothing more, and so I left him.

As I entered the corridor again, a broad meat-like man, in an apron, accosted me, and, jerking his thumb over my shoulder, said "Is that your friend?"

"Yes."

"Does he want to starve? If he does, let him live on the prison fare, that's all."

"Who are you?" asked I, not knowing what to make of such an unofficially speaking person in such a place.

"I am the grub-man. Such gentlemen as have friends here, hire me to provide them with something good to eat."

"Is this so?" said I, turning to the turnkey.

He said it was.

"Well, then," said I, slipping some silver into the grub-man's hands (for so they called him), "I want you to give particular attention to my friend there; let him have the best dinner you can get. And you must be as polite to him as possible."

"Introduce me, will you?" said the grub-man, looking at me with an expression which seemed to say he was all impatience for an opportunity to give a specimen of his breeding.

Thinking it would prove of benefit to the scrivener, I acquiesced; and, asking the grub-man his name, went up with him to Bartleby.

"Bartleby, this is a friend; you will find him very useful to you."

"Your sarvant, sir, your sarvant," said the grub-man, making a low salutation behind his apron. "Hope you find it pleasant here, sir; nice grounds — cool apartments — hope you'll stay with us some time — try to make it agreeable. What will you have for dinner to-day?"

"I prefer not to dine to-day," said Bartleby, turning away. "It would disagree with me; I am unused to dinners." So saying, he slowly moved to the other side of the inclosure, and took up a position fronting the dead-wall.

"How's this?" said the grub-man, addressing me with a stare of astonishment. "He's odd, ain't he?"

"I think he is a little deranged," said I, sadly.

"Deranged? deranged is it? Well, now, upon my word, I thought that friend of yourn was a gentleman forger; they are always pale and genteel-like, them forgers. I can't help pity 'em — can't help it, sir. Did you know Monroe Edwards?" he added, touchingly, and paused. Then, laying his hand piteously on my shoulder, sighed, "he died of consumption at Sing-Sing. So you weren't acquainted with Monroe?"

"No, I was never socially acquainted with any forgers. But I cannot stop longer. Look to my friend yonder. You will not lose by it. I will see you again."

Some few days after this, I again obtained admission to the Tombs, and went through the corridors in quest of Bartleby; but without finding him.

"I saw him coming from his cell not long ago," said a turnkey, "may be he's gone to loiter in the yards."

So I went in that direction.

"Are you looking for the silent man?" said another turnkey, passing me.

"Yonder he lies — sleeping in the yard there. 'Tis not twenty minutes since I saw him lie down."

The yard was entirely quiet. It was not accessible to the common prisoners. The surrounding walls, of amazing thickness, kept off all sounds behind them. The Egyptian character of the masonry weighed upon me with its gloom. But a soft imprisoned turf grew under foot. The heart of the eternal pyramids, it seemed, wherein, by some strange magic, through the clefts, grass-seed, dropped by birds, had sprung.

Strangely huddled at the base of the wall, his knees drawn up, and lying on his side, his head touching the cold stones, I saw the wasted Bartleby. But nothing stirred. I paused; then went close up to him; stooped over, and saw that his dim eyes were open; otherwise he seemed profoundly sleeping. Something prompted me to touch him. I felt his hand, when a tingling shiver ran up my arm and down my spine to my feet.

The round face of the grub-man peered upon me now. "His dinner is ready. Won't he dine to-day, either? Or does he live without dining?"

"Lives without dining," said I, and closed the eyes.

"Eh! — He's asleep, ain't he?"

"With kings and counselors,"° murmured I.

There would seem little need for proceeding further in this history. Imagination will readily supply the meagre recital of poor Bartleby's interment. But, ere parting with the reader, let me say, that if this little narrative has sufficiently interested him, to awaken curiosity as to who Bartleby was, and what manner of life he led prior to the present narrator's making his acquaintance, I can only reply, that in such curiosity I fully share, but am wholly unable to gratify it. Yet here I hardly know whether I should divulge one little item of rumor, which came to my ear a few months after the scrivener's decease. Upon what basis it rested, I could never ascertain; and hence, how true it is I cannot now tell. But, inasmuch as this vague report has not been without a certain suggestive interest to me, however sad, it may prove the same with some others; and so I will briefly mention it. The report was this: that Bartleby had been a subordinate clerk in the Dead Letter Office at Washington, from which he had been suddenly removed by a change in the administration. When I think over this rumor, hardly can I express the emotions which seize me. Dead letters! does it not sound like dead men? Conceive a man by nature and misfortune prone to a pallid hopelessness, can any business seem more fitted to heighten it than that of continually handling these dead letters, and assorting them for the flames? For by the cart-load they are annually burned. Sometimes from out the folded paper the pale clerk takes a ring — the finger it was meant for, perhaps, moulders in the grave; a bank-note sent in swiftest charity — he whom it would relieve, nor eats nor hungers any more; pardon for

---

With kings and counselors: A reference to Job 3:14. Job, who has lost his family and all his property and has been stricken by a terrible disease, wishes he had never been born: "then had I been at rest with kings and counselors of the earth, which built desolate places for themselves."

those who died despairing; hope for those who died unhoping; good tidings for those who died stifled by unrelieved calamities. On errands of life, these letters speed to death.

Ah, Bartleby! Ah, humanity!

⋉⋊

LORRIE MOORE *(b. 1957) was born in Glen Falls, New York, the daughter of an insurance executive and a housewife. After completing her studies at St. Lawrence University and Cornell University, where she earned an M.F.A. in 1982, Moore began teaching at the University of Wisconsin. As an undergraduate she won a* Seventeen *magazine short story contest in 1976, and she has been publishing her fiction in magazines such as* Cosmopolitan, Ms., *and* The New Yorker *ever since. In 1987 her novel* Anagrams *was published.*

Self-Help, *Moore's first collection of short stories, appeared in 1985. As the title of the book suggests, several of the humorous stories, like "How to Become a Writer," were narrated in what Moore calls "second person, mock-imperative" voices as she parodied the self-improvement manuals popular with American readers. In the book Moore included sketches to cover various situations — "The Kid's Guide to Divorce," "How to Talk to Your Mother," "How to Be an Other Woman."*

Reviewers noted that typically the fictional characters narrating Moore's stories were intelligent people whose self-knowledge only contributed to their sense of distress, so they reacted by attempting to distance themselves from their dilemmas through humor. A character in Moore's second collection, Like Life *(1990), is told, "Everything's a joke with you." She replies, "Nothing's a joke with me. It just all comes out like one." Moore has said that the stories in* Self-Help, *written between 1980 and 1983, were stylistic experiments. She thought,*

> *Let's see what happens when one eliminates the subject, leaves the verb shivering at the start of a clause; what happens when one appropriates the "how-to" form for a fiction, for an irony, for a "how-not-to" . . . the self-help proffered here, then, is perhaps only that of art itself, which, if you agree with Oscar Wilde, is quite useless.*

Moore's most recent book is Who Will Run the Frog Hospital *(1994).*

LORRIE MOORE

How to Become a Writer   *1985*

First, try to be something, anything, else. A movie star / astronaut. A movie star/missionary. A movie star/kindergarten teacher. President of the World. Fail miserably. It is best if you fail at an early age — say, fourteen. Early, critical disillusionment is necessary so that at fifteen you can write long haiku sequences about thwarted desire. It is a pond, a cherry blossom, a wind brushing against sparrow wing leaving for mountain. Count the syllables. Show it to your mom. She is tough and practical. She has a son in Vietnam and a husband who may be having an affair. She believes in wearing brown because it hides spots. She'll look briefly at your writing, then back up at you with a face blank as a donut. She'll say: "How about emptying the dishwasher?" Look away. Shove the forks in the fork drawer. Accidentally break one of the freebie gas station glasses. This is the required pain and suffering. This is only for starters.

In your high school English class look only at Mr. Killian's face. Decide faces are important. Write a villanelle about pores. Struggle. Write a sonnet. Count the syllables: nine, ten, eleven, thirteen. Decide to experiment with fiction. Here you don't have to count syllables. Write a short story about an elderly man and woman who accidentally shoot each other in the head, the result of an inexplicable malfunction of a shotgun which appears mysteriously in their living room one night. Give it to Mr. Killian as your final project. When you get it back, he has written on it: "Some of your images are quite nice, but you have no sense of plot." When you are home, in the privacy of your own room, faintly scrawl in pencil beneath his black-inked comments: "Plots are for dead people, pore-face."

Take all the babysitting jobs you can get. You are great with kids. They love you. You tell them stories about old people who die idiot deaths. You sing them songs like "Blue Bells of Scotland," which is their favorite. And when they are in their pajamas and have finally stopped pinching each other, when they are fast asleep, you read every sex manual in the house, and wonder how on earth anyone could ever do those things with someone they truly loved. Fall asleep in a chair reading Mr. McMurphy's *Playboy*. When the McMurphys come home, they will tap you on the shoulder, look at the magazine in your lap, and grin. You will want to die. They will ask you if Tracey took her medicine all right. Explain, yes, she did, that you promised her a story if she would take it like a big girl and that seemed to work out just fine. "Oh, marvelous," they will exclaim.

Try to smile proudly.

Apply to college as a child psychology major.

As a child psychology major, you have some electives. You've always liked birds. Sign up for something called "The Ornithological Field Trip." It meets Tuesdays and Thursdays at two. When you arrive at Room 134 on the first day of class, everyone is sitting around a seminar table talking about metaphors. You've heard of these. After a short, excruciating while, raise your hand and say diffidently, "Excuse me, isn't this Birdwatching One-oh-one?" The class stops and turns to look at you. They seem to all have one face — giant and blank as a vandalized clock. Someone with a beard booms out, "No, this is Creative Writing." Say: "Oh — right," as if perhaps you knew all along. Look down at your schedule. Wonder how the hell you ended up here. The computer, apparently, has made an error. You start to get up to leave and then don't. The lines at the registrar this week are huge. Perhaps you should stick with this mistake. Perhaps your creative writing isn't all that bad. Perhaps it is fate. Perhaps this is what your dad meant when he said, "It's the age of computers, Francie, it's the age of computers."

Decide that you like college life. In your dorm you meet many nice people. Some are smarter than you. And some, you notice, are dumber than you. You will continue, unfortunately, to view the world in exactly these terms for the rest of your life.

The assignment this week in creative writing is to narrate a violent happening. Turn in a story about driving with your Uncle Gordon and another one about two old people who are accidentally electrocuted when they go to turn on a badly wired desk lamp. The teacher will hand them back to you with comments: "Much of your writing is smooth and energetic. You have, however, a ludicrous notion of plot." Write another story about a man and a woman who, in the very first paragraph, have their lower torsos accidentally blitzed away by dynamite. In the second paragraph, with the insurance money, they buy a frozen yogurt stand together. There are six more paragraphs. You read the whole thing out loud in class. No one likes it. They say your sense of plot is outrageous and incompetent. After class someone asks you if you are crazy.

Decide that perhaps you should stick to comedies. Start dating someone who is funny, someone who has what in high school you called a "really great sense of humor" and what now your creative writing class calls "self-contempt giving rise to comic form." Write down all of his jokes, but don't tell him you are doing this. Make up anagrams of his old girlfriend's name and name all of your socially handicapped characters with them. Tell him his old girlfriend is in all of your stories and then watch how funny he can be, see what a really great sense of humor he can have.

Your child psychology advisor tells you you are neglecting courses in your major. What you spend the most time on should be what you're majoring in. Say yes, you understand.

In creative writing seminars over the next two years, everyone continues to smoke cigarettes and ask the same things: "But does it work?" "Why should we care about this character?" "Have you earned this cliché?" These seem like important questions.

On days when it is your turn, you look at the class hopefully as they scour your mimeographs for a plot. They look back up at you, drag deeply, and then smile in a sweet sort of way.

You spend too much time slouched and demoralized. Your boyfriend suggests bicycling. Your roommate suggests a new boyfriend. You are said to be self-mutilating and losing weight, but you continue writing. The only happiness you have is writing something new, in the middle of the night, armpits damp, heart pounding, something no one has yet seen. You have only those brief, fragile, untested moments of exhilaration when you know: you are a genius. Understand what you must do. Switch majors. The kids in your nursery project will be disappointed, but you have a calling, an urge, a delusion, an unfortunate habit. You have, as your mother would say, fallen in with a bad crowd.

Why write? Where does writing come from? These are questions to ask yourself. They are like: Where does dust come from? Or: Why is there war? Or: If there's a God, then why is my brother now a cripple?

These are questions that you keep in your wallet, like calling cards. These are questions, your creative writing teacher says, that are good to address in your journals but rarely in your fiction.

The writing professor this fall is stressing the Power of the Imagination. Which means he doesn't want long descriptive stories about your camping trip last July. He wants you to start in a realistic context but then to alter it. Like recombinant DNA. He wants you to let your imagination sail, to let it grow big-bellied in the wind. This is a quote from Shakespeare.

Tell your roommate your great idea, your great exercise of imaginative power: a transformation of Melville to contemporary life. It will be about monomania and the fish-eat-fish world of life insurance in Rochester, New York. The first line will be "Call me Fishmeal," and it will feature a menopausal suburban husband named Richard, who because he is so depressed all the time is called "Mopey Dick" by his witty wife Elaine. Say to your roommate: "Mopey Dick, get it?" Your roommate looks at you, her face blank as a large Kleenex. She comes up to you, like a buddy, and puts an arm around your burdened shoulders. "Listen, Francie," she says, slow as speech therapy. "Let's go out and get a big beer."

The seminar doesn't like this one either. You suspect they are beginning to feel sorry for you. They say: "You have to think about what is happening. Where is the story here?"

The next semester the writing professor is obsessed with writing from personal experience. You must write from what you know, from what has happened to you. He wants death, he wants camping trips. Think about what has happened to you. In three years there have been three things: you lost your virginity; your parents got divorced; and your brother came home from a forest ten miles from the Cambodian border with only half a thigh, a permanent smirk nestled into one corner of his mouth.

About the first you write: "It created a new space, which hurt and cried in a voice that wasn't mine, 'I'm not the same anymore, but I'll be okay.' "

About the second you write an elaborate story of an old married couple who stumble upon an unknown land mine in their kitchen and accidentally blow themselves up. You call it: "For Better or for Liverwurst."

About the last you write nothing. There are no words for this. Your typewriter hums. You can find no words.

At undergraduate cocktail parties, people say, "Oh, you write? What do you write about?" Your roommate, who has consumed too much wine, too little cheese, and no crackers at all, blurts: "Oh, my god, she always writes about her dumb boyfriend."

Later on in life you will learn that writers are merely open, helpless texts with no real understanding of what they have written and therefore must half-believe anything and everything that is said of them. You, however, have not yet reached this stage of literary criticism. You stiffen and say, "I do not," the same way you said it when someone in the fourth grade accused you of really liking oboe lessons and your parents really weren't just making you take them.

Insist you are not very interested in any one subject at all, that you are interested in the music of language, that you are interested in — in — syllables, because they are the atoms of poetry, the cells of the mind, the breath of the soul. Begin to feel woozy. Stare into your plastic wine cup.

"Syllables?" you will hear someone ask, voice trailing off, as they glide slowly toward the reassuring white of the dip.

Begin to wonder what you do write about. Or if you have anything to say. Or if there even is such a thing as a thing to say. Limit these thoughts to no more than ten minutes a day; like sit-ups, they can make you thin.

You will read somewhere that all writing has to do with one's genitals. Don't dwell on this. It will make you nervous.

Your mother will come visit you. She will look at the circles under your eyes and hand you a brown book with a brown briefcase on the cover. It is entitled: *How to Become a Business Executive.* She has also brought the *Names for Baby* encyclopedia you asked for; one of your characters, the aging clown–schoolteacher, needs a new name. Your mother will shake her head and say: "Francie, Francie, remember when you were going to be a child psychology major?"

Say: "Mom, I like to write."

She'll say: "Sure you like to write. Of course. Sure you like to write."

Write a story about a confused music student and title it: "Schubert Was the One with the Glasses, Right?" It's not a big hit, although your roommate likes the part where the two violinists accidentally blow themselves up in a recital room. "I went out with a violinist once," she says, snapping her gum.

Thank god you are taking other courses. You can find sanctuary in nineteenth-century ontological snags and invertebrate courting rituals. Certain globular mollusks have what is called "Sex by the Arm." The male octopus, for instance, loses the end of one arm when placing it inside the female body during intercourse. Marine biologists call it "Seven Heaven." Be glad you know these things. Be glad you are not just a writer. Apply to law school.

From here on in, many things can happen. But the main one will be this: you decide not to go to law school after all, and, instead, you spend a good, big chunk of your adult life telling people how you decided not to go to law school after all. Somehow you end up writing again. Perhaps you go to graduate school. Perhaps you work odd jobs and take writing courses at night. Perhaps you are working on a novel and writing down all the clever remarks and intimate personal confessions you hear during the day. Perhaps you are losing your pals, your acquaintances, your balance.

You have broken up with your boyfriend. You now go out with men who, instead of whispering "I love you," shout: "Do it to me, baby." This is good for your writing.

Sooner or later you have a finished manuscript more or less. People look at it in a vaguely troubled sort of way and say, "I'll bet becoming a writer was always a fantasy of yours, wasn't it?" Your lips dry to salt. Say that of all the fantasies possible in the world, you can't imagine being a writer even making the top twenty. Tell them you were going to be a child psychology major. "I bet," they always sigh, "you'd be great with kids." Scowl fiercely. Tell them you're a walking blade.

Quit classes. Quit jobs. Cash in old savings bonds. Now you have time like warts on your hands. Slowly copy all of your friends' addresses into a new address book.

Vacuum. Chew cough drops. Keep a folder full of fragments.

An eyelid darkening sideways.
World as conspiracy.
Possible plot? A woman gets on a bus.
Suppose you threw a love affair and nobody came?

At home drink a lot of coffee. At Howard Johnson's order the cole slaw. Consider how it looks like the soggy confetti of a map: where you've been, where you're going — "You Are Here," says the red star on the back of the menu.

Occasionally a date with a face blank as a sheet of paper asks you whether writers often become discouraged. Say that sometimes they do and sometimes they do. Say it's a lot like having polio.

"Interesting," smiles your date, and then he looks down at his arm hairs and starts to smooth them, all, always, in the same direction.

∞

BHARATI MUKHERJEE *(b. 1940) was born in Calcutta, India. As a young girl she lived in London with her parents and sisters, but she returned to India in 1951 and was educated at the universities of Calcutta and Baroda, where she received an M.A. in English and ancient Indian culture. While studying for her doctorate at the University of Iowa Writers Workshop, she married the novelist Clark Blaise in 1963. For several years they lived in Canada, where she published two novels,* The Tiger's Daughter *(1972) and* Wife *(1975). Mukherjee and her husband then lived for a year in India, an experience that led to their collaboration on the journal* Days *and* Nights in Calcutta *(1977). It describes their different impressions of the country — Blaise* *was fascinated by his introduction to Bengali life and culture, Mukherjee angered by the oppression of women in India.*

In 1980 Mukherjee came to live in the United States, where she began teaching at the University of Iowa. In Canada she had been conscious of racism: "I was frequently taken for a prostitute or a shoplifter, frequently assumed to be a domestic, praised by astonished auditers that I didn't have a 'singsong' accent. The society itself . . . routinely made crippling assumptions about me, and about my 'kind.' " In the United States, Mukherjee became more optimistic. She has described the note card pinned above her writing desk to give her inspiration. It quotes the showman Liberace, whom she admires as an "American original": "Too much of a good thing is simply wonderful." She feels that her writing has lost the "mordant and self-protected irony" she had adopted from her previous literary model, V. S. Naipaul. Her outlook is more tolerant in The Middleman and Other Stories *(1988), the book that established her reputation in this country.*

The critic Ann Mandel has understood that in such stories as "A Father," Mukherjee is dramatizing the immigrant's "request for recognition — the desire to be 'visible' in honorable ways, to be recognized as a person rather than as an ethnic stereotype." The characters in The Middleman *represent America's newest wave of Third World immigrants — Filipino, Salvadoran, Iraqi, Indian. Mukherjee's recent novels are* Jasmine *(1989) and* The Holder of the World *(1992).*

BHARATI MUKHERJEE

A Father   1985

One Wednesday morning in mid-May Mr. Bhowmick woke up as he usually did at 5:43 A.M., checked his Rolex against the alarm clock's digital readout, punched down the alarm (set for 5:45), then nudged his wife awake. She worked as a claims investigator for an insurance company that had an office in a nearby shopping mall. She didn't really have to leave the house until 8:30, but she liked to get up early and cook him a big breakfast. Mr. Bhowmick had to drive a long way to work. He was a naturally dutiful, cautious man, and he set the alarm clock early enough to accommodate a margin for accidents.

While his wife, in a pink nylon negligee she had paid for with her own MasterCard card, made him a new version of French toast from a clipping ("Eggs-cellent Recipes!") Scotchtaped to the inside of a kitchen cupboard, Mr. Bhowmick brushed his teeth. He brushed, he gurgled with the loud, hawking noises that he and his brother had been taught as children to make in order to flush clean not merely teeth but also tongue and palate.

After that he showered, then, back in the bedroom again, he recited prayers in Sanskrit to Kali, the patron goddess of his family, the goddess of wrath and vengeance. In the pokey flat of his childhood in Ranchi, Bihar, his mother had given over a whole bedroom to her collection of gods and goddesses. Mr. Bhowmick couldn't be that extravagant in Detroit. His daughter, twenty-six and an electrical engineer, slept in the other of the two bedrooms in his apartment. But he had done his best. He had taken Woodworking I and II at a nearby recreation center and built a grotto for the goddess. Kali-Mata was eight inches tall, made of metal and painted a glistening black so that the metal glowed like the oiled, black skin of a peasant woman. And though Kali-Mata was totally nude except for a tiny gilt crown and a garland strung together from sinners' chopped off heads, she looked warm, cozy, *pleased*, in her makeshift wooden shrine in Detroit. Mr. Bhowmick had gathered quite a crowd of admiring, fellow woodworkers in those final weeks of decoration.

"Hurry it up with the prayers," his wife shouted from the kitchen. She was an agnostic, a believer in ambition, not grace. She frequently complained that his prayers had gotten so long that soon he wouldn't have time to go to work, play duplicate bridge with the Ghosals, or play the *tabla*° in the Bengali Association's one Sunday per month musical soirees. Lately she'd begun to drain him in a wholly new way. He wasn't praying, she nagged; he was shutting her out of his life. There'd be no peace in the house until she hid Kali-Mata in a suitcase.

She nagged, and he threatened to beat her with his shoe as his father had threatened his mother: it was the thrust and volley of marriage. There was no question of actually taking off a shoe and applying it to his wife's body. She was bigger than he was. And, secretly, he admired her for having the nerve, the agnosticism, which as a college boy in backward Bihar he too had claimed.

"I have time," he shot at her. He was still wrapped in a damp terry towel.

"You have time for everything but domestic life."

It was the fault of the shopping mall that his wife had started to buy pop psychology paperbacks. These paperbacks preached that for couples who could sit down and talk about their "relationship," life would be sweet again. His engineer daughter was on his wife's side. She accused him of holding things in.

"Face it, Dad," she said. "You have an affect deficit."

But surely everyone had feelings they didn't want to talk about or talk over. He definitely did not want to blurt out anything about the sick-in-the-guts sensations that came over him most mornings and that he couldn't bubble down with Alka-Seltzer or smother with Gas-X. The women in his family were smarter than him. They were cheerful, outgoing, more American somehow.

How could he tell these bright, mocking women that in the 5:43 A.M. darkness, he sensed invisible presences: gods and snakes frolicked in the master bedroom, little white sparks of cosmic static crackled up the legs of his pajamas. Something was out there in the dark, something that could invent accidents and coincidences to remind mortals that even in Detroit they were no more than mortal. His wife would label this paranoia and dismiss it. Para-

---

tabla: An Indian musical instrument; a kind of drum.

noia, premonition: whatever it was, it had begun to undermine his composure.

Take this morning. Mr. Bhowmick had woken up from a pleasant dream
about a man taking a Club Med vacation, and the postdream satisfaction had
lasted through the shower, but when he'd come back to the shrine in the bedroom, he'd noticed all at once how scarlet and saucy was the tongue that Kali-
Mata stuck out at the world. Surely he had not lavished such alarming detail,
such admonitory colors on that flap of flesh.

Watch out, ambulatory sinners. Be careful out there, the goddess
warned him, and not with the affection of Sergeant Esterhaus,° either.

"French toast must be eaten hot-hot," his wife nagged. "Otherwise
they'll taste like rubber."

Mr. Bhowmick laid the trousers of a two-trouser suit he had bought on
sale that winter against his favorite tweed jacket. The navy stripes in the
trousers and the small, navy tweed flecks in the jacket looked quite good together. So what if the Chief Engineer had already started wearing summer cot-
tons?

"I am coming, I am coming," he shouted back. "You want me to eat hot-
hot, you start the frying only when I am sitting down. You didn't learn anything from Mother in Ranchi?"

"Mother cooked French toast from fancy recipes? I mean French Sandwich Toast with complicated filling?"

He came into the room to give her his testiest look. "You don't know the
meaning of complicated cookery. And mother had to get the coal fire of the
chula° going first."

His daughter was already at the table. "Why don't you break down and
buy her a microwave oven? That's what I mean about sitting down and talking things out." She had finished her orange juice. She took a plastic measure
of Slim-Fast out of its can and poured the powder into a glass of skim milk.
"It's ridiculous."

Babli was not the child he would have chosen as his only heir. She was
brighter certainly than the sons and daughters of the other Bengalis he knew
in Detroit, and she had been the only female student in most of her classes at
Georgia Tech, but as she sat there in her beige linen business suit, her thick
chin dropping into a polka-dotted cravat, he regretted again that she was not
the child of his dreams. Babli would be able to help him out moneywise if
something happened to him, something so bad that even his pension plans
and his insurance policies and his money market schemes wouldn't be
enough. But Babli could never comfort him. She wasn't womanly or tender
the way that unmarried girls had been in the wistful days of his adolescence.
She could sing Hindi film songs, mimicking exactly the high, artificial voice of

---

Sergeant Esterhaus: Sergeant Phil Esterhaus would begin each episode of the popular 1980s
television series *Hill Street Blues* by admonishing his officers, "Let's be careful out there."
chula: A clay oven.

Lata Mungeshkar, and she had taken two years of dance lessons at Sona Devi's Dance Academy in Southfield, but these accomplishments didn't add up to real femininity. Not the kind that had given him palpitations in Ranchi.

Mr. Bhowmick did his best with his wife's French toast. In spite of its filling of marshmallows, apricot jam and maple syrup, it tasted rubbery. He drank two cups of Darjeeling tea, said, "Well, I'm off," and took off.

All might have gone well if Mr. Bhowmick hadn't fussed longer than usual about putting his briefcase and his trenchcoat in the backseat. He got in behind the wheel of his Oldsmobile, fixed his seatbelt and was just about to turn the key in the ignition when his neighbor, Al Stazniak, who was starting up his Buick Skylark, sneezed. A sneeze at the start of a journey brings bad luck. Al Stazniak's sneeze was fierce, made up of five short bursts, too loud to be ignored.

Be careful out there! Mr. Bhowmick could see the goddess's scarlet little tongue tip wagging at him.

He was a modern man, an intelligent man. Otherwise he couldn't have had the options in life that he did have. He couldn't have given up a good job with perks in Bombay and found a better job with General Motors in Detroit. But Mr. Bhowmick was also a prudent enough man to know that some abiding truth lies bunkered within each wanton Hindu superstition. A sneeze was more than a sneeze. The heedless are carried off in ambulances. He had choices to make. He could ignore the sneeze, and so challenge the world unseen by men. Perhaps Al Stazniak had hayfever. For a sneeze to be a potent omen, surely it had to be unprovoked and terrifying, a thunderclap cleaving the summer skies. Or he could admit the smallness of mortals, undo the fate of the universe by starting over, and go back inside the apartment, sit for a second on the sofa, then re-start his trip.

Al Stazniak rolled down his window. "Everything okay?"

Mr. Bhowmick nodded shyly. They weren't really friends in the way neighbors can sometimes be. They talked as they parked or pulled out of their adjacent parking stalls. For all Mr. Bhowmick knew, Al Stazniak had no legs. He had never seen the man out of his Skylark.

He let the Buick back out first. Everything was okay, yes, please. All the same he undid his seatbelt. Compromise, adaptability, call it what you will. A dozen times a day he made these small trade-offs between new-world reasonableness and old-world beliefs.

While he was sitting in his parked car, his wife's ride came by. For fifty dollars a month, she was picked up and dropped off by a hard up, newly divorced woman who worked at a florist's shop in the same mall. His wife came out the front door in brown K-Mart pants and a burgundy windbreaker. She waved to him, then slipped into the passenger seat of the florist's rusty Japanese car.

He was a metallurgist. He knew about rust and ways of preventing it, secret ways, thus far unknown to the Japanese.

Babli's fiery red Mitsubishi was still in the lot. She wouldn't leave for work for another eight minutes. He didn't want her to know he'd been undone by a sneeze. Babli wasn't tolerant of superstitions. She played New Wave music in her tapedeck. If asked about Hinduism, all she'd ever said to her American friends was that "it's neat." Mr. Bhowmick had heard her on the phone years before. The cosmos balanced on the head of a snake was like a beachball balanced on the snout of a circus seal. "This Hindu myth stuff," he'd heard her say, "is like a series of super graphics."

He'd forgiven her. He could probably forgive her anything. It was her way of surviving high school in a city that was both native to her, and alien.

There was no question of going back where he'd come from. He hated Ranchi. Ranchi was no place for dreamers. All through his teenage years, Mr. Bhowmick had dreamed of success abroad. What form that success would take he had left vague. Success had meant to him escape from the constant plotting and bitterness that wore out India's middle class.

Babli should have come out of the apartment and driven off to work by now. Mr. Bhowmick decided to take a risk, to dash inside and pretend he'd left his briefcase on the coffee table.

When he entered the living room, he noticed Babli's spring coat and large vinyl pocketbook on the sofa. She was probably sorting through the junk jewelry on her dresser to give her business suit a lift. She read hints about dressing in women's magazines and applied them to her person with seriousness. If his luck held, he could sit on the sofa, say a quick prayer and get back to the car without her catching on.

It surprised him that she didn't shout out from her bedroom, "Who's there?" What if he had been a rapist?

Then he heard Babli in the bathroom. He heard unladylike squawking noises. She was throwing up. A squawk, a spitting, then the horrible gurgle of a waterfall.

A revelation came to Mr. Bhowmick. A woman vomiting in the privacy of the bathroom could mean many things. She was coming down with the flu. She was nervous about a meeting. But Mr. Bhowmick knew at once that his daughter, his untender, unloving daughter whom he couldn't love and hadn't tried to love, was not, in the larger world of Detroit, unloved. Sinners are everywhere, even in the bosom of an upright, unambitious family like the Bhowmicks. It was the goddess sticking out her tongue at him.

The father sat heavily on the sofa, shrinking from contact with her coat and pocketbook. His brisk, bright engineer daughter was pregnant. Someone had taken time to make love to her. Someone had thought her tender, feminine. Someone even now was perhaps mooning over her. The idea excited him. It was so grotesque and wondrous. At twenty-six Babli had found the man of her dreams; whereas at twenty-six Mr. Bhowmick had given up on truth, beauty and poetry and exchanged them for two years at Carnegie Tech.

Mr. Bhowmick's tweed-jacketed body sagged against the sofa cushions. Babli would abort, of course. He knew his Babli. It was the only possible option if she didn't want to bring shame to the Bhowmick family. All the same, he could see a chubby baby boy on the rug, crawling to his granddaddy. Shame like that was easier to hide in Ranchi. There was always a barren womb sanctified by marriage that could claim sudden fructifying by the goddess

Parvati. Babli would do what she wanted. She was headstrong and independent and he was afraid of her.

Babli staggered out of the bathroom. Damp stains ruined her linen suit. It was the first time he had seen his daughter look ridiculous, quite unprofessional. She didn't come into the living room to investigate the noises he'd made. He glimpsed her shoeless stockinged feet flip-flop on collapsed arches down the hall to her bedroom.

"Are you all right?" Mr. Bhowmick asked, standing in the hall. "Do you need Sinutab?"

She wheeled around. "What're you doing here?"

He was the one who should be angry. "I'm feeling poorly too," he said. "I'm taking the day off."

"I feel fine," Babli said.

Within fifteen minutes Babli had changed her clothes and left. Mr. Bhowmick had the apartment to himself all day. All day for praising or cursing the life that had brought him along with its other surprises an illegitimate grandchild.

It was his wife that he blamed. Coming to America to live had been his wife's idea. After the wedding, the young Bhowmicks had spent two years in Pittsburgh on his student visa, then gone back home to Ranchi for nine years. Nine crushing years. Then the job in Bombay had come through. All during those nine years his wife had screamed and wept. She was a woman of wild, progressive ideas — she'd called them her "American" ideas — and she'd been martyred by her neighbors for them. American memsahib.° Markin mem, Markin mem. ° In bazaars the beggar boys had trailed her and hooted. She'd done provocative things. She'd hired a chamar° woman who by caste rules was forbidden to cook for higher caste families, especially for widowed mothers of decent men. This had caused a blowup in the neighborhood. She'd made other, lesser errors. While other wives shopped and cooked every day, his wife had cooked the whole week's menu on weekends.

"What's the point of having a refrigerator, then?" She'd been scornful of the Ranchi women.

His mother, an old-fashioned widow, had accused her of trying to kill her by poisoning. "You are in such a hurry? You want to get rid of me quick-quick so you can go back to the States?"

Family life had been turbulent.

He had kept aloof, inwardly siding with his mother. He did not love his wife now, and he had not loved her then. In any case, he had not defended her. He felt some affection, and he felt guilty for having shunned her during those unhappy years. But he had thought of it then as revenge. He had wanted to marry a beautiful woman. Not being a young man of means, only a young man with prospects, he had had no right to yearn for pure beauty. He cursed

---

memsahib: Mrs.
Markin mem: American Mrs.
chamar: A person of one of the lower castes in the Indian caste (class) system.

his fate and after a while, settled for a barrister's daughter, a plain girl with a wide, flat plank of a body and myopic eyes. The barrister had sweetened the deal by throwing in an all-expenses-paid two years' study at Carnegie Tech to which Mr. Bhowmick had been admitted. Those two years had changed his wife from pliant girl to ambitious woman. She wanted America, nothing less.

It was his wife who had forced him to apply for permanent resident status in the U.S. even though he had a good job in Ranchi as a government engineer. The putting together of documents for the immigrant visa had been a long and humbling process. He had had to explain to a chilly clerk in the Embassy that, like most Indians of his generation, he had no birth certificate. He had to swear out affidavits, suffer through police checks, bribe orderlies whose job it was to move his dossier from desk to desk. The decision, the clerk had advised him, would take months, maybe years. He hadn't dared hope that merit might be rewarded. Merit could collapse under bad luck. It was for grace that he prayed.

While the immigration papers were being processed, he had found the job in Bombay. So he'd moved his mother in with his younger brother's family, and left his hometown for good. Life in Bombay had been lighthearted, almost fulfilling. His wife had thrown herself into charity work with the same energy that had offended the Ranchi women. He was happy to be in a big city at last. Bombay was the Rio de Janeiro of the East; he'd read that in a travel brochure. He drove out to Nariman Point at least once a week to admire the necklace of municipal lights, toss coconut shells into the dark ocean, drink beer at the Oberoi-Sheraton where overseas Indian girls in designer jeans beckoned him in sly ways. His nights were full. He played duplicate bridge, went to the movies, took his wife to Bingo nights at his club. In Detroit he was a lonelier man.

Then the green card° had come through. For him, for his wife, and for the daughter who had been born to them in Bombay. He sold what he could sell, and put in his brother's informal trust what he couldn't to save on taxes. Then he had left for America, and one more start.

All through the week, Mr. Bhowmick watched his daughter. He kept furtive notes on how many times she rushed to the bathroom and made hawking, wrenching noises, how many times she stayed late at the office, calling her mother to say she'd be taking in a movie and pizza afterwards with friends.

He had to tell her that he knew. And he probably didn't have much time. She shouldn't be on Slim-Fast in her condition. He had to talk things over with her. But what would he say to her? What position could he take? He had to choose between public shame for the family, and murder.

For three more weeks he watched her and kept his silence. Babli wore shifts to the office instead of business suits, and he liked her better in those garments. Perhaps she was dressing for her young man, not from necessity.

---

green card: American certification of an immigrant's legal resident status.

Her skin was pale and blotchy by turn. At breakfast her fingers looked stiff, and she had trouble with silverware.

Two Saturdays running, he lost badly at duplicate bridge. His wife scolded him. He had made silly mistakes. When was Babli meeting this man? Where? He must be American; Mr. Bhowmick prayed only that he was white. He pictured his grandson crawling to him, and the grandson was always fat and brown and buttery-skinned, like the infant Krishna. An American son-in-law was a terrifying notion. Why was she not mentioning men, at least, preparing the way for the major announcement? He listened sharply for men's names, rehearsed little lines like, "Hello, Bob, I'm Babli's old man," with a cracked little laugh. Bob, Jack, Jimmy, Tom. But no names surfaced. When she went out for pizza and a movie it was with the familiar set of Indian girls and their strange, unpopular, American friends, all without men. Mr. Bhowmick tried to be reasonable. Maybe she had already gotten married and was keeping it secret. "Well, Bob, you and Babli sure had Mrs. Bhowmick and me going there, heh-heh," he mumbled one night with the Sahas and Ghosals, over cards. "Pardon?" asked Pronob Saha. Mr. Bhowmick dropped two tricks, and his wife glared. "Such stupid blunders," she fumed on the drive back. A new truth was dawning; there would be no marriage for Babli. Her young man probably was not so young and not so available. He must be already married. She must have yielded to passion or been raped in the office. His wife seemed to have noticed nothing. Was he a murderer, or a conspirator? He kept his secret from his wife; his daughter kept her decision to herself.

Nights, Mr. Bhowmick pretended to sleep, but as soon as his wife began her snoring — not real snores so much as loud, gaspy gulpings for breath — he turned on his side and prayed to Kali-Mata.

In July, when Babli's belly had begun to push up against the waistless dresses she'd bought herself, Mr. Bhowmick came out of the shower one weekday morning and found the two women screaming at each other. His wife had a rolling pin in one hand. His daughter held up a *National Geographic* as a shield for her head. The crazy look that had been in his wife's eyes when she'd shooed away beggar kids was in her eyes again.

"Stop it!" His own boldness overwhelmed him. "Shut up! Babli's pregnant, so what? It's your fault, you made us come to the States."

Girls like Babli were caught between rules, that's the point he wished to make. They were too smart, too impulsive for a backward place like Ranchi, but not tough nor smart enough for sex-crazy places like Detroit.

"My fault?" his wife cried. "I told her to do hanky-panky with boys? I told her to shame us like this?"

She got in one blow with the rolling pin. The second glanced off Babli's shoulder and fell on his arm which he had stuck out for his grandson's sake.

"I'm calling the police," Babli shouted. She was out of the rolling pin's range. "This is brutality. You can't do this to me."

"Shut up! Shut your mouth, foolish woman." He wrenched the weapon from his wife's fist. He made a show of taking off his shoe to beat his wife on the face.

"What do you know? You don't know anything." She let herself down slowly on a dining chair. Her hair, curled overnight, stood in wild whorls around her head. "Nothing."

"And you do!" He laughed. He remembered her tormentors, and laughed again. He had begun to enjoy himself. Now *he* was the one with the crazy, progressive ideas.

"Your daughter is pregnant, yes," she said, "any fool knows that. But ask her the name of the father. Go, ask."

He stared at his daughter who gazed straight ahead, eyes burning with hate, jaw clenched with fury.

"Babli?"

"Who needs a man?" she hissed. "The father of my baby is a bottle and a syringe. Men louse up your lives. I just want a baby. Oh, don't worry — he's a certified fit donor. No diseases, college graduate, above average, and he made the easiest twenty-five dollars of his life — "

"Like animals," his wife said. For the first time he heard horror in her voice. His daughter grinned at him. He saw her tongue, thick and red, squirming behind her row of perfect teeth.

"Yes, yes, yes," she screamed, "like livestock. Just like animals. You should be happy — that's what marriage is all about, isn't it? Matching bloodlines, matching horoscopes, matching castes, matching, matching, matching . . ." and it was difficult to know if she was laughing or singing, or mocking and like a madwoman.

Mr. Bhowmick lifted the rolling pin high above his head and brought it down hard on the dome of Babli's stomach. In the end, it was his wife who called the police.

လ

ALICE MUNRO (*b. 1931*) *grew up on a farm in a rural community near Lake Huron in Ontario, Canada, where her father raised silver foxes. After attending the University of Western Ontario for two years, she married and moved to British Columbia. Munro remembers that she began writing things down when she was about twelve, and at age fifteen she decided she would soon write a great novel: "But I thought perhaps I wasn't ready so I would write a short story in the meantime." She began publishing her stories when she was a university student, but her writing progressed very slowly during the next several years after she remarried and raised a family. "I never intended to be a short story writer," she has explained. "I started writing them because I didn't have time to write anything else — I had three children. And then I got used to writing stories, so I saw my material that way, and now I don't think I'll ever write a novel." In 1968 Munro published her first collection of stories,* Dance of the Happy Shades, *which won the Governor General's Award in Canada. Three years later she published her second book,* Lives of Girls and Women. *Another collection of stories,* Something I've Been Meaning to Tell You, *appeared in 1974, and a series of connected stories titled* Who Do You Think You Are? *was published in 1978, giving Munro her second Governor General's Award. She won her third with*

The Progress of Love *in 1987. Her most recent book,* Friend of My Youth, *was published in 1990.*

Almost all Munro's stories are set in southern Ontario, where she grew up and now lives with her second husband. She sees herself as an anachronism, "because I write about places where your roots are and most people don't live that kind of life any more at all. Most writers, probably, the writers who are most in tune with our time, write about places that have no texture because this is where most of us live."

Although Lives of Girls and Women *was published as a novel, Munro first wrote it as a series of stories, which she later revised in a loosely patterned autobiographical structure. Frequently her narrator is a young girl, who notes in great detail what she sees around her, while conveying a poignant sense of her own subjectivity, as in "Walker Brothers Cowboy." Literary critics have observed that Munro's stories about small town life are reminiscent of the fiction of such American writers as Flannery O'Connor and Eudora Welty.*

ALICE MUNRO

Walker Brothers Cowboy 1968

After supper my father says, "Want to go down and see if the Lake's still there?" We leave my mother sewing under the dining-room light, making clothes for me against the opening of school. She has ripped up for this purpose an old suit and an old plaid wool dress of hers, and she has to cut and match very cleverly and also make me stand and turn for endless fittings, sweaty, itchy from the hot wool, ungrateful. We leave my brother in bed in the little screened porch at the end of the front verandah, and sometimes he kneels on his bed and presses his face against the screen and calls mournfully, "Bring me an ice cream cone!" but I call back, "You will be asleep," and do not even turn my head.

Then my father and I walk gradually down the long, shabby sort of street, with Silverwoods Ice Cream signs standing on the sidewalk, outside tiny, lighted stores. This is in Tuppertown, an old town on Lake Huron, an old grain port. The street is shaded, in some places, by maple trees whose roots have cracked and heaved the sidewalk and spread out like crocodiles into the bare yards. People are sitting out, men in shirt-sleeves and undershirts and women in aprons — not people we know but if anybody looks ready to nod and say, "Warm night," my father will nod too and say something the same. Children are still playing. I don't know them either because my mother keeps my brother and me in our own yard, saying he is too young to leave it and I have to mind him. I am not so sad to watch their evening games because the games themselves are ragged, dissolving. Children, of their own will, draw apart, separate into islands of two or one under the heavy trees, occupying themselves in such solitary ways as I do all day, planting pebbles in the dirt or writing in it with a stick.

Presently we leave these yards and houses behind, we pass a factory with boarded-up windows, a lumberyard whose high wooden gates are locked for the night. Then the town falls away in a defeated jumble of shreds and small junkyards, the sidewalk gives up and we are walking on a sandy path with burdocks, plantains, humble nameless weeds all around. We enter a vacant lot, a kind of park really, for it is kept clear of junk and there is one bench with a slat missing on the back, a place to sit and look at the water. Which is generally grey in the evening, under a lightly overcast sky, no sunsets, the horizon dim. A very quiet, washing noise on the stones of the beach. Further along, towards the main part of town, there is a stretch of sand, a water slide, floats bobbing around the safe swimming area, a life guard's rickety throne. Also a long dark green building, like a roofed verandah, called the Pavilion, full of farmers and their wives, in stiff good clothes, on Sundays. That is the part of the town we used to know when we lived at Dungannon and came here three or four times a summer, to the Lake. That, and the docks where we would go and look at the grain boats, ancient, rusty, wallowing, making us wonder how they got past the breakwater let alone to Fort William.

Tramps hang around the docks and occasionally on these evenings wander up the dwindling beach and climb the shifting, precarious path boys have made, hanging onto dry bushes, and say something to my father which, being frightened of tramps, I am too alarmed to catch. My father says he is a bit hard up himself. "I'll roll you a cigarette if it's any use to you," he says, and he shakes tobacco out carefully on one of the thin butterfly papers, flicks it with his tongue, seals it, and hands it to the tramp who takes it and walks away. My father also rolls and lights and smokes one cigarette of his own.

He tells me how the Great Lakes came to be. All where Lake Huron is now, he says, used to be flat land, a wide flat plain. Then came the ice, creeping down from the north, pushing deep into the low places. Like *that* — and he shows me his hand with his spread fingers pressing the rock-hard ground where we are sitting. His fingers make hardly any impression at all and he says, "Well, the old ice cap had a lot more power behind it than this hand has." And then the ice went back, shrank back towards the North Pole where it came from, and left its fingers of ice in the deep places it had gouged, and ice turned to lakes and there they were today. They were *new*, as time went. I try to see that plain before me, dinosaurs walking on it, but I am not able even to imagine the shore of the Lake when the Indians were there, before Tuppertown. The tiny share we have of time appalls me, though my father seems to regard it with tranquillity. Even my father, who sometimes seems to me to have been at home in the world as long as it has lasted, has really lived on this earth only a little longer than I have, in terms of all the time there has been to live in. He has not known a time, any more than I, when automobiles and electric lights did not at least exist. He was not alive when this century started. I will be barely alive — old, old — when it ends. I do not like to think of it. I wish the Lake to be always just a lake, with the safe-swimming floats marking it, and the breakwater and the lights of Tuppertown.

My father has a job, selling for Walker Brothers. This is a firm that sells almost entirely in the country, the back country. Sunshine, Boylesbridge,

Turnaround — that is all his territory. Not Dungannon where we used to live, Dungannon is too near town and my mother is grateful for that. He sells cough medicine, iron tonic, corn plasters, laxatives, pills for female disorders, mouth wash, shampoo, liniment, salves, lemon and orange and raspberry concentrate for making refreshing drinks, vanilla, food colouring, black and green tea, ginger, cloves and other spices, rat poison. He has a song about it, and these two lines:

> And have all linaments and oils,
> For everything from corns to boils. . . .

Not a very funny song, in my mother's opinion. A pedlar's song, and that is what he is, a pedlar knocking at backwoods kitchens. Up until last winter we had our own business, a fox farm. My father raised silver foxes and sold their pelts to the people who make them into capes and coats and muffs. Prices fell, my father hung on hoping they would get better next year, and they fell again, and he hung on one more year and one more and finally it was not possible to hang on any more, we owed everything to the feed company. I have heard my mother explain this, several times, to Mrs. Oliphant who is the only neighbour she talks to. (Mrs. Oliphant also has come down in the world, being a schoolteacher who married the janitor.) We poured all we had into it, my mother says, and we came out with nothing. Many people could say the same thing, these days, but my mother has no time for the national calamity, only ours. Fate has flung us onto a street of poor people (it does not matter that we were poor before, that was a different sort of poverty), and the only way to take this, as she sees it, is with dignity, with bitterness, with no reconciliation. No bathroom with a claw-footed tub and a flush toilet is going to comfort her, nor water on tap and sidewalks past the house and milk in bottles, not even the two movie theatres and the Venus Restaurant and Woolworths so marvellous it has live birds singing in its fan-cooled corners and fish as tiny as fingernails, as bright as moons, swimming in its green tanks. My mother does not care.

In the afternoons she often walks to Simon's Grocery and takes me with her to help carry things. She wears a good dress, navy blue with little flowers, sheer, worn over a navy-blue slip. Also a summer hat of white straw, pushed down on the side of the head, and white shoes I have just whitened on a newspaper on the back steps. I have my hair freshly done in long damp curls which the dry air will fortunately soon loosen, a stiff large hair-ribbon on top of my head. This is entirely different from going out after supper with my father. We have not walked past two houses before I feel we have become objects of universal ridicule. Even the dirty words chalked on the sidewalk are laughing at us. My mother does not seem to notice. She walks serenely like a lady shopping, like a *lady* shopping, past the housewives in loose beltless dresses torn under the arms. With me her creation, wretched curls and flaunting hair bow, scrubbed knees and white socks — all I do not want to be. I loathe even my name when she says it in public, in a voice so high, proud, and ringing, deliberately different from the voice of any other mother on the street.

My mother will sometimes carry home, for a treat, a brick of ice cream — pale Neapolitan; and because we have no refrigerator in our house we wake my brother and eat it at once in the dining room, always darkened by the wall of the house next door. I spoon it up tenderly, leaving the chocolate till last, hoping to have some still to eat when my brother's dish is empty. My mother tries then to imitate the conversations we used to have at Dungannon, going back to our earliest, most leisurely days before my brother was born, when she would give me a little tea and a lot of milk in a cup like hers and we would sit out on the step facing the pump, the lilac tree, the fox pens beyond. She is not able to keep from mentioning those days. "Do you remember when we put you in your sled and Major pulled you?" (Major our dog, that we had to leave with neighbours when we moved.) "Do you remember your sandbox outside the kitchen window?" I pretend to remember far less than I do, wary of being trapped into sympathy or any unwanted emotion.

My mother has headaches. She often has to lie down. She lies on my brother's narrow bed in the little screened porch, shaded by heavy branches. "I look up at that tree and I think I am at home," she says.

"What you need," my father tells her, "is some fresh air and a drive in the country." He means for her to go with him, on his Walker Brothers route.

That is not my mother's idea of a drive in the country.

"Can I come?"

"Your mother might want you for trying on clothes."

"I'm beyond sewing this afternoon," my mother says.

"I'll take her then. Take both of them, give you a rest."

What is there about us that people need to be given a rest from? Never mind. I am glad enough to find my brother and make him go to the toilet and get us both into the car, our knees unscrubbed, my hair unringleted. My father brings from the house his two heavy brown suitcases, full of bottles, and sets them on the back seat. He wears a white shirt, brilliant in the sunlight, a tie, light trousers belonging to his summer suit (his other suit is black, for funerals, and belonged to my uncle before he died), and a creamy straw hat. His salesman's outfit, with pencils clipped in the shirt pocket. He goes back once again, probably to say goodbye to my mother, to ask her if she is sure she doesn't want to come, and hear her say, "No. No thanks, I'm better just to lie here with my eyes closed." Then we are backing out of the driveway with the rising hope of adventure, just the little hope that takes you over the bump into the street, the hot air starting to move, turning into a breeze, the houses growing less and less familiar as we follow the short cut my father knows, the quick way out of town. Yet what is there waiting for us all afternoon but hot hours in stricken farmyards, perhaps a stop at a country store and three ice cream cones or bottles of pop, and my father singing? The one he made up about himself has a title — "The Walker Brothers Cowboy" — and it starts out like this:

Old Ned Fields, he now is dead,
So I am ridin' the route instead. . . .

Who is Ned Fields? The man he has replaced, surely, and if so he really is dead; yet my father's voice is mournful-jolly, making his death some kind of nonsense, a comic calamity. "Wisht I was back on the Rio Grande, plungin' through the dusky sand." My father sings most of the time while driving the car. Even now, heading out of town, crossing the bridge and taking the sharp turn onto the highway, he is humming something, mumbling a bit of a song to himself, just tuning up, really, getting ready to improvise, for out along the highway we pass the Baptist Camp, the Vacation Bible Camp, and he lets loose:

Where are the Baptists, where are the Baptists,
where are all the Baptists today?
They're down in the water, in Lake Huron water,
with their sins all a-gittin' washed away.

My brother takes this for straight truth and gets up on his knees trying to see down to the Lake. "I don't see any Baptists," he says accusingly. "Neither do I, son," says my father. "I told you, they're down in the Lake."

No roads paved when we left the highway. We have to roll up the windows because of dust. The land is flat, scorched, empty. Bush lots at the back of the farms hold shade, black pine-shade like pools nobody can ever get to. We bump up a long lane and at the end of it what could look more unwelcoming, more deserted than the tall unpainted farmhouse with grass growing uncut right up to the front door, green blinds down and a door upstairs opening on nothing but air? Many houses have this door, and I have never yet been able to find out why. I ask my father and he says they are for walking in your sleep. *What?* Well if you happen to be walking in your sleep and you want to step outside. I am offended, seeing too late that he is joking, as usual, but my brother says sturdily, "If they did that they would break their necks."

The nineteen-thirties. How much this kind of farmhouse, this kind of afternoon, seem to me to belong to that one decade in time, just as my father's hat does, his bright flared tie, our car with its wide running board (an Essex, and long past its prime). Cars somewhat like it, many older, none dustier, sit in the farmyards. Some are past running and have their doors pulled off, their seats removed for use on porches. No living things to be seen, chickens or cattle. Except dogs. There are dogs, lying in any kind of shade they can find, dreaming, their lean sides rising and sinking rapidly. They get up when my father opens the car door, he has to speak to them. "Nice boy, there's a boy, nice old boy." They quiet down, go back to their shade. He should know how to quiet animals, he has held desperate foxes with tongs around their necks. One gentling voice for the dogs and another, rousing, cheerful, for calling at doors. "Hello there, Missus, it's the Walker Brothers man and what are you out of today?" A door opens, he disappears. Forbidden to follow, forbidden even to leave the car, we can just wait and wonder what he says. Sometimes trying to make my mother laugh he pretends to be himself in a farm kitchen, spreading out his sample case. "Now then, Missus, are you troubled with parasitic life? Your children's scalps, I mean. All those crawly little things we're too polite to mention that show up on the heads of the best of families? Soap alone is useless, kerosene is not too nice a perfume, but I have here — " Or else,

"Believe me, sitting and driving all day the way I do I *know* the value of these fine pills. Natural relief. A problem common to old folks, too, once their days of activity are over — How about you, Grandma?" He would wave the imaginary box of pills under my mother's nose and she would laugh finally, unwillingly. "He doesn't say that really, does he?" I said, and she said no of course not, he was too much of a gentleman.

One yard after another, then, the old cars, the pumps, dogs, views of grey barns and falling-down sheds and unturning windmills. The men, if they are working in the fields, are not in any fields that we can see. The children are far away, following dry creek beds or looking for blackberries, or else they are hidden in the house, spying at us through cracks in the blinds. The car seat has grown slick with our sweat. I dare my brother to sound the horn, wanting to do it myself but not wanting to get the blame. He knows better. We play *I Spy,* but it is hard to find many colours. Grey for the barns and sheds and toilets and houses, brown for the yard and fields, black or brown for the dogs. The rusting cars show rainbow patches, in which I strain to pick out purple or green; likewise I peer at doors for shreds of old peeling paint, maroon or yellow. We can't play with letters, which would be better, because my brother is too young to spell. The game disintegrates anyway. He claims my colours are not fair, and wants extra turns.

In one house no door opens, though the car is in the yard. My father knocks and whistles, calls, "Hullo there! Walker Brothers man!" but there is not a stir of reply anywhere. This house has no porch, just a bare, slanting slab of cement on which my father stands. He turns around, searching the barnyard, the barn whose mow must be empty because you can see the sky through it, and finally he bends to pick up his suitcases. Just then a window is opened upstairs, a white pot appears on the sill, is tilted over and its contents splash down the outside wall. The window is not directly above my father's head, so only a stray splash would catch him. He picks up his suitcases with no particular hurry and walks, no longer whistling, to the car. "Do you know what that was?" I say to my brother. "*Pee.*" He laughs and laughs.

My father rolls and lights a cigarette before he starts the car. The window has been slammed down, the blind drawn, we never did see a hand or face. "Pee, pee," sings my brother ecstatically. "Somebody dumped down pee!" "Just don't tell your mother that," my father says. "She isn't liable to see the joke." "Is it in your song?" my brother wants to know. My father says no but he will see what he can do to work it in.

I notice in a little while that we are not turning in any more lanes, though it does not seem to me that we are headed home. "Is this the way to Sunshine?" I ask my father, and he answers, "No ma'am it's not." "Are we still in your territory?" He shakes his head. "We're going *fast*," my brother says approvingly, and in fact we are bouncing along through dry puddle-holes so that all the bottles in the suitcases clink together and gurgle promisingly.

Another lane, a house, also unpainted, dried to silver in the sun.

"I thought we were out of your territory."

"We are."

"Then what are we going in here for?"

"You'll see."

In front of the house a short, sturdy woman is picking up washing, which had been spread on the grass to bleach and dry. When the car stops she stares at it hard for a moment, bends to pick up a couple more towels to add to the bundle under her arm, comes across to us, and says in a flat voice, neither welcoming nor unfriendly, "Have you lost your way?"

My father takes his time getting out of the car. "I don't think so," he says. "I'm the Walker Brothers man."

"George Golley is our Walker Brothers man," the woman says, "and he was out here no more than a week ago. Oh, my Lord God," she says harshly, "it's you."

"It was, the last time I looked in the mirror," my father says. The woman gathers all the towels in front of her and holds on to them tightly, pushing them against her stomach as if it hurt. "Of all the people I never thought to see. And telling me you were the Walker Brothers man."

"I'm sorry if you were looking forward to George Golley," my father says humbly.

"And look at me, I was prepared to clean the hen-house. You'll think that's just an excuse but it's true. I don't go round looking like this every day." She is wearing a farmer's straw hat, through which pricks of sunlight penetrate and float on her face, a loose, dirty print smock, and running shoes. "Who are those in the car, Ben? They're not yours?"

"Well I hope and believe they are," my father says, and tells our names and ages. "Come on, you can get out. This is Nora, Miss Cronin. Nora, you better tell me, is it still Miss, or have you got a husband hiding in the woodshed?"

"If I had a husband that's not where I'd keep him, Ben," she says, and they both laugh, her laugh abrupt and somewhat angry. "You'll think I got no manners, as well as being dressed like a tramp," she says. "Come on in out of the sun. It's cool in the house."

We go across the yard ("Excuse me taking you in this way but I don't think the front door has been opened since Papa's funeral, I'm afraid the hinges might drop off"), up the porch steps, into the kitchen, which really is cool, high ceilinged, the blinds of course down, a simple, clean, threadbare room with waxed worn linoleum, potted geraniums, drinking-pail and dipper, a round table with scrubbed oilcloth. In spite of the cleanness, the wiped and swept surfaces, there is a faint sour smell — maybe of the dishrag or the tin dipper or the oilcloth, or the old lady, because there is one, sitting in an easy chair under the clock shelf. She turns her head slightly in our direction and says, "Nora? Is that company?"

"Blind," says Nora in a quick explaining voice to my father. Then, "You won't guess who it is, Momma. Hear his voice."

My father goes to the front of her chair and bends and says hopefully, "Afternoon, Mrs. Cronin."

"Ben Jordan," says the old lady with no surprise. "You haven't been to see us in the longest time. Have you been out of the country?"

My father and Nora look at each other.

"He's married, Momma," says Nora cheerfully and aggressively. "Married and got two children and here they are." She pulls us forward, makes each of us touch the old lady's dry, cool hand while she says our names in turn. Blind! This is the first blind person I have ever seen close up. Her eyes are closed, the eyelids sunk away down, showing no shape of the eyeball, just hollows. From one hollow comes a drop of silver liquid, a medicine, or a miraculous tear.

"Let me get into a decent dress," Nora says. "Talk to Momma. It's a treat for her. We hardly ever see company, do we Momma?"

"Not many makes it out this road," says the old lady placidly. "And the ones that used to be around here, our old neighbours, some of them have pulled out."

"True everywhere," my father says.

"Where's your wife then?"

"Home. She's not too fond of the hot weather, makes her feel poorly."

"Well." This is a habit of country people, old people, to say "well," meaning, "is that so?" with a little extra politeness and concern.

Nora's dress, when she appears again — stepping heavily on Cuban heels down the stairs in the hall — is flowered more lavishly than anything my mother owns, green and yellow on brown, some sort of floating sheer crepe, leaving her arms bare. Her arms are heavy, and every bit of her skin you can see is covered with little dark freckles like measles. Her hair is short, black, coarse, and curly, her teeth very white and strong. "It's the first time I knew there was such a thing as green poppies," my father says, looking at her dress.

"You would be surprised all the things you never knew," says Nora, sending a smell of cologne far and wide when she moves and displaying a change of voice to go with the dress, something more sociable and youthful. "They're not poppies anyway, they're just flowers. You go and pump me some good cold water and I'll make these children a drink." She gets down from the cupboard a bottle of Walker Brothers Orange syrup.

"You telling me you were the Walker Brothers man!"

"It's the truth, Nora. You go and look at my sample cases in the car if you don't believe me. I got the territory directly south of here."

"Walker Brothers? Is that a fact? You selling for Walker Brothers?"

"Yes ma'am."

"We always heard you were raising foxes over Dungannon way."

"That's what I was doing, but I kind of run out of luck in that business."

"So where're you living? How long've you been out selling?"

"We moved into Tuppertown. I been at it, oh, two, three months. It keeps the wolf from the door. Keeps him as far away as the back fence."

Nora laughs. "Well I guess you count yourself lucky to have the work. Isabel's husband in Brantford, he was out of work the longest time. I thought if he didn't find something soon I was going to have them all land in here to feed, and I tell you I was hardly looking forward to it. It's all I can manage with me and Momma."

"Isabel married," my father says. "Muriel married too?"

"No, she's teaching school out west. She hasn't been home for five years.

I guess she finds something better to do with her holidays. I would if I was her." She gets some snapshots out of the table drawer and starts showing him. "That's Isabel's oldest boy, starting school. That's the baby sitting in her carriage. Isabel and her husband. Muriel. That's her roommate with her. That's a fellow she used to go around with, and his car. He was working in a bank out there. That's her school, it has eight rooms. She teaches Grade Five." My father shakes his head. "I can't think of her any way but when she was going to school, so shy I used to pick her up on the road — I'd be on my way to see you — and she would not say one word, not even agree it was a nice day."

"She's got over that."

"Who are you talking about?" says the old lady.

"Muriel. I said she's got over being shy."

"She was here last summer."

"No Momma that was Isabel. Isabel and her family were here last summer. Muriel's out west."

"I meant Isabel."

Shortly after this the old lady falls asleep, her head on the side, her mouth open. "Excuse her manners," Nora says. "It's old age." She fixes an afghan over her mother and says we can all go into the front room where our talking won't disturb her.

"You two," my father says. "Do you want to go outside and amuse yourselves?"

Amuse ourselves how? Anyway I want to stay. The front room is more interesting than the kitchen, though barer. There is a gramophone and a pump organ and a picture on the wall of Mary, Jesus' mother — I know that much — in shades of bright blue and pink with a spiked band of light around her head. I know that such pictures are found only in the homes of Roman Catholics and so Nora must be one. We have never known any Roman Catholics at all well, never well enough to visit in their houses. I think of what my grandmother and my Aunt Tena, over in Dungannon, used to always say to indicate that somebody was a Catholic. *So-and-so digs with the wrong foot,* they would say. *She digs with the wrong foot.* That was what they would say about Nora.

Nora takes a bottle, half full, out of the top of the organ and pours some of what is in it into the two glasses that she and my father have emptied of the orange drink.

"Keep it in case of sickness?" my father says.

"Not on your life," says Nora. "I'm never sick. I just keep it because I keep it. One bottle does me a fair time, though, because I don't care for drinking alone. Here's luck!" She and my father drink and I know what it is. Whisky. One of the things my mother has told me in our talks together is that my father never drinks whisky. But I see he does. He drinks whisky and he talks of people whose names I have never heard before. But after a while he turns to a familiar incident. He tells about the chamberpot that was emptied out the window. "Picture me there," he says, "hollering my heartiest. *Oh, lady, it's your Walker Brothers man, anybody home?*" He does himself hollering, grinning absurdly, waiting, looking up in pleased expectation, and then — oh, ducking, covering his head with his arms, looking as if he begged for mercy (when he never did anything like that, I was watching), and Nora laughs, almost as hard as my brother did at the time.

"That isn't true! That's not a word true!"

"Oh, indeed it is ma'am. We have our heroes in the ranks of Walker Brothers. I'm glad you think it's funny," he says sombrely.

I ask him shyly, "Sing the song."

"What song? Have you turned into a singer on top of everything else?"

Embarrassed, my father says, "Oh, just this song I made up while I was driving around, it gives me something to do, making up rhymes."

But after some urging he does sing it, looking at Nora with a droll, apologetic expression, and she laughs so much that in places he has to stop and wait for her to get over laughing so he can go on, because she makes him laugh too. Then he does various parts of his salesman's spiel. Nora when she laughs squeezes her large bosom under her folded arms. "You're crazy," she says. "That's all you are." She sees my brother peering into the gramophone and she jumps up and goes over to him. "Here's us sitting enjoying ourselves and not giving you a thought, isn't it terrible?" she says. "You want me to put a record on, don't you? You want to hear a nice record? Can you dance? I bet your sister can, can't she?"

I say no. "A big girl like you and so good-looking and can't dance!" says Nora. "It's high time you learned. I bet you'd make a lovely dancer. Here, I'm going to put on a piece I used to dance to and even your daddy did, in his dancing days. You didn't know your daddy was a dancer, did you? Well, he is a talented man, your daddy!"

She puts down the lid and takes hold of me unexpectedly around the waist, picks up my other hand and starts making me go backwards. "This is the way, now, this is how they dance. Follow me. This foot, see. One and one-two. One and one-two. That's fine, that's lovely, don't look at your feet! Follow me, that's right, see how easy? You're going to be a lovely dancer! One and one-two. One and one-two. Ben, see your daughter dancing!" *Whispering while you cuddle near me. Whispering where no one can hear me. . . .*

Round and round the linoleum, me proud, intent, Nora laughing and moving with great buoyancy, wrapping me in her strange gaiety, her smell of whisky, cologne, and sweat. Under the arms her dress is damp, and little drops form along her upper lip, hang in the soft black hairs at the corners of her mouth. She whirls me around in front of my father — causing me to stumble, for I am by no means so swift a pupil as she pretends — and lets me go, breathless.

"Dance with me, Ben."

"I'm the world's worst dancer, Nora, and you know it."

"I certainly never thought so."

"You would now."

She stands in front of him, arms hanging loose and hopeful, her breasts, which a moment ago embarrassed me with their warmth and bulk, rising and falling under her loose flowered dress, her face shining with the exercise, and delight.

"Ben."

My father drops his head and says quietly, "Not me, Nora."

So she can only go and take the record off. "I can drink alone but I can't dance alone," she says. "Unless I am a whole lot crazier than I think I am."

"Nora," says my father smiling. "You're not crazy."

"Stay for supper."

"Oh, no. We couldn't put you to the trouble."

"It's no trouble. I'd be glad of it."

"And their mother would worry. She'd think I'd turned us over in a ditch."

"Oh, well. Yes."

"We've taken a lot of your time now."

"Time." says Nora bitterly. "Will you come by ever again."

"I will if I can," says my father.

"Bring the children. Bring your wife."

"Yes I will," says my father. "I will if I can."

When she follows us to the car he says, "You come to see us too, Nora. We're right on Grove Street, left-hand side going in, that's north, and two doors this side — east — of Baker Street."

Nora does not repeat these directions. She stands close to the car in her soft, brilliant dress. She touches the fender, making an unintelligible mark in the dust there.

On the way home my father does not buy any ice cream or pop, but he does go into a country store to get a package of licorice, which he shares with us. *She digs with the wrong foot,* I think, and the words seem sad to me as never before, dark, perverse. My father does not say anything to me about not mentioning things at home, but I know, just from the thoughtfulness, the pause when he passes the licorice, that there are things not to be mentioned. The whisky, maybe the dancing. No worry about my brother, he does not notice enough. At most he might remember the blind lady, the picture of Mary.

"Sing," my brother commands my father, but my father says gravely, "I don't know, I seem to be fresh out of songs. You watch the road and let me know if you see any rabbits."

So my father drives and my brother watches the road for rabbits and I feel my father's life flowing back from our car in the last of the afternoon, darkening and turning strange, like a landscape that has an enchantment on it, making it kindly, ordinary, and familiar while you are looking at it, but changing it, once your back is turned, into something you will never know, with all kinds of weathers, and distances you cannot imagine.

When we get closer to Tuppertown the sky becomes gently overcast, as always, nearly always, on summer evenings by the Lake.

છ૭

JOYCE CAROL OATES (b. 1938) was born in Lockport, New York, one of three children in a Roman Catholic family. She began to put picture stories down on paper even before she could write, and she remembers that her parents "dutifully"

*supplied her with lined tablets and gave her a typewriter when she was fourteen. In
1956, after Oates graduated from high school, she went on a scholarship to major in
English at Syracuse University, but she did not devote most of her time to writing until after she received her M.A. from the University of Wisconsin in 1961. Discovering
by chance that one of her stories had been cited in the honor roll of Martha Foley's annual* The Best American Short Stories, *Oates assembled the fourteen stories in her
first book,* By the North Gate *(1963). Her career was launched, and as John Updike
has speculated, she "was perhaps born a hundred years too late; she needs a lustier audience, a race of Victorian word-eaters to be worthy of her astounding productivity,
her tireless gift of self-enthrallment."*

*One of our most prolific authors, Oates has published almost seventy books, in-
cluding over a hundred stories. Recent collections of stories are* Raven's Wing *(1986)
and* The Assignation *(1988); the same year she published the essays in* (Woman)
Writer: Occasions and Opportunities. *Oates also writes poetry and literary criticism.* New Heaven, New Earth *(1974), analyzes the "visionary experience in literature" as exemplified in the work of Henry James, Virginia Woolf, Franz Kafka, D. H.
Lawrence, Flannery O'Connor, and others. As a writer, critic, and professor at Princeton University, she dedicates her life to "promoting and exploring literature. . . . I am
not conscious of being in any particular literary tradition, though I share with my
contemporaries an intense interest in the formal aspects of writing; each of my books
is an experiment of a kind, an investigation of the relationship between a certain consciousness and its formal aesthetic expression."*

*The story "Where Are You Going, Where Have You Been?" was first published
in* Epoch *in 1966; it was included in* The Best American Short Stories *of 1967 and*
Prize Stories: The O. Henry Awards 1968 *and was made into a film. Oates has said
that this story, based on an article in* Life *magazine about a Tucson, Arizona, murderer, has been "constantly misunderstood by one generation, and intuitively understood by another." She sees the story as dealing with a human being "struggling
heroically to define personal identity in the face of incredible opposition, even in the
face of death itself." The story "Heat," which recalls Katherine Anne Porter's "He," is
from her recent collection* Heat and Other Stories *(1992). Her latest collection is*
Haunted: Tales of the Grotesque *(1994), the same year she published the novel*
Foxfire: Confessions of a Girl Gang.

RELATED STORY: *Katherine Anne Porter, "He," page 601.*

JOYCE CAROL OATES

Heat

1991

It was midsummer, the heat rippling above the macadam roads. Cicadas
screaming out of the trees and the sky like pewter, glaring.

The days were the same day, like the shallow mud-brown river moving
always in the same direction but so slow you couldn't see it. Except for Sunday: church in the morning, then the fat Sunday newspaper, the color comics
and newsprint on your fingers.

Rhea and Rhoda Kunkel went flying on their rusted old bicycles, down the long hill toward the railroad yard, Whipple's Ice, the scrubby pastureland where dairy cows grazed. They'd stolen six dollars from their own grandmother who loved them. They were eleven years old, they were identical twins, they basked in their power.

Rhea and Rhoda Kunkel: it was always Rhea-and-Rhoda, never Rhoda-and-Rhea, I couldn't say why. You just wouldn't say the names that way. Not even the teachers at school would say them that way.

We went to see them in the funeral parlor where they were waked, we were made to. The twins in twin caskets, white, smooth, gleaming, perfect as plastic, with white satin lining puckered like the inside of a fancy candy box. And the waxy white lilies, and the smell of talcum powder and perfume. The room was crowded, there was only one way in and out.

Rhea and Rhoda were the same girl, they'd wanted it that way.

Only looking from one to the other could you see they were two.

The heat was gauzy, you had to push your way through like swimming. On their bicycles Rhea and Rhoda flew through it hardly noticing, from their grandmother's place on Main Street to the end of South Main where the paved road turned to gravel leaving town. That was the summer before seventh grade, when they died. Death was coming for them but they didn't know.

They thought the same thoughts sometimes at the same moment, had the same dream and went all day trying to remember it, bringing it back like something you'd be hauling out of the water on a tangled line. We watched them, we were jealous. None of us had a twin. Sometimes they were serious and sometimes, remembering, they shrieked and laughed like they were being killed. They stole things out of desks and lockers but if you caught them they'd hand them right back, it was like a game.

There were three floor fans in the funeral parlor that I could see, tall whirring fans with propellor blades turning fast to keep the warm air moving. Strange little gusts came from all directions making your eyes water. By this time Roger Whipple was arrested, taken into police custody. No one had hurt him. He would never stand trial, he was ruled mentally unfit, he would never be released from confinement.

He died there, in the state psychiatric hospital, years later, and was brought back home to be buried, the body of him I mean. His earthly remains.

Rhea and Rhoda Kunkel were buried in the same cemetery, the First Methodist. The cemetery is just a field behind the church.

In the caskets the dead girls did not look like anyone we knew really. They were placed on their backs with their eyes closed, and their mouths, the way you don't always in life when you're sleeping. Their faces were too small. Every eyelash showed, too perfect. Like angels everyone was saying and it was strange it was *so*. I stared and stared.

What had been done to them, the lower parts of them, didn't show in the caskets.

Roger Whipple worked for his father at Whipple's Ice. In the newspaper it stated he was nineteen, he'd gone to DeWitt Clinton until he was sixteen, my mother's friend Sadie taught there and remembered him from the special education class. A big slow sweet-faced boy with these big hands and feet, thighs like hams. A shy gentle boy with good manners and a hushed voice.

He wasn't simpleminded exactly, like the others in that class. He was watchful, he held back.

Roger Whipple in overalls squatting in the rear of his father's truck, one of his older brothers drove. There would come the sound of the truck in the driveway, the heavy block of ice smelling of cold, ice tongs over his shoulder. He was strong, round-shouldered like an older man. Never staggered or grunted. Never dropped anything. Pale washed-looking eyes lifting out of a big face, a soft mouth wanting to smile. We giggled and looked away. They said he'd never been the kind to hurt even an animal, all the Whipples swore.

Sucking ice, the cold goes straight into your jaws and deep into the bone.

People spoke of them as the Kunkel twins. Mostly nobody tried to tell them apart. Homely corkscrew-twisty girls you wouldn't know would turn up so quiet and solemn and almost beautiful, perfect little dolls' faces with the freckles powdered over, touches of rouge on the cheeks and mouths. I was tempted to whisper to them, kneeling by the coffins. Hey Rhea! Hey Rhoda! Wake *up!*

They had loud slip-sliding voices that were the same voice. They weren't shy. They were always first in line. One behind you and one in front of you and you'd better be wary of some trick. Flamey-orange hair and the bleached-out skin that goes with it, freckles like dirty raindrops splashed on their faces. Sharp green eyes they'd bug out until you begged them to stop.

Places meant to be serious, Rhea and Rhoda had a hard time sitting still. In church, in school, a sideways glance between them could do it. Jamming their knuckles into their mouths, choking back giggles. Sometimes laughing escaped through their fingers like steam hissing. Sometimes it came out like snorting and then none of us could hold back. The worst time was in assembly, the principal up there telling us that Miss Flagler had died, we would all miss her. Tears shining in the woman's eyes behind her goggle-glasses and one of the twins gave a breathless little snort, you could feel it like flames running down the whole row of girls, none of us could hold back.

Sometimes the word "tickle" was enough to get us going, just that word.

I never dreamt about Rhea and Rhoda so strange in their caskets sleeping out in the middle of a room where people could stare at them, shed tears and pray over them. I never dream about actual things, only things I don't know. Places I've never been, people I've never seen. Sometimes the person I am in the dream isn't me. Who it is, I don't know.

Rhea and Rhoda bounced up the drive behind. Whipple's Ice. They were laughing like crazy and didn't mind the potholes jarring their teeth, or the clouds of dust. If they'd had the same dream the night before, the hot sunlight erased it entirely.

When death comes for you you sometimes know and sometimes don't.

Roger Whipple was by himself in the barn, working. Kids went down there to beg him for ice to suck or throw around or they'd tease him, not out of meanness but for something to do. It was slow, the days not changing in the summer, heat sometimes all night long. He was happy with children that age, he was that age himself in his head, sixth grade learning abilities as the newspaper stated though he could add and subtract quickly. Other kinds of arithmetic gave him trouble.

People were saying afterward he'd always been strange. Watchful like he was, those thick soft lips. The Whipples did wrong, to let him run loose.

They said he'd always been a good gentle boy, went to Sunday school and sat still there and never gave anybody any trouble. He collected Bible cards, he hid them away under his mattress for safekeeping. Mr. Whipple started in early, disciplining him the way you might discipline a big dog or a horse. Not letting the creature know he has any power to be himself exactly. Not giving him the opportunity to test his will.

Neighbors said the Whipples worked him like a horse in fact. The older brothers were the most merciless. And why they all wore coveralls, heavy denim and long legs on days so hot, nobody knew. The thermometer above the First Midland Bank read 98°F. on noon of that day, my mother said.

Nights afterward my mother would hug me before I went to bed. Pressing my face hard against her breasts and whispering things I didn't hear, like praying to Jesus to love and protect *her* little girl and keep *her* from harm but I didn't hear, I shut my eyes tight and endured it. Sometimes we prayed together, all of us or just my mother and me kneeling by my bed. Even then I knew she was a good mother, there was this girl she loved as her daughter that was me and loved more than that girl deserved. There was nothing I could do about it.

Mrs. Kunkel would laugh and roll her eyes over the twins. In that house they were "double trouble" — you'd hear it all the time like a joke on the radio that keeps coming back. I wonder did she pray with them too. I wonder would they let her.

In the long night you forget about the day, it's like the other side of the world. Then the sun is there, and the heat. You forget.

We were running through the field behind school, a place where people dumped things sometimes and there was a dead dog there, a collie with beautiful fur but his eyes were gone from the sockets and the maggots had got him where somebody tried to lift him with her foot and when Rhea and Rhoda saw they screamed a single scream and hid their eyes.

They did nice things — gave their friends candy bars, nail polish, some novelty key chains they'd taken from somewhere, movie stars' pictures framed in plastic. In the movies they'd share a box of popcorn not noticing where one or the other of them left off and a girl who wasn't any sister of theirs sat.

Once they made me strip off my clothes where we'd crawled under the Kunkel's veranda. This was a large hollowed-out space where the earth dropped away at one end, you could sit without bumping your head, it was cool and smelled of dirt and stone. Rhea said all of a sudden, Strip! and Rhoda said at once, Strip! — come on! So it happened. They wouldn't let me out unless I took off my clothes, my shirt and shorts, yes and my panties too. Come *on* they said whispering and giggling, they were blocking the way out so I had no choice. I was scared but I was laughing too. This is to show our power over you, they said. But they stripped too just like me.

You have power over others you don't realize until you test it.

Under the Kunkels' veranda we stared at each other but we didn't touch each other. My teeth chattered because what if somebody saw us? Some boy, or Mrs. Kunkel herself? I was scared but I was happy too. Except for our faces, their face and mine, we could all be the same girl.

The Kunkel family lived in one side of a big old clapboard house by the river, you could hear the trucks rattling on the bridge, shifting their noisy gears on the hill. Mrs. Kunkel had eight children, Rhea and Rhoda were the youngest. Our mothers wondered why Mrs. Kunkel had let herself go — she had a moon-shaped pretty face but her hair was frizzed ratty, she must have weighed two hundred pounds, sweated and breathed so hard in the warm weather. They'd known her in school. Mr. Kunkel worked construction for the county. Summer evenings after work he'd be sitting on the veranda drinking beer, flicking cigarette butts out into the yard, you'd be fooled almost thinking they were fireflies. He went barechested in the heat, his upper body dark like stained wood. Flat little purplish nipples inside his chest hair the girls giggled to see. Mr. Kunkel teased us all, he'd mix Rhea and Rhoda up the way he'd mix the rest of us up like it was too much trouble to keep names straight.

Mr. Kunkel was in police custody, he didn't even come to the wake. Mrs. Kunkel was there in rolls of chin fat that glistened with sweat and tears, the makeup on her face was caked and discolored so you were embarrassed to look. It scared me, the way she grabbed me as soon as my parents and I came in. Hugging me against her big balloon breasts sobbing and all the strength went out of me, I couldn't push away.

The police had Mr. Kunkel, for his own good they said. He'd gone to the Whipples, though the murderer had been taken away, saying he would kill anybody he could get his hands on, the old man, the brothers. They were all responsible he said, his little girls were dead. Tear them apart with his bare hands he said but he had a tire iron.

Did it mean anything special, or was it just an accident, Rhea and Rhoda had taken six dollars from their grandmother an hour before? Because death was coming for them, it had to happen one way or another.

If you believe in God you believe that. And if you don't believe in God it's obvious.

Their grandmother lived upstairs over a shoe store downtown, an apartment looking out on Main Street. They'd bicycle down there for something to do and she'd give them grape juice or lemonade and try to keep them a while, a lonely old lady but she was nice, she was always nice to me, it was kind of nasty of Rhea and Rhoda to steal from her but they were like that. One was in the kitchen talking with her and without any plan or anything the other went to use the bathroom then slipped into her bedroom, got the money out of her purse like it was something she did every day of the week, that easy. On the stairs going down to the street Rhoda whispered to Rhea what did you *do?* knowing Rhea had done something she hadn't ought to have done but not knowing what it was or anyway how much money it was. They started in poking each other, trying to hold the giggles back until they were safe away.

On their bicycles they stood high on the pedals, coasting, going down the hill but not using their brakes. *What did you do! Oh what did you do!*

Rhea and Rhoda always said they could never be apart. If one didn't know exactly where the other was that one could die. Or the other could die. Or both.

Once they'd gotten some money from somewhere, they wouldn't say where, and paid for us all to go to the movies. And ice cream afterward too.

You could read the newspaper articles twice through and still not know what he did. Adults talked about it for a long time but not so we could hear. I thought probably he'd used an ice pick. Or maybe I heard somebody guess that who didn't know any more than me.

We liked it that Rhea and Rhoda had been killed, and all the stuff in the paper, and everybody talking about it, but we didn't like it that they were dead, we missed them.

Later, in the tenth grade, the Kaufmann twins moved into our school district. Doris and Diane. But it wasn't the same thing.

Roger Whipple said he didn't remember any of it. Whatever he did, he didn't remember. At first everybody thought he was lying then they had to accept it as true, or true in some way, doctors from the state hospital examined him. He said over and over he hadn't done anything and he didn't remember the twins there that afternoon but he couldn't explain why their bicycles were where they were at the foot of his stairway and he couldn't explain why he'd taken a bath in the middle of the day. The Whipples admitted that wasn't a practice of Roger's or of any of them, ever, a bath in the middle of the day.

Roger Whipple was a clean boy, though. His hands always scrubbed so you actually noticed, swinging the block of ice off the truck and, inside the kitchen, helping to set it in the ice box. They said he'd go crazy if he got bits of straw under his nails from the ice house or inside his clothes. He'd been taught to shave and he shaved every morning without fail, they said the sight of the beard growing in, the scratchy feel of it, seemed to scare him.

A few years later his sister Linda told us how Roger was built like a horse. She was our age, a lot younger than him, she made a gesture toward her crotch so we'd know what she meant. She'd happened to see him a few times she said, by accident.

There he was squatting in the dust laughing, his head lowered watching Rhea and Rhoda circle him on their bicycles. It was a rough game where the twins saw how close they could come to hitting him, brushing him with the bike fenders and he'd lunge out not seeming to notice if his fingers hit the spokes, it was all happening so fast you maybe wouldn't feel pain. Out back of the ice house where the yard blended in with the yard of the old railroad depot next door that wasn't used any more. It was burning hot in the sun, dust rose in clouds behind the girls. Pretty soon they got bored with the game though Roger Whipple even in his heavy overalls wanted to keep going. He was red-faced with all the excitement, he was a boy who loved to laugh and didn't have much chance. Rhea said she was thirsty, she wanted some ice, so Roger Whipple scrambled right up and went to get a big bag of ice cubes! — he hadn't any more sense than that.

They sucked on the ice cubes and fooled around with them. He was panting and lolling his tongue pretending to be a dog and Rhea and Rhoda cried, Here doggie! Here doggie-doggie! tossing ice cubes at Roger Whipple he tried to catch in his mouth. That went on for a while. In the end the twins just dumped the rest of the ice onto the dirt then Roger Whipple was saying he had some secret things that belonged to his brother Eamon he could show them. Hidden under his bed mattress, would they like to see what the things were?

He wasn't one who could tell Rhea from Rhoda or Rhoda from Rhea. There was a way some of us knew, the freckles on Rhea's face were a little darker than Rhoda's. Rhea's eyes were just a little darker than Rhoda's. But you'd have to see the two side by side with no clowning around to know.

Rhea said okay, she'd like to see the secret things. She let her bike fall where she was straddling it.

Roger Whipple said he could only take one of them upstairs to his room at a time, he didn't say why.

Okay said Rhea. Of the Kunkel twins Rhea always had to be first.

She'd been born first, she said. Weighed a pound or two more.

Roger Whipple's room was in a strange place — on the second floor of the Whipple house above an unheated storage space that had been added after the main part of the house was built. There was a way of getting to the room from the outside, up a flight of rickety wood stairs. That way Roger could get in and out of his room without going through the rest of the house. People said the Whipples had him live there like some animal, they didn't want him tramping through the house but they denied it. The room had an inside door too.

Roger Whipple weighed about one-hundred ninety pounds that day. In the hospital he swelled up like a balloon, people said, bloated from the drugs, his skin was soft and white as bread dough and his hair fell out. He was an old man when he died aged thirty-one.

Exactly why he died, the Whipples never knew. The hospital just told them his heart had stopped in his sleep.

Rhoda shaded her eyes watching her sister running up the stairs with Roger Whipple behind her and felt the first pinch of fear, that something was wrong, or was going to be wrong. She called after them in a whining voice that she wanted to come along too, she didn't want to wait down there all alone, but Rhea just called back to her to be quiet and wait her turn, so Rhoda waited, kicking at the ice cubes melting in the dirt, and after a while she got restless and shouted up to them — the door was shut, the shade on the window was drawn — saying she was going home, damn them she was sick of waiting she said and she was going home. But nobody came to the door or looked out the window, it was like the place was empty. Wasps had built one of those nests that look like mud in layers under the eaves and the only sound was wasps.

Rhoda bicycled toward the road so anybody who was watching would think she was going home, she was thinking she hated Rhea! hated her damn twin sister! wished she was dead and gone, God damn her! She was going home and the first thing she'd tell their mother was that Rhea had stolen six dollars from Grandma: she had it in her pocket right that moment.

The Whipple house was an old farmhouse they'd tried to modernize by putting on red asphalt siding meant to look like brick. Downstairs the rooms were big and drafty, upstairs they were small, some of them unfinished and with bare floorboards, like Roger Whipple's room which people would afterward say based on what the police said was like an animal's pen, nothing in it but a bed shoved into a corner and some furniture and boxes and things Mrs. Whipple stored there.

Of the Whipples — there were seven in the family still living at home — only Mrs. Whipple and her daughter Iris were home that afternoon. They said they hadn't heard a sound except for kids playing in the back, they swore it.

Rhoda was bent on going home and leaving Rhea behind but at the end of the driveway something made her turn her bicycle wheel back . . . so if you were watching you'd think she was just cruising around for something to do, a red-haired girl with whitish skin and freckles, skinny little body, pedaling fast, then slow, then coasting, then fast again, turning and dipping and criss-crossing her path, talking to herself as if she was angry. She hated Rhea! She was furious at Rhea! But feeling sort of scared too and sickish in the pit of her belly knowing that she and Rhea shouldn't be in two places, something might happen to one of them or to both. Some things you know.

So she pedaled back to the house. Laid her bike down in the dirt next to Rhea's. The bikes were old hand-me-downs, the kickstands were broken. But their daddy had put on new Goodyear tires for them at the start of the summer and he'd oiled them too.

You never would see just one of the twins' bicycles anywhere, you always saw both of them laid down on the ground and facing in the same direction with the pedals in about the same position.

Rhoda peered up at the second floor of the house, the shade drawn over the window, the door still closed. She called out Rhea? Hey Rhea? starting up the stairs making a lot of noise so they'd hear her, pulling on the railing as if to break it the way a boy would. Still she was scared. But making noise like that and feeling so disgusted and mad helped her get stronger, and there was Roger Whipple with the door open staring down at her flush-faced and sweaty as if he was scared too. He seemed to have forgotten her. He was wiping his hands on his overalls. He just stared, a lemony light coming up in his eyes.

Afterward he would say he didn't remember anything — didn't remember anything. Big as a grown man but round-shouldered so it was hard to judge how tall he was, or how old. His straw-colored hair falling in his eyes and his fingers twined together as if he was praying or trying with all his strength to keep his hands still. He didn't remember anything about the twins or anything in his room or in the ice house afterward but he cried a lot, he acted scared and guilty and sorry, they decided he shouldn't be put on trial, there was no point to it.

Mrs. Whipple kept to the house afterward, never went out not even to church or grocery shopping. She died of cancer just before Roger died, she'd loved him she said, she always said none of it had been his fault really, he wasn't the kind of boy even to hurt an animal, he'd loved kittens especially and was a good sweet obedient boy and religious too and whatever happened it must have been because those girls were teasing him, he'd had a lifetime of being teased and taunted by children, his heart broken by all the abuse, and something must have snapped that day, that was all.

The Whipples were the ones, though, who called the police. Mr. Whipple found the girls' bodies back in the ice house hidden under some straw and canvas.

He found them around nine that night, with a flashlight. He knew, he said. The way Roger was acting, and the fact the Kunkel girls were missing, word had gotten out. He knew but he didn't know what he knew or what he would find. Roger taking a bath like that in the middle of the day and washing his hair too and shaving for the second time and not answering when his mother spoke to him, just sitting there staring at the floor as if he was listening to something no one else could hear. He knew, Mr. Whipple said. The hardest minute of his life was in the ice house lifting that canvas to see what was under it.

He took it hard too, he never recovered. He hadn't any choice but to think what a lot of people thought — it had been his fault. He was an old-time Methodist, he took all that seriously, but none of it helped him. Believed Jesus Christ was his personal savior and He never stopped loving Roger or turned His face from him and if Roger did truly repent in his heart he would be saved and they would be reunited in Heaven, all the Whipples reunited. He believed, but none of it helped in his life.

The ice house is still there but boarded up and derelict, the Whipples' ice business ended long ago. Strangers live in the house and the yard is littered with rusting hulks of cars and pickup trucks. Some Whipples live scattered around the country but none in town. The old train depot is still there too.

After I'd been married some years I got involved with this man, I won't say his name, his name is not a name I say, but we would meet back there sometimes, back in that old lot that's all weeds and scrub trees. Wild as kids and on the edge of being drunk. I was crazy for this guy, I mean crazy like I could hardly think of anybody but him or anything but the two of us making love the way we did, with him deep inside me I wanted it never to stop just fuck and fuck and fuck I'd whisper to him and this went on for a long time, two or three years then ended the way these things do and looking back on it I'm not able to recognize that woman as if she was someone not even not-me but a crazy woman I would despise, making so much of such a thing, risking her marriage and her kids finding out and her life being ruined for such a thing, my God. The things people do.

It's like living out a story that has to go on its way.

Behind the ice house in his car I'd think of Rhea and Rhoda and what happened that day upstairs in Roger Whipple's room. And the funeral parlor with the twins like dolls laid out and their eyes like dolls' eyes too that shut when you tilt them back. One night when I wasn't asleep but wasn't awake either I saw my parents standing in the doorway of my bedroom watching me and I knew their thoughts, how they were thinking of Rhea and Rhoda and of me their daughter wondering how they could keep me from harm and there was no clear answer.

In his car in his arms I'd feel my mind drift. After we'd made love or at least after the first time. And I saw Rhoda Kunkel hesitating on the stairs a few steps down from Roger Whipple. I saw her white-faced and scared but deciding to keep going anyway, pushing by Roger Whipple to get inside the room, to find Rhea, she had to brush against him where he was standing as if he meant to block her but not having the nerve exactly to block her and he was smelling of his body and breathing hard but not in imitation of any dog now, not with his tongue flopping and lolling to make them laugh. Rhoda was asking where was Rhea? — she couldn't see well at first in the dark little cubbyhole of a room because the sunshine had been so bright outside.

Roger Whipple said Rhea had gone home. His voice sounded scratchy as if it hadn't been used in some time. She'd gone home he said and Rhoda said right away that Rhea wouldn't go home without her and Roger Whipple came toward her saying yes she did, yes she *did* as if he was getting angry she wouldn't believe him. Rhoda was calling, Rhea? Where are you? Stumbling against something on the floor tangled with the bedclothes.

Behind her was this big boy saying again and again yes she did, yes she *did*, his voice rising but it would never get loud enough so that anyone would hear and come save her.

I wasn't there, but some things you know.

JOYCE CAROL OATES

Where Are You Going, Where Have You Been?   *1966*

For Bob Dylan

Her name was Connie. She was fifteen and she had a quick nervous giggling habit of craning her neck to glance into mirrors, or checking other people's faces to make sure her own was all right. Her mother, who noticed everything and knew everything and who hadn't much reason any longer to look at her own face, always scolded Connie about it. "Stop gawking at yourself, who are you? You think you're so pretty?" she would say. Connie would raise her eyebrows at these familiar complaints and look right through her mother, into a shadowy vision of herself as she was right at that moment: she knew she was pretty and that was everything. Her mother had been pretty once too, if you could believe those old snapshots in the album, but now her looks were gone and that was why she was always after Connie.

"Why don't you keep your room clean like your sister? How've you got your hair fixed — what the hell stinks? Hair spray? You don't see your sister using that junk."

Her sister June was twenty-four and still lived at home. She was a secretary in the high school Connie attended, and if that wasn't bad enough — with her in the same building — she was so plain and chunky and steady that Connie had to hear her praised all the time by her mother and her mother's sisters. June did this, June did that, she saved money and helped clean the house and cooked and Connie couldn't do a thing, her mind was all filled with trashy daydreams. Their father was away at work most of the time and when he came home he wanted supper and he read the newspaper at supper and after supper he went to bed. He didn't bother talking much to them, but around his bent head Connie's mother kept picking at her until Connie wished her mother was dead and she herself was dead and it was all over. "She makes me want to throw up sometimes," she complained to her friends. She had a high, breathless, amused voice which made everything she said a little forced, whether it was sincere or not.

There was one good thing: June went places with girl friends of hers, girls who were just as plain and steady as she, and so when Connie wanted to do that her mother had no objections. The father of Connie's best girl friend drove the girls the three miles to town and left them off at a shopping plaza, so that they could walk through the stores or go to a movie, and when he came to pick them up again at eleven he never bothered to ask what they had done.

They must have been familiar sights, walking around that shopping plaza in their shorts and flat ballerina slippers that always scuffed the sidewalk, with charm bracelets jingling on their thin wrists; they would lean together to whisper and laugh secretly if someone passed by who amused or interested them. Connie had long dark blond hair that drew anyone's eye to it, and she wore part of it pulled up on her head and puffed out and the rest of it she let fall down her back. She wore a pullover jersey blouse that looked one way when she was at home and another way when she was away from home. Everything about her had two sides to it, one for home and one for anywhere that was not home: her walk that could be childlike and bobbing, or languid enough to make anyone think she was hearing music in her head, her mouth which was pale and smirking most of the time, but bright and pink on these evenings out, her laugh which was cynical and drawling at home — "Ha, ha, very funny" — but high-pitched and nervous anywhere else, like the jingling of the charms on her bracelet.

Sometimes they did go shopping or to a movie, but sometimes they went across the highway, ducking fast across the busy road, to a drive-in restaurant where older kids hung out. The restaurant was shaped like a big bottle, though squatter than a real bottle, and on its cap was a revolving figure of a grinning boy who held a hamburger aloft. One night in midsummer they ran across, breathless with daring, and right away someone leaned out a car window and invited them over, but it was just a boy from high school they didn't like. It made them feel good to be able to ignore him. They went up through the maze of parked and cruising cars to the bright-lit, fly-infested restaurant, their faces pleased and expectant as if they were entering a sacred building that loomed out of the night to give them what haven and what blessing they yearned for. They sat at the counter and crossed their legs at the ankles, their thin shoulders rigid with excitement and listened to the music that made everything so good: the music was always in the background like music at a church service, it was something to depend upon.

A boy named Eddie came in to talk with them. He sat backwards on his stool, turning himself jerkily around in semi-circles and then stopping and turning again, and after a while he asked Connie if she would like something to eat. She said she did and so she tapped her friend's arm on her way out — her friend pulled her face up into a brave droll look — and Connie said she would meet her at eleven, across the way. "I just hate to leave her like that," Connie said earnestly, but the boy said that she wouldn't be alone for long. So they went out to his car and on the way Connie couldn't help but let her eyes wander over the windshields and faces all around her, her face gleaming with the joy that had nothing to do with Eddie or even this place; it might have been the music. She drew her shoulders up and sucked in her breath with the pure pleasure of being alive, and just at that moment she happened to glance at a face just a few feet from hers. It was a boy with shaggy black hair, in a convertible jalopy painted gold. He stared at her and then his lips widened into a grin. Connie slit her eyes at him and turned away, but she couldn't help glancing back and there he was still watching her. He wagged a finger and laughed and said, "Gonna get you, baby," and Connie turned away again without Eddie noticing anything.

She spent three hours with him, at the restaurant where they ate hamburgers and drank Cokes in wax cups that were always sweating, and then down an alley a mile or so away, and when he left her off at five to eleven only the movie house was still open at the plaza. Her girl friend was there, talking with a boy. When Connie came up the two girls smiled at each other and Connie said, "How was the movie?" and the girl said, "*You* should know." They rode off with the girl's father, sleepy and pleased, and Connie couldn't help but look at the darkened shopping plaza with its big empty parking lot and its signs that were faded and ghostly now, and over at the drive-in restaurant where cars were still circling tirelessly. She couldn't hear the music at this distance.

Next morning June asked her how the movie was and Connie said, "So-so."

She and that girl and occasionally another girl went out several times a week that way, and the rest of the time Connie spent around the house — it was summer vacation — getting in her mother's way and thinking, dreaming, about the boys she met. But all the boys fell back and dissolved into a single face that was not even a face, but an idea, a feeling, mixed up with the urgent insistent pounding of the music and the humid night air of July. Connie's mother kept dragging her back to the daylight by finding things for her to do or saying suddenly, "What's this about the Pettinger girl?"

And Connie would say nervously, "Oh, her. That dope." She always drew thick clear lines between herself and such girls, and her mother was simple and kindly enough to believe her. Her mother was so simple, Connie thought, that it was maybe cruel to fool her so much. Her mother went scuffling around the house in old bedroom slippers and complained over the telephone to one sister about the other, then the other called up and the two of them complained about the third one. If June's name was mentioned her mother's tone was approving, and if Connie's name was mentioned it was disapproving. This did not really mean she disliked Connie and actually Connie thought that her mother preferred her to June because she was prettier, but the two of them kept up a pretense of exasperation, a sense that they were tugging and struggling over something of little value to either of them. Sometimes, over coffee, they were almost friends, but something would come up — some vexation that was like a fly buzzing suddenly around their heads — and their faces went hard with contempt.

One Sunday Connie got up at eleven — none of them bothered with church — and washed her hair so that it could dry all day long, in the sun. Her parents and sister were going to a barbecue at an aunt's house and Connie said no, she wasn't interested, rolling her eyes, to let mother know just what she thought of it. "Stay home alone then," her mother said sharply. Connie sat out back in a lawn chair and watched them drive away, her father quiet and bald, hunched around so that he could back the car out, her mother with a look that was still angry and not at all softened through the windshield, and in the back seat poor old June all dressed up as if she didn't know what a barbecue was, with all the running yelling kids and the flies. Connie sat with her eyes closed in the sun, dreaming and dazed with the warmth about her as if this were a kind of love, the caresses of love, and her mind slipped over onto thoughts of the boy she had been with the night before and how nice he had been, how sweet it always was, not the way someone like June would suppose but sweet, gentle, the way it was in movies and promised in songs; and when she opened her eyes she hardly knew where she was, the back yard ran off into weeds and a fenceline of trees and behind it the sky was perfectly blue and still. The asbestos "ranch house" that was now three years old startled her — it looked small. She shook her head as if to get awake.

It was too hot. She went inside the house and turned on the radio to drown out the quiet. She sat on the edge of her bed, barefoot, and listened for an hour and a half to a program called XYZ Sunday Jamboree, record after record of hard, fast, shrieking songs she sang along with, interspersed by exclamations from "Bobby King": "An' look here you girls at Napoleon's — Son and Charley want you to pay real close attention to this song coming up!"

And Connie paid close attention herself, bathed in a glow of slow-pulsed joy that seemed to rise mysteriously out of the music itself and lay languidly about the airless little room, breathed in and breathed out with each gentle rise and fall of her chest.

After a while she heard a car coming up the drive. She sat up at once, startled, because it couldn't be her father so soon. The gravel kept crunching all the way in from the road — the driveway was long — and Connie ran to the window. It was a car she didn't know. It was an open jalopy, painted a bright gold that caught the sun opaquely. Her heart began to pound and her fingers snatched at her hair, checking it, and she whispered "Christ. Christ," wondering how bad she looked. The car came to a stop at the side door and the horn sounded four short taps as if this were a signal Connie knew.

She went into the kitchen and approached the door slowly, then hung out the screen door, her bare toes curling down off the step. There were two boys in the car and now she recognized the driver: he had shaggy, shabby black hair that looked crazy as a wig and he was grinning at her.

"I ain't late, am I?" he said.

"Who the hell do you think you are?" Connie said.

"Toldja I'd be out, didn't I?"

"I don't even know who you are."

She spoke sullenly, careful to show no interest or pleasure, and he spoke in a fast bright monotone. Connie looked past him to the other boy, taking her time. He had fair brown hair, with a lock that fell onto his forehead. His sideburns gave him a fierce, embarrassed look, but so far he hadn't even bothered to glance at her. Both boys wore sunglasses. The driver's glasses were metallic and mirrored everything in miniature.

"You wanta come for a ride?" he said.

Connie smirked and let her hair fall loose over one shoulder.

"Don'tcha like my car? New paint job," he said. "Hey."

"What?"

"You're cute."

She pretended to fidget, chasing flies away from the door.

"Don'tcha believe me, or what?" he said.

"Look, I don't even know who you are," Connie said in disgust.

"Hey, Ellie's got a radio, see. Mine's broke down." He lifted his friend's arm and showed her the little transistor the boy was holding, and now Connie began to hear the music. It was the same program that was playing inside the house.

"Bobby King?" she said.

"I listen to him all the time. I think he's great."

"He's kind of great," Connie said reluctantly.

"Listen, that guy's *great*. He knows where the action is."

Connie blushed a little, because the glasses made it impossible for her to see just what this boy was looking at. She couldn't decide if she liked him or if he was just a jerk, and so she dawdled in the doorway and wouldn't come down or go back inside. She said, "What's all that stuff painted on your car?"

"Can'tcha read it?" He opened the door very carefully, as if he was afraid it might fall off. He slid out just as carefully, planting his feet firmly on the ground, the tiny metallic world in his glasses slowing down like gelatine hardening and in the midst of it Connie's bright green blouse. "This here is my name, to begin with," he said. ARNOLD FRIEND was written in tar-like black letters on the side, with a drawing of a round grinning face that reminded Connie of a pumpkin, except it wore sunglasses. "I wanta introduce myself, I'm Arnold Friend and that's my real name and I'm gonna be your friend, honey, and inside the car's Ellie Oscar, he's kinda shy." Ellie brought his transistor up to his shoulder and balanced it there. "Now these numbers are a secret code, honey," Arnold Friend explained. He read off the numbers 33, 19, 17 and raised his eyebrows at her to see what she thought of that, but she didn't think much of it. The left rear fender had been smashed and around it was written, on the gleaming gold background: DONE BY CRAZY WOMAN DRIVER. Connie had to laugh at that. Arnold Friend was pleased at her laughter and looked up at her. "Around the other side's a lot more — you wanta come and see them?"

"No."

"Why not?"

"Why should I?"

"Don'tcha wanta see what's on the car? Don'tcha wanta go for a ride?"

"I don't know."

"Why not?"

"I got things to do."

"Like what?"

"Things."

He laughed as if she had said something funny. He slapped his thighs. He was standing in a strange way, leaning back against the car as if he were balancing himself. He wasn't tall, only an inch or so taller than she would be if she came down to him. Connie liked the way he was dressed, which was the way all of them dressed: tight faded jeans stuffed into black, scuffed boots, a belt that pulled his waist in and showed how lean he was, and a white pullover shirt that was a little soiled and showed the hard small muscles of his arms and shoulders. He looked as if he probably did hard work, lifting and carrying things. Even his neck looked muscular. And his face was a familiar face, somehow: the jaw and chin and cheeks slightly darkened, because he hadn't shaved for a day or two, and the nose long and hawk-like, sniffing as if she were a treat he was going to gobble up and it was all a joke.

"Connie, you ain't telling the truth. This is your day set aside for a ride with me and you know it," he said, still laughing. The way he straightened and recovered from his fit of laughing showed that it had been all fake.

"How do you know what my name is?" she said suspiciously.

"It's Connie."

"Maybe and maybe not."

"I know my Connie," he said, wagging his finger. Now she remembered him even better, back at the restaurant, and her cheeks warmed at the thought of how she sucked in her breath just at the moment she passed him how she must have looked to him. And he had remembered her. "Ellie and I come out here especially for you," he said. "Ellie can sit in back. How about it?"

"Where?"

"Where what?"

"Where're we going?"

He looked at her. He took off the sunglasses and she saw how pale the skin around his eyes was, like holes that were not in shadow but instead in light. His eyes were like chips of broken glass that catch the light in an amiable way. He smiled. It was as if the idea of going for a ride somewhere, to some place, was a new idea to him.

"Just for a ride, Connie sweetheart."

"I never said my name was Connie," she said.

"But I know what it is. I know your name and all about you, lots of things," Arnold Friend said. He had not moved yet but stood still leaning back against the side of his jalopy. "I took a special interest in you, such a pretty girl, and found out all about you like I know your parents and sister are gone somewheres and I know where and how long they're going to be gone, and I know who you were with last night, and your best friend's name is Betty. Right?"

He spoke in a simple lilting voice, exactly as if he were reciting the words to a song. His smile assured her that everything was fine. In the car Ellie turned up the volume on his radio and did not bother to look around at them.

"Ellie can sit in the back seat," Arnold Friend said. He indicated his friend with a casual jerk of his chin, as if Ellie did not count and she could not bother with him.

"How'd you find out all that stuff?" Connie said.

"Listen? Betty Schultz and Tony Fitch and Jimmy Pettinger and Nancy Pettinger," he said, in a chant. "Raymond Stanley and Bob Hutter — "

"Do you know all those kids?"

"I know everybody."

"Look, you're kidding. You're not from around here."

"Sure."

"But — how come we never saw you before?"

"Sure you saw me before," he said. He looked down at his boots, as if he were a little offended. "You just don't remember."

"I guess I'd remember you," Connie said.

"Yeah?" He looked up at this, beaming. He was pleased. He began to mark time with the music from Ellie's radio, tapping his fists lightly together. Connie looked away from his smile to the car, which was painted so bright it almost hurt her eyes to look at it. She looked at that name, ARNOLD FRIEND. And up at the front fender was an expression that was familiar — MAN THE FLYING SAUCERS. It was an expression kids had used the year before, but didn't use this year. She looked at it for a while as if the words meant something to her that she did not yet know.

"What're you thinking about? Huh?" Arnold Friend demanded. "Not worried about your hair blowing around in the car, are you?"

"No."

"Think I maybe can't drive good?"

"How do I know?"

"You're a hard girl to handle. How come?" he said. "Don't you know I'm your friend? Didn't you see me put my sign in the air when you walked by?"

"What sign?"

"My sign." And he drew an X in the air, leaning out toward her. They were maybe ten feet apart. After his hand fell back to his side the X was still in the air, almost visible. Connie let the screen door close and stood perfectly still inside it, listening to the music from her radio and the boy's blend together.

She stared at Arnold Friend. He stood there so stiffly relaxed, pretending to be relaxed, with one hand idly on the door handle as if he were keeping himself up that way and had no intention of ever moving again. She recognized most things about him, the tight jeans that showed his thighs and buttocks and the greasy leather boots and the tight shirt, and even that slippery friendly smile of his, that sleepy dreamy smile that all the boys used to get across ideas they didn't want to put into words. She recognized all this and also the singsong way he talked, slightly mocking, kidding, but serious and a little melancholy, and she recognized the way he tapped one fist against the other in homage to the perpetual music behind him. But all these things did not come together.

She said suddenly, "Hey, how old are you?"

His smile faded. She could see then that he wasn't a kid, he was much older — thirty, maybe more. At this knowledge her heart began to pound faster.

"That's a crazy thing to ask. Can'tcha see I'm your own age?"

"Like hell you are."

"Or maybe a coupla years older, I'm eighteen."

"Eighteen?" she said doubtfully.

He grinned to reassure her and lines appeared at the corners of his mouth. His teeth were big and white. He grinned so broadly his eyes became slits and she saw how thick the lashes were, thick and black as if painted with a black tar-like material. Then he seemed to become embarrassed, abruptly, and looked over his shoulder at Ellie. "*Him,* he's crazy," he said. "Ain't he a riot, he's a nut, a real character." Ellie was still listening to the music. His sunglasses told nothing about what he was thinking. He wore a bright orange shirt unbuttoned halfway to show his chest, which was a pale, bluish chest and not muscular like Arnold Friend's. His shirt collar was turned up all around and the very tips of the collar pointed out past his chin as if they were protecting him. He was pressing the transistor radio up against his ear and sat there in a kind of daze, right in the sun.

"He's kinda strange," Connie said.

"Hey, she says you're kinda strange! Kinda strange!" Arnold Friend cried. He pounded on the car to get Ellie's attention. Ellie turned for the first time and Connie saw with shock that he wasn't a kid either — he had a fair, hairless face, cheeks reddened slightly as if the veins grew too close to the surface of his skin, the face of a forty-year-old baby. Connie felt a wave of dizziness rise in her at this sight and she stared at him as if waiting for something to change the shock of the moment, make it all right again. Ellie's lips kept shaping words, mumbling along with the words blasting his ear.

"Maybe you two better go away," Connie said faintly.

"What? How come?" Arnold Friend cried. "We come out here to take you for a ride. It's Sunday." He had the voice of the man on the radio now. It was the same voice, Connie thought. "Don'tcha know it's Sunday all day and honey, no matter who you were with last night today you're with Arnold Friend and don't you forget it! — Maybe you better step out here," he said, and this last was in a different voice. It was a little flatter, as if the heat was finally getting to him.

"No. I got things to do."

"Hey."

"You two better leave."

"We ain't leaving until you come with us."

"Like hell I am — "

"Connie, don't fool around with me. I mean, I mean, don't fool *around*," he said, shaking his head. He laughed incredulously. He placed his sunglasses on top of his head, carefully, as if he were indeed wearing a wig, and brought the stems down behind his ears. Connie stared at him, another wave of dizziness and fear rising in her so that for a moment he wasn't even in focus but was just a blur, standing there against his gold car, and she had the idea that he had driven up the driveway all right but had come from nowhere before that and belonged nowhere and that everything about him and even the music that was so familiar to her was only half real.

"If my father comes and sees you — "

"He ain't coming. He's at a barbecue."

"How do you know that?"

"Aunt Tillie's. Right now they're — uh — they're drinking. Sitting around," he said vaguely, squinting as if he were staring all the way to town and over to Aunt Tillie's back yard. Then the vision seemed to clear and he nodded energetically. "Yeah. Sitting around. There's your sister in a blue dress, huh? And high heels, the poor sad bitch — nothing like you, sweetheart! And your mother's helping some fat woman with the corn, they're cleaning the corn — husking the corn — "

"What fat woman?" Connie cried.

"How do I know what fat woman. I don't know every goddamn fat woman in the world!" Arnold Friend laughed.

"Oh, that's Mrs. Hornby. . . . Who invited her?" Connie said. She felt a little light-headed. Her breath was coming quickly.

"She's too fat. I don't like them fat. I like them the way you are, honey," he said, smiling sleepily at her. They stared at each other for a while, through the screen door. He said softly, "Now what you're going to do is this: you're going to come out that door. You're going to sit up front with me and Ellie's going to sit in the back, the hell with Ellie, right? This isn't Ellie's date. You're my date. I'm your lover, honey."

"What? You're crazy — "

"Yes, I'm your lover. You don't know what that is but you will," he said. "I know that too. I know all about you. But look: it's real nice and you couldn't ask for nobody better than me, or more polite. I always keep my word. I'll tell you how it is, I'm always nice at first, the first time. I'll hold you so tight you won't think you have to try to get away or pretend anything because you'll know you can't. And I'll come inside you where it's all secret and you'll give in to me and you'll love me — "

"Shut up! You're crazy!" Connie said. She backed away from the door. She put her hands against her ears as if she'd heard something terrible, something not meant for her. "People don't talk like that, you're crazy," she muttered. Her heart was almost too big now for her chest and its pumping made sweat break out all over her. She looked out to see Arnold Friend pause and then take a step toward the porch lurching. He almost fell. But, like a clever drunken man, he managed to catch his balance. He wobbled in his high boots and grabbed hold of one of the porch posts.

"Honey?" he said. "You still listening?"

"Get the hell out of here!"

"Be nice, honey. Listen."

"I'm going to call the police — "

He wobbled again and out of the side of his mouth came a fast spat curse, an aside not meant for her to hear. But even this "Christ!" sounded forced. Then he began to smile again. She watched this smile come, awkward as if he were smiling from inside a mask. His whole face was a mask, she thought wildly, tanned down onto his throat but then running out as if he had plastered make-up on his face but had forgotten about his throat.

"Honey — ? Listen, here's how it is. I always tell the truth and I promise you this: I ain't coming in that house after you."

"You better not! I'm going to call the police if you — if you don't — "

"Honey," he said, talking right through her voice, "honey, I'm not coming in there but you are coming out here. You know why?"

She was panting. The kitchen looked like a place she had never seen before, some room she had run inside but which wasn't good enough, wasn't going to help her. The kitchen window had never had a curtain, after three years, and there were dishes in the sink for her to do — probably — and if you ran your hand across the table you'd probably feel something sticky there.

"You listening, honey? Hey?"

" — going to call the police — "

"Soon as you touch the phone I don't need to keep my promise and can come inside. You won't want that."

She rushed forward and tried to lock the door. Her fingers were shaking. "But why lock it," Arnold Friend said gently, talking right into her face. "It's just a screen door. It's just nothing." One of his boots was at a strange angle, as if his foot wasn't in it. It pointed out to the left, bent at the ankle. "I mean, anybody can break through a screen door and glass and wood and iron or anything else if he needs to, anybody at all and specially Arnold Friend. If the place got lit up with a fire, honey, you'd come running out into my arms, right into my arms and safe at home — like you knew I was your lover and'd stopped fooling around, I don't mind a nice shy girl but I don't like no fooling around." Part of those words were spoken with a slight rhythmic lilt, and Connie somehow recognized them — the echo of a song from last year, about a girl rushing into her boy friend's arms and coming home again —

Connie stood barefoot on the linoleum floor, staring at him. "What do you want?" she whispered.

"I want you," he said.

"What?"

"Seen you that night and thought, that's the one, yes sir. I never needed to look any more."

"But my father's coming back. He's coming to get me. I had to wash my hair first — " She spoke in a dry, rapid voice, hardly raising it for him to hear.

"No, your daddy is not coming and yes, you had to wash your hair and you washed it for me. It's nice and shining and all for me, I thank you, sweetheart," he said, with a mock bow, but again he almost lost his balance. He had to bend and adjust his boots. Evidently his feet did not go all the way down; the boots must have been stuffed with something so that he would seem taller. Connie stared out at him and behind him Ellie in the car, who seemed to be looking off toward Connie's right, into nothing. This Ellie said, pulling the words out of the air one after another as if he were just discovering them, "You want me to pull out the phone?"

"Shut your mouth and keep it shut," Arnold Friend said, his face red from bending over or maybe from embarrassment because Connie had seen his boots. "This ain't none of your business."

"What — what are you doing? What do you want?" Connie said. "If I call the police they'll get you, they'll arrest you — "

"Promise was not to come in unless you touch that phone, and I'll keep that promise," he said. He resumed his erect position and tried to force his shoulders back. He sounded like a hero in a movie, declaring something important. He spoke too loudly and it was as if he were speaking to someone behind Connie. "I ain't made plans for coming in that house where I don't belong but just for you to come out to me, the way you should. Don't you know who I am?"

"You're crazy," she whispered. She backed away from the door but did not want to go into another part of the house, as if this would give him permission to come through the door. "What do you. . . . You're crazy, you. . . ."

"Huh? What're you saying, honey?"

Her eyes darted everywhere in the kitchen. She could not remember what it was, this room.

"This is how it is, honey: you come out and we'll drive away, have a nice ride. But if you don't come out we're gonna wait till your people come home and then they're all going to get it."

"You want that telephone pulled out?" Ellie said. He held the radio away from his ear and grimaced, as if without the radio the air was too much for him.

"I toldja shut up, Ellie." Arnold Friend said, "You're deaf, get a hearing aid, right? Fix yourself up. This little girl's no trouble and's gonna be nice to me, so Ellie keep to yourself, this ain't your date — right? Don't hem in on me. Don't hog. Don't crush. Don't bird dog. Don't trail me," he said in a rapid meaningless voice, as if he were running through all the expressions he'd learned but was no longer sure which one of them was in style, then rushing on to new ones, making them up with his eyes closed, "Don't crawl under my fence, don't squeeze in my chipmunk hole, don't sniff my glue, suck my popsicle, keep your own greasy fingers on yourself!" He shaded his eyes and peered in at Connie, who was backed against the kitchen table. "Don't mind him, honey, he's just a creep. He's a dope. Right? I'm the boy for you and like

I said you come out here nice like a lady and give me your hand, and nobody else gets hurt, I mean, your nice old bald-headed daddy and your mummy and your sister in her high heels. Because listen: why bring them in this?"

"Leave me alone," Connie whispered.

"Hey, you know that old woman down the road, the one with the chickens and stuff — you know her?"

"She's dead!"

"Dead? What? You know her?" Arnold Friend said.

"She's dead — "

"Don't you like her?"

"She's dead — she's — she isn't here any more — "

"But don't you like her, I mean, you got something against her? Some grudge or something?" Then his voice dipped as if he were conscious of rudeness. He touched the sunglasses on top of his head as if to make sure they were still there. "Now you be a good girl."

"What are you going to do?"

"Just two things, or maybe three," Arnold Friend said. "But I promise it won't last long and you'll like me that way you get to like people you're close to. You will. It's all over for you here, so come on out. You don't want your people in any trouble, do you?"

She turned and bumped against a chair or something, hurting her leg, but she ran into the back room and picked up the telephone. Something roared in her ear, a tiny roaring, and she was so sick with fear that she could do nothing but listen to it — the telephone was clammy and very heavy and her fingers groped down to the dial but were too weak to touch it. She began to scream into the phone, into the roaring. She cried out, she cried for her mother, she felt her breath start jerking back and forth in her lungs as if it were something Arnold Friend were stabbing her with again and again with no tenderness. A noisy sorrowful wailing rose all about her and she was locked inside it the way she was locked inside this house.

After a while she could hear again. She was sitting on the floor, with her wet back against the wall.

Arnold Friend was saying from the door, "That's a good girl. Put the phone back."

She kicked the phone away from her.

"No, honey. Pick it up. Put it back right."

She picked it up and put it back. The dial tone stopped.

"That's a good girl. Now you come outside."

She was hollow with what had been fear, but what was now just an emptiness. All that screaming had blasted it out of her. She sat, one leg cramped under her, and deep inside her brain was something like a pinpoint of light that kept going and would not let her relax. She thought, I'm not going to see my mother again. She thought, I'm not going to sleep in my bed again. Her bright green blouse was all wet.

Arnold Friend said, in a gentle-loud voice that was like a stage voice. "The place where you came from ain't there any more, and where you had in mind to go is cancelled out. This place you are now — inside your daddy's house — is nothing but a cardboard box I can knock down any time. You know that and always did know it. You hear me?"

She thought, I have got to think. I have to know what to do.

"We'll go out to a nice field, out in the country here where it smells so nice and it's sunny," Arnold Friend said. "I'll have my arms tight around you so you won't need to try to get away and I'll show you what love is like, what it does. The hell with this house! It looks solid all right," he said. He ran a fingernail down the screen and the noise did not make Connie shiver, as it would have the day before. "Now put your hand on your heart, honey. Feel that? That feels solid too but we know better, be nice to me, be sweet like you can because what else is there for a girl like you but to be sweet and pretty and give in? — and get away before her people come back?"

She felt her pounding heart. Her hands seemed to enclose it. She thought for the first time in her life that it was nothing that was hers, that belonged to her, but just a pounding, living thing inside this body that wasn't hers either.

"You don't want them to get hurt," Arnold Friend went on. "Now get up, honey. Get up all by yourself."

She stood.

"Now turn this way. That's right. Come over to me — Ellie, put that away, didn't I tell you? You dope. You miserable creepy dope," Arnold Friend said. His words were not angry but only part of an incantation. The incantation was kindly. "Now come out through the kitchen to me honey and let's see a smile, try it, you're a brave sweet little girl and now they're eating corn and hotdogs cooked to bursting over an outdoor fire, and they don't know one thing about you and never did and honey you're better than them because not one of them would have done this for you."

Connie felt the linoleum under her feet; it was cool. She brushed her hair back out of her eyes. Arnold Friend let go of the post tentatively and opened his arms for her, his elbows pointing up toward each other and his wrist limp, to show that this was an embarrassed embrace and a little mocking, he didn't want to make her self-conscious.

She put out her hand against the screen. She watched herself push the door slowly open as if she were safe back somewhere in the other doorway, watching this body and this head of long hair moving out into the sunlight where Arnold Friend waited.

"My sweet little blue-eyed girl," he said, in a half-sung sigh that had nothing to do with her brown eyes but was taken up just the same by the vast sunlit reaches of the land behind him and on all sides of him, so much land that Connie had never seen before and did not recognize except to know that she was going to it.

∽∾

TIM O'BRIEN (b. 1946) *was born in Austin, Minnesota, and educated at Macalester College and Harvard University. Drafted into the army during the Vietnam War, he attained the rank of sergeant and received the Purple Heart.*

O'Brien's first book, If I Die in a Combat Zone, Box Me Up and Ship Me Home *(1973), is an account of his combat experience presented as "autofiction," a mixture of autobiography and fiction. His next book,* Northern Lights *(1974), depicts a conflict between two brothers. But O'Brien produced his finest work to date in the novel* Going after Cacciato *(1978), which won the National Book Award and was judged by many critics to be the best book by an American about the Vietnam War. This was followed by* The Nuclear Age *(1985), a novel set in 1995 about the ominous future of the human race.*

"Soldiers are dreamers," a line by the English poet Siegfried Sassoon, who survived a sniper's bullet during World War I, is the epigraph for Going after Cacciato. *Dreams play an important role in all O'Brien's fiction, yet the note they sound in a story such as "The Things They Carried" is not surrealistic. The dream is always rooted so firmly in reality that it survives, paradoxically, as the most vital element in an O'Brien story. "The Things They Carried" first appeared in* Esquire *magazine and was included in* The Best American Short Stories *when Ann Beattie edited the volume in 1987. It is also included in O'Brien's recent collection* The Things They Carried *(1990). O'Brien's latest book is the novel* In the Lake of the Woods *(1994).*

TIM O'BRIEN

The Things They Carried

1986

First Lieutenant Jimmy Cross carried letters from a girl named Martha, a junior at Mount Sebastian College in New Jersey. They were not love letters, but Lieutenant Cross was hoping, so he kept them folded in plastic at the bottom of his rucksack. In the late afternoon, after a day's march, he would dig his foxhole, wash his hands under a canteen, unwrap the letters, hold them with the tips of his fingers, and spend the last hour of light pretending. He would imagine romantic camping trips into the White Mountains in New Hampshire. He would sometimes taste the envelope flaps, knowing her tongue had been there. More than anything, he wanted Martha to love him as he loved her, but the letters were mostly chatty, elusive on the matter of love. She was a virgin, he was almost sure. She was an English major at Mount Sebastian, and she wrote beautifully about her professors and roommates and midterm exams, about her respect for Chaucer and her great affection for Virginia Woolf. She often quoted lines of poetry; she never mentioned the war, except to say, Jimmy, take care of yourself. The letters weighed ten ounces. They were signed "Love, Martha," but Lieutenant Cross understood that "Love" was only a way of signing and did not mean what he sometimes pretended it meant. At dusk, he would carefully return the letters to his rucksack. Slowly, a bit distracted, he would get up and move among his men, checking the perimeter, then at full dark he would return to his hole and watch the night and wonder if Martha was a virgin.

The things they carried were largely determined by necessity. Among the necessities or near necessities were P-38 can openers, pocket knives, heat tabs, wrist watches, dog tags, mosquito repellant, chewing gum, candy, cigarettes, salt tablets, packets of Kool-Aid, lighters, matches, sewing kits, Military Payment Certificates, C rations, and two or three canteens of water. Together, these items weighed between fifteen and twenty pounds, depending upon a man's habits or rate of metabolism. Henry Dobbins, who was a big man, carried extra rations; he was especially fond of canned peaches in heavy syrup over pound cake. Dave Jensen, who practiced field hygiene, carried a toothbrush, dental floss, and several hotel-size bars of soap he'd stolen on R&R in Sydney, Australia. Ted Lavender, who was scared, carried tranquilizers until he was shot in the head outside the village of Than Khe in mid-April. By necessity, and because it was SOP,° they all carried steel helmets that weighed five pounds including the liner and camouflage cover. They carried the standard fatigue jackets and trousers. Very few carried underwear. On their feet they carried jungle boots — 2.1 pounds — and Dave Jensen carried three pairs of socks and a can of Dr. Scholl's foot powder as a precaution against trench foot. Until he was shot, Ted Lavender carried six or seven ounces of premium dope, which for him was a necessity. Mitchell Sanders, the RTO,° carried condoms. Norman Bowker carried a diary. Rat Kiley carried comic books. Kiowa, a devout Baptist, carried an illustrated New Testament that had been presented to him by his father, who taught Sunday school in Oklahoma City, Oklahoma. As a hedge against bad times, however, Kiowa also carried his grandmother's distrust of the white man, his grandfather's old hunting hatchet. Necessity dictated. Because the land was mined and booby-trapped, it was SOP for each man to carry a steel-centered, nylon-covered flak jacket, which weighed 6.7 pounds, but which on hot days seemed much heavier. Because you could die so quickly, each man carried at least one large compress bandage, usually in the helmet band for easy access. Because the nights were cold, and because the monsoons were wet, each carried a green plastic poncho that could be used as a raincoat or ground sheet or makeshift tent. With its quilted liner, the poncho weighed almost two pounds, but it was worth every ounce. In April, for instance, when Ted Lavender was shot, they used his poncho to wrap him up, then to carry him across the paddy, then to lift him into the chopper that took him away.

They were called legs or grunts.

To carry something was to "hump" it, as when Lieutenant Jimmy Cross humped his love for Martha up the hills and through the swamps. In its intransitive form, "to hump" meant "to walk," or "to march," but it implied burdens far beyond the intransitive.

Almost everyone humped photographs. In his wallet, Lieutenant Cross carried two photographs of Martha. The first was a Kodachrome snapshot signed "Love," though he knew better. She stood against a brick wall. Her eyes were gray and neutral, her lips slightly open as she stared straight-on at the camera. At night, sometimes, Lieutenant Cross wondered who had taken the picture, because he knew she had boyfriends, because he loved her so

---

SOP: Standard operating procedure.
RTO: Radiotelephone operator.

much, and because he could see the shadow of the picture taker spreading out against the brick wall. The second photograph had been clipped from the 1968 Mount Sebastian yearbook. It was an action shot — women's volleyball — and Martha was bent horizontal to the floor, reaching, the palms of her hands in sharp focus, the tongue taut, the expression frank and competitive. There was no visible sweat. She wore white gym shorts. Her legs, he thought, were almost certainly the legs of a virgin, dry and without hair, the left knee cocked and carrying her entire weight, which was just over one hundred pounds. Lieutenant Cross remembered touching that left knee. A dark theater, he remembered, and the movie was *Bonnie and Clyde*, and Martha wore a tweed skirt, and during the final scene, when he touched her knee, she turned and looked at him in a sad, sober way that made him pull his hand back, but he would always remember the feel of the tweed skirt and the knee beneath it and the sound of the gunfire that killed Bonnie and Clyde, how embarrassing it was, how slow and oppressive. He remembered kissing her good night at the dorm door. Right then, he thought, he should've done something brave. He should've carried her up the stairs to her room and tied her to the bed and touched that left knee all night long. He should've risked it. Whenever he looked at the photographs, he thought of new things he should've done.

What they carried was partly a function of rank, partly of field specialty.

As a first lieutenant and platoon leader, Jimmy Cross carried a compass, maps, code books, binoculars, and a .45-caliber pistol that weighed 2.9 pounds fully loaded. He carried a strobe light and the responsibility for the lives of his men.

As an RTO, Mitchell Sanders carried the PRC-25 radio, a killer, twenty-six pounds with its battery.

As a medic, Rat Kiley carried a canvas satchel filled with morphine and plasma and malaria tablets and surgical tape and comic books and all the things a medic must carry, including M&M's for especially bad wounds, for a total weight of nearly twenty pounds.

As a big man, therefore a machine gunner, Henry Dobbins carried the M-60, which weighed twenty-three pounds unloaded, but which was almost always loaded. In addition, Dobbins carried between ten and fifteen pounds of ammunition draped in belts across his chest and shoulders.

As PFCs or Spec 4s, most of them were common grunts and carried the standard M-16 gas-operated assault rifle. The weapon weighed 7.5 pounds unloaded, 8.2 pounds with its full twenty-round magazine. Depending on numerous factors, such as topography and psychology, the riflemen carried anywhere from twelve to twenty magazines, usually in cloth bandoliers, adding on another 8.4 pounds at minimum, fourteen pounds at maximum. When it was available, they also carried M-16 maintenance gear — rods and steel brushes and swabs and tubes of LSA oil — all of which weighed about a pound. Among the grunts, some carried the M-79 grenade launcher, 5.9 pounds unloaded, a reasonably light weapon except for the ammunition, which was heavy. A single round weighed ten ounces. The typical load was twenty-five rounds. But Ted Lavender, who was scared, carried thirty-four rounds when he was shot and killed outside Than Khe, and he went down under an exceptional burden, more than twenty pounds of ammunition, plus the flak jacket and helmet and rations and water and toilet paper and tranquilizers and all the rest, plus the unweighed fear. He was dead weight. There was no twitching or flopping. Kiowa, who saw it happen, said it was like watching a rock fall, or a big sandbag or something — just boom, then down — not like the movies where the dead guy rolls around and does fancy spins and goes ass over teakettle — not like that, Kiowa said, the poor bastard just flat-fuck fell. Boom. Down. Nothing else. It was a bright morning in mid-April. Lieutenant Cross felt the pain. He blamed himself. They stripped off Lavender's canteens and ammo, all the heavy things, and Rat Kiley said the obvious, the guy's dead, and Mitchell Sanders used his radio to report one U.S. KIA° and to request a chopper. Then they wrapped Lavender in his poncho. They carried him out to a dry paddy, established security, and sat smoking the dead man's dope until the chopper came. Lieutenant Cross kept to himself. He pictured Martha's smooth young face, thinking he loved her more than anything, more than his men, and now Ted Lavender was dead because he loved her so much and could not stop thinking about her. When the dust-off arrived, they carried Lavender aboard. Afterward they burned Than Khe. They marched until dusk, then dug their holes, and that night Kiowa kept explaining how you had to be there, how fast it was, how the poor guy just dropped like so much concrete. Boom-down, he said. Like cement.

In addition to the three standard weapons — the M-60, M-16, and M-79 — they carried whatever presented itself, or whatever seemed appropriate as a means of killing or staying alive. They carried catch-as-catch-can. At various times, in various situations, they carried M-14s and CAR-15s and Swedish Ks and grease guns and captured AK-47s and Chi-Coms and RPGs and Simonov carbines and black-market Uzis and .38-caliber Smith & Wesson handguns and 66 mm LAWs and shotguns and silencers and blackjacks and bayonets and C-4 plastic explosives. Lee Strunk carried a slingshot; a weapon of last resort, he called it. Mitchell Sanders carried brass knuckles. Kiowa carried his grandfather's feathered hatchet. Every third or fourth man carried a Claymore antipersonnel mine — 3.5 pounds with its firing device. They all carried fragmentation grenades — fourteen ounces each. They all carried at least one M-18 colored smoke grenade — twenty-four ounces. Some carried CS or tear-gas grenades. Some carried white-phosphorus grenades. They carried all they could bear, and then some, including a silent awe for the terrible power of the things they carried.

In the first week of April, before Lavender died, Lieutenant Jimmy Cross received a good-luck charm from Martha. It was a simple pebble, an ounce at most. Smooth to the touch, it was a milky-white color with flecks of orange and violet, oval-shaped, like a miniature egg. In the accompanying letter, Martha wrote that she had found the pebble on the Jersey shoreline, precisely

---

KIA: Killed in action.

where the land touched water at high tide, where things came together but also separated. It was this separate-but-together quality, she wrote, that had inspired her to pick up the pebble and to carry it in her breast pocket for several days, where it seemed weightless, and then to send it through the mail, by air, as a token of her truest feelings for him. Lieutenant Cross found this romantic. But he wondered what her truest feelings were, exactly, and what she meant by separate-but-together. He wondered how the tides and waves had come into play on that afternoon along the Jersey shoreline when Martha saw the pebble and bent down to rescue it from geology. He imagined bare feet. Martha was a poet, with the poet's sensibilities, and her feet would be brown and bare, the toenails unpainted, the eyes chilly and somber like the ocean in March, and though it was painful, he wondered who had been with her that afternoon. He imagined a pair of shadows moving along the strip of sand where things came together but also separated. It was phantom jealousy, he knew, but he couldn't help himself. He loved her so much. On the march, through the hot days of early April, he carried the pebble in his mouth, turning it with his tongue, tasting sea salts and moisture. His mind wandered. He had difficulty keeping his attention on the war. On occasion he would yell at his men to spread out the column, to keep their eyes open, but then he would slip away into daydreams, just pretending, walking barefoot along the Jersey shore, with Martha, carrying nothing. He would feel himself rising. Sun and waves and gentle winds, all love and lightness.

What they carried varied by mission.

When a mission took them to the mountains, they carried mosquito netting, machetes, canvas tarps, and extra bug juice.

If a mission seemed especially hazardous, or if it involved a place they knew to be bad, they carried everything they could. In certain heavily mined AOs,° where the land was dense with Toe Poppers and Bouncing Betties, they took turns humping a twenty-eight-pound mine detector. With its headphones and big sensing plate, the equipment was a stress on the lower back and shoulders, awkward to handle, often useless because of the shrapnel in the earth, but they carried it anyway, partly for safety, partly for the illusion of safety.

On ambush, or other night missions, they carried peculiar little odds and ends. Kiowa always took along his New Testament and a pair of moccasins for silence. Dave Jensen carried night-sight vitamins high in carotin. Lee Strunk carried his slingshot; ammo, he claimed, would never be a problem. Rat Kiley carried brandy and M&M's. Until he was shot, Ted Lavender carried the starlight scope, which weighed 6.3 pounds with its aluminum carrying case. Henry Dobbins carried his girlfriend's pantyhose wrapped around his neck as a comforter. They all carried ghosts. When dark came, they would move out single file across the meadows and paddies to their ambush coordi-

---

AOs: Areas of operations.

nates, where they would quietly set up the Claymores and lie down and spend the night waiting.

Other missions were more complicated and required special equipment. In mid-April, it was their mission to search out and destroy the elaborate tunnel complexes in the Than Khe area south of Chu Lai. To blow the tunnels, they carried one-pound blocks of pentrite high explosives, four blocks to a man, sixty-eight pounds in all. They carried wiring, detonators, and battery-powered clackers. Dave Jensen carried earplugs. Most often, before blowing the tunnels, they were ordered by higher command to search them, which was considered bad news, but by and large they just shrugged and carried out orders. Because he was a big man, Henry Dobbins was excused from tunnel duty. The others would draw numbers. Before Lavender died there were seventeen men in the platoon, and whoever drew the number seventeen would strip off his gear and crawl in head first with a flashlight and Lieutenant Cross's .45-caliber pistol. The rest of them would fan out as security. They would sit down or kneel, not facing the hole, listening to the ground beneath them, imagining cobwebs and ghosts, whatever was down there — the tunnel walls squeezing in — how the flashlight seemed impossibly heavy in the hand and how it was tunnel vision in the very strictest sense, compression in all ways, even time, and how you had to wiggle in — ass and elbows — a swallowed-up feeling — and how you found yourself worrying about odd things — will your flashlight go dead? Do rats carry rabies? If you screamed, how far would the sound carry? Would your buddies hear it? Would they have the courage to drag you out? In some respects, though not many, the waiting was worse than the tunnel itself. Imagination was a killer.

On April 16, when Lee Strunk drew the number seventeen, he laughed and muttered something and went down quickly. The morning was hot and very still. Not good, Kiowa said. He looked at the tunnel opening, then out across a dry paddy toward the village of Than Khe. Nothing moved. No clouds or birds or people. As they waited, the men smoked and drank Kool-Aid, not talking much, feeling sympathy for Lee Strunk but also feeling the luck of the draw. You win some, you lose some, said Mitchell Sanders, and sometimes you settle for a rain check. It was a tired line and no one laughed.

Henry Dobbins ate a tropical chocolate bar. Ted Lavender popped a tranquilizer and went off to pee.

After five minutes, Lieutenant Jimmy Cross moved to the tunnel, leaned down, and examined the darkness. Trouble, he thought — a cave-in maybe. And then suddenly, without willing it, he was thinking about Martha. The stresses and fractures, the quick collapse, the two of them buried alive under all that weight. Dense, crushing love. Kneeling, watching the hole, he tried to concentrate on Lee Strunk and the war, all the dangers, but his love was too much for him, he felt paralyzed, he wanted to sleep inside her lungs and breathe her blood and be smothered. He wanted her to be a virgin and not a virgin, all at once. He wanted to know her. Intimate secrets — why poetry? Why so sad? Why the grayness in her eyes? Why so alone? Not lonely, just alone — riding her bike across campus or sitting off by herself in the cafeteria.

Even dancing, she danced alone — and it was the aloneness that filled him with love. He remembered telling her that one evening. How she nodded and looked away. And how, later, when he kissed her, she received the kiss without returning it, her eyes wide open, not afraid, not a virgin's eyes, just flat and uninvolved.

Lieutenant Cross gazed at the tunnel. But he was not there. He was buried with Martha under the white sand at the Jersey shore. They were pressed together, and the pebble in his mouth was her tongue. He was smiling. Vaguely, he was aware of how quiet the day was, the sullen paddies, yet he could not bring himself to worry about matters of security. He was beyond that. He was just a kid at war, in love. He was twenty-two years old. He couldn't help it.

A few moments later Lee Strunk crawled out of the tunnel. He came up grinning, filthy but alive. Lieutenant Cross nodded and closed his eyes while the others clapped Strunk on the back and made jokes about rising from the dead.

Worms, Rat Kiley said. Right out of the grave. Fuckin' zombie.

The men laughed. They all felt great relief.

Spook City, said Mitchell Sanders.

Lee Strunk made a funny ghost sound, a kind of moaning, yet very happy, and right then, when Strunk made that high happy moaning sound, when he went *Ahhooooo*, right then Ted Lavender was shot in the head on his way back from peeing. He lay with his mouth open. The teeth were broken. There was a swollen black bruise under his left eye. The cheekbone was gone. Oh shit, Rat Kiley said, the guy's dead. The guy's dead, he kept saying, which seemed profound — the guy's dead. I mean really.

The things they carried were determined to some extent by superstition. Lieutenant Cross carried his good-luck pebble. Dave Jensen carried a rabbit's foot. Norman Bowker, otherwise a very gentle person, carried a thumb that had been presented to him as a gift by Mitchell Sanders. The thumb was dark brown, rubbery to the touch, and weighed four ounces at most. It had been cut from a VC corpse, a boy of fifteen or sixteen. They'd found him at the bottom of an irrigation ditch, badly burned, flies in his mouth and eyes. The boy wore black shorts and sandals. At the time of his death he had been carrying a pouch of rice, a rifle, and three magazines of ammunition.

You want my opinion, Mitchell Sanders said, there's a definite moral here.

He put his hand on the dead boy's wrist. He was quiet for a time, as if counting a pulse, then he patted the stomach, almost affectionately, and used Kiowa's hunting hatchet to remove the thumb.

Henry Dobbins asked what the moral was.

Moral?

You know. *Moral*.

Sanders wrapped the thumb in toilet paper and handed it across to Norman Bowker. There was no blood. Smiling, he kicked the boy's head, watched the flies scatter, and said, It's like with that old TV show — Paladin. Have gun, will travel.

Henry Dobbins thought about it.

Yeah, well, he finally said. I don't see no moral.

There it *is*, man.

Fuck off.

They carried USO stationery and pencils and pens. They carried Sterno, safety pins, trip flares, signal flares, spools of wire, razor blades, chewing tobacco, liberated joss sticks and statuettes of the smiling Buddha, candles, grease pencils, *The Stars and Stripes*, fingernail clippers, Psy Ops° leaflets, bush hats, bolos, and much more. Twice a week, when the resupply choppers came in, they carried hot chow in green Mermite cans and large canvas bags filled with iced beer and soda pop. They carried plastic water containers, each with a two-gallon capacity. Mitchell Sanders carried a set of starched tiger fatigues for special occasions. Henry Dobbins carried Black Flag insecticide. Dave Jensen carried empty sandbags that could be filled at night for added protection. Lee Strunk carried tanning lotion. Some things they carried in common. Taking turns, they carried the big PRC-77 scrambler radio, which weighed thirty pounds with its battery. They shared the weight of memory. They took up what others could no longer bear. Often, they carried each other, the wounded or weak. They carried infections. They carried chess sets, basketballs, Vietnamese-English dictionaries, insignia of rank, Bronze Stars and Purple Hearts, plastic cards imprinted with the Code of Conduct. They carried diseases, among them malaria and dysentery. They carried lice and ringworm and leeches and paddy algae and various rots and molds. They carried the land itself — Vietnam, the place, the soil — a powdery orange-red dust that covered their boots and fatigues and faces. They carried the sky. The whole atmosphere, they carried it, the humidity, the monsoons, the stink of fungus and decay, all of it, they carried gravity. They moved like mules. By daylight they took sniper fire, at night they were mortared, but it was not battle, it was just the endless march, village to village, without purpose, nothing won or lost. They marched for the sake of the march. They plodded along slowly, dumbly, leaning forward against the heat, unthinking, all blood and bone, simple grunts, soldiering with their legs, toiling up the hills and down into the paddies and across the rivers and up again and down, just humping, one step and then the next and then another, but no volition, no will, because it was automatic, it was anatomy, and the war was entirely a matter of posture and carriage, the hump was everything, a kind of inertia, a kind of emptiness, a dullness of desire and intellect and conscience and hope and human sensibility. Their principles were in their feet. Their calculations were biological. They had no sense of strategy or mission. They searched the villages without knowing what to look for, not caring, kicking over jars of rice, frisking children and

---

Psy Ops: Psychological operations.

old men, blowing tunnels, sometimes setting fires and sometimes not, then forming up and moving on to the next village, then other villages, where it would always be the same. They carried their own lives. The pressures were enormous. In the heat of early afternoon, they would remove their helmets and flak jackets, walking bare, which was dangerous but which helped ease the strain. They would often discard things along the route of march. Purely for comfort, they would throw away rations, blow their Claymores and grenades, no matter, because by nightfall the resupply choppers would arrive with more of the same, then a day or two later still more, fresh watermelons and crates of ammunition and sunglasses and woolen sweaters — the resources were stunning — sparklers for the Fourth of July, colored eggs for Easter. It was the great American war chest — the fruits of science, the smokestacks, the canneries, the arsenals at Hartford, the Minnesota forests, the machine shops, the vast fields of corn and wheat — they carried like freight trains; they carried it on their backs and shoulders — and for all the ambiguities of Vietnam, all the mysteries and unknowns, there was at least the single abiding certainty that they would never be at a loss for things to carry.

After the chopper took Lavender away, Lieutenant Jimmy Cross led his men into the village of Than Khe. They burned everything. They shot chickens and dogs, they trashed the village well, they called in artillery and watched the wreckage, then they marched for several hours through the hot afternoon, and then at dusk, while Kiowa explained how Lavender died, Lieutenant Cross found himself trembling.

He tried not to cry. With his entrenching tool, which weighed five pounds, he began digging a hole in the earth.

He felt shame. He hated himself. He had loved Martha more than his men, and as a consequence Lavender was now dead, and this was something he would have to carry like a stone in his stomach for the rest of the war.

All he could do was dig. He used his entrenching tool like an ax, slashing, feeling both love and hate, and then later, when it was full dark, he sat at the bottom of his foxhole and wept. It went on for a long while. In part, he was grieving for Ted Lavender, but mostly it was for Martha, and for himself, because she belonged to another world, which was not quite real, and because she was a junior at Mount Sebastian College in New Jersey, a poet and a virgin and uninvolved, and because he realized she did not love him and never would.

Like cement, Kiowa whispered in the dark. I swear to God — boom-down. Not a word.

I've heard this, said Norman Bowker.

A pisser, you know? Still zipping himself up. Zapped while zipping.

All right, fine. That's enough.

Yeah, but you had to see it, the guy just —

I *heard*, man. Cement. So why not shut the fuck *up*?

Kiowa shook his head sadly and glanced over at the hole where Lieutenant Jimmy Cross sat watching the night. The air was thick and wet. A warm, dense fog had settled over the paddies and there was the stillness that precedes rain.

After a time Kiowa sighed.

One thing for sure, he said. The Lieutenant's in some deep hurt. I mean that crying jag — the way he was carrying on — it wasn't fake or anything, it was real heavy-duty hurt. The man cares.

Sure, Norman Bowker said.

Say what you want, the man does care.

We all got problems.

Not Lavender.

No, I guess not, Bowker said. Do me a favor, though.

Shut up?

That's a smart Indian. Shut up.

Shrugging, Kiowa pulled off his boots. He wanted to say more, just to lighten up his sleep, but instead he opened his New Testament and arranged it beneath his head as a pillow. The fog made things seem hollow and unattached. He tried not to think about Ted Lavender, but then he was thinking how fast it was, no drama, down and dead, and how it was hard to feel anything except surprise. It seemed un-Christian. He wished he could find some great sadness, or even anger, but the emotion wasn't there and he couldn't make it happen. Mostly he felt pleased to be alive. He liked the smell of the New Testament under his cheek, the leather and ink and paper and glue, whatever the chemicals were. He liked hearing the sounds of night. Even his fatigue, it felt fine, the stiff muscles and the prickly awareness of his own body, a floating feeling. He enjoyed not being dead. Lying there, Kiowa admired Lieutenant Jimmy Cross's capacity for grief. He wanted to share the man's pain, he wanted to care as Jimmy Cross cared. And yet when he closed his eyes, all he could think was Boom-down, and all he could feel was the pleasure of having his boots off and the fog curling in around him and the damp soil and the Bible smells and the plush comfort of night.

After a moment Norman Bowker sat up in the dark.

What the hell, he said. You want to talk, *talk*. Tell it to me.

Forget it.

No, man, go on. One thing I hate, it's a silent Indian.

For the most part they carried themselves with poise, a kind of dignity. Now and then, however, there were times of panic, when they squealed or wanted to squeal but couldn't, when they twitched and made moaning sounds and covered their heads and said Dear Jesus and flopped around on the earth and fired their weapons blindly and cringed and sobbed and begged for the noise to stop and went wild and made stupid promises to themselves and to God and to their mothers and fathers, hoping not to die. In different ways, it happened to all of them. Afterward, when the firing ended, they would blink and peek up. They would touch their bodies, feeling shame, then quickly hiding it. They would force themselves to stand. As if in slow motion, frame by frame, the world would take on the old logic — absolute silence, then the wind, then sunlight, then voices. It was the burden of being alive.

Awkwardly, the men would reassemble themselves, first in private, then in groups, becoming soldiers again. They would repair the leaks in their eyes. They would check for casualties, call in dust-offs, light cigarettes, try to smile, clear their throats and spit and begin cleaning their weapons. After a time someone would shake his head and say, No lie, I almost shit my pants, and someone else would laugh, which meant it was bad, yes, but the guy had obviously not shit his pants, it wasn't that bad, and in any case nobody would ever do such a thing and then go ahead and talk about it. They would squint into the dense, oppressive sunlight. For a few moments, perhaps, they would fall silent, lighting a joint and tracking its passage from man to man, inhaling, holding in the humiliation. Scary stuff, one of them might say. But then someone else would grin or flick his eyebrows and say, Roger-dodger, almost cut me a new asshole, *almost.*

There were numerous such poses. Some carried themselves with a sort of wistful resignation, others with pride or stiff soldierly discipline or good humor or macho zeal. They were afraid of dying but they were even more afraid to show it.

They found jokes to tell.

They used a hard vocabulary to contain the terrible softness. *Greased,* they'd say. *Offed, lit up, zapped while zipping.* It wasn't cruelty, just stage presence. They were actors and the war came at them in 3-D. When someone died, it wasn't quite dying, because in a curious way it seemed scripted, and because they had their lines mostly memorized, irony mixed with tragedy, and because they called it by other names, as if to encyst and destroy the reality of death itself. They kicked corpses. They cut off thumbs. They talked grunt lingo. They told stories about Ted Lavender's supply of tranquilizers, how the poor guy didn't feel a thing, how incredibly tranquil he was.

There's a moral here, said Mitchell Sanders.

They were waiting for Lavender's chopper, smoking the dead man's dope.

The moral's pretty obvious, Sanders said, and winked. Stay away from drugs. No joke, they'll ruin your day every time.

Cute, said Henry Dobbins.

Mind-blower, get it? Talk about wiggy — nothing left, just blood and brains.

They made themselves laugh.

There it is, they'd say, over and over, as if the repetition itself were an act of poise, a balance between crazy and almost crazy, knowing without going. There it is, which meant be cool, let it ride, because oh yeah, man, you can't change what can't be changed, there it is, there it absolutely and positively and fucking well *is.*

They were tough.

They carried all the emotional baggage of men who might die. Grief, terror, love, longing — these were intangibles, but the intangibles had their own mass and specific gravity, they had tangible weight. They carried shameful memories. They carried the common secret of cowardice barely restrained, the instinct to run or freeze or hide, and in many respects this was the heaviest burden of all, for it could never be put down, it required perfect balance and perfect posture. They carried their reputations. They carried the soldier's greatest fear, which was the fear of blushing. Men killed, and died, because they were embarrassed not to. It was what had brought them to the war in the first place, nothing positive, no dreams of glory or honor, just to avoid the blush of dishonor. They died so as not to die of embarrassment. They crawled into tunnels and walked point and advanced under fire. Each morning, despite the unknowns, they made their legs move. They endured. They kept humping. They did not submit to the obvious alternative, which was simply to close the eyes and fall. So easy, really. Go limp and tumble to the ground and let the muscles unwind and not speak and not budge until your buddies picked you up and lifted you into the chopper that would roar and dip its nose and carry you off to the world. A mere matter of falling, yet no one ever fell. It was not courage, exactly; the object was not valor. Rather, they were too frightened to be cowards.

By and large they carried these things inside, maintaining the masks of composure. They sneered at sick call. They spoke bitterly about guys who had found release by shooting off their own toes or fingers. Pussies, they'd say. Candyasses. It was fierce, mocking talk, with only a trace of envy or awe, but even so, the image played itself out behind their eyes.

They imagined the muzzle against flesh. They imagined the quick, sweet pain, then the evacuation to Japan, then a hospital with warm beds and cute geisha nurses.

They dreamed of freedom birds.

At night, on guard, staring into the dark, they were carried away by jumbo jets. They felt the rush of takeoff. *Gone!* they yelled. And then velocity, wings and engines, a smiling stewardess — but it was more than a plane, it was a real bird, a big sleek silver bird with feathers and talons and high screeching. They were flying. The weights fell off, there was nothing to bear. They laughed and held on tight, feeling the cold slap of wind and altitude, soaring, thinking *It's over, I'm gone!* — they were naked, they were light and free — it was all lightness, bright and fast and buoyant, light as light, a helium buzz in the brain, a giddy bubbling in the lungs as they were taken up over the clouds and the war, beyond duty, beyond gravity and mortification and global entanglements — *Sin loi!°* they yelled, *I'm sorry, motherfuckers, but I'm out of it, I'm goofed, I'm on a space cruise, I'm gone!* — and it was a restful, disencumbered sensation, just riding the light waves, sailing that big silver freedom bird over the mountains and oceans, over America, over the farms and great sleeping cities and cemeteries and highways and the golden arches of McDonald's. It was flight, a kind of fleeing, a kind of falling, falling higher and higher, spinning off the edge of the earth and beyond the sun and through the vast, silent vacuum where there were no burdens and where everything weighed exactly

---

Sin loi!: "Sorry about that!"

nothing. *Gone!* they screamed, *I'm sorry but I'm gone!* And so at night, not quite dreaming, they gave themselves over to lightness, they were carried, they were purely borne.

On the morning after Ted Lavender died, First Lieutenant Jimmy Cross crouched at the bottom of his foxhole and burned Martha's letters. Then he burned the two photographs. There was a steady rain falling, which made it difficult, but he used heat tabs and Sterno to build a small fire, screening it with his body, holding the photographs over the tight blue flame with the tips of his fingers.

He realized it was only a gesture. Stupid, he thought. Sentimental, too, but mostly just stupid.

Lavender was dead. You couldn't burn the blame.

Besides, the letters were in his head. And even now, without photographs, Lieutenant Cross could see Martha playing volleyball in her white gym shorts and yellow T-shirt. He could see her moving in the rain.

When the fire died out, Lieutenant Cross pulled his poncho over his shoulders and ate breakfast from a can.

There was no great mystery, he decided.

In those burned letters Martha had never mentioned the war, except to say, Jimmy, take care of yourself. She wasn't involved. She signed the letters "Love," but it wasn't love, and all the fine lines and technicalities did not matter.

The morning came up wet and blurry. Everything seemed part of everything else, the fog and Martha and the deepening rain.

It was a war, after all.

Half smiling, Lieutenant Jimmy Cross took out his maps. He shook his head hard, as if to clear it, then bent forward and began planning the day's march. In ten minutes, or maybe twenty, he would rouse the men and they would pack up and head west, where the maps showed the country to be green and inviting. They would do what they had always done. The rain might add some weight, but otherwise it would be one more day layered upon all the other days.

He was realistic about it. There was that new hardness in his stomach.

No more fantasies, he told himself.

Henceforth, when he thought about Martha, it would be only to think that she belonged elsewhere. He would shut down the daydreams. This was not Mount Sebastian, it was another world, where there were no pretty poems or midterm exams, a place where men died because of carelessness and gross stupidity. Kiowa was right. Boom-down, and you were dead, never partly dead.

Briefly, in the rain, Lieutenant Cross saw Martha's gray eyes gazing back at him.

He understood.

It was very sad, he thought. The things men carried inside. The things men did or felt they had to do.

He almost nodded at her, but didn't.

Instead he went back to his maps. He was now determined to perform his duties firmly and without negligence. It wouldn't help Lavender, he knew that, but from this point on he would comport himself as a soldier. He would dispose of his good-luck pebble. Swallow it, maybe, or use Lee Strunk's slingshot, or just drop it along the trail. On the march he would impose strict field discipline. He would be careful to send out flank security, to prevent straggling or bunching up, to keep his troops moving at the proper pace and at the proper interval. He would insist on clean weapons. He would confiscate the remainder of Lavender's dope. Later in the day, perhaps, he would call the men together and speak to them plainly. He would accept the blame for what had happened to Ted Lavender. He would be a man about it. He would look them in the eyes, keeping his chin level, and he would issue the new SOPs in a calm, impersonal tone of voice, an officer's voice, leaving no room for argument or discussion. Commencing immediately, he'd tell them, they would no longer abandon equipment along the route of march. They would police up their acts. They would get their shit together, and keep it together, and maintain it neatly and in good working order.

He would not tolerate laxity. He would show strength, distancing himself.

Among the men there would be grumbling, of course, and maybe worse, because their days would seem longer and their loads heavier, but Lieutenant Cross reminded himself that his obligation was not to be loved but to lead. He would dispense with love; it was not now a factor. And if anyone quarreled or complained, he would simply tighten his lips and arrange his shoulders in the correct command posture. He might give a curt little nod. Or he might not. He might just shrug and say Carry on, then they would saddle up and form into a column and move out toward the villages of Than Khe.

ಌ

FLANNERY O'CONNOR *(1925–1964) was born in Savannah, Georgia, the only child of Roman Catholic parents. When she was thirteen her father was found to have disseminated lupus, an incurable disease in which antibodies in the immune system attack the body's own substances. After her father's death in 1941, O'Connor attended Georgia State College for Women in Milledgeville, where she also published stories and edited the literary magazine. On the strength of these stories, she was awarded a fellowship at the Writers Workshop at the University of Iowa and earned her M.F.A. degree there. Late in 1950 she became ill with what was diagnosed as lupus, and she returned to Milledgeville to start a series of treatments that temporarily arrested the disease. Living with her mother on the family's 500-acre dairy farm, O'Connor began to work again, writing from nine to twelve in the morning and spending the rest of the day resting, reading, writing letters, and raising peacocks.*

O'Connor's first book, Wise Blood, *a complex comic novel attacking the contemporary secularization of religion, was published in 1952. It was followed in 1955 by a collection of stories,* A Good Man Is Hard to Find. *O'Connor was able to see a second novel,* The Violent Bear It Away, *through to publication in 1960, but she died of lupus in 1964, having completed enough stories for a second collection,* Everything

That Rises Must Converge *(1965). Her total output of just thirty-one stories, collected in her* Complete Stories, *won the National Book Award for fiction in 1972.*

Despite her illness, O'Connor was never a recluse; she accepted as many lecture invitations as her health would permit. A volume of her lectures and occasional pieces was published in 1969 as Mystery and Manners. *It is a valuable companion to her stories and novels, because she often reflected on her writing and interpreted her fiction. As a devout Roman Catholic, O'Connor was uncompromising in her religious views: "For I am no disbeliever in spiritual purpose and no vague believer. This means that for me the meaning of life is centered in our Redemption by Christ and what I see in the world I see in relation to that." As Joyce Carol Oates recognized in her essay "The Visionary Art of Flannery O'Connor," O'Connor is one of the great religious writers of modern times, unique "in her celebration of the necessity of succumbing to the divine through violence that is immediate and irreparable. There is no mysticism in her work that is only spiritual; it is physical as well." O'Connor's stories, like the three included here, frequently involve family relationships but are not meant to be read as realistic fiction, despite her remarkable ear for dialogue. O'Connor said she wrote them as parables, as the epigraph to* A Good Man Is Hard to Find *attests.*

RELATED COMMENTARIES: *See Casebook on Flannery O'Connor, pages 847–870, including Flannery O'Connor, "From 'Letters 1954–55,'" page 847, "Writing Short Stories," page 849, "The Element of Suspense in 'A Good Man Is Hard to Find,'" page 854; V. S. Pritchett, "Flannery O'Connor: Satan Comes to Georgia," page 857; Robert H. Brinkmeyer Jr., "Flannery O'Connor and Her Readers," page 859; Dorothy Tuck McFarland, "On 'Good Country People,'" page 864; Wayne C. Booth, "A Rhetorical Reading of O'Connor's 'Everything That Rises Must Converge,'" page 867.*

FLANNERY O'CONNOR

Everything That Rises Must Converge

1961

Her doctor had told Julian's mother that she must lose twenty pounds on account of her blood pressure, so on Wednesday nights Julian had to take her downtown on the bus for a reducing class at the Y. The reducing class was designed for working girls over fifty, who weighed from 165 to 200 pounds. His mother was one of the slimmer ones, but she said ladies did not tell their age or weight. She would not ride the buses by herself at night since they had been integrated, and because the reducing class was one of her few pleasures, necessary for her health, and *free,* she said Julian could at least put himself out to take her, considering all she did for him. Julian did not like to consider all she did for him, but every Wednesday night he braced himself and took her.

She was almost ready to go, standing before the hall mirror, putting on her hat, while he, his hands behind him, appeared pinned to the door frame, waiting like Saint Sebastian for the arrows to begin piercing him. The hat was new and had cost her seven dollars and a half. She kept saying, "Maybe I shouldn't have paid that for it. No, I shouldn't have. I'll take it off and return it tomorrow. I shouldn't have bought it."

Julian raised his eyes to heaven. "Yes, you should have bought it," he said. "Put it on and let's go." It was a hideous hat. A purple velvet flap came down on one side of it and stood up on the other; the rest of it was green and looked like a cushion with the stuffing out. He decided it was less comical than jaunty and pathetic. Everything that gave her pleasure was small and depressed him.

She lifted the hat one more time and set it down slowly on top of her head. Two wings of gray hair protruded on either side of her florid face, but her eyes, sky-blue, were as innocent and untouched by experience as they must have been when she was ten. Were it not that she was a widow who had struggled fiercely to feed and clothe and put him through school and who was supporting him still, "until he got on his feet," she might have been a little girl that he had to take to town.

"It's all right, it's all right," he said. "Let's go." He opened the door himself and started down the walk to get her going. The sky was a dying violet and the houses stood out darkly against it, bulbous liver-colored monstrosities of a uniform ugliness though no two were alike. Since this had been a fashionable neighborhood forty years ago, his mother persisted in thinking they did well to have an apartment in it. Each house had a narrow collar of dirt around it in which sat, usually, a grubby child. Julian walked with his hands in his pockets, his head down and thrust forward, and his eyes glazed with the determination to make himself completely numb during the time he would be sacrificed to her pleasure.

The door closed and he turned to find the dumpy figure, surmounted by the atrocious hat, coming toward him. "Well," she said, "you only live once and paying a little more for it, I at least won't meet myself coming and going."

"Some day I'll start making money," Julian said gloomily — he knew he never would — "and you can have one of those jokes whenever you take the fit." But first they would move. He visualized a place where the nearest neighbor would be three miles away on either side.

"I think you're doing fine," she said, drawing on her gloves. "You've only been out of school a year. Rome wasn't built in a day."

She was one of the few members of the Y reducing class who arrived in hat and gloves and who had a son who had been to college. "It takes time," she said, "and the world is in such a mess. This hat looked better on me than any of the others, though when she brought it out I said, 'Take that thing back. I wouldn't have it on my head,' and she said, 'Now wait till you see it on,' and when she put it on me, I said, 'We-ull,' and she said, 'If you ask me, that hat does something for you and you do something for the hat, and besides,' she said, 'with that hat, you won't meet yourself coming and going.' "

Julian thought he could have stood his lot better if she had been selfish, if she had been an old hag who drank and screamed at him. He walked along, saturated in depression, as if in the midst of his martyrdom he had lost his faith. Catching sight of his long, hopeless, irritated face, she stopped suddenly with a grief-stricken look, and pulled back on his arm. "Wait on me," she said. "I'm going back to the house and take this thing off and tomorrow I'm going to return it. I was out of my head. I can pay the gas bill with the seven-fifty."

He caught her arm in a vicious grip. "You are not going to take it back," he said. "I like it."

"Well," she said, "I don't think I ought . . ."

"Shut up and enjoy it," he muttered, more depressed than ever.

"With the world in the mess it's in," she said, "it's a wonder we can enjoy anything. I tell you, the bottom rail is on the top."

Julian sighed.

"Of course," she said, "if you know who you are, you can go anywhere." She said this every time he took her to the reducing class. "Most of them in it are not our kind of people," she said, "but I can be gracious to anybody. I know who I am."

"They don't give a damn for your graciousness," Julian said savagely. "Knowing who you are is good for one generation only. You haven't the foggiest idea where you stand now or who you are."

She stopped and allowed her eyes to flash at him. "I most certainly do know who I am," she said, "and if you don't know who you are, I'm ashamed of you."

"Oh hell," Julian said.

"Your great-grandfather was a former governor of this state," she said. "Your grandfather was a prosperous landowner. Your grandmother was a Godhigh."

"Will you look around you," he said tensely, "and see where you are now?" and he swept his arm jerkily out to indicate the neighborhood, which the growing darkness at least made less dingy.

"You remain what you are," she said. "Your great-grandfather had a plantation and two hundred slaves."

"There are no more slaves," he said irritably.

"They were better off when they were," she said. He groaned to see that she was off on that topic. She rolled onto it every few days like a train on an open track. He knew every stop, every junction, every swamp along the way, and knew the exact point at which her conclusion would roll majestically into the station: "It's ridiculous. It's simply not realistic. They should rise, yes, but on their own side of the fence."

"Let's skip it," Julian said.

"The ones I feel sorry for," she said, "are the ones that are half white. They're tragic."

"Will you skip it?"

"Suppose we were half white. We would certainly have mixed feelings."

"I have mixed feelings now," he groaned.

"Well let's talk about something pleasant," she said. "I remember going to Grandpa's when I was a little girl. Then the house had double stairways that went up to what was really the second floor — all the cooking was done on the first. I used to like to stay down in the kitchen on account of the way the walls smelled. I would sit with my nose pressed against the plaster and take deep breaths. Actually the place belonged to the Godhighs but your grandfather Chestny paid the mortgage and saved it for them. They were in reduced circumstances," she said, "but reduced or not, they never forgot who they were."

"Doubtless that decayed mansion reminded them," Julian muttered. He never spoke of it without contempt or thought of it without longing. He had seen it once when he was a child before it had been sold. The double stairways had rotted and had been torn down. Negroes were living in it. But it remained in his mind as his mother had known it. It appeared in his dreams regularly. He would stand on the wide porch, listening to the rustle of oak leaves, then wander through the high-ceilinged hall into the parlor that opened onto it and gaze at the worn rugs and faded draperies. It occurred to him that it was he, not she, who could have appreciated it. He preferred its threadbare elegance to anything he could name and it was because of it that all the neighborhoods they had lived in had been a torment to him — whereas she had hardly known the difference. She called her insensitivity "being adjustable."

"And I remember the old darky who was my nurse, Caroline. There was no better person in the world. I've always had a great respect for my colored friends," she said. "I'd do anything in the world for them and they'd . . ."

"Will you for God's sake get off that subject?" Julian said. When he got on a bus by himself, he made it a point to sit down beside a Negro, in reparation as it were for his mother's sins.

"You're mighty touchy tonight," she said. "Do you feel all right?"

"Yes I feel all right," he said. "Now lay off."

She pursed her lips. "Well, you certainly are in a vile humor," she observed. "I just won't speak to you at all."

They had reached the bus stop. There was no bus in sight and Julian, his hands still jammed in his pockets and his head thrust forward, scowled down the empty street. The frustration of having to wait on the bus as well as ride on it began to creep up his neck like a hot hand. The presence of his mother was borne in upon him as she gave a pained sigh. He looked at her bleakly. She was holding herself very erect under the preposterous hat, wearing it like a banner of her imaginary dignity. There was in him an evil urge to break her spirit. He suddenly unloosened his tie and pulled it off and put it in his pocket.

She stiffened. "Why must you look like *that* when you take me to town?" she said. "Why must you deliberately embarrass me?"

"If you'll never learn where you are," he said, "you can at least learn where I am."

"You look like a — thug," she said.

"Then I must be one," he murmured.

"I'll just go home," she said. "I will not bother you. If you can't do a little thing like that for me . . ."

Rolling his eyes upward, he put his tie back on. "Restored to my class," he muttered. He thrust his face toward her and hissed, "True culture is in the mind, the *mind*," he said, and tapped his head, "the mind."

"It's in the heart," she said, "and in how you do things and how you do things is because of who you *are*."

"Nobody in the damn bus cares who you are."

"I care who I am," she said icily.

The lighted bus appeared on top of the next hill and as it approached, they moved out into the street to meet it. He put his hand under her elbow and hoisted her up on the creaking step. She entered with a little smile, as if she were going into a drawing room where everyone had been waiting for her. While he put in the tokens, she sat down on one of the broad front seats for three which faced the aisle. A thin woman with protruding teeth and long yellow hair was sitting on the end of it. His mother moved up beside her and left room for Julian beside herself. He sat down and looked at the floor across the aisle where a pair of thin feet in red and white canvas sandals were planted.

His mother immediately began a general conversation meant to attract anyone who felt like talking. "Can it get any hotter?" she said and removed from her purse a folding fan, black with a Japanese scene on it, which she began to flutter before her.

"I reckon it might could," the woman with the protruding teeth said, "but I know for a fact my apartment couldn't get no hotter."

"It must get the afternoon sun," his mother said. She sat forward and looked up and down the bus. It was half filled. Everybody was white. "I see we have the bus to ourselves," she said. Julian cringed.

"For a change," said the woman across the aisle, the owner of the red and white canvas sandals. "I come on one the other day and they were thick as fleas — up front and all through."

"The world is in a mess everywhere," his mother said. "I don't know how we've let it get in this fix."

"What gets my goat is all those boys from good families stealing automobile tires," the woman with the protruding teeth said. "I told my boy, I said you may not be rich but you been raised right and if I ever catch you in any such mess, they can send you on to the reformatory. Be exactly where you belong."

"Training tells," his mother said. "Is your boy in high school?"

"Ninth grade," the woman said.

"My son just finished college last year. He wants to write but he's selling typewriters until he gets started," his mother said.

The woman leaned forward and peered at Julian. He threw her such a malevolent look that she subsided against the seat. On the floor across the aisle there was an abandoned newspaper. He got up and got it and opened it out in front of him. His mother discreetly continued the conversation in a lower tone but the woman across the aisle said in a loud voice, "Well that's nice. Selling typewriters is close to writing. He can go right from one to the other."

"I tell him," his mother said, "that Rome wasn't built in a day."

Behind the newspaper Julian was withdrawing into the inner compartment of his mind where he spent most of his time. This was a kind of mental bubble in which he established himself when he could not bear to be part of what was going on around him. From it he could see out and judge but in it he was safe from any kind of penetration from without. It was the only place where he felt free of the general idiocy of his fellows. His mother had never entered it but from it he could see her with absolute clarity.

The old lady was clever enough and he thought that if she had started from any of the right premises, more might have been expected of her. She lived according to the laws of her own fantasy world, outside of which he had never seen her set foot. The law of it was to sacrifice herself for him after she had first created the necessity to do so by making a mess of things. If he had permitted her sacrifices, it was only because her lack of foresight had made them necessary. All of her life had been a struggle to act like a Chestny without the Chestny goods, and to give him everything she thought a Chestny ought to have; but since, said she, it was fun to struggle, why complain? And when you had won, as she had won, what fun to look back on the hard times! He could not forgive her that she had enjoyed the struggle and that she thought *she* had won.

What she meant when she said she had won was that she had brought him up successfully and had sent him to college and that he had turned out so well — good looking (her teeth had gone unfilled, so that his could be straightened), intelligent (he realized he was too intelligent to be a success), and with a future ahead of him (there was of course no future ahead of him). She excused his gloominess on the grounds that he was still growing up and his radical ideas on his lack of practical experience. She said he didn't yet know a thing about "life," that he hadn't even entered the real world — when already he was as disenchanted with it as a man of fifty.

The further irony of all this was that in spite of her, he had turned out so well. In spite of going to only a third-rate college, he had, on his own initiative, come out with a first-rate education; in spite of growing up dominated by a small mind, he had ended up with a large one; in spite of all her foolish views, he was free of prejudice and unafraid to face facts. Most miraculous of all, instead of being blinded by love for her as she was for him, he had cut himself emotionally free of her and could see her with complete objectivity. He was not dominated by his mother.

The bus stopped with a sudden jerk and shook him from his meditation. A woman from the back lurched forward with little steps and barely escaped falling in his newspaper as she righted herself. She got off and a large Negro got on. Julian kept his paper lowered to watch. It gave him a certain satisfaction to see injustice in daily operation. It confirmed his view that with a few exceptions there was no one worth knowing within a radius of three hundred miles. The Negro was well dressed and carried a briefcase. He looked round and then sat down on the other end of the seat where the woman with the red and white canvas sandals was sitting. He immediately unfolded a newspaper and obscured himself behind it. Julian's mother's elbow at once prodded insistently into his ribs. "Now you see why I won't ride on these buses by myself," she whispered.

The woman with the red and white canvas sandals had risen at the same time the Negro sat down and had gone further back in the bus and taken the seat of the woman who had got off. His mother leaned forward and cast her an approving look.

Julian rose, crossed the aisle, and sat down in the place of the woman with the canvas sandals. From this position, he looked serenely across at his mother. Her face had turned an angry red. He stared at her, making his eyes the eyes of a stranger. He felt his tension suddenly lift as if he had openly declared war on her.

He would have liked to get in conversation with the Negro and to talk with him about art or politics or any subject that would be above the comprehension of those around them, but the man remained entrenched behind his paper. He was either ignoring the change of seating or had never noticed it. There was no way for Julian to convey his sympathy.

His mother kept her eyes fixed reproachfully on his face. The woman with the protruding teeth was looking at him avidly as if he were a type of monster new to her.

"Do you have a light?" he asked the Negro.

Without looking away from his paper, the man reached in his pocket and handed him a packet of matches.

"Thanks," Julian said. For a moment he held the matches foolishly. A NO SMOKING sign looked down upon him from over the door. This alone would not have deterred him; he had no cigarettes. He had quit smoking some months before because he could not afford it. "Sorry," he muttered and handed back the matches. The Negro lowered the paper and gave him an annoyed look. He took the matches and raised the paper again.

His mother continued to gaze at him but she did not take the advantage of his momentary discomfort. Her eyes retained their battered look. Her face seemed to be unnaturally red, as if her blood pressure had risen. Julian allowed no glimmer of sympathy to show on his face. Having got the advantage, he wanted desperately to keep it and carry it through. He would have liked to teach her a lesson that would last her a while, but there seemed no way to continue the point. The Negro refused to come out from behind his paper.

Julian folded his arms and looked stolidly before him, facing her but as if he did not see her, as if he had ceased to recognize her existence. He visualized a scene in which, the bus having reached their stop, he would remain in his seat and when she said, "Aren't you going to get off?" he would look at her as a stranger who had rashly addressed him. The corner they got off on was usually deserted, but it was well lighted and it would not hurt her to walk by herself the four blocks to the Y. He decided to wait until the time came and then decide whether or not he would let her get off by herself. He would have to be at the Y at ten to bring her back, but he could leave her wondering if he was going to show up. There was no reason for her to think she could always depend on him.

He retired again into the high-ceilinged room sparsely settled with large pieces of antique furniture. His soul expanded momentarily but then he became aware of his mother across from him and the vision shriveled. He studied her coldly. Her feet in little pumps dangled like a child's and did not quite reach the floor. She was training on him an exaggerated look of reproach. He felt completely detached from her. At that moment he could with pleasure have slapped her as he would have slapped a particularly obnoxious child in his charge.

He began to imagine various unlikely ways by which he could teach her a lesson. He might make friends with some distinguished Negro professor or lawyer and bring him home to spend the evening. He would be entirely justified but her blood pressure would rise to 300. He could not push her to the extent of making her have a stroke, and moreover, he had never been successful at making any Negro friends. He had tried to strike up an acquaintance on the bus with some of the better types, with ones that looked like professors or ministers or lawyers. One morning he had sat down next to a distinguished-looking dark brown man who had answered his questions with a sonorous solemnity but who had turned out to be an undertaker. Another day he had sat down beside a cigar-smoking Negro with a diamond ring on his finger, but after a few stilted pleasantries, the Negro had rung the buzzer and risen, slipping two lottery tickets into Julian's hand as he climbed over him to leave.

He imagined his mother lying desperately ill and his being able to secure only a Negro doctor for her. He toyed with that idea for a few minutes and then dropped it for a momentary vision of himself participating as a sympathizer in a sit-in demonstration. This was possible but he did not linger with it. Instead, he approached the ultimate horror. He brought home a beautiful suspiciously Negroid woman. Prepare yourself, he said. There is nothing you can do about it. This is the woman I've chosen. She's intelligent, dignified, even good, and she's suffered and she hasn't thought it *fun.* Now persecute us, go ahead and persecute us. Drive her out of here, but remember, you're driving me too. His eyes were narrowed and through the indignation he had generated, he saw his mother across the aisle, purplefaced, shrunken to the dwarf-like proportions of her moral nature, sitting like a mummy beneath the ridiculous banner of her hat.

He was tilted out of his fantasy again as the bus stopped. The door opened with a sucking hiss and out of the dark a large, gaily dressed, sullen-looking colored woman got on with a little boy. The child, who might have been four, had on a short plaid suit and a Tyrolean hat with a blue feather in it. Julian hoped that he would sit down beside him and that the woman would push in beside his mother. He could think of no better arrangement.

As she waited for her tokens, the woman was surveying the seating possibilities — he hoped with the idea of sitting where she was least wanted. There was something familiar-looking about her but Julian could not place what it was. She was a giant of a woman. Her face was set not only to meet opposition but to seek it out. The downward tilt of her large lower lip was like a warning sign: DON'T TAMPER WITH ME. Her bulging figure was encased in a green crepe dress and her feet overflowed in red shoes. She had on a hideous hat. A purple velvet flap came down on one side of it and stood up on the other; the rest of it was green and looked like a cushion with the stuffing out. She carried a mammoth red pocketbook that bulged throughout as if it were stuffed with rocks.

To Julian's disappointment, the little boy climbed up on the empty seat beside his mother. His mother lumped all children, black and white, into the common category, "cute," and she thought little Negroes were on the whole cuter than little white children. She smiled at the little boy as he climbed on the seat.

Meanwhile the woman was bearing down upon the empty seat beside Julian. To his annoyance, she squeezed herself into it. He saw his mother's face change as the woman settled herself next to him and he realized with satisfaction that this was more objectionable to her than it was to him. Her face seemed almost gray and there was a look of dull recognition in her eyes, as if suddenly she had sickened at some awful confrontation. Julian saw that it was because she and the woman had, in a sense, swapped sons. Though his mother would not realize the symbolic significance of this, she would feel it. His amusement showed plainly on his face.

The woman next to him muttered something unintelligible to herself. He was conscious of a kind of bristling next to him, muted growling like that of an angry cat. He could not see anything but the red pocketbook upright on the bulging green thighs. He visualized the woman as she had stood waiting for her tokens — the ponderous figure, rising from the red shoes upward over the solid hips, the mammoth bosom, the haughty face, to the green and purple hat.

His eyes widened.

The vision of the two hats, identical, broke upon him with the radiance of a brilliant sunrise. His face was suddenly lit with joy. He could not believe that Fate had thrust upon his mother such a lesson. He gave a loud chuckle so that she would look at him and see that he saw. She turned her eyes on him slowly. The blue in them seemed to have turned a bruised purple. For a moment he had an uncomfortable sense of her innocence, but it lasted only a second before principle rescued him. Justice entitled him to laugh. His grin hardened until it said to her as plainly as if he were saying aloud: Your punishment exactly fits your pettiness. This should teach you a permanent lesson.

Her eyes shifted to the woman. She seemed unable to bear looking at him and to find the woman preferable. He became conscious again of the bristling presence at his side. The woman was rumbling like a volcano about to become active. His mother's mouth began to twitch slightly at one corner. With a sinking heart, he saw incipient signs of recovery on her face and realized that this was going to strike her suddenly as funny and was going to be no lesson at all. She kept her eyes on the woman and an amused smile came over her face as if the woman were a monkey that had stolen her hat. The little Negro was looking up at her with large fascinated eyes. He had been trying to attract her attention for some time.

"Carver," the woman said suddenly. "Come heah!"

When he saw that the spotlight was on him at last, Carver drew his feet up and turned himself toward Julian's mother and giggled.

"Carver!" the woman said. "You heah me? Come Heah!"

Carver slid down from the seat but remained squatting with his back against the base of it, his head turned slowly around toward Julian's mother, who was smiling at him. The woman reached a hand across the aisle and snatched him to her. He righted himself and hung backwards on her knees, grinning at Julian's mother. "Isn't he cute?" Julian's mother said to the woman with the protruding teeth.

"I reckon he is," the woman said without conviction.

The Negress yanked him upright but he eased out of her grip and shot across the aisle and scrambled, giggling wildly, onto the seat beside his love.

"I think he likes me," Julian's mother said, and smiled at the woman. It was the smile she used when she was being particularly gracious to an inferior. Julian saw everything lost. The lesson had rolled off her like rain on a roof.

The woman stood up and yanked the little boy off the seat as if she were snatching him from contagion. Julian could feel the rage in her at having no weapon like his mother's smile. She gave the child a sharp slap across his leg. He howled once and then thrust his head into her stomach and kicked his feet against her shins. "Behave," she said vehemently.

The bus stopped and the Negro who had been reading the newspaper got off. The woman moved over and set the little boy down with a thump between herself and Julian. She held him firmly by the knee. In a moment he put his hands in front of his face and peeped at Julian's mother through his fingers.

"I see yoooooooo!" she said and put her hand in front of her face and peeped at him.

The woman slapped his hand down. "Quit yo' foolishness," she said, "before I knock the living Jesus out of you!"

Julian was thankful that the next stop was theirs. He reached up and pulled the cord. The woman reached up and pulled it at the same time. Oh my God, he thought. He had the terrible intuition that when they got off the bus together, his mother would open her purse and give the little boy a nickel. The gesture would be as natural to her as breathing. The bus stopped and the woman got up and lunged to the front, dragging the child, who wished to stay on, after her. Julian and his mother got up and followed. As they neared the door, Julian tried to relieve her of her pocketbook.

"No," she murmured, "I want to give the little boy a nickel."

"No!" Julian hissed. "No!"

She smiled down at the child and opened her bag. The bus door opened and the woman picked him up by the arm and descended with him, hanging at her hip. Once in the street she set him down and shook him.

Julian's mother had to close her purse while she got down the bus step but as soon as her feet were on the ground, she opened it again and began to rummage inside. "I can't find but a penny," she whispered, "but it looks like a new one."

"Don't do it!" Julian said fiercely between his teeth. There was a streetlight on the corner and she hurried to get under it so that she could better see into her pocketbook. The woman was heading off rapidly down the street with the child still hanging backward on her hand.

"Oh little boy!" Julian's mother called and took a few quick steps and caught up with them just beyond the lamppost. "Here's a bright new penny for you," and she held out the coin, which shone bronze in the dim light.

The huge woman turned and for a moment stood, her shoulders lifted and her face frozen with frustrated rage, and stared at Julian's mother. Then all at once she seemed to explode like a piece of machinery that had been given one ounce of pressure too much. Julian saw the black fist swing out with the red pocketbook. He shut his eyes and cringed as he heard the woman shout, "He don't take nobody's pennies!" When he opened his eyes, the woman was disappearing down the street with the little boy staring wide-eyed over her shoulder. Julian's mother was sitting on the sidewalk.

"I told you not to do that," Julian said angrily. "I told you not to do that!"

He stood over her for a minute, gritting his teeth. Her legs were stretched out in front of her and her hat was on her lap. He squatted down and looked her in the face. It was totally expressionless. "You got exactly what you deserved," he said. "Now get up."

He picked up her pocketbook and put what had fallen out back in it. He picked the hat up off her lap. The penny caught his eye on the sidewalk and he picked that up and let it drop before her eyes into the purse. Then he stood up and leaned over and held his hands out to pull her up. She remained immobile. He sighed. Rising above them on either side were black apartment buildings, marked with irregular rectangles of light. At the end of the block a man came out of a door and walked off in the opposite direction. "All right," he said, "suppose somebody happens by and wants to know why you're sitting on the sidewalk?"

She took the hand and, breathing hard, pulled heavily up on it and then stood for a moment, swaying slightly as if the spots of light in the darkness were circling around her. Her eyes, shadowed and confused, finally settled on his face. He did not try to conceal his irritation. "I hope this teaches you a lesson," he said. She leaned forward and her eyes raked his face. She seemed trying to determine his identity. Then, as if she found nothing familiar about him, she started off with a headlong movement in the wrong direction.

"Aren't you going to the Y?" he asked.

"Home," she muttered.

"Well, are we walking?"

For answer she kept going. Julian followed along, his hands behind him. He saw no reason to let the lesson she had had go without backing it up with an explanation of its meaning. She might as well be made to understand what had happened to her. "Don't think that was just an uppity Negro woman," he said. "That was the whole colored race which will no longer take your condescending pennies. That was your black double. She can wear the same hat as you, and to be sure," he added gratuitously (because he thought it was funny), "it looked better on her than it did on you. What all this means," he said, "is that the old world is gone. The old manners are obsolete and your graciousness is not worth a damn." He thought bitterly of the house that had been lost for him. "You aren't who you think you are," he said.

She continued to plow ahead, paying no attention to him. Her hair had come undone on one side. She dropped her pocketbook and took no notice. He stopped and picked it up and handed it to her but she did not take it.

"You needn't act as if the world had come to an end," he said, "because it hasn't. From now on you've got to live in a new world and face a few realities for a change. Buck up," he said, "it won't kill you."

She was breathing fast.

"Let's wait on the bus," he said.

"Home," she said thickly.

"I hate to see you behave like this," he said. "Just like a child. I should be able to expect more of you." He decided to stop where he was and make her stop and wait for a bus. "I'm not going any farther," he said, stopping. "We're going on the bus."

She continued to go on as if she had not heard him. He took a few steps and caught her arm and stopped her. He looked into her face and caught his breath. He was looking into a face he had never seen before. "Tell Grandpa to come get me," she said.

He stared, stricken.

"Tell Caroline to come get me," she said.

Stunned, he let her go and she lurched forward again, walking as if one leg were shorter than the other. A tide of darkness seemed to be sweeping her from him. "Mother!" he cried. "Darling, sweetheart, wait!" Crumpling, she fell to the pavement. He dashed forward and fell at her side, crying, "Mamma, Mamma!" He turned her over. Her face was fiercely distorted. One eye, large and staring, moved slightly to the left as if it had become unmoored. The other remained fixed on him, raked his face again, found nothing, and closed.

"Wait here, wait here!" he cried and jumped up and began to run for help toward a cluster of lights he saw in the distance ahead of him. "Help, help!" he shouted, but his voice was thin, scarcely a thread of sound. The lights drifted farther away the faster he ran and his feet moved numbly as if they carried him nowhere. The tide of darkness seemed to sweep him back to her, postponing from moment to moment his entry into the world of guilt and sorrow.

FLANNERY O'CONNOR

Good Country People   1955

Besides the neutral expression that she wore when she was alone, Mrs. Freeman had two others, forward and reverse, that she used for all her human dealings. Her forward expression was steady and driving like the advance of a heavy truck. Her eyes never swerved to left or right but turned as the story turned as if they followed a yellow line down the center of it. She seldom used the other expression because it was not often necessary for her to retract a statement, but when she did, her face came to a complete stop, there was an almost imperceptible movement of her black eyes, during which they seemed to be receding, and then the observer would see that Mrs. Freeman, though she might stand there as real as several grain sacks thrown on top of each other, was no longer there in spirit. As for getting anything across to her when this was the case, Mrs. Hopewell had given it up. She might talk her head off. Mrs. Freeman could never be brought to admit herself wrong on any point.

She would stand there and if she could be brought to say anything, it was something like, "Well, I wouldn't of said it was and I wouldn't of said it wasn't," or letting her gaze range over the top kitchen shelf where there was an assortment of dusty bottles, she might remark, "I see you ain't ate many of them figs you put up last summer."

They carried on their most important business in the kitchen at breakfast. Every morning Mrs. Hopewell got up at seven o'clock and lit her gas heater and Joy's. Joy was her daughter, a large blonde girl who had an artificial leg. Mrs. Hopewell thought of her as a child though she was thirty-two years old and highly educated. Joy would get up while her mother was eating and lumber into the bathroom and slam the door, and before long, Mrs. Freeman would arrive at the back door. Joy would hear her mother call, "Come on in," and then they would talk a while in low voices that were indistinguishable in the bathroom. By the time Joy came in, they had usually finished the weather report and were on one or the other of Mrs. Freeman's daughters, Glynese or Carramae, Joy called them Glycerin and Caramel. Glynese, a redhead, was eighteen and had many admirers; Carramae, a blonde, was only fifteen but already married and pregnant. She could not keep anything on her stomach. Every morning Mrs. Freeman told Mrs. Hopewell how many times she had vomited since the last report.

Mrs. Hopewell liked to tell people that Glynese and Carramae were two of the finest girls she knew and that Mrs. Freeman was a *lady* and that she was never ashamed to take her anywhere or introduce her to anybody they might meet. Then she would tell how she had happened to hire the Freemans in the first place and how they were a godsend to her and how she had had them four years. The reason for her keeping them so long was that they were not trash. They were good country people. She had telephoned the man whose name they had given as a reference and he had told her that Mr. Freeman was a good farmer but that his wife was the nosiest woman ever to walk the earth. "She's got to be into everything," the man said. "If she don't get there before the dust settles, you can bet she's dead, that's all. She'll want to know all your business. I can stand him real good," he had said, "but me nor my wife neither could have stood that woman one more minute on this place." That had put Mrs. Hopewell off for a few days.

She had hired them in the end because there were no other applicants but she had made up her mind beforehand exactly how she would handle the woman. Since she was the type who had to be into everything, then, Mrs. Hopewell had decided, she would not only let her be into everything, she would *see to it* that she was into everything — she would give her the responsibility of everything, she would put her in charge. Mrs. Hopewell had no bad qualities of her own but she was able to use other people's in such a constructive way that she never felt the lack. She had hired the Freemans and she had kept them four years.

Nothing is perfect. This was one of Mrs. Hopewell's favorite sayings. Another was: that is life! And still another, the most important, was: well, other people have their opinions too. She would make these statements, usually at the table, in a tone of gentle insistence as if no one held them but her, and the large hulking Joy, whose constant outrage had obliterated every expression from her face, would stare just a little to the side of her, her eyes icy blue, with the look of someone who has achieved blindness by an act of will and means to keep it.

When Mrs. Hopewell said to Mrs. Freeman that life was like that, Mrs. Freeman would say, "I always said so myself." Nothing had been arrived at by anyone that had not first been arrived at by her. She was quicker than Mr. Freeman. When Mrs. Hopewell said to her after they had been on the place a while, "You know, you're the wheel behind the wheel," and winked, Mrs. Freeman had said, "I know it. I've always been quick. It's some that are quicker than others."

"Everybody is different," Mrs. Hopewell said.

"Yes, most people is," Mrs. Freeman said.

"It takes all kinds to make the world."

"I always said it did myself."

The girl was used to this kind of dialogue for breakfast and more of it for dinner; sometimes they had it for supper too. When they had no guest they ate in the kitchen because that was easier. Mrs. Freeman always managed to arrive at some point during the meal and to watch them finish it. She would stand in the doorway if it were summer but in the winter she would stand with one elbow on top of the refrigerator and look down on them, or she would stand by the gas heater, lifting the back of her skirt slightly. Occasionally she would stand against the wall and roll her head from side to side. At no time was she in any hurry to leave. All this was very trying on Mrs. Hopewell but she was a woman of great patience. She realized that nothing is perfect and that in the Freemans she had good country people and that if, in this day and age, you get good country people, you had better hang onto them.

She had had plenty of experience with trash. Before the Freemans she had averaged one tenant family a year. The wives of these farmers were not the kind you would want to be around you for very long. Mrs. Hopewell, who had divorced her husband long ago, needed someone to walk over the fields with her; and when Joy had to be impressed for these services, her remarks were usually so ugly and her face so glum that Mrs. Hopewell would say, "If you can't come pleasantly, I don't want you at all," to which the girl, standing square and rigid-shouldered with her neck thrust slightly forward, would reply, "If you want me, here I am — LIKE I AM."

Mrs. Hopewell excused this attitude because of the leg (which had been shot off in a hunting accident when Joy was ten). It was hard for Mrs. Hopewell to realize that her child was thirty-two now and that for more than twenty years she had had only one leg. She thought of her still as a child because it tore her heart to think instead of the poor stout girl in her thirties who had never danced a step or had any *normal* good times. Her name was really Joy but as soon as she was twenty-one and away from home, she had had it legally changed. Mrs. Hopewell was certain that she had thought and thought until she had hit upon the ugliest name in any language. Then she had gone and had the beautiful name, Joy, changed without telling her mother until after she had done it. Her legal name was Hulga.

When Mrs. Hopewell thought the name Hulga, she thought of the broad blank hull of a battleship. She would not use it. She continued to call her Joy to which the girl responded but in a purely mechanical way.

Hulga had learned to tolerate Mrs. Freeman who saved her from taking walks with her mother. Even Glynese and Carramae were useful when they occupied attention that might otherwise have been directed at her. At first she had thought she could not stand Mrs. Freeman for she had found that it was not possible to be rude to her. Mrs. Freeman would take on strange resentments and for days together she would be sullen but the source of her displeasure was always obscure; a direct attack, a positive leer, blatant ugliness to her face — these never touched her. And without warning one day, she began calling her Hulga.

She did not call her that in front of Mrs. Hopewell who would have been incensed but when she and the girl happened to be out of the house together, she would say something and add the name Hulga to the end of it, and the big spectacled Joy-Hulga would scowl and redden as if her privacy had been intruded upon. She considered the name her personal affair. She had arrived at it first purely on the basis of its ugly sound and then the full genius of its fitness had struck her. She had a vision of the name working like the ugly sweating Vulcan who stayed in the furnace and to whom, presumably, the goddess had to come when called. She saw it as the name of her highest creative act. One of her major triumphs was that her mother had not been able to turn her dust into Joy, but the greater one was that she had been able to turn it herself into Hulga. However, Mrs. Freeman's relish for using the name only irritated her. It was as if Mrs. Freeman's beady steel-pointed eyes had penetrated far enough behind her face to reach some secret fact. Something about her seemed to fascinate Mrs. Freeman and then one day Hulga realized that it was the artificial leg. Mrs. Freeman had a special fondness for the details of secret infections, hidden deformities, assaults upon children. Of diseases, she preferred the lingering or incurable. Hulga had heard Mrs. Hopewell give her the details of the hunting accident, how the leg had been literally blasted off, how she had never lost consciousness. Mrs. Freeman could listen to it any time as if it had happened an hour ago.

When Hulga stumped into the kitchen in the morning (she could walk without making the awful noise but she made it — Mrs. Hopewell was certain — because it was ugly-sounding), she glanced at them and did not speak. Mrs. Hopewell would be in her red kimono with her hair tied around her head in rags. She would be sitting at the table, finishing her breakfast and Mrs. Freeman would be hanging by her elbow outward from the refrigerator, looking down at the table. Hulga always put her eggs on the stove to boil and then stood over them with her arms folded, and Mrs. Hopewell would look at her — a kind of indirect gaze divided between her and Mrs. Freeman — and would think that if she would only keep herself up a little, she wouldn't be so bad looking. There was nothing wrong with her face that a pleasant expression wouldn't help. Mrs. Hopewell said that people who looked on the bright side of things would be beautiful even if they were not.

Whenever she looked at Joy this way, she could not help but feel that it would have been better if the child had not taken the Ph.D. It had certainly not brought her out any and now that she had it, there was no more excuse for her to go to school again. Mrs. Hopewell thought it was nice for girls to go to school to have a good time but Joy had "gone through." Anyhow, she would not have been strong enough to go again. The doctors had told Mrs. Hopewell that with the best of care, Joy might see forty-five. She had a weak heart. Joy had made it plain that if it had not been for this condition, she would be far from these red hills and good country people. She would be in a university lecturing to people who knew what she was talking about. And Mrs. Hopewell could very well picture her there, looking like a scarecrow and lecturing to more of the same. Here she went about all day in a six-year-old skirt and a yellow sweat shirt with a faded cowboy on a horse embossed on it. She thought this was funny; Mrs. Hopewell thought it was idiotic and showed simply that she was still a child. She was brilliant but she didn't have a grain of sense. It seemed to Mrs. Hopewell that every year she grew less like other people and more like herself — bloated, rude, and squint-eyed. And she said such strange things! To her own mother she had said — without warning, without excuse, standing up in the middle of a meal with her face purple and her mouth half full — "Woman! do you ever look inside? Do you ever look inside and see what you are *not*? God!" she had cried sinking down again and staring at her plate, "Malebranche was right: we are not our own light. We are not our own light!" Mrs. Hopewell had no idea to this day what brought that on. She had only made the remark, hoping Joy would take it in, that a smile never hurt anyone.

The girl had taken the Ph.D. in philosophy and this left Mrs. Hopewell at a complete loss. You could say, "My daughter is a nurse," or "My daughter is a schoolteacher," or even, "My daughter is a chemical engineer." You could not say, "My daughter is a philosopher." That was something that had ended with the Greeks and Romans. All day Joy sat on her neck in a deep chair, reading. Sometimes she went for walks but she didn't like dogs or cats or birds or flowers or nature or nice young men. She looked at nice young men as if she could smell their stupidity.

One day Mrs. Hopewell had picked up one of the books the girl had just put down and opening it at random, she read, "Science, on the other hand, has to assert its soberness and seriousness afresh and declare that it is concerned solely with what-is. Nothing — how can it be for science anything but a horror and a phantasm? If science is right, then one thing stands firm: science wishes to know nothing of nothing. Such is after all the strictly scientific approach to Nothing. We know it by wishing to know nothing of Nothing." These words had been underlined with a blue pencil and they worked on Mrs. Hopewell like some evil incantation in gibberish. She shut the book quickly and went out of the room as if she were having a chill.

This morning when the girl came in, Mrs. Freeman was on Carramae. "She thrown up four times after supper," she said, "and was up twict in the night after three o'clock. Yesterday she didn't do nothing but ramble in the bureau drawer. All she did. Stand up there and see what she could run up on."

"She's got to eat," Mrs. Hopewell muttered, sipping her coffee, while she watched Joy's back at the stove. She was wondering what the child had said to the Bible salesman. She could not imagine what kind of a conversation she could possibly have had with him.

He was a tall gaunt hatless youth who had called yesterday to sell them a Bible. He had appeared at the door, carrying a large black suitcase that weighted him so heavily on one side that he had to brace himself against the door facing. He seemed on the point of collapse but he said in a cheerful voice, "Good morning, Mrs. Cedars!" and set the suitcase down on the mat. He was not a bad-looking young man though he had on a bright blue suit and yellow socks that were not pulled up far enough. He had prominent face bones and a streak of sticky-looking brown hair falling across his forehead.

"I'm Mrs. Hopewell," she said.

"Oh!" he said, pretending to look puzzled but with his eyes sparkling, "I saw it said 'The Cedars' on the mailbox so I thought you was Mrs. Cedars!" and he burst out in a pleasant laugh. He picked up the satchel and under cover of a pant, he fell forward into her hall. It was rather as if the suitcase had moved first, jerking him after it. "Mrs. Hopewell!" he said and grabbed her hand. "I hope you are well!" and he laughed again and then all at once his face sobered completely. He paused and gave her a straight earnest look and said, "Lady, I've come to speak of serious things."

"Well, come in," she muttered, none too pleased because her dinner was almost ready. He came into the parlor and sat down on the edge of a straight chair and put the suitcase between his feet and glanced around the room as if he were sizing her up by it. Her silver gleamed on the two sideboards; she decided he had never been in a room as elegant as this.

"Mrs. Hopewell," he began, using her name in a way that sounded almost intimate, "I know you believe in Chrustian service."

"Well yes," she murmured.

"I know," he said and paused, looking very wise with his head cocked on one side, "that you're a good woman. Friends have told me."

Mrs. Hopewell never liked to be taken for a fool. "What are you selling?" she asked.

"Bibles," the young man said and his eye raced around the room before he added, "I see you have no family Bible in your parlor, I see that is the one lack you got!"

Mrs. Hopewell could not say, "My daughter is an atheist and won't let me keep the Bible in the parlor." She said, stiffening slightly, "I keep my Bible by my bedside." This was not the truth. It was in the attic somewhere.

"Lady," he said, "the word of God ought to be in the parlor."

"Well, I think that's a matter of taste," she began. "I think . . ."

"Lady," he said, "for a Chrustian, the word of God ought to be in every room in the house besides in his heart. I know you're a Chrustian because I can see it in every line of your face."

She stood up and said, "Well, young man, I don't want to buy a Bible and I smell my dinner burning."

He didn't get up. He began to twist his hands and looking down at them he said softly, "Well lady, I'll tell you the truth — not many people want to buy one nowadays and besides, I know I'm real simple. I don't know how to say a thing but to say it. I'm just a country boy." He glanced up into her unfriendly face. "People like you don't like to fool with country people like me!"

"Why!" she cried, "good country people are the salt of the earth! Besides, we all have different ways of doing, it takes all kinds to make the world go 'round. That's life!"

"You said a mouthful," he said.

"Why, I think there aren't enough good country people in the world!" she said, stirred. "I think that's what's wrong with it!"

His face had brightened. "I didn't inraduce myself," he said. "I'm Manley Pointer from out in the country around Willohobie, not even from a place, just from near a place."

"You wait a minute," she said. "I have to see about my dinner." She went out to the kitchen and found Joy standing near the door where she had been listening.

"Get rid of the salt of the earth," she said, "and let's eat."

Mrs. Hopewell gave her a pained look and turned the heat down under the vegetables. "*I* can't be rude to anybody," she murmured and went back into the parlor.

He had opened the suitcase and was sitting with a Bible on each knee. "You might as well put those up," she told him. "I don't want one."

"I appreciate your honesty," he said. "You don't see any more real honest people unless you go way out in the country."

"I know," she said, "real genuine folks!" Through the crack in the door she heard a groan.

"I guess a lot of boys come telling you they're working their way through college," he said, "but I'm not going to tell you that. Somehow," he said, "I don't want to go to college. I want to devote my life to Chrustian service. See," he said, lowering his voice, "I got this heart condition. I may not live long. When you know it's something wrong with you and you may not live long, well then, lady . . ." He paused, with his mouth open, and stared at her.

He and Joy had the same condition! She knew that her eyes were filling with tears but she collected herself quickly and murmured, "Won't you stay for dinner? We'd love to have you!" and was sorry the instant she heard herself say it.

"Yes mam," he said in an abashed voice, "I would sher love to do that!"

Joy had given him one look on being introduced to him and then throughout the meal had not glanced at him again. He had addressed several remarks to her, which she had pretended not to hear. Mrs. Hopewell could not understand deliberate rudeness, although she lived with it, and she felt she had always to overflow with hospitality to make up for Joy's lack of courtesy. She urged him to talk about himself and he did. He said he was the seventh child of twelve and that his father had been crushed under a tree when he himself was eight years old. He had been crushed very badly, in fact, almost cut in two and was practically not recognizable. His mother had got along the best she could by hard working and she had always seen that her children went to Sunday School and that they read the Bible every evening. He was now nineteen years old and he had been selling Bibles for four months. In that time he had sold seventy-seven Bibles and had the promise of two more sales. He wanted to become a missionary because he thought that was the way you could do most for people. "He who losest his life shall find it," he said simply and he was so sincere, so genuine and earnest that Mrs. Hopewell would not for the world have smiled. He prevented his peas from sliding onto the table by blocking them with a piece of bread which he later cleaned his plate with. She could see Joy observing sidewise how he handled his knife and fork and she saw too that every few minutes, the boy would dart a keen appraising glance at the girl as if he were trying to attract her attention.

After dinner Joy cleared the dishes off the table and disappeared and Mrs. Hopewell was left to talk with him. He told her again about his childhood and his father's accident and about various things that had happened to him. Every five minutes or so she would stifle a yawn. He sat for two hours until finally she told him she must go because she had an appointment in town. He packed his Bibles and thanked her and prepared to leave, but in the doorway he stopped and wrung her hand and said that not on any of his trips had he met a lady as nice as her and he asked if he could come again. She had said she would always be happy to see him.

Joy had been standing in the road, apparently looking at something in the distance, when he came down the steps toward her, bent to the side with his heavy valise. He stopped where she was standing and confronted her directly. Mrs. Hopewell could not hear what he said but she trembled to think what Joy would say to him. She could see that after a minute Joy said something and that then the boy began to speak again, making an excited gesture with his free hand. After a minute Joy said something else at which the boy began to speak once more. Then to her amazement, Mrs. Hopewell saw the two of them walk off together, toward the gate. Joy had walked all the way to the gate with him and Mrs. Hopewell could not imagine what they had said to each other, and she had not yet dared to ask.

Mrs. Freeman was insisting upon her attention. She had moved from the refrigerator to the heater so that Mrs. Hopewell had to turn and face her in order to seem to be listening. "Glynese gone out with Harvey Hill again last night," she said. "She had this sty."

"Hill," Mrs. Hopewell said absently, "is that the one who works in the garage?"

"Nome, he's the one that goes to chiropracter school," Mrs. Freeman said. "She had this sty. Been had it two days. So she says when he brought her in the other night he says, 'Lemme get rid of that sty for you,' and she says, 'How?' and he says, 'You just lay yourself down acrost the seat of that car and I'll show you.' So she done it and he popped her neck. Kept on a-popping it several times until she made him quit. This morning," Mrs. Freeman said, "she ain't got no sty. She ain't got no traces of a sty."

"I never heard of that before," Mrs. Hopewell said.

"He ast her to marry him before the Ordinary," Mrs. Freeman went on, "and she told him she wasn't going to be married in no *office*."

"Well, Glynese is a fine girl," Mrs. Hopewell said. "Glynese and Carramae are both fine girls."

"Carramae said when her and Lyman was married Lyman said it sure felt sacred to him. She said he said he wouldn't take five hundred dollars for being married by a preacher."

"How much would he take?" the girl asked from the stove.

"He said he wouldn't take five hundred dollars," Mrs. Freeman repeated.

"Well we all have work to do," Mrs. Hopewell said.

"Lyman said it just felt more sacred to him," Mrs. Freeman said. "The doctor wants Carramae to eat prunes. Says instead of medicine. Says them cramps is coming from pressure. You know where I think it is?"

"She'll be better in a few weeks," Mrs. Hopewell said.

"In the tube," Mrs. Freeman said. "Else she wouldn't be as sick as she is."

Hulga had cracked her two eggs into a saucer and was bringing them to the table along with a cup of coffee that she had filled too full. She sat down carefully and began to eat, meaning to keep Mrs. Freeman there by questions if for any reason she showed an inclination to leave. She could perceive her mother's eye on her. The first round-about question would be about the Bible salesman and she did not wish to bring it on. "How did he pop her neck?" she asked.

Mrs. Freeman went into a description of how he had popped her neck. She said he owned a '55 Mercury but that Glynese said she would rather marry a man with only a '36 Plymouth who would be married by a preacher. The girl asked what if he had a '32 Plymouth and Mrs. Freeman said what Glynese had said was a '36 Plymouth.

Mrs. Hopewell said there were not many girls with Glynese's common sense. She said what she admired in those girls was their common sense. She said that reminded her that they had had a nice visitor yesterday, a young man selling Bibles. "Lord," she said, "he bored me to death but he was so sincere and genuine I couldn't be rude to him. He was just good country people, you know," she said, " — just the salt of the earth."

"I seen him walk up," Mrs. Freeman said, "and then later — I seen him walk off," and Hulga could feel the slight shift in her voice, the slight insinuation, that he had not walked off alone, had he? Her face remained expressionless but the color rose into her neck and she seemed to swallow it down with the next spoonful of egg. Mrs. Freeman was looking at her as if they had a secret together.

"Well, it takes all kinds of people to make the world go 'round," Mrs. Hopewell said. "It's very good we aren't all alike."

"Some people are more alike than others," Mrs. Freeman said.

Hulga got up and stumped, with about twice the noise that was necessary, into her room and locked the door. She was to meet the Bible salesman at ten o'clock at the gate. She had thought about it half the night. She had started thinking of it as a great joke and then she had begun to see profound implications in it. She had lain in bed imagining dialogues for them that were insane on the surface but that reached below to depths that no Bible salesman would be aware of. Their conversation yesterday had been of this kind.

He had stopped in front of her and had simply stood there. His face was bony and sweaty and bright, with a little pointed nose in the center of it, and his look was different from what it had been at the dinner table. He was gazing at her with open curiosity, with fascination, like a child watching a new fantastic animal at the zoo, and he was breathing as if he had run a great distance to reach her. His gaze seemed somehow familiar but she could not think where she had been regarded with it before. For almost a minute he didn't say anything. Then on what seemed an insuck of breath, he whispered, "You ever ate a chicken that was two days old?"

The girl looked at him stonily. He might have just put this question up for consideration at the meeting of a philosophical association. "Yes," she presently replied as if she had considered it from all angles.

"It must have been mighty small!" he said triumphantly and shook all over with little nervous giggles, getting very red in the face, and subsiding finally into his gaze of complete admiration, while the girl's expression remained exactly the same.

"How old are you?" he asked softly.

She waited some time before she answered. Then in a flat voice she said, "Seventeen."

His smiles came in succession like waves breaking on the surface of a little lake. "I see you got a wooden leg," he said. "I think you're brave. I think you're real sweet."

The girl stood blank and solid and silent.

"Walk to the gate with me," he said. "You're a brave sweet little thing and I liked you the minute I seen you walk in the door."

Hulga began to move forward.

"What's your name?" he asked, smiling down on the top of her head.

"Hulga," she said.

"Hulga," he murmured, "Hulga. Hulga. I never heard of anybody name Hulga before. You're shy, aren't you, Hulga?" he asked.

She nodded, watching his large red hand on the handle of the giant valise.

"I like girls that wear glasses," he said. "I think a lot. I'm not like these people that a serious thought don't ever enter their heads. It's because I may die."

"I may die too," she said suddenly and looked up at him. His eyes were very small and brown, glittering feverishly.

"Listen," he said, "don't you think some people was meant to meet on account of what all they got in common and all? Like they both think serious thoughts and all?" He shifted the valise to his other hand so that the hand nearest her was free. He caught hold of her elbow and shook it a little. "I don't work on Saturday," he said. "I like to walk in the woods and see what Mother Nature is wearing. O'er the hills and far away. Pic-nics and things. Couldn't we go on a pic-nic tomorrow? Say yes, Hulga," he said and gave her a dying look as if he felt his insides about to drop out of him. He had even seemed to sway slightly toward her.

During the night she had imagined that she seduced him. She imagined that the two of them walked on the place until they came to the storage barn beyond the two back fields and there, she imagined, that things came to such a pass that she very easily seduced him and that then, of course, she had to reckon with his remorse. True genius can get an idea across even to an inferior mind. She imagined that she took his remorse in hand and changed it into a deeper understanding of life. She took all his shame away and turned it into something useful.

She set off for the gate at exactly ten o'clock, escaping without drawing Mrs. Hopewell's attention. She didn't take anything to eat, forgetting that food is usually taken on a pic-nic. She wore a pair of slacks and a dirty white shirt, and as an afterthought, she had put some Vapex on the collar of it since she did not own any perfume. When she reached the gate no one was there.

She looked up and down the empty highway and had the furious feeling that she had been tricked, that he had only meant to make her walk to the gate after the idea of him. Then suddenly he stood up, very tall, from behind a bush on the opposite embankment. Smiling, he lifted his hat which was new and wide-brimmed. He had not worn it yesterday and she wondered if he had bought it for the occasion. It was toast-colored with a red and white band around it and was slightly too large for him. He stepped from behind the bush still carrying the black valise. He had on the same suit and the same yellow socks sucked down in his shoes from walking. He crossed the highway and said, "I knew you'd come!"

The girl wondered acidly how he had known this. She pointed to the valise and asked, "Why did you bring your Bibles?"

He took her elbow, smiling down on her as if he could not stop. "You can never tell when you'll need the word of God, Hulga," he said. She had a moment in which she doubted that this was actually happening and then they began to climb the embankment. They went down into the pasture toward the woods. The boy walked lightly by her side, bouncing on his toes. The valise did not seem to be heavy today; he even swung it. They crossed half the pasture without saying anything and then, putting his hand easily on the small of her back, he asked softly, "Where does your wooden leg join on?"

She turned an ugly red and glared at him and for an instant the boy looked abashed. "I didn't mean you no harm," he said. "I only meant you're so brave and all. I guess God takes care of you."

"No," she said, looking forward and walking fast, "I don't even believe in God."

At this he stopped and whistled. "No!" he exclaimed as if he were too astonished to say anything else.

She walked on and in a second he was bouncing at her side, fanning with his hat. "That's very unusual for a girl," he remarked, watching her out of the corner of his eye. When they reached the edge of the wood, he put his hand on her back again and drew her against him without a word and kissed her heavily.

The kiss, which had more pressure than feeling behind it, produced that extra surge of adrenalin in the girl that enables one to carry a packed trunk out of a burning house, but in her, the power went at once to the brain. Even before he released her, her mind, clear and detached and ironic anyway, was regarding him from a great distance, with amusement but with pity. She had never been kissed before and she was pleased to discover that it was an unexceptional experience and all a matter of the mind's control. Some people might enjoy drain water if they were told it was vodka. When the boy, looking expectant but uncertain, pushed her gently away, she turned and walked on, saying nothing as if such business, for her, were common enough.

He came along panting at her side, trying to help her when he saw a root that she might trip over. He caught and held back the long swaying blades of thorn vine until she had passed beyond them. She led the way and he came breathing heavily behind her. Then they came out on a sunlit hillside, sloping softly into another one a little smaller. Beyond, they could see the rusted top of the old barn where the extra hay was stored.

The hill was sprinkled with small pink weeds. "Then you ain't saved?" he asked suddenly, stopping.

The girl smiled. It was the first time she had smiled at him at all. "In my economy," she said, "I'm saved and you are damned but I told you I didn't believe in God."

Nothing seemed to destroy the boy's look of admiration. He gazed at her now as if the fantastic animal at the zoo had put its paw through the bars and given him a loving poke. She thought he looked as if he wanted to kiss her again and she walked on before he had the chance.

"Ain't there somewheres we can sit down sometime?" he murmured, his voice softening toward the end of the sentence.

"In that barn," she said.

They made for it rapidly as if it might slide away like a train. It was a large two-story barn, cool and dark inside. The boy pointed up the ladder that led into the loft and said, "It's too bad we can't go up there."

"Why can't we?" she asked.

"Yer leg," he said reverently.

The girl gave him a contemptuous look and putting both hands on the ladder, she climbed it while he stood below, apparently awestruck. She pulled herself expertly through the opening and then looked down at him and said, "Well, come on if you're coming," and he began to climb the ladder, awkwardly bringing the suitcase with him.

"We won't need the Bible," she observed.

"You never can tell," he said, panting. After he had got into the loft, he was a few seconds catching his breath. She had sat down in a pile of straw. A wide sheath of sunlight, filled with dust particles, slanted over her. She lay back against a bale, her face turned away, looking out the front opening of the barn where hay was thrown from a wagon into the loft. The two pink-speckled hillsides lay back against a dark ridge of woods. The sky was cloudless and cold blue. The boy dropped down by her side and put one arm under her and the other over her and began methodically kissing her face, making little noises like a fish. He did not remove his hat but it was pushed far enough back not to interfere. When her glasses got in his way, he took them off of her and slipped them into his pocket.

The girl at first did not return any of the kisses but presently she began to and after she had put several on his cheek, she reached his lips and remained there, kissing him again and again as if she were trying to draw all the breath out of him. His breath was clear and sweet like a child's and the kisses were sticky like a child's. He mumbled about loving her and about knowing when he first seen her that he loved her, but the mumbling was like the sleepy fretting of a child being put to sleep by his mother. Her mind, throughout this, never stopped or lost itself for a second to her feelings. "You ain't said you loved me none," he whispered finally, pulling back from her. "You got to say that."

She looked away from him off into the hollow sky and then down at a black ridge and then down farther into what appeared to be two green swelling lakes. She didn't realize he had taken her glasses but this landscape could not seem exceptional to her for she seldom paid any close attention to her surroundings.

"You got to say it," he repeated. "You got to say you love me."

She was always careful how she committed herself. "In a sense," she began, "if you use the word loosely, you might say that. But it's not a word I use. I don't have illusions. I'm one of those people who see *through* to nothing."

The boy was frowning. "You got to say it. I said it and you got to say it," he said.

The girl looked at him almost tenderly. "You poor baby," she murmured. "It's just as well you don't understand," and she pulled him by the neck, face-down, against her. "We are all damned," she said, "but some of us have taken off our blindfolds and see that there's nothing to see. It's a kind of salvation."

The boy's astonished eyes looked blankly through the ends of her hair. "Okay," he almost whined, "but do you love me or don'tcher?"

"Yes," she said and added, "in a sense. But I must tell you something. There mustn't be anything dishonest between us." She lifted his head and looked him in the eye. "I am thirty years old," she said. "I have a number of degrees."

The boy's look was irritated but dogged. "I don't care," he said. "I don't care a thing about what all you done. I just want to know if you love me or don'tcher?" and he caught her to him and wildly planted her face with kisses until she said, "Yes, yes."

"Okay then," he said, letting her go. "Prove it."

She smiled, looking dreamily out on the shifty landscape. She had seduced him without even making up her mind to try. "How?" she asked, feeling that he should be delayed a little.

He leaned over and put his lips to her ear. "Show me where your wooden leg joins on," he whispered.

The girl uttered a sharp little cry and her face instantly drained of color. The obscenity of the suggestion was not what shocked her. As a child she had sometimes been subject to feelings of shame but education had removed the last traces of that as a good surgeon scrapes for cancer; she would no more have felt it over what he was asking than she would have believed in his Bible. But she was as sensitive about the artificial leg as a peacock about his tail. No one ever touched it but her. She took care of it as someone else would his soul, in private and almost with her own eyes turned away. "No," she said.

"I known it," he muttered, sitting up. "You're just playing me for a sucker."

"Oh no no!" she cried. "It joins on at the knee. Only at the knee. Why do you want to see it?"

The boy gave her a long penetrating look. "Because," he said, "it's what makes you different. You ain't like anybody else."

She sat staring at him. There was nothing about her face or her round freezing-blue eyes to indicate that this had moved her; but she felt as if her heart had stopped and left her mind to pump her blood. She decided that for the first time in her life she was face to face with real innocence. This boy, with an instinct that came from beyond wisdom, had touched the truth about her. When after a minute, she said in a hoarse high voice, "All right," it was like surrendering to him completely. It was like losing her own life and finding it again, miraculously, in his.

Very gently be began to roll the slack leg up. The artificial limb, in a white sock and brown flat shoe, was bound in a heavy material like canvas and ended in an ugly jointure where it was attached to the stump. The boy's face and his voice were entirely reverent as he uncovered it and said, "Now show me how to take it off and on."

She took it off for him and put it back on again and then he took it off himself, handling it as tenderly as if it were a real one. "See!" he said with a delighted child's face. "Now I can do it myself!"

"Put it back on," she said. She was thinking that she would run away with him and that every night he would take the leg off and every morning put it back on again. "Put it back on," she said.

"Not yet," he murmured, setting it on its foot out of her reach. "Leave it off for a while. You got me instead."

She gave a little cry of alarm but he pushed her down and began to kiss her again. Without the leg she felt entirely dependent on him. Her brain seemed to have stopped thinking altogether and to be about some other function that it was not very good at. Different expressions raced back and forth over her face. Every now and then the boy, his eyes like two steel spikes, would glance behind him where the leg stood. Finally she pushed him off and said, "Put it back on me now."

"Wait," he said. He leaned the other way and pulled the valise toward him and opened it. It had a pale blue spotted lining and there were only two Bibles in it. He took one of these out and opened the cover of it. It was hollow and contained a pocket flask of whiskey, a pack of cards, and a small blue box with printing on it. He laid these out in front of her one at a time in an evenly-spaced row, like one presenting offerings at the shrine of a goddess. He put the blue box in her hand. THIS PRODUCT TO BE USED ONLY FOR THE PREVENTION OF DISEASE, she read, and dropped it. The boy was unscrewing the top of the flask. He stopped and pointed, with a smile, to the deck of cards. It was not an ordinary deck but one with an obscene picture on the back of each card. "Take a swig," he said, offering her the bottle first. He held it in front of her, but like one mesmerized, she did not move.

Her voice when she spoke had an almost pleading sound. "Aren't you," she murmured, "aren't you just good country people?"

The boy cocked his head. He looked as if he were just beginning to understand that she might be trying to insult him. "Yeah," he said, curling his lip slightly, "but it ain't held me back none. I'm as good as you any day in the week."

"Give me my leg," she said.

He pushed it farther away with his foot. "Come on now, let's begin to have us a good time," he said coaxingly. "We ain't got to know one another good yet."

"Give me my leg!" she screamed and tried to lunge for it but he pushed her down easily.

"What's the matter with you all of a sudden?" he asked, frowning as he screwed the top on the flask and put it quickly back inside the Bible. "You just a while ago said you didn't believe in nothing. I thought you was some girl!"

Her face was almost purple. "You're a Christian!" she hissed. "You're a fine Christian! You're just like them all — say one thing and do another. You're a perfect Christian, you're . . ."

The boy's mouth was set angrily. "I hope you don't think," he said in a lofty indignant tone, "that I believe in that crap! I may sell Bibles but I know which end is up and I wasn't born yesterday and I know where I'm going!"

"Give me my leg!" she screeched. He jumped up so quickly that she barely saw him sweep the cards and the blue box into the Bible and throw the Bible into the valise. She saw him grab the leg and then she saw it for an instant slanted forlornly across the inside of the suitcase with a Bible at either side of its opposite ends. He slammed the lid shut and snatched up the valise and swung it down the hole and then stepped through himself.

When all of him had passed but his head, he turned and regarded her with a look that no longer had any admiration in it. "I've gotten a lot of interesting things," he said. "One time I got a woman's glass eye this way. And you needn't to think you'll catch me because Pointer ain't really my name. I use a different name at every house I call at and don't stay nowhere long. And I'll tell you another thing, Hulga," he said, using the name as if he didn't think much of it, "you ain't so smart. I been believing in nothing ever since I was born!" and then the toast-colored hat disappeared down the hole and the girl was left, sitting on the straw in the dusty sunlight. When she turned her churning face toward the opening, she saw his blue figure struggling successfully over the green speckled lake.

Mrs. Hopewell and Mrs. Freeman, who were in the back pasture, digging up onions, saw him emerge a little later from the woods and head across the meadow toward the highway. "Why, that looks like that nice dull young man that tried to sell me a Bible yesterday," Mrs. Hopewell said, squinting. "He must have been selling them to the Negroes back in there. He was so simple," she said, "but I guess the world would be better off if we were all that simple."

Mrs. Freeman's gaze drove forward and just touched him before he disappeared under the hill. Then she returned her attention to the evil-smelling onion shoot she was lifting from the ground. "Some can't be that simple," she said. "I know I never could."

FLANNERY O'CONNOR

A Good Man Is Hard to Find 1955

The dragon is by the side of the road, watching those who pass. Beware lest he devour you. We go to the Father of Souls, but it is necessary to pass by the dragon.

–St. Cyril of Jerusalem

The grandmother didn't want to go to Florida. She wanted to visit some of her connections in east Tennessee and she was seizing at every chance to change Bailey's mind. Bailey was the son she lived with, her only boy. He was sitting on the edge of his chair at the table, bent over the orange sports section of the *Journal*. "Now look here, Bailey," she said, "see here, read this," and she stood with one hand on her thin hip and the other rattling the newspaper at his bald head. "Here this fellow that calls himself The Misfit is aloose from the Federal Pen and headed toward Florida and you read here what it says he did to these people. Just you read it. I wouldn't take my children in any direction with a criminal like that aloose in it. I couldn't answer to my conscience if I did."

Bailey didn't look up from his reading so she wheeled around then and faced the children's mother, a young woman in slacks, whose face was as broad and innocent as a cabbage and was tied around with a green headkerchief that had two points on the top like a rabbit's ears. She was sitting on the sofa, feeding the baby his apricots out of a jar. "The children have been to Florida before," the old lady said. "You all ought to take them somewhere else for a change so they would see different parts of the world and be broad. They never have been to east Tennessee."

The children's mother didn't seem to hear her but the eight-year-old boy, John Wesley, a stocky child with glasses, said, "If you don't want to go to Florida, why dontcha stay at home?" He and the little girl, June Star, were reading the funny papers on the floor.

"She wouldn't stay at home to be queen for a day," June Star said without raising her yellow head.

"Yes and what would you do if this fellow, The Misfit, caught you?" the grandmother asked.

"I'd smack his face," John Wesley said.

"She wouldn't stay at home for a million bucks," June Star said. "Afraid she'd miss something. She has to go everywhere we go."

"All right, Miss," the grandmother said. "Just remember that the next time you want me to curl your hair."

June Star said her hair was naturally curly.

The next morning the grandmother was the first one in the car, ready to go. She had her big black valise that looked like the head of a hippopotamus in one corner, and underneath it she was hiding a basket with Pitty Sing, the cat, in it. She didn't intend for the cat to be left alone in the house for three days because he would miss her too much and she was afraid he might brush against one of the gas burners and accidentally asphyxiate himself. Her son, Bailey, didn't like to arrive at a motel with a cat.

She sat in the middle of the back seat with John Wesley and June Star on either side of her. Bailey and the children's mother and the baby sat in front and they left Atlanta at eight forty-five with the mileage on the car at 55890. The grandmother wrote this down because she thought it would be interesting to say how many miles they had been when they got back. It took them twenty minutes to reach the outskirts of the city.

The old lady settled herself comfortably, removing her white cotton gloves and putting them up with her purse on the shelf in front of the back window. The children's mother still had on slacks and still had her head tied up in a green kerchief, but the grandmother had on a navy blue straw sailor hat with a bunch of white violets on the brim and a navy blue dress with a small white dot in the print. Her collars and cuffs were white organdy trimmed with lace and at her neckline she had pinned a purple spray of cloth violets containing a sachet. In case of an accident, anyone seeing her dead on the highway would know at once that she was a lady.

She said she thought it was going to be a good day for driving, neither too hot nor too cold, and she cautioned Bailey that the speed limit was fifty-five miles an hour and that the patrolmen hid themselves behind billboards and small clumps of trees and sped out after you before you had a chance to slow down. She pointed out interesting details of the scenery: Stone Mountain; the blue granite that in some places came up to both sides of the highway; the brilliant red clay banks slightly streaked with purple; and the various crops that made rows of green lace-work on the ground. The trees were full of silver-white sunlight and the meanest of them sparkled. The children were reading comic magazines and their mother had gone back to sleep.

"Let's go through Georgia fast so we won't have to look at it much," John Wesley said.

"If I were a little boy," said the grandmother, "I wouldn't talk about my native state that way. Tennessee has the mountains and Georgia has the hills."

"Tennessee is just a hillbilly dumping ground," John Wesley said, "and Georgia is a lousy state too."

"You said it," June Star said.

"In my time," said the grandmother, folding her thin veined fingers, "children were more respectful of their native states and their parents and everything else. People did right then. Oh look at the cute little pickaninny!" she said and pointed to a Negro child standing in the door of a shack. "Wouldn't that make a picture, now?" she asked and they all turned and looked at the little Negro out of the back window. He waved.

"He didn't have any britches on," June Star said.

"He probably didn't have any," the grandmother explained. "Little niggers in the country don't have things like we do. If I could paint, I'd paint that picture," she said.

The children exchanged comic books.

The grandmother offered to hold the baby and the children's mother passed him over the front seat to her. She set him on her knee and bounced him and told him about the things they were passing. She rolled her eyes and screwed up her mouth and stuck her leathery thin face into his smooth bland one. Occasionally he gave her a faraway smile. They passed a large cotton field with five or six graves fenced in the middle of it, like a small island. "Look at the graveyard!" the grandmother said, pointing it out. "That was the old family burying ground. That belonged to the plantation."

"Where's the plantation?" John Wesley asked.

"Gone with the Wind," said the grandmother. "Ha. Ha."

When the children finished all the comic books they had brought, they opened the lunch and ate it. The grandmother ate a peanut butter sandwich and an olive and would not let the children throw the box and the paper napkins out the window. When there was nothing else to do they played a game by choosing a cloud and making the other two guess what shape it suggested. John Wesley took one the shape of a cow and June Star guessed a cow and John Wesley said, no, an automobile, and June Star said he didn't play fair, and they began to slap each other over the grandmother.

The grandmother said she would tell them a story if they would keep quiet. When she told a story, she rolled her eyes and waved her head and was very dramatic. She said once when she was a maiden lady she had been courted by a Mr. Edgar Atkins Teagarden from Jasper, Georgia. She said he was a very good-looking man and a gentleman and that he brought her a watermelon every Saturday afternoon with his initials cut in it, E. A. T. Well, one Saturday, she said, Mr. Teagarden brought the watermelon and there was nobody at home and he left it on the front porch and returned in his buggy to Jasper, but she never got the watermelon, she said, because a nigger boy ate it when he saw the initials, E. A. T.! This story tickled John Wesley's funny bone and he giggled and giggled but June Star didn't think it was any good. She said she wouldn't marry a man that just brought her a watermelon on Saturday. The grandmother said she would have done well to marry Mr. Teagarden because he was a gentleman and had bought Coca-Cola stock when it first came out and that he had died only a few years ago, a very wealthy man.

They stopped at The Tower for barbecued sandwiches. The Tower was a part stucco and part wood filling station and dance hall set in a clearing outside of Timothy. A fat man named Red Sammy Butts ran it and there were signs stuck here and there on the building and for miles up and down the highway saying, TRY RED SAMMY'S FAMOUS BARBECUE. NONE LIKE FAMOUS RED SAMMY'S! RED SAM! THE FAT BOY WITH THE HAPPY LAUGH. A VETERAN! RED SAMMY'S YOUR MAN!

Red Sammy was lying on the bare ground outside The Tower with his head under a truck while a gray monkey about a foot high, chained to a small chinaberry tree, chattered nearby. The monkey sprang back into the tree and got on the highest limb as soon as he saw the children jump out of the car and run toward him.

Inside, The Tower was a long dark room with a counter at one end and tables at the other and dancing space in the middle. They all sat down at a board table next to the nickelodeon and Red Sam's wife, a tall burnt-brown woman with hair and eyes lighter than her skin, came and took their order. The children's mother put a dime in the machine and played "The Tennessee Waltz," and the grandmother said that tune always made her want to dance. She asked Bailey if he would like to dance but he only glared at her. He didn't have a naturally sunny disposition like she did and trips made him nervous. The grandmother's brown eyes were very bright. She swayed her head from side to side and pretended she was dancing in her chair. June Star said play something she could tap to so the children's mother put in another dime and played a fast number and June Star stepped out onto the dance floor and did her tap routine.

"Ain't she cute?" Red Sam's wife said, leaning over the counter. "Would you like to come be my little girl?"

"No I certainly wouldn't," June Star said. "I wouldn't live in a broken-down place like this for a million bucks!" and she ran back to the table.

"Ain't she cute?" the woman repeated, stretching her mouth politely.

"Aren't you ashamed?" hissed the grandmother.

Red Sam came in and told his wife to quit lounging on the counter and hurry up with these people's order. His khaki trousers reached just to his hip bones and his stomach hung over them like a sack of meal swaying under his shirt. He came over and sat down at a table nearby and let out a combination sigh and yodel. "You can't win," he said. "You can't win," and he wiped his sweating red face off with a gray handkerchief. "These days you don't know who to trust," he said. "Ain't that the truth?"

"People are certainly not nice like they used to be," said the grandmother.

"Two fellers come in here last week," Red Sammy said, "driving a Chrysler. It was a old beat-up car but it was a good one and these boys looked all right to me. Said they worked at the mill and you know I let them fellers charge the gas they bought? Now why did I do that?"

"Because you're a good man!" the grandmother said at once.

"Yes'm, I suppose so," Red Sam said as if he were struck with this answer.

His wife brought the orders, carrying the five plates all at once without a tray, two in each hand and one balanced on her arm. "It isn't a soul in this green world of God's that you can trust," she said. "And I don't count nobody out of that, not nobody," she repeated, looking at Red Sammy.

"Did you read about that criminal, The Misfit, that's escaped?" asked the grandmother.

"I wouldn't be a bit surprised if he didn't attack this place right here," said the woman. "If he hears about it being here, I wouldn't be none surprised to see him. If he hears it's two cent in the cash register, I wouldn't be a tall surprised if he. . . ."

"That'll do," Red Sam said. "Go bring these people their Co'-Colas," and the woman went off to get the rest of the order.

"A good man is hard to find," Red Sammy said. "Everything is getting terrible. I remember the day you could go off and leave your screen door unlatched. Not no more."

He and the grandmother discussed better times. The old lady said that in her opinion Europe was entirely to blame for the way things were now. She said the way Europe acted you would think we were made of money and Red Sam said it was no use talking about it, she was exactly right. The children ran outside into the white sunlight and looked at the monkey in the lacy chinaberry tree. He was busy catching fleas on himself and biting each one carefully between his teeth as if it were a delicacy.

They drove off again into the hot afternoon. The grandmother took cat naps and woke up every few minutes with her own snoring. Outside of Toombsboro she woke up and recalled an old plantation that she had visited in this neighborhood once when she was a young lady. She said the house had six white columns across the front and that there was an avenue of oaks leading up to it and two little wooden trellis arbors on either side in front where you sat down with your suitor after a stroll in the garden. She recalled exactly which road to turn off to get to it. She knew that Bailey would not be willing to lose any time looking at an old house, but the more she talked about it, the more she wanted to see it once again and find out if the little twin arbors were still standing. "There was a secret panel in this house," she said craftily, not telling the truth but wishing that she were, "and the story went that all the family silver was hidden in it when Sherman came through but it was never found. . . ."

"Hey!" John Wesley said. "Let's go see it! We'll find it! We'll poke all the woodwork and find it! Who lives there? Where do you turn off at? Hey Pop, can't we turn off there?"

"We never have seen a house with a secret panel!" June Star shrieked. "Let's go to the house with the secret panel! Hey Pop, can't we go see the house with the secret panel!"

"It's not far from here, I know," the grandmother said. "It won't take over twenty minutes."

Bailey was looking straight ahead. His jaw was as rigid as a horseshoe. "No," he said.

The children began to yell and scream that they wanted to see the house with the secret panel. John Wesley kicked the back of the front seat and June Star hung over her mother's shoulder and whined desperately into her ear that they never had any fun even on their vacation, that they could never do what THEY wanted to do. The baby began to scream and John Wesley kicked the back of the seat so hard that his father could feel the blows in his kidney.

"All right!" he shouted and drew the car to a stop at the side of the road. "Will you all shut up? Will you all just shut up for one second? If you don't shut up, we won't go anywhere."

"It would be very educational for them," the grandmother murmured.

"All right," Bailey said, "but get this: this is the only time we're going to stop for anything like this. This is the one and only time."

"The dirt road that you have to turn down is about a mile back," the grandmother directed. "I marked it when we passed."

"A dirt road," Bailey groaned.

After they had turned around and were headed toward the dirt road, the grandmother recalled other points about the house, the beautiful glass over the front doorway and the candle-lamp in the hall. John Wesley said that the secret panel was probably in the fireplace.

"You can't go inside this house," Bailey said. "You don't know who lives there."

"While you all talk to the people in front, I'll run around behind and get in a window," John Wesley suggested.

"We'll all stay in the car," his mother said.

They turned onto the dirt road and the car raced roughly along in a swirl of pink dust. The grandmother recalled the times when there were no paved roads and thirty miles was a day's journey. The dirt road was hilly and there were sudden washes in it and sharp curves on dangerous embankments. All at once they would be on a hill, looking down over the blue tops of trees for miles around, then the next minute, they would be in a red depression with the dust-coated trees looking down on them.

"This place had better turn up in a minute," Bailey said, "or I'm going to turn around."

The road looked as if no one had traveled on it for months.

"It's not much farther," the grandmother said and just as she said it, a horrible thought came to her. The thought was so embarrassing that she turned red in the face and her eyes dilated and her feet jumped up, upsetting her valise in the corner. The instant the valise moved, the newspaper top she had over the basket under it rose with a snarl and Pitty Sing, the cat, sprang onto Bailey's shoulder.

The children were thrown to the floor and their mother, clutching the baby, was thrown out the door onto the ground, the old lady was thrown into the front seat. The car turned over once and landed right-side-up in a gulch off the side of the road. Bailey remained in the driver's seat with the cat gray-striped with a broad white face and an orange nose clinging to his neck like a caterpillar.

As soon as the children saw they could move their arms and legs, they scrambled out of the car, shouting, "We've had an ACCIDENT!" The grandmother was curled up under the dashboard, hoping she was injured so that Bailey's wrath would not come down on her all at once. The horrible thought she had before the accident was that the house she had remembered so vividly was not in Georgia but in Tennessee.

Bailey removed the cat from his neck with both hands and flung it out the window against the side of a pine tree. Then he got out of the car and started looking for the children's mother. She was sitting against the side of the red gutted ditch, holding the screaming baby, but she only had a cut down her face and a broken shoulder. "We've had an ACCIDENT!" the children screamed in a frenzy of delight.

"But nobody's killed," June Star said with disappointment as the grandmother limped out of the car, her hat still pinned to her head but the broken front brim standing up at a jaunty angle and the violet spray hanging off the side. They all sat down in the ditch, except the children, to recover from the shock. They were all shaking.

"Maybe a car will come along," said the children's mother hoarsely.

"I believe I have injured an organ," said the grandmother, pressing her side, but no one answered her. Bailey's teeth were clattering. He had on a yellow sport shirt with bright blue parrots designed in it and his face was as yellow as the shirt. The grandmother decided that she would not mention that the house was in Tennessee.

The road was about ten feet above and they could only see the tops of the trees on the other side of it. Behind the ditch they were sitting in there were more woods, tall and dark and deep. In a few minutes they saw a car some distance away on top of a hill, coming slowly as if the occupants were watching them. The grandmother stood up and waved both arms dramatically to attract their attention. The car continued to come on slowly, disappeared around a bend and appeared again, moving even slower, on top of the hill they had gone over. It was a big black battered hearse-like automobile. There were three men in it.

It came to a stop just over them and for some minutes, the driver looked down with a steady expressionless gaze to where they were sitting, and didn't speak. Then he turned his head and muttered something to the other two and they got out. One was a fat boy in black trousers and a red sweat shirt with a silver stallion embossed on the front of it. He moved around on the right side of them and stood staring, his mouth partly open in a kind of loose grin. The other had on khaki pants and a blue striped coat and a gray hat pulled very low, hiding most of his face. He came around slowly on the left side. Neither spoke.

The driver got out of the car and stood by the side of it, looking down at them. He was an older man than the other two. His hair was just beginning to gray and he wore silver-rimmed spectacles that gave him a scholarly look. He had a long creased face and didn't have on any shirt or undershirt. He had on blue jeans that were too tight for him and was holding a black hat and a gun. The two boys also had guns.

"We've had an ACCIDENT!" the children screamed.

The grandmother had the peculiar feeling that the bespectacled man was someone she knew. His face was as familiar to her as if she had known him all her life but she could not recall who he was. He moved away from the car and began to come down the embankment, placing his feet carefully so that he wouldn't slip. He had on tan and white shoes and no socks, and his ankles were red and thin. "Good afternoon," he said. "I see you all had you a little spill."

"We turned over twice!" said the grandmother.

"Oncet," he corrected. "We seen it happen. Try their car and see will it run, Hiram," he said quietly to the boy with the gray hat.

"What you got that gun for?" John Wesley asked. "Whatcha gonna do with that gun?"

"Lady," the man said to the children's mother, "would you mind calling them children to sit down by you? Children make me nervous. I want all you all to sit down right together there where you're at."

"What are you telling US what to do for?" June Star asked.

Behind them the line of woods gaped like a dark open mouth. "Come here," said the mother.

"Look here now," Bailey said suddenly, "we're in a predicament! We're in . . ."

The grandmother shrieked. She scrambled to her feet and stood staring. "You're The Misfit!" she said. "I recognized you at once!"

"Yes'm," the man said, smiling slightly as if he were pleased in spite of himself to be known, "but it would have been better for all of you, lady, if you hadn't of reckernized me."

Bailey turned his head sharply and said something to his mother that shocked even the children. The old lady began to cry and The Misfit reddened.

"Lady," he said, "don't you get upset. Sometimes a man says things he don't mean. I don't reckon he meant to talk to you thataway."

"You wouldn't shoot a lady, would you?" the grandmother said and removed a clean handkerchief from her cuff and began to slap at her eyes with it.

The Misfit pointed the toe of his shoe into the ground and made a little hole and then covered it up again. "I would hate to have to," he said.

"Listen," the grandmother almost screamed, "I know you're a good man. You don't look a bit like you have common blood. I know you must come from nice people!"

"Yes mam," he said, "finest people in the world." When he smiled he showed a row of strong white teeth. "God never made a finer woman than my mother and my daddy's heart was pure gold," he said. The boy with the red sweat shirt had come around behind them and was standing with his gun at his hip. The Misfit squatted down on the ground. "Watch them children, Bobby Lee," he said. "You know they make me nervous." He looked at the six of them huddled together in front of him and he seemed to be embarrassed as if he couldn't think of anything to say. "Ain't a cloud in the sky," he remarked, looking up at it. "Don't see no sun but don't see no cloud neither."

"Yes, it's a beautiful day," said the grandmother. "Listen," she said, "you shouldn't call yourself The Misfit because I know you're a good man at heart. I can just look at you and tell."

"Hush!" Bailey yelled. "Hush! Everybody shut up and let me handle this!" He was squatting in the position of a runner about to sprint forward but he didn't move.

"I pre-chate that, lady," The Misfit said and drew a little circle in the ground with the butt of his gun.

"It'll take a half a hour to fix this here car," Hiram called, looking over the raised hood of it.

"Well, first you and Bobby Lee get him and that little boy to step over yonder with you," The Misfit said, pointing to Bailey and John Wesley. "The boys want to ast you something," he said to Bailey. "Would you mind stepping back in them woods there with them?"

"Listen," Bailey began, "we're in a terrible predicament! Nobody realizes what this is," and his voice cracked. His eyes were as blue and intense as the parrots in his shirt and he remained perfectly still.

The grandmother reached up to adjust her hat brim as if she were going to the woods with him but it came off in her hand. She stood staring at it and after a second she let it fall to the ground. Hiram pulled Bailey up by the arm as if he were assisting an old man. John Wesley caught hold of his father's hand and Bobby Lee followed. They went off toward the woods and just as they reached the dark edge, Bailey turned and supporting himself against a gray naked pine trunk, he shouted, "I'll be back in a minute, Mamma, wait on me!"

"Come back this instant!" his mother shrilled but they all disappeared into the woods.

"Bailey Boy!" the grandmother called in a tragic voice but she found she was looking at The Misfit squatting on the ground in front of her. "I just know you're a good man," she said desperately. "You're not a bit common!"

"Nome, I ain't a good man," The Misfit said after a second as if he had considered her statement carefully, "but I ain't the worst in the world neither. My daddy said I was a different breed of dog from my brothers and sisters. 'You know,' Daddy said, 'it's some that can live their whole life out without asking about it and it's others has to know why it is, and this boy is one of the latters. He's going to be into everything!' " He put on his black hat and looked up suddenly and then away deep into the woods as if he were embarrassed again. "I'm sorry I don't have on a shirt before you ladies," he said, hunching his shoulders slightly. "We buried our clothes that we had on when we escaped and we're just making do until we can get better. We borrowed these from some folks we met," he explained.

"That's perfectly all right," the grandmother said. "Maybe Bailey has an extra shirt in his suitcase."

"I'll look and see terrectly," The Misfit said.

"Where are they taking him?" the children's mother screamed.

"Daddy was a card himself," The Misfit said. "You couldn't put anything over on him. He never got in trouble with the Authorities though. Just had the knack of handling them."

"You could be honest too if you'd only try," said the grandmother. "Think how wonderful it would be to settle down and live a comfortable life and not have to think about somebody chasing you all the time."

The Misfit kept scratching in the ground with the butt of his gun as if he were thinking about it. "Yes'm, somebody is always after you," he murmured.

The grandmother noticed how thin his shoulder blades were just behind his hat because she was standing up looking down at him. "Do you ever pray?" she asked.

He shook his head. All she saw was the black hat wiggle between his shoulder blades. "Nome," he said.

There was a pistol shot from the woods, followed closely by another. Then silence. The old lady's head jerked around. She could hear the wind move through the tree tops like a long satisfied insuck of breath. "Bailey Boy!" she called.

"I was a gospel singer for a while," The Misfit said. "I been most everything. Been in the arm service, both land and sea, at home and abroad, been twict married, been an undertaker, been with the railroads, plowed Mother Earth, been in a tornado, seen a man burnt alive oncet," and he looked up at the children's mother and the little girl who were sitting close together, their faces white and their eyes glassy; "I even seen a woman flogged," he said.

"Pray, pray," the grandmother began, "pray, pray. . . ."

"I never was a bad boy that I remember of," The Misfit said in an almost dreamy voice, "but somewheres along the line I done something wrong and got sent to the penitentiary. I was buried alive," and he looked up and held her attention to him by a steady stare.

"That's when you should have started to pray," she said. "What did you do to get sent to the penitentiary, that first time?"

"Turn to the right, it was a wall," The Misfit said, looking up again at the cloudless sky. "Turn to the left, it was a wall. Look up it was a ceiling, look down it was a floor. I forgot what I done, lady. I set there and set there, trying to remember what it was I done and I ain't recalled it to this day. Oncet in a while, I would think it was coming to me, but it never come."

"Maybe they put you in by mistake," the old lady said vaguely.

"Nome," he said. "It wasn't no mistake. They had the papers on me."

"You must have stolen something," she said.

The Misfit sneered slightly. "Nobody had nothing I wanted," he said. "It was a head-doctor at the penitentiary said what I had done was kill my daddy but I known that for a lie. My daddy died in nineteen ought nineteen of the epidemic flu and I never had a thing to do with it. He was buried in the Mount Hopewell Baptist churchyard and you can see for yourself."

"If you would pray," the old lady said, "Jesus would help you."

"That's right," The Misfit said.

"Well then, why don't you pray?" she asked trembling with delight suddenly.

"I don't want no hep," he said. "I'm doing all right by myself."

Bobby Lee and Hiram came ambling back from the woods. Bobby Lee was dragging a yellow shirt with bright blue parrots in it.

"Throw me that shirt, Bobby Lee," The Misfit said. The shirt came flying at him and landed on his shoulder and he put it on. The grandmother couldn't name what the shirt reminded her of. "No, lady," The Misfit said while he was buttoning it up, "I found out the crime don't matter. You can do one thing or you can do another, kill a man or take a tire off his car, because sooner or later you're going to forget what it was you done and just be punished for it."

The children's mother had begun to make heaving noises as if she couldn't get her breath. "Lady," he asked, "would you and that little girl like to step off yonder with Bobby Lee and Hiram and join your husband?"

"Yes, thank you," the mother said faintly. Her left arm dangled helplessly and she was holding the baby, who had gone to sleep, in the other. "Hep that lady up, Hiram," The Misfit said as she struggled to climb out of the ditch, "and Bobby Lee, you hold onto that little girl's hand."

"I don't want to hold hands with him," June Star said. "He reminds me of a pig."

The fat boy blushed and laughed and caught her by the arm and pulled her off into the woods after Hiram and her mother.

Alone with The Misfit, the grandmother found that she had lost her voice. There was not a cloud in the sky nor any sun. There was nothing around her but woods. She wanted to tell him that he must pray. She opened and closed her mouth several times before anything came out. Finally she found herself saying, "Jesus, Jesus," meaning, Jesus will help you, but the way she was saying it, it sounded as if she might be cursing.

"Yes'm," The Misfit said as if he agreed. "Jesus thrown everything off balance. It was the same case with Him as with me except He hadn't committed any crime and they could prove I had committed one because they had the papers on me. Of course," he said, "they never shown me my papers. That's why I sign myself now. I said long ago, you get your signature and sign everything you do and keep a copy of it. Then you'll know what you done and you can hold up the crime to the punishment and see do they match and in the end you'll have something to prove you ain't been treated right. I call myself The Misfit," he said, "because I can't make what all I done wrong fit what all I gone through in punishment."

There was a piercing scream from the woods, followed closely by a pistol report. "Does it seem right to you, lady, that one is punished a heap and another ain't punished at all?"

"Jesus!" the old lady cried. "You've got good blood! I know you wouldn't shoot a lady! I know you come from nice people! Pray! Jesus, you ought not to shoot a lady. I'll give you all the money I've got!"

"Lady," The Misfit said, looking beyond her far into the woods, "there never was a body that give the undertaker a tip."

There were two more pistol reports and the grandmother raised her head like a parched old turkey hen crying for water and called, "Bailey Boy, Bailey Boy!" as if her heart would break.

"Jesus was the only One that ever raised the dead," The Misfit continued, "and He shouldn't have done it. He thrown everything off balance. If He did what He said, then it's nothing for you to do but throw away everything and follow Him, and if He didn't, then it's nothing for you to do but enjoy the few minutes you got left the best you can by killing somebody or burning down his house or doing some other meanness to him. No pleasure but meanness," he said and his voice had become almost a snarl.

"Maybe He didn't raise the dead," the old lady mumbled, not knowing what she was saying and feeling so dizzy that she sank down in the ditch with her legs twisted under her.

"I wasn't there so I can't say He didn't," The Misfit said. "I wisht I had of been there," he said, hitting the ground with his fist. "It ain't right I wasn't there because if I had of been there I would of known. Listen lady," he said in a high voice, "if I had of been there I would of known and I wouldn't be like I am now." His voice seemed about to crack and the grandmother's head cleared for an instant. She saw the man's face twisted close to her own as if he were going to cry and she murmured, "Why you're one of my babies. You're one of my own children!" She reached out and touched him on the shoulder. The Misfit sprang back as if a snake had bitten him and shot her three times through the chest. Then he put his gun down on the ground and took off his glasses and began to clean them.

Hiram and Bobby Lee returned from the woods and stood over the ditch, looking down at the grandmother who half sat and half lay in a puddle of blood with her legs crossed under her like a child's and her face smiling up at the cloudless sky.

Without his glasses, The Misfit's eyes were red-rimmed and pale and defenseless-looking. "Take her off and throw her where you thrown the others," he said, picking up the cat that was rubbing itself against his leg.

"She was a talker, wasn't she?" Bobby Lee said, sliding down the ditch with a yodel.

"She would of been a good woman," The Misfit said, "if it had been somebody there to shoot her every minute of her life."

"Some fun!" Bobby Lee said.

"Shut up, Bobby Lee," The Misfit said. "It's no real pleasure in life."

༚

FRANK O'CONNOR *was the pseudonym for Michael Francis O'Donovan (1903–1966), who was born in Cork, Ireland. His parents were so poor that he only made it through the fourth grade at the Christian Brothers School in Cork. During the Irish struggle for independence from England (1918–21), he was briefly a member of the Irish Republican Army. For several years thereafter he worked as a librarian in Cork and Dublin; it was at this time that he began using his pseudonym so that he would not jeopardize his job as a public official. He had started to write stories as a boy, and for a while he could not decide whether to be a painter or a writer: "I discovered by the time I was sixteen or seventeen that paints cost too much money, so I became a writer because you could be a writer with a pencil and a penny notebook."*

When O'Connor was twenty-eight years old, the Atlantic Monthly *published his story "Guests of the Nation," which he later said was an imitation of Isaac Babel's stories in* Red Cavalry. *His first collection of stories appeared that same year (1931), and from then on he made his living as a writer. During the 1950s he lived in the United States, teaching at Harvard and Northwestern universities and publishing two excellent critical works,* The Mirror in the Roadway *(1956), a study of the modern novel, and* The Lonely Voice *(1963), a history of the short story. O'Connor was a prolific writer, editor, critic, and translator, with almost fifty books to his credit, including fourteen volumes of short stories. He often rewrote his stories several times, even after they were published, so many of them appear in different versions in his various volumes.*

O'Connor's greatest achievement was in the short story. Primarily indebted to Anton Chekhov, he declared himself to be an old-fashioned storyteller, believing that a story should have the sound of a person speaking. This conviction gives his fiction an engaging tone, confirming — as do Chekhov's stories — the author's basic sympathy toward his characters. In praising O'Connor's stories, the noted Irish poet William Butler Yeats said that he was "doing for Ireland what Chekhov did for Russia."

RELATED COMMENTARY: Frank O'Connor, "Style and Form in Joyce's 'The Dead,'" page 780.

FRANK O'CONNOR

Guests of the Nation

1931, 1954

I

At dusk the big Englishman, Belcher, would shift his long legs out of the ashes and say "Well, chums, what about it?" and Noble or me would say "All right, chum" (for we had picked up some of their curious expressions), and the little Englishman, Hawkins, would light the lamp and bring out the cards. Sometimes Jeremiah Donovan would come up and supervise the game and get excited over Hawkins's cards, which he always played badly, and shout at him as if he was one of our own "Ah, you divil, you, why didn't you play the tray?"

But ordinarily Jeremiah was a sober and contented poor devil like the big Englishman, Belcher, and was looked up to only because he was a fair hand at documents, though he was slow enough even with them. He wore a small cloth hat and big gaiters over his long pants, and you seldom saw him with his hands out of his pockets. He reddened when you talked to him, tilting from toe to heel and back, and looking down all the time at his big farmer's feet. Noble and me used to make fun of his broad accent, because we were from the town.

I couldn't at the time see the point of me and Noble guarding Belcher and Hawkins at all, for it was my belief that you could have planted that pair down anywhere from this to Claregalway and they'd have taken root there like a native weed. I never in my short experience seen two men to take to the country as they did.

They were handed on to us by the Second Battalion when the search for them became too hot, and Noble and myself, being young, took over with a natural feeling of responsibility, but Hawkins made us look like fools when he showed that he knew the country better than we did.

"You're the bloke they calls Bonaparte," he says to me. "Mary Brigid O'Connell told me to ask you what you done with the pair of her brother's socks you borrowed."

For it seemed, as they explained it, that the Second used to have little evenings, and some of the girls of the neighborhood turned in, and, seeing they were such decent chaps, our fellows couldn't leave the two Englishmen out of them. Hawkins learned to dance "The Walls of Limerick," "The Siege of

Ennis," and "The Waves of Tory" as well as any of them, though, naturally, he couldn't return the compliment, because our lads at that time did not dance foreign dances on principle.

So whatever privileges Belcher and Hawkins had with the Second they just naturally took with us, and after the first day or two we gave up all pretense of keeping a close eye on them. Not that they could have got far, for they had accents you could cut with a knife and wore khaki tunics and overcoats with civilian pants and boots. But it's my belief that they never had any idea of escaping and were quite content to be where they were.

It was a treat to see how Belcher got off with the old woman of the house where we were staying. She was a great warrant to scold, and cranky even with us, but before ever she had a chance of giving our guests, as I may call them, a lick of her tongue, Belcher had made her his friend for life. She was breaking sticks, and Belcher, who hadn't been more than ten minutes in the house, jumped up from his seat and went over to her.

"Allow me, madam," he says, smiling his queer little smile, "please allow me"; and he takes the bloody hatchet. She was struck too paralytic to speak, and after that, Belcher would be at her heels, carrying a bucket, a basket, or a load of turf, as the case might be. As Noble said, he got into looking before she leapt, and hot water, or any little thing she wanted, Belcher would have it ready for her. For such a huge man (and though I am five foot ten myself I had to look up at him) he had an uncommon shortness or should I say lack? of speech. It took us some time to get used to him, walking in and out, like a ghost, without a word. Especially because Hawkins talked enough for a platoon, it was strange to hear big Belcher with his toes in the ashes come out with a solitary "Excuse me, chum" or "That's right, chum." His one and only passion was cards, and I will say for him that he was a good card-player. He could have fleeced myself and Noble, but whatever we lost to him Hawkins lost to us, and Hawkins played with the money Belcher gave him.

Hawkins lost to us because he had too much old gab, and we probably lost to Belcher for the same reason. Hawkins and Noble would spit at one another about religion into the early hours of the morning, and Hawkins worried the soul out of Noble, whose brother was a priest, with a string of questions that would puzzle a cardinal. To make it worse even in treating of holy subjects, Hawkins had a deplorable tongue. I never in all my career met a man who could mix such a variety of cursing and bad language into an argument. He was a terrible man, and a fright to argue. He never did a stroke of work, and when he had no one else to talk to, he got stuck in the old woman.

He met his match in her, for one day when he tried to get her to complain profanely of the drought, she gave him a great come-down by blaming it entirely on Jupiter Pluvius (a deity neither Hawkins nor I have ever heard of, though Noble said that among the pagans it was believed that he had something to do with the rain). Another day he was swearing at the capitalists for starting the German war when the old lady laid down her iron, puckered up her little crab's mouth, and said: "Mr. Hawkins, you can say what you like about the war, and think you'll deceive me because I'm only a simple poor countrywoman, but I know what started the war. It was the Italian Count that stole the heathen divinity out of the temple in Japan. Believe me, Mr. Hawkins, nothing but sorrow and want can follow the people that disturb the hidden powers."

A queer old girl, all right.

II

We had our tea one evening, and Hawkins lit the lamp and we all sat into cards. Jeremiah Donovan came in too, and sat down and watched us for a while, and it suddenly struck me that he had no great love for the two Englishmen. It came as a great surprise to me, because I hadn't noticed anything about him before.

Late in the evening a really terrible argument blew up between Hawkins and Noble, about capitalists and priests and love of your country.

"The capitalists," says Hawkins with an angry gulp, "pays the priests to tell you about the next world so as you won't notice what the bastards are up to in this."

"Nonsense, man!" says Noble, losing his temper. "Before ever a capitalist was thought of, people believed in the next world."

Hawkins stood up as though he was preaching a sermon.

"Oh, they did, did they?" he says with a sneer. "They believed all the things you believe, isn't that what you mean? And you believe that God created Adam, and Adam created Shem, and Shem created Jehoshophat. You believe all that silly old fairytale about Eve and Eden and the apple. Well, listen to me, chum. If you're entitled to hold a silly belief — like that, I'm entitled to hold my silly belief which is that the first thing your God created was a bleeding capitalist, with morality and Rolls-Royce complete. Am I right, chum?" he says to Belcher.

"You're right, chum," says Belcher with his amused smile, and got up from the table to stretch his long legs into the fire and stroke his moustache. So, seeing that Jeremiah Donovan was going, and that there was no knowing when the argument about religion would be over, I went out with him. We strolled down to the village together, and then he stopped and started blushing and mumbling and saying I ought to be behind, keeping guard on the prisoners. I didn't like the tone he took with me, and anyway I was bored with life in the cottage, so I replied by asking him what the hell we wanted guarding them at all for. I told him I'd talked it over with Noble, and that we'd both rather be out with a fighting column.

"What use are those fellows to us?" says I.

He looked at me in surprise and said: "I thought you knew we were keeping them as hostages."

"Hostages?" I said.

"The enemy have prisoners belonging to us," he says, "and now they're talking of shooting them. If they shoot our prisoners, we'll shoot theirs."

"Shoot them?" I said.

"What else did you think we were keeping them for?" he says.

"Wasn't it very unforeseen of you not to warn Noble and myself of that in the beginning?" I said.

"How was it?" says he. "You might have known it."

"We couldn't know it, Jeremiah Donovan," says I. "How could we when they were on our hands so long?"

"The enemy have our prisoners as long and longer," says he.

"That's not the same thing at all," says I.

"What difference is there?" says he.

I couldn't tell him, because I knew he wouldn't understand. If it was only an old dog that was going to the vet's, you'd try and not get too fond of him, but Jeremiah Donovan wasn't a man that would ever be in danger of that.

"And when is this thing going to be decided?" says I.

"We might hear tonight," he says. "Or tomorrow or the next day at latest. So if it's only hanging round here that's a trouble to you, you'll be free soon enough."

It wasn't the hanging round that was a trouble to me at all by this time. I had worse things to worry about. When I got back to the cottage the argument was still on. Hawkins was holding forth in his best style, maintaining that there was no next world, and Noble was maintaining that there was; but I could see that Hawkins had had the best of it.

"Do you know what, chum?" he was saying with a saucy smile. "I think you're just as big a bleeding unbeliever as I am. You say you believe in the next world, and you know just as much about the next world as I do, which is sweet damn-all. What's heaven? You don't know. Where's heaven? You don't know. You know sweet damn-all! I ask you again, do they wear wings?"

"Very well, then," says Noble, "they do. Is that enough for you? They do wear wings."

"Where do they get them, then? Who makes them? Have they a factory for wings? Have they a sort of store where you hands in your chit and takes your bleeding wings?"

"You're an impossible man to argue with," says Noble. "Now, listen to me — " And they were off again.

It was long after midnight when we locked up and went to bed. As I blew out the candle I told Noble what Jeremiah Donovan was after telling me. Noble took it very quietly. When we'd been in bed about an hour he asked me did I think we ought to tell the Englishmen. I didn't think we should, because it was more than likely that the English wouldn't shoot our men, and even if they did, the brigade officers, who were always up and down with the Second Battalion and knew the Englishmen well, wouldn't be likely to want them plugged. "I think so too," says Noble. "It would be great cruelty to put the wind up them now."

"It was very unforeseen of Jeremiah Donovan anyhow," says I.

It was next morning that we found it so hard to face Belcher and Hawkins. We went about the house all day scarcely saying a word. Belcher didn't seem to notice; he was stretched into the ashes as usual, with his usual look of waiting in quietness for something unforeseen to happen, but Hawkins noticed and put it down to Noble's being beaten in the argument of the night before.

"Why can't you take a discussion in the proper spirit?" he says severely.

"You and your Adam and Eve! I'm a Communist, that's what I am. Communist or anarchist, it all comes to much the same thing." And for hours he went round the house, muttering when the fit took him. "Adam and Eve! Adam and Eve! Nothing better to do with their time than picking bleeding apples!"

III

I don't know how we got through that day, but I was very glad when it was over, the tea things were cleared away, and Belcher said in his peaceable way: "Well, chums, what about it?" We sat round the table and Hawkins took out the cards, and just then I heard Jeremiah Donovan's footstep on the path and a dark presentiment crossed my mind. I rose from the table and caught him before he reached the door.

"What do you want?" I asked.

"I want those two soldier friends of yours," he says, getting red.

"Is that the way, Jeremiah Donovan?" I asked.

"That's the way. There were four of our lads shot this morning, one of them a boy of sixteen."

"That's bad," I said.

At that moment Noble followed me out, and the three of us walked down the path together, talking in whispers. Feeney, the local intelligence officer, was standing by the gate.

"What are you going to do about it?" I asked Jeremiah Donovan.

"I want you and Noble to get them out; tell them they're being shifted again; that'll be the quietest way."

"Leave me out of that," says Noble under his breath.

Jeremiah Donovan looks at him hard.

"All right," he says. "You and Feeney get a few tools from the shed and dig a hole by the far end of the bog. Bonaparte and myself will be after you. Don't let anyone see you with the tools. I wouldn't like it to go beyond ourselves."

We saw Feeney and Noble go round to the shed and went in ourselves. I left Jeremiah Donovan to do the explanations. He told them that he had orders to send them back to the Second Battalion. Hawkins let out a mouthful of curses, and you could see that though Belcher didn't say anything, he was a bit upset too. The old woman was for having them stay in spite of us, and she didn't stop advising them until Jeremiah Donovan lost his temper and turned on her. He had a nasty temper, I noticed. It was pitch-dark in the cottage by this time, but no one thought of lighting the lamp, and in the darkness the two Englishmen fetched their topcoats and said good-bye to the old woman.

"Just as a man makes a home of a bleeding place, some bastard at headquarters thinks you're too cushy and shunts you off," says Hawkins, shaking her hand.

"A thousand thanks, madam," says Belcher. "A thousand thanks for everything" — as though he'd made it up.

We went round to the back of the house and down towards the bog. It was only then that Jeremiah Donovan told them. He was shaking with excitement.

"There were four of our fellows shot in Cork this morning and now you're to be shot as a reprisal."

"What are you talking about?" snaps Hawkins. "It's bad enough being mucked about as we are without having to put up with your funny jokes."

"It isn't a joke," says Donovan. "I'm sorry, Hawkins, but it's true," and begins on the usual rigmarole about duty and how unpleasant it is.

I never noticed that people who talk a lot about duty find it much of a trouble to them.

"Oh, cut it out!" says Hawkins.

"Ask Bonaparte," says Donovan, seeing that Hawkins isn't taking him seriously. "Isn't it true, Bonaparte?"

"It is," I say, and Hawkins stops.

"Ah, for Christ's sake, chum!"

"I mean it, chum," I say.

"You don't sound as if you mean it."

"If he doesn't mean it, I do," says Donovan, working himself up.

"What have you against me, Jeremiah Donovan?"

"I never said I had anything against you. But why did your people take out four of our prisoners and shoot them in cold blood?"

He took Hawkins by the arm and dragged him on, but it was impossible to make him understand that we were in earnest. I had the Smith and Wesson in my pocket and I kept fingering it and wondering what I'd do if they put up a fight for it or ran, and wishing to God they'd do one or the other. I knew if they did run for it, that I'd never fire on them. Hawkins wanted to know was Noble in it, and when we said yes, he asked us why Noble wanted to plug him. Why did any of us want to plug him? What had he done to us? Weren't we all chums? Didn't we understand him and didn't he understand us? Did we imagine for an instant that he'd shoot us for all the so-and-so officers in the so-and-so British Army?

By this time we'd reached the bog, and I was so sick I couldn't even answer him. We walked along the edge of it in the darkness, and every now and then Hawkins would call a halt and begin all over again, as if he was wound up, about our being chums, and I knew that nothing but the sight of the grave would convince him that we had to do it. And all the time I was hoping that something would happen; that they'd run for it or that Noble would take over the responsibility from me. I had the feeling that it was worse on Noble than on me.

IV

At last we saw the lantern in the distance and made towards it. Noble was carrying it, and Feeney was standing somewhere in the darkness behind him, and the picture of them so still and silent in the bogland brought it home to me that we were in earnest, and banished the last bit of hope I had.

Belcher, on recognizing Noble, said: "Hallo, chum," in his quiet way, but Hawkins flew at him at once, and the argument began all over again, only this time Noble had nothing to say for himself and stood with his head down, holding the lantern between his legs.

It was Jeremiah Donovan who did the answering. For the twentieth time, as though it was haunting his mind, Hawkins asked if anybody thought he'd shoot Noble.

"Yes, you would," says Jeremiah Donovan.

"No, I wouldn't, damn you!"

"You would, because you'd know you'd be shot for not doing it."

"I wouldn't, not if I was to be shot twenty times over. I wouldn't shoot a pal. And Belcher wouldn't — isn't that right, Belcher?"

"That's right, chum," Belcher said, but more by way of answering the question than of joining in the argument. Belcher sounded as though whatever unforeseen thing he'd always been waiting for had come at last.

"Anyway, who says Noble would be shot if I wasn't? What do you think I'd do if I was in his place, out in the middle of a blasted bog?"

"What would you do?" asks Donovan.

"I'd go with him wherever he was going, of course. Share my last bob with him and stick by him through thick and thin. No one can ever say of me that I let down a pal."

"We had enough of this," says Jeremiah Donovan, cocking his revolver. "Is there any message you want to send?"

"No, there isn't."

"Do you want to say your prayers?"

Hawkins came out with a cold-blooded remark that even shocked me and turned on Noble again.

"Listen to me, Noble," he says. "You and me are chums. You can't come over to my side, so I'll come over to your side. That show you I mean what I say? Give me a rifle and I'll go along with you and the other lads."

Nobody answered him. We knew that was no way out.

"Hear what I'm saying?" he says. "I'm through with it. I'm a deserter or anything else you like. I don't believe in your stuff, but it's no worse than mine. That satisfy you?"

Noble raised his head, but Donovan began to speak and he lowered it again without replying.

"For the last time, have you any messages to send?" says Donovan in a cool, excited sort of voice.

"Shut up, Donovan! You don't understand me, but these lads do. They're not the sort to make a pal and kill a pal. They're not the tools of any capitalist."

I alone of the crowd saw Donovan raise his Webley to the back of Hawkins's neck, and as he did so I shut my eyes and tried to pray. Hawkins had begun to say something else when Donovan fired, and as I opened my eyes at the bang, I saw Hawkins stagger at the knees and lie out flat at Noble's feet, slowly and as quiet as a kid falling asleep, with the lantern-light on his lean legs and bright farmer's boots. We all stood very still, watching him settle out in the last agony.

Then Belcher took out a handkerchief and began to tie it about his own eyes (in our excitement we'd forgotten to do the same for Hawkins), and, seeing it wasn't big enough, turned and asked for the loan of mine. I gave it to him and he knotted the two together and pointed with his foot at Hawkins.

"He's not quite dead," he says. "Better give him another."

Sure enough, Hawkins's left knee is beginning to rise. I bend down and put my gun to his head; then, recollecting myself, I get up again. Belcher understands what's in my mind.

"Give him his first," he says. "I don't mind. Poor bastard, we don't know what's happening to him now."

I knelt and fired. By this time I didn't seem to know what I was doing. Belcher, who was fumbling a bit awkwardly with the handkerchiefs, came out with a laugh as he heard the shot. It was the first time I heard him laugh and it sent a shudder down my back; it sounded so unnatural.

"Poor bugger!" he said quietly. "And last night he was so curious about it all. It's very queer, chums, I always think. Now he knows as much about it as they'll ever let him know, and last night he was all in the dark."

Donovan helped him to tie the handkerchiefs about his eyes. "Thanks, chum," he said. Donovan asked if there were any messages he wanted sent.

"No, chum," he says, "not for me. If any of you would like to write to Hawkins's mother, you'll find a letter from her in his pocket. He and his mother were great chums. But my missus left me eight years ago. Went away with another fellow and took the kid with her. I like the feeling of a home, as you may have noticed, but I couldn't start again after that."

It was an extraordinary thing, but in those few minutes Belcher said more than in all the weeks before. It was just as if the sound of the shot had started a flood of talk in him and he could go on the whole night like that, quite happily, talking about himself. We stood round like fools now that he couldn't see us any longer. Donovan looked at Noble, and Noble shook his head. Then Donovan raised his Webley, and at that moment Belcher gives his queer laugh again. He may have thought we were talking about him, or perhaps he noticed the same thing I'd noticed and couldn't understand it.

"Excuse me, chums," he says. "I feel I'm talking the hell of a lot, and so silly, about my being so handy about a house and things like that. But this thing came on me suddenly. You'll forgive me, I'm sure."

"You don't want to say a prayer?" asks Donovan.

"No, chum," he says. "I don't think it would help. I'm ready, and you boys want to get it over."

"You understand that we're only doing our duty?" says Donovan.

Belcher's head was raised like a blind man's, so that you could only see his chin and the tip of his nose in the lantern-light.

"I never could make out what duty was myself," he said. "I think you're all good lads, if that's what you mean. I'm not complaining."

Noble, just as if he couldn't bear any more of it, raised his fist at Donovan, and in a flash Donovan raised his gun and fired. The big man went over like a sack of meal, and this time there was no need of a second shot.

I don't remember much about the burying, but that it was worse than all the rest because we had to carry them to the grave. It was all mad lonely with nothing but a patch of lantern-light between ourselves and the dark, and birds hooting and screeching all round, disturbed by the guns. Noble went through Hawkins's belongings to find the letter from his mother, and then joined his hands together. He did the same with Belcher. Then, when we'd filled the grave, we separated from Jeremiah Donovan and Feeney and took our tools back to the shed. All the way we didn't speak a word. The kitchen was dark and cold as we'd left it, and the old woman was sitting over the hearth, saying her beads. We walked past her into the room, and Noble struck a match to light the lamp. She rose quietly and came to the doorway with all her cantankerousness gone.

"What did ye do with them?" she asked in a whisper, and Noble started so that the match went out in his hand.

"What's that?" he asked without turning around.

"I heard ye," she said.

"What did you hear?" asked Noble.

"I heard ye. Do ye think I didn't hear ye, putting the spade back in the houseen?"

Noble struck another match and this time the lamp lit for him.

"Was that what ye did to them?" she asked.

Then, by God, in the very doorway, she fell on her knees and began praying, and after looking at her for a minute or two Noble did the same by the fireplace. I pushed my way out past her and left them at it. I stood at the door, watching the stars and listening to the shrieking of the birds dying out over the bogs. It is so strange what you feel at times like that that you can't describe it. Noble says he saw everything ten times the size, as though there were nothing in the whole world but that little patch of bog with the two Englishmen stiffening into it, but with me it was as if the patch of bog where the Englishmen were was a million miles away, and even Noble and the old woman, mumbling behind me, and the birds and the bloody stars were all far away, and I was somehow very small and very lost and lonely like a child astray in the snow. And anything that happened to me afterwards, I never felt the same about again.

∞

TILLIE OLSEN (b. 1913) *was born in Omaha, Nebraska, the daughter of political refugees from the Russian Czarist repression after the revolution of 1905. Her father was a farmer, packing-house worker, house painter, and jack-of-all-trades; her mother was a factory worker. At the age of sixteen Olsen dropped out of high school to help support her family during the Depression. She was a member of the Young Communist League, involved in the Warehouse Union's labor disputes in Kansas City. At age nineteen she began her first novel,* Yonnondio. *Four chapters of this book about a poverty-stricken working-class family were completed in the next four years, during which time she married, gave birth to her first child, and was left with the baby by her husband because, as she later wrote in her autobiographical story "I Stand Here Ironing," he "could no longer endure sharing want" with them. In 1934 a section of the first chapter of her novel was published in* Partisan Review, *but she abandoned the unfinished book in 1937. The year before she had married Jack Olsen, with whom she had three more children; raising the children and working for political causes took up all her time. In the 1940s she was a factory worker; in the 1950s, a secretary. It was not* *until 1953, when her youngest daughter started school, that she was able to begin writing again.*

That year Olsen enrolled in a class in fiction writing at San Francisco State College. She was awarded a Stanford University creative writing fellowship for 1955 and 1956. During the 1950s she wrote the four stories collected in Tell Me a Riddle, *which established her reputation when the book was published as a paperback in 1961. Identified as a champion of the reemerging feminist movement, Olsen wrote a bio-graphical introduction to Rebecca Harding Davis's nineteenth-century proletarian novel,* Life in the Iron Mills, *published by the Feminist Press in 1972. Two years later, after several grants and creative writing fellowships, she published the still-unfinished* Yonnondio. Silences, *a collection of essays exploring the different circumstances that obstruct or silence literary creation, appeared in 1978.*

As the Canadian author Margaret Atwood has understood about Olsen,

> *Few writers have gained such wide respect on such a small body of published work. . . . Among women writers in the United States, "respect" is too pale a word: "reverence" is more like it. This is presumably because women writers, even more than their male counterparts, recognize what a heroic feat it is to have held down a job, raised four children, and still somehow managed to become and to remain a writer.*

A radical feminist, Olsen has said that she felt no personal guilt as a single parent over her daughter's predicament, as described in her confessional narrative "I Stand Here Ironing," since "guilt is a word used far too sloppily, to cover up harmful situations in society that must be changed." Her four stories have appeared in more than fifty an-thologies and have been translated into many languages. In 1994 she received the Rea Award for the Short Story, a literary prize that honors a living American author who has made "a significant contribution to the short story as an art form."

TILLIE OLSEN

I Stand Here Ironing   1961

I stand here ironing, and what you asked me moves tormented back and forth with the iron.

"I wish you would manage the time to come in and talk with me about your daughter. I'm sure you can help me understand her. She's a youngster who needs help and whom I'm deeply interested in helping."

"Who needs help." . . . Even if I came, what good would it do? You think because I am her mother I have a key, or that in some way you could use me as a key? She has lived for nineteen years. There is all that life that has hap-pened outside of me, beyond me.

And when is there time to remember, to sift, to weigh, to estimate, to to-tal? I will start and there will be an interruption and I will have to gather it all together again. Or I will become engulfed with all I did or did not do, with what should have been and what cannot be helped.

She was a beautiful baby. The first and only one of our five that was beautiful at birth. You do not guess how new and uneasy her tenancy in her now-loveliness. You did not know her all those years she was thought homely, or see her poring over her baby pictures, making me tell her over and over how beautiful she had been — and would be, I would tell her — and was now, to the seeing eye. But the seeing eyes were few or nonexistent. Including mine.

I nursed her. They feel that's important nowadays, I nursed all the children, but with her, with all the fierce rigidity of first motherhood, I did like the books then said. Though her cries battered me to trembling and my breasts ached with swollenness, I waited till the clock decreed.

Why do I put that first? I do not even know if it matters, or if it explains anything.

She was a beautiful baby. She blew shining bubbles of sound. She loved motion, loved light, loved color and music and textures. She would lie on the floor in her blue overalls patting the surface so hard in ecstasy her hands and feet would blur. She was a miracle to me, but when she was eight months old I had to leave her daytimes with the woman downstairs to whom she was no miracle at all, for I worked or looked for work and for Emily's father, who "could no longer endure" (he wrote in his good-bye note) "sharing want with us."

I was nineteen. It was pre-relief, pre-WPA world of the depression. I would start running as soon as I got off the streetcar, running up the stairs, the place smelling sour, and awake or asleep to startle awake, when she saw me she would break into a clogged weeping that could not be comforted, a weeping I can hear yet.

After a while I found a job hashing at night so I could be with her days, and it was better. But it came to where I had to bring her to his family and leave her.

It took a long time to raise the money for her fare back. Then she got chicken pox and I had to wait longer. When she finally came, I hardly knew her, walking quick and nervous like her father, looking like her father, thin, and dressed in a shoddy red that yellowed her skin and glared at the pockmarks. All the baby loveliness gone.

She was two. Old enough for nursery school they said, and I did not know then what I know now — the fatigue of the long day, and the lacerations of group life in the kinds of nurseries that are only parking places for children.

Except that it would have made no difference if I had known. It was the only place there was. It was the only way we could be together, the only way I could hold a job.

And even without knowing, I knew. I knew the teacher that was evil because all these years it has curdled into my memory, the little boy hunched in the corner, her rasp, "why aren't you outside, because Alvin hits you? that's no reason, go out, scaredy." I knew Emily hated it even if she did not clutch and implore "don't go Mommy" like the other children, mornings.

She always had a reason why we should stay home. Momma, you look sick. Momma, I feel sick. Momma, the teachers aren't there today, they're sick. Momma, we can't go, there was a fire last night. Momma, it's a holiday today, no school, they told me.

But never a direct protest, never rebellion. I think of our others in their three-, four-year-oldness — the explosions, the tempers, the denunciations, the demands — and I feel suddenly ill. I put the iron down. What in me demanded that goodness in her? And what was the cost, the cost to her of such goodness?

The old man living in the back once said in his gentle way: "You should smile at Emily more when you look at her." What *was* in my face when I looked at her? I loved her. There were all the acts of love.

It was only with the others I remembered what he said, and it was the face of joy, and not of care or tightness or worry I turned to them — too late for Emily. She does not smile easily, let alone almost always as her brothers and sisters do. Her face is closed and sombre, but when she wants, how fluid. You must have seen it in her pantomimes, you spoke of her rare gift for comedy on the stage that rouses laughter out of the audience so dear they applaud and applaud and do not want to let her go.

Where does it come from, that comedy? There was none of it in her when she came back to me that second time, after I had to send her away again. She had a new daddy now to learn to love, and I think perhaps it was a better time.

Except when we left her alone nights, telling ourselves she was old enough.

"Can't you go some other time, Mommy, like tomorrow?" she would ask. "Will it be just a little while you'll be gone? Do you promise?"

The time we came back, the front door open, the clock on the floor in the hall. She rigid awake. "It wasn't just a little while. I didn't cry. Three times I called you, just three times, and then I ran downstairs to open the door so you could come faster. The clock talked loud. I threw it away, it scared me what it talked."

She said the clock talked loud again that night I went to the hospital to have Susan. She was delirious with the fever that comes before red measles, but she was fully conscious all the week I was gone and the week after we were home when she could not come near the new baby or me.

She did not get well. She stayed skeleton thin, not wanting to eat, and night after night she had nightmares. She would call for me, and I would rouse from exhaustion to sleepily call back: "You're all right, darling, go to sleep, it's just a dream," and if she still called, in a sterner voice, "now go to sleep, Emily, there's nothing to hurt you." Twice, only twice, when I had to get up for Susan anyhow, I went in to sit with her.

Now when it is too late (as if she would let me hold her and comfort her like I do the others) I get up and go to her at once at her moan or restless stirring. "Are you awake, Emily? Can I get you something?" And the answer is always the same: "No, I'm all right, go back to sleep, Mother."

They persuaded me at the clinic to send her away to a convalescent home in the country where "she can have the kind of food and care you can't manage for her, and you'll be free to concentrate on the new baby." They still send children to that place. I see pictures on the society page of sleek young women planning affairs to raise money for it, or dancing at the affairs, or decorating Easter eggs or filling Christmas stockings for the children.

They never have a picture of the children so I do not know if the girls still wear those gigantic red bows and the ravaged looks on the every other Sunday when parents can come to visit "unless otherwise notified" — as we were notified the first six weeks.

Oh it is a handsome place, green lawns and tall trees and fluted flower beds. High up on the balconies of each cottage the children stand, the girls in their red bows and white dresses, the boys in white suits and giant red ties. The parents stand below shrieking up to be heard and the children shriek down to be heard, and between them the invisible wall "Not To Be Contaminated by Parental Germs or Physical Affection."

There was a tiny girl who always stood hand in hand with Emily. Her parents never came. One visit she was gone. "They moved her to Rose Cottage," Emily shouted in explanation. "They don't like you to love anybody here."

She wrote once a week, the labored writing of a seven-year-old. "I am fine. How is the baby. If I write my leter nicly I will have a star. Love." There never was a star. We wrote every other day, letters she could never hold or keep but only hear read — once. "We simply do not have room for children to keep any personal possessions," they patiently explained when we pieced one Sunday's shrieking together to plead how much it would mean to Emily, who loved so to keep things, to be allowed to keep her letters and cards.

Each visit she looked frailer. "She isn't eating," they told us.

(They had runny eggs for breakfast or mush with lumps, Emily said later, I'd hold it in my mouth and not swallow. Nothing ever tasted good, just when they had chicken.)

It took us eight months to get her released home, and only the fact that she gained back so little of her seven lost pounds convinced the social worker.

I used to try to hold and love her after she came back, but her body would stay stiff, and after a while she'd push away. She ate little. Food sickened her, and I think much of life too. Oh she had physical lightness and brightness, twinkling by on skates, bouncing like a ball up and down up and down over the jump rope, skimming over the hill; but these were momentary.

She fretted about her appearance, thin and dark and foreign-looking at a time when every little girl was supposed to look or thought she should look a chubby blonde replica of Shirley Temple. The doorbell sometimes rang for her, but no one seemed to come and play in the house or to be a best friend. Maybe because we moved so much.

There was a boy she loved painfully through two school semesters. Months later she told me how she had taken pennies from my purse to buy him candy. "Licorice was his favorite and I brought him some every day, but he still liked Jennifer better'n me. Why, Mommy?" The kind of question for which there is no answer.

School was a worry for her. She was not glib or quick in a world where glibness and quickness were easily confused with ability to learn. To her overworked and exasperated teachers she was an overconscientious "slow learner" who kept trying to catch up and was absent entirely too often.

I let her be absent, though sometimes the illness was imaginary. How different from my now-strictness about attendance with the others. I wasn't working. We had a new baby. I was home anyhow. Sometimes, after Susan grew old enough, I would keep her home from school, too, to have them all together.

Mostly Emily had asthma, and her breathing, harsh and labored, would fill the house with a curiously tranquil sound. I would bring the two old dresser mirrors and her boxes of collections to her bed. She would select beads and single earrings, bottle tops and shells, dried flowers and pebbles, old postcards and scraps, all sorts of oddments; then she and Susan would play Kingdom, setting up landscapes and furniture, peopling them with action.

Those were the only times of peaceful companionship between her and Susan. I have edged away from it, that poisonous feeling between them, that terrible balancing of hurts and needs I had to do between the two, and did so badly, those earlier years.

Oh there were conflicts between the others too, each one human, needing, demanding, hurting, taking — but only between Emily and Susan, no, Emily toward Susan that corroding resentment. It seems so obvious on the surface, yet it is not obvious; Susan, the second child, Susan, golden- and curly-haired and chubby, quick and articulate and assured, everything in appearance and manner Emily was not; Susan, not able to resist Emily's precious things, losing or sometimes clumsily breaking them; Susan telling jokes and riddles to company for applause while Emily sat silent (to say to me later: that was *my* riddle, Mother, I told it to Susan); Susan, who for all the five years' difference in age was just a year behind Emily in developing physically.

I am glad for that slow physical development that widened the difference between her and her contemporaries, though she suffered over it. She was too vulnerable for that terrible world of youthful competition, of preening and parading, of constant measuring of yourself against every other, of envy, "If I had that copper hair," "If I had that skin. . . ." She tormented herself enough about not looking like the others, there was enough of unsureness, the having to be conscious of words before you speak, the constant caring — what are they thinking of me? without having it all magnified by the merciless physical drives.

Ronnie is calling. He is wet and I change him. It is rare there is such a cry now. That time of motherhood is almost behind me when the ear is not one's own but must always be racked and listening for the child cry, the child call. We sit for a while and I hold him, looking out over the city spread in charcoal with its soft aisles of light. "*Shoogily*," he breathes and curls closer. I carry him back to bed, asleep. *Shoogily*. A funny word, a family word, inherited from Emily, invented by her to say: *comfort*.

In this and other ways she leaves her seal, I say aloud. And startle at my saying it. What do I mean? What did I start to gather together, to try and make coherent? I was at the terrible, growing years. War years. I do not remember them well. I was working, there were four smaller ones now, there was not time for her. She had to help be a mother, and housekeeper, and shopper. She had to get her seal. Mornings of crisis and near hysteria trying to get lunches packed, hair combed, coats and shoes found, everyone to school or Child Care on time, the baby ready for transportation. And always the paper scribbled on by a smaller one, the book looked at by Susan then mislaid, the homework not done. Running out to that huge school where she was one, she was lost, she was a drop; suffering over the unpreparedness, stammering and unsure in her classes.

There was so little time left at night after the kids were bedded down. She would struggle over books, always eating (it was in those years she developed her enormous appetite that is legendary in our family) and I would be ironing, or preparing food for the next day, or writing V-mail to Bill, or tending the baby. Sometimes, to make me laugh, or out of her despair, she would imitate happenings or types at school.

I think I said once: "Why don't you do something like this in the school amateur show?" One morning she phoned me at work, hardly understandable through the weeping: "Mother, I did it. I won, I won; they gave me first prize; they clapped and clapped and wouldn't let me go."

Now suddenly she was Somebody, and as imprisoned in her difference as she had been in anonymity.

She began to be asked to perform at other high schools, even in colleges, then at city and statewide affairs. The first one we went to, I only recognized her that first moment when thin, shy, she almost drowned herself into the curtains. Then: Was this Emily? The control, the command, the convulsing and deadly clowning, the spell, then the roaring, stamping audience, unwilling to let this rare and precious laughter out of their lives.

Afterwards: You ought to do something about her with a gift like that — but without money or knowing how, what does one do? We have left it all to her, and the gift has so often eddied inside, clogged and clotted, as been used and growing.

She is coming. She runs up the stairs two at a time with her light graceful step, and I know she is happy tonight. Whatever it was that occasioned your call did not happen today.

"Aren't you ever going to finish the ironing, Mother? Whistler painted his mother in a rocker. I'd have to paint mine standing over an ironing board." This is one of her communicative nights and she tells me everything and nothing as she fixes herself a plate of food out of the icebox.

She is so lovely. Why did you want me to come in at all? Why were you concerned? She will find her way.

She starts up the stairs to bed. "Don't get me up with the rest in the morning." "But I thought you were having midterms." "Oh, those," she comes back in, kisses me, and says quite lightly, "in a couple of years when we'll all be atom-dead they won't matter a bit."

She has said it before. She *believes* it. But because I have been dredging the past, and all that compounds a human being is so heavy and meaningful in me, I cannot endure it tonight.

I will never total it all. I will never come in to say: She was a child seldom smiled at. Her father left me before she was a year old. I had to work her first six years when there was work, or I sent her home and to his relatives. There were years she had care she hated. She was dark and thin and foreign-looking in a world where the prestige went to blondeness and curly hair and dimples, she was slow where glibness was prized. She was a child of anxious, not proud, love. We were poor and could not afford for her the soil of easy growth. I was a young mother, I was a distracted mother. There were other children pushing up, demanding. Her younger sister seemed all that she was not. There were years she did not want me to touch her. She kept too much in herself, her life was such she had to keep too much in herself. My wisdom came too late. She has much to her and probably little will come of it. She is a child of her age, of depression, of war, of fear.

Let her be. So all that is in her will not bloom but in how many does it? There is still enough left to live by. Only help her to know — help make it so there is cause for her to know — that she is more than this dress on the ironing board, helpless before the iron.

‌ಣ

GRACE PALEY (b. 1922) *was born in New York City. She studied at Hunter College and New York University, and in 1942 she married for the first time. She had two children from that marriage. In the 1950s she turned from writing poetry to short fiction. Her first book of stories,* The Little Disturbances of Man *(1959), established her reputation as a writer with a remarkably supple gift for language. As Susan Sontag has noted, "She is that rare kind of writer, a natural with a voice like no one else's — funny, sad, lean, modest, energetic, acute." When this book went out of print in 1965, its reputation survived, strengthened by the infrequent appearances of her new stories in magazines such as the* Atlantic Monthly, Esquire, *the* Noble Savage, Genesis West, *the* New American Review, Ararat, *and* Fiction.

During the 1960s and 1970s Paley was prominent as a nonviolent activist protesting the Vietnam War. She was secretary of the Greenwich Village Peace Center, spent time in jail for her antiwar activities, and visited Hanoi and Moscow as a member of peace delegations, defining herself as a "somewhat combative pacifist and cooperative anarchist." During the World Peace Congress in Moscow in 1973, she condemned the Soviet Union for silencing political dissidents; the congress disassociated itself from her statement. Paley has long been a feminist and active in the antinuclear movement. In 1974 her second volume of stories, Enormous Changes at the Last Minute, *was published — it is a quieter, more openly personal collection of seventeen stories, many of them, such as "A Conversation with My Father," autobiographical. Her third book of stories,* Later the Same Day, *appeared in 1985. In 1988 Paley was designated the first official New York State Author by an act of the state legislature.*

Paley refuses to blame her teaching jobs or her involvements as an activist for her relatively low productivity as a writer. She says she writes "from distress." What she tries to get at in her stories is "a history of everyday life," and her subject matter and prose style are unmistakable. Living in a Manhattan apartment close to the Greenwich Village School (P.S. 41), Little Tony's Unisex Haircutters, the Famous Ray's Pizza, the H & H Fruit and Vegetable Market, and the Jefferson Market Branch of the New York Public Library, Paley observes her neighbors, friends, and family with compassion, humor, and hope. In such stories as "Samuel," her spare dissection of her characters is never performed at the expense of sympathy for the human condition. It is likely that, as was true of her Russian counterpart Isaac Babel, her production of sto-

ries will be limited. As she puts it, "There is a long time in me between knowing and telling." The Collected Stories of Grace Paley was published in 1994.

RELATED COMMENTARY: *Grace Paley, "A Conversation with Ann Charters," page 782.*

GRACE PALEY

A Conversation with My Father   1974

My father is eighty-six years old and in bed. His heart, that bloody motor, is equally old and will not do certain jobs any more. It still floods his head with brainy light. But it won't let his legs carry the weight of his body around the house. Despite my metaphors, this muscle failure is not due to his old heart, he says, but to a potassium shortage. Sitting on one pillow, leaning on three, he offers last-minute advice and makes a request.

"I would like you to write a simple story just once more," he says, "the kind de Maupassant wrote, or Chekhov, the kind you used to write. Just recognizable people and then write down what happened to them next."

I say, "Yes, why not? That's possible." I want to please him, though I don't remember writing that way. I *would* like to try to tell such a story, if he means the kind that begins: "There was a woman . . ." followed by plot, the absolute line between two points which I've always despised. Not for literary reasons, but because it takes all hope away. Everyone, real or invented, deserves the open destiny of life.

Finally I thought of a story that had been happening for a couple of years right across the street. I wrote it down, then read it aloud. "Pa," I said, "how about this? Do you mean something like this?"

> Once in my time there was a woman and she had a son. They lived nicely, in a small apartment in Manhattan. This boy at about fifteen became a junkie, which is not unusual in our neighborhood. In order to maintain her close friendship with him, she became a junkie too. She said it was part of the youth culture, with which she felt very much at home. After a while, for a number of reasons, the boy gave it all up and left the city and his mother in disgust. Hopeless and alone, she grieved. We all visit her.

"O.K., Pa, that's it," I said, "an unadorned and miserable tale."

"But that's not what I mean," my father said. "You misunderstood me on purpose. You know there's a lot more to it. You know that. You left everything out. Turgenev wouldn't do that. Chekhov wouldn't do that. There are in fact Russian writers you never heard of, you don't have an inkling of, as good as anyone, who can write a plain ordinary story, who would not leave out what you have left out. I object not to facts but to people sitting in trees talking senselessly, voices from who knows where. . . ."

"Forget that one, Pa, what have I left out now? In this one?"

"Her looks, for instance."

"Oh. Quite handsome, I think. Yes."

"Her hair?"

"Dark, with heavy braids, as though she were a girl or a foreigner."

"What were her parents like, her stock? That she became such a person. It's interesting, you know."

"From out of town. Professional people. The first to be divorced in their county. How's that? Enough?" I asked.

"With you, it's all a joke," he said. "What about the boy's father? Why didn't you mention him? Who was he? Or was the boy born out of wedlock?"

"Yes," I said. "He was born out of wedlock."

"For Godsakes, doesn't anyone in your stories get married? Doesn't anyone have the time to run down to City Hall before they jump into bed?"

"No," I said. "In real life, yes. But in my stories, no."

"Why do you answer me like that?"

"Oh, Pa, this is a simple story about a smart woman who came to N.Y.C. full of interest love trust excitement very up to date, and about her son, what a hard time she had in this world. Married or not, it's of small consequence."

"It is of great consequence," he said.

"O.K.," I said.

"O.K. O.K. yourself," he said, "but listen. I believe you that she's good-looking, but I don't think she was so smart."

"That's true," I said. "Actually that's the trouble with stories. People start out fantastic. You think they're extraordinary, but it turns out as the work goes along, they're just average with a good education. Sometimes the other way around, the person's a kind of dumb innocent, but he outwits you and you can't even think of an ending good enough."

"What do you do then?" he asked. He had been a doctor for a couple of decades and then an artist for a couple of decades and he's still interested in details, craft, technique.

"Well, you just have to let the story lie around till some agreement can be reached between you and the stubborn hero."

"Aren't you talking silly now?" he asked. "Start again," he said. "It so happens I'm not going out this evening. Tell the story again. See what you can do this time."

"O.K.," I said. "But it's not a five-minute job." Second attempt:

Once, across the street from us, there was a fine handsome woman, our neighbor. She had a son whom she loved because she'd known him since birth (in helpless chubby infancy, and in the wrestling, hugging ages, seven to ten, as well as earlier and later). This boy, when he fell into the fist of adolescence, became a junkie. He was not a hopeless one. He was in fact hopeful, an ideologue and successful converter. With his busy brilliance, he wrote persuasive articles for his high-school newspaper. Seeking a wider audience, using important connections, he drummed into Lower Manhattan newsstand distribution a periodical called *Oh! Golden Horse!*

In order to keep him from feeling guilty (because guilt is the stony heart of nine tenths of all clinically diagnosed cancers in America today, she said), and because she had always believed in giving bad habits room at home where one could keep an eye on them, she too became a junkie. Her kitchen was famous for a while — a center for intellectual addicts who knew what they were doing. A few felt artistic like Coleridge° and others were scientific and revolutionary like Leary.° Although she was often high herself, certain good mothering reflexes remained, and she saw to it that there was lots of orange juice around and honey and milk and vitamin pills. However, she never cooked anything but chili, and that no more than once a week. She explained, when we talked to her, seriously, with neighborly concern, that it was her part in the youth culture and she would rather be with the young, it was an honor, than with her own generation.

One week, while nodding through an Antonioni film, this boy was severely jabbed by the elbow of a stern and proselytizing girl, sitting beside him. She offered immediate apricots and nuts for his sugar level, spoke to him sharply, and took him home.

She had heard of him and his work and she herself published, edited, and wrote a competitive journal called *Man Does Live by Bread Alone*. In the organic heat of her continuous presence he could not help but become interested once more in his muscles, his arteries, and nerve connections. In fact he began to love them, treasure them, praise them with funny little songs in *Man Does Live*. . . .

> the fingers of my flesh transcend
> my transcendental soul
> the tightness in my shoulders end
> my teeth have made me whole

To the mouth of his head (that glory of will and determination) he brought hard apples, nuts, wheat germ, and soybean oil. He said to his old friends, From now on, I guess I'll keep my wits about me. I'm going on the natch. He said he was about to begin a spiritual deep-breathing journey. How about you too, Mom? he asked kindly.

His conversion was so radiant, splendid, that neighborhood kids his age began to say that he had never been a real addict at all, only a journalist along for the smell of the story. The mother tried several times to give up what had become without her son and his friends a lonely habit. This effort only brought it to supportable levels. The boy and his girl took their electronic mimeograph and moved to the bushy edge of another borough. They were very strict. They said they would not see her again until she had been off drugs for sixty days.

At home alone in the evening, weeping, the mother read and reread the seven issues of *Oh! Golden Horse!* They seemed to her as truthful as ever. We often crossed the street to visit and console. But if we mentioned any of our children who were at college or in the hospital or dropouts at home, she would cry out, My baby! My baby! and burst into terrible, face-scarring, time-consuming tears. The End.

First my father was silent, then he said, "Number One: You have a nice sense of humor. Number Two: I see you can't tell a plain story. So don't waste

---

Coleridge: Samuel Taylor Coleridge (1772–1834), the English Romantic poet, was an opium addict.
Leary: Timothy Leary (1920–1996) was a former Harvard professor of psychology and early advocate of the use of LSD.

time." Then he said sadly, "Number Three: I suppose that means she was alone, she was left like that, his mother. Alone. Probably sick?"

I said, "Yes."

"Poor woman. Poor girl, to be born in a time of fools, to live among fools. The end. The end. You were right to put that down. The end."

I didn't want to argue, but I had to say, "Well, it is not necessarily the end, Pa."

"Yes," he said, "what a tragedy. The end of a person."

"No, Pa," I begged him. "It doesn't have to be. She's only about forty. She could be a hundred different things in this world as time goes on. A teacher or a social worker. An ex-junkie! Sometimes it's better than having a master's in education."

"Jokes," he said. "As a writer that's your main trouble. You don't want to recognize it. Tragedy! Plain tragedy! Historical tragedy! No hope. The end."

"Oh, Pa," I said. "She could change."

"In your own life, too, you have to look it in the face." He took a couple of nitroglycerin. "Turn to five," he said, pointing to the dial on the oxygen tank. He inserted the tubes into his nostrils and breathed deep. He closed his eyes and said, "No."

I had promised the family to always let him have the last word when arguing, but in this case I had a different responsibility. That woman lives across the street. She's my knowledge and my invention. I'm sorry for her. I'm not going to leave her there in that house crying. (Actually neither would Life, which unlike me has no pity.)

Therefore: She did change. Of course her son never came home again. But right now, she's the receptionist in a storefront community clinic in the East Village. Most of the customers are young people, some old friends. The head doctor has said to her, "If we only had three people in this clinic with your experiences. . . ."

"The doctor said that?" My father took the oxygen tubes out of his nostrils and said, "Jokes. Jokes again."

"No, Pa, it could really happen that way, it's a funny world nowadays."

"No," he said. "Truth first. She will slide back. A person must have character. She does not."

"No, Pa," I said. "That's it. She's got a job. Forget it. She's in that storefront working."

"How long will it be?" he asked. "Tragedy! You too. When will you look it in the face?"

GRACE PALEY

Samuel   1968

Some boys are very tough. They're afraid of nothing. They are the ones who climb a wall and take a bow at the top. Not only are they brave on the roof, but they make a lot of noise in the darkest part of the cellar where even the super hates to go. They also jiggle and hop on the platform between the locked doors of the subway cars.

Four boys are jiggling on the swaying platform. Their names are Alfred, Calvin, Samuel, and Tom. The men and the women in the cars on either side watch them. They don't like them to jiggle or jump but don't want to interfere. Of course some of the men in the cars were once brave boys like these. One of them had ridden the tail of a speeding truck from New York to Rockaway Beach without getting off, without his sore fingers losing hold. Nothing happened to him then or later. He had made a compact with other boys who preferred to watch: starting at Eighth Avenue and Fifteenth Street, he would get to some specified place, maybe Twenty-third and the river, by hopping the tops of the moving trucks. This was hard to do when one truck turned a corner in the wrong direction and the nearest truck was a couple of feet too high. He made three or four starts before succeeding. He had gotten this idea from a film at school called *The Romance of Logging.* He had finished high school, married a good friend, was in a responsible job and going to night school.

These two men and others looked at the four boys jumping and jiggling on the platform and thought, It must be fun to ride that way, especially now the weather is nice and we're out of the tunnel and way high over the Bronx. Then they thought, These kids do seem to be acting sort of stupid. They *are* little. Then they thought of some of the brave things they had done when they were boys and jiggling didn't seem so risky.

The ladies in the car became very angry when they looked at the four boys. Most of them brought their brows together and hoped the boys could see their extreme disapproval. One of the ladies wanted to get up and say, be careful you dumb kids, get off that platform or I'll call a cop. But three of the boys were Negroes and the fourth was something else she couldn't tell for sure. She was afraid they'd be fresh and laugh at her and embarrass her. She wasn't afraid they'd hit her, but she was afraid of embarrassment. Another lady thought, their mothers never know where they are. It wasn't true in this particular case. Their mothers all knew that they had gone to see the missile exhibit on Fourteenth Street.

Out on the platform, whenever the train accelerated, the boys would raise their hands and point them up to the sky to act like rockets going off, then they rat-tat-tatted the shatterproof glass pane like machine guns, although no machine guns had been exhibited.

For some reason known only to the motorman, the train began a sudden slowdown. The lady who was afraid of embarrassment saw the boys jerk forward and backward and grab the swinging guard chains. She had her own boy at home. She stood up with determination and went to the door. She slid it open and said, "You boys will be hurt. You'll be killed. I'm going to call the conductor if you don't just go into the next car and sit down and be quiet."

Two of the boys said, "Yes'm," and acted as though they were about to go. Two of them blinked their eyes a couple of times and pressed their lips together. The train resumed its speed. The door slid shut, parting the lady and the boys. She leaned against the side door because she had to get off at the next stop.

The boys opened their eyes wide at each other and laughed. The lady blushed. The boys looked at her and laughed harder. They began to pound each other's back. Samuel laughed the hardest and pounded Alfred's back until Alfred coughed and the tears came. Alfred held tight to the chain hook. Samuel pounded him even harder when he saw the tears. He said, "Why you bawling? You a baby, huh?" and laughed. One of the men whose boyhood had been more watchful than brave became angry. He stood up straight and looked at the boys for a couple of seconds. Then he walked in a citizenly way to the end of the car, where he pulled the emergency cord. Almost at once, with a terrible hiss, the pressure of air abandoned the brakes and the wheels were caught and held.

People standing in the most secure places fell forward, then backward. Samuel had let go of his hold on the chain so he could pound Tom as well as Alfred. All the passengers in the cars whipped back and forth, but he pitched only forward and fell head first to be crushed and killed between the cars.

The train had stopped hard, halfway into the station, and the conductor called at once for the trainmen who knew about this kind of death and how to take the body from the wheels and brakes. There was silence except for passengers from other cars who asked, What happened! What happened! The ladies waited around wondering if he might be an only child. The men recalled other afternoons with very bad endings. The little boys stayed close to each other, leaning and touching shoulders and arms and legs.

When the policeman knocked at the door and told her about it, Samuel's mother began to scream. She screamed all day and moaned all night, though the doctors tried to quiet her with pills.

Oh, oh, she hopelessly cried. She did not know how she could ever find another boy like that one. However, she was a young woman and she became pregnant. Then for a few months she was hopeful. The child born to her was a boy. They brought him to be seen and nursed. She smiled. But immediately she saw that this baby wasn't Samuel. She and her husband together have had other children, but never again will a boy exactly like Samuel be known.

ΩΩ

EDGAR ALLAN POE (1809–1849), *the son of poor traveling actors, was adopted by the merchant John Allan of Richmond, Virginia, after the death of Poe's mother. He was educated in Virginia and England, served two years in the army as an enlisted man, then entered the military academy at West Point, from which he was expelled after a year. When John Allan disinherited him, Poe turned to writing to earn his living. In 1833 his story "Ms. Found in a Bottle" won a fifty-dollar prize for the best story in a popular Baltimore periodical, and shortly afterward Poe became editor of the* Southern Literary Messenger. *In 1836 he married his cousin Virginia Clemm, who was thirteen years old. Poe's brilliant reviews, poems, and stories attracted wide attention, but the magazine fired him in 1837 because of his unstable temperament. His remaining years were a struggle with poverty, depression, poor health aggravated by addiction to drugs and alcohol, and — after 1847 — grief over the death of his wife. The writer Jorge Luis Borges observed that Poe's life "was short and unhappy, if unhappiness can be short."*

Most of Poe's stories can be divided into two categories: tales of terror, such as "The Cask of Amontillado" (1846) and "The Tell-Tale Heart" (1843), in which unity of effect or a single impression is of the greatest importance, and stories of intellect or reason, analytic tales that are precursors of the modern detective story. When critics accused him of imitating German romantic writers such as Heinrich von Kleist in his monologues of inspired madness, Poe answered, "Terror is not of Germany, but of the soul."

Poe is also important as one of the earliest writers to attempt to formulate an aesthetic theory about the short story form, or the "prose tale," as it was called in his time. His most extensive comments on this subject are in his reviews of Hawthorne's tales for the periodicals Graham's Magazine *in 1842 and* Godey's Lady's Book *in 1847; in these reviews he also described his own philosophy of composition. Poe believed that unity of a "single effect" was the most essential quality of all successful short fiction. He praised Hawthorne for his "invention, creation, imagination, originality" — qualities Poe himself possessed in abundance.*

RELATED COMMENTARY: *Edgar Allan Poe, "The Importance of the Single Effect in a Prose Tale," page 787.*

EDGAR ALLAN POE

The Cask of Amontillado   1846

The thousand injuries of Fortunato I had borne as I best could; but when he ventured upon insult, I vowed revenge. You, who so well know the nature of my soul, will not suppose, however, that I gave utterance to a threat. *At length* I would be avenged; this was a point definitely settled — but the very definitiveness with which it was resolved precluded the idea of risk. I must not only punish, but punish with impunity. A wrong is unredressed when retribution overtakes its redresser. It is equally unredressed when the avenger fails to make himself felt as such to him who has done the wrong.

It must be understood, that neither by word nor deed had I given Fortunato cause to doubt my good-will. I continued, as was my wont, to smile in his face, and he did not perceive that my smile *now* was at the thought of his immolation.

He had a weak point — this Fortunato — although in other regards he was a man to be respected and even feared. He prided himself on his connoisseurship in wine. Few Italians have the true virtuoso spirit. For the most part their enthusiasm is adopted to suit the time and opportunity — to practise imposture upon the British and Austrian *millionnaires.* In painting and gemmary Fortunato, like his countrymen, was a quack — but in the matter of old wines he was sincere. In this respect I did not differ from him materially: I was skilful in the Italian vintages myself, and bought largely whenever I could.

It was about dusk, one evening during the supreme madness of the carnival season, that I encountered my friend. He accosted me with excessive warmth, for he had been drinking much. The man wore motley. He had on a tight-fitting parti-striped dress, and his head was surmounted by the conical cap and bells. I was so pleased to see him, that I thought I should never have done wringing his hand.

I said to him: "My dear Fortunato, you are luckily met. How remarkably well you are looking to-day! But I have received a pipe° of what passes for Amontillado, and I have my doubts."

"How?" said he. "Amontillado? A pipe? Impossible! And in the middle of the carnival!"

"I have my doubts," I replied; "and I was silly enough to pay the full Amontillado price without consulting you in the matter. You were not to be found, and I was fearful of losing a bargain."

"Amontillado!"

"I have my doubts."

"Amontillado!"

"And I must satisfy them."

"Amontillado!"

"As you are engaged, I am on my way to Luchesi. If any one has a critical turn, it is he. He will tell me —— "

"Luchesi cannot tell Amontillado from Sherry."

"And yet some fools will have it that his taste is a match for your own."

"Come, let us go."

"Whither?"

"To your vaults."

"My friend, no; I will not impose upon your good nature. I perceive you have an engagement. Luchesi —— "

"I have no engagement; — come."

"My friend, no. It is not the engagement, but the severe cold with which I perceive you are afflicted. The vaults are insufferably damp. They are encrusted with nitre."

"Let us go, nevertheless. The cold is merely nothing. Amontillado! You have been imposed upon. And as for Luchesi, he cannot distinguish Sherry from Amontillado."

Thus speaking, Fortunato possessed himself of my arm. Putting on a mask of black silk, and drawing a *roquelaire°* closely about my person, I suffered him to hurry me to my palazzo.

There were no attendants at home; they had absconded to make merry in honor of the time. I had told them that I should not return until the morning, and had given them explicit orders not to stir from the house. These orders were sufficient, I well knew, to insure their immediate disappearance, one and all, as soon as my back was turned.

I took from their sconces two flambeaux, and giving one to Fortunato, bowed him through several suites of rooms to the archway that led into the vaults. I passed down a long and winding staircase, requesting him to be cautious as he followed. We came at length to the foot of the descent, and stood together on the damp ground of the catacombs of the Montresors.

---

pipe: A large cask or keg.
roquelaire: A short cloak.

The gait of my friend was unsteady, and the bells upon his cap jingled as he strode.

"The pipe?" said he.

"It is farther on," said I; "but observe the white web-work which gleams from these cavern walls."

He turned toward me, and looked into my eyes with two filmy orbs that distilled the rheum of intoxication.

"Nitre?" he asked, at length.

"Nitre," I replied. "How long have you had that cough?"

"Ugh! ugh! ugh! — ugh! ugh! ugh! — ugh! ugh! ugh! — ugh! ugh! ugh! — ugh! ugh! ugh!"

My poor friend found it impossible to reply for many minutes.

"It is nothing," he said, at last.

"Come," I said, with decision, "we will go back; your health is precious. You are rich, respected, admired, beloved; you are happy, as once I was. You are a man to be missed. For me it is no matter. We will go back; you will be ill, and I cannot be responsible. Besides, there is Luchesi —— "

"Enough," he said; "the cough is a mere nothing; it will not kill me. I shall not die of a cough."

"True — true," I replied; "and, indeed, I had no intention of alarming you unnecessarily; but you should use all proper caution. A draught of this Medoc will defend us from the damps."

Here I knocked off the neck of a bottle which I drew from a long row of its fellows that lay upon the mould.

"Drink," I said, presenting him the wine.

He raised it to his lips with a leer. He paused and nodded to me familiarly, while his bells jingled.

"I drink," he said, "to the buried that repose around us."

"And I to your long life."

He again took my arm, and we proceeded.

"These vaults," he said, "are extensive."

"The Montresors," I replied, "were a great and numerous family."

"I forget your arms."

"A huge human foot d'or,° in a field azure; the foot crushes a serpent rampant whose fangs are imbedded in the heel."

"And the motto?"

"Nemo me impune lacessit."°

"Good!" he said.

The wine sparkled in his eyes and the bells jingled. My own fancy grew warm with the Medoc. We had passed through walls of piled bones, with casks and puncheons intermingling into the inmost recesses of the catacombs. I paused again, and this time I made bold to seize Fortunato by an arm above the elbow.

---

d'or: Of gold.
Nemo me impune lacessit: "No one wounds me with impunity"; the motto of the royal arms of Scotland.

"The nitre!" I said; "see, it increases. It hangs like moss upon the vaults. We are below the river's bed. The drops of moisture trickle among the bones. Come, we will go back ere it is too late. Your cough —— "

"It is nothing," he said; "let us go on. But first, another draught of the Medoc."

I broke and reached him a flagon of De Grâve. He emptied it at a breath. His eyes flashed with a fierce light. He laughed and threw the bottle upward with a gesticulation I did not understand.

I looked at him in surprise. He repeated the movement — a grotesque one.

"You do not comprehend?" he said.

"Not I," I replied.

"Then you are not of the brotherhood."

"How?"

"You are not of the masons."

"Yes, yes," I said; "yes, yes."

"You? Impossible! A mason?"

"A mason," I replied.

"A sign," he said.

"It is this," I answered, producing a trowel from beneath the folds of my *roquelaire*.

"You jest," he exclaimed, recoiling a few paces. "But let us proceed to the Amontillado."

"Be it so," I said, replacing the tool beneath the cloak, and again offering him my arm. He leaned upon it heavily. We continued our route in search of the Amontillado. We passed through a range of low arches, descended, passed on, and descending again, arrived at a deep crypt, in which the foulness of the air caused our flambeaux rather to glow than flame.

At the most remote end of the crypt there appeared another less spacious. Its walls had been lined with human remains, piled to the vault overhead, in the fashion of the great catacombs of Paris. Three sides of this interior crypt were still ornamented in this manner. From the fourth the bones had been thrown down, and lay promiscuously upon the earth, forming at one point a mound of some size. Within the wall thus exposed by the displacing of the bones, we perceived a still interior recess, in depth about four feet, in width three, in height six or seven. It seemed to have been constructed for no especial use within itself, but formed merely the interval between two of the colossal supports of the roof of the catacombs, and was backed by one of their circumscribing walls of solid granite.

It was in vain that Fortunato, uplifting his dull torch, endeavored to pry into the depth of the recess. Its termination the feeble light did not enable us to see.

"Proceed," I said; "herein is the Amontillado. As for Luchesi —— "

"He is an ignoramus," interrupted my friend, as he stepped unsteadily forward, while I followed immediately at his heels. In an instant he had reached the extremity of the niche, and finding his progress arrested by the rock, stood stupidly bewildered. A moment more and I had fettered him to the granite. In its surface were two iron staples, distant from each other about two feet, horizontally. From one of these depended a short chain, from the other a padlock. Throwing the links about his waist, it was but the work of a few seconds to secure it. He was too much astounded to resist. Withdrawing the key I stepped back from the recess.

"Pass your hand," I said, "over the wall; you cannot help feeling the nitre. Indeed it is *very* damp. Once more let me *implore* you to return. No? Then I must positively leave you. But I must first render you all the little attentions in my power."

"The Amontillado!" ejaculated my friend, not yet recovered from his astonishment.

"True," I replied; "the Amontillado."

As I said these words I busied myself among the pile of bones of which I have before spoken. Throwing them aside, I soon uncovered a quantity of building stone and mortar. With these materials and with the aid of my trowel, I began vigorously to wall up the entrance of the niche.

I had scarcely laid the first tier of the masonry when I discovered that the intoxication of Fortunato had in a great measure worn off. The earliest indication I had of this was a low moaning cry from the depth of the recess. It was *not* the cry of a drunken man. There was then a long and obstinate silence. I laid the second tier, and the third, and the fourth; and then I heard the furious vibrations of the chain. The noise lasted for several minutes, during which, that I might hearken to it with the more satisfaction, I ceased my labors and sat down upon the bones. When at last the clanking subsided, I resumed the trowel, and finished without interruption the fifth, the sixth, and the seventh tier. The wall was now nearly upon a level with my breast. I again paused, and holding the flambeaux over the masonwork, threw a few feeble rays upon the figure within.

A succession of loud and shrill screams, bursting suddenly from the throat of the chained form, seemed to thrust me violently back. For a brief moment I hesitated — I trembled. Unsheathing my rapier, I began to grope with it about the recess; but the thought of an instant reassured me. I placed my hand upon the solid fabric of the catacombs, and felt satisfied. I reapproached the wall. I replied to the yells of him who clamored. I reechoed — I aided — I surpassed them in volume and in strength. I did this, and the clamorer grew still.

It was now midnight, and my task was drawing to a close. I had completed the eighth, the ninth, and the tenth tier. I had finished a portion of the last and the eleventh; there remained but a single stone to be fitted and plastered in. I struggled with its weight; I placed it partially in its destined position. But now there came from out the niche a low laugh that erected the hairs upon my head. It was succeeded by a sad voice, which I had difficulty in recognizing as that of the noble Fortunato. The voice said —

"Ha! ha! ha! — he! he! — a very good joke indeed — an excellent jest. We will have many a rich laugh about it at the palazzo — he! he! he! — over our wine — he! he! he!"

"The Amontillado!" I said.

"He! he! he! — he! he! he! — yes, the Amontillado. But is it not getting late? Will not they be awaiting us at the palazzo, the Lady Fortunato and the rest? Let us be gone."

"Yes," I said, "let us be gone."

"*For the love of God, Montresor!*"

"Yes," I said, "for the love of God!"

But to these words I hearkened in vain for a reply. I grew impatient. I called aloud:

"Fortunato!"

No answer. I called again:

"Fortunato!"

No answer still. I thrust a torch through the remaining aperture and let it fall within. There came forth in return only a jingling of the bells. My heart grew sick — on account of the dampness of the catacombs. I hastened to make an end of my labor. I forced the last stone into its position; I plastered it up. Against the new masonry I re-erected the old rampart of bones. For the half of a century no mortal has disturbed them. *In pace requiescat!*

EDGAR ALLAN POE

The Tell-Tale Heart

1843

True! — nervous — very, very dreadfully nervous I had been and am; but why *will* you say that I am mad? The disease had sharpened my senses — not destroyed — not dulled them. Above all was the sense of hearing acute. I heard all things in the heaven and in the earth. I heard many things in hell. How, then, am I mad? Hearken! and observe how healthily — how calmly I can tell you the whole story.

It is impossible to say how first the idea entered my brain; but once conceived, it haunted me day and night. Object there was none. Passion there was none. I loved the old man. He had never wronged me. He had never given me insult. For his gold I had no desire. I think it was his eye! yes, it was this! One of his eyes resembled that of a vulture — a pale blue eye, with a film over it. Whenever it fell upon me, my blood ran cold; and so by degrees — very gradually — I made up my mind to take the life of the old man, and thus rid myself of the eye for ever.

Now this is the point. You fancy me mad. Madmen know nothing. But you should have seen *me.* You should have seen how wisely I proceeded — with what caution — with what foresight — with what dissimulation I went to work! I was never kinder to the old man than during the whole week before I killed him. And every night, about midnight, I turned the latch of his door and opened it — oh, so gently! And then, when I had made an opening sufficient for my head, I put in a dark lantern, all closed, closed, so that no light shone out, and then I thrust in my head. Oh, you would have laughed to see how cunningly I thrust it in! I moved it slowly — very, very slowly, so that I might not disturb the old man's sleep. It took me an hour to place my whole head within the opening so far that I could see him as he lay upon his bed. Ha — would a madman have been so wise as this? And then, when my head was well in the room, I undid the lantern cautiously — oh, so cautiously — cautiously (for the hinges creaked) — I undid it just so much that a single thin ray fell upon the vulture eye. And this I did for seven long nights — every night just after midnight — but I found the eye always closed; and so it was impossible to do the work; for it was not the old man who vexed me, but his Evil Eye. And every morning, when the day broke, I went boldly into the chamber, and spoke courageously to him, calling him by name in a hearty tone, and inquiring how he had passed the night. So you see he would have been a very profound old man, indeed, to suspect that every night, just at twelve, I looked in upon him while he slept.

Upon the eighth night I was more than usually cautious in opening the door. A watch's minute hand moves more quickly than did mine. Never before that night had I *felt* the extent of my own powers — of my sagacity. I could scarcely contain my feelings of triumph. To think that there I was, opening the door, little by little, and he not even to dream of my secret deeds or thoughts. I fairly chuckled at the idea; and perhaps he heard me; for he moved on the bed suddenly, as if startled. Now you may think that I drew back — but no. His room was as black as pitch with the thick darkness (for the shutters were close fastened, through fear of robbers), and so I knew that he could not see the opening of the door, and I kept pushing it on steadily, steadily.

I had my head in, and was about to open the lantern, when my thumb slipped upon the tin fastening, and the old man sprang up in the bed, crying out — "Who's there?"

I kept quite still and said nothing. For a whole hour I did not move a muscle, and in the meantime I did not hear him lie down. He was still sitting up in the bed listening; — just as I have done, night after night, hearkening to the death watches in the wall.

Presently I heard a slight groan, and I knew it was the groan of mortal terror. It was not a groan of pain or of grief — oh, no! — it was the low stifled sound that arises from the bottom of the soul when overcharged with awe. I knew the sound well. Many a night, just at midnight, when all the world slept, it has welled up from my own bosom, deepening with its dreadful echo, the terrors that distracted me. I say I knew it well. I knew what the old man felt, and pitied him, although I chuckled at heart. I knew that he had been lying awake ever since the first slight noise, when he had turned in the bed. His fears had been ever since growing upon him. He had been trying to fancy them causeless, but could not. He had been saying to himself — "It is nothing but the wind in the chimney — it is only a mouse crossing the floor," or "it is merely a cricket which has made a single chirp." Yes, he has been trying to comfort himself with these suppositions; but he had found all in vain. *All in vain*; because Death, in approaching him, had stalked with his black shadow before him, and enveloped the victim. And it was the mournful influence of the unperceived shadow that caused him to feel — although he neither saw nor heard — to *feel* the presence of my head within the room.

When I had waited a long time, very patiently, without hearing him lie down, I resolved to open a little — a very, very little crevice in the lantern. So I opened it — you cannot imagine how stealthily, stealthily — until, at length, a single dim ray, like the thread of the spider, shot from out the crevice and full upon the vulture eye.

It was open — wide, wide open — and I grew furious as I gazed upon it. I saw it with perfect distinctness — all a dull blue, with a hideous veil over it that chilled the very marrow in my bones, but I could see nothing else of the old man's face or person: for I had directed the ray as if by instinct, precisely upon the damned spot.

And now have I not told you that what you mistake for madness is but over-acuteness of the senses? — now, I say, there came to my ears a low, dull, quick sound, such as a watch makes when enveloped in cotton. I knew *that* sound well too. It was the beating of the old man's heart. It increased my fury, as the beating of a drum stimulates the soldier into courage.

But even yet I refrained and kept still. I scarcely breathed. I held the lantern motionless. I tried how steadily I could maintain the ray upon the eye. Meantime the hellish tattoo of the heart increased. It grew quicker and quicker, and louder and louder every instant. The old man's terror *must* have been extreme! It grew louder, I say, louder every moment! — do you mark me well? I have told you that I am nervous: so I am. And now at the dead hour of the night, amid the dreadful silence of that old house, so strange a noise as this excited me to uncontrollable terror. Yet, for some minutes longer I refrained and stood still. But the beating grew louder, louder! I thought the heart must burst. And now a new anxiety seized me — the sound would be heard by a neighbor! The old man's hour had come! With a loud yell, I threw open the lantern and leaped into the room. He shrieked once — once only. In an instant I dragged him to the floor, and pulled the heavy bed over him. I then smiled gaily, to find the deed so far done. But, for many minutes, the heart beat on with a muffled sound. This, however, did not vex me; it would not be heard through the wall. At length it ceased. The old man was dead. I removed the bed and examined the corpse. Yes, he was stone, stone dead. I placed my hand upon the heart and held it there many minutes. There was no pulsation. He was stone dead. His eye would trouble me no more.

If still you think me mad, you will think so no longer when I describe the wise precautions I took for the concealment of the body. The night waned, and I worked hastily, but in silence. First of all I dismembered the corpse. I cut off the head and the arms and the legs.

I then took up three planks from the flooring of the chamber, and deposited all between the scantlings. I then replaced the boards so cleverly, so cunningly, that no human eye — not even *his* — could have detected anything wrong. There was nothing to wash out — no stain of any kind — no blood-spot whatever. I had been too wary for that. A tub had caught all — ha! ha!

When I had made an end of these labors, it was four o'clock — still dark as midnight. As the bell sounded the hour, there came a knocking at the street door. I went down to open it with a light heart — for what had I *now* to fear? There entered three men, who introduced themselves, with perfect suavity, as officers of the police. A shriek had been heard by a neighbor during the night;

suspicion of foul play had been aroused; information had been lodged at the police office, and they (the officers) had been deputed to search the premises.

I smiled — for *what* had I to fear? I bade the gentlemen welcome. The shriek, I said, was my own in a dream. The old man, I mentioned, was absent in the country. I took my visitors all over the house. I bade them search — search *well*. I led them, at length, to *his* chamber. I showed them his treasures, secure, undisturbed. In the enthusiasm of my confidence, I brought chairs into the room, and desired them *here* to rest from their fatigues, while I myself, in the wild audacity of my perfect triumph, placed my own seat upon the very spot beneath which reposed the corpse of the victim.

The officers were satisfied. My *manner* had convinced them. I was singularly at ease. They sat, and while I answered cheerily, they chatted familiar things. But, ere long, I felt myself getting pale and wished them gone. My head ached, and I fancied a ringing in my ears: but still they sat and still they chatted. The ringing became more distinct: — it continued and became more distinct: I talked more freely to get rid of the feeling: but it continued and gained definitiveness — until, at length, I found that the noise was *not* within my ears.

No doubt I now grew *very* pale; — but I talked more fluently, and with a heightened voice. Yet the sound increased — and what could I do? It was *a low, dull, quick sound — much such a sound as a watch makes when enveloped in cotton.* I gasped for breath — and yet the officers heard it not. I talked more quickly — more vehemently; but the noise steadily increased. I arose and argued about trifles, in a high key and with violent gesticulations, but the noise steadily increased. Why *would* they not be gone? I paced the floor to and fro with heavy strides, as if excited to fury by the observation of the men — but the noise steadily increased. Oh God! what *could* I do? I foamed — I raved — I swore! I swung the chair upon which I had been sitting, and grated it upon the boards, but the noise arose over all and continually increased. It grew louder — louder — *louder*! And still the men chatted pleasantly, and smiled. Was it possible they heard not? Almighty God! — no, no! They heard! — they suspected! — they *knew*! — they were making a mockery of my horror! — this I thought, and this I think. But any thing was better than this agony! Any thing was more tolerable than this derision! I could bear those hypocritical smiles no longer! I felt that I must scream or die! — and now — again! — hark! louder! louder! louder! *louder*! —

"Villains!" I shrieked, "dissemble no more! I admit the deed! — tear up the planks! — here, here! — it is the beating of his hideous heart!"

ℚℚ

KATHERINE ANNE PORTER *(1890–1980) was born Callie Russell Porter in Indian Creek, Texas. When she was only two her mother died. Educated at boarding schools and an Ursuline convent, Porter worked briefly as a reporter in Chicago and Denver. As a child she had wanted to be a writer, but it took fifteen years of serious writing before she trusted herself enough as a stylist to approach a publisher. Most of her life during this time was a financial struggle; she spent only 10 percent of her energy on writing, and "the other 90 percent went to keeping my head above water." She nearly* *lost her life in the influenza epidemic that swept the United States at the end of World War I, and when she recovered she went to Mexico to study Aztec and Mayan art.*

Porter achieved acclaim with her first collection of short stories, Flowering Judas and Other Stories, in 1930. Her most productive decade as a writer was the 1930s, when she published Noon Wine (1937) and Pale Horse, Pale Rider: Three Short Novels (1939). She supported herself with lecture tours and teaching jobs at various universities while she worked on her novel Ship of Fools (1962), which took more than two decades to complete. In 1965 her Collected Stories won both the Pulitzer Prize and the National Book Award.

Porter's style is not so recognizably "southern" as William Faulkner's or Flannery O'Connor's. She was a southerner by tradition and inheritance, but she had thought of herself since childhood as "always restless, always a roving spirit." She was very conscious of her own art as a storyteller, and of the art of fiction in general; she wrote personal essays on Willa Cather, Katherine Mansfield, Flannery O'Connor, Eudora Welty, and Virginia Woolf. Particularly indebted in her best stories to Mansfield, Porter attempted to dramatize a character's state of mind rather than develop a complicated plot. Her analysis of Mansfield's literary practice in the essay "The Art of Katherine Mansfield" can also be applied to a story such as "He":

> With fine objectivity, she bares a moment of experience, real experience, in the life of some one human being; she states no belief, gives no motives, airs no theories, but simply presents to the reader a situation, a place, and a character, and there it is; and the emotional content is present as implicitly as the germ is in the grain of wheat.

RELATED STORY: *Joyce Carol Oates, "Heat," page 496.*

KATHERINE ANNE PORTER

He   1927

Life was very hard for the Whipples. It was hard to feed all the hungry mouths, it was hard to keep the children in flannels during the winter, short as it was: "God knows what would become of us if we lived north," they would say: keeping them decently clean was hard. "It looks like our luck won't never let up on us," said Mr. Whipple, but Mrs. Whipple was all for taking what was sent and calling it good, anyhow when the neighbors were in earshot. "Don't ever let a soul hear us complain," she kept saying to her husband. She couldn't stand to be pitied. "No, not if it comes to it that we have to live in a wagon and pick cotton around the country," she said, "nobody's going to get a chance to look down on us."

Mrs. Whipple loved her second son, the simple-minded one, better than she loved the other two children put together. She was forever saying so, and when she talked with certain of her neighbors, she would even throw in her husband and her mother for good measure.

"You needn't keep on saying it around," said Mr. Whipple, "you'll make people think nobody else has any feelings about Him but you."

"It's natural for a mother," Mrs. Whipple would remind him. "You know yourself it's more natural for a mother to be that way. People don't expect so much of fathers, some way."

This didn't keep the neighbors from talking plainly among themselves. "A Lord's pure mercy if He should die," they said. "It's the sins of the fathers," they agreed among themselves. "There's bad blood and bad doings somewhere, you can bet on that." This behind the Whipples' back. To their faces everybody said, "He's not so bad off. He'll be all right yet. Look how He grows!"

Mrs. Whipple hated to talk about it, she tried to keep her mind off it, but every time anybody set foot in the house, the subject always came up, and she had to talk about Him first, before she could get on to anything else. It seemed to ease her mind. "I wouldn't have anything happen to Him for all the world, but it just looks like I can't keep Him out of mischief. He's so strong and active, He's always into everything; He was like that since He could walk. It's actually funny sometimes, the way He can do anything; it's laughable to see Him up to His tricks. Emly has more accidents; I'm forever tying up her bruises, and Adna can't fall a foot without cracking a bone. But He can do anything and not get a scratch. The preacher said such a nice thing once when he was here. He said, and I'll remember it to my dying day, 'The innocent walk with God — that's why He don't get hurt.'" Whenever Mrs. Whipple repeated these words, she always felt a warm pool spread in her breast, and the tears would fill her eyes, and then she could talk about something else.

He did grow and He never got hurt. A plank blew off the chicken house and struck Him on the head and He never seemed to know it. He had learned a few words, and after this He forgot them. He didn't whine for food as the other children did, but waited until it was given Him; He ate squatting in the corner, smacking and mumbling. Rolls of fat covered Him like an overcoat, and He could carry twice as much wood and water as Adna. Emly had a cold in the head most of the time — "she takes that after me," said Mrs. Whipple — so in bad weather they gave her the extra blanket off His cot. He never seemed to mind the cold.

Just the same, Mrs. Whipple's life was a torment for fear something might happen to Him. He climbed the peach trees much better than Adna and went skittering along the branches like a monkey, just a regular monkey. "Oh, Mrs. Whipple, you hadn't ought to let Him do that. He'll lose His balance sometime. He can't rightly know what He's doing."

Mrs. Whipple almost screamed out at the neighbor. "He *does* know what He's doing! He's as able as any other child! Come down out of there, you!" When He finally reached the ground she could hardly keep her hands off Him for acting like that before people, a grin all over His face and her worried sick about Him all the time.

"It's the neighbors," said Mrs. Whipple to her husband. "Oh, I do mortally wish they would keep out of our business. I can't afford to let Him do anything for fear they'll come nosing around about it. Look at the bees, now. Adna can't handle them, they sting him up so; I haven't got time to do everything, and now I don't dare let Him. But if He gets a sting He don't really mind."

"It's just because He ain't got sense enough to be scared of anything," said Mr. Whipple.

"You ought to be ashamed of yourself," said Mrs. Whipple, "talking that way about your own child. Who's to take up for Him if we don't, I'd like to know? He sees a lot that goes on, He listens to things all the time. And anything I tell Him to do He does it. Don't never let anybody hear you say such things. They'd think you favored the other children over Him."

"Well, now I don't, and you know it, and what's the use of getting all worked up about it? You always think the worst of everything. Just let Him alone, He'll get along somehow. He gets plenty to eat and wear, don't He?" Mr. Whipple suddenly felt tired out. "Anyhow, it can't be helped now."

Mrs. Whipple felt tired too, she complained in a tired voice. "What's done can't never be undone, I know that as good as anybody; but He's my child, and I'm not going to have people say anything. I get sick of people coming around saying things all the time."

In the early fall Mrs. Whipple got a letter from her brother saying he and his wife and two children were coming over for a little visit next Sunday week. "Put the big pot in the little one," he wrote at the end. Mrs. Whipple read this part out loud twice, she was so pleased. Her brother was a great one for saying funny things. "We'll just show him that's no joke," she said, "we'll just butcher one of the suckling pigs."

"It's a waste and I don't hold with waste the way we are now," said Mr. Whipple. "That pig'll be worth money by Christmas."

"It's a shame and a pity we can't have a decent meal's vittles once in a while when my own family comes to see us," said Mrs. Whipple. "I'd hate for his wife to go back and say there wasn't a thing in the house to eat. My God, it's better than buying up a great chance of meat in town. There's where you'd spend the money!"

"All right, do it yourself then," said Mr. Whipple. "Christamighty, no wonder we can't get ahead!"

The question was how to get the little pig away from his ma, a great fighter, worse than a Jersey cow. Adna wouldn't try it: "That sow'd rip my insides out all over the pen." "All right, old fraidy," said Mrs. Whipple, "He's not scared. Watch Him do it." And she laughed as though it was all a good joke and gave Him a little push towards the pen. He sneaked up and snatched the pig right away from the teat and galloped back and was over the fence with the sow raging at His heels. The little black squirming thing was screeching like a baby in a tantrum, stiffening its back and stretching its mouth to the ears. Mrs. Whipple took the pig with her face stiff and sliced its throat with one stroke. When He saw the blood He gave a great jolting breath and ran away. "But He'll forget and eat plenty, just the same," thought Mrs. Whipple. Whenever she was thinking, her lips moved making words. "He'd eat it all if I didn't stop Him. He'd eat up every mouthful from the other two if I'd let Him."

She felt badly about it. He was ten years old now and a third again as large as Adna, who was going on fourteen. "It's a shame, a shame," she kept saying under her breath, "and Adna with so much brains!"

She kept on feeling badly about all sorts of things. In the first place it was the man's work to butcher; the sight of the pig scraped pink and naked made her sick. He was too fat and soft and pitiful-looking. It was simply a shame the way things had to happen. By the time she had finished it up, she almost wished her brother would stay at home.

Early Sunday morning Mrs. Whipple dropped everything to get Him all cleaned up. In an hour He was dirty again, with crawling under fences after a possum, and straddling along the rafters of the barn looking for eggs in the hayloft. "My Lord, look at you now after all my trying! And here's Adna and Emly staying so quiet. I get tired trying to keep you decent. Get off that shirt and put on another, people will say I don't half dress you!" And she boxed Him on the ears, hard. He blinked and blinked and rubbed His head, and His face hurt Mrs. Whipple's feelings. Her knees began to tremble, she had to sit down while she buttoned His shirt. "I'm just all gone before the day starts."

The brother came with his plump healthy wife and two great roaring hungry boys. They had a grand dinner, with the pig roasted to a crackling in the middle of the table, full of dressing, a pickled peach in his mouth and plenty of gravy for the sweet potatoes.

"This looks like prosperity all right," said the brother; "you're going to have to roll me home like I was a barrel when I'm done."

Everybody laughed out loud; it was fine to hear them laughing all at once around the table. Mrs. Whipple felt warm and good about it. "Oh, we've got six more of these; I say it's as little as we can do when you come to see us so seldom."

He wouldn't come into the dining room, and Mrs. Whipple passed it off very well. "He's timider than my other two," she said. "He'll just have to get used to you. There isn't everybody He'll make up with, you know how it is with some children, even cousins." Nobody said anything out of the way.

"Just like my Alty here," said the brother's wife. "I sometimes got to lick him to make him shake hands with his own grandmammy."

So that was over, and Mrs. Whipple loaded up a big plate for Him first, before everybody. "I always say He ain't to be slighted, no matter who else goes without," she said, and carried it to Him herself.

"He can chin Himself on the top of the door," said Emly, helping along.

"That's fine. He's getting along fine," said the brother.

They went away after supper. Mrs. Whipple rounded up the dishes, and sent the children to bed and sat down and unlaced her shoes. "You see?" she said to Mr. Whipple. "That's the way my whole family is. Nice and considerate about everything. No out-of-the-way remarks — they *have* got refinement. I get awfully sick of people's remarks. Wasn't that pig good?"

Mr. Whipple said, "Yes, we're out three hundred pounds of pork, that's all. It's easy to be polite when you come to eat. Who knows what they had in their minds all along?"

"Yes, that's like you," said Mrs. Whipple. "I don't expect anything else from you. You'll be telling me next that my own brother will be saying around that we made Him eat in the kitchen! Oh, my God!" She rocked her head in her hands, a hard pain started in the very middle of her forehead. "Now it's all spoiled, and everything was so nice and easy. All right, you don't like them and you never did — all right, they'll not come here again soon, never you mind! But they *can't* say He wasn't dressed every lick as good as Adna — oh, honest, sometimes I wish I was dead!"

"I wish you'd let up," said Mr. Whipple. "It's bad enough as it is."

It was a hard winter. It seemed to Mrs. Whipple that they hadn't ever known anything but hard times, and now to cap it all a winter like this. The crops were about half of what they had a right to expect; after the cotton was in it didn't do much more than cover the grocery bill. They swapped off one of the plow horses, and got cheated, for the new one died of the heaves. Mrs. Whipple kept thinking all the time it was terrible to have a man you couldn't depend on not to get cheated. They cut down on everything, but Mrs. Whipple kept saying there are things you can't cut down on, and they cost money. It took a lot of warm clothes for Adna and Emly, who walked four miles to school during the three-months session. "He sets around the fire a lot, He won't need so much," said Mr. Whipple. "That's so," said Mrs. Whipple, "and when He does the outdoor chores He can wear your tarpaullion coat. I can't do no better, that's all."

In February He was taken sick, and lay curled up under His blanket looking very blue in the face and acting as if He would choke. Mr. and Mrs. Whipple did everything they could for Him for two days, and then they were scared and sent for the doctor. The doctor told them they must keep Him warm and give Him plenty of milk and eggs. "He isn't as stout as He looks, I'm afraid," said the doctor. "You've got to watch them when they're like that. You must put more cover onto Him, too."

"I just took off His big blanket to wash," said Mrs. Whipple, ashamed. "I can't stand dirt."

"Well, you'd better put it back on the minute it's dry," said the doctor, "or He'll have pneumonia."

Mr. and Mrs. Whipple took a blanket off their own bed and put His cot in by the fire. "They can't say we didn't do everything for Him," she said, "even to sleeping cold ourselves on His account."

When the winter broke He seemed to be well again, but He walked as if His feet hurt Him. He was able to run a cotton planter during the season.

"I got it all fixed up with Jim Ferguson about breeding the cow next time," said Mr. Whipple. "I'll pasture the bull this summer and give Jim some fodder in the fall. That's better than paying out money when you haven't got it."

"I hope you didn't say such a thing before Jim Ferguson," said Mrs. Whipple. "You oughtn't to let him know we're so down as all that."

"Godamighty, that ain't saying we're down. A man is got to look ahead sometimes. He can lead the bull over today. I need Adna on the place."

At first Mrs. Whipple felt easy in her mind about sending Him for the bull. Adna was too jumpy and couldn't be trusted. You've got to be steady around animals. After He was gone she started thinking, and after a while she could hardly bear it any longer. She stood in the lane and watched for Him. It was nearly three miles to go and a hot day, but He oughtn't to be so long about it. She shaded her eyes and stared until colored bubbles floated in her eyeballs. It was just like everything else in life, she must always worry and never know a moment's peace about anything. After a long time she saw Him turn into the side lane, limping. He came on very slowly, leading the big hulk of an animal by a ring in the nose, twirling a little stick in His hand, never looking back or sideways, but coming on like a sleepwalker with His eyes half shut.

Mrs. Whipple was scared sick of bulls; she had heard awful stories about how they followed on quietly enough, and then suddenly pitched on with a bellow and pawed and gored a body to pieces. Any second now that black monster would come down on Him, my God, He'd never have sense enough to run.

She mustn't make a sound nor a move; she mustn't get the bull started. The bull heaved his head aside and horned the air at a fly. Her voice burst out of her in a shriek, and she screamed at Him to come on, for God's sake. He didn't seem to hear her clamor, but kept on twirling His switch and limping on, and the bull lumbered along behind him as gently as a calf. Mrs. Whipple stopped calling and ran towards the house, praying under her breath: "Lord, don't let anything happen to Him. Lord, you *know* people will say we oughtn't to have sent Him. You *know* they'll say we didn't take care of Him. Oh, get Him home, safe home, safe home, and I'll look out for Him better! Amen."

She watched from the window while He led the beast in, and tied him up in the barn. It was no use trying to keep up, Mrs. Whipple couldn't bear another thing. She sat down and rocked and cried with her apron over her head.

From year to year the Whipples were growing poorer and poorer. The place just seemed to run down of itself, no matter how hard they worked. "We're losing our hold," said Mrs. Whipple. "Why can't we do like other people and watch for our best chances? They'll be calling us poor white trash next."

"When I get to be sixteen I'm going to leave," said Adna. "I'm going to get a job in Powell's grocery store. There's money in that. No more farm for me."

"I'm going to be a schoolteacher," said Emly. "But I've got to finish the eighth grade, anyhow. Then I can live in town. I don't see any chances here."

"Emly takes after my family," said Mrs. Whipple. "Ambitious every last one of them, and they don't take second place for anybody."

When fall came Emly got a chance to wait on table in the railroad eatinghouse in the town near by, and it seemed such a shame not to take it when the wages were good and she could get her food too, that Mrs. Whipple decided to let her take it, and not bother with school until the next session. "You've got plenty of time," she said. "You're young and smart as a whip."

With Adna gone too, Mr. Whipple tried to run the farm with just Him to help. He seemed to get along fine, doing His work and part of Adna's without noticing it. They did well enough until Christmas time, when one morning He slipped on the ice coming up from the barn. Instead of getting up He thrashed round and round, and when Mr. Whipple got to Him, He was having some sort of fit.

They brought Him inside and tried to make Him sit up, but He blubbered and rolled, so they put Him to bed and Mr. Whipple rode to town for the doctor. All the way there and back he worried about where the money was to come from: it sure did look like he had about all the troubles he could carry.

From then on He stayed in bed. His legs swelled up double their size, and the fits kept coming back. After four months, the doctor said, "It's no use, I think you'd better put Him in the County Home for treatment right away. I'll see about it for you. He'll have good care there and be off your hands."

"We don't begrudge Him any care, and I won't let Him out of my sight," said Mrs. Whipple. "I won't have it said I sent my sick child off among strangers."

"I know how you feel," said the doctor. "You can't tell me anything about that, Mrs. Whipple. I've got a boy of my own. But you'd better listen to me. I can't do anything more for Him, that's the truth."

Mr. and Mrs. Whipple talked it over a long time that night after they went to bed. "It's just charity," said Mrs. Whipple, "that's what we've come to, charity! I certainly never looked for this."

"We pay taxes to help support the place just like everybody else," said Mr. Whipple, "and I don't call that taking charity. I think it would be fine to have Him where He'd get the best of everything . . . and besides, I can't keep up with these doctor bills any longer."

"Maybe that's why the doctor wants us to send Him — he's scared he won't get his money," said Mrs. Whipple.

"Don't talk like that," said Mr. Whipple, feeling pretty sick, "or we won't be able to send Him."

"Oh, but we won't keep Him there long," said Mrs. Whipple. "Soon's He's better, we'll bring Him right back home."

"The doctor has told you and told you time and again He can't ever get better, and you might as well stop talking," said Mr. Whipple.

"Doctors don't know everything," said Mrs. Whipple, feeling almost happy. "But anyhow, in the summer Emly can come home for a vacation, and Adna can get down for Sundays: we'll all work together and get on our feet again, and the children will feel they've got a place to come to."

All at once she saw it full summer again, with the garden going fine, and new white roller shades up all over the house, and Adna and Emly home, so full of life, all of them happy together. Oh, it could happen, things would ease up on them.

They didn't talk before Him much, but they never knew just how much He understood. Finally the doctor set the day and a neighbor who owned a double-seated carryall offered to drive them over. The hospital would have sent an ambulance, but Mrs. Whipple couldn't stand to see Him going away looking so sick as all that. They wrapped Him in blankets, and the neighbor and Mr. Whipple lifted Him into the back seat of the carryall beside Mrs. Whipple, who had on her black shirt waist. She couldn't stand to go looking like charity.

"You'll be all right, I guess I'll stay behind," said Mr. Whipple. "It don't look like everybody ought to leave the place at once."

"Besides, it ain't as if He was going to stay forever," said Mrs. Whipple to the neighbor. "This is only for a little while."

They started away, Mrs. Whipple holding to the edges of the blankets to keep Him from sagging sideways. He sat there blinking and blinking. He worked His hands out and began rubbing His nose with His knuckles, and then with the end of the blanket. Mrs. Whipple couldn't believe what she saw; He was scrubbing away big tears that pulled out of the corners of His eyes. He sniveled and made a gulping noise. Mrs. Whipple kept saying, "Oh, honey, you don't feel so bad, do you? You don't feel so bad, do you?" for He seemed to be accusing her of something. Maybe He remembered that time she boxed His ears, maybe He had been scared that day with the bull, maybe He had slept cold and couldn't tell her about it; maybe He knew they were sending Him away for good and all because they were too poor to keep Him. Whatever it was, Mrs. Whipple couldn't bear to think of it. She began to cry, frightfully, and wrapped her arms tight around Him. His head rolled on her shoulder: she had loved Him as much as she possibly could, there were Adna and Emly who had to be thought of too, there was nothing she could do to make up to Him for His life. Oh, what a mortal pity He was ever born.

They came in sight of the hospital, with the neighbor driving very fast, not daring to look behind him.

ରେ

LESLIE MARMON SILKO *(b. 1948), a Laguna Pueblo, was born and grew up in New Mexico. She was educated at Board of Indian Affairs schools in Laguna, a Catholic school in Albuquerque, and the University of New Mexico, where she received her B.A. in English in 1969. After teaching at various colleges, she became a professor of English at the University of Arizona at Tucson. Silko's first novel, Ceremony (1977), is regarded as one of the most important books in modern Native American literature. In it she forged a connection between the shared past of the tribe and the individual life of a Native American returning home after World War II. Silko has received a National Endowment for the Arts fellowship, a Pushcart Prize, and a three-year grant from the MacArthur Foundation, which enabled her to take time off from teaching and become "a little less beholden to the everyday world."*

Storyteller (1981), a collection of tribal folktales, family anecdotes, photographs by her grandfather, and her own poems and stories, is Silko's personal anthology of the Laguna Pueblo culture. "Yellow Woman," from that collection, illustrates Silko's skill in retelling a traditional Native American legend in a realistic contemporary context that confirms its emotional truth and makes it accessible to a larger audience.

Tales about a "ka'tsina" mountain spirit who seduces the Yellow Woman away from her husband and family were first told to the fictional heroine by her grandfather. The Yellow Woman in the traditional captivity narratives can be interpreted in several ways — as a girl who runs off with men outside the tribe, as a raped and kidnapped married woman, as a spirit, as a fertility archetype. In creating fiction, Silko works with all the implied meanings of the old legends; she has said that she writes "because I like seeing how I can translate [a] sort of feeling or flavor or sense of a story that's told and heard onto the page." Her most recent books are The Almanac of the Dead *(1991) and* Sacred Water *(1993).*

RELATED COMMENTARIES: *Leslie Marmon Silko, "Language and Literature from a Pueblo Indian Perspective," page 793; Paula Gunn Allen, "Whirlwind Man Steals Yellow Woman," page 726.*

LESLIE MARMON SILKO

Yellow Woman   1974

I

My thigh clung to his with dampness, and I watched the sun rising up through the tamaracks and willows. The small brown water birds came to the river and hopped across the mud, leaving brown scratches in the alkali-white crust. They bathed in the river silently. I could hear the water, almost at our feet where the narrow fast channel bubbled and washed green ragged moss and fern leaves. I looked at him beside me, rolled in the red blanket on the white river sand. I cleaned the sand out of the cracks between my toes, squinting because the sun was above the willow trees. I looked at him for the last time, sleeping on the white river sand.

I felt hungry and followed the river south the way we had come the afternoon before, following our footprints that were already blurred by the lizard tracks and bug trails. The horses were still lying down, and the black one whinnied when he saw me but he did not get up — maybe it was because the corral was made out of thick cedar branches and the horses had not yet felt the sun like I had. I tried to look beyond the pale red mesas to the pueblo. I knew it was there, even if I could not see it, on the sand rock hill above the river, the same river that moved past me now and had reflected the moon last night.

The horse felt warm underneath me. He shook his head and pawed the sand. The bay whinnied and leaned against the gate trying to follow, and I remembered him asleep in the red blanket beside the river. I slid off the horse and tied him close to the other horse. I walked north with the river again, and the white sand broke loose in footprints over footprints.

"Wake up."

He moved in the blanket and turned his face to me with his eyes still closed. I knelt down to touch him.

"I'm leaving."

He smiled now, eyes still closed. "You are coming with me, remember?" He sat up now with his bare dark chest and belly in the sun.

"Where?"

"To my place."

"And will I come back?"

He pulled his pants on. I walked away from him, feeling him behind me and smelling the willows.

"Yellow Woman," he said.

I turned to face him. "Who are you?" I asked.

He laughed and knelt on the low, sandy bank, washing his face in the river. "Last night you guessed my name, and you knew why I had come."

I stared past him at the shallow moving water and tried to remember the night, but I could only see the moon in the water and remember his warmth around me.

"But I only said that you were him and that I was Yellow Woman — I'm not really her — I have my own name and I come from the pueblo on the other side of the mesa. Your name is Silva and you are a stranger I met by the river yesterday afternoon."

He laughed softly. "What happened yesterday has nothing to do with what you will do today, Yellow Woman."

"I know — that's what I'm saying — the old stories about the ka'tsina spirit° and Yellow Woman can't mean us."

My old grandpa liked to tell those stories best. There is one about Badger and Coyote who went hunting and were gone all day, and when the sun was going down they found a house. There was a girl living there alone, and she had light hair and eyes and she told them that they could sleep with her. Coyote wanted to be with her all night so he sent Badger into a prairie-dog hole, telling him he thought he saw something in it. As soon as Badger crawled in, Coyote blocked up the entrance with rocks and hurried back to Yellow Woman.

"Come here," he said gently.

He touched my neck and I moved close to him to feel his breathing and to hear his heart. I was wondering if Yellow Woman had known who she was — if she knew that she would become part of the stories. Maybe she'd had another name that her husband and relatives called her so that only the ka'tsina from the north and the storytellers would know her as Yellow Woman. But I didn't go on; I felt him all around me, pushing me down into the white river sand.

Yellow Woman went away with the spirit from the north and lived with him and his relatives. She was gone for a long time, but then one day she came back and she brought twin boys.

"Do you know the story?"

"What story?" He smiled and pulled me close to him as he said this. I was afraid lying there on the red blanket. All I could know was the way he felt, warm, damp, his body beside me. This is the way it happens in the stories, I was thinking, with no thought beyond the moment she meets the ka'tsina spirit and they go.

---

ka'tsina spirit: A mountain spirit of the Pueblo Indians.

"I don't have to go. What they tell in stories was real only then, back in time immemorial, like they say."

He stood up and pointed at my clothes tangled in the blanket. "Let's go," he said.

I walked beside him, breathing hard because he walked fast, his hand around my wrist. I had stopped trying to pull away from him, because his hand felt cool and the sun was high, drying the river bed into alkali. I will see someone, eventually I will see someone, and then I will be certain that he is only a man — some man from nearby — and I will be sure that I am not Yellow Woman. Because she is from out of time past and I live now and I've been to school and there are highways and pickup trucks that Yellow Woman never saw.

It was an easy ride north on horseback. I watched the change from the cottonwood trees along the river to the junipers that brushed past us in the foothills, and finally there were only piñons, and when I looked up at the rim of the mountain plateau I could see pine trees growing on the edge. Once I stopped to look down, but the pale sandstone had disappeared and the river was gone and the dark lava hills were all around. He touched my hand, not speaking, but always singing softly a mountain song and looking into my eyes.

I felt hungry and wondered what they were doing at home now — my mother, my grandmother, my husband, and the baby. Cooking breakfast, saying. "Where did she go? — maybe kidnapped," and Al going to the tribal police with the details: "She went walking along the river."

The house was made with black lava rock and red mud. It was high above the spreading miles of arroyos and long mesas. I smelled a mountain smell of pitch and buck brush. I stood there beside the black horse, looking down on the small, dim country we had passed, and I shivered.

"Yellow Woman, come inside where's it's warm."

II

He lit a fire in the stove. It was an old stove with a round belly and an enamel coffeepot on top. There was only the stove, some faded Navajo blankets, and a bedroll and cardboard box. The floor was made of smooth adobe plaster, and there was one small window facing east. He pointed at the box.

"There's some potatoes and the frying pan." He sat on the floor with his arms around his knees pulling them close to his chest and he watched me fry the potatoes. I didn't mind him watching me because he was always watching me — he had been watching me since I came upon him sitting on the river bank trimming leaves from a willow twig with his knife. We ate from the pan and he wiped the grease from his fingers on his Levis.

"Have you brought women here before?" He smiled and kept chewing, so I said, "Do you always use the same tricks?"

"What tricks?" He looked at me like he didn't understand.

"The story about being a ka'tsina from the mountains. The story about Yellow Woman."

Silva was silent; his face was calm.

"I don't believe it. Those stories couldn't happen now," I said.

He shook his head and said softly, "But someday they will talk about us, and they will say, 'Those two lived long ago when things like that happened.'"

He stood up and went out. I ate the rest of the potatoes and thought about things — about the noise the stove was making and the sound of the mountain wind outside. I remembered yesterday and the day before, and then I went outside.

I walked past the corral to the edge where the narrow trail cut through the black rim rock. I was standing in the sky with nothing around me but the wind that came down from the blue mountain peak behind me. I could see faint mountain images in the distance miles across the vast spread of mesas and valleys and plains. I wondered who was over there to feel the mountain wind on those sheer blue edges — who walks on the pine needles in those blue mountains.

"Can you see the pueblo?" Silva was standing behind me.

I shook my head. "We're too far away."

"From here I can see the world." He stepped out on the edge. "The Navajo reservation begins over there." He pointed to the east. "The Pueblo boundaries are over here." He looked below us to the south, where the narrow trail seemed to come from. "The Texans have their ranches over there, starting with that valley, the Concho Valley. The Mexicans run some cattle over there too."

"Do you ever work for them?"

"I steal from them," Silva answered. The sun was dropping behind us and shadows were filling the land below. I turned away from the edge that dropped forever into the valleys below.

"I'm cold," I said; "I'm going inside," I started wondering about this man who could speak the Pueblo language so well but who lived on a mountain and rustled cattle. I decided that this man Silva must be Navajo, because Pueblo men didn't do things like that.

"You must be a Navajo."

Silva shook his head gently. "Little Yellow Woman," he said, "you never give up, do you? I have told you who I am. The Navajo people know me, too." He knelt down and unrolled the bedroll and spread the extra blankets out on a piece of canvas. The sun was down, and the only light in the house came from outside — the dim orange light from sundown.

I stood there and waited for him to crawl under the blankets.

"What are you waiting for?" he said, and I lay down beside him. He undressed me slowly like the night before beside the river — kissing my face gently and running his hands up and down my belly and legs. He took off my pants and then he laughed.

"Why are you laughing?"

"You are breathing so hard."

I pulled away from him and turned my back to him.

He pulled me around and pinned me down with his arms and chest. "You don't understand, do you, little Yellow Woman? You will do what I want."

And again he was all around me with his skin slippery against mine, and I was afraid because I understood that his strength could hurt me. I lay underneath him and I knew that he could destroy me. But later, while he slept beside me, I touched his face and I had a feeling — the kind of feeling for him that overcame me that morning along the river. I kissed him on the forehead and he reached out for me.

When I woke up in the morning he was gone. It gave me a strange feeling because for a long time I sat there on the blankets and looked around the little house for some object of his — some proof that he had been there or maybe that he was coming back. Only the blankets and the cardboard box remained. The .30–30° that had been leaning in the corner was gone, and so was the knife I had used the night before. He was gone, and I had my chance to go now. But first I had to eat, because I knew it would be a long walk home.

I found some dried apricots in the cardboard box, and I sat down on a rock at the edge of the plateau rim. There was no wind and the sun warmed me. I was surrounded by silence. I drowsed with apricots in my mouth, and I didn't believe that there were highways or railroads or cattle to steal.

When I woke up, I stared down at my feet in the black mountain dirt. Little black ants were swarming over the pine needles around my foot. They must have smelled the apricots. I thought about my family far below me. They would be wondering about me, because this had never happened to me before. The tribal police would file a report. But if old Grandpa weren't dead he would tell them what happened — he would laugh and say, "Stolen by a ka'tsina, a mountain spirit. She'll come home — they usually do." There are enough of them to handle things. My mother and grandmother will raise the baby like they raised me. Al will find someone else, and they will go on like before, except that there will be a story about the day I disappeared while I was walking along the river. Silva had come for me; he said he had. I did not decide to go. I just went. Moonflowers blossom in the sand hills before dawn, just as I followed him. That's what I was thinking as I wandered along the trail through the pine trees.

It was noon when I got back. When I saw the stone house I remembered that I had meant to go home. But that didn't seem important any more, maybe because there were little blue flowers growing in the meadow behind the stone house and the gray squirrels were playing in the pines next to the house. The horses were standing in the corral, and there was a beef carcass hanging on the shady side of a big pine in front of the house. Flies buzzed around the clotted blood that hung from the carcass. Silva was washing his hands in a bucket full of water. He must have heard me coming because he spoke to me without turning to face me.

"I've been waiting for you."

"I went walking in the big pine trees."

I looked into the bucket full of bloody water with brown-and-white animal hairs floating in it. Silva stood there letting his hand drip, examining me intently.

.30–30: A rifle.

"Are you coming with me?"

"Where?" I asked him.

"To sell the meat in Marquez."

"If you're sure it's O.K."

"I wouldn't ask you if it wasn't," he answered.

He sloshed the water around in the bucket before he dumped it out and set the bucket upside down near the door. I followed him to the corral and watched him saddle the horses. Even beside the horses he looked tall, and I asked him again if he wasn't Navajo. He didn't say anything; he just shook his head and kept cinching up the saddle.

"But Navajos are tall."

"Get on the horse," he said, "and let's go."

The last thing he did before we started down the steep trail was to grab the .30–30 from the corner. He slid the rifle into the scabbard that hung from his saddle.

"Do they ever try to catch you?" I asked.

"They don't know who I am."

"Then why did you bring the rifle?"

"Because we are going to Marquez where the Mexicans live."

III

The trail leveled out on a narrow ridge that was steep on both sides like an animal spine. On one side I could see where the trail went around the rocky gray hills and disappeared into the southeast where the pale sandrock mesas stood in the distance near my home. On the other side was a trail that went west, and as I looked far into the distance I thought I saw the little town. But Silva said no, that I was looking in the wrong place, that I just thought I saw houses. After that I quit looking off into the distance; it was hot and the wildflowers were closing up their deep-yellow petals. Only the waxy cactus flowers bloomed in the bright sun, and I saw every color that a cactus blossom can be; the white ones and the red ones were still buds, but the purple and the yellow were blossoms, open full and the most beautiful of all.

Silva saw him before I did. The white man was riding a big gray horse, coming up the trail toward us. He was traveling fast and the gray horse's feet sent rocks rolling off the trail into the dry tumbleweeds. Silva motioned for me to stop and we watched the white man. He didn't see us right away, but finally his horse whinnied at our horses and he stopped. He looked at us briefly before he loped the gray horse across the three hundred yards that separated us. He stopped his horse in front of Silva, and his young fat face was shadowed by the brim of his hat. He didn't look mad, but his small, pale eyes moved from the blood-soaked gunny sacks hanging from my saddle to Silva's face and then back to my face.

"Where did you get the fresh meat?" the white man asked.

"I've been hunting," Silva said, and when he shifted his weight in the saddle the leather creaked.

"The hell you have, Indian. You've been rustling cattle. We've been looking for the thief for a long time."

The rancher was fat, and sweat began to soak through his white cowboy shirt and the wet cloth stuck to the thick rolls of belly fat. He almost seemed to be panting from the exertion of talking, and he smelled rancid, maybe because Silva scared him.

Silva turned to me and smiled. "Go back up the mountain, Yellow Woman."

The white man got angry when he heard Silva speak in a language he couldn't understand. "Don't try anything, Indian. Just keep riding to Marquez. We'll call the state police from there."

The rancher must have been unarmed because he was very frightened and if he had a gun he would have pulled it out then. I turned my horse around and the rancher yelled, "Stop!" I looked at Silva for an instant and there was something ancient and dark — something I could feel in my stomach — in his eyes, and when I glanced at his hand I saw his finger on the trigger of the .30–30 that was still in the saddle scabbard. I slapped my horse across the flank and the sacks of raw meat swung against my knees as the horse leaped up the trail. It was hard to keep my balance, and once I thought I felt the saddle slipping backward; it was because of this that I could not look back.

I didn't stop until I reached the ridge where the trail forked. The horse was breathing deep gasps and there was a dark film of sweat on its neck. I looked down in the direction I had come from, but I couldn't see the place. I waited. The wind came up and pushed warm air past me. I looked up at the sky, pale blue and full of thin clouds and fading vapor trails left by jets.

I think four shots were fired — I remember hearing four hollow explosions that reminded me of deer hunting. There could have been more shots after that, but I couldn't have heard them because my horse was running again and the loose rocks were making too much noise as they scattered around his feet.

Horses have a hard time running downhill, but I went that way instead of uphill to the mountain because I thought it was safer. I felt better with the horse running southeast past the round gray hills that were covered with cedar trees and black lava rock. When I got to the plain in the distance I could see the dark green patches of tamaracks that grew along the river; and beyond the river I could see the beginning of the pale sandrock mesas. I stopped the horse and looked back to see if anyone was coming; then I got off the horse and turned the horse around, wondering if it would go back to its corral under the pines on the mountain. It looked back at me for a moment and then plucked a mouthful of green tumbleweeds before it trotted back up the trail with its ears pointed forward, carrying its head daintily to one side to avoid stepping on the dragging reins. When the horse disappeared over the last hill, the gunny sacks full of meat were still swinging and bouncing.

IV

I walked toward the river on a wood-hauler's road that I knew would eventually lead to the paved road. I was thinking about waiting beside the road for someone to drive by, but by the time I got to the pavement I had decided it wasn't very far to walk if I followed the river back the way Silva and I had come.

The river water tasted good, and I sat in the shade under a cluster of silvery willows. I thought about Silva, and I felt sad at leaving him; still, there was something strange about him, and I tried to figure it out all the way back home.

I came back to the place on the river bank where he had been sitting the first time I saw him. The green willow leaves that he had trimmed from the branch were still lying there, wilted in the sand. I saw the leaves and I wanted to go back to him — to kiss him and to touch him — but the mountains were too far away now. And I told myself, because I believe it, he will come back sometime and be waiting again by the river.

I followed the path up from the river into the village. The sun was getting low, and I could smell supper cooking when I got to the screen door of my house. I could hear their voices inside — my mother was telling my grandmother how to fix the Jell-O and my husband, Al, was playing with the baby. I decided to tell them that some Navajo had kidnapped me, but I was sorry that old Grandpa wasn't alive to hear my story because it was the Yellow Woman stories he liked to tell best.

ॐ

HJALMAR SÖDERBERG *(1869–1941), one of Sweden's most important writers of fiction, was born and raised in Stockholm, the setting for many of his novels and short stories. Educated at Uppsala University, Söderberg returned to Stockholm to become a journalist and short story writer for the popular daily newspaper* Svenska Dagbladet. *His ambition was to craft "a clear, cold prose with words like sharp teeth," and he soon gained a reputation for his fearless attacks on organized religion and his honest portrayal of human sexuality. His novels* Martin Birck's Youth *(1901) and* Dr. Glas *(1905) plunged him into religious and political controversy. Moving to Copenhagen in 1917, he spent the next two decades studying and writing about the historical reality behind the Judeo-Christian tradition. With the rise of totalitarianism in Europe he returned to journalism in the late 1930s to speak out courageously in a liberal Göteborg newspaper against fascist ideology. Söderberg died soon after the German occupation of Denmark.*

The translator and critic Carl Lofmark has noted that as a story writer Söderberg

> *combines brevity with power: the shortest of [his] short stories can be full of significance and feeling, while his irony betrays the personal mood of a sceptic who has no time for romantic illusions. . . . His stories still make a strong impression today, because they treat basic questions in an honest way. . . . They seldom supply answers — for their author is a true sceptic — but they raise important questions and they provoke thought and reflection.*

One of the basic questions Söderberg asks in his short fiction is, What is the meaning of life? A freethinking author who lost the Christian faith of his childhood, he keenly felt the lack of the sense of purpose and security that accompany religious faith.

As Lofmark has observed, "Religion was not only a great political and social force in his time, it was also a strong emotional support. . . . Söderberg sustained a real loss; he could find no other emotional home, no other basis for morality and action which might replace it." This sense of loss is dramatized in "A Dog without a Master." Shortly before his death, Söderberg commented that "people have always been so fond of that story because they imagine it is about a dog."

RELATED POEMS: Lawrence Ferlinghetti, "Dog," page 1092; Louis Jenkins, "How to Tell a Wolf from a Dog," page 961.

Hjalmar Söderberg

A Dog without a Master   1894

TRANSLATED BY SAMUEL CHARTERS

A man died, and nobody, after he was dead, took care of his black dog. The dog mourned bitterly for a long time. He didn't, however, lie down to die on his master's grave, possibly because he didn't know where it was, and possibly also because he was at heart a happy, young dog who was of the opinion that he still had some unfinished business to settle with existence.

There are two kinds of dogs: dogs that have a master, and dogs that don't. On the outside there isn't much difference. A dog without a master can be just as fat as others, often fatter. No, the difference lies somewhere else. For a dog, human beings are Infinity, Providence. A master to obey, to follow, to depend on: you can say that's the meaning of a dog's life. Of course a dog doesn't think about his master every minute, and of course he doesn't always tag along at his heels; no, he often runs around by himself in a businesslike way and sniffs the corners of the houses and gets to know other dogs and snaps up a bone if he comes across one and worries about a lot of things: but the instant his master whistles, that all goes out of his doggy brain faster than the scourge of the Lord drove the moneylenders out of the temple; for he knows the one thing that must be done. And he forgets about his house corners and his dog friends and rushes to his master.

The dog, whose master died he didn't know how, and was buried he didn't know where, mourned for him a long time, but as the days passed and nothing happened to remind him of his master, he forgot about him. He didn't recognize his master's smell on the street where his master had lived any more. Often when he was tumbling on the lawn with another dog a whistling would cut through the air, and in an instant his friend would disappear like the wind. Then he would prick up his ears, but none of the whistling was like his master's. So he forgot about him more and more; he forgot that he'd ever had a master. He forgot that there had ever been a time when he wouldn't have thought it was possible for a dog to live without a master. You could say he turned into a dog that had seen better days, though that was on the inside, for on the outside things went pretty well for him. He lived the way a dog lives. Now and then on the market square he stole a good meal and got beaten, and he had romantic adventures, and lay down to sleep when he was tired. He made friends and enemies. One day he would beat up a dog that was weaker than he was, and the next day he would be beaten up by a dog that was stronger. Early in the morning you could see him running down his master's street. Out of habit he stayed there most of the time. He runs straight ahead, looking as if he has something important to do, sniffing another dog as he passes, but not bothering to follow up their meeting; afterwards he goes faster, but all of a sudden sits down and scratches behind his ear with feverish energy. The next moment he rushes across the street to chase a red cat down a cellar hole, after which, resuming his businesslike expression, he continues on his way and disappears around the corner.

So his days passed and the years followed closely upon each other, and he got older without noticing.

And so once there was a cloudy evening. It was wet and cold, and now and then there was a rain shower. The old dog had spent the whole day on an excursion into town; he came slowly up the street, limping a little. A couple of times he stopped and shook the black coat that with the years had become streaked with gray around his head and neck. As he usually did he sniffed to the right and then to the left as he walked. He detoured into a doorway and when he came out he had another dog with him. The next moment a third dog joined them. They were young, playful dogs and they wanted to coax him to play, but he was in a bad temper and the rain was coming down heavier. Then a whistle cut through the air, a long and sharp whistle. The old dog looked at the two young dogs, but they didn't pay any attention. It wasn't one of their masters who had whistled. Then the old dog without a master pricked up his ears. All at once he felt so strange. A new whistle and the old dog jumped perplexed from one side to the other. It was his master who was whistling, so he had to follow him. Someone whistled a third time, just as piercing and sharp. So where is he, which way? How could I have become separated from my master? And when did it happen? Yesterday or the day before yesterday, or maybe a little while ago? And what did my master look like, and what did he smell like and where is he, where is he? He ran around and sniffed at every one who passed by, but none of them was his master, and none of them wanted to be. Then he turned and ran down the street. He stopped at the corner and looked all around him. His master wasn't there. He bounded back down the street; the dirt splashed him and the rain dripped from his coat. He stopped at every corner, but nowhere was his master. Then he sat down at a street corner and stretched his shaggy head toward the sky and howled.

Have you ever seen or heard a forgotten dog like this — one without a master, when he stretches his neck toward the sky and howls, howls? Other dogs slink slowly away with their tails between their legs. They can't comfort him, and they can't help.

ເວເວ

SUSAN SONTAG *(b. 1933), cultural critic and woman of letters, was born in New York City, earned her undergraduate degree at the University of California at Berkeley and the University of Chicago, and received her graduate degrees in English* *and philosophy from Harvard University. She taught in various colleges until the mid-1960s, when she began to write full-time. The collection* Against Interpretation and Other Essays *(1966), especially the article "Notes on Camp," which defends "camp" art as a legitimate form because "there exists a good taste of bad taste."* Illness as Metaphor *(1978) develops the argument that society uses physical illnesses such as tuberculosis and cancer to project a sense of its own inadequacies and irrational fears. Sontag wrote this book after her own successful bout with cancer.* Styles of Radical Will *(1969),* On Photography *(1977), and* A Susan Sontag Reader *(1982) helped strengthen her reputation, as the critic Hilton Kramer has written, for possessing "an unfailing faculty for dividing intellectual opinion and inspiring a sense of outrage, consternation, and betrayal among the many readers" who disagree with her. In addition to her works of nonfiction, Sontag has published several novels — most recently* The Volcano Lover *(1992) — and screenplays and a collection of experimental short stories,* I, Etcetera *(1991).*

Sontag's fiction is fueled by her pleasure in using her mind to invent characters and situations. She admits to thinking "that the model of writing as self-expression is much too crude. If I thought that what I'm doing when I write is expressing myself, I'd junk my typewriter. . . . Writing is a much more complicated activity than that." Stories such as "The Way We Live Now" illustrate her belief that "artists are spokesmen of what in our sensibility is changing, and they choose among a number of possible different ways of rendering experience."

Sontag's way of "rendering experience" resulted in one of the first American stories about AIDS, published in the November 24, 1986, issue of The New Yorker *magazine, three years before her book* AIDS and Its Metaphors. *The writer David Leavitt has described his experience of reading "The Way We Live Now" and the strong effect the story had on him.*

RELATED COMMENTARY: *David Leavitt, "The Way I Live Now," page 766.*

SUSAN SONTAG

The Way We Live Now   *1986*

At first he was just losing weight, he felt only a little ill, Max said to Ellen, and he didn't call for an appointment with his doctor, according to Greg, because he was managing to keep on working at more or less the same rhythm, but he did stop smoking, Tanya pointed out, which suggests he was frightened, but also that he wanted, even more than he knew, to be healthy, or healthier, or maybe just to gain back a few pounds, said Orson, for he told her, Tanya went on, that he expected to be climbing the walls (isn't that what people say?) and found, to his surprise, that he didn't miss cigarettes at all and reveled in the sensation of his lungs' being ache-free for the first time in years. But did he have a good doctor, Stephen wanted to know, since it would have been crazy not to go for a checkup after the pressure was off and he was back from the conference in Helsinki, even if by then he was feeling better. And he said, to Frank, that he would go, even though he was indeed frightened, as he admitted to Jan, but who wouldn't be frightened now, though, odd as that might seem, he hadn't been worrying until recently, he avowed to Quentin, it was only in the last six months that he had the metallic taste of panic in his mouth, because becoming seriously ill was something that happened to other people, a normal delusion, he observed to Paolo, if one was thirty-eight and had never had a serious illness; he wasn't, as Jan confirmed, a hypochondriac. Of course, it was hard not to worry, everyone was worried, but it wouldn't do to panic, because, as Max pointed out to Quentin, there wasn't anything one could do except wait and hope, wait and start being careful, be careful, and hope. And even if one did prove to be ill, one shouldn't give up, they had new treatments that promised an arrest of the disease's inexorable course, research was progressing. It seemed that everyone was in touch with everyone else several times a week, checking in, I've never spent so many hours at a time on the phone, Stephen said to Kate, and when I'm exhausted after the two or three calls made to me, giving me the latest, instead of switching off the phone to give myself a respite I tap out the number of another friend or acquaintance, to pass on the news. I'm not sure I can afford to think so much about it, Ellen said, and I suspect my own motives, there's something morbid I'm getting used to, getting excited by, this must be like what people felt in London during the Blitz. As far as I know, I'm not at risk, but you never know, said Aileen. This thing is totally unprecedented, said Frank. But don't you think he ought to see a doctor, Stephen insisted. Listen, said Orson, you can't force people to take care of themselves, and what makes you think the worst, he could be just run down, people still do get ordinary illnesses, awful ones, why are you assuming it has to be that. But all I want to be sure, said Stephen, is that he understands the options, because most people don't, that's why they won't see a doctor or have the test, they think there's nothing one can do. But is there anything one can do, he said to Tanya (according to Greg), I mean what do I gain if I go to the doctor; if I'm really ill, he's reported to have said, I'll find out soon enough.

And when he was in the hospital, his spirits seemed to lighten, according to Donny. He seemed more cheerful than he had been in the last months, Ursula said, and the bad news seemed to come almost as a relief, according to Ira, as a truly unexpected blow, according to Quentin, but you'd hardly expect him to have said the same thing to all his friends, because his relation to Ira was so different from his relation to Quentin (this according to Quentin, who was proud of their friendship), and perhaps he thought Quentin wouldn't be undone by seeing him weep, but Ira insisted that couldn't be the reason he behaved so differently with each, and that maybe he was feeling less shocked, mobilizing his strength to fight for his life, at the moment he saw Ira but overcome by feelings of hopelessness when Quentin arrived with flowers, because anyway the flowers threw him into a bad mood, as Quentin told Kate, since the hospital room was choked with flowers, you couldn't have crammed another flower into that room, but surely you're exaggerating, Kate said, smiling, everybody likes flowers. Well, who wouldn't exaggerate at a time like this, Quentin said sharply. Don't you think this is an exaggeration. Of course I do, said Kate gently, I was only teasing, I mean I didn't mean to tease. I know that, Quentin said, with tears in his eyes, and Kate hugged him and said well, when I go this evening I guess I won't bring flowers, what does he want, and Quentin said, according to Max, what he likes best is chocolate. Is there anything else, asked Kate, I mean like chocolate but not chocolate. Licorice, said Quentin, blowing his nose. And besides that. Aren't you exaggerating now, Quentin said, smiling. Right, said Kate, so if I want to bring him a whole raft of stuff, besides chocolate and licorice, what else. Jelly beans, Quentin said.

He didn't want to be alone, according to Paolo, and lots of people came in the first week, and the Jamaican nurse said there were other patients on the floor who would be glad to have the surplus flowers, and people weren't afraid to visit, it wasn't like the old days, as Kate pointed out to Aileen, they're not even segregated in the hospital anymore, as Hilda observed, there's nothing on the door of his room warning visitors of the possibility of contagion, as there was a few years ago; in fact, he's in a double room and, as he told Orson, the old guy on the far side of the curtain (who's clearly on the way out, said Stephen) doesn't even have the disease, so, as Kate went on, you really should go and see him, he'd be happy to see you, he likes having people visit, you aren't not going because you're afraid, are you. Of course not, Aileen said, but I don't know what to say, I think I'll feel awkward, which he's bound to notice, and that will make him feel worse, so I won't be doing him any good, will I. But he won't notice anything, Kate said, patting Aileen's hand, it's not like that, it's not the way you imagine, he's not judging people or wondering about their motives, he's just happy to see his friends. But I never was really a friend of his, Aileen said, you're a friend, he's always liked you, you told me he talks about Nora with you, I know he likes me, he's even attracted to me, but he respects you. But, according to Wesley, the reason Aileen was so stingy with her visits was that she could never have him to herself, there were always others there already and by the time they left still others had arrived, she'd been in love with him for years, and I can understand, said Donny, that Aileen should feel bitter that if there could have been a woman friend he did more than occasionally bed, a woman he really loved, and my God, Victor said, who had known him in those years, he was crazy about Nora, what a heart-rending couple they were, two surly angels, then it couldn't have been she.

And when some of the friends, the ones who came every day, waylaid the doctor in the corridor, Stephen was the one who asked the most informed questions, who'd been keeping up not just with the stories that appeared several times a week in the *Times* (which Greg confessed to have stopped reading, unable to stand it anymore) but with articles in the medical journals published here and in England and France, and who knew socially one of the principal doctors in Paris who was doing some much-publicized research on the disease, but his doctor said little more than that the pneumonia was not life-threatening, the fever was subsiding, of course he was still weak but he was responding well to the antibiotics, that he'd have to complete his stay in the hospital, which entailed a minimum of twenty-one days on the IV, before she could start him on the new drug, for she was optimistic about the possibility of getting him into the protocol; and when Victor said that if he had so much trouble eating (he'd say to everyone when they coaxed him to eat some of the hospital meals, that food didn't taste right, that he had a funny metallic taste in his mouth) it couldn't be good that friends were bringing him all that chocolate, the doctor just smiled and said that in these cases the patient's morale was also an important factor, and if chocolate made him feel better she saw no harm in it, which worried Stephen, as Stephen said later to Donny, because they wanted to believe in the promises and taboos of today's high-tech medicine but here this reassuringly curt and silver-haired specialist in the disease, someone quoted frequently in the papers, was talking like some oldfangled country GP who tells the family that tea with honey or chicken soup may do as much for the patient as penicillin, which might mean, as Max said, that they were just going through the motions of treating him, that they were not sure about what to do, or rather, as Xavier interjected, that they didn't know what the hell they were doing, that the truth, the real truth, as Hilda said, upping the ante, was that they didn't, the doctors, really have any hope.

Oh, no, said Lewis, I can't stand it, wait a minute, I can't believe it, are you sure, I mean are they sure, have they done all the tests, it's getting so when the phone rings I'm scared to answer because I think it will be someone telling me someone else is ill; but did Lewis really not know until yesterday, Robert said testily, I find that hard to believe, everybody is talking about it, it seems impossible that someone wouldn't have called Lewis; and perhaps Lewis did know, was for some reason pretending not to know already, because, Jan recalled, didn't Lewis say something months ago to Greg, and not only to Greg, about his not looking well, losing weight, and being worried about him and wishing he'd see a doctor, so it couldn't come as a total surprise. Well, everybody is worried about everybody now, said Betsy, that seems to be the way we live, the way we live now. And, after all, they were once very close, doesn't Lewis still have the keys to his apartment, you know the way you let someone keep the keys after you've broken up, only a little because you hope the person might just saunter in, drunk or high, late some evening, but mainly because it's wise to have a few sets of keys strewn around town, if you live alone, at the top of a former commerical building that, pretentious as it is, will never acquire a doorman or even a resident superintendent, someone whom you can call on for the keys late one night if you find you've lost yours or have locked yourself out. Who else has keys, Tanya inquired, I was thinking somebody might drop by tomorrow before coming to the hospital and bring some treasures, because the other day, Ira said, he was complaining about how dreary the hospital room was, and how it was like being locked up in a motel room, which got everybody started telling funny stories about motel rooms they'd known, and at Ursula's story, about the Luxury Budget Inn in Schenectady, there was an uproar of laughter around his bed, while he watched them in silence, eyes bright with fever, all the while, as Victor recalled, gobbling that damned chocolate. But, according to Jan, whom Lewis's keys enabled to tour the swank of his bachelor lair with an eye to bringing over some art consolation to brighten up the hospital room, the Byzantine icon wasn't on the wall over his bed, and that was a puzzle until Orson remembered that he'd recounted without seeming upset (this disputed by Greg) that the boy he'd recently gotten rid of had stolen it, along with four of the *maki-e* lacquer boxes, as if these were objects as easy to sell on the street as a TV or a stereo. But he's always been very generous, Kate said quietly, and though he loves beautiful things isn't really attached to them, to things, as Orson said, which is unusual in a collector, as Frank commented, and when Kate shuddered and tears sprang to her eyes and Orson inquired anxiously if he, Orson, had said something wrong, she pointed out that they'd begun talking about him in a retrospective mode, summing up what he was like, what made them fond of him, as if he were finished, completed, already a part of the past.

Perhaps he was getting tired of having so many visitors, said Robert, who was, as Ellen couldn't help mentioning, someone who had come only twice and was probably looking for a reason not to be in regular attendance, but there could be no doubt, according to Ursula, that his spirits had dipped, not that there was any discouraging news from the doctors, and he seemed now to prefer being alone a few hours of the day; and he told Donny that he'd begun keeping a diary for the first time in his life, because he wanted to record the course of his mental reactions to this astonishing turn of events, to do something parallel to what the doctors were doing, who came every morning and conferred at his bedside about his body, and that perhaps it wasn't so important what he wrote in it, which amounted, as he said wryly to Quentin, to little more than the usual banalities about terror and amazement that this was happening to him, to him also, plus the usual remorseful assessments of his past life, his pardonable superficialities, capped by resolves to live better, more deeply, more in touch with his work and his friends, and not to care so passionately about what people thought of him, interspersed with admonitions to himself that in this situation his will to live counted more than anything else and that if he really wanted to live, and trusted life, and liked himself well enough (down, ol' debbil Thanatos!), he *would* live, he would be an exception; but perhaps all this, as Quentin ruminated, talking on the phone to Kate, wasn't the point, the point was that by the very keeping of the diary he was accumulating something to reread one day, slyly staking out his claim to a future time, in which the diary would be an object, a relic, in which he might not actually reread it, because he would want to have put this ordeal behind him, but the diary would be there in the drawer of his stupendous Majorelle desk, and he could already, he did actually say to Quentin one late sunny afternoon, propped up in the hospital bed, with the stain of chocolate framing one corner of a heartbreaking smile, see himself in the penthouse, the October sun streaming through those clear windows instead of this streaked one, and the diary, the pathetic diary, safe inside the drawer.

It doesn't matter about the treatment's side effects, Stephen said (when talking to Max), I don't know why you're so worried about that, every strong treatment has some dangerous side effects, it's inevitable, you mean otherwise the treatment wouldn't be effective, Hilda interjected, and anyway, Stephen went on doggedly, just because there *are* side effects it doesn't mean he has to get them, or all of them, each one, or even some of them. That's just a list of all the possible things that could go wrong, because the doctors have to cover themselves, so they make up a worst-case scenario, but isn't what's happening to him, and to so many other people, Tanya interrupted, a worst-case scenario, a catastrophe no one could have imagined, it's too cruel, and isn't everything a side effect, quipped Ira, even *we* are all side effects, but we're not bad side effects, Frank said, he likes having his friends around, and we're helping each other, too; because his illness sticks us all in the same glue, mused Xavier, and, whatever the jealousies and grievances from the past that have made us wary and cranky with each other, when something like this happens (the sky is falling, the sky is falling!) you understand what's really important. I agree, Chicken Little, he is reported to have said. But don't you think, Quentin observed to Max, that being as close to him as we are, making time to drop by the hospital every day, is a way of our trying to define ourselves more firmly and irrevocably as the well, those who aren't ill, who aren't going to fall ill, as if what's happened to him couldn't happen to us, when in fact the chances are that before long one of us will end up where he is, which is probably what he felt when he was one of the cohort visiting Zack in the spring (you never knew Zack, did you?), and, according to Clarice, Zack's widow, he didn't come very often, he said he hated hospitals, and didn't feel he was doing Zack any good, that Zack would see on his face how uncomfortable he was. Oh, he was one of those, Aileen said. A coward. Like me.

And after he was sent home from the hospital, and Quentin had volunteered to move in and was cooking meals and taking telephone messages and keeping the mother in Mississippi informed, well, mainly keeping her from flying to New York and heaping her grief on her son and confusing the household routine with her oppressive ministrations, he was able to work an hour or two in his study, on days he didn't insist on going out, for a meal or a movie, which tired him. He seemed optimistic, Kate thought, his appetite was good, and what he said, Orson reported, was that he agreed when Stephen advised him that the main thing was to keep in shape, he was a fighter, right, he wouldn't be who he was if he weren't, and was he ready for the big fight, Stephen asked rhetorically (as Max told it to Donny), and he said you bet, and Stephen added it could be a lot worse, you could have gotten the disease two years ago, but now so many scientists are working on it, the American team and the French team, everyone bucking for that Nobel Prize a few years down the road, that all you have to do is stay healthy for another year or two and then there will be good treatment. Yes, he said, Stephen said, my timing is good. And Betsy, who had been climbing on and rolling off macrobiotic diets for a decade, came up with a Japanese specialist she wanted him to see but thank God, Donny reported, he'd had the sense to refuse, but he did agree to see Victor's visualization therapist, although what could one possibly visualize, said Hilda, when the point of visualizing disease was to see it as an entity with contours, borders, here rather than there, something limited, something you were the host of, in the sense that you could disinvite the disease, while this was so total; or would be, Max said. But the main thing, said Greg, was to see that he didn't go the macrobiotic route, which might be harmless for plump Betsy but could only be devastating for him, lean as he'd always been, with all the cigarettes and other appetite-suppressing chemicals he'd been welcoming into his body for years; and now was hardly the time, as Stephen pointed out, to be worried about cleaning up his act, and eliminating the chemical additives and other pollutants that we're all blithely or not so blithely feasting on, blithely since we're healthy, healthy as we can be; so far, Ira said. Meat and potatoes is what I'd be happy to see him eating, Ursula said wistfully. And spaghetti and clam sauce, Greg added. And thick cholesterol-rich omelets with smoked mozzarella, suggested Yvonne, who had flown from London for the weekend to see him. Chocolate cake, said Frank. Maybe not chocolate cake, Ursula said, he's already eating so much chocolate.

   And when, not right away but still only three weeks later, he was accepted into the protocol for the new drug, which took considerable behind-the-scenes lobbying with the doctors, he talked less about being ill, according to Donny, which seemed like a good sign, Kate felt, a sign that he was not feeling like a victim, feeling not that he *had* a disease but, rather, was living *with* a disease (that was the right cliché, wasn't it?), a more hospitable arrangement, said Jan, a kind of cohabitation which implied that it was something temporary, that it could be terminated, but terminated how, said Hilda, and when you say hospitable, Jan, I hear hospital. And it was encouraging, Stephen insisted, that from the start, at least from the time he was finally persuaded to make the telephone call to his doctor, he was willing to say the name of the disease, pronounce it often and easily, as if it were just another word, like boy or gallery or cigarette or money or deal, as in no big deal, Paolo interjected, because, as Stephen continued, to utter the name is a sign of health, a sign that one has accepted being who one is, mortal, vulnerable, not exempt, not an exception after all, it's a sign that one is willing, truly willing, to fight for one's life. And we must say the name, too, and often, Tanya added, we mustn't lag behind him in honesty, or let him feel that, the effort of honesty having been made, it's something done with and he can go on to other things. One is so much better prepared to help him, Wesley replied. In a way he's fortunate, said Yvonne, who had taken care of a problem at the New York store and was flying back to London this evening, sure, fortunate, said Wesley, no one is shunning him, Yvonne went on, no one's afraid to hug him or kiss him lightly on the mouth, in London we are, as usual, a few years behind you, people I know, people who would seem to be not even remotely at risk, are just terrified, but I'm impressed by how cool and rational you all are; you find us cool, asked Quentin. But I have to say, he's reported to have said, I'm terrified, I find it very hard to read (and you know how he loves to read, said Greg; yes, reading is his television, said Paolo) or to think, but I don't feel hysterical. I feel quite hysterical, Lewis said to Yvonne. But you're able to *do* something for him, that's wonderful, how I wish I could stay longer, Yvonne answered, it's rather beautiful, I can't help thinking, this utopia of friendship you've assembled around him (this pathetic utopia, said Kate), so that the disease, Yvonne concluded, is not, anymore, out there. Yes, don't you think we're more at home here, with him, with the disease, said Tanya, because the imagined disease is so much worse than the reality of him, whom we all love, each in our fashion, having it. I know for me his getting it has quite demystified the disease, said Jan, I don't feel afraid, spooked, as I did before he became ill, when it was only news about remote acquaintances, whom I never saw again after they became ill. But you know you're not going to come down with the disease, Quentin said, to which Ellen replied, on her behalf, that's not the point, and possibly untrue, my gynecologist says that everyone is at risk, everyone who has a sexual life, because sexuality is a chain that links each of us to many others, unknown others, and now the great chain of being has become a chain of death as well. It's not the same for you, Quentin insisted, it's not the same for you as it is for me or Lewis or Frank or Paolo or Max, I'm more and more frightened, and I have every reason to be. I don't think about whether I'm at risk or not, said Hilda, I know that I was afraid to know someone with the disease, afraid of what I'd see, what I'd feel, and after the first day I came to the hospital I felt so relieved. I'll never feel that way, that fear, again; he doesn't seem different from me. He's not, Quentin said.

According to Lewis, he talked more often about those who visited more often, which is natural, said Betsy, I think he's even keeping a tally. And among those who came or checked in by phone every day, the inner circle as it were, those who were getting more points, there was still a further competition, which was what was getting on Betsy's nerves, she confessed to Jan; there's always that vulgar jockeying for position around the bedside of the gravely ill, and though we all feel suffused with virtue at our loyalty to him (speak for yourself, said Jan), to the extent that we're carving time out of every day, or almost every day, though some of us are dropping out, as Xavier pointed out, aren't we getting at least as much out of this as he is. Are we, said Jan. We're rivals for a sign from him of special pleasure over a visit, each stretching for the brass ring of his favor, wanting to feel the most wanted, the true nearest and dearest, which is inevitable with someone who doesn't have a spouse and children or an official in-house lover, hierarchies that no one would dare contest, Betsy went on, so we are the family he's founded, without meaning to, without official titles and ranks (we, we, snarled Quentin); and is it so clear, though some of us, Lewis and Quentin and Tanya and Paolo, among others, are ex-lovers and all of us more or less than friends, which one of us he prefers, Victor said (now it's us, raged Quentin), because sometimes I think he looks forward more to seeing Aileen, who has visited only three times, twice at the hospital and once since he's been home, than he does you or me; but, according to Tanya, after being very disappointed that Aileen hadn't come, now he was angry, while, according to Xavier, he was not really hurt but touchingly passive, accepting Aileen's absence as something he somehow deserved. But he's happy to have people around, said Lewis; he says when he doesn't have company he gets very sleepy, he sleeps (according to Quentin), and then perks up when someone arrives, it's important that he not feel ever alone. But, said Victor, there's one person he hasn't heard from, whom he'd probably like to hear from more than most of us; but she didn't just vanish, even right after she broke away from him, and he knows exactly where she lives now, said Kate, he told me he put in a call to her last Christmas Eve, and she said it's nice to hear from you and Merry Christmas, and he was shattered, according to Orson, and furious and disdainful, according to Ellen (what do you expect of her, said Wesley, she was burned out), but Kate wondered if maybe he hadn't phoned Nora in the middle of a sleepless night, what's the time difference, and Quentin said no, I don't think so, I think he wouldn't want her to know.

And when he was feeling even better and had regained the pounds he'd shed right away in the hospital, though the refrigerator started to fill up with organic wheat germ and grapefruit and skimmed milk (he's worried about his cholesterol count, Stephen lamented), and told Quentin he could manage by himself now, and did, he started asking everyone who visited how he looked, and everyone said he looked great, so much better than a few weeks ago, which didn't jibe with what anyone had told him at that time; but then it was getting harder and harder to know how he looked, to answer such a question honestly when among themselves they wanted to be honest, both for honesty's sake and (as Donny thought) to prepare for the worst, because he'd been looking like *this* for so long, at least it seemed so long, that it was as if he'd always been like this, how did he look before, but it was only a few months, and those words, pale and wan looking and fragile, hadn't they always applied? And one Thursday Ellen, meeting Lewis at the door of the building, said, as they rode up together in the elevator, how is he *really*? But you see how he is, Lewis said tartly, he's fine, he's perfectly healthy, and Ellen understood that of course Lewis didn't think he was perfectly healthy but that he wasn't worse, and that was true, but wasn't it, well, almost heartless to talk like that. Seems inoffensive to me, Quentin said, but I know what you mean, I remember once talking to Frank, somebody, after all, who has volunteered to do five hours a week of office work at the Crisis Center (I know, said Ellen), and Frank was going on about this guy, diagnosed almost a year ago, and so much further along, who'd been complaining to Frank on the phone about the indifference of some doctor, and had gotten quite abusive about the doctor, and Frank was saying there was no reason to be so upset, the implication being that *he*, Frank, wouldn't behave so irrationally, and I said, barely able to control my scorn, but Frank, Frank, he has every reason to be upset, he's dying, and Frank said, said according to Quentin, oh, I don't like to think about it that way.

And it was while he was still home, recuperating, getting his weekly treatment, still not able to do much work, he complained, but, according to Quentin, up and about most of the time and turning up at the office several days a week, that bad news came about two remote acquaintances, one in Houston and one in Paris, news that was intercepted by Quentin on the ground that it could only depress him, but Stephen contended that it was wrong to lie to him, it was so important for him to live in the truth; that had been one of his first victories, that he was candid, that he was even willing to crack jokes about the disease, but Ellen said it wasn't good to give him this end-of-the-world feeling, too many people were getting ill, it was becoming such a common destiny that maybe some of the will to fight for his life would be drained out of him if it seemed to be as natural as, well, death. Oh, Hilda said, who didn't know personally either the one in Houston or the one in Paris, but knew *of* the one in Paris, a pianist who specialized in twentieth-century Czech and Polish music, I have his records, he's such a valuable person, and, when Kate glared at her, continued defensively, I know every life is equally sacred, but that *is* a thought, another thought, I mean, all these valuable people who aren't going to have their normal four score as it is now, these people aren't going to be replaced, and it's such a loss to the culture. But this isn't going to go on forever, Wesley said, it can't, they're bound to come up with something (they, they, muttered Stephen), but did you ever think, Greg said, that if some people don't die, I mean even if they can keep them alive (they, they, muttered Kate), they continue to be carriers, and that means, if you have a conscience, that you can never make love, make love fully, as you'd been wont — wantonly, Ira said — to do. But it's better than dying, said Frank. And in all his talk about the future, when he allowed himself to be hopeful, according to Quentin, he never mentioned the prospect that even if he didn't die, if he were so fortunate as to be among the first generation of the disease's survivors, never mentioned, Kate confirmed, that whatever happened it was over, the way he had lived until now, but, according to Ira, he did think about it, the end of bravado, the end of folly, the end of trusting life, the end of taking life for granted, and of treating life as something that, samurai-like, he thought himself ready to throw away lightly, impudently; and Kate recalled, sighing, a brief exchange she'd insisted on having as long as two years ago, huddling on a banquette covered with steel-gray industrial carpet on an upper level of The Prophet and toking up for their next foray onto the dance floor: she'd said hesitantly, for it felt foolish asking a prince of debauchery to, well, take it easy, and she wasn't keen on playing big sister, a role, as Hilda confirmed, he inspired in many women, are you being careful, honey, you know what I mean. And he replied, Kate went on, no, I'm not, listen, I can't, I just can't, sex is too important to me, always has been (he started talking like that, according to Victor, after Nora left him), and if I get it, well, I get it. But he wouldn't talk like that now, would he, said Greg; he must feel awfully foolish now, said Betsy, like someone who went on smoking, saying I can't give up cigarettes, but when the bad X-ray is taken even the most besotted nicotine addict can stop on a dime. But sex isn't like cigarettes, is it, said Frank, and, besides, what good does it do to remember that he was reckless, said Lewis angrily, the appalling thing is that you just have to be unlucky once, and wouldn't he feel even worse if he'd stopped three years ago and had come down with it anyway, since one of the most terrifying features of the disease is that you don't know when you contracted it, it could have been ten years ago, because surely this disease has existed for years and years, long before it was recognized; that is, named. Who knows how long (I think a lot about that, said

Max) and who knows (I know what you're going to say, Stephen interrupted) how many are going to get it.

I'm feeling fine, he's reported to have said whenever someone asked him how he was, which was almost always the first question anyone asked. Or: I'm feeling better, how are you? But he said other things, too, I'm playing leapfrog with myself, he is reported to have said, according to Victor. And: There must be a way to get something positive out of this situation, he's reported to have said to Kate. How American of him, said Paolo. Well, said Betsy, you know the old American adage: When you've got a lemon, make lemonade. The one thing I'm sure I couldn't take, Jan said he said to her, is becoming disfigured, but Stephen hastened to point out the disease doesn't take that form very often anymore, its profile is mutating, and, in conversation with Ellen, wheeled up words like blood-brain barrier; I never thought there was a barrier *there*, said Jan. But he mustn't know about Max, Ellen said, that would really depress him, please don't tell him, he'll have to know, Quentin said grimly, and he'll be furious not to have been told. But there's time for that, when they take Max off the respirator, said Ellen; but isn't it incredible, Frank said, Max was fine, not feeling ill at all, and then to wake up with a fever of a hundred and five, unable to breathe, but that's the way it often starts, with absolutely no warning, Stephen said, the disease has so many forms. And when, after another week had gone by, he asked Quentin where Max was, he didn't question Quentin's account of a spree in the Bahamas, but then the number of people who visited regularly was thinning out, partly because the old feuds that had been put aside through the first hospitalization and the return home had resurfaced, and the flickering enmity between Lewis and Frank exploded, even though Kate did her best to mediate between them, and also because he himself had done something to loosen the bonds of love that united the friends around him, by seeming to take them all for granted, as if it were perfectly normal for so many people to carve out so much time and attention for him, visit him every few days, talk about him incessantly on the phone with each other; but, according to Paolo, it wasn't that he was less grateful, it was just something he was getting used to, the visits. It had become, with time, a more ordinary kind of situation, a kind of ongoing party, first at the hospital and now since he was home, barely on his feet again, it being clear, said Robert, that I'm on the B list; but Kate said, that's absurd, there's no list; and Victor said, but there is, only it's not he, it's Quentin who's drawing it up. He wants to see us, we're helping him, we have to do it the way he wants, he fell down yesterday on the way to the bathroom, he mustn't be told about Max (but he already knew, according to Donny), it's getting worse.

When I was home, he is reported to have said, I was afraid to sleep, as I was dropping off each night it felt like just that, as if I were falling down a black hole, to sleep felt like giving in to death, I slept every night with the light on; but here, in the hospital, I'm less afraid. And to Quentin he said, one morning, the fear rips through me, it tears me open; and, to Ira, it presses me together, squeezes me toward myself. Fear gives everything its hue, its high. I feel so, I don't know how to say it, exalted, he said to Quentin. Calamity is an amazing high, too. Sometimes I feel *so* well, so powerful, it's as if I could jump out of my skin. Am I going crazy, or what? Is it all this attention and coddling I'm getting from everybody, like a child's dream of being loved? Is it the drugs? I know it sounds crazy but sometimes I think this is a *fantastic* experience, he said shyly; but there was also the bad taste in the mouth, the pressure in the head and at the back of the neck, the red, bleeding gums, the painful, if pink-lobed, breathing, and his ivory pallor, color of white chocolate. Among those who wept when told over the phone that he was back in the hospital were Kate and Stephen (who'd been called by Quentin), and Ellen, Victor, Aileen, and Lewis (who were called by Kate), and Xavier and Ursula (who were called by Stephen). Among those who didn't weep were Hilda, who said that she'd just learned that her seventy-five-year-old aunt was dying of the disease, which she'd contracted from a transfusion given during her successful double bypass of five years ago, and Frank and Donny and Betsy, but this didn't mean, according to Tanya, that they weren't moved and appalled, and Quentin thought they might not be coming soon to the hospital but would send presents; the room, he was in a private room this time, was filling up with flowers, and plants, and books, and tapes. The high tide of barely suppressed acrimony of the last weeks at home subsided into the routines of hospital visiting, though more than a few resented Quentin's having charge of the visiting book (but it was Quentin who had the idea, Lewis pointed out); now, to insure a steady stream of visitors, preferably no more than two at a time (this, the rule in all hospitals, wasn't enforced here, at least on this floor; whether out of kindness or inefficiency, no one could decide), Quentin had to be called first, to get one's time slot, there was no more casual dropping by. And his mother could no longer be prevented from taking a plane and installing herself in a hotel near the hospital; but he seemed to mind her daily presence less than expected, Quentin said; said Ellen it's we who mind, do you suppose she'll stay long. It was easier to be generous with each other visiting him here in the hospital, as Donny pointed out, than at home, where one minded never being alone with him; coming here, in our twos and twos, there's no doubt about what our role is, how we should be, collective, funny, distracting, undemanding, light, it's important to be light, for in all this dread there is gaiety, too, as the poet said, said Kate. (His eyes, his glittering eyes, said Lewis.) His eyes looked dull, extinguished, Wesley said to Xavier, but Betsy said his face, not just his eyes, looked soulful, warm; whatever is there, said Kate, I've never been so aware of his eyes; and Stephen said, I'm afraid of what my eyes show, the way I watch him, with too much intensity, or a phony kind of casualness, said Victor. And, unlike at home, he was clean-shaven each morning, at whatever hour they visited him; his curly hair was always combed; but he complained that the nurses had changed since he was here the last time, and that he didn't like the change, he wanted everyone to be the same. The room was furnished now with some of his personal effects (odd word for one's things, said Ellen), and Tanya brought drawings and a letter from her nine-year-old dyslexic son, who was

writing now, since she'd purchased a computer; and Donny brought champagne and some helium balloons, which were anchored to the foot of his bed;
tell me about something that's going on, he said, waking up from a nap to
find Donny and Kate at the side of his bed, beaming at him; tell me a story,
he said wistfully, said Donny, who couldn't think of anything to say; *you're*
the story, Kate said. And Xavier brought an eighteenth-century Guatemalan
wooden statue of Saint Sebastian with upcast eyes and open mouth, and
when Tanya said what's that, a tribute to eros past, Xavier said where I come
from Sebastian is venerated as a protector against pestilence. Pestilence symbolized by arrows? Symbolized by arrows. All people remember is the body
of a beautiful youth bound to a tree, pierced by arrows (of which he always
seems oblivious, Tanya interjected), people forget that the story continues,
Xavier continued, that when the Christian women came to bury the martyr
they found him still alive and nursed him back to health. And he said, according to Stephen, I didn't know Saint Sebastian didn't die. It's undeniable,
isn't it, said Kate on the phone to Stephen, the fascination of the dying. It
makes me ashamed. We're learning how to die, said Hilda, I'm not ready to
learn, said Aileen; and Lewis, who was coming straight from the other hospital, the hospital where Max was still being kept in ICU, met Tanya getting
out of the elevator on the tenth floor, and as they walked together down the
shiny corridor past the open doors, averting their eyes from the other patients sunk in their beds, with tubes in their noses, irradiated by the bluish
light from the television sets, the thing I can't bear to think about, Tanya said
to Lewis, is someone dying with the TV on.

He has that strange, unnerving detachment now, said Ellen, that's what
upsets me, even though it makes it easier to be with him. Sometimes he was
querulous. I can't stand them coming in here taking my blood every morning,
what are they doing with all that blood, he is reported to have said; but where
was his anger, Jan wondered. Mostly he was lovely to be with, always saying
how are *you*, how are you feeling. He's so sweet now, said Aileen. He's so nice,
said Tanya. (Nice, nice, groaned Paolo.) At first he was very ill, but he was rallying, according to Stephen's best information, there was no fear of his not recovering this time, and the doctor spoke of his being discharged from the
hospital in another ten days if all went well, and the mother was persuaded to
fly back to Mississippi, and Quentin was readying the penthouse for his return. And he was still writing his diary, not showing it to anyone, though
Tanya, first to arrive one late-winter morning, and finding him dozing,
peeked, and was horrified, according to Greg, not by anything she read but by
a progressive change in his handwriting: in the recent pages, it was becoming
spidery, less legible, and some lines of script wandered and tilted about the
page. I was thinking, Ursula said to Quentin, that the difference between a
story and a painting or photograph is that in a story you can write, He's still
alive. But in a painting or a photo you can't show "still." You can just show
him being alive. He's still alive, Stephen said.

JOHN STEINBECK *(1902–1968) was born in Salinas and raised near Monterey in the fertile farm country of the Salinas Valley in California, the locale for his story "The Chrysanthemums." His mother was a former schoolteacher; his father was the county treasurer. In high school Steinbeck wrote for the school newspaper and was president of his class. He enjoyed literature from an early age and read novels by Gustave Flaubert, Fyodor Dostoevsky, and Thomas Hardy in the family library. Enrolled at Stanford University as an English major, Steinbeck dropped out before graduating and worked at odd jobs — fruit picker, caretaker, laboratory assistant — while he practiced writing fiction. Several times he took short-term jobs with the Spreckels Sugar Company and gained a perspective on labor problems, which he would later describe in his novels.*

In 1929 Steinbeck began his literary career by publishing Cup of Gold, *a fictionalized biography of Henry Morgan, the seventeenth-century Welsh pirate. His next book,* The Pastures of Heaven *(1932), is a collection of short stories about the people in a farm community in California. The critic Brian Barbour has stated that Steinbeck realized early in his career that the short story form was not congenial to his talents. He needed the more expansive form of the novel to give his characters the room for what he considered real growth. In 1936 Steinbeck wrote* In Dubious Battle, *his first major political novel. He then published four more novels and another book of short fiction before his greatest work,* The Grapes of Wrath *(1939). This book, about a family from the Dust Bowl who emigrate to California and struggle to make a living despite agricultural exploitation, won Steinbeck the Pulitzer Prize. Among his many other successful novels are* East of Eden *(1952) and* The Winter of Our Discontent *(1961). He received the Nobel Prize for literature in 1962.*

One of the most accomplished popular novelists in the United States, Steinbeck excelled — as did Ernest Hemingway — in the creation of exciting conflicts, convincing dialogue, and recognizable characters to dramatize his philosophy of life. Although his production of short stories was relatively slight, his work is often anthologized because of his clear, realistic treatment of social themes as his characters struggle to forge meaningful lives. "The Chrysanthemums" echoes the D. H. Lawrence story "Odour of Chrysanthemums" in its concerns with sexual roles and the difficulty of striking a balance between self-interest and the needs of others. Steinbeck's biographer, Jackson J. Benson, also commented that the excellence of "The Chrysanthemums" lies in "its delicate, indirect handling of a woman's emotions . . . [especially] the difficulty of the woman in finding a creative significant role in a male-dominated society."

RELATED STORY: *D. H. Lawrence, "Odour of Chrysanthemums," page 413.*

RELATED COMMENTARY: *Jay Parini, "Lawrence's and Steinbeck's 'Chrysanthemums,' " page 786.*

JOHN STEINBECK

The Chrysanthemums

1938

The high grey-flannel fog of winter closed off the Salinas Valley from the sky and from all the rest of the world. On every side it sat like a lid on the mountains and made of the great valley a closed pot. On the broad, level land floor the gang plows bit deep and left the black earth shining like metal where the shares had cut. On the foothill ranches across the Salinas River, the yellow stubble fields seemed to be bathed in pale cold sunshine, but there was no sunshine in the valley now in December. The thick willow scrub along the river flamed with sharp and positive yellow leaves.

It was a time of quiet and of waiting. The air was cold and tender. A light wind blew up from the southwest so that the farmers were mildly hopeful of a good rain before long; but fog and rain do not go together.

Across the river, on Henry Allen's foothill ranch there was little work to be done, for the hay was cut and stored and the orchards were plowed up to receive the rain deeply when it should come. The cattle on the higher slopes were becoming shaggy and rough-coated.

Elisa Allen, working in her flower garden, looked down across the yard and saw Henry, her husband, talking to two men in business suits. The three of them stood by the tractor shed, each man with one foot on the side of the little Fordson. They smoked cigarettes and studied the machine as they talked.

Elisa watched them for a moment and then went back to her work. She was thirty-five. Her face was lean and strong and her eyes were as clear as water. Her figure looked blocked and heavy in her gardening costume, a man's black hat pulled low down over her eyes, clod-hopper shoes, a figured print dress almost completely covered by a big corduroy apron with four big pockets to hold the snips, the trowel and scratcher, the seeds, and the knife she worked with. She wore heavy leather gloves to protect her hands while she worked.

She was cutting down the old year's chrysanthemum stalks with a pair of short and powerful scissors. She looked down toward the men by the tractor shed now and then. Her face was eager and mature and handsome; even her work with the scissors was overeager, overpowerful. The chrysanthemum stems seemed too small and easy for her energy.

She brushed a cloud of hair out of her eyes with the back of her glove, and left a smudge of earth on her cheek in doing it. Behind her stood the neat white farm house with red geraniums close-banked around it as high as the windows. It was a hard-swept looking little house with hard-polished windows, and a clean mud-mat on the front steps.

Elisa cast another glance toward the tractor shed. The strangers were getting into their Ford coupe. She took off a glove and put her strong fingers down into the forest of new green chrysanthemum sprouts that were growing around the old roots. She spread the leaves and looked down among the close-growing stems. No aphids were there, no sowbugs or snails or cutworms. Her terrier fingers destroyed such pests before they could get started.

Elisa started at the sound of her husband's voice. He had come near quietly, and he leaned over the wire fence that protected her flower garden from cattle and dogs and chickens.

"At it again," he said. "You've got a strong new crop coming."

Elisa straightened her back and pulled on the gardening glove again. "Yes. They'll be strong this coming year." In her tone and on her face there was a little smugness.

"You've got a gift with things," Henry observed. "Some of those yellow chrysanthemums you had this year were ten inches across. I wish you'd work out in the orchard and raise some apples that big."

Her eyes sharpened. "Maybe I could do it, too. I've a gift with things, all right. My mother had it. She could stick anything in the ground and make it grow. She said it was having planters' hands that knew how to do it."

"Well, it sure works with flowers," he said.

"Henry, who were those men you were talking to?"

"Why, sure, that's what I came to tell you. They were from the Western Meat Company. I sold thirty head of three-year-old steers. Got nearly my own price, too."

"Good," she said. "Good for you."

"And I thought," he continued, "I thought how it's Saturday afternoon, and we might go into Salinas for dinner at a restaurant, and then to a picture show — to celebrate, you see."

"Good," she repeated. "Oh, yes. That will be good."

Henry put on his joking tone. "There's fights tonight. How'd you like to go to the fights?"

"Oh, no," she said breathlessly. "No, I wouldn't like fights."

"Just fooling, Elisa. We'll go to a movie. Let's see. It's two now. I'm going to take Scotty and bring down those steers from the hill. It'll take us maybe two hours. We'll go in town about five and have dinner at the Cominos Hotel. Like that?"

"Of course I'll like it. It's good to eat away from home."

"All right, then. I'll go get up a couple of horses."

She said, "I'll have plenty of time to transplant some of these sets, I guess."

She heard her husband calling Scotty down by the barn. And a little later she saw the two men ride up the pale yellow hillside in search of the steers.

There was a little square sandy bed kept for rooting the chrysanthemums. With her trowel she turned the soil over and over, and smoothed it and patted it firm. Then she dug ten parallel trenches to receive the sets. Back at the chrysanthemum bed she pulled out the little crisp shoots, trimmed off the leaves at each one with her scissors, and laid it on a small orderly pile.

A squeak of wheels and plod of hoofs came from the road. Elisa looked up. The country road ran along the dense bank of willows and cottonwoods that bordered the river, and up this road came a curious vehicle, curiously drawn. It was an old spring-wagon, with a round canvas top on it like the corner of a prairie schooner. It was drawn by an old bay horse and a little grey-and-white burro. A big stubble-bearded man sat between the cover flaps and drove the crawling team. Underneath the wagon, between the hind wheels, a lean and rangy mongrel dog walked sedately. Words were painted on the canvas, in clumsy, crooked letters. "Pots, pans, knives, sisors, lawn mores, Fixed." Two rows of articles, and the triumphantly definitive "Fixed" below. The black paint had run down in little sharp points beneath each letter.

Elisa, squatting on the ground, watched to see the crazy, loose-jointed wagon pass by. But it didn't pass. It turned into the farm road in front of her house, crooked old wheels skirling and squeaking. The rangy dog darted from between the wheels and ran ahead. Instantly the two ranch shepherds flew out at him. Then all three stopped, and with stiff and quivering tails, with taut straight legs, with ambassadorial dignity, they slowly circled, sniffing daintily. The caravan pulled up to Elisa's wire fence and stopped. Now the newcomer dog, feeling outnumbered, lowered his tail and retired under the wagon with raised hackles and bared teeth.

The man on the seat called out, "That's a bad dog in a fight when he gets started."

Elisa laughed. "I see he is. How soon does he generally get started?"

The man caught up her laughter and echoed it heartily. "Sometimes not for weeks and weeks," he said. He climbed stiffly down, over the wheel. The horse and the donkey dropped like unwatered flowers.

Elisa saw that he was a very big man. Although his hair and beard were greying, he did not look old. His worn black suit was wrinkled and spotted with grease. The laughter had disappeared from his face and eyes the moment his laughing voice ceased. His eyes were dark, and they were full of the brooding that gets in the eyes of teamsters and of sailors. The calloused hands he rested on the wire fence were cracked, and every crack was a black line. He took off his battered hat.

"I'm off my general road, ma'am," he said. "Does this dirt road cut over across the river to the Los Angeles highway?"

Elisa stood up and shoved the thick scissors in her apron pocket. "Well, yes, it does, but it winds around and then fords the river. I don't think your team could pull through the sand."

He replied with some asperity, "It might surprise you what them beasts can pull through."

"When they get started?" she asked.

He smiled for a second. "Yes. When they get started."

"Well," said Elisa, "I think you'll save time if you go back to the Salinas road and pick up the highway there."

He drew a big finger down the chicken wire and made it sing. "I ain't in any hurry, ma'am. I go from Seattle to San Diego and back every year. Takes all my time. About six months each way. I aim to follow nice weather."

Elisa took off her gloves and stuffed them in the apron pocket with the scissors. She touched the under edge of her man's hat, searching for fugitive hairs. "That sounds like a nice kind of a way to live," she said.

He leaned confidentially over the fence. "Maybe you noticed the writing on my wagon. I mend pots and sharpen knives and scissors. You got any of them things to do?"

"Oh, no," she said, quickly. "Nothing like that." Her eyes hardened with resistance.

"Scissors is the worst thing," he explained. "Most people just ruin scissors trying to sharpen 'em, but I know how. I got a special tool. It's a little bobbit kind of thing, and patented. But it sure does the trick."

"No. My scissors are all sharp."

"All right, then. Take a pot," he continued earnestly, "a bent pot, or a pot with a hole. I can make it like new so you don't have to buy no new ones. That's a savings for you."

"No," she said shortly. "I tell you I have nothing like that for you to do."

His face fell to an exaggerated sadness. His voice took on a whining undertone. "I ain't had a thing to do today. Maybe I won't have no supper tonight. You see I'm off my regular road. I know folks on the highway clear from Seattle to San Diego. They save their things for me to sharpen up because they know I do it so good and save them money."

"I'm sorry," Elisa said irritably. "I haven't anything for you to do."

His eyes left her face and fell to searching the ground. They roamed about until they came to the chrysanthemum bed where she had been working. "What's them plants, ma'am?"

The irritation and resistance melted from Elisa's face. "Oh, those are chrysanthemums, giant whites and yellows. I raise them every year, bigger than anybody around here."

"Kind of a long-stemmed flower? Looks like a quick puff of colored smoke?" he asked.

"That's it. What a nice way to describe them."

"They smell kind of nasty till you get used to them," he said.

"It's a good bitter smell," she retorted, "not nasty at all."

He changed his tone quickly, "I like the smell myself."

"I had ten-inch-blooms this year," she said.

The man leaned farther over the fence. "Look, I know a lady down the road a piece, has got the nicest garden you ever seen. Got nearly every kind of flower but no chrysanthemums. Last time I was mending a copper-bottom washtub for her (that's a hard job but I do it good), she said to me, 'If you ever run acrost some nice chrysanthemums I wish you'd try to get me a few seeds.' That's what she told me."

Elisa's eyes grew alert and eager. "She couldn't have known much about chrysanthemums. You *can* raise them from seed, but it's much easier to root the little sprouts you see there."

"Oh," he said. "I s'pose I can't take none to her, then."

"Why yes you can," Elisa cried. "I can put some in damp sand, and you can carry them right along with you. They'll take root in the pot if you keep them damp. And then she can transplant them."

"She'd sure like to have some, ma'am. You say they're nice ones?"

"Beautiful," she said. "Oh, beautiful." Her eyes shone. She tore off the battered hat and shook out her dark pretty hair. "I'll put them in a flower pot, and you can take them right with you. Come into the yard."

While the man came through the picket gate Elisa ran excitedly along the geranium-bordered path to the back of the house. And she returned carrying a big red flower pot. The gloves were forgotten now. She kneeled on the ground by the starting bed and dug up the sandy soil with her fingers and scooped it into the bright new flower pot. Then she picked up the little pile of shoots she had prepared. With her strong fingers she pressed them into the sand and tamped around them with her knuckles. The man stood over her. "I'll tell you what to do," she said. "You remember so you can tell the lady."

"Yes, I'll try to remember."

"Well, look. These will take root in about a month. Then she must set them out, about a foot apart in good rich earth like this, see?" She lifted a handful of dark soil for him to look at. "They'll grow fast and tall. Now remember this: In July tell her to cut them down, about eight inches from the ground."

"Before they bloom?" he asked.

"Yes, before they bloom." Her face was tight with eagerness. "They'll grow right up again. About the last of September the buds will start."

She stopped and seemed perplexed. "It's the budding that takes the most care," she said hesitantly. "I don't know how to tell you." She looked deep into his eyes, searchingly. Her mouth opened a little, and she seemed to be listening. "I'll try to tell you," she said. "Did you ever hear of planting hands?"

"Can't say I have, ma'am."

"Well, I can only tell you what it feels like. It's when you're picking off the buds you don't want. Everything goes right down into your fingertips. You watch your fingers work. They do it themselves. You can feel how it is. They pick and pick the buds. They never make a mistake. They're with the plant. Do you see? Your fingers and the plant. You can feel that, right up your arm. They know. They never make a mistake. You can feel it. When you're like that you can't do anything wrong. Do you see that? Can you understand that?"

She was kneeling on the ground looking up at him. Her breast swelled passionately.

The man's eyes narrowed. He looked away self-consciously. "Maybe I know," he said. "Sometimes in the night in the wagon there — "

Elisa's voice grew husky. She broke in on him, "I've never lived as you do, but I know what you mean. When the night is dark — why, the stars are sharp-pointed, and there's quiet. Why, you rise up and up! Every pointed star gets driven into your body. It's like that. Hot and sharp and — lovely."

Kneeling there, her hand went out toward his legs in the greasy black trousers. Her hesitant fingers almost touched the cloth. Then her hand dropped to the ground. She crouched low like a fawning dog.

He said, "It's nice, just like you say. Only when you don't have no dinner, it ain't."

She stood up then, very straight, and her face was ashamed. She held the flower pot out to him and placed it gently in his arms. "Here. Put it in your wagon, on the seat, where you can watch it. Maybe I can find something for you to do."

At the back of the house she dug in the can pile and found two old and battered aluminum saucepans. She carried them back and gave them to him. "Here, maybe you can fix these."

His manner changed. He became professional. "Good as new I can fix them." At the back of his wagon he set a little anvil, and out of an oily tool box dug a small machine hammer. Elisa came through the gate to watch him while he pounded out the dents in the kettles. His mouth grew sure and knowing. At a difficult part of the work he sucked his underlip.

"You sleep right in the wagon?" Elisa asked.

"Right in the wagon, ma'am. Rain or shine I'm dry as a cow in there."

"It must be nice," she said. "It must be very nice. I wish women could do such things."

"It ain't the right kind of a life for a woman."

Her upper lip raised a little, showing her teeth. "How do you know? How can you tell?" she said.

"I don't know, ma'am," he protested. "Of course I don't know. Now here's your kettles, done. You don't have to buy no new ones."

"How much?"

"Oh, fifty cents'll do. I keep my prices down and my work good. That's why I have all them satisfied customers up and down the highway."

Elisa brought him a fifty-cent piece from the house and dropped it in his hand. "You might be surprised to have a rival some time. I can sharpen scissors, too. And I can beat the dents out of little pots. I could show you what a woman might do."

He put his hammer back in the oily box and shoved the little anvil out of sight. "It would be a lonely life for a woman, ma'am, and a scarey life, too, with animals creeping under the wagon all night." He climbed over the singletree, steadying himself with a hand on the burro's white rump. He settled himself in the seat, picked up the lines. "Thank you kindly, ma'am," he said. "I'll do like you told me; I'll go back and catch the Salinas road."

"Mind," she called, "if you're long in getting there, keep the sand damp."

"Sand, ma'am? . . . Sand? Oh, sure. You mean around the chrysanthemums. Sure I will." He clucked his tongue. The beasts leaned luxuriously into their collars. The mongrel dog took his place between the back wheels. The wagon turned and crawled out the entrance road and back the way it had come, along the river.

Elisa stood in front of her wire fence watching the slow progress of the caravan. Her shoulders were straight, her head thrown back, her eyes half-closed, so that the scene came vaguely into them. Her lips moved silently, forming the words "Good-bye — good-bye." Then she whispered, "That's a bright direction. There's a glowing there." The sound of her whisper startled her. She shook herself free and looked about to see whether anyone had been listening. Only the dogs had heard. They lifted their heads toward her from their sleeping in the dust, and then stretched out their chins and settled asleep again. Elisa turned and ran hurriedly into the house.

In the kitchen she reached behind the stove and felt the water tank. It was full of hot water from the noonday cooking. In the bathroom she tore off her soiled clothes and flung them into the corner. And then she scrubbed herself with a little block of pumice, legs and thighs, loins and chest and arms, until her skin was scratched and red. When she had dried herself she stood in front of a mirror in her bedroom and looked at her body. She tightened her stomach and threw out her chest. She turned and looked over her shoulder at her back.

After a while she began to dress, slowly. She put on her newest under-clothing and her nicest stockings and the dress which was the symbol of her prettiness. She worked carefully on her hair, penciled her eyebrows and rouged her lips.

Before she was finished she heard the little thunder of hoofs and the shouts of Henry and his helper as they drove the red steers into the corral. She heard the gate bang shut and set herself for Henry's arrival.

His step sounded on the porch. He entered the house calling, "Elisa, where are you?"

"In my room, dressing. I'm not ready. There's hot water for your bath. Hurry up. It's getting late."

When she heard him splashing in the tub, Elisa laid his dark suit on the bed, and shirt and socks and tie beside it. She stood his polished shoes on the floor beside the bed. Then she went to the porch and sat primly and stiffly down. She looked toward the river road where the willow-line was still yellow with frosted leaves so that under the high grey fog they seemed a thin band of sunshine. This was the only color in the grey afternoon. She sat unmoving for a long time. Her eyes blinked rarely.

Henry came banging out of the door, shoving his tie inside his vest as he came. Elisa stiffened and her face grew tight. Henry stopped short and looked at her. "Why — why, Elisa. You look so nice!"

"Nice? You think I look nice? What do you mean by 'nice'?"

Henry blundered on. "I don't know. I mean you look different, strong and happy."

"I am strong? Yes, strong. What do you mean 'strong'?"

He looked bewildered. "You're playing some kind of a game," he said helplessly. "It's a kind of a play. You look strong enough to break a calf over your knee, happy enough to eat it like a watermelon."

For a second she lost her rigidity. "Henry! Don't talk like that. You didn't know what you said." She grew complete again. "I'm strong," she boasted, "I never knew before how strong."

Henry looked down toward the tractor shed, and when he brought his eyes back to her, they were his own again. "I'll get out the car. You can put on your coat while I'm starting."

Elisa went into the house. She heard him drive to the gate and idle down his motor, and then she took a long time to put on her hat. She pulled it here and pressed it there. When Henry turned the motor off she slipped into her coat and went out.

The little roadster bounced along on the dirt road by the river, raising the birds and driving the rabbits into the brush. Two cranes flapped heavily over the willow-line and dropped into the river-bed.

Far ahead on the road Elisa saw a dark speck. She knew.

She tried not to look as they passed it, but her eyes would not obey. She whispered to herself sadly, "He might have thrown them off the road. That wouldn't have been much trouble, not very much. But he kept the pot," she explained. "He had to keep the pot. That's why he couldn't get them off the road."

The roadster turned a bend and she saw the caravan ahead. She swung full around toward her husband so she could not see the little covered wagon and the mismatched team as the car passed them.

In a moment it was over. The thing was done. She did not look back.

She said loudly, to be heard above the motor. "It will be good, tonight, a good dinner."

"Now you're changed again," Henry complained. He took one hand from the wheel and patted her knee. "I ought to take you in to dinner oftener. It would be good for both of us. We get so heavy out on the ranch."

"Henry," she asked, "could we have wine at dinner?"

"Sure we could. Say! That will be fine."

She was silent for a while; then she said, "Henry, at those prize fights, do the men hurt each other very much?"

"Sometimes a little, not often. Why?"

"Well, I've read how they break noses, and blood runs down their chests. I've read how the fighting gloves get heavy and soggy with blood."

He looked around at her. "What's the matter, Elisa? I didn't know you read things like that." He brought the car to a stop, then turned to the right over the Salinas River bridge.

"Do any women ever go to the fights?" she asked.

"Oh, sure, some. What's the matter Elisa? Do you want to go? I don't think you'd like it, but I'll take you if you really want to go."

She relaxed limply in the seat. "Oh, no. No. I don't want to go. I'm sure I don't." Her face was turned away from him. "It will be enough if we can have wine. It will be plenty." She turned up her coat collar so he could not see that she was crying weakly — like an old woman.

∽∾∽

AMY TAN (b. 1952) was born in Oakland, California. Her father was educated as an engineer in Beijing; her mother left China in 1949, just before the communist revolution. Tan remembers that as a child she felt like an American girl trapped in a Chinese body: "There was shame and self-hate. There is this myth that America is a melting pot, but what happens in assimilation is that we end up deliberately choosing the American things — hot dogs and apple pie — and ignoring the Chinese offerings."

After her father's death, Tan and her mother lived in Switzerland, where she attended high school. "I was a novelty," she recalls. "There were so few Asians in Europe that everywhere I went people stared. Europeans asked me out. I had never been asked out in America." After attending a small college in Oregon, she worked for IBM as a writer of computer manuals. In 1984 Tan and her mother visited China and met her relatives; there she made the important discovery, as she has said, that "I belonged to my family and my family belonged to China." A year later, back in San Francisco, Tan read Louise Erdrich's Love Medicine and was so impressed by the power of its interlocking stories about another cultural minority, American Indians, that she began to write short stories herself. One of them was published in a little magazine read by a literary agent in San Diego, who urged Tan to outline a book about the conflicts between different cultures and generations of Chinese mothers and daughters in the United States. After her agent negotiated a $50,000 advance from Putnam, Tan worked full-time on the first draft of her book The Joy Luck Club (1989) and finished it in four months.

*"Two Kinds" is an excerpt from that novel. At first Tan thought her book con-
tract was "all a token minority thing. I thought they had to fill a quota since there
weren't many Chinese Americans writing." But her book was a best-seller and was
nominated for a National Book Award. As the novelist Valerie Miner has recognized,
Tan's special gifts are her storytelling ability and her "remarkable ear for dialogue and
dialect, representing the choppy English of the mother and the sloppy California ver-
nacular of the daughter with a sensitive authenticity." At the heart of Tan's book is the
tough bond between mother and daughter. "I'm my own person," the daughter says.
"How can she be her own person," the mother answers. "When did I give her up?"
Tan has also published another novel,* The Kitchen God's Wife *(1992), and a children's book,* The Moon Lady *(1992).*

AMY TAN

Two Kinds   *1989*

My mother believed you could be anything you wanted to be in America. You could open a restaurant. You could work for the government and get
good retirement. You could buy a house with almost no money down. You
could become rich. You could become instantly famous.

"Of course you can be prodigy, too," my mother told me when I was
nine. "You can be best anything. What does Auntie Lindo know? Her daughter, she is only best tricky."

America was where all my mother's hopes lay. She had come here in
1949 after losing everything in China: her mother and father, her family home,
her first husband, and two daughters, twin baby girls. But she never looked
back with regret. There were so many ways for things to get better.

We didn't immediately pick the right kind of prodigy. At first my mother
thought I could be a Chinese Shirley Temple. We'd watch Shirley's old movies
on TV as though they were training films. My mother would poke my arm
and say, *"Ni kan"* — You watch. And I would see Shirley tapping her feet, or
singing a sailor song, or pursing her lips into a very round O while saying,
"Oh my goodness."

"Ni kan," said my mother as Shirley's eyes flooded with tears. "You already know how. Don't need talent for crying!"

Soon after my mother got this idea about Shirley Temple, she took me to
a beauty training school in the Mission district and put me in the hands of a
student who could barely hold the scissors without shaking. Instead of getting
big fat curls, I emerged with an uneven mass of crinkly black fuzz. My mother
dragged me off to the bathroom and tried to wet down my hair.

"You look like Negro Chinese," she lamented, as if I had done this on
purpose.

The instructor of the beauty training school had to lop off these soggy
clumps to make my hair even again. "Peter Pan is very popular these days,"
the instructor assured my mother. I now had hair the length of a boy's, with

straight-across bangs that hung at a slant two inches above my eyebrows. I liked the haircut and it made me actually look forward to my future fame.

In fact, in the beginning, I was just as excited as my mother, maybe even more so. I pictured this prodigy part of me as many different images, trying each one on for size. I was a dainty ballerina girl standing by the curtains, waiting to hear the right music that would send me floating on my tiptoes. I was like the Christ child lifted out of the straw manger, crying with holy indignity. I was Cinderella stepping from her pumpkin carriage with sparkly cartoon music filling the air.

In all of my imaginings, I was filled with a sense that I would soon become *perfect*. My mother and father would adore me. I would be beyond reproach. I would never feel the need to sulk for anything.

But sometimes the prodigy in me became impatient. "If you don't hurry up and get me out of here, I'm disappearing for good," it warned. "And then you'll always be nothing."

Every night after dinner, my mother and I would sit at the Formica kitchen table. She would present new tests, taking her examples from stories of amazing children she had read in *Ripley's Believe It or Not*, or *Good Housekeeping, Reader's Digest*, and a dozen other magazines she kept in a pile in our bathroom. My mother got these magazines from people whose houses she cleaned. And since she cleaned many houses each week, we had a great assortment. She would look through them all, searching for stories about remarkable children.

The first night she brought out a story about a three-year-old boy who knew the capitals of all the states and even most of the European countries. A teacher was quoted as saying the little boy could also pronounce the names of the foreign cities correctly.

"What's the capital of Finland?" my mother asked me, looking at the magazine story.

All I knew was the capital of California, because Sacramento was the name of the street we lived on in Chinatown. "Nairobi!" I guessed, saying the most foreign word I could think of. She checked to see if that was possibly one way to pronounce "Helsinki" before showing me the answer.

The tests got harder — multiplying numbers in my head, finding the queen of hearts in a deck of cards, trying to stand on my head without using my hands, predicting the daily temperatures in Los Angeles, New York, and London.

One night I had to look at a page from the Bible for three minutes and then report everything I could remember. "Now Jehoshaphat had riches and honor in abundance and . . . that's all I remember, Ma," I said.

And after seeing my mother's disappointed face once again, something inside of me began to die. I hated the tests, the raised hopes and failed expectations. Before going to bed that night, I looked in the mirror above the bathroom sink and when I saw only my face staring back — and that it would always be this ordinary face — I began to cry. Such a sad, ugly girl! I made high-pitched noises like a crazed animal, trying to scratch out the face in the mirror.

And then I saw what seemed to be the prodigy side of me — because I had never seen that face before. I looked at my reflection, blinking so I could see more clearly. The girl staring back at me was angry, powerful. This girl and I were the same. I had new thoughts, willful thoughts, or rather thoughts filled with lots of won'ts. I won't let her change me, I promised myself. I won't be what I'm not.

So now on nights when my mother presented her tests, I performed listlessly, my head propped on one arm. I pretended to be bored. And I was. I got so bored I started counting the bellows of the foghorns out on the bay while my mother drilled me in other areas. The sound was comforting and reminded me of the cow jumping over the moon. And the next day, I played a game with myself, seeing if my mother would give up on me before eight bellows. After a while I usually counted only one, maybe two bellows at most. At last she was beginning to give up hope.

Two or three months had gone by without any mention of my being a prodigy again. And then one day my mother was watching *The Ed Sullivan Show* on TV. The TV was old and the sound kept shorting out. Every time my mother got halfway up from the sofa to adjust the set, the sound would go back on and Ed would be talking. As soon as she sat down, Ed would go silent again. She got up, the TV broke into loud piano music. She sat down. Silence. Up and down, back and forth, quiet and loud. It was like a stiff embraceless dance between her and the TV set. Finally she stood by the set with her hand on the sound dial.

She seemed entranced by the music, a little frenzied piano piece with this mesmerizing quality, sort of quick passages and then teasing lilting ones before it returned to the quick playful parts.

"*Ni kan,*" my mother said, calling me over with hurried hand gestures. "Look here."

I could see why my mother was fascinated by the music. It was being pounded out by a little Chinese girl, about nine years old, with a Peter Pan haircut. The girl had the sauciness of a Shirley Temple. She was proudly modest like a proper Chinese child. And she also did this fancy sweep of a curtsy, so that the fluffy skirt of her white dress cascaded slowly to the floor like the petals of a large carnation.

In spite of these warning signs, I wasn't worried. Our family had no piano and we couldn't afford to buy one, let alone reams of sheet music and piano lessons. So I could be generous in my comments when my mother bad-mouthed the little girl on TV.

"Play note right, but doesn't sound good! No singing sound," complained my mother.

"What are you picking on her for?" I said carelessly. "She's pretty good. Maybe she's not the best, but she's trying hard." I knew almost immediately I would be sorry I said that.

"Just like you," she said. "Not the best. Because you not trying." She gave a little huff as she let go of the sound dial and sat down on the sofa.

The little Chinese girl sat down also to play an encore of "Anitra's

Dance" by Grieg. I remember the song, because later on I had to learn how to play it.

Three days after watching *The Ed Sullivan Show*, my mother told me what my schedule would be for piano lessons and piano practice. She had talked to Mr. Chong, who lived on the first floor of our apartment building. Mr. Chong was a retired piano teacher and my mother had traded house-cleaning services for weekly lessons and a piano for me to practice on every day, two hours a day, from four until six.

When my mother told me this, I felt as though I had been sent to hell. I whined and then kicked my foot a little when I couldn't stand it anymore.

"Why don't you like me the way I am? I'm *not* a genius! I can't play the piano. And even if I could, I wouldn't go on TV if you paid me a million dollars!" I cried.

My mother slapped me. "Who ask you be genius?" she shouted. "Only ask you be your best. For you sake. You think I want you be genius? Hnnh! What for! Who ask you!"

"So ungrateful," I heard her mutter in Chinese. "If she had as much talent as she has temper, she would be famous now."

Mr. Chong, whom I secretly nicknamed Old Chong, was very strange, always tapping his fingers to the silent music of an invisible orchestra. He looked ancient in my eyes. He had lost most of the hair on top of his head and he wore thick glasses and had eyes that always looked tired and sleepy. But he must have been younger than I thought, since he lived with his mother and was not yet married.

I met Old Lady Chong once and that was enough. She had this peculiar smell like a baby that had done something in its pants. And her fingers felt like a dead person's, like an old peach I once found in the back of the refrigerator; the skin just slid off the meat when I picked it up.

I soon found out why Old Chong had retired from teaching piano. He was deaf. "Like Beethoven!" he shouted to me. "We're both listening only in our head!" And he would start to conduct his frantic silent sonatas.

Our lessons went like this. He would open the book and point to different things, explaining their purpose: "Key! Treble! Bass! No sharps or flats! So this is C major! Listen now and play after me!"

And then he would play the C scale a few times, a simple chord, and then, as if inspired by an old, unreachable itch, he gradually added more notes and running trills and a pounding bass until the music was really something quite grand.

I would play after him, the simple scale, the simple chord, and then I just played some nonsense that sounded like a cat running up and down on top of garbage cans. Old Chong smiled and applauded and then said, "Very good! But now you must learn to keep time!"

So that's how I discovered that Old Chong's eyes were too slow to keep up with the wrong notes I was playing. He went through the motions in half-time. To help me keep rhythm, he stood behind me, pushing down on my right shoulder for every beat. He balanced pennies on top of my wrists so I would keep them still as I slowly played scales and arpeggios. He had me curve my hand around an apple and keep that shape when playing chords. He marched stiffly to show me how to make each finger dance up and down, staccato like an obedient little soldier.

He taught me all these things, and that was how I also learned I could be lazy and get away with mistakes, lots of mistakes. If I hit the wrong notes because I hadn't practiced enough, I never corrected myself. I just kept playing in rhythm. And Old Chong kept conducting his own private reverie.

So maybe I never really gave myself a fair chance. I did pick up the basics pretty quickly, and I might have become a good pianist at that young age. But I was so determined not to try, not to be anybody different that I learned to play only the most ear-splitting preludes, the most discordant hymns.

Over the next year, I practiced like this, dutifully in my own way. And then one day I heard my mother and her friend Lindo Jong both talking in a loud bragging tone of voice so others could hear. It was after church, and I was leaning against the brick wall wearing a dress with stiff white petticoats. Auntie Lindo's daughter, Waverly, who was about my age, was standing farther down the wall about five feet away. We had grown up together and shared all the closeness of two sisters squabbling over crayons and dolls. In other words, for the most part, we hated each other. I thought she was snotty. Waverly Jong had gained a certain amount of fame as "Chinatown's Littlest Chinese Chess Champion."

"She bring home too many trophy," lamented Auntie Lindo that Sunday. "All day she play chess. All day I have no time do nothing but dust off her winnings." She threw a scolding look at Waverly, who pretended not to see her.

"You lucky you don't have this problem," said Auntie Lindo with a sigh to my mother.

And my mother squared her shoulders and bragged: "Our problem worser than yours. If we ask Jing-mei wash dish, she hear nothing but music. It's like you can't stop this natural talent."

And right then, I was determined to put a stop to her foolish pride.

A few weeks later, Old Chong and my mother conspired to have me play in a talent show which would be held in the church hall. By then, my parents had saved up enough to buy me a secondhand piano, a black Wurlitzer spinet with a scarred bench. It was the showpiece of our living room.

For the talent show, I was to play a piece called "Pleading Child" from Schumann's *Scenes from Childhood*. It was a simple, moody piece that sounded more difficult than it was. I was supposed to memorize the whole thing, playing the repeat parts twice to make the piece sound longer. But I dawdled over it, playing a few bars and then cheating, looking up to see what notes followed. I never really listened to what I was playing. I daydreamed about being somewhere else, about being someone else.

The part I liked to practice best was the fancy curtsy: right foot out, touch the rose on the carpet with a pointed foot, sweep to the side, left leg bends, look up and smile.

My parents invited all the couples from the Joy Luck Club to witness my debut. Auntie Lindo and Uncle Tin were there. Waverly and her two older brothers had also come. The first two rows were filled with children both younger and older than I was. The littlest ones got to go first. They recited simple nursery rhymes, squawked out tunes on miniature violins, twirled Hula Hoops, pranced in pink ballet tutus, and when they bowed or curtsied, the audience would sigh in unison, "Awww," and then clap enthusiastically.

When my turn came, I was very confident. I remember my childish excitement. It was as if I knew, without a doubt, that the prodigy side of me really did exist. I had no fear whatsoever, no nervousness. I remember thinking to myself, This is it! This is it! I looked out over the audience, at my mother's blank face, my father's yawn, Auntie Lindo's stiff-lipped smile, Waverly's sulky expression. I had on a white dress layered with sheets of lace, and a pink bow in my Peter Pan haircut. As I sat down I envisioned people jumping to their feet and Ed Sullivan rushing up to introduce me to everyone on TV.

And I started to play. It was so beautiful. I was so caught up in how lovely I looked that at first I didn't worry how I would sound. So it was a surprise to me when I hit the first wrong note and I realized something didn't sound quite right. And then I hit another and another followed that. A chill started at the top of my head and began to trickle down. Yet I couldn't stop playing, as though my hands were bewitched. I kept thinking my fingers would adjust themselves back, like a train switching to the right track. I played this strange jumble through two repeats, the sour notes staying with me all the way to the end.

When I stood up, I discovered my legs were shaking. Maybe I had just been nervous and the audience, like Old Chong, had seen me go through the right motions and had not heard anything wrong at all. I swept my right foot out, went down on my knee, looked up and smiled. The room was quiet, except for Old Chong, who was beaming and shouting, "Bravo! Bravo! Well done!" But then I saw my mother's face, her stricken face. The audience clapped weakly, and as I walked back to my chair, with my whole face quivering as I tried not to cry, I heard a little boy whisper loudly to his mother, "That was awful," and the mother whispered back, "Well, she certainly tried."

And now I realized how many people were in the audience, the whole world it seemed. I was aware of eyes burning into my back. I felt the shame of my mother and father as they sat stiffly throughout the rest of the show.

We could have escaped during intermission. Pride and some strange sense of honor must have anchored my parents to their chairs. And so we watched it all: the eighteen-year-old boy with a fake mustache who did a magic show and juggled flaming hoops while riding a unicycle. The breasted girl with white makeup who sang from *Madama Butterfly* and got honorable mention. And the eleven-year-old boy who won first prize playing a tricky violin song that sounded like a busy bee.

After the show, the Hsus, the Jongs, and the St. Clairs from the Joy Luck Club came up to my mother and father.

"Lots of talented kids," Auntie Lindo said vaguely, smiling broadly.

"That was somethin' else," said my father, and I wondered if he was referring to me in a humorous way, or whether he even remembered what I had done.

Waverly looked at me and shrugged her shoulders. "You aren't a genius like me," she said matter-of-factly. And if I hadn't felt so bad, I would have pulled her braids and punched her stomach.

But my mother's expression was what devastated me: a quiet, blank look that said she had lost everything. I felt the same way, and it seemed as if everybody were now coming up, like gawkers at the scene of an accident, to see what parts were actually missing. When we got on the bus to go home, my father was humming the busy-bee tune and my mother was silent. I kept thinking she wanted to wait until we got home before shouting at me. But when my father unlocked the door to our apartment, my mother walked in and then went to the back, into the bedroom. No accusations. No blame. And in a way, I felt disappointed. I had been waiting for her to start shouting, so I could shout back and cry and blame her for all my misery.

I assumed my talent-show fiasco meant I never had to play the piano again. But two days later, after school, my mother came out of the kitchen and saw me watching TV.

"Four clock," she reminded me as if it were any other day. I was stunned, as though she were asking me to go through the talent-show torture again. I wedged myself more tightly in front of the TV.

"Turn off TV," she called from the kitchen five minutes later.

I didn't budge. And then I decided. I didn't have to do what my mother said anymore. I wasn't her slave. This wasn't China. I had listened to her before and look what happened. She was the stupid one.

She came out from the kitchen and stood in the arched entryway of the living room. "Four clock," she said once again, louder.

"I'm not going to play anymore," I said nonchalantly. "Why should I? I'm not a genius."

She walked over and stood in front of the TV. I saw her chest was heaving up and down in an angry way.

"No!" I said, and I now felt stronger, as if my true self had finally emerged. So this was what had been inside me all along.

"No! I won't!" I screamed.

She yanked me by the arm, pulled me off the floor, snapped off the TV. She was frighteningly strong, half pulling, half carrying me toward the piano as I kicked the throw rugs under my feet. She lifted me up and onto the hard bench. I was sobbing by now, looking at her bitterly. Her chest was heaving even more and her mouth was open, smiling crazily as if she were pleased I was crying.

"You want me to be someone that I'm not!" I sobbed. "I'll never be the kind of daughter you want me to be!"

"Only two kinds of daughters," she shouted in Chinese. "Those who are obedient and those who follow their own mind! Only one kind of daughter can live in this house. Obedient daughter!"

"Then I wish I wasn't your daughter. I wish you weren't my mother," I shouted. As I said these things I got scared. I felt like worms and toads and slimy things were crawling out of my chest, but it also felt good, as if this awful side of me had surfaced, at last.

"Too late change this," said my mother shrilly.

And I could sense her anger rising to its breaking point. I wanted to see it spill over. And that's when I remembered the babies she had lost in China, the ones we never talked about. "Then I wish I'd never been born!" I shouted. "I wish I were dead! Like them."

It was as if I had said the magic words, Alakazam! — and her face went blank, her mouth closed, her arms went slack, and she backed out of the room, stunned, as if she were blowing away like a small brown leaf, thin, brittle, lifeless.

It was not the only disappointment my mother felt in me. In the years that followed, I failed her so many times, each time asserting my own will, my right to fall short of expectations. I didn't get straight As. I didn't become class president. I didn't get into Stanford. I dropped out of college.

For unlike my mother, I did not believe I could be anything I wanted to be. I could only be me.

And for all those years, we never talked about the disaster at the recital or my terrible accusations afterward at the piano bench. All that remained unchecked, like a betrayal that was now unspeakable. So I never found a way to ask her why she had hoped for something so large that failure was inevitable.

And even worse, I never asked her what frightened me the most: Why had she given up hope?

For after our struggle at the piano, she never mentioned my playing again. The lessons stopped, the lid to the piano was closed, shutting out the dust, my misery, and her dreams.

So she surprised me. A few years ago, she offered to give me the piano, for my thirtieth birthday. I had not played in all those years. I saw the offer as a sign of forgiveness, a tremendous burden removed.

"Are you sure?" I asked shyly. "I mean, won't you and Dad miss it?"

"No, this your piano," she said firmly. "Always your piano. You only one can play."

"Well, I probably can't play anymore," I said. "It's been years."

"You pick up fast," said my mother, as if she knew this was certain. "You have natural talent. You could been genius if you want to."

"No I couldn't."

"You just not trying," said my mother. And she was neither angry nor sad. She said it as if to announce a fact that could never be disproved. "Take it," she said.

But I didn't at first. It was enough that she had offered it to me. And after that, every time I saw it in my parents' living room, standing in front of the bay windows, it made me feel proud, as if it were a shiny trophy I had won back.

• • •

Last week I sent a tuner over to my parents' apartment and had the piano reconditioned, for purely sentimental reasons. My mother had died a few months before and I had been getting things in order for my father, a little bit at a time. I put the jewelry in special silk pouches. The sweaters she had knitted in yellow, pink, bright orange — all the colors I hated — I put those in moth-proof boxes. I found some old Chinese silk dresses, the kind with little slits up the sides. I rubbed the old silk against my skin, then wrapped them in tissue and decided to take them home with me.

After I had the piano tuned, I opened the lid and touched the keys. It sounded even richer than I remembered. Really, it was a very good piano. Inside the bench were the same exercise notes with handwritten scales, the same secondhand music books with their covers held together with yellow tape.

I opened up the Schumann book to the dark little piece I had played at the recital. It was on the left-hand side of the page, "Pleading Child." It looked more difficult than I remembered. I played a few bars, surprised at how easily the notes came back to me.

And for the first time, or so it seemed, I noticed the piece on the right-hand side. It was called "Perfectly Contented." I tried to play this one as well. It had a lighter melody but the same flowing rhythm and turned out to be quite easy. "Pleading Child" was shorter but slower; "Perfectly Contented" was longer but faster. And after I played them both a few times, I realized they were two halves of the same song.

᠗Ꮼ

LEO TOLSTOY *(1828–1910) is generally considered the greatest Russian writer of prose fiction. Born on his parents' estate in the province of Tulu, he spent his years at the university drinking and gambling like many other noblemen, but in his twenties he joined the Russian army and began writing sketches of military life. After he left the army and traveled in Europe, he settled down to writing. He produced his two great novels,* War and Peace *and* Anna Karenina, *in 1869 and 1877, respectively. As Tolstoy grew older, he began to be dissatisfied with literature, reaching the conclusion that art is ungodly because it is founded on imagination. Vladimir Nabokov described Tolstoy's obsession thus: "Somehow, the process of seeking the Truth seemed more important to him than the easy, vivid, brilliant discovery of the illusion of truth through the medium of his artistic genius." In his eighties Tolstoy decided that by living comfortably on his country estate he was betraying his ideal of simple, saintly existence, so he wandered away from his home, heading for a monastery. He died in the waiting room of a little railway station, refusing to let his wife come near him.*

In "The Soul of the Artist" (1896), an essay about Guy de Maupassant, Tolstoy wrote:

> *The cement which binds together every work of art into a whole and thereby produces the effect of lifelike illusion, is not the unity of persons and places, but that of the author's independent moral relation to the subject. . . . Therefore, a writer who has not a clear, definite, and fresh view of the universe, and especially a writer who does not even consider this necessary, cannot produce*

a work of art. He may write much and beautifully, but a work of art will not result.

The chief theme of Tolstoy's writing, as in his great story "The Death of Ivan Ilych" (1886), is that the only certain happiness is to live for others. This helps to explain the tragedy of Ivan Ilych, who just before his death realizes that he has not lived as he should have. The story took Tolstoy two years to finish. In its first version, it was told in the first person by a colleague, who was given the diary Ivan Ilych kept during his fatal illness. The narrator begins, "It is impossible, absolutely impossible, to live as I have lived, and as we all live. I realized that as a result of the death of an acquaintance of mine, Ivan Ilych, and of the diary he left behind." Finally Tolstoy told the story in the third person, without using the diary.

RELATED COMMENTARIES: Peter Rudy, "Tolstoy's Revisions in 'The Death of Ivan Ilych,'" page 790; Leo Tolstoy, "Chekhov's Intent in 'The Darling,'" page 801; and "Shakespeare's Immoral Frame of Mind," page 2048.

Leo Tolstoy

The Death of Ivan Ilych 1886

TRANSLATED BY LOUISE MAUDE AND AYLMER MAUDE

I

During an interval in the Melvinski trial in the large building of the Law Courts, the members and public prosecutor met in Ivan Egorovich Shebek's private room, where the conversation turned on the celebrated Krasovski case. Fëdor Vasilievich warmly maintained that it was not subject to their jurisdiction, Ivan Egorovich maintained the contrary, while Peter Ivanovich, not having entered into the discussion at the start, took no part in it but looked through the *Gazette* which had just been handed in.

"Gentlemen," he said, "Ivan Ilych has died!"

"You don't say so!"

"Here, read it yourself," replied Peter Ivanovich, handing Fëdor Vasilievich the paper still damp from the press. Surrounded by a black border were the words: "Praskovya Fëdorovna Golovina, with profound sorrow, informs relatives and friends of the demise of her beloved husband Ivan Ilych Golovin, Member of the Court of Justice, which occurred on February the 4th of this year 1882. The funeral will take place on Friday at one o'clock in the afternoon."

Ivan Ilych had been a colleague of the gentlemen present and was liked by them all. He had been ill for some weeks with an illness said to be incurable. His post had been kept open for him, but there had been conjectures that in case of his death Alexeev might receive his appointment, and that either Vinnikov or Shtabel would succeed Alexeev. So on receiving the news of Ivan Ilych's death the first thought of each of the gentlemen in that private room was of the changes and promotions it might occasion among themselves or their acquaintances.

"I shall be sure to get Shtabel's place or Vinnikov's," thought Fëdor Vasilievich. "I was promised that long ago, and the promotion means an extra eight hundred rubles a year for me besides the allowance."

"Now I must apply for my brother-in-law's transfer from Kaluga," thought Peter Ivanovich. "My wife will be very glad, and then she won't be able to say that I never do anything for her relations."

"I thought he would never leave his bed again," said Peter Ivanovich aloud. "It's very sad."

"But what really was the matter with him?"

"The doctors couldn't say — at least they could, but each of them said something different. When last I saw him I thought he was getting better."

"And I haven't been to see him since the holidays. I always meant to go."

"Had he any property?"

"I think his wife had a little — but something quite trifling."

"We shall have to go to see her, but they live so terribly far away."

"Far away from you, you mean. Everything's far away from your place."

"You see, he never can forgive my living on the other side of the river," said Peter Ivanovich, smiling at Shebek. Then, still talking of the distances between different parts of the city, they returned to the Court.

Besides considerations as to the possible transfers and promotions likely to result from Ivan Ilych's death, the mere fact of the death of a near acquaintance aroused, as usual, in all who heard of it the complacent feeling that, "it is he who is dead and not I."

Each one thought or felt, "Well, he's dead but I'm alive!" But the more intimate of Ivan Ilych's acquaintances, his so-called friends, could not help thinking also that they would now have to fulfill the very tiresome demands of propriety by attending the funeral service and paying a visit of condolence to the widow.

Fëdor Vasilievich and Peter Ivanovich had been his nearest acquaintances. Peter Ivanovich had studied law with Ivan Ilych and had considered himself to be under obligations to him.

Having told his wife at dinner-time of Ivan Ilych's death and of his conjecture that it might be possible to get her brother transferred to their circuit, Peter Ivanovich sacrificed his usual nap, put on his evening clothes, and drove to Ivan Ilych's house.

At the entrance stood a carriage and two cabs. Leaning against the wall in the hall downstairs near the cloak-stand was a coffin-lid covered with cloth of gold, ornamented with gold cord and tassels, that had been polished up with metal powder. Two ladies in black were taking off their fur cloaks. Peter Ivanovich recognized one of them as Ivan Ilych's sister, but the other was a stranger to him. His colleague Schwartz was just coming downstairs, but on seeing Peter Ivanovich enter he stopped and winked at him, as if to say: "Ivan Ilych has made a mess of things — not like you and me."

Schwartz's face, with his Piccadilly whiskers and his slim figure in evening dress, had as usual an air of elegant solemnity which contrasted with the playfulness of his character and had a special piquancy here, or so it seemed to Peter Ivanovich.

Peter Ivanovich allowed the ladies to precede him and slowly followed them upstairs. Schwartz did not come down but remained where he was, and Peter Ivanovich understood that he wanted to arrange where they should play bridge that evening. The ladies went upstairs to the widow's room, and Schwartz, with seriously compressed lips but a playful look in his eyes, indicated by a twist of his eyebrows the room to the right where the body lay.

Peter Ivanovich, like everyone else on such occasions, entered feeling uncertain what he would have to do. All he knew was that at such times it is always safe to cross oneself. But he was not quite sure whether one should make obeisances while doing so. He therefore adopted a middle course. On entering the room he began crossing himself and made a slight movement resembling a bow. At the same time, as far as the motion of his head and arm allowed, he surveyed the room. Two young men — apparently nephews, one of whom was a high-school pupil — were leaving the room, crossing themselves as they did so. An old woman was standing motionless, and a lady with strangely arched eyebrows was saying something to her in a whisper. A vigorous, resolute Church Reader, in a frock-coat, was reading something in a loud voice with an expression that precluded any contradiction. The butler's assistant, Gerasim, stepping lightly in front of Peter Ivanovich, was strewing something on the floor. Noticing this, Peter Ivanovich was immediately aware of a faint odor of a decomposing body.

The last time he had called on Ivan Ilych, Peter Ivanovich had seen Gerasim in the study. Ivan Ilych had been particularly fond of him and he was performing the duty of a sick nurse.

Peter Ivanovich continued to make the sign of the cross, slightly inclining his head in an intermediate direction between the coffin, the Reader, and the icons on the table in a corner of the room. Afterwards, when it seemed to him that this movement of his arm in crossing himself had gone on too long, he stopped and began to look at the corpse.

The dead man lay, as dead men always lie, in a specially heavy way, his rigid limbs sunk in the soft cushions of the coffin, with the head forever bowed on the pillow. His yellow waxen brow with bald patches over his sunken temples was thrust up in the way peculiar to the dead, the protruding nose seeming to press on the upper lip. He was much changed and had grown even thinner since Peter Ivanovich had last seen him, but, as is always the case with the dead, his face was handsomer and above all more dignified than when he was alive. The expression on the face said that what was necessary had been accomplished, and accomplished rightly. Besides this there was in that expression a reproach and a warning to the living. This warning seemed to Peter Ivanovich out of place, or at least not applicable to him. He felt a certain discomfort and so he hurriedly crossed himself once more and turned and went out the door — too hurriedly and too regardless of propriety, as he himself was aware.

Schwartz was waiting for him in the adjoining room with legs spread wide apart and both hands toying with his top-hat behind his back. The mere sight of that playful, well-groomed, and elegant figure refreshed Peter Ivanovich. He felt that Schwartz was above all these happenings and would not surrender to any depressing influences. His very look said that this incident of a church service for Ivan Ilych could not be a sufficient reason for infringing the order of the session — in other words, that it would certainly not prevent his unwrapping a new pack of cards and shuffling them that evening while a footman placed four fresh candles on the table: in fact, that there was no reason for supposing that this incident would hinder their spending the evening agreeably. Indeed he said this in a whisper as Peter Ivanovich passed him, proposing that they should meet for a game at Fëdor Vasilievich's. But apparently Peter Ivanovich was not destined to play bridge that evening. Praskovya Fëdorovna (a short, fat woman who despite all efforts to the contrary had continued to broaden steadily from her shoulders downwards and who had the same extraordinarily arched eyebrows as the lady who had been standing by the coffin), dressed all in black, her head covered with lace, came out of her own room with some other ladies, conducted them to the room where the dead body lay, and said: "The service will begin immediately. Please go in."

Schwartz, making an indefinite bow, stood still, evidently neither accepting nor declining this invitation. Praskovya Fëdorovna, recognizing Peter Ivanovich, sighed, went close up to him, took his hand, and said: "I know you were a true friend to Ivan Ilych . . ." and looked at him awaiting some suitable response. And Peter Ivanovich knew that, just as it had been the right thing to cross himself in that room, so what he had to do here was to press her hand, sigh, and say, "Believe me. . . ." So he did all this and as he did it felt that the desired result had been achieved: that both he and she were touched.

"Come with me. I want to speak to you before it begins," said the widow. "Give me your arm."

Peter Ivanovich gave her his arm and they went to the inner rooms, passing Schwartz, who winked at Peter Ivanovich compassionately.

"That does for our bridge! Don't object if we find another player. Perhaps you can cut in when you do escape," said his playful look.

Peter Ivanovich sighed still more deeply and despondently, and Praskovya Fëdorovna pressed his arm gratefully. When they reached the drawing-room, upholstered in pink cretonne and lighted by a dim lamp, they sat down at the table — she on a sofa and Peter Ivanovich on a low pouffe, the springs of which yielded spasmodically under his weight. Praskovya Fëdorovna had been on the point of warning him to take another seat, but felt that such a warning was out of keeping with her present condition and so changed her mind. As he sat down on the pouffe Peter Ivanovich recalled how Ivan Ilych had arranged this room and had consulted him regarding this pink cretonne with green leaves. The whole room was full of furniture and knick-knacks, and on her way to the sofa the lace of the widow's black shawl caught on the carved edge of the table. Peter Ivanovich rose to detach it, and the springs of the pouffe, relieved of his weight, rose also and gave him a push. The widow began detaching her shawl herself, and Peter Ivanovich again sat down, suppressing the rebellious springs of the pouffe under him. But the widow had not quite freed herself and Peter Ivanovich got up again, and again the pouffe rebelled and even creaked. When this was all over she took out a clean cambric handkerchief and began to weep. The episode with the shawl and the struggle with the pouffe had cooled Peter Ivanovich's emotions and he sat there with a sullen look on his face. This awkward situation was interrupted by Sokolov, Ivan Ilych's butler, who came to report that the plot in the cemetery that Praskovya Fëdorovna had chosen would cost two hundred rubles. She stopped weeping and, looking at Peter Ivanovich with the air of a victim, remarked in French that it was very hard for her. Peter Ivanovich made a silent gesture signifying his full conviction that it must indeed be so.

"Please smoke," she said in a magnanimous yet crushed voice, and turned to discuss with Sokolov the price of the plot for the grave.

Peter Ivanovich while lighting his cigarette heard her inquiring very circumstantially into the price of different plots in the cemetery and finally decided which she would take. When that was done she gave instructions about engaging the choir. Sokolov then left the room.

"I look after everything myself," she told Peter Ivanovich, shifting the albums that lay on the table; and noticing that the table was endangered by his cigarette-ash, she immediately passed him an ashtray, saying as she did so: "I consider it an affectation to say that my grief prevents my attending to practical affairs. On the contrary, if anything can — I won't say console me, but — distract me, it is seeing to everything concerning him." She again took out her handkerchief as if preparing to cry, but suddenly, as if mastering her feeling, she shook herself and began to speak calmly. "But there is something I want to talk to you about."

Peter Ivanovich bowed, keeping control of the springs of the pouffe, which immediately began quivering under him.

"He suffered terribly the last few days."

"Did he?" said Peter Ivanovich.

"Oh, terribly! He screamed unceasingly, not for minutes but for hours. For the last three days he screamed incessantly. It was unendurable. I cannot understand how I bore it; you could hear him three rooms off. Oh, what I have suffered!"

"Is it possible that he was conscious all that time?" asked Peter Ivanovich.

"Yes," she whispered. "To the last moment. He took leave of us a quarter of an hour before he died, and asked us to take Vasya away."

The thought of the sufferings of this man he had known so intimately, first as a merry little boy, then as a school-mate, and later as a grown-up colleague, suddenly struck Peter Ivanovich with horror, despite an unpleasant consciousness of his own and this woman's dissimulation. He again saw that brow, and that nose pressing down on the lip, and felt afraid for himself.

"Three days of frightful suffering and then death! Why, that might suddenly, at any time, happen to me," he thought, and for a moment felt terrified. But — he did not himself know how — the customary reflection at once occurred to him that this had happened to Ivan Ilych and not to him, and that it should not and could not happen to him, and that to think that it could would be yielding to depression which he ought not to do, as Schwartz's expression plainly showed. After which reflection Peter Ivanovich felt reassured, and began to ask with interest about the details of Ivan Ilych's death, as though death was an accident natural to Ivan Ilych but certainly not to himself.

After many details of the really dreadful physical sufferings Ivan Ilych had endured (which details he learnt only from the effect those sufferings had produced on Praskoyva Fëdorovna's nerves) the widow apparently found it necessary to get to business.

"Oh, Peter Ivanovich, how hard is it! How terribly, terribly hard!" and she again began to weep.

Peter Ivanovich sighed and waited for her to finish blowing her nose. When she had done so he said, "Believe me . . ." and she again began talking and brought out what was evidently her chief concern with him — namely, to question him as to how she could obtain a grant of money from the government on the occasion of her husband's death. She made it appear that she was asking Peter Ivanovich's advice about her pension, but he soon saw that she already knew about that to the minutest detail, more even than he did himself. She knew how much could be got out of the government in consequence of her husband's death, but wanted to find out whether she could not possibly extract something more. Peter Ivanovich tried to think of some means of doing so, but after reflecting for a while and, out of propriety, condemning the government for its niggardliness, he said he thought that nothing more could be got. Then she sighed and evidently began to devise means of getting rid of her visitor. Noticing this, he put out his cigarette, rose, pressed her hand, and went out into the anteroom.

In the dining-room where the clock stood that Ivan Ilych had liked so much and had bought at an antique shop, Peter Ivanovich met a priest and a few acquaintances who had come to attend the service, and he recognized Ivan Ilych's daughter, a handsome young woman. She was in black and her slim figure appeared slimmer than ever. She had a gloomy, determined, almost angry expression, and bowed to Peter Ivanovich as though he were in some way to blame. Behind her, with the same offended look, stood a wealthy young man, an examining magistrate, whom Peter Ivanovich also knew and who was her fiancé, as he had heard. He bowed mournfully to them and was about to pass into the death-chamber, when from under the stairs appeared the figure of Ivan Ilych's schoolboy son, who was extremely like his father. He seemed a little Ivan Ilych, such as Peter Ivanovich remembered when they studied law together. His tear-stained eyes had in them the look that is seen in the eyes of boys of thirteen or fourteen who are not pure-minded. When he saw Peter Ivanovich he scowled morosely and shamefacedly. Peter Ivanovich nodded to him and entered the death-chamber. The service began: candles, groans, incense, tears, and sobs. Peter Ivanovich stood looking gloomily down at his feet. He did not look once at the dead man, did not yield to any depressing influence, and was one of the first to leave the room. There was no one in the anteroom, but Gerasim darted out of the dead man's room, rummaged with his strong hands among the fur coats to find Peter Ivanovich's, and helped him on with it.

"Well, friend Gerasim," said Peter Ivanovich, so as to say something. "It's a sad affair, isn't it?"

"It's God's will. We shall all come to it some day," said Gerasim, displaying his teeth — the even, white teeth of a healthy peasant — and, like a man in the thick of urgent work, he briskly opened the front door, called the coachman, helped Peter Ivanovich into the sledge, and sprang back to the porch as if in readiness for what he had to do next.

Peter Ivanovich found the fresh air particularly pleasant after the smell of incense, the dead body, and carbolic acid.

"Where to, sir?" asked the coachman.

"It's not too late even now. . . . I'll call round on Fëdor Vasilievich."

He accordingly drove there and found them just finishing the first rubber, so that it was quite convenient for him to cut in.

II

Ivan Ilych's life had been most simple and most ordinary and therefore most terrible.

He had been a member of the Court of Justice, and died at the age of forty-five. His father had been an official who after serving in various ministries and departments in Petersburg had made the sort of career which brings men to positions from which by reason of their long service they cannot be dismissed, though they were obviously unfit to hold any responsible position, and for whom therefore posts are specially created, which though fictitious carry salaries of from six to ten thousand rubles that are not fictitious, and in receipt of which they live on to a great age.

Such was the Privy Councillor and superfluous member of various superfluous institutions, Ilya Epimovich Golovin.

He had three sons, of whom Ivan Ilych was the second. The eldest son was following in his father's footsteps only in another department, and was already approaching that stage in the service at which a similar sinecure would be reached. The third son was a failure. He had ruined his prospects in a number of positions and was now serving in the railway department. His father and brothers, and still more their wives, not merely disliked meeting him, but avoided remembering his existence unless compelled to do so. His sister had married Baron Greff, a Petersburg official of her father's type. Ivan Ilych was *le phénix de la famille*° as people said. He was neither as cold and formal as his elder brother nor as wild as the younger, but was a happy mean between them — an intelligent, polished, lively, and agreeable man. He had studied with his younger brother at the School of Law, but the latter had failed to complete the course and was expelled when he was in the fifth class. Ivan Ilych finished the course well. Even when he was at the School of Law he was just what he remained for the rest of his life: a capable, cheerful, good-natured, and sociable man, though strict in the fulfillment of what he considered to be

---

le phénix de la famille: The pride of the family. (Unless otherwise indicated, all foreign phrases are in French — often the everyday language of middle-class and upper-class Russians of Tolstoy's time.)

his duty: and he considered his duty to be what was so considered by those in authority. Neither as a boy nor as a man was he a toady, but from early youth was by nature attracted to people of high station as a fly is drawn to the light, assimilating their ways and views of life and establishing friendly relations with them. All the enthusiasms of childhood and youth passed without leaving much trace on him; he succumbed to sensuality, to vanity, and latterly among the highest classes to liberalism, but always within limits which his instinct unfailingly indicated to him as correct.

At school he had done things which had formerly seemed to him very horrid and made him feel disgusted with himself when he did them; but when later on he saw that such actions were done by people of good position and that they did not regard them as wrong, he was able not exactly to regard them as right, but to forget about them entirely or not be at all troubled at remembering them.

Having graduated from the School of Law and qualified for the tenth rank of the civil service, and having received money from his father for his equipment, Ivan Ilych ordered himself clothes at Scharmer's, the fashionable tailor, hung a medallion inscribed *respice finem*° on his watch-chain, took leave of his professor and the prince who was patron of the school, had a farewell dinner with his comrades at Donon's first-class restaurant, and with his new and fashionable portmanteau, linen, clothes, shaving and other toilet appliances, and a traveling rug, all purchased at the best shops, he set off for one of the provinces where, through his father's influence, he had been attached to the Governor as an official for special service.

In the province Ivan Ilych soon arranged as easy and agreeable a position for himself as he had had at the School of Law. He performed his official tasks, made his career, and at the same time amused himself pleasantly and decorously. Occasionally he paid official visits to country districts, where he behaved with dignity both to his superiors and inferiors, and performed the duties entrusted to him, which related chiefly to the sectarians,° with an exactness and incorruptible honesty of which he could not but feel proud.

In official matters, despite his youth and taste for frivolous gaiety, he was exceedingly reserved, punctilious, and even severe; but in society he was often amusing and witty, and always good-natured, correct in his manner, and *bon enfant*,° as the governor and his wife — with whom he was like one of the family — used to say of him.

In the province he had an affair with a lady who made advances to the elegant young lawyer, and there was also a milliner; and there were carousals with aides-de-camp who visited the district, and after-supper visits to a certain outlying street of doubtful reputation; and there was too some obsequiousness to his chief and even to his chief's wife, but all this was done with such a tone of good breeding that no hard names could be applied to it. It all

---

respice finem: "Consider your end" — that is, your death (Latin).
sectarians: "Old Believers," dissenters from the Orthodox Church.
bon enfant: One of the boys (literally, "a good child").

came under the heading of the French saying: *"Il faut que jeunesse se passe."*° It was all done with clean hands, in clean linen, with French phrases, and above all among people of the best society and consequently with the approval of people of rank.

So Ivan Ilych served for five years and then came a change in his official life. The new and reformed judicial institutions were introduced, and new men were needed. Ivan Ilych became such a new man. He was offered the post of examining magistrate, and he accepted it though the post was in another province and obliged him to give up the connections he had formed and to make new ones. His friends met to give him a send-off; they had a group-photograph taken and presented him with a silver cigarette-case, and he set off to his new post.

As examining magistrate Ivan Ilych was just as *comme il faut*° and decorous a man, inspiring general respect and capable of separating his official duties from his private life, as he had been when acting as an official on special service. His duties now as examining magistrate were far more interesting and attractive than before. In his former position it had been pleasant to wear an undress uniform made by Scharmer, and to pass through the crowd of petitioners and officials who were timorously awaiting an audience with the governor, and who envied him as with free and easy gait he went straight into his chief's private room to have a cup of tea and a cigarette with him. But not many people had then been directly dependent on him — only police officials and the sectarians when he went on special missions — and he liked to treat them politely, almost as comrades, as if he were letting them feel that he who had the power to crush them was treating them in this simple, friendly way. There were then but few such people. But now, as an examining magistrate, Ivan Ilych felt that everyone without exception, even the most important and self-satisfied, was in his power, and that he need only write a few words on a sheet of paper with a certain heading, and this or that important, self-satisfied person would be brought before him in the role of an accused person or a witness, and if he did not choose to allow him to sit down, would have to stand before him and answer his questions. Ivan Ilych never abused his power; he tried on the contrary to soften its expression, but the consciousness of it and of the possibility of softening its effect, supplied the chief interest and attraction of his office. In his work itself, especially in his examinations, he very soon acquired a method of eliminating all considerations irrelevant to the legal aspect of the case, and reducing even the most complicated case to a form in which it would be presented on paper only in its externals, completely excluding his personal opinion of the matter, while above all observing every prescribed formality. The work was new and Ivan Ilych was one of the first men to apply the new Code of 1864.°

On taking up the post of examining magistrate in a new town, he made

---

"Il faut que jeunesse se passe": "Youth will have its day."
comme il faut: Proper (literally, "as it should be").
Code of 1864: The emancipation of the serfs in 1861 was followed by a thorough, all-round reform of judicial proceedings. [Translators' note]

new acquaintances and connections, placed himself on a new footing, and assumed a somewhat different tone. He took up an attitude of rather dignified aloofness towards the provincial authorities, but picked out the best circle of legal gentlemen and wealthy gentry living in the town and assumed a tone of slight dissatisfaction with the government, of moderate liberalism, and of enlightened citizenship. At the same time, without at all altering the elegance of his toilet, he ceased shaving his chin and allowed his beard to grow as it pleased.

Ivan Ilych settled down very pleasantly in this new town. The society there, which inclined towards opposition to the Governor, was friendly, his salary was larger, and he began to play *vint*,° which he found added not a little to the pleasure of life, for he had a capacity for cards, played good-humoredly, and calculated rapidly and astutely, so that he usually won.

After living there for two years he met his future wife, Praskovya Fëdorovna Mikhel, who was the most attractive, clever, and brilliant girl of the set in which he moved, and among other amusements and relaxations from his labors as examining magistrate, Ivan Ilych established light and playful relations with her.

While he had been an official on special service he had been accustomed to dance, but now as an examining magistrate it was exceptional for him to do so. If he danced now, he did it as if to show that though he served under the reformed order of things, and had reached the fifth official rank, yet when it came to dancing he could do it better than most people. So at the end of an evening he sometimes danced with Praskovya Fëdorovna, and it was chiefly during these dances that he captivated her. She fell in love with him. Ivan Ilych had at first no definite intention of marrying, but when the girl fell in love with him he said to himself: "Really, why shouldn't I marry?"

Praskovya Fëdorovna came of a good family, was not bad looking, and had some little property. Ivan Ilych might have aspired to a more brilliant match, but even this was good. He had his salary, and she, he hoped, would have an equal income. She was well connected, and was a sweet, pretty, and thoroughly correct young woman. To say that Ivan Ilych married because he fell in love with Praskovya Fëdorovna and found that she sympathized with his views of life would be as incorrect as to say that he married because his social circle approved of the match. He was swayed by both these considerations: the marriage gave him personal satisfaction, and at the same time it was considered the right thing by the most highly placed of his associates.

So Ivan Ilych got married.

The preparations for marriage and the beginning of married life, with its conjugal caresses, the new furniture, new crockery, and new linen, were very pleasant until his wife became pregnant — so that Ivan Ilych had begun to think that marriage would not impair the easy, agreeable, gay, and always decorous character of his life, approved of by society and regarded by himself as natural, but would even improve it. But from the first months of his wife's

---

vint: A form of bridge. [Translators' note]

pregnancy, something new, unpleasant, depressing, and unseemly, and from which there was no way of escape, unexpectedly showed itself.

His wife, without any reason — *de gaieté de coeur°* as Ivan Ilych expressed it to himself — began to disturb the pleasure and propriety of their life. She began to be jealous without any cause, expected him to devote his whole attention to her, found fault with everything, and made coarse and ill-mannered scenes.

At first Ivan Ilych hoped to escape from the unpleasantness of this state of affairs by the same easy and decorous relation to life that had served him heretofore: he tried to ignore his wife's disagreeable moods, continued to live in his usual easy and pleasant way, invited friends to his house for a game of cards, and also tried going out to his club or spending his evenings with friends. But one day his wife began upbraiding him so vigorously, using such coarse words, and continued to abuse him every time he did not fulfil her demands, so resolutely and with such evident determination not to give way till he submitted — that is, till he stayed at home and was bored just as she was — that he became alarmed. He now realized that matrimony — at any rate with Praskovya Fëdorovna — was not always conducive to the pleasures and amenities of life, but on the contrary often infringed both comfort and propriety, and that he must therefore entrench himself against such infringement. And Ivan Ilych began to seek for means of doing so. His official duties were the one thing that imposed upon Praskovya Fëdorovna, and by means of his official work and the duties attached to it he began struggling with his wife to secure his own independence.

With the birth of their child, the attempts to feed it and the various failures in doing so, and with the real and imaginary illnesses of mother and child, in which Ivan Ilych's sympathy was demanded but about which he understood nothing, the need of securing for himself an existence outside his family life became still more imperative.

As his wife grew more irritable and exacting and Ivan Ilych transferred the center of gravity of his life more and more to his official work so did he grow to like his work better and became more ambitious than before.

Very soon, within a year of his wedding, Ivan Ilych had realized that marriage, though it may add some comforts to life, is in fact a very intricate and difficult affair towards which in order to perform one's duty, that is, to lead a decorous life approved of by society, one must adopt a definite attitude just as towards one's official duties.

And Ivan Ilych evolved such an attitude towards married life. He only required of it those conveniences — dinner at home, housewife, and bed — which it could give him, and above all that propriety of external forms required by public opinion. For the rest he looked for light-hearted pleasure and propriety, and was very thankful when he found them, but if he met with antagonism and querulousness he at once retired into his separate fenced-off world of official duties, where he found satisfaction.

---

de gaieté de coeur: From sheer exuberance (literally, "from happiness of heart").

Ivan Ilych was esteemed a good official, and after three years was made Assistant Public Prosecutor. His new duties, their importance, the possibility of indicting and imprisoning anyone he chose, the publicity his speeches received, and the success he had in all these things made his work still more attractive.

More children came. His wife became more and more querulous and ill-tempered, but the attitude Ivan Ilych had adopted towards his home life rendered him almost impervious to her grumbling.

After seven years' service in that town he was transferred to another province as Public Prosecutor. They moved, but were short of money and his wife did not like the place they moved to. Though the salary was higher the cost of living was greater, besides which two of their children died and family life became still more unpleasant for him.

Praskovya Fëdorovna blamed her husband for every inconvenience they encountered in their new home. Most of the conversations between husband and wife, especially as to the children's education, led to topics which recalled former disputes, and those disputes were apt to flare up again at any moment. There remained only those rare periods of amorousness which still came to them at times but did not last long. These were islets at which they anchored for a while and then again set out upon that ocean of veiled hostility which showed itself in their aloofness from one another. This aloofness might have grieved Ivan Ilych had he considered that it ought not to exist, but he now regarded the position as normal, and even made it the goal at which he aimed in family life. His aim was to free himself more and more from those unpleasantnesses and to give them a semblance of harmlessness and propriety. He attained this by spending less and less time with his family, and when obliged to be at home he tried to safeguard his position by the presence of outsiders. The chief thing however was that he had his official duties. The whole interest of his life now centered in the official world and that interest absorbed him. The consciousness of his power, being able to ruin anybody he wished to ruin, the importance, even the external dignity of his entry into court, or meetings with his subordinates, his success with superiors and inferiors, and above all his masterly handling of cases, of which he was conscious — all this gave him pleasure and filled his life, together with chats with his colleagues, dinners, and bridge. So that on the whole Ivan Ilych's life continued to flow as he considered it should do — pleasantly and properly.

So things continued for another seven years. His eldest daughter was already sixteen, another child had died, and only one son was left, a schoolboy and a subject of dissension. Ivan Ilych wanted to put him in the School of Law, but to spite him Praskovya Fëdorovna entered him at the High School. The daughter had been educated at home and had turned out well: the boy did not learn badly either.

III

So Ivan Ilych lived for seventeen years after his marriage. He was already a Public Prosecutor of long standing, and had declined several proposed transfers while awaiting a more desirable post, when an unanticipated and unpleasant occurrence quite upset the peaceful course of his life. He was expecting to be offered the post of presiding judge in a University town, but Happe somehow came to the front and obtained the appointment instead. Ivan Ilych became irritable, reproached Happe, and quarreled both with him and with his immediate superiors — who became colder to him and again passed him over when other appointments were made.

This was in 1880, the hardest year of Ivan Ilych's life. It was then that it became evident on the one hand that his salary was insufficient for them to live on, and on the other that he had been forgotten, and not only this, but that what was for him the greatest and most cruel injustice appeared to others a quite ordinary occurrence. Even his father did not consider it his duty to help him. Ivan Ilych felt himself abandoned by everyone, and that they regarded his position with a salary of 3,500 rubles as quite normal and even fortunate. He alone knew that with the consciousness of the injustices done him, with his wife's incessant nagging, and with the debts he had contracted by living beyond his means, his position was far from normal.

In order to save money that summer he obtained leave of absence and went with his wife to live in the country at her brother's place.

In the country, without his work, he experienced *ennui* for the first time in his life, and not only *ennui* but intolerable depression, and he decided that it was impossible to go on living like that, and that it was necessary to take energetic measures.

Having passed a sleepless night pacing up and down the veranda, he decided to go to Petersburg and bestir himself, in order to punish those who had failed to appreciate him and to get transferred to another ministry.

Next day, despite many protests from his wife and her brother, he started for Petersburg with the sole object of obtaining a post with a salary of five thousand rubles a year. He was no longer bent on any particular department, or tendency, or kind of activity. All he now wanted was an appointment to another post with a salary of five thousand rubles, either in the administration, in the banks, with the railways, in one of the Empress Marya's Institutions,° or even in the customs — but it had to carry with it a salary of five thousand rubles and be in a ministry other than that in which they had failed to appreciate him.

And this quest of Ivan Ilych's was crowned with remarkable and unexpected success. At Kursk an acquaintance of his, F. I. Ilyin, got into the first-class carriage, sat down beside Ivan Ilych, and told him of a telegram just received by the Governor of Kursk announcing that a change was about to take place in the ministry: Peter Ivanovich was to be superseded by Ivan Semënovich.

The proposed change, apart from its significance for Russia, had a special significance for Ivan Ilych, because by bringing forward a new man, Peter Petrovich, and consequently his friend Zachar Ivanovich, it was highly favorable for Ivan Ilych, since Zachar Ivanovich was a friend and colleague of his.

Empress Marya's Institutions: Orphanages founded by the wife of Czar Paul I, who ruled from 1796 to 1801.

In Moscow this news was confirmed, and on reaching Petersburg Ivan Ilych found Zachar Ivanovich and received a definite promise of an appointment in his former department of Justice.

A week later he telegraphed to his wife: "Zachar in Miller's place. I shall receive appointment on presentation of report."

Thanks to this change of personnel, Ivan Ilych had unexpectedly obtained an appointment in his former ministry which placed him two stages above his former colleagues besides giving him five thousand rubles salary and three thousand five hundred rubles for expenses connected with his removal. All his ill humor towards his former enemies and the whole department vanished, and Ivan Ilych was completely happy.

He returned to the country more cheerful and contented than he had been for a long time. Praskovya Fëdorovna also cheered up and a truce was arranged between them. Ivan Ilych told of how he had been fêted by everybody in Petersburg, how all those who had been his enemies were put to shame and now fawned on him, how envious they were of his appointment, and how much everybody in Petersburg had liked him.

Praskovya Fëdorovna listened to all this and appeared to believe it. She did not contradict anything, but only made plans for their life in the town to which they were going. Ivan Ilych saw with delight that these plans were his plans, that he and his wife agreed, and that, after a stumble, his life was regaining its due and natural character of pleasant lightheartedness and decorum.

Ivan Ilych had come back for a short time only, for he had to take up his new duties on the 10th of September. Moreover, he needed time to settle into the new place, to move all his belongings from the province, and to buy and order many additional things: in a word, to make such arrangements as he had resolved on, which were almost exactly what Praskovya Fëdorovna too had decided on.

Now that everything had happened so fortunately, and that he and his wife were at one in their aims and moreover saw so little of one another, they got on together better than they had done since the first years of marriage. Ivan Ilych had thought of taking his family away with him at once, but the insistence of his wife's brother and her sister-in-law, who had suddenly become particularly amiable and friendly to him and his family, induced him to depart alone.

So he departed, and the cheerful state of mind induced by his success and by the harmony between his wife and himself, the one intensifying the other, did not leave him. He found a delightful house, just the thing both he and his wife had dreamt of. Spacious, lofty reception rooms in the old style, a convenient and dignified study, rooms for his wife and daughter, a study for his son — it might have been specially built for them. Ivan Ilych himself superintended the arrangements, chose the wallpapers, supplemented the furniture (preferably with antiques which he considered particularly *comme il faut*), and supervised the upholstering. Everything progressed and progressed and approached the ideal he had set himself: even when things were only half completed they exceeded his expectations. He saw what a refined and elegant character, free from vulgarity, it would all have when it was ready. On falling asleep he pictured to himself how the reception-room would look. Looking at the yet unfinished drawing-room he could see the fireplace, the screen, the what-not, the little chairs dotted here and there, the dishes and plates on the walls, and the bronzes, as they would be when everything was in place. He was pleased by the thought of how his wife and daughter, who shared his taste in this matter, would be impressed by it. They were certainly not expecting as much. He had been particularly successful in finding, and buying cheaply, antiques which gave a particularly aristocratic character to the whole place. But in his letters he intentionally understated everything in order to be able to surprise them. All this so absorbed him that his new duties — though he liked his official work — interested him less than he had expected. Sometimes he even had moments of absent-mindedness during the Court Sessions, and would consider whether he should have straight or curved cornices for his curtains. He was so interested in it all that he often did things himself, re-arranging the furniture, or rehanging the curtains. Once when mounting a step-ladder to show the upholsterer, who did not understand, how he wanted the hangings draped, he made a false step and slipped, but being a strong and agile man he clung on and only knocked his side against the knob of the window frame. The bruised place was painful but the pain soon passed, and he felt particularly bright and well just then. He wrote: "I feel fifteen years younger." He thought he would have everything ready by September, but it dragged on till mid-October. But the result was charming not only in his eyes but to everyone who saw it.

In reality it was just what is usually seen in the houses of people of moderate means who want to appear rich, and therefore succeed only in resembling others like themselves: there were damasks, dark wood, plants, rugs, and dull and polished bronzes — all the things people of a certain class have in order to resemble other people of that class. His house was so like the others that it would never have been noticed, but to him it all seemed to be quite exceptional. He was very happy when he met his family at the station and brought them to the newly furnished house all lit up, where a footman in a white tie opened the door into the hall decorated with plants, and when they went on into the drawing room, and the study uttering exclamations of delight. He conducted them everywhere, drank in their praises eagerly, and beamed with pleasure. At tea that evening, when Praskovya Fëdorovna among other things asked him about his fall, he laughed and showed them how he had gone flying and had frightened the upholsterer.

"It's a good thing I'm a bit of an athlete. Another man might have been killed, but I merely knocked myself, just here; it hurts when it's touched, but it's passing off already — it's only a bruise."

So they began living in their new home — in which, as always happens, when they got thoroughly settled in they found they were just one room short — and with the increased income, which as always was just a little (some five hundred rubles) too little, but it was all very nice.

Things went particularly well at first, before everything was finally arranged and while something had still to be done: this thing bought, that thing ordered, another thing moved, and something else adjusted. Though there were some disputes between husband and wife, they were both so well satisfied and had so much to do that it all passed off without any serious quarrels. When nothing was left to arrange it became rather dull and something seemed to be lacking, but they were then making acquaintances, forming habits, and life was growing fuller.

Ivan Ilych spent his mornings at the law court and came home to dinner, and at first he was generally in a good humor, though he occasionally became irritable just on account of his house. (Every spot on the tablecloth or the upholstery, and every broken windowblind string, irritated him. He had devoted so much trouble to arranging it all that every disturbance of it distressed him.) But on the whole his life ran its course as he believed life should do: easily, pleasantly, and decorously.

He got up at nine, drank his coffee, read the paper, and then put on his undress uniform and went to the law courts. There the harness in which he worked had already been stretched to fit him and he donned it without a hitch: petitioners, inquiries at the chancery, the chancery itself, and the sittings public and administrative. In all this the thing was to exclude everything fresh and vital, which always disturbs the regular course of official business, and to admit only official relations with people, and then only on official grounds. A man would come, for instance, wanting some information. Ivan Ilych, as one in whose sphere the matter did not lie, would have nothing to do with him: but if the man had some business with him in his official capacity, something that could be expressed on officially stamped paper, he would do everything, positively everything he could within the limits of such relations, and in doing so would maintain the semblance of friendly human relations, that is, would observe the courtesies of life. As soon as the official relations ended, so did everything else. Ivan Ilych possessed this capacity to separate his real life from the offical side of affairs and not mix the two, in the highest degree, and by long practice and natural aptitude had brought it to such a pitch that sometimes, in the manner of a virtuoso, he would even allow himself to let the human and official relations mingle. He let himself do this just because he felt that he could at any time he chose resume the strictly official attitude again and drop the human relation. And he did it all easily, pleasantly, correctly, and even artistically. In the intervals between the sessions he smoked, drank tea, chatted a little about politics, a little about general topics, a little about cards, but most of all about official appointments. Tired, but with the feelings of a virtuoso — one of the first violins who has played his part in an orchestra with precision — he would return home to find that his wife and daughter had been out paying calls, or had a visitor, and that his son had been to school, had done his homework with his tutor, and was duly learning what is taught at High Schools. Everything was as it should be. After dinner, if they had no visitors, Ivan Ilych sometimes read a book that was being much discussed at the time, and in the evening settled down to work, that is, read official papers, compared the depositions of witnesses, and noted paragraphs of the Code applying to them. This was neither dull nor amusing. It was dull when he might have been playing bridge, but if no bridge was available it was at any rate better than doing nothing or sitting with his wife. Ivan Ilych's chief pleasure was giving little dinners to which he invited men and women of good social position, and just as his drawing-room resembled all other drawing-rooms so did his enjoyable little parties resemble all other such parties.

Once they even gave a dance. Ivan Ilych enjoyed it and everything went off well, except that it led to a violent quarrel with his wife about the cakes and sweets. Praskovya Fëdorovna had made her own plans, but Ivan Ilych insisted on getting everything from an expensive confectioner and ordered too many cakes, and the quarrel occurred because some of those cakes were left over and the confectioner's bill came to forty-five rubles. It was a great and disagreeable quarrel. Praskovya Fëdorovna called him "a fool and an imbecile," and he clutched at his head and made angry allusions to divorce.

But the dance itself had been enjoyable. The best people were there, and Ivan Ilych had danced with Princess Trufonova, a sister of the distinguished founder of the Society "Bear My Burden."

The pleasures connected with his work were pleasures of ambition; his social pleasures were those of vanity; but Ivan Ilych's greatest pleasure was playing bridge. He acknowledged that whatever disagreeable incident happened in his life, the pleasure that beamed like a ray of light about everything else was to sit down to bridge with good players, not noisy partners, and of course to four-handed bridge (with five players it was annoying to have to stand out, though one pretended not to mind), to play a clever and serious game (when the cards allowed it), and then to have supper and drink a glass of wine. After a game of bridge, especially if he had won a little (to win a large sum was unpleasant), Ivan Ilych went to bed in specially good humor.

So they lived. They formed a circle of acquaintances among the best people and were visited by people of importance and by young folk. In their views as to their acquaintances, husband, wife, and daughter were entirely agreed, and tacitly and unanimously kept at arm's length and shook off the various shabby friends and relations who, with much show of affection, gushed into the drawing-room with its Japanese plates on the walls. Soon these shabby friends ceased to obtrude themselves and only the best people remained in the Golovins' set.

Young men made up to Lisa, and Petrishchev, an examining magistrate and Dmitri Ivanovich Petrishchev's son and sole heir, began to be so attentive to her that Ivan Ilych had already spoken to Praskovya Fëdorovna about it, and considered whether they should not arrange a party for them, or get up some private theatricals.

So they lived, and all went well, without change, and life flowed pleasantly.

IV

They were all in good health. It could not be called ill health if Ivan Ilych sometimes said that he had a queer taste in his mouth and felt some discomfort in his left side.

But this discomfort increased and, though not exactly painful, grew into a sense of pressure in his side accompanied by ill humor. And his irritability became worse and worse and began to mar the agreeable, easy, and correct life that had established itself in the Golovin family. Quarrels between husband and wife became more and more frequent, and soon the ease and amenity disappeared and even the decorum was barely maintained. Scenes again became frequent, and very few of those islets remained on which husband and wife could meet without explosion. Praskovya Fëdorovna now had good reason to say that her husband's temper was trying. With characteristic exaggeration she said he had always had a dreadful temper, and that it had needed all her good nature to put up with it for twenty years. It was true that now the quarrels were started by him. His bursts of temper always came just before dinner, often just as he began to eat his soup. Sometimes he noticed that a plate or dish was chipped, or the food was not right, or his son put his elbow on the table, or his daughter's hair was not done as he liked it, and for all this he blamed Praskovya Fëdorovna. At first she retorted and said disagreeable things to him, but once or twice he fell into such a rage at the beginning of dinner that she realized it was due to some physical derangement brought on by taking food, and so she restrained herself and did not answer, but only hurried to get the dinner over. She regarded this self-restraint as highly praiseworthy. Having come to the conclusion that her husband had a dreadful temper and made her life miserable, she began to feel sorry for herself, and the more she pitied herself the more she hated her husband. She began to wish he would die; yet she did not want him to die because then his salary would cease. And this irritated her against him still more. She considered herself dreadfully unhappy just because not even his death could save her, and though she concealed her exasperation, that hidden exasperation of hers increased his irritation also.

After one scene in which Ivan Ilych had been particularly unfair and after which he had said in explanation that he certainly was irritable but that it was due to his not being well, she said that if he was ill it should be attended to, and insisted on his going to see a celebrated doctor.

He went. Everything took place as he had expected and as it always does. There was the usual waiting and the important air assumed by the doctor, with which he was so familiar (resembling that which he himself assumed in court), and the sounding and listening, and the questions which called for answers that were foregone conclusions and were evidently unnecessary, and the look of importance which implied that "if only you put yourself in our hands we will arrange everything — we know indubitably how it has to be done, always in the same way for everybody alike." It was all just as it was in the law courts. The doctor put on just the same air towards him as he himself put on towards an accused person.

The doctor said that so-and-so indicated that there was so-and-so inside the patient, but if the investigation of so-and-so did not confirm this, then he must assume that and that. If he assumed that and that, then . . . and so on. To Ivan Ilych only one question was important: was his case serious or not? But the doctor ignored that inappropriate question. From his point of view it was not the one under consideration, the real question was to decide between a floating kidney, chronic catarrh, or appendicitis. It was not a question of Ivan Ilych's life or death, but one between a floating kidney and appendicitis. And that question the doctor solved brilliantly, as it seemed to Ivan Ilych, in favor of the appendix, with the reservation that should an examination of the urine give fresh indications the matter would be reconsidered. All this was just what Ivan Ilych had himself brilliantly accomplished a thousand times in dealing with men on trial. The doctor summed up just as brilliantly, looking over his spectacles triumphantly and even gaily at the accused. From the doctor's summing up Ivan Ilych concluded that things were bad, but that for the doctor, and perhaps for everybody else, it was a matter of indifference, though for him it was bad. And this conclusion struck him painfully, arousing in him a great feeling of pity for himself and of bitterness towards the doctor's indifference to a matter of such importance.

He said nothing of this, but rose, placed the doctor's fee on the table, and remarked with a sigh: "We sick people probably often put inappropriate questions. But tell me, in general, is this complaint dangerous, or not? . . ."

The doctor looked at him sternly over his spectacles with one eye, as if to say: "Prisoner, if you will not keep to the questions put to you, I shall be obliged to have you removed from the court."

"I have already told you what I consider necessary and proper. The analysis may show something more." And the doctor bowed.

Ivan Ilych went out slowly, seated himself disconsolately in his sledge, and drove home. All the way home he was going over what the doctor had said, trying to translate those complicated, obscure, scientific phrases into plain language and find in them an answer to the question: "Is my condition bad? Is it very bad? Or is there as yet nothing much wrong?" And it seemed to him that the meaning of what the doctor had said was that it was very bad. Everything in the streets seemed depressing. The cabmen, the houses, the passers-by, and the shops, were dismal. His ache, this dull gnawing ache that never ceased for a moment, seemed to have acquired a new and more serious significance from the doctor's dubious remarks. Ivan Ilych now watched it with a new and oppressive feeling.

He reached home and began to tell his wife about it. She listened, but in the middle of his account his daughter came in with her hat on, ready to go out with her mother. She sat down reluctantly to listen to this tedious story, but could not stand it long, and her mother too did not hear him to the end.

"Well, I am very glad," she said. "Mind now to take your medicine regularly. Give me the prescription and I'll send Gerasim to the chemist's." And she went to get ready to go out.

While she was in the room Ivan Ilych had hardly taken time to breathe, but he sighed deeply when she left it.

"Well," he thought, "perhaps it isn't so bad after all."

He began taking his medicine and following the doctor's directions, which had been altered after the examination of the urine. But then it happened that there was a contradiction between the indications drawn from the examination of the urine and the symptoms that showed themselves. It turned out that what was happening differed from what the doctor had told him, and that he had either forgotten, or blundered, or hidden something from him. He could not, however, be blamed for that, and Ivan Ilych still obeyed his orders implicitly and at first derived some comfort from doing so.

From the time of his visit to the doctor, Ivan Ilych's chief occupation was the exact fulfilment of the doctor's instructions regarding hygiene and the taking of medicine, and the observation of his pain and his excretions. His chief interests came to be people's ailments and people's health. When sickness, deaths, or recoveries were mentioned in his presence, especially when the illness resembled his own, he listened with agitation which he tried to hide, asked questions, and applied what he heard to his own case.

The pain did not grow less, but Ivan Ilych made efforts to force himself to think that he was better. And he could do this so long as nothing agitated him. But as soon as he had any unpleasantness with his wife, any lack of success in his official work, or held bad cards at bridge, he was at once acutely sensible of his disease. He had formerly borne such mischances, hoping soon to adjust what was wrong, to master it and attain success, or make a grand slam. But now every mischance upset him and plunged him into despair. He would say to himself: "There now, just as I was beginning to get better and the medicine had begun to take effect, comes this accursed misfortune, or unpleasantness. . . ." And he was furious with the mishap, or with the people who were causing the unpleasantness and killing him, for he felt that this fury was killing him but could not restrain it. One would have thought that it should have been clear to him that this exasperation with circumstances and people aggravated his illness, and that he ought therefore to ignore unpleasant occurrences. But he drew the very opposite conclusion: he said that he needed peace, and he watched for everything that might disturb it and became irritable at the slightest infringement of it. His condition was rendered worse by the fact that he read medical books and consulted doctors. The progress of his disease was so gradual that he could deceive himself when comparing one day with another — the difference was so slight. But when he consulted the doctors it seemed to him that he was getting worse, and even very rapidly. Yet despite this he was continually consulting them.

That month he went to see another celebrity, who told him almost the same as the first had done but put his questions rather differently, and the interview with this celebrity only increased Ivan Ilych's doubts and fears. A friend of a friend of his, a very good doctor, diagnosed his illness again quite differently from the others, and though he predicted recovery, his questions and suppositions bewildered Ivan Ilych still more and increased his doubts. A homoeopathist diagnosed the disease in yet another way, and prescribed medicine which Ivan Ilych took secretly for a week. But after a week, not feeling any improvement and having lost confidence both in the former doctor's treatment and in this one's, he became still more despondent. One day a lady acquaintance mentioned a cure effected by a wonder-working icon. Ivan Ilych caught himself listening attentively and beginning to believe that it had occurred. This incident alarmed him. "Has my mind really weakened to such an extent?" he asked himself. "Nonsense! It's all rubbish. I mustn't give way to nervous fears but having chosen a doctor must keep strictly to his treatment.

That is what I will do. Now it's all settled. I won't think about it, but will follow the treatment seriously till summer, and then we shall see. From now there must be no more of this wavering!" This was easy to say but impossible to carry out. The pain in his side oppressed him and seemed to grow worse and more incessant, while the taste in his mouth grew stranger and stranger. It seemed to him that his breath had a disgusting smell, and he was conscious of a loss of appetite and strength. There was no deceiving himself: something terrible, new, and more important than anything before in his life, was taking place within him of which he alone was aware. Those about him did not understand or would not understand it, but thought everything in the world was going on as usual. That tormented Ivan Ilych more than anything. He saw that his household, especially his wife and daughter who were in a perfect whirl of visiting, did not understand anything of it and were annoyed that he was so depressed and so exacting, as if he were to blame for it. Though they tried to disguise it he saw that he was an obstacle in their path, and that his wife had adopted a definite line in regard to his illness and kept to it regardless of anything he said or did. Her attitude was this: "You know," she would say to her friends, "Ivan Ilych can't do as other people do, and keep to the treatment prescribed for him. One day he'll take his drops and keep strictly to his diet and go to bed in good time, but the next day unless I watch him he'll suddenly forget his medicine, eat sturgeon — which is forbidden — and sit up playing cards till one o'clock in the morning."

"Oh, come, when was that?" Ivan Ilych would ask in vexation. "Only once at Peter Ivanovich's."

"And yesterday with Shebek."

"Well, even if I hadn't stayed up, this pain would have kept me awake."

"Be that as it may you'll never get well like that, but will always make us wretched."

Praskovya Fëdorovna's attitude to Ivan Ilych's illness, as she expressed it both to others and to him, was that it was his own fault and was another of the annoyances he caused her. Ivan Ilych felt that this opinion escaped her involuntarily — but that did not make it easier for him.

At the law courts too, Ivan Ilych noticed, or thought he noticed, a strange attitude towards himself. It sometimes seemed to him that people were watching him inquisitively as a man whose place might soon be vacant. Then again, his friends would suddenly begin to chaff him in a friendly way about his low spirits, as if the awful, horrible, and unheard-of thing that was going on within him, incessantly gnawing at him and irresistibly drawing him away, was a very agreeable subject for jests. Schwartz in particular irritated him by his jocularity, vivacity, and *savoir-faire,* which reminded him of what he himself had been ten years ago.

Friends came to make up a set and they sat down to cards. They dealt, bending the new cards to soften them, and he sorted the diamonds in his hand and found he had seven. His partner said "No trumps" and supported him with two diamonds. What more could be wished for? It ought to be jolly and lively. They would make a grand slam. But suddenly Ivan Ilych was conscious of that gnawing pain, that taste in his mouth, and it seemed ridiculous that in such circumstances he should be pleased to make a grand slam.

He looked at his partner Mikhail Mikhaylovich, who rapped the table with his strong hand and instead of snatching up the tricks pushed the cards courteously and indulgently towards Ivan Ilych that he might have the pleasure of gathering them up without the trouble of stretching out his hand for them. "Does he think I am too weak to stretch out my arm?" thought Ivan Ilych, and forgetting what he was doing he over-trumped his partner, missing the grand slam by three tricks. And what was more awful of all was that he saw how upset Mikhail Mikhaylovich was about it but did not himself care. And it was dreadful to realize why he did not care.

They all saw that he was suffering and said: "We can stop if you are tired. Take a rest." Lie down? No, he was not at all tired, and he finished the rubber. All were gloomy and silent. Ivan Ilych felt that he had diffused this gloom over them and could not dispel it. They had supper and went away, and Ivan Ilych was left alone with the consciousness that his life was poisoned and was poisoning the lives of others, and that this poison did not weaken but penetrated more and more deeply into his whole being.

With this consciousness, and with physical pain besides the terror, he must go to bed, often to lie awake the greater part of the night. Next morning he had to get up again, dress, go to the law courts, speak, and write; or if he did not go out, spend at home those twenty-four hours a day each of which was a torture. And he had to live thus all alone on the brink of an abyss, with no one who understood or pitied him.

V

So one month passed and then another. Just before the New Year his brother-in-law came to town and stayed at their house. Ivan Ilych was at the law courts and Praskovya Fëdorovna had gone shopping. When Ivan Ilych came home and entered his study he found his brother-in-law there — a healthy, florid man — unpacking his portmanteau himself. He raised his head on hearing Ivan Ilych's footsteps and looked up at him for a moment without a word. That stare told Ivan Ilych everything. His brother-in-law opened his mouth to utter an exclamation of surprise but checked himself, and that action confirmed it all.

"I have changed, eh?"

"Yes, there is a change."

And after that, try as he would to get his brother-in-law to return to the subject of his looks, the latter would say nothing about it. Praskovya Fëdorovna came home and her brother went out to her. Ivan Ilych locked the door and began to examine himself in the glass, first full face, then in profile. He took up a portrait of himself taken with his wife, and compared it with what he saw in the glass. The change in him was immense. Then he bared his arms to the elbow, looked at them, drew the sleeves down again, sat down on an ottoman, and grew blacker than night.

"No, no, this won't do!" he said to himself, and jumped up, went to the table, took up some law papers and began to read them, but could not continue. He unlocked the door and went into the reception-room. The door leading to the drawing room was shut. He approached it on tiptoe and listened.

"No, you are exaggerating!" Praskovya Fëdorovna was saying.

"Exaggerating! Don't you see it? Why, he's a dead man! Look at his eyes — there's no light in them. But what is it that is wrong with him?"

"No one knows. Nikolaevich said something, but I don't know what. And Leshchetitsky° said quite the contrary. . . ."

Ivan Ilych walked away, went to his own room, lay down, and began musing: "The kidney, a floating kidney." He recalled all the doctors had told him of how it detached itself and swayed about. And by an effort of imagination he tried to catch that kidney and arrest it and support it. So little was needed for this, it seemed to him. "No, I'll go to see Peter Ivanovich again." He rang, ordered the carriage, and got ready to go.

"Where are you going, Jean?" asked his wife, with a specially sad and exceptionally kind look.

This exceptionally kind look irritated him. He looked morosely at her. "I must go to see Peter Ivanovich."°

He went to see Peter Ivanovich, and together they went to see his friend, the doctor. He was in, and Ivan Ilych had a long talk with him.

Reviewing the anatomical and physiological details of what in the doctor's opinion was going on inside him, he understood it all.

There was something, a small thing, in the vermiform appendix. It might all come right. Only stimulate the energy of one organ and check the activity of another, then absorption would take place and everything would come right. He got home rather late for dinner, ate his dinner, and conversed cheerfully, but could not for a long time bring himself to go back to work in his room. At last, however, he went to his study and did what was necessary, but the consciousness that he had put something aside — an important, intimate matter which he would revert to when his work was done — never left him. When he had finished his work he remembered that this intimate matter was the thought of his vermiform appendix. But he did not give himself up to it, and went to the drawing-room for tea. There were callers there, including the examining magistrate who was a desirable match for his daughter, and they were conversing, playing the piano, and singing. Ivan Ilych, as Praskovya Fëdorovna remarked, spent that evening more cheerfully than usual, but he never for a moment forgot that he had postponed the important matter of the appendix. At eleven o'clock he said good-night and went to his bedroom. Since his illness he had slept alone in a small room next to his study. He undressed and took up a novel by Zola,° but instead of reading it he fell into thought, and in his imagination that desired improvement in the vermiform appendix occurred. There were the absorption and evacuation and the re-

---

Nikolaevich . . . Leshchetitsky: Two doctors, the latter a celebrated specialist. [Translators' note]
Peter Ivanovich: Ivanovich is the friend whose friend is a doctor. [Translators' note]
Zola: Émile Zola (1840–1902) was a French novelist.

establishment of normal activity. "Yes, that's it!" he said to himself. "One need only assist nature, that's all." He remembered his medicine, rose, took it, and lay down on his back watching for the beneficent action of the medicine and for it to lessen the pain. "I need only take it regularly and avoid all injurious influences. I am already feeling better, much better." He began touching his side: it was not painful to the touch. "There, I really don't feel it. It's much better already." He put out the light and turned on his side. . . . "The appendix is getting better, absorption is occurring." Suddenly he felt the old, familiar, dull, gnawing pain, stubborn and serious. There was the same familiar loathsome taste in his mouth. His heart sank and he felt dazed. "My God! My God!" he muttered. "Again, again! and it will never cease." And suddenly the matter presented itself in a quite different aspect. "Vermiform appendix! Kidney!" he said to himself. "It's not a question of appendix or kidney, but of life and . . . death. Yes, life was there and now it is going, going and I cannot stop it. Yes. Why deceive myself? Isn't it obvious to everyone but me that I'm dying, and that it's only a question of weeks, days . . . it may happen this moment. There was light and now there is darkness. I was here and now I'm going there! Where?" A chill came over him, his breathing ceased, and he felt only the throbbing of his heart.

"When I am not, what will there be? There will be nothing. Then where shall I be when I am no more? Can this be dying? No, I don't want to!" He jumped up and tried to light the candle, felt for it with trembling hands, dropped candle and candlestick on the floor, and fell back on his pillow.

"What's the use? It makes no difference," he said to himself, staring with wide-open eyes into the darkness. "Death. Yes, death. And none of them know or wish to know it, and they have no pity for me. Now they are playing." (He heard through the door the distant sound of a song and its accompaniment.) "It's all the same to them, but they will die too! Fools! I first, and they later, but it will be the same for them. And now they are merry . . . the beasts!"

Anger choked him and he was agonizingly, unbearably miserable. "It is impossible that all men have been doomed to suffer this awful horror!" He raised himself.

"Something must be wrong. I must calm myself — must think it all over from the beginning." And he again began thinking. "Yes, the beginning of my illness: I knocked my side, but I was still quite well that day and the next. It hurt a little, then rather more. I saw the doctors, then followed despondency and anguish, more doctors, and I drew nearer to the abyss. My strength grew less and I kept coming nearer and nearer, and now I have wasted away and there is no light in my eyes. I think of the appendix — but this is death! I think of mending the appendix, and all the while here is death! Can it really be death?" Again terror seized him and he gasped for breath. He leant down and began feeling for the matches, pressing with his elbow on the stand beside the bed. It was in his way and hurt him, he grew furious with it, pressed on it still harder, and upset it. Breathless and in despair he fell on his back, expecting death to come immediately.

Meanwhile the visitors were leaving. Praskovya Fëdorovna was seeing them off. She heard something fall and came in.

"What has happened?"

"Nothing. I knocked it over accidentally."

She went out and returned with a candle. He lay there panting heavily, like a man who has run a thousand yards, and stared upwards at her with a fixed look.

"What is it, Jean?"

"No . . . no . . . thing. I upset it." ("Why speak of it? She won't understand," he thought.)

And in truth she did not understand. She picked up the stand, lit his candle, and hurried away to see another visitor off. When she came back he still lay on his back, looking upwards.

"What is it? Do you feel worse?"

"Yes."

She shook her head and sat down.

"Do you know, Jean, I think we must ask Leshchetitsky to come and see you here."

This meant calling in the famous specialist, regardless of expense. He smiled malignantly and said "No." She remained a little longer and then went up to him and kissed his forehead.

While she was kissing him he hated her from the bottom of his soul and with difficulty refrained from pushing her away.

"Good-night. Please God you'll sleep."

"Yes."

VI

Ivan Ilych saw that he was dying, and he was in continual despair.

In the depth of his heart he knew he was dying, but not only was he not accustomed to the thought, he simply did not and could not grasp it.

The syllogism he had learnt from Kiezewetter's Logic:° "Caius is a man, men are mortal, therefore Caius is mortal," had always seemed to him correct as applied to Caius, but certainly not as applied to himself. That Caius — man in the abstract — was mortal, was perfectly correct, but he was not Caius, not an abstract man, but a creature quite, quite separate from all others. He had been little Vanya, with a mama and a papa, with Mitya and Volodya, with the toys, a coachman and a nurse, afterwards with Katenka and with all the joys, griefs, and delights of childhood, boyhood, and youth. What did Caius know of the smell of that striped leather ball Vanya had been so fond of? Had Caius kissed his mother's hand like that, and did the silk of her dress rustle so for Caius? Had he rioted like that at school when the pastry was bad? Had Caius been in love like that? Could Caius preside at a session as he did? "Caius really was mortal, and it was right for him to die; but for me, little Vanya, Ivan Ilych, with all my thoughts and emotions, it's altogether a different matter. It cannot be that I ought to die. That would be too terrible."

Kiezewetter's Logic: Klaus Kiezewetter (1766–1819) wrote *The Outline of Logic According to Kantian Principles,* a popular text in Russia, based on the teachings of German philosopher Immanuel Kant (1722–1804).

Such was his feeling.

"If I had to die like Caius I should have known it was so. An inner voice would have told me so, but there was nothing of the sort in me and I and all my friends felt that our case was quite different from that of Caius. And now here it is!" he said to himself. "It can't be. It's impossible! But here it is. How is this? How is one to understand it?"

He could not understand it, and tried to drive this false, incorrect, morbid thought away and to replace it by other proper and healthy thoughts. But that thought, and not the thought only but the reality itself, seemed to come and confront him.

And to replace that thought he called up a succession of others, hoping to find in them some support. He tried to get back into the former current of thoughts that had once screened the thought of death from him. But strange to say, all that formerly shut off, hidden, and destroyed, his consciousness of death, no longer had that effect. Ivan Ilych now spent most of his time in attempting to re-establish that old current. He would say to himself: "I will take up my duties again — after all I used to live by them." And banishing all doubts he would go to the law courts, enter into conversation with his colleagues, and sit carelessly as was his wont, scanning the crowd with a thoughtful look and leaning both his emaciated arms on the arms of his oak chair; bending over as usual to a colleague and drawing his papers nearer he would interchange whispers with him, and then suddenly raising his eyes and sitting erect would pronounce certain words and open the proceedings. But suddenly in the midst of those proceedings the pain in his side, regardless of the stage the proceedings had reached, would begin its own gnawing work. Ivan Ilych would turn his attention to it and try to drive the thought of it away, but without success. *It* would come and stand before him and look at him, and he would be petrified and the light would die out of his eyes, and he would again begin asking himself whether *It* alone was true. And his colleagues and subordinates would see with surprise and distress that he, the brilliant and subtle judge, was becoming confused and making mistakes. He would shake himself, try to pull himself together, manage somehow to bring the sitting to a close, and return home with the sorrowful consciousness that his judicial labors could not as formerly hide from him what he wanted them to hide, and could not deliver him from *It*. And what was worst of all was that *It* drew his attention to itself not in order to make him take some action but only that he should look at *It*, look it straight in the face: look at it and without doing anything, suffer inexpressibly.

And to save himself from this condition Ivan Ilych looked for consolations — new screens — and new screens were found and for a while seemed to save him, but then they immediately fell to pieces or rather became transparent, as if *It* penetrated them and nothing could veil *It*.

In these latter days he would go into the drawing-room he had arranged — that drawing-room where he had fallen and for the sake of which (how bitterly ridiculous it seemed) he had sacrificed his life — for he knew that his illness originated with that knock. He would enter and see that something had scratched the polished table. He would look for the cause of this and find that it was the bronze ornamentation of an album, that had got bent. He would take up the expensive album which he had lovingly arranged, and feel vexed with his daughter and her friends for their untidiness — for the album was torn here and there and some of the photographs turned upside down. He would put it carefully in order and bend the ornamentation back into position. Then it would occur to him to place all those things in another corner of the room, near the plants. He could call the footman, but his daughter or wife would come to help him. They would not agree, and his wife would contradict him, and he would dispute and grow angry. But that was all right, for then he did not think about *It*. *It* was invisible.

But then, when he was moving something himself, his wife would say: "Let the servants do it. You will hurt yourself again." And suddenly *It* would flash through the screen and he would see it. It was just a flash, and he hoped it would disappear, but he would involuntarily pay attention to his side. "It sits there as before, gnawing just the same!" And he could no longer forget *It*, but could distinctly see it looking at him from behind the flowers. "What is it all for?"

"It really is so! I lost my life over that curtain as I might have done when storming a fort. Is that possible? How terrible and how stupid. It can't be true! It can't, but it is."

He would go to his study, lie down, and again be alone with *It*: face to face with *It*. And nothing could be done with *It* except to look at it and shudder.

VII

How it happened it is impossible to say because it came about step by step, unnoticed, but in the third month of Ivan Ilych's illness, his wife, his daughter, his son, his acquaintances, the doctors, the servants, and above all he himself, were aware that the whole interest he had for other people was whether he would soon vacate his place, and at last release the living from the discomfort caused by his presence and be himself released from his sufferings.

He slept less and less. He was given opium and hypodermic injections of morphine, but this did not relieve him. The dull depression he experienced in a somnolent condition at first gave him a little relief, but only as something new, afterwards it became as distressing as the pain itself or even more so.

Special foods were prepared for him by the doctors' orders, but all those foods became increasingly distasteful and disgusting to him.

For his excretions also special arrangements had to be made, and this was a torment to him every time — a torment from the uncleanliness, the unseemliness, and the smell, and from knowing that another person had to take part in it.

But just through this most unpleasant matter, Ivan Ilych obtained comfort. Gerasim, the butler's young assistant, always came in to carry the things out. Gerasim was a clean, fresh peasant lad, grown stout on town food and always cheerful and bright. At first the sight of him, in his clean Russian peasant costume, engaged on that disgusting task embarrassed Ivan Ilych.

Once when he got up from the commode too weak to draw up his trousers, he dropped into a soft armchair and looked with horror at his bare, enfeebled thighs with the muscles so sharply marked on them.

Gerasim with a firm light tread, his heavy boots emitting a pleasant smell of tar and fresh winter air, came in wearing a clean Hessian apron, the sleeves of his print shirt tucked up over his strong bare young arms; and refraining from looking at his sick master out of consideration for his feelings, and restraining the joy of life that beamed from his face, he went up to the commode.

"Gerasim!" said Ivan Ilych in a weak voice.

Gerasim started, evidently afraid he might have committed some blunder, and with a rapid movement turned his fresh, kind, simply young face which just showed the first downy signs of a beard.

"Yes, sir?"

"That must be very unpleasant for you. You must forgive me. I am helpless."

"Oh, why, sir," and Gerasim's eyes beamed and he showed his glistening white teeth, "what's a little trouble? It's a case of illness with you, sir."

And his deft strong hands did their accustomed task, and he went out of the room stepping lightly. Five minutes later he as lightly returned.

Ivan Ilych was still sitting in the same position in the armchair.

"Gerasim," he said when the latter had replaced the freshly-washed utensil. "Please come here and help me." Gerasim went up to him. "Lift me up. It is hard for me to get up, and I have sent Dmitri away."

Gerasim went up to him, grasped his master with his strong arms deftly but gently, in the same way that he stepped — lifted him, supported him with one hand, and with the other drew up his trousers and would have set him down again, but Ivan Ilych asked to be led to the sofa. Gerasim, without an effort and without apparent pressure, led him, almost lifting him, to the sofa and placed him on it.

"Thank you. How easily and well you do it all!"

Gerasim smiled again and turned to leave the room. But Ivan Ilych felt his presence such a comfort that he did not want to let him go.

"One thing more, please move up that chair. No, the other one — under my feet. It is easier for me when my feet are raised."

Gerasim brought the chair, set it down gently in place, and raised Ivan Ilych's legs on to it. It seemed to Ivan Ilych that he felt better while Gerasim was holding up his legs.

"It's better when my legs are higher," he said. "Place that cushion under them."

Gerasim did so. He again lifted the legs and placed them, and again Ivan Ilych felt better while Gerasim held his legs. When he set them down Ivan Ilych fancied he felt worse.

"Gerasim," he said. "Are you busy now?"

"Not at all, sir," said Gerasim, who had learnt from the townsfolk how to speak to gentlefolk.

"What have you still to do?"

"What have I to do? I've done everything except chopping the logs for tomorrow."

"Then hold my legs up a bit higher, can you?"

"Of course I can. Why not?" And Gerasim raised his master's legs higher and Ivan Ilych thought that in that position he did not feel any pain at all.

"And how about the logs?"

"Don't trouble about that, sir. There's plenty of time."

Ivan Ilych told Gerasim to sit down and hold his legs, and began to talk to him. And strange to say it seemed to him that he felt better while Gerasim held his legs up.

After that Ivan Ilych would sometimes call Gerasim and get him to hold his legs on his shoulders, and he liked talking to him. Gerasim did it all easily, willingly, simply, and with a good nature that touched Ivan Ilych. Health, strength, and vitality in other people were offensive to him, but Gerasim's strength and vitality did not mortify but soothed him.

What tormented Ivan Ilych most was the deception, the lie, which for some reason they all accepted, that he was not dying but was simply ill, and that he only need keep quiet and undergo a treatment and then something very good would result. He however knew that do what they would nothing would come of it, only still more agonizing suffering and death. This deception tortured him — their not wishing to admit what they all knew and what he knew, but wanting to lie to him concerning his terrible condition, and wishing and forcing him to participate in that lie. Those lies — lies enacted over him on the eve of his death and destined to degrade this awful, solemn act to the level of their visitings, their curtains, their sturgeon for dinner — were a terrible agony for Ivan Ilych. And strangely enough, many times when they were going through their antics over him he had been within a hairbreadth of calling out to them: "Stop lying! You know and I know that I am dying. Then at least stop lying about it!" But he had never had the spirit to do it. The awful, terrible act of his dying was, he could see, reduced by those about him to the level of a casual, unpleasant, and almost indecorous incident (as if someone entered a drawing-room diffusing an unpleasant odor) and this was done by that very decorum which he had served all his life long. He saw that no one felt for him, because no one even wished to grasp his position. Only Gerasim recognized it and pitied him. And so Ivan Ilych felt at ease only with him. He felt comforted when Gerasim supported his legs (sometimes all night long) and refused to go to bed, saying, "Don't you worry, Ivan Ilych. I'll get sleep enough later on," or when he suddenly became familiar and exclaimed: "If you weren't sick it would be another matter, but as it is, why should I grudge a little trouble?" Gerasim alone did not lie; everything showed that he alone understood the facts of the case and did not consider it necessary to disguise them, but simply felt sorry for his emaciated and enfeebled master. Once when Ivan Ilych was sending him away he even said straight out: "We shall all of us die, so why should I grudge a little trouble?" — expressing the fact that he did not think his work burdensome, because he was doing it for a dying man and hoped someone would do the same for him when his time came.

Apart from this lying, or because of it, what most tormented Ivan Ilych was that no one pitied him as he wished to be pitied. At certain moments after prolonged suffering he wished most of all (though he would have been ashamed to confess it) for someone to pity him as a sick child is pitied. He longed to be petted and comforted. He knew he was an important functionary, that he had a beard turning grey, and that therefore what he longed for was impossible, but still he longed for it. And in Gerasim's attitude towards him there was something akin to what he wished for, and so that attitude comforted him. Ivan Ilych wanted to weep, wanted to be petted and cried over, and then his colleague Shebek would come, and instead of weeping and being petted, Ivan Ilych would assume a serious, severe, and profound air, and by force of habit would express his opinion on a decision of the Court of Cassation and would stubbornly insist on that view. This falsity around him and within him did more than anything else to poison his last days.

VIII

It was morning. He knew it was morning because Gerasim had gone, and Peter the footman had come and put out the candles, drawn back one of the curtains, and begun quietly to tidy up. Whether it was morning or evening, Friday or Sunday, made no difference, it was all just the same: the gnawing, unmitigated, agonizing pain, never ceasing for an instant, the consciousness of life inexorably waning but not yet extinguished, the approach of that ever dreaded and hateful Death which was the only reality, and always the same falsity. What were days, weeks, hours, in such a case?

"Will you have some tea, sir?"

"He wants things to be regular, and wishes the gentlefolk to drink tea in the morning," thought Ivan Ilych, and only said "No."

"Wouldn't you like to move onto the sofa, sir?"

"He wants to tidy up the room, and I'm in the way. I am uncleanliness and disorder," he thought, and said only:

"No, leave me alone."

The man went on bustling about. Ivan Ilych stretched out his hand. Peter came up, ready to help.

"What is it, sir?"

"My watch."

Peter took the watch which was close at hand and gave it to his master.

"Half-past eight. Are they up?"

"No, sir, except Vasily Ivanich" (the son) "who has gone to school. Praskovya Fëdorovna ordered me to wake her if you asked for her. Shall I do so?"

"No, there's no need to." "Perhaps I'd better have some tea," he thought, and added aloud: "Yes, bring me some tea."

Peter went to the door, but Ivan Ilych dreaded being left alone. "How can I keep him here? Oh yes, my medicine." "Peter, give me my medicine."

"Why not? Perhaps it may still do me some good." He took a spoonful and swallowed it. "No, it won't help. It's all tomfoolery, all deception," he decided as soon as he became aware of the familiar, sickly, hopeless taste. "No, I can't believe in it any longer. But the pain, why this pain? If it would only cease just for a moment!" And he moaned. Peter turned towards him. "It's all right. Go and fetch me some tea."

Peter went out. Left alone Ivan Ilych groaned not so much with pain, terrible though that was, as from mental anguish. Always and for ever the same, always these endless days and nights. If only it would come quicker! If only *what* would come quicker? Death, darkness? . . . No, no! Anything rather than death!

When Peter returned with the tea on a tray, Ivan Ilych stared at him for a time in perplexity, not realizing who and what he was. Peter was disconcerted by that look and his embarrassment brought Ivan Ilych to himself.

"Oh, tea! All right, put it down. Only help me to wash and put on a clean shirt."

And Ivan Ilych began to wash. With pauses for rest, he washed his hands and then his face, cleaned his teeth, brushed his hair, and looked in the glass. He was terrified by what he saw, especially by the limp way in which his hair clung to his pallid forehead.

While his shirt was being changed he knew that he would be still more frightened at the sight of his body, so he avoided looking at it. Finally he was ready. He drew on a dressing gown, wrapped himself in a plaid, and sat down in the armchair to take his tea. For a moment he felt refreshed, but as soon as he began to drink the tea he was again aware of the same taste, and the pain also returned. He finished it with an effort, and then lay down stretching out his legs, and dismissed Peter.

Always the same. Now a spark of hope flashes up, then a sea of despair rages, and always pain; always pain, always despair, and always the same. When alone he had a dreadful and distressing desire to call someone, but he knew beforehand that with others present it would be still worse. "Another dose of morphine — to lose consciousness. I will tell him, the doctor, that he must think of something else. It's impossible, impossible, to go on like this."

An hour and another pass like that. But now there is a ring at the door bell. Perhaps it's the doctor? It is. He comes in fresh, hearty, plump, and cheerful, with that look on his face that seems to say: "There now, you're in a panic about something, but we'll arrange it all for you directly!" The doctor knows this expression is out of place here, but he has put it on once for all and can't take it off — like a man who has put on a frock-coat in the morning to pay a round of calls.

The doctor rubs his hands vigorously and reassuringly.

"Brr! How cold it is! There's such a sharp frost; just let me warm myself!" he says, as if it were only a matter of waiting till he was warm, and then he would put everything right.

"Well now, how are you?"

Ivan Ilych feels that the doctor would like to say: "Well, how are our affairs?" but that even he feels that this would not do, and says instead: "What sort of a night have you had?"

Ivan Ilych looks at him as much as to say: "Are you really never ashamed of lying?" But the doctor does not wish to understand this question, and Ivan Ilych says: "Just as terrible as ever. The pain never leaves me and never subsides. If only something. . . ."

"Yes, you sick people are always like that. . . . There, now I think I am warm enough. Even Praskovya Fëdorovna, who is so particular, could find no fault with my temperature. Well, now I can say good-morning," and the doctor presses his patient's hand.

Then, dropping his former playfulness, he begins with a most serious face to examine the patient, feeling his pulse and taking his temperature, and then begins the sounding and auscultation.

Ivan Ilych knows quite well and definitely that all this is nonsense and pure deception, but when the doctor, getting down on his knee, leans over him, putting his ear first higher then lower, and performs various gymnastic movements over him with a significant expression on his face, Ivan Ilych submits to it all as he used to submit to the speeches of the lawyers, though he knew very well that they were all lying and why they were lying.

The doctor, kneeling on the sofa, is still sounding him when Praskovya Fëdorovna's silk dress rustles at the door and she is heard scolding Peter for not having let her know of the doctor's arrival.

She comes in, kisses her husband, and at once proceeds to prove that she has been up a long time already, and only owing to a misunderstanding failed to be there when the doctor arrived.

Ivan Ilych looks at her, scans her all over, sets against her the whiteness and plumpness and cleanness of her hands and neck, the gloss of her hair, and the sparkle of her vivacious eyes. He hates her with his whole soul. And the thrill of hatred he feels for her makes him suffer from her touch.

Her attitude towards him and his disease is still the same. Just as the doctor had adopted a certain relation to his patient which he could not abandon, so had she formed one towards him — that he was not doing something he ought to do and was himself to blame, and that she reproached him lovingly for this — and she could not now change that attitude.

"You see he doesn't listen to me and doesn't take his medicine at the proper time. And above all he lies in a position that is no doubt bad for him — with his legs up."

She described how he made Gerasim hold his legs up.

The doctor smiled with a contemptuous affability that said: "What's to be done? These sick people do have foolish fancies of that kind, but we must forgive them."

When the examination was over the doctor looked at his watch, and then Praskovya Fëdorovna announced to Ivan Ilych that it was of course as he pleased, but she had sent today for a celebrated specialist who would examine him and have a consultation with Michael Danilovich (their regular doctor).

"Please don't raise any objections. I am doing this for my own sake," she said ironically, letting it be felt that she was doing it all for his sake and only said this to leave him no right to refuse. He remained silent, knitting his brows. He felt that he was so surrounded and involved in a mesh of falsity that it was hard to unravel anything.

Everything she did for him was entirely for her own sake, and she told him she was doing for herself what she actually was doing for herself, as if that was so incredible that he must understand the opposite.

At half-past eleven the celebrated specialist arrived. Again the sounding began and the significant conversations in his presence and in another room, about the kidneys and the appendix, and the questions and answers, with such an air of importance that again, instead of the real question of life and death which now alone confronted him, the question arose of the kidney and appendix which were not behaving as they ought to and would now be attacked by Michael Danilovich and the specialist and forced to amend their ways.

The celebrated specialist took leave of him with a serious though not hopeless look, and in reply to the timid question Ivan Ilych, with eyes glistening with fear and hope, put to him as to whether there was a chance of recovery, said that he could not vouch for it but there was a possibility. The look of hope with which Ivan Ilych watched the doctor out was so pathetic that Praskovya Fëdorovna, seeing it, even wept as she left the room to hand the doctor his fee.

The gleam of hope kindled by the doctor's encouragement did not last long. The same room, the same pictures, curtains, wallpaper, medicine bottles, were all there, and the same aching suffering body, and Ivan Ilych began to moan. They gave him a subcutaneous injection and he sank into oblivion.

It was twilight when he came to. They brought him his dinner and he swallowed some beef tea with difficulty, and then everything was the same again and night was coming on.

After dinner, at seven o'clock, Praskovya Fëdorovna came into the room in evening dress, her full bosom pushed up by her corset, and with traces of powder on her face. She had reminded him in the morning that they were going to the theater. Sarah Bernhardt was visiting the town and they had a box, which he had insisted on their taking. Now he had forgotten about it and her toilet offended him, but he concealed his vexation when he remembered that he had himself insisted on their securing a box and going because it would be an instructive and aesthetic pleasure for the children.

Praskovya Fëdorovna came in, self-satisfied but yet with a rather guilty air. She sat down and asked how he was, but, as he saw, only for the sake of asking and not in order to learn about it, knowing that there was nothing to learn — and then went on to what she really wanted to say: that she would not on any account have gone but that the box had been taken and Helen and their daughter were going, as well as Petrishchev (the examining magistrate, their daughter's fiancé) and that it was out of the question to let them go alone; but that she would have much preferred to sit with him for a while; and he must be sure to follow the doctor's orders while she was away.

"Oh, and Fëdor Petrovich" (the fiancé) "would like to come in. May he? And Lisa?"

"All right."

Their daughter came in in full evening dress, her fresh young flesh exposed (making a show of that very flesh which in his own case caused so much suffering), strong, healthy, evidently in love, and impatient with illness, suffering, and death, because they interfered with her happiness.

Fëdor Petrovich came in too, in evening dress, his hair curled *à la Capoul,*° a tight stiff collar round his long sinewy neck, an enormous white shirt-front and narrow black trousers tightly stretched over his strong thighs. He had one white glove tightly drawn on, and was holding his opera hat in his hand.

Following him the schoolboy crept in unnoticed, in a new uniform, poor little fellow, and wearing gloves. Terribly dark shadows showed under his eyes, the meaning of which Ivan Ilych knew well.

His son had always seemed pathetic to him, and now it was dreadful to see the boy's frightened look of pity. It seemed to Ivan Ilych that Vasya was the only one besides Gerasim who understood and pitied him.

They all sat down and again asked how he was. A silence followed. Lisa asked her mother about the opera-glasses, and there was an altercation between mother and daughter as to who had taken them and where they had been put. This occasioned some unpleasantness.

Fëdor Petrovich inquired of Ivan Ilych whether he had ever seen Sarah Bernhardt. Ivan Ilych did not at first catch the question, but then replied: "No, have you seen her before?"

"Yes, in *Adrienne Lecouvreur.*"°

Praskovya Fëdorovna mentioned some rôles in which Sarah Bernhardt was particularly good. Her daughter disagreed. Conversation sprang up as to the elegance and realism of her acting — the sort of conversation that is always repeated and is always the same.

In the midst of the conversation Fëdor Petrovich glanced at Ivan Ilych and became silent. The others also looked at him and grew silent. Ivan Ilych was staring with glittering eyes straight before him, evidently indignant with them. This had to be rectified, but it was impossible to do so. The silence had to be broken, but for a time no one dared to break it and they all became afraid that the conventional deception would suddenly become obvious and the truth become plain to all. Lisa was the first to pluck up courage and break that silence, but by trying to hide what everybody was feeling, she betrayed it.

"Well, if we are going it's time to start," she said, looking at her watch, a present from her father, and with a faint and significant smile at Fëdor Petrovich relating to something known only to them. She got up with a rustle of her dress.

They all rose, said good-night, and went away.

à la Capoul: An elaborate hairstyle for men. Capoul was a famous French singer.
Adrienne Lecouvreur: Comedy by French playwrights Eugène Scribe and Ernest Legouvé.

When they had gone it seemed to Ivan Ilych that he felt better; the falsity had gone with them. But the pain remained — that same pain and that same fear that made everything monotonously alike, nothing harder and nothing easier. Everything was worse.

Again minute followed minute and hour followed hour. Everything remained the same and there was no cessation. And the inevitable end of it all became more and more terrible.

"Yes, send Gerasim here," he replied to a question Peter asked.

IX

His wife returned late at night. She came in on tiptoe, but he heard her, opened his eyes, and made haste to close them again. She wished to send Gerasim away and to sit with him herself, but he opened his eyes and said: "No, go away."

"Are you in great pain?"

"Always the same."

"Take some opium."

He agreed and took some. She went away.

Till about three in the morning he was in a state of stupefied misery. It seemed to him that he and his pain were being thrust into a narrow, deep black sack, but though they were pushed further and further in they could not be pushed to the bottom. And this, terrible enough in itself, was accompanied by suffering. He was frightened yet wanted to fall through the sack, he struggled but yet co-operated. And suddenly he broke through, fell, and regained consciousness. Gerasim was sitting at the foot of the bed dozing quietly and patiently, while he himself lay with his emaciated stockinged legs resting on Gerasim's shoulders; the same shaded candle was there and the same unceasing pain.

"Go away, Gerasim," he whispered.

"It's all right, sir. I'll stay a while."

"No. Go away."

He removed his legs from Gerasim's shoulders, turned sideways onto his arm, and felt sorry for himself. He only waited till Gerasim had gone into the next room and then restrained himself no longer but wept like a child. He wept on account of his helplessness, his terrible loneliness, the cruelty of man, the cruelty of God, and the absence of God.

"Why hast Thou done all this? Why hast Thou brought me here? Why, why dost Thou torment me so terribly?"

He did not expect an answer and yet wept because there was no answer and could be none. The pain again grew more acute, but he did not stir and did not call. He said to himself: "Go on! Strike me! But what is it for? What have I done to Thee? What is it for?"

Then he grew quiet and not only ceased weeping but even held his breath and became all attention. It was as though he were listening not to an audible voice but to the voice of his soul, to the current of thoughts arising within him.

"What is it you want?" was the first clear conception capable of expression in words, that he heard.

"What do you want? What do you want?" he repeated to himself.

"What do I want? To live and not to suffer," he answered.

And again he listened with such concentrated attention that even his pain did not distract him.

"To live? How?" asked his inner voice.

"Why, to live as I used to — well and pleasantly."

"As you lived before, well and pleasantly?" the voice repeated.

And in imagination he began to recall the best moments of his pleasant life. But strange to say none of those best moments of his pleasant life now seemed at all what they had then seemed — none of them except the first recollections of childhood. There, in childhood, there had been something really pleasant with which it would be possible to live if it could return. But the child who had experienced that happiness existed no longer, it was like a reminiscence of somebody else.

As soon as the period began which had produced the present Ivan Ilych, all that had then seemed joys now melted before his sight and turned into something trivial and often nasty.

And the further he departed from childhood and the nearer he came to the present the more worthless and doubtful were the joys. This began with the School of Law. A little that was really good was still found there — there was lightheartedness, friendship, and hope. But in the upper classes there had already been fewer of such good moments. Then during the first years of his official career, when he was in the service of the Governor, some pleasant moments again occurred: they were the memories of love for a woman. Then all became confused and there was still less of what was good; later on again there was still less that was good, and the further he went the less there was. His marriage, a mere accident, then the disenchantment that followed it, his wife's bad breath and the sensuality and hypocrisy: then the deadly official life and those preoccupations about money, a year of it, and two, and ten, and twenty, and always the same thing. And the longer it lasted the more deadly it became. "It is as if I had been going downhill while I imagined I was going up. And that is really what it was. I was going up in public opinion, but to the same extent life was ebbing away from me. And now it is all done and there is only death."

"Then what does it mean? Why? It can't be that life is so senseless and horrible. But if it really has been so horrible and senseless, why must I die and die in agony? There is something wrong!"

"Maybe I did not live as I ought to have done," it suddenly occurred to him. "But how could that be, when I did everything properly?" he replied, and immediately dismissed from his mind this, the sole solution of all the riddles of life and death, as something quite impossible.

"Then what do you want now? To live? Live how? Live as you lived in the law courts when the usher proclaimed 'The judge is coming!' The judge is coming, the judge!" he repeated to himself. "Here he is, the judge. But I am not guilty!" he exclaimed angrily. "What is it for?" And he ceased crying, but turning his face to the wall continued to ponder on the same question: Why, and for what purpose, is there all this horror? But however much he pondered he found no answer. And whenever the thought occurred to him, as it often did, that it all resulted from his not having lived as he ought to have done, he at once recalled the correctness of his whole life and dismissed so strange an idea.

X

Another fortnight passed. Ivan Ilych now no longer left his sofa. He would not lie in bed but lay on the sofa, facing the wall nearly all the time. He suffered ever the same unceasing agonies and in his loneliness pondered always on the same insoluble question: "What is this? Can it be that it is Death?" And the inner voice answered: "Yes, it is Death."

"Why these sufferings?" And the voice answered, "For no reason — they just are so." Beyond and besides this there was nothing.

From the very beginning of his illness, ever since he had first been to see the doctor, Ivan Ilych's life had been divided between two contrary and alternating moods: now it was despair and the expectation of this uncomprehended and terrible death, and now hope and an intently interested observation of the functioning of his organs. Now before his eyes there was only a kidney or an intestine that temporarily evaded its duty, and now only that incomprehensible and dreadful death from which it was impossible to escape.

These two states of mind had alternated from the very beginning of his illness, but the further it progressed the more doubtful and fantastic became the conception of the kidney, and the more real the sense of impending death.

He had but to call to mind what he had been three months before and what he was now, to call to mind with what regularity he had been going downhill, for every possibility of hope to be shattered.

Latterly during that loneliness in which he found himself as he lay facing the back of the sofa, a loneliness in the midst of a populous town and surrounded by numerous acquaintances and relations but that yet could not have been more complete anywhere — either at the bottom of the sea or under the earth — during that terrible loneliness Ivan Ilych had lived only in memories of the past. Pictures of his past rose before him one after another. They always began with what was nearest in time and then went back to what was most remote — to his childhood — and rested there. If he thought of the stewed prunes that had been offered him that day, his mind went back to the raw shrivelled French plums of his childhood, their peculiar flavor and the flow of saliva when he sucked their stones, and along with the memory of that taste came a whole series of memories of those days: his nurse, his brother, and their toys. "No, I mustn't think of that. . . . It is too painful," Ivan Ilych said to himself, and brought himself back to the present — to the button on the back of the sofa and the creases in its morocco. "Morocco is expensive, but it does not wear well: there had been a quarrel about it. It was a different kind of quarrel and a different kind of morocco that time when we tore father's portfolio and were punished, and mama brought us some tarts. . . ." And again his thoughts dwelt on his childhood, and again it was painful and he tried to banish them and fix his mind on something else.

Then again together with that chain of memories another series passed through his mind — of how his illness had progressed and grown worse. There also the further back he looked the more life there had been. There had been more of what was good in life and more of life itself. The two merged together. "Just as the pain went on getting worse and worse, so my life grew worse and worse," he thought. "There is one bright spot there at the back, at the beginning of life, and afterwards all becomes blacker and blacker and proceeds more and more rapidly — in inverse ratio to the square of the distance from death," thought Ivan Ilych. And the example of a stone falling downwards with increasing velocity entered his mind. Life, a series of increasing sufferings, flies further and further towards its end — the most terrible suffering. "I am flying. . . ." He shuddered, shifted himself, and tried to resist, but was already aware that resistance was impossible, and again with eyes weary of gazing but unable to cease seeing what was before them, he stared at the back of the sofa and waited — awaiting that dreadful fall and shock and destruction.

"Resistance is impossible!" he said to himself. "If I could only understand what it is all for! But that too is impossible. An explanation would be possible if it could be said that I have not lived as I ought to. But it is impossible to say that," and he remembered all the legality, correctitude, and propriety of his life. "That at any rate can certainly not be admitted," he thought, and his lips smiled ironically as if someone could see that smile and be taken in by it. "There is no explanation! Agony, death. . . . What for?"

XI

Another two weeks went by in this way and during that fortnight an event occurred that Ivan Ilych and his wife had desired. Petrishchev formally proposed. It happened in the evening. The next day Praskovya Fëdorovna came into her husband's room considering how best to inform him of it, but that very night there had been a fresh change for the worse in his condition. She found him still lying on the sofa but in a different position. He lay on his back, groaning and staring fixedly straight in front of him.

She began to remind him of his medicines, but he turned his eyes towards her with such a look that she did not finish what she was saying; so great an animosity, to her in particular, did that look express.

"For Christ's sake let me die in peace!" he said.

She would have gone away, but just then their daughter came in and went up to say good morning. He looked at her as he had done at his wife, and in reply to her inquiry about his health said dryly that he would soon free them all of himself. They were both silent and after sitting with him for a while went away.

"Is it our fault?" Lisa said to her mother. "It's as if we were to blame! I am sorry for papa, but why should we be tortured?"

The doctor came at his usual time. Ivan Ilych answered "Yes" and "No," never taking his angry eyes from him, and at last said: "You know you can do nothing for me, so leave me alone."

"We can ease your sufferings."

"You can't even do that. Let me be."

The doctor went into the drawing-room and told Praskovya Fëdorovna that the case was very serious and that the only resource left was opium to allay her husband's sufferings, which must be terrible.

It was true, as the doctor said, that Ivan Ilych's physical sufferings were terrible, but worse than the physical sufferings were his mental sufferings, which were his chief torture.

His mental sufferings were due to the fact that that night, as he looked at Gerasim's sleepy, good-natured face with its prominent cheek-bones, the question suddenly occurred to him: "What if my whole life has really been wrong?"

It occurred to him that what had appeared perfectly impossible before, namely that he had not spent his life as he should have done, might after all be true. It occurred to him that his scarcely perceptible attempts to struggle against what was considered good by the most highly placed people, those scarcely noticeable impulses which he had immediately suppressed, might have been the real thing, and all the rest false. And his professional duties and the whole arrangement of his life and of his family, and all his social and official interests, might all have been false. He tried to defend all those things to himself and suddenly felt the weakness of what he was defending. There was nothing to defend.

"But if that is so," he said to himself, "and I am leaving this life with the consciousness that I have lost all that was given me and it is impossible to rectify it — what then?"

He lay on his back and began to pass his life in review in quite a new way. In the morning when he saw first his footman, then his wife, then his daughter, and then the doctor, their every word and movement confirmed to him the awful truth that had been revealed to him during the night. In them he saw himself — all that for which he had lived — and saw clearly that it was not real at all, but a terrible and huge deception which had hidden both life and death. This consciousness intensified his physical suffering tenfold. He groaned and tossed about, and pulled at his clothing which choked and stifled him. And he hated them on that account.

He was given a large dose of opium and became unconscious, but at noon his sufferings began again. He drove everybody away and tossed from side to side.

His wife came to him and said:

"Jean, my dear, do this for me. It can't do any harm and often helps. Healthy people often do it."

He opened his eyes wide.

"What? Take communion? Why? It's unnecessary! However . . ."

She began to cry.

"Yes, do, my dear. I'll send for our priest. He is such a nice man."

"All right. Very well," he muttered.

When the priest came and heard his confession, Ivan Ilych was softened and seemed to feel a relief from his doubts and consequently from his sufferings, and for a moment there came a ray of hope. He again began to think of the vermiform appendix and the possibility of correcting it. He received the sacrament with tears in his eyes.

When they laid him down again afterwards he felt a moment's ease, and the hope that he might live awoke in him again. He began to think of the operation that had been suggested to him. "To live! I want to live!" he said to himself.

His wife came in to congratulate him after his communion, and when uttering the usual conventional words she added:

"You feel better, don't you?"

Without looking at her he said "Yes."

Her dress, her figure, the expression of her face, the tone of her voice, all revealed the same thing. "This is wrong, it is not as it should be. All you have lived for and still live for is falsehood and deception, hiding life and death from you." And as soon as he admitted that thought, his hatred and his agonizing physical suffering again sprang up, and with that suffering a consciousness of the unavoidable, approaching end. And to this was added a new sensation of grinding shooting pain and a feeling of suffocation.

The expression of his face when he uttered that "yes" was dreadful. Having uttered it, he looked her straight in the eyes, turned on his face with a rapidity extraordinary in his weak state and shouted:

"Go away! Go away and leave me alone!"

XII

From that moment the screaming began that continued for three days, and was so terrible that one could not hear it through two closed doors without horror. At the moment he answered his wife he realized that he was lost, that there was no return, that the end had come, the very end, and his doubts were still unsolved and remained doubts.

"Oh! Oh! Oh!" he cried in various intonations. He had begun by screaming "I won't!" and continued screaming on the letter O.

For three whole days, during which time did not exist for him, he struggled in that black sack into which he was being thrust by an invisible, resistless force. He struggled as a man condemned to death struggles in the hands of the executioner, knowing that he cannot save himself. And every moment he felt that despite all his efforts he was drawing nearer and nearer to what terrified him. He felt that his agony was due to his being thrust into that black hole and still more to his not being able to get right into it. He was hindered from getting into it by his conviction that his life had been a good one. That very justification of his life held him fast and prevented his moving forward, and it caused him most torment of all.

Suddenly some force struck him in the chest and side, making it still harder to breathe, and he fell through the hole and there at the bottom was a light. What had happened to him was like the sensation one sometimes experiences in a railway carriage when one thinks one is going backwards while one is really going forwards and suddenly becomes aware of the real direction.

"Yes, it was all not the right thing," he said to himself, "but that's no matter. It can be done. But what *is* the right thing?" he asked himself, and suddenly grew quiet.

This occurred at the end of the third day, two hours before his death. Just then his schoolboy son had crept softly in and gone up to the bedside. The dying man was still screaming desperately and waving his arms. His hand fell on the boy's head, and the boy caught it, pressed it to his lips, and began to cry.

At that very moment Ivan Ilych fell through and caught sight of the light, and it was revealed to him that though his life had not been what it should have been, this could still be rectified. He asked himself, "What *is* the right thing?" and grew still, listening. Then he felt that someone was kissing his hand. He opened his eyes, looked at his son, and felt sorry for him. His wife came up to him and he glanced at her. She was gazing at him open-mouthed, with undried tears on her nose and cheek and a despairing look on her face. He felt sorry for her too.

"Yes, I am making them wretched," he thought. "They are sorry, but it will be better for them when I die." He wished to say this but had not the strength to utter it. "Besides, why speak? I must act," he thought. With a look at his wife he indicated his son and said: "Take him away . . . sorry for him . . . sorry for you too. . . ." He tried to add, "forgive me," but said "forgo" and waved his hand, knowing that He whose understanding mattered would understand.

And suddenly it grew clear to him that what had been oppressing him and would not leave him was all dropping away at once from two sides, from ten sides, and from all sides. He was sorry for them, he must act so as not to hurt them: release them and free himself from these sufferings. "How good and how simple!" he thought. "And the pain?" he asked himself. "What had become of it? Where are you, pain?"

He turned his attention to it.

"Yes, here it is. Well, what of it? Let the pain be."

"And death . . . where is it?"

He sought his former accustomed fear of death and did not find it. "Where is it? What death?" There was no fear because there was no death.

In place of death there was light.

"So that's what it is!" he suddenly exclaimed aloud. "What joy!"

To him all this happened in a single instant, and the meaning of that instant did not change. For those present his agony continued for another two hours. Something rattled in his throat, his emaciated body twitched, then the gasping and rattle became less and less frequent.

"It is finished!" said someone near him.

He heard these words and repeated them in his soul.

"Death is finished," he said to himself. "It is no more!"

He drew in a breath, stopped in the midst of a sigh, stretched out, and died.

JOHN UPDIKE *(b. 1932) was born in Shillington, Pennsylvania, an only child. His father taught algebra in a local high school, and his mother wrote short stories and novels. His mother's consciousness of a special destiny, combined with his family's meager income — they lived with his mother's parents for the first thirteen years of Updike's life — made him "both arrogant and shy" as a teenager. He wrote stories, drew cartoons, and clowned for the approval of his peers. After getting straight A's in high school, he went to Harvard University on a full scholarship, studying English and graduating summa cum laude in 1954. He spent a year at Oxford on a fellowship, then joined the staff of* The New Yorker. *In 1959 Updike published both his first book of short fiction,* The Same Door, *and his first novel,* The Poorhouse Fair. *That year he also moved from New York City to a coastal town in Massachusetts, where he has lived most of the time since.*

In the 1960s, 1970s, and early 1980s, Updike continued to alternate novels and collections of stories, adding occasional volumes of verse, collections of essays, and one play. His novels include Rabbit, Run *(1960),* Couples *(1968),* Rabbit Redux *(1971), and* Marry Me *(1976).* Rabbit Is Rich *(1981), continuing the story of Harry "Rabbit" Angstrom, a suburban Pennsylvanian whom Updike has traced through adolescence, marriage, fatherhood, and middle age, won virtually every major American literary award for the year it appeared; Updike concluded the series with* Rabbit at Rest *(1991). Updike's collections of stories include* Pigeon Feathers *(1962),* Museums and Women *(1972), and* Problems and Other Stories *(1981). In 1983 Updike won the National Book Critics Circle Award for his collection of essays and criticism* Hugging the Shore. *In 1989 he published his memoirs,* Self-Consciousness. *Among his recent books is another collection,* Philadelphia and Other Stories, *(1995).*

Updike has said he is indebted to J. D. Salinger's stories for the literary form he adopted to describe the painful experience of adolescence: "I learned a lot from Salinger's short stories; he did remove the short narrative from the wise-guy, slice-of-life stories of the thirties and forties. Like most innovative artists, he made new room for shapelessness, for life as it is lived." Updike writes realistic narrative, believing that "fiction is a tissue of lies that refreshes and informs our sense of actuality. Reality is — chemically, atomically, biologically — a fabric of microscopic accuracies." His fiction, such as the story "A & P," concentrates on these "microscopic accuracies," tiny details of characterization and setting brilliantly described.

RELATED COMMENTARY: *John Updike, "Kafka and 'The Metamorphosis,' " page 804.*

JOHN UPDIKE

A & P

1961

In walks these three girls in nothing but bathing suits. I'm in the third checkout slot, with my back to the door, so I don't see them until they're over by the bread. The one that caught my eye first was the one in the plaid green two-piece. She was a chunky kid, with a good tan and a sweet broad soft-looking can with those two crescents of white just under it, where the sun never seems to hit, at the top of the backs of her legs. I stood there with my hand on a box of HiHo crackers trying to remember if I rang it up or not. I ring it up again and the customer starts giving me hell. She's one of these cash-register-watchers, a witch about fifty with rouge on her cheekbones and no eyebrows, and I know it made her day to trip me up. She'd been watching cash registers for fifty years and probably never seen a mistake before.

By the time I got her feathers smoothed and her goodies into a bag — she gives me a little snort in passing, if she'd been born at the right time they would have burned her over in Salem — by the time I get her on her way the girls had circled around the bread and were coming back, without a pushcart, back my way along the counters, in the aisle between the checkouts and the Special bins. They didn't even have shoes on. There was this chunky one, with the two-piece — it was bright green and the seams on the bra were still sharp and her belly was still pretty pale so I guessed she just got it (the suit) — there was this one, with one of those chubby berry-faces, the lips all bunched together under her nose, this one, and a tall one, with black hair that hadn't quite frizzed right, and one of these sunburns right across under the eyes, and a chin that was too long — you know, the kind of girl other girls think is very "striking" and "attractive" but never quite makes it, as they very well know, which is why they like her so much — and then the third one, that wasn't quite so tall. She was the queen. She kind of led them, the other two peeking around and making their shoulders round. She didn't look around, not this queen, she just walked straight on slowly, on these long white prima-donna legs. She came down a little hard on her heels, as if she didn't walk in her bare feet that much, putting down her heels and then letting the weight move along to her toes as if she was testing the floor with every step, putting a little deliberate extra action into it. You never know for sure how girls' minds work (do you really think it's a mind in there or just a little buzz like a bee in a glass jar?) but you got the idea she had talked the other two into coming in here with her, and now she was showing them how to do it, walk slow and hold yourself straight.

She had on a kind of dirty-pink — beige maybe, I don't know — bathing suit with a little nubble all over it, and what got me, the straps were down. They were off her shoulders looped loose around the cool tops of her arms, and I guess as a result the suit had slipped a little on her, so all around the top of the cloth there was this shining rim. If it hadn't been there you wouldn't have known there could have been anything whiter than those shoulders. With the straps pushed off, there was nothing between the top of the suit and the top of her head except just *her,* this clean bare plane of the top of her chest down from the shoulder bones like a dented sheet of metal tilted in the light. I mean, it was more than pretty.

She had sort of oaky hair that the sun and salt had bleached, done up in a bun that was unravelling, and a kind of prim face. Walking into the A & P with your straps down, I suppose it's the only kind of face you *can* have. She held her head so high her neck, coming up out of those white shoulders, looked kind of stretched, but I didn't mind. The longer her neck was, the more of her there was.

She must have felt in the corner of her eye me and over my shoulder Stokesie in the second slot watching, but she didn't tip. Not this queen. She kept her eyes moving across the racks, and stopped, and turned so slow it made my stomach rub the inside of my apron, and buzzed to the other two, who kind of huddled against her for relief, and then they all three of them went up the cat-and-dog-food-breakfast-cereal-macaroni-rice-raisins-season-ings-spreads-spaghetti-soft-drinks-crackers-and-cookies aisle. From the third slot I look straight up this aisle to the meat counter, and I watched them all the way. The fat one with the tan sort of fumbled with the cookies, but on second thought she put the package back. The sheep pushing their carts down the aisle — the girls were walking against the usual traffic (not that we have one-way signs or anything) — were pretty hilarious. You could see them, when Queenie's white shoulders dawned on them, kind of jerk, or hop, or hiccup, but their eyes snapped back to their own baskets and on they pushed. I bet you could set off dynamite in an A & P and the people would by and large keep reaching and checking oatmeal off their lists and muttering "Let me see, there was a third thing, began with A, asparagus, no, ah, yes, applesauce!" or whatever it is they do mutter. But there was no doubt, this jiggled them. A few houseslaves in pin curlers even looked around after pushing their carts past to make sure what they had seen was correct.

You know, it's one thing to have a girl in a bathing suit down on the beach, where what with the glare nobody can look at each other much any-way, and another thing in the cool of the A & P, under the fluorescent lights, against all those stacked packages, with her feet paddling along naked over our checkboard green-and-cream rubber-tile floor.

"Oh Daddy," Stokesie said beside me. "I feel so faint."

"Darling," I said. "Hold me tight." Stokesie's married, with two babies chalked up on his fuselage already, but as far as I can tell that's the only dif-ference. He's twenty-two, and I was nineteen this April.

"Is it done?" he asks, the responsible married man finding his voice. I forgot to say he thinks he's going to be manager some sunny day, maybe in 1990 when it's called the Great Alexandrov and Petrooshki Tea Company or something.

What he meant was, our town is five miles from a beach, with a big sum-mer colony out on the Point, but we're right in the middle of town, and the women generally put on a shirt or shorts or something before they get out of the car into the street. And anyway these are usually women with six children and varicose veins mapping their legs and nobody, including them, could care less. As I say, we're right in the middle of town, and if you stand at our front doors you can see two banks and the Congregational church and the newspa-per store and three real-estate offices and about twenty-seven old freeloaders tearing up Central Street because the sewer broke again. It's not as if we're on the Cape; we're north of Boston and there's people in this town haven't seen the ocean for twenty years.

The girls had reached the meat counter and were asking McMahon something. He pointed, they pointed, and they shuffled out of sight behind a pyramid of Diet Delight peaches. All that was left for us to see was old McMahon patting his mouth and looking after them sizing up their joints. Poor kids, I began to feel sorry for them, they couldn't help it.

Now here comes the sad part of the story, at least my family says it's sad, but I don't think it's so sad myself. The store's pretty empty, it being Thursday afternoon, so there was nothing much to do except lean on the register and wait for the girls to show up again. The whole store was like a pinball machine and I didn't know which tunnel they'd come out of. After a while they come around out of the far aisle, around the light bulbs, records at discount of the Caribbean Six or Tony Martin Sings or some such gunk you wonder they waste the wax on, sixpacks of candy bars, and plastic toys done up in cellophane that fall apart when a kid looks at them anyway. Around they come, Queenie still leading the way, and holding a little gray jar in her hand. Slots Three through Seven are unmanned and I could see her wondering between Stokes and me, but Stokesie with his usual luck draws an old party in baggy gray pants who stumbles up with four giant cans of pineapple juice (what do these bums *do* with all that pineapple juice? I've often asked myself) so the girls come to me. Queenie puts down the jar and I take it into my fingers icy cold. Kingfish Fancy Herring Snacks in Pure Sour Cream: 49¢. Now her hands are empty, not a ring or a bracelet, bare as God made them, and I wonder where the money's coming from. Still with that prim look she lifts a folded dollar bill out of the hollow at the center of her nubbled pink top. The jar went heavy in my hand. Really, I thought that was so cute.

Then everybody's luck begins to run out. Lengel comes in from haggling with a truck full of cabbages on the lot and is about to scuttle into that door marked MANAGER behind which he hides all day when the girls touch his eye. Lengel's pretty dreary, teaches Sunday school and the rest, but he doesn't miss that much. He comes over and says, "Girls, this isn't the beach."

Queenie blushes, though maybe it's just a brush of sunburn I was noticing for the first time, now that she was so close. "My mother asked me to pick up a jar of herring snacks." Her voice kind of startled me, the way voices do when you see the people first, coming out so flat and dumb yet kind of tony, too, the way it ticked over "pick up" and "snacks." All of a sudden I slid right down her voice into her living room. Her father and the other men were standing around in ice-cream coats and bow ties and the women were in sandals picking up herring snacks on toothpicks off a big glass plate and they were all holding drinks the color of water with olives and sprigs of mint in them. When my parents have somebody over they get lemonade and if it's a real racy affair Schlitz in tall glasses with "They'll Do It Every Time" cartoons stencilled on.

"That's all right," Lengel said. "But this isn't the beach." His repeating this struck me as funny, as if it had just occurred to him, and he had been thinking all these years the A & P was a great big sand dune and he was the head lifeguard. He didn't like my smiling — as I say he doesn't miss much — but he concentrates on giving the girls that sad Sunday-school-superintendent stare.

Queenie's blush is no sunburn now, and the plump one in plaid, that I liked better from the back — a really sweet can — pipes up, "We weren't do-ing any shopping. We just came in for the one thing."

"That makes no difference," Lengel tells her, and I could see from the way his eyes went that he hadn't noticed she was wearing a two-piece before. "We want you decently dressed when you come in here."

"We *are* decent," Queenie says suddenly, her lower lip pushing, getting sore now that she remembers her place, a place from which the crowd that runs the A & P must look pretty crummy. Fancy Herring Snacks flashed in her very blue eyes.

"Girls, I don't want to argue with you. After this come in here with your shoulders covered. It's our policy." He turns his back. That's policy for you. Policy is what the kingpins want. What the others want is juvenile delin-quency.

All this while, the customers had been showing up with their carts but, you know, sheep, seeing a scene, they had all bunched up on Stokesie, who shook open a paper bag as gently as peeling a peach, not wanting to miss a word. I could feel in the silence everybody getting nervous, most of all Lengel, who asks me, "Sammy, have you rung up their purchase?"

I thought and said "No" but it wasn't about that I was thinking. I go through the punches, 4, 9, GROC, TOT — it's more complicated than you think, and after you do it often enough, it begins to make a little song, that you hear words to, in my case "Hello (*bing*) there, you (*gung*) hap-py *pee*-pul (*splat*)!" — the *splat* being the drawer flying out. I uncrease the bill, tenderly as you may imagine, it just having come from between the two smoothest scoops of vanilla I had ever known were there, and pass a half and a penny into her nar-row pink palm, and nestle the herrings in a bag and twist its neck and hand it over, all the time thinking.

The girls, and who'd blame them, are in a hurry to get out, so I say "I quit" to Lengel enough for them to hear, hoping they'll stop and watch me, their unsuspected hero. They keep right on going, into the electric eye; the door flies open and they flicker across the lot to their car, Queenie and Plaid and Big Tall Goony-Goony (not that as raw material she was so bad), leaving me with Lengel and a kink in his eyebrow.

"Did you say something, Sammy?"

"I said I quit."

"I thought you did."

"You didn't have to embarrass them."

"It was they who were embarrassing us."

I started to say something that came out "Fiddle-de-doo." It's a saying of my grandmother's, and I know she would have been pleased.

"I don't think you know what you're saying," Lengel said.

"I know you don't," I said. "But I do." I pull the bow at the back of my apron and start shrugging it off my shoulders. A couple customers that had been heading for my slot begin to knock against each other, like scared pigs in a chute.

Lengel sighs and begins to look very patient and old and gray. He's been a friend of my parents for years. "Sammy, you don't want to do this to your Mom and Dad," he tells me. It's true, I don't. But it seems to me that once you begin a gesture it's fatal not to go through with it. I fold the apron, "Sammy" stitched in red on the pocket, and put it on the counter, and drop the bow tie on top of it. The bow tie is theirs, if you've ever wondered. "You'll feel this for the rest of your life," Lengel says, and I know that's true, too, but remembering how he made that pretty girl blush makes me so scrunchy inside I punch the No Sale tab and the machine whirs "pee-pul" and the drawer splats out. One advantage to this scene taking place in summer, I can follow this up with a clean exit, there's no fumbling around getting your coat and galoshes, I just saunter into the electric eye in my white shirt that my mother ironed the night before, and the door heaves itself open, and outside the sunshine is skating around on the asphalt.

I look around for my girls, but they're gone, of course. There wasn't anybody but some young married screaming with her children about some candy they didn't get by the door of a powder-blue Falcon station wagon. Looking back in the big windows, over the bags of peat moss and aluminum lawn furniture stacked on the pavement, I could see Lengel in my place in the slot, checking the sheep through. His face was dark gray and his back stiff, as if he'd just had an injection of iron, and my stomach kind of fell as I felt how hard the world was going to be to me hereafter.

ಐ

ALICE WALKER *(b. 1944) was the eighth and youngest child of Willie Lee and Minnie Lou Grant Walker, sharecroppers in Eatonton, Georgia. Walker did well in school, encouraged by her teachers and her mother, whose stories she loved as "a walking history of our community." For two years, Walker attended Spelman College in Atlanta, the oldest college for black women in the United States. Then she studied at Sarah Lawrence College in New York, where she began her writing career by publishing a book of poetry,* Once *(1968). Since that time Walker has published several collections of poetry, novels, volumes of short stories, and* Living by the Word *(1988), a book of essays. Her best-known novel,* The Color Purple *(1982), won the American Book Award and the Pulitzer Prize and has been made into a motion picture. Recent books are* The Temple of My Familiar *(1989),* Possessing the Secret of Joy *(1992), and* The Complete Stories *(1994).*

Walker's books show her commitment to the idea of radical social change. She was active in the civil rights movement in Mississippi, where she met and married a civil rights lawyer from whom she separated after the birth of their daughter. In confronting the painful struggle of black people's history, Walker asserts that the creativity of black women, the extent to which they are permitted to express themselves, is a measure of the health of the entire American society. She calls herself a "womanist," her term for a black feminist. In her definition, "womanism" is preferable to "feminism" because, as she has said,

> *Part of our tradition as black women is that we are universalists. Black children, yellow children, red children, brown children, that is the black woman's*

normal, day-to-day relationship. In my family alone, we are about four differ-
ent colors. When a black woman looks at the world, it is so different [from a
white woman] . . . when I look at the people in Iran they look like kinfolk.
When I look at the people in Cuba, they look like my uncles and nieces.

Walker credits many writers for influencing her prose style in her short fiction.
Virginia Woolf, Zora Neale Hurston, and Gabriel García Márquez seem to Walker to
be "like musicians; at one with their cultures and their historical subconscious." Her
two books of stories show a clear progression of theme. The women of In Love and
Trouble *(1973) struggle against social injustice almost in spite of themselves, as does*
the title character in "Roselily," from that collection; the heroines of You Can't Keep
a Good Woman Down *(1981) consciously challenge conventions. Walker has said,*
"Writing really helps you heal yourself. I think if you write long enough, you will be
a healthy person. That is, if you write what you need to write, as opposed to what will
make money, or what will make fame."

    RELATED COMMENTARY: *Alice Walker, "Zora Neale Hurston: A Cautionary*
Tale and a Partisan View," page 807.

ALICE WALKER

Roselily

1973

Dearly Beloved

She dreams; dragging herself across the world. A small girl in her mother's
white robe and veil, knee raised waist high through a bowl of quicksand
soup. The man who stands beside her is against this standing on the front
porch of her house, being married to the sound of cars whizzing by on highway 61.

we are gathered here

Like cotton to be weighed. Her fingers at the last minute busily removing dry
leaves and twigs. Aware it is a superficial sweep. She knows he blames Mississippi for the respectful way the men turn their heads up in the yard, the
women stand waiting and knowledgeable, their children held from mischief
by teachings from the wrong God. He glares beyond them to the occupants of
the cars, white faces glued to promises beyond a country wedding, noses
thrust forward like dogs on a track. For him they usurp the wedding.

in the sight of God

Yes, open house. That is what country black folks like. She dreams she
does not already have three children. A squeeze around the flowers in her
hands chokes off three and four and five years of breath. Instantly she is
ashamed and frightened in her superstition. She looks for the first time at the
preacher, forces humility into her eyes, as if she believes he is, in fact, a man of

God. She can imagine God, a small black boy, timidly pulling the preacher's coattail.

to join this man and this woman

She thinks of ropes, chains, handcuffs, his religion. His place of worship. Where she will be required to sit apart with covered head. In Chicago, a word she hears when thinking of smoke, from his description of what a cinder was, which they never had in Panther Burn. She sees hovering over the heads of the clean neighbors in her front yard black specks falling, clinging, from the sky. But in Chicago. Respect, a chance to build. Her children at last from underneath the detrimental wheel. A chance to be on top. What a relief, she thinks. What a vision, a view, from up so high.

in holy matrimony.

Her fourth child she gave away to the child's father who had some money. Certainly a good job. Had gone to Harvard. Was a good man but weak because good language meant so much to him he could not live with Roselily. Could not abide TV in the living room, five beds in three rooms, no Bach except from four to six on Sunday afternoons. No chess at all. She does not forget to worry about her son among his father's people. She wonders if the New England climate will agree with him. If he will ever come down to Mississippi, as his father did, to try to right the country's wrongs. She wonders if he will be stronger than his father. His father cried off and on throughout her pregnancy. Went to skin and bones. Suffered nightmares, retching and falling out of bed. Tried to kill himself. Later told his wife he found the right baby through friends. Vouched for, the sterling qualities that would make up his character.

It is not her nature to blame. Still, she is not entirely thankful. She supposes New England, the North, to be quite different from what she knows. It seems right somehow to her that people who move there to live return home completely changed. She thinks of the air, the smoke, the cinders. Imagines cinders big as hailstones; heavy, weighing on the people. Wonders how this pressure finds it way into the veins, roping the springs of laughter.

If there's anybody here that knows a reason why

But of course they know no reason why beyond what they daily have come to know. She thinks of the man who will be her husband, feels shut away from him because of the stiff severity of his plain black suit. His religion. A lifetime of black and white. Of veils. Covered head. It is as if her children are already gone from her. Not dead, but exalted on a pedestal, a stalk that has no roots. She wonders how to make new roots. It is beyond her. She wonders what one does with memories in a brand-new life. This had seemed easy, until she thought of it. "The reasons why . . . the people who" . . . she thinks, and does not wonder where the thought is from.

these two should not be joined

She thinks of her mother, who is dead. Dead, but still her mother. Joined. This is confusing. Of her father. A gray old man who sold wild mink, rabbit, fox skins to Sears, Roebuck. He stands in the yard, like a man waiting for a train. Her young sisters stand behind her in smooth green dresses, with flowers in their hands and hair. They giggle, she feels, at the absurdity of the wedding. They are ready for something new. She thinks the man beside her should marry one of them. She feels old. Yoked. An arm seems to reach out from behind her and snatch her backward. She thinks of cemeteries and the long sleep of grandparents mingling in the dirt. She believes that she believes in ghosts. In the soil giving back what it takes.

together

In the city. He sees her in a new way. This she knows, and is grateful. But is it new enough? She cannot always be a bride and virgin, wearing robes and veil. Even now her body itches to be free of satin and voile, organdy and lily of the valley. Memories crash against her. Memories of being bare to the sun. She wonders what it will be like. Not to have to go to a job. Not to work in a sewing plant. Not to worry about learning to sew straight seams in working-men's overalls, jeans, and dress pants. Her place will be in the home, he has said, repeatedly, promising her rest she had prayed for. But now she wonders. When she is rested, what will she do? They will make babies — she thinks practically about her fine brown body, his strong black one. They will be inevitable. Her hands will be full. Full of what? Babies. She is not comforted.

let him speak

She wishes she had asked him to explain more of what he meant. But she was impatient. Impatient to be done with sewing. With doing everything for three children, alone. Impatient to leave the girls she had known since childhood, their children growing up, their husbands hanging around her, already old, seedy. Nothing about them that she wanted, or needed. The fathers of her children driving by, waving, not waving; reminders of times she would just as soon forget. Impatient to see the South Side, where they would live and build and be respectable and respected and free. Her husband would free her. A romantic hush. Proposal. Promises. A new life! Respectable, reclaimed, renewed. Free! In robe and veil.

or forever hold

She does not even know if she loves him. She loves his sobriety. His refusal to sing just because he knows the tune. She loves his pride. His blackness and his gray car. She loves his understanding of her *condition*. She thinks she loves the effort he will make to redo her into what he truly wants. His love of her makes her completely conscious of how unloved she was before. This is something; though it makes her unbearably sad. Melancholy. She blinks her eyes. Remembers she is finally being married, like other girls. Like other girls, women? Something strains upward behind her eyes. She thinks of the something as a rat trapped, concerned, scurrying to and fro in her head, peering through the windows of her eyes. She wants to live for once. But doesn't know quite what that means. Wonders if she has ever done it. If she ever will. The preacher is odious to her. She wants to strike him out of the way, out of her light, with the back of her hand. It seems to her he has always been standing in front of her, barring her way.

his peace.

The rest she does not hear. She feels a kiss, passionate, rousing, within the general pandemonium. Cars drive up blowing their horns. Firecrackers go off. Dogs come from under the house and begin to yelp and bark. Her husband's hand is like the clasp of an iron gate. People congratulate. Her children press against her. They look with awe and distaste mixed with hope at their new father. He stands curiously apart, in spite of the people crowding about to grasp his free hand. He smiles at them all but his eyes are as if turned inward. He knows they cannot understand that he is not a Christian. He will not explain himself. He feels different, he looks it. The old women thought he was like one of their sons except that he had somehow got away from them. Still a son, not a son. Changed.

She thinks how it will be later in the night in the silvery gray car. How they will spin through the darkness of Mississippi and in the morning be in Chicago, Illinois. She thinks of Lincoln, the president. That is all she knows about the place. She feels ignorant, *wrong*, backward. She presses her worried fingers into his palm. He is standing in front of her. In the crush of well-wishing people, he does not look back.

இஇ

EUDORA WELTY *(b. 1909) was born in Jackson, Mississippi, where she has spent nearly her whole life. She has a predominately tranquil view of the South, so her stories and novels provide a strong contrast to the turbulent fiction of William Faulkner and Richard Wright, who also wrote about Mississippi. Welty grew up as one of three children in a close-knit family living two blocks from the state capitol. Her father was the president of an insurance company, and her mother was a thrifty housewife who kept a Jersey cow in a little pasture behind the backyard. An insatiable reader as a child, Welty began writing spontaneously and continued, without any particular encouragement or any plan to be a writer, during her years in college. In her midtwenties she started to publish stories in the* Southern Review, *but she credits the persistence of her New York literary agent with helping her get a story published in the* Atlantic Monthly *in 1941. This event led directly to the publication of her first book of stories,* A Curtain of Green, *the same year.*

During World War II Welty was a staff member of the New York Times Book Review *while she lived at home with her mother and continued to write short fiction. Another collection was published in 1943 as* The Wide Net and Other Stories. *After leaving her newspaper work, she turned a short story into her first novel,* Delta Wedding *(1946), on the advice of her agent. She has produced several other story collections over the years. Her novel* The Optimist's Daughter *won the Pulitzer Prize in 1972. In 1980* The Collected Stories of Eudora Welty *appeared, forty-one stories in all. Welty is also a fine critic of the short story. Her essays and reviews of the work of writers such as Anton Chekhov, Willa Cather, Katherine Anne Porter, Virginia Woolf, and Isak Dinesen, as well as some comments on her own work, were collected in* The Eye of the Story *(1977). Eight years later the book* Conversations with Eudora Welty *was a best-seller.*

In the preface to her collected stories, Welty stated,

> *I have been told, both in approval and in accusation, that I seem to love all my characters. What I do in writing of any character is to try to enter into the mind, heart, and skin of a human being who is not myself. Whether this happens to be a man or a woman, old or young, with skin black or white, the primary challenge lies in making the jump itself. It is the act of a writer's imagination that I set most high.*

Although Welty's fiction contains occasional sharp glances at southern people, her usual manner is a calm celebration of her characters' minor victories, as in "A Worn Path."

RELATED COMMENTARIES: *Eudora Welty, "Is Phoenix Jackson's Grandson Really Dead?" page 809; and "Plot and Character in Chekhov's 'The Darling,' " page 811.*

EUDORA WELTY

A Worn Path 1941

It was December — a bright frozen day in the early morning. Far out in the country there was an old Negro woman with her head tied in a red rag, coming along a path through the pinewoods. Her name was Phoenix Jackson. She was very old and small and she walked slowly in the dark pine shadows, moving a little from side to side in her steps, with the balanced heaviness and lightness of a pendulum in a grandfather clock. She carried a thin, small cane made from an umbrella, and with this she kept tapping the frozen earth in front of her. This made a grave and persistent noise in the still air, that seemed meditative like the chirping of a solitary little bird.

She wore a dark striped dress reaching down to her shoe tops, and an equally long apron of bleached sugar sacks, with a full pocket: all neat and tidy, but every time she took a step she might have fallen over her shoelaces, which dragged from her unlaced shoes. She looked straight ahead. Her eyes were blue with age. Her skin had a pattern all its own of numberless branching wrinkles and as though a whole little tree stood in the middle of her forehead, but a golden color ran underneath, and the two knobs of her cheeks were illumined by a yellow burning under the dark. Under the red rag her hair came down on her neck in the frailest of ringlets, still black, and with an odor like copper.

Now and then there was a quivering in the thicket. Old Phoenix said, "Out of my way, all you foxes, owls, beetles, jack rabbits, coons and wild animals! . . . Keep out from under these feet, little bobwhites. . . . Keep the big wild hogs out of my path. Don't let none of those come running my direction. I got a long way." Under her small black-freckled hand her cane, limber as a buggy whip, would switch at the brush as if to rouse up any hiding things.

On she went. The woods were deep and still. The sun made the pine needles almost too bright to look at, up where the wind rocked. The cones dropped as light as feathers. Down in the hollow was the mourning dove — it was not too late for him.

The path ran up a hill. "Seem like there is chains about my feet, time I get this far," she said, in the voice of argument old people keep to use with themselves. "Something always take a hold of me on this hill — pleads I should stay."

After she got to the top she turned and gave a full, severe look behind her where she had come. "Up through pines," she said at length. "Now down through oaks."

Her eyes opened their widest, and she started down gently. But before she got to the bottom of the hill a bush caught her dress.

Her fingers were busy and intent, but her skirts were full and long, so that before she could pull them free in one place they were caught in another. It was not possible to allow the dress to tear. "I in the thorny bush," she said. "Thorns, you doing your appointed work. Never want to let folks pass, no sir. Old eyes thought you was a pretty little *green* bush."

Finally, trembling all over, she stood free, and after a moment dared to stoop for her cane.

"Sun so high!" she cried, leaning back and looking, while the thick tears went over her eyes. "The time getting all gone here."

At the foot of this hill was a place where a log was laid across the creek. "Now comes the trial," said Phoenix.

Putting her right foot out, she mounted the log and shut her eyes. Lifting her skirt, leveling her cane fiercely before her, like a festival figure in some parade, she began to march across. Then she opened her eyes and she was safe on the other side.

"I wasn't as old as I thought," she said.

But she sat down to rest. She spread her skirts on the bank around her and folded her hands over her knees. Up above her was a tree in a pearly cloud of mistletoe. She did not dare to close her eyes, and when a little boy brought her a plate with a slice of marble-cake on it she spoke to him. "That would be acceptable," she said. But when she went to take it there was just her own hand in the air.

So she left that tree, and had to go through a barbed-wire fence. There she had to creep and crawl, spreading her knees and stretching her fingers like a baby trying to climb the steps. But she talked loudly to herself: she could not let her dress be torn now, so late in the day, and she could not pay for having her arm or her leg sawed off if she got caught fast where she was.

At last she was safe through the fence and risen up out in the clearing. Big dead trees, like black men with one arm, were standing in the purple stalks of the withered cotton field. There sat a buzzard.

"Who you watching?"

In the furrow she made her way along.

"Glad this not the season for bulls," she said, looking sideways, "and the good Lord made his snakes to curl up and sleep in the winter. A pleasure I don't see no two-headed snake coming around that tree, where it come once. It took a while to get by him, back in the summer."

She passed through the old cotton and went into a field of dead corn. It whispered and shook and was taller than her head. "Through the maze now," she said, for there was no path.

Then there was something tall, black, and skinny there, moving before her.

At first she took it for a man. It could have been a man dancing in the field. But she stood still and listened, and it did not make a sound. It was as silent as a ghost.

"Ghost," she said sharply, "who be you the ghost of? For I have heard of nary death close by."

But there was no answer — only the ragged dancing in the wind.

She shut her eyes, reached out her hand, and touched a sleeve. She found a coat and inside that an emptiness, cold as ice.

"You scarecrow," she said. Her face lighted. "I ought to be shut up for good," she said with laughter. "My senses is gone. I too old. I the oldest people I ever know. Dance, old scarecrow," she said, "while I dancing with you."

She kicked her foot over the furrow, and with mouth drawn down, shook her head once or twice in a little strutting way. Some husks blew down and whirled in streamers about her skirts.

Then she went on, parting her way from side to side with the cane, through the whispering field. At last she came to the end, to a wagon track where the silver grass blew between the red ruts. The quail were walking around like pullets, seeming all dainty and unseen.

"Walk pretty," she said. "This the easy place. This the easy going."

She followed the track, swaying through the quiet bare fields, through the little strings of trees silver in their dead leaves, past cabins silver from weather, with the doors and windows boarded shut, all like old women under a spell sitting there. "I walking in their sleep," she said, nodding her head vigorously.

In a ravine she went where a spring was silently flowing through a hollow log. Old Phoenix bent and drank. "Sweet-gum makes the water sweet," she said, and drank more. "Nobody know who made this well, for it was here when I was born."

The track crossed a swampy part where the moss hung as white as lace from every limb. "Sleep on, alligators, and blow your bubbles." Then the track went into the road.

Deep, deep the road went down between the high green-colored banks. Overhead the live-oaks met, and it was as dark as a cave.

A black dog with a lolling tongue came up out of the weeds by the ditch. She was meditating, and not ready, and when he came at her she only hit him a little with her cane. Over she went in the ditch, like a little puff of milkweed.

Down there, her senses drifted away. A dream visited her, and she reached her hand up, but nothing reached down and gave her a pull. So she lay there and presently went to talking. "Old woman," she said to herself, "that black dog come up out of the weeds to stall you off, and now there he sitting on his fine tail, smiling at you."

A white man finally came along and found her — a hunter, a young man, with his dog on a chain.

"Well, Granny!" he laughed. "What are you doing there?"

"Lying on my back like a June-bug waiting to be turned over, mister," she said, reaching up her hand.

He lifted her up, gave her a swing in the air, and set her down. "Anything broken, Granny?"

"No sir, them old dead weeds is springy enough," said Phoenix, when she had got her breath. "I thank you for your trouble."

"Where do you live, Granny?" he asked, while the two dogs were growling at each other.

"Away back yonder, sir, behind the ridge. You can't even see it from here."

"On your way home?"

"No sir, I going to town."

"Why, that's too far! That's as far as I walk when I come out myself, and I get something for my trouble." He patted the stuffed bag he carried, and there hung down a little closed claw. It was one of the bobwhites, with its beak hooked bitterly to show it was dead. "Now you go on home, Granny!"

"I bound to go to town, mister," said Phoenix. "The time come around."

He gave another laugh, filling the whole landscape. "I know you old colored people! Wouldn't miss going to town to see Santa Claus!"

But something held old Phoenix very still. The deep lines in her face went into a fierce and different radiation. Without warning, she had seen with her own eyes a flashing nickel fall out of the man's pocket onto the ground.

"How old are you, Granny?" he was saying.

"There is no telling, mister," she said, "no telling."

Then she gave a little cry and clapped her hands and said, "Git on away from here, dog! Look! Look at that dog!" She laughed as if in admiration. "He ain't scared of nobody. He a big black dog." She whispered, "Sic him!"

"Watch me get rid of that cur," said the man. "Sic him, Pete! Sic him!"

Phoenix heard the dogs fighting, and heard the man running and throwing sticks. She even heard a gunshot. But she was slowly bending forward by that time, further and further forward, the lid stretched down over her eyes, as if she were doing this in her sleep. Her chin was lowered almost to her knees. The yellow palm of her hand came out from the fold of her apron. Her fingers slid down and along the ground under the piece of money with the grace and care they would have in lifting an egg from under a setting hen. Then she slowly straightened up, she stood erect, and the nickel was in her apron pocket. A bird flew by. Her lips moved. "God watching me the whole time. I come to stealing."

The man came back, and his own dog panted about them. "Well, I scared him off that time," he said, and then he laughed and lifted his gun and pointed it at Phoenix.

She stood straight and faced him.

"Doesn't the gun scare you?" he said, still pointing it.

"No, sir, I seen plenty go off closer by, in my day, and for less than what I done," she said, holding utterly still.

He smiled, and shouldered the gun. "Well, Granny," he said, "you must be a hundred years old, and scared of nothing. I'd give you a dime if I had any money with me. But you take my advice and stay home, and nothing will happen to you."

"I bound to go on my way, mister," said Phoenix. She inclined her head in the red rag. Then they went in different directions, but she could hear the gun shooting again and again over the hill.

She walked on. The shadows hung from the oak trees to the road like curtains. Then she smelled wood-smoke, and smelled the river, and she saw a steeple and the cabins on their steep steps. Dozens of little black children whirled around her. There ahead was Natchez shining. Bells were ringing. She walked on.

In the paved city it was Christmas time. There were red and green electric lights strung and crisscrossed everywhere, and all turned on in the daytime. Old Phoenix would have been lost if she had not distrusted her eyesight and depended on her feet to know where to take her.

She paused quietly on the sidewalk where people were passing by. A lady came along in the crowd, carrying an armful of red-, green-, and silver-wrapped presents; she gave off perfume like the red roses in hot summer, and Phoenix stopped her.

"Please, missy, will you lace up my shoe?" She held up her foot.

"What do you want, Grandma?"

"See my shoe," said Phoenix. "Do all right for out in the country, but wouldn't look right to go in a big building."

"Stand still then, Grandma," said the lady. She put her packages down on the sidewalk beside her and laced and tied both shoes tightly.

"Can't lace 'em with a cane," said Phoenix. "Thank you, missy. I doesn't mind asking a nice lady to tie up my shoe, when I gets out on the street."

Moving slowly and from side to side, she went into the big building, and into a tower of steps, where she walked up and around and around until her feet knew to stop.

She entered a door, and there she saw nailed up on the wall the document that had been stamped with the gold seal and framed in the gold frame, which matched the dream that was hung up in her head.

"Here I be," she said. There was a fixed and ceremonial stiffness over her body.

"A charity case, I suppose," said an attendant who sat at the desk before her.

But Phoenix only looked above her head. There was sweat on her face, the wrinkles in her skin shone like a bright net.

"Speak up, Grandma," the woman said. "What's your name? We must have your history, you know. Have you been here before? What seems to be the trouble with you?"

Old Phoenix only gave a twitch to her face as if a fly were bothering her.

"Are you deaf?" cried the attendant.

But then the nurse came in.

"Oh, that's just old Aunt Phoenix," she said. "She doesn't come for herself — she has a little grandson. She makes these trips just as regular as clockwork. She lives away back off the Old Natchez Trace." She bent down. "Well, Aunt Phoenix, why don't you just take a seat? We won't keep you standing after your long trip." She pointed.

The old woman sat down, bolt upright in the chair.

"Now, how is the boy?" asked the nurse.

Old Phoenix did not speak.

"I said, how is the boy?"

But Phoenix only waited and stared straight ahead, her face very solemn and withdrawn into rigidity.

"Is his throat any better?" asked the nurse. "Aunt Phoenix, don't you hear me? Is your grandson's throat any better since the last time you came for the medicine?"

With her hands on her knees, the old woman waited, silent, erect and motionless, just as if she were in armor.

"You mustn't take up our time this way, Aunt Phoenix," the nurse said. "Tell us quickly about your grandson, and get it over. He isn't dead, is he?"

At last there came a flicker and then a flame of comprehension across her face, and she spoke.

"My grandson. It was my memory had left me. There I sat and forgot why I made my long trip."

"Forgot?" The nurse frowned. "After you came so far?"

Then Phoenix was like an old woman begging a dignified forgiveness for waking up frightened in the night. "I never did go to school, I was too old at the Surrender," she said in a soft voice. "I'm an old woman without an education. It was my memory fail me. My little grandson, he is just the same, and I forgot it in the coming."

"Throat never heals, does it?" said the nurse, speaking in a loud, sure voice to old Phoenix. By now she had a card with something written on it, a little list. "Yes. Swallowed lye. When was it? — January — two, three years ago — "

Phoenix spoke unasked now. "No, missy, he not dead, he just the same. Every little while his throat began to close up again, and he not able to swallow. He not get his breath. He not able to help himself. So the time come around, and I go on another trip for the soothing medicine."

"All right. The doctor said as long as you came to get it, you could have it," said the nurse. "But it's an obstinate case."

"My little grandson, he sit up there in the house all wrapped up, waiting by himself," Phoenix went on. "We is the only two left in the world. He suffer and it don't seem to put him back at all. He got a sweet look. He going to last. He wear a little patch quilt and peep out holding his mouth open like a little bird. I remembers so plain now. I not going to forget him again, no, the whole enduring time. I could tell him from all the others in creation."

"All right." The nurse was trying to hush her now. She brought her a bottle of medicine. "Charity," she said, making a check mark in a book.

Old Phoenix held the bottle close to her eyes, and then carefully put it into her pocket.

"I thank you," she said.

"It's Christmas time, Grandma," said the attendant. "Could I give you a few pennies out of my purse?"

"Five pennies is a nickel," said Phoenix stiffly.

"Here's a nickel," said the attendant.

Phoenix rose carefully and held out her hand. She received the nickel and then fished the other nickel out of her pocket and laid it beside the new one. She stared at her palm closely, with her head on one side.

Then she gave a tap with her cane on the floor.

"This is what come to me to do," she said. "I going to the store and buy my child a little windmill they sells, made out of paper. He going to find it hard to believe there such a thing in the world. I'll march myself back where he waiting, holding it straight up in this hand."

She lifted her free hand, gave a little nod, turned around, and walked out of the doctor's office. Then her slow step began on the stairs, going down.

ରେ

TENNESSEE WILLIAMS *(1911–1983) was born Thomas Lanier Williams in Columbus, Mississippi, the second child of Edwina Dakin Williams, the daughter of an Episcopal clergyman, and Cornelius Coffin Williams, a traveling salesman. Williams spent the first fifteen years of his life living with his mother and older sister, Rose, in more than sixteen homes until his father took a permanent job in St. Louis. Williams was an indifferent high school student, but he began to publish stories in school newspapers as a teenager. An English major in college, his favorite authors were Anton Chekhov, Henrik Ibsen, and August Strindberg, and he was determined to become a playwright. After attending two other universities, he enrolled at the University of Iowa in 1937, where he saw his first full-length plays produced onstage. After graduation he held different jobs to support himself while he worked on his plays, poetry, and short fiction.*

Williams wrote the story "Portrait of a Girl in Glass" in 1943. He turned the story into a play, The Gentleman Caller, *while he was under contract with M-G-M to write a script for a movie starring Lana Turner. The script was turned down, and Williams left Hollywood soon after. He then rewrote the script as* The Glass

Menagerie, *which opened in Chicago in December 1944. After a shaky start, the play ran for 561 performances in New York City and won the Drama Critics' Circle Award as the best American play of the year.*

Williams continued writing short stories in addition to plays for most of his life. "Portrait of a Girl in Glass" was published in 1948 in his first collection of short fiction, One Arm and Other Stories. *An autobiographical story, it is based on Williams's close relationship with his sister, Rose. He used his own name Tom for himself as one of the characters in the story, and he called the character based on his sister Laura. The story takes place in St. Louis in the early 1930s, during the Depression, at a time when Williams had been taken out of college by his father to work at the International Shoe Company, where his father had found a job fifteen years before.*

In Williams's autobiography, Memoirs *(1975), he described his feelings for his fragile, highly sensitive sister: "My sister and I had a close relationship, quite unsullied by any carnal knowledge . . . and yet our love was, and is, the deepest in our lives." Withdrawn and depressed, Rose suffered from a mental breakdown after Williams left home for the University of Iowa in 1937. Urged by the doctors, her parents authorized a prefrontal lobotomy — a new surgical technique at that time — without consulting Williams. Although the operation relieved Rose's anxieties, it deprived her of the ability to relate to others except in an institutional setting. Despite the passage of time, when asked how old she was, Rose always replied that she was twenty-eight and that her brother, Tom, was twenty-six. Rose Williams has outlived her brother, who established a fund for her lifetime hospital care in his will.*

RELATED PLAY: *Tennessee Williams,* The Glass Menagerie, *page 1704.*

RELATED COMMENTARIES: *Benjamin Nelson, "Problems in* The Glass Menagerie," *page 2009; Tennessee Williams, "Production Notes to* The Glass Menagerie," *page 2031.*

TENNESSEE WILLIAMS

Portrait of a Girl in Glass   1948

We lived in a third floor apartment on Maple Street in Saint Louis, on a block which also contained the Ever-ready Garage, a Chinese laundry, and a bookie shop disguised as a cigar store.

Mine was an anomalous character, one that appeared to be slated for radical change or disaster, for I was a poet who had a job in a warehouse. As for my sister Laura, she could be classified even less readily than I. She made no positive motion toward the world but stood at the edge of the water, so to speak, with feet that anticipated too much cold to move. She'd never have budged an inch, I'm pretty sure, if my mother who was a relatively aggressive sort of woman had not shoved her roughly forward, when Laura was twenty years old, by enrolling her as a student in a nearby business college. Out of her "magazine money" (she sold subscriptions to women's magazines), Mother had paid my sister's tuition for a term of six months. It did not work out. Laura tried to memorize the typewriter keyboard, she had a chart at home, she used to sit silently in front of it for hours, staring at it while she cleaned and polished her infinite number of little glass ornaments. She did this every evening after dinner. Mother would caution me to be very quiet. "Sister is looking at her typewriter chart!" I felt somehow that it would do her no good, and I was right. She would seem to know the positions of the keys until the weekly speed drill got underway, and then they would fly from her mind like a bunch of startled birds.

At last she couldn't bring herself to enter the school any more. She kept this failure a secret for a while. She left the house each morning as before and spent six hours walking around the park. This was in February, and all the walking outdoors regardless of weather brought on influenza. She was in bed for a couple of weeks with a curiously happy little smile on her face. Of course Mother phoned the business college to let them know she was ill. Whoever was talking on the other end of the line had some trouble, it seems, in remembering who Laura was, which annoyed my mother and she spoke up pretty sharply. "Laura has been attending that school of yours for two months, you certainly ought to recognize her name!" Then came the stunning disclosure. The person sharply retorted, after a moment or two, that now she *did* remember the Wingfield girl, and that she had not been at the business college *once* in about a month. Mother's voice became strident. Another person was brought to the phone to verify the statement of the first. Mother hung up and went to Laura's bedroom where she lay with a tense and frightened look in place of the faint little smile. Yes, admitted my sister, what they said was true. "I couldn't go any longer, it scared me too much, it made me sick at the stomach!"

After this fiasco, my sister stayed at home and kept in her bedroom mostly. This was a narrow room that had two windows on a dusky areaway between two wings of the building. We called this areaway Death Valley for a reason that seems worth telling. There were a great many alley cats in the neighborhood and one particularly vicious dirty white Chow who stalked them continually. In the open or on the fire escapes they could usually elude him but now and again he cleverly contrived to run some youngster among them into the cul-de-sac of this narrow areaway at the far end of which, directly beneath my sister's bedroom windows, they made the blinding discovery that what had appeared to be an avenue of escape was really a locked arena, a gloomy vault of concrete and brick with walls too high for any cat to spring, in which they must suddenly turn to spit at their death until it was hurled upon them. Hardly a week went by without a repetition of this violent drama. The areaway had grown to be hateful to Laura because she could not look out on it without recalling the screams and the snarls of killing. She kept the shades drawn down, and as Mother would not permit the use of electric current except when needed, her days were spent almost in perpetual twilight. There were three pieces of dingy ivory furniture in the room, a bed, a bureau, a chair. Over the bed was a remarkably bad religious painting, a very effeminate head of Christ with teardrops visible just below the eyes. The charm of the room was produced by my sister's collection of glass. She loved colored glass and had covered the walls with shelves of little glass articles, all of them light and delicate in color. These she washed and polished with endless care. When you entered the room there was always this soft, transparent radiance in it which came from the glass absorbing whatever faint light came through the shades on Death Valley. I have no idea how many articles there were of this delicate glass. There must have been hundreds of them. But Laura could tell you exactly. She loved each one.

She lived in a world of glass and also a world of music. The music came from a 1920 victrola and a bunch of records that dated from about the same period, pieces such as "Whispering" or "The Love Nest" or "Dardanella." These records were souvenirs of our father, a man whom we barely remembered, whose name was spoken rarely. Before his sudden and unexplained disappearance from our lives, he had made this gift to the household, the phonograph and the records, whose music remained as a sort of apology for him. Once in a while, on payday at the warehouse, I would bring home a new record. But Laura seldom cared for these new records, maybe because they reminded her too much of the noisy tragedies in Death Valley or the speed drills at the business college. The tunes she loved were the ones she had always heard. Often she sang to herself at night in her bedroom. Her voice was thin, it usually wandered off-key. Yet it had a curious child-like sweetness. At eight o'clock in the evening I sat down to write in my own mousetrap of a room. Through the closed doors, through the walls, I would hear my sister singing to herself, a piece like "Whispering" or "I Love You" or "Sleepy Time Gal," losing the tune now and then but always preserving the minor atmosphere of the music. I think that was why I always wrote such strange and sorrowful poems in those days. Because I had in my ears the wispy sound of my sister serenading her pieces of colored glass, washing them while she sang or merely looking down at them with her vague blue eyes until the points of gem-like radiance in them gently drew the arching particles of reality from her mind and finally produced a state of hypnotic calm in which she even stopped singing or washing the glass and merely sat without motion until my mother knocked at the door and warned her against the waste of electric current.

I don't believe that my sister was actually foolish. I think the petals of her mind had simply closed through fear, and it's no telling how much they had closed upon in the way of secret wisdom. She never talked very much, not even to me, but once in a while she did pop out with something that took you by surprise.

After work at the warehouse or after I'd finished my writing in the evening, I'd drop in her room for a little visit because she had a restful and soothing effect on nerves that were worn rather thin from trying to ride two horses simultaneously in two opposite directions.

I usually found her seated in the straight-back ivory chair with a piece of glass cupped tenderly in her palm.

"What are you doing? Talking to it?" I asked.

"No," she answered gravely, "I was just looking at it."

On the bureau were two pieces of fiction which she had received as Christmas or birthday presents. One was a novel called the *Rose-Garden Husband* by someone whose name escapes me. The other was *Freckles* by Gene Stratton Porter. I never saw her reading the *Rose-Garden Husband,* but the other book was one that she actually lived with. It had probably never occurred to

Laura that a book was something you read straight through and then laid aside as finished. The character Freckles, a one-armed orphan youth who worked in a lumber camp, was someone that she invited into her bedroom now and then for a friendly visit just as she did me. When I came in and found this novel open upon her lap, she would gravely remark that Freckles was having some trouble with the foreman of the lumber camp or that he had just received an injury to his spine when a tree fell on him. She frowned with genuine sorrow when she reported these misadventures of her story-book hero, possibly not recalling how successfully he came through them all, that the injury to the spine fortuitously resulted in the discovery of rich parents and that the bad-tempered foreman had a heart of gold at the end of the book. Freckles became involved in romance with a girl he called The Angel, but my sister usually stopped reading when this girl became too prominent in the story. She closed the book or turned back to the lonelier periods in the orphan's story. I only remember her making one reference to this heroine of the novel. "The Angel is nice," she said, "but seems to be kind of conceited about her looks."

Then one time at Christmas, while she was trimming the artificial tree, she picked up the Star of Bethlehem that went on the topmost branch and held it gravely toward the chandelier.

"Do stars have five points really?" she enquired.

This was the sort of thing that you didn't believe and that made you stare at Laura with sorrow and confusion.

"No," I told her, seeing she really meant it, "they're round like the earth and most of them much bigger."

She was gently surprised by this new information. She went to the window to look up at the sky which was, as usual during Saint Louis winters, completely shrouded by smoke.

"It's hard to tell," she said, and returned to the tree.

So time passed on till my sister was twenty-three. Old enough to be married, but the fact of the matter was she had never even had a date with a boy. I don't believe this seemed as awful to her as it did to Mother.

At breakfast one morning Mother said to me, "Why don't you cultivate some nice young friends? How about down at the warehouse? Aren't there some young men down there you could ask to dinner?"

This suggestion surprised me because there was seldom quite enough food on her table to satisfy three people. My mother was a terribly stringent housekeeper, God knows we were poor enough in actuality, but my mother had an almost obsessive dread of becoming even poorer. A not unreasonable fear since the man of the house was a poet who worked in a warehouse, but one which I thought played too important a part in all her calculations.

Almost immediately Mother explained herself.

"I think it might be nice," she said, "for your sister."

I brought Jim home to dinner a few nights later. Jim was a big red-haired Irishman who had the scrubbed and polished look of well-kept chinaware. His big square hands seemed to have a direct and very innocent hunger for touching his friends. He was always clapping them on your arms or shoulders and they burned through the cloth of your shirt like plates taken out of an oven. He was the best-liked man in the warehouse and oddly enough he was the only one that I was on good terms with. He found me agreeably ridiculous, I think. He knew of my secret practice of retiring to a cabinet in the lavatory and working on rhyme schemes when work was slack in the warehouse, and of sneaking up on the roof now and then to smoke my cigarette with a view across the river at the undulant open country of Illinois. No doubt I was classified as screwy in Jim's mind as much as in the others', but while their attitude was suspicious and hostile when they first knew me, Jim's was warmly tolerant from the beginning. He called me Slim, and gradually his cordial acceptance drew the others around, and while he remained the only one who actually had anything to do with me, the others had now begun to smile when they saw me as people smile at an oddly fashioned dog who crosses their path at some distance.

Nevertheless it took some courage for me to invite Jim to dinner. I thought about it all week and delayed the action till Friday noon, the last possible moment, as the dinner was set for that evening.

"What are you doing tonight?" I finally asked him.

"Not a God damn thing," said Jim. "I had a date but her Aunt took sick and she's hauled her freight to Centralia!"

"Well," I said, "why don't you come over for dinner?"

"Sure!" said Jim. He grinned with astonishing brightness.

I went outside to phone the news to Mother.

Her voice that was never tired responded with an energy that made the wires crackle.

"I suppose he's Catholic?" she said.

"Yes," I told her, remembering the tiny silver cross on his freckled chest.

"Good!" she said. "I'll bake a salmon loaf!"

And so we rode home together in his jalopy.

I had a curious feeling of guilt and apprehension as I led the lamb-like Irishman up three flights of cracked marble steps to the door of Apartment F, which was not thick enough to hold inside it the odor of baking salmon.

Never having a key, I pressed the bell.

"Laura!" came Mother's voice. "That's Tom and Mr. Delaney! Let them in!"

There was a long, long pause.

"Laura?" she called again. "I'm busy in the kitchen, you answer the door!"

Then at last I heard my sister's footsteps. They went right past the door at which we were standing and into the parlor. I heard the creaking noise of the phonograph crank. Music commenced. One of the oldest records, a march of Sousa's, put on to give her the courage to let in a stranger.

The door came timidly open and there she stood in a dress from Mother's wardrobe, a black chiffon ankle-length and high-heeled slippers on which she balanced uncertainly like a tipsy crane of melancholy plumage. Her eyes stared back at us with a glassy brightness and her delicate wing-like shoulders were hunched with nervousness.

"Hello!" said Jim, before I could introduce him.

He stretched out his hand. My sister touched it only for a second.

"Excuse me!" she whispered, and turned with a breathless rustle back to her bedroom door, the sanctuary beyond it briefly revealing itself with the tinkling, muted radiance of glass before the door closed rapidly but gently on her wraith-like figure.

Jim seemed to be incapable of surprise.

"Your sister?" he asked.

"Yes, that was her," I admitted. "She's terribly shy with strangers."

"She looks like you," said Jim, "except she's pretty."

Laura did not reappear till called to dinner. Her place was next to Jim at the drop-leaf table and all through the meal her figure was slightly tilted away from his. Her face was feverishly bright and one eyelid, the one on the side toward Jim, had developed a nervous wink. Three times in the course of the dinner she dropped her fork on her plate with a terrible clatter and she was continually raising the water glass to her lips for hasty little gulps. She went on doing this even after the water was gone from the glass. And her handling of the silver became more awkward and hurried all the time.

I thought of nothing to say.

To Mother belonged the conversational honors, such as they were. She asked the caller about his home and family. She was delighted to learn that his father had a business of his own, a retail shoe store somewhere in Wyoming. The news that he went to night school to study accounting was still more edifying. What was his heart set on beside the warehouse? Radio-engineering? My, my, my! It was easy to see that here was a very up-and-coming young man who was certainly going to make his place in the world!

Then she started to talk about her children. Laura, she said, was not cut out for business. She was domestic, however, and making a home was really a girl's best bet.

Jim agreed with all this and seemed not to sense the ghost of an implication. I suffered through it dumbly, trying not to see Laura trembling more and more beneath the incredible unawareness of Mother.

And bad as it was, excruciating in fact, I thought with dread of the moment when dinner was going to be over, for then the diversion of food would be taken away, we would have to go into the little steam-heated parlor. I fancied the four of us having run out of talk, even Mother's seemingly endless store of questions about Jim's home and his job all used up finally — the four of us, then, just sitting there in the parlor, listening to the hiss of the radiator and nervously clearing our throats in the kind of self-consciousness that gets to be suffocating.

But when the blancmange was finished, a miracle happened.

Mother got up to clear the dishes away. Jim gave me a clap on the shoulders and said, "Hey, Slim, let's go have a look at those old records in there!"

He sauntered carelessly into the front room and flopped down on the floor beside the victrola. He began sorting through the collection of worn-out records and reading their titles aloud in a voice so hearty that it shot like beams of sunlight through the vapors of self-consciousness engulfing my sister and me.

He was sitting directly under the floor-lamp and all at once my sister jumped up and said to him, "Oh — you have freckles!"

Jim grinned. "Sure that's what my folks call me — Freckles!"

"Freckles?" Laura repeated. She looked toward me as if for the confirmation of some too wonderful hope. I looked away quickly, not knowing whether to feel relieved or alarmed at the turn that things were taking.

Jim had wound the victrola and put on *Dardanella*.

He grinned at Laura.

"How about you an' me cutting the rug a little?"

"What?" said Laura breathlessly, smiling and smiling.

"Dance!" he said, drawing her into his arms.

As far as I knew she had never danced in her life. But to my everlasting wonder she slipped quite naturally into those huge arms of Jim's, and they danced round and around the small steam-heated parlor, bumping against the sofa and chairs and laughing loudly and happily together. Something opened up in my sister's face. To say it was love is not too hasty a judgment, for after all he had freckles and that was what his folks called him. Yes, he had undoubtedly assumed the identity — for all practical purposes — of the one-armed orphan youth who lived in the Limberlost, that tall and misty region to which she retreated whenever the walls of Apartment F became too close to endure.

Mother came back in with some lemonade. She stopped short as she entered the portieres.

"Good heavens! Laura? Dancing?"

Her look was absurdly grateful as well as startled.

"But isn't she stepping all over you, Mr. Delaney?"

"What if she does?" said Jim, with bearish gallantry. "I'm not made of eggs!"

"Well, well, well!" said Mother, senselessly beaming.

"She's light as a feather!" said Jim. "With a little more practice she'd dance as good as Betty!"

There was a little pause of silence.

"Betty?" said Mother.

"The girl I go out with!" said Jim.

"Oh!" said Mother.

She set the pitcher of lemonade carefully down and with her back to the caller and her eyes on me, she asked him just how often he and the lucky young lady went out together.

"Steady!" said Jim.

Mother's look, remaining on my face, turned into a glare of fury.

"Tom didn't mention that you went out with a girl!"

"Nope," said Jim. "I didn't mean to let the cat out of the bag. The boys at the warehouse'll kid me to death when Slim gives the news away."

He laughed heartily but his laughter dropped heavily and awkwardly away as even his dull senses were gradually penetrated by the unpleasant sensation the news of Betty had made.

"Are you thinking of getting married?" said Mother.

"First of next month!" he told her.

It took her several moments to pull herself together. Then she said in a dismal tone, "How nice! If Tom had only told us we could have asked you *both*!"

Jim had picked up his coat.

"Must you be going?" said Mother.

"I hope it don't seem like I'm rushing off," said Jim, "but Betty's gonna get back on the eight o'clock train an' by the time I get my jalopy down to the Wabash depot — "

"Oh, then, we mustn't keep you."

Soon as he'd left, we all sat down, looking dazed.

Laura was the first to speak.

"Wasn't he nice?" she asked. "And all those freckles!"

"Yes," said Mother. Then she turned to me.

"You didn't mention that he was engaged to be married!"

"Well, how did I know that he was engaged to be married?"

"I thought you called him your best friend down at the warehouse?"

"Yes, but I didn't know he was going to be married!"

"How peculiar!" said Mother. "How very peculiar!"

"No," said Laura gently, getting up from the sofa. "There's nothing peculiar about it."

She picked up one of the records and blew on its surface a little as if it were dusty, then set it softly back down.

"People in love," she said, "take everything for granted."

What did she mean by that? I never knew.

She slipped quietly back to her room and closed the door.

Not very long after that I lost my job at the warehouse. I was fired for writing a poem on the lid of a shoe-box. I left Saint Louis and took to moving around. The cities swept about me like dead leaves, leaves that were brightly colored but torn away from the branches. My nature changed. I grew to be firm and sufficient.

In five years' time I had nearly forgotten home. I had to forget it, I couldn't carry it with me. But once in a while, usually in a strange town before I have found companions, the shell of deliberate hardness is broken through. A door comes softly and irresistibly open. I hear the tired old music my unknown father left in the place he abandoned as faithlessly as I. I see the faint and sorrowful radiance of the glass, hundreds of little transparent pieces of it in very delicate colors. I hold my breath, for if my sister's face appears among them — the night is hers!

RICHARD WRIGHT *(1908–1960) was born on a plantation near Natchez, Mississippi, the son of a farmhand and a country schoolteacher. His home life was disrupted when his father deserted the family, and Wright later said it was only through reading that he managed to keep himself alive. As soon as he could he moved north, to Memphis, Chicago, and then to New York City, where he became involved in radical politics. He was a member of the Communist Party from 1932 to 1944. In the 1930s he worked as a reporter for* The New Masses, *a correspondent for the Harlem bureau of the* Daily Worker, *and an editor for* New Challenge, *a left-wing magazine that published his "Blueprint for Negro Writing," an effort to bridge the gap between Marxism and black nationalism, in 1938. He was also then writing the stories that appeared in* Uncle Tom's Children *(1938), which won first prize in a contest for writers in the Federal Writers' Project during the Depression. Wright's early fiction was strongly influenced by Ernest Hemingway's way of writing stories, but Wright also set himself the problem of how to use a modernist style to write about social issues:*

> *Practically all of us, young writers, were influenced by Ernest Hemingway. We liked the simple, direct way in which he wrote, but a great many of us wanted to write about social problems. The question came up: How could we write about social problems and use a simple style? Hemingway's style is so concentrated on naturalistic detail that there is no room for social comment. One boy said that one way was to dig deeper into the character and try to get something that will live. I decided to try it.*

The result was the five stories published in Uncle Tom's Children. *Next Wright turned to his first novel,* Native Son *(1940), an American classic dramatizing a brutal story of racial conflict. This was followed by* Black Boy *(1945), a brilliant autobiography written when he was not yet forty. The next year he left the United States to spend the last fourteen years of his life in Paris, feeling himself alienated from American values. In 1960, the year Wright died, he gathered for publication his second book of short stories,* Eight Men, *made up of fiction that had appeared over the years in magazines and anthologies, including "The Man Who Was Almost a Man," written in the 1930s.*

Telling stories from a realistic view of his own experience, Wright experimented with literary techniques in all his fiction. His short stories dramatize the same themes as his novels and are equally experimental. "The Man Who Was Almost a Man" weaves the black farm boy's speech so skillfully with standard English narration that most readers are unaware of the effect of the deliberate juxtaposition, but this technique brings us closer to the boy's world while making an implicit social comment about his exclusion from the exploitative white society engulfing him.

RELATED POEM: *Richard Wright, "Four Haikus," page 963.*

RICHARD WRIGHT

The Man Who Was Almost a Man
1961

Dave struck out across the fields, looking homeward through paling light. Whut's the use talkin wid em niggers in the field? Anyhow, his mother was putting supper on the table. Them niggers can't understan nothing. One of these days he was going to get a gun and practice shooting, then they couldn't talk to him as though he were a little boy. He slowed, looking at the ground. Shucks, Ah ain scareda them even ef they are biggern me! Aw, Ah know whut Ahma do. Ahm going by ol Joe's sto n git that Sears Roebuck catlog n look at them guns. Mebbe Ma will lemme buy one when she gits mah pay from ol man Hawkins. Ahma beg her t gimme some money. Ahm ol ernough to hava gun. Ahm seventeen. Almost a man. He strode, feeling his long loose-jointed limbs. Shucks, a man oughta hava little gun aftah he done worked hard all day.

He came in sight of Joe's store. A yellow lantern glowed on the front porch. He mounted steps and went through the screen door, hearing it bang behind him. There was a strong smell of coal oil and mackerel fish. He felt very confident until he saw fat Joe walk in through the rear door, then his courage began to ooze.

"Howdy, Dave! Whutcha want?"

"How yuh, Mistah Joe? Aw, Ah don wanna buy nothing. Ah jus wanted t see ef yuhd lemme look at tha catlog erwhile."

"Sure! You wanna see it here?"

"Nawsuh. Ah wants t take it home wid me. Ah'll bring it back termorrow when Ah come in from the fiels."

"You plannin on buying something?"

"Yessuh."

"Your ma lettin you have your own money now?"

"Shucks. Mistah Joe, Ahm gittin t be a man like anybody else!"

Joe laughed and wiped his greasy white face with a red bandanna.

"Whut you plannin on buyin?"

Dave looked at the floor, scratched his head, scratched his thigh, and smiled. Then he looked up shyly.

"Ah'll tell yuh, Mistah Joe, ef yuh promise yuh won't tell."

"I promise."

"Waal, Ahma buy a gun."

"A gun? What you want with a gun?"

"Ah wanna keep it."

"You ain't nothing but a boy. You don't need a gun."

"Aw, lemme have the catlog, Mistah Joe. Ah'll bring it back."

Joe walked through the rear door. Dave was elated. He looked around at barrels of sugar and flour. He heard Joe coming back. He craned his neck to see if he were bringing the book. Yeah, he's got it. Gawddog, he's got it!

"Here, but be sure you bring it back. It's the only one I got."

"Sho, Mistah Joe."

"Say, if you wanna buy a gun, why don't you buy one from me? I gotta gun to sell."

"Will it shoot?"

"Sure it'll shoot."

"Whut kind is it?"

"Oh, it's kinda old . . . a left-hand Wheeler. A pistol. A big one."

"Is it got bullets in it?"

"It's loaded."

"Kin Ah see it?"

"Where's your money?"

"What yuh wan fer it?"

"I'll let you have it for two dollars."

"Just two dollahs? Shucks, Ah could buy tha when Ah git mah pay."

"I'll have it here when you want it."

"Awright, suh. Ah be in fer it."

He went through the door, hearing it slam again behind him. Ahma git some money from Ma n buy me a gun! Only two dollahs! He tucked the thick catalogue under his arm and hurried.

"Where yuh been, boy?" His mother held a steaming dish of black-eyed peas.

"Aw, Ma, Ah jus stopped down the road t talk wid the boys."

"Yuh know bettah t keep suppah waitin."

He sat down, resting the catalogue on the edge of the table.

"Yuh git up from there and git to the well n wash yosef! Ah ain feedin no hogs in mah house!"

She grabbed his shoulder and pushed him. He stumbled out of the room, then came back to get the catalogue.

"Whut this?"

"Aw, Ma, it's jusa catlog."

"Who yuh git it from?"

"From Joe, down at the sto."

"Waal, thas good. We kin use it in the outhouse."

"Naw, Ma." He grabbed for it. "Gimme ma catlog, Ma."

She held onto it and glared at him.

"Quit hollerin at me! Whut's wrong wid yuh? Yuh crazy?"

"But Ma, please. It ain mine! It's Joe's! He tol me t bring it back t im termorrow."

She gave up the book. He stumbled down the back steps, hugging the thick book under his arm. When he had splashed water on his face and hands, he groped back to the kitchen and fumbled in a corner for the towel. He bumped into a chair; it clattered to the floor. The catalogue sprawled at his feet. When he had dried his eyes he snatched up the book and held it again under his arm. His mother stood watching him.

"Now, ef yuh gonna act a fool over that ol book, Ah'll take it n burn it up."

"Naw, Ma, please."

"Waal, set down n be still!"

He sat down and drew the oil lamp close. He thumbed page after page, unaware of the food his mother set on the table. His father came in. Then his small brother.

"Whutcha got there, Dave?" his father asked.

"Jusa catlog," he answered, not looking up.

"Yeah, here they is!" His eyes glowed at blue-and-black revolvers. He glanced up, feeling sudden guilt. His father was watching him. He eased the book under the table and rested it on his knees. After the blessing was asked, he ate. He scooped up peas and swallowed fat meat without chewing. Buttermilk helped to wash it down. He did not want to mention money before his father. He would do much better by cornering his mother when she was alone. He looked at his father uneasily out of the edge of his eye.

"Boy, how come yuh don quit foolin wid tha book n eat yo suppah?"

"Yessuh."

"How you n ol man Hawkins gitten erlong?"

"Suh?"

"Can't yuh hear? Why don yuh lissen? Ah ast yu how wuz yuh n ol man Hawkins gittin erlong?"

"Oh, swell, Pa. Ah plows mo lan than anybody over there."

"Waal, yuh oughta keep you mind on whut yuh doin."

"Yessuh."

He poured his plate full of molasses and sopped it up slowly with a chunk of cornbread. When his father and brother had left the kitchen, he still sat and looked again at the guns in the catalogue, longing to muster courage enough to present his case to his mother. Lawd, ef Ah only had tha pretty one! He could almost feel the slickness of the weapon with his fingers. If he had a gun like that he would polish it and keep it shining so it would never rust. N Ah'd keep it loaded, by Gawd!

"Ma?" His voice was hesitant.

"Hunh?"

"Ol man Hawkins give yuh mah money yit?"

"Yeah, but ain no usa yuh thinking bout throwin nona it erway. Ahm keeping tha money sos yuh kin have cloes t go to school this winter."

He rose and went to her side with the open catalogue in his palms. She was washing dishes, her head bent low over a pan. Shyly he raised the book. When he spoke, his voice was husky, faint.

"Ma, Gawd knows Ah wans one of these."

"One of whut?" she asked, not raising her eyes.

"One of these," he said again, not daring even to point. She glanced up at the page, then at him with wide eyes.

"Nigger, is yuh gone plumb crazy?"

"Aw, Ma — "

"Git outta here! Don yuh talk t me bout no gun! Yuh a fool!"

"Ma, Ah kin buy one fer two dollahs."

"Not ef Ah knows it, yuh ain!"

"But yuh promised me one — "

"Ah don care what Ah promised! Yuh ain nothing but a boy yit!"

"Ma, ef yuh lemme buy one Ah'll *never* ast yuh fer nothing no mo."

"Ah tol yuh t git outta here! Yuh ain gonna toucha penny of tha money fer no gun! Thas how come Ah has Mistah Hawkins t pay yo wages t me, cause Ah knows yuh ain got no sense."

"But, Ma, we needa gun. Pa ain got no gun. We needa gun in the house. Yuh kin never tell whut might happen."

"Now don yuh try to maka fool outta me, boy! Ef we did hava gun, yuh wouldn't have it!"

He laid the catalogue down and slipped his arm around her waist.

"Aw, Ma, Ah done worked hard alla summer n ain ast yuh fer nothing, is Ah, now?"

"Thas whut yuh spose t do!"

"But Ma, Ah wans a gun. Yuh kin lemme have two dollahs outta mah money. Please, Ma. I kin give it to Pa. . . . Please, Ma! Ah loves yuh, Ma."

When she spoke her voice came soft and low.

"What yu wan wida gun, Dave? Yuh don need no gun. Yuh'll git in trouble. N ef yo pa jus thought Ah let yuh have money t buy a gun he'd hava fit."

"Ah'll hide it, Ma. It ain but two dollahs."

"Lawd, chil, whut's wrong wid yuh?"

"Ain nothin wrong, Ma. Ahm almos a man now. Ah wans a gun."

"Who gonna sell yuh a gun?"

"Ol Joe at the sto."

"N it don cos but two dollahs?"

"Thas all, Ma. Jus two dollahs. Please, Ma."

She was stacking the plates away; her hands moved slowly, reflectively. Dave kept an anxious silence. Finally, she turned to him.

"Ah'll let yuh git tha gun ef yuh promise me one thing."

"What's tha, Ma?"

"Yuh bring it straight back t me, yuh hear? It be fer Pa."

"Yessum! Lemme go now, Ma."

She stooped, turned slightly to one side, raised the hem of her dress, rolled down the top of her stocking, and came up with a slender wad of bills.

"Here," she said. "Lawd knows yuh don need no gun. But yer pa does. Yuh bring it right back t me, yuh hear? Ahma put it up. Now ef yuh don, Ahma have yuh pa lick yuh so hard yuh won fergit it."

"Yessum."

He took the money, ran down the steps, and across the yard.

"Dave! Yuuuuuh Daaaaave!"

He heard, but he was not going to stop now. "Now, Lawd!"

The first movement he made the following morning was to reach under his pillow for the gun. In the gray light of dawn he held it loosely, feeling a sense of power. Could kill a man with a gun like this. Kill anybody, black or white. And if he were holding his gun in his hand, nobody could run over him; they would have to respect him. It was a big gun, with a long barrel and a heavy handle. He raised and lowered it in his hand, marveling at its weight.

He had not come straight home with it as his mother had asked; instead he had stayed out in the fields, holding the weapon in his hand, aiming it now and then at some imaginary foe. But he had not fired it; he had been afraid that his father might hear. Also he was not sure he knew how to fire it.

To avoid surrendering the pistol he had not come into the house until he knew that they were all asleep. When his mother had tiptoed to his bedside late that night and demanded the gun, he had first played possum; then he had told her that the gun was hidden outdoors, that he would bring it to her in the morning. Now he lay turning it slowly in his hands. He broke it, took out the cartridges, felt them, and then put them back.

He slid out of bed, got a long strip of old flannel from a trunk, wrapped the gun in it, and tied it to his naked thigh while it was still loaded. He did not go in to breakfast. Even though it was not yet daylight, he started for Jim Hawkins' plantation. Just as the sun was rising he reached the barns where the mules and plows were kept.

"Hey! That you, Dave?"

He turned. Jim Hawkins stood eying him suspiciously.

"What're yuh doing here so early?"

"Ah didn't know Ah wuz gittin up so early, Mistah Hawkins. Ah was fixin t hitch up ol Jenny n take her t the fiels."

"Good. Since you're so early, how about plowing that stretch down by the woods?"

"Suits me, Mistah Hawkins."

"O.K. Go to it!"

He hitched Jenny to a plow and started across the fields. Hot dog! This was just what he wanted. If he could get down by the woods, he could shoot his gun and nobody would hear. He walked behind the plow, hearing the traces creaking, feeling the gun tied tight to his thigh.

When he reached the woods, he plowed two whole rows before he decided to take out the gun. Finally, he stopped, looked in all directions, then untied the gun and held it in his hand. He turned to the mule and smiled.

"Know whut this is, Jenny? Naw, yuh wouldn know! Yuhs jusa ol mule! Anyhow, this is a gun, n it kin shoot, by Gawd!"

He held the gun at arm's length. Whut t hell, Ahma shoot this thing! He looked at Jenny again.

"Lissen here, Jenny! When Ah pull this ol trigger, Ah don wan yuh t run n acka fool now!"

Jenny stood with head down, her short ears pricked straight. Dave walked off about twenty feet, held the gun far out from him at arm's length, and turned his head. Hell, he told himself, Ah ain afraid. The gun felt loose in his fingers; he waved it wildly for a moment. The he shut his eyes and tightened his forefinger. Bloom! A report half deafened him and he thought his right hand was torn from his arm. He heard Jenny whinnying and galloping over the field, and he found himself on his knees, squeezing his fingers hard between his legs. His hand was numb; he jammed it into his mouth, trying to warm it, trying to stop the pain. The gun lay at his feet. He did not quite know what had happened. He stood up and stared at the gun as though it were a living thing. He gritted his teeth and kicked the gun. Yuh almos broke mah arm! He turned to look for Jenny; she was far over the fields, tossing her head and kicking wildly.

"Hol on there, ol mule!"

When he caught up with her she stood trembling, walling her big white eyes at him. The plow was far away; the traces had broken. Then Dave stopped short, looking, not believing. Jenny was bleeding. Her left side was red and wet with blood. He went closer. Lawd, have mercy! Wondah did Ah shoot this mule? He grabbed for Jenny's mane. She flinched, snorted, whirled, tossing her head.

"Hol on now! Hol on."

Then he saw the hole in Jenny's side, right between the ribs. It was round, wet, red. A crimson stream streaked down the front leg, flowing fast. Good Gawd! Ah wuzn't shootin at tha mule. He felt panic. He knew he had to stop that blood, or Jenny would bleed to death. He had never seen so much blood in all his life. He chased the mule for half a mile, trying to catch her. Finally she stopped, breathing hard, stumpy tail half arched. He caught her mane and led her back to where the plow and gun lay. Then he stopped and grabbed handfuls of damp black earth and tried to plug the bullet hole. Jenny shuddered, whinnied, and broke from him.

"Hol on! Hol on now!"

He tried to plug it again, but blood came anyhow. His fingers were hot and sticky. He rubbed dirt into his palms, trying to dry them. Then again he attempted to plug the bullet hole, but Jenny shied away, kicking her heels high. He stood helpless. He had to do something. He ran at Jenny; she dodged him. He watched a red stream of blood flow down Jenny's leg and form a bright pool at her feet.

"Jenny . . . Jenny," he called weakly.

His lips trembled. She's bleeding t death! He looked in the direction of home, wanting to go back, wanting to get help. But he saw the pistol lying in the damp black clay. He had a queer feeling that if he only did something, this would not be; Jenny would not be there bleeding to death.

When he went to her this time, she did not move. She stood with sleepy, dreamy eyes; and when he touched her she gave a low-pitched whinny and knelt to the ground, her front knees slopping in blood.

"Jenny . . . Jenny . . ." he whispered.

For a long time she held her neck erect; then her head sank, slowly. Her ribs swelled with a mighty heave and she went over.

Dave's stomach felt empty, very empty. He picked up the gun and held it gingerly between his thumb and forefinger. He buried it at the foot of a tree. He took a stick to cover the pool of blood with dirt — but what was the use? There was Jenny lying with her mouth open and her eyes walled and glassy. He could not tell Jim Hawkins he had shot his mule. But he had to tell something. Yeah, Ah'll tell em Jenny started gittin wil n fell on the joint of the plow. . . . But that would hardly happen to a mule. He walked across the field slowly, head down.

It was sunset. Two of Jim Hawkins' men were over near the edge of the woods digging a hole in which to bury Jenny. Dave was surrounded by a knot of people, all of whom were looking down at the dead mule.

"I don't see how in the world it happened," said Jim Hawkins for the tenth time.

The crowd parted and Dave's mother, father, and small brother pushed into the center.

"Where Dave?" his mother called.

"There he is," said Jim Hawkins.

His mother grabbed him.

"Whut happened, Dave? Whut yuh done?"

"Nothin."

"C mon, boy, talk," his father said.

Dave took a deep breath and told the story he knew nobody believed. "Waal," he drawled. "Ah brung ol Jenny down here sos Ah could do mah plowin. Ah plowed bout two rows, just like yuh see." He stopped and pointed at the long rows of upturned earth. "Then somethin musta been wrong wid ol Jenny. She wouldn ack right a-tall. She started snortin n kickin her heels. Ah tried t hol her, but she pulled erway, rearin n goin in. Then when the point of the plow was stickin up in the air, she swung erroun n twisted herself back on it. . . . She stuck herself n started t bleed. N fo Ah could do anything, she wuz dead."

"Did you ever hear of anything like that in all your life?" asked Jim Hawkins.

There were white and black standing in the crowd. They murmured. Dave's mother came close to him and looked hard into his face. "Tell the truth, Dave," she said.

"Looks like a bullet hole to me," said one man.

"Dave, whut yuh do wid the gun?" his mother asked.

The crowd surged in, looking at him. He jammed his hands into his pockets, shook his head slowly from left to right, and backed away. His eyes were wide and painful.

"Did he hava gun?" asked Jim Hawkins.

"By Gawd, Ah tol yuh tha wuz a gun wound," said a man, slapping his thigh.

His father caught his shoulders and shook him till his teeth rattled.

"Tell whut happened, yuh rascal! Tell whut. . . ."

Dave looked at Jenny's stiff legs and began to cry.

"Whut yuh do wid tha gun?" his mother asked.

"What wuz he doin wida gun?" his father asked.

"Come on and tell the truth," said Hawkins. "Ain't nobody going to hurt you. . . ."

His mother crowded close to him.

"Did yuh shoot tha mule, Dave?"

Dave cried, seeing blurred white and black faces.

"Ahh ddinn gggo tt sshooot hher. . . . Ah sssswear ffo Gawd Ahh ddin. . . . Ah wuz a-tryin t sssee ef the old gggun would sshoot — "

"Where yuh git the gun from?" his father asked.

"Ah got it from Joe, at the sto."

"Where yuh git the money?"

"Ma give it t me."

"He kept worryin me, Bob. Ah had t. Ah tol im t bring the gun right back t me. . . . It was fer yuh, the gun."

"But how yuh happen to shoot that mule?" asked Jim Hawkins.

"Ah wuzn shootin at the mule, Mistah Hawkins. The gun jumped when Ah pulled the trigger.... N fo Ah knowed anythin Jenny was there a-bleedin."

Somebody in the crowd laughed. Jim Hawkins walked close to Dave and looked into his face.

"Well, looks like you have bought you a mule, Dave."

"Ah swear fo Gawd, Ah didn go t kill the mule, Mistah Hawkins!"

"But you killed her!"

All the crowd was laughing now. They stood on tiptoe and poked heads over one another's shoulders.

"Well, boy, looks like yuh done bought a dead mule! Hahaha!"

"Ain tha ershame."

"Hohohohoho."

Dave stood, head down, twisting his feet in the dirt.

"Well, you needn't worry about it, Bob," said Jim Hawkins to Dave's father. "Just let the boy keep on working and pay me two dollars a month."

"Whut yuh wan fer yo mule, Mistah Hawkins?"

Jim Hawkins screwed up his eyes.

"Fifty dollars."

"Whut yuh do wid tha gun?" Dave's father demanded.

Dave said nothing.

"Yuh wan me t take a tree n beat yuh till yuh talk!"

"Nawsuh!"

"Whut yuh do wid it?"

"Ah throwed it erway."

"Where?"

"Ah . . . Ah throwed it in the creek."

"Waal, c mon home. N firs thing in the mawnin git to tha creek n fin tha gun."

"Yessuh."

"Whut yuh pay fer it?"

"Two dollahs."

"Take tha gun n git yo money back n carry it to Mistah Hawkins, yuh hear? N don fergit Ahma lam you black bottom good fer this! Now march yosef on home, suh!"

Dave turned and walked slowly. He heard people laughing. Dave glared, his eyes welling with tears. Hot anger bubbled in him. Then he swallowed and stumbled on.

That night Dave did not sleep. He was glad that he had gotten out of killing the mule so easily, but he was hurt. Something hot seemed to turn over inside him each time he remembered how they had laughed. He tossed on his bed, feeling his hard pillow. N Pa says he's gonna beat me. . . . He remembered other beatings, and his back quivered. Naw, naw, Ah sho don wan im t beat me tha way no mo. Dam em all! Nobody ever gave him anything. All he did was work. They treat me like a mule, n then they beat me. He gritted his teeth. N Ma had t tell on me.

Well, if he had to, he would take old man Hawkins that two dollars. But that meant selling the gun. And he wanted to keep that gun. Fifty dollars for a dead mule.

He turned over, thinking how he had fired the gun. He had an itch to fire it again. Ef other men kin shoota gun, by Gawd, Ah kin! He was still, listening. Mebbe they all sleepin now. The house was still. He heard the soft breathing of his brother. Yes, now! He would go down and get that gun and see if he could fire it! He eased out of bed and slipped into overalls.

The moon was bright. He ran almost all the way to the edge of the woods. He stumbled over the ground, looking for the spot where he had buried the gun. Yeah, here it is. Like a hungry dog scratching for a bone, he pawed it up. He puffed his black cheeks and blew dirt from the trigger and barrel. He broke it and found four cartridges unshot. He looked around; the fields were filled with silence and moonlight. He clutched the gun stiff and hard in his fingers. But, as soon as he wanted to pull the trigger, he shut his eyes and turned his head. Naw, Ah can't shoot wid mah eyes closed n mah head turned. With effort he held his eyes open; then he squeezed. *Blooooom!* He was stiff, not breathing. The gun was still in his hands. Dammit, he'd done it! He fired again. *Blooooom!* He smiled. *Bloooom! Blooooom! Click, click.* There! It was empty. If anybody could shoot a gun, he could. He put the gun into his hip pocket and started across the fields.

When he reached the top of a ridge he stood straight and proud in the moonlight, looking at Jim Hawkins' big white house, feeling the gun sagging in his pocket. Lawd, ef Ah had just one mo bullet Ah'd taka shot at tha house. Ah'd like t scare ol man Hawkins jusa little. . . . Jusa enough t let im know Dave Saunders is a man.

To his left the road curved, running to the tracks of the Illinois Central. He jerked his head, listening. From far off came a faint *hoooof-hoooof, huvvof-hoooof.* . . . He stood rigid. Two dollahs a mont. Les see now. . . . Tha means it'll take bout two years. Shucks! Ah'll be dam!

He started down the road, toward the tracks. Yeah, here she comes! He stood beside the track and held himself stiffly. Here she comes, erroun the ben. . . . C mon, yuh slow poke! C mon! He had his hand on his gun; something quivered in his stomach. Then the train thundered past, the gray and brown box cars rumbling and clinking. He gripped the gun tightly; then he jerked his hand out of his pocket. Ah betcha Bill wouldn't do it! Ah betcha. . . . The cars slid past, steel grinding upon steel. Ahm ridin yuh ternight, so hep me Gawd! He was hot all over. He hesitated just a moment; then he grabbed, pulled atop of a car, and lay flat. He felt his pocket; the gun was still there. Ahead the long rails were glinting in the moonlight, stretching away, away to somewhere, somewhere where he could be a man. . . .

౫౫

7

COMMENTARIES ON STORIES AND STORYTELLERS

PAULA GUNN ALLEN *is a poet and professor of literature. This story is from her book of Native American traditional tales,* Spider Woman's Granddaughters *(1989).*

PAULA GUNN ALLEN

Whirlwind Man Steals Yellow Woman   1983

Kochinnenako, Yellow Woman, was grinding corn one day with her three sisters. They looked into the water jars and saw that they were empty. They said, "We need some water." Kochinnenako said she would go, and taking the jars made her way across the mesa and went down to the spring. She climbed the rockhewn stairs to the spring that lay in a deep pool of shade. As she knelt to dip the gourd dipper into the cool shadowed water, she heard someone coming down the steps. She looked up and saw Whirlwind Man. He said, "Gutwatzi, Kochinnenako. Are you here?"

"Da'waa'e," she said, dipping water calmly into the four jars beside her. She didn't look at him.

"Put down the dipper," he said. "I want you to come with me."

"I am filling these jars with water as you can see," she said. "My sisters and I are grinding corn, and they are waiting for me."

"No," Whirlwind Man said. "You must come and go with me. If you won't come, well, I'll have to kill you." He showed her his knife.

726

Kochinnenako put the dipper down carefully. "All right," she said. "I guess I'll go with you." She got up. She went with Whirlwind Man to the other side of the world where he lived with his mother, who greeted her like his wife.

The jars stayed, tall and fat and cool in the deep shade by the shadowed spring.

That was one story. She knew they laughed about Kochinnenako. Brought her up when some woman was missing for awhile. Said she ran off with a Navajo, or maybe with a mountain spirit, "Like Kochinnenako." Maybe the name had become synonymous with "whore" at Guadalupe. Ephanie knew that Yellow was the color of woman, ritual color of faces painted in death, or for some of the dances. But there was a tone of dismissal, or derision there that she couldn't quite pin down, there anyway. No one told how Kochinnenako went with Whirlwind Man because she was forced. Said, "Then Whirlwind Man raped Kochinnenako." Rather, the story was that his mother had greeted Yellow Woman, and made her at home in their way. And that when Kochinnenako wanted to return home, had agreed, asking only that she wait while the old woman prepared gifts for Kochinnenako's sisters.

Ephanie wondered if Yellow Woman so long ago had known what was happening to her. If she could remember it or if she thought maybe she had dreamed it. If they laughed at her, or threw her out when she returned. She wondered if Kochinnenako cried.

ॐ

JULIA ALVAREZ *is a writer who teaches literature at Middlebury College. She discusses Clarice Lispector's story in the anthology* You've Got to Read This *(1994).*

JULIA ALVAREZ

On Lispector's "The Smallest Woman in the World"

1994

Stories that hold me spellbound remind me of the tale the Ancient Mariner has to tell. He finds just the person whom he knows has to hear his story, and then he holds his listener with the glittering eye of his narrative. The listener might resist at first, but when the tale is told, he feels the deep *ah yes* of having heard just the thing he needed to hear.

There are stories I admire, ones I adore, ones I wish I had written. But the story that holds me spellbound is the one I feel was written because someone like me had to read it.

I first read Clarice Lispector's story "The Smallest Woman in the World" about sixteen–seventeen years ago, before the great push in anthologies, colleges, curriculum to include "minority voices." I had been trained back in those days when you read only *the* great books — Milton, Shakespeare, Chaucer — and you went to anthropology, or in my case home to the Island, to learn about *the other*. Literature, for me, was definitely the colony of the powerful, and I was fully identified with them. When I read *The Tempest*, I too held Caliban at arm's length, never giving a thought to what his rights were to the island Prospero had conquered. When I heard the lover's plaint in the Sonnets about his dark lady's looks, I understood how a fair one would have made him feel better. In other words, I looked at *the other* with a cold, dominant Yeatsian eye, though my own personal experience, of course, negated my literary one. All the women authors I did finally read, and all the "minority" women authors that saved my work and psyche from total divorce from my own roots and culture and being, I read long after graduate school, on my own.

When I picked up the Lispector story, I was just beginning this process of reading on my own. The Ancient Mariner story is obviously compelling because the listener is ripe for the telling. Encountering that first paragraph I was all set, with my training, for Joseph Conrad and the trek into deepest Africa to encounter horror, the horror. "Imagine my surprise" when I came upon the seventeen and three-quarter inch, full-grown, black, silent, and very pregnant smallest woman in the world! I burst out laughing.

It was a heady, gleeful, refreshing laughter — aimed at myself mostly. How could I have missed her in all my reading? The answer came almost at once: of course, she is *so* small — and silent and black and pregnant — that I and, it seemed, most of western tradition had overlooked her.

It is hard to know who she really is. We are first introduced to her through the point of view of the explorer. Instantly upon meeting her, he names her, giving her a ridiculous, prettifying name, reminiscent of her obvious opposite, Saint Teresa, the Little Flower. But the explorer himself is being transformed by the encounter: as he studies her before naming her, he feels "a delicacy of feeling" of which his wife would never have thought him capable. To this sweet, deeply moving biblical moment of Adam naming in the garden, the newly baptized Little Flower responds by scratching her crotch. The explorer looks away, embarrassed, I suppose.

The story, too, looks away for a long while; instead of staying in Africa, we head back for "civilization." (Part of the transforming effect of this story is that the reader starts saying all these words with a sense of irony.) Now we hear reaction after reaction to Little Flower — all having more to do with the readers of the Sunday papers than they do with the oblivious little woman still, we assume, in deepest Africa, scratching where it itches.

I do wonder why almost all of the responders are women — except for one little boy and an absent, uneasy father, coughing behind his paper. Is it because, as the wife of the uneasy father accuses, "You're the insensitive one"? We women are the responders. It's the next best thing if we can't go on the adventures. After all, the world might not be our apple, but it can be our Rorschach, goddammit! Then, too, Little Flower is pregnant, a condition that binds her to other females. But this sense of resemblance makes the women uneasy. One woman at her mirror rolling her hair draws away from this black, crude face, placing a distance of "insuperable millenniums" between the creature and herself. "It isn't human," another mother reminds her daughter. I can understand their reluctance — they are fully identified with their dominant status as the refined and beautiful wives and daughters of the powerful.

By moving away from Little Flower into the drawing room, the story charts a common impulse: always we want to come back to what we know. To bring back the strange into the cozy safety of our living room and *respond*. To theorize and coopt it with our love and misinformed understanding, p.c.-ing her to death. And at the same time to distance ourselves from it — to respond to it but not identify with it.

The story has wandered far from the original creature herself — just as I had in my own training when I first came upon the story. As I said, it is difficult to encounter the unadulterated rare thing herself and not interpose our selves, our faces, our prejudices upon it. But finally the narrator returns us to the source. Now, we will get "the secret of her own secret": what we've wanted to know all along, Who is Little Flower? What does she mean? In other words, the story raises in the reader the same curiosity about Little Flower as symbol that the explorer and his civilized ladies felt toward the little figure herself.

But wait, Little Flower is laughing! At us? No, not really. For if she were laughing at us, we would be speaking the same language. Unlike the sad women we met in the drawing rooms who have learned — or are beginning to intuit — the wisdom that "sorrow is endless," Little Flower posits joy with her laughter. She is still close to her irreducible being, and she is joyous because she has not been eaten, and she is in love with the explorer because she likes his boots and his shiny ring. She responds to these feelings in a frankly sexual way. Little Flower is free of the cruel refinements of these feelings that must be making the other women in their little golden cages so unhappy.

Or so we understand from our author, who must be intuiting what Little Flower is feeling, for the smallest woman doesn't speak. She does finally say one word, one quoted word in the whole story, "Yes." All we hear of her is her wonderful laughter, which serves, at least for me, the same function as the Ancient Mariner's glittering eye. That laughter holds me and echoes in my head long after the story is over. And then, I realize — and I remember the shock of that first reading — that the laughter was coming from deep inside me.

Yes!

What I suddenly understood that first time I read the story — and my laughter each time I reread the story confirms it — was that I was Little Flower. *Yes*. I am really — in the hiddenmost parts of the deepest Africa in me — the smallest woman in the world. I've learned English perfectly without an accent. Due to vitamins and good nutrition, I have grown to a sizable small size and weight. I know how to throw this small weight and American voice around. I have the degrees, the training on how to respond to literature, I have a car, a house, a closest full of pretty clothes, because it is good to own, good to own.

But it's not just me who is Little Flower. Everyone who reads the story knows he or she is Little Flower, and he or she is also the overlay of responses and note-taking that keeps the little being invisible and minuscule inside us: our little pregnancy, the first atom of our being, the creature who has not been eaten. But cruel refinements interfere. And we forget the visceral first and truest response of our being to the world.

Sometimes I know I forget who I am under the overlay of Sunday papers, of work, of clothes, of the feminine, of the American girl, of netted hats, of words, words, words.

But this little story always reminds me and that is why it holds me, spellbound.

తొ

SHERWOOD ANDERSON *commented on his practice of writing short stories in his autobiography,* A Story Teller's Story, *published in 1924. This book was his first attempt to write his memoirs and authenticate his "legend" — an impoverished childhood, a revolt against business life, and an entrance into the avant-garde literary circles of Chicago, New Orleans, and New York. He was more concerned with the meaning than with the facts of his life. In his rejection of the "plot" story (a story emphasizing plot over character, setting, or theme), which he considered contrived fiction, he became a strong influence on many subsequent writers of short stories and revitalized the American short story tradition.*

SHERWOOD ANDERSON

Form, Not Plot, in the Short Story   1924

For such men as myself you must understand there is always a great difficulty about telling the tale after the scent has been picked up. . . . Having, from a conversation overheard or in some other way, got the tone of a tale, I was like a woman who has just become impregnated. Something was growing inside me. At night when I lay in my bed I could feel the heels of the tale kicking against the walls of my body. Often as I lay thus every word of the tale came to me quite clearly but when I got out of bed to write it down the words would not come.

I had constantly to seek in roads new to me. Other men had felt what I had felt, had seen what I had seen — how had they met the difficulties I faced? My father when he told his tales walked up and down the room before his audience. He pushed out little experimental sentences and watched his audience narrowly. There was a dull-eyed old farmer sitting in a corner of the room. Father had his eyes on the fellow. "I'll get him," he said to himself. He watched the farmer's eyes. When the experimental sentence he had tried did not get anywhere he tried another and kept trying. Besides words he had — to help the telling of his tales — the advantage of being able to act out those parts for which he could find no words. He could frown, shake his fists, smile, let a look of pain or annoyance drift over his face.

These were his advantages that I had to give up if I was to write my tales rather than tell them and how often I had cursed my fate.

How significant words had become to me! At about this time an American woman living in Paris, Miss Gertrude Stein, had published a book called *Tender Buttons* and it had come into my hands. How it had excited me! Here was something purely experimental and dealing in words separated from sense — in the ordinary meaning of the word sense — an approach I was sure the poets must often be compelled to make. Was it an approach that would help me? I decided to try it.

A year or two before the time of which I am now writing an American painter, Mr. Felix Russman, had taken me one day into his workshop to show me his colors. He laid them out on a table before me and then his wife called him out of the room and he stayed for half an hour. It had been one of the most exciting moments of my life. I shifted the little pans of color about, laid one color against another. I walked away and came near. Suddenly there had flashed into my consciousness, for perhaps the first time in my life, the secret inner world of the painters. Before that time I had wondered often enough why certain paintings, done by the old masters, and hung in our Chicago Art Institute, had so strange an effect upon me. Now I thought I knew. The true painter revealed all of himself in every stroke of his brush. Titian made one feel so utterly the splendor of himself; from Fra Angelico and Sandro Botticelli there came such a deep human tenderness that on some days it fairly brought tears to the eyes; in a most dreadful way and in spite of all his skill Bouguereau gave away his own inner nastiness while Leonardo made one feel all of the grandeur of his mind just as Balzac° had made his readers feel the universality and wonder of his mind.

Very well then, the words used by the tale-teller were as the colors used by the painter. Form was another matter. It grew out of the materials of the tale and the teller's reaction to them. It was the tale trying to take form that kicked about inside the tale-teller at night when he wanted to sleep.

And words were something else. Words were the surfaces, the clothes of the tale. I thought I had begun to get something a little clearer now. I had smiled to myself a little at the sudden realization of how little native American words had been used by American story-writers. When most American writers wanted to be very American they went in for slang. Surely we American scribblers had paid long and hard for the English blood in our veins. The English had got their books into our schools, their ideas of correct forms of expression were firmly fixed in our minds. Words as commonly used in our writing were in reality an army that marched in a certain array and the generals in command of the army were still English. One saw the words as marching, always just so — in books — and came to think of them so — in books.

But when one told a tale to a group of advertising men sitting in a barroom in Chicago or to a group of laborers by a factory door in Indiana one instinctively disbanded the army. There were moments then for what have

---

Balzac: Honoré de Balzac (1799–1850), French novelist, one of the earliest realists.

always been called by our correct writers "unprintable words." One got now and then a certain effect by a bit of profanity. One dropped instinctively into the vocabulary of the men about, was compelled to do so to get the full effect sought for the tale. Was the tale he was telling not just the tale of a man named Smoky Pete and how he caught his foot in the trap set for himself? — or perhaps one was giving them the Mama Geigans story. The devil. What had the words of such a tale to do with Thackeray° or Fielding?° Did the men to whom one told the tale not know a dozen Smoky Petes and Mama Geigans? Had one ventured into the classic English models for tale-telling at that moment there would have been a roar. "What the devil! Don't you go high-toning us!"

And it was sure one did not always seek a laugh from his audience. Sometimes one wanted to move the audience, make them squirm with sympathy. Perhaps one wanted to throw an altogether new light on a tale the audience already knew.

Would the common words of our daily speech in shops and offices do the trick? Surely the Americans among whom one sat talking had felt everything the Greeks had felt, everything the English felt? Deaths came to them, the tricks of fate assailed their lives. I was certain none of them lived felt or talked as the average American novel made them live feel and talk and as for the plot short stories of the magazines — those bastard children of the de Maupassant, Poe, and O. Henry° — it was certain there were no plot short stories ever lived in any life I had known anything about.

ɷ

JAMES BALDWIN *wrote this account of how he became a writer in his book* Notes of a Native Son *(1955). He admitted that "the most difficult (and most rewarding) thing in my life has been the fact that I was born a Negro and was forced, therefore, to effect some kind of truce with this reality." As his biographer Louis H. Pratt has understood, this "truce" forced Baldwin "into an open confrontation with his experience, enabling him to make an honest assessment of his past. . . . Baldwin the artist has been liberated because he has found a way to use his past and to transform those experiences resulting therefrom into art."*

JAMES BALDWIN

Autobiographical Notes   1955

I was born in Harlem thirty-one years ago. I began plotting novels at about the time I learned to read. The story of my childhood is the usual bleak

---

Thackeray: William Makepeace Thackeray (1811–1863), English novelist.
Fielding: Henry Fielding (1707–1754), one of the first English novelists.
O. Henry: The pseudonym of William Sydney Porter (1862–1910), a famous American author of short stories with elaborate plots and often "trick" endings.

fantasy, and we can dismiss it with the unrestrained observation that I certainly would not consider living it again. In those days my mother was given to the exasperating and mysterious habit of having babies. As they were born, I took them over with one hand and held a book with the other. The children probably suffered, though they have since been kind enough to deny it, and in this way I read *Uncle Tom's Cabin* and *A Tale of Two Cities* over and over and over again; in this way, in fact, I read just about everything I could get my hands on — except the Bible, probably because it was the only book I was encouraged to read. I must also confess that I wrote — a great deal — and my first professional triumph, in any case, the first effort of mine to be seen in print, occurred at the age of twelve or thereabouts, when a short story I had written about the Spanish revolution won some sort of prize in an extremely short-lived church newspaper. I remember the story was censored by the lady editor, though I don't remember why, and I was outraged.

Also wrote plays, and songs, for one of which I received a letter of congratulations from Mayor La Guardia, and poetry, about which the less said, the better. My mother was delighted by all these goings-on, but my father wasn't; he wanted me to be a preacher. When I was fourteen I became a preacher, and when I was seventeen I stopped. Very shortly thereafter I left home. For God knows how long I struggled with the world of commerce and industry — I guess they would say they struggled with *me* — and when I was about twenty-one I had enough done of a novel to get a Saxton Fellowship. When I was twenty-two the fellowship was over, the novel turned out to be unsalable, and I started waiting on tables in a Village° restaurant and writing book reviews — mostly, as it turned out, about the Negro problem, concerning which the color of my skin made me automatically an expert. Did another book, in company with photographer Theodore Pelatowski, about the storefront churches in Harlem. This book met exactly the same fate as my first — fellowship, but no sale. (It was a Rosenwald Fellowship.) By the time I was twenty-four I had decided to stop reviewing books about the Negro problem — which, by this time, was only slightly less horrible in print than it was in life — and I packed my bags and went to France, where I finished, God knows how, *Go Tell It on the Mountain.*

Any writer, I suppose, feels that the world into which he was born is nothing less than a conspiracy against the cultivation of his talent — which attitude certainly has a great deal to support it. On the other hand, it is only because the world looks on his talent with such a frightening indifference that the artist is compelled to make his talent important. So that any writer, looking back over even so short a span of time as I am here forced to assess, finds that the things which hurt him and the things which helped him cannot be divorced from each other; he could be helped in a certain way only because he was hurt in a certain way; and his help is simply to be enabled to move from one conundrum to the next — one is tempted to say that he moves from one disaster to the next. When one begins looking for influences one finds them by

---

Village: Greenwich Village, New York City.

the score. I haven't thought much about my own, not enough anyway; I hazard that the King James Bible, the rhetoric of the store-front church, something ironic and violent and perpetually understated in Negro speech — and something of Dickens' love for bravura — have something to do with me today; but I wouldn't stake my life on it. Likewise, innumerable people have helped me in many ways; but finally, I suppose, the most difficult (and most rewarding) thing in my life has been the fact that I was born a Negro and was forced, therefore, to effect some kind of truce with this reality. (Truce, by the way, is the best one can hope for.)

One of the difficulties about being a Negro writer (and this is not special pleading, since I don't mean to suggest that he has it worse than anybody else) is that the Negro problem is written about so widely. The bookshelves groan under the weight of information, and everyone therefore considers himself informed. And this information, furthermore, operates usually (generally, popularly) to reinforce traditional attitudes. Of traditional attitudes there are only two — For or Against — and I, personally, find it difficult to say which attitude has caused me the most pain. I am perfectly aware that the change from ill-will to good-will, however motivated, however imperfect, however expressed, is better than no change at all.

But it is part of the business of the writer — as I see it — to examine attitudes, to go beneath the surface, to tap the source. From this point of view the Negro problem is nearly inaccessible. It is not only written about so widely; it is written about so badly. It is quite possible to say that the price a Negro pays for becoming articulate is to find himself, at length, with nothing to be articulate about. ("You taught me the language," says Caliban to Prospero,° "and my profit on't is I know how to curse.") Consider: The tremendous social activity that this problem generates imposes on whites and Negroes alike the necessity of looking forward, of working to bring about a better day. This is fine, it keeps the waters troubled; it is all, indeed, that has made possible the Negro's progress. Nevertheless, social affairs are not generally speaking the writer's prime concern, whether they ought to be or not; it is absolutely necessary that he establish between himself and these affairs a distance that will allow, at least, for clarity, so that before he can look forward in any meaningful sense, he must first be allowed to take a long look back. In the context of the Negro problem neither whites nor blacks, for excellent reasons of their own, have the faintest desire to look back; but I think that the past is all that makes the present coherent, and further, that the past will remain horrible for exactly as long as we refuse to assess it honestly.

I know, in any case, that the most crucial time in my own development came when I was forced to recognize that I was a kind of bastard of the West; when I followed the line of my past I did not find myself in Europe but in Africa. And this meant that in some subtle way, in a really profound way, I brought to Shakespeare, Bach, Rembrandt, to the stones of Paris, to the cathedral at Chartres, and to the Empire State Building, a special attitude. These

---

Caliban . . . Prospero: In Shakespeare's *The Tempest*, the monster Caliban is a servant of the magician Prospero.

were not really my creations, they did not contain my history; I might search in them in vain forever for any reflection of myself. I was an interloper; this was not my heritage. At the same time I had no other heritage which I could possibly hope to use — I had certainly been unfitted for the jungle or the tribe. I would have to appropriate these white centuries, I would have to make them mine — I would have to accept my special attitude, my special place in this scheme — otherwise I would have no place in *any* scheme. What was the most difficult was the fact that I was forced to admit something I had always hidden from myself, which the American Negro has had to hide from himself as the price of his public progress; that I hated and feared white people. This did not mean that I loved black people; on the contrary, I despised them, possibly because they failed to produce Rembrandt. In effect, I hated and feared the world. And this meant, not only that I thus gave the world an altogether murderous power over me, but also that in such a self-destroying limbo I could never hope to write.

One writes out of one thing only — one's own experience. Everything depends on how relentlessly one forces from this experience the last drop, sweet or bitter, it can possibly give. This is the only real concern of the artist, to recreate out of the disorder of life that order which is art. The difficulty then, for me, of being a Negro writer was the fact that I was, in effect, prohibited from examining my own experience too closely by the tremendous demands and the very real dangers of my social situation.

I don't think the dilemma outlined above is uncommon. I do think, since writers work in the disastrously explicit medium of language, that it goes a little way towards explaining why, out of the enormous resources of Negro speech and life, and despite the example of Negro music, prose written by Negroes has been generally speaking so pallid and so harsh. I have not written about being a Negro at such length because I expect that to be my only subject, but only because it was the gate I had to unlock before I could hope to write about anything else. I don't think that the Negro problem in America can be even discussed coherently without bearing in mind its context; its context being the history, traditions, customs, the moral assumptions and preoccupations of the country; in short, the general social fabric. Appearances to the contrary, no one in America escapes its effects and everyone in America bears some responsibility for it. I believe this the more firmly because it is the overwhelming tendency to speak of this problem as though it were a thing apart. But in the work of Faulkner, in the general attitude and certain specific passages in Robert Penn Warren,° and, most significantly, in the advent of Ralph Ellison, one sees the beginnings — at least — of a more genuinely penetrating search. Mr. Ellison, by the way, is the first Negro novelist I have ever read to utilize in language, and brilliantly, some of the ambiguity and irony of Negro life.

About my interests: I don't know if I have any, unless the morbid desire to own a sixteen-millimeter camera and make experimental movies can be so classified. Otherwise, I love to eat and drink — it's my melancholy conviction

---

Robert Penn Warren: An American novelist, poet, and critic (1905–1989).

that I've scarcely ever had enough to eat (this is because it's *impossible* to eat enough if you're worried about the next meal) — and I love to argue with people who do not disagree with me too profoundly, and I love to laugh. I do *not* like bohemia, or bohemians, I do not like people whose principal aim is pleasure, and I do not like people who are *earnest* about anything. I don't like people who like me because I'm a Negro; neither do I like people who find in the same accident grounds for contempt. I love America more than any other country in the world, and, exactly for this reason, I insist on the right to criticize her perpetually. I think all theories are suspect, that the finest principles may have to be modified, or may even be pulverized by the demands of life, and that one must find, therefore, one's own moral center and move through the world hoping that this center will guide one aright. I consider that I have many responsibilities, but none greater than this: to last, as Hemingway says, and get my work done.

I want to be an honest man and a good writer.

ကလ

JOHN CHEEVER *wrote this article for the October 30, 1978, issue of* Newsweek. *He was newsworthy at that time because he had just published a collection of short fiction,* The Stories of John Cheever, *which had become a best-seller. Cheever humorously refers to his early financial struggles in the article, but in Susan Cheever's book about her father, she remembers that he was often deeply frustrated by how little he earned from* The New Yorker. *"The money they paid him just wasn't enough to live on — even in the years when we children were in public schools and the family in a rented house." The second part of the* Newsweek *article almost becomes a story about Cheever's suburban neighborhood. Evidently there was nothing in the contemporary scene that he could not turn into a narrative.*

JOHN CHEEVER

Why I Write Short Stories   1978

To publish a definitive collection of short stories in one's late 60s seems to me, as an American writer, a traditional and a dignified occasion, eclipsed in no way by the fact that a great many of the stories in my current collection were written in my underwear.

This is not to say that I was ever a Bohemian. Hardly a man is now alive who can remember when Harold Ross edited *The New Yorker* magazine, but I am one of these. The Ross editorial queries were genuinely eccentric. In one short story of mine, I invented a character who returned home from work and changed his clothes before dinner. Ross wrote on the galley margin, "Eh? What's this? Cheever looks to me like a one-suiter." He was so right. At the space rates he paid, I could afford exactly one suit. In the mornings, I dressed in this and took the elevator to a windowless room in the basement where I worked. Here I hung my suit on a hanger, wrote until nightfall when I dressed and returned to our apartment. A great many of my stories were written in boxer shorts.

A collection of short stories appears like a lemon in the current fiction list, which is indeed a garden of love, erotic horseplay, and lewd and ancient family history; but so long as we are possessed by experience that is distinguished by its intensity and its episodic nature, we will have the short story in our literature, and without a literature we will, of course, perish. It was F. R. Leavis who said that literature is the first distinction of a civilized man.

Who reads short stories? one is asked, and I like to think that they are read by men and women in the dentist's office, waiting to be called to the chair; they are read on transcontinental plane trips instead of watching a banal and vulgar film spin out the time between our coasts; they are read by discerning and well-informed men and women who seem to feel that narrative fiction can contribute to our understanding of one another and the sometimes bewildering world around us.

The novel, in all its greatness, demands at least some passing notice of the classical unities, preserving that mysterious link between esthetics and moral fitness; but to have this unyielding antiquity exclude the newness in our ways of life would be regrettable. This newness is known to some of us through "Star Wars," to some of us through the melancholy that follows a fielder's error in the late innings of a ball game. In the pursuit of this newness, contemporary painting seems to have lost the language of the landscape, the still-life, and — most important — the nude. Modern music has been separated from those rhythms and tonalities that are most deeply ingrained in our memories, but literature still possesses the narrative — the story — and one would defend this with one's life.

In the short stories of my esteemed colleagues — and in a few of my own — I find those rented summer houses, those one-night love affairs, and those lost key rings that confound traditional esthetics. We are not a nomadic people, but there is more than a hint of this spirit of our great country — and the short story is the literature of the nomad.

I like to think that the view of a suburban street that I imagine from my window would appeal to a wanderer or to someone familiar with loneliness. Here is a profoundly moving display of nostalgia, vision, and love, none of it more than 30 years old, including most of the trees. Here are white columns from the manorial South, brick and timber walls from Elizabethan England, saltbox houses from our great maritime past, and flat-roofed echoes of Frank Lloyd Wright° and his vision of a day when we would all enjoy solar heating, serene and commodious interiors, and peace on earth.

The lots are 1½ acres, flowers and vegetables grow in the yards, and here and there one finds, instead of tomatoes, robust stands of cannabis with its feathery leaf. Here, in this victorious domesticity, the principal crop is a hazardous drug. And what do I see hanging in the Hartshores' clothes-yard but enough seasoning marijuana to stone a regiment.

Frank Lloyd Wright: American architect (1867–1959).

Is forgetfulness some part of the mysteriousness of life? If I speak to Mr. Hartshore about his cannabis crop, will he tell me that the greatness of Chinese civilization stood foursquare on the fantasies of opium? But it is not I who will speak to Mr. Hartshore. It will be Charlie Dilworth, a very abstemious man who lives in the house next door. He has a No Smoking sign on his front lawn, and his passionate feelings about marijuana have been intelligently channeled into a sort of reverse blackmail.

I hear them litigating late one Saturday afternoon when I have come back from playing touch football with my sons. The light is going. It is autumn. Charlie's voice is loud and clear and can be heard by anyone interested. "You keep your dogs off my lawn, you cook your steaks in the house, you keep your record player down, you keep your swimming-pool filter off in the evenings, and you keep your window shades drawn. Otherwise, I'll report your drug crop to the police and with my wife's uncle sitting as judge this month you'll get at least six months in the can for criminal possession."

They part. Night falls. Here and there a housewife, apprehending the first frost, takes in her house plants while from an Elizabethan, a Nantucket, and a Frank Lloyd Wright chimney comes the marvelous fragrance of wood smoke. You can't put this scene in a novel.

ಌ

ANTON CHEKHOV *described his theories of literature and his practice as a storyteller in countless letters to his family and friends. He was not a systematic critic, and he did not necessarily follow his own advice to other writers. Brevity and concentration on a few essentials of scene and character were the essence of his technique, but he was not always as drastically laconic in his stories as his letters suggest. What is consistently clear in his advice to other writers is his own untiring compassion and his desire to speak honestly in his efforts to help them. He wrote in his notebook, "It is not the function of art to solve problems but to present them clearly."*

These letters are to his older brother, his publisher, and a younger author whose work he admired.

ANTON CHEKHOV

Technique in Writing the Short Story   *1886–99*

TRANSLATED BY CONSTANCE GARNETT

FROM A LETTER TO ALEXANDER P. CHEKHOV, 1886

In my opinion a true description of Nature should be very brief and have a character of relevance. Commonplaces such as, "the setting sun bathing in the waves of the darkening sea, poured its purple gold, etc." — "the swallows flying over the surface of the water twittered merrily" — such commonplaces one ought to abandon. In descriptions of Nature one ought to seize upon the little particulars, grouping them in such a way that, in reading, when you shut your eyes, you get a picture.

For instance, you will get the full effect of a moonlight night if you write that on the mill-dam a little glowing star-point flashed from the neck of a broken bottle, and the round, black shadow of a dog, or a wolf, emerged and ran, etc. Nature becomes animated if you are not squeamish about employing comparisons of her phenomena with ordinary human activities, etc.

In the sphere of psychology, details are also the thing. God preserve us from commonplaces. Best of all is it to avoid depicting the hero's state of mind; you ought to try to make it clear from the hero's actions. It is not necessary to portray many characters. The center of gravity should be in two persons: him and her.

FROM A LETTER TO ALEKSEY S. SUVORIN, 1890

You abuse me for objectivity, calling it indifference to good and evil, lack of ideals and ideas, and so on. You would have me, when I describe horse-thieves, say: "Stealing horses is an evil." But that has been known for ages without my saying so. Let the jury judge them; it's my job simply to show what sort of people they are. I write: You are dealing with horse-thieves, so let me tell you that they are not beggars but well-fed people, that they are people of a special cult, and that horse-stealing is not simply theft but a passion. Of course it would be pleasant to combine art with a sermon, but for me personally it is extremely difficult and almost impossible, owing to the conditions of technique. You see, to depict horse-thieves in seven hundred lines I must all the time speak and think in their tone and feel in their spirit, otherwise, if I introduce subjectivity, the image becomes blurred and the story will not be as compact as all short stories ought to be. When I write, I reckon entirely upon the reader to add for himself the subjective elements that are lacking in the story.

FROM A LETTER TO MAXIM GORKY, 1899

More advice: when reading the proofs, cross out a host of terms qualifying nouns and verbs. You have so many such terms that the reader's mind finds it a task to concentrate on them, and he soon grows tired. You understand it at once when I say, "The man sat on the grass"; you understand it because it is clear and makes no demands on the attention. On the other hand, it is not easily understood, and it is difficult for the mind, if I write, "A tall, narrow-chested, middle-sized man, with a red beard, sat on the green grass, already trampled by pedestrians, sat silently, shyly, and timidly looked about him." That is not immediately grasped by the mind, whereas good writing should be grasped at once — in a second.

෩

KATE CHOPIN *made a number of translations, mostly of stories by Guy de Maupassant, and she published several essays on literature in St. Louis periodicals. She wrote about the influence of Maupassant on her fiction in response to an invitation from the editor of the* Atlantic Monthly *in 1896. He returned her first version of the essay, however, advising her to "set forth the matter directly." Her revised version*

was later included in the magazine with the title "In the Confidence of a Story-Teller,"
but the section describing how she first encountered Maupassant's tales and the im-
pression they made on her was dropped, perhaps because she spoke so enthusiastically
about the French writer's escape "from tradition and authority." This portion of the
essay is reprinted from the manuscript included in Volume 2 of The Complete
Works of Kate Chopin *(1969).*

KATE CHOPIN

How I Stumbled upon Maupassant 1896

About eight years ago there fell accidentally into my hands a volume of
Maupassant's tales. These were new to me. I had been in the woods, in the
fields, groping around; looking for something big, satisfying, convincing, and
finding nothing but — myself; a something neither big nor satisfying but
wholly convincing. It was at this period of my emerging from the vast solitude
in which I had been making my own acquaintance, that I stumbled upon
Maupassant. I read his stories and marvelled at them. Here was life, not fiction; for where were the plots, the old fashioned mechanism and stage trapping that in a vague, unthinking way I had fancied were essential to the art of
story making? Here was a man who had escaped from tradition and authority, who had entered into himself and looked out upon life through his own
being and with his own eyes; and who, in a direct and simple way, told us
what he saw. When a man does this, he gives us the best that he can; something valuable for it is genuine and spontaneous. He gives us his impressions.
Someone told me the other day that Maupassant had gone out of fashion. I
was not grieved to hear it. He has never seemed to me to belong to the multitude, but rather to the individual. He is not one whom we gather in crowds to
listen to — whom we follow in procession — with beating of brass instruments. He does not move us to throw ourselves into the throng — having the
integral of an unthinking whole to shout his praise. I even like to think that he
appeals to me alone. You probably like to think that he reaches you exclusively. A whole multitude may be secretly nourishing the belief in regard to
him for all I know. Someway I like to cherish the delusion that he has spoken
to no one else so directly, so intimately as he does to me. He did not say, as another might have done, "do you see these are charming stories of mine? take
them into your closet — study them closely — mark their combination — observe the method, the manner of their putting together — and if ever you are
moved to write stories you can do no better than to imitate."

෴

STEPHEN CRANE *wrote about the wreck of the* Commodore *in the article*
"Stephen Crane's Own Story" in the New York Press *on January 7, 1897. At that*
time arms and provisions were being smuggled from Florida to Cuba to aid the insur-
rection against Spanish rule. Crane boarded the Commodore *in Jacksonville on De-*

*cember 31, 1896. The ship was loaded with a cargo of rifles and ammunition. As the
scholar Olov W. Fryckstedt explained, Crane "looked forward to a long period of unknown adventures and exciting dangers in the Cuban mountains. But during the
night of January 1 the ship foundered fifteen miles off the coast of Florida after a mysterious explosion in the engine room." The first part of Crane's newspaper story describes the loading of the ship, the peril of sandbars, the explosion in the engine room,
and the lowering of the lifeboats. Then, with the ship's "whistle of despair," it became
clear to everyone onboard that the situation was hopeless. The bustling action before
the shipwreck is the substance of Crane's newspaper report; his thirty desperate hours
afterward in the ten-foot dinghy became the story of "The Open Boat."*

STEPHEN CRANE

The Sinking of the Commodore   1897

A WHISTLE OF DESPAIR

Now the whistle of the *Commodore* had been turned loose, and if there
ever was a voice of despair and death, it was in the voice of this whistle. It had
gained a new tone. It was as if its throat was already choked by the water, and
this cry on the sea at night, with a wind blowing the spray over the ship, and
the waves roaring over the bow, and swirling white along the decks, was to
each of us probably a song of man's end.

It was now that the first mate showed a sign of losing his grip. To us who
were trying in all stages of competence and experience to launch the lifeboat
he raged in all terms of fiery satire and hammerlike abuse. But the boat moved
at last and swung down toward the water.

Afterward, when I went aft, I saw the captain standing, with his arm in
a sling, holding on to a stay with his one good hand and directing the launching of the boat. He gave me a five-gallon jug of water to hold, and asked me
what I was going to do. I told him what I thought was about the proper thing,
and he told me then that the cook had the same idea, and ordered me to go forward and be ready to launch the ten-foot dinghy.

IN THE TEN-FOOT DINGHY

I remember well that he turned then to swear at a colored stoker who
was prowling around, done up in life preservers until he looked like a feather
bed. I went forward with my five-gallon jug of water, and when the captain
came we launched the dinghy, and they put me over the side to fend her off
from the ship with an oar.

They handed me down the water jug, and then the cook came into the
boat, and we sat there in the darkness, wondering why, by all our hopes of future happiness, the captain was so long in coming over to the side and ordering us away from the doomed ship.

The captain was waiting for the other boat to go. Finally he hailed in the
darkness: "Are you all right, Mr. Graines?"

The first mate answered: "All right, sir."

"Shove off, then," cried the captain.

The captain was just about to swing over the rail when a dark form came forward and a voice said, "Captain, I go with you."

The captain answered: "Yes, Billy; get in."

HIGGINS LAST TO LEAVE SHIP

It was Billy Higgins, the oiler. Billy dropped into the boat and a moment later the captain followed, bringing with him an end of about forty yards of lead line. The other end was attached to the rail of the ship.

As we swung back to leeward the captain said: "Boys, we will stay right near the ship till she goes down."

This cheerful information, of course, filled us all with glee. The line kept us headed properly into the wind, and as we rode over the monstrous waves we saw upon each rise the swaying lights of the dying *Commodore.*

When came the gray shade of dawn, the form of the *Commodore* grew slowly clear to us as our little ten-foot boat rose over each swell. She was floating with such an air of buoyancy that we laughed when we had time, and said, "What a gag it would be on those other fellows if she didn't sink at all."

But later we saw men aboard of her, and later still they began to hail us.

HELPING THEIR MATES

I had forgot to mention that previously we had loosened the end of the lead line and dropped much further to leeward. The men on board were a mystery to us, of course, as we had seen all the boats leave the ship. We rowed back to the ship, but did not approach too near, because we were four men in a ten-foot boat, and we knew that the touch of a hand on our gunwale would assuredly swamp us.

The first mate cried out from the ship that the third boat had foundered alongside. He cried that they had made rafts, and wished us to tow them.

The captain said, "All right."

Their rafts were floating astern. "Jump in!" cried the captain, but there was a singular and most harrowing hesitation. There were five white men and two negroes. This scene in the gray light of morning impressed one as would a view into some place where ghosts move slowly. These seven men on the stern of the sinking *Commodore* were silent. Save the words of the mate to the captain there was no talk. Here was death, but here also was a most singular and indefinable kind of fortitude.

Four men, I remember, clambered over the railing and stood there watching the cold, steely sheen of the sweeping waves.

"Jump," cried the captain again.

The old chief engineer first obeyed the order. He landed on the outside raft and the captain told him how to grip the raft and he obeyed as promptly and as docilely as a scholar in riding school.

THE MATE'S MAD PLUNGE

A stoker followed him, and then the first mate threw his hands over his head and plunged into the sea. He had no life belt and for my part, even when he did this horrible thing, I somehow felt that I could see in the expression of his hands, and in the very toss of his head, as he leaped thus to death, that it was rage, rage, rage unspeakable that was in his heart at the time.

And then I saw Tom Smith, the man who was going to quit filibustering after this expedition, jump to a raft and turn his face toward us. On board the *Commodore* three men strode, still in silence and with their faces turned toward us. One man had his arms folded and was leaning against the deckhouse. His feet were crossed, so that the toe of his left foot pointed downward. There they stood gazing at us, and neither from the deck nor from the rafts was a voice raised. Still was there this silence.

TRIED TO TOW THE RAFTS

The colored stoker on the first raft threw us a line and we began to tow. Of course, we perfectly understood the absolute impossibility of any such thing; our dinghy was within six inches of the water's edge, there was an enormous sea running, and I knew that under the circumstances a tugboat would have no light task in moving these rafts.

But we tried it, and would have continued to try it indefinitely, but that something critical came to pass. I was at an oar and so faced the rafts. The cook controlled the line. Suddenly the boat began to go backward and then we saw this negro on the first raft pulling on the line hand over hand and drawing us to him.

He had turned into a demon. He was wild — wild as a tiger. He was crouched on this raft and ready to spring. Every muscle of him seemed to be turned into an elastic spring. His eyes were almost white. His face was the face of a lost man reaching upward, and we knew that the weight of his hand on our gunwale doomed us.

THE *COMMODORE* SINKS

The cook let go of the line. We rowed around to see if we could not get a line from the chief engineer, and all this time, mind you, there were no shrieks, no groans, but silence, silence and silence, and then the *Commodore* sank.

She lurched to windward, then swung afar back, righted and dove into the sea, and the rafts were suddenly swallowed by this frightful maw of the ocean. And then by the men on the ten-foot dinghy were words said that were still not words — something far beyond words.

The lighthouse of Mosquito Inlet stuck up above the horizon like the point of a pin. We turned our dinghy toward the shore.

The history of life in an open boat for thirty hours would no doubt be instructive for the young, but none is to be told here and now. For my part I would prefer to tell the story at once, because from it would shine the splendid manhood of Captain Edward Murphy and of William Higgins, the oiler, but let it suffice at this time to say that when we were swamped in the surf and making the best of our way toward the shore the captain gave orders amid the wildness of the breakers as clearly as if he had been on the quarter deck of a battleship.

John Kitchell of Daytona came running down the beach, and as he ran the air was filled with clothes. If he had pulled a single lever and undressed, even as the fire horses harness, he could not seem to me to have stripped with more speed. He dashed into the water and dragged the cook. Then he went after the captain, but the captain sent him to me, and then it was that he saw Billy Higgins lying with his forehead on sand that was clear of the water, and he was dead.

ɾɔɔ

RALPH ELLISON *gave an interview for the "Art of Fiction" series of the* Paris Review *that was reprinted in his volume of essays,* Shadow and Act *(1964). In the introduction to that book he said that what is basic to the fiction writer's confrontation with the world is "converting experience into symbolic action. Good fiction is made of that which is real, and reality is difficult to come by. So much of it depends upon the individual's willingness to discover his true self, upon his defining himself — for the time being at least — against his background."*

RALPH ELLISON

The Influence of Folklore on "Battle Royal"   1964

Interviewer: Can you give us an example of the use of folklore in your own novel?

Ellison: Well, there are certain themes, symbols, and images which are based on folk material. For example, there is the old saying amongst Negroes: If you're black, stay back; if you're brown, stick around; if you're white, you're right. And there is the joke Negroes tell on themselves about their being so black they can't be seen in the dark. In my book this sort of thing was merged with the meanings which blackness and light have long had in Western mythology: evil and goodness, ignorance and knowledge, and so on. In my novel the narrator's development is one through blackness to light; that is, from ignorance to enlightenment: invisibility to visibility. He leaves the South and goes North; this, as you will notice in reading Negro folktales, is always the road to freedom — the movement upward. You have the same thing again when he leaves his underground cave for the open.

It took me a long time to learn how to adapt such examples of myth into my work — also ritual. The use of ritual is equally a vital part of the creative process. I learned a few things from Eliot, Joyce, and Hemingway, but not how to adapt them. When I started writing, I knew that in both *The Waste Land°* and *Ulysses°* ancient myth and ritual were used to give form and significance to the material; but it took me a few years to realize that the myths and rites which we find functioning in our everyday lives could be used in the same

---

The Waste Land: A long, extremely influential poem (1922) by T. S. Eliot (1888–1965).
Ulysses: An experimental novel (1922) by James Joyce (1882–1941).

way. In my first attempt at a novel — which I was unable to complete — I began by trying to manipulate the simple structural unities of *beginning, middle,* and *end,* but when I attempted to deal with the psychological strata — the images, symbols, and emotional configurations — of the experience at hand, I discovered that the unities were simply cool points of stability on which one could suspend the narrative line — but beneath the surface of apparently rational human relationships there seethed a chaos before which I was helpless. People rationalize what they shun or are incapable of dealing with; these superstitions and their rationalizations become ritual as they govern behavior. The rituals become social forms, and it is one of the functions of the artist to recognize them and raise them to the level of art.

I don't know whether I'm getting this over or not. Let's put it this way: Take the "Battle Royal" passage in my novel, where the boys are blindfolded and forced to fight each other for the amusement of the white observers. This is a vital part of behavior pattern in the South, which both Negroes and whites thoughtlessly accept. It is a ritual in preservation of caste lines, a keeping of taboo to appease the gods and ward off bad luck. It is also the initiation ritual to which all greenhorns are subjected. This passage which states what Negroes will see I did not have to invent; the patterns were already there in society, so that all I had to do was present them in a broader context of meaning. In any society there are many rituals of situation which, for the most part, go unquestioned. They can be simple or elaborate, but they are the connective tissue between the work of art and the audience.

Interviewer: Do you think a reader unacquainted with this folklore can properly understand your work?

Ellison: Yes, I think so. It's like jazz; there's no inherent problem which prohibits understanding but the assumptions brought to it. We don't all dig Shakespeare uniformly, or even *Little Red Riding Hood.* The understanding of art depends finally upon one's willingness to extend one's humanity and one's knowledge of human life. I noticed, incidentally, that the Germans, having no special caste assumptions concerning American Negroes, dealt with my work simply as a novel. I think Americans will come to view it that way in twenty years — if it's around that long.

Interviewer: Don't you think it will be?

Ellison: I doubt it. It's not an important novel. I failed of eloquence, and many of the immediate issues are rapidly fading away. If it does last, it will be simply because there are things going on in its depth that are of more permanent interest than on its surface. I hope so, anyway.

ର

RICHARD ELLMANN *was the author of prize-winning biographies of the Irish writers James Joyce and Oscar Wilde. As a biographer Ellmann seemed to have possessed an encyclopedic knowledge of his subject, yet his grasp of the facts of literary production was balanced by his brilliant use of these facts to suggest his sensitive perception of how the creative process functioned in an author's life. Instead of emphasizing biographical details in his discussion of "The Dead," Ell-*

mann perceptively used the story to illuminate a stage of Joyce's development as an artist. This excerpt is from Ellmann's James Joyce: New and Revised Edition *(1982).*

RICHARD ELLMANN

A Biographical Perspective on Joyce's "The Dead"

1982

And now Gabriel and Gretta go to the Hotel Gresham, Gabriel fired by his living wife and Gretta drained by the memory of her dead lover. He learns for the first time of the young man in Galway, whose name Joyce has deftly altered from Sonny or Michael Bodkin to Michael Furey. The new name implies, like the contrast of the militant Michael and the amiable Gabriel, that violent passion is in her Galway past, not in her Dublin present. Gabriel tries to cut Michael Furey down. "What was he?" he asks, confident that his own profession of language teacher (which of course he shared with Joyce) is superior; but she replies, "He was in the gasworks," as if this profession was as good as any other. Then Gabriel tries again, "And what did he die of so young, Gretta? Consumption, was it?" He hopes to register the usual expressions of pity, but Gretta silences and terrifies him by her answer, "I think he died for me."[1] Since Joyce has already made clear that Michael Furey was tubercular, this answer of Gretta has a fine ambiguity. It asserts the egoism of passion, and unconsciously defies Gabriel's reasonable question.

Now Gabriel begins to succumb to his wife's dead lover, and becomes a pilgrim to emotional intensities outside of his own experience. From a biographical point of view, these final pages compose one of Joyce's several tributes to his wife's artless integrity. Nora Barnacle, in spite of her defects of education, was independent, unselfconscious, instinctively right. Gabriel acknowledges the same coherence in his own wife, and he recognizes in the west of Ireland, in Michael Furey, a passion he has himself always lacked. "Better pass boldly into the other world, in the full glory of some passion, than fade and wither dismally with age," Joyce makes Gabriel think. Then comes that strange sentence in the final paragraph: "The time had come for him to set out on his journey westward." The cliché runs that journeys westward are towards death, but the west has taken on a special meaning in the story. Gretta Conroy's west is the place where life has been lived simply and passionately. The context and phrasing of the sentence suggest that Gabriel is on the edge of sleep, and half-consciously accepts what he has hitherto scorned, the possibil-

---

[1] Adaline Glasheen has discovered here an echo of Yeats's nationalistic play, *Cathleen ni Houlihan* (1902), where the old woman who symbolizes Ireland sings a song of "yellow-haired Donough that was hanged in Galway." When she is asked "What was it brought him to his death?," she replies, "He died for love of me; many a man has died for love of me." [Ellmann's note]

ity of an actual trip to Connaught. What the sentence affirms, at last, on the level of feeling, is the west, the primitive, untutored, impulsive country from which Gabriel had felt himself alienated before; in the story, the west is paradoxically linked also with the past and the dead. It is like Aunt Julia Morkan who, though ignorant, old, grey-skinned, and stupefied, seizes in her song at the party "the excitement of swift and secure flight."

The tone of the sentence, "The time had come for him to set out on his journey westward," is somewhat resigned. It suggests a concession, a relinquishment, and Gabriel is conceding and relinquishing a good deal — his sense of the importance of civilized thinking, of continental tastes, of all those tepid but nice distinctions on which he has prided himself. The bubble of his self-possession is pricked; he no longer possesses himself, and not to possess oneself is in a way a kind of death. It is a self-abandonment not unlike Furey's, and through Gabriel's mind runs the imagery of Calvary. He imagines the snow on the cemetery at Oughterard, lying "thickly drifted on the crooked crosses and headstones, on the spears of the little gate, on the barren thorns." He thinks of Michael Furey who, Gretta has said, died for her, and envies him his sacrifice for another kind of love than Christ's. To some extent Gabriel too is dying for her, in giving up what he had most valued in himself, all that holds him apart from the simpler people at the party. He feels close to Gretta through sympathy if not through love; now they are both past youth, beauty, and passion; he feels close also to her dead lover, another lamb burnt on her altar, though she too is burnt now; he feels no resentment, only pity. In his own sacrifice of himself he is conscious of a melancholy unity between the living and the dead.

Gabriel, who has been sick of his own country, finds himself drawn inevitably into a silent tribute to it of much more consequence than his spoken tribute to the party. He has had illusions of the rightness of a way of life that should be outside of Ireland; but through this experience with his wife he grants a kind of bondage, of acceptance, even of admiration to a part of the country and a way of life that are most Irish. Ireland is shown to be stronger, more intense than he. At the end of *A Portrait of the Artist*, too, Stephen Dedalus, who has been so resolutely opposed to nationalism, makes a similar concession when he interprets his departure from Ireland as an attempt to forge a conscience for his race. . . .

That Joyce at the age of twenty-five and -six should have written this story ought not to seem odd. Young writers reach their greatest eloquence in dwelling upon the horrors of middle age and what follows it. But beyond this proclivity which he shared with others, Joyce had a special reason for writing the story of "The Dead" in 1906 and 1907. In his own mind he had thoroughly justified his flight from Ireland, but he had not decided the question of where he would fly *to*. In Trieste and Rome he had learned what he had unlearned in Dublin, to be a Dubliner. As he had written his brother from Rome with some astonishment, he felt humiliated when anyone attacked his "impoverished country." "The Dead" is his first song of exile.

WILLIAM FAULKNER *was writer-in-residence at the University of Virginia in 1957 and 1958. During that time he encouraged students to ask questions about his writing. He answered more than 2,000 queries on everything from spelling to the nature of man, including a series of questions about "A Rose for Emily" addressed to him at different interviews by students of Frederick Gwynn and Joseph Blotner. These professors later edited the book* Faulkner in the University *(1959), in which the following excerpt first appeared.*

WILLIAM FAULKNER

The Meaning of "A Rose for Emily" 1959

Interviewer: What is the meaning of the title "A Rose for Emily"?

Faulkner: Oh, it's simply the poor woman had had no life at all. Her father had kept her more or less locked up and then she had a lover who was about to quit her, she had to murder him. It was just "A Rose for Emily" — that's all.

Interviewer: I was wondering, one of your short stories, "A Rose for Emily," what ever inspired you to write this story . . . ?

Faulkner: That to me was another sad and tragic manifestation of man's condition in which he dreams and hopes, in which he is in conflict with himself or with his environment or with others. In this case there was the young girl with a young girl's normal aspirations to find love and then a husband and a family, who was brow-beaten and kept down by her father, a selfish man who didn't want her to leave home because he wanted a housekeeper, and it was a natural instinct of — repressed which — you can't repress it — you can mash it down but it comes up somewhere else and very likely in a tragic form, and that was simply another manifestation of man's injustice to man, of the poor tragic human being struggling with its own heart, with others, with its environment, for the simple things which all human beings want. In that case it was a young girl that just wanted to be loved and to love and to have a husband and a family.

Interviewer: And that purely came from your imagination?

Faulkner: Well, the story did but the condition is there. It exists. I didn't invent that condition, I didn't invent the fact that young girls dream of someone to love and children and a home, but the story of what her own particular tragedy was was invented, yes. . . .

Interviewer: Sir, it has been argued that "A Rose for Emily" is a criticism of the North, and others have argued saying that it is a criticism of the South. Now, could this story, shall we say, be more properly classified as a criticism of the times?

Faulkner: Now that I don't know, because I was simply trying to write about people. The writer uses environment — what he knows — and if there's a symbolism in which the lover represented the North and the woman who murdered him represents the South, I don't say that's not valid and not there, but it was no intention of the writer to say, Now let's see, I'm going to write a piece in which I will use a symbolism for the North and another symbol for the South, that he was simply writing about people, a story which he thought was tragic and true, because it came out of the human heart, the human aspiration, the human — the conflict of conscience with glands, with the Old Adam. It was a conflict not between the North and the South so much as between, well you might say, God and Satan.

Interviewer: Sir, just a little more on that thing. You say it's a conflict between God and Satan. Well, I don't quite understand what you mean. Who is — did one represent the ——

Faulkner: The conflict was in Miss Emily, that she knew that you do not murder people. She had been trained that you do not take a lover. You marry, you don't take a lover. She had broken all the laws of her tradition, her background, and she had finally broken the law of God too, which says you do not take human life. And she knew she was doing wrong, and that's why her own life was wrecked. Instead of murdering one lover, and then to go and take another and when she used him up to murder him, she was expiating her crime.

Interviewer: Was the "Rose for Emily" an idea or a character? Just how did you go about it?

Faulkner: That came from a picture of the strand of hair on the pillow. It was a ghost story. Simply a picture of a strand of hair on the pillow in the abandoned house.

ဢ

SANDRA M. GILBERT AND SUSAN GUBAR *present a feminist reading of Charlotte Perkins Gilman's "The Yellow Wallpaper" in* The Madwoman in the Attic: The Woman Writer and the Nineteenth-Century Literary Imagination *(1979). In this book they argue that a recognizable literary tradition existed in English and American literature in which the female imagination had demonstrated "the anxiety of authorship." According to Gilbert and Gubar, "Images of enclosure and escape, fantasies in which maddened doubles functioned as asocial surrogates for docile selves . . . such patterns reoccurred throughout this tradition, along with obsessive depictions of diseases like anorexia, agoraphobia, and claustrophobia." Gilman's story is securely within this tradition of the "literature of confinement," in which a woman writer, trapped by the patriarchal society, tries to struggle free "through strategic redefinitions of self, art, and society."*

SANDRA M. GILBERT
AND SUSAN GUBAR

A Feminist Reading of Gilman's "The Yellow Wallpaper"

1979

As if to comment on the unity of all these points — on, that is, the anxiety-inducing connections between what women writers tend to see as their parallel confinements in texts, houses, and maternal female bodies —

Charlotte Perkins Gilman brought them all together in 1890 in a striking story of female confinement and escape, a paradigmatic tale which (like *Jane Eyre°*) seems to tell *the* story that all literary women would tell if they could speak their "speechless woe." "The Yellow Wallpaper," which Gilman herself called "a description of a case of nervous breakdown," recounts in the first person the experiences of a woman who is evidently suffering from a severe postpartum psychosis. Her husband, a censorious and paternalistic physician, is treating her according to methods by which S. Weir Mitchell, a famous "nerve specialist," treated Gilman herself for a similar problem. He has confined her to a large garret room in an "ancestral hall" he has rented, and he has forbidden her to touch pen to paper until she is well again, for he feels, says the narrator, "that with my imaginative power and habit of story-making, a nervous weakness like mine is sure to lead to all manner of excited fancies, and that I ought to use my will and good sense to check the tendency."

The cure, of course, is worse than the disease, for the sick woman's mental condition deteriorates rapidly. "I think sometimes that if I were only well enough to write a little it would relieve the press of ideas and rest me," she remarks, but literally confined in a room she thinks is a one-time nursery because it has "rings and things" in the walls, she is literally locked away from creativity. The "rings and things," although reminiscent of children's gymnastic equipment, are really the paraphernalia of confinement, like the gate at the head of the stairs, instruments that definitively indicate her imprisonment. Even more tormenting, however, is the room's wallpaper: a sulphurous yellow paper, torn off in spots, and patterned with "lame uncertain curves" that "plunge off at outrageous angles" and "destroy themselves in unheard of contradictions." Ancient, smoldering, "unclean" as the oppressive structures of the society in which she finds herself, this paper surrounds the narrator like an inexplicable text, censorious and overwhelming as her physician husband, haunting as the "hereditary estate" in which she is trying to survive. Inevitably she studies its suicidal implications — and inevitably, because of her "imaginative power and habit of story-making," she revises it, projecting her own passion for escape into its otherwise incomprehensible hieroglyphics. "This wallpaper," she decides, at a key point in her story,

> has a kind of subpattern in a different shade, a particularly irritating one, for you can only see it in certain lights, and not clearly then.
> But in the places where it isn't faded and where the sun is just so — I can see a strange, provoking, formless sort of figure, that seems to skulk about behind that silly and conspicuous front design.

As time passes, this figure concealed behind what corresponds (in terms of what we have been discussing) to the facade of the patriarchal text becomes clearer and clearer. By moonlight the pattern of the wallpaper "becomes bars! The outside pattern I mean, and the woman behind it is as plain as can be."

Jane Eyre: The classic Victorian novel (1847) by Charlotte Brontë (1816–1855) is considered an important feminist work.

And eventually, as the narrator sinks more deeply into what the world calls madness, the terrifying implications of both the paper and the figure imprisoned behind the paper begin to permeate — that is, to *haunt* — the rented ancestral mansion in which she and her husband are immured. The "yellow smell" of the paper "creeps all over the house," drenching every room in its subtle aroma of decay. And the woman creeps too — through the house, in the house, and out of the house, in the garden and "on that long road under the trees." Sometimes, indeed, the narrator confesses, "I think there are a great many women" both behind the paper and creeping in the garden, "and sometimes only one, and she crawls around fast, and her crawling shakes [the paper] all over. . . . And she is all the time trying to climb through. But nobody could climb through that pattern — it strangles so; I think that is why it has so many heads."

Eventually it becomes obvious to both reader and narrator that the figure creeping through and behind the wallpaper is both the narrator and the narrator's double. By the end of the story, moreover, the narrator has enabled this double to escape from her textual/architectural confinement: "I pulled and she shook, I shook and she pulled, and before morning we had peeled off yards of that paper." Is the message of the tale's conclusion mere madness? Certainly the righteous Doctor John — whose name links him to the anti-hero of Charlotte Brontë's *Villette* — has been temporarily defeated, or at least momentarily stunned. "Now why should that man have fainted?" the narrator ironically asks as she creeps around her attic. But John's unmasculine swoon of surprise is the least of the triumphs Gilman imagines for her madwoman. More significant are the madwoman's own imaginings and creations, mirages of health and freedom with which her author endows her like a fairy godmother showering gold on a sleeping heroine. The woman from behind the wallpaper creeps away, for instance, creeps fast and far on the long road, in broad daylight. "I have watched her sometimes away off in the open country," says the narrator, "creeping as fast as a cloud shadow in a high wind."

Indistinct and yet rapid, barely perceptible but inexorable, the progress of that cloud shadow is not unlike the progress of nineteenth-century literary women out of the texts defined by patriarchal poetics into the open spaces of their own authority. That such an escape from the numb world behind the patterned walls of the text was a flight from disease into health was quite clear to Gilman herself. When "The Yellow Wallpaper" was published she sent it to Weir Mitchell whose strictures had kept her from attempting the pen during her own breakdown, thereby aggravating her illness, and she was delighted to learn, years later, that "he had changed his treatment of nervous prostration since reading" her story. "If that is a fact," she declared, "I have not lived in vain." Because she was a rebellious feminist besides being a medical iconoclast, we can be sure that Gilman did not think of this triumph of hers in narrowly therapeutic terms. Because she knew, with Emily Dickinson, that "Infection in the sentence breeds," she knew that the cure for female despair must be spiritual as well as physical, aesthetic as well as social. What "The Yellow Wallpaper" shows she knew, too, is that even when a supposedly "mad" woman has been sentenced to imprisonment in the "infected" house of her own body, she may discover that, as Sylvia Plath° was to put it seventy years later, she has "a self to recover, a queen."

ഇരു

CHARLOTTE PERKINS GILMAN *wrote her autobiography,* The Living of Charlotte Perkins Gilman *(1935), in the last years of her life. Her intelligence and strength of character are evident in this work, as is her modesty after a long career as an eminent American feminist. Her straightforward description of her mental breakdown nearly fifty years earlier is in marked contrast to the obsessive fantasy of her story "The Yellow Wallpaper," written shortly after her illness.*

CHARLOTTE PERKINS GILMAN

Undergoing the Cure for Nervous Prostration   1935

This was a worse horror than before, for now I saw the stark fact — that I was well while away and sick while at home — a heartening prospect! Soon ensued the same utter prostration, the unbearable inner misery, the ceaseless tears. A new tonic had been invented, Essence of Oats, which was given me, and did some good for a time. I pulled up enough to do a little painting that fall, but soon slipped down again and stayed down. An old friend of my mother's, dear Mrs. Diman, was so grieved at this condition that she gave me a hundred dollars and urged me to go away somewhere and get cured.

At that time the greatest nerve specialist in the country was Dr. S. W. Mitchell of Philadelphia. Through the kindness of a friend of Mr. Stetson's living in that city, I went to him and took "the rest cure"; went with the utmost confidence, prefacing the visit with a long letter giving "the history of the case" in a way a modern psychologist would have appreciated. Dr. Mitchell only thought it proved self-conceit. He had a prejudice against the Beechers. "I've had two women of your blood here already," he told me scornfully. This eminent physician was well versed in two kinds of nervous prostration; that of the business man exhausted from too much work, and the society woman exhausted from too much play. The kind I had was evidently behind him. But he did reassure me on one point — there was no dementia, he said, only hysteria.

I was put to bed and kept there. I was fed, bathed, rubbed, and responded with the vigorous body of twenty-six. As far as he could see there was nothing the matter with me, so after a month of this agreeable treatment he sent me home, with this prescription:

Live as domestic a life as possible. Have your child with you all the time. (Be it remarked that if I did but dress the baby it left me shaking

---

Sylvia Plath: American poet (1932–1963). See p. 1160.

and crying — certainly far from a healthy companionship for her, to say nothing of the effect on me.) Lie down an hour after each meal. Have but two hours' intellectual life a day. And never touch pen, brush, or pencil as long as you live.

I went home, followed those directions rigidly for months, and came perilously near to losing my mind. The mental agony grew so unbearable that I would sit blankly moving my head from side to side — to get out from under the pain. Not physical pain, not the least "headache" even, just mental torment, and so heavy in its nightmare gloom that it seemed real enough to dodge.

I made a rag baby, hung it on a doorknob, and played with it. I would crawl into remote closets and under beds — to hide from the grinding pressure of that profound distress. . . .

Finally, in the fall of '87, in a moment of clear vision, we agreed to separate, to get a divorce. There was no quarrel, no blame for either one, never an unkind word between us, unbroken mutual affection — but it seemed plain that if I went crazy, it would do my husband no good, and be a deadly injury to my child.

What this meant to the young artist, the devoted husband, the loving father, was so bitter a grief and loss that nothing would have justified breaking the marriage save this worse loss which threatened. It was not a choice between going and staying, but between going, sane, and staying, insane. If I had been of the slightest use to him or to the child, I would have "stuck it," as the English say. But this progressive weakening of the mind made a horror unnecessary to face; better for that dear child to have separated parents than a lunatic mother.

We had been married four years and more. This miserable condition of mind, this darkness, feebleness, and gloom, had begun in those difficult years of courtship, had grown rapidly worse after marriage, and was now threatening utter loss; whereas I had repeated proof that the moment I left home I began to recover. It seemed right to give up a mistaken marriage.

Our mistake was mutual. If I had been stronger and wiser I should never have been persuaded into it. Our suffering was mutual too, his unbroken devotion, his manifold cares and labors in tending a sick wife, his adoring pride in the best of babies, all coming to naught, ending in utter failure — we sympathized with each other but faced a bitter necessity. The separation must come as soon as possible, the divorce must wait for conditions.

If this decision could have been reached sooner it would have been much better for me, the lasting mental injury would have been less. Such recovery as I have made in forty years, and the work accomplished, seem to show that the fear of insanity was not fulfilled, but the effects of nerve bankruptcy remain to this day. So much of my many failures, of misplay and misunderstanding and "queerness" is due to this lasting weakness, and kind friends so unfailingly refuse to allow for it, to believe it, that I am now going to some length in stating the case.

JANICE HUBBARD HARRIS *wrote* The Short Fiction of D. H. Lawrence *(1984) after the scholar Mark Spilka pointed out to her in the late 1960s that there was no critical literature on Lawrence's stories. "Where were the analyses of that lively body of fiction capable, as Julian Moynahan says, of bringing light back into the eyes of the reader exhausted by* The Plumed Serpent *or fainting amid the incremental repetitions of* The Rainbow?" *Her critical approach to the stories incorporates several modes — biographical, psychological, sociological, feminist. Comparing Lawrence with his contemporaries James Joyce, Katherine Mansfield, and Virginia Woolf, Harris concludes that "Lawrence is clearly the leader in range, sheer quantity of master- pieces, and, something harder to define, in stretching the conventions of the [short story] genre to include a variety of new possibilities."*

JANICE H. HARRIS

Levels of Meaning in Lawrence's *"The Rocking-Horse Winner"*   *1984*

"The Rocking-Horse Winner" opens with the distant, singsong voice of a fairy tale: "There was a woman who was beautiful, who started with all the advantages, yet she had no luck." So begins an ancient tale. A brave young boy is challenged by his true love. He rides off into a dreamland where he struggles and succeeds at attaining secret knowledge. He brings the secret knowledge back and with it wins treasure houses of gold, giving all to his love. Undercutting this fairy tale, however, is another, which forms a grotesque shadow, a nightmare counter to the wish fulfillment narrative. The "true love" of the brave young boy is his cold-hearted mother. The quest he has embarked on is hopeless, for every success brings a new and greater trial. Like the exhausted and terrified daughter in Rumplestiltskin, this son is per- petually set the task of spinning more gold. In this tale, no magical dwarf comes to the child's aid; the boy finally spins himself out, dropping dead on his journey, his eyes turned to stone. Like all good fairy tales, this one has sev- eral complementary levels of reference: social, familial, psychological.

On the social level, the tale reads as a satire on the equation of money, love, luck, and happiness. The target of the satire, the mother, cannot be happy without an unending flow of cold, sure cash. As she sees it, luck and lucre are the same thing. Yearning for some response and real affection from her, Paul adds the term "love," making a solid, tragic construction. Quite simply, the tale concludes that these equations are deadly. The mother, representing a society run on a money ethic, has given the younger generation a murderous education.

On a familial level, the tale dramatizes an idea implied as early as *Sons and Lovers* but overtly stated only in a late autobiographical fragment and these last tales. The idea is that mothers shape their sons into the desirable opposite of their husbands. Whatever they are powerless to prevent or alter in their mates, mothers will seek to prevent or alter in their sons. In "The Rocking-Horse Winner," the woman cannot alter her husband's ineffectuality.

She herself tries to be effective in the world of commerce and money, but she fails, partly because of the lack of opportunities available to her. So she turns unconsciously to her son. In this reading, Paul's death owes less to the specific character of his mother's demands and more to the strength of those demands. He dies — cannot live, cannot grow and flourish — partly because he is too good a son, and she is a woman with unbounded desires and no way to work directly toward their gratification. In *Sons and Lovers,* the young son kills, literally and figuratively, the paralyzed and paralyzing mother. The alternative pattern, which Lawrence felt to be common among the men of his generation, is played out in "The Rocking-Horse Winner."

But the tale acts out still another nexus of meaning, one implied in both the satire on a society governed by a money ethic and in the dramatization of a mother devourer. On this level, the hobbyhorse comes more to the fore. . . . This lonely, preadolescent boy continually retreats to his own room where, in great secrecy, he mounts his play horse and rides himself into a trancelike ecstasy. His action and the result it brings powerfully echo Lawrence's description of masturbation, physical and psychic, in his essay "Pornography and Obscenity." Discussing censorship, Lawrence praises art that inspires genuine sexual arousal, that invites union with the other, whether the "other" is another person, an idea, a landscape, the sun. Obscene art is essentially solipsistic; it arouses the desire to turn inward, to chafe, to ride the self in an endless and futile circle of self-stimulation, analysis, gratification. In masturbation, there is no reciprocity, no exchange between self and other. Applying Lawrence's indictment of masturbation to Paul's situation, we see that Paul has been taught to ride himself, that is, his hobbyhorse or obsessions, obsessions he inherited from his mother. . . .

If one takes these three levels of reference and seeks out their complementarity, one sees the rich logic of the tale. The money ethic, the devouring of sons by mothers, and the preference for masturbation are parallel in cause and result. All develop and respect only the kind of knowledge that will increase one's capacity to control. For example, like any money-maker, Paul learns about the horses only to manipulate his earnings — money and love. Paul's mother, in a variation on the theme, does not bother to learn anything about her son because she does not perceive him as useful to her. Further, Paul mounts his hobbyhorse, his surrogate sexual partner, only as a way of fulfilling his own narrowly defined program for success and happiness. In no case is the object that is to be known — horse, son, sexual partner — seen to have a life of its own, an otherness to be appreciated rather than manipulated, a furtherness that can give the knower a glimpse into all that is beyond him or her. In addition, the resolution of each nexus of meaning carries the same ironic denouement: The quest for absolute control leads to the loss of control. The mother's house, which she wants to be luxurious and proper, is haunted by crass whispers. She and her son, striving to control love and fortune, are compulsive, obsessed; Paul dies and thereby loses all chance for the very human love and contact he sought. The mother loses the very means by which her fortune was assured.

JAMES HILLMAN *wrote "A Note on Story" for the journal* Children's Literature *in 1974. Later he developed his ideas in his book* Healing Fiction *(1983), where he went on to analyze the difference in the effect on us of the stories we read in books and those we watch in films and on television. Hillman realized that "screened, watched stories are different because they enter imagination via perception. . . . [A] filmed picture may be imagined and become an image, but these images usually remain linked with the visualities in which they first appeared. Word-images, however, are immediate property of imagination. . . . [T]he essence of word-images is that they are free from the perceptible world and free one from it. They take the mind home, to its poetic base, to the imaginal." As a psychotherapist, Hillman is deeply aware of the close relationship between psychology and literature.* Healing Fiction *(1983) begins with a quotation by the poet Wallace Stevens: "The final belief is to believe in a fiction, which you know to be a fiction, there being nothing else. The exquisite truth is to know that it is a fiction and that you believe in it willingly."*

JAMES HILLMAN

A Note on Story
1974

From my perspective as depth psychologist, I see that those who have a connection with story are in better shape and have a better prognosis than those to whom story must be introduced. This is a large statement and I would like to take it apart in several ways. But I do not want to diminish its apodic-tic° claim: to have "story-awareness" is *per se* psychologically therapeutic. It is good for soul.

To have had story of any sort in childhood — and here I mean oral story, those told or read (for reading has an oral aspect even if one reads to oneself) rather than watching story on screen — puts a person into a basic recognition of and familiarity with the legitimate reality of story *per se*. It is given with life, with speech and communication, and not something later that comes with learning and literature. Coming early with life, it is already a perspective to life. One integrates life as story because one has stories in the back of the mind (unconscious) as containers for organizing events into meaningful experiences. The stories are means of telling oneself into events that might not otherwise make psychological sense at all. (Economic, scientific, and historical explanations are sorts of "stories" that often fail to give the soul the kind of imaginative meaning it seeks for understanding its psychological life.)

Having had story built in with childhood, a person is usually in better relation with the pathologized material of obscene, grotesque, or cruel images which appear spontaneously in dream and fantasy. Those who hold to the rationalist and associationist theory of mind, who put reason against and superior to imagination, argue that if we did not put in such grim tales in early

---

apodictic: Showing necessary truth or absolute certainty.

impressionable years, we would have less pathology and more rationality in later years. My practice shows me rather that the more attuned and experienced is the imaginative side of personality the less threatening the irrational, the less necessity for repression, and therefore the less actual pathology acted out in literal, daily events. In other words, through story the symbolic quality of pathological images and themes finds a place, so that these images and themes are less likely to be viewed naturalistically, with clinical literalism, as signs of sickness. These images find places in story as legitimate. They *belong* to myths, legends, and fairy tales where, just as in dreams, all sorts of peculiar figures and twisted behaviours appeal. After all, "The Greatest Story Ever Told," as some are fond of calling Easter, is replete with gruesome imagery in great pathologized detail.

Story-awareness provides a better way than clinical-awareness for coming to terms with one's own case history. Case history too is a fictional form written up by thousands of hands in thousands of clinics and consulting rooms, stored away in archives and rarely published. This fictional form called "case history" follows the genre of social realism; it believes in facts and events, and takes all tales told with excessive literalism. In deep analysis, the analyst and the patient together re-write the case history into a new story, creating the "fiction" in the collaborative work of the analysis. Some of the healing that goes on, maybe even the essence of it, is this collaborative fiction, this putting all the chaotic and traumatic events of a life into a new story. Jung said that patients need "healing fictions," but we have trouble coming to this perspective unless there is already a predilection for story-awareness.

Jungian therapy, at least as I practice it, brings about an awareness that fantasy is the dominant force in a life. One learns in therapy that fantasy is a creative activity which is continually telling a person into now this story, now that one. When we examine these fantasies we discover that they reflect the great impersonal themes of mankind as represented in tragedy, epic, folktale, legend, and myth. Fantasy in our view is the attempt of the psyche itself to re-mythologize consciousness; we try to further this activity by encouraging familiarity with myth and folktale. Soul-making goes hand in hand with deliteralizing consciousness and restoring its connection to mythic and metaphorical thought patterns. Rather than interpret the stories into concepts and rational explanations, we prefer to see conceptual explanations as secondary elaborations upon basic stories which are containers and givers of vitality. As Owen Barfield and Norman Brown have written: "Literalism is the enemy." I would add: "Literalism is sickness." Whenever we are caught in a literal view, a literal belief, a literal statement, we have lost the imaginative metaphorical perspective to ourselves and our world. Story is prophylactic in that it presents itself always as "once upon a time," as an "as if," "make-believe" reality. It is the only mode of accounting or telling about that does not posit itself as real, true, factual, revealed, i.e., literal. . . .

I think children need less convincing of the importance of story than do adults. To be adult has come to mean to be adulterated with rationalist explanations, and to shun such childishness as we find in fairy stories. I have tried to show in detail how adult and child have come to be set against each other:

childhood tends to mean wonder, imagination, creative spontaneity, while adulthood, the loss of these perspectives. . . . So the first task, as I see it, is restorying the adult — the teacher and the parent and the grandparent — in order to restore the imagination to a primary place in consciousness in each of us, regardless of age.

I have come at this from a psychological viewpoint, partly because I wish to remove story from its too close association with both education and literature — something taught and something studied. My interest in story is as something lived in and lived through, a way in which the soul finds itself in life.

ဢ

Zora Neale Hurston *continued throughout her life to make what the critic Mary Helen Washington called "unorthodox and paradoxical assertions on racial issues." Often conveyed with great wit and style, Hurston's views were always passionately held, as in her essay "What White Publishers Won't Print," first published in* Negro Digest *in April 1950.*

Zora Neale Hurston

What White Publishers Won't Print   1950

I have been amazed by the Anglo-Saxon's lack of curiosity about the internal lives and emotions of the Negroes, and for that matter, any non-Anglo-Saxon peoples within our borders, above the class of unskilled labor.

This lack of interest is much more important than it seems at first glance. It is even more important at this time than it was in the past. The internal affairs of the nation have bearings on the international stress and strain, and this gap in the national literature now has tremendous weight in world affairs. National coherence and solidarity is implicit in a thorough understanding of the various groups within a nation, and this lack of knowledge about the internal emotions and behavior of the minorities cannot fail to bar our understanding. Man, like all the other animals, fears and is repelled by that which he does not understand, and mere difference is apt to connote something malign.

The fact that there is no demand for incisive and full-dress stories about Negroes above the servant class is indicative of something of vast importance to this nation. This blank is *not* filled by the fiction built around upper-class Negroes exploiting the race problem. Rather, it tends to point it up. A college-bred Negro still is not a person like other folks, but an interesting problem, more or less. It calls to mind a story of slavery time. In this story, a master with more intellectual curiosity than usual, set out to see how much he could teach a particularly bright slave of his. When he had gotten him up to higher mathematics and to be a fluent reader of Latin, he called in a neighbor to show off his brilliant slave, and to argue that Negroes had brains just like the slave-owners had, and given the same opportunities, would turn out the same.

The visiting master of slaves looked and listened, tried to trap the literate slave in Algebra and Latin, and failing to do so in both, turned to his neighbor and said:

"Yes, he certainly knows his higher mathematics, and he can read Latin better than many white men I know, but I cannot bring myself to believe that he understands a thing that he is doing. It is all an aping of our culture. All on the outside. You are crazy if you think that it has changed him inside in the least. Turn him loose, and he will revert at once to the jungle. He is still a savage, and no amount of translating Virgil and Ovid is going to change him. In fact, all you have done is to turn a useful savage into a dangerous beast."

That was in slavery time, yes, and we have come a long, long way since then, but the troubling thing is that there are still too many who refuse to believe in the ingestion and digestion of western culture as yet. Hence the lack of literature about the higher emotions and love life of upper-class Negroes and the minorities in general.

Publishers and producers are cool to the idea. Now, do not leap to the conclusion that editors and producers constitute a special class of unbelievers. That is far from true. Publishing houses and theatrical promoters are in business to make money. They will sponsor anything that they believe will sell. They shy away from romantic stories about Negroes and Jews because they feel that they know the public indifference to such works, unless the story or play involves racial tension. It can then be offered as a study in Sociology, with the romantic side subdued. They know the scepticism in general about the complicated emotions in the minorities. The average American just cannot conceive of it, and would be apt to reject the notion, and publishers and producers take the stand that they are not in business to educate, but to make money. Sympathetic as they might be, they cannot afford to be crusaders.

In proof of this, you can note various publishers and producers edging forward a little, and ready to go even further when the trial balloons show that the public is ready for it. This public lack of interest is the nut of the matter.

The question naturally arises as to the why of this indifference, not to say scepticism, to the internal life of educated minorities.

The answer lies in what we may call THE AMERICAN MUSEUM OF UNNATURAL HISTORY. This is an intangible built on folk belief. It is assumed that all non-Anglo-Saxons are uncomplicated stereotypes. Everybody knows all about them. They are lay figures mounted in the museum where all may take them in at a glance. They are made of bent wires without insides at all. So how could anybody write a book about the nonexistent?

The American Indian is a contraption of copper wires in an eternal warbonnet, with no equipment for laughter, expressionless face, and that says "How" when spoken to. His only activity is treachery leading us to massacres. Who is so dumb as not to know all about Indians, even if they have never seen one, nor talked with anyone who ever knew one?

The American Negro exhibit is a group of two. Both of these mechanical toys are built so that their feet eternally shuffle, and their eyes pop and roll.

Shuffling feet and those popping, rolling eyes denote the Negro and no characterization is genuine without this monotony. One is seated on a stump picking away on his banjo and singing and laughing. The other is a most amoral character before a share-cropper's shack mumbling about injustice. Doing this makes him out to be a Negro "intellectual." It is as simple as all that.

The whole museum is dedicated to the convenient "typical." In there is the "typical" Oriental, Jew, Yankee, Westerner, Southerner, Latin, and even out-of-favor Nordics like the German. The Englishman "I say old chappie," and the gesticulating Frenchman. The least observant American can know all at a glance. However, the public willingly accepts the untypical in Nordics, but feels cheated if the untypical is portrayed in others. The author of *Scarlet Sister Mary*° complained to me that her neighbors objected to her book on the grounds that she had the characters thinking, "and everybody know that Nigras don't think."

But for the national welfare, it is urgent to realize that the minorities do think, and think about something other than the race problem. That they are very human and internally, according to natural endowment, are just like everybody else. So long as this is not conceived, there must remain that feeling of unsurmountable difference, and difference to the average man means something bad. If people were made right, they would be just like him.

The trouble with the purely problem arguments is that they leave too much unknown. Argue all you will or may about injustice, but as long as the majority cannot conceive of a Negro or a Jew feeling and reacting inside just as they do, the majority will keep right on believing that people who do not feel like them cannot possibly feel as they do, and conform to the established pattern. It is well known that there must be a body of waived matter, let us say, things accepted and taken for granted by all in a community, before there can be that commonality of feeling. The usual phrase is having things in common. Until this is thoroughly established in respect to Negroes in America, as well as of other minorities, it will remain impossible for the majority to conceive of a Negro experiencing a deep and abiding love and not just the passion of sex. That a great mass of Negroes can be stirred by the pageants of Spring and Fall; the extravaganza of summer, and the majesty of winter. That they can and do experience discovery of the numerous subtle faces as a foundation for a great and selfless love, and the diverse nuances that go to destroy that love as with others. As it is now, this capacity, this evidence of high and complicated emotions, is ruled out. Hence the lack of interest in a romance uncomplicated by the race struggle has so little appeal.

This insistence on defeat in a story where upper-class Negroes are portrayed, perhaps says something from the subconscious of the majority. Involved in western culture, the hero or the heroine, or both, must appear frustrated and go down to defeat, somehow. Our literature reeks with it. Is it the same as saying, "You can translate Virgil, and fumble with the differential calculus, but can you really comprehend it? Can you cope with our subtleties?"

Scarlet Sister Mary: The 1928 book by Julia Mood Peterkin (1880–1961).

That brings us to the folklore of "reversion to type." This curious doctrine has such wide acceptance that it is tragic. One has only to examine the huge literature on it to be convinced. No matter how high we may *seem* to climb, put us under strain and we revert to type, that is, to the bush. Under a superficial layer of western culture, the jungle drums throb in our veins.

This ridiculous notion makes it possible for that majority who accept it to conceive of even a man like the suave and scholarly Dr. Charles S. Johnson° to hide a black cat's bone on his person, and indulge in a midnight voodoo ceremony, complete with leopard skin and drums if threatened with the loss of the presidency of Fisk University, or the love of his wife. "Under the skin . . . better to deal with them in business, etc., but otherwise keep them at a safe distance and under control. I tell you, Carl Van Vechten,° think as you like, but they are just not like us."

The extent and extravagance of this notion reaches the ultimate in nonsense in the widespread belief that the Chinese have bizarre genitals, because of that eye-fold that makes their eyes seem to slant. In spite of the fact that no biology has ever mentioned any such difference in reproductive organs makes no matter. Millions of people believe it. "Did you know that a Chinese has . . ." Consequently, their quiet contemplative manner is interpreted as a sign of slyness and a treacherous inclination.

But the opening wedge for better understanding has been thrust into the crack. Though many Negroes denounced Carl Van Vechten's *Nigger Heaven* because of the title, and without ever reading it, the book, written in the deepest sincerity, revealed Negroes of wealth and culture to the white public. It created curiosity even when it aroused scepticism. It made folks want to know. Worth Tuttle Hedden's *The Other Room* has definitely widened the opening. Neither of these well-written works take a romance of upper-class Negro life as the central theme, but the atmosphere and the background is there. These works should be followed up by some incisive and intimate stories from the inside.

The realistic story around a Negro insurance official, dentist, general practitioner, undertaker, and the like would be most revealing. Thinly disguised fiction around the well-known Negro names is not the answer, either. The "exceptional" as well as the Ol' Man Rivers has been exploited all out of context already. Everybody is already resigned to the "exceptional" Negro, and willing to be entertained by the "quaint." To grasp the penetration of western civilization in a minority, it is necessary to know how the average behaves and lives. Books that deal with people like in Sinclair Lewis' *Main Street* is the necessary metier. For various reasons, the average, struggling, non-morbid Negro is the best-kept secret in America. His revelation to the public is the thing needed to do away with that feeling of difference which inspires fear and which ever expresses itself in dislike.

Dr. Charles S. Johnson: Johnson (1893–1956) was the first African American president of Fisk University.
Carl Van Vechten: Progressive white champion and patron of African American culture (1880–1964).

It is inevitable that this knowledge will destroy many illusions and romantic traditions which America probably likes to have around. But then, we have no record of anybody sinking into a lingering death on finding out that there was no Santa Claus. The old world will take it in its stride. The realization that Negroes are no better nor no worse, and at times just as boring as everybody else, will hardly kill off the population of the nation.

Outside of racial attitudes, there is still another reason why this literature should exist. Literature and other arts are supposed to hold up the mirror to nature. With only the fractional "exceptional" and the "quaint" portrayed, a true picture of Negro life in America cannot be. A great principle of national art has been violated.

These are the things that publishers and producers, as the accredited representatives of the American people, have not as yet taken into consideration sufficiently. Let there be light!

రాజ

SHIRLEY JACKSON *wrote this "biography of a story" in 1960 as a lecture to be delivered before reading "The Lottery" to college audiences. After her death it was included in* Come Along with Me *(1968), edited by her husband, Stanley Edgar Hyman. The lecture also contained extensive quotations from letters she had received from readers who took the story literally. These so disgusted Jackson that she promised her listeners at the conclusion of her talk, "I am out of the lottery business for good."*

SHIRLEY JACKSON

The Morning of June 28, 1948, and "The Lottery"   1968

On the morning of June 28, 1948, I walked down to the post office in our little Vermont town to pick up the mail. I was quite casual about it, as I recall — I opened the box, took out a couple of bills and a letter or two, talked to the postmaster for a few minutes, and left, never supposing that it was the last time for months that I was to pick up the mail without an active feeling of panic. By the next week I had had to change my mailbox to the largest one in the post office, and casual conversation with the postmaster was out of the question, because he wasn't speaking to me. June 28, 1948, was the day *The New Yorker* came out with a story of mine in it. It was not my first published story, nor my last, but I have been assured over and over that if it had been the only story I ever wrote or published, there would be people who would not forget my name.

I had written the story three weeks before, on a bright June morning when summer seemed to have come at last, with blue skies and warm sun and no heavenly signs to warn me that my morning's work was anything but just another story. The idea had come to me while I was pushing my daughter up the hill in her stroller — it was, as I say, a warm morning, and the hill was steep, and beside my daughter the stroller held the day's groceries — and perhaps the effort of that last fifty yards up the hill put an edge to the story; at any rate, I had the idea fairly clearly in my mind when I put my daughter in her playpen and the frozen vegetables in the refrigerator, and, writing the story, I found that it went quickly and easily, moving from beginning to end without pause. As a matter of fact, when I read it over later I decided that except for one or two minor corrections, it needed no changes, and the story I finally typed up and sent off to my agent the next day was almost word for word the original draft. This, as any writer of stories can tell you, is not a usual thing. All I know is that when I came to read the story over I felt strongly that I didn't want to fuss with it. I didn't think it was perfect, but I didn't want to fuss with it. It was, I thought, a serious, straightforward story, and I was pleased and a little surprised at the ease with which it had been written; I was reasonably proud of it, and hoped that my agent would sell it to some magazine and I would have the gratification of seeing it in print.

My agent did not care for the story, but — as she said in her note at the time — her job was to sell it, not to like it. She sent it at once to *The New Yorker*, and about a week after the story had been written I received a telephone call from the fiction editor of *The New Yorker*; it was quite clear that he did not really care for the story, either, but *The New Yorker* was going to buy it. He asked for one change — that the date mentioned in the story be changed to coincide with the date of the issue of the magazine in which the story would appear, and I said of course. He then asked, hesitantly, if I had any particular interpretation of my own for the story; Mr. Harold Ross, then the editor of *The New Yorker*, was not altogether sure that he understood the story, and wondered if I cared to enlarge upon its meaning. I said no. Mr. Ross, he said, thought that the story might be puzzling to some people, and in case anyone telephoned the magazine, as sometimes happened, or wrote in asking about the story, was there anything in particular I wanted them to say? No, I said, nothing in particular; it was just a story I wrote.

I had no more preparation than that. I went on picking up the mail every morning, pushing my daughter up and down the hill in her stroller, anticipating pleasurably the check from *The New Yorker*, and shopping for groceries. The weather stayed nice and it looked as though it was going to be a good summer. Then, on June 28, *The New Yorker* came out with my story.

Things began mildly enough with a note from a friend at *The New Yorker*: "Your story has kicked up quite a fuss around the office," he wrote. I was flattered; it's nice to think that your friends notice what you write. Later that day there was a call from one of the magazine's editors; they had had a couple of people phone in about my story, he said, and was there anything I particularly wanted him to say if there were any more calls? No, I said, nothing particular; anything he chose to say was perfectly all right with me; it was just a story.

I was further puzzled by a cryptic note from another friend: "Heard a man talking about a story of yours on the bus this morning," she wrote. "Very exciting. I wanted to tell him I knew the author, but after I heard what he was saying I decided I'd better not."

One of the most terrifying aspects of publishing stories and books is the realization that they are going to be read, and read by strangers. I had never fully realized this before, although I had of course in my imagination dwelt lovingly upon the thought of the millions and millions of people who were going to be uplifted and enriched and delighted by the stories I wrote. It had simply never occurred to me that these millions and millions of people might be so far from being uplifted that they would sit down and write me letters I was downright scared to open; of the three-hundred-odd letters that I received that summer I can count only thirteen that spoke kindly to me, and they were mostly from friends. Even my mother scolded me: "Dad and I did not care at all for your story in *The New Yorker*," she wrote sternly, "it does seem, dear, that this gloomy kind of story is what all you young people think about these days. Why don't you write something to cheer people up?"

By mid-July I had begun to perceive that I was very lucky indeed to be safely in Vermont, where no one in our small town had ever heard of *The New Yorker*, much less read my story. Millions of people, and my mother, had taken a pronounced dislike to me.

The magazine kept no track of telephone calls, but all letters addressed to me care of the magazine were forwarded directly to me for answering, and all letters addressed to the magazine — some of them addressed to Harold Ross personally; these were the most vehement — were answered at the magazine and then the letters were sent me in great batches, along with carbons of the answers written at the magazine. I have all the letters still, and if they could be considered to give any accurate cross section of the reading public, or the reading public of *The New Yorker*, or even the reading public of one issue of *The New Yorker*, I would stop writing now.

Judging from these letters, people who read stories are gullible, rude, frequently illiterate, and horribly afraid of being laughed at. Many of the writers were positive that *The New Yorker* was going to ridicule them in print, and the most cautious letters were headed, in capital letters: NOT FOR PUBLICATION or PLEASE DO NOT PRINT THIS LETTER, or, at best, THIS LETTER MAY BE PUBLISHED AT YOUR USUAL RATES OF PAYMENT. Anonymous letters, of which there were a few, were destroyed. *The New Yorker* never published any comment of any kind about the story in the magazine, but did issue one publicity release saying that the story had received more mail than any piece of fiction they had ever published; this was after the newspapers had gotten into the act, in midsummer, with a front-page story in the San Francisco *Chronicle* begging to know what the story meant, and a series of columns in New York and Chicago papers pointing out that *New Yorker* subscriptions were being canceled right and left.

Curiously, there are three main themes which dominate the letters of that first summer — three themes which might be identified as bewilderment, speculation, and plain old-fashioned abuse. In the years since then, during which the story has been anthologized, dramatized, televised, and even — in one completely mystifying transformation — made into a ballet, the tenor of letters I receive has changed. I am addressed more politely, as a rule, and the letters largely confine themselves to questions like what does this story mean? The general tone of the early letters, however, was a kind of wide-eyed, shocked innocence. People at first were not so much concerned with what the story meant; what they wanted to know was where these lotteries were held, and whether they could go there and watch.

༄

D. H. LAWRENCE *rewrote early drafts of "Odour of Chrysanthemums" several times before completing the story in 1909. He first published it in* The English Review *in 1911 and revised it further when it was included in the 1914 collection* The Prussian Officer. *Here is a passage from an early draft of the story with the corresponding description and dialogue from the final published version.*

D. H. LAWRENCE

Draft Passage from "Odour of Chrysanthemums"

MANUSCRIPT VERSION

Then they heard the girl calling shrilly upstairs:

"Mother — who is it? — who is it? — Mother!"

Elizabeth caught herself up, and going towards the stairs, she called:

"Go to sleep — it's nothing — go to sleep, and don't be silly" — then she went upstairs:

"What are you calling for? It's only your father, and he won't make any noise. Go to sleep now."

"I thought it was some men come!" wailed the child.

"They only came with your father — and you must go to sleep, he won't make any noise. He's asleep."

"Is he in bed?"

"Yes. And don't wake him. Go to sleep now."

"What time is it?" — the pitiful thin voice of the half comforted girl, and the plaintive question, were too much for the men downstairs. One by one they got their caps, and stepping over the body, they tiptoed out of the house, hearing the mother answer as they went:

"Ten o'clock — There, go to sleep now." Her voice too was dreadful in its tenderness. They knew she kissed the children; and the little ones sank down again straight to sleep. So was the terror lifted off their hearts.

PUBLISHED TEXT

Then they heard the girl's voice upstairs calling shrilly: "Mother, mother — who is it? Mother, who is it?"

Elizabeth hurried to the foot of the stairs and opened the door:

"Go to sleep!" she commanded sharply. "What are you shouting about? Go to sleep at once — there's nothing — "

Then she began to mount the stairs. They could hear her on the boards, and on the plaster floor of the little bedroom. They could hear her distinctly:

"What's the matter now? — what's the matter with you, silly thing?" — her voice was much agitated, with an unreal gentleness.

"I thought it was some men come," said the plaintive voice of the child. "Has he come?"

"Yes, they've brought him. There's nothing to make a fuss about. Go to sleep now, like a good child."

They could hear her voice in the bedroom, they waited whilst she covered the children under the bedclothes.

"Is he drunk?" asked the girl, timidly, faintly.

"No! No — he's not! He — he's asleep."

"Is he asleep downstairs?"

"Yes — and don't make a noise."

There was silence for a moment, then the men heard the frightened child again:

"What's that noise?"

"It's nothing, I tell you, what are you bothering for?"

The noise was the grandmother moaning. She was oblivious of everything, sitting on her chair rocking and moaning. The manager put his hand on her arm and bade her "Sh-sh!!"

The old woman opened her eyes and looked at him. She was shocked by this interruption, and seemed to wonder.

"What time is it?" — the plaintive thin voice of the child, sinking back unhappily into sleep, asked this last question.

"Ten o'clock," answered the mother more softly. Then she must have bent down and kissed the children.

Matthews beckoned to the men to come away. They put on their caps and took up the stretcher. Stepping over the body, they tiptoed out of the house. None of them spoke till they were far from the wakeful children.

ಞ

DAVID **L**EAVITT *published his article "The Way I Live Now" in the New York Times on July 9, 1989. It is an unusually candid account of how contemporary literature continues to offer the reader "a possibility of catharsis" in troubled times. Leavitt experienced this intense psychological release after reading Susan Sontag's story "The Way We Live Now." Aristotle described the experience of catharsis in his Poetics two thousand years ago.*

D**AVID** L**EAVITT**

The Way I Live Now   1989

It used to be that when people asked me why I hadn't written about AIDS, I'd get angry. Because I had published a book of short stories and a novel that dealt with the themes of homosexuality and illness, I suppose they assumed the subject would come naturally to me. So what? I'd shout back. I'm not obligated to write about *anything*. Only if and when I was inspired to write about AIDS would I write about it.

But the truth was that AIDS scared me so much I wanted to block it out of my mind. When AIDS came up in a conversation, I'd change the subject; when a frightening headline leaped out at me from the pages of the newspaper, I'd hurriedly skim the article, and, once assured that it described no symptoms I could claim to be suffering from myself, turn the page. Only later, when people I was close to started to get sick, and I met writers who, in the panicked wake of diagnosis, didn't have the luxury of waiting for "inspiration," did I recognize the extent to which I was masking denial with self-righteousness.

I will always remember the mid-1980s, in New York City, as a time when the streets were filled with an almost palpable sense of mourning and panic. The office of the Gay Men's Health Crisis, or G.M.H.C., was a somber, silent place; it was no surprise to me that friends who did volunteer work there often mysteriously overslept the mornings they were supposed to go. The G.M.H.C.'s gray-carpeted hallways had a funereal hush that seemed the calm obverse of the dread sweeping the city: men anxiously prodding their necks for swollen lymph glands, or craning to examine mysterious pimples in the mirror. Everyone knew what the signs were, but no one knew exactly what they meant.

Then, somewhere near the end of that long corridor of anxiety, I read Susan Sontag's story "The Way We Live Now" in *The New Yorker,* and felt a sense of enormous and long-withheld release. Up to that point, reading fiction about AIDS had seemed to me akin to being shown a brick wall somewhere in the distance and then, at full speed, being hurled into it. Sontag, however, had written a story that transcended horror and grief, and which was therefore redemptive, if not of AIDS itself, then at least of the processes by which people cope with it. The story was told from the multiple points of view of the many friends of a man with AIDS; its long sentences swirled madly around the never-named disease, just as the characters — dozens of them — swirled around their suffering friend, arguing, comforting, annoying each other, giving each other their anxieties, their metaphors, their lies.

"The Way We Live Now" succeeded, for me, primarily because it offered a possibility of catharsis, and at that time, catharsis was something we all badly needed. Particularly in the early years of the epidemic, a diagnosis of AIDS carried with it a crushing burden of guilt; the knowledge that the transmission of the virus could have been avoided if one had skipped a particular sexual encounter proved to some people almost as unbearable as the sudden, distinct possibility of death, and as a result, both the sick and the "worried well" were forever rooting through their sexual histories in an obsessive effort to determine when or if they'd been infected. As Sontag would later point out in her book, *AIDS and Its Metaphors,* there was an intimate link between the mythology of the disease and a mythology of sex as something dirty, low, and indulgent; AIDS was like the "Roman Fever" of Edith Wharton's famous short story, an illness that marked the girls who suffered from it as having made the mistake of "going to the Coliseum" with Italian men.

What "The Way We Live Now" did so beautifully was to place the small tragedy of each HIV transmission into the larger context of the history of human interaction. In the age of AIDS, Sontag wrote, "the great chain of being has become a chain of death as well." And by reminding the reader that the "chain" of sexuality through which the virus had been spread was still the chain of life, Sontag managed to lift, at least partially, the moral onus of AIDS.

"The Way We Live Now" made me feel less alone in my dread, and therefore brave enough to read more. What I learned, as I read, was that of the people who were writing about AIDS regularly, some cared deeply about those who were sick, while others didn't care at all. And if anything distinguished the worthy writing about AIDS from the worthless, the discourse from the cant, it was the simple question of whether the author cared.

ひゆ

HERMAN MELVILLE *wrote an eloquent essay on Nathaniel Hawthorne's volume of short stories,* Mosses from an Old Manse, *for the New York periodical the* Literary World *in August 1850. Unlike Edgar Allan Poe in his review of Hawthorne's short fiction, Melville did not use the opportunity to theorize about the form of the short story. Instead, he conveyed his enthusiasm for Hawthorne's tragic vision, what Melville saw as the "great power of blackness" in Hawthorne's writing that derived "its force from its appeals to that Calvinistic sense of Innate Depravity and Original Sin." This was the aspect of Hawthorne's work that seemed most congenial to Melville's own genius while he continued work that summer on his novel-in-progress,* Moby-Dick.

HERMAN MELVILLE

Blackness in Hawthorne's "Young Goodman Brown"

1850

It is curious, how a man may travel along a country road, and yet miss the grandest or sweetest of prospects, by reason of an intervening hedge so like all other hedges as in no way to hint of the wide landscape beyond. So has it been with me concerning the enchanting landscape in the soul of this Hawthorne, this most excellent Man of Mosses. His Old Manse has been written now four years, but I never read it till a day or two since. I had seen it in the bookstores — heard of it often — even had it recommended to me by a tasteful friend, as a rare, quiet book, perhaps too deserving of popularity to be popular. But there are so many books called "excellent" and so much unpopular merit, that amid the thick stir of other things, the hint of my tasteful friend was disregarded; and for four years the Mosses on the Old Manse never refreshed me with their perennial green. It may be, however, that all this while, the book, like wine, was only improving in flavor and body. . . .

But it is the least part of genius that attracts admiration. Where Hawthorne is known, he seems to be deemed a pleasant writer, with a pleasant style — a sequestered, harmless man, from whom any deep and weighty thing would hardly be anticipated: a man who means no meanings. But there is no man, in whom humor and love, like mountain peaks, soar to such a rapt height, as to receive the irradiations of the upper skies; there is no man in whom humor and love are developed in that high form called genius — no such man can exist without also possessing, as the indispensable complement of these, a great, deep intellect, which drops down into the universe like a plummet. Or, love and humor are only the eyes, through which such an intellect views this world. The great beauty in such a mind is but the product of its strength. . . .

For spite of all the Indian-summer sunlight on the hither side of Hawthorne's soul, the other side — like the dark half of the physical sphere — is shrouded in a blackness, ten times black. But this darkness but gives more effect to the ever-moving dawn, that forever advances through it, and circumnavigates his world. Whether Hawthorne has simply availed himself of this mystical blackness as a means to the wondrous effects he makes it to produce in his lights and shades; or whether there really lurks in him, perhaps unknown to himself, a touch of Puritanic gloom — this I cannot altogether tell. Certain it is, however, that this great power of blackness in him derives its force from its appeals to that Calvinistic sense of Innate Depravity and Original Sin, from whose visitations, in some shape or other, no deeply thinking mind is always and wholly free. For, in certain moods, no man can weigh this world, without throwing in something, somehow like Original Sin, to strike the uneven balance. . . .

But with whatever motive, playful or profound, Nathaniel Hawthorne has chosen to entitle his pieces in the manner he has, it is certain that some of them are directly calculated to deceive — egregiously deceive — the superficial skimmer of pages. To be downright and candid once more, let me cheerfully say that two of these titles did dolefully dupe no less an eagle-eyed reader than myself; and that, too, after I had been impressed with a sense of the great depth and breadth of this American man. "Who in the name of thunder" (as the country people say in this neighborhood), "who in the name of thunder," would anticipate any marvel in a piece entitled "Young Goodman Brown"? You would of course suppose that it was a simple little tale, intended as a supplement to "Goody Two-Shoes." Whereas it is deep as Dante; nor can you finish it, without addressing the author in his own words: "It is yours to penetrate, in every bosom, the deep mystery of sin." And with Young Goodman, too, in allegorical pursuit of his Puritan wife, you cry out in your anguish,

> "Faith!" shouted Goodman Brown, in a voice of agony and desperation; and the echoes of the forest mocked him, crying — "Faith! Faith!" as if bewildered wretches were seeking her, all through the wilderness.

Now this same piece, entitled "Young Goodman Brown," is one of the two that I had not at all read yesterday; and I allude to it now, because it is, in itself, such a strong positive illustration of that blackness in Hawthorne which I had assumed from the mere occasional shadows of it, as revealed in several of the other sketches. But had I previously perused "Young Goodman Brown," I should have been at no pains to draw the conclusion which I came to at a time when I was ignorant that the book contained one such direct and unqualified manifestation of it.

১০১

J. HILLIS MILLER *analyzed the effect of what he called "Bartleby's celebrated immobility" in the critical study* Versions of Pygmalion *(1990). Miller was intent on examining "strange and unaccountable" versions of the Pygmalion myth in European literature; each story he discussed "contains a character who does something like falling in love with a statue." In Miller's view, a story like "Bartleby, the Scrivener" was an occasion for "the act of personification essential to all storytelling and story-reading."*

J. HILLIS MILLER

A Deconstructive Reading of Melville's "Bartleby, the Scrivener"

1990

After the failure of all these strategies for getting rid of Bartleby, the narrator tries another. In part through charity but in part through the notion that it is his fate to have Bartleby permanently in his chambers, he decides to try to live with Bartleby, to take him as a permanent fixture in his office. The narrator looks into two quite different books that deny man free will in determining his life, "Edwards on the Will" and "Priestly on Necessity." For Jonathan Edwards man does not have free will because everything he does is predestined by God. For Joseph Priestly, on the other hand, man is bound within the chains of a universal material necessity. Everything happens through physical causality, and therefore everything happens as it must happen, as it has been certain through all time to happen. In either case Bartleby's presence in the narrator's rooms is something predestined:

> Gradually I slid into the persuasion that these troubles of mine touch-
> ing the scrivener, had been all predestinated from eternity, and
> Bartleby was billeted upon me for some mysterious purpose of an all-
> wise Providence, which it was not for a mere mortal like me to fathom.
> Yes, Bartleby, stay there behind your screen, thought I; I shall perse-
> cute you no more; you are harmless and noiseless as any of these old
> chairs; in short, I never feel so private as when I know you are here. At
> last I see it, I feel it; I penetrate to the predestinated purpose of my life.
> I am content. Others may have loftier parts to enact; but my mission in

this world, Bartleby, is to furnish you with office-room for such period as you may see fit to remain.

This strategy fails too, when the narrator's clients and associates let him know that Bartleby's presence in his offices is scandalizing his professional reputation. It is then that the narrator, who is nothing if not logical, conceives his strangest way of dealing with Bartleby. Since Bartleby will not budge, he himself will leave. The immobility of Bartleby turns the narrator into a nomad: "No more then. Since he will not quit me, I must quit him. I will change my offices; I will move elsewhere."

When the new tenants and the landlord of his old premises come to charge the narrator with responsibility for the nuisance Bartleby is causing, "haunting the building generally, sitting upon the banisters of the stairs by day, and sleeping in the entry by night," the narrator tries first a new strategy of saying he is in no way related to Bartleby or responsible for him. But it is no use: "I was the last person known to have anything to do with him, and they held me to the terrible account."

The narrator then meets Bartleby once more face to face. He offers to set him up in a respectable position, as a clerk in a dry-goods store, a bartender, a bill collector, or a companion for young gentlemen traveling to Europe. To all these ludicrous suggestions Bartleby replies that he is not particular, but he would prefer to remain "stationary." The narrator then, and finally, offers to take Bartleby home with him, like a stray cat, and give him refuge there. This meets with the same reply. The narrator flees the building and becomes truly a vagrant, wandering for days here and there in his rockaway.

The narrator's life and work seem to have been permanently broken by the irruption of Bartleby. It is not he but his old landlord who deals effectively with the situation. He has Bartleby "removed to the Tombs as a vagrant." This is just what the more intellectually consequent narrator has not been able to bring himself to do, not just because Bartleby is not, strictly speaking, a vagrant and not just because doing such violence to Bartleby would disobey the law of charity, but because he cannot respond with violence to a resistance that has been purely passive and has thereby "disarmed" or "unmanned" any decisive action: "Turn the man out by an actual thrusting I could not; to drive him away by calling him hard names would not do; calling in the police was an unpleasant idea. . . . You will not thrust him, the poor, pale, passive mortal, — you will not thrust such a helpless creature out of your door? you will not dishonor yourself by such cruelty? No, I will not, I cannot do that."

Even after the police have been called in and society has placed Bartleby where he belongs, the narrator continues to be haunted by a sense of unfulfilled responsibility. He visits him in the Tombs, the prison so called because it was in the Egyptian Revival style of architecture, but also no doubt in response to a deeper sense of kinship between incarceration and death: "The Egyptian character of the masonry weighed upon me with its gloom. But a soft imprisoned turf grew under foot. The heart of the eternal pyramids, it seemed, wherein, by some strange magic, through the clefts, grass-seed, dropped by birds, had sprung." Bartleby is appropriately placed in the Tombs since, if the prison courtyard where Bartleby dies is green life in the midst of death, Bartleby has been death in the midst of life. In the Tombs the narrator makes his last unsuccessful attempt to deal with Bartleby in a rational manner, to reincorporate him into ordinary life. He "narrates" to the prison authorities, as he says, "all I knew" about Bartleby, telling them Bartleby does not really belong there but must stay "till something less harsh might be done — though indeed I hardly knew what." He yields at last to the accounting for Bartleby that had been used by Ginger Nut: "I think, sir, he's a little *luny*." The narrator now tells the "grub-man" in the prison, Mr. Cutlets, "I think he is a little deranged." One powerful means society has for dealing with someone who does not fit any ordinary social category is to declare him insane.

Mr. Cutlets has his own curious and by no means insignificant way of placing Bartleby. He thinks Bartleby must be a forger. "Deranged? deranged is it? Well now, upon my word, I thought that friend of yourn was a gentleman forger; they are always pale and genteel-like, them forgers. I can't help pity 'em — can't help it, sir. Did you know Monroe Edwards?" To which the narrator answers, "No, I was never socially acquainted with any forgers." In a way Mr. Cutlets has got Bartleby right, since forgery involves the exact copying of someone else's handwriting in order to make a false document that functions performatively as if it were genuine. Bartleby is a species of forger in reverse. He copies documents all right, but he does this in such a way as to deprive them of their power to make anything happen. On the other hand, when the narrator has copied documents checked, corrected, and made functional, he is himself performing an act of forgery. He may not be socially acquainted with any forgers, but he is in a manner of speaking one himself.

The arrangement he makes with Mr. Cutlets to feed Bartleby in prison is the narrator's last attempt to reincorporate Bartleby into society. There is much emphasis on eating in the story, on what the narrator's different employees eat and drink and on how little Bartleby eats, apparently nothing at all in prison: " 'I prefer not to dine to-day,' said Bartleby, turning away. 'It would disagree with me; I am unused to dinners.' So saying he slowly moved to the other side of the inclosure, and took up a position fronting the dead-wall." Eating is one of the basic ways to share our common humanity. This Bartleby refuses, or rather he says he would prefer not to share in the ritual of eating. To refuse that is in the end deadly. Bartleby's death makes him what he has been all along, a bit of death in the midst of life.

It is entirely appropriate that the narrator's account of Bartleby should end with Bartleby's death, not because any biography should end with the death of the biographee but because in death Bartleby becomes what he has always already been. As I have said, his "I would prefer not to" is strangely oriented toward the future. It opens the future, but a future of perpetual not-yet. It can only come as death, and death is that which can never be present. There, at the end, the narrator finds the corpse of Bartleby, "strangely huddled at the base of the wall, his knees drawn up, and lying on his side, his head touching the cold stones." In an earlier version, the "Bartleby" fragment in the Melville family papers in the Gansevoort-Lansing Collection at the New York Public Library, Bartleby is found by the narrator lying in a white-washed room with his head against a tombstone: "It was clean, well-lighted and scrupulously white washed. The head-stone was standing up against the wall, and stretched on a blanket at its base, his head touching the cold marble and his feet upon the threshold lay the wasted form of Bartleby."

The corpse of Bartleby is not the presence of Bartleby. It is his eternal absence. In death he becomes what he has always been, a cadaver who "lives without dining," as the narrator says to the grub-man. Bartleby returns at death, in the final version of the story, to a fetal position. He is the incursion into life of that unattainable realm somewhere before birth and after death. But the word "realm" is misleading. What Bartleby brings is not a realm in the sense of place we might go. It is the otherness that all along haunts or inhabits life from the inside. This otherness can by no method, such as the long series of techniques the narrator tries, be accounted for, narrated, rationalized, or in any other way reassimilated into ordinary life, though it is a permanent part of that ordinary life. Bartleby is the alien that may neither be thrust out the door nor domesticated, brought into the family, given citizenship papers. Bartleby is the invasion of death into life, but not death as something from outside life. He is death as the other side of life or the cohabitant with life. "Death," nevertheless, is not the proper name for this ghostly companion of life, as if it were an allegorical meaning identified at last. Nor is "Death" its generic or common name. "Death" is a catachresis for what can never be named properly.

The narrator's last method of attempting to deal with Bartleby is his narration, going all the way from "I am a rather elderly man" to "Ah Bartleby! Ah humanity!" This narration is explicitly said to be written down and addressed to a "reader." It repeats for a more indeterminate reader, that is, for whoever happens to read it, the quasi-legal deposition he has made before the proper officer of "the Tombs, or to speak more properly, the Halls of Justice." If the narrator can encompass Bartleby with words, if he can do justice to him, he may simultaneously have accounted for him, naturalized him after all, and freed himself from his unfulfilled obligation. He will have made an adequate response to the demand Bartleby has made on him. The narrator, that is, may have justified himself while doing justice to Bartleby.

This is impossible because Bartleby cannot be identified. His story cannot be told. But the reader at the end knows better just why this is so, since we have watched the narrator try one by one a whole series of strategies for accounting for someone and has seen them one by one fail. This failure leaves Bartleby still imperturbably bringing everything to a halt or indefinitely postponing everything with his "I would prefer not to." The narrator's account is not so much an account as an apology for his failure to give an adequate account.

The narrator's writing is also an attempt at a reading, a failed attempt to read Bartleby. In this sense it is the first in a long line of attempts to read Bartleby the scrivener, though the narrator's successors do this by trying to read the text written by Melville, "Bartleby, the Scrivener." Just as Bartleby by his immovable presence in the narrator's office has demanded to be read and accounted for by him, so Melville's strange story demands to be read and accounted for. Nor have readers failed to respond to the demand. A large secondary literature has grown up around "Bartleby," remarkable for its multiplicity and diversity. All claim in one way or another to have identified Bartleby and to have accounted for him, to have done him justice. They tend to exemplify that function of policing or putting things in their place which is entrusted by our society to literary studies as one realm among many of the academic forms of accounting or accounting for. In the case of the essays on "Bartleby" this accounting often takes one or the other of two main forms, as Warminski has observed. These forms could be put under the aegis of the two-pronged last paragraph of the story — "Ah Bartleby! Ah humanity!" — or they might be said to fly in the face either of Bartleby's "But I am not particular" or of the manifest failure of the narrator's attempt to draw close to Bartleby by way of "the bond of a common humanity." Many of the essays try to explain Bartleby either by making him an example of some universal type, for example "existential man," or by finding some particular original or explanatory context for him, for example one of Melville's acquaintances who worked in a law office, or some aspect of nineteenth-century capitalism in America. But Bartleby is neither general nor particular: he is neutral. As such, he disables reading by any of these strategies, any attempt to put "Bartleby, the Scrivener" in its place by answering the question, "In mercy's name, who is he?"

No doubt my own reading also claims to have identified Bartleby, in this case by defining him as the neutral in-between that haunts all thinking and living by dialectical opposition. All readings of the story, including my own, are more ways to call in the police. They are ways of trying to put Bartleby in his place, to convey him where we want to put him, to make sense of him, even if it is an accounting that defines him as the nonsense that inhabits all sense-making. All readings attempt in one way or another to fulfill what the narrator has tried and failed to do: to tell Bartleby's story in a way that will allow us to assimilate him and the story into the vast archives of rationalization that make up the secondary literature of our profession. We are institutionalized to do that work of policing for our society. None of these techniques of assimilation works any better than any of the narrator's methods, and we remain haunted by Bartleby, but haunted also by "Bartleby, the Scrivener: A Story of Wall-Street." I claim, however, that my accounting succeeds where the others fail by showing (though that is not quite the right word) why it is that "accounting for" in any of its usual senses cannot work, either for the story or for the character the story poses.

რი

VLADIMIR NABOKOV *was a skillful guide to fiction in his* Lectures on Russian Literature. *As this excerpt from his analysis of Anton Chekhov's stories shows, he blended wit, irreverence, and critical insight in his summary of the intricacies of plot and character, illuminating the artistic achievements of the author. Nabokov felt that Chekhov's books are "sad books for humorous people" — that is, only a reader with a sense of humor can really appreciate their sadness. Chekhov's sub-*

tle humor pervades the grayness of the lives he created, flickering through his prose style: "He did it," said Nabokov, "by keeping all his words in the same dim light and of the same exact tint of gray, a tint between the color of an old fence and that of a low cloud."

Vladimir Nabokov

A Reading of Chekhov's "The Lady with the Little Dog"

1981

Chekhov comes into the story "The Lady with the Little Dog" without knocking. There is no dilly-dallying. The very first paragraph reveals the main character, the young fair-haired lady followed by her white Spitz dog on the waterfront of a Crimean resort, Yalta, on the Black Sea. And immediately after, the male character Gurov appears. His wife, whom he has left with the children in Moscow, is vividly depicted: her solid frame, her thick black eyebrows, and the way she has of calling herself "a woman who thinks." One notes the magic of the trifles the author collects — the wife's manner of dropping a certain mute letter in spelling and her calling her husband by the longest and fullest form of his name, both traits in combination with the impressive dignity of her beetle-browed face and rigid poise forming exactly the necessary impression. A hard woman with the strong feminist and social ideas of her time, but one whom her husband finds in his heart of hearts to be narrow, dull-minded, and devoid of grace. The natural transition is to Gurov's constant unfaithfulness to her, to his general attitude toward women — "that inferior race" is what he calls them, but without that inferior race he could not exist. It is hinted that these Russian romances were not altogether as light-winged as in the Paris of Maupassant. Complications and problems are unavoidable with those decent hesitating people of Moscow who are slow heavy starters but plunge into tedious difficulties when once they start going.

Then with the same neat and direct method of attack, with the bridging formula "and so . . ." (or perhaps still better rendered in English by that "Now" which begins a new paragraph in straightforward fairy tales), we slide back to the lady with the dog. Everything about her, even the way her hair was done, told him that she was bored. The spirit of adventure — though he realized perfectly well that his attitude toward a lone woman in a fashionable sea town was based on vulgar stories, generally false — this spirit of adventure prompts him to call the little dog, which thus becomes a link between her and him. They are both in a public restaurant.

> He beckoned invitingly to the Spitz, and when the dog approached him, shook his finger at it. The Spitz growled; Gurov threatened it again.
> The lady glanced at him and at once dropped her eyes.
> "He doesn't bite," she said and blushed.

> "May I give him a bone?" he asked; and when she nodded he inquired affably, "Have you been in Yalta long?"
> "About five days."

They talk. The author has hinted already that Gurov was witty in the company of women; and instead of having the reader take it for granted (you know the old method of describing the talk as "brilliant" but giving no samples of the conversation), Chekhov makes him joke in a really attractive, winning way. "Bored, are you? An average citizen lives in . . . (here Chekhov lists the names of beautifully chosen, super-provincial towns) and is not bored, but when he arrives here on his vacation it is all boredom and dust. One could think he came from Granada" (a name particularly appealing to the Russian imagination). The rest of their talk, for which this sidelight is richly sufficient, is conveyed indirectly. Now comes a first glimpse of Chekhov's own system of suggesting atmosphere by the most concise details of nature, "the sea was of a warm lilac hue with a golden path for the moon"; whoever has lived in Yalta knows how exactly this conveys the impression of a summer evening there. This first movement of the story ends with Gurov alone in his hotel room thinking of her as he goes to sleep and imagining her delicate weak-looking neck and her pretty gray eyes. It is to be noted that only now, through the medium of the hero's imagination, does Chekhov give a visible and definite form to the lady, features that fit perfectly with her listless manner and expression of boredom already known to us.

> Getting into bed he recalled that she had been a schoolgirl only recently, doing lessons like his own daughter; he thought how much timidity and angularity there was still in her laugh and her manner of talking with a stranger. It must have been the first time in her life that she was alone in a setting in which she was followed, looked at, and spoken to for one secret purpose alone, which she could hardly fail to guess. He thought of her slim, delicate throat, her lovely gray eyes.
> "There's something pathetic about her, though," he thought, and dropped off.

The next movement (each of the four diminutive chapters or movements of which the story is composed is not more than four or five pages long), the next movement starts a week later with Gurov going to the pavilion and bringing the lady iced lemonade on a hot windy day, with the dust flying; and then in the evening when the sirocco subsides, they go on the pier to watch the incoming steamer. "The lady lost her lorgnette in the crowd," Chekhov notes shortly, and this being so casually worded, without any direct influence on the story — just a passing statement — somehow fits in with that helpless pathos already alluded to.

Then in her hotel room her awkwardness and tender angularity are delicately conveyed. They have become lovers. She was now sitting with her long hair hanging down on both sides of her face in the dejected pose of a sinner in some old picture. There was a watermelon on the table. Gurov cut himself a piece and began to eat unhurriedly. This realistic touch is again a typical Chekhov device.

She tells him about her existence in the remote town she comes from and Gurov is slightly bored by her naiveté, confusion, and tears. It is only now that we learn her husband's name: von Dideritz — probably of German descent. They roam about Yalta in the early morning mist.

> At Oreanda they sat on a bench not far from the church, looked down at the sea, and were silent. Yalta was barely visible through the morning mist; white clouds rested motionlessly on the mountaintops. The leaves did not stir on the trees, the crickets chirped, and the monotonous muffled sound of the sea that rose from below spoke of the peace, the eternal sleep awaiting us. So it rumbled below when there was no Yalta, no Oreanda here; so it rumbles now, and it will rumble as indifferently and hollowly when we are no more. . . . Sitting beside a young woman who in the dawn seemed so lovely, Gurov, soothed and spellbound by these magical surroundings — the sea, the mountains, the clouds, the wide sky — thought how everything is really beautiful in this world when one reflects: everything except what we think or do ourselves when we forget the higher aims of life and our own human dignity.
>
> A man strolled up to them — probably a watchman — looked at them and walked away. And this detail, too, seemed so mysterious and beautiful. They saw a steamer arrive from Feodosia, its lights extinguished in the glow of dawn.
>
> "There is dew on the grass," said Anna Sergeievna, after a silence.
>
> "Yes, it's time to go home."

Then several days pass and then she has to go back to her home town.

" 'Time for me, too, to go North,' thought Gurov as he returned after seeing her off." And there the chapter ends.

The third movement plunges us straight into Gurov's life in Moscow. The richness of a gay Russian winter, his family affairs, the dinners at clubs and restaurants, all this is swiftly and vividly suggested. Then a page is devoted to a queer thing that has happened to him: he cannot forget the lady with the little dog. He has many friends, but the curious longing he has for talking about his adventure finds no outlet. When he happens to speak in a very general way of love and women, nobody guesses what he means, and only his wife moves her dark eyebrows and says: "Stop that fatuous posing; it does not suit you."

And now comes what in Chekhov's quiet stories may be called the climax. There is something that your average citizen calls romance and something he calls prose — though both are the meat of poetry for the artist. Such a contrast has already been hinted at by the slice of watermelon which Gurov crunched in a Yalta hotel room at a most romantic moment, sitting heavily and munching away. This contrast is beautifully followed up when at last Gurov blurts out to a friend late at night as they come out of the club: If you knew what a delightful woman I met in Yalta! His friend, a bureaucratic civil servant, got into his sleigh, the horses moved, but suddenly he turned and called back to Gurov. Yes? asked Gurov, evidently expecting some reaction to what he had just mentioned. By the way, said the man, you were quite right. That fish at the club was decidedly smelly.

This is a natural transition to the description of Gurov's new mood, his feeling that he lives among savages where cards and food are life. His family, his bank, the whole trend of his existence, everything seems futile, dull, and senseless. About Christmas he tells his wife he is going on a business trip to St. Petersburg, instead of which he travels to the remote Volga town where the lady lives.

Critics of Chekhov in the good old days when the mania for the civic problem flourished in Russia were incensed with his way of describing what they considered to be trivial unnecessary matters instead of thoroughly examining and solving the problems of bourgeois marriage. For as soon as Gurov arrives in the early hours to that town and takes the best room at the local hotel, Chekhov, instead of describing his mood or intensifying his difficult moral position, gives what is artistic in the highest sense of the word: he notes the gray carpet, made of military cloth, and the inkstand, also gray with dust, with a horseman whose hand waves a hat and whose head is gone. That is all: it is nothing but it is everything in authentic literature. A feature in the same line is the phonetic transformation which the hotel porter imposes on the German name von Dideritz. Having learned the address Gurov goes there and looks at the house. Opposite was a long gray fence with nails sticking out. An unescapable fence, Gurov says to himself, and here we get the concluding note in the rhythm of drabness and grayness already suggested by the carpet, the inkstand, the illiterate accent of the porter. The unexpected little turns and the lightness of the touches are what places Chekhov, above all Russian writers of fiction, on the level of Gogol and Tolstoy.

Presently he saw an old servant coming out with the familiar little white dog. He wanted to call it (by a kind of conditional reflex), but suddenly his heart began beating fast and in his excitement he could not remember the dog's name — another delightful touch. Later on he decides to go to the local theatre, where for the first time the operetta *The Geisha* is being given. In sixty words Chekhov paints a complete picture of a provincial theatre, not forgetting the town-governor who modestly hid in his box behind a plush curtain so that only his hands were visible. Then the lady appeared. And he realized quite clearly that now in the whole world there was none nearer and dearer and more important to him than this slight woman, lost in a small-town crowd, a woman perfectly unremarkable, with a vulgar lorgnette in her hand. He saw her husband and remembered her qualifying him as a flunkey — he distinctly resembled one.

A remarkably fine scene follows when Gurov manages to talk to her, and then their mad swift walk up all kinds of staircases and corridors, and down again, and up again, amid people in the various uniforms of provincial officials. Neither does Chekhov forget "two schoolboys who smoked on the stairs and looked down at him and her."

"You must leave," Anna Sergeievna went on in a whisper. "Do you hear, Dmitri Dmitrich? I will come and see you in Moscow. I have never been happy; I am unhappy now, and I never, never shall be happy, never! So don't make me suffer still more! I swear I'll come to Moscow. But now let us part. My dear, good, precious one, let us part!"

She pressed his hand and walked rapidly downstairs, turning to look round at him, and from her eyes he could see that she really was unhappy. Gurov stood for a while, listening, then when all grew quiet, he found his coat and left the theatre.

The fourth and last little chapter gives the atmosphere of their secret meetings in Moscow. As soon as she would arrive she used to send a red-capped messenger to Gurov. One day he was on his way to her and his daughter was with him. She was going to school, in the same direction as he. Big damp snowflakes were slowly coming down.

The thermometer, Gurov was saying to his daughter, shows a few degrees above freezing point (actually 37° above, Fahrenheit), but nevertheless snow is falling. The explanation is that this warmth applies only to the surface of the earth, while in the higher layers of the atmosphere the temperature is quite different.

And as he spoke and walked, he kept thinking that not a soul knew or would ever know about these secret meetings.

What puzzled him was that all the false part of his life, his bank, his club, his conversations, his social obligations — all this happened openly, while the real and interesting part was hidden.

> He had two lives, an open one, seen and known by all who needed to know of it, full of conventional truth and conventional falsehood, exactly like the lives of his friends and acquaintances; and another life that went on in secret. And through some strange, perhaps accidental, combination of circumstances, everything that was of interest and importance to him, everything that was essential to him, everything about which he felt sincerely and did not deceive himself, everything that constituted the core of his life, was going on concealed from others; while all that was false, the shell in which he hid to cover the truth — his work at the bank for instance, his discussions at the club, his references to the "inferior race," his appearances at anniversary celebrations with his wife — all that went on in the open. Judging others by himself, he did not believe what he saw, and always fancied that every man led his real, most interesting life under cover of secrecy as under cover of night. The personal life of every individual is based on secrecy, and perhaps it is partly for that reason that civilized man is so nervously anxious that personal privacy should be respected.

The final scene is full of that pathos which has been suggested in the very beginning. They meet, she sobs, they feel that they are the closest of couples, the tenderest of friends, and he sees that his hair is getting a little gray and knows that only death will end their love.

> The shoulders on which his hands rested were warm and quivering. He felt compassion for this life, still so warm and lovely, but probably already about to begin to fade and wither like his own. Why did she love him so much? He always seemed to women different from what he was, and they loved in him not himself, but the man

whom their imagination had created and whom they had been eagerly seeking all their lives; and afterwards, when they saw their mistake, they loved him nevertheless. And not one of them had been happy with him. In the past he had met women, come together with them, parted from them, but he had never once loved; it was anything you please, but not love. And only now when his head was gray he had fallen in love, really, truly — for the first time in his life.

They talk, they discuss their position, how to get rid of the necessity of this sordid secrecy, how to be together always. They find no solution and in the typical Chekhov way the tale fades out with no definite full-stop but with the natural motion of life.

And it seemed as though in a little while the solution would be found, and then a new and glorious life would begin; and it was clear to both of them that the end was still far off, and that what was to be most complicated and difficult for them was only just beginning.

All the traditional rules of story telling have been broken in this wonderful short story of twenty pages or so. There is no problem, no regular climax, no point at the end. And it is one of the greatest stories ever written.

ಐಐ

FRANK O'CONNOR *analyzed the stories in James Joyce's* Dubliners *in the chapter "Work in Progress" in his 1963 study of the short story,* The Lonely Voice. *O'Connor addressed himself to the question of why Joyce gave up writing stories after* Dubliners; *he observed that "it is as difficult to think of a real storyteller, like Chekhov, who had experienced the thrill of the completed masterpiece, giving up short stories forever as it is to think of Keats giving up lyric poetry." The answer, for O'Connor, can be found by comparing the formal differences between the stories at the beginning of* Dubliners *and "The Dead" at the end. This is where his analysis begins.*

FRANK O'CONNOR

Style and Form in Joyce's "The Dead"   1963

"The Dead," Joyce's last story, is entirely different from all the others. It is also immensely more complicated, and it is not always easy to see what any particular episode represents, though it is only too easy to see that it represents something. The scene is the annual dance of the Misses Morkan, old music teachers on Usher's Island, and ostensibly it is no more than a report of what happened at it, except at the end, when Gabriel Conroy and his wife Gretta return to their hotel room. There she breaks down and tells him of a youthful and innocent love affair between herself and a boy of seventeen in Galway, who had caught his death of cold from standing under her bedroom window. But this final scene is irrelevant only in appearance, for in effect it is the real story, and everything that has led up to it has been simply an enormously expanded introduction, a series of themes all of which find their climax in the hotel bedroom.

The setting of the story in a warm, vivacious lighted house in the midst of night and snow is an image of life itself, but every incident, almost every speech, has a crack in it through which we perceive the presence of death all about us, as when Gabriel says that Gretta "takes three *mortal* hours to dress herself," and the aunts say that she must be "perished alive" — an Irishism that ingeniously suggests both life and death. Several times the warmth and gaiety give rise to the idea of love and marriage, but each time it is knocked dead by phrase or incident. At the very opening of the story Gabriel suggests to the servant girl, Lily, that they will soon be attending her wedding, but she retorts savagely that "the men that is now is only all palaver and what they can get out of you," the major theme of the story, for all grace is with the dead: The younger generation have not the generosity of the two old sisters, the younger singers (Caruso, for instance!) cannot sing as well as some long dead English tenor. Gabriel's aunt actually sings "Arrayed for the Bridal," but she is only an old woman who has been dismissed from her position in the local church choir.

Gabriel himself is fired by passion for his wife, but when they return to their hotel bedroom the electric light has failed, and his passion is also extinguished when she tells him the story of her love for a dead boy. Whether it is Gabriel's quarrel with Miss Ivors, who wants him to spend his summer holiday patriotically in the West of Ireland (where his wife and the young man had met), the discussion of Cistercian monks who are supposed to sleep in their coffins, "to remind them of their last end," or the reminiscences of old singers and old relatives, everything pushes Gabriel toward the ultimate dissolution of identity in which real things disappear from about us, and we are as alone as we shall be on our deathbeds.

But it is easy enough to see from "The Dead" why Joyce gave up storytelling. One of his main passions — the elaboration of style and form — had taken control, and the short story is too tightly knit to permit expansion like this. And — what is much more important — it is quite clear from "The Dead" that he had already begun to lose sight of the submerged population that was his original subject. There are little touches of it here and there, as in the sketches of Freddy Malins and his mother — the old lady who finds everything "beautiful" — "beautiful crossing," "beautiful house," "beautiful scenery," "beautiful fish" — but Gabriel does not belong to it, nor does Gretta nor Miss Ivors. They are not characters but personalities, and Joyce would never again be able to deal with characters, people whose identity is determined by their circumstances. His own escape to Trieste, with its enlargement of his own sense of identity, had caused them to fade from his mind or — to put it more precisely — had caused them to reappear in entirely different guises. This is something that is always liable to happen to the provincial storyteller when you put him into a cosmopolitan atmosphere.

GRACE PALEY *talked with Ann Charters about her experiences as a short story writer during lunch in her Greenwich Village apartment on a snowy day in February 1986. On the wall above the kitchen table hung an oil painting, a still life of vegetables painted by her father after his retirement from the practice of medicine. Paley mentions her father's interest in art in her story "A Conversation with My Father."*

GRACE PALEY

A Conversation with Ann Charters   1986

Charters: Some literary critics think that short stories are more closely related to poetry than to the novel. Would you agree?

Paley: I would say that stories are closer to poetry than they are to the novel because first they are shorter, and second they are more concentrated, more economical, and that kind of economy, the pulling together of all the information and making leaps across the information, is really close to poetry. By leaps I mean thought leaps and feeling leaps. Also, when short stories are working right, you pay more attention to language than most novelists do.

Charters: Poe said unity was an essential factor of short stories. Do you have any ideas about this in your own work?

Paley: I suppose there has to be some kind of unity, but that's true in a novel too. It seems to me that unity is form. Form is really the vessel in which the story or poem or novel exists. The reason I don't have an answer for you is that there's really no telling — sometimes I like to start a story with one thing and end it with another. I don't know where the unity is in that case. I see the word *unity* meaning that something has to be whole, even if it ends in an open way.

Charters: You mean, as you wrote in "A Conversation with My Father," that "everyone, real or invented, deserves the open destiny of life."

Paley: Yes.

Charters: You started writing poetry before short stories, and the language of your fiction is often as compressed and metaphorical as the language of poetry. Can you describe the process of how you learned to write?

Paley: Let me put it this way: I went to school to poetry — that was where I learned how to write. People learn to write by doing various things. I suppose I also wrote a lot of letters, since it was the time of the Second World War. But apart from that I wrote poems, that's what I wrote. I thought about language a lot. That was important to me. That was my teacher. My fiction teacher was poetry.

Charters: What poets did you read when you were learning how to write?

Paley: I just read all the poets. If there was an anthology of poets, I read every single one. I knew all the Victorians. I read the Imagists. At a certain point I fell in love with the Englishmen who came to America — Christopher Isherwood, Stephen Spender, and W. H. Auden. I thought Auden was the greatest. And I loved the poetry of Dylan Thomas. Yeats meant a lot to me. I paid attention to all of them and listened to all of them. Some of them must have gotten into my ear. That's not up to me to say. That's for the reader to say. The reader of my stories will tell me, "This is whom you're influenced by," but I can't say that. I feel I was influenced by everybody.

Charters: Why did you stop writing poetry and start writing stories? What did the form of the short story offer you that the poem didn't?

Paley: First of all, I began to think of certain subject matter, women's lives specifically, and what was happening around me. I was in my thirties, which I guess is the time people start to notice these things, women's and men's lives and what their relationship is. I knew lots of women with small kids, and I was developing very close relationships with a variety of women. All sorts of things began to worry me, and I began to think about them a lot. I couldn't deal with any of this subject matter in poetry; I just didn't know how. I didn't have the technique. Other people can, but I didn't want to write poems saying "I feel this" and "I feel that." That was the last thing I wanted to do.

I can give you a definition that can be proven wrong in many ways, but for me it was that in writing poetry I wanted to talk to the world, I wanted to address the world, so to speak. But writing stories, I wanted to get the world to explain itself to me, to speak to me. And for me that was the essential difference between writing poetry and stories, and it still is, in many ways. So I had to get that world to talk to me. I had to reach out to it, a very different thing than writing poems. I had to reach out to the world and get it to tell me what it was all about, because I didn't understand it. I just didn't understand. Also, I'd always been very interested in people and told funny stories, and I didn't have any room for doing that in poems, again because of my own self. My poems were too literary, that's the real reason.

Charters: What do you mean, you had to get the world to tell you what it was all about?

Paley: In the first story I ever wrote, "The Contest," I did exactly what I just told you — I got this guy to talk. That's what I did. I had a certain guy in mind. In fact, I stuck pretty close to my notion of what he was, and the story was about a contest he had told me about. The second story I wrote was about Aunt Rose in "Goodbye and Good Luck." That began with my husband's aunt visiting us, and saying exactly the sentence I used to start the story: "I was popular in certain circles." But the rest has nothing to do with her life at all. She looked at us, this aunt of his, and she felt we didn't appreciate her, so she looked at us and she said to us, "Listen," she said. "I was popular in certain circles." That statement really began that particular story. That story was about lots of older women I knew who didn't get married, and I was thinking about them. These are two examples of how I began, how I got to my own voice by hearing and using all these other voices.

Charters: I suppose "A Conversation with My Father" isn't typical of your work, because the story you make up for him isn't what he wants, the old-fashioned Chekhov or Maupassant story, and it's not really one of your "voice" stories either, is it?

Paley: No. I'm just trying to oblige him.

Charters: So that may be one of the jokes of the story?

Paley: It could be, but I never thought of it that way. I think it's a good story. People have found it useful in literature classes, which I think is funny, but nice.

Charters: Did you make up the plot of "A Conversation with My Father," or did it actually happen when you were visiting him before he died?

Paley: My father was eighty-six years old and in bed. I spent a lot of time with him. He was an artist, and he painted pictures after he retired from being a doctor. I visited him at least once a week, and we were very close. We would have discussions. I never wrote a story for him about this neighbor, but he did say to me once, "Why can't you write a regular story, for God's sake?" something like that. So that particular story is both about literature and about that particular discussion, but it's also about generational differences, about different ways of looking at life. What my father thought could be done in the world was due to his own history. What I thought could be done in the world was different, not because I was a more open person, because he was also a very open person, but because I lived in a particularly open time, the late 1960s. The story I wrote for him was about all these druggies. It was made up, but it was certainly true. I could point out people on my block whose kids became junkies. Many of them have recovered from being junkies and are in good shape now.

Charters: Did you know any mothers in Greenwich Village who became junkies to keep their kids company?

Paley: Sure. It was a very open neighborhood then, with lots of freedom. But my father was born into a very different time. He was born in Czarist Russia and came over to America when he was twenty and worked hard and studied medicine and had a profession.

Charters: When you were growing up did you read the writers your father admired — Maupassant and Chekhov?

Paley: Actually, he had never mentioned Maupassant to me before. He did mention him in that conversation. He did read a lot, he loved Chekhov. And when he came to this country, he taught himself English by reading Dickens.

Charters: So the idea for the story came to you when he mentioned Maupassant?

Paley: Well, not really. He had just read my story "Faith in a Tree," and there are a lot of voices coming from all over in that story. And so he asked me, "What is this? All those voices? Voices from who knows where?" He wasn't actually that heavy. But when I wrote about our conversation it became a fiction, and it's different from what really happened.

Charters: It must have been fun for you to make up the two versions of the story about your neighbor in "A Conversation with My Father."

Paley: I enjoyed writing that story. Some stories you don't enjoy, because they're very hard. I didn't write it right off, but I enjoyed it.

Charters: How many days did it take you to write?

Paley: There's no such thing as days with me when I write a story. More like months. I write it and I write slow, and then I rewrite, and then I put it away, and then I take it out again. It's tedious in some respects. But that's the way it works.

Charters: When do you decide it's finished?

Paley: When I've gone over it and I can't think of another thing to change.

Charters: I was looking over your book *Enormous Changes at the Last Minute,* which is where "A Conversation with My Father" appears, and I noticed you've placed it between two very dark stories, "The Little Girl," about a runaway in the Village who commits suicide after she's raped, and "The Immigrant Story," about the starvation of the young children in a Jewish family in Poland before the mother emigrates to America. I assume you did this for a reason. When you put a collection of short fiction together, how do you order the stories?

Paley: I always have something in mind. I like to put one or two at the beginning that will be readable immediately, and then I just work it out. I like to mix the long and the short, and the serious and the funny ones. But I did put those two dark stories around "A Conversation with My Father" to show him I could look tragedy in the face. Remember he asks me at the end of the story, "When will you look it in the face?"

Charters: Was that one of the things he actually said to you when you visited him?

Paley: Well, he did tend to say that I wouldn't look things in the face. That things were hard, and I wasn't looking at it. I didn't see certain problems with my kids when they were small, and he was in some degree right. In "The Immigrant Story" a man tells me, "You have a rotten rosy temperament." But then she says, "Rosiness is not a worse windowpane than gloomy gray when viewing the world." They're both just prisms to look through.

Charters: Is that what you still believe?

Paley: Well, I do believe it, but I also believe that things are bad.

Charters: A theme that some students find when reading "A Conversation with My Father" is that one of the things you don't want to look in the face that your father is trying to prepare you for is his own death. Were you conscious of that when you wrote the story?

Paley: No.

Charters: Can you see that theme in it now?

Paley: No. But maybe you're right. As I said, that's not up to me to say. Maybe the reader of a particular story knows better than the writer what it means. But I know I wasn't thinking about that when I wrote it. I wasn't thinking of his death at all. I was thinking of him being sick and trying not to get him excited.

ः०८

JAY PARINI *analyzes John Steinbeck's debt to D. H. Lawrence's story "Odour of Chrysanthemums" in his 1995 biography of Steinbeck. The result was what Parini rates as perhaps Steinbeck's best story, "The Chrysanthemums."*

JAY PARINI

Lawrence's and Steinbeck's "Chrysanthemums"

1955

The Long Valley had appeared when Steinbeck was just past the midpoint in writing *The Grapes of Wrath*. And while it did not sell quite on the same large scale as *Tortilla Flat* or *Of Mice and Men*, it made it onto the bestseller lists: an unusual thing, then and now, for a volume of stories. His movie agent, Annie Laurie Williams, wrote to Steinbeck on September 23: "*The Long Valley* is getting marvelous press."[1] Indeed, it was. Stanley Young, in the *New York Times Book Review* (September 25, 1938), predicted that Steinbeck would "become a genuinely great American writer." The next day, in *The New Yorker,* Clifton Fadiman called the book "a remarkable collection by a writer who has so far neither repeated himself nor allowed himself a single careless sentence."

The opening story, "The Chrysanthemums," sets the tone for the book.[2] It is a brilliant piece of writing, perhaps the best story Steinbeck ever wrote. In it we follow a brief period in the life of a woman, Elisa Allen, who is married to a dull but well-intentioned farmer. Steinbeck writes: "The high grey-flannel fog of winter closed off the Salinas Valley from the sky and from all the rest of the world." As in much of his fiction, this story opens with a personified landscape, a *paysage moralisé* in which the weather and geographical setting are deeply symbolic, gesturing in the direction of the story's ultimate meaning. Here, for instance, the claustrophobic world of Elisa Allen is signaled by the claustrophobic clouds pressing in on the valley. This frustrated woman will never break free.

The title of the story, as well as the theme, reflects again the author's interest in Lawrence (whose first published story was "Odour of Chrysanthemums"). For example, both writers seem to fasten intently on the idea that a new consciousness is growing under, or within, the old rotten one, and that the old must be sacrificed to the new; the apocalyptic flavor of Lawrence is rare in Steinbeck, who might be seen as a "cooler" writer, but they share an urgent belief that one version of civilization has come to an end, and that the artist must play a key role in developing the new one.

"The Chrysanthemums" is partly about the way Elisa's dreams are manipulated by a passing rogue — a man who repairs household goods. (Steinbeck's fiction is full of men like this one: there is Mac, for instance, from *In Dubious Battle*, who will do anything to win the migrant workers' confidence.) The repairman plays upon Elisa's feelings, pretending to sympathize with her love of flowers, which is all-consuming. Her passion for chrysanthemums in particular symbolizes her intimacy with the rhythms of the natural world and

---

[1] Unpublished letter from Williams to Steinbeck (September 23, 1928) in Rare Book and Manuscript Library, Columbia University.

[2] Two excellent articles that have influenced my view of this story are Mordecai Marcus's "The Lost Dream of Sex and Childbirth in 'The Chrysanthemums,' " *Modern Fiction Studies* II (Spring 1965), and Elizabeth E. McMahan's " 'The Chrysanthemums': A Study of Woman's Sexuality," *Modern Fiction Studies* 14 (Winter 1968–1969).

represents her most essential self. Only an author who was himself a gardener could have written about the process of gardening so eloquently:

> There was a little square sandy bed kept for rooting the chrysanthemums. With her trowel she turned the soil over and over, and smoothed it and patted it firm. Then she dug ten parallel trenches to receive the sets. Back at the chrysanthemum bed she pulled out the little crisp shoots, trimmed off the leaves of each one with her scissors and laid it on a small orderly pile.

Steinbeck understands the metaphor of gardening in a deeply symbolic way, using this knowledge to make his point. Elisa is finally hurt by the repairman, who was merely toying with her, but she is not broken, as Charlotte Hadella notes: "Even though, in the end, she thinks of herself as a weak, old woman, the powerful imagery of the strong, new crop of chrysanthemums waiting for rain still dominates the story."[3] She compares Elisa's disappointment to a kind of "pruning — the clipping back of the romantic 'shoots' of her imagination before they bud so that her energy can feed a strong reality and produce large, healthy blooms."

ཚྭ

EDGAR ALLAN POE *was one of the earliest writers to discuss the aesthetic qualities of the short story as a distinct prose narrative form. In his day, literary criticism was still a new field, lacking a terminology and developed concepts. His two long reviews praising the tales of Nathaniel Hawthorne were published in* Graham's Magazine *in 1842 and* Godey's Lady's Book *in 1847; they are pioneering examples of the analytic literary essay. The following excerpt is taken from the 1842 piece, in which Poe amplifies his theory of the short story and his views on the nature of originality in literature.*

EDGAR ALLAN POE

The Importance of the Single Effect in a Prose Tale

1842

But it is of [Hawthorne's] tales that we desire principally to speak. The tale proper, in our opinion, affords unquestionably the fairest field for the exercise of the loftiest talent, which can be afforded by the wide domains of mere prose. Were we bidden to say how the highest genius could be most advantageously employed for the best display of its own powers, we should answer,

---

[3] Charlotte Hadella, "Steinbeck's Cloistered Women," in *The Steinbeck Question: New Essays in Criticism,* ed. Donald R. Noble (Troy, N.Y.: Whitston, 1993), p. 61.

without hesitation — in the composition of a rhymed poem, not to exceed in length what might be perused in an hour. Within this limit alone can the highest order of true poetry exist. We need only here say, upon this topic, that, in almost all classes of composition, the unity of effect or impression is a point of the greatest importance. It is clear, moreover, that this unity cannot be thoroughly preserved in productions whose perusal cannot be completed at one sitting. We may continue the reading of a prose composition, from the very nature of prose itself, much longer than we can persevere, to any good purpose, in the perusal of a poem. This latter, if truly fulfilling the demands of the poetic sentiment, induces an exaltation of the soul which cannot be long sustained. All high excitements are necessarily transient. Thus a long poem is a paradox. And, without unity of impression, the deepest effects cannot be brought about. Epics were the offspring of an imperfect sense of Art, and their reign is no more. A poem *too* brief may produce a vivid, but never an intense or enduring impression. Without a certain continuity of effort — without a certain duration or repetition of purpose — the soul is never deeply moved. There must be the dropping of the water upon the rock. . . .

Were we called upon, however, to designate that class of composition which, next to such a poem as we have suggested, should best fulfill the demands of high genius — should offer it the most advantageous field of exertion — we should unhesitatingly speak of the prose tale, as Mr. Hawthorne has here exemplified it. We allude to the short prose narrative, requiring from a half-hour to one or two hours in its perusal. The ordinary novel is objectionable, from its length, for reasons already stated in substance. As it cannot be read at one sitting, it deprives itself, of course, of the immense force derivable from *totality*. Worldly interests intervening during the pauses of perusal, modify, annul, or counteract, in a greater or less degree, the impressions of the book. But simple cessation in reading would, of itself, be sufficient to destroy the true unity. In the brief tale, however, the author is enabled to carry out the fullness of his intention, be it what it may. During the hour of perusal the soul of the reader is at the writer's control. There are no external or extrinsic influences — resulting from weariness or interruption.

A skillful literary artist has constructed a tale. If wise, he has not fashioned his thoughts to accommodate his incidents; but having conceived, with deliberate care, a certain unique or single *effect* to be wrought out, he then invents such incidents — he then combines such events as may best aid him in establishing this preconceived effect. If his very initial sentence tend not to the outbringing of this effect, then he has failed in his first step. In the whole composition there should be no word written, of which the tendency, direct or indirect, is not to the one pre-established design. And by such means, with such care and skill, a picture is at length painted which leaves in the mind of him who contemplates it with a kindred art, a sense of the fullest satisfaction. The idea of the tale has been presented unblemished, because undisturbed; and this is an end unattainable by the novel. Undue brevity is just as exceptionable here as in the poem; but undue length is yet more to be avoided.

We have said that the tale has a point of superiority even over the poem.

In fact, while the *rhythm* of this latter is an essential aid in the development of the poem's highest idea — the idea of the Beautiful — the artificialities of this rhythm are an inseparable bar to the development of all points of thought or expression which have their basis in *Truth*. But Truth is often, and in very great degree, the aim of the tale. Some of the finest tales are tales of ratiocination. Thus the field of this species of composition, if not in so elevated a region of the mountain of Mind, is a tableland of far vaster extent than the domain of the mere poem. Its products are never so rich, but infinitely more numerous, and more appreciable by the mass of mankind. The writer of the prose tale, in short, may bring to his theme a vast variety of modes or reflections of thought and expression — (the ratiocinative, for example, the sarcastic, or the humorous) which are not only antagonistical to the nature of the poem, but absolutely forbidden by one of its most peculiar and indispensable adjuncts; we allude, of course, to rhythm. It may be added, here, *par parenthèse*, that the author who aims at the purely beautiful in a prose tale is laboring at a great disadvantage. For Beauty can be better treated in the poem. Not so with terror, or passion, or horror, or a multitude of such other points. . . .

Of Mr. Hawthorne's "Tales" we would say, emphatically, that they belong to the highest region of Art — an Art subservient to genius of a very lofty order. We have supposed, with good reason for so supposing, that he had been thrust into his present position by one of the impudent cliques which beset our literature, and whose pretensions it is our full purpose to expose at the earliest opportunity; but we have been most agreeably mistaken. We know of few compositions which the critic can more honestly commend than these "Twice-Told Tales." As Americans, we feel proud of the book.

Mr. Hawthorne's distinctive trait is invention, creation, imagination, originality — a trait which, in the literature of fiction, is positively worth all the rest. But the nature of the originality, so far as regards its manifestation in letters, is but imperfectly understood. The inventive or original mind as frequently displays itself in novelty of *tone* as in novelty of matter. Mr. Hawthorne is original in *all* points.

It would be a matter of some difficulty to designate the best of these tales; we repeat that, without exception, they are beautiful. . . . In the way of objection we have scarcely a word to say of these tales. There is, perhaps, a somewhat too general or prevalent *tone* — a tone of melancholy and mysticism. The subjects are insufficiently varied. There is not so much of *versatility* evinced as we might well be warranted in expecting from the high powers of Mr. Hawthorne. But beyond these trivial exceptions we have really none to make. The style is purity itself. Force abounds. High imagination gleams from every page. Mr. Hawthorne is a man of the truest genius.

രെ

PETER RUDY *discussed Leo Tolstoy's extensive revisions of "The Death of Ivan Ilych" in the introduction to* Darkness and Light *(1965), a collection of three short works by Tolstoy. Rudy examined Tolstoy's diaries and correspondence, as well* *as the early drafts of the story. He discovered that the suffering of a close friend, Leonid Urosov, from an incurable disease in 1885 made a strong impression on Tolstoy, who wrote, "God sentenced all of us to death at birth, but when a doctor tells us this, it strikes us as something new."*

PETER RUDY

Tolstoy's Revisions in "The Death of Ivan Ilych"

1965

This constant reminder of impending death spurred Tolstoy's interest in what he called "a description of the ordinary death of an ordinary man." In August 1885 there began a period of intensive work that lasted into October. Thereafter the pace slackened. The story was finally sent to the printer in January 1886, presumably finished. But when Tolstoy received the proofs, he made so many and such extensive changes that the copy returned to the printer amounted to a new draft. It was the latter part of March of that year before the second set of proofs was corrected and the story was ready for publication.

Since "The Death of Ivan Ilych" is so simple in structure and mode of narration, consisting as it does of a death plus a flashback described with almost Biblical simplicity, one might very easily underestimate the effort that this story cost its author. But the truth of the matter is that, after a deceptively smooth beginning, the story went through the myriad adjustments and readjustments that frequently characterized the developmental stages of Tolstoy's fiction. Two main lines of development stand out among the many convolutions: one resulting from a search for a suitable general structure, the other from a desire to give individual narrative elements their proper emphasis.

It was Tolstoy the moralist-artist who conceived the initial general plan of "The Death of Ivan Ilych"; it was Tolstoy the artist-moralist who quickly saw its inadequacies and set about reshaping it. When he started the actual writing, Tolstoy had a very definite didactic purpose in mind: He wanted to warn the Ivan Ilychs of Russia against their self-centered, self-seeking way of life. This purpose determined the general structure of the story in its initial developmental stage. The warning was to be sounded through a dying man's observations about the truth in life, and a diary seemed the ideal framework: The remarks could be of a highly intimate nature and they could range a variety of topics without any need for artificial transitional devices. Some sort of prefatory explanation would, of course, be desirable, and this was to consist of a short introductory section narrated by Mikhail Semyonovich (the future Peter Ivanovich).

At first this general plan seemed satisfactory, and the writing of the introductory section proceeded without any apparent difficulties. Mikhail Semyonovich informs the reader that he learned of Ivan Ilych's death at the courthouse, that he paid a visit to the home of the deceased, and that the widow gave him the dead man's diary. With the introduction out of the way, Tolstoy began the first entry of the diary, the main section. In it the dying Ivan Ilych reveals his "horrible, unbearable spiritual suffering." It is the consciousness of the falsehood in life that torments Ivan: "Everything about me is a lie. My wife is a lie, my children are a lie, and I myself am a lie." But Ivan still aspires toward the truth. And while he yet has the strength, he will try, for his own benefit and that of others, to describe the truth in his diary.

But before he finished this first entry, Tolstoy began to have second thoughts about the main section. His intent was to sound a warning to a sophisticated audience. But had he chosen an effective means for achieving this end? Obviously the readers he wanted to reach would dismiss the diary as a thinly disguised sermon. The project was in danger of becoming self-defeating.

It was at this point that Tolstoy the artist-moralist took firm control and began to alter the main section. He introduced a story element into it. In the final remark of the first diary entry, Ivan Ilych informs the reader that he will first give a description of "how all this happened" to him. Now the plan appeared to be moving in the direction of a pattern that Tolstoy had used successfully in "Lucerne" many years before: A character describes his experiences and follows them with an explicative commentary. But as the newly introduced story element took more definite shape in his imagination, Tolstoy began to realize its potentiality. This story element could, all by itself and without a trace of sermonizing, convey his message with extreme effectiveness. There would first be a review of Ivan Ilych's life from his law school days to the beginning of his illness. During this period of his life Ivan Ilych would be a very obvious middle-class Everyman mirroring the practical values and conventional behavior patterns of the reader. There would, however, be no effort to probe the fundamental issues. A narrative tone of good-natured, mildly mocking humor would merely flit superficially over the surface. The reader would readily admit that this was a witty and agreeable treatment of the sort of life he himself led. And then the hellish nightmare of Ivan Ilych's illness would begin, and, before it was over, the life which the reader had identified with his own would be thoroughly exposed as a horrible sham.

When Tolstoy decided to use this narrative as the main section (and this happened only after an alternative had been considered and discarded), he was forced to drop Ivan Ilych's diary as an expository device: It would hardly be in character for the dying hero to adopt and maintain an urbanely tolerant attitude toward his earlier life when he knew how terribly wrong it had been. As a result, the narrator of the introductory part, Mikhail Semyonovich, also became the narrator of the main section. Tolstoy now has Mikhail inform his readers that he read Ivan Ilych's diary, was horrified by it, collected additional information about his friend, and is now presenting the biographical account that he compiled. But then Tolstoy visualized a dramatic ending in which Ivan Ilych, no longer able to communicate with the world about him, finally arrives at a resolution of his problem. Obviously an omniscient narrator was now necessary for the main section. For the sake of consistency, the same mode of narration had to be used in the introduction, and all references to Ivan Ilych's now superfluous diary had to be eliminated.

One main aspect of the work on "The Death of Ivan Ilych" was, then, a series of changes in the general narrative structure. Frequently proceeding simultaneously with it, and often directly provoked by it, was the other main activity: a gradual, intensive refinement of the component narrative elements. And this refinement consisted of two opposing movements: exclusion and addition.

On the one hand, there was a ruthlessly thorough exclusion of material that, while interesting in itself, would have proved both superfluous and distractive as far as the principal narrative line was concerned. For example, in the first draft of the story, Ivan Ilych, after being passed over for promotion, obtains a position that involves him in a complex of almost Job-like misfortunes; also, a forced and embarrassing stay with unsympathetic relatives is developed at considerable length. The first sequence does not appear in the final draft; the second does, but it is scaled down drastically. Had these changes not been made, the narrative center of gravity in the third section would have been shifted: The image of a man efficiently overcoming all obstacles in pursuit of his ends would have been been badly marred had there been any intimation that Ivan Ilych was, at this point, capable of floundering about under the pressure of circumstances.

On the other hand, the process of refinement consisted of a progressive saturation with detail designed to heighten the intensity of various scenes and to reinforce lines of narrative exposition. Many of the elements that contribute significantly to the effectiveness of the final version are either completely absent from the first draft or else appear there in rudimentary form. The references to the odor of putrefaction in the death chamber and the pathetic figure of Ivan Ilych's son waiting for the service to begin — deft touches used to recreate the atmosphere of death — were later additions. So was the touch of humorous byplay with the recalcitrant pouffe during Peter Ivanovich's visit to the widow, an element that plays a vital role in simulating a "realistic totality." Nor does the first draft contain that initial tantalizing hint in Part I — the "rebuke or reminder to the living" in the face of the dead judge. Ivan Ilych's desire always to belong to the best social circle, his enjoyment of power over people, his impersonal attitude toward others in the performance of his duties, and his use of work as an escape from the unpleasantness of the domestic situation are facets of his behavior that existed in the first version but were built up in significance only over the course of subsequent revisions.

৩৩

LESLIE MARMON SILKO *discussed her view of her audience and her background growing up in a matriarchal society in a lecture titled "Language and Literature from a Pueblo Indian Perspective." It was originally published in* English Literature: Opening Up the Canon *(1979).*

Leslie Marmon Silko

Language and Literature from a Pueblo Indian Perspective

1979

Where I come from, the words that are most highly valued are those which are spoken from the heart, unpremeditated and unrehearsed. Among the Pueblo people, a written speech or statement is highly suspect because the true feelings of the speaker remain hidden as he reads words that are detached from the occasion and the audience. I have intentionally not written a formal paper to read to this session because of this and because I want you to hear and to experience English in a nontraditional structure, a structure that follows patterns from the oral tradition. For those of you accustomed to a structure that moves from point A to point B to point C, this presentation may be somewhat difficult to follow because the structure of Pueblo expression resembles something like a spider's web — with many little threads radiating from a center, crisscrossing each other. As with the web, the structure will emerge as it is made and you must simply listen and trust, as the Pueblo people do, that meaning will be made.

I suppose the task that I have today is a formidable one because basically I come here to ask you, at least for a while, to set aside a number of basic approaches that you have been using and probably will continue to use in approaching the study of English or the study of language; first of all, I come to ask you to see language from the Pueblo perspective, which is a perspective that is very much concerned with including the whole of creation and the whole of history and time. And so we very seldom talk about breaking language down into words. As I will continue to relate to you, even the use of a specific language is less important than the one thing — which is the "telling," or the storytelling. And so, as Simon Ortiz has written, if you approach a Pueblo person and want to talk words or, worse than that, to break down an individual word into its components, ofttimes you will just get a blank stare, because we don't think of words as being isolated from the speaker, which, of course, is one element of the oral tradition. Moreover, we don't think of words as being alone: Words are always with other words, and the other words are almost always in a story of some sort.

Today I have brought a number of examples of stories in English because I would like to get around to the question that has been raised, or the topic that has come along here, which is what changes we Pueblo writers might make with English as a language for literature. But at the same time I would like to explain the importance of storytelling and how it relates to a Pueblo theory of language.

This "essay" is an edited transcript of an oral presentation. The "author" deliberately did not read from a prepared paper so that the audience could experience firsthand one dimension of the oral tradition — nonlinear structure. Her remarks were intended to be heard, not read.

So first I would like to go back to the Pueblo Creation story. The reason I go back to that story is because it is an all-inclusive story of creation and how life began. Tséitsínako, Thought Woman, by thinking of her sisters, and together with her sisters, thought of everything which is, and this world was created. And the belief was that everything in this world was a part of the original creation, and that the people at home realized that far away there were others — other human beings. There is even a section of the story which is a prophesy — which describes the origin of the European race, the African, and also remembers the Asian origins.

Starting out with this story, with this attitude which includes all things, I would like to point out that the reason the people are more concerned with story and communication and less with a particular language is in part an outgrowth of the area [pointing to a map] where we find ourselves. Among the twenty Pueblos there are at least six distinct languages, and possibly seven. Some of the linguists argue — and I don't set myself up to be a linguist at all — about the number of distinct languages. But certainly Zuni is all alone, and Hopi is all alone, and from mesa to mesa there are subtle differences in language — very great differences. I think that this might be the reason that what particular language was being used wasn't as important as what a speaker was trying to say. And this, I think, is reflected and stems or grows out of a particular view of the story — that is, that language *is* story. At Laguna many words have stories which make them. So when one is telling a story, and one is using words to tell the story, each word that one is speaking has a story of its own too. Often the speakers or tellers go into the stories of the words they are using to tell one story so that you get stories within stories, so to speak. This structure becomes very apparent in the storytelling, and what I would like to show you later on by reading some pieces that I brought is that this structure also informs the writing and the stories which are currently coming from Pueblo people. I think what is essential is this sense of story, and story within story, and the idea that one story is only the beginning of many stories, and the sense that stories never truly end. I would like to propose that these views of structure and the dynamics of storytelling are some of the contributions which Native American cultures bring to the English language or at least to literature in the English language.

First of all, a lot of people think of storytelling as something that is done at bedtime — that it is something that is done for small children. When I use the term "storytelling," I include a far wider range of telling activity. I also do not limit storytelling to simply old stories, but to again go back to the original view of creation, which sees that it is all part of a whole; we do not differentiate or fragment stories and experiences. In the beginning, Tséitsínako, Thought Woman, thought of all these things, and all of these things are held together as one holds many things together in a single thought.

So in the telling (and today you will hear a few of the dimensions of this telling) first of all, as was pointed out earlier, the storytelling always includes the audience and the listeners, and, in fact, a great deal of the story is believed to be inside the listener, and the storyteller's role is to draw the story out of the listeners. This kind of shared experience grows out of a strong community base. The storytelling goes on and continues from generation to generation.

The Origin story functions basically as a maker of our identity — with the story we know who we are. We are the Lagunas. This is where we came from. We came this way. We came by this place. And so from the time you are very young, you hear these stories, so that when you go out into the wider world, when one asks who you are, or where are you from, you immediately know: We are the people who came down from the north. We are the people of these stories. It continues down into clans so that you are not just talking about Laguna Pueblo people, you are talking about your own clan. Within the clans there are stories which identify the clan.

In the Creation story, Antelope says that he will help knock a hole in the earth so that the people can come up, out into the next world. Antelope tries and tries, and he uses his hooves and is unable to break through; and it is then that Badger says, "Let me help you." And Badger very patiently uses his claws and digs a way through, bringing the people into the world. When the Badger clan people think of themselves, or when the Antelope people think of themselves, it is as people who are of *this* story, and this is *our* place, and we fit into the very beginning when the people first came, before we began our journey south.

So you can move, then, from the idea of one's identity as a tribal person into clan identity. Then we begin to get to the extended family, and this is where we begin to get a kind of story coming into play which some people might see as a different kind of story, though Pueblo people do not. Anthropologists and ethnologists have, for a long time, differentiated the types of oral language they find in the Pueblos. They tended to rule out all but the old and sacred and traditional stories and were not interested in family stories and the family's account of itself. But these family stories are just as important as the other stories — the older stories. These family stories are given equal recognition. There is no definite, pre-set pattern for the way one will hear the stories of one's own family, but it is a very critical part of one's childhood, and it continues on throughout one's life. You will hear stories of importance to the family — sometimes wonderful stories — stories about the time a maternal uncle got the biggest deer that was ever seen and brought back from the mountains. And so one's sense of who the family is, and who you are, will then extend from that — "I am from the family of my uncle who brought in this wonderful deer, and it was a wonderful hunt" — so you have this sort of building or sense of identity.

There are also other stories, stories about the time when another uncle, perhaps, did something that wasn't really acceptable. In other words, this process of keeping track, of telling, is an all-inclusive process which begins to create a total picture. So it is very important that you know all of the stories — both positive and not so positive — about one's own family. The reason that it is very important to keep track of all the stories in one's own family is because you are liable to hear a story from somebody else who is perhaps an enemy of the family, and you are liable to hear a version which has been changed, a version which makes your family sound disreputable — something that will taint the honor of the family. But if you have already heard the story, you know your family's version of what *really* happened that night, so when somebody else is mentioning it, you will have a version of the story to counterbalance it. Even when there is no way around it — old Uncle Pete did a terrible thing — by knowing the stories that come out of other families, by keeping very close watch, listening constantly to learn the stories about other families, one is in a sense able to deal with terrible sorts of things that might happen within one's own family. When a member of one's own family does something that cannot be excused, one always knows stories about similar things which happened in other families. And it is not done maliciously. I think it is very important to realize this. Keeping track of all the stories within the community gives a certain distance, a useful perspective which brings incidents down to a level we can deal with. If others have done it before, it cannot be so terrible. If others have endured, so can we.

The stories are always bringing us together, keeping this whole together, keeping this family together, keeping this clan together. "Don't go away, don't isolate yourself, but come here, because we have all had these kinds of experiences" — this is what the people are saying to you when they tell you these other stories. And so there is this constant pulling together to resist what seems to me to be a basic part of human nature: When some violent emotional experience takes place, people get the urge to run off and hide or separate themselves from others. And of course, if we do that, we are not only talking about endangering the group, we are also talking about the individual or the individual family never being able to recover or to survive. Inherent in this belief is the feeling that one does not recover or get well by one's self, but it is together that we look after each other and take care of each other.

In the storytelling, then, we see this process of bringing people together, and it works not only on the family level, but also on the level of the individual. Of course, the whole Pueblo concept of the individual is a little bit different from the usual Western concept of the individual. But one of the beauties of the storytelling is that when something happens to an individual, many people will come to you and take you aside, or maybe a couple of people will come and talk to you. These are occasions of storytelling. These occasions of storytelling are continuous; they are a way of life.

Storytelling lies at the heart of the Pueblo people, and so when someone comes in and says, "When did they tell the stories, or what time of day does the storytelling take place?" that is a ridiculous question. The storytelling goes on constantly — as some old grandmother puts on the shoes of a little child and tells the child the story of a little girl who didn't wear her shoes. At the same time somebody comes into the house for coffee to talk with an adolescent boy who has just been into a lot of trouble, to reassure him that *he* got into that kind of trouble, or somebody else's son got into that kind of trouble too. You have this constant ongoing process, working on many different levels.

One of the stories I like to bring up about helping the individual in crisis is a recent story, and I want to remind you that we make no distinctions between the stories — whether they are history, whether they are fact, whether they are gossip — these distinctions are not useful when we are talking about this particular experience with language. Anyway, there was a young man who, when he came back from the war in Vietnam, had saved up his Army pay and bought a beautiful red Volkswagen Beetle. He was very proud of it, and one night drove up to a place right across the reservation line. It is a very notorious place for many reasons, but one of the more notorious things about the place is a deep arroyo behind the place. This is the King's Bar. So he ran in to pick up a cold six-pack to take home, but he didn't put on his emergency brake. And his little red Volkswagen rolled back into the arroyo and was all smashed up. He felt very bad about it, but within a few days everybody had come to him and told him stories about other people who had lost cars to that arroyo. And probably the story that made him feel the best was about the time that George Day's station wagon, with his mother-in-law and kids in the back, rolled into that arroyo. So everybody was saying, "Well, at least your mother-in-law and kids weren't in the car when it rolled in," and you can't argue with that kind of story. He felt better then because he wasn't alone anymore. He and his smashed-up Volkswagen were now joined with all the other stories of cars that fell into that arroyo.

There are a great many parallels between Pueblo experiences and the remarks that have been made about South Africa and the Caribbean countries — similarities in experiences so far as language is concerned. More specifically, with the experience of English being imposed upon the people. The Pueblo people, of course, have seen intruders come and intruders go. The first they watched come were the Spaniards; while the Spaniards were there, things had to be conducted in Spanish. But as the old stories say, if you wait long enough, they'll go. And sure enough, they went. Then another bunch came in. And old stories say, well, if you wait around long enough, not so much that they'll go, but at least their ways will go. One wonders now, when you see what's happening to technocratic-industrial culture, now that we've used up most of the sources of energy, you think perhaps the old people are right.

But anyhow, our experience with English has been different because the Bureau of Indian Affairs schools were so terrible that we never heard of Shakespeare. There was Dick and Jane, and I can remember reading that the robins were heading south for winter, but I knew that all winter the robins were around Laguna. It took me a long time to figure out what was going on. I worried for quite a while about the robins because they didn't leave in the winter, not realizing that the textbooks were written in Boston. The big textbook companies are up here in Boston and *their* robins do go south in the winter. But this freed us and encouraged us to stay with our narratives. Whatever literature we received at school (which was damn little), at home the storytelling, the special regard for telling and bringing together through the telling, was going on constantly. It has continued, and so we have a great body of classical oral literature, both in the narratives and in the chants and songs.

As the old people say, "If you can remember the stories, you will be all right. Just remember the stories." And, of course, usually when they say that to you, when you are young, you wonder what in the world they mean. But when I returned — I had been away from Laguna Pueblo for a couple of years, well more than a couple of years after college and so forth — I returned to Laguna and I went to Laguna-Acoma high school to visit an English class, and I was wondering how the telling was continuing, because Laguna Pueblo, as the anthropologists have said, is one of the more acculturated pueblos. So I walked into this high school English class and there they were sitting, these very beautiful Laguna and Acoma kids. But I knew that out in their lockers they had cassette tape recorders, and I knew that at home they had stereos, and they were listening to Kiss and Led Zeppelin and all those other things. I was almost afraid, but I had to ask — I had with me a book of short fiction (it's called *The Man to Send Rain Clouds* [New York: Viking Press, 1974]), and among the stories of other Native American writers, it has stories that I have written and Simon Ortiz has written. And there is one particular story in the book about the killing of a state policeman in New Mexico by three Acoma Pueblo men. It was an act that was committed in the early fifties. I was afraid to ask, but I had to. I looked at the class and I said, "How many of you heard this story before you read it in the book?" And I was prepared to hear this crushing truth that indeed the anthropologists were right about the old traditions dying out. But it was amazing, you know, almost all but one or two students raised their hands. They had heard that story, just as Simon and I had heard it, when we were young. That was my first indication that storytelling continues on. About half of them had heard it in English, about half of them had heard it in Laguna. I think again, getting back to one of the original statements, that if you begin to look at the core of the importance of the language and how it fits in with the culture, it is the *story* and the feeling of the story which matters more than what language it's told in.

৩৫

JANE SMILEY *prefaced her view of "Gregor: My Life as a Bug," published in* Harper's Magazine *in August 1992, with three sentences summarizing the events of Kafka's story "The Metamorphosis."*

JANE SMILEY

Gregor: My Life as a Bug   1992

After some strenuous months of adjusting to and caring for the "giant dung beetle" that has unaccountably replaced their son, Gregor, the Samsa family have gone away to the country, to get some fresh air and plan for the future. The lodgers who precipitated the crisis are gone, as is the cleaning lady who has been "looking after" Gregor for the last few weeks. Gregor himself, much desiccated and weakened, but alive, has been carried out to the dustheap to ponder his metamorphosis.

• • •

All day, though sunk deeply in the stupor of profound physical weakness, Gregor had sensed the light beyond his eyelids, woven into his dreams, as it were, in the form of an uneasy awareness that soon he would wake up, that soon, all too soon, he wouldn't be able to avoid that, but it was only at dusk that he actually did rise to consciousness, and beheld the now familiar sight of his domed belly and his numerous helpless little legs glinting in the roseate shafts of sunlight that lengthened from the west down the otherwise dreary stretch of alley that ran behind the row of apartment houses.

The cleaning lady, practical and straightforward in her way, had not been much of a diagnostician and even less of an entomologist — what could she know, without education? — but the Samsas had willingly, perhaps even eagerly, accepted her certification of Gregor's death. Gregor had, too (had he not?), so disheartened was he by his sister's revulsion (you couldn't hide such a thing, a physical reaction like that, that much was crystal clear). Nor could you, Gregor reflected, die by wishing to. All too often, you had to wake up and live on. Make the best of things. Focus on the little physical pleasures of moving and eating and feeling a bit of a breeze and try to get through the rest.

With practiced ease, but somewhat slowed by lingering weakness, Gregor rolled from his back to his thorax, and lifted himself on legs that trembled but held. The dust and dirt that the cleaning lady had thrown out with him shifted and slid off his shining shell. His long feet sank into the dust, but it wasn't that hard to pull himself upward, nibbling a rind of cheese and a stale bit of cake and a brown apple core as he went. Slowly — it didn't matter; by himself, with none of that sense of anxiety that his parents and sister had communicated to him for the last months, he could move as he wished. And in the dark, too. The sunset had faded and a warm redolent breeze came to his proboscis. He got to the apex of the dustheap and remembered an advertising slogan he had seen once for a sleeping nostrum — "Knit up the ravelled sleeve of care! — with Levy's Sleeping Draught! You'll feel better in the morning!" And he did feel better, no two ways about that. Now when he thought of his sister's reaction, well, it was her problem. Clearly, out here in the alley, he had problems of his own.

He smelled, as much as saw, the delicious odor of some rotting meat — mutton, it was — but when he stepped toward it, he toppled alarmingly forward, and then, unable to catch his balance, fell farther forward until he found himself rolling head over tail down the other side of the dustheap. He did manage to pick up the bit of mutton as he went, but only at the cost of painfully wrenching his back plates. Then he rolled out onto the cobblestones, and that was unpleasant, too — bruising his head and sides, making him ache all over, in fact. But the mutton was delicious. The thing was just to enjoy it, enjoy it at his leisure, the way they had never let him do during his whole life. And he did — he relished it bite by bite, concentrating, forgetting the pain, focusing on the pleasure.

The cobblestones were big as well as hard — how did people walk on these cobblestones? — they were like hills! What were the town's engineers thinking of, building streets like this — surely people would complain. You had to walk between them, along the seams, if you wanted to get anywhere.

Gregor shook himself, and then made his way slowly, exploring with his feelers. It was a puzzle indeed, how the town had changed this way, and then he passed a large metal cavern, dark but square-shaped and raised off the stone — clearly not a door, looking more than anything like a drainpipe, but so extraordinarily large! Gregor marveled.

And then he realized. He was not nearly so large himself as they had made him out to be. Well, that was typical of them, the way they had always magnified problems. Any little change was monstrous to them. They were fearful people. He had known that, especially his mother, and his father wasn't any better, even though he hid his fear with anger. But it was hard, living at home, not to react the way they expected you to react. Well, now that was his sister's concern, too.

He skittered with great speed and grace between the cobblestones, stopping to drink from a puddle. Cool, refreshing. The sleep and food had perked him right up.

The thing was, they weren't bad people, he could see that. They did their best, given their fears, given how housebound they were — his own fears, too, why not admit that? He had expected them to change, but he hadn't really had the guts to *make* them change. It had all stayed more or less the same — everything unspoken, everything dictated by habit and duty. What did it matter, really, whether he was serving them, as he had when he was working, or they were serving him? Just the same tangle of anxiety and pressure and obligation and tedium. Sure, love was somewhere in there, but you had to get away to find it.

A silver light swelled over the cobblestones, and Gregor looked up to see the moon, calm and full as a plate, pause over his alley. He hadn't seen it in months, since before his "metamorphosis." It was different now, though, not flat but full of facets like a giant diamond. He lifted his back pair of legs and gave a triumphant buzz of joy. Sure the world held dangers, but hell, so what? What was that compared to setting out? Compared to the actual, authentic, bona fide transformation that lay ahead of him now?

Gregor looked up at the building. Perhaps those were his family's windows, just lighting up there on the third floor, as they returned from wherever they had been. He hoped they felt better. He wanted only good things for them, after all. He gazed for a moment, then raised his proboscis in a single salute. He was off now, down the alley to the street, and to many streets beyond. He stretched his young body, and headed down the road between the cobblestones.

ରଓ

LEO TOLSTOY *wrote his commentary on "The Darling" a year after his friend Anton Chekhov's death as a way of protesting what Tolstoy considered an unfair caricature of a simple, good-hearted woman, the central character in the story. That Tolstoy experienced such a strong emotional affinity with Chekhov's fictional heroine that he felt compelled to defend her is a striking testimony to Chekhov's power as a short story writer and to Tolstoy's obsessive concern with morality. Tolstoy's ar-*

gument is essentially based on the point of view of the patriarch. Chekhov's point of view in the story is much more subtle. His narrative has prompted other, very different interpretations, as evidenced by Eudora Welty's reading (see p. 811–813).

LEO TOLSTOY

Chekhov's Intent in "The Darling"   1905

TRANSLATED BY CONSTANCE GARNETT

There is a story of profound meaning in the Book of Numbers which tells how Balak, the King of the Moabites, sent for the prophet Balaam to curse the Israelites who were on his borders. Balak promised Balaam many gifts for this service, and Balaam, tempted, went to Balak, and went with him up the mountain, where an altar was prepared with calves and sheep sacrificed in readiness for the curse. Balak waited for the curse, but instead of cursing, Balaam blessed the people of Israel.

> And Balak said unto Balaam, What hast thou done unto me? I took thee to curse mine enemies, and, behold, thou hast blessed them altogether.
> And he answered and said, Must I not take heed to speak that which the Lord hath put in my mouth?
> And Balak said unto him, Come, I pray thee, with me into another place . . . and curse me them from thence.
> But again, instead of cursing, Balaam blessed. And so it was the third time also.
> And Balak's anger was kindled against Balaam, and he smote his hands together: And Balak said unto Balaam, I called thee to curse my enemies, and, behold, thou hast altogether blessed them these three times.
> Therefore now flee thee to thy place: I thought to promote thee unto great honour; but, lo, the Lord hast kept thee back from honour.
> And so Balaam departed without having received the gifts, because, instead of cursing, he had blessed the enemies of Balak. [Numbers 23: 11–13; 24:10–11]

What happened to Balaam often happens to real poets and artists. Tempted by Balak's gifts, popularity, or by false preconceived ideas, the poet does not see the angel barring his way, though the ass sees him, and he means to curse, and yet, behold, he blesses.

This is just what happened to the true poet and artist Chekhov when he wrote this charming story "The Darling."

The author evidently means to mock at the pitiful creature — as he judges her with his intellect, but not with his heart — the Darling, who after first sharing Kukin's anxiety about his theater, then throwing herself into the interests of the timber trade, then under the influence of the veterinary surgeon regarding the campaign against the foot and mouth disease as the most important matter in the world, is finally engrossed in the grammatical questions and the interests of the little schoolboy in the big cap. Kukin's surname is absurd, even his illness and the telegram announcing his death, the timber merchant with his respectability, the veterinary surgeon, even the boy — all are absurd, but the soul of the Darling, with her faculty of devoting herself with her whole being to any one she loves, is not absurd, but marvelous and holy.

I believe that while he was writing "The Darling," the author had in his mind, though not in his heart, a vague image of a new woman; of her equality with man; of a woman mentally developed, learned, working independently for the good of society as well as, if not better than, a man; of the woman who has raised and upholds the woman question; and in writing "The Darling" he wanted to show what woman ought not to be. The Balak of public opinion bade Chekhov curse the weak, submissive undeveloped woman devoted to man; and Chekhov went up the mountain, and the calves and sheep were laid upon the altar, but when he began to speak, the poet blessed what he had come to curse. In spite of its exquisite gay humor, I at least cannot read without tears some passages of this wonderful story. I am touched by the description of her complete devotion and love for Kukin and all that he cares for, and for the timber merchant and for the veterinary surgeon, and even more of her sufferings when she is left alone and has no one to love; and finally the account of how with all the strength of womanly, motherly feelings (of which she has no experience in her own life) she devotes herself with boundless love to the future man, the schoolboy in the big cap.

The author makes her love the absurd Kukin, the insignificant timber merchant, and the unpleasant veterinary surgeon, but love is no less sacred whether its object is a Kukin or a Spinoza, a Pascal, or a Schiller,° and whether the objects of it change as rapidly as with the Darling, or whether the object of it remains the same throughout the whole life.

Some time ago I happened to read in the *Novoe Vremya* an excellent article upon woman. The author has in this article expressed a remarkably clever and profound idea about woman. "Women," he says, "are trying to show us they can do everything we men can do. I don't contest it; I am prepared to admit women can do everything men can do, and possibly better than men; but the trouble is that men cannot do anything faintly approaching to what women can do."

Yes, that is undoubtedly true, and it is true not only with regard to birth, nurture, and early education of children. Men cannot do that highest, best work which brings man nearest to God — the work of love, and complete devotion to the loved object, which good women have done, do, and will do so well and so naturally. What would become of the world, what would become of us men if women had not that faculty and did not exercise it? We could get on without women doctors, women telegraph clerks, women lawyers, women

---

Spinoza ... Schiller: Baruch Spinoza (1632–1677), Dutch philosopher; Blaise Pascal (1623–1662), French scientist and philosopher; Johann Christoph Friedrich von Schiller (1759–1805), German poet, playwright, and critic.

scientists, women writers, but life would be a sorry affair without mothers, helpers, friends, comforters, who love in men the best in them, and imperceptibly instill, evoke, and support it. There would have been no Magdalen with Christ, no Claire with St. Francis; there would have been no wives of the Dekabrists° in Siberia; there would not have been among the Duhobors° those wives who, instead of holding their husbands back, supported them in their martyrdom for truth; there would not have been those thousands and thousands of unknown women — the best of all, as the unknown always are — the comforters of the drunken, the weak, and the dissolute, who, more than any, need the comfort of love. That love, whether devoted to a Kukin or to Christ, is the chief, grand, unique strength of woman.

What an amazing misunderstanding it is — all this so-called woman question, which, as every vulgar idea is bound to do, has taken possession of the majority of women, and even of men.

"Woman longs to improve herself" — what can be more legitimate and just than that?

But a woman's work is from her very vocation different from man's, and so the ideal of feminine perfection cannot be the same as the ideal of masculine perfection. Let us admit that we do not know what that ideal is; it is quite certain in any case that it is not the ideal of masculine perfection. And yet it is to the attainment of that masculine ideal that the whole and the absurd and evil activity of the fashionable woman movement, which is such a stumbling-block to woman, is directed.

I am afraid that Chekhov was under the influence of that misunderstanding when he wrote "The Darling."

He, like Balaam, intended to curse, but the god of poetry forbade him, and commanded him to bless. And he did bless, and unconsciously clothed this sweet creature in such an exquisite radiance that she will always remain a type of what a woman can be in order to be happy herself, and to make the happiness of those with whom destiny throws her.

What makes the story so excellent is that the effect is unintentional.

I learned to ride a bicycle in a hall large enough to drill a division of soldiers. At the other end of the hall a lady was learning. I thought I must be careful to avoid getting into her way, and began looking at her. And as I looked at her I began unconsciously getting nearer and nearer to her, and in spite of the fact that, noticing the danger, she hastened to retreat, I rode down upon her and knocked her down — that is, I did the very opposite of what I wanted to do, simply because I concentrated my attention upon her.

The same thing has happened to Chekhov, but in an inverse sense: He wanted to knock the Darling down, and concentrating upon her the close attention of the poet, he raised her up.

ᛒᛒ

Dekabrists: Members of the unsuccessful December 1825 uprising against Czar Nicholas I.
Duhobors: Members of the Christian sect that advocated following inner spirituality instead of church or government doctrine.

JOHN UPDIKE *wrote a foreword to* The Complete Stories of Franz Kafka *in 1983. Updike begins his essay by quoting "He," one of Kafka's aphorisms: "All that he does seems to him, it is true, extraordinarily new, but also, because of the incredible spate of new things, extraordinarily amateurish, indeed scarcely tolerable, incapable of becoming history, breaking short the chain of the generations, cutting off for the first time at its most profound source the music of the world, which before him could at least be divined. Sometimes in his arrogance he has more anxiety for the world than for himself." Updike has great sympathy for Kafka and has written about him with considerable perception.*

JOHN UPDIKE

Kafka and "The Metamorphosis"   1983

The century since Franz Kafka was born has been marked by the idea of "modernism" — a self-consciousness new among centuries, a consciousness of being new. Sixty years after his death, Kafka epitomizes one aspect of this modern mind-set: a sensation of anxiety and shame whose center cannot be located and therefore cannot be placated; a sense of an infinite difficulty within things, impeding every step; a sensitivity acute beyond usefulness, as if the nervous system, flayed of its old hide of social usage and religious belief, must record every touch as pain. In Kafka's peculiar and highly original case this dreadful quality is mixed with immense tenderness, oddly good humor, and a certain severe and reassuring formality. The combination makes him an artist; but rarely can an artist have struggled against greater inner resistance and more sincere diffidence as to the worth of his art. . . .

Kafka dated his own maturity as a writer from the long night of September 22nd–23rd, 1912, in which he wrote "The Judgment" at a single eight-hour sitting. He confided to his diary that morning, "Only *in this way* can writing be done, only with such coherence, with such a complete opening out of the body and the soul." Yet the story is not quite free of the undeclared neurotic elements that twist the earlier work; the connection between the engagement and the father seems obscure, and the old man's fury illogical. But in staring at, with his hero Georg, "the bogey conjured up by his father," Kafka broke through to a great cavern of stored emotion. He loved this story, and among friends praised — he who deprecated almost everything from his own pen — its *Zweifellosigkeit*, its "indubitableness." Soon after its composition, he wrote, in a few weeks, "The Metamorphosis," an indubitable masterpiece. It begins with a fantastic premise, whereas in "The Judgment" events become fantastic. This premise — the gigantic insect — established in the first sentence, "The Metamorphosis" unfolds with a beautiful naturalness and a classic economy. It takes place in three acts: three times the metamorphosed Gregor Samsa ventures out of his room, with tumultuous results. The members of his family — rather simpler than Kafka's own, which had three sisters

— dispose themselves around the central horror with a touching, as well as an amusing, plausibility. The father's fury, roused in defense of the fragile mother, stems directly from the action and inflicts a psychic wound gruesomely objectified in the rotting apple Gregor carries in his back; the evolutions of the sister, Grete, from shock to distasteful ministration to a certain sulky possessiveness and finally to exasperated indifference are beautifully sketched, with not a stroke too much. The terrible but terribly human tale ends with Grete's own metamorphosis, into a comely young woman. This great story resembles a great story of the nineteenth century, Tolstoy's "The Death of Ivan Ilych"; in both, a hitherto normal man lies hideously, suddenly stricken in the midst of a family whose irritated, banal daily existence flows around him. The abyss within life is revealed, but also life itself.

What kind of insect is Gregor? Popular belief has him a cockroach, which would be appropriate for a city apartment; and the creature's retiring nature and sleazy dietary preferences would seem to conform. But, as Vladimir Nabokov, who knew his entomology, pointed out in his lectures upon "The Metamorphosis" at Cornell University, Gregor is too broad and convex to be a cockroach. The charwoman calls him a "dung beetle" (*Mistkäfer*) but, Nabokov said, "it is obvious that the good woman is adding the epithet only to be friendly." Kafka's Eduard Raban of "Wedding Preparations" daydreams, walking along, "As I lie in bed I assume the shape of a big beetle, a stag beetle or a cockchafer, I think." Gregor Samsa, awaking, sees "numerous legs, which were pitifully thin compared to the rest of his bulk." If "numerous" is more than six, he must be a centipede — not an insect at all. From evidence in the story he is brown in color and about as long as the distance between a doorknob and the floor; he is broader than half a door. He has a voice at first, "but with a persistent horrible twittering squeak behind it like an undertone," which disappears as the story progresses. His jaws don't work as ours do but he has eyelids, nostrils, and a neck. He is, in short, impossible to picture except when the author wants to evoke his appearance, to bump the reader up against some astounding, poignant new aspect of Gregor's embodiment. The strange physical discomfort noted in the earlier work is here given its perfect allegorical envelope. A wonderful moment comes when Gregor, having been painfully striving to achieve human postures, drops to his feet:

> Hardly was he down when he experienced for the first time this morning a sense of physical comfort; his legs had firm ground under them; they were completely obedient, as he noted with joy; they even strove to carry him forward in whatever direction he chose; and he was inclined to believe that a final relief from all his sufferings was at hand.

When "The Metamorphosis" was to be published as a book in 1915, Kafka, fearful that the cover illustrator "might want to draw the insect itself," wrote the publisher, "Not that, please not that! . . . The insect itself cannot be depicted. It cannot even be shown from a distance." He suggested instead a scene of the family in the apartment with a locked door, or a door open and giving on darkness. Any theatrical or cinematic version of the story must founder on this point of external representation: A concrete image of the insect would be too distracting and shut off sympathy; such a version would lack the very heart of comedy and pathos which beats in the unsteady area between objective and subjective, where Gregor's insect and human selves swayingly struggle. Still half-asleep, he notes his extraordinary condition yet persists in remembering and trying to fulfill his duties as a travelling salesman and the mainstay of this household. Later, relegated by the family to the shadows of a room turned storage closet, he responds to violin music and creeps forward, covered with dust and trailing remnants of food, to claim his sister's love. Such scenes could not be done except with words. In this age that lives and dies by the visual, "The Metamorphosis" stands as a narrative absolutely literary, able to exist only where language and the mind's hazy wealth of imagery intersect.

　　"The Metamorphosis" stands also as a gateway to the world Kafka created after it. His themes and manner were now all in place. His mastery of official pomposity — the dialect of documents and men talking business — shows itself here for the first time, in the speeches of the chief clerk. Music will again be felt, by mice and dogs, as an overwhelming emanation in Kafka's later fables — a theme whose other side is the extreme sensitivity to noise, and the longing for unblemished silence, that Kafka shared with his hero in "The Burrow." Gregor's death scene, and Kafka's death wish, return in "A Hunger Artist" — the saddest, I think, of Kafka's stories, written by a dying man who was increasingly less sanguine (his correspondence reveals) about dying. The sweeping nature of the hunger artist's abstention is made plain by the opposing symbol of the panther who replaces him in his cage: "the joy of life streamed with such ardent passion from his throat that for the onlookers it was not easy to stand the shock of it." In 1920 Milena Jesenská wrote to Brod: "Frank cannot live. Frank does not have the capacity for living. . . . He is absolutely incapable of living, just as he is incapable of getting drunk. He possesses not the slightest refuge. For that reason he is exposed to all those things against which we are protected. He is like a naked man among a multitude who are dressed." After Gregor Samsa's incarnation, Kafka showed a fondness for naked heroes — animals who have complicated and even pedantic confessions to make but who also are distinguished by some keenly observed bestial traits — the ape of "A Report to an Academy" befouls himself and his fur jumps with fleas; the dog of "Investigations" recalls his young days when, very puppylike, "I believed that great things were going on around me of which I was the leader and to which I must lend my voice, things which must be wretchedly thrown aside if I did not run for them and wag my tail for them"; the mouse folk of "Josephine the Singer" pipe and multiply and are pervaded by an "unexpended, ineradicable childishness"; and the untaxonomic inhabitant of "The Burrow" represents the animal in all of us, his cheerful consumption of "small fry" existentially yoked to a terror of being consumed himself. An uncanny empathy broods above these zoömorphs, and invests them with more of their creator's soul than all but a few human characters receive. So a child, cowed and bored by the world of human adults, makes companions of pets and toy animals.

ALICE WALKER *wrote about Zora Neale Hurston in her collection* In Search of Our Mothers' Gardens: Womanist Prose *(1983). There she also looked at Flannery O'Connor, Langston Hughes, Jean Toomer, and other writers from what she called her "womanist" perspective as a radical black woman. To clarify the meaning of her term, Walker added that "womanist is to feminist as purple is to lavender."*

ALICE WALKER

Zora Neale Hurston: A Cautionary Tale and a Partisan View

1979

During the early and middle years of her career Zora was a cultural revolutionary simply because she was always herself. Her work, so vigorous among the rather pallid productions of many of her contemporaries, comes from the essence of black folk life. During her later life she became frightened of the life she had always dared bravely before. Her work too became reactionary, static, shockingly misguided and timid. (This is especially true of her last novel, *Seraphs on the Sewannee*, which is not even about black people, which is no crime, but *is* about white people for whom it is impossible to care, which is.)

A series of misfortunes battered Zora's spirit and her health. And she was broke.

Being broke made all the difference.

Without money of one's own in a capitalist society, there is no such thing as independence. This is one of the clearest lessons of Zora's life, and why I consider the telling of her life "a cautionary tale." We must learn from it what we can.

Without money, an illness, even a simple one, can undermine the will. Without money, getting into a hospital is problematic and getting out without money to pay for the treatment is nearly impossible. Without money, one becomes dependent on other people, who are likely to be — even in their kindness — erratic in their support and despotic in their expectations of return. Zora was forced to rely, like Tennessee Williams's Blanche,° "on the kindness of strangers." Can anything be more dangerous, if the strangers are forever in control? Zora, who worked so hard, was never able to make a living from her work.

She did not complain about not having money. She was not the type. (Several months ago I received a long letter from one of Zora's nieces, a bright ten-year-old, who explained to me that her aunt was so proud that the only way the family could guess she was ill or without funds was by realizing they

---

Tennessee Williams's Blanche: Neurotic Southern belle in Williams's play *A Streetcar Named Desire* (1947).

had no idea where she was. Therefore, none of the family attended either Zora's sickbed or her funeral.) Those of us who have had "grants and fellowships from 'white folks' " know this aid is extended in precisely the way welfare is extended in Mississippi. One is asked, *curtly,* more often than not: How much do you need *just to survive?* Then one is — if fortunate — given a third of that. What is amazing is that Zora, who became an orphan at nine, a runaway at fourteen, a maid and manicurist (because of necessity and not from love of the work) before she was twenty — with one dress — managed to become Zora Neale Hurston, author and anthropologist, at all.

For me, the most unfortunate thing Zora ever wrote is her autobiography. After the first several chapters, it rings false. One begins to hear the voice of someone whose life required the assistance of too many transitory "friends." A Taoist proverb states that *to act sincerely with the insincere is dangerous.* (A mistake blacks as a group have tended to make in America.) And so we have Zora sincerely offering gratitude and kind words to people one knows she could not have respected. But this unctuousness, so out of character for Zora, is also a result of dependency, a sign of her powerlessness, her inability to pay back her debts with anything but words. They must have been bitter ones for her. In her dependency, it should be remembered, Zora was not alone — because it is quite true that America does not support or honor us as human beings, let alone as blacks, women, and artists. We have taken help where it was offered because we are committed to what we do and to the survival of our work. Zora was committed to the survival of her people's cultural heritage as well.

In my mind, Zora Neale Hurston, Billie Holiday,° and Bessie Smith° form a sort of unholy trinity. Zora *belongs* in the tradition of black women singers, rather than among "the literati," at least to me. There were the extreme highs and lows of her life, her undaunted pursuit of adventure, passionate emotional and sexual experience, and her love of freedom. Like Billie and Bessie she followed her own road, believed in her own gods, pursued her own dreams, and refused to separate herself from "common" people. It would have been nice if the three of them had had one another to turn to, in times of need. I close my eyes and imagine them: Bessie would be in charge of all the money; Zora would keep Billie's masochistic tendencies in check and prevent her from singing embarrassing anything-for-a-man songs, thereby preventing Billie's heroin addiction. In return, Billie could be, along with Bessie, the family that Zora felt she never had.

We are a people. A people do not throw their geniuses away. And if they are thrown away, it is our duty *as artists and as witnesses for the future* to collect them again for the sake of our children, and, if necessary, bone by bone.

ಬಿಬಿ

Billie Holiday: African American jazz singer (1915–1959) known for her pioneering vocal style and tragic life.
Bessie Smith: Prominent African American blues singer and song writer (1898–1937), the highest paid black artist in the United States in the 1920s.

EUDORA WELTY *included this discussion of her story "The Worn Path" in her book* The Eye of the Story *(1977). It appeared in the section "On Writing," along with her most extensive essays on the art of short fiction — essays that take up general topics such as place and time in fiction and the art of reading and writing stories. Her reviews of the work of Isak Dinesen, Ralph Ellison, William Faulkner, and Virginia Woolf from the* New York Times *are also included in this collection.*

EUDORA WELTY

Is Phoenix Jackson's Grandson Really Dead?

1977

A story writer is more than happy to be read by students; the fact that these serious readers think and feel something in response to his work he finds life-giving. At the same time he may not always be able to reply to their specific questions in kind. I wondered if it might clarify something, for both the questioners and myself, if I set down a general reply to the question that comes to me most often in the mail, from both students and their teachers, after some classroom discussion. The unrivaled favorite is this: "Is Phoenix Jackson's grandson really *dead?*"

It refers to a short story I wrote years ago called "A Worn Path," which tells of a day's journey an old woman makes on foot from deep in the country into town and into a doctor's office on behalf of her little grandson; he is at home, periodically ill, and periodically she comes for his medicine; they give it to her as usual, she receives it and starts the journey back.

I had not meant to mystify readers by withholding any fact; it is not a writer's business to tease. The story is told through Phoenix's mind as she undertakes her errand. As the author at one with the character as I tell it, I must assume that the boy is alive. As the reader, you are free to think as you like, of course: The story invites you to believe that no matter what happens, Phoenix for as long as she is able to walk and can hold to her purpose will make her journey. The *possibility* that she would keep on even if he were dead is there in her devotion and its single-minded, single-track errand. Certainly the *artistic* truth, which should be good enough for the fact, lies in Phoenix's own answer to that question. When the nurse asks, "He isn't dead, is he?" she speaks for herself: "He still the same. He going to last."

The grandchild is the incentive. But it is the journey, the going of the errand, that is the story, and the question is not whether the grandchild is in reality alive or dead. It doesn't affect the outcome of the story or its meaning from start to finish. But it is not the question itself that has struck me as much as the idea, almost without exception implied in the asking, that for Phoenix's grandson to be dead would somehow make the story "better."

It's *all right*, I want to say to the students who write to me, for things to be what they appear to be, and for words to mean what they say. It's all right, too, for words and appearances to mean more than one thing — ambiguity is a fact of life. A fiction writer's responsibility covers not only what he presents as the facts of a given story but what he chooses to stir up as their implications; in the end, these implications, too, become facts, in the larger, fictional sense. But it is not all right, not in good faith, for things *not* to mean what they say.

The grandson's plight was real and it made the truth of the story, which is the story of an errand of love carried out. If the child no longer lived, the truth would persist in the "wornness" of the path. But his being dead can't increase the truth of the story, can't affect it one way or the other. I think I signal this, because the end of the story has been reached before old Phoenix gets home again: she simply starts back. To the question "Is the grandson really dead?" I could reply that it doesn't make any difference. I could also say that I did not make him up in order to let him play a trick on Phoenix. But my best answer would be: *"Phoenix is alive."*

The origin of a story is sometimes a trustworthy clue to the author — or can provide him with the clue — to its key image; maybe in this case it will do the same for the reader. One day I saw a solitary old woman like Phoenix. She was walking; I saw her, at middle distance, in a winter country landscape, and watched her slowly make her way across my line of vision. That sight of her made me write the story. I invented an errand for her, but that only seemed a living part of the figure she was herself: What errand other than for someone else could be making her go? And her going was the first thing, her persisting in her landscape was the real thing, and the first and the real were what I wanted and worked to keep. I brought her up close enough, by imagination, to describe her face, make her present to the eyes, but the full-length figure moving across the winter fields was the indelible one and the image to keep, and the perspective extending into the vanishing distance the true one to hold in mind.

I invented for my character, as I wrote, some passing adventures — some dreams and harassments and a small triumph or two, some jolts to her pride, some flights of fancy to console her, one or two encounters to scare her, a moment that gave her cause to feel ashamed, a moment to dance and preen — for it had to be a *journey*, and all these things belonged to that, parts of life's uncertainty.

A narrative line is in its deeper sense, of course, the tracing out of a meaning, and the real continuity of a story lies in this probing forward. The real dramatic force of a story depends on the strength of the emotion that has set it going. The emotional value is the measure of the reach of the story. What gives any such content to "A Worn Path" is not its circumstances but its *subject:* the deep-grained habit of love.

What I hoped would come clear was that in the whole surround of this story, the world it threads through, the only certain thing at all is the worn path. The habit of love cuts through confusion and stumbles or contrives its way out of difficulty, it remembers the way even when it forgets, for a dumfounded moment, its reason for being. The path is the thing that matters.

Her victory — old Phoenix's — is when she sees the diploma in the doctor's office, when she finds "nailed up on the wall the document that had been stamped with the gold seal and framed in the gold frame, which matched the dream that was hung up in her head." The return with the medicine is just a matter of retracing her own footsteps. It is the part of the journey, and of the story, that can now go without saying.

In the matter of function, old Phoenix's way might even do as a sort of parallel to your way of work if you are a writer of stories. The way to get there is the all-important, all-absorbing problem, and this problem is your reason for undertaking the story. Your only guide, too, is your sureness about your subject, about what this subject is. Like Phoenix, you work all your life to find your way, through all the obstructions and the false appearances and the up-sets you may have brought on yourself, to reach a meaning — using inventions of your imagination, perhaps helped out by your dreams and bits of good luck. And finally too, like Phoenix, you have to assume that what you are working in aid of is life, not death.

But you would make the trip anyway — wouldn't you? — just on hope.

ॐ

EUDORA WELTY *included her statement on Anton Chekhov's "The Darling" in her book* The Eye of the Story *(1977). In her brief reading she analyzes the elements of plot ("aware of its clear open stress, the variations all springing from Chekhov's boundless and minute perception of character"), character motivation ("maternalism: for there it is most naturally innocent of anything but formless, thoughtless, blameless* embracing; *the true innocence is in never perceiving"), and theme ("Protest to the darlings of this world will always be [delivered] — out of inward and silent rebellion alone").*

EUDORA WELTY

Plot and Character in Chekhov's "The Darling"

1977

Clearly, the fact that stories have plots in common is of no more account than that many people have blue eyes. Plots are, indeed, what the story writer sees with, and so do we as we read. The plot is the Why. Why? is asked and replied to at various depths; the fishes in the sea are bigger the deeper we go. To learn that character is a more awe-inspiring fish and (in a short story, though not, I think, in a novel) one some degrees deeper down than situation, we have only to read Chekhov. What constitutes the reality of his characters is what they reveal to us. And the possibility that they may indeed reveal everything is what makes fictional characters differ so greatly from us in real life; yet isn't it strange that they don't really *seem* to differ? This is one clue to the extraordinary magnitude of character in fiction. Characters in the plot connect us with the vastness of our secret life, which is endlessly explorable. This is their role. What happens to them is what they have been put here to show.

In his story "The Darling," the darling's first husband, the theater manager, dies suddenly *because* of the darling's sweet passivity; this is the causality of fiction. In everyday or real life he might have held on to his health for years. But under Chekhov's hand he is living and dying in dependence on, and in revelation of, Olenka's character. He can only last a page and a half. Only by force of the story's circumstance is he here at all; Olenka took him up to begin with because he lived next door. . . . Kukin proposes and they are married. . . . And when Kukin dies, Olenka's cry of heartbreak is this: "Vanitchka, my precious, my darling! Why did I ever meet you! Why did I know you and love you! Your poor brokenhearted Olenka is all alone without you!"

With variations the pattern is repeated, and we are made to feel it as plot, aware of its clear open stress, the variations all springing from Chekhov's boundless and minute perception of character. The timber-merchant, another neighbor, is the one who walks home from the funeral with Olenka. The outcome follows tenderly, is only natural. After three days, he calls. "He did not stay long, only about ten minutes, and he did not say much, but when he left, Olenka loved him — loved him so much that she lay awake all night in a perfect fever."

Olenka and Pustovalov get along very well together when they are married. . . . Even in her dreams Olenka is in the timber business, dreaming of "perfect mountains of planks and boards," and cries out in her sleep, so that Pustovalov says to her tenderly, "Olenka, what's the matter, darling? Cross yourself!" But the timber merchant inevitably goes out in the timber yard one day without his cap on; he catches cold and dies, to leave Olenka a widow once more. "I've nobody, now you've left me, my darling," she sobs after the funeral. "How can I live without you?"

And the timber merchant is succeeded by a veterinary surgeon — who gets transferred to Siberia. But the plot is not repetition — it is direction. The love which Olenka bears to whatever is nearest her reaches its final and, we discover, its truest mold in maternalism: For there it is most naturally innocent of anything but formless, thoughtless, blameless *embracing*; the true innocence is in never perceiving. Only mother love could endure in a pursuit of such blind regard, caring so little for the reality of either life involved so long as love wraps them together, Chekhov tells us — unpretentiously, as he tells everything, and with the simplest of concluding episodes. Olenka's character is seen purely then for what it is: limpid reflection, mindless and purposeless regard, love that falls like the sun and rain on all alike, vacant when there is nothing to reflect.

We know this because, before her final chance to love, Olenka is shown to us truly alone:

> [She] got thinner and plainer; and when people met her in the street they did not look at her as they used to, and did not smile to her; evidently her best years were over and left behind, and now a new sort of life had begun for her, which did not bear thinking about. . . . And what was worst of all, she had no opinions of any sort. She saw the objects about her and understood what she saw, but could not form any opinions about them, and did not know what to talk about. And how

awful it is not to have any opinions! She wanted a love that would absorb her whole being, her whole soul and reason — that would give her ideas and an object in her life, and would warm her old blood.

The answer is Sasha, the ten-year-old son of the veterinary surgeon, an unexpected blessing from Siberia — a schoolchild. The veterinarian has another wife now, but this no longer matters. "Olenka, with arms akimbo, walked about the yard giving directions. Her face was beaming, and she was brisk and alert, as though she had waked from a long sleep. . . ." "An island is a piece of land entirely surrounded by water," Sasha reads aloud. " 'An island is a piece of land,' she repeated, and this was the first opinion to which she gave utterance with positive conviction, after so many years of silence and dearth of ideas." She would follow Sasha halfway to school, until he told her to go back. She would go to bed thinking blissfully of Sasha, "who lay sound asleep in the next room, sometimes crying out in his sleep, 'I'll give it to you! Get away! Shut up!' "

The darling herself *is* the story; all else is sacrificed to her; deaths and departures are perfunctory and to be expected. The last words of the story are the child's and a protest, but they are delivered in his sleep, as indeed protest to the darlings of this world will always be — out of inward and silent rebellion alone, as this master makes plain.

8

CASEBOOKS ON STORIES AND STORYTELLERS

CASEBOOK ON RAYMOND CARVER

Raymond Carver offers a clear example of how a contemporary author has responded to the work of earlier short story writers to follow a line of thought that links him with his predecessors. Carver has credited the influence of Ernest Hemingway and John Gardner on his work, but he paid his most extensive tribute to Anton Chekhov with the story "Errand" (p. 109), about Chekhov's death, after reading Henri Troyat's biography of Chekhov. Carver considered Chekhov the greatest short story writer ever; he was impressed by the sheer number of Chekhov's stories and by what Carver called "the awesome frequency with which he produced masterpieces, stories . . . that lay bare our emotions in ways only true art can accomplish." Carver also responded to Chekhov's dedication to the craft of writing by commenting that Chekhov once scolded another writer: "Your laziness stands out between the lines of every story. You don't work on your sentences. You must, you know. That's what makes art." Also in this section, Chekhov's widow Olga Knipper and the poet Edward Sanders describe his death, Carver's editor Tom Jenks recalls Carver's explanation of the origin of "Cathedral" (p. 98), and the critic Arthur Saltzman analyzes "What We Talk About When We Talk About Love" (p. 117).

RAYMOND CARVER

On Writing   1981

Back in the mid-1960s, I found I was having trouble concentrating my attention on long narrative fiction. For a time I experienced difficulty in trying to read it as well as in attempting to write it. My attention span had gone out on me; I no longer had the patience to try to write novels. It's an involved story, too tedious to talk about here. But I know it has much to do now with why I write poems and short stories. Get in, get out. Don't linger. Go on. It could be that I lost any great ambitions at about the same time, in my late twenties. If I did, I think it was good it happened. Ambition and a little luck are good things for a writer to have going for him. Too much ambition and bad luck, or no luck at all, can be killing. There has to be talent.

Some writers have a bunch of talent; I don't know any writers who are without it. But a unique and exact way of looking at things, and finding the right context for expressing that way of looking, that's something else. *The World According to Garp* is, of course, the marvelous world according to John Irving. There is another world according to Flannery O'Connor, and others according to William Faulkner and Ernest Hemingway. There are worlds according to Cheever, Updike, Singer, Stanley Elkin, Ann Beattie, Cynthia Ozick, Donald Barthelme, Mary Robison, William Kittredge, Barry Hannah, Ursula K. Le Guin. Every great or even every very good writer makes the world over according to his own specifications.

It's akin to style, what I'm talking about, but it isn't style alone. It is the writer's particular and unmistakable signature on everything he writes. It is his world and no other. This is one of the things that distinguishes one writer from another. Not talent. There's plenty of that around. But a writer who has some special way of looking at things and who gives artistic expression to that way of looking: that writer may be around for a time.

Isak Dinesen said that she wrote a little every day, without hope and without despair. Someday I'll put that on a three-by-five card and tape it to the wall beside my desk. I have some three-by-five cards on the wall now. "Fundamental accuracy of statement is the ONE sole morality of writing." Ezra Pound. It is not everything by ANY means, but if a writer has "fundamental accuracy of statement" going for him, he's at least on the right track.

I have a three-by-five up there with this fragment of a sentence from a story by Chekhov: ". . . and suddenly everything became clear to him." I find these words filled with wonder and possibility. I love their simple clarity, and the hint of revelation that's implied. There is mystery, too. What has been unclear before? Why is it just now becoming clear? What's happened? Most of all — what now? There are consequences as a result of such sudden awakenings. I feel a sharp sense of relief — and anticipation.

I overheard the writer Geoffrey Wolff say "No cheap tricks" to a group of writing students. That should go on a three-by-five card. I'd amend it a little to "No tricks." Period. I hate tricks. At the first sign of a trick or a gimmick in a piece of fiction, a cheap trick or even an elaborate trick, I tend to look for cover. Tricks are ultimately boring, and I get bored easily, which may go along with my not having much of an attention span. But extremely clever chi-chi writing, or just plain tomfoolery writing, puts me to sleep. Writers don't need tricks or gimmicks or even necessarily need to be the smartest fellows on the block. At the risk of appearing foolish, a writer sometimes needs to be able to just stand and gape at this or that thing — a sunset or an old shoe — in absolute and simple amazement.

Some months back, in the *New York Times Book Review,* John Barth said that ten years ago most of the students in his fiction writing seminar were interested in "formal innovation," and this no longer seems to be the case. He's a little worried that writers are going to start writing mom-and-pop novels in the 1980s. He worries that experimentation may be on the way out, along with liberalism. I get a little nervous if I find myself within earshot of somber discussions about "formal innovation" in fiction writing. Too often "experimentation" is a license to be careless, silly, or imitative in the writing. Even worse, a license to try to brutalize or alienate the reader. Too often such writing gives us no news of the world, or else describes a desert landscape and that's all — a few dunes and lizards here and there, but no people; a place uninhabited by anything recognizably human, a place of interest only to a few scientific specialists.

It should be noted that real experiment in fiction is original, hard-earned and cause for rejoicing. But someone else's way of looking at things — Barthelme's, for instance — should not be chased after by other writers. It won't work. There is only one Barthelme, and for another writer to try to appropriate Barthelme's peculiar sensibility or mise en scène under the rubric of innovation is for that writer to mess around with chaos and disaster and, worse, self-deception. The real experimenters have to Make It New, as Pound urged, and in the process have to find things out for themselves. But if writers haven't taken leave of their senses, they also want to stay in touch with us, they want to carry news from their world to ours.

It's possible, in a poem or a short story, to write about commonplace things and objects using commonplace but precise language, and to endow those things — a chair, a window curtain, a fork, a stone, a woman's earring — with immense, even startling power. It is possible to write a line of seemingly innocuous dialogue and have it send a chill along the reader's spine — the source of artistic delight, as Nabokov would have it. That's the kind of writing that most interests me. I hate sloppy or haphazard writing whether it flies under the banner of experimentation or else is just clumsily rendered realism. In Isaac Babel's wonderful short story, "Guy de Maupassant," the narrator has this to say about the writing of fiction: "No iron can pierce the heart with such force as a period put just at the right place." This too ought to go on a three-by-five.

Evan Connell said once that he knew he was finished with a short story when he found himself going through it and taking out commas and then going through the story again and putting commas back in the same places. I like that way of working on something. I respect that kind of care for what is being done. That's all we have, finally, the words, and they had better be the right ones, with the punctuation in the right places so that they can best say what they are meant to say. If the words are heavy with the writer's own unbridled emotions, or if they are imprecise and inaccurate for some other reason — if the words are in any way blurred — the reader's eyes will slide right over them and nothing will be achieved. The reader's own artistic sense will simply not be engaged. Henry James called this sort of hapless writing "weak specification."

I have friends who've told me they had to hurry a book because they needed the money, their editor or their wife was leaning on them or leaving them — something, some apology for the writing not being very good. "It would have been better if I'd taken the time." I was dumbfounded when I heard a novelist friend say this. I still am, if I think about it, which I don't. It's none of my business. But if the writing can't be made as good as it is within us to make it, then why do it? In the end, the satisfaction of having done our best, and the proof of that labor, is the one thing we can take into the grave. I wanted to say to my friend, for heaven's sake go do something else. There have to be easier and maybe more honest ways to try and earn a living. Or else just do it to the best of your abilities, your talents, and then don't justify or make excuses. Don't complain, don't explain.

In an essay called, simply enough, "Writing Short Stories," Flannery O'Connor talks about writing as an act of discovery. O'Connor says she most often did not know where she was going when she sat down to work on a short story. She says she doubts that many writers know where they are going when they begin something. She uses "Good Country People" as an example of how she put together a short story whose ending she could not even guess at until she was nearly there:

> When I started writing that story, I didn't know there was going to be a Ph.D. with a wooden leg in it. I merely found myself one morning writing a description of two women I knew something about, and before I realized it, I had equipped one of them with a daughter with a wooden leg. I brought in the Bible salesman, but I had no idea what I was going to do with him. I didn't know he was going to steal that wooden leg until ten or twelve lines before he did it, but when I found out that this was what was going to happen, I realized it was inevitable.

When I read this some years ago it came as a shock that she, or anyone for that matter, wrote stories in this fashion. I thought this was my uncomfortable secret, and I was a little uneasy with it. For sure I thought this way of working on a short story somehow revealed my own shortcomings. I remember being tremendously heartened by reading what she had to say on the subject.

I once sat down to write what turned out to be a pretty good story, though only the first sentence of the story had offered itself to me when I began it. For several days I'd been going around with this sentence in my head: "He was running the vacuum cleaner when the telephone rang." I knew a story was there and that it wanted telling. I felt it in my bones, that a story belonged with that beginning, if I could just have the time to write it. I found the time, an entire day — twelve, fifteen hours even — if I wanted to make use of it. I did, and I sat down in the morning and wrote the first sentence, and other sentences promptly began to attach themselves. I made the story just as I'd make a poem; one line and then the next, and the next. Pretty soon I could see a story, and I knew it was my story, the one I'd been wanting to write.

I like it when there is some feeling of threat or sense of menace in short stories. I think a little menace is fine to have in a story. For one thing, it's good for the circulation. There has to be tension, a sense that something is imminent, that certain things are in relentless motion, or else, most often, there simply won't be a story. What creates tension in a piece of fiction is partly the way the concrete words are linked together to make up the visible action of the story. But it's also the things that are left out, that are implied, the landscape just under the smooth (but sometimes broken and unsettled) surface of things.

V. S. Pritchett's° definition of a short story is "something glimpsed from the corner of the eye, in passing." Notice the "glimpse" part of this. First the glimpse. Then the glimpse given life, turned into something that illuminates the moment and may, if we're lucky — that word again — have even further-ranging consequences and meaning. The short story writer's task is to invest the glimpse with all that is in his power. He'll bring his intelligence and literary skill to bear (his talent), his sense of proportion and sense of the fitness of things: of how things out there really are and how he sees those things — like no one else sees them. And this is done through the use of clear and specific language, language used so as to bring to life the details that will light up the story for the reader. For the details to be concrete and convey meaning, the language must be accurate and precisely given. The words can be so precise they may even sound flat, but they can still carry; if used right, they can hit all the notes.

RAYMOND CARVER

Creative Writing 101   1983

A long time ago — it was the summer of 1958 — my wife and I and our two baby children moved from Yakima, Washington, to a little town outside of Chico, California. There we found an old house and paid twenty-five dollars a month rent. In order to finance this move, I'd had to borrow a hundred and twenty-five dollars from a druggist I'd delivered prescriptions for, a man named Bill Barton.

This is by way of saying that in those days my wife and I were stone broke. We had to eke out a living, but the plan was that I would take classes at what was then called Chico State College. But for as far back as I can remember, long before we moved to California in search of a different life and our slice of the American pie, I'd wanted to be a writer. I wanted to write, and I wanted to write anything — fiction, of course, but also poetry, plays, scripts,

---

V. S. Pritchett: British master of the short story and literary critic (b. 1900).

articles for *Sports Afield, True, Argosy,* and *Rogue* (some of the magazines I was then reading), pieces for the local newspaper — anything that involved putting words together to make something coherent and of interest to someone besides myself. But at the time of our move, I felt in my bones I had to get some education in order to go along with being a writer. I put a very high premium on education then — much higher in those days than now, I'm sure, but that's because I'm older and have an education. Understand that nobody in my family had ever gone to college or for that matter had got beyond the mandatory eighth grade in high school. I didn't know *anything,* but I knew I didn't know anything.

So along with this desire to get an education, I had this very strong desire to write; it was a desire so strong that, with the encouragement I was given in college, and the insight acquired, I kept on writing long after "good sense" and the "cold facts" — the "realities" of my life told me, time and again, that I ought to quit, stop the dreaming, quietly go ahead and do something else.

That fall at Chico State I enrolled in classes that most freshman students have to take, but I enrolled as well for something called Creative Writing 101. This course was going to be taught by a new faculty member named John Gardner, who was already surrounded by a bit of mystery and romance. It was said that he'd taught previously at Oberlin College but had left there for some reason that wasn't made clear. One student said Gardner had been fired — students, like everyone else, thrive on rumor and intrigue — and another student said Gardner had simply quit after some kind of flap. Someone else said his teaching load at Oberlin, four or five classes of freshman English each semester, had been too heavy and that he couldn't find time to write. For it was said that Gardner was a real, that is to say a practicing, writer — someone who had written novels and short stories. In any case, he was going to teach CW 101 at Chico State, and I signed up.

I was excited about taking a course from a real writer. I'd never laid eyes on a writer before, and I was in awe. But where were these novels and short stories, I wanted to know. Well, nothing had been published yet. It was said that he couldn't get his work published and that he carried it around with him in boxes. (After I became his student, I was to see those boxes of manuscript. Gardner had become aware of my difficulty in finding a place to work. He knew I had a young family and cramped quarters at home. He offered me the key to his office. I see that gift now as a turning point. It was a gift not made casually, and I took it, I think, as a kind of mandate — for that's what it was. I spent part of every Saturday and Sunday in his office, which is where he kept the boxes of manuscript. The boxes were stacked up on the floor beside the desk. *Nickel Mountain,* grease-pencilled on one of the boxes, is the only title I recall. But it was in his office, within sight of his unpublished books, that I undertook my first serious attempts at writing.) . . .

For short story writers in his class, the requirement was one story, ten to fifteen pages in length. For people who wanted to write a novel — I think there must have been one or two of these souls — a chapter of around twenty pages, along with an outline of the rest. The kicker was that this one short story, or the chapter of the novel, might have to be revised ten times in the course of the semester for Gardner to be satisfied with it. It was a basic tenet of his that a writer found what he wanted to say in the ongoing process of seeing what he'd said. And this seeing, or seeing more clearly, came about through revision. He *believed* in revision, endless revision; it was something very close to his heart and something he felt was vital for writers, at whatever stage of their development. And he never seemed to lose patience rereading a student story, even though he might have seen it in five previous incarnations.

I think his idea of a short story in 1958 was still pretty much his idea of a short story in 1982; it was something that had a recognizable beginning, middle, and an end to it. Once in a while he'd go to the blackboard and draw a diagram to illustrate a point he wanted to make about rising or falling emotion in a story — peaks, valleys, plateaus, resolution, *denouement*, things like that. Try as I might, I couldn't muster a great deal of interest or really understand this side of things, the stuff he put on the blackboard. But what I did understand was the way he would comment on a student story that was undergoing class discussion. Gardner might wonder aloud about the author's reasons for writing a story about a crippled person, say, and leaving out the fact of the character's crippledness until the very end of the story. "So you think it's a good idea not to let the reader know this man is crippled until the last sentence?" His tone of voice conveyed his disapproval, and it didn't take more than an instant for everyone in class, including the author of the story, to see that it wasn't a good strategy to use. Any strategy that kept important and necessary information away from the reader in the hope of overcoming him by surprise at the end of the story was cheating.

In class he was always referring to writers whose names I was not familiar with. Or if I knew their names, I'd never read the work. . . . He talked about James Joyce and Flaubert and Isak Dinesen as if they lived just down the road, in Yuba City. He said, "I'm here to tell you who to read as well as teach you how to write." I'd leave class in a daze and make straight for the library to find books by these writers he was talking about.

Hemingway and Faulkner were the reigning authors in those days. But altogether I'd probably read at the most two or three books by these fellows. Anyway, they were so well-known and so much talked about, they couldn't be all that good, could they? I remember Gardner telling me, "Read all the Faulkner you can get your hands on, and then read all of Hemingway to clean the Faulkner out of your system."

He introduced us to the "little" or literary periodicals by bringing a box of these magazines to class one day and passing them around so that we could acquaint ourselves with their names, see what they looked like and what they felt like to hold in the hand. He told us that this was where most of the best fiction in the country and just about all of the poetry was appearing. Fiction, poetry, literary essays, book reviews of recent books, criticism of *living* authors *by* living authors. I felt wild with discovery in those days.

For the seven or eight of us who were in his class, he ordered heavy black binders and told us we should keep our written work in these. He kept his own work in such binders, he said, and of course that settled it for us. We carried our stories in those binders and felt we were special, exclusive, singled out from others. And so we were.

I don't know how Gardner might have been with other students when it came time to have conferences with them about their work. I suspect he gave everybody a good amount of attention. But it was and still is my impression that during that period he took my stories more seriously, read them closer and more carefully, than I had any right to expect. I was completely unprepared for the kind of criticism I received from him. Before our conference he would have marked up my story, crossing out unacceptable sentences, phrases, individual words, even some of the punctuation; and he gave me to understand that these deletions were not negotiable. In other cases he would bracket sentences, phrases, or individual words, and these were items we'd talk about, these cases were negotiable. And he wouldn't hesitate to add something to what I'd written — a word here and there, or else a few words, maybe a sentence that would make clear what I was trying to say. We'd discuss commas in my story as if nothing else in the world mattered more at that moment — and, indeed, it did not. He was always looking to find something to praise. When there was a sentence, a line of dialogue, or a narrative passage that he liked, something that he thought "worked" and moved the story along in some pleasant or unexpected way, he'd write "Nice" in the margin, or else "Good!" And seeing these comments, my heart would lift.

It was close, line-by-line criticism he was giving me, and the reasons behind the criticism, why something ought to be this way instead of that; and it was invaluable to me in my development as a writer. After this kind of detailed talk about the text, we'd talk about the larger concerns of the story, the "problem" it was trying to throw light on, the conflict it was trying to grapple with, and how the story might or might not fit into the grand scheme of story writing. It was his conviction that if the words in the story were blurred because of the author's insensitivity, carelessness, or sentimentality, then the story suffered from a tremendous handicap. But there was something even worse and something that must be avoided at all costs: if the words and the sentiments were dishonest, the author was faking it, writing about things he didn't care about or believe in, then nobody could ever care anything about it.

A writer's values and craft. This is what the man taught and what he stood for, and this is what I've kept by me in the years since that brief but all-important time.

RAYMOND CARVER

The Ashtray   1984

You could write a story about this ashtray, for example, and a man and a woman. But the man and woman are always the two poles of your story. The North Pole and the South. Every story has these two poles — *he* and *she*.
                                                        —A. P. CHEKHOV

They're alone at the kitchen table in her friend's
apartment. They'll be alone for another hour, and then
her friend will be back. Outside, it's raining —
the rain coming down like needles, melting last week's
snow. They're smoking and using the ashtray . . . Maybe
just one of them is smoking . . . *He's* smoking! Never
mind. Anyway, the ashtray is filling up with
cigarettes and ashes.

She's ready to break into tears at any minute.
To plead with him, in fact, though she's proud
and has never asked for anything in her life.
He sees what's coming, recognizes the signs —
a catch in her voice as she brings her fingers
to her locket, the one her mother left her.
He pushes back his chair, gets up, goes over to
the window . . . He wishes it were tomorrow and he
were at the races. He wishes he was out walking,
using his umbrella . . . He strokes his mustache
and wishes he were anywhere except here. But
he doesn't have any choice in the matter. He's got
to put a good face on this for everybody's sake.
God knows, he never meant for things to come to
this. But it's sink or swim now. A wrong
move and he stands to lose her friend, too.
Her breathing slows. She watches him but
doesn't say anything. She knows, or thinks she
knows, where this is leading. She passes a hand
over her eyes, leans forward and puts her head
in her hands. She's done this a few times
before, but has no idea it's something
that drives him wild. He looks away and grinds
his teeth. He lights a cigarette, shakes out
the match, stands a minute longer at the window.

Then walks back to the table and sits
down with a sigh. He drops the match in the ashtray.
She reaches for his hand, and he lets her
take it. Why not? Where's the harm?
Let her. His mind's made up. She covers his
fingers with kisses, tears fall onto his wrist.

He draws on his cigarette and looks at her
as a man would look indifferently on
a cloud, a tree, or a field of oats at sunset.
He narrows his eyes against the smoke. From time

to time he uses the ashtray as he waits
for her to finish weeping.

RAYMOND CARVER

On "Errand"   1988

In early 1987 an editor at E. P. Dutton sent me a copy of the newly published Henri Troyat biography, *Chekhov*. Immediately upon the book's arrival, I put aside what I was doing and started reading. I seem to recall reading the book pretty much straight through, able, at the time, to devote entire afternoons and evenings to it.

On the third or fourth day, nearing the end of the book, I came to the little passage where Chekhov's doctor — a Badenweiler physician by the name of Dr Schwöhrer, who attended Chekhov during his last days — is summoned by Olga Knipper Chekhov to the dying writer's bedside in the early morning hours of July 2, 1904. It is clear that Chekhov has only a little while to live. Without any comment on the matter, Troyat tells his readers that this Dr Schwöhrer ordered up a bottle of champagne. Nobody had asked for champagne, of course; he just took it upon himself to do it. But this little piece of human business struck me as an extraordinary action. Before I really knew what I was going to do with it, or how I was going to proceed, I felt I had been launched into a short story of my own then and there. I wrote a few lines and then a page or two more. How did Dr Schwöhrer go about ordering champagne and at that late hour at this hotel in Germany? How was it delivered to the room and by whom, etc.? What was the protocol involved when the champagne arrived? Then I stopped and went ahead to finish reading the biography.

But just as soon as I'd finished the book I once again turned my attention back to Dr Schwöhrer and that business of the champagne. I was seriously interested in what I was doing. But what *was* I doing? The only thing that was clear to me was that I thought I saw an opportunity to pay homage — if I could bring it off, do it rightly and honorably — to Chekhov, the writer who has meant so much to me for such a long time.

I tried out ten or twelve openings to the piece, first one beginning and then another, but nothing felt right. Gradually I began to move the story away from those final moments back to the occasion of Chekhov's first public hemorrhage from tuberculosis, something that occurred in a restaurant in Moscow in the company of his friend and publisher, Suvorin. Then came the hospitalization and the scene with Tolstoy, the trip with Olga to Badenweiler, the brief period of time there in the hotel together before the end, the young bellman who makes two important appearances in the Chekhov suite and, at the end, the mortician who, like the bellman, isn't to be found in the biographical account.

The story was a hard one to write, given the factual basis of the material. I couldn't stray from what had happened, nor did I want to. As much as anything, I needed to figure out how to breathe life into actions that were merely suggested or not given moment in the biographical telling. And, finally, I saw that I needed to set my imagination free and simply invent within the confines of the story. I knew as I was writing this story that it was a good deal different from anything I'd ever done before. I'm pleased, and grateful, that it seems to have come together.

Carver's widow, Tess Gallagher, has described her "personal connection" to the composition of "Errand" in a film about Raymond Carver, To Write and Keep Kind.

> *Ray had been through many, many drafts, and he said, "I just don't know how to get out of this story." I had seen a draft or two by then and was empathizing with his waiter character. I said, "That waiter is going to be looking down, and he's going to see the cork that has popped out of the champagne. I think the ending is involved with his response to the cork. He's going to bend down to get that cork, and we're going to know something from that gesture, that action."*

OLGA KNIPPER

Remembering Chekhov   1924

TRANSLATED BY CONSTANCE GARNETT

Chekhov passed quietly and peacefully into the other world. Early in the night he woke up, and for the first time in his life asked for a doctor to be fetched. The sense of something immense swooping down upon me gave to everything I did an extraordinary calm and precision, as though some one were guiding me with a sure hand. I only remember one awful moment of being overwhelmed: the sense of masses of people near me asleep in a great hotel and at the same time my complete isolation and helplessness. I remembered that two brothers, Russian students, with whom we were acquainted, were staying at the hotel, and I asked one of them to run for a doctor, and I went myself to break up ice to lay on the dying man's heart. I can hear now the sound of retreating footsteps on the crunching sand in the midst of the oppressive stillness of the unbearably sultry July night. . . .

The doctor came, and ordered champagne. Chekhov sat up and said aloud, significantly, to the doctor, "Ich sterbe . . ."° (he knew very little German). Then he took the glass, turned to me, and with his wonderful smile said, "It's a long while since I have drunk champagne." He calmly drank it to the last drop, quietly lay down on his left side, and soon afterwards sank into silence for ever. . . . And the fearful stillness of the night was only broken by a black moth of huge proportions which burst in like a whirlwind and dashed itself in terror against the electric light and fluttered about the room. . . .

The doctor went away; in the midst of the stillness and sultriness of the night the cork shot out of the unfinished champagne bottle with a terrible

---

Ich sterbe: "I am dying."

noise. . . . It began to get light, and together with awakening nature I heard
like the first requiem the tender, lovely singing of the birds and the strains of
the organ floating in from the church hard by. No sound of human voice was
heard, there was none of the bustle of daily life, nothing but peace, beauty, and
the grandeur of death. . . .

And to me, the consciousness of my sorrow, of the loss of a man like
Chekhov, came only with the first sound of awakening life, with the coming of
people, but what I felt and went through as I stood alone on the balcony and
looked now at the rising sun and the melodious awakening of nature, now at the
lovely, serene face of Anton Pavlovitch, smiling as though with the comprehension of something — this, I repeat, still remains an inscrutable mystery to me. . . .

There had been no such moment in my life, nor will be, I imagine.

EDWARD SANDERS

From *Chekhov*   1995

At 2 AM the doctor arrived,
Chekhov covered in sweat,
and spotting the doctor
Chekhov sat up,
leaned against his pillows,
and said, "Ich sterbe."

The doctor gave him a
   camphor injection
and was sending for an
   oxygen pillow

but Chekhov said,
"What's the use?
Before it arrives
   I'll be a corpse."

In response Dr. Schwöhrer
sent for champagne,
Chekhov held a glass
and said to Olga
"It's been so long since
   I've had champagne,"

and ever slowly drank it down
then lay upon his side

A black-winged moth
had come through the window

and was beating
    its wild wings
        against the lamp.

HENRI TROYAT

Chekhov's Last Days   1987

TRANSLATED BY MICHAEL HENRY HEIM

The friends who came to see [Chekhov] found him stretched out on a daybed wearing a dressing gown. He would apologize to them for the informality of his attire and force himself to make jokes and appear interested in everything, but they were all struck by his hollow cheeks, waxen complexion, and dilated pupils. Dr. Rossolimo observed that like all tubercular patients he spoke of the disease with an almost reckless indifference. With his burning hands and flushed cheeks could he really believe in a cure?

One evening Chekhov was reminiscing happily with the writer Gilyarovsky, one of the first to encourage him to write, when Gilyarovsky mentioned he had recently returned from a visit to the steppe. All at once Chekhov grew pensive: "Oh, the steppe, the steppe! What a lucky man you are! That's where the poetry is." And he closed his eyes, smiled a childlike smile, and let his head drop onto the pillow. "I am certain he dreamed of the steppe," Gilyarovsky wrote.

Towards the end of the month Chekhov's temperature went down and he felt strong enough to get out of bed. On May 31 he announced triumphantly to his sister: "Just think. Today for the first time I put on shoes and a coat [. . .] and for the first time went out for a ride." Now there was nothing to hold him back from the journey Dr. Taube had counseled. On June 3, 1904, Anton and Olga took the train for Berlin.

Although he had left Moscow in a morbid mood, Chekhov perked up at once in Berlin. A change of place always did him good. From a comfortable room at the Hotel Savoy ("the best in Berlin") he wrote Maria letter after optimistic letter: his appetite had improved; he was putting a bit of flesh on his bones; his diarrhea had subsided; his legs no longer ached; in fact, he was on his feet all day, "running around Berlin," raiding the shops, riding through the Tiergarten. It was the first time he had ever been out of Russia with Olga, and he felt all the closer to her for their being "stranded" in a foreign city; he enjoyed discovering a new world and discussing new impressions with her. He claimed jestingly that he had not seen a single good-looking woman and that German women dressed "abominably." Yet, as he admitted to Maria, "people live a comfortable existence, the food is good, life is not expensive, [. . .] the streets are clean, order reigns." In his optimism he even made plans to spend some time at the Italian lakes and return to Yalta in August via Constantinople.

Chekhov's confidence in the future was not shared by Dr. Karl Ewald, the specialist Dr. Taube had recommended. After giving Chekhov a careful examination, Dr. Ewald spread his arms in a gesture of helplessness and left without a word. The message was obvious. "It was cruel of him, of course," Dr. Altschuler later wrote, "but Ewald's attitude may be explained by the fact that he did not understand how anyone could have permitted a man so ill to undertake so long a journey — and for what?" After an interview with Chekhov the Berlin correspondent for *Russian News* reported to his editor: "I am of the opinion that Chekhov's days are numbered. He seemed mortally ill: he was terribly thin, coughed all the time, gasped for breath at the slightest movement, and was running a high temperature."

The same journalist saw the Chekhovs off at the Potsdam station, where after three days in Berlin they took the train for Badenweiler in the Black Forest. "He had trouble making his way up the small staircase at the station," he wrote, "and sat down for several minutes to catch his breath. But as the train began to pull out, he disregarded my plea and leaned out of the window to nod good-bye."

Badenweiler is a spa on the western edge of the Black Forest not far from Basel, a clean, calm, unexciting little town that seemed to Chekhov made for convalescence. Olga and he spent their first two days there in a boarding-house, then moved into a private house that took in guests. The large, well-kept garden, all gravel paths and flower beds, afforded a beautiful view of the mountains. Chekhov spent the entire day — from morning until seven in the evening — seated or reclining in a comfortable chair. In Badenweiler the sun did not burn, he wrote to his sister, it caressed the skin. The spa physician, a Dr. Schwöhrer, proved perfectly competent and easy to get on with. Besides absolute rest he prescribed a diet of cocoa, oatmeal drenched in butter, and strawberry tea ("to aid the patient's sleep"). And while Chekhov could not help grumbling about Schwöhrer's "quackery," he boasted to Maria that he was growing stronger fast. On June 13 he went so far as to write to his mother: "My health is improving, and it's likely I'll be completely cured in a week." Olga was hopeful enough to leave him on his own and go to Basel to have her teeth examined.

After a week of euphoria, however, Chekhov once more gave way to anxiety, boredom, and the need for change. "I can't get used to this German peace and quiet," he wrote to Maria. "There's not a sound inside or out except when a band with no talent strikes up at seven in the morning and noon. There's not a drop of talent, not a drop of good taste anywhere to be seen, only great quantities of order and honesty. There's a good deal more talent in Russia, to say nothing of Italy or France." Now Dr. Schwöhrer seemed wanting too: "The same stupid cocoa, the same oatmeal." Since there was no question of their leaving Badenweiler, however, they left the house they had been staying at for the Hotel Sommer, the best the spa had to offer. Chekhov would sit out on the balcony of his room for hours, watching people enter and leave the post office across the road. Or he would plan journeys, perusing timetables and requesting information on departure dates for boats en route to Odessa from Trieste or Marseilles.

Then Badenweiler was hit by a heat wave. Chekhov, his lungs half destroyed, suffered horribly. "It's caught me unawares," he wrote to Maria, "and since all I have with me is winter clothes, I'm suffocating and dream of getting out of here." In this letter, the last Chekhov ever wrote, he gives in to despair for the first time: "The food is very tasty, but it doesn't do me much good. My stomach keeps getting upset. I can't eat the kind of butter they have here. Apparently my stomach is ruined beyond all hope. About the only remedy for it is to fast, in other words, to refrain from eating entirely, and that's that. And the only remedy for short-windedness is to keep perfectly still." His letter to her crossed one of hers to him saying that since he was doing so well she and their brother Ivan had decided to go on a short tour of the Caucasus. "So take care of yourself, dear Antosha. Try to cough less and eat more. Gather your strength and come home."

On June 29 Chekhov had a sudden violent attack and Schwöhrer had to give him both morphine and oxygen, but his pulse returned to normal and he had a peaceful night. The respite was short-lived; next day he had a new attack. Two correspondents from the Russian press rushed to Badenweiler and wired back alarming reports on the state of Chekhov's health. Chekhov, meanwhile, soon over the second attack and perfectly lucid and calm, instructed his bank in Berlin to make all payments in his wife's name. When Olga asked him the reason for his concern, he replied evasively, "It's nothing really. Just in case . . ."

On July 1 he seemed to feel better and the correspondents' reports were more optimistic: his heart was doing well, the day had passed uneventfully. Towards evening he insisted that Olga, who had not left his bedside for three days, should take a walk in the hotel grounds. When she returned, she lay down on a narrow couch near the bed. He scolded her for looking so sad. To cheer her up, he started improvising a story. It took place in a fashionable watering place where the guests were all "well-fed bankers" and "rosy-cheeked English and American tourists." Every day they would work up an appetite by going on a hike, and every evening they would rush back to the hotel dreaming of the delicious meal awaiting them. One day they returned to learn that the chef had decamped and they would have no dinner. At this point Chekhov began to describe how each of the hungry gourmets reacted to the disaster. For all her anguish Olga could not help laughing.

Although the heat was still oppressive, Chekhov soon fell asleep. His breath came in spurts, but his face was calm. Then at half past twelve he sat up in bed and called for a doctor. It was the first time Olga had ever heard him do so. Suddenly she felt very much alone in their large German hotel where everyone was asleep for the night. After a moment of indecision she recalled that there were two Russian students in the room next door. She ran and woke them, and one of them immediately rushed off to fetch Dr. Schwöhrer. "I can still hear the sound of the gravel under his shoes in the silence of that stifling July night," she later wrote.

Fever had made Chekhov delirious. He went on about a sailor or asked about the Japanese, his eyes shining. But when Olga tried to place an ice bag on his chest, he suddenly regained consciousness and said, "Don't put ice on an empty stomach."

The windows were wide open, but he could not stop panting; his temples were bathed in sweat. Dr. Schwöhrer arrived at two o'clock. When Chekhov saw him, he sat up, leaned back against the pillows, and, in a final reflex of courtesy, mustered his weak German and said, "Ich sterbe."° Schwöhrer immediately gave him a camphor injection, but his heart failed to react. He was about to send for an oxygen pillow when Chekhov, lucid to the end, protested in a broken voice, "What's the use? Before it arrives, I'll be a corpse." So Dr. Schwöhrer sent for a bottle of champagne.

When it came, Chekhov took a glass and, turning to Olga, said with a smile, "It's been so long since I've had champagne." He emptied the glass slowly and lay down on his left side. A few moments later he stopped breathing. He had passed from life to death with characteristic simplicity.

It was July 2, 1904, three o'clock in the morning. A large black-winged moth had flown in through the window and was banging wildly against the lamp. The muffled sound soon grew maddeningly distracting. Dr. Schwöhrer withdrew after a few words of consolation. All at once there was a joyous explosion: the cork had popped out of the champagne bottle and foam was fizzing out after it. The moth found its way out of the window and disappeared into the sultry night. Silence returned. When day broke at last, Olga was still sitting and staring into her husband's face. It was peaceful, smiling, knowing. "There were no human voices, no everyday sounds," she wrote. "There was only beauty, peace, and the grandeur of death."

TOM JENKS

The Origin of "Cathedral"   1993

I first met Ray Carver in New York in early September 1984 at a publishing dinner to launch Gary Fisketjon's Vintage Contemporary paperback series. Many of the new VC authors and their friends were there: Richard Ford, Toby Wolff, Jay McInerney, Tom McGuane, Jim Crumley, and Ralph Beer — a distinctly male crowd, and what struck me most was that, as we geared up to move to a nightclub, Ray, amid teasing about running off somewhere to see a woman, put himself in a taxi and headed for his hotel room alone. By the ginger way he got himself into the cab and laughingly ducked the barbs all around him, there was no doubt he meant to keep himself out of trouble.

But he was fair game for the friendly taunts that followed him into the cab. We were witnessing the Good Ray, but we all knew about the Bad Ray, the one who used to be Lord Misrule himself.

Reformed, Ray was fast becoming the most famous short story writer in the world, and the facts of his life were well known, partly because they were often the stuff of his writing and because fame brings a peculiar public intimacy.

At the time, I was an editor of *Esquire* and had made Ray's acquaintance

---

Ich sterbe: "I am dying."

through the mail and on the phone. I had published some of his work and knew him somewhat, and as I watched him slip away in the cab, I imagined him going back to his hotel room (it was early yet — ten o'clock) and telephoning Tess Gallagher [Carver's wife] at their home in Syracuse. Each evening they set aside the hours beyond ten o'clock to spend with each other. He *was*, in a sense, running off to see a woman.

A year and a half later, I visited them in Syracuse. During the days, Ray and I read stories for a book we were working on and at night we watched TV. One night, we were watching a PBS version of *Wuthering Heights*,° and Ray began to tell about another night of TV: the night the blind man for whom Tess once worked had come to visit. Tess told her side, too — how Ray was uneasy about the man's visit, uncomfortable with his blindness and his familiarity with Tess, a mild jealousy rising in Ray. Their evening was slow and tedious, and ended with the three of them watching PBS, just as we were. But on the night the blind man was visiting, Tess had fallen asleep, and then a program about cathedrals came on. The blind man had no idea what a cathedral looked like, and, in the end, Ray sat on the floor with him, holding his hands, drawing a cathedral so the blind man could sense the miracle of the shape.

Ray had written this story and titled it "Cathedral." Tess, who with Ray's encouragement had recently begun writing stories, had her own version, titled "The Harvest." She gave me a copy, humorously telling Ray, "Watch out, I'm nipping at your heels." Their good-natured competition and openness was rare in my experience of writers, many of whom are cagey about the intimate, personal connections in their work.

Arthur M. Saltzman

A Reading of "What We Talk About When We Talk About Love"

1988

The volume's title story extends the theme of the heart's perpetual commotion by updating and burlesquing Plato's *Symposium*. "What We Talk About When We Talk About Love" also features the most expansive conversationalists in this collection: Mel and Terri, both of whom are married for the second time and both sporting scars from their first marriages, and Nick (the narrator) and Laura, newlyweds who are still in the throes of a mutual romantic trance. Mel and Terri carry on the bulk of the gin-induced discussion of love, whereas Nick and Laura are more equivocal and seem content to placate their friends or to reassure one another with intimate gestures.

Mel and Terri propose divergent definitions of "real love." A cardiologist who once spent five years studying in a seminary, Mel contends that love is a spiritual phenomenon whose pinnacle was and continues to be the chivalric code. Terri, on the other hand, argues that the brutality of her first husband, Ed, displayed the formidableness of his passion for her. As the conversation

---

Wuthering Heights: Classic Victorian gothic romance (1847) by Emily Brontë (1818–1848).

gains momentum, contradictions surface in their testimonies. Mel, the self-proclaimed spiritual scientist, confesses his daydreams about murdering his first wife that parallel Terri's grotesque tales of her relationship with Ed. Meanwhile, Terri grows increasingly anxious about redeeming her volatile past, even at the expense of offending her present husband: " 'He did love me though, Mel. Grant me that,' Terri said. 'That's all I'm asking. He didn't love me the way you love me. I'm not saying that. But he loved me. You can grant me that, can't you?' "

The greatest obstacle to any ideal of love turns out to be the transitoriness of love. After all, both Mel and Terri had vowed allegiance to their original partners, so what is there to prevent the same deterioration from happening again? Ironically, the "saving grace" of love is its elasticity — one can move one from divorce or tragedy and love anew — but this is further evidence against love's absolute status and hollows out current protestations of devotion. In other words, love's transient nature could be either its vindication or its vanquishment — the source of its preciousness or its untrustworthiness. Consequently, the very situation that the four friends occupy as they conduct their leisurely talking and drinking around the dinner table is shown to have the same fragile charms as the subject at hand:

> The afternoon sun was like a presence in this room, the spacious light of ease and generosity. We could have been anywhere, somewhere enchanted. We raised our glasses again and grinned at each other like children who had agreed on something forbidden.

The relative articulateness of these characters by no means enables them to reach a satisfactory conclusion, and as a result Mel suggests that "it ought to make us feel ashamed when we talk like we know what we're talking about when we talk about love." In this way, Mel echoes Pausanias' declaration in *The Symposium*: "I do not think, Phaidros, that the rules were properly laid down, I mean that we should just simply belaud Love. For if Love were one, that would do, but really he is not one; since he is not one, it is more proper to say first which we are to praise."

Mel's crowning point regarding the spiritual core of love recalls Holly's envious vision of the dignified intimacy of the old people she encountered in "Gazebo." Mel relates how, after a terrible automobile accident, an old man and woman lay barely alive in their hospital beds; they were completely covered by casts and bandages. However, despite his horrible injuries, the husband was primarily depressed because he could not see his wife through the tiny eyeholes in his bandages. By this time Mel has grown rather drunk and profane, and his testiness toward Terri belies his argument. So, too, is his chivalric hero, the medieval knight, tarnished by the admission that he often suffocated in his armor; moreover, his protective gear was also a measure of his inaccessibility. Finally, when Mel fantasizes about arriving in the guise of a beekeeper (helmeted, anonymous, and padded from head to toe) at the house of his first wife in order to release a swarm of bees, he modernizes and disqualifies the knight's noble image.

Nick and Laura come close to embodying a simple yet profound enjoyment of one another's company, but when Nick ostentatiously kisses Laura's hand, Mel and Terri find it more amusing than tender. They all toast to "true love," but Terri's gentle admonishment to Laura — "Wait awhile" — suggests that time misses no one in its assault on affection. Rating the quality of the consolation that remains at the end of the story depends upon to what extent the elusive, unpredictable, hazardous process of love compensates for the skewering of the romantic ideal (upon which the discussants cannot agree anyway). In the darkened room, silent save for "the human noise we sat there making," perhaps these moments together, deeply imbued with shared sensibilities, make up for the antagonisms, the regrets, the flirtations, the spilled gin.

∞

CASEBOOK ON SANDRA CISNEROS

Sandra Cisneros describes her childhood experiences and how they have shaped her writing in an article published in the Texas Observer. *In essays on* The House on Mango Street, *Ellen McCracken analyzes what she considers Cisneros's "double marginalization" as an author stemming from her gender and ethnicity. Julián Olivares explores the significance of Cisneros's response to Gaston Bachelard's* The Poetics of Space: *as a student in the University of Iowa's Writers Workshop, she was unable to relate to Bachelard at all and began a quest to find her own voice as a writer. Alvina E. Quintana analyzes Cisneros's use of the house as symbol in* Home Girls: Chicana Literary Voices *(1991). Finally, the literary historian Mark Zimmerman defines Latino literature in the United States and places Cisneros with her feminist contemporaries Helena María Viramontes, Denise Chávez, and Ana Castillo.*

SANDRA CISNEROS

Straw into Gold   1987

When I was living in an artists' colony in the south of France, some fellow Latin Americans who taught at the university in Aix-en-Provence invited me to share a home-cooked meal with them. I had been living abroad almost a year then on an NEA grant, subsisting mainly on French bread and lentils so that my money could last longer. So when the invitation to dinner arrived, I accepted without hesitation. Especially since they had promised Mexican food.

What I didn't realize when they made this invitation was that I was supposed to be involved in preparing the meal. I guess they assumed I knew how to cook Mexican food because I am Mexican. They wanted specifically tortillas, though I'd never made a tortilla in my life.

It's true I had witnessed my mother rolling the little armies of dough into perfect circles, but my mother's family is from Guanajuato; they are *provincianos*, country folk. They only know how to make flour tortillas. My father's family, on the other hand, is *chilango* from Mexico City. We ate corn tortillas but we didn't make them. Someone was sent to the corner tortilleria to buy some. I'd never seen anybody make corn tortillas. Ever.

Somehow my Latino hosts had gotten a hold of a packet of corn flour, and this is what they tossed my way with orders to produce tortillas. *Asi como sea*. Any ol' way, they said and went back to their cooking.

Why did I feel like the woman in the fairy tale who was locked in a room and ordered to spin straw into gold? I had the same sick feeling when I was required to write my critical essay for the M.F.A. exam — the only piece of noncreative writing necessary in order to get my graduate degree. How was I to start? There were rules involved, here, unlike writing a poem or story, which I did intuitively. There was a step-by-step process needed and I had better know it. I felt as if making tortillas — or writing a critical paper, for that matter — were tasks so impossible I wanted to break down into tears.

Somehow though, I managed to make tortillas — crooked and burnt, but edible nonetheless. My hosts were absolutely ignorant when it came to Mexican food; they thought my tortillas were delicious. (I'm glad my mama wasn't there.) Thinking back and looking at an old photograph documenting the three of us consuming those lop-sided circles, I am amazed. Just as I am amazed I could finish my M.F.A. exam.

I've managed to do a lot of things in my life I didn't think I was capable of and which many others didn't think I was capable of either. Especially because I am a woman, a Latina, an only daughter in a family of six men. My father would've liked to have seen me married long ago. In our culture men and women don't leave their father's house except by way of marriage. I crossed my father's threshold with nothing carrying me but my own two feet. A woman whom no one came for and no one chased away.

To make matters worse, I left before any of my six brothers had ventured away from home. I broke a terrible taboo. Somehow, looking back at photos of myself as a child, I wonder if I was aware of having begun already my own quiet war.

I like to think that somehow my family, my Mexicanness, my poverty, all had something to do with shaping me into a writer. I like to think my parents were preparing me all along for my life as an artist even though they didn't know it. From my father I inherited a love of wandering. He was born in Mexico City but as a young man he traveled into the United States vagabonding. He eventually was drafted and thus became a citizen. Some of the stories he has told about his first months in the United States with little or no English surface in my stories in *The House on Mango Street* as well as others I have in mind to write in the future. From him I inherited a sappy heart. (He still cries when he watches Mexican soaps — especially if they deal with children who have forsaken their parents.)

My mother was born like me — in Chicago but of Mexican descent. It would be her tough streetwise voice that would haunt all my stories and poems. An amazing woman who loves to draw and read books and can sing an opera. A smart cookie.

When I was a little girl we traveled to Mexico City so much I thought my grandparents' house on La Fortuna, number 12, was home. It was the only constant in our nomadic ramblings from one Chicago flat to another. The house on Destiny Street, number 12, in the colonia Tepeyac would be perhaps the only home I knew, and that nostalgia for a home would be a theme that would obsess me.

My brothers also figured greatly in my art. Especially the older two; I grew up in their shadows. Henry, the second oldest and my favorite, appears often in poems I have written and in stories which at times only borrow his nickname, Kiki. He played a major role in my childhood. We were bunk-bed mates. We were co-conspirators. We were pals. Until my oldest brother came back from studying in Mexico and left me odd woman out for always.

What would my teachers say if they knew I was a writer now? Who would've guessed it? I wasn't a very bright student. I didn't much like school because we moved so much and I was always new and funny looking. In my fifth-grade report card I have nothing but an avalanche of C's and D's, but I don't remember being that stupid. I was good at art and I read plenty of library books and Kiki laughed at all my jokes. At home I was fine, but at school I never opened my mouth except when the teacher called on me.

When I think of how I see myself it would have to be at age eleven. I know I'm thirty-two on the outside, but inside I'm eleven. I'm the girl in the picture with skinny arms and a crumpled skirt and crooked hair. I didn't like school because all they saw was the outside me. School was lots of rules and sitting with your hands folded and being very afraid all the time. I liked looking out the window and thinking. I liked staring at the girl across the way writing her name over and over again in red ink. I wondered why the boy with the dirty collar in front of me didn't have a mama who took better care of him.

I think my mama and papa did the best they could to keep us warm and clean and never hungry. We had birthday and graduation parties and things like that, but there was another hunger that had to be fed. There was a hunger I didn't even have a name for. Was this when I began writing?

In 1966 we moved into a house, a real one, our first real home. This meant we didn't have to change schools and be the new kids on the block every couple of years. We could make friends and not be afraid we'd have to say goodbye to them and start all over. My brothers and the flock of boys they brought home would become important characters eventually for my stories — Louie and his cousins, Meme Ortiz and his dog with two names, one in English and one in Spanish.

My mother flourished in her own home. She took books out of the library and taught herself to garden — to grow flowers so envied we had to put a lock on the gate to keep out the midnight flower thieves. My mother has never quit gardening.

This was the period in my life, that slippery age when you are both child and woman and neither I was to record in *The House on Mango Street*. I was still shy. I was a girl who couldn't come out of her shell.

How was I to know I would be recording and documenting the women who sat their sadness on an elbow and stared out a window? It would be the city streets of Chicago I would later record, as seen through a child's eyes.

I've done all kinds of things I didn't think I could do since then. I've gone to a prestigious university, studied with famous writers, and taken an M.F.A. degree. I've taught poetry in schools in Illinois and Texas. I've gotten an NEA grant and run away with it as far as my courage would take me. I've seen the bleached and bitter mountains of the Peloponnesus. I've lived on an island. I've been to Venice twice. I've lived in Yugoslavia. I've been to the famous Nice flower market behind the opera house. I've lived in a village in the pre-Alps and witnessed the daily parade of promenaders.

I've moved since Europe to the strange and wonderful country of Texas, land of polaroid-blue skies and big bugs. I met a mayor with my last name. I met famous Chicana and Chicano artists and writers and *politicos*.

Texas is another chapter in my life. It brought with it the Dobie-Paisano Fellowship, a six-month residency on a 265-acre ranch. But most important, Texas brought Mexico back to me.

In the days when I would sit at my favorite people-watching spot, the snakey Woolworth's counter across the street from the Alamo (the Woolworth's which has since been torn down to make way for progress), I couldn't think of anything else I'd rather be than a writer. I've traveled and lectured from Cape Cod to San Francisco, to Spain, Yugoslavia, Greece, Mexico, France, Italy, and now today to Texas. Along the way there has been straw for the taking. With a little imagination, it can be spun into gold.

ELLEN McCRACKEN

On Cisneros's The House on Mango Street   1989

Sandra Cisneros's *The House on Mango Street* was published by a small regional press in 1984 and reprinted in a second edition of 3,000 in 1985.[1] Difficult to find in most libraries and bookstores, it is well known among Chicano critics and scholars, but virtually unheard of in larger academic and critical circles. In May 1985 it won the Before Columbus Foundation's American Book Award,[2] but this prize has not greatly increased the volume's national visibility. Cisneros's book has not been excluded from the canon solely because of its

---

[1] For the figures on the press run see Pedro Gutiérrez-Revuelta, "Género e ideología en el libro de Sandra Cisneros: *The House on Mango Street*," *Crítica* 1 no. 3 (1986):48–59.

[2] Gutiérrez-Revuelta, "Género e ideología," 48. This critic also cites nine articles that have appeared to date on Cisneros's text. They consist primarily of reviews in Texas newspapers and articles in Chicano journals. See also Erlinda González-Berry and Tey Diana Rebolledo's "Growing up Chicano: Tomás Rivera and Sandra Cisneros," *Revista Chicano-Riqueña* 13 (1985):109–19.

publishing circumstances: major publishing houses are quick to capitalize on a Richard Rodríguez whose widely distributed and reviewed *Hunger of Memory* (1982) does not depart ideologically and semantically from the dominant discourse. They are even willing to market an Anglo writer as a Chicano, as occurred in 1983 with Danny Santiago's *Famous All Over Town*. Rather, Cisneros's text is likely to continue to be excluded from the canon because it "speaks another language altogether," one to which the critics of the literary establishment "remain blind."

Besides the double marginalization that stems from gender and ethnicity, Cisneros transgresses the dominant discourse of canonical standards ideologically and linguistically. In bold contrast to the individualistic introspection of many canonical texts, Cisneros writes a modified autobiographical novel, or *Bildungsroman*, that roots the individual self in the broader sociopolitical reality of the Chicano community. As we will see, the story of individual development is oriented outwardly here, away from the bourgeois individualism of many standard texts. Cisneros's language also contributes to the text's otherness. In opposition to the complex, hermetic language of many canonical works, *The House on Mango Street* recuperates the simplicity of children's speech, paralleling the autobiographical protagonist's chronological age in the book. Although making the text accessible to people with a wider range of reading abilities, such simple and well-crafted prose is not currently in canonical vogue.

The volume falls between traditional genre distinctions as well. Containing a group of forty-four short and interrelated stories, the book has been classified as a novel by some because, as occurs in Tomás Rivera's . . . *y no se lo tragó la tierra*, there is character and plot development throughout the episodes. I prefer to classify Cisneros's text as a collection, a hybrid genre midway between the novel and the short story. Like Sherwood Anderson's *Winesburg, Ohio*, Pedro Juan Soto's *Spiks*, Gloria Naylor's *The Women of Brewster Place*, and Rivera's text,[3] Cisneros's collection represents the writer's attempt to achieve both the intensity of the short story and the discursive length of the novel within a single volume. Unlike the chapters of most novels, each story in the collection could stand on its own if it were to be excerpted but each attains additional important meaning when interacting with the other stories in the volume. A number of structural and thematic elements link the stories of each collection together. Whereas in *Winesburg, Ohio*, one important structuring element is the town itself, in *The House on Mango Street* and . . . *y no se lo tragó la tierra* the image of the house is a central unifying motif.

On the surface the compelling desire for a house of one's own appears individualistic rather then community oriented, but Cisneros socializes the

---

[3] Sherwood Anderson, *Winesburg, Ohio* (New York: Viking Press, 1964, rpt. 1970); Pedro Juan Soto, *Spiks*, trans. Victoria Ortiz (New York: Monthly Review Press, 1973); Gloria Naylor, *The Women of Brewster Place* (New York: Penguin Books, 1983); and Tomás Rivera, . . . *y no se lo tragó la tierra / And the Earth Did Not Part* (Berkeley: Quinto Sol, 1971). Among the many specific comparisons that might be made, Naylor's "Cora Lee" has much in common with Cisneros's "There Was an Old Woman She Had So Many Children She Didn't Know What to Do."

motif of the house, showing it to be a basic human need left unsatisfied for many of the minority population under capitalism. It is precisely the lack of housing stability that motivates the image's centrality in works by writers like Cisneros and Rivera. For the migrant worker who has moved continuously because of job exigencies and who, like many others in the Chicano community, has been deprived of an adequate place to live because of the inequities of income distribution in U.S. society, the desire for a house is not a sign of individualistic acquisitiveness but rather represents the satisfaction of a basic human need. Cisneros begins her narrative with a description of the housing conditions the protagonist's family has experienced:

> We didn't always live on Mango Street. Before that we lived on Loomis on the third floor and before that we lived on Keeler. Before Keeler it was Paulina, and before that I can't remember. But what I remember most is moving a lot. . . .
> We had to leave the flat on Loomis quick. The water pipes broke and the landlord wouldn't fix them because the house was too old. . . . We were using the washroom next door and carrying water over in empty milk gallons.

Cisneros has socialized the motif of a house of one's own by showing its motivating roots to be the inadequate housing conditions in which she and others in her community lived. We learn that Esperanza, the protagonist Cisneros creates, was subjected to humiliation by her teachers because of her family's living conditions. "You live *there?*" a nun from her school had remarked when seeing Esperanza playing in front of the flat on Loomis. "*There.* I had to look where she pointed — the third floor, the paint peeling, wooden bars Papa had nailed on the windows so we wouldn't fall out. You live *there?* The way she said it made me feel like nothing. . . ." Later, after the move to the house on Mango Street that is better but still unsatisfactory, the Sister Superior at her school responds to Esperanza's request to eat lunch in the cafeteria rather than returning home by apparently humiliating the child deliberately: "You don't live far, she says. . . . I bet I can see your house from my window. Which one? . . . That one? she said pointing to a row of ugly 3-flats, the ones even the raggedy men are ashamed to go into. Yes, I nodded even though I knew that wasn't my house and started to cry. . . ." The Sister Superior is revealing her own prejudices; in effect, she is telling the child, "All you Mexicans must live in such buildings." It is in response to humiliations such as these that the autobiographical protagonist expresses her need for a house of her own. Rather than the mere desire to possess private property, Esperanza's wish for a house represents a positive objectification of the self, the chance to redress humiliation and establish a dignified sense of her own personhood.

Cisneros links this positive objectification that a house of one's own can provide to the process of artistic creation. Early on, the protagonist remarks that the dream of a white house "with trees around it, a great big yard and grass growing without a fence" structured the bedtime stories her mother told them. This early connection of the ideal house to fiction is developed throughout the collection, especially in the final two stories. In "A House of My Own," the protagonist remarks that the desired house would contain "my books and stories" and that such a house is as necessary to the writing process as paper: "Only a house quiet as snow, a space for myself to go, clean as paper before the poem." In "Mango Says Goodbye Sometimes," the Mango Street house, which falls short of the ideal dream house, becomes a symbol of the writer's attainment of her identity through artistic creation. Admitting that she both belonged and did not belong to the "sad red house" on Mango Street, the protagonist comes to terms with the ethnic consciousness that this house represents through the process of fictive creation: "I put it down on paper and then the ghost does not ache so much. I write it down and Mango says goodbye sometimes. She does not hold me with both arms. She sets me free." She is released materially to find a more suitable dwelling that will facilitate her writing; psychologically, she alleviates the ethnic anguish that she has heretofore attempted to repress. It is important, however, that she view her departure from the Mango Street house to enable her artistic production in social rather than isolationist terms: "They will know I have gone away to come back. For the ones I left behind. For the ones who cannot get out." . . .

Cisneros touches on several other important women's issues in this volume, including media images of ideal female beauty, the reifying stare of male surveyors of women, and sex roles within the family. In an effort to counter the sexual division of labor in the home, for example, Esperanza refuses one instance of women's work: "I have begun my own quiet war. Simple. Sure. I am the one who leaves the table like a man, without pulling back the chair or picking up the plate." Although this gesture calls critical attention to gender inequities in the family, Cisneros avoids the issue of who, in fact, will end up performing the household labor that Esperanza refuses here. This important and symbolic, yet somewhat adolescent gesture merely touches on the surface of the problem and is likely, in fact, to increase the work for another woman in Esperanza's household.

The majority of stories in *The House on Mango Street*, however, face important social issues head-on. The volume's simple, poetic language, with its insistence that the individual develops within a social community rather than in isolation, distances it from many accepted canonical texts.[4] Its deceptively simple, childlike prose and its emphasis on the unromanticized, nonmainstream issues of patriarchal violence and ethnic poverty, however, should serve precisely to accord it canonical status. We must work toward a broader understanding among literary critics of the importance of such issues to art in order to attain a richer, more diverse canon and to avoid the undervaluation and oversight of such valuable texts as *The House on Mango Street*.

---

[4] Other critics have argued that Esperanza's departure from Mango Street is individualistic and escapist, and that the desire for a house of her own away from the barrio represents a belief in the American Dream. See Gutiérrez-Revuelta, "Género e ideología," 52–55 and Juan Rodríguez, "*The House on Mango Street* by Sandra Cisneros," *Austin Chronicle*, 10 Aug. 1984 (cited in Gutiérrez-Revuelta, p. 52). I find that the text itself supports the opposite view, as does the author's choice of employment. Cisneros has returned to a Chicago barrio, teaching creative writing at an alternative high school for drop-outs. See "About Sandra Cisneros," *The House on Mango Street*, 103.

JULIÁN OLIVARES

The House on Mango Street *and*
the Poetics of Space

1988

In some recent essays collectively titled "From a Writer's Notebook,"[1] Sandra Cisneros talks about her development as a writer, making particular references to her award-winning book, *The House on Mango Street*.[2] She states that the nostalgia for the perfect house was impressed on her at an early age from reading many times Virginia Lee Burton's *The Little House*. It was not until her tenure at the Iowa Writers Workshop, however, that it dawned on her that a house, her childhood home, could be the subject of a book. In a class discussion of Gaston Bachelard's *The Poetics of Space*, she came to this realization: "the metaphor of a house — *a house, a house,* it hit me. What did I know except third-floor flats. Surely my classmates knew nothing about that" ("Ghosts and Voices," 72–73). Yet Cisneros's reverie and depiction of house differ markedly from Bachelard's poetic space of house. With Bachelard we note a house conceived in terms of a male-centered ideology. A man born in the upper-crust family house, probably never having to do "female" housework and probably never having been confined to the house for reason of his sex, can easily contrive states of reverie and images of a house that a woman might not have, especially an impoverished woman raised in a ghetto. Thus, for Bachelard the house is an image of "felicitous space . . . the house shelters daydreaming, the house protects the dreamer, the house allows one to dream in peace. . . . A house constitutes a body of images that give mankind proofs or illusions of stability."[3] Cisneros inverts Bachelard's nostalgic and privileged utopia, for hers is a different reality: "That's precisely what I chose to write: about third-floor flats, and fear of rats, and drunk husbands sending rocks through windows, anything as far from the poetic as possible. And this is when I discovered the voice I'd been suppressing all along without realizing it."[4]

The determination of genre for *Mango Street* has posed a problem for some critics.[5] Is *Mango Street* a novel, short stories, prose poems, vignettes? Cisneros herself states:

> I recall I wanted to write stories that were a cross between poetry and fiction. I was greatly impressed by Jorge Luis Borges' *Dreamtigers* stories for their form. I liked how he could fit so much into a page and that the last line of each story was important to the whole in much the

---

[1] "From a Writer's Notebook": "Ghosts and Voices: Writing from Obsession," "Do You Know Me? I Wrote *The House on Mango Street*," *The Americas Review* 15:1 (1987), 69–73, 77–79.

[2] *The House on Mango Street* (Houston: Arte Público Press, 1984).

[3] *The Poetics of Space*, Trans. María Jolas (Boston: Beacon Press, 1969).

[4] Although Cisneros echoes the strong family bonds that Tomás Rivera speaks of with regard to the *casa*, home, theme, her criticism of patriarchal domination offers a challenging perspective. See Rivera for his discussion of the themes of *casa, barrio,* and *lucha* in Chicano literature, in "Chicano Literature: Fiesta of the Living," *Books Abroad* 49:3 (1975), 439–52.

[5] Pedro Gutiérrez-Revuelta, "Género e ideología en el libro de Sandra Cisneros: *The House on Mango Street*," *Crítica* 1:3 (1986), 48–59.

same way that the final lines in poems resonate. Except I wanted to write a collection which could be read at any random point without having any knowledge of what came before or after. Or that could be read in a series to tell one big story. I wanted stories like poems, compact and lyrical and ending with a reverberation. ("Do You Know Me?," 78.)

She adds that if some of the stories read like poems, it is because some had been poems redone as stories or constructed from the debris of unfinished poems.[6] The focus, then, on compression and lyricism contributes to the brevity of the narratives. With regard to this generic classification, Cisneros states:

> I said once that I wrote *Mango Street* naively, that they were "lazy poems." In other words, for me each of the stories could've developed into poems, but they were not poems. They were stories, albeit hovering in that grey area between two genres. My newer work is still exploring this terrain. ("Do You Know Me?," 79.)

On a different occasion, Cisneros has called the stories "vignettes."[7] I would affirm that, although some of the narratives of *Mango Street* are "short stories," most are vignettes, that is, literary sketches, like small illustrations nonetheless "hovering in that grey area between two genres."

I should like to discuss some of these stories and vignettes in order to demonstrate the manner in which Cisneros employs her imagery as a poetics of space and, while treating an "unpoetic" subject — as she says, expresses it poetically so that she conveys another element that Bachelard notes inherent to this space, the dialectic of inside and outside, that is, *here* and *there*, integration and alienation, comfort and anxiety (211–12). However, Cisneros again inverts Bachelard's pronouncement on the poetics of space; for Cisneros the inside, the *here*, can be confinement and a source of anguish and alienation. In this discussion we will note examples of (1) how Cisneros expresses an ideological perspective of the downtrodden but, primarily, the condition of the Hispanic woman; (2) the process of a girl's growing up; and (3) the formation of the writer who contrives a special house of her own.

This book begins with the story of the same title: "The House on Mango Street." . . .

Mango Street is a street sign, a marker, that circumscribes the neighborhood to its Latino population of Puerto Ricans, Chicanos, and Mexican immigrants. This house is not the young protagonist's dream house; it is only a temporary house. The themes that we ordinarily perceive in house, and the ones that Bachelard assumes — such as comfort, security, tranquility, esteem — are lacking. This is a house that constrains, one that she wants to leave; consequently, the house sets up a dialectic of inside and outside: of living *here* and wishing to leave for *there*.

---

[6] E.g., "The Three Sisters," "Beautiful and Cruel," "A House of My Own," in "Do You Know Me?" 79.

[7] "The softly insistent voice of a poet," *Austin American Statesman* (March 11, 1986), 14–15.

The house becomes, essentially, the narrator's first universe. She begins here because it is the beginning of her conscious narrative reflection. She describes the house from the outside; this external depiction is a metonymical description and presentation of self: "I knew then I had to have a house. A real house. One I could point to." By pointing to this dilapidated house, she points to herself. House and narrator become identified as one, thereby revealing an ideological perspective of poverty and shame. Consequently, she wants to point to another house and to point to another self. And as she longs for this other house and self, she also longs for another name. But she will find that in growing up and writing, she will come to inhabit a special house and to fit into, find comfort, in her name.

In "My Name" the protagonist says: "In English my name means hope. In Spanish it means too many letters. It means sadness, it means waiting. . . . It is the Mexican records my father plays on Sunday mornings when he is shaving, songs like sobbing." In this vignette Esperanza traces the reason for the discomfiture with her name to cultural oppression, the Mexican males' suppression of their women. Esperanza was named after her Mexican great-grandmother who was wild but tamed by her husband, so that: "She looked out the window all her life, the way so many women sit their sadness on an elbow. . . . Esperanza, I have inherited her name, but I don't want to inherit her place by the window." Here we have not the space of contentment but of sadness, and a dialectic of inside/outside. The woman's place is one of domestic confinement, not one of liberation and choice. Thus, Esperanza would like to baptize herself "under a new name, a name more like the real me, the one nobody sees. Esperanza as Lisandra or Maritza or Zeze the X. Yes. Something like Zeze the X will do." That is, Esperanza prefers a name not culturally embedded in a dominating, male-centered ideology.

I do not hold with Juan Rodríguez that Cisneros's book ultimately sets forth the traditional ideology that happiness, for example, comes with the realization of the "American Dream," a house of one's own. In his review of *Mango Street*, Rodríguez states:

> That Esperanza chooses to leave Mango St[reet], chooses to move away from her social/cultural base to become more "Anglicized," more individualistic; that she chooses to move from the real to the fantasy plane of the world as the only means of accepting and surviving the limited and limiting social conditions of her barrio becomes problematic to the more serious reader.[8]

This insistence on the preference for a comforting and materialistic life ignores the ideology of a social class' liberation, particularly that of its women, to whom the book is dedicated. The house the protagonist longs for, certainly, is a house where she can have her own room[9] and one that she can point to in pride, but, as noted through this discussion of the poetics of space, it is funda-

---

[8] *"The House on Mango Street,* by Sandra Cisneros," *Austin Chronicle* (August 10, 1984), cited in Gutiérrez-Revuelta, 52.

[9] Cf. Virginia Woolf, *A Room of One's Own* (1929).

mentally a metaphor for the house of story-telling. Neither here in the house on Mango Street nor in the "fantasy plane of the world" — as Rodríguez states, does the protagonist indulge in escapism. Esperanza wants to leave but is unable, so she attains release from her confinement through her writing. Yet even here she never leaves Mango Street; because, instead of fantasizing, she writes of her reality.[10] Erlinda Gonzales and Diana Rebolledo confirm that the house is symbolic of consciousness and collective memory, and is a nourishing structure so that "the narrator comes to understand that, despite her need for a space of her own, Mango Street *is* really a part of her — an essential creative part she will never be able to leave"; consequently, she searches in (as narrator) and will return to (as author) her neighborhood "for the human and historical materials of which [her] stories will be made."[11] On the higher plane of art, then, Esperanza transcends her condition, finding another house which is the space of literature. Yet what she writes about — "third-floor flats, and fear of rats, and drunk husbands sending rocks through windows, anything as far from the poetic as possible" — reinforces her solidarity with the people, the women, of Mango Street.

We can agree, and probably Cisneros on this occasion does, with Bachelard's observation on the house as the space of daydreaming: "the places in which we have experienced daydreaming reconstitute themselves in a new daydream, and it is because our memories of former dwelling places are relived as daydreams that these dwelling places of the past remain in us for all time." The house that Esperanza lives and lived in will always be associated with the house of story-telling — "What I remember most is Mango Street"; because of it she became a writer. Esperanza will leave Mango Street but take it with her for always, for it is inscribed within her.

ALVINA E. QUINTANA

The House as Symbol　　　　　　　　　　　*1991*

Franz Fanon has outlined three stages that characterize the works of native writers who challenge colonial structures. In the first phase, "a period of unqualified assimilation," the native writer gives proof that she has assimi-

---

[10] Even were she to move away from the barrio and have her own house, Esperanza states her conviction not to forget who she is nor where she came from:

> One day I'll own my own house, but I won't forget who I am or where I came from. Passing bums will ask, Can I come in? I'll offer them the attic, ask them to stay, because I know how it is to be without a house.
> Some days after dinner, guests and I will sit in front of a fire. Floorboards will squeak upstairs. The attic grumble.
> Rats? they'll ask.
> Bums, I'll say, and I'll be happy.
> — "Bums in the Attic," 81.

[11] "Growing Up Chicano: Tomás Rivera and Sandra Cisneros," *International Studies in Honor of Tomás Rivera*, ed. Julián Olivares (Houston: Arte Público Press, 1985), 109–20.

lated the occupying power. In the second, the native writer is disturbed; "he decides to remember what he is. . . . Past happenings of the bygone days of his childhood will be brought up out of the depths of his memory; old legends will be reinterpreted in the light of a borrowed aestheticism and of a conception of the world which was discovered under other skies." Although often symptomatic of a period of distress and difficulty characterized by experiences of death and disgust, the literature of this phase is dominated by humor and allegory. (In stage three, the writer reveals a clear sense of political autonomy.)[1]

Firmly planted in Fanon's second phase, Cisneros uses her protagonist to subtly equate the assimilated mind-set with that of a naive adolescent. Her narrative strategy gives her the freedom, in the final stories, to deconstruct childish, yet mainstream, assumptions. Now we witness a change in Esperanza's attitude. She begins to develop a critical awareness of social boundaries as she modifies her cultural perspective. In "Bums in the Attic," she states:

> People who live on hills sleep so close to the stars they forget those of us who live too much on earth. They don't look down at all except to be content to live on hills. They have nothing to do with last week's garbage or fear of rats. Night comes. Nothing wakes them but the wind. One day I'll own my own house, but I won't forget who I am or where I came from. Passing bums will ask, Can I come in? I'll offer them the attic, ask them to stay, because I know how it is to be without a house.[2]

While Esperanza's reflections reveal limited social awareness, they disclose the critical sophistication and literary skill of the "real author." Through Esperanza's characterization, Cisneros depicts some of the inner conflicts that develop as marginalized individuals attempt to resolve the apparent disjunction between their desires for cultural integrity and for individual liberation.

The symbol Cisneros chooses to represent the ideological, cultural, and economic limits imposed on the marginalized woman's space is the house. For Esperanza, life becomes a struggle to secure individual success and, her ultimate aspiration, a house of her own, a home unlike her family's, which is "small and red with tight little steps in front and windows so small you'd think they were holding their breath. Bricks are crumbling in places, and the front door is so swollen you have to push hard to get in." Esperanza longs for a house like the one in her mother's bedtime stories, "white with trees around it, a great big yard and grass growing without a fence."

The narrative unfolds around this recurrent motif, introduced in its title. *The House on Mango Street* subtly suggests a series of possible readings. Even though the use of more than one language in a single phrase is common in the United States, it nonetheless represents a linguistic practice that accommo-

---

[1] Franz Fanon, *The Wretched of the Earth*, trans. Constance Farrington (New York: Grove, 1966).

[2] Sandra Cisneros, *The House on Mango Street* (Houston: Arte Publico, 1984), 81.

dates diversity. Because Cisneros's title draws on two languages, it suggests a primordial blending of two cultural systems.[3] When we also consider how the concept of house lends itself to public and private worlds, we are in a position to understand the breadth of Cisneros's narrative.

On a material level one's house symbolically reflects one's success and achievement to the outside world. Yet in more figurative terms, the word denotes the domestic sphere, a metonomy for women's space. To the private/public dialectic Cisneros adds yet another opposition: insider/outsider cultural values, the political implications of the dominant cultural system of the United States as well as the internal convictions emphasized by Mexican culture. House becomes the metaphor for success and escape from the limitations imposed on Chicanas by cultural traditions, as well as for the boundaries and limitations of poverty. The story "A House of My Own" underscores as it expands the issues raised by Virginia Woolf in *A Room of One's Own*:

> Not a flat. Not an apartment in back. Not a man's house. Not a daddy's. A house all my own. With my porch and my pillow, my pretty purple petunias. My books and my stories. My two shoes waiting beside the bed. Nobody to shake a stick at. Nobody's garbage to pick up after. Only a house quiet as snow, a space for myself to go, clean as paper before the poem.

Cisneros's poetic text defies prosaic convention; syncopated fragments punctuated as complete thoughts make us aware of the writer's experimentation with form. "A House of My Own" graphically redefines domestic spaces as effectively as it crosses genres.

MARC ZIMMERMAN

U.S. Latino Literature: History and Development 1992

LATINO POPULATIONS AND THREE PHASES
OF MIGRATION LITERATURE

Popular impressions aside, the core base of U.S. Mexican population derives not from the northward migration of people from south of the border, but from the southward and westward migration of the border itself. To this day, in spite of great waves of immigration, the bulk of Mexican-descent population growth is from birth as opposed to immigration patterns. However, in addition to the Mexican population made part of the U.S. by wars of conquest, Mexican and then Mexican *tejano* migration became a major aspect of the U.S. Mexican population base, beginning early in the twentieth century, during the Mexican Revolution, in relation to the demand for labor on the railroads, in the fields, and of course in the steel mills, canning, food-processing,

---

[3] *Mango*, a Ceylonese word, is in common use among English speakers, a practice that illustrates my point. [Quintana's note]

and meat-packing plants of the Midwest. Through ups and downs, periods of mass deportations and expanding immigration, that population base continued to grow and to be joined after World War II by a major Puerto Rican exodus — and then by Cubans, significant numbers from the Dominican Republic, Ecuador, Colombia, Chile, and elsewhere.

To be sure, many Puerto Ricans, Cubans, and others came to the East Coast, and especially to New York, in the late nineteenth century. But the Puerto Rican exodus intensified after the U.S. took the island in 1898 and especially after the developmentalist projects culminating in "Operation Bootstrap" pushed many people off the land and sent them first to San Juan, and then New York and other U.S. points in a search for work and survival. Of course the major waves of Cuban migration came immediately after the Revolution of 1959 and the exodus from the port of Mariel in 1980. Finally, since in recent years, growing numbers of Guatemalans, Salvadorans, and Nicaraguans fleeing the political and economic crises in their respective countries have added to a core Mexican–Puerto Rican–Cuban population base which continues to expand because of high birth rates and homebase economic hardships throughout the decade.

Although heterogenous, the Mexican and Puerto Rican migrations were primarily working-class, and the groups brought with them those elements of their national and Latin American culture, oral tradition, and literature available to their social class and situations. For a distinct U.S. Latino culture and literature to emerge for each group in each locale, there had to be a sufficient experience of U.S. life, culture, and language, to pressure Latin American cultural norms, and there had to be a sufficient degree of critical consciousness, generated through hardship, but articulated through institutional or extra-institutional/countercultural formations to make writing as a vehicle of cultural definition both necessary and possible. Obviously that literary expression required an adequate pooling of resources for at least minimal cultural reproduction and distribution — from self-publishing to small chapbook and literary journal production. To the degree that each emergent work of literature tended to stand in relation to broader cultural, literary and sociopsychological patterns, that work tended to follow certain general lines of "mainstream" or minority literary development dominant nationally; but the work was also marked by certain characteristics specific to its place and group of generation. This meant that each expression by each member of a national group was at least in part filtered through a particular, sometimes regional, sometimes even a more local sense of Latino identity.

Clearly the resources available would affect literary production, as would the specific characteristics of Latino populations in given areas. But, leaving aside the Latin American literature written by professionals who have come to the U.S. as part of the brain drain, U.S. Latino literature may be divided into two major categories: (1) a literature based on and extending from long-ingrained indigenous U.S. Southwest homebase traditions, and (2) a literature based on the experience of those many primarily working-class people who have migrated from Mexico, Puerto Rico, and other parts of Latin America to the U.S. during the course of the twentieth century. To be sure many of the people of the first group have virtually become part of the second by a dislocation process which has uprooted them from their Southwest homes and sent them to work and sometimes to settle in other parts of the country, so that their original cultural and literary base, rooted in eighteenth- and nineteenth-century traditions, has been influenced, affected, and at least partially merged with the newer immigrant populations, which they have in turn also influenced. . . .

Now, under the impact of deconstructionism, feminism, postmarxism, and other postmodernist modes of thought, much contemporary Chicano writing male and female seeks to break through beyond earlier narrow ethnic concerns to ones which require new modes of understanding and analysis to grasp how the writing maintains or transcends earlier patterns and identifications. The new writing is inevitably more urban, more closely woven with other Latino and non-Latino cultural strains, more distanced from a pretechnological, precapitalist world of blood bonds and sacrifices, sacramental, ritualistic, and ceremonial relations with the earth and other humans; it is also distanced from the world of confrontational violence with Rangers, cops, or rival gangs.

In line with the educational circumstance achieved by at least a sector of Chicanos in U.S. life, writers like Gary Soto, Alberto Ríos, and several others are increasingly characterized by their withdrawal from Chicano ethnic literature and from the culturalist paradigm early identified with it. As for the feminist Chicana writers, Helena María Viramontes, Denise Chávez, as well as Ana Castillo and Sandra Cisneros, seem to drift both from Bruce-Novoa's spatial identification or Saldívar's construction of machistic border and barrio defiance; they struggle ambivalently with the older paradigms as well as the repression and the inscribed role of women which they find as central to them and to at least certain dimensions of the Chicano movement they have been seen to represent. Still others, like Cecile Piñeda, Sheila Ortiz Taylor, and Laurence Gonzales (cf. his *4-4-4* [Columbia, MO: University of Missouri Press, 1977]) seem fully turned toward the mainstream without struggling with the older paradigms or being particularly centered on them.

Nevertheless, in one way or another, many contemporary Chicano writers, and especially male ones, directly or indirectly, consciously or not, project the early paradigmatic Chicano vision into contemporary settings and circumstances; and it may well be that contemporary feminist work as well as other "new wave"–tending Chicano literature can still be shown to partake, however critically, of a land-centered structural view as a necessarily regressive, precapitalist oppositional mode, now refashioned to project a more progressive, late capitalist resistant pattern. If this is the case, then we would still be able to establish the core ties of Chicano writers to a vision which is very specifically rooted in a syncretic "imaginary" where Mexican and U.S. polarities find their resolution. We would still be able to speak of a specifically "ethnic" literature, rather than a general literature written by writers who just happen to be Chicano.

This orientation may continue to have importance if we believe that even the enforcement of the new immigration laws cannot resist the pressure

created by circumstances in Mexico, and that, even as we have new generations of sophisticated Chicanos able to read and absorb the sophisticated writings of new writers, we will continue to have large, new Chicano social sectors
who must find or create a literature expressive of and suited to their own situation and experience.

ров

CASEBOOK ON FLANNERY O'CONNOR

*Flannery O'Connor is unusual among writers in that she shared with readers
her own interpretations of her stories. While acknowledging that there is usually
more than one way to read a story, she also stated that there was only one way she
could possibly have written it. O'Connor's discussion of "A Good Man Is Hard to
Find" (p. 558) can be read alongside the interpretations of "Good Country People"
(p. 543) and "Everything That Rises Must Converge" (p. 532) by academic critics
Dorothy Tuck McFarland and Wayne C. Booth. The noted English short story writer
and critic V. S. Pritchett gives his overview of O'Connor's literary achievement,
and Robert H. Brinkmeyer, Jr., considers the relationship between O'Connor and her
readers.*

FLANNERY O'CONNOR

From Letters, 1954–55   *1955*

TO SALLY FITZGERALD

26 Dec 54

. . . I have finally got off the ms. for my collection [*A Good Man Is Hard to
Find*] and it is scheduled to appear in May. Without yr kind permission I have
taken the liberty of dedicating (grand verb) it to you and Robert. This is because you all are my adopted kin and if I dedicated it to any of my blood kin
they would think they had to go into hiding. Nine stories about original sin,
with my compliments.

I have been invited to go to Greensboro to the Women's College in
March to be on an arts panel. That is where Brother Randall Jarrell° holds
forth. I accepted but I am not looking forward to it. Can you fancy me hung in
conversation with the likes of him?

When I had lunch with Giroux [O'Connor's editor] in Atlanta he told me
about Cal's escapade in Cincinnati. It seems [Cal] convinced everybody it was
Elizabeth who was going crazy. . . . Toward the end he gave a lecture at the
university that was almost pure gibberish. I guess nobody noticed, thinking it
was the new criticism. . . .

Randall Jarrell: American poet and influential critic (1914–1965).

I just got a check for $200 for the 2nd prize in the O. Henry book° this year. My ex-mentor Paul Engle does the selecting. Jean Stafford° got the first one.

I am walking with a cane these days which gives me a great air of distinction. The scientist tells me this has nothing to do with the lupus but is rheumatism. I would not believe it except that the dose of ACTH has not been increased. Besides which I now feel it makes very little difference what you call it. As the niggers say, I have the misery.

I am reading everything I can of Romano Guardini's [Italian priest and theologian]. Have you become acquainted with his work? A book called *The Lord* of his is very fine.

TO ELIZABETH McKEE

13 January 1955

The carbon of "An Exile in the East" is enclosed, but I don't know if you realize or not that this is a rewritten version of "The Geranium" originally printed in *Accent*. *Accent* didn't pay me for it and it is rather much changed, but I enclose both stories so [the editor] can see what she's doing. I don't want to go to the penitentiary for selling a story twice (but if I do I would like to get a good price for the story).

TO ROBERT GIROUX

22 January 55

Nothing has been said about a picture for the jacket of this collection *but if you have to have one*, I would be much obliged if you could use the enclosed so that I won't have to have a new picture made. This is a self-portrait with a pheasant cock, that I painted in 1953; however, I think it will do justice to the subject for some time to come.

26 February 55

I have just written a story called "Good Country People" that Allen and Caroline [Tate?] both say is the best thing I have written and should be in this collection. I told them I thought it was too late, but anyhow I am writing now to ask if it is. It is really a story that would set the whole collection on its feet. It is 27 pages and if you can eliminate the one called "A Stroke of Good Fortune," and the other called "An Afternoon in the Woods," this one would fit the available space nicely. Also I remember you said it would be good to have one that had never been published before. I could send it to you at once *on being wired*. Please let me know.

Giroux wired O'Connor that every effort would be made to include the story. After he had read it, he wrote suggesting that an appearance by the mother and Mrs. Freeman at the end might improve it. Flannery recognized the value of the suggestion and added the sentences that are now a part of the story.

O. Henry book: The O. Henry Prizes are awarded annually to outstanding American short stories, which are collected each year in a book. O. Henry was the pen name of the popular American short story writer William Sydney Porter (1862–1910).
Jean Stafford: American short story writer and novelist (1915–1979).

7 March 55

I like the suggestion about the ending of "Good Country People" and enclose a dozen or so lines that can be added on to *the present end*. I enclose them in case you can get them put on before I get the proofs. I am mighty wary of making changes on proofs. . . .

TO SALLY AND ROBERT FITZGERALD

1 April 55

We are wondering if #6 is here yet or due to arrive momentarily. Let us hear and if you need any names, I'll be glad to cable you a rich collection. I have just got back from Greensboro where I said nothing intelligent the whole time, but enjoyed myself. Mr. Randall Jarrell, wife and stepdaughters I met and et dinner with. I must say I was shocked at what a very kind man he is — that is the last impression I expected to have of him. I also met Peter Taylor,° who is more like folks. Mrs. Jarrell is writing a novel. You get the impression the two stepdaughters may be at it too and maybe the dog. Mr. Jarrell has a beard and looks like Mephistopheles (sp?) only fatter. Mrs. Jarrell is very friendly & sunkist.

The Easter rabbit is bringing my mother a three-quarter ton truck.

I trust Giroux will be sending you a copy of the book soon. I wrote a very hot story at the last minute called "Good Country People": so now there are ten.

While I was in NC I heard somebody recite a barroom ballad. I don't remember anything but the end but beinst you all are poets I will give it to you as it is mighty deathless:

> "They stacked the stiffs outside the door.
> They made, I reckon, a cord or more."

I call that real poetry.

I have put the cane up and am walking on my own very well. Let us hear. Regards to children.

FLANNERY O'CONNOR

Writing Short Stories

1961

. . . Perhaps the central question to be considered in any discussion of the short story is what do we mean by short. Being short does not mean being slight. A short story should be long in depth and should give us an experience of meaning. I have an aunt who thinks that nothing happens in a story unless somebody gets married or shot at the end of it. I wrote a story about a tramp who marries an old woman's idiot daughter in order to acquire the old woman's automobile. After the marriage, he takes the daughter off on a wedding trip in the automobile and abandons her in an eating place and drives on by himself. Now that is a complete story. There is nothing more relating to the

---

Peter Taylor: Tennessee born and bred novelist and short story writer (1917–1994).

mystery of that man's personality that could be shown through that particular dramatization. But I've never been able to convince my aunt that it's a complete story. She wants to know what happened to the idiot daughter after that.

Not long ago that story was adapted for a television play, and the adapter, knowing his business, had the tramp have a change of heart and go back and pick up the idiot daughter and the two of them ride away, grinning madly. My aunt believes that the story is complete at last, but I have other sentiments about it — which are not suitable for public utterance. When you write a story, you only have to write one story, but there will always be people who will refuse to read the story you have written.

And this naturally brings up the awful question of what kind of a reader you are writing for when you write fiction. Perhaps we each think we have a personal solution for this problem. For my own part, I have a very high opinion of the art of fiction and a very low opinion of what is called the "average" reader. I tell myself that I can't escape him, that this is the personality I am supposed to keep awake, but that at the same time, I am also supposed to provide the intelligent reader with the deeper experience that he looks for in fiction. Now actually, both of these readers are just aspects of the writer's own personality, and in the last analysis, the only reader he can know anything about is himself. We all write at our own level of understanding, but it is the peculiar characteristic of fiction that its literal surface can be made to yield entertainment on an obvious physical plane to one sort of reader while the self-same surface can be made to yield meaning to the person equipped to experience it there.

Meaning is what keeps the short story from being short. I prefer to talk about the meaning in a story rather than the theme of a story. People talk about the theme of a story as if the theme were like the string that a sack of chicken feed is tied with. They think that if you can pick out the theme, the way you pick the right thread in the chicken-feed sack, you can rip the story open and feed the chickens. But this is not the way meaning works in fiction.

When you can state the theme of a story, when you can separate it from the story itself, then you can be sure the story is not a very good one. The meaning of a story has to be embodied in it, has to be made concrete in it. A story is a way to say something that can't be said any other way, and it takes every word in the story to say what the meaning is. You tell a story because a statement would be inadequate. When anybody asks what a story is about, the only proper thing is to tell him to read the story. The meaning of fiction is not abstract meaning but experienced meaning, and the purpose of making statements about the meaning of a story is only to help you to experience that meaning more fully.

Fiction is an art that calls for the strictest attention to the real — whether the writer is writing a naturalistic story or a fantasy. I mean that we always begin with what is or with what has an eminent possibility of truth about it. Even when one writes a fantasy, reality is the proper basis of it. A thing is fantastic because it is so real, so real that it is fantastic. Graham Greene° has said

---

Graham Greene: English writer (1904–1991).

that he can't write, "I stood over a bottomless pit," because that couldn't be true, or "Running down the stairs I jumped into a taxi," because that couldn't be true either. But Elizabeth Bowen° can write about one of her characters that "she snatched at her hair as if she heard something in it," because that is eminently possible.

I would even go so far as to say that the person writing a fantasy has to be even more strictly attentive to the concrete detail than someone writing in a naturalistic vein — because the greater the story's strain on the credulity, the more convincing the properties in it have to be.

A good example of this is a story called "The Metamorphosis" by Franz Kafka. This is a story about a man who wakes up one morning to find that he has turned into a cockroach overnight, while not discarding his human nature. The rest of the story concerns his life and feelings and eventual death as an insect with human nature, and this situation is accepted by the reader because the concrete detail of the story is absolutely convincing. The fact is that this story describes the dual nature of man in such a realistic fashion that it is almost unbearable. The truth is not distorted here, but rather, a certain distortion is used to get at the truth. If we admit, as we must, that appearance is not the same thing as reality, then we must give the artist the liberty to make certain rearrangements of nature if these will lead to greater depths of vision. The artist himself always has to remember that what he is rearranging *is* nature, and that he has to know it and be able to describe it accurately in order to have the authority to rearrange it at all.

The peculiar problem of the short-story writer is how to make the action he describes reveal as much of the mystery of existence as possible. He has only a short space to do it in and he can't do it by statement. He has to do it by showing, not by saying, and by showing the concrete — so that his problem is really how to make the concrete work double time for him.

In good fiction, certain of the details will tend to accumulate meaning from the action of the story itself, and when this happens they become symbolic in the way they work. I once wrote a story called "Good Country People," in which a lady Ph.D. has her wooden leg stolen by a Bible salesman whom she has tried to seduce. Now I'll admit that, paraphrased in this way, the situation is simply a low joke. The average reader is pleased to observe anybody's wooden leg being stolen. But without ceasing to appeal to him and without making any statements of high intention, this story does manage to operate at another level of experience, by letting the wooden leg accumulate meaning. Early in the story, we're presented with the fact that the Ph.D. is spiritually as well as physically crippled. She believes in nothing but her own belief in nothing, and we perceive that there is a wooden part of her soul that corresponds to her wooden leg. Now of course this is never stated. The fiction writer states as little as possible. The reader makes this connection from things he is shown. He may not even know that he makes the connection, but the connection is there nevertheless and it has its effect on him. As the story goes

---

Elizabeth Bowen: British novelist and short story writer (1899–1973).

on, the wooden leg continues to accumulate meaning. The reader learns how the girl feels about her leg, how her mother feels about it, and how the country woman on the place feels about it; and finally, by the time the Bible salesman comes along, the leg has accumulated so much meaning that it is, as the saying goes, loaded. And when the Bible salesman steals it, the reader realizes that he has taken away part of the girl's personality and has revealed her deeper affliction to her for the first time.

If you want to say that the wooden leg is a symbol, you can say that. But it is a wooden leg first, and as a wooden leg it is absolutely necessary to the story. It has its place on the literal level of the story, but it operates in depth as well as on the surface. It increases the story in every direction, and this is essentially the way a story escapes being short.

Now a little might be said about the way in which this happens. I wouldn't want you to think that in that story I sat down and said, "I am now going to write a story about a Ph.D. with a wooden leg, using the wooden leg as a symbol for another kind of affliction." I doubt myself if many writers know what they are going to do when they start out. When I started writing that story, I didn't know there was going to be a Ph.D. with a wooden leg in it. I merely found myself one morning writing a description of two women that I knew something about, and before I realized it, I had equipped one of them with a daughter with a wooden leg. As the story progressed, I brought in the Bible salesman, but I had no idea what I was going to do with him. I didn't know he was going to steal that wooden leg until ten or twelve lines before he did it, but when I found out that this was what was going to happen, I realized that it was inevitable. This is a story that produces a shock for the reader, and I think one reason for this is that it produced a shock for the writer.

Now despite the fact that this story came about in this seemingly mindless fashion, it is a story that almost no rewriting was done on. It is a story that was under control throughout the writing of it, and it might be asked how this kind of control comes about, since it is not entirely conscious.

I think the answer to this is what Maritain° calls "the habit of art." It is a fact that fiction writing is something in which the whole personality takes part — the conscious as well as the unconscious mind. Art is the habit of the artist; and habits have to be rooted deep in the whole personality. They have to be cultivated like any other habit, over a long period of time, by experience; and teaching any kind of writing is largely a matter of helping the student develop the habit of art. I think this is more than just a discipline, although it is that; I think it is a way of looking at the created world and of using the senses so as to make them find as much meaning as possible in things.

Now I am not so naïve as to suppose that most people come to writers' conferences in order to hear what kind of vision is necessary to write stories that will become a permanent part of our literature. Even if you do wish to hear this, your greatest concerns are immediately practical. You want to know how you can actually write a good story, and further, how you can tell when

---

Maritain: Jacques Maritain (1882–1973) was a French philosopher and critic.

you've done it; and so you want to know what the form of a short story is, as if the form were something that existed outside of each story and could be applied or imposed on the material. Of course, the more you write, the more you will realize that the form is organic, that it is something that grows out of the material, that the form of each story is unique. A story that is any good can't be reduced, it can only be expanded. A story is good when you continue to see more and more in it, and when it continues to escape you. In fiction two and two is always more than four.

The only way, I think, to learn to write short stories is to write them, and then to try to discover what you have done. The time to think of technique is when you've actually got the story in front of you. The teacher can help the student by looking at his individual work and trying to help him decide if he has written a complete story, one in which the action fully illuminates the meaning.

Perhaps the most profitable thing I can do is to tell you about some of the general observations I made about these seven stories I read of yours. All of these observations will not fit any one of the stories exactly, but they are points nevertheless that it won't hurt anyone interested in writing to think about.

The first thing that any professional writer is conscious of in reading anything is, naturally, the use of language. Now the use of language in these stories was such that, with one exception, it would be difficult to distinguish one story from another. While I can recall running into several clichés, I can't remember one image or one metaphor from the seven stories. I don't mean there weren't images in them; I just mean that there weren't any that were effective enough to take away with you.

In connection with this, I made another observation that startled me considerably. With the exception of one story, there was practically no use made of the local idiom. Now this is a Southern Writers' Conference. All the addresses on these stories were from Georgia or Tennessee, yet there was no distinctive sense of Southern life in them. A few place-names were dropped, Savannah or Atlanta or Jacksonville, but these could just as easily have been changed to Pittsburgh or Passaic without calling for any other alteration in the story. The characters spoke as if they had never heard any kind of language except what came out of a television set. This indicates that something is way out of focus.

There are two qualities that make fiction. One is the sense of mystery and the other is the sense of manners. You get the manners from the texture of existence that surrounds you. The great advantage of being a Southern writer is that we don't have to go anywhere to look for manners; bad or good, we've got them in abundance. We in the South live in a society that is rich in contradiction, rich in irony, rich in contrast, and particularly rich in its speech. And yet here are six stories by Southerners in which almost no use is made of the gifts of the region.

Of course the reason for this may be that you have seen these gifts abused so often that you have become self-conscious about using them. There is nothing worse than the writer who doesn't *use* the gifts of the region, but wallows in them. Everything becomes so Southern that it's sickening, so local that it is unintelligible, so literally reproduced that it conveys nothing. The general gets lost in the particular instead of being shown through it.

However, when the life that actually surrounds us is totally ignored, when our patterns of speech are absolutely overlooked, then something is out of kilter. The writer should then ask himself if he is not reaching out for a kind of life that is artificial to him.

An idiom characterizes a society, and when you ignore the idiom, you are very likely ignoring the whole social fabric that could make a meaningful character. You can't cut characters off from their society and say much about them as individuals. You can't say anything meaningful about the mystery of a personality unless you put that personality in a believable and significant social context. And the best way to do this is through the character's own language. When the old lady in one of Andrew Lytle's stories says contemptuously that she has a mule that is older than Birmingham, we get in that one sentence a sense of a society and its history. A great deal of the Southern writers' work is done for him before he begins, because our history lives in our talk. In one of Eudora Welty's stories a character says, "Where I come from, we use fox for yard dogs and owls for chickens, but we sing true." Now there is a whole book in that one sentence; and when the people of your section can talk like that, and you ignore it, you're just not taking advantage of what's yours. The sound of our talk is too definite to be discarded with impunity, and if the writer tries to get rid of it, he is liable to destroy the better part of his creative power.

Another thing I observed about these stories is that most of them don't go very far inside a character, don't reveal very much of the character. I don't mean that they don't enter the character's mind, but they simply don't show that he has a personality. Again this goes back partly to speech. These characters have no distinctive speech to reveal themselves with; and sometimes they have no really distinctive features. You feel in the end that no personality is revealed because no personality is there. In most good stories it is the character's personality that creates the action of the story. In most of these stories, I feel that the writer has thought of some action and then scrounged up a character to perform it. You will usually be more successful if you start the other way around. If you start with a real personality, a real character, then something is bound to happen; and you don't have to know what before you begin. In fact it may be better if you don't know what before you begin. You ought to be able to discover something from your stories. If you don't, probably nobody else will.

FLANNERY O'CONNOR

The Element of Suspense in "A Good Man Is Hard to Find"   1969

A story really isn't any good unless it successfully resists paraphrase, unless it hangs on and expands in the mind. Properly, you analyze to enjoy, but it's equally true that to analyze with any discrimination, you have to have enjoyed already, and I think that the best reason to hear a story read is that it should stimulate that primary enjoyment.

I don't have any pretensions to being an Aeschylus or Sophocles and providing you in this story with a cathartic experience out of your mythic background, though this story I'm going to read certainly calls up a good deal of the South's mythic background, and it should elicit from you a degree of pity and terror, even though its way of being serious is a comic one. I do think, though, that like the Greeks you should know what is going to happen in this story so that any element of suspense in it will be transferred from its surface to its interior.

I would be most happy if you had already read it, happier still if you knew it well, but since experience has taught me to keep my expectations along these lines modest, I'll tell you that this is the story of a family of six which, on its way driving to Florida, gets wiped out by an escaped convict who calls himself the Misfit. The family is made up of the Grandmother and her son, Bailey, and his children, John Wesley and June Star and the baby, and there is also the cat and the children's mother. The cat is named Pitty Sing, and the Grandmother is taking him with them, hidden in a basket.

Now I think it behooves me to try to establish with you the basis on which reason operates in this story. Much of my fiction takes its character from a reasonable use of the unreasonable, though the reasonableness of my use of it may not always be apparent. The assumptions that underlie this use of it, however, are those of the central Christian mysteries. These are assumptions to which a large part of the modern audience takes exception. About this I can only say that there are perhaps other ways than my own in which this story could be read, but none other by which it could have been written. Belief, in my own case anyway, is the engine that makes perception operate.

The heroine of this story, the Grandmother, is in the most significant position life offers the Christian. She is facing death. And to all appearances she, like the rest of us, is not too well prepared for it. She would like to see the event postponed. Indefinitely.

I've talked to a number of teachers who use this story in class and who tell their students that the Grandmother is evil, that in fact, she's a witch, even down to the cat. One of these teachers told me that his students, and particularly his southern students, resisted this interpretation with a certain bemused vigor, and he didn't understand why. I had to tell him that they resisted it because they all had grandmothers or great-aunts just like her at home, and they knew, from personal experience, that the old lady lacked comprehension, but that she had a good heart. The southerner is usually tolerant of those weaknesses that proceed from innocence, and he knows that a taste for self-preservation can be readily combined with the missionary spirit.

This same teacher was telling his students that morally the Misfit was several cuts above the Grandmother. He had a really sentimental attachment to the Misfit. But then a prophet gone wrong is almost always more interesting than your grandmother, and you have to let people take their pleasures where they find them.

It is true that the old lady is a hypocritical old soul; her wits are no match for the Misfit's, nor is her capacity for grace equal to his; yet I think the unprejudiced reader will feel that the Grandmother has a special kind of triumph in this story which instinctively we do not allow to someone altogether bad.

I often ask myself what makes a story work, and what makes it hold up as a story, and I have decided that it is probably some action, some gesture of a character that is unlike any other in the story, one which indicates where the real heart of the story lies. This would have to be an action or a gesture which was both totally right and totally unexpected; it would have to be one that was both in character and beyond character; it would have to suggest both the world and eternity. The action or gesture I'm talking about would have to be on the anagogical level, that is, the level which has to do with the Divine life and our participation in it. It would be a gesture that transcended any neat allegory that might have been intended or any pat moral categories a reader could make. It would be a gesture which somehow made contact with mystery.

There is a point in this story where such a gesture occurs. The Grandmother is at last alone, facing the Misfit. Her head clears for an instant and she realizes, even in her limited way, that she is responsible for the man before her and joined to him by ties of kinship which have their roots deep in the mystery she has been merely prattling about so far. And at this point, she does the right thing, she makes the right gesture.

I find that students are often puzzled by what she says and does here, but I think myself that if I took out this gesture and what she says with it, I would have no story. What was left would not be worth your attention. Our age not only does not have a very sharp eye for the almost imperceptible intrusions of grace, it no longer has much feeling for the nature of the violences which precede and follow them. The devil's greatest wile, Baudelaire has said, is to convince us that he does not exist.

I suppose the reasons for the use of so much violence in modern fiction will differ with each writer who uses it, but in my own stories I have found that violence is strangely capable of returning my characters to reality and preparing them to accept their moment of grace. Their heads are so hard that almost nothing else will do the work. This idea, that reality is something to which we must be returned at considerable cost, is one which is seldom understood by the casual reader, but it is one which is implicit in the Christian view of the world.

I don't want to equate the Misfit with the devil. I prefer to think that, however unlikely this may seem, the old lady's gesture, like the mustard-seed, will grow to be a great crow-filled tree in the Misfit's heart, and will be enough of a pain to him there to turn him into the prophet he was meant to become. But that's another story.

This story has been called grotesque, but I prefer to call it literal. A good story is literal in the same sense that a child's drawing is literal. When a child draws, he doesn't intend to distort but to set down exactly what he sees, and as his gaze is direct, he sees the lines that create motion. Now the lines of motion that interest the writer are usually invisible. They are lines of spiritual motion. And in this story you should be on the lookout for such things as the action of grace in the Grandmother's soul, and not for the dead bodies.

We hear many complaints about the prevalence of violence in modern fiction, and it is always assumed that this violence is a bad thing and meant to be an end in itself. With the serious writer, violence is never an end in itself. It is the extreme situation that best reveals what we are essentially, and I believe these are times when writers are more interested in what we are essentially than in the tenor of our daily lives. Violence is a force which can be used for good or evil, and among other things taken by it is the kingdom of heaven. But regardless of what can be taken by it, the man in the violent situation reveals those qualities least dispensable in his personality, those qualities which are all he will have to take into eternity with him; and since the characters in this story are all on the verge of eternity, it is appropriate to think of what they take with them. In any case, I hope that if you consider these points in connection with the story, you will come to see it as something more than an account of a family murdered on the way to Florida.

V. S. PRITCHETT

Flannery O'Connor: Satan Comes to Georgia
1980

All the characters in the very powerful stories of Flannery O'Connor — *Everything That Rises Must Converge* — are exposed: That is to say they are plain human beings in whose fractured lives the writer has discovered an uncouth relationship with the lasting myths and the violent passions of human life. The people are rooted in their scene, but as weeds are rooted. It would be fashionable to call her stories Gothic: They certainly have the curious inner strain of fable — replacing the social interest which is a distinguishing quality of the American novel. (She herself was an invalid most of her life and died in her native Georgia in 1964 at the age of thirty-eight.) The Southern writers have sometimes tended to pure freakishness or have concentrated on the eccentricities of a decaying social life: But this rotting and tragic order has thrown up strong, if theatrical, themes. Flannery O'Connor was born too late to be affected by the romantic and nostalgic legend of the tragic South: The grotesque for its own sake means nothing to her. It is a norm. . . .

The passions are just beneath the stagnant surface in Flannery O'Connor's stories. She was an old Catholic, not a convert, in the South of the poor white of the Bible Belt and this gave her a critical skirmishing power. But the symbolism of religion, rather than the acrimonies of sectarian dispute, fed her violent imagination — the violence is itself oddly early Protestant — as if she had seen embers of the burning Bible-fed imagery in the minds of her own characters. The symbols are always ominous: At sunset a wood may be idyllic, but also look blood-sodden. They usually precede an act of violence which will introduce the character at the end of the story "into the world of guilt and sorrow." This is her ground as a fabulist or moralist. We are left with an illusion shattered, with the chilly task of facing our hatreds. . . . The essence of Flannery O'Connor's vision is that she sees terror as a purification — unwanted, of course: it is never the sadomasochist's intended indulgence. The moment of purification may actually destroy; it will certainly show someone changed.

Symbolism has been fatal to many writers: It offers a quick return of unearned meaning. . . . But . . . whenever one detects a symbol, one is impressed by Flannery O'Connor's use of it: It is concrete and native to the text. Take the title story of the book: a middle-aged widow, dressed up in an awful new hat, is seen going with her son to a slimming class in order to get her high blood pressure down. She is a "Southern lady" in reduced circumstances and now, bitterly but helplessly opposed to Negro integration, she sticks to her dignity. "If you know who you are, you can go anywhere. . . . I can be gracious to anybody. I know who I am." This is true, in a way, but it is also a cliché, as her son tells her while they travel on the integrated local bus. Here a disturbing figure appears: a Negro woman with her child. She had on a hideous hat. A purple flap came down on one side of it and stood up on the other; the rest of it was green like a cushion with the stuffing out. The hat is exactly a replica of the white woman's hat. To her son this is comical; it ought to teach his silly mother a lesson in racialism. The Negro woman's child sees the joke too. The white woman becomes gracious to the child and prepares to do a terrible, gracious thing: to give the little child a bright new penny. When they all get off the bus she does this. The huge Negro woman, seeming "to explode like a piece of machinery that had been given one ounce of pressure too much," knocks the white woman down. Her son, who has hated his mother for years, sees a reality kill his mother and his own guilt.

Many of the stories are variations of the theme of the widowed mother who has emasculated her son; or the widower who is tragically unaware of what he is doing to his child. In one instance, a widower destroys his grandchild. These stories are not arguments; they are not case histories or indignation meetings. They are selected for the claustrophobic violence which will purify but destroy. The characters are engaged in a struggle for personal power which they usually misunderstand. . . .

If these stories are antihumanist propaganda one does not notice it until afterwards. Like all Gothic writers, Flannery O'Connor has a deep sense of the Devil or rather of the multiplicity of devils, though not in any conventional religious sense. To the poor-white Gospellers, Satan has become Literature. For her the devils are forces which appear in living shape: the stray bull which kills the old farming widow whose sons let her down; the criminal child who is proud of being an irredeemable destroyer because he has been called a child of Satan, and looks forward, eagerly — it is his right — to an eternity in the flames of hell which he takes to be literal fire; the delinquent girl who has been taught by psychiatrists to regard her vice as an illness sees this as an emancipating distinction. The author is not playing the easy game of paradox which is commonly a tiresome element in the novels of Catholic converts: For her, the role of the diabolic is to destroy pride in a misconceived virtue.

A short story ought to be faultless without being mechanical. The wrong word, a misplaced paragraph, an inadequate phrase or a convenient explanation, start fatal leaks in this kind of writing which is formally very close to poetry. That closeness must be totally sustained. There are no faults of craftsmanship in Flannery O'Connor's stories. She writes a plain style: She has a remarkable ear for the talk of the poor whites, for the received ideas of the educated; and she creates emotion and the essence of people by vivid images. . . . Flannery O'Connor is at pains to make us know intimately the lives of these poor white and struggling small-town people. They are there as they live, not in the interest of their ignorant normality, but in the interest of their exposure to forces in themselves that they do not yet understand. Satan, they will discover, is not just a word. He has legs — and those legs are their own.

ROBERT H. BRINKMEYER JR.

Flannery O'Connor and Her Readers   1989

As her letters and essays clearly indicate, O'Connor was very much concerned with her reading audience. Her comments on her audience and how it affected her as an artist, however, were not entirely consistent, and it seems clear that O'Connor was of two minds on the subject.[1] One part of O'Connor downplayed the significance of the audience, saying that artists should be concerned with one thing — their art — and that they bear no responsibility to the audience. By this line of thinking writers concentrate on making their fiction — the characters and their worlds — come alive, and they make sure that the story works as a story and not as a medium for expressing an abstract statement. The meaning of a piece of fiction, O'Connor insisted, was the entire experience one has with it and was not a statement imposed on it that could then later be extracted and held up as its "message." Such thinking was central to the advice she wrote (December 11, 1956) to A. about writing fiction. O'Connor wrote that a writer should merely "start simply with a character or anything that you can make come alive." She continued, "When you have a character he will create his own situation and his situation will suggest some kind of resolution as you get into it. Wouldn't it be better to discover a meaning in what you write than to impose one?" (*HB*, 188).

Behind O'Connor's thinking is the thought of Saint Thomas Aquinas, whom O'Connor frequently cites. For Aquinas a work of art is, as O'Connor points out in "Catholic Novelists and Their Readers," "a good in itself," being "wholly concerned with the good of that which is made." As such, it "glorifies God because it reflects God," and writers have no cause to put their work to any other end; such endeavors only undermine the integrity of the vision and sully the purity of the art. Modern writers, O'Connor says in this same essay, by and large fail to heed Aquinas's lesson and instead wrench their art to

---

[1] The most extensive discussion of O'Connor's interpretation of her audience is in Carol Shloss, *Flannery O'Connor's Dark Comedies: The Limits of Inference* (Baton Rouge, 1980). [Brinkmeyer's note]

make it fit utilitarian ends. For her, in contrast, "the artist has his hands full
and does his duty if he attends to his art. He can safely leave the evangelizing
to the evangelists" (*MM*, 171, 173, 171).

Catholic writers, in O'Connor's eyes, were particularly prone to distort
their fiction for utilitarian purposes — to make it do something rather than be
something. Particularly disturbing to her were those writers, in part goaded
by the Catholic press, who wrote in pious language about the pieties of the
Church. O'Connor's attitude toward this type of fiction was sharp: "As for the
fiction," she wrote (February 19, 1956) to John Lynch, "the motto of the
Catholic press should be: We guarantee to corrupt nothing but your taste"
(*HB*, 138). In ignoring the realities of the here and now outside the Church,
such fiction was for O'Connor little more than religious propaganda, the stuff
one expects to find in the vestibules of churches but not in bookstores. These
writers, she believed, were too concerned with presenting the Church in a favorable light and tending to their readership's spiritual needs; O'Connor's
answer to them was that in writing fiction the Catholic writer "does not decide what would be good for the Christian body and proceed to deliver it"
(*MM*, 183). Instead, as we have seen O'Connor stressing, writers must work
within the limitations of their vocation to create the best story — not tract —
possible. "The writer is only free when he can tell the reader to go jump in the
lake," O'Connor said in one of her interviews, stressing the artist's independence from the audience. She added that though the writer of course wants to
communicate a personal vision, "whether [the reader] likes it or not is no concern of the writer" (*CFO*, 39).

If in this way O'Connor downplayed the significance of the audience,
she also frequently said something quite different. She argued that the audience played a crucial role in artistic creation and that writers always had to be
aware of, and to take account of, their audience. She spoke of this connection
in "Catholic Novelists and Their Readers," saying that "it takes readers as
well as writers to make literature," and she added in "The Catholic Novelist in
the Protestant South" that "it is what writer, character, and reader share that
makes it possible to write fiction at all." Elsewhere (in "Novelist and Believer") O'Connor wrote that fiction was ultimately an attempt at communication; successful writing, she added, was not merely a rendering of the
artist's vision but a rendering of it in such a way that the reader could understand it. "The novelist doesn't write to express himself, he doesn't write simply to render a vision he believes true, rather he renders his vision so it can be
transferred, as nearly whole as possible, to his reader," she wrote. "You can
safely ignore the reader's taste, but you can't ignore his nature, you can't ignore his limited patience. Your problem is going to be difficult in direct proportion as your beliefs depart from his." She echoes this observation in "Some
Aspects of the Grotesque in Southern Fiction," saying that the writer's vision
"has to be transmitted and that the limitations and blind spots of his audience
will very definitely affect the way he is able to show what he sees" (*MM*, 182,
204–205, 162, 47).

When speaking of her own audience, O'Connor almost always stressed
the great distance she felt between herself and her readers and pointed to the

ways this gulf pressured and limited her as a writer. She believed that she and other American Catholic writers lacked a significant and responsive audience, and that this situation stifled imaginative growth and artistic expression. O'Connor found several reasons for this development. Central to the Catholic writer's plight, O'Connor believed, was the fact that in America Catholic writers lacked a distinctive social and cultural heritage based on religious identity. In "The Catholic Novelist in the Protestant South" she asserts that "the writer whose themes are religious particularly needs a region where these themes find a response in the life of the people." She then adds: "The American Catholic is short on places that reflect his particular religious life and his particular problems. This country isn't exactly cut in his image." She goes on to say that even in areas where there are large numbers of Catholics, Catholic life there lacks "the significant features that result in a high degree of regional self-consciousness" and so offers the Catholic writer few "exploitable benefits." O'Connor's analysis of Catholic writers continues: "They have no great geographical extent, they have no particularly significant history, certainly no history of defeat; they have no real peasant class, and no cultural unity of the kind you find in the South." She adds that Catholics usually "blend almost imperceptibly into the general materialistic background." This lack of a strong cultural tradition and a supportive audience greatly burdens Catholic writers, impoverishing their imaginative life and art. "If the Catholic faith were central to life in America, Catholic fiction would fare better, but the Church is not central to this society." O'Connor continues: "The things that bind us together as Catholics are known only to ourselves. A secular society understands us less and less. It becomes more and more difficult in America to make belief believable" (*MM*, 200, 201).

These final words point to the second reason American Catholics lack a supportive audience: The larger society they write from and to is overwhelmingly secular and materialistic, money based rather than religious based. O'Connor, as we saw in the first chapter, was well aware of the trends in modern social and intellectual thought that since the Enlightenment have been validating and valorizing the human consciousness and rationality while undermining and reducing the significance of the religious. In a letter (October 19, 1958) to T. R. Spivey, O'Connor wrote that by and large people in today's society have "no sense of the power of God that could produce the Incarnation and the Resurrection. They are all so busy explaining away the virgin birth and such things, reducing everything to human proportions that in time they lose even the sense of the human itself, what they were aiming to reduce everything to" (*HB*, 300). Because moderns lacked a faith in transcendent values and order, O'Connor, as she said in "Some Aspects of the Grotesque in Southern Fiction," saw the age as one "which doubts both fact and value, which is swept this way and that by momentary convictions" (*MM*, 49). O'Connor found such relativism particularly disturbing, and this in part explains her strong attraction to the fundamentalist imperative that defines all values according to the simple — but total — choice of being for either Christ or the Devil.

Given these trends and developments, O'Connor saw her own position, as well as that of almost all American Catholic writers, as being particularly precarious in terms of communicating with her readership. O'Connor frequently asserted in her letters that she could consistently count on only a handful of informed readers — an assertion largely borne out by the number of vicious and misinformed readings her work received, particularly early on — and that she had to make these readers go a long way in her life as an author. O'Connor knew hers was not the type of fiction that most Catholic readers yearned to read — not, in other words, fiction that was thoroughly positive and that went out of its way to celebrate the life of the Church. She characterized the general Catholic reader as unthinking, and she said that this reader "is so busy looking for something that fits his needs, and shows him in the best possible light, that he will find suspect anything that doesn't serve such purpose" (*MM*, 182). Elsewhere, in a letter (May 4, 1963) to Sister Mariella Gable, she wrote that those Catholic readers who demand that the writer make Christianity look desirable are asking the writer to describe Christianity's essence and not what the writer actually sees. "Ideal Christianity doesn't exist, because anything the human being touches, even Christian truth, he deforms slightly in his own image," she wrote, adding a bit later that the tendency of the Catholic readers she had been discussing "is always toward the abstract and therefore toward allegory, thinness, and ultimately what they are looking for is apologetic fiction. The best of them think: make it look desirable because it is desirable. And the rest of them think: make it look desirable so I won't look like a fool for holding it" (*HB*, 516). Such readers would find little to like in O'Connor's fiction and in all likelihood would see it as a good deal more than suspect — subversive, probably.

O'Connor of course felt an even greater distance from what she saw as the thoroughly secular and unbelieving general reader, the reader to whom she claimed she primarily wrote. In "The Catholic Novelists and Their Readers" she said that Catholic readers make a great mistake in supposing that Catholic writers write exclusively for them. "Occasionally this may happen," she wrote, "but generally it is not happening today" (*MM*, 185), and O'Connor made it clear elsewhere that it was not happening in her fiction. To A., O'Connor wrote (August 2, 1955) of the audience she perceived, saying that "one of the awful things about writing when you are a Christian is that for you the ultimate reality is the Incarnation, the present reality is the Incarnation, and nobody believes in the Incarnation; that is, nobody in your audience. My audience are the people who think God is dead. At least these are the people I am conscious of writing for" (*HB*, 92). Trying to bridge this gap between believing author and unbelieving audience was a terrible burden for O'Connor, and one that haunted her throughout her career. In a review of Caroline Gordon's *The Malefactors*, O'Connor wrote that "making grace believable to the contemporary reader is the almost insurmountable problem of the novelist who writes from the standpoint of Christian orthodoxy," an observation that speaks crucially to O'Connor's own situation in communicating with her audience (*PG*, 16).

O'Connor further perceived her audience as making demands that she was not prepared to meet — ever. She complained in "Some Aspects of the

Grotesque in Southern Fiction" that her freedom as a writer was always under pressure, since everywhere "the novelist is asked to be the handmaid of his age." She wrote, "Whenever the public is heard from, it is heard demanding a literature which is balanced and which will somehow heal the ravages of our time." This literature, she said elsewhere in this essay, was based on what she called "a realism of fact" — a realism that associated "the only legitimate material for long fiction with the movement of social forces, with the typical, with the fidelity to the way things look and happen in normal life." Such realism, she added, limited both the scope of the imaginative vision of artists and their fiction. As O'Connor noted here and elsewhere, her own fiction was written with a realism of an altogether different sort — a realism that sought not to mirror the typical but to reveal the spiritual. To this end, she says in "Novelist and Believer," the writer "is bound by the reasonable possibilities, not the probabilities of his culture" (*MM*, 46, 39, 165).

If the overall critical environment established its own orthodoxy for fiction, O'Connor also saw general readers establishing their own expectations and demands for what they should experience in the act of reading. She characterized the general readers as being "tired," of wanting what she called at one point "Instant Uplift" — that is, wanting to have their spirits raised in an act of easy compassion and sentiment. This demand for uplift and the redemptive act, O'Connor notes in "Some Aspects of the Grotesque in Southern Fiction," is a characteristic human need, and one that both the storyteller and the listener find particularly compelling in narrative. What bothers O'Connor is not that the reader seeks this motion in fiction but that the reader "has forgotten the cost of it." She explains that the modern reader's "sense of evil is diluted or lacking altogether, and so he has forgotten the price of restoration. When he reads a novel, he wants either his senses tormented or his spirits raised. He wants to be transported, instantly, either to mock damnation or a mock innocence." To underscore the risks the writer takes in ignoring such readers, O'Connor writes in this same essay that there are those who "say that the serious writer doesn't have to bother about the tired reader, but he does, because they are all tired. One old lady who wants her heart uplifted wouldn't be so bad, but you multiply her two hundred and fifty thousand times and what you get is a book club" (*MM*, 165, 48–49).

ABBREVIATIONS

Abbreviations of works by Flannery O'Connor commonly cited in the text refer to the following editions:

CFO   *Conversations with Flannery O'Connor.* Edited by Rosemary M. Magee. Jackson, Miss., 1987.

HB   *The Habit of Being: Letters.* Edited by Sally Fitzgerald. New York, 1969.

MM   *Mystery and Manners: Occasional Prose.* Edited by Sally Fitzgerald and Robert Fitzgerald. New York, 1969.

PG   *The Presence of Grace and Other Book Reviews by Flannery*

O'Connor. Compiled by Leo J. Zuber. Edited by Carter W. Martin. Athens, Ga., 1983.

DOROTHY TUCK MCFARLAND

On "Good Country People"   1976

"Good Country People," the penultimate story in the collection, is something of a comic variation on "A Good Man Is Hard to Find." As the grandmother of the title story thinks of herself as a good Christian woman who believes in all the conventional platitudes, Hulga Hopewell, the Ph.D. in philosophy who is the protagonist of "Good Country People," thinks of herself as a good nihilist who energetically disbelieves in all the conventional platitudes. In their titles both stories implicitly ask the reader to consider what are good men or good people. And in both stories O'Connor uses conventional language for comic and ironic purposes, emphasizing the meaninglessness of the platitudes in the mouths of her characters, and at the same time using their words to sound the main themes of the story. For instance, Hulga's mother, Mrs. Hopewell, characteristically strings together remarks like "Everybody is different. . . . It takes all kinds to make the world. . . . Nothing is perfect." Nevertheless, she actually tolerates differences and imperfections very poorly. Two of the themes in the story grow out of the characters' attitudes toward uniqueness ("everybody is different") and imperfection.

Mrs. Hopewell and her tenant's wife, Mrs. Freeman, embody contrasting ways of looking at the world that provide the frame for the story. Whereas Mrs. Hopewell is determined always to put a smiling face on things and never look beneath the surface, the gimlet-eyed Mrs. Freeman has a fondness for hidden things: "the details of secret infections, hidden deformities, assaults upon children." She is obsessed with the physical demands and ills of the body, and in her conversation about her two daughters she dwells on the details of two major aspects of their physical being: their sexuality and their ailments. One daughter, Glynese, is being courted by several admirers, one of whom is going to chiropractor school and who cures her of a sty by popping her neck. The other daughter, Carramae, is pregnant and unable to "keep anything on her stomach."

Mrs. Hopewell's daughter, Hulga, is antagonized by her mother's platitudinous optimism to the extent that her face has come to wear a look of constant outrage that "obliterated every other expression." She finds Mrs. Freeman tolerable only on the ground that Mrs. Freeman diverts some of her mother's attention from her; otherwise, she is uncomfortable with Mrs. Freeman's fascination with the secrets of the body.

Hulga has rejected the physical world and the life of the body in preference for the life of the mind: "She didn't like dogs or cats or birds or flowers or nature or nice young men. She looked at nice young men as if she could smell their stupidity." Her rejection of the physical world stems from her awareness of its liability to imperfection. Hulga's own imperfection is gross — she lost a leg when she was ten — but O'Connor obviously intended her to be a figure of all mankind, which suffers from the imperfections of the human condition. Hulga insists on calling attention to her physical imperfection and refuses to try to improve her appearance. However, this defensive insistence that she be accepted "LIKE I AM" does not indicate that *she* has really accepted what she is; rather, it suggests that she is trying to insulate herself against the pain of difference and imperfection.

Hulga's choice of her name reflects her response to her condition. Named Joy by her mother, she could not tolerate the incongruity between the idea of joy and her knowledge that she was "dust." She therefore chose to emphasize her deformity and ugliness by assuming an ugly name — Hulga — and a rude manner, and closed herself to joy for the sake of affirming the truth about herself. The persona she creates with the name Hulga is a blind, stony, armored creature. To her mother, the name Hulga suggests the "broad blank hull of a battleship." Hulga herself is described as being "square and rigid-shouldered," and as standing "blank and solid and silent." Her face is characteristically expressionless, and her "icy blue" eyes have the "look of someone who has achieved blindness by an act of will and means to keep it." Though she believes the self she has created is her true self, this imagery suggests that her willful blindness prevents her from seeing the true nature of the human condition as much as does her mother's insistence on always looking "at the bright side of things."

Though she has rejected joy for herself, Hulga has not given up on the possibility of love, and this secret desire is her one area of vulnerability. However, she thinks the persona she has created through her name is a means of making herself invulnerable, so that she can command and control love from a position of strength. She envisions her name working "like the ugly sweating Vulcan who stayed in the furnace and to whom the goddess [of love] had to come when called."

When an apparently naive country boy appears selling Bibles, Hulga feels that he offers no threat to her and allows herself to respond to his open admiration. Despite her utter inexperience (she has never been kissed) she decides to demonstrate her command of love by seducing him. She reinforces her image of herself as a woman of intellectual superiority and worldly wisdom by imagining that the simple Bible salesman, once seduced, will suffer from remorse, whereupon she will take away his shame and "transform it into something useful."

However, the Bible salesman's simplicity seduces her. Having climbed with her into the loft of an isolated barn, the Bible salesman gets Hulga to declare (with some reservations) that she loves him. He then demands that she prove it by showing him where her wooden leg joins on. At first shocked by his proposal, Hulga resists until he tells her why: "because [the wooden leg is] what makes you different." She feels that the Bible salesman, "with an instinct that came from beyond wisdom, had touched the truth about her." She comes to the conclusion that for the first time in her life she has encountered true innocence. She is so moved by her perception of his innocence that she lets down her defenses and allows her hidden vulnerability to emerge.

This area of vulnerability O'Connor equates with Hulga's soul and symbolizes it by her wooden leg: "she was as sensitive about the artificial leg as a peacock about his tail. No one ever touched it but her. She took care of it as someone else would his soul, in private and almost with her own eyes turned away." The leg is also, as the Bible salesman cannily recognized, what makes her different — a difference which, up to now, she has worn defensively and defiantly. Now, for the first time in the story, she accepts her difference, and allows herself to be touched in what is symbolically her soul. Accepting herself, she can surrender herself, and having surrendered herself she finds herself again, in the classic progression of love. When she allows the Bible salesman to remove her leg, "it was like surrendering to him completely. It was like losing her own life and finding it again, miraculously, in his."

Significantly, she surrenders to love in a scene in which her physical grotesqueness is not only emphasized but becomes the very means of love's expression and fulfillment. Though this scene of the Bible salesman removing Hulga's wooden leg is objectively ludicrous (and O'Connor's handling of it is full of irony), Hulga herself is, for the first time, completely without irony. The boy seems to her to be "entirely reverent" as he approaches the leg, and his removal of it is clearly the psychological and emotional equivalent to Hulga of the act of love: "She was thinking that she would run away with him and that every night he would take the leg off and every morning put it back on again."

Hulga's surrender to love also makes her vulnerable to a revelation of her own blindness. She had been convinced that she can see and that others cannot, and that she knows the truth. "Woman!" she had once shouted at her mother, enraged at Mrs. Hopewell's habit of blandly papering over ugliness with smiles. "Do you ever look inside . . . and see what you are *not*?" As a philosopher, Hulga is professionally concerned with truth. She is convinced that she has no illusions, that she has seen through appearances to the nothing that is beneath. "Some of us," she informs the Bible salesman, "have taken off our blindfolds and see that there's nothing to see." And she is utterly convinced of the truth of her assessment of the Bible salesman's innocence.

The Bible salesman, however, is anything but an innocent. Having put Hulga's leg out of her reach, he takes out of his suitcase a hollowed-out Bible containing a flask of whiskey, a deck of pornographic playing cards, and a packet of contraceptives. In response to Hulga's evident dismay, he replies, "What's the matter with you all of a sudden? . . . You just a while ago said you didn't believe in nothing. I thought you was some girl!" When he sees that he will get no farther with her, he snatches up her wooden leg, thrusts it into his suitcase, and disappears down the ladder of the barn loft.

The Bible salesman's thoroughgoing nihilism shows up Hulga's claim to believe in nothing as a superficial intellectual posture. Both his actions and his words devastate her assumption of intellectual superiority: "he turned and regarded her with a look that no longer had any admiration in it. . . . 'And I'll tell you another thing, Hulga,' he said, using the name as if he didn't think much of it, 'you ain't so smart. I been believing in nothing ever since I was born!' "

Hulga is left stranded, her previously stony face "churning" with emotion. But the Bible salesman's destruction of her illusions and her defenses (like the destruction of conventional order that resulted from the grand-mother's encounter with The Misfit) may be, for Hulga, the means of her salvation. That the Bible salesman might be a kind of savior is suggested in the description of Hulga's final glimpse of him. Looking out the window of the barn loft, she sees him making his way across the pasture. O'Connor implicitly compares him to Christ walking on the water; to Hulga's blurred vision (the Bible salesman has also taken her glasses), he seems to be "struggling successfully over the green speckled lake."

The actual or implied references to Christ in *A Good Man Is Hard to Find* are numerous. The climactic moment in the title story comes about after The Misfit expresses his intense concern over the question of whether or not Jesus raised the dead. . . . The Bible salesman in "Good Country People" is implicitly compared to Christ.

Christ, as Simeon prophesied in St. Luke's gospel, is a "sign that will be contradicted," a sign of the presence of God in the world that, to many, will not seem to be a sign of God at all — will seem, rather, its opposite. The unexpected and often grotesque and incongruous ways in which O'Connor felt Christ to be present in the world is, I think, the real subject of this collection. Not only is the image of Christ suggested in unlikely places or associated with unlikely characters; but in style as well the stories embody contradiction and incongruity — in the double point of view, in the mixture of comedy and horror, in the pervasive tone of emotional flatness and irony, on the one hand, and the intimations of depth and serious meaning on the other. Thematically and stylistically, the centrality of Christ — of that which we experience as contradictory — provides *A Good Man Is Hard to Find* with a unity that makes it more than simply a random collection of stories. . . . I would add another gloss on the meaning of the title: the good man is so hard to find because he appears in such unlikely guises, because he is hidden in irony and contradiction.

WAYNE C. BOOTH

A Rhetorical Reading of O'Connor's "Everything That Rises Must Converge"   1974

This is an extremely complex story, not only in its ironic undercuttings but in its affirmations. No reading of it can be considered adequate unless it somehow relates the curious title to the various attempts to "rise" and to the failures to "converge." In the web of inference that we must create to see the story whole, our running translation of Julian's judgments into alternative judgments is only one strand. But once we have discerned that strand clearly, the rest of the story gives few difficulties.

Since Julian's is the only mind offering us opinions (except for a few observations and metaphors from the narrator, most notably the final sentence), we must sooner or later decide how far we can trust him. It is not hard to see that he is unreliable about many things. "He never spoke of it without contempt or thought of it without longing" — what kind of man is it, we ask, who always belies his true feelings? His life is full of such contradictions, showing that in his own way he is as far out of touch with reality as he takes his mother to be. His radical self-deception is perhaps clearest in the long fantasy that begins when he "withdraws into the inner compartment of his mind where he spent most of his time." No one could misread his own character more thoroughly than Julian does in thinking that he has "turned out so well," that he has a "first rate education," that he has a "large" mind, that he is "free of prejudice and unafraid to face facts" — remember, this is the boy who "did not like to consider all she did for him" and who can take pride in having "cut himself emotionally free of her." The closer we look at the disharmonies among his various opinions and actions, the more vigorously we must work in reconstructing the terrible lost young man we see behind his self-defensive rhetoric. His childish efforts to hurt his mother begin in a comic light, as he poses like a martyr and does everything he possibly can to spoil her one pleasant time of the week. But the comedy slowly gives place to pathos and horror as he runs over in his mind the possible tortures he might subject her to, then enjoys her humiliation about the duplicate hat, and finally — so wrapped up in his own petty bitterness and futility that he cannot see what is in front of his eyes — shouts irony-laden insults at the stricken woman. "You aren't who you think you are," he says, summarizing himself as much as his mother. "You've got to live in the new world and face a few realities for a change. Buck up, it won't kill you." It *is* killing her, and *he* is the one who must now begin to "face a few realities for a change."

These disharmonies are simple and clear. But the reconstruction of what "the realities" are — of what Julian must face — is not so easy. It is obviously not to be found in the "unreal," absurdly "innocent" world of the class-bound mother, nor in the equally unreal and absurd but vicious world of Julian. One kind of unmistakable reality is found in the irreducible, often harsh details of the life that Julian and his mother encounter but cannot see because of the abstractions that blur their vision. The mother does not see real "Negroes," for example, only the stereotypes that her childhood has provided her with. But Julian does not see real people either; instead he sees only the stereotypes that his liberal opinions dictate. Similarly, neither of them can see the other: Julian cannot see his mother for what she is; she cannot see what a miserable failure she has helped to create in him.

Our question then becomes: is there some ordering of values that for this story constitutes an alternative reality, one that in a sense judges everything the characters do? Our knowledge that Flannery O'Connor was known as a devout Catholic, or even that she herself talked about her stories in religious terms, can only alert us to one possible direction of interpretation. She might, after all, write one story that was entirely different from the others; for all I know, independently of my reading, she could have written this one before being converted, or after losing her faith. Even the most detailed knowledge about the author's life and statements of purpose can only alert me to certain possibilities; I must finally ask what kinds of clues the story itself provides to aid in the task of reconstructing a world of values that contrast with Julian's inanities.

The curious title is itself a kind of warning that seems to be spoken, as it were, in a special tone of voice. It simply does not harmonize easily with most of the surface, and indeed at first hardly makes sense at all. Does everything that "rises" in the story "converge"? Hardly. The black characters are "rising," but in spite of the liberal platitudes of Julian, there is no sign in the story that in their rising they will converge with the whites or with each other; one must thus ask whether or in what limited sense they are rising at all. Julian's liberal abstractions lead him to expect all Negroes to want his sympathy and interest, and to conform to his stereotyped demand that they "rise" to "talk on subjects that would be *above* the comprehension of those around him." But they insist on dwelling in a totally inaccessible world.

Julian has been "rising," too, as he obtains what he likes to think was a "first-class education." But his sense of elevation has, obviously, separated him not only from his mother but from all of his roots, without providing him with any other allegiances that could possibly support the claim of the title. What, then, can the title mean? It does not help us much to learn that it comes from the works of Teilhard de Chardin, the Catholic priest whose scientific and theological speculations earned him the accusation of heresy.

Is there any genuine change in the story that could be considered a "rising"? There is one, indeed, if we take seriously the change in Julian produced by the catastrophe. Julian is not just nasty and petty throughout the story; he is totally absorbed in his own ego. In contrast to his mother, who is "innocent," he is corrupt. Her desire is not to do ill in the world, but good, and only the limitations of what Julian calls her "fantasy world" betray her. But Julian, as we discover him behind his rationalizations, is actually malevolent, totally incapable of "converging" with the interests of any other person. His thoughts run constantly on his hatred of the world and his desire to "justify" himself in ways that he knows will hurt his mother deeply. "He would be entirely justified [in bringing home a Negro wife] but her blood pressure would rise to 300. He could not push her to the extent of making her have a stroke, and moreover, he had never been successful at making any Negro friends."

Throughout his absurd but vicious fantasies there thus run clues that prepare us for his discovery at the end. "For a moment he had an uncomfortable sense of her *innocence,* but it lasted only a second before *principle* rescued him. *Justice* entitled him to laugh." Dimly aware of her "innocence," passionately devoted to proving his own "principles" and obtaining "justice," he can be touched only by the greatest of disasters. Having never once been genuinely touched by any trouble, having in fact used his mother and her innocence as a shield against knowledge of himself, he is at last "stricken," "stunned." The change in him is as startling as the physical change produced in her by the stroke which he has helped to induce: "Darling, sweetheart, wait!" He is "crumpled," crushed into letting his defenses down and trying, too late, to call to his mother in love.

It would probably be a mistake to see anything strongly affirmative in this final dropping of all his egotistical defenses and crying "Mamma, mamma." He has not risen very far, but as he watches her destruction, falls at her side, and then runs for help, there has been, at last, a "convergence," a meeting of two human wills, that *might* presage his genuine "entry into the world of guilt and sorrow." For the Julian we have known throughout the story to experience either genuine guilt or sorrow would be a "rise" indeed, a rise based on the final convergence. The honest nightmare of his nothingness moving into "nowhere" in the final paragraph is thus a great improvement — in the light of this view of reality we now share with the implied author — over the "mental bubble" in which he established himself, where "he was safe from any kind of penetration from without." In his bubble he had been able to "see her with absolute clarity," or so he thought. Now, at the end, his bubble has been penetrated; he is swept by a "tide of darkness," and we are led to feel that he is for the first time in a position from which some sort of genuine human life is conceivable.

Whether this interpretation is sound or not, it certainly is never stated. Except for the ending, most of the words report Julian's misguided thoughts without open correction, and they must consequently be reconstructed. But they are not translated into a message.

There is perhaps no absolute need to go further than this. Readers of many different faiths and anti-faiths can presumably participate in this story of punishment and discovery, without pushing toward any special meaning for words like sin, innocence, faith, realities, guilt, and sorrow. But those of us who have read many of Flannery O'Connor's stories and studied her life will be unable to resist seeing Julian's final problematic redemption as presented in a religious light, even a specifically Roman Catholic light. Once the story is reread from this point of view, many additional ironies accumulate, ranging from Julian's name and his saintly posings at the beginning to the gratuitousness of grace at the end. But Flannery O'Connor was eager to write stories that were not mere allegories; as she intended, this story can be experienced by anyone who catches the essential contrast among the three systems of norms, Julian's, his mother's, and the cluster of traditional, conventional values we share with the author. Though it may seem thinner to those for whom Julian's self-absorption and cruelty are judged in secular terms than for a Catholic who sees him as in mortal sin, the structure of experience will be the same for both: Everyone will be forced to reject all or most of what the words seem to say. At every point we must decide on one out of many possible reconstructions, on the basis of a set of unshakable but silent beliefs that we are expected to share (however fleetingly) with the author. No one who fails to discern and feel some sympathy for these beliefs — only a few of them specifically Roman Catholic — is likely to make very much of the story.

For readers who do see behind Julian's absurd and egotistical words, the energy devoted to the act of seeing will of course increase the emotional effect and thus their estimate of the story's worth. This will not necessarily lead them to agree with me that it is a first-class story. But if they like it at all, the force of their liking will have been strengthened by the active engagement with the ironies.

PART TWO

POETRY

9

WHAT IS A POEM?

That first green night of their dreaming, asleep beneath the Tree,
God said, "Let meanings move," and there was poetry.
— MURIEL RUKEYSER, "The Sixth Night: Waking"

Just as it is important to begin reading short stories with some idea of what a short story is, we should begin reading poetry with some idea of what we mean by poetry. What is poetry and what is a poem? The poet Emily Dickinson, when she was asked in a letter how she knew something she had read was poetry, answered,

> If I read a book and it makes my whole body so cold no fire can ever warm me, I know that it is poetry. If I feel physically as if the top of my head were taken off, I know that it is poetry. These are the only ways I know it. Is there any other way?

It is not necessary for you as a reader to have such a strong emotional response to a poem in order to enjoy it, but as you begin to know more about poetry, you will also understand some of what she felt.

You will find, as you begin your study of poetry, that it is not so simple to say just what a poem is, but this is also true of other things that can give us the feeling that the tops of our heads have been taken off. Often when rock musicians are asked by interviewers to define rock and roll, they answer, without hesitation, "That's the kind of music I play." Their answer echoes the response of the American poet Robert Frost, who, when he was asked what poetry was, shrugged, "Poetry is the kind of thing that poets write."

Part of the difficulty of finding a simple definition of poetry is that there has been so much of it. Poetry is our oldest language art. Only drama, which probably emerged two centuries later, takes us as far back into antiquity. The novel, with its history of only three or four hundred years, and the short story, with its history of less than two hundred years, are newcomers compared with poetry. In Asia and in the eastern Mediterranean and Europe, poetry has had an unbroken line of expression for almost three thousand years, and the way we define poetry would have changed as societies and poetry itself changed during these millennia.

Many poets have felt the need to define poetry, and often they use the medium of poetry to describe what it is they create. In the famous poem "Ars Poetica," the American writer Archibald MacLeish tells us that poetry is not something to be explained or analyzed, that a poem can tell the story of grief simply by showing us "An empty doorway and a maple leaf."

ARCHIBALD MACLEISH

Ars Poetica   1926

A poem should be palpable and mute
As a globed fruit

Dumb
As old medallions to the thumb

Silent as the sleeve-worn stone   5
Of casement ledges where the moss has grown —

A poem should be wordless
As the flight of birds

                •

A poem should be motionless in time
As the moon climbs   10

Leaving, as the moon releases
Twig by twig the night-entangled trees,

Leaving, as the moon behind the winter leaves,
Memory by memory the mind —

A poem should be motionless in time   15
As the moon climbs

                •

A poem should be equal to:
Not true

For all the history of grief
An empty doorway and a maple leaf   20

For love
The leaning grasses and two lights above the sea —

A poem should not mean
But be.

In a poem titled simply "Poetry," Marianne Moore attempts to state her idea of what a poem should be. A poem, as she says, is "a place for the genuine," and she scolds writers who let themselves forget that it is a direct, real experience that must go into a poem. To her, the greatness of poetry is that it can cross the boundary between our inner emotions and something outside ourselves that can reawaken these emotions. In her unforgettable phrase, a poem "can present / for inspection, 'imaginary gardens with real toads in them.' . . ."

MARIANNE MOORE

Poetry   1921, 1935

I, too, dislike it: there are things that are important beyond all
        this fiddle.
  Reading it, however, with a perfect contempt for it, one
        discovers in
    it after all, a place for the genuine.
      Hands that can grasp, eyes
        that can dilate, hair that can rise   5
          if it must, these things are important not because a
high-sounding interpretation can be put upon them but because
        they are
    useful. When they become so derivative as to become
        unintelligible,
    the same thing may be said for all of us, that we
        do not admire what   10
          we cannot understand: the bat
          holding on upside down or in quest of something to
  eat, elephants pushing, a wild horse taking a roll, a tireless wolf
        under
    a tree, the immovable critic twitching his skin like a horse
        that feels a flea, the base-
ball fan, the statistician —   15
      nor is it valid
        to discriminate against "business documents and
school-books";[1] all these phenomena are important. One must
        make a distinction
    however: when dragged into prominence by half poets, the
        result is not poetry,
    nor till the poets among us can be   20
      "literalists of

---

[1] Diary of Tolstoy (Dutton), p. 84. "Where the boundary between prose and poetry lies, I shall never be able to understand. The question is raised in manuals of style, yet the answer to it lies beyond me. Poetry is verse; prose is not verse. Or else poetry is everything with the exception of business documents and school books." [Moore's note]

the imagination"[2] — above
    insolence and triviality and can present
for inspection, "imaginary gardens with real toads in them," shall
    we have
    it. In the meantime, if you demand on the one hand,   25
    the raw material of poetry in
        all its rawness and
        that which is on the other hand
        genuine, then you are interested in poetry.

In this version of her poem, however, Moore may have felt that she had given away too many of a poet's secrets, or that she might have been stating something that was too obvious to need explaining. For whatever reason, when she printed it again several years later in her *Collected Poems*, she trimmed it down to the lines she felt were essential. The poem as she published it then reads simply,

I, too, dislike it.
    Reading it, however, with a perfect contempt for it, one discovers in
        it, after all, a place for the genuine.

As Moore made very clear (and you should remember this as you study poetry), poets have their own reasons for whatever they do.

The poems we have read so far tell us something about poetry, but we still don't have a definition. Perhaps a useful way to begin is to turn to a dictionary, where we find definitions that tell us something very specific about what a poem is. A dictionary will tell us that "a poem is a metrical composition of elevated tone depicting an emotional or philosophical truth." If you keep a definition like this in mind when you begin reading poetry, you will find it is a useful tool. The term *metrical composition* tells us to expect a poem's formal structure to be based on a rhythmic pattern of words and syllables that we can hear and anticipate. The term *elevated tone* tells us that a poem can use a different kind of language, or if it uses everyday speech it can use these words in ways that give them a special — "elevated" — significance. The term *emotional or philosophical truth* tells us that poetry can touch our deepest emotions.

As you begin studying poetry you will find it helpful to separate a poem into two parts. The first part is the emotion or the insight at the heart of the poem. This is called the **theme**. You should remember, however, that the *theme* of the poem is not necessarily the **subject** of the poem. The subject of the poem may be the writer's pet cat, but the theme of the poem is the writer's pleasure in everyday things that the cat symbolizes.

The second part of what you should think of as you read poetry consists

---

[2] Yeats' *Ideas of Good and Evil* (A. H. Bullen), p. 182. "The limitation of his view was from the very intensity of his vision; he was a too literal realist of imagination, as others are of nature; and because he believed that the figures seen by the mind's eye, when exalted by inspiration, were 'eternal existences,' symbols of divine essences, he hated every grace of style that might obscure their lineaments." [Moore's note]

of the elements of formal structure and "poetic" language, what we can call the **means** of the poem. A poet's means are the rhythms and verbal wordplay, the kind of language, the poetic form, the suggestions of the other poems or paintings or music that are there for poets to use as they write. These resources are sometimes called the *elements* of poetry, but if we use the term *means*, it also suggests that these elements are what poets *use* as they write.

With these tools, the theme and the means, you will find that you can enjoy more fully any of the poems you will be reading. Remember that these two aspects of a poem work each in different ways. The themes of poems come from within the poet's own personality. They can be the poet's thoughts, dreams, disappointments, or joys, or responses to someone else's thoughts, dreams, disappointments, or joys. The themes of a poem are also our shared experience of life. Because they come from our common humanity, they are continually renewed.

The means of poetry, however, are bound into the moment in time when each poem is written. They draw from the language and the social attitudes, the poetic traditions, and the background of the poets' lives and the moments in history when they lived. This is why you will find that poems from different times with the same themes — perhaps the poet's disappointment at the end of a love affair or the definition of poetry itself — will be expressed in different languages and forms, each a reflection of its own time and place.

As we have seen, poets often turn their thoughts about poetry into poems. This poem by San Francisco writer Lawrence Ferlinghetti describes the emotions that some poets feel as they write.

LAWRENCE FERLINGHETTI

Constantly Risking Absurdity   *1955–58*

    Constantly risking absurdity
                and death
  whenever he performs
         above the heads
               of his audience   5
  the poet like an acrobat
        climbs on rime
           to a high wire of his own making
 and balancing on eyebeams
         above a sea of faces   10
  paces his way
      to the other side of day
    performing entrechats
        and slight-of-foot tricks
  and other high theatrics   15
        and all without mistaking
    any thing

for what it may not be
For he's the super realist
who must perforce perceive   20
taut truth
before the taking of each stance or step
in his supposed advance
toward that still higher perch
where Beauty stands and waits   25
with gravity
to start her death-defying leap
And he
a little charleychaplin man
who may or may not catch   30
her fair eternal form
spreadeagled in the empty air
of existence

Sometimes poets describe what they do in phrases that are poems in themselves. The English poet Percy Bysshe Shelley wrote, "A poet is a nightingale, who sits in darkness and sings to cheer its own solitude with sweet sounds." The American poet Robert Frost tells us, "The figure a poem makes. It begins in delight and ends in wisdom." When poets write about their art they usually are serious. If they are in the mood, however, they can be half-serious. Tobey Hiller, who lives and works in Oakland, California, pretends in "The Poem" that she cannot find anything useful about poems — until the last lines, in which she tells us that with a poem we can fly above the ordinary experience of everyday life. The Alice she refers to in the title is the main character in Lewis Carroll's *Alice in Wonderland*.

TOBEY HILLER

The Poem   1987

**(or, Alice's Remarks on Reading
the Fine Print on the Bottle's Label)**

Can it walk, or talk,
or do the mambo?

Will it set off, sleek,
and neigh its way to Mexico?

Provide a shade against the sun?   5
Cure freckles? Siphon sadness?

Recited right, won't it turn the curl of waves acrylic,
cast sunsets into glass,

make grass grow green
upon a desert page?   10

Perhaps you're hoping
it will turn the t.v. off.

Or make the kids grow up un-mumbling
and acquainted with the phases of the moon.

Perhaps it does a trick   15
with eyes, closing them, or opening.

But don't confuse it with a pear.
You wouldn't try to eat it, would you?

Remember that only angels can make hair and wings
and finger-nails out of the alphabet.   20

What we make is all flight.

Finally, in her "How Poems Are Made / A Discredited View," Alice
Walker, author of the novel *The Color Purple*, tells us that she makes poems out
of her need to find a place for the disappointments in her life. She calls this "A
Discredited View" because in some contemporary criticism of poetry, commentators have suggested that writing has no meaning. They argue that a
poem, short story, or play is only a linguistic construct, a series of symbols and
references. As we will see, a poem is much more than this for Walker, and for
Muriel Rukeyser, whose epigraph began this chapter, and for most other people who read and write poetry.

ALICE WALKER

How Poems Are Made /
A Discredited View   *1984*

Letting go
in order to hold on
I gradually understand
how poems are made.

There is a place the fear must go.   5
There is a place the choice must go.
There is a place the loss must go.
The leftover love.
The love that spills out
of the too full cup   10
and runs and hides
its too full self
in shame.

I gradually comprehend
how poems are made.   15
To the upbeat flight of memories.

The flagged beats of the running
heart.

I understand how poems are made.
They are the tears   20
that season the smile.
The stiff-neck laughter
that crowds the throat.
The leftover love.

I know how poems are made.   25

There is a place the loss must go.
There is a place the gain must go.
The leftover love.

RELATED COMMENTARIES: *Aristotle, "The poet himself ought to speak the least
of all," page 1233; Ralph Waldo Emerson, From "The Poet," page 1258; Plato, "On
Banishing Poets from the State," page 1292.*

10

THE ELEMENTS OF POETRY:
A POET'S MEANS

A word is dead
When it is said,
Some say.
I say it just
Begins to live
That day.
        – EMILY DICKINSON

WORDS AND THEIR SOUND

When we first read a poem it is almost always its subject and theme that
stir our interest. We ask ourselves, "What is the poem about?" If the poem is
about something that concerns us, then we will read it. There are, however,
many poems that deal with the same basic themes, since poetry draws up its
materials from the well of our deepest emotions. What is it that makes us say
one poem is beautiful and another poem is not, even if each poem describes
the same feeling or emotional mood? The pleasure is in the *means* the poet has
used to present the theme: the sound of the words, the rhythms of the lines,
the vividness of the images. If we have some familiarity with these means, or
formal elements of poetry, our understanding and enjoyment of the poem will
be greatly increased.

Alliteration and Assonance

One of the simplest — and earliest — ways poets use the sound of
words to structure their writing is what is called **alliteration**. Alliteration is
the repetition of the same sounding letters. If it is the first letter that is repeated, and the letter is a consonant, it is called **initial alliteration**. This is the
easiest form of alliteration to recognize, and people often use it for a humorous effect. "Little Lyle lies longingly on the lawn," is one example, or "Susan
sat sewing sister's smock." Poets have generally used it more subtly, but alliteration was a common effect in the earliest poetry in English. *Beowulf*, from the

beginning of the eighth century, is the first poem composed in what was to become the English language, and it uses a style based on alliteration.

Closely related to alliteration is **assonance**, the repetition of vowel sounds within a phrase. It can be an elusive effect, sometimes difficult to recognize. Its most obvious form is a phrase like "Opacity opens up rooms," with its repetition of *o* sounds, from Amy Clampitt's poem "Fog." In the hands of a skilled poet, assonance can be an effective means to shade the meaning of the poem. In the opening lines of the poem listen to the sound of the letter *o* as it is repeated several times:

> A vagueness comes over everything,
> as though proving color and contour
> alike dispensable. . . .

If you read the lines carefully, you also can hear the alliteration of the *c* consonants of "color and contour." Clampitt has used both alliteration and assonance so skillfully that you can enjoy her use of words as you read the entire poem. In the second verse, which begins "Tactile / definition, however, has not been / totally banished," she is saying that even though the fog has made everything vague, objects still can be felt, that they are "tactile." Clampitt loved to use unfamiliar words in her poetry, and here she has given us "panicled," which is a botanical term to describe the way the kernels of blossom and seed are distributed irregularly on the stem of certain grasses and grains, like oats. Georgia O'Keeffe, mentioned in the last verse, was an American painter who in some of her canvases caught the effect of a "hueless moonflower / corolla."

AMY CLAMPITT

Fog   *1985*

A vagueness comes over everything,
as though proving color and contour
alike dispensable: the lighthouse
extinct, the islands' spruce-tips
drunk up like milk in the   5
universal emulsion; houses
reverting into the lost
and forgotten; granite
subsumed, a rumor
in a mumble of ocean.   10
                    Tactile
definition, however, has not been
totally banished: hanging

tassel by tassel, panicled
foxtail and needlegrass,   15
dropseed, furred hawkweed,

and last season's rose-hips
are vested in silenced
chimes of the finest,
clearest sea-crystal.   20
                        Opacity
opens up rooms, a showcase
for the hueless moonflower
corolla, as Georgia
O'Keeffe might have seen it,   25
of foghorns; the nodding
campanula of bell buoys;
the ticking, linear
filigree of bird voices.

Onomatopoeia

Another effect that a writer can employ using the sound of words is called **onomatopoeia**. The word is derived from Greek roots, meaning "to make names," which implies that the word is made up to describe the sound. Onomatopoeia means that a word can "sound" like the noise it describes. *Bang!* is an easy example, or if you want a bigger sound, *Boom!* Comic books are a treasure trove of onomatopoeia. How about *Pow!*, *Splat!*, *Zap!*, *RaTaTat!*, *Ping!*, and *Who-o-o-sh?* One American poet who used onomatopoeia effectively was Vachel Lindsay, who performed his poetry in informal readings across the United States in the early years of the century. Read aloud the opening line of his poem about the founder of the Salvation Army, William S. Booth:

Booth led boldly with his big bass drum. . . .

Using alliteration and onomatopoeia, Lindsay catches the sound of a Salvation Army drum with the clamorous tone of the words. In a very different example, Amy Clampitt, in the last lines of "Fog," suggests the delicate sound of "the ticking, linear / filigree of bird voices."

Rhyme

Of all the means the poet has to work with that come out of the sound of words, none of them is more familiar to us than **rhyme**. For hundreds of years part of the definition of poetry was that it rhymed. When other poets began to break away from rhyme in the early part of this century, the American poet Robert Frost, who wrote in traditional rhymed styles, growled that writing poetry without rhyme was like "playing tennis with the net down." Although there is a kind of rhyme called **eye rhyme**, which means that two words look as though they would sound alike, but the sound, if spoken aloud, is different (for example, *house* and *rouse* or *tough* and *though*), the essence of rhyme is a similarity of sound.

Two kinds of rhyme — **perfect rhyme** and **near** or **slant rhyme** — define most of what we mean by the term. The type of rhyme you recognize most in your reading is perfect rhyme. Some of the most common perfect rhymes have been used so often that they have become clichés: *moon* and *June, sigh* and *cry, dream* and *scheme*. In perfect rhyme the sound of the two words is exactly alike, and if the poet can avoid the expected or the commonplace rhyme, the effect can be exciting in itself. The most familiar use of rhyme is called **end rhyme**, in which the words at the end of the line rhyme.

One of the masters of rhymed verse in English was A. E. Housman. Here are two of his best-known poems, each of which is an excellent example of the use of perfect rhyme.

A. E. HOUSMAN

Loveliest of trees, the cherry now   1896

Loveliest of trees, the cherry now
Is hung with bloom along the bough,
And stands about the woodland ride
Wearing white for eastertide.

Now, of my three score years and ten,   5
Twenty will not come again,
And take from seventy springs a score,
It only leaves me fifty more.

And since to look at things in bloom
Fifty springs are little room,   10
About the woodlands I will go
To see the cherry hung with snow.

A. E. HOUSMAN

When I was one-and-twenty   1896

When I was one-and-twenty
    I heard a wise man say,
"Give crowns and pounds and guineas
    But not your heart away;
Give pearls away and rubies   5
    But keep your fancy free."
But I was one-and-twenty,
    No use to talk to me.

When I was one-and-twenty
    I heard him say again,   10

"The heart out of the bosom
    Was never given in vain;
'Tis paid with sighs a-plenty
    And sold for endless rue."
And I am two-and-twenty,   15
    And oh, 'tis true, 'tis true.

Poets who write rhymed verse can benefit from pleasure that readers feel as they anticipate the sound of the rhyme, but this way of writing also has disadvantages. Because each line closes with a rhyme, the repeated pattern can begin to leave the reader feeling that the rhyme is interrupting the poem's flow of ideas and imagery. Perfect rhyme can become monotonous, and the need to find a rhyme can force the poet into an awkward word order or sentences that are muddy and unclear.

Poets have devised many strategies to deal with this problem, such as working with subtle differences in the sound of the rhyming words. They discovered they could vary the sound and have a little more flexibility to shape their lines if they used near rhymes or slant rhymes. With this kind of rhyme the sound of the two words is close but not exact. Examples of near rhyme are pairs of words like *read* and *red*, *seal* and *sail*, *ball* and *bell*.

In her well-known poem "Not Waving but Drowning," Stevie Smith, a modern English poet, consciously used near rhyme to mirror the pathos of a drowning man whose waving people thought was only "larking," or showing his high spirits. The truth is that his waving was a desperate signal for help.

STEVIE SMITH

Not Waving but Drowning   *1957*

Nobody heard him, the dead man,
But still he lay moaning:
I was much further out than you thought
And not waving but drowning.

Poor chap, he always loved larking   5
And now he's dead
It must have been too cold for him his heart gave way,
They said.

Oh, no, no, no, it was too cold always
(Still the dead one lay moaning)   10
I was much too far out all my life
And not waving but drowning.

Smith was a skilled poet, and she certainly could have found a perfect rhyme for the first and last stanzas of the poem, but instead she gives us "moaning," to rhyme with "drowning," a half rhyme that suggests everything that was half successful about the man's life.

Two other terms are also used in discussing rhyme: **masculine rhyme** and **feminine rhyme**. Words are pronounced in syllables, and some syllables are given more emphasis than others. The strong syllable is called an **accent**, and we will be talking more about accents when we discuss the rhythms of poetry. Masculine rhyme means that the accent on the rhyming words is on a final strong syllable. *Stay* and *away*, *bells* and *foretells*, *otherwise* and *guise* are masculine rhymes. In a feminine rhyme, the accent on the rhyming words is on a weak syllable. *Season* and *reason*, *tower* and *flower*, *thunder* and *wonder* are feminine rhymes.

You will sometimes notice that a poet uses rhyme in the middle of the line as well as the end. This is called **internal rhyme**. This example is from "Blow, Bugle, Blow" by the nineteenth-century English poet, Alfred, Lord Tennyson. The internal rhyme occurs in the first and third lines:

> The splendor *falls* on castle *walls*
> And snowy summits old in story:
> The long light *shakes* across the *lakes*
> And the wild cataract leaps in glory.

There are two other terms that help describe what happens at the ends of the lines in a poem. If the meaning of the line comes to a definite end, it is called **end-stopped**; if the meaning does not end but continues on to the next line, it is called **enjambed**. The noun for this running of one line into another line is **enjambment**. Here is an example of end-stopped lines:

> I long to hear love's gentle tune.
> I only mourn it ends so soon.

Here is an example of enjambed lines:

> Oh, to feel the soft, soft touch of spring
> again, and the April softness it will bring!

Usually the poet tries only for a rhyme with one syllable, but many multisyllabic words are also useful as rhymes, like *September* and *remember*, *despair* and *aware*. During the centuries when most poets were concerned with rhyme they often looked for complicated rhymes to show off their skill with language. A famous example is the two-line poem the English poet John Dryden sent to a patron whose family name was Cadwallader. His patron had promised to send him a rabbit for supper, and when it did not appear, Dryden sent him a note in rhyme:

> Oh thou son of great Cadwallader
> Hast thou my hare, or hast thou swallowed her?

Poems for Further Reading

SIR THOMAS WYATT

They Flee from Me   1557

They flee from me, that sometime did me seek,
With naked foot stalking in my chamber.
I have seen them, gentle, tame, and meek,
That now are wild, and do not remember
That sometime they put themselves in danger   5
To take bread at my hand; and now they range,
Busily seeking with a continual change.

Thanked be Fortune it hath been otherwise,
Twenty times better; but once in special,
In thin array, after a pleasant guise,   10
When her loose gown from her shoulders did fall,
And she me caught in her arms long and small,
And therewith all sweetly did me kiss
And softly said, "Dear heart, how like you this?"

It was no dream, I lay broad waking.   15
But all is turned, thorough° my gentleness,   *through*
Into a strange fashion of forsaking;
And I have leave to go, of her goodness,
And she also to use newfangleness.
But since that I so kindly am served,   20
I fain would know what she hath deserved.

JOHN DONNE

Song   1633

Go and catch a falling star,
   Get with child a mandrake root,°
Tell me where all past years are,
   Or who cleft the Devil's foot,
Teach me to hear mermaids singing,   5
Or to keep off envy's stinging,
     And find
     What wind
Serves to advance an honest mind.

---

2. **mandrake root:** A plant with a forked root that resembles the lower part of the female anatomy. Folk legend holds that the mandrake shrieks when uprooted and the sound is death to the hearer.

If thou beest born to strange sights,
    Things invisible to see,   10
Ride ten thousand days and nights,
    Till age snow white hairs on thee.
Thou, when thou return'st, wilt tell me
All strange wonders that befell thee,   15
        And swear
        Nowhere
Lives a woman true, and fair.

If thou find'st one, let me know,
    Such a pilgrimage were sweet;   20
Yet do not, I would not go,
    Though at next door we might meet;
Though she were true when you met her,
And last till you write your letter,
        Yet she   25
        Will be
False, ere I come, to two, or three.

ROBERT HERRICK

To the Virgins, to Make Much of Time   *1648*

Gather ye rosebuds while ye may,
    Old time is still a-flying;
And this same flower that smiles today
    Tomorrow will be dying.

The glorious lamp of heaven, the sun,   5
    The higher he's a-getting,
The sooner will his race be run,
    And nearer he's to setting.

That age is best which is the first,
    When youth and blood are warmer;   10
But being spent, the worse, and worst
    Times still succeed the former.

Then be not coy, but use your time,
    And, while ye may, go marry;
For, having lost but once your prime,   15
    You may forever tarry.

GEORGE HERBERT

Easter Wings   1633

Lord, who createdst man in wealth and store,°
   Though foolishly he lost the same,
      Decaying more and more
         Till he became
           Most poor: 5
           With thee
         O let me rise
      As larks, harmoniously,
   And sing this day thy victories:
Then shall the fall further the flight in me.   10

My tender age in sorrow did begin:
   And still with sicknesses and shame
      Thou didst so punish sin,
         That I became
           Most thin.   15
           With thee
         Let me combine,
      And feel this day thy victory;
   For, if I imp° my wing on thine,
Affliction shall advance the flight in me.   20

EDNA ST. VINCENT MILLAY

God's World   1917

O world, I cannot hold thee close enough!
     Thy winds, thy wide grey skies!
     Thy mists that roll and rise!
Thy woods, this autumn day, that ache and sag
And all but cry with colour! That gaunt crag   5
To crush! To lift the lean of that black bluff!
World, World, I cannot get thee close enough!

Long have I known a glory in it all,
     But never knew I this:
     Here such a passion is   10
As stretcheth me apart, — Lord, I do fear
Thou'st made the world too beautiful this year;
My soul is all but out of me, — let fall
No burning leaf; prithee, let no bird call.

---

1. **wealth and store:** Abundance.   19. **imp:** Graft, a term used in falconry.

E. E. CUMMINGS

when god lets my body be   1923

when god lets my body be
From each brave eye shall sprout a tree
fruit that dangles therefrom

the purpled world will dance upon
Between my lips which did sing   5
a rose shall beget the spring

that maidens whom passion wastes
will lay between their little breasts
My strong fingers beneath the snow

into strenuous birds shall go   10
my love walking in the grass

their wings will touch with her face
and all the while shall my heart be
With the bulge and nuzzle of the sea

MARIANNE MOORE

A Talisman   1921

Under a splintered mast,
torn from the ship and cast
         near her hull,

a stumbling shepherd found,
embedded in the ground,   5
         a sea-gull

of lapis lazuli,
a scarab of the sea,
         with wings spread —

curling its coral feet,   10
parting its beak to greet
         men long dead.

GENEVIEVE TAGGARD

With Child   1922

Now I am slow and placid, fond of sun,
Like a sleek beast, or a worn one,
No slim and languid girl — not glad
With the windy trip I once had,

But velvet-footed, musing of my own,
Torpid, mellow, stupid as a stone.   5

You cleft me with your beauty's pulse, and now
Your pulse has taken body. Care not how
The old grace goes, how heavy I am grown,
Big with this loneliness, how you alone   10
Ponder our love. Touch my feet and feel
How earth tingles, teeming at my heel!
Earth's urge, not mine, — my little death, not hers;
And the pure beauty yearns and stirs.

It does not heed our ecstasies, it turns   15
With secrets of its own, its own concerns,
Toward a windy world of its own, toward stark
And solitary places. In the dark,
Defiant even now, it tugs and moans
To be untangled from these mother's bones.   20

JOHN BERRYMAN

A Professor's Song   *1948*

(. . . rabid or dog-dull.) Let me tell you how
The Eighteenth Century couplet ended. Now
Tell me. Troll me the sources of that Song —
Assigned last week — by Blake.° Come, come along,
Gentlemen. (Fidget and huddle, do. Squint soon.)   5
I want to end these fellows all by noon.

"That deep romantic chasm" — an early use;
The word is from the French, by our abuse
Fished out a bit. (Red all your eyes. O when?)
"A poet is a man speaking to men":   10
But I am then a poet, am I not? —
Ha ha. The radiator, please. Well, what?

Alive now — no — Blake would have written prose,
But movement following movement crisply flows,
So much the better, better the much so,   15
As burbleth Mozart. Twelve. The class can go.
Until I meet you, then, in Upper Hell
Convulsed, foaming immortal blood: farewell.

Rhythm

If the only poetry you read is written by contemporary poets, then it might seem that you will not need to learn about the kinds of rhythm that went into the writing of verse a hundred years ago. In the politically turbulent

---

4. **Blake:** William Blake (1757–1827), English romantic poet.

years at the beginning of the twentieth century, many young poets in Europe and the United States felt that they had to break free of old poetic forms to find a new language that could reflect the enormous social changes they could see around them. What they chose to write was called **free verse**, because it looked on the page as if it were free of the restrictions of traditional poetry. Now we realize that writing poetry this way requires the same concentration and skill needed to write in traditional forms, so often we use the term **open form** instead. (Open form is discussed further in Chapter 13.) We call the traditional verse techniques **closed form**.

Accent and Meter

Like the other poetic means we have considered so far, the rhythm of a poem is built on the sound of words. When we discussed the difference between masculine and feminine rhyme we defined the term **accent**, which is the strong syllable, or syllables, in a word. This is the part of the word we emphasize with breath and tone as we say it out loud. The accents in the words give the poem its rhythm. All words with more than one syllable will have at least one **strong accent**. The other syllables are called **weak accents**. Sometimes the terms used are **stressed** and **unstressed** instead of strong and weak, but they refer to the same pattern of emphasized and unemphasized sounds.

A technical note: you should remember that one-syllable words like *a*, *the*, and *an*, which are called articles, generally are weak, unless we want to emphasize them for a special effect. One of the most common of these effects is a phrase like "There was THE Elvis Presley, standing in our own supermarket check-out line!" This same rule applies to one-syllable prepositions like *at*, *from, to, by, with*, and *of* and the conjunctions *and* and *but*.

One-syllable words like *I* and *me* are more complicated in their usage. You will find that all of these words can have strong or weak accents, depending on the words around them. Some short words have two strong accents: *uptight* is an example. Longer words can have complex patterns of strong and weak accents. Some, like *disenchanted,* stride briskly on with alternating strong and weak accents; others, like *encyclopedia,* dance to a rhythm all their own.

Two symbols are commonly used to indicate strong and weak accents: ´ (strong) and ˘ (weak). We would indicate the pattern of accents for *disenchanted* as

    ´ ˘ ´ ˘
  dis en chant ed.

The indications for *encyclopedia* would be

  ˘ ˘ ˘ ´ ˘ ˘
  en cy clo pe di a.

Marking the pattern of accents or stresses in a line of poetry will help you understand how the line achieves its effect, and it is a skill you should practice. You should, however, practice it by copying the poem into a notebook or into your word processor. If you mark a poem on the page of your text you will never be able to see the poem without the markings, and they will become small pricks that catch at your eye when you should be thinking only of the meaning and the language of the poem. The term for this kind of analysis is **scansion**, and what you are doing is scanning the poem.

The pattern set up by the regular rhythm of words in a poem is called **meter**. To have a meter we have to have more than one or two accents; this means we have to have at least three or four words to hear the meter. In some poems it is almost necessary to follow the pattern all the way to the end of the poem to decide what the meter is.

The meters you will be studying all have names, based on what is called a **foot**, one unit of the rhythmic pattern that makes up the meter. This may sound as if we have simply gone around in a circle, but it is not difficult to understand if you write down a line of the poem and mark it with the symbols for stressed and unstressed or accented and unaccented syllables. Here is an example from a sonnet by William Shakespeare:

> ˘ ˘ | ˘ ´ | ˘ ˘ | ˘ ´ | ˘ ´
> So oft | have I | invok'd | thee for | my muse

If you read the line out loud, the first syllable, *So,* is unaccented, so the pattern of weak and strong accents is weak-strong, weak-strong, weak-strong, weak-strong, weak-strong. The foot is the unit of the two syllables — a weak one and a strong one — and as you can see we marked the foot with the symbol | . A rhythm based on a foot of one weak and one strong syllable, which has the name **iamb**, is called **iambic meter**, and it is one of the basic building blocks of English poetry.

What happens if we reverse the pattern of accents, and we have a line with a stress on the first syllable?

> ´ ˘ | ´ ˘ | ´ ˘ | ´ ˘ | ´
> Does he | ever | wonder | where I | am?

Here the pattern is strong-weak, strong-weak, strong-weak, strong-weak, strong. This metrical foot is called a **trochee**, and the name for its meter is **trochaic meter**.

Two other rhythmic patterns are commonly found in poetry in English. One is a rhythmic foot of two unaccented syllables followed by a strong syllable. An example would be

> ˘ ˘ ´ | ˘ ˘ ´ | ˘ ˘ ´ | ˘ ´
> By the sea, | by the sea, | by the beau | tiful sea.

The foot is called an **anapest**, and the line produces **anapestic meter**. The other foot reverses this pattern and we have a strong syllable followed by two weak syllables:

> ´ ˘ ˘ | ´ ˘ ˘ | ´ ˘ ˘ | ´
> Down by the | sea, by the | beautiful | sea.

The foot is called a **dactyl** and its meter is **dactylic**.

As you begin using these terms and reading poems with them in mind, you should remember that poets usually do not follow the meters consistently through the poem. When the meter never varies, the poem may be considered too "sing-song." If you read through a poem and find that most of its lines are in one meter, then you will say that the poem is iambic or dactylic, trochaic or anapestic, depending on whichever foot is used most often in the poem. We call any foot that is not part of the overall meter by its own name. If you read a line like

> She watched | him walk | in the sum | mer's light

you see that the rhythm is weak-strong, weak-strong, weak-weak-strong, weak-strong. You would say that this line is iambic, with an anapestic third foot. You will also find when you analyze the meter of some lines that there is a break in the meter. It stops and starts somewhere within the line. This is called **caesura**, and it is an important term to remember, because it will help you to sort through some of the meters in more complex lines. The symbol for a caesura is | |. In this line from another of Shakespeare's sonnets the caesura occurs between *cruel* and *do:*

> Be wise | as thou | art cruel, | | do | not press

You will usually have some help in recognizing the caesura. There will often be punctuation at that point — a period, a colon, or semicolon. Even a comma can be enough to tell you that there is a break in the rhythm. Sometimes there is an unstressed syllable at the beginning of a line that does not affect the overall meter. The term for this is an **anacrusis**. In this example the meter of the line is dactylic, with the opening word *I* as an anacrusis:

> I | went to the | river to | see the sun | fade

If you have ever studied a play by Shakespeare, you've heard the term **iambic pentameter**. We already discussed the word *iambic*. *Pentameter* is derived from the Greek word *penta*, which means "five." Combined with the word *meter*, it means a meter with five units, or feet. If you consider the first line we analyzed from a sonnet by Shakespeare — "So oft have I invok'd thee for my muse" — you see that it has five strong accents. We say the line is written in iambic pentameter, as it is made up of a foot with weak-strong syllables, and it has five of them. There are terms derived from the Greek for almost all of the conceivable line lengths, and we can list them here:

> *monometer* is a line of one foot
> *dimeter*, a line of two feet
> *trimeter*, a line of three feet
> *tetrameter*, four feet
> *pentameter*, five feet
> *hexameter*, six feet
> *heptameter*, seven feet
> *octameter*, eight feet

Two strong accents together are called a **spondee** and two weak accents together are called a **pyrrhus**. There are some further refinements of the terms for poetic meter. We use the term **rising meter** for the two feet that begin with a weak syllable, iambic and anapestic, and the term **falling meter** for the two feet that begin with a strong syllable, trochaic and dactylic.

Blank Verse

In your studies of a play by Shakespeare, you would also have encountered the term **blank verse**. Blank verse is a form that utilizes the oratorical style of a long line in regular meter, but without the confines of rhyme. The meter is iambic pentameter, although writers generally allow themselves considerable metric freedom. Blank verse was the basic language of Elizabethan drama. Here is an example from Shakespeare's *Henry IV, Part I:*

> So shaken as we are, so wan with care,
> Find we a time for frighted peace to pant,
> And breathe short-winded accents of new broils
> To be commenced in stronds° afar remote.   *strands*

One of the most popular characteristics of traditional poetry is its rhythm. If we look at turn-of-the-century graduation programs, or read newspaper stories about political rallies or club meetings from the same period, it seems as though every public gathering or school program featured poetry readings. For this kind of occasion the general feeling was the more rhythm the better. Among the graduation program favorites in the United States was "The Bells," by the American poet and short story writer Edgar Allan Poe. The contemporary American poet Allen Ginsberg has singled out this poem as an important early influence on his own writing. We can ring out our discussion of poetic meter with its clang of trochees, spondees, and monosyllabic feet.

EDGAR ALLAN POE

The Bells   1848

1

Hear the sledges with the bells —
    Silver bells!
What a world of merriment their melody foretells!
    How they tinkle, tinkle, tinkle,
      In the icy air of night!   5
    While the stars that oversprinkle
    All the Heavens, seem to twinkle
      With a crystalline delight;
    Keeping time, time, time,
    In a sort of Runic rhyme,   10
To the tintinabulation that so musically wells
    From the bells, bells, bells, bells,
      Bells, bells, bells —
    From the jingling and the tinkling of the bells.

2

        Hear the mellow wedding bells —   15
           Golden bells!
What a world of happiness their harmony foretells!
      Through the balmy air of night
      How they ring out their delight! —
        From the molten-golden notes   20
           And all in tune,
        What a liquid ditty floats
To the turtle-dove that listens while she gloats
           On the moon!
        Oh, from out the sounding cells   25
What a gush of euphony voluminously wells!
           How it swells!
           How it dwells
        On the Future! — how it tells
        Of the rapture that impels   30
      To the swinging and the ringing
        Of the bells, bells, bells! —
      Of the bells, bells, bells, bells,
          Bells, bells, bells —
To the rhyming and the chiming of the bells!   35

3

        Hear the loud alarum bells —
          Brazen bells!
What tale of terror, now, their turbulency tells!
        In the startled ear of Night
      How they scream out their affright!   40
        Too much horrified to speak,
        They can only shriek, shriek,
          Out of tune,
In a clamorous appealing to the mercy of the fire —
In a mad expostulation with the deaf and frantic fire,   45
        Leaping higher, higher, higher,
        With a desperate desire
      And a resolute endeavor
      Now — now to sit, or never,
By the side of the pale-faced moon.   50
        Oh, the bells, bells, bells!
        What a tale their terror tells
          Of despair!
      How they clang and clash and roar!
      What a horror they outpour   55
In the bosom of the palpitating air!
        Yet the ear, it fully knows,
          By the twanging

And the clanging,
How the danger ebbs and flows: — 60
Yes, the ear distinctly tells,
In the jangling
And the wrangling,
How the danger sinks and swells,
By the sinking or the swelling in the anger of the bells — 65
Of the bells —
Of the bells, bells, bells, bells,
Bells, bells, bells —
In the clamor and the clangor of the bells.

4

Hear the tolling of the bells — 70
Iron bells!
What a world of solemn thought their monody compels!
In the silence of the night
How we shiver with affright
At the melancholy meaning of the tone! 75
For every sound that floats
From the rust within their throats
Is a groan.
And the people — ah, the people
They that dwell up in the steeple 80
All alone,
And who, tolling, tolling, tolling,
In that muffled monotone,
Feel a glory in so rolling
On the human heart a stone — 85
They are neither man nor woman —
They are neither brute nor human,
They are Ghouls: —
And their king it is who tolls: —
And he rolls, rolls, rolls, rolls 90
A Pæan from the bells!
And his merry bosom swells
With the Pæan of the bells!
And he dances and he yells;
Keeping time, time, time, 95
In a sort of Runic rhyme,
To the Pæan of the bells —
Of the bells: —
Keeping time, time, time,
In a sort of Runic rhyme, 100
To the throbbing of the bells —
Of the bells, bells, bells —
To the sobbing of the bells: —

Keeping time, time, time,
　　As he knells, knells, knells,   105
In a happy Runic rhyme,
　　To the rolling of the bells —
Of the bells, bells, bells: —
　　To the tolling of the bells —
Of the bells, bells, bells, bells,   110
　　Bells, bells, bells —
To the moaning and the groaning of the bells.

RELATED COMMENTARIES: *T. S. Eliot, "From 'Tradition and the Individual Talent,' " page 1253; Christopher Merrill, "Wyatt's 'They Flee from Me,' " page 1287.*

11

THE ELEMENTS OF POETRY:
A POET'S MEANINGS

No tears in the writer, no tears in the reader. No surprise for the writer, no surprise for the reader.
— ROBERT FROST, from the introduction to *Collected Poems*, 1939

WORDS AND THEIR MEANING

What we have been studying so far is how poets use the *sound* of words as part of the work they do in writing a poem. Now we will begin to discuss those elements of a poem that depend on what a word *means*.

Denotative and Connotative Meaning

The meaning of a word may seem to be simple and straightforward, but many words also have associations that alter the way we understand them. To describe this we use two terms. The first is **denotative**, or what a word denotes. This is the dictionary meaning of the word. The second term is **connotative**. This is the associated meanings that have built up around the word, or what the word connotes. As an example, let's take the word *sweat:*

The *denotative meaning*, which we find in the dictionary: "Moisture exuded from the skin, perspiration."

The *connotative meaning*, which we understand from common usage: hard work.

Someone asks you if you can do something for them, and you answer, "No sweat." What you have said, in the denotative meaning of the word, though you have shortened it considerably, is "Doing what you have asked me to do will be so easy for me that I won't even perspire while I do it." What you have said in its connotative meaning is that for you it's an easy job. Why did you use the connotations of the word *sweat?* For the same reason a writer uses connotations. These suggested or implied meanings make our language more rich and varied, and more vivid in its expression.

Many words that you can think of also have multiple meanings in their denotative sense. *Sweet* is an adjective in the United States; it can also be a term of endearment. In Britain it is a noun meaning "dessert." *Fall* can be a verb or a noun, with its denotative meaning "to descend freely." It can also mean a season of the year, autumn. You will have to be careful in your reading to recognize which meaning the writer wants.

Fall also has connotative meanings. We often use it in a phrase like "He's heading for a fall." The denotative meaning is that if he continues in the direction he is going he will fall down. The connotation of the phrase is that he is going to get into serious trouble. Sometimes the connotation of the word will be immediately obvious; sometimes you have to study the whole poem to see what the writer intended to say. For this way of reading the poem we'll be concerning ourselves with **diction** and **syntax.**

Diction

When we speak of **diction** we are describing the language that a writer has chosen to use in a poem. For us today this means looking at the poem and deciding why one word was chosen and not another one that means the same thing and that in most ways would have done just as well as the word the poet selected. For hundreds of years, however, when people used the term **diction** in discussing a poem, they meant a special kind of language for poetry that they called **poetic diction**. Poetry was considered to be such a refined art that you could only use refined words when you wrote it. In the words of Samuel Johnson, the poet and critic of the late eighteenth century who also compiled the first dictionary of the English language, poetic diction was "a system of words refined from the grossness of domestic use."

Sometimes readers make the mistake of thinking that people in the eighteenth century talked the way their poetry sounds. Except for the occasional person of conscious literary wit such as Johnson, you can be sure that ordinary conversation did not sound that way. This idea of poetic diction, which had grown out of the classical education of that time, was grounded in the study of Latin and Greek. The poets took the classic poets and the myths and legends of the older languages as models for their own poetry. As they worked with these models, their poetry almost developed a language of its own. The term *neoclassical* (or *Augustan*) is used to describe poetry written in this style. You will get an idea of this language from these lines from "Sound and Sense" by one of the most celebrated English poets of the eighteenth century, Alexander Pope:

> True ease in writing comes from art, not chance,
> As those move easiest who have learned to dance.
> 'Tis not enough no harshness gives offense,
> The sound must seem an echo to the sense:

Soft is the strain when Zephyr° gently blows,   5
And the smooth stream in smoother numbers flows;
But when loud surges lash the sounding shore,
The hoarse, rough verse should like the torrent roar.
When Ajax° strives, some rock's vast weight to throw,
The line too labors, and the words move slow;   10
Not so, when swift Camilla° scours the plain,
Flies o'er th' unbending corn, and skims along the main.

If you had said to Pope that these lines sound artificial, not at all like the way people talk, he would have bowed his head and thanked you for the compliment. What he is telling us, in his seemingly effortless iambic pentameter and perfect rhyme, is that writing poetry does not depend on spontaneity, or "chance." The best poets will use artifice or be the ones "who have learned to dance." This is almost the opposite of our own concern with spontaneity and sincerity, but we must remember that the conventions of language reflect different historical periods.

The revolution against the limitations and artificialities that began to dominate neoclassical poetry came at the end of the eighteenth century, with the group of poets we call the *romantics*. Led by the English writers William Wordsworth and Samuel Taylor Coleridge, they broke away from the old style and tried to use language closer to ordinary ways of speaking. As Wordsworth expressed it in his introduction to the first collection of poems written in the new style, he wanted to write in "the language of the middle and lower classes of society."

The poets who are associated with the first romantics — among them William Blake, Robert Burns, Percy Bysshe Shelley, John Keats, and Lord Byron — continued to open up the poetic language to new possibilities in diction and emotional directness. Their poetry was the most important influence on the kind of immediate, personal writing that we value today.

Syntax

Syntax is derived from the Greek word "to arrange together." It refers to the order of the words in writing of any kind, not only poetry. A change in natural word order can affect the way we hear or read any kind of phrase or sentence. In poetry, where each word bears so much weight, any change becomes significant. Poets will sometimes spend as much time deciding the order of the words as they do deciding on what words to use in the first place. For anyone using traditional poetic forms, which meant rhyme and meter, the most common decision about word order was often forced on the writer by the need to find a rhyme.

If you look again at the lines from Alexander Pope's "Sound and Sense," you will see that the natural word order is altered at the ends of line 8 and line 9 because of the necessities of the rhyme. Line 8 would end, in a natural word

---

5. Zephyr: The west wind.   **9. Ajax:** Mighty warrior in Homer's *Iliad*.   **11. Camilla:** Female warrior in Virgil's *Aeneid*.

order, as "should roar like the current," but line 7 ends with "shore." The change of order to bring "roar" at the end of the line solves the problem. Line 9 presents the same difficulty. The natural word order would be "to throw some rock's vast weight," but the rhyme at the end of line 10 is "slow," and here also the change in order gives us the rhyme. You might also have noticed that there is a change in word order at the beginning of line 5. Instead of "The strain is soft," we have "Soft is the strain." Here the change has been made for the sound. If you read line 4 and then follow it with "The strain is soft," you will feel that the meter of the lines is clumsy. The change in order gives us a much smoother line, and this smoothness was one of the qualities that writers such as Pope prized most in a poem.

Imagery

We are all familiar with the literal, denotative meaning of the word *image* as a picture of something. If we say that a girl is the image of her mother, we mean that she looks just like her. If we are talking about an image in a poem, however, the word has different connotations. We do not, in a literal sense, *see* anything in a poem; we just read about it. What we call an image in poetry is a concrete description of something. It can also be a description of something we hear, touch, or feel in a physical sense. There are terms to describe each of these three kinds of images: **visual images** (things we see), **aural images** (things we hear), and **tactile images** (things we touch). If we write "an old, dark green convertible," that is a visual image. If we go on to describe the convertible's "noisy, rattling roar," that is an aural image. If we imagine sitting behind the wheel and feel "the prickly upholstery" on the seat, that is a tactile image.

Being even more precise in defining images, we have two more names for different types of tactile images. One is **gustatory** (things we taste), and the other is **olfactory** (things we smell). Describing the convertible's "lingering gas fumes" is an olfactory image, and if we drive it to a fast-food restaurant and eat a hamburger that has "a greasy, half-cooked taste," that is a gustatory image.

These kinds of physical descriptions have always been part of the poet's means, because a writer's description of specific and concrete objects in a poem strengthens our sense that what we are being told is real. This is, after all, the way we perceive the world. Our information comes to us through the perceptions of our senses, which gather in the raw material that we use to decide what we are experiencing. A poem can also include words like *beauty* and *truth*, but these are not images. They have no concrete reality, however intensely we may feel them. The word we use for them is **abstractions**.

The poems you are reading may have many images, or they may have only a single image. If we are talking about all of the images within a poem, we use the term **imagery**. The connotation of the term is that the poem presents us with a series of images that relate to one another in a way that helps to shape the poem's meaning. As you read "To Autumn" by the English romantic poet John Keats, you will see that the description of autumn is filled with visual images. Although we may find the language of the poem old-fashioned, Keats's poetry seemed revolutionary to the readers of his day.

JOHN KEATS

To Autumn   1819

Season of mists and mellow fruitfulness,
   Close bosom friend of the maturing sun:
Conspiring with him how to load and bless
   With fruit the vines that round the thatch-eaves run;
To bend with apples the mossed cottage-trees,   5
   And fill all fruit with ripeness to the core;
     To swell the gourd, and plump the hazel shells
With a sweet kernel; to set budding more,
   And still more, later flowers for the bees,
   Until they think warm days will never cease,   10
     For summer has o'er-brimmed their clammy cells.

Who hath not seen thee oft amid thy store?
   Sometimes whoever seeks abroad may find
Thee sitting careless on a granary floor,
   Thy hair soft-lifted by the winnowing wind;   15
Or on a half-reaped furrow sound asleep,
   Drowsed with the fume of poppies, while thy hook
     Spares the next swath and all its twined flowers:
And sometimes like a gleaner thou dost keep,
   Steady thy laden head across a brook;   20
   Or by a cider-press, with patient look,
     Thou watchest the last oozings hours by hours.

Where are the songs of Spring? Ay, where are they?
   Think not of them, thou hast thy music too, —
While barred clouds bloom the soft-dying day,   25
   And touch the stubble-plains with rosy hue;
Then in a wailful choir the small gnats mourn
   Among the river sallows, borne aloft
     Or sinking as the light wind lives or dies;
And full-grown lambs loud bleat from hilly bourn;   30
   Hedge-crickets sing: and now with treble soft
   The red-breast whistles from a garden-croft;
     and gathering swallows twitter in the skies.

Keats is writing here about an everyday subject, the coming of autumn to a country farm, and although his language is still too elevated to be mistaken for the way ordinary people spoke, he does not break up the poem's imagery with the continual references to classical learning that writers such as Pope considered an essential element of their poetry.

The first line is an image in itself, the autumn as a "season of mists and mellow fruitfulness." Then, almost as if we are standing in the center of the farmyard, we see the vines on the cottage eaves, the "mossed cottage-trees," the flowers for the bees, and the bees, which have gathered so much honey that they've "o'er-brimmed their clammy cells," in their hives. The figure that the poet addresses as "thee" in the second verse is autumn. The term for this way of speaking to something that is inanimate is the figure of speech called **apostrophe**.

At the end of the poem, Keats does not make any larger statement about the scene in the farmyard. He does not draw any moral or lesson from it. This was also part of the revolutionary quality of his poetry. Simply to be there, at that moment, and hear the red-breast whistling from the croft and the swallows twittering in the sky was enough for him. The sallows he notices in line 28 are low willows that grow along riverbanks, and one of the poet's strongest aural images is the description of the gnats "mourning" above the brushy willows.

Many modern poets write with the same open and direct response to a natural scene as Keats wrote. In the following poem the American writer Elizabeth Bishop is also satisfied simply to look at what is before her. She is seeing it so intensely that the poem is constructed entirely around its visual images. What she is describing is a *bight*, a small bay, usually by the ocean. *Marl* is the rich deposit of soil that streams have left on the bottom of the bight, and *claves* are wooden percussion instruments used in Caribbean and South American dance music. Charles Baudelaire, who is named in line 7, was a nineteenth-century French poet who shocked many people with the frank sensuality of his writing. He also puzzled people with his theories that poetry could find the associations between the world of the sense — the physical world — and the world of the spirit. In her line about marimba music (line 8), Bishop is humorously suggesting that this is the kind of association Baudelaire would have made when he was experimenting with substances such as the gas she can smell coming out of the muck at the bottom of the bay.

ELIZABETH BISHOP

The Bight

(On My Birthday)   *1955*

At low tide like this how sheer the water is.
White, crumbling ribs of marl protrude and glare
and the boats are dry, the pilings dry as matches.
Absorbing, rather than being absorbed,
the water in the bight doesn't wet anything,   5
the color of the gas flame turned as low as possible.
One can smell it turning to gas; if one were Baudelaire
one could probably hear it turning into marimba music.
The little ochre dredge at work off the end of the dock
already plays the dry perfectly off-beat claves.   10
The birds are outsize. Pelicans crash
into this peculiar gas unnecessarily hard,
it seems to me, like pickaxes,

rarely coming up with anything to show for it,
and going off with humorous elbowings.   15
Black-and-white man-of-war birds soar
on impalpable drifts
and open their tails like scissors on the curves
or tense them like wishbones, till they tremble.
The frowsy sponge boats keep coming in   20
with the obliging air of retrievers,
bristling with jackstraw gaffs and hooks
and decorated with bobbles of sponges.
There is a fence of chicken wire along the dock
where, glinting like little plowshares,   25
the blue-gray shark tails are hung up to dry
for the Chinese-restaurant trade.
Some of the little white boats are still piled up
against each other, or lie on their sides, stove in,
and not yet salvaged, if they ever will be, from the last bad storm,   30
like torn-open, unanswered letters.
The bight is littered with old correspondences.
Click. Click. Goes the dredge,
and brings up a dripping jawful of marl.
All the untidy activity continues,   35
awful but cheerful.

As you read the poem you may have noticed some of the poetic means
that Bishop uses to bring her description of the harbor to life. In the first line
she has changed the *syntax* to tell us the most important thing about the scene.
The line in customary order would be, "How sheer the water is like this at low
tide." Instead, the first thing she tells us is that it is low tide, so we will have
that as our immediate visual image.

Sheer is not an obvious choice to describe the gleam of the water on the
mud flats, but Bishop has made a choice in the *diction* of the poem to use *sheer*
instead of another possible word, like *shiny*. *Sheer* has the connotations of silk,
and it also has an *r* sound, which relates to the *r* of water, and gives the line a
subtle *assonance*. *Sheer* also has one syllable, which smooths out the rhythm of
the last half of the line to three iambic feet.

We can see several other phrases in which Bishop has made choices in
the diction to create an even more vivid image: *ochre* instead of yellow-brown
for the color of the dredge, "dry perfectly off-beat" for the sound of the claves,
the adjective *outsize* instead of *big* for the size of the birds, *frowsy* for the
sponge boats instead of *tattered*. The poem is written without regular meter or
rhyme, but certainly, with Bishop's brilliant skill with words, she intended to
use the near rhyme of *marl* and *cheerful* that helps to bring the poem to a close.

Simile and Metaphor

As we looked closely at Bishop's poem, we realized that she had other
means of showing us the harbor. Several times she used comparisons —

phrases that began with the word *like*. The term for this is **simile**. For an image of the pelicans flapping out of the water she used the phrase "humorous elbowings," which is an indirect comparison. The term for this is **metaphor**. Both of these terms are important in understanding how poems are written.

Writers have always used simile and metaphor because language without simile is as flat as chili without chili powder. If you have studied literature, you recognized that "as flat as chili without chili powder" is a simile. Simile and metaphor are both comparisons, but a simile tells us to watch out for the comparison with the words *like, as, as if,* or *as though,* while a metaphor does not.

Writers use comparisons for several reasons. It is often easier to describe something that is not familiar by comparing it to something that is, as in the sentence "The wing of a Morpha butterfly looks like a large blue leaf." Another use of a simile is to give a tangible reality to something that is intangible. An example: "Our love is like the shine of the sun on the sea."

The use of metaphor has long been considered one of the measures of a poet's skill. The Greek philosopher Aristotle defined metaphor as "an intuitive perception of the similarity in dissimilars." A simple metaphor would be a phrase like "You are my sunshine." Most poets, however, try to find comparisons that are more unexpected, that make the reader think about what is similar in the two objects that are being drawn together in a comparison.

The Anglo-Saxon church historian the Venerable Bede included one of the first memorable extended similes in English literature (it was derived from Psalm 84) in his eighth-century *Ecclesiastical History of the English People.* Bede wrote that the brief span of our lifetime between birth and death is "as if a sparrow beaten with wind and weather" flies into a warm, lighted hall, and then, after "a short space of this fair weather," departs back outside "to return from winter to winter again."

In Elizabeth Bishop's poem we identified both similes and a metaphor. The similes are strong word pictures. The pelicans crash into the water "like pickaxes," the man-of-war birds open their tails "like scissors," "glinting like little plowshares, / the blue-gray shark tails are hung up to dry," the little white boats lie damaged on the mud "like torn-open, unanswered letters." The metaphor is a description of pelicans struggling to fly up from the water. Bishop describes them as "going off with humorous elbowings," which compares them with people using their elbows to get through a crowd.

Here are some examples of similes:

> Like as the waves make towards the pebbled shore,
> So do our minutes hasten to their end.
> – WILLIAM SHAKESPEARE, from "Sonnet 61"

> Oh, my luve is like a red, red rose,
>   That's newly sprung in June.
> – ROBERT BURNS, from "A Red, Red Rose"

> I love smooth words, like gold-enameled fish
> which circle slowly with a golden swish.
> – ELEANOR WYLIE, from "Pretty Words"

Let us go then, you and I
When the evening is spread out against the sky
Like a patient etherized upon a table.
– T. S. ELIOT, from "The Love Song of J. Alfred Prufrock"

I am scattered like
the hot shriveled seeds.
– H.D., from "Mid-day"

Love set you going like a fat gold watch.
– SYLVIA PLATH, from "Morning Song"

What happens to a dream deferred?
    Does it dry up
    like a raisin in the sun?
– LANGSTON HUGHES, from "Harlem"

I like small kindnesses.
In fact I actually prefer them to the more
substantial kindness that is always eyeing you,
like a large animal on a rug.
– LOUISE GLÜCK, from "Gratitude"

Here are some examples of metaphors:

My Rosalind, my Rosalind,
My frolic falcon, with bright eyes.
– ALFRED, LORD TENNYSON, from "Rosalind"

Your mind and you are our Sargasso Sea.
– EZRA POUND, from "Portrait d'une Femme"

Now that I have your voice by heart, I read
In the black chords upon a dulling page
Music that is not meant for music's cage,
Whose emblems mix with words that shake and bleed.
– LOUISE BOGAN, from "Song for the Last Act"

        . . . your knees
are a southern breeze.
– WILLIAM CARLOS WILLIAMS, from "Portrait of a Lady"

The corpse was bloodless. . . .
Its open staring eyes were lustreless dead-lights.
– ROBERT LOWELL, from "The Quaker Graveyard in Nantucket"

Marriage is not
a house or even a tent

it is before that, and colder.
– MARGARET ATWOOD, from "Habitation"

As a last example, in this poem Judith Rodriguez uses "Eskimo" songs as an extended metaphor for her dancing and singing as she fixes breakfast for her daughters. Notice the series of similes as she stamps like a bear, calls like the wind, and leaps like the sea.

JUDITH RODRIGUEZ

Eskimo Occasion   1973

I am in my Eskimo-hunting-song mood,
Aha!
The lawn is tundra   the car will not start
the sunlight is an avalanche   we are avalanche-struck at our breakfast
struck with sunlight through glass   me and my spoon-fed daughters   5
out of this world in our kitchen.

I will sing the song of my daughter-hunting,
Oho!
The waves lay down   the ice grew strong
I sang the song   of dark water under ice   10
the song of winter fishing   the magic for seal rising
among the ancestor masks.

I waited by water to dream new spirits,
Hoo!
The water spoke   the ice shouted   15
the sea opened   the sun made young shadows
they breathed my breathing   I took them from deep water
I brought them fur-warmed home.

I am dancing the years of the two great hunts,
Ya-hay!   20
It was I who waited   cold in the wind-break
I stamp like the bear   I call like the wind of the thaw
I leap like the sea spring-running.   My sunstruck daughters splutter
and chuckle and bang their spoons:

Mummy is singing at breakfast and dancing!   25
So big!

Figurative and Literal Language

The term **figurative language** means that the poem uses simile or
metaphor, or any of the figures of speech we will study in the next pages. The
opposite of figurative language is **literal language**, which means that each
word is being used in its denotative sense.

Symbol

We've already seen how words and phrases have connotations and associations. A word becomes a **symbol** when it has so much meaning attached
to it that we cannot hear it spoken without immediately thinking about something else at the same time. Mention of "the flag" brings up thoughts of patriotism and America. "Wall Street" could be a reference to the structure of

American capitalism. In the 1920s the poet T. S. Eliot became the center of a lengthy discussion about symbols and symbolism, because several of his most influential poems used objects like roses or yew trees as symbols for his beliefs in tradition and his religious faith. In our own period poets more often write directly what they mean, but words like *Hollywood* or *Barbie* in a poem come loaded with associations.

Figures of Speech

There are more than two hundred ways that words can be used as figures of speech, but you need to familiarize yourself with only a few that you will meet most often. If you say "The sky is crying," you are using **personification**, which is giving human characteristics to something inanimate, animal, or abstract. In this poem Ralph Waldo Emerson personifies days as "daughters of time."

RALPH WALDO EMERSON

Days   1857

Daughters of Time, the hypocritic Days,
Muffled and dumb, like barefoot dervishes,
And marching single in an endless file,
Bring diadems and fagots in their hands.
To each they offer gifts, after his will,   5
Bread, kingdoms, stars, and sky that holds them all.
I, in my pleached garden, watched the pomp,
Forgot my morning wishes, hastily
Took a few herbs and apples, and the Day
Turned and departed silent. I, too late,   10
Under her solemn fillet saw the scorn.

The term **apostrophe** means to address something intangible or someone not commonly spoken to. The opening line of this sonnet by John Donne (see p. 948) is an example of apostrophe, as the intangible presence he is crying out to is Death:

Death, be not proud, though some have callèd thee
Mighty and dreadful, for thou art not so;
For those whom thou thinks't thou dost overthrow
Die not, poor Death. . . .

Metonymy and a type of figurative speech closely related to it, **synecdoche**, are similar to metaphor. In using metonymy the writer uses the name of one thing in place of the name of something closely related to it. Instead of saying "I knew him when he was young," the line could be "I knew him in his cradle." Synecdoche is the use of part of something to stand for the whole thing. If we say someone playing baseball or softball "has a heavy bat," we are using the bat as a substitute for the whole concept, which is that the batter hits the ball well.

There are other figures of speech that you will find in your reading, but most of these concepts are used by all writers, and you are probably already familiar with them. Some of these are *paradox, oxymoron, hyperbole,* and *understatement.* By **paradox** we mean a statement that on the surface seems that it cannot possibly be true but is true after all. In the last lines of the sonnet "Death, be not proud," John Donne uses a paradox when he suggests that because of the miracle of eternal life, it is Death itself that dies at the moment of mortality:

> One short sleep past, we wake eternally
> And death shall be no more; Death, thou shalt die.

An **oxymoron** is a statement that contradicts itself. Probably the best-known modern example is the phrase "jumbo shrimp." A more literary example is "darkness visible," Milton's phrase describing hell in *Paradise Lost.* By **hyperbole** we mean exaggerated statements that we do not really intend to be taken for the truth. When the seventeenth-century American poet Anne Bradstreet writes, in "To My Dear and Loving Husband," "I prize thy love more than whole mines of gold / Or all the riches that the East doth hold," she is using hyperbole. **Understatement** is the opposite of hyperbole. Here something is deliberately described in terms that suggest it is much smaller or less important than we know it really is. The line "Life for me ain't been no crystal stair" from Langston Hughes's poem "Mother to Son" (p. 1130) is an example of understatement.

Poems for Further Reading

ANDREW MARVELL

To His Coy Mistress   1681

> Had we but world enough, and time,
> This coyness, lady, were no crime.
> We would sit down, and think which way
> To walk, and pass our long love's day.
> Thou by the Indian Ganges' side   5
> Shouldst rubies find; I by the tide
> Of Humber would complain. I would
> Love you ten years before the flood,
> And you should, if you please, refuse
> Till the conversion of the Jews.   10
> My vegetable love should grow
> Vaster than empires and more slow;
> An hundred years should go to praise
> Thine eyes, and on thy forehead gaze;

Two hundred to adore each breast, 15
But thirty thousand to the rest;
An age at least to every part,
And the last age should show your heart.
For, lady, you deserve this state,
Nor would I love at lower rate. 20
    But at my back I always hear
Time's wingèd chariot hurrying near;
And yonder all before us lie
Deserts of vast eternity.
Thy beauty shall no more be found, 25
Nor, in thy marble vault, shall sound
My echoing song; then worms shall try
That long-preserved virginity,
And your quaint honor turn to dust,
And into ashes all my lust: 30
The grave's a fine and private place,
But none, I think, do there embrace.
    Now therefore, while the youthful hue
Sits on thy skin like morning dew,
And while thy willing soul transpires°   breathes forth 35
At every pore with instant fires,
Now let us sport us while we may,
And now, like amorous birds of prey,
Rather at once our time devour
Than languish in his slow-chapped° power.   slow-jawed 40
Let us roll all our strength and all
Our sweetness up into one ball,
And tear our pleasures with rough strife
Thorough the iron gates of life:
Thus, though we cannot make our sun 45
Stand still, yet we will make him run.

LADY MARY WORTLEY MONTAGU

The Lover: A Ballad   1747

At length, by so much importunity pressed,
Take, C —— ,° at once, the inside of my breast;
This stupid indifference so often you blame
Is not owing to nature, to fear, or to shame;
I am not as cold as a Virgin in lead,° 5

---

2. C——: Probably Lady Mary's friend Richard Chandler.   **5. Virgin in lead:** A leaded
stained-glass image of the Virgin Mary.

Nor is Sunday's sermon so strong in my head;
I know but too well how time flies along,
That we live but few years and yet fewer are young.

But I hate to be cheated, and never will buy
Long years of repentance for moments of joy.   10
Oh was there a man (but where shall I find
Good sense and good nature so equally joined?)
Would value his pleasure, contribute to mine,
Not meanly would boast, nor would lewdly design,
Not over severe, yet not stupidly vain,   15
For I would have the power though not give the pain;

No pedant yet learnéd, not rakehelly gay
Or laughing because he has nothing to say,
To all my whole sex obliging and free,
Yet never be fond of any but me;   20
In public preserve the decorum that's just,
And show in his eyes he is true to his trust,
Then rarely approach, and respectfully bow,
Yet not fulsomely pert, nor yet foppishly low.

But when the long hours of public are past   25
And we meet with champagne and a chicken at last,
May every fond pleasure that hour endear,
Be banished afar both discretion and fear,
Forgetting or scorning the airs of the crowd
He may cease to be formal, and I to be proud,   30
Till lost in the joy we confess that we live,
And he may be rude, and yet I may forgive.

And that my delight may be solidly fixed,
Let the friend and the lover be handsomely mixed,
In whose tender bosom my soul might confide,   35
Whose kindness can sooth me, whose counsel could guide.
From such a dear lover as here I describe
No danger should fright me, no millions should bribe;
But till this astonishing creature I know,
As I long have lived chaste, I will keep myself so.   40

I never will share with the wanton coquette,
Or be caught by a vain affectation of wit.
The toasters and songsters may try all their art
But never shall enter the pass of my heart.
I loathe the lewd rake, the dressed fopling despise;   45
Before such pursuers the nice° virgin flies;   *fastidious*
And as Ovid has sweetly in parables told
We harden like trees, and like rivers are cold.°

---

48. harden . . . cold: In Ovid's *Metamorphosis*, the nymphs Daphne and Arethusa, fleeing the
unwanted sexual overtures of gods, turn into a laurel tree and a fountain, respectively.

ALEXANDER POPE

From *An Essay on Man*   1733

To Henry St. John, Lord Bolingbroke

EPISTLE I. OF THE NATURE AND STATE OF MAN, WITH RESPECT TO THE UNIVERSE

Awake, my St. John! leave all meaner things
To low ambition, and the pride of kings.
Let us (since life can little more supply
Than just to look about us and to die)
Expatiate free° o'er all this scene of man;   · *range freely*   5
A mighty maze! but not without a plan;
A wild, where weeds and flowers promiscuous shoot,
Or garden, tempting with forbidden fruit.
Together let us beat this ample field,
Try what the open, what the covert yield;   10
The latent tracts, the giddy heights, explore
Of all who blindly creep, or sightless soar;
Eye Nature's walks, shoot folly as it flies,
And catch the manners living as they rise;
Laugh where we must, be candid where we can;   15
But vindicate the ways of God to man.

   1. Say first, of God above, or man below,
What can we reason, but from what we know?
Of man, what see we but his station here,
From which to reason, or to which refer?   20
Through worlds unnumbered though the God be known,
'Tis ours to trace him only in our own.
He, who through vast immensity can pierce,
See worlds on worlds compose one universe,
Observe how system into system runs,   25
What other planets circle other suns,
What varied Being peoples every star,
May tell why Heaven has made us as we are.
But of this frame the bearings, and the ties,
The strong connections, nice dependencies,   30
Gradations just, has thy pervading soul
Looked through? or can a part contain the whole?
   Is the great chain, that draws all to agree,
And drawn supports, upheld by God, or thee?

ROBERT BURNS

To a Mouse   1786

**On Turning Her Up in Her Nest with
the Plow, November, 1785**

Wee, sleekit,° cow'rin', tim'rous beastie,   *sleek*
O, what a panic's in thy breastie!
Thou need na start awa sae hasty,
      Wi' bickering brattle!
I wad be laith° to rin an' chase thee   *loath*   5
      Wi' murd'ring pattle!°   *plow*

I'm truly sorry man's dominion
Has broken Nature's social union,
An' justifies that ill opinion
      Which makes thee startle   10
At me, thy poor, earth-born companion,
      An' fellow mortal!

I doubt na, whiles, but thou may thieve;
What then? poor beastie, thou maun° live!   *must*
A daimen-icker in a thrave°   15
      'S a sma' request:
I'll get a blessin' wi' the lave,°   *remainder*
      And never miss 't!

Thy wee-bit housie, too, in ruin!
Its silly° wa's the win's are strewin'!   *feeble*   20
An' naething, now, to big° a new ane,   *build*
      O' foggage° green!   *moss*
An' bleak December's winds ensuin',
      Baith snell° an' keen!   *bitter*

Thou saw the fields laid bare and waste,   25
An' weary winter comin' fast,
An' cozie here, beneath the blast,
      Thou thought to dwell,
Till crash! the cruel coulter° passed   *cutter-blade*
      Out-through thy cell.   30

That wee-bit heap o' leaves an' stibble
Has cost thee mony a weary nibble!
Now thou's turned out, for a' thy trouble,
      But° house or hald,°   *without; land*
To thole° the winter's sleety dribble,   *endure*   35
      An' cranreuch° cauld!   *frost*

---

15. daimen-icker in a thrave: An ear or so in twenty sheaves.

But Mousie, thou art no thy lane,°   *alone*
In proving foresight may be vain:
The best-laid schemes o' mice an' men
        Gang aft a-gley,°   *often go awry* 40
An' lea'e us nought but grief an' pain,
        For promised joy.

Still thou art blest compared wi' me!
The present only toucheth thee:
But och! I backward cast my e'e   45
        On prospects drear!
An' forward though I canna see,
        I guess an' fear!

WILLIAM BLAKE

Song   *1783*

How sweet I roam'd from field to field,
   And tasted all the summer's pride,
'Till I the prince of love° beheld,   *Cupid*
   Who in the sunny beams did glide!
He shew'd me lilies for my hair,   5
   And blushing roses for my brow;
He led me through his gardens fair,
   Where all his golden pleasures grow.

With sweet May dews my wings were wet,
   And Phoebus fir'd my vocal rage;   10
He caught me in his silken net,
   And shut me in his golden cage.

He loves to sit and hear me sing,
   Then, laughing, sports and plays with me;
Then stretches out my golden wing,   15
   And mocks my loss of liberty.

WILLIAM WORDSWORTH

I Wandered Lonely as a Cloud   *1804*

I wandered lonely as a cloud
That floats on high o'er vales and hills,
When all at once I saw a crowd,
A host, of golden daffodils;
Beside the lake, beneath the trees,
Fluttering and dancing in the breeze.   5

Continuous as the stars that shine
And twinkle on the milky way,
They stretched in never-ending line
Along the margin of a bay: 10
Ten thousand saw I at a glance,
Tossing their heads in sprightly dance.

The waves beside them danced; but they
Outdid the sparkling waves in glee;
A poet could not but be gay,   15
In such a jocund company;
I gazed — and gazed — but little thought
What wealth the show to me had brought:

For oft, when on my couch I lie
In vacant or in pensive mood,   20
They flash upon that inward eye
Which is the bliss of solitude;
And then my heart with pleasure fills,
And dances with the daffodils.

WILLIAM WORDSWORTH

My Heart Leaps Up   1802

My heart leaps up when I behold
  A rainbow in the sky:
So was it when my life began;
So is it now I am a man;
So be it when I shall grow old,
  Or let me die!
The Child is father of the Man;
And I could wish my days to be
Bound each to each by natural piety.

GEORGE GORDON, LORD BYRON

She Walks in Beauty   1814

1

She walks in beauty, like the night
  Of cloudless climes and starry skies;
And all that's best of dark and bright
  Meet in her aspect and her eyes:

Thus mellowed to that tender light   5
    Which heaven to gaudy day denies.

2

One shade the more, one ray the less,
    Had half impaired the nameless grace
Which waves in every raven tress,
    Or softly lightens o'er her face;   10
Where thoughts serenely sweet express
    How pure, how dear their dwelling place.

3

And on that cheek, and o'er that brow,
    So soft, so calm, yet eloquent,
The smiles that win, the tints that glow,   15
    But tell of days in goodness spent,
A mind at peace with all below,
    A heart whose love is innocent!

PERCY BYSSHE SHELLEY

When Passion's Trance Is Overpast   *1824*

When passion's trance is overpast,
If tenderness and truth could last
Or live — whilst all wild feelings keep
Some mortal slumber, dark and deep —
I should not weep, I should not weep!   5

It were enough to feel, to see
Thy soft eyes gazing tenderly . . .
And dream the rest — and burn and be
The secret food of fires unseen,
Could thou but be what thou hast been!   10

After the slumber of the year
The woodland violets reappear;
All things revive in field or grove
And sky and sea, but two, which move
And form all others — life and love. —   15

JOHN KEATS

A Thing of Beauty   *1817*

A thing of beauty is a joy for ever:
Its loveliness increases; it will never
Pass into nothingness; but still will keep

A bower quiet for us, and a sleep
Full of sweet dreams, and health, and quiet breathing.   5
Therefore, on every morrow, are we wreathing
A flowery band to bind us to the earth,
Spite of despondence, of the inhuman dearth
Of noble natures, of the gloomy days,
Of all the unhealthy and o'er-darkened ways   10
Made for our searching: yes, in spite of all,
Some shape of beauty moves away the pall
From our dark spirits. Such the sun, the moon,
Trees old, and young sprouting a shady boon
For simple sheep; and such are daffodils   15
With the green world they live in; and clear rills
'That for themselves a cooling covert make
'Gainst the hot season; the mid forest brake,
Rich with a sprinkling of fair musk-rose blooms:
And such too is the grandeur of the dooms°   judgments   20
We have imagined for the mighty dead;
All lovely tales that we have heard or read:
An endless fountain of immortal drink,
Pouring unto us from the heaven's brink.

   Nor do we merely feel these essences   25
For one short hour; no, even as the trees
That whisper round a temple become soon
Dear as the temple's self, so does the moon,
The passion poesy, glories infinite,
Haunt us till they become a cheering light   30
Unto our souls, and bound to us so fast,
That, whether there be shine, or gloom o'ercast,
They always must be with us, or we die.

RELATED COMMENTARIES: *X. J. Kennedy, "Andrew Marvell's 'To His Coy Mistress,' " page 1277; Sidney Lea, "On Keats's 'To Autumn,' " page 1280; Percy Bysshe Shelley, "From 'A Defence of Poetry,' " page 1311; William Wordsworth, "From the Introduction to* Lyrical Ballads," *page 1330.*

12

THE TYPES OF POETRY:
A POET'S FORMS

one loves only form
and form only comes
into existence when
the thing is born
       – CHARLES OLSON, from
        "I, Maximus of Gloucester"

TYPES OF VERSE

Meter and rhyme, and their complex intertwining, are at the core of all of the forms of traditional verse. For much English poetry the basic building block is a unit of two lines that end in perfect rhyme. The term for this unit is a **couplet**. The couplet appears in English poetry as early as the twelfth century. In this poem, "Hymn to Godric," two couplets are joined together to make a four-line unit called a **stanza**, or a **verse**:

Sainte Marye, Christes bur°	*shelter*
Maidenes clenhad,° moderes flur°	*purity; flower*
Dilie° min sinne, rix° in min mod°	*remove; merge; heart*
Bring me to winne° with the self God	*joy*

We do not recognize all of the words, since language and its meanings are continually changing, but the four-line stanza, written in the four-stress line called *tetrameter* or *quadrameter,* continued to be one of the most widely used poetic means in English and American poetry for hundreds of years. One of the best-known examples of perfect rhyme, A. E. Housman's "Loveliest of trees, the cherry now," is written in this same stanza:

Loveliest of trees, the cherry now
Is hung with bloom along the bough,
And stands about the woodland ride
Wearing white for Eastertide.

We mark the sequence of rhymes in a poem with a tool like the accent symbols that we used to study the meter of a line. Instead of symbols, however, each rhyme is given a letter of the alphabet. Here is an example of how we mark the rhyme pattern of a poem using the same Housman stanza:

Loveliest of trees, the cherry now	*a*
Is hung with bloom along the bough,	*a*
And stands about the woodland ride	*b*
Wearing white for Eastertide.	*b*

Another form of this same stanza has been used almost as often by many poets. The stanza also has four lines and it is written in alternating lines of tetrameter and trimeter, but instead of *aabb*, the rhyme scheme is *abab*. Here is an example.

A. E. HOUSMAN

Oh, when I was in love with you   1896

Oh, when I was in love with you,	*a*
Then I was clean and brave,	*b*
And miles around the wonder grew	*a*
How well I did behave.	*b*
And now the fancy passes by,	*c*
And nothing will remain,	*d*
And miles around they'll say that I	*c*
Am quite myself again.	*d*

A term that is also used for a group of four rhymed lines is a **quatrain**, especially when it is part of a longer unit in a poem. A group of six lines with a recurring rhyme scheme is called a **sestet**, and the term for an eight-line group is an **octave**.

Although the couplet is the basic unit for so much poetry, occasionally the writer will also use a unit of three lines, which is called a **tercet**. Tennyson, who was ingenious in his use of rhyme, included a tercet in each stanza of his long ballad poem *The Lady of Shalott*.

> A red-cross knight forever kneeled
> To a lady in his shield,
> That sparkled on the yellow field.

With these basic terms to help us, we can begin to look at some types of poetry. Whether they are written in traditional — closed — forms or in free — open — forms, poems can generally be sorted into three main types: narrative, lyric, and dramatic. A fourth type, didactic, which includes political poetry, will be discussed in Chapter 14.

NARRATIVE POETRY

A narrative poem is simply a poem that tells the story, like the one that begins " 'Twas the night before Christmas, and all through the house . . ." The oldest form of narrative poetry is the **epic**, which is probably best known today for the two epic poems, the *Iliad* and the *Odyssey*, composed by the poet Homer. The large scale of these narratives and their sweeping depiction of the lives and events of another time have given us the adjective *epic*. (You can read a section of the *Iliad* in Chapter 14, "Poets and History.")

The Ballad

Ballads, which are also narrative poems, are part of the folk tradition of every culture. Even though we know them as printed compositions, traditional ballads come from an earlier period, when they were part of an oral tradition. They tell of a death in a family, of women who were taken by spirits, of bloody quarrels where families are broken or reunited. Most ballads were probably composed by a single individual, but when they come down to us they are usually anonymous. The name of the original writer has been lost as the ballads were passed on from singer to singer. Ballads were meant to be sung, and they are composed in simple quatrains with meters that are easily followed, sometimes with a repeated line that ends every verse, which is called a **refrain**.

In the well-known folk ballad "Barbara Allan," the stanza form uses alternating lines of four and three stressed beats. As is usual in poems that are meant to be sung, there is considerable looseness in the scansion of the beats. Another characteristic of ballads like these is that rhyme is used only for the second and fourth lines of the stanza.

TRADITIONAL BALLAD

Barbara Allan

date unknown

It was in and about the Martinmas° time,   *November 11*
 When the green leaves were a-fallin',
That Sir John Graeme in the West Country
 Fell in love with Barbara Allan.

He sent his man down through the town   5
 To the place where she was dwellin':
"O haste and come to my master dear,
 Gin° ye be Barbara Allan."   *if*

O slowly, slowly rase° she up,   *rose*
 To the place where he was lyin',   10
And when she drew the curtain by:
 "Young man, I think you're dyin'."

"O it's I'm sick, and very, very sick,
    And 'tis a' for Barbara Allan."
"O the better for me ye sal° never be*date*   *shall*   15
    Though your heart's blood were a-spillin'.

"O dinna ye mind, young man," said she,
    "When ye the cups were fillin',
That ye made the healths gae round and round,
    And slighted Barbara Allan?"   20

He turned his face unto the wall,
    And death with him was dealin':
"Adieu, adieu, my dear friends all,
    And be kind to Barbara Allan."

And slowly, slowly, rase she up,   25
    And slowly, slowly left him;
And sighing said she could not stay,
    Since death of life had reft him.

She had not gane a mile but twa,
    When she heard the dead-bell knellin',   30
And every jow° that the dead-bell ga'ed   *stroke*
    It cried, "Woe to Barbara Allan."

"O mother, mother, make my bed,
    O make it soft and narrow:
Since my love died for me today,   35
    I'll die for him tomorrow."

When we read a folk ballad it is easy to forget that the words are a transcription of what someone was singing. Although the ballads of the African American culture have not often made their way into literary anthologies, they are a vital expression that tells us much about the social background that created them. The song "Gray Goose," which is sung by black work gangs in Texas prisons, is a ballad with a sly double meaning. The "gray goose" is understood by the singers to be a veiled reference to the black American who is too tough to be destroyed, despite the tragedies of slavery and segregation.

Gray Goose   *date unknown*

Well, my papa went a-hunting,
            Well, well, well . . .
You know he took along his shotgun,
            Well, well, well . . .
You know he rared the hammer 'way back,   5
            Well, well, well . . .
You know he shot at the gray goose,
            Well, well, well . . .

Well down came the gray goose,
    Well, well, well . . .   10
After six weeks a falling,
    Well, well, well . . .
Well we gave a feather picking,
    Well, well, well . . .
Was a six weeks a pickin' him,   15
    Well, well, well . . .
Well we put him on to parboil,
    Well, well, well . . .
Well we put him in the oven,
    Well, well, well . . .   20
Was a six weeks a bakin' him,
    Well, well, well . . .
Well we put him on the table,
    Well, well, well . . .
Well the knife couldn't cut him,   25
    Well, well, well . . .
Well the last time I seen him,
    Well, well, well . . .
He was flyin' across the ocean,
    Well, well, well . . .   30

The song is started by a leader, who sings the opening phrase; then the work gang answers with the refrain, "Well, well, well . . ." This version was sung by two convicts, Louis Houston and D. J. Miller, with other prisoners at Ramsey State Prison. It was recorded in 1964 by folklorist Bruce Jackson. As they performed it, each line was repeated, but it is more interesting to read it with each line sung only once. Like most songs from the folk tradition, the rhythm is counted in accents. Here there are two strong accents in each line of the verse, and the other words and syllables are given less emphasis. The strong accents in the opening lines, as the singer performs them, are "well my PA-pa went a-HUNT-ing" and "you know he TOOK along his SHOT-gun."

Ballads for Further Reading

The Three Ravens   *date unknown*

There were three ravens sat on a tree,
   Down a down, hay down, hay down,
There were three ravens sat on a tree,
   With a down,
There were three ravens sat on a tree,   5
They were as black as they might be,
   With a down, derry, derry, derry, down, down.

The one of them said to his mate,
"Where shall we our breakfast take?"

"Down in yonder green field   10
There lies a knight slain under his shield.

"His hounds they lie down at his feet,
So well they can their master keep.

"His hawks they fly so eagerly,
There's no fowl dare him come nigh."   15

Down there comes a fallow doe,
As great with young as she might go.

She lifted up his bloody head,
And kissed his wounds that were so red.

She got him up upon her back,   20
And carried him to earthen lake.°   *pit*

She buried him before the prime;°   *sunrise*
She was dead herself ere evensong time.

God send every gentleman
Such hawks, such hounds, and such a lemman.°   *lover* 25

Lord Randall   *date unknown*

"Oh where ha'e ye been, Lord Randall my son?
O where ha'e ye been, my handsome young man?"
   "I ha'e been to the wild wood: mother, make my bed soon,
   For I'm weary wi' hunting, and fain wald° lie down." *would gladly*

"Where gat ye your dinner, Lord Randall my son?   5
   Where gat ye your dinner, my handsome young man?"
   "I dined wi' my true love: mother, make my bed soon,
   For I'm weary wi' hunting, and fain wald lie down."

"What gat ye to your dinner, Lord Randall my son?
What gat ye to your dinner, my handsome young man?"   10
   "I gat eels boiled in broo:° mother, make my bed soon, *broth*
   For I'm weary wi' hunting, and fain wald lie down."

"What became of your bloodhounds, Lord Randall my son?
What became of your bloodhounds, my handsome young man?"
   "O they swelled and they died: mother, make my bed soon, 15
   For I'm weary wi' hunting, and fain wald lie down."

"O I fear ye are poisoned, Lord Randall my son!
O I fear ye are poisoned, my handsome young man!"
   "Oh yes, I am poisoned: mother, make my bed soon,
   For I'm sick at the heart, and I fain wald lie down."   20

WILLIAM WORDSWORTH

We Are Seven   1798

―――― A simple Child,
That lightly draws its breath,
And feels its life in every limb,
What should it know of death?

I met a little cottage Girl: 5
She was eight years old, she said;
Her hair was thick with many a curl
That clustered round her head.

She had a rustic, woodland air,
And she was wildly clad: 10
Her eyes were fair, and very fair;
— Her beauty made me glad.

"Sisters and brothers, little Maid,
How many may you be?"
"How many? Seven in all," she said,   15
And wondering looked at me.

"And where are they? I pray you tell."
She answered, "Seven are we;
And two of us at Conway dwell,
And two are gone to sea.   20

"Two of us in the church-yard lie,
My sister and my brother;
And, in the church-yard cottage, I
Dwell near them with my mother."

"You say that two at Conway dwell,   25
And two are gone to sea,
Yet ye are seven! I pray you tell,
Sweet Maid, how this may be."

Then did the little Maid reply,
"Seven boys and girls are we;   30
Two of us in the church-yard lie,
Beneath the church-yard tree."

"You run about, my little Maid,
Your limbs they are alive;
If two are in the church-yard laid,   35
Then ye are only five."

"Their graves are green, they may be seen,"
The little Maid replied,
"Twelve steps or more from my mother's door,
And they are side by side.   40

"My stockings there I often knit,
My kerchief there I hem;
And there upon the ground I sit,
And sing a song to them.

"And often after sun-set, Sir,   45
When it is light and fair,
I take my little porringer,°   *porridge bowl*
And eat my supper there.

"The first that died was sister Jane;
In bed she moaning lay,   50
Till God released her of her pain;
And then she went away.

"So in the church-yard she was laid;
And, when the grass was dry,
Together round her grave we played,   55
My brother John and I.

"And when the ground was white with snow,
And I could run and slide,
My brother John was forced to go,
And he lies by her side."   60

"How many are you, then," said I,
"If they two are in heaven?"
Quick was the little Maid's reply,
"O Master! we are seven."

"But they are dead; those two are dead!   65
Their spirits are in heaven!"
'Twas throwing words away; for still
The little Maid would have her will,
And said, "Nay, we are seven!"

STERLING A. BROWN

He Was a Man   1932

It wasn't about no woman,
    It wasn't about no rape,
He wasn't crazy, and he wasn't drunk,
    An' it wasn't no shooting scrape,
        He was a man, and they laid him down.   5

He wasn't no quarrelsome feller,
    And he let other folks alone,
But he took a life, as a man will do,

In a fight for to save his own,
    He was a man, and they laid him down.   10

He worked on his little homeplace
    Down on the Eastern Shore;
He had his family, and he had his friends,
    And he didn't expect much more,
        He was a man, and they laid him down.   15

He wasn't nobody's great man,
    He wasn't nobody's good,
Was a po' boy tried to get from life
    What happiness he could,
        He was a man, and they laid him down.   20

He didn't abuse Tom Wickley,
    Said nothing when the white man curst,
But when Tom grabbed his gun, he pulled his own,
    And his bullet got there first,
        He was a man, and they laid him down.   25

Didn't catch him in no manhunt,
    But they took him from a hospital bed,
Stretched on his back in the nigger ward,
    With a bullet wound in his head,
        He was a man, and they laid him down.   30

It didn't come off at midnight
    Nor yet at the break of day,
It was in the broad noon daylight,
    When they put po' Will away,
        He was a man, and they laid him down.   35

Didn't take him to no swampland,
    Didn't take him to no woods,
Didn't hide themselves, didn't have no masks,
    Didn't wear no Ku Klux hoods,
        He was a man, and they laid him down.   40

They strung him up on Main Street,
    On a tree in the Court House Square,
And people came from miles around
    To enjoy a holiday there,
        He was a man, and they laid him down.   45

They hung him and they shot him,
    They piled packing cases around,
They burnt up Will's black body,
    'Cause he shot a white man down;
        "He was a man, and we'll lay him down."   50

It wasn't no solemn business,
    Was more like a barbecue,

The crackers° yelled when the fire blazed,
   And the women and the children too —
     "He was a man, and we laid him down."   55

The Coroner and the Sheriff
   Said "Death by Hands Unknown."
The mob broke up by midnight,
   "Another uppity Nigger gone —
     He was a man, an' we laid him down."   60

HELEN ADAM

I Love My Love   *1958*

In the dark of the moon the hair rules.
         – ROBERT DUNCAN

There was a man who married a maid. She laughed as he led her home.
The living fleece of her long bright hair she combed with a golden
   comb.
He led her home through his barley fields where the saffron poppies
   grew.
She combed, and whispered, "I love my love." Her voice like a plain-
   tive coo.
Ha! Ha!   5
Her voice like a plaintive coo.

He lived alone with his chosen bride, at first their life was sweet.
Sweet was the touch of her playful hair binding his hands and feet.
When first she murmured adoring words her words did not appall.
"I love my love with a capital A. To my love I give my All.   10
Ah, Ha!
To my love I give my All."

She circled him with the secret web she wove as her strong hair grew.
Like a golden spider she wove and sang, "My love is tender and true."
She combed her hair with a golden comb and shackled him to a tree.   15
She shackled him close to the Tree of Life. "My love I'll never set free.
No, No.
My love I'll never set free."

Whenever he broke her golden bonds he was held with bonds of gold.
"Oh! cannot a man escape from love, from Love's hot smothering
   hold?"   20
He roared with fury. He broke her bonds. He ran in the light of the sun.

---

53. crackers: Derogatory term for poor white southerners.

Her soft hair rippled and trapped his feet, as fast as his feet could run,
Ha! Ha!
As fast as his feet could run.

He dug a grave, and he dug it wide. He strangled her in her sleep.   25
He strangled his love with a strand of hair, and then he buried her
    deep.
He buried her deep when the sun was hid by a purple thunder cloud.
Her helpless hair sprawled over the corpse in a pale resplendent
    shroud.
Ha! Ha!
A pale resplendent shroud.   30

Morning and night of thunder rain, and then it came to pass
That the hair sprang up through the earth of the grave, and it grew like
    golden grass.
It grew and glittered along her grave alive in the light of the sun.
Every hair had a plaintive voice, the voice of his lovely one.

"I love my love with a capital T. My love is Tender and True.   35
I'll love my love in the barley fields when the thunder cloud is blue.
My body crumbles beneath the ground but the hairs of my head will
    grow.
I'll love my love with the hairs of my head. I'll never, never let go.
Ha! Ha!
I'll never, never let go."   40

The hair sang soft, and the hair sang high, singing of loves that drown,
Till he took his scythe by the light of the moon, and he scythed that
    singing hair down.
Every hair laughed a lilting laugh, and shrilled as his scythe swept
    through.
"I love my love with a capital T. My love is Tender and True.
Ha! Ha!   45
Tender, Tender, and True."

All through the night he wept and prayed, but before the first bird woke
Around the house in the barley fields blew the hair like billowing smoke.
Her hair blew over the barley fields where the slothful poppies gape.
All day long all its voices cooed, "My love can never escape,   50
No, No!
My love can never escape."

"Be still, be still, you devilish hair. Glide back to the grave and sleep.
Glide back to the grave and wrap her bones down where I buried her
    deep.
I am the man who escaped from love, though love was my fate and
    doom.   55
Can no man ever escape from love who breaks from a woman's
    womb?"

Over his house, when the sun stood high, her hair was a dazzling
  storm,
Rolling, lashing o'er walls and roof, heavy, and soft, and warm.
It thumped on the roof, it hissed and glowed over every window pane.
The smell of the hair was in the house. It smelled like a lion's mane,   60
Ha! Ha!
It smelled like a lion's mane.

Three times round the bed of their love, and his heart lurched with de-
  spair.
In through the keyhole, elvish bright, came creeping a single hair.
Softly, softly, it stroked his lips, on his eyelids traced a sign.   65
"I love my love with a capital Z. I mark him Zero and mine.
Ha! Ha!
I mark him Zero and mine."

The hair rushed in. He struggled and tore, but wherever he tore a tress,
"I love my love with a capital Z," sang the hair of the sorceress.   70
It swarmed upon him, it swaddled him fast, it muffled his every groan.
Like a golden monster it seized his flesh, and then it sought the bone,
Ha! Ha!
And then it sought the bone.

It smothered his flesh and sought the bones. Until his bones were bare   75
There was no sound but the joyful hiss of the sweet insatiable hair.
"I love my love," it laughed as it ran back to the grave, its home.
Then the living fleece of her long bright hair, she combed with a golden
  comb.

LYRIC POETRY

> Just as my fingers on these keys
> Make music, so the selfsame sounds
> On my spirit make a music, too. . . .

> – WALLACE STEVENS,
> from "Peter Quince at the Clavier"

The word *lyric* comes from *lyre,* the small harp that the Greek poets
played to accompany their songs, and for many centuries lyric poetry was
written in the stanza forms and the rhyme schemes of a song. Now a lyric
poem is defined as a short poem that expresses the emotions and thoughts of
the poet. Often lyric poems are written in the first person, though the "I" of the
poem may be a **persona,** which is another person through whom the poet is
speaking. The term *lyrics* is still used today, but its meaning is more specifically the text of a song. Lyric poetry is highly subjective, deeply personal, and
usually intensely emotional.

Some forms of lyric poetry are defined by a set meter and rhyme
scheme, but it is best to think of lyric poetry as a way of expressing feelings.

This poem by Scottish poet Robert Burns is an example of a lyric poem that is close to the form of a song but still expresses the writer's emotions.

ROBERT BURNS

Ae Fond Kiss   *1792*

Ae fond kiss, and then we sever!
Ae farewell, and then forever!
Deep in heart-wrung tears I'll pledge thee,
Warring sighs and groans I'll wage thee.
Who shall say that Fortune grieves him,   5
While the star of hope she leaves him?
Me, nae cheerfu' twinkle lights me,
Dark despair around benights me.

I'll ne'er blame my partial fancy:
Naething could resist my Nancy!   10
But to see her was to love her,
Love but her, and love for ever.
Had we never lov'd sae kindly,
Had we never lov'd sae blindly,
Never met — or never parted —   15
We had ne'er been broken-hearted.

Fare-the-weel, thou first and fairest!
Fare-the-weel, thou best and dearest!
Thine be ilka° joy and treasure,   *every*
Peace, Enjoyment, Love and Pleasure!   20
Ae fond kiss, and then we sever!
Ae farewell, alas, for ever!
Deep in heart-wrung tears I'll pledge thee,
Warring sighs and groans I'll wage thee.

The poem's meter — it is written in trochaic tetrameter — is so skillfully done that there is no break in the rhythmic flow. There is a clearly expressed rhyme scheme (each stanza is an octave of four closed couplets), and at the same time the language of the poem, although it is in Scottish dialect, seems natural and direct. The challenge of writing lyric poetry has always been this problem of finding a form for the poem and at the same time finding phrases and sentences that people might actually speak. The best way to test how well the poet has succeeded is to read the poem aloud. This poem of Burns meets the challenge so well that it almost seems to sing itself.

A lyric poem written more than a hundred years later comes closer to the kind of direct speech that expresses the thoughts and feelings of the poet. The American poet Hilda Doolittle, who wrote under the initials H.D., was one of the first generation of poets to abandon rhyme, and even though there is still a classic tone to her poem's diction and syntax, it is a modern poem in open form.

H.D.

Mid-day

1916

The light beats upon me.
I am startled —
a split leaf crackles on the paved floor —
I am anguished — defeated.

A slight wind shakes the seed-pods —   5
my thoughts are spent
as the black seeds.
My thoughts tear me,
I dread their fever.
I am scattered in its whirl.   10
I am scattered like
the hot shrivelled seeds.

The shrivelled seeds
are split on the path —
the grass bends with dust,
the grape slips
under its crackeled leaf: 15
Yet far beyond the spent seed-pods,
and the blackened stalks of mint,
the poplar is bright on the hill,
the poplar spreads out,   20
deep-rooted among trees.

O poplar, you are great
among the hill-stones,
while I perish on the path
among the crevices of the rocks.   25

The subjectivity that is one of the characteristics of a lyric poem is much more strongly expressed if the poem is written in a style that is closer to the writer's own way of speaking. As we have already discussed in our study of rhyme and meter, certain elements of style and language are won or lost with any changes in the way poets use the means to create their poem. What the lyric poem by H.D. has lost is the musical experience of the meter and the rhyme of Burns's poem. What has been gained is a directness and immediacy of expression.

In this contemporary lyric poem by Denise Levertov, also written in open form, the language is even more direct.

Denise Levertov

The Well　　　　　　　　　　　　　　　　　　*1987*

At sixteen I believed the moonlight
could change me if it would.
　　　　　　I moved my head
on the pillow, even moved my bed
as the moon slowly　　　　　　　　　　　　　　　　　　5
crossed the open lattice.

I wanted beauty, a dangerous
gleam of steel, my body thinner,
my pale face paler.
　　　　　　　　I moonbathed　　　　　　　　　　　10
diligently, as others sunbathe.
But the moon's unsmiling stare
kept me awake. Mornings,
I was flushed and cross.

It was on the dark nights of deep sleep　　　　　　　　15
that I dreamed the most, sunk in the well
and woke rested, and if not beautiful,
filled with some other power.

The opening lines of "The Well" have the tone of a casual conversation, then the poem develops an imagery built out of successive leaps of the imagination. Levertov uses the phrase "a dangerous / gleam of steel" to describe beauty, and "the well" itself is an image of the deepest moments of sleep, suggesting the power of the unconscious.

The Ode

Among the oldest forms of lyric poetry is the ode. As a poem of praise, it is found in nearly every language and culture. For European poets, the style had a classical model, the odes written by the Greek poet Pindar to honor the victorious athletes of the Olympic Games of fifth-century Athens. His poems are often called the "Great Odes" to separate them from the imitations that followed. Pindar intended them to be performed in public ceremonies by choruses that sang or chanted the lines.

An ode is a long, serious lyric poem, addressed to a person or to an object, that presents philosophic ideas and moral concerns. Often odes were addressed to inanimate concepts, as in Percy Bysshe Shelley's "Ode to the West Wind" or objects, as in John Keats's "Ode on a Grecian Urn." In Keats's ode he looks at a half-imagined Greek vase covered with painted scenes and decorations. When he asks, in the first stanza, "What men or gods are these? What maidens loth?," he is asking about the figures painted on the sides of the urn.

In the turmoil and riot of the life that he sees there, he imagines an eternal reality.

JOHN KEATS

Ode on a Grecian Urn   1820

Thou still unravished bride of quietness,
   Thou foster-child of silence and slow time,
Sylvan historian, who canst thus express
   A flowery tale more sweetly than our rhyme:
What leaf-fringed legend haunts about thy shape   5
   Of deities or mortals, or of both,
     In Tempe or the dales of Arcady?°
   What men or gods are these? What maidens loth?
What mad pursuit? What struggle to escape?
     What pipes and timbrels? What wild ecstasy?   10

Heard melodies are sweet, but those unheard
   Are sweeter; therefore, ye soft pipes, play on;
Not to the sensual° ear, but, more endeared,   *physical*
   Pipe to the spirit ditties of no tone:
Fair youth, beneath the trees, thou canst not leave   15
   Thy song, nor ever can those trees be bare;
     Bold Lover, never, never canst thou kiss,
Though winning near the goal — yet, do not grieve;
     She cannot fade, though thou hast not thy bliss,
   For ever wilt thou love, and she be fair!   20

Ah, happy, happy boughs! that cannot shed
   Your leaves, nor ever bid the Spring adieu;
And, happy melodist, unwearièd,
   For ever piping songs for ever new;
More happy love! more happy, happy love!   25
   For ever warm and still to be enjoyed,
     For ever panting, and for ever young;
All breathing human passion far above,
   That leaves a heart high-sorrowful and cloyed,
     A burning forehead, and a parching tongue.   30

Who are these coming to the sacrifice?
   To what green altar, O mysterious priest,
Lead'st thou that heifer lowing at the skies,
   And all her silken flanks with garlands drest?
What little town by river or sea shore,   35
   Or mountain-built with peaceful citadel,
     Is emptied of this folk, this pious morn?
   And, little town, thy streets for evermore

---

7. **Tempe . . . Arcady:** Rural places in Greece.

Will silent be; and not a soul to tell
　　Why thou art desolate, can e'er return.

O Attic° shape! Fair attitude! with brede°
　Of marble men and maidens overwrough
With forest branches and the trodden weed;
　　Thou, silent form, dost tease us out of tho
As doth Eternity: Cold Pastoral!
　When old age shall this generation waste
　　Thou shalt remain, in midst of other w
　Than ours, a friend to man, to whom thou say'st,
Beauty is truth, truth beauty, — that is all
　　Ye know on earth, and all ye need to know.　　　50

"Ode to the West Wind" has none of the philosophic calm of Keats's ode. Shelley's poem is a tumultuous reflection of the personal difficulties that had almost overwhelmed him. The autumn wind is an appropriate image for his emotions, driving before it the falling leaves that mark the approach of winter. Although it is a turbulent poem with many currents of feeling, it is written with great care and subtlety. Shelley allows himself more freedom with the meter than is usual in a formal poem, but each line has five stressed beats.

The complexity lies in the rhyme scheme. The poem is written in **terza rima**. The form is a tercet in iambic pentameter, with a sequence of rhymes that crosses from one stanza to the next, binding them together. The rhyme scheme is *aba, bcb, cdc,* continuing with the same pattern. The middle line becomes the rhyme for the outer lines of the next tercet.

Terza rima is especially effective for narrative poems and for poems, like this one, with a restless, unsettled mood. To strengthen the poem's overall structure, Shelley constructs the tercets in groups of four with an added couplet that rhymes with the middle line of the fourth tercet. This is the rhyme scheme for each stanza: *aba, bcb, cdc, ded, ee.*

PERCY BYSSHE SHELLEY

Ode to the West Wind　　　　　　　　　　　　　　　　1819

I

O wild West Wind, thou breath of Autumn's being,
Thou, from whose unseen presence the leaves dead
Are driven, like ghosts from an enchanter fleeing,

Yellow, and black, and pale, and hectic red,
Pestilence-stricken multitudes: O Thou,　　　　　　　　　　　5
Who chariotest to their dark wintry bed

The winged seeds, where they lie cold and low,
Each like a corpse within its grave, until
Thine azure sister of the Spring shall blow

ion° o'er the dreaming earth, and fill   *trumpet call* 10
  ing sweet buds like flocks to feed in air)
   th living hues and odours plain and hill:

Wild Spirit, which art moving everywhere;
Destroyer and Preserver; hear, O hear!

II

Thou on whose stream, 'mid the steep sky's commotion,   15
Loose clouds like Earth's decaying leaves are shed,
Shook from the tangled boughs of Heaven and Ocean,

Angels of rain and lightning: there are spread
On the blue surface of thine aery surge,
Like the bright hair uplifted from the head   20

Of some fierce Mænad,° even from the dim verge
Of the horizon to the zenith's height,
The locks of the approaching storm. Thou Dirge

Of the dying year, to which this closing night
Will be the dome of a vast sepulchre,   25
Vaulted with all thy congregated might

Of vapours, from whose solid atmosphere
Black rain and fire and hail will burst: O hear!

III

Thou who didst waken from his summer dreams
The blue Mediterranean, where he lay,   30
Lulled by the coil of his chrystalline streams,

Beside a pumice isle in Baiæ's bay,°
And saw in sleep old palaces and towers
Quivering within the wave's intenser day,

All overgrown with azure moss and flowers   35
So sweet, the sense faints picturing them! Thou
For whose path the Atlantic's level powers

Cleave themselves into chasms, while far below
The sea-blooms and the oozy woods which wear
The sapless foliage of the ocean, know   40

Thy voice, and suddenly grow grey with fear,
And tremble and despoil themselves: O hear!

IV

If I were a dead leaf thou mightest bear;
If I were a swift cloud to fly with thee;
A wave to pant beneath thy power, and share   45

---

21. Mænad: Female worshiper of Bacchus, the Greek god of wine and revelry.   **32. Baiæ's bay:** A bay near Naples, Italy.

The impulse of thy strength, only less free
Than thou, O Uncontrollable! If even
I were as in my boyhood, and could be

The comrade of thy wanderings over Heaven,   50
As then, when to outstrip thy skiey speed
Scarce seemed a vision; I would ne'er have striven

As thus with thee in prayer in my sore need.
Oh! lift me as a wave, a leaf, a cloud!
I fall upon the thorns of life! I bleed!

A heavy weight of hours has chained and bowed   55
One too like thee: tameless, and swift, and proud.

V

Make me thy lyre, even as the forest is:
What if my leaves are falling like its own!
The tumult of thy mighty harmonies

Will take from both a deep, autumnal tone,   60
Sweet though in sadness. Be thou, Spirit fierce,
My spirit! Be thou me, impetuous one!

Drive my dead thoughts over the universe
Like withered leaves to quicken a new birth!
And, by the incantation of this verse,   65

Scatter, as from an unextinguished hearth
Ashes and sparks, my words among mankind!
Be through my lips to unawakened Earth

The trumpet of a prophecy! O Wind,
If Winter comes, can Spring be far behind?   70

Christopher Smart, an English poet who lived at the end of the eighteenth century, wrote a poem praising his cat Jeoffry, who was his companion during the years that Smart spent in mental hospitals. It is a more casual ode, with some of the feeling of a jazz improvisation, and it was an important source of inspiration for the American "Beat" poets of the 1950s.

CHRISTOPHER SMART

From *Jubilate Agno*°   1759–63

For I will consider my Cat Jeoffry.
For he is the servant of the Living God duly and daily serving him.
For at the first glance of the glory of God in the East° he worships in his
    way.

Jubilate Agno: Latin for "Rejoice in the Lord."   **3. the glory . . . East:** I.e., the rising sun.

For is this done by wreathing his body seven times round with elegant
    quickness.
For then he leaps up to catch the musk, which is the blessing of God
    upon his prayer.   5
For he rolls upon prank to work it in.
For having done duty and received blessing he begins to consider him-
    self.
For this he performs in ten degrees.
For first he looks upon his fore-paws to see if they are clean.
For secondly he kicks up behind to clear away there.   10
For thirdly he works it upon stretch with the fore-paws extended.
For fourthly he sharpens his paws by wood.
For fifthly he washes himself.
For sixthly he rolls upon wash.
For seventhly he fleas himself, that he may not be interrupted upon the
    beat.   15
For eighthly he rubs himself against a post.
For ninthly he looks up for his instructions.
For tenthly he goes in quest of food.
For having consider'd God and himself he will consider his neighbor.
For if he meets another cat he will kiss her in kindness.   20
For when he takes his prey he plays with it to give it a chance.
For one mouse in seven escapes by his dallying.
For when his day's work is done his business more properly begins.
For he keeps the Lord's watch in the night against the adversary.
For he counteracts the powers of darkness by his electrical skin & glar-
    ing eyes.   25
For he counteracts the Devil, who is death, by brisking about the life.
For in his morning orisons he loves the sun and the sun loves him.
For he is of the tribe of Tiger.
For the Cherub Cat is a term of the Angel Tiger.°
For he has the subtlety and hissing of a serpent, which in goodness he
    suppresses.   30
For he will not do destruction if he is well-fed, neither will he spit
    without provocation.
For he purrs in thankfulness, when God tells him he's a good Cat.
For he is an instrument for the children to learn benevolence upon.
For every house is incomplete without him & a blessing is lacking in
    the spirit.
For the Lord commanded Moses concerning the cats at the departure of
    the Children of Israel from Egypt.   35
For every family had one cat at least in the bag.
For the English Cats are the best in Europe.

---

29. Cherub Cat . . . Angel Tiger: As a cherub is a small angel, so is a cat a small tiger.

For he is the cleanest in the use of his fore-paws of any quadrupede.
For the dexterity of his defence is an instance of the love of God to him
    exceedingly.
For he is the quickest to his mark of any creature.   40
For he is tenacious of his point.
For he is a mixture of gravity and waggery.
For he knows that God is his Saviour.
For there is nothing sweeter than his peace when at rest.
For there is nothing brisker than his life when in motion.   45
For he is of the Lord's poor and so indeed is he called by benevolence
    perpetually — Poor Jeoffry! poor Jeoffry! the rat has bit thy throat.
For I bless the name of the Lord Jesus that Jeoffry is better.
For the divine spirit comes about his body to sustain it in complete cat.
For his tongue is exceeding pure so that it has in purity what it wants
    in music.
For he is docile and can learn certain things.   50
For he can set up with gravity, which is patience upon approbation.
For he can fetch and carry, which is patience in employment.
For he can jump over a stick, which is patience upon proof positive.
For he can spraggle upon waggle° at the word of command.
For he can jump from an eminence into his master's bosom.   55
For he can catch the cork and toss it again.
For he is hated by the hypocrite and miser.
For the former is afraid of detection.
For the latter refuses the charge.
For he camels his back to bear the first notion of business.   60
For he is good to think on, if a man would express himself neatly.
For he made a great figure in Egypt for his signal services.
For he killed the Icneumon-rat° very pernicious by land.
For his ears are so acute that they sting again.
For from this proceeds the passing quickness of his attention.   65
For by stroking of him I have found out electricity.
For I perceived God's light about him both wax and fire.
For the Electrical fire is the spiritual substance, which God sends from
    heaven to sustain the bodies both of man and beast.
For God has blessed him in the variety of his movements.
For, though he cannot fly, he is an excellent clamberer.   70
For his motions upon the face of the earth are more than any other
    quadrupede.
For he can tread to all the measures upon the music.
For he can swim for life.
For he can creep. . . .

---

54. spraggle upon waggle: Sprawl at the wave of a hand.   **63. Icneumon-rat:** Rodent sacred to ancient Egyptians.

The Elegy

An **elegy**, like an ode, is a serious poem. In its usual form it is a long lyric poem written to lament someone's death and memorialize their life. The most widely read elegy in traditional English poetry is Thomas Gray's "Elegy Written in a Country Churchyard," published in 1751.

THOMAS GRAY

Elegy Written in a Country Churchyard   *1751*

The curfew tolls the knell of parting day,
   The lowing herd wind slowly o'er the lea,
The plowman homeward plods his weary way,
   And leaves the world to darkness and to me.

Now fades the glimmering landscape on the sight,   5
   And all the air a solemn stillness holds,
Save where the beetle wheels his droning flight,
   And drowsy tinklings lull the distant folds;

Save that from yonder ivy-mantled tower
   The moping owl does to the moon complain   10
Of such, as wand'ring near her secret bower,
   Molest her ancient solitary reign.

Beneath those rugged elms, that yew tree's shade,
   Where heaves the turf in many a mold'ring heap,
Each in his narrow cell forever laid,   15
   The rude forefathers of the hamlet sleep.

The breezy call of incense-breathing morn,
   The swallow twitt'ring from the straw-built shed,
The cock's shrill clarion, or the echoing horn,°   *hunting horn*
   No more shall rouse them from their lowly bed.   20

For them no more the blazing hearth shall burn,
   Or busy housewife ply her evening care;
No children run to lisp their sire's return,
   Or climb his knees the envied kiss to share.

Oft did the harvest to their sickle yield,   25
   Their furrow oft the stubborn glebe° has broke;   *turf*
How jocund did they drive their team afield!
   How bowed the woods beneath their sturdy stroke!

Let not Ambition mock their useful toil,
   Their homely joys, and destiny obscure;   30
Nor Grandeur hear with a disdainful smile
   The short and simple annals of the poor.

The boast of heraldry, the pomp of pow'r,
   And all that beauty, all that wealth e'er gave,

Awaits alike th' inevitable hour.   35
    The paths of glory lead but to the grave.

Nor you, ye proud, impute to these the fault,
    If Mem'ry o'er their tomb no trophies raise,
Where through the long-drawn aisle and fretted vault
    The pealing anthem swells the note of praise.   40

Can storied urn or animated bust
    Back to its mansion call the fleeting breath?
Can Honor's voice provoke the silent dust,
    Or Flatt'ry soothe the dull cold ear of Death?

Perhaps in this neglected spot is laid   45
    Some heart once pregnant with celestial fire;
Hands that the rod of empire might have swayed,
    Or waked to ecstasy the living lyre.

But knowledge to their eyes her ample page
    Rich with the spoils of time did ne'er unroll;   50
Chill Penury repressed their noble rage,
    And froze the genial current of the soul.

Full many a gem of purest ray serene,
    The dark unfathomed caves of ocean bear:
Full many a flower is born to blush unseen,   55
    And waste its sweetness on the desert air.

Some village Hampden,° that with dauntless breast
    The little tyrant of his field withstood;
Some mute inglorious Milton° here may rest,
    Some Cromwell,° guiltless of his country's blood.   60

Th' applause of list'ning senates to command,
    The threats of pain and ruin to despise,
To scatter plenty o'er a smiling land,
    And read their hist'ry in a nation's eyes,

Their lot forbade; nor circumscribed alone   65
    Their growing virtues, but their crimes confined;
Forbade to wade through slaughter to a throne,
    And shut the gates of mercy on mankind,

The struggling pangs of conscious truth to hide,
    To quench the blushes of ingenuous shame,   70
Or heap the shrine of Luxury and Pride
    With incense kindled at the Muse's flame.°

---

57. Hampden: John Hampden (1594–1643) was a member of Parliament who resisted the illegal taxes on his lands that were imposed by Charles I.   **59. Milton:** John Milton (1608–1674), the English poet.   **60. Cromwell:** Oliver Cromwell (1599–1658) served as Lord Protector of England from 1653 until his death.   **71–72. heap the shrine . . . Muse's flame:** Gray is criticizing poets who write to please wealthy patrons.

Far from the madding crowd's ignoble strife,
    Their sober wishes never learned to stray;
Along the cool sequestered vale of life   75
    They kept the noiseless tenor° of their way.   *continual movement*

Yet ev'n these bones from insult to protect
    Some frail memorial still erected nigh,
With uncouth rhymes and shapeless sculpture decked,
    Implores the passing tribute of a sigh.   80

Their name, their years, spelt by th' unlettered Muse,
    The place of fame and elegy supply:
And many a holy text around she strews,
    That teach the rustic moralist to die.

For who to dumb Forgetfulness a prey,   85
    This pleasing anxious being e'er resigned,
Left the warm precincts of the cheerful day,
    Nor cast one longing ling'ring look behind?

On some fond breast the parting soul relies,
    Some pious drops the closing eye requires;   90
Ev'n from the tomb the voice of Nature cries,
    Ev'n in our ashes live their wonted fires.

For thee, who mindful of th' unhonored dead
    Dost in these lines their artless tale relate;
If chance, by lonely contemplation led,   95
    Some kindred spirit shall inquire thy fate,

Haply° some hoary-headed swain° may say,   *perchance; shepherd*
    "Oft have we seen him at the peep of dawn
Brushing with hasty steps the dews away
    To meet the sun upon the upland lawn.   100

"There at the foot of yonder nodding beech
    That wreathes its old fantastic roots so high,
His listless length at noontide would he stretch,
    And pore upon the brook that babbles by.

"Hard by yon wood, now smiling as in scorn,   105
    Mutt'ring his wayward fancies he would rove,
Now drooping, woeful wan, like one forlorn,
    Or crazed with care, or crossed in hopeless love.

"One morn I missed him, on the customed hill,
    Along the heath and near his fav'rite tree;   110
Another came; nor yet beside the rill,
    Nor up the lawn, nor at the wood was he;

"The next with dirges due in sad array
    Slow through the churchway path we saw him borne.
Approach and read (for thou canst read) the lay,°   *song or poem* 115
    Graved on the stone beneath yon aged thorn."

THE EPITAPH

Here rests his head upon the lap of Earth
    A youth to Fortune and to Fame unknown.
Fair Science frowned not on his humble birth,
    And Melancholy marked him for her own.   120

Large was his bounty, and his soul sincere,
    Heav'n did a recompense as largely send:
He gave to Mis'ry all he had, a tear,
    He gained from Heav'n ('twas all he wished) a friend.

No farther seek his merits to disclose,
    Or draw his frailties from their dread abode,   125
(There they alike in trembling hope repose),
    The bosom of His Father and his God.

The poem can seem placid and uneventful to modern readers, but at the time it was written it made a strong and disturbing political statement. The poem was unlike other elegies that had been written before it because the individual for whom the elegy was written was an ordinary person. He was simply someone who had been buried in this village's churchyard. As Gray wrote in the epitaph that ends the poem,

Here rests his head upon the lap of Earth
    A youth to Fortune and to Fame unknown.

The person buried in the churchyard is never named. What Gray is insisting is that under other circumstances this ordinary person could have been the equal of any other person in their society. In the years leading up to the revolutions in the American colonies and in France — revolutions that overthrew the rigid class lines of the old social order — these were fiery sentiments. Another stanza from the poem, the twelfth, burned itself into the consciousness of its time, with its bold idea that in the grave might lie someone who could have ruled a nation or could have written immortal poetry. The phrases were echoed again and again by poets, politicians, and writers everywhere:

Perhaps in this neglected spot is laid
    Some heart once pregnant with celestial fire;
Hands that the rod of empire might have swayed,
    Or waked to ecstasy the living lyre.

The final line of the ninth stanza of his poem has been quoted in more speeches, books, and plays than Gray could ever have imagined: "The paths of glory lead but to the grave."

Although the form and the technical means have changed, the elegy continues as part of our poetic heritage. In this elegy on the death of Martin Luther King, Jr., the African American poet Michael Harper mingles his grief with a tone of triumph. King's death, Harper tells us, has not been in vain.

MICHAEL S. HARPER

Martin's Blues   1971

He came apart in the open,
the slow motion cameras
falling quickly
neither alive nor kicking;
stone blind dead   5
on the balcony
that old melody
etched his black lips
in a pruned echo:
We shall overcome   10
some day —

Yes we did!
Yes we did!

In her elegy for the English rock musician John Lennon, Amy Clampitt
uses the name of the apartment building where Lennon lived and was murdered as the title of her poem, and in several of the lines she alludes to phrases
from "Eleanor Rigby," one of the songs he wrote as a member of the Beatles.

AMY CLAMPITT

The Dakota   1983

Grief for a generation — all
the lonely people
gone, the riffraff
out there now mainly pigeons —
steps from its limousine   5
and lights a taper
inside the brownstone catacomb
of the Dakota. Pick up
the wedding rice, take out
the face left over from   10
the funeral nobody came to,
bring flowers, leave them woven
with the lugubrious ironwork
of the Dakota. Grief
is original, but it   15
repeats itself: there's nothing
more original it can do.

The Sonnet

Although a sonnet is short — generally fourteen lines — and is written in a regular rhyme sequence, it is one of the richest and most durable forms of lyric poetry. The difference between a sonnet and other lyric poetry is in the way the poet works with its theme. At the heart of most traditional sonnets is an implied argument that muses on the philosophic implications of the sonnet's main idea. The form has been so useful to poets for so many centuries that authors today continue to write sonnets, even if they don't feel they have to restrict themselves to traditional rhyme schemes and meter. What they want to tell the reader, when they use the term *sonnet* or write in a variant of the sonnet form, is that the poem will have a seriousness that may not be characteristic of their other short lyrics.

The sonnet was perfected in Italy in the early fourteenth century. The name comes from the Italian word *sonnetto*, which means "little song." Several poets helped develop the form, but the one whose work was most influential with English poets was Francesco Petrarca, an Italian nobleman known in English as Petrarch, who lived from 1304 to 1374. His sonnets were personal poems, written to express his unhappiness over his love for a woman who did not return his affection. In structure, the individual sonnets presented a kind of short philosophical discussion, with a presentation of the theme of the poem in the opening lines, a consideration of the theme in the next lines, then a conclusion summed up in a final couplet.

The sonnet was brought to England by a courtier and diplomat named Sir Thomas Wyatt, who was sent by Henry VIII on diplomatic missions to France and Italy. Wyatt encountered the writing of Petrarch on his travels, and before his death in 1542 he translated more than a hundred Italian sonnets. The translations were circulated in manuscript through court circles, and a younger poet, also a courtier and nobleman named Henry Howard, Earl of Surrey, who often caroused through the streets of London with Wyatt's son, translated many of the same sonnets. It was Surrey who established the rhyme scheme used by William Shakespeare.

A great playwright, Shakespeare was also an accomplished sonneteer, and one of his enduring works is a collection of 154 sonnets published in 1609. This famous example, untitled but numbered 73, takes as its theme the poet's old age. In the development of its theme and the rich use of imagery and rhyme, the poem shows all the characteristics of the classic sonnet form.

WILLIAM SHAKESPEARE

That time of year thou mayst in me behold   1609

That time of year thou mayst in me behold
When yellow leaves, or none, or few, do hang
Upon those boughs which shake against the cold,
Bare ruined choirs, where late the sweet birds sang.

In me thou seest the twilight of such day   5
As after sunset fadeth in the west;
Which by and by black night doth take away,
Death's second self that seals up in all the rest.
In me thou seest the glowing of such fire,
That on the ashes of his youth doth lie,   10
As the deathbed whereon it must expire,
Consumed with that which it was nourished by.
　　This thou perceiv'st, which makes thy love more strong,
　　To love that well, which thou must leave ere long.

If we look at the meter of the poem we can see that it is in iambic pentameter. The five-foot line, which is also the line of dramatic blank verse, has a feeling of weight and substance that the more common four-foot line of other short lyric poems does not. The fourteen lines consist of three quatrains with the rhyme scheme of *abab, cdcd, efef,* and a concluding couplet, *gg.* This way of structuring the rhyme is called the *English,* or Shakespearean, sonnet. The rhyme scheme for the *Italian,* or Petrarchan sonnet, is an octave of two quatrains that rhyme *abba,* followed by a sextet with a rhyme scheme that may have some variation but is usually either *cdecde* or *cdcdcd.*

Shakespeare was so skillful that he was able to work the sonnet form into the dialogue of one of his plays. In scene 5 of the first act of *Romeo and Juliet,* the lines of dialogue between the two lovers are written as a sonnet.

ROMEO: If I profane with my unworthiest hand
　　　　This holy shrine, the gentle fine is this,
　　　　My lips, two blushing pilgrims, ready stand
　　　　To smooth that rough touch with a tender kiss.
JULIET: Good pilgrim, you do wrong your hand too much,
　　　　Which mannerly devotion shows in this;
　　　　For saints have hands that pilgrims' hands do touch,
　　　　And palm to palm is holy palmers' kiss.
ROMEO: Have not saints lips, and holy palmers too?
JULIET: Aye, pilgrim, lips that they must use in prayer.
ROMEO: Oh then, dear saint, let lips do what hands do.
　　　　Then pray. Grant thou, lest faith turn to despair.
JULIET: Saints do not move, though grant for prayers' sake.
ROMEO: Then move not while my prayer's effect I take.

(Several of Shakespeare's sonnets are gathered in Chapter 17, "Poems and Poets.")

Some poets have felt that the sonnet form is too confining, finding it difficult to write freely with so many restraints. The romantic poet William Wordsworth answered them with a sonnet of his own, which compares the small form of the poem, with its fourteen lines and well-ordered rhyme, to a convent cell. He says that the "prison" where we choose to be is not a prison at all. Solace can be found, he suggests, in the sonnet's "scanty plot of ground."

WILLIAM WORDSWORTH

Nuns Fret Not   1807

Nuns fret not at their convent's narrow room;
And hermits are contented with their cells;
And students with their pensive citadels;
Maids at the wheel, the weaver at his loom,
Sit blithe and happy; bees that soar for bloom,   5
High at the highest Peak of Furness-fells,
With murmur by the hour in foxglove bells:
In truth the prison, unto which we doom
Ourselves, no prison is: and hence for me,
In sundry moods, 'twas pastime to be bound   10
Within the Sonnet's scanty plot of ground;
Pleased if some Souls (for such there needs must be)
Who have felt the weight of too much liberty,
Should find brief solace there, as I have found.

Sonnets for Further Reading

Because of the variety of subjects and themes in the sonnet, the best way
to experience these poems is to read as many of them as you can. Try to follow
their rhyme schemes and the way each sonnet develops its theme. This gathering of sonnets will introduce you to some of the important writers from Petrarca's time to our own. Contemporary poets use the form more freely, but
the same concentration of ideas and imagery is still what makes the sonnet
unique.

FRANCESCO PETRARCA

Love's Inconsistency   1557

TRANSLATED BY SIR THOMAS WYATT

I find no peace, and all my war is done;
    I fear and hope, I burn and freeze likewise;
    I fly above the wind, yet cannot rise;
    And nought I have, yet all the world I seize on;
That looseth, nor locketh, holdeth me in prison,   5
    And holds me not, yet can I 'scape no wise;
    Nor lets me live, nor die, at my devise,
    And yet of death it giveth none occasion.
Without eyes I see, and without tongue I plain;
    I wish to perish, yet I ask for health;   10

I love another, and yet I hate myself;
I feed in sorrow, and laugh in all my pain;
   Lo, thus displeaseth me both death and life,
   And my delight is causer of my grief.

JOHN DONNE

Death, be not proud   1633

Death, be not proud, though some have callèd thee
Mighty and dreadful, for thou art not so;
·For those whom thou think'st thou dost overthrow
Die not, poor Death, nor yet canst thou kill me.
From rest and sleep, which but thy pictures be,   5
Much pleasure; then from thee much more must flow,
And soonest our best men with thee do go,
Rest of their bones, and soul's delivery.
Thou art slave to fate, chance, kings, and desperate men,
And dost with poison, war, and sickness dwell,   10
And poppy° or charms can make us sleep as well   *opium*
And better than thy stroke; why swell'st thou then?
One short sleep past, we wake eternally
And death shall be no more; Death, thou shalt die.

LADY MARY WROTH

In this strange labyrinth how shall I turn?   1621

In this strange labyrinth how shall I turn?
   Ways are on all sides, while the way I miss:
   If to the right hand, there in love I burn;
   Let me go forward, therein danger is;
If to the left, suspicion hinders bliss,   5
   Let me turn back, Shame cries I ought return,
   Nor faint though crosses with my fortunes kiss;
   Stand still is harder, although sure to mourn.
Then let me take the right- or left-hand way;
   Go forward, or stand still, or back retire;   10
   I must these doubts endure without allay
   Or help, but travail find for my best hire.
Yet that which most my troubled sense doth move
Is to leave all, and take the thread of love.

JOHN MILTON

When I consider how my light is spent   1673

When I consider how my light is spent
 Ere half my days in this dark world and wide,
  And that one talent which is death to hide
  Lodged with me useless, though my soul more bent
To serve therewith my Maker, and present   5
 My true account, lest he returning chide,
  "Doth God exact day-labor, light denied?"
  I fondly ask. But Patience, to prevent
That murmur, soon replies, "God doth not need
 Either man's work or his own gifts. Who best   10
  Bear his mild yoke, they serve him best. His state
Is kingly: thousands at his bidding speed,
 And post o'er land and ocean without rest;
  They also serve who only stand and wait."

JOHN KEATS

When I have fears that I may cease to be   1818

When I have fears that I may cease to be
 Before my pen has gleaned my teeming brain,
Before high-piled books, in charact'ry,
 Hold like rich garners the full-ripened grain;
When I behold, upon the night's starred face,   5
 Huge cloudy symbols of a high romance,
And think that I may never live to trace
 Their shadows, with the magic hand of chance;
And when I feel, fair creature of an hour!
 That I shall never look upon thee more,   10
Never have relish in the fairy power
 Of unreflecting love! — then on the shore
Of the wide world I stand alone, and think
Till love and fame to nothingness do sink.

CHRISTINA ROSSETTI

I wish I could remember that first day   1881

I wish I could remember that first day,
 First hour, first moment of your meeting me,
  If bright or dim the season, it might be

Summer or winter for aught I can say;
So unrecorded did it slip away,   5
   So blind was I to see and to foresee,
   So dull to mark the budding of my tree
That would not blossom yet for many a May.
If only I could recollect it, such
   A day of days! I let it come and go   10
   As traceless as a thaw of bygone snow;
It seemed to mean so little, meant so much;
If only now I could recall that touch,
   First touch of hand in hand — Did one but know!

ELIZABETH BARRETT BROWNING

How Do I Love Thee?   1850

How do I love thee? Let me count the ways.
I love thee to the depth and breadth and height
My soul can reach, when feeling out of sight
For the ends of Being and ideal Grace.
I love thee to the level of every day's   5
Most quiet need, by sun and candlelight.
I love thee freely, as men strive for Right;
I love thee purely, as they turn from Praise;
I love thee with the passion put to use
In my old griefs, and with my childhood's faith.   10
I love thee with a love I seemed to lose
With my lost saints — I love thee with the breath,
Smiles, tears of all my life! — and, if God choose,
I shall but love thee better after death.

EDNA ST. VINCENT MILLAY

What lips my lips have kissed,
and where, and why   1920

What lips my lips have kissed, and where, and why,
I have forgotten, and what arms have lain
Under my head till morning; but the rain
Is full of ghosts tonight, that tap and sigh
Upon the glass and listen for reply,   5
And in my heart there stirs a quiet pain
For unremembered lads that not again
Will turn to me at midnight with a cry.
Thus in the winter stands the lonely tree,
Nor knows what birds have vanished one by one,   10

Yet knows its boughs more silent than before:
I cannot say what loves have come and gone,
I only know that summer sang in me
A little while, that in me sings no more.

COUNTEE CULLEN

Yet Do I Marvel   1925

I doubt not God is good, well-meaning, kind,
And did He stoop to quibble could tell why
The little buried mole continues blind,
Why flesh that mirrors Him must some day die,
Make plain the reason tortured Tantalus°   5
Is baited by the fickle fruit, declare
If merely brute caprice dooms Sisyphus°
To struggle up a never-ending stair.
Inscrutable His ways are, and immune
To catechism by a mind too strewn   10
With petty cares to slightly understand
What awful brain compels His awful hand.
Yet do I marvel at this curious thing:
To make a poet black, and bid him sing!

E. E. CUMMINGS

goodby Betty, don't remember me   1923

goodby Betty, don't remember me
pencil your eyes dear and have a good time
with the tall tight boys at Tabari'
s, keep your teeth snowy, stick to beer and lime,
wear dark, and where your meeting breasts are round   5
have roses darling, it's all i ask of you —
but that when light fails and this sweet profound
Paris moves with lovers, two and two
bound for themselves, when passionately dusk
brings softly down the perfume of the world   10
(and just as smaller stars begin to husk
heaven) you, you exactly paled and curled

with mystic lips take twilight where i know:
proving to Death that Love is so and so.

---

5. **Tantalus:** In Hades, the Greek underworld, Tantalus was prevented from assuaging his hunger as he reached for fruit just beyond his grasp.   7. **Sisyphus:** In Greek myth, Sisyphus was condemned to roll a huge stone uphill that always rolled back down just before he reached the top.

RITA DOVE

Wiring Home   1995

Lest the wolves loose their whistles
and shopkeepers inquire,

keep moving; though your knees flush
red as two chapped apples,

keep moving, head up,   5
past the beggar's cold cup,

past fires banked under chestnuts
and the trumpeting kiosk's

tales of odyssey and heartbreak
until, turning a corner, you stand   10

staring: ambushed
by a window of canaries

bright as a thousand
golden narcissi.

The Epigram and the Limerick

Lyric poetry, by its nature, has very loosely defined boundaries or limitations, and it also has room for many forms of humorous short poetry. One of
these is the **epigram**. Epigrams are short poems, never more than a few lines
long, often rhymed, and usually funny or wryly satirical. They are intended to
make a sharp comment or witty observation. The epigram has also been popular with humorous writers of what used to be called *light verse*, short poems
usually written for magazines that dressed down-to-earth truths in funny poetic language. The American writer of light verse Ogden Nash was particularly skilled at the art of the epigram.

OGDEN NASH

Reflection on Ice-Breaking   1931

Candy
Is Dandy,
But liquor
Is Quicker.

The **limerick** is a short, humorous poem that is defined by its verse
form. It has become one of the most widespread types of folk poetry, usually

in the scatalogical and obscene forms that everyone has read or heard at some time in their lives. The form is a fixed five-line verse, and there is only a single stanza, rhyming *aabba*. It is the characteristic meter of limericks that makes them so easy to remember. Their rhythmic pattern is two rhyming lines of three strong accents, followed by two lines of two strong accents — with a different rhyme — then a final line that returns to the three accents of the first two lines, and it rhymes with them. The meter is an anapest, but the form allows for some variation.

Whatever a reader may think of limericks, there is no other kind of poetry quite like them. They are a good example of what we mean when we talk about freedom within limits. There are many limericks that aren't scatalogical or obscene, but unfortunately they usually are not as memorable as the ones that are. This is an example of a Victorian limerick, and it uses what connoisseurs of the limerick regard as the classic opening, which is a reference to the *place* where the person in the limerick comes from.

> There was a young lady from Riga
> Who smiled as she rode on a tiger:
>   They returned from the ride
>   With the lady inside,
> And the smile on the face of the tiger.
> > — Cosmo Monkhouse

Limericks may be political:

> Ronald Reagan screamed out in dismay
> When he saw his old films: "I must say
>   It's a very hard fact —
>   I must learn to act."
> And that's what he does every day.
> > — Frank Richards

Or literary:

> Did Ophelia ask Hamlet to bed?
> Was Gertrude incestuously wed?
>   Is there anything certain?
>   By the fall of the curtain
> Almost everyone's certainly dead.
> > — A. Cinna

Or ridiculous:

> A jolly young fellow from Yuma
> Told an elephant joke to a puma;
>   Now his skeleton lies
>   Beneath hot western skies —
> The puma had no sense of huma.
> > — Ogden Nash

They can make fun of their poor reputation:

> A bather whose clothing was strewed
> By winds, that left her quite nude,
>   Saw a man coming along,
>   And, unless I am wrong,
> You expected this line to be rude.
>
> – ANONYMOUS

But whatever their subject, limericks insist on being themselves, and finally they are forgiven for their offenses.

RELATED COMMENTARIES: *Rita Dove, "An Intact World," page 1252; Erica Jong, "Devouring Time: Shakespeare's Sonnets," page 1275.*

13

THE TYPES OF POETRY: OTHER POETIC FORMS

A poem is a sum of triumphs over unpredictable resistances.
– STANLEY KUNITZ, quoted in Seldon Rodman's
Tongues of Fallen Angels

Many other forms of lyric poetry have been popular in the past, and you might encounter some of their names in your reading. **Rhyme royal** is a form that, like the sonnet, also developed from Italian models. It is a seven-line stanza in iambic pentameter with a rhyme scheme of *ababbcc*. The English medieval poet Geoffrey Chaucer used it for his long poem *Troilus and Criseyde*, and Sir Thomas Wyatt's great love poem, "They Flee from Me" (p. 887), is written in rhyme royal. Another form that Wyatt first used in English was an eight-line stanza called **ottava rima**. It has a rhyme scheme of *abababcc*.

Although **terza rima**, another of the forms taken from Italian models, has been used only occasionally by poets writing in English since the fifteenth century, it is the form for Shelley's "Ode to the West Wind," which we discussed earlier in the previous chapter. The most complex stanza form in English that continued to be used by later writers was created by Edmund Spenser at the end of the sixteenth century for his epic poem *The Faerie Queen*. The **Spenserian stanza** uses eight lines of iambic pentameter and a last line of six stressed feet, which is called an **alexandrine**. The rhyme scheme is *ababbcbcc*. Here is a stanza from Spenser's epic.

> A Gentle Knight was pricking° on the plaine,   *cantering*
> Y cladd in mightie arms and silver shielde,
> Wherein old dints of deepe wounds did remaine,
> The cruell markes of many a bloudy fielde;
> Yet armes till that time did he never wield.
> His angry steede did chide his foaming bitt,

As much disdayning to the curbe to yield:
Full jolly° knight he seemd, and faire did sitt,   *gallant*
As one for knightly giusts° and fierce encounters fitt.   *jousts*

Despite its daunting complexity, Keats used the Spenserian stanza for his ballad "Eve of St. Agnes," and Shelley wrote "Adonais," his elegy on the death of Keats, in the same form.

There are several shorter forms of lyric poetry that have been used by modern poets looking for a form of verse that would have some of the usefulness of the sonnet but would have more of a songlike quality. All of these types of lyric are characterized by complicated rhyme schemes and concise patterns of meter. The rules for writing each of them seem to contradict the idea of spontaneity, which is also considered one of the essentials of lyric poetry, but poets respond to challenges from other poets. Nearly everyone who writes in traditional closed forms tries one of these rich hybrids at one time or another. Here are two of the best-known forms, the *sestina* and the *villanelle*.

The **sestina** is composed of six stanzas, each six lines long, with a concluding verse of three lines called the **envoy**. The form, which is called the "song of sixes," is from France, where it is said to have been introduced into Provençal love poetry in the thirteenth century. It is a complicated word game where the last words of the first six lines are repeated as end words of the lines of the other five stanzas, changing places in a carefully ordered procession. The final three lines must include the words, but in any order. One of the best-known modern examples of a sestina is this poem by Elizabeth Bishop.

ELIZABETH BISHOP

Sestina   1965

September rain falls on the house.
In the failing light, the old grandmother
sits in the kitchen with the child
beside the Little Marvel Stove,
reading the jokes from the almanac,   5
laughing and talking to hide her tears.

She thinks that her equinoctial tears
and the rain that beats on the roof of the house
were both foretold by the almanac,
but only known to a grandmother.   10
The iron kettle sings on the stove.
She cuts some bread and says to the child,

It's time for tea now; but the child
is watching the teakettle's small hard tears
dance like mad on the hot black stove,   15
the way the rain must dance on the house.
Tidying up, the old grandmother
hangs up the clever almanac

on its string. Birdlike, the almanac
hovers half open above the child,   20
hovers above the old grandmother
and her teacup full of dark brown tears.
She shivers and says she thinks the house
feels chilly, and puts more wood in the stove.

It was to be, says the Marvel Stove.   25
I know what I know, says the almanac.
With crayons the child draws a rigid house
and a winding pathway. Then the child
puts in a man with buttons like tears
and shows it proudly to the grandmother.   30

But secretly, while the grandmother
busies herself about the stove,
the little moons fall down like tears
from between the pages of the almanac
into the flower bed the child   35
has carefully placed in the front of the house.

Time to plant tears, says the almanac.
The grandmother sings to the marvellous stove
and the child draws another inscrutable house.

The **villanelle** is composed of five tercets and a final quatrain, written in iambic pentameter. The rhyme scheme for the tercets is *aba*, and the quatrain repeats the final rhyme, *abaa*. Like the sestina, the poem is an elaborate game in which entire lines appear again and again. The first line of the poem is used as the final line of the second and fourth tercets, and it also becomes the next to last line of the quatrain. The last line of the first tercet becomes the last line (with slight variations in this example) for the last line of the third and fifth tercets and finally ends the poem. This is an example by the modern American poet Theodore Roethke.

THEODORE ROETHKE

The Waking   *1953*

I wake to sleep, and take my waking slow.
I feel my fate in what I cannot fear.
I learn by going where I have to go.

We think by feeling. What is there to know?   5
I hear my being dance from ear to ear.
I wake to sleep and take my waking slow.

Of those so close beside me, which are you?
God bless the Ground! I shall walk softly there,
And learn by where I have to go.

Light takes the Tree, but who can tell us how?   10
The lowly worm climbs up a winding stair;
I wake to sleep, and take my waking slow.

Great Nature has another thing to do
To you and me; so take the lively air,
And, lovely, learn by going where to go.   15

This shaking keeps me steady, I should know.
What falls away is always. This is near.
I wake to sleep, and take my waking slow.
I learn by going where I have to go.

Dylan Thomas used the villanelle form for his sorrowful poem on the death of his father, "Do Not Go Gentle into That Good Night" (p. 1202).

Open Form

Like the nineteenth-century photographer Louis Daguerre, who was supposed to have cried out, when he managed to capture an image on a silver-coated plate, "From this moment, painting is dead!," many people were certain that when poetry lost its centuries-old anchors of rhyme and meter there would be no more poetry. As we know, poetry is still with us, even though we do not usually look for rhyme schemes or count the meter when we read a poem today. In the first years of the "free verse" movement, as **open form** was called then, there was some feeling that poetry could be as "free" as the wind and that a poem could take any form the writer chose. The writers found, however, that although the way they wrote had changed, the means they worked with to create a poem were still the same. Poetry written in open form had to have the concentration and the technical virtuosity of poetry written in traditional closed forms.

This poem by the American poet Galway Kinnell has the tone of ordinary conversation, but, although the poem is not rhymed, he has used many of the traditional technical means to create it.

GALWAY KINNELL

The Man Splitting Wood in the Daybreak   1985

The man splitting wood in the daybreak
looks strong, as though, if one weakened,
one could turn to him and he would help.
Gus Newland was strong. When he split wood
he struck hard, flashing the bright steel   5
through air of daybreak so fast rock maple
leapt apart — as they think marriages will
in countries about to institute divorce —
and even willow, which, though stacked

to dry a full year, on separating — 10
actually weeps — totem wood, therefore,
to the married-until-death — miseried asunder
with many small lip-smacking gasp-noises.
But Gus is dead. We could turn to our fathers,
but they protect us only through the unperplexed — 15
looking-back of the numerals cut into their headstones.
Or to our mothers, whose love, so devastated,
can't, even in spring, break through the hard earth.
Our spouses weaken at the same rate we do.
We have to hold our children up to lean on them. — 20
What about the man splitting wood in the daybreak,
who looked strong? That was years ago. That was me.

Kinnell develops an extended metaphor of splitting wood as a symbol of young strength; he uses a shift of syntax in lines like "Or to our mothers, whose love, so devastated, / can't, even in spring, break through the hard earth"; he employs the conscious awkwardness of the constructed word *miseried* set beside the more elegant-sounding *asunder.* The meter is irregular, but if you scan the opening line, "The man splitting wood in the daybreak," you are already conscious of a strong metric pulse, which Kinnell interrupts with the phrase "Gus Newland was strong" for dramatic effect at the beginning of the fourth line. You can find alliteration in the phrase "air of daybreak." Kinnell even uses an adjective that causes a problem of interpretation, "totem wood," suggesting perhaps that the wood is an emblem or symbol for a marriage that lasts "until-death."

The Prose Poem

As readers have become more used to open form, poets have continued to explore its possibilities. A form that was first developed in France but which has now spread to every other language is the **prose poem**. The term contradicts itself by telling us that this is both prose and poetry, two forms of writing we have always been told are separate, but the term also is a good description of what writers do with the form. A prose poem is a lyric poem that has all the characteristics of a lyric but is written in prose. It presents one image or, like a lyric poem in open form, a response to a single emotion.

A prose poem can have some kind of narrative, but the story line is one of the means the poet uses to illustrate the theme of the poem. Some prose poems have the effect of a **parable**, a short narrative used to point out a moral. Others have the effect of opening the mind to the possibilities of the unconscious. Even if they present us with a single, condensed image, they often leave us with the sense that what we have just read has made us conscious of something *else.* We call poetry like this **associative**. Here are three contemporary prose poems by American writers that show some of the range of the form.

R O B E R T   B L Y

The Dead Seal near McClure's Beach   1992

1

Walking north toward the point, I come on a dead seal. From a few
feet away, he looks like a brown log. The body is on its back, dead only a
few hours. I stand and look at him. A quiver in the dead flesh. My God he
is still alive. A shock goes through me, as if a wall of my room had fallen
away.   5

His head is arched back, the small eyes closed, the whiskers sometimes
rise and fall. He is dying. This is the oil. Here on its back is the oil that heats
our houses so efficiently. Wind blows fine sand back toward the ocean. The
flipper near me lies folded over the stomach, looking like an unfinished arm,
lightly glazed with sand at the edges. The other flipper lies half underneath.   10
The seal's skin looks like an old overcoat, scratched here and there . . . by
sharp mussels maybe . . .

I reach out and touch him. Suddenly he rears up, turns over. He gives
three cries, like those from Christmas toys. He lunges toward me. I am terrified and leap back, although I know there can be no teeth in that jaw. He   15
starts flopping toward the sea. But he falls over, on his face. He does not want
to go back to the sea. He looks up at the sky, and he looks like an old lady
who has lost her hair.

He puts his chin back down on the sand, arranges his flippers, and
waits for me to go. I go.   20

2

Today I go back to say goodbye; he's dead now. But he's not — he's a
quarter mile farther up the shore. Today he is thinner, squatting on his stomach, head out. The ribs show more — each vertebra on the back under the coat
now visible, shiny. He breathes in and out.

He raises himself up, and tucks his flippers under, as if to keep   25
them warm. A wave comes in, touches his nose. He turns and looks at
me — the eyes slanted, the crown of his head like a leather jacket. He is
taking a long time to die. The whiskers white as porcupine quills, the forehead slopes, goodbye brother, die in the sound of waves, forgive us if we
have killed you, long live your race, your innertube race, so uncom-   30
fortable on land, so comfortable in the sea. Be comfortable in death then,
where the sand will be out of your nostrils, and you can swim in long loops
through the pure death, ducking under as assassinations break above you.
You don't want to be touched by me. I climb the cliff and go home the other
way.   35

ROBERT HASS

A Story about the Body   1989

The young composer, working that summer at an artist's colony, had watched her for a week. She was Japanese, a painter, almost sixty, and he thought he was in love with her. He loved her work, and her work was like the way she moved her body, used her hands, looked at him directly when she made amused and considered answers to his questions. One night, walking   5 back from a concert, they came to her door and she turned to him and said, "I think you would like to have me. I would like that too, but I must tell you that I have had a double mastectomy," and when he didn't understand, "I've lost both my breasts." The radiance that he had carried around in his belly and chest cavity — like music — withered very quickly, and he made himself look   10 at her when he said, "I'm sorry. I don't think I could." He walked back to his own cabin through the pines, and in the morning he found a small blue bowl on the porch outside his door. It looked to be full of rose petals, but he found when he picked it up that the rose petals were on top; the rest of the bowl — she must have swept them from the corners of her studio — was full of dead   15 bees.

LOUIS JENKINS

How to Tell a Wolf from a Dog   1995

A wolf carries his head down, tail down. He has a look of preoccupation, or worry, you might think. He has a family to support. He probably has a couple of broken ribs from trying to bring down a moose. He's not getting workman's comp, either, and no praise for his efforts. The wolf looks unemployed, flat broke.   5

On the other hand, a dog of similar features, a husky or a malamute, has his head up, ears up, looks attentive, self-confident, cheerful and obedient. He is fully employed with an eye toward promotion. He carries his tail high, like a banner. He's part of a big organization and has the title of "man's best friend."   10

Haiku

An easy definition of haiku might be,

A Haiku
Seventeen syllable
   Japanese po-em
popular with students.

Most dictionaries insist on two syllables for the word *poem;* so our definition can claim to have the required seventeen syllables. The haiku is so well known in Japan that most of the members of an educated Japanese family would be skilled enough in writing haiku to present verses to one another. Among experienced poets the poems were usually written in a linked sequence, each poet writing a new haiku in response to the haiku that had just been written, or that they had just read.

Most haiku are written in three lines, with five syllables in the two outer lines and seven in the middle line. As with so many other things between the two languages, Japanese and English, the similarity between our syllable and the Japanese ideogram — the system of writing using pictures to represent a thing or idea — is not as close as our precise definition suggests. An ideogram can have the connotations of one or more of our words and even an entire phrase. A direct translation from a Japanese haiku sometimes means that when you read the poem in English, you are getting considerably less from it than a Japanese reader would.

Since an ideogram may be written in different ways, the poet can also allude to other haiku or to another poet by the way the ideogram is set down on the paper. Specific places or certain seasons of the year are identified with the best-known writers. With all of these possibilities, a haiku that can seem like a small, simple poem to an English reader can present a Japanese reader with a world of allusion and response. This allusion and response are the essence of a haiku. The small glimpse of a real instant should recall in the reader some moment of life, some half-forgotten memory.

There have been thousands of writers of haiku since the form was first created, but four poets are considered to be the most important. The first is Bashō, who was born in 1644 into a samurai family. Before his death in 1694, he had turned to a simple life and spent much of his time making long journeys over the Japanese countryside, traveling by foot or on horseback. The spare simplicity of his poems reflects his Zen Buddhist beliefs. Many of his haiku were written on his travels. This is a typical Bashō poem:

> A crow is perched
> Upon a leafless withered bough —
> The evening dusk.

Here are three of Bashō's linked haiku, freely interpreted by Robert Hass:

> Ripening barley —
> does it get that color
> from the skylark's tears?

> Day by day
> the barley ripens,
> the skylarks sing.

> Having no talent,
> I just want to sleep,
> you noisy birds.

Two generations after Bashō's death, his poetry was taken up by a well-educated writer and painter named Buson, who lived from 1716 to 1783. Buson revered Bashō's poetry and at the same time brought his own sensitivity to the haiku:

> The sea in springtime
> All the warm day in breathing swells —
> In breathing swells.

Although Issa lived at almost the same time as Buson, from 1763 to 1827, his poetry had a distinctive tone that came as much from his country background as it did from his poetic studies:

> Children imitating cormorants —
> more wonderful
> than cormorants.

In the century that followed Buson's death, the haiku was neglected and the form lost some of its purity, but it was once again taken up by a younger poet, Shiki, who lived from 1872 to 1923. Shiki set the tone of the modern haiku:

> The ocean freshly green
> Mountain on mountain peaked with snow
> Birds homing to the north.

The haiku has been adopted by many American poets, particularly the Beat poets of the 1950s and the 1960s, who had become Buddhists and who tried to match the severity of the Japanese poems with their own rigor and restraint. The best known of the Beat writers, Jack Kerouac, wrote dozens of haiku, sometimes jotting them down in pencil on the back pages of the paperback books he carried in his pocket when he worked on the railroad. He called what he was writing "Western Haikus."

> Birds singing
>   in the dark
>   — Rainy dawn

> The summer chair
>   rocking by itself
> In the blizzard

> In my medicine cabinet
>   the winter fly
> has died of old age

The American writer who has perhaps best caught the essence of the haiku is the African American novelist and author of short stories Richard Wright. Wright discovered the haiku in 1959, shortly before his death. As he wrote a friend, "Maybe I'm fooling around with these little poems, but I could not let them go. I was possessed by them" (quoted in *American Poetry and Japanese Culture*, Kodama, Archon Books, 1994, p. 158). Within a few months he wrote 4,000 haiku and then spent almost as much time winnowing them down into a collection describing the seasons of the year.

I would like a bell
Tolling in this soft twilight
Over willow trees

A freezing morning
I left a bit of my skin
On the broomstick handle

A soft wind at dawn
Lifts one dry leaf and lays it
Upon another

An empty sickbed
An indented white pillow
In weak winter sun

Imagism

The term *imagism* was invented by an American poet, Ezra Pound, who was living in London and closely associated with a small group of friends who were the first imagists. As a literary movement, imagism lasted only a few years, but it was widely discussed, ridiculed, and parodied, and it had an important role in the development of open form poetry. Even poets who would not think of themselves as imagists used the methods of the imagists for their own work. The imagists were trying to create poetry that was, as it was expressed by another of their founders, T. H. Hulme, "a moment of discovery or awareness, created by effective metaphor which provides the sharp, intuitive insight that is the essence of life." In the credo that opened the 1915 imagist anthology, the first point was "To use the language of common speech, but the exact word, not the nearly exact, nor the merely decorative." The fourth point was that imagist poems should "Present an image. Poetry should render particulars exactly, and not deal in vague generalities, however magnificent and sonorous."

It was the lean, hard diction of imagist poetry that was to have a lasting effect on modern poetry. Poets found that they did not have to round every poem into a generality. As William Carlos Williams, a friend of Pound's who stayed in New Jersey and wrote his poetry with his own American voice, expressed the imagist ideal, "No ideas, but in things."

This poem by Ezra Pound is perhaps the most famous of the imagist poems. Pound used it as an example of what he meant by imagism in his introduction to the first collection of his friends' poems. It is a description of people in the Paris subway on a rainy, dark night.

EZRA POUND

In a Station of the Metro   1913

The apparition of these faces in the crowd
Petals on a wet, black bough.

For a few months, when they both were students at the University of Pennsylvania, Pound had been engaged to Hilda Doolittle. When she came to London, he persuaded her to use her initials H.D. for her poetry. She and her husband, Richard Aldington, were part of the original imagist group.

H.D.

Oread°   *1914*

Whirl up, sea —
whirl your pointed pines,
splash your great pines
on our rocks,
hurl your green over us,
cover us with your pools of fir.

Although William Carlos Williams never considered himself an imagist, the poetry he wrote after the group began to publish reflected their aims. The best way to describe the effect of the imagist credo on his work is to say he wrote poems that were made possible by imagism. His poem "The Red Wheelbarrow" would be a classic imagist description of a wheelbarrow left out in the rain close to the chickens, except for his enigmatic phrase, "so much depends." What Williams seems to be suggesting in his eight short lines is that he finds something very important in this image of rain and chickens and a wheelbarrow in his backyard, but it is an image that has never given away all its secrets.

WILLIAM CARLOS WILLIAMS

The Red Wheelbarrow   *1923*

so much depends
upon

a red wheel
barrow

glazed with rain
water

beside the white
chickens

This next poem is closer to the imagist ideal.

Oread: Mountain nymph.

WILLIAM CARLOS WILLIAMS

Classic Scene 1937

A power-house
in the shape of
a red brick chair
90 feet high

on the seat of which 5
sit the figures
of two metal
stacks — aluminum —

commanding an area
of squalid shacks 10
side by side —
from one of which

buff smoke
streams while under
a grey sky 15
the other remains
passive today —

Although Wallace Stevens was an insurance executive who lived in Hartford, Connecticut, he had many associations with Williams and other young poets who were experimenting with the new style. The first and last verses of his poem "Thirteen Ways of Looking at a Blackbird" have all the characteristics of an imagist poem. The first verse also suggests the tone of a haiku, although it has too many syllables. Other verses, like the seventh, with its admonition to the men of Haddam, a small city in Connecticut, to stop thinking about imagined exotic birds and see the blackbirds walking around the ground, are more didactic.

Like Williams's poem about the red wheelbarrow, this poem has also defied easy access to its meanings. Perhaps one way to understand it is to think of it as a series of imagist poems and short enigmatic lyrics, with blackbirds suddenly flying through. It is a poem that reminds us of Marianne Moore's description of poetry as something that can present us with "imaginary gardens with real toads in them."

WALLACE STEVENS

Thirteen Ways of Looking at a Blackbird 1931

I

Among twenty snowy mountains
The only moving thing
Was the eye of the blackbird.

II

I was of three minds,
Like a tree
In which there are three blackbirds.

III

The blackbird whistled in the autumn winds.
It was a small part of the pantomime.

IV

A man and a woman
Are one.
A man and a woman and a blackbird
Are one.

V

I do not know which to prefer,
The beauty of inflections
Or the beauty of innuendoes,
The blackbird whistling
Or just after.

VI

Icicles filled the long window
With barbaric glass.
The shadow of the blackbird
Crossed it, to and fro.
The mood
Traced in the shadow
An indecipherable cause.

VII

O thin men of Haddam,
Why do you imagine golden birds?
Do you not see how the blackbird
Walks around the feet
Of the women about you?

VIII

I know noble accents
And lucid, inescapable rhythms;
But I know, too,
That the blackbird is involved
In what I know.

IX

When the blackbird flew out of sight,
It marked the edge
Of one of many circles.

X

At the sight of blackbirds
Flying in a green light,
Even the bawds of euphony   40
Would cry out sharply.

XI

He rode over Connecticut
In a glass coach.
Once, a fear pierced him,
In that he mistook   45
The shadow of his equipage
For blackbirds.

XII

The river is moving.
The blackbird must be flying.

XIII

It was evening all afternoon.
It was snowing   50
And it was going to snow.
The blackbird sat
In the cedar-limbs.

DRAMATIC POETRY

> Is it not monstrous that this player here,
> But in a fiction, in a dream of passion,
> Could force his soul so to his own conceit
> That from her working all his visage wann'd,
> Tears in his eyes, distraction in 's aspect,
> A broken voice, and his whole function suiting
> With forms to his conceit? . . .
> – WILLIAM SHAKESPEARE, *Hamlet*, act 2, scene 2

The term *dramatic poetry*, in its denotative sense, means the use of poetry in the writing of drama. If we have grown up with English as our language, when we think of poetry as dramatic dialogue we usually are hearing, in our memory, the blank verse cadences of Shakespeare and the other Elizabethan dramatists.

If we had grown up with French as our language, however, what we would hear in our memory would be the rhymed verse of Molière, who was writing for the court of Louis XIV, more than a half a century after Shakespeare. We are not used to hearing rhymed verse as dialogue from the stage, but after a moment we become so accustomed to the courtly style of the rhyme that without the sounds and rhythm of the language the play would seem as flat and unsatisfactory as stale bread. Molière's dialogue seems to *sing* from the stage. Here is an example from his play *The Misanthrope* (1666), as translated by the poet Richard Wilbur in 1955. Two suitors are trying to force the heroine to tell them which one she loves. She finally tires of their persistence and answers sharply,

> Enough: this inquisition's gone too far:
> How utterly unreasonable you are!
> Not that I couldn't make the choice with ease;
> My heart has no conflicting sympathies;
> I know full well which one of you I favor,   5
> And you'd not see me hesitate or waver.
> But how can you expect me to reveal
> So cruelly and bluntly what I feel?
> I think it altogether too unpleasant
> To choose between two men when both are present.   10

At the beginning of this century Irish playwrights used dramatic poetry as a way to present myth and legend onstage, and their dialogue had a rich imagery. Here is an example from William Butler Yeats's play *At the Hawk's Well* (1917). An old man who has been watching the well for fifty years has lit a fire close to it and speaks to the rocks, the thorn trees, and a silent girl who is guardian of the well. The form is iambic pentameter.

> OLD MAN: Why don't you speak to me? Why don't you say:
> "Are you not weary gathering those sticks?
> Are not your fingers cold?" You have not one word,
> While yesterday you spoke three times. You said:
> "The well is full of hazel leaves." You said: 5
> "The wind is from the west," And after that:
> "If there is rain it's likely there'll be mud."
> Today you are as stupid as a fish,
> No, worse, worse, being less lively and as dumb.
> Your eyes are dazed and heavy. If the Sidhe°   10
> Must have a guardian to clean out the well
> And drive the cattle off, they might choose somebody
> That can be pleasant and companionable
> Once in the day. Why do you stare like that?
> You had that glassy look about the eyes   15
> Last time it happened. Do you know anything?
> It is enough to drive an old man crazy
> To look all day upon these broken rocks,
> And ragged thorns, and that one stupid face,
> And speak and get no answer . . .   20

---

10. Sidhe: Pronounced *shee*; in Irish folklore, hills on and under which fairies are said to dwell.

The Dramatic Monologue

One form of dramatic poetry that has been popular with poets and readers for many years is the **dramatic monologue**. It is a poem written in the form of a speech or extended narration that the person who is the subject of the poem delivers to someone else. In the nineteenth century, when the form was very popular, a dramatic monologue had a definite speaker who was talking to an imaginary person; there was some implied action; and the action took place in the present. Often the subject of the more lurid monologues was someone, often a woman, who related a story about something terrible that had happened to them, and then ended the poem by hurling themselves off a cliff or into the ocean.

The dramatic monologues written by the English poet Robert Browning, however, are character studies of people who reveal themselves as they speak. One of the best known is "My Last Duchess." If you read the poem aloud, you will hear the subtlety and ease of its language. The poem perfectly fits the nineteenth-century idea of the dramatic monologue. It includes a definite speaker, the action of the duke showing his art collection, and the moment in the present when he is talking to the emissary.

ROBERT BROWNING

My Last Duchess   1842

Ferrara

That's my last Duchess painted on the wall,
Looking as if she were alive. I call
That piece a wonder, now: Frà Pandolf's° hands
Worked busily a day, and there she stands.
Will't please you sit and look at her? I said   5
"Frà Pandolf" by design, for never read
Strangers like you that pictured countenance,
The depth and passion of its earnest glance,
But to myself they turned (since none puts by
The curtain I have drawn for you, but I)   10
And seemed as they would ask me, if they durst,
How such a glance came there; so, not the first
Are you to turn and ask thus. Sir, 'twas not
Her husband's presence only, called that spot
Of joy into the Duchess' cheek: perhaps   15
Frà Pandolf chanced to say "Her mantle laps
Over my lady's wrist too much," or "Paint
Must never hope to reproduce the faint
Half-flush that dies along her throat": such stuff

---

3. **Frà Pandolf's hands:** Brother Pandolf, a fictional painter.

Was courtesy, she thought, and cause enough   20
For calling up that spot of joy. She had
A heart — how shall I say? — too soon made glad,
Too easily impressed; she liked whate'er
She looked on, and her looks went everywhere.
Sir, 'twas all one! My favor at her breast,   25
The dropping of the daylight in the West,
The bough of cherries some officious fool
Broke in the orchard for her, the white mule
She rode with round the terrace — all and each
Would draw from her alike the approving speech,   30
Or blush, at least. She thanked men, — good! but thanked
Somehow — I know not how — as if she ranked
My gift of a nine-hundred-years-old name
With anybody's gift. Who'd stoop to blame
This sort of trifling? Even had you skill   35
In speech — which I have not — to make your will
Quite clear to such an one, and say, "Just this
Or that in you disgusts me; here you miss,
Or there exceed the mark" — and if she let
Herself be lessoned so, nor plainly set   40
Her wits to yours, forsooth, and made excuse,
   — E'en then would be some stooping; and I choose
Never to stoop. Oh sir, she smiled, no doubt,
Whene'er I passed her; but who passed without
Much the same smile? This grew; I gave commands;   45
Then all smiles stopped together. There she stands
As if alive. Will't please you rise? We'll meet
The company below, then. I repeat,
The Count your master's known munificence
Is ample warrant that no just pretense   50
Of mine for dowry will be disallowed;
Though his fair daughter's self, as I avowed
At starting, is my object. Nay, we'll go
Together down, sir. Notice Neptune, though,
Taming a sea-horse, thought a rarity,   55
Which Claus of Innsbruck° cast in bronze for me!

   The dramatic monologue today, as critic Park Honan has defined it, is "a single discourse by one whose presence is indicated by the poet, but who is not the poet himself." In the modern monologue "Next Day," the American poet Randall Jarrell has chosen the persona of a middle-aged woman whose children are off at school and who suddenly understands that she is growing old. It is the day after the funeral of a friend, and her own life, at this moment, feels "commonplace and solitary."

---

56. Claus of Innsbruck: Unidentified; probably a fictional sculptor.

RANDALL JARRELL

Next Day   1965

Moving from Cheer to Joy, from Joy to All,
I take a box
And add it to my wild rice, my Cornish game hens.
The slacked or shorted, basketed, identical
Food-gathering flocks   5
Are selves I overlook. Wisdom, said William James,°

Is learning what to overlook. And I am wise
If that is wisdom.
Yet somehow, as I buy All from these shelves
And the boy takes it to my station wagon,   10
What I've become
Troubles me even if I shut my eyes.

When I was young and miserable and pretty
And poor, I'd wish
What all girls wish: to have a husband,   15
A house and children. Now that I'm old, my wish
Is womanish:
That the boy putting groceries in my car

See me. It bewilders me he doesn't see me.
For so many years   20
I was good enough to eat: the world looked at me
And its mouth watered. How often they have undressed me,
The eyes of strangers!
And, holding their flesh within my flesh, their vile

Imaginings within my imagining,   25
I too have taken
The chance of life. Now the boy pats my dog
And we start home. Now I am good.
The last mistaken,
Ecstatic, accidental bliss, the blind   30

Happiness that, bursting, leaves upon the palm
Some soap and water —
It was so long ago, back in some Gay
Twenties, Nineties, I don't know . . . Today I miss
My lovely daughter   35
Away at school, my sons away at school,

My husband away at work — I wish for them.
The dog, the maid,
And I go through the sure unvarying days

---

6. **William James:** American pragmatist, philosopher, and psychologist (1892–1910).

At home in them. As I look at my life,   40
I am afraid
Only that it will change, as I am changing:

I am afraid, this morning, of my face.
It looks at me
From the rear-view mirror, with the eyes I hate,   45
The smile I hate. Its plain, lined look
Of gray discovery
Repeats to me: "You're old." That's all, I'm old.

And yet I'm afraid, as I was at the funeral
I went to yesterday.   50
My friend's cold made-up face, granite among its flowers,
Her undressed, operated-on, dressed body
Were my face and body.
As I think of her I hear her telling me

How young I seem; I *am* exceptional;   55
I think of all I have.
But really no one is exceptional,
No one has anything, I'm anybody,
I stand beside my grave
Confused with my life, that is commonplace and solitary.   60

RELATED COMMENTARIES: *Ezra Pound, "On the Principles of Imagism," page 1297; Peter Schmitt, "Sad Heart at the Supermarket: Randall Jarrell's 'Next Day,' " page 1307; William Carlos Williams, "Ezra Pound's Language," page 1329.*

14

POETS AND HISTORY

No single poet — Dante, Goethe, or even Shakespeare — has had a more pervasive influence on the cultural foundation of the West than the shadowy figure we call Homer. His name is so familiar that it is easy to overlook just how long his work has been our heritage. Homer described events that took place, as far as we can tell, at roughly the same time as the Exodus. Before the Old Testament was complete, his works were already the basic scrolls in a cultured man's library. By the time Jesus was born, so much had been written about Homer and his work that it would be a very long time before any of the Apostles could challenge his leading position as the most intensely studied author in Western Civilization. All this Homer accomplished with just two poems — the *Iliad* and the *Odyssey*.

— TIM SEVERIN, *The Ulysses Voyage*

THE EPIC

The need to know something of its past is characteristic of every human society. Today we expect to find these accounts written in other ways — in novels or essays, sometimes even in film. Alex Haley's novel *Roots*, which tells the story of a slave taken from Africa and follows his life and the lives of his family through slavery and freedom in the United States, is a modern story that fills this need to know about the past. In its size and its sweep of history we would call this story an **epic**.

We know of the earliest epics because they were, at some moment, written down, but before they were written they were sung or chanted, and it is because of this oral tradition that we find most epics are written as poetry. With its rhythm, wordplay, and imagery, poetry is a much more exciting way for the performer to tell a story than is prose. The earliest poem that is still a living part of the Western tradition is an epic, the *Iliad*. It was written down by one person from traditional chanted narratives in about 700 B.C. The only thing known about the poet is that his name is Homer, and he was probably blind.

The story of the *Iliad*, which tells us about the beautiful Greek woman Helen, who was kidnapped by the Trojan prince Paris, and the ten-year-long Trojan War that was waged to bring her back to her husband, has become so woven into the culture of Europe and America that it is difficult for us to remember that it is not history but a poem. We have no way of knowing if anything in the *Iliad* or the *Odyssey* — Homer's second epic poem, which tells of the long journey homeward from Troy by the Greek warrior Odysseus — is true, despite evidence unearthed by the archaeologist Heinrich Schliemann in 1873 at Hissarlik, in western Turkey, that there might have been a city something like the one Homer describes close to where he said it would be.

In his famous poem "Ozymandias" (p. 2057), the English poet Percy Bysshe Shelley describes a broken statue of a once-mighty ruler now fallen in a barren waste. On its base is the arrogant sentence, spoken by the ruler, "Look on my works, ye mighty, and despair." If we think of the power of Homer's narrative — which, after almost three thousand years, is still translated, quoted, and discussed and still inspires writers in dozens of languages — what Shelley should have written was "Look on my *words*, ye mighty, and despair."

Epic poems fill such basic psychological needs for their societies that there are epics in almost every language. In Spanish there is *El Cid*; in French, *Le Chanson de Roland*; in Sanskrit, *The Ramayama*. The first poem we know of in Old English is the epic *Beowulf*, though it tells the story of German kings and princes from the fifth century A.D. and is as much a German epic as English. For the Romans, their epic was the *Aeneid*, and in Japanese there are the medieval tales of the Heike clan, the *Heike Monagatari*, recited by blind beggars in Japan today. The role of storyteller in West African societies was filled by the musician-poets we know as griots, and there are still griots who tell the long narratives of the wars between the kingdoms of Africa and the first encounters with European adventurers.

So that you can have some idea of the language and the way that stories are told in epic poetry, we will read from Homer's *Iliad* as well as from a more recent epic poem by a West African griot telling of the first sale of slaves to European slave traders.

The *Iliad*

In this section of the *Iliad* the Greek and Trojan armies have advanced toward each other, preparing to fight. Paris, the Trojan prince who caused the war by kidnaping Helen, the wife of Menelaus, pushes forward to stride up and down in front of the Trojans challenging any of the Greek warriors (the term *Argive* is also used for the Greeks) to meet him in hand-to-hand combat. Menelaus, or Atrides as he is also called, sees him and jumps out of his chariot ready to fight. When Paris recognizes who has responded to his challenge, he turns and runs back into the Trojan lines. His brother Hector, the greatest of the Trojan warriors, taunts him for his cowardice, and finally it is decided that Paris and Menelaus will fight to the death alone between the two armies. If Paris survives he will keep Helen, and if Menelaus is left alive Helen will be returned to him. Their individual combat will end the war.

HOMER

From the *Iliad*

c. 700 B.C.

TRANSLATED BY ROBERT FAGLES

Now with the squadrons marshaled, captains leading each,
the Trojans came with cries and the din of war like wildfowl
when the long hoarse cries of cranes sweep on against the sky
and the great formations flee from winter's grim ungodly storms,
flying in force, shrieking south to the Ocean gulfs, speeding   5
blood and death to the Pygmy warriors, launching at daybreak
savage battle down upon their heads. But Achaea's armies
came on strong in silence, breathing combat-fury,
hearts ablaze to defend each other to the death.

When the South Wind showers mist on the mountaintops,   10
no friend to shepherds, better than night to thieves —
you can see no farther than you can fling a stone —
so dust came clouding, swirling up from the feet of armies
marching at top speed, trampling through the plain.

Now closer, closing, front to front in the onset   15
till Paris sprang from the Trojan forward ranks,
a challenger, lithe, magnificent as a god,
the skin of a leopard slung across his shoulders,
a reflex bow at his back and battle-sword at hip
and brandishing two sharp spears tipped in bronze   20
he strode forth, challenging all the Argive best
to fight him face-to-face in mortal combat.

Soon as the warrior Menelaus marked him,
Paris parading there with his big loping strides,
flaunting before the troops, Atrides thrilled   25
like a lion lighting on some handsome carcass,
lucky to find an antlered stag or wild goat
just as hunger strikes — he rips it, bolts it down,
even with running dogs and lusty hunters rushing him.
So Menelaus thrilled at heart — princely Paris there,   30
right before his eyes. The outlaw, the adulterer . . .
"Now for revenge!" he thought, and down he leapt
from his chariot fully armed and hit the ground.

But soon as magnificent Paris marked Atrides
shining among the champions, Paris' spirit shook.   35
Backing into his friendly ranks, he cringed from death
as one who trips on a snake in a hilltop hollow
recoils, suddenly, trembling grips his knees
and pallor takes his cheeks and back he shrinks.
So he dissolved again in the proud Trojan lines,   40

dreading Atrides — magnificent, brave Paris.

                        At one glance
Hector raked his brother with insults, stinging taunts:
"Paris, appalling Paris! Our prince of beauty —
mad for women, you lure them all to ruin!
Would to god you'd never been born, died unwed.   45
That's all I'd ask. Better that way by far
than to have you strutting here, an outrage —
a mockery in the eyes of all our enemies. Why,
the long-haired Achaeans must be roaring with laughter!
They thought *you* the bravest champion we could field,   50
and just because of the handsome luster on your limbs,
but you have no pith, no fighting strength inside you.
What? — is *this* the man who mustered the oarsmen once,
who braved the seas in his racing deep-sea ships,
trafficked with outlanders, carried off a woman   55
far from her distant shores, a great beauty
wed to a land of rugged spearmen?
                        You . . .
curse to your father, your city and all your people,
a joy to our enemies, rank disgrace to yourself!
So, you can't stand up to the battling Menelaus?   60
You'd soon feel his force, that man you robbed
of his sumptuous, warm wife. No use to you then,
the fine lyre and these, these gifts of Aphrodite,
your long flowing locks and your striking looks,
not when you roll and couple with the dust.   65
What cowards, the men of Troy — or years ago
they'd have decked you out in a suit of rocky armor,
stoned you to death for all the wrongs you've done!"

    And Paris, magnificent as a god, replied,
"Ah Hector, you criticize me fairly, yes,   70
nothing unfair, beyond what I deserve.
The heart inside you is always tempered hard,
like an ax that goes through wood when a shipwright
cuts out ship timbers with every ounce of skill
and the blade's weight drives the man's stroke.   75
So the heart inside your chest is never daunted.
Still, don't fling in my face the lovely gifts
of golden Aphrodite. Not to be tossed aside,
the gifts of the gods, those glories . . .
whatever the gods give of their own free will —   80
how could we ever choose them for ourselves?
                       Now, though,
if you really want me to fight to the finish here,
have all Trojans and Argives take their seats

and pit me against Menelaus dear to Ares —
right between the lines —   85
we'll fight it out for Helen and all her wealth.
And the one who proves the better man and wins,
he'll take those treasures fairly, lead the woman home.
The rest will seal in blood their binding pacts of friendship.
Our people will live in peace on the rich soil of Troy,   90
our enemies sail home to the stallion-land of Argos,
the land of Achaea where the women are a wonder . . ."

Toolongjong

The singer-poets of West Africa are usually called *griots*, though there is a different word for *singer* in each of the languages of the countryside. In *Toolongjong*, a poem recited by the Mandingo griot Alhaji Fabala Kanuteh in The Gambia in 1974, there is the same epic sweep to the story, the same concern with naming all of the people who are part of the story, the same attention to the places in the story that we saw in the *Iliad*. Kanuteh's poem is shorter, however, because he does not have the help of the written page. There were no written languages in West Africa, until the introduction of Arabic and the languages of the European colonists. The griots have to memorize every story and every name in their narratives, and they also have to be able to improvise and change their stories to bring different families forward or to mention the name of the village where they are singing.

Kanuteh performed the poem accompanying himself on a small, hand-made xylophone, pausing from time to time to play runs on the instrument, giving himself a moment to catch his breath and to remember what happens next in his narrative. He had spent his life as a griot, beginning as a boy when he sat at the feet of another griot and tapped out the rhythm on the side of the instrument while listening to the words of the song.

Toolongjong tells the story of the first meeting between the Africans and the Portuguese, who were cruising along the coast, trying to buy slaves. The king Seneke Jammeth sent representatives to meet them, and when he found what they wanted, he attacked the neighboring village of Tambana and sold its people to the Portuguese. The Portuguese then sold the slaves to Dutch traders, the "Hollanders," and it was the Dutch who brought the first slaves to North America in the early seventeenth century. Most of the places named in the poem are villages along the banks of the Gambia River, and the building he calls the "Slave House" is a ruined stone structure on the island of Georgetown, a trading station inland on the river. When the griot finished his song, one of the men listening stood up excitedly and said, "You must have my shilling," giving him a coin as the ceremonial payment for a moving experience.

ALHAJI FABALA KANUTEH

From *Toolongjong*   1974

TRANSLATED BY SAMUEL CHARTERS

Toolongjong is the song that was sung for Sunyetta the king of Fuda.
This same Toolongjong was also sung for the great soldiers of Sunyetta.
This Toolongjong was sung for Musa Molo, the king of Fuladu,
for Seneke Jammeh, this Toolongjong was sung for Koree Danso,
for the Sang Kala Maran,   5
this Toolongjong was sung for Mansa° Demba of Berending,   *king*
this Toolongjong was sung for Wahls Mandiba.

Now I will tell you how slaves came to be sold to the Europeans.
How it came about is what I'm going to tell.
In that time Mansa Demba was the king of Nomi   10
and Seneke Jammeh was the king at Bakindi Ke.
There were two wharves, one at Jufred Tenda,
and the other at Albreda Tenda,
and anyone who went there, to Youmi Mansa, went to the king there,
that is king Mansa Demba, and to the queen called Kodending.   15
If they got hold of any slaves they took them to Mansa Demba and sold
them to him.
At this time Han Sunyetta was the ruler of the world.
He made a king for the village of Sillia,
and another king at Salum, and another king at the village of Baul.   20
Another king Marujang and Gao.
Before that Satifa Jaware and Fakolly Kumba,
and Komfatta Keying and Nana Jibril.
They were the strongest of Sunyetta's soldiers.

Then the Europeans came,   25
at that time the only Europeans were the Portuguese.

When the Portuguese came they brought their ship to Sani Munko and
they left the ship at Sani Munko and raised their flag there.
Mansa Seneke Jammeh sent people to Sani Muno to see them.
The messengers arrived at Sani Munko and they found the Portuguese   30
there and the Portuguese asked them questions.
The first man they saw was Kambi Manneh and the Europeans asked
him what was the name of the place and he told them,
"My name is Kambi"
and they wrote that down for the name of the place, Kambi.   35
And they came to this place and they found people cutting these sticks
called the "bang" and the Europeans asked them,
"What are you cutting?" and they said they were cutting the sticks
called "bangjolo," and the Europeans wrote that down for the name.

Then the Europeans said to Seneke Jammeh, "We are looking for   40
something,"
and Seneke Jammeh asked them, "What is it?"
And they told him, "We are looking for slaves."
Seneke then went to Tambana and fought with the people of Tambana,
and fought with the village of Baria.   45
When he had these slaves he went and sold these slaves to the
Europeans.

The leader of the Europeans was called Wampiya,
and he took the slaves to the city of Salamki Joya.
He went with the slaves to the Hollanders,   50
that is to the people of Holland,
and he sold the slaves to the Hollanders,
then the Hollanders took the slaves to America . . .

When the Europeans came,
when they brought their ship from Portugal,   55
the ship used to start its journey from Banjul,
then it went to Sanemunko Jammeh, and Mansa Demba Sanko,
and Samkala Marong, and Wali Mandeba, and Jata Sela.
Anyone who had slaves they collected them all together and took
them to the places called Aladabara and Jufure to sell them to the   60
Portuguese.
Then the Portuguese put them in their ship
and left there and went to Jang Jang Bure.
When they arrived there they went
right to the slave house to collect slaves there   65
and take them to the Hollanders.
Then the Hollanders collected them and sent them to America.
It is because of this
that slaves are plenty in America.

They call them American Negroes. . . .   70

POETRY AND HISTORY

The two epic poems we have just read are both historical narratives, but
we sometimes forget that *every* poem, besides expressing the emotions and attitudes of its writer, reflects the time in which it was written. Every poem contains references to the social and cultural dimensions beyond the poem's
linguistic frame. The accumulation of these references is sometimes termed
historicity and, individually, the references are categorized as **referentiality**.
Although the terms sound complex, what they are describing is usually obvious when we read a specific poem. If we read the opening lines of Thomas
Gray's "Elegy Written in a Country Churchyard" (p. 940) with these terms in
mind, we will immediately be struck by the historical references that the lines
suggest. The poem was first published in 1751.

> The curfew tolls the knell of parting day,
>   The lowing herd wind slowly o'er the lea,
>   The plowman homeward plods his weary way.

As we read these lines we are immediately drawn into a moment of history when church bells, used to signal the beginning and ending of the workday, could be heard by everyone working the land. In our modern industrial era of pen-fed cattle it is hard to recall a time when herds returned to their stalls after a day of grazing in the fields. A plowman walking back to his cottage tired and alone is a figure we now associate more with classic landscape painting than our own reality.

Many poets, especially the younger generation of writers today, are deeply engaged in their own moment of history, and this is often expressed in poetry that is specifically political. It is poetry that wants to convince us, to shock us, or to inform us, and the subject of these poems is some reference, again, outside the poem's conventions of language or style or form. **Political poetry** has been used to open prayer meetings and to lead revolutions.

If we look back at older poets we find the same political commitment, even in moments when the poetry had to be hidden, or its sentiments concealed. The English Puritan poet John Milton, who was punished by his own government for his political activities, wrote an angry sonnet protesting the slaughter of a Protestant sect by the forces of the pope in the Italian Piedmont region in 1655.

JOHN MILTON

On the Late Massacre in Piedmont   1673

> Avenge, O Lord, thy slaughtered saints, whose bones
>   Lie scattered on the Alpine mountains cold,
>   Even them who kept thy truth so pure of old
>   When all our fathers worshiped stocks and stones,
> Forget not: in thy book record their groans   5
>   Who were thy sheep and in their ancient fold
>   Slain by the bloody Piemontese that rolled
>   Mother with infant down the rocks. Their moans
> The vales redoubled to the hills, and they
>   To Heaven. Their martyred blood and ashes sow   10
>   O'er all th' Italian fields where still doth sway
> The triple tyrant:° that from these may grow
>   A hundredfold, who having learnt thy way
>   Early may fly the Babylonian woe.°

---

12. triple tyrant: The pope, wearing his tiara, a three-crowned headpiece.   **13. Babylonian woe:** In Milton's day, Protestants often referred to the Roman Catholic Church as "the whore of Babylon."

With the growth of democratic governments in the nineteenth century, poets became more openly committed to the struggle against injustice. Although we think of Harriet Beecher Stowe's novel *Uncle Tom's Cabin* as one of the strongest protests against slavery, many English and American poets were also committed to freeing the slaves. This example is from an antislavery poem by the New England Quaker poet John Greenleaf Whittier, who once had to save himself from lynching in the confusion and tumult of a demonstration by slipping into a robe and joining the anti-Abolitionist mob that was crying out for his death.

JOHN GREENLEAF WHITTIER

From *The Farewell of a Virginia Slave Mother to Her Daughter Sold into Southern Bondage*   1837

> Gone, gone, — sold and gone,
>   To the rice-swamp dank and lone
> Where the slave-whip ceaseless swings,
> Where the noisome insect stings,
> Where the fever demon strews   5
> Poison with the falling dews,
> Where the sickly sunbeams glare
> Through the hot and noisome air,
>   Gone, gone, — sold and gone,
>   To the rice-swamp dank and lone,   10
>   From Virginia's hills and waters,
>   Woe is me, my stolen daughters!

Although Stephen Crane became famous for the classic war novel *The Red Badge of Courage*, he thought of war as brutal and inhumane. This cruelly ironic poem, written in the 1890s, is one of the first American antiwar poems.

STEPHEN CRANE

War Is Kind   1896

Do not weep, maiden, for war is kind.
Because your lover threw wild hands toward the sky
And the affrighted steed ran on alone,
Do not weep.
War is kind.   5

> Hoarse, booming drums of the regiment,
> Little souls who thirst for fight,
> These men were born to drill and die.
> The unexplained glory flies above them,
> Great is the battle-god, great, and his kingdom —   10
> A field where a thousand corpses lie.

Do not weep, babe, for war is kind
Because your father tumbled in the yellow trenches,
Raged at his breast, gulped and died,
Do not weep.   15
War is kind.

    Swift blazing flag of the regiment,
    Eagle with crest of red and gold,
    These men were born to drill and die.
    Point for them the virtue of slaughter,   20
    Make plain to them the excellence of killing
    And a field where a thousand corpses lie.

Mother whose heart hung humble as a button
On the bright splendid shroud of your son,
Do not weep.   25
War is kind.

Thomas Hardy's poem "The Man He Killed" was written during the Boer
War (1899–1902). Like Stephen Crane's poem, its theme is a response to all wars.

Thomas Hardy

The Man He Killed   1902

    "Had he and I but met
      By some old ancient inn,
  We should have sat us down to wet
      Right many a nipperkin!°

    "But ranged as infantry,   5
      And staring face to face,
  I shot at him as he at me,
      And killed him in his place.

    "I shot him dead because —
      Because he was my foe,   10
  Just so: my foe of course he was:
      That's clear enough; although

    "He thought he'd 'list, perhaps,
      Off-hand-like — just as I —
  Was out of work — had sold his traps —   15
      No other reason why.

    "Yes; quaint and curious war is!
      You shoot a fellow down
  You'd treat, if met where any bar is,
      Or help to half-a-crown."   20

---

4. **nipperkin:** A measure of alcohol less than a half pint.

Randall Jarrell's poem about the death of an American airman who was killed in the turret of his bomber during a raid over Germany in World War II is a strong example of a more contemporary antiwar poem.

RANDALL JARRELL

The Death of the Ball Turret Gunner   1945

From my mother's sleep I fell into the state
And I hunched in its belly till my wet fur froze.
Six miles from earth, loosed from its dream of life,
I woke to black flak and the nightmare fighters.
When I died they washed me out of the turret with a hose.

THE POLITICAL POEM

In our complex and uneasy world, with its confrontations between ethnic groups and its distrust of government institutions, poetry is a way for many writers to make themselves heard. In this group of political poems, American writers react to prejudice, social inequality, and political corruption, and writers from Europe and the Third World react to political oppression, the Holocaust, and terrorism.

Political Poems for Further Reading

LOUISE ERDRICH

Indian Boarding School: The Runaways   1984

Home's the place we head for in our sleep.
Boxcars stumbling north in dreams
don't wait for us. We catch them on the run.
The rails, old lacerations that we love,
shoot parallel across the face and break   5
just under Turtle Mountains.° Riding scars
you can't get lost. Home is the place they cross.

The lame guard strikes a match and makes the dark
less tolerant. We watch through cracks in boards
as the land starts rolling, rolling till it hurts   10
to be here, cold in regulation clothes.
We know the sheriff's waiting at midrun
to take us back. His car is dumb and warm.
The highway doesn't rock, it only hums

---

6. **Turtle Mountains:** A range in North Dakota and Manitoba.

like a wing of long insults. The worn-down welts   15
of ancient punishment lead back and forth.

All runaways wear dresses, long green ones,
the color you would think shame was. We scrub
the sidewalks down because it's shameful work.
Our brushes cut the stone in watered arcs.   20
and in the soak frail outlines shiver clear
a moment, things us kids pressed on the dark
face before it hardened, pale, remembering
delicate old injuries, the spines of names and leaves.

PAT MORA

Border Town: 1938   *1986*

She counts cement cracks
little Esperanza with the long brown braids,
counts so as not to hear
the girls in the playground singing,
    "the farmer's in the dell   5
      the farmer's in the dell"
laughing and running round-round
while little Esperanza walks head down
eyes full of tears.
    "The nurse takes the child"   10
but Esperanza walks alone across the loud
street, through the graveyard gates
down the dirt path, walks faster,
faster . . . away
from ghosts with long arms,   15
no "hi-ho the dairy-o" here,
runs to that other school
for Mexicans
every day wanting to stay close to home,
every day wanting to be the farmer in the dell,   20
little Esperanza in the long brown braids
counts cement cracks
               ocho, nueve, diez.

AL YOUNG

Birthday Poem   *1971*

First light of day in Mississippi
son of laborer & of house wife
it says so on the official photostat
not son of fisherman & child fugitive

from cottonfields & potato patches   5
from sugarcane chickens & well-water
from kerosene lamps & watermelons
mules named jack or jenny & wagonwheels,

years of meaningless farm work
work Work WORK WORK WORK —   10
"Papa pull you outta school bout March
to stay on the place & work the crop"
— her own earliest knowledge
of human hopelessness & waste

She carried me around nine months   15
inside her fifteen year old self
before here I sit numbering it all

How I got from then to now
is the mystery that could fill a whole library
much less an arbitrary stanza   20

But of course you already know about that
from your own random suffering
& sudden inexplicable bliss

JANICE MIRIKITANI

Recipe   1987

Round eyes

Ingredients: scissors, Scotch magic transparent tape,
             eyeliner — water based, black.
             Optional: false eyelashes.

Cleanse face thoroughly.   5

For best results, powder entire face, including eyelids.
    (lighter shades suited to total effect desired)

With scissors, cut magic tape $\frac{1}{16}$" wide, $\frac{3}{4}$"–$\frac{1}{2}$" long —
depending on length of eyelid.

Stick firmly onto mid-upper eyelid area   10
    (looking down into handmirror facilitates finding
    adequate surface)

If using false eyelashes, affix first on lid, folding any
excess lid over the base of eyelash with glue.

Paint black eyeliner on tape and entire lid.   15

Do not cry.

LORNA DEE CERVANTES

Poem for the Young White Man Who Asked Me How I, an Intelligent, Well-Read Person Could Believe in the War between Races

1981

In my land there are no distinctions.
The barbed wire politics of oppression
have been torn down long ago. The only reminder
of past battles, lost or won, is a slight
rutting in the fertile fields.   5

In my land
people write poems about love,
full of nothing but contented childlike syllables.
Everyone reads Russian short stories and weeps.
There are no boundaries.   10
There is no hunger, no
complicated famine or greed.

I am not a revolutionary.
I don't even like political poems.
Do you think I can believe in a war between races?   15

I can deny it. I can forget about it
when I'm safe,
living on my own continent of harmony
and home, but I am not
there.   20

I believe in revolution
because everywhere the crosses are burning,
sharp-shooting goose-steppers round every corner,
there are snipers in the schools . . .
(I know you don't believe this.   25
You think this is nothing
but faddish exaggeration. But they
are not shooting at you.)

I'm marked by the color of my skin.
The bullets are discrete and designed to kill slowly.   30
They are aiming at my children.
These are facts.
Let me show you my wounds: my stumbling mind, my
"excuse me" tongue, and this
nagging preoccupation   35
with the feeling of not being good enough.

These bullets bury deeper than logic.
Racism is not intellectual.
I can not reason these scars away.

Outside my door   40
there is a real enemy
who hates me.

I am a poet
who yearns to dance on rooftops,
to whisper delicate lines about joy   45
and the blessings of human understanding.
I try. I go to my land, my tower of words and
bolt the door, but the typewriter doesn't fade out
the sounds of blasting and muffled outrage.
My own days bring me slaps on the face.   50
Every day I am deluged with reminders
that this is not
my land

and this is my land.

I do not believe in the war between races   55
but in this country
there is war.

MARY JO SALTER

Welcome to Hiroshima   1984

is what you first see, stepping off the train:
a billboard brought to you in living English
by Toshiba Electric. While a channel
silent in the TV of the brain

projects those flickering re-runs of a cloud   5
that brims its risen columnful like beer
and, spilling over, hangs its foamy head,
you feel a thirst for history: what year

it started to be safe to breathe the air,
and when to drink the blood and scum afloat   10
on the Ohta River. But no, the water's clear,
they pour it for your morning cup of tea

in one of the countless sunny coffee shops
whose plastic dioramas advertise
mutations of cuisine behind the glass: 15
a pancake sandwich; a pizza someone tops

with a maraschino cherry. Passing by
the Peace Park's floral hypocenter (where
how bravely, or with what mistaken cheer,
humanity erased its own erasure),   20

you enter the memorial museum
and through more glass are served, as on a dish

of blistered grass, three mannequins. Like gloves
a mother clips to coatsleeves, strings of flesh

hang from their fingertips; or as if tied   25
to recall a duty for us, *Reverence*
the dead whose mourners too shall soon be dead,
but all commemoration's swallowed up

in questions of bad taste, how re-created
horror mocks the grim original,   30
and thinking at last *They should have left it all*
you stop. This is the wristwatch of a child.

Jammed on the moment's impact, resolute
to communicate some message, although mute,
it gestures with its hands at eight-fifteen   35
and eight-fifteen and eight-fifteen again

while tables of statistics on the wall
update the news by calling on a roll
of tape, death gummed on death, and in the case
adjacent, an exhibit under glass   40

is glass itself: a shard the bomb slammed in
a woman's arm at eight-fifteen, but some
three decades on — as if to make it plain
hope's only as renewable as pain,

and as if all the unsung   45
debasements of the past may one day come
rising to the surface once again —
worked its filthy way out like a tongue.

Carolyn Forché

The Colonel   *1978*

What you have heard is true. I was in his house. His wife carried a tray
of coffee and sugar. His daughter filed her nails, his son went out for the
night. There were daily papers, pet dogs, a pistol on the cushion beside
him. The moon swung bare on its black cord over the house. On the television was a cop show. It was in English. Broken bottles were embedded   5
in the walls around the house to scoop the kneecaps from a man's legs
or cut his hands to lace. On the windows there were gratings like those
in liquor stores. We had dinner, rack of lamb, good wine, a gold bell was
on the table for calling the maid. The maid brought green mangoes, salt,
a type of bread. I was asked how I enjoyed the country. There was a brief 10
commercial in Spanish. His wife took everything away. There was some
talk then of how difficult it had become to govern. The parrot said hello
on the terrace. The colonel told it to shut up, and pushed himself from
the table. My friend said to me with his eyes: say nothing. The colonel

returned with a sack used to bring groceries home. He spilled many hu-   15
man ears on the table. They were like dried peach halves. There is no
other way to say this. He took one of them in his hands, shook it in our
faces, dropped it into a water glass. It came alive there. I am tired of fooling around he said. As for the rights of anyone, tell your people they can
go fuck themselves. He swept the ears to the floor with his arm and held   20
the last of his wine in the air. Something for your poetry, no? he said.
Some of the ears on the floor caught this scrap of his voice. Some of the
ears on the floor were pressed to the ground.

ANNA AKHMATOVA

Instead of a Preface   1917

TRANSLATED BY RICHARD MCKANE

In the terrible years of the Yezhov terror I spent seventeen months waiting in line outside the prison in Leningrad. One day somebody in the crowd
identified me. Standing behind me was a woman, with lips blue from the cold,
who had, of course, never heard me called by name before. Now she started
out of the torpor common to us all and asked me in a whisper (everyone whispered there):

"Can you describe this?"
And I said: "I can."
Then something like a smile passed fleetingly over what had once been
her face.

ANNA AKHMATOVA

Dedication   1940

Such grief might make the mountains stoop,
reverse the waters where they flow,
but cannot burst these ponderous bolts
that block us from the prison cells
crowded with mortal woe. . . .   5
For some the wind can freshly blow,
for some the sunlight fade at ease,
but we, made partners in our dread,
hear but the grating of the keys,
and heavy-booted soldiers' tread.   10
As if for early mass, we rose
and each day walked the wilderness,
trudging through silent street and square,

to congregate, less live than dead.
The sun declined, the Neva blurred,   15
and hope sang always from afar.
Whose sentence is decreed? . . . That moan,
that sudden spurt of woman's tears,
shows one distinguished from the rest,
as if they'd knocked her to the ground   20
and wrenched the heart out of her breast,
then let her go, reeling, alone.
Where are they now, my nameless friends
from those two years I spent in hell?
What specters mock them now, amid   25
the fury of Siberian snows,
or in the blighted circle of the moon?
To them I cry, Hail and Farewell!

TADEUSZ ROZEWICZ

Pigtail   1948

TRANSLATED BY ROBERT A. MAGUIRE AND MAGNUS JAN KRYNSKI

When all the women in the transport
had their heads shaved
four workmen with brooms made of birch twigs
swept up   5
and gathered up the hair

Behind clean glass
the stiff hair lies
of those suffocated in gas chambers
there are pins and side combs   10
in this hair

The hair is not shot through with light
is not parted by the breeze
is not touched by any hand
or rain or lips   15

In huge chests
clouds of dry hair
of those suffocated
and a faded plait
a pigtail with a ribbon   20
pulled at school
by naughty boys

TADEUSZ ROZEWICZ

What Happens   *1976*

TRANSLATED BY ROBERT A. MAGUIRE AND MAGNUS JAN KRYNSKI

It has happened
and it goes on happening
and will happen again
if nothing happens to stop it

The innocent know nothing   5
because they are too innocent
and the guilty know nothing
because they are too guilty

The poor do not notice
because they are too poor   10
and the rich do not notice
because they are too rich

The stupid shrug their shoulders
because they are too stupid
and the clever shrug their shoulders   15
because they are too clever

The young do not care
because they are too young
and the old do not care
because they are too old   20

That is why nothing happens
to stop it
and that is why it has happened
and goes on happening and will happen again

WISLAWA SZYMBORSKA

The Terrorist, He Watches   *1982*

TRANSLATED BY ROBERT A. MAGUIRE AND MAGNUS JAN KRYNSKI

The bomb will go off in the bar at one twenty p.m.
Now it's only one sixteen p.m.
Some will still have time to get in,
some to get out.

The terrorist has already crossed to the other side of the street.   5
The distance protects him from any danger,
and what a sight for sore eyes:

A woman in a yellow jacket, she goes in.
A man in dark glasses, he comes out.

Guys in jeans, they are talking.   10
One seventeen and four seconds.
That shorter guy's really got it made, and gets on a scooter,
and that taller one, he goes in.

One seventeen and forty seconds.
That girl there, she's got a green ribbon in her hair.   15
Too bad that bus just cut her off.
One eighteen p.m.
The girl's not there any more.
Was she dumb enough to go in, or wasn't she?
That we'll see when they carry them out.   20

One nineteen p.m.
No one seems to be going in.
Instead a fat baldy's coming out.
Like he's looking for something in his pockets and
at one nineteen and fifty seconds   25
he goes back for those lousy gloves of his.

It's one twenty p.m.
The time, how it drags.
Should be any moment now.
Not yet.   30
Yes, this is it.
The bomb, it goes off.

YUSEF KOMUNYAKAA

Boat People   1988

After midnight they load up.
A hundred shadows move about blindly.
Something close to sleep
hides low voices drifting
toward a red horizon. Tonight's   5
a blue string, the moon's pull —
this boat's headed somewhere.
Lucky to have gotten past
searchlights low-crawling the sea,
like a woman shaking water   10
from her long dark hair.

Calm over everything, a change
of heart. Twelve times in three days
they've been lucky,
clinging to each other in gray mist.   15
Now Thai fishermen gaze out across
the sea as it changes color,

hands shading their eyes
like sailors do,
minds on robbery & rape.   20
Sunlight burns blood-orange
till nothing makes sense.
Storm warnings crackle from a radio.
Gold shines in their teeth.
The Thai fishermen turn away.   25
Not enough water for the trip.
The boat people cling to each other,
their faces like yellow sea grapes,
wounded by doubt & salt air.
Dusk hangs over the water.   30
Sea sick, they daydream Jade Mountain
a whole world away, half-drunk
on what they hunger to become.

ALLEN GINSBERG

America   *1956*

America I've given you all and now I'm nothing.
America two dollars and twentyseven cents January 17, 1956.
I can't stand my own mind.
America when will we end the human war?
Go fuck yourself with your atom bomb.   5
I don't feel good don't bother me.
I won't write my poem till I'm in my right mind.
America when will you be angelic?
When will you take off your clothes?
When will you look at yourself through the grave?   10
When will you be worthy of your million Trotskyites?°
America why are your libraries full of tears?
America when will you send your eggs to India?
I'm sick of your insane demands.
When can I go into the supermarket and buy what I need with my
    good looks?   15
America after all it is you and I who are perfect not the next world.
Your machinery is too much for me.
You made me want to be a saint.
There must be some other way to settle this argument.

---

11. **Trotskyites:** Communists who continued to consider Leon Trotsky a legitimate leader.

Burroughs° is in Tangiers I don't think he'll come back it's sinister.   20
Are you being sinister or is this some form of practical joke?
I'm trying to come to the point.
I refuse to give up my obsession.
America stop pushing I know what I'm doing.
America the plum blossoms are falling.   25
I haven't read the newspapers for months, everyday somebody goes on
    trial for murder.
America I feel sentimental about the Wobblies.°
America I used to be a communist when I was a kid I'm not sorry.
I smoke marijuana every chance I get.
I sit in my house for days on end and stare at the roses in the closet.   30
When I go to Chinatown I get drunk and never get laid.
My mind is made up there's going to be trouble.
You should have seen me reading Marx.
My psychoanalyst thinks I'm perfectly right.
I won't say the Lord's Prayer.   35
I have mystical visions and cosmic vibrations.
America I still haven't told you what you did to Uncle Max after he
    came over from Russia.
I'm addressing you.
Are you going to let your emotional life be run by Time Magazine?
I'm obsessed by Time Magazine.   40
I read it every week.
Its cover stares at me every time I slink past the corner candystore.
I read it in the basement of the Berkeley Public Library.
It's always telling me about responsibility. Businessmen are serious.
    Movie producers are serious. Everybody's serious but me.
It occurs to me that I am America.   45
I am talking to myself again.

Asia is rising against me.
I haven't got a chinaman's chance.
I'd better consider my national resources.
My national resources consist of two joints of marijuana millions of
    genitals an unpublishable private literature that jetplanes 1400
    miles an hour and twentyfive-thousand mental institutions.   50
I say nothing about my prisons nor the millions of underprivileged
    who live in my flowerpots under the light of five hundred suns.
I have abolished the whorehouses of France, Tangiers is the next to go.
My ambition is to be President despite the fact that I'm a Catholic.

---

20. Burroughs: William S. Burroughs (b. 1914), an American author whose harrowing works
about life as a drug addict were written when he was an expatriate living abroad in Mexico
and Tangiers.   **27. Wobblies:** Members of the radical International Workers of the World.

America how can I write a holy litany in your silly mood?

I will continue like Henry Ford my strophes are as individual as his au- 55
tomobiles more so they're all different sexes.

America I will send you strophes $2500 apiece $500 down on your old
strophe

America free Tom Mooney°

America save the Spanish Loyalists

America Sacco & Vanzetti must not die

America I am the Scottsboro boys. 60

America when I was seven momma took me to Communist Cell meetings they sold us garbanzos a handful per ticket a ticket costs a nickel
and the speeches were free everybody was angelic and sentimental
about the workers it was all so sincere you have no idea what a good
thing the party was in 1835 Scott Nearing° was a grand old man a
real mensch Mother Bloor the Silk-strikers' Ewig-Weibliche made me
cry I once saw the Yiddish orator Israel Amter° plain. Everybody
must have been a spy.

America you don't really want to go to war.

America it's them bad Russians.

Them Russians them Russians and them Chinamen. And them Russians.

The Russia wants to eat us alive. The Russia's power mad. She wants
to take our cars from out our garages. 65

Her wants to grab Chicago. Her needs a Red *Reader's Digest*. Her wants
our auto plants in Siberia. Him big bureaucracy running our fill-
ingstations.

That no good. Ugh. Him make Indians learn read. Him need big black
niggers. Hah. Her make us all work sixteen hours a day. Help.

America this is quite serious.

America this is the impression I get from looking in the television set.

America is this correct? 70

I'd better get right down to the job.

It's true I don't want to join the Army or turn lathes in precision parts
factories, I'm nearsighted and psychopathic anyway.

America I'm putting my queer shoulder to the wheel.

---

57. Tom Mooney: Labor organizer convicted of a bombing based on perjured evidence.
60. Scott Nearing: A radical economist; **Mother Bloor . . . Israel Amter:** New York–based
leaders of the American Communist Party.

LAWRENCE FERLINGHETTI

Two Scavengers in a Truck, Two Beautiful People in a Mercedes

1979

At the stoplight waiting for the light
     Nine A.M. downtown San Francisco
 a bright yellow garbage truck
    with two garbagemen in red plastic blazers
  standing on the back stoop   5
     one on each side hanging on
  and looking down into
      an elegant open Mercedes
  with an elegant couple in it
The man   10
   in a hip three-piece linen suit
    with shoulder-length blond hair & sunglasses
The young blond woman so casually coifed
     with a short skirt and colored stockings
 on the way to his architect's office   15
And the two scavengers up since Four A.M.
      grungy from their route
   on the way home
The older of the two with grey iron hair
     and hunched back   20
   looking down like some
     gargoyle Quasimodo
And the younger of the two
     also with sunglasses & longhair
 about the same age as the Mercedes driver 25
And both scavengers gazing down
     as from a great distance
   at the cool couple
 as if they were watching some odorless TV ad
    in which everything is always possible 30
And the very red light for an instant
    holding all four close together
 as if anything at all were possible
      between them
  across that small gulf   35
    in the high seas
      of this democracy

RELATED COMMENTARIES: *Allen Ginsberg, "On His Poetic Craft," page 1260; Michael S. Harper, "On Black American and African Writing," page 1265; Robert Hayden, "On Negro Poetry," page 1266.*

15

POET TO POET

We're all writing the same poem.
– ROBERT DUNCAN

Just as we have seen that authors of stories interact with one another in ways that help us define and understand their writing, we can see that poets also relate to the work of others. The poet Adrienne Rich has described her own experience of poetry as a child:

> I thought that the poets in the anthologies were the only real poets, that their being in the anthologies was proof of this, though some were classified as "great" and others as "minor." I owed much to these anthologies: *Silver Pennies*; the constant outflow of volumes edited by Louis Untermeyer; *The Cambridge Book of Poetry for Children*; Palgrave's *Golden Treasury*; the *Oxford Book of English Verse*. . . . I still believed that poets were inspired by some transcendental authority and spoke from some extraordinary height.

Poets often respond very strongly to other poets' work. Margaret Atwood has described her emotions when she heard Rich read from her book *Diving into the Wreck* (1973): "When I first heard the author read from it, I felt as though the top of my head was being attacked, sometimes with an ice pick, sometimes with a blunter instrument: a hatchet or a hammer." Atwood, in *her* turn, reminds the reader of Emily Dickinson's description of how she knew something she read was poetry: "If I feel physically as if the top of my head were taken off, I know that it is poetry."

You will find in your reading that it is not only modern poets who are so excited by the words of another poet. When a friend introduced John Keats to the translation of Homer by the Elizabethan poet George Chapman, they stayed up all night reading to each other. As Keats walked home at dawn he was already composing his sonnet, "On First Looking into Chapman's Homer." The poem was finished and reached his friend by the first mail, only a few hours later.

JOHN KEATS

On First Looking into Chapman's Homer   1816

Much have I travell'd in the realms of gold,
    And many goodly states and kingdoms seen;
    Round many western islands have I been
Which bards in fealty to Apollo° hold.
Oft of one wide expanse had I been told   5
    That deep-browed Homer ruled as his demesne;°
    Yet never did I breathe its pure serene°
Till I heard Chapman° speak out loud and bold:
Then felt I like some watcher of the skies
    When a new planet swims into his ken;   10
Or like stout Cortez° when with eagle eyes
    He star'd at the Pacific — and all his men
Look'd at each other with a wild surmise —
    Silent upon a peak in Darien.

In his mood of exhilaration, Keats made a mistake in the name of the Spanish explorer who first saw the Pacific (it was Balboa and not "Cortez"), but critics have never felt that this diminishes the effect of his poem.

Many poets also have poets as friends, they translate one another's poems from other languages, they read their poems to each other, they send each other copies of new manuscripts, they publish magazines of each other's poetry. In the sense that living writers are part of a community, they also are an important influence on each other. To speak of a poem from an earlier generation "influencing" a younger writer, however, is more complicated. In a discussion of young painters that applies equally well to young poets, art critic Michael Baxadall has pointed out that to say a writer or a text from an earlier generation "influences" a younger writer is misleading, since a poem written by a poet who is no longer living cannot "do" anything. It is the younger writer who *does* something. Baxadall drew up a list of the things that the younger writer can do. If the young writer is moved to respond to something

---

4. Apollo: Greek god of poetry. **6. demesne:** Domain. **7. serene:** Atmosphere.
8. Chapman: George Chapman (c. 1560–1634), Elizabethan poet whose translations of Homer's Greek epics *Iliad* and *Odyssey* Keats found superior to the eighteenth-century translations with which he was familiar. **11. Cortez:** Keats mistakenly identifies Hernando Cortés, not Vasco Núñez de Balboa, as the first European to view the Pacific Ocean from Darien, a peak in Panama.

by an older writer, the younger — in just the same way that a young painter responds to the work of an older artist — can

> draw on, resort to, avail oneself of, appropriate from, have recourse to, adapt, misunderstand, refer to, pick up, take on, engage with, react to, quote, differentiate oneself from, assimilate oneself to, assimilate, align oneself with, copy, address, paraphrase, absorb, make a variation on, revive, continue, remodel, ape, emulate, travesty, parody, extract from, distort, attend to, resist, simplify, reconstitute, elaborate on, develop, face up to, master, subvert, perpetuate, reduce, promote, respond to, transform, tackle.... [E]veryone will be able to think of others.

As we have seen in Keats's response to Homer, whichever way a young poet responds to the work of another poet, the result will be poetry.

For women readers today, the early centuries of poetry in English can present a difficult hurdle. Because of social attitudes, it is not until the nineteenth century that poetry written by women begins to play an important role in the poetic tradition. However, as critic Jan Montefiore shows us in her analysis of a sonnet by Edna St. Vincent Millay, an American poet of the 1920s, women poets did not feel that they were entirely excluded from this tradition, and they did not hesitate to take it and mold it for their own work. Montefiore writes,

> Millay's best-known sequence of love sonnets, *Fatal Interview*, depends on an individual voice speaking with a poetic vocabulary (thematic as well as lexical) which is drawn from Elizabethan poetry as reread by the Romantics, as in this excerpt from sonnet VIII:
>
> > Yet in an hour to come, disdainful dust,
> > You shall be bowed and brought to bed with me.
> > While the blood roars, or when the blood is rust
> > About a broken engine, this shall be.
> > If not today, then later; if not here,
> > On the green grass, with sighing and delight,
> > Then under it, all in good time, my dear,
> > We shall be laid together in the night.
>
> The poet's confidence and ease in handling the sonnet form are immediately apparent; she slides effortlessly from the twentieth-century image of "rust / About a broken engine" to the "timeless" line "On the green grass, with sighing and delight," using the associative rhymes "rust" and "dust" and the emphatic alliteration of "bowed and brought to bed" with an effect of relish, not cliché. Her appropriation of literary tradition is equally apparent in the way that the counterposing of love and death, the brevity of human life and the sleep of the grave, recalls Shakespeare, Marvell, and Catullus in a *cantabile* lyricism formed on Yeats. This is not an allusive poem; rather its themes are smoothed with poetic handling, and it is written in a style which assumes that poetry is timeless.

The term *allusive* that Montefiore uses, which means to allude or refer to some other writing, suggests one of the ways in which a poet responds to another poem. It is one of several ways that are part of the poet's means, the tools a poet uses to make a poem. Here are some of the most common you will find in your reading.

QUOTATION

Many poets quote directly or indirectly from other poems. Sometimes the use of someone else's words is indicated by quotation marks, but more often the quotation is left without any marks to indicate it. The writer wants to leave it to the reader, whether or not the different voice in the poem is heard. One of the uses of quotation that you will find is to give the poem a more general meaning or to present the poem in a clearer historical perspective. The California poet Robert Duncan used a quote from the Greek poet Pindar as the title and the source of ideas for one of his major poems, *A Poem Beginning with a Line by Pindar*. The line from Pindar that begins the poem is "The light foot hears you and the brightness begins." In the poem, Duncan alludes to Walt Whitman's elegy on the death of Lincoln, *When Lilacs Last in the Dooryard Bloom'd:*

> What
> if lilacs last in *this* dooryard bloomd?

A few lines later he quotes directly from Whitman, using quotation marks:

> How sad "amid lanes and through old woods"
> echoes Whitman's love for Lincoln!

Marianne Moore used many quotations in her poetry. Often it was material from magazine articles or books she was reading, or phrases that she took from other poets or writers, sometimes slightly altering them. Consider these lines from the poem "The Student":

> . . . With us, a
> school — like the singing tree of which
> the leaves were mouths singing in concert
> is both a tree of knowledge
> and of liberty. . . .

Moore tells us in a note to the poem that she adapted the sentence "Each leaf was a mouth, and every leaf joined in concert" from the book *The Arabian Nights.*

A poet who was influenced by Moore, Amy Clampitt includes a note on the line in her poem *The Outer Bar* that describes the waves striking the sandbar:

> chain-gang archangels that in their prismatic
> frenzy fall, gall and gash the daylight. . . .

Clampitt's note points out that " 'fall, gall and gash the daylight' . . . derives, of course, from 'The Windhover' by Gerard Manley Hopkins."

Quotation is also used to "engage with," if we use another of the ways younger writers respond to other poems that we listed a few paragraphs ago.

In the opening lines of her poem "the closing of the south park road," Tobey Hiller uses a quotation from Emily Dickinson:

the closing of the south park road

happens every year between Thanksgiving and Christmas
just when the light grows lucid, forgiving nothing and
disappearing *into beauty,*
as Emily says

on these days the air over the water opens into a hard wise body
lying low and immortal over everything it loves.

In the same way, Langston Hughes uses the last line from the song "Dixie" for a bitter, ironic comment on racism in "Song for a Dark Girl":

Way Down South in Dixie
   (Break the heart of me)
They hung my black young lover
   To a cross roads tree.
Way Down South in Dixie
   (Bruised body high in air)
I asked the white Lord Jesus
   What was the use of prayer.

As the critic Helen Vendler writes, "All cultural production comes about from constant interchanges of past works and ideas with current ones."

PARAPHRASE

Another way that a poet may use another poet's words is to **paraphrase** a line or a stanza. The denotative meaning of paraphrase is "to render freely, or amplify, a passage, or express its sense in other words." In his poem "Journey of the Magi," T. S. Eliot paraphrased a section from a sermon by the early English religious writer Lancelot Andrewes. This is the section from Andrewes's "Nativity Sermon" XV:

It was no summer progress. A cold coming they had of it at this time
of the year, just the worst time of the year to take a journey, and specially a long journey in. The ways deep, the weather sharp, the days
short, the sun furthest off, *in solstitio brumali,* "the very dead of winter."

This is Eliot's paraphrase, which he sets off with quotation marks to show that there is a source for the lines:

"A cold coming we had of it,
Just the worst time of the year
For a journey, and such a long journey:
The ways deep and the weather sharp,
The very dead of winter."

Eliot's poems were often a maze of unidentified paraphrases and translations. He felt that this was one way to respond to the traditions behind his poetry. As he wrote in an essay on Elizabethan drama, "One of the surest tests is the way in which a poet borrows. Immature poets imitate; mature poets steal; bad poets deface what they take; and good poets make it into something better, or at least something different." You should also read the excerpt from Eliot's essay "Tradition and the Individual Talent" in Chapter 18, Commentaries on Poetry and Poets.

IMITATION

At some point in their struggle to find their own voice, young writers usually try every form of traditional poetry. Sometimes in their mature work they will casually begin to imitate the work of another poet or another poetic style. The American poet James Merrill was very skillful at slipping in and out of a wide range of poetic voices. Often he used rhyme and near rhyme for groups of lines within his poems. As an example, in his long poem *Coda: The Higher Keys,* in addition to a crowd of allusions to other writers and other poems, his elegant diction and perfect rhyme in lines 120–28 suggest that the setting of the poem is an eighteenth-century English ballroom:

> . . . A splendor
> Across lawns meets, in Sandover's tall time —
> Dappled mirrors, its own eye. Should rhyme
> Calling to rhyme awaken the odd snore,
> No harm done. I shall study to ignore
> Looks that more boldly with each session yearn
> Toward the buffet where steaming silver urn,
> Cucumber sandwiches, rum punch, fudge laced
> With hashish cater to whatever taste.

PARODY

There is a saying that "imitation is the sincerest form of flattery," and parody achieves the same result, by paying an indirect tribute to the popularity of the poet whose work is the subject of the parody. The denotative meaning of parody is "a composition in which an author's characteristics are humorously imitated." Parodies have been written of almost every well-known writer, though they often are more malicious than humorous. Here is one written in the 1920s by Hugh Kingsmill that is humorous. The writer being parodied is A. E. Housman.

HUGH KINGSMILL

What, Still Alive at Twenty-two?   1920

> What, still alive at twenty-two,
> A clean, upstanding chap like you?
> Sure, if your throat 'tis hard to slit,
> Slit your girl's, and swing for it.

Like enough, you won't be glad   5
When they come to hang you, lad:
But bacon's not the only thing
That's cured by hanging from a string.

So, when the spilt ink of the night
Spreads o'er the blotting-pad of light,   10
Lads whose job is still to do
Shall whet their knives, and think of you.

ALLUSION

The denotative meaning of **allusion** — "to allude to" — means to "refer indirectly to something presumably known to the listener or reader." It is different from quotation because it is indirect. If you allude to something, you name it, or suggest it, and readers add their own understanding of the context. In his poem "The Love Song of J. Alfred Prufrock," T. S. Eliot alludes to Shakespeare with the line "I know the voices dying with a dying fall." Shakespeare's phrase, from *Twelfth Night*, is "If music be the food of love, play on. . . . That strain again! It had a dying fall." In act 2, scene 2 of *Hamlet*, Shakespeare alludes to the *Iliad* in Hamlet's soliloquy. After listening to one of the players begin to weep as he described the grief of Hecuba, Queen of Troy, at the death of her husband, Priam, Hamlet bursts out,

> For Hecuba!
> What's Hecuba to him, or he to Hecuba,
> That he should weep for her?

Matthew Arnold, in his poem "Dover Beach" (p. 1018), alludes to the Greek dramatist Sophocles when he describes the eternal note of sadness he hears in the sea:

> Sophocles long ago
> Heard it on the Aegean.

In the titles of her poems, Adrienne Rich often alludes to other poems and writers. The title "The Demon Lover" is a phrase from Samuel Taylor Coleridge's "Kubla Khan." "A Valediction Forbidding Mourning" is also the title of a poem by John Donne, and "When We Dead Awaken" is the title of the last play by the Norwegian playwright Henrik Ibsen.

In our discussion of quotation, we have already read some examples of allusion. In your reading you will find many other poets who use allusion to develop the themes or the language of their poetry.

ADDRESS AND TRIBUTE

Another of the ways poets respond to other poets is to address them directly, and there is a long tradition of poetry written as a **tribute** from one writer to another. A well-known example is the Elizabethan dramatist and poet Ben Jonson's tribute to his friend William Shakespeare. The poem introduced the first Folio of Shakespeare's plays, published in 1623.

BEN JONSON

To the Memory of My Beloved, The Author, Mr. William Shakespeare, and What He Hath Left Us

1623

To draw no envy, Shakespeare, on thy name
    Am I thus ample to thy book and fame,
While I confess thy writings to be such
    As neither man nor Muse can praise too much.
'Tis true, and all men's suffrage. But these ways   5
    Were not the paths I meant unto thy praise;
For silliest ignorance on these may light,
    Which, when it sounds at best, but echoes right;
Or blind affection, which doth ne'er advance
    The truth, but gropes, and urgeth all by chance;   10
Or crafty malice might pretend this praise,
    And think to ruin where it seemed to raise.
These are as some infamous bawd or whore
    Should praise a matron. What could hurt her more?
But thou art proof against them, and, indeed,   15
    Above th' ill fortune of them, or the need.
I therefore will begin. Soul of the age!
    The applause! delight! the wonder of our stage!
My Shakespeare, rise; I will not lodge thee by
    Chaucer or Spenser, or bid Beaumont lie   20
A little further to make thee a room:°
    Thou art a monument without a tomb,
And art alive still while thy book doth live,
    And we have wits to read and praise to give.
That I not mix thee so, my brain excuses,   25
    I mean with great, but disproportioned Muses;
For, if I thought my judgment were of years,
    I should commit thee surely with thy peers,
And tell how far thou didst our Lyly outshine,
    Or sporting Kyd, or Marlowe's mighty line.°   30
And though thou hadst small Latin and less Greek,
    From thence to honor thee I would not seek
For names, but call forth thund'ring Aeschylus,
    Euripides, and Sophocles° to us,

20–21. Chaucer . . . Spenser . . . Beaumont: Geoffrey Chaucer, Edmund Spenser, and Francis Beaumont were buried in the poet's corner at Westminster Abbey, while Shakespeare was buried in Stratford-upon-Avon. **29–30. Lyly . . . Kyd . . . or Marlowe's mighty line:** John Lyly, Thomas Kyd, and Christopher Marlowe were fine Elizabethan dramatists who still did not measure up to Shakespeare. **33–34. Aeschylus, Euripides, . . . Sophocles:** Aeschylus, Euripides, and Sophocles were the greatest of the classic Greek tragedians.

Pacuvius, Accius, him of Cordova dead,°   35
     To life again, to hear thy buskin° tread
And shake a stage; or, when thy socks° were on,
     Leave thee alone for the comparison
Of all that insolent Greece or haughty Rome
     Sent forth, or since did from their ashes come.   40
Triumph, my Britain; thou hast one to show
     To whom all scenes of Europe homage owe.
He was not of an age, but for all time!
     And all the Muses still were in their prime
When like Apollo he came forth to warm   45
     Our ears, or like a Mercury to charm.
Nature herself was proud of his designs,
     And joyed to wear the dressing of his lines,
Which were so richly spun, and woven so fit,
     As, since, she will vouchsafe no other wit: 50
The merry Greek, tart Aristophanes,°
     Neat Terence, witty Plautus° now not please,
But antiquated and deserted lie,
     As they were not of Nature's family.
Yet must I not give Nature all; thy Art,   55
     My gentle Shakespeare, must enjoy a part.
For though the poet's matter Nature be,
     His Art doth give the fashion; and that he
Who casts to write a living line must sweat
     (Such as thine are) and strike the second heat   60
Upon the muses' anvil; turn the same,
     And himself with it, that he thinks to frame,
Or for the laurel he may gain a scorn;
     For a good poet's made as well as born.
And such wert thou! Look how the father's face   65
     Lives in his issue; even so the race
Of Shakespeare's mind and manners brightly shines
     In his well-turned and true-filed lines,
In each of which he seems to shake a lance,°
     As brandished at the eyes of ignorance.   70
Sweet swan of Avon, what a sight it were
     To see thee in our waters yet appear,
And make those flights upon the banks of Thames

---

35. Pacuvius, Accius, him of Cordova dead: In the first century AD, Seneca the Younger "of Cordova" was the greatest of the classic Latin tragedians; his second century BC predecessors Marcus Pacuvius and Lucius Accius were minor tragedians whom Jonson cites more for rhetorical effect than for genuine comparison to Shakespeare. **36. bushkin:** The footwear of actors in tragedies were buskins; hence, a buskin is a symbol of tragedy. **37. socks:** Comic actors wore socks; therefore, a sock symbolizes comedy. **51. Aristophanes:** Greek satirical writer and dramatist. **52. Terence . . . Plautus:** Roman authors of comedic plays. **69. shake a lance:** Pun on "Shakespeare."

That so did take Eliza and our James!°
But stay; I see thee in the hemisphere   75
    Advanced and made a constellation there!
Shine forth, thou star of poets, and with rage
    Or influence° chide or cheer the drooping stage,
Which, since thy flight from hence, hath mourned like night,
    And despairs day, but for thy volume's light.   80

Young writers often feel that it is important to speak directly to the older writers who have had an effect on their own work. A good example is the poem "A Pact," by the then-young American poet Ezra Pound, addressing the classic older American poet Walt Whitman.

EZRA POUND

A Pact   1913

I made a pact with you, Walt Whitman —
I have detested you long enough.
I come to you as a grown child
who has had a pig-headed father;
I am old enough now to make friends.
It was you that broke the new wood,
Now is the time for carving.
We have one sap and one root —
Let there be commerce between us.

Often the response to the other poet is a way of paying tribute to the other writer's work. In his poem "A Supermarket in California," Allen Ginsberg also addresses Walt Whitman, paying him an affectionate tribute.

ALLEN GINSBERG

A Supermarket in California   1956

What thoughts I have of you tonight, Walt Whitman, for I walked down the sidestreets under the trees with a headache self-conscious looking at the full moon.

In my hungry fatigue, and shopping for images, I went into the neon fruit supermarket, dreaming of your enumerations!

What peaches and what penumbras! Whole families shopping at night! Aisles full of husbands! Wives in the avocados, babies in the

---

74. Eliza and our James: Queen Elizabeth I and King James I. **78. constellation ... influence:** In mythology, great heroes were often transformed into star constellations upon their death, and celestial bodies were believed to exert an influence upon earthly affairs.

tomatoes! — and you, García Lorca, what were you doing down by the watermelons!

I saw you, Walt Whitman, childless, lonely old grubber, poking among the meats in the refrigerator and eyeing the grocery boys.

I heard you asking questions of each: Who killed the pork chops? What price bananas? Are you my Angel?

I wandered in and out of the brilliant stacks of cans following you, and followed in my imagination by the store detective.

We strode down the open corridors together in our solitary fancy tasting artichokes, possessing every frozen delicacy, and never passing the cashier.

Where are we going, Walt Whitman? The doors close in an hour. Which way does your beard point tonight?

(I touch your book and dream of our odyssey in the supermarket and feel absurd.)

Will we walk all night through solitary streets? The trees add shade to shade, lights out in the houses, we'll both be lonely.

Will we stroll dreaming of the lost America of love past blue automobiles in driveways, home to our silent cottage?

Ah, dear father, graybeard, lonely old courage-teacher, what America did you have when Charon quit poling his ferry and you got out on a smoking bank and stood watching the boat disappear on the black waters of Lethe?

Berkeley, 1955

The García Lorca alluded to in the poem is the Spanish poet who was murdered by the Fascists during the Spanish Civil War.

A tribute to another poet can also be casual and amusing. In his poem "Oatmeal," Galway Kinnell imagines that he is eating oatmeal with John Keats, and this gives him a chance to talk about a problem with the text of one of Keats's best-known poems. Kinnell's reference to Patrick Kavanagh in the final line is an inside joke for readers who may recognize the Irish writer whose best-known poem is titled "The Great Hunger."

GALWAY KINNELL

Oatmeal

1990

I eat oatmeal for breakfast.
I make it on the hot plate and put skimmed milk on it.
I eat it alone.
I am aware it is not good to eat oatmeal alone.
Its consistency is such that it is better for your mental health if somebody eats it with you.
That is why I often think up an imaginary companion to have breakfast with.

5

Possibly it is even worse to eat oatmeal with an imaginary companion.
Nevertheless, yesterday morning, I ate my oatmeal — porridge, as he
    called it — with John Keats.
Keats said I was absolutely right to invite him: due to its glutinous tex-
    ture, gluey lumpishness, hint of slime, and unusual willingness to
    disintegrate, oatmeal must never be eaten alone.
He said that in his opinion, however, it is perfectly OK to eat it with an
    imaginary companion,   10
and he himself had enjoyed memorable porridges with Edmund
    Spenser and John Milton.
Even if eating oatmeal with an imaginary companion is not as whole-
    some as Keats claims, still, you can learn something from it.
Yesterday morning, for instance, Keats told me about writing the "Ode
    to a Nightingale."
He had a heck of a time finishing it — those were his words — "Oi 'ad
    a 'eck of a toime," he said, more or less, speaking through his por-
    ridge.
He wrote it quickly, on scraps of paper, which he then stuck in his
    pocket,   15
but when he got home he couldn't figure out the order of the stanzas,
    and he and a friend spread the papers on a table, and they made
    some sense of them, but he isn't sure to this day if they got it right.
An entire stanza may have slipped into the lining of his jacket through
    a hole in the pocket.
He still wonders about the occasional sense of drift between stanzas,
and the way here and there a line will go into the configuration of a
    Moslem at prayer, then raise itself up and peer about, and then lay
    itself down slightly off the mark, causing the poem to move forward
    with God's reckless wobble.
He said someone told him that later in life Wordsworth heard about
    the scraps of paper on the table, and tried shuffling some stanzas of
    his own, but only made matters worse.   20
I would not have known about any of this but for my reluctance to eat
    oatmeal alone.
When breakfast was over, John recited "To Autumn."
He recited it slowly, with much feeling, and he articulated the words
    lovingly, and his odd accent sounded sweet.
He didn't offer the story of writing "To Autumn," I doubt if there is
    much of one.
But he did say the sight of a just-harvested oat field got him started
    on it,   25
and two of the lines, "For Summer has o'er-brimmed their clammy
    cells" and "Thou watchest the last oozings hours by hours," came to
    him while eating oatmeal alone.
I can see him — drawing a spoon through the stuff, gazing into the
    glimmering furrows, muttering — and it occurs to me:
maybe there is no sublime; only the shining of the amnion's tatters.

For supper tonight I am going to have a baked potato left over from
lunch.
I am aware that a leftover baked potato is damp, slippery, and simultaneously gummy and crumbly,   30
and therefore I'm going to invite Patrick Kavanagh to join me.

RELATED COMMENTARIES: *Marilyn Chin, "On the Canon," page 1249; T. S.
Eliot, From "Tradition and the Individual Talent," page 1253.*

16

READING, THINKING, AND WRITING ABOUT POETRY

It is difficult
to get the news from poems
    yet men die miserably every day
        for lack
of what is found there.
– WILLIAM CARLOS WILLIAMS, from
"Asphodel, That Greeny Flower"

Perhaps it is because poetry *looks* different on the page, or perhaps it is because poetry sometimes wears its heart on its sleeve, but for many readers the experience of reading a poem seems different from reading a short story or a play. It is easy to be put off by the formal arrangement of lines and verses and by language that describes private emotions and hidden dreams. Reading poetry, however, is an experience very similar to reading anything else. You read a poem for what you will find there, for what it tells you about yourself, your life, your world. Then you read it a second time for the pleasure you find in the way the poet uses words.

In Chapter 9, "What Is a Poem?," you learned that it will help you to understand a poem if you can separate it into two parts as you read it over. First read the poem for what it is about, its subject and its theme; then read it to appreciate further the skill and imagination the poet has used in presenting you with this theme.

Even if you are not entirely sure that you understand everything in the poem in your first reading, you can be struck by the writer's skill. If we take a very short poem as an example, you can see that it is often the poet's ability to choose one thing out of the mass of small details that brings a poem to life. Here is a haiku by the Japanese poet Buson quoted by the American writer Jack Kerouac in his introduction to his own "Western Haikus":

> The nightingale is singing,
> Its small mouth
> open.

The description "Its small mouth / open" suggests the nightingale's song so simply and yet so vividly that the group of three short lines surrounded by the white space on the page seems to reverberate like the nightingale song itself in your imagination. Other poems can suggest an emotional situation so clearly and with such intensity that you find the words stay in your memory, even if you could not write them down exactly if you were asked. This short English medieval lyric has been part of our emotional storehouse for more than four hundred years:

> Western wind, when wilt thou blow,
> The small rain down can rain?
> Christ, if my love were in my arms,
> And I in my bed again!

You do not have to be told to read poems like these more than once. Their appeal to your feelings is immediate and unforgettable. The skill of the author has been in finding the small moment that suggests the poem's theme — the wonder of experiencing nature in Buson's haiku, and the joy of love in the medieval lyric.

Longer poems can be more difficult for the reader. Sometimes the language is unfamiliar; sometimes the theme is not clear at first reading. The general rule is to read the poem straight through to the end, even if you are unsure of the meaning of all the words or phrases the first time around. Inexperienced readers often stop after just a few lines if they begin to feel confused by what the poet appears to be saying.

If this happens, you should disregard your sense that you have lost your bearings in the poem and continue reading until you have finished it. Often the whole poem will clarify the meaning of the early images or lines. Unless you give yourself the opportunity to read the entire poem, you will not have a fair chance to find out what it is saying. For example, when you begin reading the poem "since feeling is first" (1926) by the American writer E. E. Cummings, you might stumble on the word *syntax* or the phrase "syntax of things" in the third line of the poem. Do not stop reading to reach for a dictionary to help you puzzle out what the poem means by "syntax." Just continue on to the end of the poem. Reach for the dictionary, if necessary, *after* you have read it all the way through the first time.

> since feeling is first
> who pays any attention
> to the syntax of things
> will never wholly kiss you;
> wholly to be a fool   5
> while Spring is in the world
>
> my blood approves,
> and kisses are a better fate
> than wisdom
> lady I swear by all flowers. Don't cry   10
> — the best gesture of my brain is less than
> your eyelids' flutter which says

> we are for each other: then
> laugh, leaning back in my arms
> for life's not a paragraph

15

> And death I think is no parenthesis

When you go back to the beginning of the poem to give it a second reading, you will find that the last two lines illuminate the meaning of the word *syntax* that might have given you trouble on your first reading. The poet is using literary terms in a playful manner to write a love poem, making the point that life is different from literature and should be lived fully and instinctively while there is still time. The speaker in the poem is urging his lady to follow the impulse of her heart, which he tells her is worth more than his poem.

In your study of poetry, you can admire the skill with which Cummings employs his technical means of alliteration, rhythm, and paradox. Aware that the poem was published in 1926, before the sexual revolution of the 1960s, you might also understand that the poet has written it to persuade his "lady" not to wait for a wedding ring but to abandon her caution, urging her to acknowledge the physical attraction between them and become his lover right away. Despite Cummings's use of lowercase letters and the open form of his poem, you can recognize the traditional theme of *carpe diem*, the Latin words for "seize the day," in this modern poem.

It is possible, of course, for you to pay close attention as you follow the words in a poem, read it carefully straight through to the end, reread it a second time, and still find its meaning elusive. Then you might find writing a *paraphrase* of the subject of the poem helps you to understand it as you attempt to put the poem into your own words. Your paraphrase of the Cummings's poem might look something like this:

> Feeling is more important than thinking. A person who thinks too much about the meaning of life will miss the pleasure of enjoying love. When you're young, you should throw caution to the winds and follow your heart. A love affair should take precedence over everything. Don't be sad thinking it won't work out. Letting yourself feel an attraction for someone is more important than any thought you can have. Relax and enjoy being with your lover, because life is short — it isn't as long as a paragraph, it's only a sentence. And death is a full stop — it isn't a parenthesis, it's a period.

Usually the effort of trying to find your own words to express the subject of a poem will help you to understand it. Writing a paraphrase will force you to spend more time focusing on the poem to clarify your thoughts. This is the first step in the process of thinking critically about poetry.

Poems are "meter-making arguments," so they usually represent an idea or develop a series of ideas in a coherent discourse. Poems are also "language charged with meaning to the utmost degree," so you may have to unravel the ideas behind the words as patiently as you would unravel a ball of string after your cat has played with it. When you write a paraphrase of a poem, you take the chance that you might be mistaken about all or part of its meaning. But you also have a method of clarifying the subject that usually brings you closer to the theme or the central idea that you sense behind the poem's words.

The more skilled you become as a reader of poetry, the more readily your intuition will help you grapple with the experience of the poem. At first your study of the poet's means will give you insight into the different writers' resources as they use language to create a poem. Your increased sensitivity to meter and rhyme, diction and symbolism, and the other means used by the poet should help you to understand and enjoy the work. At the beginning of your study of poetry, it may not be possible to paraphrase the entire poem successfully, but any effort you make should help to bring you closer to the poem.

GUIDELINES FOR STUDYING POETRY

1. Make an entry in your notebook for each poem that is assigned in class, writing down the author's name, the title, and the date.
2. Read the poem through once in its entirety, regardless of whether you understand all the words.
3. When you read the poem a second time, use a dictionary to look up words you don't understand.
4. Copy the first lines of the poem into your notebook to scan the rhythm of the poem. Does it fall into any of the patterns you have studied?
5. Note what impresses you most about the way the poet uses language in the poem, in particular the poem's rhyme, its figurative language, and its diction.
6. Try to write a paraphrase of the subject of the poem, following the poet's argument closely as it develops throughout the lines of the poem. Does the poet use paradox, symbolism, allusion, or tribute? Summarize, if you can, the theme of the poem in a single sentence.
7. If you have difficulty understanding any parts of the poem, or the entire poem, write down specific questions about it so that you can ask them in class.
8. Review technical words about poetry that were used in class to be sure you understand them.

THINKING CRITICALLY ABOUT POETRY

Paraphrasing a poem will help you to understand its subject and its theme, a necessary step in the process of thinking critically about poetry. Identifying the various means the poet has used to create the poem will also help you to analyze the rhetorical strategies behind the author's choice of form for the poem. For example, you might ask yourself the following:

1. Who is the speaker in the poem? How does identifying the speaker contribute to your understanding of the poem?
2. How closely can we identify the speaker with the author of the poem?

3. What attitude toward the subject of the poem does the speaker convey? What does the poet's use of irony, paradox, hyperbole, or understatement tell us about the speaker's attitude?

4. How does the poet use metaphor or simile to bring together and contrast different ideas?

5. What are the different connotations of important words in the poem? Does their meaning depend on where they are placed in the poem?

6. Why did the poet choose this poetic form and not another?

7. Why did the poet write this poem?

8. What does the poet's use of language tell you about the audience for the poem? Is it addressed to a person close to the poet or to the general reader?

9. How might different readers interpret the poem from different critical perspectives — feminist, Marxist, historical, and so forth?

WRITING ABOUT POETRY

An assignment to write a paper about a poem will help you to focus your ideas about it and sharpen your critical thinking about what you have read. In the Appendix (p. 2081) is a discussion of several methods of writing essays about literature. You will also find two student essays about poetry, one explicating Langston Hughes's "The Negro Speaks of Rivers" and the other analyzing Robert Frost's "Mending Wall."

Many theoretical approaches lend themselves to developing your critical thinking about poetry. You can emphasize the reader's response to the text, investigating the personal connotations evoked by the poet's use of specific imagery, for example. Or you might consider the intertextual elements in a contemporary poem, comparing and contrasting it with an earlier text that you see related to it in some way.

All these critical approaches depend on your close reading of poetry. Understanding the poet's means will help you to reach deeper levels of response and to clarify your understanding of how the poet creates the text. The essays by poets and critics in Chapter 18, "Commentaries on Poetry and Poets," will also shed light on the critic's role in writing about poetry.

You will probably find it helpful to copy the poem you want to write about into your computer so that you can print out several copies of it to facilitate your annotation of the text. As you read and reread, make notes about your responses. Underline words that strike you as significant. Jot down your specific feelings and thoughts about the way the poet has used language. Trace the development of the argument and try to verbalize its effect on you. Are you intrigued, sympathetic, unsympathetic, or confused? Do you feel close or distant to the situation in the poem? What overall responses do you have to it?

In writing reader-response criticism to poetry, you should first concentrate on what it is about the poem that causes your response. Is it the subject or theme of the poem or the various poetic means the author uses? Second, you should analyze what it is about you as a reader that causes your response. Did you have trouble with the poem because you were unfamiliar or uncomfortable with the subject or theme? Were you responsive to it because you admired the poet's skill with language?

The Appendix on writing about literature will help you plan your essay in stages, whichever critical approach you take in writing it. You will also find information there about prewriting, first and final drafts, revision, and styling your essay.

17

POEMS AND POETS

MATTHEW ARNOLD (1822–1888) *was born in a village in the Thames Valley, just outside of London. When he was six his family moved to Rugby School where his father, a distinguished Victorian clergyman, had become headmaster. Arnold spent most of his life in an academic environment, first as a child at Rugby, then as a student at Oxford, and for thirty-five years as an inspector of schools for the British government. He traveled throughout England and Europe, studying educational systems and observing the lives of the people who were administering them.*

At Oxford he had a reputation as a dandy. The novelist Charlotte Brontë, who met him at that time, wrote, "His manner displeases, from his seeming foppery." His writing, however, had a seriousness that sometimes dissatisfied even Arnold himself. His major poems — among them "The Scholar Gypsy" and "Thyrsis," an elegy on the death of his friend and fellow poet Arthur Hugh Clough — had an important influence on the attitudes and the ideals of the Victorian era. He stopped writing poetry in his thirties, and for the rest of his life he was a widely read and influential critic of English society and culture. "Dover Beach," his best-known poem, was written in 1851.

RELATED COMMENTARIES: *Anthony Hecht, "The Dover Bitch," page 1269; Eric Trethewey, "The Virtue of Arnold's 'Dover Beach,' " page 1318.*

MATTHEW ARNOLD

Dover Beach 1867

The sea is calm tonight.
The tide is full, the moon lies fair
Upon the straits; — on the French coast the light
Gleams and is gone; the cliffs of England stand,
Glimmering and vast, out in the tranquil bay. 5
Come to the window, sweet is the night-air!
Only, from the long line of spray
Where the sea meets the moon-blanched land,
Listen! You hear the grating roar
Of pebbles which the waves draw back, and fling, 10

At their return, up the high strand,
Begin, and cease, and then again begin,
With tremulous cadence slow, and bring
The eternal note of sadness in.

Sophocles long ago 15
Heard it on the Aegean, and it brought
Into his mind the turbid ebb and flow
Of human misery;° we
Find also in the sound a thought,
Hearing it by this distant northern sea. 20

The Sea of Faith
Was once, too, at the full, and round earth's shore
Lay like the folds of a bright girdle furled.
But now I only hear
Its melancholy, long, withdrawing roar, 25
Retreating, to the breath
Of the night-wind, down the vast edges of drear
And naked shingles° of the world. *pebble beaches*

Ah, love, let us be true
To one another! for the world, which seems 30
To lie before us like a land of dreams,
So various, so beautiful, so new,
Hath really neither joy, nor love, nor light,
Nor certitude, nor peace, nor help for pain;
And we are here as on a darkling plain 35
Swept with confused alarms of struggle and flight,
Where ignorant armies clash by night.

☙

15–18. Sophocles long ago . . . misery: In *Antigone*, Sophocles compares the calamities that afflict the house of Oedipus to a rising tide.

W. H. AUDEN *(1907–1973) was born Wystan Hugh Auden in York, a large industrial city in northern England. He graduated from Oxford in 1930 and taught school for five years, but he was already publishing poetry and was considered one of the most exciting of a new, young group of English poets, which included Stephen Spender and C. Day Lewis.*

In the 1930s Auden's poetry reflected his dismay at the effect of the world depression on England, and also his leftist views. In 1937 he went to Spain to take part in the Civil War, but he was disturbed by the Loyalists' hostility to organized religion and returned to England without seeing active combat. In 1939 he moved to the United States, and in 1946 he became an American citizen. He returned to England as a professor of poetry at Oxford from 1956 to 1960, but in his last years he was part of the colorful cultural life of the Lower East Side in New York City.

Auden prided himself on his literary professionalism, and he wrote plays, the libretto for Igor Stravinsky's opera The Rake's Progress, *and considerable literary commentary. For many years he toured U.S. universities as an excellent reader of his own poetry.*

"Miss Gee" is one of the bitterly satirical poems he wrote while he was still living in England. "Musée des Beaux Arts" was also written a few months before his move to the United States. "In Memory of W. B. Yeats" was written a few days after Yeats's death in 1939.

W. H. AUDEN

Miss Gee

1937

Let me tell you a little story
    About Miss Edith Gee;
She lived in Clevedon Terrace
    At Number 83.

She'd a slight squint in her left eye,   5
    Her lips they were thin and small,
She had narrow sloping shoulders
    And she had no bust at all.

She'd a velvet hat with trimmings,
    And a dark-grey serge costume;   10
She lived in Clevedon Terrace
    In a small bed-sitting room.°

She'd a purple mac° for wet days,
    A green umbrella too to take,
She'd a bicycle with shopping basket   15
    And a harsh back-pedal brake.

The Church of Saint Aloysius
    Was not so very far;

---

12. bed-sitting room: A one-room apartment.   **13. mac:** A mackintosh or light raincoat.

She did a lot of knitting,
    Knitting for that Church Bazaar. 20

Miss Gee looked up at the starlight
    And said: "Does anyone care
That I live in Clevedon Terrace
    On one hundred pounds a year?"

She dreamed a dream one evening 25
    That she was the Queen of France
And the Vicar of Saint Aloysius
    Asked Her Majesty to dance.

But a storm blew down the palace,
    She was biking through a field of corn, 30
And a bull with the face of the Vicar
    Was charging with lowered horn.

She could feel his hot breath behind her,
    He was going to overtake;
And the bicycle went slower and slower 35
    Because of that back-pedal brake.

Summer made the trees a picture,
    Winter made them a wreck;
She bicycled to the evening service
    With her clothes buttoned up to her neck. 40

She passed by the loving couples,
    She turned her head away;
She passed by the loving couples
    And they didn't ask her to stay.

Miss Gee sat down in the side-aisle, 45
    She heard the organ play;
And the choir it sang so sweetly
    At the ending of the day.

Miss Gee knelt down in the side-aisle,
    She knelt down on her knees; 50
"Lead me not into temptation
    But make me a good girl, please."

The days and nights went by her
    Like waves round a Cornish wreck;°
She bicycled down to the doctor 55
    With her clothes buttoned up to her neck.

She bicycled down to the doctor,
    And rang the surgery bell;

54: Cornish wreck: The coast of Cornwall was the site of many shipwrecks.

"O, doctor, I've a pain inside me,
   And I don't feel very well."   60

Doctor Thomas looked her over,
   And then he looked some more;
Walked over to his wash-basin,
   Said: "Why didn't you come before?"

Doctor Thomas sat over his dinner,   65
   Though his wife was waiting to ring;
Rolling his bread into pellets,
   Said: "Cancer's a funny thing.

"Nobody knows what the cause is,
   Though some pretend they do;   70
It's like some hidden assassin
   Waiting to strike at you.

"Childless women get it,
   And men when they retire;
It's as if there had to be some outlet   75
   For their foiled creative fire."

His wife she rang for the servant,
   Said: "Don't be so morbid, dear";
He said: "I saw Miss Gee this evening
   And she's a goner, I fear."   80

They took Miss Gee to the hospital,
   She lay there a total wreck,
Lay in the ward for women
   With the bedclothes right up to her neck.

They laid her on the table,   85
   The students began to laugh;
And Mr. Rose the surgeon
   He cut Miss Gee in half.

Mr. Rose he turned to his students,
   Said: "Gentlemen, if you please,   90
We seldom see a sarcoma
   As far advanced as this."

They took her off the table,
   They wheeled away Miss Gee
Down to another department   95
   Where they study Anatomy.

They hung her from the ceiling,
   Yes, they hung up Miss Gee;
And a couple of Oxford Groupers
   Carefully dissected her knee.   100

W. H. AUDEN

Musée des Beaux Arts° 1938

About suffering they were never wrong,
The Old Masters: how well they understood
Its human position; how it takes place
While someone else is eating or opening a window or just walking
    dully along;
How, when the aged are reverently, passionately waiting 5
For the miraculous birth, there always must be
Children who did not specially want it to happen, skating
On a pond at the edge of the wood:
They never forgot
That even the dreadful martyrdom must run its course 10
Anyhow in a corner, some untidy spot
Where the dogs go on with their doggy life and the torturer's horse
Scratches its innocent behind on a tree.

In Brueghel's *Icarus,°* for instance: how everything turns away
Quite leisurely from the disaster; the plowman may 15
Have heard the splash, the forsaken cry,
But for him it was not an important failure; the sun shown
As it had to on the white legs disappearing into the green
Water; and the expensive delicate ship that must have seen
Something amazing, a boy falling out of the sky, 20
Had somewhere to get to and sailed calmly on.

W. H. AUDEN

In Memory of W. B. Yeats 1940

(d. January, 1939)

1

He disappeared in the dead of winter:
The brooks were frozen, the airports almost deserted,
And snow disfigured the public statues;
The mercury sank in the mouth of the dying day.
What instruments we have agree 5
The day of his death was a dark cold day.

Far from his illness
The wolves ran on through the evergreen forests,

Musée des Beaux Arts: The Museum of Fine Arts in Brussels.
14. Brueghel's Icarus: Refers to the painting *Landscape with the Fall of Icarus,* by Pieter Brueghel the Elder (c. 1525–69), in the Brussels museum. The painting represents the mythical Icarus as a tiny figure, dwarfed by other characters in the painting, as he falls into the sea.

The peasant river was untempted by the fashionable quays;
By mourning tongues
The death of the poet was kept from his poems.

But for him it was his last afternoon as himself,
An afternoon of nurses and rumors;
The provinces of his body revolted,
The squares of his mind were empty,
Silence invaded the suburbs,
The current of his feeling failed; he became his admirers.

Now he is scattered among a hundred cities
And wholly given over to unfamiliar affections,
To find his happiness in another kind of wood
And be punished under a foreign code of conscience.
The words of a dead man
Are modified in the guts of the living.

But in the importance and noise of tomorrow
When the brokers are roaring like beasts on the floor of the Bourse,°
And the poor have the sufferings to which they are fairly accustomed,
And each in the cell of himself is almost convinced of his freedom,
A few thousand will think of this day
As one thinks of a day when one did something slightly unusual.
What instruments we have agree
The day of his death was a dark cold day.

2

You were silly like us; your gift survived it all:
The parish of rich women, physical decay,
Yourself. Mad Ireland hurt you into poetry.
Now Ireland has her madness and her weather still,
For poetry makes nothing happen: it survives
In the valley of its making where executives
Would never want to tamper, flows on south
From ranches of isolation and the busy griefs,
Raw towns that we believe and die in; it survives,
A way of happening, a mouth.

3

Earth, receive an honored guest:
William Yeats is laid to rest.
Let the Irish vessel lie
Emptied of its poetry.

Time that is intolerant
Of the brave and innocent,
And indifferent in a week
To a beautiful physique,

10

15

20

25

30

35

40

45

---

25. Bourse: The Paris stock exchange.

Worships language and forgives   50
Everyone by whom it lives;
Pardons cowardice, conceit,
Lays its honours at their feet.

Time that with this strange excuse
Pardoned Kipling and his views,   55
And will pardon Paul Claudel,°
Pardons him for writing well.

In the nightmare of the dark
All the dogs of Europe bark,
And the living nations wait,   60
Each sequestered in its hate;

Intellectual disgrace
Stares from every human face,
And the seas of pity lie
Locked and frozen in each eye.   65

Follow, poet, follow right
To the bottom of the night,
With your unconstraining voice
Still persuade us to rejoice;

With the farming of a verse   70
Make a vineyard of the curse,
Sing of human unsuccess
In a rapture of distress;

In the deserts of the heart
Let the healing fountain start,   75
In the prison of his days
Teach the free man how to praise.

∞

ELIZABETH BISHOP (1911–1979) *was the daughter of a successful Boston building contractor and his Canadian wife, but her father died when she was a baby, and when she was four her mother was placed in a mental institution. Bishop was raised by grandparents and relatives in Nova Scotia and Massachusetts. She suffered from severe asthma, and she was unable to attend school until she was sixteen. Among her friends, when she entered Vassar College in 1930, were the writers Muriel Rukeyser and Mary McCarthy.*

Although Bishop grew up in a period in which talented women writers — among them Edna St. Vincent Millay, Elinor Wylie, and Louise Bogan — played a dominant role in American poetry, she found their work too traditional, and she took the modernist poet Marianne Moore (p. 1153) as a mentor and friend. Another strong

---

55–56. **Kipling . . . Claudel:** Rudyard Kipling (1865–1936) and Paul Claudel (1868–1955) were writers known for their right-wing views.

influence on her writing was her long friendship with poet Robert Lowell (p. 1285). A small trust fund made it possible for her to live as she wanted, and she spent several years in Key West, Florida. After reviving an old acquaintance with Lota de Macedo Soares, she moved with her to Brazil and remained there until Soares's suicide in 1977. Then Bishop returned to the United States to teach at Harvard.

Bishop was a careful, selective poet, and she achieved considerable critical success. She won the Pulitzer Prize and the National Book Award, and her final collection was awarded the National Book Critics Circle Award. "The Fish," one of her best-known poems, was included in her first collection North and South, published in 1946. "The Armadillo" is dedicated to Robert Lowell.

RELATED COMMENTARIES: Julia Alvarez, "Elizabeth Bishop's 'One Art'," page 1231; Elizabeth Bishop, from "Efforts of Affection: A Memoir of Marianne Moore," page 1236.

Elizabeth Bishop

The Fish
1946

I caught a tremendous fish
and held him beside the boat
half out of water, with my hook
fast in a corner of his mouth.
He didn't fight. 5
He hadn't fought at all.
He hung a grunting weight,
battered and venerable
and homely. Here and there
his brown skin hung in strips 10
like ancient wallpaper,
and its pattern of darker brown
was like wallpaper:
shapes like full-blown roses
stained and lost through age. 15
He was speckled with barnacles,
fine rosettes of lime,
and infested
with tiny white sea-lice,
and underneath two or three 20
rags of green weed hung down.
While his gills were breathing in
the terrible oxygen
— the frightening gills,
fresh and crisp with blood, 25
that can cut so badly —
I thought of the coarse white flesh
packed in like feathers,

the big bones and the little bones,
the dramatic reds and blacks   30
of his shiny entrails,
and the pink swim-bladder
like a big peony.
I looked into his eyes
which were far larger than mine   35
but shallower, and yellowed,
the irises backed and packed
with tarnished tinfoil
seen through the lenses
of old scratched isinglass.   40
They shifted a little, but not
to return my stare.
— It was more like the tipping
of an object toward the light.
I admired his sullen face,   45
the mechanism of his jaw,
and then I saw
that from his lower lip
— if you could call it a lip —
grim, wet, and weaponlike,   50
hung five old pieces of fish-line,
or four and a wire leader
with the swivel still attached,
with all their five big hooks
grown firmly in his mouth.   55
A green line, frayed at the end
where he broke it, two heavier lines,
and a fine black thread
still crimped from the strain and snap
when it broke and he got away.   60
Like medals with their ribbons
frayed and wavering,
a five-haired beard of wisdom
trailing from his aching jaw.
I stared and stared   65
and victory filled up
the little rented boat,
from the pool of bilge
where oil had spread a rainbow
around the rusted engine   70
to the bailer rusted orange,
the sun-cracked thwarts,
the oarlocks on their strings,
the gunnels — until everything

was rainbow, rainbow, rainbow!   75
And I let the fish go.

ELIZABETH BISHOP

The Armadillo   *1965*

for Robert Lowell

This is the time of year
when almost every night
the frail, illegal fire balloons appear.
Climbing the mountain height,

rising toward a saint   5
still honored in these parts,
the paper chambers flush and fill with light
that comes and goes, like hearts.

Once up against the sky it's hard
to tell them from the stars —   10
planets, that is — the tinted ones:
Venus going down, or Mars,

or the pale green one. With a wind,
they flare and falter, wobble and toss;
but if it's still they steer between   15
the kite sticks of the Southern Cross,

receding, dwindling, solemnly
and steadily forsaking us,
or, in the downdraft from a peak,
suddenly turning dangerous.   20

Last night another big one fell.
It splattered like an egg of fire
against the cliff behind the house.
The flame ran down. We saw the pair

of owls who nest there flying up   25
and up, their whirling black-and-white
stained bright pink underneath, until
they shrieked up out of sight.

The ancient owl's nest must have burned.
Hastily, all alone,   30
a glistening armadillo left the scene,
rose-flecked, head down, tail down,

and then a baby rabbit jumped out,
short-eared, to our surprise.

So soft! — a handful of intangible ash   35
with fixed, ignited eyes.

Too pretty, dreamlike mimicry!
O falling fire and piercing cry
and panic, and a weak mailed fist
clenched ignorant against the sky!   40

ELIZABETH BISHOP

One Art   *1976*

The art of losing isn't hard to master;
so many things seem filled with the intent
to be lost that their loss is no disaster.

Lose something every day. Accept the fluster
of lost door keys, the hour badly spent.   5
The art of losing isn't hard to master.

Then practice losing farther, losing faster:
places, and names, and where it was you meant
to travel. None of these will bring disaster.

I lost my mother's watch. And look! my last, or   10
next-to-last, of three loved houses went.
The art of losing isn't hard to master.

I lost two cities, lovely ones. And, vaster,
some realms I owned, two rivers, a continent.
I miss them, but it wasn't a disaster.   15

— Even losing you (the joking voice, a gesture
I love) I shan't have lied. It's evident
the art of losing's not too hard to master
though it may look like (*Write* it!) like disaster.

৩৫

WILLIAM BLAKE (*1757–1827*) *was born in London, one of several children of a London haberdasher. His family expected he would become a tradesman, and he was educated to be a commercial artist. He was sent to a drawing academy when he was ten, then he studied painting for a short time at the Royal Academy of Arts.*

At the age of fourteen Blake was apprenticed to an engraver, and his seven-year apprenticeship provided him with enough knowledge and experience to set up his own small engraving business. At the same time he was reading on his own and beginning to write poetry. When he was twenty-four he married Catherine Boucher, whose father delivered produce to the London markets. The next year, 1783, his first book of poems, Poetical Sketches, *was published.*

Over the next ten years he produced his two most celebrated books. Songs of Innocence *appeared in 1789, and* Songs of Innocence and of Experience *in 1794. He created the books with a method of engraving that combined the illustrations and the hand-lettered poetry on the page, then he and his wife hand-painted each page with watercolors. To do a single copy was so time-consuming that only a handful of editions were produced, but they were so unusual and so beautiful that Blake attracted the attention of a small group of connoisseurs and artists.*

In 1800, with the financial assistance of a patron, the Blakes were able to move to the country, and he continued to draw and paint, to create illustrations for books by other writers and to create his own books of prophecy and mystical inspiration. To many of his contemporaries, Blake was an exasperating eccentric with radical opinions, who often described conversations he had just had with long-dead historical figures. As he said of his habit of seeing visions, "I do not distrust my corporeal or vegetative eye any more than I would distrust a window for its sight. I see through it, not with it." He died in 1827 at the age of seventy.

The selection of Blake's poetry is taken from Songs of Innocence and of Experience. *The last two poems — "I askèd a thief" and "Never pain to tell thy love" — were found in a small book the poet used for sketching and writing notes.*

RELATED COMMENTARY: *T. S. Eliot, "From 'William Blake,' " page 1256.*

WILLIAM BLAKE

From *Songs of Innocence*   1789

Introduction

Piping down the valleys wild
Piping songs of pleasant glee
On a cloud I saw a child,
And he laughing said to me,

"Pipe a song about a Lamb";   5
So I piped with merry chear;
"Piper pipe that song again" —
So I piped, he wept to hear.

"Drop thy pipe thy happy pipe
Sing thy songs of happy chear";   10
So I sung the same again
While he wept with joy to hear.

"Piper sit thee down and write
In a book that all may read" —
So he vanish'd from my sight.   15
And I pluck'd a hollow reed,

And I made a rural pen,
And I stain'd the water clear,

And I wrote my happy songs
Every child may joy to hear.   20

WILLIAM BLAKE

The Lamb   *1789*

Little Lamb, who made thee?
    Dost thou know who made thee?
Gave thee life, and bid thee feed
By the stream and o'er the mead;
Gave thee clothing of delight,   5
Softest clothing, wooly, bright;
Gave thee such a tender voice,
Making all the vales rejoice?
    Little Lamb, who made thee?
    Dost thou know who made thee?   10

    Little Lamb, I'll tell thee,
    Little Lamb, I'll tell thee:
He is callèd by thy name,
For he calls himself a Lamb.
He is meek, and he is mild;   15
He became a little child.
I a child, and thou a lamb,
We are callèd by his name.
    Little Lamb, God bless thee!
    Little Lamb, God bless thee!   20

WILLIAM BLAKE

Holy Thursday   *1789*

'Twas on a Holy Thursday, their innocent faces clean,
The children walking two & two, in red & blue & green;
Grey headed beadles walkd before with wands as white as snow,
Till into the high dome of Paul's° they like Thames' waters flow.

O what a multitude they seemd, these flowers of London town!   5
Seated in companies they sit with radiance all their own.
The hum of multitudes was there, but multitudes of lambs,
Thousands of little boys & girls raising their innocent hands.

---

4. **Paul's:** St. Paul's Cathedral.

Now like a mighty wind they raise to heaven the voice of song,
Or like harmonious thunderings the seats of heaven among.   10
Beneath them sit the agèd men, wise guardians of the poor;
Then cherish pity, lest you drive an angel from your door.

WILLIAM BLAKE

The Little Boy Lost   *1789*

"Father, father, where are you going?
O do not walk so fast.
Speak father, speak to your little boy
Or else I shall be lost."

The night was dark, no father was there,
The child was wet with dew.
The mire was deep, & the child did weep,
And away the vapour flew.

WILLIAM BLAKE

The Little Boy Found   *1789*

The little boy lost in the lonely fen,
Led by the wand'ring light,
Began to cry, but God ever nigh
Appeard like his father in white.

He kissed the child & by the hand led
And to his mother brought,
Who in sorrow pale, thro' the lonely dale,
Her little boy weeping sought.

WILLIAM BLAKE

From *Songs of Experience*   *1794*

Introduction

Hear the voice of the Bard!
Who Present, Past, & Future sees;
Whose ears have heard
The Holy Word
That walk'd among the ancient trees;   5

Calling the lapsèd Soul
And weeping in the evening dew,
That might controll
The starry pole,
And fallen, fallen light renew!   10

"O Earth, O Earth, return!
Arise from out the dewy grass;
Night is worn,
And the morn
Rises from the slumberous mass.   15

"Turn away no more;
Why wilt thou turn away?
The starry floor
The watry shore
Is giv'n thee till the break of.day."   20

WILLIAM BLAKE

The Sick Rose   1794

O Rose, thou art sick!
The invisible worm
That flies in the night,
In the howling storm,

Has found out thy bed
Of crimson joy,
And his dark secret love
Does thy life destroy.

WILLIAM BLAKE

The Tyger   1794

Tyger! Tyger! burning bright
In the forests of the night,
What immortal hand or eye
Could frame thy fearful symmetry?

In what distant deeps or skies   5
Burnt the fire of thine eyes?
On what wings dare he aspire?
What the hand dare seize the fire?

And what shoulder, and what art,
Could twist the sinews of thy heart?   10

And when thy heart began to beat,
What dread hand? and what dread feet?

What the hammer? what the chain?
In what furnace was thy brain?
What the anvil? what dread grasp   15
Dare its deadly terrors clasp?

When the stars threw down their spears,
And watered heaven with their tears,
Did he smile his work to see?
Did he who made the Lamb make thee?   20

Tyger! Tyger! burning bright
In the forests of the night,
What immortal hand or eye
Dare frame thy fearful symmetry?

WILLIAM BLAKE

London   *1794*

I wander through each chartered° street   *defined by law*
Near where the chartered Thames does flow,
And mark in every face I meet
Marks of weakness, marks of woe.

In every cry of every man,   5
In every Infant's cry of fear,
In every voice, in every ban,
The mind-forged manacles I hear.

How the Chimney-sweeper's cry
Every black'ning Church appalls;   10
And the hapless Soldier's sigh
Runs in blood down Palace walls.

But most through midnight streets I hear
How the youthful Harlot's curse°   *syphilis*
Blasts the new-born Infant's tear,   15
And blights with plagues the Marriage hearse.

WILLIAM BLAKE

A Poison Tree   *1794*

I was angry with my friend:
I told my wrath, my wrath did end.
I was angry with my foe:
I told it not, my wrath did grow.

And I waterd it in fears,   5
Night & morning with my tears;
And I sunnèd it with smiles,
And with soft deceitful wiles.

And it grew both day and night,
Till it bore an apple bright.   10
And my foe beheld it shine,
And he knew that it was mine,

And into my garden stole,
When the night had veild the pole;
In the morning glad I see   15
My foe outstretched beneath the tree.

WILLIAM BLAKE

The Garden of Love   1794

I went to the Garden of Love,
And saw what I never had seen:
A Chapel was built in the midst,
Where I used to play on the green.

And the gates of this Chapel were shut,   5
And "Thou shalt not" writ over the door;
So I turn'd to the Garden of Love,
That so many sweet flowers bore,

And I saw it was filled with graves,
And tomb-stones where flowers should be;   10
And Priests in black gowns were walking their rounds,
And binding with briars my joys & desires.

WILLIAM BLAKE

I askèd a thief   1796

I askèd a thief to steal me a peach,
He turned up his eyes;
I ask'd a lithe lady to lie her down,
Holy & meek she cries.

As soon as I went   5
An angel came.
He wink'd at the thief
And smild at the dame —

And without one word said
Had a peach from the tree   10

And still as a maid
Enjoy'd the lady.

WILLIAM BLAKE

Never pain to tell thy love   1796

Never pain to tell thy love
Love that never told can be,
For the gentle wind does move
Silently, invisibly.

I told my love, I told my love,   5
I told her all my heart,
Trembling, cold, in ghastly fears —
Ah, she doth depart.

Soon as she was gone from me
A traveller came by   10
Silently, invisibly —
O, was no deny.

༄

ANNE BRADSTREET (c. 1612–1672) *was born in England, the daughter of
a "well borne woman" of modest wealth and a father who was the steward of the country estate of the Earl of Lincoln. Both the earl and Bradstreet's parents were Puritans,
and she was given a much better education than most young women of her time. At
sixteen she married Simon Bradstreet, also a Puritan, and two years later, in 1630,
she, her husband, and her parents sailed to the Massachusetts Bay Colony. They lived
first in Boston and in 1644 moved to North Andover, where Bradstreet lived for the
rest of her life.*

*As a girl she had already begun writing poems that she and her father read with
pleasure together. She continued to write, while she raised eight children and managed
the household for her husband, who, as governor of the colony, was away for long periods.*

*In 1650, without her knowledge, her brother-in-law took a gathering of her po-
ems to London. The collection was the first to be published by anyone living in the
North American colonies, and the book attracted considerable attention. Because of the
constraints placed on women's lives, her brother-in-law felt obliged to assure suspicious readers, in the introduction, that Bradstreet was respectable according to the
standards of the time. The poems, he wrote, were "the work of a woman, honored and
esteemed where she lives, for her gracious demeanor, her eminent parts, her pious conversation, her courteous disposition, her exact diligence in her place, and discreet
managing of her family occasions."*

*"To My Dear and Loving Husband" and "In Reference to Her Children, 23
June 1659" were both written during Bradstreet's years in North Andover.*

A N N E B R A D S T R E E T

To My Dear and Loving Husband 1678

If ever two were one, then surely we.
If ever man were loved by wife, then thee;
If ever wife was happy in a man,
Compare with me, ye women, if you can.
I prize thy love more than whole mines of gold 5
Or all the riches that the East doth hold.
My love is such that rivers cannot quench,
Nor ought but love from thee, give recompense.
Thy love is such I can no way repay,
The heavens reward thee manifold, I pray. 10
Then while we live, in love let's so persevere
That when we live no more, we may live ever.

A N N E B R A D S T R E E T

In Reference to Her Children, 23 June 1659 1678

I had eight birds hatcht in one nest,
Four cocks there were, and hens the rest,
I nurst them up with pain and care,
Nor cost, nor labor did I spare,
Till at the last they felt their wing, 5
Mounted the trees, and learn'd to sing;
Chief of the brood then took his flight,
To regions far, and left me quite.
My mournful chirps I after send,
Till he return, or I do end: 10
Leave not thy nest, thy dam and sire,
Fly back and sing amidst this choir.
My second bird did take her flight,
And with her mate flew out of sight;
Southward they both their course did bend, 15
And seasons twain they there did spend:
Till after blown by southern gales,
They norward steer'd with filled sails.
A prettier bird was no where seen,
Along the beach among the treen. 20
I have a third of color white,
On whom I plac'd no small delight;
Coupled with mate loving and true,
Hath also bid her dam adieu:
And where Aurora° first appears,   *Roman goddess of dawn* 25

She now hath percht to spend her years;
One to the academy flew
To chat among that learned crew:
Ambition moves still in his breast
That he might chant above the rest,   30
Striving for more than to do well,
That nightingales he might excel.
My fifth, whose down is yet scarce gone,
Is 'mongst the shrubs and bushes flown,
And as his wings increase in strength,   35
On higher boughs he'll perch at length,
My other three, still with me nest,
Until they're grown, then as the rest,
Or here or there, they'll take their flight,
As is ordain'd, so shall they light.   40
If birds could weep, then would my tears
Let others know what are my fears
Lest this my brood some harm should catch,
And be surpris'd for want of watch,
Whilst pecking corn, and void of care   45
They fall un'wares in fowler's snare:
Or whilst on trees they sit and sing,
Some untoward boy at them do fling:
Or whilst allur'd with bell and glass,
The net be spread, and caught, alas.   50
Or least by lime-twigs they be foil'd,°
Or by some greedy hawks be spoil'd.
Or would my young, ye saw my breast,
And knew what thoughts there sadly rest,
Great was my pain when I you bred,   55
Great was my care when I you fed,
Long did I keep you soft and warm,
And with my wings kept off all harm,
My cares are more, and fears than ever,
My throbs such now, as 'fore were never: 60
Alas my birds, you wisdom want.
Of perils you are ignorant,
Oft times in grass, on trees, in flight,
Sore accidents on you may light.
O to your safety have an eye,   65
So happy may you live and die:
Mean while my days in tunes I'll spend,
Till my weak lays° with me shall end.   *songs or poems*
In shady woods I'll sit and sing,

---

51. lime-twigs . . . foiled: A sticky "lime" was smeared on branches to catch birds.

And things that past, no mind I'll bring. 70
Once young and pleasant, as are you,
But former toys (no joys) adieu.
My age I will not once lament,
But sing, my time so near is spent.
And from the top bough take my flight, 75
Into a country beyond sight,
Where old ones instantly grow young,
And there with seraphims° set song: *an order of angels*
No seasons cold, nor storms they see,
But spring lasts to eternity. 80
When each of you shall in your nest
Among your young ones take your rest,
In chirping language, oft them tell,
You had a dam that lov'd you well,
That did what could be done for young, 85
And nurst you up till you were strong,
And 'fore she once would let you fly,
She show'd you joy and misery;
Taught what was good, and what was ill,
What would save life, and what would kill. 90
Thus gone, amongst you I may live,
And dead, yet speak, and counsel give:
Farewell, my birds, farewell adieu,
I happy am, if well with you.

ജ

GWENDOLYN BROOKS (*b. 1917*) *was born in Topeka, Kansas, but her parents moved to Chicago's South Side soon after her birth. Her father worked as a janitor, and the family was poor, but her parents encouraged her to study in school and to write poetry. She wrote her first poems when she was seven. Her childhood was so contented that she wrote later in her autobiography, "I had always felt that to be black was good."*

Brooks had had almost immediate success as a writer. She was already publishing her poetry when she was seventeen. Her first book, A Street in Bronzeville, *which appeared in 1945, won a series of prizes, and she was awarded a Guggenheim fellowship which allowed her to spend a year devoted entirely to writing. In 1949 her second poetry collection,* Annie Allen, *won the Pulitzer Prize, the first time it had been given to an African American writer. She also published a novel,* Maud Martha, *in 1953, and taught at Chicago State University, where she is a Distinguished Professor.*

In 1967 Brooks took part in the Second Black Writer's Conference at Fisk University, and she was swept up in the new militancy of the younger black poets like Amiri Baraka and don l. lee. Her poetry became more specifically political, and finally she turned to alternative publishing so she could have some control over the way her poetry was presented.

"We Real Cool" is one of her shortest poems, and it is also one of her most fa-

mous. "The Mother" is an early poem in which the woman speaker projects a scarring, personal unhappiness. Brooks herself is the mother of a son and a daughter.

RELATED COMMENTARY: Gary Smith, "On Gwendolyn Brooks's A Street in Bronzeville," page 1316.

GWENDOLYN BROOKS

We Real Cool

1960

> The Pool Players.
> Seven at the Golden Shovel.

We real cool. We
Left school. We

Lurk late. We   5
Strike straight. We

Sing sin. We
Thin gin. We

Jazz June. We
Die soon.   10

GWENDOLYN BROOKS

The Mother

1945

Abortions will not let you forget.
You remember the children you got that you did not get,
The damp small pulps with a little or with no hair,
The singers and workers that never handled the air.
You will never neglect or beat   5
Them, or silence or buy with a sweet.
You will never wind up the sucking-thumb
Or scuttle off ghosts that come.
You will never leave them, controlling your luscious sigh,
Return for a snack of them, with gobbling mother-eye.   10

I have heard in the voices of the wind the voices of my dim killed chil-
    dren.
I have contracted. I have eased
My dim dears at the breasts they could never suck.
I have said, Sweets, if I sinned, if I seized
Your luck   15
And your lives from your unfinished reach,
If I stole your births and your names,
Your straight baby tears and your games,
Your stilted or lovely loves, your tumults, your marriages, aches, and
    your deaths,

>isoned the beginnings of your breaths,   20
....ve that even in my deliberateness I was not deliberate.
....ugh why should I whine,
....ine that the crime was other than mine? —
Since anyhow you are dead.
Or rather, or instead,   25
You were never made.
But that too, I am afraid,
Is faulty: oh, what shall I say, how is the truth to be said?
You were born, you had body, you died.
It is just that you never giggled or planned or cried.   30

Believe me, I loved you all.
Believe me, I knew you, though faintly, and I loved, I loved you
All.

৩৫

ELIZABETH BARRETT BROWNING *(1806–1861) was born on her family's estate in northern England, the oldest of eleven children. Like many women of this period, she was kept at home and given a minimal education, but once she learned to read she educated herself and began writing poetry.*

When Barrett was fifteen she was injured in a riding accident and also began to suffer from what was described as "weakness of the lungs." Her doctors prescribed both morphine and laudanum, a form of opium, for the pain, and she was addicted to both drugs for the rest of her life. The family lived for a period in London, but because the city air was too dangerous for her lungs, she moved to the coast. At Torquay her favorite brother Edward drowned almost in sight of her window, and she returned to London. When she recovered from the shock she threw herself into her poetry, and she was soon contributing poems to the leading magazines in England and America.

In 1844 a two-volume collection of her poetry appeared to great success. Barrett was now the best-known English woman poet, but she was also a near-helpless invalid, spending her days in a darkened room, dependent on drugs. Then the next year a young poet, Robert Browning, wrote her a letter praising her book and asking if he could meet her. In the beginning of their courtship they only exchanged letters, but by the time they met a few months later they were already deeply in love.

Barrett's father refused to allow her to marry Browning, and for many months she also hesitated, fearing that her poor health would make it impossible for them to have a life together. Finally, in desperation, they married in secret and fled to Italy. Her father never forgave her.

The warmer Italian climate and the happiness of her marriage helped Barrett Browning to become stronger, even if she was never entirely healthy. At the age of 43, in 1849, she gave birth to a son. She wrote steadily, publishing collections of poetry and translations. Much of her work was engaged with social issues of the time, including child labor and slavery. She had also written a sequence of sonnets during the first months of their courtship. (See "How do I love thee" on p. 950.) The poems were a private diary of her growing love and also of her hesitations and confusions.

When the sonnets were published in 1850 with the title Sonnets from the Portuguese, *they caused an immediate sensation, and despite changes in fashion and style, they have been in print ever since. The title was a half-serious attempt to shield the intimacy of the sonnets, suggesting that they were translations from the "Portuguese," which was a pet name Browning had given his wife because of her dark hair and dark eyes.*

In the spring of 1861 she suffered a severe attack of bronchitis and died in her husband's arms.

The following selection of Barrett Browning's poetry includes excerpts from two poems that reflect her strong social views. The first is from "The Cry of the Children," a sequence protesting the injustice of child labor. The other is from "The Runaway Slave at Pilgrim's Point," a poem she wrote for the American antislavery movement. The other four poems reprinted here appeared in Sonnets from the Portuguese.

RELATED COMMENTARY: *Angela Leighton, "Elizabeth Barrett Browning: Woman and Poet," page 1283.*

ELIZABETH BARRETT BROWNING

From *The Cry of the Children* 1846

I

Do ye hear the children weeping, O my brothers,
    Ere the sorrow comes with years?
They are leaning their young heads against their mothers,
    And *that* cannot stop their tears.
The young lambs are bleating in the meadows,   5
    The young birds are chirping in the nest,
The young fawns are playing with the shadows,
    The young flowers are blowing toward the west —
But the young, young children, O my brothers,
    They are weeping bitterly!   10
They are weeping in the playtime of the others,
    In the country of the free. . . .

III

They look up with their pale and sunken faces,
    And their looks are sad to see,
For the man's hoary anguish draws and presses   15
    Down the cheeks of infancy;
"Your old earth," they say, "is very dreary,
    Our young feet," they say, "are very weak;
Few paces have we taken, yet are weary —
    Our grave-rest is very far to seek: 20
Ask the aged why they weep, and not the children,
    For the outside earth is cold,

And we young ones stand without, in our bewildering,
 And the graves are for the old."

IV

"True," say the children, "it may happen 25
 That we die before our time:
Little Alice died last year, her grave is shapen
 Like a snowball, in the rime.
We looked into the pit prepared to take her:
 Was no room for any work in the close clay! 30
From the sleep wherein she lieth none will wake her,
 Crying, 'Get up, little Alice! it is day.'
If you listen by that grave, in sun and shower,
 With your ear down, little Alice never cries;
Could we see her face, be sure we should not know her, 35
 For the smile has time for growing in her eyes:
And merry go her moments, lulled and stilled in
 The shroud by the kirk-chime.°   *church bell*
It is good when it happens," say the children,
 "That we die before our time."....   40

VI

"For oh," say the children, "we are weary,
 And we cannot run or leap;
If we cared for any meadows, it were merely
 To drop down in them and sleep.
Our knees tremble sorely in the stooping, 45
 We fall upon our faces, trying to go;
And, underneath our heavy eyelids drooping
 The reddest flower would look as pale as snow.
For, all day, we drag our burden tiring
 Through the coal-dark, underground; 50
Or, all day, we drive the wheels of iron
 In the factories, round and round...."

ELIZABETH **B**ARRETT **B**ROWNING

From *The Runaway Slave at Pilgrim's Point* 1846

I

I stand on the mark beside the shore
 Of the first white pilgrim's bended knee,
Where exile turned to ancestor,
 And God was thanked for liberty.

I have run through the night, my skin is as dark,   5
I bend my knee down on this mark:
   I look on the sky and the sea.

II

O pilgrim-souls, I speak to you!
   I see you come proud and slow
From the land of the spirits pale as dew   10
   And round me and round me ye go.
O pilgrims, I have gasped and run
All night long from the whips of one
   Who in your names works sin and woe! . . .

IX

I am black, I am black!   15
   But, once, I laughed in girlish glee,
For one of my color stood in the track
   Where the drivers drove, and looked at me,
And tender and full was the look he gave —
Could a slave look *so* at another slave? —   20
   I look at the sky and the sea.

X

And from that hour our spirits grew
   As free as if unsold, unbought:
Oh, strong enough, since we were two,
   To conquer the world, we thought.   25
The drivers drove us day by day;
We did not mind, we went one way,
   And no better a freedom sought. . . .

XIV

We were black, we were black,
   We had no claim to love and bliss,   30
What marvel if each went to wrack?
   They wrung my cold hands out of his,
They dragged him — where? I crawled to touch
His blood's mark in the dust . . . not much,
   Ye pilgrim-souls, though plain as *this!*   35

XV

Wrong, followed by a deeper wrong!
   Mere grief's too good for such as I:
So the white men brought the shame ere long
   To strangle the sob of my agony.
They would not leave me for my dull   40

Wet eyes! — it was too merciful
    To let me weep pure tears and die.

XVI

I am black, I am black!
    I wore a child upon my breast,
An amulet that hung too slack, 45
    And, in my unrest, could not rest:
Thus we went moaning, child and mother,
One to another, one to another,
    Until all ended for the best.

XVII

For hark! I will tell you low, low, 50
    I am black, you see, —
And the babe who lay on my bosom so,
    Was far too white, too white for me;
As white as the ladies who scorned to pray
Beside me at church but yesterday, 55
    Though my tears had washed a place for my knee.

XVIII

My own, own child! I could not bear
    To look in his face, it was so white;
I covered him up with a kerchief there,
    I covered his face in close and tight: 60
And he moaned and struggled, as well might be,
For the white child wanted his liberty —
    Ha, ha! he wanted the master-right.

XIX

He moaned and beat with his head and feet,
    His little feet that never grew; 65
He struck them out, as it was meet,
    Against my heart to break it through:
I might have sung and made him mild,
But I dared not sing to the white-faced child
    The only song I knew. 70

XX

I pulled the kerchief very close:
    He could not see the sun, I swear,
More, then, alive, than now he does
    From between the roots of the mango . . . where?
I know where. Close! A child and mother 75

Do wrong to look at one another
  When one is black and one is fair.

XXI

Why, in that single glance I had
  Of my child's face, . . . I tell you all,
I saw a look that made me mad!   80
  The *master's* look, that used to fall
On my soul like his lash . . . or worse!
And so, to save it from my curse,
  I twisted it round in my shawl.

XXII

And he moaned and trembled from foot to head,   85
  He shivered from head to foot;
Till after a time, he lay instead
  Too suddenly still and mute.
I felt, beside, a stiffening cold:
I dared to lift up just a fold,   90
  As in lifting a leaf of the mango-fruit. . . .

XXV

From the white man's house, and the black man's hut,
  I carried the little body on:
The forest's arms did round us shut,
  And silence through the trees did run: 95
They asked no question as I went,
They stood too high for astonishment,
  They could see God sit on his throne.

XXVI

My little body, kerchiefed fast,
  I bore it on through the forest, on;   100
And when I felt it was tired at last,
  I scooped a hole beneath the moon:
Through the forest-tops the angels far,
With a white sharp finger from every star,
  Did point and mock at what was done.   105

XXVII

Yet when it was all done aright, —
  Earth, 'twixt me and my baby, strewed, —
All, changed to black earth, — nothing white, —
  A dark child in the dark! — ensued
Some comfort, and my heart grew young;   110

I sate down smiling there and sung
    The song I learnt in my maidenhood.

XXVIII

And thus we two were reconciled,
    The white child and black mother, thus;
For as I sang it soft and wild,   115
    The same song, more melodious,
Rose from the grave whereon I sate:
It was the dead child singing that,
    To join the souls of both of us.

XXIX

I look on the sea and the sky.   120
    Where the pilgrims' ships first anchored lay
The free sun rideth gloriously,
    But the pilgrim-ghosts have slid away
Through the earliest streaks of the morn:
My face is black, but it glares with a scorn   125
    Which they dare not meet by day.

XXX

Ha! — in their stead, their hunter sons!
    Ha, ha! they are on me — they hunt in a ring!
Keep off! I brave you all at once,
    I throw off your eyes like snakes that sting!   130
You have killed the black eagle at nest, I think:
Did you ever stand still in your triumph, and shrink
    From the stroke of her wounded wing?

XXXI

(Man, drop that stone you dared to lift! —)
    I wish you who stand there five abreast,   135
Each, for his own wife's joy and gift,
    A little corpse as safely at rest
As mine in the mangoes! Yes, but *she*
May keep live babies on her knee,
    And sing the song she likes the best.   140

XXXII

I am not mad; I am black.
    I see you staring in my face —
I know you staring, shrinking back,
    Ye are born of the Washington-race,
And this land is the free America,   145
And this mark on my wrist — (I prove what I say)
    Ropes tied me up here to the flogging-place.

XXXIII

You think I shrieked then? Not a sound
   I hung, as a gourd hangs in the sun;
I only cursed them all around   150
   As softly as I might have done
My very own child: from these sands
Up to the mountains, lift your hands,
   O slaves, and end what I begun!

XXXIV

Whips, curses; these must answer those!   155
   For in this UNION you have set
Two kinds of men in adverse rows,
   Each loathing each; and all forget
The seven wounds in Christ's body fair,
While HE sees gaping everywhere   160
   Our countless wounds that pay no debt.

XXXV

Our wounds are different. Your white men
   Are after all, not gods indeed,
Nor able to make Christs again
   Do good with bleeding. We who bleed   165
(Stand off!) we help not in our loss!
We are too heavy for our cross,
   And fall and crush you and your seed.

XXXVI

I fall, I swoon! I look at the sky.
   The clouds are breaking on my brain;   170
I am floated along, as if I should die
   Of liberty's exquisite pain.
In the name of the white child waiting for me
In the death-dark where we may kiss and agree,
White men, I leave you all curse free   175
   In my broken heart's disdain!

ELIZABETH BARRETT BROWNING

If thou must love me, let it be for nought   1850

If thou must love me, let it be for nought
Except for love's sake only. Do not say
"I love her for her smile . . . her look . . . her way
Of speaking gently, . . . for a trick of thought
That falls in well with mine, and certes brought   5
A sense of pleasant ease on such a day" —

For these things in themselves, Belovèd, may
Be changed, or change for thee, — and love, so wrought
May be unwrought so. Neither love me for
Thine own dear pity's wiping my cheeks dry, —   10
A creature might forget to weep, who bore
Thy comfort long, and lose thy love thereby!
But love me for love's sake, that evermore
Thou may'st love on, through love's eternity.

ELIZABETH BARRETT BROWNING

Belovèd, my Belovèd, when I think   1850

Belovèd, my Belovèd, when I think
That thou wast in the world a year ago,
What time I sat alone here in the snow
And saw no footprint, heard the silence sink
No moment at thy voice, . . . but, link by link,   5
Went counting all my chains as if that so
They never could fall off at any blow
Struck by thy possible hand . . . why, thus I drink
Of life's great cup of wonder! Wonderful,
Never to feel thee thrill the day or night   10
With personal act or speech, — nor even cull
Some prescience of thee with the blossoms white
Thou sawest growing! Atheists are as dull,
Who cannot guess God's presence out of sight.

ELIZABETH BARRETT BROWNING

If I leave all for thee, wilt thou exchange   1850

If I leave all for thee, wilt thou exchange
And be all to me? Shall I never miss
Home-talk and blessing and the common kiss
That comes to each in turn, nor count it strange,
When I look up, to drop on a new range   5
Of walls and floors, . . . another home than this?
Nay, wilt thou fill that place by me which is
Filled by dead eyes too tender to know change?
That's hardest. If to conquer love, has tried,
To conquer grief, tries more . . . as all things prove,   10
For grief indeed is love and grief beside.
Alas, I have grieved so I am hard to love.
Yet love me — wilt thou? Open thine heart wide,
And fold within, the wet wings of thy dove.

Elizabeth Barrett Browning

I thought once how Theocritus had sung 1850

I thought once how Theocritus° had sung
  Of the sweet years, the dear and wished-for years,
  Who each one in a gracious hand appears
To bear a gift for mortals, old or young:
And, as I mused it in his antique tongue, 5
  I saw, in gradual vision through my tears,
  The sweet, sad years, the melancholy years,
Those of my own life, who by turns had flung
A shadow across me. Straightway I was 'ware,
  So weeping, how a mystic Shape did move 10
Behind me, and drew me backward by the hair;
  And a voice said in mastery, while I strove, —
"Guess now who holds thee?" — "Death," I said. But, there,
  The silver answer rang, — "Not Death, but Love."

ର୍ଷ୍ଠ

MARILYN MEI LING CHIN *(b. 1955) was born in Hong Kong, where her father operated a restaurant. He moved the family to Portland, Oregon, when she was a child, and changed his daughter's name from Mei Ling to Marilyn, in homage to the actress Marilyn Monroe. He also soon abandoned the family for a Caucasian woman, and this act has left a strong emotional imprint on Chin's poetry.*

Chin graduated from the University of Massachusetts in 1977 and received her M.F.A. from the University of Iowa in 1981. Her first book, Dwarf Bamboo, was published in 1987. For several years she taught at San Diego State University, which she described as an "exile." Although she has assimilated into the mainstream American culture, she is concerned that she is losing her Chinese identity. As she told television interviewer Bill Moyers in 1995, "I am afraid of losing my Chinese, losing my language, which would be like losing part of myself, losing part of my soul. Poetry seems a way to recapture that, but of course the truth is we can't recapture the past. The vector only goes one direction and that is toward the future. So the grandeur of China — the grandeur of that past of my grandfather's, of my grand-mother's, of my mother's, and so forth — that will be all lost to me. I lose inches of it every day."

"How I Got That Name" is an autobiographical poem. "Elegy for Chloe Nguyen" is a grieving portrait of a close friend.

RELATED COMMENTARY: *Marilyn Chin, "On the Canon," page 1249.*

---

1. **Theocritus:** Greek poet of the third century B.C.

MARILYN CHIN

How I Got That Name   1994

an essay on assimilation

I am Marilyn Mei Ling Chin.
Oh, how I love the resoluteness
of that first person singular
followed by that stalwart indicative
of "be," without the uncertain i-n-g   5
of "becoming." Of course,
the name had been changed
somewhere between Angel Island and the sea,
when my father the paperson
in the late 1950s   10
obsessed with a bombshell blonde
transliterated "Mei Ling" to "Marilyn."
And nobody dared question
his initial impulse — for we all know
lust drove men to greatness,   15
not goodness, not decency.
And there I was, a wayward pink baby,
named after some tragic white woman
swollen with gin and Nembutal.
My mother couldn't pronounce the "r."   20
She dubbed me "Numba one female offshoot"
for brevity: henceforth, she will live and die
in sublime ignorance, flanked
by loving children and the "kitchen deity."
While my father dithers,   25
a tomcat in Hong Kong trash —
a gambler, a petty thug,
who bought a chain of chopsuey joints
in Piss River, Oregon,
with bootlegged Gucci cash.   30
Nobody dared question his integrity given
his nice, devout daughters
and his bright, industrious sons
as if filial piety were the standard
by which all earthly men were measured.   35

Oh, how trustworthy our daughters,
how thrifty our sons!
How we've managed to fool the experts
in education, statistics and demography —
We're not very creative but not adverse to rote-learning.   40
Indeed, they can *use* us.

But the "Model Minority"° is a tease.
We know you are watching now,
so we refuse to give you any!
Oh, bamboo shoots, bamboo shoots!   45
The further west we go, we'll hit east;
the deeper down we dig, we'll find China.
History has turned its stomach
on a black polluted beach —
where life doesn't hinge   50
on that red, red wheelbarrow,°
but whether or not our new lover
in the final episode of "Santa Barbara"°
will lean over a scented candle
and call us a "bitch."   55
Oh God, where have we gone wrong?
We have no inner resources!

Then, one redolent spring morning
the Great Patriarch Chin
peered down from his kiosk in heaven   60
and saw that his descendants were ugly.
One had a squarish head and a nose without a bridge.
Another's profile — long and knobbed as a gourd.
A third, the sad, brutish one
may never, never marry.   65
And I, his least favorite —
"not quite boiled, not quite cooked,"
a plump pomfret° simmering in my juices —
too listless to fight for my people's destiny.
"To kill without resistance is not slaughter"   70
says the proverb. So, I wait for imminent death.
The fact that this death is also metaphorical
is testament to my lethargy.

So here lies Marilyn Mei Ling Chin,
married once, twice to so-and-so, a Lee and a Wong,   75
granddaughter of Jack "the patriarch"
and the brooding Suilin Fong,
daughter of the virtuous Yuet Kuen Wong
and G. G. Chin the infamous,
sister of a dozen, cousin of a million,   80

---

42. Model Minority: Asian Americans have been stereotyped as a well-behaved, industrious "model minority."   **51. red, red wheelbarrow:** A reference to William Carlos Williams's brief modernist poem "The Red Wheelbarrow" (see p. 965 in this text).   **53. Santa Barbara:** Prime-time television "soap opera" about wealthy, glamorous characters living in the California seaside city.   **68. pomfret:** A spiny, edible fish.

survived by everybody and forgotten by all.
She was neither black nor white,
neither cherished nor vanquished,
just another squatter in her own bamboo grove
minding her poetry —   85
when one day heaven was unmerciful,
and a chasm opened where she stood.
Like the jowls of a mighty white whale,
or the jaws of a metaphysical Godzilla,
it swallowed her whole.   90
She did not flinch nor writhe,
nor fret about the afterlife,
but stayed! Solid as wood, happily
a little gnawed, tattered, mesmerized
by all that was lavished upon her   95
and all that was taken away!

MARILYN CHIN

Elegy for Chloe Nguyen   1994

(1955–1988)

Chloe's father is a professor of linguistics.
Mine runs a quick-you-do-it Laundromat in Chinatown.
If not pretty, at least I'm clean.

Bipedal in five months, trilingual in a year,
at eleven she had her first lover.   5

Here's a photo of Chloe's mother in the kitchen
making petit fours, petit fours that are very pretty.
Here's my mother picking pears, picking pears
for a self-made millionaire grower.

The night when Chloe died, her father sighed,   10
"Chloe was my heart; Chloe was my life!"

One day under an earthen black sky
and the breeze brushing our adolescent pinafores,
a star fell — or was it a satellite
exploding into a bonfire at the horizon?   15
Chloe said, "This is how I want to die,
with a bang and not with a flicker."

Oh, Chloe, eternally sophomore and soporific!
Friend of remote moribund languages!
Chloe read Serbo-Croatian, the Latin of Horace.   20
She understood Egyptian hieroglyphics, the writing of the tombs.

The tongues of the living, the slangs of the dead —
in learning she had no rival.

Then came the lovers of many languages
to quell her hunger, her despair.   25
Each night they whispered, "Chloe, you are beautiful."
Then left her with an empty sky in the morning.

Chloe, can you hear me? Is it better in heaven?
Are you happier in hell? This week I don't understand the lesson
being a slow learner — except for the one about survival.   30
And Death, I know him well . . .

He followed my grandfather as a puff of opium,
my father as a brand new car.
Rowed the boat with my grandmother,
blowing gales into my mother's ear.   35
Wrapped his arms around my asthmatic sister,
but his comforting never won us over.

Yes, Death is a beautiful man,
and the poor don't need dowries to court him.
His grassy hand, his caliph — you thought you could master.   40

Chloe, we are finally Americans now. Chloe, we are here!

ॐ

LUCILLE CLIFTON (b. 1936) *was born in Depew, a small town in upstate New York. She was educated at Fredonia State Teachers College and at Howard University. As a mother of six children she has written many books for young readers, and her writing for her adult readers includes several collections of poetry and a memoir. She has been nominated for the Pulitzer Prize for three of her books, and she has received many prizes and honors, including two National Endowment for the Arts fellowships for creative writing. She now spends much of her time teaching and lecturing.*

Clifton feels deep emotional ties to her African American heritage. A great-great-grandmother, Caroline, was kidnapped in Dahomey in Africa and brought to America as a slave. Caroline's daughter was lynched, the first black woman in Virginia to be the victim of a mob. In her poetry Clifton expresses a sense of continuity with her ancestors in language that is plain and direct. As she has expressed it, she is not interested in whether anyone thinks she is "familiar with big words."

In "the thirty eighth year" Clifton reflects on her life as she feels herself growing older. "Reply" is a strong statement of pride in response to encountering racism in the United States.

LUCILLE CLIFTON

the thirty eighth year

1974

the thirty eighth year
of my life,
plain as bread
round as a cake
an ordinary woman.   5

an ordinary woman.

i had expected to be
smaller than this,
more beautiful,
wiser in afrikan ways,   10
more confident,
i had expected
more than this.

i will be forty soon.
my mother once was forty.   15

my mother died at forty four,
a woman of sad countenance
leaving behind a girl
awkward as a stork.
my mother was thick,   20
her hair was a jungle and
she was very wise
and beautiful
and sad.

i have dreamed dreams   25
for you mama
more than once.
i have wrapped me
in your skin
and made you live again   30
more than once.
i have taken the bones you hardened
and built daughters
and they blossom and promise fruit
like afrikan trees.   35
i am a woman now.
an ordinary woman.

in the thirty eighth
year of my life,
surrounded by life,   40
a perfect picture of
blackness blessed,

i had not expected this
loneliness.

if it is western,   45
if it is the final
europe in my mind,
if in the middle of my life
i am turning the final turn
into the shining dark   50
let me come to it whole
and holy
not afraid
not lonely
out of my mother's life   55
into my own.
into my own.

i had expected more than this.
i had not expected to be
an ordinary woman.   60

LUCILLE CLIFTON

Reply   *1991*

[from a letter written to Dr. W. E. B. Du Bois by Alvin Borgquest of Clark University in Massachusetts and dated April 3, 1905:

    "We are pursuing an investigation here on the subject of crying as an expression of the emotions, and should like very much to learn about its peculiarities among the colored people. We have been referred to you as a person competent to give us information on the subject. We desire especially to know about the following salient aspects: 1. Whether the Negro sheds tears . . ."]

reply
he do
she do
they live
they love   5
they try
they tire
they flee
they fight
they bleed   10
they break
they moan
they mourn
they weep
they die   15

they do
they do
they do

෨෨

SAMUEL TAYLOR COLERIDGE *(1772–1834) was born in a small village in southern England, but after the death of his father he was sent to school in London. Despite his indolence, he could also be sporadically brilliant, and at nineteen he entered Cambridge University, where his lack of discipline overwhelmed him, and he was unable to complete his degree.*

In 1794 Coleridge met the young poet Robert Southey and, filled with the fervor of the French Revolution, they decided to establish a utopian colony in Pennsylvania. Their plans fell apart, but Coleridge, as part of the plan, had married the sister of Southey's fiancée. The marriage was as unhappy as everything else Coleridge had attempted. The next year he met William Wordsworth and soon moved close to where the older poet and his sister Dorothy were living in England. Writing together, in a fever of excitement, he and Wordsworth completed the small collection titled Lyrical Ballads, *which was published in 1798. With their book they attempted to write a new kind of poetry, closer to ordinary speech and drawing from everyday emotions. Coleridge's contribution was the long supernatural narrative "The Rime of the Ancient Mariner" and several shorter poems.*

Coleridge by this time was addicted to opium, and his writing became chaotically uneven. "Kubla Khan" is the best known of his drug-influenced poems. When he later overcame his addiction he became one of the most important literary theorists and critics of the early nineteenth century. His lifelong friend, the writer Charles Lamb, described Coleridge as "an archangel, slightly damaged." "Frost at Midnight" is one of Coleridge's "conversation poems" in blank verse that moves back and forth between description of his surroundings and lofty meditation.

SAMUEL TAYLOR COLERIDGE

Kubla Khan: or, a Vision in a Dream°   1798

In Xanadu did Kubla Khan°
    A stately pleasure-dome decree:
Where Alph, the sacred river, ran
Through caverns measureless to man
    Down to a sunless sea.   5
So twice five miles of fertile ground
With walls and towers were girdled round:
And here were gardens bright with sinuous rills

Vision in a Dream: Coleridge claimed this poem came to him in a dream, but when he woke and was transcribing it, he was interrupted by a visitor and was later unable to remember the rest of the poem.
1. Kubla Khan: In Chinese history, Kubla Khan (1216–1294) founded the Mongol dynasty.

Where blossomed many an incense-bearing tree;
And there were forests ancient as the hills,   10
Enfolding sunny spots of greenery.

But oh! that deep romantic chasm which slanted
Down the green hill athwart a cedarn cover!°
A savage place! as holy and enchanted
As e'er beneath a waning moon was haunted   15
By woman wailing for her demon-lover!
And from this chasm, with ceaseless turmoil seething,
As if this earth in fast thick pants were breathing,
A mighty fountain momently was forced,
Amid whose swift half-intermitted burst   20
Huge fragments vaulted like rebounding hail,
Or chaffy grain beneath the thresher's flail:
And 'mid these dancing rocks at once and ever
It flung up momently the sacred river.
Five miles meandering with a mazy motion   25
Through wood and dale the sacred river ran,
Then reached the caverns measureless to man,
And sank in tumult to a lifeless ocean:
And 'mid this tumult Kubla heard from far
Ancestral voices prophesying war!   30
    The shadow of the dome of pleasure
    Floated midway on the waves;
    Where was heard the mingled measure
    From the fountain and the caves.
It was a miracle of rare device,   35
A sunny pleasure-dome with caves of ice!

    A damsel with a dulcimer
    In a vision once I saw:
    It was an Abyssinian maid,
    And on her dulcimer she played,   40
    Singing of Mount Abora.
    Could I revive within me
    Her symphony and song,
    To such a deep delight 'twould win me,
That with music loud and long,   45
I would build that dome in air,
That sunny dome! those caves of ice!
And all who heard should see them there,
And all should cry, Beware! Beware!
His flashing eyes, his floating hair!   50
Weave a circle round him thrice,
And close your eyes with holy dread,

---

13. athwart . . . cover: Encompassing a grove of cedar trees.

For he on honey-dew hath fed,
And drunk the milk of Paradise.

SAMUEL TAYLOR COLERIDGE

Frost at Midnight

1798

The Frost performs its secret ministry,
Unhelped by any wind. The owlet's cry
Came loud — and hark, again! loud as before.
The inmates of my cottage, all at rest,
Have left me to that solitude, which suits   5
Abstruser musings: save that at my side
My cradled infant slumbers peacefully.
'Tis calm indeed! so calm, that it disturbs
And vexes meditation with its strange
And extreme silentness. Sea, hill, and wood,   10
This populous village! Sea, and hill, and wood,
With all the numberless goings-on of life,
Inaudible as dreams! the thin blue flame
Lies on my low-burnt fire, and quivers not;
Only that film,° which fluttered on the grate,   *soot* 15
Still flutters there, the sole quiet thing.
Methinks its motion in this hush of nature
Gives it dim sympathies with me who live,
Making it a companionable form,
Whose puny flaps and freaks the idling Spirit   20
By its own moods interprets, everywhere
Echo or mirror seeking of itself,
And makes a toy of Thought.
                                    But O! how oft,
How oft, at school, with most believing mind,   25
Presageful, have I gazed upon the bars,
To watch that fluttering *stranger!* and as oft
With unclosed lids, already had I dreamt
Of my sweet birthplace, and the old church tower,
Whose bells, the poor man's only music, rang   30
From morn to evening, all the hot fair-day,
So sweetly, that they stirred and haunted me
With a wild pleasure, falling on mine ear
Most like articulate sounds of things to come!
So gazed I, till the soothing things, I dreamt,   35
Lulled me to sleep, and sleep prolonged my dreams!
And so I brooded all the following morn,
Awed by the stern preceptor's face, mine eye
Fixed with mock study on my swimming book:

Save if the door half opened, and I snatched   40
A hasty glance, and still my heart leaped up,
For still I hoped to see the *stranger's* face,
Townsman, or aunt, or sister more beloved,
My playmate when we both were clothed alike!

Dear Babe,° that sleepest cradled by my side,   *Coleridge's infant son*   45
Whose gentle breathings, heard in this deep calm,
Fill up the interspersèd vacancies
And momentary pauses of the thought!
My babe so beautiful! it thrills my heart
With tender gladness, thus to look at thee,   50
And think that thou shalt learn far other lore,
And in far other scenes! For I was reared
In the great city, pent 'mid cloisters dim,
And saw nought lovely but the sky and stars.
But *thou*, my babe! shalt wander like a breeze   55
By lakes and sandy shores, beneath the crags
Of ancient mountain, and beneath the clouds,
Which image in their bulk both lakes and shores
And mountain crags: so shalt thou see and hear
The lovely shapes and sounds intelligible   60
Of that eternal language, which thy God
Utters, who from eternity doth teach
Himself in all, and all things in himself.
Great universal Teacher! he shall mold
Thy spirit, and by giving make it ask.   65

Therefore all seasons shall be sweet to thee,
Whether the summer clothe the general earth
With greenness, or the redbreast sit and sing
Betwixt the tufts of snow on the bare branch
Of mossy apple tree, while the nigh thatch   70
Smokes in the sun-thaw; whether the eave-drops fall
Heard only in the trances of the blast,
Or if the secret ministry of frost
Shall hang them up in silent icicles,
Quietly shining to the quiet Moon.   75

∽

E. E. CUMMINGS (1894–1962) *was born Edward Estlin Cummings in Cambridge, Massachusetts. His father was a Unitarian minister who taught sociology at Harvard. As a Harvard undergraduate, Cummings wrote conventional verse, but under the influence of the poet and critic Ezra Pound (see p. 1175), his poetry became less sentimental and more sharply satiric.*

In 1917 he went to France with a friend to join the Red Cross Ambulance Corps, but he was careless in comments he made about the French Army in letters home, for-

getting that mail was censored. He was arrested by the French authorities and impris-
oned for treason. His father, however, had important government connections and
succeeded in getting Cummings released after four months of detention. The experi-
ence became the subject of Cummings's sardonic, exuberant book, The Enormous
Room, *which appeared in 1922.*

When Cummings's poetry began to appear in the mid-1920s, it incited consid-
erable controversy, not only for his experimental techniques of breaking up words and
punctuation, but also for his eroticism and his irreverence toward the heroism of
World War I. He justified his poetic experiments by saying that he was searching for
a way to express the ecstasy of life. As he described it in the introduction to his Collected Poems *(1938), "We can never be born enough." In 1933 he traveled to the So-*
viet Union, and, characteristically, he was bored and disappointed with the Soviet
social experiment.

Also a painter, Cummings spent much of his life writing and painting in a
small house in Greenwich Village. The love poem "somewhere i have never travelled"
is a brilliantly free variation on the form of the sonnet. The elegy "Buffalo Bill 's" is
one of his best-known poems. In "if there are any heavens" he creates an affectionate
portrait of his mother and father. His lyric description of spring, "in Just-," is an ex-
ample of his poetic technique at its freshest and most expressive. (See also Cummings's
"when god lets my body be" on p. 890, "goodby Betty, don't remember me" on p. 951,
and "since feeling is first" on p. 1012.)

E. E. Cummings

somewhere i have never travelled   1931

somewhere i have never travelled,gladly beyond
any experience,your eyes have their silence:
in your most frail gesture are things which enclose me,
or which i cannot touch because they are too near

your slightest look easily will unclose me   5
though i have closed myself as fingers,
you open always petal by petal myself as Spring opens
(touching skilfully,mysteriously)her first rose

or if your wish be to close me,i and
my life will shut very beautifully,suddenly,   10
as when the heart of this flower imagines
the snow carefully everywhere descending;

nothing which we are to perceive in this world equals
the power of your intense fragility:whose texture
compels me with the colour of its countries,   15
rendering death and forever with each breathing

(i do not know what it is about you that closes
and opens;only something in me understands
the voice of your eyes is deeper than all roses)
nobody,not even the rain,has such small hands   20

E. E. CUMMINGS

Buffalo Bill 's°

1923

Buffalo Bill 's
defunct
     who used to
     ride a watersmooth-silver
                stallion   5
and break onetwothreefourfive pigeonsjustlikethat
                        Jesus

he was a handsome man
              and what i want to know is
how do you like your blueeyed boy   10
Mister Death

E. E. CUMMINGS

if there are any heavens

1931

if there are any heavens my mother will(all by herself)have
one.   It will not be a pansy heaven nor
a fragile heaven of lilies-of-the-valley but
it will be a heaven of blackred roses

my father will be(deep like a rose   5
tall like a rose)

standing near my

swaying over her
(silent)
with eyes which are really petals and see   10

nothing with the face of a poet really which
is a flower and not a face with
hands
which whisper
This is my beloved my   15
               (suddenly in sunlight

he will bow,

& the whole garden will bow)

Buffalo Bill 's: William Frederick Cody (1846–1917), known as Buffalo Bill, was a frontier scout who put together a "Wild West" show that was the most popular show in America for thirty years.

E. E. CUMMINGS

in Just-   1923

in Just-
spring   when the world is mud-
luscious the little
lame balloonman

whistles   far   and wee   5

and eddieandbill come
running from marbles and
piracies and it's
spring
when the world is puddle-wonderful   10

the queer
old balloonman whistles
far   and   wee
and bettyandisbel come dancing

from hop-scotch and jump-rope and   15

it's
spring
and
   the
       goat-footed

balloonMan   whistles   20
far
and
wee

ळ

HILDA DOOLITTLE *(1886–1961), who used her initials H.D. as a writer, was born in Bethlehem, Pennsylvania. Her mother was a member of the Moravian Brotherhood and was deeply interested in mysticism. Her father was a professor of astronomy. When she was still at school she became engaged to the young poet Ezra Pound, who was studying at the University of Pennsylvania. Pound brought another friend, William Carlos Williams, to meet her, and Williams later remembered a walk when the three of them were caught in a storm. She sat down and held up her arms, saying, "Beautiful rain, welcome."*

Her engagement to Pound ended, but later, after poor grades and ill health forced her to leave Bryn Mawr College in her sophomore year, she met Pound again in London in 1911 and became a member of the literary movement he was founding, called imagism (see p. 964). When Pound sent three of her poems to Poetry Magazine in Chicago he signed them "H.D., Imagiste."

Her life in London was turbulent and unhappy. She married one of the imagist group, Richard Aldington, but he began an affair with another woman after she had a miscarriage, and she ended the marriage, desperately poor and ill. For several months she was emotionally dependent upon the writer D. H. Lawrence (see pp. 463 and 1142), but he abruptly ended the relationship. Finally, in 1919, when H.D. was pregnant after a brief affair with a new lover, she was rescued by a wealthy English writer named Winifred Ellerman, who wrote under the name of Bryher. Bryher took over her life, and they remained together, despite occasional separations, until 1946, when their relationship ended.

H.D. wrote continually, though for many years she felt she had exhausted her themes and refused to publish. In 1960 she was the first woman to receive the Award of Merit Medal for Poetry from the American Academy of Arts and Letters. "Orchard" is an early poem, while "May 1943" is an intimate glimpse of her life during the war years. (See also H.D.'s "Mid-day" on p. 932 and "Oread" on p. 965.)

RELATED COMMENTARY: Alicia Ostriker, "The Poet as Heroine: H.D.," page 1291.

H.D.

Orchard   1916

I saw the first pear
as it fell —
the honey-seeking, golden-banded,
the yellow swarm,
was not more fleet than I,   5
(spare us from loveliness!)
and I fell prostrate,
crying:
you have flayed us with your blossoms,
spare us the beauty   10
of fruit-trees!

The honey-seeking
paused not;
the air thundered their song,
and I alone was prostrate.   15

O rough-hewn
god of the orchard,
I bring you an offering —
do you, alone unbeautiful,
son of the god,   20
spare us from loveliness:

these fallen hazel-nuts,
stripped late of their green sheaths,
grapes, red-purple,
their berries   25
dripping with wine;

pomegranates already broken,
and shrunken figs,
and quinces untouched,
I bring you as offering.   30

H.D.

May 1943   *1950*

I wanted to say I was sorry,
but why should I? but anyway
I did want to say I was sorry,
but how could I? who was I?
I wanted to say, yes, we're used to it,   5
we have the advantage,
you're new to it;
we've slithered so long in the rain,
prowled like cats in the dark,
like owls in the black-out,   10
look at us — anaemic, good-natured,
for a rat in the gutter's a rat in the gutter,
consider our fellowship,
look at each one of us,
we've grown alike, slithering,   15
slipping along with fish-baskets,
grey faces, fish-faces, frog gait,
we slop, we hop,
we're off to the bread-queue,
the meat-shop, the grocery,   20
an egg? — really madam — maybe to-morrow —
one here — one there — another one over there
is heroic (who'd know it?)
heroic? no bronze face —

no   25
    no
        no
what am I saying?

ಜಲ

EMILY DICKINSON (1830–1886) *wrote in a letter,*

If I read a book and it makes my whole body so cold no fire can ever warm me, I know that it is poetry. If I feel physically as if the top of my head were taken off, I know that is poetry. These are the only ways I know it. Is there any other way?

It is difficult, though, to imagine how someone whose days seemed as quiet and uneventful as hers could feel such a strong emotion. Outwardly, so little happened in *her life that someone reading her poetry today could say that the one "event" of her life came a few days after her death, when her sister Lavinia opened a box she'd left at the foot of her bed and found the manuscripts of hundreds of unpublished poems — poems that had been her sister's life's work.*

Dickinson, the second child of Emily and Edward Dickinson, spent her life in the small Massachusetts town of Amherst, in a house where she was born and died. For the last fourteen years of her life she lived almost entirely in one room: her large, sunny front bedroom. In her last years she dressed all in white and saw only a few friends and relatives, even though her brother and his wife lived in the house beside hers. She communicated with people through notes and lines of poems, most of them so cryptic and veiled that it was hard to know what she meant. Her niece Martha, the daughter of her brother Austin, remembered that once she came into her aunt's bedroom and Dickinson pretended to lock the door behind her, saying, "Matty, here's freedom."

The reality of Emily Dickinson's life, however, is much more complicated. In her poetry there is anger and despair as well as joy. There are many poems that hint at an unhappy love affair. One, written when she was about thirty, suggests that she thought of herself as married:

> *I'm "wife" — I've finished that —*
> *That other state —*
> *I'm Czar — I'm "Woman" now —*
> *It's safer so —*

In another, possibly written a year later, there is a burst of passion:

> *Wild Nights — Wild Nights!*
> *Were I with thee*
> *Wild nights would be*
> *Our luxury!*

In 1890, four years after she had found the box of poems, Lavinia paid to have a small selection from the manuscripts published. For help with the editing she turned to her brother's lover, Mabel Loomis Todd, and the well-known writer and literary editor Thomas Wentworth Higginson. Higginson had corresponded with Emily for more than twenty years, and even journeyed to Amherst to meet her. The public response was overwhelming — there were ten printings of the book in the first year — and immediately readers began sifting through the hints and suggestions they found in the poems to try to understand what concealed events might have inspired Dickinson to write them.

Dickinson's poetry is so oblique — so "slant" in her term — that for many years it was impossible to identify the person she loved or to guess at why the relationship ended. However, when a literary scholar reconstructed her original arrangement of the poems into small hand-sewn booklets it became clear that Dickinson had fallen deeply in love in her late twenties. Her emotional attachment to a married minister named Charles Wadsworth began in 1858 and lasted until 1863. She heard him preach on a visit to Philadelphia, and when the family needed someone to help her through an emotionally difficult period in her life she was encouraged to write him. She began sending him groups of poems and in the spring of 1858 sent him the first of a series of turbulent "master" letters, describing her love and her emotional indebtedness to him. Although his own letters to her are carefully polite he came to Amherst to visit her in 1860, and in her poetry it seems clear that their relationship was physically consummated. It is from this time that she referred to herself as "wife," and she does not seem to have considered a relationship with anyone else, although letters to a family friend, Judge Otis Lord, in 1877 hint that he had proposed to her. She continued to correspond with Wadsworth, even when she realized that they could never marry, and she saw him again when he returned to Amherst in 1880.

For many years researchers suspected that the man she loved was a close family friend named Samuel Bowles, who was often a guest in the Dickinson home. Bowles was the editor of the Springfield Republican, a daily newspaper published in nearby Springfield. Bowles, it now seems certain, was one of the two or three people she used to help her send letters to Wadsworth. He published three of her poems, but in each case they were edited to smooth out what were considered to be their "irregularities." Reading her poems as a record of her love affair makes it clear that she could never consider publishing them. They were her secret diary, and she asked Lavinia to destroy them at her death. When she wrote her now-famous letter to Thomas Wentworth Higginson in 1862, asking if he could tell her if her verse was "alive" (see p. 1334), she was only asking for his opinion, not for help in finding a publisher for the poems.

Other strains and tensions are also mirrored in the poetry. Dickinson had a very complicated relationship with her father, who was a lawyer and treasurer of Amherst College. As she described her family in a letter to Higginson,

> I have a brother and sister; my mother does not care for thought, and father, too busy with his briefs to notice what we do. He buys me many books, but begs me not to read them, because he fears they joggle the mind.

In 1856 her brother married and moved into the house next door. For several years there was a warm friendliness between Dickinson and her sister-in-law, but the marriage soured, and finally the only contact between the two households was her brother's daily visit to Emily and her sister Lavinia, who also never married. In 1881, a year after Dickinson had met Wadsworth again, a young astronomy professor named David Todd moved to Amherst with his wife, Mabel. Austin Dickinson and Mabel Todd fell passionately in love, and their affair, more or less openly acknowledged, continued until his death. Lavinia carried the messages between them, and they sometimes met in Dickinson's house.

Until she was in her thirties, Dickinson still took part in Amherst life. In 1856 her bread won second prize at the Agricultural Fair, and the next year she was on the Cattle Show Committee. As she dealt with the complex emotional tensions of her relationship, she became more and more socially withdrawn, so that by 1863 Samuel Bowles referred to her in a note to Austin as "Queen recluse." In 1862 she wrote to Higginson after he'd published an article in the April Atlantic Monthly suggesting that he might be interested in hearing from young poets. He responded to her letter with interest, but he found her poems too idiosyncratic to publish. It seems clear, however, that she had already decided that her poetry would be her "letter to the World / that never wrote to me," as she said in a poem from 1862. In 1869, when Higginson wrote and asked if she would come to Boston, she answered, "I do not cross my Father's ground to any House or Town."

Higginson, however, showed the poems to a childhood friend of Dickinson's, the successful writer Helen Hunt Jackson, and Jackson immediately recognized the genius in the work and begged her to publish. In 1876 Jackson wrote her, "You are a great poet — and it is a wrong . . . that you will not sing aloud." Jackson was able to persuade her to have a poem published anonymously, but there was never any question that Dickinson would consider further publication. The themes of the poetry of her last years were death and eternity.

Dickinson's poems seemed innocent and naive to some of her early readers, but she was conscious of other poets and their work. Unlike Elizabeth Barrett Browning, who never went to school, Dickinson went first to the Amherst Academy and then spent a year, when she was seventeen, at Mount Holyoke Female Seminary, now Mount Holyoke College. It is interesting to compare her poetry to Barrett Browning's, since she admired the English writer so much that she had a portrait of her on the wall of her bedroom. She read, but certainly was not influenced in any way, by Barrett Browning's defiant novel in verse, Aurora Leigh, with its attack on the passive role forced on women in their society. When she learned that Higginson was traveling to Europe, not long after Barrett Browning's death, Dickinson wrote him "If you touch her Grave, put one hand on the Head, for me — her unmentioned mourner."

Dickinson also read the works of John Keats, whom she admired the most of the Romantics, the Brontë sisters, and Alfred, Lord Tennyson, as well as the novels of George Eliot. But she did not let herself be influenced by the technical skill of the Victorian poets. Much of her poetry is written in simple quatrains, generally in iambic tetrameter, often with only the second and fourth lines rhyming. It is close to the style of verse that filled the hymnals she used in church. Her poetry is so startling in its imagery and its revelations that there is no real parallel to it, but it is interesting that in its form it has some similarities with the poetry of Emily Brontë. Brontë, who found literary immortality with her novel Wuthering Heights, was one of the writers Dickinson read. Like Dickinson, Brontë was reclusive, spent her short life in her family home, and drew on the hymnal for the forms of her poetry. These lines by Brontë could also have been written by Dickinson:

I'm happiest when most away
I can bear my soul from its home of clay
On a windy night when the moon is bright
And the eye wander through worlds of light . . .

No coward soul is mine
No trembler in the world's storm-troubled sphere.

Higginson read Brontë's poem "Last Lines" at Dickinson's funeral. Seven of Dickinson's poems were published in her lifetime, and in each case they were edited or rewritten to suit the conventions of the time. Would she have edited them herself if Helen Hunt Jackson could have finally persuaded her to publish them? Like so much else about her life, we will never know. We do know that every revision Higginson suggested in his letters to her was gently but firmly rejected. She knew what she had accomplished. What she left was a gathering of poems so unique and unexpected that we are still trying today to measure the dimensions of her achievement.

This selection from her poetry includes many of her best-known poems, in the *transcriptions from her manuscripts published in 1948. The poems in the new edition were numbered, as Dickinson did not title them herself. They can be interpreted in many ways, and often they refer to some specific moment in the day they were written, like "I've nothing else — to bring, You know — ," which seems to be telling Charles Wadsworth that the only things that Dickinson can bring him are poems. The poems are startling in their imagery, and behind the deceptive simplicities of their lines are subtle insights. In "I'm 'wife' — I've finished that — " Dickinson describes the passage from girl to woman as "this soft eclipse." The sixth poem in this group begins with the unforgettable image " 'Hope' is the thing with feathers — / That perches in the soul." "I taste a liquor never brewed — " was one of the three poems that Bowles published in his newspaper, and it became one of the poems discussed by other writers when it was included in the first collection in 1890. The popular poet Thomas Bailey Aldrich was irritated by the imperfect rhyme of "pearl/alcohol" in the first stanza and quickly rewrote it. His "corrected" version was,*

> I taste a liquor never brewed
> In vats along the Rhine:
> No tankards scooped in pearl could yield
> An alcohol like mine.

Nothing Aldrich ever wrote, however, could match the exuberance of the poem's last image of Dickinson herself as "the little Tippler / Leaning against the — Sun."

"I'm Nobody! Who are you?" is her sardonic comment on fame, and in "Much Madness is divinest Sense — " she could be agreeing with William Blake, with his belief that society often mistakes genius for madness. "I died for Beauty — but was scarce" is one of her many poems on the subject of death, this one agreeing with John Keats's final lines of "Ode on a Grecian Urn": " 'Beauty is truth, truth beauty' — that is all / Ye know on earth, and all ye need to know." "Love — thou art high — " and "If you were coming in the Fall," are both from the last months of her relationship with Charles Wadsworth. "Mine — by the Right of the White Election!" was probably written when she realized they could never marry, although it is — as always — difficult to be certain of the circumstances of the poem. The phrase "White Election" probably means a wedding ceremony.

"Because I could not stop for Death — " and "The Only News I know" were written in the next years. The former, with its image of death as a gentle carriage ride, was one of the most widely quoted poems from the 1890 collection. The latter was not published until 1929. "Split the Lark — and you'll find the Music — " opens with an image as vivid as the first line of " 'Hope' is the thing with feathers — ." Although "I stepped from Plank to Plank" suggests that Dickinson had lived many years to gain her "Experience," she was only thirty-four. Still, she was already feeling her life closing in around her. "A narrow Fellow in the Grass," her brilliant description of a snake and the fear she feels whenever she sees one, was published in the Springfield Republican, *but she complained that it had been published without her permission. For much of her life she was troubled by her inability to accept conventional Christian dogma, but "I never saw a Moor — " is a clear statement of her religious faith. Dickinson has found her own way to eternity.*

RELATED COMMENTARIES: *See Casebook on Emily Dickinson, pages 1333–1351, including Thomas Wentworth Higginson, "Emily Dickinson's Letters," page 1334; Thomas H. Johnson, "The Text of Emily Dickinson's Poetry," page 1343;*

Richard Wilbur, "On Emily Dickinson," page 1345; Linda Gregg, "Not Understanding Emily Dickinson," page 1346; Galway Kinnell, "The Deconstruction of Emily Dickinson," page 1350.

EMILY DICKINSON

You love me — you are sure —   c. 1860

You love me — you are sure —
I shall not fear mistake —
I shall not *cheated* wake —
Some grinning morn —
to find the Sunrise left —   5
And Orchards — unbereft —
And Dollie — gone!

I need not start — you're sure —
That night will never be —
When frightened — home to Thee I run —   10
To find the windows dark —
And no more Dollie — mark —
Quite none?

Be sure you're sure — you know —
I'll bear it better now —   15
If you'll just tell me so —
Than when — a little dull Balm grown —
Over this pain of mine —
You sting — again!

EMILY DICKINSON

I'm "wife" — I've finished that —   c. 1860

I'm "wife" — I've finished that —
That other state —
I'm Czar — I'm "Woman" now —
It's safer so —

How odd the Girl's life looks   5
Behind this soft Eclipse —
I think that Earth feels so
To folks in Heaven — now —

This being comfort — then
That other kind — was pain —   10
But why compare?
I'm "Wife"! Stop there!

EMILY DICKINSON

I taste a liquor never brewed —

c. 1860

I taste a liquor never brewed —
From Tankards scooped in Pearl —
Not all the Vats upon the Rhine
Yield such an Alcohol!

Inebriate of Air — am I — 5
And Debauchee of Dew —
Reeling — thro endless summer days —
From inns of Molten Blue —

When "Landlords" turn the drunken Bee
Out of the Foxglove's door — 10
When Butterflies — renounce their "drams" —
I shall but drink the more!

Till Seraphs swing their snowy Hats —
And Saints — to windows run —
To see the little Tippler 15
Leaning against the — Sun —

EMILY DICKINSON

I've nothing else — to bring, You know —

c. 1861

I've nothing else — to bring, You know —
So I keep bringing These —
Just as the Night keeps fetching Stars
To our familiar eyes —

Maybe, we shouldn't mind them —
Unless they didn't come —
Then — maybe, it would puzzle us
To find our way Home —

EMILY DICKINSON

Wild Nights — Wild Nights!

c. 1861

Wild Nights — Wild Nights!
Were I with thee
Wild Nights should be
Our luxury!

Futile — the Winds —
To a Heart in port —
Done with the Compass —
Done with the Chart!   5

Rowing in Eden —
Ah, the Sea!   10
Might I but moor — Tonight —
In Thee!

EMILY DICKINSON

"Hope" is the thing with feathers —   *c. 1861*

"Hope" is the thing with feathers —
That perches in the soul —
And sings the tune without the words —
And never stops — at all —

And sweetest — in the Gale — is heard —   5
And sore must be the storm —
That could abash the little Bird
That kept so many warm —

I've heard it in the chillest land —
And on the strangest Sea —   10
Yet, never, in Extremity,
It asked a crumb — of Me.

EMILY DICKINSON

There's a certain Slant of light,   *c. 1861*

There's a certain Slant of light,
Winter Afternoons —
That oppresses, like the Heft
Of Cathedral Tunes —

Heavenly Hurt, it gives us —   5
We can find no scar,
But internal difference,
Where the Meanings, are —

None may teach it — Any —
'Tis the Seal Despair —   10
An imperial affliction
Sent us of the Air —

When it comes, the Landscape listens —
Shadows — hold their breath —

When it goes, 'tis like the Distance   15
On the look of Death —

EMILY DICKINSON

I'm Nobody! Who are you?   *c. 1861*

I'm Nobody! Who are you?
Are you — Nobody — Too?
Then there's a pair of us!
Don't tell! they'd advertise — you know!

How dreary — to be — Somebody!
How public — like a Frog —
To tell one's name — the livelong June —
To an admiring Bog!

EMILY DICKINSON

After great pain, a formal feeling comes —   *c. 1862*

After great pain, a formal feeling comes —
The Nerves sit ceremonious, like Tombs —
The stiff Heart questions was it He, that bore,
And Yesterday, or Centuries before?

The Feet, mechanical, go round —   5
Of Ground, or Air, or Ought —
A Wooden way
Regardless grown,
A Quartz contentment, like a stone —

This is the Hour of Lead —   10
Remembered, if outlived,
As Freezing persons, recollect the Snow —
First — Chill — then Stupor — then the letting go —

EMILY DICKINSON

Much Madness is divinest Sense —   *c. 1862*

Much Madness is divinest Sense —
To a discerning Eye —
Much Sense — the starkest Madness —
'Tis the Majority
In this, as All, prevail —

Assent — and you are sane —
Demur — you're straightway dangerous —
And handled with a Chain —

EMILY DICKINSON

I died for Beauty — but was scarce

c. 1862

I died for Beauty — but was scarce
Adjusted in the Tomb
When One who died for Truth, was lain
In an adjoining Room —

He questioned softly "Why I failed"?   5
"For Beauty," I replied —
"And I — for Truth — Themself are One —
We Brethren, are," He said —

And so, as Kinsmen, met a Night —
We talked between the Rooms —   10
Until the Moss had reached our lips —
And covered up — our names —

EMILY DICKINSON

Love — thou art high —

c. 1862

Love — thou art high —
I cannot climb thee —
But, were it Two —
Who knows but we —
Taking turns — at the Chimborazo —   5
Ducal — at last — stand up by thee —

Love — thou art deep —
I cannot cross thee —
But, were there Two
Instead of One —   10
Rower, and Yacht — some sovereign Summer —
Who knows — but we'd reach the Sun?

Love — thou art Veiled —
A few — behold thee —
Smile — and alter — and prattle — and die —   15
Bliss — were an Oddity — without thee —
Nicknamed by God —
Eternity —

EMILY DICKINSON

I heard a Fly buzz — when I died —
c. 1862

I heard a Fly buzz — when I died —
The Stillness in the Room
Was like the Stillness in the Air —
Between the Heaves of Storm —

The Eyes around — had wrung them dry —   5
And Breaths were gathering firm
For that last Onset — when the King
Be witnessed — in the Room —

I willed my Keepsakes — Signed away
What portion of me be   10
Assignable — and then it was
There interposed a Fly —

With Blue — uncertain stumbling Buzz —
Between the light — and me —
And then the Windows failed — and then   15
I could not see to see —

EMILY DICKINSON

If you were coming in the Fall,
c. 1862

If you were coming in the Fall,
I'd brush the Summer by
With half a smile, and half a spurn,
As Housewives do, a Fly.

If I could see you in a year,   5
I'd wind the months in balls —
And put them each in separate Drawers,
For fear the numbers fuse —

If only Centuries, delayed,
I'd count them on my Hand,   10
Subtracting, till my fingers dropped
Into Van Dieman's Land.°

If certain, when this life was out —
That yours and mine, should be
I'd toss it yonder, like a Rind,   15
And take Eternity —

---

12. Van Dieman's Land: The seventeenth-century Dutch navigator Abel Tasman named an
island off the coast of Australia Van Diemen's Land, which Dickinson has misspelled. Today
it is the Australian commonwealth of Tasmania.

But, now, uncertain of the length
Of this, that is between,
It goads me, like the Goblin Bee —
That will not state — its sting.   20

EMILY DICKINSON

Mine — by the Right of the White Election!

c. 1862

Mine — by the Right of the White Election!
Mine — by the Royal Seal!
Mine — by the Sign in the Scarlet prison —
Bars — cannot conceal!

Mine — here — in Vision — and in Veto!
Mine — by the Grave's Repeal —
Titled — Confirmed —
Delirious Charter!
Mine — long as Ages steal!

EMILY DICKINSON

Because I could not stop for Death —

c. 1863

Because I could not stop for Death —
He kindly stopped for me —
The Carriage held but just Ourselves —
And Immortality.

We slowly drove — He knew no haste   5
And I had put away
My labor and my leisure too,
For His Civility —

We passed the School, where Children strove
At Recess — in the Ring —   10
We passed the Fields of Gazing Grain —
We passed the Setting Sun —

Or rather — He passed Us —
The Dews drew quivering and chill —
For only Gossamer, my Gown —   15
My Tippet — only Tulle —

We paused before a House that seemed
A Swelling of the Ground —
The Roof was scarcely visible —
The Cornice — in the Ground —   20

Since then — 'tis Centuries — and yet
Feels shorter than the Day
I first surmised the Horses' Heads
Were toward Eternity —

EMILY DICKINSON

The Only News I know   *c. 1864*

The Only News I know
Is Bulletins all Day
From Immortality.

The Only Shows I see —
Tomorrow and Today —   5
Perchance Eternity —

The Only One I meet
Is God — The Only Street —
Existence — This traversed

If Other News there be —   10
Or Admirabler Show —
I'll tell it You —

EMILY DICKINSON

Split the Lark — and you'll
find the Music —   *c. 1864*

Split the Lark — and you'll find the Music —
Bulb after Bulb, in Silver rolled —
Scantily dealt to the Summer Morning
Saved for your Ear when Lutes be old.

Loose the Flood — you shall find it patent —
Gush after Gush, reserved for you —
Scarlet Experiment! Sceptic Thomas!
Now, do you doubt that your Bird was true?

EMILY DICKINSON

I stepped from Plank to Plank   *c. 1864*

I stepped from Plank to Plank
A slow and cautious way
The Stars about my Head I felt
About my Feet the Sea.

I knew not but the next
Would be my final inch —
This gave me that precarious Gait
Some call Experience.

EMILY DICKINSON

A narrow Fellow in the Grass   *c. 1865*

A narrow Fellow in the Grass
Occasionally rides —
You may have met Him — did you not
His notice sudden is —

The Grass divides as with a Comb —   5
A spotted shaft is seen —
And then it closes at your feet
And opens further on —

He likes a Boggy Acre
A Floor too cool for Corn —   10
Yet when a Boy, and Barefoot —
I more than once at Noon
Have passed, I thought, a Whip lash
Unbraiding in the Sun
When stooping to secure it   15
It wrinkled, and was gone —

Several of Nature's People
I know, and they know me —
I feel for them a transport
Of cordiality —   20

But never met this Fellow
Attended, or alone
Without a tighter breathing
And Zero at the Bone —

EMILY DICKINSON

I never saw a Moor —   *c. 1865*

I never saw a Moor —
I never saw the Sea —
Yet know I how the Heather looks
And what a Billow be.

I never spoke with God
Nor visited in Heaven —

Yet certain am I of the spot
As if the Checks were given —

❦

JOHN DONNE (1572–1631) *was born a Roman Catholic during a period in English history when Roman Catholics were harassed by the Protestant government and were barred from advancement to most major positions of influence. His father died when he was four, and he was left with enough income to live well, but not to purchase favor at the court of Queen Elizabeth. He studied at Oxford and Cambridge universities but earned no degrees.*

In his early twenties, Donne lived like many other young, ambitious courtiers. He had many mistresses, traveled extensively in Europe, and took part in two raids against the Spanish at Cadiz and in the Azores. At the same time he read voraciously and wrote some of his most vivid erotic poetry. He had renounced his Catholicism but still hesitated to join the Church of England.

In 1598, when he was twenty-six, Donne became private secretary to Sir Thomas Egerton, one of the most powerful figures in the court of Queen Elizabeth. A brilliant future seemed certain, but three years later he fell deeply in love and secretly married Ann More, the seventeen-year-old niece of Lady Egerton. He was dismissed and thrown into prison, and for a dozen years he struggled against disappointment and financial difficulties. During this period his marriage was his only source of happiness.

Because of his brilliance and his early friendships, Donne was still welcome in the court, but King James, who succeeded Elizabeth, felt that Donne could be most useful to him in the church, and refused to consider granting Donne any other position. Donne finally surrendered and in 1615 became an Anglican priest. He was as talented in the church as he had been in court life, and in 1621 he became dean of St. Paul's Cathedral in London, where he delivered sermons and wrote devotional poetry and meditations until his death.

This selection of Donne's poetry includes two early love poems, "The Good-Morrow" and "The Flea." "Good Friday, 1613. Riding Westward" was written during the years when he was struggling with the question of his religious faith. "Thou hast made me," "At the round earth's imagined corners," and "Batter my heart, three-personed God" are from his collection of "Holy Sonnets." (See also Donne's "Song" on p. 887 and "Death, be not proud" on p. 948.)

JOHN DONNE

The Good-Morrow 1633

I wonder, by my troth, what thou and I
Did, till we loved? Were we not weaned till then,
But sucked on country pleasures, childishly?
Or snorted we in the seven sleepers' den?
'Twas so; but this, all pleasures fancies be. 5

If ever any beauty I did see,
Which I desired, and got, 'twas but a dream of thee.

And now good morrow to our waking souls,
Which watch not one another out of fear;
For love all love of other sights controls,   10
And makes one little room an everywhere.
Let sea-discoverers to new worlds have gone,
Let maps to others, worlds on worlds have shown:
Let us possess one world; each hath one, and is one.

My face in thine eye, thine in mine appears,   15
And true plain hearts do in the faces rest;
Where can we find two better hemispheres,
Without sharp North, without declining West?
Whatever dies was not mixed equally;
If our two loves be one, or thou and I   20
Love so alike that none do slacken, none can die.

JOHN DONNE

The Flea   *1633*

Mark but this flea, and mark in this
How little that which thou deny'st me is;
It sucked me first, and now sucks thee,
And in this flea our two bloods mingled be;
Thou know'st that this cannot be said   5
A sin, nor shame, nor loss of maidenhead,
　　　Yet this enjoys before it woo,
　　　And pampered swells with one blood made of two,
　　　And this, alas, is more than we would do.

Oh stay, three lives in one flea spare,   10
Where we almost, yea more than, married are.
This flea is you and I, and this
Our marriage bed, and marriage temple is;
Though parents grudge, and you, we're met
And cloistered in these living walls of jet.   15
　　　Though use° make you apt to kill me,   *habit*
　　　Let not to that, self-murder added be,
　　　And sacrilege, three sins in killing three.

Cruel and sudden, hast thou since
Purpled thy nail in blood of innocence?   20
Wherein could this flea guilty be,
Except in that drop which it sucked from thee?
Yet thou triumph'st, and say'st that thou
Find'st not thyself, nor me, the weaker now;

'Tis true; then learn how false, fears be;   25
Just so much honor, when thou yield'st to me,
Will waste, as this flea's death took life from thee.

JOHN DONNE

Good Friday, 1613. Riding Westward   1633

Let man's soul be a sphere, and then, in this,
The intelligence that moves, devotion is,
And as the other spheres, by being grown
Subject to foreign motions, lose their own,
And being by others hurried every day,   5
Scarce in a year their natural form° obey;
Pleasure or business, so, our souls admit
For their first mover, and are whirled by it.
Hence is 't, that I am carried towards the West
This day, when my soul's form bends toward the East.   10
There I should see a Sun° by rising, set,
And by that setting endless day beget:
But that Christ on this cross did rise and fall,
Sin had eternally benighted all.
Yet dare I almost be glad I do not see   15
That spectacle, of too much weight for me.
Who sees God's face, that is self-life, must die;
What a death were it then to see God die?
It made his own lieutenant, Nature, shrink;
It made his footstool crack, and the sun wink.   20
Could I behold those hands which span the poles,
And tune all spheres at once, pierced with those holes?
Could I behold that endless height which is
Zenith to us, and t'our antipodes,°
Humbled below us? Or that blood which is   25
The seat of all our souls, if not of his,
Make dirt of dust, or that flesh which was worn
By God for his apparel, ragg'd and torn?
If on these things I durst not look, durst I
Upon his miserable mother cast mine eye,   30
Who was God's partner here, and furnished thus
Half of that sacrifice which ransomed us?
Though these things, as I ride, be from mine eye,
They are present yet unto my memory,
For that looks towards them; and thou look'st towards me,   35

---

6. natural form: Moving principle.   **11. There should I see a Sun:** A pun on the "Son" (i.e.,
Jesus), whose death and resurrection recounted in the Gospels commenced the Christian era
and its hope of immortality.   **24. antipodes:** Opposite ends of the earth.

O Savior, as thou hang'st upon the tree.
I turn my back to thee but to receive
Corrections, till thy mercies bid thee leave.
O think me worth thine anger; punish me;
Burn off my rusts and my deformity; 40
Restore thine image so much, by thy grace,
That thou may'st know me, and I'll turn my face.

JOHN DONNE

Thou hast made me   1633

Thou hast made me, and shall thy work decay?
Repair me now, for now mine end doth haste;
I run to death, and death meets me as fast,
And all my pleasures are like yesterday.
I dare not move my dim eyes any way, 5
Despair behind, and death before doth cast
Such terror, and my feeble flesh doth waste
By sin in it, which it towards hell doth weigh.
Only thou art above, and when towards thee
By thy leave I can look, I rise again; 10
But our old subtle foe so tempteth me
That not one hour myself I can sustain.
Thy grace may wing me to prevent his art,
And thou like adamant draw mine iron heart.

JOHN DONNE

At the round earth's imagined corners   1633

At the round earth's imagined corners, blow
Your trumpets, angels; and arise, arise°
From death, you numberless infinities
Of souls, and to your scattered bodies go:
All whom the flood did, and fire shall, o'erthrow, 5
All whom war, dearth, age, agues, tyrannies,
Despair, law, chance hath slain, and you whose eyes
Shall behold God, and never taste death's woe.
But let them sleep, Lord, and me mourn a space;
For, if above all these, my sins abound, 10
'Tis late to ask abundance of thy grace
When we are there. Here on this lowly ground,

1–2. At the round . . . arise: In the book of Revelation, angels are seen standing at the earth's
"four corners."

Teach me how to repent; for that's as good
As if thou hadst sealed my pardon with thy blood.

JOHN DONNE

Batter my heart, three-personed God   1633

Batter my heart, three-personed God; for You
As yet but knock, breathe, shine, and seek to mend;
That I may rise and stand, o'erthrow me,'and bend
Your force to break, blow, burn, and make me new.
I, like an usurped town, to'another due,   5
Labor to'admit You, but O, to no end;
Reason, Your viceroy'in me, me should defend,
But is captíved, and proves weak or untrue.
Yet dearly'I love You,'and would be lovéd fain,
But am betrothed unto Your enemy.   10
Divorce me,'untie or break that knot again;
Take me to You, imprison me, for I,
Except You'enthrall me, never shall be free,
Nor ever chaste, except You ravish me.

ॐ

RITA DOVE *(b. 1952) was born in Akron, Ohio, into a middle-class family
that encouraged her to read. As she remembered later in the introduction to her*
Selected Poems, *published in 1993, books were her life: "First and foremost, now,
then, and always, I have been passionate about books." Her father and grandfather
both worked for the Goodyear Tire and Rubber Company. Her father earned a master's
degree after she was born and became the company's first African American research
chemist.*

*Like so many other young writers, Dove first encountered poetry in an anthol-
ogy by Louis Untermeyer, and one of the first poems she remembers is Langston
Hughes's "Dream Boogie." She still never thought of herself as a poet, or even that poets were real people, until her eleventh-grade English teacher took her to a book signing by the poet John Ciardi.*

*She graduated from Miami University of Ohio, then spent two years in Ger-
many studying on a fellowship. After her return to the United States, she received an
M.F.A. from the University of Iowa writing program in 1977. Since then she has
taught poetry and literature, with occasional breaks for traveling. She is married and
has one child.*

*Although she is only in her forties, Dove has already had a career that other po-
ets can only envy. She has been the recipient of nearly every major grant and fellowship; she studied abroad as a Fulbright/Hayes scholar; her collection of short narrative
poems about her grandparents,* Thomas and Beulah, *won the Pulitzer Prize in 1987;
and in 1993 she was appointed poet laureate of the United States.*

"Belinda's Petition" is an early poem, written in the voice of a slave woman.
"Weathering Out" and "Daystar" are from Thomas and Beulah.
RELATED COMMENTARY: *Rita Dove, "An Intact World," page 1252.*

RITA DOVE

Belinda's Petition

1980

(Boston, February, 1782)

To the honorable Senate and House
of Representatives of this Country,
new born: I am Belinda, an African,
since the age of twelve a Slave.
I will not take too much of your Time,   5
but to plead and place my pitiable Life
unto the Fathers of this Nation.

Lately your Countrymen have severed
the Binds of Tyranny. I would hope
you would consider the Same for me,   10
pure Air being the sole Advantage
of which I can boast in my present Condition.

As to the Accusation that I am Ignorant:
I received Existence on the Banks
of the Rio de Valta. All my Childhood   15
I expected nothing, if that be Ignorance.
The only Travelers were the Dead who returned
from the Ridge each Evening. How might
I have known of Men with Faces like the Moon,
who would ride toward me steadily for twelve Years?   20

RITA DOVE

Weathering Out

1986

She liked mornings the best — Thomas gone
to look for work, her coffee flushed with milk,

outside autumn trees blowsy and dripping.
Past the seventh month she couldn't see her feet

so she floated from room to room, houseshoes flapping,   5
navigating corners in wonder. When she leaned

against a door jamb to yawn, she disappeared entirely.

Last week they had taken a bus at dawn
to the new airdock. The hangar slid open in segments

and the zeppelin nosed forward in its silver envelope.   10
The man walked it out gingerly, like a poodle,

then tied it to a mast and went back inside.
Beulah felt just that large and placid, a lake;

she glistened from cocoa butter smoothed in
when Thomas returned every evening nearly   15

in tears. He'd lean an ear on her belly
and say: *Little fellow's really talking,*

though to her it was more the *pok-pok-pok*
of a fingernail tapping a thick cream lampshade.

Sometimes during the night she woke and found him   20
asleep there and the child sleeping, too.

The coffee was good but too little. Outside
everything shivered in tinfoil — only the clover

between the cobblestones hung stubbornly on,
green as an afterthought. . . .   25

RITA DOVE

Daystar   1986

She wanted a little room for thinking:
but she saw diapers steaming on the line,
a doll slumped behind the door.

So she lugged a chair behind the garage
to sit out the children's naps.   5

Sometimes there were things to watch —
the pinched armor of a vanished cricket,
a floating maple leaf. Other days
she stared until she was assured
when she closed her eyes   10
she'd see only her own vivid blood.

She had an hour, at best, before Liza appeared
pouting from the top of the stairs.
And just *what* was mother doing
out back with the field mice? Why,   15

building a palace. Later
that night when Thomas rolled over and
lurched into her, she would open her eyes
and think of the place that was hers
for an hour — where   20
she was nothing,
pure nothing, in the middle of the day.

∽

R**OBERT** D**UNCAN** (1919–1988) *was born in Oakland, California, but his mother died of influenza shortly after his birth. His father was a day laborer and he was forced to give up the baby to a couple who adopted him and raised him in small towns in California's Central Valley. The couple who adopted him were Theosophists, members of a movement following Buddhist and Brahmanic theories of pantheistic evolution and reincarnation. As critic Michael Davidson has described Duncan's up-bringing, he was given a "sense of the world in which each event becomes an intimation of a story in a larger world of meanings." Duncan never lost his interest in ritual and the occult.*

He moved to the San Francisco Bay Area in the late 1930s, and he soon met and became associated with most of the writers already living there, including poets William Everson and Kenneth Rexroth. In 1944 he published a controversial article "The Homosexual in Society," and in his first book of poems, Heavenly City, Earthly City, *which appeared in 1947, he made explicit reference to his own homosexuality.*

Duncan left the Bay Area for brief periods, including a year when he taught at Black Mountain College in North Carolina, but until his death he was actively involved in the San Francisco poetry scene, as a poet, teacher, and an important influence on many younger poets. His companion in these years was the painter Jess Collins.

"Song" is an early poem written when he was in his twenties. "My Mother Would Be a Falconress" is his moving attempt to come to some understanding of his relationship with his adoptive mother.

RELATED COMMENTARY: *Samuel Charters, "On Robert Duncan's 'My Mother Would Be a Falconress,' " page 1243.*

R**OBERT** D**UNCAN**

Song

1966

How in the dark the cows lie down.
They sleep in grace, in their dumb remove.
How the dumb sheep in the grace of dark
huddle to sleep. How the winter's cold
sharpens & glisters the whispering still.   5
How each man to his beloved comes,
to his dumb, to his grace, in the evening's chill.
How, at last, to his comfort, his death,
comes even the damnd, to his final home.
Alone I lie in the hush of my beast   10
to hear upon my body's lyre
the varying discords of my desire
until the intervening nights and days,
the sheltering darks, the revealing lights,
have passt away.   15

ROBERT DUNCAN

My Mother Would Be a Falconress   1968

My mother would be a falconress,
And I, her gay falcon treading her wrist,
would fly to bring back
from the blue of the sky to her, bleeding, a prize,
where I dream in my little hood with many bells   5
jangling when I'd turn my head.

My mother would be a falconress,
and she sends me as far as her will goes.
She lets me ride to the end of her curb
where I fall back in anguish.   10
I dread that she will cast me away,
for I fall, I mis-take, I fail in her mission.

She would bring down the little birds.
And I would bring down the little birds.
When will she let me bring down the little birds,   15
pierced from their flight with their necks broken,
their heads like flowers limp from the stem?

I tread my mother's wrist and would draw blood.
Behind the little hood my eyes are hooded.
I have gone back into my hooded silence,   20
talking to myself and dropping off to sleep.

For she has muffled my dreams in the hood she has made me,
sewn round with bells, jangling when I move.
She rides with her little falcon upon her wrist.
She uses a barb that brings me to cower.   25

She sends me abroad to try my wings
and I come back to her. I would bring down
the little birds to her
I may not tear into, I must bring back perfectly.

I tear at her wrist with my beak to draw blood,   30
and her eye holds me, anguisht, terrifying.
She draws a limit to my flight.
Never beyond my sight, she says.

She trains me to fetch and to limit myself in fetching.
She rewards me with meat for my dinner.   35
But I must never eat what she sends me to bring her.

Yet it would have been beautiful, if she would have carried me,
always, in a little hood with the bells ringing,
at her wrist, and her riding
to the great falcon hunt, and me   40
flying up to the curb of my heart from her heart

to bring down the skylark from the blue to her feet,
straining, and then released for the flight.

My mother would be a falconress,
and I her gerfalcon, raised at her will,   45
from her wrist sent flying, as if I were her own
pride, as if her pride
knew no limits, as if her mind
sought in me flight beyond the horizon.

Ah, but high, high in the air I flew.   50
And far, far beyond the curb of her will,
were the blue hills where the falcons nest.
And then I saw west to the dying sun —
it seemd my human soul went down in flames.

I tore at her wrist, at the hold she had for me,   55
until the blood ran hot and I heard her cry out,
far, far beyond the curb of her will

to horizons of stars beyond the ringing hills of the world where
    the falcons nest
I saw, and I tore at her wrist with my savage beak.

I flew, as if sight flew from the anguish in her eye beyond her sight,   60
sent from my striking loose, from the cruel strike at her wrist,
striking out from the blood to be free of her.

My mother would be a falconress,
and even now, years after this,
when the wounds I left her had surely heald,   65
and the woman is dead,
her fierce eyes closed, and if her heart
were broken, it is stilld

I would be a falcon and go free.
I tread her wrist and wear the hood,   70
talking to myself, and would draw blood.

ᘍᘊ

T. S. ELIOT *(1888–1965) was born Thomas Stearns Eliot in St. Louis, Missouri. His mother was a schoolteacher who also wrote poetry, and his father was a successful businessman. Eliot was sent to finish his education at Milton Academy, south of Boston, and then attended Harvard College.*

Following his graduation from Harvard in 1910, he spent a year in France studying at the Sorbonne and became intensely interested in the writing of a brilliant group of contemporary French poets who called themselves symbolists. *When he returned to Harvard to earn his doctorate the next year, he began writing "The Love Song of J. Alfred Prufrock," a poem that included phrases and attitudes translated from the work of symbolist poets Jules Laforgue and Arthur Rimbaud. Conrad Aiken, a fellow student who was also a poet, encouraged him to publish it, but Eliot waited until he returned to Europe in 1914 and was studying at Oxford. He read the poem to Ezra Pound (p. 1175), who immediately sent it to an American magazine. It is considered by most critics to be the first modernist poem written in English.*

In 1915 Eliot suddenly married Vivian Haigh-Wood, whom he had met in England, and had to find some kind of job to support them. He was first a schoolteacher, then a bank clerk, and finally a director in a London publishing house. With the publication in 1922 of his controversial long poem The Wasteland *— a work begun during a stay in a sanatorium brought about by exhaustion, marital difficulties, and depression — he became one of the world's most widely read and discussed younger poets. His writing, both as a poet and a literary critic, had a decisive effect on nearly every poetic tradition before World War II. He became a British citizen in 1927. In 1948 he won the Nobel Prize for literature.*

RELATED COMMENTARIES: *Cleanth Brooks Jr. and Robert Penn Warren, "On Eliot's 'The Love Song of J. Alfred Prufrock,' " page 1240; T. S. Eliot, "From 'Tradition and the Individual Talent,' " page 1253; Michael Rubiner, "T. S. Eliot Interactive," page 1301.*

T. S. ELIOT

The Love Song of J. Alfred Prufrock   1917

S'io credesse che mia risposta fosse
A persona che mai tornasse al mondo,
Questa fiamma staria senza piu scosse.
Ma perciocche giammai di questo fondo
Non torno vivo alcun, s'i'odo il vero,
Sensa tema d'infamia ti rispondo.°

Let us go then, you and I,
When the evening is spread out against the sky
Like a patient etherized upon a table;
Let us go, through certain half-deserted streets,
The muttering retreats   5
Of restless nights in one-night cheap hotels
And sawdust restaurants with oyster-shells:
Streets that follow like a tedious argument
Of insidious intent
To lead you to an overwhelming question . . .   10

S'io . . . rispondo: In Dante's *Inferno*, these lines are spoken by one of the "false counselors" whose soul is hidden within a flame that moves as it speaks: "If I believed my reply were given / to one who might ever return to the earth, this fire would cease further movement. / But as from this chasm / none has ever come back alive — if what I have heard is true — / without fearing infamy will I respond to you."

Oh, do not ask, "What is it?"
Let us go and make our visit.

In the room the women come and go
Talking of Michelangelo.

The yellow fog that rubs its back upon the window-panes   15
The yellow smoke that rubs its muzzle on the window-panes
Licked its tongue into the corners of the evening,
Lingered upon the pools that stand in drains,
Let fall upon its back the soot that falls from chimneys,
Slipped by the terrace, made a sudden leap,   20
And seeing that it was a soft October night,
Curled once about the house, and fell asleep.

And indeed there will be time
For the yellow smoke that slides along the street,
Rubbing its back upon the window-panes;   25
There will be time, there will be time
To prepare a face to meet the faces that you meet;
There will be time to murder and create,
And time for all the works and days of hands
That lift and drop a question on your plate;   30
Time for you and time for me,
And time yet for a hundred indecisions,
And for a hundred visions and revisions,
Before the taking of a toast and tea.

In the room the women come and go   35
Talking of Michelangelo.

And indeed there will be time
To wonder, "Do I dare?" and, "Do I dare?"
Time to turn back and descend the stair,
With a bald spot in the middle of my hair —   40
[They will say: "How his hair is growing thin!"]
My morning coat, my collar mounting firmly to the chin,
My necktie rich and modest, but asserted by a simple pin —
[They will say: "But how his arms and legs are thin!"]
Do I dare   45
Disturb the universe?
In a minute there is time
For decisions and revisions which a minute will reverse.

For I have known them all already, known them all:
Have known the evenings, mornings, afternoons,   50
I have measured out my life with coffee spoons;
I know the voices dying with a dying fall
Beneath the music from a farther room.
    So how should I presume?

And I have known the eyes already, known them all — 55
The eyes that fix you in a formulated phrase,
And when I am formulated, sprawling on a pin,
When I am pinned and wriggling on the wall,
Then how should I begin
To spit out all the butt-ends of my days and ways? 60
   And how should I presume?

And I have known the arms already, known them all —
Arms that are braceleted and white and bare
[But in the lamplight, downed with light brown hair!]
Is it perfume from a dress 65
That makes me so digress?
Arms that lie along a table, or wrap about a shawl.
   And should I then presume?
   And how should I begin?

       . . . . .

Shall I say, I have gone at dusk through narrow streets 70
And watched the smoke that rises from the pipes
Of lonely men in shirt-sleeves, leaning out of windows? . . .

I should have been a pair of ragged claws
Scuttling across the floors of silent seas.

       . . . . .

And the afternoon, the evening, sleeps so peacefully! 75
Smoothed by long fingers,
Asleep . . . tired . . . or it malingers,
Stretched on the floor, here beside you and me.
Should I, after tea and cakes and ices,
Have the strength to force the moment to its crisis? 80
But though I have wept and fasted, wept and prayed,
Though I have seen my head [grown slightly bald] brought in upon a
    platter,°
I am no prophet — and here's no great matter;
I have seen the moment of my greatness flicker,
And I have seen the eternal Footman hold my coat, and snicker, 85
And in short, I was afraid.

And would it have been worth it, after all,
After the cups, the marmalade, the tea,
Among the porcelain, among some talk of you and me,
Would it have been worth while, 90
To have bitten off the matter with a smile,
To have squeezed the universe into a ball
To roll it toward some overwhelming question,

---

82. **upon a platter:** A reference to the martyrdom of St. John the Baptist (Matthew 14:1–12).

To say: "I am Lazarus,° come from the dead,
Come back to tell you all, I shall tell you all" — 95
If one, settling a pillow by her head,
    Should say: "That is not what I meant at all.
    That is not it, at all."

And would it have been worth it, after all,
Would it have been worth while, 100
After the sunsets and the dooryards and the sprinkled streets,
After the novels, after the teacups, after the skirts that trail along the
    floor —
And this, and so much more? —
It is impossible to say just what I mean!
But as if a magic lantern threw the nerves in patterns on a screen: 105
Would it have been worth while
If one, settling a pillow or throwing off a shawl,
And turning toward the window, should say:
    "That is not it at all,
    That is not what I meant, at all." 110

    . . . . . .

No! I am not Prince Hamlet, nor was meant to be;
Am an attendant lord, one that will do
To swell a progress, start a scene or two,
Advise the prince; no doubt, an easy tool,
Deferential, glad to be of use, 115
Politic, cautious, and meticulous;
Full of high sentence, but a bit obtuse;
At times, indeed, almost ridiculous —
Almost, at times, the Fool.

I grow old . . . I grow old . . . 120
I shall wear the bottoms of my trousers rolled.

Shall I part my hair behind? Do I dare to eat a peach?
I shall wear white flannel trousers, and walk upon the beach.
I have heard the mermaids singing, each to each.

I do not think that they will sing to me. 125

I have seen them riding seaward on the waves
Combing the white hair of the waves blown back
When the wind blows the water white and black.

We have lingered in the chambers of the sea
By sea-girls wreathed with seaweed red and brown 130
Till human voices wake us, and we drown.

         formula-symbol

---

94. "I am Lazarus": A reference to the resurrected Lazarus (John II, 12:1–2)

LAWRENCE FERLINGHETTI (*b. 1919*) *was born in Yonkers, New York, to Italian American parents. Tragically, his father died before he was born, and his mother was institutionalized. His mother's aunt took him with her to France for five years, but her own life was difficult, and following their return to the United States, Ferlinghetti was placed in an orphanage for seven months. It was only after his great-aunt became a tutor to a wealthy New York suburban family that she was able to take care of him again. He attended the Mount Hermon School in Massachusetts and then the University of North Carolina.*

Although Ferlinghetti was later to be known for his radical pacifist views, he served as a lieutenant commander in the U.S. Navy from 1941 to 1945. After the war, he studied for his doctorate at the Sorbonne in Paris. In April 1951 he married and settled in San Francisco, where he and a friend, Peter Martin, opened a small bookstore named City Lights, after the Charlie Chaplin film. The store became the center of the new Beat literary movement, which would soon coalesce in San Francisco.

Ferlinghetti began publishing a series of small books of his own and his friends' poetry, and one of his first publications was Allen Ginsberg's poem Howl. *The poem was seized by the police for obscenity, and the trial and the publicity from it helped turn the Beats into a national news event. Ferlinghetti's own book,* Starting from San Francisco, *sold several hundred thousand copies in the 1960s.*

He is often considered a Beat writer, but his writing, such as the poem "Dog," has closer affinities to the French political poetry that he translated while in Paris. "In Goya's greatest scenes we seem to see" and "Late Impressionist Dream" reflect his serious interest in painting and art. (See also Ferlinghetti's "Constantly Risking Absurdity" on p. 877 and "Two Scavengers in a Truck, Two Beautiful People in a Mercedes" on p. 997.)

RELATED STORY: *Hjalmar Söderberg, "A Dog without a Master," page 617.*
RELATED POEM: *Louis Jenkins, "How to Tell a Wolf from a Dog," page 961.*

LAWRENCE FERLINGHETTI

Dog   *1958*

The dog trots freely in the street
and sees reality
and the things he sees
are bigger than himself
and the things he sees   5
are his reality
Drunks in doorways
Moons on trees
The dog trots freely thru the street
and the things he sees   10
are smaller than himself
Fish on newsprint
Ants in holes

Chickens in Chinatown windows
their heads a block away   15
The dog trots freely in the street
and the things he smells
smell something like himself
The dog trots freely in the street
past puddles and babies   20
cats and cigars
poolrooms and policemen
He doesn't hate cops
He merely has no use for them
and he goes past them   25
and past the dead cows hung up whole
in front of the San Francisco Meat Market
He would rather eat a tender cow
than a tough policeman
though either might do   30
And he goes past the Romeo Ravioli Factory
and past Coit's Tower
and past Congressman Doyle
He's afraid of Coit's Tower
but he's not afraid of Congressman Doyle   35
although what he hears is very discouraging
very depressing
very absurd
to a sad young dog like himself
to a serious dog like himself   40
But he has his own free world to live in
His own fleas to eat
He will not be muzzled
Congressman Doyle is just another
fire hydrant   45
to him
The dog trots freely in the street
and has his own dog's life to live
and to think about
and to reflect upon   50
touching and tasting and testing everything
investigating everything
without benefit of perjury
a real realist
with a real tale to tell   55
and a real tail to tell it with
a real live
          barking
                democratic dog

engaged in real   60
                   free enterprise
with something to say
                   about ontology
something to say
                   about reality   65
                              and how to see it
                                   and how to hear it
with his head cocked sideways
                         at streetcorners
as if he is just about to have   70
                         his picture taken
                                   for Victor Records
                    listening for
                         His Master's Voice
         and looking   75
                    like a living questionmark
                                   into the
                                   great gramaphone
                                   of puzzling existence
with its wondrous hollow horn   80
         which always seems
         just about to spout forth
                         some Victorious answer
                         to everything

LAWRENCE FERLINGHETTI

In Goya's greatest scenes we seem to see   1958

In Goya's greatest scenes we seem to see

                              the people of the world
         exactly at the moment when
              they first attained the title of

                              "suffering humanity"   5
         They writhe upon the page
                    in a veritable rage
                              of adversity
              Heaped up
                   groaning with babies and bayonets   10
                              under cement skies
         in an abstract landscape of blasted trees
              bent statues bats wings and beaks
                   slippery gibbets
         cadavers and carnivorous cocks   15

and all the final hollering monsters
          of the
                    "imagination of disaster"
          they are so bloody real
                    it is as if they really still existed   20
     And they do

               Only the landscape is changed

They still are ranged along the roads
     plagued by legionnaires
                    false windmills and demented roosters   25
     They are the same people
                    only further from home
     on freeways fifty lanes wide
               on a concrete continent
                    spaced with bland billboards   30
               illustrating imbecile illusions of happiness
     The scene shows fewer tumbrils
               but more maimed citizens
                    in painted cars   35
     and they have strange license plates
     and engines
          that devour America

Lawrence Ferlinghetti

Late Impressionist Dream   1984

In a late Impressionist dream I am riding in an open touring-
car with a group of French women in summer dresses and
picture hats with uncles in grey doeskin vests and striped
shirts with armbands and everyone is laughing and chattering
in French as if no other language has yet become socially   5
accepted And we get to an outdoor cafe by the Seine on the
outskirts of Paris as in a Manet painting under an arbor by
the river drinking wine and eating a grand picnic out of
wicker hampers And at the next table a group of French intellectuals are indulging in their famous *grande logique* proving   10
that such-and-such is really an oxymoron And just then some
loud young men drift by in punts on the river looking sheepishly like young American college students singing a drinking
song about Whiffenpoofs and we go on talking French as if
nothing else in the real world were happening anywhere And   15
all the people around me turn into characters out of Marcel
Proust and we are all in Swann's Way in a budding grove
with a straight Odette chez Swann but then of a sudden Blaise

Cendrars bursts in waving a newspaper headline screaming
"L'OR! L'OR!" and gold has been discovered in California   20
and I must leave immediately to join the Gold Rush and wake
up in my cabin in Big Sur looking like a French Canuck Jack
Kerouac and hearing the sound of the sea in which the fish
still speak Breton

ॐ

ROBERT FROST *(1874–1963) Although Walt Whitman proclaimed himself
the poet of the American democracy, it is the quiet poet of the New England countryside, Robert Frost, who is the closest the United States has come to a "national" poet.
It was fitting that when President-elect John F. Kennedy was inaugurated for a presidency that he dreamed would re-create the American spirit, he chose Robert Frost to
read a new poem for the occasion. The sun shone so brightly in the poet's eyes that he
could not read the new poem he had written, so he recited an old poem from memory,
and it fit just as well into the solemn ceremony.*

*Although Robert Frost's poetry rings with the tones of New England, and the
voice of his poems is that of a New England farmer, this was the result of a conscious
artistic choice. His own background was more diverse. He was born in San Francisco
in 1874, and lived there eleven years until his father's death. His mother then moved
with Robert and his younger sister Jeanie to Lawrence, Massachusetts, where she
looked for work as a schoolteacher. Frost attended high school in Lawrence and was a
valedictorian at his graduation. Three years later, after a stormy and jealous courtship,
he married the woman who had been the other valedictorian, Elinor White. It was a
marriage with only brief moments of happiness, but Elinor gave birth to six children,
two of whom died very young. After high school Frost briefly attended Dartmouth and
Harvard, and for the next twenty years he struggled to support his family with a series of poorly paid jobs, writing poems at night and sending them to local newspapers.
One of his failed projects was an attempt to operate a chicken farm in New Hampshire,
and even though he was unsuccessful as a farmer the experience gave him the setting
for his poetry.*

*Although Frost in later years described the family's poverty during this time in
bleak terms, he was being partially supported by his grandfather. As biographer
William H. Pritchard writes,*

> *Frost had tried poultry farming in Derry, New Hampshire, the farm pur-
> chased for him by his paternal grandfather, and the indifferent results proba-
> bly had a good deal to do with the very qualified way he would later
> characterize himself as a farmer. When William Prescott Frost died in 1901,
> he gave his grandson free use of the farm for ten years, after which it would
> belong to Frost. There was, as well, an annuity of five hundred dollars for each
> of the first ten years; it would then become eight hundred for the rest of the
> grandson's life. Meanwhile, in 1906, Frost began full-time teaching at
> Pinkerton Academy, in Derry, and in 1911 taught for a year at the Plymouth
> Normal School, in Plymouth, New Hampshire. In 1911, the farm having be-
> come his to do with as he pleased, Frost sold it, and the proceeds, in addition
> to the enlarged annuity, which was now his, made the possibility of living
> away from New England for a time — with no responsibilities except literary*

and familial ones — real and attractive. (Frost: A Literary Life Reconsidered, 1984, p. 4)

In 1912, despite the support from his grandfather he was so discouraged at his failure as a writer that he was close to emotional collapse, deeply depressed, and suicidal. In an effort to wrench himself free, he took the family to England, where they lived on his annuity. He formed a close friendship with Edward Thomas, a young English literary journalist, who began writing poetry himself after he had come to know Frost. Frost said of him later that he was "the only brother I ever had." His meetings with young English poets helped him to strip his poetry of its conventional imagery, and in 1913 he was able to find a publisher for his first book, A Boy's Will. An American expatriate living in London, Ezra Pound (p. 1175), wrote enthusiastically to American publishers about Frost's poetry and helped him find a publisher for North of Boston, which appeared in 1914. Included in the book were many of the poems that would make Frost famous, and it was an immediate success. When he returned to the United States a year later, Frost was an established writer, and he was able to find work as a teacher. He taught for many years at several schools, among them Harvard University, Amherst College, Middlebury College, and Dartmouth College, as well at the Bread Loaf School, a summer writing program that he founded and led until his death.

Frost was free of the economic worries that had plagued him for so long, but his life was not free of tragedy. His son committed suicide, and one daughter had to be confined to a mental institution. None of his family's unhappiness was directly mirrored in his poetry, which became more and more positive in tone as he grew older. Disengaging himself from the political turmoil of the 1930s, he refused to join other poets in their struggles to achieve a more just American society. As he wrote in the introduction to his Collected Poems in 1939, "I have given up my democratic prejudices and now willingly set the lower classes free to be completely taken care of by the upper classes. Political freedom is nothing to me. I bestow it right and left." At the same time, he was fiercely jealous of other poets, and he was painfully conscious that the attention of his early audience had drifted to the more modern work of writers such as T. S. Eliot, or the more politically aware poetry of Archibald MacLeish. His attacks on their work often focused on their open poetic form. In the same introduction he wrote of their poetics, "It is painful to watch our sprung-rhythmists straining at the point of omitting one short from a foot for relief from monotony." In the emotional tides of World War II, Frost's poetry became a place of refuge and comfort for many readers, and despite the disillusionment of the 1950s, he never lost the place he had won in America's heart. There was mourning across the nation at his death in 1963.

"The Pasture" was written shortly after the family had moved to England, and its description of the cow and her new calf in the spring pasture may have been inspired by home-sickness for their life in New Hampshire. Like all of Frost's poems about his experience as a farmer, "The Pasture" does not describe the reality of the farm but projects a wish that the reality might have been like that. It is this conscious presentation of idealized American experience that is at the heart of Frost's enduring popularity. Also composed in England, "Mending Wall" is unrhymed, but it is written in fluent iambic pentameter, the blank verse form that Shakespeare used for his plays. If Frost ever read Walt Whitman's poetry, with its free meter and unrhymed cadences, there is no sign of it in his own work. As he said, free verse was "like playing tennis with the net down."

In his early poetry Frost also showed a strong sense of drama, and he included several long narrative poems in his first books. The poems were stark and moody, and in them can be glimpsed some of his own unhappiness. One of the best known is "The Death of the Hired Man," a sorrowful description of an old farm laborer who has outlived his usefulness. Although the opening line suggests a freer meter, the poem is written in blank verse. "The Hill Wife" is also a desolate narrative poem, although Frost chose to tell the story in five connected lyrics.

In "Birches" he returns to his characteristically skillful iambic pentameter. It is a poem that gives some hint of his desire to live his life more freely, even if it is only to swing on birch trees. As he writes, "Earth's the right place for love." The poem also has one of his most striking images, the description of the ice breaking loose from the frozen trees,

> . . . they click upon themselves
> As the breeze rises, and turn many-colored
> As the stir cracks and crazes their enamel.

"Fire and Ice" is only a little longer than an epigram, but in its few lines Frost manages to make a sardonic comment about the end of the world. His bitter lines can be read as an allusion to the image from the gospel song about the same moment of destruction, "no more water, fire next time." "To Earthward" describes the intense fire he felt in his early love, and now he finds that for him there is "no joy but lacks salt," and he longs to feel his old fervor again.

Frost's writing appears to be so effortless that many of his most popular poems seem as clear and as simple as someone describing the weather. At the same time they are complex examples of rhyme and diction. "Stopping by Woods on a Snowy Evening" is one of these familiar poems. The seemingly artless stanzas are actually tightly structured around a complicated rhyme scheme. Even if the reader's eye is not consciously analyzing the rhymes, the ear is hearing them.

"The Road Not Taken" is one of Frost's most popular poems, written in the United States a year after his return from England. Its metaphor of life as a journey, and the decision to make the journey down one of two roads, is a striking example of a metaphor that is the poem. Readers have sometimes noticed, however, that Frost makes it clear that the roads were actually so similar that each of them was worn "about the same." The poem was actually intended as a joke for his friend Edward Thomas. Thomas could never make up his mind about anything, and Frost teased him by saying, "No matter which road you take, you'll always sigh and wish you'd taken another." Frost sent the poem to Thomas in a letter, but his friend missed the joke entirely, thinking it was a poem about the decisions Frost had made in his own life. According to his biographer Lawrence Thompson, Frost never could bring himself to confess that the poem had not worked the way he had intended.

Written in England, "After Apple-Picking" is another poem in which Frost uses a metaphor taken from his half-imagined country life to describe his emotions at his own death, and it reflects the disappointments he and his family had endured. He was only forty when he wrote it, and he would live another forty-five years.

RELATED COMMENTARIES: *See Casebook on Robert Frost, pages 1351–1361, including Rose C. Field, "An Interview with Robert Frost," page 1352; Robert Frost, "The Figure a Poem Makes," page 1354; Robert Lowell, "On Robert Frost," page*

1357; Joseph Brodsky, "On Grief and Reason," page 1357; Philip L. Gerber, "On Frost's 'After Apple-Picking,' " page 1359.

ROBERT FROST

The Pasture

1913

I'm going out to clean the pasture spring;
I'll only stop to rake the leaves away
(And wait to watch the water clear, I may):
I shan't be gone long. — You come too.

I'm going out to fetch the little calf
That's standing by the mother. It's so young
It totters when she licks it with her tongue.
I shan't be gone long. — You come too.

ROBERT FROST

Mending Wall

1914

Something there is that doesn't love a wall,
That sends the frozen-ground-swell under it,
And spills the upper boulders in the sun;
And makes gaps even two can pass abreast.
The work of hunters is another thing: 5
I have come after them and made repair
Where they have left not one stone on a stone,
But they would have the rabbit out of hiding,
To please the yelping dogs. The gaps I mean,
No one has seen them made or heard them made,   10
But at spring mending-time we find them there.
I let my neighbor know beyond the hill;
And on a day we meet to walk the line
And set the wall between us once again.
We keep the wall between us as we go.   15
To each the boulders that have fallen to each.
And some are loaves and some so nearly balls
We have to use a spell to make them balance:
"Stay where you are until our backs are turned!"
We wear our fingers rough with handling them.   20
Oh, just another kind of outdoor game,
One on a side. It comes to little more:
There where it is we do not need the wall:
He is all pine and I am apple orchard.
My apple trees will never get across   25
And eat the cones under his pines, I tell him.

He only says, "Good fences make good neighbors."
Spring is the mischief in me, and I wonder
If I could put a notion in his head:
"*Why* do they make good neighbors? Isn't it   30
Where there are cows? But here there are no cows.
Before I built a wall I'd ask to know
What I was walling in or walling out,
And to whom I was like to give offense.
Something there is that doesn't love a wall,   35
That wants it down." I could say "Elves" to him,
But it's not elves exactly, and I'd rather
He said it for himself. I see him there
Bringing a stone grasped firmly by the top
In each hand, like an old-stone savage armed.   40
He moves in darkness as it seems to me,
Not of woods only and the shade of trees.
He will not go behind his father's saying,
And he likes having thought of it so well
He says again, "Good fences make good neighbors."   45

ROBERT FROST

The Death of the Hired Man   *1914*

Mary sat musing on the lamp-flame at the table
Waiting for Warren. When she heard his step,
She ran on tiptoe down the darkened passage
To meet him in the doorway with the news
And put him on his guard. "Silas is back."   5
She pushed him outward with her through the door
And shut it after her. "Be kind," she said.
She took the market things from Warren's arms
And set them on the porch, then drew him down
To sit beside her on the wooden steps.   10

"When was I ever anything but kind to him?
But I'll not have the fellow back," he said.
"I told him so last haying, didn't I?
If he left then, I said, that ended it.
What good is he? Who else will harbor him   15
At his age for the little he can do?
What help he is there's no depending on.
Off he goes always when I need him most.
He thinks he ought to earn a little pay,
Enough at least to buy tobacco with,   20
So he won't have to beg and be beholden.
'All right,' I say, 'I can't afford to pay

Any fixed wages, though I wish I could.'
'Someone else can.' 'Then someone else will have to.'
I shouldn't mind his bettering himself   25
If that was what it was. You can be certain,
When he begins like that, there's someone at him
Trying to coax him off with pocket money, —
In haying time, when any help is scarce.
In winter he comes back to us. I'm done."   30

"Sh! not so loud: he'll hear you," Mary said.
"I want him to: he'll have to soon or late."

"He's worn out. He's asleep beside the stove.
When I came up from Rowe's I found him here,
Huddled against the barn door fast asleep,   35
A miserable sight, and frightening, too —
You needn't smile — I didn't recognize him —
I wasn't looking for him — and he's changed.
Wait till you see."

       "Where did you say he'd been?"   40

"He didn't say. I dragged him to the house,
And gave him tea and tried to make him smoke.
I tried to make him talk about his travels.
Nothing would do: he just kept nodding off."

"What did he say? Did he say anything?"   45

"But little."

      "Anything? Mary, confess
He said he'd come to ditch the meadow for me."

"Warren!"

     "But did he? I just want to know."   50

"Of course he did. What would you have him say?
Surely you wouldn't grudge the poor old man
Some humble way to save his self-respect.
He added, if you really care to know,
He meant to clear the upper pasture, too.   55
That sounds like something you have heard before?
Warren, I wish you could have heard the way
He jumbled everything. I stopped to look
Two or three times — he made me feel so queer —
To see if he was talking in his sleep.   60
He ran on Harold Wilson — you remember —
The boy you had in haying four years since.
He's finished school, and teaching in his college.
Silas declares you'll have to get him back.
He says they two will make a team for work: 65
Between them they will lay this farm as smooth!
The way he mixed that in with other things.

He thinks young Wilson a likely lad, though daft
On education — you know how they fought
All through July under the blazing sun,   70
Silas up on the cart to build the load,
Harold along beside to pitch it on."

"Yes, I took care to keep well out of earshot."

"Well, those days trouble Silas like a dream.
You wouldn't think they would. How some things linger!   75
Harold's young college boy's assurance piqued him.
After so many years he still keeps finding
Good arguments he sees he might have used.
I sympathize. I know just how it feels
To think of the right thing to say too late.   80
Harold's associated in his mind with Latin.
He asked me what I thought of Harold's saying
He studied Latin, like the violin,
Because he liked it — that an argument!
He said he couldn't make the boy believe   85
He could find water with a hazel prong —
Which showed how much good school had ever done him.
He wanted to go over that. But most of all
He thinks if he could have another chance
To teach him how to build a load of hay — "   90

"I know, that's Silas' one accomplishment.
He bundles every forkful in its place,
And tags and numbers it for future reference,
So he can find and easily dislodge it
In the unloading. Silas does that well.   95
He takes it out in bunches like big birds' nests.
You never see him standing on the hay
He's trying to lift, straining to lift himself."

"He thinks if he could teach him that, he'd be
Some good perhaps to someone in the world.   100
He hates to see a boy the fool of books.
Poor Silas, so concerned for other folk,
And nothing to look backward to with pride,
And nothing to look forward to with hope,
So now and never any different."   105

Part of a moon was falling down the west,
Dragging the whole sky with it to the hills.
Its light poured softly in her lap. She saw it
And spread her apron to it. She put out her hand
Among the harp-like morning-glory strings,   110
Taut with the dew from garden bed to eaves,
As if she played unheard some tenderness

That wrought on him beside her in the night.
"Warren," she said, "he has come home to die:
You needn't be afraid he'll leave you this time."   115

"Home," he mocked gently.

                  "Yes, what else but home?
It all depends on what you mean by home.
Of course he's nothing to us, any more
Than was the hound that came a stranger to us   120
Out of the woods, worn out upon the trail."

"Home is the place where, when you have to go there,
They have to take you in."

                  "I should have called it
Something you somehow haven't to deserve."   125

Warren leaned out and took a step or two,
Picked up a little stick, and brought it back
And broke it in his hand and tossed it by.
"Silas has better claim on us you think
Than on his brother? Thirteen little miles   130
As the road winds would bring him to his door.
Silas has walked that far no doubt to-day.
Why doesn't he go there? His brother's rich,
A somebody — director in the bank."

"He never told us that."   135

              "We know it though."

"I think his brother ought to help, of course.
I'll see to that if there is need. He ought of right
To take him in, and might be willing to —
He may be better than appearances.   140
But have some pity on Silas. Do you think
If he had any pride in claiming kin
Or anything he looked for from his brother,
He'd keep so still about him all this time?"

"I wonder what's between them."   145

                "I can tell you.
Silas is what he is — we wouldn't mind him —
But just the kind that kinfolk can't abide.
He never did a thing so very bad.
He don't know why he isn't quite as good   150
As anybody. Worthless though he is,
He won't be made ashamed to please his brother."

"I can't think Si ever hurt anyone."

"No, but he hurt my heart the way he lay
And rolled his old head on that sharped-edged chair-back.   155

He wouldn't let me put him on the lounge.
You must go in and see what you can do.
I made the bed up for him there tonight.
You'll be surprised at him — how much he's broken.
His working days are done; I'm sure of it." 160

"I'd not be in a hurry to say that."

I haven't been. Go, look, see for yourself.
But, Warren, please remember how it is:
He's come to help you ditch the meadow.
He has a plan. You mustn't laugh at him. 165
He may not speak of it, and then he may.
I'll sit and see if that small sailing cloud
Will hit or miss the moon."

       It hit the moon.
Then there were three there, making a dim row, 170
The moon, the little silver cloud, and she.

Warren returned — too soon, it seemed to her,
Slipped to her side, caught up her hand and waited.
"Warren?" she questioned.

       "Dead," was all he answered. 175

ROBERT FROST

From *The Hill Wife*   *1916*

LONELINESS
HER WORD

One ought not to have to care
 So much as you and I
Care when the birds come round the house
 To seem to say good-by;

Or care so much when they come back
 With whatever it is they sing; 5
The truth being we are as much
 Too glad for the one thing

As we are too sad for the other here —
 With birds that fill their breasts
But with each other and themselves 10
 And their built or driven nests.

ROBERT FROST

Birches   *1916*

When I see birches bend to left and right
Across the lines of straighter darker trees,
I like to think some boy's been swinging them.
But swinging doesn't bend them down to stay
As ice-storms do. Often you must have seen them   5
Loaded with ice a sunny winter morning
After a rain. They click upon themselves
As the breeze rises, and turn many-colored
As the stir cracks and crazes their enamel.
Soon the sun's warmth makes them shed crystal shells   10
Shattering and avalanching on the snow-crust —
Such heaps of broken glass to sweep away
You'd think the inner dome of heaven had fallen.
They are dragged to the withered bracken by the load,
And they seem not to break; though once they are bowed   15
So low for long, they never right themselves:
You may see their trunks arching in the woods
Years afterwards, trailing their leaves on the ground
Like girls on hands and knees that throw their hair
Before them over their heads to dry in the sun.   20
But I was going to say when Truth broke in
With all her matter-of-fact about the ice-storm,
I should prefer to have some boy bend them
As he went out and in to fetch the cows —
Some boy too far from town to learn baseball,   25
Whose only play was what he found himself,
Summer or winter, and could play alone.
One by one he subdued his father's trees
By riding them down over and over again
Until he took the stiffness out of them,   30
And not one but hung limp, not one was left
For him to conquer. He learned all there was
To learn about not launching out too soon
And so not carrying the tree away
Clear to the ground. He always kept his poise   35
To the top branches, climbing carefully
With the same pains you use to fill a cup
Up to the brim, and even above the brim.
Then he flung outward, feet first, with a swish,
Kicking his way down through the air to the ground.   40

So was I once myself a swinger of birches.
And so I dream of going back to be.
It's when I'm weary of considerations,
And life is too much like a pathless wood
Where your face burns and tickles with the cobwebs   45
Broken across it, and one eye is weeping
From a twig's having lashed across it open.
I'd like to get away from earth awhile
And then come back to it and begin over.
May no fate willfully misunderstand me   50
And half grant what I wish and snatch me away
Not to return. Earth's the right place for love:
I don't know where it's likely to go better.
I'd like to go by climbing a birch tree,
And climb black branches up a snow-white trunk,   55
Toward heaven, till the tree could bear no more,
But dipped its top and set me down again.
That would be good both going and coming back.
One could do worse than be a swinger of birches.

ROBERT FROST

Fire and Ice   1923

Some say the world will end in fire,
Some say in ice.
From what I've tasted of desire
I hold with those who favor fire.
But if it had to perish twice,
I think I know enough of hate
To say that for destruction ice
Is also great
And would suffice.

ROBERT FROST

To Earthward   1923

Love at the lips was touch
As sweet as I could bear;
And once that seemed too much;
I lived on air

That crossed me from sweet things   5
The flow of — was it musk

From hidden grapevine springs
Down hill at dusk?

I had the swirl and ache
From sprays of honeysuckle
That when they're gathered shake
Dew on the knuckle.

I craved strong sweets, but those
Seemed strong when I was young;
The petal of the rose
It was that stung.

Now no joy but lacks salt
That is not dashed with pain
And weariness and fault;
I crave the stain

Of tears, the aftermark
Of almost too much love,
The sweet of bitter bark
And burning clove.

When stiff and sore and scarred
I take away my hand
From leaning on it hard
In grass and sand,

The hurt is not enough:
I long for weight and strength
To feel the earth as rough
To all my length.

ROBERT FROST

Stopping by Woods on a Snowy Evening   1923

Whose woods these are I think I know.
His house is in the village, though;
He will not see me stopping here
To watch his woods fill up with snow.

My little horse must think it queer
To stop without a farmhouse near
Between the woods and frozen lake
The darkest evening of the year.

He gives his harness bells a shake
To ask if there is some mistake.
The only other sound's the sweep
Of easy wind and downy flake.

The woods are lovely, dark and deep,
But I have promises to keep,
And miles to go before I sleep, 15
And miles to go before I sleep.

ROBERT FROST

The Road Not Taken *1916*

Two roads diverged in a yellow wood,
And sorry I could not travel both
And be one traveler, long I stood
And looked down one as far as I could
To where it bent in the undergrowth; 5

Then took the other, as just as fair,
And having perhaps the better claim,
Because it was grassy and wanted wear;
Though as for that the passing there
Had worn them really about the same, 10

And both that morning equally lay
In leaves no step had trodden black.
Oh, I kept the first for another day!
Yet knowing how way leads on to way,
I doubted if I should ever come back. 15

I shall be telling this with a sigh
Somewhere ages and ages hence:
Two roads diverged in a wood, and I —
I took the one less traveled by,
And that has made all the difference. 20

ROBERT FROST

After Apple-Picking *1914*

My long two-pointed ladder's sticking through a tree
Toward heaven still,
And there's a barrel that I didn't fill
Beside it, and there may be two or three
Apples I didn't pick upon some bough. 5
But I am done with apple-picking now.
Essence of winter sleep is on the night,
The scent of apples: I am drowsing off.
I cannot rub the strangeness from my sight
I got from looking through a pane of glass 10

I skimmed this morning from the drinking trough
And held against the world of hoary grass.
It melted, and I let it fall and break.
But I was well
Upon my way to sleep before it fell,   15
And I could tell
What form my dreaming was about to take.
Magnified apples appear and disappear,
Stem end and blossom end,
And every fleck of russet showing clear.   20
My instep arch not only keeps the ache,
It keeps the pressure of a ladder-round.
I feel the ladder sway as the boughs bend.
And I keep hearing from the cellar bin
The rumbling sound   25
Of load on load of apples coming in.
For I have had too much
Of apple-picking: I am overtired
Of the great harvest I myself desired.
There were ten thousand thousand fruit to touch,   30
Cherish in hand, lift down, and not let fall.
For all
That struck the earth,
No matter if not bruised or spiked with stubble,
Went surely to the cider-apple heap   35
As of no worth.
One can see what will trouble
This sleep of mine, whatever sleep it is.
Were he not gone,
The woodchuck could say whether it's like his   40
Long sleep, as I describe its coming on,
Or just some human sleep.

ༀ

ALLEN GINSBERG (*b. 1926–1997*) *was born in Paterson, New Jersey. His father, Louis Ginsberg, taught high school English and also wrote conventional poetry. His mother, Naomi Ginsberg, was a committed leftist who struggled against intermittent bouts of mental instability. From 1944 to 1948 Ginsberg studied at Columbia University, where he met fledgling writers Jack Kerouac and William S. Burroughs, and with them formed a loose literary underground that would emerge as the Beat Generation. His life was chaotic as he struggled with his homosexuality and his own, and his friends', drug use. In 1949 he was hospitalized at the New York State Psychiatric Institute for eight months following an arrest for possession of stolen goods, which his friends had cached in his apartment. A dean from Columbia was able to have Ginsberg's jail sentence transmuted to psychiatric rehabilitation.*

In 1954 Ginsberg traveled to San Francisco by way of Mexico and immediately became part of the artistic ferment in the city. In the fall of 1955 he organized a reading for himself and some friends at a local art gallery, with poet Kenneth Rexroth as master of ceremonies. Ginsberg read the first part of a new poem called Howl and roused such an excited response from the audience that it was clear that a new era had begun in American poetry. The poem was published in 1956 by fellow poet Lawrence Ferlinghetti's City Lights Press, and since that time it has sold nearly a million copies in different editions and has been translated into dozens of languages.

As the most famous poet of his generation, Ginsberg led peace marches in the 1960s, traveled and read his poetry incessantly, and continued to write voluminously. He has been a teacher, a guru for thousands of young students, and a poet-singer who has toured with Bob Dylan and recorded with British punk rock bands.

The following excerpt from Howl is the section that he read aloud in 1955. "Sunflower Sutra," written in the same period, describes a walk in San Francisco with Jack Kerouac, his friend from his years at Columbia University. Sutra is a Buddhist term for a precept or a discourse. (See also Ginsberg's "A Supermarket in California" on p. 1007.)

RELATED COMMENTARY: Allen Ginsberg, "On His Poetic Craft," page 1260.

ALLEN GINSBERG

From *Howl*   1956

for Carl Solomon°

I

I saw the best minds of my generation destroyed by madness, starving
        hysterical naked,
dragging themselves through the negro streets at dawn looking for an
        angry fix,
angelheaded hipsters burning for the ancient heavenly connection to
        the starry dynamo in the machinery of night,
who poverty and tatters and hollow-eyed and high sat up smoking in
        the supernatural darkness of cold-water flats floating across the tops
        of cities contemplating jazz,
who bared their brains to Heaven under the El and saw Mohammedan
        angels staggering on tenement roofs illuminated,   5
who passed through universities with radiant cool eyes hallucinating
        Arkansas and Blake-light° tragedy among the scholars of war,
who were expelled from the academies for crazy & publishing obscene
        odes on the windows of the skull,

---

for Carl Solomon: Solomon was a young poet and editor Ginsberg met as a fellow patient at the Psychiatric Institute. **6. Blake-light:** An allusion to the paintings of William Blake (1757–1827).

who cowered in unshaven rooms in underwear, burning their money
    in wastebaskets and listening to the Terror through the wall,
who got busted in their pubic beards returning through Laredo with a
    belt of marijuana for New York,
who ate fire in paint hotels or drank turpentine in Paradise Alley,
    death, or purgatoried their torsos night after night   10
    with dreams, with drugs, with waking nightmares, alcohol and cock
    and endless balls,
incomparable blind streets of shuddering cloud and lightning in the
    mind leaping toward poles of Canada & Paterson, illuminating all
    the motionless world of Time between,
Peyote solidities of halls, backyard green tree cemetery dawns, wine
    drunkenness over the rooftops, storefront boroughs of teahead
    joyride neon blinking traffic light, sun and moon and tree vibrations
    in the roaring winter dusks of Brooklyn, ashcan rantings and kind
    king light of mind,
who chained themselves to subways for the endless ride from Battery
    to holy Bronx on benzedrine until the noise of wheels and children
    brought them down shuddering mouth-wracked and battered bleak
    of brain all drained of brilliance in the drear light of Zoo,
who sank all night in submarine light of Bickford's floated out and sat
    through the stale beer afternoon in desolate Fugazzi's, listening to
    the crack of doom on the hydrogen jukebox,   15
who talked continuously seventy hours from park to pad to bar to
    Bellevue to museum to the Brooklyn Bridge,
a lost battalion of platonic conversationalists jumping down the stoops
    off fire escapes off windowsills off Empire State out of the moon,
yacketayakking screaming vomiting whispering facts and memories
    and anecdotes and eyeball kicks and shocks of hospitals and jails
    and wars,
whose intellects disgorged in total recall for seven days and nights
    with brilliant eyes, meat for the Synagogue cast on the pavement,
who vanished into nowhere Zen New Jersey leaving a trail of ambigu-
    ous picture postcards of Atlantic City Hall,   20
suffering Eastern sweats and Tangerian bone-grindings and migraines
    of China under junk-withdrawal in Newark's bleak furnished room,
who wandered around and around at midnight in the railroad yard
    wondering where to go, and went, leaving no broken hearts,
who lit cigarettes in boxcars boxcars boxcars racketing through snow
    toward lonesome farms in grandfather night,
who studied Plotinus° Poe° St. John of the Cross telepathy and bop
    kaballa because the cosmos instinctively vibrated at their feet in
    Kansas,

---

24. **Plotinus:** Roman philosopher (205–270); **Poe:** Edgar Allan Poe (1809–1849, American
writer).

who loned it through the streets of Idaho seeking visionary indian
 angels who were visionary indian angels,   25
who thought they were only mad when Baltimore gleamed in supernatural ecstasy,
who jumped in limousines with the Chinaman of Oklahoma on the impulse of winter midnight streetlight smalltown rain,
who lounged hungry and lonesome through Houston seeking jazz or
 sex or soup, and followed the brilliant Spaniard to converse about
 America and Eternity, a hopeless task, and so took ship to Africa,
who disappeared into the volcanoes of Mexico leaving behind nothing
 but the shadow of dungarees and the lava and ash of poetry scattered in fireplace Chicago,
who reappeared on the West Coast investigating the F.B.I. in beards
 and shorts with big pacifist eyes sexy in their dark skin passing out
 incomprehensible leaflets,   30
who burned cigarette holes in their arms protesting the narcotic tobacco haze of Capitalism,
who distributed Supercommunist pamphlets in Union Square weeping
 and undressing while the sirens of Los Alamos° wailed them down,
 and wailed down Wall, and the Staten Island ferry also wailed,
who broke down crying in white gymnasiums naked and trembling
 before the machinery of other skeletons,
who bit detectives in the neck and shrieked with delight in policecars
 for committing no crime but their own wild cooking pederasty and
 intoxication,
who howled on their knees in the subway and were dragged off the
 roof waving genitals and manuscripts,   35
who let themselves be fucked in the ass by saintly motorcyclists, and
 screamed with joy,
who blew and were blown by those human seraphim, the sailors,
 caresses of Atlantic and Caribbean love,
who balled in the morning in the evenings in rosegardens and the
 grass of public parks and cemeteries scattering their semen freely to
 whomever come who may,
who hiccupped endlessly trying to giggle but wound up with a sob
 behind a partition in a Turkish Bath when the blonde & naked angel
 came to pierce them with a sword,
who lost their loveboys to the three old shrews of fate the one eyed
 shrew of the heterosexual dollar the one eyed shrew that winks out
 of the womb and the one eyed shrew that does nothing but sit on
 her ass and snip the intellectual golden threads of the craftsman's
 loom,   40
who copulated ecstatic and insatiate with a bottle of beer a sweetheart
 a package of cigarettes a candle and fell off the bed, and continued

---

32. Los Alamos: The site of the New Mexico laboratory in which the first atomic bombs were
constructed.

along the floor and down the hall and ended fainting on the wall
with a vision of ultimate cunt and come eluding the last gyzym of
consciousness,
who sweetened the snatches of a million girls trembling in the sunset,
and were red eyed in the morning but prepared to sweeten the
snatch of the sunrise, flashing buttocks under barns and naked in
the lake,
who went out whoring through Colorado in myriad stolen night-cars,
N.C.,° secret hero of these poems, cocksman and Adonis of Denver
— joy to the memory of his innumerable lays of girls in empty lots
& diner backyards, moviehouses' rickety rows, on mountaintops in
caves or with gaunt waitresses in familiar roadside lonely petticoat
upliftings & especially secret gas-station solipsisms of johns, &
hometown alleys too,
who faded out in vast sordid movies, were shifted in dreams, woke on
a sudden Manhattan, and picked themselves up out of basements
hungover with heartless Tokay and horrors of Third Avenue iron
dreams & stumbled to unemployment offices,
who walked all night with their shoes full of blood on the snowbank
docks waiting for a door in the East River to open to a room full of
steamheat and opium,   45
who created great suicidal dramas on the apartment cliff-banks of the
Hudson under the wartime blue floodlight of the moon & their
heads shall be crowned with laurel in oblivion,
who ate the lamb stew of the imagination or digested the crab at the
muddy bottom of the rivers of Bowery,
who wept at the romance of the streets with their pushcarts full of
onions and bad music,
who sat in boxes breathing in the darkness under the bridge, and rose
up to build harpsichords in their lofts,
who coughed on the sixth floor of Harlem crowned with flame under
the tubercular sky surrounded by orange crates of theology,   50
who scribbled all night rocking and rolling over lofty incantations
which in the yellow morning were stanzas of gibberish,
who cooked rotten animals lung heart feet tail borsht & tortillas dreaming of the pure vegetable kingdom,
who plunged themselves under meat trucks looking for an egg,
who threw their watches off the roof to cast their ballot for Eternity
outside of Time, & alarm clocks fell on their heads every day for the
next decade,
who cut their wrists three times successively unsuccessfully, gave up
and were forced to open antique stores where they thought they
were growing old and cried,   55
who were burned alive in their innocent flannel suits on Madison

---

43. **N.C.:** Neal Cassady, a Denver dropout and hustler who was the hero of Jack Kerouac's
1957 novel, *On the Road,* and for a short period was Ginsberg's lover.

Avenue amid blasts of leaden verse & the tanked-up clatter of the
   iron regiments of fashion & the nitroglycerine shrieks of the fairies
   of advertising & the mustard gas of sinister intelligent editors, or
   were run down by the drunken taxicabs of Absolute Reality,
who jumped off the Brooklyn Bridge this actually happened and
   walked away unknown and forgotten into the ghostly daze of
   Chinatown soup alleyways & firetrucks, not even one free beer,
who sang out of their windows in despair, fell out of the subway window, jumped in the filthy Passaic, leaped on negroes, cried all over
   the street, danced on broken wineglasses barefoot smashed phonograph records of nostalgic European 1930's German jazz finished the
   whiskey and threw up groaning into the bloody toilet, moans in
   their ears and the blast of colossal steamwhistles,
who barreled down the highways of the past journeying to each other's
   hotrod-Golgotha jail-solitude watch or Birmingham jazz incarnation,
who drove crosscountry seventytwo hours to find out if I had a vision
   or you had a vision or he had a vision to find out Eternity,   60
who journeyed to Denver, who died in Denver, who came back to Denver & waited in vain, who watched over Denver & brooded & loned
   in Denver and finally went away to find out the Time, & now Denver is lonesome for her heroes,
who fell on their knees in hopeless cathedrals praying for each other's
   salvation and light and breasts, until the soul illuminated its hair for
   a second,
who crashed through their minds in jail waiting for impossible criminals with golden heads and the charm of reality in their hearts who
   sang sweet blues to Alcatraz,
who retired to Mexico to cultivate a habit, or Rocky Mount to tender
   Buddha or Tangiers to boys or Southern Pacific to the black locomotive or Harvard to Narcissus to Woodlawn to the daisychain or
   grave,
who demanded sanity trials accusing the radio of hypnotism & were
   left with their insanity & their hands & a hung jury,   65
who threw potato salad at CCNY° lectures on Dadaism and subsequently presented themselves on the granite steps of the madhouse
   with shaven heads and harlequin speech of suicide, demanding instantaneous lobotomy,
and who were given instead the concrete void of insulin metrasol electricity hydrotherapy psychotherapy occupational therapy pingpong
   & amnesia,
who in humorless protest overturned only one symbolic pingpong
   table, resting briefly in catatonia,
returning years later truly bald except for a wig of blood, and tears and
   fingers, to the visible madman doom of the wards of the madtowns
   of the East,

---

66. CCNY: City College of New York.

Pilgrim State's Rockland's and Greystone's foetid halls, bickering with
    the echoes of the soul, rocking and rolling in the midnight solitude-
    bench dolmen-realms of love, dream of life a nightmare, bodies
    turned to stone as heavy as the moon,   70
with mother finally ******, and the last fantastic book flung out of
    the tenement window, and the last door closed at 4 AM and the
    last telephone slammed at the wall in reply and the last furnished
    room emptied down to the last piece of mental furniture, a
    yellow paper rose twisted on a wire hanger in the closet, and
    even that imaginary, nothing but a hopeful little bit of hallu-
    cination —
ah, Carl, while you are not safe I am not safe, and now you're really in
    the total animal soup of time —
and who therefore ran through the icy streets obsessed with a sudden
    flash of the alchemy of the use of the ellipse the catalog the meter &
    the vibrating plane,
who dreamt and made incarnate gaps in Time & Space through images
    juxtaposed, and trapped the archangel of the soul between 2 visual
    images and joined the elemental verbs and set the noun and dash of
    consciousness together jumping with sensation of Pater Omnipotens
    Aeterna Deus
to recreate the syntax and measure of poor human prose and stand be-
    fore you speechless and intelligent and shaking with shame, rejected
    yet confessing out the soul to conform to the rhythm of thought in
    his naked and endless head,   75
the madman bum and angel beat in Time, unknown, yet putting down
    here what might be left to say in time come after death,
and rose reincarnate in the ghostly clothes of jazz in the goldhorn
    shadow of the band and blew the suffering of America's naked
    mind for love into an eli eli lamma lamma sabacthani° saxophone
    cry that shivered the cities down to the last radio
with the absolute heart of the poem of life butchered out of their own
    bodies good to eat a thousand years.

ALLEN GINSBERG

Sunflower Sutra

                           1956

I walked on the banks of the tincan banana dock and sat down under
    the huge shade of a Southern Pacific locomotive to look at the sunset
    over the box house hills and cry.
Jack Kerouac° sat beside me on a busted rusty iron pole, companion,

---

77. **eli . . . sabacthani:** Words from a chanted prayer.
2. **Jack Kerouac:** A friend of Ginsberg's and author of *On the Road* and other autobiographical novels (1922–1969).

we thought the same thoughts of the soul, bleak and blue and sad-
   eyed, surrounded by the gnarled steel roots of trees of machinery.
The oily water on the river mirrored the red sky, sun sank on top of final Frisco peaks, no fish in that stream, no hermit in those mounts,
   just ourselves rheumy-eyed and hungover like old bums on the
   riverbank, tired and wily.
Look at the Sunflower, he said, there was a dead gray shadow against
   the sky, big as a man, sitting dry on top of a pile of ancient sawdust —
— I rushed up enchanted — it was my first sunflower, memories of
   Blake° — my visions — Harlem   5
and Hells of the Eastern rivers, bridges, clanking Joes Greasy Sandwiches, dead baby carriages, black treadless tires forgotten and
   unretreaded, the poem of the riverbank, condoms & pots, steel
   knives, nothing stainless, only the dank muck and the razor sharp
   artifacts passing into the past —
and the gray Sunflower poised against the sunset, crackly bleak and
   dusty with the smut and smog and smoke of olden locomotives in
   its eye —
corolla of bleary spikes pushed down and broken like a battered
   crown, seeds fallen out of its face, soon-to-be-toothless mouth of
   sunny air, sunrays obliterated on its hairy head like a dried wire spi-
   derweb,
leaves stuck out like arms out of the stem, gestures from the sawdust
   root, broke pieces of plaster fallen out of the black twigs, a dead fly
   in its ear,
Unholy battered old thing you were, my sunflower O my soul, I loved
   you then!   10
The grime was no man's grime but death and human locomotives,
all that dress of dust, that veil of darkened railroad skin, that smog of
   cheek, that eyelid of black mis'ry, that sooty hand or phallus or pro-
   tuberance of artificial worse-than-dirt — industrial — modern — all
   that civilization spotting your crazy golden crown —
and those blear thoughts of death and dusty loveless eyes and ends
   and withered roots below, in the home-pile of sand and sawdust,
   rubber dollar bills, skin of machinery, the guts and innards of the
   weeping coughing car, the empty lonely tincans with their rusty
   tongues alack, what more could I name, the smoked ashes of some
   cock cigar, the cunts of wheelbarrows and the milky breasts of cars,
   wornout asses out of chairs & sphincters of dynamos — all these
entangled in your mummied roots — and you there standing before
   me in the sunset, all your glory in your form!

---

5. Blake: William Blake (1757–1827), English poet and author of "Ah! Sun-flower." Ginsberg
in 1948 had had a vision in which he heard Blake's voice reciting his poems.

A perfect beauty of a sunflower! a perfect excellent lovely sunflower
   existence! a sweet natural eye to the new hip moon, woke up alive
   and excited grasping in the sunset shadow sunrise golden monthly
   breeze!   15
How many flies buzzed round you innocent of your grime, while you
   cursed the heavens of the railroad and your flower soul?
Poor dead flower? when did you forget you were a flower? when did
   you look at your skin and decide you were an impotent dirty old locomotive? the ghost of a locomotive? the specter and shade of a
   once powerful mad American locomotive?
You were never no locomotive, Sunflower, you were a sunflower!
And you Locomotive, you are a locomotive, forget me not!
So I grabbed up the skeleton thick sunflower and stuck it at my side
   like a scepter,   20
and deliver my sermon to my soul, and Jack's soul too, and anyone
   who'll listen,
— We're not our skin of grime, we're not our dread bleak dusty
   imageless locomotive, we're all beautiful golden sunflowers
   inside, we're blessed by our own seed & golden hairy naked
   accomplishment-bodies growing into mad black formal sunflowers
   in the sunset, spied on by our eyes under the shadow of the mad
   locomotive riverbank sunset Frisco hilly tincan evening sitdown
   vision.

ॐ

LOUISE GLÜCK (*b. 1943*) *was born and grew up in New York City, where
her father was a business executive. She studied at Sarah Lawrence College and received her B.A. from Columbia University in 1965. She has been married twice and
has a son and is at present a faculty member at Warren Wilson College in North
Carolina.*

Glück's first book, Firstborn, *was published in 1968, and it established her
themes of family and her personal life. The critic Helen Vendler has said of Glück's
poems, "She sees experience from very far off, almost through the end of a telescope,
transparently removed in space or time. It is this removal which gives such mythological power . . . to the account of her parents' lives and of her own childhood, and
makes their family constellation into a universal one." Glück's book* Ararat, *which
was in part an emotional response to her father's death, won the Pulitzer Prize
in 1990.*

"Labor Day," from Firstborn, *is a description of an unhappy weekend date she
spent in Connecticut. "For My Mother" is one of many poems she has written in her
effort to understand her unhappy childhood. "Gratitude" includes one of her most
memorable images, the simile of a "substantial kindness," which is "like a large animal on a rug." "Brown Circle" returns to the theme of her family.*

RELATED COMMENTARY: *Helen Vendler, "On Louise Glück," page 1321.*

LOUISE GLÜCK

Labor Day   1968

Requiring something lovely on his arm
Took me to Stamford, Connecticut, a quasi-farm,
His family's; later picking up the mammoth
Girlfriend of Charlie, meanwhile trying to pawn me off
On some third guy also up for the weekend.   5
But Saturday we still were paired; spent
it sprawled across that sprawling acreage
Until the grass grew limp
With damp. Like me. Johnston-baby, I can still see
The pelted clover, burrs' prickle fur and gorged   10
Pastures spewing infinite tiny bells. You pimp.

LOUISE GLÜCK

For My Mother   1975

It was better when we were
together in one body.
Thirty years. Screened
through the green glass
of your eye, moonlight   5
filtered into my bones
as we lay
in the big bed, in the dark,
waiting for my father.
Thirty years. He closed   10
your eyelids with
two kisses. And then spring
came and withdrew from me
the absolute
knowledge of the unborn,   15
leaving the brick stoop
where you stand, shading
your eyes, but it is
night, the moon
is stationed in the beech tree,   20
round and white among
the small tin markers of the stars:
Thirty years. A marsh
grows up around the house.

Schools of spores circulate
behind the shades, drift through   25
gauze flutterings of vegetation.

LOUISE GLÜCK

Gratitude   1975

Do not think I am not grateful for your small
kindness to me.
I like small kindnesses.
In fact I actually prefer them to the more
substantial kindness, that is always eyeing you,
like a large animal on a rug,
until your whole life reduces
to nothing but waking up morning after morning
cramped, and the bright sun shining on its tusks.

LOUISE GLÜCK

Brown Circle   1990

My mother wants to know
why, if I hate
family so much,
I went ahead and
had one. I don't   5
answer my mother.
What I hated
was being a child,
having no choice about
what people I loved.   10

I don't love my son
the way I meant to love him.
I thought I'd be
the lover of orchids who finds
red trillium growing   15
in the pine shade, and doesn't
touch it, doesn't need
to possess it. What I am
is the scientist,
who comes to that flower   20
with a magnifying glass

and doesn't leave, though
the sun burns a brown
circle of grass around
the flower. Which is   25
more or less the way
my mother loved me.

I must learn
to forgive my mother,
now that I'm helpless   30
to spare my son.

ॐ

ROBERT HAYDEN *(1913–1980) was born in Detroit. When he was three his mother, Asa Sheffey, decided that she wanted to live her own life, and although she never lost contact with her son, she gave him to a working couple named Hayden to raise. His adoptive father worked when he could as a day laborer, and Hayden grew up in poverty in the Detroit ghetto. As a boy, Hayden was small and extremely near-sighted, and he spent many hours alone reading.*

By his teens, he was already absorbed by literature, and Hayden's was a generation of African Americans who no longer felt excluded from mainstream American intellectual culture. His early poetic models were the African American writer Countee Cullen and the white poet Elinor Wylie. When Hayden graduated from high school, America was entering the depression. He attended Detroit City College until 1936, then was employed by the WPA Federal Writer's Project until the war. He married in 1940 and entered the University of Michigan, where he studied under the English poet W. H. Auden (p. 1019), who had recently moved to the United States.

From 1946 until 1969 Hayden taught at Fisk University in Nashville while also writing and publishing steadily. An early book had been published in 1940, but Hayden did not achieve wide recognition until 1966, when he was awarded the Grand Prize for Poetry for A Ballad of Remembrance *at the First World Festival of Negro Arts in Senegal. At the same time he had become reluctantly involved in the debate over political consciousness that was shaking the black literary world. Younger African American writers accused him of accommodating his writing to the white culture and refused to listen to his argument that he considered himself part of a literary culture that had no racial boundaries. The angry disagreement was one of his reasons for leaving Fisk.*

Hayden was awarded many literary prizes and honors. For four years he was Consultant in Poetry to the Library of Congress, a position that now has the title of Poet Laureate. In January 1980, a month before his death, he took part in a reading at the White House.

"Those Winter Sundays" is Hayden's best-known poem, describing his father in Detroit. " 'Incense of the Lucky Virgin' " is also drawn from the experiences of his childhood. "A Letter from Phillis Wheatley" is from his last book and is an evocative portrait of the first published African American writer. (For more on Wheatley, see p. 1207.)

RELATED COMMENTARIES: *Robert Hayden, "On Negro Poetry," page 1266; David Huddle, "The 'Banked Fire' of Robert Hayden's 'Those Winter Sundays,' " page 1271.*

ROBERT HAYDEN

Those Winter Sundays

1962

Sundays too my father got up early
and put his clothes on in the blueblack cold,
then with cracked hands that ached
from labor in the weekday weather made
banked fires blaze. No one ever thanked him.   5

I'd wake and hear the cold splintering, breaking.
When the rooms were warm, he'd call,
and slowly I would rise and dress,
fearing the chronic angers of that house,

Speaking indifferently to him,   10
who had driven out the cold
and polished my good shoes as well.
What did I know, what did I know
of love's austere and lonely offices?

ROBERT HAYDEN

"Incense of the Lucky Virgin"

1966

Incense of the Lucky Virgin,
High John the Conqueror
didn't bring him home again,
didn't get his children fed,
    get his children fed.   5

I prayed and what did prayer avail?
My candles held no power.
An evening came I prayed no more
and blew my candles out,
    oh blew my candles out.   10

Put on your Sunday ribbon-bows,
Cleola, Willie Mae;
you, Garland, go
and shine your Sunday shoes,
    make haste and shine your shoes.   15

They were so happy they forgot
they were hungry, daddyless.

Except Cleola maybe — she
wasn't asking, Where we going,
    Mommy, where we going? 20

Garland was too quick for me
(he didn't yell once as he ran);
Cleola, Willie Mae
won't be hungry any more,
    oh they'll never cry and hunger any more. 25

ROBERT HAYDEN

A Letter from Phillis Wheatley   *1978*

London, 1773

Dear Obour
    Our crossing was without
event. I could not help, at times,
reflecting on that first — my Destined —
voyage long ago (I yet 5
have some remembrance of its Horrors)
and marvelling at God's Ways.
    Last evening, her Ladyship presented me
to her illustrious Friends.
I scarce could tell them anything 10
of Africa, though much of Boston
and my hope of Heaven. I read
my latest Elegies to them.
"O Sable Muse!" the Countess cried,
embracing me, when I had done. 15
I held back tears, as is my wont,
and there were tears in Dear
Nathaniel's eyes.
    At supper — I dined apart
like captive Royalty — 20
the Countess and her Guests promised
signatures affirming me
True Poetess, albeit once a slave.
Indeed, they were most kind, and spoke,
moreover, of presenting me 25
at Court (I thought of Pocahontas) —
an Honor, to be sure, but one,
I should, no doubt, as Patriot decline.
    My health is much improved;
I feel I may, if God so Wills, 30
entirely recover here.

Idyllic England! Alas, there is
no Eden without its Serpent. Under
the chiming Complaisance I hear him Hiss;
I see his flickering tongue
when foppish would-be Wits
murmur of the Yankee Pedlar
and his Cannibal Mockingbird.
     Sister, forgive th'intrusion of
my Sombreness — Nocturnal Mood   40
I would not share with any save
your trusted Self. Let me disperse,
in closing, such unseemly Gloom
by mention of an Incident
you may, as I, consider Droll: 45
Today, a little Chimney Sweep,
his face and hands with soot quite Black,
staring hard at me, politely asked:
"Does you, M'lady, sweep chimneys too?"
I was amused, but dear Nathaniel   50
(ever Solicitous) was not.
     I pray the Blessings of our Lord
and Saviour Jesus Christ be yours
Abundantly. In his Name,

                Phillis   55

ಜಃಜ

GERARD MANLEY HOPKINS (1844–1889) *was born in Essex, outside of London. As a student at Oxford he studied classic Greek and Roman literature and also was influenced by a religious revival movement that led him to convert from Protestantism to become a Roman Catholic, and eventually a Jesuit priest. His superiors were uncomfortable with his intellectual background, and he spent several years in working-class parishes until he was appointed a professor of Greek at University College in Dublin in 1877.*

Hopkins was also a talented musician and painter, but he put aside his art and writing for the church. When he was ordained, he burned all the poems he had written. He found it impossible to give up poetry, however, and he began to write again when he was in his thirties. Hopkins never pursued publication, and his poems were left in their original manuscript form when he died. It was only after they were published some thirty years later that his genius was recognized.

Since Hopkins was not interested in publishing he could experiment with rhyme and diction in his writing, and his poems still startle readers more than a hundred years after they were written. As a musician he was interested in meter, and he developed a metric form he called "sprung rhythm," which counted the accents of each line by stress rather than syllable. As he described his poetic method in a letter to a friend, "No doubt my poetry errs on the side of oddness. . . . But as air, melody, is what strikes me most of all in music, and design in painting, so design, pattern, or what I am in the habit of calling inscape *is what above all I aim at in poetry."*

"The Windhover," "Pied Beauty," "Spring and Fall," "Thou art indeed just, Lord," *and* "God's Grandeur" *were published in 1918.*

RELATED COMMENTARY: *Bernard Bergonzi, "On Hopkins's 'The Windhover,' " page 1235.*

GERARD MANLEY HOPKINS

The Windhover°

1877

To Christ Our Lord

I caught this morning morning's minion, king-
    dom of daylight's dauphin,° dapple-dawn-drawn Falcon, in his
        riding
Of the rolling level underneath him steady air, and striding
High there, how he rung upon the rein of a wimpling wing
In his ecstasy! then off, off forth on swing,   5
    As a skate's heel sweeps smooth on a bow-bend: the hurl and
        gliding
    Rebuffed the big wind. My heart in hiding
Stirred for a bird, — the achieve of, the mastery of the thing!

Brute beauty and valor and act, oh, air, pride, plume, here
    Buckle!° AND the fire that breaks from thee then, a billion   10
Times told lovelier, more dangerous, O my chevalier!

    No wonder of it: sheer plod makes plough down sillion°
Shine, and blue-bleak embers, ah my dear,
    Fall, gall themselves, and gash gold-vermillion.

GERARD MANLEY HOPKINS

Pied Beauty

1877

Glory be to God for dappled things —
    For skies of couple-color as a brinded° cow;   *reddish flecks*
        For rose-moles all in stipple° upon trout that swim;   *spotted*
Fresh-firecoal chestnut-falls; finches' wings;
    Landscape plotted and pieced — fold, fallow, and plow;   5
        And all trades, their gear and tackle and trim.
All things counter, original, spare, strange;

The Windhover: A small hawk named for its habit of hovering with its head in the wind.
2. dauphin: Heir to the throne of France.   **10. Buckle:** An exhortation for a knight to don armor; here used as a metaphor for the hawk's appearance as a "chevalier," or knight (line 11).
12. sillion: Narrow ridge between two plowed furrows.

Whatever is fickle, freckled (who knows how?)
    With swift, slow; sweet, sour; adazzle, dim;
He fathers-forth whose beauty is past change: 10
        Praise him.

GERARD MANLEY HOPKINS

Spring and Fall   1880

to a young child

Márgarét, áre you gríeving
Over Goldengrove unleaving?
Leáves líke the things of man, you
With your fresh thoughts care for, can you?
Ah! ás the heart grows older   5
It will come to such sights colder
By and by, nor spare a sigh
Though worlds of wanwood leafmeal° lie;
And yet you will weep and know why.
Now no matter, child, the name: 10
Sórrow's spríngs áre the same.
Nor mouth had, no nor mind, expressed
What heart heard of, ghost° guessed: *spirit*
It ís the blight man was born for,
It is Margaret you mourn for.   15

GERARD MANLEY HOPKINS

Thou art indeed just, Lord   1889

Thou art indeed just, Lord, if I contend
With thee; but, sir, so what I plead is just.
Why do sinners' ways prosper? and why must
Disappointment all I endeavour end?
Wert thou my enemy, O thou my friend,   5
How wouldst thou worse, I wonder, than thou dost
Defeat, thwart me? Oh, the sots and thralls of lust
Do in spare hours more thrive than I that spend,
Sir, life upon thy cause. See, banks and brakes
Now, leavèd how thick! lacèd they are again   10
With fretty chervil,° look, and fresh wind shakes   *an herb*
Them; birds build — but not I build; no, but strain,

---

8. **wanwood leafmeal:** Scattered or decaying leaves in a desolate woods.

Time's eunuch, and not breed one work that wakes.
Mine, O thou lord of life, send my roots rain.

GERARD MANLEY HOPKINS

God's Grandeur 1877

The world is charged with the grandeur of God.
  It will flame out, like shining from shook foil;°
  It gathers to a greatness, like the ooze of oil
Crushed. Why do men then now not reck his rod?°
Generations have trod, have trod, have trod;   5
  And all is seared with trade; bleared, smeared with toil;
  And wears man's smudge and shares man's smell: the soil
Is bare now, nor can foot feel, being shod.

And for all this, nature is never spent;
  There lives the dearest freshness deep down things;   10
And though the last lights off the black West went
  Oh, morning, at the brown brink eastward, springs —
Because the Holy Ghost over the bent
  World broods with warm breast and with ah! bright wings.

ॐ

LANGSTON HUGHES (1902–1967), *who was to become America's best-
known African American writer, was one of the first American poets to reach a wide
audience with a direct, personal poetic style created from the rhythms and language of
everyday black speech. When we read him today we see only the depth of his accomplishment, but it was achieved by a lifetime of dedication to his goal, which was to create a voice for the African American community. He lived for many years alone in his
small Harlem apartment, and there were years of discouraging poverty. His determination, however — and his optimism — never wavered. As his biographer Arnold
Rampersad wrote, the greatest truth of Hughes's life was that ". . . in his chronic loneliness, true satisfaction came only from the love and regard of the black race, which he
earned by placing his finest gift, his skill with language, in its service."*

*He was born in Joplin, Missouri, but his parents separated, and he spent most
of his childhood with his maternal grandmother in Lawrence, Kansas. His father, angry at racial intolerance but prejudiced himself against darker-skinned blacks, moved
to Mexico. His mother settled in Cleveland. His grandmother was emotionally reserved, and he yearned for more contact with his mother, but his grandmother gave
him a strong sense of racial pride that never left him. She was the widow of one of the*

---

2. **shook foil:** Hopkins means *foil* in its sense of leaf or tinsel.   4. **reck his rod:** Recognize his
authority.

men killed in the battle at Harpers Ferry, Virginia, in 1859, when a small group under the leadership of abolitionist John Brown attempted to ignite a rebellion in the South by capturing the federal arsenal there and seizing weapons to arm southern slaves. Hughes heard the story from her many times, and sometimes she covered him in bed with her husband's bullet-torn shawl.

Hughes's grandmother died when he was thirteen, and he went to live with his mother in Cleveland, Ohio. He was already writing poetry. He once humorously described how he was chosen to be class poet for his graduation from Central High School, where he and a girl were the only black class members.

> My classmates, knowing that a poem had to have rhythm, elected me unanimously — thinking, no doubt, that I had some, being a Negro. . . . In the first half of the poem, I said that our school had the finest teachers that there ever were. And in the latter half, I said our class was the greatest class ever graduated. Naturally everybody applauded loudly. That was the way I began to write poetry.

He was elected, however, because he was popular with other students, competed on the track team, and, as his English teacher told an interviewer when his first book appeared, he was one of the most gifted members of his class.

Following his graduation he went to live in Mexico with his father, who was impatient with his literary ambitions. In Mexico, where he stayed for several months, Hughes learned Spanish and wrote the poem "The Negro Speaks of Rivers," which was published in 1921 in The Crisis, an intellectual journal edited by the Harlem writer and activist W. E. B. Du Bois. Uncomfortable with his father, who wanted him to study to be an engineer, Hughes returned to the United States, lived in Harlem, and attended Columbia University for a year. Restless again, he drifted for several years while he struggled to find a way to write the poetry and prose he dreamed of, and to support himself doing it. He worked as a seaman, traveling to Africa and northern Europe. For some months in 1924 he shared a small apartment in Paris with a Russian ballet dancer, then after a trip to Italy he returned to the United States, painting and scrubbing the decks on a tramp steamer to earn his fare. He spent most of the next year in Washington, D.C., working first for the Association for the Study of Negro Life and History, then as a busboy in the dining room of the Wardman Park Hotel.

Although still in his early twenties Hughes was considered one of the most promising members of the cultural movement called the Harlem Renaissance, a talented gathering of writers, artists, and musicians, who were creating a new African American consciousness. A bohemian white writer, photographer, and active supporter of the movement named Carl Van Vechten became interested in Hughes's poetry and recommended him to his own publisher. Van Vechten also chose the title, The Weary Blues, for Hughes's first poetry collection. Hughes was waiting for the book to appear at the time he was working in Washington. His breakthrough as a writer came through his job. The popular poet Vachel Lindsay stayed over at the hotel on one of his reading tours, and Hughes left some of his poems at Lindsay's place in the dining room. Lindsay read them with interest and at his reading announced to his audience that he had found a poet right there at the hotel, and a Negro poet at that. The next morning reporters from several white newspapers were waiting to interview the "busboy poet."

In 1925 Hughes won his first prize as a poet, and after some months back in Harlem he returned to school, this time at Lincoln University, in Pennsylvania. He also continued to write poetry, attempted an unsuccessful collaboration on a play with Zora Neale Hurston, and he was encouraged to begin his first novel, Not without Laughter, by a wealthy white woman who had become the financial patron of several Harlem writers. In 1931 he traveled through the southern states, reading his poetry to schools and private gatherings and using his poems to encourage his audiences to live their lives as fully as they could, despite the harsh reality of racial segregation. The racism he encountered affected him so deeply that the next year he traveled to Moscow with a group of Harlem writers and actors, and when the project collapsed he stayed in the Soviet Union for almost a year. When he came back to the United States he became politically active in several groups connected to the Communist party, although he was never a party member. Many of his poems in the 1930s reflected his emotional response to these early years of the Soviet experiment. In the late 1930s he supported the Loyalist government during the Spanish Civil War, and he spent months as a war correspondent in Madrid during the siege of the city, sharing quarters with other sympathetic writers like Ernest Hemingway and John Steinbeck. When it was clear that the struggle was hopeless, he returned to the United States.

Back in Harlem, Hughes became a public figure, working as a journalist, founding black theater groups, editing anthologies of black writing, and writing poetry, plays, and essays. He actively supported the U.S. war effort when the nation entered World War II in 1941. In 1943 he created the character of Jesse B. Semple, a Harlem Everyman called "Simple" by his friends, who commented with shrewd intelligence on the world of Harlem and its place in the larger world of American society. The "Simple Stories" were first published in a Harlem newspaper, then gathered into four very successful collections. After the war Hughes was questioned about his Communist sympathies by the House Un-American Activities Committee, but he was not blacklisted, as were many Americans involved in the arts during the McCarthy era. He continued to write poetry and create works for the theater and to support the work of other African American creative artists, among them young writers, painters, and jazz musicians, until his death in 1967.

In this selection from Langston Hughes's poetry you will find many of his recurring themes. "The Negro Speaks of Rivers," written while he was still a teenager and strongly influenced by the midwestern poet Carl Sandburg, is a haunting expression of the rich sense of history in his poetry, even though the language is direct and uncomplicated. "Mother to Son" explores the theme of family and the difficulties of everyday life. "I, Too," which borrows some of its language and style from Walt Whitman, is an expression of Hughes's consciousness of his blackness and his certainty of the worth of his blackness, even if now he is forced to "eat in the kitchen." "Bound No'th Blues" is one of the many poems he wrote in the blues form. In a blues verse the first two lines are repeated, often with small variations, and a third line concludes the idea of the first two lines and rhymes with them. The first two lines of Hughes's poem represent the first line of a blues verse; then he repeats the words, with slight variations; and the last two lines of his verse represent the third line of the blues, concluding his thought and completing the rhyme. He was the first poet to use the blues form successfully, and he used it with continued skill for many years.

The tragedy of lynching is the subject of "Song for a Dark Girl," which quotes a line from the song "Dixie" as a sardonic comment on southern racism. Hughes is becoming much more engaged politically in poems like "Song for a Dark Girl," "House in the World," and "Florida Road Workers," although he is still writing in a language that is deceptively simple and immediate in its appeal. The speaker in "House in the World" despairs that he and his "dark brothers" will never be free of white domination, and the poor worker who is building the road in Florida cheers himself up by proclaiming proudly that even if it is only rich people who will get to "sweep over" his road he will "get to see 'em ride." Poems such as these are the background to his explicitly political poetry of the 1930s, poems like "Good Morning Revolution" and "Columbia." His turn away from this kind of public poetry can be marked in the simple but enigmatic poem "Personal." "Little Lyric (Of Great Importance)" reflects his response to Harlem and his neighbors' worries.

Although there was a consciousness in America in the 1960s that the problem of racism had to be faced, Hughes lived through the violence of the voter registration drives in the southern states, and the turbulence of the efforts of the "Freedom Riders," northern students who came by the busload into the south, to challenge the legality of segregated public facilities. In poems like "Merry-Go-Round" and the well-known "Theme for English B" he continues to protest against racism, though in these poems the protest is expressed in wry, half-amused terms. The protest in "Down Where I Am" is presented wearily by someone who has been fighting prejudice for a long time and insists now that if anyone wants to see them, they'll have to, as the poem says in its closing line, "come down." In his famous poem "Dream Deferred" — the source of the phrase "raisin in the sun" which Lorraine Hansberry later used as the title of her well-known play (see p. 1829) — the speaker's patience is worn thin. The "dream deferred" is the dream of racial equality, and the speaker suggests that if the dream does not come true soon, there might be an explosion. It was a prophecy that was fulfilled in the months before his death, as in one city after another the ghettoes exploded into violence and rioting.

RELATED COMMENTARIES: *See Casebook on Langston Hughes, pages 1361–1367, including Langston Hughes, "A Toast to Harlem," page 1362; Jessie Fauset, "Meeting Langston Hughes," page 1363; Richard Wright, "A Review of* The Big Sea," *page 1365; Arnold Rampersad, "Langston Hughes as Folk Poet," page 1366.*

LANGSTON HUGHES

The Negro Speaks of Rivers   *1921*

I've known rivers:
I've known rivers ancient as the world and older than the
    flow of human blood in human veins.

My soul has grown deep like the rivers.

I bathed in the Euphrates when dawns were young.
I built my hut near the Congo and it lulled me to sleep.
I looked upon the Nile and raised the Pyramids above it.

    5

I heard the singing of the Mississippi when Abe Lincoln
    went down to New Orleans, and I've seen its muddy
    bosom turn all golden in the sunset.   10

I've known rivers:
Ancient, dusky rivers.

My soul has grown deep like the rivers.

LANGSTON HUGHES

Mother to Son   1926

Well, son, I'll tell you:
Life for me ain't been no crystal stair.
It's had tacks in it,
And splinters,
And boards torn up,   5
And places with no carpet on the floor —
Bare.
But all the time
I'se been a-climbin' on,
And reachin' landin's,   10
And turnin' corners,
And sometimes goin' in the dark
Where there ain't been no light.
So boy, don't you turn back.
Don't you set down on the steps   15
'Cause you finds it's kinder hard.
Don't you fall now —
For I'se still goin', honey,
I'se still climbin',
And life for me ain't been no crystal stair.   20

LANGSTON HUGHES

I, Too   1926

I, too, sing America.

I am the darker brother.
They send me to eat in the kitchen
When company comes,
But I laugh,   5

And eat well,
And grow strong.

Tomorrow,
I'll be at the table
When company comes.   10
Nobody'll dare
Say to me,
"Eat in the kitchen,"
Then.

Besides,   15
They'll see how beautiful I am
And be ashamed —

I, too, am America.

LANGSTON HUGHES

Bound No'th Blues   1927

Goin' down the road, Lawd,
Goin' down the road.
Down the road, Lawd,
Way, way down the road.
Got to find somebody   5
To help me carry this load.

Road's in front o' me,
Nothin' to do but walk.
Road's in front o' me,
Walk . . . an' walk . . . an' walk.   10
I'd like to meet a good friend
To come along an' talk.

Hates to be lonely,
Lawd, I hates to be sad.
Says I hates to be lonely,   15
Hates to be lonely an' sad,
But ever friend you finds seems
Like they try to do you bad.

Road, road, road, O!
Road, road . . . road . . . road, road!   20
Road, road, road, O!
On the no'thern road.
These Mississippi towns ain't
Fit fer a hoppin' toad.

LANGSTON HUGHES

Song for a Dark Girl

1927

Way Down South in Dixie
    (Break the heart of me)
They hung my black young lover
    To a cross roads tree.

Way Down South in Dixie
    (Bruised body high in air)
I asked the white Lord Jesus
    What was the use of prayer.   5

Way Down South in Dixie
    (Break the heart of me)
Love is a naked shadow   10
    On a gnarled and naked tree.

LANGSTON HUGHES

House in the World

1931

I'm looking for a house
In the world
Where the white shadows
Will not fall.

There is no such house,
Dark brothers,
No such house
At all.

LANGSTON HUGHES

Florida Road Workers

1931

Hey, Buddy!
Look at me!

I'm makin' a road
For the cars to fly by on,
Makin' a road
Through the palmetto thicket   5
For light and civilization
To travel on.

I'm makin' a road
For the rich to sweep over   10
In their big cars
And leave me standin' here.

Sure,
A road helps everybody.
Rich folks ride —   15
And I get to see 'em ride.
I ain't never seen nobody
Ride so fine before.

Hey, Buddy, look!
I'm makin' a road!   20

LANGSTON HUGHES

Good Morning Revolution   *1932*

Good-morning, Revolution:
        You're the very best friend
        I ever had.
We gonna pal around together from now on.
Say, listen, Revolution: 5
You know, the boss where I used to work,
The guy that gimme the air to cut down expenses,
He wrote a long letter to the papers ABOUT you:
Said you was a trouble maker, a alien-enemy,
In other words a son-of-a-bitch.   10
He called up the police
And told 'em to watch out for a guy
Named Revolution.

You see,
The boss knows you're my friend.   15
He sees us hangin' out together.
He knows we're hungry, and ragged,
And ain't got a damn thing in this world —
And are gonna do something about it.

The boss's got all he needs, certainly,   20
        Eats swell,
        Owns a lotta houses,
        Goes vacationin',
        Breaks strikes,
        Runs politics, bribes police,   25
        Pays off congress,
        And struts all over the earth —

But me, I ain't never had enough to eat.
Me, I ain't never been warm in winter.
Me, I ain't never known security —   30
All my life, been livin' hand to mouth,
    Hand to mouth.

Listen, Revolution,
    We're buddies, see —
    Together,   35
    We can take everything:
    Factories, arsenals, houses, ships,
    Railroads, forests, fields, orchards,
    Bus lines, telegraphs, radios,
    (Jesus! Raise hell with radios!)   40
    Steel mills, coal mines, oil wells, gas,
    All the tools of production,
    (Great day in the morning!)
    Everything —
    And turn 'em over to the people who work.   45
    Rule and run 'em for us people who work.

Boy! Them radios —
Broadcasting that very first morning to USSR:
Another member the International Soviet's done come
Greetings to the Socialist Soviet Republics   50
Hey you rising workers everywhere greetings —
    And we'll sign it: *Germany*
    Sign it: *China*
    Sign it: *Africa*
    Sign it: *Poland*   55
    Sign it: *Italy*
    Sign it: *America*
    Sign it with my one name: *Worker*
On that day when no one will be hungry, cold, oppressed,
Anywhere in the world again.   60

    That's our job!

    I been starvin' too long,
    Ain't you?

    Let's go, Revolution!

LANGSTON HUGHES

Columbia   1933

Columbia,
My dear girl,
You really haven't been a virgin for so long
It's ludicrous to keep up the pretext.
You're terribly involved in world assignations   5
And everybody knows it.
You've slept with all the big powers
In military uniforms,
And you've taken the sweet life
Of all the little brown fellows   10
In loin cloths and cotton trousers.
When they've resisted,
You've yelled, "Rape,"
At the top of your voice
And called for the middies   15
To beat them up for not being gentlemen
And liking your crooked painted mouth.
(You must think the moons of Hawaii
Disguise your ugliness.)
Really,   20
You're getting a little too old,
Columbia,
To be so naive, and so coy.
Being one of the world's big vampires,
Why don't you come on out and say so   25
Like Japan, and England, and France,
And all the other nymphomaniacs of power
Who've long since dropped their
Smoke-screens of innocence
To sit frankly on a bed of bombs?   30

O, sweet mouth of India,
And Africa,
Manchuria, and Haiti.

Columbia,
You darling,   35
Don't shoot!
I'll kiss you!

LANGSTON HUGHES

Personal

1933

In an envelope marked:
   Personal
God addressed me a letter.
In an envelope marked:
   Personal.
I have given my answer.

LANGSTON HUGHES

Little Lyric (Of Great Importance)

1942

I wish the rent
Was heaven sent.

LANGSTON HUGHES

Merry-Go-Round

1942

Colored child at carnival

Where is the Jim Crow section
On this merry-go-round,
Mister, cause I want to ride?
Down South where I come from
White and colored   5
Can't sit side by side.
Down South on the train
There's a Jim Crow car.
On the bus we're put in the back —
But there ain't no back   10
To a merry-go-round!
Where's the horse
For a kid that's black?

LANGSTON HUGHES

Down Where I Am

1950

Too many years
Beatin' at the door —
I done beat my
Both fists sore.

Too many years   5
Tryin' to get up there —
Done broke my ankles down,
Got nowhere.

Too many years
Climbin' that hill,   10
'Bout out of breath.
I got my fill.

I'm gonna plant my feet
On solid ground.
If you want to see me,   15
Come down.

LANGSTON HUGHES

Theme for English B   *1949*

The instructor said,

> *Go home and write*
> *a page tonight.*
> *And let that page come out of you —*
> *Then, it will be true.*   5

I wonder if it's that simple?
I am twenty-two, colored, born in Winston-Salem.
I went to school there, then Durham, then here
to this college on the hill above Harlem.
I am the only colored student in my class.   10
The steps from the hill lead down into Harlem,
through a park, then I cross St. Nicholas,
Eighth Avenue, Seventh, and I come to the Y,
the Harlem Branch Y, where I take the elevator
up to my room, sit down, and write this page: 15

It's not easy to know what is true for you or me
at twenty-two, my age. But I guess I'm what
I feel and see and hear, Harlem, I hear you:
hear you, hear me — we two — you, me, talk on this page.
(I hear New York, too.) Me — who?   20
Well, I like to eat, sleep, drink, and be in love.
I like to work, read, learn, and understand life.
I like a pipe for a Christmas present,
or records — Bessie, bop, or Bach.
I guess being colored doesn't make me *not* like   25
the same things other folks like who are other races.
So will my page be colored that I write?
Being me, it will not be white.

But it will be
a part of you, instructor.   30
You are white —
yet a part of me, as I am a part of you.
That's American.
Sometimes perhaps you don't want to be a part of me.
Nor do I often want to be a part of you.   35
But we are, that's true!
As I learn from you,
I guess you learn from me —
although you're older — and white —
and somewhat more free.   40

This is my page for English B.

LANGSTON HUGHES

Dream Deferred   *1959*

What happens to a dream deferred?

> Does it dry up
> like a raisin in the sun?
> OR fester like a sore —
> And then run?   5
> Does it stink like rotten meat?
> Or crust and sugar over —
> like a syrupy sweet?

> Maybe it just sags
> like a heavy load.   10

> *Or does it explode?*

ɞↄ

JOHN KEATS *(1795–1821) was the oldest of five children. His mother was the wife of the head stableman in a London livery stable. In his brief school years, Keats, despite his small stature, was mostly distinguished for his numerous fist fights. He also developed a passion for reading, under the fortunate tutelage of Charles Cowden Clarke, but after the deaths of his parents he was apprenticed at age fifteen to an apothecary surgeon. When he completed a year of studies at Guy's College, he was licensed to continue his trade, but he quickly abandoned it to become a poet.*

Little of the poetry Keats had written up to this time showed any sign of genius, although he received ample encouragement from a number of older writers, including Leigh Hunt, who introduced him to Percy Bysshe Shelley. The sonnet "On First Looking into Chapman's Homer" (p. 999), written when he was twenty-one, first hinted at what he would accomplish in the short time that was left to him.

His mother had died of tuberculosis, and Keats nursed a tubercular younger brother through his dying months in 1818. Keats contracted the disease and at the same time fell hopelessly in love with an eighteen-year-old girl named Fanny Brawne. Too poor and too ill to marry, he poured his emotions into poems and letters that were suffused with his despair, his love for Brawne, and his consciousness that his life was already running out. The sonnet "When I have fears that I may cease to be" (p. 949) was written in these months.

Keats tried to fight his illness by traveling to Italy, but he was weakened by a series of hemorrhages and died in Rome at the age of twenty-six. In his last letter he apologized to a friend for writing such a clumsy good-bye. He wrote, "I always made an awkward bow."

Both "Ode to a Nightingale" and "Bright star, would I were steadfast as thou art — " were written in Keats's remarkable year of 1819, a period in which he composed other great odes, including "To Autumn" (p. 903) and "Ode on a Grecian Urn" (p. 934). "A Thing of Beauty" (p. 917) is from his 1817 poetic romance, Endymion. **RELATED COMMENTARY:** *Sydney Lea, "On Keats's 'To Autumn,' " page 1280.*

JOHN KEATS

Ode to a Nightingale

1819

I

My heart aches, and a drowsy numbness pains
 My sense, as though of hemlock° I had drunk,   *a poison*
Or emptied some dull opiate to the drains
 One minute past, and Lethe-wards° had sunk:
'Tis not through envy of thy happy lot,
 But being too happy in thine happiness —   5
  That thou, light-wingèd Dryad° of the trees,   *wood nymph*
   In some melodious plot
 Of beechen green, and shadows numberless,
  Singest of summer in full-throated ease.

                      10
II

O, for a draught of vintage! that hath been
 Cooled a long age in the deep-delvèd earth,
Tasting of Flora° and the country green,   *goddess of flowers*
 Dance, and Provençal song,° and sunburnt mirth!
O for a beaker full of the warm South,
 Full of the true, the blushful Hippocrene,°   15

---

4. Lethe-wards: Lethe is the river of forgetfulness in Greek mythology. **14. Provençal song:** Provence, in medieval France, was famous for its troubadors.

With beaded bubbles winking at the brim,
   And purple-stainèd mouth;
That I might drink, and leave the world unseen,
   And with thee fade away into the forest dim.   20

III

Fade far away, dissolve, and quite forget
   What thou among the leaves hast never known,
The weariness, the fever, and the fret
   Here, where men sit and hear each other groan;
Where palsy shakes a few, sad, last gray hairs,   25
   Where youth grows pale, and specter-thin, and dies,
     Where but to think is to be full of sorrow
      And leaden-eyed despairs,
   Where Beauty cannot keep her lustrous eyes;
     Or new Love pine at them beyond tomorrow.   30

IV

Away! away! for I will fly to thee,
   Not charioted by Bacchus and his pards,°
But on the viewless wings of Poesy,
   Though the dull brain perplexes and retards:
Already with thee! tender is the night,   35
   And haply the Queen-Moon is on her throne,
     Clustered around by all her starry Fays;°   *fairies*
      But here there is no light,
   Save what from heaven is with the breezes blown
     Through verdurous glooms and winding mossy ways.   40

V

I cannot see what flowers are at my feet,
   Nor what soft incense hangs upon the boughs,
But, in embalmèd° darkness, guess each sweet   *perfumed*
   Wherewith the seasonable month endows
The grass, the thicket, and the fruit-tree wild;   45
   What hawthorn, and the pastoral eglantine;
     Fast fading violets covered up in leaves;
      And mid-May's eldest child,
   The coming musk-rose, full of dewy wine,
     The murmurous haunt of flies on summer eves.   50

---

16. Hippocrene: Hippocrene is the fountain of the Muses, the goddesses of artistic inspiration. **32. Bacchus and his pards:** Bacchus, the god of wine, supposedly traveled in a chariot drawn by leopards.

VI

Darkling° I listen; and for many a time   *in the dark*
    I have been half in love with easeful Death,
Called him soft names in many a musèd rhyme,
    To take into the air my quiet breath;
Now more than ever seems it rich to die,   55
    To cease upon the midnight with no pain,
        While thou art pouring forth thy soul abroad
           In such an ecstasy!
    Still wouldst thou sing, and I have ears in vain —
        To thy high requiem become a sod.   60

VII

Thou wast not born for death, immortal Bird!
    No hungry generations tread thee down;
The voice I hear this passing night was heard
    In ancient days by emperor and clown:
Perhaps the selfsame song that found a path   65
    Through the sad heart of Ruth,° when, sick for home,
        She stood in tears amid the alien corn:
           The same that oft-times hath
    Charmed magic casements, opening on the foam
        Of perilous seas, in faery lands forlorn.   70

VIII

Forlorn! the very word is like a bell
    To toll me back from thee to my sole self!
Adieu! the fancy cannot cheat so well
    As she is famed to do, deceiving elf.
Adieu! adieu! thy plaintive anthem fades   75
    Past the near meadows, over the still stream,
        Up the hill side; and now 'tis buried deep
           In the next valley-glades:
    Was it a vision, or a waking dream?
        Fled is that music: — Do I wake or sleep?   80

JOHN KEATS

Bright star, would I were steadfast as thou art —   1819

Bright star, would I were steadfast as thou art —
    Nor in lone splendor hung aloft the night
And watching, with eternal lids apart,
    Like nature's patient, sleepless Eremite,°   *hermit*

---

66. **the sad heart of Ruth:** Reference to the young widow in the biblical Book of Ruth.

The moving waters at their priestlike task   5
    Of pure ablution round earth's human shores,
Or grazing on the new soft fallen mask
    Of snow upon the mountains and the moors —
No — yet still steadfast, still unchangeable,
    Pillowed upon my fair love's ripening breast,   10
To feel forever its soft fall and swell,
    Awake forever in a sweet unrest,
Still, still to hear her tender-taken breath,
And so live ever — or else swoon to death.

ཉྫ

D. H. LAWRENCE *(1885–1930) was born David Herbert Lawrence, the son of a coal miner in the industrial town of Eastwood, in Nottinghamshire, England. His mother had been a schoolteacher, and she was frustrated by the hard existence of a coal miner's wife. She fought desperately to give Lawrence a fuller life. Through her financial sacrifices and a scholarship, Lawrence was able to complete high school; he then studied to become a teacher. In 1909, shortly after he began teaching in South London, he published his first novel,* The White Peacock, *but he was not established as a major literary figure until the publication of* Sons and Lovers *in 1913. He was twenty-eight years old.*

Lawrence was a prolific writer, and at the same time that he was creating his novels he was writing a great deal of poetry, experimenting with new forms and subject matter. His first collection of poems, Love Poems and Others, *was published in 1913. In London Lawrence allied himself with a group of young literary rebels, among them the American expatriates Ezra Pound and H.D., with whom Lawrence later had an intensely emotional but physically unconsummated relationship. A virulent social critic, he was frequently harassed by censorship because his short stories, novels, and poetry were often explicitly sexual and he always felt a need to challenge conventional moral attitudes.*

To compound his difficulties, in the spring of 1912 Lawrence had fled to Germany with the wife of a professor at Nottingham University. She was older than Lawrence and abandoned her three children to follow him. They were married after her divorce from her husband in 1914, but public opinion in England never forgave either of them. A novel he published the next year, The Rainbow, *was banned by the authorities in 1915, and a collection of his paintings was taken from a public exhibition and burned.*

Lawrence suffered from tuberculosis, and he and his wife spent years wandering in Italy, Australia, Mexico, New Mexico, and southern France, seeking a warm, sunny climate. He died in France at the age of forty-four.

Lawrence's early poetry was written in conventional forms, but an important influence on his work was the American poet Walt Whitman, whose poems were composed in a freer idiom. Lawrence was continually drawn to what he felt as the mystery and the vitality of the natural world, and he responded powerfully to the harsh physical realities he found in isolated areas such as deserts of the American Southwest and northern Mexico, which is the setting for "Mountain Lion," and rural Italy, the setting for "Snake."

RELATED COMMENTARIES: *Janice H. Harris, "Levels of Meaning in Lawrence's 'The Rocking-Horse Winner,' " page 754; D. H. Lawrence, "Draft Passage from 'Odour of Chrysanthemums,' " page 765; Jay Parini, "Lawrence's and Steinbeck's 'Chrysanthemums,' " page 786.*

D. H. LAWRENCE

Mountain Lion

1923

Climbing through the January snow, into the Lobo canyon
Dark grow the spruce-trees, blue is the balsam, water sounds still
    unfrozen, and the trail is still evident.

Men!
Two men!
Men! The only animal in the world to fear!   5

They hesitate.
We hesitate.
They have a gun.
We have no gun.

Then we all advance, to meet.   10

Two Mexicans, strangers, emerging out of the dark and snow and
    inwardness of the Lobo valley.
What are they doing here on this vanishing trail?

What is he carrying?
Something yellow.
A deer?   15

Qué tiene, amigo?
León — °

He smiles, foolishly, as if he were caught doing wrong.
And we smile, foolishly, as if we didn't know.
He is quite gentle and dark-faced.   20

It is a mountain lion.
A long, long slim cat, yellow like a lioness.
Dead.

He trapped her this morning, he says, smiling foolishly.
Lift up her face,   25
Her round, bright face, bright as frost.
Her round, fine-fashioned head, with two dead ears;
And stripes in the brilliant frost of her face, sharp, fine dark rays,

---

16–17. *Qué tiene, . . . León:* "What do you have, friend? / Lion" in Spanish.

Dark, keen, fine rays in the brilliant frost of her face.
Beautiful dead eyes.   30

Hermoso es!°

They go out towards the open;
We go on into the gloom of Lobo.
And above the trees I found her lair,
A hole in the blood-orange brilliant rocks that stick up, a little cave.   35
And bones, and twigs, and a perilous ascent.

So, she will never leap up that way again, with the yellow flash of a
    mountain lion's long shoot!
And her bright striped frost-face will never watch any more, out of the
    shadow of the cave in the blood-orange rock,
Above the trees of the Lobo dark valley-mouth!

Instead, I look out.   40
And out to the dim of the desert, like a dream, never real;
To the snow of the Sangre de Cristo mountains, the ice of the moun-
    tains of Picoris,
And near across at the opposite steep of snow, green trees motionless
    standing in snow, like a Christmas toy.

And I think in this empty world there was room for me and a moun-
    tain lion.
And I think in the world beyond, how easily we might spare a million
    or two of humans   45
And never miss them.
Yet what a gap in the world, the missing white frost-face of that slim
    yellow mountain lion!

D. H. LAWRENCE

Snake   *1923*

A snake came to my water-trough
On a hot, hot day, and I in pyjamas for the heat,
To drink there.

In the deep, strange-scented shade of the great dark carob-tree
I came down the steps with my pitcher   5
And must wait, must stand and wait, for there he was at the trough
    before me.

He reached down from a fissure in the earth-wall in the gloom
And trailed his yellow-brown slackness soft-bellied down, over the
    edge of the stone trough

---

31. *Hermoso es!:* Spanish for "It's beautiful!"

And rested his throat upon the stone bottom,
And where the water had dripped from the tap, in a small clearness,   10
He sipped with his straight mouth,
Softly drank through his straight gums, into his slack long body,
Silently.

Someone was before me at my water-trough,
And I, like a second comer, waiting.   15

He lifted his head from his drinking, as cattle do,
And looked at me vaguely, as drinking cattle do,
And flickered his two-forked tongue from his lips, and mused a
    moment,
And stooped and drank a little more,
Being earth-brown, earth-golden from the burning bowels of the earth   20
On the day of Sicilian July, with Etna° smoking.

The voice of my education said to me
He must be killed,
For in Sicily the black, black snakes are innocent, the gold are
    venomous.

And voices in me said, If you were a man   25
You would take a stick and break him now, and finish him off.

But must I confess how I liked him,
How glad I was he had come like a guest in quiet, to drink at my
    water-trough
And depart peaceful, pacified, and thankless,
Into the burning bowels of this earth?   30

Was it cowardice, that I dared not kill him?
Was it perversity, that I longed to talk to him?
Was it humility, to feel so honoured?
I felt so honoured.
And yet those voices: 35
If you were not afraid, you would kill him!

And truly I was afraid, I was most afraid,
But even so, honoured still more
That he should seek my hospitality
From out the dark door of the secret earth.   40

He drank enough
And lifted his head, dreamily, as one who has drunken,
And flickered his tongue like a forked night on the air, so black,
Seeming to lick his lips,
And looked around like a god, unseeing, into the air,   45
And slowly turned his head,
And slowly, very slowly, as if thrice adream,

---

21. **Etna:** An active volcano in Sicily.

Proceeded to draw his slow length curving round
And climb again the broken bank of my wall-face.

And as he put his head into that dreadful hole,   50
And as he slowly drew up, snake-easing his shoulders, and entered
    farther,
A sort of horror, a sort of protest against his withdrawing into that
    horrid black hole,
Deliberately going into the blackness, and slowly drawing himself
    after,
Overcame me now his back was turned.

I looked round, I put down my pitcher,   55
I picked up a clumsy log
And threw it at the water-trough with a clatter.

I think it did not hit him,
But suddenly that part of him that was left behind convulsed in
    undignified haste,
Writhed like lightning, and was gone   60
Into the black hole, the earth-lipped fissure in the wall-front.
At which, in the intense still noon, I stared with fascination.

And immediately I regretted it.
I thought how paltry, how vulgar, what a mean act!
I despised myself and the voices of my accursed human education.   65

And I thought of the albatross,°
And I wished he would come back, my snake.

For he seemed to me again like a king,
Like a king in exile, uncrowned in the underworld,
Now due to be crowned again.   70

And so, I missed my chance with one of the lords
Of life.
And I have something to expiate;
A pettiness.

⚭

ROBERT LOWELL *(1917–1977) was born in Boston to a distinguished
New England family that had already produced two major poets, James Russell
Lowell (1819–1891) and Amy Lowell (1874–1925), one of the leaders of the imagist
movement (pp. 964–967). After two years at Harvard University, Lowell left
in 1937 for Kenyon College in Ohio to join a group of young poets who had gathered
around teacher and poet John Crowe Ransom. Although his father had been a Navy
officer, Lowell became a conscientious objector during World War II and was imprisoned for five months in 1943. He continued to write poetry through his per-*

---

66. **albatross:** It was thought by many societies that to kill an albatross was to invite disaster.

sonal crises, and his second book, **Lord Weary's Castle**, won the Pulitzer Prize in 1946.

Lowell published steadily, and his books were well received, but he was beginning to suffer from acute attacks of depression. Two of his three marriages were to novelists — first to Jean Stafford in 1940 and then to Elizabeth Hardwick in 1949. He was also drinking heavily and when he was drunk he was emotionally abusive. In the 1950s he visited San Francisco and experienced the excitement of the Beat Generation, the new literary movement that had sprung up there. After seeing the effect of Beat writer Allen Ginsberg's poetry on audiences (see p. 1109) and reading an emotional poem titled "Heart's Needle" by a former student named W. D. Snodgrass, he changed his way of writing. His poems became freer and more personal. His collection Life Studies, written in the new "confessional" style, was one of the most influential books published after the war, winning the National Book Award in 1959. At this same time he was teaching a poetry course at Boston University, and among his students were Sylvia Plath (p. 1160) and Anne Sexton (p. 1185), who adopted the new style in their own writing.

Finally diagnosed as manic-depressive, Lowell with medication was able to avoid some of the psychotic episodes that had periodically caused him to be hospitalized. With novelist Norman Mailer, he was involved in the struggle against the Vietnam War, and in 1972 he married for the third time and settled in England. He had written plays and literary criticism and won the Bollingen Prize for his translations. In 1977 he returned to the United States planning to teach at Harvard, but he died of a heart attack a short time later.

One of his closest friends was poet Elizabeth Bishop (p. 1024) — in emotional moments he asked her to marry him — and "Skunk Hour" is dedicated to her. His poem is a response to her "Armadillo." It reads almost like a letter, describing a scene that is familiar to both of them. "For the Union Dead" is also a description, this time of the Boston Common and the memorial statue by Augustus Saint-Gaudens to the Civil War regiment of African American soldiers that was destroyed with its young commander, Boston's Colonel Shaw. "Epilogue" was written in 1977, shortly before Lowell's death.

RELATED COMMENTARIES: Robert Lowell, "An Explication of 'Skunk Hour,' " page 1286; Robert Lowell, "Foreword to Plath's Ariel," page 1369; Louis Simpson, "On Lowell's 'Skunk Hour,' " page 1315.

ROBERT LOWELL

Skunk Hour

1959

For Elizabeth Bishop

Nautilus Island's hermit
heiress still lives through winters in her Spartan cottage;
her sheep still graze above the sea.
Her son's a bishop. Her farmer
is first selectman in our village;   5
she's in her dotage.

Thirsting for
the hierarchic privacy
of Queen Victoria's century,
she buys up all   10
the eyesores facing her shore,
and lets them fall.

The season's ill —
we've lost our summer millionaire,
who seemed to leap from an L. L. Bean°   15
catalogue. His nine-knot yawl
was auctioned off to lobstermen.
A red fox stain covers Blue Hill.

And now our fairy
decorator brightens his shop for fall;   20
his fishnet's filled with orange cork,
orange, his cobbler's bench and awl;
there is no money in his work,
he'd rather marry.

One dark night,   25
my Tudor Ford climbed the hill's skull;
I watched for love-cars. Lights turned down,
they lay together, hull to hull,
where the graveyard shelves on the town. . . .
My mind's not right.   30

A car radio bleats,
"Love, O careless Love. . . ." I hear
my ill-spirit sob in each blood cell,
as if my hand were at its throat. . . .
I myself am hell;   35
nobody's here —

only skunks, that search
in the moonlight for a bite to eat.
They march on their soles up Main Street:
white stripes, moonstruck eyes' red fire   40
under the chalk-dry and spar spire
of the Trinitarian Church.

I stand on top
of our back steps and breathe the rich air —
a mother skunk with her column of kittens swills the garbage pail.   45
She jabs her wedge-head in a cup
of sour cream, drops her ostrich tail,
and will not scare.

---

15. L. L. Bean: A Maine mail-order store known for its sporting goods and outdoor equipment.

ROBERT LOWELL

For the Union Dead

1964

"Relinquunt Omnia Servare Rem Publican."°

The old South Boston Aquarium stands
in a Sahara of snow now. Its broken windows are boarded.
The bronze weathervane cod has lost half its scales.
The airy tanks are dry.

Once my nose crawled like a snail on the glass;   5
my hand tingled
to burst the bubbles
drifting from the noses of the cowed, compliant fish.

My hand draws back. I often sigh still
for the dark downward and vegetating kingdom   10
of the fish and reptile. One morning last March,
I pressed against the new barbed and galvanized

fence on the Boston Common. Behind their cage,
yellow dinosaur steamshovels were grunting
as they cropped up tons of mush and grass   15
to gouge their underworld garage.

Parking spaces luxuriate like civic
sandpiles in the heart of Boston.
A girdle of orange, Puritan-pumpkin colored girders
braces the tingling Statehouse,   20

shaking over the excavations, as it faces Colonel Shaw
and his bell-cheeked Negro infantry
on St. Gaudens' shaking Civil War relief,
propped by a plank splint against the garage's earthquake.

Two months after marching through Boston,   25
half the regiment was dead;
at the dedication,
William James° could almost hear the bronze Negroes breathe.

Their monument sticks like a fishbone
in the city's throat.   30
Its Colonel is as lean
as a compass-needle.

He has an angry wrenlike vigilance,
a greyhound's gentle tautness;
he seems to wince at pleasure,   35
and suffocate for privacy.

Relinquunt ... Publican: "They gave up all to serve the republic." **28. William James:**
Harvard psychologist and philosopher (1842–1910).

He is out of bounds now. He rejoices in man's lovely,
peculiar power to choose life and die —
when he leads his black soldiers to death,
he cannot bend his back.   40

On a thousand small town New England greens,
the old white churches hold their air
of sparse, sincere rebellion; frayed flags
quilt the graveyards of the Grand Army of the Republic.

The stone statues of the abstract Union Soldier   45
grow slimmer and younger each year —
wasp-waisted, they doze over muskets
and muse through their sideburns . . .

Shaw's father wanted no monument
except the ditch,   50
where his son's body was thrown
and lost with his "niggers."

The ditch is nearer.
There are no statues for the last war here;
on Boylston Street, a commercial photograph   55
shows Hiroshima boiling

over a Mosler Safe, the "Rock of Ages"
that survived the blast. Space is nearer.
When I crouch to my television set,
the drained faces of Negro school-children rise like balloons. 60

Colonel Shaw
is riding on his bubble,
he waits
for the blessèd break.

The Aquarium is gone. Everywhere,   65
giant finned cars nose forward like fish;
a savage servility
slides by on grease.

ROBERT LOWELL

Epilogue   1977

Those blessèd structures, plot and rhyme —
why are they no help to me now
I want to make
something imagined, not recalled?
I hear the noise of my own voice: 5
The painter's vision is not a lens,
it trembles to caress the light.
But sometimes everything I write

with the threadbare art of my eye
seems a snapshot,   10
lurid, rapid, garish, grouped,
heightened from life,
yet paralyzed by fact.
All's misalliance.
Yet why not say what happened?   15
Pray for the grace of accuracy
Vermeer° gave to the sun's illumination
stealing like the tide across a map
to his girl solid with yearning.
We are poor passing facts,   20
warned by that to give
each figure in the photograph
his living name.

ॐ

EDNA ST. VINCENT MILLAY *(1892–1950) was born in Rockland, Maine, and in 1923, following her marriage, she moved to a farm in the Berkshires and lived there in quiet isolation. As a poet, however, she will always be remembered for her few brief years in Greenwich Village after her graduation from Vassar College in 1917. "First Fig," a quatrain she wrote in 1920, seemed to represent with its candle metaphor the carefree spirit of the era. Her first major poem, "Renascence," was published when she was nineteen, and during her Village years she wrote short stories, plays, and several collections of lyric poetry, including a number of sonnets. She won the Pulitzer Prize in 1923 for "The Harp-Weaver," and for many years she was probably the best-known and most widely read poet in the United States. Her sequence of fifty-two love sonnets,* Fatal Interview, *published in 1931, was one of the most enthusiastically reviewed books of the time. She was also a political activist and used her poetry to defend the causes she believed in so passionately.*

"Recuerdo" catches the mood of her Greenwich Village days, with its wry description of a night on the Staten Island ferry. "I too beneath your moon, almighty Sex" is a late sonnet, written in 1939. (See also Millay's "God's World" on p. 889 and "What lips my lips have kissed" on p. 950.)

EDNA ST. VINCENT MILLAY

First Fig   1920

My candle burns at both ends;
    It will not last the night;
But ah, my foes, and oh, my friends —
    It gives a lovely light!

---

17. Vermeer: Dutch painter Jan Vermeer (1632–1675).

EDNA ST. VINCENT MILLAY

Recuerdo°   *1920*

We were very tired, we were very merry —
We had gone back and forth all night on the ferry.
It was bare and bright, and smelled like a stable —
But we looked into a fire, we leaned across a table,
We lay on a hill-top underneath the moon;   5
And the whistles kept blowing, and the dawn came soon.

We were very tired, we were very merry —
We had gone back and forth all night on the ferry;
And you ate an apple, and I ate a pear,
From a dozen of each we had bought somewhere;   10
And the sky went wan, and the wind came cold,
And the sun rose dripping, a bucketful of gold.

We were very tired, we were very merry,
We had gone back and forth all night on the ferry.
We hailed, "Good morrow, mother!" to a shawl-covered head,   15
And bought a morning paper, which neither of us read;
And she wept, "God bless you!" for the apples and pears,
And we gave her all our money but our subway fares.

EDNA ST. VINCENT MILLAY

I too beneath your moon, almighty Sex   *1939*

I too beneath your moon, almighty Sex,
Go forth at nightfall crying like a cat,
Leaving the lofty tower I laboured at
For birds to foul and boys and girls to vex
With tittering chalk; and you, and the long necks   5
Of neighbours sitting where their mothers sat
Are well aware of shadowy this and that
In me, that's neither noble nor complex.
Such as I am, however, I have brought
To what it is, this tower; it is my own;   10
Though it was reared To Beauty, it was wrought
From what I had to build with: honest bone
Is there, and anguish; pride; and burning thought;
And lust is there, and nights not spent alone.

ဢ

Recuerdo: Spanish for a "memory," or "souvenir."

MARIANNE MOORE (1887–1972) *was born in St. Louis, but her father chose not to remain with his family, and eventually Moore and her mother moved to Carlisle, Pennsylvania. She graduated from Bryn Mawr College in 1909. Following her graduation, she and her mother traveled to France and England, then for five years she taught courses in office skills at the U.S. Indian School for Native Americans in Carlisle. In 1918 she and her mother moved to New York with her brother, who was a Presbyterian minister.*

She had already begun writing poetry in college, and she began submitting her work to several small experimental magazines. Her poetry immediately attracted the attention of other writers, including William Carlos Williams (p. 1217) and Wallace Stevens. Williams included her work in a small mimeographed magazine he published in the early 1920s. From 1925 to 1929 she was editor of The Dial, *a New York literary journal.*

Moore's life was quiet. She lived with her mother in Brooklyn and worked on her poetry. The poet Elizabeth Bishop (p. 1024), who was close to her for thirty-five years, remembered her conversation as "entertaining, enlightening, fascinating, and memorable; her talk, like her poetry, was quite different from anyone else in the world."

In 1951 Moore's Collected Poems *won almost every major American literary award, and her work found new audiences who were charmed by her enthusiasm for oddly named animals, racehorses, and the Brooklyn Dodgers. "The Fish" is an early poem that attracted immediate attention, and it may have inspired the poem with the same title by Bishop. "The Mind Is an Enchanting Thing" was written in the 1940s. The simile in the opening lines, comparing the enchantment in the mind to the shine of the sun on an insect's wing, is one of her most vivid images. (See also Moore's "Poetry" on p. 875 and "A Talisman" on p. 890.)*

RELATED POEM: *Anne Waldman, "Marianne Moore," page 1206.*

RELATED COMMENTARIES: *Elizabeth Bishop, "Efforts of Affection: A Memoir of Marianne Moore," page 1236; Marianne Moore, "Some Answers to Questions Posed by Howard Nemerov," page 1289.*

MARIANNE MOORE

The Fish

1921

wade
through black jade.
    Of the crow-blue mussel shells, one keeps
    adjusting the ash heaps;
        opening and shutting itself like

5

an
injured fan.
    The barnacles which encrust the side
    of the wave, cannot hide
        there for the submerged shafts of the

10

sun,
split like spun

glass, move themselves with spotlight swiftness
   into the crevices —
      in and out, illuminating   15
the
turquoise sea
   of bodies. The water drives a wedge
   of iron through the iron edge
      of the cliff; whereupon the stars,   20
pink
rice-grains, ink-
   bespattered jellyfish, crabs like green
   lilies, and submarine
      toadstools, slide each on the other.   25
All
external
   marks of abuse are present on this
   defiant edifice —
      all the physical features of   30
ac-
cident — lack
   of cornice, dynamite grooves, burns, and
   hatchet strokes, these things stand
      out on it; the chasm side is   35
dead.
Repeated
   evidence has proved that it can live
   on what can not revive
      its youth. The sea grows old in it.   40

MARIANNE MOORE

The Mind Is an Enchanting Thing   1944

is an enchanted thing
      like the glaze on a
katydid-wing
         subdivided by sun
         till the nettings are legion.
Like Gieseking playing Scarlatti;°   5

like the apteryx-awl°
      as a beak, or the

---

6. **Gieseking playing Scarlatti:** Walter Gieseking (1895–1956) was a concert pianist who included the music of Italian composer Domenico Scarlatti (1685–1757) in his repertory.
7. **apteryx-awl:** The apteryx is a flightless bird with a narrow, awl-like beak.

kiwi's rain-shawl
        of haired feathers, the mind   10
            feeling its way as though blind,
walks along with its eyes on the ground.

It has memory's ear
        that can hear without
having to hear.   15
              Like the gyroscope's fall,
              truly unequivocal
because trued by regnant certainty,

it is a power of
        strong enchantment. It   20
is like the dove-
           neck animated by
           sun; it is memory's eye;
it's conscientious inconsistency.

It tears off the veil; tears   25
        the temptation, the
mist the heart wears,
           from its eyes, — if the heart
           has a face; it takes apart
dejection. It's fire in the dove-neck's   30

iridescence; in the
        inconsistencies
of Scarlatti.
           Unconfusion submits
           its confusion to proof; it's   35
not a Herod's oath° that cannot change.

∞

SHARON OLDS (b. 1942) *was born in San Francisco and graduated from
Stanford University. She moved to New York and eventually received her Ph.D. from
Columbia University. She has published her poetry in many literary journals, and
her second book,* The Dead and the Living, *won the Lamont Prize and the National
Book Critics Circle Award in 1984. An important influence on her work was the
new "confessional" style of Robert Lowell's earlier book* Life Studies. *Also influenced by the physical openness of the poetry of Anne Sexton, Olds writes of her
body's functions with a directness that has caused considerable controversy.* The
Wellspring, *a collection published in 1996, is a sequence of poems centered on her
life from the moment of her conception in her mother's womb. In an essay titled "The
Postconfessional Lyric," the poet Gregory Orr writes that Olds "demonstrates a*

---

36. Herod's oath: King Herod's promise to give Salome whatever she asked of him.

commitment to exploring and dramatizing primary relationships in an autobiographical mode."

Olds lives in New York City and has taught at New York University and at Goldwater Hospital, a city institution for people with disabilities. In 1993 she received a Lila Wallace Reader's Digest Writer's Award.

"The Elder Sister" is a poem about her family; "Summer Solstice, New York City" describes an incident from her life in New York.

SHARON OLDS

The Elder Sister   1984

When I look at my elder sister now
I think how she had to go first, down through the
birth canal, to force her way
head-first through the tiny channel,
the pressure of Mother's muscles on her brain,   5
the tight walls scraping her skin.
Her face is still narrow from it, the long
hollow cheeks of a Crusader on a tomb,
and her inky eyes have the look of someone who has
been in prison a long time and   10
knows they can send her back. I look at her
body and think how her breasts were the first to
rise, slowly, like swans on a pond.
By the time mine came along, they were just
two more birds in the flock, and when the hair   15
rose on the white mound of her flesh, like
threads of water out of the ground, it was the
first time, but when mine came
they knew about it. I used to think
only in terms of her harshness, sitting and   20
pissing on me in bed, but now I
see I had her before me always
like a shield. I look at her wrinkles, her clenched
jaws, her frown-lines — I see they are
the dents on my shield, the blows that did not reach me.   25
She protected me, not as a mother
protects a child, with love, but as a
hostage protects the one who makes her
escape as I made my escape, with my sister's
body held in front of me.   30

SHARON OLDS

Summer Solstice, New York City 1987

By the end of the longest day of the year he could not stand it,
he went up the iron stairs through the roof of the building
and over the soft, tarry surface
to the edge, put one leg over the complex green tin cornice
and said if they came a step closer that was it. 5
Then the huge machinery of the earth began to work for his life,
the cops came in their suits blue-grey as the sky on a cloudy evening,
and one put on a bullet-proof vest,
a black shell around his own life,
life of his children's father, in case 10
the man was armed, and one, slung with a
rope like the sign of his bounden duty,
came up out of a hole in the top of the neighbouring building
like the gold hole they say is in the top of the head,
and began to lurk toward the man who wanted to die. 15
The tallest cop approached him directly,
softly, slowly, talking to him, talking, talking,
while the man's leg hung over the lip of the next world
and the crowd gathered in the street, silent, and the
hairy net with its implacable grid was 20
unfolded near the curb and spread out and
stretched as the sheet is prepared to receive at a birth.
Then they all came a little closer
where he squatted next to his death, his shirt
glowing its milky glow like something 25
growing in a dish at night in the dark in a lab and then
everything stopped
as his body jerked and he
stepped down from the parapet and went toward them
and they closed on him, I thought they were going to 30
beat him up, as a mother whose child has been
lost will scream at the child when it's found, they
took him by the arms and held him up and
leaned him against the wall of the chimney and the
tall cop lit a cigarette 35
in his own mouth, and gave it to him, and
then they all lit cigarettes, and the
red, glowing ends burned like the
tiny campfires we lit at night
back at the beginning of the world. 40

෨෨

MARGE PIERCY *(b. 1936) was born in Detroit, where her father was employed as an installation worker by Westinghouse. Her mother was the daughter of a union activist who was murdered for his efforts to organize workers. Piercy had an emotionally difficult adolescence, and a severe attack of rheumatic fever left her physically weakened. She also began writing as a teenager, however, and with the help of scholarships and prizes she graduated from the University of Michigan in 1957 and received her M.A. a year later.*

Briefly married, Piercy was divorced by the time she was twenty-three. In the 1960s she married again, and with her husband became committed to a communal lifestyle and to the protest movement against the Vietnam War and U.S. involvement in Latin America. In 1980 she married for a third time, and since then she has lived in Wellfleet, Massachusetts, on Cape Cod. Although Piercy is one of the more popular feminist poets, she is still much better known as a novelist. Her long, fictionalized accounts of her family background and her life as a radical in the 1960s have been best-sellers, and she has been able to live comfortably on the income from her fiction and her readings.

"The woman in the ordinary" was written in 1973; "Putting the good things away," a moving tribute to her mother, was written in 1985.

MARGE PIERCY

The woman in the ordinary   1973

The woman in the ordinary pudgy downcast girl
is crouching with eyes and muscles clenched.
Round and pebble smooth she effaces herself
under ripples of conversation and debate.
The woman in the block of ivory soap   5
has massive thighs that neigh,
great breasts that blare and strong arms that trumpet.
The woman of the golden fleece
laughs uproariously from the belly
inside the girl who imitates   10
a Christmas card virgin with glued hands,
who fishes for herself in other's eyes,
who stoops and creeps to make herself smaller.
In her bottled up is a woman peppery as curry,
a yam of a woman of butter and brass,   15
compounded of acid and sweet like a pineapple,
like a handgrenade set to explode,
like goldenrod ready to bloom.

MARGE PIERCY

Putting the good things away

1985

In the drawer were folded fine
batiste slips embroidered with scrolls
and posies, edged with handmade
lace too good for her to wear.

Daily she put on schmatehs°   5
fit only to wash the car
or the windows, rags
that had never been pretty

even when new: somewhere
such dresses are sold only   10
to women without money to waste
on themselves, on pleasure,

to women who hate their bodies,
to women whose lives close on them.
Such dresses come bleached by tears,   15
packed in salt like herring.

Yet she put the good things away
for the good day that must surely
come, when promises would open
like tulips their satin cups   20

for her to drink the sweet
sacramental wine of fulfillment.
The story shone in her as through
tinted glass, how the mother

gave up and did without   25
and was in the end crowned
with what? scallions? crowned
queen of the dead place

in the heart where old dreams
whistle on bone flutes,   30
where run-over pets are forgotten,
where lost stockings go?

In the coffin she was beautiful
not because of the undertaker's
garish cosmetics but because   35
that face at eighty was still

---

5. **schmatehs:** Yiddish for "rags."

her face at eighteen peering
over the drab long dress
of poverty, clutching a book.
Where did you read your dreams, Mother?   40

Because her expression softened
from the pucker of disappointment,
the grimace of swallowed rage,
she looked a white-haired girl.

The anger turned inward, the anger   45
turned inward, where
could it go except to make pain?
It flowed into me with her milk.

Her anger annealed me.
I was dipped into the cauldron   50
of boiling rage and rose
a warrior and a witch

but still vulnerable
there where she held me.
She could always wound me   55
for she knew the secret places.

She could always touch me
for she knew the pressure
points of pleasure and pain.
Our minds were woven together.   60

I gave her presents and she hid
them away, wrapped in plastic.
Too good, she said, too good.
I'm saving them. So after her death

I sort them, the ugly things   65
that were sufficient for every
day and the pretty things for which
no day of hers was ever good enough.

ରୁଦ୍ଧ

SYLVIA PLATH *(1932–1963) Sometimes writers' lives are defined less by
what they have written than by the events of their lives. Emily Dickinson is always defined by her spinsterhood, by the stark contrast between the stillness of her everyday
life and the tumult of emotions in her poetry. Robert Frost is defined by the contradictions between the sturdy, positive life he describes in his poems and the emotional
difficulties of the life he actually lived. For Sylvia Plath, the defining moment is the
morning when she put a snack beside the bed for her sleeping children, turned on the
gas in her shabby London kitchen, and committed suicide at the age of thirty-one.
Other poets have taken their own lives, but usually it is at a point when they feel that*

they are losing their creative impulse. In the months before her death, however, Plath had been writing some of the most inspired poetry that any modern writer has achieved. When these poems were published two years after her death in the collection Ariel, *there was the same excitement that greeted the first collection of Emily Dickinson's poetry.*

Plath's life had long been troubled, but in her early childhood and school years there seemed to be enough balance to pull her through. She was born and grew up in Boston. Her father, who had emigrated from a German area of Poland as a boy, taught entomology at Boston University. Their relationship, as she described it in her poetry, was complicated, but he died when she was eight, and her mother, a high school language teacher, encouraged her to write. Plath attended Smith College and graduated summa cum laude, but between her junior and senior years she suffered a nervous breakdown and attempted suicide. She had worked some casual jobs, among them a guest editorship for Mademoiselle *magazine, and she described many of the things that happened to her during that period in her novel* The Bell Jar, *which was published the year of her death under the pseudonym "Victoria Lucas."*

The psychological effects of Plath's suicide attempt were so severe that she was given insulin shock treatments, an extreme form of psychiatric therapy, and for a time she couldn't read or write. The only person she asked to see was her high school English teacher, Wilbury Crockett. He came to the hospital at least once a week, bringing an anagram game with him. As her biographer Linda Wagner-Martin wrote, "At first Sylvia could hardly recognize any letters. He would begin with a *and* n; *some days Sylvia could add a* d *to make the word* and. *Some days she could not."*

In 1955, after her graduation, she received a Fulbright grant to study in England at Cambridge University, where she met one of the most promising young English poets, Ted Hughes. They were married in 1956 and then came to the United States, where Plath had a job teaching at Smith College and Hughes later took a job at Amherst College. For some months in 1958 she audited Robert Lowell's poetry course at Boston University, where other students included the young writers Anne Sexton (p. 1185) and George Starbuck, who became close friends of Plath's. Plath had been writing poetry for several years, although at this time her ambition was also to be a successful short story writer and novelist. The next year she spent some time in residence at the Yaddo artist's colony in Massachusetts where she completed several of the poems that went into her first book, The Colossus. *She was fiercely ambitious, and some of her emotional problems were caused by her impatience at her own failure to achieve the same success with her writing that she had achieved as a student.*

Despite strains in her marriage, Plath returned to England in December 1959 to join Hughes, who was already back in the country. They had two children, a daughter born in 1960 and a son in 1962. On the surface her life seemed ideal, with a house in the English countryside, a husband who respected her writing, and the publication of her first book the same year her first child was born. The poems she was writing, however, depict her despair at her isolation and the strains of marriage to someone who was also a gifted writer and who was attractive to other women. Hughes and Plath separated in the summer of 1962, and she moved with her children into a bleak London flat. Despite near poverty and a deepening sense of isolation she began writing the poems that would go into the Ariel *collection, sometimes composing two or three poems a day, writing furiously as the hours slipped past. By February she could no longer see any way out of her situation and ended her life. As Robert Lowell wrote in an introduction to the poems, "Her art's immortality is life's disintegration."*

Her student poetry was conventional and skillful, but already as a young writer she was pushing the limits of regular rhyme and meter. In "A Winter's Tale," written when she was twenty-one, she uses a familiar ballad form. The four-line stanzas are in iambic tetrameter, with the fourth line shortened to either two or three accents. The scene she is describing — of Boston Common and the downtown shopping district a few days before Christmas — is as familiar and casually comfortable as her use of meter and rhyme. There are perfect rhymes ("Child/mild" and "crowd/loud"), but there are also slant rhymes ("star/near"), compound rhymes ("Commission/unison"), and sight rhymes ("rouse/House"). In "Black Rook in Rainy Weather," written three years later, she shifts to open form. Although she continued to write in stanzas, the stanzas are only for the eye, as all but one of them runs on to the opening line of the next stanza. Because she does not have to look for rhymes and fill out a meter, the language is tighter and terse, suggesting the poems she would write at the end of her life.

"Ella Mason and Her Eleven Cats" is a lighter poem, using a stanza form similar to the one in "Black Rook," but this time each stanza is a complete statement, consisting of six lines in a long-long-short-long-long-short pattern. Also, the poem echoes children's verse, with the final line of every stanza saying something about cats, and there is a subtle use of near rhyme and slant rhyme between the first and fourth lines and the second and third lines of each stanza. As skilled as the writing is in these poems and as pleasurable as they are to read, placed against the Ariel poems they feel like apprentice work. As her friend and fellow poet Anne Sexton described Plath's poetry at this time, "I felt she hadn't found a voice of her own, wasn't in truth, free to be herself. Yet, of course, I knew she was skilled — intense, skilled, perceptive, strange, blonde, lovely, Sylvia." (See Sexton's commentary on p. 1370.)

"Morning Song" is the first poem in Ariel. It describes the birth of Plath's second child and her first night with him. The opening line, "Love set you going like a fat gold watch," is an example of the startling use of metaphor and imagery that makes the poems so unforgettable. The image of the watch describes the days of her pregnancy, which "love . . . set going," and the preciousness of a child's life is suggested by "gold watch." "Fat" could refer to any newborn baby, but her son Nicholas was unusually large at birth. The poem is a series of images, each brilliant in itself but also broadening the picture the poet presents us of her wonder and joy at the baby's new life.

"Mirror" is an extended image of a mirror, one in which Plath sees herself "with tears and an agitation of hands" and her old age rising toward her "like a terrible fish." "The Bee Meeting" was written in the late summer of 1962, during a period of great difficulty in her marriage — Hughes had fallen in love with the wife of a friend, and he was growing careless in his efforts to conceal their affair. Plath had been tending a hive in their garden, and a few weeks before she started the poem, one in a sequence of poems about bees, she received a copy of a new book by her friend Anne Sexton. Sexton's startlingly personal style had an effect on the way the poem was written. The starting point for the theme of the poem is a meeting of a village beekeeping group that Plath had joined.

When she read "The Applicant" on BBC radio, Plath explained that the person speaking is an executive who "wants to be sure that the applicant for his marvelous product really needs it and will treat it right." In the next to last line she refers to the applicant as "my boy," giving him a gender and putting a little distance between herself and the poem.

"Daddy," written about her father, is one of the complex poems from Ariel; it has been discussed, explained, and analyzed by many critics. In her own introduction to it for the BBC reading, Plath explained,

> Here is a poem spoken by a girl with an Electra complex. Her father died while she thought he was a God. Her case is complicated by the fact that her father was also a Nazi and her mother very possibly part Jewish. In the daughter, the two strains marry and paralyse each other — she has to act out the awful little allegory once over before she is free of it.

In the phrase "I was ten when they buried you," she is combining her father's death, when she was eight, and the family's move to Wellesley, two years later. The next line, "At twenty I tried to die," refers to her first suicide attempt.

Plath completed "Daddy" on October 12, 1962, the day after Hughes finally left her and their children, and she continued to write powerful, raging, poems over the next weeks. "Lady Lazarus" was begun on October 23 and finished October 29. In it she has become a woman like Lazarus, the New Testament figure whom Jesus raised from the dead. In this poem she is jeering and strong, and she compares her survival from earlier "deaths" to a kind of circus act, with a "peanut-crunching crowd" as an audience. In her first suicide attempt Plath left a note for her mother saying that she was going for a long walk; she then crawled into a small space under the house and swallowed a large number of sleeping pills. She was unconscious for two days while there was a hysterical search throughout the neighborhood. She refers to this in the lines "They had to call and call / And pick the worms off me like sticky pearls."

"Words" was written three months later, on February 1, 1963, and it questions the power of words to change her life. By now she was living with her two children in a small London flat, and her emotional situation had become more and more desperate. On February 5 she wrote "Edge," and six days later she was dead.

RELATED COMMENTARIES: See Casebook on Sylvia Plath, pages 1367–1377, including Sylvia Plath, From the Journals, page 1368; Robert Lowell, Foreword to Plath's Ariel, page 1369; Anne Sexton, "The Barfly Ought to Sing," page 1370; Denise Levertov, "Plath as a Confessional Poet," page 1373; Joyce Carol Oates, "Sylvia Plath's Deathly Imagination," page 1375.

SYLVIA PLATH

A Winter's Tale

1958

On Boston Common a red star
Gleams, wired to a tall Ulmus
Americana.° Magi near
The domed State House.

Old Joseph holds an alpenstock.°   5
Two waxen oxen flank the Child.
A black sheep leads the shepherds' flock.
Mary looks mild.

2–3. **Ulmus Americana:** Latin name for the American elm.   5. **alpenstock:** Pointed iron staff used in mountain climbing.

Angels — more feminine and douce
Than models from Bonwit's or Jay's,   10
Haloes lustrous as Sirius —
Gilt trumpets raise.

By S. S. Pierce, by S. S. Pierce,
The red-nosed, blue-caped women ring
For money Lord, the crowds are fierce!   15
There's caroling

On Winter Street, on Temple Place.
Poodles are baking cookies in
Filene's show windows. Grant us grace,
Donner, Blitzen,   20

And all you Santa's deer who browse
By leave of the Park Commission
On grass that once fed Boston cows.
In unison

On Pinckney, Mount Vernon, Chestnut,   25
The wreathed doors open to the crowd.
Noel! Noel! No mouth is shut.
Off key and loud

The populace sings toward the sill
Of windows with odd violet panes.   30
O Little City on a Hill!
The cordial strains

Of bellringers and singers rouse
Frost-bitten pigeons, eddy forth
From Charles Street to the Custom House,   35
From South Station to North.

SYLVIA PLATH

Black Rook in Rainy Weather   *1960*

On the stiff twig up there
Hunches a wet black rook
Arranging and rearranging its feathers in the rain.
I do not expect a miracle
Or an accident   5

To set the sight on fire
In my eye, nor seek
Any more in the desultory weather some design,
But let spotted leaves fall as they fall,
Without ceremony, or portent   10

Although, I admit, I desire,
Occasionally, some backtalk

From the mute sky, I can't honestly complain:
A certain minor light may still
Leap incandescent   15

Out of kitchen table or chair
As if a celestial burning took
Possession of the most obtuse objects now and then —
Thus hallowing an interval
Otherwise inconsequent   20

By bestowing largesse, honor,
One might say love. At any rate, I now walk
Wary (for it could happen
Even in this dull, ruinous landscape); skeptical,
Yet politic; ignorant   25

Of whatever angel may choose to flare
Suddenly at my elbow. I only know that a rook
Ordering its black feathers can so shine
As to seize my senses, haul
My eyelids up, and grant   30

A brief respite from fear
Of total neutrality. With luck,
Trekking stubborn through this season
Of fatigue, I shall
Patch together a content   35

Of sorts. Miracles occur,
If you care to call those spasmodic
Tricks of radiance miracles. The wait's begun again,
The long wait for the angel,
For that rare, random descent.°   40

SYLVIA PLATH

Ella Mason and Her Eleven Cats   *1956*

Old Ella Mason keeps cats, eleven at last count,
In her ramshackle house off Somerset Terrace;
People make queries
On seeing our neighbor's cat-haunt,
Saying: "Something's addled in a woman who accommodates   5
That many cats."

Rum and red-faced as a water-melon, her voice
Long gone to wheeze and seed, Ella Mason

---

40. that rare, random descent: In Acts 2, the Holy Ghost at Pentecost is described as descending like a dove on Jesus' disciples.

For no good reason
Plays hostess to Tabby, Tom and increase,   10
With cream and chicken-gut feasting the palates
Of finical cats.

Village stories go that in olden days
Ella flounced about, minx-thin and haughty,
A fashionable beauty,   15
Slaying the dandies with her emerald eyes;
Now, run to fat, she's a spinster whose door shuts
On all but cats.

Once we children sneaked over to spy Miss Mason
Napping in her kitchen paved with saucers.   20
On antimacassars
Table-top, cupboard shelf, cats lounged brazen,
One gruff-timbred purr rolling from furred throats:
Such stentorian cats!

With poke and giggle, ready to skedaddle,   25
We peered agog through the cobwebbed door
Straight into yellow glare
Of guardian cats crouched round their idol,
While Ella drowsed whiskered with sleek face, sly wits:
Sphinx-queen of cats.   30

"Look! there she goes, Cat-Lady Mason!"
We snickered as she shambled down Somerset Terrace
To market for her dearies,
More mammoth and blowsy with every season;
"Miss Ella's got loony from keeping in cahoots   35
With eleven cats."

But now turned kinder with time, we mark Miss Mason
Blinking green-eyed and solitary
At girls who marry —
Demure ones, lithe ones, needing no lesson   40
That vain jades sulk single down bridal nights,
Accurst as wild-cats.

SYLVIA PLATH

Morning Song   *1961*

Love set you going like a fat gold watch.
The midwife slapped your footsoles, and your bald cry
Took its place among the elements.

Our voices echo, magnifying your arrival. New statue.
In a drafty museum, your nakedness   5
Shadows our safety. We stand round blankly as walls.

I'm no more your mother
Than the cloud that distils a mirror to reflect its own slow
Effacement at the wind's hand.

All night your moth-breath   10
Flickers among the flat pink roses. I wake to listen:
A far sea moves in my ear.

One cry, and I stumble from bed, cow-heavy and floral
In my Victorian nightgown.
Your mouth opens clean as a cat's. The window square   15

Whitens and swallows its dull stars. And now you try
Your handful of notes;
The clear vowels rise like balloons.

Sylvia Plath

Mirror   *1963*

I am silver and exact. I have no preconceptions
Whatever I see I swallow immediately
Just as it is, unmisted by love or dislike.
I am not cruel, only truthful —
The eye of a little god, four-cornered.   5
Most of the time I meditate on the opposite wall.
It is pink, with speckles. I have looked at it so long
I think it is a part of my heart. But it flickers.
Faces and darkness separate us over and over.

Now I am a lake. A woman bends over me,   10
Searching my reaches for what she really is.
Then she turns to those liars, the candles or the moon.
I see her back, and reflect it faithfully.
She rewards me with tears and an agitation of hands.
I am important to her. She comes and goes.   15
Each morning it is her face that replaces the darkness.
In me she has drowned a younger girl, and in me an old woman
Rises toward her day after day, like a terrible fish.

Sylvia Plath

The Bee Meeting   *1961*

Who are these people at the bridge to meet me? They are the
    villagers —
The rector, the midwife, the sexton, the agent for bees.
In my sleeveless summery dress I have no protection,

And they are all gloved and covered, why did nobody tell me?
They are smiling and taking out veils tacked to ancient hats.   5

I am nude as a chicken neck, does nobody love me?
Yes, here is the secretary of bees with her white shop smock,
Buttoning the cuffs at my wrists and the slit from my neck to my knees.
Now I am milkweed silk, the bees will not notice.
They will not smell my fear, my fear, my fear.   10

Which is the rector now, is it that man in black?
Which is the midwife, is that her blue coat?
Everybody is nodding a square black head, they are knights in visors,
Breastplates of cheesecloth knotted under the armpits.
Their smiles and their voices are changing. I am led through a bean-
     field.   15

Strips of tinfoil winking like people,
Feather dusters fanning their hands in a sea of bean flowers,
Creamy bean flowers with black eyes and leaves like bored hearts.
Is it blood clots the tendrils are dragging up that string?
No, no, it is scarlet flowers that will one day be edible.   20

Now they are giving me a fashionable white straw Italian hat
And a black veil that molds to my face, they are making me one of
     them.
They are leading me to the shorn grove, the circle of hives.
Is it the hawthorn that smells so sick?
The barren body of hawthorn, etherizing its children.   25

Is it some operation that is taking place?
It is the surgeon my neighbors are waiting for,
This apparition in a green helmet,
Shining gloves and white suit.
Is it the butcher, the grocer, the postman, someone I know?   30

I cannot run, I am rooted, and the gorse hurts me
With its yellow purses, its spiky armory,
I could not run without having to run forever.
The white hive is snug as a virgin,
Sealing off her brood cells, her honey, and quietly humming.   35

Smoke rolls and scarves in the grove.
The mind of the hive thinks this is the end of everything.
Here they come, the outriders, on their hysterical elastics.
If I stand very still, they will think I am cow-parsley,
A gullible head untouched by their animosity,   40

Not even nodding, a personage in a hedgerow.
The villagers open the chambers, they are hunting the queen.
Is she hiding, is she eating honey? She is very clever.
She is old, old, old, she must live another year, and she knows it.
While in their fingerjoint cells the new virgins   45

Dream of a duel they will win inevitably,
A curtain of wax dividing them from the bride flight,
The upflight of the murderess into a heaven that loves her.
The villagers are moving the virgins, there will be no killing.
The old queen does not show herself, is she so ungrateful?　　　　50

I am exhausted, I am exhausted ——
Pillar of white in a blackout of knives.
I am the magician's girl who does not flinch.
The villagers are untying their disguises, they are shaking hands.
Whose is that long white box in the grove, what have they accom-
　　plished, why am I cold.　　　　55

SYLVIA PLATH

The Applicant　　　　*1962*

First, are you our sort of a person?
Do you wear
A glass eye, false teeth or a crutch,
A brace or a hook,
Rubber breasts or a rubber crotch,　　　　5

Stitches to show something's missing? No, no? Then
How can we give you a thing?
Stop crying.
Open your hand.
Empty? Empty. Here is a hand　　　　10

To fill it and willing
To bring teacups and roll away headaches
And do whatever you tell it.
Will you marry it?
It is guaranteed　　　　15

To thumb shut your eyes at the end
And dissolve of sorrow,
We make new stock from the salt.
I notice you are stark naked.
How about this suit ——　　　　20

Black and stiff, but not a bad fit.
Will you marry it?
It is waterproof, shatterproof, proof
Against fire and bombs through the roof.
Believe me, they'll bury you in it.　　　　25

Now your head, excuse me, is empty.
I have the ticket for that.
Come here, sweetie, out of the closet.

Well, what do you think of *that?*
Naked as paper to start   30

But in twenty-five years she'll be silver,
In fifty, gold.
A living doll, everywhere you look.
It can sew, it can cook,
It can talk, talk, talk.   35

It works, there is nothing wrong with it.
You have a hole, it's a poultice.
You have an eye, it's an image.
My boy, it's your last resort.
Will you marry it, marry it, marry it.   40

SYLVIA PLATH

Daddy   1962

You do not do, you do not do
Any more, black shoe
In which I have lived like a foot
For thirty years, poor and white,
Barely daring to breathe or Achoo.   5

Daddy, I have had to kill you.
You died before I had time ——
Marble-heavy, a bag full of God,
Ghastly statue with one gray toe
Big as a Frisco seal   10

And a head in the freakish Atlantic
Where it pours bean green over blue
In the waters off beautiful Nauset.
I used to pray to recover you.
Ach, du.°   *Oh, you* 15

In the German tongue, in the Polish Town°
Scraped flat by the roller
Of wars, wars, wars.
But the name of the town is common.
My Polack friend   20

Says there are a dozen or two.
So I never could tell where you
Put your foot, your root,
I never could talk to you.
The tongue stuck in my jaw.   25

---

16. Polish Town: Refers to Otto Plath's birthplace, Granbow.

It stuck in a barb wire snare.
Ich, ich, ich, ich,°   *I, I, I, I*
I could hardly speak.
I thought every German was you.
And the language obscene   30

An engine, an engine
Chuffing me off like a Jew.
A Jew to Dachau, Auschwitz, Belsen.°
I began to talk like a Jew.
I think I may well be a Jew.   35

The snows of the Tyrol, the clear beer of Vienna
Are not very pure or true.
With my gypsy-ancestress and my weird luck
And my Taroc° pack and my Taroc pack
I may be a bit of a Jew.   40

I have always been scared of *you*,
With your Luftwaffe,° your gobbledygoo.
And your neat mustache
And your Aryan eye, bright blue.
Panzer-man, panzer-man,° O You —   45

Not God but a swastika
So black no sky could squeak through.
Every woman adores a Fascist,
The boot in the face, the brute
Brute heart of a brute like you.   50

You stand at the blackboard, daddy,
In the picture I have of you,
A cleft in your chin instead of your foot
But no less a devil for that, no not
Any less the black man who   55

Bit my pretty red heart in two.
I was ten when they buried you.
At twenty I tried to die
And get back, back, back to you.
I thought even the bones would do   60

But they pulled me out of the sack,
And they stuck me together with glue.
And then I knew what to do.
I made a model of you,
A man in black with a Meinkampf° look   65

---

33. Dachau . . . Belsen: Nazi death camps in World War II.   **39. Taroc:** Pack of fortune-
telling (tarot) cards.   **42. Luftwaffe:** World War II German aircorps.   **45. Panzer-man:** In
World War II, the German panzer division was that made up of armored vehicles.
65. Meinkampf: Adolf Hitler's autobiography was titled *Meinkampf,* or "My Struggle."

And a love of the rack and the screw.
And I said I do, I do.
So daddy, I'm finally through.
The black telephone's off at the root,
The voices just can't worm through.   70

If I've killed one man, I've killed two ——
The vampire who said he was you
And drank my blood for a year,
Seven years, if you want to know.
Daddy, you can lie back now.   75

There's a stake in your fat black heart
And the villagers never liked you.
They are dancing and stamping on you.
They always *knew* it was you.
Daddy, daddy, you bastard, I'm through.   80

Sylvia Plath

Lady Lazarus°   1962

I have done it again.
One year in every ten
I manage it ——

A sort of walking miracle, my skin
Bright as a Nazi lampshade,°   5
My right foot

A paperweight,
My face a featureless, fine
Jew linen.

Peel off the napkin   10
O my enemy.
Do I terrify? ——

The nose, the eye pits, the full set of teeth?
The sour breath
Will vanish in a day.   15

Soon, soon the flesh
The grave cave ate will be
At home on me

And I a smiling woman.
I am only thirty.   20
And like the cat I have nine times to die.

Lazarus: In John 11:44, Jesus resurrects Lazarus from the grave.   5. Nazi lampshade: The
Nazis used the skin of some Jewish concentration camp prisoners to make lampshades.

This is Number Three.
What a trash
To annihilate each decade.

What a million filaments.   25
The peanut-crunching crowd
Shoves in to see

Them unwrap me hand and foot ——
The big strip tease.
Gentleman, ladies,   30

These are my hands,
My knees.
I may be skin and bone,

Nevertheless, I am the same, identical woman.
The first time it happened I was ten.   35
It was an accident.

The second time I meant
To last it out and not come back at all.
I rocked shut

As a seashell.   40
They had to call and call
And pick the worms off me like sticky pearls.

Dying
Is an art, like everything else.
I do it exceptionally well.   45

I do it so it feels like hell.
I do it so it feels real.
I guess you could say I've a call.

It's easy enough to do it in a cell.
It's easy enough to do it and stay put.   50
It's the theatrical

Comeback in broad day
To the same place, the same face, the same brute
Amused shout:

"A miracle!"   55
That knocks me out.
There is a charge

For the eyeing of my scars, there is a charge
For the hearing of my heart ——
It really goes.   60

And there is a charge, a very large charge,
For a word or a touch
Or a bit of blood

Or a piece of my hair or my clothes.
So, so, Herr Doktor.   65
So, Herr Enemy.

I am your opus,
I am your valuable,
The pure gold baby

That melts to a shriek.
I turn and burn.
Do not think I underestimate your great concern.   70

Ash, ash —
You poke and stir.
Flesh, bone, there is nothing there ——   75

A cake of soap,
A wedding ring,
A gold filling.

Herr God, Herr Lucifer,
Beware   80
Beware.

Out of the ash
I rise with my red hair
And I eat men like air.

Sylvia Plath

Words   1963

Axes
After whose stroke the wood rings,
And the echoes!
Echoes traveling
Off from the center like horses.   5

The sap
Wells like tears, like the
Water striving
To re-establish its mirror
Over the rock   10

That drops and turns,
A white skull,
Eaten by weedy greens.
Years later I
Encounter them on the road ——   15

Words dry and riderless,
The indefatigable hoof-taps.
While
From the bottom of the pool, fixed stars
Govern a life.   20

SYLVIA PLATH

Edge

1963

The woman is perfected.
Her dead

Body wears the smile of accomplishment,
The illusion of a Greek necessity

Flows in the scrolls of her toga,   5
Her bare

Feet seem to be saying:
We have come so far, it is over.

Each dead child coiled, a white serpent,
One at each little   10

Pitcher of milk, now empty.
She has folded

Them back into her body as petals
Of a rose close when the garden

Stiffens and odors bleed   15
From the sweet, deep throats of the night flower.

The moon has nothing to be sad about,
Staring from her hood of bone.

She is used to this sort of thing.
Her blacks crackle and drag.   20

∞

EZRA POUND (1885–1972) *was born in Idaho but grew up in Philadelphia,*
where his father worked at the U.S. Mint. Pound was a precocious reader, already de-
termined as a teenager to become a poet. He entered the University of Pennsylvania
when he was fifteen; at sixteen he began his personal studies of comparative literature,
and at seventeen he enrolled as a special student "to avoid irrelevant subjects." He re-
ceived his B.A. from Hamilton College, then returned to Pennsylvania for an M.A. in
Romance languages. While a student there he was engaged to Hilda Doolittle
(p. 1062), a student at Bryn Mawr College. Although they never married Pound was
to become a major influence on her life. He also met a young medical student and
novice poet named William Carlos Williams (p. 1217), whom he introduced to Doolit-
tle. He was to have almost as much influence on Williams's life.

Pound taught briefly at Wabash College after his graduation but was dismissed
for breaking college rules. With eighty dollars he sailed for Europe, and after brief stays
in Spain and Italy, he moved to London, where he stayed until 1920. He had already be-
gun publishing his own poetry, and the appearance of his book, Personae, *in London*
just after his arrival in 1910 attracted the attention of several of the younger English
writers, including Wyndham Lewis, D. H. Lawrence, and Richard Aldington. For a
time he worked as secretary to the well-known Irish writer William Butler Yeats.

Pound was also acting as European editor for Poetry Magazine *in Chicago, and he brought to the magazine much of the writing of the literary avant-garde, including T. S. Eliot's "The Love Song of J. Alfred Prufrock." He helped both Williams and Robert Frost find publishers for their work, and with Hilda Doolittle, who came to London in 1911, and her husband, Richard Aldington, he founded the literary movement called imagism (see pp. 964–967).*

By 1920 London had become "barren," so Pound moved to Paris for four years, then to Italy, where he remained, except for a controversial period in a mental hospital in the United States, for the rest of his life. While still in London he had begun work on a long poem, Cantos. *Each of the sections was a complex interweaving of materials taken from many different cultures and languages, historical documents, sharply expressed opinions, and pieces from newspapers and magazines. The breadth and the ambition of the project at first fascinated readers, but as the years passed and the sections became more and more difficult to decipher, the reputation of the poem dwindled.*

What was also evident in Cantos *was that Pound was anti-Semitic and a radical social critic. When World War II broke out he was employed by the Italian government to write and deliver twice-weekly fascist propaganda broadcasts attacking the U.S. war effort. In some of the programs, he supported the destruction of European Jewry. Under U.S. law this was treason, and when the U.S. Army liberated Italy, Pound was imprisoned in a cage outside of Pisa for several months, then returned to the United States for trial.*

Influential friends managed to have him hospitalized for mental illness, and there ensued a stormy controversy among American writers over whether Pound should or should not be tried as a traitor. He remained in the mental hospital from 1946 to 1958. Finally, he was declared incompetent to stand trial and was returned to Italy. When he reached Italian soil he delivered the old fascist salute for the benefit of the photographers and went back to writing the Cantos. *In his last years he spoke only rarely and declared that his life's work was a "botch."*

"The River-Merchant's Wife: A Letter" is one of his many adaptations of earlier translations of Chinese poetry. "Hugh Selwyn Mauberley," written just before he left London, has much of the range and the emotional attitudes he was to continue and expand in Cantos. *(See also Pound's "In a Station of the Metro" on p. 964 and "A Pact" on p. 1007.)*

RELATED COMMENTARIES: *Ezra Pound, "On the Principles of Imagism," page 1297; Ezra Pound, "What I Feel about Walt Whitman," page 1300; William Carlos Williams, "Ezra Pound's Language," page 1329.*

EZRA POUND

The River-Merchant's Wife: A Letter° 1915

While my hair was still cut straight across my forehead
I played about the front gate, pulling flowers.
You came by on bamboo stilts, playing horse,
You walked about my seat, playing with blue plums.

The River-Merchant's Wife: A Letter: A loose translation of a poem by Li Po (701–762).

And we went on living in the village of Chokan: 5
Two small people, without dislike or suspicion.
At fourteen I married My Lord you.
I never laughed, being bashful.
Lowering my head, I looked at the wall.
Called to, a thousand times, I never looked back.   10

At fifteen I stopped scowling,
I desired my dust to be mingled with yours
Forever and forever and forever.
Why should I climb the lookout?

At sixteen you departed,   15
You went into far Ku-to-yen, by the river of swirling eddies,
And you have been gone five months.
The monkeys make sorrowful noise overhead.

You dragged your feet when you went out.
By the gate now, the moss is grown, the different mosses,   20
Too deep to clear them away!
The leaves fall early this autumn, in wind.
The paired butterflies are already yellow with August
Over the grass in the West garden;
They hurt me. I grow older.   25
If you are coming down through the narrows of the river Kiang,
Please let me know before hand,
And I will come out to meet you
        As far as Cho-fu-sa.

EZRA POUND

From *Hugh Selwyn Mauberley*°   1920

Life and Contacts

Vocat æstus in umbram°
– NEMESIANUS *Ec. IV.*

E. P. ODE POUR L'ELECTION DE SON SEPULCHRE°

I

For three years, out of key with his time,
He strove to resuscitate the dead art

Hugh Selwyn Mauberley: The name of a fictitious poet who is the speaker in later stanzas.
Here the speaker is Pound himself, and the poem was written as his farewell to London, shortly
before he moved to Paris. The subtitle "Life and Contacts" is an ironic allusion to the common
subtitle of literary memoirs, "Life and Letters." **Vocat . . . umbram:** Latin for "The heat draws
us into the shade," a line from an eclogue by Nemesianus, a third-century poet from Carthage.
E. P. Ode . . . Sepulchre: French for "E[zra] P[ound] On the Selection of His Tomb," an adaptation of the title of the ode by Pierre de Ronsard (1524–1585), "On the Selection of His Tomb."

Of poetry; to maintain "the sublime"
In the old sense. Wrong from the start —
No, hardly, but seeing he had been born
In a half savage country, out of date; 5
Bent resolutely on wringing lilies from the acorn;
Capaneus;° trout for factitious bait;

"Ἴδμεν γάρ τοι πάνθ', ὅσ' ἐνὶ Τροίη
Caught in the unstopped ear;°
Giving the rocks small lee-way 10
The chopped seas held him, therefore, that year.

His true Penelope° was Flaubert,
He fished by obstinate isles;
Observed the elegance of Circe's° hair 15
Rather than the mottoes on sun-dials,

Unaffected by "The march of events,"
He passed from men's memory in *l'an trentuniesme*
De son eage;° the case presents
No adjunct to the Muses' diadem. 20

II

The age demanded an image
Of its accelerated grimace,
Something for the modern stage,
Not, at any rate, an Attic grace;

Not, not certainly, the obscure reveries
Of the inward gaze; 25
Better mendacities
Than the classics in paraphrase!

The "age demanded" chiefly a mould in plaster,
Made with no loss of time,
A prose kinema,° not, not assuredly, alabaster 30
Or the "sculpture" of rhyme.

---

8. Capaneus: One of the seven great warriors who attack the city of Thebes in Aeschylus's tragedy *The Seven against Thebes* (476 B.C.). Capaneus was killed by Zeus, ruler of the gods. **9–10. . . . unstopped ears:** Greek for "For we know all the toils suffered in wide Troy." Lines 9 and 10 refer to the homeward journey of Odysseus from the war in Troy described in Homer's *Odyssey*. Odysseus "stopped" the ears of his sailors to prevent them from hearing the song of the sirens, which lured many ships onto the rocks around the island. To hear the sirens' song, Odysseus ordered his men to tie him to the mast and to keep him bound until they were past the dangerous island. **13. Penelope:** Odysseus's wife, who resisted all temptation and was faithful to him during the long year of his absence. **15. Circe's:** The enchantress Circe held Odysseus in her spell for a year. **18. l'an . . . eage:** French for "the thirtieth year of his age"; an allusion to *The Testament* by the fifteenth-century French poet François Villon and to Pound's own book *Lustra*, published in 1916. **31. kinema:** An early spelling of the word *cinema*.

III

The tea-rose tea-grown, etc.
Supplants the mousseline of Cos,°
The pianola "replaces"   35
Sappho's barbitos.°

Christ follows Dionysus,°
Phallic and ambrosial
Made way for macerations;°
Caliban casts out Ariel.°   40

All things are a flowing,
Sage Heracleitus° says;
But a tawdry cheapness
Shall outlast our days.

Even the Christian beauty   45
Defects — after Samothrace;°
We see τὸ καλόυ°
Decreed in the market place.

Faun's flesh is not to us,
Nor the saint's vision.   50
We have the press for wafer;
Franchise for circumcision.

All men, in law, are equals.
Free of Pisistratus,°
We choose a knave or an eunuch   55
To rule over us.

O bright Apollo,°
τίν' ἄυδρα, τίν' ἤρωα, τίυα θεόυ,°
What god, man, or hero
Shall I place a tin wreath upon!   60

---

34. mousseline of Cos: A delicate fabric woven on the Greek island of Cos. **36. barbitos:** The lyre played by the Greek poet Sappho (fl. 600 B.C.). **37. Dionysus:** Greek god of fertility; celebrations in the god's honor were known for drunkenness and sexual freedom. **39. macerations:** Fasting or wasting away; Pound is contrasting Christian asceticism with Dionysian licentiousness. **40. Caliban ... Ariel:** A reference to Shakespeare's play *The Tempest*, which Pound interprets as the unimaginative Caliban casting out the free spirit Ariel. **42. Heracleitus:** Greek philosopher (fl. 500 B.C.) who believed that all reality is in a state of flux. **46. Samothrace:** Greek island, site of an important Greek naval victory and the center of a number of religious mystery cults. **47.** Greek for "the beautiful, beauty." **54. Pisistratus:** Tyrant and patron of the arts who lived in Athens in the sixth century B.C. **57. Apollo:** The Greek and Roman god of sunlight, music, and poetry. **58.** Greek for "What man, what hero, what god," Pound's adaptation of a line by Pindar (c. 522– c. 438 B.C.).

IV

These fought° in any case,
and some believing,
                    pro domo,° in any case . . .

Some quick to arm,
some for adventure,
some from fear of weakness,
some from fear of censure,
some for love of slaughter, in imagination,
learning later . . .
some in fear, learning love of slaughter;

Died some, pro patria,
                    non "dulce" non "et decor" . . .°
walked eye-deep in hell
believing in old men's lies, then unbelieving
came home, home to a lie,
home to many deceits,
home to old lies and new infamy;
usury age-old and age-thick
and liars in public places.

Daring as never before, wastage as never before.
Young blood and high blood,
fair cheeks, and fine bodies;

fortitude as never before

frankness as never before,
disillusions as never told in the old days.
hysterias, trench confessions,
laughter out of dead bellies.

65

70

75

80

85

V

There died a myriad,
And of the best, among them,
For an old bitch gone in the teeth,
For a botched civilization,

Charm, smiling at the good mouth,
Quick eyes gone under earth's lid,

For two gross of broken statues,
For a few thousand battered books.

90

95

෩

---

61. **These fought . . .**: A reference to those who fought in World War I.   63. **pro domo:** Latin
for "from the home."   71–72. **pro patria . . . "dulce" . . . "et decor":** These Latin words refer
to the Roman poet Horace (65–8 B.C.) and his famous line "dulce et decorum est pro patria
mori," which means "It is sweet and fitting to give one's life for one's country." Pound, who
inserts the Latin negative *non,* is saying that these deaths were neither sweet nor fitting.

THEODORE ROETHKE *(1908–1963) was born in Saginaw, Michigan, the son of a successful operator of commercial greenhouses. Already writing poetry as an undergraduate at the University of Michigan, he began publishing his work during his graduate studies at Michigan and Harvard. His first full-time teaching position was at Lafayette College in Pennsylvania in 1931. He later taught at several other universities before going in 1947 to the University of Washington, where he taught for the rest of his life. His book* Words for the Wind: The Collected Verse, *in 1958, established his reputation.*

Roethke was a prolific writer and had a successful career as a poet, but he struggled against alcoholism and manic-depressive illness. On more than one occasion he had to be taken in handcuffs from his classroom and was hospitalized for long periods. The poet Robert Lowell (p. 1146), a close friend, described him as "a ponderous, coarse, fattish, fortyish man, well read, likes the same things I do, and is quite a competent poet."

"Big Wind" and "My Papa's Waltz" recount childhood memories. "Elegy for Jane" is about the death of one of his students. (See also Roethke's "The Waking" on p. 957.)

THEODORE ROETHKE

Big Wind

1948

Where were the greenhouses going,
Lunging into the lashing
Wind driving water
So far down the river
All the faucets stopped?   5
So we drained the manure-machine
For the steam plant,
Pumping the stale mixture
Into the rusty boilers,
Watching the pressure gauge   10
Waver over to red,
As the seams hissed
And the live steam
Drove to the far
End of the rose-house,   15
Where the worst wind was,
Creaking the cypress window-frames
Cracking so much thin glass
We stayed all night,
Stuffing the holes with burlap;   20
But she rode it out,
That old rose-house,
She hove into the teeth of it,
The core and pith of that ugly storm,

Ploughing with her stiff prow,   25
Bucking into the wind-waves
That broke over the whole of her,
Flailing her sides with spray,
Flinging long strings of wet across the roof-top,
Finally veering, wearing themselves out, merely   30
Whistling thinly under the wind-vents;
She sailed until the calm morning,
Carrying her full cargo of roses.

THEODORE ROETHKE

My Papa's Waltz   *1948*

The whiskey on your breath
Could make a small boy dizzy;
But I hung on like death:
Such waltzing was not easy.

We romped until the pans   5
Slid from the kitchen shelf;
My mother's countenance
Could not unfrown itself.

The hand that held my wrist
Was battered on one knuckle;   10
At every step you missed
My right ear scraped a buckle.

You beat time on my head
With a palm caked hard by dirt,
Then waltzed me off to bed   15
Still clinging to your shirt.

THEODORE ROETHKE

Elegy for Jane   *1953*

My Student, Thrown by a Horse

I remember the neckcurls, limp and damp as tendrils;
And her quick look, a sidelong pickerel smile;
And how, once startled into talk, the light syllables leaped for her,
And she balanced in the delight of her thought,
A wren, happy, tail into the wind,   5
Her song trembling the twigs and small branches.
The shade sang with her;
The leaves, their whispers turned to kissing;
And the mold sang in the bleached valleys under the rose.

Oh, when she was sad, she cast herself down into such a pure depth,   10
Even a father could not find her:
Scraping her cheek against straw;
Stirring the clearest water.

My sparrow, you are not here,
Waiting like a fern, making a spiny shadow.   15
The sides of wet stones cannot console me,
Nor the moss, wound with the last light.

If only I could nudge you from this sleep,
My maimed darling, my skittery pigeon.
Over this damp grave I speak the words of my love: 20
I, with no rights in this matter,
Neither father nor lover.

୨୨

CHRISTINA ROSSETTI *(1830–1894) was born in London, the daughter of
an Italian revolutionary intellectual and poet whose activities forced him to flee to
London in 1824. He found work there as a professor of Italian at the new University
of London, but later he became ill and for many years was confined to the house.*

*As a member of a creative family, Rossetti was encouraged to write. Her brother
Dante Gabriel Rossetti was one of the leaders of the Pre-Raphaelite movement in English art and writing, an attempt to return to the artistic style of pre-Renaissance Italy.
Christina Rossetti was a devout Anglican and refused two opportunities to marry because of religious differences with her suitors. Her renunciation finally weighed on the
mood and the style of her poetry.*

The title poem of her first book, Goblin Market and Other Poems *(1862), was
unlike anything else written in the Victorian era. It is a long allegorical narrative with
strongly erotic undertones about two sisters and their struggle against temptation.
Her later poetry — much of it written after she was diagnosed with Grave's disease in
1871 — was often prayerlike, and in those lyrics that dealt with her emotional disappointments, she usually concealed her unhappiness behind conventional phrases.*

*"Song," "Up-Hill," and "After Death," her best-known lyrics, were published
in her 1862 collection. (See also Rossetti's "I wish I could remember" on p. 949.)*

CHRISTINA ROSSETTI

Song

1848

When I am dead, my dearest,
    Sing no sad songs for me;
Plant thou no roses at my head,
    Nor shady cypress tree:
Be the green grass above me   5
    With showers and dewdrops wet:

And if thou wilt, remember,
    And if thou wilt, forget.

I shall not see the shadows,
    I shall not feel the rain;
I shall not hear the nightingale   10
    Sing on as if in pain:
And dreaming through the twilight
    That doth not rise nor set,
Haply I may remember,   15
    And haply may forget.

CHRISTINA ROSSETTI

After Death   *1849*

The curtains were half drawn, the floor was swept
    And strewn with rushes, rosemary and may
    Lay thick upon the bed on which I lay,
Where thro' the lattice ivy-shadows crept.
He leaned above me, thinking that I slept   5
    And could not hear him; but I heard him say:
    "Poor child, poor child": and as he turned away
Came a deep silence, and I knew he wept.
He did not touch the shroud, or raise the fold
    That hid my face, or take my hand in his,   10
      Or ruffle the smooth pillows for my head:
    He did not love me living; but once dead
    He pitied me; and very sweet it is
To know he still is warm tho' I am cold.

CHRISTINA ROSSETTI

Up-Hill   *1858*

Does the road wind up-hill all the way?
    Yes, to the very end.
Will the day's journey take the whole long day?
    From morn to night, my friend.

But is there for the night a resting-place?   5
    A roof for when the slow dark hours begin.
May not the darkness hide it from my face?
    You cannot miss that inn.

Shall I meet other wayfarers at night?
    Those who have gone before.
Then must I knock, or call when just in sight?   10
    They will not keep you standing at that door.

Shall I find comfort, travel-sore and weak?
  Of labour you shall find the sum.
Will there be beds for me and all who seek?   15
  Yea, beds for all who come.

ର୍ଥ

ANNE SEXTON *(1928–1974), the youngest of three daughters, was born in Newton, Massachusetts, a suburb of Boston, and grew up in Wellesley. She was from a well-off New England family, spending her winters in the city and her summers on Squirrel Island in Maine. When she was nineteen she eloped with a man who was, like her father, successful in the woolen industry.*

Although outwardly she conformed to her family's expectations, Sexton was unable to resolve her inner conflicts. After the birth of each of her daughters, in 1953 and 1955, she was hospitalized for psychiatric treatment. When she first attempted suicide in 1956, her doctor suggested she begin writing poetry as therapy. She enrolled in her first writing workshop the next year, where she met the writer Maxine Kumin, who would become a close friend. The following year she enrolled in Robert Lowell's poetry class at Boston University (see p. 1146). Another young poet, Sylvia Plath (p. 1160), was in the same class.

Sexton's first book, To Bedlam and Part Way Back, *published in 1960, only a year after her class with Lowell, attracted considerable attention for its powerful confessional style. She received awards and grants, and in 1967 she won the Pulitzer Prize for her book* Live or Die. *She taught at Harvard and Colgate universities, and was appointed a professor at Boston University in 1972. Despite her recognition, however, she was unable to free herself from her emotional torment. She finally succeeded in a suicide attempt in 1974.*

"All My Pretty Ones" was written after the death of her father. "The Starry Night" is a response to a painting by Vincent van Gogh.

  RELATED COMMENTARIES: *Richard Howard, "From 'Some Tribal Female Who Is Known but Forbidden: Anne Sexton,' " page 1270; Anne Sexton, "The Barfly Ought to Sing," page 1370.*

ANNE SEXTON

All My Pretty Ones   1962

>   All my pretty ones?
> Did you say all? O hell-kite! All?
> What! all my pretty chickens and their dam
> At one fell swoop? . . .
> I cannot but remember such things were,
> That were most precious to me.
>   – *Macbeth°*

All My Pretty Ones . . . : The title and epigraph come from Shakespeare's play *Macbeth*; Macduff speaks these grieving words upon hearing that his family has been slaughtered (4.3.216ff.).

Father, this year's jinx rides us apart
where you followed our mother to her cold slumber,
a second shock boiling its stone to your heart,
leaving me here to shuffle and disencumber
you from the residence you could not afford: 5
a gold key, your half of a woollen mill,
twenty suits from Dunne's, an English Ford,
the love and legal verbiage of another will,
boxes of pictures of people I do not know.
I touch their cardboard faces. They must go. 10

But the eyes, as thick as wood in this album,
hold me. I stop here, where a small boy
waits in a ruffled dress for someone to come . . .
for this soldier who holds his bugle like a toy
or for this velvet lady who cannot smile. 15
Is this your father's father, this commodore
in a mailman suit? My father, time meanwhile
has made it unimportant who you are looking for.
I'll never know what these faces are all about.
I lock them into their book and throw them out. 20

This is the yellow scrapbook that you began
the year I was born; as crackling now and wrinkly
as tobacco leaves: clippings where Hoover outran
the Democrats,° wiggling his dry finger at me
and Prohibition; news where the *Hindenburg*° went 25
down and recent years when you went flush
on war. This year, solvent but sick, you meant
to marry that pretty widow in a one-month rush.
But before you had that second chance, I cried
on your fat shoulder. Three days later you died. 30

These are the snapshots of marriage, stopped in places.
Side by side at the rail toward Nassau° now;
here, with the winner's cup at the speedboat races,
here, in tails at the Cotillion, you take a bow,
here, by our kennel of dogs with their pink eyes, 35
running like show-bred pigs in their chain-link pen;
here, at the horseshow where my sister wins a prize;
and here, standing like a duke among groups of men.
Now I fold you down, my drunkard, my navigator,
my first lost keeper, to love or look at later. 40

I hold a five-year diary that my mother kept
for three years, telling all she does not say

23–24. Hoover outran / the Democrats: Reference to Herbert Hoover's victory in the presidential election of 1928. **25. Hindenburg:** The famous zeppelin disaster of 1936. **32. Nassau:** Capital city of the Bahamas Islands.

of your alcoholic tendency. You overslept,
she writes. My God, father, each Christmas Day
with your blood, will I drink down your glass   45
of wine? The diary of your hurly-burly years°
goes to my shelf to wait for my age to pass.
Only in this hoarded span will love persevere.
Whether you are pretty or not, I outlive you.
bend down my strange face to yours and forgive you.   50

ANNE SEXTON

The Starry Night   1962

That does not keep me from having a terrible need of — shall I say the word
— religion. Then I go out at night to paint the stars.
                              – VINCENT VAN GOGH in a letter to his brother°

The town does not exist
except where one black-haired tree slips
up like a drowned woman into the hot sky.
The town is silent. The night boils with eleven stars
Oh starry starry night! This is how   5
I want to die.

It moves. They are all alive.
Even the moon bulges in its orange irons
to push children, like a god, from its eye.
The old unseen serpent swallows up the stars.   10
Oh starry starry night! This is how
I want to die:

into that rushing beast of the night,
sucked up by that great dragon, to split
from my life with no flag,   15
no belly,
no cry.

∞

---

46. hurly-burly years: In *Macbeth* 1.1.3–4, the second witch responds to the first witch's
query about when they shall meet again with "When the hurlyburly's done, / When the battle's lost and won."
Vincent van Gogh . . . to his brother: Sexton's title echoes *Starry Night on the Rhône,* a painting by the Dutch artist Vincent van Gogh (1853–1890), who eventually went mad and committed suicide; the epigraph is taken from a letter van Gogh wrote to his brother, Theo, in
1888 — at about the time he was painting *Starry Night.*

WILLIAM SHAKESPEARE (1564–1616) *is best known as a play-wright, and his life and career are presented in the drama section in this book. Almost as honored is the sequence of sonnets he wrote during the latter part of his career. A contemporary of Shakespeare's wrote in 1598 that in addition to his plays, he was known "among his private friends" for "his sugared sonnets." They were published in 1609, the year before he retired from the theater, and since then they have been the standard against which all other sonnets in the English language are measured.*

The 154 sonnets in the sequence seem to tell the story of an unhappy love affair, but, like so much else about Shakespeare's work, there is considerable confusion and continual scholarly wrangling over interpretation of the poems themselves and the story they may tell us. There is even uncertainty about the order of the sonnets. A "Dark Lady" is the central figure in many of them, and in some there is a suggestion of a love triangle between two men and a woman. Some of the early sonnets are written to a young man of great beauty, urging him to marry.

More important than these details of the possible "story" of the sequence are the sonnets themselves, many lines and phrases from which have entered into the English language. The small gathering that follows reprints some of Shakespeare's most often anthologized sonnets. (The Shakespearean sonnet form is also discussed on pp. 945–946.)

RELATED COMMENTARY: *Erica Jong, "Devouring Time: Shakespeare's Sonnets," page 1275.*

WILLIAM SHAKESPEARE

Shall I compare thee to a summer's day?

1609

Shall I compare thee to a summer's day?
Thou art more lovely and more temperate;
Rough winds do shake the darling buds of May,
And summer's lease hath all too short a date.
Sometime too hot the eye of heaven shines, 5
And often is his gold complexion dimmed;
And every fair from fair sometime declines,
By chance, or nature's changing course untrimmed.
But thy eternal summer shall not fade
Nor lose possession of that fair thou owest; 10
Nor shall Death brag thou wander'st in his shade,
When in eternal lines to time thou growest.
So long as men can breathe or eyes can see,
So long lives this and this gives life to thee.

WILLIAM SHAKESPEARE

When to the sessions of sweet silent thought

1609

When to the sessions of sweet silent thought
I summon up remembrance of things past,
I sigh the lack of many a thing I sought,
And with old woes new wail my dear time's waste:
Then can I drown an eye, unused to flow,   5
For precious friends hid in death's dateless night,
And weep afresh love's long since canceled woe,
And moan the expense of many a vanished sight:
Then can I grieve at grievances foregone,
And heavily from woe to woe tell o'er   10
The sad account of fore-bemoanèd moan,
Which I new pay as if not paid before.
But if the while I think on thee, dear friend,
All losses are restored and sorrows end.

WILLIAM SHAKESPEARE

Let me not to the marriage of true minds

1609

Let me not to the marriage of true minds
Admit impediments. Love is not love
Which alters when it alteration finds,
Or bends with the remover to remove:
O, no! it is an ever-fixèd mark   5
That looks on tempests and is never shaken;
It is the star to every wandering bark,
Whose worth's unknown, although his height be taken.
Love's not Time's fool, though rosy lips and cheeks
Within his bending sickle's compass come;   10
Love alters not with his brief hours and weeks,
But bears it out even to the edge of doom.
If this be error and upon me proved,
I never writ, nor no man ever loved.

WILLIAM SHAKESPEARE

My mistress' eyes are nothing like the sun

1609

My mistress' eyes are nothing like the sun;
Coral is far more red than her lips' red:
If snow be white, why then her breasts are dun;
If hairs be wires, black wires grow on her head.

I have seen roses damasked, red and white, 5
But no such roses see I in her cheeks;
And in some perfumes is there more delight
Than in the breath that from my mistress reeks.
I love to hear her speak, yet well I know
That music hath a far more pleasing sound; 10
I grant I never saw a goddess go;
My mistress, when she walks, treads on the ground:
And yet, by heaven, I think my love as rare
As any she belied with false compare.

❧

PERCY BYSSHE SHELLEY *(1792–1822) was born outside of London in Sussex. His grandfather was a wealthy aristocrat and his father was a politically conservative member of Parliament. Shelley attended elite schools — first Eton, then Oxford University — but being short, slightly built, and a poor athlete, he was bullied so unmercifully by the other students that he came to see all of English society as an instrument of oppression.*

He was already writing poetry and sensational novels as a teenager, but at Oxford he and a friend, Thomas Jefferson Hogg, published a small pamphlet titled The Necessity of Atheism. *When Shelley was questioned by the university authorities, he refused to repudiate the pamphlet, and both Shelley and Hogg were expelled. Shelley was only eighteen; earlier in the year he had met a young woman named Harriet Westbrook, who was sixteen. Six months after he'd been expelled, Shelley and Harriet eloped and were married in Edinburgh.*

Early the next year, in 1812, they traveled to Dublin, and Shelley published two more pamphlets, this time advocating Catholic emancipation and Irish independence. For a year he and Harriet moved from place to place while he wrote poetry, read continuously, and tried to obtain more money from his family. In 1813 he met the controversial philosopher William Godwin and found himself drawn into Godwin's family, which included a teenage daughter, Mary, and her half-sister, Jane (later Claire) Clairmont. Harriet gave birth to a daughter, but Shelley was becoming more and more involved with Mary. Godwin tried to separate them, but Shelley attempted suicide with an overdose of opium, then after his recovery he abandoned his wife and child and fled to France with both Mary, who was sixteen, and Claire, who was a few months younger.

By abandoning his wife, Shelley had burned most of his bridges, but his father, in an effort to clear the family name, paid Shelley's debts and set him up with a yearly income. Hogg joined the group when the three of them returned to England a few months later, and for a time the four of them seem to have lived in an open experiment that they termed "free-love." Shelley somehow expected Harriet to join them, but she refused. In November she gave birth to a son they had conceived before he had fled with Mary Godwin. Three months later Mary gave birth to a daughter, who died two weeks later. Shelley was now twenty-two.

Shelley, Mary, and Claire returned to Europe and joined the poet George Gordon, Lord Byron, in Switzerland, and Byron and Claire soon became lovers. A few months later, Harriet's body was found in the Serpentine Pond in Hyde Park. She had become pregnant by someone else and, in despair, had committed suicide. Mary and Shelley, who now had a son, were married three weeks later.

Through all of this turmoil, Shelley was writing the poems for which he would finally be famous, although some years had to pass before the controversy died down about his personal life. In the summer of 1822, in northern Italy, where he and Mary and their children were now living, Shelley and a friend went out in the Bay of Spezia in a new sailboat he had had built to his own specifications. The boat overturned in a storm, and their bodies washed up on the beach three days later.

"Ozymandias" was written quickly after viewing an exhibition at the British Museum with a friend, but it has become one of his best-known poems. Like "Ode to the West Wind" (p. 935), "To a Sky-Lark" was written in 1820 and is one of Shelley's his best-known lyric odes.

RELATED COMMENTARIES: Sherod Santos, "Shelley in Ruins: The Appeal of 'Ozy-mandias,' " page 1303; Percy Bysshe Shelley, From "A Defence of Poetry," page 1311.

PERCY BYSSHE SHELLEY

Ozymandias°   1818

I met a traveler from an antique land
Who said: Two vast and trunkless legs of stone
Stand in the desert . . . Near them, on the sand,
Half sunk, a shattered visage lies, whose frown,
And wrinkled lip, and sneer of cold command,   5
Tell that its sculptor well those passions read
Which yet survive, stamped on these lifeless things,
The hand that mocked them, and the heart that fed:
And on the pedestal these words appear:
"My name is Ozymandias, king of kings: 10
Look on my works, ye Mighty, and despair!"
Nothing beside remains. Round the decay
Of that colossal wreck, boundless and bare
The lone and level sands stretch far away.

PERCY BYSSHE SHELLEY

To a Sky-Lark   1820

Hail to thee, blithe Spirit!
    Bird thou never wert —
That from Heaven, or near it,
    Pourest thy full heart
In profuse strains of unpremeditated art.   5

Ozymandias: Greek name for the thirteenth-century B.C. Egyptian pharaoh Ramses II.

Higher still and higher
    From the earth thou springest
Like a cloud of fire;
    The blue deep thou wingest,
And singing still dost soar, and soaring ever singest.   10

  In the golden lightning
    Of the sunken Sun —
O'er which clouds are brightning,
    Thou dost float and run;
Like an unbodied joy whose race is just begun.   15

  The pale purple even
    Melts around thy flight,
Like a star of Heaven
    In the broad day-light
Thou art unseen, — but yet I hear thy shrill delight,   20

  Keen as are the arrows
    Of that silver sphere,°   *the morning star*
Whose intense lamp narrows
    In the white dawn clear
Until we hardly see — we feel that it is there.   25

  All the earth and air
    With thy voice is loud,
As when Night is bare
    From one lonely cloud
The moon rains out her beams — and Heaven is overflowed.   30

  What thou art we know not;
    What is most like thee?
From rainbow clouds there flow not
    Drops so bright to see
As from thy presence showers a rain of melody.   35

  Like a Poet hidden
    In the light of thought,
Singing hymns unbidden,
    Till the world is wrought
To sympathy with hopes and fears it heeded not: 40

  Like a high-born maiden
    In a palace-tower,
Soothing her love-laden
    Soul in secret hour,
With music sweet as love — which overflows her bower: 45

  Like a glow-worm golden
    In a dell of dew,
Scattering unbeholden
    Its aerial hue
Among the flowers and grass which screen it from the view: 50

Like a rose embowered
   In its own green leaves —
By warm winds deflowered —
   Till the scent it gives
Makes faint with too much sweet heavy-winged thieves: 55

   Sound of vernal showers
      On the twinkling grass,
   Rain-awakened flowers,
      All that ever was
Joyous, and clear and fresh, thy music doth surpass.   60

   Teach us, Sprite or Bird,
      What sweet thoughts are thine:
   I have never heard
      Praise of love or wine
That panted forth a flood of rapture so divine: 65

   Chorus Hymeneal°
      Or triumphal chaunt
   Matched with thine would be all
      But an empty vaunt,
A thing wherein we feel there is some hidden want.   70

   What objects are the fountains
      Of thy happy strain?
   What fields or waves or mountains?
      What shapes of sky or plain?
What love of thine own kind? what ignorance of pain?   75

   With thy clear keen joyance
      Languor cannot be —
   Shadow of annoyance
      Never came near thee;
Thou lovest — but ne'er knew love's sad satiety.   80

   Waking or asleep,
      Thou of death must deem
   Things more true and deep
      Than we mortals dream,
Or how could thy notes flow in such a chrystal stream?   85

   We look before and after,
      And pine for what is not —
   Our sincerest laughter
      With some pain is fraught —
Our sweetest songs are those that tell of saddest thought.   90

---

66. Chorus Hymeneal: Reference to Hymen, the Greek god of marriage.

Yet if we could scorn
    Hate and pride and fear;
If we were things born
    Not to shed a tear,
I know not how thy joy we ever should come near.   95

Better than all measures
    Of delightful sound —
Better than all treasures
    That in books are found —
Thy skill to poet were, thou Scorner of the ground!   100

Teach me half the gladness
    That thy brain must know,
Such harmonious madness
    From my lips would flow
The world should listen then — as I am listening now.   110

ಚಿಲಿ

GARY SNYDER *(b. 1930) was born in San Francisco, but his family moved to a farm outside of Seattle when he was two, and he grew up in the Pacific Northwest. In 1942 the family moved to Portland, Oregon, where he went to high school. In 1947 he enrolled in Reed College, and shared a house with two other young poets, Philip Whalen and Lew Welch. His first published poems appeared in the Reed literary magazine.*

In 1952 he moved to San Francisco, then rented a small cottage in Berkeley while he studied in the university's Asian language program. He soon met Beat writers Allen Ginsberg (p. 1109) and Jack Kerouac, and his cottage became one of the hangouts for the young Beat movement. Kerouac made him the hero of his novel The Dharma Bums, *naming him "Japhy Ryder." Snyder was one of the other readers the night Allen Ginsberg first read parts of* Howl. *In 1957 Snyder moved to Japan, and for the next dozen years he lived mostly in Kyoto, studying and meditating at the Daitoku-ji Zen monastery. His first book,* Riprap, *was published in 1959.*

Snyder came back to San Francisco in time for the Human Be-In in 1967, and after that he lived for many years with his wife and children in a Japanese-style house he built in the California mountains. He now teaches poetry half the year at the University of California at Davis and also lectures on ecology and the environment. He is a popular reader of his own work and often appears with friends, including Ginsberg and Lawrence Ferlinghetti (p. 1092). His collection Turtle Island *won the Pulitzer Prize in 1975.*

"Milton by Firelight" and "How to Make Stew in the Pinacate Desert" both reflect Snyder's continuing interest in the environment and the natural world.

RELATED COMMENTARY: *Samuel Charters, "On Snyder's 'How to Make Stew in the Pinacate Desert,' " page 1245.*

GARY SNYDER

Milton by Firelight 1955

"O hell, what do mine eyes
    with grief behold?"°
Working with an old
Singlejack miner, who can sense
The vein and cleavage   5
In the very guts of rock, can
Blast granite, build
Switchbacks° that last for years
Under the beat of snow, thaw, mule-hooves.
What use, Milton, a silly story   10
Of our lost general parents,
    eaters of fruit?

The Indian, the chainsaw boy,
And a string of six mules
Came riding down to camp   15
Hungry for tomatoes and green apples.
Sleeping in saddle-blankets
Under a bright night-sky
Han River slantwise by morning.
Jays squall   20
Coffee boils

In ten thousand years the Sierras
Will be dry and dead, home of the scorpion.
Ice-scratched slabs and bent trees.

No paradise, no fall,   25
Only the weathering land
The wheeling sky,
Man, with his Satan
Scouring the chaos of the mind.
Oh Hell!   30

Fire down
Too dark to read, miles from a road
The bell-mare clangs in the meadow
That packed dirt for a fill-in
Scrambling through loose rocks   35
On an old trail
All of a summer's day.

1–2. "O hell, . . . behold?": In his 1667 epic poem *Paradise Lost,* John Milton (1608–1674)
retells the biblical story of Adam and Eve's fall from grace. Satan speaks these lines when he
first spies the couple in the Garden of Eden (4:358).   **8. Switchbacks:** Roads that zigzag up
a sharp incline.

GARY SNYDER

How to Make Stew in the Pinacate Desert   1964
Recipe for Locke & Drum°

A. J. Bayless market bent wire roller basket buy up parsnips, onion,
carrot, rutabaga and potato, bell green pepper,
& nine cuts of dark beef shank.
They run there on their legs, that makes meat tasty.

Seven at night in Tucson, get some bisquick for the dumplings,   5
Have some bacon. Go to Hadley's in the kitchen right beside the frying
steak — Diana on the phone — get a little plastic bag from Drum —
Fill it up with tarragon and chili; four bay leaves; black pepper corns
and basil; powdered oregano, something free, maybe about two tea-
spoons worth of salt.   10

Now down in Sonora, Pinacate country, build a fire of Ocotillo,°
broken twigs and bits of ironwood, in an open ring of lava: rake some
coals aside (and if you're smart) to windward,
keep the other half ablaze for heat and light.
Set Drum's fourteen-inch dutch oven with three legs across the embers.   15

Now put in the strips of bacon.
In another pan have all the vegetables cleaned up and peeled and
sliced.
Cut the beef shank meat up small and set the bone aside.
Throw in the beef shank meat,
And stir it while it fries hot,   20
lots of ash and sizzle — singe your brow —

Like Locke says almost burn it — then add water from the jeep
can —
add the little bag of herbs — cook it all five minutes more — and then   25
throw in the pan of all the rest.
Cover it up with big hot lid all heavy, sit and wait, or drink budweiser
beer.

And also mix the dumpling mix aside, some water in some bisquick,
finally drop that off the spoon into the stew.   30
And let it cook ten minutes more
and lift the black pot off the fire
to set aside another good ten minutes,
Dish it up and eat it with a spoon, sitting on a poncho in the dark.

ဢ

Locke & Drum: Drummond Hadley (b. 1938) is a poet and rancher living in Arizona. He and
his wife, Locke, are close friends of Snyder.   **12. Ocotillo:** A spiny, desert bush.

GARY SOTO (*b. 1952*) *was born to Mexican American parents in Fresno, an agricultural town in California's Central Valley. He worked in the fields in the summers and in the Fresno factories. After his graduation from high school, he entered California State University at Fresno, planning to study urban planning, but classes with poet Philip Levine turned his interest to literature and writing. After graduation he went on to the University of California at Irvine for an M.F.A.*

Soto's first poems appeared when he was still a senior in college, and his first collection, The Elements of San Joaquin, *was published in 1977. He began teaching literature and Chicano studies at the University of California campus at Berkeley the same year. His work has won many awards, and he has been granted a Guggenheim fellowship. Although Soto is perhaps the best known of the new Chicano poets, his writing has a personal identity that places it directly in the American mainstream. "Mexicans Begin Jogging" is a wryly humorous memory from his youth; "Walking with Jackie, Sitting with a Dog" is about a moment he remembers when he was even younger.*

GARY SOTO

Mexicans Begin Jogging

1981

At the factory I worked
In the fleck of rubber, under the press
Of an oven yellow with flame,
Until the border patrol opened
Their vans and my boss waved for us to run.   5
"Over the fence, Soto," he shouted,
And I shouted that I was American.
"No time for lies," he said, and pressed
A dollar in my palm, hurrying me
Through the back door.   10

Since I was on his time, I ran
And became the wag to a short tail of Mexicans —
Ran past the amazed crowds that lined
The street and blurred like photographs, in rain.
I ran from that industrial road to the soft   15
Houses where people paled at the turn of an autumn sky.
What could I do but yell *vivas*
To baseball, milkshakes, and those sociologists
Who would clock me
As I jog into the next century   20
On the power of a great, silly grin.

GARY SOTO

Walking with Jackie, Sitting with a Dog   1995

Jackie on the porch, shouting for me to come out.
It's Saturday, and I am in a sweater that's
Too large, balled at the elbows, black at the collar.
Laughing, we slam the screen door on a strained
Voice, and run down the street, sticks   5
In hand, shooing pigeons and the girls
Who are all legs.
                                          We cross the gray traffic
Of Belmont, and enter an alley, its quick stream
Of glass blinking in the angled light. We blink,   10
And throw rocks at things that move,
Slow cat or bough. We grin
Like shovels, and continue on
Because it's Saturday, early as it's ever
Going to get, and we're brothers   15
To all that's heaved over fences.
Our talk is nonsense: Africa and trees splintered
Into matchsticks, handlebars and the widening targets
Of his sister's breasts, staring us down.
The scattered newspaper, cartwheeling across   20
A street, is one way to go.
                                          And we go into
Another alley, where we find a man, asleep behind
Stacked cardboard. The sun flares
Behind trees and it means little.   25
We find a dog, hungry and sad as a suitcase kicked open
And showing nothing. At a curb we drape
Him across our laps and quarter an orange
The juice runs like the tears an onion would give,
If only it opened its eye.   30
We lick our fingers and realize
That with oranges now and plums four months away,
No one need die.

పాం

ALFRED, LORD TENNYSON (1809–1892), *born in Somersby, England,
was one of twelve children, the family's fourth son. His father was the eldest son of a
wealthy landowner, but he was disinherited and forced to become a clergyman. He was
also an abusive drunkard, and the family was in continual turmoil. In 1827 Tennyson
was sent to Cambridge to attend Trinity College, but there were severe financial problems and he was forced to leave without graduating.*
   One of Tennyson's closest friends in school was a fellow poet named Arthur

Hallam, who became engaged to Tennyson's sister. Hallam's early death from a sudden illness in 1833 deeply affected Tennyson, and he expressed his grief in the long poem "In Memoriam," published in 1850. "In Memoriam" was so successful that Tennyson was finally able to marry the woman he had loved for many years. Still in this same year 1850, he was named Poet Laureate of England, succeeding William Wordsworth (p. 1221), and he settled into a productive and secluded country life.

Tennyson's books sold widely, and he was read and quoted throughout the world. Despite his shyness he was a dramatic reader of his own poetry, and in the 1880s he was one of the first English poets to be recorded. His voice can be heard, through a sea of background hiss, declaiming the first lines of "The Charge of the Light Brigade" on a wax cylinder recording: "Half a league, half a league, half a league onward / Into the valley of death rode the six hundred." There was national mourning at his death, and he is buried in the Poets' Corner of Westminster Abbey, with other great English poets.

Although the subject of the poem "Ulysses" is the wily Greek warrior of Homer's epics about the Trojan War, the Iliad and the Odyssey, the mood and themes of the poem reflect Tennyson's struggles to overcome his grief and persevere after Arthur Hallam's death. Tennyson imagines the aged Ulysses, restless in his kingdom of Ithaca after returning from the war and his travels, as he prepares to depart again in search of new adventures. "Break, Break, Break," was written a year later.

RELATED COMMENTARY: *Richard Wilbur, "Tennyson's Voyage of the Mind," page 1326.*

ALFRED, LORD TENNYSON

Ulysses   1833

It little profits that an idle king,
By this still hearth, among these barren crags,
Matched with an aged wife, I mete and dole
Unequal laws unto a savage race
That hoard, and sleep, and feed, and know not me.   5
I cannot rest from travel: I will drink
Life to the lees: all times I have enjoyed
Greatly, have suffered greatly, both with those
That loved me, and alone; on shore, and when
Through scudding drifts the rainy Hyades°   10
Vexed the dim sea: I am become a name;
For always roaming with a hungry heart
Much have I seen and known; cities of men
And manners, climates, councils, governments,
Myself not least, but honored of them all;   15
And drunk delight of battle with my peers,
Far on the ringing plains of windy Troy.
I am a part of all that I have met;
Yet all experience is an arch wherethrough

---

10. **Hyades:** A cluster of stars whose rising was thought to be a sign of rain.

Gleams that untravelled world, whose margin fades   20
For ever and for ever when I move.
How dull it is to pause, to make an end,
To rust unburnished, not to shine in use!
As though to breathe were life. Life piled on life
Were all too little, and of one to me   25
Little remains: but every hour is saved
From that eternal silence, something more,
A bringer of new things; and vile it were
For some three suns to store and hoard myself,
And this gray spirit yearning in desire   30
To follow knowledge like a sinking star,
Beyond the utmost bound of human thought.
    This is my son, mine own Telemachus,
To whom I leave the scepter and the isle —
Well-loved of me, discerning to fulfil   35
This labor, by slow prudence to make mild
A rugged people, and through soft degrees
Subdue them to the useful and the good.
Most blameless is he, centered in the sphere
Of common duties, decent not to fail   40
In offices of tenderness, and pay
Meet° adoration to my household gods   *proper*
When I am gone. He works his work, I mine.
    There lies the port: the vessel puffs her sail;
There gloom the dark broad seas. My mariners,   45
Souls that have toiled, and wrought, and thought with me —
That ever with a frolic welcome took
The thunder and the sunshine, and opposed
Free hearts, free foreheads — you and I are old;
Old age hath yet his honor and his toil;   50
Death closes all: but something ere the end,
Some work of noble note, may yet be done,
Not unbecoming men that strove with gods.
The lights begin to twinkle from the rocks:
The long day wanes: the slow moon climbs: the deep   55
Moans round with many voices. Come, my friends,
'Tis not too late to seek a newer world.
Push off, and sitting well in order smite
The sounding furrows; for my purpose holds
To sail beyond the sunset and the baths   60
Of all the western stars, until I die.
It may be that the gulfs will wash us down:
It may be we shall touch the Happy Isles°

---

63. touch the Happy Isles: In Greek mythology the Happy Isles were the home of dead warriors. In line 64, Ulysses speaks of his old comrade Achilles, who fought alongside him at Troy and was killed there.

And see the great Achilles, whom we knew.
Though much is taken, much abides; and though 65
We are not now that strength which in old days
Moved earth and heaven, that which we are, we are;
One equal temper of heroic hearts,
Made weak by time and fate but strong in will
To strive, to seek, to find, and not to yield. 70

ALFRED, LORD TENNYSON

Break, Break, Break 1834

Break, break, break,
　On thy cold gray stones, O Sea!
And I would that my tongue could utter
　The thoughts that arise in me.

O, well for the fisherman's boy,
　That he shouts with his sister at play!
O, well for the sailor lad,
　That he sings in his boat on the bay!

And the stately ships go on
　To their haven under the hill;
But O for the touch of a vanished hand,
　And the sound of a voice that is still!

Break, break, break
　At the foot of thy crags, O Sea!
But the tender grace of a day that is dead
　Will never come back to me.

❧

DYLAN THOMAS *(1914–1953) was born in Wales and spent his few rebellious school years at the grammar school in Swansea. He decided when he was still a teenager that he would become a poet, and after an unhappy year as a newspaper reporter, he eked out a precarious living for himself and his wife, Caitlin, in London by reading poetry on the air for the BBC and writing short stories and essays. His first collection,* Eighteen Poems, *was published in 1934, when he was just twenty. As a critic wrote at the time, "Thomas's poems seem not only obscure but barbaric. The lines appear to be full of wild eldritch noises, with words, screams and shouts flung out in spectacular abandon. Upon rereading, however, it is apparent that Thomas's poems, far from being disorganized, are curiously disciplined."*

He wrote a wry autobiographical novel, Portrait of the Artist as a Young Dog, *and also a brilliant radio play for voices,* Under Milk Wood. *In the play he uses the words and the language of his neighbors in his small Welsh village with tender love and insight. In the 1950s he became enormously popular in the United States, where he lived a precarious, unstable existence, reading his poetry at college campuses across the coun-*

try. He was also drinking heavily, and he died in New York City in 1953 after a bout with alcohol that was described by the doctor as "an insult to the brain."

"In My Craft or Sullen Art" was written to celebrate his craft as a poet. "Do Not Go Gentle into That Good Night" was written for his father. In a note to the publisher about the poem he wrote, "The only person I can't show the little enclosed poem to is my father, who doesn't know he's dying."

DYLAN THOMAS

In My Craft or Sullen Art   1946

In my craft or sullen art
Exercised in the still night
When only the moon rages
And the lovers lie abed
With all their griefs in their arms,   5
I labor by singing light
Not for ambition or bread
Or the strut and trade of charms
On the ivory stages
But for the common wages   10
Of their most secret heart

Not for the proud man apart
From the raging moon I write
On these spindrift° pages   *wind-driven*
Nor for the towering dead   15
With their nightingales and psalms
But for the lovers, their arms
Round the griefs of the ages,
Who pay no praise or wages
Nor heed my craft or art.   20

DYLAN THOMAS

Do Not Go Gentle into That Good Night   1951

Do not go gentle into that good night,
Old age should burn and rave at close of day;
Rage, rage against the dying of the light.

Though wise men at their end know dark is right,
Because their words had forked no lightning they   5
Do not go gentle into that good night.

Good men, the last wave by, crying how bright
Their frail deeds might have danced in a green bay,
Rage, rage against the dying of the light.

Wild men who caught and sang the sun in flight,   10
And learn, too late, they grieved it on its way,
Do not go gentle into that good night.

Grave men, near death, who see with blinding sight
Blind eyes could blaze like meteors and be gay,
Rage, rage against the dying of the light.   15

And you, my father, there on the sad height,
Curse, bless, me now with your fierce tears, I pray.
Do not go gentle into that good night.
Rage, rage against the dying of the light.

ෙෂ

ANNE WALDMAN *(b. 1945) was born in New Jersey, but her parents soon
moved to Greenwich Village, and she grew up in an atmosphere of books and poetry.
As she remembered her mother, "Poetry was the food in her life, and I think some of
that enthusiasm was passed onto me: something about the experience of poetry being
essential, like food and light."*

*Waldman left New York to attend Bennington College in Vermont, then re-
turned to Manhattan's Lower East Side, where, with poet Lewis Warsh, she began
publishing a literary magazine called* Angel Hair. *Until 1977 she was closely involved with the Poetry Project at the St. Mark's Church in New York and was director of the program for several years.*

*In 1975, with poet Allen Ginsberg (p. 1109), she founded the Jack Kerouac
School of Disembodied Poetics at the Naropa Institute in Boulder, Colorado, where she
still lives part of the year, although she is no longer involved in the daily running of
the poetry program. She travels and performs widely, and her poetry reflects not only
the scenes of her travels but also her serious commitment to Buddhism.*

*"Our Past" is a personal poem from the 1980s. In much of her writing Waldman
has positioned herself in the mainstream of women's writing, and her poem "Marianne
Moore" pays homage to one of the century's important American women poets. (See
also p. 1153.) "To the Censorious Ones" is one of her popular performance poems.*

ANNE WALDMAN

Our Past   1988

You said my life was meant to run from yours as
     streams from the river.
You are the ocean I won't run to you
We were standing on Arapahoe in front of the Silver
     Saddle Motel
They had no rooms for us
I wore the high red huaraches of Mexico & a long skirt
     of patches   5
You had traveled back from Utah

I thought of the Salt Lakes, seeing them once from a
    plane they were like blank patches in the mind or
    bandaged places of the heart
I felt chilly
I had just ridden down the mountain with a car full of
    poets, one terrified of the shifting heights, the
    dark, the mountains, he said, closing in
I said Wait for me, but I have to go here first, or, it's too
    complicated, some kind of stalling because I
    wanted you   10
You were direct, you were traveling light, your feet
    were light, your hair was light, you were attentive
Were you rushing me?
We walked by the stream, you held me, I said I have to
    get back soon because he's waiting, maybe he's
    suffering
I think the moon was waning
You walked me back along 9th Street under dark trees   15
The night we'd met, June 6, we'd come out of the New
    York Church° to observe a performer jumping over
    signposts
I was with my friend, a mentor, much older
You were introduced to him, to me
You said you'd followed me out from that night to where
    the continent divides, where my heart divided
I wrote poems to you in Santa Fe   20
You followed me all the way to Kitkitdizze°
I waited for you, when you came I was away
I drove miles to speak with you on the telephone
I met you in Nevada City after nearly turning back to
    put out a fire
We went to Alta, the lake of your childhood   25
I wanted to stay forever in the big room with all the
    little white beds, like a nursery
You were like first love
All the impossibilities were upon us
We never had enough time
In Palo Alto where they name the streets after poets I
    admired your mother's pretty oriental things   30
In San Francisco we ate hurriedly at the joint near the opera house
I lied about going to Chicago for your birthday in New York
I lied about spending Christmas with you in Cherry Valley°

---

16. the New York Church: St. Mark's Church on Ninth Street and Second Avenue in the Lower East Side.   **21. Kitkitdizze:** The home of poet Gary Snyder in the California foothills.
33. Cherry Valley: Allen Ginsberg's farm in upstate New York.

I will never forget the dance you did to the pipes of
      Finbar Furey on New Year's Day. You kept your
      torso bent to protect your heart
Then I moved to Colorado   35
We met and sat in the yard of a friend's brother's house in
      Missoula, Montana
It's wonderful the way this city turns serenely into
      country with no fuss, the city is shed, or is it the
      other way around, the country falls off into the city?
It was how I wanted us to shed our other lives at least
      when we were together
In that yard you made me feel our situation was
      intolerable
We seemed to be in constant pain   40
When we parted at the small airport early that morning
      my heart finally ripped
In the spring back in New York, things got darker
I was sick, my head was swollen
I remember reading to you about the Abidharma on a mattress
I had trouble speaking   45
I behaved badly and embarrassed you at the uptown
      party
A part of you had left me for good
You'd given your loft over to weekly parties
You were having a public life. I felt you were turning
      into me
I wanted our private romance   50
Was I being straight with you, I wondered?
I let you think things of me that weren't true. You
      thought I was wise & couldn't be hurt
      Then I had the person I lived with and what could
      be said about that?
That summer you visited my hotel in Boulder. We
      slept on separate mattresses. I felt I was trying to
      imprison you and after you left I couldn't go back
      there for days. When I did I found a dead bird had
      gotten entrapped, struggled fiercely to get out
The following winter I waited for you in subzero cold,
      wearing black. I was told you'd come & gone. You
      didn't return. We spoke on the phone a long time
I said I was going home and falling in love with someone
      else. You said It sounds like you want to   55
My mother heard my crying and came to me in the
      bathtub and said O don't, it breaks my heart! I
      told her I was going to the hell for a while I'd often
      made for others, karma works that way. Bosh
      karma she said

We've met briefly in Portland, Oregon, and New York
We've corresponded all this time, following the details
  of each other's lives and work
Your father has recently died
My baby son grows stronger   60
The last time I saw you you were standing on my
  street corner
As I came toward you you said What a youthful gait
  you have

ANNE WALDMAN

Marianne Moore   *1994*

And reading out from a manuscript
Her face, twilight beacon or alchemist's stone
Her offering was holy in us
For she offered light, and in the reading
A claim on us   5
Not negotiable
But held us in nimble wit
And danced from page to voice to ear
We listened and when she stopped
fell silent (fall, fall)   10
Eyed each other askance not wanting
To break it up
The "it" of spell, the "it" of
Impasse
She had those eyes   15
That went right through the next thing
Quickly
& music inexorably owned

ANNE WALDMAN

To the Censorious Ones   *1994*
(Jesse Helms° & others . . .)

This chant accompanied by a chorus of women flexing their muscles. First per-
formed at the Naropa Institute.

  I'm coming up out of the tomb, Men of War
 Just when you thought you had me down, in place, hidden
    I'm coming up now

Jesse Helms: Conservative senator from North Carolina.

Can you feel the ground rumble under your feet?
It's breaking apart, it's turning over, it's pushing up   5
It's thrusting into your point of view, your private property
O Men of War, Censorious Ones!
GET READY BIG BOYS GET READY
I'm coming up now
I'm coming up with all that was hidden   10
Get ready, Big Boys, get ready
I'm coming up with all you wanted buried,
All the hermetic texts with stories in them of hot & dangerous women
Women with lascivious tongues, sharp eyes & claws
I've been working out, my muscles are strong   15
I'm pushing up the earth with all you try to censor
All the iconoclasm & bravado you scorn
All the taunts against your banner & salute
I'm coming up from Hell with all you ever suppressed
All the dark fantasies, all the dregs are coming back   20
I'm leading them back up now
They're going to bark & scoff & rage & bite
I'm opening the box
BOO!

∞

PHILLIS WHEATLEY (c. 1753–1784) was kidnapped from Africa and sold in the Boston slave market in 1761, so the true year of her birth will always be a mystery. She was bought by Susanna Wheatley, a woman of some means, and welcomed more as a new member of the Wheatley household than as a slave. Phillis was precocious and quickly learned English and Latin. She began writing when she was still only a young girl, and her earliest surviving poem was written in 1767, when she was twelve or thirteen. She was formally freed by the Wheatley family when she was about twenty but remained with them until her marriage to John Peters, a free black man, in 1778.

At the same time, she tried with newspaper advertisements to solicit enough subscribers to publish a collection of her poems, but when skepticism over her racial background made this impossible, Susanna Wheatley arranged for the poems to be published in London in 1773. Poems on Various Subjects, Religious and Moral is the first book known to be published by an African American. There were at least four printings of the book in London the first year, but the publication sold poorly in Boston, again because of resistance to Wheatley's race. She was trying to gather enough subscribers for a new collection when she was suddenly taken ill and died in 1784.

Wheatley's poems are written in the conventional neoclassical style (see p. 900) of her time, but her themes are American. Her own situation is expressed poignantly in the fourth verse of "To the Right Honorable William, Earl of Dartmouth" and in the short poem "On Being Brought from Africa to America."

PHILLIS WHEATLEY

To the Right Honourable William, Earl of Dartmouth

1773

Hail, happy day, when, smiling like the morn,
Fair *Freedom* rose *New-England* to adorn:
The northern clime beneath her genial ray,
Dartmouth, congratulates thy blissful sway:
Elate with hope her race no longer mourns,   5
Each soul expands, each grateful bosom burns,
While in thine hand with pleasure we behold
The silken reins, and *Freedom's* charms unfold.
Long lost to realms beneath the northern skies
She shines supreme, while hated *faction* dies: 10
Soon as appear'd the *Goddess* long desir'd,
Sick at the view, she languish'd and expir'd;
Thus from the splendors of the morning light
The owl in sadness seeks the caves of night.
    No more, *America,* in mournful strain   15
Of wrongs, and grievance unredress'd complain,
No longer shalt thou dread the iron chain,
Which wanton *Tyranny* with lawless hand
Had made, and with it meant t' enslave the land.
    Should you, my lord, while you peruse my song,   20
Wonder from whence my love of *Freedom* sprung,
Whence flow these wishes for the common good,
By feeling hearts alone best understood,
I, young in life, by seeming cruel fate
Was snatch'd from *Afric's* fancy'd happy seat: 25
What pangs excruciating must molest,
What sorrows labour in my parent's breast?
Steel'd was that soul and by no misery mov'd
That from a father seiz'd his babe belov'd:
Such, such my case. And can I then but pray   30
Others may never feel tyrannic sway?
    For favours past, great Sir, our thanks are due,
And thee we ask thy favours to renew,
Since in thy pow'r, as in thy will before,
To sooth the griefs, which thou did'st once deplore.   35
May heav'nly grace the sacred sanction give
To all thy works, and thou for ever live
Not only on the wings of fleeting *Fame,*
Though praise immortal crowns the patriot's name,
But to conduct to heav'ns refulgent fane,   40
May fiery coursers sweep th' ethereal plain,

And bear thee upwards to that blest abode,
Where, like the prophet, thou shalt find thy God.

PHILLIS WHEATLEY

On Being Brought from Africa to America   1773

'Twas mercy brought me from my *Pagan* land,
Taught my benighted soul to understand
That there's a God, that there's a *Saviour* too:
Once I redemption neither sought nor knew.

Some view our sable race with scornful eye,
"Their colour is a diabolic die."
Remember, *Christians*, *Negros*, black as *Cain*,°
May be refin'd, and join th'angelic train.

ᔆᔆ

WALT WHITMAN *(1819–1892) was born on Long Island, close to New York City. When he was three his father moved the family to Brooklyn. Whitman went to work as an errand boy when he was eleven and the next year took a job in a newspaper office. He educated himself by reading novels and soon was contributing poems to a Manhattan newspaper. For five years, beginning when he was sixteen, he worked mostly as a country schoolmaster on Long Island, boarding with the families of his students.*

When Whitman gave up teaching, he went back to New York and Brooklyn, and for the next fifteen years he held a series of newspaper jobs, wrote a temperance novel, and published several short stories in a national magazine. By his mid-thirties he was living at home again, crowded into a shabby house in Brooklyn with his parents and his brothers and sisters. He had lost his newspaper job and was working — when he did work — as a carpenter. He spent his days walking the streets or sitting in local libraries. He was emotionally dependent on his mother, but he was careless about missing family meals, came and went as he pleased, and hid himself for hours writing poetry in the room he shared with his brother.

In the spring of 1855 Whitman arranged with a small Brooklyn print shop to bring out a book of the poems he had been writing. He titled it Leaves of Grass. *He printed enough sheets for three hundred copies, had one hundred bound in green cloth with gold stamping, and sent copies to many important American writers. Some threw their copies in the fire, but Ralph Waldo Emerson, then the leading American intellectual figure, recognized the book's genius and sent Whitman a letter that began, "I greet you at the beginning of a great career . . ."*

---

7. black as *Cain*: In Genesis 4:14, God puts a mark on Cain for having murdered his brother Abel. Some traditions hold that this "mark" is black skin.

Emerson's praise meant that the book received some attention, but Whitman's poetry confused most readers. It was unrhymed, the rhythms were so irregular that there was no way to determine the meter of the lines, and the language was as free and direct as someone shouting in the street. Readers were also confused because the only subject of the poems seemed to be Whitman himself. It was not only the form of his poems that opened the path to modern poetry. His use of himself as the persona of the poems was an important source for the tone of confession and self-examination of much twentieth-century American poetry.

Whitman spent the rest of his life trying to organize the writing that poured into his book. Each subsequent edition of Leaves of Grass contained new poems, and he also rewrote and retitled older poems. By the end of his life he was a revered literary figure whose work was read as enthusiastically in Europe as it was in the United States. Support from friends made it possible for him to buy a small house in Camden, New Jersey, where he died in 1892.

"Out of the Cradle Endlessly Rocking" was added to Leaves of Grass in the third edition of 1860. "Beat! Beat! Drums!," "By the Bivouac's Fitful Flame," and "When I Heard the Learn'd Astronomer" were first printed in 1865 in a small collection titled Drum-Taps. "A Noiseless Patient Spider," one of Whitman's most explicitly spiritual poems, was included in an edition of Leaves of Grass that he published in 1868. "Good-bye My Fancy!" was the concluding poem in Whitman's final version of his book, which he completed just before his death.

RELATED COMMENTARIES: Robert Creeley, "On Whitman's Poetry," page 1250; Ezra Pound, "What I Feel about Walt Whitman," page 1300.

WALT WHITMAN

Out of the Cradle Endlessly Rocking 1859

Out of the cradle endlessly rocking,
Out of the mocking-bird's throat, the musical shuttle,
Out of the Ninth-month midnight,
Over the sterile sands and the fields beyond, where the child leaving
    his bed wander'd alone, bareheaded, barefoot,
Down from the shower'd halo,   5
Up from the mystic play of shadows twining and twisting as if they
    were alive,
Out from the patches of briers and blackberries,
From the memories of the bird that chanted to me,
From your memories sad brother, from the fitful risings and fallings I
    heard,
From under that yellow half-moon late-risen and swollen as if with
    tears,   10
From those beginning notes of yearning and love there in the mist,
From the thousand responses of my heart never to cease,
From the myriad thence-arous'd words,
From the word stronger and more delicious than any,

From such as now they start the scene revisiting,   15
As a flock, twittering, rising, or overhead passing,
Borne hither, ere all eludes me, hurriedly,
A man, yet by these tears a little boy again,
Throwing myself on the sand, confronting the waves,
I, chanter of pains and joys, uniter of here and hereafter,   20
Taking all hints to use them, but swiftly leaping beyond them,
A reminiscence sing.

Once Paumanok,°   Long Island
When the lilac-scent was in the air and Fifth-month grass was growing,
Up this seashore in some briers,   25
Two feather'd guests from Alabama, two together,
And their nest, and four light-green eggs spotted with brown,
And every day the he-bird to and fro near at hand,
And every day the she-bird crouch'd on her nest, silent, with bright
    eyes,
And every day I, a curious boy, never too close, never disturbing them,   30
Cautiously peering, absorbing, translating.

Shine! shine! shine!
Pour down your warmth, great sun!
While we bask, we two together.

Two together!   35
Winds blow south, or winds blow north,
Day come white, or night come black,
Home, or rivers and mountains from home,
Singing all time, minding no time,
While we two keep together.   40

Till of a sudden,
May-be kill'd, unknown to her mate,
One forenoon the she-bird crouch'd not on the nest,
Nor return'd that afternoon, nor the next,
Nor ever appear'd again.   45

And thenceforward all summer in the sound of the sea,
And at night under the full of the moon in calmer weather,
Over the hoarse surging of the sea,
Or flitting from brier to brier by day,
I saw, I heard at intervals the remaining one, the he-bird,   50
The solitary guest from Alabama.

Blow! blow! blow!
Blow up sea-winds along Paumanok's shore;
I wait and I wait till you blow my mate to me.

Yes, when the stars glisten'd,   55
All night long on the prong of a moss-scallop'd stake,
Down almost amid the slapping waves,
Sat the lone singer wonderful causing tears.

He call'd on his mate,
He pour'd forth the meanings which I of all men know.   60

Yes my brother I know,
The rest might not, but I have treasur'd every note,
For more than once dimly down to the beach gliding,
Silent, avoiding the moonbeams, blending myself with the shadows,
Recalling now the obscure shapes, the echoes, the sounds and sights af-
    ter their sorts,   65
The white arms out in the breakers tirelessly tossing,
I, with bare feet, a child, the wind wafting my hair,
Listen'd long and long.

Listen'd to keep, to sing, now translating the notes,
Following you my brother.   70

Soothe! soothe! soothe!
Close on its wave soothes the wave behind,
And again another behind embracing and lapping, every one close,
But my love soothes not me, not me.

Low hangs the moon, it rose late,   75
It is lagging — O I think it is heavy with love, with love.

O madly the sea pushes upon the land,
With love, with love.

O night! do I not see my love fluttering out among the breakers?
What is that little black thing I see there in the white?   80

Loud! loud! loud!
Loud I call to you, my love!

High and clear I shoot my voice over the waves,
Surely you must know who is here, is here,
You must know who I am, my love.   85

Low-hanging moon!
What is that dusky spot in your brown yellow?
O it is the shape, the shape of my mate!
O moon do not keep her from me any longer.

Land! land! O land!   90
Whichever way I turn, O I think you could give me my mate back again if you
    only would,
For I am almost sure I see her dimly whichever way I look.

O rising stars!
Perhaps the one I want so much will rise, will rise with some of you.

O throat! O trembling throat!   95
Sound clearer through the atmosphere!
Pierce the woods, the earth,
Somewhere listening to catch you must be the one I want.

Shake out carols!
Solitary here, the night's carols!   100
Carols of lonesome love! death's carols!

Carols under that lagging, yellow, waning moon!
O under that moon where she droops almost down into the sea!
O reckless despairing carols.

But soft! sink low!   105
Soft! let me just murmur,
And do you wait a moment you husky-nois'd sea,
For somewhere I believe I heard my mate responding to me,
So faint, I must be still, be still to listen,
But not altogether still, for then she might not come immediately to me.   110

Hither my love!
Here I am! here!
With this just-sustain'd note I announce myself to you,
This gentle call is for you my love, for you.

Do not be decoy'd elsewhere,   115
That is the whistle of the wind, it is not my voice,
That is the fluttering, the fluttering of the spray,
Those are the shadows of leaves.

O darkness! O in vain!
O I am very sick and sorrowful.   120

O brown halo in the sky near the moon, drooping upon the sea!
O troubled reflection in the sea!
O throat! O throbbing heart!
And I singing uselessly, uselessly all the night.

O past! O happy life! O songs of joy!   125
In the air, in the woods, over fields,
Loved! loved! loved! loved! loved!
But my mate no more, no more with me!
We two together no more.

The aria sinking,   130
All else continuing, the stars shining,
The winds blowing, the notes of the bird continuous echoing,
With angry moans the fierce old mother incessantly moaning,
On the sands of Paumanok's shore gray and rustling,
The yellow half-moon enlarged, sagging down, drooping, the face of
    the sea almost touching,   135
The boy ecstatic, with his bare feet the waves, with his hair the atmos-
    phere dallying,
The love in the heart long pent, now loose, now at last tumultuously
    bursting,
The aria's meaning, the ears, the soul, swiftly depositing,
The strange tears down the cheeks coursing,
The colloquy there, the trio, each uttering,   140
The undertone, the savage old mother incessantly crying,
To the boy's soul's questions sullenly timing, some drown'd secret
    hissing,
To the outsetting bard.

Demon or bird! (said the boy's soul,)
Is it indeed toward your mate you sing? or is it really to me?   145
For I, that was a child, my tongue's use sleeping, now I have heard
    you,
Now in a moment I know what I am for, I awake,
And already a thousand singers, a thousand songs, clearer, louder and
    more sorrowful than yours,
A thousand warbling echoes have started to life within me, never to
    die.

O you singer solitary, singing by yourself, projecting me,   150
O solitary me listening, never more shall I cease perpetuating you,
Never more shall I escape, never more the reverberations,
Never more the cries of unsatisfied love be absent from me,
Never again leave me to be the peaceful child I was before what there
    in the night,
By the sea under the yellow and sagging moon,   155
The messenger there arous'd, the fire, the sweet hell within,
The unknown want, the destiny of me.

O give me the clew!° (it lurks in the night here somewhere,)   *clue*
O if I am to have so much, let me have more!

A word then, (for I will conquer it,)   160
The word final, superior to all,
Subtle, sent up — what is it? — I listen;
Are you whispering it, and have been all the time, you sea-waves?
Is that it from your liquid rims and wet sands?

Whereto answering, the sea,   165
Delaying not, hurrying not,
Whisper'd me through the night, and very plainly before daybreak,
Lisp'd to me the low and delicious word death,
And again death, death, death, death,
Hissing melodious, neither like the bird nor like my arous'd child's
    heart,
     170
But edging near as privately for me rustling at my feet,
Creeping thence steadily up to my ears and laving me softly all over,
Death, death, death, death, death.

Which I do not forget,
But fuse the song of my dusky demon and brother,   175
That he sang to me in the moonlight on Paumanok's gray beach,
With the thousand responsive songs at random,
My own songs awaked from that hour,
And with them the key, the word up from the waves,
The word of the sweetest song and all songs,   180
That strong and delicious word which, creeping to my feet,
(Or like some old crone rocking the cradle, swathed in sweet garments,
    bending aside,)
The sea whisper'd me.

WALT WHITMAN

Beat! Beat! Drums!   1861

Beat! beat! drums! — blow! bugles! blow!
Through the windows — through doors — burst like a ruthless force,
Into the solemn church, and scatter the congregation,
Into the school where the scholar is studying;
Leave not the bridegroom quiet — no happiness must he have now
    with his bride,   5
Nor the peaceful farmer any peace, ploughing his field or gathering his
    grain,
So fierce you whirr and pound you drums — so shrill you bugles blow.

Beat! beat! drums! — blow! bugles! blow!
Over the traffic of cities — over the rumble of wheels in the streets;
Are beds prepared for sleepers at night in the houses? no sleepers must
    sleep in those beds,   10
No bargainers' bargains by day — no brokers or speculators — would
    they continue?
Would the talkers be talking? would the singer attempt to sing?
Would the lawyer rise in the court to state his case before the judge?
Then rattle quicker, heavier drums — you bugles wilder blow.

Beat! beat! drums! — blow! bugles! blow!   15
Make no parley — stop for no expostulation,
Mind not the timid — mind not the weeper or prayer,
Mind not the old man beseeching the young man,
Let not the child's voice be heard, nor the mother's entreaties,
Make even the trestles to shake the dead where they lie awaiting the
    hearses,   20
So strong you thump O terrible drums — so loud you bugles blow.

WALT WHITMAN

By the Bivouac's Fitful Flame   1865

By the bivouac's fitful flame,
A procession winding around me, solemn and sweet and slow — but
    first I note,
The tents of the sleeping army, the fields' and woods' dim outline,
The darkness lit by spots of kindled fire, the silence,
Like a phantom far or near an occasional figure moving,   5
The shrubs and trees, (as I lift my eyes they seem to be stealthily watch-
    ing me,)
While wind in procession thoughts, O tender and wondrous thoughts,
Of life and death, of home and the past and loved, and of those that are
    far away;

A solemn and slow procession there as I sit on the ground,
By the bivouac's fitful flame.   10

WALT WHITMAN

When I Heard the Learn'd Astronomer   1865

When I heard the learn'd astronomer,
When the proofs, the figures, were ranged in columns before me,
When I was shown the charts and diagrams, to add, divide, and mea-
      sure them,
When I sitting heard the astronomer where he lectured with much ap-
      plause in the lecture-room,
How soon unaccountable I became tired and sick,
Till rising and gliding out I wander'd off by myself,
In the mystical moist night-air, and from time to time,
Look'd up in perfect silence at the stars.

WALT WHITMAN

A Noiseless Patient Spider   1868

A noiseless patient spider,
I mark'd where on a little promontory it stood isolated,
Mark'd how to explore the vacant vast surrounding,
It launch'd forth filament, filament, filament, out of itself,
Ever unreeling them, ever tirelessly speeding them.   5

And you O my soul where you stand,
Surrounded, detached, in measureless oceans of space,
Ceaselessly musing, venturing, throwing, seeking the spheres to con-
      nect them,
Till the bridge you will need be form'd, till the ductile anchor hold,
Till the gossamer thread you fling catch somewhere, O my soul.   10

WALT WHITMAN

Good-bye My Fancy!   1891

Good-bye my Fancy!
Farewell dear mate, dear love!
I'm going away, I know not where,
Or to what fortune, or whether I may ever see you again.
So Good-bye my Fancy.   5

Now for my last — let me look back a moment;
The slower fainter ticking of the clock is in me,
Exit, nightfall, and soon the heart-thud stopping.

Long have we lived, joy'd, caress'd together;
Delightful! — now separation — Good-bye my Fancy.   10

Yet let me not be too hasty,
Long indeed have we lived, slept, filter'd, become really blended into
    one;
Then if we die we die together, (yes, we'll remain one,)
If we go anywhere we'll go together to meet what happens,
May-be we'll be better off and blither, and learn something,   15
May-be it is yourself now really ushering me to the true songs, (who
    knows?)
May-be it is you the mortal knob really undoing, turning-so now fi-
    nally,
Good-bye — and hail! my Fancy.

ର

WILLIAM CARLOS WILLIAMS (1883–1963) *was born in Rutherford, New
Jersey, where he lived and practiced medicine all his life. His mother was Puerto Rican; his father was English. Although he spent his life as a pediatrician, when he was
a student at the University of Pennsylvania he was friends with Hilda Doolittle, who
became the poet H.D. (p. 1062), and the poet Ezra Pound (p. 1175). His encounter
with them encouraged his own ambitions to be a poet, and he managed to lead a double life — as a doctor and a writer — until a series of strokes forced him to give up
medicine in the 1950s.*

*Williams felt himself isolated in his small town medical practice, but he was
part of the avant-garde poetry movements of his time, and it was as an imagist (see
imagism on pp. 964–967) that he was best known when be began publishing after
World War I. During his long career he founded small magazines; contributed essays,
poems, and stories to literary journals; and also found time to write novels, plays, and
an autobiography.*

*Many of Williams's poems are short. In his autobiography he remembers that
some of them were written on his office typewriter between patients, and some first
versions of his poems were written on prescription blanks. He was the last of the modernist poets to achieve recognition, but his work became an important influence on
younger poets like Allen Ginsberg (p. 1109), who brought Jack Kerouac, among others, to visit Williams in the 1950s.*

*"Tract" was one of his first poems to be widely read, but all of his poems, in-
cluding "Spring and All," "This Is Just to Say," and "The Dance," have the same directness of speech, the personal vocabulary, and the spontaneous poetic form that he
termed the "American idiom," which was essential to his writing. (See also Williams's
"The Red Wheelbarrow" on p. 965 and "Classic Scene" on p. 966.)*

RELATED COMMENTARY: *William Carlos Williams, "Ezra Pound's Language,"
page 1329.*

WILLIAM CARLOS WILLIAMS

Tract

1917

I will teach you my townspeople
how to perform a funeral —
for you have it over a troop
of artists —
unless one should scour the world —   5
you have the ground sense necessary.

See! the hearse leads.
I begin with a design for a hearse.
For Christ's sake not black —
nor white either — and not polished!   10
Let it be weathered — like a farm wagon —
with gilt wheels (this could be
applied fresh at small expense)
or no wheels at all:
a rough dray to drag over the ground.   15

Knock the glass out!
My God — glass, my townspeople!
For what purpose? Is it for the dead
to look out or for us to see
how well he is housed or to see   20
the flowers or the lack of them —
or what?
To keep the rain and snow from him?
He will have a heavier rain soon:
pebbles and dirt and what not,   25
Let there be no glass —
and no upholstery! phew!
and no little brass rollers
and small easy wheels on the bottom —
my townspeople what are you thinking of!   30

A rough plain hearse then
with gilt wheels and no top at all.
On this the coffin lies
by its own weight.

           No wreaths please —   35
especially no hot-house flowers.
Some common memento is better,
something he prized and is known by:
his old clothes — a few books perhaps —
God knows what! You realize   40
how we are about these things,
my townspeople —
something will be found — anything —

even flowers if he had come to that.
So much for the hearse.   45

For heaven's sake though see to the driver!
Take off the silk hat! In fact
that's no place at all for him
up there unceremoniously
dragging our friend out to his own dignity!   50
Bring him down — bring him down!
Low and inconspicuous! I'd not have him ride
on the wagon at all — damn him —
the undertaker's understrapper!
Let him hold the reins   55
and walk at the side
and inconspicuously too!

Then briefly as to yourselves:
Walk behind — as they do in France,
seventh class, or if you ride   60
Hell take curtains! Go with some show
of inconvenience; sit openly —
to the weather as to grief.
Or do you think you can shut grief in?
What — from us? We who have perhaps   65
nothing to lose? Share with us
share with us — it will be money
in your pockets.
                    Go now
I think you are ready.   70

WILLIAM CARLOS WILLIAMS

Spring and All   1923

By the road to the contagious hospital,
under the surge of the blue
mottled clouds driven from the
northeast — cold wind. Beyond, the
waste of broad, muddy fields,   5
brown with dried weeds, standing and fallen,

patches of standing water,
the scattering of tall trees.

All along the road the reddish,
purplish, forked, upstanding, twiggy   10
stuff of brushes and small trees
with dead, brown leaves under them
leafless vines —

Lifeless in appearance, sluggish,
dazed spring approaches —   15

They enter the new world naked,
cold, uncertain of all
save that they enter. All about them
the cold, familiar wind —

Now the grass, tomorrow   20
the stiff curl of wild carrot leaf.

One by one objects are defined —
It quickens: clarity, outline of leaf,

But now the stark dignity of
entrance — Still, the profound change   25
has come upon them; rooted, they
grip down and begin to awaken.

WILLIAM CARLOS WILLIAMS

This Is Just to Say   1934

I have eaten
the plums
that were in
the icebox

and which
you were probably   5
saving
for breakfast

Forgive me
they were delicious   10
so sweet
and so cold

WILLIAM CARLOS WILLIAMS

The Dance   1944

In Brueghel's great picture, The Kermess,°
the dancers go round, they go round and
around, the squeal and the blare and the
tweedle of bagpipes, a bugle and fiddles

---

1. **Brueghel's . . . The Kermess:** *The Wedding Dance* by the Flemish artist Pieter Brueghel the Elder (c. 1525–1565).

tipping their bellies (round as the thick- 5
sided glasses whose wash they impound)
their hips and their bellies off balance
to turn them. Kicking and rolling about
the Fair Grounds, swinging their butts, those
shanks must be sound to bear up under such 10
rollicking measures, prance as they dance
in Brueghel's great picture, The Kermess.

ന്വ

WILLIAM WORDSWORTH *(1770–1850) was born in the north of England, close to the Lake District. After the death of his mother when he was eight, he and his three brothers were raised in the countryside and often left free to roam. He also read hungrily and was encouraged to think of becoming a poet by his school-master.*

Wordsworth had a turbulent youth. In 1790, during his summer break from St. John's College in Cambridge, he went on a long walking trip through France and Switzerland, then returned to France after his graduation the next year, hoping to im-prove his French language skills enough to qualify as a teacher. He remained in France during the period of the wildest triumphs and fervors of the French Revolution. He fell in love with Annette Vallon, daughter of a family of Royalist sympathizers. She gave birth to Wordsworth's child, but the political turmoil forced him to return to England, and Annette was unable to follow him.

In England, Wordsworth was torn between the love he had left behind him and his disillusionment with the Revolution, which was becoming increasingly violent and despotic. At this moment, when he was struggling against a complete emotional collapse, a friend died and left Wordsworth enough money to enable the poet to devote himself entirely to his art. With his sister Dorothy, and a new friend, the young poet and critic Samuel Taylor Coleridge (p. 1056), Wordsworth began a new life.

Wordsworth and Coleridge set out to create a new style of poetry — poetry that would be closer to the language of ordinary people and would deal with genuine emotions. In 1798 they published a slim book, Lyrical Ballads, *with poems by each of them. This book is considered the beginning of the romantic movement in English poetry.*

In the course of his long life, Wordsworth lost the creative fire of his early years, but at his death he was hailed as one of the most significant literary figures England had ever produced. He began "Ode: Intimations of Immortality" in his mid thirties, and it took him two years after he wrote the first four stanzas to complete the poem. He wrote to an admirer about its subject, "Nothing was more difficult for me in childhood than to admit the notion of death as a state applicable to my own being." (See also Wordsworth's "I Wandered Lonely as a Cloud" on p. 915, "My Heart Leaps Up" on p. 916, "We Are Seven" on p. 925, and "Nuns Fret Not" on p. 947.)

WILLIAM WORDSWORTH

Ode

1807

Intimations of Immortality
from Recollections of Early Childhood

The Child is Father of the Man;
And I could wish my days to be
Bound each to each by natural piety.

1

There was a time when meadow, grove, and stream,
The earth, and every common sight,
      To me did seem
      Apparelled in celestial light,
The glory and the freshness of a dream.   5
It is not now as it hath been of yore; —
      Turn wheresoe'er I may,
      By night or day,
The things which I have seen I now can see no more.

2

      The Rainbow comes and goes,   10
      And lovely is the Rose,
      The Moon doth with delight
Look round her when the heavens are bare,
      Waters on a starry night
      Are beautiful and fair;
      The sunshine is a glorious birth;   15
      But yet I know, where'er I go,
That there hath past away a glory from the earth.

3

Now, while the birds thus sing a joyous song,
      And while the young lambs bound
      As to the tabor's sound,   20
To me alone there came a thought of grief:
A timely utterance gave that thought relief,
      And I again am strong:
The cataracts blow their trumpets from the steep;   25
No more shall grief of mine the season wrong;
I hear the Echoes through the mountains throng,
The Winds come to me from the fields of sleep,
      And all the earth is gay;
      Land and sea   30
      Give themselves up to jollity,
      And with the heart of May
      Doth every Beast keep holiday; —
      Thou Child of Joy,

Shout round me, let me hear thy shouts, thou happy
   Shepherd-boy!   35

4

Ye blessed Creatures, I have heard the call
   Ye to each other make; I see
The heavens laugh with you in your jubilee;
   My heart is at your festival,
     My head hath its coronal,°   40
The fulness of your bliss, I feel — I feel it all.
     Oh evil day! if I were sullen
     While Earth herself is adorning,
       This sweet May-morning,
     And the Children are culling   45
       On every side,
     In a thousand valleys far and wide,
     Fresh flowers; while the sun shines warm,
And the Babe leaps up on his Mother's arm: —
     I hear, I hear, with joy I hear!   50
     — But there's a Tree, of many, one,
A single Field which I have looked upon,
Both of them speak of something that is gone:
       The Pansy at my feet
       Doth the same tale repeat: 55
Whither is fled the visionary gleam?
Where is it now, the glory and the dream?

5

Our birth is but a sleep and a forgetting:
The Soul that rises with us, our life's Star,
     Hath had elsewhere its setting,   60
       And cometh from afar:
     Not in entire forgetfulness,
     And not in utter nakedness,
But trailing clouds of glory do we come
     From God, who is our home: 65
Heaven lies about us in our infancy!
Shades of the prison-house begin to close
     Upon the growing Boy,
But He beholds the light, and whence it flows,
     He sees it in his joy;   70
The Youth, who daily farther from the east
     Must travel, still is Nature's Priest,
     And by the vision splendid
     Is on his way attended;

---

40. coronal: Crown of flowers worn by young shepherds in May.

At length the Man perceives it die away,   75
And fade into the light of common day.

6

Earth fills her lap with pleasures of her own;
Yearnings she hath in her own natural kind,
And, even with something of a Mother's mind,
    And no unworthy aim,   80
    The homely Nurse doth all she can
To make her Foster-child, her Inmate Man,
    Forget the glories he hath known,
And that imperial palace whence he came.

7

Behold the Child among his new-born blisses,   85
A six years' Darling of a pigmy size!
See, where 'mid work of his own hand he lies,
Fretted by sallies of his mother's kisses,
With light upon him from his father's eyes!
See, at his feet, some little plan or chart,   90
Some fragment from his dream of human life,
Shaped by himself with newly-learnèd art;
    A wedding or a festival,
    A mourning or a funeral;
      And this hath now his heart,   95
    And unto this he frames his song:
      Then will he fit his tongue
To dialogues of business, love, or strife;
    But it will not be long
    Ere this be thrown aside,   100
    And with new joy and pride
The little Actor cons another part;
Filling from time to time his "humorous stage"°
With all the Persons, down to palsied Age,
That Life brings with her in her equipage;   105
    As if his whole vocation
    Were endless imitation.

8

Thou, whose exterior semblance doth belie
    Thy Soul's immensity;
Thou best Philosopher, who yet dost keep   110
Thy heritage, thou Eye among the blind,
That, deaf and silent, read'st the eternal deep,

---

103. **"humorous stage":** Capriciousness, but also carries the sense of the classical temperaments ("humors").

Haunted for ever by the eternal mind, —
　　　　Mighty Prophet! Seer blest!
　　　　On whom those truths do rest,　　　　　　　　　　115
Which we are toiling all our lives to find,
In darkness lost, the darkness of the grave;
Thou, over whom thy Immortality
Broods like the Day, a Master o'er a Slave,
A Presence which is not to be put by;　　　　　　　　　　120
Thou little Child, yet glorious in the might
Of heaven-born freedom on thy being's height,
Why with such earnest pains dost thou provoke
The years to bring the inevitable yoke,
Thus blindly with thy blessedness at strife?　　　　　　125
Full soon thy Soul shall have her earthly freight,
And custom lie upon thee with a weight,
Heavy as frost, and deep almost as life!

9

　　　　　O joy! that in our embers
　　　　　Is something that doth live,　　　　　　　　　130
　　　　　That nature yet remembers
　　　　　What was so fugitive!
The thought of our past years in me doth breed
Perpetual benediction: not indeed
For that which is most worthy to be blest;　　　　　　135
Delight and liberty, the simple creed
Of Childhood, whether busy or at rest,
With new-fledged hope still fluttering in his breast —
　　　　　Not for these I raise
　　　　　The song of thanks and praise;　　　　　140
　　　　But for those obstinate questionings
　　　　Of sense and outward things,
　　　　Fallings from us, vanishings;
　　　　Blank misgivings of a Creature
Moving about in worlds not realised,　　　　　　　　　145
High instincts before which our mortal Nature
Did tremble like a guilty Thing surprised:
　　　　But for those first affections,
　　　　Those shadowy recollections,
　　　　Which, be they what they may,　　　　　　150
Are yet the fountain light of all our day,
Are yet a master light of all our seeing;
　　　Uphold us, cherish, and have power to make
Our noisy years seem moments in the being
Of the eternal Silence: truths that wake,　　　　　　155
　　　　To perish never;
Which neither listlessness, nor mad endeavour,

Nor Man nor Boy,
Nor all that is at enmity with joy,
Can utterly abolish or destroy!   160
   Hence in a season of calm weather
     Though inland far we be,
Our Souls have sight of that immortal sea
     Which brought us hither,
     Can in a moment travel thither,   165
And see the Children sport upon the shore,
And hear the mighty waters rolling evermore.

10

Then sing, ye Birds, sing, sing a joyous song!
     And let the young Lambs bound
     As to the tabor's sound!   170
We in thought will join your throng,
     Ye that pipe and ye that play,
     Ye that through your hearts to-day
     Feel the gladness of the May!
What though the radiance which was once so bright   175
Be now for ever taken from my sight,
   Though nothing can bring back the hour
Of splendour in the grass, of glory in the flower;
     We will grieve not, rather find
     Strength in what remains behind;   180
     In the primal sympathy
     Which having been must ever be;
     In the soothing thoughts that spring
     Out of human suffering;
     In the faith that looks through death,   185
In years that bring the philosophic mind.

11

And O, ye Fountains, Meadows, Hills, and Groves,
Forebode not any severing of our loves!
Yet in my heart of hearts I feel your might;
I only have relinquished one delight   190
To live beneath your more habitual sway.
I love the Brooks which down their channels fret,
Even more than when I tripped lightly as they;
The innocent brightness of a new-born Day
     Is lovely yet;   195
The Clouds that gather round the setting sun
Do take a sober colouring from an eye
That hath kept watch o'er man's mortality;
Another race hath been, and other palms are won.
Thanks to the human heart by which we live,   200
Thanks to its tenderness, its joys, and fears,

To me the meanest flower that blows can give
Thoughts that do often lie too deep for tears.

ཙྪ

WILLIAM BUTLER YEATS (1865–1939) *was born in Dublin, but his parents were of English descent, and he spent much of his youth in London. His father, Jack Yeats, was a gifted but struggling artist. Yeats first decided to follow his father and become a painter. He changed his mind, however, after beginning his art studies. His first published poems appeared in the* Dublin University Review *when he was twenty.*

For most of his life Yeats journeyed between England and Ireland, where he lived some of the time in Dublin and at other times with his mother's family in County Sligo, a rural area in northwest Ireland. All three of these very different environments had an effect on his writing. His early poetry often presented a soft mood of reverie, influenced by younger poets he met in London. He also drew from his Irish background in verse dramas based on Irish legends and myths. The rough countryside of County Sligo lent his poetry a sharper, less romantic tone than that of the London poets' verse.

In 1899 Yeats helped found the Irish National Theatre, but bitter struggles with the conservative middle-class audiences eventually drove him to London. The Irish Rebellion of 1916, however, when a group of Irish idealists attempted to seize power from the British occupying forces, brought him back, and when Ireland achieved partial independence in 1922 he was appointed a senator and served in the government for six years.

Yeats had a long and successful career as a writer, and he won the Nobel Prize for literature in 1923. "The Lake Isle of Innisfree" and "When You Are Old" were written almost thirty years earlier. "The Wild Swans at Coole" was written almost twenty years after Yeats's first visit to Coole, the estate of his patron, Lady Gregory. "The Second Coming" is one of his best-known visionary poems, and "Sailing to Byzantium" is one of his most famous works about the nature of art and artists. (See also Yeats's "From At the Hawk's Well" *on p. 969.)*

WILLIAM BUTLER YEATS

The Lake Isle of Innisfree 1890

I will arise and go now, and go to Innisfree,
And a small cabin build there, of clay and wattles made;
Nine bean rows will I have there, a hive for the honey bee,
    And live alone in the bee-loud glade.

And I shall have some peace there, for peace comes dropping slow, 5
Dropping from the veils of the morning to where the cricket sings;
There midnight's all a glimmer, and noon a purple glow,
    And evening full of the linnet's wings.

I will arise and go now, for always night and day
I hear lake water lapping with low sounds by the shore; 10
While I stand on the roadway, or on the pavements gray,
    I hear it in the deep heart's core.

WILLIAM BUTLER YEATS

When You Are Old

1892

When you are old and grey and full of sleep,
And nodding by the fire, take down this book,
And slowly read, and dream of the soft look
Your eyes had once, and of their shadows deep;

How many loved your moments of glad grace,   5
And loved your beauty with love false or true,
But one man loved the pilgrim soul in you,
And loved the sorrows of your changing face;

And bending down beside the glowing bars,
Murmur, a little sadly, how Love fled   10
And paced upon the mountains overhead
And hid his face amid a crowd of stars.

WILLIAM BUTLER YEATS

The Wild Swans at Coole

1917

The trees are in their autumn beauty,
The woodland paths are dry,
Under the October twilight the water
Mirrors a still sky;
Upon the brimming water among the stones   5
Are nine-and-fifty swans.

The nineteenth autumn has come upon me
Since I first made my count;
I saw, before I had well finished,
All suddenly mount   10
And scatter wheeling in great broken rings
Upon their clamorous wings.

I have looked upon those brilliant creatures,
And now my heart is sore.
All's changed since I, hearing at twilight,   15
The first time on this shore,
The bell-beat of their wings above my head,
Trod with a lighter tread.

Unwearied still, lover by lover,
They paddle in the cold   20
Companionable streams or climb the air;
Their hearts have not grown old;
Passion or conquest, wander where they will,
Attend upon them still.

But now they drift on the still water,   25
Mysterious, beautiful;
Among what rushes will they build,
By what lake's edge or pool
Delight men's eyes when I awake some day
To find they have flown away?   30

WILLIAM BUTLER YEATS

The Second Coming   *1919*

Turning and turning in the widening gyre
The falcon cannot hear the falconer;
Things fall apart; the centre cannot hold;
Mere anarchy is loosed upon the world,
The blood-dimmed tide is loosed, and everywhere   5
The ceremony of innocence is drowned;
The best lack all conviction, while the worst
Are full of passionate intensity.

Surely some revelation is at hand;
Surely the Second Coming is at hand.   10
The Second Coming! Hardly are those words out
When a vast image out of *Spiritus Mundi*°
Troubles my sight: somewhere in sands of the desert
A shape with lion body and the head of a man,
A gaze blank and pitiless as the sun,   15
Is moving its slow thighs, while all about it
Reel shadows of the indignant desert birds.
The darkness drops again; but now I know
That twenty centuries of stony sleep
Were vexed to nightmare by a rocking cradle,   20
And what rough beast, its hour come round at last,
Slouches towards Bethlehem to be born?

WILLIAM BUTLER YEATS

Sailing to Byzantium   *1926*

I

That is no country for old men. The young
In one another's arms, birds in the trees
  — Those dying generations — at their song,

---

12. *Spiritus Mundi:* Spirit of the universe.

The salmon-falls, the mackerel-crowded seas,
Fish, flesh, or fowl, commend all summer long   5
Whatever is begotten, born, and dies.
Caught in that sensual music all neglect
Monuments of unageing intellect.

II

An aged man is but a paltry thing,
A tattered coat upon a stick, unless   10
Soul clap its hands and sing, and louder sing
For every tatter in its mortal dress,
Nor is there singing school but studying
Monuments of its own magnificence;
And therefore I have sailed the seas and come   15
To the holy city of Byzantium.

III

O sages standing in God's holy fire
As in the gold mosaic of a wall,
Come from the holy fire, perne in a gyre,°
And be the singing-masters of my soul.   20
Consume my heart away; sick with desire
And fastened to a dying animal
It knows not what it is; and gather me
Into the artifice of eternity.

IV

Once out of nature I shall never take   25
My bodily form from any natural thing,
But such a form as Grecian goldsmiths make
Of hammered gold and gold enamelling
To keep a drowsy Emperor awake;
Or set upon a golden bough to sing   30
To lords and ladies of Byzantium
Of what is past, or passing, or to come.

---

19. perne in a gyre: Yeats uses the word *perne* as a noun meaning "to spin around." *Gyre* means "circle."

18

COMMENTARIES ON POETRY
AND POETS

JULIA ALVAREZ *teaches at Middlebury College in Vermont. Her most recent works of fiction are* How the Garcia Girls Lost Their Accents *(1991) and* In the Time of the Butterflies *(1994).*

JULIA ALVAREZ

Elizabeth Bishop's "One Art"   1996

The villanelle seems to me a nearly impossible form: at worst, a mother's nag that keeps coming back every time: *did you remember to wash your hands, did you put the milk back in the refrigerator, don't forget to turn off the lights and to wash your hands and put the milk back in the refrigerator;* at best, an incantory obsessive form. The villanelle is good for reviving the dead or dying, for casting spells, a form for chanting to ourselves as we journey through the baffling mysteriousness of our lives. ("Of those so close beside me, which are you?") As we read Dylan Thomas's villanelle, "Do not go gentle into that good night," we find ourselves engaged in a ritualistic life chant for a dying man: "Rage, rage against the dying of the light." And reading Theodore Roethke's "The Waking," we put ourselves in a hypnotic iambic state, our breaths and heartbeats doing exactly what the poem tells them to do, "I wake to sleep and take my waking slow. / I learn by going where I have to go." Maybe part of the reason I consider this form so hard to master is that the masters whose villanelles exemplify the form used it in its high church style, and what my ear wants is something more informal, more conversational, more in the style of the mother's nag than of the high priest shaking his fist from his sad height.

What I love about Elizabeth Bishop's "One Art" is that it does just that. With its strong enjambments, heavy caesuras, and softer feminine rhymes, this villanelle has an offhand, conversational rhythm that contrasts sharply with the incantory, end-stopped lines, strong and straight masculine rhymes of the Thomas and Roethke villanelles. If the voice isn't quite a mother's nagging one trying to teach her forgetful daughter the art of mastering losing things, it is definitely a schoolmarm's voice (at least at the start) uttering its little schoolroom maxim. Repeat after me, please, "The art of losing isn't hard to master."

The poem then proceeds to give the writer-teacher and the reader-learner a run for their money. We are about to get a lesson on how it is done, the art of mastering losses, that is, and the villanelle form will serve as the example. This is a form that refuses to lose things: the two A lines of the first stanza are supposed to be repeated throughout intact; the two rhyming sounds echo back at the ends of all nineteen lines, and if the poet wants to indulge the obsessive repetitiveness of the form, he or she can — as Thomas does in his villanelle — repeat with some variation even the beginnings of lines: *wise men, good men, wild men, grave men.*

Against this constraint, this mastery of loss embedded in the villanelle form, Bishop pits the disasters and messiness of the human voice. Its spoken rhythms — complete with asides, corrections of itself: "my last, or next-to-last"; parenthetical phrases: "(*Write* it!)" — threaten to overturn the neat metric and rubric of the form. She begins with obvious control in her first stanza as the full breathy iambic lines unfold with only a slight enjambment in the second line. But by the second stanza and onward, all but the refrain lines have heavy caesuras and strong enjambments so that the usually incantory, controlled meter of a villanelle line is fractured: we feel the voice becoming increasingly harried, on the edge of mastering the losses she speaks of, on the edge of keeping control of the form she is writing in.

The refrain lines, too, demonstrate the struggle to keep control over the losses. Her A1 refrain line stays fiercely intact throughout the poem ("the art of losing isn't hard to master") with one minor alteration in the last stanza that captures with understatement the colossal effort of mastery ("the art of losing's not too hard to master"), but the A2 refrain line is almost "lost" in each stanza: ". . . to be lost that their loss is no disaster"; ". . . to travel. None of these will bring disaster"; "I miss them, but it wasn't a disaster"; ". . . though it may look like (*Write* it!) like disaster." The rhymes are also almost lost a couple of times, but somehow Bishop pulls them off, rhyming "my last, or" with "master". I call these rhymes last-minute rhyme-rescues that bring pleasure to readers because we were sure that this time she would lose it. Also, the feminine rhymes for the A lines create a softer, less-sure rhyme sound that contrasts sharply with the assurance of the masculine rhymes of the B lines. It is almost as if Bishop wanted her readers to see the mastered, strict adherence to form (of the A1 refrain line, of the strict B-line rhymes) next to the play and possibility of loss (the almost-lost A2 refrain line, the softer feminine rhymes). After all, this is a lesson in mastery, not dominance, one that rides the edge all the way. It might be evident by the end of the poem that the art of writing this villanelle isn't *too* hard to master, but a couple of times it did look as if Bishop was headed for disaster.

There is only one art, this one of writing, and there is also only "won art," no freebies. Bishop won this villanelle (as opposed to the form having the upper hand) by writing and righting the losses she speaks of. It is her joking voice that I love, her seemingly offhand gesture of tossing off line after line. In back of this conversational, spoken voice is all the hard work of mastery, the struggle for control, losses mastered by practice.

With "One Art," Bishop provides a model of how to master a form, the villanelle. She also provides a model for writers of how to deal with our losses by writing about them.

ༀ

ARISTOTLE *wrote the* Poetics, *one of the earliest discussions of the work of poets, in pre-Christian Athens, the same era in which Plato wrote his dialogues. Already the works of Homer were considered the standard against which dramatic writing should be judged. It should be noted that in this excerpt from his longer work, Aristotle describes poetry as something that will be performed on a stage. In his day only a handful of members of the society were literate, and poetry was considered an oral art.*

ARISTOTLE

"The poet himself ought to speak the least of all"

c. 330 B.C.

TRANSLATED BY KENNETH A. TELFORD

Of that which is descriptive and imitates in meter, it is evident that the plot, as in tragedy, ought to be constructed dramatically and be of a single action which is whole and complete and which has a beginning, middle, and end, in order that it produce, like a single, whole animal, its appropriate pleasure. And it ought not to put down anything similar to our customary histories, in which, of necessity, it is not a single action which is made evident, but a single time and whatever happens in that time, to one character or many, each incident being related to the others as it happened. For just as the sea-fight at Salamis and the battle with the Carthaginians in Sicily arose at the same time, yet were not exerted to the same end, so also in a succession of time some incidents arise after others with no one end arising. Yet this is what most poets do in their poems. On this account, as we have already mentioned, in comparison with the others Homer appears divinely inspired in not attempting to make a poem of the whole war, though indeed, it had a beginning and an end. For it would have been too great and not easily seen together, or if moderated in respect of magnitude, it would have been too complicated in the variety of its incidents. As it is, while taking only one part of the war, he uses many episodes from other parts, e.g., the catalogue of ships and other episodes, to diversify his making. The others make their epics about one man, or one time, or an action which, though one, has many parts, e.g., those who made *The Cypria* and *The Little Iliad*. Accordingly, only one or two tragedies are to be made from either the *Iliad* or the *Odyssey*, while many are to be made from *The Cypria*; and from *The Little Iliad* there have been more than eight: *The Judgment of Arms, Philoktetes, Neoptolemos, Eurypylos, The Begging, The Laconian Women, The Sack of Ilion,* and *The Departure of the Fleet,* as well as *Sinon* and *The Trojan Women.*

Moreover, epic-making ought to have the same forms as those of tragedy (for it will be either simple, complex, of character, or of suffering) as well as the same [formal] parts (excluding the making of melody and spectacle). For epics also ought to have reversals, recognitions, and sufferings. Moreover, thought and diction ought to be beautifully made in epics also. All of these were first and adequately used by Homer, for of his poems the construction of the *Iliad* is simple and of suffering, while that of the *Odyssey* is complex (since there is recognition through the whole of it) and of character, and in addition to this he surpasses all others in diction and thought.

Epic-making differs from tragedy in the length of its construction and in its meter. Now what we have already mentioned is an adequate limit to length, for it ought to be possible to see the beginning and the end together. This will be so if the constructions of epics have less length than those of the ancients yet are as long as the number of tragedies put alongside one another at one hearing. In regard to extending its magnitude there is a great advantage which is proper to epic-making, because in tragedy one may not imitate many parts being done at the same time, but only that part which is on the stage and belongs to the performers, while in epic-making, because it is descriptive, one may make many parts achieved at once, and these, if appropriate, increase the mass of the poem. With a view to magnificence, changing [the attention of] the hearer, and introducing dissimilar episodes this is a good, for it is the sameness of the incidents which, by quickly satisfying the hearer, makes tragedies fail.

Trial has shown that for epic the suitable meter is the heroic. For if one were to produce a descriptive imitation in any other meter, or in many meters, the lack of fitness would be apparent. For the heroic is the most stately and massive of meters, and on this account it admits of foreign names and metaphors more than any other, for descriptive imitation is extravagant in comparison with others. Iambic and tetrameter, on the other hand, are meters of motion, the latter involved in dancing, the former in acting. Moreover, it would be even more absurd if one were to mix meters as did Chairemon. On this account no one has produced a long poetic construction in any other meter than the heroic. Rather, as we expressed above, nature itself teaches us the suitable meter to pick.

BERNARD BERGONZI *published this examination of Hopkins's poem in 1977. It was included in a chapter aptly titled "Nearly Hard Poems' King," an anagram that poet Roy Fuller made of the letters of Hopkins's name.*

BERNARD BERGONZI

On Hopkins's "The Windhover"   1977

Even the most selective remarks about the 1877 sonnets cannot ignore "The Windhover," which is probably the most famous, and certainly the most discussed and explicated. It is a magnificent poem, where Hopkins writes with unparallelled assurance and boldness, prosodically, lexically, and syntactically. The octet provides a superb mimetic sense of the bird's freedom and mastery on the wing. This much is generally recognized. Nevertheless, the poem has provoked a great deal of argument, not so much concerned with the refinements of interpretation as with establishing the basic sense of the words. This is largely because of the disabling ambiguity at a crucial point in the poem's development: "buckle" at the beginning of the twelfth line. As everyone knows, "buckle" has two senses, and they are opposed and irreconcilable, not mutually enriching. Hopkins, like other poets, enjoyed ambiguities and the multiple associations of words. But he also knew what he wanted to say, and I believe that he did not always realise the confusion he was causing by the insufficiently considered use of a simple noun with several meanings and no clue from the context. I have already referred to "World's strand, sway of the Sea" in the third line of "The Wreck of the *Deutschland*," and there is another example in "God's Grandeur," in the phrase "shining from shook foil." This could refer to a sword used in fencing, or to fine sheet metal, and either might be appropriate. In fact, we know what Hopkins intended because he told Bridges firmly enough: "I mean foil in its sense of leaf or tinsel, and no other word whatever will give the effect I want." Even the most unabashed anti-intentionalist cannot quite ignore such testimony. It is probable that, if asked, Hopkins would have been equally sure which sense of "buckle" he intended, but in the lack of similar evidence speculation has continued. "Buckle" in the sense of "fasten together" gives the sestet, and hence the whole poem, a significantly different meaning from "buckle" in the sense of "give way under pressure." I now refer to the masterly and, I think, conclusive discussion of this crux in Professor Schneider's book. She sweeps aside the idea that both meanings can somehow be accommodated under the banner of "ambiguity":

> To observe that such-and-such a word — *buckle* it is in *The Windhover*
> — or this line or that image may mean either *x* or *y* and to conclude
> without more ado that it therefore means both is to ignore the requirement of *meaningful* reconciliation, which occurs only if something
> within the poem transforms *x* and *y* together into a *z*, or when a new

enrichment of meaning *x* is produced by the presence of meaning *y*. Otherwise one is merely seeing double.[1]

(One might, of course, read the poem in a Structuralist way as an inexhaustibly "open" text, hospitable to all possible meanings, no matter how contradictory; but only at the cost of intellectual frivolity.) Professor Schneider gives very convincing reasons for reading "buckle" as "collapse" or "give way under pressure." In her reading the sense of the sestet is that all the natural qualities associated with the falcon ("Brute beauty and valour and act . . ."), splendid and praiseworthy though they are, must give way ("buckle") in the face of the far lovelier fire that breaks from "my chevalier," Christ our Lord, who is directly addressed in line 11. Professor Schneider also persuades me to read "plough" as "plough-land," the sense in which it is used in "Pied Beauty," which clears up the other troublesome crux of the poem. One then reads the words, "sheer plod makes plough down sillion / Shine," as referring to the way in which the earth gleams when broken open in the act of ploughing, a phenomenon noticed in Hopkins's journal. In short, humble actions can produce a sudden unexpected beauty, just as dull embers can break open to reveal "gold-vermillion" fire. Such lowly achievements are characteristic of human endeavour, in contrast to the spectacular freedom of the brute creation exemplified by the bird. There is still room for subtleties of interpretation, but I follow Professor Schneider in believing that the sestet is a transformation of the experience of the octet, representing a movement from, or through, the physical to the spiritual; or from the natural to the human-and-divine.

ಜಿ

ELIZABETH BISHOP *was a young student, just beginning to write poetry, when she met Marianne Moore. They became lifelong friends, and Bishop wrote this affectionate memoir of their long relationship.*

ELIZABETH BISHOP

Efforts of Affection: A Memoir of Marianne Moore — 1983

In the first edition of Marianne Moore's *Collected Poems* of 1951 there is a poem originally called "Efforts and Affection." In my copy of this book, Marianne crossed out the "and" and wrote "of" above it. I liked this change very much, and so I am giving the title "Efforts of Affection" to the whole piece.

I first met Marianne Moore in the spring of 1934 when I was a senior at Vassar College, through Miss Fanny Borden, the college librarian. A school friend and the friend's mother, both better read and more sophisticated in

---

[1] Elisabeth W. Schneider, *The Dragon in the Gate* (Berkeley: University of California Press, 1968), p. 147.

their literary tastes than I was, had told me about Marianne Moore's poetry several years earlier. I had already read every poem of Miss Moore's I could find, in back copies of *The Dial,*° "little magazines," and anthologies in the college library. I hadn't known poetry could be like that; I took to it immediately, but although I knew there was a volume of hers called *Observations,* it was not in the library and I had never seen it.

Because Miss Borden seems like such an appropriate person to have introduced me to Marianne Moore, I want to say a little about her. She was the niece of the Fall River Lizzie Borden,° and at college the rumor was that Lizzie Borden's lurid career had had a permanently subduing effect on Miss Fanny Borden's personality. She was extremely shy and reserved and spoke in such a soft voice it was hard to hear her at all. She was tall and thin; she always dressed in browns and grays, old-fashioned, muted, and distinguished-looking. She also rode a chainless bicycle. I remember watching her ride slowly up to the library, seated very high and straight on this curiosity, which somehow seemed more lady-like than a bicycle with a chain, and park it in the rack. (We didn't padlock bicycles then.) Once, after she had gone inside, I examined the bicycle, which was indeed chainless, to see if I could figure out how it worked. I couldn't. Contact with the librarian was rare; once in a long while, in search of a book, one would be sent into Miss Borden's office, shadowy and cave-like, with books piled everywhere. She weighed down the papers on her desk with smooth, round stones, quite big stones, brought from the seashore, and once when my roommate admired one of these, Miss Borden said in her almost inaudible voice, "Do you like it? You may *have* it," and handed it over, gray, round, and very heavy.

One day I was sent in to Miss Borden's office about a book, I no longer remember what. We continued talking a little, and I finally got up my courage to ask her why there was no copy of *Observations* by that wonderful poet Marianne Moore in the Vassar library. She looked ever so gently taken aback and inquired, "Do you *like* Marianne Moore's poems?" I said I certainly did, the few I'd been able to find. Miss Borden then said calmly, "I've known her since she was a little girl," and followed that with the question that was possibly to influence the whole course of my life: "Would you like to meet her?" I was painfully — no, excruciatingly — shy and I had run away many times rather than face being introduced to adults of much less distinction than Marianne Moore, but I immediately said, "Yes." Miss Borden said that she would write to Miss Moore, who lived in Brooklyn, and also that she would be glad to lend me *her* copy of *Observations.*

Miss Borden's copy of *Observations* was an eye-opener in more ways than one. Poems like "An Octopus," about a glacier, or "Peter," about a cat, or "Marriage," about marriage, struck me, as they still do, as miracles of language and construction. Why had no one ever written about things in this clear and dazzling way before? But at the same time I was astonished to discover that Miss Borden (whom I now knew to be an old family friend of the

---

The Dial: Literary magazine of the 1920s. **Lizzie Borden:** New England woman who was tried and acquitted for the ax murders of her father and stepmother.

Moores) obviously didn't share my liking for these poems. Tucked in the back of the book were quite a few reviews that had appeared when *Observations* was published, in 1924, and most of these were highly unfavorable, some simply obtuse. There was even a parody Moore poem by Franklin P. Adams. Even more revealing, Miss Borden hadn't seen fit to place a copy of her friend's book in the college library. (Later that year I found a copy for myself, on a secondhand-book table at Macy's.)

The day came when Miss Borden told me that she had heard from Miss Moore and that Miss Moore was willing to meet me in New York, on a Saturday afternoon. Years later I discovered that Marianne had agreed to do this with reluctance; in the past, it seems, dear Miss Borden had sent several Vassar girls to meet Miss Moore and sometimes her mother as well, and every one had somehow failed to please. This probably accounted for the conditions laid down for our first rendezvous: I was to find Miss Moore seated on the bench at the right of the door leading to the reading room of the New York Public Library. They might have been even more strict. I learned later that if Miss Moore really expected *not* to like would-be acquaintances, she arranged to meet them at the Information Booth in Grand Central Station — no place to sit down, and, if necessary, an instant getaway was possible. In the meantime, I had been told a little more about her by Miss Borden, who described her as a child, a strange and appealing little creature with bright red hair — playful, and, as might have been expected, fond of calling her family and friends by the names of animals.

I was very frightened, but I put on my new spring suit and took the train to New York. I had never seen a picture of Miss Moore; all I knew was that she had red hair and usually wore a wide-brimmed hat. I expected the hair to be bright red and for her to be tall and intimidating. I was right on time, even a bit early, but she was there before me (no matter how early one arrived, Marianne was always there first) and, I saw at once, not very tall and not in the least intimidating. She was forty-seven, an age that seemed old to me then, and her hair was mixed with white to a faint rust pink, and her rust-pink eyebrows were frosted with white. The large flat black hat was as I'd expected it to be. She wore a blue tweed suit that day and, as she usually did then, a man's "polo shirt," as they were called, with a black bow at the neck. The effect was quaint, vaguely Bryn Mawr 1909, but stylish at the same time. I sat down and she began to talk.

It seems to me that Marianne talked to me steadily for the next thirty-five years, but of course that is nonsensical. I was living far from New York many of those years and saw her at long intervals. She must have been one of the world's greatest talkers: entertaining, enlightening, fascinating, and memorable; her talk, like her poetry, was quite different from anyone else's in the world. I don't know what she talked about at that first meeting; I wish I had kept a diary. Happily ignorant of the poor Vassar girls before who hadn't passed muster, I began to feel less nervous and even spoke some myself. I had what may have been an inspiration, I don't know — at any rate, I attribute my great good fortune in having known Marianne as a friend in part to it. Ringling Bros. and Barnum & Bailey Circus was making its spring visit to New

York and I asked Miss Moore (we called each other "Miss" for over two years) if she would care to go to the circus with me the Saturday after next. I didn't know that she *always* went to the circus, wouldn't have missed it for anything, and when she accepted, I went back to Poughkeepsie in the grimy day coach extremely happy.

THE CIRCUS

I got to Madison Square Garden very early — we had settled on the hour because we wanted to see the animals before the show began — but Marianne was there ahead of me. She was loaded down: two blue cloth bags, one on each arm, and two huge brown paper bags, full of something. I was given one of these. They contained, she told me, stale brown bread for the elephants, because stale brown bread was one of the things they liked best to eat. (I later suspected that they might like stale white bread just as much but that Marianne had been thinking of their health.) As we went in and down to the lower level, where we could hear (and smell) the animals, she told me her preliminary plan for the circus. Her brother, Warner, had given her an elephant-hair bracelet, of which she was very fond, two or three strands of black hairs held together with gold clasps. One of the elephant hairs had fallen out and been lost. As I probably knew, elephant hairs grow only on the tops of the heads of very young elephants. In her bag, Marianne had a pair of strong nail scissors. I was to divert the adult elephants with the bread, and, if we were lucky, the guards wouldn't observe her at the end of the line where the babies were, and she could take out her scissors and snip a few hairs from a baby's head, to repair her bracelet.

She was quite right; the elephants adored stale brown bread and started trumpeting and pushing up against each other to get it. I stayed at one end of the line, putting slices of bread into the trunks of the older elephants, and Miss Moore went rapidly down to the other end, where the babies were. The large elephants were making such a to-do that a keeper did come up my way, and out of the corner of my eye I saw Miss Moore leaning forward over the rope on tiptoe, scissors in hand. Elephant hairs are tough; I thought she would never finish her haircutting. But she did, and triumphantly we handed out the rest of the bread and set off to see the other animals. She opened her bag and showed me three or four coarse, grayish hairs in a piece of Kleenex.

I hate seeing animals in cages, especially small cages, and especially circus animals, but I think that Marianne, while probably feeling the same way, was so passionately interested in them, and knew so much about them, that she could put aside any pain or outrage for the time being. That day I remember that one handsomely patterned snake, writhing about in a glass-walled cage, seemed to raise his head on purpose to look at us. "See, he knows me!" said Miss Moore. "He remembers me from last year." This was a joke, I decided, but perhaps not altogether a joke. Then we went upstairs and the six-ring affair began. The blue bags held our refreshments: Thermos jugs of orange juice, hard-boiled eggs (the yolks only), and more brown bread, but fresh this time, and buttered. I also remember of this first visit to the circus (there were to be others) that in front of us sat a father with three young children, two boys and a girl. A big circus goes on for a long time and the children began to grow restless. Marianne leaned over with the abruptness that characterized all her movements and said to the father that if the little girl wanted to go to the bathroom, she'd be glad to take her.

ဢ

CLEANTH BROOKS JR. *and* ROBERT PENN WARREN *(the literary critic and the American poet) discussed in their groundbreaking textbook* Understanding Poetry *(1938) T. S. Eliot's major early poem from the perspective of the New Criticism, an approach that emphasizes close reading of the formal properties of literary works.*

CLEANTH BROOKS JR.
AND ROBERT PENN WARREN

On Eliot's "The Love Song of J. Alfred Prufrock" 1938

The character of Prufrock, as we shall see, is really very much like that of Hamlet — a man who is apparently betrayed by his possession of such qualities as intellect and imagination. But it is particularly dangerous to attempt to portray, and make the audience believe in and take seriously, such a person as Prufrock. We are inclined to laugh at the person who is really so painfully self-conscious that he is inhibited from all action. Moreover, in so far as the poet is using Prufrock as a character typical of our age, he must in fairness to truth avoid treating him quite so heroically as a Hamlet. At the very beginning, therefore, the poet faces a difficult problem. In using the materials of the present, the desire to be accurate, to be thoroughly truthful, forces him to exhibit the character as not purely romantic or tragic. And yet there is in such a person as he describes a very real tragedy. How shall he treat him? To attempt to treat Prufrock in full seriousness is doomed to failure; on the other hand, to make him purely comic is to falsify matters too.

Faced with this problem, the poet resorts to irony, and by employing varying shades of irony he is able to do justice to the ludicrous elements in the situation and yet do justice to the serious ones also. The casual and careless reader will probably see only the comic aspects: he will be likely to fail to appreciate the underlying seriousness of the whole poem.

The title itself gives us the first clue to the fact that the poem is ironical. We think of a love song as simple and full of warm emotion. But this poem opens on a scene where the streets

> . . . follow like an argument
> Of insidious intent
> To lead you to an overwhelming question. . . .

One notices also that the character Prufrock is continually interested in stating that "there will be time" to make up his mind. But in saying that there will be time for this, he is so hopelessly unable to act that he continues in a sort of abstracted and unconscious patter to state that there will be time

> For the yellow smoke that slides along the street,
> Rubbing its back upon the windowpanes;
> There will be time, there will be time
> To prepare a face to meet the faces that you meet;
> There will be time to murder and create,
> And time for all the works and days of hands
> That lift and drop a question on your plate.

Then, caught up by the irrelevance of his patter, he goes on to say that there will be time — not for decisions — but, ironically, for a "hundred indecisions," and for a "hundred visions and revisions."

The first part of the poem, then, can be imagined as the monologue of Prufrock himself as he finds his indecisiveness reflected in the apparently aimless streets of the city and in the fog which hangs over the city. It is filled with a rather bitter self-irony, a self-irony which is reflected in some of the abrupt transitions. But in observing this ironical monologue which illuminates the character, one has missed the point entirely if he has failed to see the psychological penetration in it. Take, for example, the tone and associations of the comparison of the evening to a "patient etherized upon a table." This comparison is "in character." It is an appropriate observation for Prufrock, being what he is, though it might not be very appropriate for an entirely different character or in a poem of entirely different tone. The evening — not any evening, but this particular evening, as seen by this particular observer — does seem to have the hushed quiet of the perfectly, and yet fatally relaxed, body of a person under ether.

Or notice also the psychological penetration of the remark, "To prepare a face to meet the faces that you meet." Again, the remark must be taken in character. Yet it is possible to observe, as a general truth, that we do prepare a face, an expression, a look, to meet the various "faces" that we meet — faces which have duly undergone a like preparation. A poorer poet would have written "To put on a mask to meet the people that you meet." Eliot's line with its concentration and its slight ironical shock is far superior. . . .

After the opening sections in which the character of the speaker is to some extent established for the reader, Prufrock describes a scene in which overcultured, bored women sip tea and discuss art. It is as though he had just stepped inside after wandering alone in the streets. Here are the people of whose criticism Prufrock is most afraid, and yet, as his characterization of them abundantly shows, he sees their shallowness. But Prufrock does not attempt to treat romantically or heroically his own character: he is able to see the ludicrous aspect of himself, his timid preciseness and vanity.

> With a bald spot in the middle of my hair —
> (They will say: "How his hair is growing thin.")
> My necktie rich and modest, but asserted by a simple pin.

But what is the function of a statement so abrupt as "I have measured out my life with coffee spoons?" Here again, the line must be taken in character. But if we are willing to take it in character, we shall be able to see that it is brilliantly ironical. It would mean literally, one supposes, that he has measured out his life in little driblets, coffee spoons being tiny in size. But it carries another and more concrete meaning: namely, that he has spent his life in just such an environment as this drawing room which he is describing. The comparison makes the same ironical point, therefore, as the lines

> And time yet for a hundred indecisions,
> And for a hundred visions and revisions,
> Before the taking of a toast and tea.

The poem's sense of fidelity to the whole situation — its willingness to take into account so many apparently discordant views and points of view — is shown in the lines

> Arms that are braceleted and white and bare
> (But in the lamplight, downed with light brown hair!)

These lines give us a contrast between what might be termed loosely the romantic and the realistic attitude. The ironical comment here parallels exactly the reference to his own bald head.

The structure of the poem is, as we have noticed, that of a sort of monologue in which the poet describes this scene or that and comments on them, and, by means of them, on himself. The irrelevance, or apparent irrelevance, is exactly the sort of irrelevance and abrupt transition which is often admired in a personal essay by a writer like Charles Lamb. The structure is essentially the same here (though of course with an entirely different tone and for a different effect). But having seen what the structure is — not a logical structure, or one following the lines of a narrative, or one based on the description of a scene, but the structure of the flow of ideas — the reader is not puzzled at the rather abrupt transition from the stanza about the arms to

> Shall I say, I have gone at dusk through narrow streets,

etc. It is a scene from the beginning of the poem — or perhaps it is a scene viewed earlier and brought back to memory by the statement about the streets and the smoke in the opening lines of the poem. It is the sort of scene which has a very real poignance about it. Prufrock feels that it meant something. But he is utterly incapable of stating the meaning before the bored and sophisticated audience of the world to which he belongs. He would be laughed at as a fool. And then comes the thought — apparently irrelevant, but the sort of thought which might easily occur in such a monologue:

> I should have been a pair of ragged claws
> Scuttling across the floors of silent seas.

A crab is about as vivid a symbol as one might find, for a person who is completely self-sufficing and cannot be, and does not need to be, sociable. And there is, moreover, a secondary implication of irony here growing out of Prufrock's disgust with these people about him and with himself: the crab is at least "alive" and has, as Prufrock does not have, a meaning and a place in its world. (Observe that the poet does not use the word *crab*. Why? Because in mentioning the most prominent feature of the crab, the claws, and with the vivid description of the effect of the crab's swimming, "scuttling," he makes the point more sharply.)

There are several literary allusions in the latter part of the poem, allusions which we must know in order to understand the poem. . . . Can they be justified? And if so, how? In the first place, they are fairly commonly known: an allusion to John the Baptist's head having been cut off at Herod's orders and brought in on a platter; an allusion to the raising of Lazarus from the dead; and a reference to Shakespeare's *Hamlet*. The poet has not imposed a very heavy burden on us, therefore, in expecting that we shall know these references. But what can be said by way of justification? In the first place, all the allusions are "in character." They are comparisons which would normally occur to such a person as Prufrock, and they would naturally occur in the sort of meditation in which he indulges in this poem. In the second place, they do a great deal to sharpen the irony in the poem. Prufrock is vividly conscious of the sorry figure which he cuts in comparison with the various great figures from the past or from literature whom, in a far-off sense, he resembles. He has seen his reputation picked to pieces — his head, a slightly bald head, brought in on a platter like that of John the Baptist. But *he* is no prophet — nothing is lost. Death itself in this society can be regarded as nothing more than a liveried footman, putting on the coats of the departing, and death, like the knowing and insolent footman, is quite capable, he believes, of snickering behind his back.

ജ

SAMUEL CHARTERS's response to Duncan's poem is included in his Some Poems/Poets: Studies in American Underground Poetry *(1971). In this selection, Charters emphasizes the fascination with medievalism that is central to Duncan's poetry.*

SAMUEL CHARTERS

On Robert Duncan's "My Mother Would Be a Falconress"

1971

The title has been changed — to "My Mother Would Be a Falconress" in its collected version — but I think [Robert Duncan] has lost some of the symbolism that was in the original title "Lammas Dream Poem." Lammas? — Anglo-Saxon, from *hlammesse, hlafmaesse*, the loaf Mass, bread feast. *Hlaf* — loaf; *maesse* — Mass. The first day of August, Lammas Day, or the time of year. Duncan wrote in an introduction, ". . . And when I wrote down the hour and date, I saw it was Lammas. 'August 1, 1964,' I wrote: 'Lammas tide, 2 A.M.' " Lammas tide — around Lammas Day. The poem has no involvement with Lammas, but its symbolism is involved with the medieval sport of falconry and the word *Lammas* has an association with the medieval, with the conception of the year in ceremonies and functions.

> My mother would be a falconress
> And I, her gay falcon treading her wrist,
> would fly to bring back
> from the blue of the sky to her, bleeding, a prize.

The medieval pageantry of the falcon, of falconry, as a complex image of his relationship with his mother. It has a distant unreality, but with its entangling image of mother-son, falconress-falcon, an immediate emotional insistence. The cry is heard within us, but from — medieval, richly ornate — a complex involvement of past. A dream-of-poem image, a wakening-within-poem image. Duncan, ". . . I had awakend at two in the night with the lines repeated insistently in my mind." The immediacy of the phrase held the poem's image within it, the whole of the poem implicit in its directions.

What is a falcon concerned with? With his captivity? his captor? his prey? Who knows about falcons? Duncan's falcon has so little to do with the ferocity of the hunting falcon. His falcon has become a child, while still a bird of prey tied to a wrist:

> I dream in my little hood with many bells
> jangling when I'd turn my head

And, childlike, its involvement is with its captor:

> she sends me as far as her will goes.
> She lets me ride to the end of her curb
> where I fall back in anguish.
> I dread that she will cast me away,
> for I fall, I mis-take, I fail in her mission.

How can Duncan achieve an image of such complex physical involvement? To make himself the hawk and the hawk himself. The image has its own strength, and the brilliance of the art — the unity of the language — sustains it. There is something in the image of the son as a young hawk on his mother's wrist — lean, impatient, savage — treading the wrist waiting for the hood to be untied from its eyes — an imagination's vision of the mother-son relationship that opens and extends the reality of that relationship.

The poem moves on as the image shifts, moves from its first subtle implications to its widest circumference of meaning, and it grows as his consciousness of the image grows. At the opening of the poem he places its emphasis on the structured ritual of medieval hawking, but with himself identified as the hawk still tied to the falconer's wrist, himself as the child who must rise from the close fettering of the falconress who has bound him.

> For she has muffled my dreams in the hood she has made me,
> sewn round with bells, jangling when I move
> She uses a barb that brings me to cower.

Even in his brief moments of flight — in the soaring spiral of the hawk as it hunts — it isn't the prey, but still his captor who absorbs him.

> She sends me abroad to try my wings
> and I come back to her. I would bring down

the little birds to her
I may not tear into, I must bring back perfectly.

It is a poem of desperations, of desperate love and as desperate sadness. He must tear himself free, but he will always be entangled in their relationship.

Yet it would have been beautiful, if she had carried me,
always, in a little hood with the bells ringing,
at her wrist, and her riding
to the great falcon hunt, and me
flying up to the curb of my heart from her heart
to bring down the skylark from the blue to her feet,
straining, and then released for the flight.

He has bared them and left them to the implications of their relationship as mother and son.

ಐಐ

SAMUEL CHARTERS's *reading of Snyder's poem as a desert ceremony was included in* Some Poems/Poets: Studies in American Underground Poetry *(1971).*

SAMUEL CHARTERS

On Snyder's "How to Make Stew in the Pinacate Desert"   *1971*

A poem of simplicities — of affecting simplicities — and I am affected by it, as I am by Snyder — and I am uncertain about it, as I am uncertain about Synder. Not uncertain about his effectiveness as a poet — Snyder is brilliant and unmistakable — but I am uncertain of the innocence that could write a poem of the simplicity of "How to Make Stew in the Pinacate Desert." It is an innocence that somehow has the feeling of a stance, an attitude — which would make it not innocent — but his poem, like Snyder, has the feeling of completeness, that the poem, and he, is what it says it is. Within the poem are larger implications, but it is — simply — a recipe for cooking stew in the desert, written for some friends.

A. J. Bayless market bent wire roller basket buy up parsnips, onion,
carrot, rutabaga and potato, bell green pepper,
& nine cuts of dark beef shank.
They run there on their legs, that makes meat tasty.

Almost without art, without guile. The only suggestion of something else in its simplicity is the implied excitement in the movement of the first phrase. "A. J. Bayless market bent wire roller basket . . ." instead of "Go to the A. J. Bayless market . . ." The "bent wire roller basket" is an impression, a glimpse, an image of the market interior, not an elision of "get a bent wire basket . . ." In his hurry, in his excitement, only time for glimpses. But why excitement over cooking a stew? The simplicity is only an immediate face of the poem, an attitude that Snyder is using to direct the poem's movement. And it is a poem, even if it reads like a recipe.

> Seven at night in Tucson, get some bisquick for the dumplings.
> Have some bacon. Go to Hadley's in the kitchen right beside the frying
> steak — Diana on the phone —

It is — also — more than a poem. In its simplicities and immediacies Snyder is describing a ceremony. The definiteness of the directions, the care of the details, for the vegetables, the meat, the times, places, spaces, all the movements of a ceremony. A simple ceremony, but by the act of ceremony itself the levels of meaning have become multiple, the steps of the ceremony followed with the image of their implied meanings. A ceremony for what, to yield what? Ceremonies have a circumference beyond their immediate event that gives even their confusions a larger importance. Even Gary Snyder's ceremony for making beef stew in the desert outside of Tucson, Arizona.

> get a little plastic bag from Drum —
> Fill it up with tarragon and chili; four bay leaves; black pepper corns
> and basil; powdered oregano, something free, maybe about two tea-
> spoons worth of salt.

Snyder's ceremony is like much of his poetry, an attempt to reenact the experience of the natural environment. *Walden* written in a small hand. An American ceremony, affirmed over and over by American writers who, like Snyder, have felt the necessity of continuing this experience. They've thought of it either as a step toward a "true" environment — a positive stance — or as a step away from the "false" environment of the American city — a negative stance. For Snyder the ceremony is a step toward, a positive movement and direction, its affirmation so self-evident that he doesn't even feel the necessity of justifying it. His poetry has had this same clarity of affirmation from his earliest books. *Riprap* has as little artifice as his recipe for stew. The poems — it was his first book — almost completely outlined the spaces that his poetry has filled since. The opening poem, "Mid-August at Sourdough Mountain Lookout," ends,

> I cannot remember things I once read
> A few friends, but they are in cities.
> Drinking cold snow-water from a tin cup
> Looking down for miles
> Through high still air.

Even in a book as early as *Riprap* the innocence was directly and clearly present.

His poetry has this openness, this simplicity, but it also has a fullness, a sense of completeness. Everything in the poems comes out of his involvement with the earth in its deepest sense. In *Riprap* there is the shamanism of "Praise for Sick Women," poems from his loose wandering as a merchant seaman, poems from his life in the mountains of the Pacific Northwest, from his life in

Japan — for the "great stone garden in the sea" — the themes that have continued through his poetry. In all of it is the same innocence — the same guarded distance from the concept of a city and a crowd. Snyder would have liked to live his life as part of a tribe, without a tribe he has had to develop his own rituals toward the earth and its creatures. The years he has spent in Zen studies in Japan could have emphasized the ceremonial in a poem about a desert stew — since so much of the life in a monastery is ceremonial — but it could as well come out of his feeling of the necessity of the tribe and its ritual.

But the poetry still has a confusing element, its certainty is sometimes disquieting. The simplicity, the innocence sometimes has an overtone of obviousness, of insistence. Does Snyder mean it? Is his innocence genuine, despite the obvious complexity of his attitude toward it? Within its small frame even a poem like the stew recipe is insisting on the uniqueness of the wilderness experience, its attitudes — through his own involved feeling of tribe and earth — rooted in the Rousseauist° vision of the romantic primitive, and to its manifestation through the American philosophic ideal of an essential innocence in the wild and the untouched. A long-lived plant with deep roots, a summer sumac with its branches cut away but still growing in its roots and forcing its green swatch of leaf into the afternoon's heat. Thoreau, ranging the same ground, would have stepped further, would have related the ceremony of cooking a desert stew to his own, and intensely personal, philosophy; but Thoreau, without being conscious of it, was less innocent than Snyder. From *Walden,*

> It is hard to provide and cook so simple and clean a diet as will not offend the imagination: but this, I think, is to be fed when we feed the body: they should both sit down at the same table. Yet perhaps this may be done. The fruits eaten temperately need not make us ashamed of our appetites, nor interrupt the worthiest pursuits. But put an extra condiment into your dish, and it will poison you. It is not worth the while to live by rich cookery. Most men would feel shame if caught preparing with their own hands precisely such a dinner, whether of animal or vegetable food, as is every day prepared for them by others. Yet till this is otherwise we are not civilized, and, if gentlemen and ladies, are not true men and women . . .

In a period when nearly everybody made stew in the woods, Thoreau had to do more than list the ingredients and the kind of firewood. Snyder, at a time when very few people make stew in the desert, has only to describe the steps of his simple ceremony.

The innocence that is close to the center of the experience, the consciousness that moves Snyder's poem, is it a true innocence? It seems to have a still breath of naiveté, to be even less involved with the world at the farthest end of the railroad than Thoreau was at his pond. But Snyder's individuality has a complexity of depth and mood. He has come to it from a new concep-

---

Rousseauist: I.e., Jean-Jacques Rousseau (1712–1778), the French philosopher who idealized the innocence of humankind in nature.

tion, the concept of an innocence that builds itself through an awareness of what it has to avoid. A self-chosen innocence. Snyder has sensed that his response to much of what the American environment is forcing in on him has to be an act of rejection. His rejection is so complete that nothing of this response is even present in the poem. Nothing in his description of his stew-making ceremony suggests that he is self-conscious — even self-aware that the simplicity of the poem, in itself, has to be an expression of his own complexity. The poem, for him, is as complete within itself as a piece of stone.

> Now down in Sonora, Pinacate country, build a fire of Ocotillo,
> broken twigs and bits of ironwood, in an open ring of lava: rake
> some coals aside (and if you're smart) to windward,
> keep the other half ablaze for heat and light.
> Set Drum's fourteen-inch dutch oven with three legs across the
> embers.

The care for detail, the insistence on detail, has the same kind of concentration as a paragraph on fire building in a Boy Scout manual — even to the advice about raking the coals aside to windward — and it is as isolated in its implications. There is no movement of thought away from the fire, only movement around it. The fire, like the poem, is complete within itself. There aren't any adjectives, phrases, confusions to the simple act of building it. In its completeness, its lack of implication, it becomes an innocence so intensely felt that — as Snyder knew — it has no need of affirmation. In itself the ceremonial cooking of a stew in the desert is the assertion of innocence. The details become as bare, as sharply outlined in their clarity as the dried brushwood piled on the desert floor.

> Now put in the strips of bacon.
> In another pan have all the vegetables cleaned up and peeled and
> sliced.
> . . .
> add the little bag of herbs — cook it all five minutes more — and then
> throw in the pan of all the rest.
> Cover it up with big hot lid all heavy, sit and wait, or drink budweiser
> beer.

Budweiser beer? Was that what he drank the first time? Does he have to do everything just as he did it the first time? Indian boys, playing, trail each other across the stones and through the dry brush with a trace of a heel or a still-damp spot in a stream bed where a stone was kicked out of the way. Trailing behind to find the place where he has been before, Snyder's poem follows the marks left by bags of herbs, bits of ironwood, and cans of Budweiser beer. It is a place where other American poets have spent long years of their lives — in the dream of wilderness experience — of the relationship of the land and the trees, the sky and earth. To be there, at that place, is enough, without need of description, or perhaps can't be described. At least not by Snyder, whose innocence is complete. An innocence that knows, but denies its knowledge. The moral implication is tangled and obscure, a denial of knowledge as a form of innocence, but he would probably refuse even to consider the implication.

It could be that at this place in the American journey it is the only innocence
left to us.

> And let it cook ten minutes more
> and lift the black pot off the fire
> to set aside another good ten minutes.

As description the poem catches some of the excitement of fending for
food and warmth in the desert night — the "black pot" — blackened by the
smoky sticks used for firewood — the time sitting and waiting for the pot to
cool. And there is no question for him of the reality of the experience — or in
the reality of the innocence of which the experience is an expression. The
poem ends in the stillness of the dwindling fire and the smell of wood smoke
in the night air.

> Dish it up and eat it with a spoon, sitting on a poncho in the dark.

The dishes still have to be washed — or at least some water rinsed in the pot
so it won't be too hard to clean in the morning — and the fire banked in for the
night, but with the stew gone Snyder's small ceremony is over.

৫৩

MARILYN CHIN, *a Chinese American poet, responded to a question about
"the canon" in a 1995 interview. In recent years much discussion has centered on the
canon, the long tradition of literature that has served as the American educational
standard. Some people believe the canon defines U.S. culture; others consider it a fence
that has kept out writing by women and members of cultural minorities.*

MARILYN CHIN

On the Canon
1995

My personal psychology regarding "the canon" is this: To the outer
world I say in a devil-may-care manner "to hell with it." It's a fixed endgame:
There will always be an imperialist, Eurocentric bias. The powers-that-be who
lord over the selection process are and forevermore will be privileged white
male critics. They will decide who will be validated along with Shakespeare
and Milton and the latter-day saints of the like of Keats, Yeats, and Eliot. They
will guard that "canon" jealously with their elaborate "critical" apparatus;
and driven by their own Darwinian instinct to "survive," they will do the best
they can to "exclude" us and to promote their own monolithic vision.

But deep inside me another voice rings resolute. I am a serious poet with
a rich palette and important missive and I shall fight for the survival of my poetry. What I learned from my youth as a marginalized and isolated west coast
Asian American poet is this: It's no fun to be "excluded" . . . . as a matter of fact,
it feels like hell. What is the purpose of spending most of your adult life
hunched in a dark corner perfecting your poems, if your oeuvre will be buried

and forgotten anyway? I don't believe any poet who tells me, "No, baby, I don't give a damn about the canon." I am certain that the very same poet has his little poems all dressed up, organized and alphabetized and locked in a vault to be opened in the next century.

The poet's mission on earth is to inspire and to illuminate; and to leave behind to our glorious descendents an intricate and varied map of humanity. One way to survive is to be like Milton, who sits aloft in the great pantheon in the sky and only a very few self-flagellating geeky scholar/poets could indulge into his knotty points. Another way to survive is to be like Gwendolyn Brooks; I predict that her poem "We Real Cool" will be warm on schoolchildren's lips forever. To survive is to be like Langston Hughes, whose poem "A Raisin in the Sun" inspired the young playwright Lorraine Hansberry to write a masterpiece bearing that same name. The true test of "validation" is when one's poems can serve as inspirational models and guiding spirits for a younger generation. We must survive! We must fight to be included in "the canon," so that our voices will sing through history and the global consciousness in eternal echoes. And I'll be damned if I'm going to miss out on THAT out-of-the-body experience!

৩৫

ROBERT CREELEY *is one of the many contemporary poets who have continued to respond to the dimensions of Walt Whitman's achievement even when, in Creeley's case, it was a response that came to him late. As he writes, when he was a student it was the fashion to dismiss Whitman for his grandiosity and his optimism. This excerpt is from Creeley's introduction to a selection of Whitman's work included in a modern anthology.*

ROBERT CREELEY

On Whitman's Poetry

1973

One of the most lovely insistences in Whitman's poems seems to me his instruction that one speak for oneself. Assumedly that would be the person most involved in saying anything and yet a habit of "objective" statement argues the contrary, noting the biases and distortions and tediums of the personal that are thereby invited into the writing. Surely there is some measure possible, such would say, that can make statement a clearly defined and impersonal instance of reality, of white clouds in a blue sky, of things and feelings not distorted by any fact of one man or woman's intensive possession of them. Then there would truly be a common possibility, that all might share, and that no one would have use of more than another.

Yet if Whitman has taught me anything, and he has taught me a great deal, often against my own will, it is that the common *is* personal, intensely so, in that having no one thus to invest it, the sea becomes a curious mixture of water and table salt and the sky the chemical formula for air. It is, paradoxically, the personal which makes the common in so far as it recognizes the existence of the many in the one. In my own joy or despair, I am brought to that which others have also experienced.

My own senses of Whitman were curiously numb until I was thirty. In the forties, when I was in college, it was considered literally bad taste to have an active interest in his writing. In that sense he suffered the same fate as Wordsworth, also condemned as overly prolix and generalizing. There was a persistent embarrassment that this naively affirmative poet might affect one's own somewhat cynical wisdoms. Too, in so far as this was a time of intensively didactic criticism, what was one to do with Whitman, even if one read him? He went on and on, he seemed to lack "structure," he yielded to no "critical apparatus" then to hand. So, as students, we were herded past him as quickly as possible, and our teachers used him only as an example of "the America of that period" which, we were told, was a vast swamp of idealistic expansion and corruption. Whitman, the dupe, the dumb-bell, the pathetically regrettable instance of this country's dream and despair, the self-taught man.

That summation of Whitman and his work was a very comfortable one for all concerned. If I felt at times awkward with it, I had only to turn to Ezra Pound, whom the university also condemned, to find that he too disapproved despite the begrudging "Pact." At least he spoke of having "detested" Whitman, only publicly altering the implications of that opinion in a series of BBC interviews made in the late fifties. William Carlos Williams also seemed to dislike him, decrying the looseness of the writing, as he felt it, and the lack of a coherent prosody. He as well seemed to change his mind in age in so far as he referred to Whitman as the greatest of American poets in a public lecture on American poetry for college students. Eliot also changes his mind, as did James before him, but the point is that the heroes of my youth as well as my teachers were almost without exception extremely critical of Whitman and his influence and wanted as little as possible to do with him.

Two men, however, most dear to me, felt otherwise. The first of these was D. H. Lawrence, whose *Studies in Classic American Literature* remains the most extraordinary apprehension of the nature of American experience and writing that I know. His piece on Whitman in that book is fundamental in that he, in a decisively personal manner, first castigates Whitman for what he considers a muddling assumption of "oneness," citing "I am he that aches with amorous love . . . ." as particularly offensive, and then, with equal intensity, applauds that Whitman who is, as he puts it, "a great charger of the blood in men," a truly heroic poet whose vision and will make a place of absolute communion for others.

The second, Hart Crane, shared with Whitman my own teachers' disapproval. I remember a course which I took with F. O. Mathiessen, surely a man of deep commitment and care for his students, from which Crane had been absented. I asked for permission to give a paper on Crane, which he gave me, but I had overlooked what I should have realized would be the response of the class itself, understandably intent upon its own sophistications. How would they accept these lines, for example?

> yes, Walt,
> Afoot again, and onward without halt, —
> Not soon, nor suddenly, — no, never to let go
>   My hand
>   in yours,
>   Walt Whitman —
>   so —

If they did not laugh outright at what must have seemed to them the awkwardly stressed rhymes and sentimental camaraderie, then they tittered at
Crane's will to be one with his fellow *homosexual*. But didn't they hear, I
wanted to insist, the pacing of the rhythms of those lines, the syntax, the intently human tone, or simply the punctuation? Couldn't they read? Was Crane
to be simply another "crudity" they could so glibly be rid of? But still I myself
didn't read Whitman, more than the few poems of his that were "dealt with"
in classes or that some friend asked me to. No doubt I too was embarrassed by
my aunt's and my grandmother's ability to recite that terrible poem, "O Captain! My Captain!," banal as I felt it to be, and yet what was that specious taste
which could so distract any attention and could righteously dismiss so much
possibility, just because it didn't "like" it? Sadly, it was too much my own.

ॐ

RITA DOVE, *whose recent collection* Mother Love *(1995) is written mostly
in sonnet form, discusses the traditional verse form in the following excerpt from her
introduction.*

RITA DOVE

An Intact World   1995

"Sonnet" literally means "little song." The sonnet is a *heile Welt*, an intact
world where everything is in sync, from the stars down to the tiniest mite on
a blade of grass. And if the "true" sonnet reflects the music of the spheres, it
then follows that any variation from the strictly Petrarchan or Shakespearean
forms represents a world gone awry.

Or does it? Can't form also be a talisman against disintegration? The
sonnet defends itself against the vicissitudes of fortune by its charmed structure, its beautiful bubble. All the while, though, chaos is lurking outside the
gate.

The ancient story of Demeter and Persephone is just such a tale of a violated world. It is a modern dilemma as well — there comes a point when a
mother can no longer protect her child, when the daughter must go her own
way into womanhood. Persephone, out picking flowers with her girlfriends,
wanders off from the group. She has just stooped to pluck a golden narcissus,
when the earth opens and Hades emerges, dragging her down with him into
the Underworld. Inconsolable in her grief, Demeter neglects her duties as

goddess of agriculture, and the crops wither. The Olympians disapprove of the abduction but are more shaken by Demeter's reaction, her refusal to return to her godly work in defiance of the laws of nature; she's even left her throne in Olympus and taken to wandering about on earth disguised as a mortal. In varying degrees she is admonished or pitied by the other gods for the depth of her grief. She refuses to accept her fate, however; she strikes out against the Law, forcing Zeus to ask his brother Hades to return Persephone to her mother. Hades agrees.

But ah, can we ever really go back home, as if nothing had happened? Before returning to the surface, the girl eats a few pomegranate seeds, not realizing that anyone who partakes of the food of the dead cannot be wholly restored to the living. So she must spend half of each year at Hades' side, as Queen of the Underworld, and her mother must acquiesce: Every fall and winter Demeter is permitted to grieve for the loss of her daughter, letting vegetation wilt and die, but she is obliged to act cheerful in spring and summer, making the earth blossom and bear fruit.

Sonnets seemed the proper mode for most of [the poems in *Mother Love*] — and not only in homage and as counterpoint to Rilke's° *Sonnets to Orpheus*. Much has been said about the many ways to "violate" the sonnet in the service of American speech or modern love or whatever; I will simply say that I like how the sonnet comforts even while its prim borders (but what a pretty fence!) are stultifying; one is constantly bumping up against Order. The Demeter/Persephone cycle of betrayal and regeneration is ideally suited for this form since all three — mother-goddess, daughter-consort, and poet — are struggling to sing in their chains.

ಌ

T. S. ELIOT *first published his essay discussing literary tradition in the Lon don magazine* The Egoist *in 1919. He included it in his collection* The Sacred Wood *the following year.*

T. S. ELIOT

From "Tradition and the Individual Talent"

I

In English writing we seldom speak of tradition, though we occasionally apply its name in deploring its absence. We cannot refer to "the tradition" or to "a tradition"; at most, we employ the adjective in saying that the poetry of so-and-so is "traditional" or even "too traditional." Seldom, perhaps, does the word appear except in a phrase of censure. If otherwise, it is vaguely appro-

---

Rilke's: I.e., the German poet Rainer Maria Rilke (1875–1926).

bative, with the implication, as to the work approved, of some pleasing archaeological reconstruction. You can hardly make the word agreeable to English ears without this comfortable reference to the reassuring science of archaeology.

Certainly the word is not likely to appear in our appreciations of living or dead writers. Every nation, every race, has not only its own creative, but its own critical turn of mind; and is even more oblivious of the shortcomings and limitations of its critical habits than of those of its creative genius. We know, or think we know, from the enormous mass of critical writing that has appeared in the French language the critical method or habit of the French; we only conclude (we are such unconscious people) that the French are "more critical" than we, and sometimes even plume ourselves a little with the fact, as if the French were the less spontaneous. Perhaps they are; but we might remind ourselves that criticism is as inevitable as breathing, and that we should be none the worse for articulating what passes in our minds when we read a book and feel an emotion about it, for criticizing our own minds in their work of criticism. One of the facts that might come to light in this process is our tendency to insist, when we praise a poet, upon those aspects of his work in which he least resembles any one else. In these aspects or parts of his work we pretend to find what is individual, what is the peculiar essence of the man. We dwell with satisfaction upon the poet's difference from his predecessors, especially his immediate predecessors; we endeavour to find something that can be isolated in order to be enjoyed. Whereas if we approach a poet without this prejudice we shall often find that not only the best, but the most individual parts of his work may be those in which the dead poets, his ancestors, assert their immortality most vigorously. And I do not mean the impressionable period of adolescence, but the period of full maturity.

Yet if the only form of tradition, of handing down, consisted in following the ways of the immediate generation before us in a blind or timid adherence to its successes, "tradition" should positively be discouraged. We have seen many such simple currents soon lost in the sand; and novelty is better than repetition. Tradition is a matter of much wider significance. It cannot be inherited, and if you want it you must obtain it by great labour. It involves, in the first place, the historical sense, which we may call nearly indispensable to any one who would continue to be a poet beyond his twenty-fifth year; and the historical sense involves a perception, not only of the pastness of the past, but of its presence; the historical sense compels a man to write not merely with his own generation in his bones, but with a feeling that the whole of the literature of Europe from Homer and within it the whole of the literature of his own country has a simultaneous existence and composes a simultaneous order. This historical sense, which is a sense of the timeless as well as of the temporal and of the timeless and of the temporal together, is what makes a writer traditional. And it is at the same time what makes a writer most acutely conscious of his place in time, of his own contemporaneity.

No poet, no artist of any art, has his complete meaning alone. His significance, his appreciation is the appreciation of his relation to the dead poets and artists. You cannot value him alone; you must set him, for contrast and comparison, among the dead. I mean this as a principle of aesthetic, not merely historical, criticism. The necessity that he shall conform, that he shall cohere, is not onesided; what happens when a new work of art is created is something that happens simultaneously to all the works of art which preceded it. The existing monuments form an ideal order among themselves, which is modified by the introduction of the new (the really new) work of art among them. The existing order is complete before the new work arrives; for order to persist after the supervention of novelty, the *whole* existing order must be, if ever so slightly, altered; and so the relations, proportions, values of each work of art toward the whole are readjusted; and this is conformity between the old and the new. Whoever has approved this idea of order, of the form of European, of English literature will not find it preposterous that the past should be altered by the present as much as the present is directed by the past. And the poet who is aware of this will be aware of great difficulties and responsibilities.

In a peculiar sense he will be aware also that he must inevitably be judged by the standards of the past. I say judged, not amputated, by them; not judged to be as good as, or worse or better than, the dead; and certainly not judged by the canons of dead critics. It is a judgment, a comparison, in which two things are measured by each other. To conform merely would be for the new work not really to conform at all; it would not be new, and would therefore not be a work of art. And we do not quite say that the new is more valuable because it fits in; but its fitting in is a test of its value — a test, it is true, which can only be slowly and cautiously applied, for we are none of us infallible judges of conformity. We say: it appears to conform, and is perhaps individual, or it appears individual, and many conform; but we are hardly likely to find that it is one and not the other.

To proceed to a more intelligible exposition of the relation of the poet to the past: he can neither take the past as a lump, an indiscriminate bolus,° nor can he form himself wholly on one or two private admirations, nor can he form himself wholly upon one preferred period. The first course is inadmissible, the second is an important experience of youth, and the third is a pleasant and highly desirable supplement. The poet must be very conscious of the main current, which does not at all flow invariably through the most distinguished reputations. He must be quite aware of the obvious fact that art never improves, but that the material of art is never quite the same. He must be aware that the mind of Europe — the mind of his own country — a mind which he learns in time to be much more important than his own private mind — is a mind which changes, and that this change is a development which abandons nothing *en route*, which does not superannuate either Shakespeare, or Homer, or the rock drawing of the Magdalenian draughtsmen.° That this development, refinement perhaps, complication certainly, is not, from the point of view of the artist, any improvement. Perhaps not even an improve-

---

bolus: A large pill. **Magdalenian draughtsmen:** The artists of the Paleolithic period who drew on cave walls in La Madeleine, in the south of France.

ment from the point of view of the psychologist or not to the extent which we imagine; perhaps only in the end based upon a complication in economics and machinery. But the difference between the present and the past is that the conscious present is an awareness of the past in a way and to an extent which the past's awareness of itself cannot show.

Some one said: "The dead writers are remote from us because we *know* so much more than they did." Precisely, and they are that which we know.

I am alive to a usual objection to what is clearly part of my programme for the *métier*° of poetry. The objection is that the doctrine requires a ridiculous amount of erudition (pedantry), a claim which can be rejected by appeal to the lives of poets in any pantheon. It will even be affirmed that much learning deadens or perverts poetic sensibility. While, however, we persist in believing that a poet ought to know as much as will not encroach upon his necessary receptivity and necessary laziness, it is not desirable to confine knowledge to whatever can be put into a useful shape for examinations, drawing-rooms, or the still more pretentious modes of publicity. Some can absorb knowledge, the more tardy must sweat for it. Shakespeare acquired more essential history from Plutarch° than most men could from the whole British Museum. What is to be insisted upon is that the poet must develop or procure the consciousness of the past and that he should continue to develop this consciousness throughout his career.

What happens is a continual surrender of himself as he is at the moment to something which is more valuable. The progress of an artist is a continual self-sacrifice, a continual extinction of personality.

తిం

T. S. ELIOT, *the modernist poet was a traditionalist in his literary tastes, and it is not surprising that he was uncomfortable with some of what he felt were eccentricities in William Blake's life and work. Eliot found Blake's poetry to be profoundly free and innocent, however, even if he was honest enough to admit that Blake's freedom from what Eliot called "current opinion" was "terrifying." Eliot's essay was first published in 1930.*

T. S. ELIOT

From "William Blake" 1930

If one follows Blake's mind through the several stages of his poetic development it is impossible to regard him as a naïf, a wild man, a wild pet for the supercultivated. The strangeness is evaporated, the peculiarity is seen to be the peculiarity of all great poetry: something which is found (not everywhere) in Homer and Aeschylus and Dante and Villon, and profound and

---

Métier: French for "art" or "craft." **Plutarch:** Greek writer (c. 46–119?) whose work was used by Shakespeare as a source for his plays.

concealed in the work of Shakespeare — and also in another form in Montaigne and in Spinoza. It is merely a peculiar honesty, which, in a world too frightened to be honest, is peculiarly terrifying. It is an honesty against which the whole world conspires because it is unpleasant. Blake's poetry has the unpleasantness of great poetry. Nothing that can be called morbid or abnormal or perverse, none of the things which exemplify the sickness of an epoch or a fashion, have this quality; only those things which, by some extraordinary labour of simplification, exhibit the essential sickness or strength of the human soul. And this honesty never exists without great technical accomplishment. The question about Blake the man is the question of the circumstances that concurred to permit this honesty in his work, and what circumstances define its limitations. The favouring conditions probably include these two: that, being early apprenticed to a manual occupation, he was not compelled to acquire any other education in literature than he wanted, or to acquire it for any other reason than that he wanted it; and that, being a humble engraver, he had no journalistic-social career open to him.

There was, that is to say, nothing to distract him from his interests or to corrupt these interests: neither the ambitions of parents or wife, nor the standards of society, nor the temptations of success; nor was he exposed to imitation of himself or of any one else. These circumstances — not his supposed inspired and untaught spontaneity — are what make him innocent. His early poems show what the poems of a boy of genius ought to show, immense power of assimilation. Such early poems are not, as usually supposed, crude attempts to do something beyond the boy's capacity; they are, in the case of a boy of real promise, more likely to be quite mature and successful attempts to do something small. So with Blake, his early poems are technically admirable, and their originality is in an occasional rhythm. The verse of "Edward III" deserves study. But his affection for certain Elizabethans is not so surprising as his affinity with the very best work of his own century. He is very like Collins,° he is very eighteenth century. The poem "Whether on Ida's Shady Brow" is eighteenth-century work; the movement, the weight of it, the syntax, the choice of words:

> *The* languid *strings do scarcely move!*
> *The sound is* forc'd, *the notes are few!*

this is contemporary with Gray° and Collins, it is the poetry of a language which has undergone the discipline of prose. Blake up to twenty is decidedly a traditional.

Blake's beginnings as a poet, then, are as normal as the beginnings of Shakespeare. His method of composition, in his mature work, is exactly like that of other poets. He has an idea (a feeling, an image), he develops it by accretion or expansion, alters his verse often, and hesitates often over the final choice. The idea, of course, simply comes, but upon arrival it is subjected to prolonged manipulation. In the first phase Blake is concerned with verbal beauty; in the second he becomes the apparent naïf, really the mature intelli-

---

Collins: English poet William Collins (1721–1759). **Gray:** English poet Thomas Gray (1716–1771); see p. 940.

gence. It is only when the ideas become more automatic, come more freely and are less manipulated, that we begin to suspect their origin, to suspect that they spring from a shallower source.

The Songs of Innocence and of Experience, and the poems from the Rossetti manuscript, are the poems of a man with a profound interest in human emotions, and a profound knowledge of them. The emotions are presented in an extremely simplified, abstract form. This form is one illustration of the eternal struggle of art against education, of the literary artist against the continuous deterioration of language.

It is important that the artist should be highly educated in his own art; but his education is one that is hindered rather than helped by the ordinary processes of society which constitute education for the ordinary man. For these processes consist largely in the acquisition of impersonal ideas which obscure what we really are and feel, what we really want, and what really excites our interest. It is of course not the actual information acquired, but the conformity which the accumulation of knowledge is apt to impose, that is harmful. Tennyson is a very fair example of a poet almost wholly encrusted with opinion, almost wholly merged into his environment. Blake, on the other hand, knew what interested him, and he therefore presents only the essential, only, in fact, what can be presented, and need not be explained. And because he was not distracted, or frightened, or occupied in anything but exact statements, he understood. He was naked, and saw man naked, and from the centre of his own crystal. To him there was no more reason why Swedenborg° should be absurd than Locke.° He accepted Swedenborg, and eventually rejected him, for reasons of his own. He approached everything with a mind unclouded by current opinions. There was nothing of the superior person about him. This makes him terrifying.

ಬಿ

RALPH WALDO EMERSON's *"The Poet" appeared in his second collection titled simply* Essays *(1844) and inspired Walt Whitman to expand the limits of conventional poetic form and language. As Whitman said, "I was simmering, simmering, simmering: Emerson brought me to a boil."*

RALPH WALDO EMERSON

From *"The Poet"* 1844

The poet is the sayer, the namer, and represents beauty. He is a sovereign, and stands on the centre. For the world is not painted, or adorned, but is from the beginning beautiful; and God has not made some beautiful things, but Beauty is the creator of the universe. Therefore the poet is not any permissive potentate, but is emperor in his own right. Criticism is infested with a

---

Swedenborg: Swedish philosopher Emanuel Swedenborg (1688–1772). **Locke:** English philosopher John Locke (1632–1704).

cant of materialism, which assumes that manual skill and activity is the first merit of all men, and disparages such as say and do not, overlooking the fact, that some men namely, poets, are natural sayers, sent into the world to the end of expression, and it confounds them with those whose province is action, but who quit it to imitate the sayers. But Homer's words are as costly and admirable to Homer, as Agamemnon's victories are to Agamemnon. The poet does not wait for the hero or the sage, but, as they act and think primarily, so he writes primarily what will and must be spoken, reckoning the others, though primaries also, yet, in respect to him, secondaries and servants; as sitters or models in the studio of a painter, or as assistants who bring building materials to an architect.

For poetry was all written before time was, and whenever we are so finely organized that we can penetrate into that region where the air is music, we hear those primal warblings, and attempt to write them down, but we lose ever and anon a word, or a verse, and substitute something of our own, and thus miswrite the poem. The men of more delicate ear write down these cadences more faithfully, and these transcripts, though imperfect, become the songs of the nations. For nature is as truly beautiful as it is good, or as it is reasonable, and must as much appear, as it must be done, or be known. Words and deeds are quite indifferent modes of the divine energy. Words are also actions, and actions are a kind of words.

The sign and credentials of the poet are, that he announces that which no man foretold. He is the true and only doctor; he knows and tells; he is the only teller of news, for he was present and privy to the appearance which he describes. He is a beholder of ideas, and an utterer of the necessary and causal. We do not speak now of men of poetical talents, or of industry and skill in metre, but of the true poet. I took part in a conversation the other day, concerning a recent writer of lyrics, a man of subtle mind, whose head appeared to be a music-box of delicate tunes and rhythms, and whose skill, and command of language, we could not sufficiently praise. But when the question arose whether he were not only a lyrist, but a poet, we were obliged to confess that he is plainly a contemporary, not an eternal man. He does not stand out of our low limitations, like a Chimborazo° under the line, running up from the torrid base through all the climates of the globe, with belts of the herbage of every latitude on its high and mottled sides; but this genius is the landscape garden of a modern house, adorned with fountains and statues, with well-bred men and women standing and sitting in the walks and terraces. We hear, through all the varied music, the ground-tone of conventional life. Our poets are men of talents who sing, and not the children of music. The argument is secondary, the finish of the verses is primary.

For it is not metres, but a metre-making argument, that makes a poem, — a thought so passionate and alive, that, like the spirit of a plant or an animal, it has an architecture of its own, and adorns nature with a new thing. The thought and the form are equal in the order of time, but in the order of genesis the thought is prior to the form. The poet has a new thought: he has a

---

Chimborazo: A mountain in Ecuador.

whole new experience to unfold; he will tell us how it was with him, and all men will be the richer in his fortune. The experience of each new age requires a new confession, and the world seems always waiting for its poet. I remember, when I was young, how much I was moved one morning by tidings that genius had appeared in a youth who sat near me at table. He had left his work, and gone rambling none knew whither, and had written hundreds of lines, but could not tell whether that which was in him was therein told: he could tell nothing but that all was changed — man, beast, heaven, earth, and sea. How gladly we listened! how credulous! Society seemed to be compromised. We sat in the aurora of a sunrise which was to put out all the stars. Boston seemed to be at twice the distance it had the night before, or was much further than that. Rome, — what was Rome? Plutarch and Shakespeare were in the yellow leaf, and Homer no more should be heard of. It is much to know that poetry has been written this very day, under this very roof, by your side. What! that wonderful spirit has not expired! these stony moments are still sparkling and animated! I had fancied that the oracles were all silent, and nature had spent her fires, and behold! all night, from every pore, these fine auroras have been streaming. Every one has some interest in the advent of the poet, and no one knows how much it may concern him. We know that the secret of the world is profound, but who or what shall be our interpreter, we know not. A mountain ramble, a new style of face, a new person, may put the key into our hands. Of course, the value of genius to us is in the veracity of its report. Talent may frolic and juggle; genius realizes and adds. Mankind, in good earnest, have gone so far in understanding themselves and their work, and the foremost watchman on the peak announces his news. It is the truest word ever spoken, and the phrase will be the fittest, most musical, and the unerring voice of the world for the time.

∽∾

ALLEN GINSBERG *discusses and expands on the concepts in his writing in this 1987 interview in the* New York Quarterly.

ALLEN GINSBERG

On His Poetic Craft 1987

Interviewer: You have talked about this before, but would you begin this interview by describing the early influences on your work, or the influences on your early work?

Ginsberg: Emily Dickinson. Poe's "Bells" — "Hear the sledges with the bells — Silver Bells! . . ." Milton's long line breath in *Paradise Lost* —

> Him the almighty power
> Hurled headlong flaming from the ethereal sky
> With hideous ruin and combustion down

> To bottomless perdition, there to dwell
> In adamantine chains and penal fire,
> Who durst defy the omnipotent to arms.

Shelley's "Epipsychidion" — "one life, one death, / One Heaven, one Hell, one immortality, / And one annihilation. Woe is me! . . ." The end of Shelley's "Adonais"; and Shelley's "Ode to the West Wind" exhibits continuous breath leading to ecstatic climax.

Wordsworth's "Intimations of Immortality" —

> Our birth is but a sleep and a forgetting:
> The soul that rises with us, our life's Star,
> Hath had elsewhere its setting,

— also Wordsworth's "Tintern Abbey" exhortation, or whatever you call it:

> a sense sublime
> Of something far more deeply interfused,
> Whose dwelling is the light of setting suns,
> And the round ocean and the living air,
> And the blue sky, and in the mind of man;

That kind of poetry influenced me: a long breath poetry that has a sort of ecstatic climax.

Interviewer: What about Whitman?

Ginsberg: No, I replied very specifically. You asked me about my *first* poetry. Whitman and Blake, yes, but in terms of the *early* poems I replied specifically. When I began writing I was writing rhymed verse, stanzaic forms that I derived from my father's practice. As I progressed into that, I got more involved with Andrew Marvell.

Interviewer: Did you used to go to the Poetry Society of America meetings?

Ginsberg: Yes, I used to go with my father. It was a horrifying experience — mostly old ladies and second-rate poets.

Interviewer: Would you elaborate?

Ginsberg: That's the PSA I'm talking about. At the time it was mainly people who were enemies of, and denounced, William Carlos Williams and Ezra Pound and T. S. Eliot.

Interviewer: How long did it take you to realize they were enemies?

Ginsberg: Oh, I knew right away. I meant enemies of poetry, very specifically. Or enemies of that poetry which now by hindsight is considered sincere poetry of the time. *Their* highwater mark was, I guess, Edwin Arlington Robinson; "Eros Tyrranos" was considered, I guess, the great highwater mark of twentieth-century poetry.

Interviewer: Where did you first hear long lines in momentum?

Ginsberg: The texts I was citing were things my father taught me when I was prepubescent.

Interviewer: Did he teach them to you as beautiful words, or as the craft of poetry?

Ginsberg: I don't think people used that word "craft" in those days. It's sort of like a word that has only come into use in the last few decades. There were texts of great poetry around the house, and he would recite from memory. He never sat down and said now I am going to teach you: Capital C-R-A-F-T. Actually I don't like the use of the word craft applied to poetry, because generally along with it comes a defense of stressed iambic prosody, which I find uncraftsmanly and pedantical in its use. There are very few people in whose mouths that word makes any sense. I think Marianne Moore may have used it a few times. Pound has used it a couple of times in very specific circumstances — more often as a verb than as a general noun: "This or that poet has crafted a sestina."

Interviewer: Would you talk about later influences on your work? William Blake? Walt Whitman?

Ginsberg: Later on for open verse I was interested in Kerouac's poetry. I think that turned me on more than anyone else. I think he is a very great poet and much underrated. He hadn't been read yet by poets.

Interviewer: Most people associate Kerouac with prose, with *On the Road*, and not so much with *Mexico City Blues*. Or maybe they differentiate too strictly between prose and poetry.

Ginsberg: I think it's because people are so preoccupied with the use of the word craft and its meaning that they can't see poetry in front of them on the page. Kerouac's poetry looks like the most "uncrafted stuff" in the world. He's got a different idea of craft from most people who use the word "craft." I would say Kerouac's poetry is the craftiest of all. And as far as having the most craft of anyone, though those who talk about craft have not yet discovered it, his craft is spontaneity; his craft is having the instantaneous recall of the unconscious; his craft is the perfect executive conjunction of archetypal memorial images articulating present observation of detail and childhood epiphany fact.

Interviewer: In *Howl*, at the end of Section One, you came close to a definition of poetry, when you wrote:

Who dreamt and made incarnate gaps in Time & Space through images juxtaposed, and trapped the archangel of the soul between 2 visual images and joined the elemental verbs and set the noun and dash of consciousness together jumping with sensation of Pater Omnipotens Aeterne Deus

Ginsberg: I reparaphrased that when I was talking about Kerouac. If you heard the structure of the sentence I was composing, it was about putting present observed detail into epiphany, or catching the archangel of the soul beween two visual images. I was thinking then about what Kerouac and I thought about haiku — two visual images, opposite poles, which are connected by a lightning in the mind. In other words "Today's been a good day; let another fly come on the rice." Two disparate images, unconnected, which the mind connects.

Interviewer: Chinese poets do that. Is that what you are talking about?

Ginsberg: This is characteristic of Chinese poetry as Ezra Pound pointed out in his essay "The Chinese Written Character as a Medium for Poetry" nearly fifty years ago. Do you know that work? Well, way back when, Ezra Pound proposed Chinese hieroglyphic language as more fit for poetry, considering that it was primarily visual, than generalized language-abstraction English, with visionless words like Truth, Beauty, Craft, etc. Pound then translated some Chinese poetry and translated (from Professor Fenellossa's papers) this philosophic essay pointing to Chinese language as pictorial. There is no concrete in English, and poets could learn from Chinese to present image-detail: and out of that Pound hieroglyph rose the whole practice of imagism, the school which is referred to as "Imagism." So what you are referring to is an *old* history in twentieth-century poetry. My own thing about two visual images is just from that tradition, actually drawing from Pound's discovery and interpretation of Chinese as later practiced by Williams and everybody who studied with Pound or who understood Pound. What I'm trying to point out is that this tradition in American poetry in the twentieth century is not something *just* discovered. It was done by Pound and Williams, precisely the people that are anathema to the PSA mediocrities who were attacking Pound and Williams for not having "craft."

Interviewer: In that same section of *Howl,* in the next line, you wrote:

to recreate the syntax and measure of poor human prose and stand before you speechless and intelligent and shaking with shame, rejected yet confessing out the soul to conform to the rhythm of thought in his naked and endless head.

Ginsberg: Description of aesthetic method. Key phrases that I picked up around that time and was using when I wrote the book. I meant again that if you place two visual images side by side and let the mind connect them, the gap between the two images, the lightning in the mind illuminates. It's the *sunyata* (Buddhist term for blissful empty void) which can only be known by living creatures. So, the emptiness to which the Zen finger classically points — the ellipse — is the unspoken hair-raising awareness in between two mental visual images. I should try to make my answers a little more succinct.

Interviewer: Despite your feeling about craft, poets have developed an attitude towards your work, they have discovered certain principles of breath division in your lines —

Ginsberg: Primary fact of my writing is that I don't have any craft and don't know what I'm doing. There is absolutely no art involved, in the context of the general use of the words "art" and "craft." Such craft or art as there is, is in illuminating mental formations, and trying to observe the naked activity of my own mind. Then transcribing that activity down on paper. So the craft is being shrewd at flash lighting mental activity. Trapping the archangel of the soul, by accident, so to speak. The subject matter is the action of my mind. To put it on the most vulgar level, like on the psychoanalyst's couch is supposed to be. Now if you are thinking of "form" or even the "well-made poem" or a sonnet when you're lying on the couch, you'll never say what you have on your mind. You'd be babbling about corset styles or something *else* all the time instead of saying, "I want to fuck my mother," or whatever it is you want. So my problem is to get down the fact that I want to fuck my mother or whatever. I'm taking the most hideous image possible, so there will be no misunderstanding about what area of mind you are dealing with: what is socially unspoken, what is prophetic from the unconscious, what is universal to all men, what's the main subject of poetry, what's underneath, *inside* the mind. So, how do you get that out on the page? You observe your own mind during the time of composition and write down whatever goes through the ticker tape of mentality, or whatever you hear in the echo of your inner ear, or what flashes in picture on the eyeball while you're writing. So the subject is constantly interrupting because the mind is constantly going on vagaries — so whenever it changes I have a dash. The dashes are a function of this method of transcription of unconscious data. Now you can't write down *everything* that you've got going on — half-conscious data. You can't write down everything, you can only write down what the hand can carry. Your hand can't carry more than a twentieth of what the mind flashes, and the very fact of writing interrupts the mind's flashes and redirects attention to writing. So that the observation (for writing) impedes the function of the mind. You might say "Observation impedes Function." I get down as much as I can of genuine material, interrupting the flow of material as I get it down and when I look, I turn to the center of my brain to see the next thought, but it's probably about thirty thoughts later. So I make a dash to indicate a break, sometimes a dash plus dots. Am I making sense? — . . .

Interviewer: How much do you revise your work?

Ginsberg: As little revision as possible. The craft, the art consists in paying attention on the actual movie of the mind. Writing it down is like a byproduct of that. If you can actually keep track of your own head movie, then the writing it down is just like a secretarial job, and who gets crafty about that? Use dashes instead of semicolons. Knowing the difference between a dash — and a hyphen -. Long lines are useful at certain times, and short lines at other times. But a big notebook with lines is a helpful thing, and three pens — you have to be shrewd about that. The actual materials are important. A book at the nightstand is important — a light you can get at — or a flashlight, as Kerouac had a brakeman's lantern. That's the craft. Having the brakeman's lantern and knowing where to use the ampersand "&" for swiftness in writing. If your attention is focused all the time — as my attention was in writing "Sunflower Sutra," "TV Baby" poem later, ("Wichita Vortex Sutra" later, in a book called *Planet News*) — when attention is focused, there is no likelihood there will be much need for blue penciling revision because there'll be a sensuous continuum in the composition. So when I look over something that I've written down, I find that if my attention has lapsed from the subject, I begin to talk about myself writing about the subject or talking about my irrelevant left foot itch instead of about the giant smog factory I'm observing in Linden, New Jersey. Then I'll have to do some blue penciling, excising whatever is irrelevant: whatever I inserted self-consciously, instead of conscious of the Subject. Where self-consciousness intervenes on attention, blue pencil excision means getting rid of the dross of self-consciousness. Since the subject matter is really the operation of the mind, as in Gertrude Stein, anything that the mind passes through is proper and shouldn't be revised out, almost anything that passes through mind, anything with the exception of self-consciousness. Anything that occurs to the mind is the proper subject. So if you are making a graph of the movements of the mind, there is no point in revising it. Because then you would obliterate the actual markings of the graph. So if you're interested in writing as a form of meditation or introspective yoga, which I am, then there's no revision possible.

∽

MICHAEL S. HARPER *was interviewed by James Randall in 1984 about his thoughts on the concept of "Africa." In this excerpt, Harper talks specifically about his response to African writing.*

MICHAEL S. HARPER

On Black American and African Writing
1984

Randall: Do you think that black American writing has more vitality, more style than African writing?

Harper: I don't think I'm equipped to judge. Certainly Afro-Americans have contributed to the language and culture of this country, and much of what they've given, both internally and externally, is good. My sparse investigations in this area have shown me parallels in our experience — for example, the notion of the city and the blacks. That landscape offers incredible vitality and renewal, particularly in the period after World War II, when so much change in the society took place. Blacks have always infused the language at large with elegance and with word invention as an improvisational attitude; I grew up making words, describing events, often hostile to me, in a kind of operatic parody. We had a sense of dynamism and change. We rode the subways, went to sporting events, copied Joe Louis and Sugar Ray Robinson, and were a barometer for a way of viewing the contradictions of the world. We loved the musicians for their artistry and their élan, and we learned their coded phrasings. We became almost comfortable on the frontier. Perhaps we brought to clarity the endowments or innate gifts in all people for some types of cuisine, some attitudes of dress, some colorations and tonalities of talk. My travel to the West Indies and Africa made me pay more attention to change, made me ask questions. The artist's job is to penetrate surface gloss to find the connectives in a living tradition, what I mean when I say continuum. You build on what's come before you, you expand and extend the values implicit in the group and, in the street phrase, you *run with it.* What Walcott and Achebe seem to share, but Heaney as well,° is the sense of living tradition, the past in the present moment, and the

---

Walcott ... Heaney as well: Derek Walcott, Chinua Achebe, and Seamus Heaney are contemporary poets.

music inherent in *composition*. What the great jazz musicians meant to me was the ability to improvise upon thematic texts and make them new; they didn't start with nothing. Composition is structuring and orchestrating, revealing the hidden texts implicit in human experience. I love the challenge.

Randall: And using Marianne Moore's terms, blacks are more open, more accessible to experience than other Americans who are themselves more open to experience than Europeans. Do you feel in your own lifetime that things have improved for the black person and for the black artist?

Harper: I think any artist has to develop stamina. For blacks, the requirements of living are extreme; my own sense of urgency has not diminished over twenty-five years. I'm optimistic in attitude only because I often expect the worst — and am surprised when things work out. At the level of belief I never had any doubt that doing what I do was worthwhile. I had too much support, too many good examples, some of them connected to me and my family, to ever doubt that. We have to learn to run the risk of our own damnation, perhaps, to find transcendence. For me, race has always been a metaphor and a challenge of assertion. I never had any doubt I was good; I think others should have a "guaranteed" chance to become themselves. I've also known some gifted people whose productivity was short-lived.

Randall: Many whites also.

Harper: Absolutely. You have to fortify yourself with values, learn to study, and live your life as though you were a paradigm for the "pursuit of happiness," which isn't property, but to make of yourself an art form to be continually beautified, and made whole. I've seen too many gifted people devastated by having to live under brutal circumstances in this country.

ಇಾ

ROBERT HAYDEN's *introduction to his anthology of African American poetry discusses the tradition of "Negro poetry" which, like American poetry generally, was concerned with developing a distinctive language and form.*

ROBERT HAYDEN

On Negro Poetry 1967

The question whether we can speak with any real justification of "Negro poetry" arises often today. Some object to the term because it has been used disparagingly to indicate a kind of pseudo-poetry concerned with the race problem to the exclusion of almost everything else. Others hold that Negro poetry *per se* could only be produced in black Africa. Seen from this point of view, the poetry of the American Negro, its "specialized" content notwithstanding, is obviously not to be thought of as existing apart from the rest of our literature, but as having been shaped over some three centuries by social, moral, and literary forces essentially American.

Those who presently avow themselves "poets of the Negro revolution" argue that they do indeed constitute a separate group or school, since the purpose of their writing is to give Negroes a sense of human dignity and provide them with ideological weapons. A belligerent race pride moves these celebrants of Black Power to declare themselves not simply "poets," but "Negro poets." However, Countee Cullen, the brilliant lyricist of the Harlem Renaissance in the 1920s, insisted that he be considered a "poet," not a "Negro poet," for he did not want to be restricted to racial themes nor have his poetry judged solely on the basis of its relevance to the Negro struggle.

Cullen was aware of a peculiar risk Negro poets have had to face. The tendency of American critics has been to label the established Negro writer a "spokesman for his race." There are, as we have seen, poets who think of themselves in that role. But the effect of such labeling is to place any Negro author in a kind of literary ghetto where the standards applied to other writers are not likely to be applied to him, since he, being a "spokesman for his race," is not considered primarily a writer but a species of race-relations man, the leader of a cause, the voice of protest.

Protest has been a recurring element in the writing of American Negroes, a fact hardly to be wondered at, given the social conditions under which they have been forced to live. And the Negro poet's devotion to the cause of freedom is not in any way reprehensible, for throughout history poets have often been champions of human liberty. But bad poetry is another matter, and there is no denying that a great deal of "race poetry" is poor, because its content seems ready-made and art is displaced by argument.

Phillis Wheatley (c. 1750–1784), the first poet of African descent to win some measure of recognition, had almost nothing to say about the plight of her people. And if she resented her own ambiguous position in society, she did not express her resentment. One reason for her silence is that, although brought to Boston as a slave, she never lived as one. Another is that as a neoclassical poet she would scarcely have thought it proper to reveal much of herself in her poetry, although we do get brief glimpses of her in the poem addressed to the Earl of Dartmouth and in "On Being Brought from Africa to America." Neoclassicism emphasized reason rather than emotion and favored elegance and formality. The English poet, Alexander Pope, was the acknowledged master of this style, and in submitting to his influence Phillis Wheatley produced poetry that was as good as that of her American contemporaries. She actually wrote better than some of them.

But the poetry of Phillis Wheatley and her fellow poet, Jupiter Hammon, has historical and not literary interest for us now. The same can be said of much of eighteenth-century American poetry in general. Not until the nineteenth century did the United States begin to have literature of unqualified merit and originality. There were no Negro poets of stature in the period before the Civil War, but there were several with talent, among them George Moses Horton (1797–c. 1883) and Frances E. W. Harper (1825–1911). Didactic and sentimental, they wrote with competence and moral fervor in the manner of their times. Their poetry is remembered chiefly because it contributed to the antislavery struggle, and because it testifies to the creative efforts of Negroes under disheartening conditions. . . .

In the twentieth century Negro poets have abandoned dialect for an idiom truer to folk speech. The change has been due not only to differences in social outlook on their part but also to revolutionary developments in American poetry. The New Poetry movement, which began before the First World War and reached its definitive point in the 1920s, represented a break with the past. Free verse, diction close to everyday speech, a realistic approach to life, and the use of material once considered unpoetic — these were the goals of the movement. The Negro poet-critic, William Stanley Braithwaite, encouraged the "new" poetry through his articles in the *Boston Evening Transcript* and his yearly anthologies of magazine verse.

The New Negro movement or Negro Renaissance, resulting from the social, political, and artistic awakening of Negroes in the twenties, brought into prominence poets whose work showed the influence of the poetic revolution. Protest became more defiant, racial bitterness and racial pride more outspoken than ever before. Negro history and folklore were explored as new sources of inspiration. Spirituals, blues, and jazz suggested themes and verse patterns to young poets like Jean Toomer and Langston Hughes. Certain conventions, notably what has been called "literary Garveyism," grew out of a fervent Negro nationalism. Marcus Garvey, leader of the United Negro Improvement Association, advocated a "return" to Africa, the lost homeland, and nearly all the Renaissance poets wrote poems about their spiritual ties to Africa, about the dormant fires of African paganism in the Negro soul that the white man's civilization could never extingish. Countee Cullen's "Heritage" is one of the best of these poems, even though the Africa it presents is artificial, romanticized, and it reiterates exotic clichés in vogue during the period when it was written.

Harlem was the center of the Negro Renaissance, which for that reason is also referred to as the Harlem Renaissance. Two magazines, *The Crisis* and *Opportunity*, gave aid and encouragement to Negro writers by publishing their work and by awarding literary prizes.

In the decades since the New Negro movement, which ended with the twenties, protest and race consciousness have continued to find expression in the poetry of the American Negro. But other motivating forces are also in evidence. There are Negro poets who believe that any poet's most clearly defined task is to create with honesty and sincerity poems that will illuminate human experience — not exclusively "Negro experience." They reject the idea of poetry as racial propaganda, of poetry that functions as a kind of sociology. Their attitude is not wholly new, of course, being substantially that of Dunbar and Cullen. In counterpoise to it is the "Beat" or "nonacademic" view held by poets who are not only in rebellion against middle-class ideals and the older poetic traditions but who also advocate a militant racism in a definitely "Negro" poetry.

It has come to be expected of Negro poets that they will address themselves to the race question — and that they will all say nearly the same things about it. Such "group unity" is more apparent than real. Differences in vision and emphasis, fundamental differences in approach to the art of poetry itself, modify and give diversity to the writing of these poets, even when they employ similar themes. And certainly there is no agreement among them as to what the much debated role of the Negro poet should be.

∞

ANTHONY HECHT's *1968 parody of Matthew Arnold's "Dover Beach" (p. 1018) is not meant as an attack on the earlier poem. It is, rather, a deliberately amusing way of looking at a familiar masterpiece from another point of view.*

ANTHONY HECHT

The Dover Bitch

1968

A Criticism of Life

So there stood Matthew Arnold and this girl
With the cliffs of England crumbling away behind them,
And he said to her, "Try to be true to me,
And I'll do the same for you, for things are bad
All over, etc., etc."
Well now, I knew this girl. It's true she had read
Sophocles in a fairly good translation
And caught that bitter allusion to the sea,
But all the time he was talking she had in mind
The notion of what his whiskers would feel like
On the back of her neck. She told me later on
That after a while she got to looking out
At the lights across the channel, and really felt sad,
Thinking of all the wine and enormous beds
And blandishments in French and the perfumes.
And then she got really angry. To have been brought
All the way down from London, and then be addressed
As a sort of mournful cosmic last resort
Is really tough on a girl, and she was pretty.
Anyway, she watched him pace the room
And finger his watch-chain and seem to sweat a bit,
And then she said one or two unprintable things.
But you mustn't judge her by that. What I mean to say is,
She's really all right. I still see her once in a while
And she always treats me right. We have a drink
And I give her a good time, and perhaps it's a year
Before I see her again, but there she is,
Running to fat, but dependable as they come.
And sometimes I bring her a bottle of *Nuit d'Amour*.

ငာၛ

RICHARD HOWARD, *the poet and translator, published his important book* Alone with America *in 1980. In it he discusses some of the contradictions of Anne Sexton's poetic achievement.*

RICHARD HOWARD

From " 'Some Tribal Female Who Is Known but Forbidden': Anne Sexton"

1980

There are some areas of experience in modern life, Theodore Roethke has said, that simply cannot be rendered by either the formal lyric or straight prose. We must realize — and who could have enforced the realization upon us better than Roethke — that the writer in "freer forms" must have an even greater fidelity to his subject matter or his substance than the poet who has the support of form — of received form. He must be imaginatively "right," his rhythm must move as the mind moves, or he is lost. "On the simplest level, something must happen in this kind of poem." By which Roethke meant, I am certain, that it is not enough to report something happening in your life merely — it must be made to happen in your poem. You must begin somewhere, though, generally with your life, above all with your life when it seems to you to welter in a particular exemplary status. Such is Anne Sexton's case, and she has begun indeed with the report of her case:

> Oh! Honor and relish the facts!
> Do not think of the intense sensation
> I have as I tell you this
> but think only . . .

In fact, she has reported more than anyone else — anyone else who has set out to write poems — has ever cared or dared, and thereby she has gained, perhaps at the expense of her poetry, a kind of sacerdotal stature, the elevation of a priestess celebrating mysteries which are no less mysterious for having been conducted in all the hard glare of the marketplace and with all the explicitness mere print can afford.

Anne Sexton is the true Massachusetts heiress of little Pearl,° who as the procession of Worthies passes by asks Hester Prynne if one man in it is the same minister who kissed her by the brook. "Hold thy peace, dear little Pearl," whispers her mother. "We must not always talk in the marketplace of what happens to us in the forest." Like the sibylline, often insufferable Pearl, Anne Sexton *does* speak of such things, and in such places, and it makes her, again like Pearl, both more and less than a mere "person," something beyond a "character"; it makes her, rather, what we call a *figure*, the form of a tragic function. If you are wearing not only your heart on your sleeve, your liver on your lapel, and the other organs affixed to various articles of your attire, but also a whole alphabet in scarlet on your breast, then your poetry must bear with losing the notion of *private parts* altogether and with gaining a certain publicity that has nothing to do with the personal. Further, if you regard, as Anne Sexton does, the poem as "a lie that tells the truth" (it was Cocteau° who first spoke of himself this way), then you face the corresponding peril that the

---

Pearl: Hester Prynne's illegitimate child in Nathaniel Hawthorne's *The Scarlet Letter* (1850).
Cocteau: French writer, artist, and filmmaker Jean Cocteau (1889–1963).

truth you tell will become a lie: "there is no translating that ocean," as Miss Sexton says. And it will become a lie because you have not taken enough care to "make something happen" — in short, to lie in the way poems must lie, by devising that imaginative rightness which Roethke located primarily in rhythm, but which has everything to do as well with the consecution of images, the shape language makes as it is deposited in the reader's mind, the transactions between beginnings and endings, the *devices* — no less — of art.

"Even one alone verse sometimes makes a perfect poem," Ben Jonson declared, and so much praise (it is the kind of praise that leaves out of the reckoning a great deal of waste, a great deal of botched work) it will be easy, and what is more it will be necessary, to give Anne Sexton; like the preposterous sprite whose "demon-offspring" impulses she resumes, this poet is likely, *at any moment*, to say those oracular, outrageous things we least can bear but most require:

> Fee-fi-fo-fum
> Now I'm borrowed
> Now I'm numb

It is when she speaks beyond the moment, speaks as it were consecutively that Anne Sexton finds herself in difficulties; if we are concerned with the poem as it grows from one verse to the next, enlarging itself by means of itself, like a growing pearl, the real one (Hawthorne's, for all he tells us, never grew up), then we must discover an Anne Sexton dead set, by her third book of poems, against any such process. Hers is the truth that cancels poetry, and her career as an artist an excruciating trajectory of self-destruction, so that it is by her failures in her own enterprise that she succeeds, and by her successes as an artist that she fails herself.

ꙮ

DAVID HUDDLE *discusses Hayden's 1962 poem in his most recent book,* A David Huddle Reader *(1994). Huddle, a poet, teaches at the University of Vermont, and in 1993–94 he was acting editor of the* New England Review.

DAVID HUDDLE

The "Banked Fire" of Robert Hayden's "Those Winter Sundays"

1996

For twenty years I've been teaching Robert Hayden's most frequently anthologized poem to undergraduate poetry-writing students. By "teach," I mean that from our textbook I read the poem aloud in the classroom, I ask one of the students to read it aloud, I make some observations about it, I invite the students to make some observations about it, then we talk about it a while longer. Usually to wrap up the discussion, I'll read the poem through once more. Occasions for such teaching come up about half a dozen times a year, and so let's say that during my life I've been privileged to read this poem aloud approximately 240 times. "Those Winter Sundays" has withstood my assault upon it. It remains a poem I look forward to reading and discussing in my classroom. The poem remains alive to me, so that for hours and sometimes days after it visits my classroom, I'm hearing its lines in my mind's ear.

Though a fourteen-liner, "Those Winter Sundays" is only loosely a sonnet. Its stanzas are five, four, and five lines long. There are rhymes and near-rhymes, but no rhyme scheme. The poem's lines probably average about eight syllables. There are only three strictly iambic lines: the fourth, the eighth, and (significantly) the fourteenth. It's a poem that's powerfully informed by the sonnet form; it's a poem that "feels like" a sonnet — it has the density and gravity of a sonnet — which is to say that in its appearance on the page, in its diction and syntax, in its tone, cadence, and argumentative strategy, "Those Winter Sundays" presents the credentials of a work of literary art in the tradition of English letters. But it's also a poem that has gone its own way, a definite departure from that most conventional of all the poetic forms of English and American verse.

The abstract issue of this poem's sonnethood is of less value to my beginning poets than the tangible matter of the sounds the poem makes, especially those *k*-sounding words of the first eleven lines that one comes to associate with discomfort: "clothes . . . blueback cold . . . cracked . . . ached . . . weekday . . . banked . . . thanked . . . wake . . . cold . . . breaking . . . call . . . chronic . . . cold." What's missing from the final three lines? The *k* sounds have been driven from the poem, as the father has "driven out the cold" from the house. The sounds that have replaced those *k* sounds are the *o* sounds of "good . . . shoes . . . know . . . know . . . love . . . lonely offices." The poem lets us associate the *o* sounds with love and loneliness. Sonically the poem tells the same story the poem narrates for us. The noise of this poem moves us through its emotional journey from discomfort to lonely love. If ever there was a poem that could teach a beginning poet the viability of the element of sound-crafting, it is "Those Winter Sundays."

Quote its first two words, and a great many poets and English teachers will be able to finish the first line (if not the whole poem) from memory. Somewhat remarkably, the poem's thesis — that the office of love can be relentless, thankless, and more than a little mysterious — resides in that initially odd-sounding two-word beginning, "Sundays too." The rest of the line — the rest of the independent clause — is ordinary. Nowhere else in Anglo-American literature does the word *too* carry the weight it carries in "Those Winter Sundays."

Not as immediately apparent as its opening words but very nearly as important to the poem's overall strategy is the two-sentence engineering of the first stanza. Because they will appreciate it more if they discover it for themselves, I often maneuver Socratically to have my students describe the poem's first two sentences: long and complex, followed by short and simple. It almost always seems to me worthwhile to ask, "Why didn't Hayden begin his poem this way: 'No one ever thanked my father for getting up early on Sundays, too'? Wouldn't that be a more direct and hospitable way to bring the reader into the poem?" After I've taken my students that far, they are quick to see how that ordinary five-word unit, "No one ever thanked him," gains meaning and emotion, weight, and force, from the elaborate preparation given it by the thirty-two-word "Sundays too" first sentence.

So much depends on "No one ever thanked him" that it requires the narrative enhancement of the first four and a half lines. It is the crux of the poem. What is this poem about? It is about a son's remorse over never thanking his father not only for what he did for him but also for how (he now realizes) he felt about him. And what is the poem if not an elegantly fashioned, permanent expression of gratitude?

"Those Winter Sundays" tells a story, or it describes a circumstance, of father-son conflict, and it even makes some excuses for the son's "Speaking indifferently" to the father: there was a good deal of anger between them; "chronic angers of that house" suggests that the circumstances were complicated somewhat beyond the usual and ordinary conflict between fathers and sons. Of the father, we know that he labored outdoors with his hands. Of the son, we know that he was, in the classic manner of youth, heedless of the ways in which his father served him.

Though the evidence of his "labor" is visible in every stanza of this poem, the father himself is somewhere else. We don't see him. He is in some other room of the house than the one where our speaker is. That absence suggests the emotional distance between the father and the son as well as the current absence, through death, of the father on the occasion of this utterance. It's easy enough to imagine this poem as a graveside meditation, an elegy, and a rather impassioned one at that, "What did I know, what did I know?"

The grinding of past against present gives the poem its urgency. The story is being told with such clarity, thoughtfulness, and apparent calm that we are surprised by the outburst of the repeated question of the thirteenth line. The fourteenth line returns to a tone of tranquillity. Its diction is formal, even arch, and its phrasing suggests an extremely considered conclusion; the fourteenth line is the answer to a drastic rephrasing of the original question: *What is the precise name of what as a youth I was incapable of perceiving but that as a life-examining adult, I now suddenly understand?*

I tell my students that they may someday need this poem, they may someday be walking along downtown and find themselves asking aloud, "What did I know, what did I know?" But what I mean to suggest to them is that Hayden has made them the gift of this final phrase like a package that in ten years' time they may open and find immensely valuable: "love's austere and lonely offices." Like "the banked fires" his father made, Hayden has made a poem that will be of value to readers often years after they've first read it.

"Those Winter Sundays" has articulated a treasure of an insight and preserved it for me until I was old enough to appreciate it. The poem always has the power to move me, to make me understand something so subtle that apparently I need to be reminded of it again and again. Hayden's poem is a "banked fire" that holds its warmth and allows me to rekindle my spirits whenever I come back to read it.

"Those Winter Sundays" honors a much-criticized figure in American culture of the 1990s — the withdrawn, emotionally inexpressive, and distant (and probably unhappy and angry) father. The poem makes its way toward perceiving the emotional life of such a man. The poem *realizes* love as it lived in such a man. That my own father was somewhat similar is perhaps why the poem particularly affects me, but I have witnessed its affecting so many others that I must assume either that such fathers exist in multitudes or that the poem cuts across vast differences of background in its instruction to the reader to reconsider the lives of those who helped us make our way into adulthood.

Whenever I teach "Those Winter Sundays," I face a dilemma of personal, political, and pedagogical consequence. Do I tell my students that Hayden is an African-American poet? That fact *does* make a difference in how we read the poem: the "cracked hands that ached / from labor in the weekday weather" may be seen in a context of a racial-economic circumstance, and thus "the chronic angers of that house" may also be seen as a result of racially enforced poverty. There are, however, manual laborers and poor families of all ethnic backgrounds, and so one need not necessarily read "Those Winter Sundays" as a poem that has anything to do with racial issues. It might even be argued that to read the poem as being about race is to give the poem a racist reading.

My students are almost always white, they are only beginning to learn about modern poetry, and they aren't likely to be acquainted with any African-American poets. If I tell them that Hayden was an African American, am I practicing a subtly racist bit of pedagogy? On the other hand, if I don't tell them that the man who wrote this poem is an African American, aren't I denying them a piece of knowledge that is essential not only for the understanding of this poem but for their general poetic education? (One wonders what the equivalent might be for another poet. To omit telling students of a Robert Frost poem that he lived for most of his life in New England? To say nothing about Walt Whitman's homosexuality? To leave unmentioned Emily Dickinson's reclusiveness? Is there really any equivalent?)

I'm a teacher; I almost always look for a positive approach to such dilemmas. I see an admirable ambiguity and psychological complexity in the fact that the poem can be read in both ways, as a poem that has nothing to do with race and as a poem that is somewhat informed by the circumstance of racial injustice. I do tell my students that the author was an African American, but I tell them only after we've read it a couple of times and talked about it. That piece of information is very nearly the last thing that I tell them before I read it to them the last time, the reading in which once more I journey in my own voice through the words, the lines, the stanzas, down through the cold house into the waiting warmth it always offers me, that necessary, inspiring insight it delivers to me again and again, that the duties of love (like the duties of poetry) are often scrupulously carried out in invisible and thankless ways.

∞

ERICA JONG *first became known for her feminist novel* Fear of Flying *(1973), but she has also published several collections of poetry and a recent memoir,* Any Woman's Blues *(1991). Her essay describes her discovery of Shakespeare's sonnets when she was a college student.*

ERICA JONG

Devouring Time: Shakespeare's Sonnets   1996

My love affair with Shakespeare's sonnets began when I was in college. Looking back, it seems to me that at every stage of my adult life, the sonnets have meant something different to me — always deepening, always inexhaustible.

The most daunting challenge is to choose a favorite out of the 152 best poems in our language, since there are so many that move me deeply. I begin this impossible task by reading through the sonnets to myself silently, and then by listening to Sir John Gielgud's astonishing rendition of them, recorded in 1963, Shakespeare's quatercentenary. (I deliberately do not turn to my groaning bookshelves of Shakespeare criticism with their pointless, and ultimately snobbish, debates about the identity of "Mr. W. H." or whether or not our "Top Poet," as Auden called him, could really be a mere middle-class man of Stratford rather than the Earl of Oxford — or perhaps even the Virgin Queen herself. I want to return to the sonnets freshly — as a common reader, responding to them as a person first, a poet second.) As Gielgud's great actor's voice reawakens these dazzling poems for me, I hear again the toll of mortality in the sonnets, the elaboration of the themes of love and death and the stark repetition of their central word: "time."

Devouring time, the wastes of Time, Time's scythe, Wasteful time, in war with time, this bloody tyrant time, time's pencil, time's furrows, dear time's waste, Time's injurious hand, Time's spoils, Time's fool, a hell of time, Time's fickle glass.... It seems I cannot read or hear the sonnets without being reminded of how little time is left — which sends me to my desk to write with frenzied hand.

Time is the all-powerful, wrathful God of the sonnets. And to this awesome power, the poet opposes procreation, love, and poetry.

The first thirteen sonnets urge begetting a child to oppose death:

> Th'ou art thy mother's glass, and she in thee
> Calls back the lovely April of her prime.
>
> (Sonnet 3)

Then the theme shifts, and by Sonnet 15 the poet is comparing his own craft to procreation as a way of winning the war with time:

> And all in war with Time for love of you,
> As he takes from you, I ingraft you new.

But poetry is fired by love, so these two forms of redemption are really the same. Children redeem us from time, poetry redeems us from time, and love is the force that drives them both. As the sonnets go on to tell their twisted tale of rival loves, rival poets, love, passion, parting, obsessional sexuality, wrath, reunion, forgiveness, self-love, self-loathing, and self-forgiveness, time never ceases to be the poet's alpha and omega, the deity he both worships and despises.

And so I find myself coming back again and again to Sonnet 19, a poet's credo if ever there were one.

> Devouring Time, blunt thou the lion's paws,
> And make the earth devour her own sweet brood;
> Pluck the keen teeth from the fierce tiger's yaws,
> And burn the long-liv'd phoenix in her blood;
> Make glad and sorry seasons as thou fleet'st,
> And do whate'er thou wilt, swift-footed Time,
> To the wide world and all her fading sweets;
> But I forbid thee one most heinous crime:
> O, carve not with thy hours my love's fair brow,
> Nor draw no lines there with thine antique pen;
> Him in thy course untained do allow
> For beauty's pattern to succeeding men.
>   Yet do thy worst, old Time: despite thy wrong,
>   My love shall in my verse ever live young.

Sonnet 19 is hardly the most complex of Shakespeare's sonnets, nor the most tortured. The sonnets that recount obsessional love, jealousy, and lust are far darker and more fretted. But Sonnet 19 calls me back again and again because it is one of the few in which the poet addresses time directly and takes him on — David against Goliath.

The simplicity of the sonnet's "statement" delights me: "Time, you big bully, you think you're so great. You can make people die and tigers lose their teeth and change the seasons so fast it makes us dizzy. But spare my love. Don't scribble on him with your antique pen. On second thought, do whatever the hell you like. You have the power to destroy, but I have an even greater power: I create. And by capturing my love in poetry, I can keep my love young forever, whatever you may do to destroy him!"

There is a fluidity to this sonnet that seems to me a triumph of this difficult form. The three quatrains flow into one another and become one exhortation. The couplet argues with them all, changing the direction swiftly and ironically. The poet is standing up to the bully. Suddenly "Devouring Time" becomes "old Time," as if in the course of fourteen lines he had withered like a vampire thrown into a raging inferno. The poem itself has subdued time, made him old before his time, vanquished him. The force of poetry alone defeats time.

This theme is elaborated often in the sonnets, but seldom with such simplicity, the simplicity of a person addressing a fearsome deity without fear: the poet speaking to the gods. Throughout the sonnets, the poet addresses his love, his siren, his lust, even himself, but only in this sonnet (and once more in Sonnet 123) does he address Time directly. He throws down the gauntlet and takes Time on as if one might defeat a powerful foe simply with the force of language.

And, of course, one *can*, as Shakespeare's sonnets prove. We go back to them again and again, discovering new depths in them as time carves new depths in our hearts.

In youth, we tend to love the love poems, the poems of obsessional lust, jealousy, and rage. "Th'expense of spirit in a waste of shame" (129) reminds us of our own struggles to master lust. "So are you to my thoughts as food to life" (75) reminds us of the yearning of first love. As we age, we increasingly see Time shadowing love and the bliss of creation as the only redemption. Shakespeare's sonnets are a fugue on the theme of time. They can be read together or separately, line by line, quatrain by quatrain, or as a narrative of the power of art against decay. They prove the poet's point by their very durability.

Each time I go back to the sonnets, I find something that seemed not to be there before. Perhaps I have changed and my vision is less clouded, or else the sonnets metamorphose on the shelf. The sonnets I love best are those with sustained voices, those that sound like a person speaking. I think I hear Shakespeare's private voice in these sonnets, as if he were whispering directly in my ear.

That Shakespeare's sonnets have defeated death comforts me — for what is great poetry, after all, but the continuation of the human voice after death?

ॐ

X. J. KENNEDY *emphasizes in this discussion of Marvell's "To His Coy Mistress" that the real point of the poem is the seduction of the speaker's hesitant mistress. Kennedy's* Cross Ties: Selected Poems *was published in 1985; his most recent collection is* Dark Houses *(1992).*

X. J. KENNEDY

Andrew Marvell's "To His Coy Mistress"   *1996*

"Make it new," Ezra Pound advised his fellow poets. Few have taken a theme older and more familiar than Andrew Marvell does in "To His Coy Mistress," his most celebrated work, and rendered it with such lasting freshness. The idea of *carpe diem* ("Seize today!") resounds through the poetry of ancient Greece, Egypt, and Persia, and is a particularly favorite theme of Latin poets, notably Catullus and Horace. "Enjoy the present smiling hour," Horace counsels (in *Odes* 3.29, as translated by John Dryden), and many a later poet has urged the same policy.

Though he became a committed servant of the English Puritan party — toiling as Latin Secretary to Oliver Cromwell, the Puritan Lord Protector himself — Marvell cannot be called Puritanical. He did not resemble those American Puritans who burned witches, and (it is said) condemned the cruel sport of bearbaiting, in which dogs were turned loose upon a chained bear, not because it hurt the bear but because it gave pleasure to the spectators. Though

Marvell switched political parties over the course of his career, his biographers have found one consistent thread informing his life: a love of liberty. Marvell continually attacked censorship, wrote pamphlets urging religious freedom, and condemned those who borrowed their opinions from others — people who displayed, he said, a "party-colour'd mind." His best poems appear to hold clashing views with nearly equal sympathy; for example, though Marvell supported Oliver Cromwell, his "Horatian Ode upon Cromwell's Return from Ireland" expresses admiration for Charles I, the Stuart king whom the Puritans had deposed. Some degree of this broad-mindedness and complexity of feeling is evident in "To His Coy Mistress."

To begin, consider the title. The lady's coyness — her hesitancy, her coquetry — sets the dramatic situation. It may be a temptation to misread the word "Mistress" to mean a kept woman, but the poem makes it clear that in Marvell's time the word referred to an unmarried woman. (Were she kept, the speaker wouldn't need to argue her into bed; she would be there already.)

The poem is divided into three parts, each clearly announced by an indented line. Let me offer a few notes on what goes on in each part. The reader who already knows this poem by heart will, I hope, forgive these remarks their simplicity.

In the introductory portion of his argument, Marvell assumes that women and men naturally differ in their attitudes toward love: Women prefer to be wooed slowly, men want to forge ahead with all haste possible. The speaker pretends to consider the woman's attitude sympathetically, although (as we shall see) he is all for forging ahead. He opens his argument diplomatically, not by protesting the woman's reluctance to yield, but by suggesting that leisurely dalliance, while desirable, would be possible only in a world far larger and less hurried than the world we know. On a globe, the fact that England's River Humber is on the opposite side of the earth from the Ganges River in India throws the largest possible distance between the lovers. In imagining a vast extent of time, Marvell is equally definite. His speaker would begin the wooing back before the time of Noah, and his mistress might refuse "till the conversion of the Jews," which unlikely event, according to tradition, is to take place just before the end of the world. And so this ideal wooing would have to span human history as told in the Bible from the Old Testament book of Genesis through the New Testament book of Revelation. For "vegetable" in line 11, read "vegetative," or growing. (This line recalls one of my favorite bits of parody, author anonymous: "My vegetable love should grow / Quick as bamboo in Vigoro.") With loving playfulness, the speaker wishes that, indeed, that much world and time were available to do his lady justice. He turns a pretty compliment: "For, Lady, you deserve this state" (this slow and stately ritual). We can see his strategy. He puts the case for delay in terms so preposterous that no sensible mistress could agree to it. I find this part quietly hilarious, especially in the lines, "Two hundred, to adore each breast, / But thirty thousand to the rest." The scrupulous specificity of that number of years!

The second part begins with a magnificent "But." Then comes Marvell's awesome vision of the immense extent of death:

> But at my back I always hear
> Time's wingèd chariot hurrying near
> And yonder all before us lie
> Deserts of vast eternity.

That famous phrase "Time's wingèd chariot" may echo the classical myth of Apollo, the sun god who daily drives his fiery chariot around the sky, drawn by winged horses. How they loom large in this poem, these stressful forces — the pressure of passing time, the swift approach of eternity. This is no cheerful Christian view of eternity, but a doleful, pagan one. Foreseeing no pleasant afterlife, Marvell expects death to lead to nothing but an endless wasteland. This is a reason for lovers to leap into the sack while they still may. What's the good of keeping your maidenhead intact, he argues, just for some dumb worm in the ground to pierce (to "try," like trying a door), when (he might have added, but tactfully doesn't) you could enjoy my worm instead? Delectable is the tongue-in-cheek understatement of "The grave's a fine and private place, / But none, I think, do there embrace." Who can argue with that?

I can never read this stanza without admiring Marvell's tremendously skilled handling of meter. The rhythm of his lines has been ticking along fairly regularly in a basic iambic beat: unstressed syllables alternated with stressed ones. Then the poet hits the beginning of the line hard — "Time's wingèd." In the ensuing phrase "chariot hurrying," each word has one stressed or heavy syllable followed by two light, unstressed ones. The effect is a skipping or rippling rhythm, like a fast-moving chariot jolting over a rocky road.

In its third part the poem, with an agreeable shock, returns us to the present moment. Here we are, says the speaker, two healthy youngbloods whose vigor won't last forever. In line 34, that morning *glew* isn't Elmer's. The word, according to scholar Helge Kökeritz, is Northern English dialect for *glow*. Marvell, a Yorkshireman, may well have known it. The imagery is violent, of meateating. Time is a ravenous beast with slow, irresistible jaws; we must devour him or be devoured. Obviously, being mortal, we can't make the sun stand still as Joshua did, or Zeus, who in order to enjoy the mortal Alcmena made the night last a whole week. Some readers find a serious pun in the next-to-last line. Though the lovers cannot halt time, they can have a *son*, a child who can literally run, a living inheritance. However we read the ending, Marvell gives us a solution to the problem of fleeting time. In making love, we'll render the immediate moment as good as eternity itself — indeed, eternity being a desert, we'll render it far better.

დვ

SYDNEY LEA, *founder of the* New England Review *and a teacher at Middlebury College, considers Keats's great ode and our contemporary literary situation of "so many poets but so few great ones." Lea recently published the poetry collection* The Blainsville Testament *(1992) and also a gathering of essays called* Hunting the Whole Way Home *(1994).*

SYDNEY LEA

On Keats's "To Autumn" 1996

At many a reading in our time, this or that author will introduce a given poem in a certain way; the words of course vary, but the gist is generally as follows: "I here notice something that one of you out there might have noticed, if only you were as sensitive as I, which you're obviously not."

The premise here, that to be a poet is automatically to possess supranormal sensitivity, has never sold well with me (especially when used to defend awful behavior). Thus, even though he does so in one of my favorite works, I wince some at Wordsworth's claim that "We poets in our youth begin in gladness; / But thereof come in the end despondency and madness," wondering why this truth — if a truth at all — applies any more to poets than to other folks.

I could refer to more egregious claims by contemporaries, but why bother? I wish simply to suggest that a good writer of poems may be more sensitive to *language* than the average Joe or Jane (though not obviously more so than a good writer of prose), and that's about as far as it goes. I mention all this only because John Keats was crucial in bringing me to such an attitude, and he remains a fine corrector of the self-vaunting that I, like anyone, am utterly capable of, as man and author.

I first read Keats when I was a college boy who hoped some day to write; but I'd beforehand gotten addicted precisely to Wordsworth, trusting as shibboleth a passage from the *Recluse* fragment:

> Paradise, and groves
> Elysian, Fortunate Fields — like those of old
> Sought in the Atlantic Main — why should they be
> A history only of departed things,
> Or a mere fiction of what never was?
> For the discerning intellect of Man,
> When wedded to this goodly universe
> In love and holy passion, shall find these
> A simple produce of the common day.

At the time, I was pretty innocent even of canonical literary history, so the idea that epic or romance energies might inhere in the ordinary, that they might therefore be available to anybody, including me, felt at once like a revelation and a permission. It was also a relief: I'd been getting a lot of my poetry, as I still do, from the blues tradition in American music, and now I believed I might say, for example, that the image of sexual infidelity in Muddy Waters's "Long Distance Call," *another mule is kickin' in your stall*, rooted as it was in acute observation of the commonplace, qualified as sublime writing. If people challenged me, I'd recite to them from *The Recluse*.

Trouble was, the more I read by *The Recluse*'s creator, the more I had night thoughts: Why should this proponent of the quotidian himself seem persistently so highfalutin? I mean an epic subtitled "The Growth of a Poet's Mind"? Come *on*! Needless to say, my understanding of Wordsworth's effort was imperfect at very best, yet the poet seemed to premonish the attitude I caricatured on beginning these thoughts: Watch my mind grow, and your own pathetic little mind just might grow an inch or so, too.

And now, still convinced that in most ways Wordsworth remains the greater figure, I'm far less apt to take him up than I am the author who said in a February 1818 letter to John Reynolds that

> Wordsworth &c should have their due from us, but for the sake of a few fine imaginative or domestic passages, are we to be bullied into a certain Philosophy engendered in the whims of an Egotist[?]

This is the Keats who, in another letter to Reynolds, wrote that

> by every germ of Spirit sucking the Sap from mould ethereal every human might become great, and Humanity instead of being a wide heath of Furse and Briars with here and there a remote Oak or Pine, would become a grand democracy of Forest Trees.

Keats, in short, would at his best decline to play that more-sensitive-than-thou game. And for my money his best showed itself in "To Autumn," whose most affecting lines were for me not the celebrated closing ones but those at the start of section II:

> Who hath not seen thee oft amid thy store?
>   Sometimes whoever seeks abroad may find
> Thee sitting careless on a granary floor

The poet had seen the goddess; on the other hand, so had everyone else who made the least effort. The idea delighted me: if the great poet Keats was just another onlooker, then the other onlookers, including me, were conceivably great poets *in potentia*.

And yet, from my later perspective, the very issue of greatness seems progressively dismantled by the poem in question. Yes, "whoever seeks abroad" is prospectively an artist, an avatar of the imagination in its holiest sense, but it strikes me that "To Autumn" makes even more radical claims in pursuing its democratic mission. Not only does it dismiss individual greatness as an important aim, but it also de-emphasizes the importance of individuality itself. From the moment just cited, the author's own ego progressively cedes itself to something far broader (in this case, "To Autumn" being a so-called nature poem, the landscape), Keats thereby suggesting that the numinous really *can* inhere in the simple produce of the common day, perhaps without any great exercise of will on any single person's part.

In short, the willful and ambitious writer, the would-be prophet, of a work like *The Fall of Hyperion* seems to have recognized (and not only for "literary" reasons — recall the speed with which his health deteriorated by September of the great year) the inutility of such prophetic aspirations. Let's see how this comes about.

I am not the first to notice the absence from the opening stanza of the classical address to god or goddess. Autumn is addressed as a season, a natural phenomenon, however multifaceted. This breach of odic convention is not, admittedly, original even within Keats's own corpus: several of the other

1819 odes are similar in this way, but most do contain classical allusions or quasi-allusions at one point or another, as "To Autumn" does not. Indeed, the first stanza is a grammatical fragment (*anacoluthon* is the rhetorical term). Authorial comment on the season's presence is thus entirely elided, the only active wills within the fragment being those of the "conspiring" sun and the "thinking" bees.

Stanza two follows, a section, as I've already indicated, that asserts the omni-availability of poetic vision. And then, at the start of the final stanza, we find the one instance in which Keats, though very subtly, allows his old prophet's ego to intrude. "Where are the songs of Spring?" he asks, no doubt recalling, and a bit mournfully, the odes composed those few months earlier, "Ay, where are they?" But he quickly rallies himself: "Think not of them, thou hast thy music too." In the very act of addressing himself in the second person, the poet joins the company of *all* seekers abroad.

If that last surmise seems overwrought, note that after so minimal an egoistic intrusion, the poet becomes increasingly descriptive, even "imagist." So far from being prophecy, "To Autumn" in its closure is not even testimony. It isn't Keats, for example, who laments the fact that he is dying, as indeed he is; he notes rather that the *day* is "soft-dying." Nor is it he who mourns the demise of the day, of the year, of life itself; "small gnats" do so. The "full-grown lambs," which is to say lambs ready for slaughter, do not even mourn but simply "bleat."

We have moved quickly away from pathetic fallacy, pathos itself — largely a human construct, even in the portraiture of insects — seeming to drain from the poem entirely as it ebbs. If "bleat" struck us as a predictable verb to apply to sheep, hear how generic, almost trite, certainly colloquial, the remaining verbs in the ode become, crickets merely singing, the redbreast whistling, swallows twittering. The very vocabulary that predominates in the dramatic components — the verbs themselves — of Keats's grammar is as commonplace as any unschooled observer's might be. So much, the author implies, even for a poet's superior "sensitivity" to language.

In a song of spring like the "Ode to Psyche," Keats could write the following passage:

> So let me be thy choir, and make a moan
>   Upon the midnight hours;
> Thy voice, thy lute, thy pipe, thy incense sweet
>   From swinging censer teeming;
> Thy shrine, thy grove, thy oracle, thy heat
>   Of pale-mouth'd prophet dreaming.

Now he eschews such mighty agenda. The ego's vatic aspirations surrender themselves to something well outside the ego: in the third stanza's vision of nature, even brutes and bugs have as much right to voice themselves as does a bard.

And yet, even as he downplays the issue of the great (the "sensitive") poet, Keats leaves us "To Autumn," itself an undeniably great poem. We may be up against a paradox, though I prefer to think that the author himself would prefer to see this Septembral ode less as great than as — to choose the ubiquitous Keatsian term — beautiful.

However feckless the semantical effort to escape paradox, the power of "To Autumn" stems in the end from its modesty and from its democratic impulse. And so long as we are stuck on paradox, the ode may show our antiprophet to be prophetic after all. Ours is a poetic era often sneered at for producing so many poets but so few great ones. If, however, a progressively democratic spirit is to attend the unfolding of human history (and I for one must believe it will, so that I can remain a hopeful man), can't we conceive of our era as the excellent one forecast by Keats in his letter to Reynolds?

Can't we conceive of the world as one in which a *collective* expression of beauty will offer the vision to sustain us? Can't we take heart from the many kinds of voice that are currently chanting their way into the so-called canon? If so, then our poetry — as Keats put it in as early a poem as "Sleep and Poetry" — will "be a friend / To soothe the cares, and lift the thoughts of man." And woman, too. And all humanity.

ର

ANGELA LEIGHTON *published her feminist study of Elizabeth Barrett Browning in 1986. In this excerpt, she describes the changing attitudes toward the popular Victorian poet and her work.*

ANGELA LEIGHTON

Elizabeth Barrett Browning: Woman and Poet 1986

In April 1850, a notice appeared in the *Athenaeum* which proposed a candidate for the newly vacated post of Poet Laureate. The writer, who was probably H. F. Chorley, listed three reasons why the appointment of a woman might be appropriate: It would be "an honourable testimonial to the individual, a fitting recognition of the remarkable place which the women of England have taken in literature of the day, and a graceful compliment to the Sovereign herself." His appreciation of the female literary spirit of the age does not in itself, however, justify the appointment of a woman. He adds, scrupulously, that "there is no living poet of either sex who can prefer a higher claim than Mrs. Elizabeth Barrett Browning." At this time neither the *Sonnets from the Portuguese* nor *Aurora Leigh* were known to the public. It was Barrett Browning's 1844 collection of poems which was considered of sufficient merit to gain her this high and reputable standing as a poet. In the event, however, the successor to Wordsworth was named as Alfred Tennyson.

By 1932, when Virginia Woolf published an essay on *Aurora Leigh* in *The Common Reader*, Barrett Browning's reputation had suffered a surprising and severe decline. Woolf praises *Aurora Leigh* warmly as "a masterpiece in embryo," but her assessment of its author's fame in the early 1930s is a melancholy one. She laments that "fate has not been kind to Mrs. Browning as a writer. Nobody reads her, nobody discusses her, nobody troubles to put her in her place." The reasons for this fall into obscurity are hard to specify. One may have been the general Modernist reaction against the eminent Victorians in the 1920s and 1930s. Another may have been an intellectual reaction against that seamy and sentimental interest in Barrett Browning's life, which started with the publication of her letters at the end of the nineteenth century and was encouraged by such popularising biographical works as Rudolph Besler's play, *The Barretts of Wimpole Street*, in the early decades of the twentieth century. One other reason may have been the steep rise in Robert Browning's reputation at this time, against which his wife's was often disparagingly measured. But whatever the precise reason, it is true that Barrett Browning's fame as a poet declined steadily in the early twentieth century, and sank into obscurity, in England, for nearly fifty years after Woolf's attempt to revive it. Only with the growth of feminist publishing and criticism in the late 1970s has this tide been turned, and her poetry come to be read again, discussed, and put in its place. That its place is much higher than a century of neglect suggests, is one of the rewards of this concerted act of recuperation.

The rise and fall of Barrett Browning's reputation makes a dramatic graph of changing critical fashions and tastes. In her own lifetime, her poetry very often received high acclaim. The reviews of her first mature collection of 1844 were prestigious and encouraging. The publication of the *Sonnets from the Portuguese* in 1850 and of *Aurora Leigh* in 1856 provoked rapturous acclamations, particularly from other writers and poets. The *Sonnets* were eagerly and favourably compared with the sonnet sequences of Petrarch and Shakespeare, for instance, and *Aurora Leigh* with the epics of Homer and Milton. On the announcement of her death in 1861, there was a flood of reappraisals of her work. These were often unstintingly enthusiastic. She was hailed, for instance, as "the greatest poetess the world has ever known" and as "the Shakespeare among her sex." She was ranked "among the chief English poets of this century," and even, as one critic was prepared to testify, "with Homer, Dante, Shakespeare, Milton, Goethe, and Shelley." Her being pre-eminent among her own sex was no bar, at this time, to joining the company of the greatest male poets.

However, at the beginning of the twentieth century it is possible to detect two distinct changes of attitude in the critics. First, there is a new preoccupation with stylistic smoothness and correctness. "She is one of the most irregular of writers," Hugh Walker complained in 1910. Other critics deplored in particular her fondness for wayward colloquial metres and for half rhyme. Osbert Burdett in 1928 echoed a widespread opinion when he praised exclusively "the beautiful strictness of her sonnets." This change in taste, and its accompanying obsession with technical correctness, resulted in a depreciation of the very strengths of Barrett Browning's poetry. G. K. Chesterton's° is a rare

---

G. K. Chesterton: English journalist and author Gilbert Keith Chesterton (1874–1936).

voice at this time to applaud her "hot wit," her "high-coloured" language and "love of quaint and sustained similes."

Secondly, however, and even more damagingly, there was a new preoccupation with the criterion of womanliness among the critics. The publication of Barrett Browning's letters at the end of the nineteenth century gave impetus and encouragement to a personalised, biographical, and sexually partisan literary criticism. In 1897, Kenyon's edition of her letters, which contained many biographical notes, answered an already increasing interest in her life; while in 1899, the publication of the love letters of 1845–46 amply gratified the avidly sentimental curiosity of both critics and public. These letters in particular helped to fuel the new, heady, chivalrous admiration for the woman, which then characterises much critical writing at the turn of the century. An idealised image of the woman gradually supplants the figure of the poet in the critics' imagination, and Elizabeth Barrett Browning comes to be known, not so much as one of "the chief English poets of this century," but as the heroine of a love story. One sign of this new romanticising strain is that *Aurora Leigh* tends to be dismissed as a hectic aberration, while praise is lavished on the *Sonnets from the Portuguese*. Behind this change in literary tastes there is evidently also an ideological bias which has more to do with woman's appointed role than with the merits of poems. To love is a more womanly calling than to write.

The result of this romantic idealisation is that the woman and the poet become separate and irreconcilable figures. Furthermore, admiration for the one very often entails an implicit depreciation of the other. This prejudice in favour of the woman at the expense of the poet is ingenuously expressed by Oliver Elton at the end of his book on *The Brownings* (1924). Although this is offered as a study of both poets, Elton devotes only the last thirteen pages to Elizabeth, and these are largely a personal eulogy of the woman. "Altogether," he concludes, "we leave Mrs. Browning with a mixture of admiration and discomfort. Her faults of form and phrase are never the faults of smallness; it would have been an honour to have known her. Often we feel we would rather have known her than read her." Not only does the image of the woman contend for Elton's attention against the poems themselves; that image also provides a form of compensation for the technical shortcomings of those poems. Barrett Browning's "faults of form and phrase" are quickly excused and dismissed in the thought that "it would have been an honour to have known her." Elton's confessed predilection for the woman finally provides a reason for not reading her poetry at all: "We would rather have known her than read her."

ର୍ଯ

ROBERT LOWELL's *comments on "Skunk Hour" were a response to a discussion of the poem by fellow poets Richard Wilbur, John Frederick Nims, and John Berryman. The comments were included in the book* The Contemporary Artist as Artist and Critic *(1964), edited by Anthony Ostroff.*

ROBERT LOWELL

An Explication of "Skunk Hour" 1964

I. THE MEANING

The author of a poem is not necessarily the ideal person to explain its meaning. He is as liable as anyone else to muddle, dishonesty, and reticence. Nor is it his purpose to provide a peg for a prose essay. Meaning varies in importance from poem to poem, and from style to style, but always it is only a strand and an element in the brute flow of composition. Other elements are pictures that please or thrill for themselves, phrases that ring for their music or carry some buried suggestion. For all this the author is an opportunist, throwing whatever comes to hand into his feeling for start, continuity, contrast, climax, and completion. It is imbecile for him not to know his intentions, and unsophisticated for him to know too explicitly and fully. . . .

I am not sure whether I can distinguish between intention and interpretation. I think this is what I more or less intended. The first four stanzas are meant to give a dawdling more or less amiable picture of a declining Maine sea town. I move from the ocean inland. Sterility howls through the scenery, but I try to give a tone of tolerance, humor, and randomness to the sad prospect. The composition drifts, its direction sinks out of sight into the casual, chancy arrangements of nature and decay. Then all comes alive in stanzas V and VI. This is the dark night. I hoped my readers would remember John of the Cross's poem. My night is not gracious, but secular, puritan, and agnostical. An Existentialist night. Somewhere in my mind was a passage from Sartre or Camus° about reaching some point of final darkness where the one free act is suicide. Out of this comes the march and affirmation, an ambiguous one, of my skunks in the last two stanzas. The skunks are both quixotic and barbarously absurd, hence the tone of amusement and defiance. "Skunk Hour" is not entirely independent, but the anchor poem in its sequence. . . .

"Skunk Hour" was begun in mid-August 1957, and finished about a month later. In March of the same year, I had been giving readings on the West Coast, often reading six days a week and sometimes twice on a single day. I was in San Francisco, the era and setting of Allen Ginsberg, and all about very modest poets were waking up prophets. I became sorely aware of how few poems I had written, and that these few had been finished at the latest three or four years earlier. Their style seemed distant, symbol-ridden and willfully difficult. I began to paraphrase my Latin quotations, and to add extra syllables to a line to make it clearer and more colloquial. I felt my old poems hid what they were really about, and many times offered a stiff, humorless, and even impenetrable surface. I am no convert to the "beats." I know well too that the best poems are not necessarily poems that read aloud. Many of the greatest poems can only be read to one's self, for inspiration is no substitute for humor, shock, narrative, and a hypnotic voice, the four musts for oral performance. Still, my own poems

---

Sartre or Camus: Jean-Paul Sartre (1905–1980) and Albert Camus (1913–1960) were important modern French writers.

seemed like prehistoric monsters dragged down into the bog and death by their ponderous armor. I was reciting what I no longer felt. What influenced me more than San Francisco and reading aloud was that for some time I had been writing prose. I felt that the best style for poetry was none of the many poetic styles in English, but something like the prose of Chekhov or Flaubert.

When I returned to my home, I began writing lines in a new style. No poem, however, got finished and soon I left off and tried to forget the whole headache. Suddenly, in August, I was struck by the sadness of writing nothing, and having nothing to write, of having, at least, no language. When I began writing "Skunk Hour," I felt that most of what I knew about writing was a hindrance.

The dedication is to Elizabeth Bishop, because rereading her suggested a way of breaking through the shell of my old manner. Her rhythms, idiom, images, and stanza structure seemed to belong to a later century. "Skunk Hour" is modeled on Miss Bishop's "The Armadillo," a much better poem and one I had heard her read and had later carried around with me. Both "Skunk Hour" and "The Armadillo" use short line stanzas, start with drifting description, and end with a single animal. . . .

"Skunk Hour" was written backwards, first the last two stanzas, I think, and then the next to last two. Anyway, there was a time when I had the last four stanzas much as they now are and nothing before them. I found the bleak personal violence repellent. All was too close, though watching the lovers was not mine, but from an anecdote about Walt Whitman in his old age. I began to feel that real poetry came, not from fierce confessions, but from something almost meaningless but imagined. I was haunted by an image of a blue china doorknob. I never used the doorknob, or knew what it meant, yet somehow it started the current of images in my opening stanzas. They were written in reverse order, and at last gave my poem an earth to stand on, and space to breathe.

ಙ

CHRISTOPHER MERRILL *has most recently published the poetry collections* Workbook *(1988) and* Fevers and Tides *(1989). His discussion of Sir Thomas Wyatt's poem examines the subtleties of its meters.*

CHRISTOPHER MERRILL

Wyatt's "They Flee from Me" 1996

The conceit of comparing his beloved to a wild animal is . . . central to [Sir Thomas] Wyatt's most famous ballad, "They Flee from Me." Written in Chaucer's stanza, the popular seven-line ballad stanza that employs a rhyme royal scheme (named after King James I of Scotland, who used it in *The Kingis Quair*) and what Robert Frost might call "loose iambics," this poem has baffled strict prosodists for centuries. How to scan the second line, for example, or the fifth, without resorting to complicated metrical schemes bearing little relation to normal speech patterns is the problem facing the student of prosody. (One possible solution:

With nak | ed foot | stalk | ing in | | my cham | ber
That some | time | they put | themselves | in dan | ger)

To explain such departures from normal practice, one of his editors suggests that Wyatt "regards precision, clarity, or concentration of meaning as of primary importance." But it is more than that: such precision has its own music, which hearkens back to the stress-based prosody of Anglo-Saxon verse; that is, Wyatt is happy to sacrifice a syllable here or there in favor of rhythms buried in our ancestral memory. What better tune for the oldest subject in poetry, the lover's grief at the beloved's indifference?

In like manner, Wyatt has no fear of pulling readers up short, literally speaking, offering four-beat lines (foreshadowed in lines two and five?) when he wants to draw attention to the consequences of his loss. The emotional logic of this poem resides in moments of metrical uncertainty — "That now are wild, and do not remember," for example, or "And I have leave to go, of her goodness" — juxtaposed with the rhythmic certainty of, say, the run of pleasing pentameters in the second stanza. Here the poet celebrates one glorious night, culminating in a four-beat line — "Therewithall sweetly did me kiss" — as if to suggest the flee(t)ing nature of love: we expect to hear another beat, in the same way that the poet may have imagined he would have more nights with his beloved.

To reinforce his point, Wyatt begins the final stanza with another four-beat line: "It was no dream, I lay broad waking" is an intimate revelation, as if the poet has no choice but to confide, in the plainest tones, the nature of his loss, his sorrow. What he reveals is his bitter knowledge that nothing will ever be the same, for fortune has abandoned him. And his "strange fashion of forsaking"? This is how he bids farewell to a woman and a world. What he mourns is the loss of the certainty by which he once lived, which was embodied in the love of one woman — Anne Boleyn?° — who "softly said, 'Dear heart, how like you this?' "

"Uncertainty," according to Joseph Brodsky,° "is the mother of beauty, one of whose definitions is that it's something which isn't yours." And what was more uncertain in Renaissance England than the courtier's life? Wyatt's properties were confiscated in 1541, at which point only a pardon from the King spared him the loss of his head. More, he lived through a revolution in thinking, which began with a rival's love for his mistress and ended in the Reformation of the English Church. What makes "They Flee from Me" so poignant is that while the poet says good-bye to a woman, an age, and a world, there is such "passionate intensity" in his verse that one cannot help feeling he was in his way also greeting the new order.

Anne Boleyn: Boleyn (1507?–1536) was the second wife of Henry VIII and mother of Queen Elizabeth I of England. **Joseph Brodsky:** Soviet poet (1940–1995) exiled to the United States.

"The pass to poetry," Nadezhda Mandelstam° affirmed, "is granted only by faith in its sacramental character and a sense of responsibility for everything that happens in the world." Sir Thomas Wyatt the Elder was a poet responsible for his time and ours, which is why we may yet learn lessons from him vital to our own period of change, when the world is once again reorganizing itself day by day, stanza by stanza.

ʊʊ

MARIANNE MOORE *was one of the most skillful commentators on her own poetry and poetics. Her answers to these questions presented by poet Howard Nemerov were published in 1966.*

MARIANNE MOORE

Some Answers to Questions Posed by Howard Nemerov

1966

Nemerov: Do you see your work as having essentially changed in character or style since you began?

Moore: No, except that rhythm was my prime objective. If I succeeded in embodying a rhythm that preoccupied me, I was satisfied.

Uniform line length seemed to me essential as accrediting the satisfactory model stanza and I sometimes ended a line with a hyphen, expecting the reader to maintain the line unbroken (disregarding the hyphen). I have found readers misled by the hyphen, mistaking it as an arcane form of emphasis, so I seldom use it today.

I am today much aware of the world's dilemma. People's effect on other people results, it seems to me, in an enforced sense of responsibility — a compulsory obligation to participate in others' problems.

Nemerov: Is there, has there been, was there ever, a "revolution" in poetry, or is all that a matter of a few sleazy technical tricks? What is the relation of your work to this question, if there is a relation? Otherwise put: do you respond to such notions as The New Poetry, An American Language Distinct from English, The Collapse of Prosody, No Thoughts but in Things, The Battle between Academics and — What? — Others (A Fair Field Full of Mostly Corpses)?

Moore: The individuality and emotions of the writer should transcend modes. I recall feeling oversolitary occasionally (say in 1912) — in reflecting no "influences"; in not being able to be called an "Imagist" — but determined to put the emphasis on what mattered most to me, in a manner natural to me. I like end-stopped lines and depend on rhyme, but my rhymes are often hidden and, in being inconspicuous, escape detection. When I began writing verse, I regarded flowing continuity as indispensable.

Nadezhda Mandelstam: Widow of Soviet poet Osip Mandelstam (1891–1938).

A Jellyfish

Visible, invisible,
   a fluctuating charm
an amber-tinctured amethyst
   inhabits it, your arm
approaches and it opens
   and it closes; you had meant
to catch it and it quivers;
   you abandon your intent.

Then when I came on Charles Sorley's "The Idea" (probably in *The Egoist*, London) —

It was all my own;
   I have guarded it well from
the winds that have blown
   too bitterly

— I recognized the unaccented syllable (the light rhyme) as means for me, as in "The Jerboa":

. . . one would not be he
who has nothing but plenty.

. . . closed upper paws seeming one with the fur
in its flight from a danger.

Having written the last stanza first, I had to duplicate it, progressing backward.

Its leaps should be set
to the flageolet;
   pillar body erect
on a three-cornered smooth-working Chippendale
   claw — propped on hind legs, and tail as third toe
   between leaps to its burrow.

In "Occasionem Cognosce," the light rhyme is upside down:

. . . "Atlas"
(pressed glass)

looks best
embossed.

Poetry is a magic of pauses, as a dog-valentine contrasting "pawses" and "pauses" — sent me from Harvard where I had been discussing pauses — reminded me. I do not know what syllabic verse is. I find no appropriate application for it.

Might I say of the light rhyme that T. S. Eliot's phrase, "the greatest living master of the light rhyme," in his Introduction to my *Selected Poems* — suggesting conscious proficiency or at most a regulator art on my part, hardly deserves the term. Conscious writing can be the death of poetry.

∽∾

ALICIA OSTRIKER, *who teaches at Rutgers University, is well known both as a poet and critic. Recent poetry collections include* The Imaginary Lover *(1986) and* Green Age *(1989), and she is the author of the study* Stealing the Language: The Emergence of Women's Poetry in America *(1987). This description of H.D.'s early literary involvement with the poet Ezra Pound and imagism is included in her book* Writing Like a Woman *(1983).*

ALICIA OSTRIKER

The Poet as Heroine: H.D.

1983

War and sex, sex and war, inseparable. H.D. seems to have sought, over and over, a man whose love for her would be indistinguishable from his love for beauty and truth. What she found, too often for it to be accidental, was something more predictable.

I say she found it. But nothing in the world is so simple. I mean, really, she bought into it. Or do I? Pound of course was the first of H.D.'s failed romances. The Pound-figure in her 1927 novel *Her* "wanted Her, but he wanted a Her he called decorative." He quotes to her the line, "You are a poem though your poem's naught." She resists him, prefers another woman, loses both — they betray her with each other — and at the novel's end she is recovering from a breakdown. Thirty years later in her memoir *End to Torment*, as Pound is emerging from St. Elizabeth's, her attitude toward him as a writer is adoring, and she is filled with electric sexual memories. At the same time he is depicted as a sexual bully, a collector and discarder of female acolytes; had their engagement not been broken and Dorothy Shakespeare's fate been hers, she muses, "Ezra would have destroyed me and the center . . . of my poetry." Here is her recollection of the moment in the British Museum tea room when Ezra took from Hilda Doolittle the poem which would initiate her publishing career:

> "But Dryad . . . this is poetry." He slashed with a pencil. "Cut this out, shorten this line. 'Hermes of the Ways' is a good title. I'll send this to Harriet Monroe of *Poetry*. Have you a copy? Yes? Then we can send this, or I'll type it when I get back. Will this do?" And he scrawled "H.D. Imagiste" at the bottom of the page. (*End to Torment*, p. 18)

This is not far from girlish locker-room boasting. He said he *loved* me, girls have whispered to each other for centuries. Then consider the nuances: the "slashing" of her poem, the signing of her name for her.

He defines her. By the same token he can destroy her. He, not she, is strong, authoritative. "He" is any man she is attracted to, physically, emotionally, intellectually.

The scene in the tea room took place in October 1912. H.D. a year later married the idealistic fellow-poet and fellow-imagist, Richard Aldington. The War began the following year. In 1916 Aldington enlisted in the British Army, and H.D. took over his position as assistant editor of *The Egoist*. She had had a miscarriage which left her frail and possibly frigid. Aldington soon commenced an affair with the less intellectual and high-strung, more earthy American woman in the flat upstairs. The Aldingtons separated, although there was no legal divorce until 1938. In 1918 H.D.'s brother was killed in France. Her father suffered a stroke on hearing the news and died shortly after.

Until a definitive biography appears, we will not know how the poet reacted to the losses of a child, a husband, a brother, a father. But in the fictions H.D. wrote about this period in her life, she portrays the poet-heroine as a being who is excruciatingly passive, who depends on men to share her faith in "worlds of past beauty that were future beauty" and to cooperate in creating moments of mystic "bliss." When they fail her she does not fight, is not angry, is merely paralyzed. In *Bid Me to Live* the heroine is manipulated and rejected first by her war-coarsened husband, then by "Rico" (D. H. Lawrence), who has promised erotic and spiritual companionship. Criticizing a poem she sends him, Rico snappishly writes: "I don't like the second half of the Orpheus sequence as well as the first. Stick to the woman speaking. How can you know what Orpheus feels? It's your part to be woman, the woman vibration, Euridice should be enough." Her response, "But if he could enter, so diabolically, into the feelings of women, why should she not enter into the feelings of men?" remains unspoken and unshared. She imagines a way to escape "the biological catch" of sex roles: if two artists pair, "then the danger met the danger, the woman was man-woman, the man was woman-man." The men in the novel think otherwise. Shortly after invoking her ideal of androgynous mutuality between artist-lovers, the novelist repeats one of the novel's refrains: "The war will never be over."

∽

Plato's description of the ideal city-state, written in the form of dialogues in pre-Christian Athens, continued to cause argument and debate long into the modern historical era. His suggestion in Book 10 of the Republic *that poets should be banished from his city and his insistence, in other sections of the book, that poetry must be censored to support only the morally worthy and the brave acts of heroes can be seen as a basis for the control of the arts in modern totalitarian states. The English poet Percy Bysshe Shelley's "A Defence of Poetry" (p. 1311) was written, in part, as a refutation of Plato's ideas. The principal speaker in this selection from Book 10 is Socrates, and the other is Glaucon.*

PLATO
***

On Banishing Poets from the State
fourth century B.C.

TRANSLATED BY BENJAMIN E. JOWETT

This was the conclusion at which I was seeking to arrive when I said that painting or drawing, and imitation in general, are engaged upon productions which are far removed from truth, and are also the companions and friends and associates of a principle within us which is equally removed from reason, and that they have no true or healthy aim.

Exactly.

The imitative art is an inferior who from intercourse with an inferior has inferior offspring.

Very true.

And is this confined to the sight only, or does it extend to the hearing also, relating in fact to what we term poetry?

Probably the same would be true of poetry.

Do not rely, I said, on a probability derived from the analogy of painting; but let us once more go directly to that faculty of the mind with which imitative poetry has converse, and see whether it is good or bad.

By all means.

We may state the question thus: Imitation imitates the actions of men, whether voluntary or involuntary, on which, as they imagine, a good or bad result has ensued, and they rejoice or sorrow accordingly. Is there anything more?

No, there is nothing else.

But in all this variety of circumstances is the man at unity with himself — or rather, as in the instance of sight there was confusion and opposition in his opinions about the same things, so here also is there not strife and inconsistency in his life? Though I need hardly raise the question again, for I remember that all this has been already admitted; and the soul has been acknowledged by us to be full of these and ten thousand similar oppositions occurring at the same moment?

And we were right, he said.

Yes, I said, thus far we were right; but there was an omission which must now be supplied.

What was the omission?

Were we not saying that a good man, who has the misfortune to lose his son or anything else which is most dear to him, will bear the loss with more equanimity than another?

Yes, indeed.

But will he have no sorrow, or shall we say that although he cannot help sorrowing, he will moderate his sorrow?

The latter, he said, is the truer statement.

Tell me: will he be more likely to struggle and hold out against his sorrow when he is seen by his equals, or when he is alone in a deserted place?

The fact of being seen will make a great difference, he said.

When he is by himself he will not mind saying many things which he would be ashamed of anyone hearing, and also doing many things which he would not care to be seen doing?

True.

And doubtless it is the law and reason in him which bids him resist; while it is the affliction itself which is urging him to indulge his sorrow?

True.

But when a man is drawn in two opposite directions, to and from the same object, this, as we affirm, necessarily implies two distinct principles in him?

Certainly.

One of them is ready to follow the guidance of the law?

How do you mean?

The law would say that to be patient under calamity is best, and that we should not give way to impatience, as the good and evil in such things are not clear, and nothing is gained by impatience; also, because no human thing is of serious importance, and grief stands in the way of that which at the moment is most required.

What is most required? he asked.

That we should take counsel about what has happened, and when the dice have been thrown, according to their fall, order our affairs in the way which reason deems best; not, like children who have had a fall, keeping hold of the part struck and wasting time in setting up a howl, but always accustoming the soul forthwith to apply a remedy, raising up that which is sickly and fallen, banishing the cry of sorrow by the healing art.

Yes, he said, that is the true way of meeting the attacks of fortune.

Well then, I said, the higher principle is ready to follow this suggestion of reason?

Clearly.

But the other principle, which inclines us to recollection of our troubles and to lamentation, and can never have enough of them, we may call irrational, useless, and cowardly?

Indeed, we may.

Now does not the principle which is thus inclined to complaint, furnish a great variety of materials for imitation? Whereas the wise and calm temperament, being always nearly equable, is not easy to imitate or to appreciate when imitated, especially at a public festival when a promiscuous crowd is assembled in a theater. For the feeling represented is one to which they are strangers.

Certainly.

Then the imitative poet who aims at being popular is not by nature made, nor is his art intended, to please or to affect the rational principle in the soul; but he will appeal rather to the lachrymose and fitful temper, which is easily imitated?

Clearly.

And now we may fairly take him and place him by the side of the painter, for he is like him in two ways: first, inasmuch as his creations have an inferior degree of truth — in this, I say, he is like him; and he is also like him in being the associate of an inferior part of the soul; and this is enough to show that we shall be right in refusing to admit him into a State which is to be well ordered, because he awakens and nourishes this part of the soul, and by strengthening it impairs the reason. As in a city when the evil are permitted to wield power and the finer men are put out of the way, so in the soul of each man, as we shall maintain, the imitative poet implants an evil constitution, for he indulges the irrational nature which has no discernment of greater and less, but thinks the same thing at one time great and at another small — he is an imitator of images and is very far removed from the truth.

Exactly.

But we have not yet brought forward the heaviest count in our accusation: The power which poetry has of harming even the good (and there are very few who are not harmed) is surely an awful thing?

Yes, certainly, if the effect is what you say.

Hear and judge: The best of us, as I conceive, when we listen to a passage of Homer or one of the tragedians, in which he represents some hero who is drawling out his sorrows in a long oration, or singing, and smiting his breast — the best of us, you know, delight in giving way to sympathy, and are in raptures at the excellence of the poet who stirs our feelings most.

Yes, of course I know.

But when any sorrow of our own happens to us, then you may observe that we pride ourselves on the opposite quality — we would fain be quiet and patient; this is considered the manly part, and the other which delighted us in the recitation is now deemed to be the part of a woman.

Very true, he said.

Now can we be right in praising and admiring another who is doing that which any one of us would abominate and be ashamed of in his own person?

No, he said, that is certainly not reasonable.

Nay, I said, quite reasonable from one point of view.

What point of view?

If you consider, I said, that when in misfortune we feel a natural hunger and desire to relieve our sorrow by weeping and lamentation, and that this very feeling which is starved and suppressed in our own calamities is satisfied and delighted by the poets; the better nature in each of us, not having been sufficiently trained by reason or habit, allows the sympathetic element to break loose because the sorrow is another's; and the spectator fancies that there can be no disgrace to himself in praising and pitying anyone who, while professing to be a brave man, gives way to untimely lamentation; he thinks that the pleasure is a gain, and is far from wishing to lose it by rejection of the whole poem. Few persons ever reflect, as I should imagine, that the contagion must pass from others to themselves. For the pity which has been nourished and strengthened in the misfortunes of others is with difficulty repressed in our own.

How very true!

And does not the same hold also of the ridiculous? There are jests which you would be ashamed to make yourself, and yet on the comic stage, or indeed in private, when you hear them, you are greatly amused by them, and are not at all disgusted at their unseemliness; the case of pity is repeated; there is a principle in human nature which is disposed to raise a laugh, and this, which you once restrained by reason because you were afraid of being thought a buffoon, is now let out again; and having stimulated the risible faculty at the theater, you are betrayed unconsciously to yourself into playing the comic poet at home.

Quite true, he said.

And the same may be said of lust and anger and all the other affections, of desire and pain and pleasure, which are held to be inseparable from every

action — in all of them poetry has a like effect; it feeds and waters the passions instead of drying them up; she lets them rule, although they ought to be controlled if mankind are ever to increase in happiness and virtue.

I cannot deny it.

Therefore, Glaucon, I said, whenever you meet with any of the eulogists of Homer declaring that he has been the educator of Hellas, and that he is profitable for education and for the ordering of human things, and that you should take him up again and again and get to know him and regulate your whole life according to him, we may love and honor those who say these things — they are excellent people, as far as their lights extend; and we are ready to acknowledge that Homer is the greatest of poets and first of tragedy writers; but we must remain firm in our conviction that hymns to the gods and praises of famous men are the only poetry which ought to be admitted into our State. For if you go beyond this and allow the honeyed Muse to enter, either in epic or lyric verse, not law and the reason of mankind, which by common consent have ever been deemed best, but pleasure and pain will be the rulers in our State.

That is most true, he said.

And now since we have reverted to the subject of poetry, let this our defense serve to show the reasonableness of our former judgment in sending away out of our State an art having the tendencies which we have described; for reason constrained us. But that she may not impute to us any harshness or want of politeness, let us tell her that there is an ancient quarrel between philosophy and poetry; of which there are many proofs, such as the saying of "the yelping hound howling at her lord," or of one "mighty in the vain talk of fools," and "the mob of sages circumventing Zeus," and the "subtle thinkers who are beggars after all," and there are innumerable other signs of ancient enmity between them. Notwithstanding this, let us assure the poetry which aims at pleasure, and the art of imitation, that if she will only prove her title to exist in a well-ordered State we shall be delighted to receive her — we are very conscious of her charms; but it would not be right on that account to betray the truth. I dare say, Glaucon, that you are as much charmed by her as I am, especially when she appears in Homer?

Yes, indeed, I am greatly charmed.

Shall I propose, then, that she be allowed to return from exile, but upon this condition only — that she make a defense of herself in some lyrical or other meter?

Certainly.

ᔕᕐᒥ

EZRA POUND *was one of the founders of the short-lived but influential movement called imagism, which stressed clarity and economy of language. In this 1918 statement, which was later published under the title "A Retrospect" in a 1954 collection of his literary essays, Pound describes the imagists' aims.*

Ezra Pound

On the Principles of Imagism 1918

There has been so much scribbling about a new fashion in poetry, that I may perhaps be pardoned this brief recapitulation and retrospect.

In the spring or early summer of 1912, "H.D.," Richard Aldington, and myself decided that we were agreed upon the three principles following:

1. Direct treatment of the "thing" whether subjective or objective.

2. To use absolutely no word that does not contribute to the presentation.

3. As regarding rhythm: to compose in the sequence of the musical phrase, not in sequence of a metronome.

Upon many points of taste and of predilection we differed, but agreeing upon these three positions we thought we had as much right to a group name, at least as much right, as a number of French "schools" proclaimed by Mr Flint in the August number of Harold Monro's magazine for 1911.

This school has since been "joined" or "followed" by numerous people who, whatever their merits, do not show any signs of agreeing with the second specification. Indeed *vers libre* has become as prolix and as verbose as any of the flaccid varieties that preceded it. It has brought faults of its own. The actual language and phrasing is often as bad as that of our elders without even the excuse that the words are shovelled in to fill a metric pattern or to complete the noise of a rhyme-sound. Whether or no the phrases followed by the followers are musical must be left to the reader's decision. At times I can find a marked metre in "vers libres," as stale and hackneyed as any pseudo-Swinburnian,° at times the writers seem to follow no musical structure whatever. But it is, on the whole, good that the field should be ploughed. Perhaps a few good poems have come from the new method, and if so it is justified.

Criticism is not a circumscription or a set of prohibitions. It provides fixed points of departure. It may startle a dull reader into alertness. That little of it which is good is mostly in stray phrases; or if it be an older artist helping a younger it is in great measure but rules of thumb, cautions gained by experience.

I set together a few phrases on practical working about the time the first remarks on imagisme were published. The first use of the word "Imagiste" was in my note to T. E. Hulme's five poems, printed at the end of my "Ripostes" in the autumn of 1912. I reprint my cautions from *Poetry* for March, 1913.

A FEW DON'TS

An "Image" is that which presents an intellectual and emotional complex in an instant of time. I use the term "complex" rather in the technical

---

pseudo-Swinburnian: I.e., one who mimics the work of Algernon Charles Swinburne (1837–1909), the English poet whose poetry was noted for its romantic exaggeration.

sense employed by the newer psychologists, such as Hart, though we might not agree absolutely in our application.

It is the presentation of such a "complex" instantaneously which gives that sense of sudden liberation; that sense of freedom from time limits and space limits; that sense of sudden growth, which we experience in the presence of the greatest works of art.

It is better to present one Image in a lifetime than to produce voluminous works.

All this, however, some may consider open to debate. The immediate necessity is to tabulate A LIST OF DON'TS for those beginning to write verses. I can not put all of them into Mosaic negative.

To begin with, consider the three propositions (demanding direct treatment, economy of words, and the sequence of the musical phrase), not as dogma — never consider anything as dogma — but as the result of long contemplation, which, even if it is some one else's contemplation, may be worth consideration.

Pay no attention to the criticism of men who have never themselves written a notable work. Consider the discrepancies between the actual writing of the Greek poets and dramatists, and the theories of the Graeco-Roman grammarians, concocted to explain their metres.

LANGUAGE

Use no superfluous word, no adjective which does not reveal something.

Don't use such an expression as "dim lands *of peace*." It dulls the image. It mixes an abstraction with the concrete. It comes from the writer's not realizing that the natural object is always the *adequate* symbol.

Go in fear of abstractions. Do not retell in mediocre verse what has already been done in good prose. Don't think any intelligent person is going to be deceived when you try to shirk all the difficulties of the unspeakably difficult art of good prose by chopping your composition into line lengths.

What the expert is tired of today the public will be tired of tomorrow.

Don't imagine that the art of poetry is any simpler than the art of music, or that you can please the expert before you have spent at least as much effort on the art of verse as the average piano teacher spends on the art of music.

Be influenced by as many great artists as you can, but have the decency either to acknowledge the debt outright, or to try to conceal it.

Don't allow "influence" to mean merely that you mop up the particular decorative vocabulary of some one or two poets whom you happen to admire. A Turkish war correspondent was recently caught red-handed babbling in his despatches of "dove-grey" hills, or else it was "pearl-pale," I can not remember.

Use either no ornament or good ornament.

RHYTHM AND RHYME

Let the candidate fill his mind with the finest cadences he can discover, preferably in a foreign language,[1] so that the meaning of the words may be less likely to divert his attention from the movement; e.g. Saxon charms, Hebridean Folk Songs, the verse of Dante, and the lyrics of Shakespeare — if he can dissociate the vocabulary from the cadence. Let him dissect the lyrics of Goethe coldly into their component sound values, syllables long and short, stressed and unstressed, into vowels and consonants.

It is not necessary that a poem should rely on its music, but if it does rely on its music that music must be such as will delight the expert.

Let the neophyte know assonance and alliteration, rhyme immediate and delayed, simple and polyphonic, as a musician would expect to know harmony and counterpoint and all the minutiae of his craft. No time is too great to give to these matters or to any one of them, even if the artist seldom have need of them.

Don't imagine that a thing will "go" in verse just because it's too dull to go in prose.

Don't be "viewy" — leave that to the writers of pretty little philosophic essays. Don't be descriptive; remember that the painter can describe a landscape much better than you can, and that he has to know a deal more about it.

When Shakespeare talks of the "Dawn in russet mantle clad" he presents something which the painter does not present. There is in this line of his nothing that one can call description; he presents.

Consider the way of the scientists rather than the way of an advertising agent for a new soap.

The scientist does not expect to be acclaimed as a great scientist until he has *discovered* something. He begins by learning what has been discovered already. He goes from that point onward. He does not bank on being a charming fellow personally. He does not expect his friends to applaud the results of his freshman class work. Freshmen in poetry are unfortunately not confined to a definite and recognizable class room. They are "all over the shop." Is it any wonder "the public is indifferent to poetry?"

Don't chop your stuff into separate *iambs*. Don't make each line stop dead at the end, and then begin every next line with a heave. Let the beginning of the next line catch the rise of the rhythm wave, unless you want a definite longish pause.

In short, behave as a musician, a good musician, when dealing with that phase of your art which has exact parallels in music. The same laws govern, and you are bound by no others.

∽∾

EZRA POUND wrote this essay on Walt Whitman in 1909, only a year after he had left the United States to live permanently in Europe.

---

[1] This is for rhythm, his vocabulary must of course be found in his native tongue. [Pound's note]

EZRA POUND

What I Feel about Walt Whitman 1909

From this side of the Atlantic I am for the first time able to read Whitman, and from the vantage of my education and — if it be permitted a man of my scant years — my world citizenship: I see him America's poet. The only Poet before the artists of the Carmen-Hovey° period, or better, the only one of the conventionally recognised "American Poets" who is worth reading.

He *is* America. His crudity is an exceeding great stench, but it *is* America. He is the hollow place in the rock that echoes with his time. He *does* "chant the crucial stage" and he is the "voice triumphant." He is disgusting. He is an exceedingly nauseating pill, but he accomplishes his mission.

Entirely free from the renaissance humanist ideal of the complete man or from the Greek idealism, he is content to be what he is, and he is his time and his people. He is a genius because he has vision of what he is and of his function. He knows that he is a beginning and not a classically finished work.

I honour him for he prophesied me while I can only recognise him as a forebear of whom I ought to be proud.

In America there is much for the healing of the nations, but woe unto him of the cultured palate who attempts the dose.

As for Whitman, I read him (in many parts) with acute pain, but when I write of certain things I find myself using his rhythms. The expression of certain things related to cosmic consciousness seems tainted with this maramis.°

I am (in common with every educated man) an heir of the ages and I demand my birth-right. Yet if Whitman represented his time in language acceptable to one accustomed to my standard of intellectual-artistic living he would belie his time and nation. And yet I am but one of his "ages and ages' encrustations" or to be exact an encrustation of the next age. The vital part of my message, taken from the sap and fibre of America, is the same as his.

Mentally I am a Walt Whitman who has learned to wear a collar and a dress shirt (although at times inimical to both). Personally I might be very glad to conceal my relationship to my spiritual father and brag about my more congenial ancestry — Dante, Shakespeare, Theocritus, Villon, but the descent is a bit difficult to establish. And, to be frank, Whitman is to my fatherland (*Patriam quam odi et amo*° for no uncertain reasons) what Dante is to Italy and I at my best can only be a strife for a renaissance in America of all the lost or temporarily mislaid beauty, truth, valour, glory of Greece, Italy, England, and all the rest of it.

And yet if a man has written lines like Whitman's to *Sunset Breeze* one has to love him. I think we have not yet paid enough attention to the deliberate artistry of the man, not in details but in the large.

I am immortal even as he is, yet with a lesser vitality as I am the more in

---

Carmen-Hovey: Canadian poet William Bliss Carman (1861–1929) and American poet Richard Hovey (1864–1900) collaborated on three books of verse in their *Songs of Vagabondia* series (1894, 1896, 1901). **maramis:** Likely "marasmus," wasting away. **Patriam quam odi et amo:** Latin for "Country that I hate and love."

love with beauty (If I really do love it more than he did). Like Dante he wrote in the "vulgar tongue," in a new metric. The first great man to write in the language of his people.

Et ego Petrarca in lingua vetera scribo,° and in a tongue my people understand not.

It seems to me I should like to drive Whitman into the old world. I sledge, he drill — and to scourge America with all the old beauty. (For Beauty *is* an accusation) and with a thousand thongs from Homer to Yeats, from Theocritus to Marcel Schwob. This desire is because I am young and impatient, were I old and wise I should content myself in seeing and saying that these things will come. But now, since I am by no means sure it would be true prophecy, I am fain set my own hand to the labour.

It is a great thing, reading a man to know, not "His Tricks are not as yet my Tricks, but I can easily make them mine" but "His message is my message. We will see that men hear it."

ɾɷɿ

MICHAEL RUBINER *takes T. S. Eliot's poem "The Love Song of J. Alfred Prufrock" as the subject of modern data technology in this humorous piece he wrote for the* New York Times *in 1995.*

MICHAEL RUBINER

T. S. Eliot Interactive   1995

Let us go then
   Click on one
   you and I
   the three of us
   just the men   5
   Click on one
   When the evening is spread out against the sky
   When the morning is spread out against the sky
   Around noon
Like a patient etherized upon a table;   10
Let us go,
   Click on one
   through certain half-deserted streets
   through the souks of Marrakech
   through the fourth dimension   15

Et ego Petrarca in lingua vetera scribo: "And I, Petrarca, write in the old language." The Italian poet and scholar Francesco Petrarca (1304–1374) chose to write in Latin rather than Italian.

The muttering retreats
Of restless nights
> Click on one
> in one-night cheap hotels
> in the Sultan's Palace   20
> in Foo Ching's opium den
> Click on one
> And sawdust restaurants with oyster-shells
> And a State Dinner for the Russian Ambassador
> And a Brooklyn steakhouse that's a reputed mob hangout   25
Streets that follow
> Click on one
> like a tedious argument of insidious intent
> to a secret passageway, where the Prince and his monkey are hiding
> out
> to an abandoned building, sometime in the post-apocalyptic future,
> where a gun battle is raging   30
To lead you to an overwhelming question. . . .
Oh, do not ask,
> Click on one:
> "What is it?"
> "Where are the jewels?"   35
> "Have you ever flown one of these babies before?"
Let us go and make our visit
In the room the
> Click on one
> women   40
> K.G.B. agents
> androids
come and go
Talking of
> Click on one   45
> Michelangelo
> Detective Jack Lowry
> Spork
> Sir Gowanus
> Abu   50
I grow old. . . . I grow old. . . .
I shall
> Click on one
> wear the bottoms of my trousers rolled
> launch a nuclear strike   55
> enter the Cave of Doom

invade Carthage
go back for the boy
Shall I part my hair behind? Do I dare to
   Click on one   60
   eat a peach?
   use the flame thrower?
   use the harpoon?
   use the immobilizing ray?
I have heard the mermaids singing, each to each   65
I do not think that they will
   Click on one
   sing to me
   blow up Santiago's underwater laboratory
   find the Seventh Scroll   70
   rescue Princess Naftiya
   return to the present
   save the inhabitants of Zoltar 5
We have lingered in the chambers of the sea
By sea-girls wreathed with seaweed red and brown   75
Till human voices wake us, and we
   Click on one
   drown
   go to another poem
   end session   80

ಜ

SHEROD SANTOS *teaches at the University of Missouri, and his first collection of poetry,* Accidental Weather *(1982), was chosen for the National Poetry Series; his most recent collection is* City of Women *(1994). In this reading of Shelley's famous sonnet, Santos suggests an unusual interpretation for the figure of the broken statue in the desert.*

SHEROD SANTOS

Shelley in Ruins: The Appeal of "Ozymandias"

1996

Popular opinion of Percy Bysshe Shelley's mysterious sonnet "Ozymandias" periodically undergoes a sea change. Newman Ivey White's definitive, two-volume, fourteen hundred-page biography (1940), for instance, never even mentions the poem once, though it was included in Palgrave's *Golden Treasury* (1861), and today it is generally considered one of Shelley's finest lyric achievements — the only one of his sonnets, according to Desmond

King-Hele (1960), that "can bear comparison with Shakespeare's." The reason for this is both more and less baffling than might first appear, for the rise and fall of this poem's individual reputation seems inversely correspondent to the rise and fall of the overall reputation of Shelley's work. To put it more bluntly, those who are drawn to this poem appear to admire it, not because it's quintessential Shelley, but because it's so out of keeping with Shelley's style. Likewise, those who dislike or ignore it appear to do so for the very same reason. Where Shelley is normally oracular, extravagant, intuitional, and transportive, here he is detached, ironic, skeptical, and cool — as though the Orphean lute had been traded in for the slide rule of the metaphysical poet.

So who was Ozymandias anyway? At one level we know that this was the Greek name for Rameses II, and that inscribed on an Egyptian temple, as recorded by Diodorus Siculus, is the sentence "I am Ozymandias, king of kings." In the autumn of 1817, around the time of the poem's composition, things Egyptian were making quite a stir in England, and the British Museum had just taken in a collection of pieces from the empire of the Rameses — pieces including the Rosetta Stone and a large-scale figure of Rameses II. Following a visit to the museum with Horace Smith (the stockbroker poet who served as Shelley's London financial agent), Shelley proposed that they each compose a sonnet on the subject, and that "Ozymandias" is the wholly unimaginable result of that seemingly offhand proposal. But that information is circumstantial at best, and as such it only leads us back to itself. The more telling story lies elsewhere.

The son of a member of Parliament, Shelley was a poet who in his youth — and since he lived to be only twenty-nine, I use that term in a relative sense — believed passionately in the role of the poet as world reformer, political activist, agent of justice, and enemy of commerce, royalty, and religion. This was the poet who at eighteen sent copies of his pamphlet *The Necessity of Atheism* to all the faculty and administrators at Oxford (where he was a student at the time) and to all the bishops in the United Kingdom — a quixotic gesture for which he was duly and promptly expelled. This was the same poet who, months later in Dublin, attempted to organize the Irish into "the society of peace and love," and then, having failed at that, resettled in Wales where he sent out into the waiting world yet another hopeful pamphlet, *A Declaration of Rights,* which he launched into the air in bright balloons and onto the sea in toy boats and corked bottles. By then he was nineteen and midway through the writing of his first significant poem, *Queen Mab,* a long verse narrative studded with lectures on politics, religion, and society. In an 1812 letter to the philosopher William Godwin, he described that period of his life this way: "I could not descend to common life: the sublime interest of poetry, lofty and exalted achievements, the proselytism of the world, the equalization of its inhabitants, were to me the soul of my soul."

"Ozymandias," I think, needs to be read in light of that early, and apparently boundless, moral fervor, and in light of that age-old, ongoing, back-and-forth struggle — as germane today as then — between the social and aesthetic demands of an art. For though Shelley was only twenty-five at the time of its composition, his illimitable earlier claims on the world and his role as crusader within it, had been tested seriously by events in his life: the abandonment of his children and wife, Harriet Westbrook, to elope with Mary Godwin; the suicide of Mary's half-sister, for which Shelley felt partially responsible; the death and possible suicide of Harriet; the scandal surrounding Mary's stepsister, Claire Clairmont, pregnant by Byron though assumed by many to be pregnant by Shelley; the court's denial of custody of his children by Harriet, and his fear that he'd eventually lose custody of his children by Mary as well. The list goes on. His own small "society of peace and love" had proven to be anything but. His political aspirations had likewise come to nought. And his poetry was now generally received with a resounding public indifference. So the magnitude of his disillusionment — matched only by the vastness of his early ambitions — suffuse "Ozymandias" with a sobering retrospective self-contempt.

For though "Ozymandias" characteristically assumes Shelley's lifelong disdain for despots and kings — that "sneer of cold command" — and though the poem can be (and normally is) read as a political tract to express that disdain, it is also tempting to see the poem as a moment when Shelley steps back from himself. When, through the eyes of posterity, he observes that hopelessly failed persona — that venerated, long-suffering, super-sensitive *"Me,"* as he described it in "Julian and Maddalo," "who am as a nerve o'er which do creep / the else unfelt oppressions of this earth."

It is tempting in fact to see "Ozymandias" as an instance of the poem revising the poet, abruptly caught out in that (sometimes) painfully clarifying light that poetry and dreams will cast. It may be that there is more of Shelley in that "shattered visage" than we first perceive. For are the grand delusions of a tyrant who could boast "Look on my works, ye Mighty, and despair!" all that different from those of a poet who had once aspired to "lofty and exalted achievements, the proselytism of the world, the equalization of its inhabitants"? Perhaps pressing into being through the features of that disintegrated stone is a self Shelley now finds betrayed by destiny and lying in the rubble of his own exuberent idealism.

Yet oddly enough — and herein lies the poem's unspoken promise to the poet — within that bitter self-negation resides a deeper, more enduring affirmation. For out of "the decay / Of that colossal wreck," the world reformer will discover at last a more truly self-centering (hence, as he'd hoped, self-transcending) relationship to his art. As true for Shelley as it was for Keats, the death of the self was a prerequisite for the birth of the poet. By the time he'd write the *Defence of Poetry* — composed the year before his death, four years after "Ozymandias" — Shelley would finally come around to claim that a poet "would do ill to embody his own conceptions of right and wrong, which are usually those of his place and time, in his poetical creations, which participate in neither."

But let's go back to the beginning.

That eerie sense of detachment that distinguishes "Ozymandias" from others in the Shelley canon — and which determines for some its value as a poem — is established through a complex layering of voices, and an equally complex layering of historical times. In a prototypical modernist vein, th poem unfolds as a story within a story within a story. We have, first off, what might be called the poem's "frame," a tale recounted by the poem's anonymous narrator, who, to whatever degree, might be seen as the poet himself. His story holds a second story, as told by a "traveler from an antique land," a story before which the original narrator quickly disappears. In some faraway and long ago place, the traveler is reported to say, exists a desert in which he'd found "Two vast and trunkless legs of stone" and, nearby, "a shattered visage." And that was all, "Nothing beside remains." No trace of those achievements about which an inscription on the pedestal proudly claims, "Look on my works, ye Mighty, and despair!"

But the time the traveler refers us to points back to another time, to yet another story within *his* story, a time preceding the pedestal and the trunkless legs, a time from which a message was launched, as in a toy boat or corked bottle, onto a sea of random connections that have brought it here today. That message appears to have something to do with "those passions . . . / Which yet survive," though the artist who "mocked them" (*mocked* here means copied, not ridiculed) and the king whose heart they fed are both now reduced to "lifeless things." The message appears to exist somewhere in that pointed juxtaposition of what survives and what is swallowed up by the inexorable movement of time.

A curious thing has happened here, for the role of the artist, while linked by those passions to the role of the sovereign, is also implicitly distinguished from it. What survives of the ruler — or, in my reading, of the youthful idealist Shelley — is not, as the inscription claims, "my works," but a subordinate and reducible disposition. What survives of the artist, while reducible to neither the work nor the disposition, still of necessity contains them both (the "sneer" is inseparable from the stone on which it is carved). More significantly, the artist's making has somehow managed to outstrip time. For this reason one might assume safely that the poem has less to do with Ozymandias as an emblem of those absolute rulers Shelley deplored — after all, whether tyrant or benevolent leader, the fate of Ozymandias would remain the same — and more to do with that carefully nuanced chain of connections that has accurately "read," skillfully "mocked," and successfully kept alive "those passions."

That process, of course, only begins with the sculptor. Had it ended with him, his works, like those of Ozymandias, would have been equally lost to time. For in order to keep those passions alive, there is a second artist (whose art is telling) who has had to read and record their movement: that mysterious "traveler from an antique land," without whose story we'd know nothing of this. And then, as well, as we circle back through the layers of the poem, we are reminded of a crucial tertiary link: the poet himself, who composed the poem "Ozymandias," which contains and keeps alive both the traveler's story and the sculptor's stone.

Oddly enough, the poet proves the least present of all the figures in the poem. He ostensibly speaks only the first ten words of the sonnet, and those are directed away from himself: "I met a traveler from an antique land / Who said: . . . ." So where is he, this poet who, after a visit to the British Museum, proposed to a friend that they each attempt a sonnet on the subject? The poet who, through a mysterious confluence of events in his life, sat down to write a poem unlike anything he'd written before? It's appealing to imagine — and for some it may be instructive as well — that for the moment anyway there was no poet, that the poem was composed in that stupefying silence ("boundless and bare") between the death of one self and the birth of another; or that the poet who would be had not yet come into being, while the poet who was turned to rubble. It's appealing to imagine that at most there existed a consciousness, the faintest whisper of a consciousness, gazing back over the ruined prospect of its own past life. And what did this consciousness see? To borrow the words addressed to yet another famously uprooted statue — the great stone statue of General Du Puy in [Wallace] Stevens's *Notes Toward a Supreme Fiction* — "There never had been, never could be, such / A man."

The drama of this poem as anomaly — or more accurately as poem *donnée* — demands that we read it against the lavish backdrop of Shelley's earlier work, not as the negation or ratification of that work, but as an unwitting, and perhaps even unwanted, revelation of a spirit that had, until then, fueled that work — and would thereafter be called upon to transfigure it. "Ozymandias" serves as a cautionary tale — told by the poem to the poet midway in his writing life — about the futilities of worldly ambition and the transience of fame. But it's a poem with a darker interior as well, for at the heart of its revelation lies nothing less than a harrowing encounter with the desolate experience of self-extinction: "Round the decay / Of that colossal wreck, boundless and bare / The lone and level sands stretch far away." The shock of that experience accounts for the almost posthumous tone that attends its lines, and the effect of those lines remains one of the more urgent and unsettling and unmediated moments in Shelley's work.

ひ♋

PETER SCHMITT's *recent books include* Country Airport *and* Hazard Duty. *In his discussion of Randall Jarrell's poem, he examines the challenge of writing a poem in which the poem's central figure is a different sex from the writer.*

PETER SCHMITT

Sad Heart at the Supermarket: Randall Jarrell's "Next Day"

1996

One of the challenges for any poet, just as for a playwright or novelist, is to write convincingly in the voice of the other sex. If Randall Jarrell's dramatic monologue, or persona poem "Next Day" succeeds in this endeavor, it must do so by persuading us that this modern suburban woman's voice is entirely credible. For the poem to transcend the mere impersonation of the other gender, it must speak for humanity in general — clearly the larger of the poet's tasks.

"Next Day" begins at the supermarket, specifically in the detergent aisle: "Moving from Cheer to Joy, from Joy to All." The ironies are many in this opening line: the impossibly upbeat names on the boxes, contrasting with the speaker's own disillusionment; she is in some way trying to cleanse her life, but can't get further than her laundry; she has bypassed happiness (Cheer, Joy) for the myth of having it All, as much a fantasy today as in the prefeminist sixties when Jarrell's housewife could conceive of little in her role beyond the traditional cooking and cleaning. For her, of course, "All" turns out to be a box of soap. And ever since the rice thrown at her wedding, what remains for her that is "wild," unruly, undomesticated? Certainly not "my Cornish game hens," bred for nothing more than consumption. Her counterparts in the market, in their frisky suburban wear, are just as deprived ("slacked or shorted") despite the abundance in their carts, and one hears "basket cases" in the remainder of the fourth line. But these other women, faceless as chickens in a coop, "Are selves I overlook," the speaker claims, at least outside of the poem's relentless self-scrutiny. It's a habit she's learned from William James, this knowing when to turn away. Is Jarrell attempting to lend his poem a little academic weight, or would a long-married homemaker really know William James? It's possible, particularly if she were college educated, and if the other wives lack such a sophisticated frame of reference it only tends to make her situation rather more depressing. The internal rhyme of "selves" and "shelves" suggests that her life has indeed been "shelved" intellectually, emotionally, physically.

As the bagboy brings the groceries out to her station wagon, that comfortably suburban vehicle of domesticity, marking her "station" in life, there is at least one self she can't "overlook." Out, briefly, in the open air, her comparisons are no longer to the clucking marketgoers but to the larger world, and "What I've become / Troubles me even if I shut my eyes." Squeezing those eyes shut conjures an earlier self, "When I was young and miserable and pretty / And poor." So much for youth as a carefree time! The speaker acknowledges the conventionality of her youthful desires: "to have a husband, / A house and children" (in the usual order of attainment). "Now that I'm old," and having realized those familiar ambitions, her wish is no less conventional: "That the boy putting groceries in my car / / See me." To be favored again by youth itself. The enjambment of "See me" at the beginning of the new stanza, and its repetition at the other end of the line, force us indeed to see the phrase in all its imperative urgency: *See me!* But the bagboy, alas, does not.

It puzzles her, his lack of interest, when "For so many years / I was good enough to eat": a tasty grocery herself, the object of men's desires, when men *were* the "world" that "looked at me / And its mouth watered." (Now she looks at the world, and her *eyes* water.) Once, the eyes of others, "strangers," undressed her, like a stuffed game hen. These undressings are relegated now to the past, as are the allusions in the following lines: "holding their flesh within my flesh, their vile / / Imaginings within my imagining, / I too have taken / The chance of life." If we take this passage with at least some literalism (as we should for every line), do we assume Jarrell means her single days, sleeping with virtual strangers? Note the breath taken at the stanza break after "vile": how the "imaginings," which she herself shares, are somehow more daunting than the very acts themselves. Or has she only undressed the others with her own eyes? Taking "The chance of life" would hint otherwise — that actual, physical liaisons with others, even relative strangers, are what one must sometimes risk to gain something greater, something Jarrell quietly terms "life." It is as if she insists, *I, too, have lived, I have known desire* — if in the past.

Now, however, the speaker would settle for attracting not even men, but, from her middle-aged outlook, a "boy," who instead of giving her the eye, "pats my dog." "Now I am good," she says, if not "good enough to eat." Safe, leashed, beyond the lusts of strangers, she thinks back to "The last mistaken, / Ecstatic, accidental bliss," not necessarily sexual at all, but a "blind / / Happiness" — a filmy bubble of contentment, perhaps illusory — "that, bursting, leaves upon the palm / Some soap and water" — the detergent with which the poem began, the residue on one's hands after marriage and at least three children, now nearly grown. "It was so long ago," she reflects, "back in some Gay / Twenties" — *her* twenties? — "Nineties, I don't know." Possibly her confusion is meant to call back an imagined simpler time.

"Today," instead of an almost unlooked-for happiness, what she has is painfully felt absence, especially of her loved ones — daughter and sons away at school, husband at work — everything she once wished for and acquired, and yet she still feels alone and wishes for them still, even wishes on their behalf. The delight and pride she can take in her "accomplishments," so to speak, is limited; her daughter is "lovely," but still away from her. With only the dog and maid for company, she "go[es] through the sure unvarying days / At home in them." Home here means only routine, and yet it is precisely that safe, orderly predictability or constancy she most fears losing: "As I look at my life, / I am afraid / Only that it will change, as I am changing." What she fears, of course, is getting older and facing death.

The speaker's language is direct and exposed to the very degree that she feels exposed and vulnerable and would like to turn away but can't. "I am afraid," she repeats, "this morning, of my face." What one has known intimately all one's life now seems virtually dissociated, disembodied from the self: "It looks at me / From the rear-view mirror" just as she reviews her life. Aspects of her appearance — her eyes and smile — that have always bothered her are now, she tells us point-blank, features "I hate," even, ironically, as she smiles bravely and ruefully at her reflection. That face holds no surprises for her anymore, whatever is to be found there is "plain, lined . . . gray," bearing only one message that it repeats: "You're old." And she repeats it to herself, and for us: "That's all, I'm old." Everyone ages; how is my problem different from anyone else's? With this momentary, offhand deflection, we are all implicated in the poem.

And yet what age brings is not solely, if at all, the comforting wisdom of perspective, the wisdom of a William James. What it brings instead is a palpable fear, as the speaker repeats for the third time, "I'm afraid"; and only now do we grasp the import of the poem's title, "as I was at the funeral / I went to yesterday." We realize that the poem has been set not in the morning-after of a gratifying sexual rendezvous, but the at least as sobering *mourning* after, more frequent with age, of going to a funeral. And what frightened her so was seeing herself in the guise of her late friend, most likely another prosperous, middle-aged housewife.

"My friend's cold made-up face," rouged by morticians, is also unreal in the same way hers seems to be from that rearview mirror as she drives home. She replays touching the dead woman's face, and finding it "granite among its flowers" — that jarring juxtaposition — just as our speaker is hardened amid whatever mitigating influences her life may offer — her children, say, her house, her husband. "Her undressed, operated-on, dressed body" brings back with what one might call an almost surgical irony the earlier line, "How often they have undressed me," and the speaker spells both her lost youth and her waiting future in looking at her dead friend and conceding that what she gazed on "Were my face and body." Now it is the dead she identifies with, this self she cannot overlook. In this harsh light of mortality, even her youthful passionate encounters now dull in memory to clinical probings, mechanical exploratories that prepare us for the desolation of the poem's closing lines.

"As I think of her I hear her telling me / / How young I seem" — a voice that reaches the speaker from memory, a remembered conversation, or through imagination, out of the grave — though the stanza break's white space communicates the span of the gulf in either case. She wants to be reassured, and alongside the dead it isn't difficult to feel relatively young. And she experiences, as she has more than once in the poem, momentary relief and gratification: "I *am* exceptional; / I think of all I have." But investing the dead with the authority she herself cannot summon proves just as futile as any attempt at self-assurance: despite her seeming youth and blessings, "really no one is exceptional" (that last word repeated to dull its distinctiveness), and she continues, bleakly: "No one has anything." She rejects the worth of material advantages, or even human bonds, in the face of death, and her identification with humanity's mortal condition is now complete: "I'm anybody." Jarrell's choice of *body* over *one* emphasizes both her physical decline and refutes any claims to individuality. In fact, in this final stanza's fourth line the one indefinite pronoun that seems to be missing is *anyone* (though shadowed by the "No one"), and the speaker's terrible sense of aloneness, and not just of a momentary nature, comes fully across.

At this point in the poem we remember that she has been driving back from the supermarket, her thoughts darkening along the way, and when she says in the penultimate line, "I stand beside my grave," we know at last she has arrived home. It isn't far, the poem would seem to say, from the detergent where we began to the boxes of house and coffin. Her home, she realizes, is her grave, it's what her life, so outwardly comfortable, has come to, and little wonder it is "Confused with my life," just as she wonders how all this time her home could so completely have become her life. What Jarrell mourns here is the virtual loss of an inner life — call it intellectual, or emotional, even spiritual — when it has been so thoroughly taken over by domestic routine. But if our housewife is confused by how her life can be both "commonplace and solitary" (just like the grave), how her life has become a living death, the poem offers little consolation to us as readers, because nowhere does it suggest that our fates — however we avoid the ensnarements of routine and tedium — should be any different from hers ("I'm anybody") in its desolation and bewilderment. No matter if William James is but a solitary entry in her commonplace book, it's enough to tell us that cultivating rich interior lives brings us no closer to what the woman who has everything is missing.

With its unobtrusive rhyme scheme and midlevel diction, "Next Day" has done nothing to distract us from the voice of the speaker in all her emotional directness. Jarrell has created a persuasive woman's voice by delivering throughout a convincing *human* voice. He has somehow managed for his 1960s suburban homemaker to speak for all of us, male and female, who at one time or another find our lives more empty than complete, and so offers us the possibility that our differences as men and women may yet prove secondary to our likenesses.

৩৩

PERCY BYSSHE SHELLEY's *lyrical, impassioned defense of the poet and his art is an expression of the romantic attitude toward art and literature. In part, Shelley is defending poetry against Plato's idea that poets should be banished from the ideal city, but he is also presenting the poet and the artist as an individual who should be free of the society's constrictions.*

PERCY BYSSHE SHELLEY

From "A Defence of Poetry"   1821

A poem is the very image of life expressed in its eternal truth. There is this difference between a story and a poem, that a story is a catalogue of detached facts, which have no other bond of connexion than time, place, circumstance, cause and effect; the other is the creation of actions according to the unchangeable forms of human nature, as existing in the mind of the creator, which is itself the image of all other minds. The one is partial, and applies only to a definite period of time, and a certain combination of events which can never again recur; the other is universal, and contains within itself the germ of a relation to whatever motives or actions have place in the possible varieties of human nature. Time, which destroys the beauty and the use of the story of particular facts, stript of the poetry which should invest them, augments that of Poetry, and for ever develops new and wonderful applications of the eternal truth which it contains. Hence epitomes have been called the moths of just history; they eat out the poetry of it. The story of particular facts is as a mirror which obscures and distorts that which should be beautiful: Poetry is a mirror which makes beautiful that which is distorted.

The parts of a composition may be poetical, without the composition as a whole being a poem. A single sentence may be considered as a whole though it be found in a series of unassimilated portions; a single word even may be a spark of inextinguishable thought. And thus all the great historians, Herodotus, Plutarch, Livy, were poets; and although the plan of these writers, especially that of Livy, restrained them from developing this faculty in its highest degree, they make copious and ample amends for their subjection, by filling all the interstices of their subjects with living images.

Having determined what is poetry, and who are poets, let us proceed to estimate its effects upon society.

Poetry is ever accompanied with pleasure: all spirits on which it falls, open themselves to receive the wisdom which is mingled with its delight. In the infancy of the world, neither poets themselves nor their auditors are fully aware of the excellence of poetry: for it acts in a divine and unapprehended manner, beyond and above consciousness; and it is reserved for future generations to contemplate and measure the mighty cause and effect in all the strength and splendour of their union. Even in modern times, no living poet ever arrived at the fulness of his fame; the jury which sits in judgement upon a poet, belonging as he does to all time, must be composed of his peers: it must be impanelled by Time from the selectest of the wise of many generations. A Poet is a nightingale, who sits in darkness and sings to cheer its own solitude with sweet sounds; his auditors are as men entranced by the melody of an unseen musician, who feel that they are moved and softened, yet know not whence or why. The poems of Homer and his contemporaries were the delight of infant Greece; they were the elements of that social system which is the column upon which all succeeding civilization has reposed. Homer embodied the ideal perfection of his age in human character; nor can we doubt that those who read his verses were awakened to an ambition of becoming like to Achilles, Hector and Ulysses: the truth and beauty of friendship, patriotism and persevering devotion to an object, were unveiled to the depths in these immortal creations: the sentiments of the auditors must have been refined and enlarged by a sympathy with such great and lovely impersonations, until from admiring they imitated, and from imitation they identified themselves with the objects of their admiration. Nor let it be objected, that these characters are remote from moral perfection, and that they can by no means be considered as edifying patterns for general imitation. Every epoch under names more or less specious has deified its peculiar errors; Revenge is the naked Idol of the worship of a semi-barbarous age; and Self-deceit is the veiled Image of unknown evil before which luxury and satiety lie prostrate. But a poet considers the vices of his contemporaries as the temporary dress in which his creations must be arrayed, and which cover without concealing the eternal proportions of their beauty. An epic or dramatic personage is understood to wear them around his soul, as he may the antient armour or the modern uniform around his body; whilst it is easy to conceive a dress more graceful than either. The beauty of the internal nature cannot be so far concealed by its accidental vesture, but that the spirit of its form shall communicate itself to the very disguise, and indicate the shape it hides from the manner in which it is worn. A majestic form and graceful motions will express themselves through the most barbarous and tasteless costume. Few poets of the highest class have chosen to exhibit the beauty of their conceptions in its naked truth and splendour; and it is doubtful whether the alloy of costume, habit, etc., be not necessary to temper this planetary music for mortal ears. . . .

Poetry is indeed something divine. It is at once the centre and circumference of knowledge; it is that which comprehends all science, and that to which all science must be referred. It is at the same time the root and blossom of all other systems of thought; it is that from which all spring, and that which adorns all; and that which, if blighted, denies the fruit and the seed, and withholds from the barren world the nourishment and the succession of the scions of the tree of life. It is the perfect and consummate surface and bloom of things; it is as the odour and the colour of the rose to the texture of the elements which compose it, as the form and the splendour of unfaded beauty to the secrets of anatomy and corruption. What were Virtue, Love, Patriotism, Friendship etc. — what were the scenery of this beautiful Universe which we inhabit — what were our consolations on this side of the grave — and what were our aspirations beyond it — if Poetry did not ascend to bring light and fire from those eternal regions where the owl-winged faculty of calculation dare not ever soar? Poetry is not like reasoning, a power to be exerted according to the determination of the will. A man cannot say, "I will compose poetry." The greatest poet even cannot say it: for the mind in creation is as a fading coal which some invisible influence, like an inconstant wind, awakens to transitory brightness: this power arises from within, like the colour of a flower which fades and changes as it is developed, and the conscious portions of our natures are unprophetic either of its approach or its departure. Could this influence be durable in its original purity and force, it is impossible to predict the greatness of the results; but when composition begins, inspiration is already on the decline, and the most glorious poetry that has ever been communicated to the world is probably a feeble shadow of the original conception of the poet. I appeal to the greatest Poets of the present day, whether it be not an error to assert that the finest passages of poetry are produced by labour and study. The toil and the delay recommended by critics can be justly interpreted to mean no more than a careful observation of the inspired moments, and an artificial connexion of the spaces between their suggestions by the intertexture of conventional expressions; a necessity only imposed by the limitedness of the poetical faculty itself. For Milton conceived the Paradise Lost as a whole before he executed it in portions. We have his own authority also for the Muse having "dictated" to him the "unpremeditated song," and let this be an answer to those who would allege the fifty-six various readings of the first line of the Orlando Furioso. Compositions so produced are to poetry what mosaic is to painting. This instinct and intuition of the poetical faculty is still more observable in the plastic and pictorial arts: a great statue or picture grows under the power of the artist as a child in the mother's womb; and the very mind which directs the hands in formation is incapable of accounting to itself for the origin, the gradations, or the media of the process.

Poetry is the record of the best and happiest moments of the happiest and best minds. We are aware of evanescent visitations of thought and feeling sometimes associated with place or person, sometimes regarding our own mind alone, and always arising unforeseen and departing unbidden, but elevating and delightful beyond all expression: so that even in the desire and the regret they leave, there cannot but be pleasure, participating as it does in the nature of its object. It is as it were the interpenetration of a diviner nature through our own; but its footsteps are like those of a wind over a sea, where the coming calm erases, and whose traces remain only as on the wrinkled sand which paves it. These and corresponding conditions of being are experienced principally by those of the most delicate sensibility and the most enlarged imagination; and the state of mind produced by them is at war with every base desire. The enthusiasm of virtue, love, patriotism, and friendship is essentially linked with these emotions; and whilst they last, self appears as what it is, an atom to a Universe. Poets are not only subject to these experiences as spirits of the most refined organization, but they can colour all that they combine with the evanescent hues of this etherial world; a word, or a trait in the representation of a sense or a passion, will touch the enchanted chord, and reanimate, in those who have ever experienced these emotions, the sleeping, the cold, the buried image of the past. Poetry thus makes immortal all that is best and most beautiful in the world; it arrests the vanishing apparitions which haunt the interlunations of life, and veiling them or in language or in form sends them forth among mankind, bearing sweet news of kindred joy to those with whom their sisters abide — abide, because there is no portal of expression from the caverns of the spirit which they inhabit into the universe of things. Poetry redeems from decay the visitations of the divinity in man.

Poetry turns all things to loveliness; it exalts the beauty of that which is most beautiful, and it adds beauty to that which is most deformed; it marries exultation and horror, grief and pleasure, eternity and change; it subdues to union under its light yoke all irreconcilable things. It transmutes all that it touches, and every form moving within the radiance of its presence is changed by wondrous sympathy to an incarnation of the spirit which it breathes; its secret alchemy turns to potable gold the poisonous waters which flow from death through life; it strips the veil of familiarity from the world, and lays bare the naked and sleeping beauty which is the spirit of its forms. . . .

. . . The most unfailing herald, companion, and follower of the awakening of a great people to work a beneficial change in opinion or institution, is Poetry. At such periods there is an accumulation of the power of communicating and receiving intense and impassioned conceptions respecting man and nature. The persons in whom this power resides, may often, as far as regards many portions of their nature, have little apparent correspondence with that spirit of good of which they are the ministers. But even whilst they deny and abjure, they are yet compelled to serve, the Power which is seated upon the throne of their own soul. It is impossible to read the compositions of the most celebrated writers of the present day without being startled with the electric life which burns within their words. They measure the circumference and sound the depths of human nature with a comprehensive and all-penetrating spirit, and they are themselves perhaps the most sincerely astonished at its manifestations, for it is less their spirit than the spirit of the age. Poets are the hierophants of an unapprehended inspiration, the mirrors of the gigantic shadows which futurity casts upon the present, the words which express what they understand not; the trumpets which sing to battle, and feel not what they inspire: the influence which is moved not, but moves. Poets are the unacknowledged legislators of the World.

∞

LOUIS SIMPSON's *comments on Robert Lowell's "Skunk Hour" are particularly interesting for their contrast with the comments on the same poem by Lowell himself (see p. 1286).*

LOUIS SIMPSON

On Lowell's "Skunk Hour"   *1978*

Speaking of "Skunk Hour," one of the poems in *Life Studies*, Lowell says that he began to feel that real poetry came "not from fierce confessions, but from something almost meaningless but imagined." He was haunted by the image of a blue china doorknob. He had never used the doorknob, nor did he know what it meant, but it started the train of images in the opening stanzas.

This is a description of a process of evoking the unconscious. The doorknob performs the function of a *mandala*, the circle used in Tibetan Buddhism as an aid in meditating, the aim being to detach the self from its relations with the world. For an artist, however, the aim would be by releasing the mind from its preoccupations, to disengage the will and so enable the unconscious — or whatever one wishes to call that part of one's being that is not amenable to one's will but seems to have a will of its own — to rise to the surface.

Lowell's discovery of the unconscious as an aid in writing came as a result of the psychiatric disorder from which he suffered and the therapy he underwent in order to control it. His blue china doorknob, something "almost meaningless but imagined," is like the image a therapist chooses from his patient's speech as he associates freely, in order to pursue it and see where it leads. It is a thread into the unconscious; tugged at, it brings other images in its train.

Lowell uses the method to recreate his childhood and the lives around it. In the house on Revere Street "the vast number of remembered *things* [Lowell's emphasis] remains rocklike. Each is in its place, each has its function, its history, its drama. There, all is preserved by that motherly care that one either ignored or resented in his youth. The things and their owners come back urgent with life and meaning — because finished, they are endurable and perfect."

The resemblance to Proust is striking — it was so that the narrator of *La Recherche du Temps Perdu* set about recovering the past. Things are the repositories of an affection that one was too preoccupied to notice. One was too selfish, the equivalent in Proust of original sin. But there may come a day when the veil is lifted, and it is a thing that lifts it — things have the power to evoke, by shape or taste or smell, a time that has been lost. The senses are the house of memory, sought not for its own sake, but because to remember is to love.

"Well-adjusted" people think that people with "artistic temperament" are always dreaming of other worlds and imagining unreal things. This is not so — it is life these neurotics dream of. It is as hard for them to find the way there as it would be for a member of the Yale Club to enter Aladdin's cave. So they have a passion for facts: Proust writes to a woman of his acquaintance asking what dress she wore on a certain occasion, and Lowell pushes through the doors of "91 Revere Street." We wish to feel and express the affection we did not feel at the time — for time without affection is time lost. But with the lifting of the veil we are able to live again in a new way; this is the "philosophic mind" Wordsworth speaks of. And if we are artists we are able to point the way to others.

ನೊ

GARY SMITH *wrote this introductory note to Gwendolyn Brooks's writing for the literary quarterly* MELUS, *where it appeared in 1983. The critic Harold Bloom included it in his 1986 collection of modern critical views titled* Contemporary Poets.

GARY SMITH

On Gwendolyn Brooks's A Street in Bronzeville

1983

When Gwendolyn Brooks published her first collection of poetry, *A Street in Bronzeville* (1945), with Harper and Brothers, she already enjoyed a substantial reputation in the literary circles of Chicago. Nearly a decade earlier her mother, Keziah Brooks, had arranged meetings between her daughter and James Weldon Johnson and Langston Hughes, two of the most distinguished black writers of America's Harlem Renaissance. Determined to mold Gwendolyn into a *lady* Paul Laurence Dunbar,° Mrs. Brooks proffered poems for the famous writers to read. While Johnson's advice to the young poet was abrupt, eventually he exerted an incisive influence on her later work. In a letter and a marginal note included on the returned poems, addressed to her on 30 August 1937, Johnson praised Brooks's obvious talent and pointed her in the direction of Modernist poetry:

> My dear Miss Brooks: I have read the poems you sent me last. Of them
> I especially liked *Reunion* and *Myself*. *Reunion* is very good, and *Myself*

Paul Laurence Dunbar: Dunbar (1872–1906) was the first African American poet to achieve success with poems written in black dialect.

is good. You should, by all means, continue you[r] study and work. I shall always be glad to give you any assistance that I can. Sincerely yours. James Weldon Johnson.

Dear Miss Brooks — You have an unquestionable talent and feeling for poetry. Continue to write — at the same time, study carefully, help cultivate the highest possible standards of self-criticism. Sincerely, James Weldon Johnson.

Of course, the irony in Johnson's advice, addressed as it is to the future *lady* Dunbar, is that he actually began his own career by conspicuously imitating Dunbar's dialect poems, *Lyrics of a Lowly Life*; yet he encourages Brooks to study the work of the "best Modern poets." He was, perhaps, reacting to the latent elements of modernism already found in her poetry; but the effect was to turn Brooks momentarily away from the black aesthetic of Hughes's *Weary Blues* (1926) and Countee Cullen's *Color* (1925) toward the Modernist aesthetics of T. S. Eliot, Ezra Pound, and e. e. cummings. It is interesting to note, however, that, even though Johnson's second letter admonishes Brooks to study the Modernist poets, he cautions her "not to imitate them," but to read them with the intent of cultivating the "highest possible standards of self-criticism." Flattered by the older poet's attention and advice, Brooks embarked upon a serious attempt to absorb as much Modernist poetry as she could carry from the public library.

If Johnson played the part of literary mentor, Brooks's relationship with Hughes was more personal, warmer, and longer lasting. She was already on familiar terms with *Weary Blues,* so their first meeting was particularly inspirational. Brooks showed Hughes a packet of her poems, and he praised her talent and encouraged her to continue to write. Years later, after Brooks's reputation was firmly established by a Pulitzer prize for *Annie Allen* (1949), her relationship with Hughes blossomed into mutual admiration. Hughes dedicated his collection of short stories, *Something in Common* (1963), to her. While Hughes's poetic style had an immeasurable influence on Brooks's poetry, she also respected his personal values and lifestyle. As she noted in her autobiography, Hughes was her idol:

Langston Hughes! The words and deeds of Langston Hughes were rooted in kindness, and in pride. His point of departure was always a clear pride in his race. Race pride may be craft, art, or a music that combines the best of jazz and hymn. Langston frolicked and chanted to the measure of his own race-reverence.

He was an easy man. You could rest in his company. No one possessed a more serious understanding of life's immensities. No one was firmer in recognition of the horrors man imposes upon man, in hardy insistence on reckonings. But when those who know him remember him the memory inevitably will include laughter of an unusually warm and tender kind. The wise man, he knew, will take some juice out of this one life that is his gift.

Mightily did he use the street. He found its multiple heart, its tastes, smells, alarms, formulas, flowers, garbage and convulsions. He brought them all to his table-top. He crushed them to a writing paste. He himself became the pen.

In other words, while Johnson encouraged Brooks to find "standards for self-criticism" in Modernism, Hughes underscored the value of cultivating the ground upon which she stood. In Hughes, in both the poet and man, Brooks found standards for living: he was a model of witty candor and friendly unpretentiousness and, most importantly, a literary success. Hughes convinced Brooks that a black poet need not travel outside the realm of his own experiences to create a poetic vision and write successful poetry. Unlike the Modernist Eliot who gathered much of his poetic material from the draw-ingrooms and salons of London, Hughes found his material in the cold-water flats and backstreets of Harlem. And Brooks, as is self-evident in nearly all her poetry, learned Hughes's example by heart.

ಐಐ

ERIC TRETHEWEY *points out in this commentary that a poem as much read and discussed as Matthew Arnold's "Dover Beach" will have detractors as well as admirers. His discussion illuminates the aspects of the poem that give it its strength.*

ERIC TRETHEWEY

The Virtue of Arnold's "Dover Beach"

1996

While generally conceded to be a great, as well as canonical poem, Matthew Arnold's "Dover Beach" has not been without its detractors. Some criticisms, such as Edith Sitwell's general estimate that readers who like Arnold's poetry are precisely those who do not like poetry, amount to little more than the posturing of a minor poet with a major agenda. Other negative judgments are to be taken more seriously, being made by writers who, if they are finally led astray by a mistaken emphasis, have a genuine commitment to poetry. Examples of such critical judgments are those of Donald Hall in his essay "Ah, Love, Let Us Be True" (1959), and Douglas Bush in his *Matthew Arnold* (1971).

My own judgment is that two qualities above all stand out in Matthew Arnold's poems, of which "Dover Beach" is among the finest and most representative. One, a characteristic noted by generations of sympathetic readers, is Arnold's sustained, elegiac tone evoking loneliness and isolation, a sense, which one encounters more frequently in twentieth-century writers, of lostness in a hostile world seemingly devoid of authentic moral value. The central issue of Arnold's poems is the problem of modernity — as he phrases it in "The Scholar Gypsy," "This strange disease of modern life, / With its sick hurry, its divided aims, / It's heads o'ertaxed, its palsied hearts." The other characteristic, which has perhaps commended itself less to our own age, is Arnold's determination to resist despair and its facsimile, specious affirmation. He wrote poems hospitable to ideas, poems informed by genuinely complex thought, that were adequate representations of the pain and dislocations of modern existence, but that refused to succumb to nihilism. The difficulty he faced was how to do this without assenting to creeds outworn or fostering illusions about the human prospect. Implicitly or explicitly, Arnold's poems raise the question that he said Wordsworth had asked with "profound genuineness" in his writing; the Socratic question of how to live. "It is important, therefore, to hold fast to this," Arnold wrote in his essay on Wordsworth, "that poetry is at bottom a criticism of life; that the greatness of a poet lies in his powerful and beautiful application of ideas to life — to the question: How to live." It is a question, whatever the literary fashion of the moment, that is unlikely ever to disappear entirely from poetry.

"Dover Beach," like Wordsworth's "Lines composed a Few Miles Above Tintern Abbey," is a meditative monologue in which the character of the meditation arises organically out of the topographical situation. In the opening lines of "Dover Beach" the scene is sketched in conventionally picturesque terms. The elements of the setting are "calm," "full," "fair," "tranquil," "sweet." The lovers in the poem might be tourists at a resort hotel (Arnold and his wife spent a night at Dover on their honeymoon). But there is something more in the scene than the merely picturesque. Midway through the first stanza, the speaker begins a new sentence with an ominous "only":

> Only, from the lone line of spray
> Where the sea meets the moon-blanch'd sand,
> Listen! you hear the grating roar
> Of pebbles which the waves draw back, and fling,
> At their return, up the high strand,
> Begin, and cease, and then again begin,
> With tremulous cadence slow, and bring
> The eternal note of sadness in.

The passage constitutes a crucial turn in the poem, introducing in a single hauntingly cadenced sentence a new, unsettling sound of waveborne pebbles that the lovers hear "Begin, and cease, and then again begin." The onomatopoeia here imitates the movement of successive waves breaking on the shore. And "the grating roar" made by the pebbles being drawn back across the rocky shingle suggests to the speaker "The eternal note of sadness," a phrase that echoes, with a distinctive qualification, Wordsworth's "Still, sad music and humanity, / Nor harsh nor grating, though of ample power / To chasten and subdue." The cadence of Arnold's language, miming the motion of the water, is a rhythmic imitation of human sorrow repeating itself throughout the generations.

The allusion to Sophocles in the next stanza functions in several ways. By alluding to the lines in *Antigone* that use the sound of the sea as a figure for human misery, Arnold establishes a genealogy for his perception and connects the present with the distant past. The note of sadness is eternal. I think, however, that Arnold had something more in mind. Sophocles occupied a position in antiquity analogous to Arnold's in the nineteenth century; he was a poet with a profoundly religious sensibility, articulating a religious view of life in an age when Greek religion, the traditional forms of belief, were losing their power to compel assent. Similarly, though Arnold was at odds with Victorian orthodoxy, at the same time that he was attacking superstition, idolatry, and dogma, he was arguing for a religious, essentially poetic, mode of consciousness and fighting the debunking positivism of much contemporary liberal thought. Arnold saw in Sophocles a tragic sense of life very like his own, a sense of human isolation in a world without any sustaining code of value. The centuries of Christian consolation between Sophocles and Arnold may have given humans hope and help in bearing the inevitable, but for Arnold, the tide of faith had turned and, like the speaker in "Dover Beach," he can hear only "Its melancholy, long, withdrawing roar, / Retreating, to the breath / Of the night-wind, down the vast edges drear / And naked shingles of the world." The plangent lyricism here is characteristic of Arnold's best poems, as is the bleak evocation of an existence bereft of belief's sustaining power.

The desolation in these lines is the lowest point of the poem and gives rise to the illumination that follows. The speaker's despair before the retreat of the tide of religious faith, a retreat that weakens the bonds of community established by belief, can only be countered by an appeal to another kind of community, one based on a demythologized commitment to others, the emblem of which is the relationship between two people, grounded in love or friendship, and supported by the virtue of fidelity. Without fidelity, men and women are left in a universe emptied of ethical content to contend against one another in meaningless violence. The insight in "Dover Beach" arrives at the poem's nadir, as if to remind us, as Wallace Stevens put it in "No Possum, No Sop, No Taters," "It is only here, in this bad, that we reach / The last purity of the knowledge of good." The retreating tide of faith leaves bare in the moonlight the naked shingles of the world. The speaker, with the insight engendered by his historical situation, laments that

> the world, which *seems*
> To lie before us like a land of dreams,
> So various, so beautiful, so new,
> Hath really neither joy, nor love, nor light,
> Nor certitude, nor peace, nor help for pain [my emphasis]

The world is not a benevolent, meaningful seascape but a "darkling plain / Swept with confused alarms of struggle and flight, / Where ignorant armies clash by night." These are the last lines of the poem, clinching it in a couplet — one of only three in the poem — as if Arnold wished to leave the reader with a strong enough image of a nihilistic universe to persuade him to accept the appeal to human solidarity presented earlier.

තුඃ

HELEN VENDLER, *in her 1988 anthology titled* The Music of What Happens, *discussed what she terms the "archetypal poetry" of Louise Glück. As a critic, reviewer, and Harvard University professor, Vendler has written on most of the important contemporary poets in the United States.*

HELEN VENDLER

On Louise Glück

Louise Glück has tried in her poetry to give experience the permanent form of myth. Hers is the sort of lyric poetry that turns away from specific details and observations (names, places, dates, quotidian details — what Lowell, for instance, made the stuff of poetry) to an abstract plane, sometimes narrative, as in the Greek myths, sometimes archetypal, as in the encounter of Man with Woman. The tendency for lyric to turn mythical is often irritating to readers who yearn for biography (Who was the Fair Youth? Who was the Dark Lady? Who, for that matter, was Shakespeare?) as if facts would resolve meaning. We all began as sophomores in this respect; but we learn as we read more poetry that it is possible for novelistic detail to obscure, rather than reveal, fictive experience — that the lean shape of myth is the nakedness guaranteeing all stories.

A better argument for mythical lyric is that the beauty possible for mythical or archetypal poetry — with its own lexicon and thesaurus of images — is different from the beauty of the historical quotidian (which too has a lexicon of its own, a specific museum of images). In the treatment of Christian anecdote, for instance, there have always been what one could call artists of essence (those, for example, who painted hieratic crucifixions showing a monumental and untormented Christ in glory on the cross) and, on the other side, artists of the actual (those who painted crucifixions exhibiting a tortured corpse in a realistic social setting).

The chief obstacle in writing mythical or archetypal poetry is that the story is already known, its conclusion familiar. Interest consequently has to center almost entirely on interpretation and manner. (It is no accident that Milton, who decided to retell archetypal stories that every literate person already knew by heart, became the poet with the most highly developed manner in our history.) Glück retells, in "Mythic Fragment," Ovid's story of the myth of Daphne, saved from Apollo's advances by her father the river god Peneus, who turned her into a laurel tree. The lyric poet, facing a narrative, must choose the point at which the lyric aria will occur: Glück gives us Daphne's postmetamorphic voice. The tree, once a girl, retells the myth with the brevity proper to lyric:

> When the stern god
> approached me with his gift
> my fear enchanted him . . .
> I begged my father in the sea
> to save me. When
> the god arrived, I was nowhere,
> I was in a tree forever. Reader,
> pity Apollo: at the water's edge,
> I turned from him, I summoned
> my invisible father — as
> I stiffened in the god's arms,

of his encompassing love
my father made
no other sign from the water.

This may be the first time that the myth of Daphne has been retold as a Freudian story, the tale of a girl too much in love with her father to accept a lover. "Reader, pity Apollo," she says; we are to reflect on the many young men who lose the young women they pursue to that unacknowledged rival, the father. And pity Glück's Daphne: begging her father to save her, she imagines that the result will be Apollo repelled, herself unchanged. Instead, she stiffens into the wood of the sexually unresponsive. Her last words are, "Of his encompassing love / my father made / no other sign from the water." The blankness of that vista — as the stiffened bark looks to the silent shore — is characteristic of Glück's poems of desolation and impossibility. In this Oedipal retelling of the myth there are no compensatory moments — no laurels bound about Apollo's brow, no ecstatic, Straussian joy in leafiness. The manner of the poem has changed the manner of the myth, turning Ovid's story into a demystifying modern story of virginity, revealing its roots in incestuous desire.

Glück's poems bend erotic stereotypes into her own forms of mannerist anguish:

> I have been looking
> steadily at these elms
> and seen the process that creates
> the writhing, stationary tree
> is torment, and have understood
> it will make no forms but twisted forms.

That splendid Yeatsian close states the poetic of Glück's book: writhing, to be stationary; stationary, to be writhing. This is the poetic of myth — animating what is eternal, freezing what is temporary and vanishing. As Glück's two adjectives imply, motion does not cease, but any notion of "progress" or "advance" or "improvement" ceases. Yeats at one point called himself a marble triton growing old among the streams; that moment when a poet becomes marble is the moment of myth. Myth and archetype offer themselves as the only formally tenable vehicles for a sense of the unchangingness of writhing human experience. The older we get, the more we "progress," the more we find our situations anticipated in Ovid, in Homer, in Genesis.

It is no accident that aphorism suits archetype. Glück shows an aphoristic talent that harks back to the Greek Anthology:

> You have betrayed me, Eros.
> You have sent me
> my true love.

"Only victims," she says elsewhere, "have a destiny."

∞

WALT **WHITMAN** *used the free, rhapsodic introduction to the first edition of* Leaves of Grass *(1855) to justify the ideas and the themes in his poetry — ideas that would lead to the revolution in poetic forms that has dominated American poetry in this century.*

WALT **W**HITMAN

From the Introduction to the First Edition of Leaves of Grass

1855

The known universe has one complete lover and that is the greatest poet. He consumes an eternal passion and is indifferent which chance happens and which possible contingency of fortune or misfortune and persuades daily and hourly his delicious pay. What balks or breaks others is fuel for his burning progress to contact and amorous joy. Other proportions of the reception of pleasure dwindle to nothing to his proportions. All expected from heaven or from the highest he is rapport with in the sight of the daybreak or a scene of the winter woods or the presence of children playing or with his arm round the neck of a man or woman. His love above all love has leisure and expanse . . . . he leaves room ahead of himself. He is no irresolute or suspicious lover . . . he is sure . . . he scorns intervals. His experience and the showers and thrills are not for nothing. Nothing can jar him . . . . suffering and darkness cannot — death and fear cannot. To him complaint and jealousy and envy are corpses buried and rotten in the earth . . . . he saw them buried. The sea is not surer of the shore or the shore of the sea than he is of the fruition of his love and of all perfection and beauty.

The fruition of beauty is no chance of hit or miss . . . it is inevitable as life . . . . it is exact and plumb as gravitation. From the eyesight proceeds another eyesight and from the hearing proceeds another hearing and from the voice proceeds another voice eternally curious of the harmony of things with man. To these respond perfections not only in the committees that were supposed to stand for the rest but in the rest themselves just the same. These understand the law of perfection in masses and floods . . . that its finish is to each for itself and onward from itself . . . that it is profuse and impartial . . . that there is not a minute of the light or dark nor an acre of the earth or sea without it — nor any direction of the sky nor any trade or employment nor any turn of events. This is the reason that about the proper expression of beauty there is precision and balance . . . one part does not need to be thrust above another. The best singer is not the one who has the most lithe and powerful organ . . . the pleasure of poems is not in them that take the handsomest measure and similes and sound.

Without effort and without exposing in the least how it is done the greatest poet brings the spirit of any or all events and passions and scenes and persons some more and some less to bear on your individual character as you hear or read. To do this well is to compete with the laws that pursue and follow time. What is the purpose must surely be there and the clue of it must be there . . . . and the faintest indication is the indication of the best and then becomes the clearest indication. Past and present and future are not disjoined but joined. The greatest poet forms the consistence of what is to be from what has been and is. He drags the dead out of their coffins and stands them again on their feet . . . . he says to the past, Rise and walk before me that I may realize you. He learns the lesson . . . . he places himself where the future becomes present. The greatest poet does not only dazzle his rays over character and scenes and passions . . . he finally ascends and finishes all . . . he exhibits the pinnacles that no man can tell what they are for or what is beyond . . . . he glows a moment on the extremest verge. He is most wonderful in his last half-hidden smile or frown . . . by that flash of the moment of parting the one that sees it shall be encouraged or terrified afterward for many years. The greatest poet does not moralize or make applications of morals . . . he knows the soul. The soul has that measureless pride which consists in never acknowledging any lessons but its own. But it has sympathy as measureless as its pride and the one balances the other and neither can stretch too far while it stretches in company with the other. The inmost secrets of art sleep with the twain. The greatest poet has lain close betwixt both and they are vital in his style and thoughts.

The art of art, the glory of expression and the sunshine of the light of letters is simplicity. Nothing is better than simplicity . . . . nothing can make up for excess or for the lack of definiteness. To carry on the heave of impulse and pierce intellectual depths and give all subjects their articulations are powers neither common nor very uncommon. But to speak in literature with the perfect rectitude and insouciance of the movements of animals and the unimpeachableness of the sentiment of trees in the woods and grass by the roadside is the flawless triumph of art. If you have looked on him who has achieved it you have looked on one of the masters of the artists of all nations and times. You shall not contemplate the flight of the graygull over the bay or the mettlesome action of the blood horse or the tall leaning of sunflowers on their stalk or the appearance of the sun journeying through heaven or the appearance of the moon afterward with any more satisfaction than you shall contemplate him. The greatest poet has less a marked style and is more the channel of thoughts and things without increase or diminution, and is the free channel of himself. He swears to his art, I will not be meddlesome, I will not have in my writing any elegance or effect or originality to hang in the way between me and the rest like curtains. I will have nothing hang in the way, not the richest curtains. What I tell I tell for precisely what it is. Let who may exalt or startle or fascinate or sooth I will have purposes as health or heat or snow has and be as regardless of observation. What I experience or portray shall go from my composition without a shred of my composition. You shall stand by my side and look in the mirror with me.

The old red blood and stainless gentility of great poets will be proved by their unconstraint. A heroic person walks at his ease through and out of that custom or precedent or authority that suits him not. Of the traits of the brotherhood of writers savans musicians inventors and artists nothing is finer than silent defiance advancing from new free forms. In the need of poems philosophy politics mechanism science behaviour, the craft of art, an appropriate native grand-opera, shipcraft, or any craft, he is greatest forever and forever who contributes the greatest original practical example. The cleanest expression is that which finds no sphere worthy of itself and makes one.

The messages of great poets to each man and woman are, Come to us on equal terms, Only then can you understand us, We are no better than you, What we enclose you enclose, What we enjoy you may enjoy. Did you suppose there could be only one Supreme? We affirm there can be unnumbered Supremes, and that one does not countervail another any more than one eyesight countervails another . . . and that men can be good or grand only of the consciousness of their supremacy within them. What do you think is the grandeur of storms and dismemberments and the deadliest battles and wrecks and the wildest fury of the elements and the power of the sea and the motion of nature and of the throes of human desires and dignity and hate and love? It is that something in the soul which says, Rage on, Whirl on, I tread master here and everywhere, Master of the spasms of the sky and of the shatter of the sea, Master of nature and passion and death, And of all terror and all pain.

The American bards shall be marked for generosity and affection and for encouraging competitors . . . They shall be kosmos . . . without monopoly or secrecy . . . glad to pass any thing to any one . . . hungry for equals night and day. They shall not be careful of riches and privilege . . . . they shall be riches and privilege . . . . they shall perceive who the most affluent man is. The most affluent man is he that confronts all the shows he sees by equivalents out of the stronger wealth of himself. The American bard shall delineate no class of persons nor one or two out of the strata of interests nor love most nor truth most nor the soul most nor the body most . . . . and not be for the eastern states more than the western or the northern states more than the southern. . . .

A great poem is for ages and ages in common and for all degrees and complexions and all departments and sects and for a woman as much as a man and a man as much as a woman. A great poem is no finish to a man or woman but rather a beginning. Has any one fancied he could sit at last under some due authority and rest satisfied with explanations and realize and be content and full? To no such terminus does the greatest poet bring . . . he brings neither cessation or sheltered fatness and ease. The touch of him tells in action. Whom he takes he takes with firm sure grasp into live regions previously unattained . . . . thenceforward is no rest . . . . they see the space and ineffable sheen that turn the old spots and lights into dead vacuums. The companion of him beholds the birth and progress of stars and learns one of the meanings. Now there shall be a man cohered out of tumult and chaos . . . . the elder encourages the younger and shows him how . . . they two shall launch off fearlessly together till the new world fits an orbit for itself and looks unabashed on the lesser orbits of the stars and sweeps through the ceaseless rings and shall never be quiet again.

ოა

RICHARD WILBUR, *in this discussion, clarifies the source of Tennyson's poem in the "Inferno" section of Dante's* Divine Comedy *as well as in Homer's epic poems about the Trojan War and its aftermath, the* Iliad *and the* Odyssey.

RICHARD WILBUR

Tennyson's Voyage of the Mind   1996

Ulysses hears "many voices" in the beckoning deep, and in this complex and celebrated soliloquy there are also many voices — diverse tones, moods, assertions, and echoes that the reader is challenged to hear rightly and to attune to if he can. To be sure, a poem so handsomely written can easily be plundered for simple messages: Robert Kennedy, campaigning for the Presidency, was given to quoting, " 'Tis not too late to seek a newer world"; that phrase and others are dear to commencement speakers, while "Old age hath yet his honor and his toil" has proven useful with more mature audiences. Tennyson himself tells us that "Ulysses" may securely be taken as a heartening poem written at a time of grief and despondency. It was begun a few days after the death of his dearest friend, Arthur Hallam, whom Tennyson (and others) had regarded as a young man of "high speculative endowments," capable of addressing the intellectual and spiritual problems of the age. It was "written under the sense of loss," Tennyson said, "and gave my feeling about the need of going forward, and braving the struggle of life."

Certainly the salient echoes of the first thirty-odd lines support the idea of getting on with it, of rousing oneself to action. The "sleep, and feed" of line 5 have reminded scholars of a soliloquy of Hamlet's:

> How all occasions do inform against me
> And spur my dull revenge! What is a man,
> If the chief good and market of his time
> Be but to sleep and feed? A beast, no more.
> Sure he that made us with such large discourse,
> Looking before and after, gave us not
> That capability and godlike reason
> To fust in us unused.
>
> (IV, iv)

The sound and sense of that last phrase may also have helped to prompt lines 22–23 of "Ulysses":

> How dull it is to pause, to make an end,
> To rust unburnished, not to shine in use!

The same two lines have reminded me and others of Shakespeare's own Ulysses, in *Troilus and Cressida*, urging Achilles not to rest upon his laurels:

> Perseverance, dear my lord,
> Keeps honor bright; to have done, is to hang

Quite out of fashion, like a rusty mail,
In monumental mockery.

(III, iii, 150ff.)

In what it says and in what it echoes, the forepart of Tennyson's poem is largely the soliloquy of a heroic spirit bestirring itself to further adventure; we rightly respond to Ulysses' great appetite for life and to such splendid measures as "Far on the ringing plains of windy Troy." And yet the first five lines of the poem, which Tennyson latterly printed as a discrete paragraph, are the musings not of a hero but of a depressed island ruler who is weary of his faithful Penelope, contemptuous of his people, and too bored and lazy to improve the laws that he administers. Such attitudes cannot be appealing in a poem by Tennyson, who by 1833 was already becoming the poet of duty and social responsibility, and they jar as well with the expectations of Ulysses that we derive from Homer's *Odyssey*. But in fact the *Odyssey* is not the main and formative source of "Ulysses," which in many respects is inconsistent with Homer; for instance, if Tiresias prophesies in Homer's Book XI that Ulysses, having regained his home and beloved queen, must set forth on yet another journey, it is an inland journey from which he will return to die "after a rich old age, surrounded by a happy people."

Tennyson's version of Ulysses is chiefly based upon the twenty-sixth canto of Dante's *Inferno*, where Ulysses — the wily deviser of the Trojan horse — is found among those who, by deceit and by counseling others to deceive, have misused the high faculty of reason. Ulysses tells, in a long and beautiful speech, how on leaving Circe's island he exhorted his companions, saying, "Consider what you were born to: you were not made to live like brutes, but to pursue excellence and knowledge"; and how he sailed with them then, in a "foolish flight" (*folle volo*) through the Pillars of Hercules toward a final engulfment in the South Atlantic. "Neither fondness for my son," his narrative begins, "nor piety toward my old father, nor the due love that should have comforted Penelope, could conquer in me the yearning to know the world entire, and the good and evil ways of men."

Tennyson's poem begins also with Ulysses' culpable rejections and forsakings, and then — despite a pompous frequency of *me* and *I* unmatched except by Milton's Satan — becomes more attractive, more positive, more vigorous, more eloquent as the hero recalls his past adventures and consolidates his will to voyaging again. That the second paragraph is self-persuasive rather than fully resolved, we know by certain negative overtones that seem almost like slips of the tongue. "Yet all experience is an arch wherethrough / Gleams that untraveled world whose margin fades / Forever and forever when I move" is a way of saying that much remains to be seen; yet the weariness of "Forever and forever" seems to grant that the quest for final knowledge is vain, and that (as the voice of despair whispers in "The Two Voices") the aged seeker is doomed to "seem to find, but still to seek." The words "To follow knowledge like a sinking star," however one may parse them, have disastrous implications in a voyage-poem, and make the reader ask whether Ulysses is seeking or fleeing, and whether his goal is renewed life or suicide. The reader must try, I think, to conceive of a troubled, wavering Ulysses of whom all those things might be true.

Up to this halfway point, Ulysses has been expressing disgust with his life in Ithaca or talking himself into a last embarkation; now, as I read the poem, he imagines what he will say to the leading citizens of Ithaca when he abdicates and embarks. His tone grows accordingly politic, measured, and reassuringly colorless. There is none of the gruff dismissiveness of the poem's opening lines; the savage Ithacans, those beastly sleepers and feeders, are now merely "rugged," and Ulysses speaks with some affection of Telemachus, though condescending toward his son's merely "blameless" and "decent" capacities. In a poem responsive to the loss of Arthur Hallam, who had he lived might have been "A life in civic action warm, / A soul on highest mission sent, / A potent voice in Parliament, / A pillar steadfast in the storm," Ulysses' low regard for governance and public service, though understandable in a restless hero of action, is not in itself admirable.

In the closing paragraph of the poem, Ulysses imagines or rehearses what he will say to his mariners — how he will enlist them in a *folle volo* beyond the set limits of the known world. Homer's Odysseus returned alone to Ithaca, having lost all his companions, but Tennyson provides his hero with sailors who are veterans of Troy. Ulysses can thus magnificently appeal to their heroic memories, as he has earlier done to his own, and thereby impress them into his service. At the same time, his inspiring speech is once more peppered with discordant notes. As Christopher Ricks has brilliantly pointed out, Ulysses' discourse, though urging departure for a "newer world," exhibits a weird and near-total avoidance of the future tense. "Gloom," "dark," moaning waters, swooning rhythms, and the phrase "until I die," hint once again at a morbid wish for death. And a number of phrases, such as "strove with Gods," evoke not only Troy but Milton's war in Heaven and prepare us for a final sinister echo of Satan's "And courage never to submit or yield" (*PL*, I, 108).

It may be that some of the dissonances in "Ulysses" belong not to Tennyson's portrait of his hero but to his own inclination to be sad, slow, and sonorous regardless of the subject. I think, nonetheless, that we can derive from the poem a vivid, intelligible personality who has the vices of his virtues. Ulysses is nobly eloquent, and he is also a crafty spellbinder; he is both greathearted and egotistical; he loves bracing adventure and is a shirker of "common duties"; he vigorously defies old age and yet is depressed; he loves life and is sick of it; he is fearless but suicidal. We are left, however, with two uncertainties about him. The first is this: how far are we instructed to condemn this Ulysses, seeing as he is based on a damned soul in the *Inferno* and puts us in mind of Satan's rhetoric in Hell? In the second place, though Ulysses is clearly not some globe-trotting retiree, what sort of knowledge is he sailing after, what sort of thought does he share with his shipmates, how will he use the reason that distinguishes him from brute beasts, and what "work of noble note" is he likely to accomplish? The answers to these questions only come, I think, when we change our focus and see "Ulysses" as an allegory of the bereaved Tennyson's resolution to ponder man's place in Nature, God's purpose in the world, our grounds for faith, and our hope of immortality — great questions raised by Hallam's death, which Hallam (had he lived) might have illuminated for his time and society.

ℛℴℛ

WILLIAM CARLOS WILLIAMS, *the poet and friend of Ezra Pound, wrote this comment in a free moment during his daily medical practice and sent it in a letter dated September 25, 1940, to his publisher, James Laughlin.*

WILLIAM CARLOS WILLIAMS

Ezra Pound's Language   1940

It's easy to forget in our dislike for some of the parts Ezra Pound plays and for which there is no excuse that he is a master of language (& makes mistakes too sometimes). That goes far. It might be his only virtue and still be a mark of greatness. It is hard to appraise as it is hard to achieve, hard to isolate for criticism as for the honors earned. It is even possible that Pound himself is self deceived and performs his miracles unconsciously while he frowns over some asininity he proposes and leans upon so heavily. His language represents his last naivety, the childishness of complete sincerity discovered in the child and true poet alike.

All that is necessary to *feel* Pound's excellence in this use of language is to read the work of others — from among whom I particularly and prominently exclude E. E. Cummings. In the use of language Pound and Cummings are beyond doubt the two most distinguished American poets of today. It is the bringing over of the language of the day to the serious purposes of the poet that is the difficult thing. Both these men have evolved that ability to a high degree.

Two faulty alternatives are escaped in the achievement of this distinction. There are plenty who use the language well, fully as well as Pound, but for trivial purposes, either journalism, fiction or even verse, I mean the usual stroking of the material without penetration where anything of momentous significance is instinctively avoided. There are on the other hand poets of considerable seriousness who simply do not know what language is and unconsciously load their compositions with minute anachronisms as many as dead hairs on a mangy dog. These latter are the more pernicious, their methods well accredited by virtue of all academic teaching, simply make their work no good. They would need to go through the crises both Pound and Cummings experienced in ridding themselves of all collegiate taint.

It is impossible to praise Pound's line. The terms for such praise are lacking. There ain't none. You've got to read the line and feel first, then grasp through experience in its full significance HOW the language makes the verse live. It lives; even such unpromising cataloguing as his cantos of the chinese kings, princes and other rulers do live and become affecting under his treatment. It is the language and the language only that makes this true.

ॐ

WILLIAM WORDSWORTH *wrote two introductions to the collection of po-ems titled* Lyrical Ballads. *This is the second introduction, to the edition of 1802, which expanded and explained ideas that he had presented in the introduction to the first edition of the work in 1798.*

WILLIAM WORDSWORTH

From the Introduction to Lyrical Ballads
1802

It is supposed, that by the act of writing in verse an author makes a for-mal engagement that he will gratify certain known habits of association; that he not only thus apprizes the reader that certain classes of ideas and expres-sions will be found in his book, but that others will be carefully excluded. This exponent or symbol held forth by metrical language must in different eras of literature have excited very different expectations: for example, in the age of Catullus, Terence, and Lucretius and that of Statius or Claudian,° and in our own country, in the age of Shakespeare and Beaumont and Fletcher, and that of Donne and Cowley, or Dryden, or Pope. I will not take upon me to deter-mine the exact import of the promise which by the act of writing in verse an author, in the present day, makes to his reader; but I am certain, it will appear to many persons that I have not fulfilled the terms of an engagement thus vol-untarily contracted. They who have been accustomed to the gaudiness and inane phraseology of many modern writers, if they persist in reading this book to its conclusion, will, no doubt, frequently have to struggle with feel-ings of strangeness and awkwardness: they will look round for poetry, and will be induced to inquire by what species of courtesy these attempts can be permitted to assume that title. I hope therefore the reader will not censure me, if I attempt to state what I have proposed to myself to perform; and also (as far as the limits of a preface will permit) to explain some of the chief reasons which have determined me in the choice of my purpose: that at least he may be spared any unpleasant feeling of disappointment, and that I myself may be protected from the most dishonorable accusation which can be brought against an author, namely, that of an indolence which prevents him from en-deavouring to ascertain what is his duty, or, when this duty is ascertained, prevents him from performing it.

The principal object, then, which I proposed to myself in these poems

---

Catullus . . . Claudian: Catullus (84–54 B.C.), Terence (186–159 B.C.), and Lucretius (96–55 B.C.) were Roman poets who wrote simply, in contrast to Statius (45–96) and Claudian (370?–410?), whose work was more elaborate.

was to choose incidents and situations from common life, and to relate or describe them, throughout, as far as was possible, in a selection of language really used by men; and, at the same time, to throw over them a certain colouring of imagination, whereby ordinary things should be presented to the mind in an unusual way; and, further, and above all, to make these incidents and situations interesting by tracing in them, truly though not ostentatiously, the primary laws of our nature: chiefly, as far as regards the manner in which we associate ideas in a state of excitement. Low and rustic life was generally chosen, because in that condition, the essential passions of the heart find a better soil in which they can attain their maturity, are less under restraint, and speak a plainer and more emphatic language; because in that condition of life our elementary feelings co-exist in a state of greater simplicity, and, consequently, may be more accurately contemplated, and more forcibly communicated; because the manners of rural life germinate from those elementary feelings; and, from the necessary character of rural occupations, are more easily comprehended; and are more durable; and lastly, because in that condition the passions of men are incorporated with the beautiful and permanent forms of nature. The language, too, of these men is adopted (purified indeed from what appear to be its real defects, from all lasting and rational causes of dislike or disgust) because such men hourly communicate with the best objects from which the best part of language is originally derived; and because, from their rank in society and the sameness and narrow circle of their intercourse, being less under the influence of social vanity they convey their feelings and notions in simple and unelaborated expressions. Accordingly, such a language, arising out of repeated experience and regular feelings, is a more permanent, and a far more philosophical language, than that which is frequently substituted for it by poets, who think that they are conferring honour upon themselves and their art, in proportion as they separate themselves from the sympathies of men, and indulge in arbitrary and capricious habits of expression, in order to furnish food for fickle tastes, and fickle appetites, of their own creation.

I cannot, however, be insensible of the present outcry against the triviality and meanness both of thought and language, which some of my contemporaries have occasionally introduced into their metrical compositions; and I acknowledge, that this defect, where it exists, is more dishonorable to the writer's own character than false refinement or arbitrary innovation, though I should contend at the same time that it is far less pernicious in the sum of its consequences. From such verses the poems in these volumes will be found distinguished at least by one mark of difference, that each of them has a worthy *purpose*. Not that I mean to say, that I always began to write with a distinct purpose formally conceived; but I believe that my habits of meditation have so formed my feelings, as that my descriptions of such objects as strongly excite those feelings, will be found to carry along with them a *purpose*. If in this opinion I am mistaken, I can have little right to the name of a poet. For all good poetry is the spontaneous overflow of powerful feelings: but though this be true, poems to which any value can be attached, were never produced on any variety of subjects but by a man who, being possessed of more than usual organic sensibility, had also thought long and deeply. For our continued influxes of feeling are modified and directed by our thoughts, which are indeed the representatives of all our past feelings; and, as by contemplating the relation of these general representatives to each other we discover what is really important to men, so, by the repetition and continuance of this act, our feelings will be connected with important subjects, till at length, if we be originally possessed of much sensibility, such habits of mind will be produced, that, by obeying blindly and mechanically the impulses of those habits, we shall describe objects, and utter sentiments, of such a nature and in such connection with each other, that the understanding of the being to whom we address ourselves, if he be in a healthful state of association, must necessarily be in some degree enlightened, and his affections ameliorated. . . .

I have said that poetry is the spontaneous overflow of powerful feelings: it takes its origin from emotion recollected in tranquillity: the emotion is contemplated till by a species of reaction the tranquillity gradually disappears, and an emotion, kindred to that which was before the subject of contemplation, is gradually produced, and does itself actually exist in the mind. In this mood successful composition generally begins, and in a mood similar to this it is carried on; but the emotion, of whatever kind and in whatever degree, from various causes is qualified by various pleasures, so that in describing any passions whatsoever, which are voluntarily described, the mind will upon the whole be in a state of enjoyment. Now, if nature be thus cautious in preserving in a state of enjoyment a being thus employed, the poet ought to profit by the lesson thus held forth to him, and ought especially to take care, that whatever passions he communicates to his reader, those passions, if his reader's mind be sound and vigorous, should always be accompanied with an overbalance of pleasure. Now the music of harmonious metrical language, the sense of difficulty overcome, and the blind association of pleasure which has been previously received from works of rhyme or metre of the same or similar construction, an indistinct perception perpetually renewed of language closely resembling that of real life, and yet, in the circumstance of metre, differing from it so widely, all these imperceptibly make up a complex feeling of delight, which is of the most important use in tempering the painful feeling which will always be found intermingled with powerful descriptions of the deeper passions. This effect is always produced in pathetic and impassioned poetry; while, in lighter compositions, the ease and gracefulness with which the poet manages his numbers are themselves confessedly a principal source of the gratification of the reader. I might perhaps include all which it is *necessary* to say upon this subject by affirming, what few persons will deny, that, of two descriptions, either of passions, manners, or characters, each of them equally well executed, the one in prose and the other in verse, the verse will be read a hundred times where the prose is read once.

∽

19

CASEBOOKS ON POETRY AND POETS

CASEBOOK ON EMILY DICKINSON

This casebook on Emily Dickinson opens with material from her most important editors. Thomas Wentworth Higginson was approached by her in 1862 as a possible mentor and advisor for her writing, but Higginson found her as evasive and puzzling as she was fascinating. Higginson's description of their meeting is the only one we have of Dickinson by a contemporary who was involved in the world of literature and publishing. Following Higginson's selection is one from Thomas H. Johnson, who edited the manuscripts for the first collected edition of her poetry in 1955. Commentaries by three poets of our day follow. Richard Wilbur discusses some of the emotions he detects behind the brilliant surfaces of Dickinson's poetry. Then Linda Gregg, a California poet who first encountered Dickinson's poetry when she was in grammar school, writes about Dickinson in an essay that introduced her own poetry in the anthology 19 New American Poets of the Golden Gate, *published in 1984. Finally, a poem by Galway Kinnell describes with dismay his encounter with a deconstructed Emily Dickinson in a modern classroom.*

THOMAS WENTWORTH HIGGINSON

Emily Dickinson's Letters *1891*

On April 16, 1862, I took from the post office in Worcester, Mass., where I was then living, the following letter: —

MR. HIGGINSON, — Are you too deeply occupied to say if my verse is alive?

The mind is so near itself it cannot see distinctly, and I have none to ask.

Should you think it breathed, and had you the leisure to tell me, I should feel quick gratitude.

If I make the mistake, that you dared to tell me would give me sincerer honor toward you.

I inclose my name, asking you, if you please, sir, to tell me what is true?

That you will not betray me it is needless to ask, since honor is its own pawn.

The letter was postmarked "Amherst," and it was in a handwriting so peculiar that it seemed as if the writer might have taken her first lessons by studying the famous fossil bird-tracks in the museum of that college town. Yet it was not in the slightest degree illiterate, but cultivated, quaint, and wholly unique. Of punctuation there was little; she used chiefly dashes, and it has been thought better, in printing these letters, as with her poems, to give them the benefit in this respect of the ordinary usages; and so with her habit as to capitalization, as the printers call it, in which she followed the Old English and present German method of thus distinguishing every noun substantive. But the most curious thing about the letter was the total absence of a signature. It proved, however, that she had written her name on a card, and put it under the shelter of a smaller envelope inclosed in the larger; and even this name was written — as if the shy writer wished to recede as far as possible from view — in pencil, not in ink. The name was Emily Dickinson. Inclosed with the letter were four poems, two of which have been already printed, — "Safe in their alabaster chambers" and "I'll tell you how the sun rose," together with the two that here follow. The first comprises in its eight lines a truth so searching that it seems a condensed summary of the whole experience of a long life: —

We play at paste
Till qualified for pearl;
Then drop the paste
And deem ourself a fool.

The shapes, though, were similar
And our new hands
Learned gem-tactics,
Practicing sands.

Then came one which I have always classed among the most exquisite of her productions, with a singular felicity of phrase and an aerial lift that bears the ear upward with the bee it traces: —

The nearest dream recedes unrealized.
    The heaven we chase,
    Like the June bee
    Before the schoolboy,
    Invites the race,
    Stoops to an easy clover,
Dips — evades — teases — deploys —
Then to the royal clouds
    Lifts his light pinnace,
    Heedless of the boy
Staring, bewildered, at the mocking sky

    Homesick for steadfast honey, —
    Ah! the bee flies not
Which brews that rare variety.

The impression of a wholly new and original poetic genius was as distinct on my mind at the first reading of these four poems as it is now, after thirty years of further knowledge; and with it came the problem never yet solved, what place ought to be assigned in literature to what is so remarkable, yet so elusive of criticism. The bee himself did not evade the schoolboy more than she evaded me; and even at this day I still stand somewhat bewildered, like the boy.

    Circumstances, however, soon brought me in contact with an uncle of Emily Dickinson, a gentleman not now living; a prominent citizen of Worcester, a man of integrity and character, who shared her abruptness and impulsiveness but certainly not her poetic temperament, from which he was indeed singularly remote. He could tell but little of her, she being evidently an enigma to him, as to me. It is hard to tell what answer was made by me, under these circumstances, to this letter. It is probable that the adviser sought to gain time a little and find out with what strange creature he was dealing. I remember to have ventured on some criticism which she afterwards called "surgery," and on some questions, part of which she evaded, as will be seen, with a naïve skill such as the most experienced and worldly coquette might envy. Her second letter (received April 26, 1862), was as follows: —

    MR. HIGGINSON, — Your kindness claimed earlier gratitude, but I was ill, and write to-day from my pillow.

    Thank you for the surgery; it was not so painful as I supposed. I bring you others, as you ask, though they might not differ. While my thought is undressed, I can make the distinction; but when I put them in the gown, they look alike and numb.

    You asked how old I was? I made no verse, but one or two, until this winter, sir.

    I had a terror since September, I could tell to none; and so I sing, as the boy does of the burying ground, because I am afraid.

    You inquire my books. For poets, I have Keats, and Mr. and Mrs. Browning. For prose, Mr. Ruskin, Sir Thomas Browne, and the Revelations. I went to school, but in your manner of the phrase had no education. When a little girl, I had a friend who taught me Immortality; but venturing too near, himself, he never returned. Soon after my tutor died, and for several years my lexicon was my only companion. Then I found one more, but he was not contented I be his scholar, so he left the land.

You ask of my companions. Hills, sir, and the sundown, and a dog large as myself, that my father bought me. They are better than beings because they know, but do not tell; and the noise in the pool at noon excels my piano.

I have a brother and sister; my mother does not care for thought, and father, too busy with his briefs to notice what we do. He buys me many books, but begs me not to read them, because he fears they joggle the mind. They are religious, except me, and address an eclipse, every morning, whom they call their "Father."

But I fear my story fatigues you. I would like to learn. Could you tell me how to grow, or is it unconveyed, like melody or witchcraft?

You speak of Mr. Whitman. I never read his book, but was told that it was disgraceful.

I read Miss Prescott's Circumstance, but it followed me in the dark, so I avoided her.

Two editors of journals came to my father's house this winter, and asked me for my mind, and when I asked them "why" they said I was penurious, and they would use it for the world.

I could not weigh myself, myself. My size felt small to me. I read your chapters in the Atlantic, and experienced honor for you. I was sure you would not reject a confiding question.

Is this, sir, what you asked me to tell you? Your friend,

E. DICKINSON.

It will be seen that she had now drawn a step nearer, signing her name, and as my "friend." It will also be noticed that I had sounded her about certain American authors, then much read; and that she knew how to put her own criticisms in a very trenchant way. With this letter came some more verses, still in the same birdlike script, as for instance the following: —

> Your riches taught me poverty,
> > Myself a millionaire
> In little wealths, as girls could boast,
> > Till, broad as Buenos Ayre,
> You drifted your dominions
> > A different Peru,
> And I esteemed all poverty
> > For life's estate, with you.
>
> Of mines, I little know, myself,
> > But just the names of gems,
> The colors of the commonest,
> > And scarce of diadems
> So much that, did I meet the queen

Her glory I should know;
But this must be a different wealth,
　　To miss it, beggars so.

I'm sure 't is India, all day,
　　To those who look on you
Without a stint, without a blame,
　　Might I but be the Jew!

I'm sure it is Golconda
　　Beyond my power to deem,
To have a smile for mine, each day,
　　How better than a gem!

At least, it solaces to know
　　That there exists a gold
Although I prove it just in time
　　Its distance to behold;

Its far, far treasure to surmise
　　And estimate the pearl
That slipped my simple fingers through
　　While just a girl at school!

Here was already manifest that defiance of form, never through carelessness, and never precisely from whimsy which so marked her. The slightest
change in the order of words — the "While yet at school, a girl" — would
have given her a rhyme for this last line but no; she was intent upon her
thought and it would not have satisfied her to make the change. The other
poem further showed, what had already been visible, a rare and delicate sympathy with the life of nature: —

A bird came down the walk;
He did not know I saw;
He bit an angle-worm in halves
And ate the fellow raw.

And then he drank a dew
From a convenient grass,
And then hopped sidewise to a wall
To let a beetle pass.

He glanced with rapid eyes
That hurried all around;
They looked like frightened beads, I thought;
He stirred his velvet head

Like one in danger, cautious.
I offered him a crumb,
And he unrolled his feathers
And rowed him softer home

Than oars divide the ocean,
Too silver for a seam —

> Or butterflies, off banks of noon,
> Leap, plashless as they swim.

It is possible that in a second letter I gave more of distinct praise or encouragement, for her third is in a different mood. This was received June 8, 1862. There is something startling in its opening image: and in the yet stranger phrase that follows, where she apparently uses "mob" in the sense of chaos or bewilderment: —

DEAR FRIEND, — Your letter gave no drunkenness, because I tasted rum before. Domingo comes but once; yet I have had few pleasures so deep as your opinion, and if I tried to thank you, my tears would block my tongue.

My dying tutor told me that he would like to live till I had been a poet, but Death was much of mob as I could master, then. And when, far afterward, a sudden light on orchards, or a new fashion in the wind troubled my attention, I felt a palsy, here, the verses just relieve.

Your second letter surprised me, and for a moment, swung. I had not supposed it. Your first gave no dishonor, because the true are not ashamed. I thanked you for your justice, but could not drop the bells whose jingling cooled my tramp. Perhaps the balm seemed better, because you bled me first. I smile when you suggest that I delay "to publish," that being foreign to my thought as firmament to fin.

If fame belonged to me, I could not escape her; if she did not, the longest day would pass me on the chase, and the approbation of my dog would forsake me then. My barefoot rank is better.

You think my gait "spasmodic." I am in danger, sir. You think me "uncontrolled." I have no tribunal.

Would you have time to be the "friend" you should think I need? I have a little shape: it would not crowd your desk, nor make much racket as the mouse that dents your galleries.

If I might bring you what I do — not so frequent to trouble you — and ask you if I told it clear, 't would be control to me. The sailor cannot see the North, but knows the needle can. The "hand you stretch me in the dark" I put mine in, and turn away. I have no Saxon now: —

> As if I asked a common alms,
> And in my wondering hand
> A stranger pressed a kingdom,
> And I, bewildered, stand;
> As if I asked the Orient
> Had it for me a morn,
> And it should lift its purple dikes
> And shatter me with dawn!

But, will you be my preceptor, Mr. Higginson?

With this came the poem already published in her volume and entitled Renunciation; and also that beginning "Of all the sounds dispatched abroad," thus fixing approximately the date of those two. I must soon have written to ask her for her picture, that I might form some impression of my enigmatical correspondent. To this came the following reply, in July, 1862: —

Could you believe me without? I had no portrait, now, but am small, like the wren; and my hair is bold, like the chestnut bur; and my eyes, like the sherry in the glass, that the guest leaves. Would this do just as well?

It often alarms father. He says death might occur, and he has moulds of all the rest, but has no mould of me; but I noticed the quick wore off those things, in a few days, and forestall the dishonor. You will think no caprice of me.

You said "Dark." I know the butterfly, and the lizard, and the orchis. Are not those *your* countrymen?

I am happy to be your scholar, and will deserve the kindness I cannot repay.

If you truly consent, I recite now. Will you tell me my fault, frankly as to yourself, for I had rather wince than die. Men do not call the surgeon to commend the bone, but to set it, sir, and fracture within is more critical. And for this, preceptor, I shall bring you obedience, the blossom from my garden, and every gratitude I know.

Perhaps you smile at me. I could not stop for that. My business is circumference. An ignorance, not of customs, but if caught with the dawn, or the sunset see me, myself the only kangaroo among the beauty, sir, if you please, it afflicts me, and I thought that instruction would take it away.

Because you have much business, beside the growth of me, you will appoint, yourself, how often I shall come, without your inconvenience.

And if at any time you regret you received me, or I prove a different fabric to that you supposed, you must banish me.

When I state myself, as the representative of the verse, it does not mean me, but a supposed person.

You are true about the "perfection." To-day makes Yesterday mean.

You spoke of Pippa Passes. I never heard anybody speak of Pippa Passes before. You see my posture is benighted.

To thank you baffles me. Are you perfectly powerful? Had I a pleasure you had not, I could delight to bring it.

YOUR SCHOLAR.

This was accompanied by this strong poem, with its breathless conclusion. The title is of my own giving: —

The Saints' Rest

Of tribulation, these are they,
    Denoted by the white;
The spangled gowns, a lesser rank
    Of victors designate.

All these did conquer; but the ones
    Who overcame most times,

Wear nothing commoner than snow,
  No ornaments but palms.
"Surrender" is a sort unknown
  On this superior soil;
"Defeat" an outgrown anguish,
  Remembered as the mile
Our panting ancle barely passed
  When night devoured the road;
But we stood whispering in the house,
  And all we said, was "Saved!"

[Note by the writer of the verses.] I spelled ankle wrong.

It would seem that at first I tried a little, — a very little — to lead her in the direction of rules and traditions; but I fear it was only perfunctory, and that she interested me more in her — so to speak — unregenerate condition. Still, she recognizes the endeavor. In this case, as will be seen, I called her attention to the fact that while she took pains to correct the spelling of a word, she was utterly careless of greater irregularities. It will be seen by her answer that with her usual naive adroitness she turns my point: —

DEAR FRIEND, — Are these more orderly? I thank you for the truth.

I had no monarch in my life, and cannot rule myself; and when I try to organize, my little force explodes and leaves me bare and charred.

I think you called me "wayward." Will you help me improve?

I suppose the pride that stops the breath, in the core of woods, is not of ourself.

You say I confess the little mistake, and omit the large. Because I can see orthography; but the ignorance out of sight is my preceptor's charge.

Of "shunning men and women," they talk of hallowed things, aloud, and embarrass my dog. He and I don't object to them, if they'll exist their side. I think Carl would please you. He is dumb, and brave. I think you would like the chestnut tree I met in my walk. It hit my notice suddenly, and I thought the skies were in blossom.

Then there's a noiseless noise in the orchard that I let persons hear.

You told me in one letter you could not come to see me "now," and I made no answer; not because I had none, but did not think myself the price that you should come so far.

I do not ask so large a pleasure, lest you might deny me.

You say, "Beyond your knowledge." You would not jest with me, because I believe you; but, preceptor, you cannot mean it?

All men say "What" to me, but I thought it a fashion.

When much in the woods, as a little girl, I was told that the snake would bite me, that I might pick a poisonous flower, or goblins kidnap me; but I went along and met no one but angels, who were far shyer of me than I could be of them, so I have n't that confidence in fraud which many exercise.

I shall observe your precept, though I don't understand it, always.

I marked a line in one verse, because I met it after I made it, and never consciously touch a paint mixed by another person.

I do not let go it, because it is mine. Have you the portrait of Mrs. Browning?

Persons sent me three. If you had none, will you have mine?

YOUR SCHOLAR. . . .

At last, after many postponements, on August 16, 1870, I found myself face to face with my hitherto unseen correspondent. It was at her father's house, one of those large, square, brick mansions so familiar in our older New England towns, surrounded by trees and blossoming shrubs without, and within exquisitely neat, cool, spacious, and fragrant with flowers. After a little delay, I heard an extremely faint and pattering footstep like that of a child, in the hall, and in glided, almost noiselessly, a plain, shy little person, the face without a single good feature, but with eyes, as she herself said, "like the sherry the guest leaves in the glass," and with smooth bands of reddish chestnut hair. She had a quaint and nun-like look, as if she might be a German canoness of some religious order, whose prescribed garb was white piqué, with a blue net worsted shawl. She came toward me with two day-lilies, which she put in a childlike way into my hand, saying softly, under her breath, "These are my introduction," and adding, also under her breath, in childlike fashion, "Forgive me if I am frightened; I never see strangers, and hardly know what I say." But soon she began to talk, and thenceforward continued almost constantly; pausing sometimes to beg that I would talk instead, but readily recommencing when I evaded. There was not a trace of affectation in all this; she seemed to speak absolutely for her own relief, and wholly without watching its effect on her hearer. Led on by me, she told much about her early life, in which her father was always the chief figure, — evidently a man of the old type, *la vielle roche* of Puritanism — a man who, as she said, read on Sunday "lonely and rigorous books;" and who had from childhood inspired her with such awe, that she never learned to tell time by the clock till she was fifteen, simply because he had tried to explain it to her when she was a little child, and she had been afraid to tell him that she did not understand, and also afraid to ask any one else lest he should hear of it. Yet she had never heard him speak a harsh word, and it needed only a glance at his photograph to see how truly the Puritan tradition was preserved in him. He did not wish his children, when little, to read anything but the Bible; and when, one day, her brother brought her home Longfellow's Kavanagh, he put it secretly under the pianoforte cover, made signs to her, and they both afterwards read it. It may have been before this, however, that a student of her father's was amazed to find that she and her brother had never heard of Lydia Maria Child, then much read, and he brought Letters from New York, and hid it in the great bush of old-fashioned tree-box beside the front door. After the first book she thought in ecstasy, "This, then, is a book, and there are more of them." But she did not find so many as she expected, for she afterwards said to me, "When I lost the use of my eyes, it was a comfort to think that there were so few real books that I could easily find one to read me all of them." Afterwards, when she regained her eyes, she read Shakespeare, and thought to herself, "Why is any other book needed?"

She went on talking constantly and saying, in the midst of narrative, things quaint and aphoristic. "Is it oblivion or absorption when things pass from our minds?" "Truth is such a rare thing, it is delightful to tell it." "I find ecstasy in living; the mere sense of living is joy enough." When I asked her if she never felt any want of employment, not going off the grounds and rarely seeing a visitor, she answered, "I never thought of conceiving that I could ever have the slightest approach to such a want in all future time;" and then added, after a pause, "I feel that I have not expressed myself strongly enough," although it seemed to me that she had. She told me of her household occupations, that she made all their bread, because her father liked only hers; then saying shyly, "And people must have puddings," this very timidly and suggestively, as if they were meteors or comets. Interspersed with these confidences came phrases so emphasized as to seem the very wantonness of over-statement, as if she pleased herself with putting into words what the most extravagant might possibly think without saying, as thus: "How do most people live without any thoughts? There are many people in the world, — you must have noticed them in the street, — how do they live? How do they get strength to put on their clothes in the morning?" Or this crowning extravaganza: "If I read a book and it makes my whole body so cold no fire can ever warm me, I know that is poetry. If I feel physically as if the top of my head were taken off, I know that is poetry. These are the only ways I know it. Is there any other way?"

I have tried to describe her just as she was, with the aid of notes taken at the time; but this interview left our relation very much what it was before; — on my side an interest that was strong and even affectionate, but not based on any thorough comprehension; and on her side a hope, always rather baffled, that I should afford some aid in solving her abstruse problem of life.

The impression undoubtedly made on me was that of an excess of tension, and of an abnormal life. Perhaps in time I could have got beyond that somewhat overstrained relation which not my will, but her needs, had forced upon us. Certainly I should have been most glad to bring it down to the level of simple truth and every-day comradeship; but it was not altogether easy. She was much too enigmatical a being for me to solve in an hour's interview, and an instinct told me that the slightest attempt at direct cross-examination would make her withdraw into her shell; I could only sit still and watch, as one does in the woods; I must name my bird without a gun, as recommended by Emerson. Under this necessity I had no opportunity to see that human and humorous side of her which is strongly emphasized by her nearer friends, and which shows itself in her quaint and unique description of a rural burglary, contained in the volume of her poems. Hence, even her letters to me show her mainly on her *exaltée* side; and should a volume of her correspondence ever be printed, it is very desirable that it should contain some of her letters to friends of closer and more familiar intimacy.

After my visit came this letter: —

Enough is so vast a sweetness, I suppose it never occurs, only pathetic counterfeits.

Fabulous to me as the men of the Revelations who "shall not hunger any more." Even the possible has its insoluble particle.

After you went, I took Macbeth and turned to "Birnam Wood." Came twice "To Dunsinane." I thought and went about my work. . . .

The vein cannot thank the artery, but her solemn indebtedness to him, even the stolidest admit, and so of me who try, whose effort leaves no sound.

You ask great questions accidentally. To answer them would be events. I trust that you are safe.

I ask you to forgive me for all the ignorance I had. I find no nomination sweet as your low opinion.

Speak, if but to blame your obedient child.

You told me of Mrs. Lowell's poems. Would you tell me where I could find them, or are they not for sight? An article of yours, too, perhaps the only one you wrote that I never knew. It was about a "Latch." Are you willing to tell me? [Perhaps "A Sketch."]

If I ask too much, you could please refuse. Shortness to live has made me bold.

Abroad is close to-night and I have but to lift my hands to touch the "Heights of Abraham."   DICKINSON.

When I said, at parting, that I would come again some time, she replied, "Say, in a long time; that will be nearer. Some time is no time."

THOMAS H. JOHNSON

The Text of Emily Dickinson's Poetry   1960

At the time of her death in 1886, Emily Dickinson left in manuscript a body of verse far more extensive than anyone imagined. Cared for by a servant, Emily and her sister Lavinia had been living together in the Amherst house built by their grandfather Dickinson, alone after their mother's death in 1882. On going through her sister's effects, Lavinia discovered a small box containing about 900 poems. These were the sixty little "volumes," as Lavinia called them, "tied together with twine," that constitute the packets. Determined that she must find a publisher for them, she persuaded Mabel Loomis Todd, the wife of an Amherst professor, to undertake the task of transcribing them. Mrs. Todd enlisted the aid of Thomas Wentworth Higginson, and together they made a selection of 115 poems for publication. But Colonel Higginson was apprehensive about the willingness of the public to accept the poems as they stood. Therefore in preparing copy for the printer he undertook to smooth rhymes, regularize the meter, delete provincialisms, and substitute "sensible" metaphors. Thus "folks" became "those," "heft" became "weight," and occasionally line arrangement was altered.

The publication of *Poems by Emily Dickinson* by Roberts Brothers of Boston nevertheless proved to be one of the literary events of 1890, and the reception of the slender volume encouraged the editors to select 166 more verses, issued a year later as *Poems, Second Series*. These likewise were warmly received. In 1896 Mrs. Todd alone edited *Poems, Third Series,* bringing the total number published to 449, and together with 102 additional poems and parts of poems included in Mrs. Todd's edition of *Letters of Emily Dickinson* (1894), they constituted the Dickinson canon until 1914, when Emily Dickinson's niece and literary heir, Martha Dickinson Bianchi, issued *The Single Hound.*

By now the public had come to appreciate the quality of Dickinson's originalities, and alterations in the text of *The Single Hound* are refreshingly few. But Mrs. Bianchi sometimes had trouble reading the manuscripts, and on occasion words or phrases were misread, in that volume and in the two later ones which completed publication of all the verses in Mrs. Bianchi's possession: *Further Poems* (1929) and *Unpublished Poems* (1935). The appearance of *Bolts of Melody* (1945), from texts prepared by Mrs. Todd and her daughter, Millicent Todd Bingham, virtually completed publication of all the Dickinson poetry, and marked a new era in textual fidelity. It presented 668 poems and fragments, deriving from transcripts made by Mrs. Todd, or from manuscripts which had remained among her papers.

Clearly the time had come to present the Dickinson poetry in an unreconstructed text with some degree of chronological arrangement, and that opportunity was presented in 1950 when ownership of Emily Dickinson's literary estate was transferred to Harvard University. Editing then began on the variorum text of *The Poems of Emily Dickinson,* which I prepared for the Belknap Press of Harvard University Press (3 vols., 1955), comprising a total of 1775 poems and fragments.

The text for this edition of *The Complete Poems of Emily Dickinson* reproduces solely and completely that of the 1955 variorum edition, but intended as a reading text, it selects but one form of each poem. Inevitably therefore one is forced to make some editorial decisions about a text which never was prepared by the author as copy for the printer. Rare instances exist, notably in the poem "Blazing in gold" (228), where no text can be called "final." That poem describes a sunset which in one version stoops as low as "the kitchen window"; in another, as low as an "oriel windoe"; in a third, as low as "the Otter's Window." These copies were made over a period of five years from 1861 to 1866, and one text is apparently as "final" as another. The reader may make the choice.

Selection becomes mandatory for the semifinal drafts. Though by far the largest number of packet copies exist in but a single fair-copy version, several exist in semifinal form: those for which marginally the poet suggested an alternate reading for one word or more. In order to keep editorial construction to a bare minimum, I have followed the policy of adopting such suggestions only when they are underlined, presumably Emily Dickinson's method of indicating her own preference.

Rough drafts, of which there are relatively few, are allowed to stand as such, with no editorial tinkering.

I have silently corrected obvious misspelling (*witheld, visiter,* etc.), and misplaced apostrophes (*does'nt*). Punctuation and capitalization remain unaltered. Dickinson used dashes as a musical device, and though some may be elongated end stops, any "correction" would be gratuitous. Capitalization, though often capricious, is likewise untouched.

RICHARD WILBUR

On Emily Dickinson   1963

Emily Dickinson never lets us forget for very long that in some respects life gave her short measure; and indeed it is possible to see the greater part of her poetry as an effort to cope with her sense of privation. I think that for her there were three major privations: she was deprived of an orthodox and steady religious faith; she was deprived of love; she was deprived of literary recognition.

At the age of seventeen, after a series of revival meetings at Mount Holyoke Seminary, Emily Dickinson found that she must refuse to become a professing Christian. To some modern minds this may seem to have been a sensible and necessary step; and surely it was a step toward becoming such a poet as she became. But for her, no pleasure in her own integrity could then eradicate the feeling that she had betrayed a deficiency, a want of grace. In her letters to Abiah Root she tells of the enhancing effect of conversion on her fellow-students, and says of herself in a famous passage:

> I am one of the lingering bad ones, and so do I slink away, and pause and ponder, and ponder and pause, and do work without knowing why, not surely, for this brief world, and more sure it is not for heaven, and I ask what this message *means* that they ask for so very eagerly: *you* know of this depth and fulness, will you try to tell me about it?

There is humor in that, and stubbornness, and a bit of characteristic lurking pride: but there is also an anguished sense of having separated herself, through some dry incapacity, from spiritual community, from purpose, and from magnitude of life. As a child of evangelical Amherst, she inevitably thought of purposive, heroic life as requiring a vigorous faith. Out of such a thought she later wrote:

> The abdication of Belief
> Makes the Behavior small —
> Better an ingis fatuus
> Than no illume at all — (1551)

That hers *was* a species of religious personality goes without saying; but by her refusal of such ideas as original sin, redemption, hell, and election, she made it impossible for herself — as Professor Whicher observed — "to share the religious life of her generation." She became an unsteady congregation of one.

Her second privation, the privation of love, is one with which her poems and her biographies have made us exceedingly familiar, though some biographical facts remain conjectural. She had the good fortune, at least once, to bestow her heart on another; but she seems to have found her life, in great part, a history of loneliness, separation, and bereavement.

As for literary fame, some will deny that Emily Dickinson ever greatly desired it, and certainly there is evidence, mostly from her latter years, to support such a view. She *did* write that "Publication is the auction / Of the mind of man." And she *did* say to Helen Hunt Jackson, "How can you print a piece of your soul?" But earlier, in 1861, she had frankly expressed to Sue Dickinson the hope that "sometime" she might make her kinfolk proud of her. The truth is, I think, that Emily Dickinson knew she was good, and began her career with a normal appetite for recognition. I think that she later came, with some reason, to despair of being understood or properly valued, and so directed against her hopes of fame what was by then a well-developed disposition to renounce. That she wrote a good number of poems about fame supports my view: the subjects to which a poet returns are those which vex him.

What did Emily Dickinson do, as a poet, with her sense of privation? One thing she quite often did was to pose as the laureate and attorney of the empty-handed, and question God about the economy of His creation. Why, she asked, is a fatherly God so sparing of His presence? Why is there never a sign that prayers are heard? Why does Nature tell us no comforting news of its Maker? Why do some receive a whole loaf, while others must starve on a crumb? Where is the benevolence in shipwreck and earthquake? By asking such questions as these, she turned complaint into critique, and used her own sufferings as experiential evidence about the nature of the deity. The God who emerges from these poems is a God who does not answer, an unrevealed God whom one cannot confidently approach through Nature or through doctrine.

But there was another way in which Emily Dickinson dealt with her sentiment of lack — another emotional strategy which was both more frequent and more fruitful. I refer to her repeated assertion of the paradox that privation is more plentiful than plenty; that to renounce is to possess the more; that "The Banquet of abstemiousness / Defaces that of wine." We all know how the poet illustrated this ascetic paradox in her behavior — how in her latter years she chose to live in relative retirement, keeping the world, even in its dearest aspects, at a physical remove. She would write her friends, telling them how she missed them, then flee upstairs when they came to see her; afterward, she might send a note of apology, offering the odd explanation that "We shun because we prize." Any reader of Dickinson biographies can furnish other examples, dramatic or homely, of this prizing and shunning, this yearning and renouncing: in my own mind's eye is a picture of Emily Dickinson watching a gay circus caravan from the distance of her chamber window.

LINDA GREGG

Not Understanding Emily Dickinson   1984

Emily Dickinson was the first poet I really read. I was in the fifth or sixth grade and she seemed such a secret thing to me that I always read her in bed. I remember clearly the amazement, respect, and something maybe like horror when I read her. I still react to her that way.

I felt then and feel now that she halts me at the border of her poetry while she uses the space beyond like a landscape with many birds in it feeding on the trees after snow has fallen and now it is morning and there is a steady small rain. I didn't understand that when I was little. She was different from those I knew. For me there has always been that something in her which wanted to remain separate. I have never felt let in. Not as I feel let in by [Theodore] Roethke or [D. H.] Lawrence or Sappho or Catullus or Shakespeare. I respect it. I do not wish to approach closer than she wishes. I think of how she would stand on the upstairs landing to listen when there were guests talking downstairs in the living room. Out of respect, I do not go up those stairs after her. She called her poems her letter to the world, not her meeting or her embrace. When I went to her grave, I kept wondering what she would want me to do. I listened to the silence between us of earth and air, and of time, and to the natural silence around us. I listened for her there, and what she gave me was that silence and that distance. I accepted it gratefully, as a gift. And stayed still to be more closely where she was. I did not touch the stone.

There are still a lot of things I don't understand. The wind that seems to be in her poetry, for example. Is it her breath? I don't think so. There is very little natural breathing in her poems. I think it is something other than herself, something which halts her breath. I think she has let something like God's will into her poetry. It halts her, adds much, pushes her, even works against her feelings and body, yet is a great strength in her poems. It blows through and the words do not blow down. This doubleness in her work creates power.

One of the important ways of understanding the poetry of Emily Dickinson may be *not* understanding her. Not, at least, understanding her in the rational way. In the way we understand prose, for example. When I was a young girl, I often did not know what the poems meant. To be honest, that happened more than often. It happened almost all the time when I read her that I did not understand in the usual way. But I did understand nevertheless. Even now, I think many of her poems are successful without being understandable in a logical sense.

I want to be careful to make clear that I am not *against* understanding or explaining the poems. It gives me great pleasure when the poems suddenly yield themselves to me and become clear. I delight in people who help that to happen. I delight in the poetry whose meanings *are* clear, instantly. Lines like:

> There's a certain Slant of light
> Winter Afternoons —
> That oppresses, like the Heft
> Of Cathedral tunes —

For all of us who grew up in the country, there is a special pleasure when she speaks of a snake in the grass *wrinkling*. But one of the most important things about her poetry for the young girl I was *was* the other kind of poetry she wrote, the kind which made no logical sense to me but worked wonderfully. Lines like the ones which end that very poem about the wrinkling snake (called "A narrow fellow in the grass"):

> . . . never met this Fellow
> Attended, or alone
> Without a tighter breathing
> And Zero at the Bone —

I still don't know what "Zero at the Bone" means, not in a logical way, but it seems clear to me in another and equally important sense. This is also true for lines like:

> The deer attracts no further
> Than it resists the hound
>   (979)

Or poem 690, which begins: "Victory comes late" and ends with the fine lines:

> God keep His oath to Sparrows
> Who of little Love know how to starve.

Sometimes whole poems have this quality for me, such as poem 512:

> The Soul has Bandaged moments —
> When too appalled to stir —
> She feels some ghastly Fright come up
> And stop to look at her —
>
> Salute her — with long fingers —
> Caress her freezing hair —
> Sip, Goblin, from the very lips
> The lover — hovered — o'er —
> Unworthy, that a thought so mean
> Accost a Theme — so — fair —
>
> The Soul has moments of Escape —
> When bursting all the doors —
> She dances like a Bomb, abroad,
> And swings upon the Hours,
>
> As do the Bee — delirious borne —
> Long Dungeoned from his Rose —
> Touch Liberty — then know no more,
> But Noon, and Paradise —
>
> The Soul's retaken moments —
> When, Felon led along,
> With shackles on the plumed feet,
> And staples, in the Song,
>
> The Horror welcomes her, again,
> These, are not brayed of Tongue —

This could be explained. I can glimpse bits of meaning in among the dazzle; but to tell the truth, I am content (in this poem) not to track the meaning down by those clues. I really don't care what the exact meaning is when she speaks of:

The Soul's retaken moments —
When, Felon led along,
With shackles on the plumed feet,
And staples, in the Song.

I liked it even when I thought *plumed* was *plummed*. And I secretly hope *staples* means what we use it to mean now. Stapled Songs! It is a successful poem for me without the other kind of understanding. However, I'm not saying that I like to ride the energy, or the images. What I *am* trying to say is that there's an important way of getting to the *true* meaning which may elude analysis. I *do* understand what *the soul's bandaged moments means*. It *means* the soul's bandaged moments.

I am *not* choosing between understanding and not understanding in these poems. But I *am* trying to suggest that *sometimes* there is a legitimate way her poems communicate without needing to be decoded into logic. It is important to me and to my own work to remember that in even the greatest poetry there is often the other kind of meaning.

Anyhow, this was true for me when I read Emily Dickinson at the very beginning of my knowing about poetry. It helped me to know there is a magic at the center of poetry, a way of meaning that is different from logic. So that from the first I had the encouragement to trust my instinct in preferring metaphor to simile, image to abstractions, to trust the intuitive more than the rational in my poetry.

Of course, I am not saying this should be true for all poets. Not even for all *her* poetry, but it has *always* been how I work. Or part of how I work. And it is so partly because of Emily Dickinson. She taught me there is a difficult, hard-to-understand, hard-to-translate, hard-to-write-about-or-explain place. I knew I had that in me also. But at the same time, I learned that the difficulty or obscurity in her poetry is not because she uses images to hide a secret. Rather, it is an attempt to say something that cannot be said in a simple or direct way.

One of the amazing things about Emily Dickinson for me, when I first read her and also now, is the presence of thought in her poetry which thinks like a poem does. I remember how as a child I could almost easily understand those thoughts without understanding. Or maybe I should say understanding it *before* understanding. I remember clearly saying at that early time: "then I will have to write my own poetry. A poetry of a kind I cannot understand in the same way I cannot understand *hers*."

Understanding before understanding led me and led me toward what is magical in poetry. Maybe that is one of the most valuable things about the poetry of Emily Dickinson: to teach that there is something in poetry which cannot be handled, cannot be studied scientifically. Can only be approached, can only be honored. We can go up to the border. Can name what is there. Can know a lot. But we must remember that it is still country on the other side of the border and there are things there which we do not have good names for. We must remember there is a kind of safety in trusting the unknown. There are things beyond the border which are invisible, but if we are patient and listen hard, we can sometimes hear them.

GALWAY KINNELL

The Deconstruction of Emily Dickinson

1994

The lecture had ended when I came in,
and the professor was answering questions.
I do not know what he had been doing with her
poetry, but now he was speaking of her
as a victim of reluctant male publishers.   5
When the questions dwindled, I put up my hand.
I said the ignorant meddling of the Springfield *Daily Republican*
and the hidebound response of literary men,
and the gulf between the poetic wishfulness
then admired and her own harsh knowledge,   10
had let her see that her poems
would not be understood in her time;
and therefore, passionate to publish,
she vowed not to publish again. I said
I would recite a version of her vow,   15

    Publication – is the Auction
    Of the mind of Man –

But before I could, the professor broke in.
"Yes," he said, " 'the Auction' — 'auction,' from *augere, auctum*, to
    augment, to author . . ."
"Let's hear the poem!" "The poem!" several women,   20
who at such a moment are more outspoken than men, shouted,
but I kept still and he kept going.
"In *auctum* the economy of the signifier is split, revealing an uncon-
    scious collusion in the bourgeois commodification of con-
    sciousness. While our author says 'no,' the unreified text says
    'yes,' yes?"
He kissed his lips together and turned to me
saying, "Now, may we hear the poem?"   25
I waited a moment for full effect.
Without rising to my feet, I said,
"Professor, to understand Dickinson
it may not always be necessary to uproot her words.
Why not, first, try *listening* to her?   30
Loyalty forbids me to recite her poem now."
No, I didn't say that — I realized

she would want me to finish him off with one wallop.
So I said, "Professor, I thought you
would welcome the words of your author.   35
I see you prefer to hear yourself speak."
No, I held back — for I could hear her
urging me to put outrage into my voice
and substance into my argument.
I stood up so that everyone might see   40
the derision in my smile. "Professor," I said,
"you live in Amherst at the end of the twentieth century.
For you 'auction' means a quaint event
where somebody coaxes out the bids
on butter churns on a summer Saturday.   45
Forget etymology, this is history.
In Amherst in 1860 'auction' meant
the slave auction, you dope!"
Well, I didn't say that either,
although I have said them all,   50
many times, in the middle of the night.
In reality, I stood up and recited
like a schoolboy called upon in class.
My voice gradually weakened, and the women
who had called out for the poem   55
now looked as though they were thinking
of errands to be done on the way home.
When I finished, the professor smiled.
"Thank you. So, what at first some of us may have taken as
        a simple outcry, we all now see is an ambivalent, self-
        subversive text."
As people got up to go, I moved   60
into that sanctum within me where Emily
sometimes speaks a verse, and listened
for a sign of how she felt, such as,
"Thanks – Sweet – countryman –
for wanting – to Sing out – of Me –   65
after all that Humbug." But she was silent.

∞

CASEBOOK ON ROBERT FROST

This casebook on Robert Frost begins with a perceptive interview with the poet by Rose C. Field that appeared in the New York Times Book Review *in 1923. The next commentary is Frost's introduction to his* Selected Poems *of 1939; although he did not consider himself a critic, he did express opinions about his poetic methods in the introductions to his collections. Fellow poet Robert Lowell's sonnet suggests the more complicated reality behind the figure of the genial, wise New England bard Frost presented to his public. Nobel Prize–winning poet Joseph Brodsky's discerning response to the profoundly American poetry of Frost is from the perspective of someone who grew up in the Soviet Union and moved to the United States as an adult. Finally, Philip L. Gerber looks at Frost's "After Apple-Picking" (p. 1108) as an example of the poet's "honest duplicity," a characteristic he finds essential to all poetry.*

ROSE C. FIELD

An Interview with Robert Frost 1923

Have you ever seen a sensitive child enter a dark room, fearful of the enveloping blackness, yet more than half ashamed of the fear? That is the way Robert Frost, poet, approached the interview arranged for him with the writer. He didn't want to come, he was half afraid of coming, and he was ashamed of the fear of meeting questions.

He was met at his publisher's office at the request of his friends there. "Come and get him, please," they said. "He is a shy person — a gentle and a sensitive person — and the idea of knocking at your doors, saying, 'Here I am, come to be interviewed,' will make him run and hide." The writer came and got him.

All the way down Fifth Avenue for ten or fifteen blocks he smiled often and talked rapidly to show that he was at ease and confident. But he was not. One could see the child telling itself not to be afraid.

Arrived at the house, he took the chair offered him and sat down rigidly. Still he smiled.

"Go ahead," he said. "Ask me the questions. Let's get at it."

"There are no questions — no specific questions. Suppose you just ramble on about American poetry, about poets, about men of the past and men of the present, about where we are drifting or where we are marching. Just talk."

He looked nonplused. The rigid smile gave way to one of relief and relaxation.

"You mean to say that you're not going to fire machine-gun questions at me and expect me to answer with skyrocketing repartee. Well, I wish I'd known. Well."

The brown hand opened up on the arms of the chair and the graying head leaned back. Robert Frost began to talk. He talked of some of the poets of the past, and in his quiet, gentle manner exploded the first bombshell. He exploded many others.

"One of the real American poets of yesterday," he said, "was Longfellow. No, I am not being sarcastic. I mean it. It is the fashion nowadays to make fun of him. I come across this pose and attitude with people I meet socially, with men and women I meet in the classrooms of colleges where I teach. They laugh at his gentleness, at his lack of worldliness, at his detachment from the world and the meaning thereof.

"When and where has it been written that a poet must be a club-swinging warrior, a teller of barroom tales, a participant of unspeakable experiences? That, today, apparently is the stamp of poetic integrity. I hear people speak of men who are writing today, and their eyes light up with a deep glow of satisfaction when they can mention some putrid bit of gossip about them. 'He writes such lovely things,' they say, and in the next breath add, half worshipfully, 'He lives such a terrible life.'

"I can't see it. I can't see that a man must needs have his feet plowing through unhealthy mud in order to appreciate more fully the glowing splendor of the clouds. I can't see that a man must fill his soul with sick and miserable experiences, self-imposed and self-inflicted, and greatly enjoyed, before he can sit down and write a lyric of strange and compelling beauty. Inspiration doesn't lie in the mud; it lies in the clean and wholesome life of the ordinary man.

"Maybe I am wrong. Maybe there is something wrong with me. Maybe I haven't the power to feel, to appreciate and live the extremes of dank living and beautiful inspiration.

"Men have told me, and perhaps they are right, that I have no 'straddle.' That is the term they use: I have no straddle. That means that I cannot spread out far enough to live in filth and write in the treetops. I can't. Perhaps it is because I am so ordinary. I like the middle way, as I like to talk to the man who walks the middle way with me.

"I have given thought to this business of straddling, and there's always seemed to me to be something wrong with it, something tricky. I see a man riding two horses, one foot on the back of one horse, one foot on the other. One horse pulls one way, the other a second. His straddle is wide, Heaven help him, but it seems to me that before long it's going to hurt him. It isn't the natural way, the normal way, the powerful way to ride. It's a trick." . . .

"People do me the honor to say that I am truly a poet of America. They point to my New England background, to the fact that my paternal ancestor came here some time in the sixteen hundreds. So much is true, but what they either do not know or do not say is that my mother was an immigrant. She came to these shores from Edinburgh in an old vessel that docked at Philadelphia. But she felt the spirit of America and became part of it before she even set her foot off the boat.

"She used to tell about it when I was a child. She was sitting on the deck of the boat waiting for orders to come ashore. Near her some workmen were loading Delaware peaches on to the ship. One of them picked out one of them and dropped it into her lap.

" 'Here, take that,' he said. The way he said it and the spirit in which he gave it left an indelible impression on her mind.

" 'It was a bonny peach,' she used to say, 'and I didn't eat it. I kept it to show my friends.'

"Looking back would I say that she was less the American than my father? No. America meant something live and real and virile to her. He took it for granted. He was a Fourth-of-July American, by which I mean that he rarely failed to celebrate in the way considered proper and appropriate. She, however, was a year-around American.

"I had an aunt in New England who used to talk long and loud about the foreigners who were taking over this country. Across the way from her house stood a French Catholic church which the new people of the village had put up. Every Sunday my aunt would stand at her window, behind the curtain, and watch the steady stream of men and women pouring into church. Her mouth would twist in the way that seems peculiar to dried-up New Englanders, and she would say, 'My soul!' Just that: 'My soul!'

"All the disapproval and indignation and disgust were concentrated in these two words. She never could see why I laughed at her, but it did strike me very funny for her to be calling upon her soul for help when this mass of industrious people were going to church to save theirs. . . .

"Today almost every man who writes poetry confesses his debt to Whitman. Many have gone very much further than Whitman would have traveled with them. They are the people who believe in wide straddling.

"I, myself, as I said before, don't like it for myself. I do not write free verse; I write blank verse. I must have the pulse beat of rhythm, I like to hear it beating under the things I write.

"That doesn't mean I do not like to read a bit of free verse occasionally. I do. It sometimes succeeds in painting a picture that is very clear and startling. It's good as something created momentarily for its sudden startling effect; it hasn't the qualities, however, of something lastingly beautiful.

"And sometimes my objection to it is that it's a pose. It's not honest. When a man sets out consciously to tear up forms and rhythms and measures, then he is not interested in giving you poetry. He just wants to perform; he wants to show you his tricks. He will get an effect; nobody will deny that, but it is not a harmonious effect.

"Sometimes it strikes me that the free-verse people got their idea from incorrect proof sheets. I have had stuff come from the printers with lines half left out or positions changed about. I read the poems as they stood, distorted and half finished, and I confess I get a rather pleasant sensation from them. They make a sort of nightmarish half-sense."

As he rose to go, he said, "I am an ordinary man, I guess. That's what's the trouble with me. I like my school and I like my farm and I like people. Just ordinary, you see."

ROBERT FROST

The Figure a Poem Makes   *1939*

Abstraction is an old story with the philosophers, but it has been like a new toy in the hands of the artists of our day. Why can't we have any one quality of poetry we choose by itself? We can have in thought. Then it will go hard if we can't in practice. Our lives for it.

Granted no one but a humanist much cares how sound a poem is if it is only *a* sound. The sound is the gold in the ore. Then we will have the sound out alone and dispense with the inessential. We do till we make the discovery that the object in writing poetry is to make all poems sound as different as possible from each other, and the resources for that of vowels, consonants, punctuation, syntax, words, sentences, meter are not enough. We need the help of context — meaning — subject matter. That is the greatest help towards variety. All that can be done with words is soon told. So also with meters — particularly in our language where there are virtually but two, strict iambic and loose iambic. The ancients with many were still poor if they depended on meters for all tune. It is painful to watch our sprung-rhythmists straining at the point of omitting one short from a foot for relief from monotony. The possibilities for tune from the dramatic tones of meaning struck across the rigidity of a limited meter are endless. And we are back in poetry as merely one more art of having something to say, sound or unsound. Probably better if sound, because deeper and from wider experience.

Then there is this wildness whereof it is spoken. Granted again that it has an equal claim with sound to being a poem's better half. If it is a wild tune, it is a poem. Our problem then is, as modern abstractionists, to have the wildness pure; to be wild with nothing to be wild about. We bring up as aberrationists, giving way to undirected associations and kicking ourselves from one chance suggestion to another in all directions as of a hot afternoon in the life of a grasshopper. Theme alone can steady us down. Just as the first mystery was how a poem could have a tune in such a straightness as meter, so the second mystery is how a poem can have wildness and at the same time a subject that shall be fulfilled.

It should be of the pleasure of a poem itself to tell how it can. The figure a poem makes. It begins in delight and ends in wisdom. The figure is the same as for love. No one can really hold that the ecstasy should be static and stand still in one place. It begins in delight, it inclines to the impulse, it assumes direction with the first line laid down, it runs a course of lucky events, and ends in a clarification of life — not necessarily a great clarification, such as sects and cults are founded on, but in a momentary stay against confusion. It has denouement. It has an outcome that though unforeseen was predestined from the first image of the original mood — and indeed from the very mood. It is but a trick poem and no poem at all if the best of it was thought of first and saved for the last. It finds its own name as it goes and discovers the best waiting for it in some final phrase at once wise and sad — the happy-sad blend of the drinking song.

No tears in the writer, no tears in the reader. No surprise for the writer, no surprise for the reader. For me the initial delight is in the surprise of remembering something I didn't know I knew. I am in a place, in a situation, as if I had materialized from cloud or risen out of the ground. There is a glad recognition of the long lost and the rest follows. Step by step the wonder of unexpected supply keeps growing. The impressions most useful to my purpose seem always those I was unaware of and so made no note of at the time when taken, and the conclusion is come to that like giants we are always hurling experience ahead of us to pave the future with against the day when we may want to strike a line of purpose across it for somewhere. The line will have the more charm for not being mechanically straight. We enjoy the straight crookedness of a good walking stick. Modern instruments of precision are being used to make things crooked as if by eye and hand in the old days.

I tell how there may be a better wildness of logic than of inconsequence. But the logic is backward, in retrospect, after the act. It must be more felt than seen ahead like prophecy. It must be a revelation, or a series of revelations, as much for the poet as for the reader. For it to be that there must have been the greatest freedom of the material to move about in it and to establish relations in it regardless of time and space, previous relation, and everything but affinity. We prate of freedom. We call our schools free because we are not free to stay away from them till we are sixteen years of age. I have given up my democratic prejudices and now willingly set the lower classes free to be completely taken care of by the upper classes. Political freedom is nothing to me. I bestow it right and left. All I would keep for myself is the freedom of my material — the condition of body and mind now and then to summons aptly from the vast chaos of all I have lived through.

Scholars and artists thrown together are often annoyed at the puzzle of where they differ. Both work from knowledge; but I suspect they differ most importantly in the way their knowledge is come by. Scholars get theirs with conscientious thoroughness along projected lines of logic; poets theirs cavalierly and as it happens in and out of books. They stick to nothing deliberately, but let what will stick to them like burrs where they walk in the fields. No acquirement is on assignment, or even self-assignment. Knowledge of the second kind is much more available in the wild free ways of wit and art. A schoolboy may be defined as one who can tell you what he knows in the order in which he learned it. The artist must value himself as he snatches a thing from some previous order in time and space into a new order with not so much as a ligature clinging to it of the old place where it was organic.

More than once I should have lost my soul to radicalism if it had been the originality it was mistaken for by its young converts. Originality and initiative are what I ask for my country. For myself the originality need be no more than the freshness of a poem run in the way I have described: from delight to wisdom. The figure is the same as for love. Like a piece of ice on a hot stove the poem must ride on its own melting. A poem may be worked over once it is in being, but may not be worried into being. Its most precious quality will remain its having run itself and carried away the poet with it. Read it a hundred times: it will forever keep its freshness as a petal keeps its fragrance. It can never lose its sense of a meaning that once unfolded by surprise as it went.

ROBERT LOWELL

On Robert Frost

1969

Robert Frost at midnight, the audience gone
to vapor, the great act laid on the shelf in mothballs,
his voice musical, raw and raw — he writes in the flyleaf:
"Robert Lowell from Robert Frost, his friend in the art."
"Sometimes I feel too full of myself," I say.
And he, misunderstanding, "When I am low,
I stray away. My son wasn't your kind. The night
we told him Merrill Moore° would come to treat him,
he said, 'I'll kill him first.' One of my daughters thought things,
knew every male she met was out to make her;
the way she dresses, she couldn't make a whorehouse."
And I, "Sometimes I'm so happy I can't stand myself."
And he, "When I am too full of joy, I think
how little good my health did anyone near me."

JOSEPH BRODSKY

On Grief and Reason

1994

I should tell you that what follows is a spinoff of a seminar given four years ago at the Collège International de Philosophie, in Paris. Hence a certain breeziness to the pace; hence, too, the paucity of biographical material — irrelevant, in my view, to the analysis of a work of art in general, and particularly where a foreign audience is concerned. In any case, the pronoun "you" in these pages stands for those ignorant of or poorly acquainted with the lyrical and narrative strengths of the poetry of Robert Frost. But, first, some basics.

Robert Frost was born in 1874 and died in 1963, at the age of eighty-eight. One marriage, six children; fairly strapped when young; farming, and, later, teaching jobs in various schools. Not much travelling until late in his life; he mostly resided on the East Coast, in New England. If biography accounts for poetry, this one should have resulted in none. Yet he published nine books of poems; the second one, "North of Boston," which came out when he was forty, made him famous. This was in 1914.

After that, his sailing was a bit smoother. But literary fame is not exactly popularity. As it happens, it took the Second World War to bring Frost's work to the general public's notice. In 1943, the Council on Books in Wartime dis-

---

Merrill Moore: Poet and psychiatrist. Frost's son later committed suicide.

tributed fifty thousand copies of Frost's "Come In" to United States troops stationed overseas, as a morale-builder. By 1955, his "Selected Poems" was in its fourth edition, and one could speak of his poetry's having acquired national standing.

It did. In the course of nearly five decades following the publication of "North of Boston," Frost reaped every possible reward and honor an American poet can get; shortly before Frost's death, John Kennedy invited him to read a poem at the Inauguration ceremony. Along with recognition naturally came a great deal of envy and resentment, a substantial contribution to which emerged from the pen of Frost's own biographer. And yet both the adulation and resentment had one thing in common: a nearly total misconception of what Frost was all about.

He is generally regarded as the poet of the countryside, of rural settings — as a folksy, crusty, wisecracking old gentleman farmer, generally of positive disposition. In short, as American as apple pie. To be fair, he greatly enhanced this notion by projecting precisely this image of himself in numerous public appearances and interviews throughout his career. I suppose it wasn't that difficult for him to do, for he had those qualities in him as well. He was indeed a quintessential American poet; it is up to us, however, to find out what that quintessence is made of, and what the term "American" means as applied to poetry and, perhaps, in general.

In 1959, at a banquet thrown in New York on the occasion of Robert Frost's eighty-fifth birthday, the most prominent literary critic at that time, Lionel Trilling, rose and declared that Robert Frost was "a terrifying poet." That, of course, caused a certain stir, but the epithet was well chosen.

Now, I want you to make the distinction here between terrifying and tragic. Tragedy, as you know, is always a fait accompli, whereas terror always has to do with anticipation, with man's recognition of his own negative potential — with his sense of what he is capable of. And it is the latter that was Frost's forte, not the former. In other words, his posture is radically different from the Continental tradition of the poet as tragic hero. And that difference alone makes him — for want of a better term — American.

On the surface, he looks very positively predisposed toward his surroundings — particularly toward nature. His fluency, his "being versed in country things" alone can produce this impression. However, there is a difference between the way a European perceives nature and the way an American does. Addressing this difference, W. H. Auden, in his short essay on Frost, suggests something to the effect that when a European conceives of confronting nature, he walks out of his cottage or a little inn, filled with either friends or family, and goes for an evening stroll. If he encounters a tree, it's a tree made familiar by history, to which it's been a witness. This or that king sat underneath it, laying down this or that law — something of that sort. A tree stands there rustling, as it were, with allusions. Pleased and somewhat pensive, our man, refreshed but unchanged by that encounter, returns to his inn or cottage, finds his friends or family absolutely intact, and proceeds to have a good, merry time. Whereas when an American walks out of his house and encounters a tree it is a meeting of equals. Man and tree face each other in their respective primal power, free of references: neither has a past, and as to whose future is greater, it is a toss-up. Basically, it's epidermis meeting bark. Our man returns to his cabin in a state of bewilderment, to say the least, if not in actual shock or terror.

Now, this is obviously a romantic caricature, but it accentuates the features, and that's what I am after here. In any case, the second point could be safely billed as the gist of Robert Frost's nature poetry. Nature for this poet is neither friend nor foe, nor is it the backdrop for human drama; it is this poet's terrifying self-portrait.

PHILIP L. GERBER

On Frost's "After Apple-Picking"   1966

As an illustration of the "honest duplicity" of Frost's better verses, the early lyric "After Apple-Picking," although often analyzed, serves ideally. Some readers admire this poem because the deceptive simplicity of its surface picture has charmed them with a rich vision of idyllic New England harvest. Others treasure the poem as exemplifying the truth of John Ciardi's reminder that "a poem is never about what it seems to be about." . . .

Among the available interpretations of Frost's lyric, perhaps the most lucid and readily accessible is that based upon the Emersonian pattern of natural analogies: "things admit of being used as symbols because nature is a symbol, in the whole, and in every part." Emerson's doctrine of analogy between human life and the seasons, for instance, in which spring, summer, fall, and winter parallel the various ages of man, is seconded by Thoreau, who observed the same analogy operating within the span of the day: "The phenomena of the year take place every day in a pond on a small scale. Every morning, generally speaking, the shallow water is being warmed more rapidly than the deep, though it may not be made so warm after all, and every evening it is being cooled more rapidly until the morning. The day is an epitome of the year. The night is the winter, the morning and evening are the spring and fall, and the noon is summer." Building upon the suggestions of Emerson and Thoreau, and noting the centrality that Frost has afforded both to the yearly cycle and to the daily span, the reader begins to absorb the implications radiating from "After Apple-Picking."

On the surface of the poem, however, all seems serenely concrete and straightforward. An apple grower, eager for his awaited harvest of ripe red russets, has worked for days against the imminent arrival of autumn frost. Freezing temperatures, signs of which are already apparent, will close out his opportunities to profit fully from his year's labor. In tending his trees from springtime bud through summer growth, the man's toil has been buoyed by a tremendous stimulus of anticipation. But now the exertion of the harvest itself has wearied him. Tedium has set in. He knows he will not be allowed to pick every apple on his trees, nor does he expect to. Much more realistic now than in the spring and summer, he possibly no longer even desires to account for every piece of fruit.

The harvest has taught the apple-grower something of value. He has attempted to do more than one man can hope to do alone in a season. His excitement — as well as his weariness — has caused many apples to fall to earth. Bruised, ruined, spiked on stubble, these become relatively worthless. The energies of man and nature lavished upon bringing them to perfection seem to have been poured out for naught. Yet such accidents are to be expected in the normal course of any human scheme. It is natural also that some fruit will necessarily be left to freeze as winter closes in; for this is real, not ideal, harvest.

Sleepiness of late autumn pervades the air. All around the harvester nature is preparing herself for rest: trees are defoliating as the summer sap recedes; woodchucks are hibernating, snug in readied burrows. The harvester himself lies in bed after what he realizes may be the very last day of his harvest. He is tired to the bone, leaden-limbed; but ironically he is too fatigued to pass easily into his exhausted and well-earned slumber. His eyes swim. His feet ache from standing on the ladder rung for hours at a time. All ambition spent, he is ready to call a halt and take his rest, knowing that — like anyone totally committed to a task — he will continue the harvest of apples even in his sleep.

So accurately and so economically does Frost capture the essence of apple harvest that one cannot be faulted for finding adequate satisfaction within his portrayal of the apple-picking itself, needing no more. The sights and sounds are all there. Every sensation is recorded vigorously. No one who has used a ladder or labored long hours driven by desire, or nodded in the heady drowsiness of Indian summer, is likely to forget soon the achievement of this verse. As rural idyll, it gratifies.

Even so, the simple application of natural analogies to the poem discloses an entirely new dimension, and it does so without exertion or distortion. The explicit meaning of the poem communicates with the clarity of crystal. Just as clearly does the metaphor, camouflaged only slightly by the impressive veneer of sensory detail, make itself felt. Just as every line, detail, and word contributes to transmitting the essence of the harvest experience, so does every aspect of the poem fall into place as well within the analogies and press for their development.

One notes first that Frost selects as his setting both the night of the daily span and the winter of the yearly cycle. Either would guide the mind toward a prospect of death, but the conjunction of night and winter renders that prospect unmistakable. Numerous references to drowsiness and sleep, to strangeness of sight, and to the harvest itself all reinforce the parallel between the terminations of day, season, and existence. The span of life is embraced within the curve of season, spring to winter. But what completes the circle? Ordinarily spring again, returning after winter to bring rebirth. Hints emanate from at least two references and suggest that the resurrection of spring is probable. The first comes with an unobtrusive gesture in the poem's second line, its seemingly gratuitous reference to the ladder's pointing "toward heaven still."

Without straining the issue, the word *heaven* elicits subconscious responses involving death and immortality. The second hint occurs at the finish, as the verse concludes with a whimsical contemplation of the woodchuck's sleep, the hibernation, the little imitation of death which also will terminate in springtime "resurrection." And obviously even "just some human sleep" implies a reawakening.

Snuggling within the curve of the natural cycles is another arc, that shaped by the harvest process fulfilling itself. The harvest is awaited expectantly, with nerves atingle for rosy signals of ripeness to appear on the fruit. With the "russet showing clear," the picker goes to work, heady with grandiose visions of a bumper crop gathered to the last plump apple. The elixir of enthusiasm is steadily diluted. First come endless hours of labor. Then a weariness engulfs what energy is yet unspent. Desire wanes. Then a realization grows that the original goal will not be reached without compromise forced by circumstance. Surprisingly, it no longer seems so very critical to finish. Finally comes the letting-go, first with the hands, then with the mind, but never with the heart. The apple-picker, a sadder but wiser man, relinquishes his task altogether. Now is the time to rest from toil, to accept the verdict on his performance, to listen to himself harshly judging himself.

This harvest action, complete in itself, slips so neatly into the convenient circle created by the natural symbolism, and the whole tallies so comfortably with the surface events of the poem, that the reader arrives at the final period in a euphoria of "rightness." Surface and symbol coincide neatly.

How fortunate that Frost resisted any impulse he may have felt to press his poem into the didactic mold. A phrase or two would have shaped the verse into a substantiation of the orthodox religious view — and would have done untold violence to the lyrical purity so far sustained. But he fortuitously elected instead to suggest, to hint. Whatever sleep it is, only a woodchuck, he says fancifully, could tell for sure. The poem thus ends in deliberate ambiguity. But if a reader chooses to see "After Apple-Picking" as an allegory of man's life ascending from the eager grasping of youth to the letting-go of age, Frost will not object. Nor will he frown upon his poem viewed as a moral tale of the world having its inevitable way with human ambition. Let there be no mistake; all poetry is hinting — is metaphor. Poetry is the legitimate means of saying one thing and meaning another, an "honest duplicity."

∞

CASEBOOK ON LANGSTON HUGHES

This casebook begins with a tribute by Hughes to his beloved Harlem. The excerpt is from one of the Simple stories Hughes wrote for a Harlem newspaper in which he used the character of a Harlem Everyman, Jessie Semple — nicknamed "Simple" — as a foil for his own attitudes and opinions. The next selection is a reminiscence published in The Crisis, *an African American journal, in 1926 by the writer Jessie Fauset, a contemporary of Hughes and like him a member of the gener-*

ation of writers, artists, musicians, and critics identified as the Harlem Renaissance. There follows a review of Hughes's autobiography, The Big Sea *(1940), by Richard Wright, the most successful and controversial African American writer of the 1930s. A savagely realistic novelist and poet, Wright might have been expected to be critical of Hughes's deceptively softer and more accommodating style. Wright, however, was perceptive enough to see that in his writing Hughes "bends, but he never breaks." Finally, Arnold Rampersad, author of the first extended biography of Hughes, comments in his introduction to the collected poems about Hughes's role as a folk poet.*

LANGSTON HUGHES

A Toast to Harlem 1950

Quiet can seem unduly loud at times. Since nobody at the bar was saying a word during a lull in the bright blues-blare of the Wishing Well's usually overworked juke box, I addressed my friend Simple.

"Since you told me last night you are an Indian, explain to me how it is you find yourself living in a furnished room in Harlem, my brave buck, instead of on a reservation?"

"I am a colored Indian," said Simple.

"In other words, a Negro."

"A Black Foot Indian, daddy-o, not a red one. Anyhow, Harlem is the place I always did want to be. And if it wasn't for landladies, I would be happy. That's a fact! I love Harlem."

"What is it you love about Harlem?"

"It's so full of Negroes," said Simple. "I feel like I got protection."

"From what?"

"From white folks," said Simple. "Furthermore, I like Harlem because it belongs to me."

"Harlem does not belong to you. You don't own the houses in Harlem. They belong to white folks."

"I might not own 'em," said Simple, "but I live in 'em. It would take an atom bomb to get me out."

"Or a depression," I said.

"I would not move for no depression. No, I would not go back down South, not even to Baltimore. I am in Harlem to stay! You say the houses ain't mine. Well, the sidewalk is — and don't nobody push me off. The cops don't even say, 'Move on,' hardly no more. They learned something from them Harlem riots. They used to beat your head right in public, but now they only beat it after they get you down to the stationhouse. And they don't beat it then if they think you know a colored congressman."

"Harlem has a few Negro leaders," I said.

"Elected by my *own* vote," said Simple. "Here I ain't scared to vote — that's another thing I like about Harlem. I also like it because we've got subways and it does not take all day to get downtown, neither are you Jim

Crowed° on the way. Why, Negroes is running some of these subway trains. This morning I rode the A Train down to 34th Street. There were a Negro driving it, making ninety miles a hour. That cat *were really driving* that train! Every time he flew by one of them local stations looks like he was saying, 'Look at me! This train is mine!' That cat were gone, ole man. Which is another reason why I like Harlem! Sometimes I run into Duke Ellington on 125th Street and I say, 'What you know there, Duke?' Duke says, 'Solid, ole man.' He does not know me from Adam, but he speaks. One day I saw Lena Horne coming out of the Hotel Theresa and I said, 'Huba! Huba!' Lena smiled. Folks is friendly in Harlem. I feel like I got the world in a jug and the stopper in my hand! So drink a toast to Harlem!"

Simple lifted his glass of beer:

"Here's to Harlem!
They say Heaven is Paradise.
If Harlem ain't Heaven,
Then a mouse ain't mice!"

JESSIE FAUSET

Meeting Langston Hughes   1926

Very perfect is the memory of my first literary acquaintance with Langston Hughes. In the unforgettable days when we were publishing *The Brownies' Book* we had already appreciated a charming fragile conceit which read:

Out of the dust of dreams,
Fairies weave their garments;
Out of the purple and rose of old memories,
They make purple wings.
No wonder we find them such marvelous things.

Then one day came "The Negro Speaks of Rivers." I took the beautiful dignified creation to Dr. Du Bois and said: "What colored person is there, do you suppose, in the United States who writes like that and yet is unknown to us?" And I wrote and found him to be a Cleveland high school graduate who had just gone to live in Mexico. Already he had begun to assume that remote, so elusive quality which permeates most of his work. Before long we had the pleasure of seeing the work of the boy, whom we had sponsored, copied, and recopied in journals far and wide. "The Negro Speaks of Rivers" even appeared in translation in a paper printed in Germany.

Not very long after Hughes came to New York and not long after that he began to travel and to set down the impressions, the pictures, which his sensi-

---

Jim Crowed: Jim Crow laws were the "legal" foundation for racial discrimination in the southern states.

tive mind had registered of new forms of life and living in Holland, in France, in Spain, in Italy, and in Africa.

His poems are warm, exotic, and shot through with color. Never is he preoccupied with form. But this fault, if it is one, has its corresponding virtue, for it gives his verse, which almost always is imbued with the essence of poetry, the perfection of spontaneity. And one characteristic which makes for this bubbling-like charm is the remarkable objectivity which he occasionally achieves, remarkable for one so young, and a first step toward philosophy. Hughes has seen a great deal of the world, and this has taught him that nothing matters much but life. Its forms and aspects may vary, but living is the essential thing. Therefore make no bones about it, — "make the most of what you may spend."

Some consciousness of this must have been in him even before he began to wander for he sent us as far back as 1921:

"Shake your brown feet, honey,
Shake your brown feet, chile,
Shake your brown feet, honey,
Shake 'em swift and wil' — . . .
Sun's going down this evening —
Might never rise no mo'.
The sun's going down this very night —
Might never rise no mo' —
So dance with swift feet, honey,
(The banjo's sobbing low . . .
The sun's going down this very night —
Might never rise no mo'."

Now this is very significant, combining as it does the doctrine of the old Biblical exhortation, "eat, drink, and be merry for tomorrow ye die," Horace's "Carpe diem," the German "Freut euch des Lebens," and [Robert] Herrick's "Gather ye rosebuds while ye may." This is indeed a universal subject served Negro-style and though I am no great lover of any dialect I hope heartily that Mr. Hughes will give us many more such combinations.

Mr. Hughes is not always the calm philosopher; he has feeling a-plenty and is not ashamed to show it. He "loved his friend" who left him and so taken up is he with the sorrow of it all that he has no room for anger or resentment. While I do not think of him as a protagonist of color, — he is too much the citizen of the world for that — , I doubt if any one will ever write more tenderly, more understandingly, more humorously of the life of Harlem shot through as it is with mirth, abandon and pain. Hughes comprehends this life, has studied it and loved it. In one poem he has epitomized its essence:

Does a jazz-band ever sob?
They say a jazz-band's gay.
Yet as the vulgar dancers whirled
And the wan night wore away,

One said she heard the jazz-band sob
When the little dawn was grey.

Harlem is undoubtedly one of his great loves; the sea is another. Indeed all life is his love and his work a brilliant, sensitive interpretation of its numerous facets.

RICHARD WRIGHT

A Review of The Big Sea   1940

The double role that Langston Hughes has played in the rise of a realistic literature among the Negro people resembles in one phase the role that Theodore Dreiser° played in freeing American literary expression from the restrictions of Puritanism. Not that Negro literature was ever Puritanical, but it was timid and vaguely lyrical and folkish. Hughes's early poems, "The Weary Blues" and "Fine Clothes to the Jew," full of irony and urban imagery, were greeted by a large section of the Negro reading public with suspicion and shock when they first appeared in the middle twenties. Since then the realistic position assumed by Hughes has become the dominant outlook of all those Negro writers who have something to say.

The other phase of Hughes's role has been, for the lack of a better term, that of a cultural ambassador. Performing his task quietly and almost casually, he has represented the Negroes' case, in his poems, plays, short stories and novels, at the court of world opinion. On the other hand he has brought the experiences of other nations within the orbit of the Negro writer by his translations from the French, Russian and Spanish.

How Hughes became this forerunner and ambassador can best be understood in the cameo sequences of his own life that he gives us in his sixth and latest book, *The Big Sea*. Out of his experiences as a seaman, cook, laundry worker, farm helper, bus boy, doorman, unemployed worker, have come his writings dealing with black gals who wore red stockings and black men who sang the blues all night and slept like rocks all day.

Unlike the sons and daughters of Negro "society," Hughes was not ashamed of those of his race who had to scuffle for their bread. The jerky transitions of his own life did not admit of his remaining in one place long enough to become a slave of prevailing Negro middle-class prejudices. So beneficial does this ceaseless movement seem to Hughes that he has made it one of his life principles: six months in one place, he says, is long enough to make one's life complicated. The result has been a range of artistic interest and expression possessed by no other Negro writer of his time.

Born in Joplin, Missouri, in 1902, Hughes lived in half a dozen Midwestern towns until he entered high school in Cleveland, Ohio, where he be-

---

Theodore Dreiser: American realistic novelist (1871–1945).

gan to write poetry. His father, succumbing to that fit of disgust which overtakes so many self-willed Negroes in the face of American restrictions, went
off to Mexico to make money and proceeded to treat the Mexicans just as the
whites in America had treated him. The father yearned to educate Hughes and
establish him in business. His favorite phrase was "hurry up," and it irritated
Hughes so much that he fled his father's home.

Later he entered Columbia University, only to find it dull. He got a job
on a merchant ship, threw his books into the sea and sailed for Africa. But for
all his work, he arrived home with only a monkey and a few dollars, much to
his mother's bewilderment. Again he sailed, this time for Rotterdam, where
he left the ship and made his way to Paris. After an interval of hunger he
found a job as a doorman, then as second cook in a night club, which closed
later because of bad business. He went to Italy to visit friends and had his
passport stolen. Jobless in an alien land, he became a beachcomber until he
found a ship on which he could work his way back to New York.

The poems he had written off and on had attracted the attention of some
of his relatives in Washington and, at their invitation, he went to live with
them. What Hughes has to say about Negro "society" in Washington, relatives
and hunger are bitter poems in themselves. While living in Washington, he
won his first poetry prize; shortly afterwards Carl Van Vechten submitted a
batch of his poems to a publisher.

The rest of *The Big Sea* is literary history, most of it dealing with the
Negro renaissance, that astonishing period of prolific productivity among
Negro artists that coincided with America's "golden age" of prosperity.
Hughes writes of it with humor, urbanity and objectivity; one has the feeling that never for a moment was his sense of solidarity with those who
had known hunger shaken by it. Even when a Park Avenue patron was
having him driven about the streets of New York in her town car, he "felt
bad because he could not share his new-found comfort with his mother
and relatives." When the bubble burst in 1929, Hughes returned to the
mood that seems to fit him best. He wrote of the opening of the Waldorf-
Astoria:

> Now, won't that be charming when the last flophouse
>   has turned you down this winter?

Hughes is tough; he bends but he never breaks, and he has carried on a
manly tradition in literary expression when many of his fellow writers have
gone to sleep at their posts.

ARNOLD RAMPERSAD

Langston Hughes as Folk Poet 1994

Hughes was often called, and sometimes called himself, a folk poet. To
some people, this means that his work is almost artless and thus possibly beneath criticism. The truth indeed is that Hughes published many poems that

are doggerel. To reach his primary audience — the black masses — he was prepared to write "down" to them. Some of the pieces in this volume were intended for public recitation mainly; some started as song lyrics. Like many democratic poets, such as William Carlos Williams, he believed that the full range of his poetry should reach print as soon as possible; poetry is a form of social action. However, for Hughes, as for all serious poets, the writing of poetry was virtually a sacred commitment. And while he wished to write no verse that was beyond the ability of the masses of people to understand, his poetry, in common with that of other committed writers, is replete with allusions that must be respected and understood if it is to be properly appreciated. To respect Hughes's work, above all one must respect the African American people and their culture, as well as the American people in general and their national culture.

If Hughes kept at the center of his art the hopes and dreams, as well as the actual lived conditions, of African Americans, he almost always saw these factors in the context of the eternally embattled but eternally inspiring American democratic tradition, even as changes in the world order, notably the collapse of colonialism in Africa, redefined the experiences of African peoples around the world. Almost always, too, Hughes attempted to preserve a sense of himself as a poet beyond race and other corrosive social pressures. By his absolute dedication to his art and to his social vision, as well as to his central audience, he fused his unique vision of himself as a poet to his production of art.

"What is poetry?" Langston Hughes asked near his death. He answered, "It is the human soul entire, squeezed like a lemon or a lime, drop by drop, into atomic words." He wanted no definition of the poet that divorced his art from the immediacy of life. "A poet is a human being," he declared. "Each human being must live within his time, with and for his people, and within the boundaries of his country." Hughes constantly called upon himself for the courage and the endurance necessary to write according to these beliefs. "Hang yourself, poet, in your own words," he urged all those who would take up the mantle of the poet and dare to speak to the world. "Otherwise, you are dead."

∞

CASEBOOK ON SYLVIA PLATH

Sylvia Plath's journals are her own record of the emotional torment she experienced in the last months of her life; the excerpt that opens this casebook was edited by her husband, the poet Ted Hughes, after her suicide. The next selection is poet Robert Lowell's foreword to Plath's posthumous collection Ariel *(1966), the book that brought her international fame. It was only fitting that Lowell write the foreword: he had been Plath's poetry teacher for a short time, and the new "confessional" style of his collection* Life Studies *(1959) had been an important influence on the development of her poetry. Anne Sexton was a student in Robert Lowell's poetry class at Boston Uni-*

versity when she first met Plath; Sexton wrote this memoir in 1970, four years before her own suicide. In an interview with Sybil Estess, the poet Denise Levertov discusses the confessional mode of poetry and comments on the work and development of other confessional poets, including Robert Lowell and Sylvia Plath. Finally, the writer Joyce Carol Oates meditates on Plath's "frightened" and solipsistic imagination, concluding that Plath is one of poetry's "last romantics."

Sylvia Plath

From the Journals

Tuesday, September 29. A smoggy rainy day. Somnolent bird twitters. A weight upon me of the prose solidity of the professional storytellers: something I haven't come near. A lingering breakfast in the garage room: reminiscent of a private dormitory, an institution, a mental home. The waxed linoleum, the straight straw-backed chairs, the ashtrays and bookcases, and mammoth blue-glass grapes. Looked at the two pages of my Pillars story I wrote yesterday and felt disgust at the thinness of them. The glaze again. Prohibiting the density of feeling getting in. I must be so overconscious of markets and places to send things that I can write nothing honest and really satisfying. My feverish dreams are mere figments; I neither write nor work nor study.

Of course I depend on the mirror of the world. I have one poem I am sure of, the snake one. Other than that, no subjects. The world is a blank page. I don't even know the names of the pine trees, and, worse, make no real effort to learn. Or the stars. Or the flowers. / Read May Swenson's book yesterday. Several poems I liked: "Snow by Morning" and a fine imagist piece, "At Breakfast," on the egg. Elegant and clever sound effects, vivid images: but in the poem about artists and their shapes, textures and colors, this seems a mere virtuosity with little root. "Almanac" I liked too, about the world's history measured by the moon a hammer made on a thumbnail.

I write as if an eye were upon me. That is fatal. *The New Yorker* rejected my two exercises: as if they knew that's what they were. Are still "considering" Christmas poem, although I am sure they will not take that. The adrenaline of failure. A black hornet sits on the screen, scratching and polishing its yellowed head. Again the rains fall on rooftops the color of a pool table.

If I could cut from my brain the phantom of competition, the ego-center of self-consciousness, and become a vehicle, a pure vehicle of others, the outer world. My interest in other people is too often one of comparison, not of pure intrigue with the unique otherness of identity. Here, ideally, I should forget the outer world of appearances, publishing, checks, success. And be true to an inner heart. Yet I fight against a simplemindedness, a narcissism, a protective shell against competing, against being found wanting.

To write for itself, to do things for the joy of them. What a gift of the gods.

Robert Lowell

Foreword to Plath's Ariel   *1966*

In these poems, written in the last months of her life and often rushed out at the rate of two or three a day, Sylvia Plath becomes herself, becomes something imaginary, newly, wildly and subtly created — hardly a person at all, or a woman, certainly not another "poetess," but one of those super-real, hypnotic, great classical heroines. This character is feminine, rather than female, though almost everything we customarily think of as feminine is turned on its head. The voice is now coolly amused, witty, now sour, now fanciful, girlish, charming, now sinking to the strident rasp of the vampire — a Dido, Phaedra, or Medea, who can laugh at herself as "cow-heavy and floral in my Victorian nightgown." Though lines get repeated, and sometimes the plot is lost, language never dies in her mouth.

Everything in these poems is personal, confessional, felt, but the manner of feeling is controlled hallucination, the autobiography of a fever. She burns to be on the move, a walk, a ride, a journey, the flight of the queen bee. She is driven forward by the pounding pistons of her heart. The title *Ariel* summons up Shakespeare's lovely, though slightly chilling and androgenous spirit, but the truth is that this *Ariel* is the author's horse. Dangerous, more powerful than man, machinelike from hard training, she herself is a little like a race-horse, galloping relentlessly with risked, outstretched neck, death hurdle after death hurdle topped. She cries out for that rapid life of starting pistols, snapping tapes, and new world records broken. What is most heroic in her, though, is not her force, but the desperate practicality of her control, her hand of metal with its modest, womanish touch. Almost pure motion, she can endure "God, the great stasis in his vacuous night," hospitals, fever, paralysis, the iron lung, being stripped like a girl in the booth of a circus sideshow, dressed like a mannequin, tied down like Gulliver by the Lilliputians . . . apartments, babies, prim English landscapes, beehives, yew trees, gardens, the moon, hooks, the black boot, wounds, flowers with mouths like wounds, Belsen's lampshades made of human skin, Hitler's homicidal iron tanks clanking over Russia. Suicide, father-hatred, self-loathing — nothing is too much for the macabre gaiety of her control. Yet it is too much; her art's immortality is life's disintegration. The surprise, the shimmering, unwrapped birthday present, the transcendence "into the red eye, the cauldron of morning," and the lover, who are always waiting for her, are Death, her own abrupt and defiant death.

> He tells me how badly I photograph.
> He tells me how sweet
> The babies look in their hospital
> Icebox, a simple
>
> Frill at the neck,
> Then the flutings of their Ionian
> Death gowns,
> Then two little feet.

There is a peculiar, haunting challenge to these poems. Probably many, after reading *Ariel*, will recoil from their first overawed shock, and painfully wonder why so much of it leaves them feeling empty, evasive and inarticulate. In her lines, I often hear the serpent whisper, "Come, if only you had the courage, you too could have my rightness, audacity and ease of inspiration." But most of us will turn back. These poems are playing Russian roulette with six cartridges in the cylinder, a game of "chicken," the wheels of both cars locked and unable to swerve. Oh, for that heaven of the humble copyist, those millennia of Egyptian artists repeating their lofty set patterns! And yet Sylvia Plath's poems are not the celebration of some savage and debauched existence, that of the "damned" poet, glad to burn out his body for a few years of continuous intensity. This poetry and life are not a career; they tell that life, even when disciplined, is simply not worth it.

It is poignant, looking back, to realize that the secret of Sylvia Plath's last irresistible blaze lies lost somewhere in the checks and courtesies of her early laborious shyness. She was never a student of mine, but for a couple of months seven years ago, she used to drop in on my poetry seminar at Boston University. I see her dim against the bright sky of a high window, viewless unless one cared to look down on the city outskirts' defeated yellow brick and square concrete pillbox filling stations. She was willowy, long-waisted, sharp-elbowed, nervous, giggly, gracious — a brilliant tense presence embarrassed by restraint. Her humility and willingness to accept what was admired seemed at times to give her an air of maddening docility that hid her unfashionable patience and boldness. She showed us poems that later, more or less unchanged, went into her first book, *The Colossus*. They were somber, formidably expert in stanza structure, and had a flair for alliteration and Massachusetts' low-tide dolor.

> A mongrel working his legs to a gallop
> Hustles the gull flock to flap off the sand-spit.

Other lines showed her wit and directness.

> The pears fatten like little Buddhas.

Somehow none of it sank very deep into my awareness. I sensed her abashment and distinction, and never guessed her later appalling and triumphant fulfillment.

ANNE SEXTON

The Barfly Ought to Sing 1970

I can add, for Sylvia, only a small sketch and two poems — one poem written for her at the news of her death and the other, written a year later, written directly for both of us and for that place where we met . . . "balanced there, suicides sometimes meet. . . ."

I knew her for a while in Boston. We did grow up in the same suburban town, Wellesley, Massachusetts, but she was about four years behind me and we never met. Even if we had, I wonder if we would have become close friends, back then — she was so bright, so precocious and determined to be special while I was only a pimply boy-crazy thing, flunking most subjects, thinking I was never special. We didn't meet, at any rate, until she was married to Ted Hughes and living in Boston. We met because we were poets. Met, not for protocol, but for truth. She heard, and George Starbuck heard, that I was auditing a class at Boston University given by Robert Lowell. They kind of followed me in, joined me there and so we orbited around the class silently. If we talked at all then we were fools. We knew too much about it to talk. Silence was wiser, when we could command it. We tried, each one in his own manner; sometimes letting our own poems come up, as for a butcher, as for a lover. Both went on. We kept as quiet as possible in view of the father.

Then, after the class, we would pile into the front seat of my old Ford and I would drive quickly through the traffic to, or near, The Ritz. I would always park illegally in a LOADING ONLY ZONE, telling them gaily, "It's okay, because we are only going to get loaded!" Of we'd go, each on George's arm, into The Ritz to drink three or four or two martinis. George even has a line about this in his first book of poems, *Bone Thoughts*. He wrote, *I weave with two sweet ladies out of The Ritz*. Sylvia and I, such sleep mongers, such death mongers, were those two sweet ladies.

In the lounge-bar of The Ritz, not a typical bar at all, but very plush, deep dark red carpeting, red leather chairs around polite little tables and with waiters, white coated and awfully hushed where one knew upon stepping down the five velvet red steps that he was entering *something*, we entered. The waiters knew their job. They waited on the best of Boston, or at least, celebrities. We always hoped they'd make a mistake in our case and think us some strange Hollywood types. There had to be something to explain all our books, our snowboots, our clutter of poems, our oddness, our quick and fiery conversations — and always the weekly threesome hunched around their small but fashionable table.

Often, very often, Sylvia and I would talk at length about our first suicides; at length, in detail and in depth between the free potato chips. Suicide is, after all, the opposite of the poem. Sylvia and I often talked opposites. We talked death with burned-up intensity, both of us drawn to it like moths to an electric light bulb. Sucking on it! She told the story of her first suicide in sweet and loving detail and her description in *The Bell Jar* is just the same story. It is a wonder that we didn't depress George with our egocentricity. Instead, I think, we three were stimulated by it, even George, as if death made each of us a little more real at the moment. Thus we went on, in our fashion, ignoring Lowell and the poems left behind. Poems left behind were technique — lasting but, actually, over. We talked death and this was life for us, lasting in spite of us, or better, because of us, our intent eyes, our fingers clutching the glass, three pairs of eyes fixed on someone's — each one's gossip. I know that such fascination with death sounds strange (one does not argue that it isn't sick — one knows it *is* — there's no excuse), and that people cannot understand. They keep, every year, each year, asking me "why, why?" So here is the Why-poem, for both of us, those sweet ladies at The Ritz. I do feel somehow that it's the same answer that Sylvia would have given. She's since said it for me in so many poems — so I try to say it for us in one of mine. . . .

Wanting to Die

Since you ask, most days I cannot remember.
I walk in my clothing, unmarked by that voyage.
Then the almost unnameable lust returns.

Even then I have nothing against life.
I know well the grass blades you mention,
the furniture you have placed under the sun.

But suicides have a special language.
Like carpenters they want to know *which tools.*
They never ask *why build.*

Twice I have so simply declared myself,
have possessed the enemy, eaten the enemy,
have taken on his craft, his magic.

In this way, heavy and thoughtful,
warmer than oil or water,
I have rested, drooling at the mouth-hole.

I did not think of my body at needle point.
Even the cornea and the leftover urine were gone.
Suicides have already betrayed the body.

Still-born, they don't always die,
but dazzled, they can't forget a drug so sweet
that even children would look on and smile.

To thrust all that life under your tongue! —
that all by itself becomes a passion.
Death's a sad bone; bruised, you'd say.

and yet she waits for me, year after year,
to so delicately undo an old wound,
to empty my breath from its bad prison.

Balance there, suicides sometimes meet,
raging at the fruit, a pumped up moon,
leaving the bread they mistook for a kiss.

leaving the page of the book carelessly open,
something unsaid, the phone off the hook
and the love, whatever it was, an infection.

And balanced there we did meet and never asking *why build* — only asking *which tools.* This was our fascination. I neither could nor would give you reasons why either of us wanted *to build.* It is not my place to tell you Sylvia's why nor my desire to tell you mine. But I do say, come picture us exactly at our fragmented meetings, consumed at our passions and at our infections, as we ate five free bowls of potato chips and consumed lots of martinis.

After this we would weave out of The Ritz to spend our last pennies at The Waldorf Cafeteria — a dinner for 70 cents. George was in no hurry. He was separating from his wife. Sylvia's Ted was either able to wait or was busy enough with his own work and I had to stay in the city (I live outside of it) for a 7 P.M. appointment with my psychiatrist. A funny three.

I have heard since that Sylvia was determined from childhood to be great, a great writer at the least of it. I tell you, at the time I did not notice this in her. Something told me to bet on her but I never asked it why. I was too determined to bet on myself to actually notice where she was headed in her work. Lowell said, at the time, that he liked her work and that he felt her poems got right to the point. I didn't agree. I felt they really missed the whole point. (These were early poems of hers — poems on the way, on the working toward way.) I told Mr. Lowell that I felt she dodged the point and did so perhaps because of her preoccupation with form. Form was important for Sylvia and each really good poet has one of his own. No matter what he calls it — free verse or what. Still, it belongs to you or it doesn't. Sylvia hadn't then found a form that belonged to her. Those early poems were all in a cage (and not even her own cage at that). I felt she hadn't found a voice of her own, wasn't, in truth, free to be herself. Yet, of course, I knew she was skilled — intense, skilled, perceptive, strange, blonde, lovely, Sylvia.

DENISE LEVERTOV

Plath as Confessional Poet   1984

Sybil Estess: . . . Would you care to define what the term "confessional poetry" means to you. Do you consider yourself a confessional poet?

Denise Levertov: Confessional poetry to me means not just poetry with autobiographical elements clearly present in it but poetry which utilizes the poem as a place in which to confess parts of one's life which are troublesome — the kinds of things which require the act of confession. Although I write many poems of a personal nature, I don't consider myself a confessional writer in these terms.

Estess: You said in another interview that confessional poetry is "a poetry that isn't interested in sound or philosophical ideas, or in images as such, but in psychology. . . ." I wonder if it is possible to have good poetry which is interested *only* in psychology?

Levertov: No; I don't think that a lot of confessional poetry *is* good poetry. Sometimes poets writing in confessional modes are gifted poets, if their language instinct is good. But I think that this is the exception rather than the rule. As I understand it, the confessional poem has as its motivational force the desire to *unburden* the poet of something which he or she finds oppressive. But the danger here is reducing a work of art simply into a process of *excretion*. A poem is not *vomit!* It is not even tears. It is something very different from a bodily purge.

Estess: Does confession imply guilt? If a woman, say, writes a "confessional" poem about having had an abortion, for instance, would that not imply that she has some predisposition against abortion? Why else would she have to "confess" the abortion?

Levertov: A poem about an abortion could be confessional without being about guilt. It could simply be about pain. Or it could be exhibitionistic, since sometimes the impulse to tell the world about one's private life includes exhibitionism. On the other hand, a woman might write a poem about abortion from a highly ideological point of view; she could want to tell the world what it's like to undergo the experience. There are many different ways that one might write such a poem, none of which would involve guilt.

Estess: But would most of these really be confessional in the way we use the term for much of contemporary poetry?

Levertov: It's a very subtle, tricky point, really. Does the way in which "confessional" is used today imply guilt? I tend to think that it doesn't have to. It can just be the need to get something off your chest. Confessional in this sense is just telling a personal story and feeling better for having told it. But it could be true that when this becomes exhibitionistic, then guilt is involved. I don't know about what psychologists would say about this.

Estess: Do you think that the best confessional poetry is that which creates a myth of the self, and thus universalizes the experience. Lowell's poetry, for instance?

Levertov: Yes. Then confessional poetry transcends the merely self-therapeutic; it attains some kind of universality. And I should conclude this topic by emphasizing that what I object to most in some so-called confessional poetry is that the impulse for the works is so exclusively related to the need for the poets to unburden themselves that the aesthetic considerations are disregarded.

Estess: I wonder if you find that writing poems is particularly painful?

Levertov: Dealing with pain is not a primary function of poetry for me; that's why I say that I am not "confessional." The act of writing poetry is, to me, extremely pleasurable. I think that the whole myth of the sufferings of the poet is vanity — vanity in the Biblical sense even. The sufferings of the poet are no greater than those of any other person. Perhaps some people who are poets may be said to be more aware of some things than a lot of people are, and in that awareness they may suffer a little more than average. But there are so many other people who are just as sensitive but who don't have anything creative to *do* with their sensitivity. Since they have not found a way to incorporate their sensitivity into action, they actually suffer a great deal more than anyone who is able to create out of sensitivity.

Estess: My question concerning pain involves, partly, just what you brought up: the sense that people do suffer according to their level of consciousness, of sensitivity. Especially sensitivity concerning their own self-consciousness. The question sometimes becomes "how much sensitivity or self-consciousness can one stand?" Obviously poets such as Sylvia Plath and John Berryman felt that they could not stand any more.

Levertov: Yes. But it was not as poets that they suffered. It was as individuals who happened to have a very low threshold of suffering, of pain, that they despaired. One can say that if they had not been poets they would have suffered just as much — or more. Yes, more. And they might not have lasted as long as they did.

Estess: Berryman remarked in the last interview that he granted, published in the *Paris Review*, that he wanted to be pushed to suffer. He wanted God, as he said, to push him toward suffering in order to be able to write. His words were, "My idea is this: the artist is extremely lucky who is presented with the worst possible ordeal that will not kill him. I think that what happens to my poetic work in the future will depend upon being knocked in the face, thrown flat, given cancer, or other things of that kind. I hope to be nearly crucified." What would you remark about such an attitude?

Levertov: Whew! I would remark that there do exist in the world masochists, and that some masochists happen to be poets. It has nothing to do with the nature of the poet per se.

Estess: What about the sense of suffering in Sylvia Plath's work? We tend to think of her as a confessional poet.

Levertov: I think that she was fantastically gifted in her images; she was indeed an inspired image-maker. This saved her poems from being just therapeutic.

Estess: How much is sheer loneliness and isolation essential for the artist, if not pain?

Levertov: Loneliness is different from solitude. I think that solitude is essential, in varying degrees, for any artist. I happen to need a lot of it. And since I lead a very busy life, and am also quite sociable, I really enjoy living alone now that I do so. Because if I did not live alone, I would have an inadequate degree of solitude.

JOYCE CAROL OATES

Sylvia Plath's Deathly Imagination 1977

[D. H.] Lawrence said in *Apocalypse* that when he heard people complain of being lonely he knew their affliction: ". . . they have lost the Cosmos." It is easy to agree with Lawrence, but less easy to understand what he means. Yet if there is a way of approaching Plath's tragedy, it is only through an analysis of what Plath lost and what she was half-conscious of having lost:

> I am solitary as grass. What is it I miss?
> Shall I ever find it, whatever it is?
> ("Three Women")

We must take this loss as a real one, not a rhetorical echoing of other poets' cries; not a yearning that can be dismissed by the robust and simple-minded among us who like that formidably healthy and impossible Emerson, sought to dismiss the young people of his day "diseased" with problems of original sin, evil, predestination, and the like by contemptuously diagnosing their worries as "the soul's mumps, and measles, and whoopingcoughs" ("Spiritual Laws"). Emerson possessed a consciousness of such fluidity and explorative intelligence that any loss of the cosmos for him could seem nothing more serious than an adolescent's perverse rebelliousness, at its most profound a doubt to be answered with a few words.

These "few words" in our era are multiplied endlessly — all the books, the tradition at our disposal, the example of a perpetually renewed and self-renewing nature — and yet they are not convincing to the Sylvia Plaths of our time. For those who imagine themselves as filled with emptiness, as wounds "walking out of hospital," the pronouncements of a practical-minded, combative, "healthy" society of organized individuals are meaningless. Society, seen from the solitary individual's viewpoint, is simply an organization of the solitary, linked together materially — perhaps, in fact, crowded together but not "together," not vitally related. One of Plath's few observations about larger units of human beings is appropriately cynical:

> And then there were other faces. The faces of nations,
> Governments, parliaments, societies,
> The faceless faces of important men.
>
> It is these men I mind:
> They are so jealous of anything that is not flat! They are
>   jealous gods
> That would have the whole world flat because they are.
>   ("Three Women")

And, in a rapid associative leap that is typical of her poetry — and typical of a certain type of frightened imagination — Plath expands her sociological observation to include the mythical figures of "Father" and "Son," who conspire together to make a heaven of flatness: "Let us flatten and launder the grossness from these souls" ("Three Women"). The symbolic figures of "Father" and "Son" do not belong to a dimension of the mind exclusive, let alone transcendent, of society; and if they embody the jealous assumptions of an imagined family of "parent" and "child," they are more immediate, more terrifyingly present, than either.

"Nations, governments, parliaments, societies" conspire only in lies and cannot be trusted. Moreover, they are male in their aggression and their cynical employment of rhetoric; their counterparts cannot be women like Plath, but the creatures of "Heavy Women," who smile to themselves above their "weighty stomachs" and meditate "devoutly as the Dutch bulb," absolutely mute, "among the archetypes." Between the archetypes of jealous, ruthless power, represented by the Father/Son of religious and social tradition, and the archetypes of moronic fleshly beauty, represented by these smug mothers, there is a very small space for the creative intellect, for the employment and expansion of a consciousness that tries to transcend such limits. Before we reject Plath's definition of the artistic self as unreasonably passive, even as infantile, we should inquire why so intelligent a woman should assume these limitations, why she should not declare war against the holders of power and of the "mysteries" of the flesh — why her poetry approaches but never crosses over the threshold of an active, healthy attack upon obvious evils and injustices. The solitary ego in its prison cell is there by its own desire, its own admission of guilt in the face of even the most crazily ignorant of accusers. Like Eugene O'Neill, who lived into his sixties with this bewildering obsession of the self-annihilated-by-Others, Plath exhibits only the most remote (and rhetorical) sympathy with other people. If she tells us she may be a bit of a "Jew," it is only to define herself, her sorrows, and not to involve our sympathies for the Jews of recent European history.

Of course, the answer is that Plath did not like other people; like many who are persecuted, she identified in a perverse way with her own persecutors, and not with those who, along with her, were victims. But she did not "like" other people because she did not essentially believe that they existed; she knew intellectually that they existed, of course, since they had the power to injure her, but she did not believe they existed in the way she did, as pulsating, breathing, suffering individuals. Even her own children are objects of her perception, there for the restless scrutiny of her image-making mind, and not there as human beings with a potentiality that would someday take them beyond their immediate dependency upon her, which she sometimes enjoys and sometimes dreads.

The moral assumptions behind Plath's poetry condemned her to death, just as she, in creating this body of poems, condemned it to death. But her moral predicament is not so pathological as one may think, if conformity to an essentially sick society is taken to be — as many traditional moralists and psychologists take it — a sign of normality. Plath speaks very clearly a language we can understand. She is saying what men have been saying for many centuries, though they have not been so frank as she, and, being less sensitive as well, they have not sickened upon their own hatred for humanity: they have thrived upon it, in fact, "sublimating" it into wondrous achievements of material and mechanical splendor. Let us assume that Sylvia Plath acted out in her poetry and in her private life the deathliness of an old consciousness, the old corrupting hell of the Renaissance ideal and its "I"-ness, separate and distinct from all other fields of consciousness, which exist only to be conquered or to inflict pain upon the "I." Where at one point in civilization this very masculine, combative ideal of an "I" set against all other "I's" — and against nature as well — was necessary in order to wrench man from the hermetic contemplation of a God-centered universe and prod him into action, it is no longer necessary, its health has become a pathology, and whoever clings to its outmoded concepts will die. If romanticism and its gradually accelerating hysteria are taken as the ultimate ends of a once-vital Renaissance ideal of subject/object antagonism, then Plath must be diagnosed as one of the last romantics; and already her poetry seems to us a poetry of the past, swiftly receding into history.

PART THREE

DRAMA

20

WHAT IS A PLAY?

Suit the action to the word, the word to the action; with this special observance, that you o'erstep not the modesty of nature: for any thing so o'erdone
is from the purpose of playing, whose end, both at the first and now, was and
is, to hold, as 't were, the mirror up to nature.

HAMLET TO THE PLAYERS

In the fall of 1995, at a program celebrating the American playwright
Arthur Miller's eightieth birthday, his fellow playwright John Guare recalled
an evening in 1952 in Jackson Heights, New York, when his father took him to
see the movie version of *Death of a Salesman*, Miller's 1949 play. Guare described his father as a World War II veteran and a patriotic "commander in
charge of Americanism" in the community, a man who never questioned what
he called "the American way." Leaving the movie theater at the end of the
film, Guare's father confided to his son a secret known to no one else in the
family — he had once been a salesman in Los Angeles, and "it hadn't worked
out." The future playwright, then twelve years old, was astonished at his father's emotional response to the film: "That night was the only time I heard
him talk about that part of his life." It was also the first time Guare understood
the power of the theater, how "it could touch a man as familiar as my father in
a way that made him a stranger to me."

Of all the literary genres, drama has the greatest potential to reach the
emotions of an audience. After poetry, it is our second oldest literary form. To
define drama as a play written to be performed in a theater is true only for the
earliest plays. Later works known as "closet dramas," written in the nineteenth century by such poets as Percy Bysshe Shelley and such playwrights as
Henrik Ibsen, were meant to be performed in the solitary theater of the
reader's mind. A play can be considered a story told in dialogue, but even here
there are exceptions: the modern playwright Samuel Beckett wrote stories
without dialogue for the stage intended to be mimed by a single performer.

Today millions of viewers watch works of drama — television sitcoms, prime-time soap operas, and weekly network dramatic series — that were never intended to be performed in a theater. But for centuries *drama* meant a stage play, and it is this meaning of the word that we primarily have in mind when we speak of drama as a literary genre.

As Aristotle understood, action is the essence of drama. This is suggested in the origin of the word *drama*, which is the Greek verb *dran*, "to perform." A century after drama flourished in Greece, Aristotle wrote the *Poetics* (c. 340 B.C.), a work in which he analyzed the literary form used by Sophocles and other Greek dramatists. For Aristotle, a play was the process of imitating a significant action complete unto itself by means of language "made sensuously attractive" and spoken by the persons involved in the action, not presented through narrative. Aristotle's definition of tragedy contained six important elements: (1) plot or action, the basic principle of drama; (2) characterization, an almost equally important element; (3) the thought or theme of the play; (4) verbal expression or dialogue; (5) visual adornment or stage decoration and costumes and masks for the actors; and (6) song or music to accompany the performers' words and movement.

Because most plays are literary works meant to give an illusion of reality through their performance onstage, a playwright who has set actors in motion to tell a story cannot interrupt the action, as in a work of fiction, to offer background information about the characters or summarize events taking place over a period of time, unless, like Tennessee Williams in *The Glass Menagerie* (1945), he introduces a narrator at the beginning of the play. Usually, the playwright gives the audience information about the story through dialogue. Playwrights can also suggest the development of their story by the physical behavior of the actors onstage and by changes in lighting, sets, or costumes.

When we think of the word *drama* we have in mind an illusion of reality invented for a striking effect. To illustrate the relationship between the everyday life we live and the life we see portrayed in the theater, the director Peter Brook described a simple exercise in *The Open Door* (1993):

> Ask any volunteer to walk from one side of a space to another. Anyone can do this. The clumsiest idiot cannot fail; he just has to walk. He makes no effort and deserves no reward.
>
> Now ask him to try to imagine that he is holding a precious bowl in his hands and to walk carefully so as not to spill a drop of its contents. Here again anyone can accomplish the act of imagination that this requires and can move in a more or less convincing manner. Yet your volunteer has made a special effort, so perhaps he deserves thanks and a five-penny piece as a reward for trying.
>
> Next ask him to imagine that as he walks the bowl slips from his fingers and crashes to the ground, spilling its contents. Now he's in trouble. He tries to act and the worst kind of artificial, amateur acting will take over his body, making the expression on his face "acted" — in other words, woefully unreal.
>
> To execute this apparently simple action so that it will appear as natural as just walking demands all the skills of a highly professional

artist — an idea has to be given flesh and blood and emotional reality; it must go beyond imitation, so that an invented life is also a parallel life, which at no level can be distinguished from the real thing. Now we can see why a true actor is worth the enormous daily rate that film companies pay him for giving a plausible impression of everyday life.

One goes to the theatre to find life, but if there is no difference between life outside the theatre and life inside, then theatre makes no sense. There's no point doing it. But if we accept that life in the theatre is more visible, more vivid than on the outside, then we can see that it is simultaneously the same thing and somewhat different.

Plays are acts of make-believe — acts in which the author, actors, stage technicians, and audience are united in their participation in an imaginary world. This world onstage can mimic "real life" in such plays as Lorraine Hansberry's *A Raisin in the Sun* (1959) or Marsha Norman's *'night, Mother* (1983), with actors and sets representing contemporary everyday reality, or it can project a view of our potential experience as in a dream, in such poetic plays as Shakespeare's *Hamlet* (c. 1600) or Edward Albee's *The Sandbox* (1960).

As a story primarily told in dialogue, each play in this anthology falls into one of three conventional categories: tragedy, comedy, and tragicomedy. Broadly speaking, in **tragedy** the story ends unhappily, usually in the death of the main character, as in Sophocles' *Oedipus the King* (c. 430 B.C.). In **comedy** the story ends happily, often with a marriage symbolizing the continuation of life and the resolution of the conflict, as in Anton Chekhov's *The Bear* (1888). In **tragicomedy,** a mixture of sad and happy events, the story's resolution can take different forms, but the audience usually experiences the play as a positive statement, an affirmation of life, as in David Henry Hwang's *As the Crow Flies* (1983). This category can be further subdivided in modern plays into **dark comedy,** where the playwright's sardonic humor offers a frightening glimpse of the futility of life, as in Samuel Beckett's *Krapp's Last Tape* (1958). There is also **farce,** a short play that depends for its comic effect on exaggerated, improbable situations and slapstick action, and **parody,** a play written in deliberate imitation of another work, usually for the purpose of ridicule, such as Christopher Durang's *For Whom the Southern Belle Tolls* (1994).

Drama has experienced many innovations in form and staging in the twentieth century, even while such practitioners as the contemporary English playwright Tom Stoppard make fun of the increasing pace of our lives and the trivialization of our most cherished institutions, including the theater. In *Dogg's Hamlet* (1979), Stoppard created two short versions of Shakespeare's *Hamlet* — one that would take fifteen minutes to perform and a second, even briefer "encore" version of the play — streamlined for a production on a double-decker London bus. As short as it is, Stoppard's "encore" version of *Hamlet* as a farce (see the Casebook on Shakespeare's *Hamlet*, p. 2038) still satisfies our definition of a play — a performance by actors of a story told in dialogue. Stoppard has edited Shakespeare's words so drastically that our familiarity with the original *Hamlet* — one of the most famous plays in the European tradition — is essential to our understanding the cut version.

If the text of *Hamlet* were performed in its complete version, it would take almost six hours onstage. Every director makes some cuts in the script, but Stoppard's version is so short that he seems to be implying that contemporary audiences are so busy watching television that they have practically no time at all to sit through the long classic plays. But he also assumes that the tradition of European theater is still relevant today. The people who bought tickets when Stoppard's play was performed on the bus probably studied Shakespeare in school, where they might have become familiar with the complicated plot of *Hamlet* through reading the play or a summary of it for an English class.

If you are familiar with Shakespeare's play, Stoppard's collapsed version will remind you of what has been cut. The "encore" version of *Hamlet* conveys none of the complexity of the hero's passionate character, none of the poetry of his unforgettable soliloquies, and none of the tragedy of his dilemma. This bizarre version is meant to be only a faint, funny echo of the original.

Stoppard wrote his farce for a specific theater company in England, intending it to be seen and heard as well as read. This adds another dimension to our experience of drama. When performed in front of an audience, the text of a play is transmitted by the theatrical director, the costume and set designers, the technical staff responsible for sound and lighting, and the actors who make the play come alive. All these people work together to shape a play's meaning for the audience.

Even on a red double-decker London bus, an actor interpreting Hamlet as an aristocrat dressed in luxurious black velvet and silk ruffles will elicit a different response to the hero's personality and emotional situation than an actor who depicts Hamlet as a clown in a silly wig and circus tights or as a scruffy, leather-jacketed, metal-studded biker or as a pajama-clad patient recently escaped from a psychiatric hospital. Actors have performed the role in all these costumes, and they are all — at least in name — Hamlet. Every time an actor "plays" him, or any other character in a drama, there is the potential for interpreting the role differently.

Because drama is a collaborative effort that results in a work performed on a stage in front of an audience, we call a writer who creates plays a play-*wright*, suggesting a highly skilled craftsperson or artisan who makes something tangible. But the basic text of a play — the author's creation of dialogue and stage action and the description on the page of the setting and the characters — has a special significance. The text is the only aspect of the theater in which the writer has the last word. When we read a play, following the dialogue and the stage directions makes us conscious of how the story might take on another life when performed on a stage or in a film, but we are also aware as we follow the words on the page that reading a play puts us into a special relationship with the playwright. Like the writer, we have only words to fire our imaginations; there are no actors, costumes, or sets.

What endures is the play on the page. As Aristotle wrote about the primacy of the text in *The Poetics*, "The visual adornment of the dramatic persons can have a strong emotional effect but is the least artistic element, the least connected with the poetic art; in fact the force of tragedy can be felt even without benefit of public performance and actors, while for the production of the visual effect the property man's art is even more decisive than that of the poet's."

If a play is to survive beyond its ephemeral stage or film presentations, it depends on its text and the response of generations of readers to its story, language, structure, and deeper meaning or theme. If a play exists only in performance, it will probably not survive as literature. Reading a play in addition to seeing it performed can help you understand the work better, especially if its language or meaning is difficult to follow in the action onstage. From your seat in the theater you cannot stop a play in the middle of a scene to tell the actor, "Wait, I didn't understand that line. Please repeat it." As a reader, however, you have the luxury of being able to stop in the midst of your reading to ponder the meaning of a line or to go over an entire scene that is not immediately clear to you.

RELATED COMMENTARIES: *Edward Albee, "On Playwriting," page 1960; Aristotle, "On the Elements and General Principles of Tragedy," page 1966; Eugene O'Neill, "A Letter to Arthur Hobson Quinn," page 2019; August Wilson, "Where to Begin?," page 2033.*

21

THE ELEMENTS OF DRAMA: A PLAYWRIGHT'S MEANS

INTERVIEWER: Which playwrights did you most admire when you were young?
ARTHUR MILLER: Well, first the Greeks, for their magnificent form, the symmetry. Half the time I couldn't really repeat the story because the characters in the mythology were completely blank to me. I had no background at that time to know really what was involved in these plays, but the architecture was clear. One looks at some building of the past whose use one is ignorant of, and yet it has a modernity. It had its own specific gravity. That form has never left me; I suppose it just got burned in.

          – ARTHUR MILLER, *Paris Review* interview (1967)

Like story writers and poets, playwrights have several important means or elements at their disposal in creating dramatic works for the stage. Familiarizing yourself with these elements will help you appreciate the artistry of these creations and understand them better. Some of the terms used to analyze drama (for instance, *plot, character,* and *theme*) are similar to those used in discussing short fiction; others (*dialogue* and *staging*) refer exclusively to theater.

Even the most basic form of drama, the **monologue** — words meant to be spoken by one actor — suggests the resources available to the playwright. Consider, for example, the following fragment by Anton Chekhov. Found in his handwriting among his papers after his death, it appears to be a page that survived from one of his early attempts to rewrite his play *Uncle Vanya* (1896):

SOLOMON (alone): Oh! how dark is life! No night, when I was a child, so terrified me by its darkness as does my invisible existence. Lord, to David my father thou gavest only the gift of harmonizing words and songs, to sing and praise thee on strings, to lament sweetly, to make people weep or admire beauty; but why hast thou given me a meditative, sleepless, hungry mind? Like an insect born of the dust, I hide in darkness; and in fear and despair, all shaking and shivering, I see and hear in everything an invisible mystery. Why this morning? Why does the sun come out from behind the temple and gild the palm tree? Why this beauty of women? Where does the bird hurry, what is the meaning of its flight, if it and its young and the place to which it hastens will like myself, turn to dust? It were better I had never been born or were a stone, to which God has given neither eyes nor thoughts. In order to tire out my body by nightfall, all day yesterday, like a mere workman, I carried marble to the temple; but now the night has come and I cannot sleep. . . . I'll go and lie down. Phorses told me that if one imagines a flock of sheep running and fixes one's attention upon it, the mind gets confused and one falls asleep. I'll do it. . . . (*Exit.*)

Chekhov suggests several elements of drama in this monologue. The first word gives us the name of the **character** speaking the lines, Solomon, the son of King David, the great Hebrew poet whose psalms are included in the Old Testament. Solomon himself is a judge, not a poet, renowned throughout his kingdom for his wisdom. His first words ("Oh! how dark is life!") suggest the poetic **language** of his speech in his use of a metaphor. His next words ("No night, when I was a child, so terrified me by its darkness as does my invisible existence") suggest the subject or **theme** of his monologue, a philosophical contemplation of his own mortality. His words take on the element of **dramatic irony,** because the reader assumes that a man as wise as King Solomon would not be troubled by doubts or uncertainties.

Chekhov uses an elegant structure to present the progression of Solomon's thoughts, beginning with his statement or **exposition** of the theme. Solomon's situation is then developed in the **rising action** of the monologue, when he compares himself to his father and states the **conflict** within his personality: unlike David, he is not content to praise the Lord; he has a "sleepless, hungry mind." Next, Solomon gives specific examples of his dilemma — first his awareness of the darkness and mystery in the world, then his observation of the same mystery in sunlight and beauty. Finally, at the **climax** of his thought, when he recognizes his own mortality and the evidence all around him of the futility of all existence ("turn to dust"), he admits, "It were better I had never been born or were a stone, to which God has given neither eyes nor thoughts." He has reached bottom, accepting defeat. In the **falling action** he reminds himself about the advice he's heard from Phorses, about a method of counting sheep to put himself to sleep, and he leaves the stage determined to try it.

This monologue is a fragment, with no **resolution** other than Solomon's exit from the stage. It also lacks any physical **action** other than the speech itself, wherein Solomon meditates on mortality and attempts to fill the time before he tries to sleep. His words suggest a **plot,** telling us about what he did the previous day, trying to shake off his depression by carrying blocks of heavy marble in order to exhaust himself for sleep. **Movement** or staging of the monologue would depend on the actor saying the words onstage. We would not actually see Solomon pick up the marble slabs, but he could suggest his heavy labor — or his fatigue — by his physical stance and gestures. Each of us can imagine an appropriate **staging** for the monologue of a great Hebrew king, as ornate or as simple as we wish — a room in a realistic set that suggests a palace filled with silver and gold objects, or a symbolic bare stage furnished only with a classic plain-cloth backdrop. These choices, of course, affect how the viewer perceives the scene and the actor speaking his lines.

Plot, characterization, dialogue, and theme are the four main elements that you analyze when you think about plays as literary texts. Naturally, in plays with more than one character, playwrights can develop these elements in more complex ways. As you read the short play *Tender Offer* by the contemporary American playwright Wendy Wasserstein, be aware of how she uses plot, characterization, dialogue, and theme, as well as various physical elements of staging (for instance, the stage set and the two performers' song and dance routine), to tell a story in the words exchanged by two actors on a stage.

WENDY WASSERSTEIN

Tender Offer

1991

A girl of around nine is alone in a dance studio. She is dressed in traditional leotards and tights. She begins singing to herself, "Nothing Could Be Finer Than to Be in Carolina." She maps out a dance routine, including parts for the chorus. She builds to a finale. A man, Paul, around thirty-five, walks in. He has a sweet, though distant, demeanor. As he walks in, Lisa notices him and stops.

PAUL: You don't have to stop, sweetheart.

LISA: That's okay.

PAUL: Looked very good.

LISA: Thanks.

PAUL: Don't I get a kiss hello?

LISA: Sure.

PAUL (*embraces her*): Hi, Tiger.

LISA: Hi, Dad.

PAUL: I'm sorry I'm late.

LISA: That's okay.

PAUL: How'd it go?

LISA: Good.

PAUL: Just good?

LISA: Pretty good.

PAUL: "Pretty good." You mean you got a lot of applause or "pretty good" you could have done better.

LISA: Well, Courtney Palumbo's mother thought I was pretty good. But you know the part in the middle when everybody's supposed to freeze and the big girl comes out. Well, I think I moved a little bit.

PAUL: I thought what you were doing looked very good.

LISA: Daddy, that's not what I was doing. That was tap-dancing. I made that up.

PAUL: Oh. Well it looked good. Kind of sexy.

LISA: Yuch!

PAUL: What do you mean "yuch"?

LISA: Just yuch!

PAUL: You don't want to be sexy?

LISA: I don't care.

PAUL: Let's go, Tiger. I promised your mother I'd get you home in time for dinner.

LISA: I can't find my leg warmers.

PAUL: You can't find your what?

LISA: Leg warmers. I can't go home till I find my leg warmers.

PAUL: I don't see you looking for them.

LISA: I was waiting for you.

PAUL: Oh.

LISA: Daddy.

PAUL: What?

LISA: Nothing.

PAUL: Where do you think you left them?

LISA: Somewhere around here. I can't remember.

PAUL: Well, try to remember, Lisa. We don't have all night.

LISA: I told you. I think somewhere around here.

PAUL: I don't see them. Let's go home now. You'll call the dancing school tomorrow.

LISA: Daddy, I can't go home till I find them. Miss Judy says it's not professional to leave things.

PAUL: Who's Miss Judy?

LISA: She's my ballet teacher. She once danced the lead in *Swan Lake*, and she was a June Taylor dancer.

PAUL: Well, then, I'm sure she'll understand about the leg warmers.

LISA: Daddy, Miss Judy wanted to know why you were late today.

PAUL: Hmmmmmmmm?

LISA: Why were you late?

PAUL: I was in a meeting. Business. I'm sorry.

LISA: Why did you tell Mommy you'd come instead of her if you knew you had business?

PAUL: Honey, something just came up. I thought I'd be able to be here. I was looking forward to it.

LISA: I wish you wouldn't make appointments to see me.

PAUL: Hmmmmmmm.

LISA: You shouldn't make appointments to see me unless you know you're going to come.

PAUL: Of course I'm going to come.

LISA: No, you're not. Talia Robbins told me she's much happier living without her father in the house. Her father used to come home late and go to sleep early.

PAUL: Lisa, stop it. Let's go.

LISA: I can't find my leg warmers.

PAUL: Forget your leg warmers.

LISA: Daddy.

PAUL: What is it?

LISA: I saw this show on television, I think it was WPIX Channel 11. Well, the father was crying about his daughter.

PAUL: Why was he crying? Was she sick?

LISA: No. She was at school. And he was at business. And he just missed her, so he started to cry.

PAUL: What was the name of this show?

LISA: I don't know. I came in in the middle.

PAUL: Well, Lisa, I certainly would cry if you were sick or far away, but I know that you're well and you're home. So no reason to get maudlin.

LISA: What's maudlin?

PAUL: Sentimental, soppy. Frequently used by children who make things up to get attention.

LISA: I am sick! I am sick! I have Hodgkin's disease and a bad itch on my leg.

PAUL: What do you mean you have Hodgkin's disease? Don't say things like that.

LISA: Swoosie Kurtz, she had Hodgkin's disease on a TV movie last year, but she got better and now she's on *Love, Sidney*.

PAUL: Who is Swoosie Kurtz?

LISA: She's an actress named after an airplane. I saw her on *Live at Five*.

PAUL: You watch too much television; you should do your homework. Now, put your coat on.

LISA: Daddy, I really do have a bad itch on my leg. Would you scratch it?

PAUL: Lisa, you're procrastinating.

LISA: Why do you use words I don't understand? I hate it. You're like Daria Feldman's mother. She always talks in Yiddish to her husband so Daria won't understand.

PAUL: Procrastinating is not Yiddish.

LISA: Well, I don't know what it is.

PAUL: Procrastinating means you don't want to go about your business.

LISA: I don't go to business. I go to school.

PAUL: What I mean is you want to hang around here until you and I are late for dinner and your mother's angry and it's too late for you to do your homework.

LISA: I do not.

PAUL: Well, it sure looks that way. Now put your coat on and let's go.

LISA: Daddy.

PAUL: Honey, I'm tired. Really, later.

LISA: Why don't you want to talk to me?

PAUL: I do want to talk to you. I promise when we get home we'll have a nice talk.

LISA: No, we won't. You'll read the paper and fall asleep in front of the news.

PAUL: Honey, we'll talk on the weekend, I promise. Aren't I taking you to the theater this weekend? Let me look. (*He takes out appointment book.*) Yes. Sunday. *Joseph and the Amazing Technicolor Raincoat* with Lisa. Okay, Tiger?

LISA: Sure. It's *Dreamcoat*.

PAUL: What?

LISA: Nothing. I think I see my leg warmers. (*She goes to pick them up, and an odd-looking trophy.*)

PAUL: What's that?

LISA: It's stupid. I was second best at the dance recital, so they gave me this thing. It's stupid.

PAUL: Lisa.

LISA: What?

PAUL: What did you want to talk about?

LISA: Nothing.

PAUL: Was it about my missing your recital? I'm really sorry, Tiger. I would have liked to have been here.

LISA: That's okay.

PAUL: Honest?

LISA: Daddy, you're prostrastinating.

PAUL: I'm procrastinating. Sit down. Let's talk. So. How's school?

LISA: Fine.

PAUL: You like it?

LISA: Yup.

PAUL: You looking forward to camp this summer?

LISA: Yup.

PAUL: Is Daria Feldman going back?

LISA: Nope.

PAUL: Why not?

LISA: I don't know. We can go home now. Honest, my foot doesn't itch anymore.

PAUL: Lisa, you know what you do in business when it seems like there's nothing left to say? That's when you really start talking. Put a bid on the table.

LISA: What's a bid?

PAUL: You tell me what you want and I'll tell you what I've got to offer. Like Monopoly. You want Boardwalk, but I'm only willing to give you the Railroads. Now, because you are my daughter I'd throw in Water Works and Electricity. Understand, Tiger?

LISA: No. I don't like board games. You know, Daddy, we could get Space Invaders for our home for thirty-five dollars. In fact, we could get an Osborne System for two thousand. Daria Feldman's parents . . .

PAUL: Daria Feldman's parents refuse to talk to Daria, so they bought a computer to keep Daria busy so they won't have to speak in Yiddish. Daria will probably grow up to be a homicidal maniac lesbian prostitute.

LISA: I know what that word prostitute means.

PAUL: Good. (*Pause.*) You still haven't told me about school. Do you still like your teacher?

LISA: She's okay.

PAUL: Lisa, if we're talking try to answer me.

LISA: I am answering you. Can we go home now, please?

PAUL: Damn it, Lisa, if you want to talk to me . . . Talk to me!

LISA: I can't wait till I'm old enough so I can make my own money and never have to see you again. Maybe I'll become a prostitute.

PAUL: Young lady, that's enough.

LISA: I hate you, Daddy! I hate you! (*She throws her trophy into the trash bin.*)

PAUL: What'd you do that for?

LISA: It's stupid.

PAUL: Maybe I wanted it.

LISA: What for?

PAUL: Maybe I wanted to put it where I keep your dinosaur and the picture you made of Mrs. Kimbel with the chicken pox.

LISA: You got mad at me when I made that picture. You told me I had to respect Mrs. Kimbel because she was my teacher.

PAUL: That's true. But she wasn't my teacher. I liked her better with the chicken pox. (*Pause.*) Lisa, I'm sorry. I was very wrong to miss your recital, and you don't have to become a prostitute. That's not the type of profession Miss Judy has in mind for you.

LISA (*mumbles*): No.

PAUL: No. (*Pause.*) So Talia Robbins is really happy her father moved out?

LISA: Talia Robbins picks open the eighth-grade lockers during gym period. But she did that before her father moved out.

PAUL: You can't always judge someone by what they do or what they don't do. Sometimes you come home from dancing school and run upstairs and shut the door, and when I finally get to talk to you, everything is "okay" or "fine." Yup or nope?

LISA: Yup.

PAUL: Sometimes, a lot of times, I come home and fall asleep in front of the television. So you and I spend a lot of time being a little scared of each other. Maybe?

LISA: Maybe.

PAUL: Tell you what. I'll make you a tender offer.

LISA: What?

PAUL: I'll make you a tender offer. That's when one company publishes in the newspaper that they want to buy another company. And the company that publishes is called the Black Knight because they want to gobble up the poor little company. So the poor little company needs to be rescued. And then a White Knight comes along and makes a bigger and better offer so the shareholders won't have to tender shares to the Big Black Knight. You with me?

LISA: Sort of.

PAUL: I'll make you a tender offer like the White Knight. But I don't want to own you. I just want to make a much better offer. Okay?

LISA (*sort of understanding*): Okay. (*Pause. They sit for a moment.*) Sort of, Daddy, what do you think about? I mean, like when you're quiet what do you think about?

PAUL: Oh, business usually. If I think I made a mistake or if I think I'm doing okay. Sometimes I think about what I'll be doing five years from now and if it's what I hoped it would be five years ago. Sometimes I think about what your life will be like, if Mount Saint Helens will erupt again. What you'll become if you'll study penmanship or word processing. If you speak kindly of me to your psychiatrist when you are in graduate school. And how the hell I'll pay for your graduate school. And sometimes I try and think what it was I thought about when I was your age.

LISA: Do you ever look out your window at the clouds and try to see which kinds of shapes they are? Like one time, honest, I saw the head of Walter Cronkite in a flower vase. Really! Like look don't those kinda look like if you turn it upside down, two big elbows or two elephant trunks dancing?

PAUL: Actually still looks like Walter Cronkite in a flower vase to me. But look up a little. See the one that's still moving? That sorta looks like a whale on a thimble.

LISA: Where?

PAUL: Look up. To your right.

LISA: I don't see it. Where?

PAUL: The other way.

LISA: Oh, yeah! There's the head and there's the stomach. Yeah! (*Lisa picks up her trophy.*) Hey, Daddy.

PAUL: Hey, Lisa.

LISA: You can have this thing if you want it. But you have to put it like this, because if you put it like that it is gross.

PAUL: You know what I'd like? So I can tell people who come into my office why I have this gross stupid thing on my shelf, I'd like it if you could show me your dance recital.

LISA: Now?

PAUL: We've got time. Mother said she won't be home till late.

LISA: Well, Daddy, during a lot of it I freeze and the big girl in front dances.

PAUL: Well, how 'bout the number you were doing when I walked in?

LISA: Well, see, I have parts for a lot of people in that one, too.

PAUL: I'll dance the other parts.

LISA: You can't dance.

PAUL: Young lady, I played Yvette Mimimeux in a *Hasty Pudding Show.*°

LISA: Who's Yvette Mimimeux?

PAUL: Watch more television. You'll find out. (*Paul stands up.*) So I'm ready. (*He begins singing.*) "Nothing could be finer than to be in Carolina."

LISA: Now I go. In the morning. And now you go. Dum-da.

PAUL (*obviously not a tap dancer*): Da-da-dum.

LISA (*whines*): Daddy!

PAUL (*mimics her*): Lisa! Nothing could be finer . . .

LISA: That looks dumb.

PAUL: Oh, yeah? You think they do this better in *The Amazing Minkcoat?* No way! Now you go — da da da dum.

LISA: Da da da dum.

PAUL: If I had Aladdin's lamp for only a day, I'd make a wish . . .

Hasty Pudding Show: An all-male revue, written and staged by Harvard students and renowned for its zany humor, men in drag, and parodies of cultural icons (e.g., the mock-reference to Yvette Mimieux, a '60s movie star).

LISA: Daddy, that's maudlin!
PAUL: I know it's maudlin. And here's what I'd say:
LISA AND PAUL: I'd say that "nothing could be finer than to be in Carolina in the mooooooooooornin'."

PLOT

Plot is the structuring of the events in a play. Also called the story, plot is the essential element with which a dramatist works. If "to play," according to the dictionary definition, is to engage in mimicry, acting, or make believe, then "a play" is a literary work that mimics or imitates a complete action onstage.

The plot of *Tender Offer* is the story of how a father and his young daughter resolve their differences during a quarrel and grow closer. When Paul and Lisa finish their tap routine in the dance studio, we sense that something has been resolved between them and that the stage action is complete. The **exposition** of the plot begins with Lisa's solitary dance as the play starts and continues with the entrance of Paul, who has arrived too late to see Lisa's recital. The development of the quarrel between them is the plot's **rising action.** Paul's attempts to evade the issue of Lisa's disappointment with him and Lisa's expression of her anger lead to the **climax** of the action, when she throws her trophy away. The father's "tender offer" to his daughter is the **turning point** of the plot. Their game together finding shapes in the clouds is the **falling action,** and their final song and dance duet constitutes the **resolution** or **dénouement** of the drama. This progression of events develops a story with a beginning, a middle, and an end.

What drives the plot is usually **conflict,** and drama can be defined most simply as a progression of events that develop and resolve conflicts. Wasserstein's play continues a tradition of drama begun in the fifth century B.C. by such Greek playwrights as Sophocles and analyzed by Aristotle in *The Poetics.* Aristotle emphasized that the plot or story of a play should be unified and complete, with all aspects of the conflict resolved by the end. **Suspense** is created for the audience before the resolution of the conflict in the plot. We can see both conflict and suspense in this play.

We do not know that there is a problem between Paul and Lisa at the beginning of *Tender Offer:* all we know is that the father is so late picking up his young daughter at the dance studio that he has missed her performance at the recital. This is the dramatic situation that suggests the conflict between them. Suspense begins to build during the events of the rising action, as Wasserstein keeps us in the dark about whether Paul and Lisa will be able to resolve their differences. Lisa procrastinates about going home and suggests indirectly that she is angry with Paul by responding flatly to his opening remarks and baiting him in lines like "Talia Robbins told me she's much happier living without her father in the house." At first Paul is an authoritarian father ("Lisa, stop it. Let's go"); then, as this has no effect, he tries a softer approach ("Honey, I'm tired. Really, later").

Both characters are gentle, "tender" people, so the quarrel between them does not escalate to physical violence or a life-or-death struggle, but Wasserstein increases the tension between them when Lisa cuts through their skirmishing to confront Paul directly. She asks her father, "Why don't you want to talk to me?" When Paul responds in his customary role as the emotionally reserved parent ("I promise when we get home we'll have a nice talk"), his daughter seems to give up, delaying the resolution of the plot.

Halfway into the story, a **complication** in the plot occurs when Lisa picks up the trophy she won at the recital, and Paul begins to understand how important the afternoon has been for her. In the second half of the play, he begins to build the bridge between them that allows him to share her feelings, beginning with his next action ("Sit down. Let's talk."). Wasserstein continues to delay the resolution of the conflict and build suspense. Lisa may act calmly, but she is furious with her father. She expresses her anger in words, trying to rile him ("Can we go home now, please?", "Maybe I'll become a prostitute").

Then Wasserstein heightens the suspense: Lisa expresses her frustration by a physical action, throwing her trophy into the trash bin. Her act of hostility is the most violent event in the play, the climax or high point. It is also, of course, an act of hostility toward her father. He reacts as a concerned adult by accepting her action; he is honest enough to admit they have a problem and explains their quarrel in terms that a nine-year-old can understand ("So you and I spend a lot of time being a little scared of each other"). He defuses the tension by surprising her with his "tender offer." Taking her seriously, he shares his feelings with her, and gradually they move closer into a reconciliation symbolized by their song and dance together at the end of the play.

The action of Wasserstein's short play is very tightly constructed, exhibiting what Aristotle would call the **unity** of time and place. Its action takes less than an hour, and it occurs in one place, the dance studio. In defining the elements of classic drama, Aristotle stipulated that the action of a well-made play should be contained within a restricted period of time and a single physical place. In Sophocles' *Oedipus the King*, for example, the action occurs within one day, and the setting represents one place, the exterior of Oedipus's palace. For centuries theater critics judged playwrights according to their fidelity to Aristotle's rules about these unities, even though such brilliant writers as Shakespeare broke the rules constantly, writing plays like *Hamlet* that have complicated subplots with action occurring in different locations over extended periods of time.

Finally, in the eighteenth century, the great English critic Samuel Johnson brought some common sense to the debate. In *The Preface to Shakespeare*, Johnson wrote that Aristotle's analysis was not "an unquestionable principle":

> The truth is that the spectators [of a play in the theater] are always in their senses, and know, from the first act to the last, that the stage is only a stage, and that the players are only players. They came to hear a certain number of lines recited with just gesture and elegant modulation. The lines related to some action, and an action must be in some place; but the different actions that complete a story may be in places very remote from each other. . . . [A] lapse of years is as easily conceived as a passage of hours. In contemplation we easily contract the time of real actions, and therefore willingly permit it to be contracted when we only see their imitation.

Johnson understood that all literature, including drama, is an imitation of life. The actions we watch onstage in *Tender Offer* by the actors portraying Paul and Lisa are only imitations of what happens in a real-life relationship between father and daughter. In the play, as Johnson would have put it, these "imitations produce pain or pleasure, not because they are mistaken for realities, but because they bring realities to mind."

CHARACTERIZATION

Another important means of the playwright is **characterization,** which, as in a short story, can be the presentation of characters who play either major or minor roles in the action. Both characters in *Tender Offer* play major roles. They are also **round characters,** or fully developed human beings, a father and a daughter who are "tender" toward each other. They work through their quarrel step by step, changing their attitudes as each moves toward a better understanding of the other. In the conflict between parent and child, neither one could be called a hero or a villain. Paul was late to the recital, but he was kept busy at his office. Lisa tries to hurt him by what she says, but she enters into the spirit of his "tender offer" and invites him to look at cloud shapes outside the studio window as a prelude to joining him in their final tap dance.

In classic drama, where conflict between the characters is a confrontation between clearly delineated moral good and moral evil, the terms **protagonist** and **antagonist** are used for the hero (the central character, man or woman) and the villain, respectively. We can consider Lisa the protagonist of *Tender Offer* in that she is present on stage when the play begins, waiting for her father's arrival at the dance studio, and that the ensuing action focuses on her anger toward him. Paul could be called the antagonist because he provokes Lisa's anger, first by being late and then by not noticing she is upset. Both characters have leading roles in the short play, and both are equally complex psychological beings. When the stage directions state that Lisa "mumbles" her line and that there's a "pause" before Paul asks her a question about her friend Talia Robbins, Wasserstein is giving us subtle clues to suggest the growing tension between them.

Like short stories, plays depend on characterization to motivate the action or plot. The events occurring on stage are set in motion by the characters' personalities, and the more we understand their psychological behavior, the closer we come to understanding the play. We assume that the actions that we see on stage are plausible and consistent, within our "reading" of the different characters. We understand, for example, from the play's setting in a dance studio and from what the characters say to each other, that Lisa comes from an affluent family and seems to have a secure economic background. We factor these details into our reading of the play. As a realistic depiction of a father-daughter relationship, the characters in *Tender Offer* are solidly believable. In this short play, unlike many longer plays, there are no minor characters who exist on stage primarily to advance the action of the story or introduce subplots that complicate the main action. Minor characters usually are presented with fewer dimensions to their personalities.

The actors playing the characters can also shape our response to them. Wasserstein tells us at the beginning of *Tender Offer* that Paul has "a sweet, though distant, demeanor," but she does not give any indication of why he is "distant." It could be that while he is temperamentally reserved, he is basically honest in his dealings with his family and just happens to be so caught up in his business that he has neglected his daughter. Or we can imagine that he is "distant" because he has something to hide — for example, perhaps he missed Lisa's dance recital not because he worked late at his office but because he is having an extramarital affair. At the beginning of the play we can decide from the way the actor playing Paul speaks his lines whether we want to believe him. By the end of the play, Paul has reacted so sensitively to Lisa's feelings that we probably trust him and judge him an honest person, at least on the basis of what we have seen of his behavior onstage.

Aristotle maintained in the *Poetics* that characterization in a play was second to the element of plot or action, yet he emphasized the importance of the characters. In his ranking of the elements of drama, Aristotle was apparently as much a pragmatist as he was a theorist, judging the relative importance of plot, character, dialogue, theme, and the other elements on the basis of the literature he had actually seen and read. As evidence for his belief that structuring a good plot was the most essential element in drama, Aristotle said he noticed that beginning writers "manage to hit the mark in verbal expression and character portrayal sooner than they do in plot construction." Other critics have argued that dialogue, not characterization or plot action, is the most important element in drama. You can reach your own conclusion in this matter after you have read more plays.

DIALOGUE

Dialogue is the exchange of words between the characters in a play. In short fiction and poetry, dialogue is often set emotionally for us by the descriptive words that authors use to introduce it. They write, "He shouted," to show strong emotion, for example, or "She wailed," to show extreme unhappiness. Wasserstein tells us that Lisa "mumbles," but playwrights rely primarily on the dialogue to tell their stories.

Most critics agree that dialogue has three main functions in a play: to advance the plot, to establish the setting, and to reveal character. When we say that plot is *dialogue driven* in drama, we mean that the words of the actors advance the plot. In the exposition at the start of the play, the actors' words can also reveal important information about what has gone on before the stage action commences; dialogue continues to introduce new complications throughout the development of the plot. When Lisa greets Paul by saying "Hi, Dad," her words establish their relationship with great economy and precision. When he says, "I'm sorry I'm late" and "How'd it go?," her flat replies suggest her disappointment with him. Their exchange establishes the setting and tells what happened before the play began. In her choice of words, Lisa also hints that something is wrong.

Paul's opening dialogue presents him as a loving, if breezy, parent: "You don't have to stop, sweetheart." He's also a stickler for information, holding his daughter accountable for her actions (" 'Pretty good.' You mean you got a lot of applause or 'pretty good' you could have done better"). He puts off her question about why he's late with a noncommittal "hmmmmmmmmm," which he repeats evasively when she attempts to give him an order by saying "I wish you wouldn't make appointments to see me." Paul introduces words that Lisa doesn't understand — *maudlin* and *procrastinating* — but she is responsive to him, asking him for definitions and then deliberately misunderstanding him ("I don't go to business. I go to school"). In response, he simplifies his language as if he thinks she is stupid ("What I mean is you want to hang around here until you and I are late for dinner and your mother's angry and it's too late for you to do your homework"). This is the height of the misunderstanding between them.

When we say that Wasserstein has written realistic dialogue between the two characters in *Tender Offer* we mean that the words they speak onstage strike us as the way people could actually have a conversation. With a little thought, you realize that this is not true. Where are the pauses, incomplete sentences, rushes of words, and fillers like "like," "uh," and "you know" that creep into our usual attempts at verbal communication with another human being? We may think we are having a dialogue when we exchange words with another person, but usually it is nothing like the dialogue we hear onstage. Wasserstein has ironed out all the wrinkles in the words that Lisa and Paul exchange. Every word has been chosen for its effect on the listener. This does not mean that Wasserstein's dialogue strikes our ears as false or badly written. It is a tribute to her skill as a playwright that we believe Lisa and Paul talk in the way that people *could* have this conversation — if they were both speaking their lines onstage.

Taking Chekhov as an example, the director Peter Brook has described in *The Open Door* the way that playwrights must go beyond an imitation of life in order to create effective dialogue:

> Life in the theatre is more readable and intense because it is more concentrated. The act of reducing space and compressing time creates a concentrate.
>
> In life we speak in a chattering tumble of repetitive words, yet this quite natural way of expressing ourselves always takes a great deal of time in relation to the actual content of what one wants to say. . . . The [dramatist's] compression consists of removing everything that is not strictly necessary and intensifying what is there, such as putting a strong adjective in the place of a bland one, whilst preserving the impression of spontaneity. If this impression is maintained, we reach the point where if in life it takes two people three hours to say something, onstage it should take three minutes. . . .
>
> With Chekhov, the text gives the impression of having been recorded on tape, of taking its sentences from daily life. But there is not a phrase of Chekhov's that has not been chiseled, polished, modified, with great skill and artistry so as to give the impression that the actor is really speaking "like in daily life."
>
> However, if one tries to speak and behave just like in daily life,

one cannot play Chekhov. The actor and the director must follow the same process as the author, which is to be aware that each word, even if it appears to be innocent, is not so. It contains in itself, and in the silence that precedes and follows it, an entire unspoken complexity of energies between the characters. If one can manage to find that, and if, furthermore, one looks for the art needed to conceal it, then one succeeds in saying these simple words and giving the impression of life.

In *Tender Offer* Wasserstein also uses dialogue to be funny and lighten up the situation. As a running joke, Paul keeps giving an incorrect title (*raincoat, minkcoat*) to the musical he is going to see with his daughter, *Joseph and the Amazing Technicolor Dreamcoat*. Lisa uses colloquialisms like "kinda" and "gross," which Paul adapts into his speech to sustain their fragile bonding near the end of the play ("That sorta looks like a whale on a thimble" and "So I can tell people who come into my office why I have this gross stupid thing on my shelf"). The different levels of diction in each character's choice of words helps to enliven the dialogue, which tends to be matter of fact. This is a characteristic of realistic plays written in recent years, as opposed to the heights of poetic fancy expressed in Shakespearean dialogue. Paul tries to heighten his choice of words when he tells Lisa, "Young lady, I played Yvette Mimimeux in a *Hasty Pudding Show*," revealing in the process that he has been educated at Harvard by his casual reference to the university's drama club. Their verbal exchange is light years away from the poetry of Hamlet's words pledging obedience to his father's ghost in Act I, Scene V, of *Hamlet*:

> Remember thee!
> Yea, from the table of my memory
> I'll wipe away all trivial fond records,
> All saws of books, all forms, all pressures past
> That youth and observation copied there,
> And thy commandment all alone shall live
> Within the book and volume of my brain,
> Unmix'd with baser matter . . .

The poetic dialogues Shakespeare created in *Hamlet* are a treasury of words, not only in Hamlet's speeches to the other characters in the play but also in his **soliloquies** (speeches spoken when he is alone onstage). Wasserstein has written her dialogue in *Tender Offer* to mirror the flatter expectations of her characters. Not for them is the poetry in the lines of *Hamlet* or the passion in the anguished exchanges of August Strindberg's characters in *Miss Julie* (1888). Wasserstein is in the company of recent American playwrights like Woody Allen and David Henry Hwang.

STAGING

The staging of a play refers to the physical spectacle it presents to the audience in a performance by the actors. It takes into account such elements as the stage set, the different props and costumes used by the actors, their movement onstage, and the lighting and sound effects. *Tender Offer* is a one-set play, with its stripped-down dance-studio setting contributing to the spectator's sense of listening in on an intimate family quarrel. By entering his daughter's practice room, the father can become emotionally accessible to her in ways that he probably would not be in his office. We can read the description of the setting at the beginning of the play to locate ourselves in the world of the drama, even if the playwright gives only sparse directions (*"A girl of around nine is alone in a dance studio"*) to help us place ourselves in Lisa's story.

The transformation of a play from the page to the stage is usually a collaboration between the director; the actors; and the costume, light, and set designers. Their creativity can help the audience interpret what the dialogue reveals to them as the drama proceeds. Costumes signal aspects of character that the actors are trying to project. The lighting of the sets (now often controlled by technicians with computers transmitting hundreds of cues during a performance) helps to give the stage composition a focus. Light also casts shadows, suggesting a mood and a sense of dimensionality to the actors. The designers' work enables the viewer to *feel* a scene rather than just see it.

In most productions the director has a vision of the play that he or she communicates to the actors and the set, costume, and light designers. In the 1949 staging of Arthur Miller's *Death of a Salesman*, for example, the set designer Jo Mielziner collaborated with the author and director Elia Kazan to create a design concept centered on what he considered "the most important visual symbol in the play," the salesman's house. With great ingenuity, Mielziner constructed his set to harmonize with the effect Miller was trying to achieve in the way he told his story. Mielziner explained,

> Why should that house not be the main set, with all the other scenes — the corner of a graveyard, a hotel room in Boston, the corner of a business office, a lawyer's consultation room, and so on — played on a forestage? If I designed these little scenes in segments and fragments, with easily moved props and fluid lighting effects, I might be able, without ever lowering the curtain, to achieve the easy flow that the author clearly wanted.

The actors' movement onstage during their delivery of the dialogue is called **blocking.** Their nonverbal gestures are known as **stage business.** At times the playwright can combine the elements of movement and music to create very effective stage business, as with the tap dance symbolizing the harmony between parent and child at the end of *Tender Offer*.

A director can suggest ways for the actors to move on the set and give them stage business to further the action of the plot or support the desired illusion. When the Swedish film director Ingmar Bergman staged Henrik Ibsen's *A Doll House* in 1992, he began his production by raising the curtain to reveal the woman playing the main character Nora wearing a wine-red dress and seated on a red plush sofa. Surrounded by a clutter of toys, dolls, and doll furniture, she waited motionless for a few moments, staring out into empty space like a human doll ready to be played with.

As readers of plays we become the director, actors, designers, and musicians all in one. We may not be able to visualize Paul and Lisa's tap dance in detail or to imagine the exquisitely timed cries of the musicians accompanying a traditional Japanese Nō play or to hear the haunting backstage flute melody that Tennessee Williams specified to symbolize Laura's fragility in performances of *The Glass Menagerie*. But reading these and other plays attentively is a challenge to our imaginations to simulate the experience of seeing and hearing them brought to life in a theater.

THEME

As with short fiction and poetry, theme is the underlying meaning of a dramatic work, suggested through the dialogue spoken by the characters as they move through the action of the play. Theme must also take into account the overall effect of the different elements of drama, including the way we imagine the play staged in a theater. The theme of Wasserstein's *Tender Offer* could be expressed as the importance of a parent and child's communication with each other to build trust for their future relationship. This acknowledges the playwright's careful structure of her plot and dialogue, so that both Paul and Lisa are held accountable for the breach of good feeling between them, with Paul as a parent who has not kept his promise to attend the recital, and Lisa as a child who is acting out her disappointment. Other interpretations of the theme of *Tender Offer* are possible, of course, just as long as they do not contradict the facts in the play. For example, citing a theme of child abuse or juvenile delinquency would be to disregard what the characters do and say. Only a careless or perverse reader would come up with these faulty statements of the theme.

Awareness of the genre of a play can also help you to express its theme. Reading early plays like Sophocles' *Oedipus the King* and Shakespeare's *Hamlet*, you might find it easier to summarize the theme if you remember that these are examples of *tragedy*. Both of the title characters have a tragic flaw, or defect of character, that brings about the end of their lives as if inevitably decreed by fate. In Tom Stoppard's play *Rosencrantz and Guildenstern Are Dead* (1967), which — like his farcical *Dogg's Hamlet* — is based on Shakespeare's classic, the character of the Player gives this definition of tragedy: "We're tragedians, you see. We follow directions — there is no *choice* involved. The bad end unhappily, the good unluckily. That is what tragedy means."

Willy Russell, a contemporary of Stoppard, explored the definition of tragedy in a funny scene from his play *Educating Rita*. Here the title character, a young woman from a working-class background employed as a hairdresser who is taking classes at an English university, is so excited after seeing her first production of a Shakespeare play that she rushes back to the office of her tutor, Frank, to talk to him about it.

WILLY RUSSELL

From *Educating Rita* 1983

Frank enters carrying a briefcase and a pile of essays. He goes to the filing cabinet, takes his lecture notes from the briefcase and puts them in a drawer. He takes the sandwiches and apple from his briefcase and puts them on his desk and then goes to the window desk and dumps the essays and briefcase. He switches on the radio and then sits in the swivel chair. He opens the packet of sandwiches, takes a bite, and then picks up a book and starts reading.

Rita bursts through the door out of breath.

FRANK: What are you doing here? (*He looks at his watch.*) It's Thursday, you . . .

RITA (*moving over to the desk; quickly*): I know I shouldn't be here, it's me dinner hour, but listen, I've gorra tell someone, have y' git a few minutes, can y' spare . . . ?

FRANK (*alarmed*): My God, what is it?

RITA: I had to come an' tell y', Frank, last night, I went to the theatre! A proper one, a professional theatre.

Frank gets up and switches off the radio and then returns to the swivel chair.

FRANK (*sighing*): For God's sake, you had me worried, I thought it was something serious.

RITA: No, listen, it was. I went out an' got me ticket, it was Shakespeare, I thought it was gonna be dead borin' . . .

FRANK: Then why did you go in the first place?

RITA: I wanted to find out. But listen, it wasn't borin', it was bleedin' great, honest, ogh, it done me in, it was fantastic. I'm gonna do an essay on it.

FRANK (*smiling*): Come on, which one was it?

Rita moves upper right centre.

RITA: ". . . Out, out, brief candle!
Life's but a walking shadow, a poor player
That struts and frets his hour upon the stage
And then is heard no more. It is a tale
Told by an idiot, full of sound and fury
Signifying nothing."

FRANK (*deliberately*): Ah, *Romeo and Juliet*.

RITA (*moving towards Frank*): Tch. Frank! Be serious. I learnt that today from the book. (*She produces a copy of* Macbeth.) Look, I went out an' bought the book. Isn't it great? What I couldn't get over is how excitin' it was.

Frank puts his feet up on the desk.

RITA: Wasn't his wife a cow, eh? An' that fantastic bit where he meets Macduff an' he thinks he's all invincible. I was on the edge of me seat at that bit. I wanted to shout out an' tell Macbeth, warn him.

FRANK: You didn't, did you?

RITA: Nah. Y' can't do that in a theatre, can y'? It was dead good. It was like a thriller.

FRANK: Yes. You'll have to go and see more.

RITA: I'm goin' to. *Macbeth*'s a tragedy, isn't it?

Frank nods.

RITA: Right.

Rita smiles at Frank and he smiles back at her.

Well I just — I just had to tell someone who'd understand.

FRANK: I'm honoured that you chose me.

RITA (*moving towards the door*): Well, I better get back. I've left a customer with a perm lotion. If I don't get a move on there'll be another tragedy.

FRANK: No. There won't be a tragedy.

RITA: There will, y' know. I know this woman; she's dead fussy. If her perm doesn't come out right there'll be blood an' guts everywhere.

FRANK: Which might be quite tragic — (*He throws her the apple from his desk which she catches.*) — but it won't be a tragedy.

RITA: What?

FRANK: Well — erm — look; the tragedy of the drama has nothing to do with the sort of tragic event you're talking about. Macbeth is flawed by his ambition — yes?

RITA (*going and sitting in the chair by the desk*): Yeh. Go on. (*She starts to eat the apple.*)

FRANK: Erm — it's that flaw which forces him to take the inevitable steps towards his own doom. You see?

Rita offers him the can of soft drink. He takes it and looks at it.

FRANK (*putting the can down on the desk*): No thanks. Whereas, Rita, a woman's hair being reduced to an inch of stubble, or — or the sort of thing you read in the paper that's reported as being tragic, "Man Killed By Falling Tree," is not a tragedy.

RITA: It is for the poor sod under the tree.

FRANK: Yes, it's tragic, absolutely tragic. But it's not a tragedy in the way that *Macbeth* is a tragedy. Tragedy in dramatic terms is inevitable, preordained. Look, now, even without ever having heard the story of *Macbeth* you wanted to shout out, to warn him and prevent him going on, didn't you? But you wouldn't have been able to stop him would you?

RITA: No.

FRANK: Why?

RITA: They would have thrown me out the theatre.

FRANK: But what I mean is that your warning would have been ignored. He's warned in the play. But he can't go back. He still treads the path to doom. But the poor old fellow under the tree hasn't arrived there by following any inevitable steps has he?

RITA: No.

FRANK: There's no particular flaw in his character that has dictated his end. If he'd been warned of the consequences of standing beneath that particular tree he wouldn't have done it, would he? Understand?

RITA: So — so Macbeth brings it on himself?

FRANK: Yes. You see he goes blindly on and on and with every step he's spinning one more piece of thread which will eventually make up the network of his own tragedy. Do you see?

RITA: I think so. I'm not used to thinkin' like this.

FRANK: It's quite easy, Rita.

RITA: It is for you. I just thought it was a dead excitin' story. But the way you tell it you make me see all sorts of things in it. (*After a pause.*) It's fun, tragedy, isn't it?

Frank's explanation of why the death of "the poor old sod under the tree" is not an example of tragedy suggests the difference between tragedy and **pathos**. Pathos, according to the playwright Arthur Miller, arouses our feelings of "sadness, sympathy, identification, and even fear," while tragedy "brings us knowledge or enlightenment" about the "right way of living in the world." As Miller observed, "The reason we confuse the tragic with the pathetic, as well as why we create so few [new] tragedies, is twofold: in the first place many of our writers have given up trying to search out the right way of living, and secondly, there is not among us any commonly accepted faith in a way of life that will give us not only material gain but satisfaction."

These definitions of tragedy help us to understand the **dark comedy** or **theater of the absurd** of Samuel Beckett and Edward Albee, where the characters are presented in absurd situations that reduce the meaning or significance of their lives to zero. Comedy, on the other hand, as in Chekhov's *The Bear* or Woody Allen's screenplays, usually centers on the complications of love (if the play is a romantic comedy) or human eccentricity (if it is a comedy of manners). Like tragic plays, good comic plays are serious statements about the human situation, allowing us to laugh at ourselves after the initial shock of recognition. **Parodies,** such as Christopher Durang's *For Whom the Southern Belle Tolls,* are a particularly literary form of comedy whose intent is to find humor (not always kind) in the rewriting of an earlier work.

Another category of drama is the **didactic** play, which teaches a lesson. Although presented within the context of a comedy, Frank's explanation of tragedy in *Educating Rita* is a didactic scene. Didactic plays often teach a lesson about the best way to live, as in the fifteenth-century Japanese Nō play *Kantan* (p. 1465), whose theme is shaped by the Buddhist philosophy that influenced its playwright.

Modern plays by such authors as Henrik Ibsen, Susan Glaspell, Lorraine Hansberry, August Wilson, and Marsha Norman are realistic dramas in which the characters seem to exhibit free will in regard to their choices for future action. They are usually a mixture of comic and tragic elements. There is no end to the ways in which plays can be classified (recall Hamlet's troupe of touring actors who are proficient in acting "tragedy, comedy, history, pastoral, pastoral-comical, historical-pastoral, tragical-historical, tragical-comical-historical-pastoral, scene individable, or poem unlimited"). In each case, the way you classify the play can help you to clarify the dramatist's underlying theme.

RELATED COMMENTARIES: Leonard Mustazza, *"Generic Translation and Thematic Shift in Glaspell's* Trifles *and 'A Jury of Her Peers,' " page 2002; Sandra Saari, "Female Becomes Human: Nora Transformed in* A Doll House," *page 2021; August Strindberg, "From the Preface to* Miss Julie," *page 2024; Tennessee Williams, "Production Notes to* The Glass Menagerie," *page 2031; John Keats, "From a Letter to George and Thomas Keats, 21 December 1817," page 2048.*

22

PLAYWRIGHTS AND HISTORY

Thus the difference between the historian and the poet is not in their utterances being in verse or prose (it would be quite possible for [the historian] Herodotus's work to be translated into verse, and it would not be any the less a history with verse than it is without it); the difference lies in the fact that the historian speaks of what has happened, the poet of the kind of thing that *can* happen. Hence also poetry is a more philosophical and serious business than history; for poetry speaks more of universals, history of particulars.

           – ARISTOTLE, *Poetics*

In Aristotle's discussion of poetry in the *Poetics*, he includes the plays of Sophocles among his examples of poetry. Aristotle goes on to remark that "in tragedy [poets] still cling to the historically given names. The reason is that what is possible is persuasive. . . . Nevertheless, it is a fact that even in our tragedies, in some cases only one or two of the names are traditional, the rest being invented, and in some others none at all." The Greek playwrights' practice of mixing historical characters with imagined characters was praised by Aristotle as giving theater audiences "no less pleasure because of that." Sophocles' audiences understood that the story of Oedipus was one of the "historically given" myths of their culture, but as they watched Sophocles' play, they also accepted the imaginary characters he created, such as the Messenger and the Chorus, as effective in dramatizing the work's universal message.

Like poets and storytellers, playwrights have incorporated their society's mythology, philosophy, and history into their plays as instinctively as they have relied on their imagination in creating their work. Attentive readers will find that the Japanese culture's high regard for Buddhism in the fifteenth century is implicit in such Nō plays as *Kantan*. The new historical critic Karin S. Coddon has studied what she calls Elizabethan "religious and psychological thought" to arrive at what might have been Shakespeare's concept of mental illness in *Hamlet* (see the Casebook on Shakespeare's *Hamlet*, p. 2038).

As with stories and poems, plays can be read from several different historical contexts. This section has been organized chronologically to help give you a historical overview of this literary form as it developed in Western Europe and the United States, and it includes an example of the Japanese Nō play to suggest another influential theatrical tradition.

Our usually unexamined practice of reading plays from our own specific cultural vantage point is revealed in an essay by the anthropologist Laura Bohannon, "Shakespeare in the Bush," where she described her struggle to understand the interpretation of *Hamlet* given to her by a group of elders in a remote African village. Bohannon found that her listeners had no difficulty following the story of the play, but their different culturally determined tribal attitudes and belief in witchcraft made them skeptical of what she had always considered the "universally obvious" meaning of the drama.

For example, the African elders were unsympathetic to Hamlet's decision to avenge his father's death by killing Claudius. They explained to the anthropologist that from their point of view, "If your father's brother has killed your father, you must appeal to your father's age mates; *they* may avenge him. No man may use violence against his senior relatives." The tribal leaders did their best to clarify the play for Bohannon: "It is clear that the elders of your country have never told you what the story really means. No, don't interrupt! We believe you when you say your marriage customs are different, or your clothes and weapons. But people are the same everywhere; therefore, there are always witches and it is we, the elders, who know how witches work."

As storytellers prominent in our culture, dramatists such as Arthur Miller sometimes suggest that the meaning of their plays can be traced to the effect of their historical background. Miller's biographer, the theater critic John Lahr, has commented that "the shock of the Depression, and of the collapse of his father's power just at the moment in adolescence when Miller was trying to make an identity from his father's example, had a traumatic effect." Miller himself is more circumspect: "I've always thought of the formation of my approach to writing as springing directly out of the economic crisis of the thirties." Other playwrights, such as Tennessee Williams, were inspired to create plays from their personal story. Williams wrote *The Glass Menagerie* to communicate his devastating sense of anguish about his sister's mental illness.

Realistic plays like Henrik Ibsen's *A Doll House* and Lorraine Hansberry's *A Raisin in the Sun*, among many others in this anthology, dramatize important issues about gender and race in modern society. Experimental plays by Samuel Beckett and Edward Albee reflect postwar anomie or a breakdown of personal values. Finally, such recent plays as Tom Stoppard's slapstick version of *Hamlet* and Christopher Durang's *For Whom the Southern Belle Tolls*, which react iconoclastically to the work of earlier playwrights, suggest a larger matrix of tumultuous cultural change as our society moves uncertainly toward the next millennium.

RELATED COMMENTARIES: *Travis Bogard, "The Provincetown Players," page 1972; Sigmund Freud, "The Oedipus Complex," page 1984; David Henry Hwang, "Evolving a Multicultural Tradition," page 1987; Virginia Woolf, "What If Shakespeare Had Had a Sister?," page 2049; Anne Cheney, "The African Heritage in* A Raisin in the Sun*," page 2073.*

23

PLAYWRIGHT TO PLAYWRIGHT

It is my guess that the theater in the United States will always hew more
closely to the post–Ibsen/Chekhov tradition than does the theater in France,
let us say. It is our nature as a country, a society. But we will experiment, and
we will expect your attention.

        – EDWARD ALBEE, "Which Theater Is the Absurd One?"
        New York Times Magazine, February 25, 1962

Like short story writers and poets, dramatists also create their plays
within a tradition. The genius of Sophocles, Shakespeare, Ibsen, Strindberg,
and Chekhov is inimitable, but their plays have inspired later playwrights
to give their own interpretation of similar themes or develop their own approach based on an awareness of the earlier writers' dramatic techniques.
Writing their plays during periods when the theater flourished in ancient
Greece and Renaissance England, Sophocles and Shakespeare borrowed or
appropriated the plots of *Oedipus the King* and *Hamlet* from legend, history,
and earlier plays — a standard practice among playwrights in their historical
periods. Appropriation, or creating a new work by taking something from a
previous work, continues today as part of the legacy of our cultural heritage
of literature, music, and art. As a technique or method of working, appropriation can become a new vehicle for playwrights to express their view of the human condition.

Sophocles' and Shakespeare's versions of earlier material survive because their dramatic works reveal the fullest dimensions of their sources.
Their brilliant exploration of the characters of Oedipus and Hamlet have kept
their plays alive in theater repertoires throughout the world, whereas the literature that gave them the ideas for their plays is now known only to specialists. The essay by Francis Fergusson on *Oedipus the King* in the Commentaries
section and that by Geoffrey Bullough on *Hamlet* in the Casebook on Shakespeare's *Hamlet* will help you to understand how Sophocles and Shakespeare
transformed their sources into great works of literature.

The influence of Greek dramatists such as Sophocles has continued to the present day. When Arthur Miller was interviewed by Leonard Moss in 1980, Miller said that he "would have liked to live in Greece with the tragedies." He went on to explain the influence of earlier writers on him: "I attach myself to Ibsen because I saw him as a contemporary Greek, and I suppose it's because there was a terrific reliance in him as there was in the Greeks on the idea of the continuity between the distant past and the present. 'The birds come home to roost' — they always did; your character was your fate. I like that immensely."

Playwrights are often willing to discuss how they were influenced by earlier writers. A few years after the debut of *Death of a Salesman*, when Miller adapted Ibsen's play *An Enemy of the People* for American audiences in 1951, he wrote a preface to the published version of the play to explain the strong influence of Ibsen's work on him:

> There is one quality in Ibsen that no serious writer can afford to overlook. It lies at the very center of his force, and I found in it — as I hope others will — a profound source of strength. It is his insistence, his utter conviction, that he is going to say what he has to say, and that the audience, by God, is going to listen. It is the very same quality that makes a star actor, a great public speaker, and a lunatic. Every Ibsen play begins with the unwritten words: "Now listen here!" And these words have shown me a path through the wall of "entertainment," a path that leads beyond the formulas and dried-up precepts, the pretense and fraud, of the business of the stage. Whatever else Ibsen has to teach, this is his first and greatest contribution.

As the critic Seymour L. Flaxman observed, "The realistic drama reached the peak of its development with Ibsen, and in many ways this style continues to dominate the drama today." Ibsen extended the use of discussion and debate in the dialogues between his characters to probe their mental states, and his method of analytic exposition survives in the structure of later work by Miller and Williams as well as Lorraine Hansberry, Marsha Norman, August Wilson, and David Henry Hwang, to name only a few recent American dramatists. All of these playwrights have gone beyond Ibsen's realism to incorporate symbolic and expressionistic elements in their work, as Ibsen and Strindberg themselves did in their later plays.

Sometimes the actors who interpret a play onstage are in a special position to perceive affinities between playwrights. Geraldine Page, an actress with a special affinity for Tennessee Williams's work, has sensed the influence of Chekhov's plays on Williams. She told an interviewer that Chekhov "gives so much of the drama out of the surface noise of life. I mean in a lot of the Chekhov plays, people are sitting around talking about tea or going fishing or things that are not to do with the central drama, but to do with the way human beings express themselves and convey these things. And Tennessee uses that too."

Edward Albee often gives provocative interviews about both the positive and negative influence of earlier playwrights on him. Albee acknowledged a negative influence in Eugene O'Neill, who argued in his plays that people needed deceptions or dreams in their lives in order to live. Albee confessed that he "probably became a playwright as much as anything to refute that whole argument of O'Neill." Like the great German playwright Bertolt Brecht, Albee has what the editor Philip Kolin describes as a "combative" view of the theater, believing that it "must disturb in order to reform society." Albee explained, "I don't think you should frighten them [the audience], I think you should terrify them."

Albee has also been outspoken in his advice to aspiring playwrights. Discussing his craft in *Dramatics* magazine, he cautioned young writers about the harmful influence of reading too many great plays:

> But let me tell you one thing, if you are going to learn from other writers, don't only read the great ones, because if you do that you'll get so filled with despair and the fear that you'll never be able to do anywhere near as well as they did that you'll stop writing. I recommend that you read a lot of bad stuff, too. It's very encouraging. "Hey, I can do so much better than this." Read the greatest stuff but read the stuff that isn't so great, too. Great stuff is very discouraging. If you read only Beckett and Chekhov you'll go away and only deliver telegrams at Western Union.

Reading widely in the history of drama, you become aware that talented writers often come of age in clusters or groups, sometimes influenced by specific theaters or directors. The cluster of playwrights in Athens who created the great tragedies for the stage during the Golden Age of Greece is well known and includes Aeschylus, Euripides, and Sophocles. The Provincetown Players, an experimental theater that flourished in the early years of this century in the bohemian enclaves of Provincetown, Massachusetts, and Greenwich Village in New York City, supported another group of writers whose plays have stood the test of time — Susan Glaspell, Eugene O'Neill, and Edna St. Vincent Millay, among scores of others. The creative work of these playwrights helped establish the modern American theater, preparing the way for the gifted playwrights of the next generation.

Influence can also function as the legacy of a specific theatrical form, as in the Nō play tradition, which can be translated into the work of playwrights in various ways. The critic Yasunari Takahashi has commented on similarities between Samuel Beckett's drama and the Nō plays, and you can analyze the final scene of Hwang's short play *As the Crow Flies* (1983) to appreciate how elements of the Nō tradition appear in his work.

In our own time, parody of earlier dramatic works is a thriving form of comedy. Tom Stoppard and Christopher Durang deliberately write plays that depend for their effect on our familiarity with other plays. Durang's ridicule of Williams's characters and situation in *The Glass Menagerie* produces a far different theatrical impact from that of Stoppard's comic treatment of Shakespeare's characters and situation in *Hamlet*. As the critic William E. Gruber recognized, Stoppard's play "seems to vibrate because of the older classic," whereas Durang's play whistles like a tin horn to Williams's silver trumpet.

If time permits, you can also trace the interaction between the playwrights mentioned in the headnotes and Commentaries section but are outside the scope of this anthology. For example, the rich tradition of Irish theater has been an important influence on certain playwrights whose work is included here. Reading the plays of Sean O'Casey, you could see what Lorraine Hansberry learned from this proletarian Irish playwright whom she claimed as her major influence as a young writer.

Finally, exploring intertextual aspects of drama, you could investigate the influence of specific works of fiction and autobiography on playwrights. The literary critic Travis Bogard analyzes Eugene O'Neill's debt to Joseph Conrad's novel *The Nigger of the Narcissus* (1897) in the play *Bound East for Cardiff* (1916). David Henry Hwang discusses the influence of his contemporaries Frank Chin and Maxine Hong Kingston in his attempts at "Evolving a Multicultural Tradition." August Wilson describes the effect on him as a young playwright of hearing a blues record sung by Bessie Smith, when "the universe stuttered and everything fell to a new place." If you try to be as aware of the various literary, artistic, and musical influences in your lives as the playwrights in this anthology, you will learn a great deal about your cultural heritage and enhance your study of literature.

RELATED COMMENTARIES: *George Bernard Shaw, "On A Doll House," page 2022; Yasunari Takahashi, "Samuel Beckett and the Nō," page 2026; Jan Kott, "Bertolt Brecht's* Hamlet," *page 2055; Tom Stoppard, "Dogg's Hamlet: The Encore," page 2063; Lorraine Hansberry, "My Shakespearean Experience," page 2067.*

24

READING, THINKING, AND WRITING ABOUT DRAMA

If my tragedy makes a tragic impression on people, they have only themselves to blame.

         – AUGUST STRINDBERG, preface to *Miss Julie*

Reading a play allows you to have it both ways: you can stop the action at
any time to think about the words on the page, and you can envision what is happening in a make-believe performance in the theater of your mind. Whether you
follow a play as a passive spectator or an imaginative reader, you understand
that its author is engaged in more than an act of "let's pretend." Most playwrights are attempting to make a serious statement about how we live — both
as individuals and as members of society. Like other forms of literature, drama
takes us out of our lives and allows us access to a wider range of human thoughts
and feelings, showing us our vast potential as individuals for both good and evil.

    Having drama available as texts on the page has another advantage.
Like other writers, playwrights are conscious of themselves as contributing
to an ongoing tradition. It is possible to see many of the plays in this anthology produced onstage or as film, but they are immediately accessible within
the covers of this book. Furthermore, in Part One of this anthology, you can
read stories by Susan Glaspell and Tennessee Williams that have counterparts in their plays *Trifles* and *The Glass Menagerie*. Glaspell wrote her story
"A Jury of Her Peers" after the success of *Trifles* at the Provincetown Playhouse; Williams's "Portrait of a Girl in Glass" is an early story, written five
years before he expanded it into a play. Comparing the stories with the
plays, you will gain a deeper appreciation of the differences in the two literary genres and the different resources of playwrights and short story writers. You can also appreciate the scope of Shakespeare's extraordinary
achievement as a playwright and a poet and Chekhov's distinction as a play-

wright and a story writer by reading their selections in the different parts of this anthology.

Even in such short, relatively simple plays as *Tender Offer* you probably need two readings of the text in order to be able to discuss it in class. On the first reading, let your imagination expand and try to see the play enacted on-stage. On the second reading, be more detached from the text and try to analyze it as a work of literature by thinking about how the playwright has used the elements of drama.

For example, Wasserstein has a double meaning in mind when she uses the term *tender offer* as the title of her play. Its use in business may not be clear to every reader, but she explains it in the conversation between the father and his daughter. In your first reading you will get to understand the literal meaning of the term in business negotiations. As you follow the action on stage to its conclusion, you also see the meaning of the term enacted in the relationship between the two characters. On your second reading, you might allow the literal meaning of the play's title to take on connotative associations, symbolizing the fragile relationship between father and daughter. Then you can go on to consider how this theme is dramatized in the play's other structural elements.

Sometimes you will still have questions about the meaning of a play even after your second reading. Close the book and give yourself some time to think about it. Your effort to understand the work is a necessary part of the learning process. Remember Peter Brook's direction: "In order for something of quality to take place, an empty space needs to be created. An empty space makes it possible for a new phenomenon to come to life, for anything that touches on content, meaning, expression, language, and music can exist only if the experience is fresh and new. However, no fresh and new experience is possible if there isn't a pure, virgin space ready to receive it." If you are still confused after you have thought about the play, write down your questions and bring them to the next class discussion.

In a sense, reading drama is easier than reading poetry and short fiction because playwrights introduce you in a more leisurely fashion to the imaginative world they create on the page. For one thing, plays begin with a description of the characters who perform the action. For example, opening to the first page of Sophocles' *Oedipus the King*, you encounter a list of characters right after the title of the play. The setting or "scene" of the play is also described before you start to read the dialogue between the various characters. In *Oedipus the King* you are told that the Greek stage is meant to suggest the front of the royal house of Thebes. This is a neutral description, but then you learn that "many years have passed since Oedipus solved the riddle of the Sphinx and ascended the throne of Thebes, and now a plague has struck the city. A procession of priests enters; suppliants, broken and despondent, they carry branches wound in wool and lay them on the altar." The editor of the text of *Oedipus the King* is giving you a clue about the serious mood in which the play begins. You do not know what has caused the priests to become so unhappy, but as Oedipus comes forward with a "telltale limp" and the play starts, you read his speech in the prologue with more information to help you understand his words than you have when you begin a poem or a short story.

The opening dialogue between Oedipus and the Priest who speaks for the suppliants is an admirable illustration of the drama at the heart of a great play. There is no physical action as such between the two characters — no brawny fisticuffs, no spectacular duel, no surprising exchange of gunshots. Standing side by side, the two actors only exchange words. But the dialogue allows the reader of the play to create a personality for Oedipus and get a first sense of the conflict — or mystery — within his situation that will evoke a sense of pity and terror for him as the play unfolds.

GUIDELINES FOR STUDYING DRAMA

1. Make an entry in your notebook for each play assigned in class, writing down the author's name and the title and date of the play.
2. Use a dictionary to look up words in the headnote or in the play that you do not understand.
3. Remember that the type of theater — Greek, Elizabethan, realistic, contemporary — prevalent at the time the playwright is working can influence his or her plays.
4. When you start to read a play, note the list of characters and the playwright's description of them. Try to envision the set, if it is described at the beginning of the various scenes and acts.
5. As you read the dialogue, imagine the gestures and the costumes of the actors specified in the stage directions or suggested by what the characters say.
6. Notice what the characters *don't* say in the dialogue — their pauses and silences. Remember that their words, like those of real people, are not always to be trusted.

CRITICAL THINKING ABOUT DRAMA

As in your study of short fiction and poetry, your critical thinking about a play depends on your first having formulated an interpretation of it after reading and perhaps rereading the text. Then you can begin asking yourself questions about different aspects of the work's structure, depending on the topic given to you for a written assignment. The various elements of drama are often the focus of a critical inquiry. The questions to help you think critically about drama are similar to those asked of short fiction. The Appendix (p. 2081) lists strategies for writing about short fiction that can be applied to plays. In addition, you might consider the following topics as you read.

Plot. What is the conflict of the play? Is it developed in separate stages of rising action, complication, climax, falling action, and resolution? Can you find examples of foreshadowing? Does the play have a subplot or second plot? How is it related to the main plot? Is there any repetition of significant action? If so, what do you think the playwright intended?

Characters. Is there a protagonist and an antagonist in the play? Do you think that they are presented as round or flat, static or dynamic characters? Are they realistic or symbolic? Often in drama it helps you to think critically about characterization if you select one character for your analysis. How is this character described in stage directions? How do other characters in the play see him or her? How does the character view himself or herself? What words or actions given to this character help to define his or her personality?

Dialogue. Which is given more emphasis in the play, dialogue or physical action? Is the dialogue realistic or symbolic? To what effect does the author use poetic, colloquial, or dialect English? What is the tone of the speeches? Does the playwright use consistent patterns of imagery or metaphor in the speeches of different characters in order to suggest something important about them?

Stage Setting. How does the setting help establish the time and place of the play? Is the setting realistic or symbolic? What objects onstage are particularly important in suggesting the mood of the characters or their values? What does the setting suggest about the theme of the play? How would a different staging of the play affect your interpretation?

Irony and Symbolism. Can you find any instances of dramatic irony in the play when you (as a reader or spectator) know more about the situation than do the onstage characters? Does this make you more or less sympathetic toward the characters? What aspects of the play and its staging seem symbolic? What do they symbolize? Is the symbolism extensive enough to form an allegorical system? If so, what is the meaning implied by the allegory?

Theme. What ideas explored by the play seem most significant to you? Which of the preceding elements of the play conveys the theme most effectively? Does the playwright give a clear statement of the theme to any one of the characters? If there is no resolution of the theme in the action of the play, what emotional effect does this have on you? Is the conflict between the characters a struggle between moral good and moral evil? Is the playwright attempting to *explain* or to *explore* the issues?

WRITING ABOUT DRAMA

An assignment to write an essay about a specific play or aspect of drama will give you the opportunity to bring your ideas about what you have read into focus. The process of writing about drama will sharpen your critical analysis of the text you have chosen to discuss and will clarify your understanding of the ideas dramatized by the playwright. Because every reader's background is different, your reading of the plays will reflect the life experience that you bring to them. Using the vocabulary of the elements of drama to help you express your thoughts about the plays, you have the opportunity to articulate your interpretations clearly and forcibly to another reader.

If you have seen a play produced on film or in the theater, this experience can often help you write about it. Usually you will be expected to analyze your impressions far beyond summarizing the plot of the play. In the Appendix (p. 2081), you can find a student essay on a dramatic work that may help you to develop your ideas about the assignment.

Often, choosing a specific critical approach in your paper — biographical, historical, or reader response, for example — will give you a perspective from which to take useful notes during your second close reading of the play, clarifying your understanding of how the playwright has developed dialogue, images, and patterns of action. Finally, in the Commentaries section, you will find essays that illustrate different critical perspectives and supply background information for your paper.

RELATED COMMENTARIES: *Helge Normann Nilsen, "Marxism and the Early Plays of Arthur Miller," page 2012; Joan Templeton, "Is* A Doll House *a Feminist Text?," page 2029; Karin S. Coddon, "A New Historicist Reading of* Hamlet*," page 2065; Margaret B. Wilkerson, "Hansberry's Awareness of Culture and Gender," page 2077.*

25

PLAYS AND PLAYWRIGHTS

SOPHOCLES *(495–406 B.C.), along with Aeschylus and Euripides, was one of the three major authors of Greek tragedy. He lived for nearly ninety years through most of the turbulent events of his country during the fifth century B.C. He was only five when the Greek army turned back the invading Persians at Marathon, but he probably heard that after the battle a messenger brought word of the victory back to Athens, running the twenty-six miles between Marathon and Athens and dying of exhaustion while delivering the news. Ten years later, in 480 B.C., the Greeks won another major battle against the Persian navy at Salamis. At the victory celebration Sophocles, a teenager trained in dance, is said to have made his first public appearance dancing nude to his own lyre accompaniment.*

The period in which the Greek playwrights flourished is known as the Golden Age. Athens became rich as the city's allies paid its statesmen tribute money, and statesmen honored the gifted poets, playwrights, philosophers, architects, and scientists who thrived in the city. This great period lasted barely to the last years of the century, starting its decline when the armed forces of the Greek city-state were defeated in Sicily in 413 B.C. Six years later, just before the death of Sophocles, the Spartans destroyed the Greek navy at Aegospotami and imposed their own government in Athens, bringing the Golden Age to an end.

The earliest extant Greek play for two actors, Aeschylus's The Persians, *dates from 472 B.C. Thirty years younger than Aeschylus, Sophocles won his first prize for one of his plays in 468 B.C. at the Great Dionysia during the competition for playwrights in Athens. The Great Dionysia was the name given to the important holiday each year when the Greek plays were produced. Occurring just before the arrival of* spring, the festival honored Dionysus, the god of fertility and growth, who was mysteriously linked to Hades, the lord of the underworld and death. The celebration began in Athens with a procession carrying a statue of Dionysus from his temple to the theater at the Acropolis. It included the ritual slaying of a sacrificial bull and much drunken revelry, as Dionysus was also the god of wine in Greece.

The high point of the annual festival was the three-day competition among the playwrights, each of whom submitted four plays: three tragedies (tragedy was considered the highest form of drama by the Greeks) and a brief satyr play, which combined slapstick and erotic comedy. A comic play was also included in the performances, so although the plays were relatively short, the audience was expected to have sufficient stamina and interest to sit through several plays each day. As the British playwright Tony Harrison has observed, the Greek dramatists were "open-eyed about suffering but with a heart still open to celebration and physical affirmation." Traditionally during the Great Dionysia, a comic play began the program each day, and the tragic plays were followed by a satyr play to maintain "a kind of celebratory route in the sensual and everyday to follow the tragedy."

The dramatic performances at the Acropolis were part of a religious celebration, a public holiday rather than a commercial theater, with the entire population of the city marching in the procession and thousands of people filling the amphitheater on the slopes of the Acropolis to watch the plays. Originally the audience sat on the ground, then on wooden seats. When the weight of the crowd caused the wooden seats to collapse, they were replaced with concentric tiers of stone seats designed on the hillside to surround the stage almost completely. The high priest of Dionysus sat at the place of honor at the center of the first tier of this theater-in-the-round in Athens.

To keep order among the huge crowd, there were strict laws — apparently even the penalty of death — against taking another person's seat or engaging in fights. Tickets were expensive (almost the price of a laborer's daily wage), but funds were available so that poor people and slaves could attend. To underscore the religious importance of the event, prisoners were released from jail so they could also attend. Evidence suggests that women weren't admitted into the audience to watch Greek plays, but this is a contentious point argued by archeologists and historians.

During the three days of theater in Athens each year, it was customary for playwrights to act in their own plays. Apparently Sophocles could dance better than he could project his voice onstage (contemporary viewers describe him as having a "small voice"), and this would explain why he gave the leading role in his plays to an actor. Sophocles originated the practice of giving parts to a third actor onstage and introduced such innovations as painted scenery and a larger tragic chorus (increasing it from twelve men to fifteen). Active as a playwright in Athens for over half a century, he wrote more than a hundred plays and won first prize at the Great Dionysia eighteen times, more than any other playwright. Today only seven complete Sophoclean tragedies survive (the Oedipus trilogy and the plays Philoctetes, Ajax, Trachiniae, and Elektra) as well as a satyr play about the childhood of the god Hermes and nearly a thousand fragments of his other plays.

Sophocles and other playwrights who introduced their work during the Great Dionysia sought to arouse pity and fear among the spectators with their tragic plays about death and suffering; they sought to instill a sense of religious awe at the mysterious power of the gods, whose perfect knowledge of events stands in contrast to the *imperfect knowledge of mortal beings. In classical Greek theater, only men were actors. They wore shoes with high heels to increase their stature and masks to help amplify their voices and simulate their appearance as mythical heroes or gods. The masks and costumes also enabled them to assume the roles of women, who were often central characters in the plays that dramatized mythical stories and legends made famous by earlier poets and historians. Actors were trained in singing and dancing as well as speaking, but in the large amphitheaters they were judged by how effectively they projected their voices to suggest the emotional states of their characters. The design of the outdoor theater and the costuming and masks of the actors contributed to the audience's sense of participation in a religious ritual. The importance of respecting the oracles — and of accepting the gods' prophecy, which is often fulfilled in ways that humans do not expect — is frequently mentioned in* Oedipus the King. *At the end of the play Oedipus has learned to his sorrow that the gods are omnipotent and that he cannot escape his fate.*

Audiences watching Oedipus the King *would have known the legendary story before they came to the theater. At the beginning of the play they were aware of the tragic flaw of pride in Oedipus's character and understood the mysterious circumstances of his birth far better than he did. In the theater, the spectators' pleasure would derive from recognizing the dramatic irony in the poetic dialogue and the elegant way Sophocles structured the events of the story as Oedipus gradually uncovers the truth about his past. Unlike Aeschylian tragedy, which is essentially static, Sophocles unfolded the incident of Oedipus's past like a detective story, linking events by cause and effect and motivating them plausibly. In the process Sophocles also revealed different dimensions of his protagonist's character, his strong as well as his weak points. Oedipus exhibits a high moral character as king. He is genuinely concerned about his subjects and eager to help them during the plague that has descended on the city. Yet he is quick to suspect his loyal brother-in-law Creon of a plot to usurp his power and ready to taunt his heartbroken wife, Jocasta, when he thinks she is glorying in her "noble blood."*

Sophocles was nicknamed "the Attic Bee" because he relied on such earlier works as Homer's Iliad *and* Odyssey *for material for his plays, but he always developed his characterizations far beyond his sources and created dialogue marked by eloquence and vigor. He also gave active roles to the chorus of citizens and the messenger, who function as important characters in the play. When Sophocles began* Oedipus the King *by having the king promise the chorus of citizens to help fight the plague, the playwright knew that this detail would arouse sympathy in the Athenian audience, because plague had ravaged their city only five years before. This addition also deepens our sense of foreboding at the beginning of the play, because Sophocles was suggesting a further irony about Oedipus's character. It was believed at the time that the well-being of the state was a reflection of the health of its ruler. The Greek audience would know that, according to legend, Oedipus was a descendent of Cadmus, the founder of Thebes. The city had a disputed leadership because of a fraternal rivalry that the gods had decreed would wipe out Cadmus's entire family.* Oedipus the King *is the first of the trilogy of plays Sophocles wrote about this tragic situation. When the three plays are produced together, they are usually presented in the order that follows the chronology of events in the plot:* Oedipus the King *(first produced between 430 and 427* B.C.*),* Oedipus at Colonus *(posthumously produced in 401* B.C.*), and* Antigone *(first produced in 441* B.C.*).*

Oedipus the King *was considered such a masterpiece a century after its creation that the philosopher and critic Aristotle used it in the* Poetics *as the example on which to base his aesthetic theory of drama. Aristotle understood that Sophocles structured the story of* Oedipus the King *so that the rising action that revealed the complications of the plot led to Oedipus's moment of recognition in the second half of the play, precisely at the time the falling action began. In Aristotle's analysis, this combination of a serious character defect combined with the destiny ordained by the implacable gods constitutes a "tragic flaw." Sophocles structured his play so as to first arouse pity and fear in the spectators watching the proud and headstrong Oedipus gradually unravel the truth about his past, and then allow them to experience a purging or catharsis of their emotions at the sight of Oedipus broken by the gods' prophecy at the end of the play. Yet, paradoxically, the blinded figure of Oedipus remains heroic, because his determination to discover the truth about his own identity remains a moral victory despite the tragic outcome of his search. This dramatic illustration of the gods' power over human frailty must have been a transcendent religious experience for the audience during the festival of Dionysus.*

RELATED COMMENTARIES: *Aristotle, "On the Elements and General Principles of Tragedy," page 1966; Francis Fergusson, "Oedipus, Myth and Play," page 1977; Sigmund Freud, "The Oedipus Complex," page 1984; Bernard Knox, "Oedipus' Heroic Achievement," page 1991; Muriel Rukeyser, "Myth," page 2020.*

SOPHOCLES

Oedipus the King
c. 430 B.C.

TRANSLATED BY ROBERT FAGLES

CHARACTERS

OEDIPUS, *king of Thebes*
A PRIEST *of Zeus*
CREON, *brother of Jocasta*
A CHORUS *of Theban citizens and their* LEADER
TIRESIAS, *a blind prophet*
JOCASTA, *the queen, wife of Oedipus*
A MESSENGER *from Corinth*
A SHEPHERD
A MESSENGER *from inside the palace*
ANTIGONE, ISMENE, *daughters of Oedipus and Jocasta*
GUARDS AND ATTENDANTS
PRIESTS OF THEBES

TIME AND SCENE: *The royal house of Thebes. Double doors dominate the facade; a stone altar stands at the center of the stage.*

Many years have passed since Oedipus solved the riddle of the Sphinx° and ascended the throne of Thebes, and now a plague has struck the city. A procession of

---

the riddle of the Sphinx: The Sphinx asked, "What walks on four legs in the morning, two at noon, and three in the evening?" Oedipus replied, "Man."

*priests enters; suppliants, broken and despondent, they carry branches wound in wool
and lay them on the altar.*

    *The doors open. Guards assemble. Oedipus comes forward, majestic but for a
telltale limp, and slowly views the condition of his people.*

OEDIPUS: Oh my children, the new blood of ancient Thebes,
    why are you here? Huddling at my altar,
    praying before me, your branches wound in wool.°
    Our city reeks with the smoke of burning incense,
    rings with cries for the Healer and wailing for the dead.   5
    I thought it wrong, my children, to hear the truth
    from others, messengers. Here I am myself —
    you all know me, the world knows my fame:
    I am Oedipus.

Helping a Priest to his feet.

                  Speak up, old man. Your years,
    your dignity — you should speak for the others.   10
    Why here and kneeling, what preys upon you so?
    Some sudden fear? some strong desire?
    You can trust me; I am ready to help,
    I'll do anything. I would be blind to misery
    not to pity my people kneeling at my feet.   15
PRIEST: Oh Oedipus, king of the land, our greatest power!
    You see us before you, men of all ages
    clinging to your altars. Here are boys,
    still too weak to fly from the nest,
    and here the old, bowed down with the years,
    the holy ones — a priest of Zeus° myself — and here   20
    the picked, unmarried men, the young hope of Thebes.
    And all the rest, your great family gathers now,
    branches wreathed, massing in the squares,
    kneeling before the two temples of queen Athena°   25
    or the river-shrine where the embers glow and die
    and Apollo sees the future in the ashes.
                  Our city —
    look around you, see with your own eyes —
    our ship pitches wildly, cannot lift her head
    from the depths, the red waves of death . . .   30
    Thebes is dying. A blight on the fresh crops
    and the rich pastures, cattle sicken and die,
    and the women die in labor, children stillborn,
    and the plague, the fiery god of fever hurls down
    on the city, his lightning slashing through us —   35

---

3. **wool:** Wool was used in offerings to Apollo, the god of poetry, sun, prophecy, and healing.
21. **Zeus:** The highest Olympian deity and father of Apollo.   **25. Athena:** The goddess of
wisdom and protector of Greek cities.

raging plague in all its vengeance, devastating
the house of Cadmus!° And Black Death luxuriates
in the raw, wailing miseries of Thebes.

Now we pray to you. You cannot equal the gods,
your children know that, bending at your altar.   40
But we do rate you first of men,
both in the common crises of our lives
and face-to-face encounters with the gods.
You freed us from the Sphinx; you came to Thebes
and cut us loose from the bloody tribute we had paid   45
that harsh, brutal singer. We taught you nothing,
no skill, no extra knowledge, still you triumphed.
A god was with you, so they say, and we believe it —
you lifted up our lives.
                              So now again,
Oedipus, king, we bend to you, your power —   50
we implore you, all of us on our knees:
find us strength, rescue! Perhaps you've heard
the voice of a god or something from other men,
Oedipus . . . what do you know?
The man of experience — you see it every day —   55
his plans will work in a crisis, his first of all.
Act now — we beg you, best of men, raise up our city!
Act, defend yourself, your former glory!
Your country calls you savior now
for your zeal, your action years ago.   60
Never let us remember of your reign:
you helped us stand, only to fall once more.
Oh raise up our city, set us on our feet.
The omens were good that day you brought us joy —
be the same man today!   65
Rule our land, you know you have the power,
but rule a land of the living, not a wasteland.
Ship and towered city are nothing, stripped of men
alive within it, living all as one.

OEDIPUS: My children,
I pity you. I see — how could I fail to see   70
what longings bring you here? Well I know
you are sick to death, all of you,
but sick as you are, not one is sick as I.
Your pain strikes each of you alone, each
in the confines of himself, no other. But my spirit   75
grieves for the city, for myself and all of you.
I wasn't asleep, dreaming. You haven't wakened me —

---

37. **Cadmus:** The legendary founder of Thebes.

I've wept through the nights, you must know that,
groping, laboring over many paths of thought.
After a painful search I found one cure: 80
I acted at once. I sent Creon,
my wife's own brother, to Delphi° —
Apollo the Prophet's oracle — to learn
what I might do or say to save our city.

Today's the day. When I count the days gone by 85
it torments me . . . what is he doing?
Strange, he's late, he's gone too long.
But once he returns, then, then I'll be a traitor
if I do not do all the god makes clear.

PRIEST: Timely words. The men over there 90
are signaling — Creon's just arriving.

OEDIPUS:

Sighting Creon, then turning to the altar.

Lord Apollo,
let him come with a lucky word of rescue,
shining like his eyes!

PRIEST: Welcome news, I think — he's crowned, look,
and the laurel wreath is bright with berries. 95

OEDIPUS: We'll soon see. He's close enough to hear —

Enter Creon from the side; his face is shaded with a wreath.

Creon, prince, my kinsman, what do you bring us?
What message from the god?

CREON: Good news.
I tell you even the hardest things to bear,
if they should turn out well, all would be well. 100

OEDIPUS: Of course, but what were the god's *words*? There's no hope
and nothing to fear in what you've said so far.

CREON: If you want my report in the presence of these . . .

Pointing to the priests while drawing Oedipus toward the palace.

I'm ready now, or we might go inside.

OEDIPUS: Speak out,
speak to us all. I grieve for these, my people, 105
far more than I fear for my own life.

CREON: Very well,
I will tell you what I heard from the god.
Apollo commands us — he was quite clear —
"Drive the corruption from the land,
don't harbor it any longer, past all cure, 110
don't nurse it in your soil — root it out!"

---

82. Delphi: The shrine where the oracle of Apollo held forth.

OEDIPUS: How can we cleanse ourselves — what rites?
    What's the source of the trouble?
CREON: Banish the man, or pay back blood with blood.
    Murder sets the plague-storm on the city.
OEDIPUS: Whose murder?   115
    Whose fate does Apollo bring to light?
CREON: Our leader,
    my lord, was once a man named Laius,
    before you came and put us straight on course.
OEDIPUS: I know —
    or so I've heard. I never saw the man myself.
CREON: Well, he was killed, and Apollo commands us now —   120
    he could not be more clear,
    "Pay the killers back — whoever is responsible."
OEDIPUS: Where on earth are they? Where to find it now,
    the trail of the ancient guilt so hard to trace?
CREON: "Here in Thebes," he said.   125
    Whatever is sought for can be caught, you know,
    whatever is neglected slips away.
OEDIPUS: But where,
    in the palace, the fields or foreign soil,
    where did Laius meet his bloody death?
CREON: He went to consult an oracle, he said,   130
    and he set out and never came home again.
OEDIPUS: No messenger, no fellow-traveler saw what happened?
    Someone to cross-examine?
CREON: No,
    they were all killed but one. He escaped,
    terrified, he could tell us nothing clearly,   135
    nothing of what he saw — just one thing.
OEDIPUS: What's that?
    One thing could hold the key to it all,
    a small beginning gives us grounds for hope.
CREON: He said thieves attacked them — a whole band,
    not single-handed, cut King Laius down.
OEDIPUS: A thief,   140
    so daring, wild, he'd kill a king? Impossible,
    unless conspirators paid him off in Thebes.
CREON: We suspected as much. But with Laius dead
    no leader appeared to help us in our troubles.
OEDIPUS: Trouble? Your *king* was murdered — royal blood!   145
    What stopped you from tracking down the killer
    then and there?
CREON: The singing, riddling Sphinx.
    She . . . persuaded us to let the mystery go
    and concentrate on what lay at our feet.
OEDIPUS: No,

I'll start again — I'll bring it all to light myself!   150
Apollo is right, and so are you, Creon,
to turn our attention back to the murdered man.
Now you have *me* to fight for you, you'll see:
I am the land's avenger by all rights
and Apollo's champion too.   155
But not to assist some distant kinsman, no,
for my own sake I'll rid us of this corruption.
Whoever killed the king may decide to kill me too,
with the same violent hand — by avenging Laius
I defend myself.

To the priests.

                    Quickly, my children.   160
Up from the steps, take up your branches now.

To the guards.

One of you summon the city here before us,
tell them I'll do everything. God help us,
we will see our triumph — or our fall.

Oedipus and Creon enter the palace, followed by the guards.

PRIEST: Rise, my sons. The kindness we came for   165
Oedipus volunteers himself.
Apollo has sent his word, his oracle —
Come down, Apollo, save us, stop the plague.

The priests rise, remove their branches, and exit to the side. Enter a Chorus, the citizens of Thebes, who have not heard the news that Creon brings. They march around the altar, chanting.

CHORUS: Zeus!
Great welcome voice of Zeus, what do you bring?
What word from the gold vaults of Delphi   170
comes to brilliant Thebes? I'm racked with terror —
                    terror shakes my heart
and I cry your wild cries, Apollo, Healer of Delos°
I worship you in dread . . . what now, what is your price?
some new sacrifice? some ancient rite from the past   175
come round again each spring? —
                    what will you bring to birth?
Tell me, child of golden Hope
        warm voice that never dies!

You are the first I call, daughter of Zeus   180
deathless Athena — I call your sister Artemis,°
heart of the market place enthroned in glory,

---

173. Delos: Apollo was born on this sacred island.   **181. Artemis:** Apollo's sister, the goddess of hunting, the moon, and chastity.

guardian of our earth —
I call Apollo astride the thunderheads of heaven —
O triple shield against death, shine before me now!   185
If ever, once in the past, you stopped some ruin
launched against our walls
            you hurled the flame of pain
far, far from Thebes — you gods
      come now, come down once more!
                              No, no   190
the miseries numberless, grief on grief, no end —
too much to bear, we are all dying
O my people . . .
      Thebes like a great army dying
and there is no sword of thought to save us, no   195
and the fruits of our famous earth, they will not ripen
no and the women cannot scream their pangs to birth —
screams for the Healer, children dead in the womb
            and life on life goes down
                        you can watch them go   200
      like seabirds winging west, outracing the day's fire
down the horizon, irresistibly
            streaking on to the shores of Evening
                              Death
so many deaths, numberless deaths on deaths, no end —
Thebes is dying, look, her children   205
stripped of pity . . .
      generations strewn on the ground
unburied, unwept, the dead spreading death
and the young wives and gray-haired mothers with them
cling to the altars, trailing in from all over the city —   210
Thebes, city of death, one long cortege
            and the suffering rises
                  wails for mercy rise
            and the wild hymn for the Healer blazes out
clashing with our sobs our cries of mourning —   215
      O golden daughter of god, send rescue
      radiant as the kindness in your eyes!
Drive him back! — the fever, the god of death
                        that raging god of war
not armored in bronze, not shielded now, he burns me,   220
battle cries in the onslaught burning on —
O rout him from our borders!
Sail him, blast him out to the Sea-queen's chamber
                  the black Atlantic gulfs
      or the northern harbor, death to all   225
where the Thracian surf comes crashing.
Now what the night spares he comes by day and kills —

the god of death.
O lord of the stormcloud,
you who twirl the lightning, Zeus, Father,
thunder Death to nothing!   230

Apollo, lord of the light, I beg you —
whip your longbow's golden cord
showering arrows on our enemies — shafts of power
champions strong before us rushing on!

Artemis, Huntress,   235
torches flaring over the eastern ridges —
ride Death down in pain!

God of the headdress gleaming gold, I cry to you —
your name and ours are one, Dionysus° —
come with your face aflame with wine   240
your raving women's cries°
your army on the march! Come with the lightning
come with torches blazing, eyes ablaze with glory!
Burn that god of death that all gods hate!

Oedipus enters from the palace to address the Chorus, as if addressing the entire city of Thebes.

OEDIPUS: You pray to the gods? Let me grant your prayers.   245
Come, listen to me — do what the plague demands:
you'll find relief and lift your head from the depths.

I will speak out now as a stranger to the story,
a stranger to the crime. If I'd been present then,
there would have been no mystery, no long hunt   250
without a clue in hand. So now, counted
a native Theban years after the murder,
to all of Thebes I make this proclamation:
if any one of you knows who murdered Laius,
the son of Labdacus, I order him to reveal   255
the whole truth to me. Nothing to fear,
even if he must denounce himself,
let him speak up
and so escape the brunt of the charge —
he will suffer no unbearable punishment,   260
nothing worse than exile, totally unharmed.

Oedipus pauses, waiting for a reply.

Next,
if anyone knows the murderer is a stranger,
a man from alien soil, come, speak up.

---

239. Dionysus: The god of fertility and wine.   **241. your . . . cries:** Dionysus was attended
by female celebrants.

I will give him a handsome reward, and lay up
gratitude in my heart for him besides.   265

Silence again, no reply.

But if you keep silent, if anyone panicking,
trying to shield himself or friend or kin,
rejects my offer, then hear what I will do.
I order you, every citizen of the state
where I hold throne and power: banish this man —   270
whoever he may be — never shelter him, never
speak a word to him, never make him partner
to your prayers, your victims burned to the gods.
Never let the holy water touch his hands.
Drive him out, each of you, from every home.   275
He is the plague, the heart of our corruption,
as Apollo's oracle has revealed to me
just now. So I honor my obligations:
I fight for the god and for the murdered man.

Now my curse on the murderer. Whoever he is,   280
a lone man unknown in his crime
or one among many, let that man drag out
his life in agony, step by painful step —
I curse myself as well . . . if by any chance
he proves to be an intimate of our house,   285
here at my hearth, with my full knowledge,
may the curse I just called down on him strike me!

These are your orders: perform them to the last.
I command you, for my sake, for Apollo's, for this country
blasted root and branch by the angry heavens.   290
Even if god had never urged you on to act,
how could you leave the crime uncleansed so long?
A man so noble — your king, brought down in blood —
you should have searched. But I am the king now,
I hold the throne that he held then, possess his bed   295
and a wife who shares our seed . . . why, our seed
might be the same, children born of the same mother
might have created blood-bonds between us
if his hope of offspring hadn't met disaster —
but fate swooped at his head and cut him short.   300
So I will fight for him as if he were my father,
stop at nothing, search the world
to lay my hands on the man who shed his blood,
the son of Labdacus descended of Polydorus,
Cadmus of old and Agenor, founder of the line: 305
their power and mine are one.
                         Oh dear gods,
my curse on those who disobey these orders!

Let no crops grow out of the earth for them —
shrivel their women, kill their sons,
burn them to nothing in this plague 310
that hits us now, or something even worse.
But you, loyal men of Thebes who approve my actions,
may our champion, Justice, may all the gods
be with us, fight beside us to the end!

LEADER: In the grip of your curse, my king, I swear 315
I'm not the murderer, cannot point him out.
As for the search, Apollo pressed it on us —
he should name the killer.

OEDIPUS: Quite right,
but to force the gods to act against their will —
no man has the power.

LEADER: Then if I might mention 320
the next best thing . . .

OEDIPUS: The third best too —
don't hold back, say it.

LEADER: I still believe . . .
Lord Tiresias sees with the eyes of Lord Apollo.
Anyone searching for the truth, my king,
might learn it from the prophet, clear as day. 325

OEDIPUS: I've not been slow with that. On Creon's cue
I sent the escorts, twice, within the hour.
I'm surprised he isn't here.

LEADER: We need him —
without him we have nothing but old, useless rumors.

OEDIPUS: Which rumors? I'll search out every word. 330

LEADER: Laius was killed, they say, by certain travelers.

OEDIPUS: I know — but no one can find the murderer.

LEADER: If the man has a trace of fear in him
he won't stay silent long,
not with your curses ringing in his ears. 335

OEDIPUS: He didn't flinch at murder,
he'll never flinch at words.

*Enter Tiresias, the blind prophet, led by a boy with escorts in attendance. He remains
at a distance.*

LEADER: Here is the one who will convict him, look,
they bring him on at last, the seer, the man of god.
The truth lives inside him, him alone.

OEDIPUS: O Tiresias, 340
master of all the mysteries of our life,
all you teach and all you dare not tell,
signs in the heavens, signs that walk the earth!
Blind as you are, you can feel all the more
what sickness haunts our city. You, my lord, 345

are the one shield, the one savior we can find.

We asked Apollo — perhaps the messengers
haven't told you — he sent his answer back:
"Relief from the plague can only come one way.
Uncover the murderers of Laius,   350
put them to death or drive them into exile."
So I beg you, grudge us nothing now, no voice,
no message plucked from the birds, the embers
or the other mantic ways within your grasp.
Rescue yourself, your city, rescue me —   355
rescue everything infected by the dead.
We are in your hands. For a man to help others
with all his gifts and native strength:
that is the noblest work.
TIRESIAS: How terrible — to see the truth
when the truth is only pain to him who sees!   360
I knew it well, but I put it from my mind,
else I never would have come.
OEDIPUS: What's this? Why so grim, so dire?
TIRESIAS: Just send me home. You bear your burdens,
I'll bear mine. It's better that way,   365
please believe me.
OEDIPUS: Strange response — unlawful,
unfriendly too to the state that bred and raised you;
you're withholding the word of god.
TIRESIAS: I fail to see
that your own words are so well-timed.
I'd rather not have the same thing said of me . . .   370
OEDIPUS: For the love of god, don't turn away,
not if you know something. We beg you,
all of us on our knees.
TIRESIAS: None of you knows —
and I will never reveal my dreadful secrets,
not to say your own.   375
OEDIPUS: What? You know and you won't tell?
You're bent on betraying us, destroying Thebes?
TIRESIAS: I'd rather not cause pain for you or me.
So why this . . . useless interrogation?
You'll get nothing from me.
OEDIPUS: Nothing! You,   380
you scum of the earth, you'd enrage a heart of stone!
You won't talk? Nothing moves you?
Out with it, once and for all!
TIRESIAS: You criticize my temper . . . unaware
of the one *you* live with, you revile me.   385
OEDIPUS: Who could restrain his anger hearing you?

What outrage — you spurn the city!

TIRESIAS: What will come will come.

Even if I shroud it all in silence.

OEDIPUS: What will come? You're bound to *tell* me that. 390

TIRESIAS: I'll say no more. Do as you like, build your anger
to whatever pitch you please, rage your worst —

OEDIPUS: Oh I'll let loose, I have such fury in me —
now I see it all. You helped hatch the plot,
you did the work, yes, short of killing him 395
with your own hands — and given eyes I'd say
you did the killing single-handed!

TIRESIAS: Is that so!
I charge you, then, submit to that decree
you just laid down: from this day onward
speak to no one, not these citizens, not myself. 400
You are the curse, the corruption of the land!

OEDIPUS: You, shameless —
aren't you appalled to start up such a story?
You think you can get away with this?

TIRESIAS: I have already.
The truth with all its power lives inside me. 405

OEDIPUS: Who primed you for this? Not your prophet's trade.

TIRESIAS: You did, you forced me, twisted it out of me.

OEDIPUS: What? Say it again — I'll understand it better.

TIRESIAS: Didn't you understand, just now?
Or are you tempting me to talk? 410

OEDIPUS: No, I can't say I grasped your meaning.
Out with it, again!

TIRESIAS: I say you are the murderer you hunt.

OEDIPUS: That obscenity, twice — by god, you'll pay.

TIRESIAS: Shall I say more, so you can really rage? 415

OEDIPUS: Much as you want. Your words are nothing —
futile.

TIRESIAS: You cannot imagine . . . I tell you,
you and your loved ones live together in infamy,
you cannot see how far you've gone in guilt.

OEDIPUS: You think you can keep this up and never suffer? 420

TIRESIAS: Indeed, if the truth has any power.

OEDIPUS: It does
but not for you, old man. You've lost your power,
stone-blind, stone-deaf — senses, eyes blind as stone!

TIRESIAS: I pity you, flinging at me the very insults
each man here will fling at you so soon.

OEDIPUS: Blind, 425
lost in the night, endless night that nursed you!
You can't hurt me or anyone else who sees the light —

you can never touch me.

TIRESIAS: True, it is not your fate
to fall at my hands. Apollo is quite enough,
and he will take some pains to work this out.   430
OEDIPUS: Creon! Is this conspiracy his or yours?
TIRESIAS: Creon is not your downfall, no, you are your own.
OEDIPUS: O power —
wealth and empire, skill outstripping skill
in the heady rivalries of life,
what envy lurks inside you! Just for this,   435
the crown the city gave me — I never sought it,
they laid it in my hands — for this alone, Creon,
the soul of trust, my loyal friend from the start
steals against me . . . so hungry to overthrow me
he sets this wizard on me, this scheming quack,   440
this fortune-teller peddling lies, eyes peeled
for his own profit — seer blind in his craft!

Come here, you pious fraud. Tell me,
when did you ever prove yourself a prophet?
When the Sphinx, that chanting Fury kept her deathwatch here,   445
why silent then, not a word to set our people free?
There was a riddle, not for some passer-by to solve —
it cried out for a prophet. Where were you?
Did you rise to the crisis? Not a word,
you and your birds, your gods — nothing.   450
No, but I came by, Oedipus the ignorant,
I stopped the Sphinx! With no help from the birds,
the flight of my own intelligence hit the mark.

And this is the man you'd try to overthrow?
You think you'll stand by Creon when he's king?   455
You and the great mastermind —
you'll pay in tears, I promise you, for this,
this witch-hunt. If you didn't look so senile
the lash would teach you what your scheming means!
LEADER: I'd suggest his words were spoken in anger,   460
Oedipus . . . yours too, and it isn't what we need.
The best solution to the oracle, the riddle
posed by god — we should look for that.
TIRESIAS: You are the king no doubt, but in one respect,
at least, I am your equal: the right to reply.   465
I claim that privilege too.
I am not your slave. I serve Apollo.
I don't need Creon to speak for me in public.
                                    So,
you mock my blindness? Let me tell you this.

You with your precious eyes,   470
you're blind to the corruption of your life,
to the house you live in, those you live with —
who *are* your parents? Do you know? All unknowing
you are the scourge of your own flesh and blood,
the dead below the earth and the living here above,   475
and the double lash of your mother and your father's curse
will whip you from this land one day, their footfall
treading you down in terror, darkness shrouding
your eyes that now can see the light!
                             Soon, soon
you'll scream aloud — what haven won't reverberate?   480
What rock of Cithaeron° won't scream back in echo?
That day you learn the truth about your marriage,
the wedding-march that sang you into your halls,
the lusty voyage home to the fatal harbor!
And a load of other horrors you'd never dream   485
will level you with yourself and all your children.

There. Now smear us with insults — Creon, myself
and every word I've said. No man will ever
be rooted from the earth as brutally as you.
OEDIPUS: Enough! Such filth from him? Insufferable —   490
    what, still alive? Get out —
    faster, back where you came from — vanish!
TIRESIAS: I'd never have come if you hadn't called me here.
OEDIPUS: If I thought you'd blurt out such absurdities,
    you'd have died waiting before I'd had you summoned.   495
TIRESIAS: Absurd, am I? To you, not to your parents:
    the ones who bore you found me sane enough.
OEDIPUS: Parents — who? Wait . . . who is my father?
TIRESIAS: This day will bring your birth and your destruction.
OEDIPUS: Riddles — all you can say are riddles, murk and darkness.   500
TIRESIAS: Ah, but aren't you the best man alive at solving riddles?
OEDIPUS: Mock me for that, go on, and you'll reveal my greatness.
TIRESIAS: Your great good fortune, true, it was your ruin.
OEDIPUS: Not if I saved the city — what do I care?
TIRESIAS: Well then, I'll be going.

To his attendant.

                       Take me home, boy.   505
OEDIPUS: Yes, take him away. You're a nuisance here.
    Out of the way, the irritation's gone.

Turning his back on Tiresias, moving toward the palace.

---

481. **Cithaeron:** The mountains where Oedipus was abandoned as an infant.

TIRESIAS: I will go,
　　once I have said what I came here to say.
　　I'll never shrink from the anger in your eyes —
　　you can't destroy me. Listen to me closely: 510
　　the man you've sought so long, proclaiming,
　　cursing up and down, the murderer of Laius —
　　he is here. A stranger,
　　you may think, who lives among you,
　　he soon will be revealed a native Theban   515
　　but he will take no joy in the revelation.
　　Blind who now has eyes, beggar who now is rich,
　　he will grope his way toward a foreign soil,
　　a stick tapping before him step by step.

Oedipus enters the palace.

　　Revealed at last, brother and father both   520
　　to the children he embraces, to his mother
　　son and husband both — he sowed the loins
　　his father sowed, he spilled his father's blood!

　　Go in and reflect on that, solve that.
　　And if you find I've lied   525
　　from this day onward call the prophet blind.

Tiresias and the boy exit to the side.

CHORUS: Who —
　　who is the man the voice of god denounces
　　resounding out of the rocky gorge of Delphi?
　　　　The horror too dark to tell,
　　whose ruthless bloody hands have done the work?   530
　　His time has come to fly
　　　　to outrace the stallions of the storm
　　　　　　　　his feet a streak of speed —
　　Cased in armor, Apollo son of the Father
　　lunges on him, lightning-bolts afire!   535
　　And the grim unerring Furies°
　　　　　　　closing for the kill.
　　　　　　　　　　　　Look,
　　the word of god has just come blazing
　　flashing off Parnassus'° snowy heights!
　　　　That man who left no trace —   540
　　after him, hunt him down with all our strength!
　　Now under bristling timber
　　　　up through rocks and caves he stalks
　　　　　　　　like the wild mountain bull —

---

536. Furies: Three spirits who avenged evildoers.   **539. Parnassus:** A mountain in Greece associated with Apollo.

cut off from men, each step an agony, frenzied, racing blind   545
but he cannot outrace the dread voices of Delphi
ringing out of the heart of Earth,
   the dark wings beating around him shrieking doom
       the doom that never dies, the terror —

The skilled prophet scans the birds and shatters me with terror!   550
I can't accept him, can't deny him, don't know what to say,
I'm lost, and the wings of dark foreboding beating —
I cannot see what's come, what's still to come . . .
and what could breed a blood feud between
   Laius' house and the son of Polybus?°   555
I know of nothing, not in the past and not now,
no charge to bring against our king, no cause
to attack his fame that rings throughout Thebes —
   not without proof — not for the ghost of Laius,
   not to avenge a murder gone without a trace.   560

Zeus and Apollo know, they know, the great masters
   of all the dark and depth of human life.
But whether a mere man can know the truth,
whether a seer can fathom more than I —
there is no test, no certain proof   565
   though matching skill for skill
a man can outstrip a rival. No, not till I see
these charges proved will I side with his accusers.
We saw him then, when the she-hawk° swept against him,
saw with our own eyes his skill, his brilliant triumph —   570
   there was the test — he was the joy of Thebes!
   Never will I convict my king, never in my heart.

Enter Creon from the side.

CREON: My fellow-citizens, I hear King Oedipus
  levels terrible charges at me. I had to come.
  I resent it deeply. If, in the present crisis,   575
  he thinks he suffers any abuse from me,
  anything I've done or said that offers him
  the slightest injury, why, I've no desire
  to linger out this life, my reputation a shambles.
  The damage I'd face from such an accusation   580
  is nothing simple. No, there's nothing worse:
  branded a traitor in the city, a traitor
  to all of you and my good friends.
LEADER: True,
  but a slur might have been forced out of him,
  by anger perhaps, not any firm conviction.   585

---

555. Polybus: The King of Corinth, who is thought to be Oedipus's father. **569. she-hawk:** The Sphinx.

CREON: The charge was made in public, wasn't it?
    I put the prophet up to spreading lies?
LEADER: Such things were said . . .
    I don't know with what intent, if any.
CREON: Was his glance steady, his mind right
    when the charge was brought against me?   590
LEADER: I really couldn't say. I never look
    to judge the ones in power.

The doors open. Oedipus enters.

                     Wait,
    here's Oedipus now.
OEDIPUS: You — here? You have the gall
    to show your face before the palace gates?   595
    You, plotting to kill me, kill the king —
    I see it all, the marauding thief himself
    scheming to steal my crown and power!
                   Tell me,
    in god's name, what did you take me for,
    coward or fool, when you spun out your plot?   600
    Your treachery — you think I'd never detect it
    creeping against me in the dark? Or sensing it,
    not defend myself? Aren't you the fool,
    you and your high adventure. Lacking numbers,
    powerful friends, out for the big game of empire —   605
    you need riches, armies to bring that quarry down!
CREON: Are you quite finished? It's your turn to listen
    for just as long as you've . . . instructed me.
    Hear me out, then judge me on the facts.
OEDIPUS: You've a wicked way with words, Creon,   610
    but I'll be slow to learn — from you.
    I find you a menace, a great burden to me.
CREON: Just one thing, hear me out in this.
OEDIPUS: Just one thing,
    don't tell me you're not the enemy, the traitor.
CREON: Look, if you think crude, mindless stubbornness   615
    such a gift, you've lost your sense of balance.
OEDIPUS: If you think you can abuse a kinsman,
    then escape the penalty, you're insane.
CREON: Fair enough, I grant you. But this injury
    you say I've done you, what is it?   620
OEDIPUS: Did you induce me, yes or no,
    to send for that sanctimonious prophet?
CREON: I did. And I'd do the same again.
OEDIPUS: All right then, tell me, how long is it now
    since Laius . . .
CREON: Laius — what did *he* do?
OEDIPUS: Vanished,   625
    swept from sight, murdered in his tracks.

CREON: The count of the years would run you far back . . .
OEDIPUS: And that far back, was the prophet at his trade?
CREON: Skilled as he is today, and just as honored.
OEDIPUS: Did he ever refer to me then, at that time?
CREON: No,   630
 never, at least, when I was in his presence.
OEDIPUS: But you did investigate the murder, didn't you?
CREON: We did our best, of course, discovered nothing.
OEDIPUS: But the great seer never accused me then — why not?
CREON: I don't know. And when I don't, *I* keep quiet.   635
OEDIPUS: You do know this, you'd tell it too —
 if you had a shred of decency.
CREON: What?
 If I know, I won't hold back.
OEDIPUS: Simply this:
 if the two of you had never put heads together,
 we'd never have heard about *my* killing Laius.   640
CREON: If that's what he says . . . well, you know best.
 But now I have a right to learn from you
 as you just learned from me.
OEDIPUS: Learn your fill,
 you never will convict me of the murder.
CREON: Tell me, you're married to my sister, aren't you?   645
OEDIPUS: A genuine discovery — there's no denying that.
CREON: And you rule the land with her, with equal power?
OEDIPUS: She receives from me whatever she desires.
CREON: And I am the third, all of us are equals?
OEDIPUS: Yes, and it's there you show your stripes —   650
 you betray a kinsman.
CREON: Not at all.
 Not if you see things calmly, rationally,
 as I do. Look at it this way first:
 who in his right mind would rather rule
 and live in anxiety than sleep in peace?   655
 Particularly if he enjoys the same authority.
 Not I, I'm not the man to yearn for kingship,
 not with a king's power in my hands. Who would?
 No one with any sense of self-control.
 Now, as it is, you offer me all I need,   660
 not a fear in the world. But if I wore the crown . . .
 there'd be many painful duties to perform,
 hardly to my taste.
      How could kingship
 please me more than influence, power
 without a qualm? I'm not that deluded yet,   665
 to reach for anything but privilege outright,
 profit free and clear.

Now all men sing my praises, all salute me,
now all who request your favors curry mine.
I'm their best hope: success rests in me. 670
Why give up that, I ask you, and borrow trouble?
A man of sense, someone who sees things clearly
would never resort to treason.
No, I've no lust for conspiracy in me,
nor could I ever suffer one who does. 675

Do you want proof? Go to Delphi yourself,
examine the oracle and see if I've reported
the message word-for-word. This too:
if you detect that I and the clairvoyant
have plotted anything in common, arrest me, 680
execute me. Not on the strength of one vote,
two in this case, mine as well as yours.
But don't convict me on sheer unverified surmise.

How wrong it is to take the good for bad,
purely at random, or take the bad for good. 685
But reject a friend, a kinsman? I would as soon
tear out the life within us, priceless life itself.
You'll learn this well, without fail, in time.
Time alone can bring the just man to light;
the criminal you can spot in one short day.
LEADER: Good advice, 690
my lord, for anyone who wants to avoid disaster.
Those who jump to conclusions may be wrong.
OEDIPUS: When my enemy moves against me quickly,
plots in secret, I move quickly too, I must,
I plot and pay him back. Relax my guard a moment, 695
waiting his next move — he wins his objective,
I lose mine.
CREON: What do you want?
You want me banished?
OEDIPUS: No, I want you dead.
CREON: Just to show how ugly a grudge can . . .
OEDIPUS: So,
still stubborn? you don't think I'm serious? 700
CREON: I think you're insane.
OEDIPUS: Quite sane — in my behalf.
CREON: Not just as much in mine?
OEDIPUS: You — my mortal enemy?
CREON: What if you're wholly wrong?
OEDIPUS: No matter — I must rule.
CREON: Not if you rule unjustly.
OEDIPUS: Hear him, Thebes, my city!
CREON: My city too, not yours alone! 705

LEADER: Please, my lords.

Enter Jocasta from the palace.

> Look, Jocasta's coming,
> and just in time too. With her help
> you must put this fighting of yours to rest.

JOCASTA: Have you no sense? Poor misguided men,
> such shouting — why this public outburst?   710
> Aren't you ashamed, with the land so sick,
> to stir up private quarrels?

To Oedipus.

> Into the palace now. And Creon, you go home.
> Why make such a furor over nothing?

CREON: My sister, it's dreadful . . . Oedipus, your husband,   715
> he's bent on a choice of punishments for me,
> banishment from the fatherland or death.

OEDIPUS: Precisely. I caught him in the act, Jocasta,
> plotting, about to stab me in the back.

CREON: Never — curse me, let me die and be damned   720
> if I've done you any wrong you charge me with.

JOCASTA: Oh god, believe it, Oedipus,
> honor the solemn oath he swears to heaven.
> Do it for me, for the sake of all your people.

The Chorus begins to chant.

CHORUS: Believe it, be sensible   725
> give way, my king, I beg you!

OEDIPUS: What do you want from me, concessions?

CHORUS: Respect him — he's been no fool in the past
> and now he's strong with the oath he swears to god.

OEDIPUS: You know what you're asking?

CHORUS: I do.

OEDIPUS: Then out with it!   730

CHORUS: The man's your friend, your kin, he's under oath —
> don't cast him out, disgraced
> branded with guilt on the strength of hearsay only.

OEDIPUS: Know full well, if that's what you want
> you want me dead or banished from the land.

CHORUS: Never —   735
> no, by the blazing Sun, first god of the heavens!
>   Stripped of the gods, stripped of loved ones,
> let me die by inches if that ever crossed my mind.
> But the heart inside me sickens, dies as the land dies
> and now on top of the old griefs you pile this,   740
> your fury — both of you!

OEDIPUS: Then let him go,
> even if it does lead to my ruin, my death

or my disgrace, driven from Thebes for life.
It's you, not him I pity — your words move me.
He, wherever he goes, my hate goes with him.   745
CREON: Look at you, sullen in yielding, brutal in your rage —
you'll go too far. It's perfect justice:
natures like yours are hardest on themselves.
OEDIPUS: Then leave me alone — get out!
CREON: I'm going.
You're wrong, so wrong. These men know I'm right.   750

Exit to the side. The Chorus turns to Jocasta.

CHORUS: Why do you hesitate, my lady
        why not help him in?
JOCASTA: Tell me what's happened first.
CHORUS: Loose, ignorant talk started dark suspicions
        and a sense of injustice cut deeply too.   755
JOCASTA: On both sides?
CHORUS: Oh yes.
JOCASTA: What did they say?
CHORUS: Enough, please, enough! The land's so racked already
        or so it seems to me . . .
        End the trouble here, just where they left it.
OEDIPUS: You see what comes of your good intentions now?   760
And all because you tried to blunt my anger.
CHORUS: My king,
I've said it once, I'll say it time and again —
        I'd be insane, you know it,
senseless, ever to turn my back on you.
You who set our beloved land — storm-tossed, shattered —   765
straight on course. Now again, good helmsman,
steer us through the storm!

The Chorus draws away, leaving Oedipus and Jocasta side by side.

JOCASTA: For the love of god,
Oedipus, tell me too, what is it?
Why this rage? You're so unbending.
OEDIPUS: I will tell you. I respect you, Jocasta,   770
much more than these . . .

Glancing at the Chorus.

Creon's to blame, Creon schemes against me.
JOCASTA: Tell me clearly, how did the quarrel start?
OEDIPUS: He says *I* murdered Laius — I am guilty.
JOCASTA: How does he know? Some secret knowledge   775
or simple hearsay?
OEDIPUS: Oh, he sent his prophet in
to do his dirty work. You know Creon,
Creon keeps his own lips clean.

JOCASTA: A prophet?
Well then, free yourself of every charge!
Listen to me and learn some peace of mind: 780
no skill in the world,
nothing human can penetrate the future.
Here is proof, quick and to the point.
An oracle came to Laius one fine day
(I won't say from Apollo himself   ·   785
but his underlings, his priests) and it said
that doom would strike him down at the hands of a son,
our son, to be born of our own flesh and blood. But Laius,
so the report goes at least, was killed by strangers,
thieves, at a place where three roads meet . . . my son —   790
he wasn't three days old and the boy's father
fastened his ankles, had a henchman fling him away
on a barren, trackless mountain.
                            There, you see?
Apollo brought neither thing to pass. My baby
no more murdered his father than Laius suffered —   795
his wildest fear — death at his own son's hands.
That's how the seers and their revelations
mapped out the future. Brush them from your mind.
Whatever the god needs and seeks
he'll bring to light himself, with ease.
OEDIPUS: Strange,   800
hearing you just now . . . my mind wandered,
my thoughts racing back and forth.
JOCASTA: What do you mean? Why so anxious, startled?
OEDIPUS: I thought I heard you say that Laius
was cut down at a place where three roads meet.   805
JOCASTA: That was the story. It hasn't died out yet.
OEDIPUS: Where did this thing happen? Be precise.
JOCASTA: A place called Phocis, where two branching roads,
one from Daulia, one from Delphi,
come together — a crossroads.   810
OEDIPUS: When? How long ago?
JOCASTA: The heralds no sooner reported Laius dead
than you appeared and they hailed you king of Thebes.
OEDIPUS: My god, my god — what have you planned to do to me?
JOCASTA: What, Oedipus? What haunts you so?
OEDIPUS: Not yet.   815
Laius — how did he look? Describe him.
Had he reached his prime?
JOCASTA: He was swarthy,
and the gray had just begun to streak his temples,
and his build . . . wasn't far from yours.
OEDIPUS: Oh no no,

I think I've just called down a dreadful curse   820
    upon myself — I simply didn't know!
JOCASTA: What are you saying? I shudder to look at you.
OEDIPUS: I have a terrible fear the blind seer can see.
    I'll know in a moment. One thing more —
JOCASTA: Anything,
    afraid as I am — ask, I'll answer, all I can.   825
OEDIPUS: Did he go with a light or heavy escort,
    several men-at-arms, like a lord, a king?
JOCASTA: There were five in the party, a herald among them,
    and a single wagon carrying Laius.
OEDIPUS: Ai —
    now I can see it all, clear as day.   830
    Who told you all this at the time, Jocasta?
JOCASTA: A servant who reached home, the lone survivor.
OEDIPUS: So, could he still be in the palace — even now?
JOCASTA: No indeed. Soon as he returned from the scene
    and saw you on the throne with Laius dead and gone,   835
    he knelt and clutched my hand, pleading with me
    to send him into the hinterlands, to pasture,
    far as possible, out of sight of Thebes.
    I sent him away. Slave though he was,
    he'd earned that favor — and much more.   840
OEDIPUS: Can we bring him back, quickly?
JOCASTA: Easily. Why do you want him so?
OEDIPUS: I'm afraid,
    Jocasta, I have said too much already.
    That man — I've got to see him.
JOCASTA: Then he'll come.
    But even I have a right, I'd like to think,   845
    to know what's torturing you, my lord.
OEDIPUS: And so you shall — I can hold nothing back from you,
    now I've reached this pitch of dark foreboding.
    Who means more to me than you? Tell me,
    whom would I turn toward but you   850
    as I go through all this?

    My father was Polybus, king of Corinth.
    My mother, a Dorian, Merope. And I was held
    the prince of the realm among the people there,
    till something struck me out of nowhere,   855
    something strange . . . worth remarking perhaps,
    hardly worth the anxiety I gave it.
    Some man at a banquet who had drunk too much
    shouted out — he was far gone, mind you —
    that I am not my father's son. Fighting words!   860
    I barely restrained myself that day

but early the next I went to mother and father,
questioned them closely, and they were enraged
at the accusation and the fool who let it fly.
So as for my parents I was satisfied,   865
but still this thing kept gnawing at me,
the slander spread — I had to make my move.
                                        And so,
unknown to mother and father I set out for Delphi,
and the god Apollo spurned me, sent me away
denied the facts I came for,   870
but first he flashed before my eyes a future
great with pain, terror, disaster — I can hear him cry,
"You are fated to couple with your mother, you will bring
a breed of children into the light no man can bear to see —
you will kill your father, the one who gave you life!"   875
I heard all that and ran. I abandoned Corinth,
from that day on I gauged its landfall only
by the stars, running, always running
toward some place where I would never see
the shame of all those oracles come true.   880
And as I fled I reached that very spot
where the great king, you say, met his death.
Now, Jocasta, I will tell you all.
Making my way toward this triple crossroad
I began to see a herald, then a brace of colts   885
drawing a wagon, and mounted on the bench . . . a man,
just as you've described him, coming face-to-face,
and the one in the lead and the old man himself
were about to thrust me off the road — brute force —
and the one shouldering me aside, the driver,   890
I strike him in anger! — and the old man, watching me
coming up along his wheels — he brings down
his prod, two prongs straight at my head!
I paid him back with interest!
Short work, by god — with one blow of the staff   895
in this right hand I knock him out of his high seat,
roll him out of the wagon, sprawling headlong —
I killed them all — every mother's son!

Oh, but if there is any blood-tie
between Laius and this stranger . . .   900
what man alive more miserable than I?
More hated by the gods? *I* am the man
no alien, no citizen welcomes to his house,
law forbids it — not a word to me in public,
driven out of every hearth and home.   905
And all these curses I — no one but I
brought down these piling curses on myself!

And you, his wife, I've touched your body with these,
the hands that killed your husband cover you with blood.

Wasn't I born for torment? Look me in the eyes!   910
I am abomination — heart and soul!
I must be exiled, and even in exile
never see my parents, never set foot
on native earth again. Else I'm doomed
to couple with my mother and cut my father down ...   915
Polybus who reared me, gave me life.

                    But why, why?
Wouldn't a man of judgment say — and wouldn't he be right —
some savage power has brought this down upon my head?

Oh no, not that, you pure and awesome gods,
never let me see that day! Let me slip   920
from the world of men, vanish without a trace
before I see myself stained with such corruption,
stained to the heart.
LEADER: My lord, you fill our hearts with fear.
    But at least until you question the witness,   925
    do take hope.
OEDIPUS: Exactly. He is my last hope —
I'm waiting for the shepherd. He is crucial.
JOCASTA: And once he appears, what then? Why so urgent?
OEDIPUS: I'll tell you. If it turns out that his story
    matches yours, I've escaped the worst.   930
JOCASTA: What did I say? What struck you so?
OEDIPUS: You said *thieves* —
he told you a whole band of them murdered Laius.
So, if he still holds to the same number,
I cannot be the killer. One can't equal many.
But if he refers to one man, one alone,   935
clearly the scales come down on me:
I am guilty.
JOCASTA: Impossible. Trust me,
I told you precisely what he said,
and he can't retract it now;
the whole city heard it, not just I.   940
And even if he should vary his first report
by one man more or less, still, my lord,
he could never make the murder of Laius
truly fit the prophecy. Apollo was explicit:
my son was doomed to kill my husband ... my son,   945
poor defenseless thing, he never had a chance
to kill his father. They destroyed him first.

So much for prophecy. It's neither here nor there.
From this day on, I wouldn't look right or left.

OEDIPUS: True, true. Still, that shepherd,   950
    someone fetch him — now!
JOCASTA: I'll send at once. But do let's go inside.
    I'd never displease you, least of all in this.

Oedipus and Jocasta enter the palace.

CHORUS: Destiny guide me always
    Destiny find me filled with reverence   955
        pure in word and deed.
    Great laws tower above us, reared on high
    born for the brilliant vault of heaven —
        Olympian sky their only father,
    nothing mortal, no man gave them birth,   960
    their memory deathless, never lost in sleep:
    within them lives a mighty god, the god does not grow old.

    Pride breeds the tyrant
    violent pride, gorging, crammed to bursting
        with all that is overripe and rich with ruin —   965
    clawing up to the heights, headlong pride
    crashes down the abyss — sheer doom!
        No footing helps, all foothold lost and gone,
    But the healthy strife that makes the city strong —
    I pray that god will never end that wrestling: 970
    god, my champion, I will never let you go.

    But if any man comes striding, high and mighty
        in all he says and does,
    no fear of justice, no reverence
    for the temples of the gods —   975
        let a rough doom tear him down,
    repay his pride, breakneck, ruinous pride!
    If he cannot reap his profits fairly
        cannot restrain himself from outrage —
    mad, laying hands on the holy things untouchable!   980

        Can such a man, so desperate, still boast
        he can save his life from the flashing bolts of god?
          If all such violence goes with honor now
          why join the sacred dance?

    Never again will I go reverent to Delphi,   985
        the inviolate heart of Earth
    or Apollo's ancient oracle at Abae
    or Olympia of the fires —
        unless these prophecies all come true
    for all mankind to point toward in wonder.   990
    King of kings, if you deserve your titles
        Zeus, remember, never forget!

You and your deathless, everlasting reign.

> They are dying, the old oracles sent to Laius,
> now our masters strike them off the rolls.   995
>   Nowhere Apollo's golden glory now —
>   the gods, the gods go down.

Enter Jocasta from the palace, carrying a suppliant's branch wound in wool.

JOCASTA: Lords of the realm, it occurred to me,
just now, to visit the temples of the gods,
so I have my branch in hand and incense too.   1000

Oedipus is beside himself. Racked with anguish,
no longer a man of sense, he won't admit
the latest prophecies are hollow as the old —
he's at the mercy of every passing voice
if the voice tells of terror.   1005
I urge him gently, nothing seems to help,
so I turn to you, Apollo, you are nearest.

Placing her branch on the altar, while an old herdsman enters from the side, not the one just summoned by the king but an unexpected messenger from Corinth.

I come with prayers and offerings . . . I beg you,
cleanse us, set us free of defilement!
Look at us, passengers in the grip of fear,   1010
watching the pilot of the vessel go to pieces.

MESSENGER:

Approaching Jocasta and the Chorus.

Strangers, please, I wonder if you could lead us
to the palace of the king . . . I think it's Oedipus.
Better, the man himself — you know where he is?
LEADER: This is his palace, stranger. He's inside.   1015
But here is his queen, his wife and mother
of his children.
MESSENGER: Blessings on you, noble queen,
queen of Oedipus crowned with all your family —
blessings on you always!
JOCASTA: And the same to you, stranger, you deserve it . . .   1020
such a greeting. But what have you come for?
Have you brought us news?
MESSENGER: Wonderful news —
for the house, my lady, for your husband too.
JOCASTA: Really, what? Who sent you?
MESSENGER: Corinth.
I'll give you the message in a moment.   1025
You'll be glad of it — how could you help it? —
though it costs a little sorrow in the bargain.
JOCASTA: What can it be, with such a double edge?

MESSENGER: The people there, they want to make your Oedipus
    king of Corinth, so they're saying now.   103

JOCASTA: Why? Isn't old Polybus still in power?

MESSENGER: No more. Death has got him in the tomb.

JOCASTA: What are you saying? Polybus, dead? — dead?

MESSENGER: If not,
    if I'm not telling the truth, strike me dead too.

JOCASTA:

To a servant.

    Quickly, go to your master, tell him this!   103

    You prophecies of the gods, where are you now?
    This is the man that Oedipus feared for years,
    he fled him, not to kill him — and now he's dead,
    quite by chance, a normal, natural death,
    not murdered by his son.

OEDIPUS:

Emerging from the palace.

                                    Dearest,   104
    what now? Why call me from the palace?

JOCASTA:

Bringing the Messenger closer.

        Listen to *him,* see for yourself what all
        those awful prophecies of god have come to.

OEDIPUS: And who is he? What can he have for me?

JOCASTA: He's from Corinth, he's come to tell you   104
    your father is no more — Polybus — he's dead!

OEDIPUS:

Wheeling on the Messenger.

    What? Let me have it from your lips.

MESSENGER: Well,
    if that's what you want first, then here it is:
    make no mistake, Polybus is dead and gone.

OEDIPUS: How — murder? sickness? — what? what killed him?   105

MESSENGER: A light tip of the scales can put old bones to rest.

OEDIPUS: Sickness then — poor man, it wore him down.

MESSENGER: That,
    and the long count of years he'd measured out.

OEDIPUS: So!
    Jocasta, why, why look to the Prophet's hearth,
    the fires of the future? Why scan the birds   105
    that scream above our heads? They winged me on
    to the murder of my father, did they? That was my doom?
    Well look, he's dead and buried, hidden under the earth,
    and here I am in Thebes, I never put hand to sword —
    unless some longing for me wasted him away,   106

then in a sense you'd say I caused his death.
But now, all those prophecies I feared — Polybus
packs them off to sleep with him in hell!
They're nothing, worthless.

JOCASTA: There.
Didn't I tell you from the start?   1065

OEDIPUS: So you did. I was lost in fear.

JOCASTA: No more, sweep it from your mind forever.

OEDIPUS: But my mother's bed, surely I must fear —

JOCASTA: Fear?
What should a man fear? It's all chance,
chance rules our lives. Not a man on earth   1070
can see a day ahead, groping through the dark.
Better to live at random, best we can.
And as for this marriage with your mother —
have no fear. Many a man before you,
in his dreams, has shared his mother's bed.   1075
Take such things for shadows, nothing at all —
Live, Oedipus,
as if there's no tomorrow!

OEDIPUS: Brave words,
and you'd persuade me if mother weren't alive.
But mother lives, so for all your reassurances   1080
I live in fear, I must.

JOCASTA: But your father's death,
that, at least, is a great blessing, joy to the eyes!

OEDIPUS: Great, I know . . . but I fear *her* — she's still alive.

MESSENGER: Wait, who is this woman, makes you so afraid?

OEDIPUS: Merope, old man. The wife of Polybus.   1085

MESSENGER: The queen? What's there to fear in her?

OEDIPUS: A dreadful prophecy, stranger, sent by the gods.

MESSENGER: Tell me, could you? Unless it's forbidden
other ears to hear.

OEDIPUS: Not at all.
Apollo told me once — it is my fate —   1090
I must make love with my own mother,
shed my father's blood with my own hands.
So for years I've given Corinth a wide berth,
and it's been my good fortune too. But still,
to see one's parents and look into their eyes   1095
is the greatest joy I know.

MESSENGER: You're afraid of that?
That kept you out of Corinth?

OEDIPUS: My *father*, old man —
so I wouldn't kill my father.

MESSENGER: So that's it.
Well then, seeing I came with such good will, my king,

why don't I rid you of that old worry now?   1100

OEDIPUS: What a rich reward you'd have for that.

MESSENGER: What do you think I came for, majesty?

So you'd come home and I'd be better off.

OEDIPUS: Never, I will never go near my parents.

MESSENGER: My boy, it's clear, you don't know what you're doing.   1105

OEDIPUS: What do you mean, old man? For god's sake, explain.

MESSENGER: If you ran from *them*, always dodging home . . .

OEDIPUS: Always, terrified Apollo's oracle might come true —

MESSENGER: And you'd be covered with guilt, from both your parents.

OEDIPUS: That's right, old man, that fear is always with me.   1110

MESSENGER: Don't you know? You've really nothing to fear.

OEDIPUS: But why? If I'm their son — Merope, Polybus?

MESSENGER: Polybus was nothing to you, that's why, not in blood.

OEDIPUS: What are you saying — Polybus was not my father?

MESSENGER: No more than I am. He and I are equals.

OEDIPUS: My father —   1115

how can my father equal nothing? You're nothing to me!

MESSENGER: Neither was he, no more your father than I am.

OEDIPUS: Then why did he call me his son?

MESSENGER: You were a gift,

years ago — know for a fact he took you

from my hands.

OEDIPUS: No, from another's hands?   1120

Then how could he love me so? He loved me, deeply . . .

MESSENGER: True, and his early years without a child

made him love you all the more.

OEDIPUS: And you, did you . . .

buy me? find me by accident?

MESSENGER: I stumbled on you,

down the woody flanks of Mount Cithaeron.

OEDIPUS: So close,   1125

what were you doing here, just passing through?

MESSENGER: Watching over my flocks, grazing them on the slopes.

OEDIPUS: A herdsman, were you? A vagabond, scraping for wages?

MESSENGER: Your savior too, my son, in your worst hour.

OEDIPUS: Oh —

when you picked me up, was I in pain? What exactly?   1130

MESSENGER: Your ankles . . . they tell the story. Look at them.

OEDIPUS: Why remind me of that, that old affliction?

MESSENGER: Your ankles were pinned together; I set you free.

OEDIPUS: That dreadful mark — I've had it from the cradle.

MESSENGER: And you got your name from that misfortune too,   1135

the name's still with you.

OEDIPUS: Dear god, who did it? —

mother? father? Tell me.

MESSENGER: I don't know.

The one who gave you to me, he'd know more.
OEDIPUS: What? You took me from someone else?
    You didn't find me yourself?
MESSENGER: No sir,   1140
    another shepherd passed you on to me.
OEDIPUS: Who? Do you know? Describe him.
MESSENGER: He called himself a servant of . . .
    if I remember rightly — Laius.

Jocasta turns sharply.

OEDIPUS: The king of the land who ruled here long ago?   1145
MESSENGER: That's the one. That herdsman was *his* man.
OEDIPUS: Is he still alive? Can I see him?
MESSENGER: They'd know best, the people of these parts.

Oedipus and the Messenger turn to the Chorus.

OEDIPUS: Does anyone know that herdsman,
    the one he mentioned? Anyone seen him   1150
    in the fields, in town? Out with it!
    The time has come to reveal this once for all.
LEADER: I think he's the very shepherd you wanted to see,
    a moment ago. But the queen, Jocasta,
    she's the one to say.
OEDIPUS: Jocasta,   1155
    you remember the man we just sent for?
    Is *that* the one he means?
JOCASTA: That man . . .
    why ask? Old shepherd, talk, empty nonsense,
    don't give it another thought, don't even think —
OEDIPUS: What — give up now, with a clue like this?   1160
    Fail to solve the mystery of my birth?
    Not for all the world!
JOCASTA: Stop — in the name of god,
    if you love your own life, call off this search!
    My suffering is enough.
OEDIPUS: Courage!
    Even if my mother turns out to be a slave,   1165
    and I a slave, three generations back,
    you would not seem common.
JOCASTA: Oh no,
    listen to me, I beg you, don't do this.
OEDIPUS: Listen to you? No more. I must know it all,
    see the truth at last.
JOCASTA: No, please —   1170
    for your sake — I want the best for you!
OEDIPUS: Your best is more than I can bear.
JOCASTA: You're doomed —
    may you never fathom who you are!

OEDIPUS:

To a servant.

> Hurry, fetch me the herdsman, now!
> Leave her to glory in her royal birth.

JOCASTA: Aieeeeee —
> man of agony —
> that is the only name I have for you,
> that, no other — ever, ever, ever!

Flinging [herself] through the palace doors. A long, tense silence follows.

LEADER: Where's she gone, Oedipus?
> Rushing off, such wild grief . . .
> I'm afraid that from this silence
> something monstrous may come bursting forth.

OEDIPUS: Let it burst! Whatever will, whatever must!
> I must know my birth, no matter how common
> it may be — must see my origins face-to-face.
> She perhaps, she with her woman's pride
> may well be mortified by my birth,
> but I, I count myself the son of Chance,
> the great goddess, giver of all good things —
> I'll never see myself disgraced. She is my mother!
> And the moons have marked me out, my blood-brothers,
> one moon on the wane, the next moon great with power.
> That is my blood, my nature — I will never betray it,
> never fail to search and learn my birth!

CHORUS: Yes — if I am a true prophet
> > if I can grasp the truth,
> > by the boundless skies of Olympus,
> at the full moon of tomorrow, Mount Cithaeron
> you will know how Oedipus glories in you —
> you, his birthplace, nurse, his mountain-mother!
> And we will sing you, dancing out your praise —
> you lift our monarch's heart!
> > Apollo, Apollo, god of the wild cry
> > > may our dancing please you!
> > > > Oedipus —
> > > son, dear child, who bore you?
> Who of the nymphs who seem to live forever
> mated with Pan,° the mountain-striding Father?
> Who was your mother? who, some bride of Apollo
> the god who loves the pastures spreading toward the sun?
> > Or was it Hermes, king of the lightning ridges?
> > Or Dionysus, lord of frenzy, lord of the barren peaks —

1175

1180

1185

1190

1195

1200

1205

1210

1207. **Pan:** The god of shepherds, who was, like Hermes and Dionysus, associated with the wilderness.

did he seize you in his hands, dearest of all his lucky finds? —
    found by the nymphs, their warm eyes dancing, gift
to the lord who loves them dancing out his joy!

*Oedipus strains to see a figure coming from the distance. Attended by palace guards,
an old Shepherd enters slowly, reluctant to approach the King.*

OEDIPUS: I never met the man, my friends . . . still,.   1215
    if I had to guess, I'd say that's the shepherd,
    the very one we've looked for all along.
    Brothers in old age, two of a kind,
    he and our guest here. At any rate
    the ones who bring him in are my own men,   1220
    I recognize them.

Turning to the Leader.

            But you know more than I,
    you should, you've seen the man before.
LEADER: I know him, definitely. One of Laius' men,
    a trusty shepherd, if there ever was one.
OEDIPUS: You, I ask you first, stranger,   1225
    you from Corinth — is this the one you mean?
MESSENGER: You're looking at him. He's your man.
OEDIPUS:

To the Shepherd.

    You, old man, come over here —
    look at me. Answer all my questions.
    Did you ever serve King Laius?
SHEPHERD: So I did . . .   1230
    a slave, not bought on the block though,
    born and reared in the palace.
OEDIPUS: Your duties, your kind of work?
SHEPHERD: Herding the flocks, the better part of my life.
OEDIPUS: Where, mostly? Where did you do your grazing?
SHEPHERD: Well,   1235
    Cithaeron sometimes, or the foothills round about.
OEDIPUS: This man — you know him? ever see him there?
SHEPHERD:

Confused, glancing from the Messenger to the King.

    Doing what — what man do you mean?
OEDIPUS:

Pointing to the Messenger.

    This one here — ever have dealings with him?
SHEPHERD: Not so I could say, but give me a chance,   1240
    my memory's bad . . .
MESSENGER: No wonder he doesn't know me, master.
    But let me refresh his memory for him.
    I'm sure he recalls old times we had

on the slopes of Mount Cithaeron;   124&
he and I, grazing our flocks, he with two
and I with one — we both struck up together,
three whole seasons, six months at a stretch
from spring to the rising of Arcturus° in the fall,
then with winter coming on I'd drive my herds   1250
to my own pens, and back he'd go with his
to Laius' folds.

To the Shepherd.

      Now that's how it was,
wasn't it — yes or no?
SHEPHERD: Yes, I suppose . . .
it's all so long ago.
MESSENGER: Come, tell me,
you gave me a child back then, a boy, remember?   1255
A little fellow to rear, my very own.
SHEPHERD: What? Why rake up that again?
MESSENGER: Look, here he is, my fine old friend —
the same man who was just a baby then.
SHEPHERD: Damn you, shut your mouth — quiet!
OEDIPUS: Don't lash out at him, old man —   1260
you need lashing more than he does.
SHEPHERD: Why,
master, majesty — what have I done wrong?
OEDIPUS: You won't answer his question about the boy.
SHEPHERD: He's talking nonsense, wasting his breath.   1265
OEDIPUS: So, you won't talk willingly —
then you'll talk with pain.

The guards seize the Shepherd.

SHEPHERD: No, dear god, don't torture an old man!
OEDIPUS: Twist his arms back, quickly!
SHEPHERD: God help us, why? —
what more do you need to know?   1270
OEDIPUS: Did you give him that child? He's asking.
SHEPHERD: I did . . . I wish to god I'd died that day.
OEDIPUS: You've got your wish if you don't tell the truth.
SHEPHERD: The more I tell, the worse the death I'll die.
OEDIPUS: Our friend here wants to stretch things out, does he?   1275

Motioning to his men for torture.

SHEPHERD: No, no, I gave it to him — I just said so.
OEDIPUS: Where did you get it? Your house? Someone else's?
SHEPHERD: It wasn't mine, no, I got it from . . . someone.

1249. Arcturus: A star whose rising marked the end of summer.

OEDIPUS: Which one of them?

Looking at the citizens.

Whose house?

SHEPHERD: No — 1280
god's sake, master, no more questions!

OEDIPUS: You're a dead man if I have to ask again.

SHEPHERD: Then — the child came from the house . . .
of Laius.

OEDIPUS: A slave? or born of his own blood?

SHEPHERD: Oh no,
I'm right at the edge, the horrible truth — I've got to say it!

OEDIPUS: And I'm at the edge of hearing horrors, yes, but I must hear! 1285

SHEPHERD: All right! His son, they said it was — his son!
But the one inside, your wife,
she'd tell it best.

OEDIPUS: My wife —
she gave it to you? 1290

SHEPHERD: Yes, yes, my king.

OEDIPUS: Why, what for?

SHEPHERD: To kill it.

OEDIPUS: Her own child,
how could she? 1295

SHEPHERD: She was afraid —
frightening prophecies.

OEDIPUS: What?

SHEPHERD: They said —
he'd kill his parents.

OEDIPUS: But you gave him to this old man — why? 1300

SHEPHERD: I pitied the little baby, master,
hoped he'd take him off to his own country,
far away, but he saved him for this, this fate.
If you are the man he says you are, believe me,
you were born for pain.

OEDIPUS: O god — 1305
all come true, all burst to light!
O light — now let me look my last on you!
I stand revealed at last —
cursed in my birth, cursed in marriage,
cursed in the lives I cut down with these hands! 1310

*Rushing through the doors with a great cry. The Corinthian Messenger, the Shepherd,
and attendants exit slowly to the side.*

CHORUS: O the generations of men
the dying generations — adding the total
of all your lives I find they come to nothing . . .
does there exist, is there a man on earth
who seizes more joy than just a dream, a vision? 1315

And the vision no sooner dawns than dies
blazing into oblivion.

You are my great example, you, your life,
your destiny, Oedipus, man of misery —
I count no man blest.

     You outranged all men!   132
   Bending your bow to the breaking-point
you captured priceless glory, O dear god,
and the Sphinx came crashing down,
     the virgin, claws hooked
like a bird of omen singing, shrieking death —   132
like a fortress reared in the face of death
you rose and saved our land.

From that day on we called you king
we crowned you with honors, Oedipus, towering over all —
mighty king of the seven gates of Thebes.   133

But now to hear your story — is there a man more agonized?
More wed to pain and frenzy? Not a man on earth,
the joy of your life ground down to nothing
O Oedipus, name for the ages —
   one and the same wide harbor served you   133
     son and father both
son and father came to rest in the same bridal chamber.
How, how could the furrows your father plowed
bear you, your agony, harrowing on
in silence O so long?

     But now for all your power   134
Time, all-seeing Time has dragged you to the light,
judged your marriage monstrous from the start —
the son and the father tangling, both one —
O child of Laius, would to god
   I'd never seen you, never never!   134
   Now I weep like a man who wails the dead
and the dirge comes pouring forth with all my heart!
I tell you the truth, you gave me life
my breath leapt up in you
and now you bring down night upon my eyes.   135

Enter a Messenger from the palace.

MESSENGER: Men of Thebes, always the first in honor,
  what horrors you will hear, what you will see,
  what a heavy weight of sorrow you will shoulder . . .
  if you are true to your birth, if you still have
  some feeling for the royal house of Thebes.   135
  I tell you neither the waters of the Danube
  nor the Nile can wash this palace clean.

Such things it hides, it soon will bring to light —
terrible things, and none done blindly now,
all done with a will. The pains   1360
we inflict upon ourselves hurt most of all.
LEADER: God knows we have pains enough already.
What can you add to them?
MESSENGER: The queen is dead.
LEADER: Poor lady — how?
MESSENGER: By her own hand. But you are spared the worst,   1365
you never had to watch . . . I saw it all,
and with all the memory that's in me
you will learn what that poor woman suffered.

Once she'd broken in through the gates,
dashing past us, frantic, whipped to fury,   1370
ripping her hair out with both hands —
straight to her rooms she rushed, flinging herself
across the bridal-bed, doors slamming behind her —
once inside, she wailed for Laius, dead so long,
remembering how she bore his child long ago,   1375
the life that rose up to destroy him, leaving
its mother to mother living creatures
with the very son she'd borne.
Oh how she wept, mourning the marriage-bed
where she let loose that double brood — monsters —   1380
husband by her husband, children by her child.
                                        And then —
but how she died is more than I can say. Suddenly
Oedipus burst in, screaming, he stunned us so
we couldn't watch her agony to the end,
our eyes were fixed on him. Circling   1385
like a maddened beast, stalking, here, there
crying out to us —
                        Give him a sword! His wife,
no wife, his mother, where can he find the mother earth
that cropped two crops at once, himself and all his children?
He was raging — one of the dark powers pointing the way,   1390
none of us mortals crowding around him, no,
with a great shattering cry — someone, something leading him on —
he hurled at the twin doors and bending the bolts back
out of their sockets, crashed through the chamber.
And there we saw the woman hanging by the neck,   1395
cradled high in a woven noose, spinning,
swinging back and forth. And when he saw her,
giving a low, wrenching sob that broke our hearts,
slipping the halter from her throat, he eased her down,
in a slow embrace he laid her down, poor thing . . .   1400
then, what came next, what horror we beheld!

He rips off her brooches, the long gold pins
holding her robes — and lifting them high,
looking straight up into the points,
he digs them down the sockets of his eyes, crying, "You, 1405
you'll see no more the pain I suffered, all the pain I caused!
Too long you looked on the ones you never should have seen,
blind to the ones you longed to see, to know! Blind
from this hour on! Blind in the darkness — blind!"
His voice like a dirge, rising, over and over 1410
raising the pins, raking them down his eyes.
And at each stroke blood spurts from the roots,
splashing his beard, a swirl of it, nerves and clots —
black hail of blood pulsing, gushing down.

These are the griefs that burst upon them both, 1415
coupling man and woman. The joy they had so lately,
the fortune of their old ancestral house
was deep joy indeed. Now, in this one day,
wailing, madness and doom, death, disgrace,
all the griefs in the world that you can name, 1420
all are theirs forever.

LEADER: Oh poor man, the misery —
has he any rest from pain now?

A voice within, in torment.

MESSENGER: He's shouting,
"Loose the bolts, someone, show me to all of Thebes!
My father's murderer, my mother's — "
No, I can't repeat it, it's unholy.
Now he'll tear himself from his native earth, 1425
not linger, curse the house with his own curse.
But he needs strength, and a guide to lead him on.
This is sickness more than he can bear.

The palace doors open.

Look,
he'll show you himself. The great doors are opening — 1430
you are about to see a sight, a horror
even his mortal enemy would pity.

Enter Oedipus, blinded, led by a boy. He stands at the palace steps, as if surveying his people once again.

CHORUS: O the terror —
the suffering, for all the world to see,
the worst terror that ever met my eyes.
What madness swept over you? What god, 1435
what dark power leapt beyond all bounds,
beyond belief, to crush your wretched life? —
godforsaken, cursed by the gods!

I pity you but I can't bear to look.
I've much to ask, so much to learn, 1440
so much fascinates my eyes,
but you . . . I shudder at the sight.

OEDIPUS: Oh, Ohhh —
the agony! I am agony —
where am I going? where on earth?
            where does all this agony hurl me? 1445
where's my voice? —
            winging, swept away on a dark tide —
My destiny, my dark power, what a leap you made!

CHORUS: To the depths of terror, too dark to hear, to see.

OEDIPUS: Dark, horror of darkness 1450
my darkness, drowning, swirling around me
crashing wave on wave — unspeakable, irresistible
            headwind, fatal harbor! Oh again,
the misery, all at once, over and over
the stabbing daggers, stab of memory 1455
raking me insane.

CHORUS: No wonder you suffer
twice over, the pain of your wounds,
the lasting grief of pain.

OEDIPUS: Dear friend, still here?
Standing by me, still with a care for me,
the blind man? Such compassion, 1460
            loyal to the last. Oh it's you,
I know you're here, dark as it is
I'd know you anywhere, your voice —
it's yours, clearly yours.

CHORUS: Dreadful, what you've done . . .
how could you bear it, gouging out your eyes? 1465
What superhuman power drove you on?

OEDIPUS: Apollo, friends, Apollo —
he ordained my agonies — these, my pains on pains!
But the hand that struck my eyes was mine,
mine alone — no one else — 1470
            I did it all myself!
What good were eyes to me?
Nothing I could see could bring me joy.

CHORUS: No, no, exactly as you say.

OEDIPUS: What can I ever see?
What love, what call of the heart 1475
can touch my ears with joy? Nothing, friends.
Take me away, far, far from Thebes,
            quickly, cast me away, my friends —
this great murderous ruin, this man cursed to heaven,
the man the deathless gods hate most of all! 1480

CHORUS: Pitiful, you suffer so, you understand so much . . .
    I wish you'd never known.
OEDIPUS: Die, die —
    whoever he was that day in the wilds
    who cut my ankles free of the ruthless pins,
        he pulled me clear of death, he saved my life   1485
        for this, this kindness —
                Curse him, kill him!
    If I'd died then, I'd never have dragged myself,
    my loved ones through such hell.
CHORUS: Oh if only . . . would to god.
OEDIPUS: I'd never have come to this,   1490
    my father's murderer — never been branded
    mother's husband, all men see me now! Now,
        loathed by the gods, son of the mother I defiled
        coupling in my father's bed, spawning lives in the loins
    that spawned my wretched life. What grief can crown this grief?   1495
        It's mine alone, my destiny — I am Oedipus!
CHORUS: How can I say you've chosen for the best?
    Better to die than be alive and blind.
OEDIPUS: What I did was best — don't lecture me,
    no more advice. I, with *my* eyes,
    how could I look my father in the eyes   1500
    when I go down to death? Or mother, so abused . . .
    I've done such things to the two of them,
    crimes too huge for hanging.
                  Worse yet,
    the sight of my children, born as they were born,   1505
    how could I long to look into their eyes?
    No, not with these eyes of mine, never.
    Not this city either, her high towers,
    the sacred glittering images of her gods —
    I am misery! I, her best son, reared   1510
    as no other son of Thebes was ever reared,
    I've stripped myself, I gave the command myself.
    All men must cast away the great blasphemer,
    the curse now brought to light by the gods,
    the son of Laius — I, my father's son!   1515

    Now I've exposed my guilt, horrendous guilt,
    could I train a level glance on you, my countrymen?
    Impossible! No, if I could just block off my ears,
    the springs of hearing, I would stop at nothing —
    I'd wall up my loathsome body like a prison,   1520
    blind to the sound of life, not just the sight.
    Oblivion — what a blessing . . .
    for the mind to dwell a world away from pain.

O Cithaeron, why did you give me shelter?
Why didn't you take me, crush my life out on the spot? 1525
I'd never have revealed my birth to all mankind.

O Polybus, Corinth, the old house of my fathers,
so I believed — what a handsome prince you raised —
under the skin, what sickness to the core.
Look at me! Born of outrage, outrage to the core. 1530

O triple roads — it all comes back, the secret,
dark ravine, and the oaks closing in
where the three roads join . . .
You drank my father's blood, my own blood
spilled by my own hands — you still remember me? 1535
What things you saw me do? Then I came here
and did them all once more!

        Marriages! O marriage,
you gave me birth, and once you brought me into the world
you brought my sperm rising back, springing to light
fathers, brothers, sons — one deadly breed — 1540
brides, wives, mothers. The blackest things
a man can do, I have done them all!

          No more —
it's wrong to name what's wrong to do. Quickly,
for the love of god, hide me somewhere,
kill me, hurl me into the sea 1545
where you can never look on me again.

Beckoning to the Chorus as they shrink away.

           Closer,
it's all right. Touch the man of sorrow.
Do. Don't be afraid. My troubles are mine
and I am the only man alive who can sustain them.

Enter Creon from the palace, attended by palace guards.

LEADER: Put your requests to Creon. Here he is, 1550
    just when we need him. He'll have a plan, he'll act.
    Now that he's the sole defense of the country
    in your place.
OEDIPUS: Oh no, what can I say to him?
    How can I ever hope to win his trust?
    I wronged him so, just now, in every way. 1555
    You must see that — I was so wrong, so wrong.
CREON: I haven't come to mock you, Oedipus,
    or to criticize your former failings.

Turning to the guards.

          You there,
have you lost all respect for human feeling?

At least revere the Sun, the holy fire 1560
 that keeps us all alive. Never expose a thing
 of guilt and holy dread so great it appalls
 the earth, the rain from heaven, the light of day!
 Get him into the halls — quickly as you can.
 Piety demands no less. Kindred alone 1565
 should see a kinsman's shame. This is obscene.
OEDIPUS: Please, in god's name . . . you wipe my fears away,
 coming so generously to me, the worst of men.
 Do one thing more, for your sake, not mine.
CREON: What do you want? Why so insistent?
OEDIPUS: Drive me out of the land at once, far from sight, 1570
 where I can never hear a human voice.
CREON: I'd have done that already, I promise you.
 First I wanted the god to clarify my duties.
OEDIPUS: The god? His command was clear, every word: 1575
 death for the father-killer, the curse —
 he said destroy me!
CREON: So he did. Still, in such a crisis
 it's better to ask precisely what to do.
OEDIPUS: You'd ask the oracle about a man like me?
CREON: By all means. And this time, I assume, 1580
 even you will obey the god's decrees.
OEDIPUS: I will,
 I will. And you, I command you — I beg you . . .
 the woman inside, bury her as you see fit.
 It's the only decent thing,
 to give your own the last rites. As for me, 1585
 never condemn the city of my fathers
 to house my body, not while I'm alive, no,
 let me live on the mountains, on Cithaeron,
 my favorite haunt, I have made it famous.
 Mother and father marked out that rock 1590
 to be my everlasting tomb — buried alive.
 Let me die there, where they tried to kill me.
 Oh but this I know: no sickness can destroy me,
 nothing can. I would never have been saved
 from death — I have been saved 1595
 for something great and terrible, something strange.
 Well let my destiny come and take me on its way!

 About my children, Creon, the boys at least,
 don't burden yourself. They're men;
 wherever they go, they'll find the means to live. 1600
 But my two daughters, my poor helpless girls,
 clustering at our table, never without me
 hovering near them . . . whatever I touched,
 they always had their share. Take care of them, 1605

I beg you. Wait, better — permit me, would you?
Just to touch them with my hands and take
our fill of tears. Please . . . my king.
Grant it, with all your noble heart.
If I could hold them, just once, I'd think   1610
I had them with me, like the early days
when I could see their eyes.

Antigone and Ismene, two small children, are led in from the palace by a nurse.

                          What's that?
O god! Do I really hear you sobbing? —
my two children. Creon, you've pitied me?
Sent me my darling girls, my own flesh and blood!   1615
Am I right?

CREON: Yes, it's my doing.
I know the joy they gave you all these years,
the joy you must feel now.

OEDIPUS: Bless you, Creon!
May god watch over you for this kindness,
better than he ever guarded me.
                       Children, where are you?   1620
Here, come quickly —

Groping for Antigone and Ismene, who approach their father cautiously, then embrace him.

                     Come to these hands of mine,
your brother's hands, your own father's hands
that served his once bright eyes so well —
that made them blind. Seeing nothing, children,
knowing nothing, I became your father,   1625
I fathered you in the soil that gave me life.

How I weep for you — I cannot see you now . . .
just thinking of all your days to come, the bitterness,
the life that rough mankind will thrust upon you.
Where are the public gatherings you can join,   1630
the banquets of the clans? Home you'll come,
in tears, cut off from the sight of it all,
the brilliant rites unfinished.
And when you reach perfection, ripe for marriage,
who will he be, my dear ones? Risking all   1635
to shoulder the curse that weighs down my parents,
yes and you too — that wounds us all together.
What more misery could you want?
Your father killed his father, sowed his mother,
one, one and the selfsame womb sprang you —   1640
he cropped the very roots of his existence.
Such disgrace, and you must bear it all!
Who will marry you then? Not a man on earth.

Your doom is clear: you'll wither away to nothing,
single, without a child.

Turning to Creon.

Oh Creon,   1645
you are the only father they have now . . .
we who brought them into the world
are gone, both gone at a stroke —
Don't let them go begging, abandoned,
women without men. Your own flesh and blood!   1650
Never bring them down to the level of my pains.
Pity them. Look at them, so young, so vulnerable,
shorn of everything — you're their only hope.
Promise me, noble Creon, touch my hand.

Reaching toward Creon, who draws back.

You, little ones, if you were old enough   1655
to understand, there is much I'd tell you.
Now, as it is, I'd have you say a prayer.
Pray for life, my children,
live where you are free to grow and season.
Pray god you find a better life than mine,   1660
the father who begot you.

CREON: Enough.
You've wept enough. Into the palace now.

OEDIPUS: I must, but I find it very hard.

CREON: Time is the great healer, you will see.

OEDIPUS: I am going — you know on what condition?   1665

CREON: Tell me. I'm listening.

OEDIPUS: Drive me out of Thebes, in exile.

CREON: Not I. Only the gods can give you that.

OEDIPUS: Surely the gods hate me so much —

CREON: You'll get your wish at once.

OEDIPUS: You consent?   1670

CREON: I try to say what I mean; it's my habit.

OEDIPUS: Then take me away. It's time.

CREON: Come along, let go of the children.

OEDIPUS: No —
don't take them away from me, not now! No no no!

*Clutching his daughters as the guards wrench them loose and take them through the
palace doors.*

CREON: Still the king, the master of all things?   1675
No more: here your power ends.
None of your power follows you through life.

*Exit Oedipus and Creon to the palace. The Chorus comes forward to address the audi-
ence directly.*

CHORUS: People of Thebes, my countrymen, look on Oedipus.

He solved the famous riddle with his brilliance,
he rose to power, a man beyond all power.
Who could behold his greatness without envy?
Now what a black sea of terror has overwhelmed him.
Now as we keep our watch and wait the final day,
count no man happy till he dies, free of pain at last.

Exit in procession.

1680

ೞ

NŌ DRAMA — *the word nō means "accomplishment" or "perfect art" — achieved its classic form in Japan during the fifteenth century. Thousands of Nō plays exist, but only about two hundred of them are performed in the modern repertoire. The playwright Zeami (pronounced zay-ah-mee; 1363–1443) is credited with creating classic Nō drama. The son of the early Nō actor and playwright Kan'ami (1333–1384), Zeami was educated at court as the protégé of the shogun ruler in Kyoto. Some historians have speculated that Zeami could have written Kantan near the end of his life, but it also could be the work of his talented son-in-law, the playwright Komparu Zenchiku (1405–1468). Kantan was first performed in 1464.*

Like the classic Greek drama, Nō plays were shaped by the religious belief of their time. In medieval Japan, religion meant early Buddhism, which is concerned with spiritual or psychological wholeness. The young man in Kantan seeks enlightenment so that he will know the proper way to live. If the essential quality of Greek drama as manifest in the plays of Sophocles is a theater of action, then the Nō drama — with its formal, measured sequences of poetry, music, and dance — can be described as a theater of contemplation. The plot of a Nō play does not involve resolving opposition (as when Oedipus must come to terms with his fate) or personal conflict between individuals (as when Oedipus suspects Creon of wanting to become king). Instead, Nō is a poetic theater of symbols. The scholar Yasuo Nakamura has observed that the actors in a Nō play "invite the detached contemplation of the audience. Since they are not, in the Western sense, characters, but types (and are so conceived by the actors), sympathetic involvement, as with actors who portray 'real people,' is impossible."

Like the classic Greek actors in Sophocles' time, all roles in the Nō theater were performed by men, often artfully masked and elaborately costumed. This was an elite theater, unlike the popular theater of the Greeks and Elizabethans. The Japanese playwrights' and actors' sophisticated fusion of music, dance, and poetry was supported by wealthy patrons. Surviving with little modification to the present time, the traditional Nō stage is an indoor raised square platform about nineteen feet square bounded by four pillars, with the audience seated both at the front and side of the stage. A bridgeway runs from upstage right back to the dressing room, serving as an entrance and exit passage.

Onstage behind the actors, in view of the audience, are the musicians who accompany the performance, a flute player and two or three drummers, whose eerie cries are part of the music. The members of the speaking chorus, who describe the scene and interpret the action while never getting involved in the action (as does the chorus in a Greek play), have a stationary position seated to the right onstage. The actors' voices move around a few basic pitches, and they sing their lines of poetry in vocal patterns against the rhythms played by the musicians. During the performance the spectator senses constant, subtle changes in tempo, corresponding to the Buddhist view that the world is in a state of continual flux. Because the actors' delivery of their lines to music is slow, and the dances can be prolonged to nearly any length, a staged play can last for hours as an elegant sequence of sights and sounds, although the Nō texts are short.

In classic Nō drama the center of attention is always called the shite *(pronounced* shee-tay*), or "actor," who sings and dances his portrayal of the leading character. Other performers are the* waki *(pronounced* wah-kee*), a "person on the side" or "witness," and the* ai *(pronounced* eye*), or "interlude," who represents a minor character, often of lower social rank. Sometimes this was an actor from the comic Kyogen plays that followed the performance of the Nō plays as the Greek tragedies were followed by comic satyr plays. In* Kantan, *the woman who keeps the inn and introduces the stage action is the* ai; *the Imperial Envoy who brings news of good fortune to the young man Rosei is the* waki, *and Rosei is the masked* shite, *speaking in prose and verse and sometimes singing his lines in the meter of classical Japanese poetry. Often in a Nō play, as in* Kantan, *the* shite *is engaged in a quest to give up final attachments to worldly things, and he is helped in this quest by the* waki. *There are several different categories of Nō plays, defined by the* shite's *role as a god, a warrior, a woman, or other character.*

The Nō theater was first discovered by Western readers during the Meiji era (1868–1912), most notably when the scholar Ernest Fenollosa began to translate Japanese texts that were later finished by the American poet Ezra Pound. In 1916 the Irish poet and dramatist William Butler Yeats wrote a commentary on Certain Noble Plays of Japan, *which included an anecdote about the tradition of the classic Nō actors that Pound had found among the Fenollosa manuscripts. The story suggests that a version of Constantin Stanislavsky's "Method acting," which developed in the European theater a half century later, might have first been practiced in Japan:*

> *A young man was following a stately old woman through the streets of a Japanese town, and presently she turned to him and spoke: "Why do you follow me?" "Because you are so interesting." But he wished, he told her, to become a player of old women on the Nō stage. If he would become famous as a Nō player, she said, he must not observe life, nor put on an old voice and stint the music of his voice. He must know how to suggest an old woman and yet find it all in the heart.*

As Zeami wrote in one of his dissertations on the Nō theater, an actor must understand that the audience was an essential element in the drama. Zeami wrote that for the Nō actor, "one's figure seen from the viewpoint of the audience is the 'view from without,' while one's own figure seen with one's own eyes is the 'view from within.' " In order for the actor to observe himself with the "view from without," he must become one with the audience. At that time he "will be able to actually see himself clearly."

Kantan is one of the Nō plays set in ancient China, as the translator Royall Tyler points out, because "Chinese literature and art were important to many fifteenth-century" cultured patrons of Nō. The source of the text is a fictional work of the T'ang dynasty well known to the audience, but the Japanese playwright added his own touch by making enlightenment, not material wealth and success, the object of Rosei's quest. Tyler adds that "the moment (near the end of the play) when Rosei races

*to lie down on the pillow before he wakes is now famous, but pre-nineteenth-century
staging was much less dramatic."*

RELATED PLAYS: *Samuel Beckett,* Krapp's Last Tape, *page 1696; David Henry
Hwang,* As the Crow Flies, *page 1950.*

RELATED COMMENTARY: *Yasunari Takahashi, "Samuel Beckett and the Nō,"
page 2026.*

Kantan

c. 1464

TRANSLATED BY ROYALL TYLER

PERSONS IN ORDER OF APPEARANCE

A woman, *the* INNKEEPER	*ai*
ROSEI, *a young man* (Kantan-otoka *mask*)	*shite*
AN IMPERIAL ENVOY	*waki*
TWO PALANQUIN-BEARERS	*wakizure*
THREE IMPERIAL MINISTERS	*wakizure*
A DANCER	*kokata*

Stage assistant places a "palace" (a roofed dais) in witness square.
Enter Innkeeper, carrying the Pillow of Kantan. She stands in base square.

INNKEEPER: You see before you one whose home is the village of Kantan, in
China. Ryōsen'ō is my name.° For a long time now I have been giving
lodging to those who pass by on the road. A monk who once stayed here
was practising the arts of the Immortals and he gave me a wondrous pillow. One who merely dozes off on this pillow awakens to the truth of
past and future. I call it the Pillow of Kantan, and I offer it to travellers
for their use. If a traveller comes by, I will invite him to stay. Take heed,
good people! I will have him in to stay!

She places the pillow on the dais and withdraws to villager position.

*To music, enter Rosei, carrying a "Chinese" fan in his right hand and a rosary
in his left. He stands in base square, at first facing back of stage, then turning to face
audience to say his name.*

ROSEI: Lost on the journey of this dreary life
　　　　　lost on the journey of this dreary life,
　　　　　how long have I to tread the path of dreams?
You have before you a young man named Rosei. My home is in the land
of Shoku. Although born as a human being, I do not aspire to follow the
Buddha, but instead only fritter my life away.° However, I understand
that a holy sage resides upon Flying Sheep Mountain in the land of So. I
am therefore hastening toward Flying Sheep Mountain, to seek enlight-
ment from him.

Ryōsen'ō is my name: In modern performances (the text of this speech dates from the eighteenth century) the Innkeeper does not have a name. Ryōsen'ō is actually one of the names of
the Taoist adept who gives the seeker the pillow in some of the source versions of the story.
aspire . . . away: Buddhahood can be attained only from birth as a human being, and this
birth is supremely rare.

The home I know so well
vanishes behind me in the clouds
vanishes behind me in the clouds,
while I cross the mountains, range on range,
unsure what lies ahead. In travel wear,
I lodge where night finds me, in the fields,
among the hills or in a lonely village,
till Kantan, once simply a name,   *Mimes walking.*
lies before me, for I have arrived
lies before me, for I have arrived.

Having come so swiftly, I have already reached the village of Kantan. The sun is still high in the sky, but I will none the less seek lodging here. I beg your pardon!

Innkeeper rises and comes to first pine.

INNKEEPER: Are you a traveller? Where are you going?

ROSEI: My name is Rosei and I am from the land of Shoku. Although born as a human being, I do not aspire to follow the Buddha, but instead only fritter my life away. So I have come to find the holy sage who resides upon Flying Sheep Mountain. I wish to seek enlightenment from him.

INNKEEPER: My goodness, you have certainly come a long way! Well, once a monk stayed here. He was practising the arts of the Immortals, and he gave me a wondrous pillow called the Pillow of Kantan. One who dozes off a moment on this pillow awakens to the truth of past and future. Rest your head upon this pillow, then, and wait to dream.

Rosei steps onto the dais, goes down on one knee, and gazes at the pillow.

ROSEI: So this is the celebrated Pillow of Kantan!
Now I shall set out to know the truth,
testing this pillow and the sacred dream
that Heaven no doubt will vouchsafe to me.
Refuge I sought, from a passing shower°

CHORUS: refuge I sought, from a passing shower,
at a wayside inn, though day remained;
and now, to sleep a while and dream,
I lie down on the Pillow of Kantan
I lie down on the Pillow of Kantan.

Rosei lies down on his back, head on the pillow, and covers his face with his fan.
Enter Envoy, followed by Palanquin-Bearers. Envoy kneels, raps dais near the pillow with his fan, then retreats to centre where he kneels again and bows low.

ENVOY: Pardon me, Rosei, if you please. I have a message for you.

Rosei rises.

Refuge . . . shower: A reference to the story of Saigyō and the Harlot of Eguchi, explained in the introduction to *Eguchi.*

ROSEI: Who are you?
ENVOY: Sir, I am a royal envoy, and it is my duty to inform you that the King of
So wishes to cede you his throne.
ROSEI: What astonishing news! Why in the world should I occupy his throne?
ENVOY: How should I fathom his reasons, sir? You are to rule the kingdom. No
doubt you are endowed with certain auspicious signs. Please lose no
time. Enter this palanquin.

ROSEI:	How it gleams and sparkles, as though dew	
ENVOY:	shone in slanting sun! This palanquin,	
ROSEI:	wholly new to me, will take me now	*Sits up, drops rosary.*
ENVOY:	to glory you had never thought to gain	
ROSEI:	and lift me to the skies,	
ENVOY:	so you will feel.	
CHORUS:	Entering this jewelled palanquin	

Rosei steps off dais and comes to centre, where, in concert with Palanquin-Bearers, he mimes entering the palanquin. Envoy stands behind him.

> entering this jewelled palanquin,
> I set out on the way, yet unaware
> the flower of happy fortune is a dream,
> and wondering that I should rise above the clouds
> to reign as king.

Exeunt Envoy and Palanquin-Bearers.
> *To music, enter Dancer and Court Officials. They sit along the side of stage.*

> O how glad, how glorious a vision!
> O how glad, how glorious a vision!
> High beyond the clouds there tower now,
> bright beneath an all-illumining moon,
> the Cloud-Dragon Hall, the Abō Palace,°
> gleaming in a flood of radiance.
> And behold an equally wondrous scene:
> a park spread with gold and silver sand,
> walled in the four directions. Four jewelled gates
> admit or bid farewell to happy folk
> clothed in light. Surely, the far-famed
> City of Glory, or the Fair Citadel,°
> offer no more perfect loveliness
> than this sight so welcome to the eyes!
> Lords of a thousand or a myriad households
> pour in, bearing a thousand or a myriad gems,

Cloud-Dragon . . . Palace: "Cloud-Dragon Hall" evokes an idealized imperial residence. The Abō (A-fang) Palace belonged to China's first emperor, Ch'in-shih-huang-ti (third century B.C.).
City . . . Citadel: Palaces in the Buddha Amida's Western Paradise and in the Tōri Heaven at the summit of Mount Sumeru, the central mountain of the Buddhist cosmos.

> treasures innumerable, as offerings.
> Their banners paint the heavens, and on earth
> resound like thunder; while with mighty voice
> the multitude roars out tumultuous praise
> the multitude roars out tumultuous praise.

ROSEI: To the east, three hundred cubits high,°

CHORUS: stands a mountain all of purest silver,
> surmounted by a risen sun of gold.

ROSEI: To the west, three hundred cubits tall,

CHORUS: rises a mountain made of purest gold,
> surmounted by a risen silver sun.
> The Hall of Life Eternal harbours
> springs and autumns beyond reckoning,
> and before the Gate of Everlasting Youth,
> sun and moon barely move:
> surely these inspired the present scene!

Envoy bows to Rosei.

MINISTER: Forgive my rude interruption, Your Majesty, but you have now sat
on the throne for fifty years. Be good enough to drink this Elixir of the
Immortals, and you will enjoy a thousand years of life. I have brought
you on this occasion the Heavenly Elixir and the Goblet of Celestial
Dew.

ROSEI: This Heavenly Elixir, of which you speak,

MINISTER: is the wine that the Immortals drink.

ROSEI: And the Goblet of Celestial Dew,

MINISTER: likewise, is the cup they drain in joy.

ROSEI: And this wine confers a thousand years,

MINISTER: yes, ten thousand springs in high estate,

ROSEI: the Sovereign having wealth,

MINISTER: the people, ease,

*With his fan, Minister mimes pouring wine for Dancer, who then goes to Rosei and
does the same. Rosei receives the wine on his fan.*

CHORUS: the realm, peace, and, forever more
> the realm, peace, and, forever more,
> fullness of happy fortune,
> joy increasing through all future time:
> those blessings the chrysanthemum wine°
> brings to all. Come, pass it lightly round!

ROSEI: Pass the cup!

Below, as Chorus sings, Dancer performs a "dream dance."

To . . . high: This scene is based on a passage in *Heike monogatari* about a palace associated
with Ch'in-shih-huang-ti. The lines about the Hall of Life Eternal and the Gate of Everlasting
Youth are from a congratulatory couplet in the *Wakan rōei shū* ("A Collection of Japanese and
Chinese Poems for Chanting Aloud," 1013).

those . . . wine: The chrysanthemum is the flower of long life.

CHORUS: O pass the cup, I say,
that clear, chrysanthemum waters
speed on down the stream, till eager hands
dart from sleeves gay with chrysanthemums
to pick it up again:° a swaying dance
of graceful, sweeping gesture, as of light;
while, aloft, the round and radiant moon
circles in the everlasting sky.

DANGER: O silver dew

CHORUS: O silver dew
that from my chyrsanthemums
drops day by day,
what aeons will you need
to fill the deep?°
Never shall these blessed waters fail,
flowing as they do from healing springs
that yield all their bounty, without end.
O how they gush forth, with might renewed!
One who drinks, savours the dews of Heaven,
waxes glad, and fain would leap for joy,
as pleasure merges night into bright day.
Happiness, delight, brilliant success:
all these here attain their pinnacle.

Dancer retires to side of stage.

DANCE: *gaku* [*twenty minutes of dance*]

Rosei now performs a gaku *dance, first on the dais, then on the full stage. As text resumes, he continues dancing and miming.*

ROSEI: How long shall the spring of glory last?
Forever and a day,
and longer still.
Just so, the dawn moon lingers in the sky.

ROSEI: He of the moon dances a manly measure,
feathery cloud-sleeves billowing, manifold,
while his song of joy
resounds night-long

CHORUS: resounds night-long,
till sunrise bursts upon the world.
I had thought it night

ROSEI: yet day has dawned;

CHORUS: had thought day risen,

ROSEI: yet the moon is bright.

---

to . . . again: An evocation of *kyokusui no en* ("the feast of the meandering waters"), at which cups of wine were set floating down a stream. A participant had to compose a Chinese poem before a cup drifted past, then pluck the cup from the stream and drain it.

O silver dew . . . deep?: A poem by Fujiwara no Motosuke, from the *Shūishū,* a tenth-century imperial anthology.

CHORUS: With spring flowers blooming on the bough,
ROSEI: autumn leaves gather their deep hues.
CHORUS: Ah, here is summer!
ROSEI: No, for snow is falling.
CHORUS: So the seasons turn before my eyes.
spring and summer, autumn, winter;
trees and grasses bloom within a day.
How beautiful, how wondrous a sight!
So time passes and the years slip by
so time passes and the years slip by,
till fifty years of glory reach an end,
and melt away to nothing. They are gone,
for all these things happened in a dream.

Rosei gazes around him, races to the dais, leaps onto it, and lies down.

There upon the Pillow of Kantan,
the sleeper's dream is broken, and he wakes.

Innkeeper comes forward and raps upon the dais, by the pillow.

INNKEEPER: Wake up, traveller! The millet is ready for your meal! Get up now,
get up! *Exit through side door.*

Rosei rises. He dances and mimes as appropriate throughout the final passage.

ROSEI From his dream, Rosei now awakens
CHORUS: From his dream, Rosei now awakens,
fifty springs and falls of glory gone
as though they had not been. Dazed, he rises.
ROSEI: How many they were, before,
CHORUS: the lovely palace ladies' murmuring voices,
ROSEI: that now are wind sighing through the pines.
CHORUS: Halls, pavilions, towers
ROSEI: were a passing lodging at Kantan.
CHORUS: All that time of glory,
ROSEI: fifty years,
CHORUS: was a dream that lasted the short while
ROSEI: millet takes to cook upon a stove.
CHORUS: A wonder, yes, and a mystery!
ROSEI: Pondering at last man's condition,
CHORUS: one sees a hundred years of happiness,
once life is done, are a dream, no more.
Fifty brilliant years are over now.
Hopes for future glory or great age,
all the joys five decades offered him,
have fled, now that he has reigned on high.
All things are a dream while millet cooks.
ROSEI: All hail, the Three Treasures!°

---

the Three Treasures!: The Buddha, his teaching, and the fellowship of monks.

CHORUS: Now he understands: the sage he sought,
                  bent on liberation, was this pillow.

Kneels, presses the pillow reverently to his forehead.

                  How great the gift it gave him at Kantan!

Puts pillow down and goes to stand in base square, where he will stamp the final beat.

                  How great the gift it gave him at Kantan,
                  where he has seen the world to be a dream,
                  and, finding his hopes met, now journeys home.

ॐ

WILLIAM SHAKESPEARE *(1564–1616), the great English playwright and poet, was born in Stratford, the third of eight children of Mary Arden, daughter of a prosperous landowner, and John Shakespeare, a glovemaker. We know a little more about Shakespeare's personal life than we know about Sophocles' life two thousand years before. Some forty documents of Shakespeare's time offer details about him, commensurate with his station in life and professional activities. The register of the Stratford parish church documents Shakespeare's baptism and burial, along with the baptisms of his daughter Susanna and his twins, Judith and Hamnet. We also know that in 1582, at the age of eighteen, he married Anne Hathaway in Stratford (she was twenty-six), and that before his death he made a will leaving most of his considerable property to his two daughters (his son, Hamnet, had died at age eleven). Shakespeare willed only his "second best bed" to his wife, whom he apparently left in Stratford with his children when he went off to London to make his fortune in the theater.*

As a young man in London, Shakespeare worked as an actor and playwright, but his first publications were two books of poetry. In 1593, after an outbreak of the plague had closed the London theaters, he published his first poem, Venus and Adonis, *dedicated to his wealthy patron the Earl of Southampton. A year later he published another long narrative poem,* The Rape of Lucrece. *(A third book, his collection of sonnets, was published in 1609.) When the theaters reopened in London at the end of 1594, Shakespeare joined the new Lord Chamberlain's Company, for whom he continued to act and write plays until 1613. The literary historian François Laroque has described the astute way Shakespeare managed his career before his retirement as a wealthy man in Stratford:*

> *The Chamberlain's Men were organized in an unusual manner: the six main actors [including Shakespeare] formed an association in which each was a shareholder, directly receiving part of the takings from performances. The actors were financially independent, paying only rent to the theatre proprietor James Burbage. . . . Shakespeare never changed company, a fact rare enough to be worthy of note. From now on he worked to strengthen his position as both player and playwright. In addition to his acting he wrote an average of two plays a year until 1608, when the pace of theatrical production slackened. The decision early in his career to remain in one place, with one company, enabled him quickly to consolidate his first successes as a writer and to become in his lifetime the most highly sought after dramatist of the Elizabethan and Jacobean stage.*

The exact number of plays written by Shakespeare is unknown, as the practice of his time was for playwrights to collaborate on scripts, often reworking and adapting older material, but thirty-seven plays currently make up the Shakespeare canon. Seven years after his death, thirty-six of his plays were collected by actors in his theater company desirous to honor his memory and to protect his work from unscrupulous publishers. The table of contents in this First Folio edition of 1623 reads, "A Catalogue of the several Comedies, Histories, and Tragedies contained in this Volume." This way of organizing the plays has continued to the present day.

The comedies included, among other plays, The Tempest, The Comedy of Errors, A Midsummer Night's Dream, As You Like It, The Taming of the Shrew, and The Merchant of Venice. The history plays — most of which Shakespeare wrote early in his career, between 1590 and 1597 — included Richard II; Henry IV, Parts 1 and 2; Henry V; Henry VI, Parts 1–3; and Richard III. The tragedies included Romeo and Juliet, Macbeth, King Lear, Othello, and Hamlet. Although eighteen of Shakespeare's plays were published in his lifetime as small books called quartos, no play manuscript used by a printer in this time has survived, so we depend on the work of scholars for the editing of his texts.

The Elizabethan theater flourished during the reign of Elizabeth I and her successor, James I, having its origins in fifteenth-century religious pageants and plays such as The Second Shepherd's Play and Everyman, which were performed by actors who were part of traveling companies. The first permanent theater in England was not built until 1576, only about fifteen years before Shakespeare came to London to begin his career. Toward the end of the sixteenth century, playwrights began to glorify English history, turning to secular material for their subjects. National patriotism was stirred by the defeat of the Spanish Armada, which had failed spectacularly in its attempt to conquer England in 1588. When Shakespeare began to write plays, there were several professional acting companies in London, and we have a good idea of the design of their theaters from the foundations of the Rose Playhouse, excavated in 1988. A reconstruction of the Globe Playhouse, in which Shakespeare once held a one-tenth interest as a partner in the company of the Chamberlain's Men, is due to open in London in 1997. The original structure's thatched roof sported a globe with the Latin inscription totus mundus agit histrionem — "All the world's a stage."

Elizabethan theaters such as the Rose and the Globe, the two largest public theaters in London, were tall buildings, usually round or octagonal, with three tiers of galleries for the spectators. The Globe was located south of the Thames river in a neighborhood famous for its bearbaiting pits, gambling houses, brothels, and theaters. The Globe was the finest playhouse in London, yet its raised, covered stage, which projected into the audience, was so small that no more than a dozen actors could appear at a time. The gallery directly behind the stage was used by musicians or actors (as for the balcony scene in Romeo and Juliet). In the front section of the stage was a trapdoor used for the entrance and disappearance of devils and ghosts, or for burial scenes, as in Hamlet. Actors could also stand under the stage, as in the mention in Hamlet that the "ghost cries under the stage."

Audiences of up to eight hundred people paid a penny each to stand in the uncovered pit to watch the play, with ticket prices increasing up to six pence for a seat in the galleries, which held an additional fifteen hundred spectators. Plays were performed in these public theaters only in daylight, without artificial illumination. As in

Greek and Nō theater, only men were trained as actors, including boys who played women's roles until their voices broke. Shakespeare wrote complex parts for specific actors in his company, such as Richard Burbage, who first played the role of Hamlet. As an actor Shakespeare was not a star performer; probably he played the ghost of the murdered king in productions of Hamlet. *In theater records he was designated a "principal comedian" in 1598, a "principle tragedian" in 1603, and one of the "man players" in 1608.*

On June 29, 1613, soon after Shakespeare's retirement to Stratford, the Globe Playhouse burned to the ground during a performance of his play Henry VIII. *A volley of blank shots fired by an actor onstage set fire to the thatched roof of the galleries. Everyone in the audience escaped unharmed, with the exception of a man whose trousers caught fire in the blaze; according to spectators, he doused the fire in his clothes with a bottle of ale. Thirty years later, all the theaters in England would be torn down by order of Parliament in 1642 and 1644 under Puritan rule.*

While Shakespeare and his generation of gifted contemporaries — Christopher Marlowe, Thomas Kyd, and Ben Jonson, to name only a few — were creating their plays, audiences crammed into the theaters six days a week, eager to witness stage spectacles and listen to the players' grandiloquence. Plays such as Hamlet, *which included a ghost, stabbings, suicide, and duels, in addition to rich and complex lines of poetry, were the regular fare of the patrons of the Globe Playhouse. Shakespeare and his company of actors were so successful that they enjoyed royal patronage. They performed for Queen Elizabeth I on the average of three times a year, and it is recorded that King James I was in attendance at the first performance of* Macbeth *in 1604.*

Just as Shakespeare depended on the contemporary historian Raphael Holinshed's chronicles for the material of his English history plays, he used earlier sources as the basis for Hamlet. *He was also influenced by Kyd's* Spanish Tragedy *(c. 1587), which set the standard for a new genre of English plays called "revenge tragedies." In addition, writings by Shakespeare's contemporaries indicate that a "lost play" of* Hamlet *was known to Shakespeare before he wrote his version of the play. In creating their* **revenge tragedies** *(plays in which the plot typically centers on a spectacular attempt to avenge the murder of a family member), Shakespeare and other popular English dramatists took the early Roman playwrights as their models. The Greek playwrights were not popular at the time, but a contemporary account credited Shakespeare with being as polished a writer of comedy and tragedy as the Romans Plautus and Seneca, respectively.*

The extraordinary richness of Shakespeare's theatrical world is made evident in Hamlet. *Unlike other avengers in the revenge tragedies of his time, Hamlet is a complex figure. He plays the multiple roles of son, lover, philosopher, actor, and prince. He questions the reality of his experience, procrastinates in carrying out his promise to avenge his father's death, considers his own failure of will and emotional paralysis, and contemplates suicide. Because most of us can sympathize with his difficult situation, Hamlet is the best known and most often performed of Shakespeare's plays. Actors have offered different interpretations of the role as diverse as Sir John Gielgud's aristocratic, disillusioned Hamlet in 1934 to the young actor Mark Rylance's recent performance of a psychotic Hamlet dressed in striped pajamas, inhabiting the Danish court as if it were a psychiatric hospital. As the critic Edward*

Hubler recognized, "Tragedy of the first order is a rare phenomenon. It came into being in Greece in the fifth century B.C., where it flourished for a while, and it did not
appear again until some two thousand years later when Shakespeare wrote Hamlet
in 1600."

RELATED STORY: *Jorge Luis Borges, "Everything and Nothing," page 96.*

RELATED CASEBOOK: *Saxo Grammaticus, "The Secret Lock of Amleth's Wis-
dom," page 2039; Geoffrey Bullough, "Sources of Shakespeare's Hamlet," page 2041;
H. D. F. Kitto, "Hamlet and the Oedipus," page 2043; François Laroque, "A Review
of Shakespeare Studies," page 2045; John Keats, "From a Letter to George and Thomas
Keats, 21 December 1817," page 2048; Leo Tolstoy, "Shakespeare's Immoral Frame of
Mind," page 2048; Virginia Woolf, "What If Shakespeare Had Had a Sister?," page
2049; T. S. Eliot, "Hamlet and His Problems," page 2051; Jan Kott, "Bertolt Brecht's
Hamlet," page 2055; Bert G. Hornback, "Hamlet's Heroism," page 2057; Tom Stoppard, "Dogg's Hamlet: The Encore," page 2063; Karin S. Coddon, A New Historicist Reading of Hamlet," page 2065.*

WILLIAM SHAKESPEARE

Hamlet, Prince of Denmark

c. 1600

[DRAMATIS PERSONAE

CLAUDIUS, *King of Denmark*
HAMLET, *son to the late and nephew to the present king*
POLONIUS, *lord chamberlain*
HORATIO, *friend to Hamlet*
LAERTES, *son to Polonius*
VOLTIMAND ⎫
CORNELIUS ⎪
ROSENCRANTZ ⎬ *courtiers*
GUILDENSTERN ⎪
OSRIC ⎭
A GENTLEMAN
A PRIEST
MARCELLUS ⎫ *officers*
BERNARDO ⎭
FRANCISCO, *a soldier*
REYNALDO, *servant to Polonius*
PLAYERS
TWO CLOWNS, *grave-diggers*
FORTINBRAS, *Prince of Norway*
A CAPTAIN
ENGLISH AMBASSADORS
GERTRUDE, *Queen of Denmark, and mother to Hamlet*
OPHELIA, *daughter to Polonius*
LORDS, LADIES, OFFICERS, SOLDIERS, SAILORS, MESSENGERS, *and other* ATTENDANTS
GHOST *of Hamlet's father*

SCENE: *Denmark.*]

[ACT I

SCENE I: *Elsinore. A platform° before the castle.*]

Enter Bernardo and Francisco, two sentinels.

BERNARDO: Who's there?

FRANCISCO: Nay, answer me:° stand, and unfold yourself.

BERNARDO: Long live the king!°

FRANCISCO: Bernardo?

BERNARDO: He.   5

FRANCISCO: You come most carefully upon your hour.

BERNARDO: 'Tis now struck twelve; get thee to bed, Francisco.

FRANCISCO: For this relief much thanks: 'tis bitter cold,
    And I am sick at heart.

BERNARDO: Have you had quiet guard?

FRANCISCO: Not a mouse stirring.   10

BERNARDO: Well, good night.
    If you do meet Horatio and Marcellus,
    The rivals° of my watch, bid them make haste.

Enter Horatio and Marcellus.

FRANCISCO: I think I hear them. Stand, ho! Who is there?

HORATIO: Friends to this ground.

MARCELLUS: And liegemen to the Dane.   15

FRANCISCO: Give you° good night.

MARCELLUS: O, farewell, honest soldier:
    Who hath reliev'd you?

FRANCISCO: Bernardo hath my place.
    Give you good night.   *Exit Francisco.*

MARCELLUS: Holla! Bernardo!

BERNARDO: Say,
    What, is Horatio there?

HORATIO: A piece of him.

BERNARDO: Welcome, Horatio: welcome, good Marcellus.   20

MARCELLUS: What, has this thing appear'd again to-night?

BERNARDO: I have seen nothing.

MARCELLUS: Horatio says 'tis but our fantasy,
    And will not let belief take hold of him
    Touching this dreaded sight, twice seen of us: 25
    Therefore I have entreated him along
    With us to watch the minutes of this night;
    That if again this apparition come,
    He may approve° our eyes and speak to it.

ACT I SCENE I   **s.d. platform:** a level space on the battlements of the royal castle at Elsinore, a Danish seaport; now Helsingör. **2. me:** This is emphatic, since Francisco is the sentry. **3. Long live the king:** Either a password or greeting; Horatio and Marcellus use a different one in line 15. **13. rivals:** Partners. **16. Give you:** God give you. **29. approve:** Corroborate.

HORATIO: Tush, tush, 'twill not appear.

BERNARDO: Sit down awhile;   30
  And let us once again assail your ears,
  That are so fortified against our story
  What we have two nights seen.

HORATIO: Well, sit we down,
  And let us hear Bernardo speak of this.

BERNARDO: Last night of all,   35
  When yond same star that's westward from the pole°
  Had made his course t' illume that part of heaven
  Where now it burns, Marcellus and myself,
  The bell then beating one, —

Enter Ghost.

MARCELLUS: Peace, break thee off; look, where it comes again!   40
BERNARDO: In the same figure, like the king that's dead.
MARCELLUS: Thou art a scholar;° speak to it, Horatio.
BERNARDO: Looks 'a not like the king? mark it, Horatio.
HORATIO: Most like: it harrows° me with fear and wonder.
BERNARDO: It would be spoke to.°
MARCELLUS: Speak to it, Horatio.   45
HORATIO: What art thou that usurp'st this time of night,
  Together with that fair and warlike form
  In which the majesty of buried Denmark°
  Did sometimes march? by heaven I charge thee, speak!
MARCELLUS: It is offended.
BERNARDO: See it stalks away!   50
HORATIO: Stay! speak, speak! I charge thee, speak!   *Exit Ghost.*
MARCELLUS: 'Tis gone, and will not answer.
BERNARDO: How now, Horatio! you tremble and look pale:
  Is not this something more than fantasy?
  What think you on 't?   55
HORATIO: Before my God, I might not this believe
  Without the sensible and true avouch
  Of mine own eyes.
MARCELLUS: Is it not like the king?
HORATIO: As thou art to thyself:
  Such was the very armour he had on   60
  When he the ambitious Norway combated;
  So frown'd he once, when, in an angry parle,
  He smote° the sledded Polacks° on the ice.
  'Tis strange.

---

36. pole: Polestar. **42. scholar:** Exorcisms were performed in Latin, which Horatio, as an educated man, would be able to speak. **44. harrows:** Lacerates the feelings. **45. It . . . to:** A ghost could not speak until spoken to. **48. buried Denmark:** The buried king of Denmark. **63. smote:** Defeated; **sledded Polacks:** Polanders using sledges.

MARCELLUS: Thus twice before, and jump° at this dead hour,   65
    With martial stalk hath he gone by our watch.
HORATIO: In what particular thought to work I know not;
    But in the gross and scope° of my opinion,
    This bodes some strange eruption to our state.
MARCELLUS: Good now,° sit down, and tell me, he that knows,   70
    Why this same strict and most observant watch
    So nightly toils° the subject° of the land,
    And why such daily cast° of brazen cannon,
    And foreign mart° for implements of war;
    Why such impress° of shipwrights, whose sore task   75
    Does not divide the Sunday from the week;
    What might be toward, that this sweaty haste
    Doth make the night joint-labourer with the day:
    Who is't that can inform me?
HORATIO: That can I;
    At least, the whisper goes so. Our last king,   80
    Whose image even but now appear'd to us,
    Was, as you know, by Fortinbras of Norway,
    Thereto prick'd on° by a most emulate° pride,
    Dar'd to the combat; in which our valiant Hamlet —
    For so this side of our known world esteem'd him —   85
    Did slay this Fortinbras; who, by a seal'd compact,
    Well ratified by law and heraldry,°
    Did forfeit, with his life, all those his lands
    Which he stood seiz'd° of, to the conqueror:
    Against the which, a moiety competent°   90
    Was gaged by our king; which had return'd
    To the inheritance of Fortinbras,
    Had he been vanquisher; as, by the same comart,°
    And carriage° of the article design'd,
    His fell to Hamlet. Now, sir, young Fortinbras,   95
    Of unimproved° mettle hot and full,°
    Hath in the skirts of Norway here and there
    Shark'd up° a list of lawless resolutes,°
    For food and diet,° to some enterprise
    That hath a stomach in't; which is no other —   100
    As it doth well appear unto our state —
    But to recover of us, by strong hand

---

65. jump: Exactly.   **68. gross and scope:** General drift.   **70. Good now:** An expression denoting entreaty or expostulation.   **72. toils:** Causes or makes to toil; **subject:** People, subjects.   **73. cast:** Casting, founding.   **74. mart:** Buying and selling, traffic.   **75. impress:** Impressment.   **83. prick'd on:** Incited; **emulate:** Rivaling.   **87. law and heraldry:** Heraldic law, governing combat.   **89. seiz'd:** Possessed.   **90. moiety competent:** Adequate or sufficient portion.   **93. comart:** Joint bargain.   **94. carriage:** Import, bearing.   **96. unimproved:** Not turned to account; **hot and full:** Full of fight.   **98. Shark'd up:** Got together in haphazard fashion; **resolutes:** Desperadoes.   **99. food and diet:** No pay but their keep.

And terms compulsatory, those foresaid lands
So by his father lost: and this, I take it,
Is the main motive of our preparations,
The source of this our watch and the chief head   105
Of this post-haste and romage° in the land.

BERNARDO: I think it be no other but e'en so:
Well may it sort° that this portentous figure
Comes armed through our watch; so like the king   110
That was and is the question of these wars.

HORATIO: A mote° it is to trouble the mind's eye.
In the most high and palmy state° of Rome,
A little ere the mightiest Julius fell,
The graves stood tenantless and the sheeted dead   115
Did squeak and gibber in the Roman streets:
As stars with trains of fire° and dews of blood,
Disasters° in the sun; and the moist star°
Upon whose influence Neptune's empire° stands
Was sick almost to doomsday with eclipse: 120
And even the like precurse° of fear'd events,
As harbingers preceding still the fates
And prologue to the omen coming on,
Have heaven and earth together demonstrated
Unto our climatures and countrymen. —   125

Enter Ghost.

But soft, behold! lo, where it comes again!
I'll cross° it, though it blast me. Stay, illusion!
If thou hast any sound, or use of voice,
Speak to me!   *It° spreads his arms.*
If there be any good thing to be done,   130
That may to thee do ease and grace to me,
Speak to me!
If thou art privy to thy country's fate,
Which, happily, foreknowing may avoid,
O, speak!   135
Or if thou hast uphoarded in thy life
Extorted treasure in the womb of earth,
For which, they say, you spirits oft walk in death,   *The cock crows.*
Speak of it:° stay, and speak! Stop it, Marcellus.

MARCELLUS: Shall I strike at it with my partisan?°   140
HORATIO: Do, if it will not stand.

---

107. romage: Bustle, commotion.   **109. sort:** Suit.   **112. mote:** Speck of dust.   **113. palmy state:** Triumphant sovereignty.   **117. stars . . . fire:** I.e., comets.   **118. Disasters:** Unfavorable aspects; **moist star:** The moon, governing tides.   **119. Neptune's empire:** The sea.   **121. precurse:** Heralding.   **127. cross:** Meet, face, thus bringing down the evil influence on the person who crosses it.   **129. It:** The Ghost, or perhaps Horatio.   **133–139. If . . . it:** Horatio recites the traditional reasons why ghosts might walk.   **140. partisan:** Long-handled spear with a blade having lateral projections.

BERNARDO: 'Tis here!

HORATIO: 'Tis here!

MARCELLUS: 'Tis gone!   [*Exit Ghost.*]

    We do it wrong, being so majestical,

    To offer it the show of violence;

    For it is, as the air, invulnerable,   145

    And our vain blows malicious mockery.

BERNARDO: It was about to speak, when the cock crew.°

HORATIO: And then it started like a guilty thing

    Upon a fearful summons. I have heard,

    The cock, that is the trumpet to the morn,   150

    Doth with his lofty and shrill-sounding throat

    Awake the god of day; and, at his warning,

    Whether in sea or fire, in earth or air,

    Th' extravagant and erring° spirit hies

    To his confine:° and of the truth herein   155

    This present object made probation.°

MARCELLUS: It faded on the crowing of the cock.

    Some say that ever 'gainst° that season comes

    Wherein our Saviour's birth is celebrated,

    The bird of dawning singeth all night long: 160

    And then, they say, no spirit dare stir abroad;

    The nights are wholesome; then no planets strike,°

    No fairy takes, nor witch hath power to charm,

    So hallow'd and so gracious° is that time.

HORATIO: So have I heard and do in part believe it.   165

    But, look, the morn, in russet mantle clad,

    Walks o'er the dew of yon high eastward hill:

    Break we our watch up; and by my advice,

    Let us impart what we have seen to-night

    Unto young Hamlet; for, upon my life,   170

    This spirit, dumb to us, will speak to him.

    Do you consent we shall acquaint him with it,

    As needful in our loves, fitting our duty?

MARCELLUS: Let's do 't, I pray; and I this morning know

    Where we shall find him most conveniently.   *Exeunt.* 175

[SCENE II: *A room of state in the castle.*]

Flourish. Enter Claudius, King of Denmark, Gertrude the Queen, Councilors, Polonius and his Son Laertes, Hamlet, cum aliis° [*including Voltimand and Cornelius*].

---

147. **cock crew:** According to traditional ghost lore, spirits returned to their confines at cockcrow.   154. **extravagant and erring:** Wandering. Both words mean the same thing.   155. **confine:** Place of confinement.   156. **probation:** Proof, trial.   158. **'gainst:** Just before.   162. **planets strike:** It was thought that planets were malignant and might strike travelers by night.   164. **gracious:** Full of goodness.   SCENE II.   s.d. *cum aliis:* With others.

KING: Though yet of Hamlet our dear brother's death
  The memory be green, and that it us befitted
  To bear our hearts in grief and our whole kingdom
  To be contracted in one brow of woe,
  Yet so far hath discretion fought with nature   5
  That we with wisest sorrow think on him,
  Together with remembrance of ourselves.
  Therefore our sometime sister, now our queen,
  Th' imperial jointress° to this warlike state,
  Have we, as 'twere with a defeated joy, —   10
  With an auspicious and a dropping eye,
  With mirth in funeral and with dirge in marriage,
  In equal scale weighing delight and dole, —
  Taken to wife: nor have we herein barr'd
  Your better wisdoms, which have freely gone   15
  With this affair along. For all, our thanks.
  Now follows, that° you know, young Fortinbras,
  Holding a weak supposal° of our worth,
  Or thinking by our late dear brother's death
  Our state to be disjoint° and out of frame,°   20
  Colleagued° with this dream of his advantage,°
  He hath not fail'd to pester us with message,
  Importing° the surrender of those lands
  Lost by his father, with all bands of law,
  To our most valiant brother. So much for him.   25
  Now for ourself and for this time of meeting:
  Thus much the business is: we have here writ
  To Norway, uncle of young Fortinbras, —
  Who, impotent and bed-rid, scarcely hears
  Of this his nephew's purpose, — to suppress   30
  His further gait° herein; in that the levies,
  The lists and full proportions, are all made
  Out of his subject:° and we here dispatch
  You, good Cornelius, and you, Voltimand,
  For bearers of this greeting to old Norway;   35
  Giving to you no further personal power
  To business with the king, more than the scope
  Of these delated° articles allow.
  Farewell, and let your haste commend your duty.

CORNELIUS:
VOLTIMAND: } In that and all things will we show our duty.   40

---

9. jointress: Woman possessed of a jointure, or, joint tenancy of an estate. **17. that:** That which. **18. weak supposal:** Low estimate. **20. disjoint:** Distracted, out of joint; **frame:** Order. **21. Colleagued:** added to; **dream . . . advantage:** Visionary hope of success. **23. Importing:** Purporting, pertaining to. **31. gait:** Proceeding. **33. Out of his subject:** At the expense of Norway's subjects (collectively). **38. delated:** Expressly stated.

KING: We doubt it nothing: heartily farewell.

                             [*Exeunt Voltimand and Cornelius.*]

    And now, Laertes, what's the news with you?

    You told us of some suit; what is't, Laertes?

    You cannot speak of reason to the Dane,°

    And lose your voice:° what wouldst thou beg, Laertes,   45

    That shall not be my offer, not thy asking?

    The head is not more native° to the heart,

    The hand more instrumental° to the mouth,

    Than is the throne of Denmark to thy father.

    What wouldst thou have, Laertes?

LAERTES: My dread lord,   50

    Your leave and favour to return to France;

    From whence though willingly I came to Denmark,

    To show my duty in your coronation,

    Yet now, I must confess, that duty done,

    My thoughts and wishes bend again toward France   55

    And bow them to your gracious leave and pardon.°

KING: Have you your father's leave? What says Polonius?

POLONIUS: He hath, my lord, wrung from me my slow leave

    By laboursome petition, and at last

    Upon his will I seal'd my hard consent: 60

    I do beseech you, give him leave to go.

KING: Take thy fair hour, Laertes; time be thine,

    And thy best graces spend it at thy will!

    But now, my cousin° Hamlet, and my son, —

HAMLET [*aside*]: A little more than kin, and less than kind!°   65

KING: How is it that the clouds still hang on you?

HAMLET: Not so, my lord; I am too much in the sun.°

QUEEN: Good Hamlet, cast thy nighted colour off,

    And let thine eye look like a friend on Denmark.

    Do not for ever with thy vailed lids   70

    Seek for thy noble father in the dust:

    Thou know'st 'tis common; all that lives must die,

    Passing through nature to eternity.

HAMLET: Ay, madam, it is common.°

QUEEN: If it be,

    Why seems it so particular with thee?   75

---

44. the Dane: Danish king.   **45. lose your voice:** Speak in vain.   **47. native:** Closely connected, related.   **48. instrumental:** Serviceable.   **56. leave and pardon:** Permission to depart.   **64. cousin:** Any kin not of the immediate family.   **65. A little . . . kind:** My relation to you has become more than kinship warrants; it has also become unnatural.   **67. I am . . . sun:** The senses seem to be: I am too much out of doors, I am too much in the sun of your grace (ironical), I am too much of a son to you. Possibly an allusion to the proverb "Out of heaven's blessing into the warm sun"; i.e., Hamlet is out of house and home in being deprived of the kingship.   **74. Ay . . . common:** It is common, but it hurts nevertheless; possibly a reference to the commonplace quality of the queen's remark.

HAMLET: Seems, madam! nay, it is; I know not "seems."
    'Tis not alone my inky cloak, good mother,
    Nor customary suits° of solemn black,
    Nor windy suspiration° of forc'd breath,
    No, nor the fruitful river in the eye,   80
    Nor the dejected 'haviour of the visage,
    Together with all forms, moods, shapes of grief,
    That can denote me truly: these indeed seem,
    For they are actions that a man might play:
    But I have that within which passeth show;   85
    These but the trappings and the suits of woe.
KING: 'Tis sweet and commendable in your nature, Hamlet,
    To give these mourning duties to your father:
    But, you must know, your father lost a father;
    That father lost, lost his, and the survivor bound   90
    In filial obligation for some term
    To do obsequious° sorrow: but to persever
    In obstinate condolement° is a course
    Of impious stubbornness; 'tis unmanly grief;
    It shows a will most incorrect° to heaven,   95
    A heart unfortified, a mind impatient,
    An understanding simple and unschool'd:
    For what we know must be and is as common
    As any the most vulgar thing° to sense,
    Why should we in our peevish opposition   100
    Take it to heart? Fie! 'tis a fault to heaven,
    A fault against the dead, a fault to nature,
    To reason most absurd; whose common theme
    Is death of fathers, and who still hath cried,
    From the first corse till he that died to-day,   105
    "This must be so." We pray you, throw to earth
    This unprevailing° woe, and think of us
    As of a father: for let the world take note,
    You are the most immediate° to our throne;
    And with no less nobility° of love   110
    Than that which dearest father bears his son,
    Do I impart° toward you. For your intent
    In going back to school in Wittenberg,°
    It is most retrograde° to our desire:
    And we beseech you, bend you° to remain   115

---

78. **customary suits:** Suits prescribed by custom for mourning.   79. **windy suspiration:** Heavy sighing.   92. **obsequious:** Dutiful.   93. **condolement:** Sorrowing.   95. **incorrect:** Untrained, uncorrected.   99. **vulgar thing:** Common experience.   107. **unprevailing:** Unavailing.   109. **most immediate:** Next in succession.   110. **nobility:** High degree.   112. **impart:** The object is apparently *love* (line 110).   113. **Wittenberg:** Famous German university founded in 1502.   114. **retrograde:** Contrary.   115. **bend you:** Incline yourself; imperative.

Here, in the cheer and comfort of our eye,
Our chiefest courtier, cousin, and our son.

QUEEN: Let not thy mother lose her prayers, Hamlet:
I pray thee, stay with us; go not to Wittenberg.

HAMLET: I shall in all my best obey you, madam.   120

KING: Why, 'tis a loving and a fair reply:
Be as ourself in Denmark. Madam, come;
This gentle and unforc'd accord of Hamlet
Sits smiling to my heart: in grace whereof,
No jocund health that Denmark drinks to-day,   125
But the great cannon to the clouds shall tell,
And the king's rouse° the heaven shall bruit again,°
Re-speaking earthly thunder. Come away.

Flourish. Exeunt all but Hamlet.

HAMLET: O, that this too too sullied flesh would melt,
Thaw and resolve itself into a dew!   130
Or that the Everlasting had not fix'd
His canon 'gainst self-slaughter! O God! God!
How weary, stale, flat and unprofitable,
Seem to me all the uses of this world!
Fie on't! ah fie! 'tis an unweeded garden,   135
That grows to seed; things rank and gross in nature
Possess it merely.° That it should come to this!
But two months dead: nay, not so much, not two:
So excellent a king; that was, to this,
Hyperion° to a satyr; so loving to my mother   140
That he might not beteem° the winds of heaven
Visit her face too roughly. Heaven and earth!
Must I remember? why, she would hang on him,
As if increase of appetite had grown
By what it fed on: and yet, within a month —   145
Let me not think on't — Frailty, thy name is woman! —
A little month, or ere those shoes were old
With which she followed my poor father's body,
Like Niobe,° all tears: — why she, even she —
O God! a beast, that wants discourse of reason,°   150
Would have mourn'd longer — married with my uncle,
My father's brother, but no more like my father
Than I to Hercules: within a month:
Ere yet the salt of most unrighteous tears
Had left the flushing in her galled° eyes,   155

---

127. rouse: Draft of liquor; **bruit again:** Echo.   **137. merely:** Completely, entirely.   **140. Hyperion:** God of the sun in the older regime of ancient gods.   **141. beteem:** Allow.
149. Niobe: Tantalus's daughter, who boasted that she had more sons and daughters than Leto; for this Apollo and Artemis slew her children. She was turned into stone by Zeus or Mount Sipylus.   **150. discourse of reason:** Process or faculty of reason.   **155. galled:** Irr' tated.

She married. O, most wicked speed, to post
With such dexterity° to incestuous sheets!
It is not nor it cannot come to good:
But break, my heart; for I must hold my tongue.

Enter Horatio, Marcellus, and Bernardo.

HORATIO: Hail to your lordship!

HAMLET: I am glad to see you well: 160
    Horatio! — or I do forget myself.

HORATIO: The same, my lord, and your poor servant ever.

HAMLET: Sir, my good friend; I'll change that name with you:°
    And what make you from Wittenberg, Horatio?
    Marcellus?   165

MARCELLUS: My good lord —

HAMLET: I am very glad to see you. Good even, sir.
    But what, in faith, make you from Wittenberg?

HORATIO: A truant disposition, good my lord.

HAMLET: I would not hear your enemy say so,   170
    Nor shall you do my ear that violence,
    To make it truster of your own report
    Against yourself: I know you are no truant.
    But what is your affair in Elsinore?
    We'll teach you to drink deep ere you depart.   175

HORATIO: My lord, I came to see your father's funeral.

HAMLET: I prithee, do not mock me, fellow-student;
    I think it was to see my mother's wedding.

HORATIO: Indeed, my lord, it follow'd hard° upon.

HAMLET: Thrift, thrift, Horatio! the funeral bak'd meats°   180
    Did coldly furnish forth the marriage tables.
    Would I had met my dearest° foe in heaven
    Or ever I had seen that day, Horatio!
    My father! — methinks I see my father.

HORATIO: Where, my lord!

HAMLET: In my mind's eye, Horatio.   185

HORATIO: I saw him once; 'a° was a goodly king.

HAMLET: 'A was a man, take him for all in all,
    I shall not look upon his like again.

HORATIO: My lord, I think I saw him yesternight.

HAMLET: Saw? who?   190

HORATIO: My lord, the king your father.

HAMLET: The king my father!

HORATIO: Season your admiration° for a while
    With an attent ear, till I may deliver,

---

157. dexterity: Facility.   **163. I'll . . . you:** I'll be your servant; you shall be my friend; also explained as "I'll exchange the name of friend with you."   **179. hard:** Close.   **180. bak'd meats:** Meat pies.   **182. dearest:** Direst. The adjective *dear* in Shakespeare has two different origins: O.E. *deore*, "beloved," and O.E. *deor*, "fierce." *Dearest* is the superlative of the second.   **'a:** He.   **192. Season your admiration:** Restrain your astonishment.

    Upon the witness of these gentlemen,
    This marvel to you.
HAMLET: For God's love, let me hear.   195
HORATIO: Two nights together had these gentlemen,
    Marcellus and Bernardo, on their watch,
    In the dead waste and middle of the night,
    Been thus encount'red. A figure like your father,
    Armed at point exactly, cap-a-pe,°   200
    Appears before them, and with solemn march
    Goes slow and stately by them: thrice he walk'd
    By their oppress'd° and fear-surprised eyes,
    Within his truncheon's° length; whilst they, distill'd°
    Almost to jelly with the act° of fear,   205
    Stand dumb and speak not to him. This to me
    In dreadful secrecy impart they did;
    And I with them the third night kept the watch:
    Where, as they had deliver'd, both in time,
    Form of the thing, each word made true and good,   210
    The apparition comes: I knew your father;
    These hands are not more like.
HAMLET: But where was this?
MARCELLUS: My lord, upon the platform where we watch'd.
HAMLET: Did you not speak to it?
HORATIO: My lord, I did;
    But answer made it none: yet once methought   215
    It lifted up it° head and did address
    Itself to motion, like as it would speak;
    But even then the morning cock crew loud,
    And at the sound it shrunk in haste away,
    And vanish'd from our sight.
HAMLET: 'Tis very strange.   220
HORATIO: As I do live, my honour'd lord, 'tis true;
    And we did think it writ down in our duty
    To let you know of it.
HAMLET: Indeed, indeed, sirs, but this troubles me.
    Hold you the watch to-night?
MARCELLUS: ⎫
           ⎬   We do, my lord.   225
BERNARDO: ⎭
HAMLET: Arm'd, say you?
MARCELLUS: ⎫
           ⎬ Arm'd, my lord.
BERNARDO: ⎭
HAMLET: From top to toe?
MARCELLUS: ⎫
           ⎬   My lord, from head to foot.
BERNARDO: ⎭

---

200. cap-a-pe: From head to foot.   **203. oppress'd:** Distressed.   **204. truncheon:** Officer's
staff; **distill'd:** Softened, weakened.   **205. act:** Action.   **216. it:** Its.

HAMLET: Then saw you not his face?

HORATIO: O, yes, my lord; he wore his beaver° up.   230

HAMLET: What, look'd he frowningly?

HORATIO: A countenance more
    In sorrow than in anger.

HAMLET: Pale or red?

HORATIO: Nay, very pale.

HAMLET: And fix'd his eyes upon you?

HORATIO: Most constantly.

HAMLET: I would I had been there.

HORATIO: It would have much amaz'd you.   235

HAMLET: Very like, very like. Stay'd it long?

HORATIO: While one with moderate haste might tell a hundred.

MARCELLUS: ⎫
BERNARDO: ⎭ Longer, longer.

HORATIO: Not when I saw't.

HAMLET: His beard was grizzled, — no?

HORATIO: It was, as I have seen it in his life,   240
    A sable° silver'd.

HAMLET: I will watch to-night;
    Perchance 'twill walk again.

HORATIO: I warr'nt it will.

HAMLET: If it assume my noble father's person,
    I'll speak to it, though hell itself should gape
    And bid me hold my peace. I pray you all,   245
    If you have hitherto conceal'd this sight,
    Let it be tenable in your silence still;
    And whatsoever else shall hap to-night,
    Give it an understanding, but no tongue:
    I will requite your loves. So, fare you well: 250
    Upon the platform, 'twixt eleven and twelve,
    I'll visit you.

ALL: Our duty to your honour.

HAMLET: Your loves, as mine to you: farewell.   *Exeunt [all but Hamlet]*.
    My father's spirit in arms! all is not well;
    I doubt° some foul play: would the night were come! 255
    Till then sit still, my soul: foul deeds will rise,
    Though all the earth o'erwhelm them, to men's eyes.   *Exit.*

[SCENE III: *A room in Polonius's house.*]

Enter Laertes and Ophelia, his Sister.

LAERTES: My necessaries are embark'd: farewell:
    And, sister, as the winds give benefit

---

230. **beaver:** Visor on the helmet.   **241. sable:** Black color.   **255. doubt:** Fear.

And convoy is assistant,° do not sleep,
But let me hear from you.
OPHELIA: Do you doubt that?
LAERTES: For Hamlet and the trifling of his favour,   5
Hold it a fashion° and a toy in blood,°
A violet in the youth of primy° nature,
Forward,° not permanent, sweet, not lasting,
The perfume and suppliance of a minute;°
No more.
OPHELIA: No more but so?
LAERTES: Think it no more: 10
For nature, crescent,° does not grow alone
In thews° and bulk, but, as this temple° waxes,
The inward service of the mind and soul
Grows wide withal. Perhaps he loves you now,
And now no soil° nor cautel° doth besmirch   15
The virtue of his will: but you must fear,
His greatness weigh'd,° his will is not his own;
For he himself is subject to his birth:
He may not, as unvalued persons do,
Carve for himself; for on his choice depends   20
The safety and health of this whole state;
And therefore must his choice be circumscrib'd
Unto the voice and yielding° of that body
Whereof he is the head. Then if he says he loves you,
It fits your wisdom so far to believe it   25
As he in his particular act and place
May give his saying deed;° which is no further
Than the main voice of Denmark goes withal.
Then weigh what loss your honour may sustain,
If with too credent° ear you list his songs,   30
Or lose your heart, or your chaste treasure open
To his unmast'red° importunity.
Fear it, Ophelia, fear it, my dear sister,
And keep you in the rear of your affection,
Out of the shot and danger of desire.   35
The chariest° maid is prodigal enough,
If she unmask her beauty to the moon:
Virtue itself 'scapes not calumnious strokes:
The canker galls the infants of the spring,°

SCENE III.   **3. convoy is assistant:** Means of conveyance are available.   **6. fashion:** Custom, prevailing usage; **toy in blood:** Passing amorous fancy.   **7. primy:** In its prime.   **8. Forward:** Precocious.   **9. suppliance of a minute:** Diversion to fill up a minute.   **11. crescent:** Growing, waxing.   **12. thews:** Bodily strength; **temple:** Body.   **15. soil:** blemish; **cautel:** Crafty device.   **17. greatness weigh'd:** High position considered.   **23. voice and yielding:** Assent, approval.   **27. deed:** Effect.   **30. credent:** Credulous.   **32. unmast'red:** Unrestrained.   **36. chariest:** Most scrupulously modest.   **39. The canker ... spring:** The cankerworm destroys the young plants of spring.

Too oft before their buttons° be disclos'd,° 40
And in the morn and liquid dew° of youth
Contagious blastments° are most imminent.
Be wary then; best safety lies in fear:
Youth to itself rebels, though none else near.

OPHELIA: I shall the effect of this good lesson keep, 45
As watchman to my heart. But, good my brother,
Do not, as some ungracious° pastors do,
Show me the steep and thorny way to heaven;
Whiles, like a puff'd° and reckless libertine,
Himself the primrose path of dalliance treads, 50
And recks° not his own rede.°

Enter Polonius.

LAERTES: O, fear me not.
I stay too long: but here my father comes.
A double° blessing is a double grace;
Occasion° smiles upon a second leave.

POLONIUS: Yet here, Laertes? aboard, aboard, for shame! 55
The wind sits in the shoulder of your sail,
And you are stay'd for. There; my blessing with thee!
And these few precepts° in thy memory
Look thou character.° Give thy thoughts no tongue,
Nor any unproportion'd° thought his act. 60
Be thou familiar, but by no means vulgar.°
Those friends thou hast, and their adoption tried,
Grapple them to thy soul with hoops of steel;
But do not dull thy palm with entertainment
Of each new-hatch'd, unfledg'd° comrade. Beware 65
Of entrance to a quarrel, but being in,
Bear't that th' opposed may beware of thee.
Give every man thy ear, but few thy voice;
Take each man's censure, but reserve thy judgement.
Costly thy habit as thy purse can buy, 70
But not express'd in fancy;° rich, not gaudy;
For the apparel oft proclaims the man,
And they in France of the best rank and station
Are of a most select and generous chief in that.°
Neither a borrower nor a lender be; 75
For loan oft loses both itself and friend,

---

40. buttons: Buds; **disclos'd:** Opened.   **41. liquid dew:** I.e., time when dew is fresh.   **42. blastments:** Blights.   **47. ungracious:** Graceless.   **49. puff'd:** Bloated.   **51. recks:** Heeds; **rede:** Counsel.   **53. double:** I.e., Laertes has already bade his father good-by.   **54. Occasion:** Opportunity.   **58. precepts:** Many parallels have been found to the series of maxims which follows, one of the closer being that in Lyly's *Euphues*.   **59. character:** Inscribe.   **60. unproportion'd:** Inordinate.   **61. vulgar:** Common.   **65. unfledg'd:** Immature.   **71. express'd in fancy:** Fantastical in design.   **74. Are ... that:** *Chief* is usually taken as a substantive meaning "head," "eminence."

And borrowing dulleth edge of husbandry.°
This above all: to thine own self be true,
And it must follow, as the night the day,
Thou canst not then be false to any man.   80
Farewell: my blessing season° this in thee!
LAERTES: Most humbly do I take my leave, my lord.
POLONIUS: The time invites you; go; your servants tend.
LAERTES: Farewell, Ophelia; and remember well
    What I have said to you.
OPHELIA: 'Tis in my memory lock'd,   85
    And you yourself shall keep the key of it.
LAERTES: Farewell.   *Exit Laertes.*
POLONIUS: What is 't, Ophelia, he hath said to you?
OPHELIA: So please you, something touching the Lord Hamlet.
POLONIUS: Marry, well bethought: 90
    'Tis told me, he hath very oft of late
    Given private time to you; and you yourself
    Have of your audience been most free and bounteous:
    If it be so, as so't is put on° me,
    And that in way of caution, I must tell you,   95
    You do not understand yourself so clearly
    As it behooves my daughter and your honour.
    What is between you? give me up the truth.
OPHELIA: He hath, my lord, of late made many tenders°
    Of his affection to me.   100
POLONIUS: Affection! pooh! you speak like a green girl,
    Unsifted° in such perilous circumstance.
    Do you believe his tenders, as you call them?
OPHELIA: I do not know, my lord, what I should think.
POLONIUS: Marry, I will teach you: think yourself a baby;   105
    That you have ta'en these tenders° for true pay,
    Which are not sterling.° Tender° yourself more dearly;
    Or — not to crack the wind° of the poor phrase,
    Running it thus — you'll tender me a fool.°
OPHELIA: My lord, he hath importun'd me with love   110
    In honourable fashion.
POLONIUS: Ay, fashion° you may call it; go to, go to.
OPHELIA: And hath given countenance° to his speech, my lord,
    With almost all the holy vows of heaven.
POLONIUS: Ay, springes° to catch woodcocks.° I do know,   115
    When the blood burns, how prodigal the soul

---

77. husbandry: Thrift. **81. season:** Mature. **94. put on:** Impressed on. **99, 103. tenders:** Offers. **102. Unsifted:** Untried. **106. tenders:** Promises to pay. **107. sterling:** Legal currency; **Tender:** Hold. **108. crack the wind:** I.e., run it until it is broken-winded. **109. tender ... fool:** Show me a fool (for a daughter). **112. fashion:** Mere form, pretense. **113. countenance:** Credit, support. **115. springes:** Snares; **woodcocks:** Birds easily caught, type of stupidity.

Lends the tongue vows: these blazes, daughter,
Giving more light than heat, extinct in both,
Even in their promise, as it is a-making,
You must not take for fire. From this time 120
Be somewhat scanter of your maiden presence;
Set your entreatments° at a higher rate
Than a command to parley.° For Lord Hamlet,
Believe so much in him,° that he is young,
And with a larger tether may he walk 125
Than may be given you: in few,° Ophelia,
Do not believe his vows; for they are brokers;°
Not of that dye° which their investments° show,
But mere implorators of° unholy suits,
Breathing° like sanctified and pious bawds, 130
The better to beguile. This is for all:
I would not, in plain terms, from this time forth,
Have you so slander° any moment leisure,
As to give words or talk with the Lord Hamlet.
Look to 't, I charge you: come your ways. 135
OPHELIA: I shall obey, my lord.
                                                                    Exeunt.

[SCENE IV: *The platform.*]

Enter Hamlet, Horatio, and Marcellus.

HAMLET: The air bites shrewdly; it is very cold.
HORATIO: It is a nipping and an eager air.
HAMLET: What hour now?
HORATIO: I think it lacks of twelve.
MARCELLUS: No, it is struck.
HORATIO: Indeed? I heard it not: then it draws near the season 5
    Wherein the spirit held his wont to walk.

A flourish of trumpets, and two pieces go off.

    What does this mean, my lord?
HAMLET: The king doth wake° to-night and takes his rouse,°
    Keeps wassail,° and the swagg'ring up-spring° reels;°
    And, as he drains his draughts of Rhenish° down, 10
    The kettle-drum and trumpet thus bray out
    The triumph of his pledge.°
HORATIO: Is it a custom?

---

122. entreatments: Conversations, interviews. **123. command to parley:** Mere invitation
to talk. **124. so . . . him:** This much concerning him. **126. in few:** Briefly. **127. brokers:**
Go-betweens, procurers. **128. dye:** Color or sort; **investments:** Clothes. **129. implorators
of:** Solicitors of. **130. Breathing:** Speaking. **133. slander:** Bring disgrace or reproach
upon. SCENE IV. **8. wake:** Stay awake, hold revel; **rouse:** Carouse, drinking bout. **9.
wassail:** Carousal; **up-spring:** Last and wildest dance at German merry-makings; **reels:** Reels
through. **10. Rhenish:** Rhine wine. **12. triumph . . . pledge:** His glorious achievement as
a drinker.

HAMLET: Ay, marry, is 't:
  But to my mind, though I am native here
  And to the manner born,° it is a custom   15
  More honour'd in the breach than the observance.
  This heavy-headed revel east and west
  Makes us traduc'd and tax'd of other nations:
  They clepe° us drunkards, and with swinish phrase°
  Soil our addition;° and indeed it takes   20
  From our achievements, though perform'd at height,
  The pith and marrow of our attribute.°
  So, oft it chances in particular men,
  That for some vicious mole of nature° in them,
  As, in their birth — wherein they are not guilty,   25
  Since nature cannot choose his origin —
  By the o'ergrowth of some complexion,
  Oft breaking down the pales° and forts of reason,
  Or by some habit that too much o'er-leavens°
  The form of plausive° manners, that these men,   30
  Carrying, I say, the stamp of one defect,
  Being nature's livery,° or fortune's star,° —
  Their virtues else — be they as pure as grace,
  As infinite as man may undergo —
  Shall in the general censure take corruption   35
  From that particular fault: the dram of eale°
  Doth all the noble substance of a doubt
  To his own scandal.°

Enter Ghost.

HORATIO: Look, my lord, it comes!
HAMLET: Angels and ministers of grace° defend us!
  Be thou a spirit of health or goblin damn'd,   40
  Bring with thee airs from heaven or blasts from hell,
  Be thy intents wicked or charitable,
  Thou com'st in such a questionable° shape
  That I will speak to thee: I'll call thee Hamlet,
  King, father, royal Dane: O, answer me!   45
  Let me not burst in ignorance; but tell
  Why thy canoniz'd° bones, hearsed° in death,

---

15. to . . . born: Destined by birth to be subject to the custom in question. **19. clepe:** Call; **with swinish phrase:** By calling us swine. **20. addition:** Reputation. **22. attribute:** Reputation. **24. mole of nature:** Natural blemish in one's constitution. **28. pales:** Palings (as of a fortification). **29. o'er-leavens:** Induces a change throughout (as yeast works in bread). **30. plausive:** Pleasing. **32. nature's livery:** Endowment from nature; **fortune's star:** The position in which one is placed by fortune, a reference to astrology. The two phrases are aspects of the same thing. **36.–38. the dram . . . scandal:** A famous crux: *dram of eale* has had various interpretations, the preferred one being probably, "a dram of evil." **39. ministers of grace:** Messengers of God. **43. questionable:** Inviting question or conversation. **47. canoniz'd:** Buried according to the canons of the church; **hearsed:** Coffined.

Have burst their cerements;° why the sepulchre,
Wherein we saw thee quietly interr'd,
Hath op'd his ponderous and marble jaws,   50
To cast thee up again. What may this mean,
That thou, dead corse, again in complete steel
Revisits thus the glimpses of the moon,°
Making night hideous; and we fools of nature°
So horridly to shake our disposition   55
With thoughts beyond the reaches of our souls?
Say, why is this? wherefore? what should we do?

[Ghost] beckons [Hamlet].

HORATIO: It beckons you to go away with it,
    As if it some impartment° did desire
    To you alone.
MARCELLUS: Look, with what courteous action   60
    It waves you to a more removed° ground:
    But do not go with it.
HORATIO: No, by no means.
HAMLET: It will not speak; then I will follow it.
HORATIO: Do not, my lord!
HAMLET: Why, what should be the fear?
    I do not set my life at a pin's fee;   65
    And for my soul, what can it do to that,
    Being a thing immortal as itself?
    It waves me forth again: I'll follow it.
HORATIO: What if it tempt you toward the flood, my lord,
    Or to the dreadful summit of the cliff   70
    That beetles o'er° his base into the sea,
    And there assume some other horrible form,
    Which might deprive your sovereignty of reason°
    And draw you into madness? think of it:
    The very place puts toys of desperation,°   75
    Without more motive, into every brain
    That looks so many fathoms to the sea
    And hears it roar beneath.
HAMLET: It waves me still.
    Go on; I'll follow thee.
MARCELLUS: You shall not go, my lord.
HAMLET: Hold off your hands!   80

---

48. cerements: Grave-clothes.   **53. glimpses of the moon:** The earth by night.   **54. fools
of nature:** Mere men, limited to natural knowledge.   **59. impartment:** Communication.
61. removed: Remote.   **71. beetles o'er:** Overhangs threateningly.   **73. deprive...reason:**
Take away the sovereignty of your reason. It was thought that evil spirits would sometimes
assume the form of departed spirits in order to work madness in a human creature.   **75.
toys of desperation:** Freakish notions of suicide.

HORATIO: Be rul'd; you shall not go.
HAMLET: My fate cries out,
    And makes each petty artere° in this body
    As hardy as the Nemean lion's° nerve.°
    Still am I call'd. Unhand me, gentlemen.
    By heaven, I'll make a ghost of him that lets° me!   85
    I say, away! Go on; I'll follow thee.   *Exeunt Ghost and Hamlet.*
HORATIO: He waxes desperate with imagination.
MARCELLUS: Let's follow; 'tis not fit thus to obey him.
HORATIO: Have after. To what issue° will this come?
MARCELLUS: Something is rotten in the state of Denmark.   90
HORATIO: Heaven will direct it.°
MARCELLUS: Nay, let's follow him.   *Exeunt.*

[SCENE V: *Another part of the platform.*]

Enter Ghost and Hamlet.

HAMLET: Whither wilt thou lead me? speak; I'll go no further.
GHOST: Mark me.
HAMLET: I will.
GHOST: My hour is almost come,
    When I to sulphurous and tormenting flames
    Must render up myself.
HAMLET: Alas, poor ghost!
GHOST: Pity me not, but lend thy serious hearing   5
    To what I shall unfold.
HAMLET: Speak; I am bound to hear.
GHOST: So art thou to revenge, when thou shalt hear.
HAMLET: What?
GHOST: I am thy father's spirit,
    Doom'd for a certain term to walk the night,   10
    And for the day confin'd to fast° in fires,
    Till the foul crimes done in my days of nature
    Are burnt and purg'd away. But that I am forbid
    To tell the secrets of my prison-house,
    I could a tale unfold whose lightest word   15
    Would harrow up thy soul, freeze thy young blood,
    Make thy two eyes, like stars, start from their spheres,°
    Thy knotted° and combined° locks to part
    And each particular hair to stand an end,

---

82. artere: Artery. **83. Nemean lion's:** The Nemean lion was one of the monsters slain by Hercules; **nerve:** Sinew, tendon. The point is that the arteries which were carrying the spirits out into the body were functioning and were as stiff and hard as the sinews of the lion. **85. lets:** Hinders. **89. issue:** Outcome. **91. it:** I.e., the outcome. SCENE V. **11. fast:** Probably, do without food. It has been sometimes taken in the sense of doing general penance. **17. spheres:** Orbits. **18. knotted:** Perhaps intricately arranged; **combined:** Tied, bound.

Like quills upon the fretful porpentine:° 20
But this eternal blazon° must not be
To ears of flesh and blood. List, list, O, list!
If thou didst ever thy dear father love —

HAMLET: O God!

GHOST: Revenge his foul and most unnatural° murder. 25

HAMLET: Murder!

GHOST: Murder most foul, as in the best it is;
But this most foul, strange and unnatural.

HAMLET: Haste me to know't, that I, with wings as swift
As meditation or the thoughts of love, 30
May sweep to my revenge.

GHOST: I find thee apt;
And duller shouldst thou be than the fat weed°
That roots itself in ease on Lethe wharf,°
Wouldst thou not stir in this. Now, Hamlet, hear:
'Tis given out that, sleeping in my orchard, 35
A serpent stung me; so the whole ear of Denmark
Is by a forged process of my death
Rankly abus'd: but know, thou noble youth,
The serpent that did sting thy father's life
Now wears his crown.

HAMLET: O my prophetic soul! 40
My uncle!

GHOST: Ay, that incestuous, that adulterate° beast,
With witchcraft of his wit, with traitorous gifts, —
O wicked wit and gifts, that have the power
So to seduce! — won to his shameful lust 45
The will of my most seeming-virtuous queen:
O Hamlet, what a falling-off was there!
From me, whose love was of that dignity
That it went hand in hand even with the vow
I made to her in marriage, and to decline 50
Upon a wretch whose natural gifts were poor
To those of mine!
But virtue, as it never will be moved,
Though lewdness court it in a shape of heaven,
So lust, though to a radiant angel link'd, 55
Will sate itself in a celestial bed,
And prey on garbage.
But, soft! methinks I scent the morning air;
Brief let me be. Sleeping within my orchard,

---

20. porpentine: Porcupine.   **21. eternal blazon:** Promulgation or proclamation of eternity, revelation of the hereafter.   **25. unnatural:** I.e., pertaining to fratricide.   **32. fat weed:** Many suggestions have been offered as to the particular plant intended, including asphodel; probably a general figure for plants growing along rotting wharves and piles.   **33. Lethe wharf:** Bank of the river of forgetfulness in Hades.   **42. adulterate:** Adulterous.

My custom always of the afternoon, 60
Upon my secure° hour thy uncle stole,
With juice of cursed hebona° in a vial,
And in the porches of my ears did pour
The leperous° distilment; whose effect
Holds such an enmity with blood of man 65
That swift as quicksilver it courses through
The natural gates and alleys of the body,
And with a sudden vigour it doth posset°
And curd, like eager° droppings into milk,
The thin and wholesome blood: so did it mine; 70
And a most instant tetter bark'd about,
Most lazar-like,° with vile and loathsome crust,
All my smooth body.
Thus was I, sleeping, by a brother's hand
Of life, of crown, of queen, at once dispatch'd:° 75
Cut off even in the blossoms of my sin,
Unhous'led,° disappointed,° unanel'd,°
No reck'ning made, but sent to my account
With all my imperfections on my head:
O, horrible! O, horrible! most horrible!° 80
If thou hast nature in thee, bear it not;
Let not the royal bed of Denmark be
A couch for luxury° and damned incest.
But, howsomever thou pursues this act,
Taint not thy mind,° nor let thy soul contrive 85
Against thy mother aught: leave her to heaven
And to those thorns that in her bosom lodge,
To prick and sting her. Fare thee well at once!
The glow-worm shows the matin° to be near,
And 'gins to pale his uneffectual fire:° 90
Adieu, adieu, adieu! remember me. [*Exit.*]
HAMLET: O all you host of heaven! O earth! what else?
And shall I couple° hell? O, fie! Hold, hold, my heart;
And you, my sinews, grow not instant old,
But bear me stiffly up. Remember thee! 95
Ay, thou poor ghost, whiles memory holds a seat
In this distracted globe.° Remember thee!

---

61. secure: Confident, unsuspicious.   **62. hebona:** Generally supposed to mean henbane, conjectured *hemlock*; *ebenus,* meaning "yew."   **64. leperous:** Causing leprosy.   **68. posset:** Coagulate, curdle.   **69. eager:** Sour, acid.   **72. lazar-like:** Leperlike.   **75. dispatch'd:** Suddenly bereft.   **77. Unhous'led:** Without having received the sacrament; **disappointed:** Unready, without equipment for the last journey; **unanel'd:** Without having received extreme unction.   **80. O . . . horrible:** Many editors give this line to Hamlet; Garrick and Sir Henry Irving spoke it in that part.   **83. luxury:** Lechery.   **85. Taint . . . mind:** Probably, deprave not thy character, do nothing except in the pursuit of a natural revenge.   **89. matin:** Morning.   **90. uneffectual fire:** Cold light.   **93. couple:** Add.   **97. distracted globe:** Confused head.

Yea, from the table of my memory
I'll wipe away all trivial fond records,
All saws° of books, all forms, all pressures° past,   100
That youth and observation copied there;
And thy commandment all alone shall live
Within the book and volume of my brain,
Unmix'd with baser matter: yes, by heaven!
O most pernicious woman!   105
O villain, villain, smiling, damned villain!
My tables,° — meet it is I set it down,
That one may smile, and smile, and be a villain;
At least I am sure it may be so in Denmark: [*Writing.*]
So, uncle, there you are. Now to my word;°   110
It is "Adieu, adieu! remember me,"
I have sworn't.

Enter Horatio and Marcellus.

HORATIO: My lord, my lord —
MARCELLUS: Lord Hamlet, —
HORATIO: Heavens secure him!
HAMLET: So be it!
MARCELLUS: Hillo, ho, ho,° my lord!   115
HAMLET: Hillo, ho, ho, boy! come, bird, come.
MARCELLUS: How is't, my noble lord?
HORATIO: What news, my lord?
HAMLET: O, wonderful!
HORATIO: Good my lord, tell it.
HAMLET: No; you will reveal it.
HORATIO: Not I, my lord, by heaven.
MARCELLUS: Nor I, my lord.   120
HAMLET: How say you, then; would heart of man once think it?
     But you'll be secret?
HORATIO: ⎫
MARCELLUS: ⎰   Ay, by heaven, my lord.
HAMLET: There's ne'er a villain dwelling in all Denmark
     But he's an arrant° knave.
HORATIO: There needs no ghost, my lord, come from the grave   125
     To tell us this.
HAMLET: Why, right; you are in the right;
     And so, without more circumstance at all,
     I hold it fit that we shake hands and part:
     You, as your business and desire shall point you;
     For every man has business and desire,   130

---

100. **saws:** Wise sayings; **pressures:** Impressions stamped.   107. **tables:** Probably a small
portable writing tablet carried at the belt.   110. **word:** Watchword.   115. **Hillo, ho, ho:** A
falconer's call to a hawk in air.   124. **arrant:** Thoroughgoing.

Such as it is; and for my own poor part,
Look you, I'll go pray.

HORATIO: These are but wild and whirling words, my lord.

HAMLET: I am sorry they offend you, heartily;
Yes, 'faith, heartily.

HORATIO: There's no offence, my lord.   135

HAMLET: Yes, by Saint Patrick,° but there is, Horatio,
And much offence too. Touching this vision here,
It is an honest° ghost, that let me tell you:
For your desire to know what is between us,
O'ermaster 't as you may. And now, good friends,   140
As you are friends, scholars and soldiers,
Give me one poor request.

HORATIO: What is 't, my lord? we will.

HAMLET: Never make known what you have seen to-night.

HORATIO: } My lord, we will not.
MARCELLUS: }

HAMLET: Nay, but swear 't.

HORATIO: In faith,   145
My lord, not I.

MARCELLUS: Nor I, my lord, in faith.

HAMLET: Upon my sword.°

MARCELLUS: We have sworn, my lord, already.

HAMLET: Indeed, upon my sword, indeed.   *Ghost cries under the stage.*

GHOST: Swear.

HAMLET: Ah, ha, boy! say'st thou so? art thou there, truepenny?°   150
Come on — you hear this fellow in the cellarage —
Consent to swear.

HORATIO: Propose the oath, my lord.

HAMLET: Never to speak of this that you have seen,
Swear by my sword.

GHOST [*beneath*]: Swear.   155

HAMLET: Hic et ubique?° then we'll shift our ground.
Come hither, gentlemen,
And lay your hands again upon my sword:
Swear by my sword,
Never to speak of this that you have heard.   160

GHOST [*beneath*]: Swear by his sword.

HAMLET: Well said, old mole! canst work i' th' earth so fast?
A worthy pioner!° Once more remove, good friends.

HORATIO: O day and night, but this is wondrous strange!

HAMLET: And therefore as a stranger give it welcome.   165

---

136. Saint Patrick: St. Patrick was keeper of Purgatory and patron saint of all blunders and
confusion.   **138. honest:** I.e., a real ghost and not an evil spirit.   **147. sword:** I.e., the hilt in
the form of a cross.   **150. truepenny:** Good old boy, or the like.   **156. Hic et ubique?:** Here
and everywhere?   **163. pioner:** Digger, miner.

There are more things in heaven and earth, Horatio,
Than are dreamt of in your philosophy.
But come;
Here, as before, never, so help you mercy,
How strange or odd soe'er I bear myself,   170
As I perchance hereafter shall think meet
To put an antic° disposition on,
That you, at such times seeing me, never shall,
With arms encumb'red° thus, or this head-shake,
Or by pronouncing of some doubtful phrase,   175
As "Well, well, we know," or "We could, an if we would,"
Or "If we list to speak," or "There be, an if they might,"
Or such ambiguous giving out,° to note°
That you know aught of me: this not to do,
So grace and mercy at your most need help you,   180
Swear.
GHOST [*beneath*]: Swear.
HAMLET: Rest, rest, perturbed spirit! [*They swear.*] So, gentlemen,
With all my love I do commend me to you:
And what so poor a man as Hamlet is
May do, t' express his love and friending° to you,   185
God willing, shall not lack. Let us go in together;
And still your fingers on your lips, I pray.
The time is out of joint: O cursed spite,
That ever I was born to set it right!
Nay, come, let's go together.   *Exeunt.*   190

[ACT II

SCENE I: *A room in Polonius's house.*]

Enter old Polonius with his man [Reynaldo].

POLONIUS: Give him this money and these notes, Reynaldo.
REYNALDO: I will, my lord.
POLONIUS: You shall do marvellous wisely, good Reynaldo,
Before you visit him, to make inquire
Of his behaviour.
REYNALDO: My lord, I did intend it.   5
POLONIUS: Marry, well said; very well said. Look you, sir,
Inquire me first what Danskers° are in Paris;
And how, and who, what means, and where they keep,°
What company, at what expense; and finding
By this encompassment° and drift° of question   10

---

172. **antic**: Fantastic.   174. **encumb'red**: Folded or entwined.   178. **giving out**: Profession
of knowledge; **to note**: To give a sign.   186. **friending**: Friendliness.   ACT II, SCENE I.   7.
Danskers: Danke was a common variant for "Denmark"; hence "Dane."   8. **keep**: Dwell.
10. **encompassment**: Roundabout talking; **drift**: Gradual approach or course.

That they do know my son, come you more nearer
Than your particular demands will touch it:°
Take° you as 'twere, some distant knowledge of him;
As thus, "I know his father and his friends,
And in part him": do you mark this, Reynaldo?   15
REYNALDO: Ay, very well, my lord.
POLONIUS: "And in part him; but" you may say "not well:
But, if 't be he I mean, he's very wild;
Addicted so and so": and there put on° him
What forgeries° you please; marry, none so rank   20
As may dishonour him; take heed of that;
But, sir, such wanton,° wild and usual slips
As are companions noted and most known
To youth and liberty.
REYNALDO: As gaming, my lord.
POLONIUS: Ay, or drinking, fencing,° swearing, quarrelling,   25
Drabbing;° you may go so far.
REYNALDO: My lord, that would dishonour him.
POLONIUS: 'Faith, no; as you may season it in the charge.
You must not put another scandal on him,
That he is open to incontinency;°   30
That's not my meaning: but breathe his faults so quaintly°
That they may seem the taints of liberty°
The flash and outbreak of a fiery mind,
A savageness in unreclaimed° blood,
Of general assault.°
REYNALDO: But, my good lord, —   35
POLONIUS: Wherefore should you do this?
REYNALDO: Ay, my lord,
I would know that.
POLONIUS: Marry, sir, here's my drift;
And, I believe, it is a fetch of wit:°
You laying these slight sullies on my son,
As 'twere a thing a little soil'd i' th' working,   40
Mark you,
Your party in converse, him you would sound,
Having ever° seen in the prenominate° crimes
The youth you breathe of guilty, be assur'd

11.–12. come . . . it: I.e., you will find out more this way than by asking pointed questions
13. Take: Assume, pretend.   **19. put on:** Impute to.   **20. forgeries:** Invented tales.   **22. wanton:** Sportive, unrestrained.   **25. fencing:** Indicative of the ill repute of professional fencers and fencing schools in Elizabethan times.   **26. Drabbing:** Associating with immoral women.   **30. incontinency:** Habitual loose behavior.   **31. quaintly:** Delicately, ingeniously.   **32. taints of liberty:** Blemishes due to freedom.   **34. unreclaimed:** Untamed.   **35. general assault:** Tendency that assails all untrained youth.   **38. fetch of wit:** Clever trick.   **43. ever:** At any time; **prenominate:** Before-mentioned.

He closes with you in this consequence;°   45
"Good sir," or so, or "friend," or "gentleman,"
According to the phrase or the addition
Of man and country.

REYNALDO: Very good, my lord.

POLONIUS: And then, sir, does 'a this — 'a does — what was I about to say? By
the mass, I was about to say something: where did I leave?   50

REYNALDO: At "closes in the consequence," at "friend or so," and "gentleman."

POLONIUS: At "closes in the consequence," ay, marry;
He closes thus: "I know the gentleman;
I saw him yesterday, or t' other day,
Or then, or then; with such, or such; and, as you say,   55
There was 'a gaming; there o'ertook in 's rouse°
There falling out at tennis": or perchance,
"I saw him enter such a house of sale,"
Videlicet,° a brothel, or so forth.
See you now;   60
Your bait of falsehood takes this carp of truth:
And thus do we of wisdom and of reach,°
With windlasses° and with assays of bias,°
By indirections° find directions° out:
So by my former lecture° and advice,   65
Shall you my son. You have me, have you not?

REYNALDO: My lord, I have.

POLONIUS: God bye ye;° fare ye well.

REYNALDO: Good my lord!

POLONIUS: Observe his inclination in yourself.°

REYNALDO: I shall, my lord.   70

POLONIUS: And let him ply his music.°

REYNALDO: Well, my lord.

POLONIUS: Farewell!   *Exit Reynaldo.*

Enter Ophelia.

                   How now, Ophelia! what's the matter?

OPHELIA: O, my lord, my lord, I have been so affrighted!

POLONIUS: With what, i' th' name of God?

OPHELIA: My lord, as I was sewing in my closet,°   75
Lord Hamlet, with his doublet° all unbrac'd;°

---

45. closes . . . consequence: Agrees with you in this conclusion. **56. o'ertook in 's rouse:**
Overcome by drink. **59. Videlicet:** Namely. **62. reach:** Capacity, ability. **63. wind-
lasses:** I.e., circuitous paths; **assays of bias:** Attempts that resemble the course of the bowl,
which, being weighted on one side, has a curving motion. **64. indirections:** Devious
courses; **directions:** Straight courses, i.e., the truth. **65. lecture:** Admonition. **67. bye ye:**
Be with you. **69. Observe . . . yourself:** In your own person, not by spies; or conform your
own conduct to his inclination; or test him by studying yourself. **71. ply his music:** Probably to be taken literally. **75. closet:** Private chamber. **76. doublet:** Close-fitting coat; **unbrac'd:** Unfastened.

No hat upon his head; his stockings foul'd,
Ungart'red, and down-gyved° to his ankle;
Pale as his shirt; his knees knocking each other;
And with a look so piteous in purport   80
As if he had been loosed out of hell
To speak of horrors, — he comes before me.
POLONIUS: Mad for thy love?
OPHELIA: My lord, I do not know;
But truly, I do fear it.
POLONIUS: What said he?
OPHELIA: He took me by the wrist and held me hard;   85
Then goes he to the length of all his arm;
And, with his other hand thus o'er his brow,
He falls to such perusal of my face
As 'a would draw it. Long stay'd he so;
At last, a little shaking of mine arm   90
And thrice his head thus waving up and down,
He rais'd a sigh so piteous and profound
As it did seem to shatter all his bulk°
And end his being: that done, he lets me go:
And, with his head over his shoulder turn'd,   95
He seem'd to find his way without his eyes;
For out o' doors he went without their helps,
And, to the last, bended their light on me.
POLONIUS: Come, go with me: I will go seek the king.
This is the very ecstasy of love,   100
Whose violent property° fordoes° itself
And leads the will to desperate undertakings
As oft as any passion under heaven
That does afflict our natures. I am sorry.
What, have you given him any hard words of late?   105
OPHELIA: No, my good lord, but, as you did command,
I did repel his letters and denied
His access to me.
POLONIUS: That hath made him mad.
I am sorry that with better heed and judgement
I had not quoted° him: I fear'd he did but trifle,   110
And meant to wrack thee; but, beshrew my jealousy!°
By heaven, it is as proper to our age
To cast beyond° ourselves in our opinions
As it is common for the younger sort
To lack discretion. Come, go we to the king: 115

---

78. down-gyved: Fallen to the ankles (like gyves or fetters). **93. bulk:** Body. **101. property:** Nature; **fordoes:** Destroys. **110. quoted:** Observed. **111. beshrew my jealousy:** Curse my suspicions. **113. cast beyond:** Overshoot, miscalculate.

This must be known; which, being kept close, might move
More grief to hide than hate to utter love.°
Come.   *Exeunt.*

[SCENE II: *A room in the castle.*]

Flourish. Enter King and Queen, Rosencrantz, and Guildenstern [with others].

KING: Welcome, dear Rosencrantz and Guildenstern!
    Moreover that° we much did long to see you,
    The need we have to use you did provoke
    Our hasty sending. Something have you heard
    Of Hamlet's transformation; so call it,   5
    Sith° nor th' exterior nor the inward man
    Resembles that it was. What it should be,
    More than his father's death, that thus hath put him
    So much from th' understanding of himself,
    I cannot dream of: I entreat you both,   10
    That, being of so young days° brought up with him,
    And sith so neighbour'd to his youth and haviour,
    That you vouchsafe your rest° here in our court
    Some little time: so by your companies
    To draw him on to pleasures, and to gather,   15
    So much as from occasion you may glean,
    Whether aught, to us unknown, afflicts him thus,
    That, open'd, lies within our remedy.
QUEEN: Good gentlemen, he hath much talk'd of you;
    And sure I am two men there are not living   20
    To whom he more adheres. If it will please you
    To show us so much gentry° and good will
    As to expend your time with us awhile,
    For the supply and profit° of our hope,
    Your visitation shall receive such thanks   25
    As fits a king's remembrance.
ROSENCRANTZ: Both your majesties
    Might, by the sovereign power you have of us,
    Put your dread pleasures more into command
    Than to entreaty.
GUILDENSTERN: But we both obey,
    And here give up ourselves, in the full bent°   30
    To lay our service freely at your feet,
    To be commanded.

116.–117. might . . . love: I.e., I might cause more grief to others by hiding the knowledge of Hamlet's love to Ophelia than hatred to me and mine by telling of it. SCENE II. **2. Moreover that:** Besides the fact that. **6. Sith:** Since. **11. of . . . days:** From such early youth. **13. vouchsafe your rest:** Please to stay. **22. gentry:** Courtesy. **24. supply and profit:** Aid and successful outcome. **30. in . . . bent:** To the utmost degree of our mental capacity.

KING: Thanks, Rosencrantz and gentle Guildenstern.
QUEEN: Thanks, Guildenstern and gentle Rosencrantz:
    And I beseech you instantly to visit 35
    My too much changed son. Go, some of you,
    And bring these gentlemen where Hamlet is.
GUILDENSTERN: Heavens make our presence and our practices
    Pleasant and helpful to him!
QUEEN: Ay, amen!

      Exeunt Rosencrantz and Guildenstern [with some Attendants].

Enter Polonius.

POLONIUS: Th' ambassadors from Norway, my good lord, 40
    Are joyfully return'd.
KING: Thou still hast been the father of good news.
POLONIUS: Have I, my lord? I assure my good liege,
    I hold my duty, as I hold my soul,
    Both to my God and to my gracious king: 45
    And I do think, or else this brain of mine
    Hunts not the trail of policy so sure
    As it hath us'd to do, that I have found
    The very cause of Hamlet's lunacy.
KING: O, speak of that; that do I long to hear. 50
POLONIUS: Give first admittance to th' ambassadors;
    My news shall be the fruit to that great feast.
KING: Thyself do grace to them, and bring them in.   *[Exit Polonius.]*
    He tells me, my dear Gertrude, he hath found
    The head and source of all your son's distemper. 55
QUEEN: I doubt° it is no other but the main;°
    His father's death, and our o'erhasty marriage.
KING: Well, we shall sift him.

    Enter Ambassadors [Voltimand and Cornelius, with Polonius.]
                  Welcome, my good friends!
    Say, Voltimand, what from our brother Norway?
VOLTIMAND: Most fair return of greetings and desires. 60
    Upon our first, he sent out to suppress
    His nephew's levies; which to him appear'd
    To be a preparation 'gainst the Polack;
    But, better look'd into, he truly found
    It was against your highness: whereat griev'd, 65
    That so his sickness, age and impotence
    Was falsely borne in hand,° sends out arrests
    On Fortinbras; which he, in brief, obeys;
    Receives rebuke from Norway, and in fine°
    Makes vow before his uncle never more 70

---

56. doubt: Fear; **main:** Chief point, principal concern.   **67. borne in hand:** Deluded.   **69. in fine:** In the end.

To give th' assay° of arms against your majesty.
Whereon old Norway, overcome with joy,
Gives him three score thousand crowns in annual fee,
And his commission to employ those soldiers,
So levied as before, against the Polack: 75
With an entreaty, herein further shown, [*giving a paper.*]
That it might please you to give quiet pass
Through your dominions for this enterprise,
On such regards of safety and allowance°
As therein are set down.

KING: It likes° us well;   80
And at our more consider'd° time we'll read,
Answer, and think upon this business.
Meantime we thank you for your well-took labour:
Go to your rest; at night we'll feast together:
Most welcome home!   *Exeunt Ambassadors.*

POLONIUS: This business is well ended.   85
My liege, and madam, to expostulate
What majesty should be, what duty is,
Why day is day, night night, and time is time,
Were nothing but to waste night, day and time.
Therefore, since brevity is the soul of wit,°   90
And tediousness the limbs and outward flourishes,°
I will be brief: your noble son is mad:
Mad call I it; for, to define true madness
What is 't but to be nothing else but mad?
But let that go.

QUEEN: More matter, with less art.   95
POLONIUS: Madam, I swear I use no art at all.
That he is mad, 'tis true: 'tis true 'tis pity;
And pity 'tis 'tis true: a foolish figure;°
But farewell it, for I will use no art.
Mad let us grant him, then: and now remains   100
That we find out the cause of this effect,
Or rather say, the cause of this defect,
For this effect defective comes by cause:
Thus it remains, and the remainder thus.
Perpend.°   105
I have a daughter — have while she is mine —
Who, in her duty and obedience, mark,
Hath given me this: now gather, and surmise. [*Reads the letter.*] "To the
celestial and my soul's idol,

---

71. assay: Assault, trial (of arms).   **79. safety and allowance:** Pledges of safety to the country and terms of permission for the troops to pass.   **80. likes:** Pleases.   **81. consider'd:** Suitable for deliberation.   **90. wit:** Sound sense or judgment.   **91. flourishes:** Ostentation, embellishments.   **98. figure:** Figure of speech.   **105. Perpend:** Consider.

the most beautified Ophelia," — 110
That's an ill phrase, a vile phrase; "beautified" is a vile phrase: but you
shall hear. Thus: [*Reads.*]
"In her excellent white bosom, these, & c."
QUEEN: Came this from Hamlet to her?
POLONIUS: Good madam, stay awhile; I will be faithful. [*Reads.*] 115
       "Doubt thou the stars are fire;
          Doubt that the sun doth move;
          Doubt truth to be a liar;
          But never doubt I love.
"O dear Ophelia, I am ill at these numbers;° I have not art to reckon° my 120
groans: but that I love thee best, O most best, believe it. Adieu.
     "Thine evermore, most dear lady, whilst this machine° is to him,
                                   HAMLET."

This, in obedience, hath my daughter shown me,
And more above,° hath his solicitings,
As they fell out° by time, by means° and place, 125
All given to mine ear.
KING: But how hath she
Receiv'd his love?
POLONIUS: What do you think of me?
KING: As of a man faithful and honourable.
POLONIUS: I would fain prove so. But what might you think,
When I had seen this hot love on the wing — 130
As I perceiv'd it, I must tell you that,
Before my daughter told me — what might you,
Or my dear majesty your queen here, think,
If I had play'd the desk or table-book,°
Or given my heart a winking,° mute and dumb, 135
Or look'd upon this love with idle sight;
What might you think? No, I went round to work,
And my young mistress thus I did bespeak:°
"Lord Hamlet is a prince, out of thy star;°
This must not be": and then I prescripts gave her, 140
That she should lock herself from his resort,
Admit no messengers, receive no tokens.
Which done, she took the fruits of my advice;
And he, repelled — a short tale to make —
Fell into a sadness, then into a fast, 145
Thence to a watch,° thence into a weakness,

---

120. ill ... numbers: Unskilled at writing verses; **reckon:** Number metrically, scan.
122. machine: Bodily frame. **125. more above:** Moreover. **126. fell out:** Occurred;
means: Opportunities (of access). **135. play'd ... table-book:** I.e., remained shut up, concealed this information. **136. given ... winking:** Given my heart a signal to keep silent.
139. bespeak: Address. **140. out ... star:** Above thee in position. **147. watch:** State of
sleeplessness.

Thence to a lightness,° and, by this declension,°
Into the madness wherein now he raves,
And all we mourn for.

KING: Do you think 'tis this?   150

QUEEN: It may be, very like.

POLONIUS: Hath there been such a time — I would fain know that —
That I have positively said " 'Tis so,"
When it prov'd otherwise?

KING: Not that I know.

Polonius [*pointing to his head and shoulder*]: Take this from this, if this be other- 155
wise:
If circumstances lead me, I will find
Where truth is hid, though it were hid indeed
Within the centre.°

KING: How may we try it further?

POLONIUS: You know, sometimes he walks four hours together
Here in the lobby.

QUEEN: So he does indeed.   160

POLONIUS: At such a time I'll loose my daughter to him:
Be you and I behind an arras° then;
Mark the encounter: if he love her not
And be not from his reason fall'n thereon,°
Let me be no assistant for a state,   165
But keep a farm and carters.

KING: We will try it.

Enter Hamlet [reading on a book].

QUEEN: But, look, where sadly the poor wretch comes reading.

POLONIUS: Away, I do beseech you both, away:

                              Exeunt King and Queen [with Attendants].

I'll board° him presently. O, give me leave.
How does my good Lord Hamlet?   170

HAMLET: Well, God-a-mercy.

POLONIUS: Do you know me, my lord?

HAMLET: Excellent well; you are a fishmonger.°

POLONIUS: Not I, my lord.

HAMLET: Then I would you were so honest a man.

POLONIUS: Honest, my lord!   175

HAMLET: Ay, sir; to be honest, as this world goes, is to be one man picked out of
ten thousand.

POLONIUS: That's very true, my lord.

---

148. **lightness:** Lightheadedness; **declension:** Decline, deterioration. 158. **centre:** Middle point of the earth. 162. **arras:** Hanging, tapestry. 164. **thereon:** On that account.
169. **board:** Accost. 173. **fishmonger:** An opprobrious expression meaning "bawd," "procurer."

HAMLET: For if the sun breed maggots in a dead dog, being a good kissing car- 180
rion,° — Have you a daughter?

POLONIUS: I have, my lord.

HAMLET: Let her not walk i' the sun:° conception° is a blessing: but as your
daughter may conceive — Friend, look to 't.

POLONIUS [*aside*]: How say you by° that? Still harping on my daughter: yet he 185
knew me not at first; 'a said I was a fishmonger: 'a is far gone, far gone:
and truly in my youth I suffered much extremity for love; very near this.
I'll speak to him again. What do you read, my lord?

HAMLET: Words, words, words.

POLONIUS: What is the matter,° my lord? 190

HAMLET: Between who?°

POLONIUS: I mean, the matter that you read, my lord.

HAMLET: Slanders, sir: for the satirical rogue says here that old men have grey
beards, that their faces are wrinkled, their eyes purging° thick amber
and plum-tree gum and that they have a plentiful lack of wit, together 195
with most weak hams: all which, sir, though I most powerfully and po-
tently believe, yet I hold it not honesty° to have it thus set down, for
yourself, sir, should be old as I am, if like a crab you could go backward.

POLONIUS [ASIDE]: Though this be madness, yet there is method in 't. — Will
you walk out of the air, my lord? 200

HAMLET: Into my grave.

POLONIUS: Indeed, that's out of the air. *(Aside.)* How pregnant sometimes his
replies are! a happiness° that often madness hits on, which reason and
sanity could not so prosperously° be delivered of. I will leave him, and
suddenly contrive the means of meeting between him and my daughter. 205
— My honourable lord, I will most humbly take my leave of you.

HAMLET: You cannot, sir, take from me any thing that I will more willingly part
withal: except my life, except my life, except my life.

Enter Guildenstern and Rosencrantz.

POLONIUS: Fare you well, my lord.

HAMLET: These tedious old fools! 210

POLONIUS: You go to seek the Lord Hamlet; there he is.

ROSENCRANTZ [*to Polonius*]: God save you, sir! [*Exit Polonius.*]

GUILDENSTERN: My honoured lord!

ROSENCRANTZ: My most dear lord!

HAMLET: My excellent good friends! How dost thou, Guildenstern? Ah, Rosen- 215
crantz! Good lads, how do ye both?

ROSENCRANTZ: As the indifferent° children of the earth.

GUILDENSTERN: Happy, in that we are not over-happy;

180.–181. **good kissing carrion:** I.e., a good piece of flesh for kissing (?). 183. **i' the sun:** In
the sunshine of princely favors; **conception:** Quibble on "understanding" and "pregnancy."
185. **by:** Concerning. 190. **matter:** Substance. 191. **Between who:** Hamlet deliberately
takes *matter* as meaning "basis of dispute." 194. **purging:** discharging. 197. **honesty:** Decency. 203. **happiness:** Felicity of expression. 204. **prosperously:** Successfully. 217. **indifferent:** Ordinary.

On Fortune's cap we are not the very button.

HAMLET: Nor the soles of her shoe?   220

ROSENCRANTZ: Neither, my lord.

HAMLET: Then you live about her waist, or in the middle of her favours?

GUILDENSTERN: 'Faith, her privates° we.

HAMLET: In the secret parts of Fortune? O, most true; she is a strumpet. What's
the news?   225

ROSENCRANTZ: None, my lord, but that the world's grown honest.

HAMLET: Then is doomsday near: but your news is not true. Let me question
more in particular: what have you, my good friends, deserved at the
hands of Fortune, that she sends you to prison hither?

GUILDENSTERN: Prison, my lord!   230

HAMLET: Denmark's a prison.

ROSENCRANTZ: Then is the world one.

HAMLET: A goodly one; in which there are many confines,° wards and dun-
geons, Denmark being one o' the worst.

ROSENCRANTZ: We think not so, my lord.   235

HAMLET: Why, then, 'tis none to you; for there is nothing either good or bad,
but thinking makes it so: to me it is a prison.

ROSENCRANTZ: Why then, your ambition makes it one; 'tis too narrow for your
mind.

HAMLET: O God, I could be bounded in a nutshell and count myself a king of 240
infinite space, were it not that I have bad dreams.

GUILDENSTERN: Which dreams indeed are ambition, for the very substance of
the ambitious° is merely the shadow of a dream.

HAMLET: A dream itself is but a shadow.

ROSENCRANTZ: Truly, and I hold ambition of so airy and light a quality that it is 245
but a shadow's shadow.

HAMLET: Then are our beggars bodies, and our monarchs and outstretched heroes the beggars' shadows. Shall we to the court? for, by my fay,° I cannot reason.°

ROSENCRANTZ: ⎫
              ⎬   We'll wait upon° you.   250
GUILDENSTERN: ⎭

HAMLET: No such matter: I will not sort° you with the rest of my servants, for,
to speak to you like an honest man, I am most dreadfully attended.° But,
in the beaten way of friendship,° what make you at Elsinore?

ROSENCRANTZ: To visit you, my lord: no other occasion.

HAMLET: Beggar that I am, I am ever poor in thanks; but I thank you: and sure, 255
dear friends, my thanks are too dear a° halfpenny. Were you not sent
for? Is it your own inclining? Is it a free visitation? Come, come, deal
justly with me: come, come; nay, speak.

---

223. **privates:** I.e., ordinary men (sexual pun on *private parts*).   233. **confines:** Places of confinement.   243. **very . . . ambitious:** That seemingly most substantial thing which the ambitious pursue.   248. **fay:** Faith.   249. **reason:** Argue.   250. **wait upon:** Accompany.   251.
sort: Class.   252. **dreadfully attended:** Poorly provided with servants.   253. **in the . . .
friendship:** As a matter of course among friends.   256. **a:** I.e., at a.

GUILDENSTERN: What should we say, my lord?

HAMLET: Why, any thing, but to the purpose. You were sent for; and there is a 260
kind of confession in your looks which your modesties have not craft
enough to colour: I know the good king and queen have sent for you.

ROSENCRANTZ: To what end, my lord?

HAMLET: That you must teach me. But let me conjure° you, by the rights of our
fellowship, by the consonancy of our youth,° by the obligation of our 265
ever-preserved love, and by what more dear a better proposer° could
charge you withal, be even and direct with me, whether you were sent for,
or no?

ROSENCRANTZ [*aside to Guildenstern*]: What say you?

HAMLET [*aside*]: Nay, then, I have an eye of you. — If you love me, hold not 270
off.

GUILDENSTERN: My lord, we were sent for.

HAMLET: I will tell you why; so shall my anticipation prevent your discovery,°
and your secrecy to the king and queen moult no feather. I have of late
— but wherefore I know not — lost all my mirth, forgone all custom of 275
exercises; and indeed it goes so heavily with my disposition that this
goodly frame, the earth, seems to me a sterile promontory, this most excellent canopy, the air, look you, this brave o'erhanging firmament, this
majestical roof fretted° with golden fire, why, it appeareth nothing to me
but a foul and pestilent congregation of vapours. What a piece of work 280
is a man! how noble in reason! how infinite in faculties° in form and
moving how express° and admirable! in action how like an angel! in ap-
prehension° how like a god! the beauty of the world! the paragon of animals! And yet, to me, what is this quintessence° of dust? man delights
not me: no, nor woman neither, though by your smiling you seem to 285
say so.

ROSENCRANTZ: My lord, there was no such stuff in my thoughts.

HAMLET: Why did you laugh then, when I said "man delights not me"?

ROSENCRANTZ: To think, my lord, if you delight not in man, what lenten° entertainment the players shall receive from you: we coted° them on the way; 290
and hither are they coming, to offer you service.

HAMLET: He that plays the king shall be welcome; his majesty shall have tribute of me; the adventurous knight shall use his foil and target;° the lover
shall not sigh gratis; the humorous man° shall end his part in peace; the
clown shall make those laugh whose lungs are tickle o' the sere;° and the 295
lady shall say her mind freely, or the blank verse shall halt for 't.° What
players are they?

---

264. conjure: Adjure, entreat. **265. consonancy of our youth:** The fact that we are of the
same age. **266. better proposer:** One more skillful in finding proposals. **273. prevent
your discovery:** Forestall your disclosure. **279. fretted:** Adorned. **281. faculties:**
Capacity. **282. express:** Well-framed(?), exact(?). **282–283. apprehension:** Understanding. **284. quintessence:** The fifth essence of ancient philosophy, supposed to be the substance of the heavenly bodies and to be latent in all things. **289. lenten:** Meager. **290.
coted:** Overtook and passed beyond. **293. foil and target:** Sword and shield. **294. humorous man:** Actor who takes the part of the humor characters. **295. tickle o' the sere:**
Easy on the trigger. **295–296. the lady ... for 't:** The lady (fond of talking) shall have opportunity to talk, blank verse or no blank verse.

ROSENCRANTZ: Even those you were wont to take delight in, the tragedians of the city.

HAMLET: How chances it they travel? their residence,° both in reputation and profit, was better both ways.   300

ROSENCRANTZ: I think their inhibition° comes by the means of the late innovation.°

HAMLET: Do they hold the same estimation they did when I was in the city? are they so followed?

ROSENCRANTZ: No, indeed, are they not.   305

HAMLET: How° comes it? do they grow rusty?

ROSENCRANTZ: Nay, their endeavour keeps in the wonted pace: but there is, sir, an aery° of children, little eyases,° that cry out on the top of question,° and are most tyrannically° clapped for 't: these are now the fashion, and 310 so berattle° the common stages° — so they call them — that many wearing rapiers° are afraid of goose-quills° and dare scarce come thither.

HAMLET: What, are they children? who maintains 'em? how are they escoted?° Will they pursue the quality° no longer than they can sing?° will they not say afterwards, if they should grow themselves to common° players 315 — as it is most like, if their means are no better — their writers do them wrong, to make them exclaim against their own succession?°

ROSENCRANTZ: 'Faith, there has been much to do on both sides; and the nation holds it no sin to tarre° them to controversy: there was, for a while, no money bid for argument,° unless the poet and the player went to cuffs° 320 in the question.°

HAMLET: Is't possible?

GUILDENSTERN: O, there has been much throwing about of brains.

HAMLET: Do the boys carry it away?°

ROSENCRANTZ: Ay, that they do, my lord; Hercules and his load° too.   325

HAMLET: It is not very strange; for my uncle is king of Denmark, and those that would make mows° at him while my father lived, give twenty, forty,

---

300. **residence:** Remaining in one place.   302. **inhibition:** Formal prohibition (from acting plays in the city or, possibly, at court).   302.–303. **innovation:** The new fashion in satirical plays performed by boy actors in the "private" theaters.   307.–325. **How . . . load too:** The passage is the famous one dealing with the War of the Theatres (1599–1602); namely, the rivalry between the children's companies and the adult actors.   309. **aery:** Nest; **eyases:** Young hawks.; **cry . . . question:** Speak in a high key dominating conversation; clamor forth the height of controversy; probably "excel" (cf. line 459); perhaps intended to decry leaders of the dramatic profession.   310. **tyrannically:** Outrageously.   311. **berattle:** Berate; **common stages:** Public theaters.   311.–312. **many wearing rapiers:** Many men of fashion, who were afraid to patronize the common players for fear of being satirized by the poets who wrote for the children; **goose-quills:** I.e., pens of satirists.   313. **escoted:** Maintained.   314. **quality:** Acting profession; **no longer . . . sing:** I.e., until their voices change.   315. **common:** Regular, adult.   317. **succession:** future careers.   319. **tarre:** Set on (as dogs).   320. **argument:** Probably, plot for a play; **went to cuffs:** Came to blows.   321. **question:** Controversy.   324. **carry it away:** Win the day.   325. **Hercules . . . load:** Regarded as an allusion to the sign of the Globe Theatre, which was Hercules bearing the world on his shoulder.   327. **mows:** Grimaces.

fifty, a hundred ducats° a-piece for his picture in little.° 'Sblood, there is
something in this more than natural, if philosophy could find it out.

A flourish [of trumpets within].

GUILDENSTERN: There are the players.　　　　　　　　　　　　　　　　330

HAMLET: Gentlemen, you are welcome to Elsinore. Your hands, come then: the
appurtenance of welcome is fashion and ceremony: let me comply° with
you in this garb,° lest my extent° to the players, which, I tell you, must
show fairly outwards, should more appear like entertainment than
yours. You are welcome: but my uncle-father and aunt-mother are de- 335
ceived.

GUILDENSTERN: In what, my dear lord?

HAMLET: I am but mad north-north-west:° when the wind is southerly I know
a hawk from a handsaw.°

Enter Polonius.

POLONIUS: Well be with you, gentlemen!　　　　　　　　　　　　　　340

HAMLET: Hark you, Guildenstern; and you too: at each ear a hearer: that great
baby you see there is not yet out of his swaddling-clouts.°

ROSENCRANTZ: Happily he is the second time come to them; for they say an old
man is twice a child.

HAMLET: I will prophesy he comes to tell me of the players; mark it. — You say 345
right, sir: o' Monday morning;° 'twas then indeed.

POLONIUS: My lord, I have news to tell you.

HAMLET: My lord, I have news to tell you. When Roscius° was an actor in
Rome, —

POLONIUS: The actors are come hither, my lord.　　　　　　　　　　　350

HAMLET: Buz, buz!°

POLONIUS: Upon my honour, —

HAMLET: Then came each actor on his ass, —

POLONIUS: The best actors in the world, either for tragedy, comedy, history, pastoral, pastoral-comical, historical-pastoral, tragical-historical, tragical- 355
comical-historical-pastoral, scene individable,° or poem unlimited:°
Seneca° cannot be too heavy, nor Plautus° too light. For the law of writ
and the liberty,° these are the only men.

---

328. ducats: Gold coins worth 9s. 4d; **in little:** In miniature.　**332. comply:** Observe the for-
malities of courtesy.　**333. garb:** Manner; **extent:** Showing of kindness.　**338. I am . . .
north-north-west:** I am only partly mad, i.e., in only one point of the compass.　**339. handsaw:** A proposed reading of *hernshaw* would mean "heron"; *handsaw* may be an early corruption of *hernshaw*. Another view regards *hawk* as the variant of *hack*, a tool of the pickax
type, and *handsaw* as a saw operated by hand.　**342. swaddling-clouts:** Cloths in which to
wrap a newborn baby.　**346. o' Monday morning:** Said to mislead Polonius.　**348. Roscius:**
A famous Roman actor.　**351. Buz, buz:** An interjection used at Oxford to denote stale news.
356. scene individable: A play observing the unity of place; **poem unlimited:** A play disregarding the unities of time and place.　**357. Seneca:** Writer of Latin tragedies, model of early
Elizabethan writers of tragedy; **Plautus:** Writer of Latin comedy.　**357.–358. law . . . liberty:**
Pieces written according to rules and without rules, i.e., "classical" and "romantic" dramas.

HAMLET: O Jephthah, judge of Israel,° what a treasure hadst thou!

POLONIUS: What a treasure had he, my lord?   360

HAMLET: Why,

> "One fair daughter, and no more,
> The which he loved passing well."

POLONIUS [*aside*]: Still on my daughter.

HAMLET: Am I not i' the right, old Jephthah?   365

POLONIUS: If you call me Jephthah, my lord, I have a daughter that I love pass-
ing° well.

HAMLET: Nay, that follows not.

POLONIUS: What follows, then, my lord?

HAMLET: Why,   370

> "As by lot, God wot,"

and then, you know,

> "It came to pass, as most like° it was," —

the first row° of the pious chanson° will show you more; for look, where
my abridgement comes.°   375

Enter the Players.

You are welcome, masters; welcome, all. I am glad to see thee well. Welcome,
good friends. O, old friend! why, thy face is valanced° since I saw thee
last: comest thou to beard me in Denmark? What, my young lady and
mistress! By'r lady, your ladyship is nearer to heaven than when I saw
you last, by the altitude of a chopine.° Pray God, your voice, like a piece 380
of uncurrent° gold, be not cracked within the ring.° Masters, you are all
welcome. We'll e'en to 't like French falconers, fly at any thing we see:
we'll have a speech straight: come, give us a taste of your quality; come,
a passionate speech.

FIRST PLAYER: What speech, my good lord?   385

HAMLET: I heard thee speak me a speech once, but it was never acted; or, if it
was, not above once; for the play, I remember, pleased not the million;
'twas caviary to the general:° but it was — as I received it, and others,
whose judgements in such matters cried in the top of° mine — an excellent play, well digested in the scenes, set down with as much modesty as 390
cunning.° I remember, one said there were no sallets° in the lines to
make the matter savoury, nor no matter in the phrase that might indict°
the author of affectation; but called it an honest method, as wholesome
as sweet, and by very much more handsome than fine.° One speech in 't

---

359. Jephthah . . . Israel: Jephthah had to sacrifice his daughter; see Judges 11.   **366–367. passing:** Surpassingly.   **373. like:** Probable.   **374. row:** Stanza; **chanson:** Ballad.   **375. abridgement comes:** Opportunity comes for cutting short the conversation.   **377. valanced:** Fringed
(with a beard).   **380. chopine:** Kind of shoe raised by the thickness of the heel; worn in Italy,
particularly at Venice.   **381. uncurrent:** Not passable as lawful coinage; **cracked within the
ring:** In the center of coins were rings enclosing the sovereign's head; if the coin was cracked
within this ring, it was unfit for currency.   **388. caviary to the general:** Not relished by the multitude.   **389. cried in the top of:** Spoke with greater authority than.   **391. cunning:** Skill; **sal-
lets:** Salads: here, spicy improprieties.   **392. indict:** Convict.   **393–394. as wholesome . . . fine:**
Its beauty was not that of elaborate ornament, but that of order and proportion.

I chiefly loved: 'twas Æneas' tale to Dido;° and thereabout of it espe-   395
cially, where he speaks of Priam's slaughter: if it live in your memory,
begin at this line: let me see, let me see —
"The rugged Pyrrhus,° like th' Hyrcanian beast,"° —
'tis not so: — it begins with Pyrrhus: —
"The rugged Pyrrhus, he whose sable arms,   400
Black as his purpose, did the night resemble
When he lay couched in the ominous horse,°
Hath now this dread and black complexion smear'd
With heraldry more dismal; head to foot
Now is he total gules;° horridly trick'd°   405
With blood of fathers, mothers, daughters, sons,
Bak'd and impasted° with the parching streets,
That lend a tyrannous and a damned light
To their lord's murder: roasted in wrath and fire,
And thus o'er-sized° with coagulate gore,   410
With eyes like carbuncles, the hellish Pyrrhus
Old grandsire Priam seeks."
So, proceed you.
POLONIUS: 'Fore God, my lord, well spoken, with good accent and good discre-
tion.   415
FIRST PLAYER: "Anon he finds him
Striking too short at Greeks; his antique sword,
Rebellious to his arm, lies where it falls,
Repugnant° to command: unequal match'd,
Pyrrhus at Priam drives; in rage strikes wide;   420
But with the whiff and wind of his fell sword
Th' unnerved father falls. Then senseless Ilium,°
Seeming to feel this blow, with flaming top
Stoops to his base, and with a hideous crash
Takes prisoner Pyrrhus' ear: for, lo! his sword   425
Which was declining on the milky head
Of reverend Priam, seem'd i' th' air to stick:
So, as a painted tyrant,° Pyrrhus stood,
And like a neutral to his will and matter,°
Did nothing.   430
But, as we often see, against° some storm,
A silence in the heavens, the rack° stand still,
The bold winds speechless and the orb below

---

395. Æneas' tale to Dido: The lines recited by the player are imitated from Marlowe and
Nashe's *Dido Queen of Carthage* (II.i.214ff.). They are written in such a way that the conventionality of the play within a play is raised above that of ordinary drama.   **398. Pyrrhus:** A
Greek hero in the Trojan War; **Hyrcanian beast:** The tiger; see Virgil, *Aeneid,* IV.266.   **402.**
ominous horse: Trojan horse.   **405. gules:** Red, a heraldic term; **trick'd:** Spotted, smeared.
407. impasted: Made into a paste.   **410. o'er-sized:** Covered as with size or glue.   **419. Re-**
pugnant: Disobedient.   **422. Then senseless Ilium:** Insensate Troy.   **428. painted tyrant:**
Tyrant in a picture.   **429. matter:** Task.   **431. against:** Before.   **432. rack:** Mass of clouds.

As hush as death, anon the dreadful thunder
Doth rend the region,° so, after Pyrrhus' pause,   435
Aroused vengeance sets him new a-work;
And never did the Cyclops' hammers fall
On Mars's armour forg'd for proof eterne°
With less remorse than Pyrrhus' bleeding sword
Now falls on Priam.   440
Out, out, thou strumpet, Fortune! All you gods,
In general synod,° take away her power;
Break all the spokes and fellies° from her wheel,
And bowl the round nave° down the hill of heaven,
As low as to the fiends!"   445

POLONIUS: This is too long.

HAMLET: It shall to the barber's, with your beard. Prithee, say on: he's for a jig°
or a tale of bawdry,° or he sleeps: say on: come to Hecuba.°

FIRST PLAYER: "But who, ah woe! had seen the mobled° queen — "

HAMLET: "The mobled queen?"   450

POLONIUS: That's good; "mobled queen" is good.

FIRST PLAYER: "Run barefoot up and down, threat'ning the flames
With bisson rheum;° a clout° upon that head
Where late the diadem stood, and for a robe,
About her lank and all o'er-teemed° loins,   455
A blanket, in the alarm of fear caught up;
Who this had seen, with tongue in venom steep'd,
'Gainst Fortune's state would treason have pronounc'd:°
But if the gods themselves did see her then
When she saw Pyrrhus make malicious sport   460
In mincing with his sword her husband's limbs,
The instant burst of clamour that she made,
Unless things mortal move them not at all,
Would have made milch° the burning eyes of heaven,
And passion in the gods."   465

POLONIUS: Look, whe'r he has not turned° his colour and has tears in 's eyes.
Prithee, no more.

HAMLET: 'Tis well; I'll have thee speak out the rest soon. Good my lord, will
you see the players well bestowed? Do you hear, let them be well used;
for they are the abstract° and brief chronicles of the time: after your   470
death you were better have a bad epitaph than their ill report while you
live.

---

435. **region:** Assembly.   438. **proof eterne:** External resistance to assault.   442. **synod:** Assembly.   443. **fellies:** Pieces of wood forming the rim of a wheel.   444. **nave:** Hub.   447. **jig:** Comic performance given at the end or in an interval of a play.   448. **bawdry:** Indecency; **Hecuba:** Wife of Priam, king of Troy.   449. **mobled:** Muffled.   453. **bisson rheum:** Blinding tears; **clout:** Piece of cloth.   455. **o'er-teemed:** Worn out with bearing children.   458. **pronounc'd:** Proclaimed.   464. **milch:** Moist with tears.   466. **turned:** Changed.   470. **abstract:** Summary account.

POLONIUS: My lord, I will use them according to their desert.

HAMLET: God's bodykins,° man, much better: use every man after his desert, and who shall 'scape whipping? Use them after your own honour and   475
dignity: the less they deserve, the more merit is in your bounty. Take them in.

POLONIUS: Come, sirs.

HAMLET: Follow him, friends: we'll hear a play tomorrow. [*Aside to First Player.*] Dost thou hear me, old friend; can you play the Murder of Gon-   480
zago?

FIRST PLAYER: Ay, my lord.

HAMLET: We'll ha 't to-morrow night. You could, for a need, study a speech of some dozen or sixteen lines,° which I would set down and insert in 't, could you not?   485

FIRST PLAYER: Ay, my lord.

HAMLET: Very well. Follow that lord; and look you mock him not. — My good friends, I'll leave you till night: you are welcome to Elsinore.

Exeunt Polonius and Players.

ROSENCRANTZ: Good my lord!   *Exeunt [Rosencrantz and Guildenstern.]*

HAMLET: Ay, so, God bye to you. — Now I am alone.   490
O, what a rogue and peasant° slave am I!
Is it not monstrous that this player here,
But in a fiction, in a dream of passion,
Could force his soul so to his own conceit
That from her working all his visage wann'd,°   495
Tears in his eyes, distraction in 's aspect,
A broken voice, and his whole function suiting
With forms to his conceit?° and all for nothing!
For Hecuba!
What's Hecuba to him, or he to Hecuba,   500
That he should weep for her? What would he do,
Had he the motive and the cue for passion
That I have? He would drown the stage with tears
And cleave the general ear with horrid speech,
Make mad the guilty and appall the free,   505
Confound the ignorant, and amaze indeed
The very faculties of eyes and ears.
Yet I,
A dull and muddy-mettled° rascal, peak,°
Like John-a-dreams,° unpregnant of° my cause,   510

---

474. bodykins: Diminutive form of the oath "by God's body."   **484. dozen or sixteen lines:** Critics have amused themselves by trying to locate Hamlet's lines. Lucianus's speech III.ii.226–231 is the best guess.   **491. peasant:** Base.   **495. wann'd:** Grew pale.   **497.–498. his whole ... conceit:** His whole being responded with forms to suit his thought.   **509. muddy-mettled:** Dull-spirited; **peak:** Mope, pine.   **510. John-a-dreams:** An expression occurring elsewhere in Elizabethan literature to indicate a dreamer; **unpregnant of:** Not quickened by.

And can say nothing; no, not for a king.
Upon whose property° and most dear life
A damn'd defeat was made. Am I a coward?
Who calls me villain? breaks my pate across?
Plucks off my beard, and blows it in my face?   515
Tweaks me by the nose? gives me the lie i' th' throat,
As deep as to the lungs? who does me this?
Ha!
'Swounds, I should take it: for it cannot be
But I am pigeon-liver'd° and lack gall   520
To make oppression bitter, or ere this
I should have fatted all the region kites°
With this slave's offal: bloody, bawdy villain!
Remorseless, treacherous, lecherous, kindless° villain!
O, vengeance!   525
Why, what an ass am I! This is most brave,
That I, the son of a dear father murder'd,
Prompted to my revenge by heaven and hell,
Must, like a whore, unpack my heart with words,
And fall a-cursing, like a very drab,°   530
A stallion!°
Fie upon 't! foh! About,° my brains! Hum, I have heard
That guilty creatures sitting at a play
Have by the very cunning of the scene
Been struck so to the soul that presently   535
They have proclaim'd their malefactions;
For murder, though it have no tongue, will speak
With most miraculous organ. I'll have these players
Play something like the murder of my father
Before mine uncle: I'll observe his looks: 540
I'll tent° him to the quick: if 'a do blench,°
I know my course. The spirit that I have seen
May be the devil:° and the devil hath power
T' assume a pleasing shape; yea, and perhaps
Out of my weakness and my melancholy,   545
As he is very potent with such spirits,°
Abuses me to damn me: I'll have grounds
More relative° than this:° the play's the thing
Wherein I'll catch the conscience of the king.   *Exit.*

---

512. property: Proprietorship (of crown and life). **520. pigeon-liver'd:** The pigeon was supposed to secrete no gall; if Hamlet, so he says, had had gall, he would have felt the bitterness of oppression, and avenged it. **522. region kites:** Kites of the air. **524. kindless:** Unnatural. **530. drab:** Prostitute. **531. stallion:** Prostitute (male or female). **532. About:** About it, or turn thou right about. **541. tent:** Probe; **blench:** Quail, flinch. **543. May be the devil:** Hamlet's suspicion is properly grounded in the belief of the time. **546. spirits:** Humors. **548. relative:** Closely related, definite; **this:** I.e., the ghost's story.

[ACT III

SCENE I: *A room in the castle.*]

Enter King, Queen, Polonius, Ophelia, Rosencrantz, Guildenstern, Lords.

KING: And can you, by no drift of conference,°
    Get from him why he puts on this confusion,
    Grating so harshly all his days of quiet
    With turbulent and dangerous lunacy?
ROSENCRANTZ: He does confess he feels himself distracted;   5
    But from what cause 'a will by no means speak.
GUILDENSTERN: Nor do we find him forward° to be sounded,
    But, with a crafty madness, keeps aloof,
    When we would bring him on to some confession
    Of his true state.
QUEEN: Did he receive you well?   10
ROSENCRANTZ: Most like a gentleman.
GUILDENSTERN: But with much forcing of his disposition.°
ROSENCRANTZ: Niggard of question;° but, of our demands,
    Most free in his reply.
QUEEN: Did you assay° him
    To any pastime?   15
ROSENCRANTZ: Madam, it so fell out, that certain players
    We o'er-raught° on the way: of these we told him;
    And there did seem in him a kind of joy
    To hear of it: they are here about the court,
    And, as I think, they have already order   20
    This night to play before him.
POLONIUS: 'Tis most true:
    And he beseech'd me to entreat your majesties
    To hear and see the matter.
KING: With all my heart; and it doth much content me
    To hear him so inclin'd.   25
    Good gentlemen, give him a further edge,°
    And drive his purpose into these delights.
ROSENCRANTZ: We shall, my lord.   *Exeunt Rosencrantz and Guildenstern.*
KING: Sweet Gertrude, leave us too;
For we have closely° sent for Hamlet hither,
    That he, as 'twere by accident, may here   30
    Affront° Ophelia:
    Her father and myself, lawful espials,°
    Will so bestow ourselves that, seeing, unseen,

ACT III, SCENE I.   **1. drift of conference:** Device of conversation. **7. forward:** Willing. **12. forcing of his disposition:** I.e., against his will. **13. Niggard of question:** Sparing of conversation. **14. assay:** Try to win. **17. o'er-raught:** Overtook. **26. edge:** Incitement. **29. closely:** Secretly. **31. Affront:** Confront. **32. lawful espials:** Legitimate spies.

We may of their encounter frankly judge,
And gather by him, as he is behav'd,   35
If 't be th' affliction of his love or no
That thus he suffers for.

QUEEN: I shall obey you.
And for your part, Ophelia, I do wish
That your good beauties be the happy cause
Of Hamlet's wildness:° so shall I hope your virtues   40
Will bring him to his wonted way again,
To both your honours.

OPHELIA: Madam, I wish it may.   [*Exit Queen.*]

POLONIUS: Ophelia, walk you here. Gracious,° so please you,
We will bestow ourselves. [*To Ophelia.*] Read on this book;
That show of such an exercise° may colour°   45
Your loneliness. We are oft to blame in this, —
'Tis too much prov'd — that with devotion's visage
And pious action we do sugar o'er
The devil himself.

KING: [*aside*] O, 'tis too true!
How smart a lash that speech doth give my conscience!   50
The harlot's cheek, beautied with plast'ring art,
Is not more ugly to° the thing° that helps it
Than is my deed to my most painted word:
O heavy burthen!

POLONIUS: I hear him coming: let's withdraw, my lord.   55
                                        [*Exeunt King and Polonius.*]
Enter Hamlet.

HAMLET: To be, or not to be: that is the question:
Whether 'tis nobler in the mind to suffer
The slings and arrows of outrageous fortune,
Or to take arms against a sea° of troubles,
And by opposing end them? To die: to sleep;   60
No more; and by a sleep to say we end
The heart-ache and the thousand natural shocks
That flesh is heir to, 'tis a consummation
Devoutly to be wish'd. To die, to sleep;
To sleep: perchance to dream: ay, there's the rub;   65
For in that sleep of death what dreams may come
When we have shuffled° off this mortal coil,°
Must give us pause: there's the respect°

---

40. wildness: Madness. **43. Gracious:** Your grace (addressed to the king). **45. exercise:**
Act of devotion (the book she reads is one of devotion); **colour:** Give a plausible appearance
to. **52. to:** Compared to; **thing:** I.e., the cosmetic. **59. sea:** The mixed metaphor of this
speech has often been commented on; a later emendation *siege* has sometimes been spoken
on the stage. **67. shuffled:** Sloughed, cast; **coil:** Usually means "turmoil"; here, possibly
"body" (conceived of as wound about the soul like rope); *clay, soil, veil,* have been suggested
as emendations. **68. respect:** Consideration.

That makes calamity of so long life;°
For who would bear the whips and scorns of time,°   70
Th' oppressor's wrong, the proud man's contumely,
The pangs of despis'd° love, the law's delay,
The insolence of office° and the spurns°
That patient merit of th' unworthy takes,
When he himself might his quietus° make   75
With a bare bodkin?° who would fardels° bear,
To grunt and sweat under a weary life,
But that the dread of something after death,
The undiscover'd country from whose bourn°
No traveller returns, puzzles the will   80
And makes us rather bear those ills we have
Than fly to others that we know not of?
Thus conscience° does make cowards of us all;
And thus the native hue° of resolution
Is sicklied o'er° with the pale cast° of thought,   85
And enterprises of great pitch° and moment°
With this regard° their currents° turn awry,
And lose the name of action — Soft you now!
The fair Ophelia! Nymph, in thy orisons°
Be all my sins rememb'red.
OPHELIA: Good my lord,   90
How does your honour for this many a day?
HAMLET: I humbly thank you; well, well, well.
OPHELIA: My lord, I have remembrances of yours,
That I have longed long to re-deliver;
I pray you, now receive them.
HAMLET: No, not I;   95
I never gave you aught.
OPHELIA: My honour'd lord, you know right well you did;
And, with them, words of so sweet breath compos'd
As made the things more rich: their perfume lost,
Take these again; for to the noble mind   100
Rich gifts wax poor when givers prove unkind.
There, my lord.
HAMLET: Ha, ha! are you honest?°
OPHELIA: My lord?

---

69. of ... life: So long-lived.   **70. time:** The world.   **72. despis'd:** Rejected.   **73. office:**
Office-holders; **spurns:** Insults.   **75. quietus:** Acquittance; here, death.   **76. bare bodkin:**
Mere dagger; *bare* is sometimes understood as "unsheathed"; **fardels:** Burdens.   **79.**
bourne: Boundary.   **83. conscience:** Probably, inhibition by the faculty of reason restraining
the will from doing wrong.   **84. native hue:** Natural color; metaphor derived from the color
of the face.   **85. sicklied o'er:** Given a sticky tinge; **cast:** Shade of color.   **86. pitch:** Height
(as of a falcon's flight); **moment:** Importance.   **87. regard:** Respect, consideration; **currents:**
Courses.   **89. orisons:** Prayers.   **103.–108. are you honest ... beauty:** *Honest* meaning
"truthful" and "chaste" and *fair* meaning "just, honorable" (line 105) and "beautiful" (line
107) are not mere quibbles; the speech has the irony of a *double entendre*.

HAMLET: Are you fair? 105

OPHELIA: What means your lordship?

HAMLET: That if you be honest and fair, your honesty° should admit no discourse to° your beauty.

OPHELIA: Could beauty, my lord, have better commerce° than with honesty?

HAMLET: Ay, truly; for the power of beauty will sooner transform honesty from 110
what it is to a bawd than the force of honesty can translate beauty into
his likeness: this was sometime a paradox, but now the time° gives it
proof. I did love you once.

OPHELIA: Indeed, my lord, you made me believe so.

HAMLET: You should not have believed me; for virtue cannot so inoculate° our 115
old stock but we shall relish of it:° I loved you not.

OPHELIA: I was the more deceived.

HAMLET: Get thee to a nunnery: why wouldst thou be a breeder of sinners? I
am myself indifferent honest;° but yet I could accuse me of such things
that it were better my mother had not borne me: I am very proud, re- 120
vengeful, ambitious, with more offences at my beck° than I have
thoughts to put them in, imagination to give them shape, or time to act
them in. What should such fellows as I do crawling between earth and
heaven? We are arrant knaves, all; believe none of us. Go thy ways to a
nunnery. Where's your father? 125

OPHELIA: At home, my lord.

HAMLET: Let the doors be shut upon him, that he may play the fool no where
but in 's own house. Farewell.

OPHELIA: O, help him, you sweet heavens!

HAMLET: If thou dost marry, I'll give thee this plague for thy dowry: be thou 130
as chaste as ice, as pure as snow, thou shalt not escape calumny. Get thee to a
nunnery, go: farewell. Or, if thou wilt needs marry, marry a fool; for wise
men know well enough what monsters° you make of them. To a nunnery, go, and quickly too. Farewell.

OPHELIA: O heavenly powers, restore him! 135

HAMLET: I have heard of your° paintings too, well enough; God hath given you
one face, and you make yourselves another: you jig,° you amble, and
you lisp; you nick-name God's creatures, and make your wantonness
your ignorance.° Go to, I'll no more on 't; it hath made me mad. I say, we
will have no moe marriage: those that are married already, all but one,° 140
shall live; the rest shall keep as they are. To a nunnery, go. *Exit.*

OPHELIA: O, what a noble mind is here o'er-thrown!
The courtier's, soldier's, scholar's, eye, tongue, sword;

---

107. **your honesty:** Your chastity. 108. **discourse to:** Familiar intercourse with. 109. **commerce:** Intercourse. 112. **the time:** The present age. 115. **inoculate:** Graft (metaphorical).
116. **but . . . it:** I.e., that we do not still have about us a taste of the old stock; i.e., retain our
sinfulness. 119. **indifferent honest:** Moderately virtuous. 121. **beck:** Command. 133.
monsters: An allusion to the horns of a cuckold. 136. **your:** Indefinite use. 137. **jig:**
Move with jerky motion; probably allusion to the *jig*, or song and dance, of the current stage.
138.–139. **make . . . ignorance:** I.e., excuse your wantonness on the ground of your ignorance. 140. **one:** I.e., the king.

Th' expectancy and rose° of the fair state,
The glass of fashion and the mould of form,° 145
Th' observ'd of all observers,° quite, quite down!
And I, of ladies most deject and wretched,
That suck'd the honey of his music vows,
Now see that noble and most sovereign reason,
Like sweet bells jangled, out of time and harsh; 150
That unmatch'd form and feature of blown° youth
Blasted with ecstasy:° O, woe is me,
T' have seen what I have seen, see what I see!

Enter King and Polonius.

KING: Love! his affections do not that way tend;
Nor what he spake, though it lack'd form a little, 155
Was not like madness. There's something in his soul,
O'er which his melancholy sits on brood;
And I do doubt° the hatch and the disclose°
Will be some danger: which for to prevent,
I have in quick determination 160
Thus set it down: he shall with speed to England,
For the demand of our neglected tribute:
Haply the seas and countries different
With variable° objects shall expel
This something-settled° matter in his heart, 165
Whereon his brains still beating puts him thus
From fashion of himself.° What think you on 't?

POLONIUS: It shall do well: but yet do I believe
The origin and commencement of his grief
Sprung from neglected love. How now, Ophelia! 170
You need not tell us what Lord Hamlet said;
We heard it all. My lord, do as you please;
But, if you hold it fit, after the play
Let his queen mother all alone entreat him
To show his grief: let her be round° with him; 175
And I'll be plac'd, so please you, in the ear
Of all their conference. If she find him not,
To England send him, or confine him where
Your wisdom best shall think.

KING: It shall be so:
Madness in great ones must not unwatch'd go.   *Exeunt.* 180

---

144. **expectancy and rose:** Source of hope.   145. **The glass ... form:** The mirror of fashion and the pattern of courtly behavior.   146. **observ'd ... observers:** I.e., the center of attention in the court.   151. **blown:** Blooming.   152. **ecstasy:** Madness.   158. **doubt:** Fear; **disclose:** Disclosure or revelation (by chipping of the shell).   164. **variable:** Various.   165. **something-settled:** Somewhat settled.   167. **From ... himself:** Out of his natural manner.   175. **round:** Blunt.

[SCENE II: *A hall in the castle.*]

Enter Hamlet and three of the Players.

HAMLET: Speak the speech, I pray you, as I pronounced it to you, trippingly on the tongue: but if you mouth it, as many of your° players do, I had as lief the town-crier spoke my lines. Nor do not saw the air too much with your hand, thus, but use all gently; for in the very torrent, tempest, and, as I may say, whirlwind of your passion, you must acquire and beget a   5
temperance that may give it smoothness. O, it offends me to the soul to hear a robustious° periwig-pated° fellow tear a passion to tatters, to very rags, to split the ears of the groundlings,° who for the most part are capable of° nothing but inexplicable° dumb-shows and noise: I would have such a fellow whipped for o'er-doing Termagant;° it out-herods   10
Herod:° pray you, avoid it.

FIRST PLAYER: I warrant your honour.

HAMLET: Be not too tame neither, but let your own discretion be your tutor: suit the action to the word, the word to the action; with this special observance, that you o'er-step not the modesty of nature: for any thing so   15
overdone is from the purpose of playing, whose end, both at the first and now, was and is, to hold, as 't were, the mirror up to nature; to show virtue her own feature, scorn her own image, and the very age and body of the time his form and pressure.° Now this overdone, or come tardy off,° though it make the unskilful laugh, cannot but make the judicious   20
grieve; the censure of the which one° must in your allowance o'erweigh a whole theatre of others. O, there be players that I have seen play, and heard others praise, and that highly, not to speak it profanely, that, neither having the accent of Christians nor the gait of Christian, pagan, nor man, have so strutted and bellowed that I have thought some of nature's   25
journeymen° had made men and not made them well, they imitated humanity so abominably.

FIRST PLAYER: I hope we have reformed that indifferently° with us, sir.

HAMLET: O, reform it altogether. And let those that play your clowns speak no more than is set down for them; for there be of° them that will them-   30
selves laugh, to set on some quantity of barren° spectators to laugh too; though, in the mean time, some necessary question of the play be then to

---

SCENE II. **2. your:** Indefinite use. **7. robustious:** Violent, boisterous; **periwig-pated:** Wearing a wig. **8. groundlings:** Those who stood in the yard of the theater. **8–9. capable of:** Susceptible of being influenced by; **inexplicable:** Of no significance worth explaining. **10. Termagant:** A god of the Saracens; a character in the St. Nicholas play, where one of his worshipers, leaving him in charge of goods, returns to find them stolen; whereupon he beats the god (or idol), which howls vociferously. **11. Herod:** Herod of Jewry; a character in *The Slaughter of the Innocents* and other cycle plays. The part was played with great noise and fury. **19. pressure:** Stamp, impressed character. **19.–20. come tardy off:** Inadequately done. **21. the censure . . . one:** The judgment of even one of whom. **26. journeymen:** Laborers not yet masters in their trade. **28. indifferently:** Fairly, tolerably. **30. of:** I.e., some among them. **31. barren:** I.e., of wit.

be considered: that's villanous, and shows a most pitiful ambition in the
fool that uses it. Go, make you ready.   [*Exeunt Players.*]
Enter Polonius, Guildenstern, and Rosencrantz.

How now, my lord! will the king hear this piece of work?   35
POLONIUS: And the queen too, and that presently.
HAMLET: Bid the players make haste.   [*Exit Polonius.*]
Will you two help to hasten them?

ROSENCRANTZ: ⎫
GUILDENSTERN: ⎬   We will, my lord.   *Exeunt they two.*

HAMLET: What ho! Horatio!

Enter Horatio.

HORATIO: Here, sweet lord, at your service.   40
HAMLET: Horatio, thou art e'en as just° a man
As e'er my conversation cop'd withal.
HORATIO: O, my dear lord, —
HAMLET: Nay, do not think I flatter;
For what advancement may I hope from thee
That no revenue hast but thy good spirits,   45
To feed and clothe thee? Why should the poor be flatter'd?
No, let the candied tongue lick absurd pomp,
And crook the pregnant° hinges of the knee
Where thrift° may follow fawning. Dost thou hear?
Since my dear soul was mistress of her choice   50
And could of men distinguish her election,
S' hath seal'd thee for herself; for thou hast been
As one, in suff'ring all, that suffers nothing,
A man that fortune's buffets and rewards
Hast ta'en with equal thanks: and blest are those   55
Whose blood and judgement are so well commeddled,
That they are not a pipe for fortune's finger
To sound what stop° she please. Give me that man
That is not passion's slave, and I will wear him
In my heart's core, ay, in my heart of heart,   60
As I do thee. — Something too much of this. —
There is a play to-night before the king;
One scene of it comes near the circumstance
Which I have told thee of my father's death:
I prithee, when thou seest that act afoot,   65
Even with the very comment of thy soul°
Observe my uncle: if his occulted° guilt
Do not itself unkennel in one speech,

---

41. just: Honest, honorable.   **48. pregnant:** Pliant.   **49. thrift:** Profit.   **58. stop:** Hole in a
wind instrument for controlling the sound.   **66. very . . . soul:** Inward and sagacious criticism.   **67. occulted:** Hidden.

It is a damned° ghost that we have seen,
And my imaginations are as foul   70
As Vulcan's stithy.° Give him heedful note;
For I mine eyes will rivet to his face,
And after we will both our judgements join
In censure of his seeming.°
HORATIO: Well, my lord:
If 'a steal aught the whilst this play is playing,   75
And 'scape detecting, I will pay the theft.

Enter trumpets and kettledrums, King, Queen, Polonius, Ophelia, [Rosencrantz,
Guildenstern, and others].

HAMLET: They are coming to the play; I must be idle:° Get you a place.
KING: How fares our cousin Hamlet?
HAMLET: Excellent, i' faith; of the chameleon's dish:° I eat the air, promise-
  crammed: you cannot feed capons so.   80
KING: I have nothing with° this answer, Hamlet; these words are not mine.°
HAMLET: No, nor mine now. [*To Polonius.*] My lord, you played once i' the uni-
  versity, you say?
POLONIUS: That did I, my lord; and was accounted a good actor.
HAMLET: What did you enact?   85
POLONIUS: I did enact Julius Cæsar: I was killed i' the Capitol; Brutus killed
  me.
HAMLET: It was a brute part of him to kill so capital a calf there. Be the players
  ready?
ROSENCRANTZ: Ay, my lord; they stay upon your patience.   90
QUEEN: Come hither, my dear Hamlet, sit by me.
HAMLET: No, good mother, here's metal more attractive.
POLONIUS [*to the king*]: O, ho! do you mark that?
HAMLET: Lady, shall I lie in your lap?   [*Lying down at Ophelia's feet.*]
OPHELIA: No, my lord.   95
HAMLET: I mean, my head upon your lap?
OPHELIA: Ay, my lord.
HAMLET: Do you think I meant country° matters?
OPHELIA: I think nothing, my lord.
HAMLET: That's a fair thought to lie between maids' legs.   100
OPHELIA: What is, my lord?
HAMLET: Nothing.
OPHELIA: You are merry, my lord.
HAMLET: Who, I?
OPHELIA: Ay, my lord.   105

---

69. damned: In league with Satan.   **71. stithy:** Smithy, place of *stiths* (anvils).   **74. censure
... seeming:** Judgment of his appearance or behavior.   **77. idle:** Crazy, or not attending to
anything serious.   **79. chameleon's dish:** Chameleons were supposed to feed on air. (Hamlet deliberately misinterprets the king's "fares" as "feeds.")   **81. have . . . with:** Make nothing of; **are not mine:** Do not respond to what I ask.   **98. country:** With a bawdy pun.

HAMLET: O God, your only° jig-maker.° What should a man do but be merry?
for, look you, how cheerfully my mother looks, and my father died
within's two hours.

OPHELIA: Nay, 'tis twice two months, my lord.

HAMLET: So long? Nay then, let the devil wear black, for I'll have a suit of 110
sables.° O heavens! die two months ago, and not forgotten yet? Then
there's hope a great man's memory may outlive his life half a year: but,
by 'r lady, 'a must build churches, then; or else shall 'a suffer not thinking on,° with the hobbyhorse, whose epitaph is "For, O, for, O, the
hobbyhorse is forgot."° 115

The trumpets sound. Dumb show follows.

Enter a King and a Queen [very lovingly]; the Queen embracing him, and he
her. [She kneels, and makes show of protestation unto him.] He takes her up, and de-
clines his head upon her neck: he lies him down upon a bank of flowers: she, seeing him
asleep, leaves him. Anon comes in another man, takes off his crown, kisses it, pours
poison in the sleeper's ears, and leaves him. The Queen returns; finds the King dead,
makes passionate action. The Poisoner, with some three or four come in again, seem to
condole with her. The dead body is carried away. The Poisoner woos the Queen with
gifts: she seems harsh awhile, but in the end accepts love. [Exeunt.]

OPHELIA: What means this, my lord?

HAMLET: Marry, this is miching mallecho;° it means mischief.

OPHELIA: Belike this show imports the argument of the play.

Enter Prologue.

HAMLET: We shall know by this fellow: the players cannot keep counsel; they'll
tell all. 120

OPHELIA: Will 'a tell us what this show meant?

HAMLET: Ay, or any show that you'll show him: be not you ashamed to show,
he'll not shame to tell you what it means.

OPHELIA: You are naught, you are naught:° I'll mark the play.

PROLOGUE: For us, and for our tragedy, 125
Here stooping° to your clemency,
We beg your hearing patiently. [*Exit.*]

HAMLET: Is this a prologue, or the posy° of a ring?

OPHELIA: 'Tis brief, my lord.

HAMLET: As woman's love. 130

Enter [two Players as] King and Queen.

PLAYER KING: Full thirty times hath Phoebus' cart gone round
Neptune's salt wash° and Tellus'° orbed ground,

---

106. your only: Only your; **jig-maker:** Composer of jigs (song and dance). **110.–111. suit of**
sables: Garments trimmed with the fur of the sable, with a quibble on *sable* meaning "black."
113.–114. suffer . . . on: Undergo oblivion. **114.–115. "For . . . forgot":** Verse of a song occurring also in *Love's Labour's Lost,* III.i.30. The hobbyhorse was a character in the Morris
Dance. **117. miching mallecho:** Sneaking mischief. **124. naught:** Indecent. **126. stoop-**
ing: Bowing. **128. posy:** Motto. **132. salt wash:** The sea; **Tellus:** Goddess of the earth
(*orbed ground*).

And thirty dozen moons with borrowed° sheen
About the world have times twelve thirties been,
Since love our hearts and Hymen° did our hands   135
Unite commutual° in most sacred bands.

PLAYER QUEEN: So many journeys may the sun and moon
Make us again count o'er ere love be done!
But, woe is me, you are so sick of late,
So far from cheer and from your former state,   140
That I distrust° you. Yet, though I distrust,
Discomfort you, my lord, it nothing must:
For women's fear and love holds quantity;°
In neither aught, or in extremity.
Now, what my love is, proof hath made you know;   145
And as my love is siz'd, my fear is so:
Where love is great, the littlest doubts are fear;
Where little fears grow great, great love grows there.

PLAYER KING: 'Faith, I must leave thee, love, and shortly too;
My operant° powers their functions leave° to do: 150
And thou shalt live in this fair world behind,
Honour'd, belov'd; and haply one as kind
For husband shalt thou —

PLAYER QUEEN: O, confound the rest!
Such love must needs be treason in my breast:
In second husband let me be accurst!   155
None wed the second but who kill'd the first.

HAMLET (*aside*): Wormwood, wormwood.

PLAYER QUEEN: The instances that second marriage move
Are base respects of thrift, but none of love:
A second time I kill my husband dead,   160
When second husband kisses me in bed.

PLAYER KING: I do believe you think what now you speak;
But what we do determine oft we break.
Purpose is but the slave to memory,
Of violent birth, but poor validity: 165
Which now, like fruit unripe, sticks on the tree;
But fall, unshaken, when they mellow be.
Most necessary 'tis that we forget
To pay ourselves what to ourselves is debt:
What to ourselves in passion we propose,   170
The passion ending, doth the purpose lose.
The violence of either grief or joy
Their own enactures° with themselves destroy:

---

133. borrowed: I.e., reflected. **135. Hymen:** God of matrimony. **136. commutual:** Mutually. **141. distrust:** Am anxious about. **143. holds quantity:** Keeps proportion between. **150. operant:** Active; **leave:** Cease. **173. enactures:** Fulfillments.

Where joy most revels, grief doth most lament;
Grief joys, joy grieves, on slender accident.   175
This world is not for aye,° nor 'tis not strange
That even our loves should with our fortunes change;
For 'tis a question left us yet to prove,
Whether love lead fortune, or else fortune love.
The great man down, you mark his favourite flies;   180
The poor advanc'd makes friends of enemies.
And hitherto doth love on fortune tend;
For who° not needs shall never lack a friend,
And who in want a hollow friend doth try,
Directly seasons° him his enemy.   185
But, orderly to end where I begun,
Our wills and fates do so contrary run
That our devices still are overthrown;
Our thoughts are ours, their ends° none of our own:
So think thou wilt no second husband wed;   190
But die thy thoughts when thy first lord is dead.

PLAYER QUEEN: Nor earth to me give food, nor heaven light!
Sport and repose lock from me day and night!
To desperation turn my trust and hope!
An anchor's° cheer° in prison be my scope!   195
Each opposite° that blanks° the face of joy
Meet what I would have well and it destroy!
Both here and hence pursue me lasting strife,
If, once a widow, ever I be wife!

HAMLET: If she should break it now!   200

PLAYER KING: 'Tis deeply sworn. Sweet, leave me here awhile;
My spirits grow dull, and fain I would beguile
The tedious day with sleep.   [*Sleeps.*]

PLAYER QUEEN: Sleep rock thy brain;
And never come mischance between us twain!   *Exit.*

HAMLET: Madam, how like you this play?   205

QUEEN: The lady doth protest too much, methinks.

HAMLET: O, but she'll keep her word.

KING: Have you heard the argument? Is there no offence in 't?

HAMLET: No, no, they do but jest, poison in jest; no offence i' the world.

KING: What do you call the play?   210

HAMLET: The Mouse-trap. Marry, how? Tropically.° This play is the image of a
murder done in Vienna: Gonzago° is the duke's name; his wife, Baptista:
you shall see anon; 't is a knavish piece of work: but what o' that? your

---

176. **aye:** Ever.   183. **who:** Whoever.   185. **seasons:** Matures, ripens.   189. **ends:** Results.
195. **An anchor's:** An anchorite's; **cheer:** Fare; sometimes printed as *chair.*   196. **opposite:**
Adverse thing; **blanks:** Causes to *blanch* or grow pale.   211. **Tropically:** Figuratively, *trapi-
cally* suggests a pun on *trap* in *Mouse-trap* (line 211).   212. **Gonzago:** In 1538 Luigi Gonzago
murdered the Duke of Urbano by pouring poisoned lotion in his ears.

majesty and we that have free souls, it touches us not: let the galled jade°
winch,° our withers° are unwrung.°   215

Enter Lucianus.

This is one Lucianus, nephew to the king.

OPHELIA: You are as good as a chorus,° my lord.

HAMLET: I could interpret between you and your love, if I could see the puppets dallying.°

OPHELIA: You are keen, my lord, you are keen.   220

HAMLET: It would cost you a groaning to take off my edge.

OPHELIA: Still better, and worse.°

HAMLET: So you mistake° your husbands. Begin, murderer; pox,° leave thy
damnable faces, and begin. Come: the croaking raven doth bellow for revenge.   225

LUCIANUS: Thoughts black, hands apt, drugs fit, and time agreeing;
Confederate° season, else no creature seeing;
Thou mixture rank, of midnight weeds collected,
With Hecate's° ban° thrice blasted, thrice infected,
Thy natural magic and dire property,   230
On wholesome life usurp immediately.

[*Pours the poison into the sleeper's ears.*]

HAMLET: 'A poisons him i' the garden for his estate. His name's Gonzago: the
story is extant, and written in very choice Italian: you shall see anon how
the murderer gets the love of Gonzago's wife.

OPHELIA: The king rises.   235

HAMLET: What, frighted with false fire!°

QUEEN: How fares my lord?

POLONIUS: Give o'er the play.

KING: Give me some light: away!

POLONIUS: Lights, lights, lights!   *Exeunt all but Hamlet and Horatio.* 240

HAMLET: Why, let the strucken deer go weep,
The hart ungalled play;
For some must watch, while some must sleep:
Thus runs the world away.°
Would not this,° sir, and a forest of feathers° — if the rest of my fortunes 245

---

214. galled jade: Horse whose hide is rubbed by saddle or harness. **215. winch:** Wince;
withers: The part between the horse's shoulder blades; **unwrung:** Not wrung or twisted.
217. chorus: In many Elizabethan plays the action was explained by an actor known as the
"chorus"; at a puppet show the actor who explained the action was known as an "interpreter," as indicated by the lines following. **219. dallying:** With sexual suggestion, continued in *keen* (sexually aroused), *groaning* (i.e., in pregnancy), and *edge* (i.e., sexual desire or
impetuosity). **222. Still . . . worse:** More keen, less decorous. **223. mistake:** Err in taking;
pox: An imprecation. **227. Confederate:** Conspiring (to assist the murderer). **229.
Hecate:** The goddess of witchcraft; **ban:** Curse. **236. false fire:** Fireworks, or a blank discharge. **241.–244. Why . . . away:** Probably from an old ballad, with allusion to the popular
belief that a wounded deer retires to weep and die. Cf. *As You Like It*, II.i.66. **245. this:** I.e.,
the play; **feathers:** Allusion to the plumes which Elizabethan actors were fond of wearing.

turn Turk with° me — with two Provincial roses° on my razed° shoes,
get me a fellowship in a cry° of players,° sir?

HORATIO: Half a share.°

HAMLET: A whole one, I.

> For thou dost know, O Damon dear, 250
>   This realm dismantled° was
> Of Jove himself; and now reigns here
>   A very, very° — pajock.°

HORATIO: You might have rhymed.

HAMLET: O good Horatio, I'll take the ghost's word for a thousand pound. 255
    Didst perceive?

HORATIO: Very well, my lord.

HAMLET: Upon the talk of the poisoning?

HORATIO: I did very well note him.

HAMLET: Ah, ha! Come, some music! come, the recorders!° 260

> For if the king like not the comedy,
> Why then, belike, he likes it not, perdy.°
> Come, some music!

Enter Rosencrantz and Guildenstern.

GUILDENSTERN: Good my lord, vouchsafe me a word with you.

HAMLET: Sir, a whole history. 265

GUILDENSTERN: The king, sir, —

HAMLET: Ay, sir, what of him?

GUILDENSTERN: Is in his retirement marvellous distempered.

HAMLET: With drink, sir?

GUILDENSTERN: No, my lord, rather with choler.° 270

HAMLET: Your wisdom should show itself more richer to signify this to his doc-
    tor; for, for me to put him to his purgation would perhaps plunge him
    into far more choler.

GUILDENSTERN: Good my lord, put your discourse into some frame° and start
    not so wildly from my affair. 275

HAMLET: I am tame, sir: pronounce.

GUILDENSTERN: The queen, your mother, in most great affliction of spirit, hath
    sent me to you.

HAMLET: You are welcome.

GUILDENSTERN: Nay, good my lord, this courtesy is not of the right breed. If it 280
    shall please you to make me a wholesome° answer, I will do your

---

246. turn Turk with: Go back on; **two Provincial roses:** Rosettes of ribbon like the roses of
Provins near Paris, or else the roses of Provence; **razed:** Cut, slashed (by way of ornament).
247. cry: Pack (as of hounds); **fellowship . . . players:** Partnership in a theatrical company.
248. Half a share: Allusion to the custom in dramatic companies of dividing the ownership
into a number of shares among the householders.   **251. dismantled:** Stripped, divested.
250.–253. For . . . very: Probably from an old ballad having to do with Damon and Pythias.
253. pajock: Peacock (a bird with a bad reputation). Possibly the word was *patchock*, diminutive of *patch*, clown.   **260. recorders:** Wind instruments of the flute kind.   **262. perdy:**
Corruption of *par dieu*.   **270. choler:** Bilious disorder, with quibble on the sense "anger."
274. frame: Order.   **281. wholesome:** Sensible.

mother's commandment; if not, your pardon and my return shall be the end of my business.

HAMLET: Sir, I cannot.

GUILDENSTERN: What, my lord?   285

HAMLET: Make you a wholesome answer; my wit's diseased: but, sir, such answer as I can make, you shall command; or, rather, as you say, my mother: therefore no more, but to the matter:° my mother, you say, —

ROSENCRANTZ: Then thus she says; your behaviour hath struck her into amazement and admiration.   290

HAMLET: O wonderful son, that can so 'stonish a mother! But is there no sequel at the heels of this mother's admiration? Impart.

ROSENCRANTZ: She desires to speak with you in her closet, ere you go to bed.

HAMLET: We shall obey, were she ten times our mother. Have you any further trade with us?   295

ROSENCRANTZ: My lord, you once did love me.

HAMLET: And do still, by these pickers and stealers.°

ROSENCRANTZ: Good my lord, what is your cause of distemper? you do, surely, bar the door upon your own liberty, if you deny your griefs to your friend.   300

HAMLET: Sir, I lack advancement.

ROSENCRANTZ: How can that be, when you have the voice° of the king himself for your succession in Denmark?

HAMLET: Ay, sir, but "While the grass grows,"° — the proverb is something musty.   305

Enter the Players with recorders.

O, the recorders! let me see one. To withdraw° with you: — why do you go about to recover the wind° of me, as if you would drive me into a toil?°

GUILDENSTERN: O, my lord, if my duty be too bold, my love is too unmannerly.°   310

HAMLET: I do not well understand that. Will you play upon this pipe?

GUILDENSTERN: My lord, I cannot.

HAMLET: I pray you.

GUILDENSTFRN: Believe me, I cannot.

HAMLET: I beseech you.   315

GUILDENSTERN: I know no touch of it, my lord.

---

288. matter: Matter in hand. **297. pickers and stealers:** Hands, so called from the catechism "to keep my hands from picking and stealing." **302. voice:** Support. **304. "While . . . grows":** The rest of the proverb is "the silly horse starves." Hamlet may be destroyed while he is waiting for the succession to the kingdom. **306. withdraw:** Speak in private. **307. recover the wind:** Get to the windward side. **308. toil:** Snare. **309.–310. if . . . unmannerly:** If I am using an unmannerly boldness, it is my love which occasions it.

HAMLET: 'Tis as easy as lying: govern these ventages° with your fingers and thumb, give it breath with your mouth, and it will discourse most eloquent music. Look you, these are the stops.

GUILDENSTERN: But these cannot I command to any utterance of harmony; I 320 have not the skill.

HAMLET: Why, look you now, how unworthy a thing you make of me! You would play upon me; you would seem to know my stops; you would pluck out the heart of my mystery; you would sound me from my lowest note to the top of my compass:° and there is much music, excellent 325 voice, in this little organ;° yet cannot you make it speak. 'Sblood, do you think I am easier to be played on than a pipe? Call me what instrument you will, though you can fret° me, you cannot play upon me.

Enter Polonius.

God bless you, sir!

POLONIUS: My lord, the queen would speak with you, and presently. 330

HAMLET: Do you see yonder cloud that 's almost in shape of a camel?

POLONIUS: By the mass, and 'tis like a camel, indeed.

HAMLET: Methinks it is like a weasel.

POLONIUS: It is backed like a weasel.

HAMLET: Or like a whale? 335

POLONIUS: Very like a whale.

HAMLET: Then I will come to my mother by and by. [*Aside.*] They fool me to the top of my bent.° — I will come by and by.°

POLONIUS: I will say so. [*Exit.*]

HAMLET: By and by is easily said. 340

Leave me, friends. [*Exeunt all but Hamlet.*]

'Tis now the very witching time° of night,

When churchyards yawn and hell itself breathes out

Contagion to this world: now could I drink hot blood,

And do such bitter business as the day 345

Would quake to look on. Soft! now to my mother.

O heart, lose not thy nature; let not ever

The soul of Nero° enter this firm bosom:

Let me be cruel, not unnatural:

I will speak daggers to her, but use none; 350

My tongue and soul in this be hypocrites;

How in my words somever she be shent,°

To give them seals° never, my soul, consent! *Exit.*

---

317. ventages: Stops of the recorders. **325. compass:** Range of voice. **326. organ:** Musical instrument, i.e., the pipe. **328. fret:** Quibble on meaning "irritate" and the piece of wood, gut, or metal which regulates the fingering. **338. top of my bent:** Limit of endurance, i.e., extent to which a bow may be bent; **by and by:** Immediately. **342. witching time:** I.e., time when spells are cast. **348. Nero:** Murderer of his mother, Agrippina. **352. shent:** Rebuked. **353. give them seals:** Confirm with deeds.

[SCENE III: *A room in the castle.*]

Enter King, Rosencrantz, and Guildenstern.

KING: I like him not, nor stands it safe with us
    To let his madness range. Therefore prepare you;
    I your commission will forthwith dispatch,°
    And he to England shall along with you:
    The terms° of our estate° may not endure   5
    Hazard so near us as doth hourly grow
    Out of his brows.°

GUILDENSTERN: We will ourselves provide:
    Most holy and religious fear it is
    To keep those many many bodies safe
    That live and feed upon your majesty.   10

ROSENCRANTZ: The single and peculiar° life is bound,
    With all the strength and armour of the mind,
    To keep itself from noyance;° but much more
    That spirit upon whose weal depend and rest
    The lives of many. The cess° of majesty   15
    Dies not alone; but, like a gulf,° doth draw
    What's near it with it: it is a massy wheel,
    Fix'd on the summit of the highest mount,
    To whose huge spokes ten thousand lesser things
    Are mortis'd and adjoin'd; which, when it falls,   20
    Each small annexment, petty consequence,
    Attends° the boist'rous ruin. Never alone
    Did the king sigh, but with a general groan.

KING: Arm° you, I pray you, to this speedy voyage;
    For we will fetters put about this fear,   25
    Which now goes too free-footed.

ROSENCRANTZ: We will haste us.
        Exeunt Gentlemen [Rosencrantz and Guildenstern].

Enter Polonius.

POLONIUS: My lord, he's going to his mother's closet:
    Behind the arras° I'll convey° myself,
    To hear the process;° I'll warrant she'll tax him home:°
    And, as you said, and wisely was it said,   30
    'Tis meet that some more audience than a mother,
    Since nature makes them partial, should o'erhear
    The speech, of vantage.° Fare you well, my liege:

SCENE III. **3. dispatch:** Prepare. **5. terms:** Condition, circumstances; **estate:** State. **7. brows:** Effronteries. **11. single and peculiar:** Individual and private. **13. noyance:** Harm. **15. cess:** Decease. **16. gulf:** Whirlpool. **22. Attends:** Participates in. **24. Arm:** Prepare. **28. arras:** Screen of tapestry placed around the walls of household apartments; **convey:** Implication of secrecy, *convey* was often used to mean "steal." **29. process:** Proceedings; **tax him home:** Reprove him severely. **33. of vantage:** From an advantageous place.

I'll call upon you ere you go to bed,
And tell you what I know.
KING: Thanks, dear my lord.   *Exit [Polonius].* 35
O, my offence is rank, it smells to heaven;
It hath the primal eldest curse° upon't,
A brother's murder. Pray can I not,
Though inclination be as sharp as will:°
My stronger guilt defeats my strong intent;   40
And, like a man to double business bound,
I stand in pause where I shall first begin,
And both neglect. What if this cursed hand
Were thicker than itself with brother's blood,
Is there not rain enough in the sweet heavens   45
To wash it white as snow? Whereto serves mercy
But to confront° the visage of offence?
And what's in prayer but this two-fold force,
To be forestalled° ere we come to fall,
Or pardon'd being down? Then I'll look up;   50
My fault is past. But, O, what form of prayer
Can serve my turn? "Forgive me my foul murder"?
That cannot be: since I am still possess'd
Of those effects for which I did the murder,
My crown, mine own ambition° and my queen.   55
May one be pardon'd and retain th' offence?°
In the corrupted currents° of this world
Offence's gilded hand° may shove by justice,
And oft 'tis seen the wicked prize° itself
Buys out the law: but 'tis not so above;   60
There is no shuffling,° there the action lies°
In his true nature; and we ourselves compell'd,
Even to the teeth and forehead° of our faults,
To give in evidence. What then? what rests?°
Try what repentance can: what can it not?   65
Yet what can it when one can not repent?
O wretched state! O bosom black as death!
O limed° soul, that, struggling to be free,
Art more engag'd!° Help, angels! Make assay!°
Bow, stubborn knees; and, heart with strings of steel,   70

---

37. **primal eldest curse:** The curse of Cain, the first to kill his brother. 39. **sharp as will:** I.e.,
his desire is as strong as his determination. 47. **confront:** Oppose directly. 49. **fore-
stalled:** Prevented. 55. **ambition:** I.e., realization of ambition. 56. **offence:** Benefit accru-
ing from offense. 57. **currents:** Courses. 58. **gilded hand:** Hand offering gold as a bribe.
59. **wicked prize:** Prize won by wickedness. 61. **shuffling:** Escape by trickery; **lies:** Is sus-
tainable. 63. **teeth and forehead:** Very face. 64. **rests:** Remains. 68. **limed:** Caught as
with birdlime. 69. **engag'd:** Embedded; **assay:** Trial.

Be soft as sinews of the new-born babe!
All may be well. [*He kneels.*]

Enter Hamlet.

HAMLET: Now might I do it pat,° now he is praying;
And now I'll do't. And so 'a goes to heaven;
And so am I reveng'd. That would be scann'd:° 75
A villain kills my father; and for that,
I, his sole son, do this same villain send
To heaven.
Why, this is hire and salary, not revenge.
'A took my father grossly, full of bread;° 80
With all his crimes broad blown,° as flush° as May;
And how his audit stands who knows save heaven?
But in our circumstance and course° of thought,
'Tis heavy with him: and am I then reveng'd,
To take him in the purging of his soul, 85
When he is fit and season'd for his passage?°
No!
Up, sword; and know thou a more horrid hent:°
When he is drunk asleep,° or in his rage,
Or in th' incestuous pleasure of his bed; 90
At game, a-swearing, or about some act
That has no relish of salvation in't;
Then trip him, that his heels may kick at heaven,
And that his soul may be as damn'd and black
As hell, whereto it goes. My mother stays: 95
This physic° but prolongs thy sickly days. *Exit.*

KING: [*Rising*] My words fly up, my thoughts remain below:
Words without thoughts never to heaven go. *Exit.*

[SCENE IV: *The Queen's closet.*]

Enter [Queen] Gertrude and Polonius.

POLONIUS: 'A will come straight. Look you lay° home to him:
Tell him his pranks have been too broad° to bear with,
And that your grace hath screen'd and stood between
Much heat° and him. I'll sconce° me even here.
Pray you, be round° with him. 5
HAMLET (*within*): Mother, mother, mother!

---

73. **pat:** Opportunely. 75. **would be scann'd:** Needs to be looked into. 80. **full of bread:** Enjoying his worldly pleasures (see Ezekiel 16:49). 81. **broad blown:** In full bloom; **flush:** Lusty. 83. **in . . . course:** As we see it in our mortal situation. 86. **fit . . . passage:** I.e., reconciled to heaven by forgiveness of his sins. 88. **hent:** Seizing; or more probably, occasion of seizure. 89. **drunk asleep:** In a drunken sleep. 96. **physic:** Purging (by prayer). SCENE IV. 1. **lay:** Thrust. 2. **broad:** Unrestrained. 4. **Much heat:** I.e., the king's anger; **sconce:** Hide. 5. **round:** Blunt.

QUEEN: I'll warrant you,
    Fear me not: withdraw, I hear him coming.

                            [*Polonius hides behind the arras.*]

Enter Hamlet.

HAMLET: Now, mother, what's the matter?
QUEEN: Hamlet, thou hast thy father much offended.
HAMLET: Mother, you have my father° much offended.   10
QUEEN: Come, come, you answer with an idle tongue.
HAMLET: Go, go, you question with a wicked tongue.
QUEEN: Why, how now, Hamlet!
HAMLET: What's the matter now?
QUEEN: Have you forgot me?
HAMLET: No, by the rood,° not so:
    You are the queen, your husband's brother's wife;   15
    And — would it were not so! — you are my mother.
QUEEN: Nay, then, I'll set those to you that can speak.
HAMLET: Come, come, and sit you down; you shall not budge;
    You go not till I set you up a glass
    Where you may see the inmost part of you.   20
QUEEN: What wilt thou do? thou wilt not murder me?
    Help, help, ho!
POLONIUS [*behind*]: What, ho! help, help, help!
HAMLET [*drawing*]: How now! a rat? Dead, for a ducat, dead!

                            [*Makes a pass through the arras.*]

POLONIUS [*behind*]: O, I am slain!   [*Falls and dies.*] 25
QUEEN: O me, what hast thou done?
HAMLET: Nay, I know not:
    Is it the king?
QUEEN: O, what a rash and bloody deed is this!
HAMLET: A bloody deed! almost as bad, good mother,
    As kill a king, and marry with his brother.   30
QUEEN: As kill a king!
HAMLET: Ay, lady, it was my word.

                    [*Lifts up the arras and discovers Polonius.*]

    Thou wretched, rash, intruding fool, farewell!
    I took thee for thy better: take thy fortune;
    Thou find'st to be too busy is some danger.
    Leave wringing of your hands: peace! sit you down,   35
    And let me wring your heart; for so I shall,
    If it be made of penetrable stuff,
    If damned custom have not braz'd° it so
    That it be proof and bulwark against sense.

9.–10. thy father, my father: I.e., Claudius, the elder Hamlet.   **14. rood:** Cross.   **38. braz'd:** Brazened, hardened.

QUEEN: What have I done, that thou dar'st wag thy tongue   40
    In noise so rude against me?

HAMLET: Such an act
    That blurs the grace and blush of modesty,
    Calls virtue hypocrite, takes off the rose
    From the fair forehead of an innocent love
    And sets a blister° there, makes marriage-vows   45
    As false as dicers' oaths: O, such a deed
    As from the body of contraction° plucks
    The very soul, and sweet religion° makes
    A rhapsody° of words: heaven's face does glow
    O'er this solidity and compound mass   50
    With heated visage, as against the doom
    Is thought-sick at the act.°

QUEEN: Ay me, what act,
    That roars so loud, and thunders in the index?°

HAMLET: Look here, upon this picture, and on this.
    The counterfeit presentment° of two brothers.   55
    See, what grace was seated on this brow;
    Hyperion's° curls; the front° of Jove himself;
    An eye like Mars, to threaten and command;
    A station° like the herald Mercury
    New-lighted on a heaven-kissing hill;   60
    A combination and a form indeed,
    Where every god did seem to set his seal,
    To give the world assurance° of a man:
    This was your husband. Look you now, what follows:
    Here is your husband; like a mildew'd ear,°   65
    Blasting his wholesome brother. Have you eyes?
    Could you on this fair mountain leave to feed,
    And batten° on this moor?° Ha! have you eyes?
    You cannot call it love; for at your age
    The hey-day° in the blood is tame, it's humble,   70
    And waits upon the judgement: and what judgement
    Would step from this to this? Sense, sure, you have,
    Else could you not have motion;° but sure, that sense
    Is apoplex'd;° for madness would not err,

---

45. sets a blister: Brands as a harlot.   **47. contraction:** The marriage contract.   **48. religion:** Religious vows.   **49. rhapsody:** Senseless string.   **49.–52. heaven's . . . act:** Heaven's face blushes to look down upon this world, compounded of the four elements, with hot face as though the day of doom were near, and thought-sick at the deed (i.e., Gertrude's marriage).   **53. index:** Prelude or preface.   **55. counterfeit presentment:** Portrayed representation.   **57. Hyperion's:** The sun god's; **front:** Brow.   **59. station:** Manner of standing.   **63. assurance:** Pledge, guarantee.   **65. mildew'd ear:** See Genesis 41:5–7.   **68. batten:** Grow fat; **moor:** Barren upland.   **70. hey-day:** State of excitement.   **72.–73. Sense . . . motion:** Sense and motion are functions of the middle or sensible soul, the possession of sense being the basis of motion.   **74. apoplex'd:** Paralyzed. Mental derangement was thus of three sorts: apoplexy, ectasy, and diabolic possession.

Nor sense to ecstasy was ne'er so thrall'd°   75
But it reserv'd some quantity of choice,°
To serve in such a difference. What devil was't
That thus hath cozen'd° you at hoodman-blind?°
Eyes without feeling, feeling without sight,
Ears without hands or eyes, smelling sans° all,   80
Or but a sickly part of one true sense
Could not so mope.°
O shame! where is thy blush? Rebellious hell,
If thou canst mutine° in a matron's bones,
To flaming youth let virtue be as wax,   85
And melt in her own fire: proclaim no shame
When the compulsive ardour gives the charge,°
Since frost itself as actively doth burn
And reason pandars will.°

QUEEN: O Hamlet, speak no more:
Thou turn'st mine eyes into my very soul;   90
And there I see such black and grained° spots
As will not leave their tinct.

HAMLET: Nay, but to live
In the rank sweat of an enseamed° bed,
Stew'd in corruption, honeying and making love
Over the nasty sty, —

QUEEN: O, speak to me no more;   95
These words, like daggers, enter in mine ears;
No more, sweet Hamlet!

HAMLET: A murderer and a villain;
A slave that is not twentieth part the tithe
Of your precedent lord;° a vice of kings;°
A cutpurse of the empire and the rule,   100
That from a shelf the precious diadem stole,
And put it in his pocket!

QUEEN: No more!

Enter Ghost.

HAMLET: A king of shreds and patches,° —
Save me, and hover o'er me with your wings,
You heavenly guards! What would your gracious figure?   105
QUEEN: Alas, he's mad!

---

75. thrall'd: Enslaved.   **76. quantity of choice:** Fragment of the power to choose.   **78. coz-
en'd:** Tricked, cheated; **hoodman-blind:** Blindman's buff.   **80. sans:** Without.   **82. mope:**
Be in a depressed, spiritless state, act aimlessly.   **84. mutine:** Mutiny, rebel.   **87. gives the
charge:** Delivers the attack.   **89. reason pandars will:** The normal and proper situation was
one in which reason guided the will in the direction of good; here, reason is perverted and
leads in the direction of evil.   **91. grained:** Dyed in grain.   **93. enseamed:** Loaded with
grease, greased.   **99. precedent lord:** I.e., the elder Hamlet; **vice of kings:** Buffoon of kings; a
reference to the Vice, or clown, of the morality plays and interludes.   **103. shreds and
patches:** I.e., motley, the traditional costume of the Vice.

HAMLET: Do you not come your tardy son to chide,
    That, laps'd in time and passion,° lets go by
    Th' important° acting of your dread command?
    O, say!   110
GHOST: Do not forget: this visitation
    Is but to whet thy almost blunted purpose.
    But, look, amazement° on thy mother sits:
    O, step between her and her fighting soul:
    Conceit in weakest bodies strongest works: 115
    Speak to her, Hamlet.
HAMLET: How is it with you, lady?
QUEEN: Alas, how is 't with you,
    That you do bend your eye on vacancy
    And with th' incorporal° air do hold discourse?
    Forth at your eyes your spirits wildly peep;   120
    And, as the sleeping soldiers in th' alarm,
    Your bedded° hair, like life in excrements,°
    Start up, and stand an° end. O gentle son,
    Upon the heat and flame of thy distemper
    Sprinkle cool patience. Whereon do you look?   125
HAMLET: On him, on him! Look you, how pale he glares!
    His form and cause conjoin'd,° preaching to stones,
    Would make them capable. — Do not look upon me;
    Lest with this piteous action you convert
    My stern effects:° then what I have to do   130
    Will want true colour;° tears perchance for blood.
QUEEN: To whom do you speak this?
HAMLET: Do you see nothing there?
QUEEN: Nothing at all; yet all that is I see.
HAMLET: Nor did you nothing hear?
QUEEN: No, nothing but ourselves.
HAMLET: Why, look you there! look, how it steals away!   135
    My father, in his habit as he liv'd!
    Look, where he goes, even now, out at the portal!   *Exit Ghost.*
QUEEN: This is the very coinage of your brain:
    This bodiless creation ecstasy
    Is very cunning in.
HAMLET: Ecstasy!   140
    My pulse, as yours, doth temperately keep time,

---

108. laps'd . . . passion: Having suffered time to slip and passion to cool; also explained as "engrossed in casual events and lapsed into mere fruitless passion, so that he no longer entertains a rational purpose." **109. important:** Urgent. **113. amazement:** Frenzy, distraction. **119. incorporal:** Immaterial. **122. bedded:** Laid in smooth layers; **excrements:** The hair was considered an excrement or voided part of the body. **123. an:** On. **127. conjoin'd:** United. **129.–130. convert . . . effects:** Divert me from my stern duty. For *effects*, possibly *affects* (affections of the mind). **131. want true colour:** Lack good reason so that (with a play on the normal sense of *colour*) I shall shed tears instead of blood.

And makes as healthful music: it is not madness
That I have utt'red: bring me to the test,
And I the matter will re-word,° which madness
Would gambol° from. Mother, for love of grace,   145
Lay not that flattering unction° to your soul,
That not your trespass, but my madness speaks:
It will but skin and film the ulcerous place,
Whiles rank corruption, mining° all within,
Infects unseen. Confess yourself to heaven;   150
Repent what's past; avoid what is to come;°
And do not spread the compost° on the weeds,
To make them ranker. Forgive me this my virtue;°
For in the fatness° of these pursy° times
Virtue itself of vice must pardon beg,   155
Yea, curb° and woo for leave to do him good.
QUEEN: O Hamlet, thou hast cleft my heart in twain.
HAMLET: O, throw away the worser part of it,
And live the purer with the other half.
Good night: but go not to my uncle's bed;   160
Assume a virtue, if you have it not.
That monster, custom, who all sense doth eat,
Of habits devil, is angel yet in this,
That to the use of actions fair and good
He likewise gives a frock or livery,   165
That aptly is put on. Refrain to-night,
And that shall lend a kind of easiness
To the next abstinence: the next more easy;
For use almost can change the stamp of nature,
And either . . . the devil, or throw him out°   170
With wondrous potency. Once more, good night:
And when you are desirous to be bless'd,°
I'll blessing beg of you. For this same lord,   [*Pointing to Polonius.*]
I do repent: but heaven hath pleas'd it so,
To punish me with this and this with me,   175
That I must be their scourge and minister.
I will bestow him, and will answer well
The death I gave him. So, again, good night.
I must be cruel, only to be kind:
Thus bad begins and worse remains behind.   180
One word more, good lady.

---

144. re-word: Repeat in words.   **145. gambol:** Skip away.   **146. unction:** Ointment used medicinally or as a rite; suggestion that forgiveness for sin may not be so easily achieved.   **149. mining:** Working under the surface.   **151. what is to come:** I.e., the sins of the future.   **152. compost:** Manure.   **153. this my virtue:** My virtuous talk in reproving you.   **154. fatness:** Grossness; **pursy:** Short-winded, corpulent.   **156. curb:** Bow, bend the knee.   **170.** Defective line usually emended by inserting *master* after *either*.   **172. be bless'd:** Become blessed, i.e., repentant.

QUEEN: What shall I do?

HAMLET: Not this, by no means, that I bid you do:
    Let the bloat° king tempt you again to bed;
    Pinch wanton on your cheek; call you his mouse;
    And let him, for a pair of reechy° kisses,   185
    Or paddling in your neck with his damn'd fingers,
    Make you to ravel all this matter out,
    That I essentially° am not in madness,
    But mad in craft. 'Twere good you let him know;
    For who, that's but a queen, fair, sober, wise,   190
    Would from a paddock,° from a bat, a gib,°
    Such dear concernings° hide? who would do so?
    No, in despite of sense and secrecy,
    Unpeg the basket on the house's top,
    Let the birds fly, and, like the famous ape.°   195
    To try conclusions,° in the basket creep,
    And break your own neck down.
QUEEN: Be thou assur'd, if words be made of breath,
    And breath of life, I have no life to breathe
    What thou hast said to me.   200
HAMLET: I must to England; you know that?
QUEEN: Alack,
    I had forgot: 'tis so concluded on.
HAMLET: There's letters seal'd: and my two schoolfellows,
    Whom I will trust as I will adders fang'd,
    They bear the mandate; they must sweep my way,°   205
    And marshal me to knavery. Let it work;
    For 'tis the sport to have the enginer°
    Hoist° with his own petar:° and 't shall go hard
    But I will delve one yard below their mines,
    And blow them at the moon: O, 'tis most sweet,   210
    When in one line two crafts° directly meet.
    This man shall set me packing:°
    I'll lug the guts into the neighbour room.
    Mother, good night. Indeed this counsellor
    Is now most still, most secret and most grave,   215
    Who was in life a foolish prating knave.

---

183. bloat: Bloated.   **185. reechy:** Dirty, filthy.   **188. essentially:** In my essential nature.
191. paddock: Toad; **gib:** Tomcat.   **192. dear concernings:** Important affairs.   **195. the famous ape:** A letter from Sir John Suckling seems to supply other details of the story, otherwise not identified: "It is the story of the jackanapes and the partridges; thou starest after a
beauty till it be lost to thee, then let'st out another, and starest after that till it is gone too."
196. conclusions: Experiments.   **205. sweep my way:** Clear my path.   **207. enginer:** Con-
structor of military works, or possibly, artilleryman.   **208. Hoist:** Blown up; **petar:** Defined
as a small engine of war used to blow in a door or make a breach, and as a case filled with ex-
plosive materials.   **211. two crafts:** Two acts of guile, with quibble on the sense of "two
ships."   **212. set me packing:** Set me to making schemes, and set me to lugging (him), and,
also, send me off in a hurry.

Come, sir, to draw° toward an end with you.
Good night, mother.   *Exeunt [severally; Hamlet dragging in Polonius.]*

[ACT IV

SCENE I: *A room in the castle.*]

Enter King and Queen, with Rosencrantz and Guildenstern.

KING: There's matter in these sighs, these profound heaves:
   You must translate: 'tis fit we understand them.
   Where is your son?
QUEEN: Bestow this place on us a little while.

                              [Exeunt Rosencrantz and Guildenstern.]

   Ah, mine own lord, what have I seen to-night!
KING: What, Gertrude? How does Hamlet?   5
QUEEN: Mad as the sea and wind, when both contend
   Which is the mightier: in his lawless fit,
   Behind the arras hearing something stir,
   Whips out his rapier, cries, "A rat, a rat!"
   And, in this brainish° apprehension,° kills   10
   The unseen good old man.
KING: O heavy deed!
   It had been so with us, had we been there:
   His liberty is full of threats to all;
   To you yourself, to us, to every one.
   Alas, how shall this bloody deed be answer'd?   15
   It will be laid to us, whose providence°
   Should have kept short,° restrain'd and out of haunt,°
   This mad young man: but so much was our love,
   We would not understand what was most fit;
   But, like the owner of a foul disease,   20
   To keep it from divulging,° let it feed
   Even on the pith of life. Where is he gone?
QUEEN: To draw apart the body he hath kill'd:
   O'er whom his very madness, like some ore
   Among a mineral° of metals base,   25
   Shows itself pure; 'a weeps for what is done.
KING: O Gertrude, come away!
   The sun no sooner shall the mountains touch,
   But we will ship him hence: and this vile deed
   We must, with all our majesty and skill,   30
   Both countenance and excuse. Ho, Guildenstern!

---

217. **draw:** Come, with quibble on literal sense. ACT IV, SCENE I. **11. brainish:** Head-strong, passionate; **apprehension:** Conception, imagination. **17. providence:** Foresight.
18. short: I.e., on a short tether; **out of haunt:** Secluded. **22. divulging:** Becoming evident.
26. mineral: Mine.

Enter Rosencrantz and Guildenstern.

> Friends both, go join you with some further aid:
> Hamlet in madness hath Polonius slain,
> And from his mother's closet hath he dragg'd him: 35
> Go seek him out; speak fair, and bring the body
> Into the chapel. I pray you, haste in this.
>   [*Exeunt Rosencrantz and Guildenstern.*]
> Come, Gertrude, we'll call up our wisest friends;
> And let them know, both what we mean to do,
> And what's untimely done . . .°   40
> Whose whisper o'er the world's diameter,°
> As level° as the cannon to his blank,°
> Transports his pois'ned shot, may miss our name,
> And hit the woundless° air. O, come away!
> My soul is full of discord and dismay.   *Exeunt.* 45

[SCENE II *Another room in the castle.*]

Enter Hamlet.

HAMLET: Safely stowed.

ROSENCRANTZ: ⎫
               ⎬ (*within*) Hamlet! Lord Hamlet!
GUILDENSTERN: ⎭

HAMLET: But soft, what noise? who calls on Hamlet? O, here they come.

Enter Rosencrantz and Guildenstern.

ROSENCRANTZ: What have you done, my lord, with the dead body?

HAMLET: Compounded it with dust, whereto 'tis kin.

ROSENCRANTZ: Tell us where 'tis, that we may take it thence   5
    And bear it to the chapel.

HAMLET: Do not believe it.

ROSENCRANTZ: Believe what?

HAMLET: That I can keep your counsel° and not mine own. Besides, to be de-
    manded of a sponge! what replication° should be made by the son of a 10
    king?

ROSENCRANTZ: Take you me for a sponge, my lord?

HAMLET: Ay, sir, that soaks up the king's countenance, his rewards, his author-
    ities.° But such officers do the king best service in the end: he keeps
    them, like an ape an apple, in the corner of his jaw; first mouthed, to be 15
    last swallowed: when he needs what you have gleaned, it is but squeez-
    ing you, and, sponge, you shall be dry again.

ROSENCRANTZ: I understand you not, my lord.

HAMLET: I am glad of it: a knavish speech sleeps in a foolish ear.

---

40. Defective line; some editors add: *so, haply, slander;* others add: *for, haply, slander;* other
conjectures.   41. **diameter:** Extent from side to side.   42. **level:** Straight; **blank:** White spot
in the center of a target.   44. **woundless:** Invulnerable.   SCENE II.   9. **keep your counsel:**
Hamlet is aware of their treachery but says nothing about it.   10. **replication:** Reply.
14. **authorities:** Authoritative backing.

ROSENCRANTZ: My lord, you must tell us where the body is, and go with us to   20
   the king.
HAMLET: The body is with the king, but the king is not with the body.° The king
   is a thing —
GUILDENSTERN: A thing, my lord!
HAMLET: Of nothing: bring me to him. Hide fox, and all after.°   *Exeunt.*   25

[SCENE III: Another room in the castle.]

Enter King, and two or three.

KING: I have sent to seek him, and to find the body.
   How dangerous is it that this man goes loose!
   Yet must not we put the strong law on him:
   He's lov'd of the distracted° multitude,
   Who like not in their judgement, but their eyes;   5
   And where 'tis so, th' offender's scourge° is weigh'd,°
   But never the offence. To bear all smooth and even,
   This sudden sending him away must seem
   Deliberate pause:° diseases desperate grown
   By desperate appliance are reliev'd,   10
   Or not at all.

Enter Rosencrantz, [Guildenstern,] and all the rest.

                    How now! what hath befall'n?
ROSENCRANTZ: Where the dead body is bestow'd, my lord,
   We cannot get from him.
KING: But where is he?
ROSENCRANTZ: Without, my lord; guarded, to know your pleasure.
KING: Bring him before us.   15
ROSENCRANTZ: Ho! bring in the lord.

They enter [with Hamlet].

KING: Now, Hamlet, where's Polonius?
HAMLET: At supper.
KING: At supper! where?
HAMLET: Not where he eats, but where 'a is eaten: a certain convocation of 20
   politic° worms° are e'en at him. Your worm is your only emperor for
   diet: we fat all creatures else to fat us, and we fat ourselves for maggots:
   your fat king and your lean beggar is but variable service,° two dishes,
   but to one table: that's the end.

---

22. The body . . . body: There are many interpretations; possibly, "The body lies in death
with the king, my father; but my father walks disembodied"; or "Claudius has the bodily
possession of kingship, but kingliness, or justice of inheritance, is not with him." **25. Hide
. . . after:** An old signal cry in the game of hide-and-seek. SCENE III. **4. distracted:** I.e.,
without power of forming logical judgments. **6. scourge:** Punishment; **weigh'd:** Taken into
consideration. **9. Deliberate pause:** Considered action. **20.–21. convocation . . . worms:**
Allusion to the Diet of Worms (1521); **politic:** Crafty. **23. variable service:** A variety of
dishes.

KING: Alas, alas! 25

HAMLET: A man may fish with the worm that hath eat of a king, and eat of the
fish that hath fed of that worm.

KING: What dost thou mean by this?

HAMLET: Nothing but to show you how a king may go a progress° through the
guts of a beggar. 30

KING: Where is Polonius?

HAMLET: In heaven; send thither to see: if your messenger find him not there,
seek him i' the other place yourself. But if indeed you find him not
within this month, you shall nose him as you go up the stairs into the
lobby. 35

KING [*to some Attendants*]: Go seek him there.

HAMLET: 'A will stay till you come.   [*Exeunt Attendants.*]

KING: Hamlet, this deed, for thine especial safety, —
      Which we do tender,° as we dearly grieve
      For that which thou hast done, — must send thee hence 40
      With fiery quickness: therefore prepare thyself;
      The bark is ready, and the wind at help,
      Th' associates tend, and everything is bent
      For England.

HAMLET: For England!

KING: Ay, Hamlet.

HAMLET: Good.

KING: So is it, if thou knew'st our purposes. 45

HAMLET: I see a cherub° that sees them. But, come; for England! Farewell, dear
mother.

KING: Thy loving father, Hamlet.

HAMLET: My mother: father and mother is man and wife; man and wife is one
flesh; and so, my mother. Come, for England!   *Exit.* 50

KING: Follow him at foot;° tempt him with speed aboard;
      Delay it not; I'll have him hence to-night:
      Away! for every thing is seal'd and done
      That else leans on th' affair: pray you, make haste.

                              [*Exeunt all but the King.*]

      And, England, if my love thou hold'st at aught — 55
      As my great power thereof may give thee sense,
      Since yet thy cicatrice° looks raw and red
      After the Danish sword, and thy free awe°
      Pays homage to us — thou mayst not coldly set
      Our sovereign process; which imports at full, 60
      By letters congruing to that effect,
      The present death of Hamlet. Do it, England;

---

29. progress: Royal journey of state.   **39. tender:** Regard, hold dear.   **46. cherub:** Cheru-
bim are angels of knowledge.   **51. at foot:** Close behind, at heel.   **57. cicatrice:** Scar.   **58.
free awe:** Voluntary show of respect.

For like the hectic° in my blood he rages,
And thou must cure me: till I know 'tis done,
Howe'er my haps,° my joys were ne'er begun.   *Exit.* 65

[SCENE IV: *A plain in Denmark.*]

Enter Fortinbras with his Army over the stage.

FORTINBRAS: Go, captain, from me greet the Danish king;
    Tell him that, by his license,° Fortinbras
    Craves the conveyance° of a promis'd march
    Over his kingdom. You know the rendezvous.
    If that his majesty would aught with us,   5
    We shall express our duty in his eye;°
    And let him know so.
CAPTAIN: I will do't, my lord.
FORTINBRAS: Go softly° on.   [*Exeunt all but Captain.*]

Enter Hamlet, Rosencrantz, [Guildenstern,] &c.

HAMLET: Good sir, whose powers are these?
CAPTAIN: They are of Norway, sir.   10
HAMLET: How purpos'd, sir, I pray you?
CAPTAIN: Against some part of Poland.
HAMLET: Who commands them, sir?
CAPTAIN: The nephew to old Norway, Fortinbras.
HAMLET: Goes it against the main° of Poland, sir,   15
    Or for some frontier?
CAPTAIN: Truly to speak, and with no addition,
    We go to gain a little patch of ground
    That hath in it no profit but the name.
    To pay five ducats, five, I would not farm it;°   20
    Nor will it yield to Norway or the Pole
    A ranker rate, should it be sold in fee.°
HAMLET: Why, then the Polack never will defend it.
CAPTAIN: Yes, it is already garrison'd.
HAMLET: Two thousand souls and twenty thousand ducats   25
    Will not debate the question of this straw:°
    This is th' imposthume° of much wealth and peace,
    That inward breaks, and shows no cause without
    Why the man dies. I humbly thank you, sir.
CAPTAIN: God be wi' you, sir.   [*Exit.*]
ROSENCRANTZ: Will 't please you go, my lord?   30
HAMLET: I'll be with you straight. Go a little before.

                                        [*Exeunt all except Hamlet.*]

---

63. hectic: Fever. **65. haps:** Fortunes. SCENE IV. **2. license:** Leave. **3. conveyance:** Escort, convoy. **6. in his eye:** In his presence. **8. softly:** Slowly. **15. main:** Country itself. **20. farm it:** Take a lease of it. **22. fee:** Fee simple. **26. debate . . . straw:** Settle this trifling matter. **27. imposthume:** Purulent abscess or swelling.

How all occasions° do inform against° me,
And spur my dull revenge! What is a man,
If his chief good and market of his time°
Be but to sleep and feed? a beast, no more.   35
Sure, he that made us with such large discourse,
Looking before and after, gave us not
That capability and god-like reason
To fust° in us unus'd. Now, whether it be
Bestial oblivion, or some craven scruple   40
Of thinking too precisely on th' event,
A thought which, quarter'd, hath but one part wisdom
And ever three parts coward, I do not know
Why yet I live to say "This thing 's to do";
Sith I have cause and will and strength and means   45
To do 't. Examples gross as earth exhort me:
Witness this army of such mass and charge
Led by a delicate and tender prince,
Whose spirit with divine ambition puff'd
Makes mouths at the invisible event,   50
Exposing what is mortal and unsure
To all that fortune, death and danger dare,
Even for an egg-shell. Rightly to be great
Is not to stir without great argument,
But greatly to find quarrel in a straw   55
When honour's at the stake. How stand I then,
That have a father kill'd, a mother stain'd,
Excitements of° my reason and my blood,
And let all sleep? while, to my shame, I see
The imminent death of twenty thousand men,   60
That, for a fantasy and trick° of fame,
Go to their graves like beds, fight for a plot°
Whereon the numbers cannot try the cause,
Which is not tomb enough and continent
To hide the slain? O, from this time forth,   65
My thoughts be bloody, or be nothing worth!   *Exit.*

[SCENE V: *Elsinore. A room in the castle.*]

Enter Horatio, [Queen] Gertrude, and a Gentleman.

QUEEN: I will not speak with her.
GENTLEMAN: She is importunate, indeed distract:
    Her mood will needs be pitied.

---

32. occasions: Incidents, events; **inform against:** Generally defined as "show," "betray" (i.e.,
his tardiness); more probably *inform* means "take shape," as in *Macbeth,* II.i.48.   **34. market
of his time:** The best use he makes of his time, or, that for which he sells his time.   **39. fust:**
Grow moldy.   **58. Excitements of:** Incentives to.   **61. trick:** Toy, trifle.   **62. plot:** I.e., of
ground.

QUEEN: What would she have?

GENTLEMAN: She speaks much of her father; says she hears
    There's tricks° i' th' world; and hems, and beats her heart;°   5
    Spurns enviously at straws;° speaks things in doubt,
    That carry but half sense: her speech is nothing,
    Yet the unshaped° use of it doth move
    The hearers to collection;° they yawn° at it,
    And botch° the words up fit to their own thoughts;   10
    Which, as her winks, and nods, and gestures yield° them,
    Indeed would make one think there might be thought,
    Though nothing sure, yet much unhappily.°

HORATIO: 'Twere good she were spoken with: for she may strew
    Dangerous conjectures in ill-breeding minds.°   15

QUEEN: Let her come in.   [*Exit Gentleman.*]
    [*Aside.*] To my sick soul, as sin's true nature is,
    Each toy seems prologue to some great amiss:°
    So full of artless jealousy is guilt,
    It spills itself in fearing to be spilt.°   20

Enter Ophelia [distracted].

OPHELIA: Where is the beauteous majesty of Denmark?

QUEEN: How now, Ophelia!

OPHELIA (*she sings*): How should I your true love know
      From another one?
    By his cockle hat° and staff,   25
      And his sandal shoon.°

QUEEN: Alas, sweet lady, what imports this song?

OPHELIA: Say you? nay, pray you mark.
    (*Song*) He is dead and gone, lady,
      He is dead and gone;   30
    At his head a grass-green turf,
      At his heels a stone.
    O, ho!

QUEEN: Nay, but, Ophelia —

OPHELIA: Pray you, mark   35
    [*Sings.*] White his shroud as the mountain snow, —

Enter King.

QUEEN: Alas, look here, my lord.

OPHELIA (*Song*): Larded° all with flowers;

SCENE V. **5. tricks:** Deceptions; **heart:** I.e., breast. **6. Spurns . . . straws:** Kicks spitefully at
small objects in her path. **8. unshaped:** Unformed, artless. **9. collection:** Inference, a
guess at some sort of meaning; **yawn:** Wonder. **10. botch:** Patch. **11. yield:** Deliver, bring
forth (her words). **13. much unhappily:** Expressive of much unhappiness. **15. ill-breed-
ing minds:** Minds bent on mischief. **18. great amiss:** Calamity, disaster. **19.–20. So . . .
spilt:** Guilt is so full of suspicion that it unskillfully betrays itself in fearing to be betrayed.
25. cockle hat: Hat with cockleshell stuck in it as a sign that the wearer has been a pilgrim to
the shrine of St. James of Compostella. The pilgrim's garb was a conventional disguise for
lovers. **26. shoon:** Shoes. **38. Larded:** Decorated.

Which bewept to the grave did not go
    With true-love showers.   40

KING: How do you, pretty lady?

OPHELIA: Well, God 'ild° you! They say the owl° was a baker's daughter. Lord,
we know what we are, but know not what we may be. God be at your
table!

KING: Conceit upon her father.   45

OPHELIA: Pray let's have no words of this; but when they ask you what it
means, say you this:
    (*Song*) To-morrow is Saint Valentine's day,
        All in the morning betime,
    And I a maid at your window,
        To be your Valentine.°   50
    Then up he rose, and donn'd his clothes,
        And dupp'd° the chamber-door;
    Let in the maid, that out a maid
        Never departed more.   55

KING: Pretty Ophelia!

OPHELIA: Indeed, la, without an oath, I'll make an end on 't:
    [*Sings.*] By Gis° and by Saint Charity,
        Alack, and fie for shame!
    Young men will do 't, if they come to 't;
        By cock,° they are to blame.   60
    Quoth she, before you tumbled me,
        You promis'd me to wed.
    So would I ha' done, by yonder sun,
        An thou hadst not come to my bed.   65

KING: How long hath she been thus?

OPHELIA: I hope all will be well. We must be patient: but I cannot choose but
weep, to think they would lay him i' the cold ground. My brother shall
know of it: and so I thank you for your good counsel. Come, my coach!
Good night, ladies; good night, sweet ladies; good night, good night. 70
                                                  [*Exit.*]

KING: Follow her close; give her good watch, I pray you.   [*Exit Horatio.*]
    O, this is the poison of deep grief; it springs
    All from her father's death. O Gertrude, Gertrude,
    When sorrows come, they come not single spies,
    But in battalions. First, her father slain: 75
    Next your son gone; and he most violent author
    Of his own just remove: the people muddied,
    Thick and unwholesome in their thoughts and whispers,

---

42. God 'ild: God yield or reward; **owl:** Reference to a monkish legend that a baker's daughter was turned into an owl for refusing bread to the Savior. **51. Valentine:** This song alludes to the belief that the first girl seen by a man on the morning of this day was his valentine or true love. **53. dupp'd:** Opened. **58. Gis:** Jesus. **61. cock:** Perversion of "God" in oaths.

For good Polonius' death; and we have done but greenly,°
In hugger-mugger° to inter him: poor Ophelia   80
Divided from herself and her fair judgement,
Without the which we are pictures, or mere beasts:
Last, and as much containing as all these,
Her brother is in secret come from France;
Feeds on his wonder, keeps himself in clouds,°   85
And wants not buzzers° to infect his ear
With pestilent speeches of his father's death;
Wherein necessity, of matter beggar'd,°
Will nothing stick° our person to arraign
In ear and ear.° O my dear Gertrude, this,   90
Like to a murd'ring-piece,° in many places
Gives me superfluous death.   *A noise within.*

QUEEN: Alack, what noise is this?
KING: Where are my Switzers?° Let them guard the door.

Enter a Messenger.

What is the matter?
MESSENGER: Save yourself, my lord:
The ocean, overpeering° of his list,°   95
Eats not the flats with more impiteous haste
Than young Laertes, in a riotous head,
O'erbears your officers. The rabble call him lord;
And, as the world were now but to begin,
Antiquity forgot, custom not known,   100
The ratifiers and props of every word,°
They cry "Choose we: Laertes shall be king":
Caps, hands, and tongues, applaud it to the clouds:
"Laertes shall be king, Laertes king!"   *A noise within.*
QUEEN: How cheerfully on the false trail they cry!   105
O, this is counter,° you false Danish dogs!
KING: The doors are broke.

Enter Laertes with others.

LAERTES: Where is this king? Sirs, stand you all without.
DANES: No, let's come in.
LAERTES: I pray you, give me leave.
DANES: We will, we will.   *[They retire without the door.]* 110
LAERTES: I thank you: keep the door. O thou vile king,
Give me my father!

---

79. greenly: Foolishly. **80. hugger-mugger:** Secret haste. **85. in clouds:** Invisible.
86. buzzers: Gossipers. **88. of matter beggar'd:** Unprovided with facts. **89. nothing stick:**
Not hesitate. **90. In ear and ear:** In everybody's ears. **91. murd'ring-piece:** Small cannon or
mortar; suggestion of numerous missiles fired. **93. Switzers:** Swiss guards, mercenaries.
95. overpeering: Overflowing; **list:** Shore. **101. word:** Promise. **106. counter:** A hunting
term meaning to follow the trail in a direction opposite to that which the game has taken.

QUEEN: Calmly, good Laertes.

LAERTES: That drop of blood that's calm proclaims me bastard,
Cries cuckold to my father, brands the harlot
Even here, between the chaste unsmirched brow 115
Of my true mother.

KING: What is the cause, Laertes,
That thy rebellion looks so giant-like?
Let him go, Gertrude; do not fear our person:
There's such divinity doth hedge a king,
That treason can but peep to° what it would° 120
Acts little of his will. Tell me, Laertes,
Why thou art thus incens'd. Let him go, Gertrude.
Speak, man.

LAERTES: Where is my father?

KING: Dead.

QUEEN: But not by him.

KING: Let him demand his fill. 125

LAERTES: How came he dead? I'll not be juggled with:
To hell, allegiance! vows, to the blackest devil!
Conscience and grace, to the profoundest pit!
I dare damnation. To this point I stand,
That both the worlds I give to negligence,° 130
Let come what comes; only I'll be reveng'd
Most throughly° for my father.

KING: Who shall stay you?

LAERTES: My will,° not all the world's:
And for my means, I'll husband them so well,
They shall go far with little.

KING: Good Laertes, 135
If you desire to know the certainty
Of your dear father, is 't writ in your revenge,
That, swoopstake,° you will draw both friend and foe,
Winner and loser?

LAERTES: None but his enemies.

KING: Will you know them then? 140

LAERTES: To his good friends thus wide I'll ope my arms;
And like the kind life-rend'ring pelican,°
Repast° them with my blood.

KING: Why, now you speak
Like a good child and a true gentleman.
That I am guiltless of your father's death, 145

---

120. **peep to:** I.e., look at from afar off; **would:** Wishes to do. 130. **give to negligence:** He despises both the here and the hereafter. 132. **throughly:** thoroughly. 133. **My will:** He will not be stopped except by his own will. 138. **swoopstake:** Literally, drawing the whole stake at once, i.e., indiscriminately. 142. **pelican:** Reference to the belief that the pelican feeds its young with its own blood. 143. **Repast:** Feed.

And am most sensibly in grief for it,
It shall as level to your judgement 'pear
As day does to your eye.   *A noise within: "Let her come in."*

LAERTES: How now! what noise is that?

Enter Ophelia.

O heat,° dry up my brains! tears seven times salt,   150
Burn out the sense and virtue of mine eye!
By heaven, thy madness shall be paid with weight,
Till our scale turn the beam. O rose of May!
Dear maid, kind sister, sweet Ophelia!
O heavens! is 't possible, a young maid's wits   155
Should be as mortal as an old man's life?
Nature is fine in love, and where 'tis fine,
It sends some precious instance of itself
After the thing it loves.

OPHELIA (*Song*): They bore him barefac'd on the bier;   160
      Hey non nonny, nonny, hey nonny;
      And in his grave rain'd many a tear: —
Fare you well, my dove!

LAERTES: Hadst thou thy wits, and didst persuade revenge,
It could not move thus.   165

OPHELIA [*sings*]: You must sing a-down a-down,
      An you call him a-down-a.
O, how the wheel° becomes it! It is the false steward,° that stole his master's daughter.

LAERTES: This nothing's more than matter.   170

OPHELIA: There's rosemary,° that's for remembrance; pray you, love, remember: and there is pansies,° that's for thoughts.

LAERTES: A document° in madness, thoughts and remembrance fitted.

OPHELIA: There's fennel° for you, and columbines:° there's rue° for you; and
here's some for me: we may call it herb of grace o' Sundays: O, you must   175
wear your rue with a difference. There's a daisy:° I would give you some
violets,° but they withered all when my father died: they say 'a made a
good end, —
[*Sings.*] For bonny sweet Robin is all my joy.°

---

150. heat: Probably the heat generated by the passion of grief.   **168. wheel:** Spinning wheel
as accompaniment to the song refrain; **false steward:** The story is unknown.   **171. rosemary:** Used as a symbol of remembrance both at weddings and at funerals.   **172. pansies:**
Emblems of love and courtship. Cf. French *pensées*.   **173. document:** Piece of instruction or
lesson.   **174. fennel:** Emblem of flattery; **columbines:** Emblem of unchastity (?) or ingrati-
tude(?); **rue:** Emblem of repentance. It was usually mingled with holy water and then known
as *herb of grace*. Ophelia is probably playing on the two meanings of *rue,* "repentant" and
"even for ruth (pity)"; the former signification is for the queen, the latter for herself.
176. daisy: Emblem of dissembling, faithlessness.   **177. violets:** Emblems of faithful-
ness.   **179. For . . . joy:** Probably a line from a Robin Hood ballad.

LAERTES: Thought° and affliction, passion, hell itself,   180
    She turns to favour and to prettiness.

OPHELIA (*Song*): And will 'a not come again?°
    And will 'a not come again?
      No, no, he is dead:
      Go to thy death-bed: 185
    He never will come again.

    His beard was as white as snow,
    All flaxen was his poll:°
      He is gone, he is gone,
      And we cast away° moan:
    God ha' mercy on his soul!   190
    And of all Christian souls, I pray God. God be wi' you.   [*Exit.*]

LAERTES: Do you see this, O God?

KING: Laertes, I must commune with your grief,
    Or you deny me right.° Go but apart,   195
    Make choice of whom your wisest friends you will,
    And they shall hear and judge 'twixt you and me:
    If by direct or by collateral° hand
    They find us touch'd,° we will our kingdom give,
    Our crown, our life, and all that we call ours,   200
    To you in satisfaction; but if not,
    Be you content to lend your patience to us,
    And we shall jointly labour with your soul
    To give it due content.

LAERTES: Let this be so;
    His means of death, his obscure funeral —   205
    No trophy, sword, nor hatchment° o'er his bones,
    No noble rite nor formal ostentation —
    Cry to be heard, as 'twere from heaven to earth,
    That I must call 't in question.

KING: So you shall;
    And where th' offence is let the great axe fall.   210
    I pray you, go with me.   *Exeunt.*

[SCENE VI: *Another room in the castle.*]

Enter Horatio and others.

HORATIO: What are they that would speak with me?

GENTLEMAN: Sea-faring men, sir: they say they have letters for you.

HORATIO: Let them come in.   [*Exit Gentleman.*]
    I do not know from what part of the world
    I should be greeted, if not from lord Hamlet.   5

---

180. Thought: Melancholy thought.   **182. And . . . again:** This song appeared in the song-books as "The Merry Milkmaids' Dumps."   **188. poll:** Head.   **190. cast away:** Ship-wrecked.   **195. right:** My rights.   **198. collateral:** Indirect.   **199. touch'd:** Implicated.   **206. hatchment:** Tablet displaying the armorial bearings of a deceased person.

Enter Sailors.

FIRST SAILOR: God bless you, sir.

HORATIO: Let him bless thee too.

FIRST SAILOR: 'A shall sir, an 't please him. There's a letter for you, sir; it comes
    from the ambassador that was bound for England; if your name be Ho-
    ratio, as I am let to know it is.   10

HORATIO [*reads*]: "Horatio, when thou shalt have overlooked this, give these
    fellows some means° to the king: they have letters for him. Ere we were
    two days old at sea, a pirate of very warlike appointment gave us chase.
    Finding ourselves too slow of sail, we put on a compelled valour, and in
    the grapple I boarded them: on the instant they got clear of our ship; so 15
    I alone became their prisoner. They have dealt with me like thieves of
    mercy:° but they knew what they did; I am to do a good turn for them.
    Let the king have the letters I have sent; and repair thou to me with as
    much speed as thou wouldest fly death. I have words to speak in thine
    ear will make thee dumb; yet are they much too light for the bore° of the 20
    matter. These good fellows will bring thee where I am. Rosencrantz and
    Guildenstern hold their course for England: of them I have much to tell
    thee. Farewell.

                               "He that thou knowest thine, HAMLET."

    Come, I will give you way for these your letters;   25
    And do 't the speedier, that you may direct me
    To him from whom you brought them.   *Exeunt.*

[SCENE VII: *Another room in the castle.*]

Enter King and Laertes.

KING: Now must your conscience° my acquittance seal,
    And you must put me in your heart for friend,
    Sith you have heard, and with a knowing ear,
    That he which hath your noble father slain
    Pursued my life.

LAERTES: It well appears: but tell me   5
    Why you proceeded not against these feats,
    So criminal and so capital° in nature,
    As by your safety, wisdom, all things else,
    You mainly° were stirr'd up.

KING: O, for two special reasons;
    Which may to you, perhaps, seem much unsinew'd,°   10
    But yet to me th' are strong. The queen his mother
    Lives almost by his looks; and for myself —
    My virtue or my plague, be it either which —
    She's so conjunctive° to my life and soul,

SCENE VI. **12. means:** Means of access. **16.–17. thieves of mercy:** Merciful thieves.
20. bore: Caliber, importance. SCENE VII. **1. conscience:** Knowledge that this is true.
7. capital: Punishable by death. **9. mainly:** Greatly. **10. unsinew'd:** Weak. **14. con-
junctive:** Conformable (the next line suggesting planetary conjunction).

That, as the star moves not but in his sphere,°   15
I could not but by her. The other motive,
Why to a public count° I might not go,
Is the great love the general gender° bear him;
Who, dipping all his faults in their affection,
Would, like the spring° that turneth wood to stone,   20
Convert his gyves° to graces; so that my arrows,
Too slightly timber'd° for so loud° a wind,
Would have reverted to my bow again,
And not where I had aim'd them.

LAERTES: And so have I a noble father lost;   25
        A sister driven into desp'rate terms,°
        Whose worth, if praises may go back° again,
        Stood challenger on mount° of all the age°
        For her perfections: but my revenge will come.

KING: Break not your sleeps for that: you must not think   30
      That we are made of stuff so flat and dull
      That we can let our beard be shook with danger
      And think it pastime. You shortly shall hear more:
      I lov'd your father, and we love ourself;
      And that, I hope, will teach you to imagine —   35

Enter a Messenger with letters.

        How now! what news?

MESSENGER: Letters, my lord, from Hamlet:
      These to your majesty; this to the queen.°

KING: From Hamlet! who brought them?

MESSENGER: Sailors, my lord, they say; I saw them not:
      They were given me by Claudio;° he receiv'd them   40
      Of him that brought them.

KING: Laertes, you shall hear them.
      Leave us.   [*Exit Messenger.*]
      [*Reads.*] "High and mighty, You shall know I am set naked° on your
      kingdom. To-morrow shall I beg leave to see your kingly eyes: when I
      shall, first asking your pardon thereunto, recount the occasion of my   45
      sudden and more strange return.   "HAMLET."
      What should this mean? Are all the rest come back?
      Or is it some abuse, and no such thing?

---

15. sphere: The hollow sphere in which, according to Ptolemaic astronomy, the planets were supposed to move.   **17. count:** Account, reckoning.   **18. general gender:** Common people.
20. spring: I.e., one heavily charged with lime.   **21. gyves:** Fetters; here, faults, or possibly, punishments inflicted (on him).   **22. slightly timber'd:** Light; **loud:** Strong.   **26. terms:** State, condition.   **27. go back:** I.e., to Ophelia's former virtues.   **28. on mount:** Set up on high, *mounted* (on horseback); **of all the age:** Qualifies *challenger* and not *mount.*   **37. to the queen:** One hears no more of the letter to the queen.   **40. Claudio:** This character does not appear in the play.   **43. naked:** Unprovided (with retinue).

LAERTES: Know you the hand?

KING: 'Tis Hamlet's character. "Naked!"
    And in a postscript here, he says "alone."   50
    Can you devise° me?

LAERTES: I'm lost in it, my lord. But let him come;
    It warms the very sickness in my heart,
    That I shall live and tell him to his teeth,
    "Thus didst thou."

KING: If it be so, Laertes —   55
    As how should it be so? how otherwise?° —
    Will you be rul'd by me?

LAERTES: Ay, my lord;
    So you will not o'errule me to a peace.

KING: To thine own peace. If he be now return'd,
    As checking at° his voyage, and that he means   60
    No more to undertake it, I will work him
    To an exploit, now ripe in my device,
    Under the which he shall not choose but fall:
    And for his death no wind of blame shall breathe,
    But even his mother shall uncharge the practice°   65
    And call it accident.

LAERTES: My lord, I will be rul'd;
    The rather, if you could devise it so
    That I might be the organ.°

KING: It falls right.
    You have been talk'd of since your travel much,
    And that in Hamlet's hearing, for a quality   70
    Wherein, they say, you shine: your sum of parts
    Did not together pluck such envy from him
    As did that one, and that, in my regard,
    Of the unworthiest siege.°

LAERTES: What part is that, my lord?

KING: A very riband in the cap of youth,   75
    Yet needful too; for youth no less becomes
    The light and careless livery that it wears
    Than settled age his sables° and his weeds,
    Importing health and graveness. Two months since,
    Here was a gentleman of Normandy: —   80
    I have seen myself, and serv'd against, the French,
    And they can well° on horseback: but this gallant

---

51. devise: Explain to. **56. As . . . otherwise?** How can this (Hamlet's return) be true? (yet) how otherwise than true (since we have the evidence of his letter)? Some editors read *How should it not be so*, etc., making the words refer to Laertes' desire to meet with Hamlet. **60. checking at:** Used in falconry of a hawk's leaving the quarry to fly at a chance bird, turn aside. **65. uncharge the practice:** Acquit the stratagem of being a plot. **68. organ:** Agent, instrument. **74. siege:** Rank. **78. sables:** Rich garments. **82. can well:** Are skilled.

Had witchcraft in 't; he grew unto his seat;
And to such wondrous doing brought his horse,
As had he been incorps'd and demi-natur'd°   85
With the brave beast: so far he topp'd° my thought,
That I, in forgery° of shapes and tricks,
Come short of what he did.

LAERTES: A Norman was 't?

KING: A Norman.

LAERTES: Upon my life, Lamord.°

KING: The very same.   90

LAERTES: I know him well: he is the brooch indeed
And gem of all the nation.

KING: He made confession° of you,
And gave you such a masterly report
For art and exercise° in your defence°   95
And for your rapier most especial,
That he cried out, 'twould be a sight indeed,
If one could match you: the scrimers° of their nation,
He swore, had neither motion, guard, nor eye,
If you oppos'd them. Sir, this report of his   100
Did Hamlet so envenom with his envy
That he could nothing do but wish and beg
Your sudden coming o'er, to play° with you.
Now, out of this, —

LAERTES: What out of this, my lord?

KING: Laertes, was your father dear to you?   105
Or are you like the painting of a sorrow,
A face without a heart?

LAERTES: Why ask you this?

KING: Not that I think you did not love your father;
But that I know love is begun by time;
And that I see, in passages of proof,°   110
Time qualifies the spark and fire of it.
There lives within the very flame of love
A kind of wick or snuff that will abate it;
And nothing is at a like goodness still;
For goodness, growing to a plurisy,°   115
Dies in his own too much:° that we would do,
We should do when we would; for this "would" changes
And hath abatements° and delays as many

---

85. **incorps'd and demi-natur'd:** Of one body and nearly of one nature (like the centaur).
86. **topp'd:** Surpassed.   87. **forgery:** Invention.   90. **Lamord:** This refers possibly to Pietro
Monte, instructor to Louis XII's master of the horse.   93. **confession:** Grudging admission
of superiority.   95. **art and exercise:** Skillful exercise; **defence:** Science of defense in sword
practice.   98. **scrimers:** Fencers.   103. **play:** Fence.   110. **passages of proof:** Proved instances.   115. **plurisy:** Excess, plethora.   116. **in his own too much:** Of its own excess.
118. **abatements:** Diminutions.

As there are tongues, are hands, are accidents;°   120
And then this "should" is like a spendthrift° sigh,
That hurts by easing. But, to the quick o' th' ulcer:° —
Hamlet comes back: what would you undertake,
To show yourself your father's son in deed
More than in words?

LAERTES: To cut his throat i' th' church.

KING: No place, indeed, should murder sanctuarize;°   125
Revenge should have no bounds. But, good Laertes,
Will you do this, keep close within your chamber.
Hamlet return'd shall know you are come home:
We'll put on those shall praise your excellence
And set a double varnish on the fame   130
The Frenchman gave you, bring you in fine together
And wager on your heads: he, being remiss,
Most generous and free from all contriving,
Will not peruse the foils; so that, with ease,
Or with a little shuffling, you may choose   135
A sword unbated,° and in a pass of practice°
Requite him for your father.

LAERTES: I will do 't:
And, for that purpose, I'll anoint my sword.
I bought an unction of a mountebank,°
So mortal that, but dip a knife in it,   140
Where it draws blood no cataplasm° so rare,
Collected from all simples° that have virtue
Under the moon,° can save the thing from death
That is but scratch'd withal: I'll touch my point
With this contagion, that, if I gall° him slightly,   145
It may be death.

KING: Let's further think of this;
Weigh what convenience both of time and means
May fit us to our shape:° if this should fail,
And that our drift look through our bad performance,°
'Twere better not assay'd: therefore this project   150
Should have a back or second, that might hold,
If this should blast in proof.° Soft! let me see:
We'll make a solemn wager on your cunnings:°

---

119. accidents: Occurrences, incidents.   **120. spendthrift:** An allusion to the belief that each sigh cost the heart a drop of blood.   **121. quick o' th' ulcer:** Heart of the difficulty. **125. sanctuarize:** Protect from punishment; allusion to the right of sanctuary with which certain religious places were invested.   **136. unbated:** Not blunted, having no button; **pass of practice:** Treacherous thrust.   **139. mountebank:** Quack doctor.   **141. cataplasm:** Plaster or poultice.   **142. simples:** Herbs.   **143. Under the moon:** I.e., when collected by moonlight to add to their medicinal value.   **145. gall:** Graze, wound.   **148. shape:** Part we propose to act.   **149. drift ... performance:** Intention be disclosed by our bungling. **152. blast in proof:** Burst in the test (like a cannon).   **153. cunnings:** Skills.

I ha 't:
When in your motion you are hot and dry —   155
As make your bouts more violent to that end —
And that he calls for drink, I'll have prepar'd him
A chalice° for the nonce, whereon but sipping,
If he by chance escape your venom'd stuck,°
Our purpose may hold there. But stay, what noise?   160

Enter Queen.

QUEEN: One woe doth tread upon another's heel,
      So fast they follow: your sister's drown'd, Laertes.
LAERTES: Drown'd! O, where?
QUEEN: There is a willow° grows askant° the brook,
      That shows his hoar° leaves in the glassy stream;   165
      There with fantastic garlands did she make
      Of crow-flowers,° nettles, daisies, and long purples°
      That liberal° shepherds give a grosser name,
      But our cold maids do dead men's fingers call them:
      There, on the pendent boughs her crownet° weeds   170
      Clamb'ring to hang, an envious sliver° broke;
      When down her weedy° trophies and herself
      Fell in the weeping brook. Her clothes spread wide;
      And, mermaid-like, awhile they bore her up:
      Which time she chanted snatches of old lauds;°   175
      As one incapable° of her own distress,
      Or like a creature native and indued°
      Upon that element: but long it could not be
      Till that her garments, heavy with their drink,
      Pull'd the poor wretch from her melodious lay   180
      To muddy death.
LAERTES: Alas, then, she is drown'd?
QUEEN: Drown'd, drown'd.
LAERTES: Too much of water hast thou, poor Ophelia,
      And therefore I forbid my tears: but yet
      It is our trick;° nature her custom holds,   185
      Let shame say what it will: when these are gone,
      The woman will be out.° Adieu, my lord:
      I have a speech of fire, that fain would blaze,
      But that this folly drowns it.   *Exit.*

---

158. chalice: Cup.   159. stuck: Thrust (from *stoccado*).   164. willow: For its significance
of forsaken love; askant: Aslant.   165. hoar: White (i.e., on the underside).   167. crow-
flowers: Buttercups; long purples: Early purple orchids.   168. liberal: Probably, free-
spoken.   170. crownet: Coronet; made into a chaplet.   171. sliver: Branch.   172. weedy:
I.e., of plants.   175. lauds: Hymns.   176. incapable: Lacking capacity to apprehend.
177. indued: Endowed with qualities fitting her for living in water.   185. trick: Way.
186.–187. when . . . out: When my tears are all shed, the woman in me will be satisfied.

KING: Let's follow, Gertrude:
How much I had to do to calm his rage!   190
Now fear I this will give it start again;
Therefore let 's follow.   *Exeunt.*

[ACT V

SCENE I: *A churchyard.*]

Enter two Clowns° [with spades, &c.].

FIRST CLOWN: Is she to be buried in Christian burial when she wilfully seeks her
own salvation?

SECOND CLOWN: I tell thee she is; therefore make her grave straight:° the
crowner° hath sat on her, and finds it Christian burial.

FIRST CLOWN: How can that be, unless she drowned herself in her own defence?   5

SECOND CLOWN: Why, 'tis found so.

FIRST CLOWN: It must be "se offendendo";° it cannot be else. For here lies the
point: if I drown myself wittingly,° it argues an act: and an act hath three
branches;° it is, to act, to do, and to perform: argal,° she drowned herself
wittingly.   10

SECOND CLOWN: Nay, but hear you, goodman delver,° —

FIRST CLOWN: Give me leave. Here lies the water; good: here stands the man;
good: if the man go to this water, and drown himself, it is, will he, nill he,
he goes, — mark you that; but if the water come to him and drown him,
he drowns not himself: argal, he that is not guilty of his own death short-   15
ens not his own life.

SECOND CLOWN: But is this law?

FIRST CLOWN: Ay, marry, is 't; crowner's quest° law.

SECOND CLOWN: Will you ha' the truth on 't? If this had not been a gentle-
woman, she should have been buried out o' Christian burial.   20

FIRST CLOWN: Why, there thou say'st:° and the more pity that great folk should
have countenance° in this world to drown or hang themselves, more
than their even° Christian. Come, my spade. There is no ancient gentlemen but gardeners, ditchers, and grave-makers: they hold up° Adam's
profession.   25

SECOND CLOWN: Was he a gentleman?

FIRST CLOWN: 'A was the first that ever bore arms.

SECOND CLOWN: Why, he had none.

FIRST CLOWN: What, art a heathen? How dost thou understand the Scripture?
The Scripture says "Adam digged": could he dig without arms? I'll put   30

ACT V, SCENE I   **s.d. Clowns:** The word **clown** was used to denote peasants as well as humorous characters; here applied to the rustic type of clown.   **3. straight:** Straightway, immediately; some interpret "from east to west in a direct line, parallel with the church."
4. crowner: Coroner.   **7. "se offendendo":** For *se defendendo,* term used in verdicts of justi-
fiable homicide.   **8. wittingly:** Intentionally.   **8.–9. three branches:** Parody of legal phraseology; **argal:** Corruption of *ergo,* therefore.   **11. delver:** Digger.   **18. quest:** Inquest.
21. there thou say'st: That's right.   **22. countenance:** Privilege.   **23. even:** Fellow.
24. hold up: Maintain, continue.

another question to thee: if thou answerest me not to the purpose, confess thyself° —

SECOND CLOWN: Go to.°

FIRST CLOWN: What is he that builds stronger than either the mason, the shipwright, or the carpenter? 35

SECOND CLOWN: The gallows-maker; for that frame outlives a thousand tenants.

FIRST CLOWN: I like thy wit well, in good faith: the gallows does well; but how does it well? it does well to those that do ill: now thou dost ill to say the gallows is built stronger than the church: argal, the gallows may do well 40 to thee. To 't again, come.

SECOND CLOWN: "Who builds stronger than a mason, a shipwright, or a carpenter?"

FIRST CLOWN: Ay, tell me that, and unyoke.°

SECOND CLOWN: Marry, now I can tell. 45

FIRST CLOWN: To 't.

SECOND CLOWN: Mass,° I cannot tell.

Enter Hamlet and Horatio [at a distance].

FIRST CLOWN: Cudgel thy brains no more about it, for your dull ass will not mend his pace with beating; and, when you are asked this question next, say "a grave-maker": the houses he makes lasts till doomsday. Go, get 50 thee in, and fetch me a stoup° of liquor.

[*Exit Second Clown.*] *Song.* [*He digs.*]
In youth, when I did love, did love,
   Methought it was very sweet,
To contract — O — the time, for — a — my behove,°
   O, methought, there — a — was nothing — a — meet. 55

HAMLET: Has this fellow no feeling of his business, that 'a sings at grave-making?

HORATIO: Custom hath made it in him a property of easiness.°

HAMLET: 'Tis e'en so: the hand of little employment hath the daintier sense.

FIRST CLOWN: (*Song.*) But age, with his stealing steps, 60
   Hath claw'd me in his clutch,
And hath shipped me into the land
   As if I had never been such. [*Throws up a skull.*]

HAMLET: That skull had a tongue in it, and could sing once: how the knave jowls° it to the ground, as if 'twere Cain's jaw-bone,° that did the first 65 murder! This might be the pate of a politician,° which this ass now o'er-reaches;° one that would circumvent God, might it not?

---

32. confess thyself: "And be hanged" completes the proverb. **33. Go to:** Perhaps, "begin," or some other form of concession. **44. unyoke:** After this great effort you may unharness the team of your wits. **47. Mass:** By the Mass. **51. stoup:** Two-quart measure. **54. behove:** Benefit. **58. property of easiness:** A peculiarity that now is easy. **65. jowls:** Dashes; **Cain's jaw-bone:** Allusion to the old tradition that Cain slew Abel with the jawbone of an ass. **66. politician:** Schemer, plotter. **66–67. o'er-reaches:** Quibble on the literal sense and the sense "circumvent."

HORATIO: It might, my lord.

HAMLET: Or of a courtier; which could say "Good morrow, sweet lord! How dost thou, sweet lord?" This might be my lord such-a-one, that praised 70 my lord such-a-one's horse, when he meant to beg it; might it not?

HORATIO: Ay, my lord.

HAMLET: Why, e'en so: and now my Lady Worm's; chapless,° and knocked about the mazzard° with a sexton's spade: here's fine revolution, an we had the trick to see 't. Did these bones cost no more the breeding, but to 75 play at loggats° with 'em? mine ache to think on 't.

FIRST CLOWN: (*Song.*) A pick-axe, and a spade, a spade,
> For and° a shrouding sheet:
> O, a pit of clay for to be made
> For such a guest is meet.   [*Throws up another skull.*] 80

HAMLET: There's another: why may not that be the skull of a lawyer? Where be his quiddities° now, his quillities,° his cases, his tenures,° and his tricks? why does he suffer this mad knave now to knock him about the sconce° with a dirty shovel, and will not tell him of his action of battery? Hum! This fellow might be in 's time a great buyer of land, with his statutes, 85 his recognizances,° his fines, his double vouchers,° his recoveries:° is this the fine° of his fines, and the recovery of his recoveries, to have his fine pate full of fine dirt? will his vouchers vouch him no more of his purchases, and double ones too, than the length and breadth of a pair of indentures?° The very conveyances of his lands will scarcely lie in this 90 box; and must the inheritor° himself have no more, ha?

HORATIO: Not a jot more, my lord.

HAMLET: Is not parchment made of sheep-skins?

HORATIO: Ay, my lord, and of calf-skins° too.

HAMLET: They are sheep and calves which seek out assurance in that.° I will 95 speak to this fellow. Whose grave's this, sirrah?

FIRST CLOWN: Mine, sir.
> [*Sings.*] O, a pit of clay for to be made
> For such a guest is meet.

HAMLET: I think it be thine, indeed; for thou liest in 't.   100

FIRST CLOWN: You lie out on 't, sir, and therefore 't is not yours: for my part, I do not lie in 't, yet it is mine.

HAMLET: Thou dost lie in 't, to be in 't and say it is thine: 'tis for the dead, not for the quick; therefore thou liest.

---

73. chapless: Having no lower jaw. **74. mazzard:** Head. **76. loggats:** A game in which six sticks are thrown to lie as near as possible to a stake fixed in the ground, or block of wood on a floor. **78. For and:** And moreover. **82. quiddities:** Subtleties, quibbles; **quillities:** Verbal niceties, subtle distinctions; **tenures:** The holding of a piece of property or office or the conditions or period of such holding. **83. sconce:** Head. **85.–86. statutes, recognizances:** Legal terms connected with the transfer of land; **vouchers:** Persons called on to warrant a tenant's title; **recoveries:** Process for transfer of entailed estate. **87. fine:** The four uses of this word are as follows: (1) end, (2) legal process, (3) elegant, (4) small. **90. indentures:** Conveyances or contracts. **91. inheritor:** Possessor, owner. **94. calf-skins:** Parchments. **95. assurance in that:** Safety in legal parchments.

FIRST CLOWN: 'Tis a quick lie, sir; 'twill away again, from me to you. 105

HAMLET: What man dost thou dig it for?

FIRST CLOWN: For no man, sir.

HAMLET: What woman, then?

FIRST CLOWN: For none, neither.

HAMLET: Who is to be buried in 't? 110

FIRST CLOWN: One that was a woman, sir; but, rest her soul, she's dead.

HAMLET: How absolute° the knave is! we must speak by the card,° or equivo-
cation° will undo us. By the Lord, Horatio, these three years I have taken
note of it; the age is grown so picked° that the toe of the peasant comes
so near the heel of the courtier, he galls° his kibe.° How long hast thou 115
been a grave-maker?

FIRST CLOWN: Of all the day i' the year, I came to 't that day that our last king
Hamlet overcame Fortinbras.

HAMLET: How long is that since?

FIRST CLOWN: Cannot you tell that? every fool can tell that: it was the very day 120
that young Hamlet was born; he that is mad, and sent into England.

HAMLET: Ay, marry, why was he sent into England?

FIRST CLOWN: Why, because 'a was mad: 'a shall recover his wits there; or, if 'a
do not, 'tis no great matter there.

HAMLET: Why? 125

FIRST CLOWN: 'Twill not be seen in him there; there the men are as mad as he.

HAMLET: How came he mad?

FIRST CLOWN: Very strangely, they say.

HAMLET: How strangely?

FIRST CLOWN: Faith, e'en with losing his wits. 130

HAMLET: Upon what ground?

FIRST CLOWN: Why, here in Denmark: I have been sexton here, man and boy,
thirty years.°

HAMLET: How long will a man lie i' the earth ere he rot?

FIRST CLOWN: Faith, if 'a be not rotten before 'a die — as we have many pocky° 135
corses now-a-days, that will scarce hold the laying in — 'a will last you
some eight year or nine year: a tanner will last you nine year.

HAMLET: Why he more than another?

FIRST CLOWN: Why, sir, his hide is so tanned with his trade, that 'a will keep out
water a great while; and your water is a sore decayer of your whoreson 140
dead body. Here's a skull now hath lain you i' th' earth three and twenty
years.

HAMLET: Whose was it?

FIRST CLOWN: A whoreson mad fellow's it was: whose do you think it was?

HAMLET: Nay, I know not. 145

112–113. **absolute:** Positive, decided; **by the card:** With precision, i.e., by the mariner's card
on which the points of the compass were marked; **equivocation:** Ambiguity in the use of
terms. **114. picked:** Refined, fastidious. **115. galls:** Chafes; **kibe:** Chilblain. **133. thirty
years:** This statement with that in lines 120–121 shows Hamlet's age to be thirty years.
135. pocky: Rotten, diseased.

FIRST CLOWN: A pestilence on him for a mad rogue! 'a poured a flagon of Rhen-
    ish on my head once. This same skull, sir, was Yorick's skull, the king's
    jester.

HAMLET: This?

FIRST CLOWN: E'en that.   150

HAMLET: Let me see. [*Takes the skull.*] Alas, poor Yorick! I knew him, Horatio: a
    fellow of infinite jest, of most excellent fancy: he hath borne me on his
    back a thousand times; and now, how abhorred in my imagination it is!
    my gorge rises at it. Here hung those lips that I have kissed I know not
    how oft. Where be your gibes now? your gambols? your songs? your 155
    flashes of merriment, that were wont to set the table on a roar? Not one
    now, to mock your own grinning? quite chap-fallen? Now get you to my
    lady's chamber, and tell her, let her paint an inch thick, to this favour she
    must come; make her laugh at that. Prithee, Horatio, tell me one thing.

HORATIO: What's that, my lord?   160

HAMLET: Dost thou think Alexander looked o' this fashion i' the earth?

HORATIO: E'en so.

HAMLET: And smelt so? pah!   [*Puts down the skull.*]

HORATIO: E'en so, my lord.

HAMLET: To what base uses we may return, Horatio! Why may not imagination 165
    trace the noble dust of Alexander, till 'a find it stopping a bunghole?

HORATIO: 'Twere to consider too curiously,° to consider so.

HAMLET: No, faith, not a jot; but to follow him thither with modesty enough,
    and likelihood to lead it: as thus: Alexander died, Alexander was buried,
    Alexander returneth into dust; the dust is earth; of earth we make loam;° 170
    and why of that loam, whereto he was converted, might they not stop a
    beer-barrel?
        Imperious° Cæsar, dead and turn'd to clay,
        Might stop a hole to keep the wind away:
        O, that that earth, which kept the world in awe,   175
        Should patch a wall t'expel the winter's flaw!°
    But soft! but soft awhile! here comes the king,

Enter King, Queen, Laertes, and the Corse of [*Ophelia, in procession, with Priest,
Lords, etc.*].

    The queen, the courtiers: who is this they follow?
    And with such maimed rites? This doth betoken
    The corse they follow did with desp'rate hand   180
    Fordo° it° own life: 'twas of some estate.
    Couch° we awhile, and mark.   [*Retiring with Horatio.*]

LAERTES: What ceremony else?

HAMLET: That is Laertes,
    A very noble youth: mark.

LAERTES: What ceremony else?   185

---

167. **curiously:** Minutely.   170. **loam:** Clay paste for brickmaking.   173. **Imperious:** Imperial.   176. **flaw:** Gust of wind.   181. **Fordo:** Destroy; **it:** Its.   182. **Couch:** Hide, lurk.

FIRST PRIEST: Her obsequies have been as far enlarg'd°
    As we have warranty: her death was doubtful;
    And, but that great command o'ersways the order,
    She should in ground unsanctified have lodg'd
    Till the last trumpet; for charitable prayers,   190
    Shards,° flints and pebbles should be thrown on her:
    Yet here she is allow'd her virgin crants,°
    Her maiden strewments° and the bringing home
    Of bell and burial.°
LAERTES: Must there no more be done?
FIRST PRIEST: No more be done: 195
    We should profane the service of the dead
    To sing a requiem and such rest to her
    As to peace-parted° souls.
LAERTES: Lay her i' th' earth:
    And from her fair and unpolluted flesh
    May violets spring! I tell thee, churlish priest,   200
    A minist'ring angel shall my sister be,
    When thou liest howling.°
HAMLET: What, the fair Ophelia!
QUEEN: Sweets to the sweet: farewell!   *[Scattering flowers.]*
    I hop'd thou shouldst have been my Hamlet's wife;
    I thought thy bride-bed to have deck'd, sweet maid,   205
    And not have strew'd thy grave.
LAERTES: O, treble woe
    Fall ten times treble on that cursed head,
    Whose wicked deed thy most ingenious sense°
    Depriv'd thee of! Hold off the earth awhile,
    Till I have caught her once more in mine arms: *[Leaps into the grave.]* 210
    Now pile your dust upon the quick and dead,
    Till of this flat a mountain you have made,
    T' o'ertop old Pelion,° or the skyish head
    Of blue Olympus.
HAMLET: *[Advancing]* What is he whose grief
    Bears such an emphasis? whose phrase of sorrow   215
    Conjures the wand'ring stars,° and makes them stand
    Like wonder-wounded hearers? This is I,
    Hamlet the Dane.   *[Leaps into the grave.]*
LAERTES: The devil take thy soul!   *[Grappling with him.]*

---

186. enlarg'd: Extended, referring to the fact that suicides are not given full burial
rites. **191. Shards:** Broken bits of pottery. **192. crants:** Garlands customarily hung upon
the biers of unmarried women. **193. strewments:** Traditional strewing of flowers.
193.–194. bringing ... burial: The laying to rest of the body, to the sound of the
bell. **198. peace-parted:** Allusion to the text "Lord, now lettest thou thy servant depart in
peace." **202. howling:** I.e., in hell. **208. ingenious sense:** Mind endowed with finest
qualities. **213. Pelion:** Olympus, Pelion, and Ossa are mountains in the north of Thessaly.
216. wand'ring stars: Planets.

HAMLET: Thou pray'st not well.
    I prithee, take thy fingers from my throat;   220
    For, though I am not splenitive° and rash,
    Yet have I in me something dangerous,
    Which let thy wisdom fear: hold off thy hand.
KING: Pluck them asunder.
QUEEN: Hamlet, Hamlet!
ALL: Gentlemen, —
HORATIO: Good my lord, be quiet.   225
        [*The Attendants part them, and they come out of the grave.*]
HAMLET: Why, I will fight with him upon this theme
    Until my eyelids will no longer wag.°
QUEEN: O my son, what theme?
HAMLET: I lov'd Ophelia: forty thousand brothers
    Could not, with all their quantity° of love,   230
    Make up my sum. What wilt thou do for her?
KING: O, he is mad, Laertes.
QUEEN: For love of God, forbear° him.
HAMLET: 'Swounds,° show me what thou 'lt do:
    Woo 't° weep? woo 't fight? woo 't fast? woo 't tear thyself?   235
    Woo 't drink up eisel?° eat a crocodile?
    I'll do 't. Dost thou come here to whine?
    To outface me with leaping in her grave?
    Be buried quick with her, and so will I:
    And, if thou prate of mountains, let them throw   240
    Millions of acres on us, till our ground,
    Singeing his pate against the burning zone,°
    Make Ossa like a wart! Nay, an thou 'lt mouth,
    I'll rant as well as thou.
QUEEN: This is mere madness:
    And thus awhile the fit will work on him;   245
    Anon, as patient as the female dove.
    When that her golden couplets° are disclos'd,
    His silence will sit drooping.
HAMLET: Hear you, sir;
    What is the reason that you use me thus?
    I lov'd you ever: but it is no matter;   250
    Let Hercules himself do what he may,
    The cat will mew and dog will have his day.
KING: I pray thee, good Horatio, wait upon him.   *Exit Hamlet and Horatio.*

---

221. **splenitive:** Quick-tempered.   227. **wag:** Move (not used ludicrously).   230. **quantity:** Some suggest that the word is used in a deprecatory sense (little bits, fragments).   233. **forbear:** Leave alone.   234. **'Swounds:** Oath, "God's wounds."   235. **Woo 't:** Wilt thou.   236. **eisel:** Vinegar. Some editors have taken this to be the name of a river, such as the Yssel, the Weissel, and the Nile.   242. **burning zone:** Sun's orbit.   247. **golden couplets:** The pigeon lays two eggs; the young when hatched are covered with golden down.

[*To Laertes.*] Strengthen your patience in° our last night's speech;
We'll put the matter to the present push.°   255
Good Gertrude, set some watch over your son.
This grave shall have a living° monument:
An hour of quiet shortly shall we see;
Till then, in patience our proceeding be.   *Exeunt.*

[SCENE II: *A hall in the castle.*]

Enter Hamlet and Horatio.

HAMLET: So much for this, sir: now shall you see the other;
    You do remember all the circumstance?

HORATIO: Remember it, my lord!

HAMLET: Sir, in my heart there was a kind of fighting,
    That would not let me sleep: methought I lay
    Worse than the mutines° in the bilboes.° Rashly°   5
    And prais'd be rashness for it, let us know,
    Our indiscretion sometime serves us well,
    When our deep plots do pall:° and that should learn us
    There's a divinity that shapes our ends,
    Rough-hew° them how we will, —   10

HORATIO: That is most certain.

HAMLET: Up from my cabin,
    My sea-gown° scarf'd about me, in the dark
    Grop'd I to find out them; had my desire,
    Finger'd° their packet, and in fine° withdrew
    To mine own room again; making so bold,   15
    My fears forgetting manners, to unseal
    Their grand commission; where I found, Horatio, —
    O royal knavery! — an exact command,
    Larded° with many several sorts of reasons
    Importing Denmark's health and England's too,   20
    With, ho! such bugs° and goblins in my life,°
    That, on the supervise,° no leisure bated,°
    No, not to stay the grinding of the axe,
    My head should be struck off.

HORATIO: Is 't possible?   25

HAMLET: Here's the commission: read it at more leisure.
    But wilt thou hear me how I did proceed?

HORATIO: I beseech you.

---

254. in: By recalling. **255. present push:** Immediate test. **257. living:** Lasting; also refers
(for Laertes' benefit) to the plot against Hamlet. SCENE II. **6. mutines:** Mutineers; **bilboes:**
Shackles; **Rashly:** Goes with line 12. **9. pall:** Fail. **11. Rough-hew:** Shape roughly; it may
mean "bungle." **13. sea-gown:** "A sea-gown, or a coarse, high-collered, and short-sleeved
gowne, reaching down to the mid-leg, and used most by seamen and saylors" (Cotgrave,
quoted by Singer). **15. Finger'd:** Pilfered, filched; **in fine:** Finally. **20. Larded:** Enriched.
22. bugs: Bugbears; **such . . . life:** Such imaginary dangers if I were allowed to live. **23. supervise:** Perusal; **leisure bated:** Delay allowed.

HAMLET: Being thus be-netted round with villanies, —
    Ere I could make a prologue to my brains, 30
    They had begun the play° — I sat me down,
    Devis'd a new commission, wrote it fair:
    I once did hold it, as our statists° do,
    A baseness to write fair° and labour'd much
    How to forget that learning, but, sir, now 35
    It did me yeoman's° service: wilt thou know
    Th' effect of what I wrote?
HORATIO: Ay, good my lord.
HAMLET: An earnest conjuration from the king,
    As England was his faithful tributary,
    As love between them like the palm might flourish, 40
    As peace should still her wheaten garland° wear
    And stand a comma° 'tween their amities,
    And many such-like 'As'es° of great charge,°
    That, on the view and knowing of these contents,
    Without debatement further, more or less, 45
    He should the bearers put to sudden death,
    Not shriving-time° allow'd.
HORATIO: How was this seal'd?
HAMLET: Why, even in that was heaven ordinant.°
    I had my father's signet in my purse,
    Which was the model of that Danish seal; 50
    Folded the writ up in the form of th' other,
    Subscrib'd it, gave 't th' impression, plac'd it safely,
    The changeling never known. Now, the next day
    Was our sea-fight; and what to this was sequent°
    Thou know'st already. 55
HORATIO: So Guildenstern and Rosencrantz go to 't.
HAMLET: Why, man, they did make love to this employment;
    They are not near my conscience; their defeat
    Does by their own insinuation° grow:
    'Tis dangerous when the baser nature comes 60
    Between the pass° and fell incensed° points
    Of mighty opposites.
HORATIO: Why, what a king is this!
HAMLET: Does it not, think thee, stand° me now upon —
    He that hath kill'd my king and whor'd my mother,

30.–31. prologue . . . play: I.e., before I could begin to think, my mind had made its decision.
33. statists: Statesmen. **34. fair:** In a clear hand. **36. yeoman's:** I.e., faithful. **41. wheaten garland:** Symbol of peace. **42. comma:** Smallest break or separation. Here *amity* begins and *amity* end the period, and *peace* stands between like a dependent clause. The comma indicates continuity, link. **43. 'As'es:** The "whereases" of a formal document, with play on the word *ass;* **charge:** Import, and burden. **47. shriving-time:** Time for absolution. **48. ordinant:** Directing. **54. sequent:** Subsequent. **59. insinuation:** Interference. **61. pass:** Thrust; **fell incensed:** Fiercely angered. **63. stand:** Become incumbent.

Popp'd in between th' election° and my hopes,　　　　　　　　65
Thrown out his angle° for my proper life,
And with such coz'nage° — is 't not perfect conscience,
To quit° him with this arm? and is 't not to be damn'd,
To let this canker° of our nature come
In further evil?　　　　　　　　　　　　　　　　　　　70

HORATIO: It must be shortly known to him from England
What is the issue of the business there.

HAMLET: It will be short: the interim is mine;
And a man's life's no more than to say "One."
But I am very sorry, good Horatio,　　　　　　　　　　75
That to Laertes I forgot myself;
For, by the image of my cause, I see
The portraiture of his: I'll court his favours:
But, sure, the bravery° of his grief did put me
Into a tow'ring passion.

HORATIO:　　　　　　　　　Peace! who comes here?　　80

Enter a Courtier [Osric].

OSRIC: Your lordship is right welcome back to Denmark.

HAMLET: I humbly thank you, sir. [*To Horatio.*] Dost know this water-fly?°

HORATIO: No, my good lord.

HAMLET: Thy state is the more gracious; for 'tis a vice to know him. He hath
much land, and fertile: let a beast be lord of beasts,° and his crib shall　85
stand at the king's mess:° 'tis a chough;° but, as I say, spacious in the
possession of dirt.

OSRIC: Sweet lord, if your lordship were at leisure, I should impart a thing to
you from his majesty.

HAMLET: I will receive it, sir, with all diligence of spirit. Put your bonnet to his　90
right use; 'tis for the head.

OSRIC: I thank you lordship, it is very hot.

HAMLET: No, believe me, 'tis very cold; the wind is northerly.

OSRIC: It is indifferent° cold, my lord, indeed.

HAMLET: But yet methinks it is very sultry and hot for my complexion.　　95

OSRIC: Exceedingly, my lord; it is very sultry, — as 'twere, — I cannot tell how.
But, my lord, his majesty bade me signify to you that 'a has laid a great
wager on your head: sir, this is the matter, —

HAMLET: I beseech you, remember° — [*Hamlet moves him to put on his hat.*]

---

65. **election**: The Danish throne was filled by election.　66. **angle**: Fishing line.　67.
coz'nage: Trickery.　68. **quit**: Repay.　69. **canker**: Ulcer, or possibly the worm which
destroys buds and leaves.　79. **bravery**: Bravado.　82. **water-fly**: Vain or busily idle person.　85. **lord of beasts**: Cf. Genesis 1:26, 28.　85.–86. **his crib . . . mess**: He shall eat at the
king's table, i.e., be one of the group of persons (usually four) constituting a *mess* at a banquet.　86. **chough**: Probably, chattering jackdaw; also explained as *chuff*, provincial boor or
churl.　94. **indifferent**: Somewhat.　99. **remember**: I.e., remember thy courtesy; conventional phrase for "Be covered."

osric: Nay, good my lord; for mine ease,° in good faith. Sir, here is newly come 100
    to court Laertes; believe me, an absolute gentleman, full of most excel-
    lent differences, of very soft° society and great showing:° indeed, to
    speak feelingly° of him, he is the card° or calendar of gentry,° for you
    shall find in him the continent of what part a gentleman would see.

hamlet: Sir, his definement° suffers no perdition° in you; though, I know, to 105
    divide him inventorially° would dozy° the arithmetic of memory, and
    yet but yaw° neither, in respect of his quick sail. But, in the verity of ex-
    tolment, I take him to be a soul of great article;° and his infusion° of
    such dearth and rareness,° as, to make true diction of him, his sem-
    blable° is his mirror; and who else would trace° him, his umbrage,° 110
    nothing more.

osric: Your lordship speaks most infallibly of him.

hamlet: The concernancy,° sir? why do we wrap the gentleman in our more
    rawer breath?°

osric: Sir? 115

horatio [*aside to Hamlet*]: Is 't not possible to understand in another tongue?°
    You will do 't, sir, really.

hamlet: What imports the nomination° of this gentleman?

osric: Of Laertes?

horatio [*aside to Hamlet*]: His purse is empty already; all 's golden words are 120
    spent.

hamlet: Of him, sir.

osric: I know you are not ignorant —

hamlet: I would you did, sir; yet, in faith, if you did, it would not much ap-
    prove° me. Well, sir? 125

osric: You are not ignorant of what excellence Laertes is —

hamlet: I dare not confess that, lest I should compare with him in excellence;
    but, to know a man well, were to know himself.°

osric: I mean, sir, for his weapon; but in the imputation° laid on him by them,
    in his meed° he's unfellowed. 130

hamlet: What's his weapon?

osric: Rapier and dagger.

hamlet: That's two of his weapons: but, well.

osric: The king, sir, hath wagered with him six Barbary horses: against the
    which he has impawned,° as I take it, six French rapiers and poniards, 135

---

100. **mine ease:** Conventional reply declining the invitation of "Remember thy courtesy."
102. **soft:** Gentle; **showing:** Distinguished appearance. 103. **feelingly:** With just perception; **card:** Chart, map; **gentry:** Good breeding. 105. **definement:** Definition; **perdition:**
Loss, diminution. 106. **divide him inventorially:** I.e., enumerate his graces; **dozy:** Dizzy.
107. **yaw:** To move unsteadily (of a ship). 108. **article:** Moment or importance; **infusion:**
Infused temperament, character imparted by nature. 109. **dearth and rareness:** Rarity.
109–110. **semblable:** True likeness. 110. **trace:** Follow; **umbrage:** Shadow. 113. **concernancy:** Import. 114. **breath:** Speech. 116. **Is 't . . . tongue?:** I.e., can one converse with Osric only in this outlandish jargon? 118. **nomination:** Naming. 124–125. **approve:**
Command. 128. **but . . . himself:** But to know a man as excellent were to know Laertes.
129. **imputation:** Reputation. 130. **meed:** Merit. 135. **he has impawned:** He has wagered.

with their assigns, as girdle, hangers,° and so: three of the carriages, in faith, are very dear to fancy,° very responsive° to the hilts, most delicate° carriages, and of very liberal conceit.°

HAMLET: What call you the carriages?

HORATIO [*aside to Hamlet*]: I knew you must be edified by the margent° ere you had done. 140

OSRIC: The carriages, sir, are the hangers.

HAMLET: The phrase would be more german° to the matter, if we could carry cannon by our sides: I would it might be hangers till then. But, on: six Barbary horses against six French swords, their assigns, and three 145 liberal-conceited carriages; that's the French bet against the Danish. Why is this "impawned," as you call it?

OSRIC: The king, sir, hath laid, that in a dozen passes between yourself and him, he shall not exceed you three hits: he hath laid on twelve for nine; and it would come to immediate trial, if your lordship would vouchsafe 150 the answer.

HAMLET: How if I answer "no"?

OSRIC: I mean, my lord, the opposition of your person in trial.

HAMLET: Sir, I will walk here in the hall: if it please his majesty, it is the breathing time° of day with me; let the foils be brought, the gentleman willing, 155 and the king hold his purpose, I will win for him as I can; if not, I will gain nothing but my shame and the odd hits.

OSRIC: Shall I re-deliver you e'en so?

HAMLET: To this effect, sir; after what flourish your nature will.

OSRIC: I commend my duty to your lordship. 160

HAMLET: Yours, yours. [*Exit Osric.*] He does well to commend it himself; there are no tongues else for 's turn.

HORATIO: This lapwing° runs away with the shell on his head.

HAMLET: 'A did comply, sir, with his dug,° before 'a sucked it. Thus has he — and many more of the same breed that I know the drossy° age dotes on 165 — only got the tune° of the time and out of an habit of encounter;° a kind of yesty° collection, which carries them through and through the most fann'd and winnowed° opinions; and do but blow them to their trial, the bubbles are out.°

Enter a Lord.

---

136. hangers: Straps on the sword belt from which the sword hung.   **137. dear to fancy:** Fancifully made; **responsive:** Probably, well balanced, corresponding closely; **delicate:** I.e., in workmanship.   **138. liberal conceit:** Elaborate design.   **140. margent:** Margin of a book, place for explanatory notes.   **143. german:** Germane, appropriate.   **155. breathing time:** Exercise period.   **163. lapwing:** Peewit; noted for its wiliness in drawing a visitor away from its nest and its supposed habit of running about when newly hatched with its head in the shell; possibly an allusion to Osric's hat.   **164. did comply . . . dug:** Paid compliments to his mother's breast.   **165. drossy:** Frivolous.   **166. tune:** Temper, mood; **habit of encounter:** Demeanor of social intercourse; **yesty:** Frothy.   **168. fann'd and winnowed:** Select and refined.   **168.–169. blow . . . out:** I.e., put them to the test, and their ignorance is exposed.

LORD: My lord, his majesty commended him to you by young Osric, who brings 170
    back to him, that you attend him in the hall: he sends to know if your
    pleasure hold to play with Laertes, or that you will take longer time.

HAMLET: I am constant to my purposes; they follow the king's pleasure: if his
    fitness speaks, mine is ready; now or whensoever, provided I be so able
    as now. 175

LORD: The king and queen and all are coming down.

HAMLET: In happy time.°

LORD: The queen desires you to use some gentle entertainment to Laertes be-
    fore you fall to play.

HAMLET: She well instructs me. [*Exit Lord.*] 180

HORATIO: You will lose this wager, my lord.

HAMLET: I do not think so; since he went into France, I have been in continual
    practice; I shall win at the odds. But thou wouldst not think how ill all 's
    here about my heart: but it is no matter.

HORATIO: Nay, good my lord, — 185

HAMLET: It is but foolery; but it is such a kind of gain-giving,° as would per-
    haps trouble a woman.

HORATIO: If your mind dislike any thing, obey it: I will forestall their repair
    hither, and say you are not fit.

HAMLET: Not a whit, we defy augury: there's a special providence in the fall of 190
    a sparrow. If it be now, 'tis not to come; if it be not to come, it will be
    now; if it be not now, yet it will come: the readiness is all:° since no man
    of aught he leaves knows, what is 't to leave betimes? Let be.

A table prepared. [Enter] Trumpets, Drums, and Officers with cushions; King, Queen,
[Osric,] and all the State; foils, daggers, [and wine borne in;] and Laertes.

KING: Come, Hamlet, come, and take this hand from me.

                    [The King puts Laertes' hand into Hamlet's.]

HAMLET: Give me your pardon, sir: I have done you wrong; 195
    But pardon 't as you are a gentleman.
    This presence° knows,
    And you must needs have heard, how I am punish'd
    With a sore distraction. What I have done,
    That might your nature, honour and exception° 200
    Roughly awake, I here proclaim was madness.
    Was 't Hamlet wrong'd Laertes? Never Hamlet:
    If Hamlet from himself be ta'en away,
    And when he's not himself does wrong Laertes,
    Then Hamlet does it not, Hamlet denies it. 205
    Who does it, then? His madness: if 't be so,
    Hamlet is of the faction that is wrong'd;
    His madness is poor Hamlet's enemy.

---

177. in happy time: A phrase of courtesy. **186. gain-giving:** Misgiving. **192. all:** All that
matters. **197. presence:** Royal assembly. **200. exception:** Disapproval.

> Sir, in this audience,
> Let my disclaiming from a purpos'd evil   210
> Free me so far in your most generous thoughts,
> That I have shot mine arrow o'er the house,
> And hurt my brother.

LAERTES: I am satisfied in nature,°
> Whose motive, in this case, should stir me most
> To my revenge: but in my terms of honour   215
> I stand aloof; and will no reconcilement,
> Till by some elder masters, of known honour,
> I have a voice° and precedent of peace,
> To keep my name ungor'd. But till that time,
> I do receive your offer'd love like love,   220
> And will not wrong it.

HAMLET: I embrace it freely;
> And will this brother's wager frankly play.
> Give us the foils. Come on.

LAERTES: Come, one for me.

HAMLET: I'll be your foil,° Laertes: in mine ignorance
> Your skill shall, like a star i' th' darkest night,   225
> Stick fiery off° indeed.

LAERTES: You mock me, sir.

HAMLET: No, by this hand.

KING: Give them the foils, young Osric. Cousin Hamlet,
> You know the wager?

HAMLET: Very well, my lord;
> Your grace has laid the odds o' th' weaker side.   230

KING: I do not fear it; I have seen you both:
> But since he is better'd, we have therefore odds.

LAERTES: This is too heavy, let me see another.

HAMLET: This likes me well. These foils have all a length?

> *[They prepare to play.]*

OSRIC: Ay, my good lord.   235

KING: Set me the stoups of wine upon that table.
> If Hamlet give the first or second hit,
> Or quit in answer of the third exchange,
> Let all the battlements their ordnance fire;
> The king shall drink to Hamlet's better breath;   240
> And in the cup an union° shall he throw,
> Richer than that which four successive kings
> In Denmark's crown have worn. Give me the cups;
> And let the kettle° to the trumpet speak,

---

213. nature: I.e., he is personally satisfied, but his honor must be satisfied by the rules of the code of honor. **218. voice:** Authoritative pronouncement. **224. foil:** Quibble on the two senses: "background which sets something off," and "blunted rapier for fencing." **226. Stick fiery off:** Stand out brilliantly. **241. union:** Pearl. **244. kettle:** Kettledrum.

The trumpet to the cannoneer without, 245
The cannons to the heavens, the heavens to earth,
"Now the king drinks to Hamlet." Come begin: *Trumpets the while.*
And you, the judges, bear a wary eye.

HAMLET: Come on, sir.

LAERTES: Come, my lord.   [*They play.*]

HAMLET: One.

LAERTES: No.

HAMLET: Judgement.

OSRIC: A hit, a very palpable hit.

> *Drum, trumpets, and shot. Flourish. A piece goes off.*

LAERTES: Well; again. 250

KING: Stay; give me drink. Hamlet, this pearl° is thine;
Here's to thy health. Give him the cup.

HAMLET: I'll play this bout first; set it by awhile.
Come. [*They play.*] Another hit; what say you?

LAERTES: A touch, a touch, I do confess 't.

KING: Our son shall win. 255

QUEEN: He's fat,° and scant of breath.
Here, Hamlet, take my napkin, rub thy brows:
The queen carouses° to thy fortune, Hamlet.

HAMLET: Good madam!

KING: Gertrude, do not drink.

QUEEN: I will, my lord; I pray you, pardon me. [*Drinks.*] 260

KING [*aside*]: It is the poison'd cup: it is too late.

HAMLET: I dare not drink yet, madam; by and by.

QUEEN: Come, let me wipe thy face.

LAERTES: My lord, I'll hit him now.

KING: I do not think 't.

LAERTES [*aside*]: And yet 'tis almost 'gainst my conscience. 265

HAMLET: Come, for the third, Laertes: you but dally;
I pray you, pass with your best violence;
I am afeard you make a wanton° of me.

LAERTES: Say you so? come on.   [*They play.*]

OSRIC: Nothing, neither way. 270

LAERTES: Have at you now!

> [*Laertes wounds Hamlet; then, in scuffling, they change rapiers*°
>   *and Hamlet wounds Laertes.*]

KING: Part them; they are incens'd.

HAMLET: Nay, come again.   [*The Queen falls.*]

---

251. pearl: I.e., the poison.   **256. fat:** Not physically fit, out of training. Some earlier editors speculated that the term applied to the corpulence of Richard Burbage, who originally played the part, but the allusion now appears unlikely. *Fat* may also suggest "sweaty."   **258. carouses:** Drinks a toast.   **268. wanton:** Spoiled child.   **271. s.d. in scuffling, they change rapiers:** According to a widespread stage tradition, Hamlet receives a scratch, realizes that Laertes' sword is unbated, and accordingly forces an exchange.

OSRIC: Look to the queen there, ho!

HORATIO: They bleed on both sides. How is it, my lord?

OSRIC: How is 't, Laertes?

LAERTES: Why, as a woodcock° to mine own springe,° Osric;   275
    I am justly kill'd with mine own treachery.

HAMLET: How does the queen?

KING: She swounds° to see them bleed.

QUEEN: No, no, the drink, the drink, — O my dear Hamlet, —
    The drink, the drink! I am poison'd.   *[Dies.]*

HAMLET: O villany! Ho! let the door be lock'd: 280
    Treachery! Seek it out.   *[Laertes falls.]*

LAERTES: It is here, Hamlet: Hamlet, thou art slain;
    No med'cine in the world can do thee good;
    In thee there is not half an hour of life;
    The treacherous instrument is in thy hand,   285
    Unbated° and envenom'd: the foul practice
    Hath turn'd itself on me; lo, here I lie,
    Never to rise again: thy mother's poison'd:
    I can no more: the king, the king's to blame.

HAMLET: The point envenom'd too!   290
    Then, venom, to thy work.   *[Stabs the King.]*

ALL: Treason! treason!

KING: O, yet defend me, friends; I am but hurt.

HAMLET: Here, thou incestuous, murd'rous, damned Dane,
    Drink off this potion. Is thy union here?   295
    Follow my mother.   *[King dies.]*

LAERTES: He is justly serv'd;
    It is a poison temper'd° by himself.
    Exchange forgiveness with me, noble Hamlet:
    Mine and my father's death come not upon thee,
    Nor thine on me!   *[Dies.]* 300

HAMLET: Heaven make thee free of it! I follow thee.
    I am dead, Horatio. Wretched queen, adieu!
    You that look pale and tremble at this chance,
    That are but mutes° or audience to this act,
    Had I but time — as this fell sergeant,° Death,   305
    Is strict in his arrest — O, I could tell you —
    But let it be. Horatio, I am dead;
    Thou livest; report me and my cause aright
    To the unsatisfied.

HORATIO: Never believe it:
    I am more an antique Roman° than a Dane: 310
    Here 's yet some liquor left.

---

275. **woodcock:** As type of stupidity or as decoy; **springe:** Trap, snare. 277. **swounds:** Swoons. 286. **Unbated:** Not blunted with a button. 297. **temper'd:** Mixed. 304. **mutes:** Performers in a play who speak no words. 305. **sergeant:** Sheriff's officer. 310. **Roman:** It was the Roman custom to follow masters in death.

HAMLET: As th' art a man,
    Give me the cup: let go, by heaven, I'll ha 't.
    O God! Horatio, what a wounded name,
    Things standing thus unknown, shall live behind me!
    If thou didst ever hold me in thy heart,   315
    Absent thee from felicity awhile,
    And in this harsh world draw thy breath in pain,
    To tell my story.   *A march afar off.*
        What warlike noise is this?
OSRIC: Young Fortinbras, with conquest come from Poland,
    To the ambassadors of England gives   320
    This warlike volley.
HAMLET: O, I die, Horatio;
    The potent poison quite o'er-crows° my spirit:
    I cannot live to hear the news from England;
    But I do prophesy th' election lights
    On Fortinbras: he has my dying voice;   325
    So tell him, with th' occurrents,° more and less,
    Which have solicited.° The rest is silence.   [*Dies.*]
HORATIO: Now cracks a noble heart. Good night, sweet prince;
    And flights of angels sing thee to thy rest!
    Why does the drum come hither?   [*March within.*] 330

Enter Fortinbras, with the [English] Ambassadors [and others].

FORTINBRAS: Where is this sight?
HORATIO: What is it you would see?
    If aught of woe or wonder, cease your search.
FORTINBRAS: This quarry° cries on havoc.° O proud Death,
    What feast is toward in thine eternal cell,
    That thou so many princes at a shot   335
    So bloodily hast struck?
FIRST AMBASSADOR: The sight is dismal;
    And our affairs from England come too late:
    The ears are senseless that should give us hearing,
    To tell him his commandment is fulfill'd,
    That Rosencrantz and Guildenstern are dead: 340
    Where should we have our thanks?
HORATIO: Not from his mouth,°
    Had it th' ability of life to thank you:
    He never gave commandment for their death.
    But since, so jump° upon this bloody question,°
    You from the Polack wars, and you from England,   345
    Are here arriv'd, give order that these bodies

---

322. o'er-crows: Triumphs over. **326. occurrents:** Events, incidents. **327. solicited:** Moved, urged. **333. quarry:** Heap of dead; **cries on havoc:** Proclaims a general slaughter. **341. his mouth:** I.e., the king's. **344. jump:** Precisely; **question:** Dispute.

High on a stage° be placed to the view;
And let me speak to th' yet unknowing world
How these things came about: so shall you hear
Of carnal, bloody, and unnatural acts,   350
Of accidental judgements, casual slaughters,
Of deaths put on by cunning and forc'd cause,
And, in this upshot, purposes mistook
Fall'n on th' inventors' heads: all this can I
Truly deliver.

FORTINBRAS: Let us haste to hear it,   355
And call the noblest to the audience.
For me, with sorrow I embrace my fortune:
I have some rights of memory° in this kingdom,
Which now to claim my vantage doth invite me.

HORATIO: Of that I shall have also cause to speak,   360
And from his mouth whose voice will draw on more:°
But let this same be presently perform'd,
Even while men's minds are wild; lest more mischance,
On° plots and errors, happen.

FORTINBRAS: Let four captains
Bear Hamlet, like a soldier, to the stage;   365
For he was likely, had he been put on,
To have prov'd most royal: and, for his passage,°
The soldiers' music and the rites of war
Speak loudly for him.
Take up the bodies: such a sight as this   370
Becomes the field,° but here shows much amiss.
Go, bid the soldiers shoot.

Exeunt [marching, bearing off the dead bodies; after which a peal of ordnance is heard].

⁂⁂

HENRIK IBSEN *(1828–1906), dramatist and poet, was born the second child of a merchant in a small town in southeast Norway. After the ruin of his father's business, Ibsen was raised in extreme poverty. His familiarity with economic hardship and his long struggle to make ends meet were later reflected in his realistic dramas. As a teenager Ibsen intended to study medicine, and he helped support his family by working for six years in an apothecary shop in the seaport town of Grimstud. Self-educated, he wrote his first play, Catilina, in verse when he was twenty-one. A year later he left Grimstad to become a student in Oslo, and then in 1851 he became active in the newly formed National Theatre at Bergen, the first theater in Norway to use Norwegian actors (Danish actors had previously dominated the stage). There Ibsen gained practical*

---

347. **stage:** Platform.   358. **of memory:** Traditional, remembered.   361. **voice . . . more:** Vote will influence still others.   364. **On:** On account of, or possibly, on top of, in addition to.   367. **passage:** Death.   371. **field:** I.e., of battle.

experience designing costumes, keeping the accounts, directing, and writing. After the theater went bankrupt, he left Norway with his wife and young son in 1864 and settled in Rome. Living abroad, he wrote the historical plays Brand *(1866) and* Peer Gynt *(1867) as closet dramas, intended to be read, not acted. These plays' brilliant vision of human vocation and self-realization made Ibsen famous throughout Scandinavia when they were published, and Ibsen was awarded a government pension, although the two plays were not staged for many years.*

In 1875 Ibsen moved to Munich, where he began to experiment with a different kind of drama in The Pillars of Society *(1877), the first of his twelve realistic prose plays addressing social issues. Four years later, living in Rome and Amalfi, he wrote* A Doll House. *Its portrayal of a marriage in crisis aroused so much controversy that the play caused an immediate sensation when it was performed. His next play,* Ghosts *(1881), was also attacked for its subject matter (syphilis passed on from father to son within a respected, upper-class family), although it was staged the following year by a small experimental theater company in Chicago. In the 1880s Ibsen's plays — An* Enemy of the People *(1882) and* The Wild Duck *(1884) among them — were regarded as obscure and unconventional. The earliest major English-language production of any of his plays was in 1889 when* A Doll House *was performed in London. In 1891, after writing* Hedda Gabler *in Munich, Ibsen returned to live for the remainder of his life in Norway, where he wrote four last plays about spiritual conflicts in a new symbolic style.*

Ibsen based the plot of A Doll House *on a true story. In 1871 a young Norwegian woman named Laura Petersen sent him a sequel that she had written to his play* Brand. *Ibsen encouraged her to continue writing, calling her his "skylark." The following year she married a Danish schoolmaster who, suffering from tuberculosis, learned that he had to live in a warmer climate. The couple was poor, so Laura secretly arranged a loan to finance their trip to Italy. In 1878, after her creditor demanded repayment of the loan, she wrote a novel and sent it to Ibsen, asking him to recommend it to his publisher. Ibsen refused to endorse her book, and acting in panic, she forged a check to repay the debt. When the bank refused payment, Laura confessed to her husband what she had done. Instead of being sympathetic because she had been so concerned about his health, he accused her of being a criminal and an unfit mother for their children. Laura had a nervous breakdown, and her husband had her committed to a psychiatric hospital. After a month in the institution, she begged her husband to let her come back home for their children's sake, which he did, making it clear to her that it was against his higher moral principles. As Ibsen's biographer Michael Meyer understood, "The incident must have seemed to Ibsen to crystallize not merely woman's, but mankind's fight against conventional morality and prejudice."*

Three months after hearing that Laura Petersen had been institutionalized, Ibsen composed his "Notes for a Modern Tragedy," in which he stated the germ of the idea that he developed in A Doll House: *"There are two kinds of moral laws, two kinds of conscience, one for men and one, quite different, for women. They don't understand each other; but in practical life, woman is judged by masculine law, as though she weren't a woman but a man." Ibsen had been interested in what was then called the problem of women's rights for some time. His wife, Suzannah, championed the cause, and his friend the Norwegian novelist Camilla Collett had criticized what she considered his old-fashioned ideas about women's place in society.*

The English writer John Stuart Mill's The Subjection of Women *had been translated into Norwegian in 1869, the same year that Ibsen wrote his comedy* The League of Youth. *In this play one of the minor characters, a young wife, tells her husband, "You dressed me up like a doll; you played with me as one plays with a child." The Danish theater critic and champion of modernism Georg Brandes told Ibsen that a strong woman character like her might be a good subject for a play. In* The Pillars of Society, *which Ibsen completed just before* A Doll House, *he created two roles for women who rebel against the subordinate position dictated to them by their uncompromising patriarchal society. Yet he later insisted that in* A Doll House *he had not "worked for the Women's Rights movement. I am not even very sure what Women's Rights really are." What he really wanted to show in creating the character of Nora, he told Brandes, was a revolution of the human spirit.*

By 1879, when A Doll House *premiered at the Royal Theatre in Copenhagen, stage production had developed into the realistic theater familiar to us today. In his printed stage directions Ibsen had described the set in minute detail as a middle-class apartment, and the Danes followed his floor plan closely, adding flowering plants and a reproduction of Raphael's painting of the Madonna and child on the wall above the piano. The Royal Theatre even envisioned how to furnish Torvald's study offstage authentically with a paperweight and two candlesticks, although this view of his desk would be seen by very few people in the audience. Betty Hennings, the beautiful twenty-nine-year-old Danish actress playing Nora, was an accomplished dancer, and she was so attractive in the role that she became established as an international star. One reviewer who had come under Hennings's spell declared that in the first two acts she presented such a charming "picture of the young, inexperienced, naive, and carefree wife and mother that one truly envied" her husband for "the treasure which he possessed," thus completely missing the point of the play.*

By the end of A Doll House, *nineteenth-century audiences were nearly unanimous in their sympathy for Nora's husband, Torvald. Theater historians Frederick Marker and Lise-Lone Marker point out that in 1879, all the reviewers of this first production agreed that "the spiritual metamorphosis" that Nora undergoes in the third act of* A Doll House *from a naive wife and mother to a self-possessed independent woman was totally unconvincing. Attacked for being immoral, the play aroused so much controversy in Copenhagen that a placard reading* Her tales ikke Dukkehjem *("No* Doll House *discussions here") was sold for Danes to put in their parlors to keep the peace at home.*

Two months after the Danish premier, Ibsen rewrote the play for a German actress who refused to appear on stage unless there was a happy ending — an ending in which Nora (as a so-called normal mother) agrees to stay home to continue her marriage. This version of the play was not a success, and Ibsen restored the original ending. Later critics understood that in A Doll House *Ibsen had gone beyond the conventional idea of a "well-made play" in realistic drama to create a new type of "discussion play." Where the carefully plotted well-made play ends in a dénouement or a closed ending that resolves all the aspects of the conflict between the characters, Ibsen's discussion play culminates in an open ending without a clear resolution of the issues dramatized onstage, because the debate itself is intended to be an integral part of the dramatic action. Contemporary audiences accept Ibsen's open ending in the play, but a century ago most people were shocked by Nora's decision to leave her chil-*

dren and go off on her own. When she slammed the door of her husband's house at the end of the play, the sound reverberated round the world.

RELATED COMMENTARIES: Henrik Ibsen, "Notes for A Doll House," page 1991; Sandra Saari, "Female Becomes Human: Nora Transformed in A Doll House," page 2021; George Bernard Shaw, "On A Doll House," page 2022; Joan Templeton, "Is A Doll House a Feminist Text?," page 2029.

HENRIK IBSEN

A Doll House

1879

TRANSLATED BY ROLF FJELDE

THE CHARACTERS

TORVALD HELMER, *a lawyer*
NORA, *his wife*
DR. RANK
MRS. LINDE
NILS KROGSTAD, *a bank clerk*
The Helmers' three small children
ANNE-MARIE, *their nurse*
HELENE, *a maid*
A Delivery Boy

SCENE: *The action takes place in Helmer's residence.*

ACT I

A comfortable room, tastefully but not expensively furnished. A door to the right in the back wall leads to the entryway; another to the left leads to Helmer's study. Between these doors, a piano. Midway in the left-hand wall a door, and further back a window. Near the window a round table with an armchair and a small sofa. In the right-hand wall, toward the rear, a door, and nearer the foreground a porcelain stove with two armchairs and a rocking chair beside it. Between the stove and the side door, a small table. Engravings on the walls. An etagère with china figures and other small art objects; a small bookcase with richly bound books; the floor carpeted; a fire burning in the stove. It is a winter day.

A bell rings in the entryway; shortly after we hear the door being unlocked. Nora comes into the room, humming happily to herself; she is wearing street clothes and carries an armload of packages, which she puts down on the table to the right. She has left the hall door open; and through it a Delivery Boy is seen, holding a Christmas tree and a basket, which he gives to the Maid who let them in.

NORA: Hide the tree well, Helene. The children mustn't get a glimpse of it till this evening, after it's trimmed. (*To the Delivery Boy, taking out her purse.*) How much?

DELIVERY BOY: Fifty, ma'am.

NORA: There's a crown. No, keep the change. (*The Boy thanks her and leaves. Nora shuts the door. She laughs softly to herself while taking off her street things. Drawing a bag of macaroons from her pocket, she eats a couple, then steals over and listens at her husband's study door.*) Yes, he's home. (*Hums again as she moves to the table right.*)

HELMER (*from the study*): Is that my little lark twittering out there?

NORA (*busy opening some packages*): Yes, it is.

HELMER: Is that my squirrel rummaging around?

NORA: Yes!

HELMER: When did my squirrel get in?

NORA: Just now. (*Putting the macaroon bag in her pocket and wiping her mouth.*) Do come in, Torvald, and see what I've bought.

HELMER: Can't be disturbed. (*After a moment he opens the door and peers in, pen in hand.*) Bought, you say? All that there? Has the little spendthrift been out throwing money around again?

NORA: Oh, but Torvald, this year we really should let ourselves go a bit. It's the first Christmas we haven't had to economize.

HELMER: But you know we can't go squandering.

NORA: Oh yes, Torvald, we can squander a little now. Can't we? Just a tiny, wee bit. Now that you've got a big salary and are going to make piles and piles of money.

HELMER: Yes — starting New Year's. But then it's a full three months till the raise comes through.

NORA: Pooh! We can borrow that long.

HELMER: Nora! (*Goes over and playfully takes her by the ear.*) Are your scatter-brains off again? What if today I borrowed a thousand crowns, and you squandered them over Christmas week, and then on New Year's Eve a roof tile fell on my head and I lay there —

NORA (*putting her hand on his mouth*): Oh! Don't say such things!

HELMER: Yes, but what if it happened — then what?

NORA: If anything so awful happened, then it just wouldn't matter if I had debts or not.

HELMER: Well, but the people I'd borrowed from?

NORA: Them? Who cares about them! They're strangers.

HELMER: Nora, Nora, how like a woman! No, but seriously, Nora, you know what I think about that. No debts! Never borrow! Something of free-dom's lost — and something of beauty, too — from a home that's founded on borrowing and debt. We've made a brave stand up to now, the two of us; and we'll go right on like that the little while we have to.

NORA (*going toward the stove*): Yes, whatever you say, Torvald.

HELMER (*following her*): Now, now, the little lark's wings mustn't droop. Come on, don't be a sulky squirrel. (*Taking out his wallet.*) Nora, guess what I have here.

NORA (*turning quickly*): Money!

HELMER: There, see. (*Hands her some notes.*) Good grief, I know how costs go up in a house at Christmastime.

NORA: Ten — twenty — thirty — forty. Oh, thank you, Torvald; I can manage no end on this.

HELMER: You really will have to.

NORA: Oh yes, I promise I will! But come here so I can show you everything I bought. And so cheap! Look, new clothes for Ivar here — and a sword. Here a horse and a trumpet for Bob. And a doll and a doll's bed here for Emmy; they're nothing much, but she'll tear them to bits in no time anyway. And here I have dress material and handkerchiefs for the maids. Old Anne-Marie really deserves something more.

HELMER: And what's in that package there?

NORA (*with a cry*): Torvald, no! You can't see that till tonight!

HELMER: I see. But tell me now, you little prodigal, what have you thought of for yourself?

NORA: For myself? Oh, I don't want anything at all.

HELMER: Of course you do. Tell me just what — within reason — you'd most like to have.

NORA: I honestly don't know. Oh, listen, Torvald —

HELMER: Well?

NORA (*fumbling at his coat buttons, without looking at him*): If you want to give me something, then maybe you could — you could —

HELMER: Come on, out with it.

NORA (*hurriedly*): You could give me money, Torvald. No more than you think you can spare; then one of these days I'll buy something with it.

HELMER: But Nora —

NORA: Oh please, Torvald darling, do that! I beg you, please. Then I could hang the bills in pretty gilt paper on the Christmas tree. Wouldn't that be fun?

HELMER: What are those little birds called that always fly through their fortunes?

NORA: Oh yes, spendthrifts: I know all that. But let's do as I say, Torvald; then I'll have time to decide what I really need most. That's very sensible, isn't it?

HELMER (*smiling*): Yes, very — that is, if you actually hung onto the money I give you, and you actually used it to buy yourself something. But it goes for the house and for all sorts of foolish things, and then I only have to lay out some more.

NORA: Oh, but Torvald —

HELMER: Don't deny it, my dear little Nora. (*Putting his arm around her waist.*) Spendthrifts are sweet, but they use up a frightful amount of money. It's incredible what it costs a man to feed such birds.

NORA: Oh, how can you say that! Really, I save everything I can.

HELMER (*laughing*): Yes, that's the truth. Everything you can. But that's nothing at all.

NORA (*humming, with a smile of quiet satisfaction*): Hm, if you only knew what expenses we larks and squirrels have, Torvald.

HELMER: You're an odd little one. Exactly the way your father was. You're never at a loss for scaring up money; but the moment you have it, it runs right out through your fingers; you never know what you've done with it. Well, one takes you as you are. It's deep in your blood. Yes, these things are hereditary, Nora.

NORA: Ah, I could wish I'd inherited many of Papa's qualities.

HELMER: And I couldn't wish you anything but just what you are, my sweet little lark. But wait; it seems to me you have a very — what should I call it? — a very suspicious look today —

NORA: I do?

HELMER: You certainly do. Look me straight in the eye.

NORA (*looking at him*): Well?

HELMER (*shaking an admonitory finger*): Surely my sweet tooth hasn't been running riot in town today, has she?

NORA: No. Why do you imagine that?

HELMER: My sweet tooth really didn't make a little detour through the confectioner's?

NORA: No, I assure you, Torvald —

HELMER: Hasn't nibbled some pastry?

NORA: No, not at all.

HELMER: Not even munched a macaroon or two?

NORA: No, Torvald, I assure you, really —

HELMER: There, there now. Of course I'm only joking.

NORA (*going to the table, right*): You know I could never think of going against you.

HELMER: No, I understand that; and you *have* given me your word. (*Going over to her.*) Well, you keep your little Christmas secrets to yourself, Nora darling. I expect they'll come to light this evening, when the tree is lit.

NORA: Did you remember to ask Dr. Rank?

HELMER: No. But there's no need for that: it's assumed he'll be dining with us. All the same, I'll ask him when he stops by here this morning. I've ordered some fine wine. Nora, you can't imagine how I'm looking forward to this evening.

NORA: So am I. And what fun for the children, Torvald!

HELMER: Ah, it's so gratifying to know that one's gotten a safe, secure job, and with a comfortable salary. It's a great satisfaction, isn't it?

NORA: Oh, it's wonderful!

HELMER: Remember last Christmas? Three whole weeks before, you shut yourself in every evening till long after midnight, making flowers for the Christmas tree, and all the other decorations to surprise us. Ugh, that was the dullest time I've ever lived through.

NORA: It wasn't at all dull for me.

HELMER (*smiling*): But the outcome *was* pretty sorry, Nora.

NORA: Oh, don't tease me with that again. How could I help it that the cat came in and tore everything to shreds.

HELMER: No, poor thing, you certainly couldn't. You wanted so much to please us all, and that's what counts. But it's just as well that the hard times are past.

NORA: Yes, it's really wonderful.

HELMER: Now I don't have to sit here alone, boring myself, and you don't have to tire your precious eyes and your fair little delicate hands —

NORA (*clapping her hands*): No, is it really true, Torvald, I don't have to? Oh, how wonderfully lovely to hear! (*Taking his arm.*) Now I'll tell you just how I've thought we should plan things. Right after Christmas — (*The doorbell rings.*) Oh, the bell. (*Straightening the room up a bit.*) Somebody would have to come. What a bore!

HELMER: I'm not home to visitors, don't forget.

MAID (*from the hall doorway*): Ma'am, a lady to see you —

NORA: All right, let her come in.

MAID (*to Helmer*): And the doctor's just come too.

HELMER: Did he go right to my study?

MAID: Yes, he did.

Helmer goes into his room. The Maid shows in Mrs. Linde, dressed in traveling clothes, and shuts the door after her.

MRS. LINDE (*in a dispirited and somewhat hesitant voice*): Hello, Nora.

NORA (*uncertain*): Hello —

MRS. LINDE: You don't recognize me.

NORA: No, I don't know — but wait, I think — (*Exclaiming.*) What! Kristine! Is it really you?

MRS. LINDE: Yes, it's me.

NORA: Kristine! To think I didn't recognize you. But then, how could I? (*More quietly.*) How you've changed, Kristine!

MRS. LINDE: Yes, no doubt I have. In nine — ten long years.

NORA: Is it so long since we met! Yes, it's all of that. Oh, these last eight years have been a happy time, believe me. And so now you've come in to town, too. Made the long trip in the winter. That took courage.

MRS. LINDE: I just got here by ship this morning.

NORA: To enjoy yourself over Christmas, of course. Oh, how lovely! Yes, enjoy ourselves, we'll do that. But take your coat off. You're not still cold? (*Helping her.*) There now, let's get cozy here by the stove. No, the easy chair there! I'll take the rocker here. (*Seizing her hands.*) Yes, now you have your old look again; it was only in that first moment. You're a bit more pale, Kristine — and maybe a bit thinner.

MRS. LINDE: And much, much older, Nora.

NORA: Yes, perhaps a bit older: a tiny, tiny bit; not much at all. (*Stopping short; suddenly serious.*) Oh, but thoughtless me, to sit here, chattering away. Sweet, good Kristine, can you forgive me?

MRS. LINDE: What do you mean, Nora?

NORA (*softly*): Poor Kristine, you've become a widow.

MRS. LINDE: Yes, three years ago.

NORA: Oh, I knew it, of course: I read it in the papers. Oh, Kristine, you must believe me; I often thought of writing you then, but I kept postponing it, and something always interfered.

MRS. LINDE: Nora dear, I understand completely.

NORA: No, it was awful of me, Kristine. You poor thing, how much you must have gone through. And he left you nothing?

MRS. LINDE: No.

NORA: And no children?

MRS. LINDE: No.

NORA: Nothing at all, then?

MRS. LINDE: Not even a sense of loss to feed on.

NORA (*looking incredulously at her*): But Kristine, how could that be?

MRS. LINDE (*smiling wearily and smoothing her hair*): Oh, sometimes it happens, Nora.

NORA: So completely alone. How terribly hard that must be for you. I have three lovely children. You can't see them now; they're out with the maid. But now you must tell me everything —

MRS. LINDE: No, no, no, tell me about yourself.

NORA: No, you begin. Today I don't want to be selfish. I want to think only of you today. But there *is* something I must tell you. Did you hear of the wonderful luck we had recently?

MRS. LINDE: No, what's that?

NORA: My husband's been made manager in the bank, just think!

MRS. LINDE: Your husband? How marvelous!

NORA: Isn't it? Being a lawyer is such an uncertain living, you know, especially if one won't touch any cases that aren't clean and decent. And of course Torvald would never do that, and I'm with him completely there. Oh, we're simply delighted, believe me! He'll join the bank right after New Year's and start getting a huge salary and lots of commissions. From now on we can live quite differently — just as we want. Oh, Kristine, I feel so light and happy! Won't it be lovely to have stacks of money and not a care in the world?

MRS. LINDE: Well, anyway, it would be lovely to have enough for necessities.

NORA: No, not just for necessities, but stacks and stacks of money!

MRS. LINDE (*smiling*): Nora, Nora, aren't you sensible yet? Back in school you were such a free spender.

NORA (*with a quiet laugh*): Yes, that's what Torvald still says. (*Shaking her finger.*) But "Nora, Nora" isn't as silly as you all think. Really, we've been in no position for me to go squandering. We've had to work, both of us.

MRS. LINDE: You too?

NORA: Yes, at odd jobs — needlework, crocheting, embroidery, and such — (*Casually.*) and other things too. You remember that Torvald left the department when we were married? There was no chance of promotion in his office, and of course he needed to earn more money. But that first year he drove himself terribly. He took on all kinds of extra work that kept him going morning and night. It wore him down, and then he fell deathly ill. The doctors said it was essential for him to travel south.

MRS. LINDE: Yes, didn't you spend a whole year in Italy?

NORA: That's right. It wasn't easy to get away, you know. Ivar had just been born. But of course we had to go. Oh, that was a beautiful trip, and it saved Torvald's life. But it cost a frightful sum, Kristine.

MRS. LINDE: I can well imagine.

NORA: Four thousand, eight hundred crowns it cost. That's really a lot of money.

MRS. LINDE: But it's lucky you had it when you needed it.

NORA: Well, as it was, we got it from Papa.

MRS. LINDE: I see. It was just about the time your father died.

NORA: Yes, just about then. And, you know, I couldn't make that trip out to nurse him. I had to stay here, expecting Ivar any moment, and with my poor sick Torvald to care for. Dearest Papa, I never saw him again, Kristine. Oh, that was the worst time I've known in all my marriage.

MRS. LINDE: I know how you loved him. And then you went off to Italy?

NORA: Yes. We had the means now, and the doctors urged us. So we left a month after.

MRS. LINDE: And your husband came back completely cured?

NORA: Sound as a drum!

MRS. LINDE: But — the doctor?

NORA: Who?

MRS. LINDE: I thought the maid said he was a doctor, the man who came in with me.

NORA: Yes, that was Dr. Rank — but he's not making a sick call. He's our closest friend, and he stops by at least once a day. No, Torvald hasn't had a sick moment since, and the children are fit and strong, and I am, too. (*Jumping up and clapping her hands.*) Oh, dear God, Kristine, what a lovely thing to live and be happy! But how disgusting of me — I'm talking of nothing but my own affairs. (*Sits on a stool close by Kristine, arms resting across her knees.*) Oh, don't be angry with me! Tell me, is it really true that you weren't in love with your husband? Why did you marry him, then?

MRS. LINDE: My mother was still alive, but bedridden and helpless — and I had my two younger brothers to look after. In all conscience, I didn't think I could turn him down.

NORA: No, you were right there. But was he rich at the time?

MRS. LINDE: He was very well off, I'd say. But the business was shaky, Nora. When he died, it all fell apart, and nothing was left.

NORA: And then — ?

MRS. LINDE: Yes, so I had to scrape up a living with a little shop and a little teaching and whatever else I could find. The last three years have been like one endless workday without a rest for me. Now it's over, Nora. My poor mother doesn't need me, for she's passed on. Nor the boys, either; they're working now and can take care of themselves.

NORA: How free you must feel —

MRS. LINDE: No — only unspeakably empty. Nothing to live for now. (*Standing up anxiously.*) That's why I couldn't take it any longer out in that desolate hole. Maybe here it'll be easier to find something to do and keep my mind occupied. If I could only be lucky enough to get a steady job, some office work —

NORA: Oh, but Kristine, that's so dreadfully tiring, and you already look so tired. It would be much better for you if you could go off to a bathing resort.

MRS. LINDE (*going toward the window*): I have no father to give me travel money, Nora.

NORA (*rising*): Oh, don't be angry with me.

MRS. LINDE (*going to her*): Nora dear, don't you be angry with me. The worst of my
kind of situation is all the bitterness that's stored away. No one to work for,
and yet you're always having to snap up your opportunities. You have to
live; and so you grow selfish. When you told me the happy change in your
lot, do you know I was delighted less for your sakes than for mine?

NORA: How so? Oh, I see. You think maybe Torvald could do something for
you.

MRS. LINDE: Yes, that's what I thought.

NORA: And he will, Kristine! Just leave it to me; I'll bring it up so delicately —
find something attractive to humor him with. Oh, I'm so eager to help
you.

MRS. LINDE: How very kind of you, Nora, to be so concerned over me — dou-
bly kind, considering you really know so little of life's burdens yourself.

NORA: I — ? I know so little — ?

MRS. LINDE (*smiling*): Well, my heavens — a little needlework and such —
Nora, you're just a child.

NORA (*tossing her head and pacing the floor*): You don't have to act so superior.

MRS. LINDE: Oh?

NORA: You're just like the others. You all think I'm incapable of anything serious —

MRS. LINDE: Come now —

NORA: That I've never had to face the raw world.

MRS. LINDE: Nora dear, you've just been telling me all your troubles.

NORA: Hm! Trivia! (*Quietly.*) I haven't told you the big thing.

MRS. LINDE: Big thing? What do you mean?

NORA: You look down on me so, Kristine, but you shouldn't. You're proud that
you worked so long and hard for your mother.

MRS. LINDE: I don't look down on a soul. But it *is* true: I'm proud — and happy,
too — to think it was given to me to make my mother's last days almost
free of care.

NORA: And you're also proud thinking of what you've done for your brothers.

MRS. LINDE: I feel I've a right to be.

NORA: I agree. But listen to this, Kristine — I've also got something to be proud
and happy for.

MRS. LINDE: I don't doubt it. But whatever do you mean?

NORA: Not so loud. What if Torvald heard! He mustn't, not for anything in the
world. Nobody must know, Kristine. No one but you.

MRS. LINDE: But what is it, then?

NORA: Come here. (*Drawing her down beside her on the sofa.*) It's true — I've also
got something to be proud and happy for. I'm the one who saved Torvald's life.

MRS. LINDE: Saved — ? Saved how?

NORA: I told you about the trip to Italy. Torvald never would have lived if he
hadn't gone south —

MRS. LINDE: Of course; your father gave you the means —

NORA (*smiling*): That's what Torvald and all the rest think, but —

MRS. LINDE: But — ?

NORA: Papa didn't give us a pin. I was the one who raised the money.

MRS. LINDE: You? That whole amount?

NORA: Four thousand, eight hundred crowns. What do you say to that?

MRS. LINDE: But Nora, how was it possible? Did you win the lottery?

NORA (*disdainfully*): The lottery? Pooh! No art to that.

MRS. LINDE: But where did you get it from then?

NORA (*humming, with a mysterious smile*): Hmm, tra-la-la-la.

MRS. LINDE: Because you couldn't have borrowed it.

NORA: No? Why not?

MRS. LINDE: A wife can't borrow without her husband's consent.

NORA (*tossing her head*): Oh, but a wife with a little business sense, a wife who
    knows how to manage —

MRS. LINDE: Nora, I simply don't understand —

NORA: You don't have to. Whoever said I *borrowed* the money? I could have
    gotten it other ways. (*Throwing herself back on the sofa.*) I could have got-
    ten it from some admirer or other. After all, a girl with my ravishing ap-
    peal —

MRS. LINDE: You lunatic.

NORA: I'll bet you're eaten up with curiosity, Kristine.

MRS. LINDE: Now listen here, Nora — you haven't done something indiscreet?

NORA (*sitting up again*): Is it indiscreet to save your husband's life?

MRS. LINDE: I think it's indiscreet that without his knowledge you —

NORA: But that's the point: he mustn't know! My Lord, can't you understand?
    He mustn't ever know the close call he had. It was to *me* the doctors
    came to say his life was in danger — that nothing could save him but a
    stay in the south. Didn't I try strategy then! I began talking about how
    lovely it would be for me to travel abroad like other young wives; I
    begged and I cried; I told him please to remember my condition, to be
    kind and indulge me; and then I dropped a hint that he could easily take
    out a loan. But at that, Kristine, he nearly exploded. He said I was frivo-
    lous, and it was his duty as man of the house not to indulge me in whims
    and fancies — as I think he called them. Aha, I thought, now you'll just
    have to be saved — and that's when I saw my chance.

MRS. LINDE: And your father never told Torvald the money wasn't from him?

NORA: No, never. Papa died right about then. I'd considered bringing him into
    my secret and begging him never to tell. But he was too sick at the time —
    and then, sadly, it didn't matter.

MRS. LINDE: And you've never confided in your husband since?

NORA: For heaven's sake, no! Are you serious? He's so strict on that subject. Be-
    sides — Torvald, with all his masculine pride — how painfully humili-
    ating for him if he ever found out he was in debt to me. That would just
    ruin our relationship. Our beautiful, happy home would never be the
    same.

MRS. LINDE: Won't you ever tell him?

NORA (*thoughtfully, half smiling*): Yes — maybe sometime, years from now,
    when I'm no longer so attractive. Don't laugh! I only mean when Tor-

vald loves me less than now, when he stops enjoying my dancing and dressing up and reciting for him. Then it might be wise to have something in reserve — (*Breaking off.*) How ridiculous! That'll never happen — Well, Kristine, what do you think of my big secret? I'm capable of something too, hm? You can imagine, of course, how this thing hangs over me. It really hasn't been easy meeting the payments on time. In the business world there's what they call quarterly interest and what they call amortization, and these are always so terribly hard to manage. I've had to skimp a little here and there, wherever I could, you know. I could hardly spare anything from my house allowance, because Torvald has to live well. I couldn't let the children go poorly dressed; whatever I got for them, I felt I had to use up completely — the darlings!

MRS. LINDE: Poor Nora, so it had to come out of your own budget, then?

NORA: Yes, of course. But I was the one most responsible, too. Every time Torvald gave me money for new clothes and such, I never used more than half; always bought the simplest, cheapest outfits. It was a godsend that everything looks so well on me that Torvald never noticed. But it did weigh me down at times, Kristine. It *is* such a joy to wear fine things. You understand.

MRS. LINDE: Oh, of course.

NORA: And then I found other ways of making money. Last winter I was lucky enough to get a lot of copying to do. I locked myself in and sat writing every evening till late in the night. Ah, I was tired so often, dead tired. But still it was wonderful fun, sitting and working like that, earning money. It was almost like being a man.

MRS. LINDE: But how much have you paid off this way so far?

NORA: That's hard to say, exactly. These accounts, you know, aren't easy to figure. I only know that I've paid out all I could scrape together. Time and again I haven't known where to turn. (*Smiling.*) Then I'd sit here dreaming of a rich old gentleman who had fallen in love with me —

MRS. LINDE: What! Who is he?

NORA: Oh, really! And that he'd died, and when his will was opened, there in big letters it said, "All my fortune shall be paid over in cash, immediately, to that enchanting Mrs. Nora Helmer."

MRS. LINDE: But Nora dear — who *was* this gentleman?

NORA: Good grief, can't you understand? The old man never existed; that was only something I'd dream up time and again whenever I was at my wits' end for money. But it makes no difference now; the old fossil can go where he pleases for all I care; I don't need him or his will — because now I'm free. (*Jumping up.*) Oh, how lovely to think of that, Kristine! Carefree! To know you're carefree, utterly carefree; to be able to romp and play with the children, and to keep up a beautiful, charming home — everything just the way Torvald likes it! And think, spring is coming, with big blue skies. Maybe we can travel a little then. Maybe I'll see the ocean again. Oh yes, it *is* so marvelous to live and be happy!

The front doorbell rings.

MRS. LINDE (*rising*): There's the bell. It's probably best that I go.

NORA: No, stay. No one's expected. It must be for Torvald.

MAID (*from the hall doorway*): Excuse me, ma'am — there's a gentleman here to see Mr. Helmer, but I didn't know — since the doctor's with him —

NORA: Who is the gentleman?

KROGSTAD (*from the doorway*): It's me, Mrs. Helmer.

Mrs. Linde starts and turns away toward the window.

NORA (*stepping toward him, tense, her voice a whisper*): You? What is it? Why do you want to speak to my husband?

KROGSTAD: Bank business — after a fashion. I have a small job in the investment bank, and I hear now your husband is going to be our chief —

NORA: In other words, it's —

KROGSTAD: Just dry business, Mrs. Helmer. Nothing but that.

NORA: Yes, then please be good enough to step into the study. (*She nods indifferently as she sees him out by the hall door, then returns and begins stirring up the stove.*)

MRS. LINDE: Nora — who was that man?

NORA: That was a Mr. Krogstad — a lawyer.

MRS. LINDE: Then it really was him.

NORA: Do you know that person?

MRS. LINDE: I did once — many years ago. For a time he was a law clerk in our town.

NORA: Yes, he's been that.

MRS. LINDE: How he's changed.

NORA: I understand he had a very unhappy marriage.

MRS. LINDE: He's a widower now.

NORA: With a number of children. There now, it's burning. (*She closes the stove door and moves the rocker a bit to one side.*)

MRS. LINDE: They say he has a hand in all kinds of business.

NORA: Oh? That may be true; I wouldn't know. But let's not think about business. It's so dull.

Dr. Rank enters from Helmer's study.

Rank (*still in the doorway*): No, no really — I don't want to intrude, I'd just as soon talk a little while with your wife. (*Shuts the door, then notices Mrs. Linde.*) Oh, beg pardon. I'm intruding here too.

NORA: No, not at all. (*Introducing him.*) Dr. Rank, Mrs. Linde.

RANK: Well now, that's a name much heard in this house. I believe I passed the lady on the stairs as I came.

MRS. LINDE: Yes, I take the stairs very slowly. They're rather hard on me.

RANK: Uh-hm, some touch of internal weakness?

MRS. LINDE: More overexertion, I'd say.

RANK: Nothing else? Then you're probably here in town to rest up in a round of parties?

MRS. LINDE: I'm here to look for work.

RANK: Is that the best cure for overexertion?

MRS. LINDE: One has to live, Doctor.

RANK: Yes, there's a common prejudice to that effect.

NORA: Oh, come on, Dr. Rank — you really do want to live yourself.

RANK: Yes, I really do. Wretched as I am, I'll gladly prolong my torment indefinitely. All my patients feel like that. And it's quite the same, too, with the morally sick. Right at this moment there's one of those moral invalids in there with Helmer —

MRS. LINDE (*softly*): Ah!

NORA: Who do you mean?

RANK: Oh, it's a lawyer, Krogstad, a type you wouldn't know. His character is rotten to the root — but even he began chattering all-importantly about how he had to *live.*

NORA: Oh? What did he want to talk to Torvald about?

RANK: I really don't know. I only heard something about the bank.

NORA: I didn't know that Krog — that this man Krogstad had anything to do with the bank.

RANK: Yes, he's gotten some kind of berth down there. (*To Mrs. Linde.*) I don't know if you also have, in your neck of the woods, a type of person who scuttles about breathlessly, sniffing out hints of moral corruption, and then maneuvers his victim into some sort of key position where he can keep an eye on him. It's the healthy these days that are out in the cold.

MRS. LINDE: All the same, it's the sick who most need to be taken in.

RANK (*with a shrug*): Yes, there we have it. That's the concept that's turning society into a sanatorium.

Nora, lost in her thoughts, breaks out into quiet laughter and claps her hands.

RANK: Why do you laugh at that? Do you have any real idea of what society is?

NORA: What do I care about dreary old society? I was laughing at something quite different — something terribly funny. Tell me, Doctor — is everyone who works in the bank dependent now on Torvald?

RANK: Is that what you find so terribly funny?

NORA (*smiling and humming*): Never mind, never mind! (*Pacing the floor.*) Yes, that's really immensely amusing: that we — that Torvald has so much power now over all those people. (*Taking the bag out of her pocket.*) Dr. Rank, a little macaroon on that?

RANK: See here, macaroons! I thought they were contraband here.

NORA: Yes, but these are some that Kristine gave me.

MRS. LINDE: What? I — ?

NORA: Now, now, don't be afraid. You couldn't possibly know that Torvald had forbidden them. You see, he's worried they'll ruin my teeth. But hmp! Just this once! Isn't that so, Dr. Rank? Help yourself! (*Puts a macaroon in his mouth.*) And you too, Kristine. And I'll also have one, only a little one — or two, at the most. (*Walking about again.*) Now I'm really tremendously happy. Now there's just one last thing in the world that I have an enormous desire to do.

RANK: Well! And what's that?

NORA: It's something I have such a consuming desire to say so Torvald could hear.

RANK: And why can't you say it?

NORA: I don't dare. It's quite shocking.

MRS. LINDE: Shocking?

RANK: Well, then it isn't advisable. But in front of us you certainly can. What do you have such a desire to say so Torvald could hear?

NORA: I have such a huge desire to say — to hell and be damned!

RANK: Are you crazy?

MRS. LINDE: My goodness, Nora!

RANK: Go on, say it. Here he is.

NORA (*hiding the macaroon bag*): Shh, shh, shh!

Helmer comes in from his study, hat in hand, overcoat over his arm.

NORA (*going toward him*): Well, Torvald dear, are you through with him?

HELMER: Yes, he just left.

NORA: Let me introduce you — this is Kristine, who's arrived here in town.

HELMER: Kristine — ? I'm sorry, but I don't know —

NORA: Mrs. Linde, Torvald dear. Mrs. Kristine Linde.

HELMER: Of course. A childhood friend of my wife's, no doubt?

MRS. LINDE: Yes, we knew each other in those days.

NORA: And just think, she made the long trip down here in order to talk with you.

HELMER: What's this?

MRS. LINDE: Well, not exactly —

NORA: You see, Kristine is remarkably clever in office work, and so she's terribly eager to come under a capable man's supervision and add more to what she already knows —

HELMER: Very wise, Mrs. Linde.

NORA: And then when she heard that you'd become a bank manager — the story was wired out to the papers — then she came in as fast as she could and — Really, Torvald, for my sake you can do a little something for Kristine, can't you?

HELMER: Yes, it's not at all impossible. Mrs. Linde, I suppose you're a widow?

MRS. LINDE: Yes.

HELMER: Any experience in office work?

MRS. LINDE: Yes, a good deal.

HELMER: Well, it's quite likely that I can make an opening for you —

NORA (*clapping her hands*): You see, you see!

HELMER: You've come at a lucky moment, Mrs. Linde.

MRS. LINDE: Oh, how can I thank you?

HELMER: Not necessary. (*Putting his overcoat on.*) But today you'll have to excuse me —

RANK: Wait, I'll go with you. (*He fetches his coat from the hall and warms it at the stove.*)

NORA: Don't stay out long, dear.

HELMER: An hour; no more.

NORA: Are you going too, Kristine?

MRS. LINDE (*putting on her winter garments*): Yes, I have to see about a room now.

HELMER: Then perhaps we can all walk together.

NORA (*helping her*): What a shame we're so cramped here, but it's quite impossible for us to —

MRS. LINDE: Oh, don't even think of it! Good-bye, Nora dear, and thanks for everything.

NORA: Good-bye for now. Of course you'll be back this evening. And you too, Dr. Rank. What? If you're well enough? Oh, you've got to be! Wrap up tight now.

In a ripple of small talk the company moves out into the hall; children's voices are heard outside on the steps.

NORA: There they are! There they are! (*She runs to open the door. The children come in with their nurse, Anne-Marie.*) Come in, come in! (*Bends down and kisses them.*) Oh, you darlings — ! Look at them, Kristine. Aren't they lovely!

RANK: No loitering in the draft here.

HELMER: Come, Mrs. Linde — this place is unbearable now for anyone but mothers.

Dr. Rank, Helmer, and Mrs. Linde go down the stairs. Anne-Marie goes into the living room with the children. Nora follows, after closing the hall door.

NORA: How fresh and strong you look. Oh, such red cheeks you have! Like apples and roses. (*The children interrupt her throughout the following.*) And it was so much fun? That's wonderful. Really? You pulled both Emmy and Bob on the sled? Imagine, all together! Yes, you're a clever boy, Ivar. Oh, let me hold her a bit, Anne-Marie. My sweet little doll baby! (*Takes the smallest from the nurse and dances with her.*) Yes, yes, Mama will dance with Bob as well. What? Did you throw snowballs? Oh, if I'd only been there! No, don't bother, Anne-Marie — I'll undress them myself. Oh yes, let me. It's such fun. Go in and rest; you look half frozen. There's hot coffee waiting for you on the stove. (*The nurse goes into the room to the left. Nora takes the children's winter things off, throwing them about, while the children talk to her all at once.*) Is that so? A big dog chased you? But it didn't bite? No, dogs never bite little, lovely doll babies. Don't peek in the packages, Ivar! What is it? Yes, wouldn't you like to know. No, no, it's an ugly something. Well? Shall we play? What shall we play? Hide-and-seek? Yes, let's play hide-and-seek. Bob must hide first. I must? Yes, let me hide first. (*Laughing and shouting, she and the children play in and out of the living room and the adjoining room to the right. At last Nora hides under the table. The children come storming in, search, but cannot find her, then hear her muffled laughter, dash over to the table, lift the cloth up and find her. Wild shouting. She creeps forward as if to scare them. More shouts. Meanwhile, a knock at the hall door; no one has noticed it. Now the door half opens, and Krogstad appears. He waits a moment; the game goes on.*)

KROGSTAD: Beg pardon, Mrs. Helmer —

NORA (*with a strangled cry, turning and scrambling to her knees*): Oh! What do you want?

KROGSTAD: Excuse me. The outer door was ajar; it must be someone forgot to shut it —

NORA (*rising*): My husband isn't home, Mr. Krogstad.

KROGSTAD: I know that.

NORA: Yes — then what do you want here?

KROGSTAD: A word with you.

NORA: With — ? (*To the children, quietly.*) Go in to Anne-Marie. What? No, the strange man won't hurt Mama. When he's gone, we'll play some more. (*She leads the children into the room to the left and shuts the door after them. Then, tense and nervous:*) You want to speak to me?

KROGSTAD: Yes, I want to.

NORA: Today? But it's not yet the first of the month —

KROGSTAD: No, it's Christmas Eve. It's going to be up to you how merry a Christmas you have.

NORA: What is it you want? Today I absolutely can't —

KROGSTAD: We won't talk about that till later. This is something else. You do have a moment to spare, I suppose?

NORA: Oh yes, of course — I do, except —

KROGSTAD: Good. I was sitting over at Olsen's Restaurant when I saw your husband go down the street —

NORA: Yes?

KROGSTAD: With a lady.

NORA: Yes. So?

KROGSTAD: If you'll pardon my asking: wasn't that lady a Mrs. Linde?

NORA: Yes.

KROGSTAD: Just now come into town?

NORA: Yes, today.

KROGSTAD: She's a good friend of yours?

NORA: Yes, she is. But I don't see —

KROGSTAD: I also knew her once.

NORA: I'm aware of that.

KROGSTAD: Oh? You know all about it. I thought so. Well, then let me ask you short and sweet: is Mrs. Linde getting a job in the bank?

NORA: What makes you think you can cross-examine me, Mr. Krogstad — you, one of my husband's employees? But since you ask, you might as well know — yes, Mrs. Linde's going to be taken on at the bank. And I'm the one who spoke for her, Mr. Krogstad. Now you know.

KROGSTAD: So I guessed right.

NORA (*pacing up and down*): Oh, one does have a tiny bit of influence, I should hope. Just because I am a woman, don't think it means that — When one has a subordinate position, Mr. Krogstad, one really ought to be careful about pushing somebody who — hm —

KROGSTAD: Who has influence?

NORA: That's right.

KROGSTAD (*in a different tone*): Mrs. Helmer, would you be good enough to use your influence on my behalf?

NORA: What? What do you mean?

KROGSTAD: Would you please make sure that I keep my subordinate position in the bank?

NORA: What does that mean? Who's thinking of taking away your position?

KROGSTAD: Oh, don't play the innocent with me. I'm quite aware that your friend would hardly relish the chance of running into me again; and I'm also aware now whom I can thank for being turned out.

NORA: But I promise you —

KROGSTAD: Yes, yes, yes, to the point: there's still time, and I'm advising you to use your influence to prevent it.

NORA: But Mr. Krogstad, I have absolutely no influence.

KROGSTAD: You haven't? I thought you were just saying —

NORA: You shouldn't take me so literally. I! How can you believe that I have any such influence over my husband?

KROGSTAD: Oh, I've known your husband from our student days. I don't think the great bank manager's more steadfast than any other married man.

NORA: You speak insolently about my husband, and I'll show you the door.

KROGSTAD: The lady has spirit.

NORA: I'm not afraid of you any longer. After New Year's, I'll soon be done with the whole business.

KROGSTAD (*restraining himself*): Now listen to me, Mrs. Helmer. If necessary, I'll fight for my little job in the bank as if it were life itself.

NORA: Yes, so it seems.

KROGSTAD: It's not just a matter of income; that's the least of it. It's something else — All right, out with it! Look, this is the thing. You know, just like all the others, of course, that once, a good many years ago, I did something rather rash.

NORA: I've heard rumors to that effect.

KROGSTAD: The case never got into court; but all the same, every door was closed in my face from then on. So I took up those various activities you know about. I had to grab hold somewhere; and I dare say I haven't been among the worst. But now I want to drop all that. My boys are growing up. For their sakes, I'll have to win back as much respect as possible here in town. That job in the bank was like the first rung in my ladder. And now your husband wants to kick me right back down in the mud again.

NORA: But for heaven's sake, Mr. Krogstad, it's simply not in my power to help you.

KROGSTAD: That's because you haven't the will to — but I have the means to make you.

NORA: You certainly won't tell my husband that I owe you money?

KROGSTAD: Hm — what if I told him that?

NORA: That would be shameful of you. (*Nearly in tears.*) This secret — my joy and my pride — that he should learn it in such a crude and disgusting way — learn it from you. You'd expose me to the most horrible unpleasantness —

KROGSTAD: Only unpleasantness?

NORA (*vehemently*): But go on and try. It'll turn out the worse for you, because then my husband will really see what a crook you are, and then you'll *never* be able to hold your job.

KROGSTAD: I asked if it was just domestic unpleasantness you were afraid of?

NORA: If my husband finds out, then of course he'll pay what I owe at once, and then we'd be through with you for good.

KROGSTAD (*a step closer*): Listen, Mrs. Helmer — you've either got a very bad memory, or else no head at all for business. I'd better put you a little more in touch with the facts.

NORA: What do you mean?

KROGSTAD: When your husband was sick, you came to me for a loan of four thousand, eight hundred crowns.

NORA: Where else could I go?

KROGSTAD: I promised to get you that sum —

NORA: And you got it.

KROGSTAD: I promised to get you that sum, on certain conditions. You were so involved in your husband's illness, and so eager to finance your trip, that I guess you didn't think out all the details. It might just be a good idea to remind you. I promised you the money on the strength of a note I drew up.

NORA: Yes, and that I signed.

KROGSTAD: Right. But at the bottom I added some lines for your father to guarantee the loan. He was supposed to sign down there.

NORA: Supposed to? He did sign.

KROGSTAD: I left the date blank. In other words, your father would have dated his signature himself. Do you remember that?

NORA: Yes, I think —

KROGSTAD: Then I gave you the note for you to mail to your father. Isn't that so?

NORA: Yes.

KROGSTAD: And naturally you sent it at once — because only some five, six days later you brought me the note, properly signed. And with that, the money was yours.

NORA: Well, then; I've made my payments regularly, haven't I?

KROGSTAD: More or less. But — getting back to the point — those were hard times for you then, Mrs. Helmer.

NORA: Yes, they were.

KROGSTAD: Your father was very ill, I believe.

NORA: He was near the end.

KROGSTAD: He died soon after?

NORA: Yes.

KROGSTAD: Tell me, Mrs. Helmer, do you happen to recall the date of your father's death? The day of the month, I mean.

NORA: Papa died the twenty-ninth of September.

KROGSTAD: That's quite correct; I've already looked into that. And now we come to a curious thing — (*Taking out a paper.*) which I simply cannot comprehend.

NORA: Curious thing? I don't know —

KROGSTAD: This is the curious thing: that your father co-signed the note for your loan three days after his death.

NORA: How — ? I don't understand.

KROGSTAD: Your father died the twenty-ninth of September. But look. Here your father dated his signature October second. Isn't that curious, Mrs. Helmer? (*Nora is silent.*) Can you explain it to me? (*Nora remains silent.*) It's also remarkable that the words "October second" and the year aren't written in your father's hand, but rather in one that I think I know. Well, it's easy to understand. Your father forgot perhaps to date his signature, and then someone or other added it, a bit sloppily, before anyone knew of his death. There's nothing wrong in that. It all comes down to the signature. And there's no question about *that*, Mrs. Helmer. It really *was* your father who signed his own name here, wasn't it?

NORA (*after a short silence, throwing her head back and looking squarely at him*): No, it wasn't. *I* signed Papa's name.

KROGSTAD: Wait, now — are you fully aware that this is a dangerous confession?

NORA: Why? You'll soon get your money.

KROGSTAD: Let me ask you a question — why didn't you send the paper to your father?

NORA: That was impossible. Papa was so sick. If I'd asked him for his signature, I also would have had to tell him what the money was for. But I couldn't tell him, sick as he was, that my husband's life was in danger. That was just impossible.

KROGSTAD: Then it would have been better if you'd given up the trip abroad.

NORA: I couldn't possibly. The trip was to save my husband's life. I couldn't give that up.

KROGSTAD: But didn't you ever consider that this was a fraud against me?

NORA: I couldn't let myself be bothered by that. You weren't any concern of mine. I couldn't stand you, with all those cold complications you made, even though you knew how badly off my husband was.

KROGSTAD: Mrs. Helmer, obviously you haven't the vaguest idea of what you've involved yourself in. But I can tell you this: it was nothing more and nothing worse that I once did — and it wrecked my whole reputation.

NORA: You? Do you expect me to believe that you ever acted bravely to save your wife's life?

KROGSTAD: Laws don't inquire into motives.

NORA: Then they must be very poor laws.

KROGSTAD: Poor or not — if I introduce this paper in court, you'll be judged according to law.

NORA: This I refuse to believe. A daughter hasn't a right to protect her dying father from anxiety and care? A wife hasn't a right to save her husband's life? I don't know much about laws, but I'm sure that somewhere in the books these things are allowed. And you don't know anything about it — you who practice the law? You must be an awful lawyer, Mr. Krogstad.

KROGSTAD: Could be. But business — the kind of business we two are mixed up in — don't you think I know about that? All right. Do what you want now. But I'm telling you *this:* if I get shoved down a second time, you're going to keep me company. (*He bows and goes out through the hall.*)

NORA (*pensive for a moment, then tossing her head*): Oh, really! Trying to frighten me! I'm not so silly as all that. (*Begins gathering up the children's clothes, but soon stops.*) But — ? No, but that's impossible! I did it out of love.

THE CHILDREN (*in the doorway, left*): Mama, that strange man's gone out the door.

NORA: Yes, yes, I know it. But don't tell anyone about the strange man. Do you hear? Not even Papa!

THE CHILDREN: No, Mama. But now will you play again?

NORA: No, not now.

THE CHILDREN: Oh, but Mama, you promised.

NORA: Yes, but I can't now. Go inside; I have too much to do. Go in, go in, my sweet darlings. (*She herds them gently back in the room and shuts the door after them. Settling on the sofa, she takes up a piece of embroidery and makes some stitches, but soon stops abruptly.*) No! (*Throws the work aside, rises, goes to the hall door and calls out.*) Helene! Let me have the tree in here. (*Goes to the table, left, opens the table drawer, and stops again.*) No, but that's utterly impossible!

MAID (*with the Christmas tree*): Where should I put it, ma'am?

NORA: There. The middle of the floor.

MAID: Should I bring anything else?

NORA: No, thanks. I have what I need.

The Maid, who has set the tree down, goes out.

NORA (*absorbed in trimming the tree*): Candles here — and flowers here. That terrible creature! Talk, talk, talk! There's nothing to it at all. The tree's going to be lovely. I'll do anything to please you, Torvald. I'll sing for you, dance for you —

Helmer comes in from the hall, with a sheaf of papers under his arm.

NORA: Oh! You're back so soon?

HELMER: Yes. Has anyone been here?

NORA: Here? No.

HELMER: That's odd. I saw Krogstad leaving the front door.

NORA: So? Oh yes, that's true. Krogstad was here a moment.

HELMER: Nora, I can see by your face that he's been here, begging you to put in a good word for him.

NORA: Yes.

HELMER: And it was supposed to seem like your own idea? You were to hide it from me that he'd been here. He asked you that, too, didn't he?

NORA: Yes, Torvald, but —

HELMER: Nora, Nora, and you could fall for that? Talk with that sort of person and promise him anything? And then in the bargain, tell me an untruth.

NORA: An untruth — ?

HELMER: Didn't you say that no one had been here? (*Wagging his finger.*) My little songbird must never do that again. A songbird needs a clean beak to warble with. No false notes. (*Putting his arm about her waist.*) That's the way it should be, isn't it? Yes, I'm sure of it. (*Releasing her.*) And so, enough of that. (*Sitting by the stove.*) Ah, how snug and cozy it is here. (*Leafing among his papers.*)

NORA (*busy with the tree, after a short pause*): Torvald!

HELMER: Yes.

NORA: I'm so much looking forward to the Stenborgs' costume party, day after tomorrow.

HELMER: And I can't wait to see what you'll surprise me with.

NORA: Oh, that stupid business!

HELMER: What?

NORA: I can't find anything that's right. Everything seems so ridiculous, so inane.

HELMER: So my little Nora's come to *that* recognition?

NORA (*going behind his chair, her arms resting on its back*): Are you very busy, Torvald?

HELMER: Oh —

NORA: What papers are those?

HELMER: Bank matters.

NORA: Already?

HELMER: I've gotten full authority from the retiring management to make all necessary changes in personnel and procedure. I'll need Christmas week for that. I want to have everything in order by New Year's.

NORA: So that was the reason this poor Krogstad —

HELMER: Hm.

NORA (*still leaning on the chair and slowly stroking the nape of his neck*): If you weren't so very busy, I would have asked you an enormous favor, Torvald.

HELMER: Let's hear. What is it?

NORA: You know, there isn't anyone who has your good taste — and I want so much to look well at the costume party. Torvald, couldn't you take over and decide what I should be and plan my costume?

HELMER: Ah, is my stubborn little creature calling for a lifeguard?

NORA: Yes, Torvald, I can't get anywhere without your help.

HELMER: All right — I'll think it over. We'll hit on something.

NORA: Oh, how sweet of you. (*Goes to the tree again. Pause.*) Aren't the red flowers pretty — ? But tell me, was it really such a crime that this Krogstad committed?

HELMER: Forgery. Do you have any idea what that means?

NORA: Couldn't he have done it out of need?

HELMER: Yes, or thoughtlessness, like so many others. I'm not so heartless that I'd condemn a man categorically for just one mistake.

NORA: No, of course not, Torvald!

HELMER: Plenty of men have redeemed themselves by openly confessing their crimes and taking their punishment.

NORA: Punishment — ?

HELMER: But now Krogstad didn't go that way. He got himself out by sharp practices, and that's the real cause of his moral breakdown.

NORA: Do you really think that would — ?

HELMER: Just imagine how a man with that sort of guilt in him has to lie and cheat and deceive on all sides, has to wear a mask even with the nearest and dearest he has, even with his own wife and children. And with the children, Nora — that's where it's most horrible.

NORA: Why?

HELMER: Because that kind of atmosphere of lies infects the whole life of a home. Every breath the children take in is filled with the germs of something degenerate.

NORA (coming closer behind him): Are you sure of that?

HELMER: Oh, I've seen it often enough as a lawyer. Almost everyone who goes bad early in life has a mother who's a chronic liar.

NORA: Why just — the mother?

HELMER: It's usually the mother's influence that's dominant, but the father's works in the same way, of course. Every lawyer is quite familiar with it. And still this Krogstad's been going home year in, year out, poisoning his own children with lies and pretense; that's why I call him morally lost. (Reaching his hands out toward her.) So my sweet little Nora must promise me never to plead his cause. Your hand on it. Come, come, what's this? Give me your hand. There, now. All settled. I can tell you it'd be impossible for me to work alongside of him. I literally feel physically revolted when I'm anywhere near such a person.

NORA (withdraws her hand and goes to the other side of the Christmas tree): How hot it is here! And I've got so much to do.

HELMER (getting up and gathering his papers): Yes, and I have to think about getting some of these read through before dinner. I'll think about your costume, too. And something to hang on the tree in gilt paper, I may even see about that. (Putting his hand on her head.) Oh you, my darling little songbird. (He goes into his study and closes the door after him.)

NORA (softly, after a silence): Oh, really! It isn't so. It's impossible. It must be impossible.

ANNE-MARIE (in the doorway, left): The children are begging so hard to come in to Mama.

NORA: No, no, no, don't let them in to me! You stay with them, Anne-Marie.

ANNE-MARIE: Of course, ma'am. (Closes the door.)

NORA (pale with terror): Hurt my children — ! Poison my home? (A moment's pause; then she tosses her head.) That's not true. Never. Never in all the world.

ACT II

Same room. Beside the piano the Christmas tree now stands stripped of ornament, burned-down candle stubs on its ragged branches. Nora's street clothes lie on the sofa. Nora, alone in the room, moves restlessly about; at last she stops at the sofa and picks up her coat.

NORA (*dropping the coat again*): Someone's coming! (*Goes toward the door, listens.*) No — there's no one. Of course — nobody's coming today, Christmas Day — or tomorrow, either. But maybe — (*Opens the door and looks out.*) No, nothing in the mailbox. Quite empty. (*Coming forward.*) What nonsense! He won't do anything serious. Nothing terrible could happen. It's impossible. Why, I have three small children.

Anne-Marie, with a large carton, comes in from the room to the left.

ANNE-MARIE: Well, at last I found the box with the masquerade clothes.

NORA: Thanks. Put it on the table.

ANNE-MARIE (*does so*): But they're all pretty much of a mess.

NORA: Ahh! I'd love to rip them in a million pieces!

ANNE-MARIE: Oh, mercy, they can be fixed right up. Just a little patience.

NORA: Yes, I'll go get Mrs. Linde to help me.

ANNE-MARIE: Out again now? In this nasty weather? Miss Nora will catch cold — get sick.

NORA: Oh, worse things could happen. How are the children?

ANNE-MARIE: The poor mites are playing with their Christmas presents, but —

NORA: Do they ask for me much?

ANNE-MARIE: They're so used to having Mama around, you know.

NORA: Yes, but Anne-Marie, I *can't* be together with them as much as I was.

ANNE-MARIE: Well, small children get used to anything.

NORA: You think so? Do you think they'd forget their mother if she was gone for good?

ANNE-MARIE: Oh, mercy — gone for good!

NORA: Wait, tell me, Anne-Marie — I've wondered so often — how could you ever have the heart to give your child over to strangers?

ANNE-MARIE: But I had to, you know, to become little Nora's nurse.

NORA: Yes, but how could you *do* it?

ANNE-MARIE: When I could get such a good place? A girl who's poor and who's gotten in trouble is glad enough for that. Because that slippery fish, he didn't do a thing for me, you know.

NORA: But your daughter's surely forgotten you.

ANNE-MARIE: Oh, she certainly has not. She's written to me, both when she was confirmed and when she was married.

NORA (*clasping her about the neck*): You old Anne-Marie, you were a good mother for me when I was little.

ANNE-MARIE: Poor little Nora, with no other mother but me.

NORA: And if the babies didn't have one, then I know that you'd — What silly talk! (*Opening the carton.*) Go in to them. Now I'll have to — Tomorrow you can see how lovely I'll look.

ANNE-MARIE: Oh, there won't be anyone at the party as lovely as Miss Nora. (*She goes off into the room, left.*)

NORA (*begins unpacking the box, but soon throws it aside*): Oh, if I dared to go out. If only nobody would come. If only nothing would happen here while I'm out. What craziness — nobody's coming. Just don't think. This muff — needs a brushing. Beautiful gloves, beautiful gloves. Let it go. Let it go! One, two, three, four, five, six — (*With a cry.*) Oh, there they are! (*Poises to move toward the door, but remains irresolutely standing. Mrs. Linde enters from the hall, where she has removed her street clothes.*)

NORA: Oh, it's you, Kristine. There's no one else out there? How good that you've come.

MRS. LINDE: I hear you were up asking for me.

NORA: Yes, I just stopped by. There's something you really can help me with. Let's get settled on the sofa. Look, there's going to be a costume party tomorrow evening at the Stenborgs' right above us, and now Torvald wants me to go as a Neapolitan peasant girl and dance the tarantella that I learned in Capri.

MRS. LINDE: Really, are you giving a whole performance?

NORA: Torvald says yes, I should. See, here's the dress. Torvald had it made for me down there; but now it's all so tattered that I just don't know —

MRS. LINDE: Oh, we'll fix that up in no time. It's nothing more than the trimmings — they're a bit loose here and there. Needle and thread? Good, now we have what we need.

NORA: Oh, how sweet of you!

MRS. LINDE (*sewing*): So you'll be in disguise tomorrow, Nora. You know what? I'll stop by then for a moment and have a look at you all dressed up. But listen, I've absolutely forgotten to thank you for that pleasant evening yesterday.

NORA (*getting up and walking about*): I don't think it was as pleasant as usual yesterday. You should have come to town a bit sooner, Kristine — Yes, Torvald really knows how to give a home elegance and charm.

MRS. LINDE: And you do, too, if you ask me. You're not your father's daughter for nothing. But tell me, is Dr. Rank always so down in the mouth as yesterday?

NORA: No, that was quite an exception. But he goes around critically ill all the time — tuberculosis of the spine, poor man. You know, his father was a disgusting thing who kept mistresses and so on — and that's why the son's been sickly from birth.

MRS. LINDE (*lets her sewing fall to her lap*): But my dearest Nora, how do you know about such things?

NORA (*walking more jauntily*): Hmp! When you've had three children, then you've had a few visits from — from women who know something of medicine, and they tell you this and that.

MRS. LINDE (*resumes sewing; a short pause*): Does Dr. Rank come here every day?

NORA: Every blessed day. He's Torvald's best friend from childhood, and *my* good friend, too. Dr. Rank almost belongs to this house.

MRS. LINDE: But tell me — is he quite sincere? I mean, doesn't he rather enjoy flattering people?

NORA: Just the opposite. Why do you think that?

MRS. LINDE: When you introduced us yesterday, he was proclaiming that he'd often heard my name in this house; but later I noticed that your husband hadn't the slightest idea who I really was. So how could Dr. Rank — ?

NORA: But it's all true, Kristine. You see, Torvald loves me beyond words, and, as he puts it, he'd like to keep me all to himself. For a long time he'd almost be jealous if I even mentioned any of my old friends back home. So of course I dropped that. But with Dr. Rank I talk a lot about such things, because he likes hearing about them.

MRS. LINDE: Now listen, Nora; in many ways you're still like a child. I'm a good deal older than you, with a little more experience. I'll tell you something: you ought to put an end to all this with Dr. Rank.

NORA: What should I put an end to?

MRS. LINDE: Both parts of it, I think. Yesterday you said something about a rich admirer who'd provide you with money —

NORA: Yes, one who doesn't exist — worse luck. So?

MRS. LINDE: Is Dr. Rank well off?

NORA: Yes, he is.

MRS. LINDE: With no dependents?

NORA: No, no one. But —

MRS. LINDE: And he's over here every day?

NORA: Yes, I told you that.

MRS. LINDE: How can a man of such refinement be so grasping?

NORA: I don't follow you at all.

MRS. LINDE: Now don't try to hide it, Nora. You think I can't guess who loaned you the forty-eight hundred crowns?

NORA: Are you out of your mind? How could you think such a thing! A friend of ours, who comes here every single day. What an intolerable situation that would have been!

MRS. LINDE: Then it really wasn't him.

NORA: No, absolutely not. It never even crossed my mind for a moment — And he had nothing to lend in those days; his inheritance came later.

MRS. LINDE: Well, I think that was a stroke of luck for you, Nora dear.

NORA: No, it never would have occurred to me to ask Dr. Rank — Still, I'm quite sure that if I had asked him —

MRS. LINDE: Which you won't, of course.

NORA: No, of course not. I can't see that I'd ever need to. But I'm quite positive that if I talked to Dr. Rank —

MRS. LINDE: Behind your husband's back?

NORA: I've got to clear up this other thing; *that's* also behind his back. I've *got* to clear it all up.

MRS. LINDE: Yes, I was saying that yesterday, but —

NORA (*pacing up and down*): A man handles these problems so much better than a woman —

MRS. LINDE: One's husband does, yes.

NORA: Nonsense. (*Stopping.*) When you pay everything you owe, then you get your note back, right?

MRS. LINDE: Yes, naturally.

NORA: And can rip it into a million pieces and burn it up — that filthy scrap of paper!

MRS. LINDE (*looking hard at her, laying her sewing aside, and rising slowly*): Nora, you're hiding something from me.

NORA: You can see it in my face?

MRS. LINDE: Something's happened to you since yesterday morning. Nora, what is it?

NORA (*hurrying toward her*): Kristine! (*Listening.*) Shh! Torvald's home. Look, go in with the children a while. Torvald can't bear all this snipping and stitching. Let Anne-Marie help you.

MRS. LINDE (*gathering up some of the things*): All right, but I'm not leaving here until we've talked this out. (*She disappears into the room, left, as Torvald enters from the hall.*)

NORA: Oh, how I've been waiting for you, Torvald dear.

HELMER: Was that the dressmaker?

NORA: No, that was Kristine. She's helping me fix up my costume. You know, it's going to be quite attractive.

HELMER: Yes, wasn't that a bright idea I had?

NORA: Brilliant! But then wasn't I good as well to give in to you?

HELMER: Good — because you give in to your husband's judgment? All right, you little goose, I know you didn't mean it like that. But I won't disturb you. You'll want to have a fitting, I suppose.

NORA: And you'll be working?

HELMER: Yes. (*Indicating a bundle of papers.*) See. I've been down to the bank. (*Starts toward his study.*)

NORA: Torvald.

HELMER (*stops*): Yes.

NORA: If your little squirrel begged you, with all her heart and soul, for something — ?

HELMER: What's that?

NORA: Then would you do it?

HELMER: First, naturally, I'd have to know what it was.

NORA: Your squirrel would scamper about and do tricks, if you'd only be sweet and give in.

HELMER: Out with it.

NORA: Your lark would be singing high and low in every room —

HELMER: Come on, she does that anyway.

NORA: I'd be a wood nymph and dance for you in the moonlight.

HELMER: Nora — don't tell me it's that same business from this morning?

NORA (*coming closer*): Yes, Torvald, I beg you, please!

HELMER: And you actually have the nerve to drag that up again?

NORA: Yes, yes, you've got to give in to me; you *have* to let Krogstad keep his job in the bank.

HELMER: My dear Nora, I've slated his job for Mrs. Linde.

NORA: That's awfully kind of you. But you could just fire another clerk instead of Krogstad.

HELMER: This is the most incredible stubbornness! Because you go and give an impulsive promise to speak up for him, I'm expected to —

NORA: That's not the reason, Torvald. It's for your own sake. That man does writing for the worst papers; you said it yourself. He could do you any amount of harm. I'm scared to death of him —

HELMER: Ah, I understand. It's the old memories haunting you.

NORA: What do you mean by that?

HELMER: Of course, you're thinking about your father.

NORA: Yes, all right. Just remember how those nasty gossips wrote in the papers about Papa and slandered him so cruelly. I think they'd have had him dismissed if the department hadn't sent you up to investigate, and if you hadn't been so kind and open-minded toward him.

HELMER: My dear Nora, there's a notable difference between your father and me. Your father's official career was hardly above reproach. But mine is; and I hope it'll stay that way as long as I hold my position.

NORA: Oh, who can ever tell what vicious minds can invent? We could be so snug and happy now in our quiet, carefree home — you and I and the children, Torvald! That's why I'm pleading with you so —

HELMER: And just by pleading for him you make it impossible for me to keep him on. It's already known at the bank that I'm firing Krogstad. What if it's rumored around now that the new bank manager was vetoed by his wife —

NORA: Yes, what then — ?

HELMER: Oh yes — as long as our little bundle of stubbornness gets her way — ! I should go and make myself ridiculous in front of the whole office — give people the idea I can be swayed by all kinds of outside pressure. Oh, you can bet I'd feel the effects of that soon enough! Besides — there's something that rules Krogstad right out at the bank as long as I'm the manager.

NORA: What's that?

HELMER: His moral failings I could maybe overlook if I had to —

NORA: Yes, Torvald, why not?

HELMER: And I hear he's quite efficient on the job. But he was a crony of mine back in my teens — one of those rash friendships that crop up again and again to embarrass you later in life. Well, I might as well say it straight out: we're on a first-name basis. And that tactless fool makes no effort at all to hide it in front of others. Quite the contrary — he thinks that entitles him to take a familiar air around me, and so every other second he comes booming out with his "Yes, Torvald!" and "Sure thing, Torvald!" I tell you, it's been excruciating for me. He's out to make my place in the bank unbearable.

NORA: Torvald, you can't be serious about all this.

HELMER: Oh no? Why not?

NORA: Because these are such petty considerations.

HELMER: What are you saying? Petty? You think I'm petty!

NORA: No, just the opposite, Torvald dear. That's exactly why —

HELMER: Never mind. You call my motives petty; then I might as well be just that. Petty! All right! We'll put a stop to this for good. (*Goes to the hall door and calls.*) Helene!

NORA: What do you want?

HELMER (*searching among his papers*): A decision. (*The Maid comes in.*) Look here; take this letter; go out with it at once. Get hold of a messenger and have him deliver it. Quick now. It's already addressed. Wait, here's some money.

MAID: Yes, sir. (*She leaves with the letter.*)

HELMER (*straightening his papers*): There, now, little Miss Willful.

NORA (*breathlessly*): Torvald, what was that letter?

HELMER: Krogstad's notice.

NORA: Call it back, Torvald! There's still time. Oh, Torvald, call it back! Do it for my sake — for your sake, for the children's sake! Do you hear, Torvald; do it! You don't know how this can harm us.

HELMER: Too late.

NORA: Yes, too late.

HELMER: Nora dear, I can forgive you this panic, even though basically you're insulting me. Yes, you are! Or isn't it an insult to think that *I* should be afraid of a courtroom hack's revenge? But I forgive you anyway, because this shows so beautifully how much you love me. (*Takes her in his arms.*) This is the way it should be, my darling Nora. Whatever comes, you'll see; when it really counts, I have strength and courage enough as a man to take on the whole weight myself.

NORA (*terrified*): What do you mean by that?

HELMER: The whole weight, I said.

NORA (*resolutely*): No, never in all the world.

HELMER: Good. So we'll share it, Nora, as man and wife. That's as it should be. (*Fondling her.*) Are you happy now? There, there, there — not these frightened dove's eyes. It's nothing at all but empty fantasies — Now you should run through your tarantella and practice your tambourine. I'll go to the inner office and shut both doors, so I won't hear a thing; you can make all the noise you like. (*Turning in the doorway.*) And when Rank comes, just tell him where he can find me. (*He nods to her and goes with his papers into the study, closing the door.*)

NORA (*standing as though rooted, dazed with fright, in a whisper*): He really could do it. He will do it. He'll do it in spite of everything. No, not that, never, never! Anything but that! Escape! A way out — (*The doorbell rings.*) Dr. Rank! Anything but that! *Anything,* whatever it is! (*Her hands pass over her face, smoothing it; she pulls herself together, goes over and opens the hall door. Dr. Rank stands outside, hanging his fur coat up. During the following scene, it begins getting dark.*)

NORA: Hello, Dr. Rank. I recognized your ring. But you mustn't go in to Torvald yet; I believe he's working.

RANK: And you?

NORA: For you, I always have an hour to spare — you know that. (*He has entered, and she shuts the door after him.*)

RANK: Many thanks. I'll make use of these hours while I can.

NORA: What do you mean by that? While you can?

RANK: Does that disturb you?

NORA: Well, it's such an odd phrase. Is anything going to happen?

RANK: What's going to happen is what I've been expecting so long — but I honestly didn't think it would come so soon.

NORA (*gripping his arm*): What is it you've found out? Dr. Rank, you have to tell me!

RANK (*sitting by the stove*): It's all over for me. There's nothing to be done about it.

NORA (*breathing easier*): Is it you — then — ?

RANK: Who else? There's no point in lying to one's self. I'm the most miserable of all my patients, Mrs. Helmer. These past few days I've been auditing my internal accounts. Bankrupt! Within a month I'll probably be laid out and rotting in the churchyard.

NORA: Oh, what a horrible thing to say.

RANK: The thing itself is horrible. But the worst of it is all the other horror before it's over. There's only one final examination left; when I'm finished with that, I'll know about when my disintegration will begin. There's something I want to say. Helmer with his sensitivity has such a sharp distaste for anything ugly. I don't want him near my sickroom.

NORA: Oh, but Dr. Rank —

RANK: I won't have him in there. Under no condition. I'll lock my door to him — As soon as I'm completely sure of the worst, I'll send you my calling card marked with a black cross, and you'll know then the wreck has started to come apart.

NORA: No, today you're completely unreasonable. And I wanted you so much to be in a really good humor.

RANK: With death up my sleeve? And then to suffer this way for somebody else's sins. Is there any justice in that? And in every single family, in some way or another, this inevitable retribution of nature goes on —

NORA (*her hands pressed over her ears*): Oh, stuff! Cheer up! Please — be gay!

RANK: Yes, I'd just as soon laugh at it all. My poor, innocent spine, serving time for my father's gay army days.

NORA (*by the table, left*): He was so infatuated with asparagus tips and pâté de foie gras, wasn't that it?

RANK: Yes — and with truffles.

NORA: Truffles, yes. And then with oysters, I suppose?

RANK: Yes, tons of oysters, naturally.

NORA: And then the port and champagne to go with it. It's so sad that all these delectable things have to strike at our bones.

RANK: Especially when they strike at the unhappy bones that never shared in the fun.

NORA: Ah, that's the saddest of all.

RANK (*looks searchingly at her*): Hm.

NORA (*after a moment*): Why did you smile?

RANK: No, it was you who laughed.

NORA: No, it was you who smiled, Dr. Rank!

RANK (*getting up*): You're even a bigger tease than I'd thought.

NORA: I'm full of wild ideas today.

RANK: That's obvious.

NORA (*putting both hands on his shoulders*): Dear, dear Dr. Rank, you'll never die for Torvald and me.

RANK: Oh, that loss you'll easily get over. Those who go away are soon forgotten.

NORA (*looks fearfully at him*): You believe that?

RANK: One makes new connections, and then —

NORA: Who makes new connections?

RANK: Both you and Torvald will when I'm gone. I'd say you're well under way already. What was that Mrs. Linde doing here last evening?

NORA: Oh, come — you can't be jealous of poor Kristine?

RANK: Oh yes, I am. She'll be my successor here in the house. When I'm down under, that woman will probably —

NORA: Shh! Not so loud. She's right in there.

RANK: Today as well. So you see.

NORA: Only to sew on my dress. Good gracious, how unreasonable you are. (*Sitting on the sofa.*) Be nice now, Dr. Rank. Tomorrow you'll see how beautifully I'll dance; and you can imagine then that I'm dancing only for you — yes, and of course for Torvald, too — that's understood. (*Takes various items out of the carton.*) Dr. Rank, sit over here and I'll show you something.

RANK (*sitting*): What's that?

NORA: Look here. Look.

RANK: Silk Stockings.

NORA: Flesh-colored. Aren't they lovely? Now it's so dark here, but tomorrow — No, no, no, just look at the feet. Oh well, you might as well look at the rest.

RANK: Hm —

NORA: Why do you look so critical? Don't you believe they'll fit?

RANK: I've never had any chance to form an opinion on that.

NORA (*glancing at him a moment*): Shame on you. (*Hits him lightly on the ear with the stockings.*) That's for you. (*Puts them away again.*)

RANK: And what other splendors am I going to see now?

NORA: Not the least bit more, because you've been naughty. (*She hums a little and rummages among her things.*)

RANK (*after a short silence*): When I sit here together with you like this, completely easy and open, then I don't know — I simply can't imagine — whatever would have become of me if I'd never come into this house.

NORA (*smiling*): Yes, I really think you feel completely at ease with us.

RANK (*more quietly, staring straight ahead*): And then to have to go away from it all —

NORA: Nonsense, you're not going away.

RANK (*his voice unchanged*): — and not even be able to leave some poor show of gratitude behind, scarcely a fleeting regret — no more than a vacant place that anyone can fill.

NORA: And if I asked you now for — ? No —

RANK: For what?

NORA: For a great proof of your friendship —

RANK: Yes, yes?

NORA: No, I mean — for an exceptionally big favor —

RANK: Would you really, for once, make me so happy?

NORA: Oh, you haven't the vaguest idea what it is.

RANK: All right, then tell me.

NORA: No, but I can't, Dr. Rank — it's all out of reason. It's advice and help, too — and a favor —

RANK: So much the better. I can't fathom what you're hinting at. Just speak out. Don't you trust me?

NORA: Of course. More than anyone else. You're my best and truest friend, I'm sure. That's why I want to talk to you. All right, then, Dr. Rank: there's something you can help me prevent. You know how deeply, how inexpressibly dearly Torvald loves me; he'd never hesitate a second to give up his life for me.

RANK (*leaning close to her*): Nora — do you think he's the only one —

NORA (*with a slight start*): Who — ?

RANK: Who'd gladly give up his life for you.

NORA (*heavily*): I see.

RANK: I swore to myself you should know this before I'm gone. I'll never find a better chance. Yes, Nora, now you know. And also you know now that you can trust me beyond anyone else.

NORA (*rising, natural and calm*): Let me by.

RANK (*making room for her, but still sitting*): Nora —

NORA (*in the hall doorway*): Helene, bring the lamp in. (*Goes over to the stove.*) Ah, dear Dr. Rank, that was really mean of you.

RANK (*getting up*): That I've loved you just as deeply as somebody else? Was *that* mean?

NORA: No, but that you came out and told me. That was quite unnecessary —

RANK: What do you mean? Have you known — ?

The Maid comes in with the lamp, sets it on the table, and goes out again.

RANK: Nora — Mrs. Helmer — I'm asking you: have you known about it?

NORA: Oh, how can I tell what I know or don't know? Really, I don't know what to say — Why did you have to be so clumsy, Dr. Rank! Everything was so good.

RANK: Well, in any case, you now have the knowledge that my body and soul are at your command. So won't you speak out?

NORA (*looking at him*): After that?

RANK: Please, just let me know what it is.

NORA: You can't know anything now.

RANK: I have to. You mustn't punish me like this. Give me the chance to do whatever is humanly possible for you.

NORA: Now there's nothing you can do for me. Besides, actually, I don't need any help. You'll see — it's only my fantasies. That's what it is. Of course! (*Sits in the rocker, looks at him, and smiles.*) What a nice one you are, Dr. Rank. Aren't you a little bit ashamed, now that the lamp is here?

RANK: No, not exactly. But perhaps I'd better go — for good?

NORA: No, you certainly can't do that. You must come here just as you always have. You know Torvald can't do without you.

RANK: Yes, but *you?*

NORA: You know how much I enjoy it when you're here.

RANK: That's precisely what threw me off. You're a mystery to me. So many times I've felt you'd almost rather be with me than with Helmer.

NORA: Yes — you see, there are some people that one loves most and other people that one would almost prefer being with.

RANK: Yes, there's something to that.

NORA: When I was back home, of course I loved Papa most. But I always thought it was so much fun when I could sneak down to the maids' quarters, because they never tried to improve me, and it was always so amusing, the way they talked to each other.

RANK: Aha, so it's *their* place that I've filled.

NORA (*jumping up and going to him*): Oh, dear, sweet Dr. Rank, that's not what I meant at all. But you can understand that with Torvald it's just the same as with Papa —

The Maid enters from the hall.

MAID: Ma'am — please! (*She whispers to Nora and hands her a calling card.*)

NORA (*glancing at the card*): Ah! (*Slips it into her pocket.*)

RANK: Anything wrong?

NORA: No, no, not at all. It's only some — it's my new dress —

RANK: Really? But — there's your dress.

NORA: Oh, that. But this is another one — I ordered it — Torvald mustn't know —

RANK: Ah, now we have the big secret.

NORA: That's right. Just go in with him — he's back in the inner study. Keep him there as long as —

RANK: Don't worry. He won't get away. (*Goes into the study.*)

NORA (*to the Maid*): And he's standing waiting in the kitchen?

MAID: Yes, he came up by the back stairs.

NORA: But didn't you tell him somebody was here?

MAID: Yes, but that didn't do any good.

NORA: He won't leave?

MAID: No, he won't go till he's talked with you, ma'am.

NORA: Let him come in, then — but quietly. Helene, don't breathe a word about this. It's a surprise for my husband.

MAID: Yes, yes, I understand — (*Goes out.*)

NORA: This horror — it's going to happen. No, no, no, it can't happen, it mustn't. (*She goes and bolts Helmer's door. The Maid opens the hall door for Krogstad and shuts it behind him. He is dressed for travel in a fur coat, boots, and a fur cap.*)

NORA (*going toward him*): Talk softly. My husband's home.

KROGSTAD: Well, good for him.

NORA: What do you want?

KROGSTAD: Some information.

NORA: Hurry up, then. What is it?

KROGSTAD: You know, of course, that I got my notice.

NORA: I couldn't prevent it, Mr. Krogstad. I fought for you to the bitter end, but nothing worked.

KROGSTAD: Does your husband's love for you run so thin? He knows everything I can expose you to, and all the same he dares to —

NORA: How can you imagine he knows anything about this?

KROGSTAD: Ah, no — I can't imagine it either, now. It's not at all like my fine
Torvald Helmer to have so much guts —

NORA: Mr. Krogstad, I demand respect for my husband!

KROGSTAD: Why, of course — all due respect. But since the lady's keeping it so
carefully hidden, may I presume to ask if you're also a bit better informed than yesterday about what you've actually done?

NORA: More than you could ever teach me.

KROGSTAD: Yes, I *am* such an awful lawyer.

NORA: What is it you want from me?

KROGSTAD: Just a glimpse of how you are, Mrs. Helmer. I've been thinking
about you all day long. A cashier, a night-court scribbler, a — well, a
type like me also has a little of what they call a heart, you know.

NORA: Then show it. Think of my children.

KROGSTAD: Did you or your husband ever think of mine? But never mind. I
simply wanted to tell you that you don't need to take this thing too seriously. For the present, I'm not proceeding with any action.

NORA: Oh no, really! Well — I knew that.

KROGSTAD: Everything can be settled in a friendly spirit. It doesn't have to get
around town at all; it can stay just among us three.

NORA: My husband must never know anything of this.

KROGSTAD: How can you manage that? Perhaps you can pay me the balance?

NORA: No, not right now.

KROGSTAD: Or you know some way of raising the money in a day or two?

NORA: No way that I'm willing to use.

KROGSTAD: Well, it wouldn't have done you any good, anyway. If you stood in
front of me with a fistful of bills, you still couldn't buy your signature
back.

NORA: Then tell me what you're going to do with it.

KROGSTAD: I'll just hold onto it — keep it on file. There's no outsider who'll
even get wind of it. So if you've been thinking of taking some desperate
step —

NORA: I have.

KROGSTAD: Been thinking of running away from home —

NORA: I have!

KROGSTAD: Or even of something worse —

NORA: How could you guess that?

KROGSTAD: You can drop those thoughts.

NORA: How could you guess I was thinking of *that?*

KROGSTAD: Most of us think about *that* at first. I thought about it too, but I discovered I hadn't the courage —

NORA (*lifelessly*): I don't either.

KROGSTAD (*relieved*): That's true, you haven't the courage? You too?

NORA: I don't have it — I don't have it.

KROGSTAD: It would be terribly stupid, anyway. After that first storm at home blows out, why, then — I have here in my pocket a letter for your husband —

NORA: Telling everything?

KROGSTAD: As charitably as possible.

NORA (*quickly*): He mustn't ever get that letter. Tear it up. I'll find some way to get money.

KROGSTAD: Beg pardon, Mrs. Helmer, but I think I just told you —

NORA: Oh, I don't mean the money I owe you. Let me know how much you want from my husband, and I'll manage it.

KROGSTAD: I don't want money from your husband.

NORA: What do you want, then?

KROGSTAD: I'll tell you what. I want to recoup, Mrs. Helmer; I want to get on in the world — and there's where your husband can help me. For a year and a half I've kept myself clean of anything disreputable — all that time struggling with the worst conditions; but I was satisfied, working my way up step by step. Now I've been written right off, and I'm just not in the mood to come crawling back. I tell you, I want to move on. I want to get back in the bank — in a better position. Your husband can set up a job for me —

NORA: He'll never do that!

KROGSTAD: He'll do it. I know him. He won't dare breathe a word of protest. And once I'm in there together with him, you just wait and see! Inside of a year, I'll be the manager's right-hand man. It'll be Nils Krogstad, not Torvald Helmer, who runs the bank.

NORA: You'll never see the day!

KROGSTAD: Maybe you think you can —

NORA: I have the courage now — for *that*.

KROGSTAD: Oh, you don't scare me. A smart, spoiled lady like you —

NORA: You'll see; you'll see!

KROGSTAD: Under the ice, maybe? Down in the freezing coal-black water? There, till you float up in the spring, ugly, unrecognizable, with your hair falling out —

NORA: You don't frighten me.

KROGSTAD: Nor do you frighten me. One doesn't do these things, Mrs. Helmer. Besides, what good would it be? I'd still have him safe in my pocket.

NORA: Afterwards? When I'm no longer — ?

KROGSTAD: Are you forgetting that *I'll* be in control then over your final reputation? (*Nora stands speechless, staring at him.*) Good; now I've warned you. Don't do anything stupid. When Helmer's read my letter, I'll be waiting for his reply. And bear in mind that it's your husband himself who's forced me back to my old ways. I'll never forgive him for that. Good-bye, Mrs. Helmer. (*He goes out through the hall.*)

NORA (*goes to the hall door, opens it a crack, and listens*): He's gone. Didn't leave the letter. Oh no, no, that's impossible too! (*Opening the door more and more.*) What's that? He's standing outside — not going downstairs. He's thinking it over? Maybe he'll — ? (*A letter falls in the mailbox; then Krogstad's footsteps are heard, dying away down a flight of stairs. Nora gives a muffled cry and runs over toward the sofa table. A short pause.*) In the mail-box. (*Slips warily over to the hall door.*) It's lying there. Torvald, Torvald — now we're lost!

MRS. LINDE (*entering with costume from the room, left*): There now, I can't see any-thing else to mend. Perhaps you'd like to try —

NORA (*in a hoarse whisper*): Kristine, come here.

MRS. LINDE (*tossing the dress on the sofa*): What's wrong? You look upset.

NORA: Come here. See that letter? *There!* Look — through the glass in the mail-box.

MRS. LINDE: Yes, yes, I see it.

NORA: That letter's from Krogstad —

MRS. LINDE: Nora — it's Krogstad who loaned you the money!

NORA: Yes, and now Torvald will find out everything.

MRS. LINDE: Believe me, Nora, it's best for both of you.

NORA: There's more you don't know. I forged a name.

MRS. LINDE: But for heaven's sake — ?

NORA: I only want to tell you that, Kristine, so that you can be my witness.

MRS. LINDE: Witness? Why should I — ?

NORA: If I should go out of my mind — it could easily happen —

MRS. LINDE: Nora!

NORA: Or anything else occurred — so I couldn't be present here —

MRS. LINDE: Nora, Nora, you aren't yourself at all!

NORA: And someone should try to take on the whole weight, all of the guilt, you follow me —

MRS. LINDE: Yes, of course, but why do you think — ?

NORA: Then you're the witness that it isn't true, Kristine. I'm very much my-self; my mind right now is perfectly clear; and I'm telling you: nobody else has known about this; I alone did everything. Remember that.

MRS. LINDE: I will. But I don't understand all this.

NORA: Oh, how could you ever understand it? It's the miracle now that's going to take place.

MRS. LINDE: The miracle?

NORA: Yes, the miracle. But it's so awful, Kristine. It mustn't take place, not for anything in the world.

MRS. LINDE: I'm going right over and talk with Krogstad.

NORA: Don't go near him; he'll do you some terrible harm!

MRS. LINDE: There was a time once when he'd gladly have done anything for me.

NORA: He?

MRS. LINDE: Where does he live?

NORA: Oh, how do I know? Yes. (*Searches in her pocket.*) Here's his card. But the letter, the letter — !

HELMER (*from the study, knocking on the door*): Nora!

NORA (*with a cry of fear*): Oh! What is it? What do you want?

HELMER: Now, now, don't be so frightened. We're not coming in. You locked the door — are you trying on the dress?

NORA: Yes, I'm trying it. I'll look just beautiful, Torvald.

MRS. LINDE (*who has read the card*): He's living right around the corner.

NORA: Yes, but what's the use? We're lost. The letter's in the box.

MRS. LINDE: And your husband has the key?

NORA: Yes, always.

MRS. LINDE: Krogstad can ask for his letter back unread; he can find some excuse —

NORA: But it's just this time that Torvald usually—

MRS. LINDE: Stall him. Keep him in there. I'll be back as quick as I can. (*She hurries out through the hall entrance.*)

NORA (*goes to Helmer's door, opens it, and peers in*): Torvald!

HELMER (*from the inner study*): Well — does one dare set foot in one's own living room at last? Come on, Rank, now we'll get a look — (*In the doorway.*) But what's this?

NORA: What, Torvald dear?

HELMER: Rank had me expecting some grand masquerade.

RANK (*in the doorway*): That was my impression, but I must have been wrong.

NORA: No one can admire me in my splendor — not till tomorrow.

HELMER: But Nora dear, you look so exhausted. Have you practiced too hard?

NORA: No, I haven't practiced at all yet.

HELMER: You know, it's necessary —

NORA: Oh, it's absolutely necessary, Torvald. But I can't get anywhere without your help. I've forgotten the whole thing completely.

HELMER: Ah, we'll soon take care of that.

NORA: Yes, take care of me, Torvald, please! Promise me that? Oh, I'm so nervous. That big party — You must give up everything this evening for me. No business — don't even touch your pen. Yes? Dear Torvald, promise?

HELMER: It's a promise. Tonight I'm totally at your service — you little helpless thing. Hm — but first there's one thing I want to — (*Goes toward the hall door.*)

NORA: What are you looking for?

HELMER: Just to see if there's any mail.

NORA: No, no, don't do that, Torvald!

HELMER: Now what?

NORA: Torvald, please. There isn't any.

HELMER: Let me look, though. (*Starts out. Nora, at the piano, strikes the first notes of the tarantella. Helmer, at the door, stops.*) Aha!

NORA: I can't dance tomorrow if I don't practice with you.

HELMER (*going over to her*): Nora dear, are you really so frightened?

NORA: Yes, so terribly frightened. Let me practice right now; there's still time before dinner. Oh, sit down and play for me, Torvald. Direct me. Teach me, the way you always have.

HELMER: Gladly, if it's what you want. (*Sits at the piano.*)

NORA (*snatches the tambourine up from the box, then a long, varicolored shawl, which she throws around herself, whereupon she springs forward and cries out*): Play for me now! Now I'll dance!

Helmer plays and Nora dances. Rank stands behind Helmer at the piano and looks on.

HELMER (*as he plays*): Slower. Slow down.

NORA: Can't change it.

HELMER: Not so violent, Nora!

NORA: Has to be just like this.

HELMER (*stopping*): No, no, that won't do at all.

NORA (*laughing and swinging her tambourine*): Isn't that what I told you?

RANK: Let me play for her.

HELMER (*getting up*): Yes, go on. I can teach her more easily then.

Rank sits at the piano and plays; Nora dances more and more wildly. Helmer has sta-tioned himself by the stove and repeatedly gives her directions; she seems not to hear them; her hair loosens and falls over her shoulders; she does not notice, but goes on dancing. Mrs. Linde enters.

MRS. LINDE (*standing dumbfounded at the door*): Ah — !

NORA (*still dancing*): See what fun, Kristine!

HELMER: But Nora darling, you dance as if your life were at stake.

NORA: And it is.

HELMER: Rank, stop! This is pure madness. Stop it, I say!

Rank breaks off playing, and Nora halts abruptly.

HELMER (*going over to her*): I never would have believed it. You've forgotten everything I taught you.

NORA (*throwing away the tambourine*): You see for yourself.

HELMER: Well, there's certainly room for instruction here.

NORA: Yes, you see how important it is. You've got to teach me to the very last minute. Promise me that, Torvald?

HELMER: You can bet on it.

NORA: You mustn't, either today or tomorrow, think about anything else but me; you mustn't open any letters — or the mailbox —

HELMER: Ah, it's still the fear of that man —

NORA: Oh yes, yes, that too.

HELMER: Nora, it's written all over you — there's already a letter from him out there.

NORA: I don't know. I guess so. But you mustn't read such things now; there mustn't be anything ugly between us before it's all over.

RANK (*quietly to Helmer*): You shouldn't deny her.

HELMER (*putting his arms around her*): The child can have her way. But tomor-row night, after you've danced —

NORA: Then you'll be free.

MAID (*in the doorway, right*): Ma'am, dinner is served.

NORA: We'll be wanting champagne, Helene.

MAID: Very good, ma'am. (*Goes out.*)

HELMER: So — a regular banquet, hm?

NORA: Yes, a banquet — champagne till daybreak! (*Calling out.*) And some macaroons, Helene. Heaps of them — just this once.

HELMER (*taking her hands*): Now, now, now — no hysterics. Be my own little lark again.

NORA: Oh, I will soon enough. But go on in — and you, Dr. Rank. Kristine, help me put up my hair.

RANK (*whispering, as they go*): There's nothing wrong — really wrong, is there?

HELMER: Oh, of course not. It's nothing more than this childish anxiety I was telling you about. (*They go out, right.*)

NORA: Well?

MRS. LINDE: Left town.

NORA: I could see by your face.

MRS. LINDE: He'll be home tomorrow evening. I wrote him a note.

NORA: You shouldn't have. Don't try to stop anything now. After all, it's a wonderful joy, this waiting here for the miracle.

MRS. LINDE: What is it you're waiting for?

NORA: Oh, you can't understand that. Go in to them; I'll be along in a moment.

Mrs. Linde goes into the dining room. Nora stands a short while as if composing herself; then she looks at her watch.

NORA: Five. Seven hours to midnight. Twenty-four hours to the midnight after, and then the tarantella's done. Seven and twenty-four? Thirty-one hours to live.

HELMER (*in the doorway, right*): What's become of the little lark?

NORA (*going toward him with open arms*): Here's your lark!

ACT III

Same scene. The table, with chairs around it, has been moved to the center of the room. A lamp on the table is lit. The hall door stands open. Dance music drifts down from the floor above. Mrs. Linde sits at the table, absently paging through a book, trying to read, but apparently unable to focus her thoughts. Once or twice she pauses, tensely listening for a sound at the outer entrance.

MRS. LINDE (*glancing at her watch*): Not yet — and there's hardly any time left. If only he's not — (*Listening again.*) Ah, there he is. (*She goes out in the hall and cautiously opens the outer door. Quiet footsteps are heard on the stairs. She whispers:*) Come in. Nobody's here.

KROGSTAD (*in the doorway*): I found a note from you at home. What's back of all this?

MRS. LINDE: I just *had* to talk to you.

KROGSTAD: Oh? And it just *had* to be here in this house?

MRS. LINDE: At my place it was impossible; my room hasn't a private entrance. Come in; we're all alone. The maid's asleep, and the Helmers are at the dance upstairs.

KROGSTAD (*entering the room*): Well, well, the Helmers are dancing tonight? Really?

MRS. LINDE: Yes, why not?

KROGSTAD: How true — why not?

MRS. LINDE: All right, Krogstad, let's talk.

KROGSTAD: Do we two have anything more to talk about?

MRS. LINDE: We have a great deal to talk about.

KROGSTAD: I wouldn't have thought so.

MRS. LINDE: No, because you've never understood me, really.

KROGSTAD: Was there anything more to understand — except what's all too common in life? A calculating woman throws over a man the moment a better catch comes by.

MRS. LINDE: You think I'm so thoroughly calculating? You think I broke it off lightly?

KROGSTAD: Didn't you?

MRS. LINDE: Nils — is that what you really thought?

KROGSTAD: If you cared, then why did you write me the way you did?

MRS. LINDE: What else could I do? If I had to break off with you, then it was my job as well to root out everything you felt for me.

KROGSTAD (*wringing his hands*): So that was it. And this — all this, simply for money!

MRS. LINDE: Don't forget I had a helpless mother and two small brothers. We couldn't wait for you, Nils; you had such a long road ahead of you then.

KROGSTAD: That may be; but you still hadn't the right to abandon me for somebody else's sake.

MRS. LINDE: Yes — I don't know. So many, many times I've asked myself if I did have that right.

KROGSTAD (*more softly*): When I lost you, it was as if all the solid ground dissolved from under my feet. Look at me; I'm a half-drowned man now, hanging onto a wreck.

MRS. LINDE: Help may be near.

KROGSTAD: It was near — but then you came and blocked it off.

MRS. LINDE: Without my knowing it, Nils. Today for the first time I learned that it's you I'm replacing at the bank.

KROGSTAD: All right — I believe you. But now that you know, will you step aside?

MRS. LINDE: No, because that wouldn't benefit you in the slightest.

KROGSTAD: Not "benefit" me, hm! I'd step aside anyway.

MRS. LINDE: I've learned to be realistic. Life and hard, bitter necessity have taught me that.

KROGSTAD: And life's taught me never to trust fine phrases.

MRS. LINDE: Then life's taught you a very sound thing. But you do have to trust in actions, don't you?

KROGSTAD: What does that mean?

MRS. LINDE: You said you were hanging on like a half-drowned man to a wreck.

KROGSTAD: I've good reason to say that.

MRS. LINDE: I'm also like a half-drowned woman on a wreck. No one to suffer with; no one to care for.

KROGSTAD: You made your choice.

MRS. LINDE: There wasn't any choice then.

KROGSTAD: So — what of it?

MRS. LINDE: Nils, if only we two shipwrecked people could reach across to each other.

KROGSTAD: What are you saying?

MRS. LINDE: Two on one wreck are at least better off than each on his own.

KROGSTAD: Kristine!

MRS. LINDE: Why do you think I came into town?

KROGSTAD: Did you really have some thought of me?

MRS. LINDE: I have to work to go on living. All my born days, as long as I can remember, I've worked, and it's been my best and my only joy. But now I'm completely alone in the world; it frightens me to be so empty and lost. To work for yourself — there's no joy in that. Nils, give me something — someone to work for.

KROGSTAD: I don't believe all this. It's just some hysterical feminine urge to go out and make a noble sacrifice.

MRS. LINDE: Have you ever found me to be hysterical?

KROGSTAD: Can you honestly mean this? Tell me — do you know everything about my past?

MRS. LINDE: Yes.

KROGSTAD: And you know what they think I'm worth around here.

MRS. LINDE: From what you were saying before, it would seem that with me you could have been another person.

KROGSTAD: I'm positive of that.

MRS. LINDE: Couldn't it happen still?

KROGSTAD: Kristine — you're saying this in all seriousness? Yes, you are! I can see it in you. And do you really have the courage, then — ?

MRS. LINDE: I need to have someone to care for; and your children need a mother. We both need each other. Nils, I have faith that you're good at heart — I'll risk everything together with you.

KROGSTAD (*gripping her hands*): Kristine, thank you, thank you — Now I know I can win back a place in their eyes. Yes — but I forgot —

MRS. LINDE (*listening*): Shh! The tarantella. Go now! Go on!

KROGSTAD: Why? What is it?

MRS. LINDE: Hear the dance up there? When that's over, they'll be coming down.

KROGSTAD: Oh, then I'll go. But — it's all pointless. Of course, you don't know the move I made against the Helmers.

MRS. LINDE: Yes, Nils, I know.

KROGSTAD: And all the same, you have the courage to — ?

MRS. LINDE: I know how far despair can drive a man like you.

KROGSTAD: Oh, if I only could take it all back.

MRS. LINDE: You easily could — your letter's still lying in the mailbox.

KROGSTAD: Are you sure of that?

MRS. LINDE: Positive. But —

KROGSTAD (*looks at her searchingly*): Is that the meaning of it, then? You'll save your friend at any price. Tell me straight out. Is that it?

MRS. LINDE: Nils — anyone who's sold herself for somebody else once isn't going to do it again.

KROGSTAD: I'll demand my letter back.

MRS. LINDE: No, no.

KROGSTAD: Yes, of course. I'll stay here till Helmer comes down; I'll tell him to give me my letter again — that it only involves my dismissal — that he shouldn't read it —

MRS. LINDE: No, Nils, don't call the letter back.

KROGSTAD: But wasn't that exactly why you wrote me to come here?

MRS. LINDE: Yes, in that first panic. But it's been a whole day and night since then, and in that time I've seen such incredible things in this house. Helmer's got to learn everything; this dreadful secret has to be aired; those two have to come to a full understanding; all these lies and evasions can't go on.

KROGSTAD: Well, then, if you want to chance it. But at least there's one thing I can do, and do right away —

MRS. LINDE (*listening*): Go now, go quick! The dance is over. We're not safe another second.

KROGSTAD: I'll wait for you downstairs.

MRS. LINDE: Yes, please do; take me home.

KROGSTAD: I can't believe it; I've never been so happy. (*He leaves by way of the outer door; the door between the room and the hall stays open.*)

MRS. LINDE (*straightening up a bit and getting together her street clothes*): How different now! How different! Someone to work for, to live for — a home to build. Well, it is worth the try! Oh, if they'd only come! (*Listening.*) Ah, there they are. Bundle up. (*She picks up her hat and coat. Nora's and Helmer's voices can be heard outside; a key turns in the lock, and Helmer brings Nora into the hall almost by force. She is wearing the Italian costume with a large black shawl about her; he has on evening dress, with a black domino open over it.*)

NORA (*struggling in the doorway*): No, no, no, not inside! I'm going up again. I don't want to leave so soon.

HELMER: But Nora dear —

NORA: Oh, I beg you, please, Torvald. From the bottom of my heart, *please* — only an hour more!

HELMER: Not a single minute, Nora darling. You know our agreement. Come on, in we go; you'll catch cold out here. (*In spite of her resistance, he gently draws her into the room.*)

MRS. LINDE: Good evening.

NORA: Kristine!

HELMER: Why, Mrs. Linde — are you here so late?

MRS. LINDE: Yes, I'm sorry, but I did want to see Nora in costume.

NORA: Have you been sitting here, waiting for me?

MRS. LINDE: Yes. I didn't come early enough; you were all upstairs; and then I thought I really couldn't leave without seeing you.

HELMER (*removing Nora's shawl*): Yes, take a good look. She's worth looking at, I can tell you that, Mrs. Linde. Isn't she lovely?

MRS. LINDE: Yes, I should say —

HELMER: A dream of loveliness, isn't she? That's what everyone thought at the party, too. But she's horribly stubborn — this sweet little thing. What's to be done with her? Can you imagine, I almost had to use force to pry her away.

NORA: Oh, Torvald, you're going to regret you didn't indulge me, even for just a half hour more.

HELMER: There, you see. She danced her tarantella and got a tumultuous hand — which was well earned, although the performance may have been a bit too naturalistic — I mean it rather overstepped the proprieties of art. But never mind — what's important is, she made a success, an overwhelming success. You think I could let her stay on after that and spoil the effect? Oh no; I took my lovely little Capri girl — my capricious little Capri girl, I should say — took her under my arm; one quick tour of the ballroom, a curtsy to every side, and then — as they say in novels — the beautiful vision disappeared. An exit should always be effective, Mrs. Linde, but that's what I can't get Nora to grasp. Phew, it's hot in here. (*Flings the domino on a chair and opens the door to his room.*) Why's it dark in here? Oh yes, of course. Excuse me. (*He goes in and lights a couple of candles.*)

NORA (*in a sharp, breathless whisper*): So?

MRS. LINDE (*quietly*): I talked with him.

NORA: And — ?

MRS. LINDE: Nora — you must tell your husband everything.

NORA (*dully*): I knew it.

MRS. LINDE: You've got nothing to fear from Krogstad, but you have to speak out.

NORA: I won't tell.

MRS. LINDE: Then the letter will.

NORA: Thanks, Kristine. I know now what's to be done. Shh!

HELMER (*reentering*): Well, then, Mrs. Linde — have you admired her?

MRS. LINDE: Yes, and now I'll say good night.

HELMER: Oh, come, so soon? Is this yours, this knitting?

MRS. LINDE: Yes, thanks. I nearly forgot it.

HELMER: Do you knit, then?

MRS. LINDE: Oh yes.

HELMER: You know what? You should embroider instead.

MRS. LINDE: Really? Why?

HELMER: Yes, because it's a lot prettier. See here, one holds the embroidery so, in the left hand, and then one guides the needle with the right — so — in an easy, sweeping curve — right?

MRS. LINDE: Yes, I guess that's —

HELMER: But, on the other hand, knitting — it can never be anything but ugly. Look, see here, the arms tucked in, the knitting needles going up and down — there's something Chinese about it. Ah, that was really a glorious champagne they served.

MRS. LINDE: Yes, good night, Nora, and don't be stubborn anymore.

HELMER: Well put, Mrs. Linde!

MRS. LINDE: Good night, Mr. Helmer.

HELMER (*accompanying her to the door*): Good night, good night. I hope you get home all right. I'd be very happy to — but you don't have far to go. Good night, good night. (*She leaves. He shuts the door after her and returns.*) There, now, at last we got her out the door. She's a deadly bore, that creature.

NORA: Aren't you pretty tired, Torvald?

HELMER: No, not a bit.

NORA: You're not sleepy?

HELMER: Not at all. On the contrary, I'm feeling quite exhilarated. But you? Yes, you really look tired and sleepy.

NORA: Yes, I'm very tired. Soon now I'll sleep.

HELMER: See! You see! I was right all along that we shouldn't stay longer.

NORA: Whatever you do is always right.

HELMER (*kissing her brow*): Now my little lark talks sense. Say, did you notice what a time Rank was having tonight?

NORA: Oh, was he? I didn't get to speak with him.

HELMER: I scarcely did either, but it's a long time since I've seen him in such high spirits. (*Gazes at her a moment, then comes nearer her.*) Hm — it's marvelous, though, to be back home again — to be completely alone with you. Oh, you bewitchingly lovely young woman!

NORA: Torvald, don't look at me like that!

HELMER: Can't I look at my richest treasure? At all that beauty that's mine, mine alone — completely and utterly.

NORA (*moving around to the other side of the table*): You mustn't talk to me that way tonight.

HELMER (*following her*): The tarantella is still in your blood, I can see — and it makes you even more enticing. Listen. The guests are beginning to go. (*Dropping his voice.*) Nora — it'll soon be quiet through this whole house.

NORA: Yes, I hope so.

HELMER: You do, don't you, my love? Do you realize — when I'm out at a party like this with you — do you know why I talk to you so little, and keep such a distance away; just send you a stolen look now and then — you know why I do it? It's because I'm imagining then that you're my secret darling, my secret bride-to-be, and that no one suspects there's anything between us.

NORA: Yes, yes; oh, yes, I know you're always thinking of me.

HELMER: And then when we leave and I place the shawl over those fine young rounded shoulders — over that wonderful curving neck — then I pretend that you're my young bride, that we're just coming from the wedding, that for the first time I'm bringing you into my house — that for the first time I'm alone with you — completely alone with you, your trembling young beauty! All this evening I've longed for nothing but you. When I saw you turn and sway in the tarantella — my blood was pounding till I couldn't stand it — that's why I brought you down here so early —

NORA: Go away, Torvald! Leave me alone. I don't want all this.

HELMER: What do you mean? Nora, you're teasing me. You will, won't you? Aren't I your husband — ?

A knock at the outside door.

NORA (*startled*): What's that?

HELMER (*going toward the hall*): Who is it?

RANK (*outside*): It's me. May I come in a moment?

HELMER (*with quiet irritation*): Oh, what does he want now? (*Aloud.*) Hold
    on. (*Goes and opens the door.*) Oh, how nice that you didn't just pass
    us by!

RANK: I thought I heard your voice, and then I wanted so badly to have a look
    in. (*Lightly glancing about.*) Ah, me, these old familiar haunts. You have it
    snug and cozy in here, you two.

HELMER: You seemed to be having it pretty cozy upstairs, too.

RANK: Absolutely. Why shouldn't I? Why not take in everything in life? As much
    as you can, anyway, and as long as you can. The wine was superb —

HELMER: The champagne especially.

RANK: You noticed that too? It's amazing how much I could guzzle down.

NORA: Torvald also drank a lot of champagne this evening.

RANK: Oh?

NORA: Yes, and that always makes him so entertaining.

RANK: Well, why shouldn't one have a pleasant evening after a well-spent day?

HELMER: Well spent? I'm afraid I can't claim that.

RANK (*slapping him on the back*): But I can, you see!

NORA: Dr. Rank, you must have done some scientific research today.

RANK: Quite so.

HELMER: Come now — little Nora talking about scientific research!

NORA: And can I congratulate you on the results?

RANK: Indeed you may.

NORA: Then they were good?

RANK: The best possible for both doctor and patient — certainty.

NORA (*quickly and searchingly*): Certainty?

RANK: Complete certainty. So don't I owe myself a gay evening afterwards?

NORA: Yes, you're right, Dr. Rank.

HELMER: I'm with you — just so long as you don't have to suffer for it in the
    morning.

RANK: Well, one never gets something for nothing in life.

NORA: Dr. Rank — are you very fond of masquerade parties?

RANK: Yes, if there's a good array of odd disguises —

NORA: Tell me, what should we two go as at the next masquerade?

HELMER: You little featherhead — already thinking of the next!

RANK: We two? I'll tell you what: you must go as Charmed Life —

HELMER: Yes, but find a costume for *that!*

RANK: Your wife can appear just as she looks every day.

HELMER: That was nicely put. But don't you know what you're going to be?

RANK: Yes, Helmer, I've made up my mind.

HELMER: Well?

RANK: At the next masquerade I'm going to be invisible.

HELMER: That's a funny idea.

RANK: They say there's a hat — black, huge — have you never heard of the hat
    that makes you invisible? You put it on, and then no one on earth can see
    you.

HELMER (*suppressing a smile*): Ah, of course.

RANK: But I'm quite forgetting what I came for. Helmer, give me a cigar, one of the dark Havanas.

HELMER: With the greatest pleasure. (*Holds out his case.*)

RANK: Thanks. (*Takes one and cuts off the tip.*)

NORA (*striking a match*): Let me give you a light.

RANK: Thank you. (*She holds the match for him; he lights the cigar.*) And now good-bye.

HELMER: Good-bye, good-bye, old friend.

NORA: Sleep well, Doctor.

RANK: Thanks for that wish.

NORA: Wish me the same.

RANK: You? All right, if you like — Sleep well. And thanks for the light. (*He nods to them both and leaves.*)

HELMER (*his voice subdued*): He's been drinking heavily.

NORA (*absently*): Could be. (*Helmer takes his keys from his pocket and goes out in the hall.*) Torvald — what are you after?

HELMER: Got to empty the mailbox; it's nearly full. There won't be room for the morning papers.

NORA: Are you working tonight?

HELMER: You know I'm not. Why — what's this? Someone's been at the lock.

NORA: At the lock — ?

HELMER: Yes, I'm positive. What do you suppose — ? I can't imagine one of the maids — ? Here's a broken hairpin. Nora, it's yours —

NORA (*quickly*): Then it must be the children —

HELMER: You'd better break them of that. Hm, hm — well, opened it after all. (*Takes the contents out and calls into the kitchen.*) Helene! Helene, would you put out the lamp in the hall. (*He returns to the room shutting the hall door, then displays the handful of mail.*) Look how it's piled up. (*Sorting through them.*) Now what's this?

NORA (*at the window*): The letter! Oh, Torvald, no!

HELMER: Two calling cards — from Rank.

NORA: From Dr. Rank?

HELMER (*examining them*): "Dr. Rank, Consulting Physician." They were on top. He must have dropped them in as he left.

NORA: Is there anything on them?

HELMER: There's a black cross over the name. See? That's a gruesome notion. He could almost be announcing his own death.

NORA: That's just what he's doing.

HELMER: What! You've heard something? Something he's told you?

NORA: Yes. That when those cards came, he'd be taking his leave of us. He'll shut himself in now and die.

HELMER: Ah, my poor friend! Of course I knew he wouldn't be here much longer. But so soon — And then to hide himself away like a wounded animal.

NORA: If it has to happen, then it's best it happens in silence — don't you think so, Torvald?

HELMER (*pacing up and down*): He'd grown right into our lives. I simply can't imagine him gone. He with his suffering and loneliness — like a dark cloud setting off our sunlit happiness. Well, maybe it's best this way. For him, at least. (*Standing still.*) And maybe for us too, Nora. Now we're thrown back on each other, completely. (*Embracing her.*) Oh you, my darling wife, how can I hold you close enough? You know what, Nora — time and again I've wished you were in some terrible danger, just so I could stake my life and soul and everything, for your sake.

NORA (*tearing herself away, her voice firm and decisive*): Now you must read your mail, Torvald.

HELMER: No, no, not tonight. I want to stay with you, dearest.

NORA: With a dying friend on your mind?

HELMER: You're right. We've both had a shock. There's ugliness between us — these thoughts of death and corruption. We'll have to get free of them first. Until then — we'll stay apart.

NORA (*clinging about his neck*): Torvald — good night! Good night!

HELMER (*kissing her on the cheek*): Good night, little songbird. Sleep well, Nora. I'll be reading my mail now. (*He takes the letters into his room and shuts the door after him.*)

NORA (*with bewildered glances, groping about, seizing Helmer's domino, throwing it around her, and speaking in short, hoarse, broken whispers*): Never see him again. Never, never. (*Putting her shawl over her head.*) Never see the children either — them, too. Never, never. Oh, the freezing black water! The depths — down — Oh, I wish it were over — He has it now; he's reading it — now. Oh no, no, not yet. Torvald, good-bye, you and the children — (*She starts for the hall; as she does, Helmer throws open his door and stands with an open letter in his hand.*)

HELMER: Nora!

NORA (*screams*): Oh — !

HELMER: What is this? You know what's in this letter?

NORA: Yes, I know. Let me go! Let me out!

HELMER (*holding her back*): Where are you going?

NORA (*struggling to break loose*): You can't save me, Torvald!

HELMER (*slumping back*): True! Then it's true what he writes? How horrible! No, no, it's impossible — it can't be true.

NORA: It *is* true. I've loved you more than all this world.

HELMER: Ah, none of your slippery tricks.

NORA (*taking one step toward him*): Torvald — !

HELMER: What *is* this you've blundered into!

NORA: Just let me loose. You're not going to suffer for my sake. You're not going to take on my guilt.

HELMER: No more play-acting. (*Locks the hall door.*) You stay right here and give me a reckoning. You understand what you've done? Answer! You understand?

NORA (*looking squarely at him, her face hardening*): Yes. I'm beginning to understand everything now.

HELMER (*striding about*): Oh, what an awful awakening! In all these eight years — she who was my pride and joy — a hypocrite, a liar — worse, worse — a criminal! How infinitely disgusting it all is! The shame! (*Nora says nothing and goes on looking straight at him. He stops in front of her.*) I should have suspected something of the kind. I should have known. All your father's flimsy values — Be still! All your father's flimsy values have come out in you. No religion, no morals, no sense of duty — Oh, how I'm punished for letting him off! I did it for your sake, and you repay me like this.

NORA: Yes, like this.

HELMER: Now you've wrecked all my happiness — ruined my whole future. Oh, it's awful to think of. I'm in a cheap little grafter's hands; he can do anything he wants with me, ask for anything, play with me like a puppet — and I can't breathe a word. I'll be swept down miserably into the depths on account of a featherbrained woman.

NORA: When I'm gone from this world, you'll be free.

HELMER: Oh, quit posing. Your father had a mess of those speeches too. What good would that ever do me if you were gone from this world, as you say? Not the slightest. He can still make the whole thing known; and if he does, I could be falsely suspected as your accomplice. They might even think that I was behind it — that I put you up to it. And all that I can thank you for — you that I've coddled the whole of our marriage. Can you see now what you've done to me?

NORA (*icily calm*): Yes.

HELMER: It's so incredible, I just can't grasp it. But we'll have to patch up whatever we can. Take off the shawl. I said, take it off! I've got to appease him somehow or other. The thing has to be hushed up at any cost. And as for you and me, it's got to seem like everything between us is just as it was — to the outside world, that is. You'll go right on living in this house, of course. But you can't be allowed to bring up the children; I don't dare trust you with them — Oh, to have to say this to someone I've loved so much! Well, that's done with. From now on happiness doesn't matter; all that matters is saving the bits and pieces, the appearance — (*The doorbell rings. Helmer starts.*) What's that? And so late. Maybe the worst — ? You think he'd — ? Hide, Nora! Say you're sick. (*Nora remains standing motionless. Helmer goes and opens the door.*)

MAID (*half dressed, in the hall*): A letter for Mrs. Helmer.

HELMER: I'll take it. (*Snatches the letter and shuts the door.*) Yes, it's from him. You don't get it; I'm reading it myself.

NORA: Then read it.

HELMER (*by the lamp*): I hardly dare. We may be ruined, you and I. But — I've got to know. (*Rips open the letter, skims through a few lines, glances at an enclosure, then cries out joyfully.*) Nora! (*Nora looks inquiringly at him.*) Nora! Wait — better check it again — Yes, yes, it's true. I'm saved. Nora, I'm saved!

NORA: And I?

HELMER: You too, of course. We're both saved, both of us. Look. He's sent back your note. He says he's sorry and ashamed — that a happy development in his life — oh, who cares what he says! Nora, we're saved! No one can hurt you. Oh, Nora, Nora — but first, this ugliness all has to go. Let me see — (*Takes a look at the note.*) No, I don't want to see it; I want the whole thing to fade like a dream. (*Tears the note and both letters to pieces, throws them into the stove and watches them burn.*) There — now there's nothing left — He wrote that since Christmas Eve you — Oh, they must have been three terrible days for you, Nora.

NORA: I fought a hard fight.

HELMER: And suffered pain and saw no escape but — No, we're not going to dwell on anything unpleasant. We'll just be grateful and keep on repeating: it's over now, it's over! You hear me, Nora? You don't seem to realize — it's over. What's it mean — that frozen look? Oh, poor little Nora, I understand. You can't believe I've forgiven you. But I have, Nora; I swear I have. I know that what you did, you did out of love for me.

NORA: That's true.

HELMER: You loved me the way a wife ought to love her husband. It's simply the means that you couldn't judge. But you think I love you any the less for not knowing how to handle your affairs? No, no — just lean on me; I'll guide you and teach you. I wouldn't be a man if this feminine helplessness didn't make you twice as attractive to me. You mustn't mind those sharp words I said — that was all in the first confusion of thinking my world had collapsed. I've forgiven you, Nora; I swear I've forgiven you.

NORA: My thanks for your forgiveness. (*She goes out through the door, right.*)

HELMER: No, wait — (*Peers in.*) What are you doing in there?

NORA (*inside*): Getting out of my costume.

HELMER (*by the open door*): Yes, do that. Try to calm yourself and collect your thoughts again, my frightened little songbird. You can rest easy now; I've got wide wings to shelter you with. (*Walking about close by the door.*) How snug and nice our home is, Nora. You're safe here; I'll keep you like a hunted dove I've rescued out of a hawk's claws. I'll bring peace to your poor, shuddering heart. Gradually it'll happen, Nora; you'll see. Tomorrow all this will look different to you; then everything will be as it was. I won't have to go on repeating I forgive you; you'll feel it for yourself. How can you imagine I'd ever conceivably want to disown you — or even blame you in any way? Ah, you don't know a man's heart, Nora. For a man there's something indescribably sweet and satisfying in knowing he's forgiven his wife — and forgiven her out of a full and open heart. It's as if she belongs to him in two ways now: in a sense he's given her fresh into the world again, and she's become his wife and his child as well. From now on that's what you'll be to me — you little, bewildered, helpless thing. Don't be afraid of anything, Nora; just open your heart to me, and I'll be conscience and will to you both — (*Nora enters in her regular clothes.*) What's this? Not in bed? You've changed your dress?

NORA: Yes, Torvald, I've changed my dress.

HELMER: But why now, so late?

NORA: Tonight I'm not sleeping.

HELMER: But Nora dear —

NORA (*looking at her watch*): It's still not so very late. Sit down, Torvald; we have a lot to talk over. (*She sits at one side of the table.*)

HELMER: Nora — what is this? That hard expression —

NORA: Sit down. This'll take some time. I have a lot to say.

HELMER (*sitting at the table directly opposite her*): You worry me, Nora. And I don't understand you.

NORA: No, that's exactly it. You don't understand me. And I've never understood you either — until tonight. No, don't interrupt. You can just listen to what I say. We're closing out accounts, Torvald.

HELMER: How do you mean that?

NORA (*after a short pause*): Doesn't anything strike you about our sitting here like this?

HELMER: What's that?

NORA: We've been married now eight years. Doesn't it occur to you that this is the first time we two, you and I, man and wife, have ever talked seriously together?

HELMER: What do you mean — seriously?

NORA: In eight whole years — longer even — right from our first acquaintance, we've never exchanged a serious word on any serious thing.

HELMER: You mean I should constantly go and involve you in problems you couldn't possibly help me with?

NORA: I'm not talking of problems. I'm saying that we've never sat down seriously together and tried to get to the bottom of anything.

HELMER: But dearest, what good would that ever do you?

NORA: That's the point right there: you've never understood me. I've been wronged greatly, Torvald — first by Papa, and then by you.

HELMER: What! By us — the two people who've loved you more than anyone else?

NORA (*shaking her head*): You never loved me. You've thought it fun to be in love with me, that's all.

HELMER: Nora, what a thing to say!

NORA: Yes, it's true now, Torvald. When I lived at home with Papa, he told me all his opinions, so I had the same ones too; or if they were different I hid them, since he wouldn't have cared for that. He used to call me his doll-child, and he played with me the way I played with my dolls. Then I came into your house —

HELMER: How can you speak of our marriage like that?

NORA (*unperturbed*): I mean, then I went from Papa's hands into yours. You arranged everything to your own taste, and so I got the same taste as you — or I pretended to; I can't remember. I guess a little of both, first one, then the other. Now when I look back, it seems as if I'd lived here like a beggar — just from hand to mouth. I've lived by doing tricks for you, Torvald. But that's the way you wanted it. It's a great sin what you and Papa did to me. You're to blame that nothing's become of me.

HELMER: Nora, how unfair and ungrateful you are! Haven't you been happy
here?

NORA: No, never. I thought so — but I never have.

HELMER: Not — not happy!

NORA: No, only lighthearted. And you've always been so kind to me. But our
home's been nothing but a playpen. I've been your doll-wife here, just as
at home I was Papa's doll-child. And in turn the children have been my
dolls. I thought it was fun when you played with me, just as they
thought it fun when I played with them. That's been our marriage, Torvald.

HELMER: There's some truth in what you're saying — under all the raving exaggeration. But it'll all be different after this. Playtime's over; now for
the schooling.

NORA: Whose schooling — mine or the children's?

HELMER: Both yours and the children's, dearest.

NORA: Oh, Torvald, you're not the man to teach me to be a good wife to you.

HELMER: And you can say that?

NORA: And I — how am I equipped to bring up children?

HELMER: Nora!

NORA: Didn't you say a moment ago that that was no job to trust me with?

HELMER: In a flare of temper! Why fasten on that?

NORA: Yes, but you were so very right. I'm not up to the job. There's another
job I have to do first. I have to try to educate myself. You can't help me
with that. I've got to do it alone. And that's why I'm leaving you now.

HELMER (*jumping up*): What's that?

NORA: I have to stand completely alone, if I'm ever going to discover myself
and the world out there. So I can't go on living with you.

HELMER: Nora, Nora!

NORA: I want to leave right away. Kristine should put me up for the night —

HELMER: You're insane! You've no right! I forbid you!

NORA: From here on, there's no use forbidding me anything. I'll take with me
whatever is mine. I don't want a thing from you, either now or later.

HELMER: What kind of madness is this!

NORA: Tomorrow I'm going home — I mean, home where I came from. It'll be
easier up there to find something to do.

HELMER: Oh, you blind, incompetent child!

NORA: I must learn to be competent, Torvald.

HELMER: Abandon your home, your husband, your children! And you're not
even thinking what people will say.

NORA: I can't be concerned about that. I only know how essential this is.

HELMER: Oh, it's outrageous. So you'll run out like this on your most sacred
vows.

NORA: What do you think are my most sacred vows?

HELMER: And I have to tell you that! Aren't they your duties to your husband
and children?

NORA: I have other duties equally sacred.

HELMER: That isn't true. What duties are they?

NORA: Duties to myself.

HELMER: Before all else, you're a wife and mother.

NORA: I don't believe in that anymore. I believe that, before all else, I'm a human being, no less than you — or anyway, I ought to try to become one. I know the majority thinks you're right, Torvald, and plenty of books agree with you, too. But I can't go on believing what the majority says, or what's written in books. I have to think over these things myself and try to understand them.

HELMER: Why can't you understand your place in your own home? On a point like that, isn't there one everlasting guide you can turn to? Where's your religion?

NORA: Oh, Torvald, I'm really not sure what religion is.

HELMER: What — ?

NORA: I only know what the minister said when I was confirmed. He told me religion was this thing and that. When I get clear and away by myself, I'll go into that problem too. I'll see if what the minister said was right, or, in any case, if it's right for me.

HELMER: A young woman your age shouldn't talk like that. If religion can't move you, I can try to rouse your conscience. You do have some moral feeling? Or, tell me — has that gone too?

NORA: It's not easy to answer that, Torvald. I simply don't know. I'm all confused about these things. I just know I see them so differently from you. I find out, for one thing, that the law's not at all what I'd thought — but I can't get it through my head that the law is fair. A woman hasn't a right to protect her dying father or save her husband's life! I can't believe that.

HELMER: You talk like a child. You don't know anything of the world you live in.

NORA: No, I don't. But now I'll begin to learn for myself. I'll try to discover who's right, the world or I.

HELMER: Nora, you're sick; you've got a fever. I almost think you're out of your head.

NORA: I've never felt more clearheaded and sure in my life.

HELMER: And — clearheaded and sure — you're leaving your husband and children?

NORA: Yes.

HELMER: Then there's only one possible reason.

NORA: What?

HELMER: You no longer love me.

NORA: No. That's exactly it.

HELMER: Nora! You can't be serious!

NORA: Oh, this is so hard, Torvald — you've been so kind to me always. But I can't help it. I don't love you anymore.

HELMER (*struggling for composure*): Are you also clearheaded and sure about that?

NORA: Yes, completely. That's why I can't go on staying here.

HELMER: Can you tell me what I did to lose your love?

NORA: Yes, I can tell you. It was this evening when the miraculous thing didn't come — then I knew you weren't the man I'd imagined.

HELMER: Be more explicit; I don't follow you.

NORA: I've waited now so patiently eight long years — for, my Lord, I know miracles don't come every day. Then this crisis broke over me, and such a certainty filled me: *now* the miraculous event would occur. While Krogstad's letter was lying out there, I never for an instant dreamed that you could give in to his terms. I was so utterly sure you'd say to him: go on, tell your tale to the whole wide world. And when he'd done that —

HELMER: Yes, what then? When I'd delivered my own wife into shame and disgrace —

NORA: When he'd done that, I was so utterly sure that you'd step forward, take the blame on yourself and say: I am the guilty one.

HELMER: Nora — !

NORA: You're thinking I'd never accept such a sacrifice from you? No, of course not. But what good would my protests be against you? That was the miracle I was waiting for, in terror and hope. And to stave that off, I would have taken my life.

HELMER: I'd gladly work for you day and night, Nora — and take on pain and deprivation. But there's no one who gives up honor for love.

NORA: Millions of women have done just that.

HELMER: Oh, you think and talk like a silly child.

NORA: Perhaps. But you neither think nor talk like the man I could join myself to. When your big fright was over — and it wasn't from any threat against me, only for what might damage you — when all the danger was past, for you it was just as if nothing had happened. I was exactly the same, your little lark, your doll, that you'd have to handle with double care now that I'd turned out so brittle and frail. (*Gets up.*) Torvald — in that instant it dawned on me that for eight years I've been living here with a stranger, and that I've even conceived three children — oh, I can't stand the thought of it! I could tear myself to bits.

HELMER (*heavily*): I see. There a gulf that's opened between us — that's clear. Oh, but Nora, can't we bridge it somehow?

NORA: The way I am now, I'm no wife for you.

HELMER: I have the strength to make myself over.

NORA: Maybe — if your doll gets taken away.

HELMER: But to part! To part from you! No, Nora no — I can't imagine it.

NORA (*going out, right*): All the more reason why it has to be. (*She reenters with her coat and a small overnight bag, which she puts on a chair by the table.*)

HELMER: Nora, Nora, not now! Wait till tomorrow.

NORA: I can't spend the night in a strange man's room.

HELMER: But couldn't we live here like brother and sister —

NORA: You know very well how long that would last. (*Throws her shawl about her.*) Good-bye, Torvald. I won't look in on the children. I know they're in better hands than mine. The way I am now, I'm no use to them.

HELMER: But someday, Nora — someday — ?

NORA: How can I tell? I haven't the least idea what'll become of me.

HELMER: But you're my wife, now and wherever you go.

NORA: Listen, Torvald — I've heard that when a wife deserts her husband's house just as I'm doing, then the law frees him from all responsibility. In any case, I'm freeing you from being responsible. Don't feel yourself bound, any more than I will. There has to be absolute freedom for us both. Here, take your ring back. Give me mine.

HELMER: That too?

NORA: That too.

HELMER: There it is.

NORA: Good. Well, now it's all over. I'm putting the keys here. The maids know all about keeping up the house — better than I do. Tomorrow, after I've left town, Kristine will stop by to pack up everything that's mine from home. I'd like those things shipped up to me.

HELMER: Over! All over! Nora, won't you ever think about me?

NORA: I'm sure I'll think of you often, and about the children and the house here.

HELMER: May I write you?

NORA: No — never. You're not to do that.

HELMER: Oh, but let me send you —

NORA: Nothing. Nothing.

HELMER: Or help you if you need it.

NORA: No. I accept nothing from strangers.

HELMER: Nora — can I never be more than a stranger to you?

NORA (*picking up her overnight bag*): Ah, Torvald — it would take the greatest miracle of all —

HELMER: Tell me the greatest miracle!

NORA: You and I both would have to transform ourselves to the point that — Oh, Torvald, I've stopped believing in miracles.

HELMER: But I'll believe. Tell me! Transform ourselves to the point that — ?

NORA: That our living together could be a true marriage. (*She goes out down the hall.*)

HELMER (*sinks down on a chair by the door, face buried in his hands*): Nora! Nora! (*Looking about and rising.*) Empty. She's gone. (*A sudden hope leaps in him.*) The greatest miracle — ?

From below, the sound of a door slamming shut.

തയ

AUGUST STRINDBERG (1849–1912), *the preeminent Swedish dramatist, was astonishingly productive during a lifetime marked by periods of paranoia and emotional instability. His collected plays, novels, short stories, and essays comprise fifty-five volumes, in addition to his highly original work as an amateur painter during a period in which the arts flourished in Scandinavia. Born in Stockholm, the fourth of eleven children of a mother who was a servant and a father who was a moderately successful businessman, Strindberg later wrote that his childhood was a nightmare, torn between his pious mother's sense of inferiority and his strict father's emotional reserve. In 1867 he began to study at Uppsala University, but as his biog-*

rapher Barry Jacobs has observed, "he was too impatient to concentrate on his studies for very long and too poor to taste many of the pleasures of student life."

Strindberg became a playwright in 1869, when, at the age of twenty, he failed as an actor at the Royal Theatre in Stockholm. The story goes that he attempted suicide by taking opium, but when the effects of the drug wore off, he lay in bed wondering how he could ever face his father again. The idea for a play came to his mind, and he completed it four hours later. This play has been lost, but his other work from his first year as a writer has survived, including the full-length play The Freethinker, about a young teacher who refused to renounce the teaching of the American Unitarian reformer Theodore Parker, whose work Strindberg had read and admired. In 1872 he wrote a version of his first successful play, Master Olof, a historical drama that has become a classic in Swedish theater.

Strindberg's intellectual interests were widespread. In 1876 he, like his contemporary Henrik Ibsen, came under the influence of the Danish critic Georg Brandes, who believed that literature should deal with contemporary issues. A decade later Strindberg was fascinated by Friedrich Nietzsche's idea of the superman and the psychology of the "superior individual," before he moved on to fervent study of current scientific and occult theories of hypnotism, animal magnetism, alchemy, and psychic travel. He was pessimistic about human development, deriving his theories from his interpretation of Charles Darwin's explanation of evolution in The Origin of Species (1865). Such plays as Miss Julie (1888) contributed to a literary movement called naturalism, based on the idea that each individual was shaped more by environment and heredity than by acts of free will. Strindberg was such a brilliant playwright that, like Ibsen, his achievement in the theater it gave it new life, rescuing it from the artifice and artificiality that predominated on the stage since the beginning of the nineteenth century.

Ibsen and Strindberg contributed differently to the birth of the modern theater. In 1879 the French writer Edmond de Goncourt predicted that the novel would kill off the drama in the next fifty years, because the novel offered more subtle psychological analysis of the complex human personality than any play currently on the stage. First Ibsen, and then Strindberg, proved him wrong. In such plays as A Doll House, Ibsen primarily worked within the conventions of the realistic stage productions of his time, revolutionizing the content of his plays to introduce controversial subject matter instead of relying on banal entertainments or didactic "thesis" plays. In such plays as Miss Julie, Strindberg visualized a new kind of physical theater, free of what he considered the claptrap of elaborate scenery and costumes. He began to experiment with different kinds of long and short plays and used the symbolism inherent in the poetic use of words, music, and dance in order to suggest a deeper psychological truth about his characters.

In the last months of 1888, when Strindberg began to write Miss Julie, he was living in Copenhagen and was near the end of his marriage to his first wife, Siri von Essen, a successful actress. In previous years he had explored the theme of social mobility he was to dramatize in Miss Julie in works of fiction and autobiography such as Son of a Servant (1886) and Defense of a Madman (1887). In Copenhagen he began to write a new kind of play and tried to start his own theater company, modeled after the experimental Theatre Libre company recently opened in Paris. In this period of his life, as Strindberg wrote a friend, he wanted to "write plays that will free us from

*the necessity of dragging costumes, decorations, and props along with us." Earlier in
1888 he wrote* The Father *for this Parisian company, but it was rejected. This play
dramatized the battle between the sexes by showing how a wife could drive her husband insane by insinuating that he is not the father of their child.*

In Miss Julie *Strindberg went further in his effort to heighten dramatic conflict
on stage, creating a play with only three characters and escalating the tension between
them by introducing elements of an erotic triangle in addition to a significant difference in their social status. When the Danish censors in Copenhagen refused to allow
the first scheduled performance of* Miss Julie *on March 1, 1889, Strindberg arranged
for a private performance to be given before an audience of 150 male students and a
half-dozen women at Copenhagen University two weeks later.*

A reporter from the Stockholm paper Dagens Nyheter *was present for this premiere. He described the crowded, "depressing room" with a low ceiling and no venti-
lation and a gas light shining through the half-transparent curtain. The stage set
seemed to make more impression on the reporter than the play itself: "To our surprise,
it resembles a real kitchen. A plate-rack, a kitchen table, a speaking tube to the floor
above, a big stove with rows of copper pots above it — in short, everything is there,
presenting the living image of a real kitchen." The reporter thought little of the performance of Strindberg's wife in the title role, but his comment about her suggested the
conventional moral judgment of the time, placing all the blame on the character of
Miss Julie for what happens in the play: "She is cold, much too cold, and one gets no
impression at all of the kind of woman who would seduce a man like Jean." Strindberg
was present at the performance, but he refused to watch the stage. Instead, the reporter
observed that he "stood half-hidden behind a door, his face pale and twisted with jealousy," convinced that his wife was having an affair with the actor playing Jean.*

*Strindberg's attitude toward women was inconsistent. During his second mar-
riage he wrote in a letter that "woman is to me the earth and all its glory, the bond that
binds, and of all the evil the worst evil I have seen is the female sex." Finally, toward
the end of his life, during his third marriage, he wrote in* A Blue Book *(1901), "When
I approach a woman as a lover, I look up to her, I see something of the mother in her,
and this I respect. I assume a subordinate position, become childish and puerile, and
actually am subordinate, like most men . . . I put her on a pedestal." His always passionately held, often contradictory ideas about women made riveting drama when
translated onto the stage.*

In later works such as A Dream Play *(1902) and* The Ghost Sonata *(1907),
Strindberg developed his characters' upheavals of emotion even further than in* Miss
Julie. *In these plays he gave "free play" to his imagination, as the critic John Gassner
has observed, "calling for a kaleidoscopic succession of outdoor and indoor settings,
symbolic structures or props, and scenic transformations like the flower bud on the
roof [in* A Dream Play*] that opens into a gigantic chrysanthemum." Here Strindberg
created a new kind of expressionist drama that influenced later dramatists such as Eugene O'Neill and paved the way for experiments in absurdist and surrealistic theater
in the work of Samuel Beckett and Tennessee Williams.*

*Considering the controversial content of his plays and their often difficult stag-
ing requirements, we can understand why for most of his life Strindberg was "an author in search of an audience."* Miss Julie *was not seen in Stockholm until 1906, but
the following year, when Strindberg produced it in his own Intimate Theatre there, it*

was given 134 performances. One of the most popular modern plays, it has often been televised and filmed, most notably in 1951 by the great Swedish director Alf Sjöberg.

RELATED COMMENTARY: *August Strindberg, "From the Preface to* Miss Julie," *page 2024.*

AUGUST STRINDBERG

Miss Julie   1888

TRANSLATED BY HARRY G. CARLSON

CHARACTERS

MISS JULIE, *twenty-five years old*
JEAN, *her father's valet, thirty years old*
KRISTINE, *her father's cook, thirty-five years old*

The action takes place in the count's kitchen on midsummer eve.

SETTING

A large kitchen, the ceiling and side walls of which are hidden by draperies. The rear wall runs diagonally from down left to up right. On the wall down left are two shelves with copper, iron, and pewter utensils; the shelves are lined with scalloped paper. Visible to the right is most of a set of large, arched glass doors, through which can be seen a fountain with a statue of Cupid, lilac bushes in bloom, and the tops of some Lombardy poplars. At down left is the corner of a large tiled stove; a portion of its hood is showing. At right, one end of the servants' white pine dining table juts out; several chairs stand around it. The stove is decorated with birch branches; juniper twigs are strewn on the floor. On the end of the table stands a large Japanese spice jar, filled with lilac blossoms. An ice-box, a sink, and a washstand. Above the door is an old-fashioned bell on a spring; to the left of the door, the mouthpiece of a speaking tube is visible.

Kristine is frying something on the stove. She is wearing a light-colored cotton dress and an apron. Jean enters. He is wearing livery and carries a pair of high riding-boots with spurs, which he puts down on the floor where they can be seen by the audience.

JEAN: Miss Julie's crazy again tonight; absolutely crazy!

KRISTINE: So you finally came back?

JEAN: I took the Count to the station and when I returned past the barn I stopped in for a dance. Who do I see but Miss Julie leading off the dance with the gamekeeper! But as soon as she saw me she rushed over to ask me for the next waltz. And she's been waltzing ever since — I've never seen anything like it. She's crazy!

KRISTINE: She always has been, but never as bad as the last two weeks since her engagement was broken off.

JEAN: Yes, I wonder what the real story was there. He was a gentleman, even if he wasn't rich. Ah! These people have such romantic ideas. (*Sits at the end of the table.*) Still, it's strange, isn't it? I mean that she'd rather stay home with the servants on midsummer eve instead of going with her father to visit relatives?

KRISTINE: She's probably embarrassed after that row with her fiancé.

JEAN: Probably! He gave a good account of himself, though. Do you know how it happened, Kristine? I saw it, you know, though I didn't let on I had.

KRISTINE: No! You saw it?

JEAN: Yes, I did. ——— That evening they were out near the stable, and she was "training" him — as she called it. Do you know what she did? She made him jump over her riding crop, the way you'd teach a dog to jump. He jumped twice and she hit him each time. But the third time he grabbed the crop out of her hand, hit her with it across the cheek, and broke it in pieces. Then he left.

KRISTINE: So, that's what happened! I can't believe it!

JEAN: Yes, that's the way it went! ——— What have you got for me that's tasty, Kristine?

KRISTINE (*serving him from the pan*): Oh, it's only a piece of kidney I cut from the veal roast.

JEAN (*smelling the food*): Beautiful! That's my favorite *délice*. (*Feeling the plate.*) But you could have warmed the plate!

KRISTINE: You're fussier than the Count himself, once you start! (*She pulls his hair affectionately.*)

JEAN (*angry*): Stop it, leave my hair alone! You know I'm touchy about that.

KRISTINE: Now, now, it's only love, you know that. (*Jean eats. Kristine opens a bottle of beer.*)

JEAN: Beer? On midsummer eve? No thank you! I can do better than that. (*Opens a drawer in the table and takes out a bottle of red wine with yellow sealing wax.*) See that? Yellow seal! Give me a glass! A wine glass! I'm drinking this *pur*.

KRISTINE: (*returns to the stove and puts on a small saucepan*): God help the woman who gets you for a husband! What a fussbudget.

JEAN: Nonsense! You'd be damned lucky to get a man like me. It certainly hasn't done you any harm to have people call me your sweetheart. (*Tastes the wine.*) Good! Very good! Just needs a little warming. (*Warms the glass between his hands.*) We bought this in Dijon. Four francs a liter, not counting the cost of the bottle, or the customs duty. ——— What are you cooking now? It stinks like hell!

KRISTINE: Oh, some slop Miss Julie wants to give Diana.

JEAN: Watch your language, Kristine. But why should you have to cook for that damn mutt on midsummer eve? Is she sick?

KRISTINE: Yes, she's sick! She sneaked out with the gatekeeper's dog — and now there's hell to pay. Miss Julie won't have it!

JEAN: Miss Julie has too much pride about some things and not enough about others, just like her mother was. The Countess was most at home in the kitchen and the cowsheds, but a *one*-horse carriage wasn't elegant enough for her. The cuffs of her blouse was dirty, but she had to have her coat of arms on her cufflinks. ——— And Miss Julie won't take proper care of herself either. If you ask me, she just isn't refined. Just now, when she was dancing in the barn, she pulled the gamekeeper away from Anna and made him dance with her. *We* wouldn't behave like that, but

that's what happens when aristocrats pretend they're common people —
they get *common!* ———— But she is quite a woman! Magnificent! What
shoulders, and what — et cetera!

KRISTINE: Oh, don't overdo it! I've heard what Clara says, and she dresses her.

JEAN: Ha, Clara! You're all jealous of each other! I've been out riding with
her . . . And the way she dances!

KRISTINE: Listen, Jean! You're going to dance with me, when I'm finished here,
aren't you?

JEAN: Of course I will.

KRISTINE: Promise?

JEAN: Promise? When I say I'll do something, I do it! By the way, the kidney
was very good. (*Corks the bottle.*)

JULIE (*in the doorway to someone outside*): I'll be right back! You go ahead for
now! (*Jean sneaks the bottle back into the table drawer and gets up respectfully.
Miss Julie enters and crosses to Kristine by the stove.*) Well? Is it ready? (*Kristine indicates that Jean is present.*)

JEAN (*gallantly*): Are you ladies up to something secret?

JULIE (*flicking her handkerchief in his face*): None of your business!

JEAN: Hmm! I like the smell of violets!

JULIE (*coquettishly*): Shame on you! So you know about perfumes, too? You certainly know how to dance. Ah, ah! No peeking! Go away.

JEAN (*boldly but respectfully*): Are you brewing up a magic potion for midsummer eve? Something to prophecy by under a lucky star, so you'll catch a
glimpse of your future husband!

JULIE (*caustically*): You'd need sharp eyes to see him! (*To Kristine.*) Pour out half
a bottle and cork it well. ———— Come and dance a schottische with me,
Jean . . .

JEAN (*hesitating*): I don't want to be impolite to anyone, and I've already
promised this dance to Kristine . . .

JULIE: Oh, she can have another one — can't you Kristine? Won't you lend me
Jean?

KRISTINE: It's not up to me, ma'am. (*To Jean.*) If the mistress is so generous, it
wouldn't do for you to say no. Go on, Jean, and thank her for the honor.

JEAN: To be honest, and no offense intended, I wonder whether it's wise for
you to dance twice running with the same partner, especially since these
people are quick to jump to conclusions . . .

JULIE (*flaring up*): What's that? What sort of conclusions? What do you mean?

JEAN (*submissively*): If you don't understand, ma'am, I must speak more
plainly. It doesn't look good to play favorites with your servants. . . .

JULIE: Play favorites! What an idea! I'm astonished! As mistress of the house, I
honor your dance with my presence. And when I dance, I want to dance
with someone who can lead, so I won't look ridiculous.

JEAN: As you order, ma'am! I'm at your service!

JULIE (*gently*): Don't take it as an order! On a night like this we're all just ordinary people having fun, so we'll forget about rank. Now, take my
arm! ———— Don't worry, Kristine! I won't steal your sweetheart! (*Jean offers his arm and leads Miss Julie out.*)

MIME

The following should be played as if the actress playing Kristine were really alone. When she has to, she turns her back to the audience. She does not look toward them, nor does she hurry as if she were afraid they would grow impatient. Schottische music played on a fiddle sounds in the distance. Kristine hums along with the music. She clears the table, washes the dishes, dries them, and puts them away. She takes off her apron. From a table drawer she removes a small mirror and leans it against the bowl of lilacs on the table. She lights a candle, heats a hairpin over the flame, and uses it to set a curl on her forehead. She crosses to the door and listens, then returns to the table. She finds the handkerchief Miss Julie left behind, picks it up, and smells it. Then, preoccupied, she spreads it out, stretches it, smooths out the wrinkles, and folds it into quarters, and so forth.

JEAN (*enters alone*): God, she really *is* crazy! What a way to dance! Everybody's laughing at her behind her back. What do you make of it, Kristine?

KRISTINE: Ah! It's that time of the month for her, and she always gets peculiar like that. Are you going to dance with me now?

JEAN: You're not mad at me, are you, for leaving . . . ?

KRISTINE: Of course not! ——— Why should I be, for a little thing like that? Besides, I know my place . . .

JEAN (*puts his arm around her waist*): You're a sensible girl, Kristine, and you'd make a good wife . . .

JULIE (*entering; uncomfortably surprised; with forced good humor*): What a charming escort — running away from his partner.

JEAN: On the contrary, Miss Julie. Don't you see how I rushed back to the partner I abandoned!

JULIE (*changing her tone*): You know, you're a superb dancer! ——— But why are you wearing livery on a holiday? Take it off at once!

JEAN: Then I must ask you to go outside for a moment. You see, my black coat is hanging over here . . . (*Gestures and crosses right.*)

JULIE: Are you embarrassed about changing your coat in front of me? Well, go in your room then. Either that or stay and I'll turn my back.

JEAN: With your permission, ma'am! (*He crosses right. His arm is visible as he changes his jacket.*)

JULIE (*to Kristine*): Tell me, Kristine — you two are so close — . Is Jean your fiancé?

KRISTINE: Fiancé? Yes, if you wish. We can call him that.

JULIE: What do you mean?

KRISTINE: You had a fiancé yourself, didn't you? So . . .

JULIE: Well, we were properly engaged . . .

KRISTINE: But nothing came of it, did it? (*Jean returns dressed in a frock coat and bowler hat.*)

JULIE: *Très gentil, monsieur Jean! Très gentil!*

JEAN: *Vous voulez plaisanter, madame!*

JULIE: *Et vous voulez parler français!* Where did you learn that?

JEAN: In Switzerland, when I was wine steward in one of the biggest hotels in Lucerne!

JULIE: You look like a real gentleman in that coat! *Charmant!* (*Sits at the table.*)

JEAN: Oh, you're flattering me!

JULIE (*offended*): Flattering you?

JEAN: My natural modesty forbids me to believe that you would really compliment someone like me, and so I took the liberty of assuming that you were exaggerating, which polite people call flattering.

JULIE: Where did you learn to talk like that? You must have been to the theatre often.

JEAN: Of course. And I've done a lot of traveling.

JULIE: But you come from here, don't you?

JEAN: My father was a farm hand on the district attorney's estate nearby. I used to see you when you were little, but you never noticed me.

JULIE: No! Really?

JEAN: Sure. I remember one time especially . . . but I can't talk about that.

JULIE: Oh, come now! Why not? Just this once!

JEAN: No, I really couldn't, not now. Some other time, perhaps.

JULIE: Why some other time? What's so dangerous about now?

JEAN: It's not dangerous, but there are obstacles. ——— Her, for example. (*Indicating Kristine, who has fallen asleep in a chair by the stove.*)

JULIE: What a pleasant wife she'll make! She probably snores, too.

JEAN: No, she doesn't, but she talks in her sleep.

JULIE (*cynically*): How do *you* know?

JEAN (*audaciously*): I've heard her! (*Pause, during which they stare at each other.*)

JULIE: Why don't you sit down?

JEAN: I couldn't do that in your presence.

JULIE: But if I order you to?

JEAN: Then I'd obey.

JULIE: Sit down, then. ——— No, wait. Can you get me something to drink first?

JEAN: I don't know what we have in the ice box. I think there's only beer.

JULIE: Why do you say "only"? My tastes are so simple I prefer beer to wine. (*Jean takes a bottle of beer from the ice-box and opens it. He looks for a glass and a plate in the cupboard and serves her.*)

JEAN: Here you are, ma'am.

JULIE: Thank you. Won't you have something yourself?

JEAN: I'm not partial to beer, but if it's an order . . .

JULIE: An order? ——— Surely a gentleman can keep his lady company.

JEAN: You're right, of course. (*Opens a bottle and gets a glass.*)

JULIE: Now, drink to my health! (*He hesitates.*) What? A man of the world — and shy?

JEAN (*in mock romantic fashion, he kneels and raises his glass*): Skål to my mistress!

JULIE: Bravo! ——— Now kiss my shoe, to finish it properly. (*Jean hesitates, then boldly seizes her foot and kisses it lightly.*) Perfect! You should have been an actor.

JEAN (*rising*): That's enough now, Miss Julie! Someone might come in and see us.

JULIE: What of it?

JEAN: People talk, that's what! If you knew how their tongues were wagging just now at the dance, you'd . . .

JULIE: What were they saying? Tell me! —— Sit down!

JEAN (*sits*): I don't want to hurt you, but they were saying things —— suggestive things, that, that . . . well, you can figure it out for yourself! You're not a child. If a woman is seen drinking alone with a man — let alone a servant — at night — then . . .

JULIE: Then what? Besides, we're not alone. Kristine is here.

JEAN: Asleep!

JULIE: Then I'll wake her up. (*Rising.*) Kristine! Are you asleep? (*Kristine mumbles in her sleep.*)

JULIE: Kristine! —— She certainly can sleep!

KRISTINE (*in her sleep*): The Count's boots are brushed — put the coffee on — right away, right away — uh, huh — oh!

JULIE (*grabbing Kristine's nose*): Will you wake up!

JEAN (*severely*): Leave her alone — let her sleep!

JULIE: (*sharply*): What?

JEAN: Someone who's been standing over a stove all day has a right to be tired by now. Sleep should be respected . . .

JULIE (*changing her tone*): What a considerate thought — it does you credit — thank you! (*Offering her hand.*) Come outside and pick some lilacs for me! (*During the following, Kristine awakens and shambles sleepily off right to bed.*)

JEAN: Go with you?

JULIE: With me!

JEAN: We couldn't do that! Absolutely not!

JULIE: I don't understand. Surely you don't imagine . . .

JEAN: No, I don't, but the others might.

JULIE: What? That I've fallen in love with a servant?

JEAN: I'm not a conceited man, but such things happen — and for these people, nothing is sacred.

JULIE: I do believe you're an aristocrat!

JEAN: Yes, I am.

JULIE: And I'm stepping down . . .

JEAN: Don't step down, Miss Julie, take my advice. No one'll believe you stepped down voluntarily. People will always say you fell.

JULIE: I have a higher opinion of people than you. Come and see! —— Come! (*She stares at him broodingly.*)

JEAN: You're very strange, do you know that?

JULIE: Perhaps! But so are you! —— For that matter, everything is strange. Life, people, everything. Like floating scum, drifting on and on across the water, until it sinks down and down! That reminds me of a dream I have now and then. I've climbed up on top of a pillar. I sit there and see no way of getting down. I get dizzy when I look down, and I must get down, but I don't have the courage to jump. I can't hold on firmly, and I long to be able to fall, but I don't fall. And yet I'll have no peace until I get down, no rest unless I get down, down on the ground! And if I did get down to the ground, I'd want to be under the earth . . . Have you ever felt anything like that?

JEAN: No. I dream that I'm lying under a high tree in a dark forest. I want to get up, up on top, and look out over the bright landscape, where the sun is shining, and plunder the bird's nest up there, where the golden eggs lie. And I climb and climb, but the trunk's so thick and smooth, and it's so far to the first branch. But I know if I just reached that first branch, I'd go right to the top, like up a ladder. I haven't reached it yet, but I will, even if it's only in a dream!

JULIE: Here I am chattering with you about dreams. Come, let's go out! Just into the park! (*She offers him her arm, and they start to leave.*)

JEAN: We'll have to sleep on nine midsummer flowers, Miss Julie, to make our dreams come true! (*They turn at the door. Jean puts his hand to his eye.*)

JULIE: Did you get something in your eye?

JEAN: It's nothing — just a speck — it'll be gone in a minute.

JULIE: My sleeve must have brushed against you. Sit down and let me help you. (*She takes him by the arm and seats him. She tilts his head back and with the tip of a handkerchief tries to remove the speck.*) Sit still, absolutely still! (*She slaps his hand.*) Didn't you hear me? —— Why, you're trembling; the big, strong man is trembling! (*Feels his biceps.*) What muscles you have!

JEAN (*warning*): Miss Julie!

JULIE: Yes, *monsieur* Jean.

JEAN: Attention! Je ne suis qu'un homme!

JULIE: Will you sit still! —— There! Now it's gone! Kiss my hand and thank me.

JEAN (*rising*): Miss Julie, listen to me! —— Kristine has gone to bed! —— Will you listen to me!

JULIE Kiss my hand first!

JEAN: Listen to me!

JULIE: Kiss my hand first!

JEAN: All right, but you've only yourself to blame!

JULIE: For what?

JEAN: For what? Are you still a child at twenty-five? Don't you know that's it's dangerous to play with fire?

JULIE: Not for me. I'm insured.

JEAN (*boldly*): No, you're not! But even if you were, there's combustible material close by.

JULIE: Meaning you?

JEAN: Yes! Not because it's me, but because I'm young ——

JULIE: And handsome — what incredible conceit! A Don Juan perhaps! Or a Joseph! Yes, that's it, I do believe you're a Joseph!

JEAN: Do you?

JULIE: I'm almost afraid so. (*Jean boldly tries to put his arm around her waist and kiss her. She slaps his face.*) How dare you?

JEAN: Are you serious or joking?

JULIE: Serious.

JEAN: Then so was what just happened. You play games too seriously, and that's dangerous. Well, I'm tired of games. You'll excuse me if I get back to work. I haven't done the Count's boots yet and it's long past midnight.

JULIE: Put the boots down!

JEAN: No! It's the work I have to do. I never agreed to be your playmate, and never will. It's beneath me.

JULIE: You're proud.

JEAN: In certain ways, but not in others.

JULIE: Have you ever been in love?

JEAN: We don't use that word, but I've been fond of many girls, and once I was sick because I couldn't have the one I wanted. That's right, sick, like those princes in the Arabian Nights° — who couldn't eat or drink because of love.

JULIE: Who was she? (*Jean is silent.*) Who was she?

JEAN: You can't force me to tell you that.

JULIE: But if I ask you as an equal, as a — friend! Who was she?

JEAN: You!

JULIE (*sits*): How amusing . . .

JEAN: Yes, if you like! It was ridiculous ——— You see, that was the story I didn't want to tell you earlier. Maybe I will now. Do you know how the world looks from down below? ——— Of course you don't. Neither do hawks and falcons, whose backs we can't see because they're usually soaring up there above us. I grew up in a shack with seven brothers and sisters and a pig, in the middle of a wasteland, where there wasn't a single tree. But from our window I could see the tops of apple trees above the wall of your father's garden. That was the Garden of Eden, guarded by angry angels with flaming swords. All the same, the other boys and I managed to find our way to the Tree of Life. ——— Now you think I'm contemptible, I suppose.

JULIE: Oh, all boys steal apples.

JEAN: You say that, but you think I'm contemptible anyway. Oh well! One day I went into the Garden of Eden with my mother, to weed the onion beds. Near the vegetable garden was a small Turkish pavilion in the shadow of jasmine bushes and overgrown with honeysuckle. I had no idea what it was used for, but I'd never seen such a beautiful building. People went in and came out again, and one day the door was left open. I sneaked close and saw walls covered with pictures of kings and emperors, and red curtains with fringes at the windows — now you know the place I mean. I ——— (*Breaks off a sprig of lilac and holds it in front of Miss Julie's nose.*) ——— I'd never been inside the manor house, never seen any-

---

Arabian Nights: *The Arabian Nights' Entertainment,* also called *The Thousand and One Nights,* is a collection of Asian and Middle Eastern tales whose famous characters include Aladdin, Ali Baba, and Sinbad the Sailor.

thing except the church — but this was more beautiful. From then on, no matter where my thoughts wandered, they returned — there. And gradually I got a longing to experience, just once, the full pleasure of — *enfin*, I sneaked in, saw, and marveled! But then I heard someone coming! There was only one exit for ladies and gentlemen, but for me there was another, and I had no choice but to take it! (*Miss Julie, who has taken the lilac sprig, lets it fall on the table.*) Afterwards, I started running. I crashed through a raspberry bush, flew over a strawberry patch, and came up onto the rose terrace. There I caught sight of a pink dress and a pair of white stockings — it was you. I crawled under a pile of weeds, and I mean under — under thistles that pricked me and wet dirt that stank. And I looked at you as you walked among the roses, and I thought: if it's true that a thief can enter heaven and be with the angels, then why can't a farmhand's son here on God's earth enter the manor house garden and play with the Count's daughter?

JULIE (*romantically*): Do you think all poor children would have thought the way you did?

JEAN (*at first hesitant, then with conviction*): If *all* poor — yes — of course. Of course!

JULIE: It must be terrible to be poor!

JEAN (*with exaggerated suffering*): Oh, Miss Julie! Oh! ——— A dog can lie on the Countess's sofa, a horse can have his nose patted by a young lady's hand, but a servant ——— (*Changing his tone.*) ——— oh, I know — now and then you find one with enough stuff in him to get ahead in the world, but how often? ——— Anyhow, do you know what I did then? ——— I jumped in the millstream with my clothes on, was pulled out, and got a beating. But the following Sunday, when my father and all the others went to my grandmother's, I arranged to stay home. I scrubbed myself with soap and water, put on my best clothes, and went to church so that I could see you! I saw you and returned home, determined to die. But I wanted to die beautifully and pleasantly, without pain. And then I remembered that it was dangerous to sleep under an elder bush. We had a big one, and it was in full flower. I plundered its treasures and bedded down under them in the oat bin. Have you ever noticed how smooth oats are? — and soft to the touch, like human skin . . . ! Well, I shut the lid and closed my eyes. I fell asleep and woke up feeling very sick. But I didn't die, as you can see. What was I after? ——— I don't know. There was no hope of winning you, of course. ——— You were a symbol of the hopelessness of ever rising out of the class in which I was born.

JULIE: You're a charming storyteller. Did you ever go to school?

JEAN: A bit, but I've read lots of novels and been to the theatre often. And then I've listened to people like you talk — that's where I learned most.

JULIE: Do you listen to what we say?

JEAN: Naturally! And I've heard plenty, too, driving the carriage or rowing the boat. Once I heard you and a friend . . .

JULIE: Oh? ——— What did you hear?

JEAN: I'd better not say. But I was surprised a little. I couldn't imagine where you learned such words. Maybe at bottom there isn't such a great difference between people as we think.

JULIE: Shame on you! We don't act like you when we're engaged.

JEAN (*staring at her*): Is that true? ——— You don't have to play innocent with me, Miss . . .

JULIE: The man I gave my love to was a swine.

JEAN: That's what you all say — afterwards.

JULIE: All?

JEAN: I think so. I know I've heard that phrase before, on similar occasions.

JULIE: What occasions?

JEAN: Like the one I'm talking about. The last time . . .

JULIE (*rising*): Quiet! I don't want to hear any more!

JEAN: That's interesting — that's what *she* said, too. Well, if you'll excuse me, I'm going to bed.

JULIE (*gently*): To bed? On midsummer eve?

JEAN: Yes! Dancing with the rabble out there doesn't amuse me much.

JULIE: Get the key to the boat and row me out on the lake. I want to see the sun come up.

JEAN: Is that wise?

JULIE: Are you worried about your reputation?

JEAN: Why not? Why should I risk looking ridiculous and getting fired without a reference, just when I'm trying to establish myself. Besides, I think I owe something to Kristine.

JULIE: So, now it's Kristine . . .

JEAN: Yes, but you, too. ——— Take my advice, go up and go to bed!

JULIE: Am I to obey you?

JEAN: Just this once — for your own good! Please! It's very late. Drowsiness makes people giddy and liable to lose their heads! Go to bed! Besides — unless I'm mistaken — I hear the others coming to look for me. And if they find us together, you'll be lost!

(*The Chorus approaches, singing:*)

> The swineherd found his true love
> a pretty girl so fair,
> The swineherd found his true love
> but let the girl beware.

> For then he saw the princess
> the princess on the golden hill,
> but then saw the princess,
> so much fairer still.

> So the swineherd and the princess
> they danced the whole night through,
> and he forgot his first love,
> to her he was untrue.

> And when the long night ended,
> and in the light of day, of day,

the dancing too was ended,
and the princess could not stay.

Then the swineherd lost his true love,
and the princess grieves him still,
and never more she'll wander
from atop the golden hill.

JULIE: I know all these people and I love them, just as they love me. Let them come in and you'll see.

JEAN: No, Miss Julie, they don't love you. They take your food, but they spit on it! Believe me! Listen to them, listen to what they're singing! —— No, don't listen to them!

JULIE (*listening*): What are the singing?

JEAN: It's a dirty song! About you and me!

JULIE: Disgusting! Oh! How deceitful! ——

JEAN: The rabble is always cowardly! And in a battle like this, you don't fight; you can only run away!

JULIE: Run away? But where? We can't go out — or into Kristine's room.

JEAN: True. But there's my room. Necessity knows no rules. Besides, you can trust me. I'm your friend and I respect you.

JULIE: But suppose — suppose they look for you in there?

JEAN: I'll bolt the door, and if anyone tries to break in, I'll shoot! —— Come! (*On his knees.*) Come!

JULIE (*urgently*): Promise me . . . ?

JEAN: I swear! (*Miss Julie runs off right. Jean hastens after her.*)

BALLET

Led by a fiddler, the servants and farm people enter, dressed festively, with flowers in their hats. On the table they place a small barrel of beer and a keg of schnapps, both garlanded. Glasses are brought out, and the drinking starts. A dance circle is formed and "The Swineherd and the Princess" is sung. When the dance is finished, everyone leaves, singing.

Miss Julie enters alone. She notices the mess in the kitchen, wrings her hands, then takes out her powder puff and powders her nose.

JEAN (*enters, agitated*): There, you see? And you heard them. We can't possibly stay here now, you know that.

JULIE: Yes, I know. But what can we do?

JEAN: Leave, travel, far away from here.

JULIE: Travel? Yes, but where?

JEAN: To Switzerland, to the Italian lakes. Have you ever been there?

JULIE: No. Is it beautiful?

JEAN: Oh, an eternal summer — oranges growing everywhere, laurel trees, always green . . .

JULIE: But what'll we do there?

JEAN: I'll open a hotel — with first-class service for first-class people.

JULIE: Hotel?

JEAN: That's the life, you know. Always new faces, new languages. No time to worry or be nervous. No hunting for something to do — there's always work to do done: bells ringing night and day, train whistles blowing, carriages coming and going, and all the while gold rolling into the till! That's the life!

JULIE: Yes, it sounds wonderful. But what'll I do?

JEAN: You'll be mistress of the house: the jewel in our crown! With your looks . . . and your manner — oh — success is guaranteed! It'll be wonderful! You'll sit in your office like a queen and push an electric button to set your slaves in motion. The guests will file past your throne and timidly lay their treasures before you. ——— You have no idea how people tremble when they get their bill. ——— I'll salt the bills and you'll sweeten them with your prettiest smile. ——— Let's get away from here ——— (*Takes a timetable out of his pocket.*) ——— Right away, on the next train! ——— We'll be in Malmö six-thirty tomorrow morning, Hamburg at eight-forty; from Frankfurt to Basel will take a day, then on to Como by way of the St. Gotthard Tunnel, in, let's see, three days. Three days!

JULIE: That's all very well! But Jean — you must give me courage! ——— Tell me you love me! Put your arms around me!

JEAN (*hesitating*): I want to — but I don't dare. Not in this house, not again. I love you — never doubt that — you don't doubt it, do you Miss Julie?

JULIE (*shy; very feminine*): "Miss!" ——— Call me Julie! There are no barriers between us any more. Call me Julie!

JEAN (*tormented*): I can't! There'll always be barriers between us as long as we stay in this house. ——— There's the past and there's the Count. I've never met anyone I had such respect for. ——— When I see his gloves lying on a chair, I feel small. ——— When I hear that bell up there ring, I jump like a skittish horse. ——— And when I look at his boots standing there so stiff and proud, I feel like bowing! (*Kicking the boots.*) Superstitions and prejudices we learned as children — but they can easily be forgotten. If I can just get to another country, a republic, people will bow and scrape when they see my livery — *they'll* bow and scrape, you hear, not me! I wasn't born to cringe. I've got stuff in me, I've got character, and if I can only grab onto that first branch, you watch me climb! I'm a servant today, but next year I'll own my own hotel. In ten years I'll have enough to retire. Then I'll go to Rumania and be decorated. I could — mind you I said *could* — end up a count!

JULIE: Wonderful, wonderful!

JEAN: Ah, in Rumania you just buy your title, and so you'll be a countess after all. My countess!

JULIE: But I don't care about that — that's what I'm putting behind me! Show me you love me, otherwise — otherwise, what am I?

JEAN: I'll show you a thousand times — afterwards! Not here! And whatever you do, no emotional outbursts, or we'll both be lost! We must think this through coolly, like sensible people. (*He takes a cigar, snips the end, and lights it.*) You sit there, and I'll sit here. We'll talk as if nothing happened.

JULIE (*desperately*): Oh, my God! Have you no feelings?

JEAN: Me? No one has more feelings than I do, but I know how to control them.

JULIE: A little while ago you could kiss my shoe — and now!

JEAN (*harshly*): Yes, but that was before. Now we have other things to think about.

JULIE: Don't speak harshly to me!

JEAN: I'm not — just sensibly! We've already done one foolish thing, let's not have any more. The Count could return any minute, and by then we've got to decide what to do with our lives. What do you think of my plans for the future? Do you approve?

JULIE: They sound reasonable enough. I have only one question: for such a big undertaking you need capital — do you have it?

JEAN (*chewing on the cigar*): Me? Certainly! I have my professional expertise, my wide experience, and my knowledge of languages. That's capital enough, I should think!

JULIE: But all that won't even buy a train ticket.

JEAN: That's true. That's why I'm looking for a partner to advance me the money.

JULIE: Where will you find one quickly enough?

JEAN: That's up to you, if you want to come with me.

JULIE: But I can't; I have no money of my own. (*Pause.*)

JEAN: Then it's all off . . .

JULIE: And . . .

JEAN: Things stay as they are.

JULIE: Do you think I'm going to stay in this house as your lover? With all the servants pointing their fingers at me? Do you imagine I can face my father after this? No! Take me away from here, away from shame and dishonor ——— Oh, what have I done! My God, my God! (*She cries.*)

JEAN: Now, don't start that old song! ——— What have you done? The same as many others before you.

JULIE (*screaming convulsively*): And now you think I'm contemptible! ——— I'm falling, I'm falling!

JEAN: Fall down to my level and I'll lift you up again.

JULIE: What terrible power drew me to you? The attraction of the weak to the strong? The falling to the rising? Or was it love? Was this love? Do you know what love is?

JEAN: Me? What do you take me for? You don't think this was my first time, do you?

JULIE: The things you say, the thoughts you think!

JEAN: That's the way I was taught, and that's the way I am! Now don't get excited and don't play the grand lady, because we're in the same boat now! ——— Come on, Julie, I'll pour you a glass of something special! (*He opens a drawer in the table, takes out a wine bottle, and fills two glasses already used.*)

JULIE: Where did you get that wine?

JEAN: From the cellar.

JULIE: My father's burgundy!

JEAN: That'll do for his son-in-law, won't it?

JULIE: And I drink beer! Beer!

JEAN: That only shows I have better taste.

JULIE: Thief!

JEAN: Planning to tell?

JULIE: Oh, oh! Accomplice of a common thief! Was I drunk? Have I been walking in a dream the whole evening? Midsummer eve! A time of innocent fun!

JEAN: Innocent, eh?

JULIE (*pacing back and forth*): Is there anyone on earth more miserable than I am at this moment?

JEAN: Why should you be? After such a conquest? Think of Kristine in there. Don't you think she has feelings, too?

JULIE: I thought so awhile ago, but not any more. No, a servant is a servant . . .

JEAN: And a whore is a whore!

JULIE (*on her knees, her hands clasped*): Oh, God in Heaven, end my wretched life! Take me away from the filth I'm sinking into! Save me! Save me!

JEAN: I can't deny I feel sorry for you. When I lay in that onion bed and saw you in the rose garden, well . . . I'll be frank . . . I had the same dirty thoughts all boys have.

JULIE: And you wanted to die for me!

JEAN: In the oat bin? That was just talk.

JULIE: A lie, in other words!

JEAN (*beginning to feel sleepy*): More or less! I got the idea from a newspaper story about a chimney sweep who curled up in a firewood bin full of lilacs because he got a summons for not supporting his illegitimate child . . .

JULIE: So, that's what you're like . . .

JEAN: I had to think of something. And that's the kind of story women always go for.

JULIE: Swine!

JEAN: *Merde!*

JULIE: And now you've seen the hawk's back . . .

JEAN: Not exactly its *back* . . .

JULIE: And I was to be the first branch . . .

JEAN: But the branch was rotten . . .

JULIE: I was to be the sign on the hotel . . .

JEAN: And I the hotel . . .

JULIE: Sit at your desk, entice your customers, pad their bills . . .

JEAN: That I'd do myself . . .

JULIE: How can anyone be so thoroughly filthy?

JEAN: Better clean up then!

JULIE: You lackey, you menial, stand up, when I speak to you!

JEAN: Menial's strumpet, lackey's whore, shut up and get out of here! Who are you to lecture me on coarseness? None of my kind is ever as coarse as you were tonight. Do you think one of your maids would throw herself at a man the way you did? Have you ever seen any girl of my class offer herself like that? I've only seen it among animals and streetwalkers.

JULIE (*crushed*): You're right. Hit me, trample on me. I don't deserve any better. I'm worthless. But help me! If you see any way out of this, help me, Jean, please!

JEAN (*more gently*): I'd be lying if I didn't admit to a sense of triumph in all this, but do you think that a person like me would have dared even to look at someone like you if you hadn't invited it? I'm still amazed . . .

JULIE: And proud . . .

JEAN: Why not? Though I must say it was too easy to be really exciting.

JULIE: Go on, hit me, hit me harder!

JEAN (*rising*): No! Forgive me for what I've said! I don't hit a man when he's down, let alone a woman. I can't deny though, that I'm pleased to find out that what looked so dazzling to us from below was only tinsel, that the hawk's back was only gray, after all, that the lovely complexion was only powder, that those polished fingernails had black edges, and that a dirty handkerchief is still dirty, even if it smells of perfume . . . ! On the other hand, it hurts me to find out that what I was striving for wasn't finer, more substantial. It hurts me to see you sunk so low that you're inferior to your own cook. It hurts like watching flowers beaten down by autumn rains and turned into mud.

JULIE: You talk as if you were already above me.

JEAN: I am. You see, I could make you a countess, but you could never make me a count.

JULIE: But I'm the child of a count — something you could never be!

JEAN: That's true. But I could be the father of counts — if . . .

JULIE: But you're a thief. I'm not.

JEAN: There are worse things than being a thief! Besides, when I'm working in a house, I consider myself sort of a member of the family, like one of the children. And you don't call it stealing when a child snatches a berry off a full bush. (*His passion is aroused again.*) Miss Julie, you're a glorious woman, much too good for someone like me! You were drinking and you lost your head. Now you want to cover up your mistake by telling yourself that you love me! You don't. Maybe there was a physical attraction — but then your love is no better than mine. ———— I could never be satisfied to be no more than an animal to you, and I could never arouse real love in you.

JULIE: Are you sure of that?

JEAN: You're suggesting it's possible ———— Oh, I could fall in love with you, no doubt about it. You're beautiful, you're refined ———— (*approaching and taking her hand.*) ———— cultured, lovable when you want to be, and once you start a fire in a man, it never goes out. (*Putting his arm around her waist.*) You're like hot, spicy wine, and one kiss from you . . . (*He tries to lead her out, but she slowly frees herself.*)

JULIE: Let me go!? ———— You'll never win me like that.

JEAN: *How* then? ———— Not like that? Not with caresses and pretty speeches. Not with plans about the future or rescue from disgrace! *How* then?

JULIE: How? How? I don't know! ———— I have no idea ———— I detest you as I detest rats, but I can't escape from you.

JEAN: Escape with me!

JULIE (*pulling herself together*): Escape? Yes, we must escape! ——— But I'm so tired. Give me a glass of wine? (*Jean pours the wine. She looks at her watch.*) But we must talk first. We still have a little time. (*She drains the glass, then holds it out for more.*)

JEAN: Don't drink so fast. It'll go to your head.

JULIE: What does it matter?

JEAN: What does it matter? It's vulgar to get drunk! What did you want to tell me?

JULIE: We must escape! But first we must talk, I mean I must talk. You've done all the talking up to now. You told about your life, now I want to tell about mine, so we'll know all about each other before we go off together.

JEAN: Just a minute! Forgive me! If you don't want to regret it afterwards, you'd better think twice before revealing any secrets about yourself.

JULIE: Aren't you my friend?

JEAN: Yes, sometimes! But don't rely on me.

JULIE: You're only saying that. ——— Besides, everyone already knows my secrets. ——— You see, my mother was a commoner — very humble background. She was brought up believing in social equality, women's rights, and all that. The idea of marriage repelled her. So, when my father proposed, she replied that she would never become his wife, but he could be her lover. He insisted that he didn't want the woman he loved to be less respected than he. But his passion ruled him, and when she explained that the world's respect meant nothing to her, he accepted her conditions.

But now his friends avoided him and his life was restricted to taking care of the estate, which couldn't satisfy him. I came into the world — against my mother's wishes, as far as I can understand. She wanted to bring me up as a child of nature, and, what's more, to learn everything a boy had to learn, so that I might be an example of how a woman can be as good as a man. I had to wear boy's clothes and learn to take care of horses, but I was never allowed in the cowshed. I had to groom and harness the horses and go hunting — and even had to watch them slaughter animals — that was disgusting! On the estate men were put on women's jobs and women on men's jobs — with the result that the property became run down and we became the laughing stock of the district. Finally, my father must have awakened from his trance because he rebelled and changed everything his way. My parents were then married quietly. Mother became ill — I don't know what illness it was — but she often had convulsions, hid in the attic and in the garden, and sometimes stayed out all night. Then came the great fire, which you've heard about. The house, the stables, and the cowshed all burned down, under very curious circumstances, suggesting arson, because the accident happened the day after the insurance had expired. The quarterly premium my father sent in was delayed because of a messenger's carelessness and didn't arrive in time. (*She fills her glass and drinks.*)

JEAN: Don't drink any more!

JULIE: Oh, what does it matter. ———— We were left penniless and had to sleep in the carriages. My father had no idea where to find money to rebuild the house because he had so slighted his old friends that they had forgotten him. Then my mother suggested that he borrow from a childhood friend of hers, a brick manufacturer who lived nearby. Father got the loan without having to pay interest, which surprised him. And that's how the estate was rebuilt. ———— (*Drinks again.*) Do you know who started the fire?

JEAN: The Countess, your mother.

JULIE: Do you know who the brick manufacturer was?

JEAN: Your mother's lover?

JULIE: Do you know whose money it was?

JEAN: Wait a moment — no, I don't.

JULIE: It was my mother's.

JEAN: You mean the Count's, unless they didn't sign an agreement when they were married.

JULIE: They didn't. ———— My mother had a small inheritance which she didn't want under my father's control, so she entrusted it to her — friend.

JEAN: Who stole it!

JULIE: Exactly! He kept it. ———— All this my father found out, but he couldn't bring it to court, couldn't repay his wife's lover, couldn't prove it was his wife's money! It was my mother's revenge for being forced into marriage against her will. It nearly drove him to suicide — there was a rumor that he tried with a pistol, but failed. So, he managed to live through it and my mother had to suffer for what she'd done. You can imagine that those were a terrible five years for me. I loved my father, but I sided with my mother because I didn't know the circumstances. I learned from her to hate men — you've heard how she hated the whole male sex — and I swore to her I'd never be a slave to any man.

JEAN: But you got engaged to that lawyer.

JULIE: In order to make him my slave.

JEAN: And he wasn't willing?

JULIE: He was willing, all right, but I wouldn't let him. I got tired of him.

JEAN: I saw it — out near the stable.

JULIE: What did you see?

JEAN: I saw — how he broke off the engagement.

JULIE: That's a lie! I was the one who broke it off. Has he said that he did? That swine . . .

JEAN: He was no swine, I'm sure. So, you hate men, Miss Julie?

JULIE: Yes! ———— Most of the time! But sometimes — when the weakness comes, when passion burns! Oh, God, will the fire never die out?

JEAN: Do you hate me, too?

JULIE: Immeasurably! I'd like to have you put to death, like an animal . . .

JEAN: I see — the penalty for bestiality — the woman get two years at hard labor and the animal is put to death. Right?

JULIE: Exactly!

JEAN: But there's no prosecutor here — and no animal. So, what'll we do?

JULIE: Go away!

JEAN: To torment each other to death?

JEAN: No! To be happy for — two days, a week, as long as we can be happy, and then — die . . .

JEAN: Die? That's stupid! It's better to open a hotel!

JULIE (*without listening*): ———— on the shore of Lake Como, where the sun always shines, where the laurels are green at Christmas and the oranges glow.

JEAN: Lake Como is a rainy hole, and I never saw any oranges outside the stores. But tourists are attracted there because there are plenty of villas to be rented out to lovers, and that's a profitable business. ———— Do you know why? Because they sign a lease for six months — and then leave after three weeks!

JULIE (*naively*): Why after three weeks?

JEAN: They quarrel, of course! But they still have to pay the rent in full! And so you rent the villas out again. And that's the way it goes, time after time. There's never a shortage of love — even if it doesn't last long!

JULIE: You don't want to die with me?

JEAN: I don't want to die at all! For one thing, I like living, and for another, I think suicide is a crime against the Providence which gave us life.

JULIE: You believe in God? *You?*

JEAN: Of course I do. And I go to church every other Sunday. ———— To be honest, I'm tired of all this, and I'm going to bed.

JULIE: Are you? And do you think I can let it go at that? A man owes something to the woman he's shamed.

JEAN (*taking out his purse and throwing a silver coin on the table*): Here! I don't like owing anything to anybody.

JULIE (*pretending not to notice the insult*): Do you know what the law states . . .

JEAN: Unfortunately the law doesn't state any punishment for the woman who seduces a man!

JULIE (*as before*): Do you see any way out but to leave, get married, and then separate?

JEAN: Suppose I refuse such a *mésalliance?*

JULIE: *Mésalliance . . .*

JEAN: Yes, for me! You see, I come from better stock than you. There's no arsonist in my family.

JULIE: How do you know?

JEAN: You can't prove otherwise. We don't keep charts on our ancestors — there's just the police records! But I've read about your family. Do you know who the founder was? He was a miller who let the king sleep with his wife one night during the Danish War. I don't have any noble ancestors like that. I don't have any noble ancestors at all, but I could become one myself.

JULIE: This is what I get for opening my heart to someone unworthy, for giving my family's honor . . .

JEAN: Dishonor! ——— Well, I told you so: when people drink, they talk, and talk is dangerous!

JULIE: Oh, how I regret it! ——— How I regret it! ——— If you at least loved me.

JEAN: For the last time — what do you want? Shall I cry; shall I jump over your riding crop? Shall I kiss you and lure you off to Lake Como for three weeks, and then God knows what . . . ? What shall I do? What do you want? This is getting painfully embarrassing! But that's what happens when you stick your nose in women's business. Miss Julie! I see that you're unhappy. I know you're suffering, but I can't understand you. We don't have such romantic ideas; there's not this kind of hate between us. Love is a game we play when we get time off from work, but we don't have all day and night, like you. I think you're sick, really sick. Your mother was crazy, and her ideas have poisoned your life.

JULIE: Be kind to me. At least now you're talking like a human being.

JEAN: Be human yourself, then. You spit on me, and you won't let me wipe myself off ———

JULIE: Help me! Help Me! Just tell me what to do, where to go!

JEAN: In God's name, if I only knew myself!

JULIE: I've been crazy, out of my mind, but isn't there any way out?

JEAN: Stay here and keep calm! No one knows anything!

JULIE: Impossible! The others know and Kristine knows.

JEAN: No they don't, and they'd never believe a thing like that!

JULIE (*hesitantly*): But — it could happen again!

JEAN: That's true!

JULIE: And then?

JEAN (*frightened*): Then! ——— Why didn't I think about that? Yes, there is only one thing to do — get away from here! Right away! I can't come with you, then we'd be finished, so you'll have to go alone — away — anywhere!

JULIE: Alone? ——— Where? ——— I can't do that!

JEAN: You must! And before the Count gets back! If you stay, you know what'll happen. Once you make a mistake like this, you want to continue because the damage has already been done . . . Then you get bolder and bolder — until finally you're caught! So leave! Later you can write to the Count and confess everything — except that it was me! He'll never guess who it was, and he's not going to be eager to find out, anyway.

JULIE: I'll go if you come with me.

JEAN: Are you out of your head? Miss Julie runs away with her servant! In two days it would be in the newspapers, and that's something your father would never live through.

JULIE: I can't go and I can't stay! Help me! I'm so tired, so terribly tired. ——— Order me! Set me in motion — I can't think or act on my own . . .

JEAN: What miserable creatures you people are! You strut around with your noses in the air as if you were the lords of creation! All right, I'll order you. Go upstairs and get dressed! Get some money for the trip, and then come back down!

JULIE (*in a half-whisper*): Come up with me!

JEAN: To your room? ——— Now you're crazy again! (*Hesitates for a moment.*) No! Go, at once! (*Takes her hand to lead her out.*)

JULIE (*as she leaves*): Speak kindly to me, Jean!

JEAN: An order always sounds unkind — now you know how it feels. (*Jean, alone, sighs with relief. He sits at the table, takes out a notebook and pencil, and begins adding up figures, counting aloud as he works. He continues in dumb show until Kristine enters, dressed for church. She is carrying a white tie and shirt front.*)

KRISTINE: Lord Jesus, what a mess! What have you been up to?

JEAN: Oh, Miss Julie dragged everybody in here. You mean you didn't hear anything? You must have been sleeping soundly.

KRISTINE: Like a log.

JEAN: And dressed for church already?

KRISTINE: Of course! You remember you promised to come with me to communion today!

JEAN: Oh, yes, that's right. ——— And you brought my things. Come on, then! (*He sits down. Kristine starts to put on his shirt front and tie. Pause. Jean begins sleepily.*) What's the gospel text for today?

KRISTINE: On St. John's Day? — the beheading of John the Baptist, I should think!

JEAN: Ah, that'll be a long one, for sure. ——— Hey, you're choking me! ——— Oh, I'm sleepy, so sleepy!

KRISTINE: Yes, what have you been doing, up all night? Your face is absolutely green.

JEAN: I've been sitting here gabbing with Miss Julie.

KRISTINE: She has no idea what's proper, that one! (*Pause.*)

JEAN: You know, Kristine . . .

KRISTINE: What?

JEAN: It's really strange when you think about it. ——— Her!

KRISTINE: What's so strange?

JEAN: Everything! (*Pause.*)

KRISTINE: (*looking at the half-empty glasses standing on the table*): Have you been drinking together, too?

JEAN: Yes.

KRISTINE: Shame on you! ——— Look me in the eye!

JEAN: Well?

KRISTINE: Is it possible? Is it possible?

JEAN (*thinking it over for a moment*): Yes, it is.

KRISTINE: Ugh! I never would have believed it! No, shame on you, shame!

JEAN: You're not jealous of her, are you?

KRISTINE: No, not of her! If it had been Clara or Sofie I'd have scratched your eyes out! ——— I don't know why, but that's the way I feel. ——— Oh, it's disgusting!

JEAN: Are you angry at her, then?

KRISTINE: No, at you! That was an awful thing to do, awful! Poor girl! ——— No, I don't care who knows it — I won't stay in a house where we can't respect the people we work for.

JEAN: Why should we respect them?

KRISTINE: You're so clever, you tell me! Do you want to wait on people who can't behave decently? Do you? You disgrace yourself that way, if you ask me.

JEAN: But it's a comfort to know they aren't any better than us.

KRISTINE: Not for me. If they're no better, what do we have to strive for to better ourselves. —— And think of the Count! Think of him! As if he hasn't had enough misery in his life! Lord Jesus! No, I won't stay in this house any longer! —— And it had to be with someone like you! If it had been that lawyer, if it had been a real gentleman . . .

JEAN: What do you mean?

KRISTINE: Oh, you're all right for what you are, but there are men and gentlemen, after all! —— No, this business with Miss Julie I can never forget. She was so proud, so arrogant with men, you wouldn't have believed she could just go and give herself — and to someone like you! And she was going to have poor Diana shot for running after the gatekeeper's mutt —— Yes, I'm giving my notice, I mean it — I won't stay here any longer. On the twenty-fourth of October, I leave!

JEAN: And then?

KRISTINE: Well, since the subject has come up, it's about time you looked around for something since we're going to get married, in any case.

JEAN: Where am I going to look? I couldn't find a job like this if I was married.

KRISTINE: No, that's true. But you can find work as a porter or as a caretaker in some government office. The state doesn't pay much, I know, but it's secure, and there's a pension for the wife and children . . .

JEAN (*grimacing*): That's all very well, but it's a bit early for me to think about dying for a wife and children. My ambitions are a little higher than that.

KRISTINE: Your ambitions, yes! Well, you have obligations, too! Think about them!

JEAN: Don't start nagging me about obligations, I know what I have to do! (*Listening for something outside.*) Besides, this is something we have plenty of time to think over. Go and get ready for church.

KRISTINE: Who's that walking around up there?

JEAN: I don't know, unless it's Clara.

KRISTINE (*going*): You don't suppose it's the Count, who came home without us hearing him?

JEAN (*frightened*): The Count? No, I don't think so. He'd have rung.

KRISTINE (*going*): Well, God help us! I've never seen anything like this before. (*The sun has risen and shines through the treetops in the park. The light shifts gradually until it slants in through the windows. Jean goes to the door and signals. Miss Julie enters, dressed in travel clothes and carrying a small birdcage, covered with a cloth, which she places on a chair.*)

JULIE: I'm ready now.

JEAN: Shh! Kristine is awake.

JULIE (*very nervous during the following*): Does she suspect something?

JEAN: She doesn't know anything. But my God, you look awful!

JULIE: Why? How do I look?

JEAN: You're pale as a ghost and — excuse me, but your face is dirty.

JULIE: Let me wash up then. ——— (*She goes to the basin and washes her hands and face.*) Give me a towel! ——— Oh — the sun's coming up.

JEAN: Then the goblins will disappear.

JULIE: Yes, there must have been goblins out last night! ——— Jean, listen, come with me! I have some money now.

JEAN (*hesitantly*): Enough?

JULIE: Enough to start with. Come with me! I just can't travel alone on a day like this — midsummer day on a stuffy train — jammed in among crowds of people staring at me. Eternal delays at every station, while I'd wish I had wings. No, I can't, I can't! And then there'll be memories, memories of midsummer days when I was little. The church — decorated with birch leaves and lilacs; dinner at the big table with relatives and friends; the afternoons in the park, dancing, music, flowers, and games. Oh, no matter how far we travel, the memories will follow in the baggage car, with remorse and guilt!

JEAN: I'll go with you — but right away, before it's too late. Right this minute!

JULIE: Get dressed, then! (*Picking up the birdcage.*)

JEAN: But no baggage! It would give us away!

JULIE: No, nothing! Only what we can have in the compartment with us.

JEAN (*has taken his hat*): What've you got there? What is it?

JULIE: It's only my greenfinch. I couldn't leave her behind.

JEAN: What? Bring a birdcage with us? You're out of your head! Put it down!

JULIE: It's the only thing I'm taking from my home — the only living being that loves me, since Diana was unfaithful. Don't be cruel! Let me take her!

JEAN: Put the cage down, I said! ——— And don't talk so loudly — Kristine will hear us!

JULIE: No, I won't leave her in the hands of strangers! I'd rather you killed her.

JEAN: Bring the thing here, then, I'll cut its head off!

JULIE: Oh! But don't hurt her! Don't . . . no, I can't.

JEAN: Bring it here! I can!

JULIE (*taking the bird out of the cage and kissing it*): Oh, my little Serena, must you die and leave your mistress?

JEAN: Please don't make a scene! Your whole future is at stake! Hurry up! (*He snatches the bird from her, carries it over to the chopping block, and picks up a meat cleaver. Miss Julie turns away.*) You should have learned how to slaughter chickens instead of how to fire pistols. (*He chops off the bird's head.*) Then you wouldn't feel faint at the sight of blood.

JULIE (*screaming*): Kill me, too! Kill me! You, who can slaughter an innocent animal without blinking an eye! Oh, how I hate, how I detest you! There's blood between us now! I curse the moment I set eyes on you! I curse the moment I was conceived in my mother's womb!

JEAN: What good does cursing do? Let's go!

JULIE (*approaching the chopping block, as if drawn against her will*): No, I don't want to go yet. I can't . . . until I see . . . Shh! I hear a carriage ——— (*She listens, but her eyes never leave the cleaver and the chopping block*). Do you think I can't stand the sight of blood? You think I'm so weak . . . Oh —

I'd like to see your blood and your brains on a chopping block! — I'd like to see your whole sex swimming in a sea of blood, like my little bird . . . I think I could drink from your skull! I'd like to bathe my feet in your open chest and eat your heart roasted whole! —— You think I'm weak. You think I love you because my womb craved your seed. You think I want to carry your spawn under my heart and nourish it with my blood — bear your child and take your name! By the way, what is your family name? I've never heard it. —— Do you have one? I was to be Mrs. Bootblack — or Madame Pigsty. —— You dog, who wears my collar, you lackey, who bears my coat of arms on your buttons — do I have to share you with my cook, compete with my own servant? Oh! Oh! Oh! —— You think I'm a coward who wants to run away! No, now I'm staying — and let the storm break! My father will come home . . . to find his desk broken open — and his money gone! Then he'll ring — that bell . . . twice for his valet — and then he'll send for the police . . . and then I'll tell everything! Everything! Oh, what a relief it'll be to have it all end — if only it will end! —— And then he'll have a stroke and die . . . That'll be the end of all of us — and there'll be peace . . . quiet . . . eternal rest! —— And then our coat of arms will be broken against his coffin — the family title extinct — but the valet's line will go on in an orphanage . . . win laurels in the gutter, and end in jail!

JEAN: There's the blue blood talking! Very good, Miss Julie! Just don't let that miller out of the closet! (*Kristine enters, dressed for church, with a psalmbook in her hand.*)

JULIE (*rushing to Kristine and falling into her arms, as if seeking protection*): Help me, Kristine! Help me against this man!

KRISTINE (*unmoved and cold*): What a fine way to behave on a Sunday morning! (*Sees the chopping block.*) And look at this mess! —— What does all this mean? Why all this screaming and carrying on?

JULIE: Kristine! You're a woman and my friend! Beware of this swine!

JEAN (*uncomfortable*): While you ladies discuss this, I'll go in and shave. (*Slips off right.*)

JULIE: You must listen to me so you'll understand!

KRISTINE: No, I could never understand such disgusting behavior! Where are you off to in your traveling clothes? —— And he had his hat on. —— Well? —— Well? ——

JULIE: Listen to me, Kristine! Listen, and I'll tell you everything ——

KRISTINE: I don't want to hear it . . .

JULIE: But you must listen to me . . .

KRISTINE: What about? If it's about this silliness with Jean, I'm not interested, because it's none of my business. But if you're thinking of tricking him into running out, we'll soon put a stop to that!

JULIE (*extremely nervous*): Try to be calm now, Kristine, and listen to me! I can't stay here, and neither can Jean — so we must go away . . .

KRISTINE: Hm, hm!

JULIE (*brightening*): You see, I just had an idea —— What if all three of us go — abroad — to Switzerland and start a hotel together? —— I have money, you see — and Jean and I could run it — and I thought you, you could take care of the kitchen . . . Wouldn't that be wonderful? ———— Say yes! And come with us, and then everything will be settled! ———— Oh, do say yes! (*Embracing Kristine and patting her warmly.*)

KRISTINE (*coolly, thoughtfully*): Hm, hm!

JULIE (*presto tempo*): You've never traveled, Kristine. ———— You must get out and see the world. You can't imagine how much fun it is to travel by train — always new faces — new countries. ———— And when we get to Hamburg, we'll stop off at the zoo — you'll like that. ———— And then we'll go to the theatre and the opera — and when we get to Munich, dear, there we have museums, with Rubens and Raphael, the great painters, as you know. ———— You've heard of Munich, where King Ludwig lived — the king who went mad. ———— And then we'll see his castles — they're still there and they're like castles in fairy tales. ———— And from there it isn't far to Switzerland — and the Alps. ———— Imagine — the Alps have snow on them even in the middle of summer! ———— And oranges grow there and laurel trees that are green all year round ———— (*Jean can be seen in the wings right, sharpening his razor on a strop which he holds with his teeth and his left hand. He listens to the conversation with satisfaction, nodding now and then in approval. Miss Julie continues tempo prestissimo.*) And then we'll start a hotel — and I'll be at the desk, while Jean greets the guests . . . does the shopping . . . writes letters. ———— You have no idea what a life it'll be — the train whistles blowing and the carriages arriving and the bells ringing in the rooms and down in the restaurant. ———— And I'll make out the bills — and I know how to salt them! . . . You'll never believe how timid travelers are when they have to pay their bills! ———— And you — you'll be in charge of the kitchen. ———— Naturally, you won't have to stand over the stove yourself. ———— And since you're going to be seen by people, you'll have to wear beautiful clothes. ———— And you, with your looks — no, I'm not flattering you — one fine day you'll grab yourself a husband! ———— You'll see! ———— A rich Englishman — they're so easy to ———— (*Slowing down*) ———— catch — and then we'll get rich — and build ourselves a villa on Lake Como. ———— It's true it rains there a little now and then, but ———— (*Dully.*) ———— the sun has to shine sometimes — although it looks dark — and then . . . of course we could always come back home again ———— (*Pause.*) ———— here — or somewhere else ————

KRISTINE: Listen, Miss Julie, do you believe all this?

JULIE (*crushed*): Do I believe it?

KRISTINE: Yes!

JULIE (*wearily*): I don't know. I don't believe in anything any more. (*She sinks down on the bench and cradles her head in her arms on the table.*) Nothing! Nothing at all!

KRISTINE (*turning right to where Jean is standing*): So, you thought you'd run out!

JEAN (*embarrassed; puts the razor on the table*): Run out? That's no way to put it. You hear Miss Julie's plan, and even if she is tired after being up all night, it's still a practical plan.

KRISTINE: Now you listen to me! Did you think I'd work as a cook for that . . .

JEAN (*sharply*): You watch what you say in front of your mistress! Do you understand?

KRISTINE: Mistress!

JEAN: Yes!

KRISTINE: Listen to him! Listen to him!

JEAN: Yes, you listen! It'd do you good to listen more and talk less! Miss Julie is your mistress. If you despise her, you have to despise yourself for the same reason!

KRISTINE: I've always had enough self-respect ————

JEAN: ———— to be able to despise other people!

KRISTINE: ———— to stop me from doing anything that's beneath me. You can't say that the Count's cook has been up to something with the groom or the swineherd! Can you?

JEAN: No, you were lucky enough to get hold of a gentleman!

KRISTINE: Yes, a gentleman who sells the Count's oats from the stable.

JEAN: You should talk — taking a commission from the grocer and bribes from the butcher.

KRISTINE: What?

JEAN: And you say you can't respect your employers any longer. You, you, you!

KRISTINE: Are you coming to church with me, now? You could use a good sermon after your fine deed!

JEAN: No, I'm not going to church today. You'll have to go alone and confess what you've been up to.

KRISTINE: Yes, I'll do that, and I'll bring back enough forgiveness for you, too. The Savior suffered and died on the Cross for all our sins, and if we go to Him with faith and a penitent heart, He takes all our sins on Himself.

JEAN: Even grocery sins?

JULIE: And do you believe that, Kristine?

KRISTINE: It's my living faith, as sure as I stand here. It's the faith I learned as a child, Miss Julie, and kept ever since. "Where sin abounded, grace did much more abound!"

JULIE: Oh, if I only had your faith. If only . . .

KRISTINE: Well, you see, we can't have it without God's special grace, and that isn't given to everyone ————

JULIE: Who is it given to then?

KRISTINE: That's the great secret of the workings of grace, Miss Julie, and God is no respecter of persons, for the last shall be the first . . .

JULIE: Then He does respect the last.

KRISTINE (*continuing*): . . . and it is easier for a camel to go through the eye of a needle, than for a rich man to enter the Kingdom of God. That's how it is, Miss Julie! Anyhow, I'm going now — alone, and on the way I'm going to tell the groom not to let any horses out, in case anyone wants to leave before the Count gets back! ———— Goodbye! (*Leaves.*)

JEAN: What a witch! ———— And all this because of a greenfinch! ————

JULIE (*dully*): Never mind the greenfinch! ———— Can you see any way out of this? Any end to it?

JEAN (*thinking*): No!

JULIE: What would you do in my place?

JEAN: In your place? Let's see — as a person of position, as a woman who had — fallen. I don't know — wait, now I know.

JULIE (*taking the razor and making a gesture*): You mean like this?

JEAN: Yes! But — understand — *I* wouldn't do it! That's the difference between us!

JULIE: Because you're a man and I'm a woman? What sort of difference is that?

JEAN: The usual difference — between a man and a woman.

JULIE (*with the razor in her hand*): I want to, but I can't! ———— My father couldn't either, the time he should have done it.

JEAN: No, he shouldn't have! He had to revenge himself first.

JULIE: And now my mother is revenged again, through me.

JEAN: Didn't you ever love your father, Miss Julie?

JULIE: Oh yes, deeply, but I've hated him, too. I must have done so without realizing it! It was he who brought me up to despise my own sex, making me half woman, half man. Whose fault is what's happened? My father's, my mother's, my own? My own? I don't have anything that's my own. I don't have a single thought that I didn't get from my father, not an emotion that I didn't get from my mother, and this last idea — that all people are equal — I got that from my fiancé. ———— That's why I called him a swine! How can it be my fault? Shall I let Jesus take on the blame, the way Kristine does? ———— No, I'm too proud to do that and too sensible — thanks to my father's teachings. ———— And as for someone rich not going to heaven, that's a lie. But Kristine won't get in — how will she explain the money she has in the savings bank? Whose fault is it? ———— What does it matter whose fault it is? I'm still the one who has to bear the blame, face the consequences . . .

JEAN: Yes, but . . . (*The bell rings sharply twice. Miss Julie jumps up. Jean changes his coat.*) The Count is back! Do you suppose Kristine — (*He goes to the speaking tube, taps the lid, and listens.*)

JULIE: He's been to his desk!

JEAN: It's Jean, sir! (*Listening; the audience cannot hear the Count's voice.*) Yes, sir! (*Listening.*) Yes sir! Right away! (*Listening.*) At once, sir! (*Listening.*) I see, in half an hour!

JULIE (*desperately frightened*): What did he say? Dear Lord, what did he say?

JEAN: He wants his boots and his coffee in half an hour.

JULIE: So, in half an hour! Oh, I'm so tired. I'm not able to do anything. I can't repent, can't run away, can't stay, can't live — can't die! Help me now! Order me, and I'll obey like a dog! Do me this last service, save my honor, save his name! You know what I *should* do, but don't have the will to . . . You will it, you order me to do it!

JEAN: I don't know why ———— but now I can't either ———— I don't understand. ———— It's as if this coat made it impossible for me to order you to do anything. ———— And now, since the Count spoke to me — I — I can't really explain it — but — ah, it's the damn lackey in me! —————— I think if the Count came down here now — and ordered me to cut my throat, I'd do it on the spot.

JULIE: Then pretend you're he, and I'm you! —————— You gave such a good performance before when you knelt at my feet. —————— You were a real nobleman. —————— Or — have you ever seen a hypnotist in the theatre? (*Jean nods.*) He says to his subject: "Take the broom," and he takes it. He says: "Sweep," and he sweeps ——————

JEAN: But the subject has to be asleep.

JULIE (*ecstatically*): I'm already asleep. —————— The whole room is like smoke around me . . . and you look like an iron stove . . . shaped like a man in black, with a tall hat — and your eyes glow like coals when the fire is dying — and your face is a white patch, like ashes —————— (*The sunlight has reached the floor and now shines on Jean.*) —————— it's so warm and good —————— (*She rubs her hands as if warming them before a fire.*) —————— and bright — and so peaceful!

JEAN: (*taking the razor and putting it in her hand*): Here's the broom! Go now while it's bright — out to the barn — and . . . (*Whispers in her ear.*)

JULIE (*awake*): Thank you. I'm going now to rest! But just tell me — that those who are first can also receive the gift of grace. Say it, even if you don't believe it.

JEAN: The first? No, I can't! —————— But wait — Miss Julie — now I know! You're no longer among the first — you're now among — the last!

JULIE: That's true. —————— I'm among the very last. I'm the last one of all! Oh! —————— But now I can't go! —————— Tell me once more to go!

JEAN: No, now I can't either! I can't!

JULIE: And the first shall be the last!

JEAN: Don't think, don't think! You're taking all my strength from me, making me a coward. —————— What was that? I thought the bell moved! —————— No! Shall we stuff paper in it? - —————— To be so afraid of a bell! —————— But it isn't just a bell. —————— There's someone behind it — a hand sets it in motion — and something else sets the hand in motion. —————— Maybe if you cover your ears — cover your ears! But then it rings even louder! rings until someone answers. —————— And then it's too late! And then the police come — and — then —————— (*The bell rings twice loudly. Jean flinches, then straightens up.*) It's horrible! But there's no other way! —————— Go! (*Miss Julie walks firmly out through the door.*)

ର୍ଘ

ANTON CHEKHOV (1860–1904) *was one of the few writers to gain eminence in two literary forms: the short story and the drama. Chekhov was born in modest circumstances in Taganrog, in southwestern Russia. His grandfather had been a serf who had bought his freedom, and his father was an unsuccessful grocer who believed in his son's education. Chekhov began to write stories while he was still a medical student to help his family pay off debts. These stories were mostly humorous sketches he first published in comic journals under different pen names, thinking he would keep his own* *name for his medical articles. Chekhov qualified as a doctor in 1884, but by 1887 the first two collections of his humorous stories had sold so well that he could afford to give all his time to writing. The next year he published the long story "The Steppe" in a literary journal, establishing his reputation as a writer of serious fiction.*

At the same time Chekhov was beginning his career as a writer, he was also creating his earliest plays, both serious and comic. Apparently he decided to become a playwright after seeing a Russian touring company's performance of Uncle Tom's Cabin, *a dramatized version of Harriet Beecher Stowe's popular 1852 novel. The plays Chekhov wrote that succeeded initially onstage were entertainments he called "vaudevilles" or farces, humorous short pieces sometimes based on his stories. He subtitled* The Bear *(1888), an original play, "A Farce in One Act." According to his English translator Michael Frayn, "It made the audience laugh non-stop . . . [and] it went on to cause a 'furor' at the Alexandrinsky, the imperial theatre in St Petersburg, and then to take the provinces by storm."*

Two years later, when Chekhov journeyed thousands of miles through rural villages in Siberia on his way to the penal colony in Sakhalin to interview prisoners for a book (published in 1895), he discovered that his comic plays were widely produced by amateur dramatic groups everywhere. A decade later, according to Frayn, Chekhov complained that "practically every lady I meet begins her acquaintance with me by saying: 'I've acted in your Bear.'" Chekhov made so much money in royalties from these early humorous plays that he told another writer that "anyone possessing fifty acres and ten tolerable vaudevilles I reckon to be a made man — his widow will never die of hunger. . . . The provinces will swallow anything. Just try to see there are good parts. The simpler the setting and the smaller the cast, the more often the vaudeville will be done." His words were a mixture of flippancy and practicality characteristic of his letters to aspiring writers who came to him for advice about their careers. The Bear *has survived as a classic comedy because its dialogue is full of energy and its succinct characterizations offer challenging opportunities for the actors.*

Chekhov's reputation as an important playwright is based on four plays he wrote in the last decade of his life: The Seagull *(1895),* Uncle Vanya *(1896),* Three Sisters *(1901), and* The Cherry Orchard *(1904). These plays revolutionized traditional drama by their new form, a complex mixture of comedy and tragedy that developed over the years he was writing and rewriting them for Constantin Stanislavsky's experimental Moscow Art Theatre. Chekhov struggled to make the transition from successful writer of short fiction and comic farces to serious dramatist while suffering from the physical debilitation of advanced tuberculosis. His sympathetic detachment as a story writer, his technique of compassionately allowing his characters to express their viewpoints, served him well as a dramatist. As he wrote his publisher, Aleksey S. Suvorin, who was also his closest friend, "If you're served coffee, then don't try looking for beer in it. If I present you with a professor's thoughts, then trust me and don't look for Chekhov's thoughts in them." What interested him was not the content of his characters' ideas but "the nature of these opinions, their dependence upon external influences, and so on. They must be examined like objects, like symptoms, entirely objectively, not attempting either to agree with them or to dispute them."*

As a short story writer Chekhov insisted that the writer must not judge his characters but remain an impartial witness, taking no moral stand about their con-

flicts and desires. As a dramatist he went even further. In his last four plays he discarded the idea of the well-made play and scattered his exposition of his characters' situation throughout the acts, compressing and internalizing the physical action, creating a new impressionistic form called "a theater of mood." He intended his plays to have no moral conflicts, no heroes or villains; all the characters invite a compassionate interpretation. This was a radical step for Chekhov to take as a dramatist, because in the theater of his time, plays were supposed to simplify the world offstage, to bring coherence to the chaos of feelings in which we live, and to impose a moral (and therefore human) order on the inhuman universe.

Even in Chekhov's early play The Bear, *we can see his typically realistic treatment of his characters as contradictory people rather than sentimentalized stereotypes, in their comic battle of the sexes. In the turbulent years before the Russian Revolution of 1917, Chekhov refused to take sides on social issues. In one of his letters to the Russian poet Alexei Plescheyev, he wrote that "the people I fear are those who seek to read tendencies into what one writes, and who want to see me as straightforwardly liberal or conservative. I am not a liberal — not a conservative . . . — not an indifferentist. I should like to be a free artist, and nothing else."*

RELATED STORIES: *Anton Chekhov, "The Darling," page 136; Anton Chekhov, "The Lady with the Pet Dog," page 145; Raymond Carver, "Errand," page 109 (see also the Casebook on Raymond Carver, page 814).*

RELATED COMMENTARIES: *Peter Brook, "On Chekhov," page 1975; Anton Chekhov, "Technique in Writing the Short Story," page 738.*

ANTON CHEKHOV

The Bear   1888

A Farce in One Act

TRANSLATED BY RONALD HINGLEY

Dedicated to N. N. Solovtsov

CHARACTERS

MRS. HELEN POPOV, *a young widow with dimpled cheeks, a landowner*
GREGORY SMIRNOV, *a landowner in early middle age*
LUKE, *Mrs. Popov's old manservant*

The action takes place in the drawing-room of Mrs. Popov's country house.

SCENE 1

Mrs. Popov, in deep mourning, with her eyes fixed on a snapshot, and Luke.

LUKE: This won't do, madam, you're just making your life a misery. Cook's out with the maid picking fruit, every living creature's happy and even our cat knows how to enjoy herself — she's parading round the yard trying to pick up a bird or two. But here you are cooped up inside all day like you was in a convent cell — you never have a good time. Yes, it's true. Nigh on twelve months it is since you last set foot outdoors.

MRS. POPOV: And I'm never going out again, why should I? My life's finished. He lies in his grave, I've buried myself inside these four walls — we're both dead.

LUKE: There you go again! I don't like to hear such talk, I don't. Your husband died and that was that — God's will be done and may he rest in peace. You've shed a few tears and that'll do, it's time to call it a day — you can't spend your whole life a-moaning and a-groaning. The same thing happened to me once, when my old woman died, but what did I do? I grieved a bit, shed a tear or two for a month or so and that's all she's getting. Catch me wearing sackcloth and ashes for the rest of my days, it'd be more than the old girl was worth! [*Sighs.*] You've neglected all the neighbours — won't go and see them or have them in the house. We never get out and about, lurking here like dirty great spiders, saving your presence. The mice have been at my livery too. And it's not for any lack of nice people either — the county's full of 'em, see. There's the regiment stationed at Ryblovo and them officers are a fair treat, a proper sight for sore eyes they are. They have a dance in camp of a Friday and the brass band plays most days. This ain't right, missus. You're young, and pretty as a picture with that peaches-and-cream look, so make the most of it. Them looks won't last for ever, you know. If you wait another ten years to come out of your shell and lead them officers a dance, you'll find it's too late.

MRS. POPOV [*decisively*]: Never talk to me like that again, please. When Nicholas died my life lost all meaning, as you know. You may think I'm alive, but I'm not really. I swore to wear this mourning and shun society till my dying day, do you hear? Let his departed spirit see how I love him! Yes, I realize you know what went on — that he was often mean to me, cruel and, er, unfaithful even, but I'll be true to the grave and show him how much I can love. And he'll find me in the next world just as I was before he died.

LUKE: Don't talk like that — walk round the garden instead. Or else have Toby or Giant harnessed and go and see the neighbours.

MRS. POPOV: Oh dear! [*Weeps.*]

LUKE: Missus! Madam! What's the matter? For heaven's sake!

MRS. POPOV: He was so fond of Toby — always drove him when he went over to the Korchagins' place and the Vlasovs'. He drove so well too! And he looked so graceful when he pulled hard on the reins, remember? Oh Toby, Toby! See he gets an extra bag of oats today.

LUKE: Very good, madam.

[*A loud ring.*]

MRS. POPOV [*shudders*]: Who is it? Tell them I'm not at home.

LUKE: Very well, madam. [*Goes out.*]

SCENE 2

Mrs. Popov, alone.

MRS. POPOV [*looking at the snapshot*]: Now you shall see how I can love and forgive, Nicholas. My love will only fade when I fade away myself, when this poor heart stops beating. [*Laughs, through tears.*] Well, aren't you ashamed of yourself? I'm your good, faithful little wifie, I've locked myself up and I'll be faithful to the grave, while you — aren't you ashamed, you naughty boy? You deceived me and you used to make scenes and leave me alone for weeks on end.

SCENE 3

Mrs. Popov and Luke.

LUKE [*Comes in, agitatedly.*]: Someone's asking for you, madam. Wants to see you ——

MRS. POPOV: Then I hope you told them I haven't received visitors since the day my husband died.

LUKE: I did, but he wouldn't listen — his business is very urgent, he says.

MRS. POPOV: *I am not at home!*

LUKE: So I told him, but he just swears and barges straight in, drat him. He's waiting in the dining-room.

MRS. POPOV [*irritatedly*]: All right, ask him in here then. Aren't people rude?

[*Luke goes out.*]

MRS. POPOV: Oh, aren't they all a bore? What do they want with me, why must they disturb my peace? [*Sighs.*] Yes, I see I really shall have to get me to a nunnery. [*Reflects.*] I'll take the veil, that's it.

SCENE 4

Mrs. Popov, Luke, and Smirnov.

SMIRNOV [*coming in, to Luke*]: You're a fool, my talkative friend. An ass. [*Seeing Mrs. Popov, with dignity.*] May I introduce myself, madam? Gregory Smirnov, landed gentleman and lieutenant of artillery retired. I'm obliged to trouble you on most urgent business.

MRS. POPOV [*not holding out her hand*]: What do you require?

SMIRNOV: I had the honour to know your late husband. He died owing me twelve hundred roubles — I have his two IOUs. Now I've some interest due to the land-bank tomorrow, madam, so may I trouble you to let me have the money today?

MRS. POPOV: Twelve hundred roubles — . How did my husband come to owe you that?

SMIRNOV: He used to buy his oats from me.

MRS. POPOV [*sighing, to Luke*]: Oh yes — Luke, don't forget to see Toby has his extra bag of oats. [*Luke goes out. To Smirnov.*] Of course I'll pay if Nicholas owed you something, but I've nothing on me today, sorry. My manager will be back from town the day after tomorrow and I'll get him to pay you whatever it is then, but for the time being I can't oblige. Besides, it's precisely seven months today since my husband died and I am in no fit state to discuss money.

SMIRNOV: Well, I'll be in a fit state to go bust with a capital B if I can't pay that interest tomorrow. They'll have the bailiffs in on me.

MRS. POPOV: You'll get your money the day after tomorrow.

SMIRNOV: I don't want it the day after tomorrow, I want it now.

MRS. POPOV: I can't pay you now, sorry.

SMIRNOV: And I can't wait till the day after tomorrow.

MRS. POPOV: Can I help it if I've no money today?

SMIRNOV: So you can't pay then?

MRS. POPOV: Exactly.

SMIRNOV: I see. And that's your last word, is it?

MRS. POPOV: It is.

SMIRNOV: Your last word? You really mean it?

MRS. POPOV: It is.

SMIRNOV: Your last word? You really mean it?

MRS. POPOV: I do.

SMIRNOV [*sarcastic*]: Then I'm greatly obliged to you, I'll put it in my diary! [*Shrugs.*] And people expect me to be cool and collected! I met the local excise man on my way here just now. "My dear Smirnov," says he, "why are you always losing your temper?" But how can I help it, I ask you? I'm in desperate need of money! Yesterday morning I left home at crack of dawn. I call on everyone who owes me money, but not a soul forks out. I'm dog-tired. I spend the night in some God-awful place — by the vodka barrel in a Jewish pot-house. Then I fetch up here, fifty miles from home, hoping to see the colour of my money, only to be fobbed off with this "no fit state" stuff! How *can* I keep my temper?

MRS. POPOV: I thought I'd made myself clear. You can have your money when my manager gets back from town.

SMIRNOV: It's not your manager I'm after, it's you. What the blazes, pardon my language, do I want with your manager?

MRS. POPOV: I'm sorry, my dear man, but I'm not accustomed to these peculiar expressions and to this tone. I have closed my ears. [*Hurries out.*]

SCENE 5

Smirnov, alone.

SMIRNOV: Well, what price that! "In no fit state!" Her husband died seven months ago, if you please! Now have I got my interest to pay or not? I want a straight answer — yes or no? All right, your husband's dead, you're in no fit state and so on and so forth, and your blasted manager's hopped it. But what am I supposed to do? Fly away from my creditors by balloon, I take it! Or go and bash the old brain-box against a brick wall? I call on Gruzdev — not at home. Yaroshevich is in hiding. I have a real old slanging-match with Kuritsyn and almost chuck him out of the window. Mazutov has the belly-ache, and this creature's "in no fit state." Not one of the swine will pay. This is what comes of being too nice to them and behaving like some snivelling no-hoper or old woman. It doesn't pay to wear kid gloves with this lot! All right, just you wait — I'll give you something to remember me by! You don't make a monkey out of me, blast you! I'm staying here — going to stick around till she coughs up. Pah! I feel well and truly riled today. I'm shaking like a leaf, I'm so furious — choking I am. Phew, my God, I really think I'm going to pass out! [*Shouts.*] Hey, you there!

SCENE 6

Smirnov and Luke.

LUKE [*comes in*]: What is it?

SMIRNOV: Bring me some kvass or water, will you?

[*Luke goes out.*]

SMIRNOV: What a mentality, though! You need money so bad you could shoot yourself, but she won't pay, being "in no fit state to discuss money," if you please! There's female logic for you and no mistake! That's why I don't like talking to women. Never have. Talk to a woman — why, I'd rather sit on top of a powder magazine! Pah! It makes my flesh creep, I'm so fed up with her, her and that great trailing dress! Poetic creatures they call 'em! Why, the very sight of one gives me cramp in both legs, I get so aggravated.

SCENE 7

Smirnov and Luke.

LUKE [*comes in and serves some water*]: Madam's unwell and won't see anyone.

SMIRNOV: You clear out!

[*Luke goes out.*]

SMIRNOV: "Unwell and won't see anyone." All right then, don't! I'm staying put, chum, and I don't budge one inch till you unbelt. Be ill for a week and I'll stay a week, make it a year and a year I'll stay. I'll have my rights, lady! As for your black dress and dimples, you don't catch me that way — we know all about those dimples! [*Shouts through the window.*] Unhitch, Simon, we're here for some time — I'm staying put. Tell the stable people to give my horses oats. And you've got that animal tangled in the reins again, you great oaf! [*Imitates him.*] "I don't care." I'll give you don't care! [*Moves away from the window.*] How ghastly — it's unbearably hot, no one will pay up, I had a bad night, and now here's this female with her long black dress and her states. I've got a headache. How about a glass of vodka? That might be an idea. [*Shouts.*] Hey, you there!

LUKE [*comes in*]: What is it?

SMIRNOV: Bring me a glass of vodka.

[*Luke goes out.*]

SMIRNOV: Phew! [*Sits down and looks himself over.*] A fine specimen I am, I must say — dust all over me, my boots dirty, unwashed, hair unbrushed, straw on my waistcoat. I bet the little woman took me for a burglar. [*Yawns.*] It's not exactly polite to turn up in a drawing-room in this rig! Well, anyway, I'm not a guest here, I'm collecting money. And there's no such thing as correct wear for the well-dressed creditor.

LUKE [*comes in and gives him the vodka*]: This is a liberty, sir.

SMIRNOV [*angrily*]: What!

LUKE: I, er, it's all right, I just ——

SMIRNOV: Who do you think you're talking to? You hold your tongue!

LUKE [*aside*]: Now we'll never get rid of him, botheration take it! It's an ill wind brought him along.

[*Luke goes out.*]

SMIRNOV: Oh, I'm so furious! I could pulverize the whole world, I'm in such a rage. I feel quite ill. [*Shouts.*] Hey, you there!

SCENE 8

Mrs. Popov and Smirnov.

MRS. POPOV [*comes in, with downcast eyes*]: Sir, in my solitude I have grown unaccustomed to the sound of human speech, and I can't stand shouting. I must urgently request you not to disturb my peace.

SMIRNOV: Pay up and I'll go.

MRS. POPOV: As I've already stated quite plainly, I've no ready cash. Wait till the day after tomorrow.

SMIRNOV: I've also had the honour of stating quite plainly that I need the money today, not the day after tomorrow. If you won't pay up now, I'll have to put my head in a gas-oven tomorrow.

MRS. POPOV: Can I help it if I've no cash in hand? This is all rather odd.

SMIRNOV: So you won't pay up now, eh?

MRS. POPOV: I can't.

SMIRNOV: In that case I'm not budging, I'll stick around here till I do get my money. [*Sits down.*] You'll pay the day after tomorrow, you say? Very well, then I'll sit here like this till the day after tomorrow. I'll just stay put exactly as I am. [*Jumps up.*] I ask you — have I got that interest to pay tomorrow or haven't I? Think I'm trying to be funny, do you?

MRS. POPOV: Kindly don't raise your voice at me, sir — we're not in the stables.

SMIRNOV: I'm not discussing stables, I'm asking whether my interest falls due tomorrow. Yes or no?

MRS. POPOV: You don't know how to treat a lady.

SMIRNOV: Oh yes I do.

MRS. POPOV: Oh no you don't. You're a ride, ill-bred person. Nice men don't talk to ladies like that.

SMIRNOV: Now this *is* a surprise! How do you want me to talk then? In French, I suppose? [*In an angry, simpering voice.*] Madame, je voo pree. You won't pay me — how perfectly delightful. Oh, *pardong*, I'm sure — sorry you were troubled! Now isn't the weather divine today? And that black dress looks too, too charming! [*Bows and scrapes.*]

MRS. POPOV: That's silly. And not very clever.

SMIRNOV [*mimics her*]: "Silly, not very clever." I don't know how to treat a lady, don't I? Madam, I've seen more women in my time than you have house-sparrows. I've fought three duels over women. There have been twenty-one women in my life. Twelve times it was me broke it off, the other nine got in first. Oh yes! Time was I made an ass of myself, slobbered, mooned around, bowed and scraped, and practically crawled on my belly. I loved, I suffered, I sighed at the moon, I languished, I melted, I grew cold. I loved passionately, madly, in every conceivable fashion, damn me, burbling nineteen to the dozen about women's emancipation, and wasting half my substance on the tender passion. But now — no thank you very much! I can't be fooled any more, I've had enough. Black eyes, passionate looks, crimson lips, dimpled cheeks, moonlight, "Whispers, passion's bated breathing" — I don't give a tinker's cuss for the lot now, lady. Present company excepted, all women, large or small, are simpering, mincing, gossipy creatures. They're great haters. They're eyebrow-deep in lies. They're futile, they're trivial, they're cruel, they're outrageously illogical. And as for having anything upstairs [*Taps his forehead.*] — I'm sorry to be so blunt, but the very birds in the trees can run rings round your average blue-stocking. Take any one of these poetical creations. Oh, she's all froth and fluff, she is, she's half divine, she sends you into a million raptures. But you take a peep inside her mind, and what do you see? A common or garden crocodile! [*Clutches the back of a chair, which cracks and breaks.*] And yet this crocodile somehow thinks its great life-work, privilege, and monopoly is the tender passion — that's what really gets me! But damn and blast it, and crucify me upside down on that wall if I'm wrong — does a woman know how to love any living creature apart from lapdogs? Her love gets no further than snivelling and slobbering. The man suffers and makes sacrifices, while she just twitches the train of her dress and tries to get him squirming under her thumb, that's what her love adds up to! You must know what women are like, seeing you've the rotten luck to be one. Tell me frankly, did you ever see a sincere, faithful, true woman? You know you didn't. Only the old and ugly ones are true and faithful. You'll never find a constant woman, not in a month of Sundays you won't, not once in a blue moon!

MRS. POPOV: Well, I like that! Then who is true and faithful in love to your way of thinking? Not men by any chance?

SMIRNOV: Yes, madam. Men.

MRS. POPOV: Men! [*Gives a bitter laugh.*] Men true and faithful in love! That's rich, I must say. [*Vehemently.*] What right have you to talk like that? Men true and faithful! If it comes to that, the best man I've ever known was my late husband, I may say. I loved him passionately, with all my heart as only an intelligent young woman can. I gave him my youth, my happiness, my life, my possessions. I lived only for him. I worshipped him as an idol. And — what do you think? This best of men was shamelessly deceiving me all along the line! After his death I found a drawer in his desk full of love letters, and when he was alive — oh, what a frightful memory! — he used to leave me on my own for weeks on end, he carried on with other girls before my very eyes, he was unfaithful to me, he spent my money like water, and he joked about my feelings for him. But I loved him all the same, and I've been faithful to him. What's more, I'm still faithful and true now that he's dead. I've buried myself alive inside these four walls and I shall go round in these widow's weeds till my dying day.

SMIRNOV [*with a contemptuous laugh*]: Widow's weeds! Who do you take me for? As if I didn't know why you wear this fancy dress and bury yourself indoors! Why, it sticks out a mile! Mysterious and romantic, isn't it? Some army cadet or hack poet may pass by your garden, look up at your windows and think: "There dwells Tamara, the mysterious princess, the one who buried herself alive from love of her husband." Who do you think you're fooling?

MRS. POPOV [*flaring up*]: What! You dare to take that line with me!

SMIRNOV: Buries herself alive — but doesn't forget to powder her nose!

MRS. POPOV: You dare adopt that tone!

SMIRNOV: Don't you raise your voice to me, madam, I'm not one of your servants. Let me call a spade a spade. Not being a woman, I'm used to saying what I think. So stop shouting, pray.

MRS. POPOV: It's you who are shouting, not me. Leave me alone, would you mind?

SMIRNOV: Pay up, and I'll go.

MRS. POPOV: You'll get nothing out of me.

SMIRNOV: Oh yes I shall.

MRS. POPOV: Just to be awkward, you won't get one single copeck. And you can leave me alone.

SMIRNOV: Not having the pleasure of being your husband or fiancé, I'll trouble you not to make a scene. [*Sits down.*] I don't like it.

MRS. POPOV [*choking with rage*]: Do I see you sitting down?

SMIRNOV: You must certainly do.

MRS. POPOV: Would you mind leaving?

SMIRNOV: Give me my money. [*Aside.*] Oh, I'm in such a rage! Furious I am!

MRS. POPOV: I've no desire to bandy words with cads, sir. Kindly clear off! [*Pause.*] Well, are you going or aren't you?

SMIRNOV: No.

MRS. POPOV: No?

SMIRNOV: No!

MRS. POPOV: Very well then! [*Rings.*]

SCENE 9

The above and Luke.

MRS. POPOV: Show this gentleman out, Luke.

LUKE [*goes up to Smirnov*]: Be so good as to leave, sir, when you're told, sir. No point in ——

SMIRNOV [*Jumping up*]: You hold your tongue! Who do you think you're talking to? I'll carve you up in little pieces.

LUKE [*clutching at his heart*]: Heavens and saints above us! [*Falls into an armchair.*] Oh, I feel something terrible — fair took my breath away, it did.

MRS. POPOV: But where's Dasha? Dasha! [*Shouts.*] Dasha! Pelageya! Dasha! [*Rings.*]

LUKE: Oh, they've all gone fruit-picking. There's no one in the house. I feel faint. Fetch water.

MRS. POPOV: Be so good as to clear out!

SMIRNOV: Couldn't you be a bit more polite?

MRS. POPOV [*clenching her fists and stamping*]: You uncouth oaf! You have the manners of a bear! Think you own the place? Monster!

SMIRNOV: What! You say that again!

MRS. POPOV: I called you an ill-mannered oaf, a monster!

SMIRNOV [*advancing on her*]: Look here, what right have you to insult me?

MRS. POPOV: All right, I'm insulting you. So what? Think I'm afraid of you?

SMIRNOV: Just because you look all romantic, you can get away with anything — is that your idea? This is duelling talk!

LUKE: Heavens and saints above us! Water!

SMIRNOV: Pistols at dawn!

MRS. POPOV: Just because you have big fists and the lungs of an ox you needn't think I'm scared, see? Think you own the place, don't you!

SMIRNOV: We'll shoot it out! No one calls me names and gets away with it, weaker sex or no weaker sex.

MRS. POPOV [*trying to shout him down*]: You coarse lout!

SMIRNOV: Why should it only be us men who answer for our insults? It's high time we dropped that silly idea. If women want equality, let them damn well have equality! I challenge you, madam!

MRS. POPOV: Want to shoot it out, eh? Very well.

SMIRNOV: This very instant!

MRS. POPOV: Most certainly! My husband left some pistols, I'll fetch them instantly. [*Moves hurriedly off and comes back.*] I'll enjoy putting a bullet through that thick skull, damn your infernal cheek! [*Goes out.*]

SMIRNOV: I'll pot her like a sitting bird. I'm not one of your sentimental young puppies. She'll get no chivalry from me!

LUKE: Kind sir! [*Kneels.*] Grant me a favour, pity an old man and leave this place. First you frighten us out of our wits, now you want to fight a duel.

SMIRNOV: [*Not listening.*] A duel! There's true women's emancipation for you! That evens up the sexes with a vengeance! I'll knock her off as a matter of principle. But what a woman! [*Mimics her.*] "Damn your infernal cheek! I'll put a bullet through that thick skull." Not bad, eh? Flushed all over, flashing eyes, accepts my challenge! You know, I've never seen such a woman in my life.

LUKE: Go away, sir, and I'll say prayers for you till the day I die.

SMIRNOV: There's a regular woman for you, something I do appreciate! A proper woman — not some namby-pamby, wishy-washy female, but a really red-hot bit of stuff, a regular pistol-packing little spitfire. A pity to kill her, really.

LUKE [*weeps*]: Kind sir — do leave. Please!

SMIRNOV: I definitely like her. Definitely! Never mind her dimples, I like her. I wouldn't mind letting her off what she owes me, actually. And I don't feel angry any more. Wonderful woman!

SCENE 10

The above and Mrs. Popov.

MRS. POPOV [*comes in with the pistols*]: Here are the pistols. But before we start would you mind showing me how to fire them? I've never had a pistol in my hands before.

LUKE: Lord help us! Mercy on us! I'll go and find the gardener and coachman. What have we done to deserve this? [*Goes out.*]

SMIRNOV [*examining the pistols*]: Now, there are several types of pistol. There are Mortimer's special duelling pistols with percussion caps. Now, yours here are Smith and Wessons, triple action with extractor, centre-fired. They're fine weapons, worth a cool ninety roubles the pair. Now, you hold a revolver like this. [*Aside.*] What eyes, what eyes! She's hot stuff all right!

MRS. POPOV: Like this?

SMIRNOV: Yes, that's right. Then you raise the hammer and take aim like this. Hold your head back a bit, stretch your arm out properly. Right. And then with this finger you press this little gadget and that's it. But the great thing is — don't get excited and do take your time about aiming. Try and see your hand doesn't shake.

MRS. POPOV: All right. We can't very well shoot indoors, let's go in the garden.

SMIRNOV: Very well. But I warn you, I'm firing in the air.

MRS. POPOV: Oh, this is the limit! Why?

SMIRNOV: Because, because — . That's my business.

MRS. POPOV: Got cold feet, eh? I see. Now don't shilly-shally, sir. Kindly follow me. I shan't rest till I've put a bullet through your brains, damn you. Got the wind up, have you?

SMIRNOV: Yes.

MRS. POPOV: That's a lie. Why won't you fight?

SMIRNOV: Because, er, because you, er, I like you.

MRS. POPOV [*with a vicious laugh*]: He likes me! He dares to say he likes me! [*Points to the door.*] I won't detain you.

SMIRNOV [*puts down the revolver without speaking, picks up his peaked cap and moves off; near the door he stops and for about half a minute the two look at each other without speaking; then he speaks, going up to her hesitantly*]: Listen. Are you still angry? I'm absolutely furious myself, but you must see — how can I put it? The fact is that, er, it's this way, actually — . [*Shouts.*] Anyway, can I help it if I like you? [*Clutches the back of a chair, which cracks and breaks.*] Damn fragile stuff, furniture! I like you! Do you understand? I, er, I'm almost in love.

MRS. POPOV: Keep away from me, I loathe you.

SMIRNOV: God, what a woman! Never saw the like of it in all my born days. I'm sunk! Without trace! Trapped like a mouse!

MRS. POPOV: Get back or I shoot.

SMIRNOV: Shoot away. I'd die happily with those marvellous eyes looking at me, that's what you can't see — die by that dear little velvet hand. Oh, I'm crazy! Think it over and make your mind up now, because once I leave this place we shan't see each other again. So make your mind up. I'm a gentleman and a man of honour, I've ten thousand a year, I can put a bullet through a coin in midair, and I keep a good stable. Be my wife.

MRS. POPOV [*indignantly brandishes the revolver*]: A duel! We'll shoot it out!

SMIRNOV: I'm out of my mind! Nothing makes any sense. [*Shouts.*] Hey, you there — water!

MRS. POPOV [*shouts*]: We'll shoot it out!

SMIRNOV: I've lost my head, fallen for her like some damfool boy! [*Clutches her hand. She shrieks with pain.*] I love you! [*Kneels.*] I love you as I never loved any of my twenty-one other women — twelve times it was me broke it off, the other nine got in first. But I never loved anyone as much as you. I've gone all sloppy, soft, and sentimental. Kneeling like an imbecile, offering my hand! Disgraceful! Scandalous! I haven't been in love for five years, I swore not to, and here I am crashing head over heels, hook, line, and sinker! I offer you my hand. Take it or leave it. [*Gets up and hurries to the door.*]

MRS. POPOV: Just a moment.

SMIRNOV [*stops*]: What is it?

MRS. POPOV: Oh, never mind, just go away. But wait. No, go, go away. I hate you. Or no — don't go away. Oh, if you knew how furious I am! [*Throws the revolver on the table.*] My fingers are numb from holding this beastly thing. [*Tears a handkerchief in her anger.*] Why are you hanging about? Clear out!

SMIRNOV: Good-bye.

MRS. POPOV: Yes, yes, go away! [*Shouts.*] Where are you going? Stop. Oh, go away then. I'm so furious! Don't you come near me, I tell you.

SMIRNOV [*going up to her*]: I'm so fed up with myself! Falling in love like a schoolboy! Kneeling down! It's enough to give you the willies! [*Rudely.*] I love you! Oh, it's just what the doctor ordered, this is! There's my interest due in tomorrow, haymaking's upon us — and *you* have to come along! [*Takes her by the waist.*] I'll never forgive myself.

MRS. POPOV: Go away! You take your hands off me! I, er, hate you! We'll sh-shoot it out!

[*A prolonged kiss.*]

SCENE 11

The above, Luke with an axe, the gardener with a rake, the coachman with a pitchfork, and some workmen with sundry sticks and staves.

LUKE [*seeing the couple kissing*]: Mercy on us! [*Pause.*]

MRS. POPOV [*lowering her eyes*]: Luke, tell them in the stables — Toby gets no oats today.

Curtain

യൂ

SUSAN GLASPELL (*1876–1948*) *was born in Davenport, Iowa, into a family that had been among the state's first settlers a generation before. After her graduation from high school, she worked as a reporter and society editor for various newspapers before enrolling at Drake University in Des Moines, where she studied literature, philosophy, and history. She also edited the college newspaper and began to write short stories. In 1899 she took a job as statehouse reporter for the* Des Moines Daily News. *Years later she claimed that the discipline of newspaper work helped her to become a creative writer.*

At the age of twenty-five, Glaspell returned to Davenport to live with her family, "boldly" determined, as she said, to quit journalism and "give all my time to my own writing. I say 'boldly,' because I had to earn my living." Slowly she began to publish her own work, mostly sentimental magazine stories and an undistinguished first novel — fiction that, as her biographer C. W. E. Bigsby has noted, "suggested little of the originality and power which were to mark her work in the theater." In 1909

Glaspell met George Cram Cook, a novelist and utopian socialist from a wealthy family who divorced his second wife and left his two children to marry her.

Glaspell and Cook moved to Greenwich Village in New York City and collaborated on a short play for the experimental Washington Square Players in 1915, Suppressed Desires, *a comedy about psychoanalysis and its founder, Sigmund Freud, whom they sarcastically referred to as "the new Messiah." The simple sets and amateur performances in this off-Broadway theater company contrasted with the ostentation then prevailing on Broadway. There producers such as David Belasco went to extreme lengths in the lavishness of their sets and costumes, transferring to the stage every detail of an actual Child's Restaurant, for example, in the popular play* The Governor's Lady *in 1912. After the Players left Greenwich Village to relocate in Provincetown on Cape Cod in 1916, Cook urged Glaspell to write a new play for their fledgling theater company, renamed the Provincetown Players. When she protested that she did not know how to write plays, he told her, "Nonsense. You've got a stage, haven't you?"*

Glaspell's memory of a murder trial in Iowa that she'd covered as a newspaper reporter served as the inspiration for the short play Trifles *(1916). A decade later, in her biography of her husband,* The Road to the Temple *(1927), Glaspell recalled how she visualized the play while sitting in a ramshackle fish house at the end of a wharf in Provincetown where she and Cook were establishing a theater:*

> *So I went out on the wharf, sat alone on one of our wooden benches without a back, and looked a long time at that bare little stage. After a time the stage became a kitchen — a kitchen there all by itself. I saw just where the stove was, the table, and the steps going upstairs. Then the door at the back opened, and people all bundled up came in — two or three men, I wasn't sure which, but sure enough about the two women, who hung back, reluctant to enter that kitchen. When I was a newspaper reporter out in Iowa, I was sent down-state to do a murder trial, and I never forgot going into the kitchen of a woman locked up in town. I had meant to do it as a short story, but the stage took it for its own, so I hurried in from the wharf to write down what I had seen. Whenever I got stuck, I would run across the street to the old wharf, sit in that leaning little theater under which the sea sounded, until the play was ready to continue. Sometimes things written in my room would not form on the stage, and I must go home and cross them out.*

Glaspell finished Trifles *in ten days. It opened on August 8, 1916, with Glaspell and Cook in the cast. Glaspell went on to write ten more plays for the Provincetown Players, but* Trifles *is the one play of hers that is continually reprinted. She also published a short story version of the play, entitled "A Jury of Her Peers," in 1917. During the six years of Cook's visionary leadership, the Provincetown Players produced one hundred plays by fifty-two authors. The company's promotion of American playwrights was an important landmark in the history of theater in the United States. As the historian Barbara Ozieblo realized, the Provincetown Players "constituted a laboratory for their two stars, Eugene O'Neill and Susan Glaspell; they triumphed both in the United States and in England; they broke the hegemony of Broadway, proving the value of little theatres and their experimental work and so seeding the mature drama of America."*

RELATED STORY: *Susan Glaspell, "A Jury of Her Peers," page 243.*

RELATED COMMENTARIES: *Travis Bogard, "The Provincetown Players," page 1972; Leonard Mustazza, "Generic Translation and Thematic Shift in Susan Glaspell's* Trifles *and 'A Jury of Her Peers,' " page 2002.*

SUSAN GLASPELL

Trifles

1916

CHARACTERS

GEORGE HENDERSON, *county attorney*
HENRY PETERS, *sheriff*
LEWIS HALE, *a neighboring farmer*
MRS. PETERS
MRS. HALE

SCENE: *The kitchen in the now abandoned farmhouse of John Wright, a gloomy kitchen, and left without having been put in order — the walls covered with a faded wall paper. Down right is a door leading to the parlor. On the right wall above this door is a built-in kitchen cupboard with shelves in the upper portion and drawers below. In the rear wall at right, up two steps is a door opening onto stairs leading to the second floor. In the rear wall at left is a door to the shed and from there to the outside. Between these two doors is an old-fashioned black iron stove. Running along the left wall from the shed door is an old iron sink and sink shelf, in which is set a hand pump. Downstage of the sink is an uncurtained window. Near the window is an old wooden rocker. Center stage is an unpainted wooden kitchen table with straight chairs on either side. There is a small chair down right. Unwashed pans under the sink, a loaf of bread outside the breadbox, a dish towel on the table — other signs of incompleted work. At the rear the shed door opens and the Sheriff comes in followed by the County Attorney and Hale. The Sheriff and Hale are men in middle life, the County Attorney is a young man; all are much bundled up and go at once to the stove. They are followed by the two women — the Sheriff's wife, Mrs. Peters, first; she is a slight wiry woman, a thin nervous face. Mrs. Hale is larger and would ordinarily be called more comfortable looking, but she is disturbed now and looks fearfully about as she enters. The women have come in slowly, and stand close together near the door.*

COUNTY ATTORNEY (*at stove rubbing his hands*): This feels good. Come up to the fire, ladies.

MRS. PETERS (*after taking a step forward*): I'm not — cold.

SHERIFF (*unbuttoning his overcoat and stepping away from the stove to right of table as if to mark the beginning of official business*): Now, Mr. Hale, before we move things about, you explain to Mr. Henderson just what you saw when you came here yesterday morning.

COUNTY ATTORNEY (*crossing down to left of the table*): By the way, has anything been moved? Are things just as you left them yesterday?

SHERIFF (*looking about*): It's just about the same. When it dropped below zero last night I thought I'd better send Frank out this morning to make a fire for us — (*sits right of center table*) no use getting pneumonia with a big case on, but I told him not to touch anything except the stove — and you know Frank.

COUNTY ATTORNEY: Somebody should have been left here yesterday.

SHERIFF: Oh — yesterday. When I had to send Frank to Morris Center for that man who went crazy — I want you to know I had my hands full yester-

day. I knew you could get back from Omaha by today and as long as I
went over everything here myself ──────

COUNTY ATTORNEY: Well, Mr. Hale, tell just what happened when you came here
yesterday morning.

HALE (*crossing down to above table*): Harry and I had started to town with a load
of potatoes. We came along the road from my place and as I got here I
said, "I'm going to see if I can't get John Wright to go in with me on a
party telephone." I spoke to Wright about it once before and he put me
off, saying folks talked too much anyway, and all he asked was peace
and quiet — I guess you know about how much he talked himself; but I
thought maybe if I went to the house and talked about it before his wife,
though I said to Harry that I didn't know as what his wife wanted made
much difference to John ──────

COUNTY ATTORNEY: Let's talk about that later, Mr. Hale. I do want to talk about
that, but tell now just what happened when you got to the house.

HALE: I didn't hear or see anything; I knocked at the door, and still it was
all quiet inside. I knew they must be up, it was past eight o'clock. So
I knocked again, and I thought I heard somebody say, "Come in." I
wasn't sure, I'm not sure yet, but I opened the door — this door (*indicating the door by which the two women are still standing*) and there in that
rocker — (*pointing to it*) sat Mrs. Wright. (*They all look at the rocker down
left.*)

COUNTY ATTORNEY: What — was she doing?

HALE: She was rockin' back and forth. She had her apron in her hand and was
kind of — pleating it.

COUNTY ATTORNEY: And how did she — look?

HALE: Well, she looked queer.

COUNTY ATTORNEY: How do you mean — queer?

HALE: Well, as if she didn't know what she was going to do next. And kind of
done up.

COUNTY ATTORNEY (*takes out notebook and pencil and sits left of center table*): How
did she seem to feel about your coming?

HALE: Why, I don't think she minded — one way or other. She didn't pay much
attention. I said, "How do, Mrs. Wright, it's cold, ain't it?" And she said,
"Is it?" — and went on kind of pleating at her apron. Well, I was surprised; she didn't ask me to come up to the stove, or to set down, but just
sat there, not cven looking at me, so I said, "I want to see John." And
then she — laughed. I guess you would call it a laugh. I thought of
Harry and the team outside, so I said a little sharp: "Can't I see John?"
"No," she says, kind o' dull like. "Ain't he home?" says I. "Yes," says
she, "he's home." "Then why can't I see him?" I asked her, out of patience. " 'Cause he's dead," says she. "*Dead?*" says I. She just nodded her
head, not getting a bit excited, but rockin' back and forth. "Why —
where is he?" says I, not knowing what to say. She just pointed upstairs — like that. (*Himself pointing to the room above.*) I started for the
stairs, with the idea of going up there. I walked from there to here —

then I says, "Why, what did he die of?" "He died of a rope round his neck," says she, and just went on pleatin' at her apron. Well, I went out and called Harry. I thought I might — need help. We went upstairs and there he was lyin' ——

COUNTY ATTORNEY: I think I'd rather have you go into that upstairs, where you can point it all out. Just go on now with the rest of the story.

HALE: Well, my first thought was to get that rope off. It looked . . . (*stops; his face twitches*) . . . but Harry, he went up to him, and he said, "No, he's dead all right, and we'd better not touch anything." So we went back downstairs. She was still sitting that same way. "Has anybody been notified?" I asked. "No," says she, unconcerned. "Who did this, Mrs. Wright?" said Harry. He said it businesslike — and she stopped pleatin' of her apron. "I don't know," she says. "You don't *know?*" says Harry. "No," says she. "Weren't you sleepin' in the bed with him?" says Harry. "Yes," says she, "but I was on the inside." "Somebody slipped a rope round his neck and strangled him and you didn't wake up?" says Harry. "I didn't wake up," she said after him. We must 'a' looked as if we didn't see how that could be, for after a minute she said, "I sleep sound." Harry was going to ask her more questions but I said maybe we ought to let her tell her story first to the coroner, or the sheriff, so Harry went fast as he could to Rivers' place, where there's a telephone.

COUNTY ATTORNEY: And what did Mrs. Wright do when she knew that you had gone for the coroner?

HALE: She moved from the rocker to that chair over there (*pointing to a small chair in the down right corner*) and just sat there with her hands held together and looking down. I got a feeling that I ought to make some conversation, so I said I had come in to see if John wanted to put in a telephone, and at that she started to laugh, and then she stopped and looked at me — scared. (*The County Attorney, who has had his notebook out, makes a note.*) I dunno, maybe it wasn't scared. I wouldn't like to say it was. Soon Harry got back, and then Dr. Lloyd came and you, Mr. Peters, and so I guess that's all I know that you don't.

COUNTY ATTORNEY (*rising and looking around*): I guess we'll go upstairs first — and then out to the barn and around there. (*To the Sheriff.*) You're convinced that there was nothing important here — nothing that would point to any motive?

SHERIFF: Nothing here but kitchen things. (*The County Attorney, after again looking around the kitchen, opens the door of a cupboard closet in right wall. He brings a small chair from right — gets on it and looks on a shelf. Pulls his hand away, sticky.*)

COUNTY ATTORNEY: Here's a nice mess. (*The women draw nearer up center.*)

MRS. PETERS (*to the other woman*): Oh, her fruit; it did freeze. (*To the Lawyer.*) She worried about that when it turned so cold. She said the fire'd go out and her jars would break.

SHERIFF (*rises*): Well, can you beat the woman! Held for murder and worryin' about her preserves.

COUNTY ATTORNEY (*getting down from chair*): I guess before we're through she may have something more serious than preserves to worry about. (*Crosses down right center.*)

HALE: Well, women are used to worrying over trifles. (*The two women move a little closer together.*)

COUNTY ATTORNEY (*with the gallantry of a young politician*): And yet, for all their worries, what would we do without the ladies? (*The women do not unbend. He goes below the center table to the sink, takes a dipperful of water from the pail, and pouring it into a basin, washes his hands. While he is doing this the Sheriff and Hale cross to cupboard, which they inspect. The County Attorney starts to wipe his hands on the roller towel, turns it for a cleaner place.*) Dirty towels! (*Kicks his foot against the pans under the sink.*) Not much of a housekeeper, would you say, ladies?

MRS. HALE (*stiffly*): There's a great deal of work to be done on a farm.

COUNTY ATTORNEY: To be sure. And yet (*with a little bow to her*) I know there are some Dickson County farmhouses which do not have such roller towels. (*He gives it a pull to expose its full-length again.*)

MRS. HALE: Those towels get dirty awful quick. Men's hands aren't always as clean as they might be.

COUNTY ATTORNEY: Ah, loyal to your sex, I see. But you and Mrs. Wright were neighbors. I suppose you were friends, too.

MRS. HALE (*shaking her head*): I've not seen much of her of late years. I've not been in this house — it's more than a year.

COUNTY ATTORNEY (*crossing to women up center*): And why was that? You didn't like her?

MRS. HALE: I liked her all well enough. Farmers' wives have their hands full, Mr. Henderson. And then ——

COUNTY ATTORNEY: Yes —— ?

MRS. HALE (*looking about*): It never seemed a very cheerful place.

COUNTY ATTORNEY: No — it's not cheerful. I shouldn't say she had the home-making instinct.

MRS. HALE: Well, I don't know as Wright had, either.

COUNTY ATTORNEY: You mean that they didn't get on very well?

MRS. HALE: No, I don't mean anything. But I don't think a place'd be any cheerfuller for John Wright's being in it.

COUNTY ATTORNEY: I'd like to talk more of that a little later. I want to get the lay of things upstairs now. (*He goes past the women to up right where steps lead to a stair door.*)

SHERIFF: I suppose anything Mrs. Peters does'll be all right. She was to take in some clothes for her, you know, and a few little things. We left in such a hurry yesterday.

COUNTY ATTORNEY: Yes, but I would like to see what you take, Mrs. Peters, and keep an eye out for anything that might be of use to us.

MRS. PETERS: Yes, Mr. Henderson. (*The men leave by up right door to stairs. The women listen to the men's steps on the stairs, then look about the kitchen.*)

MRS. HALE (*crossing left to sink*): I'd hate to have men coming into my kitchen, snooping around and criticizing. (*She arranges the pans under sink which the lawyer had shoved out of place.*)

MRS. PETERS: Of course it's no more than their duty. (*Crosses to cupboard up right.*)

MRS. HALE: Duty's all right, but I guess that deputy sheriff that came out to make the fire might have got a little of this on. (*Gives the roller towel a pull.*) Wish I'd thought of that sooner. Seems mean to talk about her for not having things slicked up when she had to come away in such a hurry. (*Crosses right to Mrs. Peters at cupboard.*)

MRS. PETERS (*who has been looking through cupboard, lifts one end of towel that covers a pan*): She had bread set. (*Stands still.*)

MRS. HALE (*eyes fixed on a loaf of bread beside the breadbox, which is on a low shelf of the cupboard*): She was going to put this in there. (*Picks up loaf, abruptly drops it. In a manner of returning to familiar things.*) It's a shame about her fruit. I wonder if it's all gone. (*Gets up on the chair and looks.*) I think there's some here that's all right, Mrs. Peters. Yes — here; (*holding it toward the window*) this is cherries, too. (*Looking again.*) I declare I believe that's the only one. (*Gets down, jar in her hand. Goes to the sink and wipes it off on the outside.*) She'll feel awful bad after all her hard work in the hot weather. I remember the afternoon I put up my cherries last summer. (*She puts the jar on the big kitchen table, center of the room. With a sigh, is about to sit down in the rocking chair. Before she is seated realizes what chair it is; with a slow look at it, steps back. The chair which she has touched rocks back and forth. Mrs. Peters moves to center table and they both watch the chair rock for a moment or two.*)

MRS. PETERS (*shaking off the mood which the empty rocking chair has evoked. Now in a businesslike manner she speaks*): Well I must get those things from the front room closet. (*She goes to the door at the right but, after looking into the other room, steps back.*) You coming with me, Mrs. Hale? You could help me carry them. (*They go in the other room; reappear, Mrs. Peters carrying a dress, petticoat, and skirt, Mrs. Hale following with a pair of shoes.*) My, it's cold in there. (*She puts the clothes on the big table and hurries to the stove.*)

MRS. HALE (*right of center table examining the skirt*): Wright was close. I think maybe that's why she kept so much to herself. She didn't even belong to the Ladies' Aid. I suppose she felt she couldn't do her part, and then you don't enjoy things when you feel shabby. I heard she used to wear pretty clothes and be lively, when she was Minnie Foster, one of the town girls singing in the choir. But that — oh, that was thirty years ago. This all you want to take in?

MRS. PETERS: She said she wanted an apron. Funny thing to want, for there isn't much to get you dirty in jail, goodness knows. But I suppose just to make her feel more natural. (*Crosses to cupboard.*) She said they was in the top drawer in this cupboard. Yes, here. And then her little shawl that always hung behind the door. (*Opens stair door and looks.*) Yes, here it is. (*Quickly shuts door leading upstairs.*)

MRS. HALE (*abruptly moving toward her*): Mrs. Peters?

MRS. PETERS: Yes, Mrs. Hale? (*At up right door.*)

MRS. HALE: Do you think she did it?

MRS. PETERS (*in a frightened voice*): Oh, I don't know.

MRS. HALE: Well, I don't think she did. Asking for an apron and her little shawl. Worrying about her fruit.

MRS. PETERS (*starts to speak, glances up, where footsteps are heard in the room above. In a low voice*): Mr. Peters says it looks bad for her. Mr. Henderson is awful sarcastic in a speech and he'll make fun of her sayin' she didn't wake up.

MRS. HALE: Well, I guess John Wright didn't wake when they was slipping that rope under his neck.

MRS. PETERS (*crossing slowly to table and placing shawl and apron on table with other clothing*): No, it's strange. It must have been done awful crafty and still. They say it was such a — funny way to kill a man, rigging it all up like that.

MRS. HALE (*crossing to left of Mrs. Peters at table*): That's just what Mr. Hale said. There was a gun in the house. He says that's what he can't understand.

MRS. PETERS: Mr. Henderson said coming out that what was needed for the case was a motive; something to show anger, or — sudden feeling.

MRS. HALE (*who is standing by the table*): Well, I don't see any signs of anger around here. (*She puts her hand on the dish towel, which lies on the table, stands looking down at table, one-half of which is clean, the other half messy.*) It's wiped to here. (*Makes a move as if to finish work, then turns and looks at loaf of bread outside the breadbox. Drops towel. In that voice of coming back to familiar things.*) Wonder how they are finding things upstairs. (*Crossing below table to down right.*) I hope she had it a little more red-up up there. You know, it seems kind of *sneaking*. Locking her up in town and then coming out here and trying to get her own house to turn against her!

MRS. PETERS: But, Mrs. Hale, the law is the law.

MRS. HALE: I s'pose 'tis. (*Unbuttoning her coat.*) Better loosen up your things, Mrs. Peters. You won't feel them when you go out. (*Mrs. Peters takes off her fur tippet, goes to hang it on chair back left of table, stands looking at the work basket on floor near down left window.*)

MRS. PETERS: She was piecing a quilt. (*She brings the large sewing basket to the center table and they look at the bright pieces, Mrs. Hale above the table and Mrs. Peters left of it.*)

MRS. HALE: It's a log cabin pattern. Pretty, isn't it? I wonder if she was goin' to quilt it or just knot it? (*Footsteps have been heard coming down the stairs. The Sheriff enters followed by Hale and the County Attorney.*)

SHERIFF: They wonder if she was going to quilt it or just knot it! (*The men laugh, the women look abashed.*)

COUNTY ATTORNEY (*rubbing his hands over the stove*): Frank's fire didn't do much up there, did it? Well, let's go out to the barn and get that cleared up. (*The men go outside by up left door.*)

MRS. HALE (*resentfully*): I don't know as there's anything so strange, our takin' up our time with little things while we're waiting for them to get the evidence. (*She sits in chair right of table smoothing out a block with decision.*) I don't see as it's anything to laugh about.

MRS. PETERS (*apologetically*): Of course they've got awful important things on their minds. (*Pulls up a chair and joins Mrs. Hale at the left of the table.*)

MRS. HALE (*examining another block*): Mrs. Peters, look at this one. Here, this is the one she was working on, and look at the sewing! All the rest of it has been so nice and even. And look at this! It's all over the place! Why, it looks as if she didn't know what she was about! (*After she has said this they look at each other, then start to glance back at the door. After an instant Mrs. Hale has pulled at a knot and ripped the sewing.*)

MRS. PETERS: Oh, what are you doing, Mrs. Hale?

MRS. HALE (*mildly*): Just pulling out a stitch or two that's not sewed very good. (*Threading a needle.*) Bad sewing always made me fidgety.

MRS. PETERS (*with a glance at door, nervously*): I don't think we ought to touch things.

MRS. HALE: I'll just finish up this end. (*Suddenly stopping and leaning forward.*) Mrs. Peters?

MRS. PETERS: Yes, Mrs. Hale?

MRS. HALE: What do you suppose she was so nervous about?

MRS. PETERS: Oh — I don't know. I don't know as she was nervous. I sometimes sew awful queer when I'm just tired. (*Mrs. Hale starts to say something, looks at Mrs. Peters, then goes on sewing.*) Well, I must get these things wrapped up. They may be through sooner than we think. (*Putting apron and other things together.*) I wonder where I can find a piece of paper, and string. (*Rises.*)

MRS. HALE: In that cupboard, maybe.

MRS. PETERS (*crosses right looking in cupboard*): Why, here's a bird-cage. (*Holds it up.*) Did she have a bird, Mrs. Hale?

MRS. HALE: Why, I don't know whether she did or not — I've not been here for so long. There was a man around last year selling canaries cheap, but I don't know as she took one; maybe she did. She used to sing real pretty herself.

MRS. PETERS (*glancing around*): Seems funny to think of a bird here. But she must have had one, or why would she have a cage? I wonder what happened to it?

MRS. HALE: I s'pose maybe the cat got it.

MRS. PETERS: No, she didn't have a cat. She's got that feeling some people have about cats — being afraid of them. My cat got in her room and she was real upset and asked me to take it out.

MRS. HALE: My sister Bessie was like that. Queer, ain't it?

MRS. PETERS (*examining the cage*): Why, look at this door. It's broke. One hinge is pulled apart. (*Takes a step down to Mrs. Hale's right.*)

MRS. HALE (*looking too*): Looks as if someone must have been rough with it.

MRS. PETERS: Why, yes. (*She brings the cage forward and puts it on the table.*)

MRS. HALE (*glancing toward up left door*): I wish if they're going to find any evidence they'd be about it. I don't like this place.

MRS. PETERS: But I'm awful glad you came with me, Mrs. Hale. It would be lonesome for me sitting here alone.

MRS. HALE: It would, wouldn't it? (*Dropping her sewing.*) But I tell you what I do wish, Mrs. Peters. I wish I had come over sometimes when *she* was here. I — (*looking around the room*) — wish I had.

MRS. PETERS: But of course you were awful busy, Mrs. Hale — your house and your children.

MRS. HALE (*rises and crosses left*): I could've come. I stayed away because it weren't cheerful — and that's why I ought to have come. I — (*looking out left window*) — I've never liked this place. Maybe because it's down in a hollow and you don't see the road. I dunno what it is, but it's a lonesome place and always was. I wish I had come over to see Minnie Foster sometimes. I can see now — (*Shakes her head.*)

MRS. PETERS (*left of table and above it*): Well, you mustn't reproach yourself, Mrs. Hale. Somehow we just don't see how it is with other folks until — something turns up.

MRS. HALE: Not having children makes less work — but it makes a quiet house, and Wright out to work all day, and no company when he did come in. (*Turning from window.*) Did you know John Wright, Mrs. Peters?

MRS. PETERS: Not to know him; I've seen him in town. They say he was a good man.

MRS. HALE: Yes — good; he didn't drink, and kept his word as well as most, I guess, and paid his debts. But he was a hard man, Mrs. Peters. Just to pass the time of day with him — (*Shivers.*) Like a raw wind that gets to the bone. (*Pauses, her eye falling on the cage.*) I should think she would 'a' wanted a bird. But what do you suppose went with it?

MRS. PETERS: I don't know, unless it got sick and died. (*She reaches over and swings the broken door, swings it again, both women watch it.*)

MRS. HALE: You weren't raised round here, were you? (*Mrs. Peters shakes her head.*) You didn't know — her?

MRS. PETERS: Not till they brought her yesterday.

MRS. HALE: She — come to think of it, she was kind of like a bird herself — real sweet and pretty, but kind of timid and — fluttery. How — she — did — change. (*Silence: then as if struck by a happy thought and relieved to get back to everyday things. Crosses right above Mrs. Peters to cupboard, replaces small chair used to stand on to its original place down right.*) Tell you what, Mrs. Peters, why don't you take the quilt in with you? It might take up her mind.

MRS. PETERS: Why, I think that's a real nice idea, Mrs. Hale. There couldn't possibly be any objection to it could there? Now, just what would I take? I wonder if her patches are in here — and her things. (*They look in the sewing basket.*)

MRS. HALE (*crosses to right of table*): Here's some red. I expect this has got sewing things in it. (*Brings out a fancy box.*) What a pretty box. Looks like something somebody would give you. Maybe her scissors are in here. (*Opens box. Suddenly puts her hand to her nose.*) Why ——— (*Mrs. Peters bends nearer, then turns her face away.*) There's something wrapped up in this piece of silk.

MRS. PETERS: Why, this isn't her scissors.

MRS. HALE (*lifting the silk*): Oh, Mrs. Peters — it's ———— (*Mrs. Peters bends closer.*)

MRS. PETERS: It's the bird.

MRS. HALE: But, Mrs. Peters — look at it! Its neck! Look at its neck! It's all — other side *to.*

MRS. PETERS: Somebody — wrung — its — neck. (*Their eyes meet. A look of growing comprehension, of horror. Steps are heard outside. Mrs. Hale slips box under quilt pieces, and sinks into her chair. Enter Sheriff and County Attorney. Mrs. Peters steps down left and stands looking out of window.*)

COUNTY ATTORNEY (*as one turning from serious things to little pleasantries*): Well, ladies, have you decided whether she was going to quilt it or knot it? (*Crosses to center above table.*)

MRS. PETERS: We think she was going to — knot it. (*Sheriff crosses to right of stove, lifts stove lid, and glances at fire, then stands warming hands at stove.*)

COUNTY ATTORNEY: Well, that's interesting, I'm sure. (*Seeing the bird-cage.*) Has the bird flown?

MRS. HALE (*putting more quilt pieces over the box*): We think the — cat got it.

COUNTY ATTORNEY (*preoccupied*): Is there a cat? (*Mrs. Hale glances in a quick covert way at Mrs. Peters.*)

MRS. PETERS (*turning from window takes a step in*): Well, not *now.* They're superstitious, you know. They leave.

COUNTY ATTORNEY (*to Sheriff Peters, continuing an interrupted conversation*): No sign at all of anyone having come from the outside. Their own rope. Now let's go up again and go over it piece by piece. (*They start upstairs.*) It would have to have been someone who knew just the ———— (*Mrs. Peters sits down left of table. The two women sit there not looking at one another, but as if peering into something and at the same time holding back. When they talk now it is in the manner of feeling their way over strange ground, as if afraid of what they are saying, but as if they cannot help saying it.*)

MRS. HALE (*hesitatively and in hushed voice*): She liked the bird. She was going to bury it in that pretty box.

MRS. PETERS (*in a whisper*): When I was a girl — my kitten — there was a boy took a hatchet, and before my eyes — and before I could get there ———— (*Covers her face an instant.*) If they hadn't held me back I would have — (*catches herself, looks upstairs where steps are heard, falters weakly*) — hurt him.

MRS. HALE (*with a slow look around her*): I wonder how it would seem never to have had any children around. (*Pause.*) No, Wright wouldn't like the bird — a thing that sang. She used to sing. He killed that, too.

MRS. PETERS (*moving uneasily*): We don't know who killed the bird.

MRS. HALE: I knew John Wright.

MRS. PETERS: It was an awful thing was done in this house that night, Mrs. Hale. Killing a man while he slept, slipping a rope around his neck that choked the life out of him.

MRS. HALE: His neck. Choked the life out of him. (*Her hand goes out and rests on the bird-cage.*)

MRS. PETERS (*with rising voice*): We don't know who killed him. We don't *know*.

MRS. HALE (*her own feeling not interrupted*): If there'd been years and years of nothing, then a bird to sing to you, it would be awful — still, after the bird was still.

MRS. PETERS (*something within her speaking*): I know what stillness is. When we homesteaded in Dakota, and my first baby died — after he was two years old, and me with no other then ———

MRS. HALE (*moving*): How soon do you suppose they'll be through looking for the evidence?

MRS. PETERS: I know what stillness is. (*Pulling herself back.*) The law has got to punish crime, Mrs. Hale.

MRS. HALE (*not as if answering that*): I wish you'd seen Minnie Foster when she wore a white dress with blue ribbons and stood up there in the choir and sang. (*A look around the room.*) Oh, I *wish* I'd come over here once in a while! That was a crime! That was a crime! Who's going to punish that?

MRS. PETERS (*looking upstairs*): We mustn't — take on.

MRS. HALE: I might have known she needed help! I know how things can be — for women. I tell you, it's queer, Mrs. Peters. We live close together and we live far apart. We all go through the same things — it's all just a different kind of the same thing. (*Brushes her eyes, noticing the jar of fruit, reaches out for it.*) If I was you I wouldn't tell her her fruit was gone. Tell her it *ain't*. Tell her it's all right. Take this in to prove it to her. She — she may never know whether it was broke or not.

MRS. PETERS (*takes the jar, looks about for something to wrap it in; takes petticoat from the clothes brought from the other room, very nervously begins winding this around the jar. In a false voice*): My, it's a good thing the men couldn't hear us. Wouldn't they just laugh! Getting all stirred up over a little thing like a — dead canary. As if that could have anything to do with — with — wouldn't they *laugh*! (*The men are heard coming downstairs.*)

MRS. HALE (*under her breath*): Maybe they would — maybe they wouldn't.

COUNTY ATTORNEY: No, Peters, it's all perfectly clear except a reason for doing it. But you know juries when it comes to women. If there was some definite thing. (*Crosses slowly to above table. Sheriff crosses down right. Mrs. Hale and Mrs. Peters remain seated at either side of table.*) Something to show — something to make a story about — a thing that would connect up with this strange way of doing it ——— (*The women's eyes meet for an instant. Enter Hale from outer door.*)

HALE (*remaining by door*): Well, I've got the team around. Pretty cold out there.

COUNTY ATTORNEY: I'm going to stay awhile by myself. (*To the Sheriff.*) You can send Frank out for me, can't you? I want to go over everything. I'm not satisfied that we can't do better.

SHERIFF: Do you want to see what Mrs. Peters is going to take in? (*The Lawyer picks up the apron, laughs.*)

COUNTY ATTORNEY: Oh, I guess they're not very dangerous things the ladies have picked out. (*Moves a few things about, disturbing the quilt pieces which cover the box. Steps back.*) No, Mrs. Peters doesn't need supervising. For that matter a sheriff's wife is married to the law. Ever think of it that way, Mrs. Peters?

MRS. PETERS: Not — just that way.

SHERIFF (*chuckling*): Married to the law. (*Moves to down right door to the other room.*) I just want you to come in here a minute, George. We ought to take a look at these windows.

COUNTY ATTORNEY (*scoffingly*): Oh, windows!

SHERIFF: We'll be right out, Mr. Hale. (*Hale goes outside. The Sheriff follows the County Attorney into the room. Then Mrs. Hale rises, hands tight together, looking intensely at Mrs. Peters, whose eyes make a slow turn, finally meeting Mrs. Hale's. A moment Mrs. Hale holds her, then her own eyes point the way to where the box is concealed. Suddenly Mrs. Peters throws back quilt pieces and tries to put the box in the bag she is carrying. It is too big. She opens box, starts to take bird out, cannot touch it, goes to pieces, stands there helpless. Sound of a knob turning in the other room. Mrs. Hale snatches the box and puts it in the pocket of her big coat. Enter County Attorney and Sheriff, who remains down right.*)

COUNTY ATTORNEY (*crosses to up left door facetiously*): Well, Henry, at least we found out that she was not going to quilt it. She was going to — what is it you call it, ladies?

MRS. HALE (*standing center below table facing front, her hand against her pocket*): We call it — knot it, Mr. Henderson.

Curtain.

ॐ

EUGENE O'NEILL (*1888–1953*), *America's first major playwright, was born in a hotel room on Broadway, the third son of the popular actor James O'Neill, who toured for years in the leading role of* The Count of Monte Cristo, *and Ella Quinlan O'Neill, who followed her husband from theater to theater with their young children. After O'Neill won the Nobel Prize for Literature in 1936, he used harrowing details about his mother's addiction to morphine, his father's obsession with his acting career, and his older brother Jamie's alcoholism as the basis for his greatest play,* Long Day's Journey into Night *(written in 1939–41 but not produced until 1956).*

O'Neill's debut as a playwright with his one-act play Bound East for Cardiff *at the Provincetown Playhouse occurred after a decade of turbulent adventures as a young man. In 1906 he graduated from the Betts Academy in Connecticut, and then in fairly rapid succession he dropped out of Princeton University, traveled to Honduras to prospect (unsuccessfully) for gold, eloped with his first wife and fathered his first son, got divorced, attempted suicide, went to sea as a merchant sailor, jumped ship in Buenos Aires, returned to New York aboard a tramp steamer, tended bar in a waterfront saloon, shipped out again on voyages as an able-bodied seaman, and suffered a bout of tuberculosis. O'Neill later said that it was his reading of August Strindberg's plays in 1913 that "first gave me the vision of what modern drama could be, and first inspired me with the urge to write for the theatre myself." That year he wrote his first one-act plays about the sea, including* Bound East for Cardiff, *and spent a semester at Harvard College in a play-writing workshop taught by George Pierce Baker. Three years later, when O'Neill showed up in Provincetown, he had written eleven short plays, some of them already published in a vanity press book paid for by his father.*

Bound East for Cardiff *was the second play on the program with Susan Glaspell's* Trifles *in the summer of 1916, when the Provincetown Players began their first season in a rickety wooden building previously used for storing fish on the wharf in the coastal village. In O'Neill's play, Glaspell's husband George Cram Cook played the leading role of Yank, a sailor dying in his bunk in the forecastle of the tramp steamer SS* Glencairn. *Glaspell's description of the spellbound theater audience watching O'Neill's debut as a playwright gives a vivid sense of the scene:*

> *I may see it through memories too emotional, but it seems to me I have never sat before a more moving production than our* Bound East for Cardiff, *when Eugene O'Neill was produced for the first time on any stage. . . . The sea has been good to Eugene O'Neill. There was a fog, just as the script demanded, fog bell in the harbour. The tide was in, and it washed under us and around, spraying through the holes in the floor, giving us the rhythm and the flavor of the sea while the big dying sailor talked to his friend Drisc of the life he had always wanted deep in the land, where you'd never see a ship or smell the sea. It is not merely figurative language to say the old wharf shook with applause.*

O'Neill wrote fifteen plays for the Provincetown Playhouse, many of them — like the rest of his early plays — containing blunt racial and gender stereotypes. For example, in the opening lines of Bound East for Cardiff, *a seaman's crude boast about hitting "a bloomin' nigger" in New Guinea is met with laughter by the rest of the crew, who chide him for telling a lie, not for hitting a woman or for using the crude stereotype of a "jungle woman." O'Neill's early theater was a complex mixture of re-alism and expressionism. Like Strindberg, his theatrical experiments were extreme and unpredictable. As one of the Provincetown Players said about him, "Half the time we who knew him best did not know what kink lay behind his maddest insistences." There is little plot in* Bound East for Cardiff, *but the play relies on setting and mood to re-create the atmosphere of the seamen's cramped quarters in the forecastle of the tramp steamer, a stifling world of unattainable desires and inevitable destiny.*

During the next four years, O'Neill continued to write experimental short plays for the Provincetown Players, including a cycle of "sea plays" using characters in the crew of this same ship, the SS Glencairn. *His efforts culminated in 1920 with two very successful long plays.* Beyond the Horizon *won him the first of his four Pulitzer prizes, and* The Emperor Jones *made American theater history when Cook brought in the actor Charles Gilpin from Harlem to play the leading role, the first time an African American actor appeared in a major role in legitimate theater in the United States. The play moved from the Provincetown Players' little theater in Greenwich Village to a Broadway production, and O'Neill's career as a major playwright was launched. In the next fifteen years he produced a series of plays that, in the words of theater historian Lee Jacobus, provided audiences with "frightening visions of the soul's interior." These plays included* Anna Christie *(1921; later made into a film starring Greta Garbo);* The Hairy Ape *(1922);* Desire under the Elms *(1924),* The Great God Brown *(1926);* Marco's Millions *(1928);* Strange Interlude *(1928), a drama in nine acts that was enormously popular;* Mourning Becomes Electra *(1931), which originally took three days to perform; and* Ah! Wilderness *(1933), O'Neill's only comedy.*

From 1934 to 1946 O'Neill worked on a cycle of eleven plays covering the United States' history from the Revolutionary War to the Depression; he later destroyed nearly all of these plays. The one play in the cycle which he completed was A Touch of the Poet, produced posthumously in 1957. While much of O'Neill's work seems dated, this play and A Moon for the Misbegotten (1943), which completes the story of his mother and his brother Jamie dramatized in Long Day's Journey into Night, explore human relationships and remain accessible to today's audiences. In O'Neill's dedication, he said that Long Day's Journey into Night was "a play of old sorrow, written in tears and blood." It has been described by many critics as the highest achievement of any playwright in the American theater.

RELATED COMMENTARIES: *Travis Bogard, "The Provincetown Players," page 1972; Eugene O'Neill, "A Letter to Arthur Hobson Quinn," page 2019.*

EUGENE O'NEILL

Bound East for Cardiff   1916
A Play in One Act

DRAMATIS PERSONAE

YANK	PAUL
DRISCOLL	SMITTY
COCKY	IVAN
DAVIS	THE CAPTAIN
SCOTTY	THE SECOND MATE
OLSON	

The action of the play takes place in the years preceding the outbreak of World War I.

SCENE: *The seamen's forecastle of the British tramp steamer* Glencairn *on a foggy night midway on the voyage between New York and Cardiff. An irregular-shaped compartment, the sides of which almost meet at the far end to form a triangle. Sleeping bunks about six feet long, ranged three deep with a space of three feet separating the upper from the lower, are built against the sides. On the right above the bunks three or four port holes can be seen. In front of the bunks, rough wooden benches. Over the bunks on the left, a lamp in a bracket. In the left foreground, a doorway. On the floor near it, a pail with a tin dipper. Oilskins are hanging from a hook near the doorway.*

The far side of the forecastle is so narrow that it contains only one series of bunks.

In under the bunks a glimpse can be had of sea-chests, suit-cases, sea-boots, etc., jammed in indiscriminately.

At regular intervals of a minute or so the blast of the steamer's whistle can be heard above all the other sounds.

Five men are sitting on the benches talking. They are dressed in dirty patched suits of dungaree, flannel shirts, and all are in their stocking feet. Four of the men are pulling on pipes and the air is heavy with rancid tobacco smoke. Sitting on the top bunk in the left foreground, a Norwegian, Paul, is softly playing some folk song on a battered accordion. He stops from time to time to listen to the conversation.

In the lower bunk in the rear a dark-haired, hard-featured man is lying appar- ently asleep. One of his arms is stretched limply over the side of the bunk. His face is very pale, and drops of clammy perspiration glisten on his forehead.

It is nearing the end of the dog-watch — about ten minutes to eight in the evening.

COCKY (*a wizened runt of a man. He is telling a story. The others are listening with amused, incredulous faces, interrupting him at the end of each sentence with loud derisive guffaws*): Makin' love to me, she was! It's Gawd's truth! A bloomin' nigger! Greased all over with cocoanut oil, she was. Gawd blimey, I couldn't stand 'er. Bloody old cow, I says; and with that I fetched 'er a biff on the ear wot knocked 'er silly, an' — (*He is interrupted by a roar of laughter from the others.*)

DAVIS (*a middle-aged man with black hair and moustache*): You're a liar, Cocky.

SCOTTY (*a dark young fellow*): Ho-ho! Ye werr neverr in New Guinea in yourr life, I'm thinkin'.

OLSON (*a Swede with a drooping blond moustache — with ponderous sarcasm*): Yust tink of it! You say she wass a cannibal, Cocky?

DRISCOLL (*a brawny Irishman with the battered features of a prizefighter*): How cud ye doubt ut, Ollie? A quane av the naygurs she musta been surely. Who else wud think herself aqual to fallin' in love wid a beauthiful, divil-may- care rake av a man the loike av Cocky? (*A burst of laughter from the crowd.*)

COCKY (*indignantly*): Gaw strike me dead if it ain't true, every bleedin' word of it. 'Appened ten year ago come Christmas.

SCOTTY: 'Twas a Christmas dinner she had her eyes on.

DAVIS: He'd a been a tough old bird.

DRISCOLL: 'Tis lucky for both av ye ye escaped; for the quane av the cannibal isles wad 'a died av the belly ache the day afther Christmas, divil a doubt av ut. (*The laughter at this is long and loud.*)

COCKY (*sullenly*): Blarsted fat 'eads!

The sick man in the lower bunk in the rear groans and moves restlessly. There is a hushed silence. All the men turn and stare at him.

DRISCOLL: Ssshh! (*In a hushed whisper.*) We'd best not be talkin' so loud and him tryin' to have a bit av a sleep. (*He tiptoes softly to the side of the bunk.*) Yank! You'd be wantin' a drink av wather, maybe? (*Yank does not reply. Driscoll bends over and looks at him.*) It's asleep he is, sure enough. His breath is chokin' in his throat loike wather gurglin' in a poipe. (*He comes back qui- etly and sits down. All are silent, avoiding each other's eyes.*)

COCKY (*after a pause*): Poor devil! It's over the side for 'im, Gawd 'elp 'im.

DRISCOLL: Stop your croakin'! He's not dead yet, and, praise God, he'll have many a long day yet before him.

SCOTTY (*shaking his head doubtfully*): He's bod, mon, he's verry bod.

DAVIS: Lucky he's alive. Many a man's light woulda gone out after a fall like that.

OLSON: You saw him fall?

DAVIS: Right next to him. He and me was goin' down in number two hold to do some chippin'. He puts his leg over careless-like and misses the ladder and plumps straight down to the bottom. I was scared to look over for a minute, and then I heard him groan and I scuttled down after him. He was hurt bad inside, for the blood was drippin' from the side of his mouth. He was groanin' hard, but he never let a word out of him.

COCKY: An' you blokes remember when we 'auled 'im in 'ere. Oh, 'ell, 'e says, oh, 'ell — like that, and nothink else.

OLSON: Did the captain know where he iss hurted?

COCKY: That silly ol' josser! Wot the 'ell would 'e know abaht anythink?

SCOTTY (*scornfully*): He fiddles in his mouth wi' a bit of glass.

DRISCOLL (*angrily*): The divil's own life ut is to be out on the lonely sea wid nothin' betune you and a grave in the ocean but a spindle-shanked, grey-whiskered auld fool the loike av him. 'Twas enough to make a saint shwear to see him wid his gold watch in his hand, tryin' to look as wise as an owl on a tree, and all the toime he not knowin' whether 'twas cholery or the barber's itch was the matther wid Yank.

SCOTTY (*sardonically*): He gave him a dose of salts, na doot?

DRISCOLL: Divil a thing he gave him at all, but looked in the book he had wid him, and shook his head, and walked out widout sayin' a word, the second mate afther him no wiser than himself, God's curse on the two av him!

COCKY (*after a pause*): Yank was a good shipmate, pore beggar. Lend me four bob in Noo Yark, 'e did.

DRISCOLL (*warmly*): A good shipmate he was and is, none betther. Ye said no more than the truth Cocky. Five years and more ut is since first I shipped wid him, and we've stuck together iver since through good luck and bad. Fights we've had, God help us, but 'twas only when we'd a bit av drink taken, and we always shook hands the nixt mornin'. Whativer was his was mine, and many's the toime I'd a been on the beach or worse, but for him. And now — (*His voice trembles as he fights to control his emotion.*) Divil take me if I'm not startin' to blubber loike an auld woman, and he not dead at all, but goin' to live many a long year yet, maybe.

DAVIS: The sleep'll do him good. He seems better now.

OLSON: If he wude eat something —

DRISCOLL: Wud ye have him be eatin' in his condishun? Sure it's hard enough on the rest av us wid nothin' the matther wid our insiders to be stomachin' the skoff on this rusty lime-juicer.

SCOTTY (*indignantly*): It's a starvation ship.

DAVIS: Plenty o' work and no food — and the owner ridin' around in carriages!

OLSON: Hash, hash! Stew, stew! Marmalade, py damn! (*He spits disgustedly.*)

COCKY: Bloody swill! Fit only for swine is wot I say.

DRISCOLL: And the dishwather they disguise wid the name av tea! And the putty they call bread! My belly feels loike I'd swalleyed a dozen rivets at the thought av ut! And sea-biscuit that'd break the teeth av a lion if he had the misfortune to take a bite at one!

Unconsciously they have all raised their voices, forgetting the sick man in their sailor's delight at finding something to grumble about.

PAUL (*swings his feet over the side of his bunk, stops playing his accordion, and says slowly*): And rot-ten po-tay-toes! (*He starts in playing again. The sick man gives a groan of pain.*)

DRISCOLL (*holding up his hand*): Shut your mouths, all av you. 'Tis a hell av a thing for us to be complainin' about our guts, and a sick man maybe dyin' listenin' to us. (*Gets up and shakes his fist at the Norwegian.*) God stiffen you, ye square-head scut! Put down that organ av yours or I'll break your ugly face for you. Is that banshee schreechin' fit music for a sick man?

The Norwegian puts his accordion in the bunk and lies back and closes his eyes. Driscoll goes over and stands beside Yank. The steamer's whistle sounds particularly loud in the silence.

DAVIS: Damn this fog! (*Reaches in under a bunk and yanks out a pair of sea-boots, which he pulls on.*) My look-out next, too. Must be nearly eight bells, boys.

With the exception of Olson, all the men sitting up put on oilskins, sou'-westers, sea-boots, etc., in preparation for the watch on deck. Olson crawls into a lower bunk on the right.

SCOTTY: My wheel.

OLSON (*disgustedly*): Nothin' but yust dirty weather all dis voyage. I yust can't sleep when weestle blow. (*He turns his back to the light and is soon fast asleep and snoring.*)

SCOTTY: If this fog keeps up, I'm tellin' ye, we'll no be in Carrdiff for a week or more.

DRISCOLL: 'Twas just such a night as this the auld Dover wint down. Just about this toime ut was, too, and we all sittin' round in the fo'c'sle, Yank beside me, whin all av a suddint we heard a great slitherin' crash, and the ship heeled over till we was all in a heap on wan side. What came afther I disremimber exactly, except 'twas a hard shift to get the boats over the side before the auld teakittle sank. Yank was in the same boat wid me, and sivin morthal days we drifted wid scarcely a drop of wather or a bite to chew on. 'Twas Yank here that held me down whin I wanted to jump into the ocean, roarin' mad wid the thirst. Picked up we were on the same day wid only Yank in his senses, and him steerin' the boat.

COCKY (*protestingly*): Blimey, but you're a cheerful blighter, Driscoll! Talkin' abaht shipwrecks in this 'ere blushin' fog. (*Yank groans and stirs uneasily, opening his eyes. Driscoll hurries to his side.*)

DRISCOLL: Are ye feelin' any betther, Yank?

YANK (*in a weak voice*): No.

DRISCOLL: Sure, you must be. You look as sthrong as an ox. (*Appealing to the others.*) Am I tellin' him a lie?

DAVIS: The sleep's done you good.

COCKY: You'll be 'avin your pint of beer in Cardiff this day week.

SCOTTY: And fish and chips, mon!

YANK (*peevishly*): Wat're yuh all lyin' fur? D'yuh think I'm scared to — (*He hesitates as if frightened by the word he is about to say.*)

DRISCOLL: Don't be thinkin' such things!

The ship's bell is heard heavily tolling eight times. From the forecastle head above the voice of the look-out rises in a long wail: Aaall's welll. The men look uncertainly at Yank as if undecided whether to say good-bye or not.

YANK (*in an agony of fear*): Don't leave me, Drisc! I'm dyin', I tell yuh. I won't stay here alone with every one snorin'. I'll go out on deck. (*He makes a feeble attempt to rise, but sinks back with a sharp groan. His breath comes in wheezy gasps.*) Don't leave me, Drisc! (*His face grows white and his head falls back with a jerk.*)

DRISCOLL: Don't be worryin', Yank. I'll not move a step out av here — and let that divil av a bosun curse his black head off. You speak a word to the bosun, Cocky. Tell him that Yank is bad took and I'll be stayin' wid him a while yet.

COCKY: Right-o. (*Cocky, Davis, and Scotty go out quietly.*)

COCKY (*from the alleyway*): Gawd blimey, the fog's thick as soup.

DRISCOLL: Are ye satisfied now, Yank? (*Receiving no answer, he bends over the still form.*) He's fainted, God help him! (*He gets a tin dipper from the bucket and bathes Yank's forehead with the water. Yank shudders and opens his eyes.*)

YANK (*slowly*): I thought I was goin' then. Wha' did yuh wanta wake me up fur?

DRISCOLL (*with forced gaiety*): Is it wishful for heaven ye are?

YANK (*gloomily*): Hell, I guess.

DRISCOLL (*crossing himself involuntarily*): For the love av the saints don't be talkin' loike that! You'd give a man the creeps. It's chippin' rust on deck you'll be in a day or two wid the best av us.

Yank does not answer, but closes his eyes wearily. The seaman who has been on look-out, Smitty, a young Englishman, comes in and takes off his dripping oilskins. While he is doing this the man whose turn at the wheel has been relieved enters. He is a dark, burly fellow with a round stupid face. The Englishman steps softly over to Driscoll. The other crawls into a lower bunk.

SMITTY (*whispering*): How's Yank?

DRISCOLL: Betther. Ask him yourself. He's awake.

YANK: I'm all right, Smitty.

SMITTY: Glad to hear it, Yank. (*He crawls to an upper bunk and is soon asleep.*)

IVAN (*the stupid-faced seaman who came in after Smitty twists his head in the direction of the sick man*): You feel gude, Jank?

YANK (*wearily*): Yes, Ivan.

IVAN: Dot's gude. (*He rolls over on his side and falls asleep immediately.*)

YANK (*after a pause broken only by snores — with a bitter laugh*): Good-bye and good luck to the lot of you!

DRISCOLL: Is ut painin' you again?

YANK: It hurts like hell — here. (*He points to the lower part of his chest on the left side.*) I guess my old pump's busted. Ooohh!

A spasm of pain contracts his pale features. He presses his hand to his side and writhes on the thin mattress of his bunk. The perspiration stands out in beads on his forehead.

DRISCOLL (*terrified*): Yank! Yank! What is ut? (*Jumping to his feet.*) I'll run for the captain. (*He starts for the doorway.*)

YANK (*sitting up in his bunk, frantic with fear*): Don't leave me, Drisc! For God's
    sake don't leave me alone! (*He leans over the side of his bunk and spits.*
    Driscoll comes back to him.) Blood! Ugh!

DRISCOLL: Blood again! I'd best be gettin' the captain.

YANK: No, no, don't leave me! If yuh do I'll git up and follow you. I ain't no
    coward, but I'm scared to stay here with all of them asleep and snorin'.
    (*Driscoll, not knowing what to do, sits down on the bench beside him. He grows*
    calmer and sinks back on the mattress.) The captain can't do me no good,
    yuh know it yourself. The pain ain't so bad now, but I thought it had me
    then. It was like a buzz-saw cuttin' into me.

DRISCOLL (*fiercely*): God blarst ut!

*The Captain and the Second Mate of the steamer enter the forecastle. The Captain is
an old man with grey moustache and whiskers. The Mate is clean-shaven and middle-
aged. Both are dressed in simple blue uniforms.*

THE CAPTAIN (*taking out his watch and feeling Yank's pulse*): And how is the sick
    man?

YANK (*feebly*): All right, sir.

THE CAPTAIN: And the pain in the chest?

YANK: It still hurts, sir, worse than ever.

THE CAPTAIN (*taking a thermometer from his pocket and putting it into Yank's
    mouth*): Here. Be sure and keep this in under your tongue, not over it.

THE MATE (*after a pause*): Isn't this your watch on deck, Driscoll?

DRISCOLL: Yes, sorr, but Yank was fearin' to be alone, and —

THE CAPTAIN: That's all right, Driscoll.

DRISCOLL: Thank ye, sorr.

THE CAPTAIN (*stares at his watch for a moment or so; then takes the thermometer from
    Yank's mouth and goes to the lamp to read it. His expression grows very grave.
    He beckons the Mate and Driscoll to the corner near the doorway. Yank watches
    them furtively. The Captain speaks in a low voice to the Mate*): Way up, both
    of them. (*To Driscoll.*) Has he been spitting blood again?

DRISCOLL: Not much for the hour just past, sorr, but before that —

THE CAPTAIN: A great deal?

DRISCOLL: Yes, sorr.

THE CAPTAIN: He hasn't eaten anything?

DRISCOLL: No, sorr.

THE CAPTAIN: Did he drink that medicine I sent him?

DRISCOLL: Yes, sorr, but it didn't stay down.

THE CAPTAIN (*shaking his head*): I'm afraid — he's very weak. I can't do anything
    else for him. It's too serious for me. If this had only happened a week
    later we'd be in Cardiff in time to —

DRISCOLL: Plaze help him some way, sorr!

THE CAPTAIN (*impatiently*): But, my good man, I'm not a doctor. (*More kindly as
    he sees Driscoll's grief.*) You and he have been shipmates a long time?

DRISCOLL: Five years and more, sorr.

THE CAPTAIN: I see. Well, don't let him move. Keep him quiet and we'll hope for
    the best. I'll read the matter up and send him some medicine, something

to ease the pain, anyway. (*Goes over to Yank.*) Keep up your courage! You'll be better to-morrow. (*He breaks down lamely before Yank's steady gaze.*) We'll pull you through all right — and — hm — well — coming, Robinson? Dammit! (*He goes out hurriedly, followed by the Mate.*)

DRISCOLL (*trying to conceal his anxiety*): Didn't I tell you you wasn't half as sick as you thought you was? The Captain'll have you out on deck cursin' and swearin' loike a trooper before the week is out.

YANK: Don't lie, Drisc. I heard what he said, and if I didn't I c'd tell by the way I feel. I know what's goin' to happen. I'm goin' to — (*He hesitates for a second — then resolutely.*) I'm goin' to die, that's what, and the sooner the better!

DRISCOLL (*wildly*): No, and be damned to you, you're not. I'll not let you.

YANK: It ain't no use, Drisc. I ain't got a chance, but I ain't scared. Gimme a drink of water, will yuh, Drisc? My throat's burnin' up.

Driscoll brings the dipper full of water and supports his head while he drinks in great gulps.

DRISCOLL (*seeking vainly for some word of comfort*): Are ye feelin' more aisy loike now?

YANK: Yes — now — when I know it's all up. (*A pause.*) You mustn't take it so hard, Drisc. I was just thinkin' it ain't as bad as people think — dyin'. I ain't never took much stock in the truck them sky-pilots preach. I ain't never had religion; but I know whatever it is what comes after it can't be no worser'n this. I don't like to leave you, Drisc, but — that's all.

DRISCOLL (*with a groan*): Lad, lad, don't be talkin'.

YANK: This sailor life ain't much to cry about leavin' — just one ship after another, hard work, small pay, and bum grub; and when we git into port, just a drunk endin' up in a fight, and all your money gone, and then ship away again. Never meetin' no nice people; never gittin' outa sailor town, hardly, in any port; travellin' all over the world and never seein' none of it; without no one to care whether you're alive or dead. (*With a bitter smile.*) There ain't much in all that that'd make yuh sorry to lose it, Drisc.

DRISCOLL (*gloomily*): It's a hell av a life, the sea.

YANK (*musingly*): It must be great to stay on dry land all your life and have a farm with a house of your own with cows and pigs and chickens, 'way in the middle of the land where yuh'd never smell the sea or see a ship. It must be great to have a wife, and kids to play with at night after supper when your work was done. It must be great to have a home of your own, Drisc.

DRISCOLL (*with a great sigh*): It must, surely; but what's the use av thinkin' av ut? Such things are not for the loikes av us.

YANK: Sea-farin' is all right when you're young and don't care, but we ain't chickens no more, and somehow, I dunno, this last year has seemed rotten, and I've had a hunch I'd quit — With you, of course — and we'd save our coin, and go to Canada or Argentine or some place and git a farm, just a small one, just enough to live on. I never told yuh this cause I thought you'd laugh at me.

DRISCOLL (*enthusiastically*): Laugh at you, is ut? When I'm havin' the same thoughts myself, toime afther toime. It's a grand idea and we'll be doin' ut sure if you'll stop your crazy notion — about — about bein' so sick.

YANK (*sadly*): Too late. We shouldn'ta made this trip, and then — How'd all the fog git in here?

DRISCOLL: Fog?

YANK: Everything looks misty. Must be my eyes gittin' weak, I guess. What was we talkin' of a minute ago? Oh yes, a farm. It's too late. (*His mind wandering.*) Argentine, did I say? D'yuh remember the times we've had in Buenos Aires? The moving pictures in Barracas? Some class to them, d'yuh remember?

DRISCOLL (*with satisfaction*): I do that; and so does the piany player. He'll not be forgettin' the black eye I gave him in a hurry.

YANK: Remember the time we was there on the beach and had to go to Tommy Moore's boarding house to git shipped? And he sold us rotten oilskins and sea-boots full of holes, and shipped us on a skysail yarder round the Horn, and took two months' pay for it. And the days we used to sit on the park benches along the Paseo Colon with the vigilantes lookin' hard at us? And the songs at the Sailor's Opera where the guy played rag-time — d'yuh remember them?

DRISCOLL: I do, surely.

YANK: And La Plata — phew, the stink of the hides! I always liked Argentine — all except that booze, caña. How drunk we used to git on that, remember?

DRISCOLL: Cud I forget ut? My head pains me at the menshun av that divil's brew.

YANK: Remember the night I went crazy with the heat in Singapore? And the time you was pinched by the cops in Port Said? And the time we was both locked up in Sydney for fightin'?

DRISCOLL: I do so.

YANK: And that fight on the dock at Cape Town — (*His voice betrays great inward perturbation.*)

DRISCOLL (*hastily*): Don't be thinkin' av that now. 'Tis past and gone.

YANK: D'yuh think He'll hold it up against me?

DRISCOLL (*mystified*): Who's that?

YANK: God. They say He sees everything. He must know it was done in fair fight, in self-defence, don't yuh think?

DRISCOLL: Av course. Ye stabbed him, and be damned to him, for the skulkin' swine he was, afther him tryin' to stick you in the back, and you not suspectin'. Let your conscience be aisy. I wisht I had nothin' blacker than that on my sowl. I'd not be afraid av the angel Gabriel himself.

YANK (*with a shudder*): I c'd see him a minute ago with the blood spurtin' out of his neck. Ugh!

DRISCOLL: The fever, ut is, that makes you see such things. Give no heed to ut.

YANK (*uncertainly*): You don't think He'll hold it up agin me — God, I mean?

DRISCOLL: If there's justice in hiven, no! (*Yank seems comforted by this assurance.*)

YANK (*after a pause*): We won't reach Cardiff for a week at least. I'll be buried at
    sea.

DRISCOLL (*putting his hands over his ears*): Sshh! I won't listen to you.

YANK (*as if he had not heard him*): It's as good a place as any other, I s'pose —
    only I always wanted to be buried on dry land. But what the hell'll I
    care — then? (*Fretfully.*) Why should it be a rotten night like this with
    that damned whistle blowin' and people snorin' all round? I wish the
    stars was out, and the moon, too; I c'd lie out on deck and look at them,
    and it'd make it easier to go — somehow.

DRISCOLL: For the love av God don't be talkin' loike that!

YANK: Whatever pay's comin' to me yuh can divvy up with the rest of the boys;
    and you take my watch. It ain't worth much, but it's all I've got.

DRISCOLL: But have ye no relations at all to call your own?

YANK: No, not as I know of. One thing I forgot: You know Fanny the barmaid
    at the Red Stork in Cardiff?

DRISCOLL: Sure, and who doesn't?

YANK: She's been good to me. She tried to lend me half a crown when I was
    broke there last trip. Buy her the biggest box of candy yuh c'n find in
    Cardiff. (*Breaking down — in a choking voice.*) It's hard to ship on this voy-
    age I'm goin' on — alone! (*Driscoll reaches out and grasps his hand. There is
    a pause, during which both fight to control themselves.*) My throat's like a fur-
    nace. (*He gasps for air.*) Gimme a drink of water, will yuh, Drisc? (*Driscoll
    gets him a dipper of water.*) I wish this was a pint of beer. Oooohh!

*He chokes, his face convulsed with agony, his hands tearing at his shirt front. The dip-
per falls from his nerveless fingers.*

DRISCOLL: For the love av God, what is ut, Yank?

YANK (*speaking with tremendous difficulty*): S'long, Drisc! (*He stares straight in
    front of him with eyes starting from their sockets.*) Who's that?

DRISCOLL: Who? What?

YANK (*faintly*): A pretty lady dressed in black.

His face twitches and his body writhes in a final spasm, then straightens out rigidly.

DRISCOLL (*pale with horror*): Yank! Yank! Say a word to me for the love av
    hiven! (*He shrinks away from the bunk, making the sign of the cross. Then
    comes back and puts a trembling hand on Yank's chest, and bends closely over
    the body.*)

COCKY (*from the alleyway*): Oh, Driscoll! Can you leave Yank for arf a mo' and
    give me a 'and?

DRISCOLL (*with a great sob*): Yank! (*He sinks down on his knees beside the bunk, his
    head on his hands. His lips move in some half-remembered prayer.*)

COCKY (*enters, his oilskins and sou'-wester glistening with drops of water*): The fog's
    lifted.

*Cocky sees Driscoll and stands staring at him with open mouth. Driscoll makes the
sign of the cross again.*

COCKY (*mockingly*): Sayin' 'is prayers!

He catches sight of the still figure in the bunk and an expression of awed understanding comes over his face. He takes off his dripping sou'-wester and stands, scratching his head.

COCKY (*in a hushed whisper*): Gawd blimey!

Curtain

ಣ

SAMUEL BECKETT (*1906–1989*), *the son of a licensed surveyor, was born into an upper-middle-class Protestant family in Dublin. He was such a brilliant student of French and Italian at Trinity College that after graduation he was offered a job teaching English in Paris in 1928. There he met the Irish expatriate writer James Joyce, who shared his fascination with language, and for a brief time he helped Joyce by transcribing passages of* Finnegans Wake. *Beckett's first work appeared in Paris in the avant-garde literary magazine* transition. *In 1931 he published* Proust, *a study of the French novelist, followed in 1934 with* More Pricks than Kicks, *a book of short stories. Settled in Paris, he continued to write and publish experimental fiction in English until the outbreak of World War II.*

During the war Beckett was active in the French Resistance and was forced to evade the Gestapo by going underground as a farm laborer for two years in Vichy France. After the war he returned to Paris, where he wrote a trilogy of novels in French — Molloy, Malone Dies, *and* The Unnamable, *which he translated and published in English in 1955, 1956, and 1958, respectively. Beckett said that he originally wrote in French to help him pare down his style and to record only what was essential. The theme of these novels — a view of the human predicament as a state of existence without hope or meaning — was to be developed further when, in middle age, Beckett began writing for the theater.*

En Attendant Godot, Beckett's first theatrical production and greatest success, premiered in Paris in 1953. The play is a comedy about two tramps, Vladimir and Estragon, who amuse themselves with vaudeville routines while they wait for a mysterious man whom they call Godot to join them. The two tramps' futile conversation about a Godot character who never arrives caught the sympathy of the French audiences. Translated into English as Waiting for Godot, *the play was also an immediate success in England and the United States, even staged by prisoners in San Quentin in 1961. Beckett's drama reflected a postwar mood of disillusionment and lack of faith in the world as a comprehensible place. It contributed to a new kind of experimental theater — the theater of the absurd — expressing a sense of anguish at the futility of the human situation.*

As the critic Martin Esslin stated in The Theatre of the Absurd (*1961*), *the intent of such playwrights as Beckett and others influenced by him (for instance, Harold Pinter and Edward Albee) is to make theatergoers "aware of man's precarious position in the universe." Esslin explained,*

> As the Theater of the Absurd is not concerned with conveying information or presenting the problems of destinies of characters that exist outside the author's inner world, as it does not expound a thesis or debate ideological propo-

sitions, it is not concerned with the representation of events, the narration of the fate or the adventures of characters, but instead with the presentation of one individual's basic situation. It is a theater of situation as against a theater of events in sequence, and therefore it uses a language based on patterns of concrete images rather than argument and discursive speech. And since it is trying to present a sense of being, it can neither investigate nor solve problems of conduct or morals.

Most people who saw or read Waiting for Godot *thought Godot was a metaphor for God, but Beckett never confirmed this view. Jokingly he even replied that the play was a reflection of his experience as a secret agent during the French Resistance, waiting for a courier who never showed up. Plays like* Waiting for Godot *and* Krapp's Last Tape *(1958), in which Krapp plays tape recordings of himself from the past, were so open-ended that their meanings could be endlessly debated. Beckett's bleak vision of the world reflects his own fascination with the darkness of human folly and failure, as when Krapp realizes "that the dark" he has struggled to "keep under" is in reality his most precious ally, his true subject, the fertile world of his own subconscious.*

Beckett's pessimism about the human condition went beyond the existential philosophy of such French writers as Jean-Paul Sartre and Albert Camus. In the years immediately after the war, their books promoted atheism, but Beckett's skepticism led him in his writing to express his sense of a breakdown of all systems, including language. In his last years he wrote only short dramatic fragments of experimental theater — plays such as Breath *(1970), which runs for thirty seconds and features a rubbish heap onstage and a soundtrack of a single breath. It is ironic that, considering Beckett's loss of faith in words as an agency of communication, his vision as a playwright is so eloquent that his plays have been translated into most of the languages spoken in the world today. In 1969 he was awarded the Nobel Prize for literature.*

As the critic Hugh Kenner noted in his book about modern Irish writers, A Colder Eye *(1983), Beckett's theater was indebted to his Irish roots. When asked which playwright had influenced him, Becket answered John Millington Synge, who wrote plays for the Abbey Theatre in Dublin, where Beckett saw them produced as a boy, along with some Nō plays introduced earlier into Ireland by the poet William Butler Yeats. Synge's* The Well of the Saints *(1905) featured two old and blind actors, and his* In the Shadow of the Glen *(1903) introduced the character of the eloquent tramp whom Beckett later used in his plays. Kenner believed that in these plays of Synge,*

> *the Greeks with their music and spectacle and choric dancing never entrusted so much dramatic leverage to so little visible movement, so little variety. This principle leads from Synge's world straight into Beckett's: to* Embers *for instance, a play for radio that confines the whole of a novelistic plot and subplot within the head of a man who sits talking, talking, to drown out the sound of the sea and the sound of the remembered voices of the dead. All that confronts us, in this [Beckett's] tour de force of expressive monotony, is the wreckage of a story, a wrecked life, wrecked words: "Stories, stories, years and years of stories, till the need came on me, for someone, to be with me, anyone, a stranger, to talk to, imagine he hears me, years of that, and then, now for someone who . . . knew me, in the old days, anyone, to be with me, imagine he hears me, what I am, now."*

RELATED PLAYS: *Edward Albee,* The Sandbox, *page 1823; Nō drama,* Kantan, *page 1465.*

RELATED COMMENTARIES: *Martin Esslin, "On Krapp's Last Tape," page 1976; Yasunari Takahashi, "Samuel Beckett and the Nō," page 2026.*

SAMUEL BECKETT

Krapp's Last Tape   1958
A Play in One Act

SCENE: *A late evening in the future.*

Krapp's den. Front center a small table, the two drawers of which open towards audience. Sitting at the table, facing front, i.e. across from the drawers, a wearish old man: Krapp.

> *Rusty black narrow trousers too short for him. Rusty black sleeveless waistcoat, four capacious pockets. Heavy silver watch and chain. Grimy white shirt open at neck, no collar. Surprising pair of dirty white boots, size ten at least, very narrow and pointed.*
>
> *White face. Purple nose. Disordered gray hair. Unshaven.*
>
> *Very near-sighted (but unspectacled). Hard of hearing.*
>
> *Cracked voice. Distinctive intonation.*
>
> *Laborious walk.*
>
> *On the table a tape-recorder with microphone and a number of cardboard boxes containing reels of recorded tapes.*
>
> *Table and immediately adjacent area in strong white light. Rest of stage in darkness.*
>
> *Krapp remains a moment motionless, heaves a great sigh, looks at his watch, fumbles in his pockets, takes out an envelope, puts it back, fumbles, takes out a small bunch of keys, raises it to his eyes, chooses a key, gets up and moves to front of table. He stoops, unlocks first drawer, peers into it, feels about inside it, takes out a reel of tape, peers at it, puts it back, locks drawer, unlocks second drawer, peers into it, feels about inside it, takes out a large banana, peers at it, locks drawer, puts keys back in his pocket. He turns, advances to edge of stage, halts, strokes banana, peels it, drops skin at his feet, puts end of banana in his mouth and remains motionless, staring vacuously before him. Finally he bites off the end, turns aside, and begins pacing to and fro at edge of stage, in the light, i.e. not more than four or five paces either way, meditatively eating banana. He treads on skin, slips, nearly falls, recovers himself, stoops and peers at skin and finally pushes it, still stooping, with his foot over the edge of stage into pit. He resumes his pacing, finishes banana, returns to table, sits down, remains a moment motionless, heaves a great sigh, takes keys from his pockets, raises them to his eyes, chooses key, gets up and moves to front of table, unlocks second drawer, takes out a second large banana, peers at it, locks drawer, puts back keys in his pocket, turns, advances to edge of stage, halts, strokes banana, peels it, tosses skin into pit, puts end of banana in his mouth, and remains motionless, star-*

ing vacuously before him. Finally he has an idea, puts banana in his waistcoat pocket, the end emerging, and goes with all the speed he can muster backstage into darkness. Ten seconds. Loud pop of cork. Fifteen seconds. He comes back into light carrying an old ledger and sits down at table. He lays ledger on table, wipes his mouth, wipes his hands on the front of his waistcoat, brings them smartly together and rubs them.

KRAPP (*briskly*): Ah! (*He bends over ledger, turns the pages, finds the entry he wants, reads.*) Box . . . thrree . . . spool . . . five. (*He raises his head and stares front. With relish.*) Spool! (*Pause.*) Spooool! (*Happy smile. Pause. He bends over table, starts peering and poking at the boxes.*) Box . . . thrree . . . thrree . . . four . . . two . . . (*with surprise*) nine! good God! . . . seven . . . ah! the little rascal! (*He takes up box, peers at it.*) Box thrree. (*He lays it on table, opens it, and peers at spools inside.*) Spool . . . (*he peers at ledger*) . . . five (*he peers at spools*) . . . five . . . five! . . . ah! the little scoundrel! (*He takes out a spool, peers at it.*) Spool five. (*He lays it on table, closes box three, puts it back with the others, takes up the spool.*) Box thrree, spool five. (*He bends over the machine, looks up. With relish.*) Spooool! (*Happy smile. He bends, loads spool on machine, rubs his hands.*) Ah! (*He peers at ledger, reads entry at foot of page.*) Mother at rest at last . . . Hm . . . The black ball . . . (*He raises his head, stares blankly front. Puzzled.*) Black ball? . . . (*He peers again at ledger, reads.*) The dark nurse . . . (*He raises his head, broods, peers again at ledger, reads.*) Slight improvement in bowel condition . . . Hm . . . Memorable . . . what? (*He peers closer.*) Equinox, memorable equinox. (*He raises his head, stares blankly front. Puzzled.*) Memorable equinox? . . . (*Pause. He shrugs his shoulders, peers again at ledger, reads.*) Farewell to — (*he turns the page*) — love.

He raises his head, broods, bends over machine, switches on, and assumes listening posture; i.e. leaning forward, elbows on table, hand cupping ear towards machine, face front.

TAPE (*strong voice, rather pompous, clearly Krapp's at a much earlier time*): Thirty-nine today, sound as a — (*Settling himself more comfortably he knocks one of the boxes off the table, curses, switches off, sweeps boxes and ledger violently to the ground, winds tape back to beginning, switches on, resumes posture.*) Thirty-nine today, sound as a bell, apart from my old weakness, and intellectually I have now every reason to suspect at the . . . (*hesitates*) . . . crest of the wave — or thereabouts. Celebrated the awful occasion, as in recent years, quietly at the Winehouse. Not a soul. Sat before the fire with closed eyes, separating the grain from the husks. Jotted down a few notes, on the back of an envelope. Good to be back in my den, in my old rags. Have just eaten I regret to say three bananas and only with difficulty refrained from a fourth. Fatal things for a man with my condition. (*Vehemently.*) Cut 'em out! (*Pause.*) The new light above my table is a great improvement. With all this darkness round me I feel less alone. (*Pause.*) In a way. (*Pause.*) I love to get up and move about in it, then back here to . . . (*hesitates*) . . . me. (*Pause.*) Krapp.

Pause.

The grain, now what I wonder do I mean by that, I mean . . . *(hesitates)* . . . I suppose I mean those things worth having when all the dust has — when all *my* dust has settled. I close my eyes and try and imagine them.

Pause. Krapp closes his eyes briefly.

Extraordinary silence this evening, I strain my ears and do not hear a sound. Old Miss McGlome always sings at this hour. But not tonight. Songs of her girlhood, she says. Hard to think of her as a girl. Wonderful woman though. Connaught, I fancy. *(Pause.)* Shall I sing when I am her age, if I ever am? No. *(Pause.)* Did I sing as a boy? No. *(Pause.)* Did I ever sing? No.

Pause.

Just been listening to an old year, passages at random. I did not check in the book, but it must be at least ten or twelve years ago. At that time I think I was still living on and off with Bianca in Kedar Street. Well out of that, Jesus yes! Hopeless business. *(Pause.)* Not much about her, apart from a tribute to her eyes. Very warm. I suddenly saw them again. *(Pause.)* Incomparable! *(Pause.)* Ah well . . . *(Pause.)* These old P.M.s are gruesome, but I often find them — *(Krapp switches off, broods, switches on)* — a help before embarking on a new . . . *(hesitates)* . . . retrospect. Hard to believe I was ever that young whelp. The voice! Jesus! And the aspirations! *(Brief laugh in which Krapp joins.)* And the resolutions! *(Brief laugh in which Krapp joins.)* To drink less, in particular. *(Brief laugh of Krapp alone.)* Statistics. Seventeen hundred hours, out of the preceding eight thousand odd, consumed on licensed premises alone. More than 20%, say 40% of his waking life. *(Pause.)* Plans for a less . . . *(hesitates)* . . . engrossing sexual life. Last illness of his father. Flagging pursuit of happiness. Unattainable laxation. Sneers at what he calls his youth and thanks to God that it's over. *(Pause.)* False ring there. *(Pause.)* Shadows of the opus . . . magnum. Closing with a — *(brief laugh)* — yelp to Providence. *(Prolonged laugh in which Krapp joins.)* What remains of all that misery? A girl in a shabby green coat, on a railway-station platform? No?

Pause.

When I look —

Krapp switches off, broods, looks at his watch, gets up, goes backstage into darkness. Ten seconds. Pop of cork. Ten seconds. Second cork. Ten seconds. Third cork. Ten seconds. Brief burst of quavering song.

KRAPP *(sings):* Now the day is over,
Night is drawing nigh-igh,
Shadows — °

Now . . . Shadows: From the hymn "Now the Day Is Over" by Sabine Baring-Gould (1834–1924), author of "Onward, Christian Soldiers."

Fit of coughing. He comes back into light, sits down, wipes his mouth, switches on, resumes his listening posture.

TAPE: — back on the year that is gone, with what I hope is perhaps a glint of the old eye to come, there is of course the house on the canal where mother lay a-dying, in the late autumn, after her long viduity° (*Krapp gives a start*), and the — (*Krapp switches off, winds back tape a little, bends his ear closer to machine, switches on*) — a-dying, after her long viduity, and the —

Krapp switches off, raises his head, stares blankly before him. His lips move in the syllables of "viduity." No sound. He gets up, goes backstage into darkness, comes back with an enormous dictionary, lays it on table, sits down and looks up the word.

KRAPP (*reading from dictionary*): State — or condition of being — or remaining — a widow — or widower. (*Looks up. Puzzled.*) Being — or remaining? . . . (*Pause. He peers again at dictionary. Reading.*) "Deep weeds of viduity" . . . Also of an animal, especially a bird . . . the vidua or weaver-bird . . . Black plumage of male . . . (*He looks up. With relish.*) The vidua-bird!

Pause. He closes dictionary, switches on, resumes listening posture.

TAPE: — bench by the weir from where I could see her window. There I sat, in the biting wind, wishing she were gone. (*Pause.*) Hardly a soul, just a few regulars, nursemaids, infants, old men, dogs. I got to know them quite well — oh by appearance of course I mean! One dark young beauty I recollect particularly, all white and starch, incomparable bosom, with a big black hooded perambulator, most funereal thing. Whenever I looked in her direction she had her eyes on me. And yet when I was bold enough to speak to her — not having been introduced — she threatened to call a policeman. As if I had designs on her virtue! (*Laugh. Pause.*) The face she had! The eyes! Like . . . (*hesitates*) . . . chrysolite! (*Pause.*) Ah well . . . (*Pause.*) I was there when — (*Krapp switches off, broods, switches on again*) — the blind went down, one of those dirty brown roller affairs, throwing a ball for a little white dog, as chance would have it. I happened to look up and there it was. All over and done with, at last. I sat on for a few moments with the ball in my hand and the dog yelping and pawing at me. (*Pause.*) Moments. Her moments, my moments. (*Pause.*) The dog's moments. (*Pause.*) In the end I held it out to him and he took it in his mouth, gently, gently. A small, old, black, hard, solid rubber ball. (*Pause.*) I shall feel it, in my hand, until my dying day. (*Pause.*) I might have kept it. (*Pause.*) But I gave it to the dog.

Pause.

    Ah well . . .

Pause.

---

viduity: Widowhood.

Spiritually a year of profound gloom and indigence until that memorable night in March, at the end of the jetty, in the howling wind, never to be forgotten, when suddenly I saw the whole thing. The vision, at last. This I fancy is what I have chiefly to record this evening, against the day when my work will be done and perhaps no place left in my memory, warm or cold, for the miracle that . . . (*hesitates*) . . . for the fire that set it alight. What I suddenly saw then was this, that the belief I had been going on all my life, namely — (*Krapp switches off impatiently, winds tape forward, switches on again*) — great granite rocks the foam flying up in the light of the lighthouse and the wind-gauge spinning like a propellor, clear to me at last that the dark I have always struggled to keep under is in reality my most — (*Krapp curses, switches off, winds tape forward, switches on again*) — unshatterable association until my dissolution of storm and night with the light of the understanding and the fire — (*Krapp curses louder, switches off, winds tape forward, switches on again*) — my face in her breasts and my hand on her. We lay there without moving. But under us all moved, and moved us, gently, up and down, and from side to side.

Pause.

Past midnight. Never knew such silence. The earth might be uninhabited.

Pause.

Here I end —

Krapp switches off, winds tape back, switches on again.

— upper lake, with the punt, bathed off the bank, then pushed out into the stream and drifted. She lay stretched out on the floorboards with her hands under her head and her eyes closed. Sun blazing down, bit of a breeze, water nice and lively. I noticed a scratch on her thigh and asked her how she came by it. Picking gooseberries, she said. I said again I thought it was hopeless and no good going on, and she agreed, without opening her eyes. (*Pause.*) I asked her to look at me and after a few moments — (*pause*) — after a few moments she did, but the eyes just slits, because of the glare. I bent over her to get them in the shadow and they opened. (*Pause. Low.*) Let me in. (*Pause.*) We drifted in among the flags and stuck. The way they went down, sighing, before the stem! (*Pause.*) I lay down across her with my face in her breasts and my hand on her. We lay there without moving. But under us all moved, and moved us, gently, up and down, and from side to side.

Pause.

Past midnight. Never knew —

Krapp switches off, broods. Finally he fumbles in his pockets, encounters the banana, takes it out, peers at it, puts it back, fumbles, brings out the envelope, fumbles, puts back envelope, looks at his watch, gets up and goes backstage into darkness. Ten seconds. Sound of bottle against glass, then brief siphon. Ten seconds. Bottle against glass alone. Ten seconds. He comes back a little unsteadily into light, goes to front of table, takes out keys, raises them to his eyes, chooses key, unlocks first drawer, peers into it, feels about inside, takes out reel, peers at it, locks drawer, puts keys back in his pocket, goes and sits down, takes reel off machine, lays it on dictionary, loads virgin reel on machine, takes envelope from his pocket, consults back of it, lays it on table, switches on, clears his throat, and begins to record.

KRAPP: Just been listening to that stupid bastard I took myself for thirty years ago, hard to believe I was ever as bad as that. Thank God that's all done with anyway. *(Pause.)* The eyes she had! *(Broods, realizes he is recording silence, switches off, broods. Finally.)* Everything there, everything, all the — *(Realizes this is not being recorded, switches on.)* Everything there, everything on this old muckball, all the light and dark and famine and feasting of ... *(hesitates)* ... the ages! *(In a shout.)* Yes! *(Pause.)* Let that go! Jesus! Take his mind off his homework! Jesus! *(Pause. Weary.)* Ah well, maybe he was right. *(Pause.)* Maybe he was right. *(Broods. Realizes. Switches off. Consults envelope.)* Pah! *(Crumples it and throws it away. Broods. Switches on.)* Nothing to say, not a squeak. What's a year now? The sour cud and the iron stool. *(Pause.)* Revelled in the word spool. *(With relish.)* Spooool! Happiest moment of the past half million. *(Pause.)* Seventeen copies sold, of which eleven at trade price to free circulating libraries beyond the seas. Getting known. *(Pause.)* One pound six and something, eight I have little doubt. *(Pause.)* Crawled out once or twice, before the summer was cold. Sat shivering in the park, drowned in dreams and burning to be gone. Not a soul. *(Pause.)* Last fancies. *(Vehemently.)* Keep 'em under! *(Pause.)* Scalded the eyes out of me reading *Effie* again, a page a day, with tears again. Effie ... *(Pause.)* Could have been happy with her, up there on the Baltic, and the pines, and the dunes. *(Pause.)* Could I? *(Pause.)* And she? *(Pause.)* Pah! *(Pause.)* Fanny came in a couple of times. Bony old ghost of a whore. Couldn't do much, but I suppose better than a kick in the crutch. The last time wasn't so bad. How do you manage it, she said, at your age? I told her I'd been saving up for her all my life. *(Pause.)* Went to Vespers once, like when I was in short trousers. *(Pause. Sings.)*

Now the day is over,
Night is drawing nigh-igh,
Shadows — *(coughing, then almost inaudible)* — of the evening
Steal across the sky.

(Gasping.) Went to sleep and fell off the pew. *(Pause.)* Sometimes wondered in the night if a last effort mightn't — *(Pause.)* Ah finish your booze now and get to your bed. Go on with this drivel in the morning. Or leave it at that. *(Pause.)* Leave it at that. *(Pause.)* Lie propped up in the dark — and wander. Be again in the dingle on a Christmas Eve, gathering holly, the red-berried. *(Pause.)* Be again on Croghan on a Sunday morning, in the haze, with the bitch, stop and listen to the bells. *(Pause.)* And so on. *(Pause.)* Be again, be again. *(Pause.)* All that old misery. *(Pause.)* Once wasn't enough for you. *(Pause.)* Lie down across her.

Long pause. He suddenly bends over machine, switches off, wrenches off tape, throws it away, puts on the other, winds it forward to the passage he wants, switches on, listens staring front.

TAPE: — gooseberries, she said. I said again I thought it was hopeless and no good going on, and she agreed, without opening her eyes. (*Pause.*) I asked her to look at me and after a few moments — (*pause*) — after a few moments she did, but the eyes just slits, because of the glare. I bent over her to get them in the shadow and they opened. (*Pause. Low.*) Let me in. (*Pause.*) We drifted in among the flags and stuck. The way they went down, sighing, before the stem! (*Pause.*) I lay down across her with my face in her breasts and my hand on her. We lay there without moving. But under us all moved, and moved us, gently, up and down, and from side to side.

Pause. Krapp's lips move. No sound.

Past midnight. Never knew such silence. The earth might be uninhabited.

Pause.

Here I end this reel. Box — (*pause*) — three, spool — (*pause*) — five. (*Pause.*) Perhaps my best years are gone. When there was a chance of happiness. But I wouldn't want them back. Not with the fire in me now. No, I wouldn't want them back.

Krapp motionless staring before him. The tape runs on in silence.

Curtain

৩৩

TENNESSEE WILLIAMS (1911–1983) *was born Thomas Lanier Williams in Columbus, Mississippi, the second child of Edwina Dakin Williams, the daughter of an Episcopal clergyman, and Cornelius Coffin Williams, a traveling salesman. In the first fifteen years of his life, Williams lived with his mother and his older sister, Rose, in over sixteen homes until his father took a permanent job in St. Louis. An indifferent student, Williams began to publish stories in high school newspapers as a teenager. As an English major in college, his favorite authors were dramatists — Chekhov, Ibsen, and Strindberg — and he decided to become a playwright. After attending two other universities, he enrolled at the University of Iowa in 1937, where he saw his first full-length plays produced onstage. After graduation he held different jobs to support himself while he worked on his plays, poetry, and short fiction.*

Williams wrote the story "Portrait of a Girl in Glass" in 1943. He turned the story into a play, The Gentleman Caller, *while he was under contract with M-G-M to write a script for a movie starring Lana Turner. (Williams had a cataract in one eye, so he was exempt from military service during World War II.) The script was turned down, and Williams left Hollywood soon after. He then rewrote the script as* The Glass Menagerie, *which opened in Chicago in December 1944. After a shaky start,* the play ran for 561 performances in New York City and won the Drama Critics Circle Award as the best American play of the year.

In the introduction to Williams's Collected Stories, the writer Gore Vidal analyzed how Williams used his life as the basis of his art:

> Like most natural writers, Tennessee could not possess his own life until he had written about it. This is common. But what is not common was the way that he went about not only recapturing lost time but then regaining it in a way that far surpassed the original experience. . . . [First he turned his memories into stories, then] he would make a play of the story and then — and this is why he was so compulsive a working playwright — he would have the play produced so that he could, like God, rearrange his original experience into something that was no longer God's and unpossessable but his. The frantic lifelong desire for play-productions was not just ambition or a need to be busy, it was the only way that he ever had of being entirely alive.

In Williams's production notes to The Glass Menagerie, he calls it a "memory play" and describes his vision of a revitalized, lyrical theater of feelings. Both the play and "Portrait of a Girl in Glass" are based on Williams's memories of his close relationship with his sister, Rose, who was institutionalized after a lobotomy authorized by Williams's parents while he was a student at the University of Iowa. In his autobiographical play, he portrayed his sister and himself as victims and outsiders in the family. He used his own name for himself as the character Tom and called his sister Laura, as well as punning on her name in the phrase "Blue Roses" later in her dialogue with the gentleman caller.

When Williams turned the original short story into a play, he gave a much larger role to the figure of the mother Amanda, who tries to dominate the lives of her son and daughter. The young playwright William Inge, who met Williams just before The Glass Menagerie was produced, recalled that the play was exciting because "it enabled me to see the true dynamics between life and art. . . . I don't think any of his plays is quite as personal as the Menagerie, although Menagerie, when you see it, does not strike you as a too personal play in any way at all. It's a real work of art . . . it's not self-indulgent, is what I'm trying to say. It is out of self, but it is conceived in terms of universality."

The Glass Menagerie introduces several themes that reoccur in later Williams plays, including the fear of isolation and the need for understanding by the dispossessed. The most successful American playwright of his generation, Williams wrote several other prize-winning plays, including A Streetcar Named Desire (1948), The Rose Tattoo (1951), Cat on a Hot Tin Roof (1955), Suddenly Last Summer (1958), Sweet Bird of Youth (1959), and The Night of the Iguana (1961). All of them, like The Glass Menagerie, were made into motion pictures.

RELATED STORY: Tennessee Williams, "Portrait of a Girl in Glass," page 708.

RELATED PLAY: Christopher Durang, For Whom the Southern Belle Tolls, page 1937.

RELATED COMMENTARIES: Tennessee Williams, "Production Notes to The Glass Menagerie," page 2031; Benjamin Nelson, "Problems in The Glass Menagerie," page 2009.

TENNESSEE WILLIAMS

The Glass Menagerie   1945

nobody,not even the rain,has such small hands
— E. E. CUMMINGS

LIST OF CHARACTERS

AMANDA WINGFIELD, *the mother. A little woman of great but confused vitality clinging frantically to another time and place. Her characterization must be carefully created, not copied from type. She is not paranoiac, but her life is paranoia. There is much to admire in Amanda, and as much to love and pity as there is to laugh at. Certainly she has endurance and a kind of heroism, and though her foolishness makes her unwittingly cruel at times, there is tenderness in her slight person.*

LAURA WINGFIELD, *her daughter. Amanda, having failed to establish contact with reality, continues to live vitally in her illusions, but Laura's situation is even graver. A childhood illness has left her crippled, one leg slightly shorter than the other, and held in a brace. This defect need not be more than suggested on the stage. Stemming from this, Laura's separation increases till she is like a piece of her own glass collection, too exquisitely fragile to move from the shelf.*

TOM WINGFIELD, *her son. And the narrator of the play. A poet with a job in a warehouse. His nature is not remorseless, but to escape from a trap he has to act without pity.*

JIM O'CONNOR, *the gentleman caller. A nice, ordinary, young man.*

SCENE: *An alley in St. Louis.*
PART I: *Preparation for a Gentleman Caller.*
PART II: *The Gentleman Calls.*
TIME: *Now and the Past.*

SCENE I

The Wingfield apartment is in the rear of the building, one of those vast hivelike conglomerations of cellular living-units that flower as warty growths in overcrowded urban centers of lower middle-class population and are symptomatic of the impulse of this largest and fundamentally enslaved section of American society to avoid fluidity and differentiation and to exist and function as one interfused mass of automatism.

The apartment faces an alley and is entered by a fire-escape, a structure whose name is a touch of accidental poetic truth, for all of these huge buildings are always burning with the slow and implacable fires of human desperation. The fire-escape is included in the set — that is, the landing of it and steps descending from it.

The scene is memory and is therefore nonrealistic. Memory takes a lot of poetic license. It omits some details; others are exaggerated, according to the emotional value of the articles it touches, for memory is seated predominantly in the heart. The interior is therefore rather dim and poetic.

At the rise of the curtain, the audience is faced with the dark, grim rear wall of the Wingfield tenement. This building, which runs parallel to the footlights, is flanked on both sides by dark, narrow alleys which run into murky canyons of tangled clotheslines, garbage cans, and the sinister latticework of neighboring fire-escapes. It is up and down these side alleys that exterior entrances and exits are made, during the play. At the end of Tom's opening commentary, the dark tenement wall slowly reveals (by means of a transparency) the interior of the ground floor Wingfield apartment.

Downstage is the living room, which also serves as a sleeping room for Laura, the sofa unfolding to make her bed. Upstage, center, and divided by a wide arch or second proscenium with transparent faded portieres (or second curtain), is the dining room. In an old-fashioned what-not in the living room are seen scores of transparent glass animals. A blown-up photograph of the father hangs on the wall of the living room, facing the audience, to the left of the archway. It is the face of a very handsome young man in a doughboy's First World War cap. He is gallantly smiling, ineluctably smiling, as if to say, "I will be smiling forever."

The audience hears and sees the opening scene in the dining room through both the transparent fourth wall of the building and the transparent gauze portieres of the dining-room arch. It is during this revealing scene that the fourth wall slowly ascends, out of sight. This transparent exterior wall is not brought down again until the very end of the play, during Tom's final speech.

The narrator is an undisguised convention of the play. He takes whatever license with dramatic convention as is convenient to his purposes.

Tom enters dressed as a merchant sailor from alley, stage left, and strolls across the front of the stage to the fire-escape. There he stops and lights a cigarette. He addresses the audience.

TOM: Yes, I have tricks in my pocket, I have things up my sleeve. But I am the opposite of a stage magician. He gives you illusion that has the appearance of truth. I give you truth in the pleasant disguise of illusion. To begin with, I turn back time. I reverse it to that quaint period, the thirties, when the huge middle class of America was matriculating in a school for the blind. Their eyes had failed them, or they had failed their eyes, and so they were having their fingers pressed forcibly down on the fiery Braille alphabet of a dissolving economy. In Spain there was revolution. Here there was only shouting and confusion. In Spain there was Guernica.° Here there were disturbances of labor, sometimes pretty violent, in otherwise peaceful cities such as Chicago, Cleveland, Saint Louis. . . . This is the social background of the play.

(Music.)

The play is memory. Being a memory play, it is dimly lighted, it is sentimental, it is not realistic. In memory everything seems to happen to music. That explains the fiddle in the wings. I am the narrator of the play, and also a character in it. The other characters are my mother, Amanda, my sister, Laura, and a gentleman caller who appears in the final scenes. He is the most realistic character in the play, being an emissary from a world of reality that we were somehow set apart from. But since I have a poet's weakness for symbols, I am using this character also as a symbol; he is the long delayed but always expected something that we live

---

Guernica: A town in Spain annihilated by German bombers in 1937.

for. There is a fifth character in the play who doesn't appear except in this larger-than-life photograph over the mantel. This is our father who left us a long time ago. He was a telephone man who fell in love with long distances; he gave up his job with the telephone company and skipped the light fantastic out of town. . . . The last we heard of him was a picture post-card from Mazatlán, on the Pacific coast of Mexico, containing a message of two words — "Hello — Good-bye!" and no address. I think the rest of the play will explain itself. . . .

Amanda's voice becomes audible through the portieres.

(*Legend on screen: "Où sont les neiges."°*)
He divides the portieres and enters the upstage area.
 Amanda and Laura are seated at a drop-leaf table. Eating is indicated by gestures without food or utensils. Amanda faces the audience.
 Tom and Laura are seated in profile.
 The interior has lit up softly and through the scrim we see Amanda and Laura seated at the table in the upstage area.

AMANDA (*calling*): Tom?
TOM: Yes, Mother.
AMANDA: We can't say grace until you come to the table!
TOM: Coming, Mother. (*He bows slightly and withdraws, reappearing a few moments later in his place at the table.*)
AMANDA (*to her son*): Honey, don't *push* with your *fingers*. If you have to push with something, the thing to push with is a crust of bread. And chew — chew! Animals have sections in their stomachs which enable them to digest food without mastication, but human beings are supposed to chew their food before they swallow it down. Eat food leisurely, son, and really enjoy it. A well-cooked meal has lots of delicate flavors that have to be held in the mouth for appreciation. So chew your food and give your salivary glands a chance to function!

Tom deliberately lays his imaginary fork down and pushes his chair back from the table.

TOM: I haven't enjoyed one bite of this dinner because of your constant directions on how to eat it. It's you that makes me rush through meals with your hawklike attention to every bite I take. Sickening — spoils my appetite — all this discussion of animals' secretion — salivary glands — mastication!
AMANDA (*lightly*): Temperament like a Metropolitan star! (*He rises and crosses downstage.*) You're not excused from the table.
TOM: I am getting a cigarette.
AMANDA: You smoke too much.

Laura rises.

Où sont les neiges: Part of a line by the French poet François Villon; the complete line translates, "But where are the snows of Yesteryear?"

LAURA: I'll bring in the blanc mange.

He remains standing with his cigarette by the portieres during the following.

AMANDA (*rising*): No, sister, no, sister — you be the lady this time and I'll be the darky.

LAURA: I'm already up.

AMANDA: Resume your seat, little sister — I want you to stay fresh and pretty — for gentlemen callers!

LAURA: I'm not expecting any gentlemen callers.

AMANDA (*crossing out to kitchenette. Airily*): Sometimes they come when they are least expected! Why, I remember one Sunday afternoon in Blue Mountain — (*Enters kitchenette.*)

TOM: I know what's coming!

LAURA: Yes. But let her tell it.

TOM: Again?

LAURA: She loves to tell it.

Amanda returns with bowl of dessert.

AMANDA: One Sunday afternoon in Blue Mountain — your mother received — seventeen! — gentlemen callers! Why, sometimes there weren't chairs enough to accommodate them all. We had to send the nigger over to bring in folding chairs from the parish house.

TOM (*remaining at portieres*): How did you entertain those gentlemen callers?

AMANDA: I understood the art of conversation!

TOM: I bet you could talk.

AMANDA: Girls in those days *knew* how to talk, I can tell you.

TOM: Yes?

(*Image: Amanda as a girl on a porch greeting callers.*)

AMANDA: They knew how to entertain their gentlemen callers. It wasn't enough for a girl to be possessed of a pretty face and a graceful figure — although I wasn't slighted in either respect. She also needed to have a nimble wit and a tongue to meet all occasions.

TOM: What did you talk about?

AMANDA: Things of importance going on in the world! Never anything coarse or common or vulgar. (*She addresses Tom as though he were seated in the vacant chair at the table though he remains by portieres. He plays this scene as though he held the book.*) My callers were gentlemen — all! Among my callers were some of the most prominent young planters of the Mississippi Delta — planters and sons of planters!

Tom motions for music and a spot of light on Amanda.

Her eyes lift, her face glows, her voice becomes rich and elegiac.

(*Screen legend: "Où sont les neiges."*)

There was young Champ Laughlin who later became vice-president of the Delta Planters Bank. Hadley Stevenson who was drowned in Moon Lake and left his widow one hundred and fifty thousand in Government bonds. There were the Cutrere brothers, Wesley and Bates. Bates was one of my bright particular beaux! He got in a quarrel with that wild

Wainright boy. They shot it out on the floor of Moon Lake Casino. Bates was shot through the stomach. Died in the ambulance on his way to Memphis. His widow was also well-provided for, came into eight or ten thousand acres, that's all. She married him on the rebound — never loved her — carried my picture on him the night he died! And there was that boy that every girl in the Delta had set her cap for! That beautiful, brilliant young Fitzhugh boy from Green County!

TOM: What did he leave his widow?

AMANDA: He never married! Gracious, you talk as though all of my old admirers had turned up their toes to the daisies!

TOM: Isn't this the first you mentioned that still survives?

AMANDA: That Fitzhugh boy went North and made a fortune — came to be known as the Wolf of Wall Street! He had the Midas touch, whatever he touched turned to gold! And I could have been Mrs. Duncan J. Fitzhugh, mind you! But — I picked your *father*!

LAURA (*rising*): Mother, let me clear the table.

AMANDA: No dear, you go in front and study your typewriter chart. Or practice your shorthand a little. Stay fresh and pretty! — It's almost time for our gentlemen callers to start arriving. (*She flounces girlishly toward the kitchenette.*) How many do you suppose we're going to entertain this afternoon?

Tom throws down the paper and jumps up with a groan.

LAURA (*alone in the dining room*): I don't believe we're going to receive any, Mother.

AMANDA (*reappearing, airily*): What? No one — not one? You must be joking! (*Laura nervously echoes her laugh. She slips in a fugitive manner through the half-open portieres and draws them gently behind her. A shaft of very clear light is thrown on her face against the faded tapestry of the curtains.*) (*Music: "The Glass Menagerie" under faintly.*) (*Lightly.*) Not one gentleman caller? It can't be true! There must be a flood, there must have been a tornado!

LAURA: It isn't a flood, it's not a tornado, Mother. I'm just not popular like you were in Blue Mountain. . . . (*Tom utters another groan. Laura glances at him with a faint, apologetic smile. Her voice catching a little.*) Mother's afraid I'm going to be an old maid.

(*The scene dims out with "Glass Menagerie" music.*)

SCENE II

"Laura, Haven't You Ever Liked Some Boy?"

On the dark stage the screen is lighted with the image of blue roses.

Gradually Laura's figure becomes apparent and the screen goes out.

The music subsides.

Laura is seated in the delicate ivory chair at the small clawfoot table.

She wears a dress of soft violet material for a kimono — her hair tied back from her forehead with a ribbon.

She is washing and polishing her collection of glass.

Amanda appears on the fire-escape steps. At the sound of her ascent, Laura catches her breath, thrusts the bowl of ornaments away, and seats herself stiffly before the diagram of the typewriter keyboard as though it held her spellbound. Something has happened to Amanda. It is written in her face as she climbs to the landing: a look that is grim and hopeless and a little absurd.

She has on one of those cheap or imitation velvety-looking cloth coats with imitation fur collar. Her hat is five or six years old, one of those dreadful cloche hats that were worn in the late twenties, and she is clasping an enormous black patent-leather pocketbook with nickel clasp and initials. This is her full-dress outfit, the one she usually wears to the D.A.R.°

Before entering she looks through the door.

She purses her lips, opens her eyes wide, rolls them upward, and shakes her head.

Then she slowly lets herself in the door. Seeing her mother's expression Laura touches her lips with a nervous gesture.

LAURA: Hello, Mother, I was — (*She makes a nervous gesture toward the chart on the wall. Amanda leans against the shut door and stares at Laura with a martyred look.*)

AMANDA: Deception? Deception? (*She slowly removes her hat and gloves, continuing the swift suffering stare. She lets the hat and gloves fall on the floor — a bit of acting.*)

LAURA (*shakily*): How was the D.A.R. meeting? (*Amanda slowly opens her purse and removes a dainty white handkerchief, which she shakes out delicately and delicately touches to her lips and nostrils.*) Didn't you go to the D.A.R. meeting, Mother?

AMANDA (*faintly, almost inaudibly*): — No. — No. (*Then more forcibly.*) I did not have the strength — to go to the D.A.R. In fact, I did not have the courage! I wanted to find a hole in the ground and hide myself in it forever! (*She crosses slowly to the wall and removes the diagram of the typewriter keyboard. She holds it in front of her for a second, staring at it sweetly and sorrowfully — then bites her lips and tears it in two pieces.*)

LAURA (*faintly*): Why did you do that, Mother? (*Amanda repeats the same procedure with the chart of the Gregg Alphabet.°*) Why are you —

AMANDA: Why? Why? How old are you, Laura?

LAURA: Mother, you know my age.

AMANDA: I thought that you were an adult; it seems that I was mistaken. (*She crosses slowly to the sofa and sinks down and stares at Laura.*)

LAURA: Please don't stare at me, Mother.

Amanda closes her eyes and lowers her head. Count ten.

AMANDA: What are we going to do, what is going to become of us, what is the future?

D.A.R.: Daughters of the American Revolution, whose ancestors served the patriots' cause in the Revolutionary War. **Gregg Alphabet:** Shorthand system invented by John Robert Gregg.

Count ten.

LAURA: Has something happened, Mother? (*Amanda draws a long breath and takes out the handkerchief again. Dabbing process.*) Mother, has — something happened?

AMANDA: I'll be all right in a minute. I'm just bewildered — (*count five*) — by life. . . .

LAURA: Mother, I wish that you would tell me what's happened.

AMANDA: As you know, I was supposed to be inducted into my office at the D.A.R. this afternoon. (*Image: A swarm of typewriters.*) But I stopped off at Rubicam's Business College to speak to your teachers about your having a cold and ask them what progress they thought you were making down there.

LAURA: Oh. . . .

AMANDA: I went to the typing instructor and introduced myself as your mother. She didn't know who you were. Wingfield, she said. We don't have any such student enrolled at the school! I assured her she did, that you had been going to classes since early in January. "I wonder," she said, "if you could be talking about that terribly shy little girl who dropped out of school after only a few days' attendance?" "No," I said, "Laura, my daughter, has been going to school every day for the past six weeks!" "Excuse me," she said. She took the attendance book out and there was your name, unmistakably printed, and all the dates you were absent until they decided that you had dropped out of school. I still said, "No, there must have been some mistake! There must have been some mix-up in the records!" And she said, "No — I remember her perfectly now. Her hand shook so that she couldn't hit the right keys! The first time we gave a speed-test, she broke down completely — was sick at the stomach and almost had to be carried into the wash-room! After that morning she never showed up any more. We phoned the house but never got any answer" — while I was working at Famous and Barr, I suppose, demonstrating those — Oh! I felt so weak I could barely keep on my feet. I had to sit down while they got me a glass of water! Fifty dollars' tuition, all of our plans — my hopes and ambitions for you — just gone up the spout, just gone up the spout like that. (*Laura draws a long breath and gets awkwardly to her feet. She crosses to the Victrola, and winds it up.*) What are you doing?

LAURA: Oh! (*She releases the handle and returns to her seat.*)

AMANDA: Laura, where have you been going when you've gone out pretending that you were going to business college?

LAURA: I've just been going out walking.

AMANDA: That's not true.

LAURA: It is. I just went walking.

AMANDA: Walking? Walking? In winter? Deliberately courting pneumonia in that light coat? Where did you walk to, Laura?

LAURA: It was the lesser of two evils, Mother. (*Image: Winter scene in park.*) I couldn't go back up. I — threw up — on the floor!

AMANDA: From half past seven till after five every day you mean to tell me you walked around in the park, because you wanted to make me think that you were still going to Rubicam's Business College?

LAURA: It wasn't as bad as it sounds. I went inside places to get warmed up.

AMANDA: Inside where?

LAURA: I went in the art museum and the bird-houses at the Zoo. I visited the penguins every day! Sometimes I did without lunch and went to the movies. Lately I've been spending most of my afternoons in the Jewel-box, that big glass house where they raise the tropical flowers.

AMANDA: You did all this to deceive me, just for the deception? (*Laura looks down.*) Why?

LAURA: Mother, when you're disappointed, you get that awful suffering look on your face, like the picture of Jesus' mother in the museum!

AMANDA: Hush!

LAURA: I couldn't face it.

Pause. A whisper of strings.
(*Legend: "The Crust of Humility."*)

AMANDA (*hopelessly fingering the huge pocketbook*): So what are we going to do the rest of our lives? Stay home and watch the parades go by? Amuse ourselves with the glass menagerie, darling? Eternally play those worn-out phonograph records your father left as a painful reminder of him? We won't have a business career — we've given that up because it gave us nervous indigestion! (*Laughs wearily.*) What is there left but dependency all our lives? I know so well what becomes of unmarried women who aren't prepared to occupy a position. I've seen such pitiful cases in the South — barely tolerated spinsters living upon the grudging patronage of sister's husband or brother's wife! — stuck away in some little mousetrap of a room — encouraged by one in-law to visit another — little birdlike women without any nest — eating the crust of humility all their life! Is that the future that we've mapped out for ourselves? I swear it's the only alternative I can think of! It isn't a very pleasant alternative, is it? Of course — some girls *do* marry. (*Laura twists her hands nervously.*) Haven't you ever liked some boy?

LAURA: Yes. I liked one once. (*Rises.*) I came across his picture a while ago.

AMANDA (*with some interest*): He gave you his picture?

LAURA: No, it's in the year-book.

AMANDA (*disappointed*): Oh — a high-school boy.

(*Screen image: Jim as a high-school hero bearing a silver cup.*)

LAURA: Yes. His name was Jim. (*Laura lifts the heavy annual from the clawfoot table.*) Here he is in *The Pirates of Penzance.*

AMANDA (*absently*): The what?

LAURA: The operetta the senior class put on. He had a wonderful voice and we sat across the aisle from each other Mondays, Wednesdays, and Fridays in the Aud. Here he is with the silver cup for debating! See his grin?

AMANDA (*absently*): He must have had a jolly disposition.

LAURA: He used to call me — Blue Roses.

(*Image: Blue roses.*)

AMANDA: Why did he call you such a name as that?

LAURA: When I had that attack of pleurosis — he asked me what was the matter when I came back. I said pleurosis — he thought that I said Blue Roses! So that's what he always called me after that. Whenever he saw me, he'd holler, "Hello, Blue Roses!" I didn't care for the girl that he went out with. Emily Meisenbach. Emily was the best-dressed girl at Soldan. She never struck me, though, as being sincere. . . . It says in the Personal Section — they're engaged. That's — six years ago! They must be married by now.

AMANDA: Girls that aren't cut out for business careers usually wind up married to some nice man. (*Gets up with a spark of revival.*) Sister, that's what you'll do!

Laura utters a startled, doubtful laugh. She reaches quickly for a piece of glass.

LAURA: But, Mother —

AMANDA: Yes? (*Crossing to photograph.*)

LAURA (*in a tone of frightened apology*): I'm — crippled!

(*Image: Screen.*)

AMANDA: Nonsense! Laura, I've told you never, never to use that word. Why, you're not crippled, you just have a little defect — hardly noticeable, even! When people have some slight disadvantage like that, they cultivate other things to make up for it — develop charm — and vivacity — and — *charm*! That's all you have to do! (*She turns again to the photograph.*) One thing your father had *plenty* of — was *charm*!

Tom motions to the fiddle in the wings.
   (*The scene fades out with music.*)

SCENE III

(*Legend on the screen: "After the Fiasco — "*)
   Tom speaks from the fire-escape landing.

TOM: After the fiasco at Rubicam's Business College, the idea of getting a gentleman caller for Laura began to play a more important part in Mother's calculations. It became an obsession. Like some archetype of the universal unconscious, the image of the gentleman caller haunted our small apartment. . . . (*Image: Young man at door with flowers.*) An evening at home rarely passed without some allusion to this image, this specter, this hope. . . . Even when he wasn't mentioned, his presence hung in Mother's preoccupied look and in my sister's frightened, apologetic manner — hung like a sentence passed upon the Wingfields! Mother was a woman of action as well as words. She began to take logical steps in the planned direction. Late that winter and in the early spring — realizing that extra money would be needed to properly feather the nest and plume the bird — she conducted a vigorous campaign on the telephone, roping in subscribers to one of those magazines for matrons called *The*

Home-maker's Companion, the type of journal that features the serialized sublimations of ladies of letters who think in terms of delicate cuplike breasts, slim, tapering waists, rich, creamy thighs, eyes like wood-smoke in autumn, fingers that soothe and caress like strains of music, bodies as powerful as Etruscan sculpture.

(Screen image: Glamour *magazine cover.)*

Amanda enters with phone on long extension cord. She is spotted in the dim stage.

AMANDA: Ida Scott? This is Amanda Wingfield! We *missed* you at the D.A.R. last Monday! I said to myself: She's probably suffering with that sinus condition! How is that sinus condition? Horrors! Heaven have mercy! — You're a Christian martyr, yes, that's what you are, a Christian martyr! Well, I just now happened to notice that your subscription to the *Companion*'s about to expire! Yes, it expires with the next issue, honey! — just when that wonderful new serial by Bessie Mae Hopper is getting off to such an exciting start. Oh, honey, it's something that you can't miss! You remember how *Gone with the Wind* took everybody by storm? You simply couldn't go out if you hadn't read it. All everybody *talked* was Scarlett O'Hara. Well, this is a book that critics already compare to *Gone with the Wind.* It's the *Gone with the Wind* of the post–World War generation! — What? — Burning? — Oh, honey, don't let them burn, go take a look in the oven and I'll hold the wire! Heavens — I think she's hung up!

(Dim out.)

(Legend on screen: "You think I'm in love with Continental Shoemakers?")

Before the stage is lighted, the violent voices of Tom and Amanda are heard. They are quarreling behind the portieres. In front of them stands Laura with clenched hands and panicky expression.

A clear pool of light on her figure throughout this scene.

TOM: What in Christ's name am I —

AMANDA (*shrilly*): Don't you use that —

TOM: Supposed to do!

AMANDA: Expression! Not in my —

TOM: Ohhh!

AMANDA: Presence! Have you gone out of your senses?

TOM: I have, that's true, *driven* out!

AMANDA: What is the matter with you, you — big — big — IDIOT!

TOM: Look — I've got *no thing,* no single thing —

AMANDA: Lower your voice!

TOM: In my life here that I can call my own! Everything is —

AMANDA: Stop that shouting!

TOM: Yesterday you confiscated my books! You had the nerve to —

AMANDA: I took that horrible novel back to the library — yes! That hideous book by that insane Mr. Lawrence.° (*Tom laughs wildly.*) I cannot control

---

Mr. Lawrence: D. H. Lawrence (1885–1930), English writer who propounded free sexuality. (See pp. 401 and 1142.)

the output of diseased minds or people who cater to them — (*Tom laughs still more wildly.*) BUT I WON'T ALLOW SUCH FILTH BROUGHT INTO MY HOUSE! No, no, no, no, no!

TOM: House, house! Who pays rent on it, who makes a slave of himself to —

AMANDA (*fairly screeching*): Don't you DARE to —

TOM: No, no, I mustn't say things! *I've* got to just —

AMANDA: Let me tell you —

TOM: I don't want to hear any more! (*He tears the portieres open. The upstage area is lit with a turgid smoky red glow.*)

Amanda's hair is in metal curlers and she wears a very old bathrobe, much too large for her slight figure, a relic of the faithless Mr. Wingfield.

An upright typewriter and a wild disarray of manuscripts are on the drop-leaf table. The quarrel was probably precipitated by Amanda's interruption of his creative labor. A chair lying overthrown on the floor.

Their gesticulating shadows are cast on the ceiling by the fiery glow.

AMANDA: You *will* hear more, you —

TOM: No, I won't hear more, I'm going out!

AMANDA: You come right back in —

TOM: Out, out, out! Because I'm —

AMANDA: Come back here, Tom Wingfield! I'm not through talking to you!

TOM: Oh, go —

LAURA (*desperately*): Tom!

AMANDA: You're going to listen, and no more insolence from you! I'm at the end of my patience! (*He comes back toward her.*)

TOM: What do you think I'm at? Aren't I supposed to have any patience to reach the end of, Mother? I know, I know. It seems unimportant to you, what I'm *doing* — what I *want* to do — having a little *difference* between them! You don't think that —

AMANDA: I think you've been doing things that you're ashamed of. That's why you act like this. I don't believe that you go every night to the movies. Nobody goes to the movies night after night. Nobody in their right minds goes to the movies as often as you pretend to. People don't go to the movies at nearly midnight, and movies don't let out at two A.M. Come in stumbling. Muttering to yourself like a maniac! You get three hours' sleep and then go to work. Oh, I can picture the way you're doing down there. Moping, doping, because you're in no condition.

TOM (*wildly*): No, I'm in no condition!

AMANDA: What right have you got to jeopardize your job? Jeopardize the security of us all? How do you think we'd manage if you were —

TOM: Listen! You think I'm crazy *about* the *warehouse!* (*He bends fiercely toward her slight figure.*) You think I'm in love with the Continental Shoemakers? You think I want to spend fifty-five *years* down there in that — *celotex interior!* with — *fluorescent* — *tubes!* Look! I'd rather somebody picked up a crowbar and battered out my brains — than go back mornings! I *go!* Every time you come in yelling that God damn *"Rise and Shine!" "Rise*

and Shine!" I say to myself "How *lucky dead* people are!" But I get up. I
go! For sixty-five dollars a month I give up all that I dream of doing and
being *ever!* And you say self — *self's* all I ever think of. Why, listen, if self
is what I thought of, Mother, I'd be where he is — ! (*Pointing to father's
picture.*) As far as the system of transportation reaches! (*He starts past her.
She grabs his arm.*) Don't grab at me, Mother!

AMANDA: Where are you going?

TOM: I'm going to the *movies!*

AMANDA: I don't believe that lie!

TOM (*crouching toward her, overtowering her tiny figure. She backs away, gasping*):
I'm going to opium dens! Yes, opium dens, dens of vice and criminals'
hang-outs, Mother. I've joined the Hogan gang, I'm a hired assassin, I
carry a tommy-gun in a violin case! I run a string of cat-houses in the
Valley! They call me Killer, Killer Wingfield, I'm leading a double-life,
a simple, honest warehouse worker by day, by night a dynamic *czar* of
the *underworld, Mother.* I go to gambling casinos, I spin away fortunes
on the roulette table! I wear a patch over one eye and a false mustache,
sometimes I put on green whiskers. On those occasions they call me —
El Diablo!° Oh, I could tell you things to make you sleepless! My enemies plan to dynamite this place. They're going to blow us all sky-high
some night! I'll be glad, very happy, and so will you! You'll go up, up
on a broomstick, over Blue Mountain with seventeen gentlemen
callers! You ugly — babbling old — *witch....* (*He goes through a series of
violent, clumsy movements, seizing his overcoat, lunging to the door, pulling
it fiercely open. The women watch him, aghast. His arm catches in the sleeve
of the coat as he struggles to pull it on. For a moment he is pinioned by the
bulky garment. With an outraged groan he tears the coat off again, splitting
the shoulders of it, and hurls it across the room. It strikes against the shelf of
Laura's glass collection, there is a tinkle of shattering glass. Laura cries out as
if wounded.*)

(*Music legend: "The Glass Menagerie."*)

LAURA (*shrilly*): My glass! — menagerie.... (*She covers her face and turns away.*)

*But Amanda is still stunned and stupefied by the "ugly witch" so that she barely no-
tices this occurrence. Now she recovers her speech.*

AMANDA (*in an awful voice*): I won't speak to you — until you apologize! (*She
crosses through portieres and draws them together behind her. Tom is left with
Laura. Laura clings weakly to the mantel with her face averted. Tom stares at
her stupidly for a moment. Then he crosses to shelf. Drops awkwardly to his
knees to collect the fallen glass, glancing at Laura as if he would speak but
couldn't.*)

"The Glass Menagerie" steals in as
(*The scene dims out.*)

El Diablo: The devil (Spanish).

SCENE IV

The interior is dark. Faint light in the alley.

A deep-voiced bell in a church is tolling the hour of five as the scene commences.

Tom appears at the top of the alley. After each solemn boom of the bell in the tower, he shakes a little noise-maker or rattle as if to express the tiny spasm of man in contrast to the sustained power and dignity of the Almighty. This and the unsteadiness of his advance make it evident that he has been drinking.

As he climbs the few steps to the fire-escape landing light steals up inside. Laura appears in night-dress, observing Tom's empty bed in the front room.

Tom fishes in his pockets for the door-key, removing a motley assortment of articles in the search, including a perfect shower of movie-ticket stubs and an empty bottle. At last he finds the key, but just as he is about to insert it, it slips from his fingers. He strikes a match and crouches below the door.

TOM (*bitterly*): One crack — and it falls through!

Laura opens the door.

LAURA: Tom! Tom, what are you doing?

TOM: Looking for a door-key.

LAURA: Where have you been all this time?

TOM: I have been to the movies.

LAURA: All this time at the movies?

TOM: There was a very long program. There was a Garbo picture and a Mickey Mouse and a travelogue and a newsreel and a preview of coming attractions. And there was an organ solo and a collection for the milk-fund — simultaneously — which ended up in a terrible fight between a fat lady and an usher!

LAURA (*innocently*): Did you have to stay through everything?

TOM: Of course! And, oh, I forgot! There was a big stage show! The headliner on this stage show was Malvolio the Magician. He performed wonderful tricks, many of them, such as pouring water back and forth between pitchers. First it turned to wine and then it turned to beer and then it turned to whiskey. I know it was whiskey it finally turned into because he needed somebody to come up out of the audience to help him, and I came up — both shows! It was Kentucky Straight Bourbon. A very generous fellow, he gave souvenirs. (*He pulls from his back pocket a shimmering rainbow-colored scarf.*) He gave me this. This is his magic scarf. You can have it, Laura. You wave it over a canary cage and you get a bowl of gold-fish. You wave it over the gold-fish bowl and they fly away canaries. . . . But the wonderfullest trick of all was the coffin trick. We nailed him into a coffin and he got out of the coffin without removing one nail. (*He has come inside.*) There is a trick that would come in handy for me — get me out of this 2 by 4 situation! (*Flops onto bed and starts removing shoes.*)

LAURA: Tom — Shhh!

TOM: What you shushing me for?

LAURA: You'll wake up Mother.

TOM: Goody, goody! Pay 'er back for all those "Rise an' Shines." (*Lies down, groaning.*) You know it don't take much intelligence to get yourself into a nailed-up coffin, Laura. But who in hell ever got himself out of one without removing one nail?

As if in answer, the father's grinning photograph lights up.

(*Scene dims out.*)

Immediately following: The church bell is heard striking six. At the sixth stroke the alarm clock goes off in Amanda's room, and after a few moments we hear her calling: "Rise and Shine! Rise and Shine! Laura, go tell your brother to rise and shine!"

TOM (*sitting up slowly*): I'll rise — but I won't shine.

The light increases.

AMANDA: Laura, tell your brother his coffee is ready.

Laura slips into front room.

LAURA: Tom! it's nearly seven. Don't make Mother nervous. (*He stares at her stupidly. Beseechingly.*) Tom, speak to Mother this morning. Make up with her, apologize, speak to her!

TOM: She won't to me. It's her that started not speaking.

LAURA: If you just say you're sorry she'll start speaking.

TOM: Her not speaking — is that such a tragedy?

LAURA: Please — please!

AMANDA (*calling from kitchenette*): Laura, are you going to do what I asked you to do, or do I have to get dressed and go out myself?

LAURA: Going, going — soon as I get on my coat! (*She pulls on a shapeless felt hat with nervous, jerky movement, pleadingly glancing at Tom. Rushes awkwardly for coat. The coat is one of Amanda's, inaccurately made-over, the sleeves too short for Laura.*) Butter and what else?

AMANDA (*entering upstage*): Just butter. Tell them to charge it.

LAURA: Mother, they make such faces when I do that.

AMANDA: Sticks and stones may break my bones, but the expression on Mr. Garfinkel's face won't harm us! Tell your brother his coffee is getting cold.

LAURA (*at door*): Do what I asked you, will you, will you, Tom?

He looks sullenly away.

AMANDA: Laura, go now or just don't go at all!

LAURA (*rushing out*): Going — going! (*A second later she cries out. Tom springs up and crosses to the door. Amanda rushes anxiously in. Tom opens the door.*)

TOM: Laura?

LAURA: I'm all right. I slipped, but I'm all right.

AMANDA (*peering anxiously after her*): If anyone breaks a leg on those fire-escape steps, the landlord ought to be sued for every cent he possesses! (*She shuts door. Remembers she isn't speaking and returns to other room.*)

As Tom enters listlessly for his coffee, she turns her back to him and stands rigidly facing the window on the gloomy gray vault of the areaway. Its light on her face with its aged but childish features is cruelly sharp, satirical as a Daumier° print.

> *(Music under: "Ave Maria.")*

Tom glances sheepishly but sullenly at her averted figure and slumps at the table. The coffee is scalding hot; he sips it and gasps and spits it back in the cup. At his gasp, Amanda catches her breath and half turns. Then catches herself and turns back to window.

Tom blows on his coffee, glancing sidewise at his mother. She clears her throat. Tom clears his. He starts to rise. Sinks back down again, scratches his head, clears his throat again. Amanda coughs. Tom raises his cup in both hands to blow on it, his eyes staring over the rim of it at his mother for several moments. Then he slowly sets the cup down and awkwardly and hesitantly rises from the chair.

TOM (*hoarsely*): Mother. I — I apologize. Mother. (*Amanda draws a quick, shuddering breath. Her face works grotesquely. She breaks into childlike tears.*) I'm sorry for what I said, for everything that I said, I didn't mean it.

AMANDA (*sobbingly*): My devotion has made me a witch and so I make myself hateful to my children!

TOM: No, you *don't.*

AMANDA: I worry so much, don't sleep, it makes me nervous!

TOM (*gently*): I understand that.

AMANDA: I've had to put up a solitary battle all these years. But you're my right-hand bower! Don't fall down, don't fail!

TOM (*gently*): I try, Mother.

AMANDA (*with great enthusiasm*): Try and you will SUCCEED! (*The notion makes her breathless.*) Why, you — you're just *full* of natural endowments! Both of my children — they're *unusual* children! Don't you think I know it? I'm so — *proud!* Happy and — feel I've — so much to be thankful for but — Promise me one thing, son!

TOM: What, Mother?

AMANDA: Promise, son, you'll — never be a drunkard!

TOM (*turns to her grinning*): I will never be a drunkard, Mother.

AMANDA: That's what frightened me so, that you'd be drinking! Eat a bowl of Purina!

TOM: Just coffee, Mother.

AMANDA: Shredded wheat biscuit?

TOM: No. No, Mother, just coffee.

AMANDA: You can't put in a day's work on an empty stomach. You've got ten minutes — don't gulp! Drinking too-hot liquids makes cancer of the stomach. . . . Put cream in.

TOM: No, thank you.

AMANDA: To cool it.

TOM: No! No, thank you, I want it black.

Daumier: Honoré Daumier (1808–1879) was a French caricaturist, lithographer, and painter.

AMANDA: I know, but it's not good for you. We have to do all that we can to build ourselves up. In these trying times we live in, all that we have to cling to is — each other. . . . That's why it's so important to — Tom, I — I sent out your sister so I could discuss something with you. If you hadn't spoken I would have spoken to you. (*Sits down.*)

TOM (*gently*): What is it, Mother, that you want to discuss?

AMANDA: Laura!

Tom puts his cup down slowly.

(*Legend on screen: "Laura."*)

(*Music: "The Glass Menagerie."*)

TOM: — Oh. — Laura . . .

AMANDA (*touching his sleeve*): You know how Laura is. So quiet but — still water runs deep! She notices things and I think she — broods about them. (*Tom looks up.*) A few days ago I came in and she was crying.

TOM: What about?

AMANDA: You.

TOM: Me?

AMANDA: She has an idea that you're not happy here.

TOM: What gave her that idea?

AMANDA: What gives her any idea? However, you do act strangely. I — I'm not criticizing, understand *that!* I know your ambitions do not lie in the warehouse, that like everybody in the whole wide world — you've had to — make sacrifices, but — Tom — Tom — life's not easy, it calls for — Spartan endurance! There's so many things in my heart that I cannot describe to you! I've never told you but I — *loved* your father. . . .

TOM (*gently*): I know that, Mother.

AMANDA: And you — when I see you taking after his ways! Staying out late — and — well, you *had* been drinking the night you were in that — terrifying condition! Laura says that you hate the apartment and that you go out nights to get away from it! Is that true, Tom?

TOM: No. You say there's so much in your heart that you can't describe to me. That's true of me, too. There's so much in my heart that I can't describe to *you!* So let's respect each other's —

AMANDA: But, why — *why,* Tom — are you always so *restless?* Where do you go to, nights?

TOM: I — go to the movies.

AMANDA: Why do you go to the movies so much, Tom?

TOM: I go to the movies because — I like adventure. Adventure is something I don't have much of at work, so I go to the movies.

AMANDA: But, Tom, you go to the movies *entirely too much!*

TOM: I like a lot of adventure.

Amanda looks baffled, then hurt. As the familiar inquisition resumes he becomes hard and impatient again. Amanda slips back into her querulous attitude toward him.

(*Image on screen: Sailing vessel with Jolly Roger.*)

AMANDA: Most young men find adventure in their careers.

TOM: Then most young men are not employed in a warehouse.

AMANDA: The world is full of young men employed in warehouses and offices and factories.

TOM: Do all of them find adventure in their careers?

AMANDA: They do or they do without it! Not everybody has a craze for adventure.

TOM: Man is by instinct a lover, a hunter, a fighter, and none of those instincts are given much play at the warehouse!

AMANDA: Man is by instinct! Don't quote instinct to me! Instinct is something that people have got away from! It belongs to animals! Christian adults don't want it!

TOM: What do Christian adults want, then, Mother?

AMANDA: Superior things! Things of the mind and the spirit! Only animals have to satisfy instincts! Surely your aims are somewhat higher than theirs! Than monkeys — pigs —

TOM: I reckon they're not.

AMANDA: You're joking. However, that isn't what I wanted to discuss.

TOM (*rising*): I haven't much time.

AMANDA (*pushing his shoulders*): Sit down.

TOM: You want me to punch in red° at the warehouse, Mother?

AMANDA: You have five minutes. I want to talk about Laura.

(*Legend: "Plans and Provisions."*)

TOM: All right! What about Laura?

AMANDA: We have to be making plans and provisions for her. She's older than you, two years, and nothing has happened. She just drifts along doing nothing. It frightens me terribly how she just drifts along.

TOM: I guess she's the type that people call home girls.

AMANDA: There's no such type, and if there is, it's a pity! That is unless the home is hers, with a husband!

TOM: What?

AMANDA: Oh, I can see the handwriting on the wall as plain as I see the nose in front of my face! It's terrifying! More and more you remind me of your father! He was out all hours without explanation — Then *left! Good-bye!* And me with the bag to hold. I saw that letter you got from the Merchant Marine. I know what you're dreaming of. I'm not standing here blindfolded. Very well, then. Then *do* it! But not till there's somebody to take your place.

TOM: What do you mean?

AMANDA: I mean that as soon as Laura has got somebody to take care of her, married, a home of her own, independent — why, then you'll be free to go wherever you please, on land, on sea, whichever way the wind blows! But until that time you've got to look out for your sister. I don't say me because I'm old and don't matter! I say for your sister because she's young and dependent. I put her in business college — a dismal

---

punch in red: Show up late for work.

failure! Frightened her so it made her sick to her stomach. I took her over to the Young People's League at the church. Another fiasco. She spoke to nobody, nobody spoke to her. Now all she does is fool with those pieces of glass and play those worn-out records. What kind of a life is that for a girl to lead!

TOM: What can I do about it?

AMANDA: Overcome selfishness! Self, self, self is all that you ever think of! (*Tom springs up and crosses to get his coat. It is ugly and bulky. He pulls on a cap with earmuffs.*) Where is your muffler? Put your wool muffler on! (*He snatches it angrily from the closet and tosses it around his neck and pulls both ends tight.*) Tom! I haven't said what I had in mind to ask you.

TOM: I'm too late to —

AMANDA (*catching his arms — very importunately. Then shyly.*): Down at the warehouse, aren't there some — nice young men?

TOM: No!

AMANDA: There *must* be — *some.*

TOM: Mother —

Gesture.

AMANDA: Find out one that's clean-living — doesn't drink and — ask him out for sister!

TOM: What?

AMANDA: For *sister!* To *meet!* Get *acquainted!*

TOM (*stamping to door*): Oh, my *go-osh!*

AMANDA: Will you? (*He opens door. Imploringly.*) Will you? (*He starts down.*) Will you? *Will* you, dear?

TOM (*calling back*): YES!

Amanda closes the door hesitantly and with a troubled but faintly hopeful expression.
(*Screen image:* Glamour *magazine cover.*)
Spot Amanda at phone.

AMANDA: Ella Cartwright? This is Amanda Wingfield! How are you, honey? How is that kidney condition? (*Count five.*) Horrors! (*Count five.*) You're a Christian martyr, yes, honey, that's what you are, a Christian martyr! Well, I just happened to notice in my little red book that your subscription to the *Companion* has just run out! I knew that you wouldn't want to miss out on the wonderful serial starting in this new issue. It's by Bessie Mae Hopper, the first thing she's written since *Honeymoon for Three*. Wasn't that a strange and interesting story? Well, this one is even lovelier, I believe. It has a sophisticated society background. It's all about the horsey set on Long Island!

(*Fade out.*)

SCENE V

(*Legend on screen: "Annunciation."*) *Fade with music.*

   It is early dusk of a spring evening. Supper has just been finished in the Wingfield apartment. Amanda and Laura in light-colored dresses are removing dishes from the table, in the upstage area, which is shadowy, their movements formalized almost as a dance or ritual, their moving forms as pale and silent as moths.

Tom, in white shirt and trousers, rises from the table and crosses toward the fire-escape.

AMANDA (*as he passes her*): Son, will you do me a favor?

TOM: What?

AMANDA: Comb your hair! You look so pretty when your hair is combed! (*Tom slouches on sofa with evening paper. Enormous caption "Franco Triumphs."°*) There is only one respect in which I would like you to emulate your father.

TOM: What respect is that?

AMANDA: The care he always took of his appearance. He never allowed himself to look untidy. (*He throws down the paper and crosses to fire-escape.*) Where are you going?

TOM: I'm going out to smoke.

AMANDA: You smoke too much. A pack a day at fifteen cents a pack. How much would that amount to in a month? Thirty times fifteen is how much, Tom? Figure it out and you will be astounded at what you could save. Enough to give you a night-school course in accounting at Washington U! Just think what a wonderful thing that would be for you, son!

Tom is unmoved by the thought.

TOM: I'd rather smoke. (*He steps out on landing, letting the screen door slam.*)

AMANDA (*sharply*): I know! That's the tragedy of it. . . . (*Alone, she turns to look at her husband's picture.*)

(*Dance music: "All the World Is Waiting for the Sunrise!"*)

TOM (*to the audience*): Across the alley from us was the Paradise Dance Hall. On evenings in spring the windows and doors were open and the music came outdoors. Sometimes the lights were turned out except for a large glass sphere that hung from the ceiling. It would turn slowly about and filter the dusk with delicate rainbow colors. Then the orchestra played a waltz or a tango, something that had a slow and sensuous rhythm. Couples would come outside, to the relative privacy of the alley. You could see them kissing behind ash-pits and telephone poles. This was the compensation for lives that passed like mine, without any change or adventure. Adventure and change were imminent in this year. They were waiting around the corner for all these kids. Suspended in the mist over the Berchtesgaden,° caught in the folds of Chamberlain's° umbrella — In Spain there was Guernica! But here there was only hot swing music and liquor, dance halls, bars, and movies, and sex that hung in the

---

"Franco Triumphs": In January 1939 Francisco Franco's (1892–1975) victory over the Loyalists ended the Spanish Civil War.   **Berchtesgaden:** A resort in the German Alps where Adolf Hitler had a heavily protected villa.   **Chamberlain:** Neville Chamberlain (1869–1940) was the British prime minister who sought to avoid war with Hitler through a policy of appeasement.

gloom like a chandelier and flooded the world with brief, deceptive rainbows. . . . All the world was waiting for bombardments!

Amanda turns from the picture and comes outside.

AMANDA (*sighing*): A fire-escape landing's a poor excuse for a porch. (*She spreads a newspaper on a step and sits down, gracefully and demurely as if she were settling into a swing on a Mississippi veranda.*) What are you looking at?

TOM: The moon.

AMANDA: Is there a moon this evening?

TOM: It's rising over Garfinkel's Delicatessen.

AMANDA: So it is! A little silver slipper of a moon. Have you made a wish on it yet?

TOM: Um-hum.

AMANDA: What did you wish for?

TOM: That's a secret.

AMANDA: A secret, huh? Well, I won't tell mine either. I will be just as mysterious as you.

TOM: I bet I can guess what yours is.

AMANDA: Is my head so transparent?

TOM: You're not a sphinx.

AMANDA: No, I don't have secrets. I'll tell you what I wished for on the moon. Success and happiness for my precious children! I wish for that whenever there's a moon, and when there isn't a moon, I wish for it, too.

TOM: I thought perhaps you wished for a gentleman caller.

AMANDA: Why do you say that?

TOM: Don't you remember asking me to fetch one?

AMANDA: I remember suggesting that it would be nice for your sister if you brought home some nice young man from the warehouse. I think I've made that suggestion more than once.

TOM: Yes, you have made it repeatedly.

AMANDA: Well?

TOM: We are going to have one.

AMANDA: *What?*

TOM: A gentleman caller!

(*The Annunciation is celebrated with music.*)

Amanda rises.

(*Image on screen: Caller with bouquet.*)

AMANDA: You mean you have asked some nice young man to come over?

TOM: Yep. I've asked him to dinner.

AMANDA: You really did?

TOM: I did!

AMANDA: You did, and did he — *accept?*

TOM: He did!

AMANDA: Well, well — well, well! That's — lovely!

TOM: I thought that you would be pleased.

AMANDA: It's definite, then?

TOM: Very definite.

AMANDA: Soon?

TOM: Very soon.

AMANDA: For heaven's sake, stop putting on and tell me some things, will you?

TOM: What things do you want me to tell you?

AMANDA: Naturally I would like to know when he's *coming!*

TOM: He's coming tomorrow.

AMANDA: *Tomorrow?*

TOM: Yep. Tomorrow.

AMANDA: But, Tom!

TOM: Yes, Mother?

AMANDA: Tomorrow gives me no time!

TOM: Time for what?

AMANDA: Preparations! Why didn't you phone me at once, as soon as you asked him, the minute that he accepted? Then, don't you see, I could have been getting ready!

TOM: You don't have to make any fuss.

AMANDA: Oh, Tom, Tom, Tom, of course I have to make a fuss! I want things nice, not sloppy! Not thrown together. I'll certainly have to do some fast thinking, won't I?

TOM: I don't see why you have to think at all.

AMANDA: You just don't know. We can't have a gentleman caller in a pig-sty! All my wedding silver has to be polished, the monogrammed table linen ought to be laundered! The windows have to be washed and fresh curtains put up. And how about clothes? We have to *wear* something, don't we?

TOM: Mother, this boy is no one to make a fuss over!

AMANDA: Do you realize he's the first young man we've introduced to your sister? It's terrible, dreadful, disgraceful that poor little sister has never received a single gentleman caller! Tom, come inside! (*She opens the screen door.*)

TOM: What for?

AMANDA: I want to ask you some things.

TOM: If you're going to make such a fuss, I'll call it off, I'll tell him not to come.

AMANDA: You certainly won't do anything of the kind. Nothing offends people worse than broken engagements. It simply means I'll have to work like a Turk! We won't be brilliant, but we'll pass inspection. Come on inside. (*Tom follows, groaning.*) Sit down.

TOM: Any particular place you would like me to sit?

AMANDA: Thank heavens I've got that new sofa! I'm also making payments on a floor lamp I'll have sent out! And put the chintz covers on, they'll brighten things up! Of course I'd hoped to have these walls repapered. . . . What is the young man's name?

TOM: His name is O'Connor.

AMANDA: That, of course, means fish — tomorrow is Friday! I'll have that salmon loaf — with Durkee's dressing! What does he do? He works at the warehouse?

TOM: Of course! How else would I —

AMANDA: Tom, he — doesn't drink?

TOM: Why do you ask me that?

AMANDA: Your father *did!*

TOM: Don't get started on that!

AMANDA: He *does* drink, then?

TOM: Not that I know of!

AMANDA: Make sure, be certain! The last thing I want for my daughter's a boy who drinks!

TOM: Aren't you being a little premature? Mr. O'Connor has not yet appeared on the scene!

AMANDA: But will tomorrow. To meet your sister, and what do I know about his character? Nothing! Old maids are better off than wives of drunkards!

TOM: Oh, my God!

AMANDA: Be still!

TOM (*leaning forward to whisper*): Lots of fellows meet girls whom they don't marry!

AMANDA: Oh, talk sensibly, Tom — and don't be sarcastic! (*She has gotten a hairbrush.*)

TOM: What are you doing?

AMANDA: I'm brushing that cow-lick down! What is this young man's position at the warehouse?

TOM (*submitting grimly to the brush and the interrogation*): This young man's position is that of a shipping clerk, Mother.

AMANDA: Sounds to me like a fairly responsible job, the sort of a job *you* would be in if you just had more *get-up.* What is his salary? Have you got any idea?

TOM: I would judge it to be approximately eighty-five dollars a month.

AMANDA: Well — not princely, but —

TOM: Twenty more than I make.

AMANDA: Yes, how well I know! But for a family man, eighty-five dollars a month is not much more than you can just get by on. . . .

TOM: Yes, but Mr. O'Connor is not a family man.

AMANDA: He might be, mightn't he? Some time in the future?

TOM: I see. Plans and provisions.

AMANDA: You are the only young man that I know of who ignores the fact that the future becomes the present, the present the past, and the past turns into everlasting regret if you don't plan for it!

TOM: I will think that over and see what I can make of it.

AMANDA: Don't be supercilious with your mother! Tell me some more about this — what do you call him?

TOM: James D. O'Connor. The D. is for Delaney.

AMANDA: Irish on *both* sides! *Gracious!* And doesn't drink?

TOM: Shall I call him up and ask him right this minute?

AMANDA: The only way to find out about those things is to make discreet inquiries at the proper moment. When I was a girl in Blue Mountain and it was suspected that a young man drank, the girl whose attentions he had been receiving, if any girl *was*, would sometimes speak to the minister of his church, or rather her father would if her father was living, and sort of feel him out on the young man's character. That is the way such things are discreetly handled to keep a young woman from making a tragic mistake!

TOM: Then how did you happen to make a tragic mistake?

AMANDA: That innocent look of your father's had everyone fooled! He *smiled* — the world was *enchanted!* No girl can do worse than put herself at the mercy of a handsome appearance! I hope that Mr. O'Connor is not too good-looking.

TOM: No, he's not too good-looking. He's covered with freckles and hasn't too much of a nose.

AMANDA: He's not right-down homely, though?

TOM: Not right-down homely. Just medium homely, I'd say.

AMANDA: Character's what to look for in a man.

TOM: That's what I've always said, Mother.

AMANDA: You've never said anything of the kind and I suspect you would never give it a thought.

TOM: Don't be suspicious of me.

AMANDA: At least I hope he's the type that's up and coming.

TOM: I think he really goes in for self-improvement.

AMANDA: What reason have you to think so?

TOM: He goes to night school.

AMANDA (*beaming*): Splendid! What does he do, I mean study?

TOM: Radio engineering and public speaking!

AMANDA: Then he has visions of being advanced in the world! Any young man who studies public speaking is aiming to have an executive job some day! And radio engineering? A thing for the future! Both of these facts are very illuminating. Those are the sort of things that a mother should know concerning any young man who comes to call on her daughter. Seriously or — not.

TOM: One little warning. He doesn't know about Laura. I didn't let on that we had dark ulterior motives. I just said, why don't you come have dinner with us? He said okay and that was the whole conversation.

AMANDA: I bet it was! You're eloquent as an oyster. However, he'll know about Laura when he gets here. When he sees how lovely and sweet and pretty she is, he'll thank his lucky stars he was asked to dinner.

TOM: Mother, you mustn't expect too much of Laura.

AMANDA: What do you mean?

TOM: Laura seems all those things to you and me because she's ours and we love her. We don't even notice she's crippled any more.

AMANDA: Don't say crippled! You know that I never allow that word to be used!

TOM: But face facts, Mother. She is and — that's not all —

AMANDA: What do you mean "not all"?

TOM: Laura is very different from other girls.

AMANDA: I think the difference is all to her advantage.

TOM: Not quite all — in the eyes of others — strangers — she's terribly shy and lives in a world of her own and those things make her seem a little peculiar to people outside the house.

AMANDA: Don't say peculiar.

TOM: Face the facts. She is.

(*The dance-hall music changes to a tango that has a minor and somewhat ominous tone.*)

AMANDA: In what way is she peculiar — may I ask?

TOM (*gently*): She lives in a world of her own — a world of — little glass ornaments, Mother.... (*Gets up. Amanda remains holding brush, looking at him, troubled.*) She plays old phonograph records and — that's about all — (*He glances at himself in the mirror and crosses to door.*)

AMANDA (*sharply*): Where are you going?

TOM: I'm going to the movies. (*Out screen door.*)

AMANDA: Not to the movies, every night to the movies! (*Follows quickly to screen door.*) I don't believe you always go to the movies! (*He is gone. Amanda looks worriedly after him for a moment. Then vitality and optimism return and she turns from the door. Crossing to portieres.*) Laura! Laura! (*Laura answers from kitchenette.*)

LAURA: Yes, Mother.

AMANDA: Let those dishes go and come in front! (*Laura appears with dish towel. Gaily.*) Laura, come here and make a wish on the moon!

LAURA (*entering*): Moon — moon?

AMANDA: A little silver slipper of a moon. Look over your left shoulder, Laura, and make a wish! (*Laura looks faintly puzzled as if called out of sleep. Amanda seizes her shoulders and turns her at angle by the door.*) Now! Now, darling, *wish!*

LAURA: What shall I wish for, Mother?

AMANDA (*her voice trembling and her eyes suddenly filling with tears*): Happiness! Good Fortune!

The violin rises and the stage dims out.

SCENE VI

(*Image: High-school hero.*)

TOM: And so the following evening I brought Jim home to dinner. I had known Jim slightly in high school. In high school Jim was a hero. He had tremendous Irish good nature and vitality with the scrubbed and polished look of white chinaware. He seemed to move in a continual spotlight. He was a star in basketball, captain of the debating club, president of the senior class and the glee club and he sang the male lead in the annual light operas. He was always running or bounding, never just walking. He seemed always at the point of defeating the law of gravity. He was shooting with such velocity through his adolescence that you would logically expect him to arrive at nothing short of the White House by the time he was thirty. But Jim apparently ran into more interference after his graduation from Soldan. His speed had definitely slowed. Six years after he left high school he was holding a job that wasn't much better than mine.

(*Image: Clerk.*)

He was the only one at the warehouse with whom I was on friendly terms. I was valuable to him as someone who could remember his former glory, who had seen him win basketball games and the silver cup in debating. He knew of my secret practice of retiring to a cabinet of the washroom to work on poems when business was slack in the warehouse. He called me Shakespeare. And while the other boys in the warehouse regarded me with suspicious hostility, Jim took a humorous attitude toward me. Gradually his attitude affected the others, their hostility wore off, and they also began to smile at me as people smile at an oddly fashioned dog who trots across their paths at some distance.

I knew that Jim and Laura had known each other at Soldan, and I had heard Laura speak admiringly of his voice. I didn't know if Jim remembered her or not. In high school Laura had been as unobtrusive as Jim had been astonishing. If he did remember Laura, it was not as my sister, for when I asked him to dinner, he grinned and said, "You know, Shakespeare, I never thought of you as having folks!"

He was about to discover that I did. . . .

(*Light upstage.*)
(*Legend on screen: "The Accent of a Coming Foot."*)
Friday evening. It is about five o'clock of a late spring evening which comes "scattering poems in the sky."
A delicate lemony light is in the Wingfield apartment.
Amanda has worked like a Turk in preparation for the gentleman caller. The results are astonishing. The new floor lamp with its rose-silk shade is in place, a colored paper lantern conceals the broken light fixture in the ceiling, new billowing white curtains are at the windows, chintz covers are on chairs and sofa, a pair of new sofa pillows make their initial appearance.
Open boxes and tissue paper are scattered on the floor.
Laura stands in the middle with lifted arms while Amanda crouches before her, adjusting the hem of the new dress, devout and ritualistic. The dress is colored and designed by memory. The arrangement of Laura's hair is changed; it is softer and more becoming. A fragile, unearthly prettiness has come out in Laura: she is like a piece of translucent glass touched by light, given a momentary radiance, not actual, not lasting.

AMANDA (*impatiently*): Why are you trembling?
LAURA: Mother, you've made me so nervous!
AMANDA: How have I made you nervous?
LAURA: By all this fuss! You make it seem so important!
AMANDA: I don't understand you, Laura. You couldn't be satisfied with just sitting home, and yet whenever I try to arrange something for you, you seem to resist it. (*She gets up.*) Now take a look at yourself. No, wait! Wait just a moment — I have an idea!

LAURA: What is it now?

Amanda produces two powder puffs which she wraps in handkerchiefs and stuffs in Laura's bosom.

LAURA: Mother, what are you doing?

AMANDA: They call them "Gay Deceivers"!

LAURA: I won't wear them!

AMANDA: You will!

LAURA: Why should I?

AMANDA: Because, to be painfully honest, your chest is flat.

LAURA: You make it seem like we were setting a trap.

AMANDA: All pretty girls are a trap, a pretty trap, and men expect them to be. (*Legend: "A Pretty Trap."*) Now look at yourself, young lady. This is the prettiest you will ever be! I've got to fix myself now! You're going to be surprised by your mother's appearance! (*She crosses through portieres, humming gaily.*)

Laura moves slowly to the long mirror and stares solemnly at herself.

A wind blows the white curtains inward in a slow, graceful motion and with a faint, sorrowful sighing.

AMANDA (*offstage*): It isn't dark enough yet. (*She turns slowly before the mirror with a troubled look*).

(*Legend on screen: "This Is My Sister: Celebrate Her with Strings!" Music.*)

AMANDA (*laughing, off*): I'm going to show you something. I'm going to make a spectacular appearance!

LAURA: What is it, Mother?

AMANDA: Possess your soul in patience — you will see! Something I've resurrected from that old trunk! Styles haven't changed so terribly much after all. . . . (*She parts the portieres.*) Now just look at your mother! (*She wears a girlish frock of yellowed voile with a blue silk sash. She carries a bunch of jonquils — the legend of her youth is nearly revived. Feverishly.*) This is the dress in which I led the cotillion. Won the cakewalk twice at Sunset Hill, wore one spring to the Governor's ball in Jackson! See how I sashayed around the ballroom, Laura? (*She raises her skirt and does a mincing step around the room.*) I wore it on Sundays for my gentlemen callers! I had it on the day I met your father — I had malaria fever all that spring. The change of climate from East Tennessee to the Delta — weakened resistance — I had a little temperature all the time — not enough to be serious — just enough to make me restless and giddy! Invitations poured in — parties all over the Delta! — "Stay in bed," said Mother, "you have fever!" — but I just wouldn't. — I took quinine but kept on going, going! — Evenings, dances! — Afternoons, long, long rides! Picnics — lovely! — So lovely, that country in May. — All lacy with dogwood, literally flooded with jonquils! — That was the spring I had the craze for jonquils. Jonquils became an absolute obsession. Mother said, "Honey, there's no more room for jonquils." And still I kept bringing in more jonquils. Whenever, wherever I saw them, I'd say, "Stop! Stop! I see jonquils!" I made the young men help me gather the jonquils! It was a joke, Amanda and her jonquils! Finally there were no more vases to hold them, every available space was filled with jonquils. No vases to hold them? All right, I'll hold them myself! And then I — (*She stops in front of the picture.*) (*Music.*) met your father! Malaria fever and jonquils and then — this — boy. . . . (*She switches on the rose-colored lamp.*) I hope they get here before it starts to rain. (*She crosses upstage and places the jonquils in bowl on table.*) I gave your brother a little extra change so he and Mr. O'Connor could take the service car home.

LAURA (*with altered look*): What did you say his name was?

AMANDA: O'Connor.

LAURA: What is his first name?

AMANDA: I don't remember. Oh, yes, I do. It was — Jim!

Laura sways slightly and catches hold of a chair.
    (*Legend on screen: "Not Jim!"*)

LAURA (*faintly*): Not — Jim!

AMANDA: Yes, that was it, it was Jim! I've never known a Jim that wasn't nice!

(*Music: Ominous.*)

LAURA: Are you sure his name is Jim O'Connor?

AMANDA: Yes. Why?

LAURA: Is he the one that Tom used to know in high school?

AMANDA: He didn't say so. I think he just got to know him at the warehouse.

LAURA: There was a Jim O'Connor we both knew in high school — (*Then, with effort.*) If that is the one that Tom is bringing to dinner — you'll have to excuse me, I won't come to the table.

AMANDA: What sort of nonsense is this?

LAURA: You asked me once if I'd ever liked a boy. Don't you remember I showed you this boy's picture?

AMANDA: You mean the boy you showed me in the year-book?

LAURA: Yes, that boy.

AMANDA: Laura, Laura, were you in love with that boy?

LAURA: I don't know, Mother. All I know is I couldn't sit at the table if it was him!

AMANDA: It won't be him! It isn't the least bit likely. But whether it is or not, you will come to the table. You will not be excused.

LAURA: I'll have to be, Mother.

AMANDA: I don't intend to humor your silliness, Laura. I've had too much from you and your brother, both! So just sit down and compose yourself till they come. Tom has forgotten his key so you'll have to let them in, when they arrive.

LAURA (*panicky*): Oh, Mother — *you* answer the door!

AMANDA (*lightly*): I'll be in the kitchen — busy!

LAURA: Oh, Mother, please answer the door, don't make me do it!

AMANDA (*crossing into kitchenette*): I've got to fix the dressing for the salmon. Fuss, fuss — silliness! — over a gentleman caller!

Door swings shut. Laura is left alone.
> (*Legend:* "Terror!")
> *She utters a low moan and turns off the lamp — sits stiffly on the edge of the*
sofa, knotting her fingers together.
> (*Legend on screen:* "The Opening of a Door!")
> *Tom and Jim appear on the fire-escape steps and climb to landing. Hearing their*
approach, Laura rises with a panicky gesture. She retreats to the portieres.
> *The doorbell. Laura catches her breath and touches her throat. Low drums.*

AMANDA (*calling*): Laura, sweetheart! The door!

Laura stares at it without moving.

JIM: I think we just beat the rain.

TOM: Uh-huh. (*He rings again, nervously. Jim whistles and fishes for a cigarette.*)

AMANDA (*very, very gaily*): Laura, that is your brother and Mr. O'Connor! Will
you let them in, darling?

Laura crosses toward kitchenette door.

LAURA (*breathlessly*): Mother — you go to the door!

Amanda steps out of kitchenette and stares furiously at Laura. She points imperiously
at the door.

LAURA: Please, please!

AMANDA (*in a fierce whisper*): What is the matter with you, you silly thing?

LAURA (*desperately*): Please, you answer it, *please!*

AMANDA: I told you I wasn't going to humor you, Laura. Why have you chosen this moment to lose your mind?

LAURA: Please, please, please, you go!

AMANDA: You'll have to go to the door because I can't!

LAURA (*despairingly*): I can't either!

AMANDA: Why?

LAURA: I'm *sick!*

AMANDA: I'm sick, too — of your nonsense! Why can't you and your brother be
normal people? Fantastic whims and behavior! (*Tom gives a long ring.*)
Preposterous goings on! Can you give me one reason — (*Calls out lyri-*
cally.) COMING! JUST ONE SECOND! — why should you be afraid to open a
door? Now you answer it, Laura!

LAURA: Oh, oh, oh . . . (*She returns through the portieres. Darts to the Victrola and*
winds it frantically and turns it on.)

AMANDA: Laura Wingfield, you march right to that door!

LAURA: Yes — yes, Mother!

A faraway, scratchy rendition of "Dardanella" softens the air and gives her strength
to move through it. She slips to the door and draws it cautiously open.
> *Tom enters with the caller, Jim O'Connor.*

TOM: Laura, this is Jim. Jim, this is my sister, Laura.

JIM (*stepping inside*): I didn't know that Shakespeare had a sister!

LAURA (*retreating stiff and trembling from the door*): How — how do you do?

JIM (*heartily extending his hand*): Okay!

Laura touches it hesitantly with hers.

JIM: Your hand's *cold*, Laura!

LAURA: Yes, well — I've been playing the Victrola . . .

JIM: Must have been playing classical music on it! You ought to play a little hot swing music to warm you up!

LAURA: Excuse me — I haven't finished playing the Victrola . . .

She turns awkwardly and hurries into the front room. She pauses a second by the Victrola. Then catches her breath and darts through the portieres like a frightened deer.

JIM (*grinning*): What was the matter?

TOM: Oh — with Laura? Laura is — terribly shy.

JIM: Shy, huh? It's unusual to meet a shy girl nowadays. I don't believe you ever mentioned you had a sister.

TOM: Well, now you know. I have one. Here is the *Post Dispatch*. You want a piece of it?

JIM: Uh-huh.

TOM: What piece? The comics?

JIM: Sports! (*Glances at it.*) Ole Dizzy Dean is on his bad behavior.

TOM (*disinterest*): Yeah? (*Lights cigarette and crosses back to fire-escape door.*)

JIM: Where are *you* going?

TOM: I'm going out on the terrace.

JIM (*goes after him*): You know, Shakespeare — I'm going to sell you a bill of goods!

TOM: What goods?

JIM: A course I'm taking.

TOM: Huh?

JIM: In public speaking! You and me, we're not the warehouse type.

TOM: Thanks — that's good news. But what has public speaking got to do with it?

JIM: It fits you for — executive positions!

TOM: Awww.

JIM: I tell you it's done a helluva lot for me.

(*Image: Executive at desk.*)

TOM: In what respect?

JIM: In every! Ask yourself what is the difference between you an' me and men in the office down front? Brains? — No! — Ability? — No! Then what? Just one little thing —

TOM: What is that one little thing?

JIM: Primarily it amounts to — social poise! Being able to square up to people and hold your own on any social level!

AMANDA (*offstage*): Tom?

TOM: Yes, Mother?

AMANDA: Is that you and Mr. O'Connor?

TOM: Yes, Mother.

AMANDA: Well, you just make yourselves comfortable in there.

TOM: Yes, Mother.

AMANDA: Ask Mr. O'Connor if he would like to wash his hands.

JIM: Aw — no — no — thank you — I took care of that at the warehouse.
    Tom —

TOM: Yes?

JIM: Mr. Mendoza was speaking to me about you.

TOM: Favorably?

JIM: What do you think?

TOM: Well —

JIM: You're going to be out of a job if you don't wake up.

TOM: I am waking up —

JIM: You show no signs.

TOM: The signs are interior.

(*Image on screen: The sailing vessel with Jolly Roger again.*)

TOM: I'm planning to change. (*He leans over the rail speaking with quiet exhilaration. The incandescent marquees and signs of the first-run movie houses light
his face from across the alley. He looks like a voyager.*) I'm right at the point of
committing myself to a future that doesn't include the warehouse and
Mr. Mendoza or even a night-school course in public speaking.

JIM: What are you gassing about?

TOM: I'm tired of the movies.

JIM: Movies!

TOM: Yes, movies! Look at them — (*A wave toward the marvels of Grand Avenue.*)
All of those glamorous people — having adventures — hogging it all,
gobbling the whole thing up! You know what happens? People go to the
movies instead of *moving*! Hollywood characters are supposed to have all
the adventures for everybody in America, while everybody in America
sits in a dark room and watches them have them! Yes, until there's a war.
That's when adventure becomes available to the masses! *Everyone's* dish,
not only Gable's! Then the people in the dark room come out of the dark
room to have some adventures themselves — Goody, goody — It's our
turn now, to go to the South Sea Island — to make a safari — to be exotic, far-off — But I'm not patient. I don't want to wait till then. I'm tired
of the *movies* and I am *about* to *move*!

JIM (*incredulously*): Move?

TOM: Yes.

JIM: When?

TOM: Soon!

JIM: Where? Where?

(*Theme three: Music seems to answer the question, while Tom thinks it over. He
searches among his pockets.*)

TOM: I'm starting to boil inside. I know I seem dreamy, but inside — well, I'm
boiling! Whenever I pick up a shoe, I shudder a little thinking how short
life is and what I am doing! — Whatever that means. I know it doesn't
mean shoes — except as something to wear on a traveler's feet! (*Finds
paper.*) Look —

JIM: What?

TOM: I'm a member.

JIM (*reading*): The Union of Merchant Seamen.

TOM: I paid my dues this month, instead of the light bill.

JIM: You will regret it when they turn the lights off.

TOM: I won't be here.

JIM: How about your mother?

TOM: I'm like my father. The bastard son of a bastard! See how he grins? And he's been absent going on sixteen years!

JIM: You're just talking, you drip. How does your mother feel about it?

TOM: Shhh — Here comes Mother! Mother is not acquainted with my plans!

AMANDA (*enters portieres*): Where are you all?

TOM: On the terrace, Mother.

They start inside. She advances to them. Tom is distinctly shocked at her appearance. Even Jim blinks a little. He is making his first contact with girlish Southern vivacity and in spite of the night-school course in public speaking is somewhat thrown off the beam by the unexpected outlay of social charm.

Certain responses are attempted by Jim but are swept aside by Amanda's gay laughter and chatter. Tom is embarrassed but after the first shock Jim reacts very warmly. Grins and chuckles, is altogether won over.

(Image: Amanda as a girl.)

AMANDA (*coyly smiling, shaking her girlish ringlets*): Well, well, well, so this is Mr. O'Connor. Introductions entirely unnecessary. I've heard so much about you from my boy. I finally said to him, Tom — good gracious! — why don't you bring this paragon to supper? I'd like to meet this nice young man at the warehouse! — Instead of just hearing him sing your praises so much! I don't know why my son is so stand-offish — that's not Southern behavior! Let's sit down and — I think we could stand a little more air in here! Tom, leave the door open. I felt a nice fresh breeze a moment ago. Where has it gone? Mmm, so warm already! And not quite summer, even. We're going to burn up when summer really gets started. However, we're having — we're having a very light supper. I think light things are better fo' this time of year. The same as light clothes are. Light clothes an' light food are what warm weather calls fo'. You know our blood gets so thick during th' winter — it takes a while fo' us to *adjust* ou'selves! — when the season changes. . . . It's come so quick this year. I wasn't prepared. All of a sudden — heavens! Already summer! — I ran to the trunk an' pulled out this light dress — Terribly old! Historical almost! But feels so good — so good an' co-ol, y'know. . . .

TOM: Mother —

AMANDA: Yes, honey?

TOM: How about — supper?

AMANDA: Honey, you go ask Sister if supper is ready! You know that Sister is in full charge of supper! Tell her you hungry boys are waiting for it. (*To Jim.*) Have you met Laura?

JIM: She —

AMANDA: Let you in? Oh, good, you've met already! It's rare for a girl as sweet an' pretty as Laura to be domestic! But Laura is, thank heavens, not only pretty but also very domestic. I'm not at all. I never was a bit. I never could make a thing but angel-food cake. Well, in the South we had so many servants. Gone, gone, gone. All vestiges of gracious living! Gone completely! I wasn't prepared for what the future brought me. All of my gentlemen callers were sons of planters and so of course I assumed that I would be married to one and raise my family on a large piece of land with plenty of servants. But man proposes — and woman accepts the proposal! — To vary that old, old saying a little bit — I married no planter! I married a man who worked for the telephone company! — that gallantly smiling gentleman over there! (*Points to the picture.*) A telephone man who — fell in love with long distance! — Now he travels and I don't even know where! — But what am I going on for about my — tribulations! Tell me yours — I hope you don't have any! Tom?

TOM (*returning*): Yes, Mother?

AMANDA: Is supper nearly ready?

TOM: It looks to me like supper is on the table.

AMANDA: Let me look — (*She rises prettily and looks through portieres.*) Oh, lovely — But where is Sister?

TOM: Laura is not feeling well and she says that she thinks she'd better not come to the table.

AMANDA: What? — Nonsense! — Laura? Oh, Laura!

LAURA (*offstage, faintly*): Yes, Mother.

AMANDA: You really must come to the table. We won't be seated until you come to the table! Come in, Mr. O'Connor. You sit over there and I'll — Laura? Laura Wingfield! You're keeping us waiting, honey! We can't say grace until you come to the table!

The back door is pushed weakly open and Laura comes in. She is obviously quite faint, her lips trembling, her eyes wide and staring. She moves unsteadily toward the table.
(*Legend: "Terror!"*)
Outside a summer storm is coming abruptly. The white curtains billow inward at the windows and there is a sorrowful murmur and deep blue dusk.
Laura suddenly stumbles — She catches at a chair with a faint moan.

TOM: Laura!

AMANDA: Laura! (*There is a clap of thunder.*) (*Legend: "Ah!"*) (*Despairingly.*) Why, Laura, you *are* sick, darling! Tom, help your sister into the living room, dear! Sit in the living room, Laura — rest on the sofa. Well! (*To the gentleman caller.*) Standing over the hot stove made her ill! — I told her that it was just too warm this evening, but — (*Tom comes back in. Laura is on the sofa.*) Is Laura all right now?

TOM: Yes.

AMANDA: What *is* that? Rain? A nice cool rain has come up! (*She gives the gentleman caller a frightened look.*) I think we may — have grace — now . . . (*Tom looks at her stupidly.*) Tom, honey — you say grace!

TOM: Oh . . . "For these and all thy mercies — " (*They bow their heads, Amanda stealing a nervous glance at Jim. In the living room Laura, stretched on the sofa,*

clenches her hand to her lips, to hold back a shuddering sob.) God's Holy
Name be praised —

(*The scene dims out.*)

SCENE VII

A Souvenir

    *Half an hour later. Dinner is just being finished in the upstage area, which is
concealed by the drawn portieres.*

    *As the curtain rises Laura is still huddled upon the sofa, her feet drawn un-
der her, her head resting on a pale blue pillow, her eyes wide and mysteriously
watchful. The new floor lamp with its shade of rose-colored silk gives a soft, becoming light to her face, bringing out the fragile, unearthly prettiness which usually
escapes attention. There is a steady murmur of rain, but it is slackening and stops
soon after the scene begins; the air outside becomes pale and luminous as the moon
breaks out.*

    A moment after the curtain rises, the lights in both rooms flicker and go out.

JIM: Hey, there, Mr. Light Bulb!

Amanda laughs nervously.
    (*Legend: "Suspension of a Public Service."*)

AMANDA: Where was Moses when the lights went out? Ha-ha. Do you know
    the answer to that one, Mr. O'Connor?

JIM: No, Ma'am, what's the answer?

AMANDA: In the dark! (*Jim laughs appreciatively.*) Everybody sit still. I'll light the
    candles. Isn't it lucky we have them on the table? Where's a match?
    Which of you gentlemen can provide a match?

JIM: Here.

AMANDA: Thank you, sir.

JIM: Not at all, Ma'am!

AMANDA: I guess the fuse has burnt out. Mr. O'Connor, can you tell a burnt-out
    fuse? I know I can't and Tom is a total loss when it comes to mechanics.
    (*Sound: Getting up: Voices recede a little to kitchenette.*) Oh, be careful you
    don't bump into something. We don't want our gentleman caller to
    break his neck. Now wouldn't that be a fine howdy-do?

JIM: Ha-ha! Where is the fuse-box?

AMANDA: Right here next to the stove. Can you see anything?

JIM: Just a minute.

AMANDA: Isn't electricity a mysterious thing? Wasn't it Benjamin Franklin who
    tied a key to a kite? We live in such a mysterious universe, don't we?
    Some people say that science clears up all the mysteries for us. In my
    opinion it only creates more! Have you found it yet?

JIM: No, Ma'am. All these fuses look okay to me.

AMANDA: Tom!

TOM: Yes, Mother?

AMANDA: That light bill I gave you several days ago. The one I told you we got
    the notices about?

TOM: Oh. — Yeah.

(*Legend: "Ha!"*)

AMANDA: You didn't neglect to pay it by any chance?

TOM: Why, I —

AMANDA: Didn't! I might have known it!

JIM: Shakespeare probably wrote a poem on that light bill, Mrs. Wingfield.

AMANDA: I might have known better than to trust him with it! There's such a high price for negligence in this world!

JIM: Maybe the poem will win a ten-dollar prize.

AMANDA: We'll just have to spend the remainder of the evening in the nineteenth century, before Mr. Edison made the Mazda lamp!

JIM: Candlelight is my favorite kind of light.

AMANDA: That shows you're romantic! But that's no excuse for Tom. Well, we got through dinner. Very considerate of them to let us get through dinner before they plunged us into everlasting darkness, wasn't it, Mr. O'Connor?

JIM: Ha-ha!

AMANDA: Tom, as a penalty for your carelessness you can help me with the dishes.

JIM: Let me give you a hand.

AMANDA: Indeed you will not!

JIM: I ought to be good for something.

AMANDA: Good for something? (*Her tone is rhapsodic.*) You? Why, Mr. O'Connor, nobody, *nobody's* given me this much entertainment in years — as you have!

JIM: Aw, now, Mrs. Wingfield!

AMANDA: I'm not exaggerating, not one bit! But Sister is all by her lonesome. You go keep her company in the parlor! I'll give you this lovely old candelabrum that used to be on the altar at the church of the Heavenly Rest. It was melted a little out of shape when the church burnt down. Lightning struck it one spring. Gypsy Jones was holding a revival at the time and he intimated that the church was destroyed because the Episcopalians gave card parties.

JIM: Ha-ha.

AMANDA: And how about coaxing Sister to drink a little wine? I think it would be good for her! Can you carry both at once?

JIM: Sure. I'm Superman!

AMANDA: Now, Thomas, get into this apron!

The door of kitchenette swings closed on Amanda's gay laughter; the flickering light approaches the portieres.

 Laura sits up nervously as he enters. Her speech at first is low and breathless from the almost intolerable strain of being alone with a stranger.

 (*Legend: "I Don't Suppose You Remember Me at All!"*)

 In her first speeches in this scene, before Jim's warmth overcomes her paralyzing shyness, Laura's voice is thin and breathless as though she has run up a steep flight of stairs.

Jim's attitude is gently humorous. In playing this scene it should be stressed that while the incident is apparently unimportant, it is to Laura the climax of her secret life.

JIM: Hello, there, Laura.

LAURA (*faintly*): Hello. (*She clears her throat.*)

JIM: How are you feeling now? Better?

LAURA: Yes. Yes, thank you.

JIM: This is for you. A little dandelion wine. (*He extends it toward her with extravagant gallantry.*)

LAURA: Thank you.

JIM: Drink it — but don't get drunk! (*He laughs heartily. Laura takes the glass uncertainly; laughs shyly.*) Where shall I set the candles?

LAURA: Oh — oh, anywhere . . .

JIM: How about here on the floor? Any objections?

LAURA: No.

JIM: I'll spread a newspaper under to catch the drippings. I like to sit on the floor. Mind if I do?

LAURA: Oh, no.

JIM: Give me a pillow?

LAURA: What?

JIM: A pillow!

LAURA: Oh . . . (*Hands him one quickly.*)

JIM: How about you? Don't you like to sit on the floor?

LAURA: Oh — yes.

JIM: Why don't you, then?

LAURA: I — will.

JIM: Take a pillow! (*Laura does. Sits on the other side of the candelabrum. Jim crosses his legs and smiles engagingly at her.*) I can't hardly see you sitting way over there.

LAURA: I can — see you.

JIM: I know, but that's not fair, I'm in the limelight. (*Laura moves her pillow closer.*) Good! Now I can see you! Comfortable?

LAURA: Yes.

JIM: So am I. Comfortable as a cow. Will you have some gum?

LAURA: No, thank you.

JIM: I think that I will indulge, with your permission. (*Musingly unwraps it and holds it up.*) Think of the fortune made by the guy that invented the first piece of chewing gum. Amazing, huh? The Wrigley Building is one of the sights of Chicago. — I saw it summer before last when I went up to the Century of Progress. Did you take in the Century of Progress?

LAURA: No, I didn't.

JIM: Well, it was quite a wonderful exposition. What impressed me most was the Hall of Science. Gives you an idea of what the future will be in America, even more wonderful than the present time is! (*Pause. Smiling at her.*) Your brother tells me you're shy. Is that right, Laura?

LAURA: I — don't know.

JIM: I judge you to be an old-fashioned type of girl. Well, I think that's a pretty good type to be. Hope you don't think I'm being too personal — do you?

LAURA (*hastily, out of embarrassment*): I believe I *will* take a piece of gum, if you — don't mind. (*Clearing her throat.*) Mr. O'Connor, have you — kept up with your singing?

JIM: Singing? Me?

LAURA: Yes. I remember what a beautiful voice you had.

JIM: When did you hear me sing?

(*Voice offstage in the pause.*)

VOICE (*offstage*): O blow, ye winds, heigh-ho,
  A-roving I will go!
  I'm off to my love
  With a boxing glove —
  Ten thousand miles away!

JIM: You say you've heard me sing?

LAURA: Oh, yes! Yes, very often . . . I — don't suppose you remember me — at all?

JIM (*smiling doubtfully*): You know I have an idea I've seen you before. I had that idea soon as you opened the door. It seemed almost like I was about to remember your name. But the name that I started to call you — wasn't a name! And so I stopped myself before I said it.

LAURA: Wasn't it — Blue Roses?

JIM (*springs up, grinning*): Blue Roses! My gosh, yes — Blue Roses! That's what I had on my tongue when you opened the door! Isn't it funny what tricks your memory plays? I didn't connect you with the high school somehow or other. But that's where it was; it was high school. I didn't even know you were Shakespeare's sister! Gosh, I'm sorry.

LAURA: I didn't expect you to. You — barely knew me!

JIM: But we did have a speaking acquaintance, huh?

LAURA: Yes, we — spoke to each other.

JIM: When did you recognize me?

LAURA: Oh, right away!

JIM: Soon as I came in the door?

LAURA: When I heard your name I thought it was probably you. I knew that Tom used to know you a little in high school. So when you came in the door — Well, then I was — sure.

JIM: Why didn't you *say* something, then?

LAURA (*breathlessly*): I didn't know what to say, I was — too surprised!

JIM: For goodness' sakes! You know, this sure is funny!

LAURA: Yes! Yes, isn't it, though . . .

JIM: Didn't we have a class in something together?

LAURA: Yes, we did.

JIM: What class was that?

LAURA: It was — singing — Chorus!

JIM: Aw!

LAURA: I sat across the aisle from you in the Aud.

JIM: Aw.

LAURA: Mondays, Wednesdays, and Fridays.

JIM: Now I remember — you always came in late.

LAURA: Yes, it was so hard for me, getting upstairs. I had that brace on my leg — it clumped so loud!

JIM: I never heard any clumping.

LAURA (*wincing in the recollection*): To me it sounded like — thunder!

JIM: Well, well, well. I never even noticed.

LAURA: And everybody was seated before I came in. I had to walk in front of all those people. My seat was in the back row. I had to go clumping all the way up the aisle with everyone watching!

JIM: You shouldn't have been self-conscious.

LAURA: I know, but I was. It was always such a relief when the singing started.

JIM: Aw, yes, I've placed you now! I used to call you Blue Roses. How was it that I got started calling you that?

LAURA: I was out of school a little while with pleurosis. When I came back you asked me what was the matter. I said I had pleurosis — you thought I said Blue Roses. That's what you always called me after that!

JIM: I hope you didn't mind.

LAURA: Oh, no — I liked it. You see, I wasn't acquainted with many — people. . . .

JIM: As I remember you sort of stuck by yourself.

LAURA: I — I — never had much luck at — making friends.

JIM: I don't see why you wouldn't.

LAURA: Well, I — started out badly.

JIM: You mean being —

LAURA: Yes, it sort of — stood between me —

JIM: You shouldn't have let it!

LAURA: I know, but it did, and —

JIM: You were shy with people!

LAURA: I tried not to be but never could —

JIM: Overcome it?

LAURA: No, I — I never could!

JIM: I guess being shy is something you have to work out of kind of gradually.

LAURA (*sorrowfully*): Yes — I guess it —

JIM: Takes time!

LAURA: Yes —

JIM: People are not so dreadful when you know them. That's what you have to remember! And everybody has problems, not just you, but practically everybody has got some problems. You think of yourself as having the only problems, as being the only one who is disappointed. But just look around you and you will see lots of people as disappointed as you are. For instance, I hoped when I was going to high school that I would be further along at this time, six years later, than I am now — You remember that wonderful write-up I had in *The Torch?*

LAURA: Yes! (*She rises and crosses to table.*)

JIM: It said I was bound to succeed in anything I went into! (*Laura returns with the annual.*) Holy Jeez! *The Torch!* (*He accepts it reverently. They smile across it with mutual wonder. Laura crouches beside him and they begin to turn through it. Laura's shyness is dissolving in his warmth.*)

LAURA: Here you are in *Pirates of Penzance!*

JIM (*wistfully*): I sang the baritone lead in that operetta.

LAURA (*rapidly*): So — *beautifully!*

JIM (*protesting*): Aw —

LAURA: Yes, yes — beautifully — beautifully!

JIM: You heard me?

LAURA: All three times!

JIM: No!

LAURA: Yes!

JIM: All three performances?

LAURA (*looking down*): Yes.

JIM: Why?

LAURA: I — wanted to ask you to — autograph my program.

JIM: Why didn't you ask me to?

LAURA: You were always surrounded by your own friends so much that I never had a chance to.

JIM: You should have just —

LAURA: Well, I — thought you might think I was —

JIM: Thought I might think you was — what?

LAURA: Oh —

JIM (*with reflective relish*): I was beleaguered by females in those days.

LAURA: You were terribly popular!

JIM: Yeah —

LAURA: You had such a — friendly way —

JIM: I was spoiled in high school.

LAURA: Everybody — liked you!

JIM: Including you?

LAURA: I — yes, I — I did, too — (*She gently closes the book in her lap.*)

JIM: Well, well, well! — Give me that program, Laura. (*She hands it to him. He signs it with a flourish.*) There you are — better late than never!

LAURA: Oh, I — what a — surprise!

JIM: My signature isn't worth very much right now. But some day — maybe — it will increase in value! Being disappointed is one thing and being discouraged is something else. I am disappointed but I'm not discouraged. I'm twenty-three years old. How old are you?

LAURA: I'll be twenty-four in June.

JIM: That's not old age.

LAURA: No, but —

JIM: You finished high school?

LAURA (*with difficulty*): I didn't go back.

JIM: You mean you dropped out?

LAURA: I made bad grades in my final examinations. (*She rises and replaces the book and the program. Her voice strained.*) How is — Emily Meisenbach getting along?

JIM: Oh, that kraut-head!

LAURA: Why do you call her that?

JIM: That's what she was.

LAURA: You're not still — going with her?

JIM: I never see her.

LAURA: It said in the Personal Section that you were — engaged!

JIM: I know, but I wasn't impressed by that — propaganda!

LAURA: It wasn't — the truth?

JIM: Only in Emily's optimistic opinion!

LAURA: Oh —

(*Legend: "What Have You Done since High School?"*)

> *Jim lights a cigarette and leans indolently back on his elbows smiling at Laura with a warmth and charm which light her inwardly with altar candles. She remains by the table and turns in her hands a piece of glass to cover her tumult.*

JIM (*after several reflective puffs on a cigarette*): What have you done since high school? (*She seems not to hear him.*) Huh? (*Laura looks up.*) I said what have you done since high school, Laura?

LAURA: Nothing much.

JIM: You must have been doing something these six long years.

LAURA: Yes.

JIM: Well, then, such as what?

LAURA: I took a business course at business college —

JIM: How did that work out?

LAURA: Well, not very — well — I had to drop out, it gave me — indigestion —

Jim laughs gently.

JIM: What are you doing now?

LAURA: I don't do anything — much. Oh, please don't think I sit around doing nothing! My glass collection takes up a good deal of my time. Glass is something you have to take good care of.

JIM: What did you say — about glass?

LAURA: Collection I said — I have one — (*She clears her throat and turns away again, acutely shy.*)

JIM (*abruptly*): You know what I judge to be the trouble with you? Inferiority complex! Know what that is? That's what they call it when someone low-rates himself! I understand it because I had it, too. Although my case was not so aggravated as yours seems to be. I had it until I took up public speaking, developed my voice, and learned that I had an aptitude for science. Before that time I never thought of myself as being outstanding in any way whatsoever! Now I've never made a regular study of it, but I have a friend who says I can analyze people better than doctors that make a profession of it. I don't claim that to be necessarily true, but I can sure guess a person's psychology, Laura! (*Takes out his gum.*) Excuse me, Laura. I always take it out when the flavor is gone. I'll use this scrap of paper to wrap it in. I know how it is to get it stuck on a shoe. Yep — that's what I judge to be your principal trouble. A lack of confidence in yourself as a person. You don't have the proper amount of faith in yourself. I'm basing that fact on a number of your remarks and also on certain observations I've made. For instance that clumping you thought was so awful in high school. You say that you even dreaded to walk into class. You see what you did? You dropped out of school, you gave up an education because of a clump, which as far as I know was practically nonexistent! A little physical defect is what you have. Hardly noticeable even! Magnified thousands of times by imagination! You know what my strong advice to you is? Think of yourself as *superior* in some way!

LAURA: In what way would I think?

JIM: Why, man alive, Laura! Just look about you a little. What do you see? A world full of common people! All of 'em born and all of 'em going to die! Which of them has one-tenth of your good points! Or mine! Or anyone else's, as far as that goes — Gosh! Everybody excels in some one thing. Some in many! (*Unconsciously glances at himself in the mirror.*) All you've got to do is discover in *what*! Take me, for instance. (*He adjusts his tie at the mirror.*) My interest happened to lie in electrodynamics. I'm taking a course in radio engineering at night school, Laura, on top of a fairly responsible job at the warehouse. I'm taking that course and studying public speaking.

LAURA: Ohhhh.

JIM: Because I believe in the future of television! (*Turning back to her.*) I wish to be ready to go up right along with it. Therefore I'm planning to get in on the ground floor. In fact, I've already made the right connections and all that remains is for the industry itself to get under way! Full steam — (*His eyes are starry.*) Knowledge — Zzzzzp! Money — Zzzzzzp! — Power! That's the cycle democracy is built on! (*His attitude is convincingly dynamic. Laura stares at him, even her shyness eclipsed in her absolute wonder. He suddenly grins.*) I guess you think I think a lot of myself!

LAURA: No — o-o-o, I —

JIM: Now how about you? Isn't there something you take more interest in than anything else?

LAURA: Well, I do — as I said — have my — glass collection —

A peal of girlish laughter from the kitchen.

JIM: I'm not right sure I know what you're talking about. What kind of glass is it?

LAURA: Little articles of it, they're ornaments mostly! Most of them are little animals made out of glass, the tiniest little animals in the world. Mother calls them a glass menagerie! Here's an example of one, if you'd like to see it! This one is one of the oldest. It's nearly thirteen. (*He stretches out his hand.*) (*Music: "The Glass Menagerie."*) Oh, be careful — if you breathe, it breaks!

JIM: I'd better not take it. I'm pretty clumsy with things.

LAURA: Go on, I trust you with him! (*Places it in his palm.*) There now — you're holding him gently! Hold him over the light, he loves the light! You see how the light shines through him?

JIM: It sure does shine!

LAURA: I shouldn't be partial, but he is my favorite one.

JIM: What kind of thing is this one supposed to be?

LAURA: Haven't you noticed the single horn on his forehead?

JIM: A unicorn, huh?

LAURA: Mmm-hmmm!

JIM: Unicorns, aren't they extinct in the modern world?

LAURA: I know!

JIM: Poor little fellow, he must feel sort of lonesome.

LAURA (*smiling*): Well, if he does he doesn't complain about it. He stays on a shelf with some horses that don't have horns and all of them seem to get along nicely together.

JIM: How do you know?

LAURA (*lightly*): I haven't heard any arguments among them!

JIM (*grinning*): No arguments, huh? Well, that's a pretty good sign! Where shall I set him?

LAURA: Put him on the table. They all like a change of scenery once in a while!

JIM (*stretching*): Well, well, well, well — Look how big my shadow is when I stretch!

LAURA: Oh, oh, yes — it stretches across the ceiling!

JIM (*crossing to door*): I think it's stopped raining. (*Opens fire-escape door.*) Where does the music come from?

LAURA: From the Paradise Dance Hall across the alley.

JIM: How about cutting the rug a little, Miss Wingfield?

LAURA: Oh, I —

JIM: Or is your program filled up? Let me have a look at it. (*Grasps imaginary card.*) Why, every dance is taken! I'll have to scratch some out. (*Waltz music: "La Golondrina."*) Ahhh, a waltz! (*He executes some sweeping turns by himself then holds his arms toward Laura.*)

LAURA (*breathlessly*): I — can't dance!

JIM: There you go, that inferiority stuff!

LAURA: I've never danced in my life!

JIM: Come on, try!

LAURA: Oh, but I'd step on you!

JIM: I'm not made out of glass.

LAURA: How — how — how do we start?

JIM: Just leave it to me. You hold your arms out a little.

LAURA: Like this?

JIM: A little bit higher. Right. Now don't tighten up, that's the main thing about it — relax.

LAURA (*laughing breathlessly*): It's hard not to.

JIM: Okay.

LAURA: I'm afraid you can't budge me.

JIM: What do you bet I can't? (*He swings her into motion.*)

LAURA: Goodness, yes, you can!

JIM: Let yourself go, now, Laura, just let yourself go.

LAURA: I'm —

JIM: Come on!

LAURA: Trying.

JIM: Not so stiff — Easy does it!

LAURA: I know but I'm —

JIM: Loosen th' backbone! There now, that's a lot better.

LAURA: Am I?

JIM: Lots, lots better! (*He moves her about the room in a clumsy waltz.*)

LAURA: Oh, my!

JIM: Ha-ha!

LAURA: Goodness, yes you can!

JIM: Ha-ha-ha! (*They suddenly bump into the table. Jim stops.*) What did we hit on?

LAURA: Table.

JIM: Did something fall off it? I think —

LAURA: Yes.

JIM: I hope it wasn't the little glass horse with the horn!

LAURA: Yes.

JIM: Aw, aw, aw. Is it broken?

LAURA: Now it is just like all the other horses.

JIM: It's lost its —

LAURA: Horn! It doesn't matter. Maybe it's a blessing in disguise.

JIM: You'll never forgive me. I bet that that was your favorite piece of glass.

LAURA: I don't have favorites much. It's no tragedy, Freckles. Glass breaks so
    easily. No matter how careful you are. The traffic jars the shelves and
    things fall off them.

JIM: Still I'm awfully sorry that I was the cause.

LAURA (*smiling*): I'll just imagine he had an operation. The horn was removed
    to make him feel less — freakish! (*They both laugh.*) Now he will feel
    more at home with the other horses, the ones that don't have horns . . .

JIM: Ha-ha, that's very funny! (*Suddenly serious.*) I'm glad to see that you have
    a sense of humor. You know — you're — well — very different! Surpris-
    ingly different from anyone else I know! (*His voice becomes soft and hesi-
    tant with a genuine feeling.*) Do you mind me telling you that? (*Laura is
    abashed beyond speech.*) You make me feel sort of — I don't know how to
    put it! I'm usually pretty good at expressing things, but — This is some-
    thing that I don't know how to say! (*Laura touches her throat and clears
    it — turns the broken unicorn in her hands.*) (*Even softer.*) Has anyone ever
    told you that you were pretty?

Pause: Music.

    (*Laura looks up slowly, with wonder, and shakes her head.*) Well, you are! In a
very different way from anyone else. And all the nicer because of the difference, too. (*His voice becomes low and husky. Laura turns away, nearly faint*

with the novelty of her emotions.) I wish that you were my sister. I'd teach you to have some confidence in yourself. The different people are not like other people, but being different is nothing to be ashamed of. Because other people are not such wonderful people. They're one hundred times one thousand. You're one times one! They walk all over the earth. You just stay here. They're common as — weeds, but — you — well, you're — *Blue Roses!*

(*Image on screen: Blue Roses.*)
   (*Music changes.*)

LAURA: But blue is wrong for — roses . . .

JIM: It's right for you — You're — pretty!

LAURA: In what respect am I pretty?

JIM: In all respects — believe me! Your eyes — your hair — are pretty! Your hands are pretty! (*He catches hold of her hand.*) You think I'm making this up because I'm invited to dinner and have to be nice. Oh, I could do that! I could put on an act for you, Laura, and say lots of things without being very sincere. But this time I am. I'm talking to you sincerely. I happened to notice you had this inferiority complex that keeps you from feeling comfortable with people. Somebody needs to build your confidence up and make you proud instead of shy and turning away and — blushing — Somebody ought to — ought to — *kiss* you, Laura! (*His hand slips slowly up her arm to her shoulder.*) (*Music swells tumultuously.*) (*He suddenly turns her about and kisses her on the lips. When he releases her Laura sinks on the sofa with a bright, dazed look. Jim backs away and fishes in his pocket for a cigarette.*) (*Legend on screen: "Souvenir."*) Stumble-john! (*He lights the cigarette, avoiding her look. There is a peal of girlish laughter from Amanda in the kitchen. Laura slowly raises and opens her hand. It still contains the little broken glass animal. She looks at it with a tender, bewildered expression.*) Stumble-john! I shouldn't have done that — That was way off the beam. You don't smoke, do you? (*She looks up, smiling, not hearing the question. He sits beside her a little gingerly. She looks at him speechlessly — waiting. He coughs decorously and moves a little farther aside as he considers the situation and senses her feelings, dimly, with perturbation. Gently.*) Would you — care for a — mint? (*She doesn't seem to hear him but her look grows brighter even.*) Peppermint — Life Saver? My pocket's a regular drug store — wherever I go . . . (*He pops a mint in his mouth. Then gulps and decides to make a clean breast of it. He speaks slowly and gingerly.*) Laura, you know, if I had a sister like you, I'd do the same thing as Tom. I'd bring out fellows — introduce her to them. The right type of boys of a type to — appreciate her. Only — well — he made a mistake about me. Maybe I've got no call to be saying this. That may not have been the idea in having me over. But what if it was? There's nothing wrong about that. The only trouble is that in my case — I'm not in a situation to — do the right thing. I can't take down your number and say I'll phone. I can't call up next week and — ask for a date. I thought I had better explain the situation in case you misunderstood it and — hurt your feelings. . . . (*Pause. Slowly, very*

slowly, Laura's look changes, her eyes returning slowly from his to the orna-
ment in her palm.)

Amanda utters another gay laugh in the kitchen.

LAURA (*faintly*): You — won't — call again?

JIM: No, Laura, I can't. (*He rises from the sofa.*) As I was just explaining, I've —
got strings on me, Laura, I've — been going steady! I go out all the time
with a girl named Betty. She's a home-girl like you, and Catholic, and
Irish, and in a great many ways we — get along fine. I met her last summer on a moonlight boat trip up the river to Alton, on the *Majestic.*
Well — right away from the start it was — love! (*Legend: Love!*) (*Laura*
sways slightly forward and grips the arm of the sofa. He fails to notice, now en-
rapt in his own comfortable being.) Being in love has made a new man of
me! (*Leaning stiffly forward, clutching the arm of the sofa, Laura struggles vis-*
ibly with her storm. But Jim is oblivious, she is a long way off.) The power of
love is really pretty tremendous! Love is something that — changes the
whole world, Laura! (*The storm abates a little and Laura leans back. He no-*
tices her again.) It happened that Betty's aunt took sick, she got a wire and
had to go to Centralia. So Tom — when he asked me to dinner — I naturally just accepted the invitation, not knowing that you — that he —
that I — (*He stops awkwardly.*) Huh — I'm a stumble-john! (*He flops back*
on the sofa. The holy candles in the altar of Laura's face have been snuffed out!
There is a look of almost infinite desolation. Jim glances at her uneasily.) I wish
that you would — say something. (*She bites her lip which was trembling*
and then bravely smiles. She opens her hand again on the broken glass orna-
ment. Then she gently takes his hand and raises it level with her own. She care-
fully places the unicorn in the palm of his hand, then pushes his fingers closed
upon it.) What are you — doing that for? You want me to have him? —
Laura? (*She nods.*) What for?

LAURA: A — souvenir . . .

She rises unsteadily and crouches beside the Victrola to wind it up.

(*Legend on screen: "Things Have a Way of Turning Out So Badly."*)

(*Or image: "Gentleman caller waving good-bye! — Gaily."*)

At this moment Amanda rushes brightly back in the front room. She bears a
pitcher of fruit punch in an old-fashioned cut-glass pitcher and a plate of macaroons.
The plate has a gold border and poppies painted on it.

AMANDA: Well, well, well! Isn't the air delightful after the shower? I've made
you children a little liquid refreshment. (*Turns gaily to the gentleman*
caller.) Jim, do you know that song about lemonade?

"Lemonade, lemonade
Made in the shade and stirred with a spade —
Good enough for any old maid!"

JIM (*uneasily*): Ha-ha! No — I never heard it.

AMANDA: Why, Laura! You look so serious!

JIM: We were having a serious conversation.

AMANDA: Good! Now you're better acquainted!

JIM (*uncertainly*): Ha-ha! Yes.

AMANDA: You modern young people are much more serious-minded than my generation. I was so gay as a girl!

JIM: You haven't changed, Mrs. Wingfield.

AMANDA: Tonight I'm rejuvenated! The gaiety of the occasion, Mr. O'Connor! (*She tosses her head with a peal of laughter. Spills lemonade.*) Oooo! I'm baptizing myself!

JIM: Here — let me —

AMANDA (*setting the pitcher down*): There now. I discovered we had some maraschino cherries. I dumped them in, juice and all!

JIM: You shouldn't have gone to that trouble, Mrs. Wingfield.

AMANDA: Trouble, trouble? Why it was loads of fun! Didn't you hear me cutting up in the kitchen? I bet your ears were burning! I told Tom how outdone with him I was for keeping you to himself so long a time! He should have brought you over much, much sooner! Well, now that you've found your way, I want you to be a very frequent caller! Not just occasional but all the time. Oh, we're going to have a lot of gay times together! I see them coming! Mmm, just breathe that air! So fresh, and the moon's so pretty! I'll skip back out — I know where my place is when young folks are having a — serious conversation!

JIM: Oh, don't go out, Mrs. Wingfield. The fact of the matter is I've got to be going.

AMANDA: Going, now? You're joking! Why, it's only the shank of the evening, Mr. O'Connor!

JIM: Well, you know how it is.

AMANDA: You mean you're a young workingman and have to keep workingmen's hours. We'll let you off early tonight. But only on the condition that next time you stay later. What's the best night for you? Isn't Saturday night the best night for you workingmen?

JIM: I have a couple of time-clocks to punch, Mrs. Wingfield. One at morning, another one at night!

AMANDA: My, but you *are* ambitious! You work at night, too?

JIM: No, Ma'am, not work but — Betty! (*He crosses deliberately to pick up his hat. The band at the Paradise Dance Hall goes into a tender waltz.*)

AMANDA: Betty? Betty? Who's — Betty! (*There is an ominous cracking sound in the sky.*)

JIM: Oh, just a girl. The girl I go steady with! (*He smiles charmingly. The sky falls.*)

(*Legend: "The Sky Falls."*)

AMANDA (*a long-drawn exhalation*): Ohhhh . . . Is it a serious romance, Mr. O'Connor?

JIM: We're going to be married the second Sunday in June.

AMANDA: Ohhhh — how nice! Tom didn't mention that you were engaged to be married.

JIM: The cat's not out of the bag at the warehouse yet. You know how they are. They call you Romeo and stuff like that. (*He stops at the oval mirror to put on his hat. He carefully shapes the brim and the crown to give a discreetly dash-*

ing effect.) It's been a wonderful evening, Mrs. Wingfield. I guess this is what they mean by Southern hospitality.

AMANDA: It really wasn't anything at all.

JIM: I hope it don't seem like I'm rushing off. But I promised Betty I'd pick her up at the Wabash depot, an' by the time I get my jalopy down there her train'll be in. Some women are pretty upset if you keep 'em waiting.

AMANDA: Yes, I know — The tyranny of women! (*Extends her hand.*) Good-bye, Mr. O'Connor. I wish you luck — and happiness — and success! All three of them, and so does Laura — Don't you, Laura?

LAURA: Yes!

JIM (*taking her hand*): Good-bye, Laura. I'm certainly going to treasure that souvenir. And don't you forget the good advice I gave you. (*Raises his voice to a cheery shout.*) So long, Shakespeare! Thanks again, ladies — Good night!

He grins and ducks jauntily out.

> *Still bravely grimacing, Amanda closes the door on the gentleman caller. Then she turns back to the room with a puzzled expression. She and Laura don't dare to face each other. Laura crouches beside the Victrola to wind it.*

AMANDA (*faintly*): Things have a way of turning out so badly. I don't believe that I would play the Victrola. Well, well — well — Our gentleman caller was engaged to be married! Tom!

TOM (*from back*): Yes, Mother?

AMANDA: Come in here a minute. I want to tell you something awfully funny.

TOM (*enters with macaroon and a glass of the lemonade*): Has the gentleman caller gotten away already?

AMANDA: The gentleman caller has made an early departure. What a wonderful joke you played on us!

TOM: How do you mean?

AMANDA: You didn't mention that he was engaged to be married.

TOM: Jim? Engaged?

AMANDA: That's what he just informed us.

TOM: I'll be jiggered! I didn't know about that.

AMANDA: That seems very peculiar.

TOM: What's peculiar about it?

AMANDA: Didn't you call him your best friend down at the warehouse?

TOM: He is, but how did I know?

AMANDA: It seems extremely peculiar that you wouldn't know your best friend was going to be married!

TOM: The warehouse is where I work, not where I know things about people!

AMANDA: You don't know things anywhere! You live in a dream; you manufacture illusions! (*He crosses to door.*) Where are you going?

TOM: I'm going to the movies.

AMANDA: That's right, now that you've had us make such fools of ourselves. The effort, the preparations, all the expense! The new floor lamp, the rug, the clothes for Laura! All for what? To entertain some other girl's fiancé! Go to the movies, go! Don't think about us, a mother deserted, an unmarried sister who's crippled and has no job! Don't let anything interfere with your selfish pleasure! Just go, go, go — to the movies!

TOM: All right, I will! The more you shout about my selfishness to me the quicker I'll go, and I won't go to the movies!

AMANDA: Go, then! Then go to the moon — you selfish dreamer!

Tom smashes his glass on the floor. He plunges out on the fire-escape, slamming the door. Laura screams — cut by door.

Dance-hall music up. Tom goes to the rail and grips it desperately, lifting his face in the chill white moonlight penetrating the narrow abyss of the alley.

(Legend on screen: "And So Good-Bye . . .")

Tom's closing speech is timed with the interior pantomime. The interior scene is played as though viewed through sound-proof glass. Amanda appears to be making a comforting speech to Laura who is huddled upon the sofa. Now that we cannot hear the mother's speech, her silliness is gone and she has dignity and tragic beauty. Laura's dark hair hides her face until at the end of the speech she lifts it to smile at her mother. Amanda's gestures are slow and graceful, almost dancelike, as she comforts the daughter. At the end of her speech she glances a moment at the father's picture — then withdraws through the portieres. At close of Tom's speech, Laura blows out the candles, ending the play.

TOM: I didn't go to the moon, I went much further — for time is the longest distance between two places — Not long after that I was fired for writing a poem on the lid of a shoe-box. I left Saint Louis. I descended the steps of this fire-escape for a last time and followed, from then on, in my father's footsteps, attempting to find in motion what was lost in space — I traveled around a great deal. The cities swept about me like dead leaves, leaves that were brightly colored but torn away from the branches. I would have stopped, but I was pursued by something. It always came upon me unawares, taking me altogether by surprise. Perhaps it was a familiar bit of music. Perhaps it was only a piece of transparent glass — Perhaps I am walking along a street at night, in some strange city, before I have found companions. I pass the lighted window of a shop where perfume is sold. The window is filled with pieces of colored glass, tiny transparent bottles in delicate colors, like bits of a shattered rainbow. Then all at once my sister touches my shoulder. I turn around and look into her eyes. . . . Oh, Laura, Laura, I tried to leave you behind me, but I am more faithful than I intended to be! I reach for a cigarette, I cross the street, I run into the movies or a bar, I buy a drink, I speak to the nearest stranger — anything that can blow your candles out! (*Laura bends over the candles*) — for nowadays the world is lit by lightning! Blow out your candles, Laura — and so good-bye . . .

She blows the candles out.

(The Scene Dissolves.)

ARTHUR MILLER *(b. 1915), the son of a clothing manufacturer, was born in Manhattan but moved to Brooklyn as a teenager when his father's business collapsed during the Depression. After high school he worked for two years in an automobile parts warehouse to save money for his college tuition. He wrote his first play in 1935 as a journalism student at the University of Michigan, later recalling for a Paris Review interviewer that*

> *it was written on a spring vacation in six days. I was so young that I dared do such things, begin it and finish it in a week. I'd seen about two plays in my life, so I didn't know how long an act was supposed to be, but across the hall there was a fellow who did the costumes for the University theater and he said, "Well, it's roughly forty minutes." I had written an enormous amount of material and I got an alarm clock. It was all a lark to me, and not to be taken too seriously . . . that's what I told myself. As it turned out, the acts were longer than that, but the sense of timing was in me even from the beginning, and the play had a form right from the start.*

Miller's early plays won prizes at the University of Michigan, and he went on after graduation to write plays for radio and work for the Federal Theater Project. After failing with The Man Who Had All the Luck *in 1944, Miller had his first successful play in 1947 with* All My Sons.

In Boston during the pre-Broadway preview of this play, Miller had a chance meeting outside the Colonial Theater with his uncle Manny Newman, a traveling salesman. Their encounter suggested the idea of Death of a Salesman *to Miller a short time later. Miller recalled, "I could see his grim hotel room behind him, the long trip up from New York in his little car, the hopeless hope of the day's business. Without so much as acknowledging my greeting, he said, 'Buddy is doing very well.' " Miller understood that his uncle was a competitor at all times, and that he had taken the Colonial Theater marquee advertising Miller's new play as an irresistible challenge to assert that his own son, Buddy, was also a success. To Miller, his uncle was an absurd yet unforgettable figure, "so completely isolated from the ordinary laws of gravity, so elaborate in his fantastic inventions, and despite his ugliness so lyrically in love with fame and fortune and their inevitable descent on his family, that he possessed my imagination until I knew more or less precisely how he would react to any sign or word or idea."*

*Yet Miller was also aware that his uncle's unexpected appearance outside the Boston theater had another effect on him, cutting "through time like a knife through a layer cake." In the encounter Miller had felt himself reduced from an accomplished thirty-year-old playwright (*All My Sons *went on to win the year's Pulitzer Prize and a Drama Critics Circle Award) to an emotionally vulnerable adolescent. He decided to write a play about his uncle "without any transitions at all, dialogue that would simply leap from bone to bone of a skeleton that would not for an instant cease being added to, an organism as strictly economic as a leaf, as trim as an ant."*

In six weeks during the spring of 1948, Miller wrote the first draft of Death of a Salesman. *He credits a production of Tennessee Williams's* A Streetcar Named Desire *the previous November as another important influence that shaped his play: Williams's "words and their liberation, the joy of the writer in writing them, the radi-*

ant eloquence of its composition." The theater historian Brenda Murphy sees a link between Williams's poetic language in that play and "the poetry of the mundane that infuses Salesman." Elia Kazan, who directed both Streetcar and Salesman, recalled that Miller was also greatly impressed with the staging of Williams's play, appearing to be "full of wonder at the theatre's expressive possibilities. [Miller] told me he was amazed at how simply and successfully the non-realistic elements in the play . . . blended with the realistic ones."

Collaborating with Kazan and set designer Jo Mielziner, Miller extensively revised his preproduction script of Death of a Salesman. It was the hit of the 1948–49 Broadway season, running for 742 performances and winning the Pulitzer Prize, the Drama Critics Circle Award, the Donaldson Award, and Tony Awards for best play, best direction, best scene design, and best supporting actor. Published as a script, the play became a best-seller, and it was the only play ever to be a Book-of-the-Month Club selection. Perhaps the drama critic Brooks Atkinson summarized its appeal for audiences in his New York Times review after the premier of the play: "Mr. Miller has looked with compassion into the hearts of some ordinary Americans and quietly transferred their hope and anguish to the theatre." In the essay "Tragedy and the Common Man," Miller interpreted Willy Loman's tragedy as that of Everyman: "The Chinese reaction to my Beijing production of Salesman would confirm what had become more and more obvious over the decades in the play's hundreds of productions throughout the world: Willy was representative everywhere, in every kind of system, of ourselves in this time."

Miller has continued to write plays, most notably in The Crucible (1953) and A View from the Bridge (1956). He also wrote the screenplay of the film The Misfits for his second wife, Marilyn Monroe, from whom he was divorced in 1961. Among his later plays are After the Fall (1964), The Archbishop's Ceiling (1977), Danger: Memory! (1986), and The Last Yankee (1993). Miller has also written a memoir, Timebends (1987), and excellent essays on the theater and the craft of playwriting, many of them collected in 1978 in The Theatre Essays of Arthur Miller, edited by Robert A. Martin.

RELATED COMMENTARIES: Arthur Miller, "In Memoriam," page 1994; Arthur Miller, "On Death of a Salesman as an American Tragedy," page 1996; Arthur Miller, "From the Paris Review Interview," page 2000; Helge Normann Nilsen, "Marxism and the Early Plays of Arthur Miller," page 2012.

ARTHUR MILLER

Death of a Salesman   1949

Certain Private Conversations in Two Acts and a Requiem

CAST

WILLY LOMAN	UNCLE BEN
LINDA	HOWARD WAGNER
BIFF	JENNY
HAPPY	STANLEY
BERNARD	MISS FORSYTHE
THE WOMAN	LETTA
CHARLEY	

SCENE: *The action takes place in Willy Loman's house and yard and in various places he visits in the New York and Boston of today.*

Throughout the play, in the stage directions, left and right mean stage left and stage right.

ACT I

A melody is heard, played upon a flute. It is small and fine, telling of grass and trees and the horizon. The curtain rises.

Before us is the Salesman's house. We are aware of towering, angular shapes behind it, surrounding it on all sides. Only the blue light of the sky falls upon the house and forestage; the surrounding area shows an angry glow of orange. As more light appears, we see a solid vault of apartment houses around the small, fragile-seeming home. An air of the dream clings to the place, a dream rising out of reality. The kitchen at center seems actual enough, for there is a kitchen table with three chairs, and a refrigerator. But no other fixtures are seen. At the back of the kitchen there is a draped entrance, which leads to the living-room. To the right of the kitchen, on a level raised two feet, is a bedroom furnished only with a brass bedstead and a straight chair. On a shelf over the bed a silver athletic trophy stands. A window opens onto the apartment house at the side.

Behind the kitchen, on a level raised six and a half feet, is the boys' bedroom, at present barely visible. Two beds are dimly seen, and at the back of the room a dormer window. (This bedroom is above the unseen living-room.) At the left a stairway curves up to it from the kitchen.

The entire setting is wholly or, in some places, partially transparent. The roofline of the house is one-dimensional; under and over it we see the apartment buildings. Before the house lies an apron, curving beyond the forestage into the orchestra. This forward area serves as the back yard as well as the locale of all Willy's imaginings and of his city scenes. Whenever the action is in the present the actors observe the imaginary wall-lines, entering the house only through its door at the left. But in the scenes of the past these boundaries are broken, and characters enter or leave a room by stepping "through" a wall onto the forestage.

From the right, Willy Loman, the Salesman, enters, carrying two large sample cases. The flute plays on. He hears but is not aware of it. He is past sixty years of age, dressed quietly. Even as he crosses the stage to the doorway of the house, his exhaustion is apparent. He unlocks the door, comes into the kitchen, and thankfully lets his burden down, feeling the soreness of his palms. A word-sigh escapes his lips — it might be "Oh, boy, oh, boy." He closes the door, then carries his cases out into the living-room, through the draped kitchen doorway.

Linda, his wife, has stirred in her bed at the right. She gets out and puts on a robe, listening. Most often jovial, she has developed an iron repression of her exceptions to Willy's behavior — she more than loves him, she admires him, as though his mercurial nature, his temper, his massive dreams and little cruelties, served her only as sharp reminders of the turbulent longings within him, longings which she shares but lacks the temperament to utter and follow to their end.

LINDA (*hearing Willy outside the bedroom, calls with some trepidation*): Willy!

WILLY: It's all right. I came back.

LINDA: Why? What happened? (*Slight pause.*) Did something happen, Willy?

WILLY: No, nothing happened.

LINDA: You didn't smash the car, did you?

WILLY (*with casual irritation*): I said nothing happened. Didn't you hear me?

LINDA: Don't you feel well?

WILLY: I'm tired to the death. (*The flute has faded away. He sits on the bed beside her, a little numb.*) I couldn't make it. I just couldn't make it, Linda.

LINDA (*very carefully, delicately*): Where were you all day? You look terrible.

WILLY: I got as far as a little above Yonkers. I stopped for a cup of coffee. Maybe it was the coffee.

LINDA: What?

WILLY (*after a pause*): I suddenly couldn't drive any more. The car kept going off onto the shoulder, y'know?

LINDA (*helpfully*): Oh. Maybe it was the steering again. I don't think Angelo knows the Studebaker.

WILLY: No, it's me, it's me. Suddenly I realize I'm goin' sixty miles an hour and I don't remember the last five minutes. I'm — I can't seem to — keep my mind to it.

LINDA: Maybe it's your glasses. You never went for your new glasses.

WILLY: No, I see everything. I came back ten miles an hour. It took me nearly four hours from Yonkers.

LINDA (*resigned*): Well, you'll just have to take a rest, Willy, you can't continue this way.

WILLY: I just got back from Florida.

LINDA: But you didn't rest your mind. Your mind is overactive, and the mind is what counts, dear.

WILLY: I'll start out in the morning. Maybe I'll feel better in the morning. (*She is taking off his shoes.*) These goddam arch supports are killing me.

LINDA: Take an aspirin. Should I get you an aspirin? It'll soothe you.

WILLY (*with wonder*): I was driving along, you understand? And I was fine. I was even observing the scenery. You can imagine, me looking at scenery, on the road every week of my life. But it's so beautiful up there, Linda, the trees are so thick, and the sun is warm. I opened the windshield and just let the warm air bathe over me. And then all of a sudden I'm goin' off the road! I'm tellin' ya, I absolutely forgot I was driving. If I'd've gone the other way over the white line I might've killed somebody. So I went on again — and five minutes later I'm dreamin' again, and I nearly — (*He presses two fingers against his eyes.*) I have such thoughts, I have such strange thoughts.

LINDA: Willy, dear. Talk to them again. There's no reason why you can't work in New York.

WILLY: They don't need me in New York. I'm the New England man. I'm vital in New England.

LINDA: But you're sixty years old. They can't expect you to keep traveling every week.

WILLY: I'll have to send a wire to Portland. I'm supposed to see Brown and Morrison tomorrow morning at ten o'clock to show the line. God-dammit, I could sell them! (*He starts putting on his jacket.*)

LINDA (*taking the jacket from him*): Why don't you go down to the place tomorrow and tell Howard you've simply got to work in New York? You're
too accommodating, dear.

WILLY: If old man Wagner was alive I'd a been in charge of New York now! That
man was a prince, he was a masterful man. But that boy of his, that
Howard, he don't appreciate. When I went north the first time, the Wagner Company didn't know where New England was!

LINDA: Why don't you tell those things to Howard, dear?

WILLY (*encouraged*): I will, I definitely will. Is there any cheese?

LINDA: I'll make you a sandwich.

WILLY: No, go to sleep. I'll take some milk. I'll be up right away. The boys in?

LINDA: They're sleeping. Happy took Biff on a date tonight.

WILLY (*interested*): That so?

LINDA: It was so nice to see them shaving together, one behind the other, in the
bathroom. And going out together. You notice? The whole house smells
of shaving lotion.

WILLY: Figure it out. Work a lifetime to pay off a house. You finally own it, and
there's nobody to live in it.

LINDA: Well, dear, life is a casting off. It's always that way.

WILLY: No, no, some people — some people accomplish something. Did Biff
say anything after I went this morning?

LINDA: You shouldn't have criticized him, Willy, especially after he just got off
the train. You mustn't lose your temper with him.

WILLY: When the hell did I lose my temper? I simply asked him if he was making any money. Is that a criticism?

LINDA: But, dear, how could he make any money?

WILLY (*worried and angered*): There's such an undercurrent in him. He became a
moody man. Did he apologize when I left this morning?

LINDA: He was crestfallen, Willy. You know how he admires you. I think if he
finds himself, then you'll both be happier and not fight any more.

WILLY: How can he find himself on a farm? Is that a life? A farmhand? In the beginning, when he was young, I thought, well, a young man, it's good for
him to tramp around, take a lot of different jobs. But it's more than ten
years now and he has yet to make thirty-five dollars a week!

LINDA: He's finding himself, Willy.

WILLY: Not finding yourself at the age of thirty-four is a disgrace!

LINDA: Shh!

WILLY: The trouble is he's lazy, goddammit!

LINDA: Willy, please!

WILLY: Biff is a lazy bum!

LINDA: They're sleeping. Get something to eat. Go on down.

WILLY: Why did he come home? I would like to know what brought him
home.

LINDA: I don't know. I think he's still lost, Willy. I think he's very lost.

WILLY: Biff Loman is lost. In the greatest country in the world a young man
with such — personal attractiveness, gets lost. And such a hard worker.
There's one thing about Biff — he's not lazy.

LINDA: Never.

WILLY (*with pity and resolve*): I'll see him in the morning; I'll have a nice talk with him. I'll get him a job selling. He could be big in no time. My God! Remember how they used to follow him around in high school? When he smiled at one of them their faces lit up. When he walked down the street . . . (*He loses himself in reminiscences.*)

LINDA (*trying to bring him out of it*): Willy, dear, I got a new kind of American-type cheese today. It's whipped.

WILLY: Why do you get American when I like Swiss?

LINDA: I just thought you'd like a change —

WILLY: I don't want a change! I want Swiss cheese. Why am I always being contradicted?

LINDA (*with a covering laugh*): I thought it would be a surprise.

WILLY: Why don't you open a window in here, for God's sake?

LINDA (*with infinite patience*): They're all open, dear.

WILLY: The way they boxed us in here. Bricks and windows, windows and bricks.

LINDA: We should've bought the land next door.

WILLY: The street is lined with cars. There's not a breath of fresh air in the neighborhood. The grass don't grow any more, you can't raise a carrot in the back yard. They should've had a law against apartment houses. Remember those two beautiful elm trees out there? When I and Biff hung the swing between them?

LINDA: Yeah, like being a million miles from the city.

WILLY: They should've arrested the builder for cutting those down. They massacred the neighborhood. (*Lost.*) More and more I think of those days, Linda. This time of year it was lilac and wisteria. And then the peonies would come out, and the daffodils. What fragrance in this room!

LINDA: Well, after all, people had to move somewhere.

WILLY: No, there's more people now.

LINDA: I don't think there's more people. I think —

WILLY: There's more people! That's what's ruining this country! Population is getting out of control. The competition is maddening! Smell the stink from that apartment house! And another one on the other side . . . How can they whip cheese?

On Willy's last line, Biff and Happy raise themselves up in their beds, listening.

LINDA: Go down, try it. And be quiet.

WILLY (*turning to Linda, guiltily*): You're not worried about me, are you, sweetheart?

BIFF: What's the matter?

HAPPY: Listen!

LINDA: You've got too much on the ball to worry about.

WILLY: You're my foundation and my support, Linda.

LINDA: Just try to relax, dear. You make mountains out of molehills.

WILLY: I won't fight with him any more. If he wants to go back to Texas, let him go.

LINDA: He'll find his way.

WILLY: Sure. Certain men just don't get started till later in life. Like Thomas Edison, I think. Or B. F. Goodrich. One of them was deaf. (*He starts for the bedroom doorway.*) I'll put my money on Biff.

LINDA: And Willy — if it's warm Sunday we'll drive in the country. And we'll open the windshield, and take lunch.

WILLY: No, the windshields don't open on the new cars.

LINDA: But you opened it today.

WILLY: Me? I didn't. (*He stops.*) Now isn't that peculiar! Isn't that a remarkable — (*He breaks off in amazement and fright as the flute is heard distantly.*)

LINDA: What, darling?

WILLY: That is the most remarkable thing.

LINDA: What, dear?

WILLY: I was thinking of the Chevy. (*Slight pause.*) Nineteen twenty-eight . . . when I had that red Chevy — (*Breaks off.*) That funny? I coulda sworn I was driving that Chevy today.

LINDA: Well, that's nothing. Something must've reminded you.

WILLY: Remarkable. Ts. Remember those days? The way Biff used to simonize that car? The dealer refused to believe there was eighty thousand miles on it. (*He shakes his head.*) Heh! (*To Linda.*) Close your eyes, I'll be right up. (*He walks out of the bedroom.*)

HAPPY (*to Biff*): Jesus, maybe he smashed up the car again!

LINDA (*calling after Willy*): Be careful on the stairs, dear! The cheese is on the middle shelf! (*She turns, goes over to the bed, takes his jacket, and goes out of the bedroom.*)

Light has risen on the boys' room. Unseen, Willy is heard talking to himself, "Eighty thousand miles," and a little laugh. Biff gets out of bed, comes downstage a bit, and stands attentively. Biff is two years older than his brother Happy, well built, but in these days bears a worn air and seems less self-assured. He has succeeded less, and his dreams are stronger and less acceptable than Happy's. Happy is tall, powerfully made. Sexuality is like a visible color on him, or a scent that many women have discovered. He, like his brother, is lost, but in a different way, for he has never allowed himself to turn his face toward defeat and is thus more confused and hard-skinned, although seemingly more content.

HAPPY (*getting out of bed*): He's going to get his license taken away if he keeps that up. I'm getting nervous about him, y'know, Biff?

BIFF: His eyes are going.

HAPPY: No, I've driven with him. He sees all right. He just doesn't keep his mind on it. I drove into the city with him last week. He stops at a green light and then it turns red and he goes. (*He laughs.*)

BIFF: Maybe he's color-blind.

HAPPY: Pop? Why he's got the finest eye for color in the business. You know that.

BIFF (*sitting down on his bed*): I'm going to sleep.

HAPPY: You're not still sour on Dad, are you, Biff?

BIFF: He's all right, I guess.

WILLY (*underneath them, in the living-room*): Yes, sir, eighty thousand miles — eighty-two thousand!

BIFF: You smoking?

HAPPY (*holding out a pack of cigarettes*): Want one?

BIFF (*taking a cigarette*): I can never sleep when I smell it.

WILLY: What a simonizing job, heh!

HAPPY (*with deep sentiment*): Funny, Biff, y'know? Us sleeping in here again? The old beds. (*He pats his bed affectionately.*) All the talk that went across those two beds, huh? Our whole lives.

BIFF: Yeah. Lotta dreams and plans.

HAPPY (*with a deep and masculine laugh*): About five hundred women would like to know what was said in this room.

They share a soft laugh.

BIFF: Remember that big Betsy something — what the hell was her name — over on Bushwick Avenue?

HAPPY (*combing his hair*): With the collie dog!

BIFF: That's the one. I got you in there, remember?

HAPPY: Yeah, that was my first time — I think. Boy, there was a pig! (*They laugh, almost crudely.*) You taught me everything I know about women. Don't forget that.

BIFF: I bet you forgot how bashful you used to be. Especially with girls.

HAPPY: Oh, I still am, Biff.

BIFF: Oh, go on.

HAPPY: I just control it, that's all. I think I got less bashful and you got more so. What happened, Biff? Where's the old humor, the old confidence? (*He shakes Biff's knee. Biff gets up and moves restlessly about the room.*) What's the matter?

BIFF: Why does Dad mock me all the time?

HAPPY: He's not mocking you, he —

BIFF: Everything I say there's a twist of mockery on his face. I can't get near him.

HAPPY: He just wants you to make good, that's all. I wanted to talk to you about Dad for a long time, Biff. Something's — happening to him. He — talks to himself.

BIFF: I noticed that this morning. But he always mumbled.

HAPPY: But not so noticeable. It got so embarrassing I sent him to Florida. And you know something? Most of the time he's talking to you.

BIFF: What's he say about me?

HAPPY: I can't make it out.

BIFF: What's he say about me?

HAPPY: I think the fact that you're not settled, that you're still kind of up in the air . . .

BIFF: There's one or two other things depressing him, Happy.

HAPPY: What do you mean?

BIFF: Never mind. Just don't lay it all to me.

HAPPY: But I think if you just got started — I mean — is there any future for you out there?

BIFF: I tell ya, Hap, I don't know what the future is. I don't know — what I'm supposed to want.

HAPPY: What do you mean?

BIFF: Well, I spent six or seven years after high school trying to work myself up. Shipping clerk, salesman, business of one kind or another. And it's a measly manner of existence. To get on that subway on the hot mornings in summer. To devote your whole life to keeping stock, or making phone calls, or selling or buying. To suffer fifty weeks of the year for the sake of a two-week vacation, when all you really desire is to be outdoors, with your shirt off. And always to have to get ahead of the next fella. And still — that's how you build a future.

HAPPY: Well, you really enjoy it on a farm? Are you content out there?

BIFF (*with rising agitation*): Hap, I've had twenty or thirty different kinds of jobs since I left home before the war, and it always turns out the same. I just realized it lately. In Nebraska when I herded cattle, and the Dakotas, and Arizona, and now in Texas. It's why I came home now, I guess, because I realized it. This farm I work on, it's spring there now, see? And they've got about fifteen new colts. There's nothing more inspiring or — beautiful than the sight of a mare and a new colt. And it's cool there now, see? Texas is cool now, and it's spring. And whenever spring comes to where I am, I suddenly get the feeling, my God, I'm not gettin' anywhere! What the hell am I doing, playing around with horses, twenty-eight dollars a week! I'm thirty-four years old, I oughta be makin' my future. That's when I come running home. And now, I get here, and I don't know what to do with myself. (*After a pause.*) I've always made a point of not wasting my life, and everytime I come back here I know that all I've done is to waste my life.

HAPPY: You're a poet, you know that, Biff? You're a — you're an idealist!

BIFF: No, I'm mixed up very bad. Maybe I oughta get married. Maybe I oughta get stuck into something. Maybe that's my trouble. I'm like a boy. I'm not married. I'm not in business, I just — I'm like a boy. Are you content, Hap? You're a success, aren't you? Are you content?

HAPPY: Hell, no!

BIFF: Why? You're making money, aren't you?

HAPPY (*moving about with energy, expressiveness*): All I can do now is wait for the merchandise manager to die. And suppose I get to be merchandise manager? He's a good friend of mine, and he just built a terrific estate on Long Island. And he lived there about two months and sold it, and now he's building another one. He can't enjoy it once it's finished. And I know that's just what I would do. I don't know what the hell I'm workin' for. Sometimes I sit in my apartment — all alone. And I think of the rent I'm paying. And it's crazy. But then, it's what I always wanted. My own apartment, a car, and plenty of women. And still, goddammit, I'm lonely.

BIFF (*with enthusiasm*): Listen, why don't you come out West with me?

HAPPY: You and I, heh?

BIFF: Sure, maybe we could buy a ranch. Raise cattle, use our muscles. Men built like we are should be working out in the open.

HAPPY (*avidly*): The Loman Brothers, heh?

BIFF (*with vast affection*): Sure, we'd be known all over the counties!

HAPPY (*enthralled*): That's what I dream about, Biff. Sometimes I want to just rip my clothes off in the middle of the store and outbox that goddam merchandise manager. I mean I can outbox, outrun, and outlift anybody in that store, and I have to take orders from those common, petty sons-of-bitches till I can't stand it any more.

BIFF: I'm tellin' you, kid, if you were with me I'd be happy out there.

HAPPY (*enthused*): See, Biff, everybody around me is so false that I'm constantly lowering my ideals . . .

BIFF: Baby, together we'd stand up for one another, we'd have someone to trust.

HAPPY: If I were around you —

BIFF: Hap, the trouble is we weren't brought up to grub for money. I don't know how to do it.

HAPPY: Neither can I!

BIFF: Then let's go!

HAPPY: The only thing is — what can you make out there?

BIFF: But look at your friend. Builds an estate and then hasn't the peace of mind to live in it.

HAPPY: Yeah, but when he walks into the store the waves part in front of him. That's fifty-two thousand dollars a year coming through the revolving door, and I got more in my pinky finger than he's got in his head.

BIFF: Yeah, but you just said —

HAPPY: I gotta show some of those pompous, self-important executives over there that Hap Loman can make the grade. I want to walk into the store the way he walks in. Then I'll go with you, Biff. We'll be together yet, I swear. But take those two we had tonight. Now weren't they gorgeous creatures?

BIFF: Yeah, yeah, most gorgeous I've had in years.

HAPPY: I get that any time I want, Biff. Whenever I feel disgusted. The trouble is, it gets like bowling or something. I just keep knockin' them over and it doesn't mean anything. You still run around a lot?

BIFF: Naa. I'd like to find a girl — steady, somebody with substance.

HAPPY: That's what I long for.

BIFF: Go on! You'd never come home.

HAPPY: I would! Somebody with character, with resistance! Like Mom, y'know? You're gonna call me a bastard when I tell you this. That girl Charlotte I was with tonight is engaged to be married in five weeks. (*He tries on his new hat.*)

BIFF: No kiddin'!

HAPPY: Sure, the guy's in line for the vice-presidency of the store. I don't know what gets into me, maybe I just have an overdeveloped sense of compe-

tition or something, but I went and ruined her, and furthermore I can't
get rid of her. And he's the third executive I've done that to. Isn't that a
crummy characteristic? And to top it all, I go to their weddings! (*Indignantly, but laughing.*) Like I'm not supposed to take bribes. Manufactur-
ers offer me a hundred-dollar bill now and then to throw an order their
way. You know how honest I am, but it's like this girl, see. I hate myself
for it. Because I don't want the girl, and, still, I take it and — I love it!

BIFF: Let's go to sleep.

HAPPY: I guess we didn't settle anything, heh?

BIFF: I just got one idea that I think I'm going to try.

HAPPY: What's that?

BIFF: Remember Bill Oliver?

HAPPY: Sure, Oliver is very big now. You want to work for him again?

BIFF: No, but when I quit he said something to me. He put his arm on my
shoulder, and he said, "Biff, if you ever need anything, come to me."

HAPPY: I remember that. That sounds good.

BIFF: I think I'll go to see him. If I could get ten thousand or even seven or eight
thousand dollars I could buy a beautiful ranch.

HAPPY: I bet he'd back you. 'Cause he thought highly of you, Biff. I mean, they
all do. You're well liked, Biff. That's why I say to come back here, and we
both have the apartment. And I'm tellin' you, Biff, any babe you
want . . .

BIFF: No, with a ranch I could do the work I like and still be something. I just
wonder though. I wonder if Oliver still thinks I stole that carton of basketballs.

HAPPY: Oh, he probably forgot that long ago. It's almost ten years. You're too
sensitive. Anyway, he didn't really fire you.

BIFF: Well, I think he was going to. I think that's why I quit. I was never sure
whether he knew or not. I know he thought the world of me, though. I
was the only one he'd let lock up the place.

WILLY (*below*): You gonna wash the engine, Biff?

HAPPY: Shh!

Biff looks at Happy, who is gazing down, listening. Willy is mumbling in the parlor.

HAPPY: You hear that?

They listen. Willy laughs warmly.

BIFF (*growing angry*): Doesn't he know Mom can hear that?

WILLY: Don't get your sweater dirty, Biff!

A look of pain crosses Biff's face.

HAPPY: Isn't that terrible? Don't leave again, will you? You'll find a job here.
You gotta stick around. I don't know what to do about him, it's getting
embarrassing.

WILLY: What a simonizing job!

BIFF: Mom's hearing that!

WILLY: No kiddin', Biff, you got a date? Wonderful!

HAPPY: Go on to sleep. But talk to him in the morning, will you?

BIFF (*reluctantly getting into bed*): With her in the house. Brother!

HAPPY (*getting into bed*): I wish you'd have a good talk with him.

The light on their room begins to fade.

BIFF (*to himself in bed*): That selfish, stupid . . .

HAPPY: Sh . . . Sleep, Biff.

Their light is out. Well before they have finished speaking, Willy's form is dimly seen below in the darkened kitchen. He opens the refrigerator, searches in there, and takes out a bottle of milk. The apartment houses are fading out, and the entire house and surroundings become covered with leaves. Music insinuates itself as the leaves appear.

WILLY: Just wanna be careful with those girls, Biff, that's all. Don't make any promises. No promises of any kind. Because a girl, y'know, they always believe what you tell 'em, and you're very young, Biff, you're too young to be talking seriously to girls.

Light rises on the kitchen. Willy, talking, shuts the refrigerator door and comes downstage to the kitchen table. He pours milk into a glass. He is totally immersed in himself, smiling faintly.

WILLY: Too young entirely, Biff. You want to watch your schooling first. Then when you're all set, there'll be plenty of girls for a boy like you. (*He smiles broadly at a kitchen chair.*) That so? The girls pay for you? (*He laughs.*) Boy, you must really be makin' a hit.

Willy is gradually addressing — physically — a point offstage, speaking through the wall of the kitchen, and his voice has been rising in volume to that of a normal conversation.

WILLY: I been wondering why you polish the car so careful. Ha! Don't leave the hubcaps, boys. Get the chamois to the hubcaps. Happy, use newspaper on the windows, it's the easiest thing. Show him how to do it, Biff! You see, Happy? Pad it up, use it like a pad. That's it, that's it, good work. You're doin' all right, Hap. (*He pauses, then nods in approbation for a few seconds, then looks upward.*) Biff, first thing we gotta do when we get time is clip that big branch over the house. Afraid it's gonna fall in a storm and hit the roof. Tell you what. We get a rope and sling her around, and then we climb up there with a couple of saws and take her down. Soon as you finish the car, boys, I wanna see ya. I got a surprise for you, boys.

BIFF (*offstage*): Whatta ya got, Dad?

WILLY: No, you finish first. Never leave a job till you're finished — remember that. (*Looking toward the "big trees."*) Biff, up in Albany I saw a beautiful hammock. I think I'll buy it next trip, and we'll hang it right between those two elms. Wouldn't that be something? Just swingin' there under those branches. Boy, that would be . . .

Young Biff and Young Happy appear from the direction Willy was addressing. Happy carries rags and a pail of water. Biff, wearing a sweater with a block "S," carries a football.

BIFF (*pointing in the direction of the car offstage*): How's that, Pop, professional?

WILLY: Terrific. Terrific job, boys. Good work, Biff.

HAPPY: Where's the surprise, Pop?

WILLY: In the back seat of the car.

HAPPY: Boy! (*He runs off.*)

BIFF: What is it, Dad? Tell me, what'd you buy?

WILLY (*laughing, cuffs him*): Never mind, something I want you to have.

BIFF (*turns and starts off*): What is it, Hap?

HAPPY (*offstage*): It's a punching bag!

BIFF: Oh, Pop!

WILLY: It's got Gene Tunney's signature on it!

Happy runs onstage with a punching bag.

BIFF: Gee, how'd you know we wanted a punching bag?

WILLY: Well, it's the finest thing for the timing.

HAPPY (*lies down on his back and pedals with his feet*): I'm losing weight, you notice, Pop?

WILLY (*to Happy*): Jumping rope is good too.

BIFF: Did you see the new football I got?

WILLY (*examining the ball*): Where'd you get a new ball?

BIFF: The coach told me to practice my passing.

WILLY: That so? And he gave you the ball, heh?

BIFF: Well, I borrowed it from the locker room. (*He laughs confidentially.*)

WILLY (*laughing with him at the theft*): I want you to return that.

HAPPY: I told you he wouldn't like it!

BIFF (*angrily*): Well, I'm bringing it back!

WILLY (*stopping the incipient argument, to Happy*): Sure, he's gotta practice with a regulation ball, doesn't he? (*To Biff.*) Coach'll probably congratulate you on your initiative!

BIFF: Oh, he keeps congratulating my initiative all the time, Pop.

WILLY: That's because he likes you. If somebody else took that ball there'd be an uproar. So what's the report, boys, what's the report?

BIFF: Where'd you go this time, Dad? Gee we were lonesome for you.

WILLY (*pleased, puts an arm around each boy and they come down to the apron*): Lonesome, heh?

BIFF: Missed you every minute.

WILLY: Don't say? Tell you a secret, boys. Don't breathe it to a soul. Someday I'll have my own business, and I'll never have to leave home any more.

HAPPY: Like Uncle Charley, heh?

WILLY: Bigger than Uncle Charley! Because Charley is not — liked. He's liked, but he's not — well liked.

BIFF: Where'd you go this time, Dad?

WILLY: Well, I got on the road, and I went north to Providence. Met the Mayor.

BIFF: The Mayor of Providence!

WILLY: He was sitting in the hotel lobby.

BIFF: What'd he say?

WILLY: He said, "Morning!" And I said, "You got a fine city here, Mayor." And then he had coffee with me. And then I went to Waterbury. Waterbury is a fine city. Big clock city, the famous Waterbury clock. Sold a nice bill there. And then Boston — Boston is the cradle of the Revolution. A fine city. And a couple of other towns in Mass., and on to Portland and Bangor and straight home!

BIFF: Gee, I'd love to go with you sometime, Dad.

WILLY: Soon as summer comes.

HAPPY: Promise?

WILLY: You and Hap and I, and I'll show you all the towns. America is full of beautiful towns and fine, upstanding people. And they know me, boys, they know me up and down New England. The finest people. And when I bring you fellas up, there'll be open sesame for all of us, 'cause one thing, boys: I have friends. I can park my car in any street in New England, and the cops protect it like their own. This summer, heh?

BIFF AND HAPPY (*together*): Yeah! You bet!

WILLY: We'll take our bathing suits.

HAPPY: We'll carry your bags, Pop!

WILLY: Oh, won't that be something! Me comin' into the Boston stores with you boys carryin' my bags. What a sensation!

Biff is prancing around, practicing passing the ball.

WILLY: You nervous, Biff, about the game?

BIFF: Not if you're gonna be there.

WILLY: What do they say about you in school, now that they made you captain?

HAPPY: There's a crowd of girls behind him everytime the classes change.

BIFF (*taking Willy's hand*): This Saturday, Pop, this Saturday — just for you, I'm going to break through for a touchdown.

HAPPY: You're supposed to pass.

BIFF: I'm takin' one play for Pop. You watch me, Pop, and when I take off my helmet, that means I'm breakin' out. Then you watch me crash through that line!

WILLY (*kisses Biff*): Oh, wait'll I tell this in Boston!

Bernard enters in knickers. He is younger than Biff, earnest and loyal, a worried boy.

BERNARD: Biff, where are you? You're supposed to study with me today.

WILLY: Hey, looka Bernard. What're you lookin' so anemic about, Bernard?

BERNARD: He's gotta study, Uncle Willy. He's got Regents next week.

HAPPY (*tauntingly, spinning Bernard around*): Let's box, Bernard!

BERNARD: Biff! (*He gets away from Happy.*) Listen, Biff, I heard Mr. Birnbaum say that if you don't start studyin' math, he's gonna flunk you, and you won't graduate. I heard him!

WILLY: You better study with him, Biff. Go ahead now.

BERNARD: I heard him!

BIFF: Oh, Pop, you didn't see my sneakers! (*He holds up a foot for Willy to look at.*)

WILLY: Hey, that's a beautiful job of printing!

BERNARD (*wiping his glasses*): Just because he printed University of Virginia on his sneakers doesn't mean they've got to graduate him, Uncle Willy!

WILLY (*angrily*): What're you talking about? With scholarships to three universities they're gonna flunk him?

BERNARD: But I heard Mr. Birnbaum say —

WILLY: Don't be a pest, Bernard! (*To his boys.*) What an anemic!

BERNARD: Okay, I'm waiting for you in my house, Biff.

Bernard goes off. The Lomans laugh.

WILLY: Bernard is not well liked, is he?

BIFF: He's liked, but he's not well liked.

HAPPY: That's right, Pop.

WILLY: That's just what I mean. Bernard can get the best marks in school, y'understand, but when he gets out in the business world, y'understand, you are going to be five times ahead of him. That's why I thank Almighty God you're both built like Adonises.° Because the man who makes an appearance in the business world, the man who creates personal interest, is the man who gets ahead. Be liked and you will never want. You take me, for instance. I never have to wait in line to see a buyer. "Willy Loman is here!" That's all they have to know, and I go right through.

BIFF: Did you knock them dead, Pop?

WILLY: Knocked 'em cold in Providence, slaughtered 'em in Boston.

HAPPY (*on his back, pedaling again*): I'm losing weight, you notice, Pop?

Linda enters, as of old, a ribbon in her hair, carrying a basket of washing.

LINDA (*with youthful energy*): Hello, dear!

WILLY: Sweetheart!

LINDA: How'd the Chevy run?

WILLY: Chevrolet, Linda, is the greatest car ever built. (*To the boys.*) Since when do you let your mother carry wash up the stairs?

BIFF: Grab hold there, boy!

HAPPY: Where to, Mom?

LINDA: Hang them up on the line. And you better go down to your friends, Biff. The cellar is full of boys. They don't know what to do with themselves.

BIFF: Ah, when Pop comes home they can wait!

WILLY (*laughs appreciatively*): You better go down and tell them what to do, Biff.

BIFF: I think I'll have them sweep out the furnace room.

WILLY: Good work, Biff.

BIFF (*goes through wall-line of kitchen to doorway at back and calls down*): Fellas! Everybody sweep out the furnace room! I'll be right down!

VOICES: All right! Okay, Biff.

BIFF: George and Sam and Frank, come out back! We're hangin' up the wash! Come on, Hap, on the double! (*He and Happy carry out the basket.*)

LINDA: The way they obey him!

WILLY: Well, that's training, the training. I'm tellin' you, I was sellin' thousands and thousands, but I had to come home.

LINDA: Oh, the whole block'll be at that game. Did you sell anything?

Adonises: In Greek Mythology Adonis is a youth known for his good looks and favored by Aphrodite, the goddess of love and beauty.

WILLY: I did five hundred gross in Providence and seven hundred gross in Boston.

LINDA: No! Wait a minute, I've got a pencil. (*She pulls pencil and paper out of her apron pocket.*) That makes your commission . . . Two hundred — my God! Two hundred and twelve dollars!

WILLY: Well, I didn't figure it yet, but . . .

LINDA: How much did you do?

WILLY: Well, I — I did — about a hundred and eighty gross in Providence. Well, no — it came to — roughly two hundred gross on the whole trip.

LINDA (*without hesitation*): Two hundred gross. That's . . . (*She figures.*)

WILLY: The trouble was that three of the stores were half closed for inventory in Boston. Otherwise I woulda broke records.

LINDA: Well, it makes seventy dollars and some pennies. That's very good.

WILLY: What do we owe?

LINDA: Well, on the first there's sixteen dollars on the refrigerator —

WILLY: Why sixteen?

LINDA: Well, the fan belt broke, so it was a dollar eighty.

WILLY: But it's brand new.

LINDA: Well, the man said that's the way it is. Till they work themselves in, y'know.

They move through the wall-line into the kitchen.

WILLY: I hope we didn't get stuck on that machine.

LINDA: They got the biggest ads of any of them!

WILLY: I know, it's a fine machine. What else?

LINDA: Well, there's nine-sixty for the washing machine. And for the vacuum cleaner there's three and a half due on the fifteenth. Then the roof, you got twenty-one dollars remaining.

WILLY: It don't leak, does it?

LINDA: No, they did a wonderful job. Then you owe Frank for the carburetor.

WILLY: I'm not going to pay that man! That goddam Chevrolet, they ought to prohibit the manufacture of that car!

LINDA: Well, you owe him three and a half. And odds and ends, comes to around a hundred and twenty dollars by the fifteenth.

WILLY: A hundred and twenty dollars! My God, if business don't pick up I don't know what I'm gonna do!

LINDA: Well, next week you'll do better.

WILLY: Oh, I'll knock 'em dead next week. I'll go to Hartford. I'm very well liked in Hartford. You know, the trouble is, Linda, people don't seem to take to me.

They move onto the forestage.

LINDA: Oh, don't be foolish.

WILLY: I know it when I walk in. They seem to laugh at me.

LINDA: Why? Why would they laugh at you? Don't talk that way, Willy.

Willy moves to the edge of the stage. Linda goes into the kitchen and starts to darn stockings.

WILLY: I don't know the reason for it, but they just pass me by. I'm not noticed.

LINDA: But you're doing wonderful, dear. You're making seventy to a hundred dollars a week.

WILLY: But I gotta be at it ten, twelve hours a day. Other men — I don't know — they do it easier. I don't know why — I can't stop myself — I talk too much. A man oughta come in with a few words. One thing about Charley. He's a man of few words, and they respect him.

LINDA: You don't talk too much, you're just lively.

WILLY (*smiling*): Well, I figure, what the hell, life is short, a couple of jokes. (*To himself.*) I joke too much! (*The smile goes.*)

LINDA: Why? You're —

WILLY: I'm fat. I'm very — foolish to look at, Linda. I didn't tell you, but Christmas time I happened to be calling on F. H. Stewarts, and a salesman I know, as I was going in to see the buyer I heard him say something about — walrus. And I — I cracked him right across the face. I won't take that. I simply will not take that. But they do laugh at me. I know that.

LINDA: Darling . . .

WILLY: I gotta overcome it. I know I gotta overcome it. I'm not dressing to advantage, maybe.

LINDA: Willy, darling, you're the handsomest man in the world —

WILLY: Oh, no, Linda.

LINDA: To me you are. (*Slight pause.*) The handsomest.

From the darkness is heard the laughter of a woman. Willy doesn't turn to it, but it continues through Linda's lines.

LINDA: And the boys, Willy. Few men are idolized by their children the way you are.

Music is heard as behind a scrim, to the left of the house, The Woman, dimly seen, is dressing.

WILLY (*with great feeling*): You're the best there is, Linda, you're a pal, you know that? On the road — on the road I want to grab you sometimes and just kiss the life outa you.

The laughter is loud now, and he moves into a brightening area at the left, where The Woman has come from behind the scrim and is standing, putting on her hat, looking into a "mirror" and laughing.

WILLY: 'Cause I get so lonely — especially when business is bad and there's nobody to talk to. I get the feeling that I'll never sell anything again, that I won't make a living for you, or a business, a business for the boys. (*He talks through The Woman's subsiding laughter; The Woman primps at the "mirror."*) There's so much I want to make for —

THE WOMAN: Me? You didn't make me, Willy. I picked you.

WILLY (*pleased*): You picked me?

THE WOMAN (*who is quite proper-looking, Willy's age*): I did. I've been sitting at that desk watching all the salesmen go by, day in, day out. But you've got such a sense of humor, and we do have such a good time together, don't we?

WILLY: Sure, sure. (*He takes her in his arms.*) Why do you have to go now?

THE WOMAN: It's two o'clock . . .

WILLY: No, come on in! (*He pulls her.*)

THE WOMAN: . . . my sisters'll be scandalized. When'll you be back?

WILLY: Oh, two weeks about. Will you come up again?

THE WOMAN: Sure thing. You do make me laugh. It's good for me. (*She squeezes his arm, kisses him.*) And I think you're a wonderful man.

WILLY: You picked me, heh?

THE WOMAN: Sure. Because you're so sweet. And such a kidder.

WILLY: Well, I'll see you next time I'm in Boston.

THE WOMAN: I'll put you right through to the buyers.

WILLY (*slapping her bottom*): Right. Well, bottoms up!

THE WOMAN (*slaps him gently and laughs*): You just kill me, Willy. (*He suddenly grabs her and kisses her roughly.*) You kill me. And thanks for the stockings. I love a lot of stockings. Well, good night.

WILLY: Good night. And keep your pores open!

THE WOMAN: Oh, Willy!

The Woman bursts out laughing, and Linda's laughter blends in. The Woman disappears into the dark. Now the area at the kitchen table brightens. Linda is sitting where she was at the kitchen table, but now is mending a pair of her silk stockings.

LINDA: You are, Willy. The handsomest man. You've got no reason to feel that —

WILLY (*coming out of The Woman's dimming area and going over to Linda*): I'll make it all up to you, Linda, I'll —

LINDA: There's nothing to make up, dear. You're doing fine, better than —

WILLY (*noticing her mending*): What's that?

LINDA: Just mending my stockings. They're so expensive —

WILLY (*angrily, taking them from her*): I won't have you mending stockings in this house! Now throw them out!

Linda puts the stockings in her pocket.

BERNARD (*entering on the run*): Where is he? If he doesn't study!

WILLY (*moving to the forestage, with great agitation*): You'll give him the answers!

BERNARD: I do, but I can't on a Regents! That's a state exam! They're liable to arrest me!

WILLY: Where is he? I'll whip him, I'll whip him!

LINDA: And he'd better give back that football, Willy, it's not nice.

WILLY: Biff! Where is he? Why is he taking everything?

LINDA: He's too rough with the girls, Willy. All the mothers are afraid of him!

WILLY: I'll whip him!

BERNARD: He's driving the car without a license!

The Woman's laugh is heard.

WILLY: Shut up!

LINDA: All the mothers —

WILLY: Shut up!

BERNARD (*backing quietly away and out*): Mr. Birnbaum says he's stuck up.

WILLY: Get outa here!

BERNARD: If he doesn't buckle down he'll flunk math! (*He goes off.*)

LINDA: He's right, Willy, you've gotta —

WILLY (*exploding at her*): There's nothing the matter with him! You want him to be a worm like Bernard? He's got spirit, personality . . .

As he speaks, Linda, almost in tears, exits into the living-room. Willy is alone in the kitchen, wilting and staring. The leaves are gone. It is night again, and the apartment houses look down from behind.

WILLY: Loaded with it. Loaded! What is he stealing? He's giving it back, isn't he? Why is he stealing? What did I tell him? I never in my life told him anything but decent things.

Happy in pajamas has come down the stairs; Willy suddenly becomes aware of Happy's presence.

HAPPY: Let's go now, come on.

WILLY (*sitting down at the kitchen table*): Huh! Why did she have to wax the floors herself? Everytime she waxes the floors she keels over. She knows that!

HAPPY: Shh! Take it easy. What brought you back tonight?

WILLY: I got an awful scare. Nearly hit a kid in Yonkers. God! Why didn't I go to Alaska with my brother Ben that time! Ben! That man was a genius, that man was success incarnate! What a mistake! He begged me to go.

HAPPY: Well, there's no use in —

WILLY: You guys! There was a man started with the clothes on his back and ended up with diamond mines!

HAPPY: Boy, someday I'd like to know how he did it.

WILLY: What's the mystery? The man knew what he wanted and went out and got it! Walked into a jungle, and comes out, the age of twenty-one, and he's rich! The world is an oyster, but you don't crack it open on a mattress!

HAPPY: Pop, I told you I'm gonna retire you for life.

WILLY: You'll retire me for life on seventy goddam dollars a week? And your women and your car and your apartment, and you'll retire me for life! Christ's sake, I couldn't get past Yonkers today! Where are you guys, where are you? The woods are burning! I can't drive a car!

Charley has appeared in the doorway. He is a large man, slow of speech, laconic, immovable. In all he says, despite what he says, there is pity, and, now, trepidation. He has a robe over pajamas, slippers on his feet. He enters the kitchen.

CHARLEY: Everything all right?

HAPPY: Yeah, Charley, everything's . . .

WILLY: What's the matter?

CHARLEY: I heard some noise. I thought something happened. Can't we do something about the walls? You sneeze in here, and in my house hats blow off.

HAPPY: Let's go to bed, Dad. Come on.

Charley signals to Happy to go.

WILLY: You go ahead, I'm not tired at the moment.

HAPPY (*to Willy*): Take it easy, huh? (*He exits.*)

WILLY: What're you doin' up?

CHARLEY (*sitting down at the kitchen table opposite Willy*): Couldn't sleep good. I had a heartburn.

WILLY: Well, you don't know how to eat.

CHARLEY: I eat with my mouth.

WILLY: No, you're ignorant. You gotta know about vitamins and things like that.

CHARLEY: Come on, let's shoot. Tire you out a little.

WILLY (*hesitantly*): All right. You got cards?

CHARLEY (*taking a deck from his pocket*): Yeah, I got them. Someplace. What is it with those vitamins?

WILLY (*dealing*): They build up your bones. Chemistry.

CHARLEY: Yeah, but there's no bones in a heartburn.

WILLY: What are you talkin' about? Do you know the first thing about it?

CHARLEY: Don't get insulted.

WILLY: Don't talk about something you don't know anything about.

They are playing. Pause.

CHARLEY: What're you doin' home?

WILLY: A little trouble with the car.

CHARLEY: Oh. (*Pause.*) I'd like to take a trip to California.

WILLY: Don't say.

CHARLEY: You want a job?

WILLY: I got a job, I told you that. (*After a slight pause.*) What the hell are you offering me a job for?

CHARLEY: Don't get insulted.

WILLY: Don't insult me.

CHARLEY: I don't see no sense in it. You don't have to go on this way.

WILLY: I got a good job. (*Slight pause.*) What do you keep comin' in here for?

CHARLEY: You want me to go?

WILLY (*after a pause, withering*): I can't understand it. He's going back to Texas again. What the hell is that?

CHARLEY: Let him go.

WILLY: I got nothin' to give him, Charley, I'm clean, I'm clean.

CHARLEY: He won't starve. None a them starve. Forget about him.

WILLY: Then what have I got to remember?

CHARLEY: You take it too hard. To hell with it. When a deposit bottle is broken you don't get your nickel back.

WILLY: That's easy enough for you to say.

CHARLEY: That ain't easy for me to say.

WILLY: Did you see the ceiling I put up in the living-room?

CHARLEY: Yeah, that's a piece of work. To put up a ceiling is a mystery to me. How do you do it?

WILLY: What's the difference?

CHARLEY: Well, talk about it.

WILLY: You gonna put up a ceiling?

CHARLEY: How could I put up a ceiling?

WILLY: Then what the hell are you bothering me for?

CHARLEY: You're insulted again.

WILLY: A man who can't handle tools is not a man. You're disgusting.

CHARLEY: Don't call me disgusting, Willy.

Uncle Ben, carrying a valise and an umbrella, enters the forestage from around the right corner of the house. He is a stolid man, in his sixties, with a mustache and an authoritative air. He is utterly certain of his destiny, and there is an aura of far places about him. He enters exactly as Willy speaks.

WILLY: I'm getting awfully tired, Ben.

Ben's music is heard. Ben looks around at everything.

CHARLEY: Good, keep playing; you'll sleep better. Did you call me Ben?

Ben looks at his watch.

WILLY: That's funny. For a second there you reminded me of my brother Ben.

BEN: I only have a few minutes. (*He strolls, inspecting the place. Willy and Charley continue playing.*)

CHARLEY: You never heard from him again, heh? Since that time?

WILLY: Didn't Linda tell you? Couple of weeks ago we got a letter from his wife in Africa. He died.

CHARLEY: That so.

BEN (*chuckling*): So this is Brooklyn, eh?

CHARLEY: Maybe you're in for some of his money.

WILLY: Naa, he had seven sons. There's just one opportunity I had with that man . . .

BEN: I must make a train, William. There are several properties I'm looking at in Alaska.

WILLY: Sure, sure! If I'd gone with him to Alaska that time, everything would've been totally different.

CHARLEY: Go on, you'd froze to death up there.

WILLY: What're you talking about?

BEN: Opportunity is tremendous in Alaska, William. Surprised you're not up there.

WILLY: Sure, tremendous.

CHARLEY: Heh?

WILLY: There was the only man I ever met who knew the answers.

CHARLEY: Who?

BEN: How are you all?

WILLY (*taking a pot, smiling*): Fine, fine.

CHARLEY: Pretty sharp tonight.

BEN: Is mother living with you?

WILLY: No, she died a long time ago.

CHARLEY: Who?

BEN: That's too bad. Fine specimen of a lady, Mother.

WILLY (*to Charley*): Heh?

BEN: I'd hoped to see the old girl.

CHARLEY: Who died?

BEN: Heard anything from Father, have you?

WILLY (*unnerved*): What do you mean, who died?

CHARLEY (*taking a pot*): What're you talkin' about?

BEN (*looking at his watch*): William, it's half-past eight!

WILLY (*as though to dispel his confusion he angrily stops Charley's hand*): That's my build!

CHARLEY: I put the ace —

WILLY: If you don't know how to play the game I'm not gonna throw my money away on you!

CHARLEY (*rising*): It was my ace, for God's sake!

WILLY: I'm through, I'm through!

BEN: When did Mother die?

WILLY: Long ago. Since the beginning you never knew how to play cards.

CHARLEY (*picks up the cards and goes to the door*): All right! Next time I'll bring a deck with five aces.

WILLY: I don't play that kind of game!

CHARLEY (*turning to him*): You ought to be ashamed of yourself!

WILLY: Yeah?

CHARLEY: Yeah! (*He goes out.*)

WILLY (*slamming the door after him*): Ignoramus!

BEN (*as Willy comes toward him through the wall-line of the kitchen*): So you're William.

WILLY (*shaking Ben's hand*): Ben! I've been waiting for you so long! What's the answer? How did you do it?

BEN: Oh, there's a story in that.

Linda enters the forestage, as of old, carrying the wash basket.

LINDA: Is this Ben?

BEN (*gallantly*): How do you do, my dear.

LINDA: Where've you been all these years? Willy's always wondered why you —

WILLY (*pulling Ben away from her impatiently*): Where is Dad? Didn't you follow him? How did you get started?

BEN: Well, I don't know how much you remember.

WILLY: Well, I was just a baby, of course, only three or four years old —

BEN: Three years and eleven months.

WILLY: What a memory, Ben!

BEN: I have many enterprises, William, and I have never kept books.

WILLY: I remember I was sitting under the wagon in — was it Nebraska?

BEN: It was South Dakota, and I gave you a bunch of wild flowers.

WILLY: I remember you walking away down some open road.

BEN (*laughing*): I was going to find Father in Alaska.

WILLY: Where is he?

BEN: At that age I had a very faulty view of geography, William. I discovered after a few days that I was heading due south, so instead of Alaska, I ended up in Africa.

LINDA: Africa!

WILLY: The Gold Coast!

BEN: Principally diamond mines.

LINDA: Diamond mines!

BEN: Yes, my dear. But I've only a few minutes —

WILLY: No! Boys! Boys! (*Young Biff and Happy appear.*) Listen to this. This is your Uncle Ben, a great man! Tell my boys, Ben!

BEN: Why, boys, when I was seventeen I walked into the jungle, and when I was twenty-one I walked out. (*He laughs.*) And by God I was rich.

WILLY (*to the boys*): You see what I been talking about? The greatest things can happen!

BEN (*glancing at his watch*): I have an appointment in Ketchikan Tuesday week.

WILLY: No, Ben! Please tell about Dad. I want my boys to hear. I want them to know the kind of stock they spring from. All I remember is a man with a big beard, and I was in Mamma's lap, sitting around a fire, and some kind of high music.

BEN: His flute. He played the flute.

WILLY: Sure, the flute, that's right!

New music is heard, a high, rollicking tune.

BEN: Father was a very great and a very wild-hearted man. We would start in Boston, and he'd toss the whole family into the wagon, and then he'd drive the team right across the country; through Ohio, and Indiana, Michigan, Illinois, and all the Western states. And we'd stop in the towns and sell the flutes that he'd made on the way. Great inventor, Father. With one gadget he made more in a week than a man like you could make in a lifetime.

WILLY: That's just the way I'm bringing them up, Ben — rugged, well liked, all-around.

BEN: Yeah? (*To Biff.*) Hit that, boy — hard as you can. (*He pounds his stomach.*)

BIFF: Oh, no, sir!

BEN (*taking boxing stance*): Come on, get to me. (*He laughs.*)

WILLY: Go to it, Biff! Go ahead, show him!

BIFF: Okay! (*He cocks his fists and starts in.*)

LINDA (*to Willy*): Why must he fight, dear?

BEN (*sparring with Biff*): Good boy! Good boy!

WILLY: How's that, Ben, heh?

HAPPY: Give him the left, Biff!

LINDA: Why are you fighting?

BEN: Good boy! (*Suddenly comes in, trips Biff, and stands over him, the point of his umbrella poised over Biff's eye.*)

LINDA: Look out, Biff!

BIFF: Gee!

BEN (*patting Biff's knee*): Never fight fair with a stranger, boy. You'll never get out of the jungle that way. (*Taking Linda's hand and bowing*): It was an honor and a pleasure to meet you, Linda.

LINDA (*withdrawing her hand coldly, frightened*): Have a nice — trip.

BEN (*to Willy*): And good luck with your — what do you do?

WILLY: Selling.

BEN: Yes. Well . . . (*He raises his hand in farewell to all.*)

WILLY: No, Ben, I don't want you to think . . . (*He takes Ben's arm to show him.*) It's Brooklyn, I know, but we hunt too.

BEN: Really, now.

WILLY: Oh, sure, there's snakes and rabbits and — that's why I moved out here. Why, Biff can fell any one of these trees in no time! Boys! Go right over to where they're building the apartment house and get some sand. We're gonna rebuild the entire front stoop now! Watch this, Ben!

BIFF: Yes, sir! On the double, Hap!

HAPPY (*as he and Biff run off*): I lost weight, Pop, you notice?

Charley enters in knickers, even before the boys are gone.

CHARLEY: Listen, if they steal any more from that building the watchman'll put the cops on them!

LINDA (*to Willy*): Don't let Biff . . .

Ben laughs lustily.

WILLY: You shoulda seen the lumber they brought home last week. At least a dozen six-by-tens worth all kinds a money.

CHARLEY: Listen, if that watchman —

WILLY: I gave them hell, understand. But I got a couple of fearless characters there.

CHARLEY: Willy, the jails are full of fearless characters.

BEN (*clapping Willy on the back, with a laugh at Charley*): And the stock exchange, friend!

WILLY (*joining in Ben's laughter*): Where are the rest of your pants?

CHARLEY: My wife bought them.

WILLY: Now all you need is a golf club and you can go upstairs and go to sleep. (*To Ben*). Great athlete! Between him and his son Bernard they can't hammer a nail!

BERNARD (*rushing in*): The watchman's chasing Biff!

WILLY (*angrily*): Shut up! He's not stealing anything!

LINDA (*alarmed, hurrying off left*): Where is he? Biff, dear! (*She exits.*)

WILLY (*moving toward the left, away from Ben*): There's nothing wrong. What's the matter with you?

BEN: Nervy boy. Good!

WILLY (*laughing*): Oh, nerves of iron, that Biff!

CHARLEY: Don't know what it is. My New England man comes back and he's bleedin', they murdered him up there.

WILLY: It's contacts, Charley, I got important contacts!

CHARLEY (*sarcastically*): Glad to hear it, Willy. Come in later, we'll shoot a little casino. I'll take some of your Portland money. (*He laughs at Willy and exits.*)

WILLY (*turning to Ben*): Business is bad, it's murderous. But not for me, of course.

BEN: I'll stop by on my way back to Africa.

WILLY (*longingly*): Can't you stay a few days? You're just what I need, Ben, because I — I have a fine position here, but I — well, Dad left when I was such a baby and I never had a chance to talk to him and I still feel — kind of temporary about myself.

BEN: I'll be late for my train.

They are at opposite ends of the stage.

WILLY: Ben, my boys — can't we talk? They'd go into the jaws of hell for me, see, but I —

BEN: William, you're being first-rate with your boys. Outstanding, manly chaps!

WILLY (*hanging on to his words*): Oh, Ben, that's good to hear! Because sometimes I'm afraid that I'm not teaching them the right kind of — Ben, how should I teach them?

BEN (*giving great weight to each word, and with a certain vicious audacity*): William, when I walked into the jungle, I was seventeen. When I walked out I was twenty-one. And, by God, I was rich! (*He goes off into darkness around the right corner of the house.*)

WILLY: . . . was rich! That's just the spirit I want to imbue them with! To walk into a jungle! I was right! I was right! I was right!

Ben is gone, but Willy is still speaking to him as Linda, in nightgown and robe, enters the kitchen, glances around for Willy, then goes to the door of the house, looks out, and sees him. Comes down to his left. He looks at her.

LINDA: Willy, dear? Willy?

WILLY: I was right!

LINDA: Did you have some cheese? (*He can't answer.*) It's very late, darling. Come to bed, heh?

WILLY (*looking straight up*): Gotta break your neck to see a star in this yard.

LINDA: You coming in?

WILLY: Whatever happened to that diamond watch fob? Remember? When Ben came from Africa that time? Didn't he give me a watch fob with a diamond in it?

LINDA: You pawned it, dear. Twelve, thirteen years ago. For Biff's radio correspondence course.

WILLY: Gee, that was a beautiful thing. I'll take a walk.

LINDA: But you're in your slippers.

WILLY (*starting to go around the house at the left*): I was right! I was! (*Half to Linda, as he goes, shaking his head.*) What a man! There was a man worth talking to. I was right!

LINDA (*calling after Willy*): But in your slippers, Willy!

Willy is almost gone when Biff, in his pajamas, comes down the stairs and enters the kitchen.

BIFF: What is he doing out there?

LINDA: Sh!

BIFF: God Almighty, Mom, how long has he been doing this?

LINDA: Don't, he'll hear you.

BIFF: What the hell is the matter with him?

LINDA: It'll pass by morning.

BIFF: Shouldn't we do anything?

LINDA: Oh, my dear, you should do a lot of things, but there's nothing to do, so go to sleep.

Happy comes down the stairs and sits on the steps.

HAPPY: I never heard him so loud, Mom.

LINDA: Well, come around more often; you'll hear him. (*She sits down at the table and mends the lining of Willy's jacket.*)

BIFF: Why didn't you ever write me about this, Mom?

LINDA: How would I write to you? For over three months you had no address.

BIFF: I was on the move. But you know I thought of you all the time. You know that, don't you, pal?

LINDA: I know, dear, I know. But he likes to have a letter. Just to know that there's still a possibility for better things.

BIFF: He's not like this all the time, is he?

LINDA: It's when you come home he's always the worst.

BIFF: When I come home?

LINDA: When you write you're coming, he's all smiles, and talks about the future, and — he's just wonderful. And then the closer you seem to come, the more shaky he gets, and then, by the time you get here, he's arguing, and he seems angry at you. I think it's just that maybe he can't bring himself to — to open up to you. Why are you so hateful to each other? Why is that?

BIFF (*evasively*): I'm not hateful, Mom.

LINDA: But you no sooner come in the door than you're fighting!

BIFF: I don't know why. I mean to change. I'm tryin', Mom, you understand?

LINDA: Are you home to stay now?

BIFF: I don't know. I want to look around, see what's doin'.

LINDA: Biff, you can't look around all your life, can you?

BIFF: I just can't take hold, Mom. I can't take hold of some kind of a life.

LINDA: Biff, a man is not a bird, to come and go with the springtime.

BIFF: Your hair . . . (*He touches her hair.*) Your hair got so gray.

LINDA: Oh, it's been gray since you were in high school. I just stopped dyeing it, that's all.

BIFF: Dye it again, will ya? I don't want my pal looking old. (*He smiles.*)

LINDA: You're such a boy! You think you can go away for a year and . . . You've got to get it into your head now that one day you'll knock on this door and there'll be strange people here —

BIFF: What are you talking about? You're not even sixty, Mom.

LINDA: But what about your father?

BIFF (*lamely*): Well, I meant him too.

HAPPY: He admires Pop.

LINDA: Biff, dear, if you don't have any feeling for him, then you can't have any feeling for me.

BIFF: Sure I can, Mom.

LINDA: No. You can't just come to see me, because I love him. (*With a threat, but only a threat, of tears.*) He's the dearest man in the world to me, and I won't have anyone making him feel unwanted and low and blue. You've got to make up your mind now, darling, there's no leeway any more. Either he's your father and you pay him that respect, or else you're not to come here. I know he's not easy to get along with — nobody knows that better than me — but . . .

WILLY (*from the left, with a laugh*): Hey, hey, Biffo!

BIFF (*starting to go out after Willy*): What the hell is the matter with him? (*Happy stops him.*)

LINDA: Don't — don't go near him!

BIFF: Stop making excuses for him! He always, always wiped the floor with you. Never had an ounce of respect for you.

HAPPY: He's always had respect for —

BIFF: What the hell do you know about it?

HAPPY (*surlily*): Just don't call him crazy!

BIFF: He's got no character — Charley wouldn't do this. Not in his own house — spewing out that vomit from his mind.

HAPPY: Charley never had to cope with what he's got to.

BIFF: People are worse off than Willy Loman. Believe me, I've seen them!

LINDA: Then make Charley your father, Biff. You can't do that, can you? I don't say he's a great man. Willy Loman never made a lot of money. His name was never in the paper. He's not the finest character that ever lived. But he's a human being, and a terrible thing is happening to him. So attention must be paid. He's not to be allowed to fall into his grave like an old dog. Attention, attention must be finally paid to such a person. You called him crazy —

BIFF: I didn't mean —

LINDA: No, a lot of people think he's lost his — balance. But you don't have to be very smart to know what his trouble is. The man is exhausted.

HAPPY: Sure!

LINDA: A small man can be just as exhausted as a great man. He works for a company thirty-six years this March, opens up unheard-of territories to their trademark, and now in his old age they take his salary away.

HAPPY (*indignantly*): I didn't know that, Mom.

LINDA: You never asked, my dear! Now that you get your spending money someplace else you don't trouble your mind with him.

HAPPY: But I gave you money last —

LINDA: Christmas time, fifty dollars! To fix the hot water it cost ninety-seven fifty! For five weeks he's been on straight commission, like a beginner, an unknown!

BIFF: Those ungrateful bastards!

LINDA: Are they any worse than his sons? When he brought them business, when he was young, they were glad to see him. But now his old friends, the old buyers that loved him so and always found some order to hand him in a pinch — they're all dead, retired. He used to be able to make six, seven calls a day in Boston. Now he takes his valises out of the car and puts them back and takes them out again and he's exhausted. Instead of walking he talks now. He drives seven hundred miles, and when he gets there no one knows him any more, no one welcomes him. And what goes through a man's mind, driving seven hundred miles home without having earned a cent? Why shouldn't he talk to himself? Why? When he has to go to Charley and borrow fifty dollars a week and pretend to me that it's his pay? How long can that go on? How long? You see what I'm sitting here and waiting for? And you tell me he has no character? The man who never worked a day but for your benefit? When does he get the medal for that? Is this his reward — to turn around at the age of sixty-three and find his sons, who he loved better than his life, one a philandering bum —

HAPPY: Mom!

LINDA: That's all you are, my baby! (*To Biff.*) And you! What happened to the love you had for him? You were such pals! How you used to talk to him on the phone every night! How lonely he was till he could come home to you!

BIFF: All right, Mom. I'll live here in my room, and I'll get a job. I'll keep away from him, that's all.

LINDA: No, Biff. You can't stay here and fight all the time.

BIFF: He threw me out of this house, remember that.

LINDA: Why did he do that? I never knew why.

BIFF: Because I know he's a fake and he doesn't like anybody around who knows!

LINDA: Why a fake? In what way? What do you mean?

BIFF: Just don't lay it all at my feet. It's between me and him — that's all I have to say. I'll chip in from now on. He'll settle for half my pay check. He'll be all right. I'm going to bed. (*He starts for the stairs.*)

LINDA: He won't be all right.

BIFF (*turning on the stairs, furiously*): I hate this city and I'll stay here. Now what do you want?

LINDA: He's dying, Biff.

Happy turns quickly to her, shocked.

BIFF (*after a pause*): Why is he dying?

LINDA: He's been trying to kill himself.

BIFF (*with great horror*): How?

LINDA: I live from day to day.

BIFF: What're you talking about?

LINDA: Remember I wrote you that he smashed up the car again? In February?

BIFF: Well?

LINDA: The insurance inspector came. He said that they have evidence. That all these accidents in the last year — weren't — weren't — accidents.

HAPPY: How can they tell that? That's a lie.

LINDA: It seems there's a woman . . . (*She takes a breath as*):

    BIFF (*sharply but contained*): What woman?

    LINDA (*simultaneously*): . . . and this woman . . . .

LINDA: What?

BIFF: Nothing. Go ahead.

LINDA: What did you say?

BIFF: Nothing. I just said what woman?

HAPPY: What about her?

LINDA: Well, it seems she was walking down the road and saw his car. She says that he wasn't driving fast at all, and that he didn't skid. She says he came to that little bridge, and then deliberately smashed into the railing, and it was only the shallowness of the water that saved him.

BIFF: Oh, no, he probably just fell asleep again.

LINDA: I don't think he fell asleep.

BIFF: Why not?

LINDA: Last month . . . (*With great difficulty.*) Oh, boys, it's so hard to say a thing like this! He's just a big stupid man to you, but I tell you there's more good in him than in many other people. (*She chokes, wipes her eyes.*) I was looking for a fuse. The lights blew out, and I went down the cellar. And behind the fuse box — it happened to fall out — was a length of rubber pipe — just short.

HAPPY: No kidding?

LINDA: There's a little attachment on the end of it. I knew right away. And sure enough, on the bottom of the water heater there's a new little nipple on the gas pipe.

HAPPY (*angrily*): That — jerk.

BIFF: Did you have it taken off?

LINDA: I'm — I'm ashamed to. How can I mention it to him? Every day I go down and take away that little rubber pipe. But, when he comes home, I put it back where it was. How can I insult him that way? I don't know what to do. I live from day to day, boys. I tell you, I know every thought in his mind. It sounds so old-fashioned and silly, but I tell you he put his whole life into you and you've turned your backs on him. (*She is bent over in chair, weeping, her face in her hands.*) Biff, I swear to God! Biff, his life is in your hands!

HAPPY (*to Biff*): How do you like that damned fool!

BIFF (*kissing her*): All right, pal, all right. It's all settled now. I've been remiss. I know that, Mom. But now I'll stay, and I swear to you, I'll apply myself. (*Kneeling in front of her, in a fever of self-reproach.*) It's just — you see, Mom, I don't fit in business. Not that I won't try. I'll try, and I'll make good.

HAPPY: Sure you will. The trouble with you in business was you never tried to please people.

BIFF: I know, I —

HAPPY: Like when you worked for Harrison's. Bob Harrison said you were tops, and then you go and do some damn fool thing like whistling whole songs in the elevator like a comedian.

BIFF (*against Happy*): So what? I like to whistle sometimes.

HAPPY: You don't raise a guy to a responsible job who whistles in the elevator!

LINDA: Well, don't argue about it now.

HAPPY: Like when you'd go off and swim in the middle of the day instead of taking the line around.

BIFF (*his resentment rising*): Well, don't you run off? You take off sometimes, don't you? On a nice summer day?

HAPPY: Yeah, but I cover myself!

LINDA: Boys!

HAPPY: If I'm going to take a fade the boss can call any number where I'm supposed to be and they'll swear to him that I just left. I'll tell you something that I hate to say, Biff, but in the business world some of them think you're crazy.

BIFF (*angered*): Screw the business world!

HAPPY: All right, screw it! Great, but cover yourself!

LINDA: Hap, Hap!

BIFF: I don't care what they think! They've laughed at Dad for years, and you know why? Because we don't belong in this nuthouse of a city! We should be mixing cement on some open plain, or — or carpenters. A carpenter is allowed to whistle!

Willy walks in from the entrance of the house, at left.

WILLY: Even your grandfather was better than a carpenter. (*Pause. They watch him.*) You never grew up. Bernard does not whistle in the elevator, I assure you.

BIFF (*as though to laugh Willy out of it*): Yeah, but you do, Pop.

WILLY: I never in my life whistled in an elevator! And who in the business world thinks I'm crazy?

BIFF: I didn't mean it like that, Pop. Now don't make a whole thing out of it, will ya?

WILLY: Go back to the West! Be a carpenter, a cowboy, enjoy yourself!

LINDA: Willy, he was just saying —

WILLY: I heard what he said!

HAPPY (*trying to quiet Willy*): Hey, Pop, come on now . . .

WILLY (*continuing over Happy's line*): They laugh at me, heh? Go to Filene's, go to the Hub, go to Slattery's, Boston. Call out the name Willy Loman and see what happens! Big shot!

BIFF: All right, Pop.

WILLY: Big!

BIFF: All right!

WILLY: Why do you always insult me?

BIFF: I didn't say a word. (*To Linda.*) Did I say a word?

LINDA: He didn't say anything, Willy.

WILLY (*going to the doorway of the living-room*): All right, good night, good night.

LINDA: Willy, dear, he just decided . . .

WILLY (*to Biff*): If you get tired hanging around tomorrow, paint the ceiling I put up in the living-room.

BIFF: I'm leaving early tomorrow.

HAPPY: He's going to see Bill Oliver, Pop.

WILLY (*interestedly*): Oliver? For what?

BIFF (*with reserve, but trying, trying*): He always said he'd stake me. I'd like to go into business, so maybe I can take him up on it.

LINDA: Isn't that wonderful?

WILLY: Don't interrupt. What's wonderful about it? There's fifty men in the City of New York who'd stake him. (*To Biff.*) Sporting goods?

BIFF: I guess so. I know something about it and —

WILLY: He knows something about it! You know sporting goods better than Spalding, for God's sake! How much is he giving you?

BIFF: I don't know, I didn't even see him yet, but —

WILLY: Then what're you talkin' about?

BIFF (*getting angry*): Well, all I said was I'm gonna see him, that's all!

WILLY (*turning away*): Ah, you're counting your chickens again.

BIFF (*starting left for the stairs*): Oh, Jesus, I'm going to sleep!

WILLY (*calling after him*): Don't curse in this house!

BIFF (*turning*): Since when did you get so clean?

HAPPY (*trying to stop them*): Wait a . . .

WILLY: Don't use that language to me! I won't have it!

HAPPY (*grabbing Biff, shouts*): Wait a minute! I got an idea. I got a feasible idea. Come here, Biff, let's talk this over now, let's talk some sense here. When I was down in Florida last time, I thought of a great idea to sell sporting goods. It just came back to me. You and I, Biff — we have a line, the Loman Line. We train a couple of weeks, and put on a couple of exhibitions, see?

WILLY: That's an idea!

HAPPY: Wait! We form two basketball teams, see? Two water-polo teams. We play each other. It's a million dollars' worth of publicity. Two brothers, see? The Loman Brothers. Displays in the Royal Palms — all the hotels. And banners over the ring and the basketball court: "Loman Brothers." Baby, we could sell sporting goods!

WILLY: That is a one-million-dollar idea!

LINDA: Marvelous!

BIFF: I'm in great shape as far as that's concerned.

HAPPY: And the beauty of it is, Biff, it wouldn't be like a business. We'd be out playin' ball again . . .

BIFF (*enthused*): Yeah, that's . . .

WILLY: Million-dollar . . .

HAPPY: And you wouldn't get fed up with it, Biff. It'd be the family again. There'd be the old honor, and comradeship, and if you wanted to go off for a swim or somethin' — well, you'd do it! Without some smart cooky gettin' up ahead of you!

WILLY: Lick the world! You guys together could absolutely lick the civilized world.

BIFF: I'll see Oliver tomorrow. Hap, if we could work that out . . .

LINDA: Maybe things are beginning to —

WILLY (*wildly enthused, to Linda*): Stop interrupting! (*To Biff.*) But don't wear sport jacket and slacks when you see Oliver.

BIFF: No, I'll —

WILLY: A business suit, and talk as little as possible, and don't crack any jokes.

BIFF: He did like me. Always liked me.

LINDA: He loved you!

WILLY (*to Linda*): Will you stop! (*To Biff.*) Walk in very serious. You are not applying for a boy's job. Money is to pass. Be quiet, fine, and serious. Everybody likes a kidder, but nobody lends him money.

HAPPY: I'll try to get some myself, Biff. I'm sure I can.

WILLY: I see great things for you kids, I think your troubles are over. But remember, start big and you'll end big. Ask for fifteen. How much you gonna ask for?

BIFF: Gee, I don't know —

WILLY: And don't say "Gee." "Gee" is a boy's word. A man walking in for fifteen thousand dollars does not say "Gee!"

BIFF: Ten, I think, would be top though.

WILLY: Don't be so modest. You always started too low. Walk in with a big laugh. Don't look worried. Start off with a couple of your good stories to lighten things up. It's not what you say, it's how you say it — because personality always wins the day.

LINDA: Oliver always thought the highest of him —

WILLY: Will you let me talk?

BIFF: Don't yell at her, Pop, will ya?

WILLY (*angrily*): I was talking, wasn't I?

BIFF: I don't like you yelling at her all the time, and I'm tellin' you, that's all.

WILLY: What're you, takin' over this house?

LINDA: Willy —

WILLY (*turning on her*): Don't take his side all the time, goddammit!

BIFF (*furiously*): Stop yelling at her!

WILLY (*suddenly pulling on his cheek, beaten down, guilt ridden*): Give my best to Bill Oliver — he may remember me. (*He exits through the living-room doorway.*)

LINDA (*her voice subdued*): What'd you have to start that for? (*Biff turns away.*) You see how sweet he was as soon as you talked hopefully? (*She goes over to Biff.*) Come up and say good night to him. Don't let him go to bed that way.

HAPPY: Come on, Biff, let's buck him up.

LINDA: Please, dear. Just say good night. It takes so little to make him happy. Come. (*She goes through the living-room doorway, calling upstairs from within the living-room.*) Your pajamas are hanging in the bathroom, Willy!

HAPPY (*looking toward where Linda went out*): What a woman! They broke the mold when they made her. You know that, Biff?

BIFF: He's off salary. My God, working on commission!

HAPPY: Well, let's face it: he's no hot-shot selling man. Except that sometimes, you have to admit, he's a sweet personality.

BIFF (*deciding*): Lend me ten bucks, will ya? I want to buy some new ties.

HAPPY: I'll take you to a place I know. Beautiful stuff. Wear one of my striped shirts tomorrow.

BIFF: She got gray. Mom got awful old. Gee, I'm gonna go in to Oliver tomorrow and knock him for a —

HAPPY: Come on up. Tell that to Dad. Let's give him a whirl. Come on.

BIFF (*steamed up*): You know, with ten thousand bucks, boy!

HAPPY (*as they go into the living-room*): That's the talk, Biff, that's the first time I've heard the old confidence out of you! (*From within the living-room, fading off.*) You're gonna live with me, kid, and any babe you want just say the word . . . (*The last lines are hardly heard. They are mounting the stairs to their parents' bedroom.*)

LINDA (*entering her bedroom and addressing Willy, who is in the bathroom. She is straightening the bed for him*): Can you do anything about the shower? It drips.

WILLY (*from the bathroom*): All of a sudden everything falls to pieces! Goddam plumbing, oughta be sued, those people. I hardly finished putting it in and the thing . . . (*His words rumble off.*)

LINDA: I'm just wondering if Oliver will remember him. You think he might?

WILLY (*coming out of the bathroom in his pajamas*): Remember him? What's the matter with you, you crazy? If he'd've stayed with Oliver he'd be on top by now! Wait'll Oliver gets a look at him. You don't know the average caliber any more. The average young man today — (*he is getting into bed*) — is got a caliber of zero. Greatest thing in the world for him was to bum around.

Biff and Happy enter the bedroom. Slight pause.

WILLY (*stops short, looking at Biff*): Glad to hear it, boy.

HAPPY: He wanted to say good night to you, sport.

WILLY (*to Biff*): Yeah. Knock him dead, boy. What'd you want to tell me?

BIFF: Just take it easy, Pop. Good night. (*He turns to go.*)

WILLY (*unable to resist*): And if anything falls off the desk while you're talking to him — like a package or something — don't you pick it up. They have office boys for that.

LINDA: I'll make a big breakfast —

WILLY: Will you let me finish? (*To Biff.*) Tell him you were in the business in the West. Not farm work.

BIFF: All right, Dad.

LINDA: I think everything —

WILLY (*going right through her speech*): And don't undersell yourself. No less than fifteen thousand dollars.

BIFF (*unable to bear him*): Okay. Good night, Mom. (*He starts moving.*)

WILLY: Because you got a greatness in you, Biff, remember that. You got all kinds a greatness . . . (*He lies back, exhausted. Biff walks out.*)

LINDA (*calling after Biff*): Sleep well, darling!

HAPPY: I'm gonna get married, Mom. I wanted to tell you.

LINDA: Go to sleep, dear.

HAPPY (*going*): I just wanted to tell you.

WILLY: Keep up the good work. (*Happy exits.*) God . . . remember that Ebbets Field game? The championship of the city?

LINDA: Just rest. Should I sing to you?

WILLY: Yeah. Sing to me. (*Linda hums a soft lullaby.*) When that team came out —
he was the tallest, remember?

LINDA: Oh, yes. And in gold.

*Biff enters the darkened kitchen, takes a cigarette, and leaves the house. He comes
downstage into a golden pool of light. He smokes, staring at the night.*

WILLY: Like a young god. Hercules — something like that. And the sun, the sun
all around him. Remember how he waved to me? Right up from the
field, with the representatives of three colleges standing by? And the
buyers I brought, and the cheers when he came out — Loman, Loman,
Loman! God Almighty, he'll be great yet. A star like that, magnificent,
can never really fade away!

*The light on Willy is fading. The gas heater begins to glow through the kitchen wall,
near the stairs, a blue flame beneath red coils.*

LINDA (*timidly*): Willy dear, what has he got against you?

WILLY: I'm so tired. Don't talk any more.

Biff slowly returns to the kitchen. He stops, stares toward the heater.

LINDA: Will you ask Howard to let you work in New York?

WILLY: First thing in the morning. Everything'll be all right.

*Biff reaches behind the heater and draws out a length of rubber tubing. He is horrified
and turns his head toward Willy's room, still dimly lit, from which the strains of
Linda's desperate but monotonous humming rise.*

WILLY (*staring through the window into the moonlight*): Gee, look at the moon
moving between the buildings!

Biff wraps the tubing around his hand and quickly goes up the stairs.

Curtain

ACT II

*Music is heard, gay and bright. The curtain rises as the music fades away. Willy, in
shirt sleeves, is sitting at the kitchen table, sipping coffee, his hat in his lap. Linda is
filling his cup when she can.*

WILLY: Wonderful coffee. Meal in itself.

LINDA: Can I make you some eggs?

WILLY: No. Take a breath.

LINDA: You look so rested, dear.

WILLY: I slept like a dead one. First time in months. Imagine, sleeping till ten on
a Tuesday morning. Boys left nice and early, heh?

LINDA: They were out of here by eight o'clock.

WILLY: Good work!

LINDA: It was so thrilling to see them leaving together. I can't get over the shaving lotion in this house!

WILLY (*smiling*): Mmm —

LINDA: Biff was very changed this morning. His whole attitude seemed to be
hopeful. He couldn't wait to get downtown to see Oliver.

WILLY: He's heading for a change. There's no question, there simply are certain men that take longer to get — solidified. How did he dress?

LINDA: His blue suit. He's so handsome in that suit. He could be a — anything in that suit!

Willy gets up from the table. Linda holds his jacket for him.

WILLY: There's no question, no question at all. Gee, on the way home tonight I'd like to buy some seeds.

LINDA (*laughing*): That'd be wonderful. But not enough sun gets back there. Nothing'll grow any more.

WILLY: You wait, kid, before it's all over we're gonna get a little place out in the country, and I'll raise some vegetables, a couple of chickens . . .

LINDA: You'll do it yet, dear.

Willy walks out of his jacket. Linda follows him.

WILLY: And they'll get married, and come for a weekend. I'd build a little guest house. 'Cause I got so many fine tools, all I'd need would be a little lumber and some peace of mind.

LINDA (*joyfully*): I sewed the lining . . .

WILLY: I could build two guest houses, so they'd both come. Did he decide how much he's going to ask Oliver for?

LINDA (*getting him into the jacket*): He didn't mention it, but I imagine ten or fifteen thousand. You going to talk to Howard today?

WILLY: Yeah. I'll put it to him straight and simple. He'll just have to take me off the road.

LINDA: And Willy, don't forget to ask for a little advance, because we've got the insurance premium. It's the grace period now.

WILLY: That's a hundred . . . ?

LINDA: A hundred and eight, sixty-eight. Because we're a little short again.

WILLY: Why are we short?

LINDA: Well, you had the motor job on the car . . .

WILLY: That goddam Studebaker!

LINDA: And you got one more payment on the refrigerator . . .

WILLY: But it just broke again!

LINDA: Well, it's old, dear.

WILLY: I told you we should've bought a well-advertised machine. Charley bought a General Electric and it's twenty years old and it's still good, that son-of-a-bitch.

LINDA: But, Willy —

WILLY: Whoever heard of a Hastings refrigerator? Once in my life I would like to own something outright before it's broken! I'm always in a race with the junkyard! I just finished paying for the car and it's on its last legs. The refrigerator consumes belts like a goddam maniac. They time those things. They time them so when you finally paid for them, they're used up.

LINDA (*buttoning up his jacket as he unbuttons it*): All told, about two hundred dollars would carry us, dear. But that includes the last payment on the mortgage. After this payment, Willy, the house belongs to us.

WILLY: It's twenty-five years!

LINDA: Biff was nine years old when we bought it.

WILLY: Well, that's a great thing. To weather a twenty-five year mortgage is —

LINDA: It's an accomplishment.

WILLY: All the cement, the lumber, the reconstruction I put in this house! There ain't a crack to be found in it any more.

LINDA: Well, it served its purpose.

WILLY: What purpose? Some stranger'll come along, move in, and that's that. If only Biff would take this house, and raise a family . . . (*He starts to go.*) Good-by, I'm late.

LINDA (*suddenly remembering*): Oh, I forgot! You're supposed to meet them for dinner.

WILLY: Me?

LINDA: At Frank's Chop House on Forty-eighth near Sixth Avenue.

WILLY: Is that so! How about you?

LINDA: No, just the three of you. They're gonna blow you to a big meal!

WILLY: Don't say! Who thought of that?

LINDA: Biff came to me this morning, Willy, and he said, "Tell Dad, we want to blow him to a big meal." Be there six o'clock. You and your two boys are going to have dinner.

WILLY: Gee whiz! That's really somethin'. I'm gonna knock Howard for a loop, kid. I'll get an advance, and I'll come home with a New York job. Goddammit, now I'm gonna do it!

LINDA: Oh, that's the spirit, Willy!

WILLY: I will never get behind a wheel the rest of my life!

LINDA: It's changing, Willy, I can feel it changing!

WILLY: Beyond a question. G'by, I'm late. (*He starts to go again.*)

LINDA (*calling after him as she runs to the kitchen table for a handkerchief*): You got your glasses?

WILLY (*feels for them, then comes back in*): Yeah, yeah, got my glasses.

LINDA (*giving him the handkerchief*): And a handkerchief.

WILLY: Yeah, handkerchief.

LINDA: And your saccharine?

WILLY: Yeah, my saccharine.

LINDA: Be careful on the subway stairs.

She kisses him, and a silk stocking is seen hanging from her hand. Willy notices it.

WILLY: Will you stop mending stockings? At least while I'm in the house. It gets me nervous. I can't tell you. Please.

Linda hides the stocking in her hand as she follows Willy across the forestage in front of the house.

LINDA: Remember, Frank's Chop House.

WILLY (*passing the apron*): Maybe beets would grow out there.

LINDA (*laughing*): But you tried so many times.

WILLY: Yeah. Well, don't work hard today. (*He disappears around the right corner of the house.*)

LINDA: Be careful!

As Willy vanishes, Linda waves to him. Suddenly the phone rings. She runs across the stage and into the kitchen and lifts it.

LINDA: Hello? Oh, Biff! I'm so glad you called, I just . . . Yes, sure, I just told him. Yes, he'll be there for dinner at six o'clock, I didn't forget. Listen, I was just dying to tell you. You know that little rubber pipe I told you about? That he connected to the gas heater? I finally decided to go down the cellar this morning and take it away and destroy it. But it's gone! Imagine? He took it away himself, it isn't there! (*She listens.*) When? Oh, then you took it. Oh — nothing, it's just that I'd hoped he'd taken it away himself. Oh, I'm not worried, darling, because this morning he left in such high spirits, it was like the old days! I'm not afraid any more. Did Mr. Oliver see you? . . . Well, you wait there then. And make a nice impression on him, darling. Just don't perspire too much before you see him. And have a nice time with Dad. He may have big news too! . . . That's right, a New York job. And be sweet to him tonight, dear. Be loving to him. Because he's only a little boat looking for a harbor. (*She is trembling with sorrow and joy.*) Oh, that's wonderful, Biff, you'll save his life. Thanks, darling. Just put your arm around him when he comes into the restaurant. Give him a smile. That's the boy . . . Good-by, dear . . . You got your comb? . . . That's fine. Good-by, Biff dear.

In the middle of her speech, Howard Wagner, thirty-six, wheels in a small typewriter table on which is a wire-recording machine and proceeds to plug it in. This is on the left forestage. Light slowly fades on Linda as it rises on Howard. Howard is intent on threading the machine and only glances over his shoulder as Willy appears.

WILLY: Pst! Pst!

HOWARD: Hello, Willy, come in.

WILLY: Like to have a little talk with you, Howard.

HOWARD: Sorry to keep you waiting. I'll be with you in a minute.

WILLY: What's that, Howard?

HOWARD: Didn't you ever see one of these? Wire recorder.

WILLY: Oh. Can we talk a minute?

HOWARD: Records things. Just got delivery yesterday. Been driving me crazy, the most terrific machine I ever saw in my life. I was up all night with it.

WILLY: What do you do with it?

HOWARD: I bought it for dictation, but you can do anything with it. Listen to this. I had it home last night. Listen to what I picked up. The first one is my daughter. Get this. (*He flicks the switch and "Roll Out the Barrel" is heard being whistled.*) Listen to that kid whistle.

WILLY: That is lifelike, isn't it?

HOWARD: Seven years old. Get that tone.

Willy: Ts, ts. Like to ask a little favor if you . . .

The whistling breaks off, and the voice of Howard's daughter is heard.

HIS DAUGHTER: "Now you, Daddy."

HOWARD: She's crazy for me! (*Again the same song is whistled.*) That's me! Ha! (*He winks.*)

WILLY: You're very good!

The whistling breaks off again. The machine runs silent for a moment.

HOWARD: Sh! Get this now, this is my son.

HIS SON: "The capital of Alabama is Montgomery; the capital of Arizona is Phoenix; the capital of Arkansas is Little Rock; the capital of California is Sacramento . . ." (*and on, and on*).

HOWARD (*holding up five fingers*): Five years old, Willy!

WILLY: He'll make an announcer some day!

HIS SON (*continuing*): "The capital . . ."

HOWARD: Get that — alphabetical order! (*The machine breaks off suddenly.*) Wait a minute. The maid kicked the plug out.

WILLY: It certainly is a —

HOWARD: Sh, for God's sake!

HIS SON: "It's nine o'clock, Bulova watch time. So I have to go to sleep."

WILLY: That really is —

HOWARD: Wait a minute! The next is my wife.

They wait.

HOWARD'S VOICE: "Go on, say something." (*Pause.*) "Well, you gonna talk?"

HIS WIFE: "I can't think of anything."

HOWARD'S VOICE: "Well, talk — it's turning."

HIS WIFE (*shyly, beaten*): "Hello." (*Silence.*) "Oh, Howard, I can't talk into this . . ."

HOWARD (*snapping the machine off*): That was my wife.

WILLY: That is a wonderful machine. Can we —

HOWARD: I tell you, Willy, I'm gonna take my camera, and my bandsaw, and all my hobbies, and out they go. This is the most fascinating relaxation I ever found.

WILLY: I think I'll get one myself.

HOWARD: Sure, they're only a hundred and a half. You can't do without it. Supposing you wanna hear Jack Benny, see? But you can't be at home at that hour. So you tell the maid to turn the radio on when Jack Benny comes on, and this automatically goes on with the radio . . .

WILLY: And when you come home you . . .

HOWARD: You can come home twelve o'clock, one o'clock, any time you like, and you get yourself a Coke and sit yourself down, throw the switch, and there's Jack Benny's program in the middle of the night!

WILLY: I'm definitely going to get one. Because lots of time I'm on the road, and I think to myself, what I must be missing on the radio!

HOWARD: Don't you have a radio in the car?

WILLY: Well, yeah, but who ever thinks of turning it on?

HOWARD: Say, aren't you supposed to be in Boston?

WILLY: That's what I want to talk to you about, Howard. You got a minute? (*He draws a chair in from the wing.*)

HOWARD: What happened? What're you doing here?

WILLY: Well . . .

HOWARD: You didn't crack up again, did you?

WILLY: Oh, no. No . . .

HOWARD: Geez, you had me worried there for a minute. What's the trouble?

WILLY: Well, tell you the truth, Howard. I've come to the decision that I'd rather not travel any more.

HOWARD: Not travel! Well, what'll you do?

WILLY: Remember, Christmas time, when you had the party here? You said you'd try to think of some spot for me here in town.

HOWARD: With us?

WILLY: Well, sure.

HOWARD: Oh, yeah, yeah. I remember. Well, I couldn't think of anything for you, Willy.

WILLY: I tell ya, Howard. The kids are all grown up, y'know. I don't need much any more. If I could take home — well, sixty-five dollars a week, I could swing it.

HOWARD: Yeah, but Willy, see I —

WILLY: I tell ya why, Howard. Speaking frankly and between the two of us, y'know — I'm just a little tired.

HOWARD: Oh, I could understand that, Willy. But you're a road man, Willy, and we do a road business. We've only got a half-dozen salesmen on the floor here.

WILLY: God knows, Howard, I never asked a favor of any man. But I was with the firm when your father used to carry you in here in his arms.

HOWARD: I know that, Willy, but —

WILLY: Your father came to me the day you were born and asked me what I thought of the name of Howard, may he rest in peace.

HOWARD: I appreciate that, Willy, but there just is no spot here for you. If I had a spot I'd slam you right in, but I just don't have a single solitary spot.

He looks for his lighter. Willy has picked it up and gives it to him. Pause.

WILLY (*with increasing anger*): Howard, all I need to set my table is fifty dollars a week.

HOWARD: But where am I going to put you, kid?

WILLY: Look, it isn't a question of whether I can sell merchandise, is it?

HOWARD: No, but it's a business, kid, and everybody's gotta pull his own weight.

WILLY (*desperately*): Just let me tell you a story, Howard —

HOWARD: 'Cause you gotta admit, business is business.

WILLY (*angrily*): Business is definitely business, but just listen for a minute. You don't understand this. When I was a boy — eighteen, nineteen — I was already on the road. And there was a question in my mind as to whether selling had a future for me. Because in those days I had a yearning to go to Alaska. See, there were three gold strikes in one month in Alaska, and I felt like going out. Just for the ride, you might say.

HOWARD (*barely interested*): Don't say.

WILLY: Oh, yeah, my father lived many years in Alaska. He was an adventurous man. We've got quite a little streak of self-reliance in our family. I thought I'd go out with my older brother and try to locate him, and maybe settle in the North with the old man. And I was almost decided to go, when I met a salesman in the Parker House. His name was Dave Singleman. And he was eighty-four years old, and he'd drummed merchandise in thirty-one states. And old Dave, he'd go up to his room, y'understand, put on his green velvet slippers — I'll never forget — and pick up his phone and call the buyers, and without ever leaving his room, at the age of eighty-four, he made his living. And when I saw that, I realized that selling was the greatest career a man could want. 'Cause what could be more satisfying than to be able to go, at the age of eighty-four, into twenty or thirty different cities, and pick up a phone, and be remembered and loved and helped by so many different people? Do you know? when he died — and by the way he died the death of a salesman, in his green velvet slippers in the smoker of the New York, New Haven, and Hartford, going into Boston — when he died, hundreds of salesmen and buyers were at his funeral. Things were sad on a lotta trains for months after that. (*He stands up. Howard has not looked at him.*) In those days there was personality in it, Howard. There was respect, and comradeship, and gratitude in it. Today, it's all cut and dried, and there's no chance for bringing friendship to bear — or personality. You see what I mean? They don't know me any more.

HOWARD (*moving away, to the right*): That's just the thing, Willy.

WILLY: If I had forty dollars a week — that's all I'd need. Forty dollars, Howard.

HOWARD: Kid, I can't take blood from a stone, I —

WILLY (*desperation is on him now*): Howard, the year Al Smith° was nominated, your father came to me and —

HOWARD (*starting to go off*): I've got to see some people, kid.

WILLY (*stopping him*): I'm talking about your father! There were promises made across this desk! You mustn't tell me you've got people to see — I put thirty-four years into this firm, Howard, and now I can't pay my insurance! You can't eat the orange and throw the peel away — a man is not a piece of fruit! (*After a pause.*) Now pay attention. Your father — in 1928 I had a big year. I averaged a hundred and seventy dollars a week in commissions.

HOWARD (*impatiently*): Now, Willy, you never averaged —

WILLY (*banging his hand on the desk*): I averaged a hundred and seventy dollars a week in the year of 1928! And your father came to me — or rather, I was in the office here — it was right over this desk — and he put his hand on my shoulder —

HOWARD (*getting up*): You'll have to excuse me, Willy, I gotta see some people. Pull yourself together. (*Going out.*) I'll be back in a little while.

On Howard's exit, the light on his chair grows very bright and strange.

Al Smith: The Democratic candidate for president of the United States in 1928, Smith lost the election to Herbert Hoover.

WILLY: Pull myself together! What the hell did I say to him? My God, I was yelling at him! How could I! (*Willy breaks off, staring at the light, which occupies the chair, animating it. He approaches this chair, standing across the desk from it.*) Frank, Frank, don't you remember what you told me that time? How you put your hand on my shoulder, and Frank . . . (*He leans on the desk and as he speaks the dead man's name he accidentally switches on the recorder, and instantly:*)

HOWARD'S SON: ". . . of New York is Albany. The capital of Ohio is Cincinnati, the capital of Rhode Island is . . . " (*The recitation continues.*)

WILLY (*leaping away with fright, shouting*): Ha! Howard! Howard! Howard!

HOWARD (*rushing in*): What happened?

WILLY (*pointing at the machine, which continues nasally, childishly, with the capital cities*): Shut it off! Shut it off!

HOWARD (*pulling the plug out*): Look, Willy . . .

WILLY (*pressing his hands to his eyes*): I gotta get myself some coffee. I'll get some coffee . . .

Willy starts to walk out. Howard stops him.

HOWARD (*rolling up the cord*): Willy, look . . .

WILLY: I'll go to Boston.

HOWARD: Willy, you can't go to Boston for us.

WILLY: Why can't I go?

HOWARD: I don't want you to represent us. I've been meaning to tell you for a long time now.

WILLY: Howard, are you firing me?

HOWARD: I think you need a good long rest, Willy.

WILLY: Howard —

HOWARD: And when you feel better, come back, and we'll see if we can work something out.

WILLY: But I gotta earn money, Howard. I'm in no position to —

HOWARD: Where are your sons? Why don't your sons give you a hand?

WILLY: They're working on a very big deal.

HOWARD: This is no time for false pride, Willy. You go to your sons and you tell them that you're tired. You've got two great boys, haven't you?

WILLY: Oh, no question, no question, but in the meantime . . .

HOWARD: Then that's that, heh?

WILLY: All right, I'll go to Boston tomorrow.

HOWARD: No, no.

WILLY: I can't throw myself on my sons. I'm not a cripple!

HOWARD: Look, kid, I'm busy this morning.

WILLY (*grasping Howard's arm*): Howard, you've got to let me go to Boston!

HOWARD (*hard, keeping himself under control*): I've got a line of people to see this morning. Sit down, take five minutes, and pull yourself together, and then go home, will ya? I need the office, Willy. (*He starts to go, turns, remembering the recorder, starts to push off the table holding the recorder.*) Oh, yeah. Whenever you can this week, stop by and drop off the samples.

You'll feel better, Willy, and then come back and we'll talk. Pull yourself together, kid, there's people outside.

Howard exits, pushing the table off left. Willy stares into space, exhausted. Now the music is heard — Ben's music — first distantly, then closer, closer. As Willy speaks, Ben enters from the right. He carries valise and umbrella.

WILLY: Oh, Ben, how did you do it? What is the answer? Did you wind up the Alaska deal already?

BEN: Doesn't take much time if you know what you're doing. Just a short business trip. Boarding ship in an hour. Wanted to say good-by.

WILLY: Ben, I've got to talk to you.

BEN (*glancing at his watch*): Haven't the time, William.

WILLY (*crossing the apron to Ben*): Ben, nothing's working out. I don't know what to do.

BEN: Now, look here, William. I've bought timberland in Alaska and I need a man to look after things for me.

WILLY: God, timberland! Me and my boys in those grand outdoors!

BEN: You've a new continent at your doorstep, William. Get out of these cities, they're full of talk and time payments and courts of law. Screw on your fists and you can fight for a fortune up there.

WILLY: Yes, yes! Linda, Linda!

Linda enters as of old, with the wash.

LINDA: Oh, you're back?

BEN: I haven't much time.

WILLY: No, wait! Linda, he's got a proposition for me in Alaska.

LINDA: But you've got — (*To Ben.*) He's got a beautiful job here.

WILLY: But in Alaska, kid, I could —

LINDA: You're doing well enough, Willy!

BEN (*to Linda*): Enough for what, my dear?

LINDA (*frightened of Ben and angry at him*): Don't say those things to him! Enough to be happy right here, right now. (*To Willy, while Ben laughs.*) Why must everybody conquer the world? You're well liked, and the boys love you, and someday — (*to Ben*) — why, old man Wagner told him just the other day that if he keeps it up he'll be a member of the firm, didn't he, Willy?

WILLY: Sure, sure. I am building something with this firm, Ben, and if a man is building something he must be on the right track, mustn't he?

BEN: What are you building? Lay your hand on it. Where is it?

WILLY (*hesitantly*): That's true, Linda, there's nothing.

LINDA: Why? (*To Ben.*) There's a man eighty-four years old —

WILLY: That's right, Ben, that's right. When I look at that man I say, what is there to worry about?

BEN: Bah!

WILLY: It's true, Ben. All he has to do is go into any city, pick up the phone, and he's making his living and you know why?

BEN (*picking up his valise*): I've got to go.

WILLY (*holding Ben back*): Look at this boy!

Biff, in his high school sweater, enters carrying suitcase. Happy carries Biff's shoulder guards, gold helmet, and football pants.

WILLY: Without a penny to his name, three great universities are begging for him, and from there the sky's the limit, because it's not what you do, Ben. It's who you know and the smile on your face! It's contacts, Ben, contacts! The whole wealth of Alaska passes over the lunch table at the Commodore Hotel, and that's the wonder, the wonder of this country, that a man can end with diamonds here on the basis of being liked! (*He turns to Biff.*) And that's why when you get out on that field today it's important. Because thousands of people will be rooting for you and loving you. (*To Ben, who has again begun to leave.*) And Ben! when he walks into a business office his name will sound out like a bell and all the doors will open to him! I've seen it, Ben, I've seen it a thousand times! You can't feel it with your hand like timber, but it's there!

BEN: Good-by, William.

WILLY: Ben, am I right? Don't you think I'm right? I value your advice.

BEN: There's a new continent at your doorstep, William. You could walk out rich. Rich! (*He is gone.*)

WILLY: We'll do it here, Ben! You hear me? We're gonna do it here!

Young Bernard rushes in. The gay music of the Boys is heard.

BERNARD: Oh, gee, I was afraid you left already!

WILLY: Why? What time is it?

BERNARD: It's half-past one!

WILLY: Well, come on, everybody! Ebbets Field next stop! Where's the pennants? (*He rushes through the wall-line of the kitchen and out into the living-room.*)

LINDA (*to Biff*): Did you pack fresh underwear?

BIFF (*who has been limbering up*): I want to go!

BERNARD: Biff, I'm carrying your helmet, ain't I?

HAPPY: I'm carrying the helmet.

BERNARD: How am I going to get in the locker room?

LINDA: Let him carry the shoulder guards. (*She puts her coat and hat on in the kitchen.*)

BERNARD: Can I, Biff? 'Cause I told everybody I'm going to be in the locker room.

HAPPY: In Ebbets Field it's the clubhouse.

BERNARD: I meant the clubhouse. Biff!

HAPPY: Biff!

BIFF (*grandly, after a slight pause*): Let him carry the shoulder guards.

HAPPY (*as he gives Bernard the shoulder guards*): Stay close to us now.

Willy rushes in with the pennants.

WILLY (*handing them out*): Everybody wave when Biff comes out on the field. (*Happy and Bernard run off.*) You set now, boy?

The music has died away.

BIFF: Ready to go, Pop. Every muscle is ready.

WILLY (*at the edge of the apron*): You realize what this means?

BIFF: That's right, Pop.

WILLY (*feeling Biff's muscles*): You're comin' home this afternoon captain of the All-Scholastic Championship Team of the City of New York.

BIFF: I got it, Pop. And remember, pal, when I take off my helmet, that touchdown is for you.

WILLY: Let's go! (*He is starting out, with his arm around Biff, when Charley enters, as of old, in knickers.*) I got no room for you, Charley.

CHARLEY: Room? For what?

WILLY: In the car.

CHARLEY: You goin' for a ride? I wanted to shoot some casino.

WILLY (*furiously*): Casino! (*Incredulously.*) Don't you realize what today is?

LINDA: Oh, he knows, Willy. He's just kidding you.

WILLY: That's nothing to kid about!

CHARLEY: No, Linda, what's goin' on?

LINDA: He's playing in Ebbets Field.

CHARLEY: Baseball in this weather?

WILLY: Don't talk to him. Come on, come on! (*He is pushing them out.*)

CHARLEY: Wait a minute, didn't you hear the news?

WILLY: What?

CHARLEY: Don't you listen to the radio? Ebbets Field just blew up.

WILLY: You go to hell! (*Charley laughs. Pushing them out.*) Come on, come on! We're late.

CHARLEY (*as they go*): Knock a homer, Biff, knock a homer!

WILLY (*the last to leave, turning to Charley*): I don't think that was funny, Charley. This is the greatest day of his life.

CHARLEY: Willy, when are you going to grow up?

WILLY: Yeah, heh? When this game is over, Charley, you'll be laughing out of the other side of your face. They'll be calling him another Red Grange. Twenty-five thousand a year.

CHARLEY (*kidding*): Is that so?

WILLY: Yeah, that's so.

CHARLEY: Well, then, I'm sorry, Willy. But tell me something.

WILLY: What?

CHARLEY: Who is Red Grange?

WILLY: Put up your hands. Goddam you, put up your hands!

Charley, chuckling, shakes his head and walks away, around the left corner of the stage. Willy follows him. The music rises to a mocking frenzy.

WILLY: Who the hell do you think you are, better than everybody else? You don't know everything, you big, ignorant, stupid . . . Put up your hands!

Light rises, on the right side of the forestage, on a small table in the reception room of Charley's office. Traffic sounds are heard. Bernard, now mature, sits whistling to himself. A pair of tennis rackets and an overnight bag are on the floor beside him.

WILLY (*offstage*): What are you walking away for? Don't walk away! If you're going to say something say it to my face! I know you laugh at me behind my back. You'll laugh out of the other side of your goddam face after this game. Touchdown! Touchdown! Eighty thousand people! Touchdown! Right between the goal posts.

Bernard is a quiet, earnest, but self-assured young man. Willy's voice is coming from right upstage now. Bernard lowers his feet off the table and listens. Jenny, his father's secretary, enters.

JENNY (*distressed*): Say, Bernard, will you go out in the hall?

BERNARD: What is that noise? Who is it?

JENNY: Mr. Loman. He just got off the elevator.

BERNARD (*getting up*): Who's he arguing with?

JENNY: Nobody. There's nobody with him. I can't deal with him any more, and your father gets all upset everytime he comes. I've got a lot of typing to do, and your father's waiting to sign it. Will you see him?

WILLY (*entering*): Touchdown! Touch — (*He sees Jenny.*) Jenny, Jenny, good to see you. How're ya? Workin'? Or still honest?

JENNY: Fine. How've you been feeling?

WILLY: Not much any more, Jenny. Ha, ha! (*He is surprised to see the rackets.*)

BERNARD: Hello, Uncle Willy.

WILLY (*almost shocked*): Bernard! Well, look who's here! (*He comes quickly, guiltily, to Bernard and warmly shakes his hand.*)

BERNARD: How are you? Good to see you.

WILLY: What are you doing here?

BERNARD: Oh, just stopped by to see Pop. Get off my feet till my train leaves. I'm going to Washington in a few minutes.

WILLY: Is he in?

BERNARD: Yes, he's in his office with the accountant. Sit down.

WILLY (*sitting down*): What're you going to do in Washington?

BERNARD: Oh, just a case I've got there, Willy.

WILLY: That so? (*Indicating the rackets.*) You going to play tennis there?

BERNARD: I'm staying with a friend who's got a court.

WILLY: Don't say. His own tennis court. Must be fine people, I bet.

BERNARD: They are, very nice. Dad tells me Biff's in town.

WILLY (*with a big smile*): Yeah, Biff's in. Working on a very big deal, Bernard.

BERNARD: What's Biff doing?

WILLY: Well, he's been doing very big things in the West. But he decided to establish himself here. Very big. We're having dinner. Did I hear your wife had a boy?

BERNARD: That's right. Our second.

WILLY: Two boys! What do you know!

BERNARD: What kind of a deal has Biff got?

WILLY: Well, Bill Oliver — very big sporting-goods man — he wants Biff very badly. Called him in from the West. Long distance, carte blanche, special deliveries. Your friends have their own private tennis court?

BERNARD: You still with the old firm, Willy?

WILLY (*after a pause*): I'm — I'm overjoyed to see how you made the grade, Bernard, overjoyed. It's an encouraging thing to see a young man really — really — Looks very good for Biff — very — (*He breaks off, then.*) Bernard — (*He is so full of emotion, he breaks off again.*)

BERNARD: What is it, Willy?

WILLY (*small and alone*): What — what's the secret?

BERNARD: What secret?

WILLY: How — how did you? Why didn't he ever catch on?

BERNARD: I wouldn't know that, Willy.

WILLY (*confidentially, desperately*): You were his friend, his boyhood friend. There's something I don't understand about it. His life ended after that Ebbets Field game. From the age of seventeen nothing good ever happened to him.

BERNARD: He never trained himself for anything.

WILLY: But he did, he did. After high school he took so many correspondence courses. Radio mechanics; television; God knows what, and never made the slightest mark.

BERNARD (*taking off his glasses*): Willy, do you want to talk candidly?

WILLY (*rising, faces Bernard*): I regard you as a very brilliant man, Bernard. I value your advice.

BERNARD: Oh, the hell with the advice, Willy. I couldn't advise you. There's just one thing I've always wanted to ask you. When he was supposed to graduate, and the math teacher flunked him —

WILLY: Oh, that son-of-a-bitch ruined his life.

BERNARD: Yeah, but, Willy, all he had to do was go to summer school and make up that subject.

WILLY: That's right, that's right.

BERNARD: Did you tell him not to go to summer school?

WILLY: Me? I begged him to go. I ordered him to go!

BERNARD: Then why wouldn't he go?

WILLY: Why? Why! Bernard, that question has been trailing me like a ghost for the last fifteen years. He flunked the subject, and laid down and died like a hammer hit him!

BERNARD: Take it easy, kid.

WILLY: Let me talk to you — I got nobody to talk to. Bernard, Bernard, was it my fault? Y'see? It keeps going around in my mind, maybe I did something to him. I got nothing to give him.

BERNARD: Don't take it so hard.

WILLY: Why did he lay down? What is the story there? You were his friend!

BERNARD: Willy, I remember, it was June, and our grades came out. And he'd flunked math.

WILLY: That son-of-a-bitch!

BERNARD: No, it wasn't right then. Biff just got very angry, I remember, and he was ready to enroll in summer school.

WILLY (*surprised*): He was?

BERNARD: He wasn't beaten by it at all. But then, Willy, he disappeared from the block for almost a month. And I got the idea that he'd gone up to New England to see you. Did he have a talk with you then?

Willy stares in silence.

BERNARD: Willy?

WILLY (*with a strong edge of resentment in his voice*): Yeah, he came to Boston. What about it?

BERNARD: Well, just that when he came back — I'll never forget this, it always mystifies me. Because I'd thought so well of Biff, even though he'd always taken advantage of me. I loved him, Willy, y'know? And he came back after that month and took his sneakers — remember those sneakers with "University of Virginia" printed on them? He was so proud of those, wore them every day. And he took them down in the cellar, and burned them up in the furnace. We had a fist fight. It lasted at least half an hour. Just the two of us, punching each other down the cellar, and crying right through it. I've often thought of how strange it was that I knew he'd given up his life. What happened in Boston, Willy?

Willy looks at him as at an intruder.

BERNARD: I just bring it up because you asked me.

WILLY (*angrily*): Nothing. What do you mean, "What happened?" What's that got to do with anything?

BERNARD: Well, don't get sore.

WILLY: What are you trying to do, blame it on me? If a boy lays down is that my fault?

BERNARD: Now, Willy, don't get —

WILLY: Well, don't — don't talk to me that way! What does that mean, "What happened?"

Charley enters. He is in his vest, and he carries a bottle of bourbon.

CHARLEY: Hey, you're going to miss that train. (*He waves the bottle.*)

BERNARD: Yeah, I'm going. (*He takes the bottle.*) Thanks, Pop. (*He picks up his rackets and bag.*) Good-by, Willy, and don't worry about it. You know. "If at first you don't succeed . . ."

WILLY: Yes, I believe in that.

BERNARD: But sometimes, Willy, it's better for a man just to walk away.

WILLY: Walk away?

BERNARD: That's right.

WILLY: But if you can't walk away?

BERNARD (*after a slight pause*): I guess that's when it's tough. (*Extending his hand.*) Good-by, Willy.

WILLY (*shaking Bernard's hand*): Good-by, boy.

CHARLEY (*an arm on Bernard's shoulder*): How do you like this kid? Gonna argue a case in front of the Supreme Court.

BERNARD (*protesting*): Pop!

WILLY (*genuinely shocked, pained, and happy*): No! The Supreme Court!

BERNARD: I gotta run. 'By, Dad!

CHARLEY: Knock 'em dead, Bernard!

Bernard goes off.

WILLY (*as Charley takes out his wallet*): The Supreme Court! And he didn't even mention it!

CHARLEY (*counting out money on the desk*): He don't have to — he's gonna do it.

WILLY: And you never told him what to do, did you? You never took any interest in him.

CHARLEY: My salvation is that I never took any interest in any thing. There's
some money — fifty dollars. I got an accountant inside.

WILLY: Charley, look . . . (*With difficulty.*) I got my insurance to pay. If you can
manage it — I need a hundred and ten dollars.

Charley doesn't reply for a moment; merely stops moving.

WILLY: I'd draw it from my bank but Linda would know, and I . . .

CHARLEY: Sit down, Willy.

WILLY (*moving toward the chair*): I'm keeping an account of everything, remember. I'll pay every penny back. (*He sits.*)

CHARLEY: Now listen to me, Willy.

WILLY: I want you to know I appreciate . . .

CHARLEY (*sitting down on the table*): Willy, what're you doin'? What the hell is
goin' on in your head?

WILLY: Why? I'm simply . . .

CHARLEY: I offered you a job. You can make fifty dollars a week. And I won't
send you on the road.

WILLY: I've got a job.

CHARLEY: Without pay? What kind of a job is a job without pay? (*He rises.*)
Now, look, kid, enough is enough. I'm no genius but I know when I'm
being insulted.

WILLY: Insulted!

CHARLEY: Why don't you want to work for me?

WILLY: What's the matter with you? I've got a job.

CHARLEY: Then what're you walkin' in here every week for?

WILLY (*getting up*): Well, if you don't want me to walk in here —

CHARLEY: I am offering you a job.

WILLY: I don't want your goddam job!

CHARLEY: When the hell are you going to grow up?

WILLY (*furiously*): You big ignoramus, if you say that to me again I'll rap you
one! I don't care how big you are! (*He's ready to fight.*)

Pause.

CHARLEY (*kindly, going to him*): How much do you need, Willy?

WILLY: Charley, I'm strapped. I'm strapped. I don't know what to do. I was just
fired.

CHARLEY: Howard fired you?

WILLY: That snotnose. Imagine that? I named him. I named him Howard.

CHARLEY: Willy, when're you gonna realize that them things don't mean anything? You named him Howard, but you can't sell that. The only thing
you got in this world is what you can sell. And the funny thing is that
you're a salesman, and you don't know that.

WILLY: I've always tried to think otherwise, I guess. I always felt that if a man
was impressive, and well liked, that nothing —

CHARLEY: Why must everybody like you? Who liked J. P. Morgan? Was he impressive? In a Turkish bath he'd look like a butcher. But with his pockets

on he was very well liked. Now listen, Willy, I know you don't like me, and nobody can say I'm in love with you, but I'll give you a job because — just for the hell of it, put it that way. Now what do you say?

WILLY: I — I just can't work for you, Charley.

CHARLEY: What're you, jealous of me?

WILLY: I can't work for you, that's all, don't ask me why.

CHARLEY (*angered, takes out more bills*): You been jealous of me all your life, you damned fool! Here, pay your insurance. (*He puts the money in Willy's hand.*)

WILLY: I'm keeping strict accounts.

CHARLEY: I've got some work to do. Take care of yourself. And pay your insurance.

WILLY (*moving to the right*): Funny, y'know? After all the highways, and the trains, and the appointments, and the years, you end up worth more dead than alive.

CHARLEY: Willy, nobody's worth nothin' dead. (*After a slight pause.*) Did you hear what I said?

Willy stands still, dreaming.

CHARLEY: Willy!

WILLY: Apologize to Bernard for me when you see him. I didn't mean to argue with him. He's a fine boy. They're all fine boys, and they'll end up big — all of them. Someday they'll all play tennis together. Wish me luck, Charley. He saw Bill Oliver today.

CHARLEY: Good luck.

WILLY (*on the verge of tears*): Charley, you're the only friend I got. Isn't that a remarkable thing? (*He goes out.*)

CHARLEY: Jesus!

Charley stares after him a moment and follows. All light blacks out. Suddenly raucous music is heard, and a red glow rises behind the screen at right. Stanley, a young waiter, appears, carrying a table, followed by Happy, who is carrying two chairs.

STANLEY (*putting the table down*): That's all right, Mr. Loman, I can handle it myself. (*He turns and takes the chairs from Happy and places them at the table.*)

HAPPY (*glancing around*): Oh, this is better.

STANLEY: Sure, in the front there you're in the middle of all kinds a noise. Whenever you got a party, Mr. Loman, you just tell me and I'll put you back here. Y'know, there's a lotta people they don't like it private, because when they go out they like to see a lotta action around them because they're sick and tired to stay in the house by theirself. But I know you, you ain't from Hackensack. You know what I mean?

HAPPY (*sitting down*): So how's it coming, Stanley?

STANLEY: Ah, it's a dog's life. I only wish during the war they'd a took me in the Army. I coulda been dead by now.

HAPPY: My brother's back, Stanley.

STANLEY: Oh, he come back, heh? From the Far West.

HAPPY: Yeah, big cattle man, my brother, so treat him right. And my father's coming too.

STANLEY: Oh, your father too!

HAPPY: You got a couple of nice lobsters?

STANLEY: Hundred per cent, big.

HAPPY: I want them with the claws.

STANLEY: Don't worry, I don't give you no mice. (*Happy laughs.*) How about some wine? It'll put a head on the meal.

HAPPY: No. You remember, Stanley, that recipe I brought you from overseas? With the champagne in it?

STANLEY: Oh, yeah, sure. I still got it tacked up yet in the kitchen. But that'll have to cost a buck apiece anyways.

HAPPY: That's all right.

STANLEY: What'd you, hit a number or somethin'?

HAPPY: No, it's a little celebration. My brother is — I think he pulled off a big deal today. I think we're going into business together.

STANLEY: Great! That's the best for you. Because a family business, you know what I mean? — that's the best.

HAPPY: That's what I think.

STANLEY: 'Cause what's the difference? Somebody steals? It's in the family. Know what I mean? (*Sotto voce.°*) Like this bartender here. The boss is goin' crazy what kinda leak he's got in the cash register. You put it in but it don't come out.

HAPPY (*raising his head*): Sh!

STANLEY: What?

HAPPY: You notice I wasn't lookin' right or left, was I?

STANLEY: No.

HAPPY: And my eyes are closed.

STANLEY: So what's the — ?

HAPPY: Strudel's comin'.

STANLEY (*catching on, looks around*): Ah, no, there's no —

He breaks off as a furred, lavishly dressed girl enters and sits at the next table. Both follow her with their eyes.

STANLEY: Geez, how'd ya know?

HAPPY: I got radar or something. (*Staring directly at her profile.*) Oooooooo . . . Stanley.

STANLEY: I think that's for you, Mr. Loman.

HAPPY: Look at that mouth. Oh, God. And the binoculars.

STANLEY: Geez, you got a life, Mr. Loman.

HAPPY: Wait on her.

STANLEY (*going to the girl's table*): Would you like a menu, ma'am?

GIRL: I'm expecting someone, but I'd like a —

HAPPY: Why don't you bring her — excuse me, miss, do you mind? I sell champagne, and I'd like you to try my brand. Bring her a champagne, Stanley.

GIRL: That's awfully nice of you.

HAPPY: Don't mention it. It's all company money. (*He laughs.*)

Sotto voce: Softly, "under the breath" (Italian).

GIRL: That's a charming product to be selling, isn't it?

HAPPY: Oh, gets to be like everything else. Selling is selling, y'know.

GIRL: I suppose.

HAPPY: You don't happen to sell, do you?

GIRL: No, I don't sell.

HAPPY: Would you object to a compliment from a stranger? You ought to be on a magazine cover.

GIRL (*looking at him a little archly*): I have been.

Stanley comes in with a glass of champagne.

HAPPY: What'd I say before, Stanley? You see? She's a cover girl.

STANLEY: Oh, I could see, I could see.

HAPPY (*to the Girl*): What magazine?

GIRL: Oh, a lot of them. (*She takes the drink.*) Thank you.

HAPPY: You know what they say in France, don't you? "Champagne is the drink of the complexion" — Hya, Biff!

Biff has entered and sits with Happy.

BIFF: Hello, kid. Sorry I'm late.

HAPPY: I just got here. Uh, Miss — ?

GIRL: Forsythe.

HAPPY: Miss Forsythe, this is my brother.

BIFF: Is Dad here?

HAPPY: His name is Biff. You might've heard of him. Great football player.

GIRL: Really? What team?

HAPPY: Are you familiar with football?

GIRL: No, I'm afraid I'm not.

HAPPY: Biff is quarterback with the New York Giants.

GIRL: Well, that is nice, isn't it? (*She drinks.*)

HAPPY: Good health.

GIRL: I'm happy to meet you.

HAPPY: That's my name. Hap. It's really Harold, but at West Point they called me Happy.

GIRL (*now really impressed*): Oh, I see. How do you do? (*She turns her profile.*)

BIFF: Isn't Dad coming?

HAPPY: You want her?

BIFF: Oh, I could never make that.

HAPPY: I remember the time that idea would never come into your head. Where's the old confidence, Biff?

BIFF: I just saw Oliver —

HAPPY: Wait a minute. I've got to see that old confidence again. Do you want her? She's on call.

BIFF: Oh, no. (*He turns to look at the Girl.*)

HAPPY: I'm telling you. Watch this. (*Turning to the Girl.*) Honey? (*She turns to him.*) Are you busy?

GIRL: Well, I am . . . but I could make a phone call.

HAPPY: Do that, will you, honey? And see if you can get a friend. We'll be here for a while. Biff is one of the greatest football players in the country.

GIRL (*standing up*): Well, I'm certainly happy to meet you.

HAPPY: Come back soon.

GIRL: I'll try.

HAPPY: Don't try, honey, try hard.

The Girl exits. Stanley follows, shaking his head in bewildered admiration.

HAPPY: Isn't that a shame now? A beautiful girl like that? That's why I can't get married. There's not a good woman in a thousand. New York is loaded with them, kid!

BIFF: Hap, look —

HAPPY: I told you she was on call!

BIFF (*strangely unnerved*): Cut it out, will ya? I want to say something to you.

HAPPY: Did you see Oliver?

BIFF: I saw him all right. Now look, I want to tell Dad a couple of things and I want you to help me.

HAPPY: What? Is he going to back you?

BIFF: Are you crazy? You're out of your goddam head, you know that?

HAPPY: Why? What happened?

BIFF (*breathlessly*): I did a terrible thing today, Hap. It's been the strangest day I ever went through. I'm all numb, I swear.

HAPPY: You mean he wouldn't see you?

BIFF: Well, I waited six hours for him, see? All day. Kept sending my name in. Even tried to date his secretary so she'd get me to him, but no soap.

HAPPY: Because you're not showin' the old confidence, Biff. He remembered you, didn't he?

BIFF (*stopping Happy with a gesture*): Finally, about five o'clock, he comes out. Didn't remember who I was or anything. I felt like such an idiot, Hap.

HAPPY: Did you tell him my Florida idea?

BIFF: He walked away. I saw him for one minute. I got so mad I could've torn the walls down! How the hell did I ever get the idea I was a salesman there? I even believed myself that I'd been a salesman for him! And then he gave me one look and — I realized what a ridiculous lie my whole life has been! We've been talking in a dream for fifteen years. I was a shipping clerk.

HAPPY: What'd you do?

BIFF (*with great tension and wonder*): Well, he left, see. And the secretary went out. I was all alone in the waiting-room. I don't know what came over me, Hap. The next thing I know I'm in his office — paneled walls, everything. I can't explain it. I — Hap, I took his fountain pen.

HAPPY: Geez, did he catch you?

BIFF: I ran out. I ran down all eleven flights. I ran and ran and ran.

HAPPY: That was an awful dumb — what'd you do that for?

BIFF (*agonized*): I don't know, I just — wanted to take something, I don't know. You gotta help me, Hap, I'm gonna tell Pop.

HAPPY: You crazy? What for?

BIFF: Hap, he's got to understand that I'm not the man somebody lends that kind of money to. He thinks I've been spiting him all these years and it's eating him up.

HAPPY: That's just it. You tell him something nice.

BIFF: I can't.

HAPPY: Say you got a lunch date with Oliver tomorrow.

BIFF: So what do I do tomorrow?

HAPPY: You leave the house tomorrow and come back at night and say Oliver is thinking it over. And he thinks it over for a couple of weeks, and gradually it fades away and nobody's the worse.

BIFF: But it'll go on forever!

HAPPY: Dad is never so happy as when he's looking forward to something!

Willy enters.

HAPPY: Hello, scout!

WILLY: Gee, I haven't been here in years!

Stanley has followed Willy in and sets a chair for him. Stanley starts off but Happy stops him.

HAPPY: Stanley!

Stanley stands by, waiting for an order.

BIFF (*going to Willy with guilt, as to an invalid*): Sit down, Pop. You want a drink?

WILLY: Sure, I don't mind.

BIFF: Let's get a load on.

WILLY: You look worried.

BIFF: N-no. (*To Stanley.*) Scotch all around. Make it doubles.

STANLEY: Doubles, right. (*He goes.*)

WILLY: You had a couple already, didn't you?

BIFF: Just a couple, yeah.

WILLY: Well, what happened, boy? (*Nodding affirmatively, with a smile.*) Everything go all right?

BIFF (*takes a breath, then reaches out and grasps Willy's hand.*) Pal . . . (*He is smiling bravely, and Willy is smiling too.*) I had an experience today.

HAPPY: Terrific, Pop.

WILLY: That so? What happened?

BIFF (*high, slightly alcoholic, above the earth*): I'm going to tell you everything from first to last. It's been a strange day. (*Silence. He looks around, composes himself as best he can, but his breath keeps breaking the rhythm of his voice.*) I had to wait quite a while for him, and —

WILLY: Oliver.

BIFF: Yeah, Oliver. All day, as a matter of cold fact. And a lot of — instances — facts, Pop, facts about my life came back to me. Who was it, Pop? Who ever said I was a salesman with Oliver?

WILLY: Well, you were.

BIFF: No, Dad, I was a shipping clerk.

WILLY: But you were practically —

BIFF (*with determination*): Dad, I don't know who said it first, but I was never a salesman for Bill Oliver.

WILLY: What're you talking about?

BIFF: Let's hold on to the facts tonight, Pop. We're not going to get anywhere bullin' around. I was a shipping clerk.

WILLY (*angrily*): All right, now listen to me —

BIFF: Why don't you let me finish?

WILLY: I'm not interested in stories about the past or any crap of that kind because the woods are burning, boys, you understand? There's a big blaze going on all around. I was fired today.

BIFF (*shocked*): How could you be?

WILLY: I was fired, and I'm looking for a little good news to tell your mother, because the woman has waited and the woman has suffered. The gist of it is that I haven't got a story left in my head, Biff. So don't give me a lecture about facts and aspects. I am not interested. Now what've you got to say to me?

Stanley enters with three drinks. They wait until he leaves.

WILLY: Did you see Oliver?

BIFF: Jesus, Dad!

WILLY: You mean you didn't go up there?

HAPPY: Sure he went up there.

BIFF: I did. I — saw him. How could they fire you?

WILLY (*on the edge of his chair*): What kind of a welcome did he give you?

BIFF: He won't even let you work on commission?

WILLY: I'm out! (*Driving.*) So tell me, he gave you a warm welcome?

HAPPY: Sure, Pop, sure!

BIFF (*driven*): Well, it was kind of —

WILLY: I was wondering if he'd remember you. (*To Happy.*) Imagine, man doesn't see him for ten, twelve years and gives him that kind of a welcome!

HAPPY: Damn right!

BIFF (*trying to return to the offensive*): Pop, look —

WILLY: You know why he remembered you, don't you? Because you impressed him in those days.

BIFF: Let's talk quietly and get this down to the facts, huh?

WILLY (*as though Biff had been interrupting*): Well, what happened? It's great news, Biff. Did he take you into his office or'd you talk in the waiting-room?

BIFF: Well, he came in, see, and —

WILLY (*with a big smile*): What'd he say? Betcha he threw his arm around you.

BIFF: Well, he kinda —

WILLY: He's a fine man. (*To Happy.*) Very hard man to see, y'know.

HAPPY (*agreeing*): Oh, I know.

WILLY (*to Biff*): Is that where you had the drinks?

BIFF: Yeah, he gave me a couple of — no, no!

HAPPY (*cutting in*): He told him my Florida idea.

WILLY: Don't interrupt. (*To Biff.*) How'd he react to the Florida idea?

BIFF: Dad, will you give me a minute to explain?

WILLY: I've been waiting for you to explain since I sat down here! What happened? He took you into his office and what?

BIFF: Well — I talked. And — and he listened, see.

WILLY: Famous for the way he listens, y'know. What was his answer?

BIFF: His answer was — (*He breaks off, suddenly angry.*) Dad, you're not letting me tell you what I want to tell you!

WILLY (*accusing, angered*): You didn't see him, did you?

BIFF: I did see him!

WILLY: What'd you insult him or something? You insulted him, didn't you?

BIFF: Listen, will you let me out of it, will you just let me out of it!

HAPPY: What the hell!

WILLY: Tell me what happened!

BIFF (*to Happy*): I can't talk to him!

A single trumpet note jars the ear. The light of green leaves stains the house, which holds the air of night and a dream. Young Bernard enters and knocks on the door of the house.

YOUNG BERNARD (*frantically*): Mrs. Loman, Mrs. Loman!

HAPPY: Tell him what happened!

BIFF (*to Happy*): Shut up and leave me alone!

WILLY: No, no! You had to go and flunk math!

BIFF: What math? What're you talking about?

YOUNG BERNARD: Mrs. Loman, Mrs. Loman!

Linda appears in the house, as of old.

WILLY (*wildly*): Math, math, math!

BIFF: Take it easy, Pop!

YOUNG BERNARD: Mrs. Loman!

WILLY (*furiously*): If you hadn't flunked you'd've been set by now!

BIFF: Now, look, I'm gonna tell you what happened, and you're going to listen to me.

YOUNG BERNARD: Mrs. Loman!

BIFF: I waited six hours —

HAPPY: What the hell are you saying?

BIFF: I kept sending in my name but he wouldn't see me. So finally he . . . (*He continues unheard as light fades low on the restaurant.*)

YOUNG BERNARD: Biff flunked math!

LINDA: No!

YOUNG BERNARD: Birnbaum flunked him! They won't graduate him!

LINDA: But they have to. He's gotta go to the university. Where is he? Biff! Biff!

YOUNG BERNARD: No, he left. He went to Grand Central.

LINDA: Grand — You mean he went to Boston!

YOUNG BERNARD: Is Uncle Willy in Boston?

LINDA: Oh, maybe Willy can talk to the teacher. Oh, the poor, poor boy!

Light on house area snaps out.

BIFF (*at the table, now audible, holding up a gold fountain pen*): . . . so I'm washed up with Oliver, you understand? Are you listening to me?

WILLY (*at a loss*): Yeah, sure. If you hadn't flunked —

BIFF: Flunked what? What're you talking about?

WILLY: Don't blame everything on me! I didn't flunk math — you did! What pen?

HAPPY: That was awful dumb, Biff, a pen like that is worth —

WILLY (*seeing the pen for the first time*): You took Oliver's pen?

BIFF (*weakening*): Dad, I just explained it to you.

WILLY: You stole Bill Oliver's fountain pen!

BIFF: I didn't exactly steal it! That's just what I've been explaining to you!

HAPPY: He had it in his hand and just then Oliver walked in, so he got nervous and stuck it in his pocket!

WILLY: My God, Biff!

BIFF: I never intended to do it, Dad!

OPERATOR'S VOICE: Standish Arms, good evening!

WILLY (*shouting*): I'm not in my room!

BIFF (*frightened*): Dad, what's the matter? (*He and Happy stand up.*)

OPERATOR: Ringing Mr. Loman for you!

WILLY: I'm not there, stop it!

BIFF (*horrified, gets down on one knee before Willy*): Dad, I'll make good, I'll make good. (*Willy tries to get to his feet. Biff holds him down.*) Sit down now.

WILLY: No, you're no good, you're no good for anything.

BIFF: I am, Dad, I'll find something else, you understand? Now don't worry about anything. (*He holds up Willy's face.*) Talk to me, Dad.

OPERATOR: Mr. Loman does not answer. Shall I page him?

WILLY (*attempting to stand, as though to rush and silence the Operator*): No, no, no!

HAPPY: He'll strike something, Pop.

WILLY: No, no . . .

BIFF (*desperately, standing over Willy*): Pop, listen! Listen to me! I'm telling you something good. Oliver talked to his partner about the Florida idea. You listening? He — he talked to his partner, and he came to me . . . I'm going to be all right, you hear? Dad, listen to me, he said it was just a question of the amount!

WILLY: Then you . . . got it?

HAPPY: He's gonna be terrific, Pop!

WILLY (*trying to stand*): Then you got it, haven't you? You got it! You got it!

BIFF (*agonized, holds Willy down*): No, no. Look, Pop. I'm supposed to have lunch with them tomorrow. I'm just telling you this so you'll know that I can still make an impression, Pop. And I'll make good somewhere, but I can't go tomorrow, see?

WILLY: Why not? You simply —

BIFF: But the pen, Pop!

WILLY: You give it to him and tell him it was an oversight!

HAPPY: Sure, have lunch tomorrow!

BIFF: I can't say that —

WILLY: You were doing a crossword puzzle and accidentally used his pen!

BIFF: Listen, kid, I took those balls years ago, now I walk in with his fountain pen? That clinches it, don't you see? I can't face him like that! I'll try elsewhere.

PAGE'S VOICE: Paging Mr. Loman!

WILLY: Don't you want to be anything?

BIFF: Pop, how can I go back?

WILLY: You don't want to be anything, is that what's behind it?

BIFF (*now angry at Willy for not crediting his sympathy*): Don't take it that way! You think it was easy walking into that office after what I'd done to him? A team of horses couldn't have dragged me back to Bill Oliver!

WILLY: Then why'd you go?

BIFF: Why did I go? Why did I go! Look at you! Look at what's become of you!

Off left, The Woman laughs.

WILLY: Biff, you're going to lunch tomorrow, or —

BIFF: I can't go. I've got no appointment!

HAPPY: Biff, for . . . !

WILLY: Are you spiting me?

BIFF: Don't take it that way! Goddammit!

WILLY (*strikes Biff and falters away from the table*): You rotten little louse! Are you spiting me?

THE WOMAN: Someone's at the door, Willy!

BIFF: I'm no good, can't you see what I am?

HAPPY (*separating them*): Hey, you're in a restaurant! Now cut it out, both of you! (*The girls enter.*) Hello, girls, sit down.

The Woman laughs, off left.

MISS FORSYTHE: I guess we might as well. This is Letta.

THE WOMAN: Willy, are you going to wake up?

BIFF (*ignoring Willy*): How're ya, miss, sit down. What do you drink?

MISS FORSYTHE: Letta might not be able to stay long.

LETTA: I gotta get up very early tomorrow. I got jury duty. I'm so excited! Were you fellows ever on a jury?

BIFF: No, but I been in front of them! (*The girls laugh.*) This is my father.

LETTA: Isn't he cute? Sit down with us, Pop.

HAPPY: Sit him down, Biff!

BIFF (*going to him*): Come on, slugger, drink us under the table. To hell with it! Come on, sit down, pal.

On Biff's last insistence, Willy is about to sit.

THE WOMAN (*now urgently*): Willy, are you going to answer the door!

The Woman's call pulls Willy back. He starts right, befuddled.

BIFF: Hey, where are you going?

WILLY: Open the door.

BIFF: The door?

WILLY: The washroom . . . . the door . . . where's the door?

BIFF (*leading Willy to the left*): Just go straight down.

Willy moves left.

THE WOMAN: Willy, Willy, are you going to get up, get up, get up, get up?

Willy exits left.

LETTA: I think it's sweet you bring your daddy along.

MISS FORSYTHE: Oh, he isn't really your father!

BIFF (*at left, turning to her resentfully*): Miss Forsythe, you've just seen a prince walk by. A fine, troubled prince. A hard-working, unappreciated prince. A pal, you understand? A good companion. Always for his boys.

LETTA: That's so sweet.

HAPPY: Well, girls, what's the program? We're wasting time. Come on, Biff. Gather round. Where would you like to go?

BIFF: Why don't you do something for him?

HAPPY: Me!

BIFF: Don't you give a damn for him, Hap?

HAPPY: What're you talking about? I'm the one who —

BIFF: I sense it, you don't give a good goddamn about him. (*He takes the rolled-up hose from his pocket and puts it on the table in front of Happy.*) Look what I found in the cellar, for Christ's sake. How can you bear to let it go on?

HAPPY: Me? Who goes away? Who runs off and —

BIFF: Yeah, but he doesn't mean anything to you. You could help him — I can't! Don't you understand what I'm talking about? He's going to kill himself, don't you know that?

HAPPY: Don't I know it! Me!

BIFF: Hap, help him! Jesus . . . help him . . . Help me, help me, I can't bear to look at his face! (*Ready to weep, he hurries out, up right.*)

HAPPY (*starting after him*): Where are you going?

MISS FORSYTHE: What's he so mad about?

HAPPY: Come on, girls, we'll catch up with him.

MISS FORSYTHE (*as Happy pushes her out*): Say, I don't like that temper of his!

HAPPY: He's just a little overstrung, he'll be all right!

WILLY (*off left, as The Woman laughs*): Don't answer! Don't answer!

Letta: Don't you want to tell your father —

HAPPY: No, that's not my father. He's just a guy. Come on, we'll catch Biff, and, honey, we're going to paint this town! Stanley, where's the check! Hey, Stanley!

They exit. Stanley looks toward left.

STANLEY (*calling to Happy indignantly*): Mr. Loman! Mr. Loman!

Stanley picks up a chair and follows them off. Knocking is heard off left. The Woman enters, laughing. Willy follows her. She is in a black slip; he is buttoning his shirt. Raw, sensuous music accompanies their speech.

WILLY: Will you stop laughing? Will you stop?

THE WOMAN: Aren't you going to answer the door? He'll wake the whole hotel.

WILLY: I'm not expecting anybody.

THE WOMAN: Whyn't you have another drink, honey, and stop being so damn self-centered?

WILLY: I'm so lonely.

THE WOMAN: You know you ruined me, Willy? From now on, whenever you come to the office, I'll see that you go right through to the buyers. No waiting at my desk any more, Willy. You ruined me.

WILLY: That's nice of you to say that.

THE WOMAN: Gee, you are self-centered! Why so sad? You are the saddest, self-centeredest soul I ever did see-saw. (*She laughs. He kisses her.*) Come on inside, drummer boy. It's silly to be dressing in the middle of the night. (*As knocking is heard.*) Aren't you going to answer the door?

WILLY: They're knocking on the wrong door.

THE WOMAN: But I felt the knocking. And he heard us talking in here. Maybe the hotel's on fire!

WILLY (*his terror rising*): It's a mistake.

THE WOMAN: Then tell him to go away!

WILLY: There's nobody there.

THE WOMAN: It's getting on my nerves, Willy. There's somebody standing out there and it's getting on my nerves!

WILLY (*pushing her away from him*): All right, stay in the bathroom here, and don't come out. I think there's a law in Massachusetts about it, so don't come out. It may be that new room clerk. He looked very mean. So don't come out. It's a mistake, there's no fire.

The knocking is heard again. He takes a few steps away from her, and she vanishes into the wing. The light follows him, and now he is facing Young Biff, who carries a suitcase. Biff steps toward him. The music is gone.

BIFF: Why didn't you answer?

WILLY: Biff! What are you doing in Boston?

BIFF: Why didn't you answer? I've been knocking for five minutes, I called you on the phone —

WILLY: I just heard you. I was in the bathroom and had the door shut. Did anything happen home?

BIFF: Dad — I let you down.

WILLY: What do you mean?

BIFF: Dad . . .

WILLY: Biffo, what's this about? (*Putting his arm around Biff.*) Come on, let's go downstairs and get you a malted.

BIFF: Dad, I flunked math.

WILLY: Not for the term?

BIFF: The term. I haven't got enough credits to graduate.

WILLY: You mean to say Bernard wouldn't give you the answers?

BIFF: He did, he tried, but I only got a sixty-one.

WILLY: And they wouldn't give you four points?

BIFF: Birnbaum refused absolutely. I begged him, Pop, but he won't give me those points. You gotta talk to him before they close the school. Because if he saw the kind of man you are, and you just talked to him in your way, I'm sure he'd come through for me. The class came right before practice, see, and I didn't go enough. Would you talk to him? He'd like you, Pop. You know the way you could talk.

WILLY: You're on. We'll drive right back.

BIFF: Oh, Dad, good work! I'm sure he'll change it for you!

WILLY: Go downstairs and tell the clerk I'm checkin' out. Go right down.

BIFF: Yes, sir! See, the reason he hates me, Pop — one day he was late for class so I got up at the blackboard and imitated him. I crossed my eyes and talked with a lithp.

WILLY (*laughing*): You did? The kids like it?

BIFF: They nearly died laughing!

WILLY: Yeah? What'd you do?

BIFF: The thquare root of thixthy twee is . . . (*Willy bursts out laughing; Biff joins him.*) And in the middle of it he walked in!

Willy laughs and The Woman joins in offstage.

WILLY (*without hesitation*): Hurry downstairs and —

BIFF: Somebody in there?

WILLY: No, that was next door.

The Woman laughs offstage.

BIFF: Somebody got in your bathroom!

WILLY: No, it's the next room, there's a party —

THE WOMAN (*enters, laughing. She lisps this*): Can I come in? There's something in the bathtub, Willy, and it's moving!

Willy looks at Biff, who is staring open-mouthed and horrified at The Woman.

WILLY: Ah — you better go back to your room. They must be finished painting by now. They're painting her room so I let her take a shower here. Go back, go back . . . (*He pushes her.*)

THE WOMAN (*resisting*): But I've got to get dressed, Willy, I can't —

WILLY: Get out of here! Go back, go back . . . (*Suddenly striving for the ordinary*): This is Miss Francis, Biff, she's a buyer. They're painting her room. Go back, Miss Francis, go back . . .

THE WOMAN: But my clothes, I can't go out naked in the hall!

WILLY (*pushing her offstage*): Get outa here! Go back, go back!

Biff slowly sits down on his suitcase as the argument continues offstage.

THE WOMAN: Where's my stockings? You promised me stockings, Willy!

WILLY: I have no stockings here!

THE WOMAN: You had two boxes of size nine sheers for me, and I want them!

WILLY: Here, for God's sake, will you get outa here!

THE WOMAN (*enters holding a box of stockings*): I just hope there's nobody in the hall. That's all I hope. (*To Biff.*) Are you football or baseball?

BIFF: Football.

THE WOMAN (*angry, humiliated*): That's me too. G'night. (*She snatches her clothes from Willy, and walks out.*)

WILLY (*after a pause*): Well, better get going. I want to get to the school first thing in the morning. Get my suits out of the closet. I'll get my valise. (*Biff doesn't move.*) What's the matter? (*Biff remains motionless, tears falling.*) She's a buyer. Buys for J. H. Simmons. She lives down the hall — they're painting. You don't imagine — (*He breaks off. After a pause.*) Now listen, pal, she's just a buyer. She sees merchandise in her room and they have to keep it looking just so . . . (*Pause. Assuming command.*) All right, get my suits. (*Biff doesn't move.*) Now stop crying and do as I say. I gave you an order. Biff, I gave you an order! Is that what you do when I give you an order? How dare you cry! (*Putting his arm around Biff.*) Now look, Biff,

when you grow up you'll understand about these things. You mustn't —
you mustn't overemphasize a thing like this. I'll see Birnbaum first thing
in the morning.

BIFF: Never mind.

WILLY (*getting down beside Biff*): Never mind! He's going to give you those
points. I'll see to it.

BIFF: He wouldn't listen to you.

WILLY: He certainly will listen to me. You need those points for the U. of Virginia.

BIFF: I'm not going there.

WILLY: Heh? If I can't get him to change that mark you'll make it up in summer
school. You've got all summer to —

BIFF (*his weeping breaking from him*): Dad . . .

WILLY (*infected by it*): Oh, my boy . . .

BIFF: Dad . . .

WILLY: She's nothing to me, Biff. I was lonely, I was terribly lonely.

BIFF: You — you gave her Mama's stockings! (*His tears break through and he rises
to go.*)

WILLY (*grabbing for Biff*): I gave you an order!

BIFF: Don't touch me, you — liar!

WILLY: Apologize for that!

BIFF: You fake! You phony little fake! You fake! (*Overcome, he turns quickly and
weeping fully goes out with his suitcase. Willy is left on the floor on his knees.*)

WILLY: I gave you an order! Biff, come back here or I'll beat you! Come back
here! I'll whip you!

Stanley comes quickly in from the right and stands in front of Willy.

WILLY (*shouts at Stanley*): I gave you an order . . .

STANLEY: Hey, let's pick it up, pick it up, Mr. Loman. (*He helps Willy to his feet.*)
Your boys left with the chippies. They said they'll see you home.

A second waiter watches some distance away.

WILLY: But we were supposed to have dinner together.

Music is heard, Willy's theme.

STANLEY: Can you make it?

WILLY: I'll — sure, I can make it. (*Suddenly concerned about his clothes.*) Do I — I
look all right?

STANLEY: Sure, you look all right. (*He flicks a speck off Willy's lapel.*)

WILLY: Here — here's a dollar.

STANLEY: Oh, your son paid me. It's all right.

WILLY (*putting it in Stanley's hand*): No, take it. You're a good boy.

STANLEY: Oh, no, you don't have to . . .

WILLY: Here — here's some more, I don't need it any more. (*After a slight pause.*)
Tell me — is there a seed store in the neighborhood?

STANLEY: Seeds? You mean like to plant?

As Willy turns, Stanley slips the money back into his jacket pocket.

WILLY: Yes. Carrots, peas . . .

STANLEY: Well, there's hardware stores on Sixth Avenue, but it may be too late now.

WILLY (*anxiously*): Oh, I'd better hurry. I've got to get some seeds. (*He starts off to the right.*) I've got to get some seeds, right away. Nothing's planted. I don't have a thing in the ground.

Willy hurries out as the light goes down. Stanley moves over to the right after him, watches him off. The other waiter has been staring at Willy.

STANLEY (*to the waiter*): Well, whatta you looking at?

The waiter picks up the chairs and moves off right. Stanley takes the table and follows him. The light fades on this area. There is a long pause, the sound of the flute coming over. The light gradually rises on the kitchen, which is empty. Happy appears at the door of the house, followed by Biff. Happy is carrying a large bunch of long-stemmed roses. He enters the kitchen, looks around for Linda. Not seeing her, he turns to Biff, who is just outside the house door, and makes a gesture with his hands, indicating "Not here, I guess." He looks into the living-room and freezes. Inside, Linda, unseen, is seated, Willy's coat on her lap. She rises ominously and quietly and moves toward Happy, who backs up into the kitchen, afraid.

HAPPY: Hey, what're you doing up? (*Linda says nothing but moves toward him implacably.*) Where's Pop? (*He keeps backing to the right, and now Linda is in full view in the doorway to the living-room.*) Is he sleeping?

LINDA: Where were you?

HAPPY (*trying to laugh it off*): We met two girls, Mom, very fine types. Here, we brought you some flowers. (*Offering them to her.*) Put them in your room, Ma.

She knocks them to the floor at Biff's feet. He has now come inside and closed the door behind him. She stares at Biff, silent.

HAPPY: Now what'd you do that for? Mom, I want you to have some flowers —

LINDA (*cutting Happy off, violently to Biff*): Don't you care whether he lives or dies?

HAPPY (*going to the stairs*): Come upstairs, Biff.

BIFF (*with a flare of disgust, to Happy*): Go away from me! (*To Linda.*) What do you mean, lives or dies? Nobody's dying around here, pal.

LINDA: Get out of my sight! Get out of here!

BIFF: I wanna see the boss.

LINDA: You're not going near him!

BIFF: Where is he? (*He moves into the living-room and Linda follows.*)

LINDA (*shouting after Biff*): You invite him for dinner. He looks forward to it all day — (*Biff appears in his parents' bedroom, looks around, and exits.*) — and then you desert him there. There's no stranger you'd do that to!

HAPPY: Why? He had a swell time with us. Listen, when I — (*Linda comes back into the kitchen*) — desert him I hope I don't outlive the day!

LINDA: Get out of here!

HAPPY: Now look, Mom . . .

LINDA: Did you have to go to women tonight? You and your lousy rotten whores!

Biff re-enters the kitchen.

HAPPY: Mom, all we did was follow Biff around trying to cheer him up! (*To Biff.*) Boy, what a night you gave me!

LINDA: Get out of here, both of you, and don't come back! I don't want you tormenting him any more. Go on now, get your things together! (*To Biff.*) You can sleep in his apartment. (*She starts to pick up the flowers and stops herself.*) Pick up this stuff, I'm not your maid any more. Pick it up, you bum, you!

Happy turns his back to her in refusal. Biff slowly moves over and gets down on his knees, picking up the flowers.

LINDA: You're a pair of animals! Not one, not another living soul would have had the cruelty to walk out on that man in a restaurant!

BIFF (*not looking at her*): Is that what he said?

LINDA: He didn't have to say anything. He was so humiliated he nearly limped when he came in.

HAPPY: But, Mom, he had a great time with us —

BIFF (*cutting him off violently*): Shut up!

Without another word, Happy goes upstairs.

LINDA: You! You didn't even go in to see if he was all right!

BIFF (*still on the floor in front of Linda, the flowers in his hand; with self-loathing*): No. Didn't. Didn't do a damned thing. How do you like that, heh? Left him babbling in a toilet.

LINDA: You louse. You . . .

BIFF: Now you hit it on the nose! (*He gets up, throws the flowers in the wastebasket.*) The scum of the earth, and you're looking at him!

LINDA: Get out of here!

BIFF: I gotta talk to the boss, Mom. Where is he?

LINDA: You're not going near him. Get out of this house!

BIFF (*with absolute assurance, determination*): No. We're gonna have an abrupt conversation, him and me.

LINDA: You're not talking to him!

Hammering is heard from outside the house, off right. Biff turns toward the noise.

LINDA (*suddenly pleading*): Will you please leave him alone?

BIFF: What's he doing out there?

LINDA: He's planting the garden!

BIFF (*quietly*): Now? Oh, my God!

Biff moves outside, Linda following. The light dies down on them and comes up on the center of the apron as Willy walks into it. He is carrying a flashlight, a hoe, and handful of seed packets. He raps the top of the hoe sharply to fix it firmly, and then moves to the left, measuring off the distance with his foot. He holds the flashlight to look at the seed packets, reading off the instructions. He is in the blue of night.

WILLY: Carrots . . . quarter-inch apart. Rows . . . one-foot rows. (*He measures it off.*) One foot. (*He puts down a package and measures off.*) Beets. (*He puts down another package and measures again.*) Lettuce. (*He reads the package, puts it down.*) One foot — (*He breaks off as Ben appears at the right and moves slowly down to him.*) What a proposition, ts, ts. Terrific, terrific. 'Cause she's suffered, Ben, the woman has suffered. You understand me? A man can't go out the way he came in, Ben, a man has got to add up to something. You can't, you can't — (*Ben moves toward him as though to interrupt.*) You gotta consider, now. Don't answer so quick. Remember, it's a guaranteed twenty-thousand-dollar proposition. Now look, Ben, I want you to go through the ins and outs of this thing with me. I've got nobody to talk to, Ben, and the woman has suffered, you hear me?

BEN (*standing still, considering*): What's the proposition?

WILLY: It's twenty thousand dollars on the barrelhead. Guaranteed, gilt-edged, you understand?

BEN: You don't want to make a fool of yourself. They might not honor the policy.

WILLY: How can they dare refuse? Didn't I work like a coolie to meet every premium on the nose? And now they don't pay off? Impossible!

BEN: It's called a cowardly thing, William.

WILLY: Why? Does it take more guts to stand here the rest of my life ringing up a zero?

BEN (*yielding*): That's a point, William. (*He moves, thinking, turns.*) And twenty thousand — that *is* something one can feel with the hand, it is there.

WILLY (*now assured, with rising power*): Oh, Ben, that's the whole beauty of it! I see it like a diamond, shining in the dark, hard and rough, that I can pick up and touch in my hand. Not like — like an appointment! This would not be another damned-fool appointment, Ben, and it changes all the aspects. Because he thinks I'm nothing, see, and so he spites me. But the funeral — (*Straightening up.*) Ben, that funeral will be massive! They'll come from Maine, Massachusetts, Vermont, New Hampshire! All the old-timers with the strange license plates — that boy will be thunderstruck, Ben, because he never realized — I am known! Rhode Island, New York, New Jersey — I am known, Ben, and he'll see it with his eyes once and for all. He'll see what I am, Ben! He's in for a shock, that boy!

BEN (*coming to the edge of the garden*): He'll call you a coward.

WILLY (*suddenly fearful*): No, that would be terrible.

BEN: Yes. And a damned fool.

WILLY: No, no, he mustn't, I won't have that! (*He is broken and desperate.*)

BEN: He'll hate you William.

The gay music of the Boys is heard.

WILLY: Oh, Ben, how do we get back to all the great times? Used to be so full of light, and comradeship, the sleigh-riding in winter, and the ruddiness on his cheeks. And always some kind of good news coming up, always something nice coming up ahead. And never even let me carry the valises in the house, and simonizing, simonizing that little red car! Why, why can't I give him something and not have him hate me?

BEN: Let me think about it. (*He glances at his watch.*) I still have a little time. Remarkable proposition, but you've got to be sure you're not making a fool of yourself.

Ben drifts off upstage and goes out of sight. Biff comes down from the left.

WILLY (*suddenly conscious of Biff, turns and looks up at him, then begins picking up the packages of seeds in confusion*): Where the hell is that seed? (*Indignantly.*) You can't see nothing out here! They boxed in the whole goddamn neighborhood!

BIFF: There are people all around here. Don't you realize that?

WILLY: I'm busy. Don't bother me.

BIFF (*taking the hoe from Willy*): I'm saying good-by to you, Pop. (*Willy looks at him, silent, unable to move.*) I'm not coming back any more.

WILLY: You're not going to see Oliver tomorrow?

BIFF: I've got no appointment, Dad.

WILLY: He put his arm around you, and you've got no appointment?

BIFF: Pop, get this now, will you? Everytime I've left it's been a fight that sent me out of here. Today I realized something about myself and I tried to explain it to you and I — I think I'm just not smart enough to make any sense out of it for you. To hell with whose fault it is or anything like that. (*He takes Willy's arm.*) Let's just wrap it up, heh? Come on in, we'll tell Mom. (*He gently tries to pull Willy to left.*)

WILLY (*frozen, immobile, with guilt in his voice*): No, I don't want to see her.

BIFF: Come on! (*He pulls again, and Willy tries to pull away.*)

WILLY (*highly nervous*): No, no, I don't want to see her.

BIFF (*tries to look into Willy's face, as if to find the answer there*): Why don't you want to see her?

WILLY (*more harshly now*): Don't bother me, will you?

BIFF: What do you mean, you don't want to see her? You don't want them calling you yellow, do you? This isn't your fault; it's me, I'm a bum. Now come inside! (*Willy strains to get away.*) Did you hear what I said to you?

Willy pulls away and quickly goes by himself into the house. Biff follows.

LINDA (*to Willy*): Did you plant, dear?

BIFF (*at the door, to Linda*): All right, we had it out. I'm going and I'm not writing any more.

LINDA (*going to Willy in the kitchen*): I think that's the best way, dear. 'Cause there's no use drawing it out, you'll just never get along.

Willy doesn't respond.

BIFF: People ask where I am and what I'm doing, you don't know, and you don't care. That way it'll be off your mind and you can start brightening up again. All right? That clears it, doesn't it? (*Willy is silent, and Biff goes to him.*) You gonna wish me luck, scout? (*He extends his hand.*) What do you say?

LINDA: Shake his hand, Willy.

WILLY (*turning to her, seething with hurt*): There's no necessity to mention the pen at all, y'know.

BIFF (*gently*): I've got no appointment, Dad.

WILLY (*erupting fiercely*): He put his arm around . . . ?

BIFF: Dad, you're never going to see what I am, so what's the use of arguing? If I strike oil I'll send you a check. Meantime forget I'm alive.

WILLY (*to Linda*): Spite, see?

BIFF: Shake hands, Dad.

WILLY: Not my hand.

BIFF: I was hoping not to go this way.

WILLY: Well, this is the way you're going. Good-by.

Biff looks at him a moment, then turns sharply and goes to the stairs.

WILLY (*stops him with*): May you rot in hell if you leave this house!

BIFF (*turning*): Exactly what is it that you want from me?

WILLY: I want you to know, on the train, in the mountains, in the valleys, wherever you go, that you cut down your life for spite!

BIFF: No, no.

WILLY: Spite, spite, is the word of your undoing! And when you're down and out, remember what did it. When you're rotting somewhere beside the railroad tracks, remember, and don't you dare blame it on me!

BIFF: I'm not blaming it on you!

WILLY: I won't take the rap for this, you hear?

Happy comes down the stairs and stands on the bottom step, watching.

BIFF: That's just what I'm telling you!

WILLY (*sinking into a chair at the table, with full accusation*): You're trying to put a knife in me — don't think I don't know what you're doing!

BIFF: All right, phony! Then let's lay it on the line. (*He whips the rubber tube out of his pocket and puts it on the table.*)

HAPPY: You crazy —

LINDA: Biff! (*She moves to grab the hose, but Biff holds it down with his hand.*)

BIFF: Leave it there! Don't move it!

WILLY (*not looking at it*): What is that?

BIFF: You know goddam well what that is.

WILLY (*caged, wanting to escape*): I never saw that.

BIFF: You saw it. The mice didn't bring it into the cellar! What is this supposed to do, make a hero out of you? This supposed to make me sorry for you?

WILLY: Never heard of it.

BIFF: There'll be no pity for you, you hear it? No pity!

WILLY (*to Linda*): You hear the spite!

BIFF: No, you're going to hear the truth — what you are and what I am!

LINDA: Stop it!

WILLY: Spite!

HAPPY (*coming down toward Biff*): You cut it now!

BIFF (*to Happy*): The man don't know who we are! The man is gonna know! (*To Willy.*) We never told the truth for ten minutes in this house!

HAPPY: We always told the truth!

BIFF (*turning on him*): You big blow, are you the assistant buyer? You're one of the two assistants to the assistant, aren't you?

HAPPY: Well, I'm practically —

BIFF: You're practically full of it! We all are! And I'm through with it. (*To Willy.*) Now hear this, Willy, this is me.

WILLY: I know you!

BIFF: You know why I had no address for three months? I stole a suit in Kansas City and I was in jail. (*To Linda, who is sobbing.*) Stop crying. I'm through with it.

Linda turns away from them, her hands covering her face.

WILLY: I suppose that's my fault!

BIFF: I stole myself out of every good job since high school!

WILLY: And whose fault is that?

BIFF: And I never got anywhere because you blew me so full of hot air I could never stand taking orders from anybody! That's whose fault it is!

WILLY: I hear that!

LINDA: Don't, Biff!

BIFF: It's goddam time you heard that! I had to be boss big shot in two weeks, and I'm through with it!

WILLY: Then hang yourself! For spite, hang yourself!

BIFF: No! Nobody's hanging himself, Willy! I ran down eleven flights with a pen in my hand today. And suddenly I stopped, you hear me? And in the middle of that office building, do you hear this? I stopped in the middle of that building and I saw — the sky. I saw the things that I love in this world. The work and the food and time to sit and smoke. And I looked at the pen and said to myself, what the hell am I grabbing this for? Why am I trying to become what I don't want to be? What am I doing in an office, making a contemptuous, begging fool of myself, when all I want is out there, waiting for me the minute I say I know who I am! Why can't I say that, Willy? (*He tries to make Willy face him, but Willy pulls away and moves to the left.*)

WILLY (*with hatred, threateningly*): The door of your life is wide open!

BIFF: Pop! I'm a dime a dozen, and so are you!

WILLY (*turning on him now in an uncontrolled outburst*): I am not a dime a dozen! I am Willy Loman, and you are Biff Loman!

Biff starts for Willy, but is blocked by Happy. In his fury, Biff seems on the verge of attacking his father.

BIFF: I am not a leader of men, Willy, and neither are you. You were never anything but a hard-working drummer who landed in the ash can like all the rest of them! I'm one dollar an hour, Willy! I tried seven states and couldn't raise it. A buck an hour! Do you gather my meaning? I'm not bringing home any prizes any more, and you're going to stop waiting for me to bring them home!

WILLY (*directly to Biff*): You vengeful, spiteful mutt!

Biff breaks from Happy. Willy, in fright, starts up the stairs. Biff grabs him.

BIFF (*at the peak of his fury*): Pop, I'm nothing! I'm nothing, Pop. Can't you understand that? There's no spite in it any more. I'm just what I am, that's all.

Biff's fury has spent itself, and he breaks down, sobbing, holding on to Willy, who dumbly fumbles for Biff's face.

WILLY (*astonished*): What're you doing? What're you doing? (*To Linda.*) Why is he crying?

BIFF (*crying, broken*): Will you let me go, for Christ's sake? Will you take that phony dream and burn it before something happens? (*Struggling to contain himself, he pulls away and moves to the stairs.*) I'll go in the morning. Put him — put him to bed. (*Exhausted, Biff moves up the stairs to his room.*)

WILLY (*after a long pause, astonished, elevated*): Isn't that — isn't that remarkable? Biff — he likes me!

LINDA: He loves you, Willy!

HAPPY (*deeply moved*): Always did, Pop.

WILLY: Oh, Biff! (*Staring wildly.*) He cried! Cried to me. (*He is choking with his love, and now cries out his promise.*) That boy — that boy is going to be magnificent!

Ben appears in the light just outside the kitchen.

BEN: Yes, outstanding, with twenty thousand behind him.

LINDA (*sensing the racing of his mind, fearfully, carefully*): Now come to bed, Willy. It's all settled now.

WILLY (*finding it difficult not to rush out of the house*): Yes, we'll sleep. Come on. Go to sleep, Hap.

BEN: And it does take a great kind of a man to crack the jungle.

In accents of dread, Ben's idyllic music starts up.

HAPPY (*his arm around Linda*): I'm getting married, Pop, don't forget it. I'm changing everything. I'm gonna run that department before the year is up. You'll see, Mom. (*He kisses her.*)

BEN: The jungle is dark but full of diamonds, Willy.

Willy turns, moves, listening to Ben.

LINDA: Be good. You're both good boys, just act that way, that's all.

HAPPY: 'Night, Pop. (*He goes upstairs.*)

LINDA (*to Willy*): Come, dear.

BEN (*with greater force*): One must go in to fetch a diamond out.

WILLY (*to Linda, as he moves slowly along the edge of the kitchen, toward the door*): I just want to get settled down, Linda. Let me sit alone for a little.

LINDA (*almost uttering her fear*): I want you upstairs.

WILLY (*taking her in his arms*): In a few minutes, Linda. I couldn't sleep right now. Go on, you look awful tired. (*He kisses her.*)

BEN: Not like an appointment at all. A diamond is rough and hard to the touch.

WILLY: Go on now. I'll be right up.

LINDA: I think this is the only way, Willy.

WILLY: Sure, it's the best thing.

BEN: Best thing!

WILLY: The only way. Everything is gonna be — go on, kid, get to bed. You look so tired.

LINDA: Come right up.

WILLY: Two minutes.

Linda goes into the living-room, then reappears in her bedroom. Willy moves just outside the kitchen door.

WILLY: Loves me. (*Wonderingly.*) Always loved me. Isn't that a remarkable thing? Ben, he'll worship me for it!

BEN (*with promise*): It's dark there, but full of diamonds.

WILLY: Can you imagine that magnificence with twenty thousand dollars in his pocket?

LINDA (*calling from her room*): Willy! Come up!

WILLY (*calling into the kitchen*): Yes! Yes. Coming! It's very smart, you realize that, don't you, sweetheart? Even Ben sees it. I gotta go, baby. 'By! 'By! (*Going over to Ben, almost dancing.*) Imagine? When the mail comes he'll be ahead of Bernard again!

BEN: A perfect proposition all around.

WILLY: Did you see how he cried to me? Oh, if I could kiss him, Ben!

BEN: Time, William, time!

WILLY: Oh, Ben, I always knew one way or another we were gonna make it, Biff and I!

BEN (*looking at his watch*): The boat. We'll be late. (*He moves slowly off into the darkness.*)

WILLY (*elegiacally, turning to the house*): Now when you kick off, boy, I want a seventy-yard boot, and get right down the field under the ball, and when you hit, hit low and hit hard, because it's important, boy. (*He swings around and faces the audience.*) There's all kinds of important people in the stands, and the first thing you know . . . (*Suddenly realizing he is alone.*) Ben! Ben, where do I . . . ? (*He makes a sudden movement of search.*) Ben, how do I . . . ?

LINDA (*calling*): Willy, you coming up?

WILLY (*uttering a gasp of fear, whirling about as if to quiet her*): Sh! (*He turns around as if to find his way; sounds, faces, voices, seem to be swarming in upon him and he flicks at them, crying.*) Sh! Sh! (*Suddenly music, faint and high, stops him. It rises in intensity, almost to an unbearable scream. He goes up and down on his toes, and rushes off around the house.*) Shhh!

LINDA: Willy?

There is no answer. Linda waits. Biff gets up off his bed. He is still in his clothes. Happy sits up. Biff stands listening.

LINDA (*with real fear*): Willy, answer me! Willy!

There is the sound of a car starting and moving away at full speed.

LINDA: No!

BIFF (*rushing down the stairs*): Pop!

As the car speeds off, the music crashes down in a frenzy of sound, which becomes the soft pulsation of a single cello string. Biff slowly returns to his bedroom. He and Happy gravely don their jackets. Linda slowly walks out of her room. The music has developed into a dead march. The leaves of day are appearing over everything. Charley and Bernard, somberly dressed, appear and knock on the kitchen door. Biff and Happy slowly descend the stairs to the kitchen as Charley and Bernard enter. All stop a moment when Linda, in clothes of mourning, bearing a little bunch of roses, comes through the draped doorway into the kitchen. She goes to Charley and takes his arm. Now all move toward the audience, through the wall-line of the kitchen. At the limit of the apron, Linda lays down the flowers, kneels, and sits back on her heels. All stare down at the grave.

REQUIEM

CHARLEY: It's getting dark, Linda.

Linda doesn't react. She stares at the grave.

BIFF: How about it, Mom? Better get some rest, heh? They'll be closing the gate soon.

Linda makes no move. Pause.

HAPPY (*deeply angered*): He had no right to do that. There was no necessity for it. We would've helped him.

CHARLEY (*grunting*): Hmmm.

BIFF: Come along, Mom.

LINDA: Why didn't anybody come?

CHARLEY: It was a very nice funeral.

LINDA: But where are all the people he knew? Maybe they blame him.

CHARLEY: Naa. It's a rough world, Linda. They wouldn't blame him.

LINDA: I can't understand it. At this time especially. First time in thirty-five years we were just about free and clear. He only needed a little salary. He was even finished with the dentist.

CHARLEY: No man only needs a little salary.

LINDA: I can't understand it.

BIFF: There were a lot of nice days. When he'd come home from a trip; or on Sundays, making the stoop; finishing the cellar; putting on the new porch; when he built the extra bathroom; and put up the garage. You know something, Charley, there's more of him in that front stoop than in all the sales he ever made.

CHARLEY: Yeah. He was a happy man with a batch of cement.

LINDA: He was so wonderful with his hands.

BIFF: He had the wrong dreams. All, all, wrong.

HAPPY (*almost ready to fight Biff*): Don't say that!

BIFF: He never knew who he was.

CHARLEY (*stopping Happy's movement and reply. To Biff*): Nobody dast blame this man. You don't understand: Willy was a salesman. And for a salesman, there is no rock bottom to the life. He don't put a bolt to a nut, he don't tell you the law or give you medicine. He's a man way out there in the blue, riding on a smile and a shoeshine. And when they start not smiling back — that's an earthquake. And then you get yourself a couple of spots on your hat, and you're finished. Nobody dast blame this man. A salesman is got to dream, boy. It comes with the territory.

BIFF: Charley, the man didn't know who he was.

HAPPY (*infuriated*): Don't say that!

BIFF: Why don't you come with me, Happy?

HAPPY: I'm not licked that easily. I'm staying right in this city, and I'm gonna beat this racket! (*He looks at Biff, his chin set.*) The Loman Brothers!

BIFF: I know who I am, kid.

HAPPY: All right, boy. I'm gonna show you and everybody else that Willy Loman did not die in vain. He had a good dream. It's the only dream you can have — to come out number-one man. He fought it out here, and this is where I'm gonna win it for him.

BIFF (*with a hopeless glance at Happy, bends toward his mother*): Let's go, Mom.

LINDA: I'll be with you in a minute. Go on, Charley. (*He hesitates.*) I want to, just for a minute. I never had a chance to say good-by.

Charley moves away, followed by Happy. Biff remains a slight distance up and left of Linda. She sits there, summoning herself. The flute begins, not far away, playing behind her speech.

LINDA: Forgive me, dear. I can't cry. I don't know what it is, but I can't cry. I don't understand it. Why did you ever do that? Help me, Willy, I can't cry. It seems to me that you're just on another trip. I keep expecting you. Willy, dear, I can't cry. Why did you do it? I search and search and I search, and I can't understand it, Willy. I made the last payment on the house today. Today, dear. And there'll be nobody home. (*A sob rises in her throat.*) We're free and clear. (*Sobbing more fully, released.*) We're free. (*Biff comes slowly toward her.*) We're free . . . We're free . . .

Biff lifts her to her feet and moves out up right with her in his arms. Linda sobs quietly. Bernard and Charley come together and follow them, followed by Happy. Only the music of the flute is left on the darkening stage as over the house the hard towers of the apartment buildings rise into sharp focus, and

The Curtain Falls

ॐ

EDWARD ALBEE (*b. 1928*) *was born in Washington, D.C. When he was two weeks old he was adopted by Reed and Frances Albee, a wealthy couple in Larchmont, New York, and named after his adopted grandfather, Edward Franklin Albee, part owner of the Keith-Albee Theater Circuit, a coast-to-coast chain of vaudeville theaters. Albee's family life was unhappy, and by the time he applied for Choate preparatory school, he knew he wanted to become a playwright. At Choate he published a one-act melodrama in the literary magazine. When Albee turned twenty-one, he received from his grandmother a $100,000 trust fund, which enabled him to drop out of Trinity College in Hartford and move to New York City to write plays. Albee supplemented the income from his inheritance by working a series of odd jobs, including that of a Western Union messenger. For nearly a decade he shared a floor-through apartment in Chelsea with William Flanagan, who recalled that Albee "adored the the-*

atre from the beginning and there can't have been anything of even mild importance that we didn't see together." As an aspiring playwright, Albee admired the plays of Tennessee Williams, but when he discovered his own voice in the theater he said he recognized he was one of the "children of [Samuel] Beckett."

Shortly before Albee's thirtieth birthday, when it looked as if he might have no talent for playwriting, he sat down at the kitchen table and wrote The Zoo Story. Flanagan sent it to friends in Europe, and it was given a workshop production in German translation in Berlin in 1959, on a double bill with Beckett's one-act play Krapp's Last Tape. The following year both plays were produced in English in the off-Broadway Provincetown Playhouse. In 1960 Albee wrote a trilogy of one-act plays — The Sandbox, The Death of Bessie Smith, and Fam and Yam — which he followed in 1961 with The American Dream and Bartleby, an operatic adaptation of Herman Melville's story. The Sandbox and The American Dream were often produced on college campuses, and they made Albee's reputation until he scored his first success on Broadway with the full-length play Who's Afraid of Virginia Woolf? This won the Drama Critics Circle Award in 1962 and launched Albee's career as a major American playwright even before it was made into a successful film starring Elizabeth Taylor and Richard Burton. During the last thirty-five years Albee has won many prizes for his plays, including Pulitzer prizes for Seascape (1975) and Three Tall Women (1994).

Albee has said that The Sandbox, a fourteen-minute comedy that premiered at the Jazz Gallery in New York City, is one of his favorite works. Written in memory of his maternal grandmother and benefactor, who died in 1959 at the age of eighty-three, it is a satiric caricature of relationships within a dysfunctional family. Albee believes that playwrights have an important obligation beyond making a statement about the human condition; they must also attempt to change both their society and the theatrical forms within which their predecessors have worked. He has often been abrasive to critics who questioned the dark vision and experimental structure of his plays, as in his essay "Which Theater Is the Absurd One?":

> What of this theater? Is it, as it has been accused of being, obscure, sordid, destructive, anti-theater, perverse, and absurd (in the sense of foolish)? Or is it merely, as I have so often heard it put, that "This sort of stuff is too depressing, too . . . too mixed up; I go to the theater to relax and have a good time"?
>
> I would submit that it is this latter attitude — that the theater is a place to relax and have a good time — in conflict with the purpose of the Theater of the Absurd — which is to make a man face up to the human condition as it really is — that has produced all the brouhaha and the dissent. I would submit that the Theater of the Absurd, in the sense that it is truly the contemporary theater, facing as it does man's condition as it is, is the Realistic theater of our time; and that the supposed Realistic theater — the term used here to mean most of what is done on Broadway — in the sense that it panders to the public need for self-congratulation and reassurance and presents a false picture of ourselves to ourselves, is, with an occasional very lovely exception, really and truly the Theater of the Absurd.

RELATED COMMENTARIES: Edward Albee, "On Playwriting," page 1960; Richard Amacher, "On The Sandbox," page 1964.

EDWARD ALBEE

The Sandbox   1960

THE PLAYERS

THE YOUNG MAN, *twenty-five, a good-looking, well-built boy in a bathing suit.*
MOMMY, *fifty-five, a well-dressed, imposing woman.*
DADDY, *sixty, a small man; gray, thin.*
GRANDMA, *eighty-six, a tiny, wizened woman with bright eyes.*
THE MUSICIAN, *no particular age, but young would be nice.*

NOTE: *When, in the course of the play, Mommy and Daddy call each other by these names, there should be no suggestion of regionalism. These names are of empty affection and point up the pre-senility and vacuity of their characters.*

THE SCENE: *A bare stage, with only the following: Near the footlights, far stage-right, two simple chairs set side by side, facing the audience; near the footlights, far stage-left, a chair facing stage-right with a music stand before it; farther back, and stage-center, slightly elevated and raked, a large child's sandbox with a toy pail and shovel; the background is the sky, which alters from brightest day to deepest night.*

At the beginning, it is brightest day; the Young Man is alone on stage, to the rear of the sandbox, and to one side. He is doing calisthenics; he does calisthenics until quite at the very end of the play. These calisthenics, employing the arms only, should suggest the beating and fluttering of wings. The Young Man is, after all, the Angel of Death.

Mommy and Daddy enter from stage-left, Mommy first.

MOMMY (*motioning to Daddy*): Well, here we are; this is the beach.
DADDY (*whining*): I'm cold.
MOMMY (*dismissing him with a little laugh*): Don't be silly; it's as warm as toast.
  Look at that nice young man over there: *he* doesn't think it's cold. (*Waves to the Young Man.*) Hello.
YOUNG MAN (*with an endearing smile*): Hi!
MOMMY (*looking about*): This will do perfectly . . . don't you think so, Daddy?
  There's sand there . . . and the water beyond. What do you think,
  Daddy?
DADDY (*vaguely*): Whatever you say, Mommy.
MOMMY (*with the same little laugh*): Well, of course . . . whatever I say. Then, it's
  settled, is it?
DADDY (*shrugs*): She's *your* mother, not mine.
MOMMY: *I* know she's my mother. What do you take me for? (*A pause.*) All
  right, now; let's get on with it. (*She shouts into the wings, stage-left.*) You!
  Out there! You can come in now.

The Musician enters, seats himself in the chair, stage-left, places music on the music stand, is ready to play. Mommy nods approvingly.

MOMMY: Very nice; very nice. Are you ready, Daddy? Let's go get Grandma.
DADDY: Whatever you say, Mommy.

MOMMY (*leading the way out, stage-left*): Of course, whatever I say. (*To the Musician.*) You can begin now.

The Musician begins playing; Mommy and Daddy exit; the Musician, all the while playing, nods to the Young Man.

YOUNG MAN (*with the same endearing smile*): Hi!

After a moment, Mommy and Daddy re-enter, carrying Grandma. She is borne in by their hands under her armpits; she is quite rigid; her legs are drawn up; her feet do not touch the ground; the expression on her ancient face is that of puzzlement and fear.

DADDY: Where do we put her?

MOMMY (*the same little laugh*): Wherever I say, of course. Let me see . . . well . . . all right, over there . . . in the sandbox. (*Pause.*) Well, what are you waiting for, Daddy? . . . The sandbox!

Together they carry Grandma over to the sandbox and more or less dump her in.

GRANDMA (*righting herself to a sitting position; her voice a cross between a baby's laugh and cry*): Ahhhhhh! Graaaaa!

DADDY (*dusting himself*): What do we do now?

MOMMY (*to the Musician*): You can stop now.

The Musician stops.

> (*Back to Daddy.*) What do you mean, what do we do now? We go over there and sit down, of course. (*To the Young Man.*) Hello there.

YOUNG MAN (*again smiling*): Hi!

Mommy and Daddy move to the chairs, stage-right, and sit down. A pause.

GRANDMA (*same as before*): Ahhhhhh! Ah-haaaaaa! Graaaaaa!

DADDY: Do you think . . . do you think she's . . . comfortable?

MOMMY (*impatiently*): How would I know?

DADDY (*pause*): What do we do now?

MOMMY (*as if remembering*): We . . . wait. We . . . sit here . . . and we wait . . . that's what we do.

DADDY (*after a pause*): Shall we talk to each other?

MOMMY (*with that little laugh; picking something off her dress*): Well, *you* can talk, if you want to . . . if you can think of anything to *say* . . . if you can think of anything *new*.

DADDY (*thinks*): No . . . I suppose not.

MOMMY (*with a triumphant laugh*): Of course not!

GRANDMA (*banging the toy shovel against the pail*): Haaaaaa! Ah-haaaaaa!

MOMMY (*out over the audience*): Be quiet, Grandma . . . just be quiet, and wait.

Grandma throws a shovelful of sand at Mommy.

MOMMY (*still out over the audience*): She's throwing sand at me! You stop that, Grandma; you stop throwing sand at Mommy! (*To Daddy.*) She's throwing sand at me.

Daddy looks around at Grandma, who screams at him.

GRANDMA: GRAAAAAA!

MOMMY: Don't look at her. Just . . . sit here . . . be very still . . . and wait. (*To the Musician.*) You . . . uh . . . you go ahead and do whatever it is you do.

The Musician plays.

Mommy and Daddy are fixed, staring out beyond the audience. Grandma looks at them, looks at the Musician, looks at the sandbox, throws down the shovel.

GRANDMA: Ah-haaaaaa! Graaaaaa! (*Looks for reaction; gets none. Now ... directly to the audience.*) Honestly! What a way to treat an old woman! Drag her out of the house . . . stick her in a car . . . bring her out here from the city . . . dump her in a pile of sand . . . and leave her here to set. I'm eighty-six years old! I was married when I was seventeen. To a farmer. He died when I was thirty. (*To the Musician.*) Will you stop that, please?

The Musician stops playing.

I'm a feeble old woman . . . how do you expect anybody to hear me over that peep! peep! peep! (*To herself.*) There's no respect around here. (*To the Young Man.*) There's no respect around here!

YOUNG MAN (*same smile*): Hi!

GRANDMA (*after a pause, a mild double-take, continues, to the audience*): My husband died when I was thirty (*indicates Mommy*), and I had to raise that big cow over there all by my lonesome. You can imagine what *that* was like. Lordy! (*To the Young Man.*) Where'd they get *you?*

YOUNG MAN: Oh . . . I've been around for a while.

GRANDMA: I'll bet you have! Heh, heh, heh. Will you look at you!

YOUNG MAN (*flexing his muscles*): Isn't that something? (*Continues his calisthenics.*)

GRANDMA: Boy, oh boy; I'll say. Pretty good.

YOUNG MAN (*sweetly*): I'll say.

GRANDMA: Where ya from?

YOUNG MAN: Southern California.

GRANDMA (*nodding*): Figgers; figgers. What's your name, honey?

YOUNG MAN: I don't know. . . .

GRANDMA (*to the audience*): Bright, too!

YOUNG MAN: I mean . . . I mean, they haven't given me one yet . . . the studio . . .

GRANDMA (*giving him the once-over*): You don't say . . . you don't say. Well . . . uh, I've got to talk some more . . . don't you go 'way.

YOUNG MAN: Oh, no.

GRANDMA (*turning her attention back to the audience*): Fine; fine. (*Then, once more, back to the Young Man.*) You're . . . you're an actor, hunh?

YOUNG MAN (*beaming*): Yes. I am.

GRANDMA (*to the audience again; shrugs*): I'm smart that way. Anyhow, I had to raise . . . *that* over there all by my lonesome; and what's next to her there . . . that's what she married. Rich? I tell you . . . money, money, money. They took me off the *farm* . . . which was real decent of them . . . and they moved me into the big town house with *them* . . . fixed a nice place for me under the stove . . . gave me an army blanket . . . and my own dish . . . my very own dish! So, what have I got to complain about? Nothing, of course. I'm not complaining. (*She looks up at the sky, shouts to someone off stage.*) Shouldn't it be getting dark now, dear?

The lights dim; night comes on. The Musician begins to play; it becomes deepest night. There are spots on all the players, including the Young Man, who is, of course, continuing his calisthenics.

DADDY (*stirring*): It's nighttime.

MOMMY: Shhhh. Be still . . . wait.

DADDY (*whining*): It's so hot.

MOMMY: Shhhhhh. Be still . . . wait.

GRANDMA (*to herself*): That's better. Night. (*To the Musician.*) Honey, do you play
all through this part?

The Musician nods.

Well, keep it nice and soft; that's a good boy.

The Musician nods again; plays softly.

That's nice.

There is an off-stage rumble.

DADDY (*starting*): What was that?

MOMMY (*beginning to weep*): It was nothing.

DADDY: It was . . . it was . . . thunder . . . or a wave breaking . . . or something.

MOMMY (*whispering, through her tears*): It was an off-stage rumble . . . and you
know what *that* means. . . .

DADDY: I forget. . . .

MOMMY (*barely able to talk*): It means the time has come for poor Grandma . . .
and I can't bear it!

DADDY (*vacantly*): I . . . I suppose you've got to be brave.

GRANDMA (*mocking*): That's right, kid; be brave. You'll bear up; you'll get over
it.

Another off-stage rumble . . . louder.

MOMMY: Ohhhhhhhhhh . . . poor Grandma . . . poor Grandma. . . .

GRANDMA (*to Mommy*): I'm fine! I'm all right! It hasn't happened yet!

*A violent off-stage rumble. All the lights go out, save the spot on the Young Man; the
Musician stops playing.*

MOMMY: Ohhhhhhhhhh. . . . Ohhhhhhhhhh. . . .

Silence.

GRANDMA: Don't put the lights up yet . . . I'm not ready; I'm not quite ready.
(*Silence.*) All right, dear . . . I'm about done.

*The lights come up again, to brightest day; the Musician begins to play. Grandma is
discovered, still in the sandbox, lying on her side, propped up on an elbow, half covered, busily shoveling sand over herself.*

GRANDMA (*muttering*): I don't know how I'm supposed to do anything with
this goddam toy shovel. . . .

DADDY: Mommy! It's daylight!

MOMMY (*brightly*): So it is! Well! Our long night is over. We must put away our
tears, take off our mourning . . . and face the future. It's our duty.

GRANDMA (*still shoveling; mimicking*): . . . take off our mourning . . . face the future. . . . Lordy!

Mommy and Daddy rise, stretch. Mommy waves to the Young Man.

YOUNG MAN (*with that smile*): Hi!

Grandma plays dead. (!) Mommy and Daddy go over to look at her; she is a little more than half buried in the sand; the toy shovel is in her hands, which are crossed on her breast.

MOMMY (*before the sandbox; shaking her head*): Lovely! It's . . . it's hard to be sad . . . she looks . . . so happy. (*With pride and conviction.*) It pays to do things well. (*To the Musician.*) All right, you can stop now, if you want to. I mean, stay around for a swim, or something; it's all right with us. (*She sighs heavily.*) Well, Daddy . . . off we go.

DADDY: Brave Mommy!

MOMMY: Brave Daddy!

They exit, stage-left.

GRANDMA (*after they leave; lying quite still*): It pays to do things well. . . . Boy, oh boy! (*She tries to sit up.*) . . . well, kids . . . (*but she finds she can't*) . . . I . . . I can't get up. I . . . I can't move. . . .

The Young Man stops his calisthenics, nods to the Musician, walks over to Grandma, kneels down by the sandbox.

GRANDMA: I . . . can't move. . . .

YOUNG MAN: Shhhhh . . . be very still. . . .

GRANDMA: I . . . I can't move. . . .

YOUNG MAN: Uh . . . ma'am; I . . . I have a line here.

GRANDMA: Oh, I'm sorry, sweetie; you go right ahead.

YOUNG MAN: I am . . . uh . . .

GRANDMA: Take your time, dear.

YOUNG MAN (*prepares; delivers the line like a real amateur*): I am the Angel of Death. I am . . . uh . . . I am come for you.

GRANDMA: What . . . wha . . . (*Then, with resignation.*) . . . ohhhh . . . ohhhh, I see.

The Young Man bends over, kisses Grandma gently on the forehead.

GRANDMA (*her eyes closed, her hands folded on her breast again, the shovel between her hands, a sweet smile on her face*): Well . . . that was very nice, dear. . . .

YOUNG MAN (*still kneeling*): Shhhhhh . . . be still. . . .

GRANDMA: What I meant was . . . you did that very well, dear. . . .

YOUNG MAN (*blushing*): . . . . oh . . .

GRANDMA: No; I mean it. You've got that . . . you've got a quality.

YOUNG MAN (*with his endearing smile*): Oh . . . thank you; thank you very much . . . ma'am.

GRANDMA (*slowly; softly — as the Young Man puts his hands on top of Grandma's*): You're . . . you're welcome . . . dear.

Tableau. The Musician continues to play as the curtain slowly comes down.

Curtain

LORRAINE HANSBERRY *(1930–1965) was born in Chicago, the youngest of four children of Carl Hansberry, a successful real estate agent who founded one of the first African American banks in that city. Despite her parents' wealth, the family was forced by Chicago law to live in the ghetto on the South Side. When Hansberry was eight years old, her father bought a home in a white neighborhood. After the family moved into their new house, a mob threw a brick through the window, barely missing her. Carl Hansberry decided to stay in the house, although he had not been given clear title to it, and he began a civil rights suit to test the restrictive law. After he lost his case in the Illinois courts, he was supported by the National Association for the Advancement of Colored People (NAACP) to appeal the decision in the United States Supreme Court. The ruling was reversed, and the family continued to live in the house.*

In To Be Young, Gifted and Black *(1971), a posthumous collection of Hansberry's writing, she described how she became involved in a race riot in high school that radicalized her still further when she was seventeen. She attended officially integrated Englewood High School, but in 1947 the white students went on a strike against the blacks. Hansberry described how "the well-dressed, colored students like herself had stood amusedly around the parapet, staring, simply staring at the mob of several hundred striking whites, trading taunts and insults — but showing not the least inclination to further assert racial pride." Word about the riot at the high school spread from the affluent neighborhood to the South Side ghetto schools: "The ofays [whites]·are out on strike and beating up and raping colored girls under the viaduct." Carloads of poor black students, "waving baseball bats and shouting slogans of the charge," drove up to Englewood High School. Hansberry watched them "come, pouring out of the bowels of the ghetto, the children of the unqualified oppressed: the black working class in their costumes of pegged pants and conked heads and tight skirts and almost knee-length sweaters and — worst of all — colored anklets, held up by rubber bands! Yes, they had come and they had fought . . . She never could forget one thing:* They had fought back!"

Hansberry's ambition in high school was to become a journalist. After two years at the University of Wisconsin, she transferred to the New School for Social Research in New York City. In New York she began working as a reporter and editor for Freedom, *a monthly magazine owned by the black actor Paul Robeson. After her marriage to the playwright Robert Nemiroff in 1953, she began to write plays full-time.* A Raisin in the Sun, *her first completed work, was produced on Broadway in 1959 with money raised by her friends. Starring the then little-known Sidney Poitier as Walter Lee Younger, the play was immediately successful. Hansberry became the first black playwright to win the New York Drama Critics Circle Award, a landmark achievement in American theater in view of both her gender and race.*

Hansberry took the title of A Raisin in the Sun *from a poem by Langston Hughes, "Harlem (A Dream Deferred)." In her play she looked beneath what Hughes called "the surface of Negro color" to dramatize the human situation of her characters, fulfilling Hughes's vision in his essay "Writers: Black and White" that an African American writer would succeed by becoming a "writer first, colored second. This means losing nothing of your racial identity. It is just that in the great sense of the word, anytime, any place, good art transcends land, race, or nationality, and color drops away. If you are a good writer, in the end neither blackness nor whiteness makes a difference to readers."*

In the early 1960s Hansberry used her prominence as a successful playwright to champion civil rights causes, as in The Movement: Documentary of a Struggle for Equality *(1964), a book of photographs in support of the Student Nonviolent Coordinating Committee (SNCC). Suffering from cancer, she completed only one other full-length play,* The Sign in Sidney Brustein's Window, *produced in 1964, three months before her death. In 1972 Nemiroff edited a volume of her short plays,* Les Blancs: The Collected Last Plays of Lorraine Hansberry, *and produced a musical version of* A Raisin in the Sun *that won a Tony Award.*

RELATED COMMENTARIES: *See Casebook on Lorraine Hansberry's* A Raisin in the Sun, *pages 2066–2080, including Lorraine Hansberry, "My Shakespearean Experience," page 2067; James Baldwin, "Sweet Lorraine," page 2068; Julius Lester, "The Heroic Dimension in* A Raisin in the Sun," *page 2070; Anne Cheney, "The African Heritage in* A Raisin in the Sun," *page 2073; Steven R. Carter, "Hansberry's Artistic Misstep," page 2076; and Margaret B. Wilkerson, "Hansberry's Awareness of Culture and Gender," page 2077.*

LORRAINE HANSBERRY

A Raisin in the Sun 1959

Harlem (A Dream Deferred)

What happens to a dream deferred?

Does it dry up
Like a raisin in the sun?
Or fester like a sore —
And then run?
Does it stink like rotten meat?
Or crust and sugar over —
Like a syrupy sweet?

Maybe it just sags
Like a heavy load.

Or does it explode?
    – LANGSTON HUGHES

CHARACTERS (IN ORDER OF APPEARANCE)

RUTH YOUNGER
TRAVIS YOUNGER
WALTER LEE YOUNGER, *brother*
BENEATHA YOUNGER
LENA YOUNGER, *Mama*
JOSEPH ASAGAI
GEORGE MURCHISON
MRS. JOHNSON
KARL LINDNER
BOBO
MOVING MEN

The action of the play is set in Chicago's Southside, sometime between World War II and the present.

ACT I

SCENE I. [*Friday morning.*]

The Younger living room would be a comfortable and well-ordered room if it were not for a number of indestructible contradictions to this state of being. Its furnishings are typical and undistinguished and their primary feature now is that they have clearly had to accommodate the living of too many people for too many years — and they are tired. Still, we can see that at some time, a time probably no longer remembered by the family (except perhaps for Mama), the furnishings of this room were actually selected with care and love and even hope — and brought to this apartment and arranged with taste and pride.

That was a long time ago. Now the once loved pattern of the couch upholstery has to fight to show itself from under acres of crocheted doilies and couch covers which have themselves finally come to be more important than the upholstery. And here a table or a chair has been moved to disguise the worn places in the carpet; but the carpet has fought back by showing its weariness, with depressing uniformity, elsewhere on its surface.

Weariness has, in fact, won in this room. Everything has been polished, washed, sat on, used, scrubbed too often. All pretenses but living itself have long since vanished from the very atmosphere of this room.

Moreover, a section of this room, for it is not really a room unto itself, though the landlord's lease would make it seem so, slopes backward to provide a small kitchen area, where the family prepares the meals that are eaten in the living room proper, which must also serve as dining room. The single window that has been provided for these "two" rooms is located in this kitchen area. The sole natural light the family may enjoy in the course of a day is only that which fights its way through this little window.

At left, a door leads to a bedroom which is shared by Mama and her daughter, Beneatha. At right, opposite, is a second room (which in the beginning of the life of this apartment was probably a breakfast room) which serves as a bedroom for Walter and his wife, Ruth.

Time: Sometime between World War II and the present.

Place: Chicago's Southside.

At Rise: It is morning dark in the living room. Travis is asleep on the make-down bed at center. An alarm clock sounds from within the bedroom at right, and presently Ruth enters from that room and closes the door behind her. She crosses sleepily toward the window. As she passes her sleeping son she reaches down and shakes him a little. At the window she raises the shade and a dusky Southside morning light comes in feebly. She fills a pot with water and puts it on to boil. She calls to the boy, between yawns, in a slightly muffled voice.

Ruth is about thirty. We can see that she was a pretty girl, even exceptionally so, but now it is apparent that life has been little that she expected, and disappointment has already begun to hang in her face. In a few years, before thirty-five even, she will be known among her people as a "settled woman."

She crosses to her son and gives him a good, final, rousing shake.

RUTH: Come on now, boy, it's seven thirty! (*Her son sits up at last, in a stupor of sleepiness.*) I say hurry up, Travis! You ain't the only person in the world got to use a bathroom! (*The child, a sturdy, handsome little boy of ten or eleven, drags himself out of the bed and almost blindly takes his towels and "to-day's clothes" from drawers and a closet and goes out to the bathroom, which is in an outside hall and which is shared by another family or families on the same floor. Ruth crosses to the bedroom door at right and opens it and calls in to her husband.*) Walter Lee! . . . It's after seven thirty! Lemme see you do some waking up in there now! (*She waits.*) You better get up from there, man! It's after seven thirty I tell you. (*She waits again.*) All right, you just go ahead and lay there and next thing you know Travis be finished and Mr. Johnson'll be in there and you'll be fussing and cussing round here like a madman! And be late too! (*She waits, at the end of patience.*) Walter Lee — it's time for you to GET UP!

She waits another second and then starts to go into the bedroom, but is apparently satisfied that her husband has begun to get up. She stops, pulls the door to, and returns to the kitchen area. She wipes her face with a moist cloth and runs her fingers through her sleep-disheveled hair in a vain effort and ties an apron around her housecoat. The bedroom door at right opens and her husband stands in the doorway in his pajamas, which are rumpled and mismated. He is a lean, intense young man in his middle thirties, inclined to quick nervous movements and erratic speech habits — and always in his voice there is a quality of indictment.

WALTER: Is he out yet?

RUTH: What you mean *out?* He ain't hardly got in there good yet.

WALTER (*wandering in, still more oriented to sleep than to a new day*): Well, what was you doing all that yelling for if I can't even get in there yet? (*Stopping and thinking.*) Check coming today?

RUTH: They *said* Saturday and this is just Friday and I hopes to God you ain't going to get up here first thing this morning and start talking to me 'bout no money — 'cause I 'bout don't want to hear it.

WALTER: Something the matter with you this morning?

RUTH: No — I'm just sleepy as the devil. What kind of eggs you want?

WALTER: Not scrambled. (*Ruth starts to scramble eggs.*) Paper come? (*Ruth points impatiently to the rolled up* Tribune *on the table, and he gets it and spreads it out and vaguely reads the front page.*) Set off another bomb yesterday.

RUTH (*maximum indifference*): Did they?

WALTER (*looking up*): What's the matter with you?

RUTH: Ain't nothing the matter with me. And don't keep asking me that this morning.

WALTER: Ain't nobody bothering you. (*Reading the news of the day absently again.*) Say Colonel McCormick is sick.

RUTH (*affecting tea-party interest*): Is he now? Poor thing.

WALTER (*sighing and looking at his watch*): Oh, me. (*He waits.*) Now what is that boy doing in that bathroom all this time? He just going to have to start getting up earlier. I can't be being late to work on account of him fooling around in there.

RUTH (*turning on him*): Oh, no he ain't going to be getting up no earlier no such thing! It ain't his fault that he can't get to bed no earlier nights 'cause he got a bunch of crazy good-for-nothing clowns sitting up running their mouths in what is supposed to be his bedroom after ten o'clock at night . . .

WALTER: That's what you mad about, ain't it? The things I want to talk about with my friends just couldn't be important in your mind, could they?

He rises and finds a cigarette in her handbag on the table and crosses to the little window and looks out, smoking and deeply enjoying this first one.

RUTH (*almost matter of factly, a complaint too automatic to deserve emphasis*): Why you always got to smoke before you eat in the morning?

WALTER (*at the window*): Just look at 'em down there . . . Running and racing to work . . . (*He turns and faces his wife and watches her a moment at the stove, and then, suddenly.*) You look young this morning, baby.

RUTH (*indifferently*): Yeah?

WALTER: Just for a second — stirring them eggs. Just for a second it was — you looked real young again. (*He reaches for her; she crosses away. Then, drily.*) It's gone now — you look like yourself again!

RUTH: Man, if you don't shut up and leave me alone.

WALTER (*looking out to the street again*): First thing a man ought to learn in life is not to make love to no colored woman first thing in the morning. You all some eeeevil people at eight o'clock in the morning.

Travis appears in the hall doorway, almost fully dressed and quite wide awake now, his towels and pajamas across his shoulders. He opens the door and signals for his father to make the bathroom in a hurry.

TRAVIS (*watching the bathroom*): Daddy, come on!

Walter gets his bathroom utensils and flies out to the bathroom.

RUTH: Sit down and have your breakfast, Travis.

TRAVIS: Mama, this is Friday. (*Gleefully.*) Check coming tomorrow, huh?

RUTH: You get your mind off money and eat your breakfast.

TRAVIS (*eating*): This is the morning we supposed to bring the fifty cents to school.

RUTH: Well, I ain't got no fifty cents this morning.

TRAVIS: Teacher say we have to.

RUTH: I don't care what teacher say. I ain't got it. Eat your breakfast, Travis.

TRAVIS: I *am* eating.

RUTH: Hush up now and just eat!

The boy gives her an exasperated look for her lack of understanding, and eats grudgingly.

TRAVIS: You think Grandmama would have it?

RUTH: No! And I want you to stop asking your grandmother for money, you hear me?

TRAVIS (*outraged*): Gaaaleee! I don't ask her, she just gimme it sometimes!

RUTH: Travis Willard Younger — I got too much on me this morning to be —

TRAVIS: Maybe Daddy —
RUTH: *Travis!*

The boy hushes abruptly. They are both quiet and tense for several seconds.

TRAVIS (*presently*): Could I maybe go carry some groceries in front of the supermarket for a little while after school then?

RUTH: Just hush, I said. (*Travis jabs his spoon into his cereal bowl viciously, and rests
his head in anger upon his fists.*) If you through eating, you can get over
there and make up your bed.

*The boy obeys stiffly and crosses the room, almost mechanically, to the bed and more
or less folds the bedding into a heap, then angrily gets his books and cap.*

TRAVIS (*sulking and standing apart from her unnaturally*): I'm gone.

RUTH (*looking up from the stove to inspect him automatically*): Come here. (*He
crosses to her and she studies his head.*) If you don't take this comb and fix
this here head, you better! (*Travis puts down his books with a great sigh of
oppression, and crosses to the mirror. His mother mutters under her breath
about his "slubbornness."*) 'Bout to march out of here with that head looking just like chickens slept in it! I just don't know where you get your
slubborn ways . . . And get your jacket, too. Looks chilly out this morning.

TRAVIS (*with conspicuously brushed hair and jacket*): I'm gone.

RUTH: Get carfare and milk money — (*Waving one finger.*) — and not a single
penny for no caps, you hear me?

TRAVIS (*with sullen politeness*): Yes'm.

*He turns in outrage to leave. His mother watches after him as in his frustration he ap-
proaches the door almost comically. When she speaks to him, her voice has become a
very gentle tease.*

RUTH (*mocking; as she thinks he would say it*): Oh, Mama makes me so mad sometimes, I don't know what to do! (*She waits and continues to his back as he
stands stock-still in front of the door.*) I wouldn't kiss that woman good-bye
for nothing in this world this morning! (*The boy finally turns around and
rolls his eyes at her, knowing the mood has changed and he is vindicated; he does
not, however, move toward her yet.*) Not for nothing in this world! (*She finally laughs aloud at him and holds out her arms to him and we see that it is a
way between them, very old and practiced. He crosses to her and allows her to
embrace him warmly but keeps his face fixed with masculine rigidity. She holds
him back from her presently and looks at him and runs her fingers over the features of his face. With utter gentleness — .*) Now — whose little old angry
man are you?

TRAVIS (*the masculinity and gruffness start to fade at last*): Aw gaalee — Mama . . .

RUTH (*mimicking*): Aw — gaaaaalleeeee, Mama! (*She pushes him, with rough
playfulness and finality, toward the door.*) Get on out of here or you going to
be late.

TRAVIS (*in the face of love, new aggressiveness*): Mama, could I *please* go carry groceries?

RUTH: Honey, it's starting to get so cold evenings.

WALTER (*coming in from the bathroom and drawing a make-believe gun from a make-believe holster and shooting at his son*): What is it he wants to do?

RUTH: Go carry groceries after school at the supermarket.

WALTER: Well, let him go . . .

TRAVIS (*quickly, to the ally*): I *have* to — she won't gimme the fifty cents . . .

WALTER (*to his wife only*): Why not?

RUTH (*simply, and with flavor*): 'Cause we don't have it.

WALTER (*to Ruth only*): What you tell the boy things like that for? (*Reaching down into his pants with a rather important gesture.*) Here, son —

He hands the boy the coin, but his eyes are directed to his wife's. Travis takes the money happily.

TRAVIS: Thanks, Daddy.

He starts out. Ruth watches both of them with murder in her eyes. Walter stands and stares back at her with defiance, and suddenly reaches into his pocket again on an afterthought.

WALTER (*without even looking at his son, still staring hard at his wife*): In fact, here's another fifty cents . . . Buy yourself some fruit today — or take a taxicab to school or something!

TRAVIS: Whoopee —

He leaps up and clasps his father around the middle with his legs, and they face each other in mutual appreciation; slowly Walter Lee peeks around the boy to catch the violent rays from his wife's eyes and draws his head back as if shot.

WALTER: You better get down now — and get to school, man.

TRAVIS (*at the door*): O.K. Good-bye.

He exits.

WALTER (*after him, pointing with pride*): That's *my* boy. (*She looks at him in disgust and turns back to her work.*) You know what I was thinking 'bout in the bathroom this morning?

RUTH: No.

WALTER: How come you always try to be so pleasant!

RUTH: What is there to be pleasant 'bout!

WALTER: You want to know what I was thinking 'bout in the bathroom or not!

RUTH: I know what you thinking 'bout.

WALTER (*ignoring her*): 'Bout what me and Willy Harris was talking about last night.

RUTH (*immediately — a refrain*): Willy Harris is a good-for-nothing loudmouth.

WALTER: Anybody who talks to me has got to be a good-for-nothing loudmouth, ain't he? And what you know about who is just a good-for-nothing loudmouth? Charlie Atkins was just a "good-for-nothing loudmouth" too, wasn't he! When he wanted me to go in the dry-cleaning business with him. And now — he's grossing a hundred thousand a year. A hundred thousand dollars a year! You still call *him* a loudmouth!

RUTH (*bitterly*): Oh, Walter Lee . . .

She folds her head on her arms over the table.

WALTER (*rising and coming to her and standing over her*): You tired, ain't you? Tired of everything. Me, the boy, the way we live — this beat-up hole — everything. Ain't you? (*She doesn't look up, doesn't answer.*) So tired — moaning and groaning all the time, but you wouldn't do nothing to help, would you? You couldn't be on my side that long for nothing, could you?

RUTH: Walter, please leave me alone.

WALTER: A man needs for a woman to back him up . . .

RUTH: Walter —

WALTER: Mama would listen to you. You know she listen to you more than she do me and Bennie. She think more of you. All you have to do is just sit down with her when you drinking your coffee one morning and talking 'bout things like you do and — (*He sits down beside her and demonstrates graphically what he thinks her methods and tone should be.*) — you just sip your coffee, see, and say easy like that you been thinking 'bout that deal Walter Lee is so interested in, 'bout the store and all, and sip some more coffee, like what you saying ain't really that important to you — And the next thing you know, she be listening good and asking you questions and when I come home — I can tell her the details. This ain't no fly-by-night proposition, baby. I mean we figured it out, me and Willy and Bobo.

RUTH (*with a frown*): Bobo?

WALTER: Yeah. You see, this little liquor store we got in mind cost seventy-five thousand and we figured the initial investment on the place be 'bout thirty thousand, see. That be ten thousand each. Course, there's a couple of hundred you got to pay so's you don't spend your life just waiting for them clowns to let your license get approved —

RUTH: You mean graft?

WALTER (*frowning impatiently*): Don't call it that. See there, that just goes to show you what women understand about the world. Baby, don't *nothing* happen for you in the world 'less you pay *somebody* off!

RUTH: Walter, leave me alone! (*She raises her head and stares at him vigorously — then says, more quietly.*) Eat your eggs, they gonna be cold.

WALTER (*straightening up from her and looking off*): That's it. There you are. Man say to his woman: I got me a dream. His woman say: Eat your eggs. (*Sadly, but gaining in power.*) Man say: I got to take hold of this here world, baby! And a woman will say: Eat your eggs and go to work. (*Passionately now.*) Man say: I got to change my life, I'm choking to death, baby! And his woman say — (*In utter anguish as he brings his fists down on his thighs.*) — Your eggs is getting cold!

RUTH (*softly*): Walter, that ain't none of our money.

WALTER (*not listening at all or even looking at her*): This morning, I was lookin' in the mirror and thinking about it . . . I'm thirty-five years old; I been married eleven years and I got a boy who sleeps in the living room — (*Very, very quietly.*) — and all I got to give him is stories about how rich white people live . . .

RUTH: Eat your eggs, Walter.

WALTER (*slams the table and jumps up*): — DAMN MY EGGS — DAMN ALL
THE EGGS THAT EVER WAS!

RUTH: Then go to work.

WALTER (*looking up at her*): See — I'm trying to talk to you 'bout myself —
(*Shaking his head with the repetition.*) — and all you can say is eat them
eggs and go to work.

RUTH (*wearily*): Honey, you never say nothing new. I listen to you every day,
every night and every morning, and you never say nothing new. (*Shrugging.*) So you would rather *be* Mr. Arnold than be his chauffeur. So — I
would *rather* be living in Buckingham Palace.

WALTER: That is just what is wrong with the colored woman in this world . . .
Don't understand about building their men up and making 'em feel like
they somebody. Like they can do something.

RUTH (*drily, but to hurt*): There *are* colored men who do things.

WALTER: No thanks to the colored woman.

RUTH: Well, being a colored woman, I guess I can't help myself none.

*She rises and gets the ironing board and sets it up and attacks a huge pile of rough-
dried clothes, sprinkling them in preparation for the ironing and then rolling them
into tight fat balls.*

WALTER (*mumbling*): We one group of men tied to a race of women with small
minds!

*His sister Beneatha enters. She is about twenty, as slim and intense as her brother. She
is not as pretty as her sister-in-law, but her lean, almost intellectual face has a hand-
someness of its own. She wears a bright-red flannel nightie, and her thick hair stands
wildly about her head. Her speech is a mixture of many things; it is different from the
rest of the family's insofar as education has permeated her sense of English — and perhaps the Midwest rather than the South has finally — at last — won out in her inflection; but not altogether, because over all of it is a soft slurring and transformed use
of vowels which is the decided influence of the Southside. She passes through the room
without looking at either Ruth or Walter and goes to the outside door and looks, a little blindly, out to the bathroom. She sees that it has been lost to the Johnsons. She
closes the door with a sleepy vengeance and crosses to the table and sits down a little
defeated.*

BENEATHA: I am going to start timing those people.

WALTER: You should get up earlier.

BENEATHA (*her face in her hands. She is still fighting the urge to go back to bed*): Really — would you suggest dawn? Where's the paper?

WALTER (*pushing the paper across the table to her as he studies her almost clinically,
as though he has never seen her before*): You a horrible-looking chick at this
hour.

BENEATHA (*drily*): Good morning, everybody.

WALTER (*senselessly*): How is school coming?

BENEATHA (*in the same spirit*): Lovely. Lovely. And you know, biology is the
greatest. (*Looking up at him.*) I dissected something that looked just like
you yesterday.

WALTER: I just wondered if you've made up your mind and everything.

BENEATHA (*gaining in sharpness and impatience*): And what did I answer yesterday morning — and the day before that?

RUTH (*from the ironing board, like someone disinterested and old*): Don't be so nasty, Bennie.

BENEATHA (*still to her brother*): And the day before that and the day before that!

WALTER (*defensively*): I'm interested in you. Something wrong with that? Ain't many girls who decide —

WALTER AND BENEATHA (*in unison*): — "to be a doctor."

Silence.

WALTER: Have we figured out yet just exactly how much medical school is going to cost?

RUTH: Walter Lee, why don't you leave that girl alone and get out of here to work?

BENEATHA (*exits to the bathroom and bangs on the door*): Come on out of there, please!

She comes back into the room.

WALTER (*looking at his sister intently*): You know the check is coming tomorrow.

BENEATHA (*turning on him with a sharpness all her own*): That money belongs to Mama, Walter, and it's for her to decide how she wants to use it. I don't care if she wants to buy a house or a rocket ship or just nail it up somewhere and look at it. It's hers. Not ours — *hers.*

WALTER (*bitterly*): Now ain't that fine! You just got your mother's interest at heart, ain't you, girl? You such a nice girl — but if Mama got that money she can always take a few thousand and help you through school too — can't she?

BENEATHA: I have never asked anyone around here to do anything for me!

WALTER: No! And the line between asking and just accepting when the time comes is big and wide — ain't it!

BENEATHA (*with fury*): What do you want from me, Brother — that I quit school or just drop dead, which!

WALTER: I don't want nothing but for you to stop acting holy 'round here. Me and Ruth done made some sacrifices for you — why can't you do something for the family?

RUTH: Walter, don't be dragging me in it.

WALTER: You are in it — Don't you get up and go work in somebody's kitchen for the last three years to help put clothes on her back?

RUTH: Oh, Walter — that's not fair . . .

WALTER: It ain't that nobody expects you to get on your knees and say thank you, Brother; thank you, Ruth; thank you, Mama — and thank you, Travis, for wearing the same pair of shoes for two semesters —

BENEATHA (*dropping to her knees*): Well — I *do* — all right? — thank everybody! And forgive me for ever wanting to be anything at all! (*Pursuing him on her knees across the floor.*) FORGIVE ME, FORGIVE ME, FORGIVE ME!

RUTH: Please stop it! Your mama'll hear you.

WALTER: Who the hell told you you had to be a doctor? If you so crazy 'bout messing 'round with sick people — then go be a nurse like other women — or just get married and be quiet . . .

BENEATHA: Well — you finally got it said . . . It took you three years but you finally got it said. Walter, give up; leave me alone — it's Mama's money.

WALTER: *He was my father, too!*

BENEATHA: So what? He was mine, too — and Travis' grandfather — but the insurance money belongs to Mama. Picking on me is not going to make her give it to you to invest in any liquor stores — (*Under breath, dropping into a chair.*) — and I for one say, God bless Mama for that!

WALTER (*to Ruth*): See — did you hear? Did you hear!

RUTH: Honey, please go to work.

WALTER: Nobody in this house is ever going to understand me.

BENEATHA: Because you're a nut.

WALTER: Who's a nut?

BENEATHA: You — you are a nut. Thee is mad, boy.

WALTER (*looking at his wife and his sister from the door, very sadly*): The world's most backward race of people, and that's a fact.

BENEATHA (*turning slowly in her chair*): And then there are all those prophets who would lead us out of the wilderness — (*Walter slams out of the house.*) — into the swamps!

RUTH: Bennie, why you always gotta be pickin' on your brother? Can't you be a little sweeter sometimes? (*Door opens. Walter walks in. He fumbles with his cap, starts to speak, clears throat, looks everywhere but at Ruth. Finally:*)

WALTER (*to Ruth*): I need some money for carfare.

RUTH (*looks at him, then warms; teasing, but tenderly*): Fifty cents? (*She goes to her bag and gets money.*) Here — take a taxi!

Walter exits. Mama enters. She is a woman in her early sixties, full-bodied and strong. She is one of those women of a certain grace and beauty who wear it so unobtrusively that it takes a while to notice. Her dark-brown face is surrounded by the total whiteness of her hair, and, being a woman who has adjusted to many things in life and overcome many more, her face is full of strength. She has, we can see, wit and faith of a kind that keep her eyes lit and full of interest and expectancy. She is, in a word, a beautiful woman. Her bearing is perhaps most like the noble bearing of the women of the Hereros of Southwest Africa — rather as if she imagines that as she walks she still bears a basket or a vessel upon her head. Her speech, on the other hand, is as careless as her carriage is precise — she is inclined to slur everything — but her voice is perhaps not so much quiet as simply soft.

MAMA: Who that 'round here slamming doors at this hour?

She crosses through the room, goes to the window, opens it, and brings in a feeble little plant growing doggedly in a small pot on the window sill. She feels the dirt and puts it back out.

RUTH: That was Walter Lee. He and Bennie was at it again.

MAMA: My children and they tempers. Lord, if this little old plant don't get more sun than it's been getting it ain't never going to see spring again. (*She turns from the window.*) What's the matter with you this morning,

Ruth? You looks right peaked. You aiming to iron all them things? Leave
some for me. I'll get to 'em this afternoon. Bennie honey, it's too drafty
for you to be sitting 'round half dressed. Where's your robe?

BENEATHA: In the cleaners.

MAMA: Well, go get mine and put it on.

BENEATHA: I'm not cold, Mama, honest.

MAMA: I know — but you so thin . . .

BENEATHA (*irritably*): Mama, I'm not cold.

MAMA (*seeing the make-down bed as Travis has left it*): Lord have mercy, look at
that poor bed. Bless his heart — he tries, don't he?

She moves to the bed Travis has sloppily made up.

RUTH: No — he don't half try at all 'cause he knows you going to come along
behind him and fix everything. That's just how come he don't know
how to do nothing right now — you done spoiled that boy so.

MAMA (*folding bedding*): Well — he's a little boy. Ain't supposed to know 'bout
housekeeping. My baby, that's what he is. What you fix for his breakfast
this morning?

RUTH (*angrily*): I feed my son, Lena!

MAMA: I ain't meddling — (*Under breath; busy-bodyish.*) I just noticed all last
week he had cold cereal, and when it starts getting this chilly in the fall
a child ought to have some hot grits or something when he goes out in
the cold —

RUTH (*furious*): I gave him hot oats — is that all right!

MAMA: I ain't meddling. (*Pause.*) Put a lot of nice butter on it? (*Ruth shoots her
an angry look and does not reply.*) He likes lots of butter.

RUTH (*exasperated*): Lena —

MAMA (*to Beneatha. Mama is inclined to wander conversationally sometimes*): What
was you and your brother fussing 'bout this morning?

BENEATHA: It's not important, Mama.

*She gets up and goes to look out at the bathroom, which is apparently free, and she
picks up her towels and rushes out.*

MAMA: What was they fighting about?

RUTH: Now you know as well as I do.

MAMA (*shaking her head*): Brother still worrying hisself sick about that money?

RUTH: You know he is.

MAMA: You had breakfast?

RUTH: Some coffee.

MAMA: Girl, you better start eating and looking after yourself better. You almost thin as Travis.

RUTH: Lena —

MAMA: Un-hunh?

RUTH: What are you going to do with it?

MAMA: Now don't you start, child. It's too early in the morning to be talking
about money. It ain't Christian.

RUTH: It's just that he got his heart set on that store —

MAMA: You mean that liquor store that Willy Harris want him to invest in?

RUTH: Yes —

MAMA: We ain't no business people, Ruth. We just plain working folks.

RUTH: Ain't nobody business people till they go into business. Walter Lee say colored people ain't never going to start getting ahead till they start gambling on some different kinds of things in the world — investments and things.

MAMA: What done got into you, girl? Walter Lee done finally sold you on investing.

RUTH: No. Mama, something is happening between Walter and me. I don't know what it is — but he needs something — something I can't give him any more. He needs this chance, Lena.

MAMA (*frowning deeply*): But liquor, honey —

RUTH: Well — like Walter say — I spec people going to always be drinking themselves some liquor.

MAMA: Well — whether they drinks it or not ain't none of my business. But whether I go into business selling it to 'em *is*, and I don't want that on my ledger this late in life. (*Stopping suddenly and studying her daughter-in-law.*) Ruth Younger, what's the matter with you today? You look like you could fall over right there.

RUTH: I'm tired.

MAMA: Then you better stay home from work today.

RUTH: I can't stay home. She'd be calling up the agency and screaming at them, "My girl didn't come in today — send me somebody! My girl didn't come in!" Oh, she just have a fit . . .

MAMA: Well, let her have it. I'll just call her up and say you got the flu —

RUTH (*laughing*): Why the flu?

MAMA: 'Cause it sounds respectable to 'em. Something white people get, too. They know 'bout the flu. Otherwise they think you been cut up or something when you tell 'em you sick.

RUTH: I got to go in. We need the money.

MAMA: Somebody would of thought my children done all but starved to death the way they talk about money here late. Child, we got a great big old check coming tomorrow.

RUTH (*sincerely, but also self-righteously*): Now that's your money. It ain't got nothing to do with me. We all feel like that — Walter and Bennie and me — even Travis.

MAMA (*thoughtfully, and suddenly very far away*): Ten thousand dollars —

RUTH: Sure is wonderful.

MAMA: Ten thousand dollars.

RUTH: You know what you should do, Miss Lena? You should take yourself a trip somewhere. To Europe or South America or someplace —

MAMA (*throwing up her hands at the thought*): Oh, child!

RUTH: I'm serious. Just pack up and leave! Go on away and enjoy yourself some. Forget about the family and have yourself a ball for once in your life —

MAMA (*drily*): You sound like I'm just about ready to die. Who'd go with me? What I look like wandering 'round Europe by myself?

RUTH: Shoot — these here rich white women do it all the time. They don't think nothing of packing up they suitcases and piling on one of them big steamships and — swoosh! — they gone, child.

MAMA: Something always told me I wasn't no rich white woman.

RUTH: Well — what are you going to do with it then?

MAMA: I ain't rightly decided. (*Thinking. She speaks now with emphasis.*) Some of it got to be put away for Beneatha and her schoolin' — and ain't nothing going to touch that part of it. Nothing. (*She waits several seconds, trying to make up her mind about something, and looks at Ruth a little tentatively before going on.*) Been thinking that we maybe could meet the notes on a little old two-story somewhere, with a yard where Travis could play in the summertime, if we use part of the insurance for a down payment and everybody kind of pitch in. I could maybe take on a little day work again, few days a week —

RUTH (*studying her mother-in-law furtively and concentrating on her ironing, anxious to encourage without seeming to*): Well, Lord knows, we've put enough rent into this here rat trap to pay for four houses by now . . .

MAMA (*looking up at the words "rat trap" and then looking around and leaning back and sighing — in a suddenly reflective mood —*): "Rat trap" — yes, that's all it is. (*Smiling.*) I remember just as well the day me and Big Walter moved in here. Hadn't been married but two weeks and wasn't planning on living here no more than a year. (*She shakes her head at the dissolved dream.*) We was going to set away, little by little, don't you know, and buy a little place out in Morgan Park. We had even picked out the house. (*Chuckling a little.*) Looks right dumpy today. But Lord, child, you should know all the dreams I had 'bout buying that house and fixing it up and making me a little garden in the back — (*She waits and stops smiling.*) And didn't none of it happen.

Dropping her hands in a futile gesture.

RUTH (*keeps her head down, ironing*): Yes, life can be a barrel of disappointments, sometimes.

MAMA: Honey, Big Walter would come in here some nights back then and slump down on that couch there and just look at the rug, and look at me and look at the rug and then back at me — and I'd know he was down then . . . really down. (*After a second very long and thoughtful pause; she is seeing back to times that only she can see.*) And then, Lord, when I lost that baby — little Claude — I almost thought I was going to lose Big Walter too. Oh, that man grieved hisself! He was one man to love his children.

RUTH: Ain't nothin' can tear at you like losin' your baby.

MAMA: I guess that's how come that man finally worked hisself to death like he done. Like he was fighting his own war with this here world that took his baby from him.

RUTH: He sure was a fine man, all right. I always liked Mr. Younger.

MAMA: Crazy 'bout his children! God knows there was plenty wrong with Walter Younger — hard-headed, mean, kind of wild with women — plenty wrong with him. But he sure loved his children. Always wanted them to

have something — be something. That's where Brother gets all these notions, I reckon. Big Walter used to say, he'd get right wet in the eyes
sometimes, lean his head back with the water standing in his eyes and
say, "Seem like God didn't see fit to give the black man nothing but
dreams — but He did give us children to make them dreams seem
worthwhile." (*She smiles.*) He could talk like that, don't you know.

RUTH: Yes, he sure could. He was a good man, Mr. Younger.

MAMA: Yes, a fine man — just couldn't never catch up with his dreams, that's
all.

*Beneatha comes in, brushing her hair and looking up to the ceiling, where the sound
of a vacuum cleaner has started up.*

BENEATHA: What could be so dirty on that woman's rugs that she has to vacuum them every single day?

RUTH: I wish certain young women 'round here who I could name would take
inspiration about certain rugs in a certain apartment I could also mention.

BENEATHA (*shrugging*): How much cleaning can a house need, for Christ's
sakes.

MAMA (*not liking the Lord's name used thus*): Bennie!

RUTH: Just listen to her — just listen!

BENEATHA: Oh, God!

MAMA: If you use the Lord's name just one more time —

BENEATHA (*a bit of a whine*): Oh, Mama —

RUTH: Fresh — just fresh as salt, this girl!

BENEATHA (*drily*): Well — if the salt loses its savor —

MAMA: Now that will do. I just ain't going to have you 'round here reciting the
scriptures in vain — you hear me?

BENEATHA: How did I manage to get on everybody's wrong side by just walking into a room?

RUTH: If you weren't so fresh —

BENEATHA: Ruth, I'm twenty years old.

MAMA: What time you be home from school today?

BENEATHA: Kind of late. (*With enthusiasm.*) Madeline is going to start my guitar
lessons today.

Mama and Ruth look up with the same expression.

MAMA: Your *what* kind of lessons?

BENEATHA: Guitar.

RUTH: Oh, Father!

MAMA: How come you done taken it in your mind to learn to play the guitar?

BENEATHA: I just want to, that's all.

MAMA (*smiling*): Lord, child, don't you know what to do with yourself? How
long it going to be before you get tired of this now — like you got tired
of that little play-acting group you joined last year? (*Looking at Ruth.*)
And what was it the year before that?

RUTH: The horseback-riding club for which she bought that fifty-five-dollar
riding habit that's been hanging in the closet ever since!

MAMA (*to Beneatha*): Why you got to flit so from one thing to another, baby?

BENEATHA (*sharply*): I just want to learn to play the guitar. Is there anything wrong with that?

MAMA: Ain't nobody trying to stop you. I just wonders sometimes why you has to flit so from one thing to another all the time. You ain't never done nothing with all that camera equipment you brought home —

BENEATHA: I don't flit! I — I experiment with different forms of expression —

RUTH: Like riding a horse?

BENEATHA: — People have to express themselves one way or another.

MAMA: What is it you want to express?

BENEATHA (*angrily*): Me! (*Mama and Ruth look at each other and burst into raucous laughter.*) Don't worry — I don't expect you to understand.

MAMA (*to change the subject*): Who you going out with tomorrow night?

BENEATHA (*with displeasure*): George Murchison again.

MAMA (*pleased*): Oh — you getting a little sweet on him?

RUTH: You ask me, this child ain't sweet on nobody but herself — (*Under breath.*) Express herself!

They laugh.

BENEATHA: Oh — I like George all right, Mama. I mean I like him enough to go out with him and stuff, but —

RUTH (*for devilment*): What does *and stuff* mean?

BENEATHA: Mind your own business.

MAMA: Stop picking at her now, Ruth. (*She chuckles — then a suspicious sudden look at her daughter as she turns in her chair for emphasis.*) What DOES it mean?

BENEATHA (*wearily*): Oh, I just mean I couldn't ever really be serious about George. He's — he's so shallow.

RUTH: Shallow — what do you mean he's shallow? He's *Rich!*

MAMA: Hush, Ruth.

BENEATHA: I know he's rich. He knows he's rich, too.

RUTH: Well — what other qualities a man got to have to satisfy you, little girl?

BENEATHA: You wouldn't even begin to understand. Anybody who married Walter could not possibly understand.

MAMA (*outraged*): What kind of way is that to talk about your brother?

BENEATHA: Brother is a flip — let's face it.

MAMA (*to Ruth, helplessly*): What's a flip?

RUTH (*glad to add kindling*): She's saying he's crazy.

BENEATHA: Not crazy. Brother isn't really crazy yet — he — he's an elaborate neurotic.

MAMA: Hush your mouth!

BENEATHA: As for George. Well. George looks good — he's got a beautiful car and he takes me to nice places and, as my sister-in-law says, he is probably the richest boy I will ever get to know and I even like him sometimes — but if the Youngers are sitting around waiting to see if their little Bennie is going to tie up the family with the Murchisons, they are wasting their time.

RUTH: You mean you wouldn't marry George Murchison if he asked you someday? That pretty, rich thing? Honey, I knew you was odd —

BENEATHA: No I would not marry him if all I felt for him was what I feel now.
Besides, George's family wouldn't really like it.

MAMA: Why not?

BENEATHA: Oh, Mama — The Murchisons are honest-to-God-real-*live*-rich colored people, and the only people in the world who are more snobbish
than rich white people are rich colored people. I thought everybody
knew that. I've met Mrs. Murchison. She's a scene!

MAMA: You must not dislike people 'cause they well off, honey.

BENEATHA: Why not? It makes just as much sense as disliking people 'cause
they are poor, and lots of people do that.

RUTH (*a wisdom-of-the-ages manner. To Mama*): Well, she'll get over some of this —

BENEATHA: Get over it? What are you talking about, Ruth? Listen, I'm going to
be a doctor. I'm not worried about who I'm going to marry yet — if I
ever get married.

MAMA AND RUTH: *If!*

MAMA: Now, Bennie —

BENEATHA: Oh, I probably will ... but first I'm going to be a doctor, and
George, for one, still thinks that's pretty funny. I couldn't be bothered
with that. I am going to be a doctor and everybody around here better
understand that!

MAMA (*kindly*): 'Course you going to be a doctor, honey, God willing.

BENEATHA (*drily*): God hasn't got a thing to do with it.

MAMA: Beneatha — that just wasn't necessary.

BENEATHA: Well — neither is God. I get sick of hearing about God.

MAMA: Beneatha!

BENEATHA: I mean it! I'm just tired of hearing about God all the time. What has
He got to do with anything? Does He pay tuition?

MAMA: You 'bout to get your fresh little jaw slapped!

RUTH: That's just what she needs, all right!

BENEATHA: Why? Why can't I say what I want to around here, like everybody
else?

MAMA: It don't sound nice for a young girl to say things like that — you wasn't
brought up that way. Me and your father went to trouble to get you and
Brother to church every Sunday.

BENEATHA: Mama, you don't understand. It's all a matter of ideas, and God is
just one idea I don't accept. It's not important. I am not going out and be
immoral or commit crimes because I don't believe in God. I don't even
think about it. It's just that I get tired of Him getting credit for all the
things the human race achieves through its own stubborn effort. There
simply is no blasted God — there is only man and it is *He* who makes
miracles!

*Mama absorbs this speech, studies her daughter, and rises slowly and crosses to Be-
neatha and slaps her powerfully across the face. After, there is only silence and the
daughter drops her eyes from her mother's face, and Mama is very tall before her.*

MAMA: Now — you say after me, in my mother's house there is still God. (*There is a long pause and Beneatha stares at the floor wordlessly. Mama repeats the phrase with precision and cool emotion.*) In my mother's house there is still God.

BENEATHA: In my mother's house there is still God.

A long pause.

MAMA (*walking away from Beneatha, too disturbed for triumphant posture. Stopping and turning back to her daughter*): There are some ideas we ain't going to have in this house. Not long as I am at the head of this family.

BENEATHA: Yes, ma'am.

Mama walks out of the room.

RUTH (*almost gently, with profound understanding*): You think you a woman, Bennie — but you still a little girl. What you did was childish — so you got treated like a child.

BENEATHA: I see. (*Quietly.*) I also see that everybody thinks it's all right for Mama to be a tyrant. But all the tyranny in the world will never put a God in the heavens!

She picks up her books and goes out. Pause.

RUTH (*goes to Mama's door*): She said she was sorry.

MAMA (*coming out, going to her plant*): They frightens me, Ruth. My children.

RUTH: You got good children, Lena. They just a little off sometimes — but they're good.

MAMA: No — there's something come down between me and them that don't let us understand each other and I don't know what it is. One done almost lost his mind thinking 'bout money all the time and the other done commence to talk about things I can't seem to understand in no form or fashion. What is it that's changing, Ruth.

RUTH (*soothingly, older than her years*): Now . . . you taking it all too seriously. You just got strong-willed children and it takes a strong woman like you to keep 'em in hand.

MAMA (*looking at her plant and sprinkling a little water on it*): They spirited all right, my children. Got to admit they got spirit — Bennie and Walter. Like this little old plant that ain't never had enough sunshine or nothing — and look at it . . .

She has her back to Ruth, who has had to stop ironing and lean against something and put the back of her hand to her forehead.

RUTH (*trying to keep Mama from noticing*): You . . . sure . . . loves that little old thing, don't you? . . .

MAMA: Well, I always wanted me a garden like I used to see sometimes at the back of the houses down home. This plant is close as I ever got to having one. (*She looks out of the window as she replaces the plant.*) Lord, ain't nothing as dreary as the view from this window on a dreary day, is there? Why ain't you singing this morning, Ruth? Sing that "No Ways Tired." That song always lifts me up so — (*She turns at last to see that Ruth has slipped*

quietly to the floor, in a state of semiconsciousness.) Ruth! Ruth honey —
what's the matter with you . . . Ruth!

Curtain.

SCENE II. [*The following morning.*]

It is the following morning; a Saturday morning, and house cleaning is in progress at the Youngers'. Furniture has been shoved hither and yon and Mama is giving the kitchen-area walls a washing down. Beneatha, in dungarees, with a handkerchief tied around her face, is spraying insecticide into the cracks in the walls. As they work, the radio is on and a Southside disk-jockey program is inappropriately filling the house with a rather exotic saxophone blues. Travis, the sole idle one, is leaning on his arms, looking out of the window.

TRAVIS: Grandmama, that stuff Bennie is using smells awful. Can I go downstairs, please?

MAMA: Did you get all them chores done already? I ain't seen you doing much.

TRAVIS: Yes'm — finished early. Where did Mama go this morning?

MAMA (*looking at Beneatha*): She had to go on a little errand.

The phone rings. Beneatha runs to answer it and reaches it before Walter, who has entered from bedroom.

TRAVIS: Where?

MAMA: To tend to her business.

BENEATHA: Haylo . . . (*Disappointed.*) Yes, he is. (*She tosses the phone to Walter, who barely catches it.*) It's Willie Harris again.

WALTER (*as privately as possible under Mama's gaze*): Hello, Willie. Did you get the
papers from the lawyer? . . . No, not yet. I told you the mailman doesn't
get here till ten-thirty . . . No, I'll come there . . . Yeah! Right away. (*He
hangs up and goes for his coat.*)

BENEATHA: Brother, where did Ruth go?

WALTER (*as he exits*): How should I know!

TRAVIS: Aw come on, Grandma. Can I go outside?

MAMA: Oh, I guess so. You stay right in front of the house, though, and keep a
good lookout for the postman.

TRAVIS: Yes'm. (*He darts into bedroom for stickball and bat, reenters, and sees Beneatha on her knees spraying under sofa with behind upraised. He edges closer
to the target, takes aim, and lets her have it. She screams.*) Leave them poor
little cockroaches alone, they ain't bothering you none! (*He runs as she
swings the spraygun at him viciously and playfully.*) Grandma! Grandma!

MAMA: Look out there, girl, before you be spilling some of that stuff on that
child!

TRAVIS (*safely behind the bastion of Mama*): That's right — look out, now! (*He
exits.*)

BENEATHA (*drily*): I can't imagine that it would hurt him — it has never hurt the
roaches.

MAMA: Well, little boys' hides ain't as tough as Southside roaches. You better
get over there behind the bureau. I seen one marching out of there like
Napoleon yesterday.

BENEATHA: There's really only one way to get rid of them, Mama —

MAMA: How?

BENEATHA: Set fire to this building! Mama, where did Ruth go?

MAMA (*looking at her with meaning*): To the doctor, I think.

BENEATHA: The doctor? What's the matter? (*They exchange glances.*) You don't think —

MAMA (*with her sense of drama*): Now I ain't saying what I think. But I ain't never been wrong 'bout a woman neither.

The phone rings.

BENEATHA (*at the phone*): Hay-lo . . . (*Pause, and a moment of recognition.*) Well — when did you get back! . . . And how was it? . . . Of course I've missed you — in my way . . . This morning? No . . . house cleaning and all that and Mama hates it if I let people come over when the house is like this . . . You *have*? Well, that's different . . . What is it — Oh, what the hell, come on over . . . Right, see you then. *Arrivederci.*

She hangs up.

MAMA (*who has listened vigorously, as is her habit*): Who is that you inviting over here with this house looking like this? You ain't got the pride you was born with!

BENEATHA: Asagai doesn't care how houses look, Mama — he's an intellectual.

MAMA: *Who?*

BENEATHA: Asagai — Joseph Asagai. He's an African boy I met on campus. He's been studying in Canada all summer.

MAMA: What's his name?

BENEATHA: Asagai, Joseph. Ah-sah-guy . . . He's from Nigeria.

MAMA: Oh, that's the little country that was founded by slaves way back . . .

BENEATHA: No, Mama — that's Liberia.

MAMA: I don't think I never met no African before.

BENEATHA: Well, do me a favor and don't ask him a whole lot of ignorant questions about Africans. I mean, do they wear clothes and all that —

MAMA: Well, now, I guess if you think we so ignorant 'round here maybe you shouldn't bring your friends here —

BENEATHA: It's just that people ask such crazy things. All anyone seems to know about when it comes to Africa is Tarzan —

MAMA (*indignantly*): Why should I know anything about Africa?

BENEATHA: Why do you give money at church for the missionary work?

MAMA: Well, that's to help save people.

BENEATHA: You mean save them from *heathenism* —

MAMA (*innocently*): Yes.

BENEATHA: I'm afraid they need more salvation from the British and the French.

Ruth comes in forlornly and pulls off her coat with dejection. They both turn to look at her.

RUTH (*dispiritedly*): Well, I guess from all the happy faces — everybody knows.

BENEATHA: You pregnant?

MAMA: Lord have mercy, I sure hope it's a little old girl. Travis ought to have a sister.

Beneatha and Ruth give her a hopeless look for this grandmotherly enthusiasm.

BENEATHA: How far along are you?

RUTH: Two months.

BENEATHA: Did you mean to? I mean did you plan it or was it an accident?

MAMA: What do you know about planning or not planning?

BENEATHA: Oh, Mama.

RUTH (*wearily*): She's twenty years old, Lena.

BENEATHA: Did you plan it, Ruth?

RUTH: Mind your own business.

BENEATHA: It is my business — where is he going to live, on the *roof*? (*There is silence following the remark as the three women react to the sense of it.*) Gee — I didn't mean that, Ruth, honest. Gee, I don't feel like that at all. I — I think it is wonderful.

RUTH (*dully*): Wonderful.

BENEATHA: Yes — really.

MAMA (*looking at Ruth, worried*): Doctor say everything going to be all right?

RUTH (*far away*): Yes — she says everything is going to be fine . . .

MAMA (*immediately suspicious*): "She" — What doctor you went to?

Ruth folds over, near hysteria.

MAMA (*worriedly hovering over Ruth*): Ruth honey — what's the matter with you — you sick?

Ruth has her fists clenched on her thighs and is fighting hard to suppress a scream that seems to be rising in her.

BENEATHA: What's the matter with her, Mama?

MAMA (*working her fingers in Ruth's shoulders to relax her*): She be all right. Women gets right depressed sometimes when they get her way. (*Speaking softly, expertly, rapidly.*) Now you just relax. That's right . . . just lean back, don't think 'bout nothing at all . . . nothing at all —

RUTH: I'm all right . . .

The glassy-eyed look melts and then she collapses into a fit of heavy sobbing. The bell rings.

BENEATHA: Oh, my God — that must be Asagai.

MAMA (*to Ruth*): Come on now, honey. You need to lie down and rest awhile . . . then have some nice hot food.

They exit, Ruth's weight on her mother-in-law. Beneatha, herself profoundly disturbed, opens the door to admit a rather dramatic-looking young man with a large package.

ASAGAI: Hello, Alaiyo —

BENEATHA (*holding the door open and regarding him with pleasure*): Hello . . . (*Long pause.*) Well — come in. And please excuse everything. My mother was very upset about my letting anyone come here with the place like this.

ASAGAI (*coming into the room*): You look disturbed too . . . Is something wrong?

BENEATHA (*still at the door, absently*): Yes . . . we've all got acute ghetto-itus. (*She smiles and comes toward him, finding a cigarette and sitting.*) So — sit down! No! Wait! (*She whips the spraygun off sofa where she had left it and puts the cushions back. At last perches on arm of sofa. He sits.*) So, how was Canada?

ASAGAI (*a sophisticate*): Canadian.

BENEATHA (*looking at him*): Asagai, I'm very glad you are back.

ASAGAI (*looking back at her in turn*): Are you really?

BENEATHA: Yes — very.

ASAGAI: Why? — you were quite glad when I went away. What happened?

BENEATHA: You went away.

ASAGAI: Ahhhhhhhh.

BENEATHA: Before — you wanted to be so serious before there was time.

ASAGAI: How much time must there be before one knows what one feels?

BENEATHA (*stalling this particular conversation. Her hands pressed together, in a deliberately childish gesture*): What did you bring me?

ASAGAI (*handing her the package*): Open it and see.

BENEATHA (*eagerly opening the package and drawing out some records and the colorful robes of a Nigerian woman*): Oh Asagai! . . . You got them for me! . . . How beautiful . . . and the records too! (*She lifts out the robes and runs to the mirror with them and holds the drapery up in front of herself.*)

ASAGAI (*coming to her at the mirror*): I shall have to teach you how to drape it properly. (*He flings the material about her for the moment and stands back to look at her.*) Ah — Oh-pay-gay-day, oh-gbah-mu-shay. (*A Yoruba exclamation for admiration.*) You wear it well . . . very well . . . mutilated hair and all.

BENEATHA (*turning suddenly*): My hair — what's wrong with my hair?

ASAGAI (*shrugging*): Were you born with it like that?

BENEATHA (*reaching up to touch it*): No . . . of course not.

She looks back to the mirror, disturbed.

ASAGAI (*smiling*): How then?

BENEATHA: You know perfectly well how . . . as crinkly as yours . . . that's how.

ASAGAI: And it is ugly to you that way?

BENEATHA (*quickly*): Oh, no — not ugly . . . (*More slowly, apologetically.*) But it's so hard to manage when it's, well — raw.

ASAGAI: And so to accommodate that — you mutilate it every week?

BENEATHA: It's not mutilation!

ASAGAI (*laughing aloud at her seriousness*): Oh . . . please! I am only teasing you because you are so very serious about these things. (*He stands back from her and folds his arms across his chest as he watches her pulling at her hair and frowning in the mirror.*) Do you remember the first time you met me at school? . . . (*He laughs.*) You came up to me and you said — and I thought you were the most serious little thing I had ever seen — you said: (*He imitates her.*) "Mr. Asagai — I want very much to talk with you. About Africa. You see, Mr. Asagai, I am looking for my *identity!*"

He laughs.

BENEATHA (*turning to him, not laughing*): Yes —

Her face is quizzical, profoundly disturbed.

ASAGAI (*still teasing and reaching out and taking her face in his hands and turning her profile to him*): Well . . . it is true that this is not so much a profile of a Hollywood queen as perhaps a queen of the Nile — (*A mock dismissal of the importance of the question.*) But what does it matter? Assimilationism is so popular in your country.

BENEATHA (*wheeling, passionately, sharply*): I am not an assimilationist!

ASAGAI (*the protest hangs in the room for a moment and Asagai studies her, his laughter fading*): Such a serious one. (*There is a pause.*) So — you like the robes? You must take excellent care of them — they are from my sister's personal wardrobe.

BENEATHA (*with incredulity*): You — you sent all the way home — for me?

ASAGAI (*with charm*): For you — I would do much more . . . Well, that is what I came for. I must go.

BENEATHA: Will you call me Monday?

ASAGAI: Yes . . . We have a great deal to talk about. I mean about identity and time and all that.

BENEATHA: Time?

ASAGAI: Yes. About how much time one needs to know what one feels.

BENEATHA: You see! You never understood that there is more than one kind of feeling which can exist between a man and a woman — or, at least, there should be.

ASAGAI (*shaking his head negatively but gently*): No. Between a man and a woman there need be only one kind of feeling. I have that for you . . . Now even . . . right this moment . . .

BENEATHA: I know — and by itself — it won't do. I can find that anywhere.

ASAGAI: For a woman it should be enough.

BENEATHA: I know — because that's what it says in all the novels that men write. But it isn't. Go ahead and laugh — but I'm not interested in being someone's little episode in America or — (*With feminine vengeance.*) — one of them! (*Asagai has burst into laughter again.*) That's funny as hell, huh!

ASAGAI: It's just that every American girl I have known has said that to me. White — black — in this you are all the same. And the same speech, too!

BENEATHA (*angrily*): Yuk, yuk, yuk!

ASAGAI: It's how you can be sure that the world's most liberated women are not liberated at all. You all talk about it too much!

Mama enters and is immediately all social charm because of the presence of a guest.

BENEATHA: Oh — Mama — this is Mr. Asagai.

MAMA: How do you do?

ASAGAI (*total politeness to an elder*): How do you do, Mrs. Younger. Please forgive me for coming at such an outrageous hour on a Saturday.

MAMA: Well, you are quite welcome. I just hope you understand that our house don't always look like this. (*Chatterish.*) You must come again. I would

love to hear all about — (*Not sure of the name.*) — your country. I think
it's so sad the way our American Negroes don't know nothing about
Africa 'cept Tarzan and all that. And all that money they pour into these
churches when they ought to be helping you people over there drive out
them French and Englishmen done taken away your land.

*The mother flashes a slightly superior look at her daughter upon completion of the
recitation.*

ASAGAI (*taken aback by this sudden and acutely unrelated expression of sympathy*):
Yes . . . yes . . .

MAMA (*smiling at him suddenly and relaxing and looking him over*): How many
miles is it from here to where you come from?

ASAGAI: Many thousands.

MAMA (*looking at him as she would Walter*): I bet you don't half look after yourself, being away from your mama either. I spec you better come 'round
here from time to time to get yourself some decent homecooked
meals . . .

ASAGAI (*moved*): Thank you. Thank you very much. (*They are all quiet, then —*)
Well . . . I must go. I will call you Monday, Alaiyo.

MAMA: What's that he call you?

ASAGAI: Oh — "Alaiyo." I hope you don't mind. It is what you would call a
nickname, I think. It is a Yoruba word. I am a Yoruba.

MAMA (*looking at Beneatha*): I — I thought he was from — (*Uncertain.*)

ASAGAI (*understanding*): Nigeria is my country. Yoruba is my tribal origin —

BENEATHA: You didn't tell us what Alaiyo means . . . for all I know, you might
be calling me Little Idiot or something . . .

ASAGAI: Well . . . let me see . . . I do not know how just to explain it . . . The
sense of a thing can be so different when it changes languages.

BENEATHA: You're evading.

ASAGAI: No — really it is difficult . . . (*Thinking.*) It means . . . it means One for
Whom Bread — Food — Is Not Enough. (*He looks at her.*) Is that all right?

BENEATHA (*understanding, softly*): Thank you.

MAMA (*looking from one to the other and not understanding any of it*): Well . . . that's
nice . . . You must come see us again — Mr. —

ASAGAI: Ah-sah-guy . . .

MAMA: Yes . . . Do come again.

ASAGAI: Good-bye.

He exits.

MAMA (*after him*): Lord, that's a pretty thing just went out here! (*Insinuatingly,
to her daughter.*) Yes, I guess I see why we done commence to get so interested in Africa 'round here. Missionaries my aunt Jenny!

She exits.

BENEATHA: Oh, Mama! . . .

*She picks up the Nigerian dress and holds it up to her in front of the mirror again. She
sets the headdress on haphazardly and then notices her hair again and clutches at it*

and then replaces the headdress and frowns at herself. Then she starts to wriggle in front of the mirror as she thinks a Nigerian woman might. Travis enters and stands regarding her.

TRAVIS: What's the matter, girl, you cracking up?

BENEATHA: Shut up.

She pulls the headdress off and looks at herself in the mirror and clutches at her hair again and squinches her eyes as if trying to imagine something. Then, suddenly, she gets her raincoat and kerchief and hurriedly prepares for going out.

MAMA (*coming back into the room*): She's resting now. Travis, baby, run next door and ask Miss Johnson to please let me have a little kitchen cleanser. This here can is empty as Jacob's kettle.

TRAVIS: I just came in.

MAMA: Do as you told. (*He exits and she looks at her daughter.*) Where you going?

BENEATHA (*halting at the door*): To become a queen of the Nile!

She exits in a breathless blaze of glory. Ruth appears in the bedroom doorway.

MAMA: Who told you to get up?

RUTH: Ain't nothing wrong with me to be lying in no bed for. Where did Bennie go?

MAMA (*drumming her fingers*): Far as I could make out — to Egypt. (*Ruth just looks at her.*) What time is it getting to?

RUTH: Ten twenty. And the mailman going to ring that bell this morning just like he done every morning for the last umpteen years.

Travis comes in with the cleanser can.

TRAVIS: She say to tell you that she don't have much.

MAMA (*angrily*): Lord, some people I could name sure is tight-fisted! (*Directing her grandson.*) Mark two cans of cleanser on the list there. If she that hard up for kitchen cleanser, I sure don't want to forget to get her none!

RUTH: Lena — maybe the woman is just short on cleanser —

MAMA (*not listening*): — Much baking powder as she done borrowed from me all these years, she could of done gone into the baking business!

The bell sounds suddenly and sharply and all three are stunned — serious and silent — midspeech. In spite of all the other conversations and distractions of the morning, this is what they have been waiting for, even Travis, who looks helplessly from his mother to his grandmother. Ruth is the first to come to life again.

RUTH (*to Travis*): Get down them steps, boy!

Travis snaps to life and flies out to get the mail.

MAMA (*her eyes wide, her hand to her breast*): You mean it done really come?

RUTH (*excited*): Oh, Miss Lena!

MAMA (*collecting herself*): Well . . . I don't know what we all so excited about 'round here for. We known it was coming for months.

RUTH: That's a whole lot different from having it come and being able to hold it in your hands . . . a piece of paper worth ten thousand dollars . . . (*Travis bursts back into the room. He holds the envelope high above his head, like a little dancer, his face is radiant and he is breathless. He moves to his grandmother with sudden slow ceremony and puts the envelope into her hands. She accepts it, and then merely holds it and looks at it.)* Come on! Open it . . . Lord have mercy, I wish Walter Lee was here!

TRAVIS: Open it, Grandmama!

MAMA *(staring at it)*: Now you all be quiet. It's just a check.

RUTH: Open it . . .

MAMA *(still staring at it)*: Now don't act silly . . . We ain't never been no people to act silly 'bout no money —

RUTH *(swiftly)*: We ain't never had none before — OPEN IT!

Mama finally makes a good strong tear and pulls out the thin blue slice of paper and inspects it closely. The boy and his mother study it raptly over Mama's shoulders.

MAMA: Travis! *(She is counting off with doubt.)* Is that the right number of zeros?

TRAVIS: Yes'm . . . ten thousand dollars. Gaalee, grandmama, you rich.

MAMA *(She holds the check away from her, still looking at it. Slowly her face sobers into a mask of unhappiness)*: Ten thousand dollars. *(She hands it to Ruth.)* Put it away somewhere, Ruth. *(She does not look at Ruth; her eyes seem to be seeing something somewhere very far off.)* Ten thousand dollars they give you. Ten thousand dollars.

TRAVIS *(to his mother, sincerely)*: What's the matter with Grandmama — don't she want to be rich?

RUTH *(distractedly)*: You go on out and play now, baby. *(Travis exits. Mama starts wiping dishes absently, humming intently to herself. Ruth turns to her, with kind exasperation.)* You've gone and got yourself upset.

MAMA *(not looking at her)*: I spec if it wasn't for you all . . . I would just put that money away or give it to the church or something.

RUTH: Now what kind of talk is that. Mr. Younger would just be plain mad if he could hear you talking foolish like that.

MAMA *(stopping and staring off)*: Yes . . . he sure would. *(Sighing.)* We got enough to do with that money, all right. *(She halts then, and turns and looks at her daughter-in-law hard; Ruth avoids her eyes and Mama wipes her hands with finality and starts to speak firmly to Ruth.)* Where did you go today, girl?

RUTH: To the doctor.

MAMA *(impatiently)*: Now, Ruth . . . you know better than that. Old Doctor Jones is strange enough in his way but there ain't nothing 'bout him make somebody slip and call him "she" — like you done this morning.

RUTH: Well, that's what happened — my tongue slipped.

MAMA: You went to see that woman, didn't you?

RUTH *(defensively, giving herself away)*: What woman you talking about?

MAMA *(angrily)*: That woman who —

Walter enters in great excitement.

WALTER: Did it come?

MAMA *(quietly)*: Can't you give people a Christian greeting before you start asking about money?

WALTER (*to Ruth*): Did it come? (*Ruth unfolds the check and lays it quietly before him, watching him intently with thoughts of her own. Walter sits down and grasps it close and counts off the zeros.*) Ten thousand dollars — (*He turns suddenly, frantically to his mother and draws some papers out of his breast pocket.*) Mama — look. Old Willy Harris put everything on paper —

MAMA: Son — I think you ought to talk to your wife . . . I'll go on out and leave you alone if you want —

WALTER: I can talk to her later — Mama, look —

MAMA: Son —

WALTER: WILL SOMEBODY PLEASE LISTEN TO ME TODAY!

MAMA (*quietly*): I don't 'low no yellin' in this house, Walter Lee, and you know it — (*Walter stares at them in frustration and starts to speak several times.*) And there ain't going to be no investing in no liquor stores.

WALTER: But, Mama, you ain't even looked at it.

MAMA: I don't aim to have to speak on that again.

A long pause.

WALTER: You ain't looked at it and you don't aim to have to speak on that again? You ain't even looked at it and *you* have decided — (*Crumpling his papers.*) Well, *you* tell that to my boy tonight when you put him to sleep on the living-room couch . . . (*Turning to Mama and speaking directly to her.*) Yeah — and tell it to my wife, Mama, tomorrow when she has to go out of here to look after somebody else's kids. And tell it to *me*, Mama, every time we need a new pair of curtains and I have to watch *you* go out and work in somebody's kitchen. Yeah, you tell me then!

Walter starts out.

RUTH: Where you going?

WALTER: I'm going out!

RUTH: Where?

WALTER: Just out of this house somewhere —

RUTH (*getting her coat*): I'll come too.

WALTER: I don't want you to come!

RUTH: I got something to talk to you about, Walter.

WALTER: That's too bad.

MAMA (*still quietly*): Walter Lee — (*She waits and he finally turns and looks at her.*) Sit down.

WALTER: I'm a grown man, Mama.

MAMA: Ain't nobody said you wasn't grown. But you still in my house and my presence. And as long as you are — you'll talk to your wife civil. Now sit down.

RUTH (*suddenly*): Oh, let him go on out and drink himself to death! He makes me sick to my stomach! (*She flings her coat against him and exits to bedroom.*)

WALTER (*violently flinging the coat after her*): And you turn mine too, baby! (*The door slams behind her.*) That was my biggest mistake —

MAMA (*still quietly*): Walter, what is the matter with you?

WALTER: Matter with me? Ain't nothing the matter with *me*!

MAMA: Yes there is. Something eating you up like a crazy man. Something more than me not giving you this money. The past few years I been watching it happen to you. You get all nervous acting and kind of wild in the eyes — (*Walter jumps up impatiently at her words.*) I said sit there now, I'm talking to you!

WALTER: Mama — I don't need no nagging at me today.

MAMA: Seem like you getting to a place where you always tied up in some kind of knot about something. But if anybody ask you 'bout it you just yell at 'em and bust out the house and go out and drink somewheres. Walter Lee, people can't live with that. Ruth's a good, patient girl in her way — but you getting to be too much. Boy, don't make the mistake of driving that girl away from you.

WALTER: Why — what she do for me?

MAMA: She loves you.

WALTER: Mama — I'm going out. I want to go off somewhere and be by myself for a while.

MAMA: I'm sorry 'bout your liquor store, son. It just wasn't the thing for us to do. That's what I want to tell you about —

WALTER: I got to go out, Mama —

He rises.

MAMA: It's dangerous, son.

WALTER: What's dangerous?

MAMA: When a man goes outside his home to look for peace.

WALTER (*beseechingly*): Then why can't there never be no peace in this house then?

MAMA: You done found it in some other house?

WALTER: No — there ain't no woman! Why do women always think there's a woman somewhere when a man gets restless. (*Picks up the check.*) Do you know what this money means to me? Do you know what this money can do for us? (*Puts it back.*) Mama — Mama — I want so many things . . .

MAMA: Yes, son —

WALTER: I want so many things that they are driving me kind of crazy . . . Mama — look at me.

MAMA: I'm looking at you. You a good-looking boy. You got a job, a nice wife, a fine boy, and —

WALTER: A job. (*Looks at her.*) Mama, a job? I open and close car doors all day long. I drive a man around in his limousine and I say, "Yes, sir; no, sir; very good, sir; shall I take the Drive, sir?" Mama, that ain't no kind of job . . . that ain't nothing at all. (*Very quietly.*) Mama, I don't know if I can make you understand.

MAMA: Understand what, baby?

WALTER (*quietly*): Sometimes it's like I can see the future stretched out in front of me — just plain as day. The future, Mama. Hanging over there at the edge of my days. Just waiting for me — a big, looming blank space — full of *nothing*. Just waiting for *me*. But it don't have to be. (*Pause. Kneeling beside her chair.*) Mama — sometimes when I'm downtown and I pass them cool, quiet-looking restaurants where them white boys are sitting back and talking 'bout things . . . sitting there turning deals worth millions of dollars . . . sometimes I see guys don't look much older than me —

MAMA: Son — how come you talk so much 'bout money?

WALTER (*with immense passion*): Because it is life, Mama!

MAMA (*quietly*): Oh — (*Very quietly.*) So now it's life. Money is life. Once upon a time freedom used to be life — now it's money. I guess the world really do change . . .

WALTER: No — it was always money, Mama. We just didn't know about it.

MAMA: No . . . something has changed. (*She looks at him.*) You something new, boy. In my time we was worried about not being lynched and getting to the North if we could and how to stay alive and still have a pinch of dignity too . . . Now here come you and Beneatha — talking 'bout things we ain't never even thought about hardly, me and your daddy. You ain't satisfied or proud of nothing we done. I mean that you had a home; that we kept you out of trouble till you was grown; that you don't have to ride to work on the back of nobody's streetcar — You my children — but how different we done become.

WALTER (*a long beat. He pats her hand and gets up*): You just don't understand, Mama, you just don't understand.

MAMA: Son — do you know your wife is expecting another baby? (*Walter stands, stunned, and absorbs what his mother has said.*) That's what she wanted to talk to you about. (*Walter sinks down into a chair.*) This ain't for me to be telling — but you ought to know. (*She waits.*) I think Ruth is thinking 'bout getting rid of that child.

WALTER (*slowly understanding*): — No — no — Ruth wouldn't do that.

MAMA: When the world gets ugly enough — a woman will do anything for her family. *The part that's already living.*

WALTER: You don't know Ruth, Mama, if you think she would do that.

Ruth opens the bedroom door and stands there a little limp.

RUTH (*beaten*): Yes I would too, Walter. (*Pause.*) I gave her a five-dollar down payment.

There is total silence as the man stares at his wife and the mother stares at her son.

MAMA (*presently*): Well — (*Tightly.*) Well — son, I'm waiting to hear you say something . . . (*She waits.*) I'm waiting to hear how you be your father's son. Be the man he was . . . (*Pause. The silence shouts.*) Your wife say she going to destroy your child. And I'm waiting to hear you talk like him and say we a people who give children life, not who destroys them — (*She rises.*) I'm waiting to see you stand up and look like your daddy and say we done give up one baby to poverty and that we ain't going to give up nary another one . . . I'm waiting.

WALTER: Ruth — (*He can say nothing.*)

MAMA: If you a son of mine, tell her! (*Walter picks up his keys and his coat and walks out. She continues, bitterly.*) You . . . you are a disgrace to your father's memory. Somebody get me my hat!

Curtain.

ACT II

SCENE I

Time: Later the same day.

At rise: Ruth is ironing again. She has the radio going. Presently Beneatha's bedroom door opens and Ruth's mouth falls and she puts down the iron in fascination.

RUTH: What have we got on tonight!

BENEATHA (*emerging grandly from the doorway so that we can see her thoroughly robed in the costume Asagai brought*): You are looking at what a well-dressed Nigerian woman wears — (*She parades for Ruth, her hair completely hidden by the headdress; she is coquettishly fanning herself with an ornate oriental fan, mistakenly more like Butterfly than any Nigerian that ever was.*) Isn't it beautiful? (*She promenades to the radio and, with an arrogant flourish, turns off the good loud blues that is playing.*) Enough of this assimilationist junk! (*Ruth follows her with her eyes as she goes to the phonograph and puts on a record and turns and waits ceremoniously for the music to come up. Then, with a shout —*) OCOMOGOSIAY!

Ruth jumps. The music comes up, a lovely Nigerian melody. Beneatha listens, enraptured, her eyes far way — "back to the past." She begins to dance. Ruth is dumfounded.

RUTH: What kind of dance is that?

BENEATHA: A folk dance.

RUTH (*Pearl Bailey°*): What kind of folks do that, honey?

BENEATHA: It's from Nigeria. It's a dance of welcome.

RUTH: Who you welcoming?

BENEATHA: The men back to the village.

RUTH: Where they been?

BENEATHA: How should I know — out hunting or something. Anyway, they are coming back now . . .

RUTH: Well, that's good.

BENEATHA (*with the record*):

Alundi, alundi
Alundi alunya
Jop pu a jeepua
Ang gu soooooooooo
Ai yai yae . . .
Ayehaye — alundi . . .

Walter comes in during this performance; he has obviously been drinking. He leans against the door heavily and watches his sister, at first with distaste. Then his eyes look off— "back to the past" — as he lifts both his fists to the roof, screaming.

WALTER: YEAH . . . AND ETHIOPIA STRETCH FORTH HER HANDS AGAIN! . . .

Pearl Bailey: A popular African American singer (1918–1990).

RUTH (*drily, looking at him*): Yes — and Africa sure is claiming her own tonight. (*She gives them both up and starts ironing again.*)

WALTER (*all in a drunken, dramatic shout*): Shut up! . . . I'm diggin them drums . . . them drums move me! . . . (*He makes his weaving way to his wife's face and leans in close to her.*) In my *heart of hearts* — (*He thumps his chest.*) — I am much warrior!

RUTH (*without even looking up*): In your heart of hearts you are much drunkard.

WALTER (*coming away from her and starting to wander around the room, shouting*): Me and Jomo . . . (*Intently, in his sister's face. She has stopped dancing to watch him in this unknown mood.*) That's my man, Kenyatta.° (*Shouting and thumping his chest.*) FLAMING SPEAR! HOT DAMN! (*He is suddenly in possession of an imaginary spear and actively spearing enemies all over the room.*) OCOMOGOSIAY . . .

BENEATHA (*to encourage Walter, thoroughly caught up with this side of him*): OCO-MOGOSIAY, FLAMING SPEAR!

WALTER: THE LION IS WAKING . . . OWIMOWEH!

He pulls his shirt open and leaps up on the table and gestures with his spear.

BENEATHA: OWIMOWEH!

WALTER (*on the table, very far gone, his eyes pure glass sheets. He sees what we cannot, that he is a leader of his people, a great chief, a descendant of Chaka,° and that the hour to march has come*): Listen, my black brothers —

BENEATHA: OCOMOGOSIAY!

WALTER: — Do you hear the waters rushing against the shores of the coast-lands —

BENEATHA: OCOMOGOSIAY!

WALTER: — Do you hear the screeching of the cocks in yonder hills beyond where the chiefs meet in council for the coming of the mighty war —

BENEATHA: OCOMOGOSIAY!

And now the lighting shifts subtly to suggest the world of Walter's imagination, and the mood shifts from pure comedy. It is the inner Walter speaking: the Southside chauffeur has assumed an unexpected majesty.

WALTER: — Do you hear the beating of the wings of the birds flying low over the mountains and the low places of our land —

BENEATHA: OCOMOGOSIAY!

WALTER: — Do you hear the singing of the women, singing the war songs of our fathers to the babies in the great houses? Singing the sweet war songs! (*The doorbell rings.*) OH, DO YOU HEAR, MY *BLACK* BROTH-ERS!

BENEATHA (*completely gone*): We hear you, Flaming Spear —

Ruth shuts off the phonograph and opens the door. George Murchison enters.

Kenyatta: Jomo Kenyatta (c. 1894–1978), a Kenyan politician involved in the country's nationalist movement.   **Chaka:** Also spelled Shaka (c. 1787–1828), he became chief of the Zulu clan in 1816 and founded the great Zulu empire by conquering most of southern Africa.

WALTER: Telling us to prepare for the GREATNESS OF THE TIME! (*Lights back to normal. He turns and sees George.*) Black Brother!

He extends his hand for the fraternal clasp.

GEORGE: Black Brother, hell!

RUTH (*having had enough, and embarrassed for the family*): Beneatha, you got company — what's the matter with you? Walter Lee Younger, get down off that table and stop acting like a fool . . .

Walter comes down off the table suddenly and makes a quick exit to the bathroom.

RUTH: He's had a little to drink . . . I don't know what her excuse is.

GEORGE (*to Beneatha*): Look honey, we're going to the theater — we're not going to be *in* it . . . so go change, huh?

Beneatha looks at him and slowly, ceremoniously, lifts her hands and pulls off the headdress. Her hair is close-cropped and unstraightened. George freezes midsentence and Ruth's eyes all but fall out of her head.

GEORGE: What in the name of —

RUTH (*touching Beneatha's hair*): Girl, you done lost your natural mind? Look at your head!

GEORGE: What have you done to your head — I mean your hair!

BENEATHA: Nothing — except cut it off.

RUTH: Now that's the truth — it's what ain't been done to it! You expect this boy to go out with you with your head all nappy like that?

BENEATHA (*looking at George*): That's up to George. If he's ashamed of his heritage —

GEORGE: Oh, don't be so proud of yourself, Bennie — just because you look eccentric.

BENEATHA: How can something that's natural be eccentric?

GEORGE: That's what being eccentric means — being natural. Get dressed.

BENEATHA: I don't like that, George.

RUTH: Why must you and your brother make an argument out of everything people say?

BENEATHA: Because I hate assimilationist Negroes!

RUTH: Will somebody please tell me what assimila-whoever means!

GEORGE: Oh, it's just a college girl's way of calling people Uncle Toms — but that isn't what it means at all.

RUTH: Well, what does it mean?

BENEATHA (*cutting George off and staring at him as she replies to Ruth*): It means someone who is willing to give up his own culture and submerge himself completely in the dominant, and in this case *oppressive* culture!

GEORGE: Oh, dear, dear, dear! Here we go! A lecture on the African past! On our Great West African Heritage! In one second we will hear all about the great Ashanti empires; the great Songhay civilizations; and the great sculpture of Bénin — and then some poetry in the Bantu — and the whole monologue will end with the word *heritage*! (*Nastily.*) Let's face it, baby, your heritage is nothing but a bunch of raggedy-assed spirituals and some grass huts!

BENEATHA: GRASS HUTS! (*Ruth crosses to her and forcibly pushes her toward the bedroom.*) See there . . . you are standing there in your splendid ignorance talking about people who were the first to smelt iron on the face of the earth! (*Ruth is pushing her through the door.*) The Ashanti were performing surgical operations when the English — (*Ruth pulls the door to, with Beneatha on the other side, and smiles graciously at George. Beneatha opens the door and shouts the end of the sentence defiantly at George.*) — were still tatooing themselves with blue dragons! (*She goes back inside.*)

RUTH: Have a seat, George. (*They both sit. Ruth folds her hands rather primly on her lap, determined to demonstrate the civilization of the family.*) Warm, ain't it? I mean for September. (*Pause.*) Just like they always say about Chicago weather: if it's too hot or cold for you, just wait a minute and it'll change. (*She smiles happily at this cliché of clichés.*) Everybody say it's got to do with them bombs and things they keep setting off. (*Pause.*) Would you like a nice cold beer?

GEORGE: No, thank you. I don't care for beer. (*He looks at his watch.*) I hope she hurries up.

RUTH: What time is the show?

GEORGE: It's an eight-thirty curtain. That's just Chicago, though. In New York standard curtain time is eight forty.

He is rather proud of this knowledge.

RUTH (*properly appreciating it*): You get to New York a lot?

GEORGE (*offhand*): Few times a year.

RUTH: Oh — that's nice. I've never been to New York.

Walter enters. We feel he has relieved himself, but the edge of unreality is still with him.

WALTER: New York ain't got nothing Chicago ain't. Just a bunch of hustling people all squeezed up together — being "Eastern."

He turns his face into a screw of displeasure.

GEORGE: Oh — you've been?

WALTER: *Plenty* of times.

RUTH (*shocked at the lie*): Walter Lee Younger!

WALTER (*staring her down*): Plenty! (*Pause.*) What we got to drink in this house? Why don't you offer this man some refreshment. (*To George.*) They don't know how to entertain people in this house, man.

GEORGE: Thank you — I don't really care for anything.

WALTER (*feeling his head; sobriety coming*): Where's Mama?

RUTH: She ain't come back yet.

WALTER (*looking Murchison over from head to toe, scrutinizing his carefully casual tweed sports jacket over cashmere V-neck sweater over soft eyelet shirt and tie, and soft slacks, finished off with white buckskin shoes*): Why all you college boys wear them faggoty-looking white shoes?

RUTH: Walter Lee!

George Murchison ignores the remark.

WALTER (*to Ruth*): Well, they look crazy as hell — white shoes, cold as it is.

RUTH (*crushed*): You have to excuse him —

WALTER: No he don't! Excuse me for what? What you always excusing me for! I'll excuse myself when I needs to be excused! (*A pause.*) They look as funny as them black knee socks Beneatha wears out of here all the time.

RUTH: It's the college *style,* Walter.

WALTER: Style, hell. She looks like she got burnt legs or something!

RUTH: Oh, Walter —

WALTER (*an irritable mimic*): Oh, Walter! Oh, Walter! (*To Murchison.*) How's your old man making out? I understand you all going to buy that big hotel on the Drive? (*He finds a beer in the refrigerator, wanders over to Murchison, sipping and wiping his lips with the back of his hand, and straddling a chair backwards to talk to the other man.*) Shrewd move. Your old man is all right, man. (*Tapping his head and half winking for emphasis.*) I mean he knows how to operate. I mean he thinks *big,* you know what I mean, I mean for a *home,* you know? But I think he's kind of running out of ideas now. I'd like to talk to him. Listen, man, I got some plans that could turn this city upside down. I mean think like he does. *Big.* Invest big, gamble big, hell, lose *big* if you have to, you know what I mean. It's hard to find a man on this whole Southside who understands my kind of thinking — you dig? (*He scrutinizes Murchison again, drinks his beer, squints his eyes and leans in close, confidential, man to man.*) Me and you ought to sit down and talk sometimes, man. Man, I got me some ideas . . .

MURCHISON (*with boredom*): Yeah — sometimes we'll have to do that, Walter.

WALTER (*understanding the indifference, and offended*): Yeah — well, when you get the time, man. I know you a busy little boy.

RUTH: Walter, please —

WALTER (*bitterly, hurt*): I know ain't nothing in this world as busy as you colored college boys with your fraternity pins and white shoes . . .

RUTH (*covering her face with humiliation*): Oh, Walter Lee —

WALTER: I see you all all the time — with the books tucked under your arms — going to your (*British A — a mimic.*) "clahsses." And for what! What the hell you learning over there? Filling up your heads — (*Counting off on his fingers.*) — with the sociology and the psychology — but they teaching you how to be a man? How to take over and run the world? They teaching you how to run a rubber plantation or a steel mill? Naw — just to talk proper and read books and wear them faggoty-looking white shoes . . .

GEORGE (*looking at him with distaste, a little above it all*): You're all wacked up with bitterness, man.

WALTER (*intently, almost quietly, between the teeth, glaring at the boy*): And you — ain't you bitter, man? Ain't you just about had it yet? Don't you see no stars gleaming that you can't reach out and grab? You happy? — You contented son-of-a-bitch — you happy? You got it made? Bitter? Man, I'm a volcano. Bitter? Here I am a giant — surrounded by ants! Ants who can't even understand what it is the giant is talking about.

RUTH (*passionately and suddenly*): Oh, Walter — ain't you with nobody!

WALTER (*violently*): No! 'Cause ain't nobody with me! Not even my own
  mother!

RUTH: Walter, that's a terrible thing to say!

Beneatha enters, dressed for the evening in a cocktail dress and earrings, hair natural.

GEORGE: Well — hey — (*Crosses to Beneatha; thoughtful, with emphasis, since this
  is a reversal.*) You look great!

WALTER (*seeing his sister's hair for the first time*): What's the matter with your
  head?

BENEATHA (*tired of the jokes now*): I cut it off, Brother.

WALTER (*coming close to inspect it and walking around her*): Well, I'll be damned.
  So that's what they mean by the African bush . . .

BENEATHA: Ha ha. Let's go, George.

GEORGE (*looking at her*): You know something? I like it. It's sharp. I mean it really is. (*Helps her into her wrap.*)

RUTH: Yes — I think so, too. (*She goes to the mirror and starts to clutch at her hair.*)

WALTER: Oh no! You leave yours alone, baby. You might turn out to have a pin-
  shaped head or something!

BENEATHA: See you all later.

RUTH: Have a nice time.

GEORGE: Thanks. Good night. (*Half out the door, he reopens it. To Walter.*) Good
  night, Prometheus!°

Beneatha and George exit.

WALTER (*to Ruth*): Who is Prometheus?

RUTH: I don't know. Don't worry about it.

WALTER (*in fury, pointing after George*): See there — they get to a point where
  they can't insult you man to man — they got to go talk about something
  ain't nobody never heard of!

RUTH: How do you know it was an insult? (*To humor him.*) Maybe Prometheus
  is a nice fellow.

WALTER: Prometheus! I bet there ain't even no such thing! I bet that simple-
  minded clown —

RUTH: Walter —

She stops what she is doing and looks at him.

WALTER (*yelling*): Don't start!

RUTH: Start what?

WALTER: Your nagging! Where was I? Who was I with? How much money did
  I spend?

RUTH (*plaintively*): Walter Lee — why don't we just try to talk about it . . .

WALTER (*not listening*): I been out talking with people who understand me. People who care about the things I got on my mind.

RUTH (*wearily*): I guess that means people like Willy Harris.

WALTER: Yes, people like Willy Harris.

Prometheus: In Greek myth, a Titan who was punished by Zeus for stealing fire from the
gods and giving it to humankind.

RUTH (*with a sudden flash of impatience*): Why don't you all just hurry up and go into the banking business and stop talking about it!

WALTER: Why? You want to know why? 'Cause we all tied up in a race of people that don't know how to do nothing but moan, pray, and have babies!

The line is too bitter even for him and he looks at her and sits down.

RUTH: Oh, Walter . . . (*Softly.*) Honey, why can't you stop fighting me?

WALTER (*without thinking*): Who's fighting you? Who even cares about you?

This line begins the retardation of his mood.

RUTH: Well — (*She waits a long time, and then with resignation starts to put away her things.*) I guess I might as well go on to bed . . . (*More or less to herself.*) I don't know where we lost it . . . but we have . . . (*Then, to him.*) I — I'm sorry about this new baby, Walter. I guess maybe I better go on and do what I started . . . I guess I just didn't realize how bad things was with us . . . I guess I just didn't really realize — (*She starts out to the bedroom and stops.*) You want some hot milk?

WALTER: Hot milk?

RUTH: Yes — hot milk.

WALTER: Why hot milk?

RUTH: 'Cause after all that liquor you come home with you ought to have something hot in your stomach.

WALTER: I don't want no milk.

RUTH: You want some coffee then?

WALTER: No, I don't want no coffee. I don't want nothing hot to drink. (*Almost plaintively.*) Why you always trying to give me something to eat?

RUTH (*standing and looking at him helplessly*): What else can I give you, Walter Lee Younger?

She stands and looks at him and presently turns to go out again. He lifts his head and watches her going away from him in a new mood which began to emerge when he asked her "Who cares about you?"

WALTER: It's been rough, ain't it, baby? (*She hears and stops but does not turn around and he continues to her back.*) I guess between two people there ain't never as much understood as folks generally thinks there is. I mean like between me and you — (*She turns to face him.*) How we gets to the place where we scared to talk softness to each other. (*He waits, thinking hard himself.*) Why you think it got to be like that? (*He is thoughtful, almost as a child would be.*) Ruth, what is it gets into people ought to be close?

RUTH: I don't know, honey. I think about it a lot.

WALTER: On account of you and me, you mean? The way things are with us. The way something done come down between us.

RUTH: There ain't so much between us, Walter . . . Not when you come to me and try to talk to me. Try to be with me . . . a little even.

WALTER (*total honesty*): Sometimes . . . sometimes . . . I don't even know how to try.

RUTH: Walter —

WALTER: Yes?

RUTH (*coming to him, gently and with misgiving, but coming to him*): Honey . . . life don't have to be like this. I mean sometimes people can do things so that things are better . . . You remember how we used to talk when Travis was born . . . about the way we were going to live . . . the kind of house . . . (*She is stroking his head.*) Well, it's all starting to slip away from us . . .

He turns her to him and they look at each other and kiss, tenderly and hungrily. The door opens and Mama enters — Walter breaks away and jumps up. A beat.

WALTER: Mama, where have you been?

MAMA: My — them steps is longer than they used to be. Whew! (*She sits down and ignores him.*) How you feeling this evening, Ruth?

Ruth shrugs, disturbed at having been interrupted and watching her husband knowingly.

WALTER: Mama, where have you been all day?

MAMA (*still ignoring him and leaning on the table and changing to more comfortable shoes*): Where's Travis?

RUTH: I let him go out earlier and he ain't come back yet. Boy, is he going to get it!

WALTER: Mama!

MAMA (*as if she has heard him for the first time*): Yes, son?

WALTER: Where did you go this afternoon?

MAMA: I went downtown to tend to some business that I had to tend to.

WALTER: What kind of business?

MAMA: You know better than to question me like a child, Brother.

WALTER (*rising and bending over the table*): Where were you, Mama? (*Bringing his fists down and shouting.*) Mama, you didn't go do something with that insurance money, something crazy?

The front door opens slowly, interrupting him, and Travis peeks his head in, less than hopefully.

TRAVIS (*to his mother*): Mama, I —

RUTH: "Mama I" nothing! You're going to get it, boy! Get on in that bedroom and get yourself ready!

TRAVIS: But I —

MAMA: Why don't you all never let the child explain hisself.

RUTH: Keep out of it now, Lena.

Mama clamps her lips together, and Ruth advances toward her son menacingly.

RUTH: A thousand times I have told you not to go off like that —

MAMA (*holding out her arms to her grandson*): Well — at least let me tell him something. I want him to be the first one to hear . . . Come here, Travis (*The boy obeys, gladly.*) Travis — (*She takes him by the shoulder and looks into his face.*) — you know that money we got in the mail this morning?

TRAVIS: Yes'm —

MAMA: Well — what you think your grandmama gone and done with that money?

TRAVIS: I don't know, Grandmama.

MAMA (*putting her finger on his nose for emphasis*): She went out and she bought you a house! (*The explosion comes from Walter at the end of the revelation and he jumps up and turns away from all of them in a fury. Mama continues, to Travis.*) You glad about the house? It's going to be yours when you get to be a man.

TRAVIS: Yeah — I always wanted to live in a house.

MAMA: All right, gimme some sugar then — (*Travis puts his arms around her neck as she watches her son over the boy's shoulder. Then, to Travis, after the embrace.*) Now when you say your prayers tonight, you thank God and your grandfather — 'cause it was him who give you the house — in his way.

RUTH (*taking the boy from Mama and pushing him toward the bedroom*): Now you get out of here and get ready for your beating.

TRAVIS: Aw, Mama —

RUTH: Get on in there — (*Closing the door behind him and turning radiantly to her mother-in-law.*) So you went and did it!

MAMA (*quietly, looking at her son with pain*): Yes, I did.

RUTH (*raising both arms classically*): PRAISE GOD! (*Looks at Walter a moment, who says nothing. She crosses rapidly to her husband.*) Please, honey — let me be glad . . . you be glad too. (*She has laid her hands on his shoulders, but he shakes himself free of her roughly, without turning to face her.*) Oh, Walter . . . a home . . . a home. (*She comes back to Mama.*) Well — where is it? How big is it? How much it going to cost?

MAMA: Well —

RUTH: When we moving?

MAMA (*smiling at her*): First of the month.

RUTH (*throwing back her head with jubilance*): *Praise God!*

MAMA (*tentatively, still looking at her son's back turned against her and Ruth*): It's — it's a nice house too . . . (*She cannot help speaking directly to him. An imploring quality in her voice, her manner, makes her almost like a girl now.*) Three bedrooms — nice big one for you and Ruth . . . Me and Beneatha still have to share our room, but Travis have one of his own — and (*With difficulty.*) I figure if the — new baby — is a boy, we could get one of them double-decker outfits . . . And there's a yard with a little patch of dirt where I could maybe get to grow me a few flowers . . . And a nice big basement . . .

RUTH: Walter honey, be glad —

MAMA (*still to his back, fingering things on the table*): 'Course I don't want to make it sound fancier than it is . . . It's just a plain little old house — but it's made good and solid — and it will be *ours*. Walter Lee — it makes a difference in a man when he can walk on floors that belong to *him* . . .

RUTH: Where is it?

MAMA (*frightened at this telling*): Well — well — it's out there in Clybourne Park —

Ruth's radiance fades abruptly, and Walter finally turns slowly to face his mother with incredulity and hostility.

RUTH: Where?

MAMA (*matter-of-factly*): Four o six Clybourne Street, Clybourne Park.

RUTH: Clybourne Park? Mama, there ain't no colored people living in Clybourne Park.

MAMA (*almost idiotically*): Well, I guess there's going to be some now.

WALTER (*bitterly*): So that's the peace and comfort you went out and bought for us today!

MAMA (*raising her eyes to meet his finally*): Son — I just tried to find the nicest place for the least amount of money for my family.

RUTH (*trying to recover from the shock*): Well — well — 'course I ain't one never been 'fraid of no crackers, mind you — but — well, wasn't there no other houses nowhere?

MAMA: Them houses they put up for colored in them areas way out all seem to cost twice as much as other houses. I did the best I could.

RUTH (*struck senseless with the news, in its various degrees of goodness and trouble, she sits a moment, her fists propping her chin in thought, and then she starts to rise, bringing her fists down with vigor, the radiance spreading from cheek to cheek again*): Well — well — All I can say is — if this is my time in life — MY TIME — to say good-bye — (*And she builds with momentum as she starts to circle the room with an exuberant, almost tearfully happy release.*) — to these Goddamned cracking walls! — (*She pounds the walls.*) — and these marching roaches! — (*She wipes at an imaginary army of marching roaches.*) — and this cramped little closet which ain't now or never was no kitchen! . . . then I say it loud and good, HALLELUJAH! AND GOOD-BYE MISERY . . . I DON'T NEVER WANT TO SEE YOUR UGLY FACE AGAIN! (*She laughs joyously, having practically destroyed the apartment, and flings her arms up and lets them come down happily, slowly, reflectively, over her abdomen, aware for the first time perhaps that the life therein pulses with happiness and not despair.*) Lena?

MAMA (*moved, watching her happiness*): Yes, honey?

RUTH (*looking off*): Is there — is there a whole lot of sunlight?

MAMA (*understanding*): Yes, child, there's a whole lot of sunlight.

Long pause.

RUTH (*collecting herself and going to the door of the room Travis is in*): Well — I guess I better see 'bout Travis. (*To Mama.*) Lord, I sure don't feel like whipping nobody today!

She exits.

MAMA (*the mother and son are left alone now and the mother waits a long time, considering deeply, before she speaks*): Son — you — you understand what I done, don't you? (*Walter is silent and sullen.*) I — I just seen my family falling apart today . . . just falling to pieces in front of my eyes . . . We couldn't of gone on like we was today. We was going backwards 'stead of forwards — talking 'bout killing babies and wishing each other was dead . . . When it gets like that in life — you just got to do something different, push on out and do something bigger . . . (*She waits.*) I wish you

say something, son . . . I wish you'd say how deep inside you you think
I done the right thing —

WALTER (*crossing slowly to his bedroom door and finally turning there and speaking
measuredly*): What you need me to say you done right for? *You* the head
of this family. You run our lives like you want to. It was your money and
you did what you wanted with it. So what you need for me to say it was
all right for? (*Bitterly, to hurt her as deeply as he knows is possible.*) So you
butchered up a dream of mine — you — who always talking 'bout your
children's dreams . . .

MAMA: Walter Lee —

He just closes the door behind him. Mama sits alone, thinking heavily.
Curtain.

SCENE II

Time: Friday night, a few weeks later.

    *At rise: Packing crates mark the intention of the family to move. Beneatha and
George come in, presumably from an evening out again.*

GEORGE: O.K. . . . O.K., whatever you say . . . (*They both sit on the couch. He tries
to kiss her. She moves away.*) Look, we've had a nice evening; let's not spoil
it, huh? . . .

*He again turns her head and tries to nuzzle in and she turns away from him, not with
distaste but with momentary lack of interest; in a mood to pursue what they were talking about.*

BENEATHA: I'm *trying* to talk to you.

GEORGE: We always talk.

BENEATHA: Yes — and I love to talk.

GEORGE (*exasperated; rising*): I know it and I don't mind it sometimes . . . I want
you to cut it out, see — The moody stuff, I mean. I don't like it. You're a
nice-looking girl . . . all over. That's all you need, honey, forget the
atmosphere. Guys aren't going to go for the atmosphere — they're going to go for what they see. Be glad for that. Drop the Garbo routine.
It doesn't go with you. As for myself, I want a nice — (*Groping.*) — simple (*Thoughtfully.*) — sophisticated girl . . . not a poet — O.K.?

He starts to kiss her, she rebuffs him again and he jumps up.

BENEATHA: Why are you angry, George?

GEORGE: Because this is stupid! I don't go out with you to discuss the nature of
"quiet desperation" or to hear all about your thoughts — because the
world will go on thinking what it thinks regardless —

BENEATHA: Then why read books? Why go to school?

GEORGE (*with artificial patience, counting on his fingers*): It's simple. You read
books — to learn facts — to get grades — to pass the course — to get a
degree. That's all — it has nothing to do with thoughts.

A long pause.

BENEATHA: I see. (*He starts to sit.*) Good night, George.

George looks at her a little oddly, and starts to exit. He meets Mama coming in.

GEORGE: Oh — hello, Mrs. Younger.

MAMA: Hello, George, how you feeling?

GEORGE: Fine — fine, how are you?

MAMA: Oh, a little tired. You know them steps can get you after a day's work. You all have a nice time tonight?

GEORGE: Yes — a fine time. A fine time.

MAMA: Well, good night.

GEORGE: Good night. (*He exits. Mama closes the door behind her.*)

MAMA: Hello, honey. What you sitting like that for?

BENEATHA: I'm just sitting.

MAMA: Didn't you have a nice time?

BENEATHA: No.

MAMA: No? What's the matter?

BENEATHA: Mama, George is a fool — honest. (*She rises.*)

MAMA (*hustling around unloading the packages she has entered with. She stops*): Is he, baby?

BENEATHA: Yes.

Beneatha makes up Travis's bed as she talks.

MAMA: You sure?

BENEATHA: Yes.

MAMA: Well — I guess you better not waste your time with no fools.

Beneatha looks up at her mother, watching her put groceries in the refrigerator. Finally she gathers up her things and starts into the bedroom. At the door she stops and looks back at her mother.

BENEATHA: Mama —

MAMA: Yes, baby —

BENEATHA: Thank you.

MAMA: For what?

BENEATHA: For understanding me this time.

She exits quickly and the mother stands, smiling a little, looking at the place where Beneatha just stood. Ruth enters.

RUTH: Now don't you fool with any of this stuff, Lena —

MAMA: Oh, I just thought I'd sort a few things out. Is Brother here?

RUTH: Yes.

MAMA (*with concern*): Is he —

RUTH (*reading her eyes*): Yes.

Mama is silent and someone knocks on the door. Mama and Ruth exchange weary and knowing glances and Ruth opens it to admit the neighbor, Mrs. Johnson,° who is a rather squeaky wide-eyed lady of no particular age, with a newspaper under her arm.

Mrs. Johnson: This character and the scene of her visit were cut from the original production and early editions of the play.

MAMA (*changing her expression to acute delight and a ringing cheerful greeting*): Oh — hello there, Johnson.

JOHNSON (*this is a woman who decided long ago to be enthusiastic about EVERY-THING in life and she is inclined to wave her wrist vigorously at the height of her exclamatory comments*): Hello there, yourself! H'you this evening, Ruth?

RUTH (*not much of a deceptive type*): Fine, Mis' Johnson, h'you?

JOHNSON: Fine. (*Reaching out quickly, playfully, and patting Ruth's stomach.*) Ain't you starting to poke out none yet! (*She mugs with delight at the over familiar remark and her eyes dart around looking at the crates and packing preparation; Mama's face is a cold sheet of endurance.*) Oh, ain't we getting ready round here, though! Yessir! Lookathere! I'm telling you the Youngers is really getting ready to "move on up a little higher!" — Bless God!

MAMA (*a little drily, doubting the total sincerity of the Blesser*): Bless God.

JOHNSON: He's good, ain't He?

MAMA: Oh yes, He's good.

JOHNSON: I mean sometimes He works in mysterious ways . . . but He works, don't He!

MAMA (*the same*): Yes, he does.

JOHNSON: I'm just soooooo happy for y'all. And this here child — (*about Ruth*) looks like she could just pop open with happiness, don't she. Where's all the rest of the family?

MAMA: Bennie's gone to bed —

JOHNSON: Ain't no . . . (*the implication is pregnancy*) sickness done hit you — I hope . . . ?

MAMA: No — she just tired. She was out this evening.

JOHNSON (*all is a coo, an emphatic coo*): Aw — ain't that lovely. She still going out with the little Murchison boy?

MAMA (*drily*): Ummmm huh.

JOHNSON: That's lovely. You sure got lovely children, Younger. Me and Isaiah talks all the time 'bout what fine children you was blessed with. We sure do.

MAMA: Ruth, give Mis' Johnson a piece of sweet potato pie and some milk.

JOHNSON: Oh honey, I can't stay hardly a minute — I just dropped in to see if there was anything I could do. (*Accepting the food easily.*) I guess y'all seen the news what's all over the colored paper this week . . .

MAMA: No — didn't get mine yet this week.

JOHNSON (*lifting her head and blinking with the spirit of catastrophe*): You mean you ain't read 'bout them colored people that was bombed out their place out there?

Ruth straightens with concern and takes the paper and reads it. Johnson notices her and feeds commentary.

JOHNSON: Ain't it something how bad these here white folks is getting here in Chicago! Lord, getting so you think you right down in Mississippi! (*With a tremendous and rather insincere sense of melodrama.*) 'Course I thinks it's wonderful how our folk keeps on pushing out. You hear some of these

Negroes round here talking 'bout how they don't go where they ain't wanted and all that — but not me, honey! (*This is a lie.*) Wilhemenia Othella Johnson goes anywhere, any time she feels like it! (*With head movement for emphasis.*) Yes I do! Why if we left it up to these here crackers, the poor niggers wouldn't have nothing — (*She clasps her hand over her mouth.*) Oh, I always forgets you don't 'low that word in your house.

MAMA (*quietly, looking at her*): No — I don't 'low it.

JOHNSON (*vigorously again*): Me neither! I was just telling Isaiah yesterday when he come using it in front of me — I said, "Isaiah, it's just like Mis' Younger says all the time — "

MAMA: Don't you want some more pie?

JOHNSON: No — no thank you; this was lovely. I got to get on over home and have my midnight coffee. I hear some people say it don't let them sleep but I finds I can't close my eyes right lessen I done had that laaaast cup of coffee . . . (*She waits. A beat. Undaunted.*) My Goodnight coffee, I calls it!

MAMA (*with much eye-rolling and communication between herself and Ruth*): Ruth, why don't you give Mis' Johnson some coffee.

Ruth gives Mama an unpleasant look for her kindness.

JOHNSON (*accepting the coffee*): Where's Brother tonight?

MAMA: He's lying down.

JOHNSON: MMmmmmm, he sure gets his beauty rest, don't he? Good-looking man. Sure is a good-looking man! (*Reaching out to pat Ruth's stomach again.*) I guess that's how come we keep on having babies around here. (*She winks at Mama.*) One thing 'bout Brother, he always know how to have a *good* time. And soooooo ambitious! I bet it was his idea y'all moving out to Clybourne Park. Lord — I bet this time next month y'all's names will have been in the papers plenty — (*Holding up her hands to mark off each word of the headline she can see in front of her.*) "NEGROES IN-VADE CLYBOURNE PARK — BOMBED!"

MAMA (*she and Ruth look at the woman in amazement*): We ain't exactly moving out there to get bombed.

JOHNSON: Oh honey — you know I'm praying to God every day that don't nothing like that happen! But you have to think of life like it is — and these here Chicago peckerwoods is some baaaad peckerwoods.

MAMA (*wearily*): We done thought about all that Mis' Johnson.

Beneatha comes out of the bedroom in her robe and passes through to the bathroom. Mrs. Johnson turns.

JOHNSON: Hello there, Bennie!

BENEATHA (*crisply*): Hello, Mrs. Johnson.

JOHNSON: How is school?

BENEATHA (*crisply*): Fine, thank you. (*She goes out.*)

JOHNSON (*insulted*): Getting so she don't have much to say to nobody.

MAMA: The child was on her way to the bathroom.

JOHNSON: I know — but sometimes she act like ain't got time to pass the time of day with nobody ain't been to college. Oh — I ain't criticizing her none. It's just — you know how some of our young people gets when they get a little education. (*Mama and Ruth say nothing, just look at her.*) Yes — well. Well, I guess I better get on home. (*Unmoving.*) 'Course I can understand how she must be proud and everything — being the only one in the family to make something of herself. I know just being a chauffeur ain't never satisfied Brother none. He shouldn't feel like that, though. Ain't nothing wrong with being a chauffeur.

MAMA: There's plenty wrong with it.

JOHNSON: What?

MAMA: Plenty. My husband always said being any kind of a servant wasn't a fit thing for a man to have to be. He always said a man's hands was made to make things, or to turn the earth with — not to drive nobody's car for 'em — or — (*she looks at her own hands*) carry they slop jars. And my boy is just like him — he wasn't meant to wait on nobody.

JOHNSON (*rising, somewhat offended*): Mmmmmmmmmm. The Youngers is too much for me! (*She looks around.*) You sure one proud-acting bunch of colored folks. Well — I always thinks like Booker T. Washington said that time — "Education has spoiled many a good plow hand" —

MAMA: Is that what old Booker T. said?

JOHNSON: He sure did.

MAMA: Well, it sounds just like him. The fool.

JOHNSON (*indignantly*): Well — he was one of our great men.

MAMA: Who said so?

JOHNSON (*nonplussed*): You know, me and you ain't never agreed about some things, Lena Younger. I guess I better be going —

RUTH (*quickly*): Good night.

JOHNSON: Good night. Oh — (*Thrusting it at her.*) You can keep the paper! (*With a trill.*) 'Night.

MAMA: Good night, Mis' Johnson.

Mrs. Johnson exits.

RUTH: If ignorance was gold . . .

MAMA: Shush. Don't talk about folks behind their backs.

RUTH: You do.

MAMA: I'm old and corrupted. (*Beneatha enters.*) You was rude to Mis' Johnson, Beneatha, and I don't like it at all.

BENEATHA (*at her door*): Mama, if there are two things we, as a people, have got to overcome, one is the Klu Klux Klan — and the other is Mrs. Johnson. (*She exits.*)

MAMA: Smart aleck.

The phone rings.

RUTH: I'll get it.

MAMA: Lord, ain't this a popular place tonight.

RUTH (*at the phone*): Hello — Just a minute. (*Goes to door.*) Walter, it's Mrs. Arnold. (*Waits. Goes back to the phone. Tense.*) Hello. Yes, this is his wife speaking . . . He's lying down now. Yes . . . well, he'll be in tomorrow. He's been very sick. Yes — I know we should have called, but we were

so sure he'd be able to come in today. Yes — yes, I'm very sorry. Yes . . .
Thank you very much. (*She hangs up. Walter is standing in the doorway of
the bedroom behind her.*) That was Mrs. Arnold.

WALTER (*indifferently*): Was it?

RUTH: She said if you don't come in tomorrow that they are getting a new
man . . .

WALTER: Ain't that sad — ain't that crying sad.

RUTH: She said Mr. Arnold has had to take a cab for three days . . . Walter, you
ain't been to work for three days! (*This is a revelation to her.*) Where you
been, Walter Lee Younger? (*Walter looks at her and starts to laugh.*) You're
going to lose your job.

WALTER: That's right . . . (*He turns on the radio.*)

RUTH: Oh, Walter, and with your mother working like a dog every day —

A steamy, deep blues pours into the room.

WALTER: That's sad too — Everything is sad.

MAMA: What you been doing for these three days, son?

WALTER: Mama — you don't know all the things a man what got leisure can
find to do in this city . . . What's this — Friday night? Well — Wednesday I borrowed Willy Harris' car and I went for a drive . . . just me and
myself and I drove and drove . . . Way out . . . way past South Chicago,
and I parked the car and I sat and looked at the steel mills all day long. I
just sat in the car and looked at them big black chimneys for hours. Then
I drove back and I went to the Green Hat. (*Pause.*) And Thursday —
Thursday I borrowed the car again and I got in it and I pointed it the
other way and I drove the other way — for hours — way, way up to
Wisconsin, and I looked at the farms. I just drove and looked at the
farms. Then I drove back and I went to the Green Hat. (*Pause.*) And today — today I didn't get the car. Today I just walked. All over the Southside. And I looked at the Negroes and they looked at me and finally I just
sat down on the curb at Thirty-ninth and South Parkway and I just sat
there and watched the Negroes go by. And then I went to the Green Hat.
You all sad? You all depressed? And you know where I am going right
now —

Ruth goes out quietly.

MAMA: Oh, Big Walter, is this the harvest of our days?

WALTER: You know what I like about the Green Hat? I like this little cat they got
there who blows a sax . . . He blows. He talks to me. He ain't but 'bout
five feet tall and he's got a conked head and his eyes is always closed
and he's all music —

MAMA (*rising and getting some papers out of her handbag*): Walter —

WALTER: And there's this other guy who plays the piano . . . and they got a
sound. I mean they can work on some music . . . They got the best little
combo in the world in the Green Hat . . . You can just sit there and drink
and listen to them three men play and you realize that don't nothing
matter worth a damn, but just being there —

MAMA: I've helped do it to you, haven't I, son? Walter, I been wrong.

WALTER: Naw — you ain't never been wrong about nothing, Mama.

MAMA: Listen to me, now. I say I been wrong, son. That I been doing to you what the rest of the world been doing to you. (*She turns off the radio.*) Walter — (*She stops and he looks up slowly at her and she meets his eyes pleadingly.*) What you ain't never understood is that I ain't got nothing, don't own nothing, ain't never really wanted nothing that wasn't for you. There ain't nothing as precious to me . . . There ain't nothing worth holding on to, money, dreams, nothing else — if it means — if it means it's going to destroy my boy. (*She takes an envelope out of her hand-bag and puts it in front of him and he watches her without speaking or moving.*) I paid the man thirty-five hundred dollars down on the house. That leaves sixty-five hundred dollars. Monday morning I want you to take this money and take three thousand dollars and put it in a savings account for Beneatha's medical schooling. The rest you put in a checking account — with your name on it. And from now on any penny that come out of it or that go in it is for you to look after. For you to decide. (*She drops her hands a little helplessly.*) It ain't much, but it's all I got in the world and I'm putting it in your hands. I'm telling you to be the head of this family from now on like you supposed to be.

WALTER (*stares at the money*): You trust me like that, Mama?

MAMA: I ain't never stop trusting you. Like I ain't never stop loving you.

She goes out, and Walter sits looking at the money on the table. Finally, in a decisive gesture, he gets up, and, in mingled joy and desperation, picks up the money. At the same moment, Travis enters for bed.

TRAVIS: What's the matter, Daddy? You drunk?

WALTER (*sweetly, more sweetly than we have ever known him*): No, Daddy ain't drunk. Daddy ain't going to never be drunk again . . .

TRAVIS: Well, good night, Daddy.

The father has come from behind the couch and leans over, embracing his son.

WALTER: Son, I feel like talking to you tonight.

TRAVIS: About what?

WALTER: Oh, about a lot of things. About you and what kind of man you going to be when you grow up . . . Son — son, what do you want to be when you grow up?

TRAVIS: A bus driver.

WALTER (*laughing a little*): A what? Man, that ain't nothing to want to be!

TRAVIS: Why not?

WALTER: 'Cause, man — it ain't big enough — you know what I mean.

TRAVIS: I don't know then. I can't make up my mind. Sometimes Mama asks me that too. And sometimes when I tell her I just want to be like you — she says she don't want me to be like that and sometimes she says she does. . . .

WALTER (*gathering him up in his arms*): You know what, Travis? In seven years you going to be seventeen years old. And things is going to be very different with us in seven years, Travis. . . . One day when you are seventeen I'll come home — home from my office downtown somewhere —

TRAVIS: You don't work in no office, Daddy.

WALTER: No — but after tonight. After what your daddy gonna do tonight, there's going to be offices — a whole lot of offices. . . .

TRAVIS: What you gonna do tonight, Daddy?

WALTER: You wouldn't understand yet, son, but your daddy's gonna make a transaction . . . a business transaction that's going to change our lives. . . . That's how come one day when you 'bout seventeen years old I'll come home and I'll be pretty tired, you know what I mean, after a day of conferences and secretaries getting things wrong the way they do . . . 'cause an executive's life is hell, man — (*The more he talks the farther away he gets.*) And I'll pull the car up on the driveway . . . just a plain black Chrysler, I think, with white walls — no — black tires. More elegant. Rich people don't have to be flashy . . . though I'll have to get something a little sportier for Ruth — maybe a Cadillac convertible to do her shopping in. . . . And I'll come up the steps to the house and the gardener will be clipping away at the hedges and he'll say, "Good evening, Mr. Younger." And I'll say, "Hello, Jefferson, how are you this evening?" And I'll go inside and Ruth will come downstairs and meet me at the door and we'll kiss each other and she'll take my arm and we'll go up to your room to see you sitting on the floor with the catalogues of all the great schools in America around you. . . . All the great schools in the world! And — and I'll say, all right son — it's your seventeenth birthday, what is it you've decided? . . . Just tell me where you want to go to school and you'll go. Just tell me, what it is you want to be — and you'll *be* it. . . . Whatever you want to be — Yessir! (*He holds his arms open for Travis.*) You just name it, son . . . (*Travis leaps into them.*) and I hand you the world!

Walter's voice has risen in pitch and hysterical promise and on the last line he lifts Travis high.

Blackout.

SCENE **III**

Time: Saturday, moving day, one week later.

Before the curtain rises, Ruth's voice, a strident, dramatic church alto, cuts through the silence.

It is, in the darkness, a triumphant surge, a penetrating statement of expectation: "Oh, Lord, I don't feel no ways tired! Children, oh, glory hallelujah!"

As the curtain rises we see that Ruth is alone in the living room, finishing up the family's packing. It is moving day. She is nailing crates and tying cartons. Beneatha enters, carrying a guitar case, and watches her exuberant sister-in-law.

RUTH: Hey!

BENEATHA (*putting away the case*): Hi.

RUTH (*pointing at a package*): Honey — look in that package there and see what I found on sale this morning at the South Center. (*Ruth gets up and moves to the package and draws out some curtains.*) Lookahere — hand-turned hems!

BENEATHA: How do you know the window size out there?

RUTH (*who hadn't thought of that*): Oh — Well, they bound to fit something in the whole house. Anyhow, they was too good a bargain to pass up. (*Ruth slaps her head, suddenly remembering something.*) Oh, Bennie — I meant to put a special note on that carton over there. That's your mama's good china and she wants 'em to be very careful with it.

BENEATHA: I'll do it.

Beneatha finds a piece of paper and starts to draw large letters on it.

RUTH: You know what I'm going to do soon as I get in that new house?

BENEATHA: What?

RUTH: Honey — I'm going to run me a tub of water up to here . . . (*With her fingers practically up to her nostrils.*) And I'm going to get in it — and I am going to sit . . . and sit . . . and sit in that hot water and the first person who knocks to tell *me* to hurry up and come out —

BENEATHA: Gets shot at sunrise.

RUTH (*laughing happily*): You said it, sister! (*Noticing how large Beneatha is absent-mindedly making the note*): Honey, they ain't going to read that from no airplane.

BENEATHA (*laughing herself*): I guess I always think things have more emphasis if they are big, somehow.

RUTH (*looking up at her and smiling*): You and your brother seem to have that as a philosophy of life. Lord, that man — done changed so 'round here. You know — you know what we did last night? Me and Walter Lee?

BENEATHA: What?

RUTH (*smiling to herself*): We went to the movies. (*Looking at Beneatha to see if she understands.*) We went to the movies. You know the last time me and Walter went to the movies together?

BENEATHA: No.

RUTH: Me neither. That's how long it been. (*Smiling again.*) But we went last night. The picture wasn't much good, but that didn't seem to matter. We went — and we held hands.

BENEATHA: Oh, Lord!

RUTH: We held hands — and you know what?

BENEATHA: What?

RUTH: When we come out of the show it was late and dark and all the stores and things was closed up . . . and it was kind of chilly and there wasn't many people on the streets . . . and we was still holding hands, me and Walter.

BENEATHA: You're killing me.

Walter enters with a large package. His happiness is deep in him; he cannot keep still with his newfound exuberance. He is singing and wiggling and snapping his fingers. He puts his package in a corner and puts a phonograph record, which he has brought in with him, on the record player. As the music, soulful and sensuous, comes up he dances over to Ruth and tries to get her to dance with him. She gives in at last to his raunchiness and in a fit of giggling allows herself to be drawn into his mood. They dip and she melts into his arms in a classic, body-melting "slow drag."

BENEATHA (*regarding them a long time as they dance, then drawing in her breath for a deeply exaggerated comment which she does not particularly mean*): Talk about — olddddddddddd-fashionedddddddd — Negroes!

WALTER (*stopping momentarily*): What kind of Negroes?

He says this in fun. He is not angry with her today, nor with anyone. He starts to dance with his wife again.

BENEATHA: Old-fashioned.

WALTER (*as he dances with Ruth*): You know, when these *New Negroes* have their convention — (*Pointing at his sister.*) — that is going to be the chairman of the Committee on Unending Agitation. (*He goes on dancing, then stops.*) Race, race, race! . . . Girl, I do believe you are the first person in the history of the entire human race to successfully brainwash yourself. (*Beneatha breaks up and he goes on dancing. He stops again, enjoying his tease.*) Damn, even the N double A C P takes a holiday sometimes! (*Beneatha and Ruth laugh. He dances with Ruth some more and starts to laugh and stops and pantomimes someone over an operating table.*) I can just see that chick someday looking down at some poor cat on an operating table and before she starts to slice him, she says . . . (*Pulling his sleeves back maliciously.*) "By the way, what are your views on civil rights down there? . . ."

He laughs at her again and starts to dance happily. The bell sounds.

BENEATHA: Sticks and stones may break my bones but . . . words will never hurt me!

Beneatha goes to the door and opens it as Walter and Ruth go on with the clowning. Beneatha is somewhat surprised to see a quiet-looking middle-aged white man in a business suit holding his hat and a briefcase in his hand and consulting a small piece of paper.

MAN: Uh — how do you do, miss. I am looking for a Mrs. — (*He looks at the slip of paper.*) Mrs. Lena Younger? (*He stops short, struck dumb at the sight of the oblivious Walter and Ruth.*)

BENEATHA (*smoothing her hair with slight embarrassment*): Oh — yes, that's my mother. Excuse me. (*She closes the door and turns to quiet the other two.*) Ruth! Brother! (*Enunciating precisely but soundlessly: "There's a white man at the door!" They stop dancing, Ruth cuts off the phonograph, Beneatha opens the door. The man casts a curious quick glance at all of them.*) Uh — come in please.

MAN (*coming in*): Thank you.

BENEATHA: My mother isn't here just now. Is it business?

MAN: Yes . . . well, of a sort.

WALTER (*freely, the Man of the House*): Have a seat. I'm Mrs. Younger's son. I look after most of her business matters.

Ruth and Beneatha exchange amused glances.

MAN (*regarding Walter, and sitting*): Well — My name is Karl Lindner . . .

WALTER (*stretching out his hand*): Walter Younger. This is my wife — (*Ruth nods politely.*) — and my sister.

LINDNER: How do you do.

WALTER (*amiably, as he sits himself easily on a chair, leaning forward on his knees with interest and looking expectantly into the newcomer's face*): What can we do for you, Mr. Lindner!

LINDNER (*some minor shuffling of the hat and briefcase on his knees*): Well — I am a representative of the Clybourne Park Improvement Association —

WALTER (*pointing*): Why don't you sit your things on the floor?

LINDNER: Oh — yes. Thank you. (*He slides the briefcase and hat under the chair.*) And as I was saying — I am from the Clybourne Park Improvement Association and we have had it brought to our attention at the last meeting that you people — or at least your mother — has bought a piece of residential property at — (*He digs for the slip of paper again.*) — four o six Clybourne Street . . .

WALTER: That's right. Care for something to drink? Ruth, get Mr. Lindner a beer.

LINDNER (*upset for some reason*): Oh — no, really. I mean thank you very much, but no thank you.

RUTH (*innocently*): Some coffee?

LINDNER: Thank you, nothing at all.

Beneatha is watching the man carefully.

LINDNER: Well, I don't know how much you folks know about our organization. (*He is a gentle man; thoughtful and somewhat labored in his manner.*) It is one of these community organizations set up to look after — oh, you know, things like block upkeep and special projects and we also have what we call our New Neighbors Orientation Committee . . .

BENEATHA (*drily*): Yes — and what do they do?

LINDNER (*turning a little to her and then returning the main force to Walter*): Well — it's what you might call a sort of welcoming committee, I guess. I mean they, we — I'm the chairman of the committee — go around and see the new people who move into the neighborhood and sort of give them the lowdown on the way we do things out in Clybourne Park.

BENEATHA (*with appreciation of the two meanings, which escape Ruth and Walter*): Un-huh.

LINDNER: And we also have the category of what the association calls — (*he looks elsewhere*) — uh — special community problems . . .

BENEATHA: Yes — and what are some of those?

WALTER: Girl, let the man talk.

LINDNER (*with understated relief*): Thank you. I would sort of like to explain this thing in my own way. I mean I want to explain to you in a certain way.

WALTER: Go ahead.

LINDNER: Yes. Well. I'm going to try to get right to the point. I'm sure we'll all appreciate that in the long run.

BENEATHA: Yes.

WALTER: Be still now!

LINDNER: Well —

RUTH (*still innocently*): Would you like another chair — you don't look comfortable.

LINDNER (*more frustrated than annoyed*): No, thank you very much. Please. Well — to get right to the point, I — (*A great breath, and he is off at last.*) I am sure you people must be aware of some of the incidents which have happened in various parts of the city when colored people have moved into certain areas — (*Beneatha exhales heavily and starts tossing a piece of fruit up and down in the air.*) Well — because we have what I think is going to be a unique type of organization in American community life — not only do we deplore that kind of thing — but we are trying to do something about it. (*Beneatha stops tossing and turns with a new and quizzical interest to the man.*) We feel — (*gaining confidence in his mission because of the interest in the faces of the people he is talking to*) — we feel that most of the trouble in this world, when you come right down to it — (*he hits his knee for emphasis*) — most of the trouble exists because people just don't sit down and talk to each other.

RUTH (*nodding as she might in church, pleased with the remark*): You can say that again, mister.

LINDNER (*more encouraged by such affirmation*): That we don't try hard enough in this world to understand the other fellow's problem. The other guy's point of view.

RUTH: Now that's right.

Beneatha and Walter merely watch and listen with genuine interest.

LINDNER: Yes — that's the way we feel out in Clybourne Park. And that's why I was elected to come here this afternoon and talk to you people. Friendly like, you know, the way people should talk to each other and see if we couldn't find some way to work this thing out. As I say, the whole business is a matter of *caring* about the other fellow. Anybody can see that you are a nice family of folks, hard working and honest I'm sure. (*Beneatha frowns slightly, quizzically, her head tilted regarding him.*) Today everybody knows what it means to be on the outside of *something*. And of course, there is always somebody who is out to take advantage of people who don't always understand.

WALTER: What do you mean?

LINDNER: Well — you see our community is made up of people who've worked hard as the dickens for years to build up that little community. They're not rich and fancy people; just hard-working, honest people who don't really have much but those little homes and a dream of the kind of community they want to raise their children in. Now, I don't say we are perfect and there is a lot wrong in some of the things they want. But you've got to admit that a man, right or wrong, has the right to want to have the neighborhood he lives in a certain kind of way. And at the moment the overwhelming majority of our people out there feel that people get along better, take more of a common interest in the life of the community, when they share a common background. I want you to believe me when I tell you that race prejudice simply doesn't enter into it.

It is a matter of the people of Clybourne Park believing, rightly or wrongly, as I say, that for the happiness of all concerned that our Negro families are happier when they live in their *own* communities.

BENEATHA (*with a grand and bitter gesture*): This, friends, is the Welcoming Committee!

WALTER (*dumfounded, looking at Lindner*): Is this what you came marching all the way over here to tell us?

LINDNER: Well, now we've been having a fine conversation. I hope you'll hear me all the way through.

WALTER (*tightly*): Go ahead, man.

LINDNER: You see — in the face of all the things I have said, we are prepared to make your family a very generous offer . . .

BENEATHA: Thirty pieces and not a coin less!

WALTER: Yeah?

LINDNER (*putting on his glasses and drawing a form out of the briefcase*): Our association is prepared, through the collective effort of our people, to buy the house from you at a financial gain to your family.

RUTH: Lord have mercy, ain't this the living gall!

WALTER: All right, you through?

LINDNER: Well, I want to give you the exact terms of the financial arrangement —

WALTER: We don't want to hear no exact terms of no arrangements. I want to know if you got any more to tell us 'bout getting together?

LINDNER (*taking off his glasses*): Well — I don't suppose that you feel . . .

WALTER: Never mind how I feel — you got any more to say 'bout how people ought to sit down and talk to each other? . . . Get out of my house, man.

He turns his back and walks to the door.

LINDNER (*looking around at the hostile faces and reaching and assembling his hat and briefcase*): Well — I don't understand why you people are reacting this way. What do you think you are going to gain by moving into a neighborhood where you just aren't wanted and where some elements — well — people can get awful worked up when they feel that their whole way of life and everything they've ever worked for is threatened.

WALTER: Get out.

LINDNER (*at the door, holding a small card*): Well — I'm sorry it went like this.

WALTER: Get out.

LINDNER (*almost sadly regarding Walter*): You just can't force people to change their hearts, son.

He turns and puts his card on a table and exits. Walter pushes the door to with stinging hatred, and stands looking at it. Ruth just sits and Beneatha just stands. They say nothing. Mama and Travis enter.

MAMA: Well — this all the packing got done since I left out of here this morning. I testify before God that my children got all the energy of the *dead!* What time the moving men due?

BENEATHA: Four o'clock. You had a caller, Mama.

She is smiling, teasingly.

MAMA: Sure enough — who?

BENEATHA (*her arms folded saucily*): The Welcoming Committee.

Walter and Ruth giggle.

MAMA (*innocently*): Who?

BENEATHA: The Welcoming Committee. They said they're sure going to be glad to see you when you get there.

WALTER (*devilishly*): Yeah, they said they can't hardly wait to see your face.

Laughter.

MAMA (*sensing their facetiousness*): What's the matter with you all?

WALTER: Ain't nothing the matter with us. We just telling you 'bout the gentleman who came to see you this afternoon. From the Clybourne Park Improvement Association.

MAMA: What he want?

RUTH (*in the same mood as Beneatha and Walter*): To welcome you, honey.

WALTER: He said they can't hardly wait. He said the one thing they don't have, that they just *dying* to have out there is a fine family of fine colored people! (*To Ruth and Beneatha.*) Ain't that right!

RUTH (*mockingly*): Yeah! He left his card —

BENEATHA (*handing card to Mama*): In case.

Mama reads and throws it on the floor — understanding and looking off as she draws her chair up to the table on which she has put her plant and some sticks and some cord.

MAMA: Father, give us strength. (*Knowingly — and without fun.*) Did he threaten us?

BENEATHA: Oh — Mama — they don't do it like that any more. He talked Brotherhood. He said everybody ought to learn how to sit down and hate each other with good Christian fellowship.

She and Walter shake hands to ridicule the remark.

MAMA (*sadly*): Lord, protect us . . .

RUTH: You should hear the money those folks raised to buy the house from us. All we paid and then some.

BENEATHA: What they think we going to do — eat 'em?

RUTH: No, honey, marry 'em.

MAMA (*shaking her head*): Lord, Lord, Lord . . .

RUTH: Well — that's the way the crackers crumble. (*A beat.*) Joke.

BENEATHA (*laughingly noticing what her mother is doing*): Mama, what are you doing?

MAMA: Fixing my plant so it won't get hurt none on the way . . .

BENEATHA: Mama, you going to take *that* to the new house?

MAMA: Un-huh —

BENEATHA: That raggedy-looking old thing?

MAMA (*stopping and looking at her*): It expresses ME!

RUTH (*with delight, to Beneatha*): So there, Miss Thing!

Walter comes to Mama suddenly and bends down behind her and squeezes her in his arms with all his strength. She is overwhelmed by the suddenness of it and, though delighted, her manner is like that of Ruth and Travis.

MAMA: Look out now, boy! You make me mess up my thing here!

WALTER (*his face lit, he slips down on his knees beside her, his arms still about her*):
Mama . . . you know what it means to climb up in the chariot?

MAMA (*gruffly, very happy*): Get on away from me now . . .

RUTH (*near the gift-wrapped package, trying to catch Walter's eye*): Psst —

WALTER: What the old song say, Mama . . .

RUTH: Walter — Now?

She is pointing at the package.

WALTER (*speaking the lines, sweetly, playfully, in his mother's face*):

I got wings . . . you got wings . . .
All God's Children got wings . . .

MAMA: Boy — get out of my face and do some work . . .

WALTER:

When I get to heaven gonna put on my wings,
Gonna fly all over God's heaven . . .

BENEATHA (*teasingly, from across the room*): Everybody talking 'bout heaven ain't
going there!

WALTER (*to Ruth, who is carrying the box across to them*): I don't know, you think
we ought to give her that . . . Seems to me she ain't been very appreciative around here.

MAMA (*eying the box, which is obviously a gift*): What is that?

WALTER (*taking it from Ruth and putting it on the table in front of Mama*): Well —
what you all think? Should we give it to her?

RUTH: Oh — she was pretty good today.

MAMA: I'll good you —

She turns her eyes to the box again.

BENEATHA: Open it, Mama.

*She stands up, looks at it, turns and looks at all of them, and then presses her hands
together and does not open the package.*

WALTER (*sweetly*): Open it, Mama. It's for you. (*Mama looks in his eyes. It is the
first present in her life without its being Christmas. Slowly she opens her package and lifts out, one by one, a brand-new sparkling set of gardening tools. Walter continues, prodding.*) Ruth made up the note — read it . . .

MAMA (*picking up the card and adjusting her glasses*): "To our own Mrs. Miniver° —
Love from Brother, Ruth, and Beneatha." Ain't that lovely . . .

TRAVIS (*tugging at his father's sleeve*): Daddy, can I give her mine now?

WALTER: All right, son. (*Travis flies to get his gift.*)

MAMA: Now I don't have to use my knives and forks no more . . .

WALTER: Travis didn't want to go in with the rest of us, Mama. He got his own.
(*Somewhat amused.*) We don't know what it is . . .

Mrs. Miniver: Title character of the 1942 film about a middle-class family's struggle to survive in wartorn Britain.

TRAVIS (*racing back in the room with a large hatbox and putting it in front of his grandmother*): Here!

MAMA: Lord have mercy, baby. You done gone and bought your grandmother a hat?

TRAVIS (*very proud*): Open it!

She does and lifts out an elaborate, but very elaborate, wide gardening hat, and all the adults break up at the sight of it.

RUTH: Travis, honey, what is that?

TRAVIS (*who thinks it is beautiful and appropriate*): It's a gardening hat! Like the ladies always have on in the magazines when they work in their gardens.

BENEATHA (*giggling fiercely*): Travis — we were trying to make Mama Mrs. Miniver — not Scarlett O'Hara!

MAMA (*indignantly*): What's the matter with you all! This here is a beautiful hat! (*Absurdly.*) I always wanted me one just like it!

She pops it on her head to prove it to her grandson, and the hat is ludicrous and considerably oversized.

RUTH: Hot dog! Go, Mama!

WALTER (*doubled over with laughter*): I'm sorry, Mama — but you look like you ready to go out and chop you some cotton sure enough!

They all laugh except Mama, out of deference to Travis's feelings.

MAMA (*gathering the boy up to her*): Bless your heart — this is the prettiest hat I ever owned — (*Walter, Ruth, and Beneatha chime in — noisily, festively, and insincerely congratulating Travis on his gift.*) What are we all standing around here for? We ain't finished packin' yet. Bennie, you ain't packed one book.

The bell rings.

BENEATHA: That couldn't be the movers . . . it's not hardly two good yet —

Beneatha goes into her room. Mama starts for door.

WALTER (*turning, stiffening*): Wait — wait — I'll get it.

He stands and looks at the door.

MAMA: You expecting company, son?

WALTER (*just looking at the door*): Yeah — yeah . . .

Mama looks at Ruth, and they exchange innocent and unfrightened glances.

MAMA (*not understanding*): Well, let them in, son.

BENEATHA (*from her room*): We need some more string.

MAMA: Travis — you run to the hardware and get me some string cord.

Mama goes out and Walter turns and looks at Ruth. Travis goes to a dish for money.

RUTH: Why don't you answer the door, man?

WALTER (*suddenly bounding across the floor to embrace her*): 'Cause sometimes it hard to let the future begin! (*Stooping down in her face.*)

I got wings! You got wings!
All God's children got wings!

He crosses to the door and throws it open. Standing there is a very slight little man in a not-too-prosperous business suit and with haunted frightened eyes and a hat pulled down tightly, brim up, around his forehead. Travis passes between the men and exits. Walter leans deep in the man's face, still in his jubilance.

> When I get to heaven gonna put on my wings,
> Gonna fly all over God's heaven . . .

The little man just stares at him.

> Heaven —

Suddenly he stops and looks past the little man into the empty hallway.

> Where's Willy, man?

BOBO: He ain't with me.

WALTER (*not disturbed*): Oh — come on in. You know my wife.

BOBO (*dumbly, taking off his hat*): Yes — h'you, Miss Ruth.

RUTH (*quietly, a mood apart from her husband already, seeing Bobo*): Hello, Bobo.

WALTER: You right on time today . . . Right on time. That's the way! (*He slaps Bobo on his back.*) Sit down . . . lemme hear.

Ruth stands stiffly and quietly in back of them, as though somehow she senses death, her eyes fixed on her husband.

BOBO (*his frightened eyes on the floor, his hat in his hands*): Could I please get a drink of water, before I tell you about it, Walter Lee?

Walter does not take his eyes off the man. Ruth goes blindly to the tap and gets a glass of water and brings it to Bobo.

WALTER: There ain't nothing wrong, is there?

BOBO: Lemme tell you —

WALTER: Man — didn't nothing go wrong?

BOBO: Lemme tell you — Walter Lee. (*Looking at Ruth and talking to her more than to Walter.*) You know how it was. I got to tell you how it was. I mean first I got to tell you how it was all the way . . . I mean about the money I put in, Walter Lee . . .

WALTER (*with taut agitation now*): What about the money you put in?

BOBO: Well — it wasn't much as we told you — me and Willy — (*He stops.*) I'm sorry, Walter. I got a bad feeling about it. I got a real bad feeling about it . . .

WALTER: Man, what you telling me about all this for? . . . Tell me what happened in Springfield . . .

BOBO: Springfield.

RUTH (*like a dead woman*): What was supposed to happen in Springfield?

BOBO (*to her*): This deal that me and Walter went into with Willy — Me and Willy was going to go down to Springfield and spread some money 'round so's we wouldn't have to wait so long for the liquor license . . . That's what we were going to do. Everybody said that was the way you had to do, you understand, Miss Ruth?

WALTER: Man — what happened down there?

BOBO (*a pitiful man, near tears*): I'm trying to tell you, Walter.

WALTER (*screaming at him suddenly*): THEN TELL ME, GODDAMMIT . . . WHAT'S THE MATTER WITH YOU?

BOBO: Man . . . I didn't go to no Springfield, yesterday.

WALTER (*halted, life hanging in the moment*): Why not?

BOBO (*the long way, the hard way to tell*): 'Cause I didn't have no reasons to . . .

WALTER: Man, what are you talking about!

BOBO: I'm talking about the fact that when I got to the train station yesterday morning — eight o'clock like we planned . . . Man — *Willy didn't never show up.*

WALTER: Why . . . where was he . . . where is he?

BOBO: That's what I'm trying to tell you . . . I don't know . . . I waited six hours . . . I called his house . . . and I waited . . . six hours . . . I waited in that train station six hours . . . (*Breaking into tears.*) That was all the extra money I had in the world . . . (*Looking up at Walter with the tears running down his face.*) Man, *Willy is gone.*

WALTER: Gone, what you mean Willy is gone? Gone where? You mean he went by himself. You mean he went off to Springfield by himself — to take care of getting the license — (*Turns and looks anxiously at Ruth.*) You mean maybe he didn't want too many people in on the business down there? (*Looks to Ruth again, as before.*) You know Willy got his own ways. (*Looks back to Bobo.*) Maybe you was late yesterday and he just went on down there without you. Maybe — maybe — he's been callin' you at home tryin' to tell you what happened or something. Maybe — maybe — he just got sick. He's somewhere — he's got to be somewhere. We just got to find him — me and you got to find him. (*Grabs Bobo senselessly by the collar and starts to shake him.*) We got to!

BOBO (*in sudden angry, frightened agony*): What's the matter with you, Walter! *When a cat take off with your money he don't leave you no road maps!*

WALTER (*turning madly, as though he is looking for Willy in the very room*): Willy! . . . Willy . . . don't do it . . . Please don't do it . . . Man, not with that money . . . Man, please, not with that money . . . Oh, God . . . Don't let it be true . . . (*He is wandering around, crying out for Willy and looking for him or perhaps for help from God.*) Man . . . I trusted you . . . Man, I put my life in your hands . . . (*He starts to crumple down on the floor as Ruth just covers her face in horror. Mama opens the door and comes into the room, with Beneatha behind her.*) Man . . . (*He starts to pound the floor with his fists, sobbing wildly.*) THAT MONEY IS MADE OUT OF MY FATHER'S FLESH —

BOBO (*standing over him helplessly*): I'm sorry, Walter . . . (*Only Walter's sobs reply. Bobo puts on his hat.*) I had my life staked on this deal, too . . .

He exits.

MAMA (*to Walter*): Son — (*She goes to him, bends down to him, talks to his bent head.*) Son . . . Is it gone? Son, I gave you sixty-five hundred dollars. Is it gone? All of it? Beneatha's money too?

WALTER (*lifting his head slowly*): Mama . . . I never . . . went to the bank at all . . .

MAMA (*not wanting to believe him*): You mean . . . your sister's school money . . . you used that too . . . Walter? . . .

WALTER: Yessss! All of it . . . It's all gone . . .

There is total silence. Ruth stands with her face covered with her hands; Beneatha leans forlornly against a wall, fingering a piece of red ribbon from the mother's gift. Mama stops and looks at her son without recognition and then, quite without thinking about it, starts to beat him senselessly in the face. Beneatha goes to them and stops it.

BENEATHA: Mama!

Mama stops and looks at both of her children and rises slowly and wanders vaguely, aimlessly away from them.

MAMA: I seen . . . him . . . night after night . . . come in . . . and look at that rug . . . and then look at me . . . the red showing in his eyes . . . the veins moving in his head . . . I seen him grow thin and old before he was forty . . . working and working and working like somebody's old horse . . . killing himself . . . and you — you give it all away in a day — (*She raises her arms to strike him again.*)

BENEATHA: Mama —

MAMA: Oh, God . . . (*She looks up to Him.*) Look down here — and show me the strength.

BENEATHA: Mama —

MAMA (*folding over*): Strength . . .

BENEATHA (*plaintively*): Mama . . .

MAMA: Strength!

Curtain.

ACT III

Time: An hour later.

    At curtain, there is a sullen light of gloom in the living room, gray light not unlike that which began the first scene of Act I. At left we can see Walter within his room, alone with himself. He is stretched out on the bed, his shirt out and open, his arms under his head. He does not smoke, he does not cry out, he merely lies there, looking up at the ceiling, much as if he were alone in the world.

    In the living room Beneatha sits at the table, still surrounded by the now almost ominous packing crates. She sits looking off. We feel that this is a mood struck perhaps an hour before, and it lingers now, full of the empty sound of profound disappointment. We see on a line from her brother's bedroom the sameness of their attitudes. Presently the bell rings and Beneatha rises without ambition or interest in answering. It is Asagai, smiling broadly, striding into the room with energy and happy expectation and conversation.

ASAGAI: I came over . . . I had some free time. I thought I might help with the packing. Ah, I like the look of packing crates! A household in preparation for a journey! It depresses some people . . . but for me . . . it is another feeling. Something full of the flow of life, do you understand? Movement, progress . . . It makes me think of Africa.

BENEATHA: Africa!

ASAGAI: What kind of a mood is this? Have I told you how deeply you move me?

BENEATHA: He gave away the money, Asagai . . .

ASAGAI: Who gave away what money?

BENEATHA: The insurance money. My brother gave it away.

ASAGAI: Gave it away?

BENEATHA: He made an investment! With a man even Travis wouldn't have trusted with his most worn-out marbles.

ASAGAI: And it's gone?

BENEATHA: Gone!

ASAGAI: I'm very sorry . . . And you, now?

BENEATHA: Me? . . . Me? . . . Me, I'm nothing . . . Me. When I was very small . . . we used to take our sleds out in the wintertime and the only hills we had were the ice-covered stone steps of some houses down the street. And we used to fill them in with snow and make them smooth and slide down them all day . . . and it was very dangerous, you know . . . far too steep . . . and sure enough one day a kid named Rufus came down too fast and hit the sidewalk and we saw his face just split open right there in front of us . . . And I remember standing there looking at his bloody open face thinking that was the end of Rufus. But the ambulance came and they took him to the hospital and they fixed the broken bones and they sewed it all up . . . and the next time I saw Rufus he just had a little line down the middle of his face . . . I never got over that . . .

ASAGAI: What?

BENEATHA: That that was what one person could do for another, fix him up — sew up the problem, make him all right again. That was the most marvelous thing in the world . . . I wanted to do that. I always thought it was the one concrete thing in the world that a human being could do. Fix up the sick, you know — and make them whole again. This was truly being God . . .

ASAGAI: You wanted to be God?

BENEATHA: No — I wanted to cure. It used to be so important to me. I wanted to cure. It used to matter. I used to care. I mean about people and how their bodies hurt . . .

ASAGAI: And you've stopped caring?

BENEATHA: Yes — I think so.

ASAGAI: Why?

BENEATHA (*bitterly*): Because it doesn't seem deep enough, close enough to what ails mankind! It was a child's way of seeing things — or an idealist's.

ASAGAI: Children see things very well sometimes — and idealists even better.

BENEATHA: I know that's what you think. Because you are still where I left off. You with all your talk and dreams about Africa! You still think you can patch up the world. Cure the Great Sore of Colonialism — (*loftily, mocking it*) with the Penicillin of Independence — !

ASAGAI: Yes!

BENEATHA: Independence *and then what?* What about all the crooks and thieves and just plain idiots who will come into power and steal and plunder the same as before — only now they will be black and do it in the name of the new Independence — WHAT ABOUT THEM?!

ASAGAI: That will be the problem for another time. First we must get there.

BENEATHA: And where does it end?

ASAGAI: End? Who even spoke of an end? To life? To living?

BENEATHA: An end to misery! To stupidity! Don't you see there isn't any real progress, Asagai, there is only one large circle that we march in, around and around, each of us with our own little picture in front of us — our own little mirage that we think is the future.

ASAGAI: That is the mistake.

BENEATHA: What?

ASAGAI: What you just said — about the circle. It isn't a circle—it is simply a long line — as in geometry, you know, one that reaches into infinity. And because we cannot see the end — we also cannot see how it changes. And it is very odd but those who see the changes — who dream, who will not give up — are called idealists . . . and those who see only the circle — we call *them* the "realists"!

BENEATHA: Asagai, while I was sleeping in that bed in there, people went out and took the future right out of my hands! And nobody asked me, nobody consulted me — they just went out and changed my life!

ASAGAI: Was it your money?

BENEATHA: What?

ASAGAI: Was it your money he gave away?

BENEATHA: It belonged to all of us.

ASAGAI: But did you earn it? Would you have had it at all if your father had not died?

BENEATHA: No.

ASAGAI: Then isn't there something wrong in a house — in a world — where all dreams, good or bad, must depend on the death of a man? I never thought to see *you* like this, Alaiyo. You! Your brother made a mistake and you are grateful to him so that now you can give up the ailing human race on account of it! You talk about what good is struggle, what good is anything! Where are we all going and why are we bothering!

BENEATHA: AND YOU CANNOT ANSWER IT!

ASAGAI (*shouting over her*): I LIVE THE ANSWER! (*Pause.*) In my village at home it is the exceptional man who can even read a newspaper . . . or who ever sees a book at all. I will go home and much of what I will have to say will seem strange to the people of my village. But I will teach and work and things will happen, slowly and swiftly. At times it will seem that nothing changes at all . . . and then again the sudden dramatic events which make history leap into the future. And then quiet again. Retrogression even. Guns, murder, revolution. And I even will have moments when I wonder if the quiet was not better than all that death and hatred. But I will look about my village at the illiteracy and disease and ignorance and I will not wonder long. And perhaps . . . perhaps I will be a great man . . . I mean perhaps I will hold on to the substance of truth and find my way always with the right course . . . and perhaps for it I will be butchered in my bed some night by the servants of empire . . .

BENEATHA: *The martyr!*

ASAGAI (*he smiles*): . . . or perhaps I shall live to be a very old man, respected and esteemed in my new nation . . . And perhaps I shall hold office and this is what I'm trying to tell you, Alaiyo: perhaps the things I believe now for my country will be wrong and outmoded, and I will not understand and do terrible things to have things my way or merely to keep my power. Don't you see that there will be young men and women — not British soldiers then, but my own black countrymen — to step out of the shadows some evening and slit my then useless throat? Don't you see they have always been there . . . that they always will be. And that such a thing as my own death will be an advance? They who might kill me even . . . actually replenish all that I was.

BENEATHA: Oh, Asagai, I know all that.

ASAGAI: Good! Then stop moaning and groaning and tell me what you plan to do.

BENEATHA: Do?

ASAGAI: I have a bit of a suggestion.

BENEATHA: What?

ASAGAI (*rather quietly for him*): That when it is all over — that you come home with me —

BENEATHA (*staring at him and crossing away with exasperation*): Oh — Asagai — at this moment you decide to be romantic!

ASAGAI (*quickly understanding the misunderstanding*): My dear, young creature of the New World — I do not mean across the city — I mean across the ocean: home — to Africa.

BENEATHA (*slowly understanding and turning to him with murmured amazement*): To Africa?

ASAGAI: Yes! . . . (*Smiling and lifting his arms playfully.*) Three hundred years later the African Prince rose up out of the seas and swept the maiden back across the middle passage over which her ancestors had come —

BENEATHA (*unable to play*): To — to Nigeria?

ASAGAI: Nigeria. Home. (*Coming to her with genuine romantic flippancy.*) I will show you our mountains and our stars; and give you cool drinks from gourds and teach you the old songs and the ways of our people — and, in time, we will pretend that — (*very softly*) — you have only been away for a day. Say that you'll come — (*He swings her around and takes her full in his arms in a kiss which proceeds to passion.*)

BENEATHA (*pulling away suddenly*): You're getting me all mixed up —

ASAGAI: Why?

BENEATHA: Too many things — too many things have happened today. I must sit down and think. I don't know what I feel about anything right this minute.

She promptly sits down and props her chin on her fist.

ASAGAI (*charmed*): All right, I shall leave you. No — don't get up. (*Touching her, gently, sweetly.*) Just sit awhile and think . . . Never be afraid to sit awhile and think. (*He goes to door and looks at her.*) How often I have looked at you and said, "Ah — so this is what the New World hath finally wrought . . ."

He exits. Beneatha sits on alone. Presently Walter enters from his room and starts to rummage through things, feverishly looking for something. She looks up and turns in her seat.

BENEATHA (*hissingly*): Yes — just look at what the New World hath wrought! . . . Just look! (*She gestures with bitter disgust.*) There he is! *Monsieur le petit bourgeois noir* — himself! There he is — Symbol of a Rising Class! Entrepreneur! Titan of the system! (*Walter ignores her completely and continues frantically and destructively looking for something and hurling things to floor and tearing things out of their place in his search. Beneatha ignores the eccentricity of his actions and goes on with the monologue of insult.*) Did you dream of yachts on Lake Michigan, Brother? Did you see yourself on that Great Day sitting down at the Conference Table, surrounded by all the mighty bald-headed men in America? All halted, waiting, breathless, waiting for your pronouncements on industry? Waiting for you — Chairman of the Board! (*Walter finds what he is looking for — a small piece of white paper — and pushes it in his pocket and puts on his coat and rushes out without ever having looked at her. She shouts after him.*) I look at you and I see the final triumph of stupidity in the world!

The door slams and she returns to just sitting again. Ruth comes quickly out of Mama's room.

RUTH: Who was that?

BENEATHA: Your husband.

RUTH: Where did he go?

BENEATHA: Who knows — maybe he has an appointment at U.S. Steel.

RUTH (*anxiously, with frightened eyes*): You didn't say nothing bad to him, did you?

BENEATHA: Bad? Say anything bad to him? No — I told him he was a sweet boy and full of dreams and everything is strictly peachy keen, as the ofay kids say!

Mama enters from her bedroom. She is lost, vague, trying to catch hold, to make some sense of her former command of the world, but it still eludes her. A sense of waste overwhelms her gait; a measure of apology rides on her shoulders. She goes to her plant, which has remained on the table, looks at it, picks it up and takes it to the window sill and sits it outside, and she stands and looks at it a long moment. Then she closes the window, straightens her body with effort and turns around to her children.

MAMA: Well — ain't it a mess in here, though? (*A false cheerfulness, a beginning of something.*) I guess we all better stop moping around and get some work done. All this unpacking and everything we got to do. (*Ruth raises her head slowly in response to the sense of the line; and Beneatha in similar manner turns very slowly to look at her mother.*) One of you all better call the moving people and tell 'em not to come.

RUTH: Tell 'em not to come?

MAMA: Of course, baby. Ain't no need in 'em coming all the way here and having to go back. They charges for that too. (*She sits down, fingers to her brow, thinking.*) Lord, ever since I was a little girl, I always remembers people saying, "Lena — Lena Eggleston, you aims too high all the time. You needs to slow down and see life a little more like it is. Just slow down some." That's what they always used to say down home —

"Lord, that Lena Eggleston is a high-minded thing. She'll get her due one day!"

RUTH: No, Lena . . .

MAMA: Me and Big Walter just didn't never learn right.

RUTH: Lena, no! We gotta go. Bennie — tell her . . .

She rises and crosses to Beneatha with her arms outstretched. Beneatha doesn't respond.

> Tell her we can still move . . . the notes ain't but a hundred and twenty-five a month. We got four grown people in this house — we can work . . .

MAMA (*to herself*): Just aimed too high all the time —

RUTH (*turning and going to Mama fast — the words pouring out with urgency and desperation*): Lena — I'll work . . . I'll work twenty hours a day in all the kitchens in Chicago . . . I'll strap my baby on my back if I have to and scrub all the floors in America and wash all the sheets in America if I have to — but we got to MOVE! We got to get OUT OF HERE!!

Mama reaches out absently and pats Ruth's hand.

MAMA: No — I sees things differently now. Been thinking 'bout some of the things we could do to fix this place up some. I seen a second-hand bureau over on Maxwell Street just the other day that could fit right there. (*She points to where the new furniture might go. Ruth wanders away from her.*) Would need some new handles on it and then a little varnish and it look like something brand-new. And — we can put up them new curtains in the kitchen . . . Why this place be looking fine. Cheer us all up so that we forget trouble ever come . . . (*To Ruth.*) And you could get some nice screens to put up in your room round the baby's bassinet . . . (*She looks at both of them pleadingly.*) Sometimes you just got to know when to give up some things . . . and hold on to what you got . . .

Walter enters from the outside, looking spent and leaning against the door, his coat hanging from him.

MAMA: Where you been, son?

WALTER (*breathing hard*): Made a call.

MAMA: To who, son?

WALTER: To The Man. (*He heads for his room.*)

MAMA: What man, baby?

WALTER (*stops in the door*): The Man, Mama. Don't you know who The Man is?

RUTH: Walter Lee?

WALTER: *The Man*. Like the guys in the streets say — The Man. Captain Boss — Mistuh Charley . . . Old Cap'n Please Mr. Bossman . . .

BENEATHA (*suddenly*): Lindner!

WALTER: That's right! That's good. I told him to come right over.

BENEATHA (*fiercely, understanding*): For what? What do you want to see him for!

WALTER (*looking at his sister*): We going to do business with him.

MAMA: What you talking 'bout, son?

WALTER: Talking 'bout life, Mama. You all always telling me to see life like it is. Well — I laid in there on my back today . . . and I figured it out. Life just like it is. Who gets and who don't get. (*He sits down with his coat on and laughs.*) Mama, you know it's all divided up. Life is. Sure enough. Between the takers and the "tooken." (*He laughs.*) I've figured it out finally. (*He looks around at them.*) Yeah. Some of us always getting "tooken." (*He laughs.*) People like Willy Harris, they don't never get "tooken." And you know why the rest of us do? 'Cause we all mixed up. Mixed up bad. We get to looking 'round for the right and the wrong; and we worry about it and cry about it and stay up nights trying to figure out 'bout the wrong and the right of things all the time . . . And all the time, man, them takers is out there operating, just taking and taking. Willy Harris? Shoot — Willy Harris don't even count. He don't even count in the big scheme of things. But I'll say one thing for old Willy Harris . . . he's taught me something. He's taught me to keep my eye on what counts in this world. Yeah — (*Shouting out a little.*) Thanks, Willy!

RUTH: What did you call that man for, Walter Lee?

WALTER: Called him to tell him to come on over to the show. Gonna put on a show for the man. Just what he wants to see. You see, Mama, the man came here today and he told us that them people out there where you want us to move — well they so upset they willing to pay us *not* to move! (*He laughs again.*) And — and oh, Mama — you would of been proud of the way me and Ruth and Bennie acted. We told him to get out . . . Lord have mercy! We told the man to get out! Oh, we was some proud folks this afternoon, yeah. (*He lights a cigarette.*) We were still full of that old-time stuff . . .

RUTH (*coming toward him slowly*): You talking 'bout taking them people's money to keep us from moving in that house?

WALTER: I ain't just talking 'bout it, baby — I'm telling you that's what's going to happen!

BENEATHA: Oh, God! Where is the bottom! Where is the real honest-to-God bottom so he can't go any farther!

WALTER: See — that's the old stuff. You and that boy that was here today. You all want everybody to carry a flag and a spear and sing some marching songs, huh? You wanna spend your life looking into things and trying to find the right and the wrong part, huh? Yeah. You know what's going to happen to that boy someday — he'll find himself sitting in a dungeon, locked in forever — and the takers will have the key! Forget it, baby! There ain't no causes — there ain't nothing but taking in this world, and he who takes most is smartest — and it don't make a damn bit of difference *how*.

MAMA: You making something inside me cry, son. Some awful pain inside me.

WALTER: Don't cry, Mama. Understand. That white man is going to walk in that door able to write checks for more money than we ever had. It's important to him and I'm going to help him . . . I'm going to put on the show, Mama.

MAMA: Son — I come from five generations of people who was slaves and sharecroppers — but ain't nobody in my family never let nobody pay 'em no money that was a way of telling us we wasn't fit to walk the earth. We ain't never been that poor. (*Raising her eyes and looking at him.*) We ain't never been that — dead inside.

BENEATHA: Well — we are dead now. All the talk about dreams and sunlight that goes on in this house. It's all dead now.

WALTER: What's the matter with you all! I didn't make this world! It was give to me this way! Hell, yes, I want me some yachts someday! Yes, I want to hang some real pearls 'round my wife's neck. Ain't she supposed to wear no pearls? Somebody tell me — tell me, who decides which women is suppose to wear pearls in this world. I tell you I am a *man* — and I think my wife should wear some pearls in this world!

This last line hangs a good while and Walter begins to move about the room. The word "Man" has penetrated his consciousness; he mumbles it to himself repeatedly between strange agitated pauses as he moves about.

MAMA: Baby, how you going to feel on the inside?

WALTER: Fine! . . . Going to feel fine . . . a man . . .

MAMA: You won't have nothing left then, Walter Lee.

WALTER (*coming to her*): I'm going to feel fine, Mama. I'm going to look that son-of-a-bitch in the eyes and say — (*he falters*) — and say, "All right, Mr. Lindner — (*he falters even more*) — that's *your* neighborhood out there! You got the right to keep it like you want! You got the right to have it like you want! Just write the check and — the house is yours." And — and I am going to say — (*his voice almost breaks*) "And you — you people just put the money in my hand and you won't have to live next to this bunch of stinking niggers! . . ." (*He straightens up and moves away from his mother, walking around the room.*) And maybe — maybe I'll just get down on my black knees . . . (*He does so; Ruth and Bennie and Mama watch him in frozen horror.*) "Captain, Mistuh, Bossman — (*Groveling and grinning and wringing his hands in profoundly anguished imitation of the slow-witted movie stereotype.*) A-hee-hee-hee! Oh, yassuh boss! Yasssssuh! Great white — (*voice breaking, he forces himself to go on*) — Father, just gi' ussen de money, fo' God's sake, and we's — we's ain't gwine come out deh and dirty up yo' white folks neighborhood . . ." (*He breaks down completely.*) And I'll feel fine! Fine! FINE! (*He gets up and goes into the bedroom.*)

BENEATHA: That is not a man. That is nothing but a toothless rat.

MAMA: Yes — death done come in this here house. (*She is nodding, slowly, reflectively.*) Done come walking in my house on the lips of my children. You what supposed to be my beginning again. You — what supposed to be my harvest. (*To Beneatha.*) You — you mourning your brother?

BENEATHA: He's no brother of mine.

MAMA: What you say?

BENEATHA: I said that that individual in that room is no brother of mine.

MAMA: That's what I thought you said. You feeling like you better than he is to-day? (*Beneatha does not answer.*) Yes? What you tell him a minute ago? That he wasn't a man? Yes? You give him up for me? You done wrote his epitaph too — like the rest of the world? Well, who give you the privilege?

BENEATHA: Be on my side for once! You saw what he just did, Mama! You saw him — down on his knees. Wasn't it you who taught me to despise any man who would do that? Do what he's going to do?

MAMA: Yes — I taught you that. Me and your daddy. But I thought I taught you something else too . . . I thought I taught you to love him.

BENEATHA: Love him? There is nothing left to love.

MAMA: There is *always* something left to love. And if you ain't learned that, you ain't learned nothing. (*Looking at her.*) Have you cried for that boy today? I don't mean for yourself and for the family 'cause we lost the money. I mean for him: what he been through and what it done to him. Child, when do you think is the time to love somebody the most? When they done good and made things easy for everybody? Well then, you ain't through learning — because that ain't the time at all. It's when he's at his lowest and can't believe in hisself 'cause the world done whipped him so! When you starts measuring somebody, measure him right, child, measure him right. Make sure you done taken into account what hills and valleys he come through before he got to wherever he is.

Travis bursts into the room at the end of the speech, leaving the door open.

TRAVIS: Grandmama — the moving men are downstairs! The truck just pulled up.

MAMA (*turning and looking at him*): Are they, baby? They downstairs?

She sighs and sits. Lindner appears in the doorway. He peers in and knocks lightly, to gain attention, and comes in. All turn to look at him.

LINDNER (*hat and briefcase in hand*): Uh — hello . . .

Ruth crosses mechanically to the bedroom door and opens it and lets it swing open freely and slowly as the lights come up on Walter within, still in his coat, sitting at the far corner of the room. He looks up and out through the room to Lindner.

RUTH: He's here.

A long minute passes and Walter slowly gets up.

LINDNER (*coming to the table with efficiency, putting his briefcase on the table and starting to unfold papers and unscrew fountain pens*): Well, I certainly was glad to hear from you people. (*Walter has begun the trek out of the room, slowly and awkwardly, rather like a small boy, passing the back of his sleeve across his mouth from time to time.*) Life can really be so much simpler than people let it be most of the time. Well — with whom do I negotiate? You, Mrs. Younger, or your son here? (*Mama sits with her hands folded on her lap and her eyes closed as Walter advances. Travis goes closer to Lindner and looks at the papers curiously.*) Just some official papers, sonny.

RUTH: Travis, you go downstairs —

MAMA (*opening her eyes and looking into Walter's*): No. Travis, you stay right here. And you make him understand what you doing, Walter Lee. You teach him good. Like Willy Harris taught you. You show where our five generations done come to. (*Walter looks from her to the boy, who grins at him innocently.*) Go ahead, son — (*She folds her hands and closes her eyes.*) Go ahead.

WALTER (*at last crosses to Lindner, who is reviewing the contract*): Well, Mr. Lindner. (*Beneatha turns away.*) We called you — (*there is a profound, simple groping quality in his speech*) — because, well, me and my family (*He looks around and shifts from one foot to the other.*) Well — we are very plain people . . .

LINDNER: Yes —

WALTER: I mean — I have worked as a chauffeur most of my life — and my wife here, she does domestic work in people's kitchens. So does my mother. I mean — we are plain people . . .

LINDNER: Yes, Mr. Younger —

WALTER (*really like a small boy, looking down at his shoes and then up at the man*): And — uh — well, my father, well, he was a laborer most of his life. . . .

LINDNER (*absolutely confused*): Uh, yes — yes, I understand. (*He turns back to the contract.*)

WALTER (*a beat; staring at him*): And my father — (*With sudden intensity.*) My father almost *beat a man to death* once because this man called him a bad name or something, you know what I mean?

LINDNER (*looking up, frozen*): No, no, I'm afraid I don't —

WALTER (*a beat. The tension hangs; then Walter steps back from it*): Yeah. Well — what I mean is that we come from people who had a lot of *pride.* I mean — we are very proud people. And that's my sister over there and she's going to be a doctor — and we are very proud —

LINDNER: Well — I am sure that is very nice, but —

WALTER: What I am telling you is that we called you over here to tell you that we are very proud and that this — (*Signaling to Travis.*) Travis, come here. (*Travis crosses and Walter draws him before him facing the man.*) This is my son, and he makes the sixth generation our family in this country. And we have all thought about your offer —

LINDNER: Well, good . . . good —

WALTER: And we have decided to move into our house because my father — my father — he earned it for us brick by brick. (*Mama has her eyes closed and is rocking back and forth as though she were in church, with her head nodding the Amen yes.*) We don't want to make no trouble for nobody or fight no causes, and we will try to be good neighbors. And that's *all* we got to say about that. (*He looks the man absolutely in the eyes.*) We don't want your money. (*He turns and walks away.*)

LINDNER (*looking around at all of them*): I take it then — that you have decided to occupy . . .

BENEATHA: That's what the man said.

LINDNER (*to Mama in her reverie*): Then I would like to appeal to you, Mrs. Younger. You are older and wiser and understand things better I am sure . . .

MAMA: I am afraid you don't understand. My son said we was going to move and there ain't nothing left for me to say. (*Briskly.*) You know how these young folks is nowadays, mister. Can't do a thing with 'em! (*As he opens his mouth, she rises.*) Good-bye.

LINDNER (*folding up his materials*): Well — if you are that final about it . . . there is nothing left for me to say. (*He finishes, almost ignored by the family, who are concentrating on Walter Lee. At the door Lindner halts and looks around.*) I sure hope you people know what you're getting into.

He shakes his head and exits.

RUTH (*looking around and coming to life*): Well, for God's sake — if the moving men are here — LET'S GET THE HELL OUT OF HERE!

MAMA (*into action*): Ain't it the truth! Look at all this here mess. Ruth, put Travis' good jacket on him . . . Walter Lee, fix your tie and tuck your shirt in, you look like somebody's hoodlum! Lord have mercy, where is my plant? (*She flies to get it amid the general bustling of the family, who are deliberately trying to ignore the nobility of the past moment.*) You all start on down . . . Travis child, don't go empty-handed . . . Ruth, where did I put that box with my skillets in it? I want to be in charge of it myself . . . I'm going to make us the biggest dinner we ever ate tonight . . . Beneatha, what's the matter with them stockings? Pull them things up, girl . . .

The family starts to file out as two moving men appear and begin to carry out the heavier pieces of furniture, bumping into the family as they move about.

BENEATHA: Mama, Asagai asked me to marry him today and go to Africa —

MAMA (*in the middle of her getting-ready activity*): He did? You ain't old enough to marry nobody — (*Seeing the moving men lifting one of her chairs precariously.*) Darling, that ain't no bale of cotton, please handle it so we can sit in it again! I had that chair twenty-five years . . .

The movers sigh with exasperation and go on with their work.

BENEATHA (*girlishly and unreasonably trying to pursue the conversation*): To go to Africa, Mama — be a doctor in Africa . . .

MAMA (*distracted*): Yes, baby —

WALTER: *Africa!* What he want you to go to Africa for?

BENEATHA: To practice there . . .

WALTER: Girl, if you don't get all them silly ideas out your head! You better marry yourself a man with some loot . . .

BENEATHA (*angrily, precisely as in the first scene of the play*): What have you got to do with who I marry!

WALTER: Plenty. Now I think George Murchison —

BENEATHA: *George Murchison!* I wouldn't marry him if he was Adam and I was Eve!

Walter and Beneatha go out yelling at each other vigorously and the anger is loud and real till their voices diminish. Ruth stands at the door and turns to Mama and smiles knowingly.

MAMA (*fixing her hat at last*): Yeah — they something all right, my children . . .

RUTH: Yeah — they're something. Let's go, Lena.

MAMA (*stalling, starting to look around at the house*): Yes — I'm coming. Ruth —
RUTH: Yes?
MAMA (*quietly, woman to woman*): He finally come into his manhood today, didn't he? Kind of like a rainbow after the rain . . .
RUTH (*biting her lip lest her own pride explode in front of Mama*): Yes, Lena.

Walter's voice calls for them raucously.

WALTER (*off stage*): Y'all come on! These people charges by the hour, you know!
MAMA (waving Ruth out vaguely): All right, honey — go on down. I be down directly.

Ruth hesitates, then exits. Mama stands, at last alone in the living room, her plant on the table before her as the lights start to come down. She looks around at all the walls and ceilings and suddenly, despite herself, while the children call below, a great heaving thing rises in her and she puts her fist to her mouth to stifle it, takes a final desperate look, pulls her coat about her, pats her hat, and goes out. The lights dim down. The door opens and she comes back in, grabs her plant, and goes out for the last time. Curtain.

ಐಐ

WOODY ALLEN (*b. 1935*) *grew up in what he calls "a typical, noisy, ethnic family" in Brooklyn, New York. After graduating from high school, Allen attended and dropped out of both New York University and the City College of New York. While still a student he sold jokes to newspaper columnists, and at seventeen he was hired as an NBC staff writer for* The Colgate Comedy Hour *and* The Sid Caesar Show. *During the 1950s he wrote jokes for comedians such as Herb Shriner, Art Carney, Kaye Ballard, Buddy Hackett, and Carol Channing. After a short career as a stand-up comedian in the early 1960s, he wrote his first screenplay,* What's New Pussycat?, *in 1964; it was made into a movie the following year, with Allen playing the role of Victor Shakapopulis. In 1966 Allen's first play* Don't Drink the Water *was produced in New York City.*

Since that time, Allen has written, directed, and often starred in more than twenty films. He is one of the few major American filmmakers to insist on total control over his productions, which he equates with artistic freedom. "I'm only making films because I'm as free there as if I were writing novels. You can't create unless you're completely free." Allen's memorable roles in his own films include that of Alvy Singer in Annie Hall *(1977) and Isaac Davis in* Manhattan *(1979), from which the following monologues were taken. He also played the title roles in* Zelig *(1983) and* Broadway Danny Rose *(1984), the narrator in* Radio Days *(1987), and Oedipus Wrecks in* New York Stories *(1989), among many others. Along with his collaborator Marshall Brickman, Allen won Academy Awards for his screenplays for* Annie Hall *and* Hannah and Her Sisters *(1986). In 1986 he also won an Oscar for lifetime achievement in the motion picture industry.*

Allen's books of plays and film scripts include Death: A Comedy in One Act *(1975),* Four Screenplays *(1978),* Four Films of Woody Allen *(1982), and* Crimes and Misdemeanors *(1989). The Complete Prose of Woody Allen appeared in*

1991. As the critic Molly Haskell has observed in the Village Voice *about Allen's unique brand of comedy in his films, "Allen clings tenaciously to the worm's-eye view which is the source of his humor and his success, and which defines the limits of his vision. It is the humor of a stand-up comic, wit that plays off a given world, rather than inventing it."*

RELATED STORY: *Woody Allen, "The Kugelmass Episode," page 38.*

WOODY ALLEN

Two Monologues   1977–79

COAUTHORED BY MARSHALL BRICKMAN

ANNIE HALL

TIME: *1977*

PLACE: *Manhattan*

Alvy Singer grew up in a Jewish family in Brooklyn, in a house under the roller coaster at Coney Island. Now forty, he's become a successful comedian and comedy writer. He's seen on television and recognized on the street, whether he likes it or not. He's "arrived" but is still looking for greater meaning in his life. Alvy navigates with highly developed defenses and well-cultivated neuroses.

This monologue opens the film, as Alvy looks back on what were the best and worst of times during his love affair with Annie Hall. Shown in flashbacks, Alvy's romantic encounters with women prepared him to expect the worst. But he meets and falls in love with Annie, a refreshingly eccentric WASP in her twenties, from the middle-class Midwest. Annie's left Chippewa Falls, Wisconsin — land of frigid winters and baked hams at Christmas — to be a singer in New York — land of pastrami on rye, indoor tennis, and documentaries like The Sorrow and the Pity *playing at revival movie houses.*

Alvy and Annie enchant each other, but as the relationship develops, they find themselves pulled in conflicting directions.

ALVY: There's an old joke. Uh, two elderly women are at a Catskills mountain resort, and one of 'em says: "Boy, the food at this place is really terrible." The other one says, "Yeah, I know, and such . . . small portions." Well, that's essentially how I feel about life. Full of loneliness and misery and suffering and unhappiness, and it's all over much too quickly. The — the other important joke for me is one that's uh, usually attributed to Groucho Marx, but I think it appears originally in Freud's wit and its relation to the unconscious. And it goes like this — I'm paraphrasing. Uh . . . "I would never wanna belong to any club that would have someone like me for a member." That's the key joke of my adult life in terms of my relationships with women. Tsch, you know, lately the strangest things have been going through my mind, 'cause I turned forty, tsch, and I guess I'm going through a life crisis or something, I don't know. I, uh . . . and I'm not worried about aging. I'm not one o' those characters, you know. Although I'm balding slightly on top, that's about the worst you can say about me. I, uh, I think I'm gonna get better as I get older, you know? I think I'm gonna be the — the balding virile type, you know, as opposed to say the, uh, distinguished gray, for instance, you know? 'Less I'm neither o' those two. Unless I'm one o' those guys with saliva dribbling out of his mouth who wanders into a cafeteria with a shopping bag screaming about socialism.

Sighing.

Annie and I broke up and I — I still can't get my mind around that. You know, I — I keep sifting the pieces o' the relationship through my mind and — and examining my life and tryin' to figure out where did the screw-up come, you know, and a year ago we were . . . tsch, in love. You know, and-and-and . . . And it's funny, I'm not — I'm not a morose type. I'm not a depressive character. I — I — I, uh —

Laughing.

— you know, I was a reasonably happy kid, I guess. I was brought up in Brooklyn during World War II. . . .

MANHATTAN

TIME: 1979–1980

PLACE: *Manhattan*

Isaac (Ike) Davis, forty-two, is a successful television comedy writer attempting a novel. Divorced twice, Ike is the father of a young boy who lives with ex-wife Jill and her lesbian lover. Jill is writing a book in large part about the breakup of her marriage to Ike, causing him no end of anxiety.

Ike is having an unlikely but heartfelt love affair with Tracy, a beautiful seventeen-year-old high-school senior. His life is further complicated when he becomes involved with Mary Wilke, also divorced, a high-strung, very bright, free-lance journalist in her thirties. Mary is having an on-again off-again affair with Ike's best friend, Yale, a married academic.

At one point, Ike dictates into his tape recorder: "An idea for a short story . . . (sighing) about . . . people in Manhattan who . . . are constantly creating these real . . . unnecessary neurotic problems for themselves 'cause it keeps them from dealing with . . . more unsolvable, terrifying problems about . . . the universe."

At the beginning of the film, however, Ike tries a few upbeat openings for his novel.

IKE: "Chapter One. He adored New York City. He idolized it all out of proportion." Uh, no, make that: "He — he . . . romaticized it all out of proportion. Now . . . to him . . . no matter what the season was, this was still a town that existed in black and white and pulsated to the great tunes of George Gershwin." Ahhh, now let me start this over. "Chapter One. He was too romantic about Manhattan as he was about everything else. He thrived on the hustle . . . bustle of the crowds and the traffic. To him, New York meant beautiful women and street-smart guys who seemed to know all the angles." Nah, no . . . corny, too corny . . . for . . . my taste.

Clearing his throat.

I mean, let me try and make it more profound. "Chapter One. He adored New York City. To him, it was a metaphor for the decay of contemporary culture. The same lack of individual integrity to cause so many people to take the easy way out . . . was rapidly turning the town of his dreams in — " No, it's gonna be too preachy. I mean, you know . . . let's face it, I wanna sell some books here. "Chapter One. He adored New York City, although to him, it was a metaphor for the decay of contemporary culture. How hard it was to exist in a society desensitized by drugs, loud music, television, crime, garbage." Too angry. I don't wanna be angry. "Chapter One. He was as . . . tough and romantic as the city he loved. Behind his black-rimmed glasses was the coiled sexual power of a jungle cat." I love this. "New York was his town. And it always would be."

ನಾ

AUGUST WILSON *(b. 1945) was born in a black slum in Pittsburgh and raised with his five brothers and sisters by his mother, Daisy Wilson, who supported her children by working as a janitor downtown in the county courthouse. His father, a white man, was, as Wilson remembered, "a sporadic presence in our house." Wilson credits his mother for teaching him about black pride. He tells a story about the time she won a brand-new Speed Queen washing machine in a radio competition. When the station discovered she was black, they substituted a certificate for a secondhand washer. Wilson's mother was doing her family's laundry at the sink in her home on a scrub board, but she refused the radio's offer rather than be treated so unfairly.*

At age fifteen Wilson dropped out of school, took a job running a freight elevator, and began to spend hours in the "Negro Section" of the Pittsburgh Public Library, where he read Ralph Ellison, Langston Hughes, and James Baldwin. Back in Pittsburgh after three years in the army, he bought his first typewriter for twenty dollars and began to write poetry before gradually shifting over, on the advice of a friend, to writing plays.

Wilson later told interviewer Will Haygood that what "pained" him enough to start his writing was the idea of African Americans streaming out of the South, trying to forget their past: "My mother came from North Carolina. And all my friends were always from someplace: Alabama, Georgia. And this is what happened invariably: One of my classmates would come to school and say, 'My grandmother died. And we got some land.' I'd say, 'When you gonna move?' They'd say, 'We gonna sell it.' " It was Wilson's belief that "we should have stayed in the South. We attempted to plant what in essence was an emerging culture, a culture that had grown out of our experience of two hundred years as slaves in the South. The cities of the urban North have not been hospitable. If we had stayed in the South, we could have strengthened the culture."

In 1981 and 1982, the first professional productions of Wilson's plays were staged in little theaters in St. Paul and Pittsburgh. He also began sending his manuscripts to the Eugene O'Neill Playwrights Conference, which ran workshops to develop the talent of young American playwrights. The conference rejected his first plays but accepted his work-in-progress, Ma Rainey's Black Bottom. *"To this day," recalls Wilson, "that's about the highlight of my career."*

With Ma Rainey, Wilson *had embarked on an ambitious ten-play cycle drama-tizing different decades in the history of African Americans in the twentieth century. To date, the cycle consists of* Joe Turner's Come and Gone *(1983), set in 1911;* Ma Rainey's Black Bottom *(1981), set in 1927;* The Piano Lesson *(1986), set in 1936;* Seven Guitars *(1995), set in 1938;* Fences *(1983), set in 1957; and* Two Trains Running *(1989), set in 1969. As critic John Lahr acknowledges, "No other theatrical testament to African American life has been so popular or so poetic or so penetrating." Wilson's plays have earned him two Pulitzer Prizes, three New York Drama Critics Circle Awards, one Tony Award, and one American Theater Critics' Association Award.*

The Janitor *is a one-act play written as a fundraiser in 1985 when Wilson was a member of the New Dramatists group. He explained to theater historian Sandra G. Shannon that he*

> *came up with the idea of the janitor who is someone whom this society ignores and someone who may have some very valuable information, someone who has a vital contribution to make, and yet you have relegated him to a position where they sweep the floor. They do it for some years, and never once do we think to say, "Hey, do you have anything to say about anything? Do you have any contribution to make other than being a janitor or running an elevator or whatever?" So in that sense we really do not take advantage of all of our hu-man potential. . . . So I thought I'd show this guy here who is sweeping up the floor, and there's this microphone, and he just goes up and starts talking into the microphone.*

Wilson *has dedicated himself as a playwright to writing a new history of black America, celebrating his people's African roots and humble beginnings instead of denying them. Such plays as* The Piano Lesson *are well-crafted dramas in the tradi-tion of the European realistic theater, but Wilson also introduces elements of spon-taneity into the stage action to express what he regards as the creative genius for improvisation in black culture, as when the three male characters sit at the table and chant a Parchman prison work song. When asked by television personality Bill Moy-ers if he ever grew "weary of thinking black, writing black, being asked questions about blacks," Wilson patiently replied, "How could one grow weary of that? Whites don't get tired of thinking white or being who they are. . . . Black is not limiting. There's no idea in the world that is not contained by black life. I could write forever about the black experience in America."*

RELATED COMMENTARY: *August Wilson, "Where to Begin?" page 2033.*

AUGUST WILSON

The Janitor

1985

CHARACTERS

SAM

MR. COLLINS

SETTING: *A hotel ballroom*

Sam enters pushing a broom near the lectern. He stops and reads the sign hanging across the ballroom.

SAM: National . . . Conference . . . on . . . Youth.

He nods his approval and continues sweeping. He gets an idea, stops, and approaches the lectern. He clears his throat and begins to speak. His speech is delivered with the literacy of a janitor. He chooses his ideas carefully. He is a man who has approached life honestly, with both eyes open.

SAM: I want to thank you all for inviting me here to speak about youth. See . . . I's fifty-six years old and I knows something about youth. The first thing I knows . . . is that youth is sweet before flight . . . its odor is rife with speculation and its resilience . . . that's its bounce back . . . is remarkable. But it's that sweetness that we victims of. All of us. Its sweetness . . . and its flight. One of them fellows in that Shakespeare stuff said, "I am not what I am." See. He wasn't like Popeye. This fellow had a different understanding. "I am not what I am." Well, neither are you. You are just what you have been . . . whatever you are now. But what you are now ain't what you gonna become . . . even though it is with you now . . . it's inside you now this instant. Time . . . see, this how you get to this . . . Time ain't changed. It's just moved. Or maybe it ain't moved . . . maybe it just changed. It don't matter. We are all victims of the sweetness of youth and the time of its flight. See . . . just like you I forgot who I am. I forgot what happened first. But I know the river I step into now . . . is not the same river I stepped into twenty years ago. See. I know that much. But I have forgotten the name of the river . . . I have forgotten the names of the gods . . . and like everybody else I have tried to fool them with my dancing . . . and guess at their faces. It's the same with everybody. We don't have to mention no names. Ain't nobody innocent. We are all victims of ourselves. We have all had our hand in the soup . . . and made the music play just so. See, now . . . this what I call wrestling with Jacob's angel. You lay down at night and that angel come to wrestle with you. When you wrestling with that angel you bargaining for your future. See. And what you need to bargain with is that sweetness of youth. So . . . to the youth of the United States I says . . . don't spend that sweetness too fast! 'Cause you gonna need it. See. I's fifty-six years old and I done found that out. But it's all the same. It all comes back on you . . . just like reaping and sowing. Down and out ain't nothing but being caught up in the balance of what you put down. If you down and out and things ain't going right for you . . . you can bet you done put a down payment on your troubles. Now you got to pay up the balance. That's as true as I'm standing here. Sometimes you can't see it like that. The last note on Gabriel's horn always gets lost when you get to realizing you done heard the first. See, it's just like. . . .

MR. COLLINS (*Entering*): Come on, Sam . . . let's quit wasting time and get this floor swept. There's going to be a big important meeting here this afternoon.

SAM: Yessuh, Mr. Collins. Yessuh.

Sam goes back to sweeping as the lights go down to ——

Black

ૹ

MARSHA NORMAN (*b. 1947*), *the daughter of a fundamentalist Methodist, had a solitary childhood in Louisville, Kentucky. Her mother's religious views prohibited Norman from playing with other children and watching television and movies, and she credits her loneliness as a child as the reason she became a writer. Playing the piano, reading books, and attending the theater were permitted to her, and she saw children's plays at the Actors Theatre of Louisville, as well as later productions of Tennessee Williams's* The Glass Menagerie *and Archibald MacLeish's* J.B., *an adaptation of the Book of Job. A philosophy major at Agnes Scott College in Georgia, Norman began to work as a journalist after graduation, writing articles and reviews of books, plays, and films for the* Louisville Times.

In 1977 Norman's first play, Getting Out, *resulted from the suggestion of Jon Jory, a theater director who asked her to write a play for the Actors' Theatre. At first she felt she had no models to follow as a playwright, but then she found she could draw on her experience in a previous job working with disturbed adolescents at Kentucky Central State Hospital to create a vivid portrait of a woman parolee who served an eight-year prison sentence for robbery, kidnapping, and manslaughter.* Getting Out *was voted the best new play produced by a regional theater by the American Theatre Critics Association and appeared in a shortened version in* The Best Plays of 1977–1978.

After the success of this play, Norman moved to New York City because, as she said, she "needed to be in the world of living writers. . . . I like seeing that there are some people who do what I do, who are still alive." She wrote some one-act plays for the Actors' Theatre and another full-length play, Circus Valentine (1979), *before* 'night, Mother (1983), *which won the Pulitzer Prize in addition to several other awards and four Tony Award nominations. Four years later she published her first novel,* The Fortune Teller, *and followed it with* Four Plays (1988) *and* The Secret Garden (1991), *a Broadway musical.*

Norman described her vivid memory of writing 'night, Mother *to the interviewer David Savran:*

> *I knew going into* 'night, Mother *that it was going to be the most treacherous act of my writing life. So I went to the world of music. I was in a mad Glenn Gould state at the time — I've spent my life at the piano. Okay, I*

thought, what if I do a little sonata form, a three-act play with no intermission? You can actually feel the moment when the orchestra stops and the conductor raises his hands and Jessie says, "You talked to Agnes today," and the second movement starts. The second movement ends when Jessie goes in to get the box of presents, Mama just having said, "Don't leave me, Jessie." The actors would come on stage knowing, "We don't have to go all the way to the end. We just have to get to the Agnes section." And then you start in on Agnes and think, "Great, I'll just get to 'Don't leave me, Jessie,' then I can take a breath" — this is from Mama's point of view — "and get down and wash the floor." And then all they have to do is go to the end. 'night, Mother would be undoable if it weren't for that. . . . The first line of dialogue I wrote for 'night, Mother was Jessie's line, "We got any old towels?" As soon as I wrote it down, I understood that it was a ritual piece, that Jessie was coming in to celebrate this requiem mass. . . .

I wait until I cannot avoid it anymore and by that time, I already know what the beginning is, because of all this scribbling down. Then it's really very easy. I keep two kinds of notebooks, one that has structure and information in it and the other that has my own thoughts — "Can we really have this? What about that? What would happen if this?" I have a wonderful piece of paper upstairs that says, "Have I written something that anybody will want to see?"

Translated into several languages, 'night, Mother is frequently produced abroad. The topic of suicide is a side issue in earlier plays in this anthology, such as Shakespeare's Hamlet and Strindberg's Miss Julie, but Norman's entire play explores the issues of personal choice and motive involved in the decision to end a life. Norman does not sentimentalize the moral issues or make the topic easier for the audience to accept by giving the daughter a terminal disease. She also does not offer compelling reasons for anyone in the audience to commit suicide. Instead, 'night, Mother is a play about a middle-aged woman's attempt to prepare her mother for her decision to kill herself.

After Norman watched a performance of the play at the Uppsala State Theatre in Sweden, she protested when the director added a final scene so the audience could see the mother hold her daughter's body in her arms as the curtain descended, like the Virgin Mary holding Christ's body after the crucifixion. Norman said that the point she was trying to make in 'night, Mother was that the evening before the suicide was the holy "moment of connection" between the daughter and her mother: "Probably for the first time, Thelma [the mother] has something that is securely hers, that she does not need for anybody else to understand and would not dare tell anybody. She has a holy object: this evening that they spent together." To Norman, this "moment of connection" was the true objective of drama:

Basically, it is a moment when two people are willing to go as far as they can with each other. This doesn't happen very often, and we are lucky if we have two or three moments in our lives when we know that, with this person, we have gone as far as it is possible to go. After a lifetime of missing this daughter, of somehow just living in the same space, they finally had a moment when they actually lived together, when the issues of their lives were standing there with them in silent witness of their meeting. This is exactly the kind of meeting the theater can document, can present and preserve. In an odd way, writ-

ing for the theater is like nominating people for the archives of human history. As playwright, I select a person to nominate for permanent memory by the race. The audience, the world-wide audience, does the voting. Some of my nominations make it and some of them don't. But it seems that Jessie and Thelma are going to make it. They are going to be remembered for what they did that night.

RELATED COMMENTARY: Marsha Norman, "Interview about 'night, Mother," page 2016.

MARSHA NORMAN

'night, Mother

1983

CHARACTERS

JESSIE CATES, *in her late thirties or early forties, is pale and vaguely unsteady physically. It is only in the last year that Jessie has gained control of her mind and body, and tonight she is determined to hold on to that control. She wears pants and a long black sweater with deep pockets, which contain scraps of paper, and there may be a pencil behind her ear or a pen clipped to one of the pockets of the sweater.*

As a rule, Jessie doesn't feel much like talking. Other people have rarely found her quirky sense of humor amusing. She has a peaceful energy on this night, a sense of purpose, but is clearly aware of the time passing moment by moment. Oddly enough, Jessie has never been as communicative or as enjoyable as she is on this evening, but we must know she has not always been this way. There is a familiarity between these two women that comes from having lived together for a long time. There is a shorthand to the talk and a sense of routine comfort in the way they relate to each other physically. Naturally, there are also routine aggravations.

THELMA CATES, *"MAMA," is Jessie's mother, in her late fifties or early sixties. She had begun to feel her age and so takes it easy when she can, or when it serves her purpose to let someone help her. But she speaks quickly and enjoys talking. She believes that things are what she says they are. Her sturdiness is more a mental quality than a physical one, finally. She is chatty and nosy, and this is her house.*

The play takes place in a relatively new house built way out on a country road, with a living room and connecting kitchen, and a center hall that leads off to the bedrooms. A pull cord in the hall ceiling releases a ladder which leads to the attic. One of these bedrooms opens directly onto the hall, and its entry should be visible to everyone in the audience. It should be, in fact, the focal point of the entire set, and the lighting should make it disappear completely at times and draw the entire set into it at others. It is a point of both threat and promise. It is an ordinary door that opens onto absolute nothingness. That door is the point of all the action, and the utmost care should be given to its design and construction.

The living room is cluttered with magazines and needlework catalogues, ashtrays and candy dishes. Examples of Mama's needlework are everywhere — pillows, afghans, and quilts, doilies and rugs, and they are quite nice examples. The house is more comfortable than messy, but there is quite a lot to keep in place here. It is more personal than charming. It is not quaint. Under no circumstances should the set and its dressing make a judgment about the intelligence or taste of Jessie and Mama. It should simply indicate that they are very specific real people who happen to live in a particular part of the country. Heavy accents, which would further distance the audience from Jessie and Mama, are also wrong.

The time is the present, with the action beginning about 8:15. Clocks onstage in the kitchen and on a table in the living room should run throughout the performance and be visible to the audience.

Mama stretches to reach the cupcakes in a cabinet in the kitchen. She can't see them, but she can feel around for them, and she's eager to have one, so she's working pretty hard at it. This may be the most serious exercise Mama ever gets. She finds a cupcake, the coconut-covered, raspberry-and-marshmallow-filled kind known as a snowball, but sees that there's one missing from the package. She calls to Jessie, who is apparently somewhere else in the house.

MAMA (*unwrapping the cupcake*): Jessie, it's the last snowball, sugar. Put it on the list, O.K.? And we're out of Hershey bars, and where's that peanut brittle? I think maybe Dawson's been in it again. I ought to put a big mirror on the refrigerator door. That'll keep him out of my treats, won't it? You hear me, honey? (*Then more to herself.*) I hate it when the coconut falls off. Why does the coconut fall off?

Jessie enters from her bedroom, carrying a stack of newspapers.

JESSIE: We got any old towels?

MAMA: There you are!

JESSIE (*holding a towel that was on the stack of newspapers*): Towels you don't want anymore. (*Picking up Mama's snowball wrapper.*) How about this swimming towel Loretta gave us? Beach towel, that's the name of it. You want it? (*Mama shakes her head no.*)

MAMA: What have you been doing in there?

JESSIE: And a big piece of plastic like a rubber sheet or something. Garbage bags would do if there's enough.

MAMA: Don't go making a big mess, Jessie. It's eight o'clock already.

JESSIE: Maybe an old blanket or towels we got in a soap box sometime?

MAMA: I said don't make a mess. Your hair is black enough, hon.

JESSIE (*continuing to search the kitchen cabinets, finding two or three more towels to add to her stack*): It's not for my hair, Mama. What about some old pillows anywhere, or a foam cushion out of a yard chair would be real good.

MAMA: You haven't forgot what night it is, have you? (*Holding up her fingernails.*) They're all chipped, see? I've been waiting all week, Jess. It's Saturday night, sugar.

JESSIE: I know. I got it on the schedule.

MAMA (*crossing to the living room*): You want me to wash 'em now or are you making your mess first? (*Looking at the snowball.*) We're out of these. Did I say that already?

JESSIE: There's more coming tomorrow. I ordered you a whole case.

MAMA (*checking the* TV Guide): A whole case will go stale, Jessie.

JESSIE: They can go in the freezer till you're ready for them. Where's Daddy's gun?

MAMA: In the attic.

JESSIE: Where in the attic? I looked your whole nap and couldn't find it anywhere.

MAMA: One of his shoeboxes, I think.

JESSIE: Full of shoes. I looked already.

MAMA: Well, you didn't look good enough, then. There's that box from the ones he wore to the hospital. When he died, they told me I could have them back, but I never did like those shoes.

JESSIE (*pulling them out of her pocket*): I found the bullets. They were in an old milk can.

MAMA (*as Jessie starts for the hall*): Dawson took the shotgun, didn't he? Hand me that basket, hon.

JESSIE (*getting the basket for her*): Dawson better not've taken that pistol.

MAMA (*stopping her again*): Now my glasses, please. (*Jessie returns to get the glasses.*) I told him to take those rubber boots, too, but he said they were for fishing. I told him to take up fishing.

Jessie reaches for the cleaning spray and cleans Mama's glasses for her.

JESSIE: He's just too lazy to climb up there, Mama. Or maybe he's just being smart. That floor's not very steady.

MAMA (*getting out a piece of knitting*): It's not a floor at all, hon, it's a board now and then. Measure this for me. I need six inches.

JESSIE (*as she measures*): Dawson could probably use some of those clothes up there. Somebody should have them. You ought to call the Salvation Army before the whole thing falls in on you. Six inches exactly.

MAMA: It's plenty safe! As long as you don't go up there.

JESSIE (*turning to go again*): I'm careful.

MAMA: What do you want the gun for, Jess?

JESSIE (*not returning this time. Opening the ladder in the hall*): Protection. (*She steadies the ladder as Mama talks.*)

MAMA: You take the TV way too serious, hon. I've never seen a criminal in my life. This is way too far to come for what's out here to steal. Never seen a one.

JESSIE (*taking her first step up*): Except for Ricky.

MAMA: Ricky is mixed up. That's not a crime.

JESSIE: Get your hands washed. I'll be right back. And get 'em real dry. You dry your hands till I get back or it's no go, all right?

MAMA: I thought Dawson told you not to go up those stairs.

JESSIE (*going up*): He did.

MAMA: I don't like the idea of a gun, Jess.

JESSIE (*calling down from the attic*): Which shoebox, do you remember?

MAMA: Black.

JESSIE: The box was black?

MAMA: The shoes were black.

JESSIE: That doesn't help much, Mother.

MAMA: I'm not trying to help, sugar. (*No answer.*) We don't have anything anybody'd want, Jessie. I mean, I don't even want what we got, Jessie.

JESSIE: Neither do I. Wash your hands. (*Mama gets up and crosses to stand under the ladder.*)

MAMA: You come down from there before you have a fit. I can't come up and get you, you know.

JESSIE: I know.

MAMA: We'll just hand it over to them when they come, how's that? Whatever they want, the criminals.

JESSIE: That's a good idea, Mama.

MAMA: Ricky will grow out of this and be a real fine boy, Jess. But I have to tell you, I wouldn't want Ricky to know we had a gun in the house.

JESSIE: Here it is. I found it.

MAMA: It's just something Ricky's going through. Maybe he's in with some bad people. He just needs some time, sugar. He'll get back in school or get a job or one day you'll get a call and he'll say he's sorry for all the trouble he's caused and invite you out for supper someplace dress-up.

JESSIE (*coming back down the steps*): Don't worry. It's not for him, it's for me.

MAMA: I didn't think you would shoot your own boy, Jessie. I know you've felt like it, well, we've all felt like shooting somebody, but we don't do it. I just don't think we need . . .

JESSIE (*interrupting*): Your hands aren't washed. Do you want a manicure or not?

MAMA: Yes, I do, but . . .

JESSIE (*crossing to the chair*): Then wash your hands and don't talk to me any more about Ricky. Those two rings he took were the last valuable things *I* had, so now he's started in on other people, door to door. I hope they put him away sometime. I'd turn him in myself if I knew where he was.

MAMA: You don't mean that.

JESSIE: Every word. Wash your hands and that's the last time I'm telling you.

Jessie sits down with the gun and starts cleaning it, pushing the cylinder out, checking to see that the chambers and barrel are empty, then putting some oil on a small patch of cloth and pushing it through the barrel with the push rod that was in the box. Mama goes to the kitchen and washes her hands, as instructed, trying not to show her concern about the gun.

MAMA: I shoulda got you to bring down that milk can. Agnes Fletcher sold hers to somebody with a flea market for forty dollars apiece.

JESSIE: I'll go back and get it in a minute. There's a wagon wheel up there, too. There's even a churn. I'll get it all if you want.

MAMA (*coming over, now, taking over now*): What are you doing?

JESSIE: The barrel has to be clean, Mama. Old powder, dust gets in it . . .

MAMA: What for?

JESSIE: I told you.

MAMA (*reaching for the gun*): And I told you, we don't get criminals out here.

JESSIE (*quickly pulling it to her*): And I told you . . . (*Then trying to be calm.*) The gun is for me.

MAMA: Well, you can have it if you want. When I die, you'll get it all, anyway.

JESSIE: I'm going to kill myself, Mama.

MAMA (*returning to the sofa*): Very funny. Very funny.

JESSIE: I am.

MAMA: You are not! Don't even say such a thing, Jessie.

JESSIE: How would you know if I didn't say it? You want it to be a surprise? You're lying there in your bed or maybe you're just brushing your teeth and you hear this . . . noise down the hall?

MAMA: Kill yourself.

JESSIE: Shoot myself. In a couple of hours.

MAMA: It must be time for your medicine.

JESSIE: Took it already.

MAMA: What's the matter with you?

JESSIE: Not a thing. Feel fine.

MAMA: You feel fine. You're just going to kill yourself.

JESSIE: Waited until I felt good enough, in fact.

MAMA: Don't make jokes, Jessie. I'm too old for jokes.

JESSIE: It's not a joke, Mama.

Mama watches for a moment in silence.

MAMA: That gun's no good, you know. He broke it right before he died. He dropped it in the mud one day.

JESSIE: Seems O.K. (*She spins the chamber, cocks the pistol, and pulls the trigger. The gun is not yet loaded, so all we hear is the click, but it will definitely work. It's also obvious that Jessie knows her way around a gun. Mama cannot speak.*) I had Cecil's all ready in there, just in case I couldn't find this one, but I'd rather use Daddy's.

MAMA: Those bullets are at least fifteen years old.

JESSIE (*pulling out another box*): These are from last week.

MAMA: Where did you get those?

JESSIE: Feed store Dawson told me about.

MAMA: Dawson!

JESSIE: I told him I was worried about prowlers. He said he thought it was a good idea. He told me what kind to ask for.

MAMA: If he had any idea . . .

JESSIE: He took it as a compliment. He thought I might be taking an interest in things. He got through telling me all about the bullets and then he said we ought to talk like this more often.

MAMA: And where was I while this was going on?

JESSIE: On the phone with Agnes. About the milk can, I guess. Anyway, I asked Dawson if he thought they'd send me some bullets and he said he'd just call for me, because he knew they'd send them if he told them to. And he was absolutely right. Here they are.

MAMA: How could he do that?

JESSIE: Just trying to help, Mama.

MAMA: And then I told you where the gun was.

JESSIE (*smiling, enjoying this joke*): See? Everybody's doing what they can.

MAMA: You told me it was for protection!

JESSIE: It *is*! I'm still doing your nails, though. Want to try that new Chinaberry color?

MAMA: Well, I'm calling Dawson right now. We'll just see what he has to say about this little stunt.

JESSIE: Dawson doesn't have any more to do with this.

MAMA: He's your brother.

JESSIE: And that's all.

MAMA (*stands up, moves toward the phone*): Dawson will put a stop to this. Yes he will. He'll take the gun away.

JESSIE: If you call him, I'll just have to do it before he gets here. Soon as you hang up the phone, I'll just walk in the bedroom and lock the door. Dawson will get here just in time to help you clean up. Go ahead, call him. Then call the police. Then call the funeral home. Then call Loretta and see if *she'll* do your nails.

MAMA: You will not! This is crazy talk, Jessie!

Mama goes directly to the telephone and starts to dial, but Jessie is fast, coming up behind her and taking the receiver out of her hand, putting it back down.

JESSIE (*firm and quiet*): I said no. This is private. Dawson is not invited.

MAMA: Just me.

JESSIE: I don't want anybody else over here. Just you and me. If Dawson comes over, it'll make me feel stupid for not doing it ten years ago.

MAMA: I think we better call the doctor. Or how about the ambulance. You like that one driver, I know. What's his name, Timmy? Get you somebody to talk to.

JESSIE (*going back to her chair*): I'm through talking, Mama. You're it. No more.

MAMA: We're just going to sit around like every other night in the world and then you're going to kill yourself? (*Jessie doesn't answer.*) You'll miss. (*Again there is no response.*) You'll just wind up a vegetable. How would you like that? Shoot your ear off? You know what the doctor said about getting excited. You'll cock the pistol and have a fit.

JESSIE: I think I can kill myself, Mama.

MAMA: You're not going to kill yourself, Jessie. You're not even upset! (*Jessie smiles, or laughs quietly, and Mama tries a different approach.*) People don't really kill themselves, Jessie. No, mam, doesn't make sense, unless you're retarded or deranged, and you're as normal as they come, Jessie, for the most part. We're all *afraid* to die.

JESSIE: I'm not, Mama. I'm cold all the time, anyway.

MAMA: That's ridiculous.

JESSIE: It's exactly what I want. It's dark and quiet.

MAMA: So is the back yard, Jessie! Close your eyes. Stuff cotton in your ears. Take a nap! It's quiet in your room. I'll leave the TV off all night.

JESSIE: So quiet I don't know it's quiet. So nobody can get me.

MAMA: You don't know what dead is like. It might not be quiet at all. What if it's like an alarm clock and you can't wake up so you can't shut it off. Ever.

JESSIE: Dead is everybody and everything I ever knew, gone. Dead is dead quiet.

MAMA: It's a sin. You'll go to hell.

JESSIE: Uh-huh.

MAMA: You will!

JESSIE: Jesus was a suicide, if you ask me.

MAMA: You'll go to hell just for saying that. Jessie!

JESSIE (*with genuine surprise*): I didn't know I thought that.

MAMA: Jessie!

Jessie doesn't answer. She puts the now-loaded gun back in the box and crosses to the kitchen. But Mama is afraid she's headed for the bedroom.

MAMA (*in a panic*): You can't use my towels! They're my towels. I've had them for a long time. I like my towels.

JESSIE: I asked you if you wanted that swimming towel and you said you didn't.

MAMA: And you can't use your father's gun, either. It's mine now, too. And you can't do it in my house.

JESSIE: Oh, come on.

MAMA: No. You can't do it. I won't let you. The house is in my name.

JESSIE: I have to go in the bedroom and lock the door behind me so they won't arrest you for killing me. They'll probably test your hands for gunpowder, anyway, but you'll pass.

MAMA: Not in my house!

JESSIE: If I'd known you were going to act like this, I wouldn't have told you.

MAMA: How am I supposed to act? Tell you to go ahead? O.K. by me, sugar? Might try it myself. What took you so long?

JESSIE: There's just no point in fighting me over it, that's all. Want some coffee?

MAMA: Your birthday's coming up, Jessie. Don't you want to know what we got you?

JESSIE: You got me dusting powder, Loretta got me a new housecoat, pink probably, and Dawson got me new slippers, too small, but they go with the robe, he'll say. (*Mama cannot speak.*) Right? (*Apparently Jessie is right.*) Be back in a minute.

Jessie takes the gun box, puts it on top of the stack of towels and garbage bags, and takes them into her bedroom. Mama, alone for a moment, goes to the phone, picks up the receiver, looks toward the bedroom, starts to dial, and then replaces the receiver in its cradle as Jessie walks back into the room. Jessie wonders, silently. They have lived together for so long there is very rarely any reason for one to ask what the other was about to do.

MAMA: I started to, but I didn't. I didn't call him.

JESSIE: Good. Thank you.

MAMA (*starting over, a new approach*): What's this all about, Jessie?

JESSIE: About?

Jessie now begins the next task she had "on the schedule," which is refilling all the candy jars, taking the empty papers out of the boxes of chocolates, etc. Mama generally snitches when Jessie does this. Not tonight, though. Nevertheless, Jessie offers.

MAMA: What did I do?

JESSIE: Nothing. Want a caramel?

MAMA (*ignoring the candy*): You're mad at me.

JESSIE: Not a bit. I am worried about you, but I'm going to do what I can before I go. We're not just going to sit around tonight. I made a list of things.

MAMA: What things?

JESSIE: How the washer works. Things like that.

MAMA: I know how the washer works. You put the clothes in. You put the soap in. You turn it on. You wait.

JESSIE: You do something else. You don't just wait.

MAMA: Whatever else you find to do, you're still mainly waiting. The waiting's the worst part of it. The waiting's what you pay somebody else to do, if you can.

JESSIE (*nodding*): O.K. Where do we keep the soap?

MAMA: I could find it.

JESSIE: See?

MAMA: If you're mad about doing the wash, we can get Loretta to do it.

JESSIE: Oh, now, that might be worth staying to see.

MAMA: She'd never in her life, would she?

JESSIE: Nope.

MAMA: What's the matter with her?

JESSIE: She thinks she's better than we are. She's not.

MAMA: Maybe if she didn't wear that yellow all the time.

JESSIE: The washer repair number is on a little card taped to the side of the machine.

MAMA: Loretta doesn't ever have to come over here again. Dawson can just leave her at home when he comes. And we don't ever have to see Dawson either if he bothers you. Does he bother you?

JESSIE: Sure he does. Be sure you clean out the lint tray every time you use the dryer. But don't ever put your house shoes in, it'll melt the soles.

MAMA: What does Dawson do, that bothers you?

JESSIE: He just calls me Jess like he knows who he's talking to. He's always wondering what I do all day. I mean, I wonder that myself, but it's my day, so it's mine to wonder about, not his.

MAMA: Family is just accident, Jessie. It's nothing personal, hon. They don't mean to get on your nerves. They don't even mean to be your family, they just are.

JESSIE: They know too much.

MAMA: About what?

JESSIE: They know things about you, and they learned it before you had a chance to say whether you wanted them to know it or not. They were there when it happened and it don't belong to them, it belongs to you, only they got it. Like my mail-order bra got delivered to their house.

MAMA: By accident!

JESSIE: All the same . . . they opened it. They saw the little rosebuds on it. (*Offering her another candy.*) Chewy mint?

MAMA: (*shaking her head no*): What do they know about you? I'll tell them never to talk about it again. Is it Ricky or Cecil or your fits or your hair is falling out or you drink too much coffee or your never go out of the house or what?

JESSIE: I just don't like their talk. The account at the grocery is in Dawson's name when you call. The number's on a whole list of numbers on the back cover of the phone book.

MAMA: Well! Now we're getting somewhere. They're none of them ever setting foot in this house again.

JESSIE: It's not them, Mother. I wouldn't kill myself just to get away from them.

MAMA: You leave the room when they come over, anyway.

JESSIE: I stay as long as I can. Besides, it's you they come to see.

MAMA: That's because I stay in the room when they come.

JESSIE: It's not them.

MAMA: Then what is it?

JESSIE (*checking the list on her note pad*): The grocery won't deliver on Saturday anymore. And if you want your order the same day, you have to call before ten. And they won't deliver less than fifteen dollars' worth. What I do is tell them what we need and tell them to add on cigarettes until it gets to fifteen dollars.

MAMA: It's Ricky. You're trying to get through to him.

JESSIE: If I thought I could do that, I would stay.

MAMA: Make him sorry he hurt you, then. That's it, isn't it?

JESSIE: He's hurt me, I've hurt him. We're about even.

MAMA: You'll be telling him killing is O.K. with you, you know. Want him to start killing next? Nothing wrong with it. Mom did it.

JESSIE: Only a matter of time, anyway, Mama. When the call comes, you let Dawson handle it.

MAMA: Honey, nothing says those calls are always going to be some new trouble he's into. You could get one that he's got a job, that he's getting married, or how about he's joined the army, wouldn't that be nice?

JESSIE: If you call the Sweet Tooth before you call the grocery, that Susie will take your fudge next door to the grocery and it'll all come out together. Be sure you talk to Susie, though. She won't let them put it in the bottom of a sack like that one time, remember?

MAMA: Ricky could come over, you know. What if he calls us?

JESSIE: It's not Ricky, Mama.

MAMA: Or anybody could call us, Jessie.

JESSIE: Not on Saturday night, Mama.

MAMA: Then what is it? Are you sick? If your gums are swelling again, we can get you to the dentist in the morning.

JESSIE: No. Can you order your medicine or do you want Dawson to? I've got a note to him. I'll add that to it if you want.

MAMA: Your eyes don't look right. I thought so yesterday.

JESSIE: That was just the ragweed. I'm not sick.

MAMA: Epilepsy is sick, Jessie.

JESSIE: It won't kill me. (*A pause.*) If it would, I wouldn't have to.

MAMA: You don't *have* to.

JESSIE: No, I don't. That's what I like about it.

MAMA: Well, I won't let you!

JESSIE: It's not up to you.

MAMA: Jessie!

JESSIE: I want to hang a big sign around my neck, like Daddy's on the barn. GONE FISHING.

MAMA: You don't like it here.

JESSIE (*smiling*): Exactly.

MAMA: I meant here in my house.

JESSIE: I know you did.

MAMA: You never should have moved back in here with me. If you'd kept your little house or found another place when Cecil left you, you'd have made some new friends at least. Had a life to lead. Had your own things around you. Give Ricky a place to come see you. You never should've come here.

JESSIE: Maybe.

MAMA: But I didn't force you, did I?

JESSIE: If it was a mistake, we made it together. You took me in. I appreciate that.

MAMA: You didn't have any business being by yourself right then, but I can see how you might want a place of your own. A grown woman should . . .

JESSIE: Mama . . . I'm just not having a very good time and I don't have any reason to think it'll get anything but worse. I'm tired. I'm hurt. I'm sad. I feel used.

MAMA: Tired of what?

JESSIE: It all.

MAMA: What does that mean?

JESSIE: I can't say it any better.

MAMA: Well, you'll have to say it better because I'm not letting you alone till you do. What were those other things? Hurt . . . (*Before Jessie can answer.*) You had this all ready to say to me, didn't you? Did you write this down? How long have you been thinking about this?

JESSIE: Off and on, ten years. On all the time, since Christmas.

MAMA: What happened at Christmas?

JESSIE: Nothing.

MAMA: So why Christmas?

JESSIE: That's it. On the nose.

A pause. Mama knows exactly what Jessie means. She was there, too, after all.

JESSIE (*putting the candy sacks away*): See where all this is? Red hots up front, sour balls and horehound mixed together in this one sack. New packages of toffee and licorice right in back there.

MAMA: Go back to your list. You're hurt by what?

JESSIE (*Mama knows perfectly well*): Mama . . .

MAMA: O.K. Sad about what? There's nothing real sad going on right now. If it was after your divorce or something, that would make sense.

JESSIE (*looking at her list, then opening the drawer*): Now, this drawer has everything in it that there's no better place for. Extension cords, batteries for the radio, extra lighters, sandpaper, masking tape, Elmer's glue, thumb-tacks, that kind of stuff. The mousetraps are under the sink, but you call Dawson if you've got one and let him do it.

MAMA: Sad about what?

JESSIE: The way things are.

MAMA: Not good enough. What things?

JESSIE: Oh, everything from you and me to Red China.

MAMA: I think we can leave the Chinese out of this.

JESSIE (*crosses back into the living room*): There's extra light bulbs in a box in the hall closet. And we've got a couple of packages of fuses in the fuse box. There's candles and matches in the top of the broom closet, but if the lights go out, just call Dawson and sit tight. But don't open the refriger-ator door. Things will stay cool in there as long as you keep the door shut.

MAMA: I asked you a question.

JESSIE: I read the paper. I don't like how things are. And they're not any better out there than they are in here.

MAMA: If you're doing this because of the newspapers, I can sure fix that!

JESSIE: There's just more of it on TV.

MAMA (*kicking the television set*): Take it out, then!

JESSIE: You wouldn't do that.

MAMA: Watch me.

JESSIE: What would you do all day?

MAMA (*desperately*): Sing. (*Jessie laughs.*) I would, too. You want to watch? I'll sing till morning to keep you alive, Jessie, please!

JESSIE: No. (*Then affectionately.*) It's a funny idea, though. What do you sing?

MAMA (*has no idea how to answer this*): We've got a good life here!

JESSIE (*going back into the kitchen*): I called this morning and canceled the papers, except for Sunday, for your puzzles; you'll still get that one.

MAMA: Let's get another dog, Jessie! You liked a big dog, now, didn't you? That King dog, didn't you?

JESSIE (*washing her hands*): I did like that King dog, yes.

MAMA: I'm so dumb. He's the one run under the tractor.

JESSIE: That makes him dumb, not you.

MAMA: For bringing it up.

JESSIE: It's O.K. Handi-Wipes and sponges under the sink.

MAMA: We could get a new dog and keep him in the house. Dogs are cheap!

JESSIE (*getting big pill jars out of the cabinet*): No.

MAMA: Something for you to take care of.

JESSIE: I've had you, Mama.

MAMA (*frantically starting to fill pill bottles*): You do too much for me. I can fill pill bottles all day, Jessie, and change the shelf paper and wash the floor when I get through. You just watch me. You don't have to do another thing in this house if you don't want to. You don't have to take care of me, Jessie.

JESSIE: I know that. You've just been letting me do it so I'll have something to do, haven't you?

MAMA (*realizing this was a mistake*): I don't do it as well as you. I just meant if it tires you out or makes you feel used . . .

JESSIE: Mama, I know you used to ride the bus. Riding the bus and it's hot and bumpy and crowded and too noisy and more than anything in the world you want to get off and the only reason in the world you don't get off is it's still fifty blocks from where you're going? Well, I can get off right now if I want to, because even if I ride fifty more years and get off then, it's the same place when I step down to it. Whenever I feel like it, I can get off. As soon as I've had enough, it's my stop. I've had enough.

MAMA: You're feeling sorry for yourself!

JESSIE: The plumber's helper is under the sink, too.

MAMA: You're not having a good time! Whoever promised you a good time? Do you think I've had a good time?

JESSIE: I think you're pretty happy, yeah. You have things you like to do.

MAMA: Like what?

JESSIE: Like crochet.

MAMA: I'll teach you to crochet.

JESSIE: I can't do any of that nice work, Mama.

MAMA: Good times don't come looking for you, Jessie. You could work some puzzles or put in a garden or go to the store. Let's call a taxi and go to the A&P!

JESSIE: I shopped you up for about two weeks already. You're not going to need toilet paper till Thanksgiving.

MAMA (*interrupting*): You're acting like some little brat, Jessie. You're mad and everybody's boring and you don't have anything to do and you don't like me and you don't like going out and you don't like staying in and you never talk on the phone and you don't watch TV and you're miserable and it's your own sweet fault.

JESSIE: And it's time I did something about it.

MAMA: Not something like killing yourself. Something like . . . buying us all new dishes! I'd like that. Or maybe the doctor would let you get a driver's license now, or I know what let's do right this minute, let's rearrange the furniture.

JESSIE: I'll do that. If you want. I always thought if the TV was somewhere else, you wouldn't get such a glare on it during the day. I'll do whatever you want before I go.

MAMA (*badly frightened by those words*): You could get a job!

JESSIE: I took that telephone sales job and I didn't even make enough money to pay the phone bill, and I tried to work at the gift shop at the hospital and they said I made people real uncomfortable smiling at them the way I did.

MAMA: You could keep books. You kept your dad's books.

JESSIE: But nobody ever checked them.

MAMA: When he died, they checked them.

JESSIE: And that's when they took the books away from me.

MAMA: That's because without him there wasn't any business, Jessie!

JESSIE (*putting the pill bottles away*): You know I couldn't work. I can't do anything. I've never been around people my whole life except when I went to the hospital. I could have a seizure any time. What good would a job do? The kind of job I could get would make me feel worse.

MAMA: Jessie!

JESSIE: It's true!

MAMA: It's what you think is true!

JESSIE (*struck by the clarity of that*): That's right. It's what I think is true.

MAMA (*hysterically*): But I can't do anything about that!

JESSIE (*quietly*): No. You can't. (*Mama slumps, if not physically, at least emotionally.*) And I can't do anything either, about my life, to change it, make it better, make me feel better about it. Like it better, make it work. But I can stop it. Shut it down, turn it off like the radio when there's nothing on I want to listen to. It's all I really have that belongs to me and I'm going to say what happens to it. And it's going to stop. And I'm going to stop it. So. Let's just have a good time.

MAMA: Have a good time.

JESSIE: We can't go on fussing all night. I mean, I could ask you things I always wanted to know and you could make me some hot chocolate. The old way.

MAMA (*in despair*): It takes cocoa, Jessie.

JESSIE (*gets it out of the cabinet*): I bought cocoa, Mama. And I'd like to have a caramel apple and do your nails.

MAMA: You didn't eat a bit of supper.

JESSIE: Does that mean I can't have a caramel apple?

MAMA: Of course not. I mean . . . (*Smiling a little.*) Of course you can have a caramel apple.

JESSIE: I thought I could.

MAMA: I make the best caramel apples in the world.

JESSIE: I know you do.

MAMA: Or used to. And you don't get cocoa like mine anywhere anymore.

JESSIE: It takes time, I know, but . . .

MAMA: The salt is the trick.

JESSIE: Trouble and everything.

MAMA (*backing away toward the stove*): It's no trouble. What trouble? You put it in the pan and stir it up. All right. Fine. Caramel apples. Cocoa. O.K.

Jessie walks to the counter to retrieve her cigarettes as Mama looks for the right pan. There are brief near-smiles, and maybe Mama clears her throat. We have a truce, for the moment. A genuine but nevertheless uneasy one. Jessie, who has been in constant motion since the beginning, now seems content to sit.

Mama starts looking for a pan to make the cocoa, getting out all the pans in the cabinets in the process. It looks like she's making a mess on purpose so Jessie will have to put them all away again. Mama is buying time, or trying to, and entertaining.

JESSIE: You talk to Agnes today?

MAMA: She's calling me from a pay phone this week. God only knows why. She has a perfectly good Trimline at home.

JESSIE (*laughing*): Well, how is she?

MAMA: How is she every day, Jessie? Nuts.

JESSIE: Is she really crazy or just silly?

MAMA: No, she's really crazy. She was probably using the pay phone because she had another little fire problem at home.

JESSIE: Mother . . .

MAMA: I'm serious! Agnes Fletcher's burned down every house she ever lived in. Eight fires, and she's due for a new one any day now.

JESSIE (*laughing*): No!

MAMA: Wouldn't surprise me a bit.

JESSIE (*laughing*): Why didn't you tell me this before? Why isn't she locked up somewhere?

MAMA: 'Cause nobody ever got hurt, I guess. Agnes woke everybody up to watch the fires as soon as she set 'em. One time she set out porch chairs and served lemonade.

JESSIE (*shaking her head*): Real lemonade?

MAMA: The houses they lived in, you knew they were going to fall down anyway, so why wait for it, is all I could ever make out about it. Agnes likes a feeling of accomplishment.

JESSIE: Good for her.

MAMA (*finding the pan she wants*): Why are you asking about Agnes? One cup or two?

JESSIE: One. She's your friend. No marshmallows.

MAMA (*getting the milk, etc.*): You have to have marshmallows. That's the old way, Jess. Two or three? Three is better.

JESSIE: Three, then. Her whole house burns up? Her clothes and pillows and everything? I'm not sure I believe this.

MAMA: When she was a girl, Jess, not now. Long time ago. But she's still got it in her, I'm sure of it.

JESSIE: She wouldn't burn her house down now. Where would she go? She can't get Buster to build her a new one, he's dead. How could she burn it up?

MAMA: Be exciting, though, if she did. You never know.

JESSIE: You do too know, Mama. She wouldn't do it.

MAMA (*forced to admit, but reluctant*): I guess not.

JESSIE: What else? Why does she wear all those whistles around her neck?

MAMA: Why does she have a house full of birds?

JESSIE: I didn't know she had a house full of birds!

MAMA: Well, she does. And she says they just follow her home. Well, I know for a fact she's still paying on the last parrot she bought. You gotta keep your life filled up, she says. She says a lot of stupid things. (*Jessie laughs, Mama continues, convinced she's getting somewhere.*) It's all that okra she eats. You can't just willy-nilly eat okra two meals a day and expect to get away with it. Made her crazy.

JESSIE: She really eats okra twice a day? Where does she get it in the winter?

MAMA: Well, she eats it a lot. Maybe not two meals, but . . .

JESSIE: More than the average person.

MAMA (*beginning to get irritated*): I don't know how much okra the average person eats.

JESSIE: Do you know how much okra Agnes eats?

MAMA: No.

JESSIE: How many birds does she have?

MAMA: Two.

JESSIE: Then what are the whistles for?

MAMA: They're not real whistles. Just little plastic ones on a necklace she won playing Bingo, and I only told you about it because I thought I might get a laugh out of you for once even if it wasn't the truth, Jessie. Things don't have to be true to talk about 'em, you know.

JESSIE: Why won't she come over here?

Mama is suddenly quiet, but the cocoa and milk are in the pan now, so she lights the stove and starts stirring.

MAMA: Well now, what a good idea. We should've had more cooca. Cocoa is perfect.

JESSIE: Except you don't like milk.

MAMA (*another attempt, but not as energetic*): I hate milk. Coats your throat as bad as okra. Something just downright disgusting about it.

JESSIE: It's because of me, isn't it?

MAMA: No, Jess.

JESSIE: Yes, Mama.

MAMA: O.K. Yes, then, but she's crazy. She's as crazy as they come. She's a lunatic.

JESSIE: What is it exactly? Did I say something, sometime? Or did she see me have a fit and's afraid I might have another one if she came over, or what?

MAMA: I guess.

JESSIE: You guess what? What's she ever said? She must've given you some reason.

MAMA: Your hands are cold.

JESSIE: What difference does that make?

MAMA: "Like a corpse," she says, "and I'm gonna be one soon enough as it is."

JESSIE: That's crazy.

MAMA: That's Agnes. "Jessie's shook the hand of death and I can't take the chance it's catching, Thelma, so I ain't comin' over, and you can understand or not, but I ain't comin'. I'll come up the driveway, but that's as far as I go."

JESSIE (*laughing, relieved*): I thought she didn't like me! She's scared of me! How about that! Scared of me.

MAMA: I could make her come over here, Jessie. I could call her up right now and she could bring the birds and come visit. I didn't know you ever thought about her at all. I'll tell her she just has to come and she'll come, all right. She owes me one.

JESSIE: No, that's all right. I just wondered about it. When I'm in the hospital, does she come over here?

MAMA: Her kitchen is just a tiny thing. When she comes over here, she feels like . . . (*Toning it down a little.*) Well, we all like a change of scene, don't we?

JESSIE (*playing along*): Sure we do. Plus there's no birds diving around.

MAMA: I hate those birds. She says I don't understand them. What's there to understand about birds?

JESSIE: Why Agnes likes them, for one thing. Why they stay with her when they could be outside with the other birds. What their singing means. How they fly. What they think Agnes is.

MAMA: Why do you have to know so much about things, Jessie? There's just not that much *to* things that I could ever see.

JESSIE: That you could ever *tell*, you mean. You didn't have to lie to me about Agnes.

MAMA: I didn't lie. You never asked before!

JESSIE: You lied about setting fire to all those houses and about how many birds she has and how much okra she eats and why she won't come over here. If I have to keep dragging the truth out of you, this is going to take all night.

MAMA: That's fine with me. I'm not a bit sleepy.

JESSIE: Mama . . .

MAMA: All right. Ask me whatever you want. Here.

They come to an awkward stop, as the cocoa is ready and Mama pours it into the cups Jessie has set on the table.

JESSIE (*as Mama takes her first sip*): Did you love Daddy?

MAMA: No.

JESSIE (*pleased that Mama understands the rules better now*): I didn't think so. Were you really fifteen when you married him?

MAMA: The way he told it? I'm sitting in the mud, he comes along, drags me in the kitchen, "She's been there ever since"?

JESSIE: Yes.

MAMA: No. It was a big fat lie, the whole thing. He just thought it was funnier that way. God, this milk in here.

JESSIE: The cocoa helps.

MAMA (*pleased that they agree on this, at least*): Not enough, though, does it? You can still taste it, can't you?

JESSIE: Yeah, it's pretty bad. I thought it was my memory that was bad, but it's not. It's the milk, all right.

MAMA: It's a real waste of chocolate. You don't have to finish it.

JESSIE (*putting her cup down*): Thanks, though.

MAMA: I should've known not to make it. I knew you wouldn't like it. You never did like it.

JESSIE: You didn't ever love him, or he did something and you stopped loving him, or what?

MAMA: He felt sorry for me. He wanted a plain country woman and that's what he married, and then he held it against me the rest of my life like I was supposed to change and surprise him somehow. Like I remember this one day he was standing on the porch and I told him to get a shirt on and he went in and got one and then he said, real peaceful, but to the point, "You're right, Thelma. If God had meant for people to go around without any clothes on, they'd have been born that way."

JESSIE (*sees Mama's hurt*): He didn't mean anything by that, Mama.

MAMA: He never said a word he didn't have to, Jessie. That was probably all he'd said to me all day, Jessie. So if he said it, there was something to it, but I never did figure that one out. What did that mean?

JESSIE: I don't know. I liked him better than you did, but I didn't know him any better.

MAMA: How could I love him, Jessie. I didn't have a thing he wanted. (*Jessie doesn't answer.*) He got his share, though. You loved him enough for both of us. You followed him around like some . . . Jessie, all the man ever did was farm and sit . . . and try to think of somebody to sell the farm to.

JESSIE: Or make me a boyfriend out of pipe cleaners and sit back and smile like the stick man was about to dance and wasn't I going to get a kick out of that. Or sit up with a sick cow all night and leave me a chain of sleepy stick elephants on my bed in the morning.

MAMA: Or just sit.

JESSIE: I liked him sitting. Big old faded blue man in the chair. Quiet.

MAMA: Agnes gets more talk out of her birds than I got from the two of you. He could've had that GONE FISHING sign around his neck in that chair. I saw him stare off at the water. I saw him look at the weather rolling in. I got where I could practically see the boat myself. But you, you knew what he was thinking about and you're going to tell me.

JESSIE: I don't know, Mama! His life, I guess. His corn. His boots. Us. Things. You know.

MAMA: No, I don't know, Jessie! You had those quiet little conversations after supper every night. What were you whispering about?

JESSIE: We weren't whispering, you were just across the room.

MAMA: What did you talk about?

JESSIE: We talked about why black socks are warmer than blue socks. Is that something to go tell Mother? You were just jealous because I'd rather talk to him than wash the dishes with you.

MAMA: I was jealous because you'd rather talk to him than anything! (*Jessie reaches across the table for the small clock and starts to wind it.*) If I had died instead of him, he wouldn't have taken you in like I did.

JESSIE: I wouldn't have expected him to.

MAMA: Then what would you have done?

JESSIE: Come visit.

MAMA: Oh, I see. He died and left you stuck with me and you're mad about it.

JESSIE (*getting up from the table*): Not anymore. He didn't mean to. I didn't have to come here. We've been through this.

MAMA: He felt sorry for you, too, Jessie, don't kid yourself about that. He said you were a runt and he said it from the day you were born and he said you didn't have a chance.

JESSIE (*getting the canister of sugar and starting to refill the sugar bowl*): I know he loved me.

MAMA: What if he did? It didn't change anything.

JESSIE: It didn't have to. I miss him.

MAMA: He never really went fishing, you know. Never once. His tackle box was full of chewing tobacco and all he ever did was drive out to the lake and sit in his car. Dawson told me. And Bennie at the bait shop, he told Dawson. They all laughed about it. And he'd come back from fishing and all he'd have to show for it was . . . a whole pipe-cleaner *family* — chickens, pigs, a dog with a bad leg — it was creepy strange. It made me sick to look at them and I hid his pipe cleaners a couple of times but he always had more somewhere.

JESSIE: I thought it might be better for you after he died. You'd get interested in things. Breathe better. Change somehow.

MAMA: Into what? The Queen? A clerk in a shoe store? Why should I? Because he said to? Because you said to? (*Jessie shakes her head.*) Well I wasn't here for his entertainment and I'm not here for yours either, Jessie. I don't know what I'm here for, but then I don't think about it. (*Realizing what all this means.*) But I bet you wouldn't be killing yourself if he were still alive. That's a fine thing to figure out, isn't it?

JESSIE (*filling the honey jar now*): That's not true.

MAMA: Oh no? Then what were you asking about him for? Why did you want to know if I loved him?

JESSIE: I didn't think you did, that's all.

MAMA: Fine then. You were right. Do you feel better now?

JESSIE (*cleaning the honey jar carefully*): It feels good to be right about it.

MAMA: It didn't matter whether I loved him. It didn't matter to me and it didn't matter to him. And it didn't mean we didn't get along. It wasn't important. We didn't talk about it. (*Sweeping the pots off the cabinet.*) Take all these pots out to the porch!

JESSIE: What for?

MAMA: Just leave me this one pan. (*She jerks the silverware drawer open.*) Get me one knife, one fork, one big spoon, and the can opener, and put them out where I can get them. (*Starts throwing knives and forks in one of the pans.*)

JESSIE: Don't do that! I just straightened that drawer!

MAMA (*throwing the pan in the sink*): And throw out all the plates and cups. I'll use paper. Loretta can have what she wants and Dawson can sell the rest.

JESSIE (*calmly*): What are you doing?

MAMA: I'm not going to cook. I never liked it, anyway. I like candy. Wrapped in plastic or coming in sacks. And tuna. I like tuna. I'll eat tuna, thank you.

JESSIE (*taking the pan out of the sink*): What if you want to make apple butter? You can't make apple butter in that little pan. What if you leave carrots on cooking and burn up that pan?

MAMA: I don't like carrots.

JESSIE: What if the strawberries are good this year and you want to go picking with Agnes.

MAMA: I'll tell her to bring a pan. You said you would do whatever I wanted! I don't want a bunch of pans cluttering up my cabinets I can't get down to, anyway. Throw them out. Every last one.

JESSIE (*gathering up the pots*): I'm putting them all back in. I'm not taking them to the porch. If you want them, they'll be here. You'll bend down and get them, like you got the one for the cocoa. And if somebody else comes over here to cook, they'll have something to cook in, and that's the end of it!

MAMA: Who's going to come cook here?

JESSIE: Agnes.

MAMA: In my pots. Not on your life.

JESSIE: There's no reason why the two of you couldn't just live here together. Be cheaper for both of you and somebody to talk to. And if the birds bothered you, well, one day when Agnes is out getting her hair done, you could take them all for a walk!

MAMA (*as Jessie straightens the silverware*): So that's why you're pestering me about Agnes. You think you can rest easy if you get me a new babysitter? Well, I don't want to live with Agnes. I barely want to talk with Agnes. She's just around. We go back, that's all. I'm not letting Agnes near this place. You don't get off as easy as that, child.

JESSIE: O.K., then. It's just something to think about.

MAMA: I don't like things to think about. I like things to go on.

JESSIE (*closing the silverware drawer*): I want to know what Daddy said to you the night he died. You came storming out of his room and said I could wait it out with him if I wanted to, but you were going to watch *Gunsmoke*. What did he say to you?

MAMA: He didn't have *anything* to say to me, Jessie. That's why I left. He didn't say a thing. It was his last chance not to talk to me and he took full advantage of it.

JESSIE (*after a moment*): I'm sorry you didn't love him. Sorry for you, I mean. He seemed like a nice man.

MAMA (*as Jessie walks to the refrigerator*): Ready for your apple now?

JESSIE: Soon as I'm through here, Mama.

MAMA: You won't like the apple, either. It'll be just like the cocoa. You never liked eating at all, did you? Any of it! What have you been living on all these years, toothpaste?

JESSIE (*as she starts to clean out the refrigerator*): Now, you know the milkman comes on Wednesdays and Saturdays, and he leaves the order blank in an egg box, and you give the bills to Dawson once a month.

MAMA: Do they still make that orangeade?

JESSIE: It's not orangeade, it's just orange.

MAMA: I'm going to get some. I thought they stopped making it. You just stopped ordering it.

JESSIE: You should drink milk.

MAMA: Not anymore, I'm not. That hot chocolate was the last. Hooray.

JESSIE (*getting the garbage can from under the sink*): I told them to keep delivering a quart a week no matter what you said. I told them you'd run out of Cokes and you'd have to drink it. I told them I knew you wouldn't pour it on the ground . . .

MAMA (*finishing her sentence*): And you told them you weren't going to be ordering anymore?

JESSIE: I told them I was taking a little holiday and to look after you.

MAMA: And they didn't think something was funny about that? You who doesn't go to the front steps? You, who only sees the driveway looking down from a stretcher passed out cold?

JESSIE (*enjoying this, but not laughing*): They said it was about time, but why didn't I take you with me? And I said I didn't think you'd want to go, and they said, "Yeah, everybody's got their own idea of vacation."

MAMA: I guess you think that's funny.

JESSIE (*pulling jars out of the refrigerator*): You know there never was any reason to call the ambulance for me. All they ever did for me in the emergency room was let me wake up. I could've done that here. Now, I'll just call them out and you say yes or no. I know you like pickles. Ketchup?

MAMA: Keep it.

JESSIE: We've had this since last Fourth of July.

MAMA: Keep the ketchup. Keep it all.

JESSIE: Are you going to drink ketchup from the bottle or what? How can you want your food and not want your pots to cook it in? This stuff will all spoil in here, Mother.

MAMA: Nothing I ever did was good enough for you and I want to know why.

JESSIE: That's not true.

MAMA: And I want to know why you've lived here this long feeling the way you do.

JESSIE: You have no earthly idea how I feel.

MAMA: Well, how could I? You're real far back there, Jessie.

JESSIE: Back where?

MAMA: What's it like over there, where you are? Do people always say the right thing or get whatever they want, or what?

JESSIE: What are you talking about?

MAMA: Why do you read the newspaper? Why don't you wear that sweater I made for you? Do you remember how I used to look, or am I just any old woman now? When you have a fit, do you see stars or what? How did you fall off the horse, really? Why did Cecil leave you? Where did you put my old glasses?

JESSIE (*stunned by Mama's intensity*): They're in the bottom drawer of your dresser in an old Milk of Magnesia box. Cecil left me because he made me choose between him and smoking.

MAMA: Jessie, I know he wasn't that dumb.

JESSIE: I never understood why he hated it so much when it's so good. Smoking is the only thing I know that's always just what you think it's going to be. Just like it was the last time, right there when you want it and real quiet.

MAMA: Your fits made him sick and you know it.

JESSIE: Say seizures, not fits. Seizures.

MAMA: It's the same thing. A seizure in the hospital is a fit at home.

JESSIE: They didn't bother him at all. Except he did feel responsible for it. It *was* his idea to go horseback riding that day. It was his idea I could do *anything* if I just made up my mind to. I fell off the horse because I didn't know how to hold on. Cecil left for pretty much the same reason.

MAMA: He had a girl, Jessie. I walked right in on them in the toolshed.

JESSIE (*after a moment*): O.K. That's fair. (*Lighting another cigarette.*) Was she very pretty?

MAMA: She was Agnes's girl, Carlene. Judge for yourself.

JESSIE (*as she walks to the living room*): I guess you and Agnes had a good talk about that, huh?

MAMA: I never thought he was good enough for you. They moved here from Tennessee, you know.

JESSIE: What are you talking about? You liked him better than I did. You flirted him out here to build your porch or I'd never even met him at all. You thought maybe he'd help you out around the place, come in and get some coffee and talk to you. God knows what you thought. All that curly hair.

MAMA: He's the best carpenter I ever saw. That little house of yours will still be standing at the end of the world, Jessie.

JESSIE: You didn't need a porch, Mama.

MAMA: All right! I wanted you to have a husband.

JESSIE: And I couldn't get one on my own, of course.

MAMA: How were you going to get a husband never opening your mouth to a living soul?

JESSIE: So I was quiet about it, so what?

MAMA: So I should have let you just sit here? Sit like your daddy? Sit here?

JESSIE: Maybe.

MAMA: Well, I didn't think so.

JESSIE: Well, what did you know?

MAMA: I never said I knew much. How was I supposed to learn anything living out here? I didn't know enough to do half the things I did in my life. Things happen. You do what you can about them and you see what happens next. I married you off to the wrong man, I admit that. So I took you in when he left. I'm sorry.

JESSIE: He wasn't the wrong man.

MAMA: He didn't love you, Jessie, or he wouldn't have left.

JESSIE: He wasn't the wrong man, Mama. I loved Cecil so much. And I tried to get more exercise and I tried to stay awake. I tried to learn to ride a horse. And I tried to stay outside with him, but he always knew I was trying, so it didn't work.

MAMA: He was a selfish man. He told me once he hated to see people move into his houses after he built them. He knew they'd mess them up.

JESSIE: I loved that bridge he built over the creek in back of the house. It didn't have to be anything special, a couple of boards would have been just fine, but he used that yellow pine and rubbed it so smooth . . .

MAMA: He had responsibilities here. He had a wife and son here and he failed you.

JESSIE: Or that baby bed he built for Ricky. I told him he didn't have to spend so much time on it, but he said it had to last, and the thing ended up weighing two hundred pounds and I couldn't move it. I said, "How long does a baby bed have to last, anyway?" But maybe he thought if it was strong enough, it might keep Ricky a baby.

MAMA: Ricky is too much like Cecil.

JESSIE: He is not. Ricky is as much like me as it's possible for any human to be. We even wear the same size pants. These are his, I think.

MAMA: That's just the same size. That's not you're the same person.

JESSIE: I see it on his face. I hear it when he talks. We look out at the world and we see the same thing: Not Fair. And the only difference between us is Ricky's out there trying to get even. And he knows not to trust anybody and he got it straight from me. And he knows not to try to get work, and guess where he got that. He walks around like there's loose boards in the floor, and you know who laid that floor, I did.

MAMA: Ricky isn't through yet. You don't know how he'll turn out!

JESSIE (*going back to the kitchen*): Yes I do and so did Cecil. Ricky is the two of us together for all time in too small a space. And we're tearing each other apart, like always, inside that boy, and if you don't see it, then you're just blind.

MAMA: Give him time, Jess.

JESSIE: Oh, he'll have plenty of that. Five years for forgery, ten years for armed assault . . .

MAMA (*furious*): Stop that! (*Then pleading.*) Jessie, Cecil might be ready to try it again, honey, that happens sometimes. Go downtown. Find him. Talk to him. He didn't know what he had in you. Maybe he sees things different now, but you're not going to know that till you go see him. Or call him up! Right now! He might be home.

JESSIE: And say what? Nothing's changed, Cecil, I'd just like to look at you, if you don't mind? No. He loved me, Mama. He just didn't know how things fall down around me like they do. I think he did the right thing. He gave himself another chance, that's all. But I did beg him to take me with him. I did tell him I would leave Ricky and you and everything I loved out here if only he would take me with him, but he couldn't and I understood that. (*Pause.*) I wrote that note I showed you. I wrote it. Not Cecil. I said "I'm sorry, Jessie, I can't fix it all for you." I said I'd always love me, not Cecil. But that's how he felt.

MAMA: Then he should've taken you with him!

JESSIE (*picking up the garbage bag she has filled*): Mama, you don't pack your garbage when you move.

MAMA: You will not call yourself garbage, Jessie.

JESSIE (*taking the bag to the big garbage can near the back door*): Just a way of saying it, Mama. Thinking about my list, that's all. (*Opening the can, putting the garbage in, then securing the lid.*) Well, a little more than that. I was trying to say it's all right that Cecil left. It was . . . a relief in a way. I never was what he wanted to see, so it was better when he wasn't looking at me all the time.

MAMA: I'll make your apple now.

JESSIE: No thanks. You get the manicure stuff and I'll be right there.

Jessie ties up the big garbage bag in the can and replaces the small garbage bag under the sink, all the time trying desperately to regain her calm. Mama watches, from a distance, her hand reaching unconsciously for the phone. Then she has a better idea. Or rather she thinks of the only other thing left and is willing to try it. Maybe she is even convinced it will work.

MAMA: Jessie, I think your daddy had little . . .

JESSIE (*interrupting her*): Garbage night is Tuesday. Put it out as late as you can. The Davis's dogs get in it if you don't. (*Replacing the garbage bag in the can under the sink.*) And keep ordering the heavy black bags. It doesn't pay to buy the cheap ones. And I've got all the ties here with the hammers and all. Take them out of the box as soon as you open a new one and put them in this drawer. They'll get lost if you don't, and rubber bands or something else won't work.

MAMA: I think your daddy had fits, too. I think he sat in his chair and had little fits. I read this a long time ago in a magazine, how little fits go, just little blackouts where maybe their eyes don't even close and people just call them "thinking spells."

JESSIE (*getting the slipcover out of the laundry basket*): I don't think you want this manicure we've been looking forward to. I washed this cover for the sofa, but it'll take both of us to get it back on.

MAMA: I watched his eyes. I know that's what it was. The magazine said some people don't even know they've had one.

JESSIE: Daddy would've known if he'd had fits, Mama.

MAMA: The lady in this story had kept track of hers and she'd had eighty thousand of them in the last eleven years.

JESSIE: Next time you wash this cover, it'll dry better if you put it on wet.

MAMA: Jessie, listen to what I'm telling you. This lady had anywhere between five and five hundred fits a day and they lasted maybe fifteen seconds apiece, so that out of her life, she'd only lost about two weeks altogether, and she had a full-time secretary job and an IQ of 120.

JESSIE (*amused by Mama's approach*): You want to talk about fits, is that it?

MAMA: Yes. I do. I want to say . . .

JESSIE (*interrupting*): Most of the time I wouldn't even know I'd had one, except I wake up with different clothes on, feeling like I've been run over. Sometimes I feel my head start to turn around or hear myself scream. And sometimes there *is* this dizzy stupid feeling a little before it, but if the TV's on, well, it's easy to miss.

As Jessie and Mama replace the slipcover on the sofa and the afghan on the chair, the physical struggle somehow mirrors the emotional one in the conversation.

MAMA: I can tell when you're about to have one. Your eyes get this big! But, Jessie, you haven't . . .

JESSIE (*taking charge of this*): What do they look like? The seizures.

MAMA (*reluctant*): Different each time, Jess.

JESSIE: O.K. Pick one, then. A good one. I think I want to know now.

MAMA: There's not much to tell. You just . . . crumple, in a heap, like a puppet and somebody cut the strings all at once, or like the firing squad in some Mexican movie, you just slide down the wall, you know. You don't know what happens? How can you not know what happens?

JESSIE: I'm busy.

MAMA: That's not funny.

JESSIE: I'm not laughing. My head turns around and I fall down and then what?

MAMA: Well, your chest squeezes in and out, and you sound like you're gagging, sucking air in and out like you can't breathe.

JESSIE: Do it for me. Make the sound for me.

MAMA: I will not. It's awful-sounding.

JESSIE: Yeah. It felt like it might be. What's next?

MAMA: Your mouth bites down and I have to get your tongue out of the way fast, so you don't bite yourself.

JESSIE: Or you. I bite you, too, don't I?

MAMA: You got me once real good. I had to get a tetanus! But I know what to watch for now. And then you turn blue and the jerks start up. Like I'm standing there poking you with a cattle prod or you're sticking your finger in a light socket as fast as you can . . .

JESSIE: Foaming like a mad dog the whole time.

MAMA: It's bubbling, Jess, not foam like the washer overflowed, for God's sake; it's bubbling like a baby spitting up. I go get a wet washcloth, that's all. And then the jerks slow down and you wet yourself and it's over. Two minutes tops.

JESSIE: How do I get to the bed?

MAMA: How do you think?

JESSIE: I'm too heavy for you now. How do you do it?

MAMA: I call Dawson. But I get you cleaned up before he gets here and I make him leave before you wake up.

JESSIE: You could just leave me on the floor.

MAMA: I want you to wake up someplace nice, O.K.? (*Then making a real effort.*) But, Jessie, and this is the reason I even brought this up! You haven't had a seizure for a solid year. A whole year, do you realize that?

JESSIE: Yeah, the phenobarb's about right now, I guess.

MAMA: You bet it is. You might never have another one, ever! You might be through with it for all time!

JESSIE: Could be.

MAMA: You are. I know you are!

JESSIE: I sure am feeling good. I really am. The double vision's gone and my gums aren't swelling. No rashes or anything. I'm feeling as good as I ever felt in my life. I'm even feeling like worrying or getting mad and I'm not afraid it will start a fit if I do, I just go ahead.

MAMA: Of course you do! You can even scream at me, if you want to. I can take it. You don't have to act like you're just visiting here, Jessie. This is your house, too.

JESSIE: The best part is, my memory's back.

MAMA: Your memory's always been good. When couldn't you remember things? You're always reminding me what . . .

JESSIE: Because I've made lists for everything. But now I remember what things mean on my lists. I see "dish towels," and I used to wonder whether I was supposed to wash them, buy them, or look for them because I wouldn't remember where I put them after I washed them, but now I know it means wrap them up, they're a present for Loretta's birthday.

MAMA (*finished with the sofa now*): You used to go looking for your lists, too, I've noticed that. You always know where they are now! (*Then suddenly worried.*) Loretta's birthday isn't coming up, is it?

JESSIE: I made a list of all the birthdays for you. I even put yours on it. (*A small smile.*) So you can call Loretta and remind her.

MAMA: Let's take Loretta to Howard Johnson's and have those fried clams. I *know* you love that clam roll.

JESSIE (*slight pause*): I won't be here, Mama.

MAMA: What have we just been talking about? You'll be here. You're well, Jessie. You're starting all over. You said it yourself. You're remembering things and . . .

JESSIE: I won't be here. If I'd ever had a year like this, to think straight and all, before now, I'd be gone already.

MAMA (*not pleading, commanding*): No, Jessie.

JESSIE (*folding the rest of the laundry*): Yes, Mama. Once I started remembering, I could see what it all added up to.

MAMA: The fits are over!

JESSIE: It's not the fits, Mama.

MAMA: Then it's me for giving them to you, but I didn't do it!

JESSIE: It's not the fits! You said it yourself, the medicine takes care of the fits.

MAMA (*interrupting*): Your daddy gave you those fits, Jessie. He passed it down to you like your green eyes and your straight hair. It's not my fault!

JESSIE: So what if he had little fits? It's not inherited. I fell off the horse. It was an accident.

MAMA: The horse wasn't the first time, Jessie. You had a fit when you were five years old.

JESSIE: I did not.

MAMA: You did! You were eating a popsicle and down you went. He gave it to you. It's *his* fault, not mine.

JESSIE: Well, you took your time telling me.

MAMA: How do you tell that to a five-year-old?

JESSIE: What did the doctor say?

MAMA: He said kids have them all the time. He said there wasn't anything to do but wait for another one.

JESSIE: But I didn't have another one.

Now there is a real silence.

JESSIE: You mean to tell me I had fits all the time as a kid and you just told me I fell down or something and it wasn't till I had the fit when Cecil was

looking that anybody bothered to find out what was the matter with
me?

MAMA: It wasn't *all the time,* Jessie. And they changed when you started to
school. More like your daddy's. Oh, that was some swell time, sitting
here with the two of you turning off and on like light bulbs some nights.

JESSIE: How many fits did I have?

MAMA: You never hurt yourself. I never let you out of my sight. I caught you
every time.

JESSIE: But you didn't tell anybody.

MAMA: It was none of their business.

JESSIE: You were ashamed.

MAMA: I didn't want anybody to know. Least of all you.

JESSIE: Least of all me. Oh, right. That was mine to know, Mama, not yours. Did
Daddy know?

MAMA: He thought you were . . . you fell down a lot. That's what he thought.
You were careless. Or maybe he thought I beat you. I don't know what
he thought. He didn't think about it.

JESSIE: Because you didn't tell him!

MAMA: If I told him about you, I'd have to tell him about him!

JESSIE: I don't like this. I don't like this one bit.

MAMA: I didn't think you'd like it. That's why I didn't tell you.

JESSIE: If I'd known I was an epileptic, Mama, I wouldn't have ridden any
horses.

MAMA: Make you feel like a freak, is that what I should have done?

JESSIE: Just get the manicure tray and sit down!

MAMA (*throwing it to the floor*): I don't want a manicure!

JESSIE: Doesn't look like you do, no.

MAMA: Maybe I did drop you, you don't know.

JESSIE: If you say you didn't, you didn't.

MAMA (*beginning to break down*): Maybe I fed you the wrong thing. Maybe you
had a fever sometime and I didn't know it soon enough. Maybe it's a
punishment.

JESSIE: For what?

MAMA: I don't know. Because of how I felt about your father. Because I didn't
want any more children. Because I smoked too much or didn't eat right
when I was carrying you. It has to be something I did.

JESSIE: It does not. It's just a sickness, not a curse. Epilepsy doesn't mean anything. It just is.

MAMA: I'm not talking about the fits here, Jessie! I'm talking about this killing
yourself. It has to be me that's the matter here. You wouldn't be doing
this if it wasn't. I didn't tell you things or I married you off to the wrong
man or I took you in and let your life get away from you or all of it put
together. I don't know what I did, but I did it. I know. This is all my fault,
Jessie, but I don't know what to do about it now!

JESSIE (*exasperated at having to say this again*): It doesn't have anything to do with
you!

MAMA: Everything you do has to do with me, Jessie. You can't do *anything*, wash your face or cut your finger, without doing it to me. That's right! You might as well kill me as you, Jessie, it's the same thing. This has to do with me, Jessie.

JESSIE: Then what if it does! What if it has everything to do with you! What if you are all I have and you're not enough? What if I could take all the rest of it if only I didn't have you here? What if the only way I can get away from you for good is to kill myself? What if it is? I can *still* do it!

MAMA (*in desperate tears*): Don't leave me, Jessie! (*Jessie stands for a moment, then turns for the bedroom.*) No! (*She grabs Jessie's arm.*)

JESSIE (*carefully taking her arm away*): I have a box of things I want people to have. I'm just going to go get it for you. You . . . just rest a minute.

Jessie is gone. Mama heads for the telephone, but she can't even pick up the receiver this time and, instead, stoops to clean up the bottles that have spilled out of the manicure tray.

Jessie returns, carrying a box that groceries were delivered in. It probably says Hershey Kisses or Starkist Tuna. Mama is still down on the floor cleaning up, hoping that maybe if she just makes it look nice enough, Jessie will stay.)

MAMA: Jessie, how can I live here without you? I need you! You're supposed to tell me to stand up straight and say how nice I look in my pink dress, and drink my milk. You're supposed to go around and lock up so I know we're safe for the night, and when I wake up, you're supposed to be out there making the coffee and watching me get older every day, and you're supposed to help me die when the time comes. I can't do that by myself, Jessie. I'm not like you, Jessie. I hate the quiet and I don't want to die and I don't want you to go, Jessie. How can I . . . (*Has to stop a moment.*) How can I get up every day knowing you had to kill yourself to make it stop hurting and I was here all the time and I never even saw it. And then you gave me this chance to make it better, convince you to stay alive, and I couldn't do it. How can I live with myself after this, Jessie?

JESSIE: I only told you so I could explain it, so you wouldn't blame yourself, so you wouldn't feel bad. There wasn't anything you could say to change my mind. I didn't want you to save me. I just wanted you to know.

MAMA: Stay with me just a little longer. Just a few more years. I don't have that many more to go, Jessie. And as soon as I'm dead, you can do whatever you want. Maybe with me gone, you'll have all the quiet you want, right here in the house. And maybe one day you'll put in some begonias up the walk and get just the right rain for them all summer. And Ricky will be married by then and he'll bring your grandbabies over and you can sneak them a piece of candy when their daddy's not looking and then be real glad when they've gone home and left you to your quiet again.

JESSIE: Don't you see, Mama, everything I do winds up like this. How could I think you would understand? How could I think you would want a manicure? We could hold hands for an hour and then I could go shoot myself? I'm sorry about tonight, Mama, but it's exactly why I'm doing it.

MAMA: If you've got the guts to kill yourself, Jessie, you've got the guts to stay alive.

JESSIE: I know that. So it's really just a matter of where I'd rather be.

MAMA: Look, maybe I can't think of what you should do, but that doesn't mean there isn't something that would help. *You* find it. *You* think of it. You can keep trying. You can get brave and try some more. You don't have to give up!

JESSIE: I'm *not* giving up! This *is* the other thing I'm trying. And I'm sure there are some other things that might work, but *might* work isn't good enough anymore. I need something that *will* work. *This* will work. That's why I picked it.

MAMA: But something might happen. Something that could change everything. Who knows what it might be, but it might be worth waiting for! (*Jessie doesn't respond.*) Try it for two more weeks. We could have more talks like tonight.

JESSIE: No, Mama.

MAMA: I'll pay more attention to you. Tell the truth when you ask me. Let you have your say.

JESSIE: No, Mama! We wouldn't have more talks like tonight, because it's this next part that's made this last part so good, Mama. No, Mama. *This* is how I have my say. This is how I say what I thought about it *all* and I say no. To Dawson and Loretta and the Red Chinese and epilepsy and Ricky and Cecil and you. And me. And hope. I say no! (*Then going to Mama on the sofa.*) Just let me go easy, Mama.

MAMA: How can I let you go?

JESSIE: You can because you have to. It's what you've always done.

MAMA: You are my child!

JESSIE: I am what became of your child. (*Mama cannot answer.*) I found an old baby picture of me. And it was somebody else, not me. It was somebody pink and fat who never heard of sick or lonely, somebody who cried and got fed, and reached up and got held and kicked but didn't hurt anybody, and slept whenever she wanted to, just by closing her eyes. Somebody who mainly just laid there and laughed at the colors waving around over her head and chewed on a polka-dot whale and woke up knowing some new trick nearly every day, and rolled over and drooled on the sheet and felt your hand pulling my quilt back up over me. That's who I started out and this is who is left. (*There is no self-pity here.*) That's what this is about. It's somebody I lost, all right, it's my own self. Who I never was. Or who I tried to be and never got there. Somebody I waited for who never came. And never will. So, see, it doesn't much matter what else happens in the world or in this house, even. I'm what was worth waiting for and I didn't make it. Me . . . who might have made a difference to me . . . I'm not going to show up, so there's no reason to stay, except to keep you company, and that's . . . not reason enough because I'm not . . . very good company. (*Pause.*) Am I.

MAMA (*knowing she must tell the truth*): No. And neither am I.

JESSIE: I had this strange little thought, well, maybe it's not so strange. Anyway, after Christmas, after I decided to do this, I would wonder, sometimes, what might keep me here, what might be worth staying for, and you know what it was? It was maybe if there was something I really liked, like maybe if I really liked rice pudding or cornflakes for breakfast or something, that might be enough.

MAMA: Rice pudding is good.

JESSIE: Not to me.

MAMA: And you're not afraid?

JESSIE: Afraid of what?

MAMA: I'm afraid of it, for me, I mean. When my time comes. I know it's coming, but . . .

JESSIE: You don't know when. Like in a scary movie.

MAMA: Yeah, sneaking up on me like some killer on the loose, hiding out in the back yard just waiting for me to have my hands full someday and how am I supposed to protect myself anyhow when I don't know what he looks like and I don't know how he sounds coming up behind me like that or if it will hurt or take very long or what I don't get done before it happens.

JESSIE: You've got plenty of time left.

MAMA: I forget what for, right now.

JESSIE: For whatever happens, I don't know. For the rest of your life. For Agnes burning down one more house or Dawson losing his hair or . . .

MAMA (*quickly*): Jessie, I can't just sit here and say O.K., kill yourself if you want to.

JESSIE: Sure you can. You just did. Say it again.

MAMA (*really startled*): Jessie! (*Quiet horror.*) How dare you! (*Furious.*) How dare you! You think you can just leave whenever you want, like you're watching television here? No, you can't, Jessie. You make me feel like a fool for being alive, child, and you are so wrong! I like it here, and I will stay here until they make me go, until they drag me screaming and I mean screeching into my grave, and you're real smart to get away before then because, I mean, honey, you've never heard noise like that in your life. (*Jessie turns away.*) Who am I talking to? You're gone already, aren't you? I'm looking right through you! I can't stop you because you're already gone! I guess you think they'll all have to talk about you now! I guess you think this will really confuse them. Oh yes, ever since Christmas you've been laughing to yourself and thinking, "Boy, are they all in for a surprise." Well, nobody's going to be a bit surprised, sweetheart. This is just like you. Do it the hard way, that's my girl, all right. (*Jessie gets up and goes into the kitchen, but Mama follows her.*) You know who they're going to feel sorry for? Me! How about that! Not you, me! They're going to be *ashamed* of you. Yes. *Ashamed!* If somebody asks Dawson about it, he'll change the subject as fast as he can. He'll talk about how much he has to pay to park his car these days.

JESSIE: Leave me alone.

MAMA: It's the truth!

JESSIE: I should've just left you a note!

MAMA (*screaming*): Yes! (*Then suddenly understanding what she has said, nearly paralyzed by the thought of it, she turns slowly to face Jessie, nearly whispering.*) No. No. I . . . might not have thought of all the things you've said.

JESSIE: It's O.K., Mama.

Mama is nearly unconscious from the emotional devastation of these last few moments. She sits down at the kitchen table, hurt and angry and desperately afraid. But she looks almost numb. She is so far beyond what is known as pain that she is virtually unreachable and Jessie knows this, and talks quietly, watching for signs of recovery.

JESSIE (*washes her hands in the sink*): I remember you liked that preacher who did Daddy's, so if you want to ask him to do the service, that's O.K. with me.

MAMA (*not an answer, just a word*): What.

JESSIE (*putting on hand lotion as she talks*): And pick some songs you like or let Agnes pick, she'll know exactly which ones. Oh, and I had your dress cleaned that you wore to Daddy's. You looked real good in that.

MAMA: I don't remember, hon.

JESSIE: And it won't be so bad once your friends start coming to the funeral home. You'll probably see people you haven't seen for years, but I thought about what you should say to get you over that nervous part when they first come in.

MAMA (*simply repeating*): Come in.

JESSIE: Take them up to see their flowers, they'd like that. And when they say, "I'm so sorry, Thelma," you just say, "I appreciate your coming, Connie." And then ask how their garden was this summer or what they're doing for Thanksgiving or how their children . . .

MAMA: I don't think I should ask about their children. I'll talk about what they have on, that's always good. And I'll have some crochet work with me.

JESSIE: And Agnes will be there, so you might not have to talk at all.

MAMA: Maybe if Connie Richards does come, I can get her to tell me where she gets that Irish yarn, she calls it. I know it doesn't come from Ireland. I think it just comes with a green wrapper.

JESSIE: And be sure to invite enough people home afterward so you get enough food to feed them all and have some left for you. But don't let anybody take anything home, especially Loretta.

MAMA: Loretta will get all the food set up, honey. It's only fair to let her have some macaroni or something.

JESSIE: No, Mama. You have to be more selfish from now on. (*Sitting at the table with Mama.*) Now, somebody's bound to ask you why I did it and you just say you don't know. That you loved me and you know I loved you and we just sat around tonight like every other night of our lives, and then I came over and kissed you and said, " 'Night, Mother," and you heard me close my bedroom door and the next thing you heard was the shot. And whatever reasons I had, well, you guess I just took them with me.

MAMA (*quietly*): It was something personal.

JESSIE: Good. That's good, Mama.

MAMA: That's what I'll say, then.

JESSIE: Personal. Yeah.

MAMA: Is that what I tell Dawson and Loretta, too? We sat around, you kissed me, " 'Night, Mother"? They'll want to know more, Jessie. They won't believe it.

JESSIE: Well, then, tell them what we did. I filled up the candy jars. I cleaned out the refrigerator. We made some hot chocolate and put the cover back on the sofa. You had no idea. All right? I really think it's better that way. If they know we talked about it, they really won't understand how you let me go.

MAMA: I guess not.

JESSIE: It's private. Tonight is private, yours and mine, and I don't want any-body else to have any of it.

MAMA: O.K., then.

JESSIE (*standing behind Mama now, holding her shoulders*): Now, when you hear the shot, I don't want you to come in. First of all, you won't be able to get in by yourself, but I don't want you trying. Call Dawson, then call the police, and then call Agnes. And then you'll need something to do till somebody gets here, so wash the hot-chocolate pan. You wash that pan till you hear the doorbell ring and I don't care if it's an hour, you keep washing that pan.

MAMA: I'll make my calls and then I'll just sit. I won't need something to do. What will the police say?

JESSIE: They'll do that gunpowder test, I guess, and ask you what happened, and by that time, the ambulance will be here and they'll come in and get me and you know how that goes. You stay out here with Dawson and Loretta. You keep Dawson out here. I want the police in the room first, not Dawson, O.K.?

MAMA: What if Dawson and Loretta want me to go home with them?

JESSIE (*returning to the living room*): That's up to you.

MAMA: I think I'll stay here. All they're got is Sanka.

JESSIE: Maybe Agnes could come stay with you for a few days.

MAMA (*standing up, looking into the living room*): I'd rather be by myself, I think. (*Walking toward the box Jessie brought in earlier.*) You want me to give peo-ple those things?

JESSIE (*they sit down on the sofa, Jessie holding the box on her lap*): I want Loretta to have my little calculator. Dawson bought it for himself, you know, but then he saw one he liked better and he couldn't bring both of them home with Loretta counting every penny the way she does, so he gave the first one to me. Be funny for her to have it now, don't you think? And all my house slippers are in a sack for her in my closet. Tell her I know they'll fit and I've never worn any of them, and make sure Dawson hears you tell her that. I'm glad he loves Loretta so much, but I wish he knew not everybody has her size feet.

MAMA (*taking the calculator*): O.K.

JESSIE (*reaching into the box again*): This letter is for Dawson, but it's mostly about you, so read it if you want. There's a list of presents for you for at least twenty more Christmases and birthdays, so if you want anything special you better add it to this list before you give it to him. Or if you want to be surprised, just don't read that page. This Christmas, you're getting mostly stuff for the house, like a new rug in your bathroom and needlework, but next Christmas, you're really going to cost him next Christmas. I think you'll like it a lot and you'd never think of it.

MAMA: And you think he'll go for it?

JESSIE: I think he'll feel like a real jerk if he doesn't. Me telling him to, like this and all. Now, this number's where you call Cecil. I called it last week and he answered, so I know he still lives there.

MAMA: What do you want me to tell him?

JESSIE: Tell him we talked about him and I only had good things to say about him, but mainly tell him to find Ricky and tell him what I did, and tell Ricky you have something for him, out here, from me, and to come get it. (*Pulls a sack out of the box.*)

MAMA (*the sack feels empty*): What is it?

JESSIE (*taking it off*): My watch. (*Putting it in the sack and taking a ribbon out of the sack to tie around the top of it.*)

MAMA: He'll sell it!

JESSIE: That's the idea. I appreciate him not stealing it already. I'd like to buy him a good meal.

MAMA: He'll buy dope with it!

JESSIE: Well, then, I hope he gets some good dope with it, Mama. And the rest of this is for you. (*Handing Mama the box now. Mama picks up the things and looks at them.*)

MAMA (*surprised and pleased*): When did you do all this? During my naps, I guess.

JESSIE: I guess. I tried to be quiet about it. (*As Mama is puzzled by the presents.*) Those are just little presents. For whenever you need one. They're not bought presents, just things I thought you might like to look at, pictures or things you think you've lost. Things you didn't know you had, even. You'll see.

MAMA: I'm not sure I want them. They'll make me think of you.

JESSIE: No they won't. They're just things, like a free tube of toothpaste I found hanging on the door one day.

MAMA: Oh. All right, then.

JESSIE: Well, maybe there's one nice present in there somewhere. It's Granny's ring she gave me and I thought you might like to have it, but I didn't think you'd wear it if I gave it to you right now.

MAMA (*taking the box to a table nearby*): No. Probably not. (*Turning back to face her.*) I'm ready for my manicure, I guess. Want me to wash my hands again?

JESSIE (*standing up*): It's time for me to go, Mama.

MAMA (*starting for her*): No, Jessie, you've got all night!

JESSIE (*as Mama grabs her*): No, Mama.

MAMA: It's not even ten o'clock.

JESSIE (*very calm*): Let me go, Mama.

MAMA: I can't. You can't go. You can't do this. You didn't say it would be so soon, Jessie. I'm scared. I love you.

JESSIE (*takes her hands away*): Let go of me, Mama. I've said everything I had to say.

MAMA (*standing still a minute*): You said you wanted to do my nails.

JESSIE (*taking a small step backward*): I can't. It's too late.

MAMA: It's not too late!

JESSIE: I don't want you to wake Dawson and Loretta when you call. I want them to still be up and dressed so they can get right over.

MAMA (*as Jessie backs up, Mama moves in on her, but carefully*): They wake up fast, Jessie, if they have to. They don't matter here, Jessie. You do. I do. We're not through yet. We've got a lot of things to take care of here. I don't know where my prescriptions are and you didn't tell me what to tell Dr. Davis when he calls or how much you want me to tell Ricky or who I call to rake the leaves or . . .

JESSIE: Don't try and stop me, Mama, you can't do it.

MAMA (*grabbing her again, this time hard*): I can too! I'll stand in front of this hall and you can't get past me. (*They struggle.*) You'll have to knock me down to get away from me, Jessie. I'm not about to let you . . .

Mama struggles with Jessie at the door and in the struggle Jessie gets away from her and —

JESSIE (*almost a whisper*): 'Night, Mother. (*She vanishes into her bedroom and we hear the door lock just as Mama gets to it.*)

MAMA (*screams*): Jessie! (*Pounding on the door.*) Jessie, you let me in there. Don't you do this, Jessie. I'm not going to stop screaming until you open this door, Jessie. Jessie! Jessie! What if I don't do any of the things you told me to do! I'll tell Cecil what a miserable man he was to make you feel the way he did and I'll give Ricky's watch to Dawson if I feel like it and the only way you can make sure I do what you want is you come out here and make me, Jessie! (*Pounding again.*) Jessie! Stop this! I didn't know! I was here with you all the time. How could I know you were so alone?

And Mama stops for a moment, breathless and frantic, putting her ear to the door, and when she doesn't hear anything, she stands up straight again and screams once more.

Jessie! Please!

And we hear the shot, and it sounds like an answer, it sounds like No.

Mama collapses against the door, tears streaming down her face, but not screaming anymore. In shock now.

Jessie, Jessie, child . . . Forgive me. (*Pause.*) I thought you were mine.

And she leaves the door and makes her way through the living room, around the furniture, as though she didn't know where it was, not knowing what to do. Finally, she goes to the stove in the kitchen and picks up the hot-chocolate pan and carries it with her to the telephone, and holds on to it while she dials the number. She looks down at the pan, holding it tight like her life depended on it. She hears Loretta answer.

MAMA: Loretta, let me talk to Dawson, honey.

CHRISTOPHER DURANG (b. 1949) was born in Montclair, New Jersey, the son of an architect. After undergraduate work at Harvard University, he earned his master's degree in playwriting from the Yale School of Drama, where he also performed in stage productions at the Yale Repertory Theatre in New Haven. While still a graduate student, Durang co-wrote and performed a cabaret, I Don't Generally Like Poetry but Have You Read "Trees"?, at the Manhattan Theatre Club. He followed this play in 1973 with the comedies Better Dead than Sorry, The Idiots Karamazov (1974), and When Dinah Shore Ruled the Earth (1975), coauthored with playwright Wendy Wasserstein. The next year he taught playwriting at Yale University and then went on to write the book for the musical A History of the American Film (1978), nominated for a Tony Award. He won Obie awards for Sister Mary Ignatius Explains It All for You (1980) and The Marriage of Betty and Boo (1985).

Durang has also written screenplays, including The Nun Who Shot Liberty Valence, The House of Husbands (coauthored with Wendy Wasserstein), and Beyond Therapy (coauthored with Robert Altman). In the 1990s Durang made several appearances as an actor in films and television. His play Media Amok premiered at American Repertory Theatre in Cambridge, Massachusetts, in 1992. For Whom the Southern Belle Tolls, his parody of Tennessee Williams's The Glass Menagerie, was included in Durang Durang, a program of one-act plays that premiered in New York City in 1994. He is a frequent performer in cabaret and stage revues.

Durang's work is published in Three Short Plays (1979) and Christopher Durang Explains It All for You (1983) as well as the anthology Plays from the Contemporary American Theatre (1988). The New York Times critic Mel Gussow has described Durang's style of comedy as having "the wiggishness of the four Marxes and the malice of Jonathan Swift."

RELATED PLAY: Tennessee Williams, The Glass Menagerie, page 1704.

CHRISTOPHER DURANG

For Whom the Southern Belle Tolls
1994

CHARACTERS

AMANDA, the mother
LAWRENCE, the son
TOM, the other son
GINNY

Lights up on a fussy living room setting. Enter Amanda, the Southern belle mother.

AMANDA: Rise and shine! Rise and shine! (Calls off.) Lawrence, honey, come on out here and let me have a look at you!

Enter Lawrence, who limps across the room. He is very sensitive, and is wearing what are clearly his dress clothes. Amanda fiddles with his bow tie and stands back to admire him.

AMANDA: Lawrence, honey, you look lovely.
LAWRENCE: No, I don't mama. I have a pimple on the back of my neck.

AMANDA: Don't say the world "pimple," honey, it's common. Now your brother Tom is bringing home a girl from the warehouse for you to meet, and I want you to make a good impression, honey.

LAWRENCE: It upsets my stomach to meet people, mama.

AMANDA: Oh, Lawrence honey, you're so sensitive it makes me want to hit you.

LAWRENCE: I don't need to meet people, mama. I'm happy just by myself, playing with my collection of glass cocktail stirrers.

Lawrence limps over to a table on top of which sits a glass jar filled with glass swizzle sticks.

AMANDA: Lawrence, you are a caution. Only retarded people and alcoholics are interested in glass cocktail stirrers.

LAWRENCE (*picking up some of them*): Each one of them has a special name, mama. This one is called Stringbean because it's long and thin; and this one is called Stringbean because it's long and thin; and this one is called Blue because it's blue.

AMANDA: All my children have such imagination, why was I so blessed? Oh, Lawrence honey, how are you going to get on in the world if you just stay home all day, year after year, playing with your collection of glass cocktail stirrers?

LAWRENCE: I don't like the world, mama, I like it here in this room.

AMANDA: I know you do, Lawrence honey, that's part of your charm. Some days. But, honey, what about making a living?

LAWRENCE: I can't work, mama. I'm crippled. (*He limps over to the couch and sits.*)

AMANDA: There is nothing wrong with your leg, Lawrence honey, all the doctors have told you that. This limping thing is an affectation.

LAWRENCE: I only know how I feel, mama.

AMANDA: Oh if only I had connections in the Mafia, I'd have someone come and break both your legs.

LAWRENCE: Don't try to make me laugh, mama. You know I have asthma.

AMANDA: Your asthma, your leg, your eczema. You're just a mess, Lawrence.

LAWRENCE: I have scabs from the itching, mama.

AMANDA: That's lovely, Lawrence. You must tell us more over dinner.

LAWRENCE: Alright.

AMANDA: That was a joke, Lawrence.

LAWRENCE: Don't try to make me laugh, mama. My asthma.

AMANDA: Now, Lawrence, I don't want you talking about your ailments to the feminine caller your brother Tom is bringing home from the warehouse, honey. No nice-bred young lady likes to hear a young man discussing his eczema, Lawrence.

LAWRENCE: What else can I talk about, mama?

AMANDA: Talk about the weather. Or Red China.

LAWRENCE: Or my collection of glass cocktail stirrers?

AMANDA: I suppose so, honey, if the conversation comes to some godawful standstill. Otherwise, I'd shut up about it. Conversation is an art, Lawrence. Back at Blue Mountain, when I had seventeen gentlemen callers, I was able to converse with charm and vivacity for six hours without stop and never once mention eczema or bone cancer or vivisection. Try to emulate me, Lawrence, honey. Charm and vivacity. And charm. And vivacity. And charm.

LAWRENCE: Well, I'll try, but I doubt it.

AMANDA: Me too, honey. But we'll go through the motions anyway, won't we?

LAWRENCE: I don't know if I want to meet some girl who works in a warehouse, mama.

AMANDA: Your brother Tom says she's a lovely girl with a nice personality. And where else does he meet girls except the few who work at the warehouse? He only seems to meet men at the movies. Your brother goes to the movies entirely too much. I must speak to him about it.

LAWRENCE: It's unfeminine for a girl to work at a warehouse.

AMANDA: Lawrence, honey, if you can't go out the door without getting an upset stomach or an attack of vertigo, then we got to find some nice girl who's willing to support you. Otherwise, how am I ever going to get you out of this house and off my hands?

LAWRENCE: Why do you want to be rid of me, mama?

AMANDA: I suppose it's unmotherly of me, dear, but you really get on my nerves. Limping around the apartment, pretending to have asthma. If only some nice girl would marry you and I knew you were taken care of, then I'd feel free to start to live again. I'd join Parents Without Partners, I'd go to dinner dances, I'd have a life again. Rather than just watch you mope about this stupid apartment. I'm not bitter, dear, it's just that I hate my life.

LAWRENCE: I understand, mama.

AMANDA: Do you, dear? Oh, you're cute. Oh listen, I think I hear them.

TOM (*from offstage*): Mother, I forgot my key.

LAWRENCE: I'll be in the other room. (*Starts to limp away.*)

AMANDA: I want you to let them in, Lawrence.

LAWRENCE: Oh, I couldn't mama. She'd see I limp.

AMANDA: Then don't limp, damn it.

TOM (*from off*): Mother, are you there?

AMANDA: Just a minute, Tom, honey. Now, Lawrence, you march over to that door or I'm going to break all your swizzle sticks.

LAWRENCE: Mama, I can't.

AMANDA: Lawrence, you're a grown boy. Now you answer that door like any normal person.

LAWRENCE: I can't.

TOM: Mother, I'm going to break the door down in a minute.

AMANDA: Just be patient, Tom. Now you're causing a scene, Lawrence. I want you to answer that door.

LAWRENCE: My eczema itches.

AMANDA: I'll itch it for you in a second, Lawrence.

TOM: Alright, I'm breaking it down.

Sound of door breaking down. Enter Tom and Ginny Bennett, a vivacious girl dressed in factory clothes.

AMANDA: Oh, Tom, you got in.

TOM: Why must we go through this every night? You know the stupid fuck won't open the door, so why don't you let him alone about it? (*To Ginny.*) My kid brother has a thing about answering doors. He thinks people will notice his limp and his asthma and his eczema.

LAWRENCE: Excuse me. I think I hear someone calling me in the other room. (*Limps off, calls to imaginary person.*) Coming!

AMANDA: Now see what you've done. He's probably going to refuse to come to the table due to your insensitivity. Oh, was any woman as cursed as I? With one son who's too sensitive and another one who's this big ox. I'm sorry, how rude of me. I'm Amanda Wingvalley. You must be Virginia Bennett from the warehouse. Tom has spoken so much about you I feel you're almost one of the family, preferably a daughter-in-law. Welcome, Virginia.

GINNY (*speaking very loudly*): Call me Ginny or Gin. But just don't call me late for dinner! (*Roars with laughter.*)

AMANDA: Oh, how amusing. (*Whispers to Tom.*) Why is she shouting? Is she deaf?

GINNY: You're asking why I am speaking loudly. It's so that I can be heard! I am taking a course in public speaking, and so far we've covered organizing your thoughts and speaking good and loud so the people in the back of the room can hear you.

AMANDA: Public speaking. How impressive. You must be interested in improving yourself.

GINNY (*truly not having heard*): What?

AMANDA (*loudly*): YOU MUST BE INTERESTED IN IMPROVING YOURSELF.

GINNY (*loudly and happily*): YES I AM!

TOM: When's dinner? I want to get this over with fast if everyone's going to shout all evening.

GINNY: What?

AMANDA (*to Ginny*): Dinner is almost ready, Ginny.

GINNY: Who's Freddy?

AMANDA: Oh, Lord. No, dear. DINNER IS READY.

GINNY: Oh good. I'm as hungry as a bear! (*Growls enthusiastically.*)

AMANDA: You must be very popular at the warehouse, Ginny.

GINNY: No popsicle for me, ma'am, although I will take you up on some gin.

AMANDA (*confused*): What?

GINNY (*loudly*): I WOULD LIKE SOME GIN.

AMANDA: Well, fine. I think I'd like to get drunk too. Tom, why don't you go and make two Southern ladies some nice summer gin and tonics? And see if your sister would like a lemonade.

TOM: Sister?

AMANDA: I'm sorry, did I say sister? I meant brother.

TOM (*calling as he exits*): Hey, four eyes, you wanna lemonade?

AMANDA: Tom's so amusing. He calls Lawrence four eyes even though he doesn't wear glasses.

GINNY: And does Lawrence wear glasses?

AMANDA (*confused*): What?

GINNY: You said Tom called Lawrence four eyes even though he doesn't wear glasses, and I wondered if Lawrence wore glasses. Because that would, you see, explain it.

AMANDA (*looks at her with despair*): Ah. I don't know. I'll have to ask Lawrence someday. Speaking of Lawrence, let me go check on the supper and see if I can convince him to come out here and make conversation with you.

GINNY: No, thank you, ma'am, I'll just have the gin.

AMANDA: What?

GINNY: What?

AMANDA: Never mind. I'll be back. Or with luck I won't.

Amanda exits. Ginny looks around uncomfortably, and crosses to the table with the collection of glass cocktail stirrers.

GINNY: They must drink a lot here.

Enter Tom with a glass of gin for Ginny.

TOM: Here's some gin for Ginny.

GINNY: What?

TOM: Here's your poison.

GINNY: No, thanks, I'll just wait here.

TOM: Have you ever thought all that loud machinery at the warehouse may be affecting your hearing?

GINNY: Scenery? You mean, like trees? Yeah, I like trees.

TOM: I like trees, too.

AMANDA (*from offstage*): Now you get out of that bed this minute, Lawrence Wingvalley, or I'm going to give that overbearing girl your entire collection of glass gobbledygook — is that clear?

Amanda pushes in Lawrence, who is wearing a nightshirt.

AMANDA: I believe Lawrence would like to visit with you, Ginny.

GINNY (*shows her drink*): Tom brought me my drink already, thank you, Mrs. Wingvalley.

AMANDA: You know a hearing aid isn't really all that expensive, dear, you might look into that.

GINNY: No, if I have the gin, I don't really want any Gatorade. Never liked the stuff anyway. But you feel free.

AMANDA: Thank you, dear. I will. Come, Tom, come to the kitchen and help me prepare the dinner. And we'll let the two young people converse. Remember, Lawrence. Charm and vivacity.

TOM: I hope this dinner won't take long, mother. I don't want to get to the movies too late.

AMANDA: Oh shut up about the movies.

Amanda and Tom exit. Lawrence stands still, uncomfortable. Ginny looks at him pleasantly. Silence for a while.

GINNY: Hi.

LAWRENCE: Hi. (*Pause.*) I'd gone to bed.

GINNY: I never eat bread. It's too fattening. I have to watch my figure if I want to get ahead in the world. Why are you wearing that nightshirt?

LAWRENCE: I'd gone to bed. I wasn't feeling well. My leg hurts and I have a headache, and I have palpitations of the heart.

GINNY: I don't know. Hum a few bars, and I'll see.

LAWRENCE: We've met before, you know.

GINNY: I've never seen snow. Is it exciting?

LAWRENCE: We were in high school together. You were voted Girl Most Likely To Succeed. We sat next to one another in glee club.

GINNY: I'm sorry, I really can't hear you. You're talking too softly.

LAWRENCE (*louder*): You used to call me BLUE ROSES.

GINNY: Blue Roses? Oh yes, I remember, sort of. Why did I do that?

LAWRENCE: I had been absent from school for several months, and when I came back, you asked me where I'd been, and I said I'd been sick with viral pneumonia, but you thought I said "blue roses."

GINNY: I didn't get much of that, but I remember you now. You used to make a spectacle of yourself every day in glee class, clumping up the aisle with this great big noisy leg brace on your leg. God, you made a racket.

LAWRENCE: I was always so afraid people were looking at me, and pointing. But then eventually mama wouldn't let me wear the leg brace anymore. She gave it to the Salvation Army.

GINNY: I've never been in the army. How long were you in for?

LAWRENCE: I've never been in the army. I have asthma.

GINNY: You do? May I see it?

LAWRENCE (*confused*): See it?

GINNY: Well, sure, unless you don't want to.

LAWRENCE: Maybe you want to see my collection of glass cocktail stirrers. (*He limps to the table, and limps back to her, holding his collection.*)

LAWRENCE (*holds up a stick*): I call this one Stringbean, because it's long and thin.

GINNY: Thank you. (*Puts it in her glass and stirs it.*)

LAWRENCE (*fairly appalled*): They're not for use. (*Takes it back from her.*) They're a collection.

GINNY: Well, I guess I stirred it enough.

LAWRENCE: They're my favorite thing in the world. (*Holds up another one.*) I call this one Q-tip, because I realized it looks like a Q-tip, except it's made out of glass and doesn't have little cotton swabs at the end of it. (*She looks blank.*) Q-TIPS.

GINNY: Really? (*She takes it and puts it in her ear.*)

LAWRENCE: No! Don't put it in your ear. (*Take it back.*) Now it's disgusting.

GINNY: Well, I didn't think it was a Q-tip, but that's what you said it was.

LAWRENCE: I call it that. I think I'm going to throw it out now. (*Holds up another one.*) I call this one Pinocchio because if you hold it perpendicular to your nose it makes your nose look long. (*He holds it to his nose.*)

GINNY: Uh huh.

LAWRENCE: And I call this one Henry Kissinger, because he wears glasses and it's made of glass.

GINNY: Uh huh. (*Takes it and stirs her drink.*)

LAWRENCE: No! They're just for looking, not for stirring. Mama, she's making a mess with my collection.

AMANDA (*from off*): Oh shut up about your collection, honey, you're probably driving the poor girl bananas.

GINNY: No bananas, thank you! My nutritionist says I should avoid potassium. You know what I take your trouble to be, Lawrence?

LAWRENCE: Mama says I'm retarded.

GINNY: I know you're tired, I figured that's why you put on the nightshirt, but this won't take long. I judge you to be lacking in self-confidence. Am I right?

LAWRENCE: Well, I am afraid of people and things, and I have a lot of ailments.

GINNY: But that makes you special, Lawrence.

LAWRENCE: What does?

GINNY: I don't know. Whatever you said. And that's why you should present yourself with more confidence. Throw back your shoulders, and say, "HI! HOW YA DOIN'?" Now you try it.

LAWRENCE (*unenthusiastically, softly*): Hello, How are you?

GINNY (*looking at watch, in response to his supposed question*): I don't know, it's about 8:30, but this won't take long and then you can go to bed. Alright, now try it. (*Booming.*) "Hi! HOW YA DOIN'?"

LAWRENCE: Hi. How ya doin'?

GINNY: Now swagger a bit. (*Kinda butch.*) HI. HOW YA DOIN'?

LAWRENCE (*imitates her fairly successfully*): HI. HOW YA DOIN'?

GINNY: Good, Lawrence. That's much better, Again.

Amanda and Tom enter from behind them and watch this.

GINNY (*continued*): HI! HOW YA DOIN'?

LAWRENCE: HI! HOW YA DOIN'?

GINNY: THE BRAVES PLAYED A HELLUVA GAME, DON'TCHA THINK?

LAWRENCE: THE BRAVES PLAYED A HELLUVA GAME, DON'TCHA THINK?

AMANDA: Oh God I feel sorry for their children. Is this the only girl who works at the warehouse, Tom?

GINNY: HI, MRS. WINGVALLEY. YOUR SON LAWRENCE AND I ARE GETTING ON JUST FINE. AREN'T WE, LAWRENCE?

AMANDA: Please, no need to shout, I'm not deaf, even if you are.

GINNY: What?

AMANDA: I'm glad you like Lawrence.

GINNY: What?

AMANDA: I'M GLAD YOU LIKE LAWRENCE.

GINNY: What?

AMANDA: WHY DON'T YOU MARRY LAWRENCE?

GINNY (*looks shocked; has heard this*): Oh.

LAWRENCE: Oh, mama.

GINNY: Oh dear, I see. So that's why Shakespeare asked me here.

AMANDA (*to Tom*): Shakespeare?

TOM: The first day of work she asked my name, and I said Tom Wingvalley, and she thought I said Shakespeare.

GINNY: Oh dear, Mrs. Wingvalley, if I had a young brother as nice and as special as Lawrence is, I'd invite girls from the warehouse home to meet him too.

AMANDA: I'm sure I don't know what you mean.

GINNY: And you're probably hoping I'll say that I'll call again.

AMANDA: Really, we haven't even had dinner yet. Tom, shouldn't you be checkin' on the roast pigs feet?

TOM: I guess so. If anything interesting happens, call me. (*Exits.*)

GINNY: But I'm afraid I won't be calling on Lawrence again.

LAWRENCE: This is so embarrassing. I told you I wanted to stay in my room.

AMANDA: Hush up, Lawrence.

GINNY: But, Lawrence, I don't want you to think that I won't be calling because I don't like you. I do like you.

LAWRENCE: You do?

GINNY: Sure. I like everybody. But I got two time clocks to punch, Mrs. Wingvalley. One at the warehouse, and one at night.

AMANDA: At night? You have a second job? That is ambitious.

GINNY: Not a second job, ma'am. Betty.

AMANDA: Pardon?

GINNY: Now who's deaf, eh what? Betty. I'm involved with a girl named Betty. We've been going together for about a year. We're saving money so that we can buy a farmhouse and a tractor together. So you (*to Lawrence*) can see why I can't visit your son, though I wish I could. No hard feelings, Lawrence. You're a good kid.

LAWRENCE (*offers her another swizzle stick*): I want you to keep this. It's my very favorite one. I call it Thermometer because it looks like a thermometer.

GINNY: You want me to have this?

LAWRENCE: Yes, as a souvenir.

GINNY (*offended*) Well, there's no need to call me a queer. Fuck you and your stupid swizzle sticks. (*Throws the offered gift upstage.*)

LAWRENCE (*very upset*): You've broken it!

GINNY: What?

LAWRENCE: You've broken it. YOU'VE BROKEN IT.

GINNY: So I've broken it. Big fuckin' deal. You have twenty more of them here.

AMANDA: Well, I'm so sorry you have to be going.

GINNY: What?

AMANDA: Hadn't you better be going?

GINNY: What?

AMANDA: Go away!

GINNY: Well I guess I can tell when I'm not wanted. I guess I'll go now.

AMANDA: You and Betty must come over some evening. Preferably when we're out.

GINNY: I wasn't shouting. (*Calls off.*) So long, Shakespeare. See you at the warehouse. (*To Lawrence.*) So long, Lawrence. I hope your rash gets better.

LAWRENCE (*saddened, holding the broken swizzle stick*): You broke Thermometer.

GINNY: What?

LAWRENCE: YOU BROKE THERMOMETER!

GINNY: Well, what was a thermometer doing in with the swizzle sticks anyway?

LAWRENCE: Its name was Thermometer, you nitwit!

AMANDA: Let it go, Lawrence. There'll be other swizzle sticks. Good-bye, Virginia.

GINNY: I sure am hungry. Any chance I might be able to take a sandwich with me?

AMANDA: Certainly you can shake hands with me, if that will make you happy.

GINNY: I said I'm hungry.

AMANDA: Really, dear? What part of Hungary are you from?

GINNY: Oh never mind. I guess I'll go.

AMANDA: That's right. You have two time clocks. It must be getting near to when you punch in Betty.

GINNY: Well, so long, everybody. I had a nice time. (*Exits.*)

AMANDA: Tom, come in here please. Lawrence, I don't believe I would play the victrola right now.

LAWRENCE: What victrola?

AMANDA: Any victrola.

Enter Tom.

TOM: Yes, mother? Where's Ginny?

AMANDA: The feminine caller made a hasty departure.

TOM: Old four eyes bored her to death, huh?

LAWRENCE: Oh, drop dead.

TOM: We should have you institutionalized.

AMANDA: That's the first helpful thing you've said all evening, but first things first. You played a little joke on us, Tom.

TOM: What are you talking about?

AMANDA: You didn't mention that your friend is already spoken for.

TOM: Really? I didn't even think she liked men.

AMANDA: Yes, well. It seems odd that you know so little about a person you see everyday at the warehouse.

TOM: The warehouse is where I work, not where I know things about people.

AMANDA: The disgrace. The expense of the pigs feet, a new tie for Lawrence. And you — bringing a lesbian into this house. We haven't had a lesbian in this house since your grandmother died, and now you have the audacity to bring in that . . . that . . .

LAWRENCE: Dyke.

AMANDA: Thank you, Lawrence. That overbearing, booming-voiced bull dyke. Into a Christian home.

TOM: Oh look, who cares? No one in their right mind would marry four eyes here.

AMANDA: You have no Christian charity, or filial devotion, or fraternal affection.

TOM: I don't want to listen to this. I'm going to the movies.

AMANDA: You go to the movies to excess, Tom. It isn't healthy.

LAWRENCE: While you're out, could you stop at the liquor store and get me some more cocktail stirrers? She broke Thermometer, and she put Q-tip in her ear.

AMANDA: Listen to your brother, Tom. He's pathetic. How are we going to support ourselves once you go? And I know you want to leave. I've seen the brochure for the merchant marines in your underwear drawer. And the application to the Air Force. And your letter of inquiry to the Ballet Trockadero. So I'm not unaware of what you're thinking. But don't leave us until you fulfill your duties here, Tom. Help brother find a wife, or a job, or a doctor. Or consider euthanasia. But don't leave me here all alone, saddled with him.

LAWRENCE: Mama, don't you like me?

AMANDA: Of course, dear. I'm just making jokes.

LAWRENCE: Be careful of my asthma.

AMANDA: I'll try, dear. Now why don't you hold your breath in case you get a case of terminal hiccups?

LAWRENCE: Alright. (*Holds his breath.*)

TOM: I'm leaving.

AMANDA: Where are you going?

TOM: I'm going to the movies.

AMANDA: I don't believe you go to the movies. What did you see last night?

TOM: Hyapatia Lee in "Beaver City."

AMANDA: And the night before that?

TOM: I don't remember. "Humpy Busboys" or something.

AMANDA: Humpy what?

TOM: Nothing. Leave me alone.

AMANDA: These are not mainstream movies, Tom. Why can't you see a normal movie like "The Philadelphia Story." Or "The Bitter Tea of General Yen"?

TOM: Those movies were made in the 1930s.

AMANDA: They're still good today.

TOM: I don't want to have this conversation. I'm going to the movies.

AMANDA: That's right, go to the movies! Don't think about us, a mother alone, an unmarried brother who thinks he's crippled and has no job. Stop holding your breath, Lawrence, mama was kidding. (*Back to Tom.*) Don't let anything interfere with your selfish pleasure. Go see your pornographic trash that's worse than anything Mr. D. H. Lawrence ever envisioned. Just go, go, go — to the movies!

TOM: Alright, I will! And the more you shout about my selfishness and my taste in movies the quicker I'll go, and I won't just go to the movies!

AMANDA: Go then! Go to the moon — you selfish dreamer!

Tom exits.

AMANDA (*continued*): Oh Lawrence, honey, what's to become of us?

LAWRENCE: Tom forgot his newspaper, mama.

AMANDA: He forgot a lot more than that, Lawrence honey. He forgot his mama and brother.

Amanda and Lawrence stay in place. Tom enters down right and stands apart from them in a spot. He speaks to the audience.

TOM: I didn't go to the moon, I went to the movies. In Amsterdam. A long, lonely trip working my way on a freighter. They had good movies in Amsterdam. They weren't in English, but I didn't really care. And as for my mother and brother — well, I was adopted anyway. So I didn't miss them.

    Or at least so I thought. For something pursued me. It always came upon me unawares, it always caught me by surprise. Sometimes it would be a swizzle stick in someone's vodka glass, or sometimes it would just be a jar of pigs feet. But then all of a sudden my brother touches my shoulder, and my mother puts her hands around my neck, and everywhere I look I am reminded of them. And in all the bars I go to there are those damn swizzle sticks everywhere. I find myself thinking of my brother Lawrence. And of his collection of glass. And of my mother. I begin to think that their story would maybe make a good novel, or even a play. A mother's hopes, a brother's dreams. Pathos, humor, even tragedy. But then I lose interest. I really haven't the energy. So I'll leave them both, dimly lit, in my memory. For nowadays the world is lit by lightning, and when we get those colored lights going, it feels like I'm on LSD. Or some other drug. Or maybe it's the trick of memory, and the fact that life is very, very sad. Play with your cocktail stirrers, Lawrence. And so, good-bye.

AMANDA (*calling over in Tom's direction*): Tom, I hear you out on the porch talking. Who are you talking to?

TOM: No one, mother. I'm just on my way to the movies.

AMANDA: Well, try not to be too late, you have to work early at the warehouse tomorrow. And please don't bring home any visitors from the movies, I'm not up to it after that awful girl. Besides, if some sailor misses his boat, that's no reason you have to put him up in your room. You're too big-hearted, son.

TOM: Yes, mother. See you later. (*Exits.*)

LAWRENCE: Look at the light through the glass, mama. (*Looks through a swizzle stick.*) Isn't it amazin'?

AMANDA: Yes, I guess it is, Lawrence. Oh, but both my children are weird. What have I done, O Lord, to deserve them?

LAWRENCE: Just lucky, mama.

AMANDA: Don't make jokes, Lawrence. Your asthma. Your eczema. My life.

LAWRENCE: Don't be sad, mama. We have each other for company and amusement.

AMANDA: That's right. It's always darkest before the dawn. Or right before a typhoon sweeps up and kills everybody.

LAWRENCE: Oh, poor mama, let me try to cheer you up with my collection. Is that a good idea?

AMANDA: It's just great, Lawrence. Thank you.

LAWRENCE: I call this one Daffodil, because its yellow, and daffodils are yellow.

AMANDA: Uh huh.

LAWRENCE (*holds up another one*): And I call this one Curtain Rod because it reminds me of a curtain rod.

AMANDA: Uh huh.

LAWRENCE: And I call this one Ocean, because it's blue, and the ocean is . . .

AMANDA: I THOUGHT YOU CALLED THE BLUE ONE BLUE, YOU IDIOT CHILD! DO I HAVE TO LISTEN TO THIS PATHETIC PRATTLING THE REST OF MY LIFE??? CAN'T YOU AT LEAST BE CONSISTENT???

LAWRENCE (*pause, hurt*): No, I guess I can't.

AMANDA: Well, try, can't you? (*Silence.*) I'm sorry, Lawrence. I'm a little short-tempered today.

LAWRENCE: That's alright.

Silence.

AMANDA (*trying to make up*): Do you have any other swizzle sticks with names, Lawrence?

LAWRENCE: Yes, I do. (*Holds one up.*) I call this one "Mama." (*He throws it over his shoulder onto the floor.*)

AMANDA: Well, that's lovely, Lawrence, thank you.

LAWRENCE: I guess I can be a little short-tempered too.

AMANDA: Yes, well, whatever. I think we won't kill each other this evening, alright?

LAWRENCE: Alright.

AMANDA: I'll just distract myself from my rage and despair, and read about other people's rage and despair in the newspaper, shall I? (*Picks up Tom's newspaper.*) Your brother has the worst reading and viewing taste of any living creature. This is just a piece of filth. (*Reads.*) Man Has Sex With Chicken, Then Makes Casserole. (*Closes the paper.*) Disgusting. Oh, Lawrence honey, look — it's the Evening Star. (*She holds the paper out in front of them.*) Let's make a wish on it, honey, shall we?

LAWRENCE: Alright, mama.

Amanda holds up the newspaper, and she and Lawrence close their eyes and make a wish.

AMANDA: What did you wish for, darlin'?

LAWRENCE: More swizzle sticks.

AMANDA: You're so predictable, Lawrence. It's part of your charm, I guess.

LAWRENCE: What did you wish for, mama?

AMANDA: The same thing, honey. Maybe just a little happiness, too, but mostly just some more swizzle sticks.

Sad music. Amanda and Lawrence look up at the Evening Star. Fade to black.

ಙ

DAVID HENRY HWANG (*b. 1957*) *was born in Los Angeles and grew up as a second-generation Chinese American. His mother was a concert pianist, and his parents wanted him to study law, medicine, or business, but he found himself more attracted to the idea of becoming a writer, partly because he realized "it was something I wasn't supposed to be." At Stanford University, Hwang began reading and seeing* *productions of plays, and he found "it was a new excitement, like being in love." In the summer of 1978, while still a college student, he saw an ad in the* Los Angeles Times *for the Padua Hills Playwrights Festival, and he applied to the workshop to study playwriting with the dramatist and actor Sam Shepard. Hwang's application was accepted, and he credits Shepard as being an inspiring teacher. A year later, as a senior at Stanford University, Hwang directed his first play,* F.O.B., *in a dormitory lounge.* Family Devotions *and* The Dance and the Railroad, *the next two plays that Hwang considered part of a Chinese American trilogy along with* F.O.B., *were completed in 1981 and dedicated to Shepard.* F.O.B. *won an Obie award, and* The Dance and the Railroad, *adapted for television, won a CINE Golden Eagle award.*

As the Crow Flies (1983) is a one-act play based on the relationship between Hwang's grandmother and the woman who cleaned her house for many years. A symbolic work, the play dramatizes a theme central to Hwang's writing: the fluidity of personal identity. In an introduction to As the Crow Flies, *he explained the background of the play:*

> My grandmother is extremely stoic, kind of a tough cookie, and she does this thing that a lot of older Chinese people do. If I talk to her in English, it's no problem. But if one of my Caucasian friends talks to her in English, my grandmother never seems to understand. To the outside world she's like an odalisque, impenetrable.
>
> So I thought, well, she's had this black cleaning lady for years and there must be some relationship, some form of understanding that's developed there. And this person who cleaned for her also happened to have two identities. She had one name for work, and at home she put on a wig, used another name, and became a different person. This is actually true. I didn't make it up, it was just a matter of accurate reporting.

Hwang has said that he is acutely conscious of himself as an Asian American writing for the theater during a period of great social change in the United States.

> The Asian American theater movement has been important to me. Let's make an analogy between artistic development and one's personal development: if you grow up as a minority in this country there's a residual negativism that you take into your system, simply because of the racism in the air. You get to the point where you feel a certain amount of self-loathing and wonder if you don't measure up to certain things. One of the only ways to remedy that is for minority people to get together, segregate themselves for a while, and realize that they all have common experiences. You can sort of repair the damage that way.
>
> But once that's done I believe there's an obligation, at least if one is going to remain engaged in the American experiment, to reintegrate yourself into the larger society. In the long run, if the ethnic theaters do their jobs properly, they should phase out their own existence. I think the future is not in monoethnic theater, but in multicultural theaters that will do a black play, an Asian play, a white play, whatever.
>
> Our country's in a transitional phase now. Over the next twenty or thirty years we're really going to see the emergence of minorities, with Caucasians becoming the plurality rather than the majority. That realignment is going to be scary and hard, but this place is such a great laboratory. You have

> *people from all these different cultures who interact intimately: some hold on*
> *to their cultures, come don't, some hate other ethnic groups, some couldn't care*
> *less — it's such an interesting scheme of things. And within all the attitudes*
> *we find here there's so much to discover about how people of different nation-*
> *alities and cultures have always looked at each other, throughout history.*

In 1988 Hwang became the first Chinese American dramatist to win the Tony
Award for best play, with his Broadway hit M. Butterfly. He has written the libretto
for Philip Glass's opera The Voyage, an allegory about Christopher Columbus's ar-
rival in America, which premiered at the Metropolitan Opera in 1992. Hwang is codi-
rector of the Asian American Theater Company in San Francisco and has received
playwriting fellowships from the Rockefeller Foundation, the Guggenheim Founda-
tion, and the National Endowment for the Arts.
> **RELATED COMMENTARY:** *David Henry Hwang, "Evolving a Multicultural Tra-*
> *dition," page 1987.*

DAVID HENRY HWANG

As the Crow Flies   1983

A living room in an upper-middle-class home, owned by Mrs. Chan, a Chinese woman
in her seventies, and her husband, P.K. Up right, a door leads out to the front drive-
way. Stage left is a door leading to the rest of the house. Mrs. Chan sits in a large chair,
centerstage, looking downstage out into a garden. Around her, Hannah, a black
woman in her late sixties, cleans. She has been their cleaning woman for over a decade.

HANNAH: I guess I never told you this before, Mrs. Chan, but I think the time is
     right now. See, I'm really two different folks. You've been knowin' me as
     Hannah Carter, 'cuz when I'm over here cleanin', that's who I am. But at
     night, or when I'm outside and stuff, I turn into Sandra Smith. (*Beat.*) Is
     that all clear?
CHAN: Um. Yeah.
HANNAH: You got all that?
CHAN: When you are here, you are Hannah Carter —
HANNAH: Right.
CHAN: And, then, you go outside, and you are . . . someone . . . someone . . .
HANNAH: Sandra Smith.
CHAN: Um. Okay.

Pause.

HANNAH: You don't have any questions 'bout that?
CHAN: Hannah Carter, Sandra Smith — I understand.
HANNAH: Well, you know how you can tell the two apart?
CHAN: No. Because I have not seen Sandra — Sandra . . .
HANNAH: Smith. Well, when I'm Sandra Smith, see, I look different. First of all,
     I'm a lot younger.

CHAN: Good.

HANNAH: And, you know, since I'm younger, well, guess I'm looser, too. What I mean by that, is, when I talk, well, I use different words. Young words. And, Mrs. Chan, since I'm younger, my hair color's a lot different too. And I don't clean floors. 'Cuz young people nowadays, they don't clean floors. They stay up around the clock, and make themselves into lazy good-for-nothings, and drink a lot, and dance themselves into a state. Young people — I just don't know what's got into them. But whatever it is, the same thing's gotten into Sandra Smith. (*Pause.*) You don't think this is all a little strange?

CHAN: No.

HANNAH: Well, that's the first time . . . I remember when I told Mrs. Washburn about Sandra Smith — she just fell right over.

CHAN: So what? So you have two different people.

HANNAH: That's right. Living inside me.

CHAN: So what? My uncle had six!

HANNAH: Six people?

CHAN: Maybe even seven. Who can keep count?

HANNAH: Seven? All in one guy?

CHAN: Way back in China — my second uncle — he had seven, maybe even eight people — inside here. I don't . . . is hard to remember all their name.

HANNAH: I can believe that.

CHAN: Chan Yup Lee — he was, uh, I think, the businessman. He runs Uncle's import-export association. Good man. Very stingy. I like him. Then, I think there was another: ah, C. Y. Sing — he is the family man. Then, one man, Fat-Fingers Lew. Introduce this sport — what is the name? Ball goes through big hoop.

HANNAH: Basketball?

CHAN: Yes, yes — introduce that to our village. Then, there is Big Far Tong — collects debt for C.Y.'s company. Never talks, only fight. Then, also, one who has been to America — Morty Fong. He all the time warns us about Communists. And, then, oh, maybe two or three others that I hardly ever meet.

HANNAH: This is all one guy?

CHAN: Mmmmm.

HANNAH: Isn't that somethin'?

CHAN: No.

HANNAH: Huh?

CHAN: Whatever you can tell me — man with six persons inside, man with three heads, man who sees a flying ghost, a sitting ghost, a ghost disguise to look like his dead wife — none of these are so unusual.

HANNAH: No?

CHAN: I have lived a long time.

HANNAH: Well, so have I, Mrs. Chan, so have I. And I'm still scared of Sandra Smith.

CHAN: Scare? Why scare? Happens all the time.

HANNAH: I don't want Sandra comin' round to any of my houses that I clean.

CHAN: Aaah — do not worry.

HANNAH: Whaddya mean? Sandra's got no respect for authority.

CHAN: Do not worry. She will not come into any house.

HANNAH: What makes you so sure?

CHAN: You have to know how ghosts think. You say, Sandra appears outdoors. Therefore, she is the outside ghost. She cannot come inside.

HANNAH: Yeah? They got rules like that? In ghost-land?

CHAN: Yes — there are rules everyplace! Have you ever been someplace where there were none?

HANNAH: Well, no, but —

CHAN: You see? Ghosts cannot kill a man if there is a goldfish in the room. They will think the fish is gold, and take it instead. They cannot enter a house if there is a raised step in the doorway. Ghosts do not look, so they trip over it instead.

HANNAH: These ghosts don't sound like they got a lot on the ball.

CHAN: Some ghosts, they are smart. But most ghosts, they are like most people. When alive, they were stupid. After death, they remain the same.

HANNAH: Well, I don't think Sandra's got much respect for those rules. That's probably why she showed up at Mrs. Washburn's.

CHAN: Inside the house?

HANNAH: 'Fraid so.

CHAN: Oh. Mrs. Washburn — does she have a goldfish?

HANNAH: No, no — I don't think so.

CHAN: There — you see?

HANNAH: Anyway, Mrs. Chan, I just thought I oughta tell you about her, on account of what happened to Mrs. Washburn. I been working for all you people ten, sometimes twenty years. All my clients — they're gettin' up there. We're all startin' to show our age. Can't compete with the young girls no more.

CHAN: I never try — even when I was one.

HANNAH: Well, the older I get, the more I see of Sandra, so I just thought I oughta be warnin' you.

CHAN: I am not afraid of Sandra Smith.

HANNAH: Well, good then. Good for you.

CHAN: She comes here, I will fight her. Not like these Americans. So stupid. Never think of these things. Never think of ghost. Never think of death. Never prepare for anything. Always think, life goes on and on, forever. And so, always, it ends.

HANNAH: Okay. Glad to hear it. Guess I'll go take the slime off the shower walls.

Hannah exits, into the house. Chan just stares downstage, from her chair. Silence. P.K. enters from the driveway, golf clubs slung over his shoulder.

P.K.: Hi, Popo!

CHAN: Hello.

P.K.: Do you have a beer?

CHAN: Look in 'frigerator.

P.K.: Just return from a good game of golf!

CHAN: Ah! What are you talking about?

P.K.: Eighteen holes, Popo!

CHAN: Ai! You cannot remember anything anymore!

P.K.: So? I remember that I go to golf!

CHAN: How can this be? You do not drive!

P.K.: What do you mean? I drive the Eldorado.

CHAN: You cannot drive the Eldorado.

P.K.: I do!

CHAN: Hanh! We sell it many years ago!

P.K.: What?

CHAN: Yes! Remember? We sell it! To John, your nephew.

P.K.: Huh? How much did he pay?

CHAN: Who cares?

P.K.: I want to know!

CHAN: I always tell you, John buys the car; you always ask me, how much does
    he pay?

P.K.: It is important! It is worth — lots of money!

CHAN: Ah, not so much money.

P.K.: No! Lots!

CHAN: Not after Humphrey breaks the back window by trying to lower top
    while driving.

P.K.: Yes! I tell Humphrey — cannot lower while driving. He says, "Of course!
    Can! This is a luxury car!" How come we sell the car?

CHAN: Ah! You cannot remember anything!

P.K.: No. Gung Gung cannot remember anything anymore.

CHAN: We sell, because you can no longer drive.

P.K.: I can! I can!

CHAN: You cannot pass the test.

P.K.: Can Humphrey pass the test?

CHAN: Of course! Of course, he passes it.

P.K.: How can? He is the one who lowers top while driving!

CHAN: Gung Gung! Because he is young, so he can pass the test!

P.K.: Young, but not so smart.

CHAN: Stupid.

P.K.: Sometimes, stupid.

CHAN: Stupid does not matter. Many stupid people drive.

Pause.

P.K.: So I did not go to golf?

CHAN: No! How can you go to golf? You cannot go anyplace.

P.K. (*points to clubs*): Then, what are these?

CHAN: You just put them on your shoulder, then walk outside. Two hour later,
    you return.

P.K.: Where did I go?

CHAN: I don't know! You tell me!

P.K.: I cannot remember anything, anymore. I thought that I go to play eighteen-hole golf. But there is no golf course. So perhaps I walk into those hills. Maybe I shoot a few balls in the hills. Maybe I sink a putt into a gopher hole.

Pause.

CHAN: Gung Gung.

P.K.: Yes, Popo?

CHAN: I saw a ghost today.

P.K.: Popo! A ghost?

CHAN: Yes — a warning ghost.

P.K.: Which is this?

CHAN: They warn that another ghost will soon come. Bigger. More dangerous. Fatter.

P.K.: Oh! Popo! Why do they send this warning ghost?

CHAN: Because, they are stupid! This is how, they become dead to begin with. Because when they were living, they were too stupid to listen to the warning ghost!

P.K.: Popo! Will you die? (*He starts to cry.*) What will Gung Gung do without you?

CHAN: No.

P.K.: Without Popo, I will be completely all lost.

CHAN: No, Gung Gung.

P.K.: I will walk around all day, not know where I am going, not know where I come from, only saying, "Popo? Where is Popo? Where is — ?"

CHAN: No! Will you listen to me? You ask the question, then you will not listen to the answer! Talk, talk, talk! If I die, leave you alone, I would be lucky!

P.K.: You mean, you will not die?

CHAN: No, I will not die.

P.K.: How can this be?

CHAN: They are stupid enough to send the warning ghost. This is how I know, they will not defeat me.

P.K.: But, when the ghost come, no one can resist.

CHAN: Who says this?

P.K.: Ummm . . .

CHAN: See? Maybe, Gung Gung, *you* cannot resist.

P.K.: No. I cannot resist.

CHAN: But you have no responsibilities. I have. I have responsibility. I cannot leave you alone, Gung Gung. And also, I must watch the grandchildren grow to adults.

P.K.: Yes — this would be good.

CHAN: So, you see, I cannot die.

P.K.: This makes me so happy.

CHAN: I will defeat the ghost.

P.K.: Yes! Popo! You can do it! Popo is very smart!

CHAN: Yeah, yeah, yeah, we all know this already.

P.K.: I am fortunate to marry such a smart wife.

CHAN: Not smart. Smart is not enough.

P.K.: More than smart.

CHAN: Fight. Fight is more important. I am willing to fight. I like to fight.

Pause.

P.K.: Why do I carry these golf clubs?

CHAN: I do not know! You ask so many times already!

P.K.: Oh — I suppose — I must go to golf.

Pause.

CHAN: Yes — you must go to golf.

P.K.: Okay. I will leave now. Take the Eldorado. Bye, Popo.

CHAN: Bye, Gung Gung.

P.K.: You will have a cold can of beer in the 'frigerator, for when I return?

CHAN: I will, Gung Gung. I will.

P.K. starts to exit out the upstage door.

   Gung Gung!

P.K.: Yes, Popo?

CHAN: Have a good game, okay, Gung Gung?

P.K.: I will have a good game, okay, Popo. (*He exits.*)

CHAN: I arrive in America one day, June 16, 1976. Many times, I have come here
    before, to visit children, but on this day, I arrive to stay. All my friends,
    all the Chinese in the Philippine, they tell me, "We thought you are stu-
    pid when you send all your children to America. We even feel sorry for
    you, that you will grow old all alone — no family around you." This is
    what they tell me.

       The day I arrive in America, I do not feel sorry. I do not miss the
    Philippine, I do not look forward live in America. Just like, I do not miss
    China, when I leave it many years ago — go live in Philippine. Just like,
    I do not miss Manila, when Japanese take our home during wartime,
    and we are all have to move to Baguio, and live in haunted house. It is
    all same to me. Go, one home to the next, one city to another, nation to
    nation, across ocean big and small.

       We are born traveling. We travel — all our lives. I am not looking
    for a home. I know there is none. The day I was marry, my mother put
    many gold bracelets on my arm, and so many necklaces that the back of
    my head grows sore. "These," she tells me. "These are for the times
    when you will have to run."

*The upstage door opens. Hannah is standing there, dressed as Sandra Smith. Sandra
wears a bright orange fright wig and a tight dress, sports huge sunglasses, and swings
a small purse.*

SANDRA: Well, hello there! Howdy, howdy, howdy!

CHAN: Hi.

SANDRA: Say, you seen Hannah? Hannah Carter? I understand she works here
    on Wednesdays.

CHAN: I think, she just leave.

SANDRA: Oh, well, that's a shame. I usually don't get to visit where she works. We were supposed to go for dinner at Chicken on Fire, but, looks like we're just not connecting. Damn! Always happens, whenever I try to meet her at one of these houses.

CHAN: So, would you like to go home, now?

SANDRA: Mmmm. Guess I could, but I wouldn't mind enjoying some of your hospitality.

CHAN: What is this, hospitality?

SANDRA: You know. What you show your guests.

CHAN: We do not have guests here! Only relatives, and, ah, servants.

SANDRA: Well, what do you do when someone comes over?

CHAN: They tell me what they want. Then, they leave.

SANDRA: No time to socialize?

CHAN: What is, socialize?

SANDRA: You know. You're not gonna offer me a tea, coffee, cake, Sanka?

CHAN: No.

SANDRA: I can't hardly believe this house.

CHAN: People — they are like cats. If you feed them, they will always return.

SANDRA: What ever happened to old-fashioned manners?

CHAN: My manners — they are very old. We act like this for centuries.

SANDRA: My name's Sandra. Sandra Smith.

CHAN: This is no surprise. Are you finish, now? Hannah is not here.

SANDRA: No — I can see that. (*Pause.*) You know, I've known Hannah — well, ever since she was a little girl. She wasn't very pretty. No one in Louisville paid much attention to her. Yeah, she's had five husbands and all, okay, that's true, but my personal guess is that most of 'em married her because she was a hard-working woman who could bring home the bacon week after week. Certain men will hold their noses for a free lunch. Hannah thinks the same thing, though she hardly ever talks about it. How can she think anything else when all five of them left her as soon as they got a whiff of some girl with pipe cleaners for legs? Hard for her to think she's much more than some mule, placed on this earth to work her back. She spends most of her life wanderin' from one beautiful house to the next, knowing intimately every detail, but never layin' down her head in any of 'em. She's what they call a good woman. Men know it, rich folks know it. Everyplace is beautiful, 'cept the place where she lives. Home is a dark room, she knows it well, knows its limits. She knows she can't travel nowhere without returnin' to that room once the sun goes down. Home is fixed, it does not move, even as the rest of the world circles 'round and 'round, picking up speed.

CHAN: You are a ghost.

SANDRA: I have a good time, if that's what you mean.

CHAN: I was warned that you would come.

SANDRA: By Hannah? She's always tellin' people about me. Like I was some kinda celebrity or somethin'.

CHAN: I fight ghosts. I chase them.

SANDRA: Can't chase anything, unless you get it runnin' from ya first.

CHAN: In Baguio, we live in a haunted house.

SANDRA: In where?

CHAN: Baguio. In the Philippine.

SANDRA: I never been there.

CHAN: During the war, we live in a haunted house. I chase the ghost out, with pots and pan. So, I know I can defeat them.

SANDRA: Hannah — she lives in a haunted house right now.

CHAN: Yes — haunted with you.

SANDRA: I show her how to make her life a little easier. Someone's gotta do it, after all her sixty-some-odd years. How 'bout you? Anything I can help you with?

CHAN: Ha! I do not need a thing!

SANDRA: I'm not sure if I believe that, Mrs. . . . . Mrs. . . . . whatever. Hannah sees you sittin' here, day after day —

CHAN: I am old! Of course I sit!

SANDRA: — starin' out into that garden —

CHAN: So?

SANDRA: First off, it's mostly dirt.

CHAN: This way, easier to take care of.

SANDRA: But you stare like there's somethin' out there.

CHAN: Yes! The sun is out there!

SANDRA: Lookin' at the sun, Mrs. — ma'am? Gotta be careful you don't burn your eyeballs out.

CHAN: I only look outside because — sky, clouds, sun — they are all there — interesting to watch.

SANDRA: Real pretty, huh?

CHAN: Yes. Sometimes pretty.

SANDRA: Looks like home.

CHAN: What is this? All the time, you talk about home, home, home?

SANDRA: Just like you do.

CHAN: I never talk about home. Barely talk at all.

SANDRA: You think you keep your lips buttoned, that means all your secrets are safe inside? If they're strong enough, things make themselves known, one way or another. Hannah knows, she's not stupid. She'd never tell anyone but me. But me, I'd tell anybody. (*Pause.*) Want me to tell you?

CHAN: Tell me what?

SANDRA: What you're lookin' at out there?

Pause.

CHAN: I can defeat you. I defeat ghost before.

SANDRA: Honey, it's not a fight no more. I've been around fifteen years. I already know you. You know me. We see the same thing. Out there. (*Pause.*) There's a crow sitting on a window sill. And two kids who chase it down a steep ravine. Their path grows darker and darker, but the crow continues, and the kids don't tire, even when the blisters start to show on their feet. Mud, sleet, rain, and snow, all try to make the kids give up the chase. The crow caws — mountains fall in its wake, but still the childrcn continue. And then it becomes dark, so dark, and the crow throws disasters at their feet. Floods, droughts, wars. The children see nothing, now. They follow the crow only by the catastrophes it leaves in its path. Where there is famine, the crow must have been. Where there are earthquakes, it has rested. They run on faith now, passing through territories uncharted, following the sound of their suffering. And it is in this way that they pass through their lives. Hardly noticing that they've entered. Without stopping to note its passing. Just following a crow, with single dedication, forgetting how they started, or why they're chasing, or even what may happen if they catch it. Running without pause or pleasure, past the point of their beginning.

Over the next section, Mrs. Chan's dress slowly rises into the air. She wears a white slip beneath. She stands up from the chair, for the first time in the play, and walks over to Sandra.

I see it in the distance.

CHAN: It is waiting for me.

SANDRA: I cannot stop my running.

CHAN: I cannot rest, even for a second.

SANDRA: There's a field out in the distance.

CHAN: There's a wooden gate in that field.

SANDRA: There is a crow sitting on that gate.

CHAN: It caws.

SANDRA: It caws.

CHAN: And disaster comes.

SANDRA: Once again.

CHAN: Nothing new.

SANDRA: Nothing blue.

CHAN: Only the scent of home.

SANDRA: I don't know why I follow it.

CHAN: I don't care to know.

SANDRA: Not now.

CHAN: Not here.

SANDRA: Not ever. Perhaps someday.

CHAN: Maybe to remember.

SANDRA: Why I run.

CHAN: Why I chase.

SANDRA: Until I am so —

CHAN: So tired.

SANDRA: Another disaster.

CHAN: Another lonely child.

SANDRA: We follow the scent of home.

Sandra removes her wig, glasses, tight dress. She too wears a white slip. She is Hannah again. Mrs. Chan moves towards the door. Hannah ever so slowly lowers herself into Mrs. Chan's chair. Hannah sits in it, beams.

HANNAH: Ooooh. Nice home, Mrs. Chan.

CHAN: I see it.

HANNAH: So do I, so do I.

CHAN: I see all the way past those mountains.

HANNAH: Welcome home, Mrs. Chan.

CHAN: Welcome home, Hannah.

Mrs. Chan exits through the garden. Hannah looks around her like a kid with a new toy. Upstage, P.K. enters with golf clubs. He cannot see Hannah in the chair.

P.K.: Hi, Popo! (*Pause.*) Where is my beer?

Hannah closes her eyes, a smile on her face.

You leave a beer in the 'frigerator? (*Pause.*) Popo? Popo?

P.K. is walking towards the chair as lights fade to black.

26

COMMENTARIES ON PLAYS AND PLAYWRIGHTS

EDWARD ALBEE *often discusses various topics relating to his work as a playwright. This commentary was originally published in* Dramatics *magazine.*

EDWARD ALBEE

On Playwriting   1989

There are a couple of things you should know. I am a playwright. I've written twenty-six plays, I think, in the past thirty-three years, which makes me a little less lazy than I sometimes think I am. Some of them have been very popular, which means people have come to see them. Some have been very unpopular.

Sometimes, being a little protective of the least popular, sometimes I think the least popular ones are superior to the more popular ones. One of the things you learn very quickly in our society is that there is not necessarily much relationship between popularity and excellence. Quite often the very best stuff is participated in by the fewest people. But you mustn't fall into the trap, either, of assuming that because nobody likes what you have done it is very good. Sometimes people don't like what you've done because it is terrible. We'll talk about that possibility, too.

It is a tough racket. It can be pretty heartbreaking, and you really have to, deep down, have a toughness to yourself, or you're not going to be able to survive in the theatre.

ON WHERE THE IDEAS FOR PLAYS COME FROM

Damned if I know. All of a sudden one day I'll be going about my own business, walking around or something, and I'll suddenly realize that I must have been thinking about a play for quite a while, even though I didn't know I was thinking about it. Because by the time I become aware that I have been thinking about a play, it's coming along quite nicely. The characters are there, the situation has begun to create itself.

I'm sure the creativity, where the ideas come from, comes from the unconscious part of the mind, which as you know makes up 90 percent of the mind. I'm convinced that is where the ideas originate, they evolve and eventually enter into the conscious mind. You keep working on them, and then eventually you write them down.

ON HIS METHOD OF WORKING

When I sit down I don't know what the first line of the play is going to be. I know what the destination is, but I don't have any idea necessarily how I am going to get there. I believe in letting the characters determine that in their situation. How they behave determines where it goes.

I try to stand back and sort of push them and guide them so the thing won't go off in all sorts of directions that it shouldn't go off in. I believe that when the characters do that it's really me doing that, since the characters can't do anything unless I tell them what to do. They don't exist. They really do exist, but they don't. They can't say anything unless I write it down for them. It is a trick you play on yourself, thinking that the characters are doing your work when really you're doing it and assigning it to the various characters.

I'm not one of these playwrights — and I'm not saying you shouldn't be this kind of playwright — I'm not one of these playwrights who writes a twenty-five-page synopsis of what the play is going to be about. I don't write down histories of the natures of the characters. I don't plot out each scene before I write it.

The only thing I do is when it is ready, when it is time to start writing something down, I wait longer than most playwrights do. Sometimes I keep an idea in my head five or six years before I'll write it down. I start at the beginning and write straight through to the end. That's the way I write. It's nice that way. You have lots of surprises. You discover all sorts of things that you were planning to do that you didn't know you were going to do.

ON THE IDEAL CONDITIONS FOR WRITING

I think it is probably better to be awake, sober, and drug-free. I suspect those three conditions are probably helpful. But beyond that, I just have to feel like writing. I'm not one of these people who goes to the desk every single day and writes. I wait until my head gets filled with stuff and I have to get it out of my head.

I used to drink occasionally and take a little grass now and again back when I was real young. And I thought that I could write an awful lot better if

I did. But it wasn't very good. It seemed wonderful at the time. Marvelous. I'd look at it the next day and say, "What the hell was that all about?"

ON THE IMPORTANCE OF CONFLICT IN DRAMA

Plays are basically about something that is wrong. Plays are about people that are not getting along with each other terribly well. Situations that are wrong. Most serious plays, good plays, are about something that's wrong that should be corrected. You can't write a very good play about a bunch of people getting along with each other very, very well and there is absolutely no argument. You can't do it. It's not going to be a play. There has to be conflict. And until the conflict is resolved there is tension, because of the conflict. People in conflict with each other, people in conflict with society, their government, philosophically, politically, socially. There is conflict and conflict produces tension. And the solution to the problem releases tension and that is probably when the play should end.

ON A PLAYWRIGHT'S SOURCES OF THE DETAILS OF CHARACTER

You keep your eyes and ears open and store it away until you need it. Part of it comes from yourself. You can't write a character unless you can get inside the character and imagine the way the character thinks.

And the rest you make up. You invent. That's why you're able to write men, women, young people, old people, black, white, no matter who or what you are. It's your responsibility and your ability to be able to do all that. You have to be able to put yourself into whatever character you are writing. So you look and listen and make things up.

ON STUDYING THE WORK OF OTHER PLAYWRIGHTS

There are some twentieth-century playwrights that I think it is very important for anybody who wants to be a playwright to know about. You start with Chekhov, one of the first great playwrights of the twentieth century. Then you have Pirandello, an extraordinary playwright that not enough people know about. And there is Brecht, a real interesting playwright, and Samuel Beckett, who may be the best of the bunch. He and Chekhov may be the best of the bunch. You have those four. That's a pretty good group to study.

But let me tell you one thing, if you are going to learn from other writers, don't only read the great ones, because if you do that you'll get so filled with despair and the fear that you'll never be able to do anywhere near as well as they did that you'll stop writing. I recommend that you read a lot of bad stuff, too. It's very encouraging. "Hey, I can do so much better than this." Read the greatest stuff but read the stuff that isn't so great, too. Great stuff is very discouraging. If you read only Beckett and Chekhov you'll go away and only deliver telegrams at Western Union.

ON BEING TRUE TO ONE'S OWN VISION

They tell you that commercial plays should be a little over two hours long. A play should be as long as it needs to be. It can be ten minutes, it can be seven hours. What should the play be about? It should be about whatever you can make a stage experience, only that. Whatever you can make valid. What style should it be written in? Whatever style is right for the play.

There are no limits, you see, except succeeding at what you do. In the commercial theatre they want certain things. They want happy problems. They want the plays to be a certain length. They want everybody to be able to walk out of the theatre fairly happy. If it can be a musical, so much the better. That's what the commercial theatre is all about. If you're that kind of a writer, okay. But if you're the kind of writer who wants to write a very grim, seven-hour play, then that's what you should write. If you want to write a play so angry, so filled with rage, that it practically takes the audience and hits them in the head or slaps them in the face, then that's the kind of play you should write.

You should write exactly what the play needs to be and pay no attention to anything else. That's all that matters. The rest is commerce, the rest is compromise. You'll be asked to do a lot of that, but hold off. One of the lovely things about being a playwright is that you can do whatever you want to do. While a lot of people would rather you do something else, they can't stop you.

ON COLLABORATION

Now, if you're in rehearsal for the first time with your play and the director says to you, maybe that scene is a little long, you may want to think about cutting it. Pay a little attention; maybe the director is right.

You go back and you look at the scene and say yes, that scene seems long. Then you have to say to yourself, does this scene seem long because I wrote it too long or because of the way it is being directed? If the director directed it differently would it still seem too long? So maybe you will ask that the scene be directed differently.

If you realize the scene is too long no matter how it is directed, then you realize, gee, I wrote this scene too long, maybe I better cut it a little bit. Then you make your own cuts. You have to be very careful because sometimes suggestions are not made to help the play but to help actors or to make things easier. You have the right to not change anything, but don't be a fool. Change things if somebody else is right.

But if you do change something because somebody else is right, you must instantly take credit for it yourself. That's very important.

രു

RICHARD AMACHER *analyzed Albee's short experimental plays in the chapter entitled "Pity and Fear in Miniature" in his study* Edward Albee *(1982). Before discussing the characters in* The Sandbox, *Amacher dissected the plot of the drama. According to his scheme, Scene 1 (exposition) introduces the characters and Mommy's scheme to get rid of Grandma. Scenes 2 through 5 (rising action) show the failure of her plan. Scene 6 (climax and conclusion) brings an unexpected turn of events that ultimately satisfies our expectations.*

RICHARD AMACHER

On *The Sandbox*   *1982*

THE CHARACTERS IN CONFLICT

The five characters in the play have obviously been selected with great care and in accord with the artistic principle of economy of means. Grandma, for example, is not only the leading character, or *protagonist*, but also the *chorus*. Her mimicking of Mommy and her mocking of Daddy, as well as her early cries, some of which are like screams of antagonism or growls of disgust, reinforce the self-revealing speeches of these two unsympathetic characters, just as the chanted explanations of the Greek chorus in ancient tragedies underlined similar aspects of the characterization and the action. In one or two places Grandma also functions as the stage manager or director, for she calls out directions to the stage hand about dimming the lights and she tells the musician how to play his music — "Keep it nice and soft" — in the night scene signifying the approach of death.

Study of the conflicting forces in *The Sandbox* shows us how central the character of Grandma is. On the surface, it appears that we have two pairs of characters struggling against each other — Mommy and Daddy in the antagonist group (who are really trying to bury Grandma, as we see by their symbolic action of heartlessly dumping her into the sandbox); and Grandma and the Young Man in the protagonist group. This ostensible pairing of unsympathetic and sympathetic characters overshadows a less obvious conflict — that between Grandma, an admirable old lady full of spiritual vitality, and the Young Man, the Angel of Death. Despite the Young Man's modesty and politeness, he is, after all, the Angel of Death; and while Grandma recognizes that her life cannot go on forever, she nevertheless still has a certain spark of spunky rebelliousness and fight left in her — enough, as a matter of fact, so that the manner of her final encounter with death becomes a suspenseful question: Will she fight to the end? Or will she resign herself to the inevitable — the superior power of the Angel of Death?

Grandma struggles against the injustice of her daughter's and her son-in-law's treatment of her more than she does against the Young Man, whom she finds attractive, pleasant, sympathetic. Although his approach is gradual, he, when the time comes, accomplishes his work quickly and efficiently — even apologetically, so polite is he — with a kiss and a laying on of hands that resembles a benediction. This kind of treatment Grandma will accept. But in resentment of her daughter's and son-in-law's standing around and not only waiting for her to die but even hastening the process, she throws sand and yells at them menacingly.

In the course of the action, Grandma moves from *"puzzlement and fear"* to acceptance. When she says "You're welcome . . . dear" to the Angel of Death at the end of the play, we see her conquer her fear of the unknown and admire her all the more. We begin to sense her heroic nature, for it is death and dying she struggles against, sympathetic as the Young Man, to her surprise, and relief, finally turns out to be after her discovery of his essential nature.

Grandma is just as sensitive to the Young Man's physical power and beauty as Mommy — in fact, more so. When he flexes his muscles for her and asks, "Isn't that something?," she answers, "Boy, oh boy; I'll say. Pretty good." Her conversation with and admiration of the Young Man is interspersed with the story of her life and hard times, which arouses sympathy for her, particularly as she stresses the fact that she is neither complaining nor feeling sorry for herself.

PITY AND FEAR: AROUSAL AND PURGATION

Grandma effectively arouses pity and fear in the audience. We *pity* her because she deserves better than she has received. After the early death of her husband, after a hard life spent in sacrificing to her undeserving daughter, after being uprooted from her natural setting on the farm (her husband having been a farmer) and transported to the city, where she was treated like a dog, she deserves something more than merely dying. But it would be unrealistic for her not to die, for the expectation of her dying has been established from almost the beginning of this play when she is carried in and dumped in the sandbox.

We *fear* for Grandma because in Aristotelian terms she is a person like ourselves — neither entirely good nor bad. In addition, her fragility, because of her great age as well as because of the great powers arrayed against her — Mommy with her "imposing" vigor, Daddy with his wealth, the Young Man with his immense power as the Angel of Death — makes us sense that her position is indeed precarious. The four off-stage rumbles especially arouse in the audience a feeling of the Young Man's power; and, since we tend to identify ourselves with Grandma, fear is aroused in us. The arousal of this fear continues until the point where the Young Man kisses her; then we are fearful that he may severely hurt her. After all, there are various ways of suffering in the death of the body.

Purgation of fear and pity in *The Sandbox* results from the demonstration that Grandma is not going to suffer more — from our comprehension that death, contrary to our usual expectations, is, for her, a sweet, welcome experience. If pity and fear are not only effectively aroused but also competently purged in this play, if these are the distinctive and characteristic emotions making up the effect of the play, we must conclude that the play is a *tragedy*. And so it is — a serious tragedy — well flavored with irony and absurdity — from Grandma's juvenile antics in the sandbox and her reference to her daughter as a "big cow" to the awkward embarrassment of the Young Man. Touches like these may not exhale the high seriousness of tone that critics like [Joseph] Krutch might like to find in modern tragedy, but we must remember that we are living in the age of the "absurd."

There are, quite naturally, different kinds of tragedy. Aristotle lists two general directions that the turn of fortune may take — either from good to bad or from bad to good. In *The Sandbox* the turn seems to be the second kind, and Grandma goes from a state of querulousness and rebellion, mostly against her daughter, to one of insight, acceptance, and peace. Beyond the essential brevity of the action imitated in the play, the use of music, an equivalent of "Song" in Aristotle's list of the essential parts of tragedy (see *Poetics*), gives *The Sandbox* a certain Grecian lyrical quality.

As mentioned earlier, Grandma acts as chorus in talking directly to the audience, as she provides the exposition about her past and complains about her daughter's treatment of her. In at least two speeches Mommy also plays this role of chorus, but Albee has her talk superciliously *"out over the audience,"* when she complains about Grandma's throwing sand at her. But more important than this incidental use of the characters for chorus effects is the way both the music and the Musician, as an actual character in the play, function as chorus.

The Sandbox, Albee's second one-act tragedy, was well received. And although it may be argued that its frequent revivals have resulted from its relative ease and cheapness of production, its popularity, in our opinion, is also due to its enduring merits as a work of art.

ৡৄ

ARISTOTLE *(384–322 B.C.), the Greek philosopher, included an analysis of tragedy in* Poetics *a century after Sophocles' plays were performed during the Great Dionysia in Athens. A student of Plato, Aristotle founded his own school, called the Lyceum, where he lectured on philosophy, science, and the arts. His lectures or treatises were so insightful that they were preserved by his students, and nearly two thousand years later, they form the basis of literary criticism. As the critic Lee Jacobus points out, Aristotle's work not only provides insight into the theoretical basis of the work of the Greek playwrights, but it also "helps us see that the drama was significant enough in Greek intellectual life to warrant an examination by the most influential Greek minds."*

ARISTOTLE

On the Elements and General Principles of Tragedy

TRANSLATED BY GERALD F. ELSE

c. 340 B.C.

TRAGEDY AND ITS SIX CONSTITUENT ELEMENTS

... At present let us deal with tragedy, recovering from what has been said so far the definition of its essential nature, as it was in development. Tragedy, then, is a process of imitating an action which has serious implications, is complete, and possesses magnitude; by means of language which has been made sensuously attractive, with each of its varieties found separately in the parts; enacted by the persons themselves and not presented through narrative; through a course of pity and fear completing the purification of tragic acts which have those emotional characteristics. By "language made sensuously attractive" I mean language that has rhythm and melody, and by "its varieties found separately" I mean the fact that certain parts of the play are carried on through spoken verses alone and others the other way around, through song.

Now first of all, since they perform the imitation through action (by acting it), the adornment of their visual appearance will perforce constitute some part of the making of tragedy; and song-composition and verbal expression also, for those are the media in which they perform the imitation. By "verbal expression" I mean the actual composition of the verses, and by "song-composition" something whose meaning is entirely clear.

Next, since it is an imitation of an action and is enacted by certain people who are performing the action, and since those people must necessarily have certain traits both of character and thought (for it is thanks to these two factors that we speak of people's actions also as having a defined character, and it is in accordance with their actions that all either succeed or fail); and since the imitation of the action is the plot, for by "plot" I mean here the structuring of the events, and by the "characters" that in accordance with which we say that the persons who are acting have a defined moral character, and by "thought" all the passages in which they attempt to prove some thesis or set forth an opinion — it follows of necessity, then, that tragedy as a whole has just six constituent elements, in relation to the essence that makes it a distinct species; and they are plot, characters, verbal expression, thought, visual adornment, and song-composition. For the elements by which they imitate are two (i.e., verbal expression and song-composition), the manner in which they imitate is one (visual adornment), the things they imitate are three (plot, characters, thought), and there is nothing more beyond these. These then are the constituent forms they use.

THE RELATIVE IMPORTANCE OF THE SIX ELEMENTS

The greatest of these elements is the structuring of the incidents. For tragedy is an imitation not of men but of a life, an action, and they have moral quality in accordance with their characters but are happy or unhappy in accordance with their actions; hence they are not active in order to imitate their characters, but they include the characters along with the actions for the sake of the latter. Thus the structure of events, the plot, is the goal of tragedy, and the goal is the greatest thing of all. . . .

Again: if one strings end to end speeches that are expressive of character and carefully worked in thought and expression, he still will not achieve the result which we said was the aim of tragedy; the job will be done much better by a tragedy that is more deficient in these other respects but has a plot, a structure of events. It is much the same case as with painting: the most beautiful pigments smeared on at random will not give as much pleasure as a black-and-white outline picture. Besides, the most powerful means tragedy has for swaying our feelings, namely the peripeties and recognitions,° are elements of plot.

Again: an indicative sign is that those who are beginning a poetic career manage to hit the mark in verbal expression and character portrayal sooner

---

peripeties and recognitions: The turning-about of fortune and the recognition on the part of the tragic hero of the truth. This is, for Aristotle, a critical moment in the drama, especially if both events happen simultaneously, as they do in *Oedipus the King.* It is quite possible for these moments to happen apart from one another. [All notes are the translator's.]

than they do in plot construction; and the same is true of practically all the earliest poets.

So plot is the basic principle, the heart and soul, as it were, of tragedy, and the characters come second: . . . it is the imitation of an action and imitates the persons primarily for the sake of their action.

Third in rank is thought. This is the ability to state the issues and appropriate points pertaining to a given topic, an ability which springs from the arts of politics and rhetoric; in fact the earliest poets made their characters talk "politically," the present-day poets rhetorically. But "character" is that kind of utterance which clearly reveals the bent of a man's moral choice (hence there is no character in that class of utterances in which there is nothing at all that the speaker is choosing or rejecting), while "thought" is the passages in which they try to prove that something is so or not so, or state some general principle.

Fourth is the verbal expression of the speeches. I mean by this the same thing that was said earlier, that the "verbal expression" is the conveyance of thought through language: a statement which has the same meaning whether one says "verses" or "speeches."

The song-composition of the remaining parts is the greatest of the sensuous attractions, and the visual adornment of the dramatic persons can have a strong emotional effect but is the least artistic element, the least connected with the poetic art; in fact the force of tragedy can be felt even without benefit of public performance and actors, while for the production of the visual effect the property man's art is even more decisive than that of the poets.

GENERAL PRINCIPLES OF THE TRAGIC PLOT

With these distinctions out of the way, let us next discuss what the structuring of the events should be like, since this is both the basic and the most important element in the tragic art. We have established, then, that tragedy is an imitation of an action which is complete and whole and has some magnitude (for there is also such a thing as a whole that has no magnitude). "Whole" is that which has beginning, middle, and end. "Beginning" is that which does not necessarily follow on something else, but after it something else naturally is or happens; "end," the other way around, is that which naturally follows on something else, either necessarily or for the most part, but nothing else after it; and "middle" that which naturally follows on something else and something else on it. So, then, well-constructed plots should neither begin nor end at any chance point but follow the guidelines just laid down.

Furthermore, since the beautiful, whether a living creature or anything that is composed of parts, should not only have these in a fixed order to one another but also possess a definite size which does not depend on chance — for beauty depends on size and order; hence neither can a very tiny creature turn out to be beautiful (since our perception of it grows blurred as it approaches the period of imperceptibility) nor an excessively huge one (for then it cannot all be perceived at once and so its unity and wholeness are lost), if for example there were a creature a thousand miles long — so, just as in the case of living creatures they must have some size, but one that can be taken in a single view, so with plots: they should have length, but such that they are easy to remember. As to a limit of the length, the one is determined by the tragic competitions and the ordinary span of attention. (If they had to compete with a hundred tragedies they would compete by the water clock, as they say used to be done [?].) But the limit fixed by the very nature of the case is: the longer the plot, up to the point of still being perspicuous as a whole, the finer it is so far as size is concerned; or to put it in general terms, the length in which, with things happening in unbroken sequence, a shift takes place either probably or necessarily from bad to good fortune or from good to bad — that is an acceptable norm of length.

But a plot is not unified, as some people think, simply because it has to do with a single person. A large, indeed an indefinite number of things can happen to a given individual, some of which go to constitute no unified event; and in the same way there can be many acts of a given individual from which no single action emerges. Hence it seems clear that those poets are wrong who have composed *Heracleïds, Theseïds,* and the like. They think that since Heracles was a single person it follows that the plot will be single too. But Homer, superior as he is in all other respects, appears to have grasped this point well also, thanks either to art or nature, for in composing an *Odyssey* he did not incorporate into it everything that happened to the hero, for example how he was wounded on Mt. Parnassus° or how he feigned madness at the muster, neither of which events, by happening, made it at all necessary or probable that the other should happen. Instead, he composed the *Odyssey* — and the *Iliad* similarly — around a unified action of the kind we have been talking about.

A poetic imitation, then, ought to be unified in the same way as a single imitation in any other mimetic field, by having a single object: since the plot is an imitation of an action, the latter ought to be both unified and complete, and the component events ought to be so firmly compacted that if any one of them is shifted to another place, or removed, the whole is loosened up and dislocated; for an element whose addition or subtraction makes no perceptible extra difference is not really a part of the whole.

From what has been said it is also clear that the poet's job is not to report what has happened but what is likely to happen: that is, what is capable of happening according to the rule of probability or necessity. Thus the difference between the historian and the poet is not in their utterances being in verse or prose (it would be quite possible for Herodotus' work to be translated into verse, and it would not be any the less a history with verse than it is without it); the difference lies in the fact that the historian speaks of what has happened, the poet of the kind of thing that *can* happen. Hence also poetry is a more philosophical and serious business than history; for poetry speaks more

---

Mt. Parnassus: A mountain in central Greece traditionally sacred to Apollo. In legend, Odysseus was wounded there, but the point Aristotle is making is that the writer of epics need not include every detail of his hero's life in a given work. Homer, in writing the *Odyssey*, was working with a hero, Odysseus, whose story had been legendary long before he began writing.

of universals, history of particulars. "Universal" in this case is what kind of person is likely to do or say certain kinds of things, according to probability or necessity; that is what poetry aims at, although it gives its persons particular names afterward; while the "particular" is what Alcibiades did or what happened to him.

In the field of comedy this point has been grasped: our comic poets construct their plots on the basis of general probabilities and then assign names to the persons quite arbitrarily, instead of dealing with individuals as the old iambic poets° did. But in tragedy they still cling to the historically given names. The reason is that what is possible is persuasive; so what has not happened we are not yet ready to believe is possible, while what has happened is, we feel, obviously possible: for it would not have happened if it were impossible. Nevertheless, it is a fact that even in our tragedies, in some cases only one or two of the names are traditional, the rest being invented, and in some others none at all. It is so, for example, in Agathon's *Antheus* — the names in it are as fictional as the events — and it gives no less pleasure because of that. Hence the poets ought not to cling at all costs to the traditional plots, around which our tragedies are constructed. And in fact it is absurd to go searching for this kind of authentication, since even the familiar names are familiar to only a few in the audience and yet give the same kind of pleasure to all.

So from these considerations it is evident that the poet should be a maker of his plots more than of his verses, insofar as he is a poet by virtue of his imitations and what he imitates is actions. Hence even if it happens that he puts something that has actually taken place into poetry, he is none the less a poet; for there is nothing to prevent some of the things that have happened from being the kind of things that can happen, and that is the sense in which he is their maker.

SIMPLE AND COMPLEX PLOTS

Among simple plots and actions the episodic are the worst. By "episodic" plot I mean one in which there is no probability or necessity for the order in which the episodes follow one another. Such structures are composed by the bad poets because they are bad poets, but by the good poets because of the actors: in composing contest pieces for them, and stretching out the plot beyond its capacity, they are forced frequently to dislocate the sequence.

Furthermore, since the tragic imitation is not only of a complete action but also of events that are fearful and pathetic,° and these come about best when they come about contrary to one's expectation yet logically, one follow-

---

old iambic poets: Aristotle may be referring to Archilochus (fl. 650 B.C.) and the iambic style he developed. The iamb is a metrical foot of two syllables, a short and a long syllable, and was the most popular metrical style before the time of Aristotle. "Dealing with individuals" implies using figures already known to the audience rather than figures whose names can be arbitrarily assigned because no one knows who they are.   **fearful and pathetic:** Aristotle said that tragedy should evoke two emotions: terror and pity. The terror results from our realizing that what is happening to the hero might just as easily happen to us; the pity results from our human sympathy with a fellow sufferer. Therefore, the fearful and pathetic represent significant emotions appropriate to our witnessing drama.

ing from the other; that way they will be more productive of wonder than if they happen merely at random, by chance — because even among chance occurrences the ones people consider most marvelous are those that seem to have come about as if on purpose: for example the way the statue of Mitys at Argos killed the man who had been the cause of Mitys' death, by falling on him while he was attending the festival; it stands to reason, people think, that such things don't happen by chance — so plots of that sort cannot fail to be artistically superior.

Some plots are simple, others are complex; indeed the actions of which the plots are imitations already fall into these two categories. By "simple" action I mean one the development of which being continuous and unified in the manner stated above, the reversal comes without peripety or recognition, and by "complex" action one in which the reversal is continuous but with recognition or peripety or both. And these developments must grow out of the very structure of the plot itself, in such a way that on the basis of what has happened previously this particular outcome follows either by necessity or in accordance with probability; for there is a greater difference in whether these events happen because of those or merely after them.

"Peripety" is a shift of what is being undertaken to the opposite in the way previously stated, and that in accordance with probability or necessity as we have just been saying; as for example in the *Oedipus* the man who has come, thinking that he will reassure Oedipus, that is, relieve him of his fear with respect to his mother, by revealing who he once was, brings about the opposite; and in the *Lynceus*, as he (Lynceus) is being led away with every prospect of being executed, and Danaus pursuing him with every prospect of doing the executing, it comes about as a result of the other things that have happened in the play that *he* is executed and Lynceus is saved. And "recognition" is, as indeed the name indicates, a shift from ignorance to awareness, pointing in the direction either of close blood ties or of hostility, of people who have previously been in a clearly marked state of happiness or unhappiness.

The finest recognition is one that happens at the same time as a peripety, as is the case with the one in the *Oedipus*. Naturally, there are also other kinds of recognition: it is possible for one to take place in the prescribed manner in relation to inanimate objects and chance occurrences, and it is possible to recognize whether a person has acted or not acted. But the form that is most integrally a part of the plot, the action, is the one aforesaid; for that kind of recognition combined with peripety will excite either pity or fear (and these are the kinds of action of which tragedy is an imitation according to our definition), because both good and bad fortune will also be most likely to follow that kind of event. Since, further, the recognition is a recognition of persons, some are of one person by the other one only (when it is already known who the "other one" is), but sometimes it is necessary for both persons to go through a recognition, as for example Iphigenia is recognized by her brother through the sending of the letter, but of him by Iphigenia another recognition is required.

These then are two elements of plot: peripety and recognition; third is the *pathos*. Of these, peripety and recognition have been discussed; a *pathos* is a destructive or painful act, such as deaths on stage, paroxysms of pain, woundings, and all that sort of thing.

ॐ

TRAVIS BOGARD *discussed the theater group that, "it is now claimed, gave birth to the modern American drama" in* Contour in Time *(1972), his critical study of the plays of Eugene O'Neill.*

TRAVIS BOGARD

The Provincetown Players   1972

The story of the stagestruck amateurs who in 1915 produced two plays on a front porch in Provincetown, Massachusetts, has become part of the folklore of the American theatre. The visitor to modern Provincetown looks reluctantly on quaint gift shops, summer "cottages" and unattractive sand dunes. Nothing there, unless it be the untouched center of the sea itself, remains of the world which, it is now claimed, gave birth to the modern American drama. The activities of the Provincetown Players in their early days are wrapped in a sentimental mist, and memory is tender with them.

There is no reason not to view the Players affectionately, just as any group of theatrical amateurs may claim the charitable sympathy of their audiences. Their story is, in fact, no different from that of hundreds of others throughout the country, whose activities in some measure seem to compensate for a lack of rural folk games. Such groups are summer insects, rippling lightly the surfaces in which they drown. Their conception is in the heat of talk, and they are born amid a drumming of hammers and a frenzied splashing of sizing and stipple. Success is to them as unexpected as failure. Neither profits them substantially, for they are prey to warring temperaments, to disaffection, to economic pressures, to fatigue and, if they find strength enough to survive all these, to professionalism.

Inevitably in such a group, if the energy of idealistic enthusiasm develops into the motivation of conscious purpose, there arises the professional. His appearance spells the end of the fun, even if normal general attrition has not yet set in. The few groups that survive do so because they move rapidly toward the firm grounds of a professional organization.

In the Provincetown Players, the professional was Eugene O'Neill. Without him, they would have been long forgotten; it is doubtful that they would have survived even one season in New York City. He quickly became their most marketable commodity; his presence defined their aims for them; he was proof of their worth as an organization. Yet he was also their destroyer, for he alone moved in the course of the significant life of the group from amateur to professional.

The Players were determined amateurs. Their early criticism of the Washington Square Players, who had set them an organizational model, was that they had turned too quickly toward professionalism by hiring a director. Later, when both were operating in New York, the Provincetown tended to look down on its rival because the "professionals" kept a press book and invited critics to first nights — actions which revealed something of the business motives of Broadway itself. The attitude of the Provincetown group changed somewhat when they discovered that the Washington Square Players were being credited with the discovery of Eugene O'Neill. Then the press book was kept and the critics invited, and other minor signs of creeping professionalism became apparent.

Yet by 1916, when they moved into Macdougal Street in Greenwich Village, it was probably too late, if ever there had been hope, for them to turn professional as the Washington Square Players were to achieve metamorphosis into the Theatre Guild. A line had been sharply drawn through the center of the organization, and on either side of it stood the two men chiefly responsible for the Provincetown's survival. The extent of the quarrel between the group's leader, George Cram Cook, and Eugene O'Neill is now impossible to determine, but "Jig" Cook's summation of the Provincetown's achievement suggests strongly that he felt O'Neill's success had destroyed the Players. Although O'Neill was what Cook claimed he was seeking, an American playwright of genius, and although he cooperated with him to the full, he was temperamentally unable to come to terms with what O'Neill released in the organization. Cook's was a life of dedication to an ideal that was never fully formulated, a seeker after a shrouded goal, a man for whom the search was more important than the good being sought. Susan Glaspell rightly titled her memoir of her husband, *The Road to the Temple:* it was the road and not the temple that mattered. Speaking of Cook's particular power "to riddle, to defend, to invite," she added: "Sometimes I wish the Provincetown Players had been a magazine." The magazine, she seems to have felt, would have permitted him to experiment in endless amateurism, to live as if he had tasted Ponce de Leon's fountain and was therefore free to seek perpetually and not to find. It was O'Neill's discovery of his own power, his increasing mastery of the drama, bringing with it new needs and giving to the group new goals, that in the end sent Cook to a self-imposed exile in Greece, from where, whenever he looked back, he viewed the course of the Players with resignation and a touch of bitterness.

What moved Cook in the beginning was probably not the quest for a native playwright or for a native drama. One suspects that this idea — stated as the Players' raison d'être — was formulated to mark a difference from the predilection of the Washington Square Players for foreign plays. In the absence of interesting American playwrights, such a goal was born of necessity, but it continued as a hallmark of their activity as the Theatre Guild. The Provincetown, searching out a cause, joined the hunt for native playwrights, a quest that reaches far back into the history of this country and from time to time has assumed something of the comic proportions of the quest for the Great American Novelist. Before O'Neill, there was no reputable candidate for the dramatic honors, and his existence gave the group's devotion to native drama some validity. Later, Cook was to say that the failure of the Players was evidenced by its inability to uncover other American dramatists of a stature comparable to O'Neill's. As the group came together, however, the stated aim sufficed, and when it moved to New York, O'Neill's suggestion was followed: that the group be called "The Playwrights' Theatre." So far as Cook himself was concerned, however, the purposes of the theatre closest to his heart were less literary.

Cook's interest was caught by an idea of theatre as a community. "One man," he wrote, "cannot produce drama. True drama is born only of one feeling animating all the members of a clan — a spirit shared by all and expressed by the few for the all. If there is nothing to take the place of the common religious purpose and passion of the primitive group out of which the Dionysian dance was born, no new vital drama can arise in any people."

His animating idea clearly was not the quest for American drama or even for a theatre. His words, which were accepted as the credo of the Players, center firmly on the idea of the communal spirit. Unlike the later Group Theatre, Cook fixed no political point of rallying, nor did he advocate such localized aesthetics as gave rise to the rural drama in regional theatres a few years later. What was important was the clan, united in festal ceremony in honor of Dionysius, late sprung up in America. Cook looked upon the theatre as an inevitable ritualistic outcropping of a group so oriented, but for him the group came first, the theatre second. The theatre, he said, was "Work done in the spirit of play," a way of working that had "the only true seriousness." He remained an amateur of theatre and, in the word's French sense, of life. Throughout his active association with them, he sought to maintain the Players as an oasis of spirit in a dusty world.

Behind his amateurism lay an abiding admiration for Athenian Greece. His was not an antiquary's interest in the past, nor did professional scholarship inhibit his idealistic, visionary attempt to summon to the present, for the spiritual resuscitation of himself and others for whom he cared, something of the qualities he sensed in the Greek Idea. His associate on the board of the Provincetown Players, Edna Kenton, described his enthusiastic purpose: "Back to Greece! — that was Jig's solution for every modern ill. Back, rather, to the spirit of Greece for its lesson, and then a return to re-evoke the group spirit from modern life." In the end, his desire led him away from America, back physically to Greece, where before he died he convinced himself that he had indeed found among the shepherds of Mount Parnassus the community of feeling and endeavor that he called "Greek" and that provided the serenity of his dreams.

രെ

PETER BROOK (b. 1925), *the distinguished English director associated with the Royal Shakespeare Company, has thought deeply about Chekhov's methods as a playwright. Brook has hypothesized that Chekhov's personal awareness of death made him write comedies in which his characters were complex people passionately desirous to be alive in a world in which "nothing is stable."*

PETER BROOK

On Chekhov 1987

Chekhov always looked for what's natural; he wanted performances and productions to be as limpid as life itself. Chekhov's writing is extremely concentrated, employing a minimum of words; in a way, it is similar to Pinter or Beckett. As with them, it is construction that counts, rhythm, the purely theatrical poetry that comes not from beautiful words but from the right word at the right moment. In the theater, someone can say "yes" in such a way that the "yes" is no longer ordinary — it can become a beautiful word, because it is the perfect expression of what cannot be expressed in any other way. With Chekhov, periods, commas, points of suspension are all of a fundamental importance, as fundamental as the "pauses" precisely indicated by Beckett. If one fails to observe them, one loses the rhythm and tensions of the play. In Chekhov's work, the punctuation represents a series of coded messages which record characters' relationships and emotions, the moments at which ideas come together or follow their own course. The punctuation enables us to grasp what the words conceal.

Chekhov is like a perfect filmmaker. Instead of cutting from one image to another — perhaps from one place to another — he switches from one emotion to another just before it gets too heavy. At the precise moment when the spectator risks becoming too involved in a character, an unexpected situation cuts across: Nothing is stable. Chekhov portrays individuals and a society in a state of perpetual change, he is the dramatist of life's movement, simultaneously smiling and serious, amusing and bitter — completely free from the "music," the Slav "nostalgia" that Paris nightclubs still preserve. He often stated that his plays were comedies — this was the central issue of his conflict with Stanislavsky.

. . . Chekhov is an infinitely detailed observer of the human comedy. As a doctor, he knew the meaning of certain kinds of behavior, how to discern what was essential, to expose what he diagnosed. Although he shows tenderness and an attentive sympathy, he never sentimentalizes. One doesn't imagine a doctor shedding tears over the illnesses of his patients. He learns how to balance compassion with distance.

In Chekhov's work, death is omnipresent — he knew it well — but there is nothing negative or unsavory in its presence. The awareness of death is balanced with a desire to live. His characters possess a sense of the present moment, and the need to taste it fully. As in great tragedies, one finds a harmony between life and death.

Chekhov died young, having traveled, written, and loved enormously, having taken part in the events of his day, in great schemes of social reform. He died shortly after asking for some champagne, and his coffin was transported in a wagon bearing the inscription "Fresh Oysters." His awareness of death, and of the precious moments that could be lived, endow his work with a sense of the relative: in other words, a viewpoint from which the tragic is always a bit absurd.

In Chekhov's work, each character has its own existence: not one of them resembles another. . . . But they all burn with intense desires. They are not disillusioned, quite the contrary: In their own ways, they are all searching for a better quality of life, emotionally and socially. Their drama is that society — the outside world — blocks their energy. The complexity of their behavior is not indicated in the words, it emerges from the mosaic construction of an infinite number of details. What is essential is to see that these are not plays about lethargic people. They are hypervital people in a lethargic world, forced to dramatize the minutest happening out of a passionate desire to live. They have not given up.

తుం

MARTIN ESSLIN, *author of* Brecht: The Man and His Work *(1969), has written about the development of avant-garde contemporary drama in* The Theatre of the Absurd *(1961). Associated with the playwrights Samuel Beckett, Eugène Ionesco, Jean Genet, Harold Pinter, and Edward Albee (among many others), the theater of the absurd, according to Esslin, is like the ancient Greek theater, "intent on making its audience aware of man's precarious and mysterious position in the universe." But such plays as* Krapp's Last Tape *— in contrast to a Greek tragedy like* Oedipus the King *— offer no coherent expression of a universal system of ultimate moral values and belief. Instead, there is only the descent into the playwright's inner world.*

MARTIN ESSLIN

On *Krapp's Last Tape* 1961

In *Krapp's Last Tape,* a one-act play that has been performed with great success on the stage in Paris, London, and New York, Beckett makes use of the tape recorder to demonstrate the elusiveness of human personality. Krapp is a very old man who throughout his adult life has annually recorded an account of the past year's impressions and events onto magnetic tape. We see him, old, decrepit, and a failure (he is a writer, but only seventeen copies of his book have been sold in the current year, "eleven at trade price to free circulating libraries beyond the seas"), listening to his own voice recorded thirty years earlier. But his voice has become the voice of a stranger to him. He even has to get a dictionary to look up one of the more elaborate words used by his former self. When the tape reaches the description of the great moment of insight that then seemed a miracle to be treasured "against the day when my work will be done," he cannot be bothered to listen to it and winds the tape on. The only description that visibly arouses his attention is one of lovemaking in a punt on a lake. Having heard his earlier self's report on his thirty-ninth year, the sixty-nine-year-old Krapp proceeds to record the current year's balance sheet. "Nothing to say, not a squeak." His only moment of happiness: "Revelled in the word spool. (*With relish.*) Spoool! Happiest moment in the past half million." There are memories of lovemaking with an old hag. But then Krapp returns to the old tape. Again the voice of his former self is heard describing the love scene on the lake. The old tape ends with a summing up: "Perhaps my best years are gone. When there was a chance of happiness. But I wouldn't want them back. Not with the fire in me now. No, I wouldn't want them back." The curtain falls on old Krapp staring motionless before him, with the tape running on in silence.

Through the brilliant device of the autobiographical library of annual recorded statements, Beckett has found a graphic expression for the problem of the ever-changing identity of the self, which he had already described in his essay on Proust. In *Krapp's Last Tape*, the self at one moment in time is confronted with its earlier incarnation only to find it utterly strange. What, then, is the identity between Krapp now and Krapp then? In what sense are they the same? And if this is a problem with an interval of thirty years, it is surely only a difference in degree if the interval is reduced to one year, one month, one hour. Beckett at one time planned to write a long play of three Krapps: Krapp with his wife, Krapp with his wife and child, Krapp alone — further variations on the theme of the identity of the self. But he has now abandoned this project.

က

FRANCIS FERGUSSON, *the eminent theater critic, discussed the way Sophocles reimagined his source of the traditional myth of Oedipus in this essay from* The Idea of a Theater *(1949). Fergusson also analyzed how Sophocles developed the important role of the chorus to help the spectators of this drama form "a new perception of the immediate situation."*

FRANCIS FERGUSSON

Oedipus, Myth and Play
1949

When Sophocles came to write his play he had the myth of Oedipus to start with. Laius and Jocasta, King and Queen of Thebes, are told by the oracle that their son will grow up to kill his father and marry his mother. The infant, his feet pierced, is left on Mount Kitharon to die. But a shepherd finds him and takes care of him; at last gives him to another shepherd, who takes him to Corinth, and there the King and Queen bring him up as their own son. But Oedipus — "Clubfoot" — is plagued in his turn by the oracle; he hears that he is fated to kill his father and marry his mother; and to escape that fate he leaves Corinth never to return. On his journey he meets an old man with his servants; gets into a dispute with him, and kills him and all his followers. He comes to Thebes at the time when the Sphinx is preying upon that City; solves the riddle which the Sphinx propounds, and saves the City. He marries the widowed Queen, Jocasta; has several children by her; rules prosperously for many years. But, when Thebes is suffering under a plague and a drought, the oracle reports that the gods are angry because Laius' slayer is unpunished. Oedipus, as King, undertakes to find him; discovers that he is himself the culprit and that Jocasta is his own mother. He blinds himself and goes into exile. From this time forth he becomes a sort of sacred relic, like the bones of a saint; perilous, but "good medicine" for the community that possesses him. He dies, at last, at Athens, in a grove sacred to the Eumenides, female spirits of fertility and night.

It is obvious, even from this sketch, that the myth, which covers several generations, has as much narrative material as *Gone with the Wind*. We do not know what versions of the story Sophocles used. It is the way of myths that they generate whole progenies of elaborations and varying versions. They are so suggestive, seem to say so much, yet so mysteriously, that the mind cannot rest content with any single form, but must add, or interpret, or simplify — reduce to terms which the reason can accept. Mr. William Troy suggests that "what is possibly most in order at the moment is a thoroughgoing refurbishment of the medieval fourfold method of interpretation, which was first developed, it will be recalled, for just such a purpose — to make at least partially available to the reason that complex of human problems which are embedded, deep and imponderable, in the Myth."[1] It appears that Sophocles, in his play, succeeded in preserving the suggestive mystery of the Oedipus myth, while presenting it in a wonderfully unified dramatic form; and this drama has all the dimensions which the fourfold method was intended to explore.

Everyone knows that when Sophocles planned the plot of the play itself, he started almost at the end of the story, when the plague descends upon the City of Thebes which Oedipus and Jocasta had been ruling with great success for a number of years. The action of the play takes less than a day, and consists of Oedipus' quest for Laius' slayer — his consulting the Oracle of Apollo, his examination of the Prophet, Tiresias, and of a series of witnesses, ending with the old Shepherd who gave him to the King and Queen of Corinth. The play ends when Oedipus is unmistakably revealed as himself the culprit.

At this literal level, the play is intelligible as a murder mystery. Oedipus takes the role of District Attorney; and when he at last convicts himself, we have a twist, a *coup de théâtre*, of unparalleled excitement. But no one who sees or reads the play can rest content with its literal coherence. Questions as to its meaning arise at once: Is Oedipus really guilty, or simply a victim of the gods, or his famous complex, of fate, of original sin? How much did he know, all along? How much did Jocasta know? The first, and most deeply instinctive effort of the mind, when confronted with this play, is to endeavor to reduce its meanings to some set of rational categories.

The critics of the Age of Reason tried to understand it as a fable of the enlightened moral will, in accordance with the philosophy of that time. Voltaire's version of the play, following Corneille, and his comments upon it, may be taken as typical. He sees it as essentially a struggle between a strong and righteous Oedipus, and the malicious and very human gods, aided and

---

[1] "Myth, Method and the Future," by William Troy. *Chimera*, Spring 1946.

abetted by the corrupt priest Tiresias; he makes it an antireligious tract, with an unmistakable moral to satisfy the needs of the discursive intellect. In order to make Oedipus "sympathetic" to his audience, he elides, as much as possible, the incest motif; and he adds an irrelevant love story. He was aware that his version and interpretation were not those of Sophocles but, with the complacent provinciality of his period, he attributes the difference to the darkness of the age in which *Sophocles* lived.

Other attempts to rationalize *Oedipus Rex* are subtler than Voltaire's, and take us further toward an understanding of the play. Freud's reduction of the play to the concepts of his psychology reveals a great deal, opens up perspectives which we are still exploring. If one reads *Oedipus* in the light of Fustel de Coulanges's *The Ancient City,* one may see it as the expression of the ancient patriarchal religion of the Greeks. And other interpretations of the play, theological, philosophical, historical, are available, none of them wrong, but all partial, all reductions of Sophocles' masterpiece to an alien set of categories. For the peculiar virtue of Sophocles' presentation of the myth is that it preserves the ultimate mystery by focusing upon the tragic human at a level beneath, or prior to any rationalization whatever. The plot is so arranged that we see the action, as it were, illumined from many sides at once.

By starting the play at the end of the story, and showing on stage only the last crucial episode in Oedipus' life, the past and present action of the protagonist are revealed together; and, in each other's light, are at last felt as one. Oedipus' quest for the slayer of Laius becomes a quest for the hidden reality of his own past; and as that slowly comes into focus, like repressed material under psychoanalysis — with sensory and emotional immediacy, yet in the light of acceptance and understanding — his immediate quest also reaches its end: he comes to see himself (the Savior of the City) and the guilty one, the plague of Thebes, at once and at one.

This presentation of the myth of Oedipus constitutes, in one sense, an "interpretation" of it. What Sophocles saw as the essence of Oedipus' nature and destiny, is not what Seneca or Dryden or Cocteau saw; and one may grant that even Sophocles did not exhaust the possibilities in the materials of the myth. But Sophocles' version of the myth does not constitute a "reduction" in the same sense as the rest.

I have said that the action which Sophocles shows is a quest, the quest for Laius' slayer; and that as Oedipus' past is unrolled before us his whole life is seen as a kind of quest for his true nature and destiny. But since the object of this quest is not clear until the end, the seeking action takes many forms, as its object appears in different lights. The object, indeed, the final perception, the "truth," looks so different at the end from what it did at the beginning that Oedipus' action itself may seem not a quest, but its opposite, a flight. Thus it would be hard to say, simply, that Oedipus either succeeds or fails. He succeeds; but his success is his undoing. He fails to find what, in one way, he sought; yet from another point of view his search is brilliantly successful. The same ambiguities surround his effort to discover who and what he is. He seems to find that he is nothing; yet thereby finds himself. And what of his relation to the gods? His quest may be regarded as a heroic attempt to escape their decrees, or as an attempt, based upon some deep natural faith, to discover what their wishes are, and what true obedience would be. In one sense Oedipus suffers forces he can neither control nor understand, the puppet of fate; yet at the same time he wills and intelligently intends his every move.

The meaning, or spiritual content of the play, is not to be sought by trying to resolve such ambiguities as these. The spiritual content of the play is the tragic action which Sophocles directly presents; and this action is in its essence *zweideutig*: triumph and destruction, darkness and enlightenment, mourning and rejoicing, at any moment we care to consider it. But this action has also a shape: a beginning, middle, and end, in time. It starts with the reasoned purpose of finding Laius' slayer. But this aim meets unforeseen difficulties, evidences which do not fit, and therefore shake the purpose as it was first understood; and so the characters suffer the piteous and terrible sense of the mystery of the human situation. From this suffering or passion, with its shifting visions, a new perception of the situation emerges; and on that basis the purpose of the action is redefined, and a new movement starts. This movement, or *tragic rhythm of action*, constitutes the shape of the play as a whole; it is also the shape of each episode, each discussion between principals with the chorus following. Mr. Kenneth Burke has studied the tragic rhythm in his *Philosophy of Literary Form*, and also in *A Grammar of Motives*, where he gives the three moments traditional designations which are very suggestive: *Poiema*, *Pathema*, *Mathema*. They may also be called, for convenience, Purpose, Passion (or Suffering) and Perception. It is this tragic rhythm of action which is the substance or spiritual content of the play, and the clue to its extraordinarily comprehensive form.

In order to illustrate these points in more detail, it is convenient to examine the scene between Oedipus and Tiresias with the chorus following it. This episode, being early in the play (the first big agon), presents, as it were, a preview of the whole action and constitutes a clear and complete example of action in the tragic rhythm. . . .

The Cambridge School of Classical Anthropologists has shown in great detail that the form of Greek tragedy follows the form of a very ancient ritual, that of the *Enniautos-Daimon*, or seasonal god.[2] This was one of the most influential discoveries of the last few generations, and it gives us new insights into *Oedipus* which I think are not yet completely explored. The clue to Sophocles' dramatizing of the myth of Oedipus is to be found in this ancient ritual, which had a similar form and meaning — that is, it also moved in the "tragic rhythm."

Experts in classical anthropology, like experts in other fields, dispute innumerable questions of fact and of interpretation which the layman can only pass over in respectful silence. One of the thornier questions seems to be whether myth or ritual came first. Is the ancient ceremony merely an enact-

---

[2] See especially Jane Ellen Harrison's *Ancient Art and Ritual*, and her *Themis* which contains an "Excursus on the ritual forms preserved in Greek Tragedy" by Professor Gilbert Murray.

ment of the Ur-Myth of the year-god — Attis, or Adonis, or Osiris, or the "Fisher-King" — in any case that Hero-King-Father-High-Priest who fights with his rival, is slain and dismembered, then rises anew with the spring season? Or did the innumerable myths of this kind arise to "explain" a ritual which was perhaps mimed or danced or sung to celebrate the annual change of seasons?

For the purpose of understanding the form and meaning of *Oedipus*, it is not necessary to worry about the answer to this question of historic fact. The figure of Oedipus himself fulfills all the requirements of the scapegoat, the dismembered king or god-figure. The situation in which Thebes is presented at the beginning of the play — in peril of its life; its crops, its herds, its women mysteriously infertile, signs of a mortal disease of the City, and the disfavor of the gods — is like the withering which winter brings, and calls, in the same way, for struggle, dismemberment, death, and renewal. And this tragic sequence is the substance of the play. It is enough to know that myth and ritual are close together in their genesis, two direct imitations of the perennial experience of the race.

But when one considers *Oedipus* as a ritual one understands it in ways which one cannot by thinking of it merely as a dramatization of a story, even that story. Harrison has shown that the Festival of Dionysos, based ultimately upon the yearly vegetation ceremonies, included *rites de passage*, like that celebrating the assumption of adulthood — celebrations of the mystery of individual growth and development. At the same time, it was a prayer for the welfare of the whole City; and this welfare was understood not only as material prosperity, but also as the natural order of the family, the ancestors, the present members, and the generations still to come, and, by the same token, obedience to the gods who were jealous, each in his own province, of this natural and divinely sanctioned order and proportion.

We must suppose that Sophocles' audience (the whole population of the City) came early, prepared to spend the day in the bleachers. At their feet was the semicircular dancing-ground for the chorus, and the thrones for the priests, and the altar. Behind that was the raised platform for the principal actors, backed by the all-purpose, emblematic façade, which would presently be taken to represent Oedipus' palace in Thebes. The actors were not professionals in our sense, but citizens selected for a religious office, and Sophocles himself had trained them and the chorus.

This crowd must have had as much appetite for thrills and diversion as the crowds who assemble in our day for football games and musical comedies, and Sophocles certainly holds the attention with an exciting show. At the same time his audience must have been alert for the fine points of poetry and dramaturgy, for *Oedipus* is being offered in competition with other plays on the same bill. But the element which distinguishes this theater, giving it its unique directness and depth, is the *ritual expectancy* which Sophocles assumed in his audience. The nearest thing we have to this ritual sense of theater is, I suppose, to be found at an Easter performance of the *Mattias Passion*. We also can observe something similar in the dances and ritual mummery of the Pueblo Indians. Sophocles' audience must have been prepared, like the Indians standing around their plaza, to consider the playing, the make-believe it was about to see — the choral invocations, with dancing and chanting; the reasoned discourses and the terrible combats of the protagonists; the mourning, the rejoicing, and the contemplation of the final stage-picture of epiphany — as imitating and celebrating the mystery of human nature and destiny. And this mystery was at once that of individual growth and development, and that of the precarious life of the human City.

I have indicated how Sophocles presents the life of the mythic Oedipus in the tragic rhythm, the mysterious quest of life. Oedipus is shown seeking his own true being; but at the same time and by the same token, the welfare of the City. When one considers the ritual form of the whole play, it becomes evident that it presents the tragic but perennial, even normal, quest of the whole City for its well-being. In this larger action, Oedipus is only the protagonist, the first and most important champion. This tragic quest is realized by all the characters in their various ways; but in the development of the action as a whole it is the chorus alone that plays a part as important as that of Oedipus; its counterpart, in fact. The chorus holds the balance between Oedipus and his antagonists, marks the progress of their struggles, and restates the main theme, and its new variation, after each dialogue or agon. The ancient ritual was probably performed by a chorus alone without individual developments and variations, and the chorus, in *Oedipus*, is still the element that throws most light on the ritual form of the play as a whole.

The chorus consists of twelve or fifteen "Elders of Thebes." This group is not intended to represent literally all of the citizens either of Thebes or of Athens. The play opens with a large delegation of Theban citizens before Oedipus' palace, and the chorus proper does not enter until after the prologue. Nor does the chorus speak directly for the Athenian audience; we are asked throughout to make-believe that the theater is the agora at Thebes; and at the same time Sophocles' audience is witnessing a ritual. It would, I think, be more accurate to say that the chorus represents the point of view and the faith of Thebes as a whole, and, by analogy, of the Athenian audience. Their errand before Oedipus' palace is like that of Sophocles' audience in the theater: they are watching a sacred combat, in the issue of which they have an all-important and official stake. Thus they represent the audience and the citizens in a particular way — not as a mob formed in response to some momentary feeling, but rather as an organ of a highly self-conscious community: something closer to the "conscience of the race" than to the overheated affectivity of a mob.

According to Aristotle, a Sophoclean chorus is a character that takes an important role in the action of the play, instead of merely making incidental music between the scenes, as in the plays of Euripides. The chorus may be described as a group personality, like an old Parliament. It has its own traditions, habits of thought and feeling, and mode of being. It exists, in a sense, as a living entity, but not with the sharp actuality of an individual. It perceives; but its perception is at once wider and vaguer than that of a single man. It shares, in its way, the seeking action of the play as a whole; but it cannot act in all the modes; it depends upon the chief agonists to invent and try out the detail of policy, just as a rather helpless but critical Parliament depends upon the Prime Minister to act but, in its less specific form of life, survives his destruction.

When the chorus enters after the prologue, with its questions, its invocation of the various gods, and its focus upon the hidden and jeopardized welfare of the City — Athens or Thebes — the list of essential *dramatis personae*, as well as the elements needed to celebrate the ritual, is complete, and the main action can begin. It is the function of the chorus to mark the stages of this action, and to perform the suffering and perceiving part of the tragic rhythm. The protagonist and his antagonists develop the "purpose" with which the tragic sequence begins; the chorus, with its less than individual being, broods over the agons, marks their stages with a word (like that of the chorus leader in the middle of the Tiresias scene), and (expressing its emotions and visions in song and dance) suffers the results, and the new perception at the end of the fight.

The choral odes are lyrics but they are not to be understood as poetry, the art of words, only, for they are intended also to be danced and sung. And though each chorus has its own shape, like that of a discrete lyric — its beginning, middle, and end — it represents also one passion or pathos in the changing action of the whole. This passion, like the other moments in the tragic rhythm, is felt at so general or, rather, so deep a level that it seems to contain both the mob ferocity that Nietzsche felt in it and, at the other extreme, the patience of prayer. It is informed by faith in the unseen order of nature and the gods, and moves through a sequence of modes of suffering. This may be illustrated from the chorus I have quoted at the end of the Tiresias scene.

It begins (close to the savage emotion of the end of the fight) with images suggesting that cruel "Bacchic frenzy" which is supposed to be the common root of tragedy and of the "old" comedy: "In panoply of fire and lightning / The son of Zeus now springs upon him." In the first antistrophe these images come together more clearly as we relish the chase; and the fleeing culprit, as we imagine him, begins to resemble Oedipus, who is lame, and always associated with the rough wilderness of Kitharon. But in the second strophe, as though appalled by its ambivalent feelings and the imagined possibilities, the chorus sinks back into a more dark and patient posture of suffering, "in awe," "hovering in hope." In the second antistrophe this is developed into something like the orthodox Christian attitude of prayer, based on faith, and assuming the possibility of a hitherto unimaginable truth and answer: "Zeus and Apollo are wise," etc. The whole chorus then ends with a new vision of Oedipus, of the culprit, and of the direction in which the welfare of the City is to be sought. This vision is still colored by the chorus's human love of Oedipus as Hero, for the chorus has still its own purgation to complete, cannot as yet accept completely either the suffering in store for it, or Oedipus as scapegoat. But it marks the end of the first complete "purpose-passion-perception" unit, and lays the basis for the new purpose which will begin the next unit.

It is also to be noted that the chorus changes the scene which we, as audience, are to imagine. During the agon between Oedipus and Tiresias, our attention is fixed upon their clash, and the scene is literal, close, and immediate: before Oedipus' palace. When the fighters depart and the choral music starts, the focus suddenly widens, as though we had been removed to a distance. We become aware of the interested City around the bright arena; and beyond that, still more dimly, of Nature, sacred to the hidden gods. Mr. Burke has expounded the fertile notion that human action may be understood in terms of the scene in which it occurs, and vice versa: the scene is defined by the mode of action. The chorus's action is not limited by the sharp, rationalized purposes of the protagonist; its mode of action, more patient, less sharply realized, is cognate with a wider, if less accurate, awareness of the scene of human life. But the chorus's action, as I have remarked, is not that of passion itself (Nietzsche's cosmic void of night) but suffering informed by the faith of the tribe in a human and a divinely sanctioned natural order: "If such deeds as these are honored," the chorus asks after Jocasta's impiety, "why should I dance and sing?" Thus it is one of the most important functions of the chorus to reveal, in its widest and most mysterious extent, the theater of human life which the play, and indeed the whole Festival of Dionysos, assumed. Even when the chorus does not speak, but only watches, it maintains this theme and this perspective — ready to take the whole stage when the fighters depart.

If one thinks of the movements of the play, it appears that the tragic rhythm analyzes human action temporally into successive modes, as a crystal analyzes a white beam of light spatially into the colored bands of the spectrum. The chorus, always present, represents one of these modes, and at the recurrent moments when reasoned purpose is gone, it takes the stage with its faith-informed passion, moving through an ordered succession of modes of suffering, to a new perception of the immediate situation.

∞

SIGMUND FREUD *(1856–1939) used Sophocles' play in* The Interpretation of Dreams *(1900) to derive the term Oedipus complex, which is central to his explanation of neurosis in his theory of psychoanalysis. Freud sought to explain the drama's enduring psychological appeal for audiences despite its lack of a comtemporary religious context. He hypothesized that audiences respond to Sophocles' tragedy because they recognize that Oedipus's relationship to his parents "might have been ours" as children. According to Freud's interpretation, the incest theme is dramatized so forcefully in* Oedipus the King *that it enables us to recognize our own "primeval wishes," suppressed in our later psychological development as individuals.*

SIGMUND FREUD

The Oedipus Complex   1900

In my experience, which is already extensive, the chief part in the mental lives of all children who later become psychoneurotics is played by their parents. Being in love with the one parent and hating the other are among the essential constituents of the stock of psychical impulses which is formed at that time and which is of such importance in determining the symptoms of the later neurosis. It is not my belief, however, that psychoneurotics differ sharply in this respect from other human beings who remain normal — that they are able, that is, to create something absolutely new and peculiar to themselves. It is far more probable — and this is confirmed by occasional observations on normal children — that they are only distinguished by exhibiting on a magnified scale feelings of love and hatred to their parents which occur less obviously and less intensely in the minds of most children.

This discovery is confirmed by a legend that has come down to us from classical antiquity: a legend whose profound and universal power to move can only be understood if the hypothesis I have put forward in regard to the psychology of children has an equally universal validity. What I have in mind is the legend of King Oedipus and Sophocles' drama which bears his name.

Oedipus, son of Laius, King of Thebes, and of Jocasta, was exposed as an infant because an oracle had warned Laius that the still unborn child would be his father's murderer. The child was rescued and grew up as a prince in an alien court, until, in doubts as to his origin, he too questioned the oracle and was warned to avoid his home since he was destined to murder his father and take his mother in marriage. On the road leading away from what he believed was his home, he met King Laius and slew him in a sudden quarrel. He came next to Thebes and solved the riddle set him by the Sphinx who barred his way. Out of gratitude the Thebans made him their king and gave him Jocasta's hand in marriage. He reigned long in peace and honor, and she who, unknown to him, was his mother bore him two sons and two daughters. Then at last a plague broke out and the Thebans made inquiry once more of the oracle. It is at this point that Sophocles' tragedy opens. The messengers bring back the reply that the plague will cease when the murderer of Laius has been driven from the land.

> But he, where is he? Where shall now be read
> The fading record of this ancient guilt?[1]

The action of the play consists in nothing other than the process of revealing, with cunning delays and ever-mounting excitement — a process that can be likened to the work of a psychoanalysis — that Oedipus himself is the murderer of Laius, but further that he is the son of the murdered man and of Jocasta. Appalled at the abomination which he has unwittingly perpetrated, Oedipus blinds himself and forsakes his home. The oracle has been fulfilled.

Oedipus Rex is what is known as a tragedy of destiny. Its tragic effect is said to lie in the contrast between the supreme will of the gods and the vain attempts of mankind to escape the evil that threatens them. The lesson which, it is said, the deeply moved spectator should learn from the tragedy is submission to the divine will and realization of his own impotence. Modern drama-

---

[1] Lewis Campbell's translation (1883), lines 108ff. [Cf. lines 123–124 of the Fagles translation in this volume. — Editors' note]

tists have accordingly tried to achieve a similar tragic effect by weaving the same contrast into a plot invented by themselves. But the spectators have looked on unmoved while a curse or an oracle was fulfilled in spite of all the efforts of some innocent man: later tragedies of destiny have failed in their effect.

If *Oedipus Rex* moves a modern audience no less than it did the contemporary Greek one, the explanation can only be that its effect does not lie in the contrast between destiny and human will, but is to be looked for in the particular nature of the material on which that contrast is exemplified. There must be something which makes a voice within us ready to recognize the compelling force of destiny in the *Oedipus*, while we can dismiss as merely arbitrary such dispositions as are laid down in [Grillparzer's] *Die Ahnfrau* or other modern tragedies of destiny. And a factor of this kind is in fact involved in the story of King Oedipus. His destiny moves us only because it might have been ours — because the oracle laid the same curse upon us before our birth as upon him. It is the fate of all of us, perhaps, to direct our first sexual impulse toward our mother and our first hatred and our first murderous wish against our father. Our dreams convince us that that is so. King Oedipus, who slew his father Laius and married his mother Jocasta, merely shows us the fulfillment of our own childhood wishes. But, more fortunate than he, we have meanwhile succeeded, in so far as we have not become psychoneurotics, in detaching our sexual impulses from our mothers and in forgetting our jealousy of our fathers. Here is one in whom these primeval wishes of our childhood have been fulfilled, and we shrink back from him with the whole force of the repression by which those wishes have since that time been held down within us. While the poet, as he unravels the past, brings to light the guilt of Oedipus, he is at the same time compelling us to recognize our own inner minds, in which those same impulses, though suppressed, are still to be found. The contrast with which the closing Chorus leaves us confronted —

> . . . Fix on Oedipus your eyes,
> Who resolved the dark enigma, noblest champion and most wise.
> Like a star his envied fortune mounted beaming far and wide:
> Now he sinks in seas of anguish, whelmed beneath a raging tide . . .[2]

— strikes as a warning at ourselves and our pride, at us who since our childhood have grown so wise and so mighty in our own eyes. Like Oedipus, we live in ignorance of these wishes, repugnant to morality, which have been forced upon us by Nature, and after their revelation we may all of us well seek to close our eyes to the scenes of our childhood.[3]

There is an unmistakable indication in the text of Sophocles' tragedy itself that the legend of Oedipus sprang from some primeval dream material

---

[2] Lewis Campbell's translation, lines 1524ff. [Cf. lines 1678–1682 in the Fagles translation in this volume. — Editors' note]

[3] [*Footnote added by Freud in 1914 edition.*] None of the findings of psychoanalytic research has provoked such embittered denials, such fierce opposition — or such amusing contortions — on the part of critics as this indication of the childhood impulses toward incest which persist in the unconscious. An attempt has even been made recently to make out, in the face of all experience, that the incest should only be taken as "symbolic." — Ferenczi

which had as its content the distressing disturbance of a child's relation to his parents owing to the first stirrings of sexuality. At a point when Oedipus, though he is not yet enlightened, has begun to feel troubled by his recollection of the oracle, Jocasta consoles him by referring to a dream which many people dream, though, as she thinks, it has no meaning:

> Many a man ere now in dreams hath lain
> With her who bare him. He hath least annoy
> Who with such omens troubleth not his mind.[4]

Today, just as then, many men dream of having sexual relations with their mothers, and speak of the fact with indignation and astonishment. It is clearly the key to the tragedy and the complement to the dream of the dreamer's father being dead. The story of Oedipus is the reaction of the imagination to these two typical dreams. And just as these dreams, when dreamt by adults, are accompanied by feelings of repulsion, so too the legend must include horror and self-punishment. Its further modification originates once again in a misconceived secondary revision of the material, which has sought to exploit it for theological purposes. . . . The attempt to harmonize divine omnipotence with human responsibility must naturally fail in connection with this subject matter just as with any other.

ဢ

DAVID HENRY HWANG *discussed his attempt to integrate his Chinese American background into his plays, referring to the influence of Tom Stoppard's* Rosencrantz and Guildenstern Are Dead *(1967) on him while he was a student at Stanford University. Hwang's essay was originally published in* MELUS *(1989–90).*

DAVID HENRY HWANG

Evolving a Multicultural Tradition *1989–90*

I want to go through a sort of personal progression that has taken place in myself and is also reflected in my work. I think I evolved from a place where I had a complete and honest non-awareness of issues of people of color, to the place where I am now — which is continuing to evolve, but is closer to some sort of multicultural model.

When I first started writing plays I had no particular desire to write about myself as an Asian American or as a person of color. Perhaps as a result

---

(1912) has proposed an ingenious "overinterpretation" of the Oedipus myth, based on a passage in one of Schopenhauer's letters. [*Added 1919.*] Later studies have shown that the "Oedipus complex," which was touched upon for the first time in the above paragraphs in the *Interpretation of Dreams,* throws a light of undreamt-of importance on the history of the human race and the evolution of religion and morality.

[4] Lewis Campbell's translation, lines 982ff. [Cf. lines 1074–1078 in the Fagles translation in this volume. — Editors' note]

of that the first few plays I wrote, which are either in a drawer of mine or buried someplace, nobody's ever seen. At a certain point I started to awaken to issues of color, in the late '70s when I was an undergraduate in college. Partially this was through the awareness of works by Asian Americans who had come before me. Directly as a result of people like Frank Chin and Maxine Hong Kingston and other non-Asian writers like Ntozake Shange, I became aware of the possibility of opening up this side of myself in my work. When I wrote my first play, *F.O.B.*, to some extent it was an attempt to validate the existence of a previous Asian American literary tradition, through an exploration of two mythological characters: Fa Mu Lan, from Maxine Hong Kingston's book *The Woman Warrior,* and a character named Kwan Gung, the god of the writers, warriors, and prostitutes from Frank Chin's play *Gee, Pop.* I thought it was interesting to try to bring these two characters together in Torrance, California, in the same way that Stoppard took Rosencrantz and Guildenstern from *Hamlet* and made another play out of it, bringing about a certain cross-fertilization. At the same time I became very interested in trying to create a form which would make sense, in terms of this new content. At the time my choice was to create some kind of fusion of Asian and Western theater. Fortunately, I was working with an actor at the time named John Lone, whom you probably know from the film, *The Last Emperor,* who had been trained in the Cantonese Opera in Hong Kong and then come to the States and received Western training. Through utilizing John's resources, we were able to create the play *The Dance and the Railroad,* which was that attempt to create a cultural fusion.

After doing a few more plays in this vein I went through a period of writer's block when I didn't write anything for two years. I sort of became disenchanted with what I perceived to be sort of a nationalist model, both the advantages and the disadvantages of it. I began to wonder first of all if I was sort of creating Orientalia for the intelligentsia. I looked at my plays and some I liked and some I didn't. But the ones that seemed to be the most popular were the ones that had the Oriental things in them, like gongs and dragons. So that was a bit of a problem. I began to look at this whole idea of going through an isolationist period where one works mostly with members of one's own race, as necessary in terms of creating a certain amount of growth and understanding and making oneself whole again — but it is perhaps limited if one wants to go beyond that. I started to think that the term "ethnic theater" was not a particularly accurate term, because I think, particularly in America, we seem to have this conceptualization of there being a mainstream theater, which everybody can appreciate and which has universal value. Then there's this ethnic stuff, which has sort of a certain anthropological value, sociological value. If you're going to work in Chinatown you should maybe go see it. I think that actually really all American theater is ethnic theater to some degree, that even if you have Tennessee Williams for instance, writing primarily about whites in the South, that a lot of writers derive their authenticity from focusing on a particular group and then drawing the universality from those particular specifics.

I also wondered if a sort of literary segregation implied a cultural limitation. It's interesting to watch the history of ideas progress in the '50s, '60s, and '70s, and even today there's still a lot of vitality to the idea that people of color, women, gays are determining our own literary destiny and not having it written for us. On the other hand, I look at Hollywood now, which has adopted this idea as a sort of segregation. That is, blacks should write about blacks and women should write kind of soft personal stories. And I wonder if it isn't also true that if we want to or if we choose to, we should be able to claim a full franchise as American writers the same as other American writers have and be able to address any subjects that we want.

So I decided to write a play, *Rich Relations*, that didn't have any Asians in it. There is a bit of a miscue there. While I think it is perfectly valid for me to do that, what I did was I wrote an autobiographical play and then I just made the characters white. I think that that's probably not being exactly true to the characters either. We're currently planning a production of that same play at the Asian American Theater Company in San Francisco using a mixed Asian-Caucasian cast. Perhaps that will prove more true to the spirit of the work. Though I certainly acknowledge that the New York production of *Rich Relations* had faults, the critical reaction was so severely negative that I'm tempted to wonder whether there was also anger on their part that I was attempting to break out of their literary segregation. Only time and future non-Asian works by me will test that theory, though I must concede that the critical reaction to *1000 Airplanes on the Roof*, which was "nonethnic," was much warmer.

Now I'm attempting to evolve to a multicultural model. Not that I think it's something political that I'm forcing myself into, but it's something that I find myself interested in. When we did *M. Butterfly*, I think it was an attempt to try and expand on some of the issues that I felt as an Asian American and put them on a different type of stage. For instance, in terms of international issues, I felt certain attitudes from the mainstream society as an Asian American, and thought — is it reasonable to think that those values also influence our policy makers as they consider the world? And in the case of the play the answer is yes. I also think I learned from writing the play the interconnectedness of the "isms." Like racism, sexism, and imperialism all being manifestations of an attempt to degrade "the other," to make "the other" less than oneself. I also tried to deal with my discomfort with the perceived "exotic" elements of my work by facing it squarely. In effect, I'd like to think *Butterfly* says to an audience, "All right, we'll give you the Orientalia you seem to desire, but then we're also going to talk about why you're so attracted to this, and how that attachment to stereotypes blinds you to the truth of your own experience" — in the case of my play's deceived Frenchman, even to the extent of being unable to tell the true gender of his lover.

When I began exploring the true story on which *M. Butterfly* is based, I found an article in the *New York Times*. The actual diplomat was trying to account for the fact that he'd never seen his Chinese lover naked. He said, "I thought she was very modest, I thought it was a Chinese custom." My reaction was, "That's not a Chinese custom." It hit me that perhaps the diplomat had fallen in love, not with an actual person, but with a fantasy stereotype of the Orient. Which led me to the idea that he probably thought he'd found his Madame Butterfly. So my play attempts to deconstruct Puccini's opera, in that the diplomat begins the play fantasizing that he's Puccini's character Pinkerton who's finally found his Butterfly. By the end of the evening, though, he realizes that it's he who is Butterfly, in that the Frenchman was the one deluded by love. The Chinese spy who perpetrated that deception is therefore the real Pinkerton. One way to read the play is when we set out to degrade others, we only succeed in degrading ourselves.

Beyond *M. Butterfly* I find myself now trying to create a play that is more multicultural in the sense that now I'm trying to write about whites, Asians, and blacks. And I find that there are risks and challenges in this approach. I was at Brown University about a week ago, and I got into a very interesting discussion with an Asian student about if, as an Asian, I write about a black character, do I not risk creating the same sort of stereotypes and misperceptions that a white writer writing about a black character or an Asian character might. I certainly think those dangers exist. On the other hand, I do feel that in terms of trying to create a model that is more representative of what this country is becoming, both multicultural plays and multicultural theaters are ultimately the wave of the future. I think that there will always continue to be a need for single ethnic theaters. But fifty or sixty years down the road I would like to think that the theaters that are the most viable are those that do a black play, a Jewish play, an Asian play, whatever, in their season.

Finally, in terms of the commercial theater and my experience with *M. Butterfly*, I actually didn't find working with the commercial theater that much different than working in the nonprofit theater. There is more money at stake, but since I'm not the one who's putting up the money it doesn't really matter. I think the working process is very similar. Of course there is in the nonprofit theater a certain guarantee of a run, whereas in the commercial theater there's a possibility you can close overnight, which a lot of plays do. That of course does put a certain pressure on the product, ultimately. Certainly, opening a play in New York off-Broadway you're reviewed by Frank Rich, who determines your fate just as well as he does in the commercial theater. So I actually didn't find it that different an experience. I'd like to stress that you are reading today my ideas at a particular point in time, but I'd like to think of myself as always changing and growing, both personally and politically. Together, we are all attempting to evolve a cultural model in America which the world has never seen before.

ର୍ଷ

HENRIK IBSEN *wrote his first notes for the play that would become* A Doll House *on October 19, 1878. At first he conceived of the drama essentially as a marital conflict that would lead to Nora's destruction because of what he saw as her entrapment in a patriarchal society. This excerpt from Ibsen's notes is from the translator A. G. Chater's* From Ibsen's Workshop *(1978).*

HENRIK IBSEN

Notes for A Doll House   *1878*

There are two kinds of spiritual law, two kinds of conscience, one in man and another, altogether different, in woman. They do not understand each other; but in practical life the woman is judged by man's law, as though she were not a woman but a man.

The wife in the play ends by having no idea of what is right or wrong; natural feeling on the one hand and belief in authority on the other have altogether bewildered her.

A woman cannot be herself in the society of the present day, which is an exclusively masculine society, with laws framed by men and with a judicial system that judges feminine conduct from a masculine point of view.

She has committed forgery, and she is proud of it; for she did it out of love for her husband, to save his life. But this husband with his commonplace principles of honor is on the side of the law and looks at the question from the masculine point of view.

Spiritual conflicts. Oppressed and bewildered by the belief in authority, she loses faith in her moral right and ability to bring up her children. Bitterness. A mother in modern society, like certain insects who go away and die when she has done her duty in the propagation of the race. Love of life, of home, of husband and children and family. Now and then a womanly shaking off of her thoughts. Sudden return of anxiety and terror. She must bear it all alone. The catastrophe approaches, inexorably, inevitably. Despair, conflict, and destruction.

ಜಲ

BERNARD KNOX *wrote his analysis of Oedipus's heroic achievement in his introduction to Robert Fagles's translation of* Three Theban Plays *by Sophocles. Knox sees a great deal of ironic wordplay in the hero's name "Oidipous," which is close to the Greek word* oida *("I know"), as Oedipus determinedly searches for the truth about himself despite his subjection to fate.*

BERNARD KNOX

Oedipus' Heroic Achievement   *1982*

Oedipus' heroic achievement is the discovery of the truth, and that discovery is the most thoroughgoing and dreadful catastrophe the stage has ever presented. The hero who in his vigor, courage, and intelligence stands as a representative of all that is creative in man discovers a truth so dreadful that the chorus which sums up the results of the great calculation sees in his fall the reduction of man to nothing.

> O the generations of men
> the dying generations — adding the total
> of all your lives I find they come to nothing . . .

The existence of human freedom, dramatically represented in the *action* of Oedipus in the play, seems to be a mockery. The discovery to which it led is a catastrophe out of all proportion to the situation. Critics have tried, with contradictory results, to find some flaw in Oedipus' character that will justify his reversal. But there is nothing in his actions that can make it acceptable to us. The chorus' despairing summation, "come to nothing," echoes our own feelings as we watch Oedipus rush into the palace.

But this estimate of the situation is not the last word; in fact, it is contradicted by the final scene of the play. Oedipus' first thought, we are told by the messenger, was to kill himself — he asked for a sword — but he blinds himself instead. This action is one that the audience must have expected; it was mentioned in the earlier *Antigone*, for example, and Oedipus as the blind, exiled wanderer seems to have been one of the invariable elements in fifth-century versions of the myth. But, though the blindness was foreseen by Tiresias, Oedipus' action did not figure in the prophecies made to and about him by Apollo. When the messenger comes from inside the palace to describe the catastrophe he uses words which emphasize the independence of this action: "terrible things, and none done blindly now, / all done with a will." And as Oedipus, wearing a mask with blood running from the eye sockets, stumbles on stage, he makes the same distinction when the chorus asks him what power impelled him to attack his eyes:

> Apollo, friends, Apollo —
> he ordained my agonies — these, my pains on pains!
> But the hand that struck my eyes was mine,
> mine alone — no one else —
> I did it all myself!

These two passages suggest that in his decision to blind himself Oedipus is acting freely, that the intricate pattern of his destiny was complete when he knew the truth. To that terrible revelation some violent reaction was inevitable; the choice was left to him. He resisted the first suicidal impulse perhaps (though Sophocles is silent on the point) because of a latent conviction, fully and openly expounded in the last play (*Oedipus at Colonus*), that he was not to blame. He chose to blind himself, as he tells the chorus, because he could not bear to see the faces of his children and his fellow-citizens. But his action has, in the context of this play, an impressive rightness; the man who, proud of his far-seeing intelligence, taunted Tiresias with his blindness now realizes that all his life long he has himself been blind to the dreadful realities of his identity and action.

The messenger's description of the horrors that took place inside the palace has prepared the audience for the spectacle of a broken man. So Oedipus seems to be at first, but very soon this bloodstained, sightless figure begins to reassert that magnificent imperious personality which was his from the beginning. He reproaches the chorus for wishing him dead rather than blind, defends his decision to blind himself, issues instructions to Creon, and finally has to be reminded that he is no longer master in Thebes. The despairing summation based on the fate of Oedipus — the great example (as the chorus calls him) that man is equal to nothing — is corrected by the reemergence of Oedipus as his old forceful self. Formidable as of old he may be, but with a difference. The confident tone in which the blind man speaks so regally is based on knowledge, knowledge of his own identity and of the truth of divine prophecy. This new knowledge, won at such a terrible price, makes clear what it was in the hero that brought about the disaster. It was ignorance.

In spite of his name, *Oidipous*, with its resemblance to the Greek word *oida* ("I know") — a theme that Sophocles hammers home with continual word-play — Oedipus, who thought he knew so much, did not even know who his mother and father were. But ignorance can be remedied, the ignorant can learn, and the force with which Oedipus now reasserts his presence springs from the truth he now understands: that the universe is not a field for the play of blind chance, and that man is not its measure. This knowledge gives him a new strength which sustains him in his misery and gives him the courage needed to go on living, though he is now an outcast, a man from whom his fellow-men recoil in horror.

The play then is a tremendous reassertion of the traditional religious view that man is ignorant, that knowledge belongs only to the gods — Freud's "theological purpose." And it seems to present at first sight a view of the universe as rigid on the side of order as Jocasta's was anarchic on the side of freedom. Jocasta thought that there was no order or design in the world, that dreams and prophecies had no validity, that man had complete freedom because it made no difference what he did — nothing made any sense. She was wrong; the design was there, and when she saw what it was she hanged herself. But the play now seems to give us a view of man's position that is just as comfortless as her acceptance of a meaningless universe. What place is there in it for human freedom and meaningful action?

Oedipus did have one freedom: he was free to find out or not find out the truth. This was the element of Sophoclean sleight-of-hand that enabled him to make a drama out of the situation which the philosophers used as the classic demonstration of man's subjection to fate. But it is more than a solution to an apparently insoluble dramatic problem; it is the key to the play's tragic theme and the protagonist's heroic stature. One freedom is allowed him: the freedom to search for the truth, the truth about the prophecies, about the gods, about himself. And of this freedom he makes full use. Against the advice and appeals of others, he pushes on, searching for the truth, the whole truth, and nothing but the truth. And in this search he shows all those great qualities that we admire in him — courage, intelligence, perseverance, the qualities that make human beings great. This freedom to search, and the heroic way in which Oedipus uses it, makes the play not a picture of man's utter feebleness caught in the toils of fate, but on the contrary, a heroic example of man's dedication to the search for truth, the truth about himself. This is perhaps the only human freedom, the play seems to say, but there could be none more noble.

∞

ARTHUR MILLER *wrote the story "In Memoriam" at the age of seventeen, while working in his father's coat factory in Manhattan shortly before he graduated from high school in 1932. During the Depression Miller's family couldn't afford to send him to college, so he worked for two years to save money for his tuition at the University of Michigan. He put away the manuscript of "In Memoriam," about a middle-aged coat salesman, and forgot about it until his mother found it after his play* Death of a Salesman *opened in 1949. Miller attached a note to his story when he placed it in the Arthur Miller Archive in the Harry Ransom Library at the University of Texas: "The real Schoenzeit of the story threw himself in front of an El [subway] train the day following the incident."*

ARTHUR MILLER

In Memoriam
1932

Sitting here now, thinking of him, he seems to be a romantic figure, but really he wasn't. Yet I couldn't venture to call him "commonplace." I never knew him intimately, yet I feel as though I knew him more closely, more thoroughly, than I know myself.

His was a salesman's profession, if one may describe such dignified slavery as a profession, and though he tried to interest himself in his work he never became entirely molded into the pot of that business. His emotions were displayed at the wrong times always, and he never quite knew when to laugh. Perhaps, if I may say so, he never was complete. He had lost something vital. There was an air of quiet solitude, of cryptic wondering about both him and his name.

Although he was ever simply and immaculately dressed, I always imagined he had been dressed by someone else.

When I first heard his name, I wondered if he hadn't forgotten some other and had merely been called this by men. His last name was Schoenzeit; the first I never learned, but it had to be Alfred. He always seemed to need that name. Especially when he sat at the small glass-topped table in my father's showroom, slowly perusing the columns of the *Times*, with tears of perspiration dotting the reddened ridge that his gray felt hat had made around his head. The shined, bulgy-toed shoes placed flatly and it seemed carefully on the carpet, his overcoat folded neatly on a chair, the bow of his tie stuck so perfectly into the crevice of a starched, rounded collar completed a setting where I am sure he never belonged.

Schoenzeit, as everyone called him, often was gay. I might add "happy," but of the last I shall never be sure. He laughed as superciliously as any of the others when someone was the object of a quip. But these occasions were rare and never lasted, as far as he was concerned. Always he returned to his fogged manner, and after the joke had faded from his mind the light which seemed to brighten his countenance, too, disappeared, and he was once more enigmatic and incomprehensible.

I had, on several occasions, been alone with him, and may truthfully say I deeply pitied such a dejected soul. At one time it was necessary for him to go to the Bronx to interview a large retail drygoods store, and I was instructed to carry his samples. It was late spring, the sky was cloudless and blue, a yellow sun was slowly warming the cool morning air, and the usual city hurriers were plying their trade.

I had six coats in my arms, holding them against my chest, while he walked, leaning very slightly forward, by my side. His feet must have hurt him, for he pointed them outward, laying them flat on the ground at every step. When walking, he seemed to be striving against a stiff wind, his eyebrows peaked together, forming tiny creases at the bridge of his nose. His hat, placed straight on his head, shaded his eyes, which gazed seekingly ahead.

It was necessary to walk from Eighth to Third Avenue in order to reach the Elevated, and he offered many times to rest. I must have looked tired, because he turned to me once and laughed, saying in his cracked yet resonant baritone, "Hard work, eh, kid? Some business . . ." Of course, I didn't admit my weariness, and pitching my head to one side, raising my eyebrows and smiling, assured him that I was enjoying it as much as he was.

In due time, we approached the El, and about a block away he slowly and lightly touched my arm and, still looking ahead, he asked, "Arthur, do you get paid from the firm for carfare?" He said this in a low tone, as though he were trying to hide his point until it was absolutely necessary to take the plunge.

I thought for a moment and answered, "Well, whenever I have to go anywhere out of walking distance I am given money to ride, but I have no standing allowance for such purposes." He seemed to falter, and flushed a trifle before answering, and for a second I felt both rage and pity for this decrepit soul, who, it seemed, aged many years as he turned to me. I knew then that he felt as though his life were ended, that he was merely being pushed by outside forces. And though his body went on as before, the soul inside had crumpled and broken beyond repair.

He was asking me now for carfare. I knew he would rather have been pulled apart by a tiger, but he was asking me for carfare, a nickel to hold out to a corpulent, uninterested machine for his fare. My heart bled for him at that moment, and as we mounted the long stairway to the trains I realized that as low and shakingly embarrassed as I felt, his senses were that much more tormented and destroyed. And I marvelled at his poise under the circumstances. The coats were warm now against me, and I was thankful to God himself for this refuge for my gawky body which, with the expression of my eyes, must reveal to him my sensations.

I tried as best I could to make this situation seem as if it were commonplace — I who had carried samples for so many salesmen. And when we reached the turnstile, I balanced my burden on one knee while I dipped my free hand into my pocket. Behind my throat, I cursed myself for not having the change. I turned from him in order to get the nickels required, and when I lifted my eyes to his figure I prayed, until my temples seemed to burst, for his salvation. At that moment, he looked so broken, so dejected and lost that I hastily lowered my gaze. He appeared to me then, as he stood there at the turnstile, like a small dog who has messed in the house, standing now, after his beating, waiting for his master to open the door to the back yard.

During the entire ride uptown, we two spoke but sparingly. The bright streets below changed constantly as we racketed past, and the windows of the houses facing the trains offered a haven for my confused and weary imagination.

He sold nothing that day and was profusely maltreated by the attending force at the buying office who, by virtue of their superior intelligence and ties to match, were vindicated even when they were consciously adding to the vicissitudes of a seller's life.

On the return trip, Alfred, as I subconsciously called him, became more voluble and questioned me as to my ambitions and my occupations in my leisure time. Upon hearing that I owned an old car, he immediately became interested and spoke a little less haltingly than was his wont. From constant rebuff, he was loath to venture an opinion, and often embarrassed us both by ending a bountiful conversation unexpectedly.

He accompanied me to my father's place and, placing his hand on the small of my back, patted me lightly, and said with a faint smile, "Thanks, Arthur — and I'll . . . see you tomorrow."

With that farewell, he was off into the crowd, and his restless body faded slowly into the dark overcoats of unknowns as it willingly shrank from my sight.

I never saw him again and had forgotten him entirely when I heard of his death.

"Schoenzeit is dead," and my only recollection of that second when I heard those words is a slow exhaling of my breath and a cool, soft, glowing smile within my soul.

৩৫

ARTHUR MILLER *analyzed the tragic dimension in Willy Loman's character when* Death of a Salesman *was published by Viking Press in 1957. In his introduction to the play, Williams discussed how his view of a tragic hero differed from Aristotle's formulation in the* Poetics. *Miller then went on to describe his dramatic method of calling Willy Loman's values into question by presenting him with what Miller called "an opposing system" of love within the family to counter his society's false ideals of power and success. As Miller remarked during a symposium on his play the following year, "The trouble with Willy Loman is that he has tremendously powerful ideals. . . . [I]f Willy Loman, for instance, had not had a very profound sense that his life as lived had left him hollow, he would have died contentedly polishing his car on some Sunday afternoon at a ripe old age. The fact is he has values. The fact that they cannot be realized is what is driving him mad."*

ARTHUR MILLER

On Death of a Salesman *as an American Tragedy*

1957

I set out not to "write a tragedy" in this play, but to show the truth as I saw it. However, some of the attacks upon it as a pseudo-tragedy contain ideas so misleading, and in some cases so laughable, that it might be in place here to deal with a few of them.

Aristotle having spoken of a fall from the heights, it goes without saying that someone of the common mold cannot be a fit tragic hero. It is now many centuries since Aristotle lived. There is no more reason for falling down in a faint before his *Poetics* than before Euclid's geometry, which has been amended numerous times by men with new insights; nor, for that matter, would I choose to have my illness diagnosed by Hippocrates rather than the most ordinary graduate of an American medical school, despite the Greek's genius. Things do change, and even a genius is limited by his time and the nature of his society.

I would deny, on grounds of simple logic, this one of Aristotle's contentions if only because he lived in a slave society. When a vast number of people are divested of alternatives, as slaves are, it is rather inevitable that one will not be able to imagine drama, let alone tragedy, as being possible for any but the higher ranks of society. There is a legitimate question of stature here, but none of rank, which is so often confused with it. So long as the hero may be said to have had alternatives of a magnitude to have materially changed the course of his life, it seems to me that in this respect at least, he cannot be debarred from the heroic role.

The question of rank is significant to me only as it reflects the question of the social application of the hero's career. There is no doubt that if a character is shown on the stage who goes through the most ordinary actions, and is suddenly revealed to be the President of the United States, his actions immediately assume a much greater magnitude, and pose the possibilities of much greater meaning, than if he is the corner grocer. But at the same time, his stature as a hero is not so utterly dependent upon his rank that the corner grocer cannot outdistance him as a tragic figure — providing, of course, that the grocer's career engages the issues of, for instance, the survival of the race, the relationships of man to God — the questions, in short, whose answers define humanity and the right way to live so that the world is a home, instead of a battleground or a fog in which disembodied spirits pass each other in an endless twilight.

In this respect *Death of a Salesman* is a slippery play to categorize because nobody in it stops to make a speech objectively stating the great issues which I believe it embodies. If it were a worse play, less closely articulating its meanings with its actions, I think it would have more quickly satisfied a certain kind of criticism. But it was meant to be less a play than a fact; it refused admission to its author's opinions and opened itself to a revelation of process and the operations of an ethic, of social laws of action no less powerful in their effects upon individuals than any tribal law administered by gods with names. I need not claim that this play is a genuine solid gold tragedy for my opinions on tragedy to be held valid. My purpose here is simply to point out a historical fact which must be taken into account in any consideration of tragedy, and it is the sharp alteration in the meaning of rank in society between the present time and the distant past. More important to me is the fact that this particular kind of argument obscures much more relevant considerations.

One of these is the question of intensity. It matters not at all whether a modern play concerns itself with a grocer or a president if the intensity of the hero's commitment to his course is less than the maximum possible. It matters not at all whether the hero falls from a great height or a small one, whether he is highly conscious or only dimly aware of what is happening, whether his pride brings the fall or an unseen pattern written behind clouds; if the intensity, the human passion to surpass his given bounds, the fanatic insistence upon his self-conceived role — if these are not present there can only be an outline of tragedy but no living thing. I believe, for myself, that the lasting appeal of tragedy is due to our need to face the fact of death in order to strengthen ourselves for life, and that over and above this function of the tragic viewpoint there are and will be a great number of formal variations which no single definition will ever embrace.

Another issue worth considering is the so-called tragic victory, a question closely related to the consciousness of the hero. One makes nonsense of this if a "victory" means that the hero makes us feel some certain joy when, for instance, he sacrifices himself for a "cause," and unhappy and morose because he dies without one. To begin at the bottom, a man's death is and ought to be an essentially terrifying thing and ought to make nobody happy. But in a great variety of ways even death, the ultimate negative, can be, and appear to be, an assertion of bravery, and can serve to separate the death of man from the death of animals; and I think it is this distinction which underlies any conceptions of a victory in death. For a society of faith, the nature of the death can prove the existence of the spirit, and posit its immortality. For a secular society it is perhaps more difficult for such a victory to document itself and to make itself felt, but, conversely, the need to offer greater proofs of the humanity of man can make that victory more real. It goes without saying that in a society where there is basic disagreement as to the right way to live, there can hardly be agreement as to the right way to die, and both life and death must be heavily weighted with meaningless futility.

It was not out of any deference to a tragic definition that Willy Loman is filled with a joy, however broken-hearted, as he approaches his end, but simply that my sense of his character dictated his joy, and even what I felt was an exultation. In terms of his character, he has achieved a very powerful piece of knowledge, which is that he is loved by his son and has been embraced by him and forgiven. In this he is given his existence, so to speak — his fatherhood, for which he has always striven and which until now he could not achieve. That he is unable to take this victory thoroughly to his heart, that it closes the circle for him and propels him to his death, is the wage of his sin, which was to have committed himself so completely to the counterfeits of dignity and the false coinage embodied in his idea of success that he can prove his existence only by bestowing "power" on his posterity, a power deriving from the sale of his last asset, himself, for the price of his insurance policy.

I must confess here to a miscalculation, however. I did not realize while writing the play that so many people in the world do not see as clearly, or would not admit, as I thought they must, how futile most lives are; so there could be no hope of consoling the audience for the death of this man. I did not realize either how few would be impressed by the fact that this man is actually a very brave spirit who cannot settle for half but must pursue his dream of himself to the end. Finally, I thought it must be clear, even obvious, that this was no dumb brute heading mindlessly to his catastrophe.

I have no need to be Willy's advocate before the jury which decides who is and who is not a tragic hero. I am merely noting that the lingering ponderousness of so many ancient definitions has blinded students and critics to the facts before them, and not only in regard to this play. Had Willy been unaware of his separation from values that endure he would have died contentedly while polishing his car, probably on a Sunday afternoon with the ball game coming over the radio. But he was agonized by his awareness of being in a false position, so constantly haunted by the hollowness of all he had placed his faith in, so aware, in short, that he must somehow be filled in his spirit or fly apart, that he staked his very life on the ultimate assertion. That he had not the intellectual fluency to verbalize his situation is not the same thing as saying that he lacked awareness, even an overly intensified consciousness that the life he had made was without form and inner meaning.

To be sure, had he been able to know that he was as much the victim of his beliefs as their defeated exemplar, had he known how much of guilt he ought to bear and how much to shed from his soul, he would be more conscious. But it seems to me that there is of necessity a severe limitation of self-awareness in any character, even the most knowing, which serves to define him as a character, and more, that this very limit serves to complete the tragedy and, indeed, to make it at all possible. Complete consciousness is possible only in a play about forces, like *Prometheus*,° but not in a play about people. I think that the point is whether there is a sufficient awareness in the hero's career to make the audience supply the rest. Had Oedipus, for instance, been more conscious and more aware of the forces at work upon him he must surely have said that he was not really to blame for having cohabited with his mother since neither he nor anyone else knew she was his mother. He must surely decide to divorce her, provide for their children, firmly resolve to investigate the family background of his next wife, and thus deprive us of a very fine play and the name for a famous neurosis. But he is conscious only up to a point, the point at which guilt begins. Now he is inconsolable and must tear out his eyes. What is tragic about this? Why is it not even ridiculous? How can we respect a man who goes to such extremities over something he could in no way help or prevent? The answer, I think, is not that we respect the man, but that we respect the Law he has so completely broken, wittingly or not, for it is that Law which, we believe, defines us as men. The confusion of some critics viewing *Death of a Salesman* in this regard is that they do not see that Willy Loman has broken a law without whose protection life is insupportable if not incomprehensible to him and to many others; it is the law which says that a failure in society and in business has no right to live. Unlike the law against incest, the law of success is not administered by statute or church, but it is very nearly as powerful in its

---

Prometheus: *Prometheus Bound* by the Greek tragedian Aeschylus (c. 525–456 B.C.).

grip upon men. The confusion increases because, while it is a law, it is by no means a wholly agreeable one even as it is slavishly obeyed, for to fail is no longer to belong to society, in his estimate. Therefore, the path is opened for those who wish to call Willy merely a foolish man even as they themselves are living in obedience to the same law that killed him. Equally, the fact that Willy's law — the belief, in other words, which administers guilt to him — is not a civilizing statute whose destruction menaces us all; it is, rather, a deeply believed and deeply suspect "good" which, when questioned as to its value, as it is in this play, serves more to raise our anxieties than to reassure us of the existence of an unseen but humane metaphysical system in the world. My attempt in the play was to counter this anxiety with an opposing system which, so to speak, is in a race for Willy's faith, and it is the system of love which is the opposite of the law of success. It is embodied in Biff Loman, but by the time Willy can perceive his love it can serve only as an ironic comment upon the life he sacrificed for power and for success and its tokens.

ကာ

ARTHUR MILLER *spoke about the dramatic portrayal of father-son relationships and the tragic hero in a* Paris Review *interview in 1966 at his farmhouse in Litchfield County, Connecticut. An astute commentator on American drama, Miller referred to the radical political theater of the 1930s, the absurd theater of the 1960s, and the then-recent play* Cat on a Hot Tin Roof *by his contemporary Tennessee Williams.*

ARTHUR MILLER

From the Paris Review Interview   1967

Interviewer: Many of your plays have that father-son relationship as the dominant theme. Were you very close to your father?

Miller: I was. I still am, but I think, actually, that my plays don't reflect directly my relationship to him. It's a very primitive thing in my plays. That is, the father was really a figure who incorporated both power and some kind of a moral law which he had either broken himself or had fallen prey to. He figures as an immense shadow. . . . I didn't expect that of my own father, literally, but of his position, apparently I did. The reason that I was able to write about the relationship, I think now, was because it had a mythical quality to me. If I had ever thought that I was writing about my father, I suppose I never could have done it. My father is, literally, a much more realistic guy than Willy Loman, and much more successful as a personality. And he'd be the last man in the world to ever commit suicide. Willy is based on an individual whom I knew very little, who was a salesman; it was years later that I realized I had only seen that man about a total of four hours in twenty years. He gave one of those impressions that is basic, evidently. When I thought of him, he would simply be a mute man: he said no more than two hundred words to me. I was a kid. Later on, I had another of that kind of contact, with a man whose fantasy was always overreaching his real outline. I've always been aware of that kind of an agony, of someone who has some driving, implacable wish in him which never goes away, which he can never block out. And it broods over him, it makes him happy sometimes or it makes him suicidal, but it never leaves him. Any hero whom we even begin to think of as tragic is obsessed, whether it's Lear or Hamlet or the women in the Greek plays.

Interviewer: Do any of the younger playwrights create heroes — in your opinion?

Miller: I tell you, I may be working on a different wave length, but I don't think they are looking at character any more, at the documentation of facts about people. All experience is looked at now from a schematic point of view. These playwrights won't let the characters escape for a moment from their preconceived scheme of how dreadful the world is. It is very much like the old strike plays. The scheme then was that someone began a play with a bourgeois ideology and got involved in some area of experience which had a connection to the labor movement — either it was actually a strike or, in a larger sense, it was the collapse of capitalism — and he ended the play with some new positioning vis-à-vis that collapse. He started without an enlightenment and he ended with some kind of enlightenment. And you could predict that in the first five minutes. Very few of those plays could be done any more, because they're absurd now. I've found over the years that a similar thing has happened with the so-called absurd theater. Predictable.

Interviewer: In other words, the notion of tragedy about which you were talking earlier is absent from this preconceived view of the world.

Miller: Absolutely. The tragic hero was supposed to join the scheme of things by his sacrifice. It's a religious thing, I've always thought. He threw some sharp light upon the hidden scheme of existence, either by breaking one of its profoundest laws, as Oedipus breaks a taboo, and therefore proves the existence of the taboo, or by proving a moral world at the cost of his own life. And that's the victory. We need him, as the vanguard of the race. We need his crime. That crime is a civilizing crime. Well, *now* the view is that it's an inconsolable universe. Nothing is proved by a crime excepting that some people are freer to produce crime than others, and usually they are more honest than the others. There is no final reassertion of a community at all. There isn't the kind of communication that a child demands. The best you could say is that it is intelligent.

Interviewer: Then it's aware —

Miller: It's aware, but it will not admit into itself any moral universe at all. Another thing that's missing is the positioning of the author in relation to power. I always assumed that underlying any story is the question of who should wield power. See, in *Death of a Salesman* you have two viewpoints. They show what would happen if we all took Willy's viewpoint toward the world, or if we all took Biff's. And took it seriously, as almost a political fact. I'm debating really which way the world ought to be run; I'm speaking of psychology and the spirit, too. For example, a play that isn't usually linked with this kind of problem is Tennessee Williams's *Cat on a Hot Tin Roof*. It struck me sharply that what is at stake there is the father's great power. He's the owner, literally, of an empire of land and farms. And he wants to immortalize that power, he wants to hand it on, because he's dying. The son has a much finer appreciation of justice and human relations than the father. The father is rougher, more Philistine; he's cruder; and when we speak of the fineness of emotions, we would probably say the son has them and the father lacks them. When I saw the play I thought, This is going to be simply marvelous because the person with the sensitivity will be presented with power and what is he going to do about it? But it never gets to that. It gets deflected onto a question of personal neurosis. It comes to a dead end. If we're talking about tragedy, the Greeks would have done something miraculous with that idea. They would have stuck the son with the power, and faced him with the racking conflicts of the sensitive man having to rule. And then you would throw light on what the tragedy of power is.

Interviewer: Which is what you were getting at in *Incident at Vichy*.

Miller: That's exactly what I was after. But I feel today's stage turns away from any consideration of power, which always lies at the heart of tragedy. I use Williams's play as an example because he's that excellent that his problems are symptomatic of the time — *Cat* ultimately came down to the mendacity of human relations. It was a most accurate personalization but it bypasses the issue which the play seems to me to raise, namely the mendacity in social relations. I still believe that when a play questions, even threatens, our social arrangement, that is when it really shakes us profoundly and dangerously, and that is when you've got to be great; good isn't enough.

Interviewer: Do you think that people in general now rationalize so, and have so many euphemisms for death, that they can't face tragedy?

Miller: I wonder whether there isn't a certain — I'm speaking now of all classes of people — you could call it a softness, or else a genuine inability to face the tough decisions and the dreadful results of error.

ဏ

LEONARD MUSTAZZA *considers the similarities and differences between Glaspell's play and short story. This essay was published in the literary journal* Studies in Short Fiction.

LEONARD MUSTAZZA

Generic Translation and Thematic Shift in Glaspell's Trifles *and "A Jury of Her Peers"* 1989

Commentators on Susan Glaspell's classic feminist short story, "A Jury of Her Peers" (1917), and the one-act play from which it derives, *Trifles* (1916), have tended to regard the two works as essentially alike. And even those few who have noticed the changes that Glaspell made in the process of generic translation have done so only in passing. In his monograph on Glaspell, Arthur Waterman, who seems to have a higher regard for the story than for the play, suggests that the story is a "moving fictional experience" because of the progressive honing of the author's skills, the story's vivid realism owing to her work as a local-color writer for the *Des Moines Daily News*, and its unified plot due to its dramatic origin.[1] More specifically, Elaine Hedges appropriately notes the significance of Glaspell's change in titles from *Trifles*, which emphasizes the supposedly trivial household items with which the women "acquit" their accused peer, to "A Jury of Her Peers," which emphasizes the question of legality. In 1917, Hedges observes, women were engaged in the final years of their fight for the vote, and Glaspell's change in titles thus "emphasizes the story's contemporaneity, by calling attention to its references to the issue of women's legal place in American society."[2] Apart from these and a few other passing remarks, however, critics have chosen to focus on one work or the other. Indeed, thematic criticisms of the respective pieces are virtually indistinguishable, most of these commentaries focusing on the question of assumed "roles" in the works.[3]

On one level, there is good reason for this lack of differentiation. Not only is the overall narrative movement of the works similar, but Glaspell incorporated in the short story virtually every single line of the dialogue from *Trifles*.[4] By the same token, though, she also added much to the short story, which is about twice as long as the play. The nature of these additions is

---

[1] Arthur E. Waterman, *Susan Glaspell* (New York: Twayne, 1966), pp. 29–30.

[2] Elaine Hedges, "Small Things Reconsidered: Susan Glaspell's 'A Jury of Her Peers,' " *Women's Studies*, 12, No. 1 (1986), 106.

[3] Rachel France notes that *Trifles* reveals "the dichotomy between men and women in rural life," an important feature of that dichotomy being the men's "proclivity for the letter of the law" as opposed to the women's more humane understanding of justice ("Apropos of Women and the Folk Play," in *Women in American Theatre: Careers, Images, Movements*, ed. Helen Krich Chinoy and Linda Walsh Jenkins [New York: Crown, 1981], p. 151). Karen Alkalay-Gut observes three polarities in "Jury": the opposition between the large external male world and the women's more circumscribed place within the home; the attitudes of men and women generally; and the distinction between *law*, which is identified with "the imposition of abstractions on individual circumstances," and *justice*, "the extrapolation of judgment from individual circumstances" ("Jury of Her Peers: The Importance of *Trifles*," *Studies in Short Fiction*, 21 [Winter 1984], 2). Karen Stein calls the play "an anomaly in the murder mystery genre, which is predominantly a male tour de force." By bonding together, she goes on, the women act in a manner that is "diametrically opposed to the solo virtuosity usually displayed by male detectives" ("The Women's World of Glaspell's *Trifles*," in *Women in American Theatre*, ed. Helen Krich Chinoy and Linda Walsh Jenkins [New York: Crown, 1981], p. 254). Judith Fetterly also advances an interesting and imaginative interpretation. She sees the characters in "Jury" as readers and the trivial household items as their text. The men fail to read the same meanings in that text that the women do because they are committed to "the equation of textuality with masculine subject matter and masculine point of view" ("Reading about Reading: 'A Jury of Her Peers,' 'The Murders in the Rue Morge,' and 'The Yellow Wallpaper,' " in *Gender and Reading: Essays on Readers, Texts and Contexts*, ed. Elizabeth A. Flynn and Patrocinio P. Schweickart [Baltimore: Johns Hopkins Univ. Press, 1986], pp. 147–48).

[4] Elaine Hedges notes that one reference included in the play but omitted from "Jury" is Mrs. Hale's lament that, because of Mr. Wright's parsimony, Minnie could not join the Ladies' Aid, a society in which women cooperated with the local church to make items like carpets and quilts. These items were then sold to support ministers' salaries and to aid foreign missions. Minnie is thus denied not only the company of other women but also one of the few public roles that farm women were allowed to play ("Small Things Reconsidered," p. 102). In this regard, the story reveals, as Jeannie McKnight suggests, "a kind of classic 'cabin fever' as motivation for the homicide . . ." ("American Dream, Nightmare Underside: Diaries, Letters, and Fiction of Women on the American Frontier," in *Women, Women Writers, and the West*, ed. L. L. Lee and Merrill Lewis [Troy, NY: Whitson, 1979], p. 31).

twofold, the first and most obvious being her descriptions of locales, modes of utterance, characters, props, and so on — the kinds of descriptions that the prose writer's form will allow but the dramatist's will not. The other type of alteration is more subtle, and it involves the revisions, embellishments, and redirections that occur when an existent story is retold. When, for instance, a novel is turned into a film or a play, the best that can be said about the generic translation is that it is "faithful," but never is it identical. So it is with "Jury." It is certainly faithful to the play, but it is also different in a variety of ways, and it is these differences, which took place in the act of generic translation, that I would like to consider here.

In her article on *Trifles*, Beverly Smith makes an interesting observation. Noting that the women in the play, Mrs. Hale and Mrs. Peters, function as defense counsel for and jury of their accused peer, Minnie Foster Wright, she goes on to suggest that the men's role, their official capacities notwithstanding, are comparable to that of a Greek Chorus, "the voice of the community's conscience," entering at various points to reiterate their major themes — Minnie's guilt and the triviality of the women's occupations, avocations, and preoccupations.[5] This equation is, I think, quite useful, for the periodic entries, commentaries, and exits of the male characters in both Glaspell works do in fact mark the progressive stages of the narrative, which primarily concerns the women, including the absent Minnie Foster.[6] Though not on stage for the entire drama, as is the Greek Chorus, the men nevertheless function in much the same way, providing commentary and separating the major movements of the narrative. What is more, if we regard the men's exits from the stage as marking these movements, we will recognize the first principal difference between the play and the story — namely, that the latter contains twice as many movements as the former and is therefore necessarily a more developed and complex work.

Trifles opens with Mr. Hale's account of what he found when he arrived at the Wright farm the day before. Of the women themselves, we know almost nothing beyond their general appearances as described in the opening stage directions — that Mrs. Peters, the sheriff's wife, is "a slight wiry woman [with] a thin nervous face"; and that Mrs. Hale, the witness's wife, is larger than Mrs. Peters and "comfortable looking," though now appearing fearful and disturbed as she enters the scene of the crime. Standing close together as they enter the Wrights' home, the women remain almost completely undifferentiated until, some time later, they begin to speak. Thus, Glaspell underscores here the male/female polarities that she will explore in the course of the play.

Her entire narrative technique is different in the prose version. That

---

[5] Beverly A. Smith, "Women's Work — Trifles? The Skill and Insight of Playwright Susan Glaspell," *International Journal of Women's Studies*, 5 (March–April 1982), 175.

[6] Cynthia Sutherland aptly observes that the story's effect depends to a large extent upon the removal of Minnie from the sight of the audience, thus focussing our attention on the facts of her plight rather than on her appearance and mannerisms ("American Women Playwrights as Mediators of the 'Woman Problem,'" *Modern Drama*, 21 [September 1978], 323).

story begins in Mrs. Hale's disordered kitchen, which will later serve as a point of comparison with the major scene of the story, Mrs. Wright's kitchen. Annoyed at being called away from her housework, she nevertheless agrees to Sheriff Peters's request that she come along to accompany Mrs. Peters, who is there to fetch some personal effects for the jailed woman. Quite unlike the play's opening, which emphasizes the physical closeness of and the attitudinal similarities between the women, "Jury," taking us as it does into Mrs. Hale's thoughts, emphasizes the women's apartness:

> She had met Mrs. Peters the year before at the county fair, and the thing she remembered about her was that *she didn't seem to like the sheriff's wife.* She was small and thin and didn't have a strong voice. Mrs. Gorman, the sheriff's wife before Gorman went out and Peters came in, had a voice that somehow seemed to be backing up the law with every word. But if Mrs. Peters didn't look like a sheriff's wife, Peters made up for it in looking like a sheriff. . . . a heavy man with a big voice, who was particularly genial with the law-abiding, as if to make it plain that he knew the difference between criminals and non-criminals. (emphasis added)

Interestingly, for all the added material here, Glaspell omits mention of what the women look like. In fact, we will get no explicit statements on their appearance.

On the other hand, what we do get in this revised opening is much that sharply differentiates the story from the play. In the latter, we are provided with no indication of Mrs. Hale's bad feelings about the sheriff's wife, and, if anything, their close physical proximity leads us to conclude the opposite. Although the women in the story will later assume this same protective stance when they enter the accused's kitchen and then again when the county attorney criticizes Mrs. Wright's kitchen, the movement together there is little more than reflexive. Elaine Hedges has argued that the latter movement together begins the process of establishing "their common bonds with each other and with Minnie."[7] This may be so of their physical proximity in the play, where no distance is established between the women at the outset, but the story presents a different situation altogether, for any emotional closeness we might infer from their act is undercut by our knowledge of Mrs. Hale's lack of respect for Mrs. Peters, particularly by comparison with her predecessor, Mrs. Gorman.

Ironically, however despite her seeming mismatch with her husband, her lack of corporal "presence," Mrs. Peters turns out to be more suited to her assumed public role than Mrs. Hale had suspected — all too suited, in fact, since she perfectly assumes her male-approved role. "Of course Mrs. Peters is one of us," the county attorney asserts prior to getting on with his investigation of the house, and that statement turns out to be laden with meaning in the story. In *Trifles,* when the men leave to go about their investigative business, the women, we are told, "listen to the men's steps, then look about the

---

[7] "Small Things Reconsidered," p. 98.

kitchen." In "Jury," however, we get much more. Again here, the women stand motionless, listening to the men's footsteps, but this momentary stasis is followed by a significant gesture: "Then, *as if releasing herself from something strange,* Mrs. Hale began to arrange the dirty pans under the sink, which the county attorney's disdainful push of the foot had deranged" (emphasis added). One is prompted here to ask: what is this "something strange" from which she releases herself? Though the actions described in the play and the story are the same, why does Glaspell not include in the stage directions to the play an indication of Mrs. Hale's facial expression?

The answer, I think, lies again in the expanded and altered context of "Jury," where the author continually stresses the distance between the women. If Mrs. Peters is, as the county attorney has suggested, one of "them," Mrs. Hale certainly is not, and she distances herself from her male-approved peer in word and deed. The something strange from which she releases herself is, in this context, her reflexive movement towards Mrs. Peters. Mrs. Hale is, in fact, both extricating herself from the male strictures placed upon all of the women and asserting her intellectual independence. Karen Alkalay-Gut has correctly observed that, to the men, the disorder of Mrs. Wright's kitchen implies her "potential homicidal tendencies, inconceivable in a good wife."[8] For her part, Mrs. Hale is rejecting the men's specious reasoning, complaining about the lawyer's disdainful treatment of the kitchen things and asserting, "I'd hate to have men comin' into my kitchen, snoopin' round and criticizin'," obviously recalling the disorder in her kitchen and resenting the conclusions about her that could be drawn. Lacking that opening scene, the play simply does not resonate so profoundly.

Even more telling is a subtle but important change that Glaspell made following Mrs. Hale's testy assertion. In both the play and the story, Mrs. Peters offers the meek defense, "Of course it's no more than their duty," and then the two works diverge. In *Trifles,* Mrs. Peters manages to change the subject. Noticing some dough that Mrs. Wright had been preparing the day before, she says flatly, "she had set bread," and that statement directs Mrs. Hale's attention to the half-done and ruined kitchen chores. In effect, the flow of conversation is mutually directed in the play, and the distance between the women is thus minimized. When she wrote the play, however, Glaspell omitted mention of the bread and instead took us into Mrs. Hale's thoughts, as she does at the beginning of the story:

> She thought of the flour in her kitchen at home — half sifted, half not sifted. She had been interrupted, and had left things half done. What had interrupted Minnie Foster? Why had that work been left half done? She made a move as if to finish it, — unfinished things always bothered her, — and then she glanced around and saw that Mrs. Peters was watching her — and she didn't want Mrs. Peters to get that feeling she got of work begun and then — for some reason — not finished.
> "It's a shame about her fruit," she said. . . .

---

[8] "Jury of Her Peers: The Importance of *Trifles*" p. 3.

Although mention of the ruined fruit preserves is included in the play as well, two significant additions are made in the above passage. First, there is the continual comparison between Mrs. Hale's life and Mrs. Wright's. Second, and more important, we get the clear sense here of Mrs. Hale's suspicion of Mrs. Peters, her not wanting to call attention to the unfinished job for fear that the sheriff's wife will get the wrong idea — or, in this case, the right idea, for the evidence of disturbance, however circumstantial, is something the men may be able to use against Mrs. Wright. In other words, unlike the play, the story posits a different set of polarities, with Mrs. Peters presumably occupying a place within the official party and Mrs. Hale taking the side of the accused against all of them.

We come at this point to a crossroads in the story. Mrs. Hale can leave things as they are and keep information to herself, or she can recruit Mrs. Peters as a fellow "juror" in the case, moving the sheriff's wife away from her sympathy for her husband's position and towards identification with the accused woman. Mrs. Hale chooses the latter course and sets about persuading Mrs. Peters to emerge, in Alkalay-Gut's words, "as an individual distinct from her role as sheriff's wife." Once that happens, "her identification with Minnie is rapid and becomes complete."[9]

The persuasive process begins easily but effectively, with Mrs. Hale reflecting upon the change in Minnie Foster Wright over the thirty or so years she has known her — the change, to use the metaphor that Glaspell will develop, from singing bird to muted caged bird. She follows this reminiscence with a direct question to Mrs. Peters about whether the latter thinks that Minnie killed her husband. "Oh, I don't know," is the frightened response in both works, but, as always, the story provides more insight and tension than does the drama. Still emphasizing in her revision the distance between the women, Glaspell has Mrs. Hale believe that her talk of the youthful Minnie has fallen on deaf ears: "Much difference it makes to her whether Minnie Foster had pretty clothes when she was a girl." This sense of the other woman's indifference to such irrelevant trivialities is occasioned not only by Mrs. Hale's persistent belief in the other woman's official role but also by an odd look that crosses Mrs. Peters's face. At second glance, however, Mrs. Hale notices something else that melts her annoyance and undercuts her suspicions about the sheriff's wife: "Then she looked again, and she wasn't so sure; in fact, she hadn't at any time been perfectly sure about Mrs. Peters. She had that shrinking manner, and yet her eyes looked as if they could see a long way into things." Whereas the play shows the women meandering towards concurrence, the short story is here seen to evolve — and part of that evolution, we must conclude, is due to Mrs. Hale's ability to persuade her peer to regard the case from her perspective. The look that she sees in Mrs. Peters's eyes suggests to her that she might be able to persuade her, that the potential for identification is there. Hence, when she asks whether Mrs. Peters thinks Minnie is guilty, the question resonates here in ways the play does not.

---

[9] "Jury of Her Peers: The Importance of *Trifles*" p. 6.

Accordingly, Mrs. Hale will become much more aggressive in her arguments hereafter, taking on something of the persuader's hopeful hostility, which, in the case of the story, stands in marked contrast to the hostility she felt for Mrs. Peters's official role earlier. Thus, when Mrs. Peters tries to retreat into a male argument, weakly asserting that "the law is the law," the Mrs. Hale of the short story does not let the remark pass, as the one in *Trifles* does: "the law is the law — and a bad stove is a bad stove. How'd you like to cook on this?" Even she, however, is startled by Mrs. Peters's immediate response to her homey analogy and *ad hominem* attack: "A person gets discouraged — and loses heart," Mrs. Peters says — "That look of seeing . . . through a thing to something else" back on her face.

As far as I am concerned, the addition of this passage is the most important change that Glaspell made in her generic translation. Having used this direct personal attack and having noted the ambivalence that Mrs. Peters feels for her role as sheriff's wife, Mrs. Hale will now proceed to effect closure of the gap between them — again, a gap that is never this widely opened in *Trifles*. Now Mrs. Hale will change her entire mode of attack, pushing the limits, doing things she hesitated doing earlier, assailing Mrs. Peters whenever she lapses into her easy conventional attitudes. For instance, when Mrs. Peters objects to Mrs. Hale's repair of a badly knitted quilt block — in effect, tampering with circumstantial evidence of Minnie's mental disturbance of the day before — Mrs. Hale proceeds to do it anyway. As a measure of how much she has changed, we have only to compare this act with her earlier hesitation to finish another chore for fear of what Mrs. Peters might think. She has no reason to be distrustful of Mrs. Peters any longer, for the process of identification is now well underway.

That identification becomes quite evident by the time the women find the most compelling piece of circumstantial evidence against Mrs. Wright — the broken bird cage and the dead bird, its neck wrung and its body placed in a pretty box in Mrs. Wright's sewing basket. When the men notice the cage and Mrs. Hale misleadingly speculates that a cat may have been at it, it is Mrs. Peters who confirms the matter. Asked by the county attorney whether a cat was on the premises, Mrs. Peters — fully aware that there is no cat and never has been — quickly and evasively replies, "Well, not *now*. . . . They're superstitious, you know; they leave." Not only is Mrs. Peters deliberately lying here, but, more important, she is assuming quite another role from the one she played earlier. Uttering a banality, she plays at being the shallow woman who believes in superstitions, thus consciously playing one of the roles the men expect her to assume and concealing her keen intellect from them, her ability to extrapolate facts from small details.

From this point forward, the play and the short story are essentially the same. Mrs. Hale will continue her persuasive assault, and Mrs. Peters will continue to struggle inwardly. The culmination of this struggle occurs when, late in the story, the county attorney says that "a sheriff's wife is married to the law," and she responds, "Not — just that way." In "Jury," however, this protest carries much greater force than it does in *Trifles* for the simple reason that it is a measure of how far Mrs. Peters has come in the course of the short story.

Appropriately enough, too, Mrs. Hale has the final word in both narratives. Asked derisively by the county attorney what stitch Mrs. Wright had been using to make her quilt, Mrs. Hale responds with false sincerity, "We call it — knot it, Mr. Henderson." Most critics have read this line as an ironic reference to the women's solidarity at this point.[10] That is quite true, but, as I have been suggesting here, the progress towards this solidarity varies subtly but unmistakably in the two narratives. Whereas *Trifles,* opening as it does with the women's close physical proximity, reveals the dichotomy between male and female concepts of justice and social roles, "A Jury of Her Peers" is much more concerned with the separateness of the women themselves and their self-injurious acquiescence in male-defined roles. Hence, in her reworking of the narrative, Glaspell did much more than translate the material from one genre to another. Rather, she subtly changed its theme, and, in so doing, she wrote a story that is much more interesting, resonant, and disturbing than the slighter drama from which it derives.

ตฉว

BENJAMIN NELSON *discussed what he considered the strengths and weaknesses of* The Glass Menagerie *in his critical study* Tennessee Williams: The Man and His Work *(1961). Nelson asked himself whether or not the play can be defined as a tragedy, and drew his conclusion after referring to Williams's short fiction.*

BENJAMIN NELSON

Problems in The Glass Menagerie   *1961*

The Glass Menagerie exhibits several of Williams's weaknesses as well as his strengths as a playwright. The great strength of the play is of course the delicate, sympathetic, yet objective creation of meaningful people in a meaningful situation. Williams has caught a decisive and desperate moment in the lives of four individuals and given it illumination and a sense of deep meaning — no small feat for any writer.

His characterizations are not equally realized. He has been unable to create Laura on more than a single dimension, while Amanda is overwhelming in her multi-faceted delineation. On a more technical level the play manifests a doubt on the part of its author toward the power of the written word. As a backdrop for *The Glass Menagerie,* Williams originally wished to use a screen to register emotions and present images from the past, present, and future. For

---

[10] Beverly Smith sees "the bond among women [as] the essential knot" ("Women's Work," p. 179). Cynthia Sutherland regards the reference to knotting as "a subdued, ironic, and grisly reminder of the manner in which a stifled wife has enacted her desperate retaliation" ("American Women Playwrights," p. 323). And Elaine Hedges argues that the reference has three meanings: the rope that Minnie knotted around her husband's neck; the bond among the women; and the fact that the women have tied the men in knots ("Small Things Reconsidered," p. 107).

example, when Jim O'Connor confesses to the family that he is going steady with another girl, the legend on the screen is to read, "The Sky Falls." Fortunately, [actor-director] Eddie Dowling deleted these touches of the poet from his production, but the play still abounds with a number of pretentious statements on the part of Tom as Narrator.

I assume that the final scene between Amanda and Laura is played in pantomime because Williams wished to portray Amanda's dignity through her gestures and her daughter's reaction, rather than through the mother's speech, which during the course of the drama has been either shrill, simpering, or saucy. But in relegating this scene to background silence while Tom makes a self-conscious statement about drifting like a dead leaf "attempting to find in motion what was lost in space," he has substituted a painfully pretentious narration for what could have been an intense and luminous moment between the two women.

Again, on the credit side of the author, his play presents genuine situation, motivation, and, as Joseph Wood Krutch has noted, "a hard substantial core of shrewd observation and deft, economical characterization." But Mr. Krutch also noted that "this hard core is enveloped in a fuzzy haze of pretentious, sentimental, pseudo-poetic verbiage."[1] In *The Glass Menagerie*, the strained lyricism runs parallel with dialogue that is fresh, alive, and highly characteristic, particularly in the speech of Amanda. This dialogue fortunately dominates the proceedings, but the excess of self-conscious "poetical" passages is quite apparent and is a fault of which Williams is to be guilty in much of his later work.

But the great weakness of *The Glass Menagerie* does not lie in its author's artistic or technical deficiencies. The weakness lies at the core of the play and evolves out of what is to become the playwright's hardening philosophical commitment. We can begin to comprehend this when we ask ourselves whether or not *The Glass Menagerie* is a tragedy. It presents a tragic situation and characters who, despite their moodiness and foolishness and self-deception, possess a sense of the tragic. With the possible exception of Laura, they are intensely genuine and the destruction of their dreams and aspirations bears the illusion of great importance. But the play is not a tragedy. The universe of *The Glass Menagerie* does not allow tragedy.

Everyone in the play is a failure and in the course of their drama they all perish a little. Amanda, the most heroic of the quartet, is pitiful but not tragic because from the outset she is doomed to failure despite her desperate struggle to right things. None of these people are given the opportunity to triumph against a fate which is as malignant as it is implacable. Their struggle is a rearguard action against life, a continuous retreat. This retreat may be moving, pathetic, melodramatic, or boisterous, but it is always a withdrawal. After all, what is the world outside the glass menagerie?

> There was only hot swing music and liquor, dance halls, bars, and movies, and sex that hung in the gloom like a chandelier and flooded

---

[1] Joseph Wood Krutch, *The Nation* 14 April 1945: 24.

the world with brief, deceptive rainbows. . . . All the world was waiting for bombardments!

The world outside the Wingfield apartment is a world of illusions, also, even more deceptive and destructive than those held by Amanda and Laura. It is the world of *Stairs to the Roof* and this time the escape is not to a new star but into the individual and personal illusions fostered by each of the characters as his private defense against destruction. Jim waits for the day when his "zzzzzp!" will at last disperse his fear and uncertainty; Laura creates her own sparkling, cold world which gives the illusion of warmth but is as eternal in its unreality as the glass from which it is composed; Amanda strikes out with all her power against her fate by clinging to the past as to a shield; and Tom, recognizing the plight of his family, can do no more than drift away from them, rudderless, frightened, and never really as far from Amanda and Laura as he knows he should be.

Not one of these individuals can cope with his situation. They struggle and their hopes and the destruction of these hopes possess a sense of great importance because Williams has created genuine people in an intensely genuine situation, but they lack the completeness to truly cope with their dilemma. They are not responsible for what has happened to them and they are much too helpless to do more than delay the inevitable. And destruction is inevitable because it is implicit in the universe of Tennessee Williams.

> For the sins of the world are really only its partialities, and these are what sufferings must atone for. . . . The nature of man is full of such makeshift arrangements, devised by himself to cover his incompletion. He feels a part of himself to be like a missing wall or a room left unfurnished and he tries as well as he can to make up for it. The use of imagination, resorting to dreams or the loftier purpose of art, is a mask he devises to cover his incompletion. Or violence such as a war, between two men or among a number of nations, is also a blind and senseless compensation for that which is not yet formed in human nature. Then there is still another compensation. This one is found in the principle of atonement, the surrender of self to violent treatment by others with the idea of thereby cleansing one's self of his guilt.[2]

This statement emanates from the core of Williams's thought and is perhaps his most illuminating commentary about himself and his work. It represents a philosophy, or let us say an attitude toward man in his universe, which is to manifest itself in all his work. It is taken from his short story, "Desire and the Black Masseur," which deals with the final compensation cited in the above quotation: purification through violence. In this tale, a man atones for what the author feels is cosmic fragmentation and guilt by allowing — and actually furthering — his destruction by a cannibal. In *Battle of Angels* and *The Purification*, we find this same kind of violent cleansing.

The Glass Menagerie is a far cry from any of these works; it is the most

---

[2] Tennessee Williams, "Desire and the Black Masseur," *One Arm and Other Stories* (New York, 1948), 85.

nonviolent drama written by Williams. Nevertheless it adheres to the belief set forth in the short story. The underlying belief in *The Glass Menagerie* is that there is very little, if any, reason for living. Man is by nature incomplete because his universe is fragmented. There is nothing to be done about this condition because nothing *can* be done about it. Human guilt becomes a corollary of universal guilt and man's life is an atonement for the human condition. In each character in *The Glass Menagerie* there is a part "like a missing wall or a room left unfurnished and he tries as well as he can to make up for it." The mask devised by Laura and Amanda and Tom and Jim is "the use of imagination, resorting to dreams." The Wingfields are broken, fragmented people because "the sins of the world are really only its partialities." They are really not at all responsible for their condition, and thus are in no way able to cope with it. They are trapped in a determined universe. Without some kind of responsibility on the part of the protagonist there is opportunity neither for tragic elevation nor tragic fall. The Wingfields were doomed the moment they were born. At best their struggles will allow them to survive . . . for a time. They will never be allowed to triumph. Thus their struggles, their hopes, and even their eventual destruction can never move far beyond pathos. The beauty and magic of *The Glass Menagerie* is that this pathos is genuine, objective, and deeply moving.

ॐ

HELGE NORMANN NILSEN *examines the influence of Marxist theory on Miller's* Death of a Salesman. *This commentary is excerpted from an essay that appeared in the journal* English Studies.

HELGE NORMANN NILSEN

Marxism and the Early Plays of Arthur Miller

1994

During the period from the nineteen-thirties through the forties Marxism exercised a controlling influence on Arthur Miller's work. This is evident in several of his earliest, unpublished plays, propaganda pieces advocating the overthrow of capitalism and the establishment of a socialist system.[1] The political tendency of these plays is too obvious to be ignored, but it has escaped the attention of most readers that the same message is embodied in the first three plays that Miller published. These are *The Man Who Had All the Luck* (1944), *All My Sons* (1947) and *Death of a Salesman* (1949), his most famous work.

---

[1] Miller has described his own and his friends' early adoption of Marxism in his autobiography: "We enjoyed a certain unity within ourselves by virtue of a higher consciousness bestowed by our expectation of a socialist evolution of the planet," *Timebends: A Life* (New York, 1987), p. 70.

If one compares the unpublished plays with the published ones, the common features emerge. American capitalism is criticized and rejected, and an alternative, socialist community and system of values are pointed to. The message is implicit rather than explicit in the printed works, but the political agenda remains the same. The most important reason behind Miller's commitment to radicalism is that the Great Depression created in him a lasting and traumatic impression of the devastating power of economic forces in the shaping of people's lives. This also meant that, in the early plays, he portrayed and analyzed his major characters as products of the American capitalist society and its influence.[2] At the same time he managed to give them individuality and persuasiveness as characters.

Miller's political attitudes at the time emerge mainly in the plays in question, but are also described in his autobiography. They fall within the tradition of analysis and criticism of capitalism established by Marx and the movements building on his theories. Miller's critique can be summed up as follows: capitalism is inhuman in its glorification of private property and its exclusive orientation toward profitmaking. Human beings are sacrificed to economic interests in ways that are not only immoral, but even criminal in nature. In business, ruthless competition is the norm. People's moral character is threatened. They may become scoundrels, or rendered insane and suicidal. Egocentric individualism reigns supreme, and society fosters no sense of responsibility to anyone beyond self and family. There is an unjust concentration of financial power into a few hands, making all others powerless and bereft of economic security. The capitalists also control most of the cultural life of society and the media, spreading their conservative political views. No institution or aspect of society can escape this influence. The false values of materialism and the cult of success threaten to extinguish human love and caring. Conformism rules, turning people into mere cogs in the machine of production, and genuine individualism and even enjoyment of life become hard to obtain. The coming socialist society, on the other hand, will be built on solidarity, human brotherhood, and the ownership of the workers and citizens of the means of production.[3] . . .

Death of a Salesman is . . . rooted in the playwright's early, agonized reactions to the Depression. Marxism had taught him that this disaster was one of the vagaries of capitalism, and his early, militant stance is suggested in an observation recorded in a notebook containing an early version of the play: "The

---

[2] In the early forties Miller attended a Marxist study group and was proposed for membership in the American Communist Party. In *The New York Times*, May 25, 1947, his name appeared on a list of sponsors of the World Youth Festival, organized by the communist World Federation of Democratic Youth. See J. Schlueter and J. K. Flanagan, *Arthur Miller* (New York, 1987), pp. 6, 146.

[3] Interpreting Marx, R. W. Miller states that: "under socialism and communism, most people are less dominated, more in possession of their lives, since they are better able to develop their capacities in light of their own assessments of their needs. Moreover, their interactions will be governed to a greater extent than now by mutual well-wishing and concern," "Marx and Morality," in *Marxism*, ed. J. R. Pennock and J. W. Chapman (New York, 1983), p. 60.

restrictions, like all tyrannies, exist by default of revolutionary resistance."[4] The reference is to formal conventions in drama, but the choice of words reveals a political radicalism also.

As in the other plays, victimization by the free play of economic forces is the main theme of *Death of a Salesman*. It is suggested in the initial stage direction: "A melody is heard, played upon a flute. It is small and fine, telling of grass and trees and the horizon. Before us is the salesman's house. We are aware of towering, angular shapes behind it, surrounding it on all sides." The people in the house are threatened and overwhelmed by the tall buildings, symbols of the crushing power of those who win out in a capitalist struggle that has no room for failures and losers.

Willy Loman, the aging salesman, is worn out to the point of breakdown by his many years on the road. But he remains a firm believer in capitalist values and has transferred his hope of success to his son Biff. Willy is a dreamer, and the play contrasts his dreams with the harsh realities of failure and mediocrity that he tries to shut out of his mind. Corrupted, or brainwashed by the system, Willy is blind to its destructiveness and is obsessed by his plans for Biff.

Biff, however, has begun to rebel against his father's ideas and to feel his way towards different standards, meaning those that Miller associates with the socialist society. Unlike his brother Happy, he has "allowed himself to turn his face toward defeat," and even this becomes a possible source of strength for him. His lack of conventional success is slowly teaching him, not that he is worthless, but that he may not be cut out for a business career and may actually be better off without it. He is trying to understand himself and discover his real identity, this also being an aim of socialism as Miller understood it. But Biff is not yet sure of himself, in the first part of the play, and still feels guilty for not being a success. He has returned to his parents in a last attempt to fulfill his father's dreams.

Happy, who has a good job and wants to get further ahead, also has doubts about his own careerism but cannot find anything to put in its place. Biff struggles with this issue, searching for and finally finding another path for himself. However, his father remains a man whose self-respect depends entirely on his role as a breadwinner and useful cog in the production machine. He worships the memory of Ben, the youth who walked into the jungle of Africa at the age of seventeen and came out rich at twenty-one, a powerful *entrepreneur*. What Willy fails to realize is that only a very few can hope to be that successful. His greatest illusion is his belief in the capitalist myth that every man can succeed in business if he only uses his opportunities. Willy is also haunted by the equally superhuman success ideal embodied in his grandfather, a heroic pioneer figure who drove across America with his family, supporting them all by selling flutes that he made himself.

The scene in which Willy is fired by his young boss Howard is a perfect illustration of the logic of the capitalist economic mechanism. Willy has been

---

[4] Notebook, in longhand, undated, in the Harry Ransom Humanities Research Center.

with the firm since before Howard was born, but the almost familiar relationship between these two still counts for nothing. Mortally afraid of ruin, like Keller, Willy appeals to Howard's conscience, reminding him how long and faithfully he has worked for the company, but to no avail. Howard is not evil, however; he is even able to sympathize with Willy's plight, but this in no way interferes with his decision to fire an aging employee who can no longer ring up any sales. Howard, like Ben or Charley, a businessman who is Willy's friend and neighbor, abides by the law of profitability first that is supreme in the world of capitalist business. He is impersonal about it, again like Charley or Ben, regarding it as a law of nature.[5]

Wanting to help Willy, Charley offers him a job, but the former refuses to take it, feeling that it would be a kind of charity and would violate the image he has of himself as a self-reliant, honorable individual who does not depend on others. Rugged individualism is the ideology of the *laissez-faire* capitalism that he believes in so deeply. But the facts are that Willy's failure is destroying him and that Biff's similar fate makes his father reject him. The all-important success ideal prevents Willy from perceiving Biff as a person and an individual. Capitalist values distort and destroy what should have been a rewarding human relationship between father and son.

The horrifying consequences of a blind adherence to these values emerge in Willy's decision to commit suicide so that his life insurance payment will enable Biff to rise in the world. But Biff, like Chris Keller, instead becomes the vehicle through which Miller subtly introduces his alternative socialist perceptions and values into his work. Biff thus becomes the only character in the drama who really understands the destructive nature of capitalist priorities and feels pity and concern for his father, exclaiming: "I can't bear to look at his face!" He tries to make Willy understand the realities of their situation, which is that their lives have been dominated by a dream that is no better than a lie. Biff has realized that the whole family are victims, in various ways and like most people, of capitalist oppression and false standards. They are basically downtrodden people, "a dime a dozen." But this, of course, is the very thing that Willy refuses to admit, and he denies it furiously. Biff tries to impress upon him that they ought to lower their expectations and rely on the comforts of love and human caring. Willy, however, is not willing to correct his capitalist hierarchy of values and accuses Biff of betrayal. His son, he says, is "vengeful" and "spiteful." But Biff continues his attempt to break through to his father's feelings and establish a genuine connection and respect between them. Hence his plaintive cry: "Pop, I'm nothing . . . I'm just what I am, that's all."

In this central scene, Willy does perceive that his son wants to show him his love, but is unable to respond to this in a simple way. Instead, and in keep-

---

[5] Brian Parker argues that because Howard and Charley, both capitalists, are ordinary men and not evil, *Death of a Salesman* cannot be an anti-capitalist play. But the fact that these are not bad men does not change the workings of the system that they represent. See "Point of View in Arthur Miller's *Death of a Salesman*," *Arthur Miller: A Collection of Critical Essays* (Englewood Cliffs, 1969), p. 99.

ing with his blinkered vision, he grotesquely interprets Biff's love as yet another sign of his potentially glorious future, or as a part of the fine personality that will help making him rich: "That boy — that boy is going to be magnificent!" The insurance money will yet secure Biff's success, he thinks, and is deluded enough to assume that his son will be thankful for the sacrifice he is making.

But at Willy Loman's grave it is capitalism and the dreams it is responsible for that are indicted. Looking back on his father's life, Biff firmly declares: "He had the wrong dreams. All, all wrong." *Death of a Salesman* suggests that the right dreams are opposed to rapacious capitalism and that they are about justice, love, and genuine selfhood as envisaged by Marxism.

. . . In *Death of a Salesman* the jobless Willy Loman has become mentally disturbed, his suicide for the sake of money an eloquent testimony to the corrosive effects of the tyrannical success ideal extolled by his society. Willy is a victim, both directly and indirectly, of the logic of a capitalism which says that human worth is proportional to economic achievement. Taken as a whole, these dramas build a powerful indictment against the American capitalist system that Miller knew, but they do not stop at that point. Whether openly or more discreetly, they suggest the possibility of another, just and humane society. This new, socialist world will be built on the principles of love, mutual concern, and sharing rather than competition.

ဆ

MARSHA NORMAN's *interview commenting on* 'night, Mother *was included in Kathleen Betsko and Rachel Koenig's* Interviews with Contemporary Women Playwrights *(1987).*

MARSHA NORMAN

Interview about 'night, Mother   1987

Interviewer: You've said the main character must want something. Is *'night, Mother,* then, Thelma's play? It seems that Jessie, the suicidal daughter, has lost all desire.

Norman: Well, Jessie certainly doesn't want to have anything more to do with *her* life, but she does want Mama to be able to go on, and that's a very strong desire on Jessie's part. She *wants* Mama to be able to do the wash and know where everything is. She wants Mama to live, and to live free of the guilt that Mama might have felt had Jessie just left her a note. Jessie's desires are so strong in the piece. The play exists because Jessie wants something for Mama. Then, of course, Mama wants Jessie to stay. So you have two conflicting goals. And at that point it is a real struggle. It might as well be armed warfare. Only very late in the piece do they realize that both goals are achievable given some moderation. What Mama does understand, finally, is that there wasn't anything she could do. And so Jessie does win. Mama certainly loses in the battle to keep her alive, but Mama does gain other things in the course of the evening.

Interviewer: For instance?

Norman: They have never been so close as they are on this evening. It is calling the question that produces the closeness.

Interviewer: What happens to a woman like Thelma Cates after her daughter has committed suicide?

Norman: Well, what's very clear about Thelma from the beginning is that she lives in an intense network of both things and people. Her friend Agnes says, "You have to keep your life filled up." That's what Thelma has done. She is devoted to her candy and her *TV Guide* and her handwork; she loves talking on the phone to her friends. After Jessie's suicide, Thelma's physical life continues pretty much the way it always was. Thelma is not weak and sick and old. She has only seemed weak and sick and old so that Jessie would feel useful. Jessie, of course, saw right through that. One of the things I think is new in Thelma's life is the experience of this evening, which will belong only to her forever. Probably for the first time, Thelma has something that is securely hers, that she does not need for anybody else to understand and would not dare tell anybody. She has a holy object: this evening that they spent together. And that probably makes for some change in Thelma. But it's probably not a change any of her friends would notice.

Interviewer: Is the holy object The Truth?

Norman: It's the moment of connection between them. Basically, it is a moment when two people are willing to go as far as they can with each other. That doesn't happen very often, and we are lucky if we have two or three moments in our lives when we know that, with this person, we have gone as far as it is possible to go. After a lifetime of missing this daughter, of somehow just living in the same space, they finally had a moment when they actually lived together, when the issues of their lives were standing there with them, in silent witness of their meeting. This is exactly the kind of meeting the theater can document, can present and preserve. In an odd way, writing for the theater is like nominating people for the archives of human history. As playwright, I select a person to nominate for permanent memory by the race. The audience, the worldwide audience, does the voting. Some of my nominations make it and some of them don't. But it seems that Jessie and Thelma are going to make it. They are going to be remembered for what they did that night.

Interviewer: Writing for the theater is an attempt to immortalize your characters?

Norman: Preserve is more like it. We preserve valuable things because they will be needed, because they are the heritage of the people who come after us. We have benefited from that preservation effort up till now — I am grateful that King Lear was preserved, that he is here for me, and I can look at his life and know what he did. We all have a responsibility to preserve those people from our own time who deserve to be remembered or must be remembered for some reason. It's the struggle that makes them memorable. Because on that night, Thelma does as good a job as anybody could do. It's that effort that gives her a place.

Interviewer: Why doesn't Thelma go a bit further? Why doesn't she attack her daughter physically to prevent the suicide?

Norman: Well, there is that final moment at the door, and it posed an interesting dilemma. At that moment in the script, Thelma is reaching for something to hit Jessie with. In the early versions of the script, there was a line that said, "I'll knock you out cold before I'll let you . . ." In my mind I saw Thelma reaching for the frying pan. Like, "I am going to hurt you now. And we will straighten this out when you wake up." [Laughter] Then Tom Moore, the director, pointed out that while it may be tragedy to pick up a frying pan, it is farce when you put it down.

Interviewer: You weren't willing then to risk humor at that point?

Norman: Right. And you can't leave Thelma standing there at the door holding the frying pan.

Interviewer: But did you try it that way during rehearsal?

Norman: We tried to make the fight as violent as we could. Thelma only has one thing left to try and that is physical harm. But I don't know if the audience ever understands that effort.

Interviewer: Did the fact that you could not demonstrate Thelma's passion in a physical way put more weight on her final verbal plea to Jessie?

Norman: The struggle at the door is one of the most difficult moments for both of them. The actress, Anne Pitoniak, as a human being inside that character, realizes she must fight and she must lose.

Interviewer: Does she let go of Jessie in that moment?

Norman: Thelma's crucial letting go has occurred earlier in the piece. This fight is pure instinct. This has nothing to do with thinking or feeling, this is just physical. This is that last moment when you realize you're cornered, and you're not going to try to talk to the grizzly bear anymore. . . . She *does* know that she has lost. Jessie is simply too powerful. But that doesn't mean that Thelma is just going to stand there.

Interviewer: You've said it's important to you to confront life and death issues. Many writers have done it through metaphor, while you confronted it literally. Not that the play is without metaphor — but the central issue is very concrete. How did you come to that decision?

Norman: Suicide is not a new issue on stage. I had seen a couple of pieces that treated it obliquely. Pieces that did not have, for example, the person that loved you most standing there across the room saying *No* to you. I felt that if you were going to talk about suicide, there was really no way to talk about it without having someone argue back. It wasn't that I wanted to work in such a naturalistic way, it was that the issue required it. We're talking about a real gun, a real fight, a real death. One of the interesting attempts that I had seen was a play that a friend of mine, Vaughan McBride, had written. Vaughan and I both had seen a newspaper article about a man who knew that he had terminal cancer and was going to commit suicide. This man went to stay with his friend over a weekend, the idea being that they would spend this weekend talking and being together; then on Sunday morning the friend would go off to get milk and the paper, he would come back, and the other man would have had his opportunity to kill himself. Vaughan showed the evening of talking, the going to bed, and the friend going off to get the newspaper in the morning. Then the man who was going to kill himself walked back up the stairs and the play was over. There was never a mention of the suicide or the friend's agreement to this plan. There was a note in the program that said the man killed himself the next morning, and this had all been arranged. I found it unsatisfying, because I wanted them to deal with it. I didn't want to read it in the program. What I came to with *'night, Mother* was a kind of final submission to the naturalistic form. I simply felt that the subject required that it be treated in a naturalistic manner.

Interviewer: The play is due to go to Japan soon, where I believe that suicide is considered a civil right. I should think the audiences there will experience your story very differently than a Western audience.

Norman: It's going to be fascinating, isn't it? I thought the same thing. I have no idea. Americans have a life-at-all-costs attitude. It's a very privileged point of view, actually.

ৎৎ

EUGENE O'NEILL *wrote a striking letter to the theater critic Arthur Hobson Quinn; in it he described his debt to the Greek tragic playwrights. Published in the second volume of Quinn's* A History of the American Drama *(1945), O'Neill's letter referred to the plays* The Emperor Jones *(1920),* The Hairy Ape *(1921),* All God's Chillun *(1923), and* Desire under the Elms *(1924) as works (like* Bound East for Cardiff*) in which the author hoped to show what he called the "nobility of tragedy" in characters who represented the most common American lives.*

EUGENE O'NEILL

A Letter to Arthur Hobson Quinn   1945

It's not in me to pose much as a "misunderstood one," but it does seem discouragingly (that is, if one lacked a sense of ironic humor!) evident to me that most of my critics don't want to see what I'm trying to do or how I'm trying to do it, although I flatter myself that end and means are characteristic, individual and positive enough not to be mistaken for anyone's else, or for those of any "modern" or "pre-modern" school. To be called a "sordid realist" one day, a "grim, pessimistic Naturalist" the next, a "lying Moral Romanticist" the next, etc., is quite perplexing — not to add the *Times* editorial that settled *Desire* once and for all by calling it a "Neo-Primitive," a Matisse of the drama, as it were! So I'm really longing to explain and try and convince some sympathetic ear that I've tried to make myself a melting pot for all these methods, seeing some virtues for my ends in each of them, and thereby, if there is enough real fire in me, boil down to my own technique. But where I feel myself most neglected is just where I set most store by myself — as a bit of a poet, who has labored with the spoken word to evolve original rhythms of beauty, where beauty apparently isn't — *Jones, Ape, God's Chillun, Desire,* etc. — and to see the transfiguring nobility of tragedy, in as near the Greek sense as one can grasp it, in seemingly the most ignoble, debased lives. And just here is where

I am a most confirmed mystic, too, for I'm always, always trying to interpret Life in terms of lives, never just lives in terms of character. I'm always acutely conscious of the Force behind — Fate, God, our biological past creating our present, whatever one calls it — Mystery certainly — and of the one eternal tragedy of Man in his glorious, self-destructive struggle to make the Force express him instead of being, as an animal is, an infinitesimal incident in its expression. And my profound conviction is that this is the only subject worth writing about and that it is possible — or can be — to develop a tragic expression in terms of transfigured modern values and symbols in the theatre which may to some degree bring home to members of a modern audience their ennobling identity with the tragic figures on the stage. Of course, this is very much of a dream, but where the theatre is concerned, one must have a dream, and the Greek dream in tragedy is the noblest ever!

ಎಎ

MURIEL **R**UKEYSER *(1913–1980) was an outspoken feminist in her poetry, plays, and novels. Her wryly humorous prose poem "Myth" about Oedipus's meeting with the Sphinx, included in her book* Breaking Open *(1973), imagines a second encounter between them. Rukeyser offers a new perspective on the meaning of their exchange and suggests that Oedipus's tactless answer to the winged female monster when he first answers her riddle (and not Freud's hypothesis of the incest taboo) is the explanation of the Greek king's tragic fate.*

M**URIEL** R**UKEYSER**

Myth   1973

Long afterward, Oedipus, old and blinded, walked the
roads.   He smelled a familiar smell.   It was
the Sphinx.   Oedipus said, "I want to ask one question.
Why didn't I recognize my mother?" "You gave the
wrong answer," said the Sphinx.   "But that was what   5
made everything possible," said Oedipus.   "No," she said.
"When I asked, What walks on four legs in the morning,
two at noon, and three in the evening, you answered,
Man.   You didn't say anything about woman."
"When you say Man," said Oedipus, "you include women   10
too. Everyone knows that."   She said, "That's what
you think."

ಎಎ

SANDRA **S**AARI, *a Norwegian critic, has compared the first draft of Ibsen's* A Doll House *with the published version and concluded that the playwright significantly changed the conflict between Nora and Torvald in his revision of his play. In the "Final Copy" of* A Doll House, *Ibsen transformed Nora into a mature person who be-*

comes capable of defining reality for herself by the end of the drama. Saari's close reading of the two versions helps us understand Ibsen's refusal to say that he had deliberately worked for the cause of women's rights in A Doll House. *In Saari's explanation, Ibsen believed "that the essential definition of a person is humanness, not gender, and that what cause things to appear otherwise are social constructs." Saari's article appeared in volume six of* Contemporary Approaches to Ibsen, *published in Oslo by Norwegian University Press in 1988.*

SANDRA SAARI

Female Becomes Human: Nora Transformed in A Doll House

1988

In his first notes for the play, Ibsen conceived of the conflict leading to complete confusion and finally to destruction. In the Final Copy, the conflict leads to Nora's clear, rational perception of reality and consequently to her rejection of the child-wife role. When the miracle doesn't happen, Nora is no longer willing to base her actions toward Torvald on the ideal of love. From the beginning of the play, Nora perceives that Torvald has faults such as egotism and jealousy, but, understanding that "miracles don't happen every day," she discounts these faults as being superficial, not essential. There is good reason for her to interpret them thus. Torvald describes himself as having great inner strength in a crisis, and he explicitly espouses love as his highest value.

In the Draft, Nora says Torvald forfeited her love when she saw that he wasn't better than she was. In the Final Copy, she says he forfeited her love when the miracle didn't happen. "The miracle," the approach of which Nora had already announced to an uncomprehending Mrs. Linde in Act 2, has the ring of unrealistic fantasy. But it is, in fact, a further development in the Final Copy, of Nora's ability to see things in a rational and ordered manner. What she means by "miracle" is: an action in the real world that confirms beyond all doubt her belief that their marriage is based on the shared ideal of love, in particular, that Torvald loves her, as she loves him, above all else, above even life itself. When the miracle doesn't happen, when what happens is instead a disconfirmation of her belief, then she relinquishes her belief.

The disconfirmation is unarguable. Upon receiving Krogstad's first letter, revealing the forgery and blackmail, Torvald responds with unmistakable self-centeredness. He dismisses Nora's protestations of having done it because "I have loved you above all else in the world," as mere "idiotic alibis." He berates Nora as "a hypocrite, a liar, and, even worse, a criminal," the social offense being for him the worst. He blames her father for her lack of proper upbringing, and her, for destroying all his own happiness, after all he has done for her. And it virtually goes without saying that he capitulates immediately to the blackmail and focuses all his concern on how to preserve appearances in the eyes of the world. There is never the slightest hint of any self-sacrifice to protect Nora. At Torvald's core is more of the petty egotism whose manifestations Nora had inaccurately interpreted as merely superficial.

But, it is not this evidence Nora cites in describing what makes Torvald a stranger to her. He is someone with whom she is no longer able to associate herself because of his hypocrisy. "After your terror was over," she says, "and when all danger was past, then for you, it was as though nothing at all had happened. I was, precisely as before, your little songbird, your doll, about whom you had to be twice as protective from now on." If Torvald can complacently return to their former relationship, if his actions don't strike him as highly anomalous in view of his professed ideals, then all along his professed ideals were a form of hypocrisy, were mere superficial rhetoric and not the description of his essential self that Nora had taken them to be. If that which would make them equal in essence — the mutuality of ideal love — doesn't inform the husband-wife relationship, then the form — male-dominated, hierarchical — in fact turns out to be the essence of the marriage. If Torvald's first duty isn't to her, then Nora's first duty is to herself.

At the end of Act 2, Nora had "danced herself free," to use Daniel Haakonsen's felicitous phrase, in response to a reality that didn't conform to Torvald's instruction. At the end of Act 3, Nora has rationally thought herself into freedom from Torvald's interpretation of reality. She then sets out to define reality for herself.

ळळ

GEORGE BERNARD SHAW (1856–1950), *the British playwright, was one of the first authors to recognize the importance of Ibsen's work in the theater. In* The Quintessence of Ibsenism (1891; rev. ed. 1913) *Shaw summarized the plot of the play and analyzed Nora's character with great sensitivity to the social issues that Ibsen had raised in the drama.*

GEORGE BERNARD SHAW

On *A Doll House*   1891

In the famous [*Doll*] *House*, the pillar of society who owns the doll is a model husband, father, and citizen. In his little household, with the three darling children and the affectionate little wife, all on the most loving terms with one another, we have the sweet home, the womanly woman, the happy family life of the idealist's dream. Mrs. Nora Helmer is happy in the belief that she has attained a valid realization of all these illusions; that she is an ideal wife and mother; and that Helmer is an ideal husband who would, if the necessity arose, give his life to save her reputation. A few simply contrived incidents disabuse her effectually on all these points. One of her earliest acts of devotion to her husband has been the secret raising of a sum of money to enable him to make a tour which was necessary to restore his health. As he would have broken down sooner than go into debt, she has had to persuade him that the money was a gift from her father. It was really obtained from a moneylender, who refused to make her the loan unless she induced her father to endorse the promissory note. This being impossible, as her father was dying at the time, she took the shortest way out of the difficulty by writing the name herself, to the entire satisfaction of the moneylender, who, though not at all duped, knew that forged bills are often the surest to be paid. Since then she has slaved in secret at scrivener's work until she has nearly paid off the debt.

At this point Helmer is made manager of the bank in which he is employed; and the moneylender, wishing to obtain a post there, uses the forged bill to force Nora to exert her influence with Helmer on his behalf. But she, having a hearty contempt for the man, cannot be persuaded by him that there was any harm in putting her father's name on the bill, and ridicules the suggestion that the law would not recognize that she was right under the circumstances. It is her husband's own contemptuous denunciation of a forgery formerly committed by the moneylender himself that destroys her self-satisfaction and opens her eyes to her ignorance of the serious business of the world to which her husband belongs: the world outside the home he shares with her. When he goes on to tell her that commercial dishonesty is generally to be traced to the influence of bad mothers, she begins to perceive that the happy way in which she plays with the children, and the care she takes to dress them nicely, are not sufficient to constitute her a fit person to train them. To redeem the forged bill, she resolves to borrow the balance due upon it from an intimate friend of the family. She has learnt to coax her husband into giving her what she asks by appealing to his affection for her: that is, by playing all sorts of pretty tricks until he is wheedled into an amorous humor. This plan she has adopted without thinking about it, instinctively taking the line of least resistance with him. And now she naturally takes the same line with her husband's friend. An unexpected declaration of love from him is the result; and it at once explains to her the real nature of the domestic influence she has been so proud of.

All her illusions about herself are now shatterd. She sees herself as an ignorant and silly woman, a dangerous mother, and a wife kept for her husband's pleasure merely; but she clings all the harder to her illusion about him: He is still the ideal husband who would make any sacrifice to rescue her from ruin. She resolves to kill herself rather than allow him to destroy his own career by taking the forgery on himself to save her reputation. The final disillusion comes when he, instead of at once proposing to pursue this ideal line of conduct when he hears of the forgery, naturally enough flies into a vulgar rage and heaps invective on her for disgracing him. Then she sees that their whole family life has been a fiction: their home a mere doll's house in which they have been playing at ideal husband and father, wife and mother. So she leaves him then and there and goes out into the real world to find out its reality for herself, and to gain some position not fundamentally false, refusing to see her children again until she is fit to be in charge of them, or to live with him until she and he become capable of a more honorable relation to one another. He at first cannot understand what has happened, and flourishes the shattered ideals over her as if they were as potent as ever. He presents the course most agreeable to him — that of her staying at home and avoiding a scandal — as her duty to her husband, to her children, and to her religion; but the magic of these disguises is gone; and at last even he understands what has really happened, and sits down alone to wonder whether that more honorable relation can ever come to pass between them.

ॐ

AUGUST STRINDBERG *wrote his preface to* Miss Julie *after finishing the play in 1888. The preface was his first explanation of "naturalistic drama," his theory that life is a struggle between the strong and the weak, and that human problems arise from our instincts and desires. The following year he developed these ideas further in his influential essay "On Modern Drama and Modern Theater." Strindberg found evidence of his theory all around him. Writing to his Danish friend Georg Brandes in September 1888, shortly after beginning* Miss Julie, *Strindberg referred to a recent scandal reported in the newspaper about an aristocratic lady's affair with her father's servant. In Strindberg's letter, he summarized his clear-eyed view of his stage heroine: "That the daughter of a count commits suicide after sexual intercourse with a lower creature and theft is extremely likely! And if she doesn't do so right away, she becomes a waitress in a bar at Hasselbacken [a fancy restaurant in Copenhagen] as the real Julie became!"*

AUGUST STRINDBERG

From the Preface to Miss Julie   1888

TRANSLATED BY HARRY G. CARLSON

Miss Julie is a modern character. Not that the man-hating half-woman has not existed in all ages but because now that she has been discovered, she has come out in the open to make herself heard. The half-woman is a type who pushes her way ahead, selling herself nowadays for power, decorations, honors, and diplomas, as formerly she used to do for money. The type implies a retrogressive step in evolution, an inferior species who cannot endure. Unfortunately, they are able to pass on their wretchedness; degenerate men seem unconsciously to choose their mates from among them. And so they breed, producing an indeterminate sex for whom life is a torture. Fortunately, the offspring go under either because they are out of harmony with reality or because their repressed instincts break out uncontrollably or because their hopes of achieving equality with men are crushed. The type is tragic, revealing the drama of a desperate struggle against Nature, tragic as the romantic heritage now being dissipated by naturalism, which has a contrary aim: happiness, and happiness belongs only to the strong and skillful species.

But Miss Julie is also: a relic of the old warrior nobility now giving way to a new nobility of nerve and intellect, a victim of her own flawed constitution, a victim of the discord caused in a family by a mother's "crime," a victim of the delusions and conditions of her age — and together these are the equivalent of the concept of Destiny, or Universal Law, of antiquity. Guilt has been abolished by the naturalist, along with God, but the consequences of an action — punishment, imprisonment or the fear of it — that he cannot erase, for the simple reason that they remain, whether he pronounces acquittal or not. Those who have been injured are not as kind and understanding as an unscathed outsider can afford to be. Even if her father felt constrained not to seek revenge, his daughter would wreak vengeance upon herself, as she does here, out of an innate or acquired sense of honor, which the upper classes inherit — from where? From barbarism, from the ancient Aryan home of the race, from medieval chivalry. It is a beautiful thing, but nowadays a hindrance to the survival of the race. It is the nobleman's harikari, which compels him to slit open his own stomach when someone insults him and which survives in a modified form in the duel, that privilege of the nobility. That is why Jean, the servant, lives, while Miss Julie cannot live without honor. The slave's advantage over the nobleman is that he lacks this fatal preoccupation with honor. But in all of us Aryans there is something of the nobleman, or a Don Quixote. And so we sympathize with the suicide, whose act means a loss of honor. We are noblemen enough to be pained when we see the mighty fallen and as superfluous as a corpse, yes, even if the fallen should rise again and make amends through an honorable act. The servant Jean is a race-founder, someone in whom the process of differentiation can be detected. Born the son of a tenant farmer, he has educated himself in the things a gentleman should know. He has been quick to learn, has finely developed senses (smell, taste, sight) and a feeling for what is beautiful. He is already moving up in the world and is not embarrassed about using other people's help. He is alienated from his fellow servants, despising them as parts of a past he has already put behind him. He fears and flees them because they know his secrets, pry into his intentions, envy his rise, and look forward eagerly to his fall. Hence his dual, indecisive nature, vacillating between sympathy for people in high social positions and hatred for those who currently occupy those positions. He is an aristocrat, as he himself says, has learned the secrets of good society, is polished on the surface but coarse beneath, wears a frock coat tastefully but without any guarantee that his body is clean.

He has respect for Miss Julie, but is afraid of Kristine because she knows his dangerous secrets. He is sufficiently callous not to let the night's events disturb his plans for the future. With both a slave's brutality and a master's lack of squeamishness, he can see blood without fainting and shake off misfortune easily. Consequently, he comes through the struggle unscathed and will probably end up an innkeeper. And even if *he* does not become a Rumanian count, his son will become a university student and possibly a county police commissioner. . . .

Apart from the fact that Jean is rising in the world, he is superior to Miss Julie because he is a man. Sexually, he is an aristocrat because of his masculine strength, his more keenly developed senses, and his capacity for taking the initiative. His sense of inferiority is mostly due to the social circumstances in which he happens to be living, and he can probably shed it along with his valet's jacket.

His slave mentality expresses itself in the fearful respect he has for the Count (the boots) and his religious superstition; but he respects the Count mainly as the occupant of the kind of high position to which he himself aspires; and the respect remains even after he has conquered the daughter of the house and seen how empty the lovely shell was.

I do not believe that love in any "higher" sense can exist between two people of such different natures, and so I have Miss Julie's love as something she fabricates in order to protect and excuse herself; and I have Jean suppose himself capable of loving her under other social circumstances. I think it is the same with love as with the hyacinth, which must take root in darkness *before* it can produce a sturdy flower. Here a flower shoots up, blooms, and goes to seed all at once, and that is why it dies so quickly.

⚬⚬

YASUNARI TAKAHASHI *analyzed the similarities between the structure of* Krapp's Last Tape *and a* Nō *play in a 1982 article in* Encounter *about what he called "the Theatre of Mind." Takahashi found echoes in Beckett's play of the traditional roles of* shite *(the protagonist),* waki *(the secondary character), and the chorus in the* Nō *drama. He also compared Beckett's place in theater history with the achievement of the great fourteenth-century Nō playwright Zeami.*

YASUNARI TAKAHASHI

Samuel Beckett and the Nō   1982

If a Nō play is no play, or if the Nō drama is not a drama, then what is it? The most succinct definition of the Nō drama in contradistinction to the Western concept of drama is given by Paul Claudel, the French playwright who also was the French ambassador to Japan in the 1920s: *"Le drame, c'est quelque chose qui arrive; le Nô, c'est quelqu'un qui arrive."* (In drama, something happens; in Nō, someone arrives.) I would tentatively paraphrase this dictum of Claudel in the following way. In the Western drama, the driving force is the conflict between man and gods or destiny, between man and man, between man and his environment, etc., and the theatre is a space in which we witness some action taking place out of this conflict and developing according to the more or less complex laws of cause and effect towards the final denouement. On the other hand, a Nō play starts at the point where everything has already happened, and what we see on the stage is not the action in its process of happening but the arrival of someone, actually a ghost out of the past, who relates and re-enacts things that happened a long time ago. . . .

Another point to be stressed is the importance of Waki, the secondary character, and of the chorus. Although the Nō drama is overwhelmingly dominated by the presence of Shite (protagonist), yet Waki is also indispensable, albeit in an indirect way. From the structural point of view, it is through his shamanic power, or (if you prefer a chemical metaphor) it is through his catalytic function, that the supernatural Shite is brought forth on the stage, taking flesh first as a village woman, then in her true identity as a ghost. Or it may be truer to say that the central action of a Nō play, i.e. the "coming" of Shite in the second part, really takes place in a dream of Waki, which is indeed the reason why the play is called a "Dream Nō." This is also a reminder that Shite in the second part exists in a totally different spatio-temporal dimension from Waki, in spite of the fact that Waki is apparently watching and listening to Shite's dance and songs, so that there is no possibility of dialogue taking place between them.

From the psychological point of view, too, Waki is crucially important, because it is with him that the audience identifies itself. In an atmosphere of great tension, the audience, together with Waki, waits for the apparition, tastes that thrill of epiphanic moment which you must see to believe, and then watches the terrifying and fascinating stranger from the other world dance out her undying fire of passion, finally to experience a catharsis of fear and pity, be it Aristotelian or not.

But it is not simply identification that matters here, for the audience sees both Shite and Waki at the same time, which fact distances the audience in a sense from either of them, thus enabling it to experience the coexistence of two different dimensions.

This dual consciousness of the audience, not unlike [Bertolt] Brecht's alienation effect, is related also to the way the chorus functions, which you may find rather curious and irrational. The chorus, by definition, should be a pure objective commentator, or at the most a mouthpiece for the feelings of the people of the community, as in Greek tragedy or in [T. S.] Eliot's *Murder in the Cathedral*. In Nō, it is much more than that. The chorus of course narrates the story objectively, but it also sometimes speaks in unison with Shite, sometimes speaks for Shite, using the first person singular, while she dances silently. . . .

Armed with this much knowledge of the Nō drama, let us now confront our subject. We may be fools rushing in where angels fear to tread, for unlike [William Butler] Yeats or Claudel or Brecht, Beckett is on his own evidence uninfluenced by this theatre form of the Far East. I asked when I met him in Paris last summer if he had been influenced by Nō, and he said, "Not consciously," which is a very tantalising answer, just like the answer he gave to Deidre Bair, who asked his permission to work on his biography: he said to her, "I will neither help you nor hinder you." In my case, however, I shall simply take his words as they are and proceed on the hypothesis that the absence of conscious influence should be all the more interesting if it could be shown that the two theatre forms, with a vast temporal and spatial distance between them, do share some fundamental characteristics. We could perhaps take courage from the fact that Yeats's play, *Purgatory*, ostensibly uninfluenced by Nō, is the finest fruit of the lessons he learnt from it, definitely a better one than the four earlier plays in which he consciously tried to steal from the wealth of the Japanese theatre. Incidentally, Beckett confirmed to me that he had a great admiration for Yeats's later poetry and plays. . . .

[*Krapp's Last Tape*] presents the old Krapp on stage as Shite (protagonist), but in this seeming monodrama, he also plays the role of Waki — he does so at least while he is straining his ears to his own voices taped in his younger days. And it is these voices that take over the role of Shite during these moments. Of course, there is a world of difference between, on the one hand, the disembodied voices which, coming out of a modern machine, and with mechanical repetition, narrate the stories of past passions ("pseudo-passions" at that), and on the other hand the overwhelming physical presence of Shite in Nō, who both narrates and beautifully dances out her old but still-too-real passion. It is also difficult to identify the half-crazy forgetful old man listening to his own voice with the sane and intelligent priest in Nō who watches and listens to the "other" character. It goes without saying that Krapp is utterly incapable of exorcising or laying the unquiet ghost which is his former self. Nevertheless, we find in *Krapp* the first unmistakable emergence in Beckett's *oeuvre* of an essentially Nō-like structure — or more strictly speaking, a structure resembling the second part of Nō, namely, the voice as Shite arriving out of an alien time-space dimension versus the character as Waki listening to that voice, without any possibility of dialogue between them.

. . . Samuel Beckett started writing plays at the point in the history of Western theatre where most of the realistic conventions of drama, together with the underlying metaphysical world-view, broke down. Or one should perhaps say that he himself was among the greatest subversive forces which brought about this collapse. In his ruthless efforts to strip the theatre of everything that is not absolutely necessary, Beckett has created something unprecedented in Western theatre, a new form of theatre which might best be called "the theatre of mind."

My argument is that, in his very originality, this twentieth-century avant-garde playwright from the westernmost island of Europe has arrived somewhere close to the point at which Zeami arrived in the fourteenth century on the easternmost island of Asia.

In both Zeami's theatre and Beckett's, nothing happens, everything has already happened (hence the complaint of "How boring!"), but someone emerges out of an unknown country. This country, which Beckett in *Ohio Impromptu* calls "the profounds of mind," is at once unknown and half-remembered. The "someone" who arrives in Nō is certainly "the other" to oneself, but anybody who has been really moved by a performance of Nō will understand that this "someone" is also the deepest self of the audience, buried under the deepest layer of culture, not necessarily Japanese culture alone.

In Beckett, the "otherness" of the "someone" is far more ambiguously and viciously entangled with one's own self. Under the malediction undreamt of by Zeami, Beckett must scrutinise modern self-consciousness and pursue it to the point where it threatens to turn into solipsism, autism, depersonalisation, or schizophrenia ("That way lies madness"). And at the end of his play,

Beckett *must* refuse to quiet the tortured soul of the hero, let alone absolve it — although one has a feeling sometimes, especially in his latest plays, that the Beckettian endgame can approach an end, that Beckett can come close to giving a quietus to the hero's sufferings. Be that as it may, it is a triumph of his art that he has incorporated the very structure of the split soul of modern man into a perfect theatrical form.

The striking affinity, despite all the obvious differences, between Beckett and Nō might be described as the conjunction of opposites; but I am personally rather attracted towards the image of the great wheel of the history of some universal drama (if such a thing exists) having come full circle, or again the image of that mythical serpent, Ouroboros, which, like a Möbius strip, has its tail in its mouth. It is interesting to know in passing that the affinity has been testified to by contemporary actors and directors, both East and West. Several of Beckett's plays have been performed successfully by Nō actors in Japan, and a number of Western directors and actors have affirmed that training in Nō theatre is one of the best approaches to performing Beckett's plays.

Finally, I would stress that Zeami's ideal of theatre consisted in "transmitting a *hana* (flower) from mind to mind." It may be true that what is transmitted in Beckett's theatre from mind to mind is something too bleak to be called a "flower." And yet we are grateful to him for creating a theatre so profoundly concerned with the agonies of a human soul, which today surely needs calming, and if possible release, just as badly as it did six hundred years ago.

ಬಿ

JOAN TEMPLETON *prepared her ironic summary of the responses of a dozen critics writing about Ibsen's theme in his famous play for the* Publication of the Modern Language Association. *After reading the critics, you may find Templeton's conclusion surprises you in its uncompromising statement of uncommon sense.*

JOAN TEMPLETON

Is A Doll House *a Feminist Text?*   1989

> A Doll House *is no more about women's rights than Shakespeare's* Richard II *is about the divine right of kings, or* Ghosts *about syphilis. . . . Its theme is the need of every individual to find out the kind of person he or she is and to strive to become that person.*[1]

Ibsen has been resoundingly saved from feminism, or, as it was called in his day, "the woman question." His rescuers customarily cite a statement the dramatist made on 26 May 1898 at a seventieth-birthday banquet given in his honor by the Norwegian Women's Rights League:

---

[1] Michael Meyer, *Ibsen* (Garden City: Doubleday, 1971), 457.

I thank you for the toast, but must disclaim the honor of having consciously worked for the women's rights movement. . . . True enough, it is desirable to solve the woman problem, along with all the others; but that has not been the whole purpose. My task has been the description of humanity.[2]

Ibsen's champions like to take this disavowal as a precise reference to his purpose in writing *A Doll House* twenty years earlier, his "original intention," according to Maurice Valency.[3] Ibsen's biographer Michael Meyer urges all reviewers of *Doll House* revivals to learn Ibsen's speech by heart,[4] and James McFarlane, editor of *The Oxford Ibsen*, includes it in his explanatory material on *A Doll House*, under "Some Pronouncements of the Author," as though Ibsen had been speaking of the play.[5] Whatever propaganda feminists may have made of *A Doll House*, Ibsen, it is argued, never meant to write a play about the highly topical subject of women's rights; Nora's conflict represents something other than, or something more than, woman's. In an article commemorating the half century of Ibsen's death, R. M. Adams explains, "*A Doll House* represents a woman imbued with the idea of becoming a person, but it proposes nothing categorical about women becoming people; in fact, its real theme has nothing to do with the sexes."[6] Over twenty years later, after feminism had resurfaced as an international movement, Einar Haugen, the doyen of American Scandinavian studies, insisted that "Ibsen's Nora is not just a woman arguing for female liberation; she is much more. She embodies the comedy as well as the tragedy of modern life."[7] In the Modern Language Association's *Approaches to Teaching* A Doll House, the editor speaks disparagingly of "reductionist views of [*A Doll House*] as a feminist drama." Summarizing a "major theme" in the volume as "the need for a broad view of the play and a condemnation of a static approach," she warns that discussions of the play's "connection with feminism" have value only if they are monitored, "properly channeled and kept firmly linked to Ibsen's text."[8]

Removing the woman question from *A Doll House* is presented as part of a corrective effort to free Ibsen from his erroneous reputation as a writer of thesis plays, a wrongheaded notion usually blamed on Shaw, who, it is claimed, mistakenly saw Ibsen as the nineteenth century's greatest iconoclast and offered that misreading to the public as *The Quintessence of Ibsenism*. Ibsen, it is now de rigueur to explain, did not stoop to "issues." He was a poet of the truth of the human soul. That Nora's exit from her dollhouse has long been the

---

[2] Henrik Ibsen, *Letters and Speeches*, ed. and trans. Evert Sprinchorn (New York: Hill, 1964), 337.

[3] Maurice Valency, *The Flower and the Castle: An Introduction to Modern Drama* (New York: Schocken, 1982), 151.

[4] Meyer, 774.

[5] James McFarlane, "*A Doll's House*: Commentary" in *The Oxford Ibsen*, ed. McFarlane (Oxford UP, 1961), V, 456.

[6] R. M. Adams, "The Fifty-First Anniversary," *Hudson Review* 10 (1957), 416.

[7] Einar Haugen, *Ibsen's Drama: Author to Audience* (Minneapolis: U of Minnesota P, 1979), vii.

[8] Yvonne Shafer, ed., *Approaches to Teaching Ibsen's* A Doll House (New York: MLA, 1985), 32.

principal international symbol for women's issues, including many that far exceed the confines of her small world, is irrelevant to the essential meaning of *A Doll House*, a play, in Richard Gilman's phrase, "pitched beyond sexual difference."[9] Ibsen, explains Robert Brustein, "was completely indifferent to (the woman question) except as a metaphor for individual freedom."[10] Discussing the relation of *A Doll House* to feminism, Halvdan Koht, author of the definitive Norwegian Ibsen life, says in summary, "Little by little the topical controversy died away; what remained was the work of art, with its demand for truth in every human relation."[11]

Thus, it turns out, the *Uncle Tom's Cabin* of the women's rights movement is not really about women at all. "Fiddle-faddle," pronounced R. M. Adams, dismissing feminist claims for the play.[12] Like angels, Nora has no sex. Ibsen meant her to be Everyman.

ಐಐ

TENNESSEE WILLIAMS *published his notes describing how he envisioned an ideal production of* The Glass Menagerie *on the stage in 1945, soon after the play had survived its shaky premiere at the Civic Theatre in Chicago. Jo Mielziner designed the sets and Paul Bowles composed the music for the original production. The play caught on with audiences because in the first three weeks of its run it was championed almost daily in laudatory articles by the* Chicago Tribune *theater critic Claudia Cassidy. As Donald Spoto wrote in* The Kindness of Strangers: The Life of Tennessee Williams *(1985), "In an unusual example of journalistic salvation, a play was for once not lost but kept alive because of critical support."*

TENNESSEE WILLIAMS

Production Notes
to The Glass Menagerie   1945

Being a "memory play," *The Glass Menagerie* can be presented with unusual freedom of convention. Because of its considerably delicate or tenuous material, atmospheric touches and subtleties of direction play a particularly important part. Expressionism and all other unconventional techniques in drama have only one valid aim, and that is a closer approach to truth. When a play employs unconventional techniques, it is not, or certainly shouldn't be, trying to escape its responsibility of dealing with reality, or interpreting experience, but is actually or should be attempting to find a closer approach, a more penetrating and vivid expression of things as they are. The straight realistic play with its genuine Frigidaire and authentic ice cubes, its characters

---

[9] Richard Gilman, *The Making of Modern Drama* (New York: Farrar, 1972), 65.
[10] Robert Brustein, *The Theatre of Revolt* (New York: Little, 1962), 105.
[11] Halvdan Koht, *Life of Ibsen* (New York: Blom, 1971), 323.
[12] Adams, 416.

that speak exactly as its audience speaks, corresponds to the academic landscape and has the same virtue of a photographic likeness. Everyone should know nowadays the unimportance of the photographic in art: that truth, life, or reality is an organic thing which the poetic imagination can represent or suggest, in essence, only through transformation, through changing into other forms than those which were merely present in appearance.

These remarks are not meant as a preface only to this particular play. They have to do with a conception of a new, plastic theater which must take the place of the exhausted theater of realistic conventions if the theater is to resume vitality as a part of our culture.

The Screen Device. There is *only one important difference between the original and acting version of the play* and that is the *omission* in the latter of the device which I tentatively included in my *original* script. This device was the use of a screen on which were projected magic-lantern slides bearing images or titles. I do not regret the omission of this device from the present Broadway production. The extraordinary power of Miss Taylor's° performance made it suitable to have the utmost simplicity in the physical production. But I think it may be interesting to some readers to see how this device was conceived. So I am putting it into the published manuscript. These images and legends, projected from behind, were cast on a section of wall between the front-room and dining-room areas, which should be indistinguishable from the rest when not in use.

The purpose of this will probably be apparent. It is to give accent to certain values in each scene. Each scene contains a particular point (or several) which is structurally the most important. In an episodic play, such as this, the basic structure or narrative line may be obscured from the audience; the effect may seem fragmentary rather than architectural. This may not be the fault of the play so much as a lack of attention in the audience. The legend or image upon the screen will strengthen the effect of what is merely allusion in the writing and allow the primary point to be made more simply and lightly than if the entire responsibility were on the spoken lines. Aside from this structural value, I think the screen will have a definite emotional appeal, less definable but just as important. An imaginative producer or director may invent many other uses for this device than those indicated in the present script. In fact the possibilities of the device seem much larger to me than the instance of this play can possibly utilize.

The Music. Another extra-literary accent in this play is provided by the use of music. A single recurring tune, "The Glass Menagerie," is used to give emotional emphasis to suitable passages. This tune is like circus music, not when you are on the grounds or in the immediate vicinity of the parade, but when you are at some distance and very likely thinking of something else. It seems under those circumstances to continue almost interminably and it

---

Miss Taylor's: Laurette Taylor (1884–1946) played the role of Amanda in the original Broadway production.

weaves in and out of your preoccupied consciousness; then it is the lightest, most delicate music in the world and perhaps the saddest. It expresses the surface vivacity of life with the underlying strain of immutable and inexpressible sorrow. When you look at a piece of delicately spun glass you think of two things: how beautiful it is and how easily it can be broken. Both of those ideas should be woven into the recurring tune, which dips in and out of the play as if it were carried on a wind that changes. It serves as a thread of connection and allusion between the narrator with his separate point in time and space and the subject of his story. Between each episode it returns as reference to the emotion, nostalgia, which is the first condition of the play. It is primarily Laura's music and therefore comes out most clearly when the play focuses upon her and the lovely fragility of glass which is her image.

The Lighting. The lighting in the play is not realistic. In keeping with the atmosphere of memory, the stage is dim. Shafts of light are focused on selected areas or actors, sometimes in contradistinction to what is the apparent center. For instance, in the quarrel scene between Tom and Amanda, in which Laura has no active part, the clearest pool of light is on her figure. This is also true of the supper scene, when her silent figure on the sofa should remain the visual center. The light upon Laura should be distinct from the others, having a peculiar pristine clarity such as light used in early religious portraits of female saints or madonnas. A certain correspondence to light in religious paintings, such as El Greco's,° where the figures are radiant in atmosphere that is relatively dusky, could be effectively used throughout the play. (It will also permit a more effective use of the screen.) A free, imaginative use of light can be of enormous value in giving a mobile, plastic quality to plays of a more or less static nature.

∞

AUGUST WILSON *described how he became a playwright in the introduction to his collection* Three Plays, *published by the University of Pittsburgh Press in 1991.*

AUGUST WILSON

Where to Begin?

1991

"Where to begin?" is among the first questions an artist asks himself. I have always told anyone who asks for my advice to begin anywhere, and that beginning will lead them, whether backward or forward, to the place they want to go. That the place where they arrive may be a place they have wanted to go to unknowingly or perhaps even unwillingly is the crucible in which many a work of art is fired. Romare Bearden has said art is born out of, among

---

El Greco: Painter (1541–1614) known for the uncanny lighting in his large canvases.

other things, necessity. One always knows his wants better than his needs. Each of these plays was a journey. At the end of each, out of necessity, emerged an artifact that is representative, the way a travel photo is representative, of the journey itself. It is the only record.

I have said elsewhere and will repeat here that writing a play is for me like walking down the landscape of the self, unattended, unadorned, exploring what D. H. Lawrence called "the dark forest of the soul." It is a place rife with shadows, a place of suspect quality and occasional dazzling brightness. What you encounter there are your demons which you have occasionally fed, trying, as Hansel, to make your way back home. You find false trails, roads closed for repairs, impregnable fortresses, scouts, armies of memory, and impossible cartography. It is a place where the cartographers labor night and day remaking the maps. The road is sometimes welcoming and its wide passages offer endearment with each step only to narrow to a footpath that has led you, boatless, to the edge of a vast and encompassing ocean. Occasionally, if you are willing to negotiate the perils, you arrive strong, brighter of spirit, to a place that sprouts yams and bolls of cotton at your footfall.

So I will begin this preface where these plays began, in 1965, with a twenty-year-old poet wrestling with the world and his place in it, having discovered the joy and terror of remaking the world in his own image through the act of writing.

To write is to fix language, to get it down and fix it to a spot and have it have meaning and be fat with substance. It is in many ways a remaking of the self in which all of the parts have been realigned, redistributed, and reassembled into a new being of sense and harmony. You have wrought something into being, and what you have wrought is what you have learned about life, and what you have learned is always pointed toward moving the harborless parts of your being closer to home. To write is to forever circle the maps, marking it all down, the latitude and longitude of each specific bearing, giving new meaning to something very old and very sacred — life itself.

As a twenty-year-old poet faced with how little you know about life, you profess to know everything. What you know most assuredly is that you are going to live until you die. What you have, almost without knowing you have it, is a sense of immortality that allows you to approach the mine fields with the blind faith of innocence and the assurance of an indefatigable spirit that rivals St. George in his willingness to slay the dragon. *If only you could get those damn words down on paper!*

I lived in a rooming house in Pittsburgh in those early days, and as I bedded down each night with my immortal self the guns of social history and responsibility that went boom in the night and called the warriors to their stations were largely ignored. If I heard them at all they had no relation to my bearing as a poet determined to answer the question of how many angels could sit on the head of a pin, despite the fact that I was having trouble identifying the angels and the size of the pin.

Most of the truly important moments in our lives go by unnoticed. We recognize them only in retrospect after we have chosen one road or another and have seen where it has taken us. Only after we have kissed the woman for the last time unknowingly, or have left her final nakedness and been marked by the unsurety and the bruise, do these moments have any resonance.

Sometimes you are privileged to recognize these moments when they occur, and from one day to the next, life, in a single stroke of gluttony, has knocked over the lamps and rearranged the maps. One night in the fall of 1965 I put a typewritten yellow-labeled record titled "Nobody in Town Can Bake a Sweet Jellyroll Like Mine," by someone named Bessie Smith, on the turntable of my 78 rpm phonograph, and the universe stuttered and everything fell to a new place.

Although the business of poetry is to enlarge the sayable, I cannot describe or even relate what I felt. Suffice it to say it was a birth, a baptism, a resurrection, and a redemption all rolled up in one. It was the beginning of my consciousness that I was a representative of a culture and the carrier of some very valuable antecedents. With my discovery of Bessie Smith and the blues I had been given a world that contained my image, a world at once rich and varied, marked and marking, brutal and beautiful, and at crucial odds with the larger world that contained it and preyed and pressed it from every conceivable angle.

"Youth is sweet before flight, and a mighty furnace is its kiln," I have written my daughter as she approaches her twenty-first birthday and wrestles, in her becoming womanhood, with the social welter of America in the nineties. My own youth is fired in the kiln of black cultural nationalism as exemplified by Amiri Baraka° in the sixties. It posited black Americans as coming from a long line of honorable people with a cultural and political history, a people of manners with a strong moral personality that had to be reclaimed by strengthening the elements of the culture that made it unique and by developing institutions for preserving and promoting it. The ideas of self-determination, self-respect, and self-defense which it espoused are still very much a part of my life as I sit down to write. I have stood them up in the world of Bessie Smith on the ground captured by the blues. Having started my beginning consciousness there it is no surprise that I would mature and my efforts at writing would come to fruition on the same ground. I saw the blues as a cultural response of a nonliterate people whose history and culture were rooted in the oral tradition. The response was to a world that was not of their making, in which the idea of themselves as a people of imminent worth that belied their recent history was continually assaulted. It was a world that did not recognize their gods, their manners, their mores. It despised their ethos and refused to even recognize humanity. In such an environment the blues was a flag bearer of self-definition, and within the scope of the larger world which lay beyond its doorstep, it carved out a life, set down rules, and urged a manner of being that corresponded to the temperament and sensibilities of its creators. It was a spiritual conduit that gave spontaneous expression to the spirit that was locked in combat and devising new strategies for engaging life

---

Amiri Baraka: African American poet and playwright (b. 1934) who led the black cultural nationalist movement in the 1960s and founded the Black Arts Repertory Theater.

and enlarging itself. It was a true and articulate literature that was in the fore-front of the development of both character and consciousness.

I turned my ear, my heart, and whatever analytical tools I possessed to embrace this world. I elevated it, rightly or wrongly, to biblical status. I rooted out the ideas and attitudes expressed in the music, charted them and bent and twisted and stretched them. I tested them on the common ground of experi-ence and evidence and gave my whole being, muscle and bone and sinew and flesh and spirit, over to the emotional reference provided by the music. I learned to read between the lines and tried to fill in the blank spaces. This was life being lived in all its timbre and horrifics, with zest and purpose and the af-firmation of the self as worthy of the highest possibilities and the highest cel-ebration. What more fertile ground could any artist want?

Though my discovery of Bessie Smith and the blues provided me with an aesthetic with which to frame my growing ideas of myself as part of some-thing larger, it was not until I discovered the art of Romare Bearden that I was able to turn it into a narrative that would encompass all of the elements of cul-ture and tradition, what [James] Baldwin had so eloquently called "the field of manners and ritual of intercourse" that sustains black American life. Bearden had accomplished in painting an expression as full and varied as the blues. My discovery of his work was akin to my discovery of Bessie Smith, a moment of privilege and exaltation that comes from recognizing yourself as a vital part of a much larger world than you had imagined. "I try to explore, in terms of the life I know best, those things which are common to all cultures," Bearden had said. I took it as my credo and sought to answer Baldwin's call for a pro-found articulation of the black tradition that could sustain a man once he left his father's house. Armed with Bearden and the blues I began to look at my-self in ways I hadn't thought of before and in which I have never ceased to think of since. I began to work with the idea that I would try to put in my work all the things I saw in his, the spirit and texture and substance and grace and elegance. But how?

Many writers anxious to see results often ignore the very thing that can produce them — craft with all its tentacles, its many facets and applications. As I was a poet and writer of short fiction, the crafting of a play was new to me. I didn't know the rules, the elements, or the tools. But, since I had been writing for fifteen years, I was not without discipline. I knew that to write and to write well one must be uncompromising and make choices based on one's heart and mind and execute them with craft. But what craft? The craft I knew was the craft of poetry and fiction. To my mind, they had to connect and in-tercept with the craft of playwrighting at some point and all I had to do was find that point. Fiction was a story told through character and dialogue, and a poem was a distillation of language and images designed to reveal an emotive response to phenomena that brought it into harmony with one's knowledge and experience. Why couldn't a play be both?

I thought that in order to accomplish that I had to look at black life with an anthropological eye, use language, character, and image to reveal its cul-tural flashpoints and in the process tell a story that further illuminated them. This is what the blues did. Why couldn't I? I was, after all, a bluesman. Never mind that I couldn't play a guitar or carry a tune in a bucket. I was cut out of the same cloth and I was on the same field of manners and endeavor — to articulate the cultural response of black Americans to the world in which they found themselves. And so I began, not tentatively, but straight ahead, unswerving, unmitigating. I had, after all, nothing to lose.

An artist who stands before a blank canvas is Picasso (or Matisse, since Picasso himself said "There is no one but Matisse"), until proven otherwise. Artists have the same tools: color, line, mass, form, and their own hearts beating, their own demons, and their own necessity. When I sat down to write I realized I was sitting in the same chair as Eugene O'Neill, Tennessee Williams, Arthur Miller, Henrik Ibsen, Amiri Baraka, and Ed Bullins.° I felt empowered by the chair. I was confronted by the same blank piece of paper, the same problems of art and craft — how to invest the characters with a life and history, how to invent situations that challenged the characters' beliefs, forced them into action, and prompted them to stand beside the consequences ready to reengage life on the new field of memory and observable phenomena. Feeling that sense of power, there were no rules. I was on a new adventure, with the blues and what I call the blood's memory as my only guide and companion. These plays are the result.

Ed Bullins: African American playwright (b. 1935).

27

CASEBOOKS ON PLAYS AND PLAYWRIGHTS

CASEBOOK ON WILLIAM SHAKESPEARE'S *HAMLET*

This Casebook on Shakespeare's Hamlet *contains twelve items to help you understand the play. The section begins with "The Secret Lock of Amleth's Wisdom," an excerpt from the earliest printed version of what scholars refer to as the "Amleth saga," compiled by Saxo Grammaticus, a Danish collector of legends at the end of the twelfth century. As the editor Geoffrey Bullough writes in* Narrative and Dramatic Sources of Shakespeare *(volume 7), "The Amleth saga belongs to a common type of revenge-story in which the hero feigns insanity or stupidity to save his life and gain an opportunity for a coup." The excerpt included here from Saxo is the account of Amleth's meeting with his mother and his murder of the courtier (Polonius in Shakespeare's play) who had been placed by Feng (Claudius) to eavesdrop on their conversation.*

The second commentary is by Bullough, who discusses other treatments of this basic plot closer to Shakespeare's time, one by the French historian François de Belleforest (1530–1583) and the other by the Elizabethan playwright Thomas Kyd (1558–1594), whose play The Spanish Tragedy *was the most popular revenge tragedy in the London theater before Shakespeare's* Hamlet. *Bullough speculates that one of the plays Kyd wrote shortly before Shakespeare created his version of the popular story, might have been the original* Hamlet. *The text of this play (nicknamed "the Ur-Hamlet" by modern historians) unfortunately has not survived. Bullough's discussion of the role of the ghost in* Hamlet *is continued by the critic H. D. F. Kitto, whose reading analyzes the similarities between Shakespeare's play and Sophocles'* Oedipus the King.

Next, the critic François Laroque gives an overview of the main trends in Shakespeare criticism during the past two centuries in his book Shakespeare: Court, Crowd and Playhouse *(1993). The excerpt from the letter by the English Romantic poet John Keats to his brothers on December 21, 1817, contains his comments on what he calls Shakespeare's "negative capability." This term has been widely discussed by generations of critics since the publication of Keats's letter. Some interpret it as Shakespeare's ability as a dramatist to lose his identity in the creation of a wide range of characters. Others believe that Keats meant that as a poet Shakespeare was able to deal with uncertainty, that he did not adhere (as did Milton in* Paradise Lost, *for example) to the strict tenets of religion or moral philosophy, trusting his "sense of Beauty" instead. In a 1906 commentary, Russian writer Leo Tolstoy offers another point of view when he attacks Shakespeare for having what he considered an "immoral frame of mind."*

Virginia Woolf's speculation about what would have happened if Shakespeare had a sister is from her book A Room of One's Own *(1929). Woolf's description of how a woman's life differed from a man's life in Elizabethan England helps us understand how this brilliant playwright, possibly the most articulate person ever to create works of literature in English, could be the father of two daughters who signed legal documents with an "X" and probably were illiterate. (See historian S. Schoenbaum's* William Shakespeare: A Compact Documentary Life *[1977].)*

T. S. Eliot's controversial analysis of "Hamlet and His Problems" was published in 1934. In this essay Eliot introduced his term objective correlative, *often used by later critics. Eliot defines the term as referring to a specific "set of objects, a situation, a chain of events" in a literary work that suggests to the reader a particular emotion the writer wishes to evoke. Then Eliot goes on to criticize the play for lacking sufficient physical events in the plot to motivate Hamlet's deep feelings.*

The final four commentaries are contemporary responses to Hamlet. *The selection by the Polish director Jan Kott includes the German playwright Bertolt Brecht's Marxist analysis of the play. Then the academic critic Bert G. Hornback defends what he calls "Hamlet's Heroism" against detractors in an article written for the* Colby Quarterly *(1994). The English playwright Tom Stoppard included a farcical version of Shakespeare's* Hamlet *to be performed as an "encore" in his two-part play* Dogg's Hamlet, Cahoot's Macbeth *(1979). Finally, in a 1989 essay from* Renaissance Studies, *the New Historicist critic Karin S. Coddon takes Hamlet's madness as her topic, focusing on the play's Elizabethan context to emphasize the difficulty in Shakespeare's time of distinguishing madness from treason.*

SAXO GRAMMATICUS

The Secret Lock of Amleth's Wisdom   c. 1200

. . . None could open the secret lock of [Amleth's] wisdom. But a friend of Feng, gifted more with assurance than judgment, declared that the unfathomable cunning of such a mind could not be detected by any vulgar plot, for the man's obstinacy was so great that it ought not to be assailed with any mild measures; there were many sides to his wiliness, and it ought not to be entrapped by any one method. Accordingly, said he, his own profounder acuteness had hit on a more delicate way, which was well fitted to be put in practice, and would effectually discover what they desired to know. Feng was purposely to absent himself, pretending affairs of great import. Amleth should be closeted alone with his mother in her chamber; but a man should first be commissioned to place himself in a concealed part of the room and listen heedfully to what they talked about. For if the son had any wits at all he would not hesitate to speak out in the hearing of his mother, or fear to trust himself to the fidelity of her who bore him. The speaker, loth to seem readier to devise than to carry out the plot, zealously proffered himself as the agent of the eavesdropping. Feng rejoiced at the scheme, and departed on pretense of a long journey. Now he who had given this counsel repaired privily to the room where Amleth was shut up with his mother, and lay down skulking in the straw. But Amleth had his antidote for the treachery. Afraid of being overheard by some eavesdropper, he at first resorted to his usual imbecile ways, and crowed like a noisy cock, beating his arms together to mimic the flapping of wings. Then he mounted the straw and begain to swing his body and jump again and again, wishing to try if aught lurked there in hiding. Feeling a lump beneath his feet, he drove his sword into the spot, and impaled him who lay hid. Then he dragged him from his concealment and slew him. Then, cutting his body into morsels, he seethed it in boiling water, and flung it through the mouth of an open sewer for the swine to eat, bestrewing the stinking mire with his hapless limbs. Having in this wise eluded the snare, he went back to the room. Then his mother set up a great wailing, and began to lament her son's folly to his face; but he said:

> Most infamous of women! dost thou seek with such lying lamentations to hide thy most heavy guilt? Wantoning like a harlot, thou hast entered a wicked and abominable state of wedlock, embracing with incestuous bosom thy husband's slayer, and wheedling with filthy lures of blandishment him who had slain the father of thy son. This, forsooth, is the way that the mares couple with the vanquishers of their mates; for brute beasts are naturally incited to pair indiscriminately; and it would seem that thou, like them, hast clean forgot thy first husband. As for me, not idly do I wear the mask of folly; for I doubt not that he who destroyed his brother will riot as ruthlessly in the blood of his kindred. Therefore it is better to choose the garb of dullness than that of sense, and to borrow some protection from a show of utter frenzy. Yet the passion to avenge my father still burns in my heart; but I am watching the chances, I await the fitting hour. There is a place for all things; against so merciless and dark a spirit must be used the deeper devices of the mind. And thou, who hadst been better employed in lamenting thine own disgrace, know it is superfluity to bewail my witlessness; thou shouldst weep for the blemish in thine own mind, not for that in another's. On the rest see thou keep silence.

With such reproaches he rent the heart of his mother and redeemed her to walk in the ways of virtue; teaching her to set the fires of the past above the seductions of the present.

When Feng returned, nowhere could he find the man who had suggested the treacherous espial; he searched for him long and carefully, but none said they had seen him anywhere. Amleth, among others, was asked in jest if he had come on any trace of him, and replied that the man had gone to the sewer, but had fallen through its bottom and been stifled by the floods of filth, and that he had been devoured by the swine that came up all about that place. This speech was flouted by those who heard; for it seemed senseless, though really it expressly avowed the truth.

GEOFFREY BULLOUGH

Sources of Shakespeare's Hamlet   1973

There was no Ghost in Saxo [Grammaticus] or [François de] Belleforest, but it was the feature of the *Ur-Hamlet* which most affected spectators and lingered on in public memory, so that in 1596 Thomas Lodge (in *Wits Miserie*) described a devil looking "as pale as the Visard of the ghost which cried so miserably at the Theatre, like an oister-wife, Hamlet, revenge."

When [Thomas] Kyd, or whoever else wrote it, adapted Belleforest's tale in terms of Senecan drama,° he dealt only with the first part of Amleth's life until his triumph over Feng, and changed the climax of that to make it tragic and (no doubt) easier to stage. The main factors shaping the altered plot were the secrecy of Amleth's father's murder and the introduction of his Ghost to incite the hero to revenge. Whereas in *The Spanish Tragedy* the Ghost of Andrea (killed before the play opens) accompanies Revenge to watch the action and "serve for Chorus in this tragedie," taking no part in the action save to express impatience at the slowness with which punishment falls on the wicked, in the *Ur-Hamlet* the father's Ghost really had some reason for demanding vengeance, and presumably started off the action by revealing it. This was a new departure in ghostly behaviour,[1] and it makes me believe that *Hamlet* was written after *The Spanish Tragedy*.

Seneca's dramas lacked the religious attitude of Greek tragedy and the theme of personal revenge superseded divine retribution; horror became a dominant effect, and the Senecan Chorus contributed to this.[2] Thus at the beginning of *Agamemnon*, Thyestes' Ghost rises from Hell to describe his own adultery with his brother Atreus' wife, and how Atreus took revenge by feasting him on the flesh of his own son; tells too how he raped his own daughter Pelopea (who later married Atreus) and had by her a son, Aegysthus, who is now Clytemnestra's paramour and will shortly help her murder Thyestes' nephew, her husband Agamemnon. The Ghost does not interfere in the action; it expounds the past

---

Senecan drama: Tragedies by the Roman playwright and Stoic philosopher Seneca (4 B.C.–A.D. 65).

[1] Cf. F. T. Bowers, *Elizabethan Revenge Tragedy*, Gloucester, Mass., 1940; E. Prosser, *Hamlet and Revenge*, Stanford, 1967.

[2] H. B. Charlton, *The Senecan Tradition in Renaissance Tragedy*, 1946.

and prepares the atmosphere of horror. The *Agamemnon* also has a scene in which Electra accuses her mother of adultery and murder — a striking anticipation of the closet-scene in *Hamlet*. The Amleth saga was in this tradition of fraternal hate and incest; hence no doubt its appeal to Elizabethan Senecan playwrights.

In *Troades* Talthybius tells how the Ghost of Achilles demanded the sacrifice of Polyxena (whom he had loved while living) before the Greek fleet could sail from Troy. In the Latin play this ghost did not appear in person, but Jasper Heywood introduced it in Act II of his translation, craving revenge on the Trojans.[3] Ignoring this proof of survival after death, Seneca's Chorus later doubts whether the soul lives on. There is a resemblance here to the apparent inconsistency in *Hamlet* where, soon after accepting the Ghost as his "father's spirit," the hero speaks of "the undiscover'd country from whose bourn / No traveller returns."

Professor Eleanor Prosser's study of the ghosts in Elizabethan drama shows that many act as Chorus or Prologue, or as the retributory voices of conscience, and that these are almost all pagan ghosts risen from Hades.[4] Few ghosts show Christian characteristics. After *Hamlet* three or four mingle Christian and pagan qualities. Only Andrugio in *Antonio's Revenge* (probably derived from the *Ur-Hamlet*) and the Ghost in *Hamlet* "appear to a protagonist to command blood revenge." (This occasionally occurred in Italian Senecan tragedies.) Andrugio's Ghost comes from his coffin to demand that his son

> Invent some stratagem of vengeance
> Which, but to think on, may like lightning glide
> With horror through thy breast.

He combines delight in the most awful tortures with assurances that he is in league with Heaven. But the play is so confused in tone that some critics have regarded it as a parody. Old Hamlet's Ghost is unique in the problems it posits, and "Shakespeare may well have intended to jolt his audience into a fresh response to what had become a hackneyed convention."[5] It is extremely unlikely that the inventor of Andrea in *The Spanish Tragedy* also created a spirit so complex as that in *Hamlet* Q2.

This is not a suitable place in which to enter the debate about the nature of this ghost. W. W. Greg's suggestion that it is a figment of Hamlet's imagination was countered by E. Stoll who thought it an objectivation of Elizabethan popular lore. For J. D. Wilson it was an occasion for Shakespeare to present three different attitudes to ghosts: the Catholic view (of Marcellus and Bernardo) that a soul could come from Purgatory; the sceptical view of Horatio (like Reginald Scot's) but soon changed to belief; and Hamlet's Protestant view (held by L. Lavater and James VI) that ghosts were probably devils but might be angels, never the souls of men. Another school of thought, including Roy W. Battenhouse and Miss Prosser, argues that the Ghost is a damned spirit come to mislead Hamlet into offending against the divine injunction against revenge.

---

[3] Cf. G. Ll. Evans, "Shakespeare, Seneca and the Kingdom of Violence," in *Roman Drama*, ed. T. A. Dorey and D. R. Dudley, 1965.

[4] E. Prosser, *op. cit.* Appendix A.

[5] Prosser, *op. cit.* pp. 101–102.

My own view is nearer to that of I. J. Semper who saw the Ghost as a visitant from Purgatory and that of Sister Miriam who sees Hamlet as justifiably doubting and testing it. But we should not exaggerate the doctrinal strictness of Shakespeare's approach or assume that he was a Catholic because he used the idea of Purgatory. P. N. Siegel was right to insist: "The Hamlet Ghost is a compound of the Senecan revenge ghost, the Catholic purgatorial spirit and the popular graveyard spook, created for an audience prepared by theatrical tradition, by what Cardinal Newman called "floating religious opinions" (as against official dogma) and by current folklore to give it dramatic credence."[6] The pagan element appears in the Ghost's insistence on quasi-physical horrors unspeakable and the reference to "Lethe wharf"; its purgatorial quality in [act 1, scene 5]. It has an almost Miltonic apprehension of virtue and vice; it loves the Sacraments and deeply regrets having died. "Unhousel'd, disappointed, unaneal'd." Its folklore features include the hour when it walks and when it disappears, and its knocking underground.

H. D. F. KITTO

Hamlet *and the* Oedipus   1956

The Oedipus Tyrannus° begins by describing twice, once in dialogue and once in lyrics, the plague which is afflicting Thebes. The cause of the plague is the presence in the city of a man who has done two things foul and unnatural above all others: he has killed his own father, and he is living incestuously with his own mother. The details of the plague are so described that we can see how its nature is strictly proportioned to its cause: to death is added sterility; the soil of Thebes, the animals, and the human kind are all barren. The meaning is obvious — unless we make it invisible by reducing the play to the stature of Tragedy of Character: what Oedipus has done is an affront to what we should call Nature, to what Sophocles calls Dikê; and since it is the first law of Nature, or Dikê, that she cannot indefinitely tolerate what is . . . contrary to Nature, she rises at last against these unpurged affronts. The plague of sterility is the outcome of the unnatural things which Oedipus has done to his parents.

Hamlet begins in the same way. The two soldiers Marcellus and Bernardo, and Horatio, who is both a soldier and a scholar, are almost terrified out of their wits by something so clean contrary to the natural order that

> I might not this believe
> Without the sensible and true avouch
> Of mine own eyes.

Professor Dover Wilson, learned in sixteenth-century demonology, has explained that the eschatology of Horatio and Hamlet is Protestant, that the Ghost is a Catholic ghost, and that Bernardo and Marcellus are plain untheo-

---

[6] P. N. Siegel, "Discerning the Ghost in *Hamlet*," *PMLA*, lxxviii, 1963, p. 148.
Oedipus Tyrannus: "Oedipus the Tyrant," another name for Sophocles' play.

logical Elizabethans. On this it would be impertinent for an ignoramus to express an opinion, but it does seem that if the "statists" in Shakespeare's audience, and scholars from the Inns of Court, saw and savoured theological *expertise* in this scene, they would be in danger of missing the main point: that the repeated appearances of the Ghost are something quite outside ordinary experience. Horatio the scholar has heard of something similar, in ancient history, "a little ere the mightiest Julius fell." So perhaps this present unnatural terror "bodes some strange eruption to our state"; or — a less disturbing thought — perhaps the ghost is concerned for some uphoarded treasure hidden in the womb of the Earth.

But at this point Shakespeare decides to write some poetry — and he is never so dangerous as when he is writing poetry:

> It faded on the crowing of the cock.
> Some say that ever 'gainst that season comes
> Wherein our Saviour's birth is celebrated,
> The bird of dawning singeth all night long:
> And then, they say, no spirit dare stir abroad,
> The nights are wholesome; then no planets strike,
> No fairy takes, nor witch hath power to charm,
> So hallowed and so gracious is the time.

Pretty good, for a simple soldier. The intense and solemn beauty of these verses lifts us, and was designed to lift us, high above the level of Horatio's conjectures. The night "wherein our Saviour's birth is celebrated" is holy and pure beyond all others; therefore these nights which the Ghost makes hideous by rising so incredibly from the grave, are impure beyond most. Unless Greek Tragedy has bemused me, this passage does more than "give a religious background to the supernatural happenings" of the scene;[1] they give the "background," that is, the logical and dynamic centre, of the whole play. We are in the presence of evil. Hamlet's own prophetic soul recognises this as soon as he hears of the Ghost:

> Foul deeds will rise,
> Though all the earth o'erwhelm them, to men's eyes.

If we may assume that Shakespeare had not read Sophocles — and that Hamlet had not read him, at Wittenberg, behind Shakespeare's back — the parallel with the *Oedipus* becomes the more interesting; for when Oedipus has at last discovered the truth the Chorus observes:

> Time sees all, and it has found you out, in your own despite. It exacts
> Dikê from you for that unnatural marriage that united mother with
> son.

"Foul deeds will rise": there are evils so great that Nature will not allow them to lie unpurged. So, returning to the battlements with Hamlet, and enquiring with him

---

[1] Dover Wilson, *What Happens in "Hamlet,"* p. 67.

Why thy canonized bones, hearsed in death,
Have burst their cerements; why the sepulchre
Wherein we saw thee quietly inurned
Hath o'ped his ponderous and marble jaws
To cast thee up again —

we learn the cause: fratricide, incest, "Murder most foul, strange and un-natural."

Here, most emphatically stated, are the very foundations and framework of the tragedy. We can, of course, neglect these, and erect a framework of our own which we find more interesting or more congenial to us. We can say, with Dr. Gregg, that the Ghost is all my eye; or, with Professor Dover Wilson, that the first act, "a little play of itself," is "an epitome of the ghost-lore of the age" — in which case it becomes something of a learned Prologue to the real play;[2] or, like Dr de Madariaga, we can neglect this encircling presence of evil, and substitute what we know of sixteenth-century Court manners; or, again without constant reference to the background which Shakespeare himself erected, we can subtly anatomise the soul and mind of Hamlet, on the assumption that Hamlet is the whole play. But if we do these things, let us not then complain that Shakespeare attempted a task too difficult for him, or conclude that the play is an ineffable mystery. Turning it into "secular" tragedy we shall be using the wrong focus. The correct focus is one which will set the whole action against a background of Nature and Heaven; for this is the background which the dramatist himself has provided.

FRANÇOIS LAROQUE

A Review of Shakespeare Studies   1993

Shakespeare criticism began in England with the work of the neoclassical writers Alexander Pope and Samuel Johnson, who won credence for the idea that the playwright's genius allowed him to rise above the rules drawn up by Aristotle in his *Poetics* — an idea to which Voltaire, who made Shakespeare known on the European continent, did not subscribe. German men of letters Johann Wolfgang von Goethe, Friedrich von Schlegel, and Johann Ludwig Tieck waxed enthusiastic over Shakespeare's work. In England William Wordsworth expressed the belief that the *Sonnets* held the key to Shakespeare's heart. John Keats identified in a letter what he termed his "negative capability": "that is, when a man is capable of being in uncertainties, mysteries, doubts, without any irritable reaching after fact and reason." And Samuel Taylor Coleridge wrote numerous essays on the plays, emphasizing the often remarkable qualities of his female characters. For him, Shakespeare was as mysterious and elusive as Proteus, god of the sea and metamorphosis. In

---

[2] Or, if it is not this, let it be shown what its organic function is. Shakespeare, having a capacious mind, may well have been keenly interested in contemporary ghost-lore, but our first question is: what has he done with it as a creative artist? Or has he done nothing with it?

France, Stendhal expressed great admiration for Shakespeare, whom he saw as the master of prose drama, while Victor Hugo, whose plays show the undeniable influence of the great Elizabethan, was even more strongly impressed by him. Hugo acclaimed the universality of Shakespeare's genius in his work *William Shakespeare*, written in 1864.

In the twentieth century criticism was dominated by A. C. Bradley, who in 1904 published a series of lectures devoted to the psychological study of the main characters in the great tragedies (*Hamlet, Othello, King Lear,* and *Macbeth*) under the title *Shakespearean Tragedy.* After the war a Cambridge professor, L. C. Knights, wrote ironically about the tendency of critics to treat fictitious characters as if they were entirely real human beings in a famous article published in 1933, entitled *How Many Children Had Lady Macbeth?* He articulated the idea that Shakespeare was, first and foremost, a dramatic poet and that his work had to be analyzed through its images and words. This aspect of his writing then drew greater critical attention, specifically in Caroline Spurgeon's book *Shakespeare's Imagery, and What It Tells Us* (1935) and the many essays published by George Wilson Knight (1933).

The trend in the 1930s and 1940s was to return to the study of historical background, for example in the work of E. M. W. Tillyard, *The Elizabethan World Picture* (1943). In his eyes, Shakespeare was complying with Tudor ideology when he wrote his historical dramas, presenting the Duke of Richmond (Henvy VII), for example, in his official light as providential savior of an English nation torn apart by the horrors of civil war. These theories are heavily disputed today, particularly by those who think in terms of cultural materialism, and see Shakespeare, contrarily, as a writer who sympathized with the oppressed (women and the poor) and whose superficial allegiances masked criticism of the mechanisms of power.

In France Shakespeare criticism found its expression in the work of Henri Fluchère, *Shakespeare dramaturge élisabéthain* ("Shakespeare, Elizabethan Dramatist"), published in 1947. A disciple of the Cambridge school led by L. C. Knights and F. R. Leavis, and influenced by T. S. Eliot's essays, Fluchère concentrated on analysis of the poetic quality of Shakespeare's work rather than of the author's life and the psychology of his characters: "It is only the man's work and not his actions and behavior that concern us. . . . The man and the mystery about him have relegated his work to second place for too long." Meanwhile, in England, Allardyce Nicoll and Glynne Wickham studied the organization of the theaters and companies; Kenneth Muir and Geoffrey Bullough did research on the sources of the plays which helped extend the traditional approach to Shakespeare's work and gave access to new information, both historical and iconographic, throwing light on Shakespeare's contribution to the theater of his time.

The Cold War period and the rise of existentialism and Marxism gave birth to materialist analyses of Shakespeare's drama, such as *Shakespeare Our Contemporary* (1964) by the Polish writer Jan Kott. His ideas greatly influenced the productions of the 1960s, in particular those of Peter Brook, who drew on them considerably. In Kott's eyes there were no good or bad kings, only the implacable steamroller of history crushing individuals like an inhuman machine. This materialist critical approach, influenced predominantly by Karl Marx and Bertolt Brecht, developed significantly with the work of Robert Weimann, *Shakespeare and Popular Tradition in the Theatre*, published in German in 1967 and in English translation in 1978, inviting comparison with *Rabelais and Popular Culture in the Middle Ages and the Renaissance* (1970) by the Russian Mikhail Bakhtin.

Psychoanalysts have also taken a great interest in Shakespeare's writing, starting with Sigmund Freud himself, who numbered the playwright's works among his bedside books, often referred to him, and even wrote important articles on his plays. Freud's disciple Ernest Jones explained Hamlet's puzzling hesitation in enacting the vengeance demanded by his dead father in terms of the Oedipus complex: Hamlet hated Claudius and at the same time envied him for occupying the place by Queen Gertrude's side that he himself secretly desired. In the aftermath of this now classic study, essays and articles from the psychoanalytic standpoint have multiplied. Among the more recent are Jacques Lacan's articles on *Hamlet*, Bernard Sichère's *Le Nom de Shakespeare* ("The Name of Shakespeare"), and *Avec Shakespeare* ("With Shakespeare") by the psychoanalyst Daniel Sibony.

In the last fifteen years Shakespeare criticism has been enlivened, not to say disturbed, by a variety of schools of thought: feminism, Deconstructionism (notably the theories of the French philosopher Jacques Derrida), and the New Historicism. The latter movement, spearheaded by Stephen Greenblatt, author of *Renaissance Self-Fashioning* (1980), aims to situate Shakespeare's work in its historical context, in relation to his contemporaries and as part of the European Renaissance. These new currents of thought have between them produced a proliferation of articles, books, and new editions of Shakespeare. Less eyecatching, but no less important, are the advances in textual criticism made by scholars examining the different technical processes behind the texts of the different editions of Shakespeare, culminating in the publication of the *New Oxford Shakespeare*, edited by Stanley Wells and Gary Taylor (*A Textual Companion*, 1987, and *The Complete Works*, 1986). Though opinion on the investigations of these two specialists is divided, the immensity of the task accomplished makes the edition an essential tool of reference.

In *Shakespeare, Les Feux de l'Envie* ("Shakespeare, the Fires of Desire") published in 1990, René Girard discusses a number of Shakespeare's plays in terms of the theory elaborated in his earlier works, the principle of mimetic desire and the rites of violence in primitive societies. Girard's book has not been unanimously well received by university critics — evidence of the extent to which, as James Joyce suggested in *Ulysses*, Shakespeare is being used as an ideological pawn.

More recent British and American criticism has tended to become increasingly specialized and increasingly written in a technical language not easily accessible to the layman. The most radical theorists have abandoned the quest for "truth" altogether, and believe that "meaning" fluctuates with time and culture and that Shakespeare's plays today are necessarily part of today's ideological strategies. Terence Hawkes, for instance, in *Meaning by Shakespeare*, claims that we "use" *Hamlet*, rather as Hamlet "used" *The Murder of Gonzago*, to prove something to ourselves in our world. "Perhaps," he says, "its probing of the relation between art and social life, role-playing on stage and role-playing in society, appears so powerfully to offer an adequate account of important aspects of our own experience that it ends by constructing them. In other words, *Hamlet* crucially helps to determine how we perceive and respond to the world in which we live."

JOHN KEATS

From a Letter to George and Thomas Keats, 21 December 1817

Hampstead Sunday

My dear Brothers,

I must crave your pardon for not having written ere this. . . .

. . . Brown and Dilke walked with me and back from the Christmas pantomime. I had not a dispute but a disquisition, with Dilke on various subjects; several things dove-tailed in my mind, and at once it struck me what quality went to form a Man of Achievement, especially in Literature and which Shakespeare possessed so enormously — I mean *Negative Capability*, that is, when a man is capable of being in uncertainties, mysteries, doubts, without any irritable reaching after fact and reason — [Samuel Taylor] Coleridge, for instance, would let go by a fine isolated verisimilitude caught from the Penetralium of mystery, from being incapable of remaining content with half-knowledge. This pursued through volumes would perhaps take us no further than this, that with a great poet the sense of Beauty overcomes every other consideration, or rather obliterates all consideration.

[Percy Bysshe] Shelley's poem is out, and there are words about its being objected to as much as "Queen Mab" was. Poor Shelley, I think he has his Quota of good qualities, in sooth la!! Write soon to your most sincere friend and affectionate Brother

John.

LEO TOLSTOY

Shakespeare's Immoral Frame of Mind

1906

I remember the astonishment I felt when I first read Shakespeare. I expected to receive a powerful aesthetic pleasure, but having read, one after the other, works regarded as his best, *King Lear, Romeo and Juliet, Hamlet,* and *Macbeth,* not only did I feel no delight, but I felt an irresistible repulsion and tedium, and doubted as to whether I was senseless in feeling works regarded as the summit of perfection by the whole of the civilized world to be trivial and positively bad, or whether the significance which this civilized world attributes to the works of Shakespeare was itself senseless. My consternation was increased by the fact that I always keenly felt the beauties of poetry in every form; then why should artistic works recognized by the whole world as those of a genius — the works of Shakespeare — not only fail to please me, but be disagreeable to me? . . .

All his characters speak, not their own, but always one and the same Shakespearean pretentious and unnatural language, in which not only they could not speak, but in which no living man ever has spoken or does speak. . . . From his first words, exaggeration is seen: the exaggeration of events, the exaggeration of emotion, and the exaggeration of effects. One sees at once that he does not believe in what he says, that it is of no necessity to him, that he invents the events he describes and is indifferent to his characters — that he has conceived them only for the stage and therefore makes them do and say only what may strike his public, and so we do not believe either in the events or in the actions or in the sufferings of the characters.

He alone can write a drama who has got something to say to men, and that something of the greatest importance for them: about man's relation to God, to the Universe, to the All, the Eternal, the Infinite. But when, thanks to the German theories about objective art, the idea was established that for the drama this was quite unnecessary, then it became obvious how a writer like Shakespeare — who had not got developed in his mind the religious convictions proper to his time, who, in fact, had no convictions at all, but heaped up in his drama all possible events, horrors, fooleries, discussions, and effects — could appear to be a dramatic writer of the greatest genius.

But these are all external reasons. The fundamental inner cause of Shakespeare's fame was and is this — that his dramas . . . corresponded to the irreligious and immoral frame of mind of the upper classes of his time and ours.

VIRGINIA WOOLF

What If Shakespeare Had Had a Sister?   1929

Let me imagine, since facts are so hard to come by, what would have happened had Shakespeare had a wonderfully gifted sister, called Judith, let us say. Shakespeare himself went, very probably — his mother was an heiress — to the grammar school, where he may have learnt Latin — Ovid, Virgil and Horace — and the elements of grammar and logic. He was, it is well known, a wild boy who poached rabbits, perhaps shot a deer, and had, rather sooner than he should have done, to marry a woman in the neighborhood, who bore him a child rather quicker than was right. That escapade sent him to seek his fortune in London. He had, it seemed, a taste for the theater; he began by holding horses at the stage door. Very soon he got work in the theater, became a successful actor, and lived at the hub of the universe, meeting everybody, knowing everybody, practicing his art on the boards, exercising his wits in the streets, and even getting access to the palace of the queen. Meanwhile his extraordinarily gifted sister, let us suppose, remained at home. She was as adventurous, as imaginative, as agog to see the world as he was. But she was not sent to school. She had no chance of learning grammar and logic, let alone of reading Horace and Virgil. She picked up a book now and then, one of her brother's perhaps, and read a few pages. But then her parents came in and told her to mend the stockings or mind the stew and not moon about with books and papers. They would have spoken sharply but kindly, for they were substantial people who knew the conditions of life for a woman and loved their daughter — indeed, more likely than not she was the apple of her father's eye. Perhaps she scribbled some pages up in an apple loft on the sly, but was careful to hide them or set fire to them. Soon, however, before she was out of her teens, she was to be betrothed to the son of a neighboring wool-stapler. She cried out that marriage was hateful to her, and for that she was severely beaten by her father. Then he ceased to scold her. He begged her instead not to hurt him, not to shame him in this matter of her marriage. He would give her a chain of beads or a fine petticoat, he said; and there were tears in his eyes. How could she disobey him? How could she break his heart? The force of her own gift alone drove her to it. She made up a small parcel of her belongings, let herself down by a rope one summer's night, and took the road to London. She was not seventeen. The birds that sang in the hedge were not more musical than she was. She had the quickest fancy, a gift like her brother's, for the tune of words. Like him, she had a taste for the theater. She stood at the stage door; she wanted to act, she said. Men laughed in her face. The manager — a fat, loose-lipped man — guffawed. He bellowed something about poodles dancing and women acting — no woman, he said, could possibly be an actress. He hinted — you can imagine what. She could get no training in her craft. Could she even seek her dinner in a tavern or roam the streets at midnight? Yet her genius was for fiction and lusted to feed abundantly upon the lives of men and women and the study of their ways. At last — for she was very young, oddly like Shakespeare the poet in her face, with the same grey eyes and rounded brows — at last Nick Greene the actor-manager took pity on her; she found herself with child by that gentleman and so — who shall measure the heat and violence of the poet's heart when caught and tangled in a woman's body? — killed herself one winter's night and lies buried at some cross-roads where the omnibuses now stop outside the Elephant and Castle.

That, more or less, is how the story would run, I think, if a woman in Shakespeare's day had had Shakespeare's genius. . . . Any woman born with a great gift in the sixteenth century would certainly have gone crazed, shot herself, or ended her days in some lonely cottage outside the village, half witch, half wizard, feared and mocked at. . . . To have lived a free life in London in the sixteenth century would have meant for a woman who was poet and playwright a nervous stress and dilemma which might well have killed her. Had she survived, whatever she had written would have been twisted and deformed, issuing from a strained and morbid imagination. And undoubtedly, I thought, looking at the shelf where there are no plays by women, her work would have gone unsigned.

T. S. ELIOT

Hamlet and His Problems 1934

Few critics have ever admitted that *Hamlet* the play is the primary problem, and Hamlet the character only secondary. And Hamlet the character has had an especial temptation for that most dangerous type of critic: the critic with a mind which is naturally of the creative order, but which through some weakness in creative power exercises itself in criticism instead. These minds often find in Hamlet a vicarious existence for their own artistic realization. Such a mind had Goethe, who made of Hamlet a Werther; and such had [Samuel Taylor] Coleridge who made of Hamlet a Coleridge; and probably neither of these men in writing about Hamlet remembered that his first business was to study a work of art. The kind of criticism that Goethe and Coleridge produced, in writing of Hamlet, is the most misleading kind possible. For they both possessed unquestionable critical insight, and both make their critical aberrations the more plausible by the substitution — of their own Hamlet for Shakespeare's — which their creative gift effects. We should be thankful that Walter Pater° did not fix his attention on this play.

Two writers of our time, Mr. J. M. Robertson and Professor Stoll of the University of Minnesota, have issued small books which can be praised for moving in the other direction. Mr. Stoll performs a service in recalling to our attention the labors of the critics of the seventeenth and eighteenth centuries, observing that

> they knew less about psychology than more recent Hamlet critics, but they were nearer in spirit to Shakespeare's art; and as they insisted on the importance of the effect of the whole rather than on the importance of the leading character, they were nearer, in their old-fashioned way, to the secret of dramatic art in general.

Qua work of art, the work of art cannot be interpreted; there is nothing to interpret; we can only criticize it according to standards, in comparison to other works of art; and for "interpretation" the chief task is the presentation of relevant historical facts which the reader is not assumed to know. Mr. Robertson points out, very pertinently, how critics have failed in their "interpretation" of *Hamlet* by ignoring what ought to be very obvious: that *Hamlet* is a stratification, that it represents the efforts of a series of men, each making what he could out of the work of his predecessors. The *Hamlet* of Shakespeare will appear to us very differently if, instead of treating the whole action of the play as due to Shakespeare's design, we perceive his *Hamlet* to be superposed upon much cruder material which persists even in the final form.

We know that there was an older play by Thomas Kyd, that extraordinary dramatic (if not poetic) genius who was in all probability the author of two plays so dissimilar as the *Spanish Tragedy* and *Arden of Feversham;* and

---

Walter Pater: English writer and critic (1839–1894) known for his complex, ornate style.

what this play was like we can guess from three clues: from the *Spanish Tragedy* itself, from the tale of Belleforest upon which Kyd's *Hamlet* must have been based, and from a version acted in Germany in Shakespeare's lifetime which bears strong evidence of having been adapted from the earlier, not from the later, play. From these three sources it is clear that in the earlier play the motive was a revenge motive simply; that the action or delay is caused, as in the *Spanish Tragedy*, solely by the difficulty of assassinating a monarch surrounded by guards; and that the "madness" of Hamlet was feigned in order to escape suspicion, and successfully. In the final play of Shakespeare, on the other hand, there is a motive which is more important than that of revenge, and which explicitly "blunts" the latter; the delay in revenge is unexplained on grounds of necessity or expediency; and the effect of the "madness" is not to lull but to arouse the king's suspicion. The alteration is not complete enough, however, to be convincing. Furthermore, there are verbal parallels so close to the *Spanish Tragedy* as to leave no doubt that in places Shakespeare was merely *revising* the text of Kyd. And finally there are unexplained scenes — the Polonius-Laertes and the Polonius-Reynaldo scenes — for which there is little excuse; these scenes are not in the verse style of Kyd, and not beyond doubt in the style of Shakespeare. These Mr. Robertson believes to be scenes in the original play of Kyd reworked by a third hand, perhaps Chapman,° before Shakespeare touched the play. And he concludes, with very strong show of reason, that the original play of Kyd was, like certain other revenge plays, in two parts of five acts each. The upshot of Mr. Robertson's examination is, we believe, irrefragable: that Shakespeare's *Hamlet*, so far as it is Shakespeare's, is a play dealing with the effect of a mother's guilt upon her son, and that Shakespeare was unable to impose this motive successfully upon the "intractable" material of the old play.

Of the intractibility there can be no doubt. So far from being Shakespeare's masterpiece, the play is most certainly an artistic failure. In several ways the play is puzzling, and disquieting as is none of the others. Of all the plays it is the longest and is possibly the one on which Shakespeare spent most pains; and yet he has left in it superfluous and inconsistent scenes which even hasty revision should have noticed. The versification is variable. Lines like

> Look, the morn, in russet mantle clad,
> Walks o'er the dew of yon high eastern hill,

are of the Shakespeare of *Romeo and Juliet*. The lines in act V, scene II,

> Sir, in my heart there was a kind of fighting
> That would not let me sleep . . .
> Up from my cabin,
> My sea-grown scarf'd about me, in the dark
> Grop'd I to find out them: had my desire;
> finger'd their packet;

are of his quite mature. Both workmanship and thought are in an unstable position. We are surely justified in attributing the play, with that other pro-

---

Chapman: George Chapman (1559?–1634), Renaissance poet and playwright.

foundly interesting play of "intractable" material and astonishing versification, *Measure for Measure*, to a period of crisis, after which follow the tragic successes which culminate in *Coriolanus*. *Coriolanus* may be not as "interesting" as *Hamlet*, but it is, with *Antony and Cleopatra*, Shakespeare's most assured artistic success. And probably more people have thought *Hamlet* a work of art because they found it interesting, than have found it interesting because it is a work of art. It is the *Mona Lisa* of literature.

The grounds of *Hamlet*'s failure are not immediately obvious. Mr. Robertson is undoubtedly correct in concluding that the essential emotion of the play is the feeling of a son toward a guilty mother:

> [Hamlet's] tone is that of one who has suffered tortures on the score of his mother's degradation. . . . The guilt of a mother is an almost intolerable motive for drama, but it had to be maintained and emphasized to supply a psychological solution, or rather a hint of one.

This, however, is by no means the whole story. It is not merely the "guilt of a mother" that cannot be handled as Shakespeare handled the suspicion of Othello, the infatuation of Antony, or the pride of Coriolanus. The subject might conceivably have expanded into a tragedy like these, intelligible, self-complete, in the sunlight. *Hamlet*, like the sonnets, is full of some stuff that the writer could not drag to light, contemplate, or manipulate into art. And when we search for this feeling, we find it, as in the sonnets, very difficult to localize. You cannot point to it in the speeches; indeed, if you examine the two famous soliloquies you see the versification of Shakespeare, but a content which might be claimed by another, perhaps by the author of the *Revenge of Bussy d'Ambois*,° act V, scene I. We find Shakespeare's *Hamlet* not in the action, not in any quotations that we might select, so much as in an unmistakable tone which is unmistakably not in the earlier play.

The only way of expressing emotion in the form of art is by finding an "objective correlative"; in other words, a set of objects, a situation, a chain of events which shall be the formula of that *particular* emotion; such that when the external facts, which must terminate in sensory experience, are given, the emotion is immediately evoked. If you examine any of Shakespeare's more successful tragedies, you will find this exact equivalence; you will find that the state of mind of Lady Macbeth walking in her sleep has been communicated to you by a skillful accumulation of imagined sensory impressions; the words of Macbeth on hearing of his wife's death strike us as if, given the sequence of events, these words were automatically released by the last event in the series. The artistic "inevitability" lies in this complete adequacy of the external to the emotion; and this is precisely what is deficient in *Hamlet*. Hamlet (the man) is dominated by an emotion which is inexpressible, because it is in *excess* of the facts as they appear. And the supposed identity of Hamlet with his author is genuine to this point: that Hamlet's bafflement at the absence of objective equivalent to his feelings is a prolongation of the bafflement of his creator in the face of his artistic problem. Hamlet is up against the difficulty

---

Revenge of Bussy d'Ambois: Tragedy (1610–11) by George Chapman.

that his disgust is occasioned by his mother, but that his mother is not an adequate equivalent for it; his disgust envelops and exceeds her. It is thus a feeling which he cannot understand; he cannot objectify it, and it therefore remains to poison life and obstruct action. None of the possible actions can satisfy it; and nothing that Shakespeare can do with the plot can express Hamlet for him. And it must be noticed that the very nature of the *données*° of the problem precludes objective equivalence. To have heightened the criminality of Gertrude would have been to provide the formula for a totally different emotion in Hamlet; it is just *because* her character is so negative and insignificant that she arouses in Hamlet the feeling which she is incapable of representing.

The "madness" of Hamlet lay to Shakespeare's hand; in the earlier play a simple ruse, and to the end, we may presume, understood as a ruse by the audience. For Shakespeare it is less than madness and more than feigned. The levity of Hamlet, his repetition of phrase, his puns, are not part of a deliberate plan of dissimulation, but a form of emotional relief. In the character Hamlet it is the buffoonery of an emotion which can find no outlet in action; in the dramatist it is the buffoonery of an emotion which he cannot express in art. The intense feeling, ecstatic or terrible, without an object or exceeding its object, is something which every person of sensibility has known; it is doubtless a subject of study for pathologists. It often occurs in adolescence: the ordinary person puts these feelings to sleep, or trims down his feelings to fit the business world; the artist keeps them alive by his ability to intensify the world to his emotions. The Hamlet of Laforgue° is an adolescent; the Hamlet of Shakespeare is not, he has not that explanation and excuse. We must simply admit that here Shakespeare tackled a problem which proved too much for him. Why he attempted it at all is an insoluble puzzle; under compulsion of what experience he attempted to express the inexpressibly horrible, we cannot ever know. We need a great many facts in his biography; and we should like to know whether, and when, and after or at the same time as what personal experience, he read Montaigne's *Apologie de Raimond Sebond.*° We should have, finally, to know something which is by hypothesis unknowable, for we assume it to be an experience which, in the manner indicated, exceeded the facts. We should have to understand things which Shakespeare did not understand himself.

---

données: Term employed by the American novelist Henry James to refer to the "givens" about a narrative — the assumptions and motifs from which it proceeds.   **Laforgue:** Jules Laforgue (1860–1887), French poet.   **Montaigne's *Apologie de Raimond Sebond:*** Michel de Montaigne (1533–1592), whose "apology" for the fifteenth-century Spaniard served as Montaigne's own defense of his opinion on the futility of reason.

JAN KOTT

Bertolt Brecht's Hamlet

1966

TRANSLATED BY BOLESLAW TABORSKI

Hamlet is like a sponge. Unless it is produced in a stylized or antiquarian fashion, it immediately absorbs all the problems of our time. It is the strangest play ever written, by its very imperfections. *Hamlet* is a great scenario, in which every character has a more or less tragic and cruel part to play, and has magnificent things to say. Every character has an irrevocable task to fulfill, a task imposed by the author. This scenario is independent of the characters; it has been devised earlier. It defines the situations, as well as the mutual relations of the characters; it dictates their words and gestures. But it does not say who the characters are. It is something external in relation to them. And that is why the scenario of *Hamlet* can be played by different sorts of characters.

An actor always enters a ready part, written not only for him. In this respect *Hamlet* does not, of course, differ from other plays. At the first rehearsal the actors sit at a table. "You will be the king," says the producer. "You will be Ophelia, and you will be Laertes. We shall now read the play." So far so good. But in the play itself similar things happen. Hamlet, Laertes, Ophelia also have to play parts imposed on them, parts against which they revolt. They are actors in a drama they do not always wholly understand, in which they have become involved. The scenario dictates actions of the *dramatis personae*, but does not dictate motives underlying the actions, i.e. the psychology. This is true of life, as well as of the theatre.

A secret organization is preparing an action. The plan has been carefully worked out: place, time-table, direction of retreat. Then the parts have to be distributed. You will stand on that corner and raise your handkerchief when you see the grey car. You will go to Z. and bring a case with grenades to the house No. 12. You will shoot in direction W. and escape in direction M. The tasks have been allotted, the parts taught. Even gestures have been defined. But the evening before, the boy who is to shoot in direction W. could have read Rimbaud or drunk vodka, or both. He may be a young philosopher, or just a teddy-boy. The girl who is to bring grenades may be having an unhappy love affair, or may be a good-time girl, or possibly both. The plan of action will not be altered because of that. The scenario remains unchanged.

Hamlet can be summarised in a number of ways: as an historical chronicle, as a thriller, or as a philosophical drama. They will probably be three different plays, though all three have been written by Shakespeare. But if the summary is fair, scenarios of the three plays will be the same. Except that every time there will be a different Ophelia, or Hamlet, or Laertes. The parts are the same, but performed by different actors.

Let us have a look at the scenario. For, after all, Shakespeare had written, or rather re-written, an old scenario, and the parts in it. But he did not distribute the parts. This has been done anew in every age. Every age has its own

Poloniuses, Fortinbrases, Hamlets, and Ophelias. Before they enter the stage, they have to go to dressing rooms. But let them not stay there too long. They may put on huge wigs, shave off their moustaches, or stick on beards, put on medieval-looking tights, or throw Byronic capes over their shoulders; they may play in armour or in tails. This does not really make much difference, on condition that their make-up is not overdone; for they must have modern faces. Otherwise they would perform a costume piece, instead of *Hamlet*.

Bertolt Brecht wrote in his *Little Organum for the Theatre:*

> . . . The theatre should always be mindful of the needs of its time. Let us take, as an example, the old play of *Hamlet*. I believe that in view of the bloody and gloomy times in which I am writing this, in view of the criminal ruling classes and general despair of reason, . . . the story of this play may be read thus: It is a time of war. Hamlet's father, the king of Denmark, had, in a victorious war of plunder, killed the king of Norway. While the latter's son, Fortinbras, is preparing himself for a new war, the king of Denmark is also killed, by his brother. The brothers of the dead kings, having become kings themselves, conclude peace with each other. Norwegian troops, on their way to a war of plunder against Poland, have been permitted to cross Danish territory. Just at this time, the warlike father's ghost asks young Hamlet to revenge the crime committed on himself. After some hesitation as to whether he should add one bloody deed to another, Hamlet — willing even to go into exile — meets at the sea shore young Fortinbras and his troops on their way to Poland. Following his example he turns back, and, in a scene of barbaric slaughter, kills his uncle, his mother, and himself, leaving Denmark to the Norwegians. Thus we observe how, in these circumstances, the young man, already somewhat stout, badly misuses his new knowledge acquired at Wittenberg University. This knowledge gets in the way when it comes to resolving conflicts of the feudal world. His reason is impractical when faced with irrational reality. He falls a tragic victim to the discrepancy between his reasoning and his action.

Brecht was writing his *Little Organum* in the years of the Second World War. No wonder that in Shakespeare's tragedy he saw, above all, armies devastating the country, wars of aggression, the powerlessness of reason. Hamlet's personal drama, or Ophelia's misfortunes were made insignificant by the events of history. Brecht was sensitive to the politics in *Hamlet*. He was more interested in the sequences of historical conflict than in the depths of the Prince of Denmark's soul. The point of departure of Polish productions of *Hamlet* in 1956 and 1959 was very similar, however they might have differed from Brecht's concepts. *Hamlet* was a political play in 1956, and remained such in 1959, although the Prince of Denmark became by then a much more complex personality and passed through new experiences.

Bert G. Hornback

Hamlet's Heroism 1994

Of course Hamlet isn't "delaying." Despite our critical heritage, that's utter silliness. To suggest that Shakespeare's great play is about such is to malign — by misreading — his most noble character. And part of Shakespeare's greatness, here as elsewhere, is that he makes characters clear to us. "Delaying" is no more Hamlet's "tragic flaw" — whatever that means — than obesity is: but then E. Vale Blake was being satirical when he wrote "The Impediment of Adipose"[1] — and the object of his satire was, surely, our critical heritage.

The reader who says that Hamlet's problem is procrastination must think that Hamlet eventually will — or should — commit revenge. But Hamlet rejects revenge: his play is not a revenger's drama at all. Hamlet isn't delaying, out of laziness or cowardice; he is refusing — on principle — to commit an act which he considers wrong. Our understanding this is essential to our understanding his character and our making sense of Shakespeare's play.

Hamlet is a young man who abhors violence. That's why his murder of poor, stupid Polonius is such a painful thing, and why the cruelly capital trick he plays on Rosencrantz and Guildenstern is so disturbing. In some lesser play — in any of the "revenge" plays popular on the Elizabethan stage — we might see the trick that gets Rosencrantz and Guildenstern killed as examples of a grimly just or morally serious wit; but in this play, Hamlet's claim of something like poetic justice is unacceptable. The callousness with which he sends them to their deaths is an aberration: he acts *out* of character — and, despite their falseness to him, his act is wrong.

In a simpler play, Hamlet's murder of Polonius might have had some melodramatic shock value. But for it to have such, the dramatist would have had to let us see the violence, experience the act. Shakespeare is capable, certainly, of creating such a scene: consider, for example, the blinding of Gloucester in *King Lear*. But Shakespeare writes the murder of Polonius differently, so that the horror of the deed has as its focus, not the act of murder or Polonius' death, but Hamlet's response to what he has done. What Shakespeare asks us to consider — and try to understand — is the effect of this act on Hamlet.

The young man who has so earnestly, so poignantly refused to obey his dead father's ghost and enact revenge, who has argued with himself so carefully to keep from doing what — on principle — he doesn't want to do, murders Polonius without thinking, impulsively. A voice cries out from behind the arras, and Hamlet strikes. "Is it the King?" he asks. If it had been Claudius, Hamlet would — or could — have excused the act: it would not have been re-

---

[1] E. Vale Blake, "The Impediment of Adipose," *Popular Science Monthly* 17 (May 1880), reprinted in *Hamlet: Enter Critic*, ed. Claire Sacks and Edgar Whan (New York, 1960), 8–15.

venge, but something like self-defense. And without violating his own conscience, he would have satisfied his father.

But no: his thoughtless act has not been so lucky. He has murdered poor, stupid Polonius.

> For this same lord,
> I do repent; but heaven hath pleas'd it so,
> To punish me with this, and this with me.
> . . . .
> I will bestow him, and will answer well
> The death I gave him.

And then: "Thus bad begins," he says, "and worse remains behind" (III, iv, 179). He can't excuse what he has done by blaming Polonius, though he will later try such a tactic to justify his sending Rosencrantz and Guildenstern off to death in England.

But Hamlet knows — feels in his mind — that he has done a terrible thing, a "bad" thing, in rashly drawing his sword and stabbing blindly through that drapery. And he fears that the next step will be his succumbing to his father's ghost's demand for intentional, calculated revenge: an even "worse" thing.

When the ghost appears after the murder of Polonius, it says it comes "to whet [Hamlet's] almost blunted purpose." Hamlet knows as much even before the ghost speaks:

> Do you come your tardy son to chide,
> That, laps'd in time and passion, lets go by
> Th' important acting of your dread command?

He fears that his father's ghost will make him change his mind: that the ghost, with his "pale . . . glares" and "piteous action," will "convert" Hamlet's principled intentions.

At the end of Act I, Hamlet complains bitterly at what is asked of him. "The time is out of joint," he says, recognising the evil that has been done, and that it goes unpunished. But then, understanding what he is expected to do, he cries, "O cursed spite / That ever I was born to set it right!" As Kittredge noted, Hamlet's words indicate that "he is too highly civilized to welcome the duty that the savage code of his nation and time imposes."[2]

Hamlet's response to his father's demand for revenge is at first to find excuses not to follow that "savage code." To understand what is called his "delaying" — and to credit it properly for what it is, a thoughtful and principled young man's earnest defense of his own conscience — we need only compare it to Laertes' later response to Claudius. Claudius goads him — Hamlet has murdered Laertes' father — and Laertes is immediately eager for revenge.

---

[2] George Lyman Kittredge, ed., *The Complete Works of Shakespeare* (New York, 1936). Kittredge's note for *Hamlet* (I, v. 189–90) reads: "Hamlet is resolved to avenge his father, but he is too highly civilized to welcome the duty that the savage code of his nation and time imposes."

Laertes, however, is a fool. At the beginning of the play he is headed off to Paris to live; Hamlet wants to go back to Wittenberg — to study. And whereas Hamlet works to understand things, Laertes — according to Claudius — "Feeds on his wonder, keeps himself in clouds." Laertes is a typical revenger: when he returns to Elsinore he is wound up and ready for violence. Whereas Hamlet, sworn to revenge, questions the moral validity of his oath, Laertes rejects "conscience," and in order to "be reveng'd" will "dare damnation."

Laertes is a fool, a dangerous young man available in his foolishness to be used. Hamlet is a thoughtful young man whose determination to protect his own honor — to maintain his morality — becomes, for Shakespeare, the heroic *social* triumph of the play.

Hamlet is Shakespeare's absolute hero. He is heroic even in the Greek sense: he is larger than life. Though "Something [was] rotten in the state of Denmark" at the beginning of the play, all that rottenness is dead at the end — and Hamlet's story remains. By his *act* of refusing to become the revenger he saves the idea of society, raises us above that "savage code."

And his refusing to become a revenger is indeed an act: an act of principle. In a play so much about thoughtfulness, an act of consciousness and conscience is most certainly an act. To live a life of principle is not to be inactive. Hamlet's life becomes meaning: it becomes the tragic "story" which *he* insists be told.

Everybody in Denmark knows when Hamlet was born. We don't find out, as readers or viewers, until late in the play, when the clown casually reminds Hamlet that everyone knows that date: "the day that our last king Hamlet overcame Fortinbras" was the "very day that young Hamlet was born." But why should either Dane or Shakespeare's audience need to know this? What does the date of Hamlet's birth have to do with this tragic story? And why should Shakespeare bother to tell us that Hamlet is thirty years old?

Let me take the long way around in trying to answer these questions.

In Act Two, the players arrive in the midst of Hamlet's playing, first with Rosencrantz and Guildenstern and then with Polonius. From his ironic teasing of Polonius, Hamlet turns to serious plotting. The scene is a long one — nearly six hundred lines. It begins with Claudius importuning Rosencrantz and Guildenstern to spy on Hamlet, and Polonius volunteering to spy. It concludes with Hamlet — "rogue and peasant slave" — planning to spy on Claudius.

Claudius' plot has as its motive self-defense: he is afraid of Hamlet, and looking for an excuse to remove him from Elsinore in one way or another. Polonius' plot is simpler: he thinks Hamlet is mad, and would prove it. Hamlet's plot proves both his sanity and his morality: he wants to prove — to himself — Claudius' guilt. Through his use of the players, he will "catch the conscience of the King."

In this long soliloquy which takes fifty-eight lines — "To be or not to be" and "How all occasions" are both thirty-four, "O that this too too solid flesh" thirty-one, " 'Tis now the very witching time" but twelve — Hamlet considers his failure to enact the revenge required of him by his father, but rejects the self-accusation of cowardice: "Fie upon 't. About, my brains!" And then, using his brains to act, he creates the plot to "observe" Claudius, and "test him to the quick."

When the players expose Claudius and he runs, "frighted" — accused, and known — Hamlet has the evidence he needed, or claimed to need, of Claudius' guilt, and is free in conscience to fulfill his oath: "Now could I drink hot blood / And do such bitter business as the day / Would quake to look on." But he knows what such revenge would mean, or be: the reference for his immediately preceding remark that "hell itself breathes out / Contagion to this world" is the act of revenge which now — according to the "savage code" — is justified.

But Hamlet doesn't enact revenge — and that is what is most startling and wonderful about this play. Midway through the third act Hamlet knows, most certainly, that Claudius murdered his father. And he knows that Claudius knows he knows it. But Hamlet makes no effort to kill his father's murderer, uses his "brains" to conceive no plan for revenge: threatens Claudius' life in no way.

Why?

Hamlet is not Laertes — nor is Laertes Shakespeare's hero. Stupid, mad impulsiveness is not heroic: it is stupid, and mad. Shakespeare's hero is thoughtful — he is, we remember, a student — and because of and through his thoughtfulness he is heroic.

Once Hamlet has proved, to himself, that Claudius is his father's murderer, he should be ready to fulfill his oath. But he doesn't even try. True, in the next scene but one he kills Polonius; the thrust of his sword is impulsive, however, not intentional. That it could have meant revenge — had Polonius been the King — is but an aspirant afterthought.

Hamlet berates himself for the "craven scruple / Of thinking too precisely," and calls such scrupulosity "one part wisdom / And . . . three parts coward." But the occasion which would "spur [his] dull revenge" is young Fortinbras' arrival, on his way to attack Poland — and Hamlet is disgustedly critical of Fortinbras' war. Asking himself to think — for God "gave us not . . . godlike reason / To fust in us unus'd" — he sees "examples" for such violence as he is sworn to, but finds them "gross as earth," not heroic. The context for his ironic cry, "O, from this time forth, / My thoughts be bloody, or be nothing worth!" is his caustic and belittling representation of war's senseless carnage: Fortinbras' adventure means but "The imminent death of twenty thousand men / That for a fantasy and trick of fame / Go to their graves."

When Hamlet has explained Claudius' villainy to Horatio, he asks, rhetorically, "is 't not perfect conscience / To quit him with this arm?" He must be "damn'd," he says, if he allows Claudius to commit "further evil."

Immediately after this, Osric arrives. For several moments — for ninety-five lines — Hamlet plays with this "waterfly." When Osric is finally allowed to say what he has come to say — that Claudius invites Hamlet to "play" with Laertes — Hamlet accepts: he will fence with Laertes, for the amusement of the king.

Why? Why should Hamlet play, to please Claudius? Hamlet understands full well that Claudius isn't interested in play: after all, Claudius knows that Hamlet knows his guilt, and Hamlet has but now avoided one plot on Claudius' part to kill him. Hamlet is fully aware that the game is but another such plot — yet all he says is that "the readiness is all." He does not try to defend himself, nor does he plot to do any harm to either Laertes or Claudius. He makes no move "to quit" Claudius, or to prohibit by force his enacting "further evil." Rather, it seems that he *submits* to "further evil," knowingly, in acceding to Claudius' request that he "play" with Laertes.

And yet Hamlet does, in a sense, avenge his father's death before he, too, dies. When Laertes, dying, explains how the one rapier's point has been "envenom'd" as part of Claudius' plot, Hamlet turns upon the king. He merely says, "Then, venom, to thy work." It is not passion that Hamlet speaks, but logic. And he doesn't attack Claudius, or run him through as he did poor Polonius. Shakespeare's stage direction says that Hamlet "Hurts the King" — no more. A prick is all that's called for, a touch — as though this were but a game, after all, mere "play" at fencing. Claudius cowers; Hamlet extends the foil, and poisons Claudius with his own poison, kills him with his own villainy. To double the effect, Hamlet also requires Claudius to drink his own poison: "Drink off this potion!"

Shakespeare has made Claudius his own punishment, and thereby lets Hamlet save his own principled, moral honor and at the same time bring to justice his father's murderer. But that's not the same thing as revenge — and *Hamlet* is not a revenger's story. Shakespeare could easily have written a revenge play, but he didn't. Unless we recognise this, we lose perhaps his most beautiful and important work.

Hamlet's story needs to be told — as Hamlet himself insists. He won't let Horatio commit suicide, to join his friend in death. "Thou liv'st," he insists; "report me and my cause aright." Again: "in this harsh world draw thy breath in pain, / To tell my story."

Hamlet dies, Fortinbras enters, and Horatio outlines the story he will tell:

> you shall hear
> Of carnal, bloody, and unnatural acts;
> Of accidental judgments, casual slaughters;
> Of deaths put on by cunning and forc'd cause.

But that's not the story of this play: it is neither the story Hamlet wants told nor the story Shakespeare has given us. Horatio — alas — has missed the point. The story he will tell is one of meaningless violence, and would fit much better one of the many bloody revenge tragedies written by Shakespeare's contemporaries.

Hamlet needs to have *his* story told. Without it, since all the actors from his father's time are now dead, history will collapse upon itself. Unless Hamlet's story is told — unless a story is told that is worth the telling, and worth our remembering — the Hamlet part of Danish history will disappear. And the thirty years from the old King's triumph over the elder Fortinbras on the day of Hamlet's birth to the entrance of the younger Fortinbras, reclaiming

Denmark on the day of Hamlet's death: that thirty years will disappear from history.

But Hamlet insists — and so does his creator — that something important has happened between Fortinbras and Fortinbras. That something is Hamlet's thoughtfulness, his moral, civilized, principled response to violence. By refusing to enact simple revenge, Hamlet has *changed* history — if only we will listen, and understand.

Hamlet's story is one of civilized *human* triumph over evil. Maybe that is why the play is so hard for us to read, and why we have spent so much time and energy (particularly in this modern age) trying to simplify it. Meaning is hard to pay attention to when we don't want to understand. The thoughtful, principled individual is hardly the hero in our time — and therefore we resist Shakespeare. His *Hamlet* is too difficult for us; in our silliness, we prefer the simple thrills of Horatio's version.

The lesson of Shakespeare's play is clear, if we will see it. The Hamlet who complained at the beginning of the play about the evil in Denmark which he was required "to set . . . right" — who saw murder as "bad" and revenge as "worse" — has managed to make evil judge itself, and punish itself. The "savage code" that Kittredge remarked on is superseded, in the end, by the greater, nobler example of Hamlet's principled moral courage. Or, rather, it could be — if we would only pay attention, and agree.

In Aeschylus' *Oresteia* it takes the intervention of the god, Athena, to stop the tumbling dominoes of revenge in the House of Atreus. In Christian mythology the god comes himself to teach against revenge: his text (which we ignore) is "turn the other cheek."[3] Instead of responding to violence with violence — instead of letting corruption corrupt its victim — the Christian god accepts injustice in order to preserve his own integrity, and by that example to teach us ours.

Hamlet is not a god; he is a student. He is one of humanity's greatest students. What he learns — on his own, without divine intervention — in his thirty years makes that short time a significant part of human history.

When we think of students, we usually make them somewhat younger than thirty years old: twenty, perhaps, or twenty-one. The same was true in Shakespeare's day. Most of us, however, haven't learned everything by the time we reach twenty or twenty-one. In making Hamlet thirty — a fulcrum time for our age as well as for an earlier age, perhaps — Shakespeare makes this play not just a young man's play but a sort of everyman's play.

Hamlet is what we all could be, if we would think, and live, according to our best thoughts. Hamlet's heroism is in his careful thoughtfulness, in his valiant determination to live by principle rather than by passion.

The one poet whose work best compares with Shakespeare's is Homer. But Homer never wrote a *Hamlet*. In the *Iliad*, Achilleus — a young man, maybe twenty years old — learns the folly of violence, the futility of revenge, but he can't keep his learning. At the end of the poem, after the truce which he

---

[3] Matthew 5:39.

declares for Hektor's funeral, he will go back to fighting. The last line of the *Il-iad* is pathetic: "Thus was the funeral of Hektor, the breaker of horses."[4] Homer stops there — because, I suspect, the next line was too painful to think of: "And then they began to fight again."

In the *Odyssey*, Odysseus — forty, perhaps? — comes home, having lost a whole generation of Ithakans through his adventuring. Then, avenging himself, he slaughters all their younger brothers in clearing his palace of Penelope's suitors. In the final scene of the poem he tries to kill their doddering fathers, the old men who have come protesting against him. He chases them, despite Athena's warning to stop. At last Zeus casts a thunderbolt at him to make him quit his violence.[5] Odysseus, reputed to be the wise man, hasn't learned a thing.

But Hamlet learns, and remains true to his learning. Shakespeare's vision is different from Homer's. Homer's seemingly cynical irony pushes *us* to learn what his heroes can't keep or comprehend. In *Hamlet*, Shakespeare's hero teaches us by his example. Hamlet lives — and dies — by his wisdom. "To thine own self be true" was silly Polonius' advice to his son: good advice, to be sure, if the self is worth being true to! Hamlet's self is thus worthy: his self is thoughtful, principled, and wise. And he remains nobly, heroically true to it.

The great thing about *Hamlet* is that it won't submit to our smaller morality, our simple-minded reading, our easy-headed acceptance of the "savage code" of revenge. *Hamlet* stands — between Fortinbras and Fortinbras, two soldiers — waiting for us to understand it and its thoughtful hero's greatness.

Hamlet isn't "delaying" — and that isn't at all what his play is about. But we have been delaying for years and years. In doing so we have been as false to Hamlet as Horatio was.

TOM STOPPARD

Dogg's Hamlet: The Encore   1979

SCENE: *Staging the play on a double-decker London bus, Stoppard gave directions for two folding screens to be placed left and right at the back of the playing area. The screen on the left had a bolt through the top for a cut-out sun, moon, and crown on hinges to be swung in and out of sight. The other screen had a two-dimensional grave for Ophelia.*

Flourish of trumpets, crown hinges up. Enter Claudius and Gertrude.

CLAUDIUS: Our sometime sister, now our Queen,
    (*Enter Hamlet.*)
    Have we taken to wife.

---

[4] *Iliad*, Book 24.
[5] *Odyssey*, Book 24.

(Crown hinges down.)

HAMLET: That it should come to this!
(Exit Claudius and Gertrude. Wind noise. Moon hinges up. Enter Horatio above.)

HORATIO: My lord, I saw him yesternight —
The King, your father.

HAMLET: Angels and ministers of grace defend us!
(Exit, running, through rest of speech.)
Something is rotten in the state of Denmark.
(Enter Ghost above.)

GHOST: I am thy father's spirit.
The serpent that did sting thy father's life
(Enter Hamlet above.)
Now wears his crown.

HAMLET: O my prophetic soul!
Hereafter I shall think meet
To put an antic disposition on.
(Moon hinges down. Exeunt. Short flourish of trumpets. Enter Polonius below, running. Crown hinges up.)

POLONIUS: Look where sadly the poor wretch comes.
(Exit Polonius, running, Enter Hamlet.)

HAMLET: I have heard that guilty creatures sitting at a play
Have by the very cunning of the scene been struck.
(Enter Claudius, Gertrude, Ophelia, Marcellus, and Horatio joking. All sit to watch imaginary play, puppets appear above screen.)
If he but blench, I know my course.
(Masque music. Claudius rises.)
The King rises!

ALL: Give o'er the play!
(Exeunt all except Gertrude and Hamlet. Crown hinges down.)

HAMLET: I'll take the ghost's word for a thousand pounds.
(Enter Polonius, goes behind arras. Short flourish of trumpets.)
Mother, you have my father much offended.

GERTRUDE: Help!

POLONIUS: Help, Ho!

HAMLET: *(Stabs Polonius.)* Dead for a ducat, dead!
(Polonius falls dead offstage. Exit Gertrude and Hamlet. Short flourish of trumpets. Enter Claudius followed by Hamlet.)

CLAUDIUS: Hamlet, this deed must send thee hence
(Exit Hamlet.)
Do it, England.
(Exit Claudius. Enter Ophelia, falls to ground. Rises and pulls gravestone to cover herself. Bell tolls twice. Enter Gravedigger and Hamlet.)

HAMLET: A pirate gave us chase. I alone became their prisoner.
(Takes skull from Gravedigger.)
Alas poor Yorick — but soft *(Returns skull to Gravedigger.)*
— This is I,

Hamlet the Dane!
(Exit Gravedigger. Enter Laertes.)
LAERTES: The devil take thy soul!
(They grapple, then break. Enter Osric between them with swords. They draw. Crown hinges up. Enter Claudius and Gertrude with goblets.)
HAMLET: Come on, Sir!
(Laertes and Hamlet fight.)
OSRIC: A hit, a very palpable hit!
CLAUDIUS: Give him the cup. Gertrude, do not drink!
GERTRUDE: I am poisoned! *(Dies.)*
LAERTES: Hamlet, thou art slain! *(Dies.)*
HAMLET: Then venom to thy work! *(Kills Claudius. Crown hinges down.)*
The rest is silence. *(Dies.)*
(Two shots offstage. End.)

KARIN S. CODDON

A New Historicist Reading of Hamlet   *1989*

Madness in *Hamlet*, . . . while engaging and even subjecting subjectivity, is not contained within it. As a particular mode of discourse it continually threatens to be construed — or misconstrued — into an incitement of social and political disorder. The metonymic markers for order — moderation, stoicism, obedience — are undermined throughout the play by the dangerous if impenetrable subjectivity of the hero. When Claudius urges Hamlet to give over his obdurate mourning, he invokes a series of maxims on authority and obedience to natural and divine order. . . .

. . . Claudius may be "a little more than kin, and less than kind," but his reasoning articulates views about mourning and self-government that were commonplaces of Elizabethan religious as well as psychological thought. The Protestant emphasis on an all-encompassing providence identified the will of God in all human experience regardless of how apparently arbitrary or unpleasant, while the government of passions was particularly imperative in a culture with more than its share of life-threatening hazards. Similarly, Claudius's insinuation that such mourning is effeminate tacitly genders melancholy; it is worth noting that Ophelia's madness, with its "unshaped" content of sexual and political allusions, doubles and even parodies Hamlet's distraction. That Claudius is so eager to attribute Ophelia's madness to "the poison of deep grief," indeed, the filial grief for which he upbraids Hamlet in act 1, scene 2, suggests that the feminization of madness in later periods has its seeds in the cultural construction of the rational, obedient male subject.[1]

But while madness addresses and reproduces the problematics of au-

---

[1] See Michel Foucault, *History of Sexuality,* vol. 1, trans. Robert Hurley (New York: Pantheon, 1978) 104, 121.

thority, the internalization of disobedience precludes taking arms against a sea of troubles. The radical inutility of unreason divides subjectivity and agency, and hence the question of Hamlet's "delay" should be considered in light of the more pervasive antagonism between inwardness and authority. The appearance of the ghost does not counter the vacuity of the preceding exercises in patriarchal authority but rather duplicates and even literalizes it in the equivocal space of the supernatural. Hamlet's initial address to the ghost identifies its ambivalence:

> Be thou a spirit of health, or goblin damn'd,
> Bring with thee airs from heaven, or blasts from hell,
> Be thy intents wicked, or charitable,
> Thou com'st in such a questionable shape
> That I will speak to thee.

As a figure of boundless semiotic ambiguity the ghost is aligned with madness and "breaking down the pales and forts of reason." Horatio, the paradigmatic reasonable man, is even more ineffectual than Claudius against unreason:

> What if it tempt you toward the flood, my lord,
> Or to the dread summit of the cliff
> That beetles o'er his base into the sea,
> And there assume some other horrible form,
> Which might deprive your sovereignty of reason,
> And draw you into madness?

The threat of madness or demonic possession, like Claudius's admonishment of unnatural grief bound up in the ideology of self-vigilance, holds no sway over the prince, who "waxes desperate with [imagination]."

ॐ

CASEBOOK ON LORRAINE HANSBERRY'S *A RAISIN IN THE SUN*

Lorraine Hansberry wrote about her "Shakespearean Experience" in high school in To Be Young, Gifted and Black, *which was published four years after her death in 1965. Hansberry began to shape her memoir of her high school English teacher nicknamed "Pale Hecate" as an essay, but within a few paragraphs she was so deeply involved in her memories of adolescence that she dramatized them in dialogue form as a series of imaginary exchanges between the teacher and her students.*

James Baldwin described his impressions of Hansberry in "Sweet Lorraine," his introduction to the 1969 edition of To Be Young, Gifted and Black. *Julius Lester analyzed "the heroic dimension" of A Raisin in the Sun in his introduction to an early edition of Hansberry's* Les Blancs: The Collected Last Plays *(1972).*

Anne Cheney discussed the African heritage in A Raisin in the Sun *in her 1984 critical study of Hansberry for Twayne's United States Authors Series. Steven*

R. Carter commented on Hansberry's "artistic misstep" in A Raisin in the Sun in his critical study Hansberry's Drama, winner of the American Book Award in 1992. Finally, Margaret B. Wilkerson considered Hansberry's "awareness of culture and gender" in a new introduction to Les Blancs published in 1994.

LORRAINE HANSBERRY

My Shakespearean Experience

1969

1

My High School Yearbook bears the dedication: "Englewood High trains for citizenship in a world of many different peoples. Who could better appreciate this wonderful country than our forefathers who traveled hundreds of miles from every known nation, seeking a land of freedom from discrimination of race, color, or creed." And in illustration, there is this:

> The Great Branches of Man at Englewood High: in front, Mangolia Ali of East Indian Mohammedan descent; second couple, Nancy Diagre and Harold Bradley, Negroid; middle couple, Rosalind Sherr and William Krugman, Jewish religion, not a racial stock; next, Eleanor Trester and Theodore Flood, Caucasoid; extreme right, Lois Lee and Barbara Nomura, Mongoloid; rear, left, Mr. Thompson, principal.

2

I was reminded of Englewood by a questionnaire which came from *Show* magazine the other day. . . .

THE SHAKESPEAREAN EXPERIENCE
SHOW POLL #5, February 1964
Some Questions Answered by: Robert Bolt, Jean Cocteau, T. S. Eliot, Tyrone Guthrie, Lorraine Hansberry, Joan Littlewood, Harold Pinter, Alain Robbe-Grillet, Igor Stravinsky, Harry S Truman

QUESTION: *What was your first contact with Shakespeare?*

High School. English literature classwork. We had to read and memorize speeches from *Macbeth* and *Julius Caesar* all under the auspices of a strange and bewigged teacher who we, after this induction, naturally and cruelly christened "Pale Hecate" — God rest her gentle, enraptured, and igniting soul!

Pale Hecate enters, ruler in hand, and takes her place in the classroom. She surveys the class. They come to attention as her eye falls on each in turn.

PALE HECATE: Y'do not read, nor speak, nor write the English language! I suspect that y'do not even *think* in it! God only knows in what language y'do think, or if you think at all. 'Tis true the *English* have done little enough with the tongue, but being the English I expect it was the best they could do. (*They giggle.*) In any case, I'll have it learned properly before a living one of y'll pass out of this class. That I will! (*Waving a composition book and indicating the grade marked in red at the top.*) As for *you,*

Miss — as for you, indeed, surely you will recognize the third letter of
the alphabet when y'have seen it?

STUDENT: "C."

PALE HECATE: Aye, a "C" it 'tis! You're a bright and clever one now after all,
aren't y'lass? (*The class snickers.*) And now, my brilliance, would you also
be informing us as to what a grade signifies when it is thus put upon the
page?

STUDENT: Average.

PALE HECATE: "Average." Yes, yes — and what else in your case, my iridescence?
Well then, I'll be tellin' you in fine order. It stands for "cheat," my luminous one! (*The class sobers.*) For them that will do *half* when *all* is called for;
for them that will slip and slide through life at the edge of their minds,
never once pushing into the interior to see what wonders are hiding there
— content to drift along on whatever gets them by, *cheating* themselves,
cheating the world, *cheating* Nature! That is what the "C" means, my dear
child — (*she smiles*) — my pet (*they giggle; in rapid order she raps each on the
head with her ruler*) — my laziest *Queen of the Ethiopes!*

She exits or dims out.

QUESTION: *Which is your favorite Shakespeare play and why?*

Favorite? It is like choosing the "superiority" of autumn days; mingling
titles permits a reply: *Othello* and *Hamlet*. Why? There is a sweetness in the former that lingers long after the tragedy is done. A kind of possibility that we
suspect in man wherein even its flaw is a tribute. The latter because there remains a depth in the Prince that, as we all know, constantly re-engages as we
mature. And it does seem that the wit remains the brightest and most instructive in all dramatic literature.

QUESTION: *What is the most important result of your familiarity with
Shakespeare? What has he given you?*

Comfort and agitation so bound together that they are inseparable. Man,
as set down in the plays, is large. Enormous. Capable of anything at all. And
yet fragile, too, this view of the human spirit; one feels it ought be respected
and protected and loved rather fiercely.

Rollicking times, Shakespeare has given me. I love to laugh and his humor is that of everyday; of every man's foible at no man's expense. Language.
At thirteen a difficult and alien tedium, those Elizabethan cadences; but soon
a balm, a thrilling source of contact with life.

JAMES BALDWIN

Sweet Lorraine   1969

That's the way I always felt about her, and so I won't apologize for calling
her that now. *She* understood it: in that far too brief a time when we walked and

talked and laughed and drank together, sometimes in the streets and bars and restaurants of the Village, sometimes at her house, sometimes at my house, sometimes gracelessly fleeing the houses of others; and sometimes seeming, for anyone who didn't know us, to be having a knockdown, drag-out battle. We spent a lot of time arguing about history and tremendously related subjects in her Bleecker Street and, later, Waverly Place flat. And often, just when I was certain that she was about to throw me out, as being altogether too rowdy a type, she would stand up, her hands on her hips (for these down-home sessions she always wore slacks) and pick up my empty glass as though she intended to throw it at me. Then she would walk into the kitchen, saying, with a haughty toss of her head, "Really, Jimmy. You ain't *right*, child!" With which stern putdown, she would hand me another drink and launch into a brilliant analysis of just why I wasn't "right." I would often stagger down her stairs as the sun came up, usually in the middle of a paragraph and always in the middle of a laugh. That marvelous laugh. That marvelous face. I loved her, she was my sister and my comrade. Her going did not so much make me lonely as make me realize how lonely we were. We had that respect for each other which perhaps is only felt by people on the same side of the barricades, listening to the accumulating thunder of the hooves of horses and the treads of tanks.

The first time I ever saw Lorraine was at the Actors' Studio, in the winter of '57–58. She was there as an observer of the Workshop Production of *Giovanni's Room*.° She sat way up in the bleachers, taking on some of the biggest names in the American theater because she had liked the play and they, in the main, hadn't. I was enormously grateful to her, she seemed to speak for me; and afterwards she talked to me with a gentleness and generosity never to be forgotten. A small, shy, determined person, with that strength dictated by absolutely impersonal ambition: she was not trying to "make it" — she was trying to keep the faith.

We really met, however, in Philadelphia, in 1959, when *A Raisin in the Sun* was at the beginning of its amazing career. Much has been written about this play; I personally feel that it will demand a far less guilty and constricted people than the present-day Americans to be able to assess it at all; as an historical achievement, anyway, no one can gainsay its importance. What is relevant here is that I had never in my life seen so many black people in the theater. And the reason was that never before, in the entire history of the American theater, had so much of the truth of black people's lives been seen on the stage. Black people ignored the theater because the theater had always ignored them.

But, in *Raisin*, black people recognized that house and all the people in it — the mother, the son, the daughter, and the daughter-in-law, and supplied the play with an interpretative element which could not be present in the minds of white people: a kind of claustrophobic terror, created not only by their knowledge of the house but by their knowledge of the streets. And when the curtain came down, Lorraine and I found ourselves in the backstage alley,

---

Giovanni's Room: Baldwin's 1956 novel about a young American in Paris dealing with issues of his sexual identity.

where she was immediately mobbed. I produced a pen and Lorraine handed me her handbag and began signing autographs. "It only happens once," she said. I stood there and watched. I watched the people, who loved Lorraine for what she had brought to them; and watched Lorraine, who loved the people for what they brought to *her*. It was not, for her, a matter of being admired. She was being corroborated and confirmed. She was wise enough and honest enough to recognize that black American artists are a very special case. One is not merely an artist and one is not judged merely as an artist: the black people crowding around Lorraine, whether or not they considered her an artist, assuredly considered her a witness. This country's concept of art and artists has the effect, scarcely worth mentioning by now, of isolating the artist from the people. One can see the effect of this in the irrelevance of so much of the work produced by celebrated white artists; but the effect of this isolation on a black artist is absolutely fatal. He *is*, already, as a black American citizen, isolated from most of his white countrymen. At the crucial hour, he can hardly look to his artistic peers for help, for they do not know enough about him to be able to correct him. To continue to grow, to remain in touch with himself, he needs the support of that community from which, however, all of the pressures of American life incessantly conspire to remove him. And when he is effectively removed, he falls silent — and the people have lost another hope.

Much of the strain under which Lorraine worked was produced by her knowledge of this reality, and her determined refusal to be destroyed by it. She was a very young woman, with an overpowering vision, and fame had come to her early — she must certainly have wished, often enough, that fame had seen fit to drag its feet a little. For fame and recognition are not synonymous, especially not here, and her fame was to cause her to be criticized very harshly, very loudly, and very often by both black and white people who were unable to believe, apparently, that a really serious intention could be contained in so glamorous a frame. She took it all with a kind of astringent good humor, refusing, for example, even to consider defending herself when she was being accused of being a "slum-lord" because of her family's real-estate holdings in Chicago. I called her during that time, and all she said — with a wry laugh — was, "My God, Jimmy, do you realize you're only the second person who's called me today? And you know how my phone kept ringing *before!*" She was not surprised. She was devoted to the human race, but she was not romantic about it.

Julius Lester

The Heroic Dimension in A Raisin in the Sun
1972

A Raisin in the Sun is no intellectual abstraction about upward mobility and conspicuous consumption. It goes right to the core of practically every black family in the ghettos of Chicago, New York, Los Angeles, and elsewhere. Whether they have a picture of Jesus, Martin Luther King, or Malcolm X on the lead-painted walls of their rat-infested tenement, all of them want to get the hell out of there as quickly as they can. Maybe black militants don't know it, or don't want to admit it, but Malcolm X made a down payment on a house in a suburban community a few weeks before he was murdered. And one surely can't accuse Malcolm of bourgeois aspirations. He merely wanted what every black wants — a home of his own adequate to his needs, at a minimum, and the fulfillment of his desires, at the most. . . . *A Raisin in the Sun* is most definitely about "human dignity" because Lorraine Hansberry is concerned with the attitude we must have toward material things if we are to be their master and not their slave. Is that attitude to be Mama's? Or is it to be Walter's? And, for blacks, locked out from these things for so long, the question is a crucial one. As blacks acquire more and more of America's material offerings, are they, too, going to be transformed by their acquisitions into mindless consumers like the majority of whites? Or are they going to continue to walk in the path of righteousness like their forebears? Lorraine Hansberry summarized it well when, in a letter, she wrote of the play:

> . . . we cannot . . . very well succumb to monetary values and know the survival of certain interior aspects of man which . . . must remain if we are to loom larger than other creatures on this planet. . . . Our people fight daily and magnificently for a more comfortable material base for their lives; they desperately need and hourly sacrifice for clean homes, decent food, personal and group dignity and the abolition of terroristic violence as their children's heritage. So, in that sense, I am certainly a materialist in the first order.
>
> However, the distortion of this aspiration surrounds us in the form of an almost maniacal lusting for "acquisitions." It seems to have absorbed the national mentality and Negroes, to be sure, have certainly been affected by it. The young man in the play, Walter Lee, is meant to symbolize their number. Consequently, in the beginning, he dreams not so much of being comfortable and imparting the most meaningful gifts to his son (education in depth, humanist values, a worship of dignity) but merely of being what it seems to him the "successful" portion of humankind is — "rich." Toward this end he is willing to make an old trade; urgently willing. On the fact that some aspect of his society has brought him to this point, the core of the drama hangs.

Walter blames himself, his wife, and his mother for what he sees as his personal failure. And only at the end of the play does it become possible for him to realize that there is a puppeteer manipulating him, a puppeteer who brought him dangerously close to destroying his family and himself.

The climax of the play comes after Walter's deal to get a liquor license falls through. Mama Younger has made a $3500 down payment on a house and gives the remaining money to Walter to do with as he wishes after he deposits $2500 in a savings account for Beneatha's education. Walter, however, takes the entire $6500 and gives it to one of his two future "partners." One of the "partners" absconds with the money. A Mr. Lindner, a white man from the neighborhood into which they are to move, comes and offers to buy the house from them for more than they would eventually pay. The whites in the neighborhood do not want a black family moving in. Previously, Walter had scornfully turned the man down. However, when he learns that his money has been stolen, he calls Mr. Lindner on the phone and tells him that they will sell the house. Mr. Lindner comes over and Walter finds that he is unable to go through with it. There is something in him — a little bit of self-respect is still left; he tells Mr. Lindner that they are going to move in. And with Walter making his first step toward being a man, a *black* man, the play ends.

Few see the heroism in Walter's simple act of assertion. Indeed, how many who have seen the play or the movie have not thought that Walter was a fool for *not* accepting the money? How one views Walter's act is a direct reflection of how much one accepts the American dream. And there is the significance of the fact that the play ends with the Youngers moving into a "white" neighborhood. To see this as a confirmation of the American dream is to accept the myth that blacks have wanted nothing more than to be integrated with whites. In actuality, the fact that the neighborhood is white is the least important thing about it. It merely happened to be the neighborhood in which Mama Younger could find a nice house she could afford. And it is this simple, practical element which has always been mistaken by whites as a desire on the part of blacks to be "integrated." But why, the question could be raised, would the Youngers persist in moving into a neighborhood where they are not wanted, where they may be subjected to harassment or even physical violence? They persist, as all blacks persist, not because it is any great honor to live among whites, but because one cannot consider himself a human being as long as he acquiesces to restrictions placed upon him by others, particularly if those restrictions are based solely on race or religion. If Walter had accepted the money, he would have been saying, in graphic language, You are right, we are niggers and don't have the right to live where we can afford to. But, with that earthy eloquence of a black still close to his roots, Walter says, "We have decided to move into our house because my father — my father — he earned it." And, in that realization, Walter learns also that it was not a black woman who castrated him. It was America and his own acceptance of America's values. No woman can make him a man. He has to do it himself.

He is a hero, a twentieth-century hero. We still long, of course, for the heroes who seemed to ride history as if it were a bronco and they were champion rodeo riders. But those heroes -- if they were ever real — come from a time when life, perhaps, was somewhat less complex. But the problems that face man in the latter twentieth century are large, larger than any one of us, and the sword of a knight in armor is laughable to the dragons roaming our countryside. Our heroes are more difficult to recognize only because they appear so small beside the overwhelming enemies they must slay. But because they appear small does not mean that they are, and it does not make their acts less heroic. Walter Lee Younger has his contemporary historic counterpart in the person of a small, quiet black woman named Rosa Parks who refused to get out of a seat on a bus in Montgomery, Alabama. It would have been so easy for her to have relinquished her seat to a white person that day — as it would have been easy for Walter to have taken the money. But something in her, as in him, said No. And in that quiet dissent, both of them said Yes to human dignity. They said No to those who would define them and thereby deny their existence, and by saying No, they began to define themselves. There have been many Rosa Parks, but few of them have mysteriously set in motion a whole movement for social change. Walter Lee Younger is one of those whose act probably set nothing in motion. And that only increases its heroic dimension. In an article in *The Village Voice*, which compared Walter to Willy Loman, Lorraine Hansberry described the hero she saw in Walter Younger:

> For if there are no waving flags and marching songs at the barricades as Walter marches out with his little battalion, it is not because the battle lacks nobility. On the contrary, he has picked up in his way, still imperfect and wobbly in his small view of human destiny, what I believe Arthur Miller once called "the golden thread of history." He becomes, in spite of those who are too intrigued with despair and hatred of man to see it, King Oedipus refusing to tear out his eyes, but attacking the Oracle instead. He is that last Jewish patriot manning his rifle in the burning ghetto at Warsaw; he is that young girl who swam into sharks to save a friend a few weeks ago; he is Anne Frank, still believing in people; he is the nine small heroes of Little Rock; he is Michelangelo creating David, and Beethoven bursting forth with the Ninth Symphony. He is all those things because he has finally reached out in his tiny moment and caught that sweet essence which is human dignity, and it shines like the old star-touched dream that is in his eyes.

ANNE CHENEY

The African Heritage in A Raisin in the Sun

1984

A moving testament to the strength and endurance of the human spirit, *A Raisin in the Sun* is a quiet celebration of the black family, the importance of African roots, the equality of women, the vulnerability of marriage, the true value of money, the survival of the individual, and the nature of man's dreams. A well-made play, *Raisin* at first seems a plea for racial tolerance or a fable of man's overcoming an insensitive society, but the simple eloquence of the characters elevates the play into a universal representation of all people's hopes, fears, and dreams.

On January 19, 1959, a timid Lorraine Hansberry wrote her mother about *Raisin*: "Mama, it is a play that tells the truth about people, Negroes and life and I think it will help a lot of people to understand how we are just as complicated as they are . . . people who are the very essence of human dignity. . . . I hope it will make you very proud."[1] Indeed, *A Raisin in the Sun* made not only Nannie Perry Hansberry proud but also artists — both black and white. *Raisin* was the first play by a black writer ever to win the prestigious New York Drama Critics' Circle Award. The play would become "an Ameri-

---

[1] Lorraine Hansberry, *To Be Young, Gifted and Black: Lorraine Hansberry in Her Own Words*, adapted by Robert Nemiroff (New York: New American Library, 1970), p. 109.

can classic, published and produced in some thirty languages abroad and in thousands of productions across the country. . . . James Baldwin [said]: "Never before in the entire history of the American theatre had so much of the truth of Black people's lives been seen on the stage."[2] Despite the earlier contributions of Langston Hughes, David Littlejohn wrote, "It would not be unfair in dating the emergence of a serious and mature Negro theater in America from 1959, the date of Lorraine Hansberry's *A Raisin in the Sun*."[3] . . .

Today some black critics feel that *A Raisin in the Sun* is a play whose time has passed — a simplistic, halting treatment of race relations. Some are confused by Hansberry's professed nationalism, when she seems to favor integration. Harold Cruse even calls *Raisin* a "cleverly written piece of glorified soap opera." Hansberry used the traditional form of the well-made play in *Raisin*, especially observing the unities of action, place, and time. The action of the play is carefully delineated: act 1 serves as the beginning, act 2 as the middle, and act 3 as the tightly knit end. Furthermore, all action is carefully and causally related. Hansberry strictly abides by the unity of place: all action transpires in one room of the Youngers' South Side Chicago apartment. Stretching the unity of time from one day to one month (not unusual for a modern dramatist), Hansberry still maintains unity of impression with the central emotional concerns of the Younger family: Walter's search for a dream, Lena's faith in God and the family, Beneatha's hope for a new world.

Hansberry needed this rather traditional form to control the innovative ideas and themes of *Raisin*. Far from being a stereotyped or romanticized treatment of black life, the play embodies ideas that have been uncommon on the Broadway stage in any period. Resurrecting the ideas of the Harlem Renaissance and anticipating the new thinking of the 1960s, Hansberry examines the importance of African roots, traditional versus innovative women, the nature of marriage, the real meaning of money, the search for human dignity. Most significantly, she addresses the sensitive question of to what extent people, in liberating themselves from the burdens of discrimination, should aspire to a white middle-class way of life.

During her *Freedom* years, Lorraine Hansberry continued to study African history with encouragement from Paul Robeson, W. E. B. Du Bois, and Louis Burnham.° "She had spent hours of her younger years poring over maps of the African continent. . . . She was at one, texture, blood . . . with the sound of a mighty Congo drum."[4] She imaginatively knew the lions, drumbeats, quiet sandy nights, respected the antiquity of Ethiopia founded in 1000 B.C. Stirred by Kenya and Ghana wresting control from Europe and England, Hansberry inevitably incorporated her knowledge of Africa in her first play.

---

[2] Robert Nemiroff, "Lorraine Hansberry Biography," unpublished paper.
[3] David Littlejohn, *Black on White: A Critical Survey of Writings by American Negroes* (New York: Grossman Publishers, 1966), p. 79.
Robeson . . . Burnham: African American authors and intellectuals associated with the Harlem Renaissance.
[4] *Young, Gifted and Black,* p. 75.

More than earlier playwrights, Hansberry made Africa a serious, yet natural, issue on Broadway.

In *Raisin* even George Murchison, Beneatha's beau, has an awareness of his African past. In the fever of Walter Lee's and Beneatha's mock African dance in act 2, George remarks sarcastically: "In one second we will hear all about the great Ashanti empires; the great Songhay civilizations; and the great sculpture of Benin — and then some poetry in the Bantu." George had probably learned in a college atmosphere that the Songhai empire was a powerful western African kingdom, which garnered wealth from its export of ivory and gold between 850 and 1500 A.D. (Mali and Ghana — not to be confused with the modern state of Ghana — were equally old and powerful empires.) Along the coast of Nigeria, Benin was another expansive empire, noted for its bronze and gold art objects, that came to power around 1500. Coming to power about 1700, Ashanti was still another western kingdom famous for its heroic warriors.[5]

In the stage directions, Hansberry writes that Lena has "the noble bearing of the women of the Hereros of Southwest Africa," who were essentially a pastoral people. Thus Hansberry identifies Lena as an "earth mother," one who nurtures both her family and her plant as well as she can. But Lena reveals her total ignorance of African history by a parroting of Beneatha's earlier remarks in her politely naive, unwittingly humorous speech to Joseph Asagai, the young Nigerian visitor: "I think it's so sad the way our American Negroes don't know nothing about Africa 'cept Tarzan and all that. And all that money they pour into these churches when they ought to be helping you people over there drive out them French and Englishmen done taken away your Land."

Most of the African material in *A Raisin in the Sun*, however, surfaces in conversations between Beneatha and Joseph Asagai. Touched by Beneatha's beauty and idealism, Asagai lovingly nicknames her Alaiyo — a Yoruban word for "One for Whom Bread — Food — Is Not Enough." In act 3, after Walter Lee has been duped out of his $6,500, Asagai visits an embittered, distraught Beneatha. Speaking of his beloved Nigeria, Asagai reveals his basic philosophy of life, of Africa: "A household in preparation for a journey . . . it is another feeling. Something full of the flow of life. . . . Movement, progress. . . . It makes me think of Africa." Perhaps he sees in Beneatha a microcosmic America — one struggling to overthrow the limitations imposed on her by an alien culture.

Asagai's village in Nigeria is one where most people cannot read, where many have not even seen a book. In the village, there are mountains and stars, cool drinks from gourds at the well, old songs, people who move slowly, anciently. But Nigeria also has guns, murder, revolution, illiteracy, disease, ignorance. Asagai understands the inevitability of change and progress in Africa; he imagines for a moment the consequences should he betray the movement. "Don't you see that . . . young men and women . . . my own black countrymen . . . [may] . . . step out of the shadows some evening and slit my then use-

---

[5] A. Adu Boahen, "Kingdoms of West Africa," in *History of Africa* (New York: McGraw-Hill, 1971), pp. 177–88.

less throat?" Rebuking Beneatha for becoming discouraged over one small frustration (Walter's losing the money), Asagai views his possible death as an advance toward freedom for himself and his people. "They who might kill me even . . . actually replenish me." Asagai's beliefs certainly contribute to Beneatha's transition from brittle idealist to a more tolerant human being.

In an interview with Studs Terkel (Chicago, May 2, 1959), Lorraine Hansberry referred to Joseph Asagai as her "favorite character" in *Raisin*. He represents the "true intellectual" with no pretense, no illusions. A revolutionary and nationalist, he realizes that initially black African leaders may be as corrupt as their white predecessors (Idi Amin of Uganda bore out this theory in the 1970s). Nevertheless, he shares Hansberry's conviction that "before you can start talking about what's wrong with independence, get it." More the idealist than the practical, effective leader — compared to Kenyatta and Nkrumah° — Asagai is willing to die at the hands of his countrymen for the general good and freedom. (Harold Issacs suggests that his name derives from the Zulu word *asegai*, "sawed-off spear.")[6] On a more obvious level, Asagai certainly refutes the stage stereotype of the African with "a bone through his nose, or his ears."[7]

In *A Raisin in the Sun*, then, Africa becomes a symbol of a proud heritage and a troublesome but hopeful future. To Hansberry's great credit, Africa is a natural, at times humorous, element in the Younger family — as Walter Lee shouts "HOT DAMN! FLAMING SPEAR," as Beneatha dresses in Nigerian robes, as Mama speaks of Tarzan, churches, and Englishmen.

STEVEN R. CARTER

Hansberry's Artistic Misstep

1991

Unfortunately, Hansberry's vigorous, sharp, and usually intriguing characterization of Beneatha is slightly marred by her one serious artistic misstep in *A Raisin in the Sun*. This occurs when Beneatha tells Lena and Ruth about the guitar lessons she has just started and they remind her about "the horseback-riding club for which she bought that fifty-five dollar riding habit that's been hanging in the closet ever since!" On the whole, this scene portrays Beneatha's striving for self-expression with warm humor and a touch of self-mockery that almost always please audiences. The problem is that only a short time earlier Walter had angrily demanded that Beneatha show more gratitude for the financial sacrifices he and Ruth have made for her, and Ruth had denied her son the 50 cents he requested for school. It is inconceivable that a woman who could refuse such a small sum to a dearly beloved son would so

---

Kenyatta and Nkrumah: Jomo Kenyatta (1894–1978) and Kwame Nkrumah (1909–1972), respectively, former presidents of Kenya and Ghana.

[6] Harold Issacs, "Five Writers and Their African Ancestors, Part II," *Phylon* 21 (Winter 1960):330.

[7] Lorraine Hansberry in interview with Studs Terkel, Chicago, May 2, 1959.

casually accept the squandering of a much larger contribution to a mere sister-in-law, and even if, by some miracle, she were able to accept it out of an all-embracing feminist sisterhood (which doesn't fit Ruth's overall character), she could not do so with such ease. Worse still, lightly tossing away all this money in the face of the family's dire need makes Beneatha seem monstrously selfish rather than mildly selfish as Hansberry had intended. Granted, Hansberry's main concern in the scene was the general relationship between the two older women and Beneatha, particularly their fond amusement at the younger woman's forms of self-expression, which are so different from anything they have ever done, and their vicarious delight at her ability to break free from restrictions, including that of having to weigh the cost of everything. However, on this rare occasion, by concentrating exclusively on the moment and neglecting to see its relation to previous parts of the play, Hansberry, to a small but disconcerting extent, damages the whole.

MARGARET B. WILKERSON

Hansberry's Awareness of Culture and Gender

1994

As a black writer, Hansberry was caught in a paradox of expectations. She was expected to write about that which she "knew best," the black experience, and yet that expression was doomed to be called parochial and narrow. Hansberry, however, challenged these facile categories and forced a redefinition of the term "universality," one which would include the dissonant voice of an oppressed American minority. As a young college student, she had wandered into a rehearsal of Sean O'Casey's *Juno and the Paycock*. Hearing in the wails and moans of the Irish characters a universal cry of human misery, she determined to capture that sound in the idiom of her own people — so that it could be heard by all. "One of the most sound ideas in dramatic writing," she would later conclude, "is that in order to create the universal, you must pay very great attention to the specific. Universality, I think, emerges from truthful identity of what is. . . . In other words, I think people, to the extent we accept them and believe them as who they're supposed to be, to that extent they can become everybody."[1] Such a choice by a black writer posed an unusual challenge to the literary establishment and a divided society ill-prepared to comprehend its meaning.

"All art is ultimately social: that which agitates and that which prepares the mind for slumber," Hansberry argued, attacking another basic tenet held by traditional critics. One of the most fundamental illusions of her time and culture, she believed, is the idea that art is not and should not make a social statement. The belief in "l'art pour l'art" permeates literary and theatrical criticism, denying the integral relationship between society and art. "The writer

---

[1] Lorraine Hansberry, *To Be Young, Gifted and Black: Lorraine Hansberry in Her Own Words.* Adapted by Robert Nemiroff (New York: New American Library, 1970), p. 128.

is deceived who thinks he has some other choice. The question is not whether one will make a social statement in one's work — but only *what* the statement will say, for if it says anything at all, it will be social."[2]

It would have been impossible for a person of her background and sensitivity to divorce herself from the momentous social and political events of the 1950s and 1960s. This period witnessed the beginning of a Cold War between the U.S. and Soviet superpowers, a rising demand by blacks for civil rights at home, and a growing intransigence by colonized peoples throughout the world. Isolation is the enemy of black writers, Hansberry believed; they are obligated to participate in the intellectual and social affairs of humankind everywhere.

This abhorrence for narrowness and parochialism led her to examine the hidden alliance between racism and sexism long before it was popular to do so, and to shape a vision cognizant of the many dimensions of colonialism and oppression. Anticipating the women's movement of the 1970s, Hansberry was already aware of the peculiar oppression under which women lived and the particular devastation visited upon women of color.

With the statement "I was born black and a female,"[3] Hansberry immediately established the basis for a tension that informed her world view. Her consciousness, of both ethnicity and gender from the very beginning, brought awareness of two key forces of conflict and oppression in the contemporary world. Because she embraced these dual truths despite their implicit competition for her attention (a competition exacerbated by external pressures), her vision was expansive enough to contain and even synthesize what to others would be contradictions. Thus, she was amused in 1955 at progressive friends who protested whenever she posed "so much as an itsy-bitsy analogy between the situation, say, of the Negro people in the U.S. — and women." She was astonished to be accused by a woman of being bitter and of thinking that men are beasts simply because she expressed the view that women are oppressed. "Must I hate 'men' any more than I hate 'white people' — because some of them are savage and others commit savage acts," she asked herself. "Of course not!" she answered vehemently.[4]

This recognition of the tension implicit in her blackness and femaleness was the starting point for her philosophical journey from the South Side of Chicago to the world community. The following quote charts that journey and the expansion of Hansberry's consciousness, which is unconstrained by culture and gender, but which at the same time refuses to diminish the importance of either.

> I was born on the South Side of Chicago. I was born black and a
> female. I was born in a depression after one world war, and came into
> my adolescence during another. While I was still in my teens the first

---

[2] Lorraine Hansberry, "The Negro Writer and His Roots: Toward a New Romanticism," *The Black Scholar,* Volume 12, Number 2, March/April, 1981, p. 5.
[3] Ibid., p. 11.
[4] Excerpted from Lorraine Hansberry's unpublished, untitled notes. New York City, November 16, 1955.

atom bombs were dropped on human beings at Nagasaki and Hiroshima. And by the time I was twenty-three years old, my government and that of the Soviet Union had entered actively into the worst conflict of nerves in human history — the Cold War.

I have lost friends and relatives through cancer, lynching, and war. I have been personally the victim of physical attack which was the offspring of racial and political hysteria. I have worked with the handicapped and seen the ravages of congenital diseases that we have not yet conquered, because we spend our time and ingenuity in far less purposeful wars; I have known persons afflicted with drug addiction and alcoholism and mental illness. I see daily on the streets of New York, street gangs and prostitutes and beggars. I have, like all of you, on a thousand occasions seen indescribable displays of man's very real inhumanity to man, and I have come to maturity, as we all must, knowing that greed and malice and indifference to human misery and bigotry and corruption, brutality, and perhaps above all else, ignorance — the prime ancient and persistent enemy of man — abound in this world.

I say all of this to say that one cannot live with sighted eyes and feeling heart and not know and react to the miseries which afflict this world.[5]

Her "sighted eyes and feeling heart" were what enabled her to hear the wail of her own people in O'Casey's *Juno and the Paycock*, a play steeped in Irish history and tradition. And those eloquent moans sent her forth to capture that collective cry in a black idiom.

Hansberry's cognizance of being black and female formed the basis for her comprehensive world-view. Just as she could accept fully the implications and responsibility of both blackness and femaleness, so was she also aware of the many other competing and equally legitimate causes which grow out of humankind's misery. The one issue that deeply concerned her but that she did not address publicly was homosexuality. The repressive atmosphere of the 1950s, coupled with the homophobia of the general society, including politically left organizations, caused her to suppress her writings that explored issues of sexuality and gender relations. Nevertheless, she pushed and teased these boundaries by probing the nature of the individual within the specifics of culture, ethnicity, and gender. In the midst of her expansiveness, she refused to diminish the pain, suffering, or truths of any one group in order to benefit another, a factor which made her plays particularly rich and her characters thoroughly complex. Hence, she could write authentically about a black family in *A Raisin in the Sun* and yet produce, in the same instance, a play which appealed to both blacks and whites, bridging for a moment the historical and cultural gaps between them.

Her universalism, which redefines that much abused term, grew out of a deep, complex encounter with the specific terms of human experience as it occurs for blacks, women, whites, and many other groups of people. Her uni-

---

[5] Ibid., pp. 11–12.

versalism was not facile, nor did it gloss over the things that divide people. She engaged those issues, worked through them to find whatever may be, *a priori*, the human commonality that lies beneath. It was as if she believed that one can understand and embrace the human family (with all its familial warfare) only to the extent that one can engage the truths (however partisan they may seem) of a social, cultural individual. "We must turn our eyes outward," she wrote, "but to do so we must also turn them inward toward our people and their complex and still transitory culture."[6] When she turned inward, she saw not only color but gender as well — a prism of humanity.

---

[6] Ibid., p. 7.

Appendix

WRITING ABOUT LITERATURE

Reading literature expands our view of the world, allowing us to share the perspective of gifted storytellers, poets, and dramatists who have used their literary craft to entertain, instruct, and perhaps enchant us. When given the assignment to write an essay about literature, you have the opportunity to explain the effect that writers have had on you. Investigating how writers have used the elements of fiction, poetry, and drama to create literature can help you think critically about it.

When you write essays about literature, you present and clarify your ideas about what you have read. Writing about stories, poems, and plays reveals what Ernest Hemingway referred to as "the measure of what you brought to the reading." As soon as you ask the smallest question about the meaning or the structure of a literary work and begin to clarify your ideas in a written response, you have begun a process that engages you both emotionally and intellectually.

Good ideas are essential to a successful essay. How do you develop your initial emotional response to a story, poem, or play to get ideas about it that you can present in a paper? The chapters in this book about reading, thinking, and writing about the different genres of literature encouraged you to become actively involved in your classroom assignments. There is no specific formula or recipe to follow that guarantees a good essay, since all writers must find their own way and learn to do it for themselves. Becoming conscious of ideas is hard work, but take courage from Franz Kafka's words, "A book should be an axe for the frozen sea within us."

Turning yourself from a relatively alert reader into a fully active writer takes time. If you understand and follow the various steps involved, the writing process can become much easier. As the essayist Alex Johnson has observed, writing is always a challenge, but thinking about it does not always have to be a chore. In "Having a Bad Morning," she confessed uncertainty as to "how to get the thinking out":

> It took me years of trial and error to learn the obvious: writing is best and most satisfying done in stages. . . . I now know and trust completely that writing happens long before I ever type a word; that my best thinking and writing will happen before and after the first draft but not necessarily during it; that by seeing writing as a process, I now know the pleasure of making connections: ruminating on a subject, seeing patterns emerge, watching an argument evolve, evidence cohere. In short, that glorious territoriality of staking and claiming a subject as my own.

The best way to write an essay about literature is to take it in stages, understanding that good writing is as much a process as it is an end result. You can use literature to help you improve your writing by investigating the techniques authors have used to create their stories, poems, and plays. When you are fully engaged in this endeavor, you will also discover that the process turns you into a better reader, exercising your sensitivity and intelligence as you proceed with the various stages toward your final draft.

Assume, for example, that your instructor has told you that your first writing assignment will be a short (250 to 350 words) essay analyzing how Eudora Welty's voice as a storyteller draws you into the story in "A Worn Path" (p. 701). You have one week to turn in your paper. Everyone works differently, but here is a description of how you might budget your time most efficiently during the week, instead of waiting for the day before it is due to start your paper and pulling an all-nighter in a desperate effort to get the work finished. Ideally, if you have the time, you'd give a day to each step of the process.

STEP ONE: KEEP A JOURNAL OR NOTEBOOK

As a first step, the journal or notebook in which you record your responses to your reading can help you to generate ideas for the essays your instructor assigns in class. In her essay "On Keeping a Notebook," the writer Joan Didion said that the main reason writers keep a record of their experience is that "we forget all too soon the things we thought we could never forget. . . . Keeping in touch is what notebooks are all about." Recording your impressions right after reading the class assignment helps you to remember what you thought about it. Usually the earliest stage in becoming aware of your response to the literary work occurs when you feel the impulse to underline words or phrases that instinctively strike you as significant when you read the text. (Remember to *restrain* your impulse to highlight or underline when you are reading books that are not your own, especially library books. Most borrowers will find marked-up library books distracting and irritating.)

Keeping a journal gives you the opportunity to set aside the time necessary to find words for your first "gut" reactions to passages that seem to leap out at you from the printed page. After your initial impulses prompt you to underline and annotate the text, you could try to phrase your response as a specific idea. This involves focusing your thoughts about what you have read and finding the language to express those thoughts.

For most students, a journal of responses to literature is an important stage in the journey of transforming yourself from a reader to a writer. Once you become aware of how you are reading a text, you have begun the process of finding your own words to describe what there is about a story, a play, or a poem that elicits your response to it. This is the beginning of your journey of discovering and communicating to others "the measure of what you brought to the reading."

STEP TWO: REVIEW YOUR JOURNAL ENTRY AND LET IDEAS SURFACE

In your journal you have noted your responses after your first (or second) reading of Welty's story. They might look something like this:

JOURNAL ENTRY

Eudora Welty's "A Worn Path" . . . First paragraph "there was" and "she" suggests a third person point of view. Welty starts right in on the story introducing an old Negro woman named Phoenix Jackson, who's taking a long walk by herself on a December afternoon in the country perhaps rural Mississippi, where Welty is from. Author knows the setting very well--lots of specific details of trees, bushes, hills, and creek--Phoenix talks to herself but she's a feisty old thing. Has trouble seeing, but she picks up and hides a nickel belonging to a hunter she meets on the trail--the old lady's conscience bothers her, but she doesn't let on--he speaks so condescendingly to her that I think she's entitled to take his money--it's just a nickel--wait--did he drop the nickel or did she just see it on the ground? yes, Welty says it fell out of his pocket--so she could have given it back to him. The old lady gets tired but she keeps going and finally arrives at Natchez. Then she goes into a building in town where "she walked up and around and around until her feet knew to stop." So she's been there often before. It seems to be a nurses' office--and she's so old and tired she forgets why she's there-- then remembers that she's come to get medicine for her grandson. Horrible--the little boy swallowed lye. He lives with Phoenix, and she makes the long walk to town for his sake every year. The nurse likes Phoenix--gives her a nickel as a Christmas present. Phoenix really loves her grandson--she tells the nurse she's going to buy him a present--a paper windmill--with her dime before she starts the long walk home.

You will notice that in your journal you spent most of your time summarizing the plot in your own words. That is the first response of most students when faced with the task of writing about literature. Your journal notes will help you to review the story efficiently when you reread them before an exam. But your instructor has asked you to write an essay, so how do you use your notes to help you find an idea about Welty's voice as a storyteller?

Look over the journal entry again. Notice that among the words summarizing the plot you included a passage that impressed you so much that you copied it into your notebook: "she walked up and around and around until her feet knew to stop." Welty has chosen the third-person point of view to narrate the story (not Phoenix Jackson's first-person "I" point of view), but when you think about the passage, you notice that in this quotation Welty seems to be using language the way Phoenix Jackson would use it to express her thoughts. Make a written note of this idea in the margin of your journal or on a separate card. You will discover later that it is an important clue about the way Welty has shaped her narrative voice in "A Worn Path." You have begun to think critically about the story.

Perhaps you recall that Robert Frost once said, "To learn to write is to learn to have ideas." Recognizing an idea and recording it so it does not disappear is essential in the writing process. In the first twenty-four hours after you have been assigned your paper, let ideas surface about the story. Jot them down in your notebook or on cards so that you will not forget them, but let your subconscious work for you. This is the time to give yourself a chance to notice memorable details that stand out in your reading of the story, or strong feelings that you have about plot, setting, characterization, or other elements. These details and feelings can lead to ideas that you can develop in an essay.

If you do not find ideas you would like to develop in your journal or early responses to the story, then go on to Step Three.

STEP THREE: GENERATE IDEAS BY BRAINSTORMING, FREEWRITING, LISTING, AND ASKING QUESTIONS

Generating ideas for the assignment can be done in a variety of ways, either as a solitary process of jotting down ideas on paper or as a communal process of talking over your ideas with a friend or classmate who has also read the story. If you follow the latter course, be sure to write down your ideas as your conversation progresses so that they do not evaporate in the general glow of good company.

Brainstorming for Ideas

Assume that you are so intrigued by the notion that Welty writes her story in Phoenix Jackson's voice that you decide to brainstorm by yourself.

Record the thoughts that occur to you while you look over the story again. Pay particular attention to the first paragraph, imagining the choices Welty made when she selected her words for the opening sentences of her story. Don't worry about completing sentences or following one idea. Begin by free-associating about whatever comes to mind:

> Simple language in the first sentence, telling the month and day and
> time. Welty's so logical --big (month) to small (morning) time units.
>
> So where's the place? It's left kind of vague--"far out in the country."
>
> Description of main character next, obviously respectable ("an old
> Negro woman") but not dull with "her head tied in a red rag."

Thinking about the assignment as you brainstorm further, you might write the following adjectives:

> respectful, warm, sympathetic, humane, compassionate, a little funny
> but gently so--Welty never makes a joke at Phoenix's expense. She's
> "neat and tidy," but still human--her shoelaces drag and she hasn't
> bothered to lace her shoes. Is it because she's too old to bend down to
> lace them? Or maybe her feet hurt and she can't buy another pair.

At this point you might discover that brainstorming has put your imagination to work on the story. Your brief vision of the figure of Phoenix Jackson so frail with age that she is unable to bend over to tie her own shoes has made her become almost as real to you as your own grandmother. This might amuse you and cause you to realize that you have learned something about the magic of literature: writing about it can make you a more active participant in it. Remember the assignment: How does Welty's voice as a storyteller draw you into her tale?

This might be a good time to review your notes. Can you find a pattern in the details Welty has given you about Phoenix Jackson? If you have been as conscious of your thoughts about the story as Phoenix was aware of the path she was following through the woods, you might begin to sense Welty building something in her careful choice of descriptive details. She seems to suggest one thing and then to continue on to its opposite. Phoenix is "an old Negro woman" (respectable), but "her head tied in a red rag" (poor, shabby). She is compared to "a pendulum in a grandfather clock" (expensive, substantial), but she is holding "a thin, small cane made from an umbrella" (cheap, homemade, recycled broken umbrella). She is "neat and tidy," but her shoelaces drag. And so on. Why does Welty do this?

At this point there are several ways to proceed with your preparation for the paper, depending on the time you have and your personal preference for the method that has worked best for you in the past. You could start organizing your ideas into a list or a tentative outline. If you do not feel ready to attempt an outline, another technique that can help you focus your thoughts is an exercise called freewriting.

Freewriting

Like brainstorming, focused freewriting can help you locate an idea worth developing when you begin to think critically about literature. In a freewriting session, you state everything that comes to mind when you try to answer a question relating to the subject of your paper. Do not stop to think of forming complete sentences or using correct grammar or spelling. Give yourself a set time — perhaps ten or fifteen minutes or even longer if you feel inspired — to spill out all your associations about the topic. You can use a scratch pad, a typewriter, or a computer — whatever you have at hand. Keep the story beside you as you write, so that you can refer to it as necessary. Then go back and underline ideas in your writing that you think could be organized into a coherent outline and developed further in an essay. Here is an example of freewriting about "A Worn Path."

> What is Welty's voice in the story? Does she tease or is she serious? What does she do that makes me want to read on, one word following the next, until I'm hooked and *want* to know "what happens next"? First of all, she makes Phoenix into a complicated character. Simple to begin with, but more there than obviously meets the eye. Not a lot of dramatic action but a soft tone, almost as if she wanted to make you bend closer to her to hear her better. Serious, simple tone to begin the story. Then that business about the red rag. Does that do it? Or is it the choice of words, so simple and down-to-earth. Just like the character Welty's trying to describe. She's like anybody's granny in the country--even if it's Mississippi by the end of the story. Think about it. The way she uses alliteration, "red rag" and "path through the pinewoods," so her voice sounds good--it's very musical and rhythmic prose. Wait-- she's creating the rhythm of Phoenix's walk, "the balanced heaviness and lightness." Welty tells and shows at the same time--amazing writer.

Focused freewriting can make many students conscious of ideas they did not know they had, like the thought that Welty's voice as a storyteller is so musical and rhythmic that it suggests the pace of Phoenix's physical movements as she makes her slow way along the worn, familiar path to town. Brainstorming ideas and freewriting can often help you to think critically about a literary work. At this point you might find yourself wanting to make a list of all the things you have discovered about the story so far. That could help you begin to set your thoughts in order before you attempt to formulate a thesis and organize an outline for your rough draft.

Listing

Another useful technique in the preliminary stage of the writing process is making lists. You are probably experienced at doing this whenever you try to keep several things in mind at once, especially if you are planning to use the list later on, as for grocery shopping or organizing "things to do" over the days of a busy weekend. Listing also can become a way to help you develop your thoughts about literature. Making a list is more focused than brainstorming or freewriting; first you must be clear about what you want to list.

For example, if you would like to develop the idea that what attracts you about Welty's storytelling voice is its musical quality, you could comb "A Worn Path" for more instances of memorable alliteration (like "red rag") in the words describing the protagonist. Or you may be tempted to list the adventures Phoenix has along the way to see if Welty organizes them in any particular order, testing an idea that has just struck you that Welty might be holding your interest in the story by increasing the suspense of her plot. (You will probably find that — strangely enough — once your brain starts to go to work analyzing literature, one idea seems to stimulate another during the writing process.) If you decide to follow this trail, be careful not to let your list degenerate into a plot summary. Always keep in mind that you are testing the incidents for their inherent quality of suspense, summarizing their emotional effect on you.

Your first idea to list examples of musical alliteration in the story seems closer to the assigned topic. As you begin to scan the story again, you suddenly notice the beautiful simile that Welty uses in the second paragraph to describe Phoenix's wrinkled face: "as though a whole little tree stood in the middle of her forehead." You see that Welty emphasizes the vitality and beauty of Phoenix's skin color — "golden." And this detail is followed at the end of the paragraph by another compliment, that her hair falls "in the frailest of ringlets, still black, and with an odor like copper." What is "an odor like copper?" you ask yourself. Is it a good smell or a bad one? This makes you remember an early idea when you started thinking about the assignment, that Welty blends positive and negative attributes into her description of Phoenix Jackson. Could that be how she keeps her story about the old woman from becoming too sentimental?

You have gotten a little sidetracked, but that is no matter, because your thoughts about the second paragraph have carried you further along on your idea about Welty's method of drawing you into the story by her poetic description of Phoenix Jackson's face. Return to the story to find the examples that you started looking for, of musical alliteration. They are as easy to find in the opening paragraph as ripe red strawberries in June:

> red rag
> side to side in her steps
> sugar sacks

When you begin to notice examples of assonance, like the sound of the *o*'s in "odor of copper," you could start to make another list. You could also jot down a third list of examples of inverted word order that Welty has used in her sentences to achieve musical effect, such as "On she went." And you could create a fourth list for examples of the regular rhythm of sentences she (or Phoenix) chants using the melody of parallel structure: "Up through pines. . . . Now down through oaks."

Asking Questions

If you have followed these preliminary steps in the writing process — annotating the text, keeping a journal, brainstorming, freewriting, and making lists — you probably have collected a surfeit of ideas and details about the story to develop in your essay. But if you are stuck, as sometimes happens despite the preliminary work (especially if you simply do not feel yourself responding to the story), there is another way to jump-start your thinking process: ask questions about it.

In the chapters on reading, thinking, and writing about each literary genre in the earlier part of this book, you may have seen questions to stimulate critical thinking about short stories (p. 29), poetry (p. 1014), and drama (p. 1413). These questions focus on the structures of the story or the way the author has used the elements or means inherent in each form. Often you can find a direction to pursue for your paper by looking over these pages and answering the questions that set your mind working. For example, if your assignment is to analyze Welty's voice as a storyteller, you might consider the questions regarding style suggested in Chapter 5: Does she use irony? What is the effect of her use of colloquial speech? Does she call attention to the way she uses words, or is her literary style inconspicuous?

If you still cannot rise to the challenge, then try to analyze your lack of interest in the story. Ask questions to help you be as specific as possible about your negative response. What *exactly* do you dislike about it? What is it about Welty's way of telling a story that bores or annoys or disappoints you so much? You may be surprised at what happens when you admit your response honestly instead of trying to disguise it under platitudes in your essay or avoid it through procrastination in starting your paper. Working up a good case for your criticism of the way an author has mishandled (at least in your judgment) the elements of fiction, poetry, and drama can stimulate your ideas.

STEP FOUR: ORGANIZE YOUR NOTES TO GENERATE A PRELIMINARY THESIS SENTENCE AND OUTLINE

After you have allotted yourself sufficient time to think critically about the assignment, you should be ready to begin to organize your thoughts about what you intend to write on the topic. A common mistake is to begin typing the first draft of the paper too soon. If you take time to organize your ideas before you start to write, you can save yourself considerable anxiety and several false starts, not to mention hours staring in frustration at a blank computer screen or collecting a pile of discarded pages with jumbled thoughts printed out on them — a sacrifice to the agony of unfocused rough drafts.

An essay about literature can take various forms and be various lengths, depending on the nature of the assignment. Whether you are writing an essay of only a few paragraphs or a research paper of several thousand words, the basic requirement is always the same. An essay on any subject is a type of expository writing, and *expository* means "serving to clarify, set forth, or explain in detail" an idea about the subject.

Writing essays about literature helps you clarify your ideas. If you want your essay to communicate these ideas clearly to a reader, you must understand that it always requires two things to be effective: a strong thesis sentence or central idea about your topic (usually stated early in the paper), and an adequate development of your thesis sentence. How you organize your paper will depend on the way you choose to develop your central idea. The three principal ways of organizing compositions about literature — explication, analysis, and comparison and contrast — will be taken up after a discussion of the ways to find a thesis sentence and write a short paper.

Which of your notes about Welty's story is the best candidate to serve you as thesis sentence? It should express the central point of your essay. Consider it a preliminary thesis at this point, subject to revision as you write your paper. The topic for your essay was how Welty's voice as a storyteller draws you into "A Worn Path." After some thought, you might come up with the following thesis sentences:

1. *Welty's voice as a narrator is interesting.* This is a common, quick, and facile solution to the problem of formulating a thesis statement for a writing assignment. It is much too general to be helpful to you when you attempt to evolve an argument by marshalling your evidence in the paper. Keep thinking until you come up with a more specific idea about your topic.

2. *Welty's voice as a narrator draws the reader into the story.* You have rephrased the topic slightly, but do not assume that by doing so you have created the perfect thesis sentence. A moment of reflection will reveal that a topic is not the same as a thesis. A topic is a general subject, but a thesis makes a statement about a topic. It is usually the result of thinking about the topic and narrowing it down to focus on some relationship of the topic to the story, poem, or play as a whole. A good thesis sentence has two important functions. First, it suggests a specific way for you to write about the topic. Second, it makes clear to your reader the approach you have taken toward the topic.

3. *The way Welty uses language as a storyteller suggests the way Phoenix Jackson would use it to express her thoughts.* This was your first insight into Welty's way of telling her story. It could serve you as a preliminary thesis, because it suggests that you have analyzed the story. The test of a thesis sentence is whether your subject ("The way Welty uses language as a storyteller") is followed by a clearly focused predicate ("suggests

the way Phoenix Jackson would use it to express her thoughts"). Then you have the statement of an idea you can develop in your essay. This one is not specifically focused on the assigned topic, but you could start writing with it and then develop your idea as one of the reasons why Welty's voice as a storyteller draws you into the narrative.

4. *Welty uses language the way a poet does to keep readers interested in her story.* This idea came out of your list of responses to the story. You can find examples of Welty's use of alliteration, assonance, and rhetorical structure to show that, like a poet, she achieves an appealing musicality in her tone of voice while telling her story. This idea relates specifically to the assignment. It could serve as a trial thesis sentence for your rough draft. You could draft a preliminary outline for an essay developing this idea, or you could begin with the previous thesis sentence and come back to this idea as you work on your paper.

Assume you take the third choice, because this was your original insight about the story and you like the idea best. You may think that you are ready to write your paper, but remember that sketching a quick outline before you start can help you see the direction to take more clearly. It does not have to be a traditional outline. Shape it in any way that will help you remember the points you intend to make if you are interrupted in the writing process. Start by writing down your preliminary thesis sentence. Then assemble the evidence you have found to support it.

> The way Welty uses language as a storyteller suggests the way Phoenix Jackson would use it to express her thoughts.
>
> 1. Simple, down-to-earth vocabulary
> 2. Poetic and musical phrases.

Because your assignment is a short paper, this initial thesis and outline will get you started on your first draft. You have followed the first manageable steps of the writing process and now you are ready to begin your essay. Once more, remember the assigned topic and compare your outline to it (if you do not have an assigned topic, you can proceed freely). Do not worry if the topic and your outline are not a perfect fit at this point. As you write your essay, try to give your thesis a sharper focus. As Alex Johnson has observed, the object of this first draft is to shape your thesis sentence into what she calls a "controlling idea":

> The most common misconception is that the first draft is about writing *per se*. It's not. It's about thinking. If you've managed to turn out felicitous phrasing, I always tell students, it's icing on the cake. The real concern is how your idea evolves and sharpens, how its deeper structure emerges. To help this process along, don't agonize over word choice. Underline a word or simply leave a space and go back in the revision stage to get it right. Use momentum. Gag your internal critic and perfectionist when they report, correctly, that the draft seems sketchy. That's why it's called a first draft.

STEP FIVE: WRITE THE FIRST DRAFT

If you begin the first paragraph of your rough draft with a strong thesis sentence, it can start ideas flowing as you concentrate on the best way to present your supporting evidence. You will often discover further possibilities for refining a preliminary thesis while using it to interpret the text. That is one reason you should allow plenty of time to complete a writing assignment. It is an unusual first draft in which the central idea is developed coherently and fully enough to be turned in as the finished paper. Revision usually stimulates further thought, sharpening and refining your argument.

Try not to become discouraged by visualizing some distant, final product — a well-organized essay, neatly typed on clean white paper, shimmering on the page in what looks to your fond eye like pristine perfection. Remember that it takes time for it to get that way. Most essays originate in half-formed, often confused thoughts that have to be coaxed to arrange themselves into coherent paragraphs linked by transitions that only much later appear to be inevitable to you.

More often than not, the 250 or 500 words you might think are a perfect essay when you turn in your final paper will be the end result — if you took enough time and care in writing — of winnowing many more words from your rough drafts. For a successful essay, you must amplify and clarify your thesis, editing your sentences and paragraphs so that each one relates coherently to your central idea. Then your essay will express your insights about the story so clearly that they can be understood by your reader as you intended.

SAMPLE FIRST DRAFT OF AN ESSAY ON
EUDORA WELTY'S "A WORN PATH"

An author's   a   point to consider about
~~A storyteller's~~ voice is key ~~to understanding~~ the way she tells
            ^   ^

     From   's choice of words, we can hear that she
her story. Eudora Welty ~~is a warm and sympathetic~~
       ^   ^

  is a warm and sympathetic
~~ ~~narrator in "A Worn Path." She uses language so simply and
^

          interests us
concretely that she   ~~makes us interested~~ immediately in the journey
                       ^

      named Phoenix Jackson
of an old woman   as she walks through the pinewoods to Natchez to
                ^

                In fact,
get medicine for her grandson. Welty uses language the way
                         ^

                            when she comes to the city
Phoenix uses it to express her thoughts, because ~~at the end of the story~~
                                        ^

we are told that "she walked up and around and around until her feet

knew to stop."

                    captures the reader's attention.
This simple, down-to-earth vocabulary ~~grounds us~~. It is as
                                    ^

Welty   *is creating*
if ~~the author~~ could read the mind of the character she ~~has created~~
  ^   ^
                                                              mind
on the page. We all would like to be able to get inside the ~~thoughts~~ of
                                                                          ^
          and   *thoughts,*
another person, ~~to~~ share their most private ~~interior world~~, so we
                        ^   ^

want to read further. This could be considered a trick, since Welty's

own voice (and mind) could not be exactly the same as the uneducated

                                      fictional
Phoenix, but Welty's ~~sincere~~ feeling for her character shines through
                                              ^

the story. Her voice is sincere.

Welty's voice interests us for another reason. She chooses

                                      a prose story,
words the way a poet would. She's writing ~~a short story,~~ but she
                                                      ^
    her
chooses words like a poet. There are many examples of alliteration
    ^
                opening   *first*
and assonance in the ~~first~~ paragraph of her story, when she must
                        ^   ^
                                      compares the pattern of wrinkles on
capture our interest. In the second paragraph, she ~~gives~~ Phoenix's
                                                              ^
                                      and poetic
~~wrinkled~~ face to a "whole little tree." This is a fresh image to help us
                                                                  ^

visualize the old woman's appearance. The plot and characterization of

Phoenix later in the story shows us how resourceful and loving she is

as a person. As a storyteller, Welty speaks of her heroine with great

affection. She blends telling and showing in "A Worn Path."

STEP SIX: REVISE

Ideally, if you have the time, you should put your rough draft away for
a day or so, and then read it again with fresh eyes. Before you return to it, you
might want to reread the literature you are writing about, looking for more details to support your thesis statement. If there are commentaries on the work
in this book, you should check to see if you can find any ideas in them relevant
to your paper.

Revision is the writing stage where you get the chance to do the best
work on your paper. You can refine your argument by clarifying your sentences, strengthening your evidence, and tying together loose ends. Most students are surprised to find how rough and unfinished their first drafts appear

after time away from the essay. Always read your work with a pen or pencil in hand. You can see from the example above how extensively the short essay on "A Worn Path" was revised. In its final version, the student also added a sentence referring to Welty's essay "Is Phoenix Jackson's Grandson Really Dead?" discovered among the commentaries in the short fiction section of the anthology (p. 809).

SAMPLE REVISED DRAFT

The Voice of the Storyteller
in Welty's "A Worn Path"

An author's voice is a key point to consider about the effect of the story on her reader. From Eudora Welty's choice of words in "A Worn Path," we can tell she's a warm and sympathetic narrator. She uses language so simply and concretely that she makes us interested in the journey of an old woman named Phoenix Jackson as she walks through the pinewoods to Natchez to get medicine for her grandson. In fact, Welty uses language the way that Phoenix would use it to express her thoughts, because when she comes to the city we are told that "she walked up and around and around until her feet knew to stop."

This simple, down-to-earth vocabulary captures the reader's attention. It is as if the author could read the mind of her character. We all would like to be able to get inside the mind of another person, to share his or her private thoughts and feelings, so we want to read further. Welty has admitted in her commentary on "A Worn Path" that "the story is told through Phoenix's mind." This could be considered a trick, since Welty's own voice (and mind) could not be exactly the same as uneducated, unsophisticated Phoenix, but Welty's respect for her imaginary character shines through her story. We think the sound of her voice is sincere, so we trust her.

Welty's voice attracts us for another reason. She's writing prose, but she chooses words like a poet. There are many examples of alliteration and assonance in the first paragraph, where her use of language must get our attention to entice us into the story. In the second paragraph, she uses a poetic simile to compare the pattern of wrinkles on Phoenix's face to a "whole little tree." This comparison helps us visualize the old woman's appearance. It's also so down-to-earth that it could even have occurred to Phoenix herself if we imagine her looking at her reflection in a forest stream or a shop window. We are irresistibly drawn into the story by the skillful voice of Eudora Welty in "A Worn Path."

STEP SEVEN: FINAL CHECK OF THE FINISHED ESSAY

Before you turn in your essay, you should check the quotations you have used to make sure that you have copied them accurately. If you have used a computer to write your paper, you should also run a spell-check. The following guide can help you in the final preparation of your essay:

1. Be sure to include your name, date, and class section on the paper.
2. Check your title. Ideally, it should suggest an idea of your approach to the assigned topic. If you include the author's name or title of the work here, be sure you have spelled it correctly and have used quotation marks or underlining appropriately.
3. Include the name of the author and title of the work you are writing about in your opening paragraph so that the reader knows what you plan to discuss. Often, at least in short essays, the reader expects you to state your thesis sentence in the first paragraph. It should relate to the class assignment.
4. Review your organization. Does your essay offer solid evidence to support your thesis statement? Does it develop ideas clearly and coherently? For effective emphasis, do your paragraphs proceed from the least important to the most important point? Can some of the longer paragraphs be divided into shorter units to clarify your main points? Are your short paragraphs adequately developed? Does each sentence relate to the one before? Have you supplied transitional sentences between paragraphs?
5. Include quotations from the work you are discussing to add variety to the vocabulary you customarily use. Such a practice also offers a change of pace to the reader of your paper, as well as a reminder of the pleasures of the original text.
6. Check that your punctuation and grammar are correct throughout your essay, and that you have written varied and complete sentences, not sentence fragments. If you spot unintentional verbal repetitions, find fresh words to replace them or revise the sentence to eliminate wordiness.
7. Look for the conclusion to your essay. If it is a short paper, you can phrase your conclusion as a sentence or two in the final paragraph. In a longer paper, you could devote at least an entire final paragraph to a statement of your conclusion.

Peer Review

Before turning in your essay, you could exchange papers with another student to check each other's work. Your instructor might also include a peer review of rough drafts or finished papers during class time, allowing you the benefit of other readers' suggestions for improvement. This could help you clarify your ideas and strengthen your argument. If you are given another student's paper, read it twice. In the first reading, enjoy the expression of its critical thought; in the second, check the various points in the list above.

TYPES OF LITERARY PAPERS

Explication

The word *explication* is derived from a Latin word that means "unfolding." When you explicate a text, you unfold its meaning in an essay, proceeding carefully to interpret it passage by passage, sometimes even line by line or word by word. A good explication concentrates on details, quoting the text of the story, poem, or play to bring the details to the attention of a reader who might have missed them approaching the text from a different perspective.

An entire story, poem, or play is usually too long to explicate completely — the explication would be far longer than the original work. You usually select a short passage or section that relates to the idea you are developing. If a poem is brief, you can explicate all of it, as in the following student essay on Langston Hughes's poem "The Negro Speaks of Rivers" (p. 1129). In a play, you could choose to explicate a key scene or a crucial dialogue. In a story, you could concentrate on the opening or closing paragraph, where you might suggest the implications of the text to develop the central idea of your essay.

Explication does not usually concern itself with the author's life or times, but his or her historical period may determine the definitions of words or the meaning of concepts that appear in the passage you are interpreting. If the literary work is a century or more old, the meanings of some words may have changed. The explication is supposed to reveal what the author might have meant when he or she wrote the poem, story, or play (not assuming conscious intentions but explicating possibilities).

For older literature, you will have to do a little research if the passage you choose for explication contains words whose meanings have changed. The *Oxford English Dictionary*, available in the reference section of your college library, will give you the meaning of a word in a particular era. The philosophical, religious, scientific, or political beliefs of the author or of his or her historical time may also enter into your interpretation of the text. The main emphasis in explication, however, is on the meaning of the words — both *denotative* and *connotative* — and the way those words affect you.

SAMPLE EXPLICATION OF A POEM

An Interpretation of Langston Hughes's

"The Negro Speaks of Rivers"

In the poem "The Negro Speaks of Rivers," Langston

Hughes uses elements of the blues to suggest the history of

blacks from ancient Egypt to the twentieth century through

the extended metaphor of the river. He explores the cultural

identity and endurance of his people, emphasizing his racial uniqueness by his rejection of traditional European writing styles.

At the beginning of "The Negro Speaks of Rivers," Hughes is searching for his cultural identity. The poem is written in plain-spoken free verse, with an emphasis on spoken rhythm and an intimate, blues-like tone as opposed to a structured rhyme and formal rhythmic scheme. A statement of his situation in the first line ("I've known rivers") is repeated in the second, as in a blues lyric, but extended so it can be followed with a third line that stands alone as well as comments on the first two. With this third line ("My soul has grown deep like the rivers"), Hughes begins a brief historical account as the voice of the African American race.

This history celebrates the transition from slavery to freedom, suggesting the strength of his race by connecting it to the image of the river. The representation of rivers and pyramids in the next lines of the poem suggests the endurance of the human spirit through time, mystically connecting his heritage to something "older than the flow of human blood in human veins." As the rivers continue to flow, so do his people continue to thrive through the changing times and the slow acceptance of racial differences.

Hughes then moves from this portrayal of his race in the bondage of slavery from the old world to the new, where Abraham Lincoln symbolizes the progressive movement from slavery to freedom. Hughes's pride and love for his race can be seen as the water of the Mississippi turns "all golden in the sunset." The last three lines of the poem suggest the sadness and complexity of the racial situation in Hughes's somber conclusion. As in a blues lyric, he ends by repeating the line that introduced his historical panorama of African American history: "My soul has grown deep like the rivers."

On the next page is an example of a longer student paper explicating a section of Nathaniel Hawthorne's "Young Goodman Brown" (p. 268) to develop a central idea in an essay. Whether you accept the student's interpretation of the scene with the pink ribbon or not, it is a good example of the use of explication to show a way to read the text that develops the central idea of an essay. The thesis statement is clearly presented in the opening paragraph, so the reader knows what the essay will be about.

At first the student approached the explication with the idea that Goodman Brown's essential weakness was his pride in trusting his senses more than his faith in God. The student felt from the start that the entire scene with the ribbon was a hallucination. Rereading the story, he found evidence in Hawthorne's words to support this interpretation. Then, in writing the essay, he developed this thesis a step further, concluding the paper with two sentences about the "short step from believing in the devil to being taken in by him." This is an example of how the writing process itself can clarify and stimulate closely related ideas.

SAMPLE EXPLICATION OF A SHORT STORY

The Devil's Tricks in Hawthorne's

"Young Goodman Brown"

Use quotes for titles of stories.

Nathaniel Hawthorne's "Young Goodman Brown" is the story of a man whose life is ruined because of the sin of pride, which makes him lose his faith in God. Goodman Brown agrees to meet the devil in the forest, and his faith is destroyed when he sees a pink ribbon fluttering to earth. He believes this ribbon could only have fallen from his beloved wife's cap. It is this scene in the story that reveals his weakness. His pride makes him trust the evidence of his own senses more than his faith in God.

Start with general thesis sentence.

Narrow the thesis to show specific direction your paper will take.

Hawthorne begins the scene in which Goodman Brown loses his faith by leaving him without other characters around him for the first time in the story. Alone with his soul, he has only himself to depend on. The devil has abandoned him in the middle of the dark woods with the maple staff that became a witch's broomstick when it was borrowed by Goody Cloyse earlier in the evening. Thus the reader has already seen the devil's tricks.

Transition: repeat key words of thesis.

Suggest background of scene before you begin explication.

Other black magic is in store for Goodman Brown. Gazing upward "into the deep arch of the firmament," he lifts his hands to pray. The word "firmament," with its biblical connotations, suggests that Goodman Brown has set his mind on God. He has scarcely begun his prayer; however, when his concentration is broken: "a cloud, though no wind was stirring, hurried across the zenith and hid the brightening stars." The devil's magic show has begun, although Goodman Brown is not aware of it.

Start to quote from the story. Do not set off short quote.

He accepts the appearance of the "black mass" of the cloud overhead and forgets his prayer, listening instead to a "<u>confused</u> and <u>doubtful</u> sound of voices. . . . The next moment, so <u>indistinct</u> were the sounds, he doubted whether he had heard aught. . . ." The adjectives and verbs I have underlined

Main section of the explication: text quoted in the order it appears.

in Hawthorne's description suggest the lack of substance in
what Goodman Brown hears and sees; he is, after all, standing under a dark cloud. The next moment he believes he
hears the voice "of a young woman, uttering lamentations,
yet with an <u>uncertain</u> sorrow, and entreating for some favor,
which, <u>perhaps</u>, it would grieve her to obtain; and all the unseen multitude, both saints and sinners, seemed to encourage
her onward."

OK to use "I"; italics are not in original.

Good active verbs.

At this point Goodman Brown believes not only that he
hears the voice of a young woman, but also that the woman is
his wife, Faith. By now he is completely deluded. When he
shouts his wife's name he is mocked by the ghosts he senses
around him: "The <u>echoes</u> of the forest mocked him crying,
'Faith! Faith!' <u>as if bewildered</u> wretches were seeking her all
through the wilderness." Here Hawthorne has built his description out of thin air. The echoes of Goodman Brown's
voice sound as if bewildered, which is certainly ironic, since
he himself is truly bewildered here.

Paragraph concludes with a strong idea about Hawthorne's use of irony in the scene.

Goodman Brown's temptation leads to his fall in the
next paragraph, when "the dark cloud swept away, leaving
the clear and silent sky above Goodman Brown. But something fluttered lightly down through the air and caught on the
branch of a tree. The young man seized it, and <u>beheld</u> a pink
ribbon." Hawthorne's language has changed, becoming simple
and stark. It suggests the physicality of what it describes.
Goodman Brown might have doubted the evidence of his eyes
and ears if he stopped to reflect on what he had been shown
in the "clear and silent sky" above his head, but before he
could reflect, the devil gave him what he took to be something
tangible to hold onto, something that looks like a pink
ribbon.

Good insight into change in language.

Thoughtful analysis of character's motiva- tion.

On the evidence of what he sees as a ribbon, Goodman
Brown jumps to the conclusion that Faith has joined in the
worship of the devil. He surrenders his trust in God forever.
He becomes a victim of his own pride, believing in the evidence of his own senses more than in God. As a Puritan,
Goodman Brown believes in the devil as much as he believes
in God. Hawthorne might be suggesting that his belief contributed to his downfall. The story shows that it is but a short
step from believing in the devil to being taken in by him.

End explication; start conclusion, tying back to thesis.

Conclusion goes one step further, to a wider implication of the thesis (logically connected).

Analysis

An *analysis* of a literary work is the result of the process of separating it into its parts in order to study the whole. Analysis is commonly applied in thinking about almost any complex subject. When you are asked to analyze literature, you must break it down into various parts and then usually select a single aspect for close study. Often what you are analyzing is one of the elements of fiction, poetry, or drama — an aspect of style, characterization, dialogue, setting, or symbolism, for example.

Whereas explication deals with a specific section of the text, analysis can range further, discussing details through the story, poem, or play that are related to your thesis. You cannot possibly analyze every word of a literary work any more than you would attempt to explicate all of it. You might begin with a general idea, or arrive at one by thinking about some smaller detail that catches your attention, as the student did by analyzing the storyteller's voice in "A Worn Path."

Suppose you are given an assignment to write an analysis of any aspect of Hawthorne's "Young Goodman Brown" that interests you. You could begin by noticing the description of the path through the forest as you reread the story, sensing a connection of the path with the effect of "blackness" you feel building up in the narrative. This single detail of the setting can lead to a central idea for your paper. Regardless of where you start to think critically, you will usually begin to write an essay that is developed through analysis by moving from a general thesis statement to the particular part of the story being analyzed. The following essay, "The Path toward Evil," is an example of how a student has analyzed "Young Goodman Brown" by tracking Hawthorne's references to the path through the forest.

Here the thesis sentence opens the essay, and the analysis follows from it. The student separated the story into various parts, analyzing the way the path figured at each stage of narration. You will notice that explication also plays a role in this essay. Even when analysis is your chosen method of developing your central idea, you should quote examples from the story to support your main points. Each time you use a quotation, comment on it to integrate it smoothly into your discussion.

SAMPLE ANALYSIS OF A SHORT STORY

The Path toward Evil

The path's purpose in "Young Goodman Brown" is to show that "evil is the nature of mankind," which is the dominant theme of Nathaniel Hawthorne's story. It is a very black theme, as Herman Melville realized in his 1850 review of Hawthorne's <u>Mosses from an Old Manse</u>. Satan has been with the Puritans since they came to America. The "dreary . . . narrow" path Goodman Brown follows through the gloomy

Thesis sentence, supported by evidence from supplementary reading.

forest is proof that human beings have frequently walked with the devil in the new land. Goodman Brown's journey on the path makes him realize that there are two kinds of evil: social and personal. He meets social evil first, and is confused by it. Then he meets the "blackness" that is the evil within himself, and he is totally destroyed.

Analysis narrows thesis and points to direction of paper's development.

When he begins to walk on the path with the devil, Goodman Brown is too innocent to understand what he hears. He does not realize that the religious intolerance of the early Puritan settlers is wrong. So his companion, the devil, enlightens him further, telling him about present-day corruption in the community. The church deacons have drunk the communion wine, and the lawyers "are firm supporters of my interest." Now Goodman Brown is horrified because he understands the meaning of the devil's remarks. He takes the first step along the path from innocence to disillusionment when he recognizes hypocrisy in the respected village elders.

Analysis is coherent — organized from beginning of story to end.

Quote from story to illustrate idea.

He proceeds a step further when he sees his own catechism teacher, the deacon, and the minister on the forest path, too. He does not understand what they are doing there. He asks himself, "Whither, then, could these holy men be journeying so deep into the heathen wilderness?" While Goodman Brown now recognizes social evil, he does not understand it. He must go further along the path to discover his own evil nature.

Good transition: one step leads to another.

Quote evidence for assertion.

End of first part (social evil).

Goodman Brown finds the answer to his question in the story's climax. The path takes him and the "holy men" to the same destination. After he has come to believe that his wife is about to become one of the devil's accomplices, he runs desperately down the path, which "grew wilder and drearier and more faintly traced, and vanished at length, leaving him in the heart of the dark wilderness, still rushing onward with the instinct that guides mortal man to evil." Although the trail is a path toward evil, it is, paradoxically, his last connection with the familiar Puritan life that has sustained him. When it stops, he is lost.

Begin second part (personal evil).

Good comment on the quote — relates it to central idea.

The path terminates in the forest clearing, with its altar dedicated to the worship of Satan. Here he learns "to behold the whole earth one stain of guilt, one mighty blood spot." There are no paths out of the wilderness now for Good-

Evidence to support the analysis of the personal evil in Goodman Brown.

man Brown. The whole earth is bathed in blood, with no firm ground upon which to fix a path that will lead him safely home. Overwhelmed by his visions in the forest, he is a lost soul. He has realized his own evil nature.

As Hawthorne knew, the Puritan settlers of Salem felt the forest was evil. They had to make paths in order to live in it. They would have died of exposure if left alone in the woods, and they needed paths to other nearby settlements. To journey alone in the forest was, as Goodman Brown learned, to leave the clearly defined, if hypocritical, moral path of the established religious community and so to invite damnation. Hawthorne dramatized his dark theme of man's essentially evil nature by showing Goodman Brown's fate. He leaves the apparently straight and narrow path of the religious settlement for the twisting, crooked path of the forest. It is a dark journey of his soul to meet "the deep mystery" of original sin.

Begin conclusion: historical background relates to particular details of the story.

Restatement of thesis.

Most students find that when they are asked to write an essay analyzing a poem, they can come closer to the poem by copying it out double-spaced into a computer or writing it in longhand on paper. Then you can scribble your observations about the poem in the margins of your paper, brainstorming alongside the text itself. To analyze Robert Frost's poem "Mending Wall" (p. 1099), for example, you could write a list of adjectives and uses for a wall — *to hide, block out, a barrier, protection, a blockade, safety, security, separation,* and so on — to familiarize yourself with the "walled" metaphor of the poem. You could also annotate Frost's use of language and the technical means of poetry. You could consider the title, weighing its various connotations in your mind after you've studied the poem. When one student tried freewriting about her response to the poem, she was reminded of a photograph of Ireland on a travel poster. This memory inspired her opening paragraph in the following essay, "Nature and Neighbors in Robert Frost's 'Mending Wall.' "

SAMPLE ANALYSIS OF A POEM

Nature and Neighbors
in Robert Frost's "Mending Wall"

Ireland is known for its rolling green countryside. Without forests, the land appears to be a sea of green stretching to a sea of blue. The land, however, is not uninterrupted; there are a few roads and homes floating in that green sea,

Funnel paragraph, narrows down to focus on assigned topic of paper.

and they are even further outnumbered by Ireland's stone
walls. They streak across every grazing field, surround the
family farmhouses, and never seem to be in need of repair.
The reason these walls remain has little to do with the skill of
their original builders. Years of maintenance keeps them
strong. Why the walls are maintained, despite the fact that
few sheep graze within their boundaries, can be explained by
examining Robert Frost's poem "Mending Wall."

The wall is in need of repair as the narrator and his
neighbor meet to fill in the gaps a cold winter has made. As
the two walk along the wall at "spring mending time" one on
each side, they replace the fallen stones and rebuild the
tumbled-down boundaries. As the stones are restored to their
places in the wall, the chaos of nature is replaced by a man-
made sense of order.

*Summary of poem's
subject.*

The neighbors "set the wall between [them] once again,"
and in doing so, they strengthen the order a year of freedom
has weakened. As they repair the wall, they are restoring
order to the natural world in which they live and work and to
their emotional worlds, where the relationships they have
with one another reside. In both cases, the wall symbolizes
the control the two men wish to possess over unpredictable
forces in their lives.

*Summary of poem's
theme.*

As a control over nature, the wall has many weaknesses. When nature does not work against the wall in New
England, sending "the frozen ground swell under it," hunters
come through, leaving "not one stone on a stone." Each year
in an annual ritual, the two neighbors must meet again to repair the damage not because they enjoy the endless process of
rebuilding the wall, but because the wall's presence gives
them some sense of control over the chaos of nature. The wall
divides the wilderness into manageable segments that are far
easier to maintain than an endless expanse of farmland. In a
visible and tangible way, the wall reminds the two that,
despite nature's awesome power, they can in some, though
impermanent, way check that power.

*Beginning of analysis
— ritual as a sense of
control over nature.*

The borders the wall forms also indicate where the
responsibility of one person ends and the duty of another
begins. It is in this way that the wall crosses from control
over nature to a controlling factor in the neighbors' relation-

*Ritual as a state-
ment of the neighbors'
relationship — use of
quotations.*

ship. Despite the fact that the wall separates two plots of trees, and the "apple trees will never get across and eat the cones under [the] pines," the wall is necessary in maintaining their friendly and mutually beneficial relationship. As the neighbor states, in the most memorable line of the poem, "Good fences make good neighbors." And in answer to the narrator's question of "Why do they make good neighbors?," one can look to the final image of the poem, a comparison of the neighbor to "an old stone savage armed."

In addition to illustrating the idea of ancient property rights, this image turns the neighbor into a threatening creature; revealing anything to him could prove dangerous. "He moves in darkness"—not the darkness caused by the shade a tree casts on a sunny day but a deeper darkness that holds the power to damage emotions that the wall symbolically protects. Therefore, the wall is a wise protection against a potentially hostile invader. It is for this reason that a wall, in this case a mental wall or symbolic sense of limits, is essential in the relationship.

Analysis of poetic imagery as it relates to the theme of the poem.

Below the surface of any human being is the potential to do harm, just as in the distance, on a clear day, a storm may be brewing. Though it is not the trusting thing to do, both neighbors understand the necessity of the wall in separating their properties and respecting personal space. The narrator begins to question his faith in the wall and the distrust it perpetuates, but in the end, as is evident by his repetition of the line "Good fences make good neighbors," he realizes the truth in such a motto. For the symbolic protection it affords and its ability to give some order to chaos, the wall has become a part of their lives.

Fresh comparison to a natural phenomenon.

Beginning of conclusion.

In Ireland, as in New England, the old stone walls remain, climbing to the tops of mountains and disappearing over the ridge. They seem to hold the green sea of grasses down as a row of stones might hold down a blanket on a breezy day. In the walls the neighbors find a sense of control over their wild land, restraining the endless landscape in manageable squares and rectangles, keeping each neighbor's overgrown field of nettles within the walls and allowing responsibility to begin and end with the stone borders. In a way the good relations between neighbors are maintained with as

Conclusion refers back to opening paragraph and restates thesis sentence.

much devotion as the walls have been maintained over the
years.

Comparison and Contrast

If you were to write about two works of literature in this anthology, you would probably use the technique of comparison and contrast. When making a comparison, you place the two works side by side and comment on their similarities. When contrasting them, you point out their differences. It is always more meaningful to compare and contrast two literary works that have something in common than two that are unrelated. As you work on your essay you will find that if there are not important similarities between the two works, your discussion will be as strained and pointless as an attempt to link closely any two dissimilar objects, like elephants and oranges.

If you decide to use the method of comparison and contrast to develop the ideas in your essay, it is usually smoother to mingle them as you go along, rather than using contrast in the first half of your paper and comparison in the second half. The result of such a fifty-fifty split is rarely a unified essay. Rather, it tends to give the impression of two separate analyses linked together at the last minute.

The following student paper uses the method of comparison and contrast in developing an idea about two stories by Edgar Allan Poe and Nathaniel Hawthorne.

In his essay, the student shaped the first paragraph as a funnel leading to his central idea. Next he compared the ways in which the two stories were similar. Then he went on in the rest of his paper to analyze the differences between them. Throughout, elements of both stories were compared and contrasted side by side, sometimes with general analytic comments, at other times with explication and interpretation of the text.

SAMPLE COMPARISON-AND-CONTRAST PAPER
ON TWO STORIES

The Single Effect in

Hawthorne's "Young Goodman Brown"

and Poe's "The Cask of Amontillado"

In addition to writing short fiction, Edgar Allan Poe   *General background*
                                                          information on topic.
published literary criticism, in which he explained his own

standards for prose tales. Poe stated that the primary goal in

creating works in this literary genre should be the

development of a "certain . . . single effect." According to Poe,   *Summary of most*
                                                                     important facts about
an author invents such incidents in the story as will establish   *topic.*

this "preconceived effect." Poe introduced this theory in one

of his reviews of a collection of Nathaniel Hawthorne's tales.

The theory was conceived by Poe and based on the work of
Hawthorne, so the stories of both men emphasize the creation
of such a "single effect."

Topic narrowed to thesis sentence.

   Hawthorne's "Young Goodman Brown" and Poe's "The
Cask of Amontillado" show each author's use of the method of
"single effect." Poe's story examines the psychological
processes in a madman's plot for revenge, and Hawthorne's
story describes a man's fall from innocence, but both tales are
constructed similarly. The action of both stories features a
single character. Both stories are unified by a central theme.
Every word, phrase, and image used by the author moves the
theme closer to complete development. Neither story is
realistic--that is, the events described are not plausible as real-
life experiences. When Goodman Brown walks with a flesh-and-
blood devil, for example, it is immediately clear that the story
is a fantasy, because flesh-and-blood devils did not exist in
Puritan Salem. A similar world of fantasy operates in "The
Cask of Amontillado." The ease with which the narrator is able
to lead Fortunato to his death is not true to life as we know it.

Important similarities.

Single protagonist.

Central theme.
Not realistic.

Specific examples.

   Both stories feature a single character, and both
emphasize a unity of single effect in developing their themes,
but there are some fundamental differences between the
stories. The first is created by the nature of the two literary
forms the authors use. Hawthorne was writing a moral
allegory. Every aspect of the story symbolizes something else.
Goodman Brown's wife, for example, is the embodiment of
morality and simple faith; even her name, "Faith,"
contributes to this symbolic meaning. The story would have a
different effect if she were named "Gertrude." Poe was
writing a psychological fantasy. Fortunato is shown dressed
in a cap similar to one that would be worn by a court jester.
By calling attention to his outfit, the narrator, Montresor,
adds to the degradation of Fortunato, which is part of the aim
of his plan for revenge. Poe's fantasy is based on human
emotions, while Hawthorne's allegory is based on intellect.

Begin analyzing differences.

Hawthorne's form.

Good example.

Contrast with Poe's form.

Summarize differences.

   There is another major difference in the style of the
two stories. Poe said that the first sentence of any tale should
bring out the effect on which the rest depends. Although Poe
set up the rules, Hawthorne did not keep to them. The
opening sentence of "Young Goodman Brown" is in no hurry:

Another feature of Poe's theory related to another difference in the stories.

"Young Goodman Brown came forth at sunset into the street at Salem village; but put his head back, after crossing the threshold, to exchange a parting kiss with his young wife." Goodman Brown is going on a journey, but the nature of the journey--which is central to the theme--is not clear. The concise opening of Poe's tale, however, reveals the theme: "The thousand injuries of Fortunato I had borne as I best could; but when he ventured upon insult, I vowed revenge." This sentence leaves no doubt in the reader's mind about the meaning of the story. The narrator declares that revenge is foremost in his mind, and the action that follows develops the idea of a character obsessed by the desire for revenge.

Quote to give evidence of difference.

Contrast with Hawthorne.

Both Poe and Hawthorne were artists deeply interested in creating works of fiction. Despite their differences of form and literary style, both created unified stories based on a "single effect," as shown in the two classic tales "Young Goodman Brown" and "The Cask of Amontillado."

Concluding summary clear, but a little brief.

The method of comparison and contrast works especially well when you are thinking about two or more works by a single writer. Here is a paper analyzing the differences in Tennessee Williams's characterization of Laura in his story "Portrait of a Girl in Glass" (p. 708) and his play *The Glass Menagerie* (p. 1704). This student used quotations from the texts skillfully to help the reader get a clearer idea of the general points he wanted to make in his essay.

SAMPLE COMPARISON-AND-CONTRAST PAPER
ON A STORY AND A PLAY

Laura's Masks

Tennessee Williams's play The Glass Menagerie and short story "Portrait of a Girl in Glass" present strikingly different portrayals of Laura, the helpless daughter of the family. In her first incarnation in the story, Laura is presented as a withdrawn, childlike, mentally ill woman. In The Glass Menagerie, she is recast as an overbearingly shy and fearful wreck. With changes in her environment, degree of mental illness, and overall personality, Williams transforms this character dramatically. Laura evolves from an ill, undecipherable enigma to a predictable and much more realistic victim.

Focus on topic of paper.

Summary of argument.

Thesis sentence.

In both story and play, Laura is the crippled, exces-

Important similarities.

sively shy woman who is trapped in the mind-set of a child. She is a private person who doesn't express extreme emotions--she carries herself quietly through both works. In both, she shows the same weakness to the outside world: "I couldn't go [to business school] any longer, it scared me too much, it made me sick at the stomach!" At home is the only place where this socially immature woman can function.

But Laura functions quite differently between the two genres, and her living environment reflects this. In the story, Laura spends much of her time in her room--a social cocoon. An unwholesome ambience lurks in Laura's room: a portrait of a weeping Christ and the "perpetual twilight" that the closed shades create. They are closed to keep out the horrors of Death Valley, the alley where stray cats are destroyed by "one particularly vicious dirty white Chow." To escape all the Chows of the world, Laura secludes herself in her room surrounded by small colored glass articles that nurture her with a radiating glow. Often her brother, Tom, enters the room and finds Laura lovingly holding an article of glass, like a Madonna and Child.

Beginning of contrast — story first.

In the play version, Laura doesn't have any such sanctuary. The physical representation of herself takes the form of "an old-fashioned what-not in the living room," where she keeps "scores of transparent glass animals." Here Laura lacks a haven of her own. She must live and sleep in the living room, constantly exposed to Amanda's onslaughts of fear and worry for their future as well as her conflicts with Tom. Laura's sensitive nerves cannot possibly find much relief here.

Contrast with the play version.

Laura is presented as a much more intellectually pathetic character in the story version. While trimming the tree one Christmas, the Star of Bethlehem stirs within Laura a curiosity about the intricacies of the universe: "Do stars have five points really?" She is prone to such inquiries, as Tom describes this as "the sort of thing that you don't believe and that made you stare at Laura with sorrow and confusion." Even after Tom answers her, Laura approaches the window for confirmation in the smoke-shrouded sky. "It's hard to tell," she replies. Indeed, Laura cannot see the real world outside of the apartment. With the Death Valley horrors outside of her bedroom window, and the cloud of smoke coating her

Analysis returns to story and its strength of presentation.

vision with mystery, staying at home appears to be a very safe and sane choice to a childlike mind.

When an element of that outside world comes over for dinner one night, the two Lauras have different reactions. In the story, Laura has never met Jim before. After Amanda calls on her to answer the door twice, there is a "long, long pause," and Laura relies on "a march of Sousa's, put on to give her the courage to let in a stranger," to complete this task. The play version displays a much more insecure Laura, who is not so easily moved to greet the dinner guest. Before Tom and Jim arrive, when Laura realizes that the gentleman caller is the same boy that she had had a crush on in high school, Laura bails out of the scheme immediately: "All I know is that I couldn't sit at the table if it was him." When the doorbell does eventually ring, she loses all confidence and calls for her mother, whining: "Mother, please, you go to the door!" "Please, you answer it, please." "I can't [get the door]." "I'm sick." Once she does get the door open, she hides herself behind it, away from Tom and Jim. Courage does not become her.

Comparison of story with the play version.

Use of specific quotes as evidence for generalizations.

One of the most apparent differences between the two Lauras is displayed in their encounters with Jim following dinner. In the play, Tennessee Williams gives notes indicating how Laura should act: "Her speech at first is low and breathless from the almost intolerable strain of being alone with a stranger. In her speeches in this scene, before Jim's warmth overcomes her paralyzing shyness, Laura's voice is thin and breathless." In the beginning Jim is doing all the talking by asking questions and trying to urge conversation out of Laura, who gives only one-word replies. She gradually relaxes, so much so that she agrees to dance with him, though reluctantly at first. Then just as she seems to give in completely, they knock over her favorite glass animal. The unicorn has been damaged, and, amazingly, Laura isn't crushed: "Oh, it doesn't matter--." It is quite possible that Jim is already beginning to take the place of the glass menagerie in her life. Laura has obviously become fond of Jim when he announces that he is engaged--she utters only two brief lines for the rest of the play.

Contrast continues.

Analysis focuses on play.

If the glass menagerie is Laura's life, then she gives herself away to Jim when she presents him the damaged unicorn as a "souvenir." Then Jim, followed by Tom, disappear out of her life. The final view that we have of Laura is as she is blowing out the candles in the living room--making herself disappear from view. Her menagerie broken and given away, Jim's affection revealed as nonexistent, and the support from her brother gone, there is nothing left for Laura but to blow out her candles and vanish herself.

A much more eccentric Laura is portrayed in "Portrait of a Girl in Glass." This Laura possesses a fearlessness quite opposite from her dramatized counterpart. She is not timid in the least. "Oh--you have freckles!" she has the nerve to exclaim to Jim. Then when he asks her to dance, it is quite clear that she is in love as she responds "breathlessly, smiling and smiling." As she slips "quite naturally into those huge arms of Jim's," Tom claims that "to say it was love is not too hasty a judgment." Yet it is impossible for the reader to forget that this is the same girl who was so incapable of interacting with any aspect of the outside world beyond her glass-fortified social cocoon. Laura's behavior in this episode appears totally out of character with what we have seen of her thus far. Who is this person?

Analysis continues by contrasting Laura's actions in the story.

If the glass menagerie was the manifestation of Laura's life in the play, then it is mirrored by the novel <u>Freckles</u> in the story. This is the book that Laura, alone in her room, would read over and over up to the point where the hero became romantically involved--then she would lose interest. But now she has found a real-life Freckles of her own, with whom she can live out the rest of the story. After Jim announces his engagement and leaves, it appears that her joy has been extinguished. It must not be forgotten, however, that this is the Laura who thinks that stars have five points, not the weak, predictable Laura of the play. To this Laura, she has just had a very pleasurable experience; the idea that she should feel hurt never crosses her simple mind. As Tom and Amanda sit down dazed, she is the first to speak. "Wasn't he nice? And all those freckles!" She displays no signs of a broken heart.

Tie-in with point made earlier in the essay, and continuation of analysis with new evidence.

When Amanda announces how peculiar it is that Tom didn't know that Jim was engaged, we see yet another puzzling side of Laura. She replies, "No, there's nothing peculiar about it. . . . People in love take everything for granted." Is she expressing a unique philosophical insight into the situation? Is she just speaking nonsense? As if to answer our question, Tom immediately comments, "What did she mean by that? I never knew." Just as a real cloud can obstruct this Laura's view of the sun, so does the cloud of her mental illness hide her from us.

"Portrait of a Girl in Glass" presents a bizarre Laura-- giddy woman-child, creative thinker, and eternal optimist--all at once. The Glass Menagerie, however, presents a much more consistent character. Here Laura is always wary and her actions are predictable. We can believe that it is these traits that Williams ultimately wanted in her character, as they are the ones that survived the transition between literary genres.

Concluding paragraph of comparison and contrast ends by restating thesis.

WRITING ABOUT THE CONTEXT OF LITERATURE

In addition to developing an idea by explication, analysis, or comparison and contrast — all methods primarily involving a close reading of the text — there are other ways to write about literature. The *context* of stories, poems, and plays is important to our understanding and appreciation of the text, as you have learned from reading the headnotes to each author's work in this anthology. The context of literature is usually defined as the biographical and historical background of the work. Literature does not exist in a vacuum. Created by a human being at some particular time in history, it is intended to speak to other human beings about ideas that have human relevance. Any critical method that clarifies the meaning and the pattern of literature is valuable, and often literary critics use more than one method in their approach to a text.

A paper on the context of literature is also an expository essay based on the development of a central idea or thesis statement. Usually this kind of critical essay develops the thesis of the paper by suggesting the connection of *cause and effect*. That is, you maintain that the story, poem, or play has characteristics that originate from causes or sources in the author's background — personal life, historical period, or literary influences. For example, you can use Kate Chopin's statement on her discovery of Maupassant's stories (on p. 740) to show something about her own method of writing short fiction. To establish this connection between the life and work of a writer, you could also analyze or explicate a Chopin story, or compare one of her stories with one of Maupassant's. The amount of time you spend on the context or the text of the story will depend on the emphasis you wish to make in your paper.

You have probably written papers about literature in a biographical context. A favorite high school term paper project is to assign an author to write about, requiring library research into his or her life or historical period. If you ever wrote this kind of a paper, you may have organized your material chronologically, tracing the life of your author and briefly describing his or her most important literary works, often with no clearly defined thesis in mind. In writing an essay based on a unified central idea, by contrast, you must ask yourself how knowing the facts of an author's life can help you to understand that author's story. You should never assume a connection between a writer's life and the literary work. A poem, play, or story can reflect the life of the man or woman who wrote it, but there are often disparities between the work and the realities of the life that are as important as the connections you can draw between them. If you plan to give a biographical analysis of Melville's "Bartleby, the Scrivener," for example, showing how it illustrates Melville's decision to stop earning his living as a writer, you must remember that he wrote the story in 1853, several years before he decided to give up writing fiction for a popular audience. In 1853, Bartleby's "I would prefer not to" was not yet Melville's conscious choice. This particular biographical reading of the story will not take you very far in your interpretation of its psychological, sociological, or philosophical complexities.

A biographical approach to literature requires at least as much care as textual criticism of the story — care in discovering and presenting the facts of an author's life and in using a sensitive interpretation of them to show relevant connections between a writer and a story. Writers often employ their own experience as the basis for literature. Richard Ellmann's biographical perspective on James Joyce's "The Dead" in the Commentaries section of Part One (p. 746) is a masterful example of the application of this particular critical strategy.

You will usually be proceeding on firmer ground when you combine biographical facts with a discussion of an author's thematic or aesthetic intentions and then relate this material to specific stories, poems, or plays. Here, again, be cautious. Statements by writers about how and why they created short stories are not necessarily the same as what a given story may show. Use your judgment carefully. Poe wrote model stories based on his theory of the "single effect," but Anton Chekhov did not always follow his own advice about how to write fiction. In "The Lady with the Pet Dog" (p. 145) he wrote beautifully about the physical setting of Yalta, instead of restricting himself to the barest description, as he advised another writer to do in his letters (p. 738).

The contexts supplied by the writers themselves in the Commentaries sections included in this anthology are meant to stimulate ideas for your essays. They give the historical and biographical backgrounds of the works. These excerpts can furnish a perspective from which you may view the individual stories, poems, and plays, as did the students who used the quotations of Melville and Poe in two of the sample essays here. Or you can write about the Commentaries as a subject in themselves, part of the wider context of literature. You can report on the entire books they came from (Frank O'Connor's study of the short story form, for example, or Eudora Welty's *The Eye of the Story*) if these books are available in your college library.

Other Perspectives

Material from other classes can also be used in papers about literature. If you major in history or psychology, for example, you can investigate the way stories, poems, or plays are sometimes read to give valuable historical or psychological information about the world they describe. You are not limited to writing about remote times when considering essays that take this approach. Joyce Carol Oates's story "Where Are You Going, Where Have You Been?" is about modern teenage life. A paper about it could investigate the connection between Oates's fantasy and psychological theories about adolescence in contemporary America. Characters in literature are often used in psychological and sociological textbooks to illustrate pathological symptoms or complexes. Sociology textbooks, for example, cite Oates's fictional characters as representing current tendencies toward *anomie*, a condition in which normative standards of conduct have weakened or disappeared. It is possible in writing about literature to illustrate philosophical, historical, sociological, or psychological material you are familiar with through your work in other college courses.

Finally, you can argue a particular ideological point of view in writing about literature. Different approaches can help you to think critically about literature. If you look up critical articles in the Commentaries sections of this anthology or in your college library, you will find that academic critics usually write about literature using a particular strategy. The more traditional approaches before 1970 tended to be formalist or biographical and historical (and occasionally Marxist). In the past twenty years more innovative contemporary theory has been developed by feminist, gender, reader-response, and deconstructionist critics, among others.

At times the background of the author can suggest an ideological approach: Richard Wright was a communist, Tillie Olsen is a feminist, Flannery O'Connor was a Catholic, and so forth. At other times an ideology held by the student but not necessarily by the author can lead to a fresh reading of a story. Depending on what you as a reader bring to "The Metamorphosis," for example, there is a "Freudian Kafka, an existentialist Kafka, a Catholic Kafka, a Marxist Kafka, a Zionist Kafka," and so forth, as suggested by the critic Hans Eichner.

Proceed with your literary analysis according to your ideology with great care, realizing that you might become insensitive to nuances of meaning other than those you are predisposed to find in a doctrinaire interpretation of the text. (The Commentaries sections and Casebooks in this anthology include examples of different critical approaches, including deconstructionist, rhetorical, biographical, feminist, psychoanalytic, and New Historicist.) At the same time an ideological approach can illuminate aspects of literature that are particularly valid and relevant for contemporary readers. A feminist interpretation of "Young Goodman Brown," for example, must not take the story literally, because Hawthorne wrote it as a moral allegory, but a feminist could use the story to argue provocatively about implied sexual stereotyping in Hawthorne's characterization of women. As the following student essay on Hawthorne's story demonstrates, a feminist perspective can illuminate how a critic can use fiction to examine and critique gender stereotypes embedded in American culture.

SAMPLE ANALYSIS FROM A FEMINIST PERSPECTIVE

Woman as Victim in "Young Goodman Brown"

A feminist reader can accuse Hawthorne of portraying his female characters not as powerful individuals but rather as gullible victims. In "Young Goodman Brown," the women characters are clearly powerless to prevent the eventual destruction of the protagonist, Goodman Brown.

Introduction to thesis statement.

While Hawthorne never intended any of the characters in his moral allegory to be read realistically (their names clearly indicate that they function on an abstract, symbolic level of meaning in the story), his attitude toward women as weak and pitiful creatures is apparent in every scene in which they appear. In the exposition of the story, Goodman Brown is kissing his Faith good-bye. It is no coincidence that he then begins his journey to the forest, where he loses his faith in humankind. Faith is described as sweet and pretty. The pinkness of her cap ribbons blatantly advertises her youth and innocence. When she pleads with her husband to remain home with her, he speaks to her as if she were a small child and bids her say her bedtime prayers. Then, to add insult to injury, Hawthorne describes her as "peeping" (not looking) after him with a dependent, "melancholy air," as if she were incapable of spending a night alone. This marriage is plainly not one of equals. Goodman Brown seems more like a father than like a newlywed husband in this scene. "Poor little Faith!" he thinks, the diminutive "little" emphasizing his attitude that a wife is someone to be looked after, not listened to.

Narrow thesis.

Begin analysis.

Quote and interpretation.

Even when "sweet" Faith is surrounded by the unholy coven later in the story, she is not portrayed as being evil. She utters lamentations "with an uncertain sorrow." Has this married woman no mind of her own? Doesn't she, like her husband, have to agree to come to this meeting on her own? Instead, she is portrayed as an innocent victim, which makes sense on an allegorical level, but hardly does credit to women in general.

Repetition of central idea.

Finally, at the end of the story, when Goodman Brown   *More evidence.*
is busy living out his life in gloomy thought, Faith's happy nature has absolutely no power to combat his cynicism. How
could she be hapy to live the rest of her life with such a man?
Hawthorne never explained how Faith reacted to her husband's changed outlook after his night in the forest. Are we to
believe that she merely accepted his change, docile as ever?

     Two other women appear in the story--Goody Cloyse   *Analysis of minor*
and Goodman Brown's mother--but neither is portrayed as   *characters.*
powerful or worthy of more than brief consideration. Goody
Cloyse was shown to be so frail that she has to enlist the help
of a male (the devil) to get to the meeting. Goodman Brown's
mother, who "threw out her hand to warn him back" at the
witches' coven, has no more power over him than poor little
Faith. These three women nourish the brief portion of this   *Conclusion.*
earthly life that Goodman Brown enjoyed, but are unable to
save his blind masculine soul in the end. Taking the longer
view, who were the true victims--the women in the story or
Goodman Brown?

     A feminist approach can produce an insightful reading of a Hawthorne
story. Arguments about the interpretation of literature are acceptable as long
as they are supported by evidence from the text. Writers do not intend their
readers to worship literature. Take courage, and try to express your own point
of view. In the Commentaries section of Part One, Leo Tolstoy's attempt to
read his own philosophy into Anton Chekhov's "The Darling" (p. 801) is an
example of an iconoclastic but well-presented interpretation of a great short
story. Literary critics and scholars are revising the canon of accepted masterpieces as changes in society and the influence of new critical theory alter our
expectations of what we look for in literature. Interpretations of great works
change, as we enlarge and redefine the canon to reflect our hopes for a changing society and a more enlightened community of readers.

     You misread literature if you think of it as absolute, perfect, final state-
ments far removed from the commonplaces of life. It needs the reader's involvement to come alive. Through their aesthetic patterns, stories, poems, and
plays show us what life is like. What they are ultimately saying, in their affirmation of life and human creativity, is — in the words of Henry James —
"Live! Live!"

SOME COMMON PROBLEMS IN WRITING ABOUT LITERATURE

Interpret, don't summarize. Summarizing the contents of a story, poem, or play in an essay is not the same as giving insights into the work's pattern and meaning. Occasionally you can summarize the plot in a sentence if you are making a transition from one part of your paper to another, but keep in mind that the reader of your paper is usually your teacher, who has already read the work and will get the impression that you do not know much about what you are doing if you merely summarize it.

Write about how you read the story, poem, or play. Try to express your own ideas through the text. If you find yourself summarizing it in more than a couple of sentences, it is probably because you did not organize your essay around a strong thesis. Your impressions and ideas are the measure of your encounter with literature. Writing encourages your clarification of these ideas. Be sure to state your central idea in a sentence in your paper. It does not matter where it appears, although if you include it in your opening paragraph it will help you keep to the point in your discussion.

Avoid long personal anecdotes. Writing on the basis of your personal experience can result in a fine memoir, but such an essay is usually not about the literature you were asked to discuss. You may want to introduce an analysis of D. H. Lawrence's "The Rocking-Horse Winner" with a short anecdote about a relevant experience you had as a child with a rocking horse, but make sure your anecdote goes on for only a few sentences before you connect it explicitly with your central idea about Lawrence's story.

Use the text to check your interpretation. Opinions about literature can be wrong. Do not insist on ideas that will not fit the details of the work. You may stumble on a central idea for your paper with an intuitive leap or a hunch about the story's meaning, but be sure the specific details of the story support your interpretation. The student who had an intuition that Goodman Brown was being tricked by the devil in the scene with the pink ribbon went back to Hawthorne's words for evidence to support his theory (see p. 2097). You may decide that Hawthorne's story is a heavily veiled nineteenth-century treatment of a wife's infidelity and her husband's resulting nervous breakdown, but can you prove it by quoting from the text? "Whatever I discover in the work is right for me," you may say, but that will not take you very far when writing a paper for an English class. Works of literature are tough, tangible constructions of language, not shifting tea leaves in the bottom of an empty cup into which you can project whatever meaning you like.

Make good use of quotations. You must quote from the text to give evidence of your interpretation. Usually a sentence should introduce and follow each quotation, linking it to the idea being developed in your paper. In the comparison-and-contrast essay on page 2104, for example, the student discussed the opening sentences of the Hawthorne and Poe tales to make a point about the differences. Each time he quoted, he introduced the quotation and followed it by a comment of his own to explain how the quotation related to his main idea. Never drop quotations into the body of your essay without a comment.

Be careful not to quote too much. Use only those passages that are relevant to your discussion. Overquoting can weaken an essay, easily turning it into a string of short quotations choppily connected by a few insufficient words from you. Be sure to make it clear to the reader why the passage you are quoting is important.

When the quotation is short (four lines or less), it should be enclosed in quotation marks and included within the regular text, as you have seen in the sample essays. When typing a quotation longer than four lines, separate it from the preceding typewritten line with double space. Then indent ten spaces, *omit quotation marks,* and type with a double spacing (unless your instructor tells you differently). If you had a reason to include the opening paragraph of "Young Goodman Brown" in your essay, for example, you would indent it like this:

> Young Goodman Brown came forth at sunset into the street at Salem
> village; but put his head back, after crossing the threshold, to exchange
> a parting kiss with his young wife. And Faith, as the wife was aptly
> named, thrust her own pretty head into the street, letting the wind
> play with the pink ribbons of her cap while she called to Goodman
> Brown.

In a shorter passage in which you use a quotation within a quotation, such as a line of dialogue inside an excerpt from a story, use double and single quotation marks: "The echoes of the forest mocked him, crying, 'Faith! Faith!' as if bewildered wretches were seeking her all through the wilderness."

If you wish to leave out words in a quoted passage, use ellipsis points, that is, three periods (or four periods if the omitted material includes the end of a sentence): "And Faith . . . thrust her own pretty head into the street. . . ."

Always quote the exact wording, punctuation, and capitalization of the original text. If you underline words in a quotation for emphasis, say that you have done so, as the writer of "The Devil's Tricks in 'Young Goodman Brown' " did in his explication of Hawthorne's text (see p. 2097).

If you find an error, for example a misspelled word in a quotation, indicate that the error is in the original by inserting *sic,* a Latin word meaning "thus," in brackets after the error itself.

Last but not least, punctuate sentences that appear in quotation marks correctly. Commas and periods always belong *inside* the quotation marks, whether or not they appeared in the original text. Semicolons, question marks, colons, and exclamation points, however, belong *outside* the quotation marks, unless they are part of the quoted material.

Avoid plagiarism.　Any material you borrow from other sources and include in your paper must be documented. If you present someone else's material (other than factual information) as if it were your own, you may be open to the charge of plagiarism. Even with factual information, if you use the exact wording of a source, you must indicate that it is a quotation. To be on the safe side, it is always better to footnote your original source, or give credit by working into your essay the name of the author and the title of the work in which you found the material you cited.

The one exception of this principle is information that is considered *common knowledge*. Common knowledge is material that is repeated in a number of sources, so that it is difficult to tell what the original source might have been. Such items as the basic biographical facts about an author or information about the publication of literary works do not need footnoting, unless you quote someone's exact words at length in your essay.

Know when and how to document the sources in your bibliography. Include the name of the author and the page number in a parenthetical citation or in the text itself:

> In Richard J. Jacobson's study, we learn that Hawthorne feared the
> artist might become "insulated from the common business of life" (27).

If you cite from more than one book by an author, mention the title in the text or include a shortened form of the title in the citation:

> We learn that Hawthorne feared the artist might become "insulated
> from the common business of life" (Jacobson, Hawthorne's Conception
> 27).

If your instructor asks you to use footnotes or endnotes, instead of parenthetical citation, you may place notes at the bottom of the page on which the reference appears, or they may be gathered together on a separate *notes* page at the end of your essay. When you footnote a source, indent the first line of each footnote five spaces before listing the author's first and last name; the title of the book; the city of publication, publisher, and date in parentheses; and the page number cited:

> [1] Richard J. Jacobson, Hawthorne's Conception of the Creative Process
> (Cambridge, MA: Harvard UP, 1965) 27.

Instructions for basic documentation form for different sources — books, magazines, encyclopedias, and so on — appear in every handbook and guide to writing college papers. They may also be found in various manuals of style and style sheets that should be available in the reference section of your college library.

GUIDELINES: HOW TO WRITE AN ESSAY ABOUT LITERATURE

1. DO NOT WAIT UNTIL THE LAST MINUTE TO START. Allow plenty of time to write and revise.

2. BE SURE YOU HAVE A CLEAR IDEA OF WHAT YOU WANT TO SAY ABOUT THE WORK. Can you state this idea as a sharply focused thesis sentence? Remember that all expository writing serves to clarify, set forth, or explain in detail an idea about a topic.

3. READ THE WORK OVER AGAIN. Check the notes in your journal and take notes that will help you amplify your central idea. If necessary, try to generate ideas by brainstorming, freewriting, listing, and asking questions. It might help at this point to assemble a short outline, to stake out the ground you intend your essay to cover. Look for an approach that is distinctive enough to be worth your time and effort yet manageable enough to be handled in a paper of the length you are assigned.

4. DECIDE HOW YOU WANT TO PROCEED TO DEVELOP YOUR THESIS. Will you use explication, analysis, or comparison and contrast? Is it appropriate to show a cause in an author's life or times and its effect on the work? If you have notes from your reading or research, assemble and number them in the order you intend to use them to develop your central idea.

5. WRITE A ROUGH DRAFT OF YOUR ESSAY. Be sure to state your central idea as a thesis sentence somewhere — preferably at the beginning of your essay. If you are using an outline, try to follow it, but allow yourself the possibility of discovering something new that you did not know you had to say while you are writing. If you have taken notes or jotted down quotations from your reading, try to introduce such material smoothly into your discussion. Remember that the heart of literary criticism is good quotation. Brief, accurate examples from the text that illustrate the points you are trying to make about your thesis are essential in writing about literature.

6. ALLOW SOME TIME TO PASS BEFORE YOU LOOK OVER YOUR ROUGH DRAFT — AT LEAST A DAY. THEN MAKE AT LEAST ONE THOROUGH REVISION BEFORE YOU COPY OR TYPE A FINISHED DRAFT OF YOUR PAPER. Some students find they need several revisions before they are satisfied with what they have written. When you review your rough draft, concentrate and read critically. Remember that the Russian writer Isaac Babel would sometimes write a hundred drafts of a story before he was satisfied. Let your words stimulate a flow of ideas about your topic; this will lead you to find more ways to illustrate your thesis or develop your train of thought. Fill out paragraphs that seem thin. Be sure transitions between paragraphs are smooth and quotations are integrated into the discussion. If you sense that your sentences are wordy, try to be more concise. Eliminate repetition. Be sure your general organization is coherent and your discussion proceeds in a clear, logical order.

7. CHECK OVER YOUR PAPER ONE LAST TIME. Make sure you have always used complete sentences and correct spelling and punctuation. Avoid sentence fragments and exclamation points, unless they are part of a quotation.

8. TYPE THE PAPER OR WRITE IT NEATLY IN ITS FINAL FORM. If your instructor requires some particular style for class papers, such as extra-wide margins or triple spacing, follow those instructions. Use 8½-by-11-inch paper. Type if you can, double spacing between lines. If you write by hand, use ink and write on only one side of each piece of paper. Leave generous margins at the top, bottom, and sides. Number the pages, beginning with the number 2 (not the word *two*) in the upper-right-hand corner of the second page. (Your title on the first page will indicate that it is the first page.) Clip and staple your pages together in the upper-left-hand corner. Be sure your name, your instructor's name, your class and section number, and the date appear on your paper.

9. READ YOUR ESSAY OVER ONE LAST TIME FOR TYPOGRAPHICAL ERRORS. Make legible corrections in ink. Have you put quotation marks around titles of short stories ("A Rose for Emily") and underlined the titles of books (Collected Stories of William Faulkner)? Have you placed commas and periods *within* quotation marks in the titles and quotations that appear in your essay? Have you inadvertently left out any words or sentences when you went from the rough draft to the final version of your essay?

10. FINALLY, MAKE A COPY OF YOUR PAPER. If you have typed the paper, make a photocopy of it before handing it in; if you wrote it on a computer, be sure to save a copy of it on disk. It is a good idea to save your notes and rough drafts as well, in case the accuracy of a quotation or the originality of your work is called into question.

What do you do after you hand in your paper? You have probably spent so much time on it — thinking, organizing, writing, and rewriting — that you feel you may never want to read it again. The act of writing the essay will have clarified your thinking and brought you closer to the literary work, so you carry with you the intangible benefit of something learned in the writing process. Returning to your essay in the future might have one final benefit: Your paper will refresh your memory, reminding you of what you did not know you knew, about both yourself and literature.

Acknowledgments (continued from p. iv)

James Baldwin. "Sonny's Blues" from *Going to Meet the Man* (New York: Dial Press, 1957). Originally published in *The Partisan Review*. Copyright © 1957 and renewed 1985 by James Baldwin. Reprinted with the permission of The James Baldwin Estate.

Toni Cade Bambara. "The Lesson" from *Gorilla, My Love*. Copyright © 1972 by Toni Cade Bambara. Reprinted with the permission of Random House, Inc.

Jorge Luis Borges. "Everything and Nothing," translated by Mildred Boyer and Howard Morland, from *Dreamtigers*. Copyright © 1964 and renewed 1992 by Howard Morland and Mildred Boyer. Reprinted with the permission of the University of Texas Press.

Raymond Carver. "Cathedral" from *Cathedral*. Copyright © 1983 by Raymond Carver. Reprinted with the permission of Alfred A. Knopf, Inc. "Errand" from *Where I'm Calling From: New and Selected Stories* (Boston: Atlantic Monthly Press, 1988). Copyright © 1986, 1987, 1988 by Tess Gallagher. Reprinted with the permission of International Creative Management. "What We Talk About When We Talk About Love" from *What We Talk About When We Talk About Love*. Copyright © 1983 by Raymond Carver. Reprinted with the permission of Alfred A. Knopf, Inc.

John Cheever. "The Swimmer" from *The Stories of John Cheever*. Originally in *The New Yorker* (July 15, 1964). Copyright © 1964 by John Cheever. Reprinted with the permission of Alfred A. Knopf, Inc.

Anton Chekhov. "The Lady with the Pet Dog" from *The Portable Chekhov*, edited and translated by Avrahm Yarmolinsky. Copyright 1947, © 1968 by The Viking Press, Inc. Copyright © 1975 by Avrahm Yarmolinsky. Reprinted with the permission of Viking Penguin, a division of Penguin Books USA Inc.

Sandra Cisneros. "The House on Mango Street," "Hairs," "My Name," "The Monkey Garden," and "Mango Says Goodbye Sometimes" from *The House on Mango Street* (New York: Alfred A. Knopf, 1984). Originally published in *The Village Voice Literary Supplement*. Copyright © 1984 by Sandra Cisneros. Reprinted with the permission of Susan Bergholz Literary Services, New York.

Ralph Ellison. "Battle Royal" from *Invisible Man*. Copyright 1948 by Ralph Ellison. Reprinted with the permission of Random House, Inc.

Louise Erdrich. "The Red Convertible" from *Love Medicine, New and Expanded Version*. Copyright © 1984, 1993 by Louise Erdrich. Reprinted with the permission of Henry Holt and Company, Inc.

William Faulkner. "A Rose for Emily" and "That Evening Sun" from *Collected Stories of William Faulkner*. Copyright 1930, 1931 and renewed © 1958, 1959 by William Faulkner. Reprinted with the permission of Random House, Inc.

Gabriel García Márquez. "A Very Old Man with Enormous Wings," translated by Gregory Rabassa, from *Leaf Storm and Other Stories*. Copyright © 1971 by Gabriel García Márquez. Reprinted with the permission of HarperCollins Publishers, Inc.

Susan Glaspell. "A Jury of Her Peers" from *Everyweek* (March 5, 1917). Copyright 1917 by Susan Glaspell. Reprinted with the permission of the Estate of Susan Glaspell.

Nadine Gordimer. "The Kindest Thing to Do" from *The Soft Voice of the Serpent* (New York: Penguin Books, 1962). Copyright 1952 and renewed © 1980 by Nadine Gordimer. Reprinted with the permission of Russell and Volkening, Inc.

Bessie Head. "Looking for a Rain God" from *The Collector of Treasures* (London: Wm. Heinemann, 1977). Copyright © 1977 by the Estate of Bessie Head. Reprinted with the permission of John Johnson, Authors' Agent, Ltd. and William Heinemann, Ltd.

Ernest Hemingway. "Hills Like White Elephants" from *The Short Stories of Ernest Hemingway*. Copyright 1927 by Charles Scribner's Sons, renewed © 1955 by Ernest Hemingway. Reprinted with the permission of Scribner, a division of Simon & Schuster, Inc.

Zora Neale Hurston. "Sweat" from *Spunk: The Selected Stories* (Berkeley: Turtle Island Foundation, 1985). First published in 1926 as part of "The Eatonville Anthology." Copyright 1926 by Zora Neale Hurston. Reprinted with the permission of Lucy Hurston.

Shirley Jackson. "The Lottery" from *The Lottery and Other Stories*. Copyright 1948, 1949 by Shirley Jackson, renewed © 1976, 1977 by Lawrence Hyman, Barry Hyman, Mrs. Sarah Webster, and Mrs. Joanne Schnurer. Reprinted with the permission of Farrar, Straus & Giroux, Inc.

Charles Johnson. "Menagerie, A Child's Fable" from *The Sorcerer's Apprentice* (New York: Atheneum Publishers, 1986). Originally published in *Indiana Review* (1984). Copyright © 1984 by Charles Johnson. Reprinted with the permission of Scribner, a division of Simon & Schuster, Inc.

Franz Kafka. "The Metamorphosis," translated by Willa and Edwin Muir, from *Franz Kafka: The Complete Stories*, edited by Nahum N. Glatzer. Copyright 1948 by Schocken Books, Inc. Reprinted with the permission of Schocken Books, published by Pantheon Books, a division of Random House, Inc.

Jamaica Kincaid. "Girl" from *At the Bottom of the River*. Copyright © 1978, 1983 by Jamaica Kincaid. Reprinted with the permission of Farrar, Straus & Giroux, Inc.

D. H. Lawrence. "The Rocking-Horse Winner" and "Odour of Chrysanthemums" from *Complete Short Stories of D. H. Lawrence*. Copyright 1922 by Thomas B. Seltzer, Inc., renewed 1950 by Frieda Lawrence. Reprinted with the permission of Viking Penguin, a division of Penguin Books USA Inc.

Clarice Lispector. "The Smallest Woman in the World," translated by Elizabeth Bishop, from *Family Ties*. Copyright © 1960 by Elizabeth Bishop. Reprinted with the permission of the Estate of Elizabeth Bishop and Farrar, Straus & Giroux, Inc.

Katherine Mansfield. "Miss Brill" from *The Short Stories of Katherine Mansfield*. Originally collected in *The Garden Party* (New York: The Modern Library, 1922). Copyright 1922 by Alfred A. Knopf, Inc., renewed 1950 by John Middleton Murray. Reprinted with the permission of the publisher.

Guy de Maupassant. "The Necklace," translated by Marjorie Laurie from *Short Stories of Guy de Maupassant* (New York: E. P. Dutton, 1934). Reprinted with the permission of Everyman's Library/David Campbell Publishers.

Lorrie Moore. "How to Become a Writer" from *Self-Help*. Copyright © 1985 by M. L. Moore. Reprinted with the permission of Alfred A. Knopf, Inc.

Bharati Mukherjee. "A Father" from *Darkness*. Copyright © 1985 by Bharati Mukherjee. Reprinted with the permission of Janklow & Nesbitt Associates and Penguin Books Canada Limited.

Alice Munro. "Walker Brothers Cowboy" from *Dance of the Happy Shades*. Copyright © 1968 by Alice Munro. Reprinted with the permission of the Virginia Barber Literary Agency, Inc. and McGraw-Hill Ryerson, Ltd.

Joyce Carol Oates. "Heat" from the *Paris Review* (1991). Copyright © 1988 by The Ontario Review, Inc. "Where Are You Going, Where Have You Been?" from *The Wheel of Love and Other Stories* (New York: Vanguard, 1970). Copyright © 1970 by Joyce Carol Oates. Both reprinted with the permission of John Hawkins Associates, Inc.

Tim O'Brien. "The Things They Carried" from *The Things They Carried*. Originally published in *Esquire* (August 1986). Copyright © 1989 by Tim O'Brien. Reprinted with the permission of Houghton Mifflin Company.

FICTION COMMENTARIES

POETRY

Anna Akhmatova. "Instead of a Preface" and "Dedication," translated by Richard McKane, from *Selected Poems.* Copyright © 1967 by Richard McKane. Reprinted with the permission of Bloodaxe Books Ltd.

W. H. Auden. "Miss Gee," "Musée des Beaux Arts," and "In Memory of W. B. Yeats" from *W. H. Auden: Collected Poems,* edited by Edward Mendelson. Copyright 1940, 1941, 1951, 1952 and renewed © 1968, 1969 by W. H. Auden. Copyright © 1976 by Edward Mendelson, William Meredith, and Monroe K. Spears. Reprinted with the permission of Random House, Inc.

Bashō. "Ripening barley —," "Day by Day," and "Having no talent," translated by Etsuko Terasaki, from the Twenty-third Day of *The Saga Diary* from "The Saga Diary of Matsuo Bashō: Introduction and Translation" in *Literature East and West* 15–16 (1971). Copyright © 1971 by Etsuko Terasaki. Reprinted with the permission of the translator.

John Berryman. "A Professor's Song" from *John Berryman Collected Poems, 1937–1971,* edited by Charles Thornbury. Copyright © 1989 by Kate Donahue Berryman. Reprinted with the permission of the author.

Elizabeth Bishop. "One Art," "The Bight (On My Birthday)," "Sestina," "The Fish," and "The Armadillo" from *The Complete Poems 1927–1979.* Copyright © 1979, 1983 by Alice Helen Methfessel. Reprinted with the permission of Farrar, Straus & Giroux, Inc.

Robert Bly. "The Dead Seal near McClure's Beach" from *What Have I Ever Lost by Dying.* Copyright © 1992 by Robert Bly. Reprinted with the permission of HarperCollins Publishers, Inc.

Louise Bogan. "Song for the Last Act" (excerpt) from *The Blue Estuaries: Poems 1923–1968.* Copyright © 1968 by Louise Bogan. Reprinted with the permission of Farrar, Straus & Giroux, Inc.

Gwendolyn Brooks. "We Real Cool" and "The Mother" from *Blacks* (Chicago, Ill: Third World Press, 1987). Copyright © 1987 by Gwendolyn Brooks Blakely. Reprinted with the permission of the author.

Sterling A. Brown. "He Was a Man" from *The Collected Poems of Sterling A. Brown,* edited by Michael S. Harper. Copyright © 1980 by Sterling A. Brown. Reprinted with the permission of HarperCollins Publishers, Inc.

Lorna Dee Cervantes. "Poem for the Young White Man Who Asked Me How I, an Intelligent, Well-Read Person Could Believe in the War between the Races" from *Emplumada.* Copyright © 1981 by Lorna Dee Cervantes. Reprinted with the permission of University of Pittsburgh Press.

Marilyn Chin. "How I Got That Name" and "Elegy for Chloe Nguyen" from *The Phoenix Gone, The Terrace Empty.* Copyright © 1994 by Marilyn Chin. Reprinted with the permission of Milkweed Editions.

A. Cinna. "Did Ophelia ask Hamlet to bed?" from *The Penguin Book of Limericks* (New York: Viking Penguin, 1983). Reprinted by permission.

Amy Clampitt. "Fog," "The Dakota," and "The Outer Bar" from *The Kingfisher.* Copyright © 1983 by Amy Clampitt. Reprinted with the permission of Alfred A. Knopf, Inc.

Lucille Clifton. "The thirty eighth year" from *good woman: poems and a memoir 1969–1980.* Copyright © 1987 by Lucille Clifton. "Reply" from *quilting: poems 1987–1990.* Copyright © 1991 by Lucille Clifton. Both reprinted with the permission of BOA Editions, Ltd., 260 East Avenue, Rochester, NY 14604.

Countee Cullen. "Yet Do I Marvel" from *Color.* Copyright 1925 by Harper & Brothers, renewed 1953 by Ida M. Cullen. Reprinted with the permission of GRM Associates, Inc. as agents for the Estate of Ida M. Cullen.

E. E. Cummings. "when god lets my body be," "goodby Betty," "since feeling is first," "somewhere i have never travelled," "Buffalo Bill's," "if there are any heavens" and "In Just-" from *Complete Poems 1904–1962,* edited by George J. Firmage. Copyright 1923, 1925, 1926, 1931, 1935, 1938, 1939, 1940, 1944, 1945, 1946, 1947, 1948, 1949, 1950, 1951, 1952, 1953, 1954, © 1955, 1956, 1957, 1958, 1959, 1960, 1961, 1962, 1963, 1966, 1967, 1968, 1972, 1973, 1973, 1975, 1976, 1977, 1978, 1979, 1980, 1981, 1982, 1983, 1984, 1985, 1986, 1987, 1988, 1989, 1990, 1991 by the Trustees for the E. E. Cummings Trust. Copyright © 1973, 1976, 1978, 1979, 1981, 1983, 1985, 1991 by George James Firmage. Reprinted with the permission of Liveright Publishing Corporation.

H.D. (Hilda Doolittle). "Mid-day," "Oread," "Orchard," and "May 1943" (Part IV only) from *Collected Poems 1912–1944,* edited by Louis L. Martz. Copyright © 1983 by the Estate of Hilda Doolittle. Reprinted with the permission of New Directions Publishing Corporation.

Emily Dickinson. #199/"I'm 'wife' — I've finished that —," #214/"I taste a liquor never brewed —," #224/"I've nothing else — to bring, You know —," #249/"Wild Nights — Wild Nights!," #254/"'Hope' is the thing with feathers," #258/"There's a certain Slant of light," #288/"I'm Nobody! Who are you?," #341/"After great pain, a formal feeling comes," #435/"Much Madness is divinest Sense," #449/"I died for Beauty — but was scarce," #453/"Love — thou are high —," #465/"I heard a Fly buzz — when I died," #511/"If you were coming in the Fall," #528/"Mine — by the right of the White Election!," #712/"Because I could not stop for Death," #827/"The Only News I know," #861/"Split the Lark — and you'll find the Music —," #875/"I stepped from Plank to Plank," #986/"A narrow Fellow in the Grass," and #1052/"I never saw a Moor —" from *The Complete Poems of Emily Dickinson,* edited by Thomas H. Johnson. Copyright 1929, 1935 by Martha Dickinson Bianchi, renewed © 1957, 1963 by Mary L. Hampson. Reprinted with the permission of The Belknap Press of Harvard University Press, Little, Brown and Company.

Rita Dove. "Wiring Home" from *Mother Love.* Copyright © 1995 by Rita Dove. Reprinted with the permission of the author and W. W. Norton & Company, Inc. "Belinda's Petition" from *Selected Poems* (New York: Pantheon Books, 1993). Copyright © 1980, 1983 by Rita Dove. Reprinted with the permission of the author. "Weathering Out" and "Daystar" from *Thomas and Beulah* (Pittsburgh: Carnegie-Mellon University Press, 1987). Copyright © 1987 by Rita Dove. Reprinted with the permission of the author.

Robert Duncan. "Song (How in the dark the cows lie down)" from *The Years as Catches* (Berkeley: Oyez, 1966). Copyright © 1966 by Robert Duncan. Reprinted by permission. "My Mother Would Be a Falconress" from *Bending the Bow.* Copyright © 1966 by Robert Duncan. Originally published in the *Paris Review.* Reprinted with the permission of New Directions Publishing Corporation.

T. S. Eliot. "Journey of the Magi" (excerpt) from *T. S. Eliot: The Complete Poems and Plays 1909–1950.* Copyright 1936 Harcourt Brace & World, renewed © 1964, 1963 by T. S. Eliot. Reprinted with the permission of Harcourt Brace & Company and Faber and Faber, Ltd. "The Love Song of J. Alfred Prufrock" from *T. S. Eliot: The Complete Poems and Plays 1909–1950.* Copyright 1917 by T. S. Eliot. Reprinted with the permission of Faber and Faber, Ltd.

Louise Erdrich. "Indian Boarding School: The Runaways" from *Jacklight.* Copyright © 1984 by Louise Erdrich. Reprinted with the permission of Henry Holt and Company, Inc.

Lawrence Ferlinghetti. "Constantly Risking Absurdity," "In Goya's greatest scenes we seem to see," and "Dog" from *A Coney Island of the Mind.* Copyright © 1958 by Lawrence Ferlinghetti. "Two Scavengers in a Truck, Two Beautiful People in a Mercedes" from *Landscapes of Living and Dying.* Copyright © 1979 by Lawrence Ferlinghetti. "Late Impressionist Dream" from *European Poems & Transitions.* Copyright © 1982 by Lawrence Ferlinghetti. All reprinted with the permission of New Directions Publishing Corporation.

Carolyn Forché. "The Colonel" from *The Country Between Us.* Copyright © 1981 by Carolyn Forché. Reprinted with the permission of HarperCollins Publishers, Inc.

Robert Frost. Two line poem ("No tears in the writer, . . . ") from the Introduction to *Collected Poems.* Copyright 1939 by Robert Frost. "The Pasture," "Mending Wall," "The Death of the Hired Man," "The Hill Wife," "Birches," "Fire and

Pat Mora. "Border Town: 1938" from *Borders*. Copyright © 1986 by Pat Mora. Reprinted with the permission of Arte Publico Press, University of Houston.

Ogden Nash. "Reflection on Ice-Breaking" and "A jolly young fellow from Yuma" from *Verses from 1929 On*. Copyright 1936 and renewed © 1964 by Ogden Nash. Reprinted with the permission of Little, Brown and Company.

Sharon Olds. "The Elder Sister" from *The Dead and the Living*. Copyright © 1983 by Sharon Olds. Reprinted with the permission of Alfred A. Knopf, Inc. "Summer Solstice, New York City" from *The Gold Cell*. Copyright © 1987 by Sharon Olds. Both reprinted with the permission of Alfred A. Knopf, Inc.

Charles Olson. "I, Maximus of Gloucester" (excerpt) from *Collected Poetry of Charles Olson*, translated and edited by George Butterick. Copyright © 1987 by University of Connecticut. Reprinted with the permission of University of California Press.

Marge Piercy. "The woman in the ordinary" from *Circles on the Water*. Copyright © 1973 by Marge Piercy. "Putting the good things away" from *My Mother's Body*. Copyright © 1985 by Marge Piercy. Both reprinted with the permission of Alfred A. Knopf, Inc.

Sylvia Plath. "A Winter's Tale" and "Ella Mason and Her Eleven Cats" from *The Collected Poems of Sylvia Plath*. "A Winter's Tale" originally published in *The New Yorker*. Copyright © 1957, 1959 by Ted Hughes. "Black Rook in Rainy Weather" and "Mirror" from *Crossing the Water*. Copyright © 1960, 1963 by Ted Hughes. "Morning Song," "The Bee Meeting," "The Applicant," "Daddy," "Lady Lazarus," "Words," and "Edge" from *Ariel*. Copyright © 1961, 1963, 1966 by Ted Hughes. All reprinted with the permission of HarperCollins Publishers, Inc. and Faber and Faber, Ltd.

Ezra Pound. "A Pact," "The River-Merchant's Wife: A Letter," and "Hugh Selwyn Mauberley: Life and Contacts" (Parts I–IV only) from *Personae*. Copyright 1926 by Ezra Pound. Reprinted with the permission of New Directions Publishing Corporation.

Frank Richards. "Ronald Reagan screamed out in dismay" as found in E. O. Parrett, ed., *The Penguin Book of Limericks* (New York: Viking Penguin, 1983). Reprinted with the permission of the author.

Judith Rodriguez. "Eskimo Occasion" from *Water Life*. Copyright © 1976 by Judith Rodriguez. Reprinted with the permission of the University of Queensland Press.

Theodore Roethke. "The Waking," "Big Wind," "Elegy for Jane," and "My Papa's Waltz" from *The Collected Poems of Theodore Roethke*. Copyright 1942 by Hearst Magazines, Inc. Copyright 1947 by The United Chapters of Phi Beta Kappa. Copyright 1950, 1953 by Theodore Roethke. Reprinted with the permission of Doubleday, a division of Bantam Doubleday Dell Publishing Group, Inc.

Tadeusz Rozewicz. "Pigtail," translated by Adam Czerniawski, from *They Came to See a Poet*. Copyright © 1976 by Princeton University Press. "What Happens," translated by Robert A. Maguire and Magnus Jan Krynski, from *The Survivor and Other Poems*. Copyright © 1991 by Anvil Poetry Press. Both reprinted with the permission of Princeton University Press.

Muriel Rukeyser. "The Sixth Night: Waking" from *A Muriel Rukeyser Reader*, edited by Jan Heller Levi (New York: W. W. Norton & Company, 1994). Copyright © 1958 by Muriel Rukeyser. Reprinted with the permission of William L. Rukeyser.

Mary Jo Salter. "Welcome to Hiroshima" from *Henry Purcell in Japan*. Copyright © 1984 by Mary Jo Salter. Reprinted with the permission of Alfred A. Knopf, Inc.

Anne Sexton. "All My Pretty Ones" and "The Starry Night" from *All My Pretty Ones*. Copyright © 1962 by Anne Sexton, renewed 1990 by Linda Sexton. Reprinted with the permission of Houghton Mifflin Company.

Stevie Smith. "Not Waving but Drowning" from *The Collected Poems of Stevie Smith*. Copyright © 1972 by Stevie Smith. Reprinted with the permission of New Directions Publishing Corporation.

Gary Snyder. "How to Make Stew in the Pinacate Desert: Recipe for Lock & Drum" from *The Back Country*. Copyright © 1968 by Gary Snyder. Reprinted with the permission of New Directions Publishing Corporation. "Milton by Firelight" from *No Nature*. Copyright © 1992 by Gary Snyder. Reprinted with the permission of North Point Press, a division of Farrar, Straus & Giroux, Inc.

Gary Soto. "Mexicans Begin Jogging" and "Walking with Jackie, Sitting with a Dog" from *New and Selected Poems*. Copyright © 1995 by Gary Soto. Reprinted with the permission of Chronicle Books, San Francisco.

Wallace Stevens. "Peter Quince at the Clavier" (excerpt) from *The Collected Poems of Wallace Stevens*. Copyright 1923 and renewed 1951 by Wallace Stevens. "Thirteen Ways of Looking at a Blackbird" from *The Collected Poems of Wallace Stevens*. Copyright 1923 and renewed 1951 by Wallace Stevens. Both reprinted with the permission of Alfred A. Knopf, Inc.

Wislawa Szymborska. "The Terrorist, He Watches," translated by Robert Maguire and Magnus Jan Krynski, from *Sounds, Feelings, Thoughts: Seventy Poems by Wislawa Szymborska*. Copyright © 1981 by Princeton University Press. Reprinted with the permission of the publishers.

Genevieve Taggard. "With Child" from *Collected Poems 1918–1938*. Copyright 1938 by Harper & Row Publishers, Inc., renewed © 1966. Reprinted with the permission of Marcia D. Liles.

Dylan Thomas. "In My Craft or Sullen Art" and "Do Not Go Gentle into That Good Night" from *The Poems of Dylan Thomas*. Copyright 1939, 1946 by New Directions Publishing Corporation. Reprinted with the permission of New Directions Publishing Corporation and David Higham Associates, London as agents for the Trustees of the Copyrights of Dylan Thomas.

Anne Waldman. "Marianne Moore," "Our Past," and "To the Censorious Ones" from *Kill or Cure*. Copyright © 1994 by Anne Waldman. Reprinted with the permission of Viking Penguin, a division of Penguin Books USA Inc.

Alice Walker. "How Poems Are Made / A Discredited View" from *Horses Make a Landscape Look More Beautiful*. Copyright © 1984 by Alice Walker. Reprinted with the permission of Harcourt Brace & Company.

William Carlos Williams. "The Red Wheelbarrow," "Classic Scene," "Spring and All," "This Is Just to Say," and "Tract" from *The Collected Poems of William Carlos Williams, Volume I, 1909–1939*, edited by Christopher MacGowan. Copyright 1938, 1944, 1945 by New Directions Publishing Corporation. "The Dance" ("In Brueghel's great picture") from *The Collected Poems of William Carlos Williams, Volume II, 1939–1962*, edited by Christopher MacGowan. Copyright 1944 by New Directions Publishing Corporation. All reprinted with the permission of the publishers.

Richard Wright. "I would like a bell," "An empty sickbed," "A freezing morning," and "A soft wind at dawn" from Ellen Wright and Michel Fabre, eds., *The Richard Wright Reader*. Copyright © 1978 by Richard Wright. Reprinted with the permission of John Hawkins Associates, Inc.

Elinor Wylie. "Madman's Song" from *Collected Poems*. Copyright 1921 by Alfred A. Knopf, Inc., renewed 1949 by William Rose Benet. Reprinted with the permission of Alfred A. Knopf, Inc.

W. B. Yeats. "The Second Coming" and "Sailing to Byzantium" from *The Poems of W. B. Yeats: A New Edition*, edited by Richard J. Finneran. Copyright 1924, 1928 by Macmillan Publishing Company, renewed 1952, © 1956, by Georgie Yeats. Reprinted with the permission of Simon & Schuster, Inc.

Coy Mistress") from Robert Pack and Jay Parini, eds., *Touchstones: American Poets on a Favorite Poem*. Copyright © 1996 by the President and Fellows of Middlebury College. Reprinted with the permission of University Press of New England.

Sydney Lea. "On Keats's 'To Autumn' " from Robert Pack and Jay Parini, eds., *Touchstones: American Poets on a Favorite Poem*. Copyright © 1996 by the President and Fellows of Middlebury College. Reprinted with the permission of University Press of New England.

Angela Leighton. "Elizabeth Barrett Browning: Woman and Poet" from *Elizabeth Barrett Browning*. Copyright © 1986 by Angela Leighton. Reprinted with the permission of Harvester Wheatsheaf/Paramount Publishing International.

Denise Levertov. "Plath as a Confessional Poet" (editors' title) excerpted from an interview by Sybil P. Estess in Joe David Bellamy, ed., *American Poetry Observed: Poets on Their Work*. Copyright © 1984 by The Board of Trustees of the University of Illinois. Reprinted with the permission of Sybil P. Estess.

Robert Lowell. "An Explanation of Skunk Hour" (editors' title) from Anthony Ostroff, ed., *The Contemporary Poet as Artist and Critic*. Copyright © 1964 by Little, Brown and Company. Reprinted with the permission of the publishers. " 'Robert Frost' " from *Notebook, Third Edition*. Copyright © 1970 by Robert Lowell. Reprinted with the permission of Farrar, Straus & Giroux, Inc. Foreword to Sylvia Plath, *Ariel*. Copyright © 1963 and renewed 1991 by Ted Hughes. Reprinted with the permission of HarperCollins Publishers, Inc.

Christopher Merrill. "Wyatt's 'They Flee from Me' " (editors' title) from Robert Pack and Jay Parini, eds., *Touchstones: American Poets on a Favorite Poem*. Copyright © 1996 by the President and Fellows of Middlebury College. Reprinted with the permission of University Press of New England.

Marianne Moore. "Some Answers to Questions Posed by Howard Nemerov" from Howard Nemerov, ed., *Poets on Poetry*. Copyright © 1966 by Basic Books, Inc., renewed 1984 by Margaret Nemerov. Reprinted with the permission of Basic-Books, a division of HarperCollins Publishers, Inc.

Joyce Carol Oates. "Sylvia Plath's Deathly Imagination" (editors' title) from Edward Butscher, ed., *Sylvia Plath: The Woman and the Work* (New York: Dodd, Mead & Co., 1977). Copyright © 1977 by Joyce Carol Oates. Reprinted with the permission of John Hawkins Associates, Inc.

Alicia Ostriker. "The Poet as Heroine: H.D." (editors' title) from *Writing Like a Woman*. Copyright © 1983 by University of Michigan. Reprinted with the permission of The University of Michigan Press.

Sylvia Plath. Journal entry, from Ted Hughes, consulting editor, and Frances McCullough, ed., *The Journals of Sylvia Plath*. Copyright © 1982 by Ted Hughes as Executor of the Estate of Sylvia Plath. Reprinted with the permission of Doubleday, a division of Bantam Doubleday Dell Publishing Group, Inc.

Plato. "On Banishing Poets from the State" (editors' title) from *The Republic*, translated by G. M. A. Grube. Copyright © 1974. Reprinted with the permission of Hackett Publishing Company, Inc.

Ezra Pound. "On the Principles of Imagism" (editors' title, originally titled, and excerpted from, "A Retrospect") from T. S. Eliot, ed., *Literary Essays of Ezra Pound*. Copyright 1935 by Ezra Pound. " 'What I Feel about Walt Whitman' " from *Selected Prose 1909–1965*, edited by William Cookson. Copyright © 1955 by Ezra Pound. Copyright © 1973 by The Estate of Ezra Pound. Both reprinted with the permission of New Directions Publishing Corporation and Faber and Faber, Ltd.

Arnold Rampersad. "Langston Hughes as Folk Poet" (editors' title) from the Introduction to Arnold Rampersad and David Roessel, eds., *The Collected Poems of Langston Hughes*. Copyright © 1994 by the Estate of Langston Hughes. Reprinted with the permission of Alfred A. Knopf, Inc.

Michael Rubiner. "T. S. Eliot Interactive" from *The New York Times Magazine* (June 18, 1995). Copyright © 1995 by Michael Rubiner. Reprinted with the permission of the author.

Sherod Santos. "Shelly in Ruins. The Appeal of 'Ozymandias' " from Robert Pack and Jay Parini, eds., *Touchstones: American Poets on a Favorite Poem* (Hanover: Middlebury College Press, 1996). Copyright © 1996 by the President and Fellows of Middlebury College. Reprinted with the permission of University Press of New England.

Peter Schmitt. "Sad Heart at the Supermarket: Randall Jarrell's 'Next Day' " from Robert Pack and Jay Parini, eds., *Touchstones: American Poets on a Favorite Poem* (Hanover: Middlebury College Press, 1996). Copyright © 1996 by the President and Fellows of Middlebury College. Reprinted with the permission of University Press of New England.

Anne Sexton. "The Barfly Ought to Sing" from Charles Newman, ed., *The Art of Sylvia Plath: A Symposium* (Bloomington: Indiana University Press, 1970). Copyright © 1970 by Anne Sexton. Reprinted with the permission of Sterling Lord Literistic, Inc. This essay includes the previously uncollected Sylvia Plath poem "Wanting to Die." Reprinted with the permission of Faber and Faber, Ltd.

Louis Simpson. "On Lowell's 'Skunk Hour' " (editors' title) from *A Revolution in Taste: Studies of W. H. Auden, Dylan Thomas, Allen Ginsberg, Sylvia Plath, and Robert Lowell*. Copyright © 1978 by Louis Simpson. Reprinted with the permission of Simon & Schuster, Inc.

Gary Smith. "On Gwendolyn Brooks' A Street in Bronzeville" (editors' title, originally titled "Gwendolyn Brooks' *A Street in Bronzeville*, The Harlem Renaissance and the Mythologies of Black Women") from *MELUS* 10.3 (Fall 1983). Copyright © 1983 by The Society for the Study of Multi-Ethnic Literature in the United States. Reprinted with the permission of the publisher.

Eric Trethewey. "The Virtue of Arnold's 'Dover Beach' " from Robert Pack and Jay Parini, eds., *Touchstones: American Poets on a Favorite Poem*. Copyright © 1996 by the President and Fellows of Middlebury College. Reprinted with the permission of University Press of New England.

Helen Vendler. "On Louise Glück" (editors' title) from *The Music of What Happens*. Copyright © 1988 by The President and Fellows of Harvard College. Reprinted with the permission of Harvard University Press.

Richard Wilbur. "Tennyson's Voyage of the Mind" from Robert Pack and Jay Parini, eds., *Touchstones: American Poets on a Favorite Poem* (Hanover: Middlebury College Press, 1996). Copyright © 1996 by the President and Fellows of Middlebury College. Reprinted with the permission of University Press of New England. "On Emily Dickinson" (editors' title, originally titled, and excerpted from, "Sumptuous Destitution") from Richard Wilbur, Louise Bogan, and Archibald MacLeish, *Emily Dickinson: Three Views* (Amherst, Mass.: Amherst College Press, 1960). This piece was later reprinted in *Responses* (New York: Harcourt Brace, 1976). Copyright © 1960 by Richard Wilbur. Reprinted with the permission of the author.

William Carlos Williams. "Ezra Pound's Language" (editors' title) from a letter to James Laughlin September 25, 1940, from Hugh Witemeyer, ed., *William Carlos Williams and James Laughlin: Selected Letters*. Copyright © 1989 by the Estate of William Carlos Williams. Reprinted with the permission of W. W. Norton & Company, Inc.

Richard Wright. "A Review of The Big Sea" (editors' title, originally titled "Forerunner and Ambassador") from *The New Republic* 103 (October 18, 1940). Copyright 1940 by Richard Wright. Reprinted with the permission of John Hawkins Associates, Inc.

DRAMA

Woody Allen. Monologue from "Annie Hall." Copyright © 1977 by United Artists Corporation. Monologue from "Manhattan." Copyright © 1979 by United Artists Corporation. Both reprinted with the permission of Sinclair Tenenbaum Olesiuk & Emanuel. All rights reserved.

Edward Albee. *The Sandbox* from *The Zoo Story, The Death of Bessie Smith and The Sandbox: Three Plays* (New York: Coward-McCann, 1960). Copyright © 1959 and renewed 1987 by Edward Albee. Reprinted with the permission of William Morris Agency.

Samuel Beckett. *Krapp's Last Tape*. Copyright © 1958 by Samuel Beckett. First appeared in *Evergreen Review* (Summer 1958). Reprinted with the permission of Grove/Atlantic, Inc.

Anton Chekhov. *The Bear*, translated by Ronald Hingley, from *Twelve Plays*. Copyright © 1992 by Ronald Hingley. Reprinted with the permission of Oxford University Press, Inc.

Christopher Durang. *For Whom the Southern Belle Tolls*. Copyright © 1993 by Christopher Durang. Reprinted with the permission of Helen Merrill, Ltd. All amateur and professional stage performance rights (other than first class rights) for *For Whom the Southern Belle Tolls* are controlled exclusively by Dramatists Play Service, 440 Park Avenue South, New York, NY 10016. No professional or nonprofessional performance of the play may be given without obtaining in advance the written permission of Dramatists Play Service, and paying the requisite fee. Inquiries concerning all other rights should be addressed to the author's representative: Helen Merrill, Ltd., 435 West 23rd Street, Suite 1A, New York, NY 10011, USA.

Susan Glaspell. *Trifles*. (New York: Frank Shay, 1916). Copyright 1916 by Susan Glaspell. Reprinted with the permission of the Estate of Susan Glaspell.

Lorraine Hansberry. *A Raisin in the Sun*. Copyright © 1958 by Robert Nemiroff as an unpublished work. Copyright © 1959, 1966, 1984 by Robert Nemiroff. Reprinted with the permission of Random House, Inc.

Langston Hughes. "Harlem (A Dream Deferred)" from *The Panther and the Lash: Poems of Our Times*. Copyright 1951 by Langston Hughes. Reprinted with the permission of Alfred A. Knopf, Inc.

David Henry Hwang. *As the Crow Flies*. Copyright © 1983 by David Henry Hwang. Reprinted with the permission of Writers and Artists. All inquiries concerning rights should be addressed to the author's representative: William Craver, Writers and Artists, 19 West 44th Street, Suite 100, New York, NY 10036, USA.

Henrik Ibsen. *A Doll House* from *The Complete Major Prose Plays of Henrik Ibsen*, translated by Rolf Fjelde. Copyright © 1965, 1970, 1978 by Rolf Fjelde. Reprinted with the permission of Dutton Signet, a division of Penguin Books USA Inc.

Kantan from *Japanese Nō Dramas*, edited and translated by Royall Tyler. Copyright © 1991 by Royall Tyler. Reprinted with the permission of Penguin Books, Ltd.

Arthur Miller. *Death of a Salesman*. Copyright 1949 and renewed © 1977 by Arthur Miller. Reprinted with the permission of Viking Penguin, a division of Penguin Books USA Inc.

Marsha Norman. *'night, Mother*. Copyright © 1983 by Marsha Norman. Reprinted with the permission of Hill and Wang, a division of Farrar, Straus & Giroux, Inc. CAUTION: Professionals and amateurs are hereby warned that *'night, Mother*, being fully protected under the Copyright Laws of the United States of America and all other countries of the Berne and Universal Copyright conventions, is subject to a royalty. All rights including, but not limited to, professional, amateur, motion picture, recitation, lecturing, public reading, radio and television broadcasting, video or sound taping, photocopying, all other forms of mechanical or electronic reproduction, and the rights of translation into foreign languages are expressly reserved. All inquiries concerning rights should be addressed to the author's agent: William Morris Agency.

Eugene O'Neill. *Bound East for Cardiff: A Play in One Act* from *Plays*. Copyright 1919 and renewed 1947 by Eugene O'Neill. Reprinted with the permission of Random House, Inc.

Willy Russell. Excerpt from act 1, scene 6 of *Educating Rita* (New York: Samuel French, 1981). Copyright © 1981 by Willy Russell. Reprinted with the permission of Samuel French, Inc.

William Shakespeare. Footnotes to accompany *Hamlet, Prince of Denmark* from Hardin Craig and David Bevington, eds., *An Introduction to Shakespeare, Revised Edition*. Copyright 1951, 1952, © 1961, 1973, 1975 by Scott, Foresman and Company. Reprinted with the permission of Addison-Wesley Educational Publishers, Inc.

Sophocles. *Oedipus* from *Three Theban Plays*, translated by Robert Fagles. Copyright © 1982 by Robert Fagles. Reprinted with the permission of Penguin Books USA Inc.

August Strindberg. *Miss Julie*, translated by Harry G. Carlson, from *Strindberg: Five Plays*. Copyright © 1983 by The Regents of the University of California. Reprinted with the permission of University of California Press.

Wendy Wasserstein. *Tender Offer* as found in *Antaeus* 66 (Spring 1991): 452–58, issue titled "Plays in One Act." Copyright © 1991 by Wendy Wasserstein. Reprinted with the permission of Rosenstone/Wender. No part of this material may be reproduced in whole or in part without the express written permission of the author or her agent.

Tennessee Williams. *The Glass Menagerie* from *The Theatre of Tennessee Williams, Volume 1*. Copyright 1945 by Tennessee Williams and Edwina D. Williams, renewed © 1971 by Tennessee Williams. Reprinted with the permission of Random House, Inc.

August Wilson. *The Janitor* from *In Short: Pieces from the New Dramatists* (New York: Broadway Play Pub., 1985). Copyright © 1985 by August Wilson. Reprinted with the permission of the author.

DRAMA COMMENTARIES

Edward Albee. "On Playwriting" from *Dramatics*. Copyright by Edward Albee. Reprinted with the permission of the William Morris Agency.

Richard Amacher. "On 'The Sandbox'" (editor's title, section originally titled "The Characters in Conflict") from *Edward Albee*. Copyright © 1969 by Twayne Publishers, Inc. Reprinted with the permission of Twayne Publishers, an imprint of Simon & Schuster Macmillan.

Aristotle. "On the Elements and General Principles of Tragedy" (editors' title), translated by Gerald F. Else, from *Poetics*, pp. 25–37. Copyright © 1967. Reprinted with the permission of The University of Michigan Press.

James Baldwin. "Sweet Lorraine" from the Introduction to Lorraine Hansberry, *To Be Young, Gifted and Black: Lorraine Hansberry in Her Own Words*. Originally published in *Esquire* (1969). Copyright © 1969 by James Baldwin. Reprinted with the permission of the James Baldwin Estate.

Travis Bogard. "The Provincetown Players" from *Contour in Time: The Plays of Eugene O'Neill*. Copyright © 1972 by Travis Bogard. Reprinted with the permission of Oxford University Press, Inc.

Peter Brook. "On Chekhov" from *The Shifting Point*. Copyright © 1987 by Peter Brook. Reprinted with the permission of HarperCollins Publishers, Inc.

Leo Tolstoy. "Shakespeare's Immoral Frame of Mind" from François Laroque, ed., *Shakespeare: Court, Crowd and Playhouse* (London: Thames & Hudson, 1993). Copyright © 1993 by François Laroque. Reprinted with the permission of Editions Gallimard, Paris.

August Wilson. "Where to Begin?" (editors' title) from the Preface to *Three Plays*. Copyright © 1991 by University of Pittsburgh Press. Reprinted with the permission of the publishers.

Tennessee Williams. "Production Notes to 'The Glass Menagerie'" from *The Theatre of Tennessee Williams, Volume 1*. Copyright © 1945 by Tennessee Williams and Edwin D. Williams. Reprinted with the permission of New Directions Publishing Corporation.

Margaret B. Wilkerson. "Hansberry's Awareness of Culture and Gender" (editors' title) from Robert Nemiroff, ed., *Les Blancs: The Collected Last Plays of Lorraine Hansberry*. Copyright © 1972 by Margaret B. Wilkerson. Reprinted with the permission of Random House, Inc.

Virginia Woolf. "What If Shakespeare Had Had a Sister" from *A Room of One's Own*. Copyright © 1929 by Harcourt Brace & World, Inc., renewed © 1957 by Leonard Woolf. Reprinted with the permission of the publisher.

INDEX OF FIRST LINES

INDEX OF AUTHORS
AND TITLES